INDEX 1947-1983

NATIONAL GEOGRAPHIC

INDEX 1947-1983

COLUMBIA BLASTS OFF ON THE SPACE SHUTTLE'S 1981 MAIDEN FLIGHT. JON SCHNEEBERGER, TED JOHNSON, JR., AND ANTHONY PERITORE, ALL NGS

A publication of the National Geographic Society
Gilbert M. Grosvenor, *President* Melvin M. Payne, *Chairman*
Wilbur E. Garrett, *Editor*
Robert L. Breeden, *Vice President, Publications*

CONTENTS

7 OUR OWN GREAT AGE OF EXPLORATION
Michael Collins, Trustee, National Geographic Society

8 THE MAGAZINE TODAY
Wilbur E. Garrett, Editor, National Geographic Magazine

84 THE SOCIETY TODAY
Gilbert M. Grosvenor, President, National Geographic Society

124 MEDALS AND AWARDS

129 INDEX TO NATIONAL GEOGRAPHIC
With entries for Society maps, books, and television specials

575 SOCIETY-SPONSORED RESEARCH
Melvin M. Payne, Chairman, Board of Trustees, and Chairman, Committee for Research and Exploration

STAFF FOR THIS BOOK:

Editor: Wilbur E. Garrett

Index: Jolene M. Blozis, Manager, Indexing Division

Project Editors: Editorial, David Jeffery; Illustrations, Robert S. Patton; Design, Constance H. Phelps

Typographic Design and Production: Howard E. Paine, Betty Clayman-DeAtley, Charles C. Uhl

Director of Manufacturing: Robert W. Messer

Production Manager: Mary A. Bennett

Indexing: Jeffrey A. Brown, George I. Burneston, III, Martha K. Hightower, Dianne L. Hosmer, Charles M. Israel, Anne K. McCain, Brit A. Peterson, Teresa S. Purvis, Catherine Warford, Michael G. Young

Editorial: Rowe Findley, Lesley B. Rogers; Legends, Joan Straker Hazell, Abigail A. Tipton; Werner L. Janney

Illustrations: Elaine Rice Ames, Bentley Andrews-Garfield, Marisa K. Domeyko; Layout, Louisa C. Clayton; Library, Eudora L. Babyak, R. Gary Colbert, Robert A. Henry, Richard A. White

Research: Ann K. Wendt, Bette J. Goss, Jan Holderness, Anne A. Jamison, Eve G. Kadick, Mary R. Lamberton, Kathy B. Maher, Jean B. McConville, Miriam R. Miller, Frances W. Shaffer

Administration: Tracey L. Blanton, George I. Burneston, Jr., Giomar Cabrales, Cynthia Collins, Dianne Craven, Victoria C. Ducheneaux, Maureen Flynn, Allison Hargraves, John Lea, Liisa Maurer, Katherine P. McGown, Mary Anne McMillen, Stuart E. Pfitzinger, Ann Salazar, Nancy Simson

Phototype: Bernard G. Quarrick, Martin G. Anderson, Jill Beves, Dennis J. Collins, Stephany J. Freedman, Walter A. Lee, Dennis R. Leonard, John R. Reap

Engraving and Printing: David V. Showers, George V. White

Library of Congress CIP Data: page 606

FLOATING FREE IN SPACE, BRUCE McCANDLESS II CUTS MAN'S LAST UMBILICAL TO MOTHER EARTH. ROBERT L. GIBSON, NASA

The Great Age of Exploration Is Our Own

By MICHAEL COLLINS TRUSTEE, NATIONAL GEOGRAPHIC SOCIETY

TWO VINTAGE YEARS: 1947, the year of supersonic flight, and 1983, the year of supersolar flight, bracket this Index. On October 14, 1947, Capt. Charles "Chuck" Yeager piloted a Bell X-1 rocket plane past the sound barrier; on June 13, 1983, the Pioneer 10 spacecraft passed the orbits of Neptune and Pluto. Yeager's feat, deemed impossible by some aerodynamicists, opened up the jet age. NASA calls Pioneer 10, the first man-made object to escape from our solar system, "a calling card announcing our existence to any other intelligences in the universe." Are these two flights the overriding achievements of these 37 years, or even worthy of mention? They have some competition, such as the launch of the space age in 1957 with the orbiting of Sputnik 1. But perhaps this talk of jet and space ages overlooks a more fundamental description.

Undeniably, the 20th century has been violent, one of world wars and genocide, and certainly the interval between 1947 and 1983 has had its share of horror, from Vietnam and Cambodia to Idi Amin in Uganda. The bomb, not used since 1945, nonetheless casts a long and awesome shadow over this period.

While man's inhumanity to man unfortunately seems a historical constant, the past third of a century may be truly special in a more optimistic way—the amount of new scientific information made available to us, the cornucopia of new facts discovered. From the cells of the human body to the rings of Saturn, we have recently seen things—and seen them clearly—that we could only guess at before. We can stand on the moon, penetrate the oceans, measure continental drift, live with artificial heart valves.

Our capability for seeing, measuring, and changing our inner and outer world has grown dramatically. We can go more places, but more important, we can *see* more places, via microscope and telescope. Orbiting telescopes, high above the obscuring gases of our atmosphere, will be increasingly important, probing in the X-ray and infrared bands as well as in the visible spectrum. Even our concept of matter has changed dramatically. When I was a student in 1947, the atom was believed to be composed of protons, neutrons, and electrons. Today we have quarks, leptons, and bosons. We continue to discover new particles, and the list has grown beyond the basic three into the hundreds, many of whose life spans are far shorter than an eye blink. In 1947 the big bang theory was only one of several scientific explanations of the origin of the universe; today physicists analyze this explosion microsecond by microsecond.

In 1947 the digital computer was in its infancy. It required an entire room full of fragile, temperamental, hot vacuum tubes to perform calculations that today (thanks to the silicon chip, an educated grain of sand) can be done with greater speed and reliability by matchbook-size computers—and at a fraction of the cost. A cost spiral in reverse—that is a rarity to savor! This quantum jump in electronics not only helps us explore inner and outer space but is also a powerful tool in changing our daily lives: our bank accounts, our automobile ignition systems, our wristwatches.

Turning the pages of this Index confirms the fecundity of the period. The more than 2,500 NATIONAL GEOGRAPHIC articles listed here convincingly document an explosion of knowledge, resulting in advances on all fronts. Truly, the great age of exploration is our own. □

MICHAEL COLLINS (OPPOSITE); ROBERT W. MADDEN

***Coming home: Michael Collins aboard the command module* Columbia *photographed the lunar module* Eagle *(opposite) as the vehicles rendezvoused after the first manned moon landing. Collins (above, center) and fellow astronauts Neil A. Armstrong, at left, and Edwin E. Aldrin, Jr., later celebrated aboard U.S.S.* Hornet.**

TORCHBEARERS CELEBRATE THE 30TH ANNIVERSARY OF THE PEOPLE'S REPUBLIC OF CHINA. BRUCE DALE, NGS

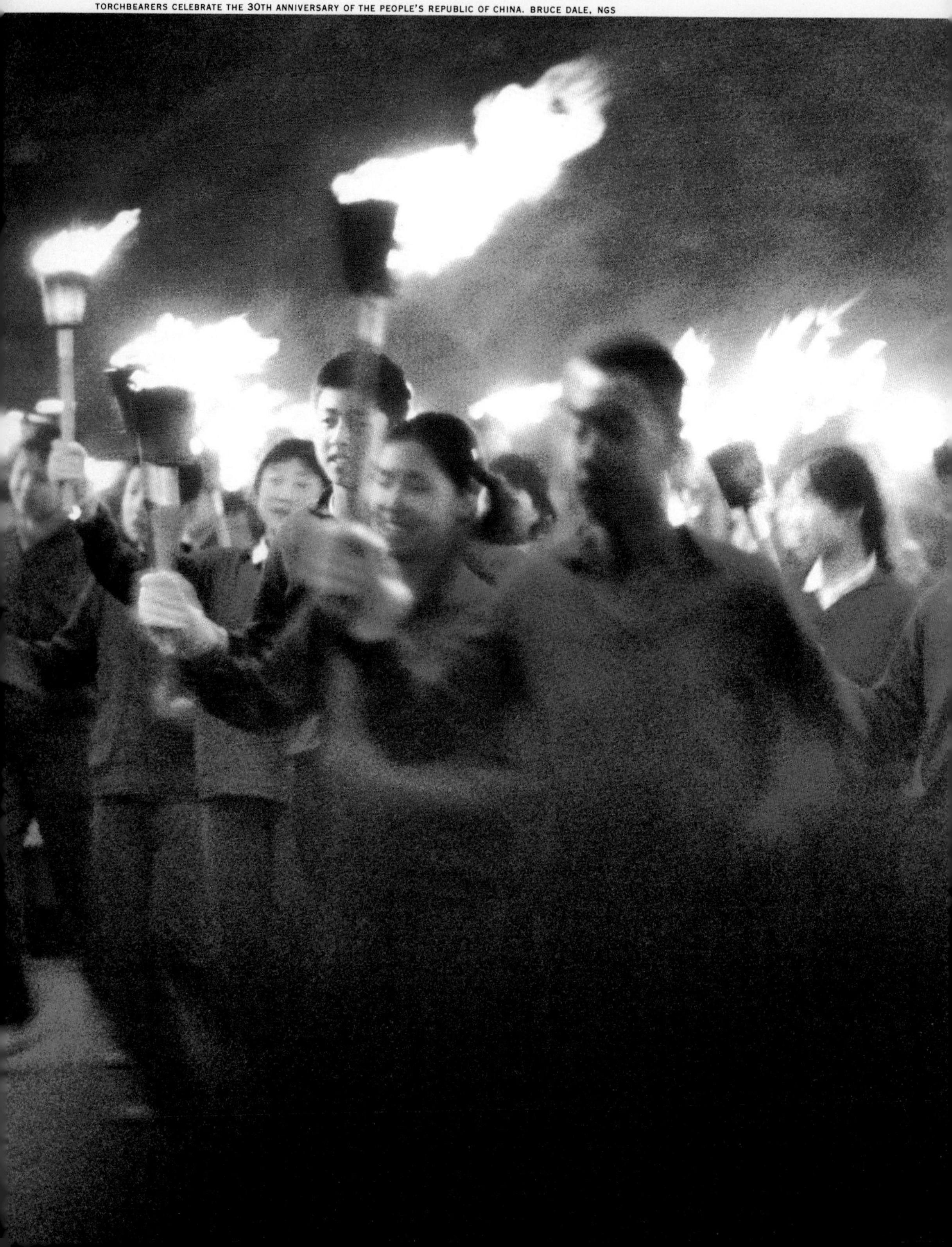

THE MAGAZINE TODAY

By WILBUR E. GARRETT EDITOR, NATIONAL GEOGRAPHIC

MAYNARD OWEN WILLIAMS, NGS

"All the world is watching how the rest of the world lives," wrote GEOGRAPHIC journalist Maynard Owen Williams in 1921, having persuaded a Chinese Buddhist monk (above) to look through a camera's viewfinder.

The gesture of a Russian child (opposite) might feed speculation on the nature of friendship and caution. Yet the magazine's function remains not speculation but, as the Editor writes, to capture the fleeting present "with as little distortion as possible" so that it may enhance our knowledge of the past and our sense of the future.

CONSIDER A SNOWFLAKE as it touches your hand—intricate, delicate, beautiful. For one small moment it is present; then it melts into the past. Yet if you had caught the snowflake on a chilled glass slide and photographed it, that image would always live in the present, permitting you to study and enjoy it at your leisure—enhancing your appreciation of all future snowflakes.

That is the essence of what the GEOGRAPHIC has been trying to do since 1888—capture and preserve significant present moments with as little distortion as possible. This Index—a guide whose memory never dims—will take you easily back to those moments of the past 37 years and in so doing turn a collection of magazines into a useful reference work.

For me this Index is more than a reference tool. It calls into sharp focus my 30 years of photographing, writing, and editing for the GEOGRAPHIC. It reminds me that they were years of loss of innocence for the world, the United States, and the NATIONAL GEOGRAPHIC. The end of World War II brought a burst of enthusiasm and idealism—nations would live in peace, their people would all enjoy the Four Freedoms, and the new United Nations would settle all disputes and guarantee a good life for all.

The first article to be indexed for this volume, the lead for January 1947, was "Cuba—American Sugar Bowl." The Korean War was three years in the future; Israel was not yet a nation, the cold war was just beginning, there was no Berlin Wall, and Vietnam was not yet a daily headline. The article, full of hope, gave little hint of the forces and problems even then incubating in Cuba that would soon lead this seemingly semicolonial island nation to become a focus of concern and frustration for United States Latin American policy for decades and even to this day. Yet Cuba was only symptomatic of the postwar storm of change that would toss nations, colonies, and continents like rag dolls in the hands of angry children. Sweeping change was overtaking the map of Africa. Iron, bamboo, and no-name curtains cut off hundreds of millions of people from one another.

Through that period the author of the Cuba article learned his lessons well. Ten years later Melville Bell Grosvenor became Editor and President of the National Geographic Society. His enthusiastic, intuitive, and brilliant leadership spanned ten dramatic years of changes, growth, and improvement in the magazine. The changes were not without controversy.

When he decided to leave our printer of sixty years for more modern presses, MBG, as he was called, announced to the staff: "This will be the first magazine to print color on every page." A less imaginative officer *(Continued on page 20)*

DEAN CONGER, NGS

Joined in the elemental bond of human affection, Muhammad Diab and his wife are united for a moment beyond all custom and all politics. Despite state incentives to take

JAMES L. STANFIELD, NGS

up a sedentary farming life, they and others in the tribes of the camel hold to their ancestral Bedouin ways, crossing and recrossing the desert lands of Syria.

A terrible thing had just happened. While on assignment in Peru, William Albert Allard photographed a shepherd boy (above) moments after a taxi had rounded a blind curve and destroyed six of his family's flock of sheep, a sharp economic blow.

Published in March 1982, the photograph so moved our members that, without being asked, they contributed more than $4,000 to replace the sheep. Staff writer Harvey Arden contacted CARE, whose Peruvian branch found the boy, Eduardo Condor Ramos.

When Ronald Burkard, assistant executive director of CARE, presented the new sheep, hundreds of Andean villagers came for the ceremony, and Eduardo (opposite) broke into tears—this time of joy. "God will pay you," he said.

In two years donations grew to $6,800 and became a Peruvian Children's Fund.

WILLIAM ALBERT ALLARD

NILS LINDQUIST, CARE

Eduardo not only had his sheep, but his village of Ichu near Lake Titicaca also had new schoolrooms, school supplies, a playground, and a motorized water pump.

Editor Bill Garrett wrote that perhaps a school "in Eduardo's district should be named Escuela Allard."

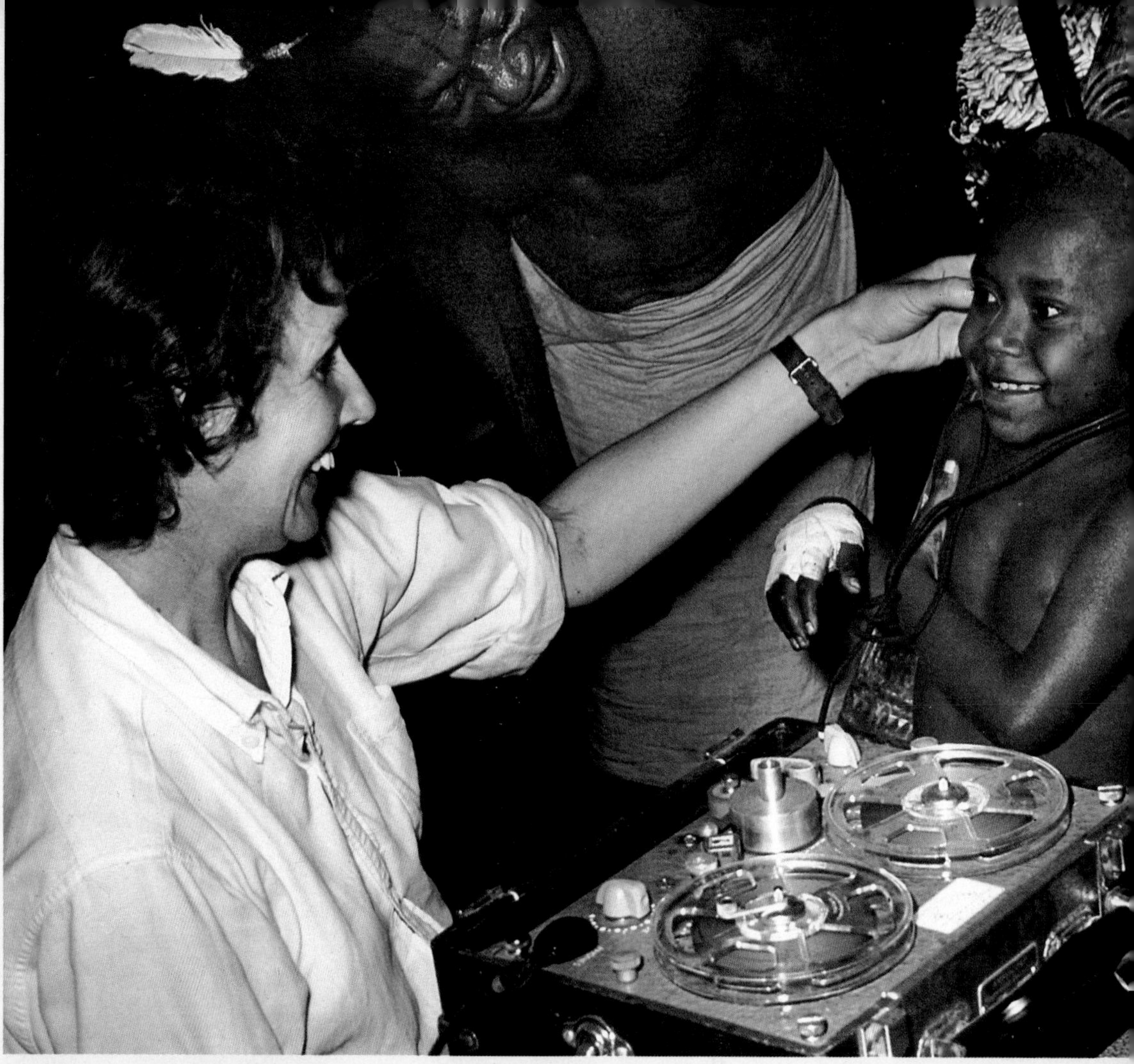

1

JOHN SCOFIELD, NGS

2

When carried into the remote niches of the world, the artifacts of Western society can at first seem alien. Yet two worlds meet quite comfortably in the tropical rain forest of New Britain **(1)** *as native dancers hear their own voices on a tape recorder for the first time. Margaret Gilliard and her husband, explorer-scientist E. Thomas Gilliard, came to study and photograph life on this remote island in the southwestern Pacific. The expedition was jointly sponsored by the Society, the Explorers Club, and the American Museum of Natural History.*

In the mountain realm of Bhutan, a royal bodyguard **(2)** *takes time out for a soft drink. Perched between India and the People's Republic of China, Bhutan has a modern, efficient army but outfits her medieval guards with their centuries-old iron helmets and shields of rhinoceros hide.*

A mail-order catalog supplied the battery-operated model cars and track set **(3)** *for a resident of Canada's Northwest Territories. His close-knit community preserves a hunting-and-*

Exotic diets, customs, and tools—

E. THOMAS GILLIARD

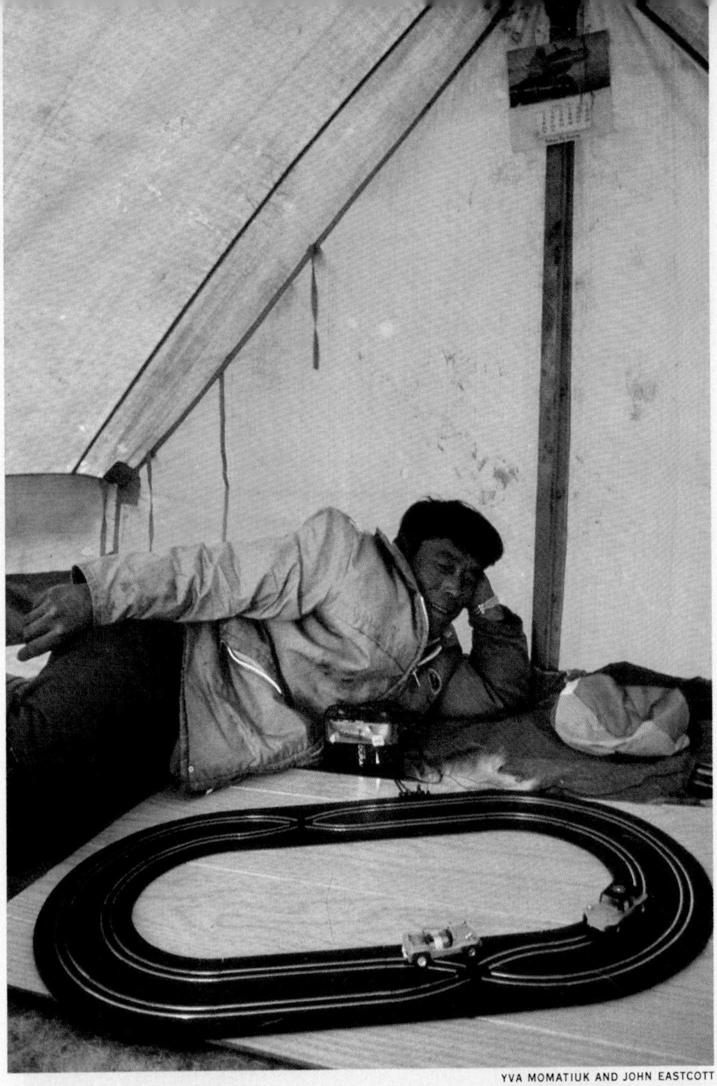

3

YVA MOMATIUK AND JOHN EASTCOTT

ROBERT AZZI, WOODFIN CAMP & ASSOCIATES

4

fishing way of life that is fast disappearing elsewhere in the Arctic. Known to the outside world as Eskimos, they call themselves Inuit, meaning "the people."

Pickup-truck mobility* (4) *links many Bedouin in Saudi Arabia with their seasonal grazing areas and still beloved herds of camels, sheep, and goats. Oil wealth almost beyond imagining has come to this nomadic, long-impoverished society. The fantastic inrush of riches has brought a whirlwind clash of tradition and change.

a look in the mirror

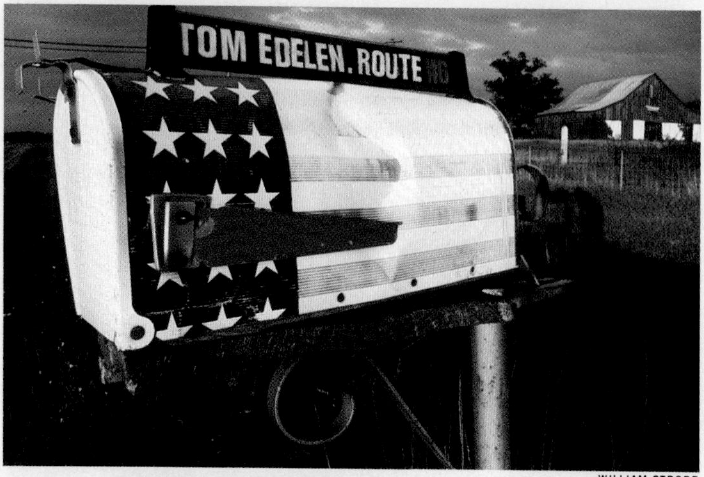

1

WILLIAM STRODE

2

C. C. LOCKWOOD

3

4

The epic ordinaries of daily life,

NICHOLAS DEVORE III

WILLIAM ALBERT ALLARD

The American land unrolls in an endless ribbon of stories documented in the GEOGRAPHIC.

The Stars and Stripes (1) *deck a mailbox in rural Kentucky. Wheat growers* (2) *reap record harvests in wide-open spaces of Montana.*

Deep in the semiwilderness of bayou country, a southern Louisiana swamp dweller (3) *feeds her flock of chickens.*

Huge draft horses (4) *provide pulling power on a Pennsylvania Amish child's family farm where religious beliefs restrict mechanization.*

"Crabbing" it's called, but a Tangier Island boy (5) *is for once on the victim's end. The isolated islanders are born to the life of a waterman, searching Chesapeake Bay for seafood prized by mainlanders.*

5

DAVID ALAN HARVEY

an American chronicle

(Continued from page 10) moaned that this was the end of the GEOGRAPHIC: "He'll break the Society." When MBG began putting photographs on the cover and initiated the phased removal of the ornate oak-and-laurel-leaf border, many predicted we were witnessing the beginning of the end. Instead, he more than doubled Society membership, began a dynamic book program, published our first world atlas and globe, and launched television's longest running documentary series. More important, he left a legacy of curiosity, imagination, and integrity that still motivates the staff.

An example: In 1964 when Canada planned to name a

NATHAN BENN

mountain for the late President John F. Kennedy, MBG looked up the one being considered and declared, "It's just a pimple—not worthy of Kennedy." He had become very fond of the first family when he joined them in launching as a public service the now famous books on the White House that have sold more than four million copies. He telephoned a top Canadian official to suggest that a more prominent peak be chosen. So the change was made to a much higher mountain; it was near the U. S.-Canadian border, and it had never been climbed. And it became Mount Kennedy.

MBG immediately reassembled *(Continued on page 30)*

Close reaching near landfall in Newfoundland, skipper Timothy Severin and his crew proved in 1977 that Irish vessels with leather hulls and flaxen sails, such as theirs, could have crossed the Atlantic Ocean in the early Middle Ages. Severin named his craft for the voyaging St. Brendan.

PAINTING BY PAUL CALLE

Near disaster strikes the first expedition organized by the Society (left), as a rain-triggered Alaskan avalanche demolishes a tent. Led by geologist Israel C. Russell, the 1890 party explored and mapped Mount St. Elias on the then little-known borderlands of southern Alaska and discovered Mount Logan, Canada's loftiest peak. Russell's first-person account enlivened an early issue of NATIONAL GEOGRAPHIC, setting a pattern for objective, eyewitness accounts that would characterize the magazine's reporting.

Struggling to the summit of the world—29,028-foot Mount Everest—Luther Jerstad (above) climbs just ahead of GEOGRAPHIC staff man Barry Bishop. The epic 1963

One foot and then the other

BARRY C. BISHOP, NGS

MOUNT EVEREST FOUNDATION

American Mount Everest Expedition, of which the Society was a major sponsor, had planted the U. S. flag on top three weeks earlier.

First to the earth's highest point, Sherpa Tenzing Norgay (left), climbing with Sir Edmund Hillary, attained Everest in 1953. Flags of the United Nations, United Kingdom, Nepal, and India flutter from his ice ax. Their lungs and legs at home in high altitudes, Sherpas became world renowned as intrepid Himalayan porters.

Seated so that penetrating 70-mile-an-hour gusts would not topple him, Barry Bishop (right) holds the U. S. and Society flags he carried to the top of Everest. "If you have to crawl on hands and knees, you're going to get there," he had told himself. Extreme conditions on the climb took their toll: Losing all his toes to limb-threatening frostbite, Bishop had to be evacuated from Base Camp by Sherpas.

LUTHER G. JERSTAD

to the apex of the world

1
RICHARD H. STEWART, NGS

2
RICHARD HANCE, WINZEN RESEARCH, INC.

3

Inside the gondola of Explorer II, *Capts. Orvil Anderson and Albert Stevens* (1) *rose almost 14 miles in 1935. The Society and the U. S. Army Air Corps sponsored their record flight. From its aircraft-carrier launching platform* (2), *the U. S. Navy's* Strato-Lab High 5 *crew and balloon set a new record by flying more than 21 miles high in 1961.* Kitty Hawk, *piloted by Maxie and Kris Anderson* (3), *soars on the first nonstop balloon crossing of North America in 1980.*

Society funds aided Comdr. Robert E. Peary (4) *and his men in their 1909 expedition, the first to reach the North Pole. Japanese adventurer Naomi Uemura* (5) *made the first solo trek to that Pole in 1978, where he strung up flags of nations in which he had found support.*

The GEOGRAPHIC *published first-person accounts of these pioneer journeys.*

4
ROBERT E. PEARY COLLECTION

5

Adventure: for the science

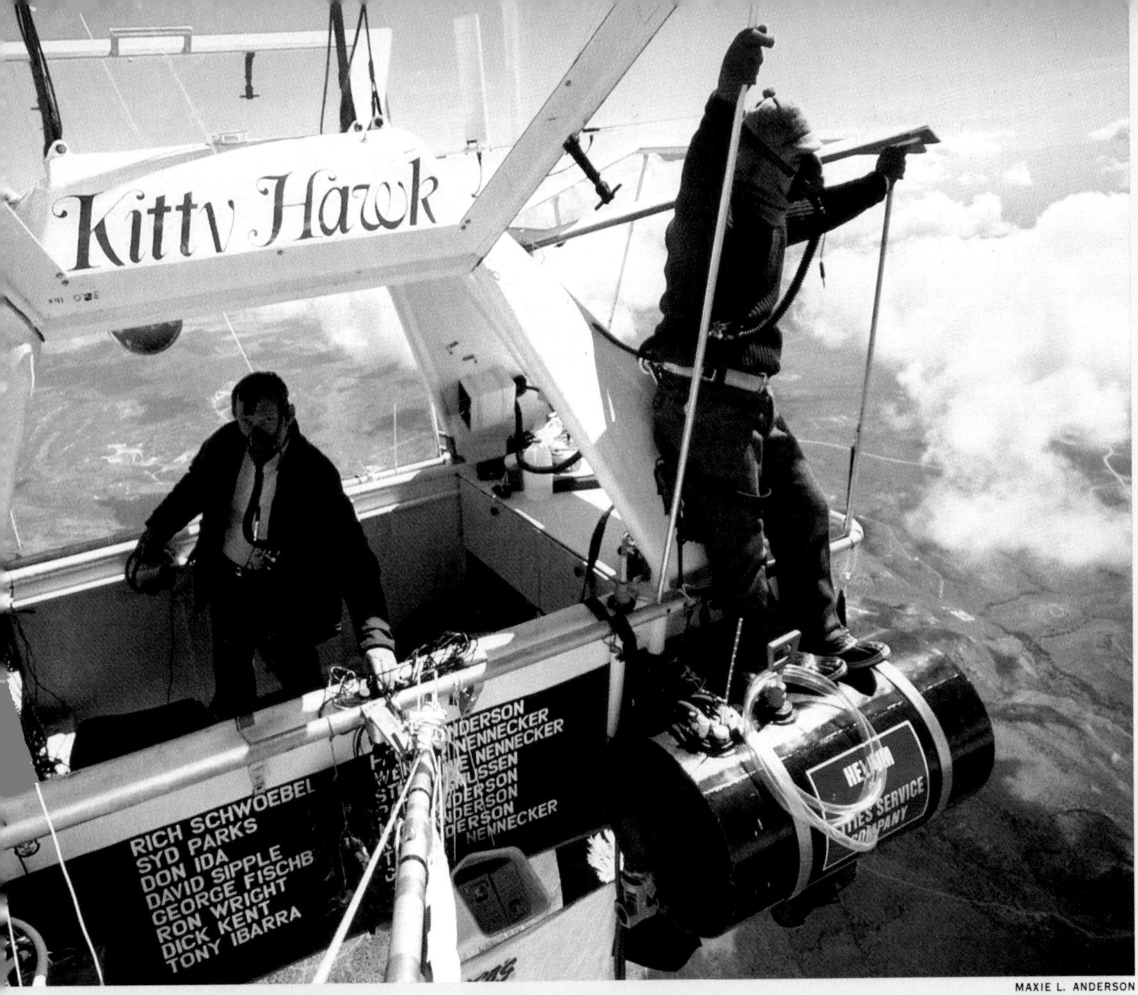

MAXIE L. ANDERSON

NAOMI UEMURA

and for the sheer doing

BOTH BY CHARLES O'REAR

The heart of the Grand Canyon had never been mapped in detail until 1970, when eminent cartographer Bradford Washburn, then director of the Boston Museum of Science, joined with the Society to take on the monumental task. It required seven years and nearly 700 helicopter landings on remote sites to plot the jagged terrain in this national park (right) carved across Arizona's northwest corner.

Although techniques such as aerial stereographic photography yielded the most detail, precise measurements had to be made on the scene. Atop Dana Butte (left) Washburn and his wife take one such reading. For pinpoint precision, a laser (below) beamed from a far shelf boomerangs from reflecting prisms in the foreground and records the distance to the centimeter.

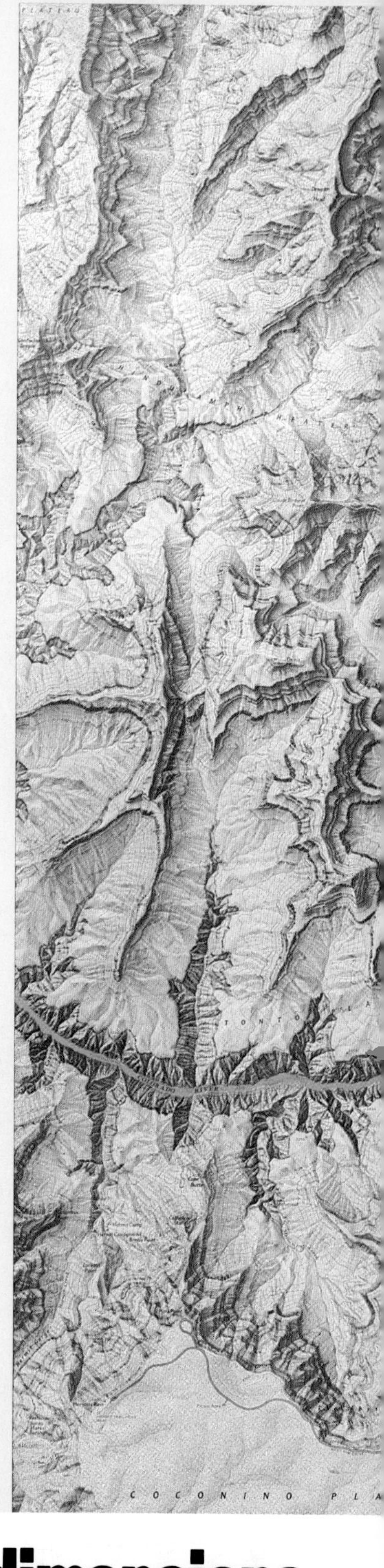

Mapping the exact dimensions

of the glorious chasm

BOTH BY U. S. ARMY AIR SERVICE

High-altitude aviator Army Lt. Albert Stevens (above) exhibits the equipment employed in setting a 1924 world's record. The GEOGRAPHIC *published his photograph (below) –*

remarkable for its day – of the city of Dayton, Ohio, from an altitude of more than six miles. Stevens, wearing the oxygen mask he used on the flight, crouches between the high-altitude camera and oxygen tank.

More than half a century later, as part of the July 1976 issue (inset) in celebration of the Bicentennial of the U. S., the magazine published a special supplement map, Portrait U.S.A. *(above), the first coast-to-coast satellite color-enhanced photomosaic of the 48 contiguous states. This unprecedented view of the country was made by Landsats 1 and 2, NASA satellites gathering earth-resource data on a global scale. They orbited 570 miles up, their images free of most of the distortion found in lower-altitude aerial photographs.*

To create Portrait U.S.A., *technicians screened more than 30,000 images taken during 3,500 orbits. They selected 569 of these to form a virtually cloudless panorama revealing details beyond the scope of conventional aerial photography. Before Landsat, producing comparable maps was costly, and the time required was such that they quickly went out of date.*

Instead of photographic cameras, the Landsats used an instrument called a multispectral scanner – MSS.

To see earth from far

PRODUCED BY THE NATIONAL GEOGRAPHIC SOCIETY FROM NASA LANDSAT IMAGERY WITH THE GENERAL ELECTRIC COMPANY BELTSVILLE PHOTOGRAPHIC ENGINEERING LABORATORY

An oscillating mirror scanned the earth and a telescope focused visible and near-infrared light waves reflected from the earth into the satellite's radiation detectors, which measured the light intensities of 1.1-acre picture elements in four different spectral bands. These values were converted into computer-digestible numbers and transmitted back to earth at the rate of 15 million units each second.

Ground stations received Landsat's stream of numbers, recorded them on magnetic tape for use by computers and then on film.

Sweeping Landsat views find a growing variety of uses: managing land and water resources, monitoring of crops and the environment, and aiding in the discovery of new energy and mineral sources. They help geologists, hydrologists, agriculturists, and planners to keep up with rapidly changing conditions on earth.

Apart from the technology that runs it and the practical uses it serves, Landsat has provided the clearest views ever of our home planet.

beyond the range of eagles

"Cleared to land," a Lockheed TriStar jet touches down at Palmdale, California. To make this image for a 1977 article on air safety, staff photographer Bruce Dale arranged to have a camera mounted on the airplane's tail fin so that the shutter could be tripped by remote control.

(Continued from page 21) members of the team that he had backed for the first American ascent of Everest and sent them to climb the new Mount Kennedy. Robert F. Kennedy accepted an invitation to join the ascent and was first to the 13,905-foot summit. MBG should have had another of his many GEOGRAPHIC exclusives, except that Robert Kennedy's film somehow reached *Life* magazine. With its shorter lead time, *Life* was out with the story within two weeks. Typically, MBG shrugged off the loss and published later, including a tribute written by Senator Kennedy. "We'll do it better," he said. And we did.

BRUCE DALE, NGS

As for the Cuba story—exactly 30 years later we published another article, this one not so hopeful, by Fred Ward. Fred, a frequent contributor, wrote the text and took every photograph, except for one of himself snapped during an interview with Cuba's leader. Following our standing policy, we properly credited that photograph—to Fidel Castro.

Perhaps because the GEOGRAPHIC has been a family institution in so many homes for generations, some longtime readers may feel uneasy at the thought that it is now somehow different. As Editor I'm often asked if the GEOGRAPHIC isn't changing. I certainly hope so. *(Continued on page 36)*

NASA

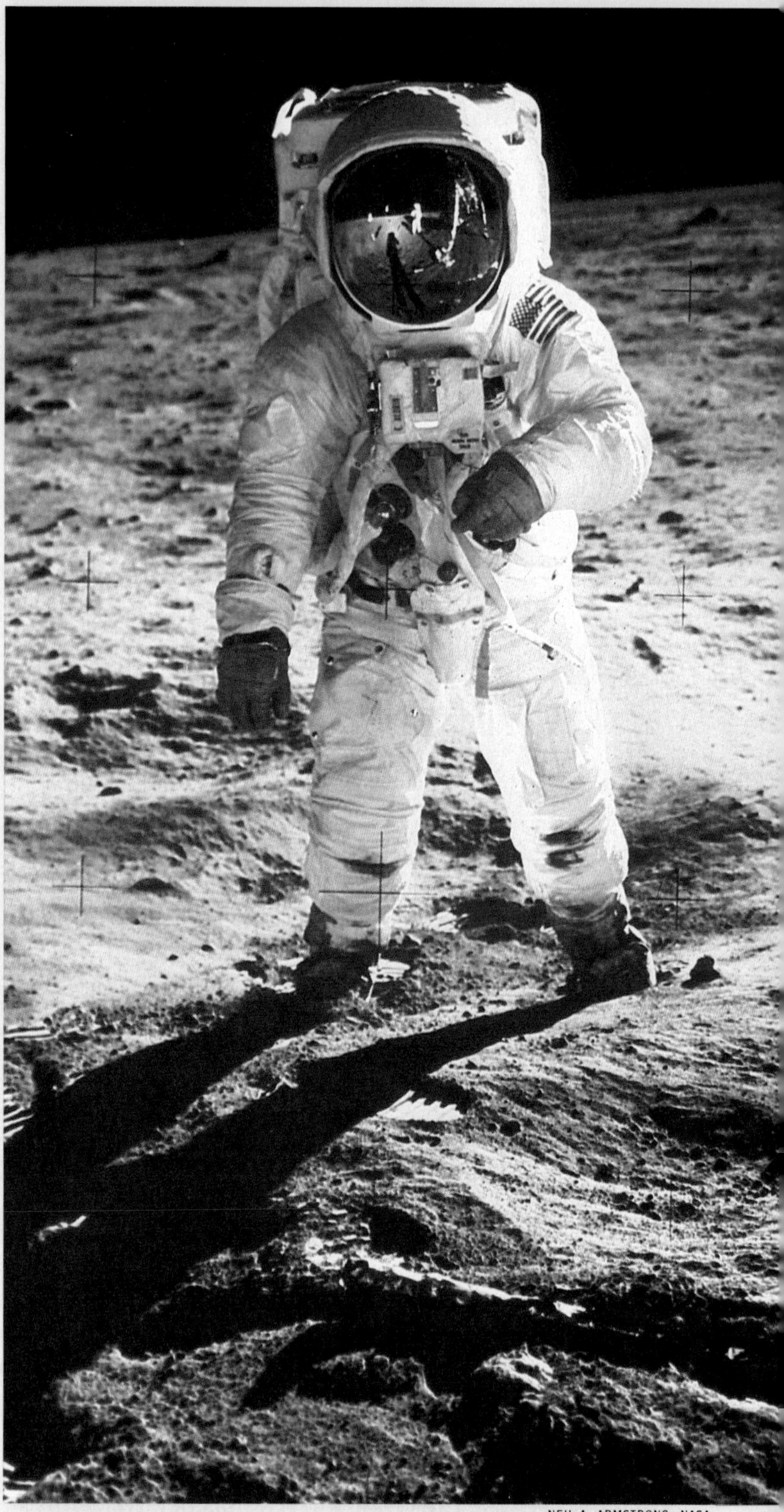

NEIL A. ARMSTRONG, NASA

With a roar of rockets, Apollo 11 (above) blasts off for the moon, July 16, 1969. Excess liquid oxygen vented at lift-off swirls about the tail.

Its five gigantic first-stage engines spewed a column of flame while generating the 7.6 million pounds of thrust necessary to boost the spacecraft from the launchpad at Kennedy Space Center.

The three-man crew carried with them the flag of the National Geographic Society on this, the first voyage to the

A record of man's first

BY EUGENE A. CERNAN, NASA

surface of the moon.

Safely down, astronaut Edwin Aldrin (left) strides across a small crater while he explores the lunar landscape. His visor reflects the U. S. flag planted by the first moon walkers, the white figure of fellow astronaut Neil Armstrong, a solar-wind collector, and their landing craft, the lunar module.

"A geologist's paradise," said Harrison Schmitt, first astronaut-geologist to examine lunar formations. The crew of the 1972 Apollo 17 mission discovered this giant boulder (above) nearly fifty feet across, while exploring the floor of the Taurus-Littrow Valley. Before being dislodged, probably by a meteorite, it had perched above on the high ridge called North Massif.

Schmitt was photographed while retrieving an indicator placed to show color, scale, and angle for photographs. The battery-powered lunar rover, loaded with television camera and scientific equipment, stands at right.

To get a comprehensive record on film, the astronauts were instructed to photograph overlapping sections of terrain (top) by standing in one spot and then rotating as they took a series of pictures with their chest-mounted cameras.

National Geographic technicians used darkroom processes to transform these separate NASA photographs into a nearly distortion-free composite of a broad swath of lunar landscape.

footfalls beyond mother earth

Covering a third of a century in space...

On a launchpad for photography, one of several remote platforms used by the GEOGRAPHIC, staff members prepare for a space shuttle lift-off in 1982. Illustrations editor Jon Schneeberger mounts the ladder as technicians Ted Johnson and Anthony Peritore adjust the sound-triggered camera under NASA escort. Such intense and continuing coverage has produced an extensive archive dating to the early days of manned spaceflight. Space activities have been well documented, as sample entries from this Index (right) attest.

SOYUZ-APOLLO MISSION:
- Apollo-Soyuz: Handclasp in Space. By Thomas Y. Canby. 183-187, Feb. 1976

SPACE COLONIES:
- The Next Frontier? By Isaac Asimov. Paintings by Pierre Mion. 76-89, July 1976

SPACE FLIGHTS AND RESEARCH:
- Awesome Views of the Forbidding Moonscape. 233-239, Feb. 1969
- Behold the Computer Revolution. By Peter T. White. Photos by Bruce Dale and Emory Kristof. 593-633, Nov. 1970
- I Fly the X-15. By Joseph A. Walker. Photos by Dean Conger. 428-450, Sept. 1962
- The Long, Lonely Leap. By Joseph W. Kittinger, Jr. Photos by Volkmar Wentzel. 854-873, Dec. 1960

◆ *Man's Conquest of Space.* Announced. 844-849, June 1968
● Satellites That Serve Us. By Thomas Y. Canby. Included: A portfolio: Images of Earth. 281-335, Sept. 1983
Spacelab 1: *Columbia.* By Michael E. Long. 301-307
● The Sun. By Herbert Friedman. Included: U. S. Naval Research Laboratory studies. 713-743, Nov. 1965
● We Saw the World From the Edge of Space. By Malcolm D. Ross. Ground photos by Walter Meayers Edwards. 671-685, Nov. 1961
● *See also* Apollo Missions; Gemini Missions; Mariner Missions; Mercury Missions; Pioneer Probes; Ranger Spacecraft; Rockets; Satellites; Skylab Missions; Space Shuttles; Spacelab; Surveyor Spacecraft; Viking Spacecraft Missions; Voyager

SPACE MEDICINE:
● Aviation Medicine on the Threshold of Space. By Allan C. Fisher, Jr. Photos by Luis Marden. 241-278, Aug. 1955
● The Flight of *Freedom 7.* By Carmault B. Jackson, Jr. 416-431, Sept. 1961
● The Making of an Astronaut. By Robert R. Gilruth. 122-144, Jan. 1965
● School for Space Monkeys. 725-729, May 1961
● Skylab, Outpost on the Frontier of Space. By Thomas Y. Canby. Photos by the nine mission astronauts. 441-469, Oct. 1974
● Spacelab 1: *Columbia.* By Michael E. Long. 301-307, Sept. 1983
● We Saw the World From the Edge of Space. By Malcolm D. Ross. Ground photos by Walter Meayers Edwards. 671-685, Nov. 1961
● *See also* Biorhythm Research; Tektite II

SPACE PIONEERS of NASA Journey Into Tomorrow. By Allan C. Fisher, Jr. Photos by Dean Conger. 48-89, July 1960

SPACE RENDEZVOUS, Milestone on the Way to the Moon. By Kenneth F. Weaver. 539-553, Apr. 1966

SPACE SATELLITES. *See* Satellites

SPACE SHUTTLES:
● *Columbia's* Astronauts' Own Story: Our Phenomenal First Flight. By John W. Young and Robert L. Crippen. Paintings by Ken Dallison. 478-503, Oct. 1981
● *Columbia's* Landing Closes a Circle. By Tom Wolfe. 474-477, Oct. 1981
● Heat Paints *Columbia's* Portrait. By Cliff Tarpy. 650-653, Nov. 1982
● Satellites That Serve Us. By Thomas Y. Canby. Included: A portfolio: Images of Earth. 281-335, Sept. 1983
Spacelab 1: *Columbia.* By Michael E. Long. 301-307
● When the Space Shuttle Finally Flies. By Rick Gore. Photos by Jon Schneeberger. Paintings by Ken Dallison. Note: The space shuttle *Columbia* will be joined in the future by *Challenger, Discovery,* and *Atlantis.* 317-347, Mar. 1981

SPACE STATIONS:
● The Next Frontier? By Isaac Asimov. Paintings by Pierre Mion. 76-89, July 1976
● Solar Energy, the Ultimate Powerhouse. By John L. Wilhelm. Photos by Emory Kristof. 381-397, Mar. 1976
● *See also* Skylab Missions

SPACE WALK:
● America's 6,000-mile Walk in Space. 440-447, Sept. 1965

SPACECRAFT:
● Of Air and Space (National Air and Space Museum). By Michael Collins. 819-837, June 1978
Picture portfolio by Nathan Benn, Robert S. Oakes, and Joseph D. Lavenburg, with text by Michael E. Long. 825-837
● *See also* Apollo Missions; Gemini Missions; Mariner Missions; Mercury Missions; Pioneer Probes; Ranger Spacecraft; Skylab Missions; Space Shuttles; Spacelab; Surveyor Spacecraft; Viking Spacecraft Missions; Voyager; *and* Satellites: DODGE Satellite; Nimbus I (Extraordinary); Telstar; *Tiros I*

SPACELAB:
● Spacelab 1: *Columbia.* By Michael E. Long. 301-307, Sept. 1983
● When the Space Shuttle Finally Flies. By Rick Gore. Photos by Jon Schneeberger. Paintings by Ken Dallison. Note: Spacelab is a European-built laboratory for use aboard the space shuttle. 317-347, Mar. 1981

W. ALLAN ROYCE, NGS

It may have been the most astonishing view of the solar system since Galileo first saw the moons of Jupiter. The Voyager 1 spacecraft had detected on Io (right), closest large moon to Jupiter, a volcano spewing sulfur some 280 kilometers—175 miles—high. Later analysis showed the fiery satellite, torn by gravity, to be the most volcanically active object in the solar system, thereby putting earth in second place.

On their flights to the outer planets, the two Voyagers sent back immense streams of data and mind-bending views, such as a close-up of Saturn (facing page).

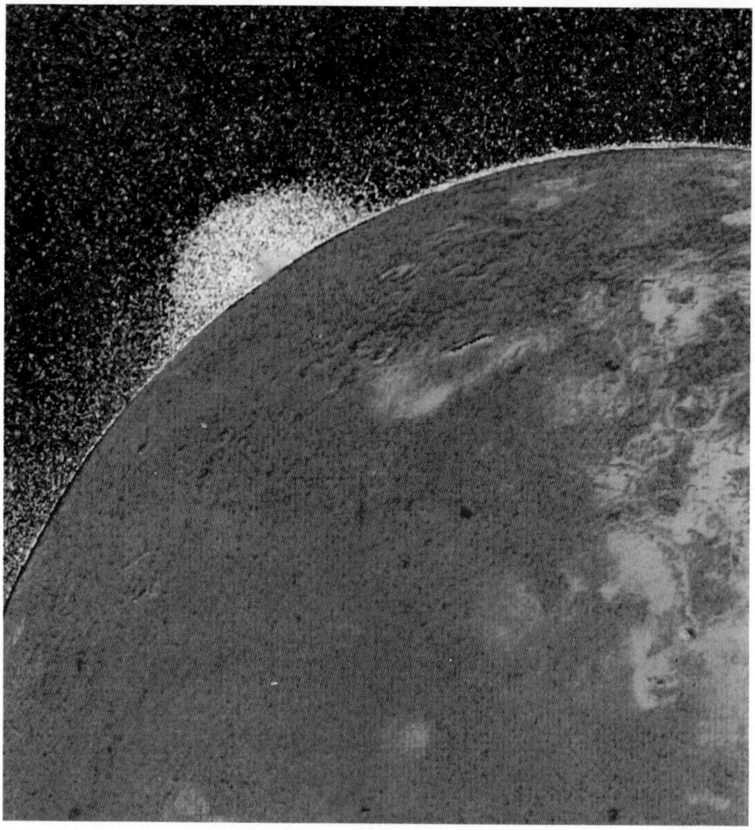

BOTH BY NASA

(Continued from page 31) As the world and all living things change, so do we. There's a saying that when the apple is through ripening, it starts rotting. We're still ripening.

Readers will have noticed that words like threatened, polluted, imperiled, and endangered began appearing in our titles with regularity under Editor Frederick G. Vosburgh (1967-70) and increased during the ten-year editorship of Gilbert M. Grosvenor (1970-80), now Society President.

The state of the natural world became headline news in the '60s and '70s, but it had long been a concern of the GEOGRAPHIC. The times had caught up to us as much as we had caught up to the times. We reported on chemical pollution, acid rain, pesticides, nuclear power, oil spills, and other environmental issues calmly and as accurately as we could. To the extent that all of us recognize those threats, improvement is more likely. We remember that as recently as the 1950s nuclear bombs were being tested in Nevada with troops present. Agent Orange hadn't been invented, and DDT was still a hero in the war against insect pests.

Changing content aside, a certain amount of misunderstanding surrounds the GEOGRAPHIC. The masthead page on the inside front cover refers to it as both a magazine and a journal. Many readers don't realize that they are not merely

Recent GEOGRAPHIC articles have undertaken explanations of the "hard" sciences—how, for instance, three-dimensional mapping by computer-assisted imaging (below) can aid in custom forming artificial limbs or in detecting spinal deformation.

How did life evolve on infant earth? About four billion years ago sunlight, storms, and volcanic eruptions (right) may have fused simple molecules into complex ones at the sea's margins. Development may have gone from primitive proteins to self-replicating DNA to life.

Physicists believe our universe (its history shown diagrammatically below) began about 15 billion years

COMPUTER IMAGING BY BIOSTEREOMETRICS LABORATORY, TEXAS INSTITUTE FOR REHABILITATION AND RESEARCH

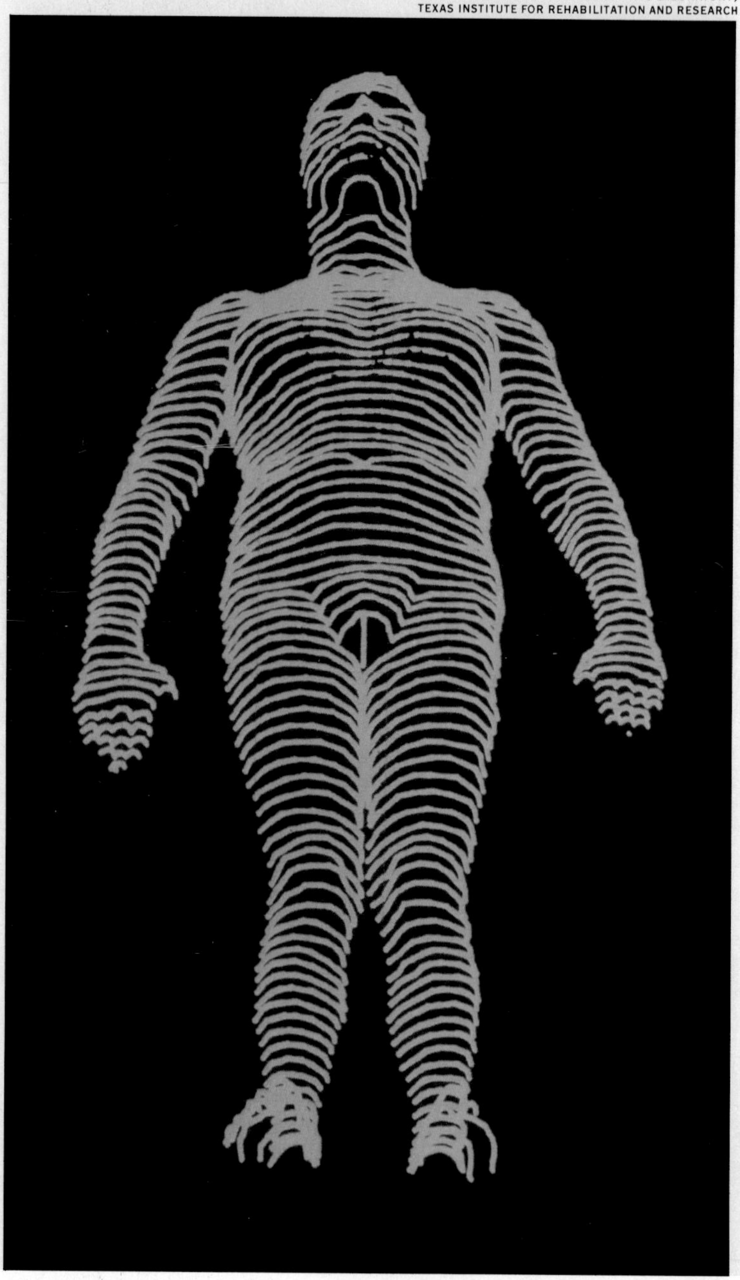

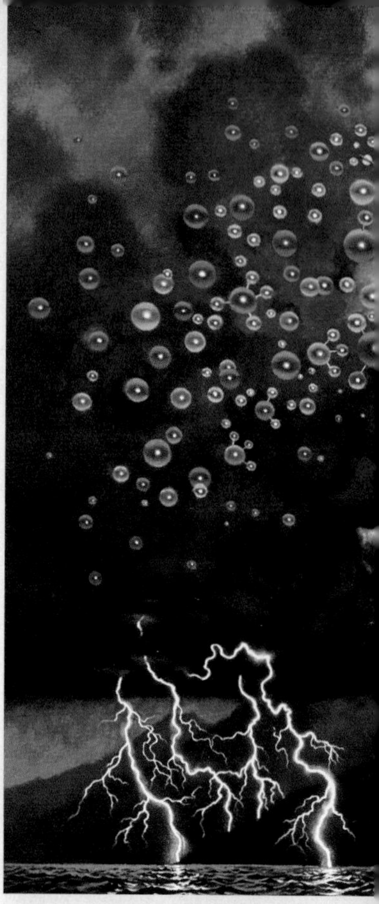

Journeys into life, space,

PAINTING BY DAVIS MELTZER

ago in a big bang that created space and time, matter and energy. Telltale radiation from that blast pervades all space in every direction of the still expanding universe.

PAINTING BY BARRON STOREY

time, and the universe within

subscribers but members of the National Geographic Society and that the magazine is its journal.

Since it is not sold on U. S. newsstands, some may have forgotten that the old yellow-bordered magazine still exists. Those who do know it are the most loyal of readers. The renewal rate among those who have been Society members for three years or more exceeds 90 percent. For those who have been members 20 years the rate is 95 percent, and for 30-year-and-above members the rate is 96 percent. (To follow this curve to an illogical conclusion: If you're a member long enough, you'll live forever!)

Because the price is so reasonable for 12 quality magazines and six map supplements a year, some people think we are a subsidized government publication. Not so; the Society is a wholly private, nonprofit educational organization largely dependent on the annual dues of members. There are no shareholders and no dividends. No Society editor or officer receives a bonus or a stock option. As one former editor said when nearing retirement, *(Continued on page 46)*

THOMAS J. ABERCROMBIE, NGS

Broaching the surface, Jacques Piccard and Lt. Don Walsh, USN, salute success in 1960 (above). They had taken the bathyscaphe Trieste *down nearly seven miles to the bottom of the Mariana Trench, deepest known oceanic abyss.*

"A submarine that you wear," called WASP (below), encases diver Doug Osborne in 1983 as he probes the wreck of the British ship Breadalbane, *lost to the Arctic Ocean in 1853.*

EMORY KRISTOF, NGS

Joining Capt. Jacques-Yves Cousteau aboard his research vessel Calypso *(1) in 1955,* GEOGRAPHIC *staff member Luis Marden, at right, spent four months in the Indian Ocean and Red Sea making the first extensive series of color pictures ever taken of that undersea world.*

Sunken treasure of ancient wine jars (2) lured a Calypso *crewman to the remains of a Greek ship wrecked in the Mediterranean Sea more than 2,000 years ago. Scientists and scholars hailed the 1952 project as the first important underwater excavation. The Society collaborated with Cousteau in many of his major projects of the period.*

Remains of the Bounty *(3) emerge in 1957 after 167 years on the seafloor. Luis Marden discovered the spot in the turbulent waters off Pitcairn Island where the famous mutineers burned the vessel to prevent detection by Britain's Royal Navy.*

Off the coast of Cyprus in 1967 (4) nautical archaeologists, aided by Society funds, surveyed, inventoried, and ultimately raised an even older wreck—a small Greek merchant ship dating from the fourth century B.C.

1 PIERRE GOUPIL

2 JACQUES ERTAUD

3 THOMAS CHRISTIAN

The sea: a preserver

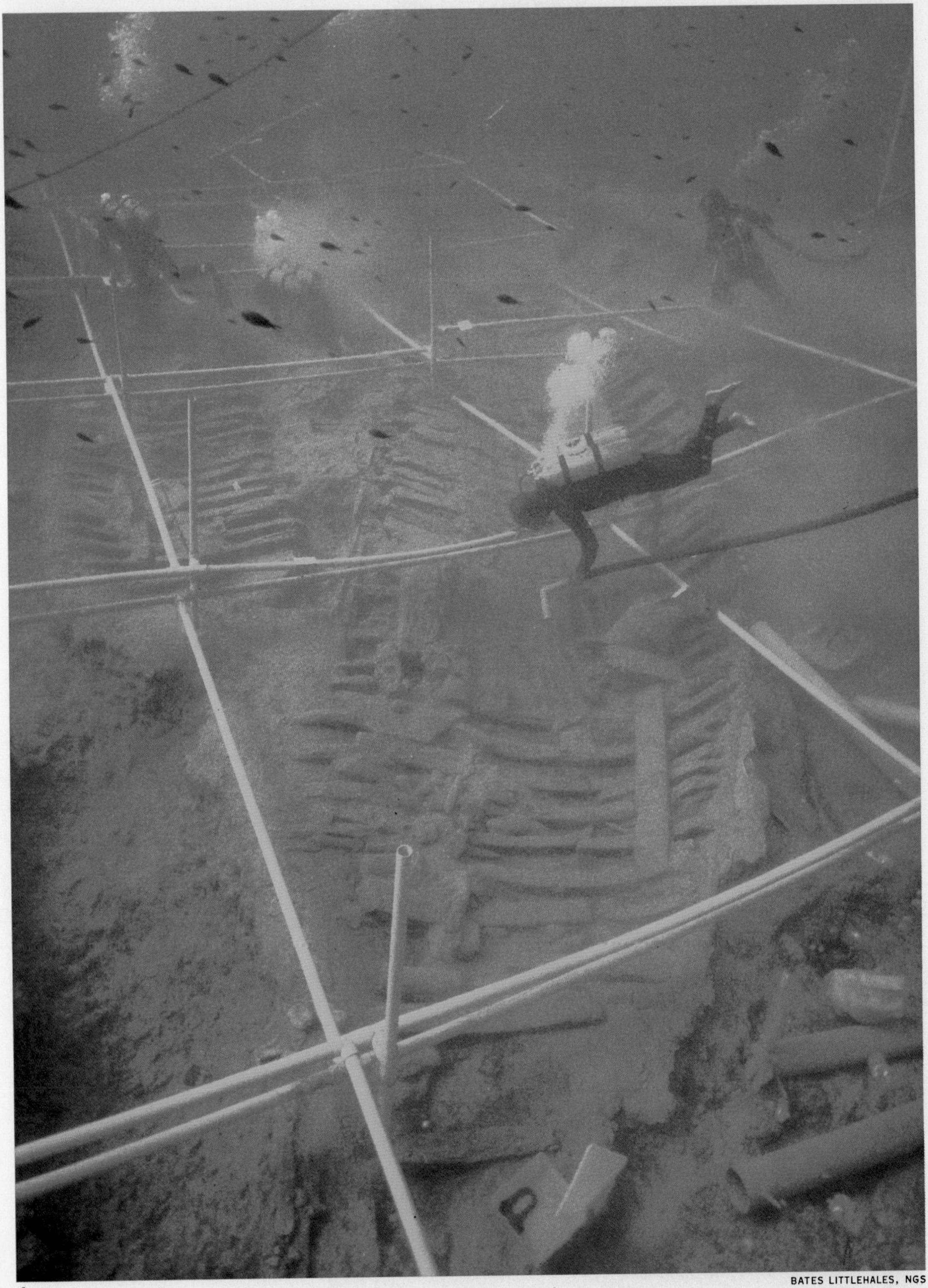

4

BATES LITTLEHALES, NGS

# of our sunken past...

1

DAVID KNUDSEN

PAINTING BY ELSE BOSTELMANN

2
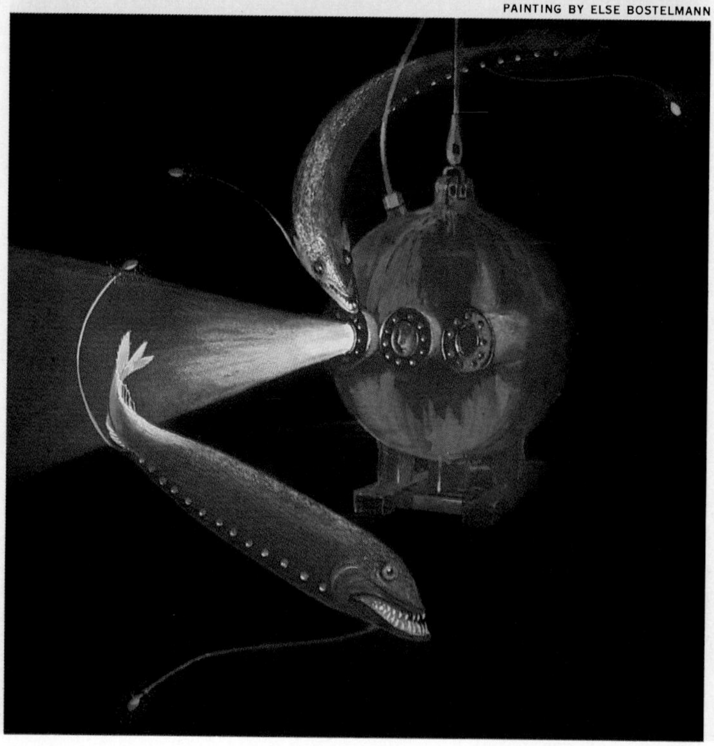

Oceanographic naturalist William Beebe (1) *emerged headfirst from the bathysphere diving chamber that in 1934 carried him to a record depth of 3,028 feet on a Society-supported descent off Bermuda.*

Oddities of the deep never before seen swam into Beebe's view. At 2,000 feet he sighted six-foot-long creatures (2) *that were later given the whimsical designation* Bathysphaera intacta, *or "untouchable bathysphere fish."*

To photograph a hogfish (3) *and other Florida reef life before the development of reliable underwater lighting, it was necessary to fire blinding explosions of flash powder above the water. The* GEOGRAPHIC *published this and other natural-color photographs in 1927—the first ever made beneath the sea.*

Inventor of the high-speed flash, Harold E. Edgerton (4) *used a swimming pool in 1959 to test one of his many*

3

W. H. LONGLEY AND CHARLES MARTIN, NGS

creations, a stroboscopic deep-sea camera. Eventually the camera dangled at the end of a seven-mile-long cable to give GEOGRAPHIC *readers a glimpse of the bottom of the 36,000-foot-deep Mariana Trench.*

In manned submersibles such as the Alvin (5), *a series of expeditions has studied seafloor rifts and spreading*

...and a dark window

4

B. ANTHONY STEWART, NGS

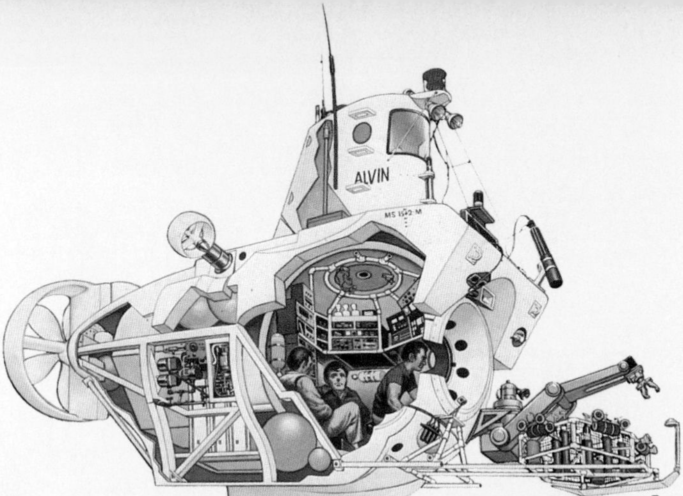

PAINTING BY DAVIS MELTZER **5**

centers. Scientists (6) aboard found hydrothermal vents gushing nutrient-rich minerals to support a teeming animal kingdom ranging from primitive bacteria to colonies of crabs. Huge blood red worms (7) protruded from forests of white plasticlike sheaths.

By major research grants, by providing cameras, film, and photographic expertise, and by operating color laboratories aboard surface ships, the Society has greatly extended scientists' ability to see and record phenomena in the sunless abyss.

Yet the sea remains earth's least explored frontier, perhaps less well documented than the surface of Mars. In coming decades as the land's resources become more depleted, the sea's importance can only increase.

7

6

EMORY KRISTOF, NGS (ABOVE AND LEFT)

on unsuspected life

(Continued from page 40) "When I leave here, I'll take nothing, not even my desk."

The GEOGRAPHIC's reasonable price comes both from the Society's nonprofit status and from the fact that our large circulation permits efficiencies that keep the unit cost down.

One member even suggested that we raise the dues because he feared we might go out of business. Not likely. With a circulation of 10.6 million we are America's third largest magazine and reach 160 of the world's 169 nations. We will enter our 97th year during 1984, and we've never been healthier.

Why has this enterprise been so successful? I believe it is primarily because we still fill the same need felt by that small group of thoughtful men who gave us our start almost a century ago—a need to address the insatiable human curiosity to know what makes this world tick.

And over the decades editors have resisted the temptation to be trendy. The magazine has kept the same size and the

ROBERT W. MADDEN, NGS

CLAUDE E. PETRONE, NGS

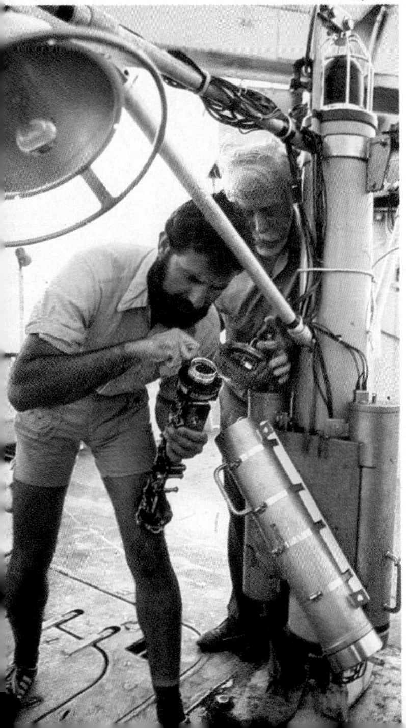

"The perfect wave" may be a surfer's dream, but the perfect, or nearly so, photograph of a surfer is possible—given imagination, technology, and patience. Bobbing under a wave, photographer Bill McCausland caught a surfer "shooting the tube" off Sydney, Australia (above). He protected his camera—while still being able to change focus and exposures—in a flexible watertight jacket developed by Luther Dillon (right) and others in the Society's custom equipment shop.

To probe depths where pressures can exceed 5,000 pounds per square inch, photographer Emory Kristof (left, at left) collaborates with Society photo-engineer Al Chandler, who designs mechanical assemblies and some of the electronics of the huge undersea camera packages.

ROBERT W. MADDEN, NGS

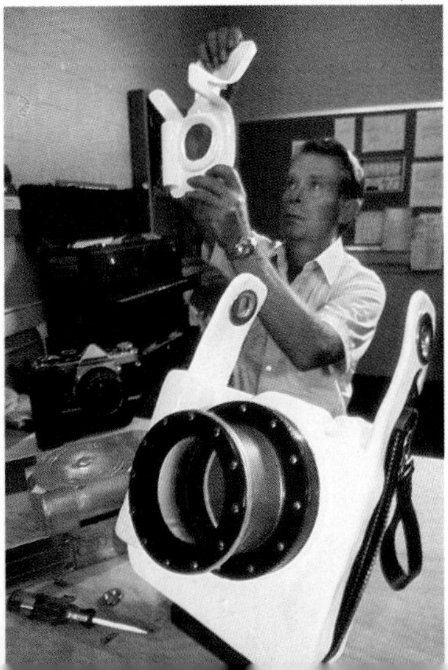

Escorted by a squadron of pilot fish, a whale shark as big as a bus cruises the waters off Baja California. Coasting in for a closer view, Eugenie Clark, at right, found the

DAVID DOUBILET

docile plankton feeder to be both female and pregnant. A leading researcher on sharks and other marine life, marine biologist Clark has reported notable findings in the GEOGRAPHIC.

same reputation for objectivity and accuracy demanded by the young Society's second President and leading benefactor, Alexander Graham Bell, and perpetuated by his son-in-law Gilbert Hovey Grosvenor—Editor for 55 years.

One of the more astute of young Grosvenor's decisions, when the magazine was still struggling, was to ignore the advice of the very successful New York City publisher S. S. McClure. McClure suggested giving up the idea of membership and changing the magazine's name, because people hate geography. He said the magazine's future could be assured only by relying on advertising revenue and newsstand sales, and by moving from Washington, D. C., to New York. Most of the major magazines that have folded since then—including long-gone *McClure's*—were published there. Most of the successful new ones have been launched elsewhere.

When the printing of color photographs became possible

RICK WEYERHAEUSER

Stained by vulture droppings, African elephants slaughtered in the aftermath of Idi Amin's overthrow rot in Uganda (right). War, poaching, farming, and exploding human populations have ravaged elephant herds.

Caged in a Bangkok market, an endangered leopard cat (opposite) snarls futilely. Illegal wildlife trade respects no animals, however rare.

GEOGRAPHIC coverage on such indiscriminate destruction of our natural heritage has helped institute remedial action.

early in this century, Editor Grosvenor quickly developed the distinctive look and outlook of the GEOGRAPHIC, which, despite all the changes since, still remains a guiding template. With the magazine's heritage of excellence, none of us can help but be intimidated by the responsibility of building on that tradition.

Yet if you'll permit a small arrogance, I feel that over the years the staff has taken that format and polished the style to the point that we can offer our readers a truer perception, a deeper understanding, a greater appreciation of this magnificent world than they could find in any other magazine.

I say this with no objectivity—but with the conviction that I work with the finest, most dedicated photographers, writers, editors, researchers, cartographers, artists, and

STEVE RAYMER, NGS

A breeding herd of African elephants finds drink and sanctuary at Agab water hole in Namibia's Etosha National Park. This semi-arid reserve can just accommodate its

DES AND JEN BARTLETT

present wildlife. For now, the animals are little disturbed by the press of human demands or the political contest for control of Namibia. For now, Etosha is a kind of ark.

Destroying its own summit, Mount St. Helens erupts in 1980 (opposite). Such earth-shattering volcanism, now dreaded for its killing power, was responsible for creating earth's early atmosphere some 4 billion years ago.

designers, and with engravers and printers who produce the magazine on superb presses using quality paper and inks.

A great deal of care is taken with all of this, sometimes with unexpected results. Soon after the crew of Apollo 11 returned from the first moon landing, staff member Lou Mazzatenta, wanting to be absolutely correct in our color reproduction of the lunar landscape, sent prints to astronaut Neil Armstrong for comment. One day Lou's telephone rang. On the other end was Neil Armstrong, perhaps the most celebrated human being in the world at that time. He hesitated for a moment, then he said, "Shucks, you folks at the GEOGRAPHIC know more about this stuff than I do."

If there is a rule we live by editorially, it is: Be There. Good intentions and armchair objectivity cannot make a story or a photograph. Only direct involvement on the scene can accomplish that, whether in the malarial forests of Central America, the rubble-strewn streets of Beirut, or the clean upland meadows of the Rockies.

We were there in 1960 when Lt. Don Walsh, USN, and Jacques Piccard rode a two-man submersible to the deepest ocean floor. In 1935 we sponsored as well as reported the highest balloon flight. We reported Sir Edmund Hillary's pioneer climb of Everest and then sponsored the American expedition in 1963. NATIONAL GEOGRAPHIC photographer Barry Bishop—now a Ph.D. in geography and a vice chairman of our Committee for Research and Exploration—was one of six to reach the summit. He came back with the pictures but lost all ten toes to frostbite.

Working in the field is often lonely, hard, dirty, and frustrating. And "being there" involves risk. In 1958 Assistant Editor George Long was aboard a seaplane that vanished en route to the Madeira Islands.

While Jim Amos was photographing the Great Salt Lake, his helicopter crashed, killing the pilot and severely injuring Jim. Just six weeks later, his first day out of the hospital and on crutches, he rented another aircraft, and finished the job.

Emory Kristof took a piece of shrapnel in his eye while photographing in Vietnam. He recovered with remarkably little loss of vision. Free lance Dickey Chapelle did not

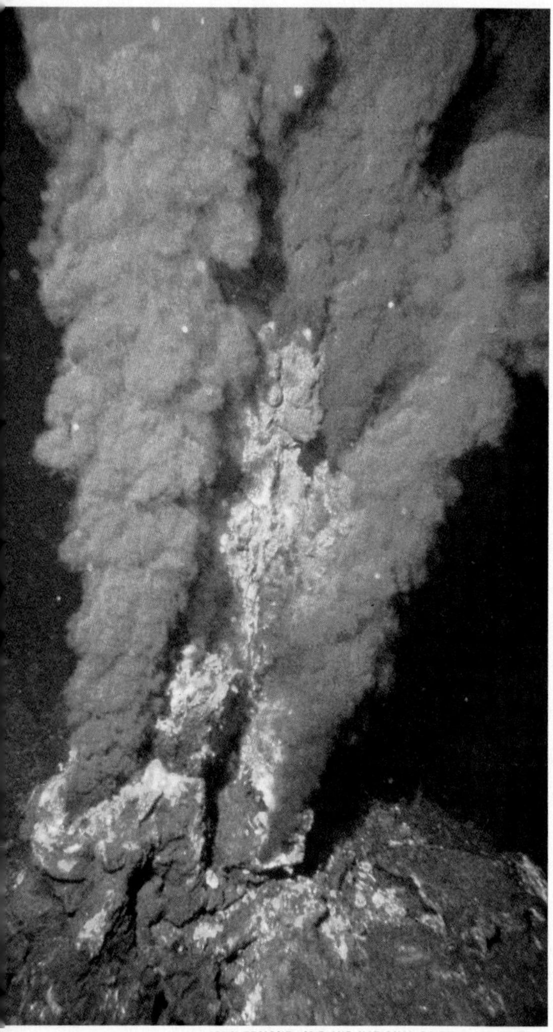

JOHN EDMOND, MIT AND NATIONAL SCIENCE FOUNDATION

Undersea "black smokers," disgorging minerals from hydrothermal vents on the East Pacific Rise, support bacteria, perhaps similar to earth's first organisms, thought to have developed in the sea, protected from then lethal sunlight.

ROGER WERTH, WOODFIN CAMP & ASSOCIATES

recover. Her final story for the GEOGRAPHIC—her second on Vietnam—was published posthumously. She was killed by a booby trap while on patrol with U. S. Marines.

Some of the danger in being there is not at first obvious. Jim Stanfield is legendary for his tenacity in making just the right photograph. He was working 8,000 feet underground in a South African gold mine, and things were not going well. The drenching humidity in the almost unbearable heat kept firing his strobe lights randomly.

Jim was down there seven arduous hours before he could solve his technical problems, in the meantime losing three cameras to spray from water-cooled drills. Jammed into a

BOTH BY MICHAEL LAWTON

three-foot-high space, he finally got the image he wanted. Two weeks later, a fire in a nearby mine killed 26 miners and hospitalized dozens.

Most of the risks of being there are more routine, but the presence of cameras attracts special attention that can be annoying and worse. While being jostled in a sea of Hindus pitching and surging in the darkness and nearly hysterical with excitement for fire-walking ceremonies in Rangoon, Burma, I felt the strap on my spare camera go slack on my shoulder. I whirled just in time to grab it back from the man who had neatly sliced the strap with a razor.

Later that same night, while I was photographing people

Mount St. Helens was the centerpiece of a national forest (top). Four months later, its top blown away, it gaped above a naked landscape where 26 lakes and 150 miles of fishing streams had been destroyed. The GEOGRAPHIC (opposite) covered the story before, during, and after the eruption.

J. SCOTT APPLEWHITE, MIAMI HERALD

All the power and fury of earth's weather explodes across the pages of the GEOGRAPHIC. *Palms (left) bent to the force of 1979's Hurricane David as it passed offshore of Miami Beach, having already devastated islands in the Caribbean.*

A tornado funnel (above) roars across an Oklahoma wheat field, its vortex darkened by churning debris. Hundreds of such twisters tear across the Great Plains yearly. An avalanche (right) bursts over Juneau, Alaska, in 1972. Taking its chances with the effects of such slides, the state's capital has permitted expansion into potential avalanche pathways.

When the earth sighs, we call

WAYNE C. CARLSON

JONATHAN GRAY

it disaster and take cover

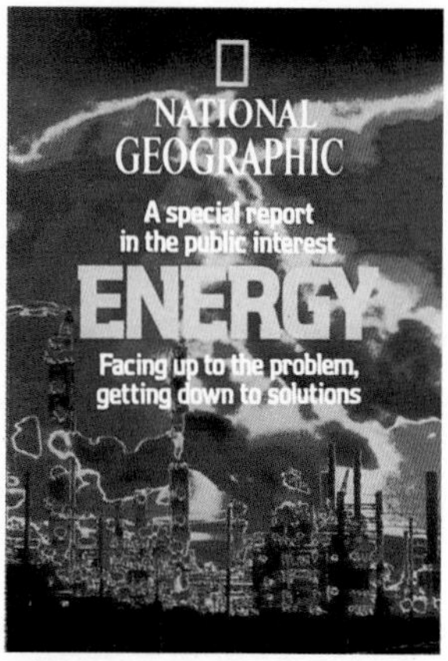

walking calmly across a pit of glowing coals, my wife, Lucille, was being molested from behind by one of the mob as she held a remote electronic flash on the opposite side of the fire pit from me. Rather than risk our losing the pictures, she held her ground with one foot while with the other she kicked backward into the dark like a Missouri mule. We got the pictures, and she thinks she got her man.

It is not always necessary to take such forceful action. On one of his many assignments to the Middle East, Tom Abercrombie, with his wife, Lynn, met a Bedouin so taken with her beauty that he wanted to buy her as a bride. He

offered six camels—all he had. Tom, not wanting to offend his host—or Lynn—replied tactfully, "Not enough camels."

In 1969 members of a Beirut mob attacked George Mobley. Less conspicuous without a camera, his teammate, writer Bill Ellis, tucked himself into the crowd shouting, "Get the photographer!" as George fled over fences and rooftops.

On the other hand, having cameras sometimes can get you out of trouble. While working in Laos during the 1973 fighting, John Everingham and I encountered a Communist patrol along a jungle trail.

Two days later—after a lot of *(Continued on page 66)*

Broken-backed and gushing crude oil,* Amoco Cadiz *foundered off the coast of Brittany in March 1978, in an era when the world tried to combat pollution while coping with oil shortages. The outlook for energy resources and technologies was reported in a special 115-page supplement to* NATIONAL GEOGRAPHIC *in 1981 (opposite).

MARTIN ROGERS

The year before the GEOGRAPHIC'S 1970 special feature on "Our Ecological Crisis" (below), Ohio's Cuyahoga River (1) *had become so polluted with oil and debris that it caught fire. This six-mile stretch in*

Cleveland was choked with industrial, municipal, and agricultural wastes. Today at the same location (2)*, people are returning to the river's banks to fish its waters, one result of a national commitment to clean up major waterways.*

The whole job is far from done, however. In an Adirondack stream (3) *brook trout confined in a wire cage succumb to asphyxiation, their water polluted by rain- and snow-borne sulfuric and nitric acids. Acid rain has eliminated fish in hundreds of lakes in the U. S. and Canada and thousands in Scandinavia, while causing international disputes as to causes and indemnification.*

Swedes pump lime (4) *into a lake to neutralize acidity and permit restocking of fish. By 1985 Sweden expects to spend 40 million dollars yearly on the program.*

1

2

TED SPIEGEL, BLACK STAR

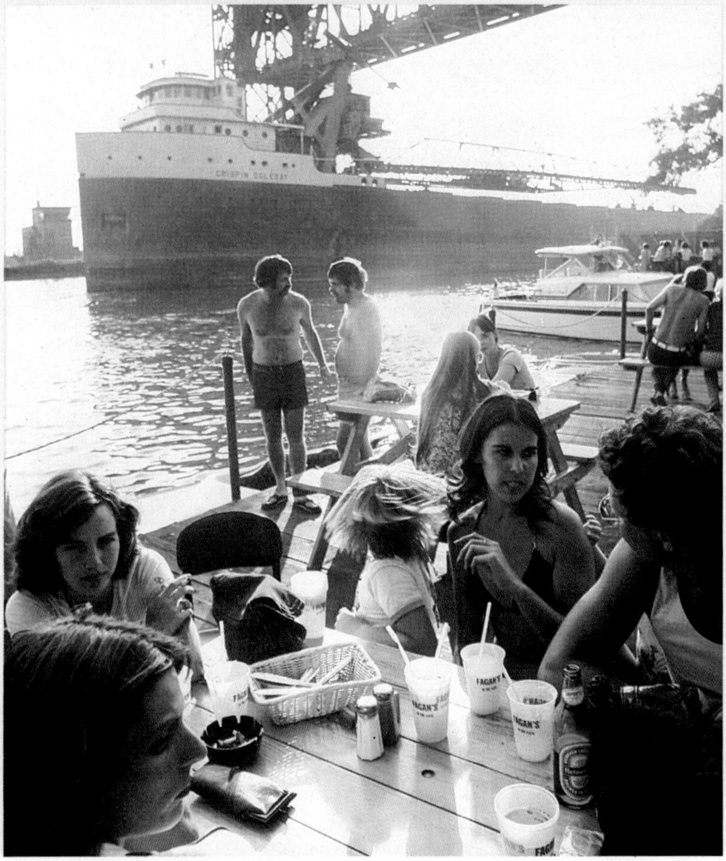

Pollution: disasters, successes,

JAMES P. BLAIR, NGS

3

TED SPIEGEL, BLACK STAR (ABOVE AND BELOW)

4

and unanswered questions

Sentry to a monument he cannot truly guard, a Kampuchean militiaman stands before Angkor Wat—national symbol of Cambodia, stone likeness of the Hindu universe, and 12th-century centerpiece of the great complex of Angkor with its 72 major monuments built by the Khmer civilization.

War has surged across Angkor, but neglect more than bullets threatens its survival. Editor Bill Garrett, writer Peter White, and photographer Dave Harvey have been among the very few Western journalists to visit the site in recent years and document the destruction.

Despite the lethal political stalemate in Kampuchea, Editor Garrett felt that some start should be made to save Angkor. He and designer Connie Phelps mounted an extensive photographic exhibit that was first displayed at the United Nations in New York City and later in the Society's Washington, D. C., museum, Explorers Hall, where it opened with traditional dances by former members of the Cambodian Royal Ballet, now expatriates (right). A Paris showing began a tour of European and Asian cities.

The hope: When the spectacular glories of Angkor are shown widely, more sentiment will build for an international effort to maintain the temples before the jungle tears them apart with probing roots, branches, and vines.

WILBUR E. GARRETT, NGS

JOSEPH H. BAILEY, NGS

(*Continued from page 61*) questioning—we were released. I believe the cameras helped convince them that we really were correspondents and not downed American pilots trying to escape. After he let us go, the officer in charge ran after us down to the Mekong River bank and asked if I'd like to photograph the prettiest girl in the village before we left. Though fearful of a trick, I couldn't resist. She was pretty and, I suspect, was the officer's girlfriend. Before leaving, I was also allowed to photograph the rest of the village, including guerrillas building a school. Later I sent prints of the prettiest girl to her admirer through diplomatic channels.

EVERY GEOGRAPHIC photographer and writer has a long evening's worth of such stories to tell. By no means do all make it into the magazine.

"If only we had the room"—that is the writer's constant complaint. The job of tackling big subjects in small spaces is a constant challenge. Photography and other illustration take up about three-fourths of each magazine. Often text, whether on the universe or, for that matter, on Delaware, cannot easily fit with clarity and grace in the available space. Sometimes I think the GEOGRAPHIC writer is like a second son in an Old World family. No matter how good the writing may be, the bulk of the space will go to the photographer.

The photography *is* superb, and the design and printing of the magazine give it a gallery showcase. In the past 15 years the GEOGRAPHIC has seven times won "Best Use of Photographs by a Magazine," and ten times its photographers have been named "Magazine Photographer of the Year."

Yet the writing is equally outstanding. Your letters, scores of national awards, and international recognition speak to our writers' skills. For some, writing is more than a daily job. In 1983 Associate Editor Joseph Judge was invited to read his *Plain Spoken Poems of Alaska* at the United Arts Club of Dublin during the James Joyce festival in Ireland's capital—a great honor. The club later published them. Long one of our most valuable free-lance contributors and now a Senior Assistant Editor, Charles McCarry—best known for *The Tears of Autumn*—has seen three of his novels selected by the Book of the Month Club.

Obviously staff members are not the only contributors to follow the "be there" philosophy. Many of the magazine's best stories have been ones (*Continued on page 74*)

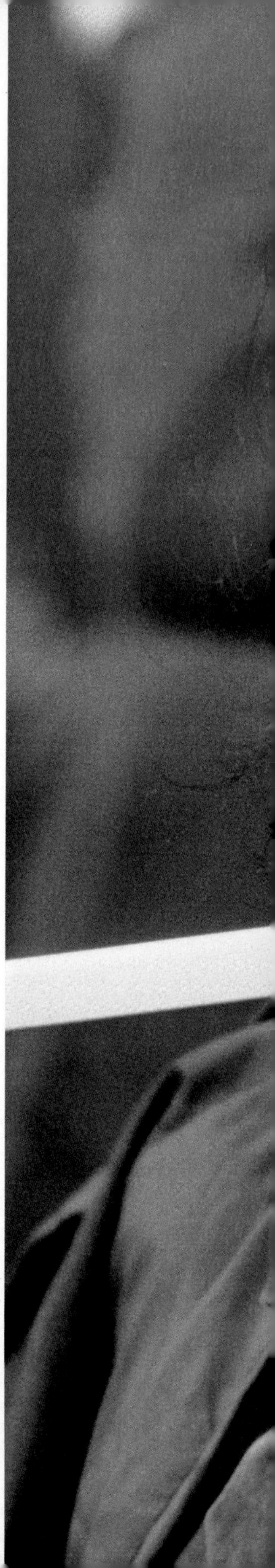

WILLIAM ALBERT ALLARD

She might have become a seamstress in Hong Kong, but 20-year-old Lau Ying Siu was caught and fettered as an illegal alien and returned to China. Refugees still stream across many borders, motivated by despair, or by hope.

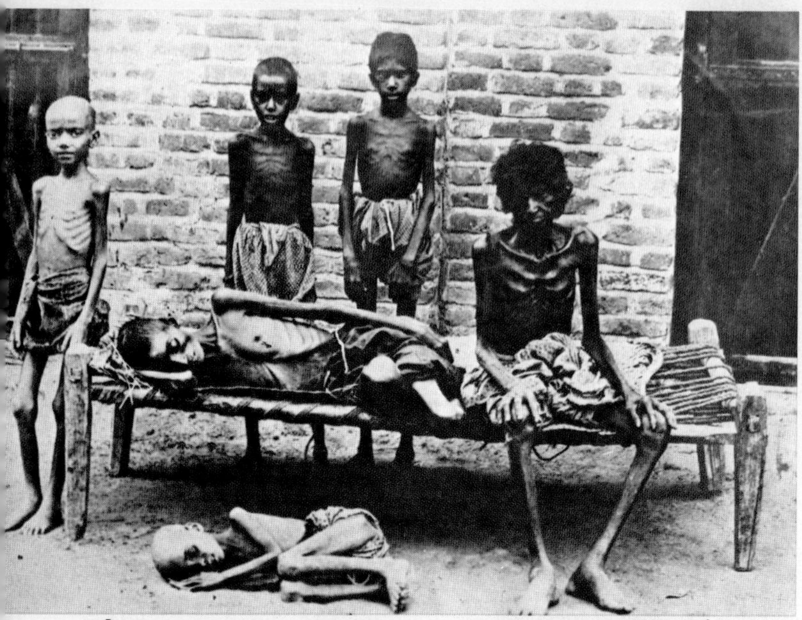

1

UNDERWOOD & UNDERWOOD

When war and natural disaster have inflicted human tragedy, the magazine has reported the stark facts in words and telling photographs.

The ravages of famine on an Indian family were documented in a 1917 issue **(1)**. *The article estimated that some three hundred million people faced starvation worldwide.*

In Namibia, where guerrillas and South Africa fought for control, a boy **(2)** *who had lost both arms while playing with a live grenade was fitted with prosthetic limbs.*

Severe malnutrition eventually killed this African infant **(3)**. *In 1980 he was one of more than a million refugees crowding camps in Somalia, a nation doubly beset by drought and border war.*

Another young victim of war **(4)** *clung to his sister as a nurse dressed foot and head wounds at a hospital in South Vietnam. The child was hit by shrapnel as U. S. Marines and Vietcong battled for Da Nang.*

A Bengali girl **(5)** *waited for relief food during a famine that ravaged Bangladesh in*

2

JIM BRANDENBURG

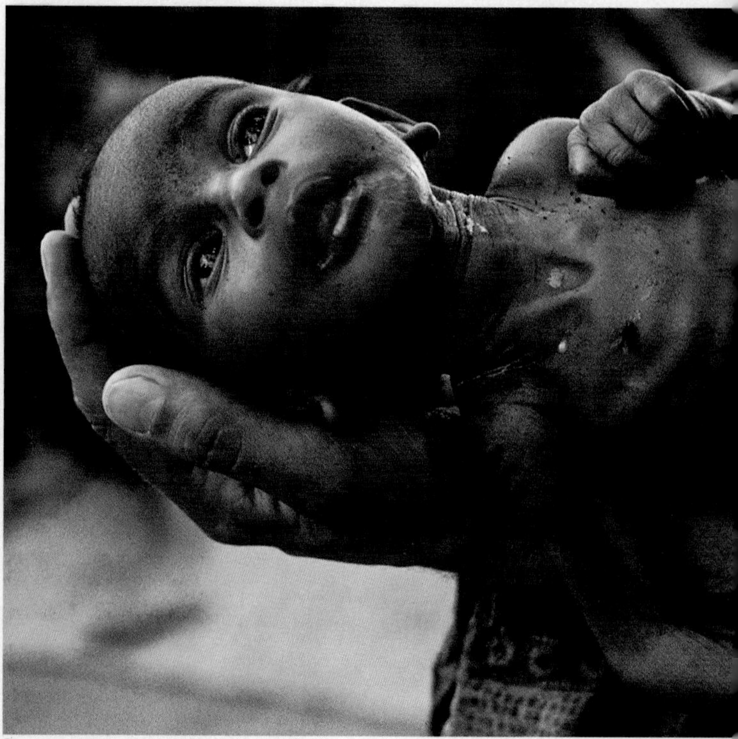

3

The hardest thing is

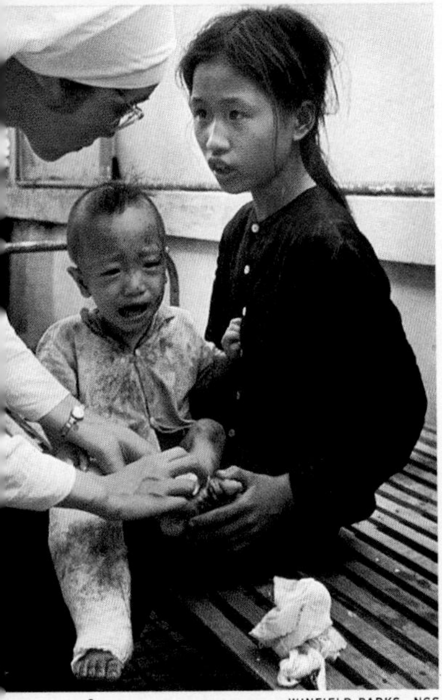

4 WINFIELD PARKS, NGS

1974. Her young country, one of the earth's most densely populated, lives in the shadow of chronic hunger.

KEVIN FLEMING

5 STEVE RAYMER, NGS

to see the children suffer

The essence of GEOGRAPHIC *journalism is reporting at first hand. In Alabama, Howard La Fay* **(1)** *takes notes during a delicate operation at University Hospital, Birmingham, to repair the flawed heart of a six-year-old Italian boy. Result: success. In*

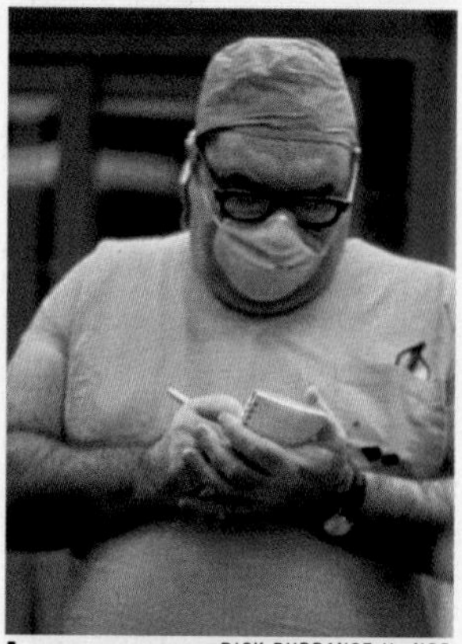

1 DICK DURRANCE II, NGS

5

3 STEVE RAYMER, NGS

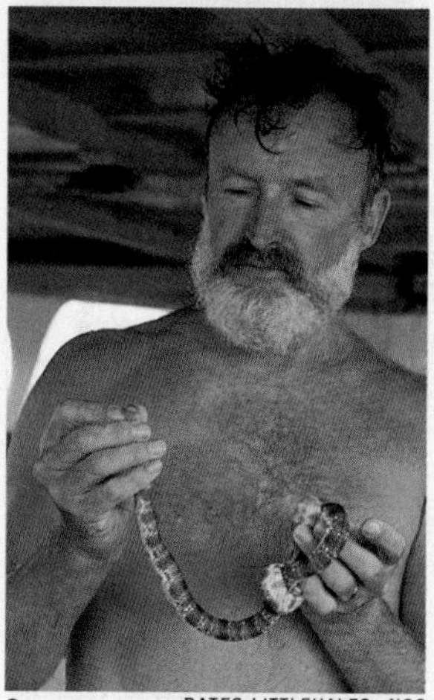

2 BATES LITTLEHALES, NGS

another delicate operation Ken MacLeish **(2)** *holds a lethal sea snake he brought from Australia's Great Barrier Reef for a zoo's collection.*

Bryan Hodgson **(3)** *interviews Alaska pipeline workers in a bar at the height of the boom when they were making $2,000 a week in a rush as wild as any forty-niner ever knew. Tom Canby* **(4)** *holds up several braces of rats during coverage of the ubiquitous rodent. Rats had destroyed most of the rice on the Philippine farm, and it was slim justice that these ended as a deep-fried dinner.*

Rowe Findley **(5)** *notes the inscription on a memorial*

4 JAMES L. STANFIELD, NGS

6

Writers: plunging into

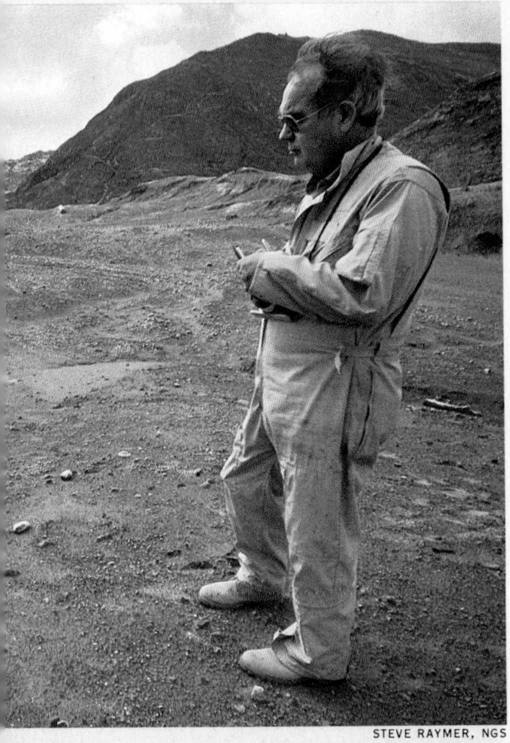

STEVE RAYMER, NGS

to crusty innkeeper Harry Truman, who, with his lodge, was buried by the eruption of Mount St. Helens. The two men, wholly different in demeanor, had earlier become friends.

In North Yemen, Noel Grove **(6)** *comes across a celebration of men carving the air with their curved daggers. Invited, he joins the dance, waving his equivalent, notebook and camera. With equal intensity but minus facial camouflage, Bart McDowell* **(7)** *accompanies members of a U. S. Marine strike force in the Indian Ocean, critical to the world's oil-supply routes.*

In the backcountry of Brunei, then moving toward independence from Britain, Joe Judge **(8)** *and an escort of troops pass through territory contested by Communist insurgents.*

7

STEVE RAYMER, NGS

STEVE RAYMER, NGS

8

DEAN CONGER, NGS

the life of the world...

Beyond the call of former duty, ex-Marine fighter pilot Mike Long (1) *sits drained midway through a spine-rattling Baja California desert auto race. Drawn by music into a park in Lanzhou, western China, Rick Gore* (2) *finds his running shoes more admired than his dancing style.*

Temporarily in the slammer at Alcatraz, Bill Graves (3) *laces his fingers around the very bars that once held Al Capone. A sort of confinement, supposedly good for one's health, buries Bill Ellis* (4) *in hot sand at Beppu on Japan's island of Kyushu.*

Trekking through utterly wild, lushly green, and thoroughly leech-infested southwestern Tasmania, Carolyn Patterson (5) *pushes ahead toward an encounter with the boulder-choked Franklin River.*

Certainly no genie and not even the bottom is visible to Allen Boraiko (6) *as he peers into a silver water jug in Jaipur, India, one of a pair each weighing 10,000 ounces, pure.*

It had warmed up—to minus 58°F—the day Bob Jordan took a test ride on a reindeer near Omyakon in

1 WILBUR E. GARRETT, NGS

2

3 JAMES L. STANFIELD, NGS

4 JAMES L. STANFIELD, NGS

...and living to the full the

BRUCE DALE, NGS

northeastern Siberia **(7)**. *The herder lived with his wife in a tent heated by a wood-burning stove, and the hardy life seemed to agree with him at age 71.*

It has long been the GEOGRAPHIC*'s policy to treat the world's people with "sympathetic understanding." And when freezing, broiling, hiking, dancing, and being otherwise engaged with them, that understanding flows naturally.*

6

FRED WARD, BLACK STAR

5

MELINDA BERGE

7

DEAN CONGER, NGS

stories they document

(Continued from page 66) we didn't plan—the stories that come from the sharing of an unusual talent, a unique trip, or a scientific or geographic discovery. Nine astronauts have told us what it was like to travel in space or walk on the moon. Jacques-Yves Cousteau shared the excitement of his undersea discoveries. Louis S. B. Leakey kept us posted on his search for prehistoric man. Jane Goodall has captivated us for two decades with her continuing study of wild chimpanzees. Eugenie Clark has brought us vicarious terror and fascinating discoveries through her shark studies. This list goes on—and we hope it always will.

Perhaps the most memorable tales of recent years were told by two young men who followed their dreams. One set sail in 1965 at age 16 to circle the world alone. Five years and three articles later, Robin Lee Graham sailed home, a man who had found the world, a wife—and a love for solid land. He settled in Montana, well out of sight of the oceans.

The other came to our offices in 1973 in walking garb and announced that he and his half-malamute dog were walking across the United States. He was disillusioned by his native land, and if he didn't find what he liked, he might leave it. Peter Gorton Jenkins found more than he bargained for. He found religion, and he found a wife, and they walked on together. He found many friends and a renewed love for his country, which he shared with us in two articles.

BUT OUR LONG TRADITION of firsthand reporting is now in some jeopardy. The vast majority of the world's people live under varying degrees of press censorship or harassment—and that percentage grows as authoritarian states take the power of the press into their own hands.

Even with experienced authors, truly being there can be difficult. In 1982 free-lance writer-photographer Loren McIntyre was jailed in a remote Venezuelan town because of a misunderstanding with local officials. If he hadn't slipped out a note to a friend, he might still be locked away.

Also, even being present does not automatically guarantee accuracy, although it's not from our lack of trying. Yes, we can get things wrong, despite the best efforts of our research staff to verify everything—*everything*—before publication. Researchers are meticulous and independent. Some of the staff may even think them ruthless on occasion. One of our best writers, having gone through the research wringer for years, finally said in exasperation as one of his stories went to press, "You never finish a story, you *abandon* it."

Despite this rigorous checking—the most thorough, we think, of any magazine—the recent addition of our Members Forum column was in part an (Continued on page 83)

JAMES L. STANFIELD, NGS

For a story on gold, writer Peter White, front, and photographer Jim Stanfield dunk in a Japanese hotel's 313.5-pound gold tub. The bath is reputed to prolong life. White reports he felt "no effect one way or another." Stanfield felt "old almost instantly."

1 TOM SENNETT

2

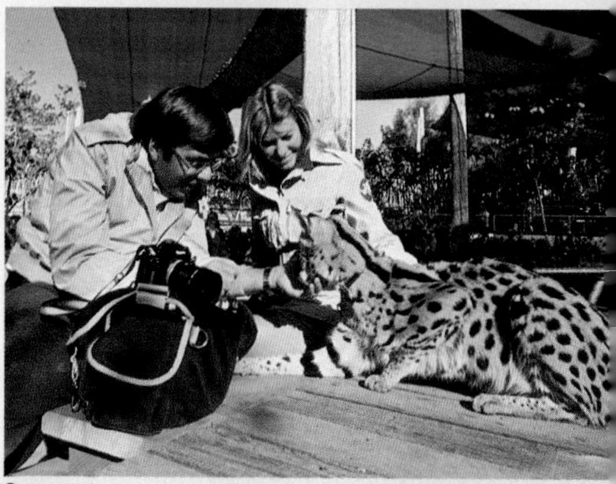

3 DAVID FALCONER

4 BO RADER

To be a GEOGRAPHIC *photographer is: to shepherd mounds of gear through endless airports; to roll out of bed before dawn weeks on end to catch the early light; to endure long separations from family and friends; to wait and wait and wait for the right moment; to keep calm in storm, riot, and other chaos—and to practice the craft at its limits.*

To get an overhead shot of the Suez Canal being cleared in 1974, Jonathan Blair (1) *hitches a ride on an Egyptian dredge. At the time, Americans were less than popular, and the operator swung him over the canal and then into it up to his feet, his knees, and his waist before setting him ashore to mutual laughter and handshakes.*

In Japan Dave Harvey (2)

Photographers: pushing

MASAAKI OKADA

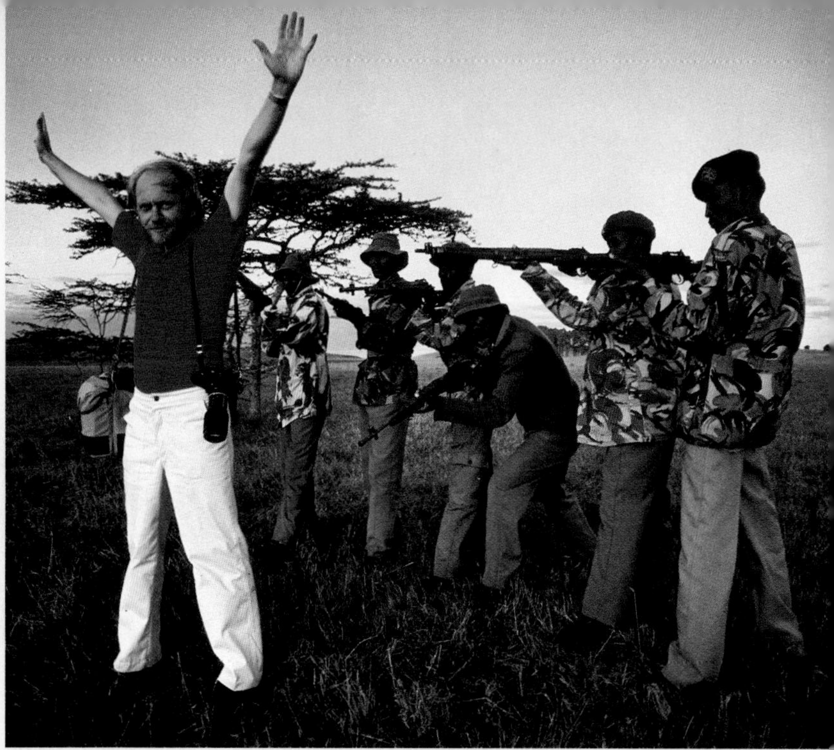

6 ESMOND BRADLEY MARTIN

is, for a change, a momentary subject during a kite-fighting festival. While covering a story on illegal trade in wildlife, Steve Raymer (3) *makes tentative friends with a serval cat confiscated by U. S. Customs and given to the San Diego Wild Animal Park. Natural science photographer Bob Sisson* (4) *shares a moment with a domestic cat while photographing one of his series on minicreatures.*

Hanging out and hanging semitough, Bob Madden (5) *checks out the streets of Brooklyn. Soon enough, Madden and Brooklyn found common ground in street savvy and laughter.*

Just kidding, of course, Jim Brandenburg (6) *tells himself while just posing, he hopes, with Kenyan game wardens during an assignment to photograph rhinos that continued to be more endangered than Jim.*

Being a thoroughgoing professional does not mean losing your humanity, and for Win Parks (7) *nothing could be more natural than bandaging the foot of an injured child in Sulawesi, Indonesia.*

5 DEVON JACKLIN

7 FROM WINFIELD PARKS, NGS

talent and technique...

1 KENNETH MACLEISH, NGS

2

It is, for the moment, a time for joy as Dean Conger (1) *steps out to photograph a native dance on the island of Mindanao in the Philippines. Much of the rest of the early 1970s assignment was less happy. Booming population and frontier mentality had pitted settlers, miners, and lumbermen against primitive native peoples without defense beyond Panamin, the small government agency that had taken up their cause.*

George Mobley (2), *second from right, learns to eat, sleep, dress, herd, and think like a Lapp during a month with a group from Norway as they follow their reindeer's migration from the interior to summer pastures on the coast.*

Tom Abercrombie (3) *is in Ladakh, a remote region of conflict between India, China, and Pakistan. As he patiently waits for the right moment to photograph the lamasery of Tikse in the Indus River Valley, young women passing by wander up for a look through his telephoto lens.*

While photographing a story on national wildlife refuges, Bates Littlehales (4) *comes muzzle to muzzle over a piece of bread with a tamed but free-ranging deer at the National Bison Range in Montana.*

Between assignments there is some time to catch a breath at headquarters and do maintenance before going back into the field. Jodi Cobb (5) *tests cameras—halfway to the middle of anywhere being no place to discover your gear isn't working.*

Crowds can present

3 LYNN ABERCROMBIE

...to the far limits of

KAREN ANNA GAUP

6 BRUCE DALE, NGS

4 LUTHER GOLDMAN

several kinds of problems. Bruce Dale (6) is surrounded by the curious in northern China, where Americans had not been since before the Communist revolution. The professional camouflage that photographers need to remain inconspicuous is of no use, as the Chinese press in to observe and to touch the congenial alien.

For Joe Scherschel (7) the problem is more familiar – how to frame the subject and get the photograph with a Guatemalan crowd jostling past during a religious festival.

5 SISSE BRIMBERG

7 DIEGO MOLINA

patience and involvement

PAT FIELD, NGS

O. LOUIS MAZZATENTA, NGS

Visitors flock to admire a full-size photomural of Leonardo da Vinci's "Last Supper" (above, right) at the National Gallery of Art in Washington, D. C.

Rex Stucky, veteran GEOGRAPHIC *phototechnician (upper left), directed the reproduction from staff photographer Vic Boswell's eight-by-ten-inch color transparency. The process involved delicate color control and matching of 36 photographic prints that compose the photomural.*

It was produced by the Society to draw attention to the major cleaning and restoration efforts under way on the original in Milan.

Painted about five hundred years ago on a monastery wall, Leonardo's famous work began to decay almost immediately. His experimental method of applying pigment, painting slowly over a lead-white primer—rather than

A life–size replica takes

COTTON COULSON

quickly on wet plaster, the traditional fresco technique—proved unstable, and much of the original pigment has since been lost.

With cleaning agents, brush, and an array of scientific techniques, restorer Dr. Pinin Brambilla Barcilon (lower left) removes centuries of dirt, glue, mold, and layers of misguided overpainting. In a typical week of meticulous work, she may be able to treat an area the size of a postage stamp, having spent three years in testing before beginning the actual restoration. "You have to think like the artist," she says.

Previous restorations repainted the mural in somber tones, darkened it with oil, and destroyed Leonardo's paint with harsh solvents. That Napoleon's troops stabled their horses in the hall, that an Allied bomb almost destroyed the monastery in World War II, and that even today humidity and pollution controls are not adequate have all contributed to the destruction.

Present restoration scaffolding is visible in the photomural. In the quarter of the painting already cleaned, much detail has reemerged, and dingy colors have given way to the brilliant palette of Leonardo. This monumental project was chronicled in an 1983 issue of the GEOGRAPHIC.

shape at the National Gallery

(*Continued from page 74*) admission of our fallibility. It offers readers a chance to correct our mistakes and, just as important, to add other relevant information.

At least 55 readers wrote us about what they thought was a mistake in Rick Gore's "Once and Future Universe"—the greatest number of letters contesting any one statement in the magazine since the Forum began. The article was correct, but we failed to note that a statement about the expanding universe seemed to contradict Einstein's theories of relativity. Astute readers pointed out our lapse. An explanation appeared in the October 1983 Members Forum.

Though we try to avoid partisan politics and bring facts to our readers, the facts often get us in trouble. From dealers who trade in endangered wildlife or archaeological treasures to nations that trade in terror, we've been accused of being pro-this or anti-that. But for consistent dissatisfaction, none can surpass the nameless censors who ten times have banned the magazine from Czechoslovakia in the past three years with never an explanation.

The events of nearly four decades covered by this Index have made a GEOGRAPHIC reporter's job an odyssey through the greatest epoch of discovery and change. Those of us who have lived through this dynamic period are the first generations to have to contend with the atomic age, when, for the first time, a single act—deliberate or mistaken—could lead to destruction of the world. And ironically, as technology permits us to probe deeper into the seemingly endless universe, our awareness grows that this beautiful, yet fragile planet may be the only one hospitable to mankind.

Like the gambler who keeps raising the stakes, our continuing mastery of technology can lead to our destruction or to a much finer life for all. As we run our fingers and our recollections through the 25,000 entries that follow, we trace a trail of adventure and discovery, growth and destruction, pathos and joy, folly and progress. Yet taken together, they give hope that mankind will win the gamble with technology. Either way, we will be there to report what happens. ☐

The mule insisted, and Editor Bill Garrett obliged. They shared an apple (below) during a break from exploring the Grand Canyon. Garrett's 1978 report was part celebration of what may be America's best loved park (opposite) – and part documentation of what that love has meant

DAVID C. OCHSNER

in terms of the overcrowding of campsites, hiking trails, and even that architect of the canyon itself, the scouring Colorado River.

He ended by writing: "I hope I left no scars on the canyon that won't heal, because there are a lot of people coming to see it. They should always find it unimpaired."

WILBUR E. GARRETT, NGS

RICHARD LEAKEY AND KENYAN COMPANIONS RIDE TO A RENDEZVOUS WITH THE REMAINS OF EARLY MAN. GORDON W. GAHAN

THE SOCIETY TODAY

By GILBERT M. GROSVENOR PRESIDENT, NATIONAL GEOGRAPHIC SOCIETY

Tradition and change meet near the North Pole as Gilbert M. Grosvenor (opposite) sits on the rim of a diving hole drilled through six feet of ice. He holds a flag that accompanied Comdr. Robert E. Peary on Society-sponsored arctic exploration in the early 1900s. Beyond are Joe MacInnis, at right, and Steve Blasco of LOREX, a Canadian expedition devoted to basic research.

Mr. Grosvenor, Editor of NATIONAL GEOGRAPHIC from 1970 to 1980 and President since then, has led the Society into new fields of book and magazine publishing, education, research, and services to members. His goal is to increase these in scope and variety as the Society prepares for its 1988 centennial.

SOME THINGS that happen in a lifetime make one truly stop and think. One of those moments for me came in 1979 when I slid through a diving hole in the ice of the Arctic Ocean and found myself in that strange world prowled only by the occasional seal—and, it occurred to me, the occasional nuclear submarine.

I was a few miles from the North Pole, the geographic center of the top of the world, where all lines of longitude meet and every direction is south. What an all-consuming goal it had been for men like ourselves only a brief 75 years ago. How they had struggled to reach it, for their own and their nation's honor. In fact, I had with me a sentimental token from that era, a flag carried by Comdr. Robert E. Peary during exploration supported by the National Geographic Society, of which I am now President.

I had reached the polar region in a few days of air travel. Our pilot could tell us exactly where the Pole was by glancing at his instruments. What explorers like Peary had sacrificed years for was now easily reachable; it was simply a matter of wanting to go.

Information once traveled by word of mouth. Now it is technically possible for any person to communicate with any other person anytime, anywhere, posing a formidable challenge to us whose mission is to convey reliable information.

What will it be like, I wondered, 75 years from now? When will a scientist unfurl the National Geographic flag at a space station? When will the first copy of our journal be delivered to the moon? Will we still be printing magazines, books, and maps, or will the information move on laser beams by way of machines not yet invented? Will our worldwide membership have instantaneous access to our entire compendium of the past—this Index, for example, contained in a chip the size of my fingernail?

The present always has two faces. The one facing the future sees that the next millennium, the year 2000, is a scant 16 years away, less than half the time span of this Index. The centennial of our Society is only four years from now.

We have come a very long way.

In 1947 the Society relied almost entirely on its journal for expression of its mission to "increase and diffuse geographic knowledge." Today, as President and chief executive officer of the Society, I deal not only with the magazine but also with book departments, videotape, film, and television operations, news and radio divisions, units that produce teaching materials, and many others. All have something in common—the tradition of quality that has become a Geographic trademark, delivered to the largest number of people at the lowest possible price. *(Continued on page 92)*

EMORY KRISTOF, NGS

New building on headquarters block

With a bold sweep and terraced setbacks, the Society's new building—here nearing completion—echoes with suggestions of Maya architecture. The monumental yet inviting structure completes the Society's Washington, D. C., headquarters complex five blocks north of the White House (visible in line with the Washington Monument):

(1) *Hubbard Memorial Hall, occupied in 1903, in recent years has held archives and small offices. It will be restored to its former simple elegance. Murals by N. C. Wyeth line its spacious stairwell.*

(2) *The 16th Street building, with its neoclassical facade, has been refurbished inside to accommodate much needed office space.*

(3) *The Melville Bell Grosvenor Building, dedicated by President Lyndon B. Johnson in 1964, will retain its most notable feature—Explorers Hall, a museum with imaginative exhibits, a favorite of visiting Society members.*

(4) *The new building will contain the Cartographic Division, the library, and a 400-seat theater with the latest in audiovisual equipment; it will be made available for use by other organizations devoted to education. With its plaza and greenery, the new building should be an ornament to the nation's capital.*

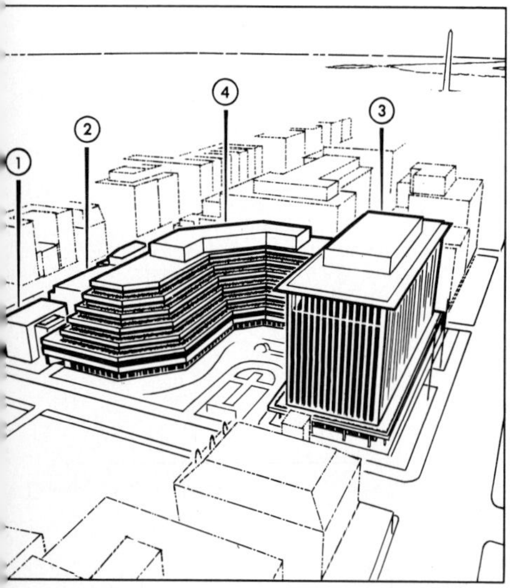

JAMES A. SUGAR, BLACK STAR

ROBERT S. PATTON, NGS

Stretching back to the vanishing point (above), two 365-ton Motter gravure presses print editorial sections of 11 million monthly NATIONAL GEOGRAPHICS *on paper brought in by 55 freight cars to the W. F. Hall plant in Corinth, Mississippi—a facility specially built to produce the magazine. A continuous web of paper runs through the presses at 1,800*

High tech speeds production

ROBERT S. PATTON, NGS

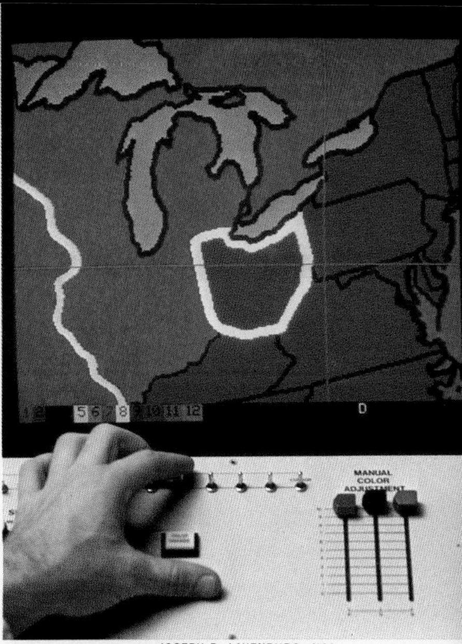

JOSEPH D. LAVENBURG, NGS

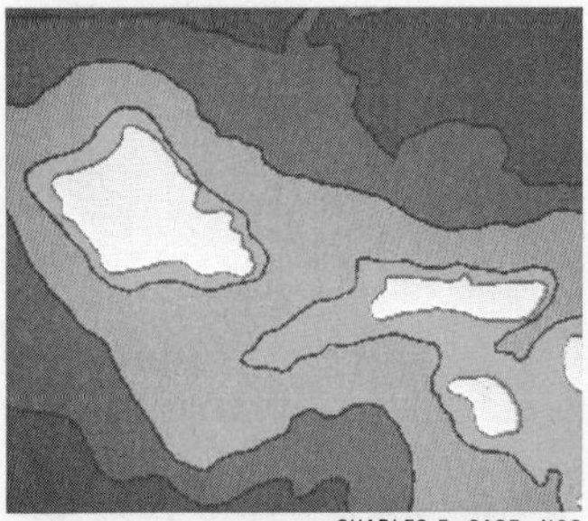

CHARLES F. CASE, NGS

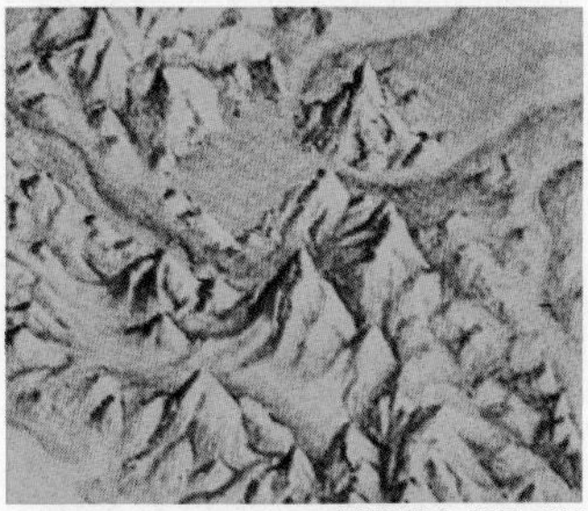

CHARLES F. CASE, NGS

feet a minute, absorbing 23,000 gallons of ink per issue. Each month's run equals 13,500 linear miles of paper.

Units of the magazine, called signatures, are collated, bound, and moved by conveyor (left) for final trimming. Speed, automation, and technology help make each copy as nearly perfect as possible.

Technology has also been applied to mapmaking, always a distinctive feature of the GEOGRAPHIC. The very first issue reported on the great blizzard of 1888. That article was supplemented by four foldout weather charts printed in color. To computerize mapmaking, the Society has recently adapted a system originally developed to design fabric patterns for the textile industry. It includes a drum scanner, two editing consoles, and a laser plotter—all powered by four minicomputers. The system eliminates much tedious handwork and saves time and film. Editors at the consoles (above, top to bottom) can electronically place state boundaries or rivers, draw topographical features, alter such artwork as depiction of mountain ranges, and even paint features or change colors.

# of printing and cartography

(Continued from page 86) There are few persons in the United States who have not had their knowledge of the world shaped in some degree by a magazine, atlas, globe, book, film, filmstrip, or television program produced by the National Geographic Society.

Thus, while our mission remains the same, while NATIONAL GEOGRAPHIC is still bordered in yellow and we continue to be a familiar institution, the Society of 1984 is vastly different than it was.

During these years the Society evolved through three phases, each roughly a decade in length. The first was one of reporting on a planet still recovering from the effects of World War II. The GEOGRAPHIC, long a pioneer in color printing, used color increasingly. At a time when color television was still experimental, the magazine was a primary source in showing the world as it truly appeared. We continued to publish books, but only on an occasional basis, as we had since the 1890s. Support for scientific research was gradually expanded to include pioneering efforts like the early undersea explorations of Jacques-Yves Cousteau.

In the next decade any tendency to accept the status quo was blown away by the whirlwind enthusiasm of Melville Bell Grosvenor, who became Editor and President in 1957. Under his leadership, Society membership more than doubled. Ambitious book-publishing programs began. Atlases and globes were launched. National Geographic Specials were telecast. We opened *(Continued on page 100)*

A ParaPlane (right) circles the Membership Center Building in Gaithersburg, Maryland, for a story on ultralight flying machines. Situated in a parklike setting, the building houses 1,100 employees who maintain all phases of communication with Society members, processing 343.5 million pieces of mail annually (left). A largely automated computer operation gives immediate answers to members' inquiries.

The Society considers these to be private communications, and, unlike many organizations, does not make members' names available for promotions or mailing lists.

JOSEPH H. BAILEY, NGS (ABOVE); CHARLES O'REAR

Meeting in Washington, D.C.– the 33 eminent men who founded the National Geographic Society

Responding to an invitation to organize "a society for the increase and diffusion of geographical knowledge," the founding members met on January 13, 1888, at the Cosmos Club.

Artist Stanley Meltzoff based this re-creation on individual photographs. Key at right identifies (1) *Charles J. Bell, banker;* (2) *Israel C. Russell, geologist;* (3) *Commodore George W. Melville, USN;* (4) *Frank Baker, anatomist;* (5) *W. B. Powell, educator;* (6) *Brig. Gen. A. W. Greely, USA, polar explorer;* (7) *Grove Karl Gilbert, geologist and a future President of the Society;* (8) *John Wesley Powell, naturalist and explorer of the Colorado River;* (9) *Gardiner Greene Hubbard, Boston lawyer*

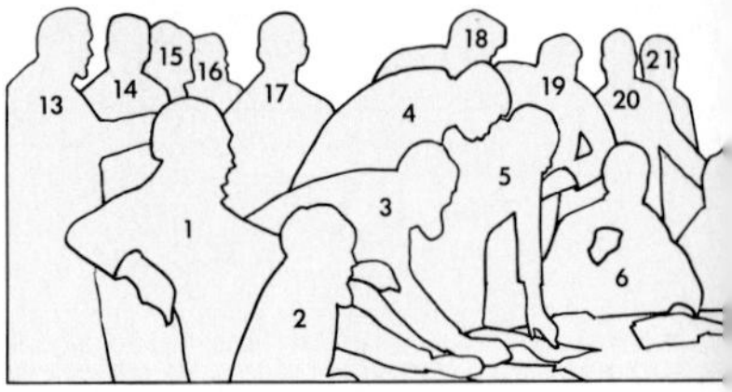

PAINTING BY STANLEY MELTZOFF

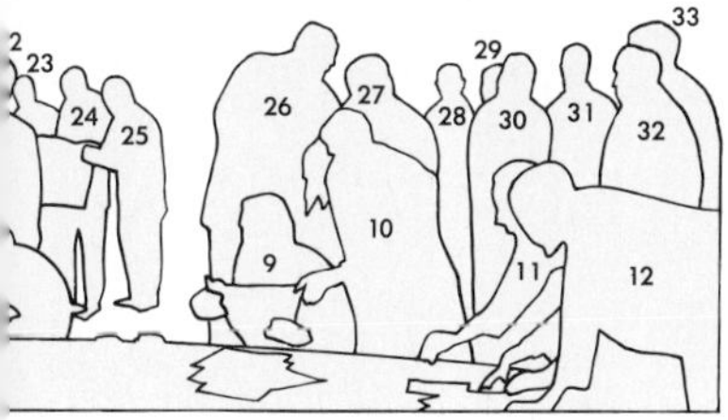

and first President of the Society, who helped finance the telephone experiments of Alexander Graham Bell; (10) *Henry Gannett, geographer and a future Society President;* (11) *William H. Dall, naturalist;* (12) *Edward E. Hayden, meteorologist;* (13) *Herbert G. Ogden, topographer;* (14) *Arthur P. Davis, civil engineer;* (15) *Gilbert Thompson, topographer;* (16) *Marcus Baker, cartographer;* (17) *George Kennan, author, lecturer, and explorer of Arctic Siberia;* (18) *James Howard Gore, educator;* (19) *O. H. Tittmann, geodesist and a future President of the Society;* (20) *Henry W. Henshaw, naturalist;* (21) *George Brown Goode, naturalist and author;* (22) *Cleveland Abbe, meteorologist;* (23) *Comdr. John R. Bartlett, USN;* (24) *Henry Mitchell, engineer;* (25) *Robert Muldrow II, geologist;* (26) *Comdr. Winfield S. Schley, USN;* (27) *Capt. C. E. Dutton, USA;* (28) *W. D. Johnson, topographer;* (29) *James C. Welling, journalist and educator;* (30) *C. Hart Merriam, Chief, U. S. Biological Survey;* (31) *Capt. Rogers Birnie, Jr., USA;* (32) *A. H. Thompson, geographer;* (33) *Samuel S. Gannett, geographer.*

Board of Trustees

Called the Board of Managers until 1920, the Board of Trustees of the National Geographic Society elects its membership, sets policy, appoints officers, and oversees all aspects of the Society's activities.

Chairman of the Board since 1976 and Chairman of the Society's Committee for Research and Exploration, Melvin M. Payne (left), a trustee since 1958, joined the Society's staff in 1932, advancing to the presidency in 1967. He has drawn upon his wealth of scientific, legal, and business experience to guide the Society and has been involved in such activities as balloon ascensions, undersea exploration, early-man research, and book editing and publishing.

The other trustees as of February 1, 1984, are pictured on these pages, in the order of their election.

Thomas W. McKnew, *Advisory Chairman, joined the Society in 1932, having served in the U. S. Navy in World War I and as a construction executive. Holder of several Society positions, he was formerly Board Chairman.*

Curtis E. LeMay, *former Chief of Staff, U. S. Air Force, had earlier led the Air Force Strategic Air Command and, in 1948, had organized the Berlin Airlift to relieve the blockaded city. He joined the Board in 1951.*

Conrad L. Wirth, *former Director, National Park Service, helped lead the expansion of park facilities during the 1960s. A student of landscape architecture, he has favored more recreation areas "close to the people."*

Laurance S. Rockefeller, *Chairman, Memorial Sloan-Kettering Cancer Center, business executive and philanthropist, has given long and distinguished service in the cause of conservation.*

James H. Wakelin, Jr., *former Assistant Secretary of Commerce for Science and Technology, was trained as a physicist and pursued a career in naval research. He has also helped to advance international oceanography.*

Gilbert M. Grosvenor, *President, National Geographic Society, joined the editorial staff in 1954 and worked in various capacities until his appointment as Editor, NATIONAL GEOGRAPHIC, a position he held from 1970 to 1980.*

Arthur B. Hanson, *an authority on laws governing the press, is a Major General, U. S. Marine Corps Reserve, Retired, and has served as trustee for various educational institutions.*

Lloyd H. Elliott, *Vice Chairman, has had broad experience in both public and private higher education. He has been President, University of Maine, and, since 1966, President, George Washington University.*

Robert C. Seamans, Jr., *Henry R. Luce Professor of Environment and Public Policy, MIT, has been active in the aeronautics and missile fields since 1941 and served as Deputy Administrator of NASA.*

Carlisle H. Humelsine, *Chairman of the Board, the Colonial Williamsburg Foundation, and regent, Smithsonian Institution, served under four Secretaries of State and earlier as assistant to Gen. George C. Marshall.*

Mrs. Lyndon B. Johnson, *founder of the National Wildflower Research Center, has received numerous high honors and earned the gratitude of Americans for her beautification efforts across the nation.*

Warren E. Burger, *Chief Justice of the United States since 1969, was appointed in 1956 to a seat on the Court of Appeals for the District of Columbia. He is Chancellor, Board of Regents, Smithsonian Institution.*

Frank Borman, *Chairman of the Board and President, Eastern Airlines, was commander in 1965 of the earth-orbiting Gemini 7 flight and in 1968 of the Apollo 8 spacecraft, first manned mission to orbit the moon.*

J. Carter Brown, *Director, National Gallery of Art, is Chairman of the Commission of Fine Arts and a trustee of the John F. Kennedy Center for the Performing Arts and the National Trust for Historic Preservation.*

George M. Elsey, *President Emeritus, American Red Cross, served as an administrative assistant in the White House and as a special assistant to the Secretary of Defense. He is a trustee of the Brookings Institution.*

Jerome H. Holland, *former Ambassador to Sweden, was President of Delaware State College and Hampton Institute. An educational trustee and corporate director, he is a fellow of the American Academy of Arts and Sciences.*

Thomas E. Bolger, *Chairman of the Board, Bell Atlantic, began his career with the Bell System while still in high school, continuing after service in World War II and graduation from college as an electrical engineer.*

Owen R. Anderson, *Vice Chairman and Executive Vice President, National Geographic Society, began his career in 1946, rising to responsibility for all communications with the Society's millions of members.*

Wilbur E. Garrett, *Editor, NATIONAL GEOGRAPHIC, joined the staff in 1954 and has received many editorial awards, including a citation for "Distinguished Service in Journalism" from the University of Missouri.*

Michael Collins, *Vice President, LTV Aerospace and Defense Company, has been Director, National Air and Space Museum, author, and command module pilot, Apollo 11, first manned mission to the moon's surface.*

A. Leon Higginbotham, Jr., *Judge, U. S. Court of Appeals for the Third Circuit, has had a distinguished career as a law professor, author, jurist, and public servant. He is a regent of the Smithsonian Institution.*

Robert L. Breeden, *Vice President, National Geographic Society, directs the organization's book publishing and educational media divisions, including WORLD and TRAVELER magazines. He joined the Society's staff in 1955.*

Trustees Emeritus

Robert E. Doyle, *former Vice Chairman and President, National Geographic Society*

Crawford H. Greenewalt, *a director and former President of E. I. du Pont de Nemours & Company*

Caryl P. Haskins, *former President, Carnegie Institution of Washington*

Wm. McChesney Martin, Jr., *former Chairman, Board of Governors, Federal Reserve System*

Frederick G. Vosburgh, *former Editor, NATIONAL GEOGRAPHIC*

James E. Webb, *former Administrator, National Aeronautics and Space Administration*

Louis B. Wright, *former Director, Folger Shakespeare Library*

HORACE ALBRIGHT, THE GROSVENOR COLLECTION

DAVID ALAN HARVEY, NGS

Generations of leadership and concern

Moved to ponder the "majesty and friendliness" that radiated from California's giant sequoias, Gilbert Hovey Grosvenor (left) camped the night under this one in 1915 and went on to influence creation of the National Park Service. His son, Melville Bell Grosvenor (below left), later also Editor and President of the Society, spearheaded a successful effort to save some of the finest remaining stands of the West's coastal redwoods, campaigning for creation of Redwood National Park.

When Gilbert Grosvenor began his career with the Society in 1899, its membership numbered 1,000, and its magazine was devoted to lengthy treatises by gentlemen scholars. Although subtitled "An Illustrated Monthly," the magazine had only a scattering of photographs and mostly technical maps. The whole enterprise was in debt and in danger of foundering. He worked to increase the publication of photographs, simplify the writing style without sacrificing accuracy, and broaden the membership beyond the professionally learned to anyone who had an interest in the world and its peoples. These strategies succeeded, and by 1910 he was able to print 24 pages of colored photographs, the largest collection published in any magazine to that date. Because color reproduction had not been perfected, the images of Korea and China were hand tinted based on the photographer's notes.

Many firsts followed, and the membership continued to grow. When Melville Grosvenor became Editor and President in 1957 after long apprenticeship, the Society and magazine were familiar institutions. Yet as his father had rescued the organization in its early years, he greatly expanded its scope. Under his leadership the membership more than doubled. The Society expanded its book publishing and produced atlases and globes. It increased contributions to research and exploration and began the highly acclaimed series of documentaries on television.

Although father and son had distinctive leadership styles – Gilbert was reserved, while Melville was gregarious – both delighted in travel and in the natural world, Gilbert as an inveterate birder, Melville as an avid sailor. Perhaps most fundamentally, both had an abiding respect and sympathy for people of all conditions everywhere. Both dedicated their lives to the Society and loved what they did.

(Continued from page 92) a new ten-story headquarters, recently named the Melville Bell Grosvenor Building.

Following the editorship of Frederick G. Vosburgh, who kept our momentum going and broke new ground, my tenure as Editor of the magazine proved to be ten of the most interesting and enjoyable years of my life. I had the satisfaction of watching our membership almost double again and pass the ten million mark; the evolution of the Society was continuing. Our members were faced with new concerns based on new awareness. In 1967 Ted Vosburgh had called attention to Everglades National Park and water problems posed by development in the area; he concluded his service with a landmark issue on the pollution threatening our air and water. By 1977 the magazine was discussing our entire wild and scenic rivers system, and in 1979 we devoted a whole issue to our national parks.

Our writers, photographers, and filmmakers were finding change everywhere they traveled, as timeless lands of nomads in the Middle East became battle zones and once romantic jungle trails became highways to war in Southeast Asia and Africa. Virtually all of Africa had changed from colonial rule to self-rule; the Middle East caught fire again and again; Asia was in turmoil. The need for geographic knowledge and understanding to help interpret these events grew with each year, as did our ability to meet the challenge.

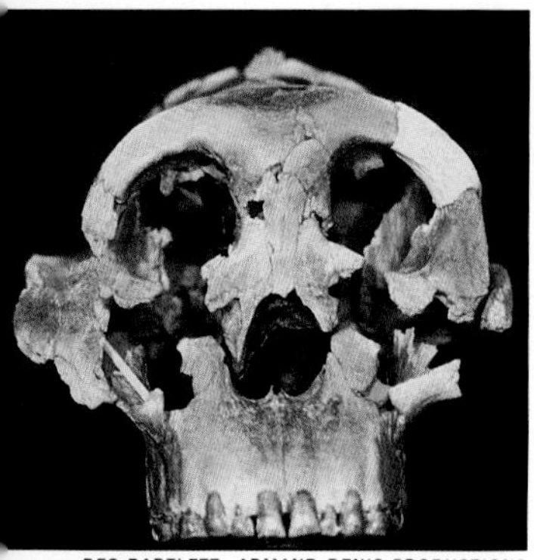

DES BARTLETT, ARMAND DENIS PRODUCTIONS

In five decades of fossil hunting and analysis, unearthing bones of hominids and animals in East Africa, the late Louis S. B. Leakey (opposite) filled major gaps in the record of early man. He displays the broken molar of a deinothere, an extinct tusked mammal, found at Olduvai Gorge in Tanzania. On his hat rests a million-year-old elephant tooth.

Leakey's 1959 discovery of the skull from a manlike creature he called Zinjanthropus (above) was shown by dating tests to have lived 1.75 million years ago.

OUR FLEDGLING BOOK PROGRAM blossomed into one of the largest publishing operations of its kind in the world, reaching new levels of quality each year. Our annual series of four Special Publications continues to be an excellent value, reaching half a million members at a price below that of many magazine subscriptions.

Our large-format books have drawn both critical and, most important to us, membership approval. It is hard for me to choose which ones to single out, but *We Americans,* published in time for the United States Bicentennial, *The World of the American Indian,* and *Journey Into China* have been among the most memorable.

Peoples and Places of the Past, a cultural atlas of the human experience from its earliest traces to the Renaissance, has certainly been the Society's most ambitious book. The result is a singular combination of text, photography, cartography, and illustration, a work that is at once a comprehensive reference and an intriguing chairside companion.

Also in 1983 the Society published *The Wonder of Birds.* The combination of a large illustrated book of essays on bird behavior, four records of bird sounds, a supplement map and text on bird migration, and a comprehensive *Field*

MELVILLE BELL GROSVENOR, NGS

1

ROBERT F. SISSON, NGS

At Olduvai Gorge (1) in Tanzania, Louis and Mary D. Leakey and their son Philip examine a habitation site for evidence of early man. The gorge has been a productive location, erosion having stripped away layers of soil that otherwise would have deeply overlaid significant deposits of fossil bones.

Primitive manlike beings (2), perhaps a family group that trekked the Laetoli plain of East Africa some 3.6 million years ago, left footprints in volcanic ash that Mary Leakey uncovered.

Sifting through gravel at Olduvai (3), Mary and crew search for fragments of an early skull.

Sharing knowledge, Louis Leakey and son Richard (4) study a fossil. Along Kenya's Lake Turkana, the younger Leakey uncovered the skull of an Australopithecus, a creature both apelike and manlike who lived about 2.6 million years ago.

On a barren ridge in northeastern Ethiopia (5) Donald C. Johanson holds aloft one of the oldest remains of man ever found, a bone from a group of an early species that died together three million years ago.

Johanson also unearthed the most complete skeleton (6) of

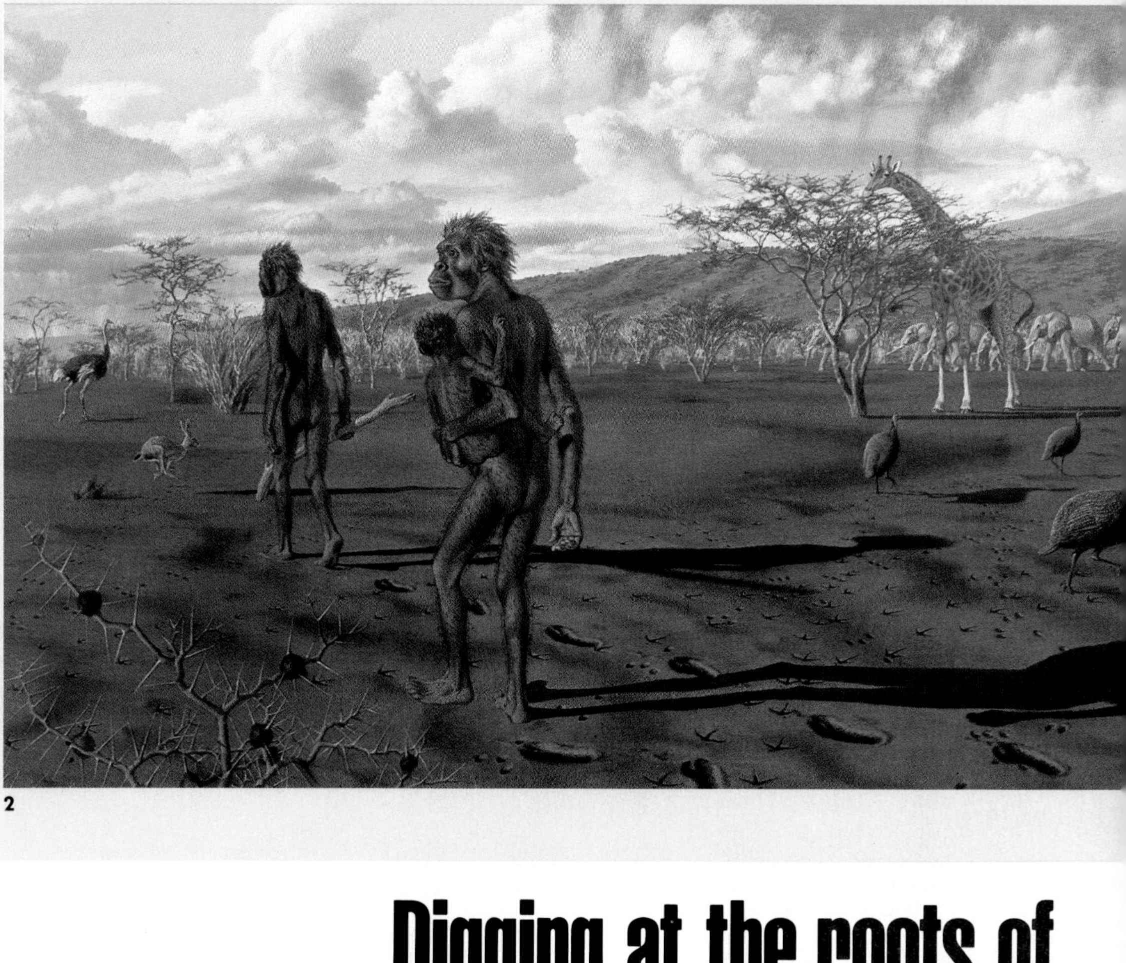

2

Digging at the roots of

3

MELVILLE BELL GROSVENOR, NGS

4

GORDON W. GAHAN

early near man yet known, a female Australopithecus less than four feet tall, dubbed "Lucy" for a Beatles song then popular.

Society support aids these and other scientists in their quests to push back the horizons of prehistory in many parts of the world and more clearly establish the development of man.

PAINTING BY JAY H. MATTERNES

5 DAVID BRILL

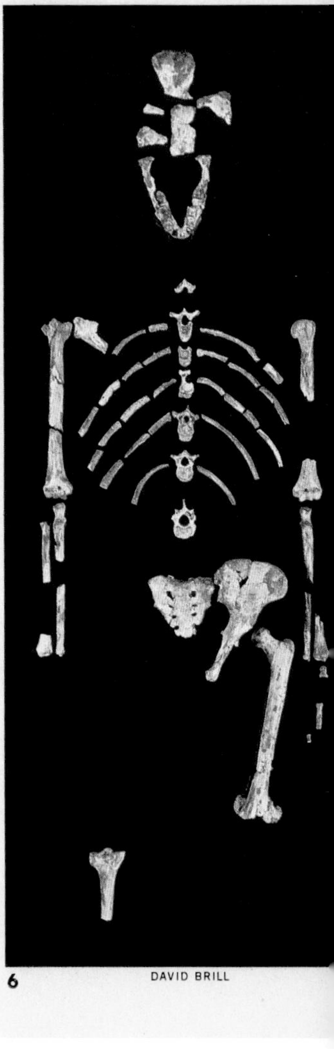

6 DAVID BRILL

the family tree of man

Guide to the Birds of North America with specially commissioned paintings was the result of prodigious scholarship and editorial imagination.

With the Fifth Edition of our *Atlas of the World,* we continued to fulfill our mission at the most fundamental level. Recently reprinted, the Fifth Edition has earned wide praise indeed, being consistently mentioned as one of the most useful and important reference works of our times.

In this period of rapid, then sustained growth, one technological problem persisted: how to maintain the high standards of color printing that had long been a GEOGRAPHIC hallmark. Our experience in book publishing proved that offset printing could give excellent results, and offset was used for some of the magazine's contents.

Yet, as we looked ahead, it was clear that to get the highest quality at a reasonable cost, we would have to reevaluate

DEREK BRYCESON

DRAWING BY DAVID BYGOTT

our printing methods. After much research and experimentation, we settled on high-speed gravure printing in a facility specially built and run by W. F. Hall Company and began producing the GEOGRAPHIC on huge new presses in 1977. It was a very large step, and, as might be expected with any such change, we had some anxious moments. While the quality of any printing depends upon many variables, we feel the results have been excellent. Especially in the darker range of colors, gravure gives an almost uncanny sense of richness and depth, and the printed photograph can convey a startling, almost three-dimensional effect. The ultimate judges of this are, of course, Society members, who see the monthly result.

The decade of the 1970s was the age of runaway inflation; and almost nothing was immune from rising prices, not

In the domain of her subjects, Jane Goodall (opposite) has lived among the chimpanzees of Tanzania's Gombe Stream National Park since 1960. Society grants have helped support the continuing chronicle of chimp behavior by this pioneer observer, the leading authority on these apes in the wild.

Of major importance has been her discovery that the normally gentle primates can, on occasion, become killers and cannibals, traits perhaps all too human.

Eyes glaring, a Gombe female (above) killed an infant chimp and shared the grisly feast with her own offspring.

With a desperate leap a mother chimp (above right) carries her twins to safety, foiling an attack by another female.

BARON HUGO VAN LAWICK

BOB CAMPBELL

ROD BRINDAMOUR

To gain acceptance by a mountain gorilla (above), Dian Fossey scratches herself vigorously, a gesture the animal finds reassuring. Largest of the great apes, gorillas were widely feared when in 1967 this zoologist began her long-term study of their life cycle and behavior. By living with them on the forested mountain slopes of Rwanda, Fossey has proved that they are among the gentlest of creatures.

In the Bornean rain forest (right) orangutans engulf anthropologist Biruté M. F. Galdikas. Indonesian law forbids capture of these endangered primates; officials have confiscated contraband apes over the years and placed dozens under the care of Galdikas.

She raises young orangutans at camp in her study area before releasing them back into the wild.

Taught by researcher Francine Patterson, Koko, a young "talking" gorilla (upper

Primate research: a certain

RONALD H. COHN

SELF-PORTRAIT BY KOKO

left), learned to communicate at a computer console by typing statements on a specially designed keyboard connected to a voice synthesizer that produced spoken words when she pressed keys.

Each key is painted with a simple, geometric pattern that represents words for objects, feelings, and actions, as well as parts of speech.

Here Patterson holds a banana and signs "fruit," as Koko keys a response, sometimes a statement such as, "Want apple eat want."

Koko has responded to and asked questions, referred to past and future events, shown an impish sense of humor, argued, lied, and even traded insults with her human friend.

This project, partly funded by the Society, taught Koko to produce spoken English for the many words she had already learned to recognize. These utterances have been transferred to a computer data file. Koko has responded to hundreds of spoken words independently of the auditory keyboard.

Koko has also mastered hundreds of words in Ameslan—American Sign Language, the hand speech used by the deaf. That language consists of gestures, each of which signifies a word or idea.

In a standard test the gorilla's IQ placed only slightly below the average for a human child. She has used signs in combinations similar to those employed by children during their first stages of learning to talk.

An aspiring photographer (lower left), one of whose pictures appeared on the cover of NATIONAL GEOGRAPHIC, the young gorilla has delighted in manipulating the controls of a 35mm camera.

kinship with humanity

gasoline or groceries, certainly not paper or postage. Holding costs down became a major priority. Our business departments performed wonders in jobs that got little recognition and less glory.

Our policy of diversification and lateral growth led us into an area in which I have taken a special personal interest. As the members of the "baby boom" of the 1940s and 1950s passed through school and into maturity, children seemed somehow to go out of fashion as a major topic of continuing national discussion. School enrollments were dropping, and in some parts of the country schools that had been rushed to completion in an era of temporary classrooms were left empty of laughter, learning, and students. Even though there were fewer children, they were still a market. Much television was aimed at them, sometimes with excellent programming, more often not.

The Society had for half a century published the weekly *School Bulletin*, but I felt we could reach more children better with a different sort of publication. In 1975 we published the first issue of National Geographic WORLD, a monthly magazine for children eight years old and up. Besides its fine editorial staff, WORLD makes use of excellent consultants—educators, to be sure, and children, its severest critics. Since the first issue, WORLD has attained the largest circulation of any magazine of its kind.

Through our hundreds of educational filmstrips, films, videotapes, and multimedia kits, the Society has made available to schools high-quality materials in a broad variety of subjects at very reasonable costs. We have begun publishing two annual series of children's books, for "young explorers" up to age eight and for "world explorers" to age thirteen.

OUR PROGRAM of funding research and exploration has grown by more than half during the past eight years. We have been able to support the work of more researchers in fields related to our mission and to increase the total dollar amounts dedicated to such research. Melvin M. Payne, Chairman of the Board of Trustees, introduces a summary of the program elsewhere in this volume. At the least, the Society has taken up some of the slack at a time when government and other private support for basic research has been less generous than it once was. We, of course, take pride in this, but the real credit goes to the members, whose annual dues make the entire funding possible.

In 1984 we are finally acting on the long-expressed desires of our membership for travel information that is at once educational and entertaining. We have just begun publication of the Society's first new *(Continued on page 114)*

Although frowning, Snowflake (opposite) enjoys his notoriety at the Barcelona zoo. The only known example of pure albinism among gorillas furrows his brow to help shield his eyes, which are easily irritated by light because of their abnormally low pigmentation.

Arthur J. Riopelle found Snowflake in the Republic of Equatorial Guinea, where the scientist was conducting Society-sponsored research of lowland gorillas. With support from the Society and the National Institutes of Health, Dr. Riopelle has directed a detailed follow-up study of the albino.

MICHAEL KUH

Songs of the humpback whale

To supplement a two-part article in 1979 on humpback whales, a sound sheet, or phonograph record (left), of their songs was bound in the magazine to make available what cannot be truly described—the chirpy, eerie, booming whale symphony.

Whale researcher Roger Payne (right, at left) and Society audiovisual technical director Jon Larimore worked at a sound-mixing console to produce the master tape.

Breaching belly-up in Alaska's Glacier Bay (above), a humpback may be

JOSEPH H. BAILEY, NGS

AL GIDDINGS, SEA FILMS, INC. (ABOVE AND BELOW)

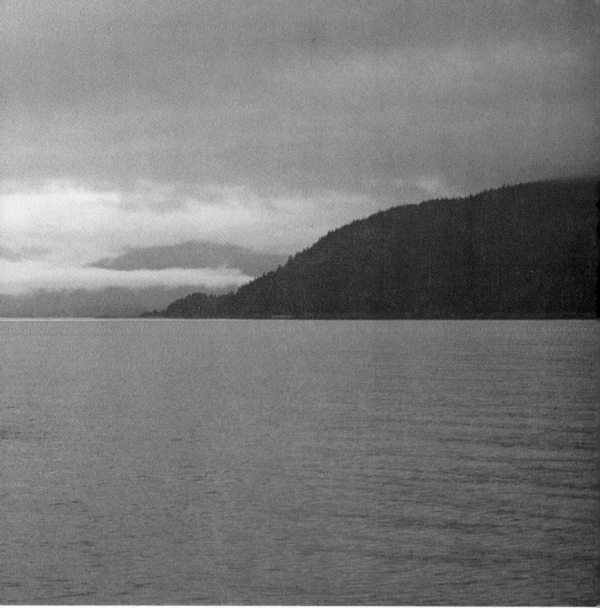

communicating with other whales or displaying strength in response to some threat. Distinctive markings on flukes (right) enable researchers to track the migrations of humpbacks from one ocean to another as they move to tropical waters to calve in winter and return to cold water to feed in summer.

Forty-five feet of gentleness that feeds on oceanic plankton, the humpback is now protected from whaling but can be disturbed by whale-watchers in boats. A sampling of the humpback song is outbound to the Milky Way aboard the Voyager 2 *spacecraft and could turn out to be more intelligible to denizens of other planets than the language of man.*

The Society, which has published some of the most remarkable photographs and paintings of the great cetaceans, has a continuing commitment to support research on whales.

BATES LITTLEHALES, NGS

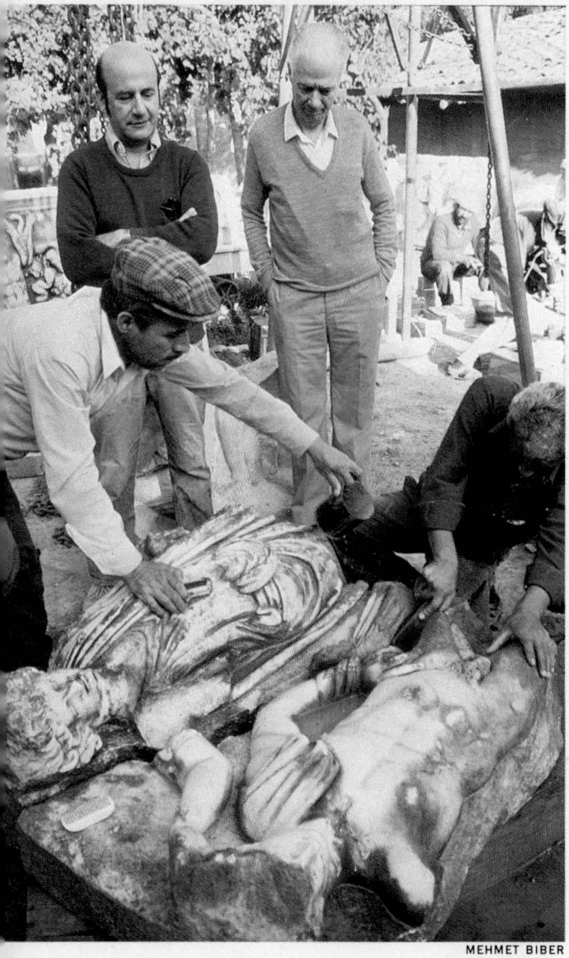

MEHMET BIBER

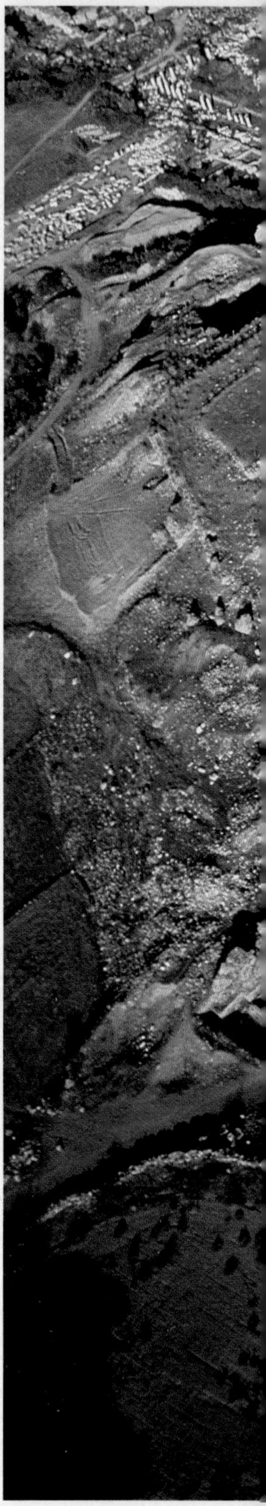

After a 1,300-year intermission, the great theater of Aphrodisias (above) emerged as the overburden of centuries was removed. More than 20 years of excavation have revealed the artistic and architectural opulence within the city (right), but much is still buried.

Sheltered in an isolated valley of southwestern Turkey, Aphrodisias thrived as a Bronze Age, Greek, Roman, and Byzantine center before succumbing to a series of earthquakes and invasions.

The city's gifted artists created a renowned school of sculpture, and demand for their works spread across the Roman world. As workmen (left) cleaned a marble panel, Society Board Chairman Melvin M. Payne, at right, and excavation director Kenan T. Erim inspected the results. Treasures from Aphrodisias are housed in a museum built by the Turkish government and the Society.

Understanding the classical world

DAVID BRILL

to better understand our own

(Continued from page 108) magazine for adults since 1888—NATIONAL GEOGRAPHIC TRAVELER. (This may be an extreme example of our caution in undertaking new projects.) TRAVELER's merits remain to be proved, but members will be quick to give us the benefit of their opinions, for in their own travels they will judge our efforts directly and personally.

ANOTHER PROJECT, now in final stages, is a new building to complete our headquarters site in Washington, D. C. The building, with its state-of-the-art auditorium and audiovisual facilities, will be a useful ornament to the city.

So the Society has not been a stranger to planning for the future. From the vantage point of 1984 I see ours as continuing in the direction of diversification of services to members. The technologies now available or under development will doubtless come to the fore in that future. Some of them may become obvious, such as satellite or cable television.

Many people are, of course, simply curious about technology and would be interested to know that with our new computer mapping equipment the Society, whose most distinctive service may be cartography, has automated the mapmaking process. What had been long, tedious handwork to assemble and fix into position much of the detailed information that must go on a map can now be accomplished by one operator at a single electronic-editing console.

Though the Society's TV documentaries, winners of nine Emmys since 1965, were very popular on commercial channels, we entered nine years ago into partnership with Gulf Oil Corporation and WQED/Pittsburgh to produce quality programs for showing on Public Broadcasting Service stations. By any measure, the programs have been enormously successful. They have won the industry's highest awards, and they have been among the most watched offerings on PBS. In fact, National Geographic Specials hold half of the top 25 places in PBS ratings over the period and now regularly reach more than 16 million viewers in their first showings. What is more important than ratings, however, is that the Society's mission has been more broadly accomplished.

Our television partnership has been necessary because the Society, acting by itself, could simply not afford to produce the programs. Television, even bad television, is extraordinarily expensive. Yet its appetite for programming is ravenous. The temptation might be to shave quality in order to have more frequent broadcasts. Whatever the Society may do in future television, we will not do that.

Some technologies, though less obvious than television, are no less important. Our writing and editing are done on

Aphrodite, goddess of love born of the sea, returns to water for a gentle cleaning. The marble statue of the patroness of the city of Aphrodisias dates from the second century A.D., when sculptors fashioned falls of marble drapery equaling the soft textured look of the cloth here wrapped around the goddess to hold in moisture.

Aphrodisian statuary was in demand throughout the Roman world, and examples have been found in Spain and North Africa. Unlike most artists of their day, the sculptors proudly signed their work, much of which is now being unearthed, restored, and displayed.

ALBERT MOLDVAY, NGS

Sunlight streams past a bowl (above) lifted through the rebuilt door of a kiva, or ceremonial room, in the cliff dwellings of Colorado's Mesa Verde National Park. The village once sheltered a tribe of Indians who disappeared 700 years ago. An archaeological expedition—the National Geographic Society-National Park Service Wetherill Mesa Project—explored the ruins and reconstructed much of the ancient complex.

In a remote Guatemalan cavern, staff archaeologist George Stuart and his son David (right) examine inscriptions and paintings made 1,200 years ago. Here Maya Indians recorded messages in columns of elegant hieroglyphs. An extraordinary archive—untouched and unknown for more than a millennium—it survives from the most brilliant age of Maya civilization, when great cities and temples arose in the now sparsely populated lowland. This most advanced pre-Columbian writing system provides a record of names, dates, and events. Many such glyphs can only be partly deciphered; others remain enigmatic. Although guards now protect the cavern, looters seeking salable artifacts have mutilated the stonework.

"El Rey" (opposite)—biggest of 11 huge heads found in southern Mexico—has his colossal face scrubbed. More than a thousand years ago, Olmec Indians sculptured this 30-ton basalt image, discovered in 1946 during a joint Society-Smithsonian Institution expedition.

WILBUR E. GARRETT, NGS

The discovery of America,

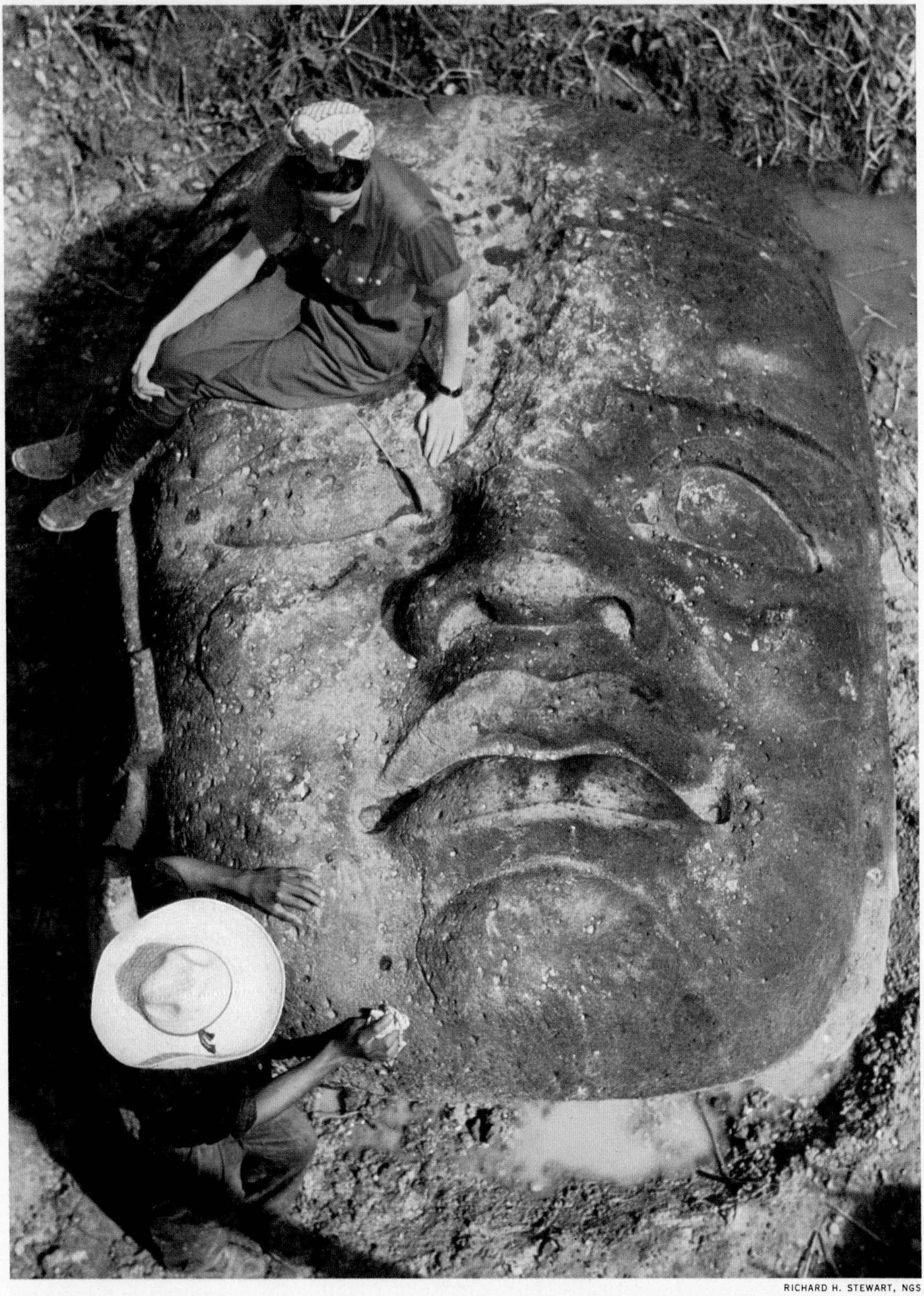

RICHARD H. STEWART, NGS

a continuing exploration

computer terminals; copy is typeset by computer and printed on electronically controlled presses. That has all become routine. An epoch that began with Johannes Gutenberg has nearly vanished.

We have arrived at that time when the convergence of new technologies—the combination of extraordinary discoveries—will change society's ways of doing things, the ways man thinks about his world. Few of these technologies are inherently new, but brought together, they have a powerful implication for the privacy, the peace, the security, and the development of the person.

Together they represent the dawn of the information age.

JOSEPH F. ROCK

The first Westerner to reach remote districts of Tibet, Joseph F. Rock (above left, at center) in the 1920s led several Society expeditions into parts of China where few Han, the ethnic majority, had ever been. His armed escorts — devout Buddhists and bandits — stood with him before Mount Jambeyang, the "peerless pyramid."

Articles on China appeared in the magazine as early as 1900, when an author dismissed, perhaps prematurely, the notion of the "Chinese paradox" in diplomatic relations with Western powers.

Just as the steam engine, the factory concept, the interchangeable part opened the industrial age, so the silicon chip, the satellite, and fiber optics announce the age of information. And—like all other ages of man—it is filled with pitfalls and disappointment as well as opportunity and gratification.

The engine of this new age is the ability to transmit enormous amounts of information at incredible speeds. It was a task of several years to hand-set the Gutenberg Bible letter by letter in movable type. Today a beam of light is capable of transmitting the entire Bible from one place to any other place on this planet in less than a second.

That same beam theoretically could carry every telephone call, radio report, and television broadcast in the United States *simultaneously*. Already telephone calls—in the form of pulses of light—are transmitted through hair-fine strands of pure glass by lasers no larger than grains of salt.

LOWELL GEORGIA

JODI COBB, NGS

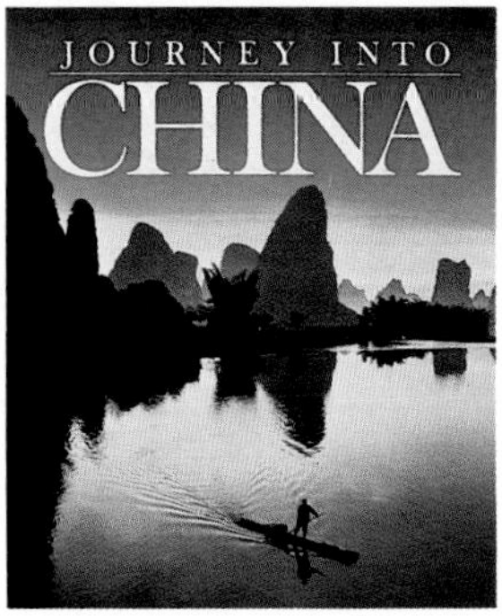

From roller-skating in Kunming (left) to the great sculpture of Buddha Vairocana, symbol of creation (top), in the caves of Longmen above the Yi River, a 1982 Society book (above) explored ancient and modern China.

The Society's television Specials came full circle in 1984. The inaugural program in 1965 showed the first "Americans on Everest." A program aired in 1984, the ninth year of partnership with WQED/Pittsburgh and Gulf Oil Corporation for broadcast on PBS TV, marked the "Return to Everest" of Sir Edmund Hillary who, with Sherpa Tenzing Norgay, was the first to stand atop the world's highest mountain.

Hillary was repeatedly drawn back to the Sherpas and their families. Although the children were bright and eager to learn (1)*, they had no school. "Our children have eyes, but still they are blind," said one Sherpa. Hillary helped them build a school, "the beginning of an avalanche," he says, that grew to 21 more schools. On one of his frequent visits to Nepal, Hillary* (2)*, at center, was filmed with his son Peter, at right. The Sherpas celebrated the return by wrapping katas, or ceremonial scarves, around Hillary's neck* (3) *and honored him with traditional dances* (4).

The aim in Society Specials has been to show the world in all its diversity and demonstrate that a popular medium can be both entertaining and instructive.

1

2

3

Television as truth: real

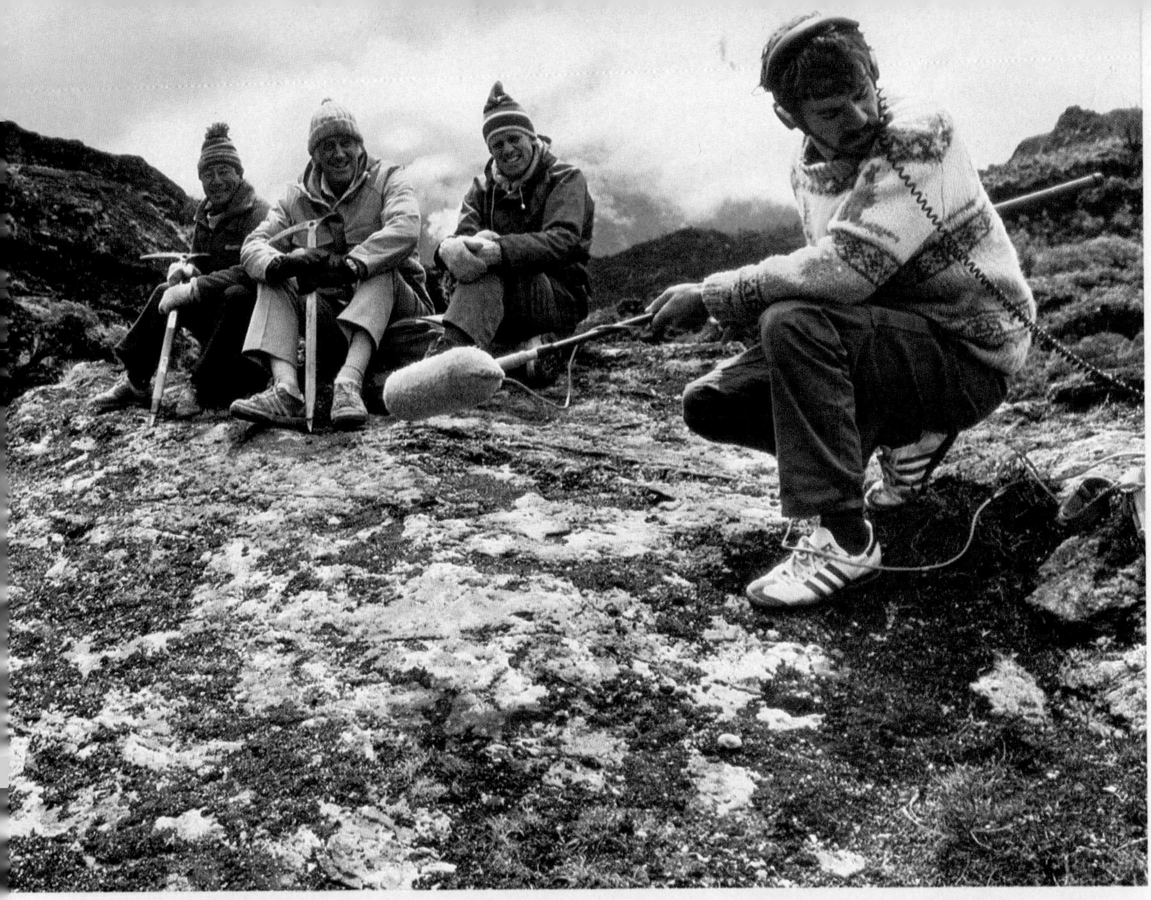

ALL BY ANNE B. K. KRUMBHAAR, NGS

4

dramas of the real world

Students give the marks when ideas are tested for National Geographic WORLD magazine. Barbara Steinwurtzel (above) gets reactions to a story from third graders at Janney Elementary School in Washington, D. C. For every ten ideas shown to children, only about two make the grade.

Editing one of the Society's more than 100 educational films (left), division director Sidney Platt, at right, and Carl Ziebe review footage. With titles ranging across the curriculum, the films help schools enrich their programs with quality material at reasonable cost.

A student at Potomac School in McLean, Virginia (right), assembles a cut-out bird, part of a Wonders of Learning Kit series. The kits promote learning flexibility, since children work at their own pace.

These and other educational media help fulfill the Society's mission by reaching children as young as kindergarten age.

ALL BY JOSEPH H. BAILEY, NGS

In the home a single 12-inch disc is capable of storing 16,000 300-page books or 108,000 full-color television images, along with two channels of high-fidelity sound.

The technology is here today that would permit a person to own a small set of such discs that could store every page and every photograph of every NATIONAL GEOGRAPHIC since 1888. At the touch of a control you could recall this information in any sequence you desired. You could even have the entire contents of the Library of Congress available on the shelves of your study.

THERE ARE OTHER GENIES loose in the world today than the one in the pure glass thread. There is the cable system that receives data from a satellite and not only beams news and entertainment into your home but can also allow you to bank, to shop, to learn, to communicate without ever leaving your chair.

The microwave emissions that are caught by your antenna enable a person or an institution to send you a menu of programming without the aid of a nationwide broadcasting company or a local station or even a cable system. Now one can—and in fact some do—print a national newspaper as easily as a local one; a world newspaper, for that matter, is entirely feasible.

The troubling question is *what* are we going to transmit? What will be the content of these ethereal messages descending upon us from space?

Certainly our Society will find a place in this new age of information. Our new building is fully equipped and wired for anticipated advances in audiovisual, computer, and electronic capabilities. For the past two years I have devoted considerable time to a careful assessment of the new broadcasting technologies, both cable and direct. The educational and cultural opportunities are almost staggering—but so too, for the moment, are the practical and economic problems to be overcome. I can only say that we will overcome them in the years ahead, for I feel that the Society is fully prepared to take advantage of these opportunities.

We will not, however, be lured into technology for its own sake.

For I keep asking this question: What technological product is "user friendly," easily portable, requires no internal or external power source, can be optically scanned at variable speeds, provides the highest quality graphics, can survive hard use, even a fair degree of abuse, and costs less than most portable radios or pocket calculators? There is still much to recommend the book or the magazine—if what is between the covers has merit. □

ROBERT S. OAKES, NGS

TO ENCOURAGE exploration, to promote scientific advance, and to recognize outstanding service to geography, the National Geographic Society presents medals, awards, and prizes for exceptional achievement. The dozens of distinguished recipients of these honors are listed here.

MEDALS

Nine Presidents and three Vice Presidents of the United States have presented National Geographic Society medals, beginning with Theodore Roosevelt in 1906. Medals represent the highest honors the Society bestows.

They are:

The Hubbard Medal, named for Gardiner Greene Hubbard, first President of the Society, awarded for distinction in exploration, discovery, and research.

The Alexander Graham Bell Medal, named for the inventor and second Society President, awarded for extraordinary achievement in geographic research, broadly construed.

The Grosvenor Medal, named for Gilbert Hovey Grosvenor, the 55-year Society President and Editor, awarded for exceptional service to geography by a Society officer or employee.

The John Oliver La Gorce Medal, named for a former Society President and Editor, awarded for accomplishment in geographic exploration, or in the sciences, or for public service to advance international understanding (formerly the Special Gold Medal).

HARRIS & EWING

Peary met Amundsen at NGS, 1913.

COMDR. ROBERT E. PEARY, 1906, Hubbard Medal: Arctic explorations. 1909, Special Medal of Honor: Discovery of North Pole.

CAPT. ROALD AMUNDSEN, 1907, Hubbard Medal: Traverse of Northwest Passage. 1913, Special Gold Medal: Discovery of South Pole.

CAPT. ROBERT A. BARTLETT, 1909, Hubbard Medal: Far-north explorations with Peary's 1909 expedition.

GROVE KARL GILBERT, 1909, Hubbard Medal: Thirty years of achievements in physical geography.

SIR ERNEST H. SHACKLETON, 1910, Hubbard Medal: Antarctic explorations and farthest south, 88° 23′.

COL. GEORGE W. GOETHALS, 1914, Special Gold Medal: Directing completion of Panama Canal.

VILHJALMUR STEFANSSON, 1919, Hubbard Medal: Discoveries in Canadian Arctic.

LT. COMDR. RICHARD E. BYRD, JR., 1926, Hubbard Medal: First to reach North Pole by airplane. 1930, Special Medal of Honor: First to attain South Pole by air.

FLOYD BENNETT, 1926, Special Gold Medal: Flight to North Pole with Richard E. Byrd.

COL. CHARLES A. LINDBERGH, 1927, Hubbard Medal: New York-Paris solo flight.

HUGO ECKENER, 1930, Special Medal of Honor: First global navigation of an airship.

ROY CHAPMAN ANDREWS, 1931, Hubbard Medal: Geographic discoveries in Central Asia.

AMELIA EARHART, 1932, Special Gold Medal: First solo Atlantic flight by a woman.

ANNE MORROW LINDBERGH, 1934, Hubbard Medal: Notable flights, as copilot, on Charles Lindbergh's aerial surveys.

CAPTS. ALBERT W. STEVENS AND ORVIL A. ANDERSON, 1935, Hubbard Medals: World altitude record of 72,395 feet in balloon *Explorer II*.

LINCOLN ELLSWORTH, 1936, Hubbard Medal: Extraordinary achievements in polar exploration.

THOMAS C. POULTER, 1937, Special Gold Medal: Achievements, Byrd Antarctic Expedition.

Medals and Awards

GEN. H. H. ARNOLD, 1945, Hubbard Medal: Contributions to aviation.

GILBERT H. GROSVENOR, 1949, Grosvenor Medal: Outstanding service to geography as Editor of NATIONAL GEOGRAPHIC.

COMDR. DONALD B. MACMILLAN, 1953, Hubbard Medal: Arctic explorations, 1908-52.

BRITISH EVEREST EXPEDITION, 1954, Hubbard Medal: Ascent of Mount Everest.

MRS. ROBERT E. PEARY, 1955, Special Gold Medal: Contributions to husband's polar explorations.

JOHN OLIVER LA GORCE, 1955, Grosvenor Medal: Outstanding service to the increase and diffusion of geographic knowledge, 1905-55.

PRINCE PHILIP, DUKE OF EDINBURGH, 1957, Special Gold Medal: Promoting science and better understanding among the world's peoples.

PAUL A. SIPLE, 1958, Hubbard Medal: For 30 years of Antarctic explorations, including leadership of first group to winter at the South Pole.

U. S. NAVY ANTARCTIC EXPEDITIONS, 1959, Hubbard Medal: Antarctic research and exploration, 1955-59.

SIR VIVIAN FUCHS, 1959, Hubbard Medal: Leadership of British trans-Antarctic expedition.

CAPT. JACQUES-YVES COUSTEAU, 1961, Special Gold Medal: Undersea exploration.

DR. AND MRS. LOUIS S. B. LEAKEY, 1962, Hubbard Medal: Anthropological discoveries in East Africa.

LT. COL. JOHN H. GLENN, JR., 1962, Hubbard Medal: Space exploration.

AMERICAN MOUNT EVEREST EXPEDITION, 1963, Hubbard Medal: Contributions to geography and high-altitude research through conquest of earth's highest mountain.

AMERICAN ANTARCTIC MOUNTAINEERING EXPEDITION, 1967, John Oliver La Gorce Medal: First ascent of Antarctica's highest peak, 1966-67.

JUAN T. TRIPPE, 1967, Hubbard Medal: Contributions to aviation.

HAROLD E. EDGERTON, 1968, John Oliver La Gorce Medal: Contributions to photographic and geophysical technology.

PHILIP VAN HORN WEEMS, 1968, John Oliver La Gorce Medal: Contributions to marine, air, and space navigation.

APOLLO 8 ASTRONAUTS COL. FRANK BORMAN, USAF, CAPT. JAMES A. LOVELL, JR., USN, AND LT. COL. WILLIAM A. ANDERS, USAF, 1969, Hubbard Medal: Space exploration; first to orbit the moon.

APOLLO 11 ASTRONAUTS NEIL A. ARMSTRONG, COL. EDWIN E. ALDRIN, JR., USAF, AND LT. COL. MICHAEL COLLINS, USAF, 1970, Hubbard Medal: Space exploration; first moon landing.

MELVILLE BELL GROSVENOR, 1974, Grosvenor Medal: Outstanding service to geography.

ALEXANDER WETMORE, 1975, Hubbard Medal: Contributions to ornithology.

BRUCE CHARLES HEEZEN, MARIE THARP, 1978, Hubbard Medal: Contributions to knowledge of the ocean floor.

JAMES E. WEBB, 1978, Hubbard Medal: Outstanding contribution to manned lunar landings.

BEN L. ABRUZZO, MAXIE L. ANDERSON, AND LARRY NEWMAN, 1979, John Oliver La Gorce Medal: In recognition of the first manned transatlantic balloon flight.

JOHN J. CRAIGHEAD AND FRANK C. CRAIGHEAD, JR., 1979, John Oliver La Gorce Medal: For pioneer use of biotelemetry to extend knowledge of wildlife behavior, life history, and ecology.

GEORGE F. BASS, 1979, John Oliver La Gorce Medal: For advancing the science of nautical archaeology.

THOMAS WILLSON McKNEW, 1980, Grosvenor Medal: For 48 years of dedicated service to the Society.

BARBARA AND BRADFORD WASHBURN, 1980, Alexander Graham Bell Medal: For unique and notable contributions to geography and cartography.

JOHN W. YOUNG AND CAPT. ROBERT L. CRIPPEN, USN, 1981, Hubbard Medal: For contributions to space science as crew of the space shuttle *Columbia*.

MELVIN MONROE PAYNE, 1982, Grosvenor Medal: For 50 years of dedicated service to the Society.

AWARDS

JANE M. SMITH AWARD

Jane McGrew Smith directed that her bequest to the Society be used to establish an award in recognition of notable contributions to geography. The award was discontinued in 1977.

ALFRED H. BROOKS, 1917, Geologist

HIRAM BINGHAM, 1917, Historian, explorer

HENRY PITTIER, 1917, Agriculturist

GEORGE KENNAN, 1917, Authority on Russia

FRANK G. CARPENTER, 1919, Journalist

WILLIAM H. DALL, 1919, Naturalist

WILLIAM H. HOLMES, 1919, Art curator

STEPHEN T. MATHER, 1919, Park Service Director

EDWARD W. NELSON, 1919, Biologist

WALTER T. SWINGLE, 1919, Plant explorer

ROBERT F. GRIGGS, 1919, Botanist

O. F. COOK, 1919, Plant explorer

JOSEPH STRAUSS, 1919, Rear Admiral, USN

J. B. TYRRELL, 1921, Canadian explorer

HERBERT E. GREGORY, 1921, Geologist

FRANK M. CHAPMAN, 1921, Ornithologist

R. G. McCONNELL, 1921, Canadian explorer

DONALD B. MACMILLAN, 1921, Explorer, Lieutenant, USNR

CHARLES SHELDON, 1925, Alaska explorer

ROBERT A. BARTLETT, 1925, Far-north explorer

NEIL M. JUDD, 1925, Archaeologist

JOSEPH F. ROCK, 1925, Plant explorer

PHILIP SIDNEY SMITH, 1925, Geologist

WILLIAM BROOKS CABOT, 1925, Author, engineer

KNUD RASMUSSEN, 1926, Greenland explorer

CHARLES A. LINDBERGH, 1927, Transatlantic flight pioneer

CURTIS D. WILBUR, 1929, Secretary of the Navy, retired

ANDREW E. DOUGLASS, 1929, Astronomer, dendrochronologist

HERBERT PUTNAM, 1929, Librarian of Congress

CORNELIUS A. PUGSLEY, 1929, Banker, conservationist

SIR WILFRED GRENFELL, 1930, Surgeon, missionary, author

ASHLEY C. McKINLEY, 1931, Captain, USA, aerial photographer

DOUGLAS W. JOHNSON, 1931, Physiographer

ANDRÉ CITROËN, 1931, French industrialist

ALBERT W. STEVENS, 1931, Captain, USA, aerial photographer

LAURENCE M. GOULD, 1931, Biologist

WILLIAM H. HOBBS, 1933, Geologist

EUGENE EDWARD BUCK, 1934, President, American Society of Composers, Authors & Publishers

VERNON BAILEY, 1934, Field naturalist

JAMES P. THOMSON, 1934, Royal Geographical Society of Australia

CHARLES F. MARVIN, 1934, Meteorologist

W. COLEMAN NEVILS, S. J., 1934, Classicist, President, Georgetown University

CLIFFORD K. BERRYMAN, 1934, Political cartoonist

LEONHARD STEJNEGER, 1935, Biologist

JOSEPH P. CONNOLLY, 1935, Geologist, college president

WILLIAM R. POPE, 1935, Colonel, USA

LAWRENCE J. BURPEE, 1936, Canadian commissioner

RANDOLPH P. WILLIAMS, 1936, Captain, U. S. Army Air Corps

ROGERS BIRNIE, JR., 1936, Retired Army officer

SAMUEL S. GANNETT, 1936, Geographer

HERBERT HOLLICK-KENYON, 1936, Pilot, Canadian Airways

HIS MAJESTY KING LEOPOLD, 1936, Brussels, Belgium

A. E. MURLIN, 1936, U. S. Geological Survey, retired

H. L. BALDWIN, 1936, U. S. Geological Survey, retired

ROBERT MULDROW, 1936, U. S. Geological Survey, retired

W. J. PETERS, 1936, U. S. Geological Survey, retired

PRINCE IYESATO TOKUGAWA, 1937, Tokyo, Japan

WEB HILL, 1937, Merchant

STEPHEN R. CAPPS, 1938, Geologist

FRANKLIN ADAMS, 1938, Authority on Latin America

GEORGE W. GODDARD, 1940, Major, USAF, aerial photographer

J. FRED ESSARY, 1941, Journalist

CHARLES H. DEETZ, 1942, Cartographer, U. S. Coast & Geodetic Survey

SAMUEL WHITTEMORE BOGGS, 1943, Department of State geographer

ALEXANDER M. PATCH, 1943, Major General, USA

ELI HELMICK, 1943, Major General, USA, retired

HARRY WARNER FRANTZ, 1943, Journalist

EDMUND W. STARLING, 1943, U. S. Secret Service

MRS. WILLIAM G. PADEN, 1943, Author

CHRISTOVA LEITE DE CASTRO, 1944, Brazilian geographer

FRANK B. JEWETT, 1945, President, National Academy of Sciences

FRANK M. MacFARLAND, 1945, President, California Academy of Sciences

S. S. VISHER, 1945, Geographer

SALVADOR MASSIP, 1946, Geographer

CHESTER W. NIMITZ, 1946, Fleet Admiral, USN, Chief of Naval Operations

MALCOLM J. PROUDFOOT, 1947, Geographer

GEOFFREY T. HELLMAN, 1947, Essayist

MAURICE EWING, 1947, Geologist

NICHOLAS H. DARTON, 1948, Geologist

BENJAMIN R. HOFFMAN, 1948, Geographical Society of Philadelphia

JOHN O'KEEFE, 1949, U. S. Army Map Service

GEORGE J. MILLER, 1949, Editor, *Journal of Geography*

EARL B. SHAW, 1949, President, Council of Geography Teachers

MRS. ALBERT W. STEVENS, 1950, Smith life member

MRS. HENRY H. ARNOLD, 1950, Smith life member

ALBERT E. GIESECKE, 1951, Government adviser, Peru

HUGH L. DRYDEN, 1951, Director, National Advisory Committee for Aeronautics

HERBERT FRIEDMANN, 1951, Curator of Birds, U. S. National Museum

MRS. J. R. HILDEBRAND, 1951, Widow of Assistant Editor, NATIONAL GEOGRAPHIC

MRS. RUTH B. SHIPLEY, 1951, Passport Office, Department of State

ANDREW GEORGE LATTA McNAUGHTON, 1952, General, Canadian Army, retired

MAYNARD OWEN WILLIAMS, 1953, Chief of Foreign Staff, NATIONAL GEOGRAPHIC

ROBERT B. ANDERSON, 1953, Secretary of the Navy

MRS. FRANKLIN L. FISHER, 1953, Widow of Illustrations Editor, NATIONAL GEOGRAPHIC

KENNETH H. GIBSON, 1953, Colonel, U. S. Air Force

IRA S. BOWEN, 1955, Astronomer

ARDITO DESIO, 1955, Leader, K-2 Expedition

CHARLES P. MOUNTFORD, 1956, Anthropologist, Australia

SIR VIVIAN FUCHS, 1959, British geologist, explorer

ALBERT A. STANLEY, 1959, U. S. Coast & Geodetic Survey

P. V. H. WEEMS, 1959, Captain, USN, retired

EDWIN A. LINK, 1959, Inventor and undersea pioneer

SIR BRUCE INGRAM, 1959, Editor, *Illustrated London News*

ARLEIGH A. BURKE, 1960, Admiral, USN, Chief of Naval Operations

LYNDON B. JOHNSON, 1962, Vice President of the United States

DR. CALVIN H. PLIMPTON, 1964, President, Amherst College

FRANKLIN L. BURR AWARD

Mary C. Burr bequeathed a fund to the Society in memory of her father. Income is used to award cash prizes to leaders in the Society's expeditions and researches for especially meritorious work in the field of geographic science.

CAPT. ALBERT W. STEVENS, 1933, 1936, Aeronaut

CAPT. ORVIL A. ANDERSON, 1936, Aeronaut

CAPT. RANDOLPH P. WILLIAMS, 1936, Aeronaut

DR. AND MRS. WILLIAM M. MANN, 1938, Zoologists

BRADFORD WASHBURN, 1939, 1965, Geographer

MATTHEW W. STIRLING, 1939, 1941, 1957, Archaeologist

MRS. MATTHEW W. STIRLING, 1941, Archaeologist

ALEXANDER WETMORE, 1944, Ornithologist

THOMAS A. JAGGER, 1945, Engineer

LYMAN J. BRIGGS, 1945, 1954, 1962, Chairman, Committee for Research and Exploration, National Geographic Society

GEORGE VAN BIESBROECK, 1947, 1948, 1953, Astronomer

EDWARD A. HALBACH, FRANCIS J. HEYDEN, S. J., CARL W. MILLER, CHARLES H. SMILEY, 1948, Astronomers

ARTHUR A. ALLEN, 1948, Ornithologist

CHARLES P. MOUNTFORD, 1950, Anthropologist

BOB CAMPBELL

Dian Fossey frolics with two young mountain gorillas, the primate species that she has lived with intimately and studied definitively.

FRANK M. SETZLER, 1950, Anthropologist

HAROLD E. EDGERTON, 1952, Electrical engineer

NEIL M. JUDD, 1955, 1963, Archaeologist

MRS. ROBERT E. PEARY, 1955, Scientific collaborator

MRS. MARIE PEARY STAFFORD, 1955, Scientific collaborator

ROBERT F. GRIGGS, 1956, Geographer

CARL F. MILLER, 1959, Archaeologist

LOUIS S. B. LEAKEY AND MARY D. LEAKEY, 1961, Anthropologists

JANE GOODALL, 1962, 1964, Zoologist

REAR ADM. DONALD B. MACMILLAN, 1963, Polar explorer

BARRY C. BISHOP, 1963, Mountaineer and glaciologist

HELGE INGSTAD AND ANNE STINE INGSTAD, 1964, Archaeologists

RICHARD E. LEAKEY, 1965, 1973, Anthropologist

NORMAN G. DYHRENFURTH, 1965, Mountaineer

MAYNARD M. MILLER, 1967, Glaciologist

DIAN J. FOSSEY, 1973, Zoologist

KENAN T. ERIM, 1973, Classical archaeologist

JARED M. DIAMOND, 1979, Ornithologist

FRED A. URQUHART AND NORAH R. URQUHART, 1979, Entomologists

BIRUTÉ M. F. GALDIKAS, 1981, Anthropologist

OTHER SOCIETY AWARDS

HERBERT FRIEDMANN, WILLIAM J. MORRIS, Arnold Guyot Memorial Award, 1968, Paleontologists

ROBERT W. WILSON, Arnold Guyot Memorial Award, 1974, Paleontologist

RICHARD L. HAY, Arnold Guyot Memorial Award, 1978, Geologist

MARY R. DAWSON, ROBERT M. WEST, Arnold Guyot Memorial Award, 1981, Vertebrate Paleontologists

HESLON MUKIRI GITHUA, Special National Geographic Society Award, 1968, Scientific collaborator

NATIONAL GEOGRAPHIC INDEX 1947-1983

This Index covers the issues of January 1947 through December 1983. A companion Index covers October 1888 through December 1946. Together the two volumes provide a complete listing of all articles that have appeared in NATIONAL GEOGRAPHIC by subject, by author, and by photographer. As an additional service, this volume lists books, map supplements, television films, and other educational materials of the Society, but they are entered only by medium and subject. The Society also publishes semiannually for each six-month volume of the magazine a free detailed index, available on request to members.

A

ABACO (Island), Bahama Islands:
• The Loyalists. By Kent Britt. Photos by Ted Spiegel. 510-539, Apr. 1975

ABALONE:
• Goggle Fishing in California Waters. By David Hellyer. Photos by Lamar Boren. 615-632, May 1949

ABBEY, EDWARD: Author:
• Guadalupe's Trails in Summer (Guadalupe Mountains National Park, Texas). 135-141, July 1979

ABBOT, J. LLOYD, Jr.: Author:
• Flight Into Antarctic Darkness. Photos by David S. Boyer. 732-738, Nov. 1967

ABBOTSBURY SWANNERY, England:
• The Swans of Abbotsbury. By Michael Moynihan. Photos by Barnet Saidman. 563-570, Oct. 1959

ABBOTT RANCH, Cherry County, Nebraska:
• Land of Long Sunsets: Nebraska's Sand Hills. By John Madson. Photos by Jodi Cobb. 493-517, Oct. 1978

ABDUL GHAFUR:
Author-Photographer:
• From America to Mecca on Airborne Pilgrimage. 1-60, July 1953

ABDUL-RAUF, MUHAMMAD: Author:
• Pilgrimage to Mecca. Photos by Mehmet Biber. 581-607, Nov. 1978

ABELL, GEORGE O.: Author:
• Exploring the Farthest Reaches of Space. 782-790, Dec. 1956

ABELL, SAM: Photographer:
• The Bonanza Bean–Coffee. By Ethel A. Starbird. 388-405, Mar. 1981
• Herbs for All Seasons. By Lonnelle Aikman. Picture portfolio text by Larry Kohl. 386-409, Mar. 1983
• Long Island's Quiet Side (East End). By Jane Snow. 662-685, May 1980
• Newfoundland Trusts in the Sea. By Gary Jennings. 112-141, Jan. 1974
• Ontario, Canada's Keystone. By David S. Boyer. Photos by Sam Abell and the author. 760-795, Dec. 1978
• Our Wild and Scenic Rivers: The Noatak. By John M. Kauffmann. 52-59, July 1977
• Yellowstone at 100: A Walk Through the Wilderness. By Karen and Derek Craighead. 579-603, May 1972

ABERCROMBIE, LYNN: Photographer:
• Oman: Guardian of the Gulf. By Thomas J. Abercrombie. Photos by the author and Lynn Abercrombie. 344-377, Sept. 1981

ABERCROMBIE, THOMAS J.:
• Editorial. By Gilbert M. Grosvenor. 291, Mar. 1977
• National Geographic Photographers Win Top Magazine Awards. 830-831, June 1959
Author:
• Bahrain: Hub of the Persian Gulf. Photos by Steve Raymer. 300-329, Sept. 1979
• Islam's Heartland, Up in Arms. 335-345, Sept. 1980
• Minneapolis and St. Paul. Photos by Annie Griffiths. 665-691, Nov. 1980
• Perth–Fair Winds and Full Sails. Photos by Cary Wolinsky. 638-667, May 1982
Author-Photographer:
• Afghanistan: Crossroad of Conquerors. 297-345, Sept. 1968
• Algeria: Learning to Live With Independence. 200-233, Aug. 1973
• Behind the Veil of Troubled Yemen. 403-445, Mar. 1964
• Cambodia: Indochina's "Neutral" Corner. 514-551, Oct. 1964
• Egypt: Change Comes to a Changeless Land. 312-343, Mar. 1977
• Ice Fishing's Frigid Charms. 861-872, Dec. 1958
• Kansai, Japan's Historic Heartland. 295-339, Mar. 1970
• Ladakh–The Last Shangri-la. 332-359, Mar. 1978
• Morocco, Land of the Farthest West. 834-865, June 1971
• Nomad in Alaska's Outback. 540-567, Apr. 1969

The microprocessor, or computer on a chip (left), is in the vanguard of proven technologies that promise easier, faster, and wider access to information. Someday a reference such as this Index may be commonly packaged in the same tiny space.

• Oman: Guardian of the Gulf. Photos by the author and Lynn Abercrombie. 344-377, Sept. 1981
• Saudi Arabia: Beyond the Sands of Mecca. 1-53, Jan. 1966
• Switzerland, Europe's High-rise Republic. 68-113, July 1969
• The Sword and the Sermon. 3-45, July 1972
• Venezuela Builds on Oil. 344-387, Mar. 1963
• Young-old Lebanon Lives by Trade. 479-523, Apr. 1958
Photographer:
• Alaska Proudly Joins the Union. By Ernest Gruening. 43-83, July 1959
• Brasília, Metropolis Made to Order. By Hernane Tavares de Sá. 704-724, May 1960
• Captain Smith of Jamestown. By Bradford Smith. 581-620, May 1957
• Easter Island and Its Mysterious Monuments. By Howard La Fay. 90-117, Jan. 1962
• Enchantress! By Theodore H. Reed. 628-641, May 1961
• Man's Deepest Dive. By Jacques Piccard. 224-239, Aug. 1960
• Man's First Winter at the South Pole. By Paul A. Siple. 439-478, Apr. 1958
• The Mighty *Enterprise*. By Nathaniel T. Kenney. 431-448, Mar. 1963
• Old-New Iran, Next Door to Russia. By Edward J. Linehan. 44-85, Jan. 1961
• Underwater Archeology: Key to History's Warehouse. By George F. Bass. Photos by Thomas J. Abercrombie and Robert B. Goodman. 138-156, July 1963
• You and the Obedient Atom. By Allan C. Fisher, Jr. Photos by B. Anthony Stewart and Thomas J. Abercrombie. 303-353, Sept. 1958

ABIDJAN, Ivory Coast:
• The Ivory Coast–African Success Story. By Michael and Aubine Kirtley. 94-125, July 1982

ABKHAZIAN A.S.S.R., U.S.S.R.:
• "Every Day Is a Gift When You Are Over 100." By Alexander Leaf. Photos by John Launois. 93-119, Jan. 1973

ABOARD the N. S. *Savannah:* World's First Nuclear Merchantman. By Alan Villiers. Photos by John E. Fletcher. 280-298, Aug. 1962

"ABOMINABLE SNOWMAN":
• Wintering on the Roof of the World. By Barry C. Bishop. 503-547, Oct. 1962

ABORIGINALS:
• "The Alice" in Australia's Wonderland. By Alan Villiers. Photos by Jeff Carter and David Moore. 230-257, Feb. 1966
• Arnhem Land Aboriginals Cling to Dreamtime. By Clive Scollay. Photos by Penny Tweedie. 644-663, Nov. 1980
• An Arnhem Land Adventure. By Donald F. Thomson. 403-430, Mar. 1948
Arnhem Land Expedition of 1948. NGS research grant. 430
• Australia. By Alan Villiers. 309-385, Sept. 1963
I. The West and the South. 309-345; II. The Settled East, the Barrier Reef, the Center. 347-385
• Cruise to Stone Age Arnhem Land. By Howell Walker. NGS research grant. 417-430, Sept. 1949
• Expedition to the Land of the Tiwi (Melville Island). By Charles P. Mountford. 417-440, Mar. 1956
• Exploring Stone Age Arnhem Land. By Charles P. Mountford. Photos by Howell Walker. NGS research grant. 745-782, Dec. 1949
• From Spear to Hoe on Groote Eylandt. By Howell Walker. 131-142, Jan. 1953
• In the Wake of Darwin's *Beagle*. By Alan Villiers. Photos by James L. Stanfield. 449-495, Oct. 1969
• The Journey of Burke and Wills. By Joseph Judge. Photos by Joseph J. Scherschel. 152-191, Feb. 1979
• Perth–Fair Winds and Full Sails. By Thomas J. Abercrombie. Photos by Cary Wolinsky. 638-667, May 1982
• Queensland: Young Titan of Australia's Tropic North. By Kenneth MacLeish. Photos by Winfield Parks. 593-639, Nov. 1968
• Rock Paintings of the Aborigines. By Kay and Stanley Breeden. 174-187, Feb. 1973
• The Top End of Down Under. By Kenneth MacLeish. Photos by Thomas Nebbia. 145-174, Feb. 1973
• Western Australia, the Big Country. By Kenneth MacLeish. Photos by James L. Stanfield. 150-187, Feb. 1975

ABRAHAM, the Friend of God. By Kenneth MacLeish. Photos by Dean Conger. 739-789, Dec. 1966

ABRAMS, AL: Author-Photographer:
• Our Life on a Border Kibbutz. By Carol and Al Abrams. 364-391, Sept. 1970

ABRAMS, CAROL: Author:
• Our Life on a Border Kibbutz. By Carol and Al Abrams. Photos by Al Abrams. 364-391, Sept. 1970

ABRIGO DO SOL (Archaeological Site), Brazil:
• Man in the Amazon: Stone Age Present Meets Stone Age Past. By W. Jesco von Puttkamer. NGS research grant. 60-83, Jan. 1979

ABRUZZO, BEN L.: Author:
• *Double Eagle II* Has Landed! Crossing the Atlantic by Balloon. By Ben L. Abruzzo, with Maxie L. Anderson and Larry Newman. 858-882, Dec. 1978
• First Across the Pacific: The Flight of *Double Eagle V*. 513-521, Apr. 1982

ABU DHABI, United Arab Emirates:
• The Arab World, Inc. By John J. Putman. Photos by Winfield Parks. 494-533, Oct. 1975
• Desert Sheikdoms of Arabia's Pirate Coast. By Ronald Codrai. 65-104, July 1956

ABU LATT (Island), Red Sea:
• Fish Men Explore a New World Undersea. By Jacques-Yves Cousteau. 431-472, Oct. 1952

ABU SIMBEL, Egypt:
• Abu Simbel's Ancient Temples Reborn. By Georg Gerster. 724-744, May 1969
• Saving the Ancient Temples at Abu Simbel. By Georg Gerster. Paintings by Robert W. Nicholson. 694-742, May 1966
• Threatened Treasures of the Nile. By Georg Gerster. 587-621, Oct. 1963

ABUNDANT Life in a Desert Land. By Walter Meayers Edwards. 424-436, Sept. 1973

ACADIA (Parish), Louisiana:
• Cajunland, Louisiana's French-speaking Coast. By Bern Keating. Photos by Charles Harbutt and Franke Keating. 353-391, Mar. 1966

ACAPULCO, Mexico:
• Mexico in Motion. By Bart McDowell. Photos by Kip Ross. 490-537, Oct. 1961
• A New Riviera: Mexico's West Coast. By Nathaniel T. Kenney. Photos by Charles O'Rear. 670-699, Nov. 1973
• The Two Acapulcos. By James Cerruti. Photos by Thomas Nebbia. 848-878, Dec. 1964

ACID RAIN–How Great a Menace? By Anne LaBastille. Photos by Ted Spiegel. 652-681, Nov. 1981

ACOMA INDIANS:
• Pueblo Pottery–2,000 Years of Artistry. By David L. Arnold. 593-605, Nov. 1982

ACROPOLIS, Athens:
• Athens: Her Golden Past Still Lights the World. By Kenneth F. Weaver. Photos by Phillip Harrington. 100-137, July 1963

ACROSS Australia by Sunpower. By Hans Tholstrup and Larry Perkins. Photos by David Austen. 600-607, Nov. 1983

ACROSS Canada by Mackenzie's Track. By Ralph Gray. 191-239, Aug. 1955

ACROSS the Alps in a Wicker Basket. By Phil Walker. 117-131, Jan. 1963

ACROSS the Frozen Desert to Byrd Station. By Paul W. Frazier. Photos by Calvin L. Larsen. 383-398, Sept. 1957

ACROSS the Pacific by Balloon: The Flight of *Double Eagle V*. By Ben L. Abruzzo. 513-521, Apr. 1982

ACROSS the Potomac From Washington. By Albert W. Atwood. 1-33, Jan. 1953

ACROSS the Ridgepole of the Alps. By Walter Meayers Edwards. 410-419, Sept. 1960

ADAMS, ABIGAIL:
• Patriots in Petticoats. By Lonnelle Aikman. Paintings by Louis S. Glanzman. 475-493, Oct. 1975

ADAMS, JOHN:
• The Living White House. By Lonnelle Aikman. 593-643, Nov. 1966
• Patriots in Petticoats. By Lonnelle Aikman. Paintings by Louis S. Glanzman. 475-493, Oct. 1975
• Profiles of the Presidents: I. The Presidency and How It Grew. By Frank Freidel. 642-687, Nov. 1964

ADAMS, JOHN QUINCY:
• The Living White House. By Lonnelle Aikman. 593-643, Nov. 1966
• Profiles of the Presidents: I. The Presidency and How It Grew. By Frank Freidel. 642-687, Nov. 1964

ADAMS, SAMUEL:
• Firebrands of the Revolution. By Eric F. Goldman. Photos by George F. Mobley. 2-27, July 1974

ADAMS FAMILY:
• Literary Landmarks of Massachusetts. By William H. Nicholas. Photos by B. Anthony Stewart and John E. Fletcher. 279-310, Mar. 1950

ADDIS ABABA, Ethiopia:
• Ethiopia: Revolution in an Ancient Empire. By Robert Caputo. 614-645, May 1983
• Ethiopian Adventure. By Nathaniel T. Kenney. Photos by James P. Blair. 548-582, Apr. 1965

ADELAIDE, Australia:
• South Australia, Gateway to the Great Outback. By Howell Walker. Photos by Joseph J. Scherschel. 441-481, Apr. 1970

ADEN PROTECTORATE, now Democratic Yemen:
• Along the Storied Incense Roads of Aden. By Hermann F. Eilts. Photos by Brian Brake. 230-254, Feb. 1957
• Sailing with Sindbad's Sons. By Alan Villiers. 675-688, Nov. 1948

ADENA CULTURE. *See* Mound Builders

ADIRONDACK MOUNTAINS, New York:
• My Backyard, the Adirondacks. By Anne LaBastille. Photos by David Alan Harvey. 616-639, May 1975

ADMIRAL of the Ends of the Earth. By Melville Bell Grosvenor. 36-48, July 1957

ADOBE New Mexico. By Mason Sutherland. Photos by Justin Locke. 783-830, Dec. 1949

"THE ADORATION OF THE MAGI," painting supplement. Jan. 1952

ADRIATIC REGION. *See* Trieste; Venice; Yugoslavia

ADRIFT on a Raft of Sargassum. Photos by Robert F. Sisson. 188-199, Feb. 1976

ADVENTURE in Western China. By Ned Gillette. Photos by the author and Galen Rowell. 174-199, Feb. 1981
Skiing From the Summit of China's Ice Mountain. 192-199

ADVENTURES in Lololand. By Rennold L. Lowy. 105-118, Jan. 1947

ADVENTURES in the Search for Man. By Louis S. B. Leakey. Photos by Hugo van Lawick. 132-152, Jan. 1963

ADVENTURES With South Africa's Black Eagles. By Jeanne Cowden. Photos by author and Arthur Bowland. 533-543, Oct. 1969

ADVENTURES with the Survey Navy. By Irving Johnson. 131-148, July 1947

ADVENTURING Along the South's Surprising Coast: Sea Islands. By James Cerruti. Photos by Thomas Nebbia and James L. Amos. 366-393, Mar. 1971

AEGEAN ISLANDS:
• The Aegean Isles: Poseidon's Playground. By Gilbert M. Grosvenor. 733-781, Dec. 1958
▲ *Classical Lands of the Mediterranean*, supplement. Dec. 1949
• Drama of Death in a Minoan Temple. By Yannis Sakellarakis and Efi Sapouna-Sakellaraki. Photos by Otis Imboden and Spyros Tsavdaroglou. 205-222, Feb. 1981
▲ *Greece and the Aegean*, Atlas series supplement. Dec. 1958
• The Isles of Greece: Aegean Birthplace of Western Culture. By Melville Bell Grosvenor. Photos by Edwin Stuart Grosvenor and Winfield Parks. 147-193, Aug. 1972
• Minoans and Mycenaeans: Greece's Brilliant Bronze Age. By Joseph Judge. Photos by Gordon W. Gahan. Paintings by Lloyd K. Townsend. 142-185, Feb. 1978
• On the Winds of the Dodecanese. By Jean and Franc Shor. 351-390, Mar. 1953
• *See also* Thera

AEGEAN REGION. *See* Aegean Islands; Greece; Turkey

AEGEAN SEA:
• Glass Treasure From the Aegean. By George F. Bass. Photos by Jonathan Blair. 768-793, June 1978
• New Tools for Undersea Archeology. By George F. Bass. Photos by Charles R. Nicklin, Jr. 403-423, Sept. 1968
• Thirty-three Centuries Under the Sea. By Peter Throckmorton. 682-703, May 1960
• Underwater Archeology: Key to History's Warehouse. By George F. Bass. Photos by Thomas J. Abercrombie and Robert B. Goodman. 138-156, July 1963

AEPYORNIS (Extinct Bird):
• Madagascar: Island at the End of the Earth. By Luis Marden. Photos by Albert Moldvay. 443-487, Oct. 1967
• Re-creating Madagascar's Giant Extinct Bird. By Alexander Wetmore. 488-493, Oct. 1967

GALEN ROWELL

Adventure in China: Kirgiz horseman

NATIONAL ARCHAEOLOGICAL MUSEUM, ATHENS, BY GORDON W. GAHAN, NGS

Minoans and Mycenaeans: "Mask of Agamemnon"

AERODYNAMICS:
● The Air-Safety Challenge. By Michael E. Long. Photos by Bruce Dale. 209-235, Aug. 1977
● Sailors of the Sky. By Gordon Young. Photos by Emory Kristof and Jack Fields. Paintings by Davis Meltzer. 49-73, Jan. 1967
● They're Redesigning the Airplane. By Michael E. Long. Photos by James A. Sugar. 76-103, Jan. 1981
● *See also* Wind Power

AERONAUTICS. *See* Aviation

AF CHAPMAN (Youth Hostel Ship):
● Thumbs Up Round the North Sea's Rim. By Frances James. Photos by Erica Koch. 685-704, May 1952

AFAR TRIBE. *See* Danakil

AFGHAN REFUGEES:
● Pakistan Under Pressure. By William S. Ellis. Photos by James L. Stanfield. 668-701, May 1981

AFGHANISTAN:
● Afghanistan: Crossroad of Conquerors. By Thomas J. Abercrombie. 297-345, Sept. 1968
● American Family in Afghanistan. By Rebecca Shannon Cresson. Photos by Osborne C. Cresson. 417-432, Sept. 1953
● Bold Horsemen of the Steppes. By Sabrina and Roland Michaud. 634-669, Nov. 1973
● In the Footsteps of Alexander the Great. By Helen and Frank Schreider. Paintings by Tom Lovell. 1-65, Jan. 1968
● Islam's Heartland, Up in Arms. By Thomas J. Abercrombie. 335-345, Sept. 1980
● Sky Road East. By Tay and Lowell Thomas, Jr. 71-112, Jan. 1960
● We Took the Highroad in Afghanistan. By Jean and Franc Shor. 673-706, Nov. 1950
● West from the Khyber Pass. By William O. Douglas. Photos by Mercedes H. Douglas and author. 1-44, July 1958
● When the President Goes Abroad (Eisenhower Tour). By Gilbert M. Grosvenor. 588-649, May 1960
● Winter Caravan to the Roof of the World. By Sabrina and Roland Michaud. 435-465, Apr. 1972

AFLOAT on the Untamed Buffalo. By Harvey Arden. Photos by Matt Bradley. 344-359, Mar. 1977

AFO-A-KOM: A Sacred Symbol Comes Home. By William S. Ellis. Photos by James P. Blair. 141-148, July 1974

AFOOT in Roadless Nepal. By Toni Hagen. 361-405, Mar. 1960

AFRAN ZODIAC (Supertanker):
● Giants That Move the World's Oil: Superships. By Noel Grove. Photos by Martin Rogers. 102-124, July 1978

AFRICA:
● Adventures in the Search for Man. By Louis S. B. Leakey. Photos by Hugo van Lawick. NGS research grant. 132-152, Jan. 1963
▲ *Africa,* Atlas series supplement. Sept. 1960
▲ *Africa; Africa, Its Political Development,* double-sided supplement. Feb. 1980
▲ *Africa: Countries of the Nile,* Atlas series supplement. Oct. 1963
● Africa: The Winds of Freedom Stir a Continent. By Nathaniel T. Kenney. Photos by W. D. Vaughn. Contents: Angola; Belgian Congo (Congo Republic); Cabinda; Egypt; Ethiopia; Ghana; Kenya; Liberia; Rhodesia and Nyasaland, Federation of; South Africa. 303-359, Sept. 1960
▲ *Africa and the Arabian Peninsula,* supplement. Mar. 1950
● Africa's Bushman Art Treasures. By Alfred Friendly. Photos by Alex R. Willcox. 848-865, June 1963
● Ambassadors of Good Will: The Peace Corps. By Sargent Shriver and Peace Corps Volunteers. Included: Gabon; Tanganyika. 297-345, Sept. 1964
● Atlantic Odyssey: Iceland to Antarctica. By Newman Bumstead. Photos by Volkmar Wentzel. 725-780, Dec. 1955
● Britain Tackles the East African Bush. By W. Robert Moore. 311-352, Mar. 1950
● Bushmen of the Kalahari. By Elizabeth Marshall Thomas. Photos by Laurence K. Marshall. 866-888, June 1963
■ Bushmen of the Kalahari. 578A-578B, Apr. 1973; 732A-732B, May 1974
● Carefree People of the Cameroons. Photos by Pierre Ichac. 233-248, Feb. 1947
● The Desert: An Age-old Challenge Grows. By Rick Gore. Photos by Georg Gerster and Bruce Dale. 586-639, Nov. 1979
● Editorials. By Gilbert M. Grosvenor. 585, May 1975; 725, June 1977
● Exploring 1,750,000 Years Into Man's Past. By L. S. B. Leakey. Photos by Robert F. Sisson. NGS research grant. 564-589, Oct. 1961
● Finding the World's Earliest Man. By L. S. B. Leakey. Photos by Des Bartlett. NGS research grant. 420-435, Sept. 1960
● Finding West Africa's Oldest City. By Susan and Roderick McIntosh. Photos by Michael and Aubine Kirtley. Contents: Jenne-jeno (site), Mali. 396-418, Sept. 1982
● Flight to Adventure. By Tay and Lowell Thomas, Jr. 49-112, July 1957
● Footprints in the Ashes of Time. By Mary D. Leakey. NGS research grant. 446-457, Apr. 1979
● Freedom Speaks French in Ouagadougou. By John Scofield. Contents: Cameroon; Central African Republic; Chad; Dahomey; Gambia; Guinea; Ivory Coast; Mali; Mauritania; Niger; Senegal; Togo; Upper Volta. 153-203, Aug. 1966
● Freedom's Progress South of the Sahara. By Howard La Fay. Photos by Joseph J. Scherschel. Contents: Burundi; Congo, Democratic Republic of the; Congo, People's Republic of the; Kenya; Mozambique; Rhodesia and Nyasaland, Federation of; Rwanda; South Africa; Tanganyika. 603-637, Nov. 1962
● How Fruit Came to America. By J. R. Magness. Paintings by Else Bostelmann. 325-377, Sept. 1951
● Hunting Musical Game in West Africa. By Arthur S. Alberts. 262-282, Aug. 1951
● Into the Heart of Africa. By Gertrude S. Weeks. NGS research grant. 257-263, Aug. 1956
● Journey Into the Great Rift: the Northern Half. By Helen and Frank Schreider. 254-290, Aug. 1965
● The Leakeys of Africa: Family in Search of Prehistoric Man. By Melvin M. Payne. 194-231, Feb. 1965
■ Man of the Serengeti. 179A-179B, Feb. 1972
● Mountains of the Moon (Ruwenzori). By Paul A. Zahl. 412-434, Mar. 1962
● My Life With Africa's Little People. By Anne Eisner Putnam. 278-302, Feb. 1960
● The Niger: River of Sorrow, River of Hope. By Georg Gerster. 152-189, Aug. 1975
▲ *Northern Africa,* supplement. Dec. 1954
▲ *Northwestern Africa,* Atlas series supplement. Aug. 1966
● Our Vegetable Travelers. By Victor R. Boswell. Paintings by Else Bostelmann. Included: An African Native of World Popularity (Watermelon); Okra, or "Gumbo," from Africa. 145-217, Aug. 1949
▲ *The Peoples of Africa; The Heritage of Africa,* supplement. Dec. 1971
● Preserving the Treasures of Olduvai Gorge. By Melvin M. Payne. Photos by Joseph J. Scherschel. NGS research grant. 701-709, Nov. 1966
● Safari from Congo to Cairo. By Elsie May Bell Grosvenor. Photos by Gilbert Grosvenor. 721-771, Dec. 1954
● Safari Through Changing Africa. By Elsie May Bell Grosvenor. Photos by Gilbert Grosvenor. 145-198, Aug. 1953
● Salt–The Essence of Life. By Gordon Young. Photos by Volkmar Wentzel and Georg Gerster. Included: Deposits and caravans in Ethiopia and Mali. 381-401, Sept. 1977
▲ *Southern Africa,* Atlas series supplement. Nov. 1962
● The Sword and the Sermon (Islam). By Thomas J. Abercrombie. 3-45, July 1972
● Theodore Roosevelt: a Centennial Tribute. By Bart McDowell. 572-590, Oct. 1958
● Tropical Rain Forests: Nature's Dwindling Treasures. By Peter T. White. Photos by James P. Blair. Paintings by Barron Storey. 2-47, Jan. 1983
▲ *Two Centuries of Conflict in the Middle East; Mideast in Turmoil,* double-sided supplement. Included: Egypt, Ethiopia, Libya, Somalia, and Sudan; Islam's spread to northern Africa. Sept. 1980
● When the President Goes Abroad (Eisenhower Tour). By Gilbert M.

Grosvenor. Included: Casablanca, Morocco; Tunis, Tunisia. 588-649, May 1960
● The World in Your Garden (Flowers). By W. H. Camp. Paintings by Else Bostelmann. Included: The Dutch and South Africa (Calla, Bird-of-Paradise Flower, Impatiens); A "Jolly Botanical Band" from Africa (Poker-plant, Gerbera, Cape Marigold, Lobelia, Castor-oil plant); More Africans, "Brought Back Alive" (Fringed hibiscus, Pelargonium or "Geranium," Gladiolus, African-violet). 1-65, July 1947
● Zulu King Weds a Swazi Princess. By Volkmar Wentzel. 47-61, Jan. 1978
● *See also* Algeria; Angola; Cameroon; Djibouti; Egypt; Ethiopia; Ivory Coast; Kenya; Liberia; Mali; Morocco; Mozambique; Namibia; Niger; Nigeria; Nile; Río Muni; Rwanda; Sahara; Sierra Leone; Sinai; Somalia; South Africa; Sudan; Suez Canal; Tanzania; Tunisia; Uganda; Upper Volta; Zaire; Zimbabwe; *and* African Wildlife; Diamonds; Phoenicians; Plate Tectonics

AFRICAN WILDLIFE:
● African Termites, Dwellers in the Dark. By Glenn D. Prestwich. 532-547, Apr. 1978
● African Wildlife: Man's Threatened Legacy. By Allan C. Fisher, Jr. Photos by Thomas Nebbia. 147-187, Feb. 1972
A Continent's Living Treasure. Paintings by Ned Seidler. 164-167
● Africa's Elephants: Can They Survive? By Oria Douglas-Hamilton. Photos by Oria and Iain Douglas-Hamilton. 568-603, Nov. 1980
● Africa's Gentle Giants (Giraffes). By Bristol Foster. Photos by Bob Campbell and Thomas Nebbia. 402-417, Sept. 1977
● Africa's Uncaged Elephants. Photos by Quentin Keynes. 371-382, Mar. 1951
◆ *Animals of East Africa.* Announced. 844-849, June 1968
● A Bad Time to Be a Crocodile. By Rick Gore. Photos by Jonathan Blair. 90-115, Jan. 1978
● Editorial. By Wilbur E. Garrett. 287, Mar. 1983
● Etosha: Namibia's Kingdom of Animals. By Douglas H. Chadwick. Photos by Des and Jen Bartlett. 344-385, Mar. 1983
■ Etosha: Place of Dry Water. 703, Dec. 1980
● Face to Face With Gorillas in Central Africa. By Paul A. Zahl. 114-137, Jan. 1960
● Family Life of Lions. By Des and Jen Bartlett. Included: Lions, Wildebeests, Zebras. 800-819, Dec. 1982
■ Gorilla. 703, Dec. 1980
● Hunting Africa's Smallest Game (Insects). By Edward S. Ross. NGS research grant. 406-419, Mar. 1961
● The Imperiled Mountain Gorilla. By Dian Fossey. NGS research grant. 501-523, Apr. 1981
Death of Marchessa. Photos by Peter G. Veit. 508-511
● In Quest of the World's Largest Frog. By Paul A. Zahl. 146-152, July 1967
● Jackals of the Serengeti. By Patricia D. Moehlman. NGS research grant. 840-850, Dec. 1980
● The Last Great Animal Kingdom. 390-409, Sept. 1960
■ Last Stand in Eden. 1, Jan. 1979
● Life and Death at Gombe (Chimpanzees). By Jane Goodall. NGS research grant. 592-621, May 1979
● Life With the King of Beasts. By George B. Schaller. 494-519, Apr. 1969
■ The Living Sands of Namib. 439, Oct. 1977; cover, Mar. 1978; 1, Jan. 1979
● The Living Sands of the Namib. By William J. Hamilton III. Photos by Carol and David Hughes. 364-377, Sept. 1983
● Locusts: "Teeth of the Wind." By Robert A. M. Conley. Photos by Gianni Tortoli. 202-227, Aug. 1969
● Making Friends With Mountain Gorillas. By Dian Fossey. Photos by Robert M. Campbell. NGS research grant. 48-67, Jan. 1970
■ Miss Goodall and the Wild Chimpanzees. 831A-831B, Dec. 1965
● More Years With Mountain Gorillas. By Dian Fossey. Photos by Robert M. Campbell. NGS research grant. 574-585, Oct. 1971
◆ *My Friends the Wild Chimpanzees.* Announced. 408-417, Mar. 1966
● My Life Among Wild Chimpanzees. By Jane Goodall. Photos by Baron Hugo van Lawick and author. NGS research grant. 272-308, Aug. 1963
● Mzima, Kenya's Spring of Life. By Joan and Alan Root. 350-373, Sept. 1971
● Namibia: Nearly a Nation? By Bryan Hodgson. Photos by Jim Brandenburg. 755-797, June 1982
● New Discoveries Among Africa's Chimpanzees. By Baroness Jane van Lawick-Goodall. Photos by Baron Hugo van Lawick. NGS research grant. 802-831, Dec. 1965
● A New Look at Kenya's "Treetops." By Quentin Keynes. 536-541, Oct. 1956
● Orphans of the Wild (Animal Orphanage, Uganda). By Bruce G. Kinloch. 683-699, Nov. 1962
● Rescuing the Rothschild. By Carolyn Bennett Patterson. 419-421, Sept. 1977
● Roaming Africa's Unfenced Zoos. By W. Robert Moore. 353-380, Mar. 1950
◆ *Safari!* 1982
● Safari from Congo to Cairo. By Elsie May Bell Grosvenor. Photos by Gilbert Grosvenor. 721-771, Dec. 1954
● Safari Through Changing Africa. By Elsie May Bell Grosvenor. Photos by Gilbert Grosvenor. 145-198, Aug. 1953
■ Search for the Great Apes. cover, Jan. 1976
● "Snowflake," the World's First

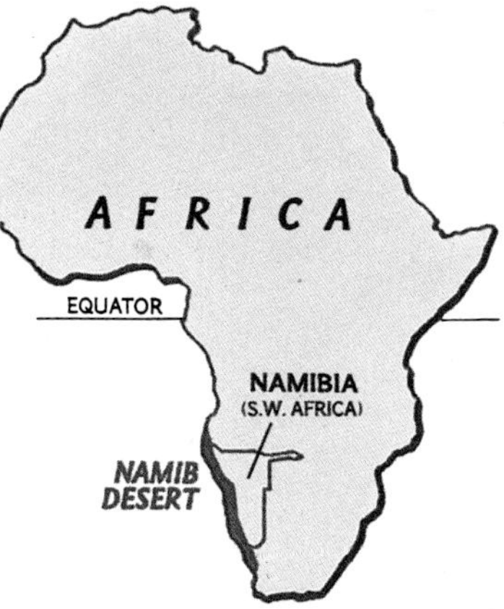

JIM BRANDENBURG

Namibia: a Herero woman

White Gorilla. By Arthur J. Riopelle. Photos by Paul A. Zahl. NGS research grant. 443-448, Mar. 1967
• Spearing Lions with Africa's Masai. By Edgar Monsanto Queeny. 487-517, Oct. 1954
• Stalking Central Africa's Wildlife. By T. Donald Carter. Paintings by Walter A. Weber. NGS research grant. 264-286, Aug. 1956
• Tanzania Marches to Its Own Drum. By Peter T. White. Photos by Emory Kristof. 474-509, Apr. 1975
• Where Elephants Have Right of Way. By George and Jinx Rodger. Included: Buffaloes; Giraffes; Hippopotamuses; Lyrehorned ankoles; Rhinoceroses. 363-389, Sept. 1960
• *See also* Baboons; Black Eagles; Cattle Egret; Cheetahs; Egyptian Vulture; Flamingos; Honey-Guide; Hornbills; Hyenas

AFRICANIZED HONEYBEES:
• Those Fiery Brazilian Bees. By Rick Gore. Photos by Bianca Lavies. 491-501, Apr. 1976

AFTER an Empire . . . Portugal. By William Graves. Photos by Bruno Barbey. 804-831, Dec. 1980

AFTER Rhodesia, a Nation Named Zimbabwe. By Charles E. Cobb, Jr. Photos by James L. Stanfield and LeRoy Woodson, Jr. 616-651, Nov. 1981

AGA KHAN:
• Weighing the Aga Khan in Diamonds. Photos by David J. Carnegie. 317-324, Mar. 1947

AGAIN–the Olympic Challenge. By Alan J. Gould. 488-513, Oct. 1964

The **AGE** of Sail Lives On at Mystic. By Alan Villiers. Photos by Weston Kemp. 220-239, Aug. 1968

AGELESS Splendors of Our Oldest Park: Yellowstone at 100. 604-615, May 1972

AGNEW, SPIRO T.:
• First Moon Explorers (Apollo 11) Receive the Society's Hubbard Medal. Included: Vice President Agnew's presentation of medal to Apollo 8 astronauts. 859-861, June 1970

AGOGINO, GEORGE: Author:
• Wyoming Muck Tells of Battle: Ice Age Man vs. Mammoth. By Cynthia Irwin, Henry Irwin, and George Agogino. 828-837, June 1962

AGRA, India. *See* Taj Mahal

AGRICULTURAL AND BOTANICAL EXPLORERS:
• American Wild Flower Odyssey. By P. L. Ricker. 603-634, May 1953
• Caught in the Assam-Tibet Earthquake. By F. Kingdon-Ward. 403-416, Mar. 1952
• The Exquisite Orchids. By Luis Marden. 485-513, Apr. 1971
• Nature's Gifts to Medicine. By Lonnelle Aikman. Paintings by Lloyd K. Townsend and Don Crowley. 420-440, Sept. 1974
• Patent Plants Enrich Our World. By Orville H. Kneen. 357-378, Mar. 1948
• Puya, the Pineapple's Andean Ancestor. By Mulford B. Foster. 463-480, Oct. 1950
• Spices, the Essence of Geography. By Stuart E. Jones. 401-420, Mar. 1949
• The World in Your Garden (Flowers). By W. H. Camp. Paintings by Else Bostelmann. 1-65, July 1947
◆ *The World in Your Garden.* Announced. 729-730, May 1957

AGRICULTURE:
• Beltsville Brings Science to the Farm. By Samuel W. Matthews. 199-218, Aug. 1953
• California's Surprising Inland Delta. By Judith and Neil Morgan. Photos by Charles O'Rear. 409-430, Sept. 1976
• Can the World Feed Its People? By Thomas Y. Canby. Photos by Steve Raymer. 2-31, July 1975
• Down on the Farm, Soviet Style–a 4-H Adventure. By John Garaventa. Photos by James Tobin and Carol Schmidt. 768-797, June 1979
• Erosion, Trojan Horse of Greece. By F. G. Renner. 793-812, Dec. 1947
• The Family Farm Ain't What It Used To Be. By James A. Sugar. 391-411, Sept. 1974
• Following the Ladybug Home. By Kenneth S. Hagen. Photos by Robert F. Sisson. Included: Study by California entomologists to control aphid pests with the introduction of ladybugs. 543-553, Apr. 1970
• 4-H Boys and Girls Grow More Food. By Frederick Simpich. 551-582, Nov. 1948
• Iowa, America's Middle Earth. By Harvey Arden. Photos by Craig Aurness. 603-629, May 1981
• Iowa's Enduring Amana Colonies. By Laura Longley Babb. Photos by Steve Raymer. 863-878, Dec. 1975
• Israel: Land of Promise. By John Scofield. Photos by B. Anthony Stewart. Included: Grains, dairying, citrus and other fruits, vegetables. 395-434, Mar. 1965
• Lanzarote, the Strangest Canary. By Stephanie Dinkins. Included: Cinder farming. 117-139, Jan. 1969
• The Maya. Note: Maya agriculturists built raised fields above swampland, constructed terraces, and dammed waterways with hand labor and stone tools. 729-811, Dec. 1975
I. Children of Time. By Howard La Fay. Photos by David Alan Harvey. 729-767; II. Riddle of the Glyphs. By George E. Stuart. Photos by Otis Imboden. 768-791; III. Resurrecting the Grandeur of Tikal. By William R. Coe. 792-798; IV. A Traveler's Tale of Ancient Tikal. Paintings by Peter Spier. Text by Alice J. Hall. 799-811
• Our Most Precious Resource: Water. By Thomas Y. Canby. Photos by Ted Spiegel. 144-179, Aug. 1980
• Our Vegetable Travelers. By Victor R. Boswell. Paintings by Else Bostelmann. 145-217, Aug. 1949
• A Paradise Called the Palouse. By Barbara Austin. Photos by Phil Schofield. Included: Hill farming techniques. 798-819, June 1982
• Rediscovering America's Forgotten Crops. By Noel D. Vietmeyer. Photos by Burgess Blevins. Paintings by Paul M. Breeden. 702-712, May 1981
• The Revolution in American Agriculture. By Jules B. Billard. Photos by James P. Blair. Included: Farm of the future (painting). 147-185, Feb. 1970
• This Land of Ours–How Are We Using It? By Peter T. White. Photos by Emory Kristof. 20-67, July 1976
• Tropical Rain Forests: Nature's Dwindling Treasures. By Peter T. White. Photos by James P. Blair. Paintings by Barron Storey. Included: Slash-and-burn farming, Tree plantations, Soil-management project. 2-47, Jan. 1983
• What's Happening to Our Climate? By Samuel W. Matthews. Included: The relationship between climatic change and cultivation. 576-615, Nov. 1976
• The Year the Weather Went Wild. By Thomas Y. Canby. Included: The severe drought in the northern plains and the western United States. 799-829, Dec. 1977
• *See also* Cattle Raising; Coffee; Cotton and Cotton Industry; Farms; Fruit and Fruit Growing; Horticulture; Livestock; Pest Control; Potatoes and Potato Growing; Rice Growing; Sheep Raising; Sugar Industry; Wheat and Wheat Growing

AGUNG, Mount, Bali, Indonesia:
• Disaster in Paradise. Photos by Robert F. Sisson. 436-458, Sept. 1963
I. Eruption of Mount Agung. By Windsor P. Booth. 436-447; II. Devastated Land and Homeless People. By Samuel W. Matthews. 447-458

AHA! It Really Works! By Robert F. Sisson. 143-147, Jan. 1974

AI APAEC (Mochica Warrior-Priest):
• Finding the Tomb of a Warrior-God. By William Duncan Strong. Photos by Clifford Evans, Jr. 453-482, Apr. 1947

AIARI RIVER, Brazil:
• Jungle Jaunt on Amazon Headwaters. By Bernice M. Goetz. 371-388, Sept. 1952

AIKMAN, LONNELLE: Author:
• Census 1960: Profile of the Nation. By Albert W. Atwood and Lonnelle Aikman. 697-714, Nov. 1959
• The DAR Story. Photos by B. Anthony Stewart and John E. Fletcher. 565-598, Nov. 1951
• Herbs for All Seasons. Photos by Sam Abell. Picture portfolio text by Larry Kohl. 386-409, Mar. 1983
• Inside the White House. Photos by B. Anthony Stewart and Thomas Nebbia. 3-43, Jan. 1961
• The Lights Are Up at Ford's Theatre. 392-401, Mar. 1970

• The Living White House. 593-643, Nov. 1966
• Mount Vernon Lives On. 651-682, Nov. 1953
• Nature's Gifts to Medicine. Paintings by Lloyd K. Townsend and Don Crowley. 420-440, Sept. 1974
• New Stars for Old Glory. 86-121, July 1959
• Patriots in Petticoats. Paintings by Louis S. Glanzman. 475-493, Oct. 1975
• Perfume, the Business of Illusion. 531-550, Apr. 1951
• Under the Dome of Freedom: The United States Capitol. Photos by George F. Mobley. 4-59, Jan. 1964
• U. S. Capitol, Citadel of Democracy. 143-192, Aug. 1952

AINU (People):
• Hokkaido, Japan's Last Frontier. By Douglas Lee. Photos by Michael S. Yamashita. 62-93, Jan. 1980
• Japan's "Sky People," the Vanishing Ainu. By Mary Inez Hilger. Photos by Eiji Miyazawa. NGS research grant. 268-296, Feb. 1967

AÏR (Region), Niger:
• The Inadan: Artisans of the Sahara. By Michael and Aubine Kirtley. 282-298, Aug. 1979

AIR Age Brings Life to Canton Island. By Howell Walker. 117-132, Jan. 1955

AIR AND SPACE MUSEUM, Smithsonian Institution, Washington, D. C.:
• Of Air and Space. By Michael Collins. 819-837, June 1978
Picture Portfolio by Nathan Benn, Robert S. Oakes, and Joseph D. Lavenburg, with text by Michael E. Long. 825-837

AIR BASES:
• Alaska's Warmer Side. By Elsie May Bell Grosvenor. Included: Eielson Air Force Base, Ladd Air Force Base. 737-775, June 1956
• Artists Roam the World of the U. S. Air Force. By Curtis E. LeMay. 650-673, May 1960
• Crosscurrents Sweep the Indian Ocean. By Bart McDowell. Photos by Steve Raymer. 422-457, Oct. 1981
• Flying in the "Blowtorch" Era. By Frederick G. Vosburgh. Contents: Andrews Air Force Base, Maryland; Carswell Air Force Base, Texas; Edwards Air Force Base, California; Eglin Air Force Base, Florida; Langley Air Force Base, Virginia; Larson Air Force Base, Washington; March Air Force Base, California; Moffett Naval Air Station, California; Williams Air Force Base, Arizona; Wright-Patterson Air Force Base, Ohio. 281-322, Sept. 1950
• Four-ocean Navy in the Nuclear Age. By Thomas W. McKnew. 145-187, Feb. 1965
• Here Come the Marines. By Frederick Simpich. Included: Anacostia Naval Air Station, Washington, D. C.; Cherry Point Air Station, North Carolina; El Toro Air Station, California. 647-672, Nov. 1950
• Of Planes and Men. By Kenneth F. Weaver. Photos by Emory Kristof and Albert Moldvay. 298-349, Sept. 1965
• Okinawa, Pacific Outpost. 538-552, Apr. 1950
• Our Navy in the Far East. By Arthur W. Radford. Photos by J. Baylor Roberts. 537-577, Oct. 1953
• *See also* Canton Island; Edwards Air Force Base; Stead Air Force Base; Thule Air Base

AIR PLANTS. *See* Bromeliads; Orchids

AIR POLLUTION:
• Acid Rain–How Great a Menace? By Anne LaBastille. Photos by Ted Spiegel. 652-681, Nov. 1981
• Laboratory in a Dirty Sky. By Rudolf J. Engelmann and Vera Simons. NGS research grant. 616-621, Nov. 1976
• The Mediterranean–Sea of Man's Fate. By Rick Gore. Photos by Jonathan Blair. 694-737, Dec. 1982
• Mexico, the City That Founded a Nation. By Louis de la Haba. Photos by Albert Moldvay. 638-669, May 1973
• Pollution, Threat to Man's Only Home. By Gordon Young. Photos by James P. Blair. 738-781, Dec. 1970
• Those Successful Japanese. By Bart McDowell. Photos by Fred Ward. Included: Air pollution in Tokyo and Yokkaichi. 323-359, Mar. 1974
• Venice Fights for Life. By Joseph Judge. Photos by Albert Moldvay. 591-631, Nov. 1972
• What's Happening to Our Climate? By Samuel W. Matthews. 576-615, Nov. 1976

AIR RESCUE SQUADRONS:
• Air Rescue Behind Enemy Lines. By Howard Sochurek. 346-369, Sept. 1968
• First American Ascent of Mount St. Elias. By Maynard M. Miller. 229-248, Feb. 1948
• Seeking the Secret of the Giants. By Frank M. Setzler. Photos by Richard H. Stewart. 390-404, Sept. 1952

The **AIR-SAFETY** Challenge. By Michael E. Long. Photos by Bruce Dale. 209-235, Aug. 1977

AIR SHOWS:
• Oshkosh: America's Biggest Air Show. By Michael E. Long. Photos by James A. Sugar and the author. Contents: The annual convention of the Experimental Aircraft Association. 365-375, Sept. 1979
• World War I Aircraft Fly Again in Rhinebeck's Rickety Rendezvous. By Harvey Arden. Photos by Howard Sochurek. 578-587, Oct. 1970
• *See also* Ultralight Aircraft

AIRBORNE UNDERSEA EXPEDITIONS:
• Inflatable Ship *(Amphitrite)* Opens Era of Airborne Undersea Expeditions. By Jacques-Yves Cousteau. 142-148, July 1961

AIRCRAFT. *See* Air Shows; Aircraft Carriers; Aviation; Balloons; Helicopters; Jet Aircraft; Recreational Aircraft; Space Shuttles; U. S. Air Force

AIRCRAFT CARRIERS:
• Four-ocean Navy in the Nuclear Age. By Thomas W. McKnew. 145-187, Feb. 1965
• The Mighty *Enterprise*. By Nathaniel T. Kenney. Photos by Thomas J. Abercrombie. 431-448, Mar. 1963
• Our Navy Explores Antarctica. By Richard E. Byrd. U. S. Navy official photos. 429-522, Oct. 1947
• Our Navy in the Far East. By Arthur W. Radford. Photos by J. Baylor Roberts. 537-577, Oct. 1953
• Pacific Fleet: Force for Peace. By Franc Shor. Photos by W. E. Garrett. 283-335, Sept. 1959
• Sailors in the Sky: Fifty Years of Naval Aviation. By Patrick N. L. Bellinger. 276-296, Aug. 1961

AIRCRAFT INDUSTRY:
• Flying in the "Blowtorch" Era. By Frederick G. Vosburgh. 281-322, Sept. 1950
• Long Island Outgrows the Country. By Howell Walker. Photos by B. Anthony Stewart. Included: Airborne Instruments Laboratory; Sperry Gyroscope Company; Fairchild, Grumman, Liberty, and Republic aircraft companies. 279-326, Mar. 1951
• They're Redesigning the Airplane. By Michael E. Long. Photos by James A. Sugar. 76-103, Jan. 1981
• *See also* Space Shuttles; Ultralight Aircraft

AIRLIFT to Berlin. 595-614, May 1949

AIRPORTS:
• Newfoundland, Canada's New Province. By Andrew H. Brown. Photos by author and Robert F. Sisson. Included: Gander, Torbay, Harbour Grace, and other sites which were jumping-off points for early transoceanic flights. 777-812, June 1949
• Skyway Below the Clouds. By Carl R. Markwith. Photos by Ernest J. Cottrell. 85-108, July 1949
• *See also* Arlington County, for Washington National Airport

AIT HADIDDOU (Berber Tribe):
• Berber Brides' Fair. By Carla Hunt. Photos by Nik Wheeler. 119-129, Jan. 1980

AJANTA, India:
• India's Sculptured Temple Caves. By Volkmar Wentzel. 665-678, May 1953

AKHENATEN TEMPLE PROJECT, Egypt:
• Computer Helps Scholars Re-create an Egyptian Temple. By Ray Winfield Smith. Photos by Emory Kristof. NGS research grant. 634-655, Nov. 1970

ALABAMA:
● Alabama, Dixie to a Different Tune. By Howard La Fay. Photos by Dick Durrance II. 534-569, Oct. 1975
● Around the "Great Lakes of the South." By Frederick Simpich. Photos by J. Baylor Roberts. 463-491, Apr. 1948
● Dixie Spins the Wheel of Industry. By William H. Nicholas. Photos by J. Baylor Roberts. 281-324, Mar. 1949
● Hurricane! By Ben Funk. Photos by Robert W. Madden. 346-379, Sept. 1980
● A Walk Across America. By Peter Gorton Jenkins. 466-499, Apr. 1977
● Whatever Happened to TVA? By Gordon Young. Photos by Emory Kristof. 830-863, June 1973
● *See also* Mobile; Russell Cave

ALAMO, San Antonio, Texas:
● San Antonio: "Texas, Actin' Kind of Natural." By Fred Kline. Photos by David Hiser. 524-549, Apr. 1976

ALAN VILLIERS' Tribute to Captain Cook: The Man Who Mapped the Pacific. By Alan Villiers. Photos by Gordon W. Gahan. 297-349, Sept. 1971

ÅLAND ISLANDS, Finland:
● Baltic Cruise of the *Caribbee.* By Carleton Mitchell. 605-646, Nov. 1950

ALASKA:
▲ *Alaska,* supplement. June 1956
◆ *Alaska.* 1969; Announced. 880-884, June 1969
■ Alaska! 215A-215B, Feb. 1967
◆ *Alaska: High Roads to Adventure.* 1976; Announced. 860-864, June 1976
● Alaska: Rising Northern Star. By Joseph Judge. Photos by Bruce Dale. Included: Alaska's land-use plan. 730-767, June 1975
● Alaska, Seward's Icebox, Became a Treasure Chest. 766-767, June 1953
● Alaska, the Big Land. By W. Robert Moore. 776-807, June 1956
● Alaska Proudly Joins the Union. By Ernest Gruening. Photos by Thomas J. Abercrombie. 43-83, July 1959
● Alaskan Family Robinson. By Nancy Robinson. Photos by John Metzger and Peter Robinson. 55-75, Jan. 1973
● An Alaskan Family's Night of Terror (Earthquake). By Tay Pryor Thomas. 142-156, July 1964
◆ *Alaskan Glacier Studies* (1914). 196, Feb. 1967
● Alaska's Automatic Lake Drains Itself (Lake George). 835-844, June 1951
● Alaska's Marine Highway. By W. E. Garrett. 776-819, June 1965
● Alaska's Mighty Rivers of Ice. By Maynard M. Miller. Photos by Christopher G. Knight. NGS research grant. 194-217, Feb. 1967
● Alaska's Russian Frontier: Little Diomede. Photos by Audrey and Frank Morgan. 551-562, Apr. 1951
● Alaska's Warmer Side. By Elsie May Bell Grosvenor. 737-775, June 1956
● Along the Yukon Trail. By Amos Burg. 395-416, Sept. 1953
▲ *America's Federal Lands; The United States,* double-sided supplement. Sept. 1982
● Among Alaska's Brown Bears. By Allan L. Egbert and Michael H. Luque. NGS research grant. 428-442, Sept. 1975
● Bikepacking Across Alaska and Canada. By Dan Burden. 682-695, May 1973
● Birds of the Alaskan Tundra. 322-327, Mar. 1972
▲ *Canada, Alaska, and Greenland,* supplement. June 1947
● Caribou: Hardy Nomads of the North. By Jim Rearden. 858-878, Dec. 1974
● Charting Our Sea and Air Lanes. By Stuart E. Jones. Photos by J. Baylor Roberts. 189-209, Feb. 1957
▲ *Close-up: U.S.A., Alaska,* supplement. Text on reverse. June 1975
● The Curlew's Secret. By Arthur A. Allen. NGS research grant. 751-770, Dec. 1948
● DEW Line, Sentry of the Far North. By Howard La Fay. 128-146, July 1958
● Earthquake! By William P. E. Graves. 112-139, July 1964
● Editorials. By Gilbert M. Grosvenor. 729, June 1975; 147, Aug. 1977; 733, Dec. 1979; By Wilbur E. Garrett. 557, Nov. 1983
● *Endeavour* Sails the Inside Passage. By Amos Burg. 801-828, June 1947
● "Ice Age Mammals of the Alaskan Tundra," supplement. Mar. 1972
● John Muir's Wild America. By Harvey Arden. Photos by Dewitt Jones. 433-461, Apr. 1973
● The Last U. S. Whale Hunters. By Emory Kristof. 346-353, Mar. 1973
"Ocean mammals are to us what the buffalo was to the Plains Indian." By Lael Morgan. 354-355
● Mammals of the Alaskan Tundra. 329-337, Mar. 1972
● Nomads of the Far North. By Matthew W. Stirling. 471-504, Oct. 1949
Hearty Folk Defy Arctic Storms. Paintings by W. Langdon Kihn. 479-494
● *North Star* Cruises Alaska's Wild West. By Amos Burg. 57-86, July 1952
● Our Bald Eagle: Freedom's Symbol Survives. By Thomas C. Dunstan. Photos by Jeff Foott. NGS research grant. 186-199, Feb. 1978
● Our Restless Earth (Earthquakes). By Maynard M. Miller. 140-141, July 1964
● Peoples of the Arctic. 144-223, Feb. 1983
I. Introduction by Joseph Judge. 144-149; II. Hunters of the Lost Spirit. By Priit J. Vesilind. Photos by David Alan Harvey. 150-173; III. Where Magic Ruled: Art of the Bering Sea.

EMORY KRISTOF, NGS
Last U. S. Whale Hunters: Eskimo crew

Race to Nome: author waves to fan
KERBY SMITH

By William W. Fitzhugh and Susan A. Kaplan. Photos by Sisse Brimberg. 198-205; IV. People of the Long Spring (Chukchis). By Yuri Rytkheu. Photos by Dean Conger. 206-223
▲ *Peoples of the Arctic; Arctic Ocean,* double-sided supplement. Feb. 1983
● Photographing Northern Wild Flowers. By Virginia L. Wells. 809-823, June 1956
● Plants of the Alaskan Tundra. 315-321, Mar. 1972
● Portrait of a Fierce and Fragile Land. By Paul A. Zahl. 303-314, Mar. 1972
● Preserving America's Last Great Wilderness. By David Jeffery. 769-791, June 1975
● Risk and Reward on Alaska's Violent Gulf. By Boyd Gibbons. Photos by Steve Raymer. 237-267, Feb. 1979
● Sharing Alaska: How Much for Parks? Opposing views by Jay S. Hammond and Cecil D. Andrus. 60-65, July 1979
▲ *State of Alaska,* Atlas series supplement. July 1959
● Thousand-mile Race to Nome: A Woman's Icy Struggle. By Susan Butcher. Photos by Kerby Smith. Contents: Iditarod Sled Dog Race. 411-422, Mar. 1983
● Timber: How Much Is Enough? By John J. Putman. Photos by Bruce Dale. 485-511, Apr. 1974
▲ *Top of the World,* Atlas series supplement. Nov. 1965
▲ *The Top of the World,* supplement. Oct. 1949
● Trek Across Arctic America. By Colin Irwin. 295-321, Mar. 1974
● When Giant Bears Go Fishing. By Cecil E. Rhode. 195-205, Aug. 1954
● Where Can the Wolf Survive? By L. David Mech. 518-537, Oct. 1977
● *See also* Aleutian Islands; Arctic National Wildlife Range; Diomede Islands; Fairbanks; Glacier Bay; Juneau; Katmai National Monument; King Island; Mount McKinley National Park; Nikolaevsk; Noatak River; North Slope; Pribilof Islands; St. Elias, Mount; Yukon (River); *and Manhattan,* S.S.

ALASKA KING CRAB:
● The Crab That Shakes Hands. By Clarence P. Idyll. Photos by Robert F. Sisson. 254-271, Feb. 1971

ALASKA PIPELINE:
● Alaska: Rising Northern Star. By Joseph Judge. Photos by Bruce Dale. 730-767, June 1975
● Oil, the Dwindling Treasure. By Noel Grove. Photos by Emory Kristof. 792-825, June 1974
● The Pipeline: Alaska's Troubled Colossus. By Bryan Hodgson. Photos by Steve Raymer. Included: Diagram, Anatomy of the pipeline; map showing potential and producing oil and gas areas. 684-717, Nov. 1976
● Will Oil and Tundra Mix? Alaska's North Slope Hangs in the Balance. By William S. Ellis. Photos by Emory Kristof. 485-517, Oct. 1971

ALASKA RANGE, Alaska:
● Mount McKinley Conquered by New Route. By Bradford Washburn. 219-248, Aug. 1953
● New Mount McKinley Challenge–Trekking Around the Continent's Highest Peak. By Ned Gillette. 66-79, July 1979
● Wildlife of Mount McKinley National Park. By Adolph Murie. Paintings by Walter A. Weber. 249-270, Aug. 1953

ALASKAN AIR COMMAND, U. S. Air Force:
● Three Months on an Arctic Ice Island. By Joseph O. Fletcher. 489-504, Apr. 1953

ALBANIA, Alone Against the World. By Mehmet Biber. 530-557, Oct. 1980

ALBANY, New York:
● Henry Hudson's River. By Willard Price. Photos by Wayne Miller. 364-403, Mar. 1962
● The Mighty Hudson. By Albert W. Atwood. Photos by B. Anthony Stewart. 1-36, July 1948

ALBATROSSES:
● The Gooney Birds of Midway. By John W. Aldrich. 839-851, June 1964
● Penguins and Their Neighbors. By Roger Tory Peterson. Photos by Des and Jen Bartlett. 237-255, Aug. 1977

ALBEMARLE COUNTY, Virginia:
● Mr. Jefferson's Charlottesville. By Anne Revis. 553-592, May 1950
● *See also* Monticello

ALBERTA (Province), Canada:
● Alberta Unearths Her Buried Treasures. By David S. Boyer. 90-119, July 1960
● Canada's Heartland, the Prairie Provinces. By W. E. Garrett. 443-489, Oct. 1970
● Canada's "Now" Frontier. By Robert Paul Jordan. Photos by Lowell Georgia. 480-511, Oct. 1976
● Canadian Rockies, Lords of a Beckoning Land. By Alan Phillips. Photos by James L. Stanfield. 353-393, Sept. 1966
▲ *Close-up, Canada: British Columbia, Alberta, Yukon Territory,* supplement. Text on reverse. Apr. 1978
● From Sun-clad Sea to Shining Mountains. By Ralph Gray. Photos by James P. Blair. 542-589, Apr. 1964
● Heart of the Canadian Rockies. By Elizabeth A. Moize. Photos by Jim Brandenburg. 757-779, June 1980
● Oil, the Dwindling Treasure. By Noel Grove. Photos by Emory Kristof. 792-825, June 1974
● On the Ridgepole of the Rockies. By Walter Meayers Edwards. 745-780, June 1947
Canada's Rocky Mountain Playground. 755-770
● *See also* Bikepacking; Great Divide Trail; Waterton-Glacier International Peace Park

ALBERTS, ARTHUR S.:
Author-Photographer:
● Hunting Musical Game in West Africa. 262-282, Aug. 1951

ALBINO ANIMALS:
● Enchantress! (Tigress). By Theodore H. Reed. Photos by Thomas J. Abercrombie. 628-641, May 1961
● Growing Up With Snowflake (Gorilla). By Arthur J. Riopelle. Photos by Michael Kuh. NGS research grant. 491-503, Oct. 1970
● "Snowflake," the World's First White Gorilla. By Arthur J. Riopelle. Photos by Paul A. Zahl. NGS research grant. 443-448, Mar. 1967
● White Tiger in My House. By Elizabeth C. Reed. Photos by Donna K. Grosvenor. 482-491, Apr. 1970

ALBUQUERQUE, New Mexico:
● New Mexico: The Golden Land. By Robert Laxalt. Photos by Adam Woolfitt. 299-345, Sept. 1970

ALCOTT, LOUISA MAY:
● Literary Landmarks of Massachusetts. By William H. Nicholas. Photos by B. Anthony Stewart and John E. Fletcher. 279-310, Mar. 1950

ALDANA E., GUILLERMO:
Author-Photographer:
● Mesa del Nayar's Strange Holy Week. 780-795, June 1971
Photographer:
● The Disaster of El Chichón. By Boris Weintraub. Photos by Guillermo Aldana E. and Kenneth Garrett. 654-684, Nov. 1982
Volcanic Cloud May Alter Earth's Climate. By Robert I. Tilling. 672-675
● The Huichols, Mexico's People of Myth and Magic. By James Norman. 832-853, June 1977

ALDERNEY (Island), English Channel:
● Britain's "French" Channel Islands. By James Cerruti. Photos by James L. Amos. 710-740, May 1971

ALDO LEOPOLD: "A Durable Scale of Values." By Boyd Gibbons. Photos by Jim Brandenburg. 682-708, Nov. 1981

ALDRICH, JOHN W.: Author:
● The Gooney Birds of Midway. 839-851, June 1964

ALDRIN, EDWIN E., Jr.:
● First Explorers on the Moon: The Incredible Story of Apollo 11. 735-797, Dec. 1969
I. Man Walks on Another World. By Neil A. Armstrong, Edwin E. Aldrin, Jr., and Michael Collins. 738-749; II. Sounds of the Space Age, From Sputnik to Lunar Landing. A record narrated by Frank Borman. 750-751; III. The Flight of Apollo 11: "One giant leap for mankind." By Kenneth F. Weaver. 752-787
● First Moon Explorers (Apollo 11) Receive the Society's Hubbard Medal. 859-861, June 1970

ALEKSIUK, MICHAEL: Author:
● Manitoba's Fantastic Snake Pits. Photos by Bianca Lavies. 715-723, Nov. 1975

ALEUTIAN ISLANDS, Alaska:
● The Aleutians: Alaska's Far-out Islands. By Lael Morgan. Photos by Steven C. Wilson. Note: 95 percent

ART BY TOM MCNEELY FROM PHOTOGRAPH, NATIONAL ANTHROPOLOGICAL ARCHIVES, SMITHSONIAN

Peoples of the Arctic: Aleut hunter

of the islands are claimed by the federal government as wildlife refuges and military sites. 336-363, Sept. 1983
- Exploring Aleutian Volcanoes. By G. D. Robinson. 509-528, Oct. 1948
- Operation Eclipse: 1948. By William A. Kinney. NGS research grant. 325-372, Mar. 1949
- *See also* Atka

ALEUTIAN RANGE, Alaska:
- Lonely Wonders of Katmai (National Monument). By Ernest Gruening. Photos by Winfield Parks. 800-831, June 1963

ALEUTS (People):
- The Aleutians: Alaska's Far-out Islands. By Lael Morgan. Photos by Steven C. Wilson. 336-363, Sept. 1983
- Atka, Rugged Home of My Aleut Friends. By Lael Morgan. 572-583, Oct. 1974
- The Fur Seal Herd Comes of Age. By Victor B. Scheffer and Karl W. Kenyon. 491-512, Apr. 1952
- New Day for Alaska's Pribilof Islanders. By Susan Hackley Johnson. Photos by Tim Thompson. 536-552, Oct. 1982
- Peoples of the Arctic. Introduction by Joseph Judge. 144-149, Feb. 1983
- ▲ *Peoples of the Arctic; Arctic Ocean,* double-sided supplement. Feb. 1983

ALEXANDER THE GREAT:
- In the Footsteps of Alexander the Great. By Helen and Frank Schreider. Paintings by Tom Lovell. 1-65, Jan. 1968

ALEXANDER, HOPE: Photographer:
- Friend of the Wind: The Common Tern. By Ian Nisbet. 234-247, Aug. 1973

ALEXANDER GRAHAM BELL MUSEUM, Baddeck, Nova Scotia:
- Alexander Graham Bell Museum: Tribute to Genius. By Jean Lesage. 227-256, Aug. 1956
- Bell Museum, Baddeck, Nova Scotia. 256, 257, 259, 261, Aug. 1959; 358-359, 361, 362, Mar. 1975
- Down East to Nova Scotia. By Winfield Parks. 853-879, June 1964

ALEXANDRIA, Virginia:
- Across the Potomac From Washington. By Albert W. Atwood. 1-33, Jan. 1953

ALFRED THE GREAT:
- The British Way. By Sir Evelyn Wrench. 421-541, Apr. 1949

ALGAE:
- Adrift on a Raft of Sargassum. Photos by Robert F. Sisson. 188-199, Feb. 1976
- Algae: the Life-givers. By Paul A. Zahl. 361-377, Mar. 1974
- Can We Save Our Salt Marshes? By Stephen W. Hitchcock. Photos by William R. Curtsinger. 729-765, June 1972
- Giant Kelp, Sequoias of the Sea. By Wheeler J. North. Photos by Bates Littlehales. 251-269, Aug. 1972
- Life Springs From Death in Truk Lagoon. By Sylvia A. Earle. Photos by Al Giddings. Included: More than a hundred species of green, red, and brown algae, including 15 previously unknown in Micronesia. 578-613, May 1976
- Teeming Life of a Pond. By William H. Amos. 274-298, Aug. 1970
- Those Marvelous, Myriad Diatoms. By Richard B. Hoover. 871-878, June 1979
- Undersea World of a Kelp Forest. By Sylvia A. Earle. Photos by Al Giddings. 411-426, Sept. 1980

ALGÅRD, GÖRAN: Photographer:
- Iceland Tapestry. By Deena Clark. 599-630, Nov. 1951
- Lapland's Reindeer Roundup. 109-116, July 1949

ALGERIA:
- Algeria: Learning to Live With Independence. By Thomas J. Abercrombie. 200-233, Aug. 1973
- Dry-land Fleet Sails the Sahara. By Jean du Boucher. Photos by Jonathan S. Blair. 696-725, Nov. 1967
- France's Stepchild, Problem and Promise. By Howard La Fay. Photos by Robert F. Sisson. 768-795, June 1960
- Oasis-hopping in the Sahara. By Maynard Owen Williams. 209-236, Feb. 1949
- Sand in My Eyes (Motor Trip). By Jinx Rodger. 664-705, May 1958

ALGONQUIAN INDIANS:
- Indian Life Before the Colonists Came. By Stuart E. Jones. Engravings by Theodore de Bry, 1590. 351-368, Sept. 1947

ALGONQUIAN LINGUISTIC STOCK:
- Nomads of the Far North. By Matthew W. Stirling. 471-504, Oct. 1949
Hearty Folk Defy Arctic Storms. Paintings by W. Langdon Kihn. 479-494

ALHAMBRA (Fortress-Palace), Granada, Spain:
- Andalusia, the Spirit of Spain. By Howard La Fay. Photos by Joseph J. Scherschel. 833-857, June 1975
- The Changing Face of Old Spain. By Bart McDowell. Photos by Albert Moldvay. 291-339, Mar. 1965
- Speaking of Spain. By Luis Marden. 415-456, Apr. 1950

ALICE SPRINGS, Australia:
- "The Alice" in Australia's Wonderland. By Alan Villiers. Photos by Jeff Carter and David Moore. 230-257, Feb. 1966

ALL-AMERICA ROSE SELECTION (AARS). *See* Portrait Rose

ALL-GIRL Team Tests the Habitat (Tektite II). By Sylvia A. Earle. Paintings by Pierre Mion. 291-296, Aug. 1971

ALL-OUT Assault on Antarctica. By Richard E. Byrd. 141-180, Aug. 1956

AB

ALLAGASH WILDERNESS WATERWAY, Maine:
- Autumn Flames Along the Allagash. By François Leydet. Photos by Farrell Grehan. 177-187, Feb. 1974

ALLARD, WILLIAM ALBERT:
Author-Photographer:
- Chief Joseph. 409-434, Mar. 1977
- Chinatown, the Gilded Ghetto (San Francisco). 627-643, Nov. 1975
- Cowpunching on the Padlock Ranch. 478-499, Oct. 1973
- The Hutterites, Plain People of the West. 98-125, July 1970
- Two Wheels Along the Mexican Border (U. S.-Mexico). 591-635, May 1971
- Yellowstone Wildlife in Winter. 637-661, Nov. 1967

Photographer:
- Amish Folk: Plainest of Pennsylvania's Plain People. By Richard Gehman. 227-253, Aug. 1965
- Canada's Mount Kennedy: The First Ascent. By James W. Whittaker. 11-33, July 1965
- Hong Kong's Refugee Dilemma. By William S. Ellis. 709-732, Nov. 1979
- Houston, Prairie Dynamo. By Stuart E. Jones. 338-377, Sept. 1967
- I See America First. By Lynda Bird Johnson. 874-904, Dec. 1965
- Land of the Ancient Basques. By Robert Laxalt. 240-277, Aug. 1968
- New Zealand's Cook Islands: Paradise in Search of a Future. By Maurice Shadbolt. 203-231, Aug. 1967
- The Two Souls of Peru. By Harvey Arden. 284-321, Mar. 1982
- The U. S. Virgin Islands. By Thomas J. Colin. Photos by William Albert Allard and Cary Wolinsky. 225-243, Feb. 1981

ALLEMAN, IRVIN E.: Artist:
- Flags of the Americas. By Elizabeth W. King. 633-657, May 1949
- Flags of the United Nations. By Elizabeth W. King. 213-238, Feb. 1951

ALLEN, ARTHUR A.:
Author-Photographer:
- The Bird's Year. 791-816, June 1951
- The Curlew's Secret. 751-770, Dec. 1948
- Duck Hunting With a Color Camera. 514-539, Oct. 1951
- A New Light Dawns on Bird Photography. 774-790, June 1948
- Sapsucker Woods, Cornell University's Exciting New Bird Sanctuary. 530-551, Apr. 1962
- Sea Bird Cities Off Audubon's Labrador. 755-774, June 1948
- Split Seconds in the Lives of Birds. 681-706, May 1954
- Voices of the Night. 507-522, Apr. 1950

ALLEN, BRYAN:
- The Flight of the *Gossamer Condor*. By Michael E. Long. 130-140, Jan. 1978

Author:
- Winged Victory of *Gossamer Albatross*. 640-651, Nov. 1979

ALLEN, DAVID G.: Photographer:
- The Quetzal, Fabulous Bird of Maya Land. By Anne LaBastille Bowes. 141-150, Jan. 1969

ALLEN, DURWARD L.: Author:
- Wolves Versus Moose on Isle Royale. By Durward L. Allen and L. David Mech. 200-219, Feb. 1963

ALLEN, JERRY: Author:
- Tom Sawyer's Town (Hannibal, Missouri). 121-140, July 1956

ALLEN, ROBERT PORTER: Author:
- Our Only Native Stork, the Wood Ibis. Photos by Frederick Kent Truslow. 294-306, Feb. 1964
- Roseate Spoonbills, Radiant Birds of the Gulf Coast. Photos by Frederick Kent Truslow. 274-288, Feb. 1962
- Whooping Cranes Fight for Survival. Photos by Frederick Kent Truslow. 650-669, Nov. 1959

ALLEN-WARNER VALLEY ENERGY SYSTEM, Utah: Proposed:
- Coal vs. Parklands. By François Leydet. Photos by Dewitt Jones. 776-803, Dec. 1980

ALLIGATOR REEF, Florida:
- Marvels of a Coral Realm. By Walter A. Starck II. NGS research grant. 710-738, Nov. 1966
- Photographing the Night Creatures of Alligator Reef. By Robert E. Schroeder. Photos by author and Walter A. Starck II. NGS research grant. 128-154, Jan. 1964

ALLIGATORS:
- Alligators: Dragons in Distress. By Archie Carr. Photos by Treat Davidson and Laymond Hardy. 133-148, Jan. 1967
- A Bad Time to Be a Crocodile. By Rick Gore. Photos by Jonathan Blair. Included: American and Chinese alligators. 90-115, Jan. 1978
- Twilight Hope for Big Cypress. By Rick Gore. Photos by Patricia Caulfield. 251-273, Aug. 1976
- *See also* Caimans; *and* Everglades (Region)

ALLMON, CHARLES:
Author-Photographer:
- Barbados, Outrider of the Antilles. 363-392, Mar. 1952
- Happy-go-lucky Trinidad and Tobago. 35-75, Jan. 1953
- Shores and Sails in the South Seas (Marquesas Islands). 73-104, Jan. 1950

Photographer:
- Bermuda, Cradled in Warm Seas. By Beverley M. Bowie. 203-238, Feb. 1954
- Martinique: A Tropical Bit of France. By Gwen Drayton Allmon. 255-283, Feb. 1959
- Rubber-cushioned Liberia. By Henry S. Villard. 201-228, Feb. 1948
- Spectacular Rio de Janeiro. By Hernane Tavares de Sá. 289-328, Mar. 1955
- Virgin Islands: Tropical Playland, U.S.A. By John Scofield. 201-232, Feb. 1956

FREDERICK KENT TRUSLOW

Roseate Spoonbills: adult on its perch

JONATHAN BLAIR

Alligators: Nile crocodile snaps at frog

• The *Yankee*'s Wander-world. By Irving and Electa Johnson. 1-50, Jan. 1949

ALLMON, GWEN DRAYTON: Author:
• Martinique: A Tropical Bit of France. Photos by Charles Allmon. 255-283, Feb. 1959

ALLYN, RUBE: Author:
• Cruising Florida's Western Waterways. Photos by Bates Littlehales. 49-76, Jan. 1955

ALONE Across the Outback. By Robyn Davidson. Photos by Rick Smolan. 581-611, May 1978

ALONE to Antarctica. By David Lewis. Drawings by Noel Sickles. 808-821, Dec. 1973

ALONG the Great Divide. By Mike Edwards. Photos by Nicholas DeVore III. 483-515, Oct. 1979

ALONG the Post Road Today. Photos by B. Anthony Stewart. 206-233, Aug. 1962

ALONG the Storied Incense Roads of Aden. By Hermann F. Eilts. Photos by Brian Brake. 230-254, Feb. 1957

ALONG the Yangtze, Main Street of China. By W. Robert Moore. 325-356, Mar. 1948

ALONG the Yukon Trail. By Amos Burg. 395-416, Sept. 1953

ALPINE MEADOWS, California:
• Avalanche! "I'm OK, I'm Alive!" By David Cupp. Photos by Lanny Johnson and Andre Benier. 282-289, Sept. 1982

ALPS (Mountains), Europe:
• Across the Alps in a Wicker Basket *(Bernina)*. By Phil Walker. 117-131, Jan. 1963
• Across the Ridgepole of the Alps. By Walter Meayers Edwards. Included: Map of cableway between Chamonix, France, and La Palud, Italy. 410-419, Sept. 1960
◆ *The Alps.* 1973. Announced. 870-874, June 1972
▲ *The Alps–Europe's Backbone,* double-sided Atlas series supplement. Sept. 1965
• The Alps: Man's Own Mountains. By Ralph Gray. Photos by Walter Meayers Edwards and William Eppridge. Included: Map of world's longest highway tunnel, Mont Blanc. 350-395, Sept. 1965
• The Great St. Bernard Hospice Today. By George Pickow. 49-62, Jan. 1957
• Liechtenstein: A Modern Fairy Tale. By Robert Booth. Photos by John Launois. 273-284, Feb. 1981
• Occupied Austria, Outpost of Democracy. By George W. Long. Photos by Volkmar Wentzel. 749-790, June 1951
• Sheep Trek in the French Alps. By Maurice Moyal. Photos by Marcel Coen. 545-564, Apr. 1952
• Soaring on Skis in the Swiss Alps. By Carolyn Bennett Patterson. Photos by Kathleen Revis. 94-121, Jan. 1961
• Surprising Switzerland. By Jean and Franc Shor. 427-478, Oct. 1956
• Switzerland, Europe's High-rise Republic. By Thomas J. Abercrombie. 68-113, July 1969
• Switzerland Guards the Roof of Europe. By William H. Nicholas. Photos by Willard R. Culver 205-246, Aug. 1950
• *See also* Bavaria; Dolomites; Saint Véran; Salzkammergut; Tirol; Val d'Hérens

ALSOP, JOSEPH: Author:
• Joseph Alsop: A Historical Perspective (on Minoan Human Sacrifice). 223, Feb. 1981
• Warriors From a Watery Grave (Bronze Sculptures). 821-827, June 1983

ALUMINUM:
• Aluminum, the Magic Metal. By Thomas Y. Canby. Photos by James L. Amos. 186-211, Aug. 1978
• Kitimat–Canada's Aluminum Titan. By David S. Boyer. 376-398, Sept. 1956

AL 'UQAYR, Saudi Arabia. *See* Gerrha

ALVIN (Research Submersible):
• Incredible World of the Deep-sea Rifts. 680-705, Nov. 1979
I. Strange World Without Sun. The Editor. 680-688; II. Return to Oases of the Deep. By Robert D. Ballard and J. Frederick Grassle. 689-705
• Oases of Life in the Cold Abyss (Galapagos Rift). By John B. Corliss and Robert D. Ballard. 441-453, Oct. 1977
• Project FAMOUS. 586-615, May 1975
I. Where the Earth Turns Inside Out. By J. R. Heirtzler. Photos by Emory Kristof. 586-603; II. Dive Into the Great Rift. By Robert D. Ballard. Photos by Emory Kristof. 604-615
• Window on Earth's Interior. By Robert D. Ballard. Photos by Emory Kristof. 228-249, Aug. 1976

AMA, Sea Nymphs of Japan. By Luis Marden. 122-135, July 1971

AMA DABLAM (Mountain), Nepal:
• Wintering on the Roof of the World. By Barry C. Bishop. 503-547, Oct. 1962

AMALFI, Italy's Divine Coast. By Luis Marden. 472-509, Oct. 1959

AMANA COLONIES, Iowa:
• Iowa's Enduring Amana Colonies. By Laura Longley Babb. Photos by Steve Raymer. 863-878, Dec. 1975

AMARANTH:
• Rediscovering America's Forgotten Crops. By Noel D. Vietmeyer. Photos by Burgess Blevins. Paintings by Paul M. Breeden. 702-712, May 1981

AMARNATH CAVE, Kashmir:
• Himalayan Pilgrimage. By Christopher Rand. 520-535, Oct. 1956

AMATEUR Gardener Creates a New Rose. By Elizabeth A. Moize. Photos by Farrell Grehan. 286-294, Aug. 1972

The **AMAZING** Frog-Eating Bat. By Merlin D. Tuttle. 78-91, Jan. 1982

AMAZON BASIN, South America:
• The Amazon. Photos by Loren McIntyre. 445-455, Oct. 1972
■ Amazon. 295A-295B, Feb. 1968
• Amazon–The River Sea. By Loren McIntyre. 456-495, Oct. 1972
• Brazil's Wild Frontier. By Loren McIntyre. 684-719, Nov. 1977
◆ *Exploring the Amazon.* Announced. 880-884, June 1969
• Giant Insects of the Amazon. By Paul A. Zahl. 632-669, May 1959
• Jari: A Billion-dollar Gamble. By Loren McIntyre. Contents: Daniel K. Ludwig's paper-pulp and food-production enterprise in Brazil's Amazon basin. 686-711, May 1980
• Jungle Jaunt on Amazon Headwaters. By Bernice M. Goetz. 371-388, Sept. 1952
• Sea Fever. By John E. Schultz. 237-268, Feb. 1949
• Tropical Rain Forests: Nature's Dwindling Treasures. By Peter T. White. Photos by James P. Blair. Paintings by Barron Storey. 2-47, Jan. 1983
• *See also* Brazil; Colombia; Ecuador

AMAZON BASIN INDIANS:
• Amazon–The River Sea. By Loren McIntyre. 456-495, Oct. 1972
• Brazil's Wild Frontier. By Loren McIntyre. Included: Mato Grosso tribes: Erigpactsã, Kabano Iáras and Kabano Pomons of the Cintas Largas, Xingu. 684-719, Nov. 1977
• Indians of the Amazon Darkness. By Harald Schultz. NGS research grant. 737-758, May 1964
• Man in the Amazon: Stone Age Present Meets Stone Age Past. By W. Jesco von Puttkamer. Included: Paleo-Indians; Wasúsus of the Nambicuara confederation. NGS research grant. 60-83, Jan. 1979
• What Future for the Wayana Indians? By Carole Devillers. 66-83, Jan. 1983
• *See also* Cinta Larga; Erigbaagtsa; Kraho; Kreen-Akarores; Machiguenga; Suyá; Tchikao; Tukuna; Txukahameis; Waurá

AMBASSADORS of Good Will: The Peace Corps. By Sargent Shriver and Peace Corps Volunteers. 297-345, Sept. 1964

AMBER:
• Exploring the World of Gems. By W. F. Foshag. 779-810, Dec. 1950
• Golden Window on the Past. Photos by Paul A. Zahl. Text by Thomas J. O'Neill. 423-435, Sept. 1977

AMERICA. *See* The Americas

AMERICA Enters the Modern Era. By Frank Freidel. 537-577, Oct. 1965

AMERICA Goes to the Fair. By Samuel W. Matthews. 293-333, Sept. 1954

AMERICAN and Geographic Flags Top Everest. By Melvin M. Payne. Photos by Barry C. Bishop. 157-157C, Aug. 1963

AMERICAN ANTARCTIC MOUNTAINEERING EXPEDITION:
● First Conquest of Antarctica's Highest Peaks. By Nicholas B. Clinch. NGS research grant. 836-863, June 1967
● First La Gorce Medal Honors Antarctic Expedition. 864-867, June 1967

An **AMERICAN** Energy Chronology. 5, *Special Report on Energy* (Feb. 1981)

AMERICAN Family in Afghanistan. By Rebecca Shannon Cresson. Photos by Osborne C. Cresson. 417-432, Sept. 1953

An **AMERICAN** 4-H Exchange: Down on the Farm in the U.S.S.R. By John Garaventa. Photos by James Tobin and Carol Schmidt. 768-797, June 1979

The **AMERICAN** Giant Comes of Age. By Frank Freidel. 660-711, May 1965

An **AMERICAN** in Russia's Capital. By Thomas T. Hammond. Photos by Dean Conger. 297-351, Mar. 1966

An **AMERICAN** Indian's View: This Land of Ours. By N. Scott Momaday. 13-19, July 1976

The **AMERICAN** Lobster, Delectable Cannibal. By Luis Marden. Photos by David Doubilet. 462-487, Apr. 1973

AMERICAN Masters in the National Gallery. By John Walker. 295-324, Sept. 1948

An **AMERICAN** Moslem Explores the Arab Past: The Sword and the Sermon. By Thomas J. Abercrombie. 3-45, July 1972

AMERICAN MOUNT EVEREST EXPEDITION:
● American and Geographic Flags Top Everest. By Melvin M. Payne. Photos by Barry C. Bishop. 157-157C, Aug. 1963
■ Americans on Everest. 448-452, Sept. 1965; 575, Nov. 1976
● America's First Everest Expedition. NGS research grant. 460-515, Oct. 1963
I. Six to the Summit. By Norman G. Dyhrenfurth. Photos by Barry C. Bishop. 460-473; II. How We Climbed Everest. By Barry C. Bishop. 477-507; III. The First Traverse. By Thomas F. Hornbein and William F. Unsoeld. 509-513; IV. President Kennedy Presents the Hubbard Medal. 514-515
● Mount Rainier: Testing Ground for Everest. By Barry C. Bishop. NGS research grant. 688-711, May 1963

AMERICAN MUSEUM OF NATURAL HISTORY, New York:
Expeditions:
● Dinosaur expedition to Texas. 710, 715, 717, May 1954
● *See also* American Museum-Armand Denis Expedition; Edgar M. Queeny-American Museum of Natural History Expedition; Gilliard Expeditions; Weeks Expedition
Museum:
● Behind New York's Window on Nature: The American Museum of Natural History. By James A. Oliver. Photos by Robert F. Sisson. 220-259, Feb. 1963
● Dinosaur Hall: *Brontosaurus*. 707, 719, 721, 722, May 1954
● Gem collection. 786, 797, 799, 801, Dec. 1950
Study Grant:
● Western Grebes. 626, May 1982
● *See also* Lerner Marine Laboratory

AMERICAN MUSEUM-ARMAND DENIS EXPEDITION:
● New Guinea's Rare Birds and Stone Age Men. By E. Thomas Gilliard. 421-488, Apr. 1953

AMERICAN POINT ISLAND, Minnesota:
● Men, Moose, and Mink of Northwest Angle. By William H. Nicholas. 265-284, Aug. 1947

AMERICAN PRIMITIVE ART. *See* Garbisch Collection

AMERICAN Processional: History on Canvas. By John and Blanche Leeper. 173-212, Feb. 1951

AMERICAN RED CROSS:
● The American Red Cross: A Century of Service. By Louise Levathes. Photos by Annie Griffiths. 777-791, June 1981
● Scenes of Postwar Finland. By La Verne Bradley. Photos by Jerry Waller. 233-264, Aug. 1947

An **AMERICAN** Retraces "Travels With a Donkey." By Carolyn Bennett Patterson. Photos by Cotton Coulson. 535-561, Oct. 1978

AMERICAN REVOLUTION:
● Benjamin Franklin, Philosopher of Dissent. By Alice J. Hall. Photos by Linda Bartlett. 93-123, July 1975
● Firebrands of the Revolution. By Eric F. Goldman. Photos by George F. Mobley. 2-27, July 1974
● From Sword to Scythe in Champlain Country. By Ethel A. Starbird. Photos by B. Anthony Stewart and Emory Kristof. 153-201, Aug. 1967
● George Washington: The Man Behind the Myths. By Howard La Fay. Photos by Ted Spiegel. 90-111, July 1976
● History and Beauty Blend in a Concord Iris Garden. By Robert T. Cochran, Jr. Photos by M. Woodbridge Williams. 705-719, May 1959
● I'm From New Jersey. By John T. Cunningham. Photos by Volkmar Wentzel. 1-45, Jan. 1960
● The Loyalists. By Kent Britt. Photos by Ted Spiegel. 510-539, Apr. 1975
● Massachusetts Builds for Tomorrow. By Robert de Roos. Photos by B. Anthony Stewart. 790-843, Dec. 1966
● New Stars for Old Glory. By Lonnelle Aikman. 86-121, July 1959
● North Through History Aboard *White Mist*. By Melville Bell Grosvenor. Photos by Edwin Stuart Grosvenor. 1-55, July 1970

PAINTING BY LOUIS S. GLANZMAN

American Revolution: Patrick Henry

• Patriots in Petticoats. By Lonnelle Aikman. Paintings by Louis S. Glanzman. Contents: Abigail Adams, Sarah Franklin Bache, Anne Bailey, Kate Moore Barry, Martha Bell, Margaret Cochran Corbin, Lydia Darragh, Mary Katherine Goddard, Elizabeth Hager, Nancy Hart, Elizabeth Hutchinson Jackson, Dicey Langston, Sybil Ludington, Rebecca Motte, Molly Pitcher (Mary Hays), Esther Reed, Deborah Sampson, Jane Thomas, Mercy Otis Warren, Martha Washington, Phillis Wheatley, Elizabeth Zane. 475-493, Oct. 1975
• Philadelphia Houses a Proud Past. By Harold Donaldson Eberlein. Photos by Thomas Nebbia. 151-191, Aug. 1960
• Profiles of the Presidents: I. The Presidency and How It Grew. By Frank Freidel. 642-687, Nov. 1964
◆ *The Revolutionary War: America's Fight for Freedom.* Announced. 868-875, June 1967
• Thomas Jefferson: Architect of Freedom. By Mike W. Edwards. Photos by Linda Bartlett. 231-259, Feb. 1976
• U. S. Capitol, Citadel of Democracy. By Lonnelle Aikman. Included: Paintings and frescoes of the Revolution by John Trumbull and Constantino Brumidi. 143-192, Aug. 1952
• Washington Lives Again at Valley Forge. By Howell Walker. 197-202, Feb. 1954
• *See also* Boston Post Roads; Daughters of the American Revolution

AMERICAN SAMOA (Island), Pacific Ocean:
• Problems in Paradise. By Mary and Laurance S. Rockefeller. Photos by Thomas Nebbia. 782-793, Dec. 1974

AMERICAN Skiers Find Adventure in Western China. By Ned Gillette. Photos by the author and Galen Rowell. 174-199, Feb. 1981
Skiing From the Summit of China's Ice Mountain. 192-199

AMERICAN Special Forces in Action in Viet Nam. By Howard Sochurek. 38-65, Jan. 1965

AMERICAN TELEPHONE AND TELEGRAPH COMPANY: Research. *See* Telstar

AMERICAN Wild Flower Odyssey. By P. L. Ricker. 603-634, May 1953

AMERICANS Afoot in Rumania. By Dan Dimancescu. Photos by Dick Durrance II and Christopher G. Knight. 810-845, June 1969

AMERICANS Climb K2. Photos by members of the expedition. 623-649, May 1979
I. The Ultimate Challenge. By James W. Whittaker. 624-639; II. On to the Summit. By James Wickwire. 641-649

The **AMERICAS:**
▲ *Bird Migration in the Americas; The Americas,* double-sided supplement. Aug. 1979
▲ *Colonization and Trade in the New World,* supplement. Painting and text on reverse. Dec. 1977
◆ *Discovering Man's Past in the Americas.* Announced. 880-884, June 1969
• Editorials. By Gilbert M. Grosvenor. 147, Aug. 1977; 723, Dec. 1977; By Wilbur E. Garrett. 1, July 1982
▲ Eight Maps of Discovery: America in the Discovery Age: the Molineaux-Wright Chart.–America Emerges: The Thirteen Original States.–Capt. John Smith's Map of Virginia.–The Opening of the American West: Burr's 1840 Map.–Captain Smith's New England.–The Pilgrims' Cape Cod.–Alaska, Seward's Icebox, Became a Treasure Chest.–George Washington's Travels, Traced on the Arrowsmith Map. 757-769, June 1953
• Flags of the Americas. By Elizabeth W. King. Contents: The Flag of the United States and the Jack; Flags of the President, the Vice President, and Heads of Executive Departments of the United States; Flags of the United States Armed Forces and Government Agencies; Flags of the Latin-American Republics. 633-657, May 1949
• Mysteries of Bird Migration. By Allan C. Fisher, Jr. Photos by Jonathan Blair. 154-193, Aug. 1979
• Reach for the New World. By Mendel Peterson. Photos by David L. Arnold. Paintings by Richard Schlecht. 724-767, Dec. 1977
• The Search for the First Americans. By Thomas Y. Canby. Photos by Kerby Smith. Paintings by Roy Andersen. 330-363, Sept. 1979
• The Voyage of *Brendan.* By Timothy Severin. Photos by Cotton Coulson. 770-797, Dec. 1977
• Who Discovered America? A New Look at an Old Question. The Editor. 769, Dec. 1977
• *See also* Central America; Colonial America; North America; South America

AMERICA's Auto Mania. By David Jeffery. Photos by Bruce Dale. 24-31, *Special Report on Energy* (Feb. 1981)

***AMERICA's** Federal Lands; The United States,* double-sided map supplement. Sept. 1982

AMERICA's First Painters: Indians. By Dorothy Dunn. 349-377, Mar. 1955

AMERICA's First Undersea Park. By Charles M. Brookfield. Photos by Jerry Greenberg. 58-69, Jan. 1962

AMERICA's Forgotten Crops. By Noel D. Vietmeyer. Photos by Burgess Blevins. Paintings by Paul M. Breeden. 702-712, May 1981

AMERICA's Little Mainstream. By Harvey Arden. Photos by Matt Bradley. 344-359, Mar. 1977

AMERICA's "Meat on the Hoof." By William H. Nicholas. 33-72, Jan. 1952

AMERICA's 6,000-mile Walk in Space. 440-447, Sept. 1965

AMERICA's Wilderness: How Much Can We Save? By Gilbert M. Grosvenor, François Leydet, and Joseph Judge. Photos by Farrell Grehan. 151-205, Feb. 1974

AMHARAS (People):
• Ethiopia: Revolution in an Ancient Empire. By Robert Caputo. 614-645, May 1983

AMHERST, Massachusetts:
• Literary Landmarks of Massachusetts. By William H. Nicholas. Photos by B. Anthony Stewart and John E. Fletcher. 279-310, Mar. 1950

AMIABLE Amsterdam. By William Davenport. Photos by Adam Woolfitt. 683-705, May 1974

AMID the Mighty Walls of Zion. By Lewis F. Clark. 37-70, Jan. 1954

AMISH SECT:
• Amish Folk: Plainest of Pennsylvania's Plain People. By Richard Gehman. Photos by William Albert Allard. 227-253, Aug. 1965
• Artists Look at Pennsylvania. By John Oliver La Gorce. 37-56, July 1948
• Pennsylvania: Faire Land of William Penn. By Gordon Young. Photos by Cary Wolinsky. 731-767, June 1978

AMMAN, Jordan:
• Home to the Holy Land. By Maynard Owen Williams. 707-746, Dec. 1950

AMOCO CADIZ (Oil Tanker):
• Superspill: Black Day for Brittany. Photos by Martin Rogers. Text by Noel Grove. 124-135, July 1978

AMONG Alaska's Brown Bears. By Allan L. Egbert and Michael H. Luque. 428-442, Sept. 1975

AMOS, JAMES L.: Photographer:
• Aluminum, the Magic Metal. By Thomas Y. Canby. 186-211, Aug. 1978
• Atlanta, Pacesetter City of the South. By William S. Ellis. 246-281, Feb. 1969
• Britain's "French" Channel Islands. By James Cerruti. 710-740, May 1971
• Buffalo Bill and the Enduring West. By Alice J. Hall. 76-103, July 1981
• Chincoteague: Watermen's Island Home. By Nathaniel T. Kenney. 810-829, June 1980
• Colorado, the Rockies' Pot of Gold. By Edward J. Linehan. 157-201, Aug. 1969
• The Great Lakes: Is It Too Late? By Gordon Young. Photos by James L. Amos and Martin Rogers. 147-185, Aug. 1973
• Great Smokies National Park: Solitude for Millions. By Gordon Young. 522-549, Oct. 1968
• Leonardo da Vinci: A Man for All Ages. By Kenneth MacLeish. 296-329, Sept. 1977
• The Miracle Metal–Platinum. By Gordon Young. 686-706, Nov. 1983

• New Zealand's Bountiful South Island. By Peter Benchley. 93-123, Jan. 1972
• The Original Boston: St. Botolph's Town (England). By Veronica Thomas. 382-389, Sept. 1974
• San Diego, California's Plymouth Rock. By Allan C. Fisher, Jr. 114-147, July 1969
• Sea Islands: Adventuring Along the South's Surprising Coast. By James Cerruti. Photos by Thomas Nebbia and James L. Amos. 366-393, Mar. 1971
• The Two Worlds of Michigan. By Noel Grove. 802-843, June 1979
• Utah's Shining Oasis. By Charles McCarry. 440-473, Apr. 1975
• Williamsburg, City for All Seasons. By Joseph Judge. 790-823, Dec. 1968
• The World of Martin Luther. By Merle Severy. 418-463, Oct. 1983

AMOS, WILLIAM H.:
Author-Photographer:
• Life on a Rock Ledge. 558-566, Oct. 1980
• The Living Sand. 820-833, June 1965
• Teeming Life of a Pond. 274-298, Aug. 1970
• Unseen Life of a Mountain Stream. 562-580, Apr. 1977

AMPHIBIANS:
◆ *Creepy Crawly Things: Reptiles and Amphibians.* Announced. 728-730, Nov. 1974
• In the Wilds of a City Parlor. By Paul A. Zahl. Included: Frogs, salamanders. 645-672, Nov. 1954
▪ Reptiles and Amphibians. 875A-875B, Dec. 1968
• Strange Animals of Australia. By David Fleay. Photos by Stanley Breeden. Included: Frogs, corroborees, toads. 388-411, Sept. 1963
• *See also* Frogs; Salamanders; Toads

AMPHITRITE (Inflatable Ship):
• Inflatable Ship Opens Era of Airborne Undersea Expeditions. By Jacques-Yves Cousteau. NGS research grant. 142-148, July 1961

AMSTERDAM, The Netherlands:
• Amiable Amsterdam. By William Davenport. Photos by Adam Woolfitt. 683-705, May 1974
• Mid-century Holland Builds Her Future. By Sydney Clark. 747-778, Dec. 1950
• The Netherlands: Nation at War With the Sea. By Alan Villiers. Photos by Adam Woolfitt. 530-571, Apr. 1968

AMUSEMENT PARKS. *See* Disneyland; Tivoli; Walt Disney World

AN LAC, Viet Nam:
• Viet Nam's Montagnards. By Howard Sochurek. 443-487, Apr. 1968

ANABAPTIST GROUPS. *See* Amish; Hutterites; Mennonites

ANABLEPS. *See* Four-eyed Fish

ANASAZI (Early Indians):
• The Anasazi–Riddles in the Ruins. By Thomas Y. Canby. Photos by Dewitt Jones and David Brill. Paintings by Roy Andersen. 554-592, Nov. 1982
• Ancient Cliff Dwellers of Mesa Verde. By Don Watson. Photos by Willard R. Culver. 349-376, Sept. 1948
• Pueblo Pottery–2,000 Years of Artistry. By David L. Arnold. 593-605, Nov. 1982
• Searching for Cliff Dwellers' Secrets. By Carroll A. Burroughs. 619-625, Nov. 1959
• Solving the Riddles of Wetherill Mesa. By Douglas Osborne. Paintings by Peter V. Bianchi. 155-195, Feb. 1964
▲ *The Southwest,* The Making of America series. Nov. 1982
• Your Society to Seek New Light on the Cliff Dwellers. 154-156, Jan. 1959

ANATOLIA (Region), Turkey:
• Ancient Aphrodisias and Its Marble Treasures. By Kenan T. Erim. Photos by Jonathan S. Blair. NGS research grant. 280-294, Aug. 1967
• Ancient Aphrodisias Lives Through Its Art. By Kenan T. Erim. Photos by David Brill. NGS research grant. 527-551, Oct. 1981
• Aphrodisias, Awakened City of Ancient Art. By Kenan T. Erim. Photos by Jonathan Blair. NGS research grant. 766-791, June 1972
• Keeping House in a Cappadocian Cave. By Jonathan S. Blair. 127-146, July 1970
• Peasants of Anatolia. By Alfred Marchionini. 57-72, July 1948

ANATOMY of a Burmese Beauty Secret. By John M. Keshishian. 798-801, June 1979

ANCHORAGE, Alaska:
• An Alaskan Family's Night of Terror (Earthquake). By Tay Pryor Thomas. 142-156, July 1964
• Earthquake! By William P. E. Graves. 112-139, July 1964

ANCIENT Aphrodisias and Its Marble Treasures. By Kenan T. Erim. Photos by Jonathan S. Blair. 280-294, Aug. 1967

ANCIENT Aphrodisias Lives Through Its Art. By Kenan T. Erim. Photos by David Brill. 527-551, Oct. 1981

ANCIENT Ashfall Creates a Pompeii of Prehistoric Animals. By Michael R. Voorhies. Photos by Annie Griffiths. Paintings by Jay Matternes. 66-75, Jan. 1981

ANCIENT Bulgaria's Golden Treasures. By Colin Renfrew. Photos by James L. Stanfield. Paintings by Jean-Leon Huens. 112-129, July 1980

ANCIENT CIVILIZATIONS. *See* Early Civilizations

ANCIENT Cliff Dwellers of Mesa Verde. By Don Watson. Photos by Willard R. Culver. 349-376, Sept. 1948

JORGEN BISCH

Burmese Beauty: Padaung woman

JOSEPH J. SCHERSCHEL, NGS

Andalusia: Zaharans play dominoes

ANCIENT Ebla Opens a New Chapter of History. By Howard La Fay. Photos by James L. Stanfield. Paintings by Louis S. Glanzman. 730-759, Dec. 1978

ANCIENT Europe Is Older Than We Thought. By Colin Renfrew. Photos by Adam Woolfitt. 615-623, Nov. 1977

ANCIENT Glory in Stone (Angkor). By Peter T. White. Photos by Wilbur E. Garrett. 552-589, May 1982

ANCIENT Mesopotamia: A Light That Did Not Fail. By E. A. Speiser. Paintings by H. M. Herget. 41-105, Jan. 1951

ANCIENT Shipwreck Yields New Facts–and a Strange Cargo. By Peter Throckmorton. Photos by Kim Hart and Joseph J. Scherschel. 282-300, Feb. 1969

ANCIENT "Skyscrapers" of the Yemen. Photos by Richard H. Sanger. 645-668, Nov. 1947

AND Now to Touch the Moon's Forbidding Face. By Kenneth F. Weaver. 633-635, May 1969

ANDALUSIA (Region), Spain:
● Andalusia, the Spirit of Spain. By Howard La Fay. Photos by Joseph J. Scherschel. 833-857, June 1975
● The Changing Face of Old Spain. By Bart McDowell. Photos by Albert Moldvay. 291-339, Mar. 1965
● Gypsy Cave Dwellers of Andalusia. 572-582, Oct. 1957
● Holy Week and the Fair in Sevilla. By Luis Marden. 499-530, Apr. 1951
● Speaking of Spain. By Luis Marden. 415-456, Apr. 1950

ANDAMAN ISLANDS, India:
● The Last Andaman Islanders. By Raghubir Singh. 66-91, July 1975

ANDEAN CONDORS:
● The Condor, Soaring Spirit of the Andes. By Jerry McGahan. Photos by Libby McGahan. 684-709, May 1971

ANDEREGG, FRED: Photographer:
● Mount Sinai's Holy Treasures (St. Catherine's Monastery). By Kurt Weitzmann. 109-127, Jan. 1964

ANDERS, WILLIAM A.:
● Hubbard Medal recipient. 861, June 1970
● "A Most Fantastic Voyage": The Story of Apollo 8's Rendezvous With the Moon. By Sam C. Phillips. 593-631, May 1969

ANDERSEN, HANS CHRISTIAN:
● The Magic World of Hans Christian Andersen. By Harvey Arden. Photos by Sisse Brimberg. 825-849, Dec. 1979

ANDERSEN, ROY: Artist:
● The Anasazi–Riddles in the Ruins. By Thomas Y. Canby. Photos by Dewitt Jones and David Brill. 554-592, Nov. 1982
▲ "Australia, Land of Living Fossils," painting supplement. Map on reverse. Feb. 1979
● A New Look at Dinosaurs. By John H. Ostrom. 152-185, Aug. 1978
● The Search for the First Americans. By Thomas Y. Canby. Photos by Kerby Smith. 330-363, Sept. 1979

ANDERSON, GEORGE W., Jr.:
Author:
● Our Nuclear Navy. 449-450, Mar. 1963

ANDERSON, KRISTIAN: Author:
● *Kitty Hawk* Floats Across North America. By Maxie and Kristian Anderson. 260-271, Aug. 1980

ANDERSON, MAXIE:
● Editorial. By Wilbur E. Garrett. 707, Dec. 1983
● A Wild, Ill-fated Balloon Race. 778-797, Dec. 1983
I. Wild Launch. 778-787; II. The Fantastic Flight of *Cote d'Or*. By Cynthia Shields. 789-793; III. Last Ascent of a Heroic Team (Maxie Anderson and Don Ida). 794-797
Author:
● *Double Eagle II* Has Landed! Crossing the Atlantic by Balloon. By Ben L. Abruzzo, with Maxie L. Anderson and Larry Newman. 858-882, Dec. 1978
● *Kitty Hawk* Floats Across North America. By Maxie and Kristian Anderson. 260-271, Aug. 1980

ANDERSON, NIKE: Author:
● October Holiday on the Outer Banks. Photos by J. Baylor Roberts. 501-529, Oct. 1955

ANDERSON, RON J.: Author:
● The Kiwi, New Zealand's Wonder Bird. 395-398, Sept. 1955

ANDERSON, SALLY: Author:
● Norway's Reindeer Lapps. Photos by Erik Borg. 364-379, Sept. 1977

ANDERSON, STEWART:
Author-Photographer:
● The West Through Boston Eyes. 733-776, June 1949

ANDERSON, WILLIAM R.:
● Submarine Through the North Pole. By William G. Lalor, Jr. Photos by John J. Krawczyk. 1-20, Jan. 1959
Author:
● The Arctic as a Sea Route of the Future. 21-24, Jan. 1959

ANDES (Mountains), South America:
● At Home in the High Andes. By Harry Tschopik, Jr. 133-146, Jan. 1955
● Avalanche! (Peru). By Bart McDowell. Photos by John E. Fletcher. 855-880, June 1962
● El Sangay, Fire-breathing Giant of the Andes. By G. Edward Lewis. 117-138, Jan. 1950
● In Quest of the Rarest Flamingo. By William G. Conway. Photos by Bates Littlehales. 91-105, July 1961
● The Incredible Potato. By Robert E. Rhoades. Photos by Martin Rogers. Included: The International Potato Center in Lima, Peru; The World Potato Collection in a research station at Huancayo, Peru; Cultivation and worship of potatoes by early Peruvian Indians. 668-694, May 1982

▲ *Indians of South America; Archaeology of South America,* double-sided supplement. Mar. 1982
● Parks, Plans, and People: How South America Guards Her Green Legacy. By Mary and Laurance Rockefeller. Photos by George F. Mobley. Included: Christ of the Andes; Lake District; Moreno Glacier; Mount Aconcagua; Nahuel Huapí National Park. 74-119, Jan. 1967
● Peru, Homeland of the Warlike Inca. By Kip Ross. 421-462, Oct. 1950
● Peru's Pilgrimage to the Sky. By Robert Randall. Photos by Loren McIntyre and Ira Block. 60-69, July 1982
● Puya, the Pineapple's Andean Ancestor. By Mulford B. Foster. 463-480, Oct. 1950
● Sky-high Bolivia. 481-496, Oct. 1950
● To Torre Egger's Icy Summit. By Jim Donini. 813-823, Dec. 1976
● The Two Souls of Peru. By Harvey Arden. Photos by William Albert Allard. 284-321, Mar. 1982

ANDORRA:
● The Enduring Pyrenees. By Robert Laxalt. Photos by Edwin Stuart Grosvenor. 794-819, Dec. 1974
● Incredible Andorra. By Lawrence L. Klingman. Photos by B. Anthony Stewart. 262-290, Aug. 1949

ANDREWS, E. WYLLYS: Author:
● Dzibilchaltun: Lost City of the Maya. 91-109, Jan. 1959

ANDRONICOS, MANOLIS: Author:
● Regal Treasures From a Macedonian Tomb. Photos by Spyros Tsavdaroglou. 55-77, July 1978

ANDROS ISLAND, Bahama Islands:
● Flamingos' Last Stand on Andros Island. By Paul A. Zahl. 635-652, May 1951
● Probing the Deep Reefs' Hidden Realm. By Walter A. Starck II and Jo D. Starck. 867-886, Dec. 1972
● *See also* Blue Holes

ANDRUS, CECIL D.: Author:
● Sharing Alaska: How Much for Parks? Opposing views by Jay S. Hammond and Cecil D. Andrus. 60-65, July 1979

ANEMOSPILIA (Area), Crete:
● Drama of Death in a Minoan Temple. By Yannis Sakellarakis and Efi Sapouna-Sakellaraki. Photos by Otis Imboden and Spyros Tsavdaroglou. 205-222, Feb. 1981

ANGEL FALLS, Venezuela:
● Jungle Journey to the World's Highest Waterfall. By Ruth Robertson. 655-690, Nov. 1949

ANGKOR, Kampuchea:
● Angkor, Jewel of the Jungle. By W. Robert Moore. Paintings by Maurice Fiévet. 517-569, Apr. 1960
● Cambodia: Indochina's "Neutral" Corner. By Thomas J. Abercrombie. 514-551, Oct. 1964
● Portrait of Indochina. By W. Robert Moore and Maynard Owen Williams. Paintings by Jean Despujols. 461-490, Apr. 1951
● The Temples of Angkor. 548-589, May 1982
I. Ancient Glory in Stone. By Peter T. White. Photos by Wilbur E. Garrett. 552-589; II. Will They Survive? Introduction by Wilbur E. Garrett. 548-551

ANGOLA, Unknown Africa. By Volkmar Wentzel. 347-383, Sept. 1961

ANIMAL BEHAVIOR. *See* Animals

ANIMAL EYES:
● Nature's Alert Eyes. By Constance P. Warner. 558-569, Apr. 1959
● *See also* Four-eyed Fish; *Photoblepharon*

ANIMAL INTRODUCTION:
● Florida, Noah's Ark for Exotic Newcomers. By Rick Gore. Photos by David Doubilet. 538-559, Oct. 1976
● New Tricks Outwit Our Insect Enemies. By Hal Higdon. Photos by Robert F. Sisson and Emory Kristof. 380-399, Sept. 1972
● *See also* Africanized Honeybees; Cattle Egret; Fig Wasps; Orioles; Walking Catfish

ANIMAL ORPHANAGE, Entebbe, Uganda:
● Orphans of the Wild. By Bruce G. Kinloch. 683-699, Nov. 1962

ANIMAL-PRODUCT TRADE:
● Wild Cargo: the Business of Smuggling Animals. By Noel Grove. Photos by Steve Raymer. 287-315, Mar. 1981

ANIMAL SACRIFICE:
● Inside the Sacred Hopi Homeland. By Jake Page. Photos by Susanne Page. Included: Golden eagle sacrifice ceremony. 607-629, Nov. 1982

ANIMAL SAFARI to British Guiana. By David Attenborough. Photos by Charles Lagus and author. 851-874, June 1957

ANIMALS:
◆ *Amazing Animal Groups.* 1981
◆ *Animals Helping People.* 1983
◆ *Animals in Winter.* 1982
■ The Animals Nobody Loved. Cover, Feb. 1976
◆ *Animals of East Africa: The Wild Realm.* 1969. Announced. 844-849, June 1968
◆ *Animals That Build Their Homes.* Announced. 718-720, Nov. 1976
◆ *Animals That Travel.* 1982
◆ *Creatures Small and Furry.* 1983
◆ *Giants From the Past.* 1983
◆ *How Animals Hide.* Announced. 726-728, Nov. 1973
◆ *The Marvels of Animal Behavior.* 1972; Announced. 588-590, Oct. 1972
■ The Mystery of Animal Behavior. 592A-592B, Oct. 1969
◆ *Secrets of Animal Survival.* 1983
● Teeming Life of a Rain Forest. By Carol and David Hughes. 49-65, Jan. 1983
◆ *Tricks Animals Play.* Announced. 724-726, Nov. 1975
◆ *Ways Animals Sleep.* 1983
● *See also* Albino Animals; Amphibians; Animal Introduction; Birds; Camouflage; Circus; Communication, Animal; Corals and Coral Reefs; Crustaceans; Endangered and Threatened Species; Extinct Species; Fishes; Frogs; Game Preserves; Insects; Mammals; Mammals, Prehistoric; Marine Biology; Microorganisms; Migration; Mollusks; Nocturnal Animals; Reptiles; Scorpions; Spiders; Tool-using Animals; Wildlife; Wildlife Refuges; Worms and Wormlike Animals; Zoos; *and* listings under Arthropods; Cephalopods

ANIMATION:
● The Magic Worlds of Walt Disney. By Robert de Roos. Photos by Thomas Nebbia. 159-207, Aug. 1963
Animation: Mickey Mouse Explains the Art to Mr. G. O. Graphic. 168-171

ANIMISM:
● Beyond the Bight of Benin. By Jeannette and Maurice Fiévet. Included: Cameroon and Nigerian tribal rites. 221-253, Aug. 1959
● Foxes Foretell the Future in Mali's Dogon Country. By Pamela Johnson Meyer. 431-448, Mar. 1969
● Inside the Sacred Hopi Homeland. By Jake Page. Photos by Susanne Page. Included: Kachinas; Golden eagle sacrifice. 607-629, Nov. 1982
● The Ivory Coast–African Success Story. By Michael and Aubine Kirtley. 94-125, July 1982
● Kachinas: Masked Dancers of the Southwest. By Paul Coze. 219-236, Aug. 1957
● Living Theater in New Guinea's Highlands. By Gillian Gillison. Photos by David Gillison. 147-169, Aug. 1983
● Rock Paintings of the Aborigines. By Kay and Stanley Breeden. 174-187, Feb. 1973
● Spirits of Change Capture the Karens. By Peter Kunstadter. 267-285, Feb. 1972
● Taboos and Magic Rule Namba Lives. By Kal Muller. 57-83, Jan. 1972
● Trek to Nepal's Sacred Crystal Mountain. By Joel F. Ziskin. 500-517, Apr. 1977
● Where Magic Ruled: Art of the Bering Sea. By William W. Fitzhugh and Susan A. Kaplan. Photos by Sisse Brimberg. 198-205, Feb. 1983
● *See also* Shamanism; Sorcery; Voodoo

ANKARA, Turkey:
● Turkey Paves the Path of Progress. By Maynard Owen Williams. 141-186, Aug. 1951
● When the President Goes Abroad (Eisenhower Tour). By Gilbert M. Grosvenor. 588-649, May 1960

ANN, Cape, Massachusetts:
● Windjamming Around New England. By Tom Horgan. Photos by Robert F. Sisson. 141-169, Aug. 1950

ANNAPOLIS, Maryland:
● Maryland on the Half Shell. By Stuart E. Jones. Photos by Robert W. Madden. 188-229, Feb. 1972

ANNAPURNA I (Mountain), Nepal:
• Triumph and Tragedy on Annapurna. By Arlene Blum. 295-311, Mar. 1979
On the Summit. By Irene Miller, with Vera Komarkova. 312-313

ANNA'S HUMMINGBIRDS:
• Hummingbirds: The Nectar Connection. By Paul W. Ewald. Photos by Robert A. Tyrrell. 223-227, Feb. 1982

ANOTHER Crossroads for Turkey. By Robert Paul Jordan. Photos by Gordon W. Gahan. 88-123, July 1977

ANTARCTIC REGIONS:
• Alone to Antarctica. By David Lewis. Drawings by Noel Sickles. 808-821, Dec. 1973
• Atlantic Odyssey: Iceland to Antarctica. By Newman Bumstead. Photos by Volkmar Wentzel. 725-780, Dec. 1955
• *Ice Bird* Ends Her Lonely Odyssey. By David Lewis. 216-233, Aug. 1975
• Off the Beaten Track of Empire (Prince Philip's Tour). By Beverley M. Bowie. Photos by Michael Parker. 584-626, Nov. 1957
• Penguins and Their Neighbors. By Roger Tory Peterson. Photos by Des and Jen Bartlett. 237-255, Aug. 1977
• Voyage to the Antarctic. By David Lewis. 544-562, Apr. 1983
• What's Happening to Our Climate? By Samuel W. Matthews. 576-615, Nov. 1976
• *See also* Antarctica; South Georgia Island

ANTARCTICA:
• Across the Frozen Desert to Byrd Station. By Paul W. Frazier. Photos by Calvin L. Larsen. 383-398, Sept. 1957
• Admiral of the Ends of the Earth (Richard E. Byrd). By Melville Bell Grosvenor. 38-48, July 1957
• All-out Assault on Antarctica. By Richard E. Byrd. 141-180, Aug. 1956
• Antarctic Scientist (Paul A. Siple) Honored by The Society. 792-793, June 1958
▲ *Antarctica,* Atlas series supplement. Feb. 1963
▲ *Antarctica,* supplement. Sept. 1957
• Antarctica: Icy Testing Ground for Space. By Samuel W. Matthews. Photos by Robert W. Madden. 569-592, Oct. 1968
• Antarctica's Nearer Side. By Samuel W. Matthews. Photos by William R. Curtsinger. 622-655, Nov. 1971
• Circling Earth From Pole to Pole. By Sir Ranulph Fiennes. Included: Antarctica's Awesome Challenge. 464-481, Oct. 1983
• The Crossing of Antarctica. By Sir Vivian Fuchs. Photos by George Lowe. 25-47, Jan. 1959
• Exploring Antarctica's Phantom Coast. By Edwin A. McDonald. Photos by W. D. Vaughn. 251-273, Feb. 1962

ROBERT W. MADDEN

Antarctica: cross at Hut Point

Loneliest Continent: Edward Oliver studies ice

ALBERT MOLDVAY, NGS

• First Conquest of Antarctica's Highest Peaks. By Nicholas B. Clinch. NGS research grant. 836-863, June 1967
• First Flight Across the Bottom of the World. By James R. Reedy. Photos by Otis Imboden. 454-464, Mar. 1964
• First La Gorce Medal Honors Antarctic Expedition. Note: Melvin M. Payne guided the design of the medal, which was executed by Peter V. Bianchi and Howard E. Paine. NGS research grant. 864-867, June 1967
• Flight Into Antarctic Darkness. By J. Lloyd Abbot, Jr. Photos by David S. Boyer. 732-738, Nov. 1967
• Man's First Winter at the South Pole (Amundsen-Scott IGY South Pole Station). By Paul A. Siple. 439-478, Apr. 1958
• New Era in the Loneliest Continent. By David M. Tyree. Photos by Albert Moldvay. Included: Byrd Station; McMurdo Station. 260-296, Feb. 1963
• Our Navy Explores Antarctica. By Richard E. Byrd. U. S. Navy official photos. 429-522, Oct. 1947
• Society Honors the Conquerors of Antarctica. 589-590, Apr. 1959
• Stalking Seals Under Antarctic Ice. By Carleton Ray. 54-65, Jan. 1966
• This Changing Earth. By Samuel W. Matthews. 1-37, Jan. 1973
• To the Men at South Pole Station. By Richard E. Byrd. 1-4, July 1957
• Voyage to the Antarctic. By David Lewis. 544-562, Apr. 1983
• We Are Living at the South Pole (IGY station). By Paul A. Siple. Photos by David S. Boyer. 5-35, July 1957
• What We've Accomplished in Antarctica. By George J. Dufek. 527-557, Oct. 1959
• Year of Discovery Opens in Antarctica. By David S. Boyer. 339-381, Sept. 1957

ANTELOPES:
• Etosha: Namibia's Kingdom of Animals. By Douglas H. Chadwick. Photos by Des and Jen Bartlett. Included: Cape elands, dik-diks, gemsbok, kudus, roans, sables, springboks, tsessebes, wildebeest. 344-385, Mar. 1983
• Roaming Africa's Unfenced Zoos. By W. Robert Moore. Included: Dik-dik, Duiker, Eland, Hartebeest, Impala, Inyala, Klipspringer, Kudu, Oryx, Roan Antelope, Sable Antelope, Sitatunga, Steenbok, Tsessebe, Waterbuck, Wildebeest (Gnu). 353-380, Mar. 1950

ANTHROPOLOGY, Cultural. *See* Ethnology

ANTHROPOLOGY, Physical:
• Adventures in the Search for Man. By Louis S. B. Leakey. Photos by Hugo van Lawick. NGS research grant. 132-152, Jan. 1963
• A Bold New Look at Our Past. The Editor. NGS research grant. 62-63, Jan. 1975
▪ Dr. Leakey and the Dawn of Man. 703A-703B, Nov. 1966

• Ethiopia Yields First "Family" of Early Man. By Donald C. Johanson. Photos by David Brill. NGS research grant. 790-811, Dec. 1976
• Exploring 1,750,000 Years Into Man's Past. By L. S. B. Leakey. Photos by Robert F. Sisson. NGS research grant. 564-589, Oct. 1961
• Exploring the Mind of Ice Age Man. By Alexander Marshack. NGS research grant. 64-89, Jan. 1975
• Finding the World's Earliest Man *(Zinjanthropus boisei)*. By L. S. B. Leakey. Photos by Des Bartlett. NGS research grant. 420-435, Sept. 1960
• Footprints in the Ashes of Time. By Mary D. Leakey. NGS research grant. 446-457, Apr. 1979
• Ice Age Man, the First American. By Thomas R. Henry. Paintings by Andre Durenceau. 781-806, Dec. 1955
• In Search of Man's Past at Lake Rudolf. By Richard E. Leakey. Photos by Gordon W. Gahan. NGS research grant. 712-734, May 1970
• The Leakey Tradition Lives On. By Melvin M. Payne. NGS research grant. 143-144, Jan. 1973
• The Leakeys of Africa: Family in Search of Prehistoric Man. By Melvin M. Payne. Included: *Homo habilis, Kenyapithecus, Proconsul, Zinjanthropus*. NGS research grant. 194-231, Feb. 1965
▪ The Legacy of L. S. B. Leakey. 439, Oct. 1977; cover, Jan. 1978
• Lifelike Man Preserved 2,000 Years in Peat. By P. V. Glob. 419-430, Mar. 1954
• Mexico's Window on the Past (National Museum). By Bart McDowell. Photos by B. Anthony Stewart. 492-519, Oct. 1968
◆ *Nomads of the World*. Announced. 882-886, June 1971
• Preserving the Treasures of Olduvai Gorge. By Melvin M. Payne. Photos by Joseph J. Scherschel. Included: *Homo erectus, Homo habilis, Kenyapithecus, Zinjanthropus*. NGS research grant. 701-709, Nov. 1966
◆ *Primitive Worlds*. Announced. 865-868, June 1973
• The Search for the First Americans. By Thomas Y. Canby. Photos by Kerby Smith. Paintings by Roy Andersen. 330-363, Sept. 1979
• Skull 1470. By Richard E. Leakey. Photos by Bob Campbell. NGS research grant. 819-829, June 1973
• Twelve National Geographic Society Scientific Projects Under Way. NGS research grant. 869-870, June 1954
• Vanished Mystery Men of Hudson Bay. By Henry B. Collins. Included: Dorset Eskimos, Sadlermiuts. 669-687, Nov. 1956
◆ *Vanishing Peoples of the Earth*. Announced. 844-849, June 1968
• Wyoming Muck Tells of Battle: Ice Age Man vs. Mammoth. By Cynthia Irwin, Henry Irwin, and George Agogino. 828-837, June 1962
• *See also* Russell Cave, Alabama, for Stone Age; *and* Archaeology; Archeomagnetism Dating; Ethnology; Potassium-Argon Dating; Radiocarbon Dating

ANTIGUA, Guatemala:
• Easter Week in Indian Guatemala. By John Scofield. 406-417, Mar. 1960
• Guatemala, Maya and Modern. By Louis de la Haba. Photos by Joseph J. Scherschel. 661-689, Nov. 1974

ANTIGUA (Island), West Indies:
• A Fresh Breeze Stirs the Leewards. By Carleton Mitchell. Photos by Winfield Parks. 488-537, Oct. 1966

ANTILLES, Greater. *See* Cuba; Dominican Republic; Haiti; Jamaica; Puerto Rico

ANTILLES, Lesser. *See* Barbados; Leeward Islands; Martinique; Netherlands Antilles; Tobago; Trinidad; Virgin Islands; Windward Islands

ANTIOCHUS I, King (Commagene):
• Throne Above the Euphrates. By Theresa Goell. 390-405, Mar. 1961

ANTS:
• At Home With the Bulldog Ant. By Robert F. Sisson. 62-75, July 1974
Face-to-Face With a World of Ants. 72-75
• The Enigma of Bird Anting. By Hance Roy Ivor. 105-119, July 1956
• Living Honey Jars of the Ant World. By Ross E. Hutchins. 405-411, Mar. 1962
• The Pesticide Dilemma. By Allen A. Boraiko. Photos by Fred Ward. Included: Fire ants. 145-183, Feb. 1980
• Teeming Life of a Rain Forest. By Carol and David Hughes. 49-65, Jan. 1983

ANTWERP, Belgium:
• Belgium: One Nation Divisible. By James Cerruti. Photos by Martin Rogers. 314-341, Mar. 1979

ANTZE, PAUL: Author:
• Round the World School. Photos by William Eppridge. 96-127, July 1962

ANYEMAQEN (Peak), Qinghai Province, China:
• Nomads of China's West. By Galen Rowell. Photos by the author and Harold A. Knutson. 244-263, Feb. 1982

APACHE:
• The White Mountain Apache. 260-290, Feb. 1980
I. At Peace With the Past, In Step With the Future. By Ronnie Lupe. 260-261; II. Coming of Age the Apache Way. By Nita Quintero. Photos by Bill Hess. 262-271; III. Seeking the Best of Two Worlds. By Bill Hess. 272-290

APARTHEID:
• South Africa's Lonely Ordeal. By William S. Ellis. Photos by James P. Blair. 780-819, June 1977
• The Zulus: Black Nation in a Land of Apartheid. By Joseph Judge. Photos by Dick Durrance II. 738-775, Dec. 1971

APES:
• The Ape (Gibbon) With Friends in Washington. By Margaretta Burr Wells. 61-74, July 1953
▪ Monkeys, Apes, and Man. 585A-585B, Oct. 1971
▪ Search for the Great Apes. Cover, Jan. 1976
• *See also* Chimpanzees; Gorillas; Orangutans

APHIDS:
• Following the Ladybug Home. By Kenneth S. Hagen. Photos by Robert F. Sisson. 543-553, Apr. 1970
• Rose Aphids. By Treat Davidson. 851-859, June 1961

APHRODISIAS (Ruins), Turkey:
• Ancient Aphrodisias and Its Marble Treasures. By Kenan T. Erim. Photos by Jonathan S. Blair. NGS research grant. 280-294, Aug. 1967
• Ancient Aphrodisias Lives Through Its Art. By Kenan T. Erim. Photos by David Brill. NGS research grant. 527-551, Oct. 1981
• Aphrodisias, Awakened City of Ancient Art. By Kenan T. Erim. Photos by Jonathan Blair. NGS research grant. 766-791, June 1972

APOLLO MISSIONS:
• And Now to Touch the Moon's Forbidding Face. By Kenneth F. Weaver. 633-635, May 1969
• Apollo 15 Explores the Mountains of the Moon. By Kenneth F. Weaver. Photos from NASA. 233-265, Feb. 1972
• Apollo Missions. 289-331, Sept. 1973
I. Summing Up Mankind's Greatest Adventure. By Gilbert M. Grosvenor. 289; II. Exploring Taurus-Littrow. By Harrison H. Schmitt. Photos by the crew of Apollo 17. 290-307; III. Have We Solved the Mysteries of the Moon? By Kenneth F. Weaver. Paintings by William H. Bond. 309-325; IV. What Is It Like to Walk on the Moon? By David R. Scott. 326-331; V. "Teammates in Mankind's Greatest Adventure," painting supplement
• Apollo 16 Brings Us Visions From Space. 856-865, Dec. 1972
• The Climb Up Cone Crater (Apollo 14). By Alice J. Hall. Photos by Edgar D. Mitchell and Alan B. Shepard, Jr. 136-148, July 1971
• First Explorers on the Moon: The Incredible Story of Apollo 11. 735-797, Dec. 1969
I. Man Walks on Another World. By Neil A. Armstrong, Edwin E. Aldrin, Jr., and Michael Collins. 738-749; II. Sounds of the Space Age, From Sputnik to Lunar Landing. A record narrated by Frank Borman. 750-751; III. The Flight of Apollo 11: "One giant leap for mankind." By Kenneth F. Weaver. 752-787; IV. What the Moon Rocks Tell Us. By Kenneth F. Weaver. 788-791

• First Moon Explorers (Apollo 11) Receive the Society's Hubbard Medal. Included: Previous presentation of medal to Apollo 8 astronauts. 859-861, June 1970
• Footprints on the Moon. By Hugh L. Dryden. Paintings by Davis Meltzer and Pierre Mion. 357-401, Mar. 1964
• The Making of an Astronaut. By Robert R. Gilruth. 122-144, Jan. 1965
• "A Most Fantastic Voyage": The Story of Apollo 8's Rendezvous With the Moon. By Sam C. Phillips. 593-631, May 1969

APOLLO-SOYUZ MISSION:
• Apollo-Soyuz: Handclasp in Space. By Thomas Y. Canby. 183-187, Feb. 1976

APPALACHIA (Region), U. S.:
• Appalachian Valley Pilgrimage. By Catherine Bell Palmer. Photos by Justin Locke. 1-32, July 1949
• Chattooga River Country: Wild Water, Proud People. By Don Belt. Photos by Steve Wall. 458-477, Apr. 1983
• My Neighbors Hold to Mountain Ways. By Malcolm Ross. Photos by Flip Schulke. 856-880, June 1958
• The People of Cumberland Gap. By John Fetterman. Photos by Bruce Dale. 591-621, Nov. 1971
• Wrestlin' for a Livin' With King Coal. By Michael E. Long. Photos by Michael O'Brien. 793-819, June 1983
• *See also* Cades Cove, Tennessee; West Virginia

APPALACHIAN MOUNTAINS, U. S.:
• Skyline Trail from Maine to Georgia. By Andrew H. Brown. Photos by Robert F. Sisson. 219-251, Aug. 1949
• *See also* Adirondack Mountains; Berkshires; Blue Ridge Mountains; Cumberland Country; Cumberland Valley; Great Smoky Mountains; Great Smoky Mountains National Park; Green Mountains; White Mountains, New Hampshire

APPALACHIAN TRAIL, U. S.:
◆ *The Appalachian Trail.* Announced. 870-874, June 1972
• Pack Trip Through the Smokies. By Val Hart. Photos by Robert F. Sisson. 473-502, Oct. 1952
• Skyline Trail from Maine to Georgia. By Andrew H. Brown. Photos by Robert F. Sisson. 219-251, Aug. 1949

APPEL, FREDRIC C.: Author:
• The Coming Revolution in Transportation. Photos by Dean Conger. 301-341, Sept. 1969

APPENNINES (Mountains), Italy:
• Carrara Marble: Touchstone of Eternity. By Cathy Newman. Photos by Pierre Boulat. 42-59, July 1982

APPIAN WAY, Italy:
• Down the Ancient Appian Way. By James Cerruti. Photos by O. Louis Mazzatenta. 714-747, June 1981

APPLE GROWING:
• Washington's Yakima Valley. By Mark Miller. Photos by Sisse Brimberg. 609-631, Nov. 1978

APPLE TREE:
• The World of My Apple Tree. By Robert F. Sisson. 836-847, June 1972

APPLEBY FAIR, Appleby, England:
• When Gypsies Gather at Appleby Fair. Photos by Bruce Dale. 848-869, June 1972

APPLIED PHYSICS LABORATORY, Johns Hopkins University. *See* DODGE Satellite

APPOMATTOX COURT HOUSE, Virginia:
• Appomattox: Where Grant and Lee Made Peace With Honor a Century Ago. By Ulysses S. Grant 3rd. Photos by Bruce Dale. 435-469, Apr. 1965

APUAN ALPS, Italy:
• Carrara Marble: Touchstone of Eternity. By Cathy Newman. Photos by Pierre Boulat. 42-59, July 1982

AQABA, Gulf of:
• The Other Side of Jordan. By Luis Marden. 790-825, Dec. 1964
• The Red Sea's Gardens of Eels. By Eugenie Clark. Photos by James L. Stanfield and David Doubilet. 724-735, Nov. 1972
• The Red Sea's Sharkproof Fish. By Eugenie Clark. Photos by David Doubilet. 718-727, Nov. 1974

AQUACULTURE:
• Giant Kelp, Sequoias of the Sea. By Wheeler J. North. Photos by Bates Littlehales. 251-269, Aug. 1972
• Plight of the Bluefin Tuna. By Michael J. A. Butler. Photos by David Doubilet. Paintings by Stanley Meltzoff. 220-239, Aug. 1982
• Shrimp Nursery: Science Explores New Ways to Farm the Sea. By Clarence P. Idyll. Photos by Robert F. Sisson. NGS research grant. 636-659, May 1965

AQUALUNG:
• Fish Men Discover a 2,200-year-old Greek Ship. By Jacques-Yves Cousteau. 1-36, Jan. 1954
• Fish Men Explore a New World Undersea. By Jacques-Yves Cousteau. 431-472, Oct. 1952
• *See also* Divers and Diving

AQUARIUMS. *See* Marineland (Florida)

AQUARIUMS, Home:
• In the Wilds of a City Parlor. By Paul A. Zahl. 645-672, Nov. 1954

AQUASCOPE:
• One Hundred Hours Beneath the Chesapeake. By Gilbert C. Klingel. Photos by Willard R. Culver. NGS research grant. 681-696, May 1955

AQUEDUCTS. *See* Los Angeles Aqueduct

AQUICULTURE. *See* Aquaculture

AQUIFERS:
• Our Most Precious Resource: Water. By Thomas Y. Canby. Photos by Ted Spiegel. 144-179, Aug. 1980

AQUITAINE (Historical Region), France:
• Bordeaux: Fine Wines and Fiery Gascons. By William Davenport. Photos by Adam Woolfitt. 233-259, Aug. 1980

ARAB-ISRAELI CONFLICT:
• Beirut–Up From the Rubble. By William S. Ellis. Photos by Steve McCurry. 262-286, Feb. 1983
• Cairo, Troubled Capital of the Arab World. By William S. Ellis. Photos by Winfield Parks. 639-667, May 1972
• Damascus, Syria's Uneasy Eden. By Robert Azzi. 512-535, Apr. 1974
• Eternal Sinai. By Harvey Arden. Photos by David Doubilet and Kevin Fleming. 420-461, Apr. 1982
Egyptian Sector. Photos by Kevin Fleming. 430-443; Israeli Sector. Photos by David Doubilet. 444-461
• Eyewitness to War in the Holy Land. By Charles Harbutt. 782-795, Dec. 1967
• Islam's Heartland, Up in Arms. By Thomas J. Abercrombie. 335-345, Sept. 1980
• Israel–The Seventh Day. By Joseph Judge. Photos by Gordon W. Gahan. 816-855, Dec. 1972
• New Life for the Troubled Suez Canal. By William Graves. Photos by Jonathan Blair. 792-817, June 1975
• Our Life on a Border Kibbutz. By Carol and Al Abrams. Photos by Al Abrams. 364-391, Sept. 1970
• Syria Tests a New Stability. By Howard La Fay. Photos by James L. Stanfield. 326-361, Sept. 1978
• This Year in Jerusalem. By Joseph Judge. Photos by Jodi Cobb. 479-515, Apr. 1983
▲ *Two Centuries of Conflict in the Middle East; Mideast in Turmoil,* double-sided supplement. Sept. 1980

ARAB NATIONS:
• The Arab World. 712-732, Nov. 1958
• The Arab World, Inc. By John J. Putman. Photos by Winfield Parks. Included: Kuwait; Oman; Saudi Arabia; United Arab Emirates. 494-533, Oct. 1975
• Desert Sheikdoms of Arabia's Pirate Coast. By Ronald Codrai. 65-104, July 1956
• Editorials. By Gilbert M. Grosvenor. 1, Jan. 1975; 443, Oct. 1975
• Oil, the Dwindling Treasure. By Noel Grove. Photos by Emory Kristof. 792-825, June 1974
▲ *The Peoples of the Middle East,* supplement. Text on reverse. July 1972
• Station Wagon Odyssey: Baghdad to Istanbul. By William O. Douglas. 48-87, Jan. 1959
• The Sword and the Sermon (Islam). By Thomas J. Abercrombie. 3-45, July 1972
• Troubled Waters East of Suez. By Ernest M. Eller. 483-522, Apr. 1954
▲ *Two Centuries of Conflict in the Middle East; Mideast in Turmoil,* double-sided supplement. Sept. 1980

• West from the Khyber Pass. By William O. Douglas. Photos by Mercedes H. Douglas and author. 1-44, July 1958
• *See also* Aden Protectorate; Algeria; Bahrain; Egypt; Iraq; Jordan; Kuwait; Lebanon; Morocco; Oman; Saudi Arabia; Sudan; Syria; Tunisia; Yemen Arab Republic

ARABIAN DESERT:
• The Desert: An Age-old Challenge Grows. By Rick Gore. Photos by Georg Gerster and Bruce Dale. 586-639, Nov. 1979

ARABIAN GULF. *See* Persian Gulf

THE ARABIAN NIGHTS ENTERTAINMENTS *(The Thousand and One Nights):*
• In the Wake of Sindbad. By Tim Severin. Photos by Richard Greenhill. 2-41, July 1982

ARABIAN PENINSULA:
▲ *Africa and the Arabian Peninsula,* supplement. Mar. 1950
• In Search of Arabia's Past. By Peter Bruce Cornwall. 493-522, Apr. 1948
• *See also* Bahrain; Kuwait; Oman; Saudi Arabia; United Arab Emirates; Yemen Arab Republic

ARACHNIDS. *See* Scorpions; Spiders

ARAN ISLANDS, Ireland:
• The Arans, Ireland's Invincible Isles. By Veronica Thomas. Photos by Winfield Parks. 545-573, Apr. 1971
• I Walked Some Irish Miles. By Dorothea Sheats. 653-678, May 1951

ARANSAS NATIONAL WILDLIFE REFUGE, Texas:
• Where Oil and Wildlife Mix. By Steven C. Wilson and Karen C. Hayden. 145-173, Feb. 1981
• Whooping Cranes Fight for Survival. By Robert Porter Allen. Photos by Frederick Kent Truslow. 650-669, Nov. 1959

ARAUCANA CHICKENS:
• Easter Egg Chickens. By Frederick G. Vosburgh. Photos by B. Anthony Stewart. 377-387, Sept. 1948

ARCHAEOLOGY:
• Abraham, the Friend of God. By Kenneth MacLeish. Photos by Dean Conger. 739-789, Dec. 1966
• The Anasazi–Riddles in the Ruins. By Thomas Y. Canby. Photos by Dewitt Jones and David Brill. Paintings by Roy Andersen. 554-592, Nov. 1982
• Ancient Aphrodisias and Its Marble Treasures. By Kenan T. Erim. Photos by Jonathan S. Blair. NGS research grant. 280-294, Aug. 1967
• Ancient Aphrodisias Lives Through Its Art. By Kenan T. Erim. Photos by David Brill. NGS research grant. 527-551, Oct. 1981
• Ancient Bulgaria's Golden Treasures. By Colin Renfrew. Photos by James L. Stanfield. Paintings by Jean-Leon Huens. 112-129, July 1980
• Ancient Europe Is Older Than We Thought. By Colin Renfrew. Photos by Adam Woolfitt. 615-623, Nov. 1977
• Angkor, Jewel of the Jungle. By W. Robert Moore. Paintings by Maurice Fiévet. 517-569, Apr. 1960
• Aphrodisias, Awakened City of Ancient Art. By Kenan T. Erim. Photos by Jonathan Blair. NGS research grant. 766-791, June 1972
▲ *Archeological Map of Middle America, Land of the Feathered Serpent,* supplement. Text on reverse. Oct. 1968
• An Archeologist Looks at Palestine. By Nelson Glueck. 739-752, Dec. 1947
• The Aztecs. 704-775, Dec. 1980
I. The Aztecs. By Bart McDowell. Photos by David Hiser. Paintings by Felipe Dávalos. 714-751; II. The Building of Tenochtitlan. By Augusto F. Molina Montes. Paintings by Felipe Dávalos. 753-765; III. New Finds in the Great Temple. By Eduardo Matos Moctezuma. Photos by David Hiser. 767-775
• A Bold New Look at Our Past. The Editor. NGS research grant. 62-63, Jan. 1975
• Bringing Old Testament Times to Life. By G. Ernest Wright. Paintings by Henry J. Soulen. 833-864, Dec. 1957
• A Buried Roman Town Gives Up Its Dead (Herculaneum). By Joseph Judge. Photos by Jonathan Blair. NGS research grant. 687-693, Dec. 1982
• China Unveils Her Newest Treasures. Photos by Robert W. Madden. 848-857, Dec. 1974
• China's Incredible Find. By Audrey Topping. Paintings by Yang Hsien-min. Contents: The first emperor's burial mound, with guardian army of terra-cotta men and horses. 440-459, Apr. 1978
◆ *Clues to America's Past.* 1976; Announced. 860-864, June 1976
• Computer Helps Scholars Re-create an Egyptian Temple. By Ray Winfield Smith. Photos by Emory Kristof. NGS research grant. 634-655, Nov. 1970
• Darius Carved History on Ageless Rock. By George G. Cameron. 825-844, Dec. 1950
◆ *Discovering Man's Past in the Americas.* 1969; Announced. 880-884, June 1969
• Drama of Death in a Minoan Temple. By Yannis Sakellarakis and Efi Sapouna-Sakellaraki. Photos by Otis Imboden and Spyros Tsavdaroglou. 205-222, Feb. 1981
• Ebla: Splendor of an Unknown Empire. By Howard La Fay. Photos by James L. Stanfield. Paintings by Louis S. Glanzman. 730-759, Dec. 1978
• Editorials. By Wilbur E. Garrett. 137, Aug. 1981; 283, Mar. 1982; 1, July 1982
• Eskimo and Viking Finds in the High Arctic: Ellesmere Island. By Peter Schledermann. Photos by Sisse

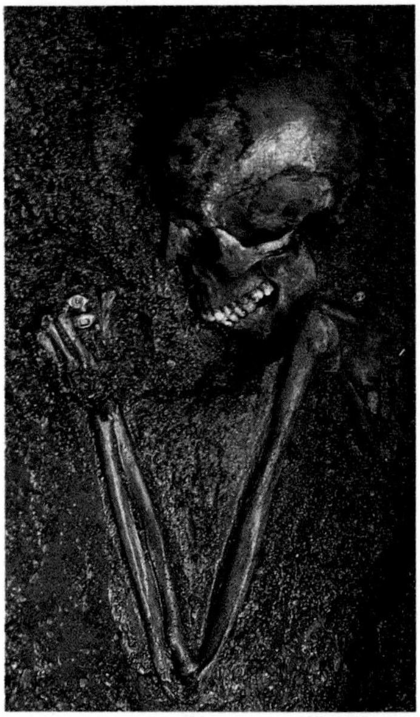

JONATHAN BLAIR

Herculaneum: skeleton of Roman lady

Ebla: statue of King Itur-Shamagan

NATIONAL MUSEUM, DAMASCUS, BY JAMES L. STANFIELD, NGS

Brimberg. Included: Artifacts of the Norse, the Dorset, the Thule. 575-601, May 1981
• Exploring Ancient Panama by Helicopter. By Matthew W. Stirling. Photos by Richard H. Stewart. Included: Archaeological sites in provinces of Chiriquí and Veraguas. NGS research grant. 227-246, Feb. 1950
• Exploring the Past in Panama. By Matthew W. Stirling. Photos by Richard H. Stewart. Included: Azuero Peninsula, Tambor region. NGS research grant. 373-399, Mar. 1949
• Finding the Tomb of a Warrior-God. By William Duncan Strong. Photos by Clifford Evans, Jr. 453-482, Apr. 1947
• Finding West Africa's Oldest City. By Susan and Roderick McIntosh. Photos by Michael and Aubine Kirtley. Contents: Jenne-jeno (site), Mali. 396-418, Sept. 1982
• First Look at a Lost Virginia Settlement (Martin's Hundred). By Ivor Noël Hume. Photos by Ira Block. Paintings by Richard Schlecht. NGS research grant. 735-767, June 1979
• The Five Worlds of Peru. By Kenneth F. Weaver. Photos by Bates Littlehales. Included: Machu Picchu, Nazca Lines, Sacsahuamán. 213-265, Feb. 1964
• Fresh Treasures from Egypt's Ancient Sands. By Jefferson Caffery. Photos by David S. Boyer. 611-650, Nov. 1955
• The Ghosts of Jericho. By James L. Kelso. 825-844, Dec. 1951
• Guatemala, Maya and Modern. By Louis de la Haba. Photos by Joseph J. Scherschel. Included: Altar de Sacrificios, Monte Alto, San Jerònimo, Seibal, Tikal. 661-689, Nov. 1974
• Hashemite Jordan, Arab Heartland. By John Scofield. Included: 'Ammān, ancient Philadelphia; Gerasa; Jericho; Petra; Qasr 'Amra; Qasr el Kharana; Copper scrolls; "Dead Sea scrolls". 841-856, Dec. 1952
• The Hohokam: First Masters of the American Desert. By Emil W. Haury. Photos by Helga Teiwes. 670-695, May 1967
• Hunting Prehistory in Panama Jungles. By Matthew W. Stirling. Photos by Richard H. Stewart. NGS research grant. 271-290, Aug. 1953
• In Search of Arabia's Past. By Peter Bruce Cornwall. 493-522, Apr. 1948
▲ *Indians of South America; Archaeology of South America,* double-sided supplement. Mar. 1982
• Indonesia Rescues Ancient Borobudur. By W. Brown Morton III. Photos by Dean Conger. 126-142, Jan. 1983
• Iraq–Where Oil and Water Mix. By Jean and Franc Shor. Included: Babylon, Nineveh, Ur. 443-489, Oct. 1958
• Jericho Gives Up Its Secrets. By Kathleen M. Kenyon and A. Douglas Tushingham. Photos by Nancy Lord. 853-870, Dec. 1953

IRA BLOCK
Martin's Hundred: restored helmets

• Joseph Alsop: A Historical Perspective (on Minoan Human Sacrifice). 223, Feb. 1981
• A Lady From China's Past. Photos from *China Pictorial.* Text by Alice J. Hall. 660-681, May 1974
• Last Moments of the Pompeians. By Amedeo Maiuri. Photos by Lee E. Battaglia. Paintings by Peter V. Bianchi. 651-669, Nov. 1961
• The Last Thousand Years Before Christ. By G. Ernest Wright. Paintings by H. J. Soulen and Peter V. Bianchi. 812-853, Dec. 1960
• Life Among the Wai Wai Indians. By Clifford Evans and Betty J. Meggers. 329-346, Mar. 1955
• Life 8,000 Years Ago Uncovered in an Alabama Cave. By Carl F. Miller. NGS research grant. 542-558, Oct. 1956
• Lost Outpost of the Egyptian Empire (Deir el-Balah, Gaza). By Trude Dothan. Photos by Sisse Brimberg. Paintings by Lloyd K. Townsend. 739-769, Dec. 1982
• Magnetic Clues Help Date the Past. By Kenneth F. Weaver. 696-701, May 1967
• Man in the Amazon: Stone Age Present Meets Stone Age Past. By W. Jesco von Puttkamer. NGS research grant. 60-83, Jan. 1979
• Man's Eighty Centuries in Veracruz. By S. Jeffrey K. Wilkerson. Photos by David Hiser. Paintings by Richard Schlecht. NGS research grant. 203-231, Aug. 1980
• The Maya. 729-811, Dec. 1975
I. Children of Time. By Howard La Fay. Photos by David Alan Harvey. 729-767; II. Riddle of the Glyphs. By George E. Stuart. Photos by Otis Imboden. 768-791; III. Resurrecting the Grandeur of Tikal. By William R. Coe. 792-798; IV. A Traveler's Tale of Ancient Tikal. Paintings by Peter Spier. Text by Alice J. Hall. 799-811
• Maya Art Treasures Discovered in Cave. By George E. Stuart. Photos by Wilbur E. Garrett. 220-235, Aug. 1981
• The Men Who Hid the Dead Sea Scrolls. By A. Douglas Tushingham. Paintings by Peter V. Bianchi. 785-808, Dec. 1958
• Mexico's Window on the Past (National Museum). By Bart McDowell. Photos by B. Anthony Stewart. 492-519, Oct. 1968
• Minoans and Mycenaeans: Greece's Brilliant Bronze Age. By Joseph Judge. Photos by Gordon W. Gahan. Paintings by Lloyd K. Townsend. 142-185, Feb. 1978
• The Mystery of the Shroud. By Kenneth F. Weaver. Note: Advanced archaeological techniques are used to study the Shroud of Turin. 730-753, June 1980
• New Clues to an Old Mystery (Virginia's Wolstenholme Towne). By Ivor Noël Hume. Photos by Ira Block. Paintings by Richard Schlecht. NGS research grant. 53-77, Jan. 1982
• New Light on a Forgotten Past (Southeast Asia). By Wilhelm G. Solheim II. 330-339, Mar. 1971

▲ *North America Before Columbus,* double-sided supplement. Dec. 1972
● On the Trail of La Venta Man. By Matthew W. Stirling. Photos by Richard H. Stewart. NGS research grant. 137-172, Feb. 1947
Hunting Mexico's Buried Temples. 145-168
● The Other Side of Jordan. By Luis Marden. Included: Jarash, Petra, Umm Qays. 790-825, Dec. 1964
● Periscope on the Etruscan Past. By Carlo M. Lerici. 337-350, Sept. 1959
● The Phoenicians, Sea Lords of Antiquity. By Samuel W. Matthews. Photos by Winfield Parks. Paintings by Robert C. Magis. Included: Excavation of the Phoenician cities of Byblos, Carthage, Kerkouane, Kition, Motya, Sarepta (Zarephath), Sidon, and Tyre; and the restoration of the Kyrenia ship and a Punic warship. 149-189, Aug. 1974
● President's Report to Members: An Exciting Year of Discovery. By Gilbert M. Grosvenor. 820-824, Dec. 1982
● "Pyramids" of the New World. By Neil Merton Judd. NGS research grant. 105-128, Jan. 1948
● Regal Treasures From a Macedonian Tomb. By Manolis Andronicos. Photos by Spyros Tsavdaroglou. 55-77, July 1978
● Russell Cave: New Light on Stone Age Life. By Carl F. Miller. NGS research grant. 427-437, Mar. 1958
● Saving the Ancient Temples at Abu Simbel. By Georg Gerster. Paintings by Robert W. Nicholson. 694-742, May 1966
● The Search for the First Americans. By Thomas Y. Canby. Photos by Kerby Smith. Paintings by Roy Andersen. Included: Date-coded maps locating habitation sites of prehistoric man of northern Asia and the Americas. 330-363, Sept. 1979
● Searching for Cliff Dwellers' Secrets. By Carroll A. Burroughs. NGS research grant. 619-625, Nov. 1959
◆ *Secrets From the Past.* 1979
● Solving the Riddles of Wetherill Mesa. By Douglas Osborne. Paintings by Peter V. Bianchi. NGS research grant. 155-195, Feb. 1964
● Stonehenge–New Light on an Old Riddle. By Harold E. Edgerton. Paintings by Brian Hope-Taylor. 846-866, June 1960
● Tanzania's Stone Age Art. By Mary D. Leakey. Photos by John Reader. 84-99, July 1983
● The Temples of Angkor. 548-589, May 1982
I. Ancient Glory in Stone. By Peter T. White. Photos by Wilbur E. Garrett. 552-589; II. Will They Survive? Introduction by Wilbur E. Garrett. 548-551
● Thera, Key to the Riddle of Minos. By Spyridon Marinatos. Photos by Otis Imboden. 702-726, May 1972
● Threatened Treasures of the Nile. By Georg Gerster. Included: Abu Simbel temples. 587-621, Oct. 1963
● Throne Above the Euphrates. By Theresa Goell. 390-405, Mar. 1961

GEORG GERSTER

Abu Simbel: stone pharaoh's head

DAVID ALAN HARVEY, NGS

Angkor: head of divinity, Angkor Thom

● The Tower of the Winds. By Derek J. de Solla Price. Paintings by Robert C. Magis. NGS research grant. 587-596, Apr. 1967
● Treasure From a Celtic Tomb. By Jörg Biel. Photos by Volkmar Wentzel. 428-438, Mar. 1980
● Tutankhamun's Golden Trove. By Christiane Desroches Noblecourt. Photos by F. L. Kenett. 625-646, Oct. 1963
● Twelve National Geographic Society Scientific Projects Under Way. Included: Eskimo ruins on Southampton and Coats Islands in Hudson Bay, Canada. NGS research grant. 869-870, June 1954
● 20th-century Indians Preserve Customs of the Cliff Dwellers. Photos by William Belknap, Jr. Included: Artifacts of Mesa Verde. NGS research grant. 196-211, Feb. 1964
● Unearthing the Oldest Known Maya. By Norman Hammond. Photos by Lowell Georgia and Martha Cooper. NGS research grant. 126-140, July 1982
● Vanished Mystery Men of Hudson Bay. By Henry B. Collins. NGS research grant. 669-687, Nov. 1956
● The Vikings. By Howard La Fay. Photos by Ted Spiegel. 492-541, Apr. 1970
● Vinland Ruins Prove Vikings Found the New World. By Helge Ingstad. NGS research grant. 708-734, Nov. 1964
▲ *Visitor's Guide to the Aztec World; Mexico and Central America,* double-sided supplement. Dec. 1980
● Who Were the "Mound Builders"? By George E. Stuart. 783-801, Dec. 1972
● Young-old Lebanon Lives by Trade. By Thomas J. Abercrombie. Included: Ba'albek; Byblos; Sidon; Tyre. 479-523, Apr. 1958
● Your Society to Seek New Light on the Cliff Dwellers (Wetherill Mesa). NGS research grant. 154-156, Jan. 1959
● *See also* Chan Chan; Easter Island; Glass; Gravel Pictographs; Lascaux Cave; La Venta, Mexico; Machu Picchu, Peru; Mesa Verde National Park, Colorado; Mesopotamia; Petra, Jordan; Roman Empire; Scilly, Isles of; Temple Caves; Zimbabwe (Ruins); *and* Anthropology, Physical; Archaeology, Underwater; Potassium-Argon Dating; Radiocarbon Dating; Tree-ring Dating

ARCHAEOLOGY, Underwater:
● Ancient Shipwreck Yields New Facts–and a Strange Cargo. By Peter Throckmorton. Photos by Kim Hart and Joseph J. Scherschel. 282-300, Feb. 1969
● Drowned Galleons Yield Spanish Gold. By Kip Wagner. Photos by Otis Imboden. 1-37, Jan. 1965
● Dzibilchaltun. NGS research grant. 91-129, Jan. 1959
I. Lost City of the Maya. By E. Wyllys Andrews. 91-109; II. Up from the Well of Time. By Luis Marden. 110-129

JONATHAN BLAIR

Galleons: diver on *Tolosa* wreck

• Exploring a 140-year-old Ship Under Arctic Ice *(Breadalbane)*. By Joseph B. MacInnis. Photos by Emory Kristof. 104A-104D, July 1983
• Exploring the Drowned City of Port Royal (Jamaica). By Marion Clayton Link. Photos by Luis Marden. NGS research grant. 151-183, Feb. 1960
• Fish Men Discover a 2,200-year-old Greek Ship. By Jacques-Yves Cousteau. NGS research grant. 1-36, Jan. 1954
• Ghost Ships of the War of 1812: *Hamilton* and *Scourge*. By Daniel A. Nelson. Photos by Emory Kristof. Paintings by Richard Schlecht. 289-313, Mar. 1983
The Incredible Crawl of Ned Myers. 300-305
• Glass Treasure From the Aegean. By George F. Bass. Photos by Jonathan Blair. NGS research grant. 768-793, June 1978
• Graveyard of the Quicksilver Galleons. By Mendel Peterson. Photos by Jonathan Blair. 850-876, Dec. 1979
• Henry VIII's Lost Warship: *Mary Rose*. By Margaret Rule. Introduction and picture text by Peter Miller. Paintings by Richard Schlecht. 646-675, May 1983
▲ "History Salvaged From the Sea," painting supplement. Map on reverse. Dec. 1977
• How We Found the *Monitor*. By John G. Newton. NGS research grant. 48-61, Jan. 1975
• Into the Well of Sacrifice (Chichén Itzá). NGS research grant. 540-561, Oct. 1961
I. Return to the Sacred Cenote. By Eusebio Dávalos Hurtado. 540-549; II. Treasure Hunt in the Deep Past. By Bates Littlehales. 550-561
• Last Harbor for the Oldest Ship. By Susan W. and Michael L. Katzev. NGS research grant. 618-625, Nov. 1974
• The Lost Fleet of Kublai Khan. By Torao Mozai. Photos by Koji Nakamura. Paintings by Issho Yada. 634-649, Nov. 1982
• New Tools for Undersea Archeology. By George F. Bass. Photos by Charles R. Nicklin, Jr. NGS research grant. 403-423, Sept. 1968
• Oldest Known Shipwreck Yields Bronze Age Cargo (Cape Gelidonya wreck). By Peter Throckmorton. NGS research grant. 697-711, May 1962
• The Phoenicians, Sea Lords of Antiquity. By Samuel W. Matthews. Photos by Winfield Parks. Paintings by Robert C. Magis. Included: The restoration of the Kyrenia ship and a Punic warship. 149-198, Aug. 1974
• Reach for the New World. By Mendel Peterson. Photos by David L. Arnold. Paintings by Richard Schlecht. 724-767, Dec. 1977
• Relics From the Rapids. By Sigurd F. Olson. Photos by David S. Boyer. 413-435, Sept. 1963
• Resurrecting the Oldest Known Greek Ship. By Michael L. Katzev. Photos by Bates Littlehales. NGS research grant. 841-857, June 1970
• The Sunken Treasure of St. Helena. By Robert Sténuit. Photos by Bates Littlehales. 562-576, Oct. 1978
• Treasure From the Ghost Galleon: *Santa Margarita*. By Eugene Lyon. Photos by Don Kincaid. 228-243, Feb. 1982
• Underwater Archeology: Key to History's Warehouse. By George F. Bass. Photos by Thomas J. Abercrombie and Robert B. Goodman. NGS research grant. 138-156, July 1963
• Warriors From a Watery Grave (Bronze Sculptures). By Joseph Alsop. 821-827, June 1983
• Yellow Sea Yields Shipwreck Trove. Photos by H. Edward Kim. Introduction by Donald H. Keith. 231-243, Aug. 1979
• *See also* Aegean Sea; *Atocha; Girona;* Kyrenia Ship; *Monitor; Slot ter Hooge;* Truk Lagoon; *Vasa;* Yassi Ada

ARCHEOLOGICAL SOCIETY OF ATHENS: Study Grant:
• Macedonian Tomb. 63, July 1978

ARCHEOMAGNETISM:
• Magnetic Clues Help Date the Past. By Kenneth F. Weaver. 696-701, May 1967

ARCHES, Natural. *See* Arches National Monument; Canyonlands National Park, Utah; Escalante Canyon, for Grosvenor Arch *and* La Gorce Arch; Natural Bridges National Monument; Rainbow Bridge National Monument; Zion National Park

ARCHES NATIONAL MONUMENT, Utah:
• Utah's Arches of Stone. By Jack Breed. 173-192, Aug. 1947

ARCHIMÈDE (Bathyscaphe):
• Where the Earth Turns Inside Out (Project FAMOUS). By J. R. Heirtzler. Photos by Emory Kristof. 586-603, May 1975

ARCHITECT of Freedom: Thomas Jefferson. By Mike W. Edwards. Photos by Linda Bartlett. 231-259, Feb. 1976

ARCHITECTURE:
• Conservation: Can We Live Better on Less? By Rick Gore. Included: Free-form house, Geohouse, solar architecture, mirrored surfaces. 34-57, *Special Report on Energy* (Feb. 1981)
• A Most Uncommon Town: Columbus, Indiana. By David Jeffery. Photos by J. Bruce Baumann. Included: Many contemporary buildings designed by master architects. 383-397, Sept. 1978
• The National Gallery's New Masterwork on the Mall. By J. Carter Brown. Photos by James A. Sugar. Contents: East Building, designed by I. M. Pei. 680-701, Nov. 1978
• Pompidou Center, Rage of Paris. By Cathy Newman. Photos by Marc Riboud. 469-477, Oct. 1980
◆ *Preserving America's Past*. 1983
• *See also* Angkor; Castles; Churches; Houses

ARCTIC INSTITUTE OF NORTH AMERICA: Expedition. *See* Curlews

ARCTIC NATIONAL WILDLIFE RANGE, Alaska:
● Our Wildest Wilderness: Alaska's Arctic National Wildlife Range. By Douglas H. Chadwick. Photos by Lowell Georgia. 737-769, Dec. 1979

ARCTIC OCEAN:
● The Arctic as a Sea Route of the Future. By William R. Anderson. 21-24, Jan. 1959
▲ *Arctic Ocean; Arctic Ocean Floor,* supplement. Oct. 1971
● Diving Beneath Arctic Ice. By Joseph B. MacInnis. Photos by William R. Curtsinger. 248-267, Aug. 1973
● Life or Death for the Harp Seal. By David M. Lavigne. Photos by William R. Curtsinger. 129-142, Jan. 1976
▲ *Peoples of the Arctic; Arctic Ocean,* double-sided supplement. Feb. 1983
● Scientists Ride Ice Islands on Arctic Odysseys. By Lowell Thomas, Jr. Photos by Ted Spiegel. 670-691, Nov. 1965
● Submarine Through the North Pole *(Nautilus)*. By William G. Lalor, Jr. Photos by John J. Krawczyk. 1-20, Jan. 1959
● Three Months on an Arctic Ice Island. By Joseph O. Fletcher. 489-504, Apr. 1953
● Tracking Danger With the Ice Patrol. By William S. Ellis. Photos by James R. Holland. 780-793, June 1968
● Up Through the Ice of the North Pole *(Skate)*. By James F. Calvert. 1-41, July 1959

ARCTIC REGIONS:
● Admiral of the Ends of the Earth (Richard E. Byrd). By Melville Bell Grosvenor. 36-48, July 1957
● Arctic Odyssey. By John Bockstoce. Photos by Jonathan Wright. Paintings by Jack Unruh. 100-127, July 1983
● Banks Island: Eskimo Life on the Polar Sea. By William O. Douglas. Photos by Clyde Hare. 703-735, May 1964
▲ *Canada, Alaska, and Greenland,* supplement. June 1947
● Circling Earth From Pole to Pole. By Sir Ranulph Fiennes. 464-481, Oct. 1983
● DEW Line, Sentry of the Far North. By Howard La Fay. 128-146, July 1958
● Domesticating the Wild and Woolly Musk Ox. By John J. Teal, Jr. Photos by Robert W. Madden. 862-879, June 1970
● Eskimo and Viking Finds in the High Arctic: Ellesmere Island. By Peter Schledermann. Photos by Sisse Brimberg. 575-601, May 1981
● Exploring a 140-year-old Ship Under Arctic Ice *(Breadalbane)*. By Joseph B. MacInnis. Photos by Emory Kristof. 104A-104D, July 1983
● Far North with "Captain Mac." By Miriam MacMillan. 465-513, Oct. 1951
● First Woman Across Greenland's Ice. By Myrtle Simpson. Photos by Hugh Simpson. 264-279, Aug. 1967
● Friendly Flight to Northern Europe. By Lyndon B. Johnson. Photos by Volkmar Wentzel. 268-293, Feb. 1964
● I Live With the Eskimos (Canadian). By Guy Mary-Rousseliere. 188-217, Feb. 1971
■ Journey to the High Arctic. 590A-590B, Apr. 1971
● Learning the Ways of the Walrus. By G. Carleton Ray. Photos by Bill Curtsinger. 565-580, Oct. 1979
● Milestones in My Arctic Journeys. By Willie Knutsen. 543-570, Oct. 1949
● Nomads of the Far North. By Matthew W. Stirling. 471-504, Oct. 1949
Hearty Folk Defy Arctic Storms. Paintings by W. Langdon Kihn. 479-494
● North for Oil: *Manhattan* Makes the Historic Northwest Passage. By Bern Keating. Photos by Tomas Sennett. 374-391, Mar. 1970
● North Toward the Pole on Skis. By Bjørn O. Staib. NGS research grant. 254-281, Feb. 1965
● Norway's Strategic Arctic Islands (Svalbard). By Gordon Young. Photos by Martin Rogers. 267-283, Aug. 1978
● Our Wildest Wilderness: Alaska's Arctic National Wildlife Range. By Douglas H. Chadwick. Photos by Lowell Georgia. 737-769, Dec. 1979
● The Peary Flag Comes to Rest. By Marie Peary Stafford. 519-532, Oct. 1954
● Peoples of the Arctic. 144-223, Feb. 1983
I. Introduction by Joseph Judge. 144-149; II. Hunters of the Lost Spirit: Alaskans, Canadians, Greenlanders, Lapps. By Priit J. Vesilind. Photos by David Alan Harvey, Ivars Silis, and Sisse Brimberg. 150-197; III. Where Magic Ruled: Art of the Bering Sea. By William W. Fitzhugh and Susan A. Kaplan. Photos by Sisse Brimberg. 198-205; IV. People of the Long Spring (Chukchis). By Yuri Rytkheu. Photos by Dean Conger. 206-223
▲ *Peoples of the Arctic; Arctic Ocean,* double-sided supplement. Feb. 1983
● Polar Bear: Lonely Nomad of the North. By Thor Larsen. 574-590, Apr. 1971
● The Society's Hubbard Medal Awarded to Commander MacMillan. 563-564, Apr. 1953
● Solo to the Pole. By Naomi Uemura. Photos by the author and Ira Block. 298-325, Sept. 1978
● Still Eskimo, Still Free: The Inuit of Umingmaktok. By Yva Momatiuk and John Eastcott. 624-647, Nov. 1977
▲ *Top of the World,* Atlas series supplement. Nov. 1965
▲ *The Top of the World,* supplement. Oct. 1949
● Trek Across Arctic America. By Colin Irwin. 295-321, Mar. 1974
● A Visit to the Living Ice Age. By Rutherford Platt. 525-545, Apr. 1957
● We Followed Peary to the Pole. By Gilbert Grosvenor and Thomas W. McKnew. 469-484, Oct. 1953
● Weather From the White North. By Andrew H. Brown. Photos by John E. Fletcher. 543-572, Apr. 1955
● *See also* Arctic Ocean; Greenland; Greenland Icecap; King Island, Alaska; Lapland; Noatak River; North Pole; North Slope, Alaska; Spitsbergen; *and* Caribou

ARCTIC SMALL TOOL CULTURE:
● Eskimo and Viking Finds in the High Arctic: Ellesmere Island. By Peter Schledermann. Photos by Sisse Brimberg. Included: Artifacts of the Norse, the Dorset, the Thule. 575-601, May 1981
● *See also* Thule Inuit

ARDASTRA GARDENS, Nassau, Bahamas:
● Ballerinas in Pink (Flamingos). By Carleton Mitchell. Photos by B. Anthony Stewart. 553-571, Oct. 1957

ARDEN, HARVEY: Author:
● America's Little Mainstream (Buffalo National River). Photos by Matt Bradley. 344-359, Mar. 1977
● Chicago! Photos by Steve Raymer. 463-493, Apr. 1978
● Eternal Sinai. Photos by David Doubilet and Kevin Fleming. 420-461, Apr. 1982
Egyptian Sector. Photos by Kevin Fleming. 430-443; Israeli Sector. Photos by David Doubilet. 444-461
● In Search of Moses. Photos by Nathan Benn. 2-37, Jan. 1976
● Iowa, America's Middle Earth. Photos by Craig Aurness. 603-629, May 1981
● John Muir's Wild America. Photos by Dewitt Jones. 433-461, Apr. 1973
● The Living Dead Sea. Photos by Nathan Benn. 225-245, Feb. 1978
● The Magic World of Hans Christian Andersen. Photos by Sisse Brimberg. 825-849, Dec. 1979
● The Pious Ones (Brooklyn's Hasidic Jews). Photos by Nathan Benn. 276-298, Aug. 1975
● A Sumatran Journey. Photos by David Alan Harvey. 406-430, Mar. 1981
● Troubled Odyssey of Vietnamese Fishermen. Photos by Steve Wall. 378-395, Sept. 1981
● The Two Souls of Peru. Photos by William Albert Allard. 284-321, Mar. 1982
● World War I Aircraft Fly Again in Rhinebeck's Rickety Rendezvous. Photos by Howard Sochurek. 578-587, Oct. 1970

ARGENTINA:
● Argentina: Young Giant of the Far South. By Jean and Franc Shor. 297-352, Mar. 1958
● Argentina Protects Its Wildlife Treasures. By William F. Conway. Photos by Des and Jen Bartlett. 290-297, Mar. 1976

• Buenos Aires, Argentina's Melting-pot Metropolis. By Jules B. Billard. Photos by Winfield Parks. 662-695, Nov. 1967
• The Gauchos, Last of a Breed. By Robert Laxalt. Photos by O. Louis Mazzatenta. 478-501, Oct. 1980
• Parks, Plans, and People: How South America Guards Her Green Legacy. By Mary and Laurance Rockefeller. Photos by George F. Mobley. 74-119, Jan. 1967
• Which Way Now for Argentina? By Loren McIntyre. 296-333, Mar. 1975
• *See also* Patagonia; Tierra del Fuego; Torre Egger

ARGUS (Fishing Schooner):
• I Sailed With Portugal's Captains Courageous. By Alan Villiers. 565-596, May 1952

ARGYLL (Yawl):
• Baltic Cruise of the *Caribbee*. By Carleton Mitchell. 605-646, Nov. 1950

ARIZONA:
• Arizona: Booming Youngster of the West. By Robert de Roos. Photos by Robert F. Sisson. 299-343, Mar. 1963
• Arizona Sheep Trek. By Francis R. Line. 457-478, Apr. 1950
• Arizona's Operation Beaver Lift. By Willis Peterson. 666-680, May 1955
• Arizona's Suburbs of the Sun. By David Jeffery. Photos by H. Edward Kim. 486-517, Oct. 1977
• Arizona's Window on Wildlife (Desert Museum). By Lewis Wayne Walker. 240-250, Feb. 1958
• Desert River Through Navajo Land. By Alfred M. Bailey. Photos by author and Fred G. Brandenburg. 149-172, Aug. 1947
• From Sun-clad Sea to Shining Mountains. By Ralph Gray. Photos by James P. Blair. 542-589, Apr. 1964
• From Tucson to Tombstone. By Mason Sutherland. 343-384, Sept. 1953
• The Hohokam: First Masters of the American Desert. By Emil W. Haury. Photos by Helga Teiwes. 670-695, May 1967
• Inside the Sacred Hopi Homeland. By Jake Page. Photos by Susanne Page. 607-629, Nov. 1982
• Kachinas: Masked Dancers of the Southwest. By Paul Coze. 219-236, Aug. 1957
• Land of the Havasupai. By Jack Breed. 655-674, May 1948
• Magnetic Clues Help Date the Past. By Kenneth F. Weaver. 696-701, May 1967
• A Map Maker Looks at the United States. By Newman Bumstead. Included: Grand Canyon; Hoover Dam; Lake Mead; Mount Sinyala; Painted Desert. 705-748, June 1951
• The Mexican Americans: A People on the Move. By Griffin Smith, Jr. Photos by Stephanie Maze. 780-809, June 1980
• Pueblo Pottery–2,000 Years of Artistry. By David L. Arnold. 593-605, Nov. 1982
• Rediscovering America's Forgotten Crops. By Noel D. Vietmeyer. Photos by Burgess Blevins. Paintings by Paul M. Breeden. 702-712, May 1981
• Scorpions: Living Fossils of the Sands. By Paul A. Zahl. 436-442, Mar. 1968
• Seeking the Secret of the Giants. By Frank M. Setzler. Photos by Richard H. Stewart. 390-404, Sept. 1952
• Shooting Rapids in Reverse! By William Belknap, Jr. 552-565, Apr. 1962
• Skyway Below the Clouds. By Carl R. Markwith. Photos by Ernest J. Cottrell. Included: Douglas; Falcon Field; International Airport, Nogales; Kinsley Ranch; Mesa; Tucson. 85-108, July 1949
• Two Wheels Along the Mexican Border. By William Albert Allard. 591-635, May 1971
• *See also* Colorado River and Basin; Fort Apache Reservation; Four Corners Country; Grand Canyon; Havasupai Indian Reservation; Mazatzal Wilderness; Monument Valley; Navajo National Monument; Organ Pipe Cactus National Monument; Powell, Lake; *and* Navajos

ARKANSAS:
• Easygoing, Hardworking Arkansas. By Boyd Gibbons. Photos by Matt Bradley. 396-427, Mar. 1978
• An Ozark Family Carves a Living and a Way of Life. Photos by Bruce Dale. 124-133, July 1975
• Through Ozark Hills and Hollows. By Mike W. Edwards. Photos by Bruce Dale. 656-689, Nov. 1970
• *See also* Buffalo National River

ARKHANES, Crete:
• Drama of Death in a Minoan Temple. By Yannis Sakellarakis and Efi Sapouna-Sakellaraki. Photos by Otis Imboden and Spyros Tsavdaroglou. 205-222, Feb. 1981

ARLINGTON COUNTY, Virginia:
• Across the Potomac from Washington. By Albert W. Atwood. 1-33, Jan. 1953

ARLINGTON NATIONAL CEMETERY, Virginia:
• 'Known but to God' (Unknown Heroes). By Beverley M. Bowie. 593-605, Nov. 1958
• The Last Full Measure (Tribute to President Kennedy). By Melville Bell Grosvenor. 307-355, Mar. 1964

ARLIS II (Ice Island), Arctic Region:
• North Toward the Pole on Skis. By Bjørn O. Staib. 254-281, Feb. 1965
• Scientists Ride Ice Islands on Arctic Odysseys. By Lowell Thomas, Jr. Photos by Ted Spiegel. 670-691, Nov. 1965

ARLIS III (Ice Island), Arctic Region:
• Scientists Ride Ice Islands on Arctic Odysseys. By Lowell Thomas, Jr. Photos by Ted Spiegel. 670-691, Nov. 1965

ARMADA. *See* Spanish Armada

ARMADILLOS:
• The Astonishing Armadillo. By Eleanor E. Storrs. Photos by Bianca Lavies. 820-830, June 1982

ARMAGEDDON. *See* Megiddo, Israel

ARMED FORCES. *See* U. S. Armed Forces

ARMENIANS:
• The Proud Armenians. By Robert Paul Jordan. Photos by Harry N. Naltchayan. 846-873, June 1978

ARMSTRONG, NEIL A.:
• First Explorers on the Moon: The Incredible Story of Apollo 11. 735-797, Dec. 1969
I. Man Walks on Another World. By Neil A. Armstrong, Edwin E. Aldrin, Jr., and Michael Collins. 738-749; II. Sounds of the Space Age, From Sputnik to Lunar Landing. A record narrated by Frank Borman. 750-751; III. The Flight of Apollo 11: "One giant leap for mankind." By Kenneth F. Weaver. 752-787
• First Moon Explorers (Apollo 11) Receive the Society's Hubbard Medal. 859-861, June 1970

ARNHEM LAND, Australia:
• Arnhem Land Aboriginals Cling to Dreamtime. By Clive Scollay. Photos by Penny Tweedie. 644-663, Nov. 1980
• An Arnhem Land Adventure. By Donald F. Thomson. 403-430, Mar. 1948
Arnhem Land Expedition of 1948. NGS research grant. 430
• Cruise to Stone Age Arnhem Land. By Howell Walker. NGS research grant. 417-430, Sept. 1949
• Exploring Stone Age Arnhem Land. By Charles P. Mountford. Photos by Howell Walker. NGS research grant. 745-782, Dec. 1949
• From Spear to Hoe on Groote Eylandt. By Howell Walker. 131-142, Jan. 1953
• The Top End of Down Under. By Kenneth MacLeish. Photos by Thomas Nebbia. 145-174, Feb. 1973

ARNO (River), Italy:
• Florence Rises From the Flood. By Joseph Judge. 1-43, July 1967

ARNOLD, DAVID L.:
Author-Photographer:
• Pueblo Pottery–2,000 Years of Artistry. 593-605, Nov. 1982
Photographer:
• The Civilizing Seine. By Charles McCarry. 478-511, Apr. 1982
• Reach for the New World. By Mendel Peterson. Paintings by Richard Schlecht. 724-767, Dec. 1977
• Yesterday Lingers Along the Connecticut. By Charles McCarry. 334-369, Sept. 1972

ARNOLD, HENRY H.:
• Fledgling Wings of the Air Force. By Thomas W. McKnew. 266-271, Aug. 1957
• Giant Effigies of the Southwest. By George C. Marshall. 389, Sept. 1952
• Memorial Tribute to General of the Air Force H. H. Arnold. 400, Mar. 1950
Author:
• My Life in the Valley of the Moon. Photos by Willard R. Culver. 689-716, Dec. 1948
• Wildlife In and Near the Valley of the Moon. Photos by Paul J. Fair. 401-414, Mar. 1950

ARNOLD, RUDY: Photographer:
• Flying in the "Blowtorch" Era. By Frederick G. Vosburgh. 281-322, Sept. 1950

AROOSTOOK COUNTY, Maine:
• Aroostook County, Maine, Source of Potatoes. By Howell Walker. 459-478, Oct. 1948
• The Incredible Potato. By Robert E. Rhoades. Photos by Martin Rogers. 668-694, May 1982

AROUND the "Great Lakes of the South." By Frederick Simpich. Photos by J. Baylor Roberts. 463-491, Apr. 1948

AROUND the World and the Calendar with the Geographic: The President's Annual Message. By Melville Bell Grosvenor. 832-866, Dec. 1959

"**AROUND** the World in Eighty Days." By Newman Bumstead. 705-750, Dec. 1951

ARRAN, Island of, Scotland:
• Home to Arran, Scotland's Magic Isle. By J. Harvey Howells. 80-99, July 1965

ARROWS Speak Louder Than Words: The Last Andaman Islanders. By Raghubir Singh. 66-91, July 1975

ARROWSMITH, AARON:
• Eight Maps of Discovery. Included: George Washington's Travels, Traced on the Arrowsmith Map. 757-769, June 1953

ART:
Aegean:
• The Aegean Isles: Poseidon's Playground. By Gilbert M. Grosvenor. 733-781, Dec. 1958
• Drama of Death in a Minoan Temple. By Yannis Sakellarakis and Efi Sapouna-Sakellaraki. Photos by Otis Imboden and Spyros Tsavdaroglou. 205-222, Feb. 1981
• Minoans and Mycenaeans: Greece's Brilliant Bronze Age. By Joseph Judge. Photos by Gordon W. Gahan. Paintings by Lloyd K. Townsend. 142-185. Feb. 1978
African:
• Afo-A-Kom: A Sacred Symbol Comes Home. By William S. Ellis. Photos by James P. Blair. 141-148, July 1974
• Africa's Bushman Art Treasures. By Alfred Friendly. Photos by Alex R. Willcox. 848-865, June 1963
• Freedom Speaks French in Ouagadougou. By John Scofield. Included: Wood carvings, textiles, wall murals, applique, masks, jewelry. 153-203, Aug. 1966
• *See also* Egyptian, *following*
American:
• American Masters in the National Gallery. By John Walker. 295-324, Sept. 1948
• American Processional: History on Canvas. By John and Blanche Leeper. 173-212, Feb. 1951
• America's First Painters: Indians. By Dorothy Dunn. 349-377, Mar. 1955
• Artists Look at Pennsylvania. By John Oliver La Gorce. 37-56, July 1948
• Audubon "On the Wing." By David Jeffery. Photos by Bates Littlehales. 149-177, Feb. 1977
• Early America Through the Eyes of Her Native Artists. By Hereward Lester Cooke, Jr. 356-389, Sept. 1962
• Goal at the End of the Trail: Santa Fe. By William S. Ellis. Photos by Gordon W. Gahan and Otis Imboden. Included: Art community and business. 323-345, Mar. 1982
• Profiles of the Presidents. By Frank Freidel. Included: White House portraits; American paintings and engravings.
I. The Presidency and How It Grew. 642-687, Nov. 1964; II. A Restless Nation Moves West. 80-121, Jan. 1965; III. The American Giant Comes of Age. 660-711, May 1965; IV. America Enters the Modern Era. 537-577, Oct. 1965; V. The Atomic Age: Its Problems and Promises. 66-119, Jan. 1966
• So Long, St. Louis, We're Heading West. By William C. Everhart. Included: American paintings of the West. 643-669, Nov. 1965
• Under the Dome of Freedom: The United States Capitol. By Lonnelle Aikman. Photos by George F. Mobley. 4-59, Jan. 1964
• U. S. Capitol, Citadel of Democracy. By Lonnelle Aikman. 143-192, Aug. 1952
• *See also* Pre-Hispanic, *following*
Ancient Europe:
• Ancient Bulgaria's Golden Treasures. By Colin Renfrew. Photos by James L. Stanfield. Paintings by Jean-Leon Huens. 112-129, July 1980
• Ancient Europe Is Older Than We Thought. By Colin Renfrew. Photos by Adam Woolfitt. 615-623, Nov. 1977
• The Celts. By Merle Severy. Photos by James P. Blair. Paintings by Robert C. Magis. 582-633, May 1977
Arctic:
• Eskimo and Viking Finds in the High Arctic: Ellesmere Island. By Peter Schledermann. Photos by Sisse Brimberg. 575-601, May 1981
• Where Magic Ruled: Art of the Bering Sea. By William W. Fitzhugh and Susan A. Kaplan. Photos by Sisse Brimberg. 198-205, Feb. 1983

NEW-YORK HISTORICAL SOCIETY

Audubon: female gyrfalcons

AUDREY TOPPING

China's Find: terra-cotta guardian

Asian:
• Angkor, Jewel of the Jungle. By W. Robert Moore. Paintings by Maurice Fiévet. 517-569, Apr. 1960
• Indonesia Rescues Ancient Borobudur. By W. Brown Morton III. Photos by Dean Conger. 126-142, Jan. 1983
• Pagan, on the Road to Mandalay. By W. E. Garrett. 343-365, Mar. 1971
• The Temples of Angkor. 548-589, May 1982
I. Ancient Glory in Stone. By Peter T. White. Photos by Wilbur E. Garrett. 552-589; II. Will They Survive? Introduction by Wilbur E. Garrett. 548-551
• *See also* Byzantine; Chinese; Islamic; Japanese; Middle Eastern, *following*
Byzantine:
• Athens to Istanbul. By Jean and Franc Shor. 37-76, Jan. 1956
• The Byzantine Empire. 709-777, Dec. 1983
I. Rome of the East. By Merle Severy. Photos by James L. Stanfield. 709-767; II. Mount Athos. 739-745; III. Eternal Easter in a Greek Village. By Maria Nicolaidis-Karanikolas. Photos by James L. Stanfield. 768-777
• Island of Faith in the Sinai Wilderness (St. Catherine's Monastery). By George H. Forsyth. Photos by Robert F. Sisson. 82-106, Jan. 1964
• Mount Sinai's Holy Treasures (St. Catherine's Monastery). By Kurt Weitzmann. Photos by Fred Anderegg. 109-127, Jan. 1964
• A New Look at Medieval Europe. By Kenneth M. Setton. Paintings by Andre Durenceau and Birney Lettick. 799-859, Dec. 1962
Chinese:
• The Caves of the Thousand Buddhas. By Franc and Jean Shor. 383-415, Mar. 1951
• China Unveils Her Newest Treasures. Photos by Robert W. Madden. 848-857, Dec. 1974
• China's Incredible Find. By Audrey Topping. Paintings by Yang Hsien-min. Included: The first emperor's burial mound, with guardian army of terra-cotta men and horses. 440-459, Apr. 1978
• A Lady From China's Past. Photos from *China Pictorial.* Text by Alice J. Hall. Included: Treasures from a noblewoman's tomb. 660-681, May 1974
Egyptian:
• Abu Simbel's Ancient Temples Reborn. By Georg Gerster. 724-744, May 1969
• Computer Helps Scholars Re-create an Egyptian Temple. By Ray Winfield Smith. Photos by Emory Kristof. NGS research grant. 634-655, Nov. 1970
• Egypt: Legacy of a Dazzling Past. By Alice J. Hall. 293-311, Mar. 1977
• Fresh Treasures from Egypt's Ancient Sands. By Jefferson Caffery. Photos by David S. Boyer. 611-650, Nov. 1955
• Lost Outpost of the Egyptian Empire. By Trude Dothan. Photos by Sisse Brimberg. Paintings by Lloyd K. Townsend. NGS research grant. 739-769, Dec. 1982
• Saving the Ancient Temples at Abu Simbel. By Georg Gerster. Paintings by Robert W. Nicholson. 694-742, May 1966
• Threatened Treasures of the Nile. By Georg Gerster. 587-621, Oct. 1963
• Tutankhamun's Golden Trove. By Christiane Desroches Noblecourt. Photos by F. L. Kenett. 625-646, Oct. 1963
• *Yankee* Cruises the Storied Nile. By Irving and Electa Johnson. Photos by Winfield Parks. 583-633, May 1965
European:
• Belgium: One Nation Divisible. By James Cerruti. Photos by Martin Rogers. Included: Flemish oil-painting techniques. 314-341, Mar. 1979
• The British Way. By Sir Evelyn Wrench. Included: William Hogarth, Hans Holbein, Sir Edwin Landseer, Sir Joshua Reynolds, Benjamin West. 421-541, Apr. 1949
• The Kress Collection: A Gift to the Nation. By Guy Emerson. 823-865, Dec. 1961
• The Louvre, France's Palace of the Arts. By Hereward Lester Cooke, Jr. 796-831, June 1971
• Masterpieces on Tour. By Harry A. McBride. 717-750, Dec. 1948
• The National Gallery After a Quarter Century. By John Walker. 348-371, Mar. 1967
• The Nation's Newest Old Masters (National Gallery of Art). By John Walker. Paintings from Kress Collection. 619-657, Nov. 1956
• Our Search for British Paintings. By Franklin L. Fisher. 543-550, Apr. 1949
• Periscope on the Etruscan Past. By Carlo M. Lerici. 337-350, Sept. 1959
• Toledo–El Greco's Spain Lives On. By Louise E. Levathes. Photos by James P. Blair. 726-753, June 1982
The Genius of El Greco. Introduction by J. Carter Brown. 736-744
• The Vienna Treasures and Their Collectors. By John Walker. 737-776, June 1950
• Your National Gallery of Art After 10 Years. By John Walker. Paintings from Kress Collection. 73-103, Jan. 1952
• *See also* Aegean; Ancient Europe; Byzantine, *preceding;* Greek; Impressionist; Medieval; Modern Art; Renaissance; Roman, *following*
Greek:
• Athens: Her Golden Past Still Lights the World. By Kenneth F. Weaver. Photos by Phillip Harrington. 100-137, July 1963
• Regal Treasures From a Macedonian Tomb. By Manolis Andronicos. Photos by Spyros Tsavdaroglou. 55-77, July 1978

• Warriors From a Watery Grave (Bronze Sculptures). By Joseph Alsop. 821-827, June 1983

Impressionist:

• Great Masters of a Brave Era in Art. By Hereward Lester Cooke, Jr. 661-697, May 1961

• In Quest of Beauty. By Paul Mellon. 372-385, Mar. 1967

Islamic:

• The Arab World. 712-732, Nov. 1958

• Glass Treasure From the Aegean. By George F. Bass. Photos by Jonathan Blair. NGS research grant. 768-793, June 1978

• Iran: Desert Miracle. By William Graves. Photos by James P. Blair. 2-47, Jan. 1975

• Iran's Shah Crowns Himself and His Empress. By Franc Shor. Photos by James L. Stanfield and Winfield Parks. 301-321, Mar. 1968

• Saudi Arabia: Beyond the Sands of Mecca. By Thomas J. Abercrombie. 1-53, Jan. 1966

• Saudi Arabia: The Kingdom and Its Power. By Robert Azzi. 286-333, Sept. 1980

• The Sword and the Sermon. By Thomas J. Abercrombie. 3-45, July 1972

• *See also* Mosques

Japanese:

• Human Treasures of Japan. By William Graves. Photos by James L. Stanfield. Contents: Ryujo Hori, doll maker; Gonroku Matsuda, lacquer artist; Tesshi Nagano, ironcaster; Utaemon Nakamura, Kabuki actor; Sadaichi Tsukiyama, samurai swordsmith. 370-379, Sept. 1972

• Kyoto and Nara: Keepers of Japan's Past. By Charles McCarry. Photos by George F. Mobley. 836-851, June 1976

• The Lost Fleet of Kublai Khan. By Torao Mozai. Photos by Koji Nakamura. Paintings by Issho Yada. 634-649, Nov. 1982

Medieval:

• Chartres: Legacy From the Age of Faith. By Kenneth MacLeish. Photos by Dean Conger. 857-882, Dec. 1969

• 900 Years Ago: the Norman Conquest. By Kenneth M. Setton. Photos by George F. Mobley. The complete Bayeux Tapestry photographed by Milton A. Ford and Victor R. Boswell, Jr. 206-251, Aug. 1966

• Searching Out Medieval Churches in Ethiopia's Wilds. By Georg Gerster. 856-884, Dec. 1970

Middle Eastern:

• Darius Carved History on Ageless Rock. By George G. Cameron. 825-844, Dec. 1950

• Ebla: Splendor of an Unknown Empire. By Howard La Fay. Photos by James L. Stanfield. Paintings by Louis S. Glanzman. 730-759, Dec. 1978

• The Phoenicians, Sea Lords of Antiquity. By Samuel W. Matthews. Photos by Winfield Parks. Paintings by Robert C. Magis. 149-189, Aug. 1974

• Throne Above the Euphrates. By Theresa Goell. 390-405, Mar. 1961

Modern Art:

• Chelsea, London's Haven of Individualists. By James Cerruti. Photos by Adam Woolfitt. 28-55, Jan. 1972

• The Fascinating World of Trash. By Peter T. White. Photos by Louie Psihoyos. 424-457, Apr. 1983

• The National Gallery After a Quarter Century. By John Walker. 348-371, Mar. 1967

• Pompidou Center, Rage of Paris. By Cathy Newman. Photos by Marc Riboud. 469-477, Oct. 1980

Pre-Hispanic:

• The Aztecs. 704-775, Dec. 1980
I. The Aztecs. By Bart McDowell. Photos by David Hiser. Paintings by Felipe Dávalos. 714-751; II. The Building of Tenochtitlan. By Augusto F. Molina Montes. Paintings by Felipe Dávalos. 753-765; III. New Finds in the Great Temple. By Eduardo Matos Moctezuma. Photos by David Hiser. 767-775

• Chan Chan, Peru's Ancient City of Kings. By Michael E. Moseley and Carol J. Mackey. Photos by David Brill. 318-345, Mar. 1973

• Finding the Tomb of a Warrior-God. By William Duncan Strong. Photos by Clifford Evans, Jr. 453-482, Apr. 1947

• Giant Effigies of the Southwest. By George C. Marshall. 389, Sept. 1952

• Gold, the Eternal Treasure. By Peter T. White. Photos by James L. Stanfield. 1-51, Jan. 1974

• Indian Life Before the Colonists Came. By Stuart E. Jones. Engravings by Theodore de Bry, 1590. 351-368, Sept. 1947

• The Lost Empire of the Incas. By Loren McIntyre. Art by Ned and Rosalie Seidler. 729-787, Dec. 1973
A Pictorial Chronicle of the Incas. 747-753

• The Maya. NGS research grant. 729-811, Dec. 1975
I. Children of Time. By Howard La Fay. Photos by David Alan Harvey. 729-767; II. Riddle of the Glyphs. By George E. Stuart. Photos by Otis Imboden. 768-791; III. Resurrecting the Grandeur of Tikal. By William R. Coe. 792-798; IV. A Traveler's Tale of Ancient Tikal. Paintings by Peter Spier. Text by Alice J. Hall. 799-811

• Maya Art Treasures Discovered in Cave. By George E. Stuart. Photos by Wilbur E. Garrett. 220-235, Aug. 1981

• Mexico's Booming Capital. By Mason Sutherland. Photos by Justin Locke. 785-824, Dec. 1951

• Mexico's Window on the Past (National Museum). By Bart McDowell. Photos by B. Anthony Stewart. 492-519, Oct. 1968

• Mystery of the Ancient Nazca Lines. By Loren McIntyre. NGS research grant. 716-728, May 1975

• On the Trail of La Venta Man. By Matthew W. Stirling. Photos by Richard H. Stewart. NGS research grant. 137-172, Feb. 1947
Hunting Mexico's Buried Temples. 145-168

Renaissance:

• "The Adoration of the Magi," painting supplement. Jan. 1952

• Carrara Marble: Touchstone of Eternity. By Cathy Newman. Photos by Pierre Boulat. 42-59, July 1982

• Escorting Mona Lisa to America. By Edward T. Folliard. 838-847, June 1963

• Florence Rises From the Flood. By Joseph Judge. 1-43, July 1967

• Leonardo da Vinci: A Man for All Ages. By Kenneth MacLeish. Photos by James L. Amos. 296-329, Sept. 1977

◆ *The Renaissance: Maker of Modern Man.* Announced. 588-592, Oct. 1970; rev. ed. 1977

• The Renaissance Lives On in Tuscany. By Luis Marden. Photos by Albert Moldvay. 626-659, Nov. 1974

• Restoration Reveals the "Last Supper." By Carlo Bertelli. Photos by Victor R. Boswell, Jr. 664-685, Nov. 1983

• Venice Fights for Life. By Joseph Judge. Photos by Albert Moldvay. 591-631, Nov. 1972

• When in Rome. . . . By Stuart E. Jones. Photos by Winfield Parks. 741-789, June 1970

Roman:

• Ancient Aphrodisias and Its Marble Treasures. By Kenan T. Erim. Photos by Jonathan S. Blair. NGS research grant. 280-294, Aug. 1967

• Ancient Aphrodisias Lives Through Its Art. By Kenan T. Erim. Photos by David Brill. NGS research grant. 527-551, Oct. 1981

• Aphrodisias, Awakened City of Ancient Art. By Kenan T. Erim. Photos by Jonathan Blair. NGS research grant. 766-791, June 1972

• Down the Ancient Appian Way. By James Cerruti. Photos by O. Louis Mazzatenta. 714-747, June 1981

• Last Moments of the Pompeians. By Amedeo Maiuri. Photos by Lee E. Battaglia. Paintings by Peter V. Bianchi. 651-669, Nov. 1961

• Roman Life in 1,600-year-old Color Pictures. By Gino Vinicio Gentili. Photos by Duncan Edwards. 211-229, Feb. 1957

• *See also* Animation; Architecture; listing under Art Galleries; Ceramics; Crafts; Folk Art; Glass; Metalwork; Mosaics; Painting; Pottery; Rock Art; Sculpture

ART GALLERIES. *See* Dresden Treasures; Hermitage; Huntington; Kunsthistorisches Museum; Louvre; National Gallery of Art; National Museum of Anthropology, Mexico City; Vizcaya; *and* Vatican City

ART RESTORATION:

• Florence Rises From the Flood. By Joseph Judge. 1-43, July 1967

• Restoration Reveals the "Last Supper." By Carlo Bertelli. Photos by Victor R. Boswell, Jr. 664-685, Nov. 1983

• Thera, Key to the Riddle of Minos. By Spyridon Marinatos. Photos by Otis Imboden. 702-726, May 1972

• Venice Fights for Life. By Joseph Judge. Photos by Albert Moldvay. 591-631, Nov. 1972
Venice's Golden Legacy. Photos by Victor R. Boswell, Jr. 609-619
• Warriors From a Watery Grave (Bronze Sculptures). By Joseph Alsop. 821-827, June 1983

ARTHROPODS. *See* Crustaceans; Insects; Scorpions; Spiders

ARTHUR, CHESTER A.:
• Inside the White House. By Lonnelle Aikman. Photos by B. Anthony Stewart and Thomas Nebbia. 3-43, Jan. 1961
• Profiles of the Presidents: III. The American Giant Comes of Age. By Frank Freidel. 660-711, May 1965

ARTISANS. *See* Crafts; Folk Art

ARTISTS:
• American Masters in the National Gallery. By John Walker. Contents: George Bellows, Mary Cassatt, William Merritt Chase, John Singleton Copley, Thomas Eakins, Chester Harding, Childe Hassam, Winslow Homer, George Inness, Rembrandt Peale, John Quidor, Edward Savage, Christian Schussele, Gilbert Stuart, Thomas Sully, James Abbott McNeill Whistler. 295-324, Sept. 1948
• American Processional: History on Canvas. By John and Blanche Leeper. Contents: John and Victor Audubon, George Caleb Bingham, David G. Blythe, James E. Butterworth, James H. Cafferty, Conrad Wise Chapman, John Singleton Copley, Robert Dudley, Thomas Eakins, J. G. Evans, Ambroise Louis Garneray, Henry Gilder, William Hahn, George Peter Alexander Healy, Winslow Homer, Thomas Hovenden, Frederick Kemmelmeyer, Edward Moran, Linton Park, Charles Willson Peale, Adrian Persac, Frederick Remington, C. Riess, Charles G. Rosenberg, John Searle, Dominique Serres, John Stevens, Louis Comfort Tiffany, John Trumbull, Charles F. Ulrich, Benjamin West. 173-212, Feb. 1951
• America's First Painters: Indians. By Dorothy Dunn. 349-377, Mar. 1955
• Artists Look at Pennsylvania. By John Oliver La Gorce. Contents: Aaron Bohrod, Adolf Dehn, Ernest Fiene, William Gropper, Fletcher Martin, Hobson Pittman, Paul Sample. 37-56, July 1948
• Audubon "On the Wing." By David Jeffery. Photos by Bates Littlehales. 149-177, Feb. 1977
• Belgium: One Nation Divisible. By James Cerruti. Photos by Martin Rogers. Included: How the Flemings brought depth to painting. 314-341, Mar. 1979
• The British Way. By Sir Evelyn Wrench. Included: William Hogarth, Hans Holbein, Sir Edwin Landseer, Sir Joshua Reynolds, Benjamin West. 421-541, Apr. 1949
• Chelsea, London's Haven of Individualists. By James Cerruti. Photos by Adam Woolfitt. Included: Sir Jacob Epstein, Anthony Gray, Walter Greaves, Edward Halliday, Augustus John, Guy Roddon, Dante Gabriel Rossetti, John Singer Sargent, William Thomson, Joseph Mallord William Turner, James McNeill Whistler. 28-55, Jan. 1972
• Early America Through the Eyes of Her Native Artists. By Hereward Lester Cooke, Jr. Contents: Francis Alexander, Winthrop Chandler, James Evans, George A. Hayes, Edward Hicks, Joseph H. Hidley, H. Knight, Hyacinthe Laclotte, Linton Park, H.M.T. Powell, Charles S. Raleigh, A. Tapy, John Toole, Benjamin West, J. Wiess. 356-389, Sept. 1962
• Goal at the End of the Trail: Santa Fe. By William S. Ellis. Photos by Gordon W. Gahan and Otis Imboden. 323-345, Mar. 1982
• Great Masters of a Brave Era in Art (Impressionist). By Hereward Lester Cooke, Jr. Contents: Eugene Boudin, Mary Cassatt, Paul Cézanne, Jean-Baptiste-Camille Corot, Honoré Daumier, Edgar Degas, Eugène Delacroix, Henri Fantin-Latour, Paul Gauguin, Vincent van Gogh, Édouard Manet, Claude Monet, Berthe Morisot, Camille Pissarro, Auguste Renoir, Henri Rousseau, Henri de Toulouse-Lautrec. 661-697, May 1961
• In Quest of Beauty. By Paul Mellon. Contents: Frédéric Bazille, Pierre Bonnard, Mary Cassatt, Paul Cézanne, Edgar Degas, Paul Gauguin, Vincent van Gogh, Édouard Manet, Claude Monet, Berthe Morisot, Pablo Picasso, Auguste Renoir, Henri Rousseau, Georges Seurat, Henri de Toulouse-Lautrec. 372-385, Mar. 1967
• The Kress Collection: A Gift to the Nation. By Guy Emerson. Contents: Giovanni Bellini, Bernardo Bellotto, Abraham Van Beyeren, Paris Bordone, Canaletto (Antonio Canale), Bernardino Fungai, El Greco, Francesco Guardi, Frans Hals, Pieter de Hooch, Lorenzo Lotto, Master of the Braunschweig Diptych, The Montaione Master, Neroccio de' Landi, Piero di Cosimo, Rembrandt Van Rijn, Jusepe de Ribera, Cosimo Rosselli, Peter Paul Rubens, Jan Steen, Bernardo Strozzi, Giovanni Battista Tiepolo, Jacopo Tintoretto, Titian, Sir Anthony Van Dyck, Domenico Veneziano, Paolo Veronese, Elisabeth Vigée-Lebrun, Simon Vouet. 823-865, Dec. 1961
• Leonardo da Vinci: A Man for All Ages. By Kenneth MacLeish. Photos by James L. Amos. 296-329, Sept. 1977
• The Louvre, France's Palace of the Arts. By Hereward Lester Cooke, Jr. Included: Paul Cézanne, Jean-Baptiste Chardin, Jean Clouet, Honoré Daumier, Jacques-Louis David, Eugène Delacroix, Jan van Eyck, Charles Le Brun, Édouard Manet, Andrea Mantegna, Gabriel Metsu, Michelangelo, François Perrier, Rembrandt, Hyacinthe Rigaud, Georges Seurat, Leonardo da Vinci, Jean Antoine Watteau, James Abbott McNeill Whistler. 796-831, June 1971
• Masterpieces on Tour. By Harry A. McBride. Contents: Hans Baldung, Alessandro Botticelli, Pieter Bruegel the Elder, Andrea del Castagno, Jean Baptiste Siméon Chardin, Albrecht Dürer, Jan Van Eyck, Frans Hals, Meindert Hobbema, Hans Holbein the Younger, Georges de La Tour, Lucas Van Leyden, Édouard Manet, Raphael, Rembrandt, Peter Paul Rubens, Jan Steen, Bernardo Strozzi, Gerard Ter Borch, Titian, Jan Vermeer, Antoine Watteau, Rogier Van der Weyden. 717-750, Dec. 1948
• The National Gallery After a Quarter Century. By John Walker. 348-371, Mar. 1967
• The Nation's Newest Old Masters (National Gallery of Art). By John Walker. Paintings from Kress Collection. Contents: Nicolò dell' Abate and Denys Calvaert, Albrecht Altdorfer, Sandro Botticelli, Cima da Conegliano, François Clouet, Jacques-Louis David, Juan de Flandes, Jean-Honoré Fragonard, Orazio Gentileschi, El Greco, Lucas Van-Leyden, Hans Memling, Pieter Jansz. Saenredam, St. Bartholomew Master, Jacopo Tintoretto, Titian, Juan van der Hamen y Leon, Sir Anthony Van Dyck, Paolo Veronese, Leonardo da Vinci. 619-657, Nov. 1956
• Our Search for British Paintings. By Franklin L. Fisher. 543-550, Apr. 1949
• Restoration Reveals the "Last Supper." By Carlo Bertelli. Photos by Victor R. Boswell, Jr. 664-685, Nov. 1983
• Toledo–El Greco's Spain Lives On. By Louise E. Levathes. Photos by James P. Blair. 726-753, June 1982
The Genius of El Greco. Introduction by J. Carter Brown. 736-744
• Under the Dome of Freedom: The United States Capitol. By Lonnelle Aikman. Photos by George F. Mobley. 4-59, Jan. 1964
• U. S. Capitol, Citadel of Democracy. By Lonnelle Aikman. 143-192, Aug. 1952
• Venice Fights for Life. By Joseph Judge. Photos by Albert Moldvay. 591-631, Nov. 1972
Venice's Golden Legacy. Photos by Victor R. Boswell, Jr. Included: Giovanni Bellini, Giorgione, Giuseppe Heintz, Jacopo Tintoretto, Titian, Paolo Veronese, Andrea del Verrocchio, Leonardo da Vinci. 609-619
• The Vienna Treasures and Their Collectors. By John Walker. Contents: Michelangelo Merisi da Caravaggio, Domenico Feti, Albrecht Dürer, Francesco Guardi, Jacob Jordaens, Lorenzo Lotto, Jusepe de Ribera, Peter Paul Rubens, Jan Steen,

Jacopo Tintoretto, Titian, Sir Anthony Van Dyck, Diego Rodriguez de Silva y Velázquez, Jan Vermeer, Paolo Veronese. 737-776, June 1950
• Your National Gallery of Art After 10 Years. By John Walker. Paintings from Kress Collection. Contents: Pieter Bruegel the Elder, Canaletto, Philippe de Champagne, Jean Baptiste Siméon Chardin, Albrecht Dürer, Benozzo Gozzoli, Jean Auguste Dominique Ingres, Giovanni Battista Piazzetta, Hubert Robert, Girolamo Romanino, Master of St. Gilles, Sebastiano del Piombo, Luca Signorelli, Sodoma, Bernardo Strozzi, Titian, Sir Anthony Van Dyck. 73-103, Jan. 1952

ARTS AND CRAFTS. *See* Crafts; Folk Art

ARUBA (Island), Netherlands Antilles:
• The Netherlands Antilles: Holland in the Caribbean. By James Cerruti. Photos by Emory Kristof. 115-146, Jan. 1970

ASCALON (Ashkelon), Israel:
• An Archeologist Looks at Palestine. By Nelson Glueck. 739-752, Dec. 1947

ASCENSION ISLAND, Atlantic Ocean:
• St. Helena: the Forgotten Island. By Quentin Keynes. 265-280, Aug. 1950

ASHERAH (Research Submarine):
• New Tools for Undersea Archeology. By George F. Bass. Photos by Charles R. Nicklin, Jr. 403-423, Sept. 1968

ASHKELON (Ruins), Israel. *See* Ascalon

ASHUR (Ancient City):
• Ancient Mesopotamia: A Light That Did Not Fail. By E. A. Speiser. Paintings by H. M. Herget. 41-105, Jan. 1951

ASIA:
• Ambassadors of Good Will: The Peace Corps. By Sargent Shriver and Peace Corps Volunteers. Included: Sarawak, Turkey. 297-345, Sept. 1964
• Around the World and the Calendar with the Geographic: The President's Annual Message. By Melville Bell Grosvenor. Included: Cambodia, Hong Kong, India, Japan, Pakistan, Thailand, Viet Nam. 832-866, Dec. 1959
• "Around the World in Eighty Days." By Newman Bumstead. Included: China, India, Iraq, Japan, Pakistan, Thailand, Turkey. 705-750, Dec. 1951
▲ *Asia; The Peoples of Mainland Southeast Asia,* supplement. Mar. 1971
▲ *Asia and Adjacent Areas,* Atlas series supplement. Dec. 1959
▲ *Asia and Adjacent Areas,* supplement. Mar. 1951
• Asian Insects in Disguise. By Edward S. Ross. 433-439, Sept. 1965
• A Bad Time to Be a Crocodile. By Rick Gore. Photos by Jonathan Blair. Included: The critically endangered Chinese alligator; the false gharial of Malaysia; the long-nosed gharial, or gavial, of the Indian subcontinent; India's mugger crocodile; and the Siamese crocodile. 90-115, Jan. 1978
• Cane Bridges of Asia. Photos from Paul Popper. 243-250, Aug. 1948
• The Desert: An Age-old Challenge Grows. By Rick Gore. Photos by Georg Gerster and Bruce Dale. Included: The Arabian Desert; Gobi Desert, China-Mongolia; Iranian Desert, Iran-Afghanistan-Pakistan; Negev Desert, Israel; Takla Makan Desert, China; Thar (Great Indian Desert), India-Pakistan; and the Turkestan Desert, U.S.S.R. 586-639, Nov. 1979
▲ *The Far East,* supplement. Sept. 1952
• Flight to Adventure. By Tay and Lowell Thomas, Jr. 49-112, July 1957
• How Fruit Came to America. By J. R. Magness. Paintings by Else Bostelmann. Included: Two Stone Fruits from the Orient (Apricots, Japanese Plums); Plums and Prunes from Europe and West Asia. 325-377, Sept. 1951
• In the Footsteps of Alexander the Great. By Helen and Frank Schreider. Paintings by Tom Lovell. 1-65, Jan. 1968
• Islam's Heartland, Up in Arms. By Thomas J. Abercrombie. Included: Afghanistan, Iraq, Israel, Jerusalem, Lebanon, Saudi Arabia, Soviet Central Asia. 335-345, Sept. 1980
• The Lands and Peoples of Southeast Asia. 295-365, Mar. 1971
I. Mosaic of Cultures. By Peter T. White. Photos by W. E. Garrett. 296-329; II. New Light on a Forgotten Past. By Wilhelm G. Solheim II. 330-339; III. Pagan, on the Road to Mandalay. By W. E. Garrett. 343-365
• New Guinea to Bali in *Yankee*. By Irving and Electa Johnson. Included: Cambodia, Indonesia, Laos, Thailand. 767-815, Dec. 1959
• Our Navy in the Far East. By Arthur W. Radford. Photos by J. Baylor Roberts. 537-577, Oct. 1953
• Our Vegetable Travelers. By Victor R. Boswell. Paintings by Else Bostelmann. Included: Native vegetables from India and the Orient. 145-217, Aug. 1949
• The Proud Armenians. By Robert Paul Jordan. Photos by Harry N. Naltchayan. Included: Armenian S.S.R., Lebanon, Turkey. 846-873, June 1978
• The Rat, Lapdog of the Devil. By Thomas Y. Canby. Photos by James L. Stanfield. Included: Burma, India, Pakistan, Philippines. 60-87, July 1977
• Round the World School (ISA). By Paul Antze. Photos by William Eppridge. Included: Hong Kong, India, Japan, Thailand. 96-127, July 1962
• The Search for the First Americans. By Thomas Y. Canby. Photos by Kerby Smith. Paintings by Roy Andersen. Included: Cultural and racial links between Paleo-Indians and Asians. 330-363, Sept. 1979
• Sky Road East (Southwest Asia). By Tay and Lowell Thomas, Jr. 71-112, Jan. 1960
▲ *Southeast Asia,* Atlas series supplement. May 1961
▲ *Southeast Asia,* supplement. Sept. 1955
▲ *Southeast Asia,* supplement. Dec. 1968
▲ *Southwest Asia,* Atlas series supplement. May 1963
▲ *Southwest Asia, including India, Pakistan, and Northeast Africa,* supplement. June 1952
• Station Wagon Odyssey: Baghdad to Istanbul. By William O. Douglas. 48-87, Jan. 1959
▲ *Viet Nam, Cambodia, Laos, and Eastern Thailand,* supplement. Text on reverse. Jan. 1965
▲ *Viet Nam, Cambodia, Laos, and Thailand,* supplement. Feb. 1967
• West from the Khyber Pass. By William O. Douglas. Photos by Mercedes H. Douglas and author. 1-44, July 1958
• When the President Goes Abroad (Eisenhower Tour). By Gilbert M. Grosvenor. Included: Afghanistan, India, Iran, Pakistan, Turkey. 588-649, May 1960
• The World in Your Garden (Flowers). By W. H. Camp. Paintings by Else Bostelmann. Included: Native flower species from Southeasten Asia, China, and Japan. 1-65, July 1947
• YWCA: International Success Story. By Mary French Rockefeller. Photos by Otis Imboden. 904-933, Dec. 1963
• *See also* Bahrain; Bali; Bangladesh, People's Republic of; Burma; China, People's Republic of; China, Republic of; Hong Kong; India; Indian Ocean; Indonesia; Iraq; Israel; Japan; Jordan; Kampuchea; Korea, Democratic People's Republic of; Korea, Republic of; Ladakh; Lebanon; Malaysia; Middle East, Nepal; Oman; Pakistan; Philippines; Saudi Arabia; Sinai Peninsula; Singapore; Sri Lanka; Syria; Taiwan; Thailand; Tibet; Turkey; Union of Soviet Socialist Republics; Yemen Arab Republic; *and* Himalayas; Holy Land; Karakoram Range; Mekong River; Pacific Fleet, U. S.; Red Sea

ASIA MINOR:
• Our Vegetable Travelers. By Victor R. Boswell. Paintings by Else Bostelmann. 145-217, Aug. 1949
• *See also* Turkey

ASIMOV, ISAAC: Author:
• Five Noted Thinkers Explore the Future. 72-73, July 1976
• The Next Frontier? Paintings by Pierre Mion. 76-89, July 1976

ASMAT (People):
• The Asmat of New Guinea, Headhunters in Today's World. By Malcolm S. Kirk. 376-409, Mar. 1972
• Netherlands New Guinea: Bone of Contention in the South Pacific. By John Scofield. 584-603, May 1962

ASPEN, Colorado:
• Colorado, the Rockies' Pot of Gold. By Edward J. Linehan. Photos by James L. Amos. 157-201, Aug. 1969
• A Town . . . a Mountain . . . a Way of Life. By Jill Durrance and Dick Durrance II. 788-807, Dec. 1973

ASPHALT:
• Happy-go-lucky Trinidad and Tobago. By Charles Allmon. 35-75, Jan. 1953

ASSAM (State), India:
• Cane Bridges of Asia. Photos from Paul Popper. 243-250, Aug. 1948
• Caught in the Assam-Tibet Earthquake. By F. Kingdon-Ward. 403-416, Mar. 1952
• Stalking the Great Indian Rhino. By Lee Merriam Talbot. 389-398, Mar. 1957
• *See also* Naga Hills

ASSATEAGUE ISLAND, Maryland-Virginia:
• Chincoteague: Watermen's Island Home. By Nathaniel T. Kenney. Photos by James L. Amos. 810-829, June 1980
◆ *The Wild Ponies of Assateague Island.* Announced. 724-726, Nov. 1975

ASSUMPTION ISLAND, Indian Ocean:
• Camera Under the Sea. By Luis Marden. 162-200, Feb. 1956

ASSYRIA (Ancient Empire):
• Ancient Mesopotamia: A Light That Did Not Fail. By E. A. Speiser. Paintings by H. M. Herget. 41-105, Jan. 1951

ASTEROIDS:
• Our Universe Unfolds New Wonders. By Albert G. Wilson. 245-260, Feb. 1952
• Voyage to the Planets. By Kenneth F. Weaver. Paintings by Ludek Pesek. 147-193, Aug. 1970

ASTON, WILLIAM J.: Author:
• Midshipmen's Cruise. By William J. Aston and Alexander G. B. Grosvenor. 711-754, June 1948

The **ASTONISHING** Armadillo. By Eleanor E. Storrs. Photos by Bianca Lavies. 820-830, June 1982

ASTRONAUTS:
• America's 6,000-mile Walk in Space. Contents: The Gemini flight of James A. McDivitt and Edward H. White II. 440-447, Sept. 1965
• Apollo 15 Explores the Mountains of the Moon. By Kenneth F. Weaver. Photos from NASA. Note: David R. Scott and James B. Irwin landed on the moon in *Falcon,* while command module pilot Alfred M. Worden orbited in *Endeavour.* 233-265, Feb. 1972
• Apollo 16 Brings Us Visions From Space. Included: Charles M. Duke, Jr. and John W. Young, who landed on the moon while Thomas K. Mattingly II orbited in the command module. 856-865, Dec. 1972

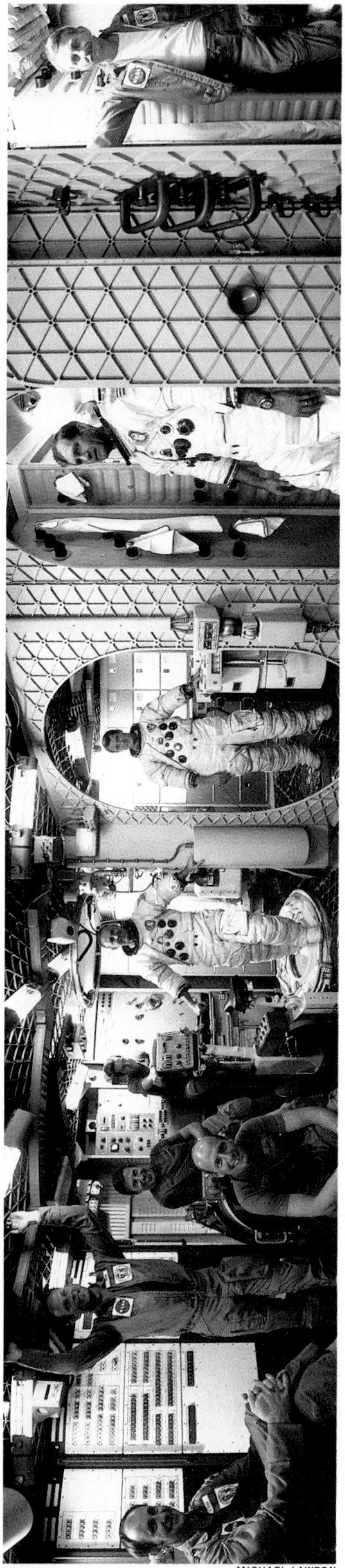

MICHAEL LAWTON

Skylab: members of the three crews

• Apollo-Soyuz: Handclasp in Space. By Thomas Y. Canby. Included: American astronauts Thomas P. Stafford, Vance D. Brand, and Donald K. "Deke" Slayton and Soviet cosmonauts Aleksey A. Leonov and Valeriy Kubasov. 183-187, Feb. 1976
• The Climb Up Cone Crater (Apollo 14). By Alice J. Hall. Photos by Edgar D. Mitchell and Alan B. Shepard, Jr. Note: Alan B. Shepard, Jr. and Edgar D. Mitchell landed on the moon in *Antares,* while Stuart A. Roosa orbited in command module *Kitty Hawk.* 136-148, July 1971
• *Columbia*'s Astronauts' Own Story: Our Phenomenal First Flight. By John W. Young and Robert L. Crippen. Paintings by Ken Dallison. Contents: The first flight in space shuttle *Columbia* by John W. Young, and Robert L. Crippen; also included are astronauts Joe H. Engle and Richard H. Truly who will test *Columbia*'s second flight. 478-503, Oct. 1981
• *Columbia*'s Landing Closes a Circle. By Tom Wolfe. Contents: John W. Young and Robert L. Crippen return the first space shuttle to Edwards Air Force Base in California. 474-477, Oct. 1981
• Countdown for Space. By Kenneth F. Weaver. Contents: Project Mercury astronauts in training (Malcolm Scott Carpenter, John H. Glenn, Jr., Virgil I. Grissom, Walter M. Schirra, Jr., and Alan B. Shepard, Jr.). 702-734, May 1961
• The Earth From Orbit. By Paul D. Lowman, Jr. Contents: Color photographs by American astronauts Charles Conrad, Jr., Leroy Gordon Cooper, Jr., James A. McDivitt, Walter Schirra, and Edward H. White. 645-671, Nov. 1966
• Exploring Taurus-Littrow. By Harrison H. Schmitt. Photos by the crew of Apollo 17. Contents: Harrison H. Schmitt and Eugene A. Cernan landed on the moon in *Challenger,* while Ronald E. Evans orbited in command module *America.* 290-307, Sept. 1973
• Exploring Tomorrow With the Space Agency. By Allan C. Fisher, Jr. Photos by Dean Conger. Included: Mercury astronauts Malcolm Scott Carpenter, Leroy Gordon Cooper, Jr., John H. Glenn, Jr., Virgil I. Grissom, Donald K. Slayton, Walter M. Schirra, Jr., and Alan B. Shepard, Jr. 48-89, July 1960
• First Explorers on the Moon: The Incredible Story of Apollo 11. Contents: Neil A. Armstrong and Edwin E. Aldrin, Jr. landed on the moon July 20, 1969 in *Eagle,* while Michael Collins orbited the moon in command module *Columbia.* 735-797, Dec. 1969
I. Man Walks on Another World. By Neil A. Armstrong, Edwin E. Aldrin, Jr., and Michael Collins. 738-749; II. Sounds of the Space Age, From Sputnik to Lunar Landing. A record narrated by Frank Borman. 750-751; III. The Flight of Apollo 11:

"One giant leap for mankind." By Kenneth F. Weaver. 752-787; IV. What the Moon Rocks Tell Us. By Kenneth F. Weaver. 788-791
- First Moon Explorers (Apollo 11) Receive the Society's Hubbard Medal. Contents: Neil A. Armstrong, Edwin E. Aldrin, Jr., and Michael Collins; previous presentation of medal to Apollo 8 astronauts Frank Borman, James A. Lovell, Jr., and William A. Anders. 859-861, June 1970
- The Flight of *Freedom 7*. By Carmault B. Jackson, Jr. Included: Mercury astronaut Alan B. Shepard, Jr. 416-431, Sept. 1961
- Footprints on the Moon. By Hugh L. Dryden. Paintings by Davis Meltzer and Pierre Mion. Included: Neil A. Armstrong, Frank Borman, Charles Conrad, Jr., Leroy Gordon Cooper, Jr., James A. Lovell, Jr., James A. McDivitt, Elliot M. See, Jr., Donald K. Slayton, Thomas P. Stafford, Edward H. White II, and John W. Young. 357-401, Mar. 1964
- John Glenn Receives the Society's Hubbard Medal. 827, June 1962; 904-906, Dec. 1962
- John Glenn's Three Orbits in *Friendship 7:* A Minute-by-Minute Account of America's First Orbital Space Flight. By Robert B. Voas. 792-827, June 1962

◆ *Let's Go to the Moon.* 1977
- The Making of an Astronaut. By Robert R. Gilruth. Contents: Edwin E. Aldrin, Jr., William A. Anders, Neil A. Armstrong, Charles A. Bassett II, Alan L. Bean, Frank Borman, James Brickle, Eugene A. Cernan, Michael Collins, Charles Conrad, Jr., Theodore C. Freeman, Virgil I. Grissom, Walter M. Schirra, Jr., Russel L. Schweickart, and John W. Young. 122-144, Jan. 1965

◆ *Man's Conquest of Space.* Announced. 844-849, June 1968
- "A Most Fantastic Voyage": The Story of Apollo 8's Rendezvous With the Moon. By Sam C. Phillips. Included: James A. Lovell, Jr., Frank Borman, and William A Anders. 593-631, May 1969
- The Pilot's Story. By Alan B. Shepard, Jr. Photos by Dean Conger. Contents: The flight of Alan B. Shepard, Jr. in *Freedom 7*. 432-444, Sept. 1961
- Skylab. Photos by the nine mission astronauts. Contents: The flights of three Skylab crews: Charles "Pete" Conrad, Jr., Joseph P. Kerwin, and Paul J. Weitz; Alan L. Bean, Owen K. Garriott, and Jack R. Lousma; Gerald P. Carr, Edward G. Gibson, and William R. Pogue. 441-503, Oct. 1974
I. Outpost in Space. By Thomas Y. Canby. 441-469; II. Its View of Earth. 471-493; III. The Sun Unveiled. By Edward G. Gibson. 494-503
- Space Rendezvous, Milestone on the Way to the Moon. By Kenneth F. Weaver. Note: James A. Lovell, Jr. and Frank Borman in Gemini 7 met in space with Walter M. Schirra, Jr. and Thomas P. Stafford in Gemini 6. 539-553, Apr. 1966
- Spacelab 1: *Columbia.* By Michael E. Long. Included: John W. Young, Brewster H. Shaw, Jr., Owen K. Garriott, Robert A. R. Parker, Byron K. Lichtenberg, and Ulf Merbold. 301-307, Sept. 1983
- "Teammates in Mankind's Greatest Adventure," supplement. Contents: Apollo crews. Sept. 1973
- Tracking America's Man in Orbit. By Kenneth F. Weaver. Photos by Robert F. Sisson. Included: M. Scott Carpenter, John H. Glenn, Jr., Walter M. Schirra, Jr., and Donald K. Slayton. 184-217, Feb. 1962
- What Is It Like to Walk on the Moon? By David R. Scott. Included: David R. Scott, James B. Irwin, Harrison H. Schmitt, and Eugene A. Cernan. 326-331, Sept. 1973
- When the Space Shuttle Finally Flies. By Rick Gore. Photos by Jon Schneeberger. Paintings by Ken Dallison. Included: Vance Brand, Dan Brandenstein, Robert L. Crippen, Anna Fisher, Gordon Fullerton, Michael Lampton, Byron Lichtenberg, Shannon Lucid, Judith Resnik, Sally Ride, Rhea Seddon, Donald K. "Deke" Slayton, Kathryn Sullivan, Richard H. Truly, John W. Young, and Europeans Wubbo Ockels, Ulf Merbold, and Claude Nicollier. 317-347, Mar. 1981

ASTRONOMY:

◆ *The Amazing Universe.* Announced. 870-874, June 1975
- Completing the Atlas of the Universe (National Geographic Society-Palomar Observatory Sky Survey). By Ira Sprague Bowen. NGS research grant. 185-190, Aug. 1955
Sky Survey Plates Unlock Secrets of the Stars. 186-187
- Current Scientific Projects of the National Geographic Society. Included: Cosmic ray research; Sky Survey. NGS research grant. 143-144, July 1953
- Exploring the Farthest Reaches of Space. By George O. Abell. Contents: National Geographic-Palomar Sky Survey. 782-790, Dec. 1956
- Eyes of Science. By Rick Gore. Photos by James P. Blair. Included: Studies made by astronomers and scientists at the Jet Propulsion Laboratory in California, the Kitt Peak National Observatory in Arizona, and the U. S. Geological Survey. 360-389, Mar. 1978
- First Color Portraits of the Heavens. By William C. Miller. 670-679, May 1959
- First Photographs of Planets and Moon Taken with Palomar's 200-inch Telescope. By Milton L. Humason. 125-130, Jan. 1953

◆ *Hidden Worlds.* 1981
- The Incredible Universe. By Kenneth F. Weaver. Photos by James P. Blair. 589-625, May 1974
Pioneers in Man's Search for the Universe. Paintings by Jean-Leon Huens. Text by Thomas Y. Canby. Contents: Nicolaus Copernicus, Albert Einstein, Galileo Galilei, William Herschel, Edwin Hubble, Johannes Kepler, Isaac Newton. 627-633

▲ *Journey Into the Universe Through Time and Space; National Geographic-Palomar Sky Survey Charting the Heavens,* double-sided supplement. June 1983

▲ *A Map of the Heavens,* supplement. Star charts on reverse. Dec. 1957

▲ *Map of the Heavens,* supplement. Star charts on reverse. Aug. 1970
- Mapping the Unknown Universe. By F. Barrows Colton. NGS research grant. 401-420, Sept. 1950
- The Once and Future Universe. By Rick Gore. Photos by James A. Sugar. Paintings by Barron Storey. Picture text by David Jeffery. 704-749, June 1983
- Our Universe Unfolds New Wonders (National Geographic-Palomar Sky Survey). By Albert G. Wilson. NGS research grant. 245-260, Feb. 1952

◆ *Picture Atlas of Our Universe.* 1980
- Sky Survey Charts the Universe. By Ira Sprague Bowen. NGS research grant. 780-781, Dec. 1956
- Split-second Time Runs Today's World. By F. Barrows Colton and Catherine Bell Palmer. Included: Study by astronomers at the Naval Observatory determines the world's measure of time. 399-428, Sept. 1947
- Twelve National Geographic Society Scientific Projects Under Way. Included: Aurora Borealis, Cosmic rays, Mars expedition, Sky Survey, Zodiacal light observations. NGS research grant. 869-870, June 1954
- *See also* Aurora Borealis; Comets; Moon; Planets; Solar System; Stars; Sun; *and* Space Shuttles; Voyager

ASTRONOMY, Ancient:
- The Maya, Riddle of the Glyphs. By George E. Stuart. Photos by Otis Imboden. Included: The two-cycle Maya calendar. 768-791, Dec. 1975
- *See also* Medicine Wheels; Stonehenge; "Sun Dagger"

ASTROPHYSICS:
- The Once and Future Universe. By Rick Gore. Photos by James A. Sugar. Paintings by Barron Storey. Picture text by David Jeffery. 704-749, June 1983
- The Sun. By Herbert Friedman. 713-743, Nov. 1965
- *See also* Geology, Lunar; Mariner Missions

ASUNCIÓN, Paraguay:
- Paraguay, Paradox of South America. By Gordon Young. Photos by O. Louis Mazzatenta. 240-269, Aug. 1982

ASWÂN HIGH DAM, Nile River:
- Threatened Treasures of the Nile. By Georg Gerster. 587-621, Oct. 1963

• *Yankee* Cruises the Storied Nile. By Irving and Electa Johnson. Photos by Winfield Parks. 583-633, May 1965

AT Home in the High Andes. By Harry Tschopik, Jr. 133-146, Jan. 1955

AT Home in the Sea. By Jacques-Yves Cousteau. 465-507, Apr. 1964

AT Home With Right Whales. By Roger Payne. Photos by Des and Jen Bartlett. 322-339, Mar. 1976

AT Home With the Bulldog Ant. By Robert F. Sisson. 62-75, July 1974

AT My Limit–I Climbed Everest Alone. By Reinhold Messner. Photos by the author and Nena Holguín. 552-566, Oct. 1981

AT Peace With the Past, In Step With the Future (Apache). By Ronnie Lupe. 260-261, Feb. 1980

AT World's End in Hunza. By Jean and Franc Shor. 485-518, Oct. 1953

ATACAMA DESERT, Chile:
• Chile, Republic on a Shoestring. By Gordon Young. Photos by George F. Mobley. 437-477, Oct. 1973

ATATÜRK, KEMAL:
• Turkey Paves the Path of Progress. By Maynard Owen Williams. 141-186, Aug. 1951
• *Yankee* Cruises Turkey's History-haunted Coast. By Irving and Electa Johnson. Photos by Joseph J. Scherschel. 798-845, Dec. 1969

ATCHAFALAYA BASIN, Louisiana:
• Trouble in Bayou Country. By Jack and Anne Rudloe. Photos by C. C. Lockwood. 377-397, Sept. 1979

ATEN TEMPLE. *See* Akhenaten Temple Project

ATHAPASCAN LINGUISTIC STOCK:
• Nomads of the Far North. By Matthew W. Stirling. 471-504, Oct. 1949
Hearty Folk Defy Arctic Storms. Paintings by W. Langdon Kihn. 479-494

ATHENS, Greece:
• "Around the World in Eighty Days." By Newman Bumstead. 705-750, Dec. 1951
• Athens: Her Golden Past Still Lights the World. By Kenneth F. Weaver. Photos by Phillip Harrington. 100-137, July 1963
• Athens to Istanbul. By Jean and Franc Shor. 37-76, Jan. 1956
• Erosion, Trojan Horse of Greece. By F. G. Renner. 793-812, Dec. 1947
• Greece: "To Be Indomitable, To Be Joyous." By Peter T. White. Photos by James P. Blair. 360-393, Mar. 1980
• The Tower of the Winds. By Derek J. de Solla Price. Paintings by Robert C. Magis. NGS research grant. 587-596, Apr. 1967
• War-torn Greece Looks Ahead. By Maynard Owen Williams. 711-744, Dec. 1949

ATHOS, Mount, Greece:
• The Byzantine Empire. 709-777, Dec. 1983
I. Rome of the East. By Merle Severy. Photos by James L. Stanfield. 709-767; II. Mount Athos. 739-745

ATITLÁN, Lake, Guatemala:
• Guatemala Revisited. By Luis Marden. 525-564, Oct. 1947

ATKA (Island), Alaska:
• Atka, Rugged Home of My Aleut Friends. By Lael Morgan. 572-583, Oct. 1974

ATKESON, RAY: Photographer:
• From Sagebrush to Roses on the Columbia. By Leo A. Borah. 571-611, Nov. 1952

ATKINSON, AGNES AKIN: Author:
• Br'er Possum, Hermit of the Lowlands. Photos by Charles Philip Fox. 405-418, Mar. 1953

ATLANTA, Georgia:
• Atlanta, Pacesetter City of the South. By William S. Ellis. Photos by James L. Amos. 246-281, Feb. 1969
• Georgia, Unlimited. By Alice J. Hall. Photos by Bill Weems. 212-245, Aug. 1978
• The Greener Fields of Georgia. By Howell Walker. Photos by author and B. Anthony Stewart. 287-330, Mar. 1954

ATLANTIC COAST, U. S.:
▲ *Atlantic Gateways,* The Making of America series. Included: Delaware, Maryland, New Jersey, New York, Pennsylvania, northern Virginia, West Virginia, and in Canada, southern Ontario and southern Quebec. On reverse: Indians and Trade, Nation in the Making, Peopling of the Gateways, Race for the Hinterlands, Growth of Industry, Spreading Urban Corridors. Mar. 1983
• Can We Save Our Salt Marshes? By Stephen W. Hitchcock. Photos by William R. Curtsinger. 729-765, June 1972
• Our Changing Atlantic Coastline. By Nathaniel T. Kenney. Photos by B. Anthony Stewart. 860-887, Dec. 1962
• Savannah to Charleston–A Good Life in the Low Country. By John J. Putman. Photos by Annie Griffiths. 798-829, Dec. 1983

ATLANTIC CONTINENTAL SHELF, U. S.:
• The Continental Shelf: Man's New Frontier. By Luis Marden. Photos by Ira Block. 495-531, Apr. 1978

ATLANTIC MISSILE RANGE:
• Cape Canaveral's 6,000-mile Shooting Gallery. By Allan C. Fisher, Jr. Photos by Luis Marden and Thomas Nebbia. 421-471, Oct. 1959

ATLANTIC OCEAN:
▲ *Atlantic Ocean,* supplement. Dec. 1955
▲ *Atlantic Ocean; Atlantic Ocean Floor,* Atlas series supplement. June 1968
• Atlantic Odyssey: Iceland to Antarctica. By Newman Bumstead. Photos by Volkmar Wentzel. 725-780, Dec. 1955
• *Calypso* Explores an Undersea Canyon. By Jacques-Yves Cousteau. Photos by Bates Littlehales. NGS research grant. 373-396, Mar. 1958
• Diving Into the Blue Holes of the Bahamas. By George J. Benjamin. Included: Tongue of the Ocean. 347-363, Sept. 1970
• Exploring the Mid-Atlantic Ridge. By Maurice Ewing. 275-294, Sept. 1948
• Four Years of Diving to the Bottom of the Sea (Bathyscaph). By Georges S. Houot. 715-731, May 1958
• Hurricane! By Ben Funk. Photos by Robert W. Madden. 346-379, Sept. 1980
Dominica. By Fred Ward. 357-359; Dynamics of a Hurricane. 370-371; Into the Eye of David. By John L. Eliot. 368-369; Paths of Fury–This Century's Worst American Storms. 360-361
• New Discoveries on the Mid-Atlantic Ridge. By Maurice Ewing. Photos by Robert F. Sisson. 611-640, Nov. 1949
• New World of the Ocean. By Samuel W. Matthews. 792-832, Dec. 1981
• Our Changing Atlantic Coastline (U. S.). By Nathaniel T. Kenney. Photos by B. Anthony Stewart. 860-887, Dec. 1962
• Project FAMOUS. 586-615, May 1975
I. Where the Earth Turns Inside Out. By J. R. Heirtzler. Photos by Emory Kristof. 586-603; II. Dive Into the Great Rift. By Robert D. Ballard. Photos by Emory Kristof. 604-615
• Search Operations. *See Thresher*
• This Changing Earth. By Samuel W. Matthews. 1-37, Jan. 1973
• Tracking Danger With the Ice Patrol. By William S. Ellis. Photos by James R. Holland. 780-793, June 1968
• Two and a Half Miles Down. By Georges S. Houot. 80-86, July 1954
• *See also* Grand Banks; Ilha Nova; Romanche Trench; Surtsey; U. S. Coast Guard; Weather Stations and Research; *and* Atlantic Ocean Crossings

ATLANTIC OCEAN CROSSINGS:
• Braving the Atlantic by Balloon. By Arnold Eiloart. 123-146, July 1959
• By Square-rigger from Baltic to Bicentennial. By Kenneth Garrett. Contents: Tall-ship race from Plymouth, England to Newport, Rhode Island via Canary Islands and Bermuda. 824-857, Dec. 1976
• Christopher Columbus and the New World He Found. By John Scofield. Photos by Adam Woolfitt. 584-625, Nov. 1975
• *Double Eagle II* Has Landed! Crossing the Atlantic by Balloon. By Ben L. Abruzzo, with Maxie L. Anderson and Larry Newman. 858-882, Dec. 1978

• How We Sailed the New *Mayflower* to America. By Alan Villiers. 627-672, Nov. 1957
• I Sailed with Portugal's Captains Courageous. By Alan Villiers. 565-596, May 1952
• The Longest Manned Balloon Flight *(Silver Fox)*. By Ed Yost. 208-217, Feb. 1977
• Magellan: First Voyage Around the World. By Alan Villiers. Photos by Bruce Dale. 721-753, June 1976
• Midshipmen's Cruise. By William J. Aston and Alexander G. B. Grosvenor. 711-754, June 1948
• Off the Beaten Track of Empire (Prince Philip's Tour). By Beverley M. Bowie. Photos by Michael Parker. Included: *Britannia's* visit to the South Atlantic Ocean islands of Falkland, South Georgia, Gough, Tristan da Cunha, St. Helena, and Ascension. 584-626, Nov. 1957
• Sir Francis Drake. By Alan Villiers. Photos by Gordon W. Gahan. 216-253, Feb. 1975
• To Europe with a Racing Start *(Finisterre)*. By Carleton Mitchell. 758-791, June 1958
• *Triton* Follows Magellan's Wake. By Edward L. Beach. Photos by J. Baylor Roberts. 585-615, Nov. 1960
• Under Canvas in the Atomic Age. By Alan Villiers. 49-84, July 1955
• The Vikings. By Howard La Fay. Photos by Ted Spiegel. 492-541, Apr. 1970
• The Voyage of *Brendan*. By Timothy Severin. Photos by Cotton Coulson. 770-797, Dec. 1977
• The Voyage of *Ra II*. By Thor Heyerdahl. Photos by Carlo Mauri and Georges Sourial. 44-71, Jan. 1971
• We're Coming Over on the *Mayflower*. By Alan Villiers. 708-728, May 1957
• Who Discovered America? A New Look at an Old Question. The Editor. 769, Dec. 1977
• World-roaming Teen-ager Sails On. By Robin Lee Graham. 449-493, Apr. 1969

ATLANTIC OCEAN ISLANDS:
◆ *America's Atlantic Isles*. 1981
• Off the Beaten Track of Empire (Prince Philip's Tour). By Beverley M. Bowie. Photos by Michael Parker. Included: The islands of Falkland, South Georgia, Gough, Tristan da Cunha, St. Helena, and Ascension. 584-626, Nov. 1957
• *See also* Azores; Bermuda; Falkland Islands; Ilha Nova; St. Helena; South Georgia Island; Surtsey; West Indies

ATLANTIC SALMON:
• Atlantic Salmon: The "Leaper" Struggles to Survive. By Art Lee. Photos by Bianca Lavies. 600-615, Nov. 1981

ATLAS MOUNTAINS, Africa. *See* High Atlas

An **ATLAS** of Energy Resources. Contents: Maps locating major resources of oil, natural gas, coal, geothermal energy, uranium, and solar energy in North America. 58-69, *Special Report on Energy* (Feb. 1981)

ATLASES, NGS:
United States Atlases:
◆ *Atlas of the Fifty United States* announced. 130-133, July 1960; 885, Dec. 1960
◆ *Picture Atlas of Our Fifty States*. 1978
Universe Atlas:
◆ *Picture Atlas of Our Universe*. 1980
World Atlases:
◆ *Atlas of the World* announced. 889, 899-900, Dec. 1962; 832-837, June 1963; 270, 275, Aug. 1982
Second edition. 819-821, June 1966; 580-581, Oct. 1967; Third edition. 735-736, Nov. 1970; Fourth edition, with annual update. 583, Nov. 1975; Fifth edition. 1981; 849, 851A-851B, Dec. 1981
◆ Cultural atlas of the ancient world, *Peoples and Places of the Past*. 1983; 824, Dec. 1982
• Microfilmed copy placed in Time Capsule, New York World's Fair, 1964-65. 525, Apr. 1965
◆ *Picture Atlas of Our World*. 1979

ATOCHA:
• *Atocha,* Tragic Treasure Galleon of the Florida Keys. By Eugene Lyon. 787-809, June 1976
■ Treasure! 575, Nov. 1976; cover, Dec. 1976
• Treasure From the Ghost Galleon: *Santa Margarita*. By Eugene Lyon. Photos by Don Kincaid. 228-243, Feb. 1982

ATOM:
• Man's New Servant, the Friendly Atom. By F. Barrows Colton. Photos by Volkmar Wentzel. 71-90, Jan. 1954
• You and the Obedient Atom. By Allan C. Fisher, Jr. 303-353, Sept. 1958
• *See also* Cosmic Rays

The **ATOMIC** Age: Its Problems and Promises. By Frank Freidel. 66-119, Jan. 1966

ATOMIC BOMB TESTS:
• Nevada Learns to Live with the Atom. By Samuel W. Matthews. 839-850, June 1953
• Operation Crossroads. Photos by Joint Task Force I. Paintings by Charles Bittinger. 519-530, Apr. 1947

ATOMIC ENERGY. *See* Nuclear Energy

ATTENBOROUGH, DAVID:
Author-Photographer:
• Animal Safari to British Guiana. Photos by Charles Lagus and author. 851-874, June 1957

ATWOOD, ALBERT W.: Author:
• Across the Potomac from Washington. 1-33, Jan. 1953
• Census 1960: Profile of the Nation. By Albert W. Atwood and Lonnelle Aikman. 697-714, Nov. 1959
• The Eternal Flame. 540-564, Oct. 1951
• The Fire of Heaven: Electricity Revolutionizes the Modern World. 655-674, Nov. 1948

EDGERTON, GERMESHAUSEN, AND GRIER, INC., FOR AEC

Atom Bomb Tests: house razed by blast, *above;* troops dig in, *below*

U.S. ARMY

NICHOLAS CHEVALIER, NATIONAL LIBRARY OF AUSTRALIA, CANBERRA

Burke and Wills: at Cooper's Creek

Australia: view of Sydney's harbor

ROBERT W. MADDEN, NGS

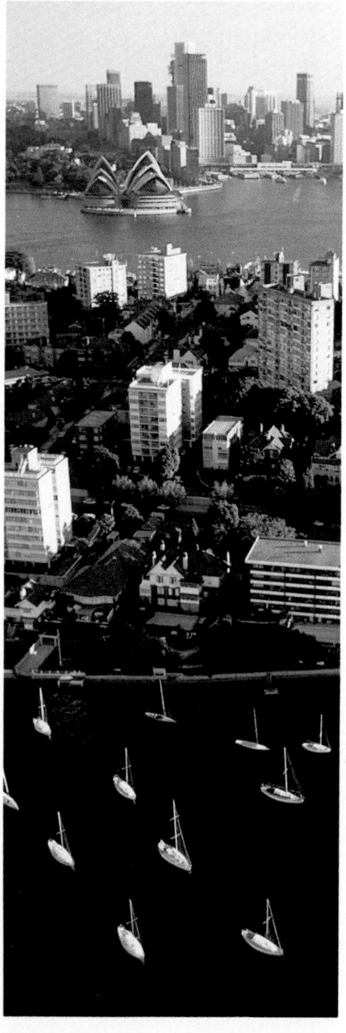

• Gilbert Grosvenor's Golden Jubilee. 253-261, Aug. 1949
• Immigrants Still Flock to Liberty's Land. 708-724, Nov. 1955
• The Merrimack: River of Industry and Romance. Photos by B. Anthony Stewart. 106-140, Jan. 1951
• The Mighty Hudson. Photos by B. Anthony Stewart. 1-36, July 1948
• The Nation's Library (Library of Congress). 663-684, May 1950
• Pittsburgh: Workshop of the Titans. 117-144, July 1949
• Stately Homes of Old Virginia. 787-802, June 1953
• Steel: Master of Them All. Photos by Willard R. Culver. 415-452, Apr. 1947
• Today on the Delaware, Penn's Glorious River. Photos by Robert F. Sisson. 1-40, July 1952
• Washington: Home of the Nation's Great. 699-738, June 1947

AUCKLAND, New Zealand:
• New Zealand: Gift of the Sea. By Maurice Shadbolt. Photos by Brian Brake. 465-511, Apr. 1962
• New Zealand, Pocket Wonder World. By Howell Walker. 419-460, Apr. 1952

AUDUBON, JOHN JAMES:
• Audubon "On the Wing." By David Jeffery. Photos by Bates Littlehales. 149-177, Feb. 1977
• Blizzard of Birds: The Tortugas Terns. By Alexander Sprunt, Jr. 213-230, Feb. 1947

AURNESS, CRAIG: Photographer:
• Iowa, America's Middle Earth. By Harvey Arden. 603-629, May 1981
• New Mexico's Mountains of Mystery. By Robert Laxalt. 416-436, Sept. 1978
• The People Who Made Saskatchewan. By Ethel A. Starbird. 651-679, May 1979
• The Pony Express. By Rowe Findley. 45-71, July 1980
• The Troubled Waters of Mono Lake. By Gordon Young. 504-519, Oct. 1981

AURORA BOREALIS:
• Unlocking Secrets of the Northern Lights. By Carl W. Gartlein. Paintings by William Crowder. NGS research grant. 673-704, Nov. 1947

AUSTEN, DAVID: Photographer:
• Across Australia by Sunpower. By Hans Tholstrup and Larry Perkins. 600-607, Nov. 1983
• Papua New Guinea. By Robert J. Gordon and François Leydet. 143-171, Aug. 1982

AUSTIN, BARBARA: Author:
• A Paradise Called the Palouse. Photos by Phil Schofield. 798-819, June 1982

AUSTRALIA:
• Across Australia by Sunpower. By Hans Tholstrup and Larry Perkins. Photos by David Austen. 600-607, Nov. 1983
• Alone Across the Outback. By Robyn Davidson. Photos by Rick Smolan. 581-611, May 1978
• Arnhem Land Expedition of 1948. NGS research grant. 430, Mar. 1948
• Australia. By Alan Villiers. 309-385, Sept. 1963
I. The West and the South. 309-345; II. The Settled East, the Barrier Reef, the Center. 347-385
◆ *Australia.* Announced. 844-849, June 1968
▲ *Australia; Land of Living Fossils,* double-sided supplement. Feb. 1979
▲ *Australia,* Atlas series supplement. Sept. 1963
▲ *Australia,* supplement. Mar. 1948
■ Australia: The Timeless Land. 300A-300B, Feb. 1969
• Australia's Amazing Bowerbirds. By Norman Chaffer. 866-873, Dec. 1961
■ Australia's Animal Mysteries. 824, Dec. 1982; Cover, Feb. 1983
• Australia's Bizarre Wild Flowers. By Paul A. Zahl. 858-868, Dec. 1976
• Australia's Great Barrier Reef. 630-663, May 1981
I. A Marine Park Is Born. By Soames Summerhays. Photos by Ron and Valerie Taylor. 630-635; II. Paradise Beneath the Sea. By Ron and Valerie Taylor. 636-663
• A Bad Time to Be a Crocodile. By Rick Gore. Photos by Jonathan Blair. 90-115, Jan. 1978
• Captain Cook: The Man Who Mapped the Pacific. By Alan Villiers. Photos by Gordon W. Gahan. 297-349, Sept. 1971
• The Desert: An Age-old Challenge Grows. By Rick Gore. Photos by Georg Gerster and Bruce Dale. 586-639, Nov. 1979
• Expedition to the Land of the Tiwi. By Charles P. Mountford. NGS research grant. 417-440, Mar. 1956
• Flight of the Platypuses. By David Fleay. 512-525, Oct. 1958
• In the Wake of Darwin's *Beagle.* By Alan Villiers. Photos by James L. Stanfield. 449-495, Oct. 1969
• A Jawbreaker for Sharks. By Valerie Taylor. 664-667, May 1981
• The Journey of Burke and Wills. By Joseph Judge. Photos by Joseph J. Scherschel. 152-191, Feb. 1979
◆ *Koalas and Kangaroos: Strange Animals of Australia.* 1981
• The Making of a New Australia. By Howell Walker. 233-259, Feb. 1956
• Off the Beaten Track of Empire (Prince Philip's Tour). By Beverley M. Bowie. Photos by Michael Parker. 584-626, Nov. 1957
• The Satin Bowerbird, Australia's Feathered Playboy. By Philip Green. 865-872, Dec. 1977
• Skylab's Fiery Finish. By Tom Riggert. 581-584, Oct. 1979
• Strange Animals of Australia. By David Fleay. Photos by Stanley Breeden. 388-411, Sept. 1963
• Those Kangaroos! They're a Marvelous Mob. By Geoffrey B. Sharman. Photos by Des and Jen Bartlett. 192-209, Feb. 1979
• The World in Your Garden (Flowers). By W. H. Camp. Paintings by

Else Bostelmann. Included: Australian Plants and Geography (Eucalyptus or Gum-tree, Bottle-brush, Strawflower, Swan River Daisy, Blue laceflower). 1-65, July 1947
• *See also* Alice Springs; Arnhem Land; Currumbin; Great Barrier Reef; Melbourne; Melville Island; New South Wales; Norfolk Island; Northern Territory; Perth; Queensland; South Australia; Sydney; Tasmania; Victoria; Western Australia; *and* Kangaroos; Lyrebird

AUSTRALIAN NEW GUINEA (now Papua New Guinea):
• Australian New Guinea. By John Scofield. 604-637, May 1962
• Change Ripples New Guinea's Sepik River. By Malcolm S. Kirk. 354-381, Sept. 1973
• Fertility Rites and Sorcery in a New Guinea Village (Gimi People). By Gillian Gillison. Photos by David Gillison. 124-146, July 1977
• Journey Into Stone Age New Guinea. By Malcolm S. Kirk. 568-592, Apr. 1969
• Living Theater in New Guinea's Highlands. By Gillian Gillison. Photos by David Gillison. 147-169, Aug. 1983
• New Guinea. The Editor. 583, May 1962
• New Guinea Festival of Faces. By Malcolm S. Kirk. 148-156, July 1969
• New Guinea to Bali in *Yankee*. By Irving and Electa Johnson. 767-815, Dec. 1959
• New Guinea's Paradise of Birds. By E. Thomas Gilliard. 661-688, Nov. 1951
• New Guinea's Rare Birds and Stone Age Men. By E. Thomas Gilliard. NGS research grant. 421-488, Apr. 1953
• Off the Beaten Track of Empire (Prince Philip's Tour). By Beverley M. Bowie. Photos by Michael Parker. 584-626, Nov. 1957
• Papua New Guinea. 143-171, Aug. 1982
I. Nation in the Making. By Robert J. Gordon. Photos by David Austen. 143-149; II. Journey Through Time. By François Leydet. Photos by David Austen. 150-171.
• Sheep Airlift in New Guinea. Photos by Ned Blood. Contents: The Hallstrom Trust's Nondugl Sheep Station in Australian New Guinea. 831-844, Dec. 1949
• To the Land of the Head-hunters. By E. Thomas Gilliard. NGS research grant. 437-486, Oct. 1955
• Tropical Rain Forests: Nature's Dwindling Treasures. By Peter T. White. Photos by James P. Blair. Paintings by Barron Storey. 2-47, Jan. 1983
• *Yankee* Roams the Orient. By Irving and Electa Johnson. 327-370, Mar. 1951
• *See also* New Britain

AUSTRALOPITHECUS:
• Ethiopia Yields First "Family" of Early Man. By Donald C. Johanson. Photos by David Brill. 790-811, Dec. 1976
• In Search of Man's Past at Lake Rudolf. By Richard E. Leakey. Photos by Gordon W. Gahan. 712-734, May 1970

AUSTRIA:
• The Alps: Man's Own Mountains. By Ralph Gray. Photos by Walter Meayers Edwards and William Eppridge. 350-395, Sept. 1965
• Building a New Austria. By Beverley M. Bowie. Photos by Volkmar Wentzel. 172-213, Feb. 1959
• The Danube: River of Many Nations, Many Names. By Mike Edwards. Photos by Winfield Parks. 455-485, Oct. 1977
• Down the Danube by Canoe. By William Slade Backer. Photos by Richard S. Durrance and Christopher G. Knight. 34-79, July 1965
• Occupied Austria, Outpost of Democracy. By George W. Long. Photos by Volkmar Wentzel. 749-790, June 1951
• Salzkammergut, Austria's Alpine Playground. By Beverley M. Bowie. Photos by Volkmar Wentzel. 246-275, Aug. 1960
• A Stroll to Venice. By Isobel Wylie Hutchison. 378-410, Sept. 1951
▲ *Switzerland, Austria, and Northern Italy,* double-sided Atlas series supplement. Sept. 1965
• Tirol, Austria's Province in the Clouds. By Peter T. White. Photos by Volkmar Wentzel. 107-141, July 1961
• *See also* Vienna

AUTOMOBILE RACE:
• Rocks, Ruts, and Sand: Driving the Mexican 1000. By Michael E. Long. 569-575, Oct. 1972

AUTOMOBILES:
• Across Australia by Sunpower. By Hans Tholstrup and Larry Perkins. Photos by David Austen. 600-607, Nov. 1983
• America's Auto Mania. By David Jeffery. Photos by Bruce Dale. 24-31, *Special Report on Energy* (Feb. 1981)
• The Auto: Problem Child With a Promising Future. 32-33, *Special Report on Energy* (Feb. 1981)
• Editorial. By Wilbur E. Garrett. 1, July 1983
• Swing Low, Sweet Chariot! By Noel Grove. Photos by Bruce Dale. 2-35, July 1983

AUTOMOTIVE INDUSTRY:
• Swing Low, Sweet Chariot! By Noel Grove. Photos by Bruce Dale. 2-35, July 1983

AUTUMN:
• Autumn Flames Along the Allagash. By François Leydet. Photos by Farrell Grehan. 177-187, Feb. 1974
• Autumn–Season of the Smokies. By Gordon Young. 142-147, July 1979
◆ *What Happens in the Autumn.* 1982

AUVERGNE (Region), France:
• Lafayette's Homeland, Auvergne. By Howell Walker. 419-436, Sept. 1957

AUYÁN-TEPUÍ (Devil Mountain), Venezuela:
• Jungle Journey to the World's Highest Waterfall. By Ruth Robertson. 655-690, Nov. 1949

AVALANCHES:
• Avalanche! By David Cupp. 280-305, Sept. 1982
I. Winter's White Death. 280-281; II. "I'm OK, I'm Alive!" Photos by Lanny Johnson and Andre Benier. 282-289; III. Battling the Juggernaut. 290-305
• Avalanche! (Peru). By Bart McDowell. Photos by John E. Fletcher. 855-880, June 1962
• *See also* Mudslides

AVIATION:
• The Air-Safety Challenge. By Michael E. Long. Photos by Bruce Dale. 209-235, Aug. 1977
• Alexander Graham Bell Museum: Tribute to Genius. By Jean Lesage. 227-256, Aug. 1956
• Aviation Looks Ahead on Its 50th Birthday. By Emory S. Land. 721-739, Dec. 1953
• The Bird Men (Ultralight Fliers). By Luis Marden. Photos by Charles O'Rear. 198-217, Aug. 1983
• Charting Our Sea and Air Lanes (U. S. Coast and Geodetic Survey). By Stuart E. Jones. Photos by J. Baylor Roberts. 189-209, Feb. 1957
• *Columbia*'s Astronauts' Own Story: Our Phenomenal First Flight. By John W. Young and Robert L. Crippen. Paintings by Ken Dallison. 478-503, Oct. 1981
• *Columbia*'s Landing Closes a Circle. By Tom Wolfe. 474-477, Oct. 1981
• The Coming Revolution in Transportation. By Fredric C. Appel. Photos by Dean Conger. 301-341, Sept. 1969
• Fact Finding for Tomorrow's Planes. By Hugh L. Dryden. Photos by Luis Marden. 757-780, Dec. 1953
• Fifty Years of Flight. 740-756, Dec. 1953
• First Flight Across the Bottom of the World. By James R. Reedy. Photos by Otis Imboden. 454-464, Mar. 1964
• Flying in the "Blowtorch" Era. By Frederick G. Vosburgh. 281-322, Sept. 1950
• The Gooney Birds of Midway. By John W. Aldrich. 839-851, June 1964
• Happy Birthday, Otto Lilienthal! By Russell Hawkes. Photos by James Collison. 286-292, Feb. 1972
• I Fly the X-15. By Joseph A. Walker. Photos by Dean Conger. 428-450, Sept. 1962
• MATS: America's Long Arm of the Air. By Beverley M. Bowie. Photos by Robert F. Sisson. 283-317, Mar. 1957
• National Geographic Society Honors Air Pioneer Juan Trippe. 584-586, Apr. 1968
• Of Air and Space (National Air and Space Museum). By Michael Collins. 819-837, June 1978
Picture portfolio by Nathan Benn,

Robert S. Oakes, and Joseph D. Lavenburg, with text by Michael E. Long. 825-837
• Of Planes and Men. By Kenneth F. Weaver. Photos by Emory Kristof and Albert Moldvay. 298-349, Sept. 1965
• Our Air Age Speeds Ahead. By F. Barrows Colton. 249-272, Feb. 1948
• Sailors in the Sky: Fifty Years of Naval Aviation. By Patrick N. L. Bellinger. 276-296, Aug. 1961
• Sailors of the Sky. By Gordon Young. Photos by Emory Kristof and Jack Fields. Paintings by Davis Meltzer. 49-73, Jan. 1967
• Skyway Below the Clouds. By Carl R. Markwith. Photos by Ernest J. Cottrell. 85-108, July 1949
• They're Redesigning the Airplane. By Michael E. Long. Photos by James A. Sugar. 76-103, Jan. 1981
• When the Space Shuttle Finally Flies. By Rick Gore. Photos by Jon Schneeberger. Paintings by Ken Dallison. Contents: The space shuttle *Columbia* will be joined by *Challenger, Discovery,* and *Atlantis.* 317-347, Mar. 1981
• World War I Aircraft Fly Again in Rhinebeck's Rickety Rendezvous. By Harvey Arden. Photos by Howard Sochurek. 578-587, Oct. 1970
• You and the Obedient Atom. By Allan C. Fisher, Jr. Photos by B. Anthony Stewart and Thomas J. Abercrombie. Included: Nuclear aircraft. 303-353, Sept. 1958
• *See also* Aircraft; Aircraft Carriers; Balloons; Civil Air Patrol; Helicopters; Parachute Jumps; Parachute Rigger School; Recreational Aircraft; Space Shuttles; U. S. Air Force

AVIATION MEDICINE:
• Aviation Medicine on the Threshold of Space. By Allan C. Fisher, Jr. Photos by Luis Marden. 241-278, Aug. 1955
• Our Air Age Speeds Ahead. By F. Barrows Colton. 249-272, Feb. 1948
• *See also* Military Air Transport Service; Space Medicine; *Strato-Lab*

AWESOME Views of the Forbidding Moonscape. 233-239, Feb. 1969

The **AWESOME** Worlds Within a Cell. By Rick Gore. Photos by Bruce Dale. Paintings by Davis Meltzer. 355-395, Sept. 1976

AYMARÁ INDIANS:
• At Home in the High Andes. By Harry Tschopik, Jr. 133-146, Jan. 1955
• Flamboyant Is the Word for Bolivia. By Loren McIntyre. 153-195, Feb. 1966
• The Lost Empire of the Incas. By Loren McIntyre. Art by Ned and Rosalie Seidler. 729-787, Dec. 1973
• Puya, the Pineapple's Andean Ancestor. By Mulford B. Foster. 463-480, Oct. 1950
• Titicaca, Abode of the Sun. By Luis Marden. Photos by Flip Schulke. 272-294, Feb. 1971

AZALEAS:
• Nautical Norfolk Turns to Azaleas. By William H. Nicholas. Photos by B. Anthony Stewart. 606-614, May 1947

AZORES (Islands), Atlantic Ocean:
• The Azores, Nine Islands in Search of a Future. By Don Moser. Photos by O. Louis Mazzatenta. 261-288, Feb. 1976
• New Discoveries on the Mid-Atlantic Ridge. By Maurice Ewing. Photos by Robert F. Sisson. 611-640, Nov. 1949
• A New Volcano Bursts from the Atlantic. By John Scofield. Photos by Robert F. Sisson. 735-757, June 1958
• To Europe with a Racing Start. By Carleton Mitchell. 758-791, June 1958

AZTECS:
▲ *Archeological Map of Middle America, Land of the Feathered Serpent,* supplement. Text on reverse. Oct. 1968
• The Aztecs. 704-775, Dec. 1980
I. The Aztecs. By Bart McDowell. Photos by David Hiser. Paintings by Felipe Dávalos. 714-751; II. The Building of Tenochtitlan. By Augusto F. Molina Montes. Paintings by Felipe Dávalos. 753-765; III. New Finds in the Great Temple. By Eduardo Matos Moctezuma. Photos by David Hiser. 767-775
• Mexico, the City That Founded a Nation. By Louis de la Haba. Photos by Albert Moldvay. 638-669, May 1973
• Mexico's Booming Capital. By Mason Sutherland. Photos by Justin Locke. 785-824, Dec. 1951
• Mexico's Window on the Past (National Museum). By Bart McDowell. Photos by B. Anthony Stewart. 492-519, Oct. 1968
◆ *The Mighty Aztecs.* 1981
• "Pyramids" of the New World. By Neil Merton Judd. 105-128, Jan. 1948
▲ *Visitor's Guide to the Aztec World; Mexico and Central America,* double-sided supplement. Dec. 1980

AZZI, ROBERT: Author-Photographer:
• Damascus, Syria's Uneasy Eden. 512-535, Apr. 1974
• Oman, Land of Frankincense and Oil. 205-229, Feb. 1973
• Saudi Arabia: The Kingdom and Its Power. 286-333, Sept. 1980

B

B-36 (Jet Bomber):
• Flying in the "Blowtorch" Era. By Frederick G. Vosburgh. 281-322, Sept. 1950

B-50. *See* Superfortresses

BAALBEK, Lebanon:
• Journey Into the Great Rift: the Northern Half. By Helen and Frank Schreider. 254-290, Aug. 1965
• Young-old Lebanon Lives by Trade. By Thomas J. Abercrombie. 479-523, Apr. 1958

BABB, LAURA LONGLEY: Author:
• Iowa's Enduring Amana Colonies. Photos by Steve Raymer. 863-878, Dec. 1975

BABBLERS (Birds). *See* Spiny Babbler

BABCOCK, RICHARD F.: Author:
• Five Noted Thinkers Explore the Future. 70-71, July 1976

BABOONS:
• Life with the "Pumphouse Gang": New Insights Into Baboon Behavior. By Shirley C. Strum. Photos by Timothy W. Ransom. 672-691, May 1975

BABYLON (Ancient City):
• Ancient Mesopotamia: A Light That Did Not Fail. By E. A. Speiser. Paintings by H. M. Herget. 41-105, Jan. 1951

BACK to the Historic Black Hills. By Leland D. Case. Photos by Bates Littlehales. 479-509, Oct. 1956

BACK-YARD Monsters in Color. By Paul A. Zahl. 235-260, Aug. 1952

BACKER, OLE FRIELE:
Author-Photographer:
• Seal Hunting Off Jan Mayen. 57-72, Jan. 1948
Photographer:
• Norway Cracks Her Mountain Shell. By Sydney Clark. Photos by Gilbert Grosvenor and Ole Friele Backer. 171-211, Aug. 1948

BACKER, WILLIAM SLADE: Author:
• Down the Danube by Canoe. Photos by Richard S. Durrance and Christopher G. Knight. 34-79, July 1965

BACKPACKING. *See* Hiking Trips

BACKWOODS Japan During American Occupation. By M. A. Huberman. 491-518, Apr. 1947

BACON, EDMUND N.: Author:
• Five Noted Thinkers Explore the Future. 74, July 1976

BACTERIA:
• The Wild World of Compost. By Cecil E. Johnson. Photos by Bianca Lavies. Included: Actinomycetes; Aerobic bacteria. 273-284, Aug. 1980

BAD Days for the Brown Pelican. By Ralph W. Schreiber. Photos by William R. Curtsinger and author. 111-123, Jan. 1975

A **BAD** Time to Be a Crocodile. By Rick Gore. Photos by Jonathan Blair. 90-115, Jan. 1978

BADDECK, Nova Scotia, Canada:
• Canada's Winged Victory: the *Silver Dart.* By Gilbert M. Grosvenor. 254-267, Aug. 1959
• Down East to Nova Scotia. By Winfield Parks. 853-879, June 1964
• Miracle Men of the Telephone. By F. Barrows Colton. Included: Photographs of Dr. Alexander Graham Bell and members of his family at their home in Baddeck. 273-316, Mar. 1947
• *See also* Bell Museum

BADEN-WÜRTTEMBERG (State), West Germany:
● Treasure From a Celtic Tomb. By Jörg Biel. Photos by Volkmar Wentzel. 428-438, Mar. 1980

BADLANDS, North and South Dakota:
● Big Game Hunting (Paleontology) in the Land of Long Ago. By Joseph P. Connolly and James D. Bump. NGS research grant. 589-605, May 1947
● North Dakota Comes into Its Own. By Leo A. Borah. Photos by J. Baylor Roberts. 283-322, Sept. 1951
● South Dakota Keeps Its West Wild. By Frederick Simpich. 555-588, May 1947
● South Dakota's Badlands: Castles in Clay. By John Madson. Photos by Jim Brandenburg. 524-539, Apr. 1981
● The West Through Boston Eyes. By Stewart Anderson. 733-776, June 1949

BAEKELAND, G. BROOKS:
Author-Photographer:
● By Parachute Into Peru's Lost World. Photos by author and Peter R. Gimbel. 268-296, Aug. 1964

BAFFIN ISLAND, Northwest Territories, Canada:
● Far North with "Captain Mac." By Miriam MacMillan. Included: Brevoort Island; Pond Inlet. 465-513, Oct. 1951
● I Live With the Eskimos. By Guy Mary-Rousseliere. 188-217, Feb. 1971
● Milestones in My Arctic Journeys. By Willie Knutsen. Included: Airfield at Frobisher Bay and the activities of the Arctic Search and Rescue section of the Air Force. 543-570, Oct. 1949

BAGANDA (Tribe):
● Return to Uganda. By Jerry and Sarah Kambites. Photos by Sarah Leen. 73-89, July 1980

BAGGARA (People):
● With the Nuba Hillmen of Kordofan. By Robin Strachan. 249-278, Feb. 1951

BAGHDAD, Iraq:
● "Around the World in Eighty Days." By Newman Bumstead. 705-750, Dec. 1951
● Iraq–Where Oil and Water Mix. By Jean and Franc Shor. 443-489, Oct. 1958
● Station Wagon Odyssey: Baghdad to Istanbul. By William O. Douglas. 48-87, Jan. 1959

BAHAMA ISLANDS, Atlantic Ocean:
● The Bahamas: Boom Times and Buccaneering. By Peter Benchley. Photos by Bruce Dale. 364-395, Sept. 1982
● The Bahamas, Isles of the Blue-green Sea. By Carleton Mitchell. Photos by B. Anthony Stewart. 147-203, Feb. 1958
● Blue-water Plankton: Ghosts of the Gulf Stream. By William M. Hamner. NGS research grant. 530-545, Oct. 1974

GUY MARY-ROUSSELIERE

With the Eskimos: Pelly Bay families

● Cape Canaveral's 6,000-mile Shooting Gallery. By Allan C. Fisher, Jr. Photos by Luis Marden and Thomas Nebbia. 421-471, Oct. 1959
● More of Sea Than of Land: The Bahamas. By Carleton Mitchell. Photos by James L. Stanfield. 218-267, Feb. 1967
● *See also* Abaco; Andros Island; Bimini Islands; Great Bahama Bank; Great Inagua; Nassau

BAHRAIN:
● Bahrain: Hub of the Persian Gulf. By Thomas J. Abercrombie. Photos by Steve Raymer. 300-329, Sept. 1979
● In Search of Arabia's Past. By Peter Bruce Cornwall. 493-522, Apr. 1948
● Troubled Waters East of Suez. By Ernest M. Eller. 483-522, Apr. 1954

BAILEY, ALFRED M.:
Author-Photographer:
● Desert River Through Navajo Land. Photos by author and Fred G. Brandenburg. 149-172, Aug. 1947

BAJA CALIFORNIA (Peninsula), Mexico:
● Baja California's Rugged Outback. By Michael E. Long. 543-567, Oct. 1972
● Baja's Murals of Mystery. By Harry Crosby. Photos by Charles O'Rear. 692-702, Nov. 1980
● Hunting the Heartbeat of a Whale. By Paul Dudley White and Samuel W. Matthews. 49-64, July 1956
● Rocks, Ruts, and Sand: Driving the Mexican 1000. By Michael E. Long. 569-575, Oct. 1972
● *See also* Raza, Isla; Scammon Lagoon

BAJAUS (People):
● Sea Gypsies of the Philippines. By Anne de Henning Singh. Photos by Raghubir Singh. 659-677, May 1976

BAKER, BETTY HAYNES: Artist:
● Flags of the Americas. By Elizabeth W. King. 633-657, May 1949
● Flags of the United Nations. By Elizabeth W. King. 213-238, Feb. 1951

BAKER, JOHN H.: Author:
● Saving Man's Wildlife Heritage. Photos by Robert F. Sisson. 581-620, Nov. 1954

BAKHTIARI (Tribespeople):
● I Become a Bakhtiari. By Paul Edward Case. 325-358, Mar. 1947

BALD EAGLES, American:
● Editorial. By Wilbur E. Garrett. 695, June 1982
● Eye to Eye With Eagles. By Frederick Kent Truslow. 123-148, Jan. 1961
● Our Bald Eagle: Freedom's Symbol Survives. By Thomas C. Dunstan. Photos by Jeff Foott. NGS research grant. 186-199, Feb. 1978

BALEARIC ISLANDS, Mediterranean Sea:
● The Balearics Are Booming. By Jean and Franc Shor. 621-660, May 1957

• Spain's Sun-blest Pleasure Isles. By Ethel A. Starbird. Photos by James A. Sugar. 679-701, May 1976

BALI (Island), Indonesia:
• Bali by the Back Roads. By Donna K. and Gilbert M. Grosvenor. 657-697, Nov. 1969
• Bali Celebrates a Festival of Faith. By Peter Miller. Photos by Fred and Margaret Eiseman. 416-427, Mar. 1980
• Bali's Sacred Mountain Blows Its Top. Photos by Robert F. Sisson. 436-458, Sept. 1963
I. Disaster in Paradise. By Windsor P. Booth. 436-447; II. Devastated Land and Homeless People. By Samuel W. Matthews. 447-458
• Indonesia, the Young and Troubled Island Nation. By Helen and Frank Schreider. 579-625, May 1961
• New Guinea to Bali in *Yankee*. By Irving and Electa Johnson. 767-815, Dec. 1959
• Republican Indonesia Tries Its Wings. By W. Robert Moore. 1-40, Jan. 1951
• This Young Giant, Indonesia. By Beverley M. Bowie. Photos by J. Baylor Roberts. 351-392, Sept. 1955
• *Yankee* Roams the Orient. By Irving and Electa Johnson. 327-370, Mar. 1951

The **BALKANS:**
▲ *The Balkans,* Atlas series supplement. Feb. 1962
▲ *Central Europe, including the Balkan States,* supplement. Sept. 1951
• *See also* Albania; Bulgaria; Greece; Romania; Yugoslavia

BALLARD, ROBERT D.: Author:
• Dive Into the Great Rift (Project FAMOUS). Photos by Emory Kristof. 604-615, May 1975
• Incredible World of the Deep-sea Rifts. 680-705, Nov. 1979
I. Strange World Without Sun. The Editor. 680-688; II. Return to Oases of the Deep. By Robert D. Ballard and J. Frederick Grassle. 689-705
• Oases of Life in the Cold Abyss (Galapagos Rift). By John B. Corliss and Robert D. Ballard. 441-453, Oct. 1977
• Window on Earth's Interior. Photos by Emory Kristof. 228-249, Aug. 1976

BALLERINAS in Pink. By Carleton Mitchell. Photos by B. Anthony Stewart. 553-571, Oct. 1957

BALLOON RACES:
• A Wild, Ill-fated Balloon Race. 778-797, Dec. 1983
I. Wild Launch. 778-787; II. The Fantastic Flight of *Cote d'Or*. By Cynthia Shields. 789-793; III. Last Ascent of a Heroic Team (Maxie Anderson and Don Ida). 794-797

BALLOONS:
• Across the Alps in a Wicker Basket *(Bernina)*. By Phil Walker. 117-131, Jan. 1963
• Braving the Atlantic by Balloon *(Small World)*. By Arnold Eiloart. 123-146, July 1959

ALAIN DEJEAN, SYGMA

MARC BULKA, SIPA PRESS/BLACK STAR

Double Eagle II:* balloon over England, *top*; crew celebrates, *above

• *Double Eagle II* Has Landed! Crossing the Atlantic by Balloon. By Ben L. Abruzzo, with Maxie L. Anderson and Larry Newman. 858-882, Dec. 1978
• First Across the Pacific: The Flight of *Double Eagle V*. By Ben L. Abruzzo. 513-521, Apr. 1982
• Hot-air Balloons Race on Silent Winds. By William R. Berry. Photos by Don W. Jones. 392-407, Mar. 1966
• *Kitty Hawk* Floats Across North America. By Maxie and Kristian Anderson. 260-271, Aug. 1980
• Laboratory in a Dirty Sky. By Rudolf J. Engelmann and Vera Simons. Contents: Project Da Vinci's manned research balloon. NGS research grant. 616-621, Nov. 1976
• The Long, Lonely Leap. By Joseph W. Kittinger, Jr. Photos by Volkmar Wentzel. 854-873, Dec. 1960
• The Longest Manned Balloon Flight *(Silver Fox)*. By Ed Yost. 208-217, Feb. 1977
• Rockets Explore the Air Above Us. By Newman Bumstead. 562-580, Apr. 1957
• To 76,000 Feet by *Strato-Lab* Balloon. By Malcolm D. Ross and M. Lee Lewis. 269-282, Feb. 1957
• Trailing Cosmic Rays in Canada's North. By Martin A. Pomerantz. NGS research grant. 99-115, Jan. 1953
• We Saw the World From the Edge of Space. By Malcolm D. Ross. Photos by Walter Meayers Edwards. 671-685, Nov. 1961
• A Wild, Ill-fated Balloon Race. 778-797, Dec. 1983
I. Wild Launch. 778-787; II. The Fantastic Flight of *Cote d'Or*. By Cynthia Shields. 789-793; III. Last Ascent of a Heroic Team (Maxie Anderson and Don Ida). 794-797

BALTIC SEA REGION, Europe:
• Amber: Golden Window on the Past. Photos by Paul A. Zahl. Text by Thomas J. O'Neill. 423-435, Sept. 1977
• Baltic Cruise of the *Caribbee*. By Carleton Mitchell. 605-646, Nov. 1950

BALTIC STATES. *See* Estonian S.S.R., U.S.S.R.

BALTIMORE, Maryland:
• Baltimore: The Hidden City. By Fred Kline. Photos by Martin Rogers. 188-215, Feb. 1975
• Chesapeake Country. By Nathaniel T. Kenney. Photos by Bates Littlehales. 370-411, Sept. 1964
• Maryland on the Half Shell. By Stuart E. Jones. Photos by Robert W. Madden. 188-229, Feb. 1972
• Spices, the Essence of Geography. By Stuart E. Jones. Included: McCormick and Company. 401-420, Mar. 1949
• *See also* Sherwood Gardens; Sparrows Point

BALTISTAN (Region), Kashmir:
• Trek to Lofty Hunza–and Beyond. By Sabrina and Roland Michaud. 644-669, Nov. 1975

BALUCHISTAN:
● Pakistan, New Nation in an Old Land. By Jean and Franc Shor. 637-678, Nov. 1952

BAMBOO:
● Bamboo, the Giant Grass. By Luis Marden. Photos by Jim Brandenburg. 502-529, Oct. 1980

BANARAS, India:
● The Ganges, River of Faith. By John J. Putman. Photos by Raghubir Singh. 445-483, Oct. 1971

BAND, GEORGE: Photographer:
● Triumph on Everest. 1-63, July 1954
I. Siege and Assault. By Sir John Hunt. 1-43; II. The Conquest of the Summit. By Sir Edmund Hillary. 45-63

BANDELIER NATIONAL MONUMENT, New Mexico:
● Adobe New Mexico. By Mason Sutherland. Photos by Justin Locke. 783-830, Dec. 1949

BANDING, Bird:
● Tireless Voyager, the Whistling Swan. By William J. L. Sladen. Photos by Bianca Lavies. NGS research grant. 134-147, July 1975

BANFF NATIONAL PARK, Alberta, Canada:
● Canadian Rockies, Lords of a Beckoning Land. By Alan Phillips. Photos by James L. Stanfield. 353-393, Sept. 1966
● Heart of the Canadian Rockies. By Elizabeth A. Moize. Photos by Jim Brandenburg. 757-779, June 1980
● Hiking the Backbone of the Rockies: Canada's Great Divide Trail. By Mike W. Edwards. Photos by Lowell Georgia. 795-817, June 1973
● On the Ridgepole of the Rockies. By Walter Meayers Edwards. 745-780, June 1947

BANGKOK, Thailand:
● "Around the World in Eighty Days." By Newman Bumstead. 705-750, Dec. 1951
● Bangkok, City of Angels. By William Graves. Photos by John Launois. 96-129, July 1973
● Hopes and Fears in Booming Thailand. By Peter T. White. Photos by Dean Conger. 76-125, July 1967
● Operation Eclipse: 1948. By William A. Kinney. NGS research grant. 325-372, Mar. 1949
● Scintillating Siam. By W. Robert Moore. 173-200, Feb. 1947
● Thailand: Luck of a Land in the Middle. By Bart McDowell. Photos by Steve Raymer. 500-535, Oct. 1982
● Thailand Bolsters Its Freedom. By W. Robert Moore. 811-849, June 1961
● Thailand's Working Royalty. Photos by John Everingham. 486-499, Oct. 1982
● *Yankee* Roams the Orient. By Irving and Electa Johnson. 327-370, Mar. 1951

BANGLADESH, People's Republic of:
● Bangladesh: Hope Nourishes a New Nation. By William S. Ellis. Photos by Dick Durrance II. 295-333, Sept. 1972
● Bangladesh: The Nightmare of Famine. Photos by Steve Raymer. 33-39, July 1975
● The Peaceful Mrus of Bangladesh. By Claus-Dieter Brauns. 267-286, Feb. 1973
● *See also* former name, East Pakistan

BANKS ISLAND, Northwest Territories, Canada:
● Banks Island: Eskimo Life on the Polar Sea. By William O. Douglas. Photos by Clyde Hare. 703-735, May 1964

BANTU (Tribespeople):
● My Life With Africa's Little People. By Anne Eisner Putnam. 278-302, Feb. 1960

BARBADOS (Island), Lesser Antilles:
● Barbados, Outrider of the Antilles. By Charles Allmon. 363-392, Mar. 1952
● Robin Sails Home. By Robin Lee Graham. 504-545, Oct. 1970

BARBEY, BRUNO: Photographer:
● After an Empire...Portugal. By William Graves. 804-831, Dec. 1980
▲ *The Face and Faith of Poland,* map, photo and essay supplement. By Peter Miller. Essay by Czesław Miłosz. Apr. 1982
● Fátima: Beacon for Portugal's Faithful. By Jane Vessels. 832-839, Dec. 1980
● Nigeria Struggles With Boom Times. By Noel Grove. 413-444, Mar. 1979

BARCELONA ZOO, Barcelona, Spain:
● Growing Up With Snowflake (White Gorilla). By Arthur J. Riopelle. Photos by Michael Kuh. NGS research grant. 491-503, Oct. 1970

BAREHANDED Battle to Cleanse the Bay. By Peter T. White. Photos by Jonathan S. Blair. 866-881, June 1971

BARGES:
● The Civilizing Seine. By Charles McCarry. Photos by David L. Arnold. 478-511, Apr. 1982
● The Danube: River of Many Nations, Many Names. By Mike Edwards. Photos by Winfield Parks. 455-485, Oct. 1977
● Inside Europe Aboard *Yankee*. By Irving and Electa Johnson. Photos by Joseph J. Scherschel. 157-195, Aug. 1964
● Paris to Antwerp with the Water Gypsies. By David S. Boyer. 530-559, Oct. 1955
● St. Louis: New Spirit Soars in Mid-America's Proud Old City. By Robert Paul Jordan. Photos by Bruce Dale. Included: Mississippi River barge traffic. 605-641, Nov. 1965
● That Dammed Missouri River. By Gordon Young. Photos by David Hiser. 374-413, Sept. 1971
● *See also* Intracoastal Waterways; Ohio (River); Rhine (River)

BARK (Ship). *See Breadalbane*

BARNACLES:
● Friendless Squatters of the Sea. By Ethel A. Starbird. Photos by Robert F. Sisson. 623-633, Nov. 1973

BARNUM & BAILEY CIRCUS. *See* Ringling Bros. and Barnum & Bailey Circus

BARRA (Island), Scotland:
● From Barra to Butt in the Hebrides. By Isobel Wylie Hutchison. 559-580, Oct. 1954
● Hunting Folk Songs in the Hebrides. By Margaret Shaw Campbell. 249-272, Feb. 1947
● Isles on the Edge of the Sea: Scotland's Outer Hebrides. By Kenneth MacLeish. Photos by Thomas Nebbia. 676-711, May 1970
The Thrush on the Island of Barra. By Archibald MacLeish. 692-693
● Scotland From Her Lovely Lochs and Seas. By Alan Villiers. Photos by Robert F. Sisson. 492-541, Apr. 1961

BARRO COLORADO ISLAND, Panama:
● The Amazing Frog-Eating Bat. By Merlin D. Tuttle. NGS research grant. 78-91, Jan. 1982

BARROW, Alaska:
● Peoples of the Arctic. 144-223, Feb. 1983
I. Introduction by Joseph Judge. 144-149; II. Hunters of the Lost Spirit: Alaskans. By Priit J. Vesilind. Photos by David Alan Harvey. 150-173
● Will Oil and Tundra Mix? Alaska's North Slope Hangs in the Balance. By William S. Ellis. Photos by Emory Kristof. 485-517, Oct. 1971

BARTKO, BOHDAN:
● Precious Corals, Hawaii's Deep-sea Jewels. By Richard W. Grigg. Photos by David Doubilet. 719-732, May 1979

BARTLETT, DES:
Author-Photographer:
● Beavers, Nature's Aquatic Engineers. By Des and Jen Bartlett. 716-732, May 1974
● Beyond the North Wind With the Snow Goose. By Des and Jen Bartlett. 822-843, Dec. 1973
. . . And Then There was Fred. . . . 843-847
● Family Life of Lions. By Des and Jen Bartlett. 800-819, Dec. 1982
Photographer:
● Etosha: Namibia's Kingdom of Animals. By Douglas H. Chadwick. 344-385, Mar. 1983
● Finding the World's Earliest Man. By L.S.B. Leakey. 420-435, Sept. 1960
● Patagonia. 290-339, Mar. 1976
I. Argentina Protects Its Wildlife Treasures. By William G. Conway. 290-297; II. Where Two Worlds Meet. 298-321; III. At Home With Right Whales. By Roger Payne. 322-339
● Penguins and Their Neighbors. By Roger Tory Peterson. 237-255, Aug. 1977

• Those Kangaroos! They're a Marvelous Mob. By Geoffrey B. Sharman. 192-209, Feb. 1979

BARTLETT, JEN:
Author-Photographer:
• Beavers, Nature's Aquatic Engineers. By Des and Jen Bartlett. 716-732, May 1974
• Beyond the North Wind With the Snow Goose. By Des and Jen Bartlett. 822-843, Dec. 1973
. . . And Then There was Fred. . . . 843-847
• Family Life of Lions. By Des and Jen Bartlett. 800-819, Dec. 1982
Photographer:
• Etosha: Namibia's Kingdom of Animals. By Douglas H. Chadwick. 344-385, Mar. 1983
• Patagonia. 290-339, Mar. 1976
I. Argentina Protects Its Wildlife Treasures. By William G. Conway. 290-297; II. Where Two Worlds Meet. 298-321; III. At Home With Right Whales. By Roger Payne. 322-339
• Penguins and Their Neighbors. By Roger Tory Peterson. 237-255, Aug. 1977
• Those Kangaroos! They're a Marvelous Mob. By Geoffrey B. Sharman. 192-209, Feb. 1979

BARTLETT, LINDA: Photographer:
• Benjamin Franklin, Philosopher of Dissent. By Alice J. Hall. 93-123, July 1975
• Exploring England's Canals. By Bryan Hodgson. 76-111, July 1974
• Irish Ways Live On in Dingle. By Bryan Hodgson. 551-576, Apr. 1976
• Montenegro: Yugoslavia's "Black Mountain." By Bryan Hodgson. 663-683, Nov. 1977
• Mountain Voices, Mountain Days (West Virginia). By Bryan Hodgson. 118-146, July 1972
• Thomas Jefferson: Architect of Freedom. By Mike W. Edwards. 231-259, Feb. 1976

BARTLETT, ROBERT A.:
• Newfoundland, Canada's New Province. By Andrew H. Brown. Photos by author and Robert F. Sisson. 777-812, June 1949

BARTON, CLARA:
• The American Red Cross: A Century of Service. By Louise Levathes. Photos by Annie Griffiths. 777-791, June 1981

BARUNTSE (Peak), Himalayas:
• Beyond Everest. By Sir Edmund Hillary. 579-610, Nov. 1955

BASEL, Switzerland:
• The Rhine: Europe's River of Legend. By William Graves. Photos by Bruce Dale. 449-499, Apr. 1967

BASILIQUE DE LA SAINTE MARIE MADELEINE, Vézelay, France:
• Vézelay, Hill of the Pilgrims. By Melvin Hall. 229-247, Feb. 1953

BASIN REGION, Utah-Nevada. *See* Great Basin

BASKET MAKERS (Indians):
• Ancient Cliff Dwellers of Mesa Verde. By Don Watson. Photos by Willard R. Culver. 349-376, Sept. 1948
• 20th-century Indians Preserve Customs of the Cliff Dwellers. Photos by William Belknap, Jr. NGS research grant. 196-211, Feb. 1964

BASQUES:
• The Enduring Pyrenees. By Robert Laxalt. Photos by Edwin Stuart Grosvenor. 794-819, Dec. 1974
• Land of the Ancient Basques. By Robert Laxalt. Photos by William Albert Allard. 240-277, Aug. 1968
• Life in the Land of the Basques. By John E. H. Nolan. Photos by Justin Locke. 147-186, Feb. 1954
• Lonely Sentinels of the American West: Basque Sheepherders. By Robert Laxalt. Photos by William Belknap, Jr. 870-888, June 1966
• Pigeon Netting–Sport of Basques. Photos by Irene Burdette-Scougall. 405-416, Sept. 1949

BASS, GEORGE F.: Author:
• Glass Treasure From the Aegean. Photos by Jonathan Blair. 768-793, June 1978
• New Tools for Undersea Archeology. Photos by Charles R. Nicklin, Jr. 403-423, Sept. 1968
• Underwater Archeology: Key to History's Warehouse. Photos by Thomas J. Abercrombie and Robert B. Goodman. 138-156, July 1963

BASS ISLANDS, Ohio:
• Yesterday Lingers on Lake Erie's Bass Islands. By Terry and Lyntha Eiler. 86-101, July 1978

BASTAR (Region), India:
• New Life for India's Villagers. By Anthony and Georgette Dickey Chapelle. 572-588, Apr. 1956

BASTOGNE, Belgium:
• Belgium Comes Back. By Harvey Klemmer. Photos by Maynard Owen Williams. 575-614, May 1948

BATAVIA, Java. *See* Djakarta

BATES, MARSTON:
Author-Photographer:
• Ifalik, Lonely Paradise of the South Seas. 547-571, Apr. 1956
Photographer:
• Keeping House for a Biologist in Colombia. By Nancy Bell Fairchild Bates. 251-274, Aug. 1948

BATES, NANCY BELL FAIRCHILD:
Author:
• Keeping House for a Biologist in Colombia. Photos by Marston Bates. 251-274, Aug. 1948

BATHYSCAPHS:
• Deep Diving off Japan. By Georges S. Houot. NGS research grant. 138-150, Jan. 1960
• Diving Through an Undersea Avalanche. By Jacques-Yves Cousteau. NGS research grant. 538-542, Apr. 1955
• Down to *Thresher* by Bathyscaph. By Donald L. Keach. 764-777, June 1964
• Four Years of Diving to the Bottom of the Sea. By Georges S. Houot. NGS research grant. 715-731, May 1958
• Man's Deepest Dive *(Trieste).* By Jacques Piccard. Photos by Thomas J. Abercrombie. 224-239, Aug. 1960
• Photographing the Sea's Dark Underworld. By Harold E. Edgerton. NGS research grant. 523-537, Apr. 1955
• To the Depths of the Sea by Bathyscaphe. By Jacques-Yves Cousteau. NGS research grant. 67-79, July 1954
• Two and a Half Miles Down. By Georges S. Houot. NGS research grant. 80-86, July 1954
• *See also Archimède*

BATS:
• The Amazing Frog-Eating Bat. By Merlin D. Tuttle. NGS research grant. 78-91, Jan. 1982
• Bats Aren't All Bad. By Alvin Novick. Photos by Bruce Dale. 615-637, May 1973
• How Bats Hunt With Sound. By J. J. G. McCue. 571-578, Apr. 1961

BATTAGLIA, LEE E.:
Author-Photographer:
• Wedding of Two Worlds (Sikkim). 708-727, Nov. 1963
Photographer:
• History Revealed in Ancient Glass. By Ray Winfield Smith. Photos by B. Anthony Stewart and Lee E. Battaglia. 346-369, Sept. 1964
• Last Moments of the Pompeians. By Amedeo Maiuri. Paintings by Peter V. Bianchi. 651-669, Nov. 1961

BATTLE MONUMENTS. *See* War Memorials

BATTLE OF THE BULGE:
• Belgium Comes Back. By Harvey Klemmer. Photos by Maynard Owen Williams. 575-614, May 1948
• Luxembourg, Survivor of Invasions. By Sydney Clark. Photos by Maynard Owen Williams. 791-810, June 1948
• Luxembourg, the Quiet Fortress. By Robert Leslie Conly. Photos by Ted H. Funk. 69-97, July 1970

BATTLEFIELDS:
▲ *Battlefields of the Civil War,* double-sided Atlas series supplement. Apr. 1961
• Gettysburg and Vicksburg: the Battle Towns Today. By Robert Paul Jordan. Map notes by Carolyn Bennett Patterson. Included: Annotated maps charting course of battles. 4-57, July 1963
• *See also* names of battles and wars, *as:* American Revolution; Hastings, Battle of

BATTLESHIPS:
• Henry VIII's Lost Warship: *Mary Rose.* By Margaret Rule. Introduction and picture text by Peter Miller. Paintings by Richard Schlecht. 646-675, May 1983
• Midshipmen's Cruise. By William J. Aston and Alexander G. B. Grosvenor. Included: *New Jersey; Wisconsin.* 711-754, June 1948

BATTLING the Juggernaut: Avalanche! By David Cupp. 290-305, Sept. 1982

BAUMANN, J. BRUCE: Photographer:
- An Eye for an Eye: Pakistan's Wild Frontier. By Mike W. Edwards. 111-139, Jan. 1977
- Heart of the Bluegrass. By Charles McCarry. 634-659, May 1974
- Indiana's Self-reliant Uplanders. By James Alexander Thom. 341-363, Mar. 1976
- A Most Uncommon Town: Columbus, Indiana. By David Jeffery. 383-397, Sept. 1978
- The Other Nevada. By Robert Laxalt. 733-761, June 1974

BAUXITE:
- Aluminum, the Magic Metal. By Thomas Y. Canby. Photos by James L. Amos. 186-211, Aug. 1978

BAVARIA (State), West Germany:
- Bavaria: Mod, Medieval–and Bewitching. By Gary Jennings. Photos by George F. Mobley. 409-431, Mar. 1974
- *See also* Dinkelsbühl

"BAY OF FIRE." *See* Phosphorescent Bay

BAYEUX TAPESTRY:
- 900 Years Ago: the Norman Conquest. By Kenneth M. Setton. Photos by George F. Mobley. The complete Bayeux Tapestry photographed by Milton A. Ford and Victor R. Boswell, Jr. 206-251, Aug. 1966

BAYKAL, Lake, U.S.S.R.:
- Siberia: Russia's Frozen Frontier. By Dean Conger. 297-345, Mar. 1967

"BE Ye Men of Valour." By Howard La Fay. 159-197, Aug. 1965

BEACH, EDWARD L.: Author:
- *Triton* (Nuclear Submarine) Follows Magellan's Wake. Photos by J. Baylor Roberts. 585-615, Nov. 1960

BEAGLE, H.M.S.:
- In the Wake of Darwin's *Beagle*. By Alan Villiers. Photos by James L. Stanfield. 449-495, Oct. 1969

BEAN, ALAN L.:
- Skylab, Outpost on the Frontier of Space. By Thomas Y. Canby. Photos by the nine mission astronauts. 441-469, Oct. 1974

BEAR MOUNTAIN, New York:
- Skyline Trail (Appalachian Trail) from Maine to Georgia. By Andrew H. Brown. Photos by Robert F. Sisson. 219-251, Aug. 1949

BEAR RIVER MIGRATORY BIRD REFUGE, Utah:
- The Dauntless Little Stilt. By Frederick Kent Truslow. 241-245, Aug. 1960
- Island, Prairie, Marsh, and Shore. By Charlton Ogburn. Photos by Bates Littlehales. 350-381, Mar. 1979

BEARD, DANIEL B.: Author:
- Wildlife of Everglades National Park. Paintings by Walter A. Weber. 83-116, Jan. 1949

MILTON A. FORD AND VICTOR R. BOSWELL, JR., NGS, BY SPECIAL PERMISSION OF THE CITY OF BAYEUX

Bayeux Tapestry: Normans attack

BEARS. *See* Black Bears; Brown Bears; Grizzly Bears; Polar Bears

La **BEAUCE** (Plain), France:
- Chartres: Legacy from the Age of Faith. By Kenneth MacLeish. Photos by Dean Conger. 857-882, Dec. 1969

BEAUFORT SEA:
- Arctic Odyssey. By John Bockstoce. Photos by Jonathan Wright. Paintings by Jack Unruh. 100-127, July 1983

BEAUHARNAIS, JOSÉPHINE DE. *See* Joséphine, Empress (France)

BEAUTY and Bounty of Southern State Trees. By William A. Dayton. Paintings by Walter A. Weber. 508-552, Oct. 1957

BEAVERS:
- Arizona's Operation Beaver Lift. By Willis Peterson. 666-680, May 1955
- Beavers, Nature's Aquatic Engineers. By Des and Jen Bartlett. 716-732, May 1974
- The Romance of American Furs. By Wanda Burnett. 379-402, Mar. 1948

BECAUSE It Rains on Hawaii. By Frederick Simpich, Jr. 571-610, Nov. 1949

BECKER, JIM: Author:
- Look What's Happened to Honolulu! Photos by Bates Littlehales. 500-531, Oct. 1969

BECKET, THOMAS À:
- Canterbury Cathedral. By Kenneth MacLeish. Photos by Thomas Nebbia. 364-379, Mar. 1976

BECKWITH, CAROL:
Author-Photographer:
- Niger's Wodaabe: "People of the Taboo." 483-509, Oct. 1983

BEDI, NARESH: Photographer:
- The Cobra, India's "Good Snake." By Harry Miller. 393-409, Sept. 1970

BEDI, RAJESH: Photographer:
- The Cobra, India's "Good Snake." By Harry Miller. 393-409, Sept. 1970
- India Struggles to Save Her Wildlife. By John J. Putman. 299-343, Sept. 1976

BEDOUIN:
- Abraham, the Friend of God. By Kenneth MacLeish. Photos by Dean Conger. 739-789, Dec. 1966
- Arab Land Beyond the Jordan. Photos by Frank Hurley. 753-768, Dec. 1947
- Eternal Sinai. By Harvey Arden. Photos by David Doubilet and Kevin Fleming. 420-461, Apr. 1982
Egyptian Sector. Photos by Kevin Fleming. 430-443; Israeli Sector. Photos by David Doubilet. 444-461
- Holy Land, My Country. By His Majesty King Hussein of Jordan. 784-789, Dec. 1964
- In Search of Moses. By Harvey Arden. Photos by Nathan Benn. 2-37, Jan. 1976

Honeybee: queen and her guards

TREAT DAVIDSON

ROBERT F. SISSON, NGS

Ladybug: female deposits egg cluster

• Jerusalem, My Home. By Bertha Spafford Vester. 826-847, Dec. 1964
• Morocco, Land of the Farthest West. By Thomas J. Abercrombie. 834-865, June 1971
• The Other Side of Jordan. By Luis Marden. 790-825, Dec. 1964
• Report from the Locust Wars. By Tony and Dickey Chapelle. 545-562, Apr. 1953
• Saudi Arabia: Beyond the Sands of Mecca. By Thomas J. Abercrombie. 1-53, Jan. 1966
• The Sword and the Sermon (Islam). By Thomas J. Abercrombie. 3-45, July 1972

BEEBE, WILLIAM: Author:
• The High World of the Rain Forest. Paintings by Guy Neale. 838-855, June 1958

BEECHEY ISLAND, Canada:
• Exploring a 140-year-old Ship Under Arctic Ice *(Breadalbane).* By Joseph B. MacInnis. Photos by Emory Kristof. 104A-104D, July 1983

BEES:
• Crossroads of the Insect World. By J. W. MacSwain. Photos by Edward S. Ross. 844-857, Dec. 1966
◆ *Honeybees.* 1973
• Inside the World of the Honeybee. By Treat Davidson. 188-217, Aug. 1959
• Those Fiery Brazilian Bees. By Rick Gore. Photos by Bianca Lavies. 491-501, Apr. 1976

BEETLES:
• Following the Ladybug Home. By Kenneth S. Hagen. Photos by Robert F. Sisson. 543-553, Apr. 1970
• Larvae. *See* Glowworms; Railroad Worms
• The Living Sands of the Namib. By William J. Hamilton III. Photos by Carol and David Hughes. Included: Water-using strategies of desert beetles. 364-377, Sept. 1983
• *See also* Fireflies

BEHIND New York's Window on Nature: The American Museum of Natural History. By James A. Oliver. Photos by Robert F. Sisson. 220-259, Feb. 1963

BEHIND the Headlines: The Panama Canal Today. By Bart McDowell. Photos by George F. Mobley. 279-294, Feb. 1978

BEHIND the Headlines in Viet Nam. By Peter T. White. Photos by Winfield Parks. 149-189, Feb. 1967

BEHIND the Veil of Troubled Yemen. By Thomas J. Abercrombie. 403-445, Mar. 1964

BEHOLD the Computer Revolution. By Peter T. White. Photos by Bruce Dale and Emory Kristof. 593-633, Nov. 1970

BEIJING, China. *See* former spelling, Peking

BEINN BHREAGH, Cape Breton Island, Nova Scotia:
• Down East to Nova Scotia. By Winfield Parks. 853-879, June 1964

BEIRUT, Lebanon:
• Beirut–Up From the Rubble. By William S. Ellis. Photos by Steve McCurry. 262-286, Feb. 1983
• Editorial. By Wilbur E. Garrett. 143, Feb. 1983
• Lebanon, Little Bible Land in the Crossfire of History. By William S. Ellis. Photos by George F. Mobley. 240-275, Feb. 1970
• Young-old Lebanon Lives by Trade. By Thomas J. Abercrombie. 479-523, Apr. 1958

BELAU, Republic of:
• Strange World of Palau's Salt Lakes. By William M. Hamner. Photos by David Doubilet. 264-282, Feb. 1982

BELDEN, CHARLES J.:
Author-Photographer:
• Dinkelsbühl Rewards Its Children. 255-268, Feb. 1957
Photographer:
• The Palio of Siena. By Edgar Erskine Hume. 231-244, Aug. 1951

BELFAST, Northern Ireland:
• War and Peace in Northern Ireland. By Bryan Hodgson. Photos by Cary Wolinsky. 470-499, Apr. 1981

BELGIAN CONGO. *See* Zaire

BELGIUM:
• Belgium: One Nation Divisible. By James Cerruti. Photos by Martin Rogers. 314-341, Mar. 1979
• Belgium Comes Back. By Harvey Klemmer. Photos by Maynard Owen Williams. 575-614, May 1948
• Belgium Welcomes the World (1958 World's Fair). By Howell Walker. 795-837, June 1958
▲ *France, Belgium, and the Netherlands,* Atlas series supplement. June 1960
• Inside Europe Aboard *Yankee.* By Irving and Electa Johnson. Photos by Joseph J. Scherschel. 157-195, Aug. 1964
• Paris to Antwerp with the Water Gypsies. By David S. Boyer. 530-559, Oct. 1955
• Thumbs Up Round the North Sea's Rim. By Frances James. Photos by Erica Koch. 685-704, May 1952
• *See also* Bruges

BELGRADE, Yugoslavia:
• Yugoslavia, Between East and West. By George W. Long. Photos by Volkmar Wentzel. 141-172, Feb. 1951
• Yugoslavia: Six Republics in One. By Robert Paul Jordan. Photos by James P. Blair. 589-633, May 1970

BELIZE (formerly British Honduras):
• Belize, the Awakening Land. By Louis de la Haba. Photos by Michael E. Long. Included: Belize City; Belmopan. 124-146, Jan. 1972
• Troubled Times for Central America. By Wilbur E. Garrett, Editor. 58-61, July 1981
• Unearthing the Oldest Known Maya. By Norman Hammond. Photos by Lowell Georgia and Martha Cooper. 126-140, July 1982

BELKNAP, WILLIAM, Jr.:
Author-Photographer:
• Man on the Moon in Idaho (Craters of the Moon National Monument). 505-525, Oct. 1960
• Nature Carves Fantasies in Bryce Canyon. 490-511, Oct. 1958
• New Mexico's Great White Sands. 113-137, July 1957
• Shooting Rapids in Reverse! Jet Boats Climb the Colorado's Torrent Through the Grand Canyon. 552-565, Apr. 1962
Photographer:
• Lonely Sentinels of the American West: Basque Sheepherders. By Robert Laxalt. 870-888, June 1966
• 20th-century Indians Preserve Customs of the Cliff Dwellers. 196-211, Feb. 1964
• Where Falcons Wear Air Force Blue, United States Air Force Academy. By Nathaniel T. Kenney. 845-873, June 1959

BELL, ALEXANDER GRAHAM:
• Alexander Graham Bell Museum: Tribute to Genius. By Jean Lesage. 227-256, Aug. 1956
• Canada's Winged Victory: the *Silver Dart*. By Gilbert M. Grosvenor. 254-267, Aug. 1959
• Clarke School for the Deaf, Northampton, Massachusetts: Active for 51 years as teacher, consultant, researcher, and president of the board. 379, 385, Mar. 1955
• 1898: The Bells on Sable. Photos by Arthur W. McCurdy. 408-409, 416-417, Sept. 1965
• Miracle Men of the Telephone. By F. Barrows Colton. 273-316, Mar. 1947
• President of NGS (1898-1903). 273, Mar. 1947; 270, 272, 273, Aug. 1982
• The Romance of the Geographic: National Geographic Magazine Observes Its Diamond Anniversary. By Gilbert Hovey Grosvenor. 516-585, Oct. 1963
• To Gilbert Grosvenor: a Monthly Monument 25 Miles High. By Frederick G. Vosburgh and the staff of the National Geographic Society. 445-487, Oct. 1966
• Washington's Historic Georgetown. By William A. Kinney. 513-544, Apr. 1953

BELL, CARL S.: Photographer:
• Sky-high Bolivia. 481-496, Oct. 1950

BELL MAKING:
• Mid-century Holland Builds Her Future. By Sydney Clark. 747-778, Dec. 1950

BELL MUSEUM, Baddeck, Nova Scotia:
• Alexander Graham Bell Museum: Tribute to Genius. By Jean Lesage. Photos by members of the Bell and Grosvenor families. 227-256, Aug. 1956
• Bell Museum, Baddeck, Nova Scotia. 256, 257, 259, 261, Aug. 1959; 358-359, 361, 362, Mar. 1975
• Down East to Nova Scotia. By Winfield Parks. 853-879, June 1964

BELL RINGING (Change Ringing):
• By Cotswold Lanes to Wold's End. By Melville Bell Grosvenor. 615-654, May 1948

BELL TELEPHONE COMPANY:
President, First: Gardiner Greene Hubbard. 273, Mar. 1947

BELL TELEPHONE LABORATORIES:
• Miracle Men of the Telephone. By F. Barrows Colton. Included: Birthplace of Telephone Magic. Photos by Willard R. Culver. 273-316, Mar. 1947
• New Miracles of the Telephone Age. By Robert Leslie Conly. 87-120, July 1954
• Telephone a Star: the Story of Communications Satellites. By Rowe Findley. 638-651, May 1962

BELL X-1 (Rocket Ship):
• Flying in the "Blowtorch" Era. By Frederick G. Vosburgh. 281-322, Sept. 1950

BELLINGER, PATRICK N. L.:
Author:
• Sailors in the Sky: Fifty Years of Naval Aviation. 276-296, Aug. 1961

BELT, DON: Author:
• Chattooga River Country: Wild Water, Proud People. Photos by Steve Wall. 458-477, Apr. 1983

BELTSVILLE, Maryland:
• Beltsville Brings Science to the Farm. By Samuel W. Matthews. Contents: Agricultural Research Center. 199-218, Aug. 1953
• Song of Hope for the Bluebird. By Lawrence Zeleny. Photos by Michael L. Smith. 855-865, June 1977

BELUGAS (White Whales):
• Three Whales That Flew. By Carleton Ray. Photos by W. Robert Moore. 346-359, Mar. 1962

BENCHLEY, PETER: Author:
• The Bahamas: Boom Times and Buccaneering. Photos by Bruce Dale. 364-395, Sept. 1982
• Bermuda–Balmy, British, and Beautiful. Photos by Emory Kristof. 93-121, July 1971
• Life's Tempo on Nantucket. Photos by James L. Stanfield. 810-839, June 1970
• New Zealand's Bountiful South Island. Photos by James L. Amos. 93-123, Jan. 1972
• A Strange Ride in the Deep (on Manta Rays). 200-203, Feb. 1981

The **BENDS** (Caisson Disease):
• At Home in the Sea. By Jacques-Yves Cousteau. 465-507, Apr. 1964
• Dzibilchaltun: Up from the Well of Time. By Luis Marden. 110-129, Jan. 1959
• Fish Men Explore a New World Undersea. By Jacques-Yves Cousteau. 431-472, Oct. 1952
• Underwater Archeology: Key to History's Warehouse. By George F. Bass. Photos by Thomas J. Abercrombie and Robert B. Goodman. 138-156, July 1963

BENEDICTINES:
• Mont Saint Michel. By Kenneth MacLeish. Photos by Cotton Coulson. 820-831, June 1977

BENELUX NATIONS. *See* Belgium; Luxembourg; Netherlands

BENIER, ANDRE: Photographer:
• Avalanche! "I'm OK, I'm Alive!" By David Cupp. Photos by Lanny Johnson and Andre Benier. 282-289, Sept. 1982

BENJAMIN, GEORGE J.:
Author-Photographer:
• Diving Into the Blue Holes of the Bahamas. 347-363, Sept. 1970

BENJAMIN BOWRING (Research Ship):
• Circling Earth From Pole to Pole. By Sir Ranulph Fiennes. 464-481, Oct. 1983

BENJAMIN FRANKLIN, Philosopher of Dissent. By Alice J. Hall. Photos by Linda Bartlett. 93-123, July 1975

BENN, NATHAN: Photographer:
• Cuba's Exiles Bring New Life to Miami. By Edward J. Linehan. 68-95, July 1973
• Florida–A Time for Reckoning. By William S. Ellis. Photos by Nathan Benn and Kevin Fleming. 172-219, Aug. 1982
• In Search of Moses. By Harvey Arden. 2-37, Jan. 1976
• The Living Dead Sea. By Harvey Arden. 225-245, Feb. 1978
• Massachusetts' North Shore: Harboring Old Ways. By Randall S. Peffer. 568-590, Apr. 1979
• New York's Land of Dreamers and Doers (Finger Lakes Region). By Ethel A. Starbird. 702-724, May 1977
• Of Air and Space (National Air and Space Museum). By Michael Collins. 819-837. Picture portfolio by Nathan Benn, Robert S. Oakes, and Joseph D. Lavenburg, with text by Michael E. Long. 825-837. June 1978
• Old Prague in Winter. By Peter T. White. 546-567, Apr. 1979
• The Pious Ones (Brooklyn's Hasidic Jews). By Harvey Arden. 276-298, Aug. 1975
• Vermont–a State of Mind and Mountains. By Ethel A. Starbird. 28-61, July 1974

BENNETT, FLOYD:
Floyd Bennett awarded Gold Medal; presentation by President Coolidge. 868, Dec. 1957

BERBERS (Tribespeople):
• Berber Brides' Fair. By Carla Hunt. Photos by Nik Wheeler. 119-129, Jan. 1980
• Trek by Mule Among Morocco's Berbers. By Victor Englebert. 850-875, June 1968

BERGE, MELINDA: Photographer:
• Pitcairn and Norfolk–The Saga of *Bounty*'s Children. By Ed Howard. Photos by David Hiser and Melinda Berge. 510-541, Oct. 1983
Pitcairn Island. 512-529; Norfolk Island. 530-541

• A Walk and Ride on the Wild Side: Tasmania. By Carolyn Bennett Patterson. Photos by David Hiser and Melinda Berge. 676-693, May 1983

BERGEN, Norway:
• Norway, Land of the Generous Sea. By Edward J. Linehan. Photos by George F. Mobley. 1-43, July 1971
• Norway Cracks Her Mountain Shell. By Sydney Clark. Photos by Gilbert Grosvenor and Ole Friele Backer. 171-211, Aug. 1948

BERING SEA PEOPLE. *See* Old Bering Sea People

BERING SEA REGION:
• Alaska's Russian Frontier: Little Diomede. Photos by Audrey and Frank Morgan. 551-562, Apr. 1951
• The Aleutians: Alaska's Far-out Islands. By Lael Morgan. Photos by Steven C. Wilson. 336-363, Sept. 1983
• Editorial. By Gilbert M. Grosvenor. 147, Aug. 1977
• Ice Age Man, the First American. By Thomas R. Henry. Paintings by Andre Durenceau. 781-806, Dec. 1955
• Learning the Ways of the Walrus. By G. Carleton Ray. Photos by Bill Curtsinger. 565-580, Oct. 1979
• New Day for Alaska's Pribilof Islanders. By Susan Hackley Johnson. Photos by Tim Thompson. 536-552, Oct. 1982
▲ *Peoples of the Arctic; Arctic Ocean,* double-sided supplement. Feb. 1983
• The Search for the First Americans. By Thomas Y. Canby. Photos by Kerby Smith. Paintings by Roy Andersen. 330-363, Sept. 1979
• Where Magic Ruled: Art of the Bering Sea. By William W. Fitzhugh and Susan A. Kaplan. Photos by Sisse Brimberg. 198-205, Feb. 1983
• *See also* King Island; Pribilof Islands

BERKSHIRES (Mountains), Massachusetts:
• Home to the Enduring Berkshires. By Charles McCarry. Photos by Jonathan S. Blair. 196-221, Aug. 1970
• Massachusetts Builds for Tomorrow. By Robert de Roos. Photos by B. Anthony Stewart. 790-843, Dec. 1966
• Mountains Top Off New England. By F. Barrows Colton. Photos by Robert F. Sisson. 563-602, May 1951

BERLIN, Germany:
• Airlift to Berlin. 595-614, May 1949
• Berlin, Island in a Soviet Sea. By Frederick G. Vosburgh. Photos by Volkmar Wentzel. 689-704, Nov. 1951
• Berlin, on Both Sides of the Wall. By Howard Sochurek. 1-47, Jan. 1970
• Modern Miracle, Made in Germany. By Robert Leslie Conly. Photos by Erich Lessing. 735-791, June 1959
• What I Saw Across the Rhine. By J. Frank Dobie. 57-86, Jan. 1947

BERLIN, East, East Germany:
• East Germany: The Struggle to Succeed. By John J. Putman. Photos by Gordon W. Gahan. 295-329, Sept. 1974
• Two Berlins–A Generation Apart. By Priit J. Vesilind. Photos by Cotton Coulson. 2-51, Jan. 1982

BERLIN, West:
• Life in Walled-off West Berlin. By Nathaniel T. Kenney and Volkmar Wentzel. Photos by Thomas Nebbia. 735-767, Dec. 1961
• Two Berlins–A Generation Apart. By Priit J. Vesilind. Photos by Cotton Coulson. 2-51, Jan. 1982

BERLIN WALL:
• Two Berlins–A Generation Apart. By Priit J. Vesilind. Photos by Cotton Coulson. 2-51, Jan. 1982

BERMUDA (Islands), Atlantic Ocean:
• Bermuda–Balmy, British, and Beautiful. By Peter Benchley. Photos by Emory Kristof. 93-121, July 1971
• Bermuda, Cradled in Warm Seas. By Beverley M. Bowie. Photos by Charles Allmon. 203-238, Feb. 1954
• By Square-rigger from Baltic to Bicentennial. By Kenneth Garrett. Included: Collision of tall ships in Bermuda waters. 824-857, Dec. 1976
• Reach for the New World. By Mendel Peterson. Photos by David L. Arnold. Paintings by Richard Schlecht. Included: Salvaged shipwreck treasure. 724-767, Dec. 1977
• To Europe with a Racing Start. By Carleton Mitchell. 758-791, June 1958

BERN, Switzerland:
• Surprising Switzerland. By Jean and Franc Shor. 427-478, Oct. 1956
• Switzerland, Europe's High-rise Republic. By Thomas J. Abercrombie. 68-113, July 1969
• Switzerland Guards the Roof of Europe. By William H. Nicholas. Photos by Willard R. Culver. 205-246, Aug. 1950

BERNINA (Balloon):
• Across the Alps in a Wicker Basket. By Phil Walker. 117-131, Jan. 1963

BERRIES:
• How Fruit Came to America. By J. R. Magness. Paintings by Else Bostelmann. 325-377, Sept. 1951
• *See also* Cranberries

BERRY, WILLIAM R.: Author:
• Hot-air Balloons Race on Silent Winds. Photos by Don W. Jones. 392-407, Mar. 1966

BERTELLI, CARLO: Author:
• Restoration Reveals the "Last Supper." Photos by Victor R. Boswell, Jr. 664-685, Nov. 1983

BESIDE the Persian Gulf. Photos by Maynard Owen Williams. 341-356, Mar. 1947

The **BEST** of Our Land (National Parks). By Gilbert M. Grosvenor. 1-2, July 1979

BETELGEUSE (Ketch):
• Chesapeake Country. By Nathaniel T. Kenney. Photos by Bates Littlehales. 370-411, Sept. 1964

BETHLEHEM:
• Hashemite Jordan, Arab Heartland. By John Scofield. 841-856, Dec. 1952
• Pilgrims Follow the Christmas Star. By Maynard Owen Williams. 831-840, Dec. 1952

BETTER Days for the Navajos. By Jack Breed. Photos by Charles W. Herbert. 809-847, Dec. 1958

BEYOND Everest. By Sir Edmund Hillary. 579-610, Nov. 1955

BEYOND the Bight of Benin (Nigeria; Cameroons). By Jeannette and Maurice Fiévet. 221-253, Aug. 1959

BEYOND the North Wind With the Snow Goose. By Des and Jen Bartlett. 822-843, Dec. 1973

BHAVNANI, ENAKSHI: Author:
• A Journey to "Little Tibet." Photos by Volkmar Wentzel. 603-634, May 1951

BHOTIAS (Tribespeople):
• High Adventure in the Himalayas. By Thomas Weir. 193-234, Aug. 1952

BHUMIBOL ADULYADEJ, King of Thailand:
• Thailand: Luck of a Land in the Middle. By Bart McDowell. Photos by Steve Raymer. 500-535, Oct. 1982
• Thailand's Working Royalty. Photos by John Everingham. 486-499, Oct. 1982

BHUTAN:
• Bhutan, Land of the Thunder Dragon. By Burt Kerr Todd. 713-754, Dec. 1952
• Bhutan: Mountain Kingdom Between Tibet and India. By Desmond Doig. 384-415, Sept. 1961
• Bhutan Crowns a New Dragon King. Photos by John Scofield. 546-571, Oct. 1974
• Life Slowly Changes in Remote Bhutan. By John Scofield. 658-683, Nov. 1976

BIAMI (People):
• Journey Into Stone Age New Guinea. By Malcolm S. Kirk. 568-592, Apr. 1969

BIANCHI, PETER V.: Artist:
• Last Moments of the Pompeians. By Amedeo Maiuri. Photos by Lee E. Battaglia. 651-669, Nov. 1961
• The Last Thousand Years Before Christ. By G. Ernest Wright. Paintings by H. J. Soulen and Peter V. Bianchi. 812-853, Dec. 1960
• The Men Who Hid the Dead Sea Scrolls. By A. Douglas Tushingham. 785-808, Dec. 1958
• Solving the Riddles of Wetherill Mesa. By Douglas Osborne. 155-195, Feb. 1964

BIBER, MEHMET:
Author-Photographer:
• Albania, Alone Against the World. 530-557, Oct. 1980

Photographer:
• Pilgrimage to Mecca. By Muhammad Abdul-Rauf. 581-607, Nov. 1978

BIBLE:
• The British Way. By Sir Evelyn Wrench. Included: James I and the translation of the Bible. 421-541, Apr. 1949
• The Men Who Hid the Dead Sea Scrolls. By A. Douglas Tushingham. Paintings by Peter V. Bianchi. 785-808, Dec. 1958

BIBLE LANDS. *See* Holy Land

BICENTENNIAL, U. S.:
• Benjamin Franklin, Philosopher of Dissent. By Alice J. Hall. Photos by Linda Bartlett. 93-123, July 1975
• By Square-rigger from Baltic to Bicentennial (Operation Sail). By Kenneth Garrett. 824-857, Dec. 1976
• Editorial. By Gilbert M. Grosvenor. 1, July 1976
• Firebrands of the Revolution. By Eric F. Goldman. Photos by George F. Mobley. 2-27, July 1974
• The Loyalists. By Kent Britt. Photos by Ted Spiegel. 510-539, Apr. 1975
• The Nation's 200th Birthday. By Gilbert M. Grosvenor. 1, July 1974
• Patriots in Petticoats. By Lonnelle Aikman. Paintings by Louis S. Glanzman. 475-493, Oct. 1975
• This Land of Ours. 1-158, July 1976
A Portfolio: "This land is your land . . ." 2-11; A First American Views His Land. By N. Scott Momaday. 13-19; This Land of Ours–How Are We Using It? By Peter T. White. Photos by Emory Kristof. 20-67; Five Noted Thinkers Explore the Future. 68-75; The Next Frontier? By Isaac Asimov. Paintings by Pierre Mion. 76-89; George Washington: The Man Behind the Myths. By Howard La Fay. Photos by Ted Spiegel. 90-111
• Thomas Jefferson: Architect of Freedom. By Mike W. Edwards. Photos by Linda Bartlett. 231-259, Feb. 1976

BICYCLING:
• Bicycles Are Back–and Booming! By Noel Grove. Photos by Michael Pfleger. 671-681, May 1973
• Bikepacking Across Alaska and Canada. By Dan Burden. 682-695, May 1973
• Europe Via the Hostel Route. By Joseph Nettis. 124-154, July 1955

BIEL, JÖRG: Author:
• Treasure From a Celtic Tomb. Photos by Volkmar Wentzel. 428-438, Mar. 1980

BIERWAGEN, OTTMAR:
Photographer:
• Quebec's Northern Dynamo. By Larry Kohl. 406-418, Mar. 1982

BIFOCAL FISH. *See* Four-eyed Fish

BIG BANG:
• The Once and Future Universe. By Rick Gore. Photos by James A. Sugar. Paintings by Barron Storey. Picture text by David Jeffery. 704-749, June 1983

BIG BEND NATIONAL PARK, Texas:
• Big Bend: Jewel in the Texas Desert. By Nathaniel T. Kenney. Photos by James L. Stanfield. 104-133, Jan. 1968

BIG CYPRESS SWAMP, Florida:
• The Imperiled Everglades. By Fred Ward. 1-27, Jan. 1972
• Twilight Hope for Big Cypress. By Rick Gore. Photos by Patricia Caulfield. 251-273, Aug. 1976

BIG GAME. *See* Game Preserves; Hunting

BIG Game Hunting in the Land of Long Ago. By Joseph P. Connolly and James D. Bump. 589-605, May 1947

BIG-LIPPED PEOPLE. *See* Sara; Suyá Indians

BIG NAMBAS (Tribespeople):
• Taboos and Magic Rule Namba Lives. By Kal Muller. 57-83, Jan. 1972
• *Yankee* Roams the Orient. By Irving and Electa Johnson. 327-370, Mar. 1951

"BIG SCHMIDT" (Telescope):
• Mapping the Unknown Universe. By F. Barrows Colton. 401-420, Sept. 1950
• *See also* Sky Survey

BIG SUR (Region), California:
• California's Land Apart–the Monterey Peninsula. By Mike W. Edwards. 682-703, Nov. 1972

BIG THICKET (Region), Texas:
• Big Thicket of Texas. By Don Moser. Photos by Blair Pittman. 504-529, Oct. 1974

BIGGEST Worm Farm Caters to Platypuses. By W. H. Nicholas. 269-280, Feb. 1949

BIGHORN MEDICINE WHEEL, Wyoming:
• Probing the Mystery of the Medicine Wheels. By John A. Eddy. Photos by Thomas E. Hooper. 140-146, Jan. 1977

BIGHORN SHEEP:
• Last Stand for the Bighorn. By James K. Morgan. 383-399, Sept. 1973

BIHARIS (People):
• Bangladesh: Hope Nourishes a New Nation. By William S. Ellis. Photos by Dick Durrance II. 295-333, Sept. 1972

BIKEPACKING Across Alaska and Canada. By Dan Burden. 682-695, May 1973

BIKINI (Atoll), Marshall Islands:
• Operation Crossroads. Photos by Joint Task Force I. Paintings by Charles Bittinger. 519-530, Apr. 1947

BILLARD, JULES B.: Author:
• Buenos Aires, Argentina's Melting-pot Metropolis. Photos by Winfield Parks. 662-695, Nov. 1967

JAMES L. STANFIELD, NGS

Big Bend: Texas desert panorama

• Canada's Window on the Pacific: The British Columbia Coast. Photos by Ted Spiegel. 338-375, Mar. 1972
• Guantánamo: Keystone in the Caribbean. Photos by W. E. Garrett and Thomas Nebbia. 420-436, Mar. 1961
• Macao Clings to the Bamboo Curtain. Photos by Joseph J. Scherschel. 521-539, Apr. 1969
• Montreal Greets the World (Expo 67). 600-621, May 1967
• Okinawa, the Island Without a Country. Photos by Winfield Parks and David Moore. 422-448, Sept. 1969
• Panama, Link Between Oceans and Continents. Photos by Bruce Dale. 402-440, Mar. 1970
• The Revolution in American Agriculture. Photos by James P. Blair. 147-185, Feb. 1970

BILLINGS, Montana:
• The Untamed Yellowstone. By Bill Richards. Photos by Dean Krakel II. 257-278, Aug. 1981

BILLION-DOLLAR Gamble in Brazil. By Loren McIntyre. 686-711, May 1980

BILOXI, Mississippi:
• Troubled Odyssey of Vietnamese Fishermen. By Harvey Arden. Photos by Steve Wall. 378-395, Sept. 1981

BIMINI ISLANDS, Bahama Islands:
• Man-of-war Fleet Attacks Bimini. By Paul A. Zahl. 185-212, Feb. 1952
• *See also* Lerner Marine Laboratory

BINGHAM, HIRAM:
• Peru, Homeland of the Warlike Inca. By Kip Ross. 421-462, Oct. 1950

BIOCHEMISTRY:
• The Awesome Worlds Within a Cell. By Rick Gore. Photos by Bruce Dale. Paintings by Davis Meltzer. 355-395, Sept. 1976
• The Wild World of Compost. By Cecil E. Johnson. Photos by Bianca Lavies. 273-284, Aug. 1980
• *See also* Bioluminescence

BIOGRAPHIES. *See* Abraham; Alexander the Great; Andersen, Hans Christian; Audubon, John James; Burke, Robert; Byrd, Richard E.; Cather, Willa; Churchill, Winston; Clark, William; Cody, William (Buffalo Bill); Columbus, Christopher; Cook, James; Dickens, Charles; Disney, Walt; Drake, Sir Francis; Eisenhower, Dwight D.; Elizabeth I; Elizabeth II; Franklin, Benjamin; Frost, Robert; El Greco; Grosvenor, Elsie May Bell; Grosvenor, Gilbert H.; Grosvenor, Melville Bell; Henry, Prince; Jefferson, Thomas; Jesus; Joseph, Chief; Kamehameha the Great; Leakey Family; Leopold, Aldo; Lewis, Meriwether; Lilienthal, Otto; Lincoln, Abraham; Luther, Martin; Magellan, Ferdinand; Moses; Muir, John; Napoleon I; Roosevelt, Theodore; Shakespeare, William; Smith, John; Thoreau, Henry D.; Twain, Mark; Vinci, Leonardo da; Washington, George; Wills, William

BIOLOGY:
• Algae: the Life-givers. By Paul A. Zahl. 361-377, Mar. 1974
• Antarctica's Nearer Side. By Samuel W. Matthews. Photos by William R. Curtsinger. Included: Laboratory studies of Antarctic land and marine life. 622-655, Nov. 1971
• Editorial. By Gilbert M. Grosvenor. 297, Sept. 1976
• Life in a "Dead" Sea–Great Salt Lake. By Paul A. Zahl. 252-263, Aug. 1967
• The New Biology. 355-407, Sept. 1976
I. The Awesome Worlds Within a Cell. By Rick Gore. Photos by Bruce Dale. Paintings by Davis Meltzer. 355-395; II. The Cancer Puzzle. By Robert F. Weaver. 396-399; III. Seven Giants Who Led the Way. Paintings by Ned Seidler. Text by Rick Gore. Contents: Francis Crick, Charles Darwin, Anton van Leeuwenhoek, Gregor Mendel, Thomas Hunt Morgan, Louis Pasteur, James D. Watson. 401-407
• *See also* Birds; Insects; Mammals; Marine Biology; Plants; Scorpions; Spiders; *and* Ecosystems

BIOLUMINESCENCE:
• Fishing in the Whirlpool of Charybdis. By Paul A. Zahl. 579-618, Nov. 1953
• Nature's Night Lights: Probing the Secrets of Bioluminescence. By Paul A. Zahl. 45-69, July 1971
• Sailing a Sea of Fire (Phosphorescent Bay). By Paul A. Zahl. 120-129, July 1960
• *See also* Fireflies; Hatchetfish; *Photoblepharon;* Railroad Worm

BIOMES. *See* Ecosystems

BIORHYTHM RESEARCH:
• Six Months Alone in a Cave. By Michel Siffre. 426-435, Mar. 1975

BIRD, ROLAND T.: Author:
• We Captured a 'Live' Brontosaur. 707-722, May 1954

BIRD ANTING:
• The Enigma of Bird Anting. By Hance Roy Ivor. 105-119, July 1956

BIRD DOGS:
• Born Hunters, the Bird Dogs. By Roland Kilbon. Paintings by Walter A. Weber. 369-398, Sept. 1947

The **BIRD** Men. By Luis Marden. Photos by Charles O'Rear. 198-217, Aug. 1983

BIRD ROCK, Santa Catalina Island, California:
• Undersea World of a Kelp Forest. By Sylvia A. Earle. Photos by Al Giddings. 411-426, Sept. 1980

BIRD SANCTUARIES AND ROOKERIES:
▲ *America's Federal Lands; The United States,* double-sided supplement. Sept. 1982
• Beyond the North Wind With the Snow Goose. By Des and Jen Bartlett. Included: De Soto, Missouri River; Sand Lake, South Dakota; Squaw Creek, Missouri. 822-843, Dec. 1973
• Duck Hunting with a Color Camera. By Arthur A. Allen. Contents: Bear River Marshes, Utah; Bombay Hook, Delaware; Cayuga Lake, New York; Horseshoe Lake Island, Illinois; Lower Souris, North Dakota; Roaches Run, Virginia. 514-539, Oct. 1951
• Hawaii's Far-flung Wildlife Paradise. By John L. Eliot. Photos By Jonathan Blair. Contents: Hawaiian National Wildlife Refuge. 670-691, May 1978
• Island, Prairie, Marsh, and Shore. By Charlton Ogburn. Photos by Bates Littlehales. Contents: Bear River Migratory Bird Refuge, Utah; Farallon Islands Refuge, California; Lostwood Wildlife Refuge, North Dakota; Merritt Island National Wildlife Refuge, Florida. 350-381, Mar. 1979
• The Japanese Crane, Bird of Happiness. By Tsuneo Hayashida. Included: Kushiro marshland refuge. 542-556, Oct. 1983
• New Scarlet Bird in Florida Skies. By Paul A. Zahl. Included: Caroni Swamp Sanctuary, Trinidad; Greynolds Park Rookery, North Miami Beach. 874-882, Dec. 1967
• Our Only Native Stork, the Wood Ibis. By Robert Porter Allen. Photos by Frederick Kent Truslow. Included: Bear Island Rookery; Corkscrew Swamp Sanctuary; Cuthbert Lake Rookery. 294-306, Feb. 1964
• The Pink Birds of Texas. By Paul A. Zahl. Contents: Roseate spoonbills and the National Audubon Society's sanctuary system on the Texas bird islands along the Gulf of Mexico. 641-654, Nov. 1949
• Roosevelt Country: T. R.'s Wilderness Legacy. By John L. Eliot. Photos by Farrell Grehan. 340-363, Sept. 1982
• Saving Man's Wildlife Heritage. By John H. Baker. Photos by Robert F. Sisson. Included: The National Audubon Society's sanctuaries in Texas, Florida, and Louisiana. 581-620, Nov. 1954
• Sea Bird Cities Off Audubon's Labrador. By Arthur A. Allen. Contents: Bradore Bay Sanctuary; Fog Island Sanctuary; Mecatina Bird Sanctuary; St. Augustin Sanctuary; St. Mary Islands Sanctuary. 755-774, June 1948
• Sea Birds of Isla Raza. By Lewis Wayne Walker. 239-248, Feb. 1951
• Tireless Voyager, the Whistling Swan. By William J. L. Sladen. Photos by Bianca Lavies. Included: Back Bay, Virginia; Blackwater, Maryland; Eastern Neck, Maryland; Mattamuskeet, North Carolina; Pungo, North Carolina; Upper Mississippi River Wild Life and Fish Refuge, Minnesota. 134-147, July 1975
• Where Oil and Wildlife Mix. By Steven C. Wilson and Karen C. Hayden. Included: Aransas National Wildlife Refuge, Texas; Padre Island National Seashore, Texas. 145-173, Feb. 1981

• Wildlife of Everglades National Park. By Daniel B. Beard. Paintings by Walter A. Weber. Included: Cuthbert Lake Rookery; East River Rookery. 83-116, Jan. 1949

• *See also* Abbotsbury Swannery, England; Aransas National Wildlife Refuge, Texas; Bear River Migratory Bird Refuge, Utah; Corkscrew Swamp, Florida; Currumbin, Australia; Everglades (Region), Florida; Las Marismas (Marshes), Spain; Little Tobago (Island); Mono Lake, California; Red Rock Lakes National Wildlife Refuge, Montana; Sapsucker Woods; Wichita Mountains Wildlife Refuge, Oklahoma

BIRDS:

• An Artist's Glimpses of Our Roadside Wildlife. Paintings by Walter A. Weber. Included: Avocets, Bald eagles, Blue-winged teals, Coots, Evening grosbeaks, Fish hawks (Ospreys), Gadwalls, Holboell's grebes, Kingbirds, Magpies, Marsh hawks, Mountain chickadees, Oregon juncos, Pine grosbeaks, Prairie falcons, Pygmy owls, Ravens, Red-breasted nuthatches, Redhead ducks, Red-tailed hawks, Ring-necked pheasants, Scissor-tailed flycatchers, Shovelers, Townsend warblers, Trumpeter swans, Vermilion flycatchers. 16-32, July 1950

• Audubon "On the Wing." By David Jeffery. Photos by Bates Littlehales. 149-177, Feb. 1977

▲ *Australia; Land of Living Fossils,* double-sided supplement. Included: Paintings by Roy Andersen. Feb. 1979

◆ *Baby Birds and How They Grow.* 1983

• Barehanded Battle to Cleanse the Bay. By Peter T. White. Photos by Jonathan S. Blair. Included: Oil-crippled birds. 866-881, June 1971

▲ *Bird Migration in the Americas: The Americas,* double-sided supplement. Included: 67 paintings by Arthur Singer. Aug. 1979

• Birds of the Alaskan Tundra. 322-327, Mar. 1972

• The Bird's Year. By Arthur A. Allen. Contents: American bittern, Avocet, Baltimore oriole, Black-crowned night heron, Blue-headed vireo, Bronze turkey, Brown thrasher, Cardinal, Cedar waxwing, Chestnut-sided warbler, Coot, Cowbird, Eared grebe, Evening grosbeak, Gila woodpecker, Golden-fronted woodpecker, Hoary redpoll, Indigo bunting, Kentucky warbler, Least bittern, Loon, Magnolia warbler, Mourning warbler, Ovenbird, Phoebe, Puffin, Purple martin, Red-bellied woodpecker, Redpoll, Redstart, Rio Grande turkey, Ruby-throated hummingbird, Ruffed grouse, Sabine's gull, Sennett's oriole, Short-billed marsh wren, Snowy heron, Sparrow hawk, Starling, White-throated sparrow, White-winged dove, Yellow-headed blackbird. 791-816, June 1951

Migration: bird's migratory cues

PAINTING BY BARRON STOREY

FREDERICK KENT TRUSLOW

Businessman in the Bush: a black skimmer fishes

• Businessman in the Bush. By Frederick Kent Truslow. 634-675, May 1970

• Can We Save Our Salt Marshes? By Stephen W. Hitchcock. Photos by William R. Curtsinger. 729-765, June 1972

• Corkscrew Swamp–Florida's Primeval Show Place. By Melville Bell Grosvenor. 98-113, Jan. 1958

• The Curlew's Secret. By Arthur A. Allen. Included: Alaska longspur, Alaska yellow wagtail, Baird's sandpiper, Black-bellied plover, Bristle-thighed curlew, Cackling goose, Cranes, Ducks, Emperor goose, Frigate bird, Geese, Golden plover, Hoary redpoll, Hudsonian curlew, Little brown crane, Northern phalarope, Old-squaw, Pacific godwit, Parasitic jaeger, Pectoral sandpiper, Ruddy turnstone, Sabine's gull, Savannah sparrow, Snow bunting, Spectacled eider, Tree sparrow, Varied thrush, Western sandpiper, Whistling swan, White-fronted goose, Wilson's snipe. 751-770, Dec. 1948

• Eden in the Outback. By Kay and Stanley Breeden. 189-203, Feb. 1973

• Editorial. By Gilbert M. Grosvenor. 151, Aug. 1975

• The Enigma of Bird Anting. By Hance Roy Ivor. 105-119, July 1956

• Etosha: Namibia's Kingdom of Animals. By Douglas H. Chadwick. Photos by Des and Jen Bartlett. Included: Blue cranes, Cape penduline tit, doves, greater and lesser flamingos, guinea fowl, marabou storks, masked weaverbird, ostriches, pied crow vultures. 344-385, Mar. 1983

• Exotic Birds in Manhattan's Bowery. By Paul A. Zahl. 77-98, Jan. 1953

• Exploring Stone Age Arnhem Land. By Charles P. Mountford. Photos by Howell Walker. 745-782, Dec. 1949

◆ *Field Guide to the Birds of North America.* 1983

• Florida, Noah's Ark for Exotic Newcomers. By Rick Gore. Photos by David Doubilet. Included: The introduction of tropical birds: budgerigar, bulbul, myna, parakeet, and parrot. 538-559, Oct. 1976

• The Galapagos, Eerie Cradle of New Species. By Roger Tory Peterson. Photos by Alan and Joan Root. 541-585, Apr. 1967

• London's Zoo of Zoos. By Thomas Garner James. 771-786, June 1953

• Lundy, Treasure Island of Birds. By P.T. Etherton. Photos by J. Allan Cash. 675-698, May 1947

• Mysteries of Bird Migration. By Allan C. Fisher, Jr. Photos by Jonathan Blair. 154-193, Aug. 1979
Tracking the Shore Dwellers: From Canada to Suriname. 175-179

• Nature's Alert Eyes. By Constance P. Warner. 558-569, Apr. 1959

• New Guinea's Paradise of Birds. By E. Thomas Gilliard. Contents: Princess Stephanie bird of paradise, Ribbon-tailed bird of paradise, *Harpyopsis* eagle, *Salvadorina* duck,

E. THOMAS GILLIARD AND HENRY KALTENTHALER, AMERICAN MUSEUM-ARMAND DENIS EXPEDITION

New Guinea: feathered dancers, *above;* lesser bird of paradise, *below*

E. THOMAS GILLIARD, AMERICAN MUSEUM-ARMAND DENIS EXPEDITION

Archboldia bowerbird, *Cnemophilus macgregorii* bowerbird, and a new bowerbird named for Leonard C. Sanford. 661-688, Nov. 1951

• New Guinea's Rare Birds and Stone Age Men. By E. Thomas Gilliard. NGS research grant. 421-488, Apr. 1953

• A New Light Dawns on Bird Photography. By Arthur A. Allen. Included: Dynamics of bird flight. 774-790, June 1948

• Our National Wildlife Refuges. 342-381, Mar. 1979
I. A Chance to Grow. By Robert E. Doyle. 342-349; II. Island, Prairie, Marsh, and Shore. By Charlton Ogburn. Photos by Bates Littlehales. 350-381

• Peerless Nepal–A Naturalist's Paradise. By S. Dillon Ripley. Photos by Volkmar Wentzel. Included: National Geographic Society-Yale University-Smithsonian Institution Expedition's rediscovery of the Spiny babbler and unsuccessful search for the Mountain quail; other birds noted and collected: Bush larks, Darjeeling woodpeckers, Flycatchers, Hedge sparrows, Hill partridges, Mergansers, Rose finches, Rufous-chinned laughing thrushes, Slaty-headed parakeets, Warblers, White-throated laughing thrushes, Yellow-billed blue magpies. 1-40, Jan. 1950

• Penguins and Their Neighbors. By Roger Tory Peterson. Photos by Des and Jen Bartlett. Included: Albatrosses, Penguins, Wilson's storm petrel. 237-255, Aug. 1977

• Peru Profits from Sea Fowl. By Robert Cushman Murphy. Photos by author and Grace E. Barstow Murphy. 395-413, Mar. 1959

• Pilgrimage to Holy Island and the Farnes. By John E. H. Nolan. Included: Cormorants, Guillemots, St. Cuthbert's duck (Eider), Terns. 547-570, Oct. 1952

• Rare Birds Flock To Spain's Marismas. By Roger Tory Peterson. 397-425, Mar. 1958

• Safari Through Changing Africa. By Elsie May Bell Grosvenor. Photos by Gilbert Grosvenor. 145-198, Aug. 1953

• Saving Man's Wildlife Heritage. By John H. Baker. Photos by Robert F. Sisson. 581-620, Nov. 1954

• Sea Bird Cities Off Audubon's Labrador. By Arthur A. Allen. NGS research grant. 755-774, June 1948

• Sea Birds of Isla Raza. By Lewis Wayne Walker. 239-248, Feb. 1951

• Seeing Birds as Real Personalities. By Hance Roy Ivor. Contents: Albino robins, Blue jays, Bluebirds, Cardinals, Chickadees, Cowbirds, European blackbirds, Mourning doves, Orioles, Robins, Rose-breasted grosbeaks, Thrushes, Waxwings, White doves. 523-530, Apr. 1954
Bluebirds on the Wing in Color. Photos by Bernard Corby and author. 527-530

• Seeking Mindanao's Strangest Creatures. By Charles Heizer Wharton. Included: Crested serpent eagle, Hornbill, Monkey-eating eagle. 389-408, Sept. 1948

◆ *Song and Garden Birds of North America.* Announced. 553-557, Oct. 1964

• Split Seconds in the Lives of Birds. By Arthur A. Allen. 681-706, May 1954

• Sri Lanka's Wildlife. 254-278, Aug. 1983
I. Sri Lanka's Wildlife Heritage: A Personal Perspective. By Arthur C. Clarke. 254-255; II. Legacy of Lively Treasures. By Dieter and Mary Plage. 256-273; III. A Nation Rises to the Challenge. By Lyn de Alwis. Photos by Dieter and Mary Plage. 274-278

◆ *Stalking Birds with Color Camera.* 1951

• Stalking Central Africa's Wildlife. By T. Donald Carter. Paintings by Walter A. Weber. NGS research grant. 264-286, Aug. 1956

• Teamwork Helps the Whooping Crane. By Roderick C. Drewien, with Ernie Kuyt. Included: Greater sandhill cranes and Whooping cranes. 680-693, May 1979

• Threatened Glories of Everglades National Park. By Frederick Kent Truslow and Frederick G. Vosburgh. Photos by Frederick Kent Truslow and Otis Imboden. 508-553, Oct. 1967

◆ *Water, Prey, and Game Birds of North America.* Announced. 529-535, Oct. 1965

• Where Oil and Wildlife Mix. By Steven C. Wilson and Karen C. Hayden. 145-173, Feb. 1981

• Where Two Worlds Meet (Patagonia). Photos by Des and Jen Bartlett. 298-321, Mar. 1976

• Wildlife In and Near the Valley of the Moon. By H. H. Arnold. Photos by Paul J. Fair. 401-414, Mar. 1950

• Wildlife of Everglades National Park. By Daniel B. Beard. Paintings by Walter A. Weber. 83-116, Jan. 1949

• Wildlife of Mount McKinley National Park. By Adolph Murie. Paintings by Walter A. Weber. 249-270, Aug. 1953

▪ Winged World. 877A-877B, Dec. 1967

◆ *Wonder of Birds.* 1983

• *See also Aepyornis*; Albatrosses; Andean Condors; Araucana Chickens; Bald Eagles; Birds of Paradise; Black Eagles; Bluebirds; Bowerbirds; Brown Pelicans; Cocks-of-the-Rock; Cooper's Hawk; Cranes; Ducks; Eagles; Egrets; Egyptian Vulture; Flamingos; Fowl, Japanese Long-tailed; Geese; Golden Eagles; Herons; Hoatzin; Honey-Guide; Hornbills; Hummingbirds; Ibises; Kingfishers; Kites; Kiwi; Limpkin; Lorikeets; Lyrebird; Nene; Oilbirds; Orioles; Ospreys; Owls; Penguins; Philippine Eagles; Pigeons; Poorwill; Puffins; Quetzal; Roadrunners; Roseate Spoonbills; Scarlet Ibis; Seabirds; Snow Geese; Spiny Babbler; Stilts; Storks; Swans; Takahe; Terns; Western Grebes; Whistling Swans;

Whooping Cranes; Wilson's Phalarope; Wood Storks; Woodpeckers; *and* Bird Sanctuaries and Rookeries; Exotic-Bird Trade

BIRDS OF PARADISE:
• Feathered Dancers of Little Tobago. By E. Thomas Gilliard. Photos by Frederick Kent Truslow. NGS research grant. 428-440, Sept. 1958
• New Guinea's Paradise of Birds. By E. Thomas Gilliard. 661-688, Nov. 1951
• New Guinea's Rare Birds and Stone Age Men. By E. Thomas Gilliard. NGS research grant. 421-488, Apr. 1953
• Strange Courtship of Birds of Paradise. By S. Dillon Ripley. Paintings by Walter A. Weber. 247-278, Feb. 1950
• To the Land of the Head-hunters. By E. Thomas Gilliard. NGS research grant. 437-486, Oct. 1955

BIRTHPLACE of Telephone Magic. Photos by Willard R. Culver. 289-312, Mar. 1947

BISCH, JØRGEN:
Author-Photographer:
• This Is the China I Saw. 591-639, Nov. 1964

BISHOP, BARRY C.:
• President Kennedy Presents the Hubbard Medal. 514-515, Oct. 1963
Author:
• Landsat Looks at Hometown Earth. 140-147, July 1976
Author-Photographer:
• How We Climbed Everest. 477-507, Oct. 1963
• Karnali, Roadless World of Western Nepal. By Lila M. and Barry C. Bishop. 656-689, Nov. 1971
• Mount Rainier: Testing Ground for Everest. 688-711, May 1963
• Wintering on the Roof of the World (Himalayas). 503-547, Oct. 1962
Photographer:
• American and Geographic Flags Top Everest. By Melvin M. Payne. 157-157C, Aug. 1963
• Six to the Summit (Everest). By Norman G. Dyhrenfurth. 460-473, Oct. 1963
• We Climbed Utah's Skyscraper Rock. By Huntley Ingalls. Photos by author and Barry C. Bishop. 705-721, Nov. 1962

BISHOP, LILA M.:
Author-Photographer:
• Karnali, Roadless World of Western Nepal. By Lila M. and Barry C. Bishop. 656-689, Nov. 1971

BISITUN, Mount, Iran:
• Darius Carved History on Ageless Rock. By George G. Cameron. 825-844, Dec. 1950

BISMARCK ARCHIPELAGO. *See* New Britain

BISON, American:
• Bison Kill By Ice Age Hunters. By Dennis Stanford. NGS research grant. 114-121, Jan. 1979
• Buffalo Bill and the Enduring West. By Alice J. Hall. Photos by James L. Amos. 76-103, July 1981
• Hays, Kansas, at the Nation's Heart. By Margaret M. Detwiler. Photos by John E. Fletcher. 461-490, Apr. 1952
• Springtime Comes to Yellowstone National Park. By Paul A. Zahl. 761-779, Dec. 1956
• The Wichitas: Land of the Living Prairie. By M. Woodbridge Williams. 661-697, May 1957
• Yellowstone Wildlife in Winter. By William Albert Allard. 637-661, Nov. 1967

A **BIT** of Old Russia Takes Root in Alaska: Nikolaevsk. By Jim Rearden. Photos by Charles O'Rear. 401-425, Sept. 1972

The **BITTERSWEET** Waters of the Lower Colorado. By Rowe Findley. Photos by Charles O'Rear. 540-569, Oct. 1973

BITTINGER, CHARLES: Artist:
• Operation Crossroads. Photos by Joint Task Force I. 519-530, Apr. 1947

BIZARRE Dragons of the Sea. Photos by Paul A. Zahl. 838-845, June 1978

BIZARRE World of the Fungi. By Paul A. Zahl. 502-527, Oct. 1965

BLACK AMERICANS:
• Brooklyn: The Other Side of the Bridge. By Alice J. Hall. Photos by Robert W. Madden. 580-613, May 1983
• Savannah to Charleston–A Good Life in the Low Country. By John J. Putman. Photos by Annie Griffiths. 798-829, Dec. 1983
• To Live in Harlem. . . . By Frank Hercules. Photos by LeRoy Woodson, Jr. 178-207, Feb. 1977
• Washington, D. C.: Hometown Behind the Monuments. By Henry Mitchell. Photos by Adam Woolfitt. 84-125, Jan. 1983

BLACK-BACKED JACKALS:
• Jackals of the Serengeti. By Patricia D. Moehlman. 840-850, Dec. 1980

BLACK BEARS:
• Studying Wildlife by Satellite. By Frank Craighead, Jr. and John Craighead. NGS research grant. 120-123, Jan. 1973

BLACK Day for Brittany. Photos by Martin Rogers. Text by Noel Grove. 124-135, July 1978

BLACK EAGLES:
• Adventures With South Africa's Black Eagles. By Jeanne Cowden. Photos by author and Arthur Bowland. 533-543, Oct. 1969

BLACK-FOOTED FERRETS:
• Last of the Black-footed Ferrets? By Tim W. Clark. Photos by Franz J. Camenzind and the author. NGS research grant. 828-838, June 1983

BLACK HILLS, South Dakota:
• Back to the Historic Black Hills. By Leland D. Case. Photos by Bates Littlehales. 479-509, Oct. 1956
• South Dakota Keeps Its West Wild. By Frederick Simpich. 555-588, May 1947
Over Plains and Hills of South Dakota. Photos by J. Baylor Roberts. 563-586

BLACK HOLES:
• The Once and Future Universe. By Rick Gore. Photos by James A. Sugar. Paintings by Barron Storey. Picture text by David Jeffery. 704-749, June 1983

BLACKBEARD (Island), Georgia:
• Sea Islands: Adventuring Along the South's Surprising Coast. By James Cerruti. Photos by Thomas Nebbia and James L. Amos. 366-393, Mar. 1971

BLACKBURN, REID:
Photographer:
• Eruption of Mount St. Helens. By Rowe Findley. Note: Reid Blackburn lost his life covering the eruption of Mount St. Helens. 3-65, Jan. 1981
I. Mountain With a Death Wish. 3-33; II. In the Path of Destruction. 35-49

BLACKSTONE, WILLIAM:
• The British Way. By Sir Evelyn Wrench. 421-541, Apr. 1949

BLAIR, JAMES P.:
Author-Photographer:
• Home to Lonely Tristan da Cunha. 60-81, Jan. 1964
Photographer:
• Afo-A-Kom: A Sacred Symbol Comes Home. By William S. Ellis. 141-148, July 1974
• Ambassadors of Good Will: The Peace Corps. By Sargent Shriver and Peace Corps Volunteers. 297-345, Sept. 1964
• California, the Golden Magnet: II. Nature's North. By William Graves. Photos by James P. Blair and Jonathan S. Blair. 641-679, May 1966
• California's San Andreas Fault. By Thomas Y. Canby. 38-53, Jan. 1973
• Cape Cod's Circle of Seasons. By Tom Melham. 40-65, July 1975
• The Celts. By Merle Severy. Paintings by Robert C. Magis. 582-633, May 1977
• Crystals, Magical Servants of the Space Age. By Kenneth F. Weaver. 278-296, Aug. 1968
• Czechoslovakia: The Dream and the Reality. By Edward J. Linehan. 151-193, Feb. 1968
• Ethiopian Adventure. By Nathaniel T. Kenney. 548-582, Apr. 1965
• Eyes of Science. By Rick Gore. 360-389, Mar. 1978
• The Fair Reopens (New York World's Fair, 1964-1965). Text by Carolyn Bennett Patterson. 505-529, Apr. 1965
• Florida Rides a Space-age Boom. By Benedict Thielen. Photos by Winfield Parks and James P. Blair. 858-903, Dec. 1963
• Freedom Speaks French in Ouagadougou. By John Scofield. 153-203, Aug. 1966

JAMES P. BLAIR, NGS

Yugoslavia: villagers from Montenegro

• From Sun-clad Sea to Shining Mountains. By Ralph Gray. 542-589, Apr. 1964
• Gettysburg and Vicksburg: the Battle Towns Today. By Robert Paul Jordan. Map notes by Carolyn Bennett Patterson. 4-57, July 1963
• Greece: "To Be Indomitable, To Be Joyous." By Peter T. White. 360-393, Mar. 1980
• In the Crusaders' Footsteps. By Franc Shor. Photos by Thomas Nebbia and James P. Blair. 731-789, June 1962
• The Incredible Universe. By Kenneth F. Weaver. 589-625, May 1974
• India's Energetic Sikhs. By John E. Frazer. 528-541, Oct. 1972
• Iran: Desert Miracle. By William Graves. 2-47, Jan. 1975
• The Man Who Talks to Hummingbirds. By Luis Marden. 80-99, Jan. 1963
• Martha's Vineyard. By William P. E. Graves. 778-809, June 1961
• New Grandeur for Flowering Washington. By Joseph Judge. 500-539, Apr. 1967
• New National Park Proposed: The Spectacular North Cascades. By Nathaniel T. Kenney. 642-667, May 1968
• One Man's London. By Allan C. Fisher, Jr. 743-791, June 1966
• Orissa, Past and Promise in an Indian State. By Bart McDowell. 546-577, Oct. 1970
• Pollution, Threat to Man's Only Home. By Gordon Young. 738-781, Dec. 1970
• The Revolution in American Agriculture. By Jules B. Billard. 147-185, Feb. 1970
• Rotterdam–Reborn From Ruins. By Helen Hill Miller. 526-553, Oct. 1960
• South Africa's Lonely Ordeal. By William S. Ellis. 780-819, June 1977
• Springtime of Hope in Poland. By Peter T. White. 467-501, Apr. 1972
• Toledo–El Greco's Spain Lives On. By Louise E. Levathes. 726-753, June 1982
• Tropical Rain Forests: Nature's Dwindling Treasures. By Peter T. White. Paintings by Barron Storey. 2-47, Jan. 1983
• Wild Elephant Roundup in India. By Harry Miller. Photos by author and James P. Blair. 372-385, Mar. 1969
• Will Coal Be Tomorrow's "Black Gold"? By Gordon Young. 234-259, Aug. 1975
• Yugoslavia: Six Republics in One. By Robert Paul Jordan. 589-633, May 1970

BLAIR, JONATHAN:

Author-Photographer:
• Keeping House in a Cappadocian Cave. 127-146, July 1970

Photographer:
• Ancient Aphrodisias and Its Marble Treasures. By Kenan T. Erim. 280-294, Aug. 1967
• Aphrodisias, Awakened City of Ancient Art. By Kenan T. Erim. 766-791, June 1972
• A Bad Time to Be a Crocodile. By Rick Gore. 90-115, Jan. 1978
• Barehanded Battle to Cleanse the Bay. By Peter T. White. 866-881, June 1971
• A Buried Roman Town Gives Up Its Dead (Herculaneum). By Joseph Judge. 687-693, Dec. 1982
• California, the Golden Magnet: II. Nature's North. By William Graves. Photos by James P. Blair and Jonathan S. Blair. 641-679, May 1966
• Cyprus Under Four Flags: A Struggle for Unity. By Kenneth MacLeish. 356-383, Mar. 1973
• Dry-land Fleet Sails the Sahara. By Jean du Boucher. 696-725, Nov. 1967
• Florida's Booming–and Beleaguered–Heartland. By Joseph Judge. 585-621, Nov. 1973
• Glass Treasure From the Aegean. By George F. Bass. 768-793, June 1978
• Graveyard of the Quicksilver Galleons. By Mendel Peterson. 850-876, Dec. 1979
• Hawaii's Far-flung Wildlife Paradise. By John L. Eliot. 670-691, May 1978
• Home to the Enduring Berkshires. By Charles McCarry. 196-221, Aug. 1970
• Madeira, Like Its Wine, Improves With Age. By Veronica Thomas. 488-513, Apr. 1973
• The Mediterranean–Sea of Man's Fate. By Rick Gore. 694-737, Dec. 1982
• Mysteries of Bird Migration. By Allan C. Fisher, Jr. 154-193, Aug. 1979
• New Life for the Troubled Suez Canal. By William Graves. 792-817, June 1975
• On the Road With an Old-time Circus. By John Fetterman. 410-434, Mar. 1972
• Riding the Outlaw Trail. By Robert Redford. 622-657, Nov. 1976
• Sicily, Where All the Songs Are Sad. By Howard La Fay. 407-436, Mar. 1976
• Stockholm, Where "Kvalitet" Is a Way of Life. By James Cerruti. Photos by Albert Moldvay and Jonathan Blair. 43-69, Jan. 1976
• Synfuels: Fill 'er Up! With What? By Thomas Y. Canby. 74-95, *Special Report on Energy* (Feb. 1981)
• Yellowstone at 100: The Pitfalls of Success. By William S. Ellis. 616-631, May 1972

BLESSING OF THE FLEET:
• Gloucester Blesses Its Portuguese Fleet. By Luis Marden. 75-84, July 1953

BLEVINS, BURGESS: Photographer:
• Rediscovering America's Forgotten Crops. By Noel D. Vietmeyer. Paintings by Paul M. Breeden. 702-712, May 1981

BLIGH, WILLIAM:
• Huzza for Otaheite! By Luis Marden. 435-459, Apr. 1962
• I Found the Bones of the *Bounty*. By Luis Marden. 725-789, Dec. 1957

● Pitcairn and Norfolk–The Saga of *Bounty*'s Children. By Ed Howard. Photos by David Hiser and Melinda Berge. 510-541, Oct. 1983
Pitcairn Island. 512-529; Norfolk Island. 530-541
● Tahiti, "Finest Island in the World." By Luis Marden. 1-47, July 1962

BLINDS, Floating (Concealments):
● Western Grebes: The Birds That Walk on Water. By Gary L. Nuechterlein. 624-637, May 1982

BLIZZARD of Birds: The Tortugas Terns. By Alexander Sprunt, Jr. 213-230, Feb. 1947

BLOCK, IRA: Photographer:
● The Continental Shelf: Man's New Frontier. By Luis Marden. 495-531, Apr. 1978
● First Look at a Lost Virginia Settlement (Martin's Hundred). By Ivor Noël Hume. Paintings by Richard Schlecht. 735-767, June 1979
● New Clues to an Old Mystery (Virginia's Wolstenholme Towne). By Ivor Noël Hume. Paintings by Richard Schlecht. 53-77, Jan. 1982
● Peru's Pilgrimage to the Sky. By Robert Randall. Photos by Loren McIntyre and Ira Block. 60-69, July 1982
● Solo to the Pole. By Naomi Uemura. Photos by the author and Ira Block. 298-325, Sept. 1978

BLOOD, NED: Photographer:
● Sheep Airlift in New Guinea. 831-844, Dec. 1949

BLOOD SERVICES:
● The American Red Cross: A Century of Service. By Louise Levathes. Photos by Annie Griffiths. 777-791, June 1981

BLOSSOMS That Defy the Seasons. By Geneal Condon. Photos by David S. Boyer. 420-427, Sept. 1958

BLOWGUN Hunters of the South Pacific. By Jane C. Goodale. Photos by Ann Chowning. 793-817, June 1966

BLUE CRABS:
● Can We Save Our Salt Marshes? By Stephen W. Hitchcock. Photos by William R. Curtsinger. 729-765, June 1972
● This Is My Island, Tangier (Virginia). By Harold G. Wheatley. Photos by David Alan Harvey. 700-725, Nov. 1973

BLUE-EYED Indian: A City Boy's Sojourn with Primitive Tribesmen in Central Brazil. By Harald Schultz. 65-89, July 1961

BLUE HOLES, Great Bahama Bank:
● Diving Into the Blue Holes of the Bahamas. By George J. Benjamin. 347-363, Sept. 1970

BLUE RIDGE (Mountains), U. S.:
● Appalachian Valley Pilgrimage. By Catherine Bell Palmer. Photos by Justin Locke. 1-32, July 1949
● Chattooga River Country: Wild Water, Proud People. By Don Belt. Photos by Steve Wall. 458-477, Apr. 1983
● My Neighbors Hold to Mountain Ways. By Malcolm Ross. Photos by Flip Schulke. 856-880, June 1958
● Shenandoah, I Long to Hear You. By Mike W. Edwards. Photos by Thomas Anthony DeFeo. 554-588, Apr. 1970
● Skyline Trail from Maine to Georgia. By Andrew H. Brown. Photos by Robert F. Sisson. 219-251, Aug. 1949
● The Virginians. By Mike W. Edwards. Photos by David Alan Harvey. 588-617, Nov. 1974
● Wrestlin' for a Livin' With King Coal. By Michael E. Long. Photos by Michael O'Brien. 793-819, June 1983

BLUE-WATER Life by Night. By Kenneth Brower. Photos by William R. Curtsinger and Chris Newbert. 834-847, Dec. 1981

BLUE-WATER Plankton: Ghosts of the Gulf Stream. By William M. Hamner. 530-545, Oct. 1974

BLUE WHALES:
◆ *The Blue Whale.* 1977
● Killer Whale Attack! Text by Cliff Tarpy. Contents: Blue whale attacked by thirty killer whales. 542-545, Apr. 1979

BLUEBIRDS:
● Seeing Birds as Real Personalities. By Hance Roy Ivor. Included: Bluebirds on the Wing in Color. Photos by Bernard Corby and author. 523-530, Apr. 1954
● Song of Hope for the Bluebird. By Lawrence Zeleny. Photos by Michael L. Smith. 855-865, June 1977

BLUEFIN TUNA:
● Plight of the Bluefin Tuna. By Michael J. A. Butler. Photos by David Doubilet. Paintings by Stanley Meltzoff. 220-239, Aug. 1982

BLUEGRASS (Region), Kentucky:
● Heart of the Bluegrass. By Charles McCarry. Photos by J. Bruce Baumann. 634-659, May 1974

BLUM, ARLENE: Author:
● Triumph and Tragedy on Annapurna. 295-311, Mar. 1979

BOAT PEOPLE:
● Florida–A Time for Reckoning. By William S. Ellis. Photos by Nathan Benn and Kevin Fleming. Included: Refugees from the 1980 Cuban boatlift and from Haiti. 172-219, Aug. 1982
● Hong Kong's Refugee Dilemma. By William S. Ellis. Photos by William Albert Allard. 709-732, Nov. 1979
● Troubled Odyssey of Vietnamese Fishermen. By Harvey Arden. Photos by Steve Wall. 378-395, Sept. 1981

BOAT RACES:
● By Square-rigger from Baltic to Bicentennial. By Kenneth Garrett. 824-857, Dec. 1976
● Down East to Nova Scotia. By Winfield Parks. Included: Marblehead-Halifax race; Bras d'Or Lakes 15-mile race for the McCurdy Cup; Jones Trophy for Canadian yachts. 853-879, June 1964
● The Thames: That Noble River. By Ethel A. Starbird. Photos by O. Louis Mazzatenta. Included: Cambridge vs. Oxford; Henley Royal Regatta. 750-791, June 1983
● To Europe with a Racing Start. By Carleton Mitchell. Included: Newport-to-Bermuda race. 758-791, June 1958
● *See also* Yachting

BOATS:
● California's Surprising Inland Delta. By Judith and Neil Morgan. Photos by Charles O'Rear. 409-430, Sept. 1976
● "Delmarva," Gift of the Sea. By Catherine Bell Palmer. Included: Chesapeake Bay boats: Bugeyes, Hampton-class sloops, Log canoes, Skipjacks. 367-399, Sept. 1950
● Here's New York Harbor. By Stuart E. Jones. Photos by Robert F. Sisson and David S. Boyer. 773-813, Dec. 1954
● Inflatable Ship *(Amphitrite)* Opens Era of Airborne Undersea Expeditions. By Jacques-Yves Cousteau. 142-148, July 1961
● The Lower Mississippi. By Willard Price. Photos by W. D. Vaughn. 681-725, Nov. 1960
● Massachusetts' North Shore: Harboring Old Ways. By Randall S. Peffer. Photos by Nathan Benn. Included: Fishing boats, boatbuilding, and sail-making. 568-590, Apr. 1979
● On the Winds of the Dodecanese. By Jean and Franc Shor. 351-390, Mar. 1953
● Ships Through the Ages: A Saga of the Sea. By Alan Villiers. Included: Small craft, precursors of the ship. 494-545, Apr. 1963
● Shooting Rapids in Reverse! Jet Boats Climb the Colorado's Torrent Through the Grand Canyon. By William Belknap, Jr. 552-565, Apr. 1962
● The Thames: That Noble River. By Ethel A. Starbird. Photos by O. Louis Mazzatenta. 750-791, June 1983
● The Thames Mirrors England's Varied Life. By Willard Price. Photos by Robert F. Sisson. 45-93, July 1958
● Trawling the China Seas. Photos by J. Charles Thompson. Contents: Junks, Sampans. 381-395, Mar. 1950
● The Upper Mississippi. By Willard Price. 651-699, Nov. 1958
● Windjamming Around New England. By Tom Horgan. Photos by Robert F. Sisson. Contents: "Brutal Beasts," Cape Cod Baby Knockabouts, Dinghies, International 210-class sloops, Lightning-class sloops. 141-169, Aug. 1950
● *See also* Barges; Canoe Trips; Coracles; Cruises and Voyages; Dhows; Dories; Dugout Canoes; Ferries; Fishing Industry; Foldboats; Hydrofoil Boats; Kayaks; Sailing Vessels; Ships; Steamboats; Towboats; Umiaks; listings under Yachts; Yawls; *and Brendan; Hickory; J. W. Westcott; River Gypsy; Tigris*

BOCAIUVA, Brazil:
• Eclipse Hunting in Brazil's Ranchland. By F. Barrows Colton. NGS research grant. 285-324, Sept. 1947

BOCKSTOCE, JOHN: Author:
• Arctic Odyssey. Photos by Jonathan Wright. Paintings by Jack Unruh. 100-127, July 1983

BODIE ISLAND, North Carolina:
• Lonely Cape Hatteras, Besieged by the Sea. By William S. Ellis. Photos by Emory Kristof. 393-421, Sept. 1969

BODY DECORATION:
• Living Theater in New Guinea's Highlands. By Gillian Gillison. Photos by David Gillison. 147-169, Aug. 1983
• Niger's Wodaabe: "People of the Taboo." By Carol Beckwith. 483-509, Oct. 1983

BOLD Horsemen of the Steppes. By Sabrina and Roland Michaud. 634-669, Nov. 1973

A **BOLD** New Look at Our Past. The Editor. 62-63, Jan. 1975

BOLIVIA:
• Amazon–The River Sea. By Loren McIntyre. 456-495, Oct. 1972
• Ambassadors of Good Will: The Peace Corps. By Sargent Shriver and Peace Corps Volunteers. 297-345, Sept. 1964
Bolivia. By Edward S. Dennison. 315-319
• Flamboyant Is the Word for Bolivia. By Loren McIntyre. 153-195, Feb. 1966
• In Quest of the Rarest Flamingo. By William G. Conway. Photos by Bates Littlehales. 91-105, July 1961
• Puya, the Pineapple's Andean Ancestor. By Mulford B. Foster. 463-480, Oct. 1950
• Sky-high Bolivia. 481-496, Oct. 1950
• *See also* Titicaca, Lake

BOLL WEEVILS:
• The Pesticide Dilemma. By Allen A. Boraiko. Photos by Fred Ward. 145-183, Feb. 1980

BOMBAY, India:
• Bombay, the Other India. By John Scofield. Photos by Raghubir Singh. 104-129, July 1981

BOMBERS:
• Flying in the "Blowtorch" Era. By Frederick G. Vosburgh. 281-322, Sept. 1950
• Fun Helped Them Fight. By Stuart E. Jones. 95-104, Jan. 1948
• Our Air Age Speeds Ahead. By F. Barrows Colton. 249-272, Feb. 1948

BONAIRE (Island), Netherlands Antilles:
• The Netherlands Antilles: Holland in the Caribbean. By James Cerruti. Photos by Emory Kristof. 115-146, Jan. 1970

The **BONANZA** Bean–Coffee. By Ethel A. Starbird. Photos by Sam Abell. 388-405, Mar. 1981

BONAPARTE, NAPOLEON. *See* Napoleon I

BOND, WILLIAM H.: Artist:
• Have We Solved the Mysteries of the Moon? By Kenneth F. Weaver. 309-325, Sept. 1973
▲ "How Man Pollutes His World," painting supplement. Text notes by Gordon Young. World map on reverse. Dec. 1970

BONDAS (Tribespeople):
• Orissa, Past and Promise in an Indian State. By Bart McDowell. Photos by James P. Blair. 546-577, Oct. 1970

BONE WORKING:
• The Search for the First Americans. By Thomas Y. Canby. Photos by Kerby Smith. Paintings by Roy Andersen. 330-363, Sept. 1979

BONIN ISLANDS, North Pacific Ocean:
• The Bonins and Iwo Jima Go Back to Japan. By Paul Sampson. Photos by Joe Munroe. 128-144, July 1968

BOOBIES:
• Peru Profits from Sea Fowl. By Robert Cushman Murphy. Photos by author and Grace E. Barstow Murphy. 395-413, Mar. 1959

BOOKS, NGS:
◆ *The Age of Chivalry.* Announced. 544-551, Oct. 1969; 592, Oct. 1970
◆ *Alaska.* Announced. 880-884, June 1969
◆ *Alaska: High Roads to Adventure.* Announced. 860-864, June 1976
◆ *Alaskan Glacier Studies* (1914). 196, Feb. 1967
◆ *Along the Continental Divide.* 1981
◆ *The Alps.* 1973. Announced. 870-874, June 1972
◆ *The Amazing Universe.* Announced. 870-874, June 1975
◆ *The American Cowboy in Life and Legend.* 1972. Announced. 882-886, June 1971
◆ *American Mountain People.* Announced. 865-868, June 1973
◆ *America's Atlantic Isles.* 1981
◆ *America's Beginnings: The Wild Shores.* Announced. 870-874, June 1974
◆ *America's Hidden Corners.* 1983
◆ *America's Historylands, Landmarks of Liberty.* Announced. 360-363, Mar. 1962; rev. ed. 1967
◆ *America's Inland Waterway.* Announced. 865-868, June 1973
◆ *America's Magnificent Mountains.* 1980
◆ *America's Majestic Canyons.* 1979
◆ *America's Spectacular Northwest.* 1982
◆ *America's Sunset Coast.* 1978
◆ *America's Wild and Scenic Rivers.* 1983
◆ *America's Wonderlands, the National Parks.* Announced. 558-561, Oct. 1959; 562-563, Oct. 1961; rev. eds. 1975, 1980
◆ *Ancient Egypt.* 1978
◆ *Animals of East Africa: The Wild Realm.* 1969. Announced. 844-849, June 1968
◆ *The Appalachian Trail.* Announced. 870-874, June 1972
◆ *As We Live and Breathe: The Challenge of Our Environment.* Announced. 882-886, June 1971
◆ *Australia.* Announced. 844-849, June 1968
◆ *Back Roads America.* 1980
◆ *The Book of Birds,* 2 vols. (1932). 328, Sept. 1948; 576, 578, Oct. 1963; 554, Oct. 1964; 480, Oct. 1966
◆ *The Book of Dogs.* Note: The title of the 1966 edition is *Man's Best Friend.* Announced. 441-442, Sept. 1958
◆ *The Book of Fishes* (1952). 418, Mar. 1957; 440, Mar. 1960; 563, Oct. 1961
◆ *Canada's Wilderness Lands.* 1982
◆ *The Civil War.* Announced. 880-884, June 1969
◆ *Clues to America's Past.* Announced. 860-864, June 1976
◆ *The Craftsman in America.* Announced. 870-874, June 1975
◆ *The Desert Realm, Lands of Majesty and Mystery.* 1982
◆ *Discovering Man's Past in the Americas.* Announced. 880-884, June 1969
◆ *Everyday Life in Ancient Times* (1951). 766, June 1954; 563, Oct. 1961
◆ *Everyday Life in Bible Times.* Announced. 494-507, Oct. 1967; rev. ed. 1977
◆ *Exploring America's Backcountry.* 1979
◆ *Exploring Canada From Sea to Sea.* Announced. 868-875, June 1967
◆ *Exploring Our Living Planet.* 1983. Announced. 822-824, Dec. 1982
◆ *Exploring the Amazon.* 1970. Announced. 880-884, June 1969
◆ *Exploring the Deep Frontier.* 1980
◆ *Field Guide to the Birds of North America.* 1983
◆ *Great Adventures With National Geographic.* Announced. 729-733, Nov. 1963
◆ *Great American Deserts.* Announced. 870-874, June 1972
◆ *Great Religions of the World.* Announced. 587-590, Oct. 1971
◆ *The Great Southwest.* 1980
◆ *Greece and Rome: Builders of Our World.* Announced. 550-567, Oct. 1968; 592, Oct. 1970
◆ *Gypsies, Wanderers of the World.* Announced. 880-884, June 1970
◆ *Hawaii.* Announced. 880-884, June 1970
◆ *Hunting Wild Life with Camera and Flashlight* (1935). 296, Mar. 1952
◆ *Images of the World: Photography at the National Geographic Society.* Announced. 709, 851, Dec. 1981
◆ *In the Footsteps of Lewis and Clark.* Announced. 880-884, June 1970
◆ *The Incredible Incas and Their Timeless Land.* Announced. 870-874, June 1975
◆ *Indians of the Americas* (1955). 418, Mar. 1957; 781, June 1959
◆ *Into the Wilderness.* 1978
◆ *Isles of the Caribbean.* 1980
◆ *Isles of the Caribbees.* Announced. 408-417, Mar. 1966

◆ *Isles of the South Pacific*. 1968. Announced. 868-875, June 1967
◆ *John Muir's Wild America*. Announced. 860-864, June 1976
◆ *Journey Across Russia: The Soviet Union Today*. 1977
◆ *Journey Into China*. 1982
◆ *Life in Rural America*. Announced. 870-874, June 1974
◆ *Lost Empires, Living Tribes*. 1982
◆ *The Majestic Rocky Mountains*. 1976. Announced. 870-874, June 1975
◆ *Man's Best Friend*. 1958; rev. ed. 1966
◆ *Man's Conquest of Space*. Announced. 844-849, June 1968
◆ *The Marvels of Animal Behavior*. Announced. 588-590, Oct. 1972
◆ *Men, Ships, and the Sea*. Announced. 552-555, Oct. 1962; rev. ed. 1973
◆ *The Mighty Aztecs*. 1981
◆ *The Mighty Mississippi*. Announced. 882-886, June 1971
◆ *My Friends the Wild Chimpanzees*. 1967. Announced. 408-417, Mar. 1966
◆ *Mysteries of the Ancient World*. 1979
◆ *The Mysterious Maya*. 1977
◆ *The National Geographic Society and Its Magazine: A History*. Announced. 582A, Oct. 1957; 408, Sept. 1959; 880, Dec. 1964
◆ *Nature's Healing Arts*. 1977
◆ *Nature's World of Wonders*. 1983
◆ *The New America's Wonderlands: Our National Parks*. Announced. 436-438, Mar. 1975; rev. ed. 1980
◆ *Nomads of the World*. Announced. 882-886, June 1971
◆ *The Ocean Realm*. 1978
◆ *On the Brink of Tomorrow: Frontiers of Science*. 1982
◆ *Our Continent: A Natural History of North America*. Announced. 572-574, Oct. 1976
◆ *Our Country's Presidents*. Announced. 408-417, Mar. 1966; rev. ed. 1981
◆ *The Pacific Crest Trail*. 1975. Announced. 870-874, June 1974
◆ *Peoples and Places of the Past: The National Geographic Illustrated Atlas of the Ancient World*. 1983; Announced. 824, Dec. 1982
◆ *Powers of Nature*. 1978
◆ *Preserving America's Past*. 1983
◆ *Primitive Worlds*. Announced. 865-868, June 1973
◆ *Railroads: The Great American Adventure*. 1977. Announced. 860-864, June 1976
◆ *The Renaissance: Maker of Modern Man*. Announced. 588-592, Oct. 1970; rev. ed. 1977
◆ *The Revolutionary War: America's Fight for Freedom*. Announced. 868-875, June 1967
◆ *The River Nile*. 408-417, Mar. 1966
◆ *Romance of the Sea*. 1981
◆ *Secret Corners of the World*. 1982
◆ *Song and Garden Birds of North America*. Announced. 553-557, Oct. 1964; rev. ed. 1975
◆ *Special Report on Energy*. 1981
◆ *Splendors of the Past: Lost Cities of the Ancient World*. 1981
◆ *Stalking Birds with Color Camera* (1951). 437, Oct. 1955; 562-563, Oct. 1961; 532, Apr. 1962; 147, Jan. 1969
◆ *Still Waters, White Waters*. 1977
◆ *This England*. Announced. 539-543, Oct. 1966
◆ *Those Inventive Americans*. 1971. Announced. 880-884, June 1970
◆ *Trails West*. 1979
◆ *Undersea Treasures*. Announced. 870-874, June 1974
◆ *Vacationland U.S.A.* Announced. 734-740, May 1970; 573, Apr. 1973
◆ *Vanishing Peoples of the Earth*. Announced. 844-849, June 1968
◆ *Vanishing Wildlife of North America*. 1974. Announced. 865-868, June 1973
◆ *The Vikings*. 870-874, June 1972
◆ *Visiting Our Past: America's Historylands*. 1977
◆ *Voyages to Paradise: Exploring in the Wake of Captain Cook*. 1981
◆ *Water, Prey, and Game Birds of North America*. Announced. 529-535, Oct. 1965
◆ *We Americans*. Announced. 580-582, Oct. 1975; rev. ed. 1981
◆ *Wild Animals of North America*. Announced. 554-557, Oct. 1960
◆ *Wild Animals of North America*. 1979
◆ *Wilderness U.S.A.* Announced. 582-584, Oct. 1973
◆ *Wonder of Birds*. 1983
◆ *Wondrous World of Fishes*. Announced. 388-393, Mar. 1965; rev. ed. 1969
◆ *World Beneath the Sea*. Announced. 868-875, June 1967
◆ *The World in Your Garden*. Announced. 729-730, May 1957
◆ *The World of the American Indian*. Announced. 584-586, Oct. 1974

Children's Books:
◆ *Amazing Animal Groups*. 1981
◆ *Amazing Animals of the Sea*. 1981
◆ *Amazing Mysteries of the World*. 1983
◆ *Animals Helping People*. 1983
◆ *Animals in Danger: Trying to Save Our Wildlife*. 1978
◆ *Animals in Winter*. 1982
◆ *Animals that Build their Homes*. Announced. 718-720, Nov. 1976
◆ *Animals that Live in the Sea*. 1978
◆ *Animals that Travel*. 1982
◆ *Baby Birds and How They Grow*. 1983
◆ *The Blue Whale*. 1977
◆ *Book of Mammals* (2 volumes). Announced. 851, Dec. 1981
◆ *Camping Adventure*. Announced. 718-720, Nov. 1976
◆ *Cats: Little Tigers in Your House*. Announced. 728-730, Nov. 1974
◆ *Cowboys*. Announced. 724-726, Nov. 1975
◆ *Creatures of the Night*. 1977
◆ *Creatures Small and Furry*. 1983
◆ *Creepy Crawly Things: Reptiles and Amphibians*. Announced. 728-730, Nov. 1974
◆ *A Day in the Woods*. Announced. 724-726, Nov. 1975
◆ *Dinosaurs*. 736-738, Nov. 1972
◆ *Dogs Working for People*. Announced. 736-738, Nov. 1972
◆ *Explore a Spooky Swamp*. 1978
◆ *Far-Out Facts*. 1980
◆ *Giants From the Past: The Age of Mammals*. 1983
◆ *Hidden Worlds*. 1981
◆ *Honeybees*. Announced. 726-728, Nov. 1973
◆ *How Animals Hide*. Announced. 726-728, Nov. 1973
◆ *How Things Are Made*. 1981
◆ *How Things Work*. 1983
◆ *Koalas and Kangaroos: Strange Animals of Australia*. 1981
◆ *Let's Go to the Moon*. 1977
◆ *Life in Ponds and Streams*. 1981
◆ *Lion Cubs*. Announced. 736-738, Nov. 1972
◆ *More Far-Out Facts*. 1982
◆ *The Mysterious Undersea World*. 1980
◆ *Namu: Making Friends With a Killer Whale*. Announced. 726-728, Nov. 1973
◆ *National Geographic Picture Atlas of Our Fifty States*. 1978
◆ *National Geographic Picture Atlas of Our Universe*. 1980
◆ *National Geographic Picture Atlas of Our World*. 1979
◆ *Our Violent Earth*. 1982
◆ *Pandas*. Announced. 726-728, Nov. 1973
◆ *The Playful Dolphins*. Announced. 718-720, Nov. 1976
◆ *Puppies*. 1982
◆ *Safari!* 1982
◆ *Secrets From the Past*. 1979
◆ *Secrets of Animal Survival*. 1983
◆ *Spiders*. 728-730, Nov. 1974
◆ *Three Little Indians*. Announced. 728-730, Nov. 1974
◆ *Treasures in the Sea*. Announced. 736-738, Nov. 1972
◆ *Tricks Animals Play*. Announced. 724-726, Nov. 1975
◆ *Ways Animals Sleep*. 1983
◆ *What Happens in the Autumn*. 1982
◆ *What Happens in the Spring*. 1977
◆ *Wild Cats*. 1981
◆ *The Wild Ponies of Assateague Island*. Announced. 724-726, Nov. 1975
◆ *Wilderness Challenge*. 1980
◆ *Wildlife Alert: The Struggle to Survive*. 1980
◆ *Wonders of the Desert World*. Announced. 718-720, Nov. 1976
◆ *Your Wonderful Body!* 1982
◆ *Zoo Babies*. 1978
◆ *Zoos Without Cages*. 1981

Public Service Books:
◆ *Equal Justice Under Law*, Supreme Court book. Published in cooperation with The Foundation of the Federal Bar Association. Announced. 411, Mar. 1966; 586, Oct. 1967; rev. ed. 1982
◆ *The First Ladies*. Published in cooperation with the White House Historical Association. 1975; rev. ed. 1983
◆ *George Washington–Man and Monument*. Published in cooperation with the Washington National Monument Association. Announced. 586, Oct. 1967; rev. ed. 1973

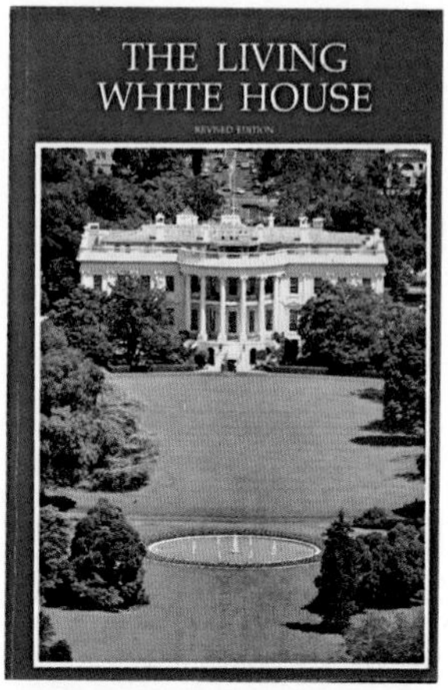

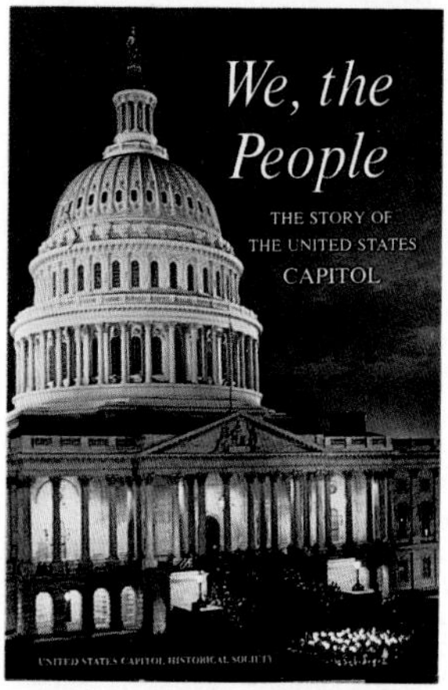

◆*The Living White House*. Published in cooperation with the White House Historical Association. Announced. 641, Nov. 1966; 586, Oct. 1967; rev. ed. 1982

◆*A Tribute to Lyndon B. Johnson, Conservationist*. Published in cooperation with The Eastern National Park and Monument Association. 1977

◆*We, the People*, Capitol guidebook. Published in cooperation with the United States Capitol Historical Society. Announced. 1, 2, Jan. 1964; 411, Mar. 1966; 586, Oct. 1967; rev. ed. 1981

◆*The White House*, guidebook. Published in cooperation with the White House Historical Association. Announced. 888-893, Dec. 1962; 1, Jan. 1964; 331, Mar. 1964; 642, Nov. 1964; 108, Jan. 1966; 411, Mar. 1966; 59, July 1966; 585, 586, Oct. 1967; rev. ed. 1982

Research Reports:

◆*1890-1954 Projects*. Announced. 442, Sept. 1975

◆*1955-1960 Projects*. Announced. 444, Sept. 1972

◆*1961-1962 Projects*. 1970

◆*1963 Projects*. Announced. 296, Aug. 1968

◆*1964 Projects*. Announced. 300, Aug. 1969

◆*1965 Projects*. Announced. 148, July 1971

◆*1966 Projects*. Announced. 146, July 1973

◆*1967 Projects*. Announced. 148, July 1974

◆*1968 Projects*. Announced. 296, Aug. 1976

◆*1969 Projects*. Announced. 294, Feb. 1978

◆*1970 Projects*. Announced. 298, Aug. 1979

◆*1971 Projects*. 1980. Announced. 480, Mar. 1981

◆*1972 Projects*. 1981. Announced. 830, June 1982

◆*1973 Projects*. Announced. 706, Nov. 1983

◆*1974 Projects*. Announced. 706, Nov. 1983

• *See also* Atlases; National Geographic Magazine: Indexes

BOOM on San Francisco Bay. By Franc Shor. Photos by David S. Boyer. 181-226, Aug. 1956

BOOM Time in Kuwait. By Paul Edward Case. 783-802, Dec. 1952

BOOM Times and Buccaneering: The Bahamas. By Peter Benchley. Photos by Bruce Dale. 364-395, Sept. 1982

The **BOOMING** Sport of Water Skiing. By Wilbur E. Garrett. 700-711, Nov. 1958

BOOMS. *See* Dhows

BOOTH, JOHN WILKES:

• The Lights Are Up at Ford's Theatre. By Lonnelle Aikman. 392-401, Mar. 1970

BOOTH, ROBERT: Author:

• Contrary New Hampshire. Photos by Sandy Felsenthal. 770-799, Dec. 1982

• Liechtenstein: A Modern Fairy Tale. Photos by John Launois. 273-284, Feb. 1981

• Yukon Fever: Call of the North. Photos by George F. Mobley. 548-578, Apr. 1978

BOOTH, WINDSOR P.: Author:

• Disaster in Paradise (Bali). Photos by Robert F. Sisson. 436-447, Sept. 1963

BOOTHBAY HARBOR, Maine:

• Seashore Summer. By Arline Strong. 436-444, Sept. 1960

BOOZ, ELISABETH B.: Author:

• Letter From Kunming: Two American Teachers in China. Photos by Thomas Nebbia. 793-813, June 1981

BOOZ, PATRICK R.:

• Letter From Kunming: Two American Teachers in China. By Elisabeth B. Booz. Photos by Thomas Nebbia. 793-813, June 1981

BORAH, LEO A.: Author:

• From Sagebrush to Roses on the Columbia. 571-611, Nov. 1952

• Illinois–Healthy Heart of the Nation. Photos by B. Anthony Stewart and Willard R. Culver. 781-820, Dec. 1953

• Landmarks of Literary England. Photos by Kathleen Revis. 295-350, Sept. 1955

• Montana, Shining Mountain Treasureland. 693-736, June 1950

• North Dakota Comes into Its Own. Photos by J. Baylor Roberts. 283-322, Sept. 1951

• Ohio Makes Its Own Prosperity. Photos by B. Anthony Stewart. 435-484, Apr. 1955

BORAIKO, ALLEN A.: Author:

• The Chip: Electronic Mini-marvel. Photos by Charles O'Rear. 421-457, Oct. 1982

• Fiber Optics: Harnessing Light by a Thread. Photos by Fred Ward. 516-535, Oct. 1979

• The Indomitable Cockroach. Photos by Bates Littlehales. 130-142, Jan. 1981

• The Pesticide Dilemma. Photos by Fred Ward. 145-183, Feb. 1980

• Silver: A Mineral of Excellent Nature. Photos by Fred Ward. 280-313, Sept. 1981

BORDEAUX (Region), France:

• Bordeaux: Fine Wines and Fiery Gascons. By William Davenport. Photos by Adam Woolfitt. 233-259, Aug. 1980

BOREN, LAMAR: Photographer:

• Goggle Fishing in California Waters. By David Hellyer. 615-632, May 1949

BORG, ERIK: Photographer:

• Norway's Reindeer Lapps. By Sally Anderson. 364-379, Sept. 1977

BORMAN, FRANK:

• Hubbard Medal recipient. 861, June 1970

• "A Most Fantastic Voyage": The Story of Apollo 8's Rendezvous With the Moon. By Sam C. Phillips. 593-631, May 1969
• Sounds of the Space Age, from Sputnik to Lunar Landing. Record narrated by Frank Borman. 750-751, Dec. 1969
• Space Rendezvous, Milestone on the Way to the Moon. By Kenneth F. Weaver. 539-553, Apr. 1966

BORN Hunters, the Bird Dogs. By Roland Kilbon. Paintings by Walter A. Weber. 369-398, Sept. 1947

BORNEO (Island), Indonesia-Malaysia. *See* Brunei; Sabah (North Borneo); Sarawak; Tanjung Puting Reserve

BORNHOLM (Island), Denmark:
• Baltic Cruise of the *Caribbee*. By Carleton Mitchell. 605-646, Nov. 1950
• 2,000 Miles Through Europe's Oldest Kingdom. By Isobel Wylie Hutchison. Photos by Maynard Owen Williams. 141-180, Feb. 1949

BOROBUDUR (Temple), Java, Indonesia:
• Indonesia Rescues Ancient Borobudur. By W. Brown Morton III. Photos by Dean Conger. 126-142, Jan. 1983

BORTON, NAN and JAMES W.: Authors:
• Ambassadors of Good Will: The Peace Corps. By Sargent Shriver and Peace Corps Volunteers. 297-345, Sept. 1964
Turkey. 331-333

BOSNIA-HERCEGOVINA (Republic), Yugoslavia:
• Yugoslavia: Six Republics in One. By Robert Paul Jordan. Photos by James P. Blair. 589-633, May 1970

BOSTELMANN, ELSE: Artist:
• How Fruit Came to America. By J. R. Magness. 325-377, Sept. 1951
• Our Vegetable Travelers. By Victor R. Boswell. 145-217, Aug. 1949
• The World in Your Garden (Flowers). By W. H. Camp. 1-65, July 1947

BOSTON, England:
• The Original Boston: St. Botolph's Town. By Veronica Thomas. Photos by James L. Amos. 382-389, Sept. 1974

BOSTON, Massachusetts:
• Benjamin Franklin, Philosopher of Dissent. By Alice J. Hall. Photos by Linda Bartlett. 93-123, July 1975
• Firebrands of the Revolution. By Eric F. Goldman. Photos by George F. Mobley. 2-27, July 1974
• Literary Landmarks of Massachusetts. By William H. Nicholas. Photos by B. Anthony Stewart and John E. Fletcher. 279-310, Mar. 1950
• Massachusetts Builds for Tomorrow. By Robert de Roos. Photos by B. Anthony Stewart. 790-843, Dec. 1966
• The Post Road Today. Photos by B. Anthony Stewart. 206-233, Aug. 1962
• Those Proper and Other Bostonians. By Joseph Judge. Photos by Ted Spiegel. 352-381, Sept. 1974
• The Wonder City That Moves by Night (Circus). By Francis Beverly Kelley. 289-324, Mar. 1948

BOSTON POST ROADS:
• The Old Boston Post Roads. By Donald Barr Chidsey. 189-205, Aug. 1962
• The Post Road Today. Photos by B. Anthony Stewart. 206-233, Aug. 1962

BOSWELL, VICTOR R.: Author:
• Our Vegetable Travelers. Paintings by Else Bostelmann. 145-217, Aug. 1949

BOSWELL, VICTOR R., Jr.: Photographer:
• The Magic Lure of Sea Shells. By Paul A. Zahl. Photos by Victor R. Boswell, Jr. and author. 386-429, Mar. 1969
• 900 Years Ago: the Norman Conquest. By Kenneth M. Setton. Photos by George F. Mobley. The complete Bayeux Tapestry photographed by Milton A. Ford and Victor R. Boswell, Jr. 206-251, Aug. 1966
• Restoration Reveals the "Last Supper." By Carlo Bertelli. 664-685, Nov. 1983
• Treasures of Dresden. By John L. Eliot. 702-717, Nov. 1978
• Venice's Golden Legacy. 609-619, Nov. 1972

BOTANICAL EXPLORERS. *See* Agricultural and Botanical Explorers

BOTANICAL GARDENS:
• Herbs for All Seasons. By Lonnelle Aikman. Photos by Sam Abell. Picture portfolio text by Larry Kohl. Included: Caprilands, Chelsea Physic Garden, Colonial gardens, Hampton Court Palace Gardens, Huntington Botanical Gardens, Jacqueline Kennedy Garden, National Herb Garden, New York Botanical Garden, Oxford University Garden, Royal Botanical Gardens at Kew, Shakespeare Elizabethan Garden, Taylor's Herb Garden, Williamsburg gardens, Willow Oak Flower and Herb Farm. 386-409, Mar. 1983
• *See also* Longwood Gardens; Royal Botanic Gardens

BOTTLENOSE DOLPHINS:
• The Trouble With Dolphins. By Edward J. Linehan. Photos by Bill Curtsinger. 506-541, Apr. 1979

BOTTOM SCRATCHERS CLUB:
• Goggle Fishing in California Waters. By David Hellyer. Photos by Lamar Boren. 615-632, May 1949

BOUCHAGE, LUC: Author:
• Mysore Celebrates the Death of a Demon. Photos by Ylla. 706-711, May 1958

BOUCHER, JEAN DU: Author:
• Dry-land Fleet Sails the Sahara. Photos by Jonathan S. Blair. 696-725, Nov. 1967

BOULAT, PIERRE: Photographer:
• Carrara Marble: Touchstone of Eternity. By Cathy Newman. 42-59, July 1982

BOUNTY, H. M. S.:
• *Bounty* Descendants Live on Remote Norfolk Island. By T. C. Roughley. Photos by J. Baylor Roberts. 559-584, Oct. 1960
• Huzza for Otaheite! By Luis Marden. 435-459, Apr. 1962
• I Found the Bones of the *Bounty*. By Luis Marden. 725-789, Dec. 1957
• Pitcairn and Norfolk–The Saga of *Bounty*'s Children. By Ed Howard. Photos by David Hiser and Melinda Berge. 510-541, Oct. 1983
Pitcairn Island. 512-529; Norfolk Island. 530-541

BOUNTY, H.M.S. (Replica):
• Huzza for Otaheite! By Luis Marden. 435-459, Apr. 1962
• Tahiti, "Finest Island in the World." By Luis Marden. 1-47, July 1962

BOURDILLON, TOM:
• Triumph on Everest. 1-63, July 1954
I. Siege and Assault. By Sir John Hunt. 1-43; II. The Conquest of the Summit. By Sir Edmund Hillary. 45-63

BOW (River), Canada:
• On the Ridgepole of the Rockies. By Walter Meayers Edwards. 745-780, June 1947

BOWDEN, TRACY:
• Graveyard of the Quicksilver Galleons. By Mendel Peterson. Photos by Jonathan Blair. 850-876, Dec. 1979

BOWDITCH, NATHANIEL:
• Literary Landmarks of Massachusetts. By William H. Nicholas. Photos by B. Anthony Stewart and John E. Fletcher. 279-310, Mar. 1950

BOWEN, IRA SPRAGUE: Author:
• Completing the Atlas of the Universe. 185-190, Aug. 1955
Sky Survey Plates Unlock Secrets of the Stars. 186-187
• Sky Survey Charts the Universe. 780-781, Dec. 1956

BOWERBIRDS:
• Australia's Amazing Bowerbirds. By Norman Chaffer. 866-873, Dec. 1961
• The Satin Bowerbird, Australia's Feathered Playboy. By Philip Green. 865-872, Dec. 1977

BOWES, ANNE LaBASTILLE: Author:
• The Quetzal, Fabulous Bird of Maya Land. Photos by David G. Allen. 141-150, Jan. 1969
• *See also* LaBastille, Anne

BOWHEAD WHALES:
• The Last U. S. Whale Hunters. By Emory Kristof. 346-355, Mar. 1973
"Ocean mammals are to us what the buffalo was to the Plains Indian." By Lael Morgan. 354-355

JOHN E. FLETCHER, NGS

Unknown Heroes: war dead in Capitol

BOWIE, BEVERLEY M.:
- Memorial Tribute to Beverley M. Bowie (1914-1958). 214, Feb. 1959

Author:
- Bermuda, Cradled in Warm Seas. Photos by Charles Allmon. 203-238, Feb. 1954
- Building a New Austria. Photos by Volkmar Wentzel. 172-213, Feb. 1959
- 'Known but to God' (Unknown Heroes). 593-605, Nov. 1958
- MATS: America's Long Arm of the Air. Photos by Robert F. Sisson. 283-317, Mar. 1957
- New England, a Modern Pilgrim's Pride. 733-796, June 1955
- Off the Beaten Track of Empire (Prince Philip's Tour). Photos by Michael Parker. 584-626, Nov. 1957
- The Past Is Present in Greenfield Village (Henry Ford Museum). Photos by Neal P. Davis and Willard R. Culver. 96-127, July 1958
- Salzkammergut, Austria's Alpine Playground. Photos by Volkmar Wentzel. 246-275, Aug. 1960
- This Young Giant, Indonesia. Photos by J. Baylor Roberts. 351-392, Sept. 1955
- Triumph on Everest: II. The Conquest of the Summit. By Sir Edmund Hillary. Note: Sir Edmund related his personal narrative to Beverley M. Bowie. 45-63, July 1954
- The White Horses of Vienna. Photos by Volkmar Wentzel. 400-419, Sept. 1958
- Williamsburg: Its College and Its Cinderella City. 439-486, Oct. 1954
- Wisconsin, Land of the Good Life. Photos by Volkmar Wentzel. 141-187, Feb. 1957

BOWLAND, ARTHUR: Photographer:
- Adventures With South Africa's Black Eagles. By Jeanne Cowden. Photos by author and Arthur Bowland. 533-543, Oct. 1969

BOY SCOUTS:
- Philmont Scout Ranch Helps Boys Grow Up. By Andrew H. Brown. 399-416, Sept. 1956
- Washington Lives Again at Valley Forge. By Howell Walker. Included: Boy Scout Jamboree. 187-202, Feb. 1954

BOYER, DAVID S.: Author:
- Golden Gate–Of City, Ships, and Surf (Golden Gate National Recreation Area, California). 98-105, July 1979
- Huntington Library, California Treasure House. 251-276, Feb. 1958
- Micronesia: The Americanization of Eden. 702-744, May 1967
- Portugal's Gem of the Ocean: Madeira. 364-394, Mar. 1959

Author-Photographer:
- Alberta Unearths Her Buried Treasures. 90-119, July 1960
- British Columbia: Life Begins at 100. 147-189, Aug. 1958
- The Canadian North: Emerging Giant. 1-43, July 1968
- Geographical Twins (Holy Land and Utah) a World Apart. 848-859, Dec. 1958
- The Glittering World of Rockhounds. 276-294, Feb. 1974
- Jerusalem to Rome in the Path of St. Paul. 707-759, Dec. 1956
- Kitimat–Canada's Aluminum Titan. 376-398, Sept. 1956
- Minnesota, Where Water Is the Magic Word. Photos by author and David Brill. 200-229, Feb. 1976
- Ontario, Canada's Keystone. Photos by Sam Abell and the author. 760-795, Dec. 1978
- Our Wild and Scenic Rivers: The St. Croix. 30-37, July 1977
- Our Wild and Scenic Rivers: The Skagit. 38-45, July 1977
- Over and Under Chesapeake Bay. 593-612, Apr. 1964
- Paris to Antwerp with the Water Gypsies. 530-559, Oct. 1955
- Petra, Rose-red Citadel of Biblical Edom. 853-870, Dec. 1955
- Powerhouse of the Northwest (Columbia River). 821-847, Dec. 1974
- Rhododendron Glories of Southwest Scotland. Photos by B. Anthony Stewart and author. 641-664, May 1954
- Warm Springs Indians Carve Out a Future. 494-505, Apr. 1979
- Wyoming: High, Wide, and Windy. 554-594, Apr. 1966
- Year of Discovery Opens in Antarctica. 339-381, Sept. 1957

Photographer:
- Ambassadors of Good Will: The Peace Corps. By Sargent Shriver and Peace Corps Volunteers. 297-345, Sept. 1964
- Blossoms That Defy the Seasons (Flower Preservation). By Geneal Condon. 420-427, Sept. 1958
- Boom on San Francisco Bay. By Franc Shor. 181-226, Aug. 1956
- Canada, My Country. By Alan Phillips. Photos by David S. Boyer and Walter Meayers Edwards. 769-819, Dec. 1961
- Crusader Lands Revisited. By Harold Lamb. 815-852, Dec. 1954
- Eastman of Rochester: Photographic Pioneer. By Allan C. Fisher, Jr. 423-438, Sept. 1954
- Flight Into Antarctic Darkness. By J. Lloyd Abbot, Jr. 732-738, Nov. 1967
- Fresh Treasures from Egypt's Ancient Sands. By Jefferson Caffery. 611-650, Nov. 1955
- Here's New York Harbor. By Stuart E. Jones. Photos by Robert F. Sisson and David S. Boyer. 773-813, Dec. 1954
- In the London of the New Queen. By H. V. Morton. 291-342, Sept. 1953
- Lake District, Poets' Corner of England. By H. V. Morton. 511-545, Apr. 1956
- London's Zoo of Zoos. By Thomas Garner James. 771-786, June 1953
- Our Navy's Long Submarine Arm. By Allan C. Fisher, Jr. Photos by David S. Boyer and author. 613-636, Nov. 1952
- Relics from the Rapids. By Sigurd F. Olson. 413-435, Sept. 1963
- A Stroll to John o'Groat's. By Isobel Wylie Hutchison. 1-48, July 1956

• We Are Living at the South Pole. By Paul A. Siple. 5-35, July 1957

BOYLE, ROBERT:
• The British Way. By Sir Evelyn Wrench. 421-541, Apr. 1949

BRADFORD, ERNLE: Author:
• Democracy's Fortress: Unsinkable Malta. Photos by Ted H. Funk. 852-879, June 1969
• The Faeroes, Isles of Maybe. Photos by Adam Woolfitt. 410-442, Sept. 1970

BRADLEY, LA VERNE: Author:
• Scenes of Postwar Finland. Photos by Jerry Waller. 233-264, Aug. 1947

BRADLEY, MATT: Photographer:
• America's Little Mainstream (Buffalo National River). By Harvey Arden. 344-359, Mar. 1977
• Easygoing, Hardworking Arkansas. By Boyd Gibbons. 396-427, Mar. 1978
• Nahanni: Canada's Wilderness Park. By Douglas H. Chadwick. 396-420, Sept. 1981

BRADSTREET, ANNE:
• Literary Landmarks of Massachusetts. By William H. Nicholas. Photos by B. Anthony Stewart and John E. Fletcher. 279-310, Mar. 1950

BRAGG, JOHN: Photographer:
• To Torre Egger's Icy Summit. By Jim Donini. 813-823, Dec. 1976

BRAHUI (Tribespeople):
• Pakistan, New Nation in an Old Land. By Jean and Franc Shor. 637-678, Nov. 1952

BRAINTREE, England. *See* New Mills

BRAKE, BRIAN: Photographer:
• Along the Storied Incense Roads of Aden. By Hermann F. Eilts. 230-254, Feb. 1957
• The Emperor's Private Garden: Kashmir. By Nigel Cameron. 606-647, Nov. 1958
• Jerusalem, the Divided City. By John Scofield. 492-531, Apr. 1959
• New Zealand: Gift of the Sea. By Maurice Shadbolt. 465-511, Apr. 1962
• Peking: a Pictorial Record. 194-197, 199-223, Aug. 1960
• Progress and Pageantry in Changing Nigeria. By W. Robert Moore. 325-365, Sept. 1956

BRAND, VANCE D.:
• Apollo-Soyuz: Handclasp in Space. By Thomas Y. Canby. 183-187, Feb. 1976

BRANDENBURG, FRED G.:
Photographer:
• Desert River (San Juan) Through Navajo Land. By Alfred M. Bailey. Photos by author and Fred G. Brandenburg. 149-172, Aug. 1947

BRANDENBURG, JIM: Photographer:
• Aldo Leopold: "A Durable Scale of Values." By Boyd Gibbons. 682-708, Nov. 1981
• Bamboo, the Giant Grass. By Luis Marden. 502-529, Oct. 1980

BOTH BY JIM BRANDENBURG

Canadian Rockies: nesting osprey, *above;* hiker near Banff, *below*

• Heart of the Canadian Rockies. By Elizabeth A. Moize. 757-779, June 1980
• Namibia: Nearly a Nation? By Bryan Hodgson. 755-797, June 1982
• South Dakota's Badlands: Castles in Clay. By John Madson. 524-539, Apr. 1981
• The Tallgrass Prairie: Can It Be Saved? By Dennis Farney. 37-61, Jan. 1980

BRANDING:
• Cowpunching on the Padlock Ranch. By William Albert Allard. 478-499, Oct. 1973

BRAS D'OR LAKES, Nova Scotia, Canada:
• Canada's Winged Victory: the *Silver Dart*. By Gilbert M. Grosvenor. 254-267, Aug. 1959
• Down East to Nova Scotia. By Winfield Parks. 853-879, June 1964
• Nova Scotia, the Magnificent Anchorage. By Charles McCarry. Photos by Gordon W. Gahan. 334-363, Mar. 1975

BRASÍLIA, Brazil:
• Brasília, Metropolis Made to Order. By Hernane Tavares de Sá. Photos by Thomas J. Abercrombie. 704-724, May 1960
• Brazil, Ôba! By Peter T. White. Photos by Winfield Parks. 299-353, Sept. 1962

BRAUNS, CLAUS-DIETER:
Author-Photographer:
• The Peaceful Mrus of Bangladesh. 267-286, Feb. 1973

BRAVING the Atlantic by Balloon. By Arnold Eiloart. 123-146, July 1959

BRAVO (Malamute-Husky):
• Antarctic Scientist Honored by The Society. Note: Bravo is proclaimed a VID (Very Important Dog) and is given an honorable discharge from the U. S. Navy. 792-793, June 1958
• Man's First Winter at the South Pole. By Paul A. Siple. 439-478, Apr. 1958

BRAVO (Weather Patrol), North Atlantic:
• Rugged Is the Word for Bravo. By Philip M. Swatek. 829-843, Dec. 1955

BRAZIL:
• The Amazon. Photos by Loren McIntyre. 445-455, Oct. 1972
▪ Amazon. 295A-295B, Feb. 1968
• Amazon–The River Sea. By Loren McIntyre. 456-495, Oct. 1972
• Blue-eyed Indian: A City Boy's Sojourn with Primitive Tribesmen in Central Brazil. By Harald Schultz. 65-89, July 1961
• The Bonanza Bean–Coffee. By Ethel A. Starbird. Photos by Sam Abell. 388-405, Mar. 1981
• Brasília, Metropolis Made to Order. By Hernane Tavares de Sá. Photos by Thomas J. Abercrombie. 704-724, May 1960
• Brazil, Ôba! By Peter T. White. Photos by Winfield Parks. 299-353, Sept. 1962

NICHOLAS DEVORE III

Brazil: lighted city of Rio de Janeiro

Amazon: Nambicuara Indian

W. JESCO VON PUTTKAMER

• Brazil Protects Her Cinta Larga Indians. By W. Jesco von Puttkamer. 420-444, Sept. 1971
• Brazil's Beleaguered Indians. By W. Jesco von Puttkamer. 254-283, Feb. 1975
I. Requiem for a Tribe? (Kreen-Akarores). 254-269; II. Good-bye to the Stone Age (Txukahameis). 270-283
• Brazil's Big-lipped Indians (Suyá). By Harald Schultz. 118-133, Jan. 1962
• Brazil's Golden Beachhead. By Bart McDowell. Photos by Nicholas DeVore III. 246-277, Feb. 1978
• Brazil's Land of Minerals. By W. Robert Moore. 479-508, Oct. 1948
• Brazil's Wild Frontier. By Loren McIntyre. 684-719, Nov. 1977
• Children of the Sun and Moon (Kraho Indians). By Harald Schultz. 340-363, Mar. 1959
• Drought Bedevils Brazil's Sertão. By John Wilson. Photos by Gordon W. Gahan. 704-723, Nov. 1972
• Eclipse Hunting in Brazil's Ranchland. By F. Barrows Colton. Photos by Richard H. Stewart and Guy W. Starling. NGS research grant. 285-324, Sept. 1947
◆ *Exploring the Amazon.* Announced. 880-884, June 1969
• The Gauchos, Last of a Breed. By Robert Laxalt. Photos by O. Louis Mazzatenta. 478-501, Oct. 1980
• Giant Insects of the Amazon. By Paul A. Zahl. NGS research grant. 632-669, May 1959
• Indians of the Amazon Darkness. By Harald Schultz. NGS research grant. 737-758, May 1964
• Jari: A Billion-dollar Gamble. By Loren McIntyre. Contents: Daniel K. Ludwig's paper-pulp and food-production enterprise in Brazil's Amazon basin. 686-711, May 1980
• Jungle Jaunt on Amazon Headwaters. By Bernice M. Goetz. 371-388, Sept. 1952
• The Jungle Was My Home. By Sasha Siemel. 695-712, Nov. 1952
• Man in the Amazon: Stone Age Present Meets Stone Age Past. By W. Jesco von Puttkamer. NGS research grant. 60-83, Jan. 1979
• Parks, Plans, and People: How South America Guards Her Green Legacy. By Mary and Laurance Rockefeller. Photos by George F. Mobley. 74-119, Jan. 1967
• Saving Brazil's Stone Age Tribes from Extinction. By Orlando and Claudio Villas Boas. Photos by W. Jesco von Puttkamer. 424-444, Sept. 1968
• Sea Fever. By John E. Schultz. 237-268, Feb. 1949
• Those Fiery Brazilian Bees. By Rick Gore. Photos by Bianca Lavies. 491-501, Apr. 1976
• Tropical Rain Forests: Nature's Dwindling Treasures. By Peter T. White. Photos by James P. Blair. Paintings by Barron Storey. 2-47, Jan. 1983
• Tukuna Maidens Come of Age. By Harald Schultz. 629-649, Nov. 1959
• The Waurá: Brazilian Indians of the Hidden Xingu. By Harald Schultz. 130-152, Jan. 1966
• Your Society Observes Eclipse in Brazil. NGS research grant. 661, May 1947
• *See also* Rio de Janeiro

BRAZILIAN BEES:
• Those Fiery Brazilian Bees. By Rick Gore. Photos by Bianca Lavies. 491-501, Apr. 1976

BRAZILIAN OTTERS:
• Giant Otters: "Big Water Dogs" in Peril. By Nicole Duplaix. Photos by the author and Bates Littlehales. NGS research grant. 130-142, July 1980

BREADALBANE (British Bark):
• Exploring a 140-year-old Ship Under Arctic Ice. By Joseph B. MacInnis. Photos by Emory Kristof. 104A-104D, July 1983

BREADFRUIT:
• Huzza for Otaheite! By Luis Marden. 435-459, Apr. 1962
• Tahiti, "Finest Island in the World." By Luis Marden. 1-47, July 1962

BREAKTHROUGH in Wildlife Studies. By John Craighead. NGS research grant. 148-158, July 1976

BRECKENFELD, GURNEY:
Photographer:
• Sierra High Trip. By David R. Brower. 844-868, June 1954

BREED, JACK: Author:
• Better Days for the Navajos. Photos by Charles W. Herbert. 809-847, Dec. 1958
Author-Photographer:
• First Motor Sortie into Escalante Land. 369-404, Sept. 1949
• Land of the Havasupai. 655-674, May 1948
• Roaming the West's Fantastic Four Corners. 705-742, June 1952
• Shooting Rapids in Dinosaur Country. Photos by author and Justin Locke. 363-390, Mar. 1954
• Utah's Arches of Stone. 173-192, Aug. 1947
Photographer:
• Colorado's Friendly Topland (Rocky Mountains). By Robert M. Ormes. 187-214, Aug. 1951
• Windjamming Around New England. By Tom Horgan. 141-169, Aug. 1950

BREEDEN, KAY:
Author-Photographer:
• Eden in the Outback. By Kay and Stanley Breeden. 189-203, Feb. 1973
• Rock Paintings of the Aborigines. By Kay and Stanley Breeden. 174-187, Feb. 1973

BREEDEN, PAUL M.: Artist:
• Rediscovering America's Forgotten Crops. By Noel D. Vietmeyer. Photos by Burgess Blevins. 702-712, May 1981

BREEDEN, STANLEY:
Author-Photographer:
• Eden in the Outback. By Kay and Stanley Breeden. 189-203, Feb. 1973

• Rock Paintings of the Aborigines. By Kay and Stanley Breeden. 174-187, Feb. 1973
Photographer:
• India Struggles to Save Her Wildlife. By John J. Putman. 299-343, Sept. 1976
• Strange Animals of Australia. By David Fleay. 388-411, Sept. 1963

BREEDER REACTORS:
• The Promise and Peril of Nuclear Energy. By Kenneth F. Weaver. Photos by Emory Kristof. 459-493, Apr. 1979

BRENDAN, Saint:
• The Voyage of *Brendan*. By Timothy Severin. Photos by Cotton Coulson. 770-797, Dec. 1977
• Who Discovered America? A New Look at an Old Question. The Editor. 769, Dec. 1977

BRENDAN (Leather-hulled Sailboat):
• The Voyage of *Brendan*. By Timothy Severin. Photos by Cotton Coulson. 770-797, Dec. 1977
• Who Discovered America? A New Look at an Old Question. The Editor. 769, Dec. 1977

BR'ER Possum, Hermit of the Lowlands. By Agnes Akin Atkinson. Photos by Charles Philip Fox. 405-418, Mar. 1953

BREWER, NADINE: Author:
• Home to the Heart of Kentucky. Photos by William Strode. 522-546, Apr. 1982

BREWERIES:
• Milwaukee: More Than Beer. By Louise Levathes. Photos by Michael Mauney. 180-201, Aug. 1980

BRIDES' FAIR:
• Berber Brides' Fair. By Carla Hunt. Photos by Nik Wheeler. 119-129, Jan. 1980

BRIDGE CONSTRUCTION:
• A Century Old, the Wonderful Brooklyn Bridge. By John G. Morris. Photos by Donal F. Holway. 565-579, May 1983

BRIDGES:
• Cane Bridges of Asia. Photos from Paul Popper. 243-250, Aug. 1948
• A Century Old, the Wonderful Brooklyn Bridge. By John G. Morris. Photos by Donal F. Holway. 565-579, May 1983
• Over and Under Chesapeake Bay. By David S. Boyer. Contents: The Chesapeake Bay Bridge-Tunnel. 593-612, Apr. 1964
• *See also* Delaware (River), for Delaware Memorial Bridge; Languedoc (Region), France, for Pont du Gard; San Francisco (City and Bay), California, for Golden Gate Bridge

BRIDGES, Natural, and Arches. *See* Arches National Monument; Canyonlands National Park; Escalante Canyon; Natural Bridges National Monument; Rainbow Bridge National Monument; Zion National Park

BRIGANTINE. *See Yankee*

BRIGGS, LYMAN J.:
• Eclipse Hunting in Brazil's Ranchland. By F. Barrows Colton. Photos by Richard H. Stewart and Guy W. Starling. NGS research grant. 285-324, Sept. 1947
Author:
• How Old Is It? (Radiocarbon Dating). By Lyman J. Briggs and Kenneth F. Weaver. 234-255, Aug. 1958
• Uncle Sam's House of 1,000 Wonders (National Bureau of Standards). By Lyman J. Briggs and F. Barrows Colton. 755-784, Dec. 1951
• When Mt. Mazama Lost Its Top: The Birth of Crater Lake. 128-133, July 1962

BRIGHT Dyes Reveal Secrets of Canada Geese. By John and Frank Craighead. 817-832, Dec. 1957

BRILL, DAVID: Photographer:
• The Anasazi–Riddles in the Ruins. By Thomas Y. Canby. Photos by Dewitt Jones and David Brill. Paintings by Roy Andersen. 554-592, Nov. 1982
• Ancient Aphrodisias Lives Through Its Art. By Kenan T. Erim. 527-551, Oct. 1981
• Chan Chan, Peru's Ancient City of Kings. By Michael E. Moseley and Carol J. Mackey. 318-345, Mar. 1973
• Ethiopia Yields First "Family" of Early Man. By Donald C. Johanson. 790-811, Dec. 1976
• Minnesota, Where Water Is the Magic Word. By David S. Boyer. Photos by author and David Brill. 200-229, Feb. 1976

BRIMBERG, SISSE: Photographer:
• Eskimo and Viking Finds in the High Arctic: Ellesmere Island. By Peter Schledermann. Included: Artifacts of the Norse, the Dorset, the Thule. 575-601, May 1981
• Hunters of the Lost Spirit: Lapps. By Priit J. Vesilind. 194-197, Feb. 1983
• Lost Outpost of the Egyptian Empire. By Trude Dothan. Paintings by Lloyd K. Townsend. 739-769, Dec. 1982
• The Magic World of Hans Christian Andersen. By Harvey Arden. 825-849, Dec. 1979
• Washington Cathedral: "House of Prayer for All People." By Robert Paul Jordan. 552-573, Apr. 1980
• Washington's Yakima Valley. By Mark Miller. 609-631, Nov. 1978
• Where Magic Ruled: Art of the Bering Sea. By William W. Fitzhugh and Susan A. Kaplan. 198-205, Feb. 1983

BRINDAMOUR, ROD: Photographer:
• Living with the Great Orange Apes: Indonesia's Orangutans. By Biruté M. F. Galdikas. 830-853, June 1980
• Orangutans, Indonesia's "People of the Forest." By Biruté Galdikas-Brindamour. 444-473, Oct. 1975

BRINGING Old Testament Times to Life. By G. Ernest Wright. Paintings by Henry J. Soulen. 833-864, Dec. 1957

BRISTLE-THIGHED CURLEW:
• The Curlew's Secret. By Arthur A. Allen. NGS research grant. 751-770, Dec. 1948

BRISTLECONE PINE, Oldest Known Living Thing. By Edmund Schulman. Photos by W. Robert Moore. 355-372, Mar. 1958

BRISTOL, HORACE:
Author-Photographer:
• Pescadores, Wind-swept Outposts of Formosa. 265-284, Feb. 1956
Photographer:
• Changing Formosa, Green Island of Refuge. By Frederick Simpich, Jr. 327-364, Mar. 1957
• Roaming Korea South of the Iron Curtain. By Enzo de Chetelat. 777-808, June 1950

BRITAIN. *See* Great Britain

BRITAIN Tackles the East African Bush. By W. Robert Moore. 311-352, Mar. 1950

The **BRITAIN** That Shakespeare Knew. By Louis B. Wright. Photos by Dean Conger. 613-665, May 1964

BRITAIN'S "French" Channel Islands. By James Cerruti. Photos by James L. Amos. 710-740, May 1971

BRITANNIA (Royal Yacht):
• Off the Beaten Track of Empire (Prince Philip's Tour). By Beverley M. Bowie. Photos by Michael Parker. 584-626, Nov. 1957

BRITISH BROADCASTING CORPORATION (B.B.C.): Expedition:
• Animal Safari to British Guiana. By David Attenborough. Photos by Charles Lagus and author. 851-874, June 1957

BRITISH Castles, History in Stone. By Norman Wilkinson. 111-129, July 1947

BRITISH COLUMBIA (Province), Canada:
• Across Canada by Mackenzie's Track. By Ralph Gray. 191-239, Aug. 1955
• Along the Yukon Trail. By Amos Burg. 395-416, Sept. 1953
• British Columbia: Life Begins at 100. By David S. Boyer. 147-189, Aug. 1958
• British Columbia's Cold Emerald Sea. Photos by David Doubilet. Text by Larry Kohl. 526-551, Apr. 1980
• Canada's Window on the Pacific: The British Columbia Coast. By Jules B. Billard. Photos by Ted Spiegel. 338-375, Mar. 1972
• Canadian Rockies, Lords of a Beckoning Land. By Alan Phillips. Photos by James L. Stanfield. 353-393, Sept. 1966
▲ *Close-up, Canada: British Columbia, Alberta, Yukon Territory,* supplement. Text on reverse. Apr. 1978
• *Endeavour* Sails the Inside Passage. By Amos Burg. 801-828, June 1947
• From Sun-clad Sea to Shining Mountains. By Ralph Gray. Photos by James P. Blair. 542-589, Apr. 1964

• *See also* Columbia River and Basin; Great Divide Trail; Kitimat; Vancouver; *and* Bikepacking

BRITISH COMMONWEALTH OF NATIONS:
• H.R.H. The Prince Philip, Duke of Edinburgh, Introduces to Members the Narrative of His Round-the-world Tour. 583-584, Nov. 1957
• Off the Beaten Track of Empire (Prince Philip's Tour). By Beverley M. Bowie. Photos by Michael Parker. 584-626, Nov. 1957

BRITISH COMMONWEALTH TRANS-ANTARCTIC EXPEDITION:
• The Crossing of Antarctica. By Sir Vivian Fuchs. Photos by George Lowe. 25-47, Jan. 1959
• Man's First Winter at the South Pole. By Paul A. Siple. 439-478, Apr. 1958
• Society Honors the Conquerors of Antarctica. 589-590, Apr. 1959

BRITISH EAST AFRICA. *See* present names: Kenya; Tanzania; Uganda

BRITISH GUIANA:
• Animal Safari to British Guiana. By David Attenborough. Photos by Charles Lagus and author. 851-874, June 1957
• Life Among the Wai Wai Indians. By Clifford Evans and Betty J. Meggers. 329-346, Mar. 1955
• Strange Courtship of the (Golden) Cock-of-the-Rock. By E. Thomas Gilliard. NGS research grant. 134-140, Jan. 1962
• Strange Little World of the Hoatzin. By J. Lear Grimmer. Photos by M. Woodbridge Williams. NGS research grant. 391-401, Sept. 1962

BRITISH HONDURAS. *See* Belize

BRITISH ISLES:
▲ *British Isles,* Atlas series supplement. July 1958
▲ *The British Isles,* supplement. Apr. 1949
▲ *British Isles; Medieval England,* double-sided supplement. Oct. 1979
▲ *A Traveler's Map of the British Isles,* supplement. Text on reverse. Apr. 1974
• *See also* Arran, Island of; Caldy; Channel Islands; Great Britain; Hebrides; Ireland; Lundy; Man, Isle of; Orkney Islands; St. Michael's Mount; Scilly, Isles of; Shetland Islands; Skomer; *and* The Renaissance; Vikings

BRITISH MOUNT EVEREST EXPEDITION:
• Triumph on Everest. 1-64, July 1954
I. Siege and Assault. By Sir John Hunt. 1-43; II. The Conquest of the Summit. By Sir Edmund Hillary. 45-63; III. President Eisenhower Presents the Hubbard Medal to Everest's Conquerors. 64

BRITISH TRANSGLOBE EXPEDITION:
• Circling Earth From Pole to Pole. By Sir Ranulph Fiennes. 464-481, Oct. 1983

The **BRITISH** Way: Great Britain's Major Gifts to Freedom, Democratic Government, Science, and Society. By Sir Evelyn Wrench. Paintings from British and American artists. 421-541, Apr. 1949

BRITT, KENT: Author:
• Costa Rica Steers the Middle Course. 32-57, July 1981
• The Joy of Pigs. Photos by George F. Mobley. 398-415, Sept. 1978
• The Loyalists. Photos by Ted Spiegel. 510-539, Apr. 1975
• Pennsylvania's Old-time Dutch Treat. Photos by H. Edward Kim. 564-578, Apr. 1973

BRITTANY (Region), France:
• France Meets the Sea in Brittany. By Howell Walker. 470-503, Apr. 1965
• Here Rest in Honored Glory . . . The United States Dedicates Six New Battle Monuments in Europe to Americans Who Gave Their Lives During World War II. Included: Brittany American Cemetery and Memorial. By Howell Walker. 739-768, June 1957
• Superspill: Black Day for Brittany. Photos by Martin Rogers. Text by Noel Grove. 124-135, July 1978
• *See also* Celts

BRITTON, WRIGHT: Author:
• Sailing Iceland's Rugged Coasts. Photos by James A. Sugar. 228-265, Aug. 1969

BROADSTAIRS, England:
• The England of Charles Dickens. By Richard W. Long. Photos by Adam Woolfitt. Included: Dickens Festival; "Bleak House," Dickens's summer home. 443-483, Apr. 1974

BROMELIADS:
• Hidden Worlds in the Heart of a Plant. By Paul A. Zahl. 389-397, Mar. 1975
• Puya, the Pineapple's Andean Ancestor. By Mulford B. Foster. 463-480, Oct. 1950

BRONTOSAURS:
• We Captured a 'Live' Brontosaur. By Roland T. Bird. 707-722, May 1954

BRONX ZOO. *See* New York Zoological Park

BRONZE AGE:
• Drama of Death in a Minoan Temple. By Yannis Sakellarakis and Efi Sapouna-Sakellaraki. Photos by Otis Imboden and Spyros Tsavdaroglou. 205-222, Feb. 1981
• Ebla: Splendor of an Unknown Empire. By Howard La Fay. Photos by James L. Stanfield. Paintings by Louis S. Glanzman. 730-759, Dec. 1978
• Lost Outpost of the Egyptian Empire. By Trude Dothan. Photos by Sisse Brimberg. Paintings by Lloyd K. Townsend. NGS research grant. 739-769, Dec. 1982
• Minoans and Mycenaeans: Greece's Brilliant Bronze Age. By Joseph Judge. Photos by Gordon W. Gahan. Paintings by Lloyd K. Townsend. 142-185, Feb. 1978
• Oldest Known Shipwreck Yields Bronze Age Cargo. By Peter Throckmorton. NGS research grant. 697-711, May 1962
• Thirty-three Centuries Under the Sea (Shipwreck). By Peter Throckmorton. 682-703, May 1960
• *See also* Hoabinhian Culture; Minoan Civilization

BRONZES:
• China Unveils Her Newest Treasures. Photos by Robert W. Madden. 848-857, Dec. 1974
• Mosaic of Cultures (Southeast Asia). By Peter T. White. Photos by W. E. Garrett. 296-329, Mar. 1971
• Warriors From a Watery Grave (Bronze Sculptures). By Joseph Alsop. 821-827, June 1983
• *See also* Dreyfus Collection

BROOK LIFE:
• Unseen Life of a Mountain Stream. By William H. Amos. 562-580, Apr. 1977

BROOKFIELD, CHARLES M.: Author:
• An Exotic New Oriole Settles in Florida. By Charles M. Brookfield and Oliver Griswold. 261-264, Feb. 1956
• Key Largo Coral Reef: America's First Undersea Park. Photos by Jerry Greenberg. 58-69, Jan. 1962

BROOKLYN (Borough), New York, N. Y.:
• Brooklyn: The Other Side of the Bridge. By Alice J. Hall. Photos by Robert W. Madden. 580-613, May 1983
• Long Island Outgrows the Country. By Howell Walker. Photos by B. Anthony Stewart. 279-326, Mar. 1951
• The Pious Ones (Brooklyn's Hasidic Jews). By Harvey Arden. Photos by Nathan Benn. 276-298, Aug. 1975

BROOKLYN BRIDGE, New York, N. Y.:
• A Century Old, the Wonderful Brooklyn Bridge. By John G. Morris. Photos by Donal F. Holway. 565-579, May 1983
• Editorial. By Wilbur E. Garrett. 563, May 1983

BROOKS, RHODA and EARLE: Authors:
• Ambassadors of Good Will: The Peace Corps. By Sargent Shriver and Peace Corps Volunteers. 297-345, Sept. 1964
Ecuador. 339-345

BROOKS RANGE, Alaska:
• Our Wildest Wilderness: Alaska's Arctic National Wildlife Range. By Douglas H. Chadwick. Photos by Lowell Georgia. 737-769, Dec. 1979

BROWER, DAVID R.: Author:
• Sierra High Trip. 844-868, June 1954

BROWER, KENNETH: Author:
• In Hawaii's Crystal Sea, A Galaxy of Life Fills the Night. Photos by William R. Curtsinger and Chris Newbert. 834-847, Dec. 1981

BROWER, WARD, Jr.:
• Easter Egg Chickens. By Frederick G. Vosburgh. Photos by B. Anthony Stewart. 377-387, Sept. 1948

BROWN, ANDREW H.: Author:
• Men Against the Hurricane. 537-560, Oct. 1950
• New St. Lawrence Seaway Opens the Great Lakes to the World. 299-339, Mar. 1959
• Newfoundland, Canada's New Province. Photos by Robert F. Sisson. 777-812, June 1949
• Ontario, Pivot of Canada's Power. Photos by B. Anthony Stewart and Bates Littlehales. 823-852, Dec. 1953
• Quebec's Forests, Farms, and Frontiers. 431-470, Oct. 1949
• Skyline Trail from Maine to Georgia. Photos by Robert F. Sisson. 219-251, Aug. 1949
• Sno-Cats Mechanize Oregon Snow Survey. Photos by John E. Fletcher. 691-710, Nov. 1949
• Sweden, Quiet Workshop for the World. 451-491, Apr. 1963
• Versatile Wood Waits on Man. 109-140, July 1951
• Weather from the White North. Photos by John E. Fletcher. 543-572, Apr. 1955
Author-Photographer:
• Haunting Heart of the Everglades. Photos by author and Willard R. Culver. 145-173, Feb. 1948
• Labrador Canoe Adventure. By Andrew Brown and Ralph Gray. 65-99, July 1951
• Norway's Fjords Pit Men Against Mountains. 96-122, Jan. 1957
• Philmont Scout Ranch Helps Boys Grow Up. 399-416, Sept. 1956
• Saving Earth's Oldest Living Things (Sequoias). Photos by Raymond Moulin and author. 679-695, May 1951
• Work-hard, Play-hard Michigan. 279-320, Mar. 1952
Photographer:
• All-out Assault on Antarctica. By Richard E. Byrd. 141-180, Aug. 1956
• Native's Return to Norway. By Arnvid Nygaard. 683-691, Nov. 1953
• Stop-and-Go Sail Around South Norway. By Edmond J. Moran. Photos by Randi Kjekstad Bull and Andrew H. Brown. 153-192, Aug. 1954

BROWN, J. CARTER: Author:
• The Genius of El Greco. 736-744, June 1982
• The National Gallery's New Masterwork on the Mall. Photos by James A. Sugar. 680-701, Nov. 1978

BROWN, JOHN:
• History Awakens at Harpers Ferry. By Volkmar Wentzel. 399-416, Mar. 1957

BROWN, ROLAND W.: Author:
• Fossils Lift the Veil of Time. By Harry S. Ladd and Roland W. Brown. 363-386, Mar. 1956

BROWN BEARS:
• Among Alaska's Brown Bears. By Allan L. Egbert and Michael H. Luque. NGS research grant. 428-442, Sept. 1975
• When Giant Bears Go Fishing. By Cecil E. Rhode. 195-205, Aug. 1954

BROWN PELICANS:
• Bad Days for the Brown Pelican. By Ralph W. Schreiber. Photos by William R. Curtsinger and author. 111-123, Jan. 1975

BRUCE, AILSA MELLON: Art Collection:
• In Quest of Beauty. Text by Paul Mellon. 372-385, Mar. 1967

BRUGES, Belgium:
• Belgium Comes Back. By Harvey Klemmer. Photos by Maynard Owen Williams. 575-614, May 1948
• Belgium Welcomes the World (1958 World's Fair). By Howell Walker. 795-837, June 1958
• Bruges, the City the Sea Forgot. By Luis Marden. 631-665, May 1955

BRUNEI (Sultanate), Borneo:
• Brunei, Borneo's Abode of Peace. By Joseph Judge. Photos by Dean Conger. 207-225, Feb. 1974
• In Storied Lands of Malaysia. By Maurice Shadbolt. Photos by Winfield Parks. 734-783, Nov. 1963
• Magellan: First Voyage Around the World. By Alan Villiers. Photos by Bruce Dale. 721-753, June 1976

BRUSSELS, Belgium:
• Belgium: One Nation Divisible. By James Cerruti. Photos by Martin Rogers. 314-341, Mar. 1979
• Belgium Comes Back. By Harvey Klemmer. Photos by Maynard Owen Williams. 575-614, May 1948
• Belgium Welcomes the World (1958 World's Fair). By Howell Walker. 795-837, June 1958

BRY, THEODORE DE: Engravings by (1590):
• Indian Life Before the Colonists Came. By Stuart E. Jones. 351-368, Sept. 1947

BRYANT, WILLIAM CULLEN:
• Literary Landmarks of Massachusetts. By William H. Nicholas. Photos by B. Anthony Stewart and John E. Fletcher. 279-310, Mar. 1950

BRYCE CANYON NATIONAL PARK, Utah:
• Nature Carves Fantasies in Bryce Canyon. By William Belknap, Jr. 490-511, Oct. 1958
• The West Through Boston Eyes. By Stewart Anderson. 733-776, June 1949

BUCHANAN, JAMES:
• The Living White House. By Lonnelle Aikman. 593-643, Nov. 1966
• Profiles of the Presidents: II. A Restless Nation Moves West. By Frank Freidel. 80-121, Jan. 1965

BUCK ISLAND REEF NATIONAL MONUMENT, St. Croix, Virgin Islands:
• Buck Island–Underwater Jewel. By Jerry and Idaz Greenberg. 677-683, May 1971

ALLAN L. EGBERT

Brown Bears: bear captures salmon

WILLIAM R. CURTSINGER

Brown Pelican: pelican scoops up fish

DAVID ALAN HARVEY

Buddhism: hands joined in worship

A **BUCKAROO** Stew of Fact and Legend: The Pony Express. By Rowe Findley. Photos by Craig Aurness. 45-71, July 1980

BUDAPEST, Hungary:
- The Danube: River of Many Nations, Many Names. By Mike Edwards. Photos by Winfield Parks. 455-485, Oct. 1977
- Hungary: Changing Homeland of a Tough, Romantic People. By Bart McDowell. Photos by Albert Moldvay and Joseph J. Scherschel. 443-483, Apr. 1971
- Hungary's New Way: A Different Communism. By John J. Putman. Photos by Bill Weems. 225-261, Feb. 1983

BUDDHISM:
- Burma, Gentle Neighbor of India and Red China. By W. Robert Moore. 153-199, Feb. 1963
- Cambodia: Indochina's "Neutral" Corner. By Thomas J. Abercrombie. 514-551, Oct. 1964
- The Caves of the Thousand Buddhas. By Franc and Jean Shor. 383-415, Mar. 1951
- Ceylon, the Resplendent Land. By Donna K. and Gilbert M. Grosvenor. 447-497, Apr. 1966
- In Long-Forbidden Tibet. By Fred Ward. 218-259, Feb. 1980
- India's Sculptured Temple Caves. By Volkmar Wentzel. 665-678, May 1953
- Indonesia Rescues Ancient Borobudur. By W. Brown Morton III. Photos by Dean Conger. Contents: World's largest Buddhist monument. 126-142, Jan. 1983
- Kathmandu's Remarkable Newars. By John Scofield. 269-285, Feb. 1979
- Kunming Pilgrimage. 213-226, Feb. 1950
- The Lands and Peoples of Southeast Asia. 295-365, Mar. 1971
  1. Mosaic of Cultures. By Peter T. White. Photos by W. E. Garrett. 296-329; 2. New Light on a Forgotten Past. By Wilhelm G. Solheim II. 330-339; 3. Pagan, on the Road to Mandalay. By W. E. Garrett. 343-365
- Nomads of China's West. By Galen Rowell. Photos by the author and Harold A. Knutson. 244-263, Feb. 1982
- Scintillating Siam. By W. Robert Moore. 173-200, Feb. 1947
- Sri Lanka: Time of Testing for an Ancient Land. By Robert Paul Jordan. Photos by Raghubir Singh. 123-150, Jan. 1979
- The Temples of Angkor. 548-589, May 1982
  I. Ancient Glory in Stone. By Peter T. White. Photos by Wilbur E. Garrett. 552-589; II. Will They Survive? Introduction by Wilbur E. Garrett. 548-551
- Thailand Bolsters Its Freedom. By W. Robert Moore. 811-849, June 1961
- *See also* Tibetan Buddhism; Zen Buddhism

BUENAVENTURA, Colombia:
- Cruising Colombia's "Ol' Man River." By Amos Burg. 615-660, May 1947

BUENOS AIRES, Argentina:
- Argentina: Young Giant of the Far South. By Jean and Franc Shor. 297-352, Mar. 1958
- Buenos Aires, Argentina's Melting-pot Metropolis. By Jules B. Billard. Photos by Winfield Parks. 662-695, Nov. 1967
- Which Way Now for Argentina? By Loren McIntyre. 296-333, Mar. 1975

BUFFALO. *See* Bison, American; Water Buffalo

BUFFALO BILL and the Enduring West. By Alice J. Hall. Photos by James L. Amos. 76-103, July 1981

BUFFALO NATIONAL RIVER, Arkansas:
- America's Little Mainstream. By Harvey Arden. Photos by Matt Bradley. Note: In 1972, Congress created the Buffalo National River, a unique administrative unit. 344-359, Mar. 1977

BUILDING a New Austria. By Beverley M. Bowie. Photos by Volkmar Wentzel. 172-213, Feb. 1959

The **BUILDING** of Tenochtitlan. By Augusto F. Molina Montes. Paintings by Felipe Dávalos. 753-765, Dec. 1980

BULGARIA:
- Ancient Bulgaria's Golden Treasures. By Colin Renfrew. Photos by James L. Stanfield. Paintings by Jean-Leon Huens. 112-129, July 1980
- The Bulgarians. By Boyd Gibbons. Photos by James L. Stanfield. 91-111, July 1980
- The Danube: River of Many Nations, Many Names. By Mike Edwards. Photos by Winfield Parks. 455-485, Oct. 1977
- Down the Danube by Canoe. By William Slade Backer. Photos by Richard S. Durrance and Christopher G. Knight. 34-79, July 1965

BULGE, Battle of the:
- Belgium Comes Back. By Harvey Klemmer. Photos by Maynard Owen Williams. 575-614, May 1948
- Luxembourg, Survivor of Invasions. By Sydney Clark. Photos by Maynard Owen Williams. 791-810, June 1948
- Luxembourg, the Quiet Fortress. By Robert Leslie Conly. Photos by Ted H. Funk. 69-97, July 1970

BULL, RANDI KJEKSTAD:
Photographer:
- Stop-and-Go Sail Around South Norway. By Edmond J. Moran. Photos by Randi Kjekstad Bull and Andrew H. Brown. 153-192, Aug. 1954

BULL DERBY: Madura (Island), Java:
- Postwar Journey Through Java. By Ronald Stuart Kain. 675-700, May 1948

BULLDOG ANTS:
● At Home With the Bulldog Ant. By Robert F. Sisson. 62-75, July 1974
Face-to-Face with a World of Ants. 72-75

BULLFIGHTS. *See* Andalusia (Region), Spain; Camargue (Region), France; Mexico City; Portugal at the Crossroads; Tijuana, Mexico

BULLFROG Ballet Filmed in Flight. By Treat Davidson. 791-799; June 1963

BUMP, JAMES D.: Author:
● Big Game Hunting in the Land of Long Ago. By Joseph P. Connolly and James D. Bump. 589-605, May 1947

BUMSTEAD, NEWMAN:
● Developed further the photo-composing machine invented by his father, Albert H. Bumstead. 419, Mar. 1953
Author:
● "Around the World in Eighty Days." 705-750, Dec. 1951
● Atlantic Odyssey: Iceland to Antarctica. Photos by Volkmar Wentzel. 725-780, Dec. 1955
● Children's Art Around the World. 365-387, Mar. 1957
● A Map Maker Looks at the United States. 705-748, June 1951
● Rockets Explore the Air Above Us. 562-580, Apr. 1957

BUNDI, India:
● Feudal Splendor Lingers in Rajputana. By Volkmar Wentzel. 411-458, Oct. 1948

BUNDY, CARTER:
● New Scarlet Bird in Florida Skies. By Paul A. Zahl. 874-882, Dec. 1967

BUNLAP, Pentecost Island:
● Land Diving With the Pentecost Islanders. By Kal Muller. 799-817, Dec. 1970

BURDEN, DAN: Author-Photographer:
● Bikepacking Across Alaska and Canada. 682-695, May 1973

BURDETT-SCOUGALL, IRENE:
Photographer:
● Pigeon Netting–Sport of Basques. 405-416, Sept. 1949

BUREAU OF STANDARDS. *See* National Bureau of Standards

BURG, AMOS: Author:
● *Endeavour* Sails the Inside Passage. 801-828, June 1947
Author-Photographer:
● Along the Yukon Trail. 395-416, Sept. 1953
● Cruising Colombia's "Ol' Man River." 615-660, May 1947
● *North Star* Cruises Alaska's Wild West. 57-86, July 1952

BURGUNDY (Region), France:
● Living the Good Life in Burgundy. By William Davenport. Photos by Robert Freson. 794-817, June 1978

BURIAL CUSTOMS:
● Ancient Mesopotamia: A Light That Did Not Fail. By E. A. Speiser. Paintings by H. M. Herget. 41-105, Jan. 1951
● China Unveils Her Newest Treasures. Photos by Robert W. Madden. 848-857, Dec. 1974
● Fresh Treasures from Egypt's Ancient Sands. By Jefferson Caffery. Photos by David S. Boyer. 611-650, Nov. 1955
● A Lady From China's Past. Photos from *China Pictorial.* Text by Alice J. Hall. 660-681, May 1974
● Life and Death in Tana Toradja. By Pamela and Alfred Meyer. 793-815, June 1972
● Lifelike Man Preserved 2,000 Years in Peat. By P. V. Glob. 419-430, Mar. 1954
● Periscope on the Etruscan Past. By Carlo M. Lerici. 337-350, Sept. 1959
● Tutankhamun's Golden Trove. By Christiane Desroches Noblecourt. Photos by F. L. Kenett. 625-646, Oct. 1963
● *See also* Funerals

BURIAL MOUNDS. *See* Bahrain; Ch'angsha; Indian Mounds; Tombs; Ur

A **BURIED** Roman Town Gives Up Its Dead (Herculaneum). By Joseph Judge. Photos by Jonathan Blair. NGS research grant. 687-693, Dec. 1982

BURKE, ARLEIGH A.:
● Hubbard Medal recipient. 589-590, Apr. 1959

BURKE, ROBERT O'HARA:
● The Journey of Burke and Wills: First Across Australia. By Joseph Judge. Photos by Joseph J. Scherschel. 152-191, Feb. 1979

BURMA:
● Anatomy of a Burmese Beauty Secret. By John M. Keshishian. 798-801, June 1979
● Burma, Gentle Neighbor of India and Red China. By W. Robert Moore. 153-199, Feb. 1963
● Burma's Leg Rowers and Floating Farms. Photos by W. E. Garrett. Text by David Jeffery. 826-845, June 1974
● Cane Bridges of Asia. Photos from Paul Popper. 243-250, Aug. 1948
● The Lands and Peoples of Southeast Asia. 295-365, Mar. 1971
I. Mosaic of Cultures. By Peter T. White. Photos by W. E. Garrett. 296-329; II. New Light on a Forgotten Past. By Wilhelm G. Solheim II. 330-339; III. Pagan, on the Road to Mandalay. By W. E. Garrett. 343-365
● Operation Eclipse: 1948. By William A. Kinney. NGS research grant. 325-372, Mar. 1949

BURNETT, WANDA: Author:
● The Romance of American Furs. 379-402, Mar. 1948

BURNS, ROBERT:
● Poets' Voices Linger in Scottish Shrines. By Isobel Wylie Hutchison. Photos by Kathleen Revis. 437-488, Oct. 1957

BURNS, ROBERT K., Jr.:
Author-Photographer:
● Saint Véran, France's Highest Village. 571-588, Apr. 1959

BURR PRIZE (Franklin L. Burr Prize):
● Burr Prizes Awarded to Dr. Edgerton and Dr. Van Biesbroeck. 705-706, May 1953; 523, Apr. 1955

BURROS, Wild:
● Getting to Know the Wild Burros of Death Valley. By Patricia des Roses Moehlman. Photos by Ira S. Lerner and author. NGS research grant. 502-517, Apr. 1972

BURROUGHS, CARROLL A.: Author:
● Searching for Cliff Dwellers' Secrets (Wetherill Mesa). 619-625, Nov. 1959

BURTON, CHARLES:
● Circling Earth From Pole to Pole. By Sir Ranulph Fiennes. 464-481, Oct. 1983

BUS TRIPS:
● Oasis-hopping in the Sahara. By Maynard Owen Williams. 209-236, Feb. 1949
● You Can't Miss America by Bus. By Howell Walker. Paintings by Walter A. Weber. 1-42, July 1950

BUSHMEN:
● Africa's Bushman Art Treasures. By Alfred Friendly. Photos by Alex R. Willcox. 848-865, June 1963
● Bushmen of the Kalahari. By Elizabeth Marshall Thomas. Photos by Laurence K. Marshall. 866-888, June 1963
■ Bushmen of the Kalahari. 578A-578B, Apr. 1973; 732A-732B, May 1974
● Namibia: Nearly a Nation? By Bryan Hodgson. Photos by Jim Brandenburg. 755-797, June 1982

BUSINESSMAN in the Bush. By Frederick Kent Truslow. 634-675, May 1970

BUSY Fairbanks Sets Alaska's Pace. By Bruce A. Wilson. 505-523, Oct. 1949

BUTCHER, SUSAN: Author:
● Thousand-mile Race to Nome: A Woman's Icy Struggle. Photos by Kerby Smith. 411-422, Mar. 1983

BUTLER, MICHAEL J. A.: Author:
● Plight of the Bluefin Tuna. Photos by David Doubilet. Paintings by Stanley Meltzoff. 220-239, Aug. 1982

BUTTERFLIES:
● The High World of the Rain Forest. By William Beebe. Paintings by Guy Neale. 838-855, June 1958
● Keeping House for Tropical Butterflies. By Jocelyn Crane. Photos by M. Woodbridge Williams. NGS research grant. 193-217, Aug. 1957
● *See also* Monarch Butterfly

BUTTRICK GARDEN, Concord, Massachusetts:
● History and Beauty Blend in a Concord Iris Garden. By Robert T. Cochran, Jr. Photos by M. Woodbridge Williams. 705-719, May 1959

***BUZ KASHI*:**
● Bold Horsemen of the Steppes (Turkomans). By Sabrina and Roland Michaud. 634-669, Nov. 1973

BY Cotswold Lanes to Wold's End. By Melville Bell Grosvenor. 615-654, May 1948

BY Full-rigged Ship to Denmark's Fairyland. By Alan Villiers. Photos by Alexander Taylor and author. 809-828, Dec. 1955

BY Parachute Into Peru's Lost World. By G. Brooks Baekeland. Photos by author and Peter R. Gimbel. NGS research grant. 268-296, Aug. 1964

BY Square-rigger from Baltic to Bicentennial. By Kenneth Garrett. 824-857, Dec. 1976

BYELORUSSIAN S.S.R., U.S.S.R.:
• Down on the Farm, Soviet Style–a 4-H Adventure. By John Garaventa. Photos by James Tobin and Carol Schmidt. 768-797, June 1979

BYRD, RICHARD EVELYN:
• Admiral of the Ends of the Earth. By Melville Bell Grosvenor. 36-48, July 1957
• The Nation Honors Admiral Richard E. Byrd. 567-578, Apr. 1962
• The Society's Hubbard Medal Awarded to Commander MacMillan. Note: Tribute was paid to the MacMillans by Admiral Byrd. 563-564, Apr. 1953
Author:
• All-out Assault on Antarctica. 141-180, Aug. 1956
• Our Navy Explores Antarctica. U. S. Navy official photos. 429-522, Oct. 1947
• To the Men at South Pole Station. 1-4, July 1957

BYZANTINE ART:
• Athens to Istanbul. By Jean and Franc Shor. 37-76, Jan. 1956
• Island of Faith in the Sinai Wilderness (St. Catherine's Monastery). By George H. Forsyth. Photos by Robert F. Sisson. 82-106, Jan. 1964
• Mount Sinai's Holy Treasures (St. Catherine's Monastery). By Kurt Weitzmann. Photos by Fred Anderegg. 109-127, Jan. 1964

BYZANTINE EMPIRE:
• Athens to Istanbul. By Jean and Franc Shor. 37-76, Jan. 1956
• The Byzantine Empire. 709-777, Dec. 1983
I. Rome of the East. By Merle Severy. Photos by James L. Stanfield. 709-767; II. Mount Athos. 739-745; III. Eternal Easter in a Greek Village. By Maria Nicolaidis-Karanikolas. Photos by James L. Stanfield. 768-777
▲ *Europe; Historical Map of Europe,* double-sided supplement. Dec. 1983
• A New Look at Medieval Europe. By Kenneth M. Setton. Paintings by Andre Durenceau and Birney Lettick. 799-859, Dec. 1962
• *Yankee* Cruises Turkey's History-haunted Coast. By Irving and Electa Johnson. Photos by Joseph J. Scherschel. 798-845, Dec. 1969

C

C & O CANAL. *See* Chesapeake and Ohio Canal

CABLE CONSTRUCTION (Wire):
• A Century Old, the Wonderful Brooklyn Bridge. By John G. Morris. Photos by Donal F. Holway. 565-579, May 1983

CABLEWAY:
• Across the Ridgepole of the Alps. By Walter Meayers Edwards. 410-419, Sept. 1960

CABOT, JOHN:
• The British Way. By Sir Evelyn Wrench. 421-541, Apr. 1949

CACAO:
• Happy-go-lucky Trinidad and Tobago. By Charles Allmon. 35-75, Jan. 1953

CACTUS CULT. *See* Huichol Indians

CACTUSES:
• Abundant Life in a Desert Land. By Walter Meayers Edwards. 424-436, Sept. 1973
• American Wild Flower Odyssey. By P. L. Ricker. 603-634, May 1953

CADES COVE, Tennessee:
• The People of Cades Cove. By William O. Douglas. Photos by Thomas Nebbia and Otis Imboden. 60-95, July 1962

CAERNARVON CASTLE, Caernarvonshire, Wales:
• The Investiture of Great Britain's Prince of Wales. By Allan C. Fisher, Jr. Photos by James L. Stanfield and Adam Woolfitt. 698-715, Nov. 1969

CAFFERY, JEFFERSON: Author:
• Fresh Treasures from Egypt's Ancient Sands. Photos by David S. Boyer. 611-650, Nov. 1955

CAIMANS:
• In the Wilds of a City Parlor. By Paul A. Zahl. 645-672, Nov. 1954

CAIRNS, ROBERT: Author:
• Sunny Corsica: French Morsel in the Mediterranean. Photos by Joseph J. Scherschel. 401-423, Sept. 1973

CAIRO, Egypt:
• "Around the World in Eighty Days." By Newman Bumstead. 705-750, Dec. 1951
• Cairo, Troubled Capital of the Arab World. By William S. Ellis. Photos by Winfield Parks. 639-667, May 1972
• Safari from Congo to Cairo. By Elsie May Bell Grosvenor. Photos by Gilbert Grosvenor. 721-771, Dec. 1954
• *See also* Akhenaten Temple Project

CAISSON DISEASE. *See* The Bends

CAJUNS:
• Cajunland, Louisiana's French-speaking Coast. By Bern Keating. Photos by Charles Harbutt and Franke Keating. 353-391, Mar. 1966
• Trouble in Bayou Country: Louisiana's Atchafalaya. By Jack and Anne Rudloe. Photos by C. C. Lockwood. 377-397, Sept. 1979

CALAVERAS BIG TREES STATE PARK, California:
• Saving Earth's Oldest Living Things. By Andrew H. Brown. Photos by Raymond Moulin and author. 679-695, May 1951

CALCUTTA, India:
• Calcutta, India's Maligned Metropolis. By Peter T. White. Photos by Raghubir Singh. 534-563, Apr. 1973
• From the Hair of Siva. By Helen and Frank Schreider. 445-503, Oct. 1960
• The Ganges, River of Faith. By John J. Putman. Photos by Raghubir Singh. 445-483, Oct. 1971

CALDY, the Monks' Island (Wales). By John E. H. Nolan. 564-578, Oct. 1955

CALENDARS:
• A Bold New Look at Our Past. The Editor. NGS research grant. 62-63, Jan. 1975
• Editorial. By Gilbert M. Grosvenor. 727, Dec. 1975
• Exploring the Mind of Ice Age Man. By Alexander Marshack. NGS research grant. 64-89, Jan. 1975
• The Maya: Riddle of the Glyphs. By George E. Stuart. Photos by Otis Imboden. 768-791, Dec. 1975

CALGARY, Alberta, Canada:
• Canada's Heartland, the Prairie Provinces. By W. E. Garrett. 443-489, Oct. 1970

CALIFORNIA:
• Avalanche! By David Cupp. 280-305, Sept. 1982
I. Winter's White Death. 280-281; II. "I'm OK, I'm Alive!" Photos by Lanny Johnson and Andre Benier. 282-289; III. Battling the Juggernaut. 290-305
• Bristlecone Pine, Oldest Known Living Thing. By Edmund Schulman. Photos by W. Robert Moore. 355-372, Mar. 1958
• California, Horn of Plenty. By Frederick Simpich. Photos by Willard R. Culver. 553-594, May 1949
• California, the Golden Magnet. By William Graves. 595-679, May 1966
I. The South. Photos by Thomas Nebbia. 595-639; II. Nature's North. Photos by James P. Blair and Jonathan S. Blair. 641-679
• Californians Escape to the Desert. By Mason Sutherland. Photos by Charles W. Herbert. 675-724, Nov. 1957
• California's Parched Oasis, the Owens Valley. By Judith and Neil Morgan. Photos by Jodi Cobb and Galen Rowell. 98-127, Jan. 1976

● California's San Andreas Fault. By Thomas Y. Canby. Photos by James P. Blair. 38-53, Jan. 1973
● California's Silicon Valley. By Moira Johnston. Photos by Charles O'Rear. 459-477, Oct. 1982
● California's Surprising Inland Delta. By Judith and Neil Morgan. Photos by Charles O'Rear. 409-430, Sept. 1976
● California's Wonderful One (State Highway No. 1). By Frank Cameron. Photos by B. Anthony Stewart. 571-617, Nov. 1959
▲ *Close-up: U.S.A., California and Nevada,* supplement. Text on reverse. June 1974
● The Desert: An Age-old Challenge Grows. By Rick Gore. Photos by Georg Gerster and Bruce Dale. 586-639, Nov. 1979
● Editorial. By Wilbur E. Garrett. 421, Oct. 1981
● Finding the Mt. Everest of All Living Things (Redwood Tree). By Paul A. Zahl. 10-51, July 1964
● The Friendly Train Called Skunk. By Dean Jennings. Photos by B. Anthony Stewart. 720-734, May 1959
● Geothermal Energy: The Power of Letting Off Steam. By Kenneth F. Weaver. 566-579, Oct. 1977
● Giant Sequoias Draw Millions to California Parks. By John Michael Kauffmann. Photos by B. Anthony Stewart. 147-187, Aug. 1959
● Goggle Fishing in California Waters. By David Hellyer. Photos by Lamar Boren. 615-632, May 1949
■ The Great Mojave Desert. 1971
● Here Come the Marines. By Frederick Simpich. Included: San Diego; and Camps Del Mar, Pendleton, and El Toro, in southern California. 647-672, Nov. 1950
● How Fruit Came to America. By J. R. Magness. Paintings by Else Bostelmann. Included: Date culture; Orange and lemon production. 325-377, Sept. 1951
● Hummingbirds: The Nectar Connection. By Paul W. Ewald. Photos by Robert A. Tyrrell. 223-227, Feb. 1982
● Indians of the Far West. By Matthew W. Stirling. Paintings by W. Langdon Kihn. 175-200, Feb. 1948
● John Muir's Wild America. By Harvey Arden. Photos by Dewitt Jones. 433-461, Apr. 1973
● A Long History of New Beginnings (National Parks). By Melville Bell Grosvenor. 18-29, July 1979
● The Lure of the Changing Desert. 817-824, June 1954
● The Magic Worlds of Walt Disney. By Robert de Roos. Photos by Thomas Nebbia. 159-207, Aug. 1963
● A Map Maker Looks at the United States. By Newman Bumstead. Included: Bakersfield; Central Valley; Lake Tahoe; Los Angeles; McCloud River; Mojave Desert; Mount Shasta; Pit River; Sacramento River; San Francisco; Shasta Dam; Sierra Nevada; Tulare; Yosemite Valley. 705-748, June 1951
▲ *A Map of California,* supplement. June 1954
● The Mexican Americans: A People on the Move. By Griffin Smith, Jr. Photos by Stephanie Maze. 780-809, June 1980
● Mono Lake: A Vital Way Station for the Wilson's Phalarope. By Joseph R. Jehl, Jr. NGS research grant. 520-525, Oct. 1981
● My Life in the Valley of the Moon. By H. H. Arnold. Photos by Willard R. Culver. 689-716, Dec. 1948
● Napa, California's Valley of the Vine. By Moira Johnston. Photos by Charles O'Rear. 695-717, May 1979
● New Rush to Golden California. By George W. Long. 723-802, June 1954
▲ *Northern California; Southern California,* double-sided U. S. Atlas series supplement. May 1966
● Orange, a Most California County. By Judith and Neil Morgan. Photos by Vince Streano. 750-779, Dec. 1981
◆ *Our Violent Earth.* 1982
● A Park to Save the Tallest Trees. By Melville Bell Grosvenor. 62-64, July 1966
● The Pesticide Dilemma. By Allen A. Boraiko. Photos by Fred Ward. 145-183, Feb. 1980
● The Proud Armenians. By Robert Paul Jordan. Photos by Harry N. Naltchayan. 846-873, June 1978
● Rediscovering America's Forgotten Crops. By Noel D. Vietmeyer. Photos by Burgess Blevins. Paintings by Paul M. Breeden. 702-712, May 1981
● Redwoods, Rain, and Lots of Room: California's North Coast. By Judith and Neil Morgan. Photos by Dewitt Jones. 330-363, Sept. 1977
● The Revolution in American Agriculture. By Jules B. Billard. Photos by James P. Blair. 147-185, Feb. 1970
● San Francisco Bay: The Beauty and the Battles. By Cliff Tarpy. Photos by James A. Sugar. 814-845, June 1981
● Saving Earth's Oldest Living Things. By Andrew H. Brown. Photos by Raymond Moulin and author. Contents: Calaveras Big Trees State Park; Giant Forest, Sequoia National Park; South Calaveras Grove. 679-695, May 1951
● Seeking the Secret of the Giants. By Frank M. Setzler. Photos by Richard H. Stewart. 390-404, Sept. 1952
Giant Effigies of the Southwest. By George C. Marshall. 389
● Shells Take You Over World Horizons. By Rutherford Platt. 33-84, July 1949
● Skiing in the United States. By Kathleen Revis. 216-254, Feb. 1959
● Skyway Below the Clouds. By Carl R. Markwith. Photos by Ernest J. Cottrell. Included: Blythe; Cahuenga Pass; Corona; Dume Point; Long Beach; Los Angeles; Palm Springs; Palos Verdes Point; Salton Sea; San Bernardino Mountains; San Gorgonio Pass; San Jacinto Mountains; Santa Monica; Santa Monica Mountains. 85-108, July 1949

JAMES A. SUGAR
San Francisco: city skyline

California: harvesting grapes for wine
THOMAS NEBBIA, NGS

CD

Gulf of California: diver rides manta

HOWARD HALL

FLIP SCHULKE, BLACK STAR

Gray Whale: female shakes down food

• Timber: How Much Is Enough? By John J. Putman. Photos by Bruce Dale. 485-511, Apr. 1974
• The Troubled Waters of Mono Lake. By Gordon Young. Photos by Craig Aurness. 504-519, Oct. 1981
• Two Wheels Along the Mexican Border. By William Albert Allard. 591-635, May 1971
• The West Through Boston Eyes. By Stewart Anderson. 733-776, June 1949
• Wildlife In and Near the Valley of the Moon. By H. H. Arnold. Photos by Paul J. Fair. 401-414, Mar. 1950
• World's Tallest Tree Discovered. By Melville Bell Grosvenor. Photos by George F. Mobley. 1-9, July 1964
• The Year the Weather Went Wild. By Thomas Y. Canby. 799-829, Dec. 1977
• *See also* Death Valley National Monument; Edwards Air Force Base; Farallon Islands Refuge; Henry E. Huntington Library and Art Gallery; Golden Gate National Recreation Area; La Jolla; Lompoc Valley; Los Angeles; Mojave Desert; Monterey Peninsula; Newport Beach; Pacific Crest Trail; Pacific Grove; Palomar Observatory; San Diego; San Francisco (City and Bay); Santa Barbara Islands; Santa Catalina Island; Sierra Nevada; Tournament of Roses; Yosemite National Park

CALIFORNIA, Baja. *See* Baja California

CALIFORNIA, Gulf of:
• A Strange Ride in the Deep (on Manta Rays). By Peter Benchley. 200-203, Feb. 1981
• *See also* Raza, Isla

CALIFORNIA ACADEMY OF SCIENCES: Expeditions and Research:
• Galapagos Scientific Project. 545, Apr. 1967
• Kelp study. 414, Sept. 1980
• NGS grant in entomology to Dr. Edward S. Ross. 408, Mar. 1961; 15,16, Jan. 1963; 282, Feb. 1965; 433, 437, Sept. 1965

CALIFORNIA DELTA:
• California's Surprising Inland Delta. By Judith and Neil Morgan. Photos by Charles O'Rear. 409-430, Sept. 1976
• San Francisco Bay: The Beauty and the Battles. By Cliff Tarpy. Photos by James A. Sugar. 814-845, June 1981

The **CALIFORNIA** Gray Whale Comes Back. By Theodore J. Walker. 394-415, Mar. 1971

CALIFORNIA INSTITUTE OF TECHNOLOGY:
• Can We Predict Quakes? By Thomas Y. Canby. Included: Seismological Laboratory of CIT. 830-835, June 1976
• Jet Propulsion Laboratory. *See* Mariner Missions; Ranger Spacecraft; Surveyor Spacecraft
• *See also* Sky Survey

CALIFORNIA STATE HIGHWAY NO. 1:
• California's Wonderful One. By Frank Cameron. Photos by B. Anthony Stewart. 571-617, Nov. 1959

CALIFORNIA WESTERN RAILROAD:
• The Friendly Train Called Skunk. By Dean Jennings. Photos by B. Anthony Stewart. 720-734, May 1959

CALLISTO (Jovian Satellite):
• What Voyager Saw: Jupiter's Dazzling Realm. By Rick Gore. Photos by NASA. 2-29, Jan. 1980

CALVERT, JAMES F.: Author:
• Up Through the Ice of the North Pole *(Skate)*. 1-41, July 1959

CALYPSO (Ship):
• At Home in the Sea. By Jacques-Yves Cousteau. 465-507, Apr. 1964
• *Calypso* Explores an Undersea Canyon (Romanche Trench). By Jacques-Yves Cousteau. Photos by Bates Littlehales. NGS research grant. 373-396, Mar. 1958
• *Calypso* Explores for Underwater Oil. By Jacques-Yves Cousteau. NGS research grant. 155-184, Aug. 1955
• Camera Under the Sea. By Luis Marden. NGS research grant. 162-200, Feb. 1956
• Exploring Davy Jones's Locker with *Calypso*. By Jacques-Yves Cousteau. Photos by Luis Marden. NGS research grant. 149-161, Feb. 1956
• Fish Men Discover a 2,200-year-old Greek Ship. By Jacques-Yves Cousteau. NGS research grant. 1-36, Jan. 1954
• Fish Men Explore a New World Undersea. By Jacques-Yves Cousteau. 431-472, Oct. 1952
• Photographing the Sea's Dark Underworld. By Harold E. Edgerton. NGS research grant. 523-537, Apr. 1955

CAMARACOTO INDIANS:
• Jungle Journey to the World's Highest Waterfall. By Ruth Robertson. 655-690, Nov. 1949

CAMARGUE (Region), France:
• The Camargue, Land of Cowboys and Gypsies. By Eugene L. Kammerman. 667-699, May 1956
• France's Wild, Watery South, the Camargue. By William Davenport. 696-726, May 1973

CAMBODIA:
• Angkor, Jewel of the Jungle. By W. Robert Moore. Paintings by Maurice Fiévet. 517-569, Apr. 1960
• Cambodia: Indochina's "Neutral" Corner. By Thomas J. Abercrombie. 514-551, Oct. 1964
• Indochina Faces the Dragon. By George W. Long. Photos by J. Baylor Roberts. 287-328, Sept. 1952
• The Lands and Peoples of Southeast Asia. 295-365, Mar. 1971
I. Mosaic of Cultures. By Peter T. White. Photos by W. E. Garrett. 296-329; II. New Light on a Forgotten Past. By Wilhelm G. Solheim II. 330-339

• The Mekong, River of Terror and Hope. By Peter T. White. Photos by W. E. Garrett. 737-787, Dec. 1968
• Portrait of Indochina. By W. Robert Moore and Maynard Owen Williams. Paintings by Jean Despujols. 461-490, Apr. 1951
• Strife-torn Indochina. By W. Robert Moore. 499-510, Oct. 1950
▲ *Viet Nam, Cambodia, Laos, and Eastern Thailand,* supplement. Text on reverse. Jan. 1965
▲ *Viet Nam, Cambodia, Laos, and Thailand,* supplement. Feb. 1967
• *See also* present name, Kampuchea

CAMBODIAN REFUGEES:
• Thailand: Refuge From Terror. By W. E. Garrett. 633-642, May 1980

CAMBRIDGE, England:
• Here Rest in Honored Glory: The United States Dedicates Six New Battle Monuments in Europe to Americans Who Gave Their Lives During World War II. By Howell Walker. Included: Cambridge American Cemetery and Memorial. 739-768, June 1957
• Our War Memorials Abroad: A Faith Kept. By George C. Marshall. Included: Cambridge American Cemetery and Memorial. 731-737, June 1957

CAMBRIDGE, Massachusetts:
• Literary Landmarks of Massachusetts. By William H. Nicholas. Photos by B. Anthony Stewart and John E. Fletcher. 279-310, Mar. 1950

CAMEL CARAVANS:
• I Joined a Sahara Salt Caravan. By Victor Englebert. 694-711, Nov. 1965
• Winter Caravan to the Roof of the World. By Sabrina and Roland Michaud. 435-465, Apr. 1972

CAMELIDS. *See* Guanacos

CAMELS:
• Alone Across the Outback (Australia). By Robyn Davidson. Photos by Rick Smolan. 581-611, May 1978

CAMENZIND, FRANZ J.:
Photographer:
• Last of the Black-footed Ferrets? By Tim W. Clark. Photos by Franz J. Camenzind and the author. 828-838, June 1983

CAMERA Under the Sea. By Luis Marden. 162-200, Feb. 1956

CAMERAS. *See* Photography

CAMERON, FRANK: Author:
• California's Wonderful One (State Highway No. 1). Photos by B. Anthony Stewart. 571-617, Nov. 1959

CAMERON, GEORGE G.:
Author-Photographer:
• Darius Carved History on Ageless Rock. 825-844, Dec. 1950

CAMERON, NIGEL: Author:
• The Emperor's Private Garden: Kashmir. Photos by Brian Brake. 606-647, Nov. 1958

CAMEROON:
• Afo-A-Kom: A Sacred Symbol Comes Home. By William S. Ellis. Photos by James P. Blair. 141-148, July 1974
• Beyond the Bight of Benin. By Jeannette and Maurice Fiévet. 221-253, Aug. 1959
• Carefree People of the Cameroons. Photos by Pierre Ichac. 233-248, Feb. 1947
• Freedom Speaks French in Ouagadougou. By John Scofield. 153-203, Aug. 1966
• *See also* Weeks Expedition

CAMOUFLAGE:
• Asian Insects in Disguise. By Edward S. Ross. NGS research grant. 433-439, Sept. 1965
• Deception: Formula for Survival. By Robert F. Sisson. Included: Grass shrimp, insects, plants, and sea horses. 394-415, Mar. 1980
• Hidden Life of an Undersea Desert. By Eugenie Clark. Photos by David Doubilet. 129-144, July 1983
◆ *How Animals Hide.* Announced. 726-728, Nov. 1973
◆ *Secrets of Animal Survival.* 1983
• *See also* Decoy Fish; Sargassum Fish

CAMP, W. H.: Author:
• The World in Your Garden (Flowers). Paintings by Else Bostelmann. 1-65, July 1947

CAMP CARSON, Colorado:
• School for Survival. By Curtis E. LeMay. 562-602, May 1953

CAMP CENTURY, Greenland:
• Nuclear Power for the Polar Regions. By George J. Dufek. 712-730, May 1962

CAMP DAVID ACCORDS:
• Eternal Sinai. By Harvey Arden. Photos by David Doubilet and Kevin Fleming. Included: Israeli withdrawal from the Sinai Peninsula by April 25, 1982, as part of the Camp David accords. 420-461, Apr. 1982
Egyptian Sector. Photos by Kevin Fleming. 430-443; Israeli Sector. Photos by David Doubilet. 444-461

CAMP LEJEUNE MARINE BASE, North Carolina:
• Here Come the Marines. By Frederick Simpich. 647-672, Nov. 1950

CAMP PENDLETON MARINE BASE, California:
• Here Come the Marines. By Frederick Simpich. 647-672, Nov. 1950

CAMPBELL, MARGARET SHAW:
Author-Photographer:
• Hunting Folk Songs in the Hebrides. 249-272, Feb. 1947

CAMPBELL, MARJORIE WILKINS:
Author:
• Canada's Dynamic Heartland, Ontario. Photos by Winfield Parks. 58-97, July 1963

CAMPBELL, ROBERT M.:
Photographer:
• Africa's Gentle Giants (Giraffes). By Bristol Foster. Photos by Bob Campbell and Thomas Nebbia. 402-417, Sept. 1977
• Making Friends With Mountain Gorillas. By Dian Fossey. 48-67, Jan. 1970
• More Years With Mountain Gorillas. By Dian Fossey. 574-585, Oct. 1971
• Skull 1470. By Richard E. Leakey. 819-829, June 1973

CAMPBELL, WILLIAM W., III:
Photographer:
• The President's Music Men (U. S. Marine Band). By Stuart E. Jones. 752-766, Dec. 1959

CAMPING TRIPS. *See* Bikepacking; Hiking Trips; Mountain Climbing; Pack Trips; Philmont Scout Ranch

CAMPS, Summer:
◆ *Camping Adventure.* Announced. 718-720, Nov. 1976
• In Touch With Nature. Text by Elizabeth A. Moize. Photos by Steve Raymer. Contents: Camps near Eagle River, Wisconsin. 537-543, Apr. 1974

CAN the Atlantic Salmon Survive? By Art Lee. Photos by Bianca Lavies. 600-615, Nov. 1981

CAN the Cooper's Hawk Survive? By Noel Snyder. Photos by author and Helen Snyder. 433-442, Mar. 1974

CAN the Tallgrass Be Saved? By Dennis Farney. Photos by Jim Brandenburg. 37-61, Jan. 1980

CAN the World Feed Its People? By Thomas Y. Canby. Photos by Steve Raymer. 2-31, July 1975

CAN We Harness the Wind? By Roger Hamilton. Photos by Emory Kristof. 812-829, Dec. 1975

CAN We Live Better on Less? By Rick Gore. 34-57, *Special Report on Energy* (Feb. 1981)

CAN We Predict Quakes? By Thomas Y. Canby. 830-835, June 1976

CAN We Save Our Salt Marshes? By Stephen W. Hitchcock. Photos by William R. Curtsinger. 729-765, June 1972

CANAAN:
• Abraham, the Friend of God. By Kenneth MacLeish. Photos by Dean Conger. 739-789, Dec. 1966

CANAANITES. *See* Phoenicians

CANADA:
• Across Canada by Mackenzie's Track. By Ralph Gray. 191-239, Aug. 1955
• Along the Yukon Trail. By Amos Burg. 395-416, Sept. 1953
▲ *Atlantic Gateways,* The Making of America series. Included: Delaware, Maryland, New Jersey, New York, Pennsylvania, northern Virginia, West Virginia, and in Canada, southern Ontario and southern Quebec. On reverse: Indians and Trade, Nation in the Making, Peopling of the Gateways, Race for the Hinterlands, Growth of Industry, Spreading Urban Corridors. Mar. 1983
• Avalanche! Battling the Juggernaut. By David Cupp. 290-305, Sept. 1982

C D

Canada: descending Devil's Thumb

DAVID S. BOYER, NGS

● Bikepacking Across Alaska and Canada. By Dan Burden. Included: Alberta; British Columbia; Yukon Territory. 682-695, May 1973

▲ *Canada,* Atlas series supplement. Dec. 1961

▲ *Canada,* supplement. Painting on reverse. Mar. 1972

▲ *Canada, Alaska, and Greenland,* supplement. June 1947

● Canada, My Country. By Alan Phillips. Photos by David S. Boyer and Walter Meayers Edwards. 769-819, Dec. 1961

● Canada Counts Its Caribou. 261-268, Aug. 1952

● Canada Marks Her First Century. By Melville Bell Grosvenor. 597-599, May 1967

● Canada's Caribou Eskimos (Padlermiut). By Donald B. Marsh. 87-104, Jan. 1947

● Canada's Heartland, the Prairie Provinces. By W. E. Garrett. Contents: Alberta; Manitoba; Saskatchewan. 443-489, Oct. 1970

● Canada's "Now" Frontier. By Robert Paul Jordan. Photos by Lowell Georgia. Included: Oil exploration in Alberta and the Northwest Territories. 480-511, Oct. 1976

◆ *Canada's Wilderness Lands.* 1982

● Canada's Winged Victory: the *Silver Dart.* By Gilbert M. Grosvenor. 254-267, Aug. 1959

● The Canadian North: Emerging Giant. By David S. Boyer. 1-43, July 1968

● Canadian Rockies, Lords of a Beckoning Land. By Alan Phillips. Photos by James L. Stanfield. 353-393, Sept. 1966

▲ *Central Canada,* Atlas series supplement. July 1963

● The Changing World of Canada's Crees. By Fred Ward. 541-569, Apr. 1975

▲ *Close-up: Canada, Maine, with the Maritime Provinces of Canada,* supplement. Text on reverse. Mar. 1975

▲ *Close-up, Canada: British Columbia, Alberta, Yukon Territory,* supplement. Text on reverse. Apr. 1978

▲ *Close-up, Canada: Ontario,* supplement. Text on reverse. Dec. 1978

▲ *Close-up, Canada: Quebec, Newfoundland,* supplement. Text on reverse, inset Southern Quebec. May 1980

▲ *Close-up, Canada: Saskatchewan, Manitoba, Northwest Territories,* supplement. Text on reverse. May 1979

● DEW Line, Sentry of the Far North. By Howard La Fay. 128-146, July 1958

▲ *Eastern Canada,* Atlas series supplement. May 1967

● Editorials. By Gilbert M. Grosvenor. 435, Apr. 1977; 585, May 1980

◆ *Exploring Canada from Sea to Sea.* Announced. 868-875, June 1967

● Far North with "Captain Mac." By Miriam MacMillan. 465-513, Oct. 1951

● From Sun-clad Sea to Shining Mountains. By Ralph Gray. Photos by James P. Blair. Included: Alberta; British Columbia. 542-589, Apr. 1964

● Ghost Ships of the War of 1812: *Hamilton* and *Scourge.* By Daniel A. Nelson. Photos by Emory Kristof. Paintings by Richard Schlecht. 289-313, Mar. 1983

● The Giant Tides of Fundy. By Paul A. Zahl. 153-192, Aug. 1957

▲ *The Great Lakes Region of the United States and Canada,* supplement. Dec. 1953

● Heart of the Canadian Rockies. By Elizabeth A. Moize. Photos by Jim Brandenburg. 757-779, June 1980

● Henry Hudson's Changing Bay. By Bill Richards. Photos by David Hiser. 380-405, Mar. 1982

● Hiking the Backbone of the Rockies: Canada's Great Divide Trail. By Mike W. Edwards. Photos by Lowell Georgia. Contents: Alberta; British Columbia. 795-817, June 1973

● I Live With the Eskimos. By Guy Mary-Rousseliere. 188-217, Feb. 1971

■ Journey to the High Arctic. 1971

● The Loyalists. By Kent Britt. Photos by Ted Spiegel. 510-539, Apr. 1975

● Men, Moose, and Mink of Northwest Angle. By William H. Nicholas. Photos by J. Baylor Roberts. 265-284, Aug. 1947

● Nahanni: Canada's Wilderness Park. By Douglas H. Chadwick. Photos by Matt Bradley. 396-420, Sept. 1981

▲ *National Parks, Monuments and Shrines of the United States and Canada,* Atlas series supplement. Text on reverse. May 1958

● New Era on the Great Lakes. By Nathaniel T. Kenney. 439-490, Apr. 1959

● New St. Lawrence Seaway Opens the Great Lakes to the World. By Andrew H. Brown. 299-339, Mar. 1959

● Niagara Falls, Servant of Good Neighbors. Photos by Walter Meayers Edwards. 574-587, Apr. 1963

● Nomads of the Far North. By Matthew W. Stirling. 471-504, Oct. 1949
Hearty Folk Defy Arctic Storms. Paintings by W. Langdon Kihn. 479-494

● North for Oil: *Manhattan* Makes the Historic Northwest Passage. By Bern Keating. Photos by Tomas Sennett. 374-391, Mar. 1970

● North Through History Aboard *White Mist.* By Melville Bell Grosvenor. Photos by Edwin Stuart Grosvenor. 1-55, July 1970

▲ *Northwestern United States and Neighboring Canadian Provinces,* supplement. June 1950

● On the Ridgepole of the Rockies. By Walter Meayers Edwards. 745-780, June 1947
Canada's Rocky Mountain Playground. 755-770

● One Canada–or Two? By Peter T. White. Photos by Winfield Parks. 436-465, Apr. 1977

- The Peary Flag Comes to Rest. By Marie Peary Stafford. 519-532, Oct. 1954
- Peoples of the Arctic. 144-223, Feb. 1983
I. Introduction by Joseph Judge. 144-149; II. Hunters of the Lost Spirit: Canadians. By Priit J. Vesilind. Photos by David Alan Harvey. 150-156
▲ *Peoples of the Arctic; Arctic Ocean,* double-sided supplement. Feb. 1983
- Playing 3,000 Golf Courses in Fourteen Lands. By Ralph A. Kennedy. 113-132, July 1952
- Quebec's Northern Dynamo. By Larry Kohl. Photos by Ottmar Bierwagen. 406-418, Mar. 1982
- Queen of Canada (Elizabeth II). By Phyllis Wilson. Photos by Kathleen Revis. 825-829, June 1959
- Relics from the Rapids (Voyageurs). By Sigurd F. Olson. Photos by David S. Boyer. 413-435, Sept. 1963
- The St. Lawrence, River Key to Canada. By Howard La Fay. Photos by John Launois. 622-667, May 1967
- The St. Lawrence River: Canada's Highway to the Sea. By William S. Ellis. Photos by Bruce Dale. 586-623, May 1980
- Song of Hope for the Bluebird. By Lawrence Zeleny. Photos by Michael L. Smith. Note: Canada boasts the world's longest bluebird nesting-box trail, 2,000 miles in length. 855-865, June 1977
- Trailing Cosmic Rays in Canada's North. By Martin A. Pomerantz. NGS research grant. 99-115, Jan. 1953
- Trek Across Arctic America. By Colin Irwin. 295-321, Mar. 1974
▲ *Vacationlands of the United States and Southern Canada,* supplement. Text on reverse. July 1966
- We Followed Peary to the Pole. By Gilbert Grosvenor and Thomas W. McKnew. 469-484, Oct. 1953
- Weather from the White North. By Andrew H. Brown. Photos by John E. Fletcher. 543-572, Apr. 1955
▲ *Western Canada,* Atlas series supplement. Sept. 1966
- Western Grebes: The Birds That Walk on Water. By Gary L. Nuechterlein. NGS research grant. 624-637, May 1982
- Yukon Fever: Call of the North. By Robert Booth. Photos by George F. Mobley. 548-578, Apr. 1978
- *See also* Alberta; Beechey Island; British Columbia; Manitoba; New Brunswick; Newfoundland; Northwest Territories; Nova Scotia; Ontario (Province); Quebec (Province); Saskatchewan; Yukon Territory; *and* Ellesmere Island; Kennedy, Mount; Resolute Bay; St. Elias, Mount; Waterton-Glacier International Peace Park

CANADA COUNCIL: Study Grants:
- Anthropology: Papua New Guinea. 128, July 1977

CANADA GEESE:
- Bright Dyes Reveal Secrets of Canada Geese. By John and Frank Craighead. 817-832, Dec. 1957

CANADIAN WILDLIFE SERVICE:
- Teamwork Helps the Whooping Crane. By Roderick C. Drewien, with Ernie Kuyt. Contents: A U. S.-Canadian effort to establish a second breeding flock of wild whoopers among close-kin sandhill cranes. 680-693, May 1979
- Tracking the Shore Dwellers (Sandpipers): From Canada to Suriname. 175-179, Aug. 1979

CANAL ZONE:
- Panama, Link Between Oceans and Continents. By Jules B. Billard. Photos by Bruce Dale. 402-440, Mar. 1970
- The Panama Canal Today. By Bart McDowell. Photos by George F. Mobley. 279-294, Feb. 1978

CANALS:
- Exploring England's Canals. By Bryan Hodgson. Photos by Linda Bartlett. 76-111, July 1974
- The Imperiled Everglades. By Fred Ward. 1-27, Jan. 1972
- Inside Europe Aboard *Yankee*. By Irving and Electa Johnson. Photos by Joseph J. Scherschel. 157-195, Aug. 1964
- Mexico's Little Venice. By W. E. Garrett. 876-888, June 1968
- North Through History Aboard *White Mist*. By Melville Bell Grosvenor. Photos by Edwin Stuart Grosvenor. 1-55, July 1970
- Paris to Antwerp with the Water Gypsies. By David S. Boyer. 530-559, Oct. 1955
- Twilight Hope for Big Cypress. By Rick Gore. Photos by Patricia Caulfield. 251-273, Aug. 1976
- *See also* Chesapeake and Ohio Canal; New York State Barge Canal; Panama Canal; Suez Canal; Sweden (Baltic Cruise), for Göta Canal; *and* Amsterdam, Netherlands; Bangkok, Thailand; Bruges, Belgium; Mekong River; Venice

CANARY ISLANDS, Atlantic Ocean:
- Lanzarote, the Strangest Canary. By Stephanie Dinkins. 117-139, Jan. 1969
- Spain's "Fortunate Isles," the Canaries. By Jean and Franc Shor. 485-522, Apr. 1955

CANAVERAL, Cape, Florida:
- Cape Canaveral's 6,000-mile Shooting Gallery. By Allan C. Fisher, Jr. Photos by Luis Marden and Thomas Nebbia. 421-471, Oct. 1959
- *Columbia*'s Astronauts' Own Story: Our Phenomenal First Flight. By John W. Young and Robert L. Crippen. Paintings by Ken Dallison. 478-503, Oct. 1981
- When the Space Shuttle Finally Flies. By Rick Gore. Photos by Jon Schneeberger. Paintings by Ken Dallison. 317-347, Mar. 1981

CANBY, THOMAS Y.: Author:
- Aluminum, the Magic Metal. Photos by James L. Amos. 186-211, Aug. 1978
- The Anasazi–Riddles in the Ruins. Photos by Dewitt Jones and David Brill. Paintings by Roy Andersen. 554-592, Nov. 1982

JAMES L. AMOS, NGS

Aluminum: velvet and aluminum coat

• Apollo-Soyuz: Handclasp in Space. 183-187, Feb. 1976
• California's San Andreas Fault. Photos by James P. Blair. 38-53, Jan. 1973
• Can the World Feed Its People? Photos by Steve Raymer. 2-31, July 1975
• Can We Predict Quakes? 830-835, June 1976
• Our Most Precious Resource: Water. Photos by Ted Spiegel. 144-179, Aug. 1980
• Pioneers in Man's Search for the Universe. Paintings by Jean-Leon Huens. 627-633, May 1974
• The Rat, Lapdog of the Devil. Photos by James L. Stanfield. 60-87, July 1977
• Satellites That Serve Us. 281-335, Sept. 1983
• The Search for the First Americans. Photos by Kerby Smith. Paintings by Roy Andersen. 330-363, Sept. 1979
• Skylab, Outpost on the Frontier of Space. Photos by the nine mission astronauts. 441-469, Oct. 1974
• Synfuels: Fill 'er Up! With What? Photos by Jonathan Blair. 74-95, *Special Report on Energy* (Feb. 1981)
• The Year the Weather Went Wild. 799-829, Dec. 1977

CANCER RESEARCH:
• The Cancer Puzzle. By Robert F. Weaver. 396-399, Sept. 1976
• You and the Obedient Atom. By Allan C. Fisher, Jr. 303-353, Sept. 1958

CANE BRIDGES of Asia. Photos from Paul Popper. 243-250, Aug. 1948

CANNIBALISM, Chimpanzee:
• Life and Death at Gombe. By Jane Goodall. NGS research grant. 592-621, May 1979

CANNIBALISM, Human. *See* Asmat; Biami; Erigbaagtsa

CANOE RACE:
• Winter Brings Carnival Time to Quebec. By Kathleen Revis. 69-97, Jan. 1958

CANOE TRIPS:
• Across Canada by Mackenzie's Track. By Ralph Gray. 191-239, Aug. 1955
• America's Little Mainstream (Buffalo National River). By Harvey Arden. Photos by Matt Bradley. 344-359, Mar. 1977
• Autumn Flames Along the Allagash. By François Leydet. Photos by Farrell Grehan. 177-187, Feb. 1974
• A Canoe Helps Hawaii Recapture Her Past. By Herb Kawainui Kane. Photos by David Hiser. 468-489, Apr. 1976
• Down the Danube by Canoe. By William Slade Backer. Photos by Richard S. Durrance and Christopher G. Knight. 34-79, July 1965
• Down the Potomac by Canoe. By Ralph Gray. Photos by Walter Meayers Edwards. 213-242, Aug. 1948
• Down the Susquehanna by Canoe. By Ralph Gray. Photos by Walter Meayers Edwards. 73-120, July 1950
• *Hokule'a* Follows the Stars to Tahiti. By David Lewis. Photos by Nicholas deVore III. 512-537, Oct. 1976
• Isles of the Pacific. 732-793, Dec. 1974
I. The Coming of the Polynesians. By Kenneth P. Emory. 732-745; II. The Pathfinders. Paintings by Herb Kawainui Kane. 756-769
• Jungle Jaunt on Amazon Headwaters. By Bernice M. Goetz. 371-388, Sept. 1952
• Jungle Journey to the World's Highest Waterfall. By Ruth Robertson. 655-690, Nov. 1949
• Kayak Odyssey: From the Inland Sea to Tokyo. By Dan Dimancescu. Photos by Christopher G. Knight. 295-337, Sept. 1967
• Kayaks Down the Nile. By John M. Goddard. 697-732, May 1955
• Labrador Canoe Adventure. By Andrew Brown and Ralph Gray. 65-99, July 1951
• Okefenokee, the Magical Swamp. By François Leydet. Photos by Farrell Grehan. 169-175, Feb. 1974
• Relics from the Rapids. By Sigurd F. Olson. Photos by David S. Boyer. 413-435, Sept. 1963
• Sea Fever. By John E. Schultz. 237-268, Feb. 1949
◆ *Still Waters, White Waters.* 1977
• Trek Across Arctic America. By Colin Irwin. 295-321, Mar. 1974
▪ Voyage of the *Hokule'a*. 575, Nov. 1976

CANOEIROS (Indians). *See* Erigbaagtsa

CANTERBURY CATHEDRAL, Canterbury, England:
• Canterbury Cathedral. By Kenneth MacLeish. Photos by Thomas Nebbia. 364-379, Mar. 1976

CANTON ISLAND, Phoenix, Islands, Pacific Ocean:
• Air Age Brings Life to Canton Island. By Howell Walker. 117-132, Jan. 1955

CANYONLANDS NATIONAL PARK, Utah:
• Canyonlands, Realm of Rock and the Far Horizon. By Rowe Findley. Photos by Walter Meayers Edwards. 71-91, July 1971
• Cities of Stone in Utah's Canyonland. By W. Robert Moore. 653-677, May 1962

CANYONS:
◆ *America's Majestic Canyons.* 1979
• Nahanni: Canada's Wilderness Park. By Douglas H. Chadwick. Photos by Matt Bradley. Included: Canada's deepest canyon system. 396-420, Sept. 1981
• *See also* Bryce Canyon National Park, Utah; Chaco Canyon, New Mexico; Dinosaur National Monument, Colorado-Utah; Escalante Canyon, Utah; Grand Canyon, Arizona; Havasupai Indian Reservation, Arizona; Navajo National Monument, Arizona; Sierra Nevada (Mountains), California (Fabulous Sierra Nevada); Zion National Park, Utah; *and* listing under Gorges

CAODAISM:
• Indochina Faces the Dragon. By George W. Long. Photos by J. Baylor Roberts. 287-328, Sept. 1952

CAPE BRETON ISLAND, Nova Scotia, Canada:
• Nova Scotia, the Magnificent Anchorage. By Charles McCarry. Photos by Gordon W. Gahan. 334-363, Mar. 1975
• *See also* Baddeck

CAPE CANAVERAL, Florida. *See* Canaveral, Cape

CAPE COD, Massachusetts:
• Cape Cod, Where Sea Holds Sway Over Man and Land. By Nathaniel T. Kenney. Photos by Dean Conger. 149-187, Aug. 1962
• Cape Cod's Circle of Seasons. By Tom Melham. Photos by James P. Blair. 40-65, July 1975
• Captain Smith's New England . . . and the Pilgrims' Cape Cod. 764-765, June 1953
• Massachusetts Builds for Tomorrow. By Robert de Roos. Photos by B. Anthony Stewart. 790-843, Dec. 1966
• Windjamming Around New England. By Tom Horgan. Photos by Robert F. Sisson. 141-169, Aug. 1950

CAPE HATTERAS NATIONAL SEASHORE, North Carolina:
• Lonely Cape Hatteras, Besieged by the Sea. By William S. Ellis. Photos by Emory Kristof. 392-421, Sept. 1969

CAPE OF GOOD HOPE PROVINCE, Republic of South Africa:
• Safari Through Changing Africa. By Elsie May Bell Grosvenor. Photos by Gilbert Grosvenor. 145-198, Aug. 1953

CAPE TOWN, Republic of South Africa:
• Africa: The Winds of Freedom Stir a Continent. By Nathaniel T. Kenney. Photos by W. D. Vaughn. 303-359, Sept. 1960
• Safari Through Changing Africa. By Elsie May Bell Grosvenor. Photos by Gilbert Grosvenor. 145-198, Aug. 1953
• South Africa Close-up. By Kip Ross. 641-681, Nov. 1962

CAPITOL, U. S. *See* U. S. Capitol

CAPITOL REEF NATIONAL PARK, Utah. *See* Escalante Canyon

CAPPADOCIA (Region), Turkey:
• Cappadocia: Turkey's Country of Cones. Photos by Marc Riboud. 122-146, Jan. 1958
• Keeping House in a Cappadocian Cave. By Jonathan S. Blair. 127-146, July 1970

CAPRI, Italy's Enchanted Rock. By Carleton Mitchell. Photos by David F. Cupp. 795-809, June 1970

CAPRICORNIA REGION, Australia. *See* Heron Island

CAPRON, LOUIS: Author:
● Florida's Emerging Seminoles. Photos by Otis Imboden. 716-734, Nov. 1969
● Florida's "Wild" Indians, the Seminole. Photos by Willard R. Culver. 819-840, Dec. 1956

CAPTAIN Cook: The Man Who Mapped the Pacific. By Alan Villiers. Photos by Gordon W. Gahan. 297-349, Sept. 1971

CAPT. John Smith's Map of Virginia. 760-761, June 1953

CAPTAIN Smith of Jamestown. By Bradford Smith. 581-620, May 1957

CAPTAIN Smith's New England . . . and the Pilgrims' Cape Cod. 764-765, June 1953

The **CAPTURE** of Jerusalem. By Franc Shor. Photos by Thomas Nebbia. 839-855, Dec. 1963

CAPTURING Strange Creatures in Colombia. By Marte Latham. Photos by Tor Eigeland. 682-693, May 1966

CAPUTO, ROBERT:
Author-Photographer:
● Ethiopia: Revolution in an Ancient Empire. 614-645, May 1983
● Sudan: Arab-African Giant. 346-379, Mar. 1982

CARACAS, Venezuela:
● Venezuela's Crisis of Wealth. By Noel Grove. Photos by Robert W. Madden. 175-209, Aug. 1976

CARAVAGGIO, MICHELANGELO MERISI DA:
● The Vienna Treasures and Their Collectors. By John Walker. 737-776, June 1950

CARAVANS, Camel:
● I Joined a Sahara Salt Caravan. By Victor Englebert. 694-711, Nov. 1965
● Winter Caravan to the Roof of the World. By Sabrina and Roland Michaud. 435-465, Apr. 1972

CARAVANS, Trailer:
● I See America First. By Lynda Bird Johnson. Photos by William Albert Allard. 874-904, Dec. 1965
● Through Europe by Trailer Caravan. By Norma Miller. Photos by Ardean R. Miller III. 769-816, June 1957

CARBON 14. *See* Radiocarbon Dating

CARDINALS:
● The Bird's Year. By Arthur A. Allen. 791-816, June 1951

CAREFREE People of the Cameroons. Photos by Pierre Ichac. 233-248, Feb. 1947

CARGO CULTS:
● Change Ripples New Guinea's Sepik River. By Malcolm S. Kirk. 354-381, Sept. 1973
● Tanna Awaits the Coming of John Frum. By Kal Muller. 706-715, May 1974

BOTH BY KAL MULLER

Tanna: islander wearing World War II relic, *top;* followers of John Frum, *above*

CARIA (Ancient Division), Asia Minor:
● Ancient Aphrodisias Lives Through Its Art. By Kenan T. Erim. Photos by David Brill. NGS research grant. 527-551, Oct. 1981

CARIB Cruises the West Indies. By Carleton Mitchell. 1-56, Jan. 1948

CARIB INDIANS. *See* Wayana Indians

CARIBBEAN Green Turtle: Imperiled Gift of the Sea. By Archie Carr. Photos by Robert E. Schroeder. 876-890, June 1967

CARIBBEAN REGION:
● Cape Canaveral's 6,000-mile Shooting Gallery. By Allan C. Fisher, Jr. Photos by Luis Marden and Thomas Nebbia. Included: Antigua; Dominican Republic; Mayagüez, Puerto Rico; St. Lucia. 471, Oct. 1959
● The Caribbean: Sun, Sea, and Seething. By Noel Grove. Photos by Steve Raymer. 244-271, Feb. 1981
● Christopher Columbus and the New World He Found. By John Scofield. Photos by Adam Woolfitt. 584-625, Nov. 1975
▲ *Countries of the Caribbean, including Mexico, Central America, and the West Indies,* supplement. Oct. 1947
● Hurricane! By Ben Funk. Photos by Robert W. Madden. 346-379, Sept. 1980
Dominica. By Fred Ward. 357-359; Dynamics of a Hurricane. 370-371; Into the Eye of David. By John L. Eliot. 368-369; Paths of Fury–This Century's Worst American Storms. 360-361
● Imperiled Gift of the Sea: Caribbean Green Turtle. By Archie Carr. Photos by Robert E. Schroeder. 876-890, June 1967
◆ *Isles of the Caribbean.* 1980
◆ *Isles of the Caribbees.* Announced. 408-417, Mar. 1966
● Reach for the New World. By Mendel Peterson. Photos by David L. Arnold. Paintings by Richard Schlecht. 724-767, Dec. 1977
● Robin Sails Home. By Robin Lee Graham. Included: Barbados; Panama; Virgin Islands. 504-545, Oct. 1970
● St. Vincent, the Grenadines, and Grenada: Taking It as It Comes. By Ethel A. Starbird. Photos by Cotton Coulson. 399-425, Sept. 1979
▲ *Tourist Islands of the West Indies; West Indies and Central America,* double-sided supplement. Feb. 1981
● *See also* Cayman Trough; Central America; Venezuela; West Indies

CARIBBEE (Yawl):
● Baltic Cruise of the *Caribbee.* By Carleton Mitchell. 605-646, Nov. 1950

CARIBOU:
● Canada Counts Its Caribou. 261-268, Aug. 1952
● Caribou: Hardy Nomads of the North. By Jim Rearden. 858-878, Dec. 1974

• Our Wildest Wilderness: Alaska's Arctic National Wildlife Range. By Douglas H. Chadwick. Photos by Lowell Georgia. 737-769, Dec. 1979
• Trek Across Arctic America. By Colin Irwin. 295-321, Mar. 1974
• Wildlife of Mount McKinley National Park. By Adolph Murie. Paintings by Walter A. Weber. 249-270, Aug. 1953

CARIBOU ESKIMOS. *See* Padlermiut

CARLIN GOLD MINE, Nevada:
• Nevada's Mountain of Invisible Gold. By Samuel W. Matthews. Photos by David F. Cupp. 668-679, May 1968

CARLSBAD CAVERNS, New Mexico:
• Carlsbad Caverns in Color. By Mason Sutherland. Photos by E. "Tex" Helm. 433-468, Oct. 1953

CARMEL, California:
• California's Land Apart–the Monterey Peninsula. By Mike W. Edwards. 682-703, Nov. 1972
• California's Wonderful One. By Frank Cameron. Photos by B. Anthony Stewart. 571-617, Nov. 1959

CARMICHAEL, LEONARD:
• Leonard Carmichael: An Appreciation. By Melvin M. Payne. 871-874, Dec. 1973
• NGS Board of Trustees member. 419, 420, 423, Mar. 1957; 592, May 1957; 834, Dec. 1959; 796-797, June 1960; 881, 883, Dec. 1960
• NGS Committee for Research and Exploration: Chairman. 882, Dec. 1961; 903, Dec. 1962; 9, 136, 146, 150, Jan. 1963; 626, Oct. 1963; 582, Oct. 1967; 230, Aug. 1970; 274, Aug. 1982
• NGS Vice President for Research and Exploration. 525, Apr. 1965
Author:
• The Smithsonian, Magnet on the Mall. Photos by Volkmar Wentzel. 796-845, June 1960

CARNEGIE, DAVID J.: Photographer:
• Weighing the Aga Khan in Diamonds. 317-324, Mar. 1947

CARNIVAL (Pre-Lenten Festival):
• Brazil, Ôba! By Peter T. White. Photos by Winfield Parks. 299-353, Sept. 1962
• Carnival in Trinidad. By Howard La Fay. Photos by Winfield Parks. 693-701, Nov. 1971
• Spectacular Rio de Janeiro. By Hernane Tavares de Sá. Photos by Charles Allmon. 289-328, Mar. 1955
• *See also* Mardi Gras

CARNIVALS. *See* Fairs; Festivals

CARNIVOROUS PLANTS:
• Malaysia's Giant Flowers and Insect-trapping Plants. By Paul A. Zahl. 680-701, May 1964
• Plants That Eat Insects. By Paul A. Zahl. 643-659, May 1961

CAROLINE ISLANDS, Pacific Ocean:
• Micronesia: The Americanization of Eden. By David S. Boyer. 702-744, May 1967
• Pacific Wards of Uncle Sam. By W. Robert Moore. 73-104, July 1948
• *See also* Ifalik; Kapingamarangi; Truk Lagoon; Ulithi; Yap Islands

CARONI SWAMP SANCTUARY, Trinidad:
• New Scarlet Bird in Florida Skies. By Paul A. Zahl. 874-882, Dec. 1967

CARPATHIAN MOUNTAINS, Europe:
• Americans Afoot in Rumania. By Dan Dimancescu. Photos by Dick Durrance II and Christopher G. Knight. 810-845, June 1969
• *See also* Tatra Mountains

CARR, ARCHIE: Author:
• Alligators: Dragons in Distress. Photos by Treat Davidson and Laymond Hardy. 133-148, Jan. 1967
• Imperiled Gift of the Sea: Caribbean Green Turtle. Photos by Robert E. Schroeder. 876-890, June 1967

CARR, GERALD P.:
• Skylab, Outpost on the Frontier of Space. By Thomas Y. Canby. Photos by the nine mission astronauts. 441-469, Oct. 1974

CARRAO, Río, Venezuela:
• Jungle Journey to the World's Highest Waterfall. By Ruth Robertson. 655-690, Nov. 1949

CARRARA MARBLE:
• Carrara Marble: Touchstone of Eternity. By Cathy Newman. Photos by Pierre Boulat. 42-59, July 1982

CARS. *See* Automobiles

CARSON, Camp, Colorado:
• School for Survival. By Curtis E. LeMay. 565-602, May 1953

CARTER, JEFF: Photographer:
• "The Alice" in Australia's Wonderland. By Alan Villiers. Photos by Jeff Carter and David Moore. 230-257, Feb. 1966

CARTER, T. DONALD: Author:
• Stalking Central Africa's Wildlife. Paintings by Walter A. Weber. 264-286, Aug. 1956

CARTER'S GROVE, Virginia:
• First Look at a Lost Virginia Settlement (Martin's Hundred). By Ivor Noël Hume. Photos by Ira Block. Paintings by Richard Schlecht. 735-767, June 1979
• New Clues to an Old Mystery (Virginia's Wolstenholme Towne). By Ivor Noël Hume. Photos by Ira Block. Paintings by Richard Schlecht. 53-77, Jan. 1982

CARTHAGE (Ancient City), North Africa:
• The Phoenicians, Sea Lords of Antiquity. By Samuel W. Matthews. Photos by Winfield Parks. Paintings by Robert C. Magis. 149-189, Aug. 1974

CARTIER, JACQUES:
• North Through History Aboard *White Mist.* By Melville Bell Grosvenor. Photos by Edwin Stuart Grosvenor. 1-55, July 1970

CARTOGRAPHERS:
• Eight Maps of Discovery. 757-769, June 1953
• *See also* Bumstead, Newman; Chamberlin, Wellman; NGS: Cartographic Division

CARTOGRAPHY:
• Editorials. By Gilbert M. Grosvenor. 583, Nov. 1975; 729, Dec. 1978; 1, July 1980; By Wilbur E. Garrett. 685, Dec. 1982; 145, Aug. 1983
• How We Mapped the Moon. By David W. Cook. 240-245, Feb. 1969
• Landsat Looks at Hometown Earth. By Barry C. Bishop. Contents: How the color photomosaic supplement *Portrait U.S.A.* was made from Landsat imagery. 140-147, July 1976
• Remote Sensing: New Eyes to See the World. By Kenneth F. Weaver. 46-73, Jan. 1969
• The Round Earth on Flat Paper. By Wellman Chamberlin. 399, Mar. 1950
• Science Explores the Monsoon Sea. By Samuel W. Matthews. Photos by Robert F. Sisson. 554-575, Oct. 1967
• *See also* Globes; Inter-American Geodetic Survey; NGS: Cartographic Division; U. S. Coast and Geodetic Survey

CARTOONS, Animated:
• The Magic Worlds of Walt Disney. By Robert de Roos. Photos by Thomas Nebbia. 159-207, Aug. 1963

CARTOONS AND COMIC STRIPS:
• The Celts. By Merle Severy. Photos by James P. Blair. Paintings by Robert C. Magis. Included: An Astérix strip by Uderzo and Goscinny. 582-633, May 1977
• Fun Helped Them Fight. By Stuart E. Jones. 95-104, Jan. 1948

CASABLANCA, Morocco:
• From Sea to Sahara in French Morocco. By Jean and Franc Shor. 147-188, Feb. 1955
• Morocco, Land of the Farthest West. By Thomas J. Abercrombie. 834-865, June 1971

CASÇADE RANGE, U. S.:
• Forest Fire: The Devil's Picnic. By Stuart E. Jones and Jay Johnston. 100-127, July 1968
• Mexico to Canada on the Pacific Crest Trail. By Mike W. Edwards. Photos by David Hiser. 741-779, June 1971
• New National Park Proposed: The Spectacular North Cascades. By Nathaniel T. Kenney. Photos by James P. Blair. 642-667, May 1968
• Sno-Cats Mechanize Oregon Snow Survey. By Andrew H. Brown. Photos by John E. Fletcher. 691-710, Nov. 1949
• Washington Wilderness, the North Cascades. By Edwards Park. Photos by Kathleen Revis. 335-367, Mar. 1961
• *See also* Rainier, Mount; St. Helens, Mount

CASE, LE AND D.: Author:
• Back to the Historic Black Hills. Photos by Bates Littlehales. 479-509, Oct. 1956

CASE, PAUL EDWARD: Author:
- Boom Time in Kuwait. 783-802, Dec. 1952
- I Become a Bakhtiari. 325-358, Mar. 1947

The **CASE** of the Killer Caterpillars. By Steven L. Montgomery. Photos by Robert F. Sisson. 219-225, Aug. 1983

CASH, J. ALLAN: Photographer:
- From Barra to Butt in the Hebrides. By Isobel Wylie Hutchison. 559-580, Oct. 1954
- Lundy, Treasure Island of Birds. By P. T. Etherton. 675-698, May 1947

CASSIDY, BUTCH:
- Riding the Outlaw Trail. By Robert Redford. Photos by Jonathan Blair. 622-657, Nov. 1976

CASTE SYSTEM. *See* Hinduism

CASTERET, NORBERT: Author:
- Lascaux Cave, Cradle of World Art. Photos by Maynard Owen Williams. 771-794, Dec. 1948

Author-Photographer:
- Probing Ice Caves of the Pyrenees. Included: Casteret Grotto. 391-404, Mar. 1953

CASTILLO DE SAN MARCOS, St. Augustine, Florida:
- St. Augustine, Nation's Oldest City, Turns 400. By Robert L. Conly. 196-229, Feb. 1966

CASTLES:
- Baltic Cruise of the *Caribbee*. By Carleton Mitchell. Included: Bohus, Hammershus, Kalmar Nyckel, Karlsten Fortress, and Stegeborg. 605-646, Nov. 1950
- The Britain That Shakespeare Knew. By Louis B. Wright. Photos by Dean Conger. Included: Baynard's, Berkeley, Cawdor, Glamis, Middleham, Tower of London, Windsor. 613-665, May 1964
- British Castles, History in Stone. By Norman Wilkinson. 111-129, July 1947
- Building a New Austria. By Beverley M. Bowie. Photos by Volkmar Wentzel. Included: Bernstein, Dürnstein, Forchtenstein, Güssing, Hofburg, Raabs, Riegersburg, Rosenburg, Schönbrunn, Schreckenwald. 172-213, Feb. 1959
- California's Wonderful One (State Highway No. 1). By Frank Cameron. Photos by B. Anthony Stewart. Included: Hearst San Simeon Historical Monument. 571-617, Nov. 1959
- Crusader Lands Revisited. By Harold Lamb. Photos by David S. Boyer. Included: Krak des Chevaliers, Margat, and Sidon. 815-852, Dec. 1954
- Cyprus, Idyllic Island in a Troubled Sea. By Jean and Franc Shor. Included: Castle of Kyrenia, St. Hilarion Castle. 627-664, May 1952
- Fabled Mount of St. Michael. By Alan Villiers. Photos by Bates Littlehales. 880-898, June 1964

WYOMING STATE ARCHIVES AND HISTORICAL DEPARTMENT

COURTESY PINKERTON'S, INC.

Outlaw Trail: Butch Cassidy, 1894, *top*; Etta Place and Sundance, *above*

- Hungary: Changing Homeland of a Tough, Romantic People. By Bart McDowell. Photos by Albert Moldvay and Joseph J. Scherschel. Included: Buda, Eger, Eszterházy, Köszeg, Royal Palace, Siklós, Székesfehérvar. 443-483, Apr. 1971
- The Investiture of Great Britain's Prince of Wales. By Allan C. Fisher, Jr. Photos by James L. Stanfield and Adam Woolfitt. Included: Caernarvon Castle. 698-715, Nov. 1969
- Luxembourg, the Quiet Fortress. By Robert Leslie Conly. Photos by Ted H. Funk. Included: Lucilinburhuc on the Bock, Vianden. 69-97, July 1970
- Modern Miracle, Made in Germany. By Robert Leslie Conly. Photos by Erich Lessing. Included: Gutenfels, Heidelberg, Katz, Maus, Sababurg, Schönburg. 735-791, June 1959
- Over the Sea to Scotland's Skye. By Robert J. Reynolds. Included: Dunvegan Castle. 87-112, July 1952
- Poets' Voices Linger in Scottish Shrines. By Isobel Wylie Hutchison. Photos by Kathleen Revis. Included: Caerlaverock, Duart, Dunnotar, Dunvegan, Edinburgh, Glamis. 437-488, Oct. 1957
- The Rhine: Europe's River of Legend. By William Graves. Photos by Bruce Dale. Included: "Cat Castle," Gutenberg, Munot, and Schönburg Castles. 449-499, Apr. 1967
- Rhododendron Glories of Southwest Scotland. By David S. Boyer. Photos by B. Anthony Stewart and author. Included: Castle Kennedy, Culzean, Lochinch. 641-664, May 1954
- Scotland From Her Lovely Lochs and Seas. By Alan Villiers. Photos by Robert F. Sisson. Included: Coll, Dunvegan, Edinburgh, Inverlochy, Kisimul, Urquhart. 492-541, Apr. 1961
- Silkworms in England Spin for the Queen. By John E. H. Nolan. Included: Lullingstone Castle's silk farm. 689-704, May 1953
- A Stroll to John o'Groat's. By Isobel Wylie Hutchison. Included: Balmoral, Belmont, Edinburgh, Falkland, Girnigoe, Invercauld, Sinclair Haunt. 1-48, July 1956
- Tirol, Austria's Province in the Clouds. By Peter T. White. Photos by Volkmar Wentzel. Included: Ambras, Hasegg, Hilltop, Lichtwert, and Weissenstein Castles. 107-141, July 1961
- Windsor Castle. By Anthony Holden. Photos by James L. Stanfield. 604-631, Nov. 1980

  The Grandeur of Windsor. Text by David Jeffery. 616-625
- *See also* Chateaux

CASTRO, FIDEL:
- Inside Cuba Today. By Fred Ward. 32-69, Jan. 1977

CATALINA ISLAND, California. *See* Santa Catalina

CATERPILLARS:
● The Case of the Killer Caterpillars. By Steven L. Montgomery. Photos by Robert F. Sisson. Contents: Predatory inchworms found only in the Hawaiian Islands. 219-225, Aug. 1983

CATFISH:
● New Florida Resident, the Walking Catfish. By Clarence P. Idyll. Photos by Robert F. Sisson. 847-851, June 1969

CATHEDRALS. *See* Canterbury Cathedral; Chartres; Notre Dame de Paris; Ste. Cécile; Washington Cathedral

CATHER, WILLA:
● The Country of Willa Cather. By William Howarth. Photos by Farrell Grehan. 71-93, July 1982

CATHOLICISM. *See* Roman Catholic Church

CATS:
■ The Big Cats. 442A-442B, Mar. 1974
◆ *Cats: Little Tigers in Your House.* Announced. 728-730, Nov. 1974
● The Cats in Our Lives. By Adolph Suehsdorf. Photos by Walter Chandoha. 508-541, Apr. 1964
◆ *Wild Cats.* 1981
● *See also* Cheetahs; Jaguar Hunting; Lions; Mountain Lions; Snow Leopards; Tigers

CATSKINS:
● Wild Cargo: the Business of Smuggling Animals. By Noel Grove. Photos by Steve Raymer. 287-315, Mar. 1981

CATTLE EGRET:
● A New Bird Immigrant Arrives. By Roger Tory Peterson. 281-292, Aug. 1954

CATTLE RAISING:
● America's "Meat on the Hoof." By William H. Nicholas. 33-72, Jan. 1952
King Ranch, Cattle Empire in Texas. 41-64
● Buffalo Bill and the Enduring West. By Alice J. Hall. Photos by James L. Amos. 76-103, July 1981
● Cowpunching on the Padlock Ranch. By William Albert Allard. 478-499, Oct. 1973
● 4-H Boys and Girls Grow More Food. By Frederick Simpich. 551-582, Nov. 1948
● The Gauchos, Last of a Breed. By Robert Laxalt. Photos by O. Louis Mazzatenta. 478-501, Oct. 1980
● Land of Long Sunsets: Nebraska's Sand Hills. By John Madson. Photos by Jodi Cobb. 493-517, Oct. 1978
● South in the Sudan. By Harry Hoogstraal. Included: Zebu cattle. 249-272, Feb. 1953
● The Wichitas: Land of the Living Prairie. By M. Woodbridge Williams. Included: Longhorns. 661-697, May 1957

CAUCASUS. *See* Abkhazian A.S.S.R.

CAUGHT in the Assam-Tibet Earthquake. By F. Kingdon-Ward. 403-416, Mar. 1952

CAULFIELD, PATRICIA: Photographer:
● The Hard Life of the Prairie Dog. By Tim W. Clark. 270-281, Aug. 1979
● Twilight Hope for Big Cypress. By Rick Gore. 251-273, Aug. 1976

CAVE ART:
● Baja's Murals of Mystery. By Harry Crosby. Photos by Charles O'Rear. 692-702, Nov. 1980
● A Bold New Look at Our Past. The Editor. NGS research grant. 62-63, Jan. 1975
● The Caves of the Thousand Buddhas (Tunhwang, China). By Franc and Jean Shor. 383-415, Mar. 1951
● Exploring Stone Age Arnhem Land (Australia). By Charles P. Mountford. Photos by Howell Walker. Included: Cave paintings of Oenpelli and Groote Eylandt. NGS research grant. 745-782, Dec. 1949
● Exploring the Mind of Ice Age Man. By Alexander Marshack. NGS research grant. 64-89, Jan. 1975
● India's Sculptured Temple Caves. By Volkmar Wentzel. 665-678, May 1953
● Lascaux Cave, Cradle of World Art. By Norbert Casteret. Photos by Maynard Owen Williams. Contents: La Baume Ladrone, La Henne Morte, La Mouthe, Lascaux, Montespan, Niaux, Trois Frères, Tuc D'Audoubert, in France; and Altamira in Spain. 771-794, Dec. 1948
● Maya Art Treasures Discovered in Cave. By George E. Stuart. Photos by Wilbur E. Garrett. 220-235, Aug. 1981
● Utah's Rock Art: Wilderness Louvre. A picture essay by Gary Smith, with Michael E. Long. 97-117, Jan. 1980

CAVE DWELLERS:
● Gypsy Cave Dwellers of Andalusia. 572-582, Oct. 1957
● *See also* Cliff Dwellers; Cones and Cone Dwellers; Tarahumara; Tasaday Tribe

CAVES:
● Bats Aren't All Bad. By Alvin Novick. Photos by Bruce Dale. 615-637, May 1973
● Birds That "See" in the Dark With Their Ears. By Edward S. Ross. 282-290, Feb. 1965
● Exploring America Underground. By Charles E. Mohr. 803-837, June 1964
● Life and Death in Tana Toradja. By Pamela and Alfred Meyer. 793-815, June 1972
● Nahanni: Canada's Wilderness Park. By Douglas H. Chadwick. Photos by Matt Bradley. Included: Grotte Mickey, Grotte Valerie, Ice Gallery. 396-420, Sept. 1981
● Nature's Night Lights: Probing the Secrets of Bioluminescence. By Paul A. Zahl. Included: Glowworms in Waitomo Caves, New Zealand. 45-69, July 1971
● On the Trail of La Venta Man (Mexico). By Matthew W. Stirling. Included: Cave of Guayabal. NGS research grant. 137-172, Feb. 1947
● Six Months Alone in a Cave (Biorhythm Research). By Michel Siffre. 426-435, Mar. 1975
● *See also* Amarnath Cave, Kashmir; Carlsbad Caverns, New Mexico; Caves, Underwater; Ice Caves; Khirbat Qumrān; National Parks (U. S.: Heritage); Russell Cave, Alabama; *and* Cave Art; Cave Dwellers

CAVES, Underwater:
● Diving Into the Blue Holes of the Bahamas. By George J. Benjamin. 347-363, Sept. 1970
● Into the Lairs of "Sleeping" Sharks. By Eugenie Clark. Photos by David Doubilet. NGS research grant. 570-584, Apr. 1975

CAYMAN TROUGH, Caribbean Sea:
● Window on Earth's Interior. By Robert D. Ballard. Photos by Emory Kristof. 228-249, Aug. 1976

CAYMANS. *See* Caimans

CELEBES (Island). *See* Sulawesi

CELLINI, BENVENUTO:
● Golden Masterpieces. 29-39, Jan. 1974

CELLS:
● The Awesome Worlds Within a Cell. By Rick Gore. Photos by Bruce Dale. Paintings by Davis Meltzer. Included: Foldout showing geography of the cell. 355-395, Sept. 1976

CELLULOSE:
● Versatile Wood Waits on Man. By Andrew H. Brown. 109-140, July 1951

CELTS:
● The Celts. By Merle Severy. Photos by James P. Blair. Paintings by Robert C. Magis. 582-633, May 1977
● Editorial. By Gilbert M. Grosvenor. 581, May 1977
▲ *Europe; Celtic Europe,* double-sided supplement. May 1977
● Treasure From a Celtic Tomb. By Jörg Biel. Photos by Volkmar Wentzel. 428-438, Mar. 1980

CEMETERIES, Military. *See* Arlington National Cemetery, Virginia; War Memorials

CENOTES. *See* Chichén Itzá; Dzibilchaltun

CENSUS 1960: Profile of the Nation. By Albert W. Atwood and Lonnelle Aikman. 697-714, Nov. 1959

CENTENARIANS. *See* Oldest People

CENTRAL AFRICAN REPUBLIC:
● Freedom Speaks French in Ouagadougou. By John Scofield. 153-203, Aug. 1966

CENTRAL AMERICA:
▲ *Archeological Map of Middle America, Land of the Feathered Serpent,* supplement. Text on reverse. Oct. 1968
▲ *Central America; Mexico,* double-sided supplement. May 1973
▲ *Countries of the Caribbean, including Mexico, Central America, and the West Indies,* supplement. Oct. 1947

• Flags of the Americas. By Elizabeth W. King. 633-657, May 1949
• How Fruit Came to America. By J. R. Magness. Paintings by Else Bostelmann. Included: Banana industry; Native fruits. 325-377, Sept. 1951
▲ *Mexico and Central America,* Atlas series supplement. Oct. 1961
▲ *Mexico and Central America,* supplement. Mar. 1953
• Our Vegetable Travelers. By Victor R. Boswell. Paintings by Else Bostelmann. Included: Native beans, common and lima. 145-217, Aug. 1949
• The Quetzal, Fabulous Bird of Maya Land. By Anne LaBastille Bowes. Photos by David G. Allen. 141-150, Jan. 1969
▲ *Tourist Islands of the West Indies; West Indies and Central America,* double-sided supplement. Feb. 1981
• Troubled Times for Central America. By Wilbur E. Garrett, Editor. Included: Belize, Costa Rica, El Salvador, Guatemala, Honduras, Nicaragua, Panama. 58-61, July 1981
• Unearthing the Oldest Known Maya. By Norman Hammond. Photos by Lowell Georgia and Martha Cooper. NGS research grant. 126-140, July 1982
▲ *Visitor's Guide to the Aztec World; Mexico and Central America,* double-sided supplement. Dec. 1980
▲ *West Indies and Central America,* supplement. Jan. 1970
• *See also* Belize; Costa Rica; El Salvador; Guatemala; Honduras; Nicaragua; Panama; Panama Canal; *and* Indians of Central America

CENTRAL PARK: Manhattan's Big Outdoors. By Stuart E. Jones. Photos by Bates Littlehales. 781-811, Dec. 1960

"The **CENTRE**" (Region), Australia:
• Australia. II. The Settled East, the Barrier Reef, the Center. By Alan Villiers. 347-385, Sept. 1963
• *See also* Alice Springs

CENTURY, Camp, Greenland:
• Nuclear Power for the Polar Regions. By George J. Dufek. 712-730, May 1962

A **CENTURY** Old, the Wonderful Brooklyn Bridge. By John G. Morris. Photos by Donal F. Holway. 565-579, May 1983

CEPHALONIA (Island), Greece:
• Homeward With Ulysses. By Melville Bell Grosvenor. Photos by Edwin Stuart Grosvenor. 1-39, July 1973

CEPHALOPODS. *See* Chambered Nautilus; Octopuses; Squids

CERAMICS:
• The Sunken Treasure of St. Helena. By Robert Sténuit. Photos by Bates Littlehales. Included: Ming porcelain. 562-576, Oct. 1978
• Yellow Sea Yields Shipwreck Trove. Photos by H. Edward Kim. Introduction by Donald H. Keith. Included: Earthenware, porcelain, and stoneware. 231-243, Aug. 1979
• *See also* Pottery

CERNAN, EUGENE A.:
• Exploring Taurus-Littrow. By Harrison H. Schmitt. 290-307, Sept. 1973

CERRUTI, JAMES: Author:
• Belgium: One Nation Divisible. Photos by Martin Rogers. 314-341, Mar. 1979
• Britain's "French" Channel Islands. Photos by James L. Amos. 710-740, May 1971
• Chelsea, London's Haven of Individualists. Photos by Adam Woolfitt. 28-55, Jan. 1972
• The Cotswolds, "Noicest Parrt o'England." Photos by Adam Woolfitt. 846-869, June 1974
• The Dominican Republic: Caribbean Comeback. Photos by Martin Rogers. 538-565, Oct. 1977
• Down the Ancient Appian Way. Photos by O. Louis Mazzatenta. 714-747, June 1981
• Edinburgh: Capital in Search of a Country. Photos by Adam Woolfitt. 274-296, Aug. 1976
• Gotland: Sweden's Treasure Island. Photos by Albert Moldvay. 268-288, Aug. 1973
• Jamaica Goes It Alone. Photos by Thomas Nebbia. 843-873, Dec. 1967
• The Netherlands Antilles: Holland in the Caribbean. Photos by Emory Kristof. 115-146, Jan. 1970
• Sea Islands: Adventuring Along the South's Surprising Coast. Photos by Thomas Nebbia and James L. Amos. 366-393, Mar. 1971
• Stockholm, Where "Kvalitet" Is a Way of Life. Photos by Albert Moldvay and Jonathan Blair. 43-69, Jan. 1976
• The Two Acapulcos. Photos by Thomas Nebbia. 848-878, Dec. 1964

CETACEANS. *See* Porpoises; Whales

CÉVENNES (Mountains), France:
• France's Past Lives in Languedoc. By Walter Meayers Edwards. 1-43, July 1951
• Travels With a Donkey–100 Years Later. By Carolyn Bennett Patterson. Photos by Cotton Coulson. 535-561, Oct. 1978

CEYLON:
• Ceylon, Island of the "Lion People." By Helen Trybulowski Gilles. 121-136, July 1948
• Ceylon, the Resplendent Land. By Donna K. and Gilbert M. Grosvenor. 447-497, Apr. 1966
• Troubled Waters East of Suez. By Ernest M. Eller. 483-522, Apr. 1954
• *See also* present name, Sri Lanka

CHACO (Region), Paraguay:
• Paraguay, Paradox of South America. By Gordon Young. Photos by O. Louis Mazzatenta. 240-269, Aug. 1982

CHACO CANYON, New Mexico:
• The Anasazi–Riddles in the Ruins. By Thomas Y. Canby. Photos by Dewitt Jones and David Brill. Paintings by Roy Andersen. 554-592, Nov. 1982

CHAD:
• Freedom Speaks French in Ouagadougou. By John Scofield. 153-203, Aug. 1966

CHADWICK, DOUGLAS H.: Author:
• Etosha: Namibia's Kingdom of Animals. Photos by Des and Jen Bartlett. 344-385, Mar. 1983
• Nahanni: Canada's Wilderness Park. Photos by Matt Bradley. 396-420, Sept. 1981
• Our Wild and Scenic Rivers: The Flathead. Photos by Lowell Georgia. 13-19, July 1977
• Our Wildest Wilderness: Alaska's Arctic National Wildlife Range. Photos by Lowell Georgia. 737-769, Dec. 1979
• Spring Comes Late to Glacier (Glacier National Park, Montana). 125-133, July 1979
Author-Photographer:
• Mountain Goats: Daring Guardians of the Heights. 284-296, Aug. 1978

CHAFFER, NORMAN:
Author-Photographer:
• Australia's Amazing Bowerbirds. 866-873, Dec. 1961

CHAGNON, NAPOLEON A.:
Author-Photographer:
• Yanomamo, the True People. 211-223, Aug. 1976

CHAKRI DYNASTY:
• Thailand's Working Royalty. Photos by John Everingham. 486-499, Oct. 1982

CHALLACOMBE, J. R.: Author:
• The Fabulous Sierra Nevada. 825-843, June 1954

The **CHALLENGE** of Air Safety. By Michael E. Long. Photos by Bruce Dale. 209-235, Aug. 1977

CHALLENGER DEEP. *See* Mariana Trench

The **CHAMBERED NAUTILUS,** Exquisite Living Fossil. Photos by Douglas Faulkner. 38-41, Jan. 1976

CHAMBERLIN, WELLMAN:
• Cartographer, NGS. 431, Mar. 1948
• Cartographic innovations. 488, Apr. 1956; 808, Dec. 1957; 49, July 1960; 698, May 1961; 875, Dec. 1961; 897, Dec. 1962; 95, July 1966; 243, Feb. 1967
• Chamberlin Trimetric Projection. 841, June 1947; 431, Mar. 1948; 826, June 1949; 399, Mar. 1950; 417, Mar. 1952; 591, Apr. 1964
• Grandson of noted explorer, Walter Wellman. 347, Mar. 1967

CHAMPA, Kingdom of:
• Mosaic of Cultures. By Peter T. White. Photos by W. E. Garrett. 296-329, Mar. 1971

CHAMPLAIN, SAMUEL DE:
• North (U. S. and Canada) Through History Aboard *White Mist.* By Melville Bell Grosvenor. Photos by Edwin Stuart Grosvenor. 1-55, July 1970

CHANG SHUHUA

Orchid Island: silver-helmeted islander

Hungary: woman weeding sugar beets

JOSEPH J. SCHERSCHEL, NGS

CHAMPLAIN, Lake, Canada-U. S.:
- From Sword to Scythe in Champlain Country. By Ethel A. Starbird. Photos by B. Anthony Stewart and Emory Kristof. 153-201, Aug. 1967
- North Through History Aboard *White Mist.* By Melville Bell Grosvenor. Photos by Edwin Stuart Grosvenor. 1-55, July 1970

CHAN CHAN, Peru's Ancient City of Kings. By Michael E. Moseley and Carol J. Mackey. Photos by David Brill. NGS research grant. 318-345, Mar. 1973

CHANDOHA, WALTER: Photographer:
- The Cats in Our Lives. By Adolph Suehsdorf. 508-541, Apr. 1964

CHANG SHUHUA: Photographer:
- The Gentle Yamis of Orchid Island. 98-109, Jan. 1977

CHANGCHUN, China:
- In Manchuria Now. By W. Robert Moore. 389-414, Mar. 1947

CHANGE Comes to a Changeless Land. By Thomas J. Abercrombie. 312-343, Mar. 1977

The **CHANGE** in Spain. By Peter T. White. Photos by David Alan Harvey. 297-331, Mar. 1978

CHANGE Ripples New Guinea's Sepik River. By Malcolm S. Kirk. 354-381, Sept. 1973

The **CHANGELESS** Horseshoe Crab. By Anne and Jack Rudloe. Photos by Robert F. Sisson. 562-572, Apr. 1981

The **CHANGING** Face of Old Spain. By Bart McDowell. Photos by Albert Moldvay. 291-339, Mar. 1965

CHANGING Formosa, Green Island of Refuge. By Frederick Simpich, Jr. Photos by Horace Bristol. 327-364, Mar. 1957

CHANGING Homeland of a Tough, Romantic People: Hungary. By Bart McDowell. Photos by Albert Moldvay and Joseph J. Scherschel. 443-483, Apr. 1971

The **CHANGING** World of Canada's Crees. By Fred Ward. 541-569, Apr. 1975

CH'ANGSHA, Hunan Province, People's Republic of China:
- A Lady From China's Past. Photos from *China Pictorial.* Text by Alice J. Hall. 660-681, May 1974

CHANNEL Cruise to Glorious Devon. By Alan Villiers. Photos by Bates Littlehales. 208-259, Aug. 1963

CHANNEL ISLANDS, California. *See* Santa Barbara Islands

CHANNEL ISLANDS, English Channel:
- Britain's "French" Channel Islands. By James Cerruti. Photos by James L. Amos. 710-740, May 1971

CHAO, JOHN: Photographer:
- Taiwan Confronts a New Era. By Noel Grove. 93-119, Jan. 1982

CHAPELLE, ANTHONY: Author:
- Report from the Locust Wars. By Tony and Dickey Chapelle. 545-562, Apr. 1953

Author-Photographer:
- New Life for India's Villagers. By Anthony and Georgette Dickey Chapelle. 572-588, Apr. 1956

CHAPELLE, DICKEY:
- What Was a Woman Doing There? (Memorial Tribute). By W. E. Garrett. 270-271, Feb. 1966

Author:
- Report from the Locust Wars. By Tony and Dickey Chapelle. 545-562, Apr. 1953

Author-Photographer:
- Helicopter War in South Viet Nam. 723-754, Nov. 1962
- New Life for India's Villagers. By Anthony and Georgette Dickey Chapelle. 572-588, Apr. 1956
- Water War in Viet Nam. 272-296, Feb. 1966

CHARACTER Marks the Coast of Maine. By John Scofield. Photos by B. Anthony Stewart. 798-843, June 1968

CHARLES, Prince of Wales:
- The Investiture of Great Britain's Prince of Wales. By Allan C. Fisher, Jr. Photos by James L. Stanfield and Adam Woolfitt. 698-715, Nov. 1969
- Windsor Castle. By Anthony Holden. Photos by James L. Stanfield. 604-631, Nov. 1980

CHARLES W. MORGAN (Whaler):
- The Age of Sail Lives On at Mystic. By Alan Villiers. Photos by Weston Kemp. 220-239, Aug. 1968

CHARLESTON, South Carolina:
- Patriots in Petticoats. By Lonnelle Aikman. Paintings by Louis S. Glanzman. 475-493, Oct. 1975
- Savannah to Charleston–A Good Life in the Low Country. By John J. Putman. Photos by Annie Griffiths. 798-829, Dec. 1983
- South Carolina Rediscovered. By Herbert Ravenel Sass. 281-321, Mar. 1953

CHARLOTTE AMALIE, Virgin Islands:
- Our Virgin Islands, 50 Years Under the Flag. By Carleton Mitchell. Photos by James L. Stanfield. 67-103, Jan. 1968
- Virgin Islands: Tropical Playland, U.S.A. By John Scofield. Photos by Charles Allmon. 201-232, Feb. 1956

CHARLOTTESVILLE, Virginia:
- Mr. Jefferson's Charlottesville. By Anne Revis. 553-592, May 1950
- *See also* Monticello

CHARTING Our Sea and Air Lanes. By Stuart E. Jones. Photos by J. Baylor Roberts. 189-209, Feb. 1957

CHARTRES, Cathedral of, France:
- Chartres: Legacy From the Age of Faith. By Kenneth MacLeish. Photos by Dean Conger. 857-882, Dec. 1969

CHARYBDIS (Whirlpool and Legendary Monster). *See* Messina, Strait of

CHATEAUX:
● Bordeaux: Fine Wines and Fiery Gascons. By William Davenport. Photos by Adam Woolfitt. Included: Beynac, de Fontgraves, d'Yquem, Haut-Brion, La Brède, Lafite-Rothschild, Latour, Margaux, Montaigne, Mouton-Rothschild, Palmer, Pétrus, Prieuré-Lichine. 233-259, Aug. 1980
● France's Past Lives in Languedoc. By Walter Meayers Edwards. Included: Cité (Fortress), Carcassonne; Polignac. 1-43, July 1951
● Lafayette's Homeland, Auvergne. By Howell Walker. Included: Aix, Chavaniac, Du Motier, La Grange, St. Romain, Tournoël. 419-436, Sept. 1957
● River of Counts and Kings: The Loire. By Kenneth MacLeish. Photos by Dean Conger. Included: Amboise, Angers, Arlempdes, Azay-le-Rideau, Blois, Chambord, Chaumont, Chenonceaux, Cheverny, Chinon, Gien, Langeais, Saumur, Sully, Ussé. 822-869, June 1966

CHATTOOGA RIVER, Georgia-North Carolina-South Carolina:
● Chattooga River Country: Wild Water, Proud People. By Don Belt. Photos by Steve Wall. 458-477, Apr. 1983

CHATURVEDI, M. D.: Author:
● The Elephant and I. 489-507, Oct. 1957

CHAUCER, GEOFFREY:
● The British Way. By Sir Evelyn Wrench. 421-541, Apr. 1949

CHEESE MAKING:
● Deep in the Heart of "Swissconsin." By William H. Nicholas. Photos by J. Baylor Roberts. 781-800, June 1947
● The Goats of Thunder Hill. By Elizabeth Nicholds. Photos by Robert F. Sisson. 625-640, May 1954
● Helping Holland Rebuild Her Land. By Gilbert M. Grosvenor and Charles Neave. 365-413, Sept. 1954
● Switzerland, Europe's High-rise Republic. By Thomas J. Abercrombie. 68-113, July 1969

CHEETAHS: In a Race for Survival. By George W. and Lory Herbison Frame. 712-728, May 1980

CHEKIANG (Province), China:
● Operation Eclipse: 1948. By William A. Kinney. NGS research grant. 325-372, Mar. 1949

CHELLEAN CULTURE:
● Exploring 1,750,000 Years Into Man's Past. By L. S. B. Leakey. Photos by Robert F. Sisson. NGS research grant. 564-589, Oct. 1961

CHELSEA, London's Haven of Individualists. By James Cerruti. Photos by Adam Woolfitt. 28-55, Jan. 1972

CHEMICAL INDUSTRY:
● Delaware–Who Needs to Be Big? By Jane Vessels. Photos by Kevin Fleming. 171-197, Aug. 1983
● Today on the Delaware, Penn's Glorious River. By Albert W. Atwood. Photos by Robert F. Sisson. 1-40, July 1952

CHEMICAL POLLUTION:
● Acid Rain–How Great a Menace? By Anne LaBastille. Photos by Ted Spiegel. 652-681, Nov. 1981
● The Pesticide Dilemma. By Allen A. Boraiko. Photos by Fred Ward. 145-183, Feb. 1980
● Pollution, Threat to Man's Only Home. By Gordon Young. Photos by James P. Blair. 738-781, Dec. 1970
● Quicksilver and Slow Death. By John J. Putman. Photos by Robert W. Madden. 507-527, Oct. 1972

CHEMISTRY:
● The British Way. By Sir Evelyn Wrench. 421-541, Apr. 1949
● The Romance of American Furs. By Wanda Burnett. Included: The plasticizing of furs, developed by Dr. José B. Calva. 379-402, Mar. 1948
● Uncle Sam's House of 1,000 Wonders (National Bureau of Standards). By Lyman J. Briggs and F. Barrows Colton. 755-784, Dec. 1951
● *See also* Biochemistry; Perfume

CHEMOSYNTHESIS:
● Incredible World of the Deep-sea Rifts. NGS research grant. 680-705, Nov. 1979
I. Strange World Without Sun. The Editor. 680-688; II. Return to Oases of the Deep. By Robert D. Ballard and J. Frederick Grassle. 689-705
● Oases of Life in the Cold Abyss (Galapagos Rift). By John B. Corliss and Robert D. Ballard. 441-453, Oct. 1977

CHEROKEE INDIANS:
● Pack Trip Through the Smokies. By Val Hart. Photos by Robert F. Sisson. 473-502, Oct. 1952

CHERRY COUNTY, Nebraska:
● Land of Long Sunsets: Nebraska's Sand Hills. By John Madson. Photos by Jodi Cobb. 493-517, Oct. 1978

CHESAPEAKE AND OHIO CANAL:
● Waterway to Washington, the C & O Canal. By Jay Johnston. 419-439, Mar. 1960

CHESAPEAKE BAY, and Region:
● Chesapeake Country. By Nathaniel T. Kenney. Photos by Bates Littlehales. 370-411, Sept. 1964
● "Delmarva," Gift of the Sea. By Catherine Bell Palmer. 367-399, Sept. 1950
● Maryland on the Half Shell. By Stuart E. Jones. Photos by Robert W. Madden. 188-229, Feb. 1972
● My Chesapeake–Queen of Bays. By Allan C. Fisher, Jr. Photos by Lowell Georgia. 428-467, Oct. 1980
● One Hundred Hours Beneath the Chesapeake. By Gilbert C. Klingel. Photos by Willard R. Culver. NGS research grant. 681-696, May 1955
▲ *Round About the Nation's Capital,* supplement. Apr. 1956
● Roving Maryland's Cavalier Country. By William A. Kinney. 431-470, Apr. 1954
● The Sailing Oystermen of Chesapeake Bay. By Luis Marden. 798-819, Dec. 1967
● This Is My Island, Tangier. By Harold G. Wheatley. Photos by David Alan Harvey. 700-725, Nov. 1973
● *See also* Eastern Shore; Virginia (Captain Smith; History Keeps House); *and* Chesapeake Bay Bridge-Tunnel; Intracoastal Waterway

CHESAPEAKE BAY BRIDGE-TUNNEL:
● Over and Under Chesapeake Bay. By David S. Boyer. 593-612, Apr. 1964

CHESSMEN Come to Life in Marostica. By Alexander Taylor. 658-668, Nov. 1956

CHESTER DALE COLLECTION:
● Great Masters of a Brave Era in Art (Impressionist). By Hereward Lester Cooke, Jr. 661-697, May 1961

CHETELAT, ENZO DE: Author:
● Roaming Korea South of the Iron Curtain. 777-808, June 1950

CHIANG KAI-SHEK:
● Eyes on the China Coast. By George W. Long. 505-512, Apr. 1953
● Taiwan: The Watchful Dragon. By Helen and Frank Schreider. 1-45, Jan. 1969

CHIAPAS (State), Mexico:
● The Disaster of El Chichón. By Boris Weintraub. Photos by Guillermo Aldana E. and Kenneth Garrett. 654-684, Nov. 1982
Volcanic Cloud May Alter Earth's Climate. By Robert I. Tilling. 672-675
● The Maya. 729-811, Dec. 1975
I. Children of Time. By Howard La Fay. Photos by David Alan Harvey. Included: Bonampak; Chamula; Palenque. 729-767; II. Riddle of the Glyphs. By George E. Stuart. Photos by Otis Imboden. Included: Palenque; Yaxchilán. 768-791
● *See also* Piedra Parada

CHICAGO, Illinois:
● Chicago! By Harvey Arden. Photos by Steve Raymer. 463-493, Apr. 1978
● The Great Lakes: Is It Too Late? By Gordon Young. Photos by James L. Amos and Martin Rogers. 147-185, Aug. 1973
● Illinois–Healthy Heart of the Nation. By Leo A. Borah. Photos by B. Anthony Stewart and Willard R. Culver. 781-820, Dec. 1953
● Illinois: The City and the Plain. By Robert Paul Jordan. Photos by James L. Stanfield and Joseph J. Scherschel. 745-797, June 1967
● Mapping the Nation's Breadbasket. By Frederick Simpich. 831-849, June 1948

CHICHÉN ITZÁ, Yucatán, Mexico:
● Into the Well of Sacrifice. NGS research grant. 540-561, Oct. 1961
I. Return to the Sacred Cenote. By Eusebio Dávalos Hurtado. 540-549; II. Treasure Hunt in the Deep Past. By Bates Littlehales. 550-561

GUILLERMO ALDANA E.

El Chichón: villagers endure volcanic ashfall

• The Maya, Children of Time. By Howard La Fay. Photos by David Alan Harvey. 729-767, Dec. 1975

CHICHICASTENANGO, Guatemala:
• Easter Week in Indian Guatemala. By John Scofield. 406-417, Mar. 1960
• Guatemala Revisited. By Luis Marden. 525-564, Oct. 1947

El **CHICHÓN** (Volcano), Mexico:
• The Disaster of El Chichón. By Boris Weintraub. Photos by Guillermo Aldana E. and Kenneth Garrett. 654-684, Nov. 1982
Volcanic Cloud May Alter Earth's Climate. By Robert I. Tilling. 672-675

CHICKENS:
• Easter Egg Chickens. By Frederick G. Vosburgh. Photos by B. Anthony Stewart. 377-387, Sept. 1948
• *See also* Onagadori

CHIDSEY, DONALD BARR: Author:
• The Old Boston Post Roads. 189-205, Aug. 1962

CHIEF JOSEPH. By William Albert Allard. 409-434, Mar. 1977

CHIHUAHUA (State), Mexico:
• The Tarahumaras: Mexico's Long Distance Runners. By James Norman. Photos by David Hiser. 702-718, May 1976

CHIHUAHUAN DESERT, Mexico-U. S. *See* Guadalupe Mountains National Park, Texas

CHILDHOOD Summer on the Maine Coast. By Arline Strong. 436-444, Sept. 1960

CHILDREN:
• Blue-eyed Indian: A City Boy's Sojourn with Primitive Tribesmen in Central Brazil. By Harald Schultz. 65-89, July 1961
• Children's Art Around the World. By Newman Bumstead. 365-387, Mar. 1957
• Dinkelsbühl Rewards Its Children. By Charles Belden. 255-268, Feb. 1957
• The Family: A Mormon Shrine. 459-463, Apr. 1975
• 4-H Boys and Girls Grow More Food. By Frederick Simpich. 551-582, Nov. 1948
• The GI and the Kids of Korea. By Robert H. Mosier. 635-664, May 1953
• In Touch With Nature. Text by Elizabeth A. Moize. Photos by Steve Raymer. 537-543, Apr. 1974
• The Magic World of Hans Christian Andersen. By Harvey Arden. Photos by Sisse Brimberg. 825-849, Dec. 1979
• Norway Cracks Her Mountain Shell. By Sydney Clark. Photos by Gilbert Grosvenor and Ole Friele Backer. Included: Constitution Day celebration; Legislation favorable to children; School gardens. 171-211, Aug. 1948
• Seashore Summer: One Mother's Recipe for Smallboy Bliss. By Arline Strong. 436-444, Sept. 1960
• Uncle Sam Bends a Twig in Germany. By Frederick Simpich. Photos by J. Baylor Roberts. 529-550, Oct. 1948
• We Build a School for Sherpa Children. By Sir Edmund Hillary. 548-551, Oct. 1962
• Zoo Animals Go to School. By Marion P. McCrane. Photos by W. E. Garrett. 694-706, Nov. 1956
• *See also* Boy Scouts; Children's Village; Children's Zoo; Clarke School for the Deaf; Little Tibet in Switzerland; Spafford Memorial Children's Hospital

CHILDREN of the Sun and Moon. By Harald Schultz; translated from German by Curtis T. Everett. 340-363, Mar. 1959

CHILDREN'S BOOKS. *See* Books, NGS: Children's Books

CHILDREN'S MAGAZINES, NGS. *See* School Bulletin; *WORLD*

CHILDREN'S VILLAGE in Switzerland, Pestalozzi. Photos by Alfred Lammer. 268-282, Aug. 1959

CHILDREN'S ZOO, Regent's Park, London:
• London's Zoo of Zoos. By Thomas Garner James. 771-786, June 1953

CHILE:
• Atlantic Odyssey: Iceland to Antarctica. By Newman Bumstead. Photos by Volkmar Wentzel. 725-780, Dec. 1955
• Chile, Republic on a Shoestring. By Gordon Young. Photos by George F. Mobley. 437-477, Oct. 1973
• Chile, the Long and Narrow Land. By Kip Ross. 185-235, Feb. 1960
• Guanacos: Wild Camels of South America. By William L. Franklin. NGS research grant. 63-75, July 1981
• The Lost Empire of the Incas. By Loren McIntyre. Art by Ned and Rosalie Seidler. 729-787, Dec. 1973
A Pictorial Chronicle of the Incas. 747-753
• Parks, Plans, and People: How South America Guards Her Green Legacy. By Mary and Laurance Rockefeller. Photos by George F. Mobley. 74-119, Jan. 1967
• *See also* Easter Island; Patagonia; Torre Egger; Valparaíso

CHILIN (Kirin), China:
• In Manchuria Now. By W. Robert Moore. 389-414, Mar. 1947

CHIMOR EMPIRE:
• Chan Chan, Peru's Ancient City of Kings. By Michael E. Moseley and Carol J. Mackey. Photos by David Brill. NGS research grant. 318-345, Mar. 1973

CHIMPANZEES:
• Life and Death at Gombe. By Jane Goodall. NGS research grant. 592-621, May 1979
▥ Miss Goodall and the Wild Chimpanzees. 831A-831B, Dec. 1965
◆ *My Friends the Wild Chimpanzees.* 1967. Announced. 408-417, Mar. 1966

• My Life Among Wild Chimpanzees. By Jane Goodall. Photos by Baron Hugo van Lawick and author. NGS research grant. 272-308, Aug. 1963
• New Discoveries Among Africa's Chimpanzees. By Baroness Jane van Lawick-Goodall. Photos by Baron Hugo van Lawick. NGS research grant. 802-831, Dec. 1965
• School for Space Monkeys. 725-729, May 1961

CHIMU (People). *See* Chimor Empire

CH'IN SHIH HUANG TI, Emperor (China):
• China's Incredible Find. By Audrey Topping. Paintings by Yang Hsien-min. 440-459, Apr. 1978

CHINA, People's Republic of:
• Adventures in Lololand. By Rennold L. Lowy. 105-118, Jan. 1947
• Along the Yangtze, Main Street of China. By W. Robert Moore. 325-356, Mar. 1948
• American Skiers Find Adventure in Western China. By Ned Gillette. Photos by the author and Galen Rowell. 174-199, Feb. 1981
Skiing From the Summit of China's Ice Mountain. 192-199
• Bamboo, the Giant Grass. By Luis Marden. Photos by Jim Brandenburg. 502-529, Oct. 1980
• The Caves of the Thousand Buddhas. By Franc and Jean Shor. 383-415, Mar. 1951
▲ *China,* Atlas series supplement. Nov. 1964
▲ *China Coast and Korea,* supplement. Oct. 1953
• China Unveils Her Newest Treasures. Photos by Robert W. Madden. 848-857, Dec. 1974
• China's Incredible Find. By Audrey Topping. Paintings by Yang Hsien-min. Included: The first emperor's burial mound, with guardian army of terra-cotta men and horses. 440-459, Apr. 1978
• China's Opening Door. By John J. Putman. Photos by H. Edward Kim. Contents: Special Economic Zones. 64-83, July 1983
• Editorials. By Gilbert M. Grosvenor. 1, July 1980; By Wilbur E. Garrett. 143, Feb. 1981
• Eyes on the China Coast. By George W. Long. 505-512, Apr. 1953
• Guilin, China's Beauty Spot. By W. E. Garrett. 536-563, Oct. 1979
• How Fruit Came to America. By J. R. Magness. Paintings by Else Bostelmann. Included: Two Stone Fruits from the Orient (Apricots; Japanese plums). 325-377, Sept. 1951
• How the Kazakhs Fled to Freedom. By Milton J. Clark. 621-644, Nov. 1954
• In Manchuria Now. By W. Robert Moore. 389-414, Mar. 1947
◆ *Journey Into China.* 1982
• Journey to China's Far West. By Rick Gore. Photos by Bruce Dale. 292-331, Mar. 1980
• A Lady From China's Past. Photos from *China Pictorial.* Text by Alice J. Hall. 660-681, May 1974

WILBUR E. GARRETT, NGS

Guilin: farmers plowing vetch under

• Letter From Kunming: Two American Teachers in China. By Elisabeth B. Booz. Photos by Thomas Nebbia. 793-813, June 1981
• The Lost Fleet of Kublai Khan. By Torao Mozai. Photos by Koji Nakamura. Paintings by Issho Yada. 634-649, Nov. 1982
• Nomads of China's West. By Galen Rowell. Photos by the author and Harold A. Knutson. 244-263, Feb. 1982
• Operation Eclipse: 1948. By William A. Kinney. NGS research grant. 325-372, Mar. 1949
• Our Vegetable Travelers. By Victor R. Boswell. Paintings by Else Bostelmann. Included: Chinese cabbage. 145-217, Aug. 1949
• Pandas in the Wild. By George B. Schaller. 735-749, Dec. 1981
▲ *The People's Republic of China; The Peoples of China,* double-sided supplement. July 1980
• Père David's Deer Saved From Extinction. By Larry Kohl. Photos by Bates Littlehales. 478-485, Oct. 1982
• Return to Changing China. By Audrey Topping. 801-833, Dec. 1971
■ Save the Panda. 824, Dec. 1982
• Shanghai: Born-again Giant. By Mike Edwards. Photos by Bruce Dale. 2-43, July 1980
"Muscle and smoke, commerce and crowds." A Shanghai Portfolio by Bruce Dale. 2-13
• This Is the China I Saw. By Jørgen Bisch. Included: Canton; Hangchow; Peking; Shanghai; Sian; Tatung; Yun Kang Caves. 591-639, Nov. 1964
• Those Outlandish Goldfish! By Paul A. Zahl. Included: China's 1960 postage stamp series. 514-533, Apr. 1973
• Trawling the China Seas. Photos by J. Charles Thompson. 381-395, Mar. 1950
• The World in Your Garden (Flowers). By W. H. Camp. Paintings by Else Bostelmann. Included: Chinese Mountainsides Yield Treasures (Regal Lily, Abelia, Peony); More Plants from Age-old China (Camellia, Hollyhock, China Aster, Blackberry-lily, Chrysanthemum, Clematis, Forsythia). 1-65, July 1947
• *See also* Everest; K2; Kunming; Peking; Tibet

CHINA, Republic of (Taiwan):
• Changing Formosa, Green Island of Refuge. By Frederick Simpich, Jr. Photos by Horace Bristol. 327-364, Mar. 1957
▲ *China,* Atlas series supplement. Nov. 1964
• Eyes on the China Coast. By George W. Long. 505-512, Apr. 1953
• Formosa–Hot Spot of the East. By Frederick G. Vosburgh. Photos by J. Baylor Roberts. 139-176, Feb. 1950
• The Gentle Yamis of Orchid Island. Photos by Chang Shuhua. 98-109, Jan. 1977
• Our Navy in the Far East. By Arthur W. Radford. Photos by J. Baylor Roberts. 537-577, Oct. 1953

• Taiwan: The Watchful Dragon. By Helen and Frank Schreider. 1-45, Jan. 1969
• Taiwan Confronts a New Era. By Noel Grove. Photos by John Chao. 93-119, Jan. 1982
• *See also* Formosa Strait; Pescadores

CHINATOWN, the Gilded Ghetto. By William Albert Allard. 627-643, Nov. 1975

CHINCHILLAS:
• The Romance of American Furs. By Wanda Burnett. 379-402, Mar. 1948

CHINCOTEAGUE ISLAND, Virginia:
• Chincoteague: Watermen's Island Home. By Nathaniel T. Kenney. Photos by James L. Amos. 810-829, June 1980

CHINESE REFUGEES:
• Hong Kong's Refugee Dilemma. By William S. Ellis. Photos by William Albert Allard. Included: Ethnic Chinese refugees expelled from Vietnam. 709-732, Nov. 1979

CHIPPEWA NATIONAL FOREST, Minnesota:
• Our Bald Eagle: Freedom's Symbol Survives. By Thomas C. Dunstan. Photos by Jeff Foott. NGS research grant. 186-199, Feb. 1978

CHIPS (Integrated Circuits):
• California's Silicon Valley. By Moira Johnston. Photos by Charles O'Rear. 459-477, Oct. 1982
• The Chip: Electronic Mini-marvel. By Allen A. Boraiko. Photos by Charles O'Rear. 421-457, Oct. 1982

CHIRIQUÍ (Province), Panama:
• Exploring Ancient Panama by Helicopter. By Matthew W. Stirling. Photos by Richard H. Stewart. NGS research grant. 227-246, Feb. 1950
• Panama, Link Between Oceans and Continents. By Jules B. Billard. Photos by Bruce Dale. 402-440, Mar. 1970

CHISOS MOUNTAINS, Texas:
• Big Bend: Jewel in the Texas Desert. By Nathaniel T. Kenney. Photos by James L. Stanfield. 104-133, Jan. 1968

CHITTAGONG HILL TRACTS, Bangladesh:
• Bangladesh: Hope Nourishes a New Nation. By William S. Ellis. Photos by Dick Durrance II. 295-333, Sept. 1972
• The Peaceful Mrus of Bangladesh. By Claus-Dieter Brauns. 267-286, Feb. 1973

CHIYODA, Japan:
• Day of the Rice God (Festival). Photos by H. Edward Kim. Text by Douglas Lee. 78-85, July 1978

CHLOROPHYLL:
• How the Sun Gives Life to the Sea (Photosynthesis). By Paul A. Zahl. 199-225, Feb. 1961

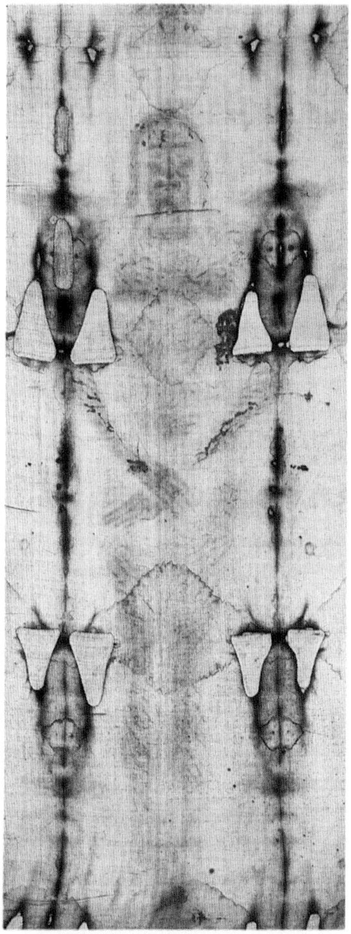

VERNON MILLER, PRINT BY REX A. STUCKY, NGS

Shroud: body image appears on cloth

CHOCÓ (Region), Colombia:
• Capturing Strange Creatures in Colombia. By Marte Latham. Photos by Tor Eigeland. 682-693, May 1966

CHOLLA CACTUS:
• Abundant Life in a Desert Land. By Walter Meayers Edwards. 424-436, Sept. 1973

CHOLO INDIANS:
• Capturing Strange Creatures in Colombia. By Marte Latham. Photos by Tor Eigeland. 682-693, May 1966

CHONG, JERRY: Photographer:
• Saving the Nene, World's Rarest Goose. By S. Dillon Ripley. 745-754, Nov. 1965

CHOU EN-LAI:
• Return to Changing China. By Audrey Topping. 801-833, Dec. 1971

CHOWNING, ANN: Photographer:
• Blowgun Hunters of the South Pacific. By Jane C. Goodale. 793-817, June 1966

CHRISTCHURCH, New Zealand:
• New Zealand, Pocket Wonder World. By Howell Walker. 419-460, Apr. 1952
• New Zealand's Bountiful South Island. By Peter Benchley. Photos by James L. Amos. 93-123, Jan. 1972

CHRISTIANITY:
• Ethiopia: Revolution in an Ancient Empire. By Robert Caputo. Included: Ethiopian Orthodox Church. 614-645, May 1983
• The Ghosts of Jericho. By James L. Kelso. 825-844, Dec. 1951
◆ *Great Religions of the World.* Announced. 587-590, Oct. 1971
• Hashemite Jordan, Arab Heartland. By John Scofield. Included: The shrines of Bethlehem and Jerusalem; Latrun Monastery. 841-856, Dec. 1952
▲ *Holy Land Today.* Atlas series supplement. Dec. 1963
• Jerusalem to Rome in the Path of St. Paul. By David S. Boyer. 707-759, Dec. 1956
• The Land of Galilee. By Kenneth MacLeish. Photos by B. Anthony Stewart. 832-865, Dec. 1965
▲ *Lands of the Bible Today,* supplement. Dec. 1956
▲ *Lands of the Bible Today,* supplement. Dec. 1967
• The Mystery of the Shroud. By Kenneth F. Weaver. Contents: The Shroud of Turin, believed by some to be Christ's burial cloth. 730-753, June 1980
• The Other Side of Jordan. By Luis Marden. 790-825, Dec. 1964
• Pilgrims Follow the Christmas Star. By Maynard Owen Williams. 831-840, Dec. 1952
• Searching Out Medieval Churches in Ethiopia's Wilds. By Georg Gerster. 856-884, Dec. 1970
• This Year in Jerusalem. By Joseph Judge. Photos by Jodi Cobb. 479-515, Apr. 1983

• Vézelay, Hill of the Pilgrims. By Melvin Hall. 229-247, Feb. 1953
• Where Jesus Walked. By Howard La Fay. Photos by Charles Harbutt. 739-781, Dec. 1967
• The World of Martin Luther. By Merle Severy. Photos by James L. Amos. 418-463, Oct. 1983
• *See also* Eastern Orthodoxy; Protestantism; Roman Catholicism

CHRISTIANSØ (Island), Denmark. *See* Baltic Cruise of the *Caribbee*

CHRISTMAS:
• "The Adoration of the Magi," painting supplement. Jan. 1952
• Christmas in Cookie Tree Land. By Louise Parker La Gorce. Photos by B. Anthony Stewart. 844-851, Dec. 1955
• Editorial. By Gilbert M. Grosvenor. 727, Dec. 1975
• Old Salem, Morning Star of Moravian Faith. By Rowe Findley. Photos by Robert W. Madden. 818-837, Dec. 1970
• Pilgrims Follow the Christmas Star. By Maynard Owen Williams. 831-840, Dec. 1952
• Williamsburg, City for All Seasons. By Joseph Judge. Photos by James L. Amos. 790-823, Dec. 1968

CHRISTOPHER COLUMBUS and the New World He Found. By John Scofield. Photos by Adam Woolfitt. 584-625, Nov. 1975

CHUBB CRATER, Quebec, Canada:
• Solving the Riddle of Chubb Crater. By V. Ben Meen. Photos by Richard H. Stewart. NGS research grant. 1-32, Jan. 1952

CHUBUT PROVINCE, Argentina:
• Patagonia. Photos by Des and Jen Bartlett. 290-339, Mar. 1976
I. Argentina Protects Its Wildlife Treasures. By William G. Conway. 290-297; II. Where Two Worlds Meet. 298-321; III. At Home With Right Whales. By Roger Payne. 322-339

CHUKCHIS:
• People of the Long Spring. By Yuri Rytkheu. Photos by Dean Conger. 206-223, Feb. 1983
▲ *Peoples of the Arctic; Arctic Ocean,* double-sided supplement. Feb. 1983

CHUCKWALLA MOUNTAINS, California:
• Poorwill Sleeps Away the Winter. By Edmund C. Jaeger. 273-280, Feb. 1953

CHUGACH MOUNTAINS, Alaska:
• Alaska's Automatic Lake Drains Itself (Lake George). 835-844, June 1951

CHURCH, RON: Photographer:
• *Deepstar* Explores the Ocean Floor. 110-129, Jan. 1971

CHURCH OF JESUS CHRIST OF LATTER-DAY SAINTS. *See* Mormons

CHURCH OF THE NATIVITY, Bethlehem:
• Hashemite Jordan, Arab Heartland. By John Scofield. 841-856, Dec. 1952

CHURCHES:
• Searching Out Medieval Churches in Ethiopia's Wilds. By Georg Gerster. 856-884, Dec. 1970
• *See also* Basilique de la Sainte Marie Madeleine; Missions; Mont Saint Michel, for La Merveille; St. Catherine's Monastery; St. Peter's; Westminster Abbey; *and* listing under Cathedrals

CHURCHILL, SIR WINSTON:
• The British Way. By Sir Evelyn Wrench. 421-541, Apr. 1949
• Tribute to Sir Winston. 153-225, Aug. 1965
I. The Churchill I Knew. By Dwight D. Eisenhower. 153-157; II. "Be Ye Men of Valour." By Howard La Fay. 159-197; III. The Funeral of Sir Winston Churchill, with Excerpts from His Speeches. Phonograph record. 198-198B; IV. The Final Tribute. Text by Carolyn Bennett Patterson. 199-225

CHURCHILL, Manitoba, Canada:
• Canada's Heartland, the Prairie Provinces. By W. E. Garrett. 443-489, Oct. 1970
• Henry Hudson's Changing Bay. By Bill Richards. Photos by David Hiser. 380-405, Mar. 1982
■ Polar Bear Alert. 395, cover, Mar. 1982
• Rockets Explore the Air Above Us. By Newman Bumstead. 562-580, Apr. 1957
• Trailing Cosmic Rays in Canada's North. By Martin A. Pomerantz. NGS research grant. 99-115, Jan. 1953

CHURCHILL DOWNS, Louisville, Kentucky:
• Heart of the Bluegrass. By Charles McCarry. Photos by J. Bruce Baumann. 634-659, May 1974

CICADAS:
• Rip Van Winkle of the Underground (Periodical Cicada). By Kenneth F. Weaver. 133-142, July 1953

CINDER FARMING. *See* Lanzarote

CINTA LARGA INDIANS:
• Brazil Protects Her Cinta Larga Indians. By W. Jesco von Puttkamer. 420-444, Sept. 1971

CIRCLING Earth From Pole to Pole. By Sir Ranulph Fiennes. 464-481, Oct. 1983

CIRCUS:
• On the Road With an Old-time Circus. By John Fetterman. Photos by Jonathan Blair. 410-434, Mar. 1972
• The Wonder City That Moves by Night. By Francis Beverly Kelley. 289-324, Mar. 1948
Circus Action in Color. By Harold E. Edgerton. 305-308

CITÉ, Île de la, Paris:
• Île de la Cité, Birthplace of Paris. By Kenneth MacLeish. Photos by Bruce Dale. 680-719, May 1968
• The More Paris Changes. . . . By Howell Walker. Photos by Gordon W. Gahan. 64-103, July 1972

CITIES Like Worcester Make America. By Howell Walker. 189-214, Feb. 1955

CITIES of Stone in Utah's Canyonland. By W. Robert Moore. 653-677, May 1962

CITRUS FRUITS:
• Florida Rides a Space-age Boom. By Benedict Thielen. Photos by Winfield Parks and James P. Blair. 858-903, Dec. 1963
• How Fruit Came to America. By J. R. Magness. Paintings by Else Bostelmann. Included: Grapefruit, Lemon, Lime, Orange. 325-377, Sept. 1951

"The **CITY**"–London's Storied Square Mile. By Allan C. Fisher, Jr. 735-777, June 1961

The **CITY** Around Red Square: Moscow. By John J. Putman. Photos by Gordon W. Gahan. 2-45, Jan. 1978

CITY Astride Two Continents: Istanbul. By William S. Ellis. Photos by Winfield Parks. 501-533, Oct. 1973

CITY PLANNING. *See* Brasília; Rotterdam; *and* listing under Urban Renewal

The **CITY** They Call Red China's Showcase. By Franc Shor. 193-223, Aug. 1960

CITY UNIVERSITY OF NEW YORK: Study Grants:
• Anthropology: Papua New Guinea. 128, July 1977

CIVIL AIR PATROL:
• Minutemen of the Civil Air Patrol. By Allan C. Fisher, Jr. Photos by John E. Fletcher. 637-665, May 1956

CIVIL WAR, U. S.:
• Appomattox: Where Grant and Lee Made Peace With Honor a Century Ago. By Ulysses S. Grant 3rd. Photos by Bruce Dale. 435-469, Apr. 1965
▲ *Battlefields of the Civil War,* double-sided Atlas series supplement. Apr. 1961
• The Civil War. By Ulysses S. Grant 3rd. 437-449, Apr. 1961
◆ *The Civil War.* Announced. 880-884, June 1969
• Echoes of Shiloh (Shiloh National Military Park, Tennessee). By Shelby Foote. 106-111, July 1979
• Gettysburg and Vicksburg: the Battle Towns Today. By Robert Paul Jordan. Map notes by Carolyn Bennett Patterson. 4-57, July 1963
• How We Found the *Monitor.* By John G. Newton. 48-61, Jan. 1975
• Just a Hundred Years Ago. By Carl Sandburg. 1-3, July 1963
• Lincoln, Man of Steel and Velvet. By Carl Sandburg. 239-241, Feb. 1960

• Our Land Through Lincoln's Eyes. By Carolyn Bennett Patterson. Photos by W. D. Vaughn. 243-277, Feb. 1960
• The Virginians. By Mike W. Edwards. Photos by David Alan Harvey. 588-617, Nov. 1974
• Witness to a War: British Correspondent Frank Vizetelly. By Robert T. Cochran, Jr. 453-491, Apr. 1961
• *See also* American Processional: History on Canvas; Atlanta; Harpers Ferry; Mobile; South Carolina Rediscovered

CIVILIZATIONS, Early. *See* Early Civilizations

The **CIVILIZING** Seine. By Charles McCarry. Photos by David L. Arnold. 478-511, Apr. 1982

CLARK, DEENA: Author:
• The Flowers That Say "Aloha." Photos by Robert B. Goodman. 121-131, Jan. 1967
• Home Life in Paris Today. 43-72, July 1950
• Iceland Tapestry. 599-630, Nov. 1951
• La Jolla, a Gem of the California Coast. Photos by J. Baylor Roberts. 755-782, Dec. 1952

CLARK, EUGENIE: Author:
• Flashlight Fish of the Red Sea. Photos by David Doubilet. 719-728, Nov. 1978
• Hidden Life of an Undersea Desert. Photos by David Doubilet. 129-144, July 1983
• Into the Lairs of "Sleeping" Sharks. Photos by David Doubilet. 570-584, Apr. 1975
• The Red Sea's Gardens of Eels. Photos by James L. Stanfield and David Doubilet. 724-735, Nov. 1972
• The Red Sea's Sharkproof Fish. Photos by David Doubilet. 718-727, Nov. 1974
• Sharks: Magnificent and Misunderstood. Photos by David Doubilet. 138-187, Aug. 1981
• The Strangest Sea. Photos by David Doubilet. 338-343, Sept. 1975

CLARK, HARLAN B.: Author:
• Yemen–Southern Arabia's Mountain Wonderland. 631-672, Nov. 1947

CLARK, LEWIS F.: Author:
• Amid the Mighty Walls of Zion (Zion National Park). 37-70, Jan. 1954

CLARK, MILTON J.:
Author-Photographer:
• How the Kazakhs Fled to Freedom. 621-644, Nov. 1954

CLARK, ROBERT: Photographer:
• Rafting Down the Yukon. By Keith Tryck. 830-861, Dec. 1975

CLARK, RONALD W.: Author:
• Liechtenstein Thrives on Stamps. 105-112, July 1948

CLARK, SYDNEY: Author:
• Luxembourg, Survivor of Invasions. Photos by Maynard Owen Williams. 791-810, June 1948
• Mid-century Holland Builds Her Future. 747-778, Dec. 1950
• Norway Cracks Her Mountain Shell. Photos by Gilbert Grosvenor and Ole Friele Backer. 171-211, Aug. 1948

CLARK, TIM W.: Author:
• The Hard Life of the Prairie Dog. Photos by Patricia Caulfield. 270-281, Aug. 1979
Author-Photographer:
• Last of the Black-footed Ferrets? Photos by Franz J. Camenzind and the author. 828-838, June 1983

CLARK, WILLIAM:
• Following the Trail of Lewis and Clark. By Ralph Gray. 707-750, June 1953

CLARKE, ARTHUR C.: Author:
• Sri Lanka's Wildlife Heritage: A Personal Perspective. 254-255, Aug. 1983

CLARKE SCHOOL FOR THE DEAF, Northampton, Massachusetts:
• Deaf Children Learn to Talk at Clarke School. By Lilian Grosvenor. Photos by Willard R. Culver. 379-397, Mar. 1955

CLASSICAL LANDS:
▲ *Classical Lands of the Mediterranean,* supplement. Dec. 1949
• *See also* Greece; Roman Empire

CLAY TABLETS. *See* Cuneiform

CLEARWATER (River), Idaho:
• Idaho Loggers Battle a River. 117-130, July 1951

CLEMENS, SAMUEL LANGHORNE. *See* Twain, Mark

CLEVELAND, GROVER:
• Inside the White House. By Lonnelle Aikman. Photos by B. Anthony Stewart and Thomas Nebbia. 3-34, Jan. 1961
• The Living White House. By Lonnelle Aikman. 593-643, Nov. 1966
• Profiles of the Presidents: III. The American Giant Comes of Age. By Frank Freidel. 660-711, May 1965

CLIFF DWELLERS:
• The Anasazi–Riddles in the Ruins. By Thomas Y. Canby. Photos by Dewitt Jones and David Brill. Paintings by Roy Andersen. 554-592, Nov. 1982
• Ancient Cliff Dwellers of Mesa Verde. By Don Watson. Photos by Willard R. Culver. 349-376, Sept. 1948
• Cities of Stone in Utah's Canyonland. By W. Robert Moore. 653-677, May 1962
• Cliff Dwellers of the Bering Sea. By Juan Muñoz. Contents: Ukivok (village), King Island, Alaska. 129-146, Jan. 1954
• Foxes Foretell the Future in Mali's Dogon Country. By Pamela Johnson Meyer. 431-448, Mar. 1969
• Navajo Ranger Interprets–Our People, Our Past. By Albert Laughter. 81-85, July 1979
• Searching for Cliff Dwellers' Secrets (Wetherill Mesa). By Carroll A. Burroughs. NGS research grant. 619-625, Nov. 1959
• Solving the Riddles of Wetherill Mesa. By Douglas Osborne. Paintings by Peter V. Bianchi. NGS research grant. 155-195, Feb. 1964
▲ *The Southwest,* The Making of America series. Included: Arizona, New Mexico, and parts of California, Colorado, Texas, Utah; and in Mexico: Baja California Norte, Chihuahua, Sonora. On reverse: 12,000 Years of History; Spanish Conquest; Anglo-American Entry and Occupancy. Nov. 1982
• 20th-century Indians Preserve Customs of the Cliff Dwellers. Photos by William Belknap, Jr. NGS research grant. 196-211, Feb. 1964
• Your Society to Seek New Light on the Cliff Dwellers. NGS research grant. 154-156, Jan. 1959

CLIFF PAINTINGS. *See* Rock Art

CLIFFORD E. LEE FOUNDATION: Study Grant:
• Humpback Whales. 466, Apr. 1982

CLIMATE:
• Acid Rain–How Great a Menace? By Anne LaBastille. Photos by Ted Spiegel. 652-681, Nov. 1981
• Alaska's Mighty Rivers of Ice. By Maynard M. Miller. Photos by Christopher G. Knight. 194-217, Feb. 1967
• Volcanic Cloud May Alter Earth's Climate. By Robert I. Tilling. 672-675, Nov. 1982
• What's Happening to Our Climate? By Samuel W. Matthews. 576-615, Nov. 1976
• The Year the Weather Went Wild. By Thomas Y. Canby. 799-829, Dec. 1977
• *See also* Weather

The **CLIMB** Up Cone Crater. By Alice J. Hall. Photos by Edgar D. Mitchell and Alan B. Shepard, Jr. 136-148, July 1971

CLIMBING Half Dome the Hard Way. By Galen Rowell. 782-791, June 1974

CLIMBING Our Northwest Glaciers. Photos by Bob and Ira Spring. 103-114, July 1953

CLINCH, NICHOLAS B.:
• First La Gorce Medal Honors Antarctic Expedition. 864-867, June 1967
Author:
• First Conquest of Antarctica's Highest Peaks. 836-863, June 1967

A **CLINICAL** Look at Burma's Long-necked Women. By John M. Keshishian. 798-801, June 1979

A **CLOCK** for the Ages: Potassium-Argon. By Garniss H. Curtis. 590-592, Oct. 1961

CLOCKS AND CLOCKMAKING:
• Split-second Time Runs Today's World. By F. Barrows Colton and Catherine Bell Palmer. 399-428, Sept. 1947
• The Tower of the Winds. By Derek J. de Solla Price. Paintings by Robert C. Magis. NGS research grant. 587-596, Apr. 1967

CLOSE-UP MAP SERIES:
● Close-up: U.S.A.–A Fresh Look at Our Land and Its Heritage. By Gilbert M. Grosvenor. 287-289, Mar. 1973
▲ *Close-up: U.S.A., Alaska,* supplement. Text on reverse. June 1975
▲ *Close-up: U.S.A., California and Nevada,* supplement. Text on reverse. June 1974
▲ *Close-up: U.S.A., Florida, with U.S. Virgin Islands and Puerto Rico,* supplement. Text on reverse. Nov. 1973
▲ *Close-up: U.S.A., Hawaii,* supplement. Text on reverse. Apr. 1976
▲ *Close-up: U.S.A., Illinois, Indiana, Ohio, and Kentucky,* supplement. Text on reverse. Feb. 1977
▲ *Close-up: U.S.A., Maine, with the Maritime Provinces of Canada,* supplement. Text on reverse. Mar. 1975
▲ *Close-up: U.S.A., The Mid-Atlantic States,* supplement. Text on reverse. Included: Delaware, Maryland, Virginia, West Virginia. Oct. 1976
▲ *Close-up: U.S.A., The North Central States,* supplement. Text on reverse. Included: Iowa, Kansas, Minnesota, Missouri, Nebraska, North Dakota, South Dakota. Mar. 1974
▲ *Close-up: U.S.A., The Northeast,* supplement. Text on reverse. Included: New Jersey, New York, Pennsylvania. Jan. 1978
▲ *Close-up: U.S.A., The Northwest,* supplement. Text on reverse. Included: Idaho, Montana, Oregon, Washington, Wyoming. Mar. 1973
▲ *Close-up: U.S.A., The South Central States,* supplement. Text on reverse. Included: Arkansas, Louisiana, Oklahoma, Texas. Oct. 1974
▲ *Close-up: U.S.A., The Southeast,* supplement. Text on reverse. Included: Alabama, Georgia, Mississippi, North Carolina, South Carolina, Tennessee. Oct. 1975
▲ *Close-up: U.S.A., The Southwest,* supplement. Text on reverse. Included: Arizona, Colorado, New Mexico, Utah. Oct. 1977
▲ *Close-up: U.S.A., Western New England,* supplement. Text on reverse. Included: Connecticut, Massachusetts, New Hampshire, Rhode Island, Vermont. July 1975
▲ *Close-up: U.S.A., Wisconsin, Michigan, and the Great Lakes,* supplement. Text on reverse. Aug. 1973

CLOSE-UP OF CANADA MAP SERIES:
▲ *British Columbia, Alberta, Yukon Territory.* Close-up series. Text on reverse. Apr. 1978
▲ *Maine, with the Maritime Provinces of Canada.* Close-up series. Text on reverse. Included: New Brunswick, Nova Scotia, Prince Edward Island. Mar. 1975
▲ *Ontario.* Close-up series. Text on reverse. Dec. 1978
▲ *Quebec, Newfoundland.* Close-up series. Text on reverse, inset of Southern Quebec. May 1980
▲ *Saskatchewan, Manitoba, Northwest Territories.* Close-up series. Text on reverse. May 1979

CLOUD FORMATIONS:
● Historic Color Portrait of Earth From Space. By Kenneth F. Weaver. Photos by DODGE Satellite. 726-731, Nov. 1967

CLOUD Gardens in the Tetons. By Frank and John Craighead. 811-830, June 1948

CLOVE-SCENTED Zanzibar. By W. Robert Moore. 261-278, Feb. 1952

CLOWN of the Desert–The Roadrunner. By Martha A. Whitson. Photos by Bruce Dale. 694-702, May 1983

CLYDE, ROBERT, Family:
● The Family: A Mormon Shrine. 459-463, Apr. 1975

COACHELLA VALLEY, California:
● The Lure of the Changing Desert. 817-824, June 1954

COAL:
▲ *America's Federal Lands; The United States,* double-sided supplement. Included: An inset map of natural resources, public and private, among them, coal regions. Sept. 1982
● An Atlas of Energy Resources. Included: Map locating coal resources of North America. 58-69, *Special Report on Energy.* (Feb. 1981)
● Coal Makes the Saar a Prize. By Franc Shor. 561-576, Apr. 1954
● Coal vs. Parklands. By François Leydet. Photos by Dewitt Jones. 776-803, Dec. 1980
● Illinois–Healthy Heart of the Nation. By Leo A. Borah. Photos by B. Anthony Stewart and Willard R. Culver. 781-820, Dec. 1953
● In Manchuria Now. By W. Robert Moore. 389-414, Mar. 1947
● Mountain Voices, Mountain Days (West Virginia). By Bryan Hodgson. Photos by Linda Bartlett. 118-146, July 1972
● Pennsylvania: Faire Land of William Penn. By Gordon Young. Photos by Cary Wolinsky. 731-767, June 1978
● Pittsburgh: Workshop of the Titans. By Albert W. Atwood. 117-144, July 1949
● Powder River Basin: New Energy Frontier. By Bill Richards. Photos by Louie Psihoyos. 96-113, *Special Report on Energy* (Feb. 1981)
● The Search for Tomorrow's Power. By Kenneth F. Weaver. Photos by Emory Kristof. 650-681, Nov. 1972
● Spitsbergen Mines Coal Again. 113-120, July 1948
● Synfuels: Fill 'er Up! With What? By Thomas Y. Canby. Photos by Jonathan Blair. 74-95, *Special Report on Energy* (Feb. 1981)
● This Land of Ours–How Are We Using It? By Peter T. White. Photos by Emory Kristof. 20-67, July 1976
● Turnaround Time in West Virginia. By Elizabeth A. Moize. Photos by Jodi Cobb. 755-785, June 1976

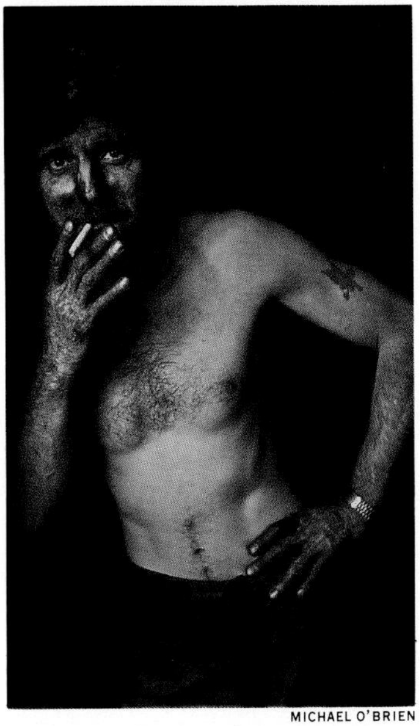
MICHAEL O'BRIEN

King Coal: miner after morning shift

MICHAEL HAYMAN

Coast Guard: rescuing a boater, *above;* monitoring an oil-well blaze, *below*

JOHN MESSINA, BLACK STAR

• The Untamed Yellowstone. By Bill Richards. Photos by Dean Krakel II. 257-278, Aug. 1981
• Will Coal Be Tomorrow's "Black Gold"? By Gordon Young. Photos by James P. Blair. 234-259, Aug. 1975
• Wrestlin' for a Livin' With King Coal. By Michael E. Long. Photos by Michael O'Brien. 793-819, June 1983

COAST, U. S. *See* Atlantic Coast; Gulf Coast; Pacific Coast

COAST AND GEODETIC SURVEY. *See* U. S. Coast and Geodetic Survey

The **COAST GUARD:** Small Service With a Big Mission. By William S. Ellis. 113-139, July 1974
• *See also* U. S. Coast Guard

COATS OF ARMS:
• Flags of the Americas. By Elizabeth W. King. Included: Coats of arms of: Argentina; Bolivia; Brazil; Chile; Colombia; Costa Rica; Cuba; Dominican Republic; Ecuador; El Salvador; Guatemala; Haiti; Honduras; Mexico; Nicaragua; Panama; Paraguay; Peru; Uruguay; Venezuela. 633-657, May 1949
• Flags of the United Nations. By Elizabeth W. King. Included: Coats of arms of: Bolivia; Chile; Colombia; Costa Rica; Denmark; Dominican Republic; Ecuador; El Salvador; Greece; Guatemala; Haiti; Honduras; Iceland; Mexico; Nicaragua; Paraguay; Peru; Sweden; United Kingdom; Uruguay; Venezuela. 213-238, Feb. 1951

COBB, CHARLES E., Jr.: Author:
• After Rhodesia, a Nation Named Zimbabwe. Photos by James L. Stanfield and LeRoy Woodson, Jr. 616-651, Nov. 1981

COBB, JODI:
• Editorial. By Wilbur E. Garrett. 553, Nov. 1982
Photographer:
• California's Parched Oasis, the Owens Valley. By Judith and Neil Morgan. Photos by Jodi Cobb and Galen Rowell. 98-127, Jan. 1976
• Cumberland, My Island for a While. By John Pennington. 649-661, Nov. 1977
• Helsinki: City With Its Heart in the Country. By Priit J. Vesilind. 237-255, Aug. 1981
• Land of Long Sunsets: Nebraska's Sand Hills. By John Madson. 493-517, Oct. 1978
• Los Angeles: City in Search of Itself. By William S. Ellis. 26-59, Jan. 1979
• Our Wild and Scenic Rivers: The Suwannee. By Jack and Anne Rudloe. 20-29, July 1977
• There's More to Nashville than Music. By Michael Kernan. 692-711, May 1978
• This Year in Jerusalem. By Joseph Judge. 479-515, Apr. 1983
• Turnaround Time in West Virginia. By Elizabeth A. Moize. 755-785, June 1976

COBRAS:
• The Cobra, India's "Good Snake." By Harry Miller. Photos by author and Naresh and Rajesh Bedi. 393-409, Sept. 1970

COCHRAN, DORIS M.: Author:
• Nature's Tank, the Turtle. Paintings by Walter A. Weber. 665-684, May 1952
• Our Snake Friends and Foes. Paintings by Walter A. Weber. 334-364, Sept. 1954

COCHRAN, ROBERT T., Jr.: Author:
• History and Beauty Blend in a Concord Iris Garden. Photos by M. Woodbridge Williams. 705-719, May 1959
• Witness to a War: British Correspondent Frank Vizetelly. 453-491, Apr. 1961

COCKROACHES:
• The Indomitable Cockroach. By Allen A. Boraiko. Photos by Bates Littlehales. 130-142, Jan. 1981

COCKS-OF-THE-ROCK:
• Cock-of-the-Rock: Jungle Dandy. By Pepper W. Trail. NGS research grant. 831-839, Dec. 1983
• Strange Courtship of the Cock-of-the-Rock. By E. Thomas Gilliard. NGS research grant. 134-140, Jan. 1962

COCLÉ INDIAN CULTURE:
• Exploring the Past in Panama. By Matthew W. Stirling. Photos by Richard H. Stewart. NGS research grant. 373-399, Mar. 1949

COCOS (Keeling) **ISLANDS,** Indian Ocean:
• *Yankee* Roams the Orient. By Irving and Electa Johnson. 327-370, Mar. 1951

COD, Cape, Massachusetts. *See* Cape Cod

COD FISHING:
• Dory on the Banks: A Day in the Life of a Portuguese Fisherman. By James H. Pickerell. 573-583, Apr. 1968
• Fishing in the Lofotens. Photos by Lennart Nilsson. 377-388, Mar. 1947
• I Sailed with Portugal's Captains Courageous. By Alan Villiers. 565-596, May 1952
▥ The Lonely Dorymen. 579A-579B, Apr. 1968
• Newfoundland, Canada's New Province. By Andrew H. Brown. Photos by Robert F. Sisson. 777-812, June 1949

CODRAI, RONALD:
Author-Photographer:
• Desert Sheikdoms of Arabia's Pirate Coast. 65-104, July 1956

CODY, WILLIAM F.:
• Buffalo Bill and the Enduring West. By Alice J. Hall. Photos by James L. Amos. 76-103, July 1981
• Hays, Kansas, at the Nation's Heart. By Margaret M. Detwiler. Photos by John E. Fletcher. 461-490, Apr. 1952

CODY, Wyoming:
• Buffalo Bill and the Enduring West. By Alice J. Hall. Photos by James L. Amos. 76-103, July 1981

COE, WILLIAM R.: Author:
• The Maya: Resurrecting the Grandeur of Tikal. 792-798, Dec. 1975

COEN, MARCEL: Photographer:
• Sheep Trek in the French Alps. By Maurice Moyal. 545-564, Apr. 1952

COFFEE:
• Behind the Veil of Troubled Yemen. By Thomas J. Abercrombie. Included: The origin of coffee drinking. 403-445, Mar. 1964
• The Bonanza Bean–Coffee. By Ethel A. Starbird. Photos by Sam Abell. 388-405, Mar. 1981
• *See also* Brazil (Brazil, Ôba!); Colombia; Costa Rica; Guatemala

COGNAT, ANDRÉ:
• What Future for the Wayana Indians? By Carole Devillers. 66-83, Jan. 1983

COHN, RONALD H.: Photographer:
• Conversations With a Gorilla. By Francine Patterson. 438-465, Oct. 1978

COLIN, THOMAS J.: Author:
• The U. S. Virgin Islands. Photos by William Albert Allard and Cary Wolinsky. 225-243, Feb. 1981

COLLECTIVE FARMS:
• Down on the Farm, Soviet Style–a 4-H Adventure. By John Garaventa. Photos by James Tobin and Carol Schmidt. 768-797, June 1979
• *See also* Kibbutzim

COLLEGES. *See* Universities

COLLINS, HENRY B.: Author:
• Vanished Mystery Men of Hudson Bay. 669-687, Nov. 1956

COLLINS, LORENCE G.:
Author-Photographer:
• Finding Rare Beauty in Common Rocks. 121-129, Jan. 1966

COLLINS, MICHAEL:
• First Explorers on the Moon: The Incredible Story of Apollo 11. 735-797, Dec. 1969
I. Man Walks on Another World. By Neil A. Armstrong, Edwin E. Aldrin, Jr., and Michael Collins. 738-749; II. Sounds of the Space Age, From Sputnik to Lunar Landing. A record narrated by Frank Borman. 750-751; III. The Flight of Apollo 11: "One giant leap for mankind." By Kenneth F. Weaver. 752-787
• First Moon Explorers (Apollo 11) Receive the Society's Hubbard Medal. 859-861, June 1970
Author:
• Man Walks on Another World. By Neil A. Armstrong, Edwin E. Aldrin, Jr., and Michael Collins. 738-749, Dec. 1969
• Of Air and Space (National Air and Space Museum). 819-837, June 1978
Picture portfolio by Nathan Benn, Robert S. Oakes, and Joseph D. Lavenburg, with text by Michael E. Long. 825-837

COLLISON, JAMES: Photographer:
• Happy Birthday, Otto Lilienthal! By Russell Hawkes. 286-292, Feb. 1972

COLOMBIA:
• Capturing Strange Creatures in Colombia. By Marte Latham. Photos by Tor Eigeland. 682-693, May 1966
• Colombia, from Amazon to Spanish Main. By Loren McIntyre. 235-273, Aug. 1970
• Cruising Colombia's "Ol' Man River." By Amos Burg. 615-660, May 1947
• Jungle Jaunt on Amazon Headwaters. By Bernice M. Goetz. 371-388, Sept. 1952
• Keeping House for a Biologist in Colombia. By Nancy Bell Fairchild Bates. Photos by Marston Bates. 251-274, Aug. 1948
• *See also* Andean Condors; Gems; Gold; Orchids

COLOMBO, Sri Lanka:
• Ceylon, the Resplendent Land. By Donna K. and Gilbert M. Grosvenor. 447-497, Apr. 1966
• Sri Lanka: Time of Testing For an Ancient Land. By Robert Paul Jordan. Photos by Raghubir Singh. 123-150, Jan. 1979

COLONIAL AMERICA:
◆ *America's Beginnings.* Announced. 870-874, June 1974
▲ *Atlantic Gateways,* The Making of America series. Included: Delaware, Maryland, New Jersey, New York, Pennsylvania, northern Virginia, West Virginia, and in Canada, southern Ontario and southern Quebec. On reverse: Indians and Trade, Nation in the Making, Peopling of the Gateways, Race for the Hinterlands, Growth of Industry, Spreading Urban Corridors. Mar. 1983
• Benjamin Franklin, Philosopher of Dissent. By Alice J. Hall. Photos by Linda Bartlett. 93-123, July 1975
▲ *Colonization and Trade in the New World,* supplement. Painting and text on reverse. Dec. 1977
▲ *Deep South,* The Making of America series. Included: Alabama, Florida, Georgia, Louisiana, Mississippi, South Carolina, and parts of Arkansas, North Carolina, and Tennessee. On reverse: Indian Legacy, Imperial Footholds, Three Empires and Three Races, Cotton Kingdom, Postbellum, New Deep South, Subtropical Playground. Aug. 1983
• First Look at a Lost Virginia Settlement (Martin's Hundred). By Ivor Noël Hume. Photos by Ira Block. Paintings by Richard Schlecht. 735-767, June 1979
• Founders of New England. By Sir Evelyn Wrench. Photos by B. Anthony Stewart. 803-838, June 1953
• Founders of Virginia. By Sir Evelyn Wrench. Photos by B. Anthony Stewart. 433-462, Apr. 1948
• From Sword to Scythe in Champlain Country. By Ethel A. Starbird. Photos by B. Anthony Stewart and Emory Kristof. 153-201, Aug. 1967
• Herbs for All Seasons. By Lonnelle Aikman. Photos by Sam Abell. Picture portfolio text by Larry Kohl. 386-409, Mar. 1983
• Massachusetts Builds for Tomorrow. By Robert de Roos. Photos by B. Anthony Stewart. Included: Boston, Concord, Duxbury, Plymouth, Sudbury. 790-843, Dec. 1966
• New Clues to an Old Mystery (Virginia's Wolstenholme Towne). By Ivor Noël Hume. Photos by Ira Block. Paintings by Richard Schlecht. 53-77, Jan. 1982
• Reach for the New World. By Mendel Peterson. Photos by David L. Arnold. Paintings by Richard Schlecht. 724-767, Dec. 1977
• Roving Maryland's Cavalier Country. By William A. Kinney. 431-470, Apr. 1954
• The St. Lawrence, River Key to Canada. By Howard La Fay. Photos by John Launois. 622-667, May 1967
▲ *The Southwest,* The Making of America series. Included: Arizona, New Mexico, and parts of California, Colorado, Texas, Utah; and in Mexico: Baja California Norte, Chihuahua, Sonora. On reverse: 12,000 Years of History; Spanish Conquest; Anglo-American Entry and Occupancy. Nov. 1982
• They'd Rather Be in Philadelphia. By Ethel A. Starbird. Photos by Ted Spiegel. 314-343, Mar. 1983
• Thomas Jefferson: Architect of Freedom. By Mike W. Edwards. Photos by Linda Bartlett. 231-259, Feb. 1976
◆ *Visiting Our Past: America's Historylands.* 1977
• *See also* Boston Post Roads; Concord, Massachusetts; Deerfield, Massachusetts; Jamestown, Virginia; Maryland (Roving); Philadelphia, Pennsylvania; Roanoke Island, for Lost Colony; St. Augustine, Florida; Williamsburg, Virginia

COLONIZATION:
• The British Way. By Sir Evelyn Wrench. 421-541, Apr. 1949
• Capt. John Smith's Map of Virginia. 760-761; Captain Smith's New England . . . and the Pilgrims' Cape Cod. 764-765, June 1953
▲ *Colonization and Trade in the New World,* supplement. Painting and text on reverse. Dec. 1977
• Editorial. By Gilbert M. Grosvenor. 723, Dec. 1977
• Founders of New England. By Sir Evelyn Wrench. Photos by B. Anthony Stewart. 803-838, June 1953
• Founders of Virginia. By Sir Evelyn Wrench. Photos by B. Anthony Stewart. 433-462, Apr. 1948
• Reach for the New World. By Mendel Peterson. Photos by David L. Arnold. Paintings by Richard Schlecht. 724-767, Dec. 1977
• The Vikings. By Howard La Fay. Photos by Ted Spiegel. 492-541, Apr. 1970
• *See also* Colonial America; Jamestown, Virginia; Mozambique, for Limpopo Colonato; Roanoke Island, for Lost Colony; St. Augustine, Florida; Vinland

C D

COLORADO:
● Along the Great Divide. By Mike Edwards. Photos by Nicholas DeVore III. 483-515, Oct. 1979
● Bison Kill By Ice Age Hunters. By Dennis Stanford. 114-121, Jan. 1979
▲ *Close-up: U.S.A., The Southwest,* supplement. Text on reverse. Oct. 1977
● Colorado, the Rockies' Pot of Gold. By Edward J. Linehan. Photos by James L. Amos. 157-201, Aug. 1969
● Colorado by Car and Campfire. By Kathleen Revis. 207-248, Aug. 1954
● Colorado's Friendly Topland (Rocky Mountains). By Robert M. Ormes. 187-214, Aug. 1951
● A Map Maker Looks at the United States. By Newman Bumstead. Included: Antero (peak); Arkansas River; Canon City; Colorado Springs; Denver; Grand Junction; Gunnison; Monarch Pass; Montrose; Ouray (peak); Pikes Peak; Pueblo; Royal Gorge; Sawatch Mountains. 705-748, June 1951
● Oil, the Dwindling Treasure. By Noel Grove. Photos by Emory Kristof. 792-825, June 1974
● Shooting Rapids in Dinosaur Country. By Jack Breed. Photos by author and Justin Locke. 363-390, Mar. 1954
● Skiing in the United States. By Kathleen Revis. 216-254, Feb. 1959
● Stalking the West's Wild Foods. By Euell Gibbons. Photos by David Hiser. 186-199, Aug. 1973
● A Walk Across America: Part II. By Peter and Barbara Jenkins. 194-229, Aug. 1979
● *See also* Aspen; Carson, Camp; Colorado Plateau; Denver; Four Corners Country; Mesa Verde National Park; U. S. Air Force Academy; Wetherill Mesa

COLORADO DESERT, California:
● Poorwill Sleeps Away the Winter. By Edmund C. Jaeger. 273-280, Feb. 1953

COLORADO PLATEAU, U. S.:
● Hunting Uranium Around the World. By Robert D. Nininger. Photos by Volkmar Wentzel. Note: The Colorado Plateau region of Colorado, Utah, Arizona, and New Mexico contains one of the richest sources of uranium in the United States. 533-558, Oct. 1954

COLORADO RIVER AND BASIN, U. S.:
● The Bittersweet Waters of the Lower Colorado. By Rowe Findley. Photos by Charles O'Rear. 540-569, Oct. 1973
● Canyonlands, Realm of Rock and the Far Horizon. By Rowe Findley. Photos by Walter Meayers Edwards. 71-91, July 1971
● Colorado's Friendly Topland (Rocky Mountains). By Robert M. Ormes. 187-214, Aug. 1951
● Desert River Through Navajo Land. By Alfred M. Bailey. Photos by author and Fred G. Brandenburg. 149-172, Aug. 1947
● First Motor Sortie into Escalante Land. By Jack Breed. 369-404, Sept. 1949
● Grand Canyon: Are We Loving It to Death? By W. E. Garrett. 16-51, July 1978
● Grand Canyon: Nature's Story of Creation. By Louis Schellbach. Photos by Justin Locke. 589-629, May 1955
● Lake Powell: Waterway to Desert Wonders. By Walter Meayers Edwards. 44-75, July 1967
● Our Most Precious Resource: Water. By Thomas Y. Canby. Photos by Ted Spiegel. 144-179, Aug. 1980
● Retracing John Wesley Powell's Historic Voyage Down the Grand Canyon. By Joseph Judge. Photos by Walter Meayers Edwards. 668-713, May 1969
● Seeking the Secret of the Giants. By Frank M. Setzler. Photos by Richard H. Stewart. 390-404, Sept. 1952
Giant Effigies of the Southwest. By George C. Marshall. 389
● Shooting Rapids in Reverse! Jet Boats Climb the Colorado's Torrent Through the Grand Canyon. By William Belknap, Jr. 552-565, Apr. 1962
● Three Roads to Rainbow. By Ralph Gray. 547-561, Apr. 1957

COLOUREDS (People):
● Namibia: Nearly a Nation? By Bryan Hodgson. Photos by Jim Brandenburg. 755-797, June 1982

COLTON, F. BARROWS: Author:
● Eclipse Hunting in Brazil's Ranchland. Photos by Richard H. Stewart and Guy W. Starling. 285-324, Sept. 1947
● Lightning in Action. 809-828, June 1950
● Man's New Servant, the Friendly Atom. Photos by Volkmar Wentzel. 71-90, Jan. 1954
● Mapping the Unknown Universe. 401-420, Sept. 1950
● Miracle Men of the Telephone. 273-316, Mar. 1947
● Mountains Top Off New England. Photos by Robert F. Sisson. 563-602, May 1951
● Our Air Age Speeds Ahead. 249-272, Feb. 1948
● Our Home-town Planet, Earth. 117-139, Jan. 1952
● Split-second Time Runs Today's World. By F. Barrows Colton and Catherine Bell Palmer. 399-428, Sept. 1947
● Uncle Sam's House of 1,000 Wonders (National Bureau of Standards). By Lyman J. Briggs and F. Barrows Colton. 755-784, Dec. 1951
● Water for the World's Growing Needs. By Herbert B. Nichols and F. Barrows Colton. 269-286, Aug. 1952

COLUMBIA, South Carolina:
● South Carolina Rediscovered. By Herbert Ravenel Sass. Photos by Robert F. Sisson. 281-321, Mar. 1953

COLUMBIA (Space Shuttle):
● *Columbia*'s Astronauts' Own Story: Our Phenomenal First Flight. By John W. Young and Robert L. Crippen. Paintings by Ken Dallison. 478-503, Oct. 1981
● *Columbia*'s Landing Closes a Circle. By Tom Wolfe. 474-477, Oct. 1981
● Heat Paints *Columbia*'s Portrait. By Cliff Tarpy. 650-653, Nov. 1982
● Satellites That Serve Us. By Thomas Y. Canby. 281-335, Sept. 1983
Spacelab 1: *Columbia*. By Michael E. Long. 301-307
● When the Space Shuttle Finally Flies. By Rick Gore. Photos by Jon Schneeberger. Paintings by Ken Dallison. 317-347, Mar. 1981

COLUMBIA RIVER AND BASIN, U. S.-Canada:
● The Columbia River, Powerhouse of the Northwest. By David S. Boyer. 821-847, Dec. 1974
● Following the Trail of Lewis and Clark. By Ralph Gray. 707-750, June 1953
● From Sagebrush to Roses on the Columbia. By Leo A. Borah. 571-611, Nov. 1952
● A Map Maker Looks at the United States. By Newman Bumstead. 705-748, June 1951
● Oregon's Many Faces. By Stuart E. Jones. Photos by Bates Littlehales. 74-115, Jan. 1969

COLUMBIA RIVER INDIANS. *See* Warm Springs Indians, Confederated Tribes of

COLUMBIA UNIVERSITY: Expeditions and Research:
● Archaeological Expedition: Virú, Peru. 453, 454, 455, 457, 463, 466, Apr. 1947
● Mid-Atlantic Ridge. 275, 279, 285, 293, Sept. 1948; 611, 636, Nov. 1949; 147, July 1950; 14, 29, Jan. 1963

COLUMBUS, CHRISTOPHER:
● Christopher Columbus and the New World He Found. By John Scofield. Photos by Adam Woolfitt. 584-625, Nov. 1975

COLUMBUS, Indiana:
● A Most Uncommon Town: Columbus, Indiana. By David Jeffery. Photos by J. Bruce Baumann. 383-397, Sept. 1978

COMANCHE (Mountain), Bolivia:
● Puya, the Pineapple's Andean Ancestor. By Mulford B. Foster. 463-480, Oct. 1950

COMANCHE INDIANS:
● Big Bend: Jewel in the Texas Desert. By Nathaniel T. Kenney. Photos by James L. Stanfield. 104-133, Jan. 1968

COMBINES (Harvesting Machines). *See* Agriculture (The Revolution); Wheat (North With the Wheat Cutters)

COMEBACK in the Caribbean–The Dominican Republic. By James Cerruti. Photos by Martin Rogers. 538-565, Oct. 1977

COMETS:
• Giant Comet (Ikeya-Seki) Grazes the Sun. By Kenneth F. Weaver. Included: Halley's comet. 259-261, Feb. 1966
• How to Catch a Passing Comet (Kohoutek). By Kenneth F. Weaver. 148-150, Jan. 1974
• What You Didn't See in Kohoutek. By Kenneth F. Weaver. 214-223, Aug. 1974

COMEX: Expedition Grant:
• Underwater Salvage: *Witte Leeuw*. 566, Oct. 1978

COMING of Age the Apache Way. By Nita Quintero. Photos by Bill Hess. 262-271, Feb. 1980

The **COMING** of the Polynesians. By Kenneth P. Emory. 732-745, Dec. 1974

The **COMING** Revolution in Transportation. By Fredric C. Appel. Photos by Dean Conger. 301-341, Sept. 1969

COMMAGENE (Ancient Country):
• Throne Above the Euphrates. By Theresa Goell. 390-405, Mar. 1961

COMMON TERNS:
• Friend of the Wind: The Common Tern. By Ian Nisbet. Photos by Hope Alexander. 234-247, Aug. 1973

COMMONWEALTH BAY, Antarctica:
• Voyage to the Antarctic. By David Lewis. 544-562, Apr. 1983

COMMONWEALTH OF NATIONS. *See* former name, British Commonwealth of Nations

COMMUNAL LIVING:
• From Spear to Hoe on Groote Eylandt. By Howell Walker. 131-142, Jan. 1953
• Old Salem, Morning Star of Moravian Faith. By Rowe Findley. Photos by Robert W. Madden. 818-837, Dec. 1970
• Return to Changing China. By Audrey Topping. 801-833, Dec. 1971
• *See also* Amana Colonies; Hutterites; Kibbutzim; Old Believers; Padanaram; Saint Véran; Shakers; Tasaday Tribe

COMMUNICATION, Animal:
• Conversations With a Gorilla. By Francine Patterson. Photos by Ronald H. Cohn. NGS research grant. 438-465, Oct. 1978
• Humpback Whales. NGS research grant. 2-25, Jan. 1979
I. The Gentle Giants. By Sylvia A. Earle. Photos by Al Giddings. 2-17; II. Their Mysterious Songs. By Roger Payne. Photos by Al Giddings. 18-25; III. Symphony of the Deep: "Songs of the Humpback Whale" (Sound sheet). 24-24B
• New Light on the Singing Whales. Introduction by Roger Payne. Photos by Flip Nicklin. NGS research grant. 463-477, Apr. 1982
• Western Grebes: The Birds That Walk on Water. By Gary L. Nuechterlein. NGS research grant. 624-637, May 1982

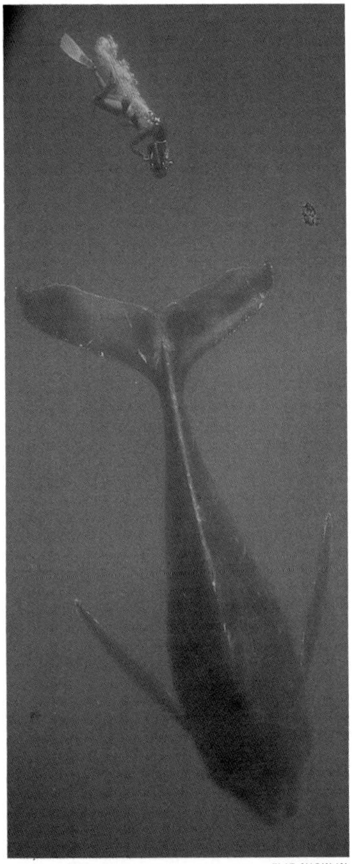

FLIP NICKLIN

Singing Whales: tracking a humpback

COMMUNICATIONS:
• DEW Line, Sentry of the Far North. By Howard La Fay. 128-146, July 1958
• Fiber Optics: Harnessing Light by a Thread. By Allen A. Boraiko. Photos by Fred Ward. 516-535, Oct. 1979
• The Flying Telegraph (Homing Pigeon). By Joseph F. Spears. Official U. S. Army Signal Corps photos. 531-554, Apr. 1947
• How Man-made Satellites Can Affect Our Lives. By Joseph Kaplan. 791-810, Dec. 1957
• Miracle Men of the Telephone. By F. Barrows Colton. 273-316, Mar. 1947
• New Miracles of the Telephone Age. By Robert Leslie Conly. 87-120, July 1954
• Satellites That Serve Us. By Thomas Y. Canby. 281-335, Sept. 1983
• Telephone a Star: the Story of Communications Satellites. By Rowe Findley. 638-651, May 1962

COMMUNITY DEVELOPMENT PROGRAMS. *See* Bastar, India; *and* Peace Corps; YWCA

COMO, Lake, Italy:
• Lombardy's Lakes, Blue Jewels in Italy's Crown. By Franc Shor. Photos by Joseph J. Scherschel. 58-99, July 1968

COMORO ISLANDS, Indian Ocean:
• Crosscurrents Sweep the Indian Ocean. By Bart McDowell. Photos by Steve Raymer. 422-457, Oct. 1981

COMPOST:
• The Wild World of Compost. By Cecil E. Johnson. Photos by Bianca Lavies. 273-284, Aug. 1980

COMPUTER APPLICATIONS:
• *Columbia*'s Astronauts' Own Story: Our Phenomenal First Flight. By John W. Young and Robert L. Crippen. Paintings by Ken Dallison. 478-503, Oct. 1981
• *Columbia*'s Landing Closes a Circle. By Tom Wolfe. 474-477, Oct. 1981
• The Coming Revolution in Transportation. By Fredric C. Appel. Photos by Dean Conger. 301-341, Sept. 1969
• Computer Helps Scholars Re-create an Egyptian Temple. By Ray Winfield Smith. Photos by Emory Kristof. 634-655, Nov. 1970
• Eyes of Science. By Rick Gore. Photos by James P. Blair. 360-389, Mar. 1978
• Heat Paints *Columbia*'s Portrait. By Cliff Tarpy. 650-653, Nov. 1982
• The Once and Future Universe. By Rick Gore. Photos by James A. Sugar. Paintings by Barron Storey. Picture text by David Jeffery. 704-749, June 1983
• Satellites That Serve Us. By Thomas Y. Canby. Included: A portfolio, Images of Earth. 281-335, Sept. 1983
Spacelab 1: *Columbia*. By Michael E. Long. 301-307

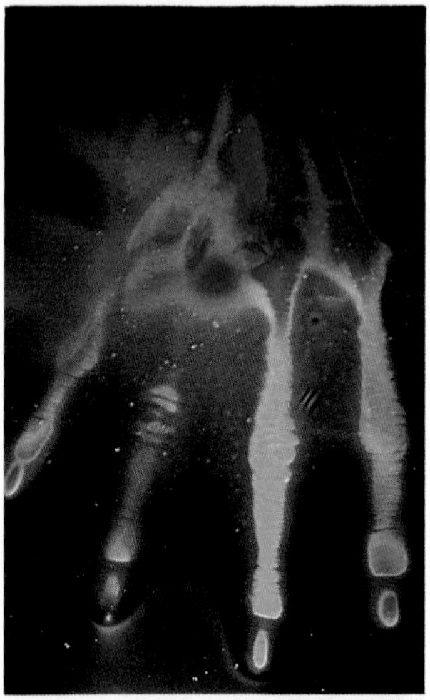

ROBERT W. MADDEN

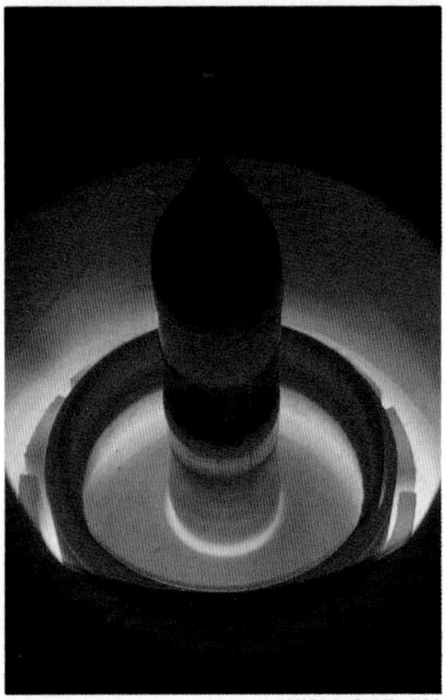

JAMES P. BLAIR, NGS

Crystals: liquid-crystal experiment registers temperature differences, *top*; growth of a silicon ingot, *above*

• We're Doing Something About the Weather! By Walter Orr Roberts. 518-555, Apr. 1972
• When the Space Shuttle Finally Flies. By Rick Gore. Photos by Jon Schneeberger. Paintings by Ken Dallison. 317-347, Mar. 1981
• *See also* Landsat; Space Flights and Research

COMPUTER TECHNOLOGY:
• Behold the Computer Revolution. By Peter T. White. Photos by Bruce Dale and Emory Kristof. 593-633, Nov. 1970
• California's Silicon Valley. By Moira Johnston. Photos by Charles O'Rear. 459-477, Oct. 1982
• The Chip: Electronic Mini-marvel. By Allen A. Boraiko. Photos by Charles O'Rear. 421-457, Oct. 1982
• Crystals, Magical Servants of the Space Age. By Kenneth F. Weaver. Photos by James P. Blair. 278-296, Aug. 1968
• Editorial. By Wilbur E. Garrett. 419, Oct. 1982

A **CONCISE** Guide to National Parks (United States). 111-123, July 1979

CONCORD, Massachusetts:
• History and Beauty Blend in a Concord Iris Garden. By Robert T. Cochran, Jr. Photos by M. Woodbridge Williams. 705-719, May 1959
• Literary Landmarks of Massachusetts. By William H. Nicholas. Photos by B. Anthony Stewart and John E. Fletcher. 279-310, Mar. 1950
• Thoreau, a Different Man. By William Howarth. Photos by Farrell Grehan. 349-387, Mar. 1981

CONCORD, New Hampshire:
• The Merrimack: River of Industry and Romance. By Albert W. Atwood. Photos by B. Anthony Stewart. 106-140, Jan. 1951

CONDON, GENEAL: Author:
• Blossoms That Defy the Seasons (Flower Preservation). Photos by David S. Boyer. 420-427, Sept. 1958

The **CONDOR,** Soaring Spirit of the Andes. By Jerry McGahan. Photos by Libby McGahan. 684-709, May 1971

CONES AND CONE DWELLERS:
• Cappadocia: Turkey's Country of Cones. Photos by Marc Riboud. 122-146, Jan. 1958
• Keeping House in a Cappadocian Cave. By Jonathan S. Blair. 127-146, July 1970

CONGER, CLEMENT E.:
Author-Photographer:
• Portugal Is Different. 583-622, Nov. 1948

CONGER, DEAN:
Author-Photographer:
• Five Times to Yakutsk. 256-269, Aug. 1977
• Siberia: Russia's Frozen Frontier. 297-345, Mar. 1967
Photographer:
• Abraham, the Friend of God. By Kenneth MacLeish. 739-789, Dec. 1966
• An American in Russia's Capital. By Thomas T. Hammond. 297-351, Mar. 1966
• The Britain That Shakespeare Knew. By Louis B. Wright. 613-665, May 1964
• Brunei, Borneo's Abode of Peace. By Joseph Judge. 207-225, Feb. 1974
• Cape Cod, Where Sea Holds Sway Over Man and Land. By Nathaniel T. Kenney. 149-187, Aug. 1962
• Chartres: Legacy From the Age of Faith. By Kenneth MacLeish. 857-882, Dec. 1969
• The Coming Revolution in Transportation. By Fredric C. Appel. 301-341, Sept. 1969
• Exploring Tomorrow With the Space Agency. By Allan C. Fisher, Jr. 48-89, July 1960
• From Sea to Shining Sea: A Cross Section of the United States Along Historic Route 40. By Ralph Gray. Photos by Dean Conger and author. 1-61, July 1961
• Help for Philippine Tribes in Trouble. By Kenneth MacLeish. 220-255, Aug. 1971
• High-stepping Idaho. By William S. Ellis. 290-317, Mar. 1973
• Hopes and Fears in Booming Thailand. By Peter T. White. 76-125, July 1967
• I Fly the X-15. By Joseph A. Walker. 428-450, Sept. 1962
• Indonesia Rescues Ancient Borobudur. By W. Brown Morton III. 126-142, Jan. 1983
• Java–Eden in Transition. By Kenneth MacLeish. 1-43, Jan. 1971
• Journey to Outer Mongolia. By William O. Douglas. 289-345, Mar. 1962
• Mr. Jefferson's Monticello. By Joseph Judge. Photos by Dean Conger and Richard S. Durrance. 426-444, Sept. 1966
• The Other Yosemite. By Nathaniel T. Kenney. 762-781, June 1974
• People of the Long Spring. By Yuri Rytkheu. 206-223, Feb. 1983
• The Pilot's Story: Astronaut Shepard's Firsthand Account of His Flight. 432-444, Sept. 1961
• River of Counts and Kings: The Loire. By Kenneth MacLeish. 822-869, June 1966
• Siberia's Empire Road, the River Ob. By Robert Paul Jordan. 145-181, Feb. 1976
• Singapore: Mini-size Superstate. By Bryan Hodgson. 540-561, Apr. 1981

CONGO, Democratic Republic of the (formerly Belgian Congo, now Zaire):
• Africa: The Winds of Freedom Stir a Continent. By Nathaniel T. Kenney. Photos by W. D. Vaughn. 303-359, Sept. 1960
• Freedom's Progress South of the Sahara. By Howard La Fay. Photos by Joseph J. Scherschel. 603-637, Nov. 1962
• My Life With Africa's Little People. By Anne Eisner Putnam. 278-302, Feb. 1960

• Roaming Africa's Unfenced Zoos. By W. Robert Moore. 353-380, Mar. 1950
• Safari from Congo to Cairo. By Elsie May Bell Grosvenor. Photos by Gilbert Grosvenor. 721-771, Dec. 1954
• White Magic in the Belgian Congo. By W. Robert Moore. 321-362, Mar. 1952
• *See also* National Parks (Africa); Ruwenzori; Virunga Mountains; Zaire

CONGO, People's Republic of the:
• Freedom's Progress South of the Sahara. By Howard La Fay. Photos by Joseph J. Scherschel. 603-637, Nov. 1962

CONGO RIVER, Africa:
• White Magic in the Belgian Congo. By W. Robert Moore. 321-362, Mar. 1952

CONGRESS, U. S. *See* U. S. Congress

CONKLIN, PAUL: Photographer:
• Ambassadors of Good Will: The Peace Corps. By Sargent Shriver and Peace Corps Volunteers. 297-345, Sept. 1964

CONLEY, ROBERT A. M.: Author:
• Locusts: "Teeth of the Wind." Photos by Gianni Tortoli. 202-227, Aug. 1969

CONLY, ROBERT LESLIE: Author:
• Luxembourg, the Quiet Fortress. Photos by Ted H. Funk. 69-97, July 1970
• Men Who Measure the Earth. Photos by John E. Fletcher. 335-362, Mar. 1956
• Modern Miracle, Made in Germany. Photos by Erich Lessing. 735-791, June 1959
• The Mohawks Scrape the Sky. Photos by B. Anthony Stewart. 133-142, July 1952
• New Miracles of the Telephone Age. 87-120, July 1954
• Northern Ireland: From Derry to Down. 232-267, Aug. 1964
• Porpoises: Our Friends in the Sea. Photos by Thomas Nebbia. 396-425, Sept. 1966
• St. Augustine, Nation's Oldest City, Turns 400. 196-229, Feb. 1966

CONNECTICUT:
• The Age of Sail Lives On at Mystic. By Alan Villiers. Photos by Weston Kemp. 220-239, Aug. 1968
• *Nomad* Sails Long Island Sound. By Thomas Horgan. 295-338, Sept. 1957
• The Old Boston Post Roads. By Donald Barr Chidsey. 189-205, Aug. 1962
• The Post Road Today. Photos by B. Anthony Stewart. 206-233, Aug. 1962
• Windjamming Around New England. By Tom Horgan. Photos by Robert F. Sisson. Included: Mystic; Stonington. 141-169, Aug. 1950
• *See also* Connecticut River and Valley; New London

CONNECTICUT RIVER AND VALLEY:
• Deerfield Keeps a Truce With Time. By Bart McDowell. Photos by Robert W. Madden. 780-809, June 1969
• Yesterday Lingers Along the Connecticut. By Charles McCarry. Photos by David L. Arnold. 334-369, Sept. 1972

CONNOLLY, JOSEPH P.: Author:
• Big Game Hunting in the Land of Long Ago. By Joseph P. Connolly and James D. Bump. 589-605, May 1947

CONQUEST of the Holy City. By Franc Shor. Photos by Thomas Nebbia. 839-855, Dec. 1963

CONRAD, ANNA:
• Avalanche! By David Cupp. 280-305, Sept. 1982
I. Winter's White Death. 280-281; II. "I'm OK, I'm Alive!" Photos by Lanny Johnson and Andre Benier. Note: Anna Conrad was rescued five days after the Alpine Meadows, California avalanche. 282-289; III. Battling the Juggernaut. 290-305

CONRAD, CHARLES, Jr.:
• Skylab, Outpost on the Frontier of Space. By Thomas Y. Canby. Photos by the nine mission astronauts. 441-469, Oct. 1974

CONSERVATION:
• African Wildlife: Man's Threatened Legacy. By Allan C. Fisher, Jr. Photos by Thomas Nebbia. Paintings by Ned Seidler. 147-187, Feb. 1972
• Aldo Leopold: "A Durable Scale of Values." By Boyd Gibbons. Photos by Jim Brandenburg. 682-708, Nov. 1981
▲ *America's Federal Lands; The United States,* double-sided supplement. Sept. 1982
• Australia's Great Barrier Reef. 630-663, May 1981
I. A Marine Park Is Born. By Soames Summerhays. Photos by Ron and Valerie Taylor. 630-635; II. Paradise Beneath the Sea. By Ron and Valerie Taylor. 636-663
• Can We Save Our Salt Marshes? By Stephen W. Hitchcock. Photos by William R. Curtsinger. 729-765, June 1972
• Conservation: Can We Live Better on Less? By Rick Gore. 34-57, *Special Report on Energy* (Feb. 1981)
• Escalante Canyon–Wilderness at the Crossroads. By Jon Schneeberger. 270-285, Aug. 1972
• India Struggles to Save Her Wildlife. By John J. Putman. 299-343, Sept. 1976
• Jackson Hole: Good-bye to the Old Days? By François Leydet. Photos by Jonathan Wright. 768-789, Dec. 1976
• John Muir's Wild America. By Harvey Arden. Photos by Dewitt Jones. 433-461, Apr. 1973
• Man's Wildlife Heritage Faces Extinction. By H.R.H. The Prince Philip, Duke of Edinburgh. 700-703, Nov. 1962
• Minnesota, Where Water is the Magic Word. By David S. Boyer. Photos by author and David Brill. 200-229, Feb. 1976
• On the Trail of Wisconsin's Ice Age. By Anne LaBastille. Photos by Cary Wolinsky. Included: Future 600- to 800-mile trail along glacial features. 182-205, Aug. 1977
• Our Most Precious Resource: Water. By Thomas Y. Canby. Photos by Ted Spiegel. 144-179, Aug. 1980
• Parks, Plans, and People: How South America Guards Her Green Legacy. By Mary and Laurance Rockefeller. Photos by George F. Mobley. 74-119, Jan. 1967
• Portrait of a Fierce and Fragile Land. By Paul A. Zahl. 303-314, Mar. 1972
■ Rain Forest. 824, Dec. 1982
• Roosevelt Country: T. R.'s Wilderness Legacy. By John L. Eliot. Photos by Farrell Grehan. 340-363, Sept. 1982
• San Francisco Bay: The Beauty and the Battles. By Cliff Tarpy. Photos by James A. Sugar. 814-845, June 1981
• Saving Man's Wildlife Heritage (National Audubon Society). By John H. Baker. Photos by Robert F. Sisson. 581-620, Nov. 1954
• Seeking the Best of Two Worlds (Apache). By Bill Hess. Included: Forestry, solar collectors, waste-burning power plant, watershed maintenance, wildlife management; and patrolling of outdoor recreation areas. 272-290, Feb. 1980
• Shrimp Nursery: Science Explores New Ways to Farm the Sea. By Clarence P. Idyll. Photos by Robert F. Sisson. NGS research grant. 636-659, May 1965
• The Tallgrass Prairie: Can It Be Saved? By Dennis Farney. Photos by Jim Brandenburg. 37-61, Jan. 1980
• Thoreau, a Different Man. By William Howarth. Photos by Farrell Grehan. 349-387, Mar. 1981
• Threatened Glories of Everglades National Park. By Frederick Kent Truslow and Frederick G. Vosburgh. Photos by Frederick Kent Truslow and Otis Imboden. 508-553, Oct. 1967
• Timber: How Much Is Enough? By John J. Putman. Photos by Bruce Dale. 485-511, Apr. 1974
• Tropical Rain Forests. 2-65, Jan. 1983
Nature's Dwindling Treasures. By Peter T. White. Photos by James P. Blair. Paintings by Barron Storey. 2-47; Teeming Life of a Rain Forest. By Carol and David Hughes. 49-65
• Twilight Hope for Big Cypress. By Rick Gore. Photos by Patricia Caulfield. 251-273, Aug. 1976
• A Walk and Ride on the Wild Side: Tasmania. By Carolyn Bennett Patterson. Photos by David Hiser and Melinda Berge. 676-693, May 1983
• Wild Cargo: the Business of Smuggling Animals. By Noel Grove. Photos by Steve Raymer. 287-315, Mar. 1981

• Will Oil and Tundra Mix? Alaska's North Slope Hangs in the Balance. By William S. Ellis. Photos by Emory Kristof. 485-517, Oct. 1971
• Yellowstone Wildlife in Winter. By William Albert Allard. 637-661, Nov. 1967
• *See also* Bird Sanctuaries and Rookeries; Buffalo National River; Connecticut River and Valley; Hudson (River); National Forests; National Monuments; National Parks; Netherlands, for land reclamation; Sea Islands, Georgia-South Carolina; Texas (Fabulous State); U. S. Soil Conservation Service; Wild Rivers; Wilderness; Wildlife Refuges; Willamette River and Valley

CONSHELF BASES:
• At Home in the Sea. By Jacques-Yves Cousteau. 465-507, Apr. 1964
• Working for Weeks on the Sea Floor. By Jacques-Yves Cousteau. Photos by Philippe Cousteau and Bates Littlehales. NGS research grant. 498-537, Apr. 1966
▪ The World of Jacques-Yves Cousteau. 529A-529B, Apr. 1966

CONSIDER the Sponge. . . . Photos by David Doubilet. Text by Michael E. Long. 392-407, Mar. 1977

CONSTANTINOPLE:
• The Byzantine Empire: Rome of the East. By Merle Severy. Photos by James L. Stanfield. 709-767, Dec. 1983
▲ *Europe; Historical Map of Europe*, double-sided supplement. Dec. 1983

CONSTELLATIONS:
▲ *A Map of the Heavens,* supplement. Star charts on reverse. Dec. 1957
▲ *Map of the Heavens,* supplement. Star charts on reverse. Aug. 1970
• Unlocking Secrets of the Northern Lights. By Carl W. Gartlein. Paintings by William Crowder. Included: Pleiades, Southern Cross, Taurus. NGS research grant. 673-704, Nov. 1947

CONSTITUTION HALL, Washington, D. C.:
• The DAR Story. By Lonnelle Aikman. Photos by B. Anthony Stewart and John E. Fletcher. 565-598, Nov. 1951
• Gilbert Grosvenor's Golden Jubilee. By Albert W. Atwood. 253-261, Aug. 1949

The **CONTENTED** Land: New Zealand's North Island. By Charles McCarry. Photos by Bates Littlehales. 190-213, Aug. 1974

CONTINENTAL DIVIDE NATIONAL SCENIC TRAIL, U. S.:
◆ *Along the Continental Divide.* 1981
• Along the Great Divide. By Mike Edwards. Photos by Nicholas DeVore III. 483-515, Oct. 1979

CONTINENTAL DRIFT. *See* Plate Tectonics

CONTINENTAL SHELF RESEARCH:
• The Continental Shelf: Man's New Frontier. By Luis Marden. Photos by Ira Block. 495-531, Apr. 1978
• The Deepest Days. By Robert Sténuit. NGS research grant. 534-547, Apr. 1965
• Outpost Under the Ocean. By Edwin A. Link. Photos by Bates Littlehales. NGS research grant. 530-533, Apr. 1965
• Tomorrow on the Deep Frontier. By Edwin A. Link. NGS research grant. 778-801, June 1964
• *See also* Conshelf Bases

A **CONTINENT'S** Living Treasure. Paintings by Ned Seidler. 164-167, Feb. 1972

CONTRARY New Hampshire. By Robert Booth. Photos by Sandy Felsenthal. 770-799, Dec. 1982

CONVERSATIONS With a Gorilla. By Francine Patterson. Photos by Ronald H. Cohn. NGS research grant. 438-465, Oct. 1978

CONWAY, WILLIAM G.: Author:
• Argentina Protects Its Wildlife Treasures. Photos by Des and Jen Bartlett. 290-297, Mar. 1976
• In Quest of the Rarest Flamingo. Photos by Bates Littlehales. 91-105, July 1961

COOBER PEDY, South Australia:
• Coober Pedy: Opal Capital of Australia's Outback. By Kenny Moore. Photos by Penny Tweedie. 560-571, Oct. 1976

COOK, JAMES:
• The British Way. By Sir Evelyn Wrench. 421-541, Apr. 1949
• Captain Cook: The Man Who Mapped the Pacific. By Alan Villiers. Photos by Gordon W. Gahan. 297-349, Sept. 1971
◆ *Voyages to Paradise: Exploring in the Wake of Captain Cook.* 1981

COOK ISLANDS, South Pacific Ocean:
• New Zealand's Cook Islands: Paradise in Search of a Future. By Maurice Shadbolt. Photos by William Albert Allard. 203-231, Aug. 1967

COOKE, HEREWARD LESTER, Jr.: Author:
• Early America Through the Eyes of Her Native Artists. 356-389, Sept. 1962
• Great Masters of a Brave Era in Art (Impressionist). 661-697, May 1961
• The Louvre, France's Palace of the Arts. 796-831, June 1971

COOKE, HOPE:
• Wedding of Two Worlds. By Lee E. Battaglia. 708-727, Nov. 1963

COOKE, RICHARD A., III: Photographer:
• Molokai–Forgotten Hawaii. By Ethel A. Starbird. 188-219, Aug. 1981

COOKIES:
• Christmas in Cookie Tree Land. By Louise Parker La Gorce. Photos by B. Anthony Stewart. 844-851, Dec. 1955

COOLIDGE, CALVIN:
• Inside the White House. By Lonnelle Aikman. Photos by B. Anthony Stewart and Thomas Nebbia. 3-43, Jan. 1961
• The Living White House. By Lonnelle Aikman. 593-643, Nov. 1966
• Profiles of the Presidents: IV. America Enters the Modern Era. By Frank Freidel. 537-577, Oct. 1965

COOPER, MARTHA: Photographer:
• Unearthing the Oldest Known Maya. By Norman Hammond. Photos by Lowell Georgia and Martha Cooper. 126-140, July 1982

COOPER RIVER WATER PROJECT:
• South Carolina Rediscovered. By Herbert Ravenel Sass. Photos by Robert F. Sisson. 281-321, Mar. 1953

COOPERATIVE FARMS. *See* Amana Colonies; China (Return); Groote Eylandt (From Spear to Hoe); Hutterites; Kibbutzim; Old Believers; Old Salem; Padanaram; Saint Véran

COOPER'S HAWK:
• Can the Cooper's Hawk Survive? By Noel Snyder. Photos by author and Helen Snyder. NGS research grant. 433-442, Mar. 1974

COPENHAGEN, Denmark:
• "Around the World in Eighty Days." By Newman Bumstead. 705-750, Dec. 1951
• Baltic Cruise of the *Caribbee.* By Carleton Mitchell. 605-646, Nov. 1950
• Copenhagen, Wedded to the Sea. By Stuart E. Jones. Photos by Gilbert M. Grosvenor. 45-79, Jan. 1963
• Denmark, Field of the Danes. By William Graves. Photos by Thomas Nebbia. 245-275, Feb. 1974
• Friendly Flight to Northern Europe. By Lyndon B. Johnson. Photos by Volkmar Wentzel. 268-293, Feb. 1964
• The Magic World of Hans Christian Andersen. By Harvey Arden. Photos by Sisse Brimberg. 825-849, Dec. 1979
• Thumbs Up Round the North Sea's Rim. By Frances James. Photos by Erica Koch. 685-704, May 1952
• 2,000 Miles Through Europe's Oldest Kingdom. By Isobel Wylie Hutchison. Photos by Maynard Owen Williams. 141-180, Feb. 1949
• Under Canvas in the Atomic Age. By Alan Villiers. 49-84, July 1955

COPERNICUS, NICOLAUS:
◆ *The Amazing Universe.* Announced. 870-874, June 1975
◆ *Picture Atlas of Our Universe.* 1980
• Pioneers in Man's Search for the Universe. Paintings by Jean-Leon Huens. Text by Thomas Y. Canby. 627-633, May 1974

COPPER:
• Ancient Mesopotamia: A Light That Did Not Fail. By E. A. Speiser. Paintings by H. M. Herget. 41-105, Jan. 1951

• From Tucson to Tombstone. By Mason Sutherland. 343-384, Sept. 1953
• Montana, Shining Mountain Treasureland. By Leo A. Borah. Included: Anaconda Copper Mining Company. 693-736, June 1950
• "Rockhounds" Uncover Earth's Mineral Beauty. By George S. Switzer. Included: Ontonagon copper boulder. 631-660, Nov. 1951
• *See also* Mines and Mining (Congo; Michigan); *and* Alaska, the Big Land

COPRA:
• Clove-scented Zanzibar. By W. Robert Moore. 261-278, Feb. 1952
• Copra-ship Voyage to Fiji's Outlying Islands. By Marjory C. Thomas. 121-140, July 1950
• Pacific Wards of Uncle Sam. By W. Robert Moore. 73-104, July 1948
• Shores and Sails in the South Seas. By Charles Allmon. 73-104, Jan. 1950

CORA INDIANS:
• Mesa del Nayar's Strange Holy Week. By Guillermo Aldana E. 780-795, June 1971

CORACLES:
• Wales, Land of Bards. By Alan Villiers. Photos by Thomas Nebbia. 727-769, June 1965

CORALS AND CORAL REEFS:
• Australia's Great Barrier Reef. 630-663, May 1981
I. A Marine Park Is Born. By Soames Summerhays. Photos by Ron and Valerie Taylor. 630-635; II. Paradise Beneath the Sea. By Ron and Valerie Taylor. 636-663
• Dazzling Corals of Palau. By Thomas O'Neill. Photos by Douglas Faulkner. 136-150, July 1978
• Fish Men Explore a New World Undersea. By Jacques-Yves Cousteau. 431-472, Oct. 1952
• Fluorescent Gems from Davy Jones's Locker. By Paul A. Zahl. 260-271, Aug. 1963
• Life Cycle of a Coral. By Robert F. Sisson. 780-793, June 1973
• Life Springs From Death in Truk Lagoon. By Sylvia A. Earle. Photos by Al Giddings. 578-613, May 1976
From Graveyard to Garden. 604-613
• Man-of-war Fleet Attacks Bimini. By Paul A. Zahl. 185-212, Feb. 1952
• Photographing the Night Creatures of Alligator Reef. By Robert E. Schroeder. Photos by author and Walter A. Starck II. NGS research grant. 128-154, Jan. 1964
• Precious Corals, Hawaii's Deep-sea Jewels. By Richard W. Grigg. 719-732, May 1979
• Probing the Deep Reefs' Hidden Realm. By Walter A. Starck II and Jo D. Starck. NGS research grant. 867-886, Dec. 1972
• Rainbow World Beneath the Red Sea. Photos by David Doubilet. 344-365, Sept. 1975
• Starfish Threaten Pacific Reefs. By James A. Sugar. 340-353, Mar. 1970

BOTH BY DAVID DOUBILET

Red Sea: a refuge to great concentrations of marine life, *top;* coral shelter for hawkfish, *above*

• Strange World of Palau's Salt Lakes. By William M. Hamner. Photos by David Doubilet. 264-282, Feb. 1982
• The Strangest Sea (Red Sea). By Eugenie Clark. Photos by David Doubilet. 338-343, Sept. 1975
• Tektite II: Part One. Science's Window on the Sea. By John G. VanDerwalker. Photos by Bates Littlehales. 256-289, Aug. 1971
• Unsung Beauties of Hawaii's Coral Reefs (Nudibranchs). By Paul A. Zahl. 510-525, Oct. 1959
• *See also* Alligator Reef; Buck Island Reef National Monument; Great Barrier Reef; John Pennekamp Coral Reef State Park; Key Largo Coral Reef; Sha'ab Rūmi (Roman Reef); *and* Aqaba, Gulf of; Bermuda; Fiji Islands; Tuamotu Archipelago

CORBY, BERNARD: Photographer:
• Bluebirds on the Wing in Color. Photos by Bernard Corby and Hance Roy Ivor. 527-530, Apr. 1954

CORCA DHUIBHNE. *See* Dingle Peninsula, Ireland

CORCORAN GALLERY OF ART, Washington, D. C.:
• American Processional: History on Canvas. By John and Blanche Leeper. 173-212, Feb. 1951

CORCOVADO NATIONAL PARK, Costa Rica:
• Teeming Life of a Rain Forest. By Carol and David Hughes. 49-65, Jan. 1983

CORDILLERA ORIENTAL, Andes Mountains. *See* Oriental, Cordillera

CORDOBA, Spain:
• Andalusia, the Spirit of Spain. By Howard La Fay. Photos by Joseph J. Scherschel. 833-857, June 1975
• Holy Week and the Fair in Sevilla. By Luis Marden. 499-530, Apr. 1951

CORFU (Island), Greece:
• Homeward With Ulysses. By Melville Bell Grosvenor. Photos by Edwin Stuart Grosvenor. 1-39, July 1973

CORK INDUSTRY:
• Portugal Is Different. By Clement E. Conger. 583-622, Nov. 1948

CORKSCREW SWAMP–Florida's Primeval Show Place. By Melville Bell Grosvenor. 98-113, Jan. 1958

CORLISS, JOHN B.: Author:
• Oases of Life in the Cold Abyss (Galapagos Rift). By John B. Corliss and Robert D. Ballard. 441-453, Oct. 1977

CORMORANTS:
• Peru Profits from Sea Fowl. By Robert Cushman Murphy. Photos by author and Grace E. Barstow Murphy. 395-413, Mar. 1959
• Sea Bird Cities Off Audubon's Labrador. By Arthur A. Allen. NGS research grant. 755-774, June 1948

CORN GROWING:
• The Family Farm Ain't What It Used To Be. By James A. Sugar. 391-411, Sept. 1974

JAMES JARCHÉ

New Queen: Elizabeth II is crowned

Iran: Shah Mohammad Reza Pahlavi

JAMES L. STANFIELD, NGS

- Iowa, America's Middle Earth. By Harvey Arden. Photos by Craig Aurness. 603-629, May 1981

CORNELL UNIVERSITY: Expeditions and Research:
- Aurora borealis. 869, June 1954
- Curlew Expedition in 1948 to Alaska. 751, 761, Dec. 1948
- "Library of Natural Sounds." 508, 511, Apr. 1950; 545, Apr. 1962; 14, Jan. 1963
- Mysteries of Bird Migration. By Allan C. Fisher, Jr. Photos by Jonathan Blair. 154-193, Aug. 1979
- Peru Project. 246, 247, Feb. 1964
- Sapsucker Woods, Cornell University's Exciting New Bird Sanctuary. By Arthur A. Allen. 530-551, Apr. 1962

CORNING GLASS WORKS FOUNDATION: Study Grant:
- Underwater Archaeology. 774, June 1978

CORNING MUSEUM OF GLASS, Corning, New York:
- History Revealed in Ancient Glass. By Ray Winfield Smith. Photos by B. Anthony Stewart and Lee E. Battaglia. 346-369, Sept. 1964

CORNWALL, PETER BRUCE: Author:
- In Search of Arabia's Past. 493-522, Apr. 1948

CORNWALL (County), England:
- Cowes to Cornwall. By Alan Villiers. Photos by Robert B. Goodman. 149-201, Aug. 1961
- *See also* St. Michael's Mount

CORONATIONS:
- Bhutan Crowns a New Dragon King. Photos by John Scofield. 546-571, Oct. 1974
- Coronation in Katmandu (Mahendra, King of Nepal). By E. Thomas Gilliard. Photos by Marc Riboud. 139-152, July 1957
- Coronations a World Apart. By the Editor. 299, Mar. 1968
- In the London of the New Queen (Elizabeth II). By H. V. Morton. 291-342, Sept. 1953
- Iran's Shah Crowns Himself and His Empress. By Franc Shor. Photos by James L. Stanfield and Winfield Parks. 301-321, Mar. 1968
- Silkworms in England Spin for the Queen. By John E. H. Nolan. 689-704, May 1953
- South Seas' Tonga Hails a King (Taufa'ahau Tupou IV). By Melville Bell Grosvenor. Photos by Edwin Stuart Grosvenor. 322-343, Mar. 1968

CORPUS CHRISTI CELEBRATION:
- Lanzarote, the Strangest Canary. By Stephanie Dinkins. 117-139, Jan. 1969
- Peru's Pilgrimage to the Sky. By Robert Randall. Photos by Loren McIntyre and Ira Block. 60-69, July 1982
- Spain's "Fortunate Isles," the Canaries. By Jean and Franc Shor. 485-522, Apr. 1955

CORSICA (Island), France:
- Sunny Corsica: French Morsel in the Mediterranean. By Robert Cairns. Photos by Joseph J. Scherschel. 401-423, Sept. 1973

COSMIC RAYS:
- Trailing Cosmic Rays in Canada's North. By Martin A. Pomerantz. NGS research grant. 99-115, Jan. 1953

COSMOLOGY:
- The Once and Future Universe. By Rick Gore. Photos by James A. Sugar. Paintings by Barron Storey. Picture text by David Jeffery. 704-749, June 1983

COSMONAUTS:
- Apollo-Soyuz: Handclasp in Space. By Thomas Y. Canby. Contents: The rendezvous in space of cosmonauts Aleksey A. Leonov and Valeriy Kubasov with astronauts Thomas P. Stafford, Vance D. Brand, and Donald K. "Deke" Slayton. 183-187, Feb. 1976

COSTA DEL SOL, Spain:
- Andalusia, the Spirit of Spain. By Howard La Fay. Photos by Joseph J. Scherschel. 833-857, June 1975

COSTA RICA:
- Costa Rica, Free of the Volcano's Veil. By Robert de Roos. 125-152, July 1965
- Costa Rica Steers the Middle Course. By Kent Britt. 32-57, July 1981
- Nature's Living, Jumping Jewels. By Paul A. Zahl. 130-146, July 1973
- Rain Forest. 824, Dec. 1982
- Teeming Life of a Rain Forest. By Carol and David Hughes. 49-65, Jan. 1983
- Troubled Times for Central America. By Wilbur E. Garrett, Editor. 58-61, July 1981
- *See also* Ostional Beach

COTE D'OR (Balloon):
- The Fantastic Flight of *Cote d'Or*. By Cynthia Shields. 789-793, Dec. 1983

COTSWOLD HILLS, England:
- By Cotswold Lanes to Wold's End. By Melville Bell Grosvenor. 615-654, May 1948
- The Cotswolds, "Noicest Parrt o'England." By James Cerruti. Photos by Adam Woolfitt. 846-869, June 1974
- The Thames Mirrors England's Varied Life. By Willard Price. Photos by Robert F. Sisson. 45-93, July 1958

COTTAGE INDUSTRIES:
- Domesticating the Wild and Wooly Musk Ox. By John J. Teal, Jr. Photos by Robert W. Madden. 862-879, June 1970
- From Barra to Butt in the Hebrides. By Isobel Wylie Hutchison. 559-580, Oct. 1954
- Isles on the Edge of the Sea: Scotland's Outer Hebrides. By Kenneth MacLeish. Photos by Thomas Nebbia. 676-711, May 1970

- ● Mountain Voices, Mountain Days. By Bryan Hodgson. Photos by Linda Bartlett. 118-146, July 1972
- ● An Ozark Family Carves a Living and a Way of Life. Photos by Bruce Dale. 124-133, July 1975

COTTON AND COTTON INDUSTRY:
- ● Alabama, Dixie to a Different Tune. By Howard La Fay. Photos by Dick Durrance II. 534-569, Oct. 1975
- ● Dixie Spins the Wheel of Industry. By William H. Nicholas. Photos by J. Baylor Roberts. 281-324, Mar. 1949
- ● The Greener Fields of Georgia. By Howell Walker. Photos by author and B. Anthony Stewart. 287-330, Mar. 1954
- ● The Merrimack: River of Industry and Romance. By Albert W. Atwood. Photos by B. Anthony Stewart. 106-140, Jan. 1951
- ● South Carolina Rediscovered. By Herbert Ravenel Sass. Photos by Robert F. Sisson. 281-321, Mar. 1953

COTTRELL, ERNEST J.:
Photographer:
- ● Skyway Below the Clouds. By Carl R. Markwith. 85-108, July 1949

COUGARS. *See* Mountain Lions

COULSON, COTTON: Photographer:
- ● Mont Saint Michel. By Kenneth MacLeish. 820-831, June 1977
- ● A New Day for Ireland. By John J. Putman. 442-469, Apr. 1981
- ● Oregon's Lovely, Lonely Coast. By Mark Miller. 798-823, Dec. 1979
- ● Return to Estonia. By Priit J. Vesilind. 485-511, Apr. 1980
- ● St. Vincent, the Grenadines, and Grenada: Taking It as It Comes. By Ethel A. Starbird. 399-425, Sept. 1979
- ● The Travail of Ireland. By Joseph Judge. 432-441, Apr. 1981
- ● Travels With a Donkey–100 Years Later. By Carolyn Bennett Patterson. 535-561, Oct. 1978
- ● Two Berlins–A Generation Apart. By Priit J. Vesilind. 2-51, Jan. 1982
- ● The Voyage of *Brendan*. By Timothy Severin. 770-797, Dec. 1977

COUNTDOWN For Space. By Kenneth F. Weaver. 702-734, May 1961

The **COUNTRY** of Willa Cather. By William Howarth. Photos by Farrell Grehan. 71-93, July 1982

COUNTY FAIR. *See* Neshoba County Fair, Mississippi

COUSTEAU, JACQUES-YVES:
- ● Jacques-Yves Cousteau Receives National Geographic Society Medal at White House. 146-147, July 1961
- ■ The World of Jacques-Yves Cousteau. 529A-529B, Apr. 1966

Author:
- ● At Home in the Sea. 465-507, Apr. 1964
- ● *Calypso* Explores an Undersea Canyon (Romanche Trench). Photos by Bates Littlehales. 373-396, Mar. 1958
- ● *Calypso* Explores for Underwater Oil. 155-184, Aug. 1955
- ● Diving Saucer *(Denise)* Takes to the Deep. 571-586, Apr. 1960
- ● Diving Through an Undersea Avalanche. 538-542, Apr. 1955
- ● Exploring Davy Jones's Locker with *Calypso*. Photos by Luis Marden. 149-161, Feb. 1956
- ● Fish Men Discover a 2,200-year-old Greek Ship. 1-36, Jan. 1954
- ● Fish Men Explore a New World Undersea. 431-472, Oct. 1952
- ● Inflatable Ship *(Amphitrite)* Opens Era of Air-borne Undersea Expeditions. 142-148, July 1961
- ● The Ocean. 780-791, Dec. 1981
- ● To the Depths of the Sea by Bathyscaphe. 67-79, July 1954
- ● Working for Weeks on the Sea Floor. Photos by Philippe Cousteau and Bates Littlehales. 498-537, Apr. 1966

COUSTEAU, PHILIPPE: Photographer:
- ● Working for Weeks on the Sea Floor. By Jacques-Yves Cousteau. Photos by Philippe Cousteau and Bates Littlehales. 498-537, Apr. 1966

COWBIRDS:
- ● The Bird's Year. By Arthur A. Allen. 791-816, June 1951

COWBOYS:
- ◆ *The American Cowboy in Life and Legend*. Announced. 882-886, June 1971
- ● British Columbia: Life Begins at 100. By David S. Boyer. 147-189, Aug. 1958
- ● Buffalo Bill and the Enduring West. By Alice J. Hall. Photos by James L. Amos. 76-103, July 1981
- ◆ *Cowboys*. Announced. 724-726, Nov. 1975
- ● Cowpunching on the Padlock Ranch. By William Albert Allard. 478-499, Oct. 1973
- ● The Fabulous State of Texas. By Stanley Walker. Photos by B. Anthony Stewart and Thomas Nebbia. 149-195, Feb. 1961
- ● *See also Gardians;* Gauchos; *and* Ranches

COWDEN, JEANNE:
Author-Photographer:
- ● Adventures With South Africa's Black Eagles. Photos by author and Arthur Bowland. 533-543, Oct. 1969

COWES, Isle of Wight:
- ● The British Way. By Sir Evelyn Wrench. 421-541, Apr. 1949
- ● Cowes to Cornwall. By Alan Villiers. Photos by Robert B. Goodman. 149-201, Aug. 1961

COWPUNCHING on the Padlock Ranch. By William Albert Allard. 478-499, Oct. 1973

COWS. *See* Cattle Raising

COYOTES:
- ■ The Animals Nobody Loved. cover. Feb. 1976
- ● The "Lone" Coyote Likes Family Life. By Hope Ryden. Photos by author and David Hiser. 278-294, Aug. 1974

COZE, PAUL: Author-Photographer:
- ● Kachinas: Masked Dancers of the Southwest. 219-236, Aug. 1957

COZUMEL ISLAND, Mexico:
- ● Probing the Deep Reefs' Hidden Realm. By Walter A. Starck II and Jo D. Starck. NGS research grant. 867-886, Dec. 1972

CRABS:
- ● Can We Save Our Salt Marshes? By Stephen W. Hitchcock. Photos by William R. Curtsinger. 729-765, June 1972
- ● The Changeless Horseshoe Crab. By Anne and Jack Rudloe. Photos by Robert F. Sisson. Note: These arthropods are not true crabs. 562-572, Apr. 1981
- ● The Crab That Shakes Hands. By Clarence P. Idyll. Photos by Robert F. Sisson. 254-271, Feb. 1971
- ● This Is My Island, Tangier (Virginia). By Harold G. Wheatley. Photos by David Alan Harvey. 700-725, Nov. 1973

CRAFTS:
- ◆ *The Craftsman in America*. Announced. 870-874, June 1975
- ● Human Treasures of Japan. By William Graves. Photos by James L. Stanfield. 370-379, Sept. 1972
- ● Kyoto and Nara: Keepers of Japan's Past. By Charles McCarry. Photos by George F. Mobley. 836-851, June 1976
- ● The Past Is Present in Greenfield Village. By Beverley M. Bowie. Photos by Neal P. Davis and Willard R. Culver. 96-127, July 1958
- ● Williamsburg, City for All Seasons. By Joseph Judge. Photos by James L. Amos. 790-823, Dec. 1968
- ● Williamsburg: Its College and Its Cinderella City. By Beverley M. Bowie. 439-486, Oct. 1954
- ● *See also* Embroidery; Folk Art; Goldsmithing; Pottery; Ship Crafting; Weaving; Wood Carving

CRAIGHEAD, CHARLES:
Photographer:
- ● Sharing the Lives of Wild Golden Eagles. By John Craighead. Photos by Charles and Derek Craighead. 420-439, Sept. 1967

CRAIGHEAD, DEREK: Author:
- ● Yellowstone at 100: A Walk Through the Wilderness. By Karen and Derek Craighead. Photos by Sam Abell. 579-603, May 1972

Photographer:
- ● Sharing the Lives of Wild Golden Eagles. By John Craighead. Photos by Charles and Derek Craighead. 420-439, Sept. 1967

CRAIGHEAD, FRANK, Jr.:
- ■ Grizzly! 639A-639B, Nov. 1967

Author-Photographer:
- ● Bright Dyes Reveal Secrets of Canada Geese. 817-832, Dec. 1957
- ● Cloud Gardens in the Tetons. 811-830, June 1948
- ● Knocking Out Grizzly Bears For Their Own Good. 276-291, Aug. 1960
- ● Studying Wildlife by Satellite. 120-123, Jan. 1973

C
D

• Trailing Yellowstone's Grizzlies by Radio. 252-267, Aug. 1966
• We Survive on a Pacific Atoll. 73-94, Jan. 1948
• White-water Adventure on Wild Rivers of Idaho. 213-239, Feb. 1970
• Wildlife Adventuring in Jackson Hole. 1-36, Jan. 1956

CRAIGHEAD, JOHN:
Grizzly! 639A-639B, Nov. 1967
Author:
• Sharing the Lives of Wild Golden Eagles. Photos by Charles and Derek Craighead. 420-439, Sept. 1967
• Studying Grizzly Habitat by Satellite. 148-158, July 1976
Author-Photographer:
• Bright Dyes Reveal Secrets of Canada Geese. 817-832, Dec. 1957
• Cloud Gardens in the Tetons. 811-830, June 1948
• Knocking Out Grizzly Bears For Their Own Good. 276-291, Aug. 1960
• Studying Wildlife by Satellite. 120-123, Jan. 1973
• Trailing Yellowstone's Grizzlies by Radio. 252-267, Aug. 1966
• We Survive on a Pacific Atoll. 73-94, Jan. 1948
• White-water Adventure on Wild Rivers of Idaho. 213-239, Feb. 1970
• Wildlife Adventuring in Jackson Hole. 1-36, Jan. 1956

CRAIGHEAD, KAREN: Author:
• Yellowstone at 100: A Walk Through the Wilderness. By Karen and Derek Craighead. Photos by Sam Abell. 579-603, May 1972

CRANBERRIES:
• The People of New Jersey's Pine Barrens. By John McPhee. Photos by William R. Curtsinger. 52-77, Jan. 1974

CRANE, JOCELYN: Author:
• Keeping House for Tropical Butterflies. Photos by M. Woodbridge Williams. 193-217, Aug. 1957

CRANES (Birds):
• And Then There Was Fred. . . . Contents: Sandhill crane. 843-847, Dec. 1973
• The Japanese Crane, Bird of Happiness. By Tsuneo Hayashida. Contents: Red-crowned crane. 542-556, Oct. 1983
• Teamwork Helps the Whooping Crane. By Roderick C. Drewien, with Ernie Kuyt. Contents: A U. S.-Canadian effort to establish a second breeding flock of wild whoopers among close-kin sandhill cranes. 680-693, May 1979
• Where Oil and Wildlife Mix. By Steven C. Wilson and Karen C. Hayden. Included: Whooping cranes. 145-173, Feb. 1981
• Whooping Cranes Fight for Survival. By Robert Porter Allen. Photos by Frederick Kent Truslow. 650-669, Nov. 1959

CRATER LAKE, Oregon:
• Crater Lake Summer. By Walter Meayers Edwards. 134-148, July 1962
• When Mt. Mazama Lost Its Top: The Birth of Crater Lake. By Lyman J. Briggs. 128-133, July 1962

DICK DURRANCE II, NGS

Rivers of Idaho: the Craigheads ride Salmon River rapids

CRATERS OF THE MOON NATIONAL MONUMENT, Idaho:
• Man on the Moon in Idaho. By William Belknap, Jr. 505-525, Oct. 1960

La **CRAU** (Plain), France:
• Sheep Trek in the French Alps. By Maurice Moyal. Photos by Marcel Coen. 545-564, Apr. 1952

CRAWFISH. *See* Crayfish

CRAYFISH:
• Trouble in Bayou Country: Louisiana's Atchafalaya. By Jack and Anne Rudloe. Photos by C. C. Lockwood. 377-397, Sept. 1979
• *See also* Spiny Lobsters

CREATURES That Deceive to Survive. By Robert F. Sisson. 394-415, Mar. 1980

CREE INDIANS:
• The Changing World of Canada's Crees. By Fred Ward. 541-569, Apr. 1975
• Nomads of the Far North. By Matthew W. Stirling. 471-504, Oct. 1949
Hearty Folk Defy Arctic Storms. Paintings by W. Langdon Kihn. 479-494
• Quebec's Northern Dynamo. By Larry Kohl. Photos by Ottmar Bierwagen. 406-418, Mar. 1982

CRESSON, OSBORNE C.:
Photographer:
• American Family in Afghanistan. By Rebecca Shannon Cresson. 417-432, Sept. 1953

CRESSON, REBECCA SHANNON:
Author:
• American Family in Afghanistan. Photos by Osborne C. Cresson. 417-432, Sept. 1953
• We Lived in Turbulent Tehran. 707-720, Nov. 1953

CRETAN CIVILIZATION. *See* Minoan Civilization

CRETE (Island), Greece:
• The Aegean Isles: Poseidon's Playground. By Gilbert M. Grosvenor. 733-781, Dec. 1958
• Crete, Cradle of Western Civilization. By Maynard Owen Williams. 693-706, Nov. 1953
• Drama of Death in a Minoan Temple. By Yannis Sakellarakis and Efi Sapouna-Sakellaraki. Photos by Otis Imboden and Spyros Tsavdaroglou. 205-222, Feb. 1981
• Joseph Alsop: A Historical Perspective (on Minoan Human Sacrifice). 223, Feb. 1981
• Minoans and Mycenaeans: Greece's Brilliant Bronze Age. By Joseph Judge. Photos by Gordon W. Gahan. Paintings by Lloyd K. Townsend. 142-185, Feb. 1978
• War-torn Greece Looks Ahead. By Maynard Owen Williams. 711-744, Dec. 1949

CRICKETS, Nature's Expert Fiddlers. By Catherine Bell Palmer. 385-394, Sept. 1953

CRIME DETECTION:
• The FBI: Public Friend Number One. By Jacob Hay. Photos by Robert F. Sisson. 860-886, June 1961

CRIMEAN PENINSULA, U.S.S.R.:
• Down on the Farm, Soviet Style–a 4-H Adventure. By John Garaventa. Photos by James Tobin and Carol Schmidt. 768-797, June 1979

CRIPPEN, ROBERT L.:
• *Columbia*'s Landing Closes a Circle. By Tom Wolfe. 474-477, Oct. 1981
• NGS Hubbard Medal Recipient. 852, Dec. 1981
• When the Space Shuttle Finally Flies. By Rick Gore. Photos by Jon Schneeberger. Paintings by Ken Dallison. 317-347, Mar. 1981
Author:
• *Columbia*'s Astronauts' Own Story: Our Phenomenal First Flight. By John W. Young and Robert L. Crippen. Paintings by Ken Dallison. 478-503, Oct. 1981

CROATIA (Republic), Yugoslavia:
• Yugoslavia: Six Republics in One. By Robert Paul Jordan. Photos by James P. Blair. 589-633, May 1970

CROCODILIANS:
• A Bad Time to Be a Crocodile. By Rick Gore. Photos by Jonathan Blair. 90-115, Jan. 1978
• Wild Cargo: the Business of Smuggling Animals. By Noel Grove. Photos by Steve Raymer. Included: Saltwater crocodile; and crocodile-hide trade, crocodile ranching. 287-315, Mar. 1981
• Wildlife of Everglades National Park. By Daniel B. Beard. Paintings by Walter A. Weber. Included: Alligators; Crocodiles. 83-116, Jan. 1949
• *See also* Alligators; Caimans

CRO-MAGNON MAN:
• A Bold New Look at Our Past. The Editor. NGS research grant. 62-63, Jan. 1975
• Exploring the Mind of Ice Age Man. By Alexander Marshack. NGS research grant. 64-89, Jan. 1975

CROMWELL, EATON: Photographer:
• Switzerland's Enchanted Val d'Hérens. By Georgia Engelhard Cromwell. 825-848, June 1955

CROMWELL, GEORGIA ENGELHARD:
Author:
• Switzerland's Enchanted Val d'Hérens. 825-848, June 1955

CROMWELL, OLIVER:
• The British Way. By Sir Evelyn Wrench. 421-541, Apr. 1949

CROPP, BEN: Photographer:
• Diving With Sea Snakes. By Kenneth MacLeish. 565-578, Apr. 1972

CROPS:
• Rediscovering America's Forgotten Crops. By Noel D. Vietmeyer. Photos by Burgess Blevins. Paintings by Paul M. Breeden. 702-712, May 1981
• *See also* Coffee; Potatoes; Wheat

CROSBY, HARRY: Author:
• Baja's Murals of Mystery. Photos by Charles O'Rear. 692-702, Nov. 1980

CROSS, JOHN W., Jr.: Author:
• Westminster, World Series of Dogdom. 91-116, Jan. 1954

CROSS FIRE at an Ancient Crossroads. By Robert Paul Jordan. Photos by Gordon W. Gahan. 88-123, July 1977

CROSSCURRENTS Sweep the Indian Ocean. By Bart McDowell. Photos by Steve Raymer. 422-457, Oct. 1981

The **CROSSING** of Antarctica. By Sir Vivian Fuchs. Photos by George Lowe. 25-47, Jan. 1959

CROSSING the Atlantic by Balloon. By Ben L. Abruzzo, with Maxie L. Anderson and Larry Newman. 858-882, Dec. 1978

CROSSROADS of the Insect World. By J. W. MacSwain. Photos by Edward S. Ross. 844-857, Dec. 1966

CROWDER, WILLIAM: Artist:
• Unlocking Secrets of the Northern Lights. By Carl W. Gartlein. 673-704, Nov. 1947

CROWLEY, DON: Artist:
• Nature's Gifts to Medicine. By Lonnelle Aikman. Paintings by Lloyd K. Townsend and Don Crowley. 420-440, Sept. 1974

CROWN JEWELS:
• Imperial Russia's Glittering Legacy. 24-33, Jan. 1978
• In the London of the New Queen (Elizabeth II). By H. V. Morton. 291-342, Sept. 1953
• The Incredible Crystal: Diamonds. By Fred Ward. Included: Iran. 85-113, Jan. 1979
• Iran's Shah Crowns Himself and His Empress. By Franc Shor. Photos by James L. Stanfield and Winfield Parks. 301-321, Mar. 1968
• The Many-sided Diamond. By George S. Switzer. Included: Great Britain's Imperial State Crown, the French crown jewels, and the Orloff Diamond of the tsarist empire. 568-586, Apr. 1958
• Questing for Gems. By George S. Switzer. Included: Great Britain; Iran; Tsarist Russia. 835-863, Dec. 1971

CRUISE to Stone Age Arnhem Land. By Howell Walker. 417-430, Sept. 1949

CRUISES AND VOYAGES:
• Adventures with the Survey Navy. By Irving Johnson. 131-148, July 1947
• The Aegean Isles: Poseidon's Playground. By Gilbert M. Grosvenor. 733-781, Dec. 1958
• Alone to Antarctica. By David Lewis. Drawings by Noel Sickles. 808-821, Dec. 1973
• Arctic Odyssey. By John Bockstoce. Photos by Jonathan Wright. Paintings by Jack Unruh. 100-127, July 1983
• Atlantic Odyssey: Iceland to Antarctica. By Newman Bumstead. Photos by Volkmar Wentzel. 725-780, Dec. 1955
• Baltic Cruise of the *Caribbee*. By Carleton Mitchell. 605-646, Nov. 1950
• A Canoe Helps Hawaii Recapture Her Past. By Herb Kawainui Kane. Photos by David Hiser. 468-489, Apr. 1976
• Captain Cook: The Man Who Mapped the Pacific. By Alan Villiers. Photos by Gordon W. Gahan. 297-349, Sept. 1971
• *Carib* Cruises the West Indies. By Carleton Mitchell. 1-56, Jan. 1948
• Channel Cruise to Glorious Devon. By Alan Villiers. Photos by Bates Littlehales. 208-259, Aug. 1963
• Christopher Columbus and the New World He Found. By John Scofield. Photos by Adam Woolfitt. 584-625, Nov. 1975
• Circling Earth From Pole to Pole. By Sir Ranulph Fiennes. 464-481, Oct. 1983
• Cowes to Cornwall. By Alan Villiers. Photos by Robert B. Goodman. 149-201, Aug. 1961
• Cruising Colombia's "Ol' Man River." By Amos Burg. 615-660, May 1947
• Cruising Florida's Western Waterways. By Rube Allyn. Photos by Bates Littlehales. 49-76, Jan. 1955
• Cruising Japan's Inland Sea. By Willard Price. 619-650, Nov. 1953
▲ *Discoverers of the Pacific; Islands of the Pacific,* double-sided supplement. Dec. 1974
• Down East to Nova Scotia. By Winfield Parks. 853-879, June 1964
• Editorials. By Gilbert M. Grosvenor. 149, Feb. 1975; 431, Oct. 1976
• *Endeavour* Sails the Inside Passage. By Amos Burg. 801-828, June 1947
• Exploring England's Canals. By Bryan Hodgson. Photos by Linda Bartlett. 76-111, July 1974
• Far North with "Captain Mac." By Miriam MacMillan. 465-513, Oct. 1951
• *Finisterre* Sails the Windward Islands. By Carleton Mitchell. Photos by Winfield Parks. 755-801, Dec. 1965
• French Riviera: Storied Playground on the Azure Coast. By Carleton Mitchell. Photos by Thomas Nebbia. 798-835, June 1967
• A Fresh Breeze Stirs the Leewards. By Carleton Mitchell. Photos by Winfield Parks. 488-537, Oct. 1966
• H.R.H. The Prince Philip, Duke of Edinburgh, Introduces to Members the Narrative of His Round-the-World Tour. 583-584, Nov. 1957
• *Hokule'a* Follows the Stars to Tahiti. By David Lewis. Photos by Nicholas deVore III. 512-537, Oct. 1976
• Homeward With Ulysses. By Melville Bell Grosvenor. Photos by Edwin Stuart Grosvenor. 1-39, July 1973

• How We Sailed the New *Mayflower* to America. By Alan Villiers. 627-672, Nov. 1957
• Huzza for Otaheite! *(Bounty* Voyage). By Luis Marden. 435-459, Apr. 1962
• I Sailed with Portugal's Captains Courageous. By Alan Villiers. 565-596, May 1952
• *Ice Bird* Ends Her Lonely Odyssey. By David Lewis. 216-233, Aug. 1975
• In the Wake of Sindbad. By Tim Severin. Photos by Richard Greenhill. 2-41, July 1982
• Inside Europe Aboard *Yankee*. By Irving and Electa Johnson. Photos by Joseph J. Scherschel. 157-195, Aug. 1964
• The Isles of Greece: Aegean Birthplace of Western Culture. By Melville Bell Grosvenor. Photos by Edwin Stuart Grosvenor and Winfield Parks. 147-193, Aug. 1972
• Lost World of the Galapagos (*Yankee* Cruise). By Irving and Electa Johnson. 681-703, May 1959
• Magellan: First Voyage Around the World. By Alan Villiers. Photos by Bruce Dale. 721-753, June 1976
• Midshipmen's Cruise. By William J. Aston and Alexander G. B. Grosvenor. 711-754, June 1948
• More of Sea Than of Land: The Bahamas. By Carleton Mitchell. Photos by James L. Stanfield. 218-267, Feb. 1967
• New Guinea to Bali in *Yankee*. By Irving and Electa Johnson. 767-815, Dec. 1959
• North for Oil: *Manhattan* Makes the Historic Northwest Passage. By Bern Keating. Photos by Tomas Sennett. 374-391, Mar. 1970
• *North Star* Cruises Alaska's Wild West. By Amos Burg. 57-86, July 1952
• North Through History Aboard *White Mist*. By Melville Bell Grosvenor. Photos by Edwin Stuart Grosvenor. 1-55, July 1970
• Off the Beaten Track of Empire (Prince Philip's Tour). By Beverley M. Bowie. Photos by Michael Parker. 584-626, Nov. 1957
• Penguins and Their Neighbors. By Roger Tory Peterson. Photos by Des and Jen Bartlett. Contents: Journey of the M.S. *Lindblad Explorer* in Antarctic Regions. 237-255, Aug. 1977
• Robin Sails Home. By Robin Lee Graham. 504-545, Oct. 1970
◆ *Romance of the Sea*. 1981
• 'Round the Horn by Submarine. By Paul C. Stimson. 129-144, Jan. 1948
• Safe Landing on Sable, Isle of 500 Shipwrecks. By Melville Bell Grosvenor. 398-431, Sept. 1965
• Saga of a Ship, the *Yankee* (Brigantine). By Luis Marden. 263-269, Feb. 1966
• Sailing Iceland's Rugged Coasts. By Wright Britton. Photos by James A. Sugar. 228-265, Aug. 1969
• Sailing with Sindbad's Sons. By Alan Villiers. 675-688, Nov. 1948
• Scotland from Her Lovely Lochs and Seas. By Alan Villiers. Photos by Robert F. Sisson. 492-541, Apr. 1961
• Sea Fever. By John E. Schultz. 237-268, Feb. 1949
• Sir Francis Drake. By Alan Villiers. Photos by Gordon W. Gahan. 216-253, Feb. 1975
• Slow Boat to Florida. By Dorothea and Stuart E. Jones. 1-65, Jan. 1958
▪ The Superliners: Twilight of an Era. 1, Jan. 1980; cover, Apr. 1980
• A Teen-ager Sails the World Alone. By Robin Lee Graham. 445-491, Oct. 1968
▪ The *Tigris* Expedition. 826, Dec. 1978; 1, Jan. 1979; Cover, Apr. 1979
• *Tigris* Sails Into the Past. By Thor Heyerdahl. Photos by Carlo Mauri and the crew of the *Tigris*. 806-827, Dec. 1978
• To Europe with a Racing Start *(Finisterre)*. By Carleton Mitchell. 758-791, June 1958
• Trawling the China Seas. Photos by J. Charles Thompson. 381-395, Mar. 1950
• *Triton* Follows Magellan's Wake. By Edward L. Beach. Photos by J. Baylor Roberts. 585-615, Nov. 1960
• Twilight of the Arab Dhow. By Marion Kaplan. 330-351, Sept. 1974
• Under Canvas in the Atomic Age. By Alan Villiers. 49-84, July 1955
• The Vikings. By Howard La Fay. Photos by Ted Spiegel. 492-541, Apr. 1970
▪ The Volga. 575, Nov. 1976
• The Voyage of *Brendan*. By Timothy Severin. Photos by Cotton Coulson. 770-797, Dec. 1977
• The Voyage of *Ra II*. By Thor Heyerdahl. Photos by Carlo Mauri and Georges Sourial. 44-71, Jan. 1971
▪ The Voyage of the Brigantine *Yankee*. 265A-265B, Feb. 1966
▪ Voyage of the *Hokule'a*. 575, Nov. 1976
▪ Voyage of the *Tigris*. 826, Dec. 1978; 1, Jan. 1979; cover, Apr. 1979
• Voyage to the Antarctic. By David Lewis. 544-562, Apr. 1983
◆ *Voyages to Paradise: Exploring in the Wake of Captain Cook*. 1981
• *White Mist* Cruises to Wreck-haunted St. Pierre and Miquelon. By Melville Bell Grosvenor. 378-419, Sept. 1967
• Who Discovered America? A New Look at an Old Question. The Editor. 769, Dec. 1977
• Windjamming Around New England. By Tom Horgan. Photos by Robert F. Sisson. 141-169, Aug. 1950
• World-roaming Teen-ager Sails On. By Robin Lee Graham. 449-493, Apr. 1969
• *Yankee* Cruises the Storied Nile. By Irving and Electa Johnson. Photos by Winfield Parks. 583-633, May 1965
• *Yankee* Cruises Turkey's History-haunted Coast. By Irving and Electa Johnson. Photos by Joseph J. Scherschel. 798-845, Dec. 1969
• *Yankee* Roams the Orient. By Irving and Electa Johnson. 327-370, Mar. 1951
• The *Yankee*'s Wander-world. By Irving and Electa Johnson. 1-50, Jan. 1949
• *See also* Boats; Canoe Trips; Ferries; Kayaks; Rivers and River Trips; Sailing Vessels; Ships; U. S. Navy

CRUSADES:
• Crusader Lands Revisited. By Harold Lamb. Photos by David S. Boyer. 815-852, Dec. 1954
• Crusader Road to Jerusalem. By Franc Shor. Photos by Thomas Nebbia. 797-855, Dec. 1963
I. Desert Ordeal of the Knights. 797-837; II. Conquest of the Holy City. 839-855
• In the Crusaders' Footsteps. By Franc Shor. Photos by Thomas Nebbia and James P. Blair. 731-789, June 1962

CRUSTACEANS:
• Diving Beneath Arctic Ice. By Joseph B. MacInnis. Photos by William R. Curtsinger. 248-267, Aug. 1973
• Life in a "Dead" Sea–Great Salt Lake. By Paul A. Zahl. 252-263, Aug. 1967
• Man-of-war Fleet Attacks Bimini. By Paul A. Zahl. 185-212, Feb. 1952
• Photographing the Night Creatures of Alligator Reef. By Robert E. Schroeder. Photos by author and Walter A. Starck II. NGS research grant. 128-154, Jan. 1964
• *See also* Barnacles; Crabs; Crayfish; Lobsters and Lobstering; Plankton; Shrimp; Shrimp Fishing; Spiny Lobsters

CRUZEN, RICHARD H.:
• Our Navy Explores Antarctica. By Richard E. Byrd. U. S. Navy official photos. 429-522, Oct. 1947

CRYSTAL MOUNTAIN, Nepal:
• Trek to Nepal's Sacred Crystal Mountain. By Joel F. Ziskin. 500-517, Apr. 1977

CRYSTAL RIVER, Florida:
• Florida's Manatees, Mermaids in Peril. By Daniel S. Hartman. Photos by James A. Sugar. NGS research grant. 342-353, Sept. 1969

CRYSTALS:
• Crystals, Magical Servants of the Space Age. By Kenneth F. Weaver. Photos by James P. Blair. 278-296, Aug. 1968
• The Laser's Bright Magic. By Thomas Meloy. Photos by Howard Sochurek. 858-881, Dec. 1966
• *See also* Diamonds; Frost; Gems; Rocks; Salt; Snowflakes; *and* Chips

CUBA:
• The Caribbean: Sun, Sea, and Seething. By Noel Grove. Photos by Steve Raymer. 244-271, Feb. 1981
• Cuba–American Sugar Bowl. By Melville Bell Grosvenor. 1-56, Jan. 1947
• Editorial. By Gilbert M. Grosvenor. 1, Jan. 1977
• Guantánamo: Keystone in the Caribbean. By Jules B. Billard. Photos by W. E. Garrett and Thomas Nebbia. 420-436, Mar. 1961

• Inside Cuba Today. By Fred Ward. 32-69, Jan. 1977

CUBAN REFUGEES:
• Cuba's Exiles Bring New Life to Miami. By Edward J. Linehan. Photos by Nathan Benn. 63-95, July 1973
• Florida–A Time for Reckoning. By William S. Ellis. Photos by Nathan Benn and Kevin Fleming. 172-219, Aug. 1982

CUBEOS (Indians):
• Jungle Jaunt on Amazon Headwaters. By Bernice M. Goetz. 371-388, Sept. 1952

CUELLO (Archaeological Site), Belize:
• Unearthing the Oldest Known Maya. By Norman Hammond. Photos by Lowell Georgia and Martha Cooper. NGS research grant. 126-140, July 1982

CUEVA DE LAS LECHUZAS, Peru:
• Birds That "See" in the Dark With Their Ears. By Edward S. Ross. 282-290, Feb. 1965

CULTURAL ATLAS:
◆ *Peoples and Places of the Past: The National Geographic Illustrated Atlas of the Ancient World.* 1983; Announced. 824, Dec. 1982

CULVER, WILLARD R.: Photographer:
• Ancient Cliff Dwellers of Mesa Verde. By Don Watson. 349-376, Sept. 1948
• Birthplace of Telephone Magic. 289-312, Mar. 1947
• California, Horn of Plenty. By Frederick Simpich. 553-594, May 1949
• Deaf Children Learn to Talk at Clarke School. By Lilian Grosvenor. 379-397, Mar. 1955
• Dragonflies–Rainbows on the Wing. By James G. Needham. 215-229, Aug. 1951
• El Morro: Story in Stone. By Edwards Park. 237-244, Aug. 1957
• Florida's "Wild" Indians, the Seminole. By Louis Capron. 819-840, Dec. 1956
• Haunting Heart of the Everglades. By Andrew H. Brown. Photos by author and Willard R. Culver. 145-173, Feb. 1948
• History Repeats in Old Natchez. By William H. Nicholas. 181-208, Feb. 1949
• Home Life in Paris Today. By Deena Clark. 43-72, July 1950
• Illinois–Healthy Heart of the Nation. By Leo A. Borah. Photos by B. Anthony Stewart and Willard R. Culver. 781-820, Dec. 1953
• Land of Louisiana Sugar Kings. By Harnett T. Kane. 531-567, Apr. 1958
• Man's Mightiest Ally. 423-450, Apr. 1947
• My Life in the Valley of the Moon. By H. H. Arnold. 689-716, Dec. 1948
• New Miracles of the Telephone Age. By Robert Leslie Conly. 87-120, July 1954
• One Hundred Hours Beneath the Chesapeake. By Gilbert C. Klingel. 681-696, May 1955
• The Past Is Present in Greenfield Village. By Beverley M. Bowie. Photos by Neal P. Davis and Willard R. Culver. 96-127, July 1958
• Rhode Island, Modern City-State. By George W. Long. 137-170, Aug. 1948
• "Rockhounds" Uncover Earth's Mineral Beauty. By George S. Switzer. 631-660, Nov. 1951
• Switzerland Guards the Roof of Europe. By William H. Nicholas. 205-246, Aug. 1950
• Uncle Sam's House of 1,000 Wonders (National Bureau of Standards). By Lyman J. Briggs and F. Barrows Colton. 755-784, Dec. 1951
• U. S. Capitol, Citadel of Democracy. By Lonnelle Aikman. 143-192, Aug. 1952
• Westminster, World Series of Dogdom. By John W. Cross, Jr. 91-116, Jan. 1954

CUMBERLAND COUNTRY, Kentucky-Tennessee:
• The People of Cumberland Gap. By John Fetterman. Photos by Bruce Dale. 591-621, Nov. 1971

CUMBERLAND ISLAND, Georgia:
• Cumberland, My Island for a While. By John Pennington. Photos by Jodi Cobb. Note: Designated a national seashore in 1972. 649-661, Nov. 1977
• Sea Islands: Adventuring Along the South's Surprising Coast. By James Cerruti. Photos by Thomas Nebbia and James L. Amos. 366-393, Mar. 1971

CUMBERLAND VALLEY, Pennsylvania:
• Appalachian Valley Pilgrimage. By Catherine Bell Palmer. Photos by Justin Locke. 1-32, July 1949

CUNEIFORM:
• Darius Carved History on Ageless Rock. By George G. Cameron. 825-844, Dec. 1950
• Ebla: Splendor of an Unknown Empire. By Howard La Fay. Photos by James L. Stanfield. Paintings by Louis S. Glanzman. 730-759, Dec. 1978

CUNNINGHAM, JOHN T.: Author:
• I'm From New Jersey. Photos by Volkmar Wentzel. 1-45, Jan. 1960
• Staten Island Ferry, New York's Seagoing Bus. By John T. Cunningham and Jay Johnston. Photos by W. D. Vaughn. 833-843, June 1959

CUPP, DAVID: Author:
• Avalanche! 280-305, Sept. 1982
I. Winter's White Death. 280-281; II. "I'm OK, I'm Alive!" Photos by Lanny Johnson and Andre Benier. 282-289
Author-Photographer:
• Avalanche! Battling the Juggernaut. 290-305, Sept. 1982
Photographer:
• Capri, Italy's Enchanted Rock. By Carleton Mitchell. 795-809, June 1970
• Denver, Colorado's Rocky Mountain High. By John J. Putman. 383-411, Mar. 1979

BRUCE DALE, NGS

Cumberland Gap: rural mail delivery

WILLIAM R. CURTSINGER

Salt Marshes: Louisiana heron chick

• Kuwait, Aladdin's Lamp of the Middle East. By John E. Frazer. 636-667, May 1969
• Nevada's Mountain of Invisible Gold. By Samuel W. Matthews. 668-679, May 1968
• Our National Forests: Problems in Paradise. By Rowe Findley. 306-339, Sept. 1982
• Solving the Mystery of Mexico's Great Stone Spheres. By Matthew W. Stirling. 295-300, Aug. 1969

CURAÇAO (Island), Netherlands Antilles:
• The Netherlands Antilles: Holland in the Caribbean. By James Cerruti. Photos by Emory Kristof. 115-146, Jan. 1970

CURE RIVER VALLEY, France. *See* Vézelay

CURITIBA, Brazil:
• Brazil's Golden Beachhead. By Bart McDowell. Photos by Nicholas DeVore III. 246-277, Feb. 1978

CURLEWS:
• The Curlew's Secret. By Arthur A. Allen. NGS research grant. 751-770, Dec. 1948

CURLING:
• Winter Brings Carnival Time to Quebec. By Kathleen Revis. 69-97, Jan. 1958

CURRENT Scientific Projects of the National Geographic Society. 143-144, July 1953

CURRENTS, Ocean. *See* Gulf Stream; Map Supplements

CURRUMBIN, Australia:
• Honey Eaters of Currumbin (Lorikeets). By Paul A. Zahl. 510-519, Oct. 1956

CURTIS, GARNISS H.: Author:
• A Clock for the Ages: Potassium-Argon. 590-592, Oct. 1961

CURTSINGER, WILLIAM R.: Photographer:
• Antarctica's Nearer Side. By Samuel W. Matthews. 622-655, Nov. 1971
• Bad Days for the Brown Pelican. By Ralph W. Schreiber. Photos by William R. Curtsinger and author. 111-123, Jan. 1975
• Can We Save Our Salt Marshes? By Stephen W. Hitchcock. 729-765, June 1972
• Diving Beneath Arctic Ice. By Joseph B. MacInnis. 248-267, Aug. 1973
• In Hawaii's Crystal Sea, A Galaxy of Life Fills the Night. By Kenneth Brower. Photos by William R. Curtsinger and Chris Newbert. 834-847, Dec. 1981
• Learning the Ways of the Walrus. By G. Carleton Ray. 565-580, Oct. 1979
• Life or Death for the Harp Seal. By David M. Lavigne. 129-142, Jan. 1976
• The People of New Jersey's Pine Barrens. By John McPhee. 52-77, Jan. 1974
• Swimming With Patagonia's Right Whales. By Roger Payne. Photos by William R. Curtsinger and Charles R. Nicklin, Jr. 576-587, Oct. 1972
• The Treasure of Porto Santo. By Robert Sténuit. Photos by author and William R. Curtsinger. 260-275, Aug. 1975
• The Trouble With Dolphins. By Edward H. Linehan. 506-541, Apr. 1979

CUSCO, Peru. *See* Cuzco

CUSS I (Drilling Barge). *See* Mohole, Project

CUSTER, GEORGE A.:
• I See America First. By Lynda Bird Johnson. Photos by William Albert Allard. 874-904, Dec. 1965
• North Dakota Comes into Its Own. By Leo A. Borah. Photos by J. Baylor Roberts. 283-322, Sept. 1951

CUZCO (Cusco), Peru:
• The Five Worlds of Peru. By Kenneth F. Weaver. Photos by Bates Littlehales. 213-265, Feb. 1964
• The Lost Empire of the Incas. By Loren McIntyre. Art by Ned and Rosalie Seidler. Included: A pictorial chronicle of the Incas. 729-787, Dec. 1973
• Peru, Homeland of the Warlike Inca. By Kip Ross. 421-462, Oct. 1950

CYANA (Diving Saucer):
• Where the Earth Turns Inside Out (Project FAMOUS). By J. R. Heirtzler. Photos by Emory Kristof. 586-603, May 1975

CYCLADES (Islands), Greece:
• The Isles of Greece: Aegean Birthplace of Western Culture. By Melville Bell Grosvenor. Photos by Edwin Stuart Grosvenor and Winfield Parks. 147-193, Aug. 1972
• *See also* Thera

CYPRESS GARDENS, Florida:
• The Booming Sport of Water Skiing. By Wilbur E. Garrett. 700-711, Nov. 1958

CYPRESS SWAMP. *See* Big Cypress Swamp

CYPRUS (Island), Mediterranean Sea:
• Cyprus, Geography's Stepchild. By Franc Shor. 873-884, June 1956
• Cyprus, Idyllic Island in a Troubled Sea. By Jean and Franc Shor. 627-664, May 1952
• Cyprus Under Four Flags: A Struggle for Unity. By Kenneth MacLeish. Photos by Jonathan Blair. 356-383, Mar. 1973
• *See also* Kyrenia Ship

CZECHOSLOVAKIA:
• Czechoslovakia: The Dream and the Reality. By Edward J. Linehan. Photos by James P. Blair. 151-193, Feb. 1968
• The Danube: River of Many Nations, Many Names. By Mike Edwards. Photos by Winfield Parks. 455-485, Oct. 1977
• Down the Danube by Canoe. By William Slade Backer. Photos by Richard S. Durrance and Christopher G. Knight. 34-79, July 1965

• Old Prague in Winter. By Peter T. White. Photos by Nathan Benn. 546-567, Apr. 1979
▲ *Poland and Czechoslovakia,* Atlas series supplement. Sept. 1958

D

The **DAR** Story. By Lonnelle Aikman. Photos by B. Anthony Stewart and John E. Fletcher. 565-598, Nov. 1951

DNA (Deoxyribonucleic Acid):
• The Awesome Worlds Within a Cell. By Rick Gore. Photos by Bruce Dale. Paintings by Davis Meltzer. 355-395, Sept. 1976

DS-2 (Diving Saucer):
• At Home in the Sea. By Jacques-Yves Cousteau. 465-507, Apr. 1964

DACCA, Bangladesh:
• Bangladesh: Hope Nourishes a New Nation. By William S. Ellis. Photos by Dick Durrance II. 295-333, Sept. 1972
• Bangladesh: The Nightmare of Famine. Photos by Steve Raymer. 33-39, July 1975
• East Pakistan Drives Back the Jungle. By Jean and Franc Shor. 399-426, Mar. 1955

DADE COUNTY, Florida. *See* Miami

DAIRY FARMS. *See* Family Farms; 4-H Clubs; Thunder Hill Goat Farm

DAIRY INDUSTRY. *See* Cheese Making

DAK PEK, Viet Nam:
• Viet Nam's Montagnards. By Howard Sochurek. 443-487, Apr. 1968

DALAI LAMA:
• In Long-Forbidden Tibet. By Fred Ward. 218-259, Feb. 1980
• Little Tibet in Switzerland. By Laura Pilarski. Photos by Fred Mayer. 711-727, Nov. 1968
• My Life in Forbidden Lhasa. By Heinrich Harrer. 1-48, July 1955

DALE, BRUCE: Photographer:
• The Air-Safety Challenge. By Michael E. Long. 209-235, Aug. 1977
• Alaska: Rising Northern Star. By Joseph Judge. 730-767, June 1975
• America's Auto Mania. By David Jeffery. 24-31, *Special Report on Energy* (Feb. 1981)
• Appomattox: Where Grant and Lee Made Peace With Honor a Century Ago. By Ulysses S. Grant 3rd. 435-469, Apr. 1965
• The Awesome Worlds Within a Cell. By Rick Gore. Paintings by Davis Meltzer. 355-395, Sept. 1976
• The Bahamas: Boom Times and Buccaneering. By Peter Benchley. 364-395, Sept. 1982
• Bats Aren't All Bad. By Alvin Novick. 615-637, May 1973
• Behold the Computer Revolution. By Peter T. White. Photos by Bruce Dale and Emory Kristof. 593-633, Nov. 1970
• The Desert: An Age-old Challenge Grows. By Rick Gore. Photos by Georg Gerster and Bruce Dale. 586-639, Nov. 1979
• Freedom Speaks French in Ouagadougou. By John Scofield. 153-203, Aug. 1966
• Hong Kong, Saturday's Child. By Joseph Judge. 541-573, Oct. 1971
• Île de la Cité, Birthplace of Paris. By Kenneth MacLeish. 680-719, May 1968
• Journey to China's Far West. By Rick Gore. 292-331, Mar. 1980
• Kenya Says *Harambee!* By Allan C. Fisher, Jr. 151-205, Feb. 1969
• Magellan: First Voyage Around the World. By Alan Villiers. 721-753, June 1976
• The Navajos. By Ralph Looney. 740-781, Dec. 1972
• An Ozark Family Carves a Living and a Way of Life. 124-133, July 1975
• Panama, Link Between Oceans and Continents. By Jules B. Billard. 402-440, Mar. 1970
• The People of Cumberland Gap. By John Fetterman. 591-621, Nov. 1971
• The Philippines: Better Days Still Elude an Old Friend. By Don Moser. 360-391, Mar. 1977
• The Rhine: Europe's River of Legend. By William Graves. 449-499, Apr. 1967
• The Roadrunner–Clown of the Desert. By Martha A. Whitson. 694-702, May 1983
• The St. Lawrence River: Canada's Highway to the Sea. By William S. Ellis. 586-623, May 1980
• St. Louis: New Spirit Soars in Mid-America's Proud Old City. By Robert Paul Jordan. 605-641, Nov. 1965
• Shanghai: Born-again Giant. By Mike Edwards. 2-43, July 1980
"Muscle and smoke, commerce and crowds." A Shanghai Portfolio by Bruce Dale. 2-13
• Snow-mantled Stehekin: Where Solitude Is in Season. By Pat Hutson. 572-588, Apr. 1974
• Southern California's Trial by Mud and Water. By Nathaniel T. Kenney. 552-573, Oct. 1969
• Swing Low, Sweet Chariot! By Noel Grove. 2-35, July 1983
• Through Ozark Hills and Hollows. By Mike W. Edwards. 656-689, Nov. 1970
• Timber: How Much Is Enough? By John J. Putman. 485-511, Apr. 1974
• Washington: The City Freedom Built. By William Graves. Photos by Bruce Dale and Thomas Nebbia. 735-781, Dec. 1964
• When Gypsies Gather at Appleby Fair. 848-869, June 1972
• *White Mist* Cruises to Wreck-haunted St. Pierre and Miquelon. By Melville Bell Grosvenor. 378-419, Sept. 1967

DALE COLLECTION. *See* Chester Dale Collection

DALLAS, Texas:
• The Fabulous State of Texas. By Stanley Walker. Photos by B. Anthony Stewart and Thomas Nebbia. 149-195, Feb. 1961
• Texas! By Howard La Fay. Photos by Gordon W. Gahan. 440-483, Apr. 1980

DALLISON, KEN: Artist:
• *Columbia's* Astronauts' Own Story: Our Phenomenal First Flight. By John W. Young and Robert L. Crippen. 478-503, Oct. 1981
• When the Space Shuttle Finally Flies. By Rick Gore. Photos by Jon Schneeberger. 317-347, Mar. 1981

DALMATIA (Region), Yugoslavia:
• Yugoslavia, Between East and West. By George W. Long. Photos by Volkmar Wentzel. 141-172, Feb. 1951
• Yugoslavia: Six Republics in One. By Robert Paul Jordan. Photos by James P. Blair. 589-633, May 1970
• Yugoslavia's Window on the Adriatic. By Gilbert M. Grosvenor. 219-247, Feb. 1962

DALRYMPLE-HAMILTON, SIR FREDERICK:
• Rhododendron Glories of Southwest Scotland. By David S. Boyer. Photos by B. Anthony Stewart and author. 641-664, May 1954

DAMASCUS, Syria:
• Damascus, Syria's Uneasy Eden. By Robert Azzi. 512-535, Apr. 1974
• Jerusalem to Rome in the Path of St. Paul. By David S. Boyer. 707-759, Dec. 1956
• The Sword and the Sermon (Islam). By Thomas J. Abercrombie. 3-45, July 1972

DAMS:
• Along the Yangtze, Main Street of China. By W. Robert Moore. 325-356, Mar. 1948
• Around the "Great Lakes of the South." By Frederick Simpich. Photos by J. Baylor Roberts. Contents: TVA system. 463-491, Apr. 1948
• The Bittersweet Waters of the Lower Colorado. By Rowe Findley. Photos by Charles O'Rear. 540-569, Oct. 1973
• Britain Tackles the East African Bush. By W. Robert Moore. Included: Dam for Lake Victoria, just below Owen Falls. 311-352, Mar. 1950
• The Canadian North: Emerging Giant. By David S. Boyer. 1-43, July 1968
• Following the Trail of Lewis and Clark. By Ralph Gray. 707-750, June 1953
• From Sagebrush to Roses on the Columbia. By Leo A. Borah. Included: Dams completed and dams under construction: Albeni Falls, American Falls, Anderson Ranch, Bonneville, Chief Joseph, The Dalles, Detroit, Grand Coulee, Hungry Horse, Lookout Point, McNary, Minidoka, Palisades, Rock Island. 571-611, Nov. 1952

● A Map Maker Looks at the United States. By Newman Bumstead. Included: Grand Coulee, Hoover, Jackson Lake, Shasta. 705-748, June 1951
● The Mekong, River of Terror and Hope. By Peter T. White. Photos by W. E. Garrett. 737-787, Dec. 1968
● Our Most Precious Resource: Water. By Thomas Y. Canby. Photos by Ted Spiegel. 144-179, Aug. 1980
● Paraguay, Paradox of South America. By Gordon Young. Photos by O. Louis Mazzatenta. Included: Itaipú Hydroelectric Development. 240-269, Aug. 1982
● Powerhouse of the Northwest (Columbia River). By David S. Boyer. 821-847, Dec. 1974
● Quebec's Northern Dynamo. By Larry Kohl. Photos by Ottmar Bierwagen. 406-418, Mar. 1982
● That Dammed Missouri River. By Gordon Young. Photos by David Hiser. 374-413, Sept. 1971
● Whatever Happened to TVA? By Gordon Young. Photos by Emory Kristof. 830-863, June 1973
● *See also* Aswân High Dam; Powell, Lake, for Glen Canyon Dam; St. Lawrence Seaway

The **DANAKIL:** Nomads of Ethiopia's Wasteland. By Victor Englebert. 186-211, Feb. 1970

DANAKIL DEPRESSION, Ethiopia:
● The Danakil: Nomads of Ethiopia's Wasteland. By Victor Englebert. 186-211, Feb. 1970

DA NANG, Viet Nam:
● Behind the Headlines in Viet Nam. By Peter T. White. Photos by Winfield Parks. 149-189, Feb. 1967

DANUBE (River), Europe:
● The Danube: River of Many Nations, Many Names. By Mike Edwards. Photos by Winfield Parks. 455-485, Oct. 1977
● Down the Danube by Canoe. By William Slade Backer. Photos by Richard S. Durrance and Christopher G. Knight. 34-79, July 1965

DAR ES SALAAM, Tanzania:
● Tanzania Marches to Its Own Drum. By Peter T. White. Photos by Emory Kristof. 474-509, Apr. 1975
● Weighing the Aga Khan in Diamonds. Photos by David J. Carnegie. 317-324, Mar. 1947

DAR POMORZA:
● By Square-rigger from Baltic to Bicentennial. By Kenneth Garrett. 824-857, Dec. 1976

DARIÉN GAP, Panama
● We Drove Panama's Darién Gap. By Kip Ross. 368-389, Mar. 1961

DARIUS THE GREAT, King (Persia):
● Darius Carved History on Ageless Rock. By George G. Cameron. 825-844, Dec. 1950
● In the Footsteps of Alexander the Great. By Helen and Frank Schreider. Paintings by Tom Lovell. 1-65, Jan. 1968

DARIUSLEUT (Sect):
● The Hutterites, Plain People of the West. By William Albert Allard. 98-125, July 1970

DARLEY, JAMES M.:
● Chief Cartographer, NGS. 875, Dec. 1961; 897, Dec. 1962; 108, 109, July 1964
Author:
● New Atlas Maps Announced by the Society: Expanded Map Program, Marking National Geographic's 70th Year, Will Bring to Members Plates for a Big New Atlas. 66-68, Jan. 1958

DARWIN, CHARLES:
● The British Way. By Sir Evelyn Wrench. 421-541, Apr. 1949
● The Galapagos, Eerie Cradle of New Species. By Roger Tory Peterson. Photos by Alan and Joan Root. 541-585, Apr. 1967
● In the Wake of Darwin's *Beagle.* By Alan Villiers. Photos by James L. Stanfield. 449-495, Oct. 1969
● Lost World of the Galapagos. By Irving and Electa Johnson. 681-703, May 1959

DARWIN, Australia:
● The Top End of Down Under. By Kenneth MacLeish. Photos by Thomas Nebbia. 145-174, Feb. 1973

DASARA (Festival): Mysore, India:
● Mysore Celebrates the Death of a Demon. By Luc Bouchage. Photos by Ylla. 706-711, May 1958

DASSEN ISLAND, South Africa:
● Oil and Penguins Don't Mix. Photos by Mike Holmes. 384-397, Mar. 1973

DATA PROCESSING, Electronic:
● Behold the Computer Revolution. By Peter T. White. Photos by Bruce Dale and Emory Kristof. 593-633, Nov. 1970
● Computer Helps Scholars Re-create an Egyptian Temple. By Ray Winfield Smith. Photos by Emory Kristof. NGS research grant. 634-655, Nov. 1970
● *See also* Computer Applications; Computer Technology

DATE LINE: United Nations, New York. By Carolyn Bennett Patterson. Photos by B. Anthony Stewart and John E. Fletcher. 305-331, Sept. 1961

DATE RAISING:
● The Lure of the Changing Desert (California). 817-824, June 1954

DATING METHODS:
● The Anasazi–Riddles in the Ruins. By Thomas Y. Canby. Photos by Dewitt Jones and David Brill. Paintings by Roy Andersen. Included: Archaeomagnetism; radiocarbon dating; tree-ring dating. 554-592, Nov. 1982
● Ancient Europe Is Older Than We Thought. By Colin Renfrew. Photos by Adam Woolfitt. Included: Radiocarbon dating; tree-ring dating. 615-623, Nov. 1977
● The Search for the First Americans. By Thomas Y. Canby. Photos by Kerby Smith. Paintings by Roy Andersen. Included: Radiocarbon dating; amino acid racemization; dentition; stratigraphy. 330-363, Sept. 1979
● This Changing Earth. By Samuel W. Matthews. Included: Carbon 14 dating; fossil dating; paleomagnetics; potassium-argon dating; radioactive-isotope dating. 1-37, Jan. 1973
● What's Happening to Our Climate? By Samuel W. Matthews. Included: Ice-core dating; Sea-core dating; Tree-ring dating. 576-615, Nov. 1976
● *See also* Archeomagnetism; Potassium-Argon Dating; Radiocarbon Dating; Tree-ring Dating

DAUFUSKIE (Island), South Carolina:
● Sea Islands: Adventuring Along the South's Surprising Coast. By James Cerruti. Photos by Thomas Nebbia and James L. Amos. 366-393, Mar. 1971

DAUGHTERS OF THE AMERICAN REVOLUTION:
● The DAR Story. By Lonnelle Aikman. Photos by B. Anthony Stewart and John E. Fletcher. 565-598, Nov. 1951

The **DAUNTLESS** Little Stilt. By Frederick Kent Truslow. 241-245, Aug. 1960

DÁVALOS, FELIPE: Artist:
● The Aztecs. By Bart McDowell. Photos by David Hiser. 714-751, Dec. 1980
● The Building of Tenochtitlan. By Augusto F. Molina Montes. 753-765, Dec. 1980

DÁVALOS HURTADO, EUSEBIO:
Author:
● Into the Well of Sacrifice. I. Return to the Sacred Cenote. 540-549, Oct. 1961

DAVENPORT, WILLIAM: Author:
● Amiable Amsterdam. Photos by Adam Woolfitt. 683-705, May 1974
● Bordeaux: Fine Wines and Fiery Gascons. Photos by Adam Woolfitt. 233-259, Aug. 1980
● France's Wild, Watery South, the Camargue. 696-726, May 1973
● Living the Good Life in Burgundy. Photos by Robert Freson. 794-817, June 1978
● Provence, Empire of the Sun. Photos by James A. Sugar. 692-715, May 1975

DAVIDSON, ROBYN: Author:
● Alone Across the Outback (Australia). Photos by Rick Smolan. 581-611, May 1978

DAVIDSON, TREAT:
Author-Photographer:
● Bullfrog Ballet Filmed in Flight. 791-799, June 1963
● Freezing the Trout's Lightning Leap. 525-530, Apr. 1958
● Inside the World of the Honeybee. 188-217, Aug. 1959
● Rose Aphids. 851-859, June 1961

• Tree Snails, Gems of the Everglades. 372-387, Mar. 1965
Photographer:
• Alligators: Dragons in Distress. By Archie Carr. Photos by Treat Davidson and Laymond Hardy. 133-148, Jan. 1967
• Moths That Behave Like Hummingbirds. 770-775, June 1965

DA VINCI, Project:
• Laboratory in a Dirty Sky. By Rudolf J. Engelmann and Vera Simons. NGS research grant. 616-621, Nov. 1976

DAVIS, MALCOLM: Author:
• Nature's Clown, the Penguin. By David Hellyer and Malcolm Davis. 405-428, Sept. 1952

DAVIS, NEAL P.: Photographer:
• The Past Is Present in Greenfield Village. By Beverley M. Bowie. Photos by Neal P. Davis and Willard R. Culver. 96-127, July 1958

DAVIS STRAIT, North America-Greenland:
• I Sailed with Portugal's Captains Courageous. By Alan Villiers. 565-596, May 1952

DAVY, SIR HUMPHRY:
• The British Way. By Sir Evelyn Wrench. 421-541, Apr. 1949

DAWSON, Canada:
• Along the Yukon Trail. By Amos Burg. 395-416, Sept. 1953
• Yukon Fever: Call of the North. By Robert Booth. Photos by George F. Mobley. 548-578, Apr. 1978

DAY of the Rice God. Photos by H. Edward Kim. Text by Douglas Lee. 78-85, July 1978

The **DAY** the Sky Fell. By Rowe Findley. 50-65, Jan. 1981

DAYTON, WILLIAM A.: Author:
• Beauty and Bounty of Southern State Trees. Paintings by Walter A. Weber. 508-552, Oct. 1957
• Wealth and Wonder of Northern State Trees. Paintings by Walter A. Weber. 651-691, Nov. 1955

DAZZLING Corals of Palau. By Thomas O'Neill. Photos by Douglas Faulkner. 136-150, July 1978

DAZZLING Legacy of an Ancient Quest. By Alice J. Hall. 293-311, Mar. 1977

DEAD, Rites for the. *See* Burial Customs; Funerals

DEAD SEA, Israel-Jordan:
• Abraham, the Friend of God. By Kenneth MacLeish. Photos by Dean Conger. 739-789, Dec. 1966
• Geographical Twins (Holy Land and Utah) a World Apart. By David S. Boyer. 848-859, Dec. 1958
• The Living Dead Sea. By Harvey Arden. Photos by Nathan Benn. Included: Map showing Israeli-occupied territory, water fluctuations of Dead Sea, diagram comparing Dead Sea water level with sea level. 225-245, Feb. 1978

DEAD SEA SCROLLS:
• The Men Who Hid the Dead Sea Scrolls. By A. Douglas Tushingham. Paintings by Peter V. Bianchi. 785-808, Dec. 1958

The **DEADLY** Fisher. By Charles E. Lane. 388-397, Mar. 1963

The **DEAF,** Schools for:
• Deaf Children Learn to Talk at Clarke School. By Lilian Grosvenor. Photos by Willard R. Culver. 379-397, Mar. 1955
• Washington's Historic Georgetown. By William A. Kinney. Included: Volta Bureau. 513-544, Apr. 1953

De ALWIS, LYN: Author:
• Sri Lanka's Wildlife: A Nation Rises to the Challenge. Photos by Dieter and Mary Plage. 274-278, Aug. 1983

DEARBORN, Michigan. *See* Henry Ford Museum

DEATH of an Island, Tristan da Cunha. By P.J.F. Wheeler. 678-695, May 1962

DEATH of Marchessa. Photos by Peter G. Veit. 508-511, Apr. 1981

DEATH VALLEY NATIONAL MONUMENT, California:
• Death Valley, the Land and the Legend. By Rowe Findley. Photos by David Hiser. 69-103, Jan. 1970
• Getting to Know the Wild Burros of Death Valley. By Patricia des Roses Moehlman. Photos by Ira S. Lerner and author. NGS research grant. 502-517, Apr. 1972
■ The Great Mojave Desert 294A-294B, Feb. 1971
• *See also* Los Angeles Aqueduct

De BEERS CONSOLIDATED MINES, Ltd.:
• The Incredible Crystal: Diamonds. By Fred Ward. 85-113, Jan. 1979

De BRY, THEODORE. *See* Bry, Theodore de

A **DECADE** of Innovation, a Lifetime of Service (Melville Bell Grosvenor). By Bart McDowell. 270-278, Aug. 1982

DECEPTION: Formula for Survival. By Robert F. Sisson. 394-415, Mar. 1980

DECEPTION ISLAND, Antarctica:
• Antarctica's Nearer Side. By Samuel W. Matthews. Photos by William R. Curtsinger. 622-655, Nov. 1971

DECOY FISH:
• Something's Fishy About That Fin! Photos by Robert J. Shallenberger and William D. Madden. 224-227, Aug. 1974

DECOYS:
• Humble Masterpieces: Decoys. By George Reiger. Photos by Kenneth Garrett. 639-663, Nov. 1983

DEEP DIVER (Submarine):
• A Taxi for the Deep Frontier. By Kenneth MacLeish. Photos by Bates Littlehales. 139-150, Jan. 1968

DEEP Diving off Japan. By Georges S. Houot. 138-150, Jan. 1960

DEEP in the Heart of "Swissconsin." By William H. Nicholas. Photos by J. Baylor Roberts. 781-800, June 1947

DEEP SEA DRILLING PROJECT:
• This Changing Earth. By Samuel W. Matthews. 1-37, Jan. 1973

DEEP-SEA RIFTS. *See* Rifts, Oceanfloor

DEEP-SEA Window Into the Earth. By Robert D. Ballard. Photos by Emory Kristof. 228-249, Aug. 1976

DEEP SOUTH, The Making of America map series. Included: Alabama, Florida, Georgia, Louisiana, Mississippi, South Carolina, and parts of Arkansas, North Carolina, and Tennessee. On reverse: Indian Legacy, Imperial Footholds, Three Empires and Three Races, Cotton Kingdom, Postbellum, New Deep South, Subtropical Playground. Aug. 1983

DEEP SUBMERGENCE SYSTEMS REVIEW GROUP (DSSRG). *See* Tomorrow on the Deep Frontier

The **DEEPEST** Days. By Robert Sténuit. 534-547, Apr. 1965

DEEPSTAR Explores the Ocean Floor. Photos by Ron Church. 110-129, Jan. 1971

DEER:
• Père David's Deer Saved From Extinction. By Larry Kohl. Photos by Bates Littlehales. 478-485, Oct. 1982
• *See also* Caribou; Reindeer

DEERFIELD, Massachusetts:
• Deerfield Keeps a Truce With Time. By Bart McDowell. Photos by Robert W. Madden. 780-809, June 1969

DEERING, JAMES: Estate:
• Vizcaya: An Italian Palazzo in Miami. By William H. Nicholas. Photos by Justin Locke. 595-604, Nov. 1950

DeFEO, THOMAS A.: Photographer:
• Satellites Gave Warning of Midwest Floods. By Peter T. White. 574-592, Oct. 1969
• Shenandoah, I Long to Hear You. By Mike W. Edwards. 554-588, Apr. 1970

DEFOE, DANIEL:
• The British Way. By Sir Evelyn Wrench. 421-541, Apr. 1949

DEFORESTATION:
• Park at the Top of the World: Mount Everest National Park. By Rick Ridgeway. Photos by Nicholas DeVore III. Note: Sagarmatha National Park was established to preserve Khumbu district forests, which have been thinned by demands of climbers and trekkers for firewood. 704-725, June 1982
Preserving a Mountain Heritage. By Sir Edmund Hillary. 696-703
■ Rain Forest. 824, Dec. 1982
• Tropical Rain Forests: Nature's Dwindling Treasures. By Peter T. White. Photos by James P. Blair. Paintings by Barron Storey. 2-47, Jan. 1983

DEGEN, ALAN R.: Photographer:
• Saving the Philippine Eagle. By Robert S. Kennedy. Photos by Alan R. Degen, Neil L. Rettig, and Wolfgang A. Salb. 847-856, June 1981

DEIR EL-BALAH (Site), Israeli-occupied Gaza Strip:
• Lost Outpost of the Egyptian Empire. By Trude Dothan. Photos by Sisse Brimberg. Paintings by Lloyd K. Townsend. NGS research grant. 739-769, Dec. 1982

DE LA HABA, LOUIS: Author:
• Belize, the Awakening Land. Photos by Michael E. Long. 124-146, Jan. 1972
• Guatemala, Maya and Modern. Photos by Joseph J. Scherschel. 661-689, Nov. 1974
• Mexico, the City That Founded a Nation. Photos by Albert Moldvay. 638-669, May 1973

DELAWARE:
• Delaware–Who Needs to Be Big? By Jane Vessels. Photos by Kevin Fleming. 171-197, Aug. 1983
• "Delmarva," Gift of the Sea. By Catherine Bell Palmer. 367-399, Sept. 1950
• Our Changing Atlantic Coastline. By Nathaniel T. Kenney. Photos by B. Anthony Stewart. Included: Dewey Beach; Rehoboth Beach. 860-887, Dec. 1962
• Today on the Delaware, Penn's Glorious River. By Albert W. Atwood. Photos by Robert F. Sisson. 1-40, July 1952
• *See also* Henlopen Dunes; Noxontown Pond

DELAWARE (River), U. S.:
• Today on the Delaware, Penn's Glorious River. By Albert W. Atwood. Photos by Robert F. Sisson. 1-40, July 1952

DELHI, India:
• Delhi, Capital of a New Dominion. By Phillips Talbot. 597-630, Nov. 1947
• *See also* New Delhi

DELIGHT (Yawl):
• Sailing Iceland's Rugged Coasts. By Wright Britton. Photos by James A. Sugar. 228-265, Aug. 1969

DE'LISLE, GORDON: Photographer:
• Australia. By Alan Villiers. 309-385, Sept. 1963
The West and the South. 309-345; The Settled East, the Barrier Reef, the Center. 347-385

DELMARVA PENINSULA (Delaware-Maryland-Virginia):
• "Delmarva," Gift of the Sea. By Catherine Bell Palmer. 367-399, Sept. 1950

DELOS (Island), Greece:
• Fish Men Discover a 2,200-year-old Greek Ship. By Jacques-Yves Cousteau. NGS research grant. 1-36, Jan. 1954
• The Isles of Greece: Aegean Birthplace of Western Culture. By Melville Bell Grosvenor. Photos by Edwin Stuart Grosvenor and Winfield Parks. 147-193, Aug. 1972

DELTA, Inland. *See* California Delta

DELTA MARSH, Manitoba, Canada:
• Western Grebes: The Birds That Walk on Water. By Gary L. Nuechterlein. NGS research grant. 624-637, May 1982

DELTA WATERFOWL RESEARCH STATION, Manitoba, Canada: Study Grant:
• Western Grebes. 629, May 1982

DEMOCRACY'S Fortress: Unsinkable Malta. By Ernle Bradford. Photos by Ted H. Funk. 852-879, June 1969

DEMOCRATIC PEOPLE'S REPUBLIC OF KOREA. *See* Korea, Democratic People's Republic of (North Korea)

DENE NATION:
• Peoples of the Arctic. 144-223, Feb. 1983
I. Introduction by Joseph Judge. 144-149; II. Hunters of the Lost Spirit: Canadians. By Priit J. Vesilind. Photos by David Alan Harvey. 174-189

DENIS, ARMAND:
• New Guinea's Rare Birds and Stone Age Men. By E. Thomas Gilliard. Note: Armand Denis was the leader of the American Museum-Armand Denis Expedition. NGS research grant. 421-488, Apr. 1953

DENISE (Diving Saucer):
• Diving Saucer Takes to the Deep. By Jacques-Yves Cousteau. NGS research grant. 571-586, Apr. 1960

DENISON, Cape, Antarctica:
• Voyage to the Antarctic. By David Lewis. 544-562, Apr. 1983

DENKER, DEBRA: Author:
• Pakistan's Kalash: People of Fire and Fervor. Photos by Steve McCurry. 458-473, Oct. 1981

DENMARK:
• Baltic Cruise of the *Caribbee.* By Carleton Mitchell. 605-646, Nov. 1950
• By Full-rigged Ship to Denmark's Fairyland. By Alan Villiers. Photos by Alexander Taylor and author. 809-828, Dec. 1955
• Denmark, Field of the Danes. By William Graves. Photos by Thomas Nebbia. 245-275, Feb. 1974
• Friendly Flight to Northern Europe. By Lyndon B. Johnson. Photos by Volkmar Wentzel. 268-293, Feb. 1964
• Lifelike Man Preserved 2,000 Years in Peat. By P. V. Glob. 419-430, Mar. 1954
• The Magic World of Hans Christian Andersen. By Harvey Arden. Photos by Sisse Brimberg. Included: Copenhagen; Odense. 825-849, Dec. 1979
• Thumbs Up Round the North Sea's Rim. By Frances James. Photos by Erica Koch. 685-704, May 1952
• 2,000 Miles Through Europe's Oldest Kingdom. By Isobel Wylie Hutchison. Photos by Maynard Owen Williams. 141-180, Feb. 1949
• Under Canvas in the Atomic Age (U. S. Coast Guard). By Alan Villiers. 49-84, July 1955
• The Vikings. By Howard La Fay. Photos by Ted Spiegel. 492-541, Apr. 1970
• *See also* Copenhagen; Faeroe Islands; Greenland

DENNISON, EDWARD S.: Author:
• Ambassadors of Good Will: The Peace Corps. By Sargent Shriver and Peace Corps Volunteers. 297-345, Sept. 1964
Bolivia. 315-319

DENTON, IVAN, Family:
• An Ozark Family Carves a Living and a Way of Life. Photos by Bruce Dale. 124-133, July 1975

DENVER, Colorado:
• Colorado, the Rockies' Pot of Gold. By Edward J. Linehan. Photos by James L. Amos. 157-201, Aug. 1969
• Colorado by Car and Campfire. By Kathleen Revis. 207-248, Aug. 1954
• Denver, Colorado's Rocky Mountain High. By John J. Putman. Photos by David Cupp. 383-411, Mar. 1979

DEOXYRIBONUCLEIC ACID (DNA):
• The Awesome Worlds Within a Cell. By Rick Gore. Photos by Bruce Dale. Paintings by Davis Meltzer. Included: "Language of Life" foldout showing the replication of DNA and the manufacture of RNA and proteins. 355-395, Sept. 1976

DE ROOS, ROBERT: Author:
• Arizona: Booming Youngster of the West. Photos by Robert F. Sisson. 299-343, Mar. 1963
• Costa Rica, Free of the Volcano's Veil. 125-152, July 1965
• The Flower Seed Growers: Gardening's Color Merchants. Photos by Jack Fields. 720-738, May 1968
• Los Angeles, City of the Angels. Photos by Thomas Nebbia. 451-501, Oct. 1962
• The Magic Worlds of Walt Disney. Photos by Thomas Nebbia. 159-207, Aug. 1963
• Massachusetts Builds for Tomorrow. Photos by B. Anthony Stewart. 790-843, Dec. 1966
• New England's "Lively Experiment," Rhode Island. Photos by Fred Ward. 370-401, Sept. 1968
• The Philippines, Freedom's Pacific Frontier. Photos by Ted Spiegel. 301-351, Sept. 1966

DESERT MUSEUM, Arizona:
• Arizona's Window on Wildlife. By Lewis Wayne Walker. 240-250, Feb. 1958

DESERT Ordeal of the Knights (First Crusade). By Franc Shor. Photos by Thomas Nebbia. 797-837, Dec. 1963

DESERT River Through Navajo Land. By Alfred M. Bailey. Photos by author and Fred G. Brandenburg. 149-172, Aug. 1947

DESERT Sheikdoms of Arabia's Pirate Coast. By Ronald Codrai. 65-104, July 1956

DESERTIFICATION:
● The Desert: An Age-old Challenge Grows. By Rick Gore. Photos by Georg Gerster and Bruce Dale. 586-639, Nov. 1979

DESERTS:
● Abundant Life in a Desert Land. By Walter Meayers Edwards. 424-436, Sept. 1973
● Alone Across the Outback (Australia). By Robyn Davidson. Photos by Rick Smolan. 581-611, May 1978
● The Desert: An Age-old Challenge Grows. By Rick Gore. Photos by Georg Gerster and Bruce Dale. 586-639, Nov. 1979
◆ *The Desert Realm, Lands of Majesty and Mystery.* 1982
● Egypt's Desert of Promise. By Farouk El-Baz. Photos by Georg Gerster. 190-221, Feb. 1982
◆ *Great American Deserts.* Announced. 870-874, June 1972
● The Hohokam: First Masters of the American Desert. By Emil W. Haury. Photos by Helga Teiwes. 670-695, May 1967
● In Search of Arabia's Past. By Peter Bruce Cornwall. 493-522, Apr. 1948
● Journey to China's Far West. By Rick Gore. Photos by Bruce Dale. 292-331, Mar. 1980
● Lake Powell: Waterway to Desert Wonders. By Walter Meayers Edwards. 44-75, July 1967
● The Lure of the Changing Desert. 817-824, June 1954
● Magnetic Clues Help Date the Past. By Kenneth F. Weaver. 696-701, May 1967
● Rediscovering America's Forgotten Crops. By Noel D. Vietmeyer. Photos by Burgess Blevins. Paintings by Paul M. Breeden. 702-712, May 1981
● Report from the Locust Wars. By Tony and Dickey Chapelle. 545-562, Apr. 1953
● The Roadrunner–Clown of the Desert. By Martha A. Whitson. Photos by Bruce Dale. 694-702, May 1983
● Scorpions: Living Fossils of the Sands. By Paul A. Zahl. 436-442, Mar. 1968
◆ *Wonders of the Desert World.* Announced. 718-720, Nov. 1976
● *See also* Atacama Desert, Chile; Baja California; Big Bend National Park, Texas; Chubut Province, Argentina; Colorado Desert; Coober Pedy, South Australia; Death Valley National Monument; Four Corners Country; Gobi; Great Rift Valley; Guadalupe Mountains National Park; Iran; Mazatzal Wilderness, Arizona; Mojave Desert; Namib Desert; Oman; Organ Pipe Cactus National Monument; Sahara; Saudi Arabia; Sinai; Sonoran Desert

DESERTS, Salt. *See* Danakil Depression, Ethiopia

DESPUJOLS, JEAN: Artist:
● Portrait of Indochina. By W. Robert Moore and Maynard Owen Williams. 461-490, Apr. 1951

BRUCE DALE, NGS

Desert: signature of a sidewinder

DETROIT, Michigan:
● Swing Low, Sweet Chariot! By Noel Grove. Photos by Bruce Dale. 2-35, July 1983
● The Two Worlds of Michigan. By Noel Grove. Photos by James L. Amos. 802-843, June 1979
● Work-hard, Play-hard Michigan. By Andrew H. Brown. 279-320, Mar. 1952

DETROIT (River), Michigan-Ontario:
● *J. W. Westcott,* Postman for the Great Lakes. By Cy La Tour. 813-824, Dec. 1950

DETWILER, MARGARET M.: Author:
● Hays, Kansas, at the Nation's Heart. Photos by John E. Fletcher. 461-490, Apr. 1952

DEVASTATED Land and Homeless People (Bali). By Samuel W. Matthews. Photos by Robert F. Sisson. 447-458, Sept. 1963

DEVEREUX, WALTER B.: Author:
● New York Again Hails the Horse. 697-720, Nov. 1954

DEVIL DANCE:
● A Journey to "Little Tibet." By Enakshi Bhavnani. Photos by Volkmar Wentzel. 603-634, May 1951
● A Woman Paints the Tibetans. By Lafugie. 659-692, May 1949

DEVIL MOUNTAIN, Venezuela. *See* Auyán-tepuí

DEVILLERS, CAROLE E.:
Author-Photographer:
● Oursi, Magnet in the Desert (Upper Volta). 512-525, Apr. 1980
● What Future for the Wayana Indians? 66-83, Jan. 1983

DEVIL'S ISLAND, Îles du Salut, French Guiana:
● *Yankee* Roams the Orient. By Irving and Electa Johnson. 327-370, Mar. 1951

DEVONSHIRE, England:
● Channel Cruise to Glorious Devon. By Alan Villiers. Photos by Bates Littlehales. 208-259, Aug. 1963

DEVORE, NICHOLAS, III:
Photographer:
● Along the Great Divide. By Mike Edwards. 483-515, Oct. 1979
● Brazil's Golden Beachhead. By Bart McDowell. 246-277, Feb. 1978
● *Hokule'a* Follows the Stars to Tahiti. By David Lewis. 512-537, Oct. 1976
● Park at the Top of the World: Mount Everest National Park. By Rick Ridgeway. 704-725, June 1982
● Should They Build a Fence Around Montana? By Mike W. Edwards. 614-657, May 1976
Growing Up in Montana. 650-657
● Trek Across Arctic America. By Colin Irwin. 295-321, Mar. 1974
● Wind, Wave, Star, and Bird. By David Lewis. 747-781, Dec. 1974

DEW LINE (Distant Early Warning Line), Sentry of the Far North. By Howard La Fay. 128-146, July 1958

JAMES L. STANFIELD, VICTOR R. BOSWELL, JR., BOTH NGS

Questing for Gems: Hope Diamond

DHAHRAN (Aẓ Ẓahrān), Saudi Arabia:
• In Search of Arabia's Past. By Peter Bruce Cornwall. 493-522, Apr. 1948
• Saudi Arabia: Beyond the Sands of Mecca. By Thomas J. Abercrombie. 1-53, Jan. 1966

DHANI NIVAT, Prince. *See* Sonakul, D.

DHOFAR PROVINCE, Oman:
• Oman: Guardian of the Gulf. By Thomas J. Abercrombie. Photos by the author and Lynn Abercrombie. 344-377, Sept. 1981

DHOWS:
• Clove-scented Zanzibar. By W. Robert Moore. 261-278, Feb. 1952
• In the Wake of Sindbad. By Tim Severin. Photos by Richard Greenhill. 2-41, July 1982
• Sailing with Sindbad's Sons. By Alan Villiers. Contents: *Bayan; Sheikh Mansur;* and Baggalas, Booms, Sambuks, Zarooks. 675-688, Nov. 1948
• Twilight of the Arab Dhow. By Marion Kaplan. 330-351, Sept. 1974

DIABLE, Île du, French Guiana. *See* Devil's Island

DIAMOND JUBILEE:
• Weighing the Aga Khan in Diamonds. Photos by David J. Carnegie. 317-324, Mar. 1947

DIAMOND ROCK ("H.M.S. Diamond Rock"), Martinique:
• *Carib* Cruises the West Indies. By Carleton Mitchell. 1-56, Jan. 1948

DIAMONDS:
• Britain Tackles the East African Bush. By W. Robert Moore. Included: Williamson mine in Tanganyika. 311-352, Mar. 1950
• Exploring the World of Gems. By W. F. Foshag. 779-810, Dec. 1950
• The Incredible Crystal: Diamonds. By Fred Ward. 85-113, Jan. 1979
• The Jungle Was My Home. By Sasha Siemel. 695-712, Nov. 1952
• The Many-sided Diamond. By George S. Switzer. 568-586, Apr. 1958
• Namibia: Nearly a Nation? By Bryan Hodgson. Photos by Jim Brandenburg. 755-797, June 1982
• Questing for Gems. By George S. Switzer. 835-863, Dec. 1971
• Weighing the Aga Khan in Diamonds. Photos by David J. Carnegie. 317-324, Mar. 1947
• White Magic in the Belgian Congo. By W. Robert Moore. 321-362, Mar. 1952

DIARY of the President's Daughter: I See America First. By Lynda Bird Johnson. Photos by William Albert Allard. 874-904, Dec. 1965

DIATOMS:
• Those Marvelous, Myriad Diatoms. By Richard B. Hoover. 871-878, June 1979

DICK SMITH EXPLORER (Schooner):
• Voyage to the Antarctic. By David Lewis. 544-562, Apr. 1983

DICKENS, CHARLES:
• The British Way. By Sir Evelyn Wrench. 421-541, Apr. 1949
• The England of Charles Dickens. By Richard W. Long. Photos by Adam Woolfitt. 443-483, Apr. 1974

DICKEY CHAPELLE Killed in Action. By W. E. Garrett. 270-271, Feb. 1966

DICKINSON, EMILY:
• Literary Landmarks of Massachusetts. By William H. Nicholas. Photos by B. Anthony Stewart and John E. Fletcher. 279-310, Mar. 1950

DIEGO GARCIA (Island), Indian Ocean:
• Crosscurrents Sweep the Indian Ocean. By Bart McDowell. Photos by Steve Raymer. 422-457, Oct. 1981

DIETZ, ROBERT S.: Author:
• The Explosive Birth of Myojin Island. 117-128, Jan. 1954

DIFFENDERFER, HOPE A.: Author:
• Okinawa, the Island Rebuilt. 265-288, Feb. 1955

A **DIFFERENT** Communism: Hungary's New Way. By John J. Putman. Photos by Bill Weems. 225-261, Feb. 1983

The **DIFFIDENT** Truffle, France's Gift to Gourmets. 419-426, Sept. 1956

DIKES AND LEVEES:
• California's Surprising Inland Delta. By Judith and Neil Morgan. Photos by Charles O'Rear. Included: Map showing the 1,100 miles of levees that rim the 55 islands reclaimed from marshland. 409-430, Sept. 1976
• Helping Holland Rebuild Her Land. By Gilbert M. Grosvenor and Charles Neave. 365-413, Sept. 1954
▪ Holland Against the Sea. 1970
• The Lower Mississippi. By Willard Price. Photos by W. D. Vaughn. 681-725, Nov. 1960
• Mississippi Delta: The Land of the River. By Douglas Lee. Photos by C. C. Lockwood. 226-253, Aug. 1983

DILMUN (Ancient Civilization):
• Bahrain: Hub of the Persian Gulf. By Thomas J. Abercrombie. Photos by Steve Raymer. 300-329, Sept. 1979

DIMANCESCU, DAN: Author:
• Americans Afoot in Rumania. Photos by Dick Durrance II and Christopher G. Knight. 810-845, June 1969
• Kayak Odyssey: From the Inland Sea to Tokyo. Photos by Christopher G. Knight. 295-337, Sept. 1967

DINGLE PENINSULA, Ireland:
• Irish Ways Live On in Dingle. By Bryan Hodgson. Photos by Linda Bartlett. 551-576, Apr. 1976

DINKELSBÜHL (Germany) Rewards Its Children. By Charles Belden. 255-268, Feb. 1957

DINKINS, STEPHANIE:
Author-Photographer:
• Lanzarote, the Strangest Canary. 117-139, Jan. 1969

DINOSAUR NATIONAL MONUMENT, Colorado-Utah:
● Shooting Rapids in Dinosaur Country. By Jack Breed. Photos by author and Justin Locke. 363-390, Mar. 1954

DINOSAURS:
◆ *Dinosaurs.* Announced. 736-738, Nov. 1972
● A New Look at Dinosaurs. By John H. Ostrom. Paintings by Roy Andersen. NGS research grant. 152-185, Aug. 1978
● We Captured a 'Live' Brontosaur. By Roland T. Bird. 707-722, May 1954
● *See also* Dinosaur National Monument

DIOMEDE ISLANDS, Bering Strait:
● Alaska's Russian Frontier: Little Diomede. Photos by Audrey and Frank Morgan. 551-562, Apr. 1951
● Nomad in Alaska's Outback. By Thomas J. Abercrombie. 540-567, Apr. 1969
● *North Star* Cruises Alaska's Wild West. By Amos Burg. 57-86, July 1952

DIOXIN:
● The Pesticide Dilemma. By Allen A. Boraiko. Photos by Fred Ward. 145-183, Feb. 1980

DISASTER in Paradise (Bali). 436-458, Sept. 1963
I. Eruption of Mount Agung. By Windsor P. Booth. Photos by Robert F. Sisson. 436-447; II. Devastated Land and Homeless People. By Samuel W. Matthews. Photos by Robert F. Sisson. 447-458

The **DISASTER** of El Chichón. By Boris Weintraub. Photos by Guillermo Aldana E. and Kenneth Garrett. 654-684, Nov. 1982
Volcanic Cloud May Alter Earth's Climate. By Robert I. Tilling. 672-675

DISASTER RELIEF:
● The American Red Cross: A Century of Service. By Louise Levathes. Photos by Annie Griffiths. 777-791, June 1981

DISCOVERED: the Monarch's Mexican Haven. By Fred A. Urquhart. Photos by Bianca Lavies. NGS research grant. 161-173, Aug. 1976

DISCOVERERS. *See* Explorers, Discoverers, and Navigators

DISCOVERY. *See* Exploration and Discovery

The **DISCUS FISH** Yields a Secret. By Gene Wolfsheimer. 675-681, May 1960

DISEASE:
● Mosquitoes, the Mighty Killers. By Lewis T. Nielsen. Included: Dengue fever, dog heartworm, encephalitis, filariasis, malaria, and yellow fever. 427-440, Sept. 1979
● The Rat, Lapdog of the Devil. By Thomas Y. Canby. Photos by James L. Stanfield. Included: Map showing plague areas of the Americas, Africa, and Asia; the number of reported cases in 1975. 60-87, July 1977
● *See also* Cancer Research; Hansen's Disease; Smallpox; *and* Medicine and Health

DISNEY, WALT:
● The Magic Worlds of Walt Disney. By Robert de Roos. Photos by Thomas Nebbia. 159-207, Aug. 1963
● Walt Disney: Genius of Laughter and Learning. By Melville Bell Grosvenor. 157D, Aug. 1963

DISNEY WORLD, Florida:
● Florida's Booming–and Beleaguered–Heartland. By Joseph Judge. Photos by Jonathan Blair. 585-621, Nov. 1973

DISNEYLAND, Anaheim, California:
● The Magic Worlds of Walt Disney. By Robert de Roos. Photos by Thomas Nebbia. 159-207, Aug. 1963

The **DISPOSSESSED** (Somali Refugees). By Larry Kohl. 756-763, June 1981

DISTANT EARLY WARNING LINE. *See* DEW Line

DISTRICT OF COLUMBIA. *See* Washington, D. C.

DIVE Into the Great Rift. By Robert D. Ballard. Photos by Emory Kristof. 604-615, May 1975

DIVERS, Land: New Hebrides. *See* Land Divers

DIVERS AND DIVING:
● Ama, Sea Nymphs of Japan. By Luis Marden. 122-135, July 1971
● At Home in the Sea. By Jacques-Yves Cousteau. 465-507, Apr. 1964
● Australia's Great Barrier Reef. Photos by Valerie and Ron Taylor. 728-741, June 1973
● The Deepest Days. By Robert Sténuit. NGS research grant. 534-547, Apr. 1965
● Diving Beneath Arctic Ice. By Joseph B. MacInnis. Photos by William R. Curtsinger. 248-267, Aug. 1973
● Diving Saucer Takes to the Deep. By Jacques-Yves Cousteau. NGS research grant. 571-586, Apr. 1960
◆ *Exploring the Deep Frontier.* 1980
● Goggle Fishing in California Waters. By David Hellyer. Photos by Lamar Boren. 615-632, May 1949
● A Jawbreaker for Sharks. By Valerie Taylor. Contents: A chain-mail diving suit. 664-667, May 1981
● Outpost Under the Ocean. By Edwin A. Link. Photos by Bates Littlehales. NGS research grant. 530-533, Apr. 1965
● Sharks: Magnificent and Misunderstood. By Eugenie Clark. Photos by David Doubilet. Included: Antishark cages. NGS research grant. 138-187, Aug. 1981
● Stalking Seals Under Antarctic Ice. By Carleton Ray. 54-65, Jan. 1966
● A Taxi for the Deep Frontier. By Kenneth MacLeish. Photos by Bates Littlehales. 139-150, Jan. 1968
● Tektite II. 256-296, Aug. 1971
I. Science's Window on the Sea. By John G. VanDerwalker. Photos by Bates Littlehales. 256-289; II. All-girl Team Tests the Habitat. By Sylvia A. Earle. Paintings by Pierre Mion. 291-296
● Tomorrow on the Deep Frontier. By Edwin A. Link. NGS research grant. 778-801, June 1964
● Twenty Fathoms Down for Mother-of-Pearl. By Winston Williams. Photos by Bates Littlehales. 512-529, Apr. 1962
● A Walk in the Deep. By Sylvia A. Earle. Photos by Al Giddings and Chuck Nicklin. Included: First open ocean use of diving suit "Jim" for scientific research; deepest solo exploration of its kind yet made. 624-631, May 1980
● Working for Weeks on the Sea Floor. By Jacques-Yves Cousteau. Photos by Philippe Cousteau and Bates Littlehales. NGS research grant. 498-537, Apr. 1966
◆ *World Beneath the Sea.* Announced. 868-875, June 1967
▮ The World of Jacques-Yves Cousteau. 529A-529B, Apr. 1966
● *See also* Archaeology, Underwater; Diving Cylinder; Diving Saucers; Sponge-fishing Industry; Underwater Exploration

DIVING BELL (Rescue Compartment):
● Our Navy's Long Submarine Arm. By Allan C. Fisher, Jr. 613-636, Nov. 1952

DIVING BIRDS:
● Western Grebes: The Birds That Walk on Water. By Gary L. Nuechterlein. NGS research grant. 624-637, May 1982

DIVING CYLINDER:
● The Long, Deep Dive. By Lord Kilbracken. Photos by Bates Littlehales. NGS research grant. 718-731, May 1963
● Our Man-in-Sea Project. By Edwin A. Link. NGS research grant. 713-717, May 1963

DIVING SAUCERS:
● Diving Saucer *(Denise)* Takes to the Deep. By Jacques-Yves Cousteau. NGS research grant. 571-586, Apr. 1960
● *See also Cyana; DS-2; Deepstar*

DIVING With Sea Snakes. By Kenneth MacLeish. Photos by Ben Cropp. 565-578, Apr. 1972

DIXIE Spins the Wheel of Industry. By William H. Nicholas. Photos by J. Baylor Roberts. 281-324, Mar. 1949

DJAKARTA (Batavia), Java:
● Java–Eden in Transition. By Kenneth MacLeish. Photos by Dean Conger. 1-43, Jan. 1971
● Postwar Journey Through Java. By Ronald Stuart Kain. 675-700, May 1948

DJIBOUTI, Republic of:
● Djibouti, Tiny New Nation on Africa's Horn. By Marion Kaplan. 518-533, Oct. 1978

C
D

DJOKJAKARTA, Java, Indonesia:
- Postwar Journey Through Java. By Ronald Stuart Kain. 675-700, May 1948
- *See also* Jogjakarta

A **DO-IT-YOURSELF** Gardener Creates a New All-America Rose. By Elizabeth A. Moize. Photos by Farrell Grehan. 286-294, Aug. 1972

DOBIE, J. FRANK: Author:
- What I Saw Across the Rhine. 57-86, Jan. 1947

DODECANESE (Islands), Aegean Sea:
- The Isles of Greece: Aegean Birthplace of Western Culture. By Melville Bell Grosvenor. Photos by Edwin Stuart Grosvenor and Winfield Parks. 147-193, Aug. 1972
- On the Winds of the Dodecanese. By Jean and Franc Shor. 351-390, Mar. 1953

DODGE SATELLITE:
- Historic Color Portrait of Earth From Space. By Kenneth F. Weaver. Photos by DODGE Satellite. 726-731, Nov. 1967

DODO (Bird):
- Mauritius, Island of the Dodo. By Quentin Keynes. 77-104, Jan. 1956

DOG SHOWS:
- Dog Mart Day in Fredericksburg. By Frederick G. Vosburgh. 817-832, June 1951
- Westminster, World Series of Dogdom. By John W. Cross, Jr. 91-116, Jan. 1954

DOGON (People):
- Foxes Foretell the Future in Mali's Dogon Country. By Pamela Johnson Meyer. 431-448, Mar. 1969

DOGS:
- ◆ *Book of Dogs*. Announced. Note: The title of the revised edition (1966) is *Man's Best Friend*. 441-442, Sept. 1958
- Born Hunters, the Bird Dogs. By Roland Kilbon. Paintings by Walter A. Weber. Contents: American Cocker Spaniel, American Water Spaniel, Brittany Spaniel, Chesapeake Bay Retriever, Clumber Spaniel, Curly-coated Retriever, English Cocker Spaniel, English Setter, English Springer Spaniel, Flat-coated Retriever, German Short-haired Pointer, Golden Retriever, Gordon Setter, Irish Setter, Irish Water Spaniel, Labrador Retriever, Pointer, Sussex Spaniel, Weimaraner, Welsh Springer Spaniel, Wire-haired Pointing Griffon. 369-398, Sept. 1947
- Dogs Work for Man. By Edward J. Linehan. Paintings by Edwin Megargee and R. E. Lougheed. 190-233, Aug. 1958
- ◆ *Dogs Working for People*. Announced. 736-738, Nov. 1972
- ◆ *Puppies*. 1982
- *See also* Bravo (Malamute-Husky); Dog Shows; St. Bernard Dogs; Sled Dogs

DOGSLED RACE. *See* Sled Dog Race

DOIG, DESMOND: Author:
- Sherpaland, My Shangri-La. 545-577, Oct. 1966
- Sikkim. 398-429, Mar. 1963

Author-Photographer:
- Bhutan: Mountain Kingdom Between Tibet and India. 384-415, Sept. 1961

DOLGANS (People):
- People of the Long Spring. By Yuri Rytkheu. Photos by Dean Conger. 206-223, Feb. 1983

DOLLHOUSE:
- Royal House for Dolls. By David Jeffery. Photos by James L. Stanfield. 632-643, Nov. 1980

DOLLS:
- The World in Dolls. By Samuel F. Pryor. Photos by Kathleen Revis. 817-831, Dec. 1959
- *See also* Dzibilchaltun, for Temple of the Seven Dolls; Kachinas

DOLOMITES (Mountains), Italy:
- A Stroll to Venice. By Isobel Wylie Hutchison. Note: The author walked from Innsbruck, Austria, through the Tyrol and Dolomites, to Venice, Italy. 378-410, Sept. 1951

DOLPHINS:
- ◆ *The Playful Dolphins*. Announced. 718-720, Nov. 1976
- The Trouble With Dolphins. By Edward J. Linehan. Photos by Bill Curtsinger. 506-541, Apr. 1979
- *See also* Killer Whales; Porpoises

DOLPO (Region), Nepal:
- Trek to Nepal's Sacred Crystal Mountain. By Joel F. Ziskin. 500-517, Apr. 1977

DOMESTICATING the Wild and Woolly Musk Ox. By John J. Teal, Jr. Photos by Robert W. Madden. 862-879, June 1970

DOMINICA (Island), Leeward Islands, West Indies:
- *Finisterre* Sails the Windward Islands. By Carleton Mitchell. Photos by Winfield Parks. 755-801, Dec. 1965
- Hurricane! By Ben Funk. Photos by Robert W. Madden. 346-379, Sept. 1980
  Dominica. By Fred Ward. 357-359; Dynamics of a Hurricane. 370-371; Into the Eye of David. By John L. Eliot. 368-369; Paths of Fury–This Century's Worst American Storms. 360-361

DOMINICAN REPUBLIC:
- Amber: Golden Window on the Past. Photos by Paul A. Zahl. Text by Thomas J. O'Neill. 423-435, Sept. 1977
- The Dominican Republic: Caribbean Comeback. By James Cerruti. Photos by Martin Rogers. 538-565, Oct. 1977
- Graveyard of the Quicksilver Galleons. By Mendel Peterson. Photos by Jonathan Blair. Note: The *Nuestra Señora de Guadalupe* and the *Conde de Tolosa* sank off the coast of the Dominican Republic in 1724 while carrying a cargo of mercury to the New World. 850-876, Dec. 1979

DONINI, JIM: Author-Photographer:
- To Torre Egger's Icy Summit. 813-823, Dec. 1976

DONKEYS:
- Travels With a Donkey–100 Years Later. By Carolyn Bennett Patterson. Photos by Cotton Coulson. 535-561, Oct. 1978
- *See also* Burros, Wild

DONNELLEY, R. R., & SONS COMPANY, Chicago, Illinois:
- Exploring an Epic Year: A Message from Your Society's President and Editor. By Melville Bell Grosvenor. 874-886, Dec. 1960

DOOR PENINSULA, Wisconsin:
- Wisconsin's Door Peninsula. By William S. Ellis. Photos by Ted Rozumalski. 347-371, Mar. 1969

DORDOGNE (Department), France:
- Exploring the Mind of Ice Age Man. By Alexander Marshack. Included: The caves of La Roche, Lascaux, Pech-Merle, Rouffignac, and the Blanchard rock shelter. NGS research grant. 64-89, Jan. 1975
- *See also* Lascaux Cave

DORIES:
- Dory on the Banks: A Day in the Life of a Portuguese Fisherman. By James H. Pickerell. 573-583, Apr. 1968
- I Sailed With Portugal's Captains Courageous. By Alan Villiers. 565-596, May 1952
- ▥ The Lonely Dorymen. 579A-579B, Apr. 1968
- *See also* Blessing of the Fleet

DORSET INUIT:
- Eskimo and Viking Finds in the High Arctic: Ellesmere Island. By Peter Schledermann. Photos by Sisse Brimberg. 575-601, May 1981
- Vanished Mystery Men of Hudson Bay. By Henry B. Collins. NGS research grant. 669-687, Nov. 1956

DORSETSHIRE, England. *See* Abbotsbury Swannery

DORYMEN (Portuguese Fishermen):
- Dory on the Banks: A Day in the Life of a Portuguese Fisherman. By James H. Pickerell. 573-583, Apr. 1968
- I Sailed with Portugal's Captains Courageous. By Alan Villiers. 565-596, May 1952
- ▥ The Lonely Dorymen. 579A-579B, Apr. 1968
- *See also* Blessing of the Fleet

DORZE (People):
- Ethiopia's Artful Weavers. By Judith Olmstead. Photos by James A. Sugar. 125-141, Jan. 1973

DOTHAN, TRUDE: Author:
- Lost Outpost of the Egyptian Empire. Photos by Sisse Brimberg. Paintings by Lloyd K. Townsend. 739-769, Dec. 1982

DOTIALS (Tribespeople):
- High Adventure in the Himalayas. By Thomas Weir. 193-234, Aug. 1952

DOUBILET, DAVID: Photographer:
- The American Lobster, Delectable Cannibal. By Luis Marden. 462-487, Apr. 1973
- British Columbia's Cold Emerald Sea. Text by Larry Kohl. 526-551, Apr. 1980
- Consider the Sponge. . . . Text by Michael E. Long. 392-407, Mar. 1977
- Eternal Sinai. By Harvey Arden. Photos by David Doubilet and Kevin Fleming. 420-461, Apr. 1982
Egyptian Sector. Photos by Kevin Fleming. 430-443; Israeli Sector. Photos by David Doubilet. 444-461
- Flashlight Fish of the Red Sea. By Eugenie Clark. 719-728, Nov. 1978
- Florida, Noah's Ark for Exotic Newcomers. By Rick Gore. 538-559, Oct. 1976
- Hidden Life of an Undersea Desert. By Eugenie Clark. 129-144, July 1983
- Into the Lairs of "Sleeping" Sharks. By Eugenie Clark. 570-584, Apr. 1975
- Loch Ness: The Lake and the Legend. By William S. Ellis. Photos by Emory Kristof and David Doubilet. 759-779, June 1977
- Plight of the Bluefin Tuna. By Michael J. A. Butler. Paintings by Stanley Meltzoff. 220-239, Aug. 1982
- Precious Corals, Hawaii's Deep-sea Jewels. By Richard W. Grigg. 719-732, May 1979
- Rainbow World Beneath the Red Sea. 344-365, Sept. 1975
- The Red Sea's Gardens of Eels. By Eugenie Clark. Photos by James L. Stanfield and David Doubilet. 724-735, Nov. 1972
- The Red Sea's Sharkproof Fish. By Eugenie Clark. 718-727, Nov. 1974
- Sharks: Magnificent and Misunderstood. By Eugenie Clark. 138-187, Aug. 1981
- Strange World of Palau's Salt Lakes. By William M. Hamner. 264-282, Feb. 1982
- The Strangest Sea (Red Sea). By Eugenie Clark. 338-343, Sept. 1975
- Undersea Wonders of the Galapagos. By Gerard Wellington. 363-381, Sept. 1978

DOUBLE EAGLE II Has Landed! Crossing the Atlantic by Balloon. By Ben L. Abruzzo, with Maxie L. Anderson and Larry Newman. 858-882, Dec. 1978

DOUBLE EAGLE V (Manned Helium Balloon):
- First Across the Pacific: The Flight of *Double Eagle V*. By Ben L. Abruzzo. 513-521, Apr. 1982

DOUGLAS, MERCEDES H.:
Photographer:
- Station Wagon Odyssey: Baghdad to Istanbul. By William O. Douglas. Photos by author, Mercedes H. Douglas, and W. Robert Moore. 48-87, Jan. 1959
- West from the Khyber Pass. By William O. Douglas. Photos by Mercedes H. Douglas and author. 1-44, July 1958

DOUGLAS, WILLIAM O.: Author:
- Banks Island: Eskimo Life on the Polar Sea. Photos by Clyde Hare. 703-735, May 1964
- The Friendly Huts of the White Mountains. Photos by Kathleen Revis. 205-239, Aug. 1961
- Journey to Outer Mongolia. Photos by Dean Conger. 289-345, Mar. 1962
- The People of Cades Cove. Photos by Thomas Nebbia and Otis Imboden. 60-95, July 1962

Author-Photographer:
- Station Wagon Odyssey: Baghdad to Istanbul. Photos by author, Mercedes H. Douglas, and W. Robert Moore. 48-87, Jan. 1959
- West from the Khyber Pass. Photos by Mercedes H. Douglas and author. 1-44, July 1958

DOUGLAS-HAMILTON, IAIN:
Photographer:
- Africa's Elephants: Can They Survive? By Oria Douglas-Hamilton. Photos by Oria and Iain Douglas-Hamilton. 568-603, Nov. 1980

DOUGLAS-HAMILTON, ORIA:
Author-Photographer:
- Africa's Elephants: Can They Survive? Photos by Oria and Iain Douglas-Hamilton. 568-603, Nov. 1980

DOVE (Sloop):
- Robin Sails Home. By Robin Lee Graham. 504-545, Oct. 1970
- A Teen-ager Sails the World Alone. By Robin Lee Graham. 445-491, Oct. 1968
- World-roaming Teen-ager Sails On. By Robin Lee Graham. 449-493, Apr. 1969

DOWN East Cruise. By Tom Horgan. Photos by Luis Marden. 329-369, Sept. 1952

DOWN East to Nova Scotia. By Winfield Parks. 853-879, June 1964

DOWN Mark Twain's River on a Raft. By Rex E. Hieronymus. 551-574, Apr. 1948

DOWN on the Farm, Soviet Style–a 4-H Adventure. By John Garaventa. Photos by James Tobin and Carol Schmidt. 768-797, June 1979

DOWN the Ancient Appian Way. By James Cerruti. Photos by O. Louis Mazzatenta. 714-747, June 1981

DOWN the Danube by Canoe. By William Slade Backer. Photos by Richard S. Durrance and Christopher G. Knight. 34-79, July 1965

DOWN the Grand Canyon 100 Years After Powell. By Joseph Judge. Photos by Walter Meayers Edwards. 668-713, May 1969

DOWN the Potomac by Canoe. By Ralph Gray. Photos by Walter Meayers Edwards. 213-242, Aug. 1948

DOWN the Susquehanna by Canoe. By Ralph Gray. Photos by Walter Meayers Edwards. 73-120, July 1950

WINFIELD PARKS, NGS

Banks Island: Eskimo with sled-dog pups

DOWN to *Thresher* by Bathyscaph. By Donald L. Keach. 764-777, June 1964

DOYLE, ROBERT E.:
• Board of Trustees, Vice Chairman (1980-). 427, Oct. 1980
• Board of Trustees member (1975). 225, Aug. 1976
• President of NGS (1976-1980). 159, 224-226, Aug. 1976; 1, Jan. 1978; 427, Oct. 1980; 276, Aug. 1982
• Secretary (1967). 577, 581, 587, 590, Oct. 1967
• Secretary, Assistant (1951). 225, Aug. 1976
• Secretary, Associate (1958), for Membership of NGS. 225, Aug. 1976
• Vice President of NGS (1961). 577, 587, Oct. 1967
Author:
• Our National Wildlife Refuges: A Chance to Grow. 342-349, Mar. 1979
• Rivers Wild and Pure: A Priceless Legacy. 2-11, July 1977

DRAGON Lizards of Komodo. By James A. Kern. 872-880, Dec. 1968

DRAGONFLIES:
• Dragonflies–Rainbows on the Wing. By James G. Needham. Contents: Blue Backs, Damsons, *Didymops, Eponina, Erythrodiplax umbrata,* Golden Wings, *Gomphus,* Green Darners, Green Jackets, Hoolets, *Libellula axillena, Libellula pulchella, Progomphus alachuensis,* Saddlebags, Seminoles, Sky Pilots. 215-229, Aug. 1951

DRAGONS of the Deep. Photos by Paul A. Zahl. 838-845, June 1978

DRAGUIGNAN, France:
• Here Rest in Honored Glory. . . . The United States Dedicates Six New Battle Monuments in Europe to Americans Who Gave Their Lives During World War II. By Howell Walker. Included: Rhône American Cemetery and Memorial. 739-768, June 1957

DRAKE, SIR FRANCIS:
• The British Way. By Sir Evelyn Wrench. 421-541, Apr. 1949
• Editorial. By Gilbert M. Grosvenor. 149, Feb. 1975
• Sir Francis Drake. By Alan Villiers. Photos by Gordon W. Gahan. 216-253, Feb. 1975
• The World of Elizabeth I. By Louis B. Wright. Photos by Ted Spiegel. Included: Historical map based on the Hondius Map of 1589, showing Drake's voyage around the world. 668-709, Nov. 1968

DRAKENSBERG RANGE, South Africa:
• Africa's Bushman Art Treasures. By Alfred Friendly. Photos by Alex R. Willcox. 848-865, June 1963
• *See also* Black Eagles

DRAMA. *See* Theater

DRAMA of Death in a Minoan Temple. By Yannis Sakellarakis and Efi Sapouna-Sakellaraki. Photos by Otis Imboden and Spyros Tsavdaroglou. 205-222, Feb. 1981

VICTOR R. BOSWELL, JR., NGS

Dresden: emerald-bearing servant

DREAM On, Vancouver. By Mike Edwards. Photos by Charles O'Rear. 467-491, Oct. 1978

DRESDEN, DONALD WILLIAM:
Author:
• Paris, Home Town of the World. Photos by Justin Locke. 767-804, June 1952

DRESDEN TREASURES:
• Treasures of Dresden. By John L. Eliot. Photos by Victor R. Boswell, Jr. 702-717, Nov. 1978

DREWIEN, RODERICK C.: Author:
• Teamwork Helps the Whooping Crane. By Roderick C. Drewien, with Ernie Kuyt. 680-693, May 1979

DREYFUS COLLECTION (Renaissance Bronzes):
• Your National Gallery of Art After 10 Years. By John Walker. 73-103, Jan. 1952

DRILLING, Undersea. *See Glomar Challenger;* Mohole, Project

DRIVING the Mexican 1000: Rocks, Ruts, and Sand. By Michael E. Long. 569-575, Oct. 1972

DROUGHT:
• Drought Bedevils Brazil's Sertão. By John Wilson. Photos by Gordon W. Gahan. 704-723, Nov. 1972
• Drought Threatens the Tuareg World. By Victor Englebert. 544-571, Apr. 1974
• Etosha: Namibia's Kingdom of Animals. By Douglas H. Chadwick. Photos by Des and Jen Bartlett. 344-385, Mar. 1983
• The Imperiled Everglades. By Fred Ward. 1-27, Jan. 1972
• The Living Sands of the Namib. By William J. Hamilton III. Photos by Carol and David Hughes. 364-377, Sept. 1983
• The Niger: River of Sorrow, River of Hope. By Georg Gerster. 152-189, Aug. 1975
• Oklahoma, the Adventurous One. By Robert Paul Jordan. Photos by Robert W. Madden. 149-189, Aug. 1971
• Our Most Precious Resource: Water. By Thomas Y. Canby. Photos by Ted Spiegel. 144-179, Aug. 1980
• Somalia's Hour of Need. By Robert Paul Jordan. Photos by Michael S. Yamashita and Kevin Fleming. 748-775, June 1981
Encampments of the Dispossessed. By Larry Kohl. 756-763
• The Top End of Down Under. By Kenneth MacLeish. Photos by Thomas Nebbia. 145-174, Feb. 1973
• What's Happening to Our Climate? By Samuel W. Matthews. 576-615, Nov. 1976
• The Year the Weather Went Wild. By Thomas Y. Canby. Included: The severe drought in the northern plains and the western United States. 799-829, Dec. 1977
• *See also* Desertification

DROWNED Galleons Yield Spanish Gold. By Kip Wagner. Photos by Otis Imboden. 1-37, Jan. 1965

DRUCKER, PHILIP: Author:
● Gifts for the Jaguar God. By Philip Drucker and Robert F. Heizer. NGS research grant. 367-375, Sept. 1956

DRUGS:
● The Astonishing Armadillo. By Eleanor E. Storrs. Photos by Bianca Lavies. Included: Immunology research with leprosy bacilli provided by armadillos. 820-830, June 1982
● Nature's Gifts to Medicine. By Lonnelle Aikman. Paintings by Lloyd K. Townsend and Don Crowley. 420-440, Sept. 1974
◆ *Nature's Healing Arts.* 1977
● *See also* Medicine and Health

DRUGS, ILLEGAL:
● Florida–A Time for Reckoning. By William S. Ellis. Photos by Nathan Benn and Kevin Fleming. Note: Illegal drug traffic is a multi-billion dollar business in Florida. 172-219, Aug. 1982

DRUIDS:
● The Celts. By Merle Severy. Photos by James P. Blair. Paintings by Robert C. Magis. 582-633, May 1977
● *See also* Stonehenge

DRUMS to Dynamos on the Mohawk. By Frederick G. Vosburgh. Photos by B. Anthony Stewart. 67-110, July 1947

DRY-LAND Fleet Sails the Sahara. By Jean du Boucher. Photos by Jonathan S. Blair. 696-725, Nov. 1967

DRY TORTUGAS (Islands), Florida:
● Blizzard of Birds: The Tortugas Terns. By Alexander Sprunt, Jr. 213-230, Feb. 1947
● Shrimp Nursery: Science Explores New Ways to Farm the Sea. By Clarence P. Idyll. Photos by Robert F. Sisson. NGS research grant. 636-659, May 1965

DRYDEN, HUGH L.: Author:
● Fact Finding for Tomorrow's Planes. Photos by Luis Marden. 757-780, Dec. 1953
● Footprints on the Moon. Paintings by Davis Meltzer and Pierre Mion. 357-401, Mar. 1964
● The International Geophysical Year: Man's Most Ambitious Study of His Environment. 285-298, Feb. 1956

DUBAI, United Arab Emirates:
● The Arab World, Inc. By John J. Putman. Photos by Winfield Parks. 494-533, Oct. 1975

DUBLIN, Ireland:
● Dublin's Historic Horse Show. By Maynard Owen Williams. 115-132, July 1953
● The Friendly Irish. By John Scofield. Photos by James A. Sugar. 354-391, Sept. 1969
● I Walked Some Irish Miles. By Dorothea Sheats. 653-678, May 1951
● A New Day for Ireland. By John J. Putman. Photos by Cotton Coulson. 442-469, Apr. 1981

DU BOUCHER, JEAN: Author:
● Dry-land Fleet Sails the Sahara. Photos by Jonathan S. Blair. 696-725, Nov. 1967

DUBROVNIK (Ragusa), Yugoslavia:
● Yugoslavia's Window on the Adriatic. By Gilbert M. Grosvenor. 219-247, Feb. 1962

DUCK RAISING:
● Long Island Outgrows the Country. By Howell Walker. Photos by B. Anthony Stewart. 279-326, Mar. 1951

DUCKBILLS. *See* Platypuses

DUCKS:
● Duck Hunting with a Color Camera. By Arthur A. Allen. Contents: Baldpates; Black Ducks; Buffleheads; Canvasbacks; Eiders; Gadwalls; Golden-eyes; Mallards; Mergansers; Muscovy Ducks; Old squaws; Pintails; Redheads; Ring necks; Ruddy Ducks; Scaups, Greater and Lesser; Shovellers; Teals, Blue-winged, and Cinnamon; Widgeons, European; Wood Ducks. 514-539, Oct. 1951
● Humble Masterpieces: Decoys. By George Reiger. Photos by Kenneth Garrett. 639-663, Nov. 1983
● *See also* Duck Raising

DUFEK, GEORGE J.:
● Hubbard Medal recipient. 589-590, Apr. 1959; 530, Oct. 1959
Author:
● Nuclear Power for the Polar Regions. 712-730, May 1962
● What We've Accomplished in Antarctica. 527-557, Oct. 1959

DUGOUT CANOES:
● Jungle Journey to the World's Highest Waterfall. By Ruth Robertson. 655-690, Nov. 1949
● Sea Fever. By John E. Schultz. 237-268, Feb. 1949

DULUTH, Minnesota:
● Minnesota Makes Ideas Pay. By Frederick G. Vosburgh. Photos by John E. Fletcher and B. Anthony Stewart. 291-336, Sept. 1949

DUMAS, FRÉDÉRIC:
● Fish Men Explore a New World Undersea. By Jacques-Yves Cousteau. 431-472, Oct. 1952

DUMPS:
● The Fascinating World of Trash. By Peter T. White. Photos by Louie Psihoyos. 424-457, Apr. 1983

DUNCAN, DAVID D.: Photographer:
● Power Comes Back to Peiping. By Nelson T. Johnson and W. Robert Moore. 337-368, Sept. 1949

DUNKIRK, France:
● Thumbs Up Round the North Sea's Rim. By Frances James. Photos by Erica Koch. 685-704, May 1952

DUNN, DOROTHY: Author:
● America's First Painters: Indians. 349-377, Mar. 1955

DUNSTAN, THOMAS C.: Author:
● Our Bald Eagle: Freedom's Symbol Survives. Photos by Jeff Foott. 186-199, Feb. 1978

DUPLAIX, NICOLE:
Author-Photographer:
● Giant Otters: "Big Water Dogs" in Peril. Photos by the author and Bates Littlehales. 130-142, July 1980

DU PONT, PIERRE S.: Estate:
● Wonderland in Longwood Gardens. By Edward C. Ferriday, Jr. 45-64, July 1951

DU PONT DE NEMOURS, E. I., & COMPANY, Wilmington, Delaware:
● Delaware–Who Needs to Be Big? By Jane Vessels. Photos by Kevin Fleming. 171-197, Aug. 1983
● *Gossamer Albatross* sponsor. 645, Nov. 1979
● Today on the Delaware, Penn's Glorious River. By Albert W. Atwood. Photos by Robert F. Sisson. 1-40, July 1952

"A **DURABLE** Scale of Values." By Boyd Gibbons. Photos by Jim Brandenburg. 682-708, Nov. 1981

DURBAN, South Africa:
● Safari Through Changing Africa. By Elsie May Bell Grosvenor. Photos by Gilbert Grosvenor. 145-198, Aug. 1953

DURBAR GATHERING:
● Progress and Pageantry in Changing Nigeria. By W. Robert Moore. 325-365, Sept. 1956

DURENCEAU, ANDRE: Artist:
● Ice Age Man, the First American. By Thomas R. Henry. 781-806, Dec. 1955
● A New Look at Medieval Europe. By Kenneth M. Setton. Paintings by Andre Durenceau and Birney Lettick. 799-859, Dec. 1962

DURRANCE, DICK, II:
Author-Photographer:
● A Town . . . a Mountain . . . a Way of Life. By Jill Durrance and Dick Durrance II. 788-807, Dec. 1973
Photographer:
● Alabama, Dixie to a Different Tune. By Howard La Fay. 534-569, Oct. 1975
● Americans Afoot in Rumania. By Dan Dimancescu. Photos by Dick Durrance II and Christopher G. Knight. 810-845, June 1969
● Bangladesh: Hope Nourishes a New Nation. By William S. Ellis. 295-333, Sept. 1972
● Down the Danube by Canoe. By William Slade Backer. Photos by Richard S. Durrance and Christopher G. Knight. 34-79, July 1965
● Leningrad, Russia's Window on the West. By Howard La Fay. 636-673, May 1971
● Library of Congress: The Nation's Bookcase. By Fred Kline. 671-687, Nov. 1975
● Mr. Jefferson's Monticello. By Joseph Judge. Photos by Dean Conger and Richard S. Durrance. 426-444, Sept. 1966
● On the Track of the West's Wild Horses. By Hope Ryden. Photos by author and Dick Durrance II. 94-109, Jan. 1971

• Striking It Rich in the North Sea. By Rick Gore. 519-549, Apr. 1977
• White-water Adventure on Wild Rivers of Idaho. By Frank Craighead, Jr. and John Craighead. 213-239, Feb. 1970
• The Zulus: Black Nation in a Land of Apartheid. By Joseph Judge. 738-775, Dec. 1971

DURRANCE, JILL:
Author-Photographer:
• A Town . . . a Mountain . . . a Way of Life. By Jill Durrance and Dick Durrance II. 788-807, Dec. 1973

DUTCH EAST INDIA COMPANY: Ships. *See Slot ter Hooge; Witte Leeuw*

DUTCH WEST INDIES. *See* Netherlands Antilles

DWELLERS in the Dark (Termites). By Glenn D. Prestwich. 532-547, Apr. 1978

DYGERT, RUTH E.: Author:
• Ambassadors of Good Will: The Peace Corps. By Sargent Shriver and Peace Corps Volunteers. 297-345, Sept. 1964
Tanganyika. 321-323

DYHRENFURTH, NORMAN G.:
Author:
• Six to the Summit (Everest). Photos by Barry C. Bishop. 460-473, Oct. 1963
• *See also* American Mount Everest Expedition

DYNAMIC Ontario. By Marjorie Wilkins Campbell. Photos by Winfield Parks. 58-97, July 1963

DYNAMICS of a Hurricane. 370-371, Sept. 1980

DZIBILCHALTUN, Yucatán, Mexico:
• Dzibilchaltun. NGS research grant. 91-129, Jan. 1959
I. Lost City of the Maya. By E. Wyllys Andrews. 91-109; II. Up from the Well of Time. By Luis Marden. 110-129

E

ECA. *See* Economic Cooperation Administration

EPA. *See* Environmental Protection Agency

EAGLE (Lunar Module):
• The Flight of Apollo 11: "One giant leap for mankind." By Kenneth F. Weaver. 752-787, Dec. 1969

EAGLE (Training Ship):
• Under Canvas in the Atomic Age (U. S. Coast Guard Cadets). By Alan Villiers. 49-84, July 1955
• *See also* Operation Sail

EAGLES:
• Seeking Mindanao's Strangest Creatures. By Charles Heizer Wharton. Included: Crested Serpent Eagle, Monkey-eating Eagle. 389-408, Sept. 1948
• *See also* Bald Eagles, American; Black Eagles; Golden Eagles; Philippine Eagles

EARLE, SYLVIA A.: Author:
• All-girl Team Tests the Habitat. Paintings by Pierre Mion. 291-296, Aug. 1971
• Humpbacks: The Gentle Whales. Photos by Al Giddings. 2-17, Jan. 1979
• Life Springs From Death in Truk Lagoon. Photos by Al Giddings. 578-603, May 1976
• Undersea World of a Kelp Forest. Photos by Al Giddings. 411-426, Sept. 1980
• A Walk in the Deep. Photos by Al Giddings and Chuck Nicklin. 624-631, May 1980

EARLIEST Geographics to Be Reprinted. By Melvin M. Payne. 688-689, Nov. 1964

EARLY AMERICA Through the Eyes of Her Native Artists. By Hereward Lester Cooke, Jr. 356-389, Sept. 1962

EARLY CIVILIZATIONS:
◆ *Amazing Mysteries of the World.* 1983
◆ *Everyday Life in Ancient Times* (1951). 766, June 1954; 563, Oct. 1961
◆ *Mysteries of the Ancient World.* 1979
◆ *Peoples and Places of the Past: The National Geographic Illustrated Atlas of the Ancient World.* Announced. 824, Dec. 1982
◆ *Secrets From the Past.* 1979
◆ *Splendors of the Past: Lost Cities of the Ancient World.* 1981
Africa:
• Finding West Africa's Oldest City. By Susan and Roderick McIntosh. Photos by Michael and Aubine Kirtley. Contents: Jenne-jeno site in Mali. 396-418, Sept. 1982
• *See also* Egypt, Ancient
Asia, Eastern:
• China Unveils Her Newest Treasures. Photos by Robert W. Madden. 848-857, Dec. 1974
• China's Incredible Find. By Audrey Topping. Paintings by Yang Hsien-min. Included: The first emperor's burial mound, with guardian army of terra-cotta men and horses. 440-459, Apr. 1978
• A Lady From China's Past. Photos from *China Pictorial.* Text by Alice J. Hall. 660-681, May 1974
• The Lands and Peoples of Southeast Asia. 295-365, Mar. 1971
Mosaic of Cultures. By Peter T. White. Photos by W. E. Garrett. 296-329; New Light on a Forgotten Past. By Wilhelm G. Solheim II. 330-339
Europe:
• Ancient Bulgaria's Golden Treasures. By Colin Renfrew. Photos by James L. Stanfield. Paintings by Jean-Leon Huens. 112-129, July 1980
• Ancient Europe Is Older Than We Thought. By Colin Renfrew. Photos by Adam Woolfitt. 615-623, Nov. 1977
• *See also* Celts; Minoan Civilization; Mycenaean Civilization
Middle East:
◆ *Everyday Life in Bible Times.* Announced. 494-507, Oct. 1967; rev. ed. 1977
• Jericho Gives Up Its Secrets. By Kathleen M. Kenyon and A. Douglas Tushingham. Photos by Nancy Lord. 853-870, Dec. 1953
▲ *Middle East, Eastern Mediterranean; Early Civilizations of the Middle East,* double-sided supplement. Sept. 1978
• *See also* Ebla; Mesopotamia; Phoenicians
North America:
◆ *Discovering Man's Past in the Americas.* 880-884, June 1969
• Man's Eighty Centuries in Veracruz. By S. Jeffrey K. Wilkerson. Photos by David Hiser. Paintings by Richard Schlecht. NGS research grant. 203-231, Aug. 1980
• *See also* Anasazi; Hohokam Culture; Mound Builders; Olmecs
South America:
◆ *Discovering Man's Past in the Americas.* 880-884, June 1969
• Finding the Tomb of a Warrior-God. By William Duncan Strong. Photos by Clifford Evans, Jr. 453-482, Apr. 1947
• *See also* Chan Chan

EARLY MAN. *See* Man, Prehistoric

EARTH:
• Apollo 16 Brings Us Visions From Space. 856-865, Dec. 1972
• The Earth From Orbit. By Paul D. Lowman, Jr. 645-671, Nov. 1966
• "The Earth from Space," photo supplement. Apollo astronauts on reverse. Sept. 1973
• Editorial. By Gilbert M. Grosvenor. 143, Aug. 1980
◆ *Exploring Our Living Planet.* 824, Dec. 1982
• Extraordinary Photograph Shows Earth Pole to Pole. Photos by Nimbus I. 190-193, Feb. 1965
• Geothermal Energy: The Power of Letting Off Steam. By Kenneth F. Weaver. 566-579, Oct. 1977
• Have We Solved the Mysteries of the Moon? By Kenneth F. Weaver. Paintings by William H. Bond. Included: The moon compared with earth. 309-325, Sept. 1973
• Historic Color Portrait of Earth From Space. By Kenneth F. Weaver. Photos by DODGE Satellite. 726-731, Nov. 1967
▲ "How Man Pollutes His World," painting supplement. Map of the World. Dec. 1970
• Our Earth as a Satellite Sees It. By W. G. Stroud. 293-302, Aug. 1960
• Our Home-town Planet, Earth. By F. Barrows Colton. 117-139, Jan. 1952
◆ *Our Violent Earth.* 1982
• Pollution, Threat to Man's Only Home. By Gordon Young. Photos by James P. Blair. 738-781, Dec. 1970
• Satellites That Serve Us. By Thomas Y. Canby. Included: Images of Earth. 281-335, Sept. 1983

● Scientists Drill at Sea to Pierce Earth's Crust (Project Mohole). By Samuel W. Matthews. Photos by J. Baylor Roberts. 686-697, Nov. 1961
● Seeing the Earth from 80 Miles Up. By Clyde T. Holliday. 511-528, Oct. 1950
● Skylab Looks at Earth. 471-493, Oct. 1974
● This Changing Earth. By Samuel W. Matthews. 1-37, Jan. 1973
▪ The Violent Earth. 286A-286B, Feb. 1973
● Voyage to the Planets. By Kenneth F. Weaver. Paintings by Ludek Pesek. 147-193, Aug. 1970
● Voyager's Historic View of Earth and Moon. 53, July 1978
● What's Happening to Our Climate? By Samuel W. Matthews. 576-615, Nov. 1976
● *See also* Plate Tectonics

EARTHQUAKES:
● An Alaskan Family's Night of Terror. By Tay Pryor Thomas. 142-156, July 1964
▪ Born of Fire. 824, Dec. 1982
● California's San Andreas Fault. By Thomas Y. Canby. Photos by James P. Blair. 38-53, Jan. 1973
● Can We Predict Quakes? By Thomas Y. Canby. 830-835, June 1976
● Caught in the Assam-Tibet Earthquake. By F. Kingdon-Ward. 403-416, Mar. 1952
● Death of an Island, Tristan da Cunha. By P.J.F. Wheeler. 678-695, May 1962
● Earthquake! (Alaska, 1964). By William P. E. Graves. 112-139, July 1964
● Earthquake in Guatemala. By Bart McDowell. Photos by W. E. Garrett and Robert W. Madden. 810-829, June 1976
● Editorial. By Gilbert M. Grosvenor. 719, June 1976
◆ *Exploring Our Living Planet*. 824, Dec. 1982
● Exploring the Drowned City of Port Royal. By Marion Clayton Link. Photos by Luis Marden. NGS research grant. 151-183, Feb. 1960
● The Night the Mountains Moved (Montana). By Samuel W. Matthews. Photos by J. Baylor Roberts. 329-359, Mar. 1960
● Our Home-town Planet, Earth. By F. Barrows Colton. 117-139, Jan. 1952
● Our Restless Earth. By Maynard M. Miller. 140-141, July 1964
◆ *Our Violent Earth*. 1982
● Peru, Homeland of the Warlike Inca. By Kip Ross. Included: Cusco earthquake of May 21, 1950. 421-462, Oct. 1950
◆ *Powers of Nature*. 1978
● This Changing Earth. By Samuel W. Matthews. 1-37, Jan. 1973
▪ The Violent Earth. 286A-286B, Feb. 1973
● Volcano and Earthquake Show Nature's Awesome Power. The Editor. 303, Mar. 1960
● Yugoslavia: Six Republics in One. By Robert Paul Jordan. Photos by James P. Blair. Included: Earthquake, 1963. 589-633, May 1970

MAC'S FOTO SERVICE

Night of Terror: quake's destruction

EARTH'S Richest Nation–A Tiny Pacific Islet. By Mike Holmes. 344-353, Sept. 1976

EARTHWATCH: Study Grant:
● Rhesus monkeys in temples of Nepal. 576, 577, Apr. 1980

EARTHWORMS:
● Biggest Worm Farm Caters to Platypuses. By W. H. Nicholas. 269-280, Feb. 1949
● Capturing Strange Creatures in Colombia. By Marte Latham. Photos by Tor Eigeland. 682-693, May 1966

The **EAST** (Region), U. S.:
● The Parks in Your Backyard. By Conrad L. Wirth. 647-707, Nov. 1963
The East. 675-689
● *See also* New England

EAST AFRICA:
◆ *Animals of East Africa: The Wild Realm*. Announced. 844-849, June 1968
● East Africa's Majestic Flamingos. Photos by M. Philip Kahl. NGS research grant. 276-294, Feb. 1970
● The Leakey Tradition Lives On. By Melvin M. Payne. NGS research grant. 143-144, Jan. 1973
● *See also* Ethiopia; Kenya; Tanzania; Uganda

EAST From Bali by Seagoing Jeep to Timor. By Helen and Frank Schreider. 236-279, Aug. 1962

EAST GERMANY. *See* German Democratic Republic

EAST INDIA COMPANY, Dutch. *See Slot ter Hooge; Witte Leeuw*

EAST PAKISTAN:
● East Pakistan Drives Back the Jungle. By Jean and Franc Shor. 399-426, Mar. 1955
● Pakistan: Problems of a Two-part Land. By Bern Keating. Photos by Albert Moldvay. 1-47, Jan. 1967
● *See also* Bangladesh

EAST RIVER (Strait), New York:
● A Century Old, the Wonderful Brooklyn Bridge. By John G. Morris. Photos by Donal F. Holway. 565-579, May 1983

EAST ST. LOUIS, Illinois:
● "Pyramids" of the New World. By Neil Merton Judd. 105-128, Jan. 1948

EASTCOTT, JOHN:
Author-Photographer:
● New Zealand's High Country. By Yva Momatiuk and John Eastcott. 246-265, Aug. 1978
● Poland's Mountain People. By Yva Momatiuk and John Eastcott. 104-129, Jan. 1981
● Still Eskimo, Still Free: The Inuit of Umingmaktok. By Yva Momatiuk and John Eastcott. 624-647, Nov. 1977

EASTER:
● Easter Greetings From the Ukrainians. By Robert Paul Jordan. Photos by James A. Sugar. 556-563, Apr. 1972

E F

JAMES L. STANFIELD, NGS

Byzantine Empire: Romanian fresco

• Easter Week in Indian Guatemala. By John Scofield. 406-417, Mar. 1960
• Eternal Easter in a Greek Village. By Maria Nicolaidis-Karanikolas. Photos by James L. Stanfield. 768-777, Dec. 1983
• Nikolaevsk: A Bit of Old Russia Takes Root in Alaska. By Jim Rearden. Photos by Charles O'Rear. 401-425, Sept. 1972
• *See also* Holy Week

"**EASTER** Egg" Chickens. By Frederick G. Vosburgh. Photos by B. Anthony Stewart. 377-387, Sept. 1948

EASTER ISLAND, Pacific Ocean:
• Easter Island and Its Mysterious Monuments. By Howard La Fay. Photos by Thomas J. Abercrombie. 90-117, Jan. 1962
• The *Yankee*'s Wander-world. By Irving and Electa Johnson. 1-50, Jan. 1949

EASTERN MEDITERRANEAN LANDS:
▲ *Lands of the Eastern Mediterranean,* Atlas series supplement. Jan. 1959
• *See also* Cyprus; Egypt; Israel; Jerusalem; Jordan; Lebanon; Sinai Peninsula; Syria; Turkey

EASTERN ORTHODOXY:
• The Byzantine Empire. 709-777, Dec. 1983
I. Rome of the East. By Merle Severy. Photos by James L. Stanfield. 709-767; II. Mount Athos. 739-745; III. Eternal Easter in a Greek Village. By Maria Nicolaidis-Karanikolas. Photos by James L. Stanfield. 768-777
• Hashemite Jordan, Arab Heartland. By John Scofield. 841-856, Dec. 1952
• Home to the Holy Land. By Maynard Owen Williams. 707-746, Dec. 1950
• On the Winds of the Dodecanese. By Jean and Franc Shor. 351-390, Mar. 1953
• The Proud Armenians. By Robert Paul Jordan. Photos by Harry N. Naltchayan. 846-873, June 1978
• Sponge Fishermen of Tarpon Springs. By Jennie E. Harris. Included: Greek Orthodox "Feast of Lights" (Epiphany). 119-136, Jan. 1947
• *See also* Old Believers; St. Catherine's Monastery

EASTERN SHORE, Maryland-Virginia:
• Chesapeake Country. By Nathaniel T. Kenney. Photos by Bates Littlehales. 370-411, Sept. 1964
• "Delmarva," Gift of the Sea. By Catherine Bell Palmer. 367-399, Sept. 1950
• Maryland on the Half Shell. By Stuart E. Jones. Photos by Robert W. Madden. 188-229, Feb. 1972
• Roving Maryland's Cavalier Country. By William A. Kinney. 431-470, Apr. 1954
• Tireless Voyager, the Whistling Swan. By William J. L. Sladen. Photos by Bianca Lavies. NGS research grant. 134-147, July 1975
• *See also* Chesapeake Bay (The Sailing Oystermen); Chesapeake Bay Bridge-Tunnel

EASTMAN, GEORGE:
• Eastman of Rochester: Photographic Pioneer. By Allan C. Fisher, Jr. 423-438, Sept. 1954

EASYGOING, Hardworking Arkansas. By Boyd Gibbons. Photos by Matt Bradley. 396-427, Mar. 1978

EBERLEIN, HAROLD DONALDSON:
Author:
• Philadelphia Houses a Proud Past. Photos by Thomas Nebbia. 151-191, Aug. 1960

EBLA (Ancient City):
• Ebla: Splendor of an Unknown Empire. By Howard La Fay. Photos by James L. Stanfield. Paintings by Louis S. Glanzman. 730-759, Dec. 1978

ECHOES of Shiloh (Shiloh National Military Park, Tennessee). By Shelby Foote. 106-111, July 1979

ECHOLOCATION:
• Stalking Seals Under Antarctic Ice. By Carleton Ray. 54-65, Jan. 1966
• *See also* Bats; Dolphins; Killer Whales; Oilbirds; Porpoises

ECLIPSES, Solar:
• Burr Prizes Awarded to Dr. Edgerton and Dr. Van Biesbroeck. 705-706, May 1953; 523, Apr. 1955
• Eclipse Hunting in Brazil's Ranchland. By F. Barrows Colton. Photos by Richard H. Stewart and Guy W. Starling. NGS research grant. 285-324, Sept. 1947
• Operation Eclipse: 1948. By William A. Kinney. Contents: Eclipse observation stations in Burma; Thailand; China; Korea; Japan; Aleutian Islands. NGS research grant. 325-372, Mar. 1949
• Solar Eclipse, Nature's Super Spectacular. By Donald H. Menzel and Jay M. Pasachoff. NGS research grant. 222-233, Aug. 1970
• The Solar Eclipse From a Jet. By Wolfgang B. Klemperer. Included: Path of totality of eclipse from Hokkaido, Japan, to beyond Bar Harbor, Maine. NGS research grant. 785-796, Nov. 1963
• South in the Sudan. By Harry Hoogstraal. Included: Khartoum, 1952 eclipse site (total eclipse of the sun, February 25). 249-272, Feb. 1953
• The Sun. By Herbert Friedman. 713-743, Nov. 1965
• Your Society Observes Eclipse in Brazil. NGS research grant. 661, May 1947

ECOLOGY:
• African Wildlife: Man's Threatened Legacy. By Allan C. Fisher, Jr. Photos by Thomas Nebbia. Paintings by Ned Seidler. 147-187, Feb. 1972
• Aldo Leopold: "A Durable Scale of Values." By Boyd Gibbons. Photos by Jim Brandenburg. 682-708, Nov. 1981

◆ *As We Live and Breathe: The Challenge of Our Environment.* Announced. 882-886, June 1971
● Florida, Noah's Ark for Exotic Newcomers. By Rick Gore. Photos by David Doubilet. 538-559, Oct. 1976
● The Imperiled Everglades. By Fred Ward. 1-27, Jan. 1972
● Our Ecological Crisis. 737-795, Dec. 1970
I. Pollution, Threat to Man's Only Home. By Gordon Young. Photos by James P. Blair. 738-781; II. The Fragile Beauty All About Us. Photos by Harry S. C. Yen. 785-795
▲ *The World; How Man Pollutes His World;* supplement. Dec. 1980
● *See also* Bighorn Sheep; Corals and Coral Reefs; Giant Kelp; Giant Tortoises; Lions; Ospreys; Tundra; Walking Catfish; Willamette River and Valley; *and* Ecosystems; Photosynthesis

ECONOMIC COOPERATION ADMINISTRATION:
● Roaming Korea South of the Iron Curtain. By Enzo de Chetelat. 777-808, June 1950
● War-torn Greece Looks Ahead. By Maynard Owen Williams. 711-744, Dec. 1949
● With Uncle Sam and John Bull in Germany. By Frederick Simpich. 117-140, Jan. 1949

ECONOMIC ZONES: People's Republic of China:
● China's Opening Door. By John J. Putman. Photos by H. Edward Kim. 64-83, July 1983

ECONOMICS:
● Five Noted Thinkers Explore the Future. Included: Isaac Asimov, Richard F. Babcock, Edmund N. Bacon, Buckminster Fuller, Gerard Piel. 68-75, July 1976

ECOSYSTEMS:
● Abundant Life in a Desert Land. By Walter Meayers Edwards. 424-436, Sept. 1973
● Australia's Great Barrier Reef. 630-663, May 1981
I. A Marine Park Is Born. By Soames Summerhays. Photos by Ron and Valerie Taylor. 630-635; II. Paradise Beneath the Sea. By Ron and Valerie Taylor. 636-663
● Can We Save Our Salt Marshes? By Stephen W. Hitchcock. Photos by William R. Curtsinger. 729-765, June 1972
● Etosha: Namibia's Kingdom of Animals. By Douglas H. Chadwick. Photos by Des and Jen Bartlett. 344-385, Mar. 1983
● Hidden Life of an Undersea Desert. By Eugenie Clark. Photos by David Doubilet. 129-144, July 1983
● Hidden Worlds in the Heart of a Plant (Bromeliad). By Paul A. Zahl. 389-397, Mar. 1975
● In Hawaii's Crystal Sea, A Galaxy of Life Fills the Night. By Kenneth Brower. Photos by William R. Curtsinger and Chris Newbert. 834-847, Dec. 1981
● Incredible World of the Deep-sea Rifts. NGS research grant. 680-705, Nov. 1979
I. Strange World Without Sun. The Editor. 680-688; II. Return to Oases of the Deep. By Robert D. Ballard and J. Frederick Grassle. 689-705
● Life on a Rock Ledge. By William H. Amos. 558-566, Oct. 1980
● The Living Sand. By William H. Amos. 820-833, June 1965
● The Living Sands of the Namib. By William J. Hamilton III. Photos by Carol and David Hughes. 364-377, Sept. 1983
● Miracle of the Potholes. By Rowe Findley. Photos by Robert F. Sisson. 570-579, Oct. 1975
● Mzima, Kenya's Spring of Life. By Joan and Alan Root. 350-373, Sept. 1971
● Strange World of Palau's Salt Lakes. By William M. Hamner. Photos by David Doubilet. 264-282, Feb. 1982
● The Tallgrass Prairie: Can It Be Saved? By Dennis Farney. Photos by Jim Brandenburg. 37-61, Jan. 1980
● Teeming Life of a Pond. By William H. Amos. 274-298, Aug. 1970
● The Tree Nobody Liked (Red Mangrove). By Rick Gore. Photos by Bianca Lavies. 669-689, May 1977
● Tropical Rain Forests. 2-65, Jan. 1983
Nature's Dwindling Treasures. By Peter T. White. Photos by James P. Blair. Paintings by Barron Storey. 2-47; Teeming Life of a Rain Forest. By Carol and David Hughes. 49-65
● The Troubled Waters of Mono Lake. By Gordon Young. Photos by Craig Aurness. NGS research grant. 504-519, Oct. 1981
● Undersea World of a Kelp Forest. By Sylvia A. Earle. Photos by Al Giddings. 411-426, Sept. 1980
● Unseen Life of a Mountain Stream. By William H. Amos. 562-580, Apr. 1977
● The Wild World of Compost. By Cecil E. Johnson. Photos by Bianca Lavies. 273-284, Aug. 1980
● The World of My Apple Tree. By Robert F. Sisson. 836-847, June 1972

ECUADOR:
● Ambassadors of Good Will: The Peace Corps. By Sargent Shriver and Peace Corps Volunteers. 297-345, Sept. 1964
Ecuador. By Rhoda and Earle Brooks. 339-345
● Ecuador–Low and Lofty Land Astride the Equator. By Loren McIntyre. 259-298, Feb. 1968
● El Sangay, Fire-breathing Giant of the Andes. By G. Edward Lewis. 117-138, Jan. 1950
● Sea Fever. By John E. Schultz. 237-268, Feb. 1949
● *See also* Galapagos Islands; Vilcabamba

EDDY, JOHN A.: Author:
● Probing the Mystery of the Medicine Wheels. Photos by Thomas E. Hooper. 140-146, Jan. 1977

EDDY, WILLIAM A.:
● Saudi Arabia, Oil Kingdom. Photos by Maynard Owen Williams. 497-512, Apr. 1948

EDEN in the Outback. By Kay and Stanley Breeden. 189-203, Feb. 1973

EDGAR M. QUEENY-AMERICAN MUSEUM OF NATURAL HISTORY EXPEDITION:
● Spearing Lions with Africa's Masai. By Edgar Monsanto Queeny. 487-517, Oct. 1954

EDGEØYA (Island), Svalbard:
● Polar Bear: Lonely Nomad of the North. By Thor Larsen. 574-590, Apr. 1971

EDGERTON, GLEN E.: Author:
● An Engineer's View of the Suez Canal. 123-140, Jan. 1957

EDGERTON, HAROLD E.:
● Burr Prizes Awarded to Dr. Edgerton and Dr. Van Biesbroeck. Note: Electronic flashlight for ultra-high-speed photography invented by Dr. Edgerton. 705-706, May 1953; 523, Apr. 1955; 467, Oct. 1955; 847, June 1960
Author:
● Circus Action in Color. 305-308, Mar. 1948
● Stonehenge–New Light on an Old Riddle. Paintings by Brian Hope-Taylor. 846-866, June 1960
Author-Photographer:
● Freezing the Flight of Hummingbirds. By Harold E. Edgerton, R. J. Niedrach, and Walker Van Riper. NGS research grant. 245-261, Aug. 1951
● Hummingbirds in Action. 221-232, Aug. 1947
● Photographing the Sea's Dark Underworld. NGS research grant. 523-537, Apr. 1955
Photographer:
● *Calypso* Explores an Undersea Canyon (Romanche Trench). By Jacques-Yves Cousteau. Photos by Bates Littlehales and Harold E. Edgerton. NGS research grant. 373-396, Mar. 1958
● Fish Men Discover a 2,200-year-old Greek Ship. By Jacques-Yves Cousteau. NGS research grant. 1-36, Jan. 1954
● To the Depths of the Sea by Bathyscaphe. By Jacques-Yves Cousteau. NGS research grant. 67-79, July 1954
● The Wonder City That Moves by Night (Circus). By Francis Beverly Kelley. 289-324, Mar. 1948

EDINBURGH, Scotland:
● Edinburgh: Capital in Search of a Country. By James Cerruti. Photos by Adam Woolfitt. 274-296, Aug. 1976
● Midshipmen's Cruise. By William J. Aston and Alexander G. B. Grosvenor. 711-754, June 1948
● Poets' Voices Linger in Scottish Shrines. By Isobel Wylie Hutchison. Photos by Kathleen Revis. 437-488, Oct. 1957

EF

EDISON, THOMAS ALVA: Laboratory and Buildings. *See* Greenfield Village

EDITOR's Postscript. By Wilbur E. Garrett. 115, *Special Report on Energy* (Feb. 1981)

EDMONTON, Alberta, Canada:
• Canada's "Now" Frontier. By Robert Paul Jordan. Photos by Lowell Georgia. 480-511, Oct. 1976

EDUCATIONAL AIDS, NGS. *See* Atlases; Books; Films and Filmstrips; Globes; Map Supplements; NGM: Indexes; Recordings; *WORLD*

EDWARDS, DUNCAN: Photographer:
• Roman Life in 1,600-year-old Color Pictures (Mosaics). By Gino Vinicio Gentili. 211-229, Feb. 1957

EDWARDS, MIKE W.: Author:
• Along the Great Divide. Photos by Nicholas DeVore III. 483-515, Oct. 1979
• California's Land Apart–the Monterey Peninsula. 682-703, Nov. 1972
• The Danube: River of Many Nations, Many Names. Photos by Winfield Parks. 455-485, Oct. 1977
• Dream On, Vancouver. Photos by Charles O'Rear. 467-491, Oct. 1978
• An Eye for an Eye: Pakistan's Wild Frontier. Photos by J. Bruce Baumann. 111-139, Jan. 1977
• Hiking the Backbone of the Rockies: Canada's Great Divide Trail. Photos by Lowell Georgia. 795-817, June 1973
• Honduras: Eye of the Storm. Photos by David Alan Harvey. 608-637, Nov. 1983
• Mexico: "A Very Beautiful Challenge." Photos by Thomas Nebbia. 612-647, May 1978
• Mexico to Canada on the Pacific Crest Trail. Photos by David Hiser. 741-779, June 1971
• Shanghai: Born-again Giant. Photos by Bruce Dale. 2-43, July 1980
• Shenandoah, I Long to Hear You. Photos by Thomas Anthony DeFeo. 554-588, Apr. 1970
• Should They Build a Fence Around Montana? Photos by Nicholas deVore III. 614-649, May 1976
• Thomas Jefferson: Architect of Freedom. Photos by Linda Bartlett. 231-259, Feb. 1976
• Through Ozark Hills and Hollows. Photos by Bruce Dale. 656-689, Nov. 1970
• Tunisia: Sea, Sand, Success. Photos by David Alan Harvey. 184-217, Feb. 1980
• The Virginians. Photos by David Alan Harvey. 588-617, Nov. 1974

EDWARDS, WALTER MEAYERS:
Author-Photographer:
• Abundant Life in a Desert Land. 424-436, Sept. 1973
• Across the Ridgepole of the Alps. 410-419, Sept. 1960
• Crater Lake Summer. 134-148, July 1962
• Eternal France. 725-764, June 1960
• France's Past Lives in Languedoc. 1-43, July 1951
• Lake Powell: Waterway to Desert Wonders. 44-75, July 1967
• On the Ridgepole of the Rockies. 745-780, June 1947
Canada's Rocky Mountain Playground. 755-770
Photographer:
• The Alps: Man's Own Mountains. By Ralph Gray. Photos by Walter Meayers Edwards and William Eppridge. 350-395, Sept. 1965
• The Camargue, Land of Cowboys and Gypsies. By Eugene L. Kammerman. 667-699, May 1956
• Canada, My Country. By Alan Phillips. Photos by David S. Boyer and Walter Meayers Edwards. 769-819, Dec. 1961
• Canyonlands, Realm of Rock and the Far Horizon. By Rowe Findley. 71-91, July 1971
• Down the Potomac by Canoe. By Ralph Gray. 213-242, Aug. 1948
• Down the Susquehanna by Canoe. By Ralph Gray. 73-120, July 1950
• Micronesia: The Americanization of Eden. By David S. Boyer. 702-744, May 1967
• Retracing John Wesley Powell's Historic Voyage Down the Grand Canyon. By Joseph Judge. 668-713, May 1969
• We Saw the World From the Edge of Space. By Malcolm D. Ross. 671-685, Nov. 1961

EDWARDS AIR FORCE BASE, California:
• *Columbia*'s Landing Closes a Circle. By Tom Wolfe. 474-477, Oct. 1981
• Fact Finding for Tomorrow's Planes. By Hugh L. Dryden. Photos by Luis Marden. 757-780, Dec. 1953

EELS:
• Night Life in the Gulf Stream. By Paul A. Zahl. 391-418, Mar. 1954
• The Red Sea's Gardens of Eels. By Eugenie Clark. Photos by James L. Stanfield and David Doubilet. NGS research grant. 724-735, Nov. 1972

EFFIGIES, Indian. *See* Gravel Pictographs

EGBERT, ALLAN L.:
Author-Photographer:
• Among Alaska's Brown Bears. By Allan L. Egbert and Michael H. Luque. NGS research grant. 428-442, Sept. 1975

EGGS:
• Easter Egg Chickens. By Frederick G. Vosburgh. Photos by B. Anthony Stewart. 377-387, Sept. 1948
• Easter Greetings From the Ukrainians. By Robert Paul Jordan. Photos by James A. Sugar. 556-563, Apr. 1972
• *See also Aepyornis;* Cooper's Hawk; Ospreys; Scarlet Ibis

EGRETS:
• Saving Man's Wildlife Heritage. By John H. Baker. Photos by Robert F. Sisson. 581-620, Nov. 1954
• Wildlife of Everglades National Park. By Daniel B. Beard. Paintings by Walter A. Weber. 83-116, Jan. 1949
• *See also* Cattle Egret

EGYPT:
▲ *Africa: Countries of the Nile,* Atlas series supplement. Oct. 1963
• Africa: The Winds of Freedom Stir a Continent. By Nathaniel T. Kenney. Photos by W. D. Vaughn. 303-359, Sept. 1960
• "Around the World in Eighty Days." By Newman Bumstead. Included: Cairo, Giza, Ismailia, Port Said, Suez Canal. 705-750, Dec. 1951
• Editorial. By Gilbert M. Grosvenor. 291, Mar. 1977
• Egypt: Two Perspectives. 293-343, Mar. 1977
I. Legacy of a Dazzling Past. By Alice J. Hall. 293-311; II. Omens for a Better Tomorrow. By Thomas J. Abercrombie. 312-343
• Egypt's Desert of Promise. By Farouk El-Baz. Photos by Georg Gerster. 190-221, Feb. 1982
• Eternal Sinai. By Harvey Arden. Photos by David Doubilet and Kevin Fleming. Included: Egyptian control of the Sinai is returned as part of the Camp David accords. 420-461, Apr. 1982
Egyptian Sector. Photos by Kevin Fleming. 430-443; Israeli Sector. Photos by David Doubilet. 444-461
• Eyewitness to War in the Holy Land. By Charles Harbutt. 782-795, Dec. 1967
• Island of Faith in the Sinai Wilderness (St. Catherine's Monastery). By George H. Forsyth. Photos by Robert F. Sisson. 82-106, Jan. 1964
• Journey Into the Great Rift: the Northern Half. By Helen and Frank Schreider. 254-290, Aug. 1965
• Kayaks Down the Nile. By John M. Goddard. 697-732, May 1955
• The Mediterranean–Sea of Man's Fate. By Rick Gore. Photos by Jonathan Blair. 694-737, Dec. 1982
• Mount Sinai's Holy Treasures (St. Catherine's Monastery). By Kurt Weitzmann. Photos by Fred Anderegg. 109-127, Jan. 1964
◆ *The River Nile.* Announced. 408-417, Mar. 1966
• Round the World School (ISA). By Paul Antze. Photos by William Eppridge. 96-127, July 1962
• Safari from Congo to Cairo. By Elsie May Bell Grosvenor. Photos by Gilbert Grosvenor. 721-771, Dec. 1954
• Sinai Sheds New Light on the Bible. By Henry Field. Photos by William B. and Gladys Terry. Included: St. Catherine's Monastery. 795-815, Dec. 1948
• Troubled Waters East of Suez. By Ernest M. Eller. 483-522, Apr. 1954
• YWCA: International Success Story. By Mary French Rockefeller. Photos by Otis Imboden. 904-933, Dec. 1963
• *Yankee* Cruises the Storied Nile. By Irving and Electa Johnson. Photos by Winfield Parks. 583-633, May 1965
• *See also* Abu Simbel; Cairo; Suez Canal

EGYPT, Ancient:
● Abraham, the Friend of God. By Kenneth MacLeish. Photos by Dean Conger. Included: Abraham's sojourn in Egypt. 739-789, Dec. 1966
◆ *Ancient Egypt.* 1978
● Computer Helps Scholars Re-create an Egyptian Temple. By Ray Winfield Smith. Photos by Emory Kristof. Contents: Akhenaten Temple Project. 634-655, Nov. 1970
■ Egypt, Quest for Eternity. cover, Feb. 1982
● Fresh Treasures from Egypt's Ancient Sands. By Jefferson Caffery. Photos by David S. Boyer. 611-650, Nov. 1955
● Gold, the Eternal Treasure. By Peter T. White. Photos by James L. Stanfield. Included: Gold from Egyptian tombs. 1-51, Jan. 1974
● In Search of Moses. By Harvey Arden. Photos by Nathan Benn. 2-37, Jan. 1976
● Legacy of a Dazzling Past. By Alice J. Hall. 293-311, Mar. 1977
● Lost Outpost of the Egyptian Empire. By Trude Dothan. Photos by Sisse Brimberg. Paintings by Lloyd K. Townsend. NGS research grant. 739-769, Dec. 1982
▲ *Nile Valley, Land of the Pharaohs,* Atlas series supplement. Text on reverse. May 1965
◆ *The River Nile.* Announced. 408-417, Mar. 1966
● Sinai Sheds New Light on the Bible. By Henry Field. Photos by William B. and Gladys Terry. 795-815, Dec. 1948
● Tutankhamun's Golden Trove. By Christiane Desroches Noblecourt. Photos by F. L. Kenett. 625-646, Oct. 1963
● *See also* Abu Simbel

EGYPTIAN VULTURE:
● Tool-using Bird: The Egyptian Vulture. By Baroness Jane van Lawick-Goodall. Photos by Baron Hugo van Lawick. 631-641, May 1968

EIGELAND, TOR: Photographer:
● Capturing Strange Creatures in Colombia. By Marte Latham. 682-693, May 1966

EIGHT Maps of Discovery. 757-769, June 1953

1898: The Bells on Sable. Photos by Arthur W. McCurdy. 408-409, 416-417, Sept. 1965

EIGHTY Centuries of Veracruz. By S. Jeffrey K. Wilkerson. Photos by David Hiser. Paintings by Richard Schlecht. NGS research grant. 203-231, Aug. 1980

EILER, LYNTHA:
Author-Photographer:
● Yesterday Lingers on Lake Erie's Bass Islands. By Terry and Lyntha Eiler. 86-101, July 1978

EILER, TERRY:
Author-Photographer:
● Yesterday Lingers on Lake Erie's Bass Islands. By Terry and Lyntha Eiler. 86-101, July 1978

SEE "THE VOLGA" TUESDAY, MARCH 8, ON PBS TV

VICTOR R. BOSWELL, JR., NGS

Legacy: Egyptian slate carving, 3100 B.C.

Photographer:
● Indian Shangri-La of the Grand Canyon. By Jay Johnston. 355-373, Mar. 1970

EILOART, ARNOLD: Author:
● Braving the Atlantic by Balloon *(Small World).* 123-146, July 1959

EILTS, HERMANN F.: Author:
● Along the Storied Incense Roads of Aden. Photos by Brian Brake. 230-254, Feb. 1957

ÉIRE. *See* Ireland, Republic of

EISEMAN, FRED and MARGARET:
Photographers:
● Bali Celebrates a Festival of Faith. By Peter Miller. 416-427, Mar. 1980

EISENHOWER, DWIGHT D.:
● The Eisenhower Story. By Howard La Fay. 1-39, July 1969
● Inside the White House. By Lonnelle Aikman. Photos by B. Anthony Stewart and Thomas Nebbia. 3-43, Jan. 1961
● The Living White House. By Lonnelle Aikman. 593-643, Nov. 1966
● President Eisenhower Presents the Hubbard Medal to Everest's Conquerors (British). 64, July 1954
● President Eisenhower Presents the Society's Hubbard Medal to the Conquerors of Antarctica. 589-590, Apr. 1959
● President Eisenhower Presents to Prince Philip the National Geographic Society's Medal. 865-868, Dec. 1957
● Profiles of the Presidents: V. The Atomic Age: Its Problems and Promises. By Frank Freidel. 66-119, Jan. 1966
● When the President Goes Abroad. By Gilbert M. Grosvenor. 588-649, May 1960
● World's Last Salute to a Great American. By William Graves and other members of the National Geographic staff. 40-51, July 1969
Author:
● The Churchill I Knew. 153-157, Aug. 1965
● A Message From the President of the United States. 587, May 1960

EISENHOWER, MAMIE GENEVA DOUD:
● The Eisenhower Story. By Howard La Fay. 1-39, July 1969
Author:
● Introduction to article, "Inside the White House." 1, Jan. 1961

EISTEDDFODS:
● Wales, Land of Bards. By Alan Villiers. Photos by Thomas Nebbia. 727-769, June 1965

EKA DASA RUDRA (Festival):
● Bali Celebrates a Festival of Faith. By Peter Miller. Photos by Fred and Margaret Eiseman. 416-427, Mar. 1980

EL-BAZ, FAROUK: Author:
● Egypt's Desert of Promise. Photos by Georg Gerster. 190-221, Feb. 1982

ELBOWROOM for the Millions. By Louise Levathes. 86-97, July 1979

EL CHICHÓN (Volcano), Mexico:
• The Disaster of El Chichón. By Boris Weintraub. Photos by Guillermo Aldana E. and Kenneth Garrett. 654-684, Nov. 1982
Volcanic Cloud May Alter Earth's Climate. By Robert I. Tilling. 672-675

ELDFELL (Volcano), Heimaey, Iceland:
• Vestmannaeyjar: Up From the Ashes. By Noel Grove. Photos by Robert S. Patton. 690-701, May 1977
• *See also* former name, Kirkjufell

ELECTRICITY:
• Can We Harness the Wind? By Roger Hamilton. Photos by Emory Kristof. 812-829, Dec. 1975
• The Fire of Heaven. By Albert W. Atwood. 655-674, Nov. 1948
• Lightning in Action. By F. Barrows Colton. 809-828, June 1950
• The Search for Tomorrow's Power. By Kenneth F. Weaver. Photos by Emory Kristof. 650-681, Nov. 1972
• Solar Energy, the Ultimate Powerhouse. By John L. Wilhelm. Photos by Emory Kristof. 381-397, Mar. 1976
• Uncle Sam's House of 1,000 Wonders (National Bureau of Standards). By Lyman J. Briggs and F. Barrows Colton. 755-784, Dec. 1951
• Whatever Happened to TVA? By Gordon Young. Photos by Emory Kristof. 830-863, June 1973
• *See also* Hydroelectric Power; Nuclear Energy

ELECTRON MICROSCOPY:
• At Home With the Bulldog Ant. By Robert F. Sisson. 62-75, July 1974
Face-to-Face With a World of Ants (Electron Micrographs). 72-75
• Electronic Voyage Through an Invisible World. By Kenneth F. Weaver. Included: Field ion microscope, scanning electron microscope, transmission electron microscope. 274-290, Feb. 1977
▪ The Invisible World. 1, Jan. 1980; cover, Mar. 1980

ELECTRONIC Mini-marvel That Is Changing Your Life: The Chip. By Allen A. Boraiko. Photos by Charles O'Rear. 421-457, Oct. 1982

ELECTRONICS:
• New Miracles of the Telephone Age. By Robert Leslie Conly. 87-120, July 1954
• *See also* Computer Applications; Computer Technology; DEW Line; Electron Microscopy; Infrared Radiation; Lasers; Microelectronics; Radar; Satellites; Sonar

ELEPHANT BIRD. *See Aepyornis*

ELEPHANT SEALS. *See* Sea Elephants

ELEPHANTS:
• Africa's Elephants: Can They Survive? By Oria Douglas-Hamilton. Photos by Oria and Iain Douglas-Hamilton. 568-603, Nov. 1980

LEE LYON
Elephants: African matriarch charges

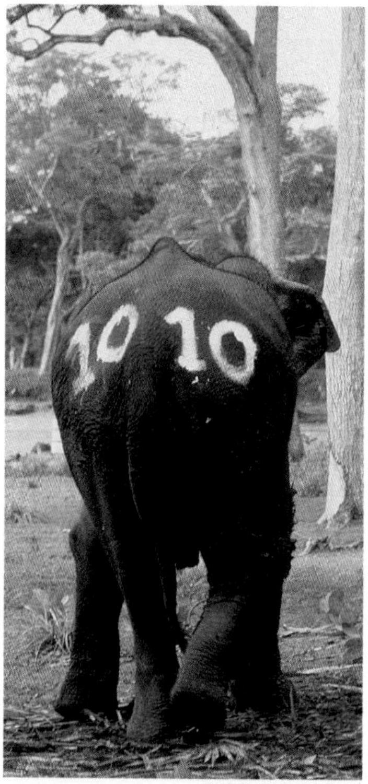

DIETER AND MARY PLAGE
Sri Lanka's Wildlife: new arrival in park

• Africa's Uncaged Elephants. Photos by Quentin Keynes. 371-382, Mar. 1951
• Bhutan, Land of the Thunder Dragon. By Burt Kerr Todd. 713-754, Dec. 1952
• Editorial. By Wilbur E. Garrett. 285, Mar. 1981
• The Elephant and I. By M. D. Chaturvedi. 489-507, Oct. 1957
• Etosha: Namibia's Kingdom of Animals. By Douglas H. Chadwick. Photos by Des and Jen Bartlett. 344-385, Mar. 1983
▪ Last Stand in Eden. 1, Jan. 1979
• On the Road With an Old-time Circus. By John Fetterman. Photos by Jonathan Blair. 410-434, Mar. 1972
• Sri Lanka's Wildlife: A Nation Rises to the Challenge. By Lyn de Alwis. Photos by Dieter and Mary Plage. 274-278, Aug. 1983
• Where Elephants Have Right of Way (Africa). By George and Jinx Rodger. Photos by George Rodger. 363-389, Sept. 1960
• Wild Elephant Roundup in India. By Harry Miller. Photos by author and James P. Blair. 372-385, Mar. 1969
• *See also* Mammoth

El **GRECO:**
• Toledo–El Greco's Spain Lives on. By Louise E. Levathes. Photos by James P. Blair. Introduction by J. Carter Brown. 726-753, June 1982

EL HATILLO CULTURE:
• Exploring the Past in Panama. By Matthew W. Stirling. Photos by Richard H. Stewart. NGS research grant. 373-399, Mar. 1949

ELIOT, JOHN L.: Author:
• Hawaii's Far-flung Wildlife Paradise. Photos by Jonathan Blair. 670-691, May 1978
• Into the Eye of David (Hurricane). 368-369, Sept. 1980
• Japan's Warriors of the Wind. Photos by David Alan Harvey. 551-561, Apr. 1977
• Roosevelt Country: T. R.'s Wilderness Legacy. Photos by Farrell Grehan. 340-363, Sept. 1982
• Treasures of Dresden. Photos by Victor R. Boswell, Jr. 702-717, Nov. 1978

ELISABETHVILLE, Democratic Republic of the Congo:
• White Magic in the Belgian Congo. By W. Robert Moore. 321-362, Mar. 1952

ELISOFON, ELIOT: Photographer:
• Yesterday's Congo, Today's Zaire. By John J. Putman. 398-432, Mar. 1973

ELIZABETH I, Queen (England):
• The British Way. By Sir Evelyn Wrench. 421-541, Apr. 1949
• Founders of Virginia. By Sir Evelyn Wrench. Photos by B. Anthony Stewart. 433-462, Apr. 1948
• The World of Elizabeth I. By Louis B. Wright. Photos by Ted Spiegel. 668-709, Nov. 1968

ELIZABETH II, Queen (Great Britain and Northern Ireland):
● In the London of the New Queen. By H. V. Morton. 291-342, Sept. 1953
● The Investiture of Great Britain's Prince of Wales. By Allan C. Fisher, Jr. Photos by James L. Stanfield and Adam Woolfitt. 698-715, Nov. 1969
● Queen Elizabeth Opens Parliament. By W. E. Roscher. Photos by Robert B. Goodman. 699-707, Nov. 1961
● Queen of Canada. By Phyllis Wilson. Photos by Kathleen Revis. 825-829, June 1959
● Silkworms in England Spin for the Queen. By John E. H. Nolan. 689-704, May 1953
● Windsor Castle. By Anthony Holden. Photos by James L. Stanfield. 604-631, Nov. 1980

ELIZABETHAN AGE:
● The British Way. By Sir Evelyn Wrench. 421-541, Apr. 1949
● Folger: Biggest Little Library in the World. By Joseph T. Foster. Photos by B. Anthony Stewart and John E. Fletcher. Note: The Folger Collection, which includes the Renaissance library of Sir R. Leicester Harmsworth, forms the Western World's most valuable historical library on English civilization of the 16th and early 17th centuries. 411-424, Sept. 1951
● *See also* Drake, Sir Francis; Elizabeth I; Shakespeare, William

ELIZALDE, MANUEL, Jr.:
● First Glimpse of a Stone Age Tribe. 881-882, Dec. 1971
● Help for Philippine Tribes in Trouble. By Kenneth MacLeish. Photos by Dean Conger. 220-255, Aug. 1971
● The Tasadays, Stone Age Cavemen of Mindanao. By Kenneth MacLeish. Photos by John Launois. 219-249, Aug. 1972

ELK:
● Jackson Hole: Good-bye to the Old Days? By François Leydet. Photos by Jonathan Wright. Included: National Elk Refuge, Wyoming. 768-789, Dec. 1976
● Yellowstone Wildlife in Winter. By William Albert Allard. 637-661, Nov. 1967

ELK MOUNTAINS, Colorado:
● Colorado's Friendly Topland. By Robert M. Ormes. 187-214, Aug. 1951

ELLER, ERNEST M.: Author:
● Troubled Waters East of Suez. 483-522, Apr. 1954

ELLESMERE ISLAND, Canada:
● Domesticating the Wild and Woolly Musk Ox. By John J. Teal, Jr. Photos by Robert W. Madden. 862-879, June 1970
● Eskimo and Viking Finds in the High Arctic: Ellesmere Island. By Peter Schledermann. Photos by Sisse Brimberg. 575-601, May 1981
● Far North with "Captain Mac." By Miriam MacMillan. Included: Cape Sabine; Fort Conger; Wade Point. 465-513, Oct. 1951
● North Toward the Pole on Skis. By Bjørn O. Staib. 254-281, Feb. 1965
● The Peary Flag Comes to Rest. By Marie Peary Stafford. 519-532, Oct. 1954
● Three Months on an Arctic Ice Island. By Joseph O. Fletcher. 489-504, Apr. 1953
● We Followed Peary to the Pole. By Gilbert Grosvenor and Thomas W. McKnew. 469-484, Oct. 1953

ELLICE ISLANDS, Pacific Ocean:
● Adventures with the Survey Navy. By Irving Johnson. 131-148, July 1947

ELLIS, MELVIN R.: Author:
● Raccoon: Amiable Rogue in a Black Mask. 841-854, Dec. 1956
● Skunks Want Peace–or Else! Photos by Charles Philip Fox. 279-294, Aug. 1955

ELLIS, WILLIAM S.: Author:
● Afo-A-Kom: A Sacred Symbol Comes Home. Photos by James P. Blair. 141-148, July 1974
● Atlanta, Pacesetter City of the South. Photos by James L. Amos. 246-281, Feb. 1969
● Bangladesh: Hope Nourishes a New Nation. Photos by Dick Durrance II. 295-333, Sept. 1972
● Beirut–Up From the Rubble. Photos by Steve McCurry. 262-286, Feb. 1983
● Cairo, Troubled Capital of the Arab World. Photos by Winfield Parks. 639-667, May 1972
● The Coast Guard: Small Service With a Big Mission. 113-139, July 1974
● Florida–A Time for Reckoning. Photos by Nathan Benn and Kevin Fleming. 172-219, Aug. 1982
● Goal at the End of the Trail: Santa Fe. Photos by Gordon W. Gahan and Otis Imboden. 323-345, Mar. 1982
● High-stepping Idaho. Photos by Dean Conger. 290-317, Mar. 1973
● Hong Kong's Refugee Dilemma. Photos by William Albert Allard. 709-732, Nov. 1979
● Istanbul, the City That Links Europe and Asia. Photos by Winfield Parks. 501-533, Oct. 1973
● Japan's Amazing Inland Sea. Photos by James L. Stanfield. 830-863, Dec. 1977
● Lebanon, Little Bible Land in the Crossfire of History. Photos by George F. Mobley. 240-275, Feb. 1970
● Loch Ness: The Lake and the Legend. Photos by Emory Kristof and David Doubilet. 759-779, June 1977
● Lonely Cape Hatteras, Besieged by the Sea. Photos by Emory Kristof. 393-421, Sept. 1969
● Los Angeles: City in Search of Itself. Photos by Jodi Cobb. 26-59, Jan. 1979
● Malaysia: Youthful Nation With Growing Pains. Photos by David Alan Harvey. 635-667, May 1977
● Pakistan Under Pressure. Photos by James L. Stanfield. 668-701, May 1981
● Romania: Maverick on a Tightrope. Photos by Winfield Parks. 688-713, Nov. 1975
● The St. Lawrence River: Canada's Highway to the Sea. Photos by Bruce Dale. 586-623, May 1980
● South Africa's Lonely Ordeal. Photos by James P. Blair. 780-819, June 1977
● Tracking Danger With the Ice Patrol. Photos by James R. Holland. 780-793, June 1968
● Will Oil and Tundra Mix? Alaska's North Slope Hangs in the Balance. Photos by Emory Kristof. 485-517, Oct. 1971
● Wisconsin's Door Peninsula. Photos by Ted Rozumalski. 347-371, Mar. 1969
● Yellowstone at 100: The Pitfalls of Success. Photos by Jonathan Blair. 616-631, May 1972

ELLSWORTH HIGHLAND TRAVERSE:
● Exploring Antarctica's Phantom Coast. By Edwin A. McDonald. Photos by W. D. Vaughn. 251-273, Feb. 1962

ELLSWORTH MOUNTAINS, Antarctica. *See* Sentinel Range

EL MORRO: Story in Stone (New Mexico). By Edwards Park. 237-244, Aug. 1957

EL SALVADOR:
● Troubled Times for Central America. By Wilbur E. Garrett, Editor. 58-61, July 1981

EL SANGAY, Fire-breathing Giant of the Andes. By G. Edward Lewis. 117-138, Jan. 1950

ELSIE (Yawl):
● Down East to Nova Scotia. By Winfield Parks. 853-879, June 1964

EL TAJÍN (Archaeological Site), Mexico:
● Man's Eighty Centuries in Veracruz. By S. Jeffrey K. Wilkerson. Photos by David Hiser. Paintings by Richard Schlecht. 203-231, Aug. 1980

EMBROIDERY:
● Madeira, Like Its Wine, Improves With Age. By Veronica Thomas. Photos by Jonathan Blair. 488-513, Apr. 1973

EMERALDS:
● Questing for Gems. By George S. Switzer. 835-863, Dec. 1971

EMERSON, GILBERT: Artist:
● How Man-made Satellites Can Affect Our Lives. By Joseph Kaplan. 791-810, Dec. 1957

EMERSON, GUY: Author:
● The Kress Collection: A Gift to the Nation. 823-865, Dec. 1961

EMERSON, RALPH WALDO:
● Literary Landmarks of Massachusetts. By William H. Nicholas. Photos by B. Anthony Stewart and John E. Fletcher. 279-310, Mar. 1950

E F

EMORY, KENNETH P.: Author:
• The Coming of the Polynesians. 732-745, Dec. 1974

The **EMPEROR'S** Private Garden: Kashmir. By Nigel Cameron. Photos by Brian Brake. 606-647, Nov. 1958

ENCAMPMENTS of the Dispossessed (Somalis). By Larry Kohl. 756-763, June 1981

ENCHANTRESS! (White Tigress). By Theodore H. Reed. Photos by Thomas J. Abercrombie. 628-641, May 1961

ENCYCLOPAEDIA BRITANNICA EDUCATIONAL CORPORATION:
• The World in Geographic Filmstrips. By Melvin M. Payne. 134-137, Jan. 1968

ENDANGERED AND THREATENED SPECIES:
• African Wildlife: Man's Threatened Legacy. By Allan C. Fisher, Jr. Photos by Thomas Nebbia. Paintings by Ned Seidler. 147-187, Feb. 1972
◆ *Animals in Danger.* 1978
• Editorials. By Gilbert M. Grosvenor. 1, Jan. 1976; By Wilbur E. Garrett. 285, Mar. 1981; 703, June 1983
• India Struggles to Save Her Wildlife. By John J. Putman. Paintings by Ned Seidler. 299-343, Sept. 1976
• The Japanese Crane, Bird of Happiness. By Tsuneo Hayashida. 542-556, Oct. 1983
• The Last Great Animal Kingdom: A Portfolio of Africa's Vanishing Wildlife. 390-409, Sept. 1960
• Last of the Black-footed Ferrets? By Tim W. Clark. Photos by Franz J. Camenzind and the author. NGS research grant. 828-838, June 1983
• Saving Man's Wildlife Heritage. By John H. Baker. Photos by Robert F. Sisson. 581-620, Nov. 1954
• Threatened Glories of Everglades National Park. By Frederick Kent Truslow and Frederick G. Vosburgh. Photos by Frederick Kent Truslow and Otis Imboden. 508-553, Oct. 1967
• The Tree Nobody Liked (Red Mangrove). By Rick Gore. Photos by Bianca Lavies. Note: Many imperiled tropical birds find sanctuary among Florida's mangroves; and the Key deer has made a comeback. 669-689, May 1977
• Tropical Rain Forests. 2-65, Jan. 1983
Nature's Dwindling Treasures. By Peter T. White. Photos by James P. Blair. Paintings by Barron Storey. 2-47; Teeming Life of a Rain Forest. By Carol and David Hughes. 49-65
◆ *Vanishing Wildlife of North America.* Announced. 865-868, June 1973
• Where Oil and Wildlife Mix. By Steven C. Wilson and Karen C. Hayden. 145-173, Feb. 1981
• Wild Cargo: the Business of Smuggling Animals. By Noel Grove. Photos by Steve Raymer. 287-315, Mar. 1981
◆ *Wildlife Alert!* 1980
• Wildlife of Everglades National Park. By Daniel B. Beard. Paintings by Walter A. Weber. 83-116, Jan. 1949
• *See also* Andean Condors; Atlantic Salmon; Bald Eagles; Bighorn Sheep; Bluebirds; Bluefin Tuna; Brown Pelicans; Cheetahs; Crocodilians; Elephants; Giant Brazilian Otters; Giant Tortoises; Gorillas; Grizzly Bears; Harp Seals; Horses, Wild; Humpback Whales; Orangutans; Pandas, Giant; Philippine Eagles; Polar Bears; Rothschild's Giraffe; Snow Leopards; Tree Snails; Trumpeter Swans; Vicuñas; Whales; Whooping Cranes; Wolves; Wood Storks

ENDEAVOUR (Bark):
• Captain Cook: The Man Who Mapped the Pacific. By Alan Villiers. Photos by Gordon W. Gahan. 297-349, Sept. 1971

ENDEAVOUR (Cutter) Sails the Inside Passage. By Amos Burg. 801-828, June 1947

The **ENDURING** Pyrenees. By Robert Laxalt. Photos by Edwin Stuart Grosvenor. 794-819, Dec. 1974

ENERGY:
• America's Auto Mania. By David Jeffery. Photos by Bruce Dale. 24-31, *Special Report on Energy* (Feb. 1981)
• An Atlas of Energy Resources. 58-69, *Special Report on Energy* (Feb. 1981)
I. Oil: Lifeblood and Liability. 58-59; II. Natural Gas: Clean, Convenient, and Cheap. 60-61; III. Coal: Abundant Resource, Abundant Problems. 62-63; IV. Geothermal: Tapping the Earth's Furnace. 64-65; V. Uranium: Too Hot to Handle? 66-67; VI. Solar Energy: Ours for the Taking. 68-69
• The Auto: Problem Child With a Promising Future. 32-33, *Special Report on Energy* (Feb. 1981)
• Conservation: Can We Live Better on Less? By Rick Gore. 34-57, *Special Report on Energy* (Feb. 1981)
I. Harnessing the Wind. 38; II. Electricity From the Sun. 40-41; III. Modern House, Ancient Architecture. 42-43; IV. The Fusion Solution. 45; V. A Visit From House Doctors. 48-49; VI. The Promise of Ocean Energy. 51; VII. Where Do Society Members Stand? 52-53
• Editorials. By Gilbert M. Grosvenor. 289, Mar. 1976; 577, Nov. 1978; By Wilbur E. Garrett. 143, Feb. 1981
• Editor's Postscript. By Wilbur E. Garrett. 115, *Special Report on Energy* (Feb. 1981)
• Energy Source Book: Where To Go For Help. Contents: A list of books, agencies, and *National Geographic* articles dealing with energy. 114, *Special Report on Energy* (Feb. 1981)
• Energy Terms. 23, *Special Report on Energy* (Feb. 1981)
• Our Energy Predicament. By Kenneth F. Weaver. 2-23, *Special Report on Energy* (Feb. 1981)
• Powder River Basin: New Energy Frontier. By Bill Richards. Photos by Louie Psihoyos. 96-113, *Special Report on Energy* (Feb. 1981)
• Synfuels: Fill 'er Up! With What? By Thomas Y. Canby. Photos by Jonathan Blair. 74-95, *Special Report on Energy* (Feb. 1981)
Wresting Oil From Reluctant Rock. 78-79
• The Unbalanced World. By NGS President Gilbert M. Grosvenor. 1, *Special Report on Energy* (Feb. 1981)
• What Six Experts Say. Contents: Statements from John F. O'Leary, John F. O'Leary Associates, Inc.; Hans H. Landsberg, Center for Energy Policy Research, Resources for the Future; Steven C. Wilson, Entheos Mountain Agriculture Institute; Robert B. Stobaugh, Harvard Graduate School of Business Administration; Fred L. Hartley, Chairman and President, Union Oil Company and President, American Petroleum Institute; Amory B. Lovins, Friends of the Earth. 70-73, *Special Report on Energy* (Feb. 1981)

ENERGY SOURCES:
• Can We Harness the Wind? By Roger Hamilton. Photos by Emory Kristof. 812-829, Dec. 1975
• The Fascinating World of Trash. By Peter T. White. Photos by Louie Psihoyos. 424-457, Apr. 1983
• The Fire of Heaven: Electricity Revolutionizes the Modern World. By Albert W. Atwood. 655-674, Nov. 1948
• Five Noted Thinkers Explore the Future. Included: Isaac Asimov, Richard F. Babcock, Edmund N. Bacon, Buckminster Fuller, Gerard Piel. 68-75, July 1976
• Hunting Uranium Around the World. By Robert D. Nininger. Photos by Volkmar Wentzel. 533-558, Oct. 1954
• The Search for Tomorrow's Power. By Kenneth F. Weaver. Photos by Emory Kristof. 650-681, Nov. 1972
◆ *Special Report on Energy.* 1981
• This Land of Ours–How Are We Using It? By Peter T. White. Photos by Emory Kristof. 20-67, July 1976
• *See also* Coal; Forest Products; Geothermal Energy; Hydroelectric Power; Natural Gas; Nuclear Energy; Ocean Energy; Oil; Solar Energy; Wind Power

ENGELMANN, RUDOLF J.: Author:
• Laboratory in a Dirty Sky. By Rudolf J. Engelmann and Vera Simons. 616-621, Nov. 1976

ENGINEERING:
• Abu Simbel's Ancient Temples Reborn. By Georg Gerster. 724-744, May 1969
• Saving the Ancient Temples at Abu Simbel. By Georg Gerster. Paintings by Robert W. Nicholson. 694-742, May 1966
• Threatened Treasures of the Nile. By Georg Gerster. 587-621, Oct. 1963

• *See also* Borobudur (Temple), Indonesia; Bridges; Dams; Pipelines, Natural Gas; Pipelines, Oil; Thames Barrier; Tunnels; *and* St. Lawrence Seaway; Suez Canal; Tennessee Valley Authority

ENGLAND:

• "Around the World in Eighty Days." By Newman Bumstead. Included: Canterbury; Eton; London; and Thames River. 705-750, Dec. 1951

• "Be Ye Men of Valour" (Churchill's Life; Funeral). By Howard La Fay. 159-197, Aug. 1965

• The Bonanza Bean–Coffee. By Ethel A. Starbird. Photos by Sam Abell. 388-405, Mar. 1981

• The Britain That Shakespeare Knew. By Louis B. Wright. Photos by Dean Conger. 613-665, May 1964

• British Castles, History in Stone. By Norman Wilkinson. 111-129, July 1947

▲ *British Isles,* Atlas series supplement. July 1958

▲ *The British Isles,* supplement. Apr. 1949

• The British Way: Great Britain's Major Gifts to Freedom, Democratic Government, Science, and Society. By Sir Evelyn Wrench. 421-541, Apr. 1949

• The Celts. By Merle Severy. Photos by James P. Blair. Paintings by Robert C. Magis. 582-633, May 1977

• Editorial. By Gilbert M. Grosvenor. 441, Oct. 1979

• The England of Charles Dickens. By Richard W. Long. Photos by Adam Woolfitt. 443-483, Apr. 1974

• Exploring England's Canals. By Bryan Hodgson. Photos by Linda Bartlett. 76-111, July 1974

• The Final Tribute (Churchill Funeral). Text by Carolyn Bennett Patterson. 199-225, Aug. 1965

• Founders of New England. By Sir Evelyn Wrench. Photos by B. Anthony Stewart. 803-838, June 1953

• Founders of Virginia. By Sir Evelyn Wrench. Photos by B. Anthony Stewart. 433-462, Apr. 1948

• Henry VIII's Lost Warship: *Mary Rose.* By Margaret Rule. Introduction and picture text by Peter Miller. Paintings by Richard Schlecht. 646-675, May 1983

• Landmarks of Literary England. By Leo A. Borah. Photos by Kathleen Revis. 295-350, Sept. 1955

▲ *Medieval England; British Isles,* double-sided supplement. Oct. 1979

• Midshipmen's Cruise. By William J. Aston and Alexander G. B. Grosvenor. 711-754, June 1948

• A New Look at Medieval Europe. By Kenneth M. Setton. Paintings by Andre Durenceau and Birney Lettick. 799-859, Dec. 1962

• 900 Years Ago: The Norman Conquest. By Kenneth M. Setton. Photos by George F. Mobley. 206-251, Aug. 1966

• The Original Boston: St. Botolph's Town. By Veronica Thomas. Photos by James L. Amos. 382-389, Sept. 1974

• Our Search for British Paintings. By Franklin L. Fisher. 543-550, Apr. 1949

• Père David's Deer Saved From Extinction. By Larry Kohl. Photos by Bates Littlehales. Included: Woburn Abbey Safari Park. 478-485, Oct. 1982

• Pilgrimage to Holy Island and the Farnes. By John E. H. Nolan. 547-570, Oct. 1952

• Queen Elizabeth Opens Parliament. By W. E. Roscher. Photos by Robert B. Goodman. 699-707, Nov. 1961

• Reach for the New World. By Mendel Peterson. Photos by David L. Arnold. Paintings by Richard Schlecht. Included: English ships and salvaged artifacts. 724-767, Dec. 1977

• Round the World School (ISA). By Paul Antze. Photos by William Eppridge. 96-127, July 1962

▲ *Shakespeare's Britain,* supplement. May 1964

• Silkworms in England Spin for the Queen. By John E. H. Nolan. 689-704, May 1953

• A Stroll to London. By Isobel Wylie Hutchison. Photos by B. Anthony Stewart. 171-204, Aug. 1950

• The Thames: That Noble River. By Ethel A. Starbird. Photos by O. Louis Mazzatenta. 750-791, June 1983

• The Thames Mirrors England's Varied Life. By Willard Price. Photos by Robert F. Sisson. 45-93, July 1958

■ This Britain: Heritage of the Sea. 583, Nov. 1975; cover, Dec. 1975

◆ *This England.* Announced. 539-543, Oct. 1966

• Thumbs Up Round the North Sea's Rim. By Frances James. Photos by Erica Koch. 685-704, May 1952

▲ *A Traveler's Map of the British Isles,* supplement. Text on reverse. Apr. 1974

• Two Englands. By Allan C. Fisher, Jr. Photos by Cary Wolinsky. 442-481, Oct. 1979

• The World of Elizabeth I. By Louis B. Wright. Photos by Ted Spiegel. 668-709, Nov. 1968

• *See also* Abbotsbury Swannery; Appleby Fair; Cambridge; Canterbury Cathedral; Cornwall; Cotswold Hills; Devonshire; Kew; Lake District; London; Portsmouth; Stonehenge; *and* Elizabethan Age; *Mayflower II;* Windsor Castle

ENGLEBERT, VICTOR:

Author-Photographer:

• The Danakil: Nomads of Ethiopia's Wasteland. 186-211, Feb. 1970

• Drought Threatens the Tuareg World. 544-571, Apr. 1974

• I Joined a Sahara Salt Caravan. 694-711, Nov. 1965

• Trek by Mule Among Morocco's Berbers. 850-875, June 1968

ENGLISH CHANNEL:

• Channel Cruise to Glorious Devon. By Alan Villiers. Photos by Bates Littlehales. 208-259, Aug. 1963

Elizabeth I: court portrait of the Queen

COURTESY THE MARQUESS OF SALISBURY

CARY WOLINSKY, STOCK, BOSTON

Two Englands: beefeater dons uniform

• Cowes to Cornwall. By Alan Villiers. Photos by Robert B. Goodman. 149-201, Aug. 1961
• Winged Victory of *Gossamer Albatross*. By Bryan Allen. 640-651, Nov. 1979
• *See also* Channel Islands; St. Michael's Mount

ENGLISH SETTLERS. *See* Founders of New England; Founders of Virginia; Roanoke Island, for Lost Colony; Williamsburg, Virginia; Wolstenholme Towne (Site), Virginia; *and* Victoria, Kansas (19th Century)

The **ENIGMA** of Bird Anting. By Hance Roy Ivor. 105-119, July 1956

ENTEBBE ANIMAL REFUGE, Uganda:
• Orphans of the Wild. By Bruce G. Kinloch. 683-699, Nov. 1962

ENTERPRISE (Nuclear Carrier):
• The Mighty *Enterprise*. By Nathaniel T. Kenney. Photos by Thomas J. Abercrombie. 431-448, Mar. 1963

ENTOMOLOGY. *See* Insects

ENVIRONMENTAL CONCERNS. *See* Air Pollution; Chemical Pollution; Conservation; Desertification; Ecology; Endangered and Threatened Species; Energy; Erosion; Land Use; Oil Spills; Pesticide Pollution; Pollution; Radioactive Wastes; Rain Forests; Strip Mining; Waste Disposal; Water Pollution; Water Resources

ENVIRONMENTAL PROTECTION AGENCY:
• The Pesticide Dilemma. By Allen A. Boraiko. Photos by Fred Ward. 145-183, Feb. 1980

ÉPINAL, France:
• Here Rest in Honored Glory . . . The United States Dedicates Six New Battle Monuments in Europe to Americans Who Gave Their Lives During World War II. By Howell Walker. Included: Épinal American Cemetery and Memorial. 739-768, June 1957

EPITAPH for a Killer? By Donald A. Henderson. Photos by Marion Kaplan. 796-805, Dec. 1978

EPPRIDGE, WILLIAM: Photographer:
• The Alps: Man's Own Mountains. By Ralph Gray. Photos by Walter Meayers Edwards and William Eppridge. 350-395, Sept. 1965
• Round the World School. By Paul Antze. 96-127, July 1962

EQUATORIAL GUINEA, Republic of. *See* Río Muni

ERIE, Lake, Canada-U. S.:
• The Great Lakes: Is It Too Late? By Gordon Young. Photos by James L. Amos and Martin Rogers. 147-185, Aug. 1973
• Yesterday Lingers on Lake Erie's Bass Islands. By Terry and Lyntha Eiler. 86-101, July 1978

ERIGBAAGTSA (Indians):
• Indians of the Amazon Darkness. By Harald Schultz. NGS research grant. 737-758, May 1964

ERIM, KENAN T.: Author:
• Ancient Aphrodisias and Its Marble Treasures. Photos by Jonathan S. Blair. 280-294, Aug. 1967
• Ancient Aphrodisias Lives Through Its Art. Photos by David Brill. 527-551, Oct. 1981
• Aphrodisias, Awakened City of Ancient Art. Photos by Jonathan Blair. 766-791, June 1972

ERONGARÍCUARO, Mexico:
• Lost Kingdom in Indian Mexico (Tarascan). By Justin Locke. 517-546, Oct. 1952

EROSION:
• Erosion, Trojan Horse of Greece. By F. G. Renner. 793-812, Dec. 1947
• Grand Canyon: Are We Loving It to Death? By W. E. Garrett. 16-51, July 1978
▲ *The Grand Canyon,* double-sided supplement. Text. NGS research grant. July 1978
• Water for the World's Growing Needs. By Herbert B. Nichols and F. Barrows Colton. 269-286, Aug. 1952
• *See also* Forests and Reforestation; Mud Slides; This Land of Ours; U. S. Soil Conservation Service

ERTAUD, JACQUES: Photographer:
• Fish Men Discover a 2,200-year-old Greek Ship. By Jacques-Yves Cousteau. 1-36, Jan. 1954
• Fish Men Explore a New World Undersea. By Jacques-Yves Cousteau. 431-472, Oct. 1952

ERUPTION of Mount St. Helens. By Rowe Findley. 3-65, Jan. 1981
I. Mountain With a Death Wish. 3-33; II. In the Path of Destruction. 35-49; III. The Day the Sky Fell. 50-65

ERZURUM, Turkey:
• Turkey Paves the Path of Progress. By Maynard Owen Williams. 141-186, Aug. 1951
• Where Turk and Russian Meet. By Ferdinand Kuhn. 743-766, June 1952

ESCALANTE CANYON, Utah:
• Escalante: Utah's River of Arches. By W. Robert Moore. 399-425, Sept. 1955
• Escalante Canyon–Wilderness at the Crossroads. By Jon Schneeberger. 270-285, Aug. 1972
• First Motor Sortie into Escalante Land. By Jack Breed. 369-404, Sept. 1949

ESCORTING Mona Lisa to America. By Edward T. Folliard. 838-847, June 1963

ESKIMAUAN LINGUISTIC STOCK:
• Nomads of the Far North. By Matthew W. Stirling. 471-504, Oct. 1949
Hearty Folk Defy Arctic Storms. Paintings by W. Langdon Kihn. 479-494

ESKIMOS:
• Alaska: Rising Northern Star. By Joseph Judge. Photos by Bruce Dale. Included: Inupiat and Nunamiut Eskimos; also Eskimos of Nunapitchuk, Selawik, and Wainwright. 730-767, June 1975
• Alaska Proudly Joins the Union. By Ernest Gruening. Photos by Thomas J. Abercrombie. 43-83, July 1959
• Alaska's Russian Frontier: Little Diomede. Photos by Audrey and Frank Morgan. 551-562, Apr. 1951
• Caribou: Hardy Nomads of the North. By Jim Rearden. 858-878, Dec. 1974
• Cliff Dwellers of the Bering Sea. By Juan Muñoz. 129-146, Jan. 1954
• Domesticating the Wild and Wooly Musk Ox. By John J. Teal, Jr. Photos by Robert W. Madden. 862-879, June 1970
• Eskimo and Viking Finds in the High Arctic: Ellesmere Island. By Peter Schledermann. Photos by Sisse Brimberg. 575-601, May 1981
• Far North with "Captain Mac." By Miriam MacMillan. Included: Eskimos of Baffin Island, Greenland, Labrador; Polar Eskimos. 465-513, Oct. 1951
• Greenland Feels the Winds of Change. By John J. Putman. Photos by George F. Mobley. Included: Polar Eskimos of northwest Greenland, last of the true Eskimos. 366-393, Sept. 1975
• Hunters of the Lost Spirit: Alaskans, Canadians, Greenlanders. By Priit J. Vesilind. Photos by David Alan Harvey and Ivars Silis. 156-193, Feb. 1983
▲ *Indians of North America,* double-sided supplement. Included: Central Eskimos; Copper Eskimos. Dec. 1972
• The Last U. S. Whale Hunters. By Emory Kristof. 346-355, Mar. 1973
"Ocean mammals are to us what the buffalo was to the Plains Indian." By Lael Morgan. 354-355
• Milestones in My Arctic Journeys. By Willie Knutsen. 543-570, Oct. 1949
• Nomad in Alaska's Outback. By Thomas J. Abercrombie. 540-567, Apr. 1969
• Nomads of the Far North. By Matthew W. Stirling. 471-504, Oct. 1949
Hearty Folk Defy Arctic Storms. Paintings by W. Langdon Kihn. 479-494
• *North Star* Cruises Alaska's Wild West. By Amos Burg. 57-86, July 1952
▲ *Peoples of the Arctic; Arctic Ocean,* double-sided supplement. Feb. 1983
• Trek Across Arctic America. By Colin Irwin. 295-321, Mar. 1974
• A Visit to the Living Ice Age. By Rutherford Platt. 525-545, Apr. 1957
• Weather from the White North. By Andrew H. Brown. Photos by John E. Fletcher. 543-572, Apr. 1955
• Where Magic Ruled: Art of the Bering Sea. By William W. Fitzhugh and Susan A. Kaplan. Photos by Sisse Brimberg. 198-205, Feb. 1983
• Will Oil and Tundra Mix? Alaska's North Slope Hangs in the Balance. By William S. Ellis. Photos by Emory Kristof. 485-517, Oct. 1971

ESKIMOS, Canadian. *See* Inuit

ESSAY SUPPLEMENT:
▲ *The Face and Faith of Poland,* map, photo, and essay supplement. By Peter Miller. Essay by Czesław Miłosz. Photos by Bruno Barbey. Apr. 1982

The **ESSENCE** of Life–Salt. By Gordon Young. Photos by Volkmar Wentzel and Georg Gerster. 381-401, Sept. 1977

ESSENES:
● The Men Who Hid the Dead Sea Scrolls. By A. Douglas Tushingham. Paintings by Peter V. Bianchi. 785-808, Dec. 1958

ESTATES AND PLANTATIONS:
● California's Wonderful One (State Highway No. 1). By Frank Cameron. Photos by B. Anthony Stewart. Included: Hearst San Simeon State Historical Monument. 571-617, Nov. 1959
● The Greener Fields of Georgia. By Howell Walker. Photos by author and B. Anthony Stewart. 287-330, Mar. 1954
● History and Beauty Blend in a Concord Iris Garden. By Robert T. Cochran, Jr. Photos by M. Woodbridge Williams. Contents: Buttrick estate. 705-719, May 1959
● History Keeps House in Virginia. By Howell Walker. 441-484, Apr. 1956
● History Repeats in Old Natchez. By William H. Nicholas. Photos by Willard R. Culver. 181-208, Feb. 1949
● Huntington Library, California Treasure House. By David S. Boyer. 251-276, Feb. 1958
● Land of Louisiana Sugar Kings. By Harnett T. Kane. Photos by Willard R. Culver. 531-567, Apr. 1958
● Mount Vernon Lives On. By Lonnelle Aikman. 651-682, Nov. 1953
● Philadelphia Houses a Proud Past. By Harold Donaldson Eberlein. Photos by Thomas Nebbia. 151-191, Aug. 1960
● Rhododendron Glories of Southwest Scotland. By David S. Boyer. Photos by B. Anthony Stewart and author. 641-664, May 1954
● Roving Maryland's Cavalier Country. By William A. Kinney. 431-470, Apr. 1954
● South Carolina Rediscovered. By Herbert Ravenel Sass. Photos by Robert F. Sisson. 281-321, Mar. 1953
● Stately Homes of Old Virginia. By Albert W. Atwood. 787-802, June 1953
● Vizcaya: An Italian Palazzo in Miami. By William H. Nicholas. Photos by Justin Locke. 595-604, Nov. 1950
● Wonderland in Longwood Gardens. By Edward C. Ferriday, Jr. Contents: Du Pont estate. 45-64, July 1951
● *See also* Monticello

ESTES, RICHARD D.: Author:
● The Flamingo Eaters of Ngorongoro (Hyenas). 535-539, Oct. 1973

KEVIN FLEMING

Somalia: child at refugee camp

ESTONIAN S.S.R., U.S.S.R:
● Editorial. By Gilbert M. Grosvenor. 439, Apr. 1980
● Return to Estonia. By Priit J. Vesilind. Photos by Cotton Coulson. 485-511, Apr. 1980

ETERNAL Easter in a Greek Village. By Maria Nicolaidis-Karanikolas. Photos by James L. Stanfield. 768-777, Dec. 1983

The **ETERNAL** Flame. By Albert W. Atwood. 540-564, Oct. 1951

ETERNAL France. By Walter Meayers Edwards. 725-764, June 1960

ETERNAL Sinai. By Harvey Arden. Photos by David Doubilet and Kevin Fleming. 420-461, Apr. 1982
Egyptian Sector. Photos by Kevin Fleming. 430-443; Israeli Sector. Photos by David Doubilet. 444-461

The **ETERNAL** Treasure, Gold. By Peter T. White. Photos by James L. Stanfield. 1-51, Jan. 1974

ETHERTON, P. T.: Author:
● Lundy, Treasure Island of Birds. Photos by J. Allan Cash. 675-698, May 1947

ETHIOPIA:
● Africa: The Winds of Freedom Stir a Continent. By Nathaniel T. Kenney. Photos by W. D. Vaughn. 303-359, Sept. 1960
● The Danakil: Nomads of Ethiopia's Wasteland. By Victor Englebert. 186-211, Feb. 1970
● Ethiopia: Revolution in an Ancient Empire. By Robert Caputo. 614-645, May 1983
■ Ethiopia: The Hidden Empire. 884A-884B, Dec. 1970
● Ethiopia Yields First "Family" of Early Man. By Donald C. Johanson. Photos by David Brill. NGS research grant. 790-811, Dec. 1976
● Ethiopian Adventure. By Nathaniel T. Kenney. Photos by James P. Blair. 548-582, Apr. 1965
● Ethiopia's Artful Weavers. By Judith Olmstead. Photos by James A. Sugar. 125-141, Jan. 1973
● Locusts: "Teeth of the Wind." By Robert A. M. Conley. Photos by Gianni Tortoli. 202-227, Aug. 1969
● Safari from Congo to Cairo. By Elsie May Bell Grosvenor. Photos by Gilbert Grosvenor. 721-771, Dec. 1954
● Salt–The Essence of Life. By Gordon Young. Photos by Volkmar Wentzel and Georg Gerster. 381-401, Sept. 1977
● Searching Out Medieval Churches in Ethiopia's Wilds. By Georg Gerster. 856-884, Dec. 1970
● Somalia's Hour of Need. By Robert Paul Jordan. Photos by Michael S. Yamashita and Kevin Fleming. Note: The Ogaden, an area historically peopled by Somalis, is claimed by Ethiopia. 748-775, June 1981
Encampments of the Dispossessed. By Larry Kohl. 756-763

ETHNOLOGY:
◆ *Primitive Worlds.* Announced. 865-868, June 1973

◆ *Vanishing Peoples of the Earth.* Announced. 844-849, June 1968
● *See also* Gypsies; Nomads
Africa:
▲ *The Peoples of Africa,* double-sided supplement. Dec. 1971
● Tanzania's Stone Age Art. By Mary D. Leakey. Photos by John Reader. 84-99, July 1983
● *See also* Bedouin; Berbers; Bushmen; Danakil; Dogon; Inadan; Lotuka; Masai; Nuba; Pokot People; Pygmies; Tuareg; Wodaabe; Zulus; *and* Oursi for Fulani and Tuareg
Americas:
● *See* Aleuts; Eskimos; Indians; Inuit
Asia:
▲ *The Peoples of China,* double-sided supplement. July 1980
▲ *The Peoples of Mainland Southeast Asia,* double-sided supplement. Mar. 1971
● *See also* Ainu; Bajaus; Bakhtiari; Bedouin; Gologs; Iban; Intha; Kalash; Karens; Kashgais; Kazaks; Kirghiz; Kurds; Lolos; Lua; Ma'dan; Montagnards; Mru Tribe; Muria Gonds; Newars; Padaung; Pathans; Tasadays; T'boli; Tharus; Turkomans; Ubo Tribe; Yamis; *and* Andaman Islands; Bhutan; Hunza; Ladakh; Naga Hills; Tibet; Wakhi
Australia:
● *See* Aboriginals
Europe:
● *See* Basques; Lapland
Middle East:
▲ *The Peoples of the Middle East,* supplement. Text on reverse. July 1972
Pacific Islands:
▲ *Discoverers of the Pacific,* double-sided supplement. Dec. 1974
● *See also* New Britain; New Guinea; New Hebrides
Union of Soviet Socialist Republics:
▲ *Peoples of the Soviet Union,* double-sided supplement. Feb. 1976

ETOSHA NATIONAL PARK, Namibia:
● Etosha: Namibia's Kingdom of Animals. By Douglas H. Chadwick. Photos by Des and Jen Bartlett. 344-385, Mar. 1983
■ Etosha: Place of Dry Water. 703, Dec. 1980
● Family Life of Lions. By Des and Jen Bartlett. 800-819, Dec. 1982
● Namibia: Nearly a Nation? By Bryan Hodgson. Photos by Jim Brandenburg. 755-797, June 1982

ETRUSCANS:
● Periscope on the Etruscan Past. By Carlo M. Lerici. 337-350, Sept. 1959

EUPHRATES (River), Asia:
● Throne Above the Euphrates. By Theresa Goell. 390-405, Mar. 1961

EUROPA (Jovian Satellite):
● What Voyager Saw: Jupiter's Dazzling Realm. By Rick Gore. Photos by NASA. 2-29, Jan. 1980

EUROPE:
● Across the Ridgepole of the Alps. By Walter Meayers Edwards. 410-419, Sept. 1960

BOTH BY WINFIELD PARKS, NGS

Danube: driver at Volksfest in Kelheim, *top;* dance class at Vienna school, *above*

◆ *The Age of Chivalry.* Announced. 544-551, Oct. 1969
▲ *The Alps–Europe's Backbone,* Atlas series double-sided supplement. Sept. 1965
● The Alps: Man's Own Mountains. By Ralph Gray. Photos by Walter Meayers Edwards and William Eppridge. 350-395, Sept. 1965
● Ancient Europe Is Older Than We Thought. By Colin Renfrew. Photos by Adam Woolfitt. 615-623, Nov. 1977
● "Around the World in Eighty Days." By Newman Bumstead. 705-750, Dec. 1951
● Atlantic Odyssey: Iceland to Antarctica. By Newman Bumstead. Photos by Volkmar Wentzel. 725-780, Dec. 1955
● Baltic Cruise of the *Caribbee.* By Carleton Mitchell. 605-646, Nov. 1950
● A Bold New Look at Our Past. The Editor. NGS research grant. 62-63, Jan. 1975
● The Byzantine Empire. 709-777, Dec. 1983
I. Rome of the East. By Merle Severy. Photos by James L. Stanfield. 709-767; II. Mount Athos. 739-745; III. Eternal Easter in a Greek Village. By Maria Nicolaidis-Karanikolas. Photos by James L. Stanfield. 768-777
● The Celts. By Merle Severy. Photos by James P. Blair. Paintings by Robert C. Magis. 582-633, May 1977
▲ *Central Europe, including the Balkan States,* supplement. Sept. 1951
▲ *Classical Lands of the Mediterranean,* supplement. Dec. 1949
● The Danube: River of Many Nations, Many Names. By Mike Edwards. Photos by Winfield Parks. 455-485, Oct. 1977
● Down the Danube by Canoe. By William Slade Backer. Photos by Richard S. Durrance and Christopher G. Knight. 34-79, July 1965
▲ *Europe,* Atlas series supplement. June 1962
▲ *Europe,* supplement. June 1957
▲ *Europe,* supplement. June 1969
▲ *Europe; Celtic Europe,* double-sided supplement. May 1977
▲ *Europe; Historical Map of Europe,* double-sided supplement. Dec. 1983
▲ *Europe and the Near East,* supplement. June 1949
● Europe Via the Hostel Route. By Joseph Nettis. 124-154, July 1955
● Exploring the Mind of Ice Age Man. By Alexander Marshack. NGS research grant. 64-89, Jan. 1975
● Friendly Flight to Northern Europe. By Lyndon B. Johnson. Photos by Volkmar Wentzel. 268-293, Feb. 1964
● Here Rest in Honored Glory. . . . (War Memorials). By Howell Walker. Included: The following memorial cemeteries: Brittany; Cambridge; Épinal; Normandy; Rhône; Sicily-Rome. 739-768, June 1957
▲ *The Historic Mediterranean; The Mediterranean Seafloor,* double-sided supplement. Dec. 1982

• How Fruit Came to America. By J. R. Magness. Paintings by Else Bostelmann. Included: Plums and Prunes from Europe and West Asia; Olives, Oil-bearing Fruit from Southern Europe. 325-377, Sept. 1951
• In the Crusaders' Footsteps. By Franc Shor. Photos by Thomas Nebbia and James P. Blair. 731-789, June 1962
• The Incredible Potato. By Robert E. Rhoades. Photos by Martin Rogers. 668-694, May 1982
• Inside Europe Aboard *Yankee*. By Irving and Electa Johnson. Photos by Joseph J. Scherschel. 157-195, Aug. 1964
• The Mediterranean–Sea of Man's Fate. By Rick Gore. Photos by Jonathan Blair. 694-737, Dec. 1982
• Napoleon. By John J. Putman. Photos by Gordon W. Gahan. 142-189, Feb. 1982
• A New Look at Medieval Europe. By Kenneth M. Setton. Paintings by Andre Durenceau and Birney Lettick. 799-859, Dec. 1962
▲ *Northern Europe,* supplement. Aug. 1954
• Our Vegetable Travelers. By Victor R. Boswell. Paintings by Else Bostelmann. Included: Kohlrabi and Brussels Sprouts Are European. 145-217, Aug. 1949
• Our War Memorials Abroad: A Faith Kept. By George C. Marshall. 731-737, June 1957
• The Rat, Lapdog of the Devil. By Thomas Y. Canby. Photos by James L. Stanfield. 60-87, July 1977
• Reach for the New World. By Mendel Peterson. Photos by David L. Arnold. Paintings by Richard Schlecht. Included: Trade and colonization by England, France, the Netherlands, Spain. 724-767, Dec. 1977
◆ *The Renaissance: Maker of Modern Man.* Announced. 588-590, Oct. 1970
• The Rhine: Europe's River of Legend. By William Graves. Photos by Bruce Dale. 449-499, Apr. 1967
• Round the World School (ISA). By Paul Antze. Photos by William Eppridge. Included: Berlin; England; Greece; Italy; Paris. 96-127, July 1962
• Striking It Rich in the North Sea. By Rick Gore. Photos by Dick Durrance II. 519-549, Apr. 1977
• A Stroll to Venice. By Isobel Wylie Hutchison. Contents: The author's trek from Innsbruck, Austria, through the Tyrol and Dolomites, to Venice, Italy. 378-410, Sept. 1951
• Through Europe by Trailer Caravan. By Norma Miller. Photos by Ardean R. Miller III. Included: Austria; France; Germany; Italy; Netherlands; Switzerland. 769-816, June 1957
• Thumbs Up Round the North Sea's Rim. By Frances James. Photos by Erica Koch. Included: Belgium; Denmark; England; France; Germany; Sweden. 685-704, May 1952
• To Europe with a Racing Start (*Finisterre*). By Carleton Mitchell. 758-791, June 1958
• The Vikings. By Howard La Fay. Photos by Ted Spiegel. 492-541, Apr. 1970
▲ *Western Europe,* supplement. Dec. 1950
• What's Happening to Our Climate? By Samuel W. Matthews. 576-615, Nov. 1976
• When the President Goes Abroad (Eisenhower Tour). By Gilbert M. Grosvenor. Included: France; Greece; Italy; Spain. 588-649, May 1960
• White Storks, Vanishing Sentinels of the Rooftops. By Roger Tory Peterson. 838-853, June 1962
• A Wild, Ill-fated Balloon Race. 778-797, Dec. 1983
I. Wild Launch. 778-787; II. The Fantastic Flight of *Cote d'Or*. By Cynthia Shields. 789-793; III. Last Ascent of a Heroic Team (Maxie Anderson and Don Ida). 794-797
• The World in Your Garden (Flowers). By W. H. Camp. Paintings by Else Bostelmann. Included: From Medieval European Gardens (Bellflower, Daisy, Pansy or Heartsease, Pot Marigold, Primrose, Rose); Europe Contributed Flowers and Words (Foxglove, Stock or Gilliflower, Sweet Scabious, Wallflower); European Meadows and Our Lawns (Snakeshead or Checkered Lily, Snowdrop, Spring Crocus). 1-65, July 1947
• The World of Martin Luther. By Merle Severy. Photos by James L. Amos. 418-463, Oct. 1983
■ *Yankee* Sails Across Europe. 469A-469B, Apr. 1967
• *See also* Albania; Andorra; Austria; Belgium; Bulgaria; Czechoslovakia; Denmark; Finland; France; German Democratic Republic; Germany; Germany, Federal Republic of; Gibraltar; Greece; Hungary; Iceland; Italy; Liechtenstein; Luxembourg; Malta; Monaco; Netherlands; Norway; Poland; Portugal; Romania; San Marino; Spain; Sweden; Switzerland; Turkey (part); listing under United Kingdom; Union of Soviet Socialist Republics (part); Vatican City; Yugoslavia

EUROPEAN SPACE AGENCY (ESA):
• Spacelab 1: *Columbia*. By Michael E. Long. 301-307, Sept. 1983

EUROPE'S Shy and Spectacular Kingfisher. Photos by Carl-Johan Junge and Emil Lütken. 413-419, Sept. 1974

EVANGELINE COUNTRY, Louisiana:
• Cajunland, Louisiana's French-speaking Coast. By Bern Keating. Photos by Charles Harbutt and Franke Keating. 353-391, Mar. 1966

EVANS, CHARLES:
• Triumph on Everest. 1-63, July 1954
I. Siege and Assault. By Sir John Hunt. 1-43; II. The Conquest of the Summit. By Sir Edmund Hillary. 45-63

EVANS, CLIFFORD:
Author-Photographer:
• Life Among the Wai Wai Indians. By Clifford Evans and Betty J. Meggers. 329-346, Mar. 1955
Photographer:
• Finding the Tomb of a Warrior-God. By William Duncan Strong. 453-482, Apr. 1947

EVANS, RONALD E.:
• Exploring Taurus-Littrow. By Harrison H. Schmitt. Photos by the crew of Apollo 17. 290-307, Sept. 1973

EVEREST, Mount, Nepal-Tibet:
• American and Geographic Flags Top Everest. By Melvin M. Payne. Photos by Barry C. Bishop. NGS research grant. 157-157C, Aug. 1963
■ Americans on Everest. 448-452, Sept. 1965; 575, Nov. 1976
• At My Limit–I Climbed Everest Alone. By Reinhold Messner. Photos by the author and Nena Holguín. 552-566, Oct. 1981
• The First Traverse. By Thomas F. Hornbein and William F. Unsoeld. NGS research grant. 509-513, Oct. 1963
• How We Climbed Everest. By Barry C. Bishop. NGS research grant. 477-507, Oct. 1963
• Park at the Top of the World: Mount Everest National Park. By Rick Ridgeway. Photos by Nicholas DeVore III. 704-725, June 1982
Preserving a Mountain Heritage. By Sir Edmund Hillary. 696-703
• Six to the Summit. By Norman G. Dyhrenfurth. Photos by Barry C. Bishop. NGS research grant. 460-473, Oct. 1963
• Triumph on Everest. 1-63, July 1954
I. Siege and Assault. By Sir John Hunt. 1-43; II. The Conquest of the Summit. By Sir Edmund Hillary. 45-63

EVERETT, CURTIS T.:
• Children of the Sun and Moon (Kraho Indians). By Harald Schultz; translated from German by Curtis T. Everett. 340-363, Mar. 1959

EVERGLADES (Region), Florida:
• Businessman in the Bush. By Frederick Kent Truslow. 634-675, May 1970
• Eye to Eye With Eagles. By Frederick Kent Truslow. 123-148, Jan. 1961
• Florida Rides a Space-age Boom. By Benedict Thielen. Photos by Winfield Parks and James P. Blair. 858-903, Dec. 1963
• Florida's Emerging Seminoles. By Louis Capron. Photos by Otis Imboden. Contents: Seminole and Miccosukee reservations and settlements. 716-734, Nov. 1969
• Florida's "Wild" Indians, the Seminole. By Louis Capron. Photos by Willard R. Culver. 819-840, Dec. 1956
• Haunting Heart of the Everglades. By Andrew H. Brown. Photos by author and Willard R. Culver. 145-173, Feb. 1948

E F

• The Imperiled Everglades. By Fred Ward. 1-27, Jan. 1972
• Our Only Native Stork, the Wood Ibis. By Robert Porter Allen. Photos by Frederick Kent Truslow. 294-306, Feb. 1964
• Saving Man's Wildlife Heritage. By John H. Baker. Photos by Robert F. Sisson. 581-620, Nov. 1954
• Shrimp Nursery: Science Explores New Ways to Farm the Sea. By Clarence P. Idyll. Photos by Robert F. Sisson. NGS research grant. 636-659, May 1965
• The Swallow-tailed Kite: Graceful Aerialist of the Everglades. 496-505, Oct. 1972
• Threatened Glories of Everglades National Park. By Frederick Kent Truslow and Frederick G. Vosburgh. Photos by Frederick Kent Truslow and Otis Imboden. Included: Drainage from Lake Okeechobee in 1880, 1920, and 1967. 508-553, Oct. 1967
• The Tree Nobody Liked (Red Mangrove). By Rick Gore. Photos by Bianca Lavies. 669-689, May 1977
• Tree Snails, Gems of the Everglades. By Treat Davidson. 372-387, Mar. 1965
• When Disaster Struck a Woodpecker's Home. By Frederick Kent Truslow. 882-884, Dec. 1966
• Wildlife of Everglades National Park. By Daniel B. Beard. Paintings by Walter A. Weber. 83-116, Jan. 1949

EVERHART, WILLIAM C.: Author:
• So Long, St. Louis, We're Heading West. 643-669, Nov. 1965

EVERINGHAM, JOHN:
Author-Photographer:
• One Family's Odyssey to America. 642-661, May 1980
Photographer:
• Thailand's Working Royalty. 486-499, Oct. 1982

"**EVERY** Day Is a Gift When You Are Over 100." By Alexander Leaf. Photos by John Launois. 93-119, Jan. 1973

EVERYONE'S Servant, the Post Office. By Allan C. Fisher, Jr. Photos by Volkmar Wentzel. 121-152, July 1954

EVOLUTION:
• Editorial. By Gilbert M. Grosvenor. 297, Sept. 1976
• The Galapagos, Eerie Cradle of New Species. By Roger Tory Peterson. Photos by Alan and Joan Root. 541-585, Apr. 1967
• In the Wake of Darwin's *Beagle*. By Alan Villiers. Photos by James L. Stanfield. 449-495, Oct. 1969
• The New Biology. 355-407, Sept. 1976
I. The Awesome Worlds Within a Cell. By Rick Gore. Photos by Bruce Dale. Paintings by Davis Meltzer. 355-395; II. The Cancer Puzzle. By Robert F. Weaver. 396-399; III. Seven Giants Who Led the Way. Paintings by Ned Seidler. Text by Rick Gore. 401-407
• *See also* Paleontology

EWALD, PAUL W.: Author:
• Hummingbirds: The Nectar Connection. Photos by Robert A. Tyrrell. 223-227, Feb. 1982

EWING, MAURICE: Author:
• Exploring the Mid-Atlantic Ridge. 275-294, Sept. 1948
• New Discoveries on the Mid-Atlantic Ridge. Photos by Robert F. Sisson. 611-640, Nov. 1949

An **EXCITING** Year of Discovery: President's Report to Members. By Gilbert M. Grosvenor. 820-824, Dec. 1982

The **EXODUS:**
• Eternal Sinai. By Harvey Arden. Photos by David Doubilet and Kevin Fleming. 420-461, Apr. 1982
• In Search of Moses. By Harvey Arden. Photos by Nathan Benn. Included: Map of Sinai Peninsula indicating two possible routes. 2-37, Jan. 1976
• Lost Outpost of the Egyptian Empire. By Trude Dothan. Photos by Sisse Brimberg. Paintings by Lloyd K. Townsend. 739-769, Dec. 1982

EXOTIC-BIRD TRADE:
• Wild Cargo: the Business of Smuggling Animals. By Noel Grove. Photos by Steve Raymer. 287-315, Mar. 1981

EXOTIC Birds in Manhattan's Bowery. By Paul A. Zahl. 77-98, Jan. 1953

An **EXOTIC** New Oriole Settles in Florida. By Charles M. Brookfield and Oliver Griswold. 261-264, Feb. 1956

EXPEDITION to the Land of the Tiwi. By Charles P. Mountford. 417-440, Mar. 1956

EXPEDITIONS AND RESEARCH. *See* listing of NGS expeditions and scientific researches, following this index; *and* names of universities and laboratories

EXPÉDITIONS POLAIRES FRANÇAISES:
• Wringing Secrets from Greenland's Icecap. By Paul-Emile Victor. 121-147, Jan. 1956

EXPERIMENT in International Living. By Hugh M. Hamill, Jr. 323-350, Mar. 1953

EXPERIMENTAL AIRCRAFT:
• The Bird Men. By Luis Marden. Photos by Charles O'Rear. Contents: Ultralights. 198-217, Aug. 1983
• Electricity From the Sun. Contents: The solar-powered aircraft, *Gossamer Penguin*. 40-41, *Special Report on Energy* (Feb. 1981)
• The Flight of the *Gossamer Condor*. By Michael E. Long. Contents: Human-powered aircraft. 130-140, Jan. 1978
• Happy Birthday, Otto Lilienthal! By Russell Hawkes. Photos by James Collison. Contents: Hang gliders. 286-292, Feb. 1972
• Oshkosh: America's Biggest Air Show. By Michael E. Long. Photos by James A. Sugar and the author. Contents: The annual convention of the Experimental Aircraft Association. 365-375, Sept. 1979
• Sailors of the Sky. By Gordon Young. Photos by Emory Kristof and Jack Fields. Paintings by Davis Meltzer. Contents: Sailplanes. 49-73, Jan. 1967
• The Thousand-mile Glide. By Karl Striedieck. Photos by Otis Imboden. Contents: Sailplanes. 431-438, Mar. 1978
• Winged Victory of *Gossamer Albatross*. By Bryan Allen. Contents: Human-powered aircraft. 640-651, Nov. 1979
• World War I Aircraft Fly Again in Rhinebeck's Rickety Rendezvous. By Harvey Arden. Photos by Howard Sochurek. 578-587, Oct. 1970

EXPLORATION AND DISCOVERY:
▲ *Arctic Ocean,* double-sided supplement. Included: Notes on explorations from earliest searches for the Northwest Passage to present-day voyages and the finding of petroleum reserves. Oct. 1971
▲ *Atlantic Gateways,* The Making of America series. Included: Delaware, Maryland, New Jersey, New York, Pennsylvania, northern Virginia, West Virginia, and in Canada, southern Ontario and southern Quebec. On reverse: Indians and Trade, Nation in the Making, Peopling of the Gateways, Race for the Hinterlands, Growth of Industry, Spreading Urban Corridors. Mar. 1983
▲ *Deep South,* The Making of America series. Included: Alabama, Florida, Georgia, Louisiana, Mississippi, South Carolina, and parts of Arkansas, North Carolina, and Tennessee. On reverse: Indian Legacy, Imperial Footholds, Three Empires and Three Races, Cotton Kingdom, Postbellum, New Deep South, Subtropical Playground. Aug. 1983
• Editorials. By Gilbert M. Grosvenor. 729, June 1975; 297, Sept. 1978; 151, Feb. 1979; 585, Nov. 1979
• Eight Maps of Discovery. 757-769, June 1953
◆ *Great Adventures With National Geographic.* Announced. 729-733, Nov. 1963
▲ *Historical Map of the United States,* supplement. Included: A legend of exploration. June 1953
• 75 Years Exploring Earth, Sea, and Sky: National Geographic Society Observes Its Diamond Anniversary. By Melvin M. Payne. 1-43, Jan. 1963
▲ *The Southwest,* The Making of America series. Included: Arizona, New Mexico, and parts of California, Colorado, Texas, Utah; and in Mexico: Baja California Norte, Chihuahua, Sonora. On reverse: 12,000 Years of History; Spanish Conquest; Anglo-American Entry and Occupancy. Nov. 1982
• The World of Elizabeth I. By Louis B. Wright. Photos by Ted Spiegel. 668-709, Nov. 1968

• *See also* Antarctica; Explorers, Discoverers, and Navigators; North Pole; Space Flights and Research; Speleology; Underwater Exploration

EXPLORER I (Stratosphere Balloon):
• NGS-U. S. Army Air Corps balloon flight (1934). 427, Apr. 1949; 14, *22-23, 24-25*, Jan. 1963; 477, Oct. 1966; 578, 579, 588, Oct. 1967; *226*, Aug. 1976

EXPLORER II (Stratosphere Balloon):
• NGS-U. S. Army Air Corps balloon flight (1935). 562, 586, May 1947; 249, Feb. 1948; 850, June 1948; 345, Sept. 1948; 427, 525, Apr. 1949; 511, Oct. 1950; 102, Jan. 1953; 262, Aug. 1955; 707, Nov. 1955; 496, Apr. 1956; 494, 495, Oct. 1956; 269, 273-274, 276, 282, Feb. 1957; 271, 281, Aug. 1957; 807, Dec. 1957; 648, Nov. 1958; 856, Dec. 1960; 5, 14, 22, 24, 26-27, Jan. 1963; 580, Oct. 1963; 294, Sept. 1965; 477, Oct. 1966; 578, 579, 588, Oct. 1967; 849, June 1968; *226*, Aug. 1976
• Twentieth Anniversary of the Epoch-making Stratosphere Flight by *Explorer II*. NGS research grant. 707, Nov. 1955

EXPLORERS (Senior Scouts):
• Philmont Scout Ranch Helps Boys Grow Up. By Andrew H. Brown. 399-416, Sept. 1956

EXPLORERS, DISCOVERERS, AND NAVIGATORS:
• Arctic Odyssey. By John Bockstoce. Photos by Jonathan Wright. Paintings by Jack Unruh. Contents: Umiak expedition along the path of Thule migration. 100-127, July 1983
• The British Way. By Sir Evelyn Wrench. Included: Cabot's Discovery of North America (1497); Francis Drake and the Elizabethan Seamen (1588); James Cook (1728-79); A Very Gallant Gentleman–Lawrence Edward Grace Oates (1880-1912). 421-541, Apr. 1949
• Circling Earth From Pole to Pole. By Sir Ranulph Fiennes. 464-481, Oct. 1983
▲ "History Salvaged From the Sea," painting supplement. Map on reverse. Dec. 1977
◆ *Into the Wilderness*. 1978
• The Journey of Burke and Wills: First Across Australia. By Joseph Judge. Photos by Joseph J. Scherschel. 152-191, Feb. 1979
• North for Oil: *Manhattan* Makes the Historic Northwest Passage. By Bern Keating. Photos by Tomas Sennett. Included: Roald Amundsen, John Cabot, Sir John Franklin, Henry Hudson,. Henry A. Larsen, Robert McClure, George P. Steele. 374-391, Mar. 1970
• North (U. S. and Canada) Through History Aboard *White Mist*. By Melville Bell Grosvenor. Photos by Edwin Stuart Grosvenor. Included: Jacques Cartier, Samuel de Champlain, Henry Hudson. 1-55, July 1970
• Our Navy Explores Antarctica. By Richard E. Byrd. U. S. Navy official photos. Includes, in addition to members of this expedition: Capt. James Cook, Sir James Clark Ross, Capt. Robert F. Scott, Sir Ernest Shackleton, Fabian Gottlieb von Bellingshausen, and J. Dumont D'Urville. 429-522, Oct. 1947
• Reach for the New World. By Mendel Peterson. Photos by David L. Arnold. Paintings by Richard Schlecht. 724-767, Dec. 1977
• Three Months on an Arctic Ice Island. By Joseph O. Fletcher. 489-504, Apr. 1953
• Trek Across Arctic America. By Colin Irwin. Included: Roald Amundsen, Knud Rasmussen. 295-321, Mar. 1974
• Voyage to the Antarctic. By David Lewis. Included: Australian Antarctic explorers Sir Douglas Mawson (1911-1914 expeditions) and David Lewis (1981-1982 expedition). 544-562, Apr. 1983
◆ *Voyages to Paradise: Exploring in the Wake of Captain Cook*. 1981
• *See also* Anderson, William R.; Beach, Edward L.; Bligh, William; Brendan, Saint; Byrd, Richard Evelyn; Calvert, James F.; Columbus, Christopher; Cook, James; Cousteau, Jacques-Yves; Darwin, Charles; Davidson, Robyn; Drake, Sir Francis; Dufek, George J.; Eiloart, Arnold; Fuchs, Sir Vivian; Henry, Prince; Heyerdahl, Thor; Houot, Georges S.; Lalor, William G., Jr.; Lewis, M. Lee; Lewis and Clark Expedition; McDonald, Edwin A.; McDonald, Eugene F., Jr.; Mackenzie, Alexander; MacMillan, Donald Baxter; Magellan, Ferdinand; Mudie, Colin; Peary, Robert E.; Piccard, Jacques; Prather, Victor A., Jr.; Raleigh, Sir Walter; Roosevelt, Theodore; Ross, Malcolm D.; Severin, Timothy; Sindbad the Sailor; Siple, Paul A.; Smith, John; Uemura, Naomi; *and* Agricultural and Botanical Explorers; listing under Astronauts; Balloons, for Ben L. Abruzzo, Maxie L. Anderson, Larry Newman, Ed Yost; Basques (Life in the Land of), for Juan Sebastián del Cano; Divers and Diving; Founders of New England; Founders of Virginia; Mountain Climbing; Phoenicians; Polynesians; Vikings

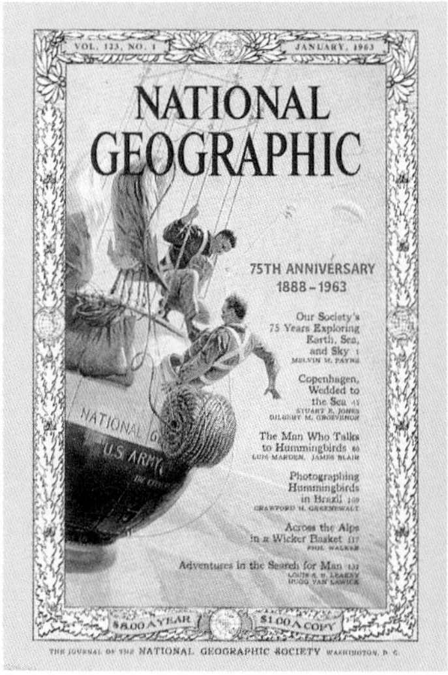

H. LEE WELLS, JR.

***Explorer II* minutes before lift-off**

EXPLORERS CLUB of New York: Expeditions:
• Exploring New Britain's Land of Fire. By E. Thomas Gilliard. NGS research grant. 260-292, Feb. 1961
• First Motor Sortie into Escalante Land. By Jack Breed. 369-404, Sept. 1949
• New Guinea's Paradise of Birds. By E. Thomas Gilliard. Note: The true summit of Mount Wilhelm was reached and flag No. 128 of the Explorers Club was unfurled. 661-668, Nov. 1951

EXPLORERS HALL, National Geographic Society:
• Curator: T. Keilor Bentley. 578, Oct. 1967
• Dedication of 17th Street Headquarters. 669, 670-675, 677, May 1964; 659, May 1965

• Display of *Aepyornis* egg from Madagascar. 479, 487, 492-493, Oct. 1967
• Display of Mount Everest Expedition equipment. 451, Sept. 1965
• Displays. 741-742, Dec. 1964; 505, Oct. 1968
• Emperor Haile Selassie I (Ethiopia) signs guest book. 555, Apr. 1965
• Globe, Great. 673-675, 677, 679, May 1964; 880, Dec. 1964; 578-579, Oct. 1967
• NGS flag, taken to moon and back by Apollo 11 astronauts, now on display in Explorers Hall. 859, 860, June 1970
• Picturephone. 750, Dec. 1964
• Presentation of Hubbard Medal to Juan T. Trippe. 584, Apr. 1968
• Visitors, number of. 669, May 1964

EXPLORING a 140-year-old Ship Under Arctic Ice. By Joseph B. MacInnis. Photos by Emory Kristof. 104A-104D, July 1983

EXPLORING Aleutian Volcanoes. By G. D. Robinson. 509-528, Oct. 1948

EXPLORING America Underground (Caves). By Charles E. Mohr. 803-837, June 1964

EXPLORING America's Great Sand Barrier Reef. By Eugene R. Guild. Photos by John E. Fletcher and author. 325-350, Sept. 1947

EXPLORING an Epic Year. By Melville Bell Grosvenor. 874-886, Dec. 1960

EXPLORING Ancient Panama by Helicopter. By Matthew W. Stirling. Photos by Richard H. Stewart. 227-246, Feb. 1950

EXPLORING Antarctica's Phantom Coast. By Edwin A. McDonald. Photos by W. D. Vaughn. 251-273, Feb. 1962

EXPLORING Australia's Coral Jungle. By Kenneth MacLeish. 743-779, June 1973

EXPLORING Canyonlands National Park. By Rowe Findley. Photos by Walter Meayers Edwards. 71-91, July 1971

EXPLORING Davy Jones's Locker with *Calypso*. By Jacques-Yves Cousteau. Photos by Luis Marden. 149-161, Feb. 1956

EXPLORING England's Canals. By Bryan Hodgson. Photos by Linda Bartlett. 76-111, July 1974

EXPLORING New Britain's Land of Fire. By E. Thomas Gilliard. 260-292, Feb. 1961

EXPLORING 1,750,000 Years Into Man's Past. By L.S.B. Leakey. Photos by Robert F. Sisson. 564-589, Oct. 1961

EXPLORING Ottawa. By Bruce Hutchison. 565-596, Nov. 1947

EXPLORING Our Neighbor World, the Moon. By Donald H. Menzel. 277-296, Feb. 1958

EXPLORING Stone Age Arnhem Land. By Charles P. Mountford. Photos by Howell Walker. 745-782, Dec. 1949

EXPLORING Taurus-Littrow. By Harrison H. Schmitt. Photos by the crew of Apollo 17. 290-307, Sept. 1973

EXPLORING the Drowned City of Port Royal (Jamaica). By Marion Clayton Link. Photos by Luis Marden. 151-183, Feb. 1960

EXPLORING the Farthest Reaches of Space. By George O. Abell. 782-790, Dec. 1956

EXPLORING the Lives of Whales. By Victor B. Scheffer. 752-767, Dec. 1976

EXPLORING the Mid-Atlantic Ridge. By Maurice Ewing. 275-294, Sept. 1948

EXPLORING the Mind of Ice Age Man. By Alexander Marshack. NGS research grant. 64-89, Jan. 1975

EXPLORING the New Biology. 355-407, Sept. 1976
I. The Awesome Worlds Within a Cell. By Rick Gore. Photos by Bruce Dale. Paintings by Davis Meltzer. 355-395; II. The Cancer Puzzle. By Robert F. Weaver. 396-399; III. Seven Giants Who Led the Way. Paintings by Ned Seidler. Text by Rick Gore. 401-407

EXPLORING the Past in Panama. By Matthew W. Stirling. Photos by Richard H. Stewart. NGS research grant. 373-399, Mar. 1949

EXPLORING the World of Gems. By W. F. Foshag. 779-810, Dec. 1950

EXPLORING Tomorrow With the Space Agency. By Allan C. Fisher, Jr. Photos by Dean Conger. 48-89, July 1960

The **EXPLOSIVE** Birth of Myojin Island. By Robert S. Dietz. 117-128, Jan. 1954

EXPO 67:
• Montreal Greets the World. By Jules B. Billard. 600-621, May 1967

EXPO '70:
• Kansai, Japan's Historic Heartland. By Thomas J. Abercrombie. 295-339, Mar. 1970

EXPOSITIONS. *See* Fairs

EXQUISITE Living Fossil, the Chambered Nautilus. Photos by Douglas Faulkner. 38-41, Jan. 1976

The **EXQUISITE** Orchids. By Luis Marden. 485-513, Apr. 1971

EXTINCT SPECIES:
• Editorial. By Wilbur E. Garrett. 703, June 1983
• Exploring the Mind of Ice Age Man. By Alexander Marshack. NGS research grant. 64-89, Jan. 1975
◆ *Giants From the Past: The Age of Mammals.* 1983
▲ "Ice Age Mammals of the Alaskan Tundra," painting supplement. Map on reverse. Mar. 1972
• *See also Aepyornis;* Dinosaurs; Mammals, Prehistoric

EXTRAORDINARY Photograph Shows Earth Pole to Pole. Photos by Nimbus I. 190-193, Feb. 1965

EXTRAORDINARY Photographs of Earth Taken by Satellite *Tiros*. By W. G. Stroud. 293-302, Aug. 1960

EXUMA CAYS, Bahama Islands:
• The Bahamas, Isles of the Blue-green Sea. By Carleton Mitchell. Photos by B. Anthony Stewart. 147-203, Feb. 1958
• More of Sea Than of Land: The Bahamas. By Carleton Mitchell. Photos by James L. Stanfield. 218-267, Feb. 1967

An **EYE** for an Eye: Pakistan's Wild Frontier. By Mike W. Edwards. Photos by J. Bruce Baumann. 111-139, Jan. 1977

EYE to Eye With Eagles. By Frederick Kent Truslow. 123-148, Jan. 1961

EYES:
• Flashlight Fish of the Red Sea *(Photoblepharon).* By Eugenie Clark. Photos by David Doubilet. 719-728, Nov. 1978
• The Four-eyed Fish Sees All. Photos by Paul A. Zahl. Text by Thomas O'Neill. 390-395, Mar. 1978
• Nature's Alert Eyes (Animal Eyes). By Constance P. Warner. 558-569, Apr. 1959

EYES of Science. By Rick Gore. Photos by James P. Blair. 360-389, Mar. 1978

EYES on the China Coast. By George W. Long. 505-512, Apr. 1953

EYEWITNESS to War in the Holy Land. By Charles Harbutt. 782-795, Dec. 1967

F

FAO. *See* United Nations Food and Agriculture Organization

The **FBI:** Public Friend Number One. By Jacob Hay. Photos by Robert F. Sisson. 860-886, June 1961

F.N.R.S. 3 (Bathyscaph):
• Deep Diving off Japan. By Georges S. Houot. NGS research grant. 138-150, Jan. 1960
• Diving Through an Undersea Avalanche. By Jacques-Yves Cousteau. NGS research grant. 538-542, Apr. 1955
• Four Years of Diving to the Bottom of the Sea. By Georges S. Houot. NGS research grant. 715-731, May 1958
• Photographing the Sea's Dark Underworld. By Harold E. Edgerton. NGS research grant. 523-537, Apr. 1955
• To the Depths of the Sea by Bathyscaphe. By Jacques-Yves Cousteau. NGS research grant. 67-79, July 1954

• Two and a Half Miles Down. By Georges S. Houot. NGS research grant. 80-86, July 1954

FABLED Mount of St. Michael. By Alan Villiers. Photos by Bates Littlehales. 880-898, June 1964

The **FABULOUS** Sierra Nevada. By J. R. Challacombe. 825-843, June 1954

The **FABULOUS** State of Texas. By Stanley Walker. Photos by B. Anthony Stewart and Thomas Nebbia. 149-195, Feb. 1961

*The **FACE** and Faith of Poland,* map, photo, and essay supplement. By Peter Miller. Essay by Czesław Miłosz. Photos by Bruno Barbey. Apr. 1982

FACE to Face With Gorillas in Central Africa. By Paul A. Zahl. 114-137, Jan. 1960

FACT Finding for Tomorrow's Planes. By Hugh L. Dryden. Photos by Luis Marden. 757-780, Dec. 1953

FAEROE ISLANDS, North Atlantic Ocean:
• The Faeroes, Isles of Maybe. By Ernle Bradford. Photos by Adam Woolfitt. 410-422, Sept. 1970
▪ The Last Vikings. 434A-434B, Mar. 1972

FAIR, PAUL J.: Photographer:
• Wildlife In and Near the Valley of the Moon. By H. H. Arnold. 401-414, Mar. 1950

FAIR of the Berber Brides. By Carla Hunt. Photos by Nik Wheeler. 119-129, Jan. 1980

FAIR Winds and Full Sails. By Thomas J. Abercrombie. Photos by Cary Wolinsky. 638-667, May 1982

FAIRBANKS, Alaska:
• Busy Fairbanks Sets Alaska's Pace. By Bruce A. Wilson. 505-523, Oct. 1949

FAIRS:
• America Goes to the Fair. By Samuel W. Matthews. 293-333, Sept. 1954
• Australian New Guinea. By John Scofield. Included: Intertribal Fair. 604-637, May 1962
• Belgium Welcomes the World (World's Fair). By Howell Walker. 795-837, June 1958
• The Fair Reopens (New York World's Fair). Photos by James P. Blair. Text by Carolyn Bennett Patterson. Included: Visitors' guide. 505-529, Apr. 1965
• 4-H Boys and Girls Grow More Food. By Frederick Simpich. 551-582, Nov. 1948
• Holy Week and the Fair in Sevilla (Spain). By Luis Marden. 499-530, Apr. 1951
• I Walked Some Irish Miles. By Dorothea Sheats. Included: Galway Fair; Killorglin's Puck Fair. 653-678, May 1951
• Kansai, Japan's Historic Heartland. By Thomas J. Abercrombie. Included: Expo '70. 295-339, Mar. 1970

THOMAS J. ABERCROMBIE, NGS

Kansai: geisha trainee on Kyoto street

• Montreal Greets the World. By Jules B. Billard. Included: Expo 67. 600-621, May 1967
• Russia as I Saw It. By Richard M. Nixon. Photos by B. Anthony Stewart. Included: American National Exhibition at Sokolniki Park in Moscow. 715-750, Dec. 1959
• Seattle Fair Looks to the 21st Century (World's Fair). By Carolyn Bennett Patterson. Photos by Thomas Nebbia. 402-427, Sept. 1962
• When Gypsies Gather at Appleby Fair. Photos by Bruce Dale. 848-869, June 1972
• A Woman Paints the Tibetans. By Lafugie. Included: Himis Fair. 659-692, May 1949
• *See also* Brides' Fair; Dog Shows; Horse Shows; Neshoba County Fair; Pennsylvania Dutch; Sing-Sing

FAIRY TALES:
• The Magic World of Hans Christian Andersen. By Harvey Arden. Photos by Sisse Brimberg. 825-849, Dec. 1979

FAIRY TERNS:
• What a Place to Lay an Egg! By Thomas R. Howell. NGS research grant. 414-419, Sept. 1971

FALCONRY:
• A New Light Dawns on Bird Photography. By Arthur A. Allen. 774-790, June 1948

FALI (Tribespeople):
• Carefree People of the Cameroons. Photos by Pierre Ichac. 233-248, Feb. 1947

FALKLAND ISLANDS AND DEPENDENCIES:
• Off the Beaten Track of Empire (Prince Philip's Tour). By Beverley M. Bowie. Photos by Michael Parker. 584-626, Nov. 1957
• People and Penguins of the Faraway Falklands. By Olin Sewall Pettingill, Jr. 387-416, Mar. 1956
• 'Round the Horn by Submarine. By Paul C. Stimson. 129-144, Jan. 1948

FAMILY FARMS:
• The Family Farm Ain't What It Used To Be. By James A. Sugar. 391-411, Sept. 1974
• Home to the Heart of Kentucky. By Nadine Brewer. Photos by William Strode. 522-546, Apr. 1982

FAMILY in Search of Prehistoric Man: The Leakeys of Africa. By Melvin M. Payne. 194-231, Feb. 1965

FAMILY ISLANDS, Bahamas:
• The Bahamas: Boom Times and Buccaneering. By Peter Benchley. Photos by Bruce Dale. 364-395, Sept. 1982

FAMILY LIFE:
• The Family: a Mormon Shrine. 459-463, Apr. 1975
• Growing Up in Montana. Photos by Nicholas deVore III. 650-657, May 1976
• Home to the Heart of Kentucky. By Nadine Brewer. Photos by William Strode. 522-546, Apr. 1982

● An Ozark Family Carves a Living and a Way of Life. Photos by Bruce Dale. 124-133, July 1975

FAMILY Life of Lions. By Des and Jen Bartlett. 800-819, Dec. 1982

FAMINE:
● Bangladesh: The Nightmare of Famine. Photos by Steve Raymer. 33-39, July 1975
● Can the World Feed Its People? By Thomas Y. Canby. Photos by Steve Raymer. 2-31, July 1975
● Drought Bedevils Brazil's Sertão. By John Wilson. Photos by Gordon W. Gahan. 704-723, Nov. 1972
● Drought Threatens the Tuareg World. By Victor Englebert. 544-571, Apr. 1974
● The Niger: River of Sorrow, River of Hope. By Georg Gerster. 152-189, Aug. 1975
● Report from the Locust Wars. By Tony and Dickey Chapelle. 545-562, Apr. 1953
● Somalia's Hour of Need. By Robert Paul Jordan. Photos by Michael S. Yamashita and Kevin Fleming. 748-775, June 1981
Encampments of the Dispossessed. By Larry Kohl. 756-763

FAMOUS (French-American Mid-Ocean Undersea Study):
● Project FAMOUS–Man's First Voyages Down to the Mid-Atlantic Ridge. By J. R. Heirtzler and Robert D. Ballard. Photos by Emory Kristof. 586-615, May 1975

FANCH'ENG, People's Republic of China:
● Return to Changing China. By Audrey Topping. 801-833, Dec. 1971

The **FANTASTIC** Flight of *Cote d'Or.* By Cynthia Shields. 789-793, Dec. 1983

FAR EAST:
▲ *The Far East,* supplement. Sept. 1952
● Our Navy in the Far East. By Arthur W. Radford. Photos by J. Baylor Roberts. 537-577, Oct. 1953
● Pacific Fleet: Force for Peace. By Franc Shor. Photos by W. E. Garrett. 283-335, Sept. 1959
● *Yankee* Roams the Orient. By Irving and Electa Johnson. 327-370, Mar. 1951
● *See also* Burma; China, People's Republic of; China, Republic of (Taiwan); Hong Kong; Indonesia; Japan; Korea, Democratic People's Republic of; Korea, Republic of; Macao; Malaysia; Philippines; Quemoy; Singapore; Southeast Asia; Thailand

FAR-FLUNG Search for the First Americans. By Thomas Y. Canby. Photos by Kerby Smith. Paintings by Roy Andersen. 330-363, Sept. 1979

FAR-FLYING Phalaropes. By Joseph R. Jehl, Jr. 520-525, Oct. 1981

FAR NORTH with "Captain Mac." By Miriam MacMillan. 465-513, Oct. 1951

FAR-OUT FACTS:
◆ *Far-Out Facts.* 1980
◆ *More Far-Out Facts.* 1982

WILLIAM STRODE

Kentucky: Heart of Kentucky map, *top;* Alice Clark ties tobacco, *above*

FARADAY, MICHAEL:
● The British Way. By Sir Evelyn Wrench. 421-541, Apr. 1949

FARALLON ISLANDS REFUGE, California:
● Island, Prairie, Marsh, and Shore. By Charlton Ogburn. Photos by Bates Littlehales. 350-381, Mar. 1979

FARMS:
● Burma's Leg Rowers and Floating Farms. Photos by W. E. Garrett. Text by David Jeffery. 826-845, June 1974
● Chattooga River Country: Wild Water, Proud People. By Don Belt. Photos by Steve Wall. 458-477, Apr. 1983
● Down on the Farm, Soviet Style–a 4-H Adventure. By John Garaventa. Photos by James Tobin and Carol Schmidt. 768-797, June 1979
● The Family Farm Ain't What It Used To Be. By James A. Sugar. 391-411, Sept. 1974
● The Goats of Thunder Hill. By Elizabeth Nicholds. Photos by Robert F. Sisson. 625-640, May 1954
● Home to the Heart of Kentucky. By Nadine Brewer. Photos by William Strode. 522-546, Apr. 1982
◆ *Life in Rural America.* Announced. 870-874, June 1974
● The Revolution in American Agriculture. By Jules B. Billard. Photos by James P. Blair. Included: Farm of the future (painting). 147-185, Feb. 1970
● The World of My Apple Tree. By Robert F. Sisson. Included: Harmony Hollow Farm. 836-847, June 1972
● *See also* Agriculture; Aquaculture; Estates and Plantations; Ranches

FARNE ISLANDS, England:
● Pilgrimage to Holy Island and the Farnes. By John E. H. Nolan. 547-570, Oct. 1952

FARNEY, DENNIS: Author:
● The Tallgrass Prairie: Can It Be Saved? Photos by Jim Brandenburg. 37-61, Jan. 1980

The **FASCINATING** World of Trash. By Peter T. White. Photos by Louie Psihoyos. 424-457, Apr. 1983

FÁTIMA, Portugal:
● Fátima: Beacon for Portugal's Faithful. By Jane Vessels. Photos by Bruno Barbey. 832-839, Dec. 1980

FAULKNER, DOUGLAS:
Author-Photographer:
● Finned Doctors of the Deep. 867-873, Dec. 1965
Photographer:
● The Chambered Nautilus, Exquisite Living Fossil. 38-41, Jan. 1976
● Dazzling Corals of Palau. By Thomas O'Neill. 136-150, July 1978

FAULTS AND FAULTING:
● Incredible World of the Deep-sea Rifts. NGS research grant. 680-705, Nov. 1979
I. Strange World Without Sun. The Editor. 680-688; II. Return to Oases of the Deep. By Robert D. Ballard and J. Frederick Grassle. 689-705

• Oases of Life in the Cold Abyss. By John B. Corliss and Robert D. Ballard. 441-453, Oct. 1977
• This Changing Earth. By Samuel W. Matthews. 1-37, Jan. 1973
• *See also* Great Rift Valley; Ocean Floors; San Andreas Fault

FAYAL (Island), Azores:
• A New Volcano Bursts From the Atlantic. By John Scofield. Photos by Robert F. Sisson. 735-757, June 1958

FEAST Day in Kapingamarangi. By W. Robert Moore. 523-537, Apr. 1950

FEATHERED Dancers of Little Tobago. By E. Thomas Gilliard. Photos by Frederick Kent Truslow. 428-440, Sept. 1958

FEDERAL BUREAU OF INVESTIGATION:
• The FBI: Public Friend Number One. By Jacob Hay. Photos by Robert F. Sisson. 860-886, June 1961

FEDERAL LANDS:
• The Aleutians: Alaska's Far-out Islands. By Lael Morgan. Photos by Steven C. Wilson. Note: 95 percent of the islands are claimed by the federal government as wildlife refuges and military sites. 336-363, Sept. 1983
▲ *America's Federal Lands; The United States,* double-sided supplement. Sept. 1982
• Roosevelt Country: T. R.'s Wilderness Legacy. By John L. Eliot. Photos by Farrell Grehan. 340-363, Sept. 1982
• *See also* National Forests; National Military Parks; National Monuments; National Parks; National Wild and Scenic Rivers System; National Wildlife Refuges; *and listings under* National Recreation Areas; National Scenic Trails; National Seashores

FEDERAL REPUBLIC OF GERMANY. *See* Germany, Federal Republic of (West Germany)

FELSENTHAL, SANDY: Photographer:
• Contrary New Hampshire. By Robert Booth. 770-799, Dec. 1982

FERRAR, NICHOLAS and JOHN:
• Founders of Virginia. By Sir Evelyn Wrench. Photos by B. Anthony Stewart. 433-462, Apr. 1948

FERRETS. *See* Black-footed Ferrets

FERRIDAY, EDWARD C., Jr.: Author:
• Wonderland in Longwood Gardens. 45-64, July 1951

FERRIES:
• Alaska's Marine Highway: Ferry Route to the North. By W. E. Garrett. 776-819, June 1965
• Hydrofoil Ferry "Flies" the Strait of Messina. By Gilbert Grosvenor. 493-496, Apr. 1957
• Staten Island Ferry, New York's Seagoing Bus. By John T. Cunningham and Jay Johnston. Photos by W. D. Vaughn. 833-843, June 1959

FERTILITY CULT:
• Fertility Rites and Sorcery in a New Guinea Village. By Gillian Gillison. Photos by David Gillison. 124-146, July 1977

FÈS, Morocco. *See* Fez

FESTIVALS:
• Belgium Welcomes the World. By Howell Walker. Included: Bayard Festival, Ath; Begonia Festival, Lochristi; Blessing of the Sea, Heist; Bruegel Festival, Wingene. 795-837, June 1958
• Brazil's Land of Minerals. By W. Robert Moore. Included: Holy Week. 479-508, Oct. 1948
• Brazil's Txukahameis: Good-bye to the Stone Age. Photos by W. Jesco von Puttkamer. Included: Tribal rites of the Txukahameis. 270-283, Feb. 1975
• Carnival in San Antonio. By Mason Sutherland. Photos by J. Baylor Roberts. Included: Fiesta de San Jacinto. 813-844, Dec. 1947
• Day of the Rice God. Photos by H. Edward Kim. Text by Douglas Lee. Contents: Rice-transplanting festival in Chiyoda, Japan. 78-85, July 1978
• Dinkelsbühl Rewards Its Children. By Charles Belden. Contents: Kinderzeche (Children's Treat). 255-268, Feb. 1957
• Edinburgh: Capital in Search of a Country. By James Cerruti. Photos by Adam Woolfitt. Included: Edinburgh International Festival. 274-296, Aug. 1976
• Exploring Stone Age Arnhem Land. By Charles P. Mountford. Photos by Howell Walker. Included: Balnuknuk and other corroborees. NGS research grant. 745-782, Dec. 1949
• Feudal Splendor Lingers in Rajputana. By Volkmar Wentzel. Included: Gangor Festival and the wedding of the Prince of Jodhpur to the Princess of Jaisalmer. 411-458, Oct. 1948
• Focusing on the Tournament of Roses. By B. Anthony Stewart and J. Baylor Roberts. 805-816, June 1954
• Home to the Enduring Berkshires. By Charles McCarry. Photos by Jonathan S. Blair. Included: Berkshire Music Festival. 196-221, Aug. 1970
• The Ivory Coast–African Success Story. By Michael and Aubine Kirtley. Included: Dipri festival. 94-125, July 1982
• Japan's Warriors of the Wind. Photos by David Alan Harvey. Text by John Eliot. Contents: Kite festival in Hamamatsu, Japan. 551-561, Apr. 1977
• Life and Death in Tana Toradja. By Pamela and Alfred Meyer. Contents: Funeral observance in Toradjaland, Sulawesi, Indonesia. 793-815, June 1972
• Living Theater in New Guinea's Highlands. By Gillian Gillison. Photos by David Gillison. 147-169, Aug. 1983
• New Guinea Festival of Faces. By Malcolm S. Kirk. 148-156, July 1969
• Niger's Wodaabe: "People of the Taboo." By Carol Beckwith. Included: Worso, a celebration of the year's marriages and births; Geerewol, a display of male beauty; Courtship dances. 483-509, Oct. 1983
• Norway Cracks Her Mountain Shell. By Sydney Clark. Photos by Gilbert Grosvenor and Ole Friele Backer. Included: Constitution Day. 171-211, Aug. 1948
• Pennsylvania Dutch Folk Festival. By Maynard Owen Williams. Contents: Kutztown Folk Festival. 503-516, Oct. 1952
• Pennsylvania's Old-time Dutch Treat. By Kent Britt. Photos by H. Edward Kim. Contents: Kutztown Folk Festival. 564-578, Apr. 1973
• San Antonio: "Texas, Actin' Kind of Natural." By Fred Kline. Photos by David Hiser. Included: Fiesta. 524-549, Apr. 1976
• Spearing Lions with Africa's Masai. By Edgar Monsanto Queeny. Included: Unoto, a Masai ceremony. 487-517, Oct. 1954
• Switzerland's Once-in-a-generation Festival (Vevey). By Jean and Franc Shor. Contents: Fête de Vignerons (Feast of the Winegrowers). 563-571, Oct. 1958
• A Town . . . a Mountain . . . a Way of Life. By Jill Durrance and Dick Durrance II. Included: Aspen Music Festival; Winterskol. 788-807, Dec. 1973
• Tukuna Maidens Come of Age. By Harald Schultz. Contents: Puberty rites. 629-649, Nov. 1959
• Viking Festival in the Shetlands. Photos by Karl W. Gullers. Contents: Up Helly Aa. 853-862, Dec. 1954
• Wales, Land of Bards. By Alan Villiers. Photos by Thomas Nebbia. Included: Eisteddfods. 727-769, June 1965
• *See also* Carnivals; Coronations; Fairs; Mardi Gras; Palio; Winter Festivals; *and* Religious Ceremonies and Festivals

FETTERMAN, JOHN: Author:
• On the Road With an Old-time Circus. Photos by Jonathan Blair. 410-434, Mar. 1972
• The People of Cumberland Gap. Photos by Bruce Dale. 591-621, Nov. 1971

FEUDAL Splendor Lingers in Rajputana. By Volkmar Wentzel. 411-458, Oct. 1948

FEZ (Fès), Morocco:
• From Sea to Sahara in French Morocco. By Jean and Franc Shor. 147-188, Feb. 1955
• Morocco, Land of the Farthest West. By Thomas J. Abercrombie. 834-865, June 1971

FIBER OPTICS: Harnessing Light by a Thread. By Allen A. Boraiko. Photos by Fred Ward. 516-535, Oct. 1979

FIELD, HENRY: Author:
• Sinai Sheds New Light on the Bible. Photos by William B. and Gladys Terry. 795-815, Dec. 1948

E F

FIELDS, JACK: Photographer:
• The Flower Seed Growers: Gardening's Color Merchants. By Robert de Roos. 720-738, May 1968
• Micronesia: The Americanization of Eden. By David S. Boyer. 702-744, May 1967
• Sailors of the Sky. By Gordon Young. Photos by Emory Kristof and Jack Fields. Paintings by Davis Meltzer. 49-73, Jan. 1967

FIENNES, SIR RANULPH: Author:
• Circling Earth From Pole to Pole. 464-481, Oct. 1983

FIESTAS. *See* Festivals

FIÉVET, JEANNETTE:
Author-Illustrator:
• Beyond the Bight of Benin. By Jeannette and Maurice Fiévet. 221-253, Aug. 1959

FIÉVET, MAURICE: Artist:
• Angkor, Jewel of the Jungle. By W. Robert Moore. 517-569, Apr. 1960
Author-Illustrator:
• Beyond the Bight of Benin. By Jeannette and Maurice Fiévet. 221-253, Aug. 1959

FIFTH ARMY, U. S.:
• Italy Smiles Again. By Edgar Erskine Hume. 693-732, June 1949

FIFTY Years of Flight. 740-756, Dec. 1953

FIG WASPS:
• The Wasp That Plays Cupid to a Fig. By Robert F. Sisson. 690-697, Nov. 1970

FIGHTING Forest Fires. 328-331, Sept. 1982

FIJI ISLANDS, Pacific Ocean:
• Copra-ship Voyage to Fiji's Outlying Islands. By Marjory C. Thomas. Included: Kava ceremony and the fire walkers of Mbengga. 121-140, July 1950
• The Islands Called Fiji. By Luis Marden. 526-561, Oct. 1958
• A Teen-ager Sails the World Alone. By Robin Lee Graham. 445-491, Oct. 1968

FILLMORE, MILLARD:
• Profiles of the Presidents: II. A Restless Nation Moves West. By Frank Freidel. 80-121, Jan. 1965

FILMS AND FILMSTRIPS, NGS:
• Film-strip service planned. 581, Oct. 1967; 583, Nov. 1975
• More than 50 films are available covering dozens of subjects in the fields of science and social studies. 583, Nov. 1975
• The World in Geographic Filmstrips. By Melvin M. Payne. 134-137, Jan. 1968
• *See also* Television Films, NGS

The **FINAL** Flight (Exploring Taurus-Littrow). By Harrison H. Schmitt. Photos by the crew of Apollo 17. 290-307, Sept. 1973

The **FINAL** Tribute (Churchill Funeral). Text by Carolyn Bennett Patterson. 199-225, Aug. 1965

FINCHES:
• Exotic Birds in Manhattan's Bowery. By Paul A. Zahl. 77-98, Jan. 1953
• The Galapagos, Eerie Cradle of New Species. By Roger Tory Peterson. Photos by Alan and Joan Root. 541-585, Apr. 1967

FINDING an "Extinct" New Zealand Bird. By R. V. Francis Smith. 393-401, Mar. 1952

FINDING Rare Beauty in Common Rocks. By Lorence G. Collins. 121-129, Jan. 1966

FINDING the Ghost Ships of War. By Daniel A. Nelson. Photos by Emory Kristof. Paintings by Richard Schlecht. 289-313, Mar. 1983

FINDING the Mt. Everest of All Living Things (Redwood Tree). By Paul A. Zahl. 10-51, July 1964

FINDING the Tomb of a Warrior-God. By William Duncan Strong. Photos by Clifford Evans, Jr. 453-482, Apr. 1947

FINDING the World's Earliest Man. By L.S.B. Leakey. Photos by Des Bartlett. 420-435, Sept. 1960

FINDING West Africa's Oldest City. By Susan and Roderick McIntosh. Photos by Michael and Aubine Kirtley. Contents: The Jenne-jeno site in Mali. 396-418, Sept. 1982

FINDLEY, ROWE: Author:
• The Bittersweet Waters of the Lower Colorado. Photos by Charles O'Rear. 540-569, Oct. 1973
• Canyonlands, Realm of Rock and the Far Horizon. Photos by Walter Meayers Edwards. 71-91, July 1971
• Death Valley, the Land and the Legend. Photos by David Hiser. 69-103, Jan. 1970
• Eruption of Mount St. Helens. 3-65, Jan. 1981
I. Mountain With a Death Wish. 3-33; II. In the Path of Destruction. 35-49; III. The Day the Sky Fell. 50-65
• Kansas City, Heartland U.S.A. Photos by Ted Spiegel. 112-139, July 1976
• Miracle of the Potholes. Photos by Robert F. Sisson. 570-579, Oct. 1975
• Mount St. Helens Aftermath: The Mountain That Was–and Will Be. Photos by Steve Raymer. 713-733, Dec. 1981
• Old Salem, Morning Star of Moravian Faith. Photos by Robert W. Madden. 818-837, Dec. 1970
• Our National Forests: Problems in Paradise. Photos by David Cupp. 306-339, Sept. 1982
• The Pony Express. Photos by Craig Aurness. 45-71, July 1980
• Telephone a Star: the Story of Communications Satellites. 638-651, May 1962

FINE ARTS. *See* Painting ; Sculpture; *and listing under* Art Galleries

FINGER LAKES, and Region, New York:
• New York's Land of Dreamers and Doers. By Ethel A. Starbird. Photos by Nathan Benn. Included: Canandaigua; Cayuga; Keuka; Owasco; Seneca; Skaneateles. 702-724, May 1977

FINISTERRE (Yawl):
• The Bahamas, Isles of the Blue-green Sea. By Carleton Mitchell. Photos by B. Anthony Stewart. 147-203, Feb. 1958
• *Finisterre* Sails the Windward Islands. By Carleton Mitchell. Photos by Winfield Parks. 755-801, Dec. 1965
• A Fresh Breeze Stirs the Leewards. By Carleton Mitchell. Photos by Winfield Parks. 488-537, Oct. 1966
• More of Sea Than of Land: The Bahamas. By Carleton Mitchell. Photos by James L. Stanfield. 218-267, Feb. 1967
• To Europe with a Racing Start. By Carleton Mitchell. 758-791, June 1958

FINLAND:
• Baltic Cruise of the *Caribbee*. By Carleton Mitchell. 605-646, Nov. 1950
• Finland: Plucky Neighbor of Soviet Russia. By William Graves. Photos by George F. Mobley. 587-629, May 1968
• Friendly Flight to Northern Europe. By Lyndon B. Johnson. Photos by Volkmar Wentzel. 268-293, Feb. 1964
• Helsinki: City With Its Heart in the Country. By Priit J. Vesilind. Photos by Jodi Cobb. 237-255, Aug. 1981
• North With Finland's Lapps. By Jean and Franc Shor. 249-280, Aug. 1954
• Scenes of Postwar Finland. By La Verne Bradley. Photos by Jerry Waller. 233-264, Aug. 1947

FINNED Doctors of the Deep (Wrasses). By Douglas Faulkner. 867-873, Dec. 1965

FIRE and Ash, Darkness at Noon: El Chichón. By Boris Weintraub. Photos by Guillermo Aldana E. and Kenneth Garrett. 654-684, Nov. 1982
Volcanic Cloud May Alter Earth's Climate. By Robert I. Tilling. 672-675

FIRE ANTS:
• The Pesticide Dilemma. By Allen A. Boraiko. Photos by Fred Ward. 145-183, Feb. 1980

FIRE FIGHTING:
• Forest Fire: The Devil's Picnic. By Stuart E. Jones and Jay Johnston. 100-127, July 1968

The **FIRE** of Heaven: Electricity Revolutionizes the Modern World. By Albert W. Atwood. 655-674, Nov. 1948

FIRE WALKING:
• Copra-ship Voyage to Fiji's Outlying Islands. By Marjory C. Thomas. 121-140, July 1950
• The Islands Called Fiji. By Luis Marden. 526-561, Oct. 1958

FIREBRANDS of the Revolution. By Eric F. Goldman. Photos by George F. Mobley. 2-27, July 1974

FIREFLIES:
● Nature's Night Lights: Probing the Secrets of Bioluminescence. By Paul A. Zahl. 45-69, July 1971
● Torchbearers of the Twilight. By Frederick G. Vosburgh. 697-704, May 1951
● Wing-borne Lamps of the Summer Night. By Paul A. Zahl. 48-59, July 1962

FIRST Across the Pacific: The Flight of *Double Eagle V*. By Ben L. Abruzzo. 513-521, Apr. 1982

FIRST AID:
● The American Red Cross: A Century of Service. By Louise Levathes. Photos by Annie Griffiths. 777-791, June 1981

FIRST American Ascent of Mount St. Elias. By Maynard M. Miller. 229-248, Feb. 1948

A **FIRST** American Views His Land. By N. Scott Momaday. 13-19, July 1976

The **FIRST** Americans. By Thomas Y. Canby. Photos by Kerby Smith. Paintings by Roy Andersen. 330-363, Sept. 1979

FIRST Colony in Space. By Isaac Asimov. Paintings by Pierre Mion. 76-89, July 1976

FIRST Color Photographs on the Moon's Rocky Face. By Homer E. Newell. 578-592, Oct. 1966

FIRST Color Portraits of the Heavens. By William C. Miller. 670-679, May 1959

FIRST Color Record of the Life Cycle of a Coral. By Robert F. Sisson. 780-793, June 1973

FIRST Conquest of Antarctica's Highest Peaks. By Nicholas B. Clinch. 836-863, June 1967

FIRST Crossings of the Ends of the Earth. The Editor. 1, Jan. 1959

The **FIRST** Emperor's Army: China's Incredible Find. By Audrey Topping. Paintings by Yang Hsien-min. 440-459, Apr. 1978

FIRST Explorers on the Moon: The Incredible Story of Apollo 11. 735-797, Dec. 1969

FIRST Flight Across the Bottom of the World. By James R. Reedy. Photos by Otis Imboden. 454-464, Mar. 1964

FIRST Glimpse of a Stone Age Tribe. 881-882, Dec. 1971

FIRST Lady of the National Geographic (Elsie May Bell Grosvenor). By Gilbert Hovey Grosvenor. 101-121, July 1965

FIRST La Gorce Medal Honors Antarctic Expedition. 864-867, June 1967

FIRST Look at a Lost Virginia Settlement (Martin's Hundred). By Ivor Noël Hume. Photos by Ira Block. Paintings by Richard Schlecht. 735-767, June 1979

FIRST Masters of the American Desert: The Hohokam. By Emil W. Haury. Photos by Helga Teiwes. 670-695, May 1967

FIRST Moon Explorers (Apollo 11) Receive the Society's Hubbard Medal. 859-861, June 1970

FIRST Motor Sortie into Escalante Land. By Jack Breed. 369-404, Sept. 1949

FIRST Photographs of Planets and Moon Taken With Palomar's 200-inch Telescope. By Milton L. Humason. 125-130, Jan. 1953

FIRST Photographs of Snow Leopards in the Wild. By George B. Schaller. 702-707, Nov. 1971

The **FIRST** Traverse (Mount Everest). By Thomas F. Hornbein and William F. Unsoeld. 509-513, Oct. 1963

FIRST Voyage Around the World (Magellan). By Alan Villiers. Photos by Bruce Dale. 721-753, June 1976

FIRST Woman Across Greenland's Ice. By Myrtle Simpson. Photos by Hugh Simpson. 264-279, Aug. 1967

FIRSTHAND Look at the Soviet Union. By Thomas T. Hammond. Photos by Erich Lessing. 352-407, Sept. 1959

FISH-BAITING ANIMALS:
● Aha! It Really Works! (Heron). By Robert F. Sisson. 143-147, Jan. 1974
● Something's Fishy About That Fin! (Decoy Fish). Photos by Robert J. Shallenberger and William D. Madden. 224-227, Aug. 1974

FISH FARMING:
● Shrimp Nursery: Science Explores New Ways to Farm the Sea. By Clarence P. Idyll. Photos by Robert F. Sisson. NGS research grant. 636-659, May 1965

FISH Men Discover a 2,200-year-old Greek Ship. By Jacques-Yves Cousteau. NGS research grant. 1-36, Jan. 1954

FISH Men Explore a New World Undersea. By Jacques-Yves Cousteau. 431-472, Oct. 1952

The **FISH** With Bifocals. Photos by Paul A. Zahl. Text by Thomas O'Neill. 390-395, Mar. 1978

FISHER, ALLAN C., Jr.: Author:
● African Wildlife: Man's Threatened Legacy. Photos by Thomas Nebbia. Paintings by Ned Seidler. 147-187, Feb. 1972
● Australia's Pacesetter State, Victoria. Photos by Thomas Nebbia. 218-253, Feb. 1971
● Aviation Medicine on the Threshold of Space. Photos by Luis Marden. 241-278, Aug. 1955
● Cape Canaveral's 6,000-mile Shooting Gallery. Photos by Luis Marden and Thomas Nebbia. 421-471, Oct. 1959
● "The City"–London's Storied Square Mile. 735-777, June 1961
● Eastman of Rochester: Photographic Pioneer. 423-438, Sept. 1954
● Everyone's Servant, the Post Office. Photos by Volkmar Wentzel. 121-152, July 1954
● Exploring Tomorrow With the Space Agency. Photos by Dean Conger. 48-89, July 1960
● The Investiture of Great Britain's Prince of Wales. Photos by James L. Stanfield and Adam Woolfitt. 698-715, Nov. 1969
● Kenya Says *Harambee!* Photos by Bruce Dale. 151-205, Feb. 1969
● Minutemen of the Civil Air Patrol. Photos by John E. Fletcher. 637-665, May 1956
● My Chesapeake–Queen of Bays. Photos by Lowell Georgia. 428-467, Oct. 1980
● Mysteries of Bird Migration. Photos by Jonathan Blair. 154-193, Aug. 1979
● The Nation's River. Photos by James L. Stanfield. 432-469, Oct. 1976
● One Man's London. Photos by James P. Blair. 743-791, June 1966
● Our Navy's Long Submarine Arm. 613-636, Nov. 1952
● Reaching for the Moon. Photos by Luis Marden. 157-171, Feb. 1959
● Rhodesia, a House Divided. Photos by Thomas Nebbia. 641-671, May 1975
● San Diego, California's Plymouth Rock. Photos by James L. Amos. 114-147, July 1969
● Two Englands. Photos by Cary Wolinsky. 442-481, Oct. 1979
● Where the River Shannon Flows. Photos by Adam Woolfitt. 652-679, Nov. 1978
● You and the Obedient Atom. 303-353, Sept. 1958

FISHER, FRANKLIN L.:
● Memorial Tribute to Franklin L. Fisher. 692, Nov. 1953
Author:
● Our Search for British Paintings. 543-550, Apr. 1949

FISHER, MELVIN A.:
● *Atocha,* Tragic Treasure Galleon of the Florida Keys. By Eugene Lyon. 787-809, June 1976
● Treasure From the Ghost Galleon: *Santa Margarita*. By Eugene Lyon. Photos by Don Kincaid. 228-243, Feb. 1982

FISHER TOWERS, Utah:
● We Climbed Utah's Skyscraper Rock. By Huntley Ingalls. Photos by author and Barry C. Bishop. 705-721, Nov. 1962

FISHERMEN:
● Dory on the Banks: A Day in the Life of a Portuguese Fisherman. By James H. Pickerell. 573-583, Apr. 1968
● Fishing in the Lofotens. Photos by Lennart Nilsson. 377-388, Mar. 1947
● Gloucester Blesses Its Portuguese Fleet. By Luis Marden. 75-84, July 1953

E F

• I Sailed with Portugal's Captains Courageous. By Alan Villiers. 565-596, May 1952
▪ The Lonely Dorymen. 579A-579B, Apr. 1968
• The Sailing Oystermen of Chesapeake Bay. By Luis Marden. 798-819, Dec. 1967
• Shad in the Shadow of Skyscrapers. By Dudley B. Martin. Photos by Luis Marden. 359-376, Mar. 1947
• Trawling the China Seas. Photos by J. Charles Thompson. 381-395, Mar. 1950
• Troubled Odyssey of Vietnamese Fishermen. By Harvey Arden. Photos by Steve Wall. 378-395, Sept. 1981
• *See also* Goggle Fishing; Lobsters and Lobstering; Sea Gypsies; Sponge-fishing Industry; Tuna; Watermen; Yamis

FISHERWOMEN:
• Ama, Sea Nymphs of Japan. By Luis Marden. 122-135, July 1971

FISHES:
• An Artist's Glimpses of Our Roadside Wildlife. Paintings by Walter A. Weber. Included: Black bass, Cutthroat trout, Eastern brook trout, Golden trout, Northern pike, Rainbow trout, Yellow perch. 16-32, July 1950
• Australia's Great Barrier Reef. 630-663, May 1981
I. A Marine Park Is Born. By Soames Summerhays. Photos by Ron and Valerie Taylor. 630-635; II. Paradise Beneath the Sea. By Ron and Valerie Taylor. 636-663
◆ *The Book of Fishes* (1952). 418, Mar. 1957; 440, Mar. 1960; 563, Aug. 1961
• The Continental Shelf: Man's New Frontier. By Luis Marden. Photos by Ira Block. 495-531, Apr. 1978
• Exploring Stone Age Arnhem Land. By Charles P. Mountford. Photos by Howell Walker. NGS research grant. 745-782, Dec. 1949
• Finned Doctors of the Deep (Wrasses). By Douglas Faulkner. 867-873, Dec. 1965
• Fish Men Explore a New World Undersea. By Jacques-Yves Cousteau. 431-472, Oct. 1952
• Fishing in the Whirlpool of Charybdis. By Paul A. Zahl. 579-618, Nov. 1953
• Florida, Noah's Ark for Exotic Newcomers. By Rick Gore. Photos by David Doubilet. 538-559, Oct. 1976
• Hidden Life of an Undersea Desert. By Eugenie Clark. Photos by David Doubilet. 129-144, July 1983
• In Hawaii's Crystal Sea, A Galaxy of Life Fills the Night. By Kenneth Brower. Photos by William R. Curtsinger and Chris Newbert. 834-847, Dec. 1981
• In the Wilds of a City Parlor. By Paul A. Zahl. 645-672, Nov. 1954
• Lake Sunapee's Golden Trout. Photos by Robert F. Sisson. 529-536, Oct. 1950
• Man-of-war Fleet Attacks Bimini. By Paul A. Zahl. 185-212, Feb. 1952
• Marineland, Florida's Giant Fish Bowl. By Gilbert Grosvenor La Gorce. Photos by Luis Marden. 679-694, Nov. 1952
• Marvels of a Coral Realm. By Walter A. Starck II. NGS research grant. 710-738, Nov. 1966
• Nature's Alert Eyes. By Constance P. Warner. 558-569, Apr. 1959
• Night Life in the Gulf Stream. By Paul A. Zahl. 391-418, Mar. 1954
• One Hundred Hours Beneath the Chesapeake. By Gilbert C. Klingel. Photos by Willard R. Culver. NGS research grant. 681-696, May 1955
• Photographing the Night Creatures of Alligator Reef (Florida). By Robert E. Schroeder. Photos by author and Walter A. Starck II. NGS research grant. 128-154, Jan. 1964
• Rainbow World Beneath the Red Sea. Photos by David Doubilet. 344-365, Sept. 1975
• The Strangest Sea (Red Sea). By Eugenie Clark. Photos by David Doubilet. 338-343, Sept. 1975
• Undersea Wonders of the Galapagos. By Gerard Wellington. Photos by David Doubilet. 363-381, Sept. 1978
◆ *Wondrous World of Fishes*. Announced. 388-393, Mar. 1965; rev. ed. 1969
• *See also* Decoy Fish; Discus Fish; Eels; Four-eyed Fish; Goldfish; Grunion; Hatchetfish; Herring; Menhaden; Mudskippers; *Photoblepharon;* Piranhas; Sailfish; Salmon; Sargassum Fish; Scorpionfish; Sea Dragons; Sea Horses; Shad; Sharks; Skates; Sole; Trout; Tuna; Walking Catfish

FISHING (Industry):
• The Aleutians: Alaska's Far-out Islands. By Lael Morgan. Photos by Steven C. Wilson. 336-363, Sept. 1983
• Atlantic Salmon: The "Leaper" Struggles to Survive. By Art Lee. Photos by Bianca Lavies. 600-615, Nov. 1981
• Chesapeake Country. By Nathaniel T. Kenney. Photos by Bates Littlehales. 370-411, Sept. 1964
• Chincoteague: Watermen's Island Home. By Nathaniel T. Kenney. Photos by James L. Amos. 810-829, June 1980
• The Continental Shelf: Man's New Frontier. By Luis Marden. Photos by Ira Block. 495-531, Apr. 1978
• The Crab That Shakes Hands. By Clarence P. Idyll. Photos by Robert F. Sisson. 254-271, Feb. 1971
• "Delmarva," Gift of the Sea. By Catherine Bell Palmer. 367-399, Sept. 1950
• Down East Cruise. By Tom Horgan. Photos by Luis Marden. 329-369, Sept. 1952
• Gloucester Blesses Its Portuguese Fleet. By Luis Marden. 75-84, July 1953
• Golden Beaches of Portugal. By Alan Villiers. 673-696, Nov. 1954
• The Hudson: "That River's Alive." By Alice J. Hall. Photos by Ted Spiegel. 62-89, Jan. 1978
• I Sailed with Portugal's Captains Courageous. By Alan Villiers. 565-596, May 1952
• Life's Tempo on Nantucket. By Peter Benchley. Photos by James L. Stanfield. 810-839, June 1970
• Maryland on the Half Shell. By Stuart E. Jones. Photos by Robert W. Madden. 188-229, Feb. 1972
• Massachusetts' North Shore: Harboring Old Ways. Photos by Nathan Benn. Included: Gloucester fishermen, lobstering, and clamming. 568-590, Apr. 1979
• Menhaden–Uncle Sam's Top Commercial Fish. By Leonard C. Roy. Photos by Robert F. Sisson. 813-823, June 1949
• My Chesapeake–Queen of Bays. By Allan C. Fisher, Jr. Photos by Lowell Georgia. 428-467, Oct. 1980
• New Day for Alaska's Pribilof Islanders. By Susan Hackley Johnson. Photos by Tim Thompson. 536-552, Oct. 1982
• New World of the Ocean. By Samuel W. Matthews. 792-832, Dec. 1981
• Newfoundland Trusts in the Sea. By Gary Jennings. Photos by Sam Abell. 112-141, Jan. 1974
• Peoples of the Arctic. 144-223, Feb. 1983
I. Introduction by Joseph Judge. 144-149; II. Hunters of the Lost Spirit: Alaskans, Canadians, Greenlanders, Lapps. By Priit J. Vesilind. Photos by David Alan Harvey, Ivars Silis, and Sisse Brimberg. 150-197
• Plight of the Bluefin Tuna. By Michael J. A. Butler. Photos by David Doubilet. Paintings by Stanley Meltzoff. 220-239, Aug. 1982
• Quicksilver and Slow Death. By John J. Putman. Photos by Robert W. Madden. Included: Mercury contamination of fish in Japan and the United States. 507-527, Oct. 1972
• Risk and Reward on Alaska's Violent Gulf. By Boyd Gibbons. Photos by Steve Raymer. 237-267, Feb. 1979
• Shad in the Shadow of Skyscrapers. By Dudley B. Martin. Photos by Luis Marden. 359-376, Mar. 1947
• Sicily the Three-Cornered. By Luis Marden. 1-48, Jan. 1955
• This Is My Island, Tangier (Virginia). By Harold G. Wheatley. Photos by David Alan Harvey. Included: Crabbing. 700-725, Nov. 1973
• Trawling the China Seas. Photos by J. Charles Thompson. 381-395, Mar. 1950
• *See also* Cod Fishing; Herring; Lobsters and Lobstering; Oyster Fleet; Shrimp Fishing; Tuna

FISHING (Sport):
• Goggle Fishing in California Waters. By David Hellyer. Photos by Lamar Boren. 615-632, May 1949
• *See also* Ice Fishing; Trout

FISHING, Night (Marine Biology Studies):
• Night Life in the Gulf Stream. By Paul A. Zahl. 391-418, Mar. 1954

FISHING in the Whirlpool of Charybdis. By Paul A. Zahl. 579-618, Nov. 1953

FISHING VESSELS. *See* Fishing (Industry)

FITCH, CLYDE:
• Literary Landmarks of Massachusetts. By William H. Nicholas. Photos by B. Anthony Stewart and John E. Fletcher. 279-310, Mar. 1950

FITZ ROY, ROBERT:
• In the Wake of Darwin's *Beagle*. By Alan Villiers. Photos by James L. Stanfield. 449-495, Oct. 1969

FITZHUGH, WILLIAM W.: Author:
• Where Magic Ruled: Art of the Bering Sea. By William W. Fitzhugh and Susan A. Kaplan. Photos by Sisse Brimberg. 198-205, Feb. 1983

FIVE Noted Thinkers Explore the Future. 68-75, July 1976

FIVE Times to Yakutsk. By Dean Conger. 256-269, Aug. 1977

The **FIVE** Worlds of Peru. By Kenneth F. Weaver. Photos by Bates Littlehales. 213-265, Feb. 1964

FJORDS:
• Norway's Fjords Pit Men Against Mountains. By Andrew H. Brown. 96-122, Jan. 1957

FLAGS:
• American and Geographic Flags Top Everest. By Melvin M. Payne. Photos by Barry C. Bishop. 157-157C, Aug. 1963
• Flags of the Americas. By Elizabeth W. King. Contents: The Flag of the United States and the Jack; Flags of the President, the Vice President, and Heads of Executive Departments of the United States; Flags of the United States Armed Forces and Government Agencies; Flags of the Latin-American Republics. 633-657, May 1949
• Flags of the United Nations (60 Member Countries). By Elizabeth W. King. 213-238, Feb. 1951
• Flags of the United Nations (99 Members). 332-345, Sept. 1961
• New Stars for Old Glory. By Lonnelle Aikman. 86-121, July 1959
• The Palio of Siena. By Edgar Erskine Hume. Contents: The standard of Siena; ward and guild banners; also, the performances of the *giuocatori di bandiera,* skilled flag manipulators. 231-244, Aug. 1951
• The Peary Flag (U. S. Flag) Comes to Rest. By Marie Peary Stafford. 519-532, Oct. 1954
• *See also* NGS: Flag

FLAMBOYANT Is the Word for Bolivia. By Loren McIntyre. 153-195, Feb. 1966

FLAMINGOS:
• Ballerinas in Pink. By Carleton Mitchell. Photos by B. Anthony Stewart. 553-571, Oct. 1957
• East Africa's Majestic Flamingos. By M. Philip Kahl. Included: Greater flamingo; Lesser flamingo. NGS research grant. 276-294, Feb. 1970
• The Flamingo Eaters of Ngorongoro. By Richard D. Estes. Contents: Flamingos as hyenas' prey. 535-539, Oct. 1973
• Flamingos' Last Stand on Andros Island. By Paul A. Zahl. 635-652, May 1951
• Freeing Flamingos From Anklets of Death. By John G. Williams. Photos by Alan Root. 934-944, Dec. 1963
• In Quest of the Rarest Flamingo (James's Flamingo). By William G. Conway. Photos by Bates Littlehales. 91-105, July 1961

FLANDERS (Region), Belgium:
• Belgium: One Nation Divisible. By James Cerruti. Photos by Martin Rogers. 314-341, Mar. 1979

FLASHLIGHT Fish of the Red Sea. By Eugenie Clark. Photos by David Doubilet. 719-728, Nov. 1978

FLAT TOP COALFIELD, West Virginia:
• Mountain Voices, Mountain Days. By Bryan Hodgson. Photos by Linda Bartlett. 118-146, July 1972

FLATHEAD RIVER, Canada-U. S.:
• Our Wild and Scenic Rivers: The Flathead. By Douglas H. Chadwick. Photos by Lowell Georgia. 13-19, July 1977

FLEA MARKET, Paris, France:
• Paris Flea Market. By Franc Shor. Photos by Alexander Taylor. 318-326, Mar. 1957

FLEAY, DAVID: Author:
• Strange Animals of Australia. Photos by Stanley Breeden. 388-411, Sept. 1963
Author-Photographer:
• Flight of the Platypuses. 512-525, Oct. 1958

FLEDGLING Wings of the Air Force. By Thomas W. McKnew. 266-271, Aug. 1957

FLEMING, SIR ALEXANDER:
• The British Way. By Sir Evelyn Wrench. 421-541, Apr. 1949

FLEMING, KEVIN: Photographer:
• Delaware–Who Needs to Be Big? By Jane Vessels. 171-197, Aug. 1983
• Eternal Sinai. By Harvey Arden. Photos by David Doubilet and Kevin Fleming. 420-461, Apr. 1982
Egyptian Sector. Photos by Kevin Fleming. 430-443; Israeli Sector. Photos by David Doubilet. 444-461
• Florida–A Time for Reckoning. By William S. Ellis. Photos by Nathan Benn and Kevin Fleming. 172-219, Aug. 1982
• Somalia's Hour of Need. By Robert Paul Jordan. Photos by Michael S. Yamashita and Kevin Fleming. 748-775, June 1981

FLEMING, ROBERT V.:
• Memorial tribute: Robert V. Fleming, 1890-1967. By Melville Bell Grosvenor. 526-529, Apr. 1968
• NGS Board of Trustees member. 706, May 1953; 81, Jan. 1957
• Treasurer of NGS. 260, 261, Aug. 1949; 64, 65A-65B, 65D, July 1954; 419, 420, 421, 423, Mar. 1957
• Vice President of NGS. 882, 883, Dec. 1960; 585, Oct. 1963; 672, May 1964; 589, Oct. 1967

M. PHILIP KAHL

Flamingos: lesser flamingos in Kenya

FLEMINGS:
• Belgium: One Nation Divisible. By James Cerruti. Photos by Martin Rogers. 314-341, Mar. 1979

FLETCHER, JOHN E.:
Author-Photographer:
• Graduation by Parachute (Parachute Rigger School). 833-846, June 1952
Photographer:
• Aboard the N.S. *Savannah:* World's First Nuclear Merchantman. By Alan Villiers. 280-298, Aug. 1962
• All-out Assault on Antarctica. By Richard E. Byrd. 141-180, Aug. 1956
• America Goes to the Fair. By Samuel W. Matthews. 293-333, Sept. 1954
• Avalanche! (Peru). By Bart McDowell. 855-880, June 1962
• Beltsville Brings Science to the Farm. By Samuel W. Matthews. 199-218, Aug. 1953
• The DAR Story. By Lonnelle Aikman. Photos by B. Anthony Stewart and John E. Fletcher. 565-598, Nov. 1951
• Date Line: United Nations, New York. By Carolyn Bennett Patterson. Photos by B. Anthony Stewart and John E. Fletcher. 305-331, Sept. 1961
• "Delmarva," Gift of the Sea. By Catherine Bell Palmer. 367-399, Sept. 1950
• Dog Mart Day in Fredericksburg. By Frederick G. Vosburgh. 817-832, June 1951
• Exploring America's Great Sand Barrier Reef. By Eugene R. Guild. Photos by John E. Fletcher and author. 325-350, Sept. 1947
• Exploring Ottawa. By Bruce Hutchison. 565-596, Nov. 1947
• Folger: Biggest Little Library in the World. By Joseph T. Foster. Photos by B. Anthony Stewart and John E. Fletcher. 411-424, Sept. 1951
• Hays, Kansas, at the Nation's Heart. By Margaret M. Detwiler. 461-490, Apr. 1952
• Literary Landmarks of Massachusetts. By William H. Nicholas. Photos by B. Anthony Stewart and John E. Fletcher. 279-310, Mar. 1950
• Mardi Gras in New Orleans. By Carolyn Bennett Patterson. Photos by Robert F. Sisson and John E. Fletcher. 726-732, Nov. 1960
• Men Who Measure the Earth. By Robert Leslie Conly. 335-362, Mar. 1956
• The Merrimack: River of Industry and Romance. By Albert W. Atwood. 106-140, Jan. 1951
• Minnesota Makes Ideas Pay. By Frederick G. Vosburgh. Photos by John E. Fletcher and B. Anthony Stewart. 291-336, Sept. 1949
• Minutemen of the Civil Air Patrol. By Allan C. Fisher, Jr. 637-665, May 1956
• Mount Vernon Lives On. By Lonnelle Aikman. 651-682, Nov. 1953

JAMES A. SUGAR
Oshkosh: Red Devils aerobatic display

• Pittsburgh: Workshop of the Titans. By Albert W. Atwood. 117-144, July 1949
• Quebec's Forests, Farms, and Frontiers. By Andrew H. Brown. 431-470, Oct. 1949
• Sea to Lakes on the St. Lawrence. By George W. Long. Photos by B. Anthony Stewart and John E. Fletcher. 323-366, Sept. 1950
• Sno-Cats Mechanize Oregon Snow Survey. By Andrew H. Brown. 691-710, Nov. 1949
• Stately Homes of Old Virginia. By Albert W. Atwood. 787-802, June 1953
• The United Nations: Capital of the Family of Man. By Adlai E. Stevenson. Photos by B. Anthony Stewart and John E. Fletcher. 297-303, Sept. 1961
• Washington's Historic Georgetown. By William A. Kinney. 513-544, Apr. 1953
• Weather From the White North. By Andrew H. Brown. 543-572, Apr. 1955

FLETCHER, JOSEPH O.: Author:
• Three Months on an Arctic Ice Island. 489-504, Apr. 1953

FLETCHER'S ICE ISLAND, Arctic Region. *See* T-3

FLIGHT. *See* Aviation; Balloons; Space Flights and Research

FLIGHT Into Antarctic Darkness. By J. Lloyd Abbot, Jr. Photos by David S. Boyer. 732-738, Nov. 1967

The **FLIGHT** of Apollo 11. By Kenneth F. Weaver. 752-787, Dec. 1969

The **FLIGHT** of *Freedom 7.* By Carmault B. Jackson, Jr. 416-431, Sept. 1961

The **FLIGHT** of the *Gossamer Condor.* By Michael E. Long. 130-140, Jan. 1978

FLIGHT of the *Kitty Hawk.* By Maxie and Kristian Anderson. 260-271, Aug. 1980

FLIGHT of the Platypuses. By David Fleay. 512-525, Oct. 1958

FLIGHT to Adventure. By Tay and Lowell Thomas, Jr. 49-112, July 1957

FLIGHT to Adventure: Sky Road East. By Tay and Lowell Thomas, Jr. 71-112, Jan. 1960

FLIGHT to Venus and Mercury. By Kenneth F. Weaver. 858-869, June 1975

FLIGHTS of Fancy at Oshkosh. By Michael E. Long. Photos by James A. Sugar and the author. Contents: The annual convention of the Experimental Aircraft Association held at Oshkosh, Wisconsin. 365-375, Sept. 1979

FLINT HILLS, Kansas:
• The Tallgrass Prairie: Can It Be Saved? By Dennis Farney. Photos by Jim Brandenburg. 37-61, Jan. 1980

FLOATING FARMS:
• Burma's Leg Rowers and Floating Farms. Photos by W. E. Garrett. Text by David Jeffery. 826-845, June 1974

FLOODS AND FLOOD CONTROL:
• Alaska's Automatic Lake Drains Itself (Lake George). 835-844, June 1951
• Florence Rises From the Flood. By Joseph Judge. 1-43, July 1967
• The Imperiled Everglades. By Fred Ward. Included: South Florida's canal system. 1-27, Jan. 1972
• The Lower Mississippi. By Willard Price. Photos by W. D. Vaughn. 681-725, Nov. 1960
• The Mekong, River of Terror and Hope. By Peter T. White. Photos by W. E. Garrett. 737-787, Dec. 1968
• The Netherlands: Nation at War With the Sea. By Alan Villiers. Photos by Adam Woolfitt. 530-571, Apr. 1968
• Our Most Precious Resource: Water. By Thomas Y. Canby. Photos by Ted Spiegel. 144-179, Aug. 1980
◆ *Our Violent Earth*. 1982
• Satellites Gave Warning of Midwest Floods. By Peter T. White. Photos by Thomas A. DeFeo. 574-592, Oct. 1969
• Shawneetown Forsakes the Ohio. By William H. Nicholas. Photos by J. Baylor Roberts. 273-288, Feb. 1948
• Southern California's Trial by Mud and Water. By Nathaniel T. Kenney. Photos by Bruce Dale. 552-573, Oct. 1969
• Threatened Glories of Everglades National Park. By Frederick Kent Truslow and Frederick G. Vosburgh. Photos by Frederick Kent Truslow and Otis Imboden. 508-553, Oct. 1967
• Trouble in Bayou Country: Louisiana's Atchafalaya. By Jack and Anne Rudloe. Photos by C. C. Lockwood. 377-397, Sept. 1979
• Venice Fights for Life. By Joseph Judge. Photos by Albert Moldvay. 591-631, Nov. 1972
• *See also* Dams; Dikes and Levees; Snow Survey

FLORENCE, Italy:
• Florence Rises From the Flood. By Joseph Judge. 1-43, July 1967
• Italy Smiles Again. By Edgar Erskine Hume. 693-732, June 1949
• Leonardo da Vinci: A Man for All Ages. By Kenneth MacLeish. Photos by James L. Amos. 296-329, Sept. 1977
• The Renaissance Lives On in Tuscany. By Luis Marden. Photos by Albert Moldvay. 626-659, Nov. 1974

FLORES (Island), Lesser Sunda Islands:
• East From Bali by Seagoing Jeep to Timor. By Helen and Frank Schreider. 236-279, Aug. 1962

FLORICULTURE:
• Amateur Gardener Creates a New Rose. By Elizabeth A. Moize. Photos by Farrell Grehan. 286-294, Aug. 1972
• The Exquisite Orchids. By Luis Marden. 485-513, Apr. 1971
• The Flower Seed Growers: Gardening's Color Merchants. By Robert de Roos. Photos by Jack Fields. 720-738, May 1968
• Patent Plants Enrich Our World. By Orville H. Kneen. 357-378, Mar. 1948
• *See also* Longwood Gardens; Royal Botanic Gardens

FLORIDA:
• American Wild Flower Odyssey. By P. L. Ricker. 603-634, May 1953
• *Atocha,* Tragic Treasure Galleon of the Florida Keys. By Eugene Lyon. Included: The State of Florida's supervision of treasure trove–search, salvage, and distribution. 787-809, June 1976
• A Bad Time to Be a Crocodile. By Rick Gore. Photos by Jonathan Blair. 90-115, Jan. 1978
• The Booming Sport of Water Skiing. By Wilbur E. Garrett. 700-711, Nov. 1958
▲ *Close-up U.S.A., Florida, with Puerto Rico and U. S. Virgin Islands,* supplement. Text on reverse. Close-up series. Nov. 1973
• Cruising Florida's Western Waterways. By Rube Allyn. Photos by Bates Littlehales. 49-76, Jan. 1955
• Drowned Galleons Yield Spanish Gold. By Kip Wagner. Photos by Otis Imboden. 1-37, Jan. 1965
• An Exotic New Oriole Settles in Florida. By Charles M. Brookfield and Oliver Griswold. 261-264, Feb. 1956
• Florida–A Time for Reckoning. By William S. Ellis. Photos by Nathan Benn and Kevin Fleming. 172-219, Aug. 1982
• Florida, Noah's Ark for Exotic Newcomers. By Rick Gore. Photos by David Doubilet. 538-559, Oct. 1976
• Florida Rides a Space-age Boom. By Benedict Thielen. Photos by Winfield Parks and James P. Blair. 858-903, Dec. 1963
• Florida's Booming–and Beleaguered–Heartland. By Joseph Judge. Photos by Jonathan Blair. 585-621, Nov. 1973
• Florida's Manatees, Mermaids in Peril. By Daniel S. Hartman. Photos by James A. Sugar. 342-353, Sept. 1969
• How Fruit Came to America. By J. R. Magness. Paintings by Else Bostelmann. Included: Orange, lime, and grapefruit production. 325-377, Sept. 1951
• Hurricane! By Ben Funk. Photos by Robert W. Madden. 346-379, Sept. 1980
Dominica. By Fred Ward. 357-359; Dynamics of a Hurricane. 370-371; Into the Eye of David. By John L. Eliot. 368-369; Paths of Fury–This Century's Worst American Storms. 360-361
• Indian Life Before the Colonists Came. By Stuart E. Jones. Engravings by Theodore de Bry, 1590. 351-368, Sept. 1947
• Limpkin, the "Crying Bird" That Haunts Florida Swamps. By Frederick Kent Truslow. 114-121, Jan. 1958
• Little Horses of the Sea (Sea Horses). By Paul A. Zahl. Included: Key Largo; Sanibel Island; Tarpon Springs. 131-153, Jan. 1959
• Men Against the Hurricane. By Andrew H. Brown. 537-560, Oct. 1950
• Our Wild and Scenic Rivers: The Suwannee. By Jack and Anne Rudloe. Photos by Jodi Cobb. 20-29, July 1977
• Reach for the New World. By Mendel Peterson. Photos by David L. Arnold. Paintings by Richard Schlecht. Included: Shipwrecks off the Florida coast. 724-767, Dec. 1977
• St. Augustine, Nation's Oldest City, Turns 400. By Robert L. Conly. 196-229, Feb. 1966
• Saving Man's Wildlife Heritage. By John H. Baker. Photos by Robert F. Sisson. 581-620, Nov. 1954
• Shrimp Nursery: Science Explores New Ways to Farm the Sea. By Clarence P. Idyll. Photos by Robert F. Sisson. NGS research grant. 636-659, May 1965
• Slow Boat to Florida *(Tradewinds).* By Dorothea and Stuart E. Jones. 1-65, Jan. 1958
• *See also* Big Cypress Swamp; Canaveral, Cape; Corkscrew Swamp; Crystal River; Everglades; Florida Keys; Marineland; Marquesas Keys; Merritt Island National Wildlife Refuge; Miami; Tampa; Tarpon Springs

FLORIDA ISLAND, Solomon Islands:
• Adventures with the Survey Navy. By Irving Johnson. 131-148, July 1947

FLORIDA KEYS, Florida:
• The Lower Keys, Florida's "Out Islands." By John Scofield. Photos by Emory Kristof and Bates Littlehales. 72-93, Jan. 1971
▒ Treasure! 575, Nov. 1976; cover, Dec. 1976
• *See also* Alligator Reef; Dry Tortugas; John Pennekamp Coral Reef State Park; Key West; Tarpon Key

FLOUR:
• Rediscovering America's Forgotten Crops. By Noel D. Vietmeyer. Photos by Burgess Blevins. Paintings by Paul M. Breeden. Included: Amaranth-seed flour. 702-712, May 1981

FLOWER PRESERVATION:
• Blossoms That Defy the Seasons. By Geneal Condon. Photos by David S. Boyer. 420-427, Sept. 1958

FLOWERS:
• American Wild Flower Odyssey. By P. L. Ricker. 603-634, May 1953
• Britain's "French" Channel Islands. By James Cerruti. Photos by James L. Amos. 710-740, May 1971
• Cloud Gardens in the Tetons. By Frank and John Craighead. 811-830, June 1948
• Crossroads of the Insect World. By J. W. MacSwain. Photos by Edward S. Ross. 844-857, Dec. 1966

• England's Scillies, the Flowering Isles. By Alan Villiers. Photos by Bates Littlehales. 126-145, July 1967
• The Flower Seed Growers: Gardening's Color Merchants. By Robert de Roos. Photos by Jack Fields. Included: The World of Flowers. Painting by Ned M. Seidler. 720-738, May 1968
• The Flowers That Say "Aloha." By Deena Clark. Photos by Robert B. Goodman. 121-131, Jan. 1967
• Herbs for All Seasons. By Lonnelle Aikman. Photos by Sam Abell. Picture portfolio text by Larry Kohl. 386-409, Mar. 1983
• Hummingbirds: The Nectar Connection. By Paul W. Ewald. Photos by Robert A. Tyrrell. Included: Pollination of fuchsia, tree tobacco, wooly blue curls. 223-227, Feb. 1982
• In the Gardens of Olympus (Washington). By Paul A. Zahl. 85-123, July 1955
• Jerusalem, My Home. By Bertha Spafford Vester. Included: Wild flower paintings. 826-847, Dec. 1964
• Malaysia's Giant Flowers and Insect-trapping Plants. By Paul A. Zahl. 680-701, May 1964
• The Netherlands: Nation at War With the Sea. By Alan Villiers. Photos by Adam Woolfitt. Included: Flower bulb industry. 530-571, Apr. 1968
• Patent Plants Enrich Our World. By Orville H. Kneen. Photos from U. S. Plant Patents. 357-378, Mar. 1948
• Photographing Northern Wild Flowers. By Virginia L. Wells. 809-823, June 1956
• Saving Man's Wildlife Heritage. By John H. Baker. Photos by Robert F. Sisson. 581-620, Nov. 1954
• A Visit to the Living Ice Age. By Rutherford Platt. 525-545, Apr. 1957
• The World in Your Garden. By W. H. Camp. Paintings by Else Bostelmann. Contents: Abelia, African-Violet, Azalea, Bellflower, Bird-of-Paradise Flower, Blackberry-Lily, Blanket-Flower, Bleeding Heart, Blue Lace-Flower, Bottle-Brush, California Poppy, Calla, Camellia, Candytuft, Canna, Cape Marigold, Castor-Oil-Plant, Catawba Rhododendron, China Aster, Chrysanthemum, Clarkia, Clematis, Common Hyacinth, Cosmos, Crown Imperial, Crown-of-Thorns, Cup-Flower, Cypress Vine, Dahlia, Daisy, East Indian Lotus, Eucalyptus (Gum-Tree), Flamboyant (Royal) Poinciana, Flame Azalea, Forsythia, Foxglove, Frangipani, French and African Marigolds, Fringed Hibiscus, Fuchsia, Garden Verbena, Gerbera, Gladiolus, Grape-Hyacinth, Hibiscus, Hollyhock, Impatiens, Japanese Iris, Japanese Wisteria, Lobelia, Lupine, Michaelmas Daisies, Morning Glory, Nasturtium, Oleander, Oriental Poppy, Oswego Tea, Pansy (Heartsease), Pelargonium ("Geranium"), Peony, Petunia, Poinsettia, Poker-Plant, Pot Marigold, Primrose, Regal Lily, Rose, Scarlet Sage, Snakes-Head (Checkered-Lily), Snapdragon, Snowdrop, Spider Flower, Spring Crocus, Star-of-Bethlehem, Stock (Gilliflower), Strawflower, Summer Perennial Phlox, Swan River Daisy, Sweet Scabious, Tiger-Flower, Travelers-Tree, Tulip, Victoria Waterlily, Wallflower, Zinnia. 1-65, July 1947
◆ *World in Your Garden.* Announced. 729-730, May 1957
• *See also* Azaleas; Bromeliads; Flower Preservation; Gardens; Irises; Orchids; Patent Plants; Puya; Rhododendrons; Roses; Tulips; Wild Flowers

FLUORESCENT Gems From Davy Jones's Locker. By Paul A. Zahl. 260-271, Aug. 1963

FLYING in the "Blowtorch" Era. By Frederick G. Vosburgh. 281-322, Sept. 1950

FLYING MAMMALS:
• "Flying" Squirrels, Nature's Gliders. By Ernest P. Walker. 663-674, May 1947
• Seeking Mindanao's Strangest Creatures. By Charles Heizer Wharton. 389-408, Sept. 1948
• Strange Animals of Australia. By David Fleay. Photos by Stanley Breeden. 388-411, Sept. 1963
• *See also* Bats

The **FLYING** Telegraph (Pigeons). By Joseph F. Spears. Official U. S. Army Signal Corps photos. 531-554, Apr. 1947

FOCUSING on the Tournament of Roses. By B. Anthony Stewart and J. Baylor Roberts. 805-816, June 1954

FOLDBOATS:
• Squaws Along the Yukon. By Ginny Hill Wood. 245-265, Aug. 1957

FOLGER: Biggest Little Library in the World. By Joseph T. Foster. Photos by B. Anthony Stewart and John E. Fletcher. 411-424, Sept. 1951

FOLK ART:
• Better Days for the Navajos. By Jack Breed. Photos by Charles W. Herbert. 809-847, Dec. 1958
• Early America Through the Eyes of Her Native Artists. By Hereward Lester Cooke, Jr. Paintings by American primitive artists. 356-389, Sept. 1962
• Easter Greetings From the Ukrainians. By Robert Paul Jordan. Photos by James A. Sugar. 556-563, Apr. 1972
• From Sea to Sahara in French Morocco. By Jean and Franc Shor. 147-188, Feb. 1955
• Haiti–West Africa in the West Indies. By John Scofield. 226-259, Feb. 1961
• Human Treasures of Japan. By William Graves. Photos by James L. Stanfield. Contents: Ryujo Hori, doll maker; Gonroku Matsuda, lacquer artist; Tesshi Nagano, ironcaster; Utaemon Nakamura, Kabuki actor; Sadaichi Tsukiyama, samurai swordsmith. 370-379, Sept. 1972
• Humble Masterpieces: Decoys. By George Reiger. Photos by Kenneth Garrett. 639-663, Nov. 1983
• The Inadan: Artisans of the Sahara. By Michael and Aubine Kirtley. 282-298, Aug. 1979
• Japan, the Exquisite Enigma. By Franc Shor. Photos by John Launois. 733-777, Dec. 1960
• Kyoto and Nara: Keepers of Japan's Past. By Charles McCarry. Photos by George F. Mobley. 836-851, June 1976
• Mexican Folk Art. By Fernando Horcasitas. Photos by David Hiser. 648-669, May 1978
• Mountain Voices, Mountain Days (West Virginia). By Bryan Hodgson. Photos by Linda Bartlett. 118-146, July 1972
• An Ozark Family Carves a Living and a Way of Life. Photos by Bruce Dale. 124-133, July 1975
• Pennsylvania's Old-time Dutch Treat. By Kent Britt. Photos by H. Edward Kim. 564-578, Apr. 1973
• Pueblo Pottery–2,000 Years of Artistry. By David L. Arnold. 593-605, Nov. 1982
• To the Land of the Head-hunters. By E. Thomas Gilliard. NGS research grant. 437-486, Oct. 1955
• Where Magic Ruled: Art of the Bering Sea. By William W. Fitzhugh and Susan A. Kaplan. Photos by Sisse Brimberg. 198-205, Feb. 1983
• The World in Dolls. By Samuel F. Pryor. Photos by Kathleen Revis. 817-831, Dec. 1959
• *See also* Embroidery; Junk Sculpture; Weaving

FOLK SONGS:
• Hunting Folk Songs in the Hebrides. By Margaret Shaw Campbell. 249-272, Feb. 1947
• Hunting Musical Game in West Africa. By Arthur S. Alberts. 262-282, Aug. 1951
• *See also* Ozark Plateau

FOLLIARD, EDWARD T.: Author:
• Escorting Mona Lisa to America. 838-847, June 1963

FOLLOWING the Ladybug Home. By Kenneth S. Hagen. Photos by Robert F. Sisson. 543-553, Apr. 1970

FOLLOWING the Reindeer With Norway's Lapps. By Sally Anderson. Photos by Erik Borg. 364-379, Sept. 1977

FOLLOWING the Tracks of a Different Man (Thoreau). By William Howarth. Photos by Farrell Grehan. 349-387, Mar. 1981

FOLLOWING the Trail of Lewis and Clark. By Ralph Gray. 707-750, June 1953

FOOD:
• Can the World Feed Its People? By Thomas Y. Canby. 2-31, July 1975
• Editorial. By Gilbert M. Grosvenor. 1, July 1975
• Erosion, Trojan Horse of Greece. By F. G. Renner. 793-812, Dec. 1947
• 4-H Boys and Girls Grow More Food. By Frederick Simpich. 551-582, Nov. 1948

• Herbs for All Seasons. By Lonnelle Aikman. Photos by Sam Abell. Picture portfolio text by Larry Kohl. 386-409, Mar. 1983
• Keeping House in London. By Frances James. 769-792, Dec. 1947
• Rediscovering America's Forgotten Crops. By Noel D. Vietmeyer. Photos by Burgess Blevins. Paintings by Paul M. Breeden. Included: Amaranth seeds; groundnuts; tepary beans. 702-712, May 1981
• The Revolution in American Agriculture. By Jules B. Billard. Photos by James P. Blair. 147-185, Feb. 1970
• Salt–The Essence of Life. By Gordon Young. Photos by Volkmar Wentzel and Georg Gerster. 381-401, Sept. 1977
• School for Survival. By Curtis E. LeMay. 565-602, May 1953
• Shad in the Shadow of Skyscrapers. By Dudley B. Martin. Photos by Luis Marden. 359-376, Mar. 1947
• *See also* Cheese Making; Coffee; Corn Growing; Fruit and Fruit Growing; Potatoes and Potato Growing; Truffles; Vegetables; Wild Foods; *and* Trucks and Trucking, for food transport

FOOD CHAIN:
• Algae: the Life-givers. By Paul A. Zahl. 361-377, Mar. 1974
• Can We Save Our Salt Marshes? By Stephen W. Hitchcock. Photos by William R. Curtsinger. 729-765, June 1972
▲ "How Man Pollutes His World," painting supplement. Map of the World. Dec. 1970
• Life Springs From Death in Truk Lagoon. By Sylvia A. Earle. Photos by Al Giddings. 578-613, May 1976
• Mzima, Kenya's Spring of Life. By Joan and Alan Root. 350-373, Sept. 1971
• Quicksilver and Slow Death (Mercury). By John J. Putman. Photos by Robert W. Madden. 507-527, Oct. 1972
• Teeming Life of a Pond. By William H. Amos. 274-298, Aug. 1970

FOOTE, SHELBY: Author:
• Echoes of Shiloh (Shiloh National Military Park, Tennessee). 106-111, July 1979

FOOTPRINTS in the Ashes of Time. By Mary D. Leakey. 446-457, Apr. 1979

FOOTPRINTS on the Moon. By Hugh L. Dryden. Paintings by Davis Meltzer and Pierre Mion. 357-401, Mar. 1964

FOOTT, JEFF: Photographer:
• Our Bald Eagle: Freedom's Symbol Survives. By Thomas C. Dunstan. 186-199, Feb. 1978

FORAGING. *See* Wild Foods

FORD, HENRY, MUSEUM, Dearborn, Michigan:
• The Past Is Present in Greenfield Village. By Beverley M. Bowie. Photos by Neal P. Davis and Willard R. Culver. 96-127, July 1958

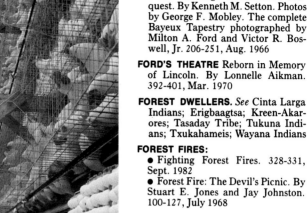

JAMES P. BLAIR, NGS

Revolution in Agriculture: egg factory

FORD, MILTON A.: Photographer:
• 900 Years Ago: The Norman Conquest. By Kenneth M. Setton. Photos by George F. Mobley. The complete Bayeux Tapestry photographed by Milton A. Ford and Victor R. Boswell, Jr. 206-251, Aug. 1966

FORD'S THEATRE Reborn in Memory of Lincoln. By Lonnelle Aikman. 392-401, Mar. 1970

FOREST DWELLERS. *See* Cinta Larga Indians; Erigbaagtsa; Kreen-Akarores; Tasaday Tribe; Tukuna Indians; Txukahameis; Wayana Indians

FOREST FIRES:
• Fighting Forest Fires. 328-331, Sept. 1982
• Forest Fire: The Devil's Picnic. By Stuart E. Jones and Jay Johnston. 100-127, July 1968

FOREST PRODUCTS:
• Brazil's Wild Frontier. By Loren McIntyre. 684-719, Nov. 1977
• Tropical Rain Forests: Nature's Dwindling Treasures. By Peter T. White. Photos by James P. Blair. Paintings by Barron Storey. 2-47, Jan. 1983
• *See also* Lumber Industry; Paper and Pulp Industry

FOREST SERVICE. *See* U. S. Forest Service

FORESTS AND REFORESTATION:
• Adobe New Mexico. By Mason Sutherland. Photos by Justin Locke. Included: Carson National Forest; Santa Fe National Forest. 783-830, Dec. 1949
▲ *America's Federal Lands; The United States,* double-sided supplement. Sept. 1982
• Backwoods Japan During American Occupation. By M. A. Huberman. 491-518, Apr. 1947
◆ *A Day in the Woods.* 1975
• Editorial. By Wilbur E. Garrett. 279, Sept. 1982
• Erosion, Trojan Horse of Greece. By F. G. Renner. 793-812, Dec. 1947
• The Friendly Train Called Skunk. By Dean Jennings. Photos by B. Anthony Stewart. 720-734, May 1959
• From Sagebrush to Roses on the Columbia. By Leo A. Borah. 571-611, Nov. 1952
• A Map Maker Looks at the United States. By Newman Bumstead. Photos by U. S. Air Force. Included: Rain forests, Olympic Peninsula (Washington); Gifford Pinchot National Forest (Washington); the Tillamook (Oregon) burn of 1933; and the Sierra Nevada forests. 705-748, June 1951
• Our Green Treasury, the National Forests. By Nathaniel T. Kenney. Photos by J. Baylor Roberts. 287-324, Sept. 1956
• Our National Forests: Problems in Paradise. By Rowe Findley. Photos by David Cupp. 306-339, Sept. 1982
• Roosevelt Country: T. R.'s Wilderness Legacy. By John L. Eliot. Photos by Farrell Grehan. 340-363, Sept. 1982

• Timber: How Much Is Enough? By John J. Putman. Photos by Bruce Dale. 485-511, Apr. 1974
• Tropical Rain Forests. 2-65, Jan. 1983
Nature's Dwindling Treasures. By Peter T. White. Photos by James P. Blair. Paintings by Barron Storey. 2-47; Teeming Life of a Rain Forest. By Carol and David Hughes. 49-65
• *See also* Giant Forest; Inyo National Forest; Ituri Forest; Jackson Hole, Wyoming; Jari River Region, Brazil; New Hampshire; Olympic National Park; Sarawak; *and* Forest Fires; Lumber Industry; National Forests; Paper and Pulp Industry; Rain Forests; Redwoods; *Sequoia gigantea*

FORMOSA. *See* Taiwan

FORMOSA STRAIT, China:
• Patrolling Troubled Formosa Strait. 573-588, Apr. 1955
• *See also* Pescadores; Quemoy; Taiwan

FORNEY RANCH, Sheridan County, Nebraska:
• Land of Long Sunsets: Nebraska's Sand Hills. By John Madson. Photos by Jodi Cobb. 493-517, Oct. 1978

FORSYTH, GEORGE H.: Author:
• Island of Faith in the Sinai Wilderness (St. Catherine's Monastery). Photos by Robert F. Sisson. 82-106, Jan. 1964

FORT APACHE RESERVATION, Arizona:
• The White Mountain Apache. 260-290, Feb. 1980
I. At Peace With the Past, In Step With the Future. By Ronnie Lupe. 260-261; II. Coming of Age the Apache Way. By Nita Quintero. Photos by Bill Hess. 262-271; III. Seeking the Best of Two Worlds. By Bill Hess. 272-290

FORT CHURCHILL, Manitoba, Canada:
• Rockets Explore the Air Above Us. By Newman Bumstead. 562-580, Apr. 1957
• Trailing Cosmic Rays in Canada's North. By Martin A. Pomerantz. 99-115, Jan. 1953

FORT DE FRANCE, Martinique:
• Martinique: Liberté, Egalité, and Uncertainty in the Caribbean. By Kenneth MacLeish. Photos by John Launois. 124-148, Jan. 1975

FORT JEFFERSON NATIONAL MONUMENT, Florida:
• The Lower Keys, Florida's "Out Islands." By John Scofield. Photos by Emory Kristof and Bates Littlehales. 72-93, Jan. 1971

FORT TERNAN, Kenya:
• Adventures in the Search for Man. By Louis S. B. Leakey. Photos by Hugo van Lawick. 132-152, Jan. 1963

FORT TICONDEROGA, New York:
• From Sword to Scythe in Champlain Country. By Ethel A. Starbird. Photos by B. Anthony Stewart and Emory Kristof. 153-201, Aug. 1967

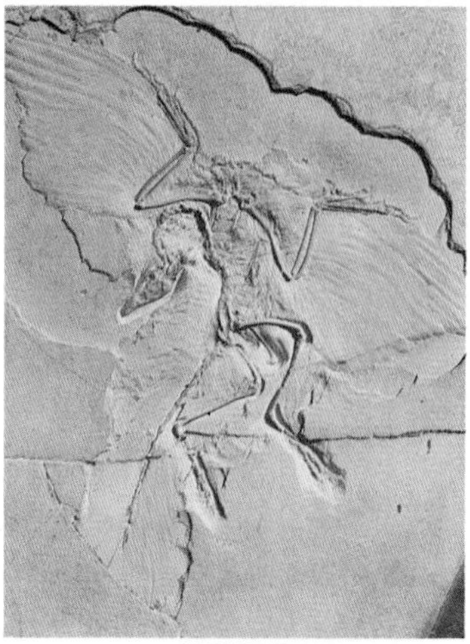

MUSEUM FUR NATURKUNDE AN DER HUMBOLDT-UNIVERSITÄT, DDR, BERLIN

Dinosaurs: *Archaeopteryx* fossil

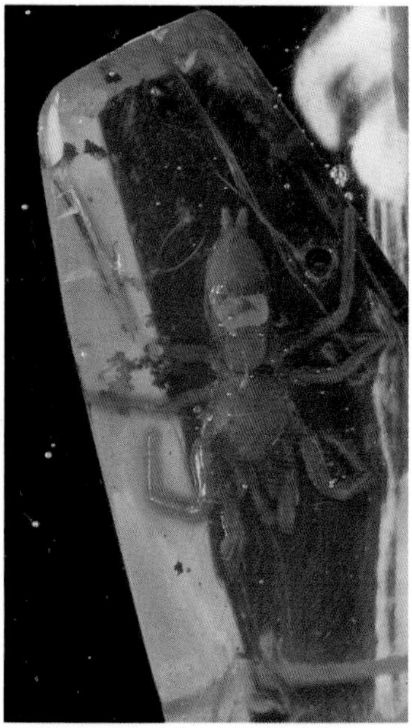

PAUL A. ZAHL

Amber: entombed spider

• North Through History Aboard *White Mist.* By Melville Bell Grosvenor. Photos by Edwin Stuart Grosvenor. 1-55, July 1970

FORTRESSES. *See* Alhambra; Castillo de San Marcos; Castles; Kremlin; Louisbourg; St. Catherine's Monastery; St. Michael's Mount; Vizcaya (Fortress-Palace); *and* Jaisalmer; Languedoc (Region), France, for Carcassonne; Luxembourg; Peru (The Five Worlds), for Sacsahuamán; Quebec (City)

FORTUNATE ISLANDS. *See* Canary Islands

FORTUNATE ISLES. *See* Scilly, Isles of

FORTUNE TELLING. *See* Dogon

FORTY-NINERS. *See* Golden Ghosts; *and* Death Valley National Monument

FOSFORESCENTE, Bahía, Puerto Rico. *See* Phosphorescent Bay

FOSHAG, W. F.: Author:
• Exploring the World of Gems. 779-810, Dec. 1950

FOSSEY, DIAN:
Gorilla. 703, Dec. 1980; cover, Apr. 1981
Search for the Great Apes. cover, Jan. 1976
Author:
• The Imperiled Mountain Gorilla. 501-523, Apr. 1981
Death of Marchessa. Photos by Peter G. Veit. 508-511
• Making Friends With Mountain Gorillas. Photos by Robert M. Campbell. 48-67, Jan. 1970
• More Years With Mountain Gorillas. Photos by Robert M. Campbell. 574-585, Oct. 1971

FOSSIL FUELS. *See* Coal; Natural Gas; Oil

FOSSILS:
• Amber: Golden Window on the Past. Photos by Paul A. Zahl. Text by Thomas J. O'Neill. 423-435, Sept. 1977
• Ancient Ashfall Creates a Pompeii of Prehistoric Animals. By Michael R. Voorhies. Photos by Annie Griffiths. Paintings by Jay Matternes. NGS research grant. 66-75, Jan. 1981
• Bison Kill By Ice Age Hunters. By Dennis Stanford. NGS research grant. 114-121, Jan. 1979
• Footprints in the Ashes of Time. By Mary D. Leakey. NGS research grant. 446-457, Apr. 1979
• Fossils Lift the Veil of Time. By Harry S. Ladd and Roland W. Brown. 363-386, Mar. 1956
• In the Wake of Darwin's *Beagle.* By Alan Villiers. Photos by James L. Stanfield. Included: Extinct mammal fossils: mastodon, machcrauchenia, megatherium, mylodon, toxodon. 449-495, Oct. 1969
• A New Look at Dinosaurs. By John H. Ostrom. Paintings by Roy Andersen. NGS research grant. 152-185, Aug. 1978

• The Search for the First Americans. By Thomas Y. Canby. Photos by Kerby Smith. Paintings by Roy Andersen. 330-363, Sept. 1979
• South Dakota's Badlands: Castles in Clay. By John Madson. Photos by Jim Brandenburg. Included: Oligocene mammal fossils; Fossilized turtles. 524-539, Apr. 1981
• *See also* Paleontology

FOSTER, BRISTOL: Author:
• Africa's Gentle Giants (Giraffes). Photos by Bob Campbell and Thomas Nebbia. 402-417, Sept. 1977

FOSTER, JOSEPH T.: Author:
• Folger: Biggest Little Library in the World. Photos by B. Anthony Stewart and John E. Fletcher. 411-424, Sept. 1951

FOSTER, MULFORD B.: Author-Photographer:
• Puya, the Pineapple's Andean Ancestor. 463-480, Oct. 1950

FOUND–a Lost Virginia Settlement (Martin's Hundred). By Ivor Noël Hume. Photos by Ira Block. Paintings by Richard Schlecht. 735-767, June 1979

FOUND at Last: the Monarch's Winter Home. By Fred A. Urquhart. Photos by Bianca Lavies. NGS research grant. 161-173, Aug. 1976

FOUNDERS of New England. By Sir Evelyn Wrench. Photos by B. Anthony Stewart. 803-838, June 1953

FOUNDERS of Virginia. By Sir Evelyn Wrench. Photos by B. Anthony Stewart. 433-462, Apr. 1948

FOUNTAIN of Fire in Hawaii. By Frederick Simpich, Jr. Photos by Robert B. Goodman and Robert Wenkam. 303-327, Mar. 1960

FOUR CORNERS COUNTRY (Arizona-Colorado-New Mexico-Utah):
• The Anasazi–Riddles in the Ruins. By Thomas Y. Canby. Photos by Dewitt Jones and David Brill. Paintings by Roy Andersen. 554-592, Nov. 1982
• Inside the Sacred Hopi Homeland. By Jake Page. Photos by Susanne Page. 607-629, Nov. 1982
• Pueblo Pottery–2,000 Years of Artistry. By David L. Arnold. 593-605, Nov. 1982
• Roaming the West's Fantastic Four Corners. By Jack Breed. 705-742, June 1952
▲ *The Southwest,* The Making of America series. Included: Arizona, New Mexico, and parts of California, Colorado, Texas, Utah; and in Mexico: Baja California Norte, Chihuahua, Sonora. On reverse: 12,000 Years of History; Spanish Conquest; Anglo-American Entry and Occupancy. Nov. 1982
• Stalking the West's Wild Foods. By Euell Gibbons. Photos by David Hiser. 186-199, Aug. 1973
• *See also* Mesa Verde National Park; Rainbow Bridge National Monument; *and* Navajos

The **FOUR-EYED** Fish Sees All. Photos by Paul A. Zahl. Text by Thomas O'Neill. 390-395, Mar. 1978

4-H CLUBS:
• America Goes to the Fair. By Samuel W. Matthews. 293-333, Sept. 1954
• Down on the Farm, Soviet Style–a 4-H Adventure. By John Garaventa. Photos by James Tobin and Carol Schmidt. 768-797, June 1979
• 4-H Boys and Girls Grow More Food. By Frederick Simpich. 551-582, Nov. 1948

FOUR-OCEAN Navy in the Nuclear Age. By Thomas W. McKnew. 145-187, Feb. 1965

A **FOUR-PART** Look at the Isles of the Pacific. 732-793, Dec. 1974

FOUR Years of Diving to the Bottom of the Sea. By Georges S. Houot. 715-731, May 1958

"1470 MAN." *See* Skull 1470

A **14TH-CENTURY** Cargo Makes Port at Last. Photos by H. Edward Kim. Introduction by Donald H. Keith. 231-243, Aug. 1979

FOWL, Japanese Long-Tailed:
• Scientist Studies Japan's Fantastic Long-tailed Fowl. By Frank X. Ogasawara. Photos by Eiji Miyazawa. NGS research grant. 845-855, Dec. 1970

FOX, CHARLES J.:
• Portrait of Gilbert H. Grosvenor. 252, 258, Aug. 1949

FOX, CHARLES PHILIP: Photographer:
• Br'er Possum, Hermit of the Lowlands. By Agnes Akin Atkinson. 405-418, Mar. 1953
• Skunks Want Peace–or Else! By Melvin R. Ellis. 279-294, Aug. 1955

FOXES:
• Foxes Foretell the Future in Mali's Dogon Country. By Pamela Johnson Meyer. 431-448, Mar. 1969
• The Romance of American Furs. By Wanda Burnett. 379-402, Mar. 1948

The **FRAGILE** Beauty All About Us. Photos by Harry S. C. Yen. 785-795, Dec. 1970

FRAGILE Nurseries of the Sea: Can We Save Our Salt Marshes? By Stephen W. Hitchcock. Photos by William R. Curtsinger. 729-765, June 1972

FRAME, GEORGE W. and LORY HERBISON: Author-Photographers:
• Cheetahs: In a Race for Survival. 712-728, May 1980

FRANCE:
• Across the Ridgepole of the Alps. By Walter Meayers Edwards. 410-419, Sept. 1960
• The Alps: Man's Own Mountains. By Ralph Gray. Photos by Walter Meayers Edwards and William Eppridge. Included: Mont Blanc highway tunnel, from Haute Savoie, France, to Valle d'Aosta, Italy. 350-395, Sept. 1965
• "Around the World in Eighty Days." By Newman Bumstead. Included: Avignon; Corsica; Lyon; Marseille; Mont Blanc; Montpellier; Paris. 705-750, Dec. 1951
• Bordeaux: Fine Wines and Fiery Gascons. By William Davenport. Photos by Adam Woolfitt. 233-259, Aug. 1980
• The Celts. By Merle Severy. Photos by James P. Blair. Paintings by Robert C. Magis. 582-633, May 1977
• The Civilizing Seine. By Charles McCarry. Photos by David L. Arnold. 478-511, Apr. 1982
• The Diffident Truffle, France's Gift to Gourmets. 419-426, Sept. 1956
• The Enduring Pyrenees. By Robert Laxalt. Photos by Edwin Stuart Grosvenor. 794-819, Dec. 1974
• Eternal France. By Walter Meayers Edwards. 725-764, June 1960
• Exploring the Mind of Ice Age Man. By Alexander Marshack. 64-89, Jan. 1975
▲ *France, Belgium, and the Netherlands,* Atlas series supplement. June 1960
• France's Past Lives in Languedoc. By Walter Meayers Edwards. 1-43, July 1951
• French Riviera: Storied Playground on the Azure Coast. By Carleton Mitchell. Photos by Thomas Nebbia. 798-835, June 1967
• Here Rest in Honored Glory . . . The United States Dedicates Six New Battle Monuments in Europe to Americans Who Gave Their Lives During World War II. By Howell Walker. Included: Brittany, Épinal, Normandy, and Rhône monuments. 739-768, June 1957
• High Road in the Pyrenees. By H. V. Morton. Photos by Justin Locke. 299-334, Mar. 1956
• The Incredible Potato. By Robert E. Rhoades. Photos by Martin Rogers. Included: Académie Parmentier, Limonest, a gastronomic society devoted to honoring the potato. 668-694, May 1982
• Inside Europe Aboard *Yankee.* By Irving and Electa Johnson. Photos by Joseph J. Scherschel. 157-195, Aug. 1964
• Land of the Ancient Basques. By Robert Laxalt. Photos by William Albert Allard. 240-277, Aug. 1968
• Life in the Land of the Basques. By John E. H. Nolan. Photos by Justin Locke. 147-186, Feb. 1954
• Living the Good Life in Burgundy. By William Davenport. Photos by Robert Freson. 794-817, June 1978
• Napoleon. By John J. Putman. Photos by Gordon W. Gahan. 142-189, Feb. 1982
• A New Look at Medieval Europe. By Kenneth M. Setton. Paintings by Andre Durenceau and Birney Lettick. 799-859, Dec. 1962
• 900 Years Ago: The Norman Conquest. By Kenneth M. Setton. Photos by George F. Mobley. 206-251, Aug. 1966

E F

• Paris to Antwerp with the Water Gypsies. By David S. Boyer. 530-559, Oct. 1955
• Pigeon Netting–Sport of Basques. Photos by Irene Burdett-Scougall. 405-416, Sept. 1949
• Sheep Trek in the French Alps. By Maurice Moyal. Photos by Marcel Coen. 545-564, Apr. 1952
▲ *A Traveler's Map of France,* supplement. Text on reverse. June 1971
• Travels With a Donkey–100 Years Later. By Carolyn Bennett Patterson. Photos by Cotton Coulson. Contents: A walking tour of the Cévennes. 535-561, Oct. 1978
• When the President Goes Abroad (Eisenhower Tour). By Gilbert M. Grosvenor. 588-649, May 1960
• *See also* Auvergne; Brittany; Camargue (Region); Chartres; Corsica; English Channel; Ice Caves (Pyrenees); Lascaux Cave; Loire River and Valley; Martinique; Mont Saint Michel; Normandy; Ouessant, Ile d'; Paris; Provence; Réunion (Island); St. Pierre and Miquelon; Saint Véran; Strasbourg; Vézelay; *and* Crusades; French Impressionists; Transatlantic Balloon Flight

FRANCOPHONES, Canada-U. S.:
• Madawaska: Down East With a French Accent. By Perry Garfinkel. Photos by Cary Wolinsky. 380-409, Sept. 1980

FRANKLIN, BENJAMIN:
• Benjamin Franklin, Philosopher of Dissent. By Alice J. Hall. Photos by Linda Bartlett. 93-123, July 1975

FRANKLIN, WILLIAM L.:
Author-Photographer:
• Guanacos: Wild Camels of South America. 63-75, July 1981
• High, Wild World of the Vicuña. 77-91, Jan. 1973

FRANKLIN L. BURR PRIZE:
• Burr Prizes Awarded to Dr. Edgerton and Dr. Van Biesbroeck. 705-706, May 1953

FRANKLIN RIVER, Tasmania:
• A Walk and Ride on the Wild Side: Tasmania. By Carolyn Bennett Patterson. Photos by David Hiser and Melinda Berge. 676-693, May 1983

FRANZÉN, ANDERS: Author:
• Ghost From the Depths: the Warship *Vasa.* 42-57, Jan. 1962

FRASER, LAURA GARDIN:
• Designer of NGS Medals: Grosvenor Medal. 255, 261, Aug. 1949; 422, Mar. 1957; 516, Oct. 1963; Hubbard Medal. 564, Apr. 1953; Special Medal of Honor. 45, July 1957

FRAZER, JOHN E.: Author:
• India's Energetic Sikhs. Photos by James P. Blair. 528-541, Oct. 1972
• Kuwait, Aladdin's Lamp of the Middle East. Photos by David F. Cupp. 636-667, May 1969

FRAZIER, PAUL W.: Author:
• Across the Frozen Desert to Byrd Station. Photos by Calvin L. Larsen. 383-398, Sept. 1957

FREDERICK G. VOSBURGH Retires as Editor; Gilbert M. Grosvenor Succeeds Him. By Melvin M. Payne. 838-843, Dec. 1970

FREDERICKSBURG, Virginia:
• Dog Mart Day in Fredericksburg. By Frederick G. Vosburgh. 817-832, June 1951

FREEDOM Flight from Hungary. Photos by Robert F. Sisson. 424-436, Mar. 1957

FREEDOM 7 (Spacecraft). *See* Mercury Missions

FREEDOM Speaks French in Ouagadougou. By John Scofield. 153-203, Aug. 1966

FREEDOM TRAIN Tours America. 529-542, Oct. 1949

FREEDOM'S Progress South of the Sahara. By Howard La Fay. Photos by Joseph J. Scherschel. 603-637, Nov. 1962

FREEING Flamingos From Anklets of Death. By John G. Williams. Photos by Alan Root. 934-944, Dec. 1963

FREETOWN, Sierra Leone:
• The Loyalists. By Kent Britt. Photos by Ted Spiegel. Note: Slaves of Patriot colonists, liberated by the British during the American Revolution, founded Freetown after the war. 510-539, Apr. 1975

FREEZING the Flight of Hummingbirds. By Harold E. Edgerton, R. J. Niedrach, and Walker Van Riper. NGS research grant. 245-261, Aug. 1951

FREEZING the Trout's Lightning Leap. By Treat Davidson. 525-530, Apr. 1958

FREHSEE, RICK: Photographer:
• Strange March of the Spiny Lobster. By William F. Herrnkind. Photos by Rick Frehsee and Bruce Mounier. 819-831, June 1975

FREIDEL, FRANK B., Jr.: Author:
Profiles of the Presidents:
• Part I. The Presidency and How It Grew. 642-687, Nov. 1964
• Part II. A Restless Nation Moves West. 80-121, Jan. 1965
• Part III. The American Giant Comes of Age. 660-711, May 1965
• Part IV. America Enters the Modern Era. 537-577, Oct. 1965
• Part V. The Atomic Age: Its Problems and Promises. 66-119, Jan. 1966

FRENCH-AMERICAN MID-OCEAN UNDERSEA STUDY. *See* FAMOUS

FRENCH-CANADIAN PROVINCES. *See* New Brunswick; Quebec

FRENCH EQUATORIAL AFRICA:
• Freedom Speaks French in Ouagadougou. By John Scofield. Included: Central African Republic; Chad; Gabon. 153-203, Aug. 1966

FRENCH GUIANA:
• What Future for the Wayana Indians? By Carole Devillers. 66-83, Jan. 1983

FRENCH IMPRESSIONISTS:
• Great Masters of a Brave Era in Art. By Hereward Lester Cooke, Jr. 661-697, May 1961
• In Quest of Beauty. Text by Paul Mellon. 372-385, Mar. 1967

FRENCH POLYNESIA. *See* Marquesas Islands; Society Islands; Tuamotu Archipelago

FRENCH RIVIERA: Storied Playground on the Azure Coast. By Carleton Mitchell. Photos by Thomas Nebbia. 798-835, June 1967

FRENCH SUDAN. *See* Mali

FRENCH WEST AFRICA:
• Freedom Speaks French in Ouagadougou. By John Scofield. Included: Dahomey; Guinea; Ivory Coast; Mali; Mauritania; Niger; Senegal. 153-203, Aug. 1966
• *See also* Mali; Mauritania; Niger; *and* Tuareg

FRESCOES. *See* Cappadocia; Cave Art; Etruscans; Minoan Civilization; Sistine Chapel

A **FRESH** Breeze Stirs the Leewards. By Carleton Mitchell. Photos by Winfield Parks. 488-537, Oct. 1966

FRESH Treasures from Egypt's Ancient Sands. By Jefferson Caffery. Photos by David S. Boyer. 611-650, Nov. 1955

FRESHWATER PRESERVE, Proposed. *See* Big Cypress Swamp, Florida

FRESON, ROBERT: Photographer:
• Living the Good Life in Burgundy. By William Davenport. 794-817, June 1978

FRIEDMAN, HERBERT: Author:
• The Sun. 713-743, Nov. 1965

FRIEDMANN, HERBERT: Author:
• Honey-Guide: The Bird That Eats Wax. Paintings by Walter A. Weber. 551-560, Apr. 1954

FRIEND of the Wind: The Common Tern. By Ian Nisbet. Photos by Hope Alexander. 234-247, Aug. 1973

FRIENDLESS Squatters of the Sea. By Ethel A. Starbird. Photos by Robert F. Sisson. 623-633, Nov. 1973

FRIENDLY, ALFRED: Author:
• Africa's Bushman Art Treasures. Photos by Alex R. Willcox. 848-865, June 1963

FRIENDLY Flight to Northern Europe. By Lyndon B. Johnson. Photos by Volkmar Wentzel. 268-293, Feb. 1964

The **FRIENDLY** Huts of the White Mountains. By William O. Douglas. Photos by Kathleen Revis. 205-239, Aug. 1961

The **FRIENDLY** Irish. By John Scofield. Photos by James A. Sugar. 354-391, Sept. 1969

The **FRIENDLY** Isles of Tonga. By Luis Marden. 345-367, Mar. 1968

The **FRIENDLY** Train Called Skunk. By Dean Jennings. Photos by B. Anthony Stewart. 720-734, May 1959

FRIENDSHIP 7 (Spacecraft). *See* Mercury Missions

FROBISHER BAY, Canada. *See* Baffin Island

FROGS:
- The Amazing Frog-Eating Bat. By Merlin D. Tuttle. Included: Bullfrogs, Mud-puddle frogs, Pug-nosed tree frogs, Poisonous frogs, and Toads. NGS research grant. 78-91, Jan. 1982
- Bullfrog Ballet Filmed in Flight. By Treat Davidson. 791-799, June 1963
- Capturing Strange Creatures in Colombia. By Marte Latham. Photos by Tor Eigeland. 682-693, May 1966
- Eden in the Outback. By Kay and Stanley Breeden. 189-203, Feb. 1973
- In Quest of the World's Largest Frog. By Paul A. Zahl. 146-152, July 1967
- Life Around a Lily Pad. Photos by Bianca Lavies. Text by Charles R. Miller. 131-142, Jan. 1980
- Nature's Living, Jumping Jewels. By Paul A. Zahl. Contents: Miniature tropical frogs of Costa Rica. 130-146, July 1973
- Teeming Life of a Pond. By William H. Amos. 274-298, Aug. 1970
- Teeming Life of a Rain Forest. By Carol and David Hughes. 49-65, Jan. 1983
- Voices of the Night. By Arthur A. Allen. Contents: Anderson's tree frog, Barking tree frog, Bird-voiced tree frog, Bullfrog, Canadian toad, Carpenter frog, Common toad, Common tree toad, Green frog, Green tree frog, Leopard or Meadow frog, Oak toad, Peeper, Pickerel frog, Pygmy swamp cricket frog, Spadefoot toad, Squirrel tree frog, Western toad. 507-522, Apr. 1950

FROM Amazon to Spanish Main: Colombia. By Loren McIntyre. 235-273, Aug. 1970

FROM America to Mecca on Airborne Pilgrimage. By Abdul Ghafur Sheikh. 1-60, July 1953

FROM Baltic to Bicentennial by Square Rigger. By Kenneth Garrett. 824-857, Dec. 1976

FROM Barra to Butt in the Hebrides. By Isobel Wylie Hutchison. 559-580, Oct. 1954

FROM Graveyard to Garden (Truk Lagoon). Photos by Al Giddings. 604-613, May 1976

FROM Indian Canoes to Submarines at Key West. By Frederick Simpich. Photos by J. Baylor Roberts. 41-72, Jan. 1950

FROM Sagebrush to Roses on the Columbia. By Leo A. Borah. 571-611, Nov. 1952

FROM Sea to Sahara in French Morocco. By Jean and Franc Shor. 147-188, Feb. 1955

TREAT DAVIDSON

Bullfrog: air-breathing frog in water

FROM Sea to Shining Sea: A Cross Section of the United States Along Historic Route 40. By Ralph Gray. Photos by Dean Conger and author. 1-61, July 1961

FROM Spear to Hoe on Groote Eylandt. By Howell Walker. 131-142, Jan. 1953

FROM Sun-clad Sea to Shining Mountains. By Ralph Gray. Photos by James P. Blair. 542-589, Apr. 1964

FROM Sword to Scythe in Champlain Country. By Ethel A. Starbird. Photos by B. Anthony Stewart and Emory Kristof. 153-201, Aug. 1967

FROM the Bahamas to Belize: Probing the Deep Reefs' Hidden Realm. By Walter A. Starck II and Jo D. Starck. 867-886, Dec. 1972

FROM the Hair of Siva. By Helen and Frank Schreider. 445-503, Oct. 1960

FROM Tucson to Tombstone. By Mason Sutherland. 343-384, Sept. 1953

FRONTIER, 19th-Century, U. S.:
- ◆ *The American Cowboy in Life and Legend*. 1972. Announced. 882-886, June 1971
- Buffalo Bill and the Enduring West. By Alice J. Hall. Photos by James L. Amos. 76-103, July 1981
- Chief Joseph. By William Albert Allard. 409-434, Mar. 1977
- ◆ *Cowboys*. Announced. 724-726, Nov. 1975
- From Tucson to Tombstone. By Mason Sutherland. 343-384, Sept. 1953
- Hays, Kansas, at the Nation's Heart. By Margaret M. Detwiler. Photos by John E. Fletcher. 461-490, Apr. 1952
- The Pony Express. By Rowe Findley. Photos by Craig Aurness. 45-71, July 1980
- A Restless Nation Moves West. By Frank Freidel. Paintings from the White House Collection. 80-121, Jan. 1965
- Riding the Outlaw Trail. By Robert Redford. Photos by Jonathan Blair. 622-657, Nov. 1976
- So Long, St. Louis, We're Heading West. By William C. Everhart. 643-669, Nov. 1965
- ◆ *Trails West*. 1979

FROST, ROBERT:
- Editorial. By Gilbert M. Grosvenor. 437, Apr. 1976
- Robert Frost and New England. By Archibald MacLeish. 438-467, Apr. 1976
  Look of a Land Beloved. Photos by Dewitt Jones. 444-467

FROST, Nature's Icing. By Robert F. Sisson. 398-405, Mar. 1976

FRUIT AND FRUIT GROWING:
- California, Horn of Plenty. By Frederick Simpich. Photos by Willard R. Culver. 553-594, May 1949
- Florida Rides a Space-age Boom. By Benedict Thielen. Photos by Winfield Parks and James P. Blair. 858-903, Dec. 1963

• How Fruit Came to America. By J. R. Magness. Paintings by Else Bostelmann. Contents: American Plum, Apple, Apricot, Avocado, Banana, Blackberry, Blueberry, Cherry, Cranberry, Currant, Date, Fig, Gooseberry, Grape, Grapefruit, Japanese Plum, Lemon, Lime, Mango, Olive, Orange, Papaya, Peach, Pear, Persimmon, Pineapple, Plum, Prune, Quince, Raspberry, Strawberry. 325-377, Sept. 1951
• The Lure of the Changing Desert (California). Included: Date raising. 817-824, June 1954
• Our Life on a Border Kibbutz. By Carol and Al Abrams. Photos by Al Abrams. 364-391, Sept. 1970
• Our Vegetable Travelers. By Victor R. Boswell. Paintings by Else Bostelmann. Included: Watermelon, Muskmelon. 145-217, Aug. 1949
• Patent Plants Enrich Our World. By Orville H. Kneen. Photos from U. S. Plant Patents. 357-378, Mar. 1948
• Washington's Yakima Valley. By Mark Miller. Photos by Sisse Brimberg. Included: Apple growing. 609-631, Nov. 1978
• The Wasp That Plays Cupid to a Fig. By Robert F. Sisson. 690-697, Nov. 1970
◆ *The World in Your Garden.* Announced. 729-730, May 1957
• *See also* Citrus Fruits; Grapes and Grape Culture; Pineapples and Pineapple Growing

FUCHS, SIR VIVIAN:
• Society Honors the Conquerors of Antarctica. 589-590, Apr. 1959
Author:
• The Crossing of Antarctica. Photos by George Lowe. 25-47, Jan. 1959

FUEGIAN INDIANS:
• In the Wake of Darwin's *Beagle.* By Alan Villiers. Photos by James L. Stanfield. 449-495, Oct. 1969

FULANI (Tribespeople):
• The Niger: River of Sorrow, River of Hope. By Georg Gerster. 152-189, Aug. 1975
• Oursi, Magnet in the Desert. By Carole E. Devillers. 512-525, Apr. 1980

FULLER, BUCKMINSTER: Author:
• Five Noted Thinkers Explore the Future. 72-73, July 1976

FULLER, R. STEVEN:
Author-Photographer:
• Winterkeeping in Yellowstone. 829-857, Dec. 1978

FUN Helped Them Fight (Bombing Squadrons). By Stuart E. Jones. 95-104, Jan. 1948

FUNAI. *See* listing under National Foundation for the Indian

FUNAN, Kingdom of:
• Mosaic of Cultures (Southeast Asia). By Peter T. White. Photos by W. E. Garrett. 296-329, Mar. 1971
• *See also* Angkor, for Khmers

FUNCHAL, Madeira:
• Madeira, Like Its Wine, Improves With Age. By Veronica Thomas. Photos by Jonathan Blair. 488-513, Apr. 1973

FUNDY, Bay of, Canada:
• The Giant Tides of Fundy. By Paul A. Zahl. 153-192, Aug. 1957

FUNERALS:
• Expedition to the Land of the Tiwi. By Charles P. Mountford. Note: Australian Aboriginal artistic and social activities are centered on funeral ceremonies. NGS research grant. 417-440, Mar. 1956
• The Ganges, River of Faith. By John J. Putman. Photos by Raghubir Singh. Included: Hindu funeral. 445-483, Oct. 1971
• Gangtok, Cloud-wreathed Himalayan Capital. By John Scofield. Included: Funeral of Princess Sonam Padaun. 698-713, Nov. 1970
• Life and Death in Tana Toradja. By Pamela and Alfred Meyer. 793-815, June 1972
• New Orleans and Her River. By Joseph Judge. Photos by James L. Stanfield. Included: Jazz funeral. 151-187, Feb. 1971
• Taboos and Magic Rule Namba Lives. By Kal Muller. 57-83, Jan. 1972
• *See also* Burial Customs

FUNERALS, State. *See* Churchill, Sir Winston; Eisenhower, Dwight D.; Kennedy, John F.

FUNGI:
• Bizarre World of the Fungi. By Paul A. Zahl. 502-527, Oct. 1965
• Slime Mold: The Fungus That Walks. By Douglas Lee. Photos by Paul A. Zahl. Note: This protoplasm is not a true fungus. 131-136, July 1981
• The Wild World of Compost. By Cecil E. Johnson. Photos by Bianca Lavies. 273-284, Aug. 1980
• *See also* Truffles

FUNK, BEN: Author:
• Hurricane! By Ben Funk. Photos by Robert W. Madden. 346-379, Sept. 1980

FUNK, TED H.: Photographer:
• Democracy's Fortress: Unsinkable Malta. By Ernle Bradford. 852-879, June 1969
• Luxembourg, the Quiet Fortress. By Robert Leslie Conly. 69-97, July 1970
• The Manx and Their Isle of Man. By Veronica Thomas. 426-444, Sept. 1972
• San Marino, Little Land of Liberty. By Donna Hamilton Shor. 233-251, Aug. 1967

FUR SEALS:
• New Day for Alaska's Pribilof Islanders. By Susan Hackley Johnson. Photos by Tim Thompson. 536-552, Oct. 1982

FURS:
• The Fur Seal Herd Comes of Age. By Victor B. Scheffer and Karl W. Kenyon. 491-512, Apr. 1952
• Life or Death for the Harp Seal. By David M. Lavigne. Photos by William R. Curtsinger. 129-142, Jan. 1976
• Men, Moose, and Mink of Northwest Angle. By William H. Nicholas. Photos by J. Baylor Roberts. 265-284, Aug. 1947
• New Day for Alaska's Pribilof Islanders. By Susan Hackley Johnson. Photos by Tim Thompson. 536-552, Oct. 1982
• The Romance of American Furs. By Wanda Burnett. 379-402, Mar. 1948
• Wild Cargo: the Business of Smuggling Animals. By Noel Grove. Photos by Steve Raymer. 287-315, Mar. 1981

FUSION:
• The Fusion Solution. 45, *Special Report on Energy* (Feb. 1981)

FUTAGAMI JIMA (Island), Japan:
• Living in a Japanese Village. By William Graves. Photos by James L. Stanfield. 668-693, May 1972

FYN (Island), Denmark:
• By Full-rigged Ship to Denmark's Fairyland. By Alan Villiers. Photos by Alexander Taylor and author. 809-828, Dec. 1955

G

The **GI** and the Kids of Korea. By Robert H. Mosier. 635-664, May 1953

GABON:
• Ambassadors of Good Will: The Peace Corps. By Sargent Shriver and Peace Corps Volunteers. 297-345, Sept. 1964
Gabon. By John F. Murphy, Jr. 325-329

GAELS:
• The Highlands, Stronghold of Scottish Gaeldom. By Kenneth MacLeish. Photos by Winfield Parks. 398-435, Mar. 1968
• Isles on the Edge of the Sea: Scotland's Outer Hebrides. By Kenneth MacLeish. Photos by Thomas Nebbia. 676-711, May 1970
• Scotland's Inner Hebrides: Isles of the Western Sea. By Kenneth MacLeish. Photos by R. Stephen Uzzell III. 690-717, Nov. 1974
• *See also* Celts

GAHAN, GORDON W.: Photographer:
• Captain Cook: The Man Who Mapped the Pacific. By Alan Villiers. 297-349, Sept. 1971
• Drought Bedevils Brazil's Sertão. By John Wilson. 704-723, Nov. 1972
• East Germany: The Struggle to Succeed. By John J. Putman. 295-329, Sept. 1974
• Goal at the End of the Trail: Santa Fe. By William S. Ellis. Photos by Gordon W. Gahan and Otis Imboden. 323-345, Mar. 1982

• In Search of Man's Past at Lake Rudolf. By Richard E. Leakey. 712-734, May 1970
• Israel–The Seventh Day. By Joseph Judge. 816-855, Dec. 1972
• Maui, Where Old Hawaii Still Lives. By Kenneth F. Weaver. 514-543, Apr. 1971
• Minoans and Mycenaeans: Greece's Brilliant Bronze Age. By Joseph Judge. Paintings by Lloyd K. Townsend. 142-185, Feb. 1978
• The More Paris Changes. . . . By Howell Walker. 64-103, July 1972
• Moscow: The City Around Red Square. By John J. Putman. 2-45, Jan. 1978
• Napoleon. By John J. Putman. 142-189, Feb. 1982
• Nova Scotia, the Magnificent Anchorage. By Charles McCarry. 334-363, Mar. 1975
• Sir Francis Drake. By Alan Villiers. 216-253, Feb. 1975
• Texas! By Howard La Fay. 440-483, Apr. 1980
• Turkey: Cross Fire at an Ancient Crossroads. By Robert Paul Jordan. 88-123, July 1977

GALAPAGOS ISLANDS, Pacific Ocean:
• The Galapagos, Eerie Cradle of New Species. By Roger Tory Peterson. Photos by Alan and Joan Root. 541-585, Apr. 1967
• Giant Tortoises: Goliaths of the Galapagos. By Craig MacFarland. Photos by author and Jan MacFarland. Included: Española; Isabela; Pinzón; Santa Cruz. 632-649, Nov. 1972
• In the Wake of Darwin's *Beagle*. By Alan Villiers. Photos by James L. Stanfield. 449-495, Oct. 1969
• Lost World of the Galapagos. By Irving and Electa Johnson. 681-703, May 1959
• Robin Sails Home. By Robin Lee Graham. 504-545, Oct. 1970
• Undersea Wonders of the Galapagos. By Gerard Wellington. Photos by David Doubilet. 363-381, Sept. 1978
• The *Yankee*'s Wander-world. By Irving and Electa Johnson. 1-50, Jan. 1949

GALAPAGOS RIFT, Pacific Ocean:
■ Dive to the Edge of Creation: Galapagos II Expedition. 682, Nov. 1979; 1, cover, Jan. 1980
• Incredible World of the Deep-sea Rifts. NGS research grant. 680-705, Nov. 1979
I. Strange World Without Sun. The Editor. 680-688; II. Return to Oases of the Deep. By Robert D. Ballard and J. Frederick Grassle. 689-705
• Oases of Life in the Cold Abyss. By John B. Corliss and Robert D. Ballard. 441-453, Oct. 1977

GALAXIES:
▲ *Journey Into the Universe Through Time and Space; National Geographic-Palomar Sky Survey Charting the Heavens,* double-sided supplement. June 1983
• The Once and Future Universe. By Rick Gore. Photos by James A. Sugar. Paintings by Barron Storey. Picture text by David Jeffery. 704-749, June 1983

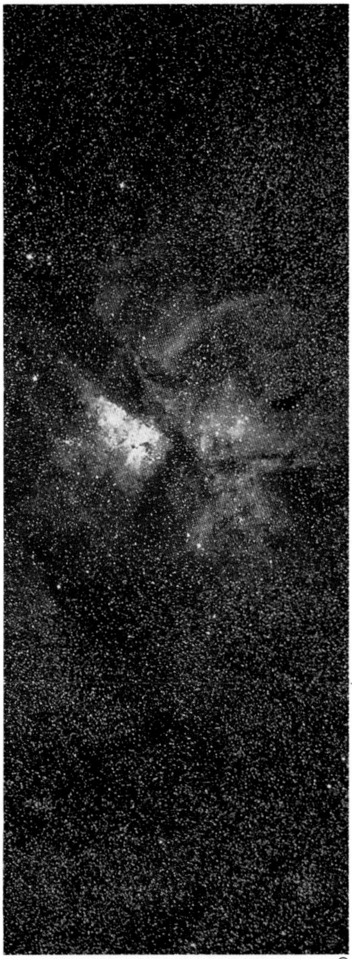

CERRO TOLOLO INTER-AMERICAN OBSERVATORY, © AURA, INC.

Universe: the Carina Nebula

A **GALAXY** of Life Fills the Night. By Kenneth Brower. Photos by William R. Curtsinger and Chris Newbert. 834-847, Dec. 1981

GALDIKAS, BIRUTE M. F.: Author:
• Living with the Great Orange Apes: Indonesia's Orangutans. Photos by Rod Brindamour. 830-853, June 1980
• Orangutans, Indonesia's "People of the Forest." Photos by Rod Brindamour. 444-473, Oct. 1975

GALILEE (Region), Israel:
• The Land of Galilee. By Kenneth MacLeish. Photos by B. Anthony Stewart. 832-865, Dec. 1965
• Where Jesus Walked. By Howard La Fay. Photos by Charles Harbutt. 739-781, Dec. 1967

GALILEO GALILEI:
• The Renaissance Lives On in Tuscany. By Luis Marden. Photos by Albert Moldvay. 626-659, Nov. 1974

GALLATIN COUNTY, Illinois. *See* Shawneetown

GALLEONS AND GALLEASSES:
• *Atocha,* Tragic Treasure Galleon of the Florida Keys. By Eugene Lyon. Included: *Santa Margarita* wreck. 787-809, June 1976
• Drowned Galleons Yield Spanish Gold. By Kip Wagner. Photos by Otis Imboden. 1-37, Jan. 1965
• Graveyard of the Quicksilver Galleons. By Mendel Peterson. Photos by Jonathan Blair. Included: *Nuestra Señora de Guadalupe; Conde de Tolosa.* 850-876, Dec. 1979
▲ "History Salvaged From the Sea," painting supplement. Map on reverse. Included: Cutaway painting of a galleon. Dec. 1977
• Priceless Relics of the Spanish Armada. By Robert Sténuit. Photos by Bates Littlehales. Included: The galleass *Girona.* 745-777, June 1969
• Reach for the New World. By Mendel Peterson. Photos by David L. Arnold. Paintings by Richard Schlecht. 724-767, Dec. 1977
■ Treasure! 575, Nov. 1976; cover, Dec. 1976
• Treasure From the Ghost Galleon: *Santa Margarita.* By Eugene Lyon. Photos by Don Kincaid. Included: *Atocha; Santa Margarita.* 228-243, Feb. 1982

GALLINAZO CULTURE:
• Finding the Tomb of a Warrior-God. By William Duncan Strong. Photos by Clifford Evans, Jr. 453-482, Apr. 1947

The **GAMBIA:**
• Freedom Speaks French in Ouagadougou. By John Scofield. 153-203, Aug. 1966

GAME FISH. *See* Sailfish; Salmon; Trout

GAME PRESERVES:
• Roaming Africa's Unfenced Zoos. By W. Robert Moore. 353-380, Mar. 1950

RAGHUBIR SINGH

Ganges: woman carries flour

• Safari from Congo to Cairo. By Elsie May Bell Grosvenor. Photos by Gilbert Grosvenor. 721-771, Dec. 1954
• Safari Through Changing Africa. By Elsie May Bell Grosvenor. Photos by Gilbert Grosvenor. 145-198, Aug. 1953
• White Magic in the Belgian Congo. By W. Robert Moore. 321-362, Mar. 1952
• *See also* National Parks; Wildlife Refuges

GAMES:
• Chessmen Come to Life in Marostica. By Alexander Taylor. 658-668, Nov. 1956
• Pennsylvania Dutch Folk Festival. By Maynard Owen Williams. 503-516, Oct. 1952
• *See also* Highland Games; Olympic Games; Sports

GANDHI, MOHANDAS KARAMCHAND:
• Delhi, Capital of a New Dominion. By Phillips Talbot. Photos by Volkmar Wentzel. 597-630, Nov. 1947

GANGES (River), India-Pakistan:
• From the Hair of Siva. By Helen and Frank Schreider. 445-503, Oct. 1960
• The Ganges, River of Faith. By John J. Putman. Photos by Raghubir Singh. 445-483, Oct. 1971

GANGTOK, Sikkim:
• Gangtok, Cloud-wreathed Himalayan Capital. By John Scofield. 689-713, Nov. 1970
• Sikkim. By Desmond Doig. 398-429, Mar. 1963
• Wedding of Two Worlds. By Lee E. Battaglia. 708-727, Nov. 1963

GANNETS:
• Sea Bird Cities Off Audubon's Labrador. By Arthur A. Allen. NGS research grant. 755-774, June 1948

GANYMEDE (Jovian Satellite):
• What Voyager Saw: Jupiter's Dazzling Realm. By Rick Gore. Photos by NASA. 2-29, Jan. 1980

GARAVENTA, JOHN: Author:
• Down on the Farm, Soviet Style–a 4-H Adventure. Photos by James Tobin and Carol Schmidt. 768-797, June 1979

GARBAGE:
• The Fascinating World of Trash. By Peter T. White. Photos by Louie Psihoyos. 424-457, Apr. 1983

GARBISCH COLLECTION:
• Early America Through the Eyes of Her Native Artists. By Hereward Lester Cooke, Jr. Paintings by American primitive artists. 356-389, Sept. 1962

GARDENING'S Color Merchants: The Flower Seed Growers. By Robert de Roos. Photos by Jack Fields. 720-738, May 1968

GARDENS:
• Ballerinas in Pink (Flamingos). By Carleton Mitchell. Photos by B. Anthony Stewart. Included: Ardastra Gardens. 553-571, Oct. 1957
• Herbs for All Seasons. By Lonnelle Aikman. Photos by Sam Abell. Picture portfolio text by Larry Kohl. Included: National Herb Garden. 386-409, Mar. 1983
• History and Beauty Blend in a Concord Iris Garden. By Robert T. Cochran, Jr. Photos by M. Woodbridge Williams. Included: Buttrick Garden. 705-719, May 1959
• Kew: The Commoners' Royal Garden. By Thomas Garner James. Photos by B. Anthony Stewart. 479-506, Apr. 1950
• Maytime Miracle in Sherwood Gardens. By Nathaniel T. Kenney. 700-709, May 1956
• Nautical Norfolk Turns to Azaleas. By William H. Nicholas. Photos by B. Anthony Stewart. 606-614, May 1947
• Our Vegetable Travelers. By Victor R. Boswell. Paintings by Else Bostelmann. 145-217, Aug. 1949
• Rhododendron Glories of Southwest Scotland. By David S. Boyer. Photos by B. Anthony Stewart and author. 641-664, May 1954
• Rose Aphids. By Treat Davidson. 851-859, June 1961
• South Carolina Rediscovered. By Herbert Ravenel Sass. Included: Cypress Gardens; Magnolia Gardens; Middleton Gardens; Swan Lake Gardens. 281-321, Mar. 1953
• Tropical Gardens of Key West. By Luis Marden. 116-124, Jan. 1953
• Wonderland in Longwood Gardens. By Edward C. Ferriday, Jr. 45-64, July 1951
• The World in Your Garden (Flowers). By W. H. Camp. Paintings by Else Bostelmann. Contents: Gardens of Africa, Australia, China, Colonial America, Egypt, England, France, Greece, Holland, India, Japan, the Mediterranean region, Mexico, Persia, Rome, South America, Spain; *and* Alpine meadow gardens; Botanical gardens; Buddhist gardens; Hanging gardens; Informal gardens; Moslem gardens; Renaissance gardens; Rock gardens; Victory gardens. 1-65, July 1947
◆ *The World in Your Garden.* Announced. 729-730, May 1957

GARDIANS (French Cowboys):
• The Camargue, Land of Cowboys and Gypsies. By Eugene L. Kammerman. 667-699, May 1956
• France's Wild, Watery South, the Camargue. By William Davenport. 696-726, May 1973

GARDNER, Mount, Antarctica:
• First Conquest of Antarctica's Highest Peaks. By Nicholas B. Clinch. NGS research grant. 836-863, June 1967

GARFIELD, JAMES A.:
• The Living White House. By Lonnelle Aikman. 593-643, Nov. 1966
• Profiles of the Presidents: III. The American Giant Comes of Age. By Frank Freidel. 660-711, May 1965

GARFINKEL, PERRY: Author:
• Madawaska: Down East With a French Accent. Photos by Cary Wolinsky. 380-409, Sept. 1980

GARRETT, KENNETH:
Author-Photographer:
• By Square-rigger from Baltic to Bicentennial. 824-857, Dec. 1976
Photographer:
• The Disaster of El Chichón. By Boris Weintraub. Photos by Guillermo Aldana E. and Kenneth Garrett. 654-684, Nov. 1982
• Humble Masterpieces: Decoys. By George Reiger. 639-663, Nov. 1983

GARRETT, WILBUR E.:
• Editor (1980-). 427, Oct. 1980; 567, Nov. 1980; 222, 234, Aug. 1981; 849, 851, Dec. 1981; 585, 589, May 1982; 270, 276, 278, Aug. 1982
• National Geographic Photographers Win Top Magazine Awards. 830-831, June 1959
Author:
• Editor's Postscript. 115, *Special Report on Energy* (Feb. 1981)
• The Making of America: 17 New Maps Tie the Nation to Its Past. 630-633, Nov. 1982
• Troubled Times for Central America. 58-61, July 1981
Author-Photographer:
• Alaska's Marine Highway: Ferry Route to the North. 776-819, June 1965
• The Booming Sport of Water Skiing. 700-711, Nov. 1958
• Canada's Heartland, the Prairie Provinces. 443-489, Oct. 1970
• Grand Canyon: Are We Loving It to Death? 2-51, July 1978
• Guilin, China's Beauty Spot. 536-563, Oct. 1979
• The Hmong of Laos: No Place to Run. 78-111, Jan. 1974
• Mexico's Little Venice. 876-888, June 1968
• Mountaintop War in Remote Ladakh. 664-687, May 1963
• Pagan, on the Road to Mandalay. 343-365, Mar. 1971
• South to Mexico City. 145-193, Aug. 1968
• The Temples of Angkor: Will They Survive? 548-551, May 1982
• Thailand: Refuge From Terror. 633-642, May 1980
Photographer:
• Burma's Leg Rowers and Floating Farms. Text by David Jeffery. 826-845, June 1974
• Earthquake in Guatemala. By Bart McDowell. Photos by W. E. Garrett and Robert W. Madden. 810-829, June 1976
• Guantánamo: Keystone in the Caribbean. By Jules B. Billard. Photos by W. E. Garrett and Thomas Nebbia. 420-436, Mar. 1961
• Life under Shellfire on Quemoy. By Franc Shor. 415-438, Mar. 1959
• Maya Art Treasures Discovered in Cave. By George E. Stuart. 220-235, Aug. 1981
• The Mekong, River of Terror and Hope. By Peter T. White. 737-787, Dec. 1968
• Mosaic of Cultures. By Peter T. White. 296-329, Mar. 1971
• Pacific Fleet: Force for Peace. By Franc Shor. 283-335, Sept. 1959

BOTH BY WILBUR E. GARRETT, NGS

Hmong: Laotian girls face uncertainty

Mexico City: Day of the Dead ritual

• Report on Laos. By Peter T. White. 241-275, Aug. 1961
• Saigon: Eye of the Storm. By Peter T. White. 834-872, June 1965
• South Viet Nam Fights the Red Tide. By Peter T. White. 445-489, Oct. 1961
• The Temples of Angkor: Ancient Glory in Stone. By Peter T. White. 552-589, May 1982
• *White Mist* Cruises to Wreck-haunted St. Pierre and Miquelon. By Melville Bell Grosvenor. 378-419, Sept. 1967
• Zoo Animals Go to School. By Marion P. McCrane. 694-706, Nov. 1956

GARRIOTT, OWEN K.:
• Skylab, Outpost on the Frontier of Space. By Thomas Y. Canby. Photos by the nine mission astronauts. 441-469, Oct. 1974

GARTER SNAKES:
• Manitoba's Fantastic Snake Pits. By Michael Aleksiuk. Photos by Bianca Lavies. 715-723, Nov. 1975

GARTLEIN, CARL W.: Author:
• Unlocking Secrets of the Northern Lights. Paintings by William Crowder. 673-704, Nov. 1947

GAS, Natural. *See* Natural Gas

GASCONY (Historical Region), France:
• Bordeaux: Fine Wines and Fiery Gascons. By William Davenport. Photos by Adam Woolfitt. 233-259, Aug. 1980

GASPARILLA CELEBRATION: Tampa, Florida:
• America Goes to the Fair. By Samuel W. Matthews. 293-333, Sept. 1954

GASPÉ PENINSULA, Canada:
• Quebec's Forests, Farms, and Frontiers. By Andrew H. Brown. 431-470, Oct. 1949
• The St. Lawrence, River Key to Canada. By Howard La Fay. Photos by John Launois. 622-667, May 1967
• Sea to Lakes on the St. Lawrence. By George W. Long. Photos by B. Anthony Stewart and John E. Fletcher. 323-366, Sept. 1950

GATES, THOMAS S., Jr.:
• Secretary of the Navy Thomas S. Gates, Jr. accepts Hubbard Medal for the U. S. Navy Antarctic Expeditions, 1955-1959. 589-590, Apr. 1959

GATEWAY NATIONAL RECREATION AREA, New Jersey-New York:
• Gateway–Elbowroom for the Millions. By Louise Levathes. 86-97, July 1979

GATEWAY to Westward Expansion. By William C. Everhart. 643-669, Nov. 1965

GAUCHOS:
• Argentina: Young Giant of the Far South. By Jean and Franc Shor. 297-352, Mar. 1958
• Brazil, Ôba! By Peter T. White. Photos by Winfield Parks. 299-353, Sept. 1962

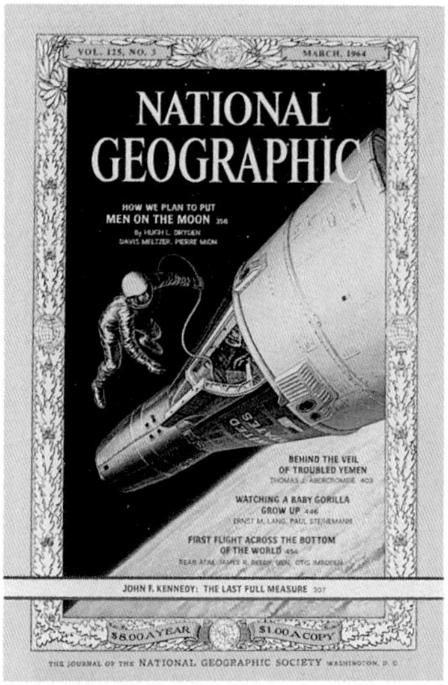

ROBERT GOMEL

Gemini: astronauts Edward H. White and James A. McDivitt after safe return

- The Gauchos, Last of a Breed. By Robert Laxalt. Photos by O. Louis Mazzatenta. 478-501, Oct. 1980
- The Purple Land of Uruguay. By Luis Marden. 623-654, Nov. 1948

GAULS. *See* Celts

GAVIALS. *See* Gharials

GAZA STRIP, Israeli-occupied Egypt:
- Lost Outpost of the Egyptian Empire. By Trude Dothan. Photos by Sisse Brimberg. Paintings by Lloyd K. Townsend. 739-769, Dec. 1982

GEESE:
- Beyond the North Wind With the Snow Goose. By Des and Jen Bartlett. 822-843, Dec. 1973
- Bright Dyes Reveal Secrets of Canada Geese. By John and Frank Craighead. 817-832, Dec. 1957
- Saving the Nene, World's Rarest Goose. By S. Dillon Ripley. Photos by Jerry Chong. 745-754, Nov. 1965

GEHMAN, RICHARD: Author:
- Amish Folk: Plainest of Pennsylvania's Plain People. Photos by William Albert Allard. 227-253, Aug. 1965

GEISHA:
- Kansai, Japan's Historic Heartland. By Thomas J. Abercrombie. 295-339, Mar. 1970

GELIDONYA, Cape, Turkey:
- Oldest Known Shipwreck Yields Bronze Age Cargo. By Peter Throckmorton. NGS research grant. 697-711, May 1962

GEMINI MISSIONS:
- America's 6,000-mile Walk in Space. 440-447, Sept. 1965
- The Earth From Orbit. By Paul D. Lowman, Jr. 645-671, Nov. 1966
- Footprints on the Moon. By Hugh L. Dryden. Paintings by Davis Meltzer and Pierre Mion. 357-401, Mar. 1964
- The Making of an Astronaut. By Robert R. Gilruth. 122-144, Jan. 1965
- Space Rendezvous, Milestone on the Way to the Moon. By Kenneth F. Weaver. 539-553, Apr. 1966

GEMS:
- Brazil's Land of Minerals. By W. Robert Moore. Contents: Amethyst, Aquamarine, Citrine, Diamond, Emerald, Morganite, Topaz, Tourmaline. 479-508, Oct. 1948
- Exploring the World of Gems. By W. F. Foshag. 779-810, Dec. 1950
- The Glittering World of Rockhounds. By David S. Boyer. 276-294, Feb. 1974
- Imperial Russia's Glittering Legacy. 24-33, Jan. 1978
- Precious Corals, Hawaii's Deep-sea Jewels. By Richard W. Grigg. 719-732, May 1979
- The Purple Land of Uruguay. By Luis Marden. Included: Agates, Amethysts, Quartz. 623-654, Nov. 1948
- Questing for Gems. By George S. Switzer. Included: Gem mining in Africa, Brazil, and Colombia; samplings of the Crown Jewel collections of Great Britain, Iran, and tsarist Russia; the history of the Koh-i-noor, Hope, and Orloff diamonds. 835-863, Dec. 1971
- *See also* Amber, a gemlike fossil resin; Diamonds; Lapidary Work; Opal Mining

GENERAL ELECTRIC COMPANY:
- Drums to Dynamos on the Mohawk. By Frederick G. Vosburgh. Photos by B. Anthony Stewart. 67-110, July 1947
- Landsat Looks at Hometown Earth. By Barry C. Bishop. Note: GE's Photographic Engineering Laboratory's color-mosaic expertise was combined with Landsat imagery to produce *Portrait U.S.A.*, first color photomosaic of the 48 contiguous states. 140-147, July 1976
- Studying Grizzly Habitat by Satellite. By John Craighead. Included: GE Image 100 computer system, used with Landsat imagery to produce satellite-computer maps of grizzly bear habitat. 148-158, July 1976
- *See also* Tektite II, for undersea equipment

GENERAL MILLS, INC.: Research and Engineering. *See Strato-Lab*

The **GENERAL SHERMAN:** Earth's Biggest Living Thing (Sequoia). 605-608, May 1958

GENERATORS, Wind-driven:
- Can We Harness the Wind? By Roger Hamilton. Photos by Emory Kristof. 812-829, Dec. 1975

GENETIC RESEARCH:
- The Awesome Worlds Within a Cell. By Rick Gore. Photos by Bruce Dale. Paintings by Davis Meltzer. 355-395, Sept. 1976
- The Incredible Potato. By Robert E. Rhoades. Photos by Martin Rogers. Included: The study of fusing two botanical cousins, the potato and tomato, and research in "true seed" adaptation. 668-694, May 1982

GENEVA, Switzerland:
- "Around the World in Eighty Days." By Newman Bumstead. 705-750, Dec. 1951
- Switzerland, Europe's High-rise Republic. By Thomas J. Abercrombie. 68-113, July 1969
- Switzerland Guards the Roof of Europe. By William H. Nicholas. Photos by Willard R. Culver. 205-246, Aug. 1950

The **GENIUS** of El Greco. Introduction by J. Carter Brown. 736-744, June 1982

GENOA, Italy:
- Italian Riviera, Land That Winter Forgot. By Howell Walker. 743-789, June 1963

GENTILI, GINO VINICIO: Author:
- Roman Life in 1,600-year-old Color Pictures (Mosaics). Photos by Duncan Edwards. 211-229, Feb. 1957

The **GENTLE** Yamis of Orchid Island. Photos by Chang Shuhua. 98-109, Jan. 1977

GIANT EFFIGIES of the Southwest. By George C. Marshall. 389, Sept. 1952

GIANT FOREST, Sequoia National Park, California:
● Giant Sequoias Draw Millions to California Parks. By John Michael Kauffmann. Photos by B. Anthony Stewart. 147-187, Aug. 1959
● Saving Earth's Oldest Living Things. By Andrew H. Brown. Photos by Raymond Moulin and author. 679-695, May 1951

GIANT FROGS:
● In Quest of the World's Largest Frog. By Paul A. Zahl. 146-152, July 1967

GIANT INSECTS of the Amazon. By Paul A. Zahl. 632-669, May 1959

GIANT KELP:
● Giant Kelp, Sequoias of the Sea. By Wheeler J. North. Photos by Bates Littlehales. 251-269, Aug. 1972
● Undersea World of a Kelp Forest. By Sylvia A. Earle. Photos by Al Giddings. 411-426, Sept. 1980

GIANT SEQUOIAS Draw Millions to California Parks. By John Michael Kauffmann. Photos by B. Anthony Stewart. 147-187, Aug. 1959

The **GIANT TIDES** of Fundy. By Paul A. Zahl. 153-192, Aug. 1957

GIANT TORTOISES: Goliaths of the Galapagos. By Craig MacFarland. Photos by author and Jan MacFarland. 632-649, Nov. 1972

GIANTS That Move the World's Oil: Superships. By Noel Grove. Photos by Martin Rogers. 102-124, July 1978

GIBBONS, BOYD: Author:
● Aldo Leopold: "A Durable Scale of Values." Photos by Jim Brandenburg. 682-708, Nov. 1981
● The Bulgarians. Photos by James L. Stanfield. 91-111, July 1980
● Easygoing, Hardworking Arkansas. Photos by Matt Bradley. 396-427, Mar. 1978
● Risk and Reward on Alaska's Violent Gulf. Photos by Steve Raymer. 237-267, Feb. 1979

GIBBONS, EUELL: Author:
● Stalking the West's Wild Foods. Photos by David Hiser. 186-199, Aug. 1973
● Stalking Wild Foods on a Desert Isle. Photos by David Hiser. 47-63, July 1972

GIBBONS:
● The Ape With Friends in Washington. By Margaretta Burr Wells. 61-74, July 1953

GIBRALTAR:
● Gibraltar–Rock of Contention. By Howard La Fay. Photos by Bates Littlehales. 102-121, July 1966
● The Mediterranean–Sea of Man's Fate. By Rick Gore. Photos by Jonathan Blair. 694-737, Dec. 1982

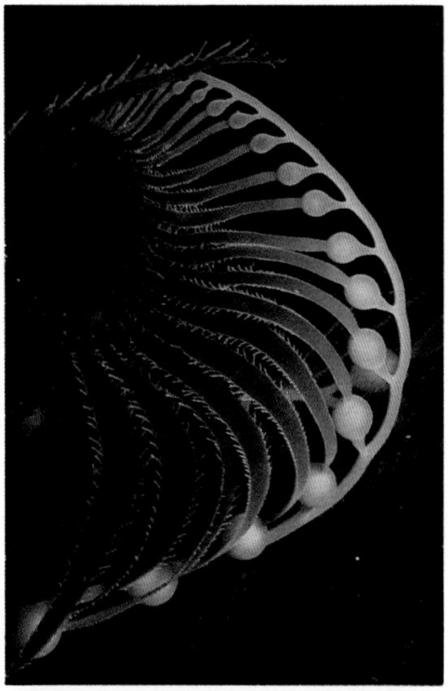

BOTH BY BATES LITTLEHALES, NGS

Kelp: gas-filled bladders support kelp, *top;* nudibranch searches for hydroids, *above*

GIBSON, EDWARD G.:
● Skylab, Outpost on the Frontier of Space. By Thomas Y. Canby. Photos by the nine mission astronauts. 441-469, Oct. 1974
Author:
● The Sun As Never Seen Before. 494-503, Oct. 1974

GIDDINGS, AL: Photographer:
● Humpback Whales. 2-25, Jan. 1979
I. The Gentle Giants. By Sylvia A. Earle. 2-17; II. Their Mysterious Songs. By Roger Payne. 18-25
● Life Springs From Death in Truk Lagoon. By Sylvia A. Earle. 578-613, May 1976
From Graveyard to Garden. 604-613
● Undersea World of a Kelp Forest. By Sylvia A. Earle. 411-426, Sept. 1980
● A Walk in the Deep. By Sylvia A. Earle. Photos by Al Giddings and Chuck Nicklin. 624-631, May 1980

GIFTS for the Jaguar God. By Philip Drucker and Robert F. Heizer. 367-375, Sept. 1956

The **GIFTS** of Golden Byzantium. By Merle Severy. Photos by James L. Stanfield. 722-767, Dec. 1983

GILBERT, SIR WILLIAM:
● The British Way. By Sir Evelyn Wrench. 421-541, Apr. 1949

GILBERT GROSVENOR Is Elected Chairman of the Board, John Oliver La Gorce Chosen President and Editor of the National Geographic Society. 65, 65A-65H, 66, July 1954
● *See also* Grosvenor, Gilbert Hovey

GILBERT GROSVENOR'S Golden Jubilee. By Albert W. Atwood. 253-261, Aug. 1949

GILBERT H. GROSVENOR VISITOR CENTER, Russell Cave, Alabama:
● Russell Cave Dedicated; New Visitor Center Named for Gilbert H. Grosvenor. NGS research grant. 440-442, Sept. 1967

GILBERT ISLANDS, Pacific Ocean. *See* Tarawa

GILGAMESH, Epic of:
● Ancient Mesopotamia: A Light That Did Not Fail. By E. A. Speiser. Paintings by H. M. Herget. 41-105, Jan. 1951

GILGIT, Kashmir:
● Pakistan, New Nation in an Old Land. By Jean and Franc Shor. 637-678, Nov. 1952

GILKA, ROBERT E.: Photographer:
● New Zealand's Milford Track: "Walk of a Lifetime." By Carolyn Bennett Patterson. 117-129, Jan. 1978

GILL, WILLIAM J.: Author:
● Pittsburgh, Pattern for Progress. Photos by Clyde Hare. 342-371, Mar. 1965

GILLES, HELEN TRYBULOWSKI:
Author:
● Ceylon, Island of the "Lion People." 121-136, July 1948

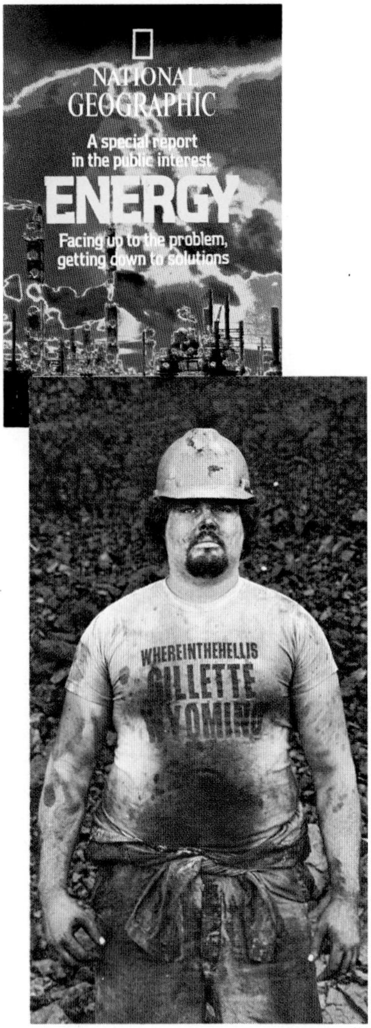

LOUIE PSIHOYOS

Gillette, Wyoming: a miner's opinion

GILLETTE, NED:
Author-Photographer:
• American Skiers Find Adventure in Western China. Photos by the author and Galen Rowell. 174-199, Feb. 1981
Skiing From the Summit of China's Ice Mountain. 192-199
• New Mount McKinley Challenge–Trekking Around the Continent's Highest Peak. 66-79, July 1979

GILLETTE, Wyoming:
• Powder River Basin: New Energy Frontier. By Bill Richards. Photos by Louie Psihoyos. 96-113, *Special Report on Energy* (Feb. 1981)

GILLIARD, E. THOMAS: Author:
• Coronation in Katmandu. Photos by Marc Riboud. 139-152, July 1957
• Feathered Dancers of Little Tobago. Photos by Frederick Kent Truslow. 428-440, Sept. 1958
Author-Photographer:
• Exploring New Britain's Land of Fire. 260-292, Feb. 1961
• New Guinea's Paradise of Birds. 661-688, Nov. 1951
• New Guinea's Rare Birds and Stone Age Men. 421-488, Apr. 1953
• Strange Courtship of the Cock-of-the-Rock. 134-140, Jan. 1962
• To the Land of the Head-hunters. 437-486, Oct. 1955

GILLIARD, MARGARET:
Photographer:
• New Guinea's Rare Birds and Stone Age Men. By E. Thomas Gilliard. Photos by E. Thomas and Margaret Gilliard. 421-488, Apr. 1953

GILLIARD EXPEDITIONS:
• Exploring New Britain's Land of Fire. By E. Thomas Gilliard. NGS research grant. 260-292, Feb. 1961
• Feathered Dancers of Little Tobago. By E. Thomas Gilliard. Photos by Frederick Kent Truslow. NGS research grant. 428-440, Sept. 1958
• New Guinea's Paradise of Birds. By E. Thomas Gilliard. 661-688, Nov. 1951
• To the Land of the Head-hunters. By E. Thomas Gilliard. 437-486, Oct. 1955

GILLISON, DAVID: Photographer:
• Fertility Rites and Sorcery in a New Guinea Village. By Gillian Gillison. 124-146, July 1977
• Living Theater in New Guinea's Highlands. By Gillian Gillison. 147-169, Aug. 1983

GILLISON, GILLIAN: Author:
• Fertility Rites and Sorcery in a New Guinea Village. Photos by David Gillison. 124-146, July 1977
• Living Theater in New Guinea's Highlands. Photos by David Gillison. 147-169, Aug. 1983

GILMAN, RAE: Photographer:
• Roaming Korea South of the Iron Curtain. By Enzo de Chetelat. 777-808, June 1950

GILRUTH, ROBERT R.: Author:
• The Making of an Astronaut. 122-144, Jan. 1965

GIMBEL, PETER R.: Photographer:
• By Parachute Into Peru's Lost World. By G. Brooks Baekeland. Photos by author and Peter R. Gimbel. 268-296, Aug. 1964

GIMBEL BROTHERS:
• Artists Look at Pennsylvania. By John Oliver La Gorce. 37-56, July 1948

GIMIS (People):
• Fertility Rites and Sorcery in a New Guinea Village. By Gillian Gillison. Photos by David Gillison. 124-146, July 1977
• Living Theater in New Guinea's Highlands. By Gillian Gillison. Photos by David Gillison. 147-169, Aug. 1983

GIRAFFES:
• Africa's Gentle Giants. By Bristol Foster. Photos by Bob Campbell and Thomas Nebbia. 402-417, Sept. 1977
• Rescuing the Rothschild. By Carolyn Bennett Patterson. 419-421, Sept. 1977

GIRONA (Armada Galleass):
• Priceless Relics of the Spanish Armada. By Robert Sténuit. Photos by Bates Littlehales. 745-777, June 1969

GIRONDE (Department), France:
• Bordeaux: Fine Wines and Fiery Gascons. By William Davenport. Photos by Adam Woolfitt. 233-259, Aug. 1980

GIZA, Pyramids of, Egypt:
• Fresh Treasures from Egypt's Ancient Sands. By Jefferson Caffery. Photos by David S. Boyer. 611-650, Nov. 1955

GLACIER BAY, Alaska:
• Humpbacks: The Gentle Whales. By Sylvia A. Earle. Photos by Al Giddings. NGS research grant. 2-17, Jan. 1979
• *See also* Glacier Bay National Monument

GLACIER BAY NATIONAL MONUMENT, Alaska:
• John Muir's Wild America. By Harvey Arden. Photos by Dewitt Jones. 433-461, Apr. 1973

GLACIER NATIONAL PARK, Montana:
• Many-splendored Glacierland. By George W. Long. Photos by Kathleen Revis. 589-636, May 1956
• Montana, Shining Mountain Treasureland. By Leo A. Borah. 693-736, June 1950
• Spring Comes Late to Glacier. By Douglas H. Chadwick. 125-133, July 1979
• The West Through Boston Eyes. By Stewart Anderson. 733-776, June 1949

GLACIERS:
• Alaska's Automatic Lake Drains Itself (Lake George). 835-844, June 1951
• Avalanche! (Peru). By Bart McDowell. Photos by John E. Fletcher. 855-880, June 1962

• Climbing Our Northwest Glaciers. Photos by Bob and Ira Spring. 103-114, July 1953
• Far North with "Captain Mac." By Miriam MacMillan. 465-513, Oct. 1951
• First American Ascent of Mount St. Elias. By Maynard M. Miller. 229-248, Feb. 1948
• On the Ridgepole of the Rockies. By Walter Meayers Edwards. 745-780, June 1947
Canada's Rocky Mountain Playground. 755-770
• On the Trail of Wisconsin's Ice Age. By Anne LaBastille. Photos by Cary Wolinsky. Included: Glacial landforms; map showing Wisconsin's future Ice Age Trail along the terminal moraine. 182-205, Aug. 1977
• Our Navy Explores Antarctica. By Richard E. Byrd. U. S. Navy official photos. 429-522, Oct. 1947
• *See also* Alps; Annapurna I; Everest, Mount; Glacier National Park; Greenland; Himalayas; Ice Ages; Ice Caves (Pyrenees); K2; McKinley, Mount; Olympic National Park; Ruwenzori

GLACIOLOGY:
• Alaska's Mighty Rivers of Ice. By Maynard M. Miller. Photos by Christopher G. Knight. NGS research grant. 194-217, Feb. 1967
• Antarctica's Nearer Side. By Samuel W. Matthews. Photos by William R. Curtsinger. Included: Glaciological studies of Deception Island. NGS research grant. 622-655, Nov. 1971
• What's Happening to Our Climate? By Samuel W. Matthews. 576-615, Nov. 1976
• Voyage to the Antarctic. By David Lewis. 544-562, Apr. 1983

GLANZMAN, LOUIS S.: Artist:
• Ebla: Splendor of an Unknown Empire. By Howard La Fay. Photos by James L. Stanfield. 730-759, Dec. 1978
• Patriots in Petticoats. By Lonnelle Aikman. 475-493, Oct. 1975

GLASS:
• Glass Treasure From the Aegean. By George F. Bass. Photos by Jonathan Blair. NGS research grant. 768-793, June 1978
• Graveyard of the Quicksilver Galleons. By Mendel Peterson. Photos by Jonathan Blair. Included: Glassware recovered from the *Nuestra Señora de Guadalupe* and the *Conde de Tolosa*. 850-876, Dec. 1979
• History Revealed in Ancient Glass. By Ray Winfield Smith. Photos by B. Anthony Stewart and Lee E. Battaglia. 346-369, Sept. 1964

GLASS Menageries of the Sea. By Paul A. Zahl. 797-822, June 1955

GLEN CANYON NATIONAL RECREATION AREA, Arizona-Utah:
• Lake Powell: Waterway to Desert Wonders. By Walter Meayers Edwards. 44-75, July 1967

GLENDORA, California:
• Southern California's Trial by Mud and Water. By Nathaniel T. Kenney. Photos by Bruce Dale. 552-573, Oct. 1969

GLENN, JOHN H., Jr.:
• John Glenn Receives the Society's Hubbard Medal. 827, June 1962
• John Glenn's Three Orbits in *Friendship 7:* A Minute-by-Minute Account of America's First Orbital Space Flight. By Robert B. Voas. 792-827, June 1962

GLIDERS. *See* Sailplanes

The **GLITTERING** World of Rockhounds. By David S. Boyer. 276-294, Feb. 1974

GLOB, P. V.: Author:
• Lifelike Man Preserved 2,000 Years in Peat. 419-430, Mar. 1954

GLOBAL POSITIONING SYSTEM (GPS):
• Satellites That Serve Us. By Thomas Y. Canby. 281-335, Sept. 1983
Spacelab 1: *Columbia.* By Michael E. Long. 301-307

GLOBE, Great: Explorers Hall, NGS:
• 12-foot globe. 673-675, 677, 679, May 1964; 880, Dec. 1964; 578-579, Oct. 1967

GLOBES, NGS:
• Axis-free globe. 270, Aug. 1982
• First. 698-701, 716, May 1961; 580, 581, Oct. 1967; 275, Aug. 1982
• Manufacturer of NGS globes. 874-875, 876-878, Dec. 1961
• National Geographic Physical Globe announced. 736, Nov. 1971
• 16-inch globe and 12-inch globe. 897, Dec. 1962
• 16-inch globe presented to Mrs. Lyndon B. Johnson. 676, 679, May 1964; 584, Oct. 1967

GLOMAR CHALLENGER (Deep Sea Drilling Project Ship):
• This Changing Earth. By Samuel W. Matthews. 1-37, Jan. 1973

GLORIOUS Bronzes of Ancient Greece: Warriors From a Watery Grave. By Joseph Alsop. 821-827, June 1983

GLOUCESTER, Massachusetts:
• Gloucester Blesses Its Portuguese Fleet. By Luis Marden. 75-84, July 1953
• Windjamming Around New England. By Tom Horgan. Photos by Robert F. Sisson. 141-169, Aug. 1950

GLOWWORMS (Beetle Larvae):
• Nature's Night Lights: Probing the Secrets of Bioluminescence. By Paul A. Zahl. 45-69, July 1971

GLUECK, NELSON: Author:
• An Archeologist Looks at Palestine. 739-752, Dec. 1947

GLYPHS:
• The Maya. 729-811, Dec. 1975
I. Children of Time. By Howard La Fay. Photos by David Alan Harvey. 729-767; II. Riddle of the Glyphs. By George E. Stuart. Photos by Otis Imboden. 768-791
• Maya Art Treasures Discovered in Cave. By George E. Stuart. Photos by Wilbur E. Garrett. 220-235, Aug. 1981
◆ *The Mysterious Maya.* 1977
• *See also* Petroglyphs

GOAL at the End of the Trail: Santa Fe. By William S. Ellis. Photos by Gordon W. Gahan and Otis Imboden. 323-345, Mar. 1982

GOATS:
• The Goats of Thunder Hill. By Elizabeth Nicholds. Photos by Robert F. Sisson. 625-640, May 1954
• Mountain Goats: Daring Guardians of the Heights. By Douglas H. Chadwick. 284-296, Aug. 1978
• Sheep Trek in the French Alps. By Maurice Moyal. Photos by Marcel Coen. 545-564, Apr. 1952

GOBI (Desert), Asia:
• The Caves of the Thousand Buddhas. By Franc and Jean Shor. 383-415, Mar. 1951
• Journey to Outer Mongolia. By William O. Douglas. Photos by Dean Conger. 289-345, Mar. 1962

GODDARD, JOHN M.: Author:
• Kayaks Down the Nile. 697-732, May 1955

GODIVA, LADY:
• The British Way. By Sir Evelyn Wrench. 421-541, Apr. 1949

GODLEY, JOHN, Third Baron Kilbracken. *See* Kilbracken, Lord

GODWIN AUSTEN (Peak), China-Pakistan. *See* K2

GOELL, THERESA:
Author-Photographer:
• Throne Above the Euphrates. 390-405, Mar. 1961

GOETHALS, GEORGE W.:
• NGS Special Gold Medal recipient. 141, Feb. 1978

GOETZ, BERNICE M.:
Author-Photographer:
• Jungle Jaunt on Amazon Headwaters. 371-388, Sept. 1952

GOGGLE FISHING in California Waters. By David Hellyer. Photos by Lamar Boren. 615-632, May 1949

GOLD:
• Ancient Bulgaria's Golden Treasures. By Colin Renfrew. Photos by James L. Stanfield. Paintings by Jean-Leon Huens. 112-129, July 1980
• *Atocha,* Tragic Treasure Galleon of the Florida Keys. By Eugene Lyon. Included: *Santa Margarita* wreck. 787-809, June 1976
• Drowned Galleons Yield Spanish Gold. By Kip Wagner. Photos by Otis Imboden. 1-37, Jan. 1965
▪ Gold! 1, Jan. 1979
• Gold, the Eternal Treasure. By Peter T. White. Photos by James L. Stanfield. 1-51, Jan. 1974
Golden Masterpieces. 29-39
• Imperial Russia's Glittering Legacy. 24-33, Jan. 1978

• Minoans and Mycenaeans: Greece's Brilliant Bronze Age. By Joseph Judge. Photos by Gordon W. Gahan. Paintings by Lloyd K. Townsend. 142-185. Feb. 1978
• Priceless Relics of the Spanish Armada. By Robert Sténuit. Photos by Bates Littlehales. 745-777, June 1969
• Reach for the New World. By Mendel Peterson. Photos by David L. Arnold. Paintings by Richard Schlecht. Included: Gold artifacts from salvaged cargoes. 724-767, Dec. 1977
• Regal Treasures From a Macedonian Tomb. By Manolis Andronicos. Photos by Spyros Tsavdaroglou. 55-77, July 1978
• Treasure From the Ghost Galleon: *Santa Margarita*. By Eugene Lyon. Photos by Don Kincaid. 228-243, Feb. 1982
• *See also* Gold Mining

GOLD COAST, West Africa:
• Hunting Musical Game in West Africa. By Arthur S. Alberts. 262-282, Aug. 1951
• *See also* Ghana

GOLD MEDAL, NGS. *See* Special Gold Medal

GOLD MEDAL Awarded to Mrs. Robert E. Peary. 148, Jan. 1956

GOLD MINING:
• Along the Yukon Trail. By Amos Burg. 395-416, Sept. 1953
• Brazil's Wild Frontier. By Loren McIntyre. 684-719, Nov. 1977
• Busy Fairbanks Sets Alaska's Pace. By Bruce A. Wilson. Photos by O. C. Sweet. 505-523, Oct. 1949
• Gold, the Eternal Treasure. By Peter T. White. Photos by James L. Stanfield. 1-51, Jan. 1974
Golden Masterpieces. 29-39
• Golden Ghosts of the Lost Sierra. By Robert Laxalt. Photos by David Hiser. 332-353, Sept. 1973
• Nevada's Mountain of Invisible Gold. By Samuel W. Matthews. Photos by David F. Cupp. 668-679, May 1968
• Yukon Fever: Call of the North. By Robert Booth. Photos by George F. Mobley. 548-578, Apr. 1978

GOLDEN Beaches of Portugal. By Alan Villiers. 673-696, Nov. 1954

GOLDEN COCKS-OF-THE-ROCK:
• Cock-of-the-Rock: Jungle Dandy. By Pepper W. Trail. NGS research grant. 831-839, Dec. 1983
• Strange Courtship of the Cock-of-the-Rock. By E. Thomas Gilliard. NGS research grant. 134-140, Jan. 1962

GOLDEN EAGLES:
• Inside the Sacred Hopi Homeland. By Jake Page. Photos by Susanne Page. Included: Sacrifice of a golden eagle. 607-629, Nov. 1982
• Scotland's Golden Eagles at Home. By C. Eric Palmar. 273-286, Feb. 1954
• Sharing the Lives of Wild Golden Eagles. By John Craighead. Photos by Charles and Derek Craighead. 420-439, Sept. 1967

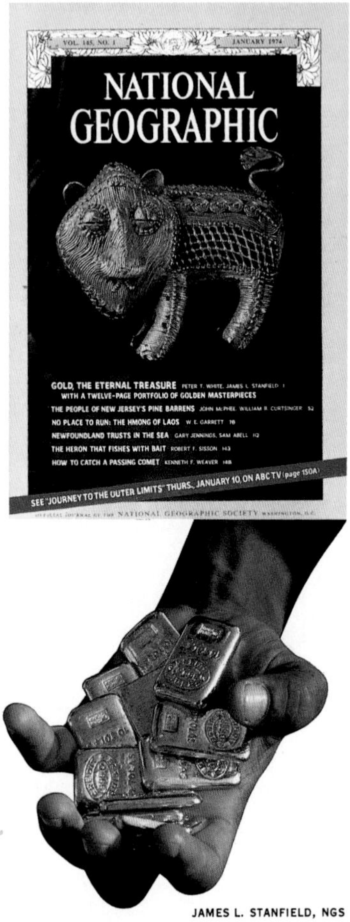

JAMES L. STANFIELD, NGS

Gold: ingots destined for India

GOLDEN GATE NATIONAL RECREATION AREA, California:
• Golden Gate–Of City, Ships, and Surf. By David S. Boyer. 98-105, July 1979

GOLDEN Ghosts of the Lost Sierra. By Robert Laxalt. Photos by David Hiser. 332-353, Sept. 1973

GOLDEN HIND (Sailing Ship):
• Sir Francis Drake. By Alan Villiers. Photos by Gordon W. Gahan. 216-253, Feb. 1975

GOLDEN JACKALS:
• Jackals of the Serengeti. By Patricia D. Moehlman. NGS research grant. 840-850, Dec. 1980

GOLDEN JUBILEES:
• Gilbert Grosvenor's Golden Jubilee. By Albert W. Atwood. 253-261, Aug. 1949
• La Gorce, John Oliver: Golden Jubilee. 422, 423, Mar. 1957; 442, Mar. 1960

GOLDEN TROUT:
• Lake Sunapee's Golden Trout. Photos by Robert F. Sisson. 529-536, Oct. 1950

GOLDEN Window on the Past. Photos by Paul A. Zahl. Text by Thomas J. O'Neill. 423-435, Sept. 1977

GOLDFISH:
• Those Outlandish Goldfish! By Paul A. Zahl. 514-533, Apr. 1973

GOLDMAN, ERIC F.: Author:
• Firebrands of the Revolution. Photos by George F. Mobley. 2-27, July 1974

GOLDSMITHING:
• Gold, the Eternal Treasure. By Peter T. White. Photos by James L. Stanfield. 1-51, Jan. 1974
Golden Masterpieces. 29-39

GOLF:
• California's Land Apart–the Monterey Peninsula. By Mike W. Edwards. Included: Cypress Point Golf Links; Monterey Peninsula Country Club; Pacific Grove Municipal Golf Links; Pebble Beach Golf Links; Spyglass Hill Golf Course. 682-703, Nov. 1972
• Playing 3,000 Golf Courses in Fourteen Lands. By Ralph A. Kennedy. 113-132, July 1952

GOLIATH FROGS. *See* Giant Frogs

GOLIATHS of the Galapagos (Giant Tortoises). By Craig MacFarland. Photos by author and Jan MacFarland. 632-649, Nov. 1972

GOLOGS (People):
• Nomads of China's West. By Galen Rowell. Photos by the author and Harold A. Knutson. 244-263, Feb. 1982

GOMBE STREAM NATIONAL PARK, Tanzania:
• Life and Death at Gombe. By Jane Goodall. NGS research grant. 592-621, May 1979

• My Life Among Wild Chimpanzees. By Jane Goodall. Photos by Baron Hugo van Lawick and author. NGS research grant. 272-308, Aug. 1963
• New Discoveries Among Africa's Chimpanzees. By Baroness Jane van Lawick-Goodall. Photos by Baron Hugo van Lawick. NGS research grant. 802-831, Dec. 1965

GONDS (Tribespeople). *See* Muria Gonds

GOOD-BYE to the Stone Age: Brazil's Txukahameis. Photos by W. Jesco von Puttkamer. 270-283, Feb. 1975

GOOD HOPE, Cape of, South Africa:
• *Yankee* Roams the Orient. By Irving and Electa Johnson. 327-370, Mar. 1951

A **GOOD** Life in the Low Country–Savannah to Charleston. By John J. Putman. Photos by Annie Griffiths. 798-829, Dec. 1983

A **GOOD** Life on the Potomac. By James L. Stanfield. 470-479, Oct. 1976

GOOD Times and Bad in Appalachia: Wrestlin' for a Livin' With King Coal. By Michael E. Long. Photos by Michael O'Brien. 793-819, June 1983

GOOD-WILL Ambassadors of the U. S. Navy Win Friends in the Far East. By Franc Shor. Photos by W. E. Garrett. 283-335, Sept. 1959

GOODALE, JANE C.: Author:
• Blowgun Hunters of the South Pacific. Photos by Ann Chowning. 793-817, June 1966
Photographer:
• Expedition to the Land of the Tiwi. By Charles P. Mountford. 417-440, Mar. 1956

GOODALL, JANE:
• Editorials. By Gilbert M. Grosvenor. 437, Oct. 1978; 591, May 1979
■ Miss Goodall and the Wild Chimpanzees. 831A-831B, Dec. 1965
Author:
• Life and Death at Gombe. 592-621, May 1979
◆ *My Friends the Wild Chimpanzees.* Announced. 408-417, Mar. 1966
• New Discoveries Among Africa's Chimpanzees. Photos by Baron Hugo van Lawick. 802-831, Dec. 1965
• Tool-using Bird: The Egyptian Vulture. Photos by Baron Hugo van Lawick. 631-641, May 1968
Author-Photographer:
• My Life Among Wild Chimpanzees. Photos by Baron Hugo van Lawick and author. 272-308, Aug. 1963

GOODALL, RAE NATALIE P.: Author:
• Housewife at the End of the World. Photos by James L. Stanfield. 130-150, Jan. 1971

GOODMAN, ROBERT B.:
Photographer:
• Australia. By Alan Villiers. 309-385, Sept. 1963
• Cowes to Cornwall (England). By Alan Villiers. 149-201, Aug. 1961
• The Flowers That Say "Aloha." By Deena Clark. 121-131, Jan. 1967
• Fountain of Fire in Hawaii. By Frederick Simpich, Jr. Photos by Robert B. Goodman and Robert Wenkam. 303-327, Mar. 1960
• Queen Elizabeth Opens Parliament. By W. E. Roscher. 699-707, Nov. 1961
• Underwater Archeology: Key to History's Warehouse. By George F. Bass. Photos by Thomas J. Abercrombie and Robert B. Goodman. 138-156, July 1963
• Western Samoa, the Pacific's Newest Nation. By Maurice Shadbolt. 573-602, Oct. 1962

The **GOONEY BIRDS** of Midway. By John W. Aldrich. 839-851, June 1964

GOOSE BAY, Labrador, Newfoundland:
• Milestones in My Arctic Journeys. By Willie Knutsen. Included: Activities of the Search and Rescue section of the Air Force. 543-570, Oct. 1949

GÓRALE (People):
• Poland's Mountain People. By Yva Momatiuk and John Eastcott. 104-129, Jan. 1981

GORDON, ROBERT J.: Author:
• Nation in the Making: Papua New Guinea. Photos by David Austen. 143-149, Aug. 1982

GORE, RICK: Author:
• The Awesome Worlds Within a Cell. Photos by Bruce Dale. Paintings by Davis Meltzer. 355-395, Sept. 1976
• A Bad Time to Be a Crocodile. Photos by Jonathan Blair. 90-115, Jan. 1978
• Conservation: Can We Live Better on Less? 34-57, *Special Report on Energy* (Feb. 1981)
• The Desert: An Age-old Challenge Grows. Photos by Georg Gerster and Bruce Dale. 586-639, Nov. 1979
• Eyes of Science. Photos by James P. Blair. 360-389, Mar. 1978
• Florida, Noah's Ark for Exotic Newcomers. Photos by David Doubilet. 538-559, Oct. 1976
• Journey to China's Far West. Photos by Bruce Dale. 292-331, Mar. 1980
• The Mediterranean–Sea of Man's Fate. Photos by Jonathan Blair. 694-737, Dec. 1982
• The Once and Future Universe. Photos by James A. Sugar. Paintings by Barron Storey. Picture text by David Jeffery. 704-749, June 1983
• Seven Giants Who Led the Way. Paintings by Ned Seidler. 401-407, Sept. 1976
• Sifting for Life in the Sands of Mars. 9-31, Jan. 1977
• Striking It Rich in the North Sea. Photos by Dick Durrance II. 519-549, Apr. 1977
• Those Fiery Brazilian Bees. Photos by Bianca Lavies. 491-501, Apr. 1976
• The Tree Nobody Liked (Red Mangrove). Photos by Bianca Lavies. 669-689, May 1977
• Twilight Hope for Big Cypress. Photos by Patricia Caulfield. 251-273, Aug. 1976
• Voyager 1 at Saturn: Riddles of the Rings. Photos by NASA. 3-31, July 1981
• What Voyager Saw: Jupiter's Dazzling Realm. Photos by NASA. 2-29, Jan. 1980
• When the Space Shuttle Finally Flies. Photos by Jon Schneeberger. Paintings by Ken Dallison. 317-347, Mar. 1981

GORGES:
• Cane Bridges of Asia. Photos from Paul Popper. 243-250, Aug. 1948
• *See also* Dinosaur National Monument; Languedoc (Region), France, for Gorges du Tarn; Olduvai Gorge; Yangtze; *and* Canyons

GORILLAS:
• Conversations With a Gorilla. By Francine Patterson. Photos by Ronald H. Cohn. NGS research grant. 438-465, Oct. 1978
• Face to Face With Gorillas in Central Africa. By Paul A. Zahl. 114-137, Jan. 1960
■ Gorilla. 703, Dec. 1980
• Growing Up With Snowflake. By Arthur J. Riopelle. Photos by Michael Kuh. NGS research grant. 491-503, Oct. 1970
• The Imperiled Mountain Gorilla. By Dian Fossey. NGS research grant. 501-523, Apr. 1981
Death of Marchessa. Photos by Peter G. Veit. 508-511
• Jambo–First Gorilla Raised by Its Mother in Captivity. By Ernst M. Lang. Photos by Paul Steinemann. 446-453, Mar. 1964
• Making Friends With Mountain Gorillas. By Dian Fossey. Photos by Robert M. Campbell. NGS research grant. 48-67, Jan. 1970
• More Years With Mountain Gorillas. By Dian Fossey. Photos by Robert M. Campbell. NGS research grant. 574-585, Oct. 1971
■ Search for the Great Apes. Cover, Jan. 1976
• "Snowflake," the World's First White Gorilla. By Arthur J. Riopelle. Photos by Paul A. Zahl. NGS research grant. 443-448, Mar. 1967

GOSSAMER ALBATROSS (Man-powered Aircraft):
• Winged Victory of *Gossamer Albatross*. By Bryan Allen. 640-651, Nov. 1979

GOSSAMER CONDOR (Man-powered Aircraft):
• The Flight of the *Gossamer Condor*. By Michael E. Long. 130-140, Jan. 1978

GOSSAMER PENGUIN (Solar-powered Aircraft):
• Electricity From the Sun. 40-41, *Special Report on Energy* (Feb. 1981)

GOTLAND (Island), Sweden:
• Gotland: Sweden's Treasure Island. By James Cerruti. Photos by Albert Moldvay. 268-288, Aug. 1973

GOULD, ALAN J.: Author:
• Again–the Olympic Challenge. 488-513, Oct. 1964

GOVERNMENT:
• The British Way: Great Britain's Major Gifts to Freedom, Democratic Government, Science, and Society. By Sir Evelyn Wrench. 421-541, Apr. 1949
• *See also* names of countries

GRADUATION by Parachute. By John E. Fletcher. 833-846, June 1952

GRAHAM, ROBIN LEE:
Author-Photographer:
• Robin Sails Home. 504-545, Oct. 1970
• A Teen-ager Sails the World Alone. 445-491, Oct. 1968
• World-roaming Teen-ager Sails On. 449-493, Apr. 1969

GRAN SABANA (Region), Venezuela:
• Jungle Journey to the World's Highest Waterfall. By Ruth Robertson. 655-690, Nov. 1949

GRANADA, Spain:
• Andalusia, the Spirit of Spain. By Howard La Fay. Photos by Joseph J. Scherschel. 833-857, June 1975
• The Changing Face of Old Spain. By Bart McDowell. Photos by Albert Moldvay. 291-339, Mar. 1965
• Speaking of Spain. By Luis Marden. 415-456, Apr. 1950

GRAND BANKS, Atlantic Ocean:
• Dory on the Banks: A Day in the Life of a Portuguese Fisherman. By James H. Pickerell. 573-583, Apr. 1968
• I Sailed with Portugal's Captains Courageous. By Alan Villiers. 565-596, May 1952
▥ The Lonely Dorymen. 579A-579B, Apr. 1968
• Newfoundland Trusts in the Sea. By Gary Jennings. Photos by Sam Abell. 112-141, Jan. 1974

GRAND CANYON, Arizona:
• Grand Canyon. Photos by W. E. Garrett. 2-15, July 1978
• Grand Canyon: Are We Loving It to Death? By W. E. Garrett. 16-51, July 1978
• Grand Canyon: Nature's Story of Creation. By Louis Schellbach. Photos by Justin Locke. 589-629, May 1955
▲ *The Grand Canyon,* double-sided supplement. Text. NGS research grant. July 1978
• Inside the Sacred Hopi Homeland. By Jake Page. Photos by Susanne Page. 607-629, Nov. 1982
• Retracing John Wesley Powell's Historic Voyage Down the Grand Canyon. By Joseph Judge. Photos by Walter Meayers Edwards. 668-713, May 1969
• Shooting Rapids in Reverse! Jet Boats Climb the Colorado's Torrent Through the Grand Canyon. By William Belknap, Jr. 552-565, Apr. 1962
• *See also* Havasupai Indian Reservation

GRAND CANYON NATIONAL PARK, Arizona:
• Grand Canyon. Photos by W. E. Garrett. 2-15, July 1978
• Grand Canyon: Are We Loving It to Death? By W. E. Garrett. 16-51, July 1978
• Grand Canyon: Nature's Story of Creation. By Louis Schellbach. Photos by Justin Locke. 589-629, May 1955
▲ *The Grand Canyon,* double-sided supplement. Text. NGS research grant. July 1978
• The West Through Boston Eyes. By Stewart Anderson. 733-776, June 1949

GRAND CONGLOUÉ (Island), Mediterranean Sea:
• Fish Men Discover a 2,200-year-old Greek Ship. By Jacques-Yves Cousteau. NGS research grant. 1-36, Jan. 1954

GRAND COULEE DAM, Washington:
• From Sagebrush to Roses on the Columbia. By Leo A. Borah. 571-611, Nov. 1952
• Powerhouse of the Northwest (Columbia River). By David S. Boyer. 821-847, Dec. 1974

GRAND TETON NATIONAL PARK, Wyoming:
• Cloud Gardens in the Tetons. By Frank and John Craighead. 811-830, June 1948
• Grand Teton–A Winter's Tale. By François Leydet. 148-152, July 1979
• I See America First. By Lynda Bird Johnson. Photos by William Albert Allard. 874-904, Dec. 1965
• Jackson Hole: Good-bye to the Old Days? By François Leydet. Photos by Jonathan Wright. 768-789, Dec. 1976
• The West Through Boston Eyes. By Stewart Anderson. 733-776, June 1949
• Wildlife Adventuring in Jackson Hole. By Frank and John Craighead. 1-36, Jan. 1956
• Wyoming: High, Wide, and Windy. By David S. Boyer. 554-594, Apr. 1966

The **GRANDEUR** of Windsor. By Anthony Holden. Photos by James L. Stanfield. 604-631, Nov. 1980
Portfolio text by David Jeffery. 616-625

GRANT, ULYSSES S.:
• Appomattox: Where Grant and Lee Made Peace With Honor a Century Ago. By Ulysses S. Grant 3rd. Photos by Bruce Dale. 435-469, Apr. 1965
• Profiles of the Presidents: III. The American Giant Comes of Age. By Frank Freidel. 660-711, May 1965

GRANT, ULYSSES S., 3rd: Author:
• Appomattox: Where Grant and Lee Made Peace With Honor a Century Ago. Photos by Bruce Dale. 435-469, Apr. 1965
• The Civil War. 437-449, Apr. 1961

GRAPES AND GRAPE CULTURE:
• Bordeaux: Fine Wines and Fiery Gascons. By William Davenport. Photos by Adam Woolfitt. 233-259, Aug. 1980
• How Fruit Came to America. By J. R. Magness. Paintings by Else Bostelmann. 325-377, Sept. 1951
• Living the Good Life in Burgundy. By William Davenport. Photos by Robert Freson. 794-817, June 1978
• My Life in the Valley of the Moon (California). By H. H. Arnold. Photos by Willard R. Culver. 689-716, Dec. 1948
• Napa, California's Valley of the Vine. By Moira Johnston. Photos by Charles O'Rear. 695-717, May 1979

GRASS-SKIRTED Yap. By W. Robert Moore. 805-830, Dec. 1952

GRASSES:
• The Tallgrass Prairie: Can It Be Saved? By Dennis Farney. Photos by Jim Brandenburg. Included: Bluestem, Cordgrass, Indian grass; and aliens, Fescue, Kentucky bluegrass. 37-61, Jan. 1980
• *See also* Bamboo

GRASSHOPPERS:
• Back-yard Monsters in Color. By Paul A. Zahl. 235-260, Aug. 1952

GRASSHOPPERS, Migratory. *See* Locusts

GRASSLANDS. *See* Prairie

GRASSLE, J. FREDERICK: Author:
• Incredible World of the Deep-sea Rifts. 680-705, Nov. 1979
I. Strange World Without Sun. The Editor. 680-688; II. Return to Oases of the Deep. By Robert D. Ballard and J. Frederick Grassle. 689-705

GRAVEL PICTOGRAPHS:
• Giant Effigies of the Southwest. By George C. Marshall. 389, Sept. 1952
• Seeking the Secret of the Giants. By Frank M. Setzler. Photos by Richard H. Stewart. Included: Map of Colorado River Basin, showing sites near Blythe, Ripley, Topock; the Hâ-âk lying site near Gila River Indian Reservation. 390-404, Sept. 1952

's **GRAVENHAGE** (The Hague), Netherlands:
• Mid-century Holland Builds Her Future. By Sydney Clark. 747-778, Dec. 1950

GRAVES, WILLIAM: Author:
• After an Empire . . . Portugal. Photos by Bruno Barbey. 804-831, Dec. 1980
• Bangkok, City of Angels. Photos by John Launois. 96-129, July 1973
• California, the Golden Magnet. 595-679, May 1966
I. The South. Photos by Thomas Nebbia. 595-639; II. Nature's North. Photos by James P. Blair and Jonathan S. Blair. 641-679
• Denmark, Field of the Danes. Photos by Thomas Nebbia. 245-275, Feb. 1974
• Earthquake! (Alaska, 1964). 112-139, July 1964

• Finland: Plucky Neighbor of Soviet Russia. Photos by George F. Mobley. 587-629, May 1968
• Human Treasures of Japan. Photos by James L. Stanfield. 370-379, Sept. 1972
• The Imperiled Giants (Whales). 722-751, Dec. 1976
• Iran: Desert Miracle. Photos by James P. Blair. 2-47, Jan. 1975
• Living in a Japanese Village. Photos by James L. Stanfield. 668-693, May 1972
• Maine's Lobster Island, Monhegan. Photos by Kosti Ruohomaa. 285-298, Feb. 1959
• Martha's Vineyard. Photos by James P. Blair. 778-809, June 1961
• Mobile, Alabama's City in Motion. Photos by Joseph J. Scherschel and Robert W. Madden. 368-397, Mar. 1968
• New Life for the Troubled Suez Canal. Photos by Jonathan Blair. 792-817, June 1975
• Puget Sound, Sea Gate of the Pacific Northwest. Photos by David Alan Harvey. 71-97, Jan. 1977
• The Rhine: Europe's River of Legend. Photos by Bruce Dale. 449-499, Apr. 1967
• San Francisco Bay, the Westward Gate. Photos by James L. Stanfield. 593-637, Nov. 1969
• Tokyo, the Peaceful Explosion. Photos by Winfield Parks. 445-487, Oct. 1964
• Washington: The City Freedom Built. Photos by Bruce Dale and Thomas Nebbia. 735-781, Dec. 1964
• World's Last Salute to a Great American (Dwight D. Eisenhower). By William Graves and other members of the National Geographic staff. 40-51, July 1969

GRAVEYARD of the Quicksilver Galleons. By Mendel Peterson. Photos by Jonathan Blair. 850-876, Dec. 1979

GRAY, RALPH: Author:
• The Alps: Man's Own Mountains. Photos by Walter Meayers Edwards and William Eppridge. 350-395, Sept. 1965
• Down the Potomac by Canoe. Photos by Walter Meayers Edwards. 213-242, Aug. 1948
• Down the Susquehanna by Canoe. Photos by Walter Meayers Edwards. 73-120, July 1950
• From Sun-clad Sea to Shining Mountains. Photos by James P. Blair. 542-589, Apr. 1964
• Rhododendron Time on Roan Mountain. 819-828, June 1957
Author-Photographer:
• Across Canada by Mackenzie's Track. 191-239, Aug. 1955
• Following the Trail of Lewis and Clark. 707-750, June 1953
• From Sea to Shining Sea: A Cross Section of the United States Along Historic Route 40. Photos by Dean Conger and author. 1-61, July 1961
• Labrador Canoe Adventure. By Andrew Brown and Ralph Gray. 65-99, July 1951
• Three Roads to Rainbow. 547-561, Apr. 1957
• Vacation Tour Through Lincoln Land. 141-184, Feb. 1952

GRAY WHALES:
• The California Gray Whale Comes Back. By Theodore J. Walker. 394-415, Mar. 1971

GRAY WOLF:
• Where Can the Wolf Survive? By L. David Mech. 518-537, Oct. 1977

GRAYS LAKE NATIONAL WILDLIFE REFUGE, Idaho:
• Teamwork Helps the Whooping Crane. By Roderick C. Drewien, with Ernie Kuyt. 680-693, May 1979

GREAT ANDAMANESE (Negrito Tribe):
• The Last Andaman Islanders. By Raghubir Singh. 66-91, July 1975

GREAT BAHAMA BANK, Bahama Islands:
• Diving Into the Blue Holes of the Bahamas. By George J. Benjamin. 347-363, Sept. 1970
• Strange March of the Spiny Lobster. By William F. Herrnkind. Photos by Rick Frehsee and Bruce Mounier. NGS research grant. 819-831, June 1975

GREAT BARRIER REEF, Australia:
• Australia. II. The Settled East, the Barrier Reef, the Center. By Alan Villiers. 347-385, Sept. 1963
• Australia's Great Barrier Reef. Photos by Valerie and Ron Taylor. 728-741, June 1973
• Australia's Great Barrier Reef. 630-663, May 1981
I. A Marine Park Is Born. By Soames Summerhays. Photos by Ron and Valerie Taylor. 630-635; II. Paradise Beneath the Sea. By Ron and Valerie Taylor. 636-663
• Exploring Australia's Coral Jungle. By Kenneth MacLeish. 743-779, June 1973
• Life Cycle of a Coral. By Robert F. Sisson. 780-793, June 1973
• On Australia's Coral Ramparts. By Paul A. Zahl. 1-48, Jan. 1957
• Queensland: Young Titan of Australia's Tropic North. By Kenneth MacLeish. Photos by Winfield Parks. 593-639, Nov. 1968

GREAT BASIN, U. S.:
• Indians of the Far West. By Matthew W. Stirling. Paintings by W. Langdon Kihn. 175-200, Feb. 1948
• *See also* Death Valley National Monument; Great Salt Lake; Mojave Desert

GREAT BRITAIN:
• "Be Ye Men of Valour" (Churchill's Life and Funeral). By Howard La Fay. 159-197, Aug. 1965
• The Britain That Shakespeare Knew. By Louis B. Wright. Photos by Dean Conger. 613-665, May 1964
• British Castles, History in Stone. By Norman Wilkinson. 111-129, July 1947
▲ *British Isles,* Atlas series supplement. July 1958
▲ *The British Isles,* supplement. Apr. 1949

ROLLIE OSTERMICK

Wolf: gray wolf peers from scrub bush

G H

• The British Way: Great Britain's Major Gifts to Freedom, Democratic Government, Science, and Society. By Sir Evelyn Wrench. 421-541, Apr. 1949
• Editorial. By Gilbert M. Grosvenor. 441, Oct. 1979
▲ *Europe; Historical Map of Europe,* double-sided supplement. Dec. 1983
• The Final Tribute (Churchill Funeral). By Carolyn Bennett Patterson. 199-225, Aug. 1965
• The Investiture of Great Britain's Prince of Wales. By Allan C. Fisher, Jr. Photos by James L. Stanfield and Adam Woolfitt. 698-715, Nov. 1969
▲ *Medieval England; British Isles,* double-sided supplement. Oct. 1979
• Our Search for British Paintings. By Franklin L. Fisher. 543-550, Apr. 1949
• Questing for Gems. By George S. Switzer. Included: The Crown Jewels of Great Britain. 835-863, Dec. 1971
▲ *Shakespeare's Britain,* supplement. May 1964
▪ This Britain. 583, Nov. 1975; cover, Dec. 1975
▲ *A Traveler's Map of the British Isles,* supplement. Text on reverse. Apr. 1974
• *See also* England; Scotland; Wales; *and* Arran, Island of; Caldy (Island); Channel Islands; Hebrides; Ireland, Northern; Lundy (Island); Man, Isle of; Orkney Islands; St. Michael's Mount; Scilly, Isles of; Shetland Islands; Skomer (Island); Skye, Isle of

GREAT BRITAIN II (Ketch):
• By Square-rigger from Baltic to Bicentennial. By Kenneth Garrett. 824-857, Dec. 1976

GREAT DIVIDE TRAIL, Alberta-British Columbia, Canada:
• Hiking the Backbone of the Rockies: Canada's Great Divide Trail. By Mike W. Edwards. Photos by Lowell Georgia. Included: Banff, Jasper, Kootenay, and Yoho National Parks; Mount Assiniboine, Mount Robson, and Willmore Wilderness Provincial Parks. 795-817, June 1973
• *See also* Continental Divide

GREAT INAGUA (Island), Bahamas:
• *Carib* Cruises the West Indies. By Carleton Mitchell. 1-56, Jan. 1948

GREAT INDIAN DESERT, India-Pakistan:
• The Desert: An Age-old Challenge Grows. By Rick Gore. Photos by Georg Gerster and Bruce Dale. 586-639, Nov. 1979

GREAT LAKES, and Region, U. S.-Canada:
▲ *Close-up: U.S.A., Wisconsin, Michigan, and the Great Lakes,* supplement. Text on reverse. Aug. 1973
• The Great Lakes: Is It Too Late? By Gordon Young. Photos by James L. Amos and Martin Rogers. 147-185, Aug. 1973
▲ *The Great Lakes Region of the United States and Canada,* supplement. Dec. 1953
• *J. W. Westcott,* Postman for the Great Lakes. By Cy La Tour. 813-824, Dec. 1950
• New Era on the Great Lakes. By Nathaniel T. Kenney. 439-490, Apr. 1959
• New St. Lawrence Seaway Opens the Great Lakes to the World. By Andrew H. Brown. 299-339, Mar. 1959
▲ *Northeastern United States, including the Great Lakes Region,* Atlas series supplement. Apr. 1959
• Relics from the Rapids (Voyageurs). By Sigurd F. Olson. Photos by David S. Boyer. 413-435, Sept. 1963
• *See also* Erie, Lake; Ontario, Lake; *and* Illinois; Indiana; Michigan; Minnesota; New York; Ohio; Ontario; Wisconsin

GREAT LAMESHUR BAY, St. John (Island), U. S. Virgin Islands. *See* Tektite II

GREAT Masters of a Brave Era in Art. By Hereward Lester Cooke, Jr. 661-697, May 1961

GREAT PLAINS, U. S. *See* Midwest

GREAT RIFT VALLEY, Africa-Asia:
• Journey Into the Great Rift: the Northern Half. By Helen and Frank Schreider. 254-290, Aug. 1965
• *See also* Aqaba, Gulf of; Danakil Depression, Ethiopia; Dead Sea; Olduvai Gorge, Tanzania; Red Sea; Rudolf, Lake, Kenya

The **GREAT ST. BERNARD HOSPICE** Today. By George Pickow. 49-62, Jan. 1957

GREAT SALT LAKE, Utah:
• Geographical Twins a World Apart. By David S. Boyer. Included: Great Salt Lake and the Dead Sea. 848-859, Dec. 1958
• Life in a "Dead" Sea–Great Salt Lake. By Paul A. Zahl. Included: Ancient inland sea, Lake Bonneville. 252-263, Aug. 1967
• Utah's Shining Oasis. By Charles McCarry. Photos by James L. Amos. 440-473, Apr. 1975

GREAT SAND BARRIER REEF, North Carolina-Virginia:
• Exploring America's Great Sand Barrier Reef. By Eugene R. Guild. Photos by John E. Fletcher and author. 325-350, Sept. 1947
• How We Found the *Monitor.* By John G. Newton. NGS research grant. 48-61, Jan. 1975
• Lonely Cape Hatteras, Besieged by the Sea. By William S. Ellis. Photos by Emory Kristof. 393-421, Sept. 1969
• October Holiday on the Outer Banks. By Nike Anderson. Photos by J. Baylor Roberts. 501-529, Oct. 1955
• Our Changing Atlantic Coastline. By Nathaniel T. Kenney. Photos by B. Anthony Stewart. 860-887, Dec. 1962

GREAT SMOKY MOUNTAINS, North Carolina-Tennessee:
• Around the "Great Lakes of the South." By Frederick Simpich. Photos by J. Baylor Roberts. 463-491, Apr. 1948
• The People of Cades Cove. By William O. Douglas. Photos by Thomas Nebbia and Otis Imboden. 60-95, July 1962
• *See also* Great Smoky Mountains National Park

GREAT SMOKY MOUNTAINS NATIONAL PARK, North Carolina-Tennessee:
• Autumn–Season of the Smokies. By Gordon Young. 142-147, July 1979
• Great Smokies National Park: Solitude for Millions. By Gordon Young. Photos by James L. Amos. 522-549, Oct. 1968
• Pack Trip Through the Smokies. By Val Hart. Photos by Robert F. Sisson. 473-502, Oct. 1952
• Skyline Trail from Maine to Georgia. By Andrew H. Brown. Photos by Robert F. Sisson. 219-251, Aug. 1949

GREAT TEMPLE OF TENOCHTITLAN:
• The Aztecs. 704-775, Dec. 1980
I. The Aztecs. By Bart McDowell. Photos by David Hiser. Paintings by Felipe Dávalos. 714-751; II. The Building of Tenochtitlan. By Augusto F. Molina Montes. Paintings by Felipe Dávalos. 753-765; III. New Finds in the Great Temple. By Eduardo Matos Moctezuma. Photos by David Hiser. 767-775
▲ *Visitor's Guide to the Aztec World; Mexico and Central America,* double-sided supplement. Dec. 1980

GREAT WHITE SHARK:
• Sharks: Magnificent and Misunderstood. By Eugenie Clark. Photos by David Doubilet. NGS research grant. 138-187, Aug. 1981

GREATER BIRDS OF PARADISE:
• Feathered Dancers of Little Tobago. By E. Thomas Gilliard. Photos by Frederick Kent Truslow. NGS research grant. 428-440, Sept. 1958

GREATER SANDHILL CRANES:
• Teamwork Helps the Whooping Crane. By Roderick C. Drewien, with Ernie Kuyt. Contents: A U. S.-Canadian effort to establish a second breeding flock of wild whoopers among close-kin sandhill cranes. 680-693, May 1979

GREBES:
• Western Grebes: The Birds That Walk on Water. By Gary L. Nuechterlein. NGS research grant. 624-637, May 1982

El **GRECO:**
• Toledo–El Greco's Spain Lives On. By Louise E. Levathes. Photos by James P. Blair. 726-753, June 1982
The Genius of El Greco. Introduction by J. Carter Brown. 736-744

GRECO-ROMAN CULTURE:
◆ *Greece and Rome: Builders of Our World.* Announced. 550-567, Oct. 1968
• *See also* Aphrodisias

GREECE:
• The Aegean Isles: Poseidon's Playground. By Gilbert M. Grosvenor. 733-781, Dec. 1958
• "Around the World in Eighty Days." By Newman Bumstead. Included: Athens, Corinth, Gulf of Korinthiakós, Gulf of Patraïkós, Kallithéa, Piraiévs. 705-750, Dec. 1951
• Athens: Her Golden Past Still Lights the World. By Kenneth F. Weaver. Photos by Phillip Harrington. 100-137, July 1963
• Athens to Istanbul. By Jean and Franc Shor. 37-76, Jan. 1956
▲ *Classical Lands of the Mediterranean,* supplement. Dec. 1949
• Crete, Cradle of Western Civilization. By Maynard Owen Williams. 693-706, Nov. 1953
• Editorial. By Gilbert M. Grosvenor. 291, Mar. 1980
• Erosion, Trojan Horse of Greece. By F. G. Renner. 793-812, Dec. 1947
• Eternal Easter in a Greek Village. By Maria Nicolaidis-Karanikolas. Photos by James L. Stanfield. 768-777, Dec. 1983
• Greece: "To Be Indomitable, To Be Joyous." By Peter T. White. Photos by James P. Blair. 360-393, Mar. 1980
▲ *Greece and the Aegean,* Atlas series supplement. Dec. 1958
• Homeward With Ulysses (Ionian Islands). By Melville Bell Grosvenor. Photos by Edwin Stuart Grosvenor. 1-39, July 1973
• The Isles of Greece: Aegean Birthplace of Western Culture. By Melville Bell Grosvenor. Photos by Edwin Stuart Grosvenor and Winfield Parks. 147-193, Aug. 1972
• Mount Athos. 739-745, Dec. 1983
• On the Winds of the Dodecanese. By Jean and Franc Shor. 351-390, Mar. 1953
• Round the World School (ISA). By Paul Antze. Photos by William Eppridge. 96-127, July 1962

GREECE, Ancient:
• Again–the Olympic Challenge. By Alan J. Gould. 488-513, Oct. 1964
• Athens: Her Golden Past Still Lights the World. By Kenneth F. Weaver. Photos by Phillip Harrington. 100-137, July 1963
• Drama of Death in a Minoan Temple. By Yannis Sakellarakis and Efi Sapouna-Sakellaraki. Photos by Otis Imboden and Spyros Tsavdaroglou. 205-222, Feb. 1981
◆ *Greece and Rome: Builders of Our World.* Announced. 550-567, Oct. 1968
• In the Footsteps of Alexander the Great. By Helen and Frank Schreider. Paintings by Tom Lovell. 1-65, Jan. 1968
• Jerusalem to Rome in the Path of St. Paul. By David S. Boyer. 707-759, Dec. 1956
• Joseph Alsop: A Historical Perspective (on Minoan Human Sacrifice). 223, Feb. 1981
• Minoans and Mycenaeans: Greece's Brilliant Bronze Age. By Joseph Judge. Photos by Gordon W. Gahan. Paintings by Lloyd K. Townsend. 142-185, Feb. 1978
• Regal Treasures From a Macedonian Tomb. By Manolis Andronicos. Photos by Spyros Tsavdaroglou. 55-77, July 1978
• Thera, Key to the Riddle of Minos. By Spyridon Marinatos. Photos by Otis Imboden. 702-726, May 1972
• The Tower of the Winds. By Derek J. de Solla Price. Paintings by Robert C. Magis. NGS research grant. 587-596, Apr. 1967

GREEK ART AND ARCHITECTURE:
• Athens: Her Golden Past Still Lights the World. By Kenneth F. Weaver. Photos by Phillip Harrington. 100-137, July 1963
• Athens to Istanbul. By Jean and Franc Shor. 37-76, Jan. 1956
• The Tower of the Winds. By Derek J. de Solla Price. Paintings by Robert C. Magis. NGS research grant. 587-596, Apr. 1967
• Warriors From a Watery Grave (Bronze Sculptures). By Joseph Alsop. 821-827, June 1983

GREEK ORTHODOX CHURCH:
• The Byzantine Empire. 709-777, Dec. 1983
I. Rome of the East. By Merle Severy. Photos by James L. Stanfield. 709-767; II. Mount Athos. 739-745; III. Eternal Easter in a Greek Village. By Maria Nicolaidis-Karanikolas. Photos by James L. Stanfield. 768-777
• Hashemite Jordan, Arab Heartland. By John Scofield. 841-856, Dec. 1952
• Home to the Holy Land. By Maynard Owen Williams. 707-746, Dec. 1950
• Island of Faith in the Sinai Wilderness (St. Catherine's Monastery). By George H. Forsyth. Photos by Robert F. Sisson. 82-106, Jan. 1964
• Mount Sinai's Holy Treasures (St. Catherine's Monastery). By Kurt Weitzmann. Photos by Fred Anderegg. 109-127, Jan. 1964
• On the Winds of the Dodecanese. By Jean and Franc Shor. 351-390, Mar. 1953
• Sinai Sheds New Light on the Bible. By Henry Field. Photos by William B. and Gladys Terry. 795-815. Dec. 1948
• Sponge Fishermen of Tarpon Springs. By Jennie E. Harris. 119-136, Jan. 1947

GREEKS:
• Cyprus Under Four Flags: A Struggle for Unity. By Kenneth MacLeish. Photos by Jonathan Blair. 356-383, Mar. 1973
• Sponge Fishermen of Tarpon Springs (Florida). By Jennie E. Harris. 119-136, Jan. 1947

GREELY, A. W.:
• Far North with "Captain Mac." By Miriam MacMillan. Included: Greely Arctic Expedition of 1881-1884. 465-513, Oct. 1951

JAMES L. STANFIELD, NGS
Greek Easter: villagers at meal

GREEN, PHILIP:
Author-Photographer:
• The Satin Bowerbird, Australia's Feathered Playboy. 865-872, Dec. 1977

GREEN, RAY O., Jr.: Photographer:
• The Swallow-tailed Kite: Graceful Aerialist of the Everglades. 496-505, Oct. 1972

GREEN BAY, Wisconsin:
• Wisconsin's Door Peninsula. By William S. Ellis. Photos by Ted Rozumalski. 347-371, Mar. 1969

GREEN COUNTY, Kentucky:
• Home to the Heart of Kentucky. By Nadine Brewer. Photos by William Strode. 522-546, Apr. 1982

GREEN MOUNTAINS, Vermont:
• Mountains Top Off New England. By F. Barrows Colton. Photos by Robert F. Sisson. 563-602, May 1951
• Sugar Weather in the Green Mountains. By Stephen Greene. Photos by Robert F. Sisson. 471-482, Apr. 1954

GREEN RIVER, Wyoming-Colorado-Utah:
• Shooting Rapids in Dinosaur Country. By Jack Breed. Photos by author and Justin Locke. 363-390, Mar. 1954

GREEN TURTLES:
• Australia's Great Barrier Reef. 630-663, May 1981
I. A Marine Park Is Born. By Soames Summerhays. Photos by Ron and Valerie Taylor. 630-635; II. Paradise Beneath the Sea. By Ron and Valerie Taylor. 636-663
• Imperiled Gift of the Sea: Caribbean Green Turtle. By Archie Carr. Photos by Robert E. Schroeder. 876-890, June 1967

GREENBERG, IDAZ:
Author-Photographer:
• Buck Island–Underwater Jewel. By Jerry and Idaz Greenberg. 677-683, May 1971

GREENBERG, JERRY:
Author-Photographer:
• Buck Island–Underwater Jewel. By Jerry and Idaz Greenberg. 677-683, May 1971
• Florida's Coral City Beneath the Sea. 70-89, Jan. 1962
Photographer:
• Key Largo Coral Reef: America's First Undersea Park. By Charles M. Brookfield. 58-69, Jan. 1962
• Sharks: Wolves of the Sea. By Nathaniel T. Kenney. 222-257, Feb. 1968

GREENE, STEPHEN: Author:
• Sugar Weather in the Green Mountains. Photos by Robert F. Sisson. 471-482, Apr. 1954

The **GREENER** Fields of Georgia. By Howell Walker. Photos by author and B. Anthony Stewart. 287-330, Mar. 1954

GREENEWALT, CRAWFORD H.:
Author-Photographer:
• The Hummingbirds. 658-679, Nov. 1960

BOTH BY GEORGE F. MOBLEY, NGS

Greenland: ice-choked Augpilagtoq harbor, *top;* Siorapaluk child, *above*

• The Marvelous Hummingbird Rediscovered. 98-101, July 1966
• Photographing Hummingbirds in Brazil. 100-115, Jan. 1963

GREENFIELD VILLAGE, Michigan:
• The Past Is Present in Greenfield Village (Henry Ford Museum). By Beverley M. Bowie. Photos by Neal P. Davis and Willard R. Culver. 96-127, July 1958

GREENHILL, RICHARD: Photographer:
• In the Wake of Sindbad. By Tim Severin. 2-41, July 1982

GREENHOUSES. *See* Kew (Royal Botanic Gardens); Longwood Gardens (Du Pont Estate); Scilly, Isles of; *and* Flowers (Flower Seed Growers)

GREENLAND:
▲ *Canada, Alaska, and Greenland,* supplement. June 1947
• Far North with "Captain Mac." By Miriam MacMillan. Included: Cape Morris Jesup, Cape York, Disko Island, Etah, Godhavn, Godthaab, Holsteinsborg, Jakobshavn, Nugâtsiaq, Qutdligssat, Refuge Harbor, Sioropaluk, Sukkertoppen, Thule. 465-513, Oct. 1951
• Greenland Feels the Winds of Change. By John J. Putman. Photos by George F. Mobley. 366-393, Sept. 1975
• Greenland's "Place by the Icebergs." By Mogens Bloch Poulsen. Photos by Thomas Nebbia. 849-869, Dec. 1973
• Hunters of the Lost Spirit: Greenlanders. By Priit J. Vesilind. Photos by Ivars Silis. 191-193, Feb. 1983
• I Sailed with Portugal's Captains Courageous. By Alan Villiers. 565-596, May 1952
• Milestones in My Arctic Journeys. By Willie Knutsen. 543-570, Oct. 1949
• The Peary Flag Comes to Rest. By Marie Peary Stafford. 519-532, Oct. 1954
▲ *Peoples of the Arctic; Arctic Ocean,* double-sided supplement. Feb. 1983
• Vinland Ruins Prove Vikings Found the New World. By Helge Ingstad. NGS research grant. 708-734, Nov. 1964
• A Visit to the Living Ice Age. By Rutherford Platt. 525-545, Apr. 1957
• We Followed Peary to the Pole. By Gilbert Grosvenor and Thomas W. McKnew. 469-484, Oct. 1953
• What's Happening to Our Climate? By Samuel W. Matthews. 576-615, Nov. 1976
• *See also* Greenland Icecap; Thule Air Base; *and* Vikings

GREENLAND ICECAP:
• First Woman Across Greenland's Ice. By Myrtle Simpson. Photos by Hugh Simpson. 264-279, Aug. 1967
• Nuclear Power for the Polar Regions. By George J. Dufek. 712-730, May 1962
• Wringing Secrets from Greenland's Icecap. By Paul-Emile Victor. 121-147, Jan. 1956

GREGORY, ALFRED: Photographer:
- Triumph on Everest. 1-63, July 1954
I. Siege and Assault. By Sir John Hunt. 1-43; II. The Conquest of the Summit. By Sir Edmund Hillary. 45-63

GREHAN, FARRELL: Photographer:
- Amateur Gardener Creates a New Rose. By Elizabeth A. Moize. 286-294, Aug. 1972
- Autumn Flames Along the Allagash. By François Leydet. 177-187, Feb. 1974
- The Country of Willa Cather. By William Howarth. 71-93, July 1982
- The Mazatzal's Harsh but Lovely Land Between. By François Leydet. 161-167, Feb. 1974
- Okefenokee, the Magical Swamp. By François Leydet. 169-175, Feb. 1974
- The Olympics: Northwest Majesty. By François Leydet. 188-197, Feb. 1974
- Roosevelt Country: T. R.'s Wilderness Legacy. By John L. Eliot. 340-363, Sept. 1982
- Thoreau, a Different Man. By William Howarth. 349-387, Mar. 1981
- Tulips: Holland's Beautiful Business. By Elizabeth A. Moize. 712-728, May 1978
- Wales, the Lyric Land. By Bryan Hodgson. 36-63, July 1983

GRENADA (Island), West Indies:
- *Carib* Cruises the West Indies. By Carleton Mitchell. 1-56, Jan. 1948
- *Finisterre* Sails the Windward Islands. By Carleton Mitchell. Photos by Winfield Parks. 755-801, Dec. 1965
- St. Vincent, the Grenadines, and Grenada: Taking It as It Comes. By Ethel A. Starbird. Photos by Cotton Coulson. 399-425, Sept. 1979

The **GRENADINES** (Islands), West Indies:
- *Finisterre* Sails the Windward Islands. By Carleton Mitchell. Photos by Winfield Parks. 755-801, Dec. 1965
- St. Vincent, the Grenadines, and Grenada: Taking It as It Comes. By Ethel A. Starbird. Photos by Cotton Coulson. 399-425, Sept. 1979

GREYNOLDS PARK, North Miami Beach, Florida:
- New Scarlet Bird in Florida Skies. By Paul A. Zahl. 874-882, Dec. 1967

GRIFFIN, EDWARD I.: Author:
- Making Friends With a Killer Whale. 418-446, Mar. 1966

GRIFFITHS, ANNIE: Photographer:
- The American Red Cross: A Century of Service. By Louise Levathes. 777-791, June 1981
- Ancient Ashfall Creates a Pompeii of Prehistoric Animals. By Michael R. Voorhies. 66-75, Jan. 1981
- High-Flying Tulsa. By Robert Paul Jordan. 378-403, Sept. 1983
- Minneapolis and St. Paul. By Thomas J. Abercrombie. 665-691, Nov. 1980
- Savannah to Charleston–A Good Life in the Low Country. By John J. Putman. 798-829, Dec. 1983

GRIGG, RICHARD W.: Author:
- Precious Corals, Hawaii's Deep-sea Jewels. Photos by David Doubilet. 719-732, May 1979

A **GRIM** Struggle for Survival: The Imperiled Mountain Gorilla. By Dian Fossey. NGS research grant. 501-523, Apr. 1981
Death of Marchessa. Photos by Peter G. Veit. 508-511

GRIMMER, J. LEAR: Author:
- Strange Little World of the Hoatzin. Photos by M. Woodbridge Williams. 391-401, Sept. 1962

GRISWOLD, OLIVER: Author:
- An Exotic New Oriole Settles in Florida. By Charles M. Brookfield and Oliver Griswold. 261-264, Feb. 1956

GRIT and Glory: The Pony Express. By Rowe Findley. Photos by Craig Aurness. 45-71, July 1980

GRIZZLY BEARS:
- ▪ Grizzly! 639A-639B, Nov. 1967
- Knocking Out Grizzly Bears For Their Own Good. By Frank and John Craighead. NGS research grant. 276-291, Aug. 1960
- Studying Grizzly Habitat by Satellite. By John Craighead. NGS research grant. 148-158, July 1976
- Trailing Yellowstone's Grizzlies by Radio. By Frank Craighead, Jr. and John Craighead. NGS research grant. 252-267, Aug. 1966

GROOTE EYLANDT (Island), Australia:
- Exploring Stone Age Arnhem Land. By Charles P. Mountford. Photos by Howell Walker. NGS research grant. 745-782, Dec. 1949
- From Spear to Hoe on Groote Eylandt. By Howell Walker. 131-142, Jan. 1953

GROSVENOR, ALEXANDER G. B.:
Author:
- Midshipmen's Cruise. By William J. Aston and Alexander G. B. Grosvenor. 711-754, June 1948

GROSVENOR, ANNE REVIS. *See* Revis, Anne, for article by

GROSVENOR, DONNA KERKAM:
Author-Photographer:
- Bali by the Back Roads. By Donna K. and Gilbert M. Grosvenor. 657-697, Nov. 1969
- Ceylon, the Resplendent Land. By Donna K. and Gilbert M. Grosvenor. 447-497, Apr. 1966
- Miniature Monaco. By Gilbert M. and Donna Kerkam Grosvenor. 546-573, Apr. 1963
Photographer:
- What's Black and White and Loved All Over? By Theodore H. Reed. 803-815, Dec. 1972
- White Tiger in My House. By Elizabeth C. Reed. 482-491, Apr. 1970

GROSVENOR, EDWIN AUGUSTUS:
- Literary Landmarks of Massachu-

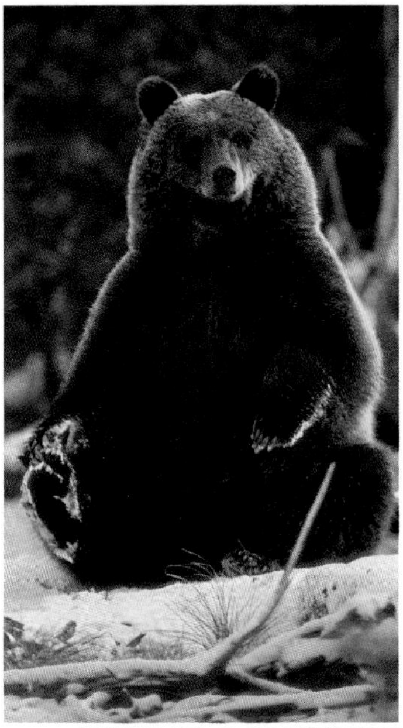

FRANK CRAIGHEAD, JR., AND JOHN CRAIGHEAD

Grizzlies: the feared *Ursus horribilis*

setts. By William H. Nicholas. Photos by B. Anthony Stewart and John E. Fletcher. 279-310, Mar. 1950

GROSVENOR, EDWIN STUART:

Photographer:

- The Enduring Pyrenees. By Robert Laxalt. 794-819, Dec. 1974
- Homeward With Ulysses. By Melville Bell Grosvenor. 1-39, July 1973
- The Isles of Greece: Aegean Birthplace of Western Culture. By Melville Bell Grosvenor. Photos by Edwin Stuart Grosvenor and Winfield Parks. 147-193, Aug. 1972
- North Through History Aboard *White Mist.* By Melville Bell Grosvenor. 1-55, July 1970
- South Seas' Tonga Hails a King. By Melville Bell Grosvenor. 322-343, Mar. 1968

GROSVENOR, ELSIE MAY BELL:

- First Lady of the National Geographic. By Gilbert Hovey Grosvenor. 101-121, July 1965
- Flag of the National Geographic Society designed by. 637, May 1949; 145, Aug. 1953; 516, 557, 564, Oct. 1963; 100, 101, 118, July 1965
- To Gilbert Grosvenor: a Monthly Monument 25 Miles High. By Frederick G. Vosburgh and the staff of the National Geographic Society. 445-487, Oct. 1966

Author:

- Alaska's Warmer Side. Photos by Gilbert Grosvenor and W. Robert Moore. 737-775, June 1956
- Safari from Congo to Cairo. Photos by Gilbert Grosvenor. 721-771, Dec. 1954
- Safari Through Changing Africa. Photos by Gilbert Grosvenor. 145-198, Aug. 1953

GROSVENOR, GILBERT HOVEY:

- Board of Trustees, Chairman (1954-1966). 65, 65B, 65D, July 1954; 445, 464, 485, Oct. 1966
- Editor (1899-1954). 65, 65B, July 1954; 459, 518, 529, 560, 561, 581, Oct. 1963; 445, Oct. 1966; 143, Feb. 1980; 848, Dec. 1981; 270, 272, 276, Aug. 1982
- Geographic sites named for. 370, 371, 373, Sept. 1949; 570, Oct. 1949; 416, 418, Sept. 1955; 737, 753, June 1956; 552, Apr. 1957; 46, July 1957; 578, Apr. 1962; 807, 826-827, June 1963; 447, 450-451, 478, Oct. 1966
- Gilbert Grosvenor's Golden Jubilee. By Albert W. Atwood. 253-261, Aug. 1949
- Grosvenor Medal Presented to Dr. Grosvenor by Charles F. Kettering. 253-255, 260, 261, Aug. 1949; 65G, July 1954; 449, 481, Oct. 1966
- President of NGS (1920-1954). 65, 65B, July 1954; 270, 276, Aug. 1982
- Russell Cave Dedicated; New Visitor Center Named for Gilbert H. Grosvenor. 440-442, Sept. 1967
- To Gilbert Grosvenor: a Monthly Monument 25 Miles High. By Frederick G. Vosburgh and the staff of the National Geographic Society. 445-487, Oct. 1966

VOL. 117, NO. 5 MAY, 1960

NATIONAL GEOGRAPHIC

A Message From the President of the United States on His Travels
DWIGHT D. EISENHOWER

When the President Goes Abroad
GILBERT M. GROSVENOR

Artists Roam the World of the U. S. Air Force
GEN. CURTIS E. LEMAY, WITH 21 PAINTINGS BY NOTED AMERICAN ILLUSTRATORS

Secret of the Discus Fish GENE WOLFSHEIMER

Oldest Shipwreck Ever Found PETER THROCKMORTON

Brasília, Metropolis Made to Order HERNANE TAVARES DE SÁ, THOMAS J. ABERCROMBIE

$8.00 A YEAR $1.00 A COPY

THE JOURNAL OF THE NATIONAL GEOGRAPHIC SOCIETY WASHINGTON, D. C.

President Abroad: Eisenhower in India with Prime Minister Nehru

GILBERT M. GROSVENOR, NGS

- ◆The two-volume *Book of Birds,* edited by Gilbert H. Grosvenor and Alexander Wetmore. 328, Sept. 1948; 576, 578, Oct. 1963; 554, Oct. 1964; 480, Oct. 1966

Author:

- First Lady of the National Geographic (Elsie May Bell Grosvenor). 101-121, July 1965
- Hydrofoil Ferry "Flies" the Strait of Messina. 493-496, Apr. 1957
- ◆*The National Geographic Society and Its Magazine: A History.* Announced. 582A, Oct. 1957; 880, Dec. 1964
- The Romance of the Geographic: National Geographic Magazine Observes Its Diamond Anniversary. 516-585, Oct. 1963

Author-Photographer:

- We Followed Peary to the Pole. By Gilbert Grosvenor and Thomas W. McKnew. 469-484, Oct. 1953

Photographer:

- Alaska's Warmer Side. By Elsie May Bell Grosvenor. 737-775, June 1956
- Alexander Graham Bell Museum: Tribute to Genius. By Jean Lesage. 227-256, Aug. 1956
- Norway Cracks Her Mountain Shell. By Sydney Clark. Photos by Gilbert Grosvenor and Ole Friele Backer. 171-211, Aug. 1948
- Safari from Congo to Cairo. By Elsie May Bell Grosvenor. 721-771, Dec. 1954
- Safari Through Changing Africa. By Elsie May Bell Grosvenor. 145-198, Aug. 1953
- Turkey Paves the Path of Progress. By Maynard Owen Williams. 141-186, Aug. 1951

GROSVENOR, MRS. GILBERT HOVEY. *See* Grosvenor, Elsie May Bell

GROSVENOR, GILBERT M.:

- Associate Editor (1967-1970). 576, 583, 584, 586-588, Oct. 1967; 843, Dec. 1970; 226, Aug. 1976
- Board of Trustees member (1966-). 485, Oct. 1966; 584, 588, Oct. 1967; 843, Dec. 1970; 226, Aug. 1976
- Editor (1970-1980). 838-843, Dec. 1970; 226, Aug. 1976; 1, Jan. 1978; 427, Oct. 1980; 567, Nov. 1980; 848, Dec. 1981; 276, 278, Aug. 1982
- President of NGS (1980-). 427, Oct. 1980; 567, Nov. 1980; 276, 278, Aug. 1982
- Vice President of NGS (1967-1980). 576, 584, 587, 588, Oct. 1967; 843, Dec. 1970

Author:

- The Best of Our Land (National Parks). 1-2, July 1979
- President's Report to Members: An Exciting Year of Discovery. 820-824, Dec. 1982
- President's Report to Members. It's Been a Banner Year! 848-852, Dec. 1981
- The Unbalanced World. 1, *Special Report on Energy* (Feb. 1981)

Author-Photographer:

- The Aegean Isles: Poseidon's Playground. 733-781, Dec. 1958
- Bali by the Back Roads. By Donna K. and Gilbert M. Grosvenor. 657-697, Nov. 1969

• Canada's Winged Victory: the *Silver Dart*. 254-267, Aug. 1959
• Ceylon, the Resplendent Land. By Donna K. and Gilbert M. Grosvenor. 447-497, Apr. 1966
• Helping Holland Rebuild Her Land. By Gilbert M. Grosvenor and Charles Neave. 365-413, Sept. 1954
• Miniature Monaco. By Gilbert M. and Donna Kerkam Grosvenor. 546-573, Apr. 1963
• When the President Goes Abroad (Eisenhower Tour). 588-649, May 1960
• Yugoslavia's Window on the Adriatic. 219-247, Feb. 1962
Photographer:
• Copenhagen, Wedded to the Sea. By Stuart E. Jones. 45-79, Jan. 1963
• Italian Riviera, Land That Winter Forgot. By Howell Walker. 743-789, June 1963
• The Leakeys of Africa: Family in Search of Prehistoric Man. By Melvin M. Payne. 194-231, Feb. 1965

GROSVENOR, LILIAN: Author:
• Deaf Children Learn to Talk at Clarke School. Photos by Willard R. Culver. 379-397, Mar. 1955

GROSVENOR, MELVILLE BELL:
• Board of Trustees, Chairman (1967-1976). 576-577, 584-589, Oct. 1967; 442, Sept. 1970
• Board of Trustees, Chairman Emeritus (1976-1982). 225, 226, Aug. 1976
• Board of Trustees, member (1945-1967). 65, 65B, 65D, July 1954; 835, Dec. 1959; 882, 883, Dec. 1960; 583, 584, Oct. 1967
• Editor (1957-1967). 419-423, Mar. 1957; 270-278, Aug. 1982
• Editor Emeritus (1977-1982)
• Editor-in-Chief (1967-1977). 576-577, 584, 586, 589, Oct. 1967; 225, 226, Aug. 1976
• Melville Bell Grosvenor, A Decade of Innovation, a Lifetime of Service. By Bart McDowell. 270-278, Aug. 1982
• President of NGS (1957-1967). 419-423, Mar. 1957; 270-278, Aug. 1982
Author:
• Admiral of the Ends of the Earth (Richard E. Byrd). 36-48, July 1957
• Articles, number of (26). 275, Aug. 1982
• Exploring an Epic Year. By Melville Bell Grosvenor. 874-886, Dec. 1960
• Homeward With Ulysses. Photos by Edwin Stuart Grosvenor. 1-39, July 1973
• The Isles of Greece: Aegean Birthplace of Western Culture. Photos by Edwin Stuart Grosvenor and Winfield Parks. 147-193, Aug. 1972
• The Last Full Measure (Tribute to President Kennedy). 307-355, Mar. 1964
• A Long History of New Beginnings (National Parks). 18-29, July 1979
• The Nation Honors Admiral Richard E. Byrd (Byrd Memorial Dedication). 567-578, Apr. 1962
• National Geographic Society Presents Russell Cave to the American People. 438, Mar. 1958
• North Through History Aboard *White Mist*. Photos by Edwin Stuart Grosvenor. 1-55, July 1970
• Our Society Welcomes Its 3,000,000th Member. 579-582, Apr. 1962
• A Park to Save the Tallest Trees. 62-64, July 1966
• Robert V. Fleming, 1890-1967. 526-529, Apr. 1968
• Safe Landing on Sable, Isle of 500 Shipwrecks. 398-431, Sept. 1965
• South Seas' Tonga Hails a King. Photos by Edwin Stuart Grosvenor. 322-343, Mar. 1968
• *White Mist* Cruises to Wreck-haunted St. Pierre and Miquelon. 378-419, Sept. 1967
• World's Tallest Tree Discovered. Photos by George F. Mobley. 1-9, July 1964
• Your Society Takes Giant New Steps: The President's Annual Message to Members. By Melville Bell Grosvenor. 874-886, Dec. 1961
• Your Society's President Reports: A Year of Widening Horizons. By Melville Bell Grosvenor. 888-906, Dec. 1962
Author-Photographer:
• Around the World and the Calendar with the Geographic: The President's Annual Message. 832-866, Dec. 1959
• By Cotswold Lanes to Wold's End. 615-654, May 1948
• Corkscrew Swamp–Florida's Primeval Show Place. 98-113, Jan. 1958
• Cuba–American Sugar Bowl. 1-56, Jan. 1947
Photographer:
• The Leakeys of Africa: Family in Search of Prehistoric Man. By Melvin M. Payne. 194-231, Feb. 1965

GROSVENOR, MRS. MELVILLE BELL. *See* Revis, Anne, for article by

GROSVENOR ARCH, Utah. *See* Escalante Canyon

GROSVENOR MEDAL:
• Designed by Laura Gardin Fraser. 255, 261, Aug. 1949; 422, Mar. 1957; 516, Oct. 1963
Recipients:
Grosvenor, Gilbert H.:
• First Grosvenor Medal recipient. 253, 254, 255, 260, 261, Aug. 1949; 65G, July 1954; 449, 481, Oct. 1966
• Gilbert Grosvenor's Golden Jubilee. By Albert W. Atwood. 253-261, Aug. 1949
La Gorce, John Oliver:
• John Oliver La Gorce Is Elected Vice-Chairman of the Board, Melville Bell Grosvenor President and Editor of the National Geographic Society. 419-423, Mar. 1957
• Presentation of medal by Gilbert H. Grosvenor. 422, 423, 442, Mar. 1960; 449, Oct. 1966

GROTTOES:
• Probing Ice Caves of the Pyrenees. By Norbert Casteret. Included: Casteret Grotto. 391-404, Mar. 1953
• *See also* Caves

GROUNDNUT SCHEME: East Africa:
• Britain Tackles the East African Bush. By W. Robert Moore. 311-352, Mar. 1950

GROUNDNUTS:
• Rediscovering America's Forgotten Crops. By Noel D. Vietmeyer. Photos by Burgess Blevins. Paintings by Paul M. Breeden. 702-712, May 1981

GROUNDWATER. *See* Aquifers

GROVE, NOEL: Author:
• Bicycles Are Back–and Booming! Photos by Michael Pfleger. 671-681, May 1973
• The Caribbean: Sun, Sea, and Seething. Photos by Steve Raymer. 244-271, Feb. 1981
• Giants That Move the World's Oil: Superships. Photos by Martin Rogers. 102-124, July 1978
• Mark Twain: Mirror of America. Photos by James L. Stanfield. 300-337, Sept. 1975
• Nigeria Struggles With Boom Times. Photos by Bruno Barbey. 413-444, Mar. 1979
• North With the Wheat Cutters. Photos by James A. Sugar. 194-217, Aug. 1972
• North Yemen. Photos by Steve Raymer. 244-269, Aug. 1979
• Oil, the Dwindling Treasure. Photos by Emory Kristof. 792-825, June 1974
• Superspill: Black Day for Brittany. Photos by Martin Rogers. 124-135, July 1978
• Swing Low, Sweet Chariot! Photos by Bruce Dale. 2-35, July 1983
• Taiwan Confronts a New Era. Photos by John Chao. 93-119, Jan. 1982
• The Two Worlds of Michigan. Photos by James L. Amos. 802-843, June 1979
• Venezuela's Crisis of Wealth. Photos by Robert W. Madden. 175-209, Aug. 1976
• Vestmannaeyjar: Up From the Ashes. Photos by Robert S. Patton. 690-701, May 1977
• A Village Fights for Its Life. 40-67, July 1973
• Wild Cargo: the Business of Smuggling Animals. Photos by Steve Raymer. 287-315, Mar. 1981

GROWING Pains Beset Puerto Rico. By William H. Nicholas. Photos by Justin Locke. 419-460, Apr. 1951

GROWING Up in Montana. Photos by Nicholas deVore III. 650-657, May 1976

GROWING Up With Snowflake (White Gorilla). By Arthur J. Riopelle. Photos by Michael Kuh. NGS research grant. 491-503, Oct. 1970

GRUENING, ERNEST: Author:
• Alaska Proudly Joins the Union. Photos by Thomas J. Abercrombie. 43-83, July 1959
• Lonely Wonders of Katmai. Photos by Winfield Parks. 800-831, June 1963

GRUNION, the Fish That Spawns on Land. By Clarence P. Idyll. Photos by Robert F. Sisson. 714-723, May 1969

GUADALAJARA, Mexico:
- The Most Mexican City, Guadalajara. By Bart McDowell. Photos by Volkmar Wentzel. 412-441, Mar. 1967

GUADALUPE, NUESTRA SEÑORA DE (Spanish Galleon):
- Graveyard of the Quicksilver Galleons. By Mendel Peterson. Photos by Jonathan Blair. 850-876, Dec. 1979

GUADALUPE MOUNTAINS NATIONAL PARK, Texas:
- Guadalupe's Trails in Summer. By Edward Abbey. 135-141, July 1979

GUADELOUPE (Island), West Indies:
- A Fresh Breeze Stirs the Leewards. By Carleton Mitchell. Photos by Winfield Parks. 488-537, Oct. 1966

GUAM (Island), Pacific Ocean:
- Magellan: First Voyage Around the World. By Alan Villiers. Photos by Bruce Dale. 721-753, June 1976
- Starfish Threaten Pacific Reefs. By James A. Sugar. 340-353, Mar. 1970
- *See also* Pacific Fleet

GUANA (Island), Virgin Islands:
- *Carib* Cruises the West Indies. By Carleton Mitchell. 1-56, Jan. 1948

GUANACOS: Wild Camels of South America. By William L. Franklin. NGS research grant. 63-75, July 1981

GUANAJUATO, Mexico:
- Experiment in International Living. By Hugh M. Hamill, Jr. 323-350, Mar. 1953

GUAÑAPE CULTURE:
- Finding the Tomb of a Warrior-God. By William Duncan Strong. Photos by Clifford Evans, Jr. 453-482, Apr. 1947

GUANO AND GUANO INDUSTRY:
- Peru Profits from Sea Fowl. By Robert Cushman Murphy. Photos by author and Grace E. Barstow Murphy. 395-413, Mar. 1959

GUANTÁNAMO: Keystone in the Caribbean. By Jules B. Billard. Photos by W. E. Garrett and Thomas Nebbia. 420-436, Mar. 1961

GUARDIAN of the Gulf. By Thomas J. Abercrombie. Photos by the author and Lynn Abercrombie. 344-377, Sept. 1981

GUATEMALA:
- Earthquake in Guatemala. By Bart McDowell. Photos by W. E. Garrett and Robert W. Madden. 810-829, June 1976
- Easter Week in Indian Guatemala. By John Scofield. 406-417, Mar. 1960
- Editorials. By Gilbert M. Grosvenor. 719, June 1976. By Wilbur E. Garrett. 137, Aug. 1981
- Guatemala, Maya and Modern. By Louis de la Haba. Photos by Joseph J. Scherschel. 661-689, Nov. 1974
- Guatemala Revisited. By Luis Marsden. 525-564, Oct. 1947
- The Maya. 729-811, Dec. 1975
I. Children of Time. By Howard La Fay. Photos by David Alan Harvey. 729-767; II. Riddle of the Glyphs. By George E. Stuart. Photos by Otis Imboden. 768-791; III. Resurrecting the Grandeur of Tikal. By William R. Coe. 792-798; IV. A Traveler's Tale of Ancient Tikal. Paintings by Peter Spier. Text by Alice J. Hall. 799-811
- Maya Art Treasures Discovered in Cave. By George E. Stuart. Photos by Wilbur E. Garrett. 220-235, Aug. 1981
- ◆ *The Mysterious Maya.* 1977
- The Quetzal, Fabulous Bird of Maya Land. By Anne LaBastille Bowes. Photos by David G. Allen. 141-150, Jan. 1969
- "Pyramids" of the New World. By Neil Merton Judd. Included: Piedras Negras, Tikal. 105-128, Jan. 1948
- Troubled Times for Central America. By Wilbur E. Garrett, Editor. 58-61, July 1981
- Who Were the "Mound Builders"? By George E. Stuart. 783-801, Dec. 1972

GUAYAQUIL, Ecuador:
- Ecuador–Low and Lofty Land Astride the Equator. By Loren McIntyre. 259-298, Feb. 1968

GUAYMAS, Mexico:
- Tracking America's Man in Orbit. By Kenneth F. Weaver. Photos by Robert F. Sisson. 184-217, Feb. 1962

GUAYMI INDIANS:
- Exploring the Past in Panama. By Matthew W. Stirling. Photos by Richard H. Stewart. NGS research grant. 373-399, Mar. 1949

GUAYULE:
- Rediscovering America's Forgotten Crops. By Noel D. Vietmeyer. Photos by Burgess Blevins. Paintings by Paul M. Breeden. Included: Rubber from the guayule. 702-712, May 1981

GUERNSEY (Island), English Channel:
- Britain's "French" Channel Islands. By James Cerruti. Photos by James L. Amos. 710-740, May 1971

GUIANAN COCKS-OF-THE-ROCK:
- Cock-of-the-Rock: Jungle Dandy. By Pepper W. Trail. NGS research grant. 831-839, Dec. 1983
- Strange Courtship of the Cock-of-the-Rock. By E. Thomas Gilliard. NGS research grant. 134-140, Jan. 1962

A **GUIDE** to Parklands (United States National Parks System). 111-123, July 1979

GUIDED MISSILES:
- Cape Canaveral's 6,000-mile Shooting Gallery. By Allan C. Fisher, Jr. Photos by Luis Marden and Thomas Nebbia. 421-471, Oct. 1959

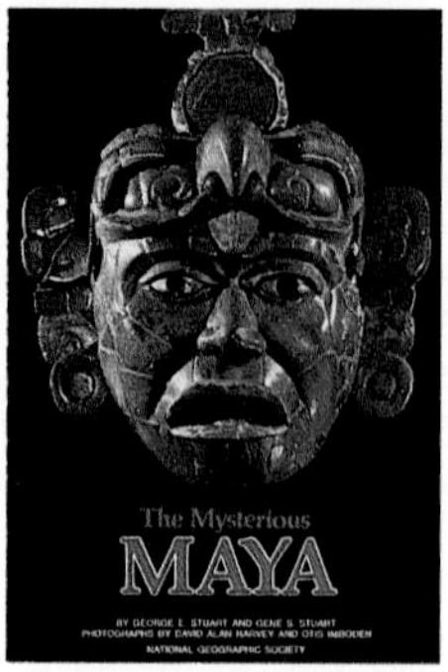

JOSEPH J. SCHERSCHEL, NGS

Guatemala: idol during Holy Week

• Our Air Age Speeds Ahead. By F. Barrows Colton. 249-272, Feb. 1948
• Seeing the Earth from 80 Miles Up. By Clyde T. Holliday. 511-528, Oct. 1950
• *See also* Nike

GUILD, EUGENE R.:
Author-Photographer:
• Exploring America's Great Sand Barrier Reef. Photos by John E. Fletcher and author. 325-350, Sept. 1947

GUILIN, China's Beauty Spot. By W. E. Garrett. 536-563, Oct. 1979

GUINEA:
• Freedom Speaks French in Ouagadougou. By John Scofield. 153-203, Aug. 1966

GUINEA, Gulf of:
• *Calypso* Explores an Undersea Canyon. By Jacques-Yves Cousteau. Photos by Bates Littlehales. Included: Islands: Annobón, Príncipe, São Tomé. NGS research grant. 373-396, Mar. 1958

GUINEY, LOUISE IMOGEN:
• Literary Landmarks of Massachusetts. By William H. Nicholas. Photos by B. Anthony Stewart and John E. Fletcher. 279-310, Mar. 1950

GULF COAST, U. S.:
• Cajunland, Louisiana's French-speaking Coast. By Bern Keating. Photos by Charles Harbutt and Franke Keating. 353-391, Mar. 1966
• Cruising Florida's Western Waterways. By Rube Allyn. Photos by Bates Littlehales. 49-76, Jan. 1955
• The Gulf's Workaday Waterway. By Gordon Young. Photos by Charles O'Rear. Included: The Gulf Intracoastal Waterway. 200-223, Feb. 1978
• Hurricane! By Ben Funk. Photos by Robert W. Madden. 346-379, Sept. 1980
• Louisiana Trades with the World. By Frederick Simpich. Photos by J. Baylor Roberts. 705-738, Dec. 1947
• The Lower Mississippi. By Willard Price. Photos by W. D. Vaughn. 681-725, Nov. 1960
• Oil, the Dwindling Treasure. By Noel Grove. Photos by Emory Kristof. Included: Plans for superports in Alabama, Louisiana, and Texas. 792-825, June 1974
• The Pink Birds of Texas. By Paul A. Zahl. 641-654, Nov. 1949
• Roseate Spoonbills, Radiant Birds of the Gulf Coast. By Robert Porter Allen. Photos by Frederick Kent Truslow. 274-288, Feb. 1962
• Troubled Odyssey of Vietnamese Fishermen. By Harvey Arden. Photos by Steve Wall. 378-395, Sept. 1981
• Where Oil and Wildlife Mix. By Steven C. Wilson and Karen C. Hayden. 145-173, Feb. 1981
• *See also* Houston; Key West; Mississippi River Delta; Mobile; New Orleans; Tampa Bay

GULF OF CALIFORNIA. *See* Raza, Isla

GULF STREAM:
• Blue-water Plankton: Ghosts of the Gulf Stream. By William M. Hamner. NGS research grant. 530-545, Oct. 1974
• Night Life in the Gulf Stream. By Paul A. Zahl. 391-418, Mar. 1954
• Strange Babies of the Sea (Plankton). By Hilary B. Moore. Paintings by Craig Phillips and Jacqueline Hutton. NGS research grant. 41-56, July 1952

GULL ISLAND, Quebec, Canada:
• Sea Bird Cities Off Audubon's Labrador. By Arthur A. Allen. NGS research grant. 755-774, June 1948

GULLERS, KARL W.: Photographer:
• Viking Festival in the Shetlands. 853-862, Dec. 1954

GULLS:
• Sea Bird Cities Off Audubon's Labrador. By Arthur A. Allen. Included: Black-backed Gull, Herring Gull, Ring-billed Gull. NGS research grant. 755-774, June 1948
• Sea Birds of Isla Raza. By Lewis Wayne Walker. Included: Yellow-footed and Heermann's Gulls. NGS research grant. 239-248, Feb. 1951

GUNBOATS, Ironclad:
• How We Found the *Monitor.* By John G. Newton. NGS research grant. 48-61, Jan. 1975

GUT, Silkworm:
• Spain's Silkworm Gut. By Luis Marden. 100-108, July 1951

GUTHRIE, RUSSELL D.: Author:
• Re-creating a Vanished World. 294-301, Mar. 1972

GUTMANN, JOHN: Photographer:
• Kunming Pilgrimage. 213-226, Feb. 1950

GUYANA. *See* former name, British Guiana

GYANGTSE, Tibet:
• A Woman Paints the Tibetans. By Lafugie. 659-692, May 1949

GYPSIES:
• The Camargue, Land of Cowboys and Gypsies. By Eugene L. Kammerman. 667-699, May 1956
• France's Wild, Watery South, the Camargue. By William Davenport. 696-726, May 1973
◆ *Gypsies, Wanderers of the World.* Announced. 880-884, June 1970
• Gypsy Cave Dwellers of Andalusia (Spain). 572-582, Oct. 1957
• Hungary: Changing Homeland of a Tough, Romantic People. By Bart McDowell. Photos by Albert Moldvay and Joseph J. Scherschel. 443-483, Apr. 1971
• Speaking of Spain. By Luis Marden. 415-456, Apr. 1950
• When Gypsies Gather at Appleby Fair. Photos by Bruce Dale. 848-869, June 1972

GYPSY MOTH:
• New Tricks Outwit Our Insect Enemies. By Hal Higdon. Photos by Robert F. Sisson and Emory Kristof. 380-399, Sept. 1972

H

HD-4:
• Hydrofoil boat, *HD-4,* designed by Alexander Graham Bell. 493, 495, 496, Apr. 1957; 257, 264, Aug. 1959; 554-555, Oct. 1963

H.R.H. Philip, Prince, Duke of Edinburgh, Introduces to Members the Narrative of His Round-the-World Tour. 583-584, Nov. 1957
• *See also* Philip, Prince, Duke of Edinburgh

HA ON (Kibbutz), Israel:
• Our Life on a Border Kibbutz. By Carol and Al Abrams. Photos by Al Abrams. 364-391, Sept. 1970

HÂ-ÂK VÂ-ÂK (Hâ-âk Lying Site), Arizona:
• Seeking the Secret of the Giants. By Frank M. Setzler. Photos by Richard H. Stewart. 390-404, Sept. 1952

HABER, HEINZ: Author:
• Space Satellites, Tools of Earth Research. Paintings by William N. Palmstrom. 487-509, Apr. 1956

HABITAT DESTRUCTION:
▪ Rain Forest. Cover, 49, Jan. 1983
• Tropical Rain Forests. 2-65, Jan. 1983
Nature's Dwindling Treasures. By Peter T. White. Photos by James P. Blair. Paintings by Barron Storey. 2-47; Teeming Life of a Rain Forest. By Carol and David Hughes. 49-65

HABSBURGS (Rulers):
• The Vienna Treasures and Their Collectors. By John Walker. Included: Kunsthistorisches Museum. 737-776, June 1950

HADAR, Ethiopia:
• Ethiopia Yields First "Family" of Early Man. By Donald C. Johanson. Photos by David Brill. NGS research grant. 790-811, Dec. 1976

HADJ. *See* Hajj

HAGEN, KENNETH S.: Author:
• Following the Ladybug Home. Photos by Robert F. Sisson. 543-553, Apr. 1970

HAGEN, TONI: Author-Photographer:
• Afoot in Roadless Nepal. 361-405, Mar. 1960

HAGERSTOWN VALLEY, Maryland:
• Appalachian Valley Pilgrimage. By Catherine Bell Palmer. Photos by Justin Locke. 1-32, July 1949

The **HAGUE** ('s Gravenhage), Netherlands:
• Mid-century Holland Builds Her Future. By Sydney Clark. 747-778, Dec. 1950
• The Netherlands: Nation at War With the Sea. By Alan Villiers. Photos by Adam Woolfitt. 530-571, Apr. 1968

HAIFA, Israel:
• An Archeologist Looks at Palestine. By Nelson Glueck. 739-752, Dec. 1947

G-H

HAILE SELASSIE I, Emperor (Ethiopia):
• Ethiopian Adventure. By Nathaniel T. Kenney. Photos by James P. Blair. 548-582, Apr. 1965

HAITI, Republic of:
• The Caribbean: Sun, Sea, and Seething. By Noel Grove. Photos by Steve Raymer. 244-271, Feb. 1981
• Haiti: Beyond Mountains, More Mountains. By Carolyn Bennett Patterson. Photos by Thomas Nebbia. 70-97, Jan. 1976
• Haiti–West Africa in the West Indies. By John Scofield. 226-259, Feb. 1961

HAJJ:
• From America to Mecca on Airborne Pilgrimage. By Abdul Ghafur. 1-60, July 1953
• Pilgrimage to Mecca. By Muhammad Abdul-Rauf. Photos by Mehmet Biber. 581-607, Nov. 1978
• Saudi Arabia: Beyond the Sands of Mecca. By Thomas J. Abercrombie. 1-53, Jan. 1966
• The Sword and the Sermon. By Thomas J. Abercrombie. 3-45, July 1972

HAKLUYT, RICHARD:
• Founders of Virginia. By Sir Evelyn Wrench. Photos by B. Anthony Stewart. 433-462, Apr. 1948

HALE, SARAH JOSEPHA:
• Literary Landmarks of Massachusetts. By William H. Nicholas. Photos by B. Anthony Stewart and John E. Fletcher. 279-310, Mar. 1950

HALEAKALA NATIONAL PARK, Hawaii:
• Maui, Where Old Hawaii Still Lives. By Kenneth F. Weaver. Photos by Gordon W. Gahan. 514-543, Apr. 1971

HALF DOME (Massif), Yosemite National Park, California:
• Climbing Half Dome the Hard Way. By Galen Rowell. 782-791, June 1974

HALIFAX RACE (Marblehead-Halifax):
• Down East to Nova Scotia. By Winfield Parks. 853-879, June 1964

HALL, ALICE J.: Author:
• Benjamin Franklin, Philosopher of Dissent. Photos by Linda Bartlett. 93-123, July 1975
• Brooklyn: The Other Side of the Bridge. Photos by Robert W. Madden. 580-613, May 1983
• Buffalo Bill and the Enduring West. Photos by James L. Amos. 76-103, July 1981
• The Climb Up Cone Crater. Photos by Edgar D. Mitchell and Alan B. Shepard, Jr. 136-148, July 1971
• Dazzling Legacy of an Ancient Quest (Egypt). 293-311, Mar. 1977
• Georgia, Unlimited. Photos by Bill Weems. 212-245, Aug. 1978
• The Hudson: "That River's Alive." Photos by Ted Spiegel. 62-89, Jan. 1978
• A Lady From China's Past. Photos from *China Pictorial.* 660-681, May 1974
• A Traveler's Tale of Ancient Tikal. Paintings by Peter Spier. 799-811, Dec. 1975

HALL, MELVIN: Author-Photographer:
• Vézelay, Hill of the Pilgrims. 229-247, Feb. 1953

HALL, ROSS: Photographer:
• Idaho Loggers Battle a River. 117-130, July 1951

The **HALLOWED** Isle, Mont Saint Michel. By Kenneth MacLeish. Photos by Cotton Coulson. 820-831, June 1977

HALLSTROM, E. J. L.:
• Sheep Airlift in New Guinea. Photos by Ned Blood. 831-844, Dec. 1949

HAMAMATSU, Japan:
• Japan's Warriors of the Wind. Photos by David Alan Harvey. Text by John Eliot. Contents: Annual kite festival. 551-561, Apr. 1977

HAMI, Sinkiang:
• The Caves of the Thousand Buddhas. By Franc and Jean Shor. 383-415, Mar. 1951

HAMILL, HUGH M., Jr.:
Author-Photographer:
• Experiment in International Living. 323-350, Mar. 1953

HAMILTON, ROGER: Author:
• Can We Harness the Wind? Photos by Emory Kristof. 812-829, Dec. 1975

HAMILTON, WILLIAM J., III: Author:
• The Living Sands of the Namib. Photos by Carol and David Hughes. 364-377, Sept. 1983

HAMILTON (River), Labrador, Newfoundland:
• Labrador Canoe Adventure. By Andrew Brown and Ralph Gray. 65-99, July 1951

HAMILTON and *Scourge:* Ghost Ships of the War of 1812. By Daniel A. Nelson. Photos by Emory Kristof. Paintings by Richard Schlecht. 289-313, Mar. 1983

HAMMARSKJÖLD, DAG:
Author-Photographer:
• A New Look at Everest. 87-93, Jan. 1961

HAMMOND, JAY S.: Author:
• Sharing Alaska: How Much for Parks? Opposing views by Jay S. Hammond and Cecil D. Andrus. 60-65, July 1979

HAMMOND, NORMAN: Author:
• Unearthing the Oldest Known Maya. Photos by Lowell Georgia and Martha Cooper. 126-140, July 1982

HAMMOND, THOMAS T.: Author:
• An American in Russia's Capital. Photos by Dean Conger. 297-351, Mar. 1966
• Firsthand Look at the Soviet Union. Photos by Erich Lessing. 352-407, Sept. 1959

HAMMURAPI, King (Babylon):
• Ancient Mesopotamia: A Light That Did Not Fail. By E. A. Speiser. Paintings by H. M. Herget. 41-105, Jan. 1951

HAMNER, WILLIAM M.: Author:
• Blue-water Plankton: Ghosts of the Gulf Stream. NGS research grant. 530-545, Oct. 1974
• Strange World of Palau's Salt Lakes. Photos by David Doubilet. 264-282, Feb. 1982

HAN DYNASTY TOMBS:
• China Unveils Her Newest Treasures. Photos by Robert W. Madden. 848-857, Dec. 1974
• A Lady From China's Past. Photos from *China Pictorial.* Text by Alice J. Hall. 660-681, May 1974

HANDCLASP in Space: Apollo-Soyuz. By Thomas Y. Canby. 183-187, Feb. 1976

HANDICRAFTS. *See* Crafts; Folk Art

HANG GLIDERS:
• Happy Birthday, Otto Lilienthal! By Russell Hawkes. Photos by James Collison. 286-292, Feb. 1972

HANKOW, China:
• Along the Yangtze, Main Street of China. By W. Robert Moore. 325-356, Mar. 1948

HANNIBAL, Missouri:
• Mark Twain: Mirror of America. By Noel Grove. Photos by James L. Stanfield. 300-337, Sept. 1975
• Tom Sawyer's Town. By Jerry Allen. 121-140, July 1956
• The West Through Boston Eyes. By Stewart Anderson. 733-776, June 1949

HANSEN'S DISEASE:
• The Astonishing Armadillo. By Eleanor E. Storrs. Photos by Bianca Lavies. Included: Immunology research with leprosy bacilli cultivated in armadillos. 820-830, June 1982
• Molokai–Forgotten Hawaii. By Ethel A. Starbird. Photos by Richard A. Cooke III. Included: Kalaupapa lepers' colony. 188-219, Aug. 1981

HAPPY Birthday, Otto Lilienthal! By Russell Hawkes. Photos by James Collison. 286-292, Feb. 1972

HAPPY-GO-LUCKY Trinidad and Tobago. By Charles Allmon. 35-75, Jan. 1953

HAPSBURGS (Rulers). *See* Habsburgs

HARBERTON, Estancia, Tierra del Fuego:
• Housewife at the End of the World. By Rae Natalie P. Goodall. Photos by James L. Stanfield. 130-150, Jan. 1971

HARBIN, China:
• In Manchuria Now. By W. Robert Moore. 389-414, Mar. 1947

HARBUTT, CHARLES:
Author-Photographer:
• Eyewitness to War in the Holy Land. 782-795, Dec. 1967
Photographer:
• Cajunland, Louisiana's French-speaking Coast. By Bern Keating. Photos by Charles Harbutt and Franke Keating. 353-391, Mar. 1966
• Today Along the Natchez Trace, Pathway Through History. By Bern Keating. 641-667, Nov. 1968

• Where Jesus Walked. By Howard La Fay. 739-781, Dec. 1967

The **HARD** Life of the Prairie Dog. By Tim W. Clark. Photos by Patricia Caulfield. NGS research grant. 270-281, Aug. 1979

HARDING, WARREN GAMALIEL:
• The Living White House. By Lonnelle Aikman. 593-643, Nov. 1966
• Profiles of the Presidents: IV. America Enters the Modern Era. By Frank Freidel. 537-577, Oct. 1965

HARDY, LAYMOND: Photographer:
• Alligators: Dragons in Distress. By Archie Carr. Photos by Treat Davidson and Laymond Hardy. 133-148, Jan. 1967

HARE, CLYDE: Photographer:
• Banks Island: Eskimo Life on the Polar Sea. By William O. Douglas. 703-735, May 1964
• Pittsburgh, Pattern for Progress. By William J. Gill. 342-371, Mar. 1965

HARGRAVE, THOMAS J.:
Author-Photographer:
• Photographing a Volcano in Action. 561-563, Oct. 1955

HARLEM, New York, New York:
• Editorial. By Gilbert M. Grosvenor. 147, Feb. 1977
• To Live in Harlem. . . . By Frank Hercules. Photos by LeRoy Woodson, Jr. 178-207, Feb. 1977

HARMONY HOLLOW (Farm), Virginia:
• The World of My Apple Tree. By Robert F. Sisson. 836-847, June 1972

HARMSWORTH, SIR LEICESTER: Renaissance Library:
• Folger: Biggest Little Library in the World. By Joseph T. Foster. Photos by B. Anthony Stewart and John E. Fletcher. 411-424, Sept. 1951

HARNESSING the Wind. 38, *Special Report on Energy* (Feb. 1981)

HAROLD II, King (England):
• 900 Years Ago: the Norman Conquest. By Kenneth M. Setton. Photos by George F. Mobley. 206-251, Aug. 1966

HARP SEALS:
• Life or Death for the Harp Seal. By David M. Lavigne. Photos by William R. Curtsinger. 129-142, Jan. 1976

HARPERS FERRY, West Virginia:
• History Awakens at Harpers Ferry. By Volkmar Wentzel. 399-416, Mar. 1957

HARRER, HEINRICH:
Author-Photographer:
• My Life in Forbidden Lhasa. 1-48, July 1955

HARRINGTON, PHILLIP:
Photographer:
• Athens: Her Golden Past Still Lights the World. By Kenneth F. Weaver. 100-137, July 1963

HARRIS, JENNIE E.: Author:
• Sponge Fishermen of Tarpon Springs. 119-136, Jan. 1947

JAMES A. SUGAR

Manatees: Orville, a half-ton manatee

HARRISON, BENJAMIN:
• Profiles of the Presidents: III. The American Giant Comes of Age. By Frank Freidel. 660-711, May 1965

HARRISON, WILLIAM HENRY:
• Profiles of the Presidents: II. A Restless Nation Moves West. By Frank Freidel. 80-121, Jan. 1965

HARRY FRANK GUGGENHEIM FOUNDATION: Study Grant:
• Jackals of the Serengeti. NGS research grant. 840, Dec. 1980

HART, KIM: Photographer:
• Ancient Shipwreck Yields New Facts–and a Strange Cargo. By Peter Throckmorton. Photos by Kim Hart and Joseph J. Scherschel. 282-300, Feb. 1969

HART, VAL: Author:
• Pack Trip Through the Smokies. Photos by Robert F. Sisson. 473-502, Oct. 1952

HART DYKE, ZOË, LADY:
• Silkworms in England Spin for the Queen. By John E. H. Nolan. 689-704, May 1953

HARTLEY, FRED L.:
• What Six Experts Say. 70-73, *Special Report on Energy* (Feb. 1981)

HARTMAN, DANIEL S.: Author:
• Florida's Manatees, Mermaids in Peril. Photos by James A. Sugar. 342-353, Sept. 1969

HARTZ, JIM: Author:
• New Jersey: A State of Surprise. Photos by Bob Krist and Michael S. Yamashita. 568-599, Nov. 1981

HARTZOG, GEORGE B., Jr.: Author:
• The Next 100 Years: A Master Plan for Yellowstone. 632-637, May 1972
• Parkscape, U.S.A.: Tomorrow in Our National Parks. 48-93, July 1966

HARVESTING:
• North With the Wheat Cutters. By Noel Grove. Photos by James A. Sugar. 194-217, Aug. 1972

HARVEY, DAVID ALAN:
Photographer:
• Honduras: Eye of the Storm. By Mike Edwards. 608-637, Nov. 1983
• Hunters of the Lost Spirit: Alaskans, Canadians. By Priit J. Vesilind. 150-189, Feb. 1983
• Japan's Warriors of the Wind. Text by John Eliot. 551-561, Apr. 1977
• Kampuchea Wakens From a Nightmare. By Peter T. White. 590-623, May 1982
• Malaysia: Youthful Nation With Growing Pains. By William S. Ellis. 635-667, May 1977
• The Maya, Children of Time. By Howard La Fay. 729-767, Dec. 1975
• My Backyard, the Adirondacks. By Anne LaBastille. 616-639, May 1975
• Our National Parks. 1-152, July 1979

G-H

• Puget Sound, Sea Gate of the Pacific Northwest. By William Graves. 71-97, Jan. 1977
• Spain: It's a Changed Country. By Peter T. White. 297-331, Mar. 1978
• A Sumatran Journey. By Harvey Arden. 406-430, Mar. 1981
• This Is My Island, Tangier. By Harold G. Wheatley. 700-725, Nov. 1973
• Tunisia: Sea, Sand, Success. By Mike Edwards. 184-217, Feb. 1980
• The Virginians. By Mike W. Edwards. 588-617, Nov. 1974

HARVEY, WILLIAM:
• The British Way. By Sir Evelyn Wrench. 421-541, Apr. 1949

HASHEMITE Jordan, Arab Heartland. By John Scofield. 841-856, Dec. 1952

HASIDIC JEWS:
• The Pious Ones (Brooklyn's Hasidic Jews). By Harvey Arden. Photos by Nathan Benn. 276-298, Aug. 1975

HASTINGS, Battle of (1066):
• 900 Years Ago: The Norman Conquest. By Kenneth M. Setton. Photos by George F. Mobley. 206-251, Aug. 1966

HATCH RIVER EXPEDITIONS:
• Shooting Rapids in Dinosaur Country. By Jack Breed. Photos by author and Justin Locke. 363-390, Mar. 1954

HATCHETFISH, Torchbearers of the Deep. By Paul A. Zahl. 713-714, May 1958

HATTERAS, Cape, North Carolina:
• Exploring America's Great Sand Barrier Reef. By Eugene R. Guild. Photos by John E. Fletcher and author. 325-350, Sept. 1947
• How We Found the *Monitor.* By John G. Newton. Contents: Search in two expeditions for the wreck of the first ironclad gunboat, lost off Cape Hatteras during the Civil War. NGS research grant. 48-61, Jan. 1975
• Lonely Cape Hatteras, Besieged by the Sea. By William S. Ellis. Photos by Emory Kristof. 393-421, Sept. 1969
• October Holiday on the Outer Banks. By Nike Anderson. Photos by J. Baylor Roberts. 501-529, Oct. 1955

HAUN, DECLAN: Photographer:
• Quebec: French City in an Anglo-Saxon World. By Kenneth MacLeish. Photos by James L. Stanfield and Declan Haun. 416-442, Mar. 1971

HAUNTING Heart of the Everglades. By Andrew H. Brown. Photos by author and Willard R. Culver. 145-173, Feb. 1948

HAURY, EMIL W.: Author:
• The Hohokam: First Masters of the American Desert. Photos by Helga Teiwes. 670-695, May 1967

HAVANA (Habana), Cuba:
• Cuba–American Sugar Bowl. By Melville Bell Grosvenor. 1-56, Jan. 1947

ROBERT W. MADDEN, NGS

Kauai: waterfalls cascade down mile-high Waialeale

• Inside Cuba Today. By Fred Ward. 32-69, Jan. 1977

HAVASUPAI INDIAN RESERVATION, Grand Canyon, Arizona:
• Indian Shangri-La of the Grand Canyon. By Jay Johnston. Photos by Terry Eiler. 355-373, Mar. 1970
• Land of the Havasupai. By Jack Breed. 655-674, May 1948

HAVE Excavations on the Island of Thera Solved the Riddle of the Minoans? By Spyridon Marinatos. Photos by Otis Imboden. 702-726, May 1972

HAVE We Solved the Mysteries of the Moon? By Kenneth F. Weaver. Paintings by William H. Bond. 309-325, Sept. 1973

HAWAII:
• Because It Rains on Hawaii. By Frederick Simpich, Jr. 571-610, Nov. 1949
• A Canoe Helps Hawaii Recapture Her Past. By Herb Kawainui Kane. Photos by David Hiser. 468-489, Apr. 1976
• Captain Cook: The Man Who Mapped the Pacific. By Alan Villiers. Photos by Gordon W. Gahan. 297-349, Sept. 1971
• The Case of the Killer Caterpillars. By Steven L. Montgomery. Photos by Robert F. Sisson. Contents: Predatory inchworms found only in the Hawaiian Islands. 219-225, Aug. 1983
▲ *Close-up: U.S.A., Hawaii,* supplement. Text on reverse. Apr. 1976
• Editorial. By Wilbur E. Garrett. 557, Nov. 1983
• The Flowers That Say "Aloha." By Deena Clark. Photos by Robert B. Goodman. 121-131, Jan. 1967
◆ *Hawaii.* Announced. 880-884, June 1970
▲ *Hawaii,* Atlas series supplement. July 1960
• Hawaii, Island of Fire and Flowers. By Gordon Young. Photos by Robert W. Madden. 399-425, Mar. 1975
▲ *Hawaii,* The Making of America series. Included: Polynesian Arrival, Hawaii in Transition, Labor for Sugar, Hawaii as Territory, Hawaii as State. Nov. 1983
• Hawaii, U.S.A. By Frederick Simpich, Jr. Photos by Thomas Nebbia. 1-45, July 1960
• Hawaii's Far-flung Wildlife Paradise. By John L. Eliot. Photos by Jonathan Blair. Contents: Hawaiian Islands National Wildlife Refuge. 670-691, May 1978
• *Hokule'a* Follows the Stars to Tahiti. By David Lewis. Photos by Nicholas deVore III. 512-537, Oct. 1976
• Humpbacks: The Gentle Whales. By Sylvia A. Earle. Photos by Al Giddings. NGS research grant. 2-17, Jan. 1979
• In Hawaii's Crystal Sea, A Galaxy of Life Fills the Night. By Kenneth Brower. Photos by William R. Curtsinger and Chris Newbert. 834-847, Dec. 1981

● Isles of the Pacific. 732-793, Dec. 1974
I. The Coming of the Polynesians. By Kenneth P. Emory. 732-745; II. Wind, Wave, Star, and Bird. By David Lewis. Photos by Nicholas deVore III. 747-781; III. The Pathfinders. Paintings by Herb Kawainui Kane. 756-769; IV. Problems in Paradise. By Mary and Laurance S. Rockefeller. Photos by Thomas Nebbia. 782-793
● Kamehameha–Hawaii's Warrior King. By Louise E. Levathes. Photos by Steve Raymer. Paintings by Herb Kawainui Kane. 558-599, Nov. 1983
● New Light on the Singing Whales. Introduction by Roger Payne. Photos by Flip Nicklin. NGS research grant. 463-477, Apr. 1982
● Precious Corals, Hawaii's Deep-sea Jewels. By Richard W. Grigg. Photos by David Doubilet. 719-732, May 1979
● Saving the Nene, World's Rarest Goose. By S. Dillon Ripley. Photos by Jerry Chong. 745-754, Nov. 1965
● Unsung Beauties of Hawaii's Coral Reefs (Nudibranchs). By Paul A. Zahl. 510-525, Oct. 1959
● YWCA: International Success Story. By Mary French Rockefeller. Photos by Otis Imboden. 904-933, Dec. 1963
● *See also* Honolulu; Kauai; Maui; Molokai; Oahu

HAWAII VOLCANOES NATIONAL PARK, Hawaii:
● Fountain of Fire in Hawaii (Kilauea Iki Crater). By Frederick Simpich, Jr. Photos by Robert B. Goodman and Robert Wenkam. 303-327, Mar. 1960
● Hawaii, Island of Fire and Flowers. By Gordon Young. Photos by Robert W. Madden. 399-425, Mar. 1975
● Photographing a Volcano in Action. By Thomas J. Hargrave. 561-563, Oct. 1955
● Volcanic Fires of the 50th State: Hawaii National Park. By Paul A. Zahl. 793-823, June 1959

HAWAIIAN ISLANDS NATIONAL WILDLIFE REFUGE:
● Hawaii's Far-flung Wildlife Paradise. By John L. Eliot. Photos by Jonathan Blair. 670-691, May 1978

HAWKES, RUSSELL: Author:
● Happy Birthday, Otto Lilienthal! Photos by James Collison. 286-292, Feb. 1972

HAWKS:
● Can the Cooper's Hawk Survive? By Noel Snyder. Photos by author and Helen Snyder. NGS research grant. 433-442, Mar. 1974
● A New Light Dawns on Bird Photography. By Arthur A. Allen. Included: Cooper's hawk, Peregrine falcon, Red-tailed hawk, Sparrow hawk; and Falconry. 774-790, June 1948

HAWTHORNE, NATHANIEL:
● Literary Landmarks of Massachusetts. By William H. Nicholas. Photos by B. Anthony Stewart and John E. Fletcher. 279-310, Mar. 1950

HAY, JACOB: Author:
● The FBI: Public Friend Number One. Photos by Robert F. Sisson. 860-886, June 1961

HAYASHIDA, TSUNEO: **Author-Photographer:**
● The Japanese Crane, Bird of Happiness. 542-556, Oct. 1983

HAYDEN, CARL: Author:
● The Nation's Capitol Revealed as Never Before. 1-3, Jan. 1964

HAYDEN, KAREN C.: **Author-Photographer:**
● Where Oil and Wildlife Mix. By Steven C. Wilson and Karen C. Hayden. 145-173, Feb. 1981

HAYDON, Mount, Alaska:
● First American Ascent of Mount St. Elias. By Maynard M. Miller. 229-248, Feb. 1948

HAYES, RUTHERFORD B.:
● Profiles of the Presidents: III. The American Giant Comes of Age. By Frank Freidel. 660-711, May 1965

HAYS, Kansas, at the Nation's Heart. By Margaret M. Detwiler. Photos by John E. Fletcher. 461-490, Apr. 1952

HEADHUNTERS:
● Roaming India's Naga Hills. By S. Dillon Ripley. Included: Angami, Kalyo Kengyu, and Rengma tribes. 247-264, Feb. 1955
● To the Land of the Head-hunters (New Guinea). By E. Thomas Gilliard. Included: Sepik River tribes of Gaikarobi, Iatmul, Kanganaram, Malingai, and Telefolmin. NGS research grant. 437-486, Oct. 1955
● *See also* Asmat; Iban

HEARST SAN SIMEON STATE HISTORICAL MONUMENT, California:
● California's Wonderful One (State Highway No. 1). By Frank Cameron. Photos by B. Anthony Stewart. 571-617, Nov. 1959

HEART of the Bluegrass. By Charles McCarry. Photos by J. Bruce Baumann. 634-659, May 1974

HEART of the Canadian Rockies. By Elizabeth A. Moize. Photos by Jim Brandenburg. 757-779, June 1980

HEART RESEARCH:
● Hunting the Heartbeat of a Whale. By Paul Dudley White and Samuel W. Matthews. NGS research grant. 49-64, July 1956
● Making Friends With a Killer Whale ("Namu"). By Edward I. Griffin. 418-446, Mar. 1966

HEARTY Folk Defy Arctic Storms. Paintings by W. Langdon Kihn. 479-494, Oct. 1949

HEAT Paints *Columbia*'s Portrait. By Cliff Tarpy. 650-653, Nov. 1982

HEAVENS:
● First Color Portraits of the Heavens. By William C. Miller. 670-679, May 1959
▲ *A Map of the Heavens,* supplement. Star charts on reverse. NGS research grant. Dec. 1957
▲ *Map of the Heavens,* supplement. Star charts on reverse. NGS research grant. Aug. 1970
● *See also* Universe

HEBREWS:
● Abraham, the Friend of God. By Kenneth MacLeish. Photos by Dean Conger. 739-789, Dec. 1966
● Bringing Old Testament Times to Life. By G. Ernest Wright. Paintings by Henry J. Soulen. 833-864, Dec. 1957
● The Last Thousand Years Before Christ. By G. Ernest Wright. Paintings by H. J. Soulen and Peter V. Bianchi. 812-853, Dec. 1960
● *See also* Moses

HEBRIDES (Islands), Scotland:
● Scotland From Her Lovely Lochs and Seas. By Alan Villiers. Photos by Robert F. Sisson. 492-541, Apr. 1961
● *See also* Inner Hebrides; Outer Hebrides

HEIMAEY (Island), Westmann Islands, Iceland:
● Vestmannaeyjar: Up From the Ashes. By Noel Grove. Photos by Robert S. Patton. 690-701, May 1977
● A Village Fights for Its Life. By Noel Grove. 40-67, July 1973

HEIRTZLER, JAMES R.: Author:
● Where the Earth Turns Inside Out. Photos by Emory Kristof. 586-603, May 1975

HEIZER, ROBERT F.: Author:
● Gifts for the Jaguar God. By Philip Drucker and Robert F. Heizer. 367-375, Sept. 1956

HELICOPTERS:
● Air Rescue Behind Enemy Lines (North Viet Nam). By Howard Sochurek. 346-369, Sept. 1968
● Aviation Looks Ahead on Its 50th Birthday. By Emory S. Land. 721-739, Dec. 1953
● Everyone's Servant, the Post Office. By Allan C. Fisher, Jr. Photos by Volkmar Wentzel. 121-152, July 1954
● Exploring Ancient Panama by Helicopter. By Matthew W. Stirling. Photos by Richard H. Stewart. NGS research grant. 227-246, Feb. 1950
● Flying in the "Blowtorch" Era. By Frederick G. Vosburgh. 281-322, Sept. 1950
● Helicopter War in South Viet Nam. By Dickey Chapelle. 723-754, Nov. 1962
● The Incredible Helicopter. By Peter T. White. 533-557, Apr. 1959
● Our Air Age Speeds Ahead. By F. Barrows Colton. 249-272, Feb. 1948

HELLYER, DAVID: Author:
● Goggle Fishing in California Waters. Photos by Lamar Boren. 615-632, May 1949
● Nature's Clown, the Penguin. By David Hellyer and Malcolm Davis. 405-428, Sept. 1952

HELM, ENNIS CREED ("Tex"): **Photographer:**
● Carlsbad Caverns in Color. By Mason Sutherland. 433-468, Oct. 1953

GH

HELP for Philippine Tribes in Trouble. By Kenneth MacLeish. Photos by Dean Conger. 220-255, Aug. 1971

HELPING Holland Rebuild Her Land. By Gilbert M. Grosvenor and Charles Neave. 365-413, Sept. 1954

HELSINKI, Finland:
• Baltic Cruise of the *Caribbee*. By Carleton Mitchell. 605-646, Nov. 1950
• Finland: Plucky Neighbor of Soviet Russia. By William Graves. Photos by George F. Mobley. 587-629, May 1968
• Helsinki: City With Its Heart in the Country. By Priit J. Vesilind. Photos by Jodi Cobb. 237-255, Aug. 1981

HENDERSON, DONALD A.: Author:
• Smallpox–Epitaph for a Killer? Photos by Marion Kaplan. 796-805, Dec. 1978

HENLEY ON THAMES, England:
• The Thames: That Noble River. By Ethel A. Starbird. Photos by O. Louis Mazzatenta. 750-791, June 1983

HENLOPEN DUNES, Delaware:
• The Living Sand. By William H. Amos. 820-833, June 1965

HENRY VIII, King (England):
• The British Way. By Sir Evelyn Wrench. 421-541, Apr. 1949

HENRY VIII's Lost Warship: *Mary Rose*. By Margaret Rule. Introduction and picture text by Peter Miller. Paintings by Richard Schlecht. 646-675, May 1983

HENRY, Prince, the Navigator:
• Prince Henry, the Explorer Who Stayed Home. By Alan Villiers. Photos by Thomas Nebbia. 616-656, Nov. 1960

HENRY, PATRICK:
• Firebrands of the Revolution. By Eric F. Goldman. Photos by George F. Mobley. 2-27, July 1974

HENRY, THOMAS R.: Author:
• Ice Age Man, the First American. Paintings by Andre Durenceau. 781-806, Dec. 1955
• The Smithsonian Institution. 325-348, Sept. 1948

HENRY, Cape, Virginia:
• Exploring America's Great Sand Barrier Reef. By Eugene R. Guild. Photos by John E. Fletcher and author. 325-350, Sept. 1947

HENRY E. HUNTINGTON LIBRARY AND ART GALLERY, San Marino, California:
• Huntington Library, California Treasure House. By David S. Boyer. 251-276, Feb. 1958

HENRY FORD MUSEUM, Dearborn, Michigan:
• The Past Is Present in Greenfield Village. By Beverley M. Bowie. Photos by Neal P. Davis and Willard R. Culver. 96-127, July 1958

HENRY HUDSON'S Changing Bay. By Bill Richards. Photos by David Hiser. 380-405, Mar. 1982

HENRY HUDSON'S River. By Willard Price. Photos by Wayne Miller. 364-403, Mar. 1962

HERALDRY. *See* Coats of Arms

HERBAL MEDICINE:
• Herbs for All Seasons. By Lonnelle Aikman. Photos by Sam Abell. Picture portfolio text by Larry Kohl. 386-409, Mar. 1983
• Karnali, Roadless World of Western Nepal. By Lila M. and Barry C. Bishop. NGS research grant. 656-689, Nov. 1971
• Nature's Gifts to Medicine. By Lonnelle Aikman. Paintings by Lloyd K. Townsend and Don Crowley. 420-440, Sept. 1974
◆ *Nature's Healing Arts*. 1977
• The People of Cumberland Gap. By John Fetterman. Photos by Bruce Dale. 591-621, Nov. 1971

HERBERT, CHARLES W.:
Photographer:
• Better Days for the Navajos. By Jack Breed. 809-847, Dec. 1958
• Californians Escape to the Desert. By Mason Sutherland. 675-724, Nov. 1957
• Sonora Is Jumping. By Mason Sutherland. 215-246, Feb. 1955

HERBICIDES:
• The Pesticide Dilemma. By Allen A. Boraiko. Photos by Fred Ward. 145-183, Feb. 1980

HERBS:
• Herbs for All Seasons. By Lonnelle Aikman. Photos by Sam Abell. Picture portfolio text by Larry Kohl. 386-409, Mar. 1983
• *See also* Bromeliads; Herbal Medicine; *and* Kew

HERCULANEUM, Italy:
• A Buried Roman Town Gives Up Its Dead. By Joseph Judge. Photos by Jonathan Blair. NGS research grant. 687-693, Dec. 1982

HERCULES, FRANK: Author:
• To Live in Harlem. . . . Photos by LeRoy Woodson, Jr. 178-207, Feb. 1977

HERE Come the Marines. By Frederick Simpich. 647-672, Nov. 1950

HERE Rest in Honored Glory . . . (War Memorials). By Howell Walker. 739-768, June 1957

HÉRENS, Val d', Switzerland:
• Switzerland's Enchanted Val d'Hérens. By Georgia Engelhard Cromwell. 825-848, June 1955

HEREROS (People):
• Namibia: Nearly a Nation? By Bryan Hodgson. Photos by Jim Brandenburg. 755-797, June 1982

HERE'S New York Harbor. By Stuart E. Jones. Photos by Robert F. Sisson and David S. Boyer. 773-813, Dec. 1954

HERE'S to Milwaukee. By Louise Levathes. Photos by Michael Mauney. 180-201, Aug. 1980

HERGET, H. M.: Artist:
• Ancient Mesopotamia: A Light That Did Not Fail. By E. A. Speiser. 41-105, Jan. 1951
How the Herget Paintings Were Composed. 57

HERITAGE of Beauty and History (U. S. National Parks). By Conrad L. Wirth. 587-661, May 1958

HERM (Island), English Channel:
• Britain's "French" Channel Islands. By James Cerruti. Photos by James L. Amos. 710-740, May 1971

HERMES, R. C.: Photographer:
• The Solemn, Sociable Puffins. By R. M. Lockley. 414-422, Sept. 1954

HERMITAGE (State Museum), Leningrad, U.S.S.R.:
• Leningrad, Russia's Window on the West. By Howard La Fay. Photos by Dick Durrance II. 636-673, May 1971

HERO (Research Vessel):
• Antarctica's Nearer Side. By Samuel W. Matthews. Photos by William R. Curtsinger. 622-655, Nov. 1971

HEROD THE GREAT, King (Judea):
• The Ghosts of Jericho. By James L. Kelso. 825-844, Dec. 1951

HERON ISLAND, Australia:
• Australia's Great Barrier Reef. 630-663, May 1981
I. A Marine Park Is Born. By Soames Summerhays. Photos by Ron and Valerie Taylor. 630-635; II. Paradise Beneath the Sea. By Ron and Valerie Taylor. 636-663

HERONS:
• Aha! It Really Works! By Robert F. Sisson. Contents: Green heron that fishes with bait. 143-147, Jan. 1974
• Wildlife of Everglades National Park. By Daniel B. Beard. Paintings by Walter A. Weber. 83-116, Jan. 1949

HERRING:
• Scenes of Postwar Finland. By La Verne Bradley. Photos by Jerry Waller. 233-264, Aug. 1947
• *See also* Menhaden

HERRNKIND, WILLIAM F.: Author:
• Strange March of the Spiny Lobster. Photos by Rick Frehsee and Bruce Mounier. 819-831, June 1975

HERZ FOUNDATION: Study Grant:
• Orangutans. 835, June 1980

HESS, BILL: Author-Photographer:
• Seeking the Best of Two Worlds (Apache). 272-290, Feb. 1980
Photographer:
• Coming of Age the Apache Way. By Nita Quintero. 262-271, Feb. 1980

HEYDEN, FRANCIS J.:
• Eclipse Hunting in Brazil's Ranchland. By F. Barrows Colton. Photos by Richard H. Stewart and Guy W. Starling. 285-324, Sept. 1947

HEYERDAHL, THOR:
▪ The *Tigris* Expedition. 826, Dec. 1978; 1, Jan. 1979; cover, Apr. 1979

Author:
• *Tigris* Sails Into the Past. Photos by Carlo Mauri and the crew of the *Tigris*. 806-827, Dec. 1978
• The Voyage of *Ra II*. Photos by Carlo Mauri and Georges Sourial. 44-71, Jan. 1971

HIBERNATION. *See* Grizzly Bears; Poorwill

HICKORY (Salvage Ship):
• Graveyard of the Quicksilver Galleons. By Mendel Peterson. Photos by Jonathan Blair. 850-876, Dec. 1979

HIDDEN Life of an Undersea Desert. By Eugenie Clark. Photos by David Doubilet. 129-144, July 1983

HIDDEN Worlds in the Heart of a Plant (Bromeliad). By Paul A. Zahl. 389-397, Mar. 1975

HIDES AND SKINS:
• New Day for Alaska's Pribilof Islanders. By Susan Hackley Johnson. Photos by Tim Thompson. 536-552, Included: Fur seal harvest by Aleuts. Oct. 1982
• Wild Cargo: the Business of Smuggling Animals. By Noel Grove. Photos by Steve Raymer. 287-315, Mar. 1981

HIEROGLYPHS:
• Computer Helps Scholars Re-create an Egyptian Temple. By Ray Winfield Smith. Photos by Emory Kristof. NGS research grant. 634-655, Nov. 1970
• *See also* Glyphs, for Maya glyphs

HIERONYMUS, REX E.: Author:
• Down Mark Twain's River on a Raft. 551-574, Apr. 1948

HIGAONON TRIBE:
• Help for Philippine Tribes in Trouble. By Kenneth MacLeish. Photos by Dean Conger. 220-255, Aug. 1971

HIGDON, HAL: Author:
• New Tricks Outwit Our Insect Enemies. Photos by Robert F. Sisson and Emory Kristof. 380-399, Sept. 1972

HIGH, Wild World of the Vicuña. By William L. Franklin. 77-91, Jan. 1973

HIGH Adventure in the Himalayas. By Thomas Weir. 193-234, Aug. 1952

HIGH ATLAS (Mountains), Africa:
• Berber Brides' Fair. By Carla Hunt. Photos by Nik Wheeler. 119-129, Jan. 1980
• Morocco, Land of the Farthest West. By Thomas J. Abercrombie. 834-865, June 1971
• Trek by Mule Among Morocco's Berbers. By Victor Englebert. 850-875, June 1968

HIGH-FLYING Tulsa. By Robert Paul Jordan. Photos by Annie Griffiths. 378-403, Sept. 1983

HIGH Road in the Pyrenees. By H. V. Morton. Photos by Justin Locke. 299-334, Mar. 1956

HIGH-STEPPING Idaho. By William S. Ellis. Photos by Dean Conger. 290-317, Mar. 1973

HIGH Tech, High Risk, and High Life in Silicon Valley. By Moira Johnston. Photos by Charles O'Rear. 459-477, Oct. 1982

HIGH Trail Through the Canadian Rockies. By Mike W. Edwards. Photos by Lowell Georgia. 795-817, June 1973

The **HIGH** World of the Rain Forest. By William Beebe. Paintings by Guy Neale. 838-855, June 1958

HIGHLAND GAMES:
• Over the Sea to Scotland's Skye. By Robert J. Reynolds. 87-112, July 1952

The **HIGHLANDS,** Stronghold of Scottish Gaeldom. By Kenneth MacLeish. Photos by Winfield Parks. 398-435, Mar. 1968

HIGHWAYS AND ROADS:
• Amalfi, Italy's Divine Coast. By Luis Marden. 472-509, Oct. 1959
• California's Wonderful One (State Highway No. 1). By Frank Cameron. Photos by B. Anthony Stewart. 571-617, Nov. 1959
• From Sea to Shining Sea: A Cross Section of the United States Along Historic Route 40. By Ralph Gray. Photos by Dean Conger and author. 1-61, July 1961
• From Sun-clad Sea to Shining Mountains. By Ralph Gray. Photos by James P. Blair. Contents: "International 89": Mexico's West Coast Highway; U. S. 89; Canada's Coleman-Kananaskis Road and Banff-Jasper Highway. 542-589, Apr. 1964
• The Old Boston Post Roads. By Donald Barr Chidsey. 189-205, Aug. 1962
• Our Growing Interstate Highway System. By Robert Paul Jordan. 195-219, Feb. 1968
• The Post Road Today. Photos by B. Anthony Stewart. 206-233, Aug. 1962
• Trucks Race the Clock From Coast to Coast. By James A. Sugar. 226-243, Feb. 1974
• *See also* Appian Way; Natchez Trace; New York State Thruway; Pan American Highway

HIKING TRIPS:
• Afoot in Roadless Nepal. By Toni Hagen. 361-405, Mar. 1960
• Along the Great Divide. By Mike Edwards. Photos by Nicholas DeVore III. 483-515, Oct. 1979
• Americans Afoot in Rumania. By Dan Dimancescu. Photos by Dick Durrance II and Christopher G. Knight. 810-845, June 1969
◆ *The Appalachian Trail.* Announced. 870-874, June 1972
• The Friendly Huts of the White Mountains. By William O. Douglas. Photos by Kathleen Revis. 205-239, Aug. 1961
• Hiking the Backbone of the Rockies: Canada's Great Divide Trail. By Mike W. Edwards. Photos by Lowell Georgia. 795-817, June 1973

JAMES A. SUGAR

Trucks: wheeling through L.A.

Our Growing Interstate: tunnel on I-80

WINFIELD PARKS, NGS

• Karnali, Roadless World of Western Nepal. By Lila M. and Barry C. Bishop. NGS research grant. 656-689, Nov. 1971
• Mexico to Canada on the Pacific Crest Trail. By Mike W. Edwards. Photos by David Hiser. 741-779, June 1971
• New Mount McKinley Challenge–Trekking Around the Continent's Highest Peak. By Ned Gillette. 66-79, July 1979
• New Zealand's Milford Track: "Walk of a Lifetime." By Carolyn Bennett Patterson. Photos by Robert E. Gilka. 117-129, Jan. 1978
◆ *The Pacific Crest Trail.* Announced. 870-874, June 1974
• Pack Trip Through the Smokies. By Val Hart. Photos by Robert F. Sisson. 473-502, Oct. 1952
• Park at the Top of the World: Mount Everest National Park. By Rick Ridgeway. Photos by Nicholas DeVore III. 704-725, June 1982
Preserving a Mountain Heritage. By Sir Edmund Hillary. 696-703
• Sierra High Trip. By David R. Brower. 844-868, June 1954
• Skyline Trail from Maine to Georgia. By Andrew H. Brown. Photos by Robert F. Sisson. 219-251, Aug. 1949
• Thumbs Up Round the North Sea's Rim. By Frances James. Photos by Erica Koch. 685-704, May 1952
• Travels With a Donkey–100 Years Later. By Carolyn Bennett Patterson. Photos by Cotton Coulson. 535-561, Oct. 1978
• A Walk Across America. By Peter Gorton Jenkins. 466-499, Apr. 1977
• A Walk Across America: Part II. By Peter and Barbara Jenkins. 194-229, Aug. 1979
• A Walk and Ride on the Wild Side: Tasmania. By Carolyn Bennett Patterson. Photos by David Hiser and Melinda Berge. 676-693, May 1983
• Yellowstone at 100: A Walk Through the Wilderness. By Karen and Derek Craighead. Photos by Sam Abell. 579-603, May 1972
• *See also* Pilgrimages; Walking Tours

HILDEBRAND, JESSE RICHARDSON:
• Memorial Tribute to Jesse Richardson Hildebrand. 104, Jan. 1952

HILGER, MARY INEZ: Author:
• Japan's "Sky People," the Vanishing Ainu. Photos by Eiji Miyazawa. 268-296, Feb. 1967

HILLARY, SIR EDMUND:
• The Crossing of Antarctica. By Sir Vivian Fuchs. Photos by George Lowe. 25-47, Jan. 1959
• President Eisenhower Presents the Hubbard Medal to Everest's Conquerors. 64, July 1954
• Triumph on Everest. 1-63, July 1954
Author:
• Beyond Everest. 579-610, Nov. 1955
• The Conquest of the Summit. 45-63, July 1954
• Preserving a Mountain Heritage (Mount Everest National Park). 696-703, June 1982
• We Build a School for Sherpa Children. 548-551, Oct. 1962

HILO, Hawaii:
• Hawaii, Island of Fire and Flowers. By Gordon Young. Photos by Robert W. Madden. 399-425, Mar. 1975

HILTON HEAD (Island), South Carolina:
• Sea Islands: Adventuring Along the South's Surprising Coast. By James Cerruti. Photos by Thomas Nebbia and James L. Amos. 366-393, Mar. 1971

HIMALAYAS (Mountains), Asia:
• Beyond Everest. By Sir Edmund Hillary. 579-610, Nov. 1955
• Caught in the Assam-Tibet Earthquake. By F. Kingdon-Ward. 403-416, Mar. 1952
• High Adventure in the Himalayas. By Thomas Weir. 193-234, Aug. 1952
• Himalayan Pilgrimage. By Christopher Rand. 520-535, Oct. 1956
• A New Look at Everest. By Dag Hammarskjöld. 87-93, Jan. 1961
• Triumph and Tragedy on Annapurna. By Arlene Blum. 295-311, Mar. 1979
On the Summit. By Irene Miller, with Vera Komarkova. 312-313
• Wintering on the Roof of the World. By Barry C. Bishop. NGS research grant. 503-547, Oct. 1962
Slow Death Threatens Man in the Thin Air of 19,000 Feet. 530-531
• A Woman Paints the Tibetans. By Lafugie. 659-692, May 1949
• *See also* Bhutan; Everest; Kashmir; Ladakh; Mustang; Nepal; Sikkim; Tibet

HIMBAS (People):
• Namibia: Nearly a Nation? By Bryan Hodgson. Photos by Jim Brandenburg. 755-797, June 1982

HIMIS MONASTERY, Ladakh:
• A Journey to "Little Tibet." By Enakshi Bhavnani. Photos by Volkmar Wentzel. 603-634, May 1951
• A Woman Paints the Tibetans. By Lafugie. 659-692, May 1949

HINDUISM:
• Bangladesh: Hope Nourishes a New Nation. By William S. Ellis. Photos by Dick Durrance II. 295-333, Sept. 1972
• Bombay, the Other India. By John Scofield. Photos by Raghubir Singh. 104-129, July 1981
• The Cobra, India's "Good Snake." By Harry Miller. 393-409, Sept. 1970
• Delhi, Capital of a New Dominion. By Phillips Talbot. 597-630, Nov. 1947
• From the Hair of Siva. By Helen and Frank Schreider. 445-503, Oct. 1960
• The Ganges, River of Faith. By John J. Putman. Photos by Raghubir Singh. 445-483, Oct. 1971
• Himalayan Pilgrimage. By Christopher Rand. 520-535, Oct. 1956
• The Idyllic Vale of Kashmir. By Volkmar Wentzel. 523-550, Apr. 1948
• India in Crisis. By John Scofield. 599-661, May 1963
• India's Sculptured Temple Caves. By Volkmar Wentzel. 665-678, May 1953
• Karnali, Roadless World of Western Nepal. By Lila M. and Barry C. Bishop. NGS research grant. 656-689, Nov. 1971
• Kathmandu's Remarkable Newars. By John Scofield. 269-285, Feb. 1979
• The Lands and Peoples of Southeast Asia. 295-365, Mar. 1971
• Orissa, Past and Promise in an Indian State. By Bart McDowell. Photos by James P. Blair. 546-577, Oct. 1970
• Purdah in India: Life Behind the Veil. By Doranne Wilson Jacobson. Included: Hindu purdah of Nimkhera, India. 270-286, Aug. 1977
• Royal Wedding at Jaisalmer. By Marilyn Silverstone. 66-79, Jan. 1965
• The Temples of Angkor. 548-589, May 1982
I. Ancient Glory in Stone. By Peter T. White. Photos by Wilbur E. Garrett. 552-589; II. Will They Survive? Introduction by Wilbur E. Garrett. 548-551
• *See also* Bali, for Hindu-animist beliefs

HIPPOPOTAMUSES:
• Mzima, Kenya's Spring of Life. Photos by Joan and Alan Root. 350-373, Sept. 1971

HISER, DAVID: Photographer:
• The Aztecs. By Bart McDowell. Paintings by Felipe Dávalos. 714-775, Dec. 1980
• A Canoe Helps Hawaii Recapture Her Past. By Herb Kawainui Kane. 468-489, Apr. 1976
• Death Valley, the Land and the Legend. By Rowe Findley. 69-103, Jan. 1970
• Golden Ghosts of the Lost Sierra. By Robert Laxalt. 332-353, Sept. 1973
• Henry Hudson's Changing Bay. By Bill Richards. 380-405, Mar. 1982
• The "Lone" Coyote Likes Family Life. By Hope Ryden. Photos by author and David Hiser. 278-294, Aug. 1974
• Man's Eighty Centuries in Veracruz. By S. Jeffrey K. Wilkerson. Paintings by Richard Schlecht. 203-231, Aug. 1980
• Mexican Folk Art. By Fernando Horcasitas. 648-669, May 1978
• Mexico to Canada on the Pacific Crest Trail. By Mike W. Edwards. 741-779, June 1971
• New Finds in the Great Temple. By Eduardo Matos Moctezuma. 767-775, Dec. 1980
• Pitcairn and Norfolk–The Saga of *Bounty*'s Children. By Ed Howard. Photos by David Hiser and Melinda Berge. 510-541, Oct. 1983
Pitcairn Island. 512-529; Norfolk Island. 530-541

● San Antonio: "Texas, Actin' Kind of Natural." By Fred Kline. 524-549, Apr. 1976
● Stalking the West's Wild Foods. By Euell Gibbons. 186-199, Aug. 1973
● Stalking Wild Foods on a Desert Isle. By Euell Gibbons. 47-63, July 1972
● The Tarahumaras: Mexico's Long Distance Runners. By James Norman. 702-718, May 1976
● That Dammed Missouri River. By Gordon Young. 374-413, Sept. 1971
● A Walk and Ride on the Wild Side: Tasmania. By Carolyn Bennett Patterson. Photos by David Hiser and Melinda Berge. 676-693, May 1983
● A Way of Life Called Maine. By Ethel A. Starbird. 727-757, June 1977

HISPANIOLA (Island), West Indies:
● Christopher Columbus and the New World He Found. By John Scofield. Photos by Adam Woolfitt. 584-625, Nov. 1975
● *See also* Dominican Republic; Haiti

HISTORIC Color Portrait of Earth From Space. By Kenneth F. Weaver. Photos by DODGE Satellite. 726-731, Nov. 1967

HISTORY, Ancient:
◆ *Discovering Man's Past in the Americas.* Announced. 880-884, June 1969
◆ *Everyday Life in Ancient Times* (1951). 766, June 1954; 563, Oct. 1961
◆ *Everyday Life in Bible Times.* Announced. 494-507, Oct. 1967; rev. ed. 1977
◆ *Mysteries of the Ancient World.* 1979
◆ *Peoples and Places of the Past: The National Geographic Illustrated Atlas of the Ancient World.* 1983; Announced. 824, Dec. 1982
◆ *Splendors of the Past: Lost Cities of the Ancient World.* 1981
● *See also* Early Civilizations; Egypt, Ancient; Greece, Ancient; Mesopotamia; Pre-Columbian Civilizations; Pre-Hispanic Culture; Roman Empire; *and* names of ancient peoples, *as:* Essenes; Etruscans; Phoenicians

HISTORY, European:
● Ancient Europe Is Older Than We Thought. By Colin Renfrew. Photos by Adam Woolfitt. 615-623, Nov. 1977
▲ *Europe; Historical Map of Europe,* double-sided supplement. Dec. 1983
● Napoleon. By John J. Putman. Photos by Gordon W. Gahan. 142-189, Feb. 1982
● The World of Martin Luther. By Merle Severy. Photos by James L. Amos. 418-463, Oct. 1983
● *See also* Celts; Medieval Europe; The Renaissance

HISTORY, Medieval. *See* Byzantine Empire; Medieval Europe

HISTORY, U. S.:
● American Processional: History on Canvas. By John and Blanche Leeper. 173-212, Feb. 1951
◆ *America's Historylands, Landmarks of Liberty.* Announced. 360-363, Mar. 1962
● Buffalo Bill and the Enduring West. By Alice J. Hall. Photos by James L. Amos. 76-103, July 1981
● Chief Joseph. By William Albert Allard. 409-434, Mar. 1977
◆ *Clues to America's Past.* Announced. 860-864, June 1976
● Early America Through the Eyes of Her Native Artists. By Hereward Lester Cooke, Jr. 356-389, Sept. 1962
● Eight Maps of Discovery. 757-769, June 1953
● Following the Trail of Lewis and Clark. By Ralph Gray. 707-750, June 1953
● From Sea to Shining Sea: A Cross Section of the United States Along Historic Route 40. By Ralph Gray. Photos by Dean Conger and author. 1-61, July 1961
▲ *Historical Map of the United States,* supplement. June 1953
◆ *In the Footsteps of Lewis and Clark.* Announced. 880-884, June 1970
◆ *Into the Wilderness.* 1978
● New Stars for Old Glory. By Lonnelle Aikman. 86-121, July 1959
● North Through History Aboard *White Mist.* By Melville Bell Grosvenor. Photos by Edwin Stuart Grosvenor. 1-55, July 1970
● The Pony Express. By Rowe Findley. Photos by Craig Aurness. 45-71, July 1980
◆ *Railroads: The Great American Adventure.* Announced. 860-864, June 1976
● Riding the Outlaw Trail. By Robert Redford. Photos by Jonathan Blair. 622-657, Nov. 1976
● Shrines of Each Patriot's Devotion. By Frederick G. Vosburgh. 51-82, Jan. 1949
● So Long, St. Louis, We're Heading West. By William C. Everhart. 643-669, Nov. 1965
● Thoreau, a Different Man. By William Howarth. Photos by Farrell Grehan. 349-387, Mar. 1981
● Today Along the Natchez Trace, Pathway Through History. By Bern Keating. Photos by Charles Harbutt. 641-667, Nov. 1968
◆ *Trails West.* 1979
● The Virginians. By Mike W. Edwards. Photos by David Alan Harvey. 588-617, Nov. 1974
◆ *Visiting Our Past: America's Historylands.* 1977
◆ *We Americans.* Announced. 580-582, Oct. 1975
● *See also* The Americas; Bicentennial; Colonial America; *and* American Revolution; Civil War, U. S.; Frontier; The Making of America Map series; Presidents, U. S.; War of 1812; World War II; *also* U. S. Capitol; White House; *and* the states, and historical cities and sites, *as:* Boston; Concord; Deerfield; Harpers Ferry; Jamestown; Mystic Seaport; Natchez; Philadelphia; Roanoke Island; St. Augustine; Washington, D. C.; Williamsburg

HISTORY and Beauty Blend in a Concord Iris Garden. By Robert T. Cochran, Jr. Photos by M. Woodbridge Williams. 705-719, May 1959

HISTORY Awakens at Harpers Ferry. By Volkmar Wentzel. 399-416, Mar. 1957

HISTORY Keeps House in Virginia. By Howell Walker. 441-484, Apr. 1956

HISTORY Repeats in Old Natchez. By William H. Nicholas. Photos by Willard R. Culver. 181-208, Feb. 1949

HISTORY Revealed in Ancient Glass. By Ray Winfield Smith. Photos by B. Anthony Stewart and Lee E. Battaglia. 346-369, Sept. 1964

HISTORY Written in the Skies (U. S. Air Force). 273-294, Aug. 1957

HITCHCOCK, STEPHEN W.: Author:
● Can We Save Our Salt Marshes? Photos by William R. Curtsinger. 729-765, June 1972

HLUHLUWE GAME RESERVE, South Africa:
● Roaming Africa's Unfenced Zoos. By W. Robert Moore. 353-380, Mar. 1950
● Safari Through Changing Africa. By Elsie May Bell Grosvenor. Photos by Gilbert Grosvenor. 145-198, Aug. 1953

HMONG REFUGEES:
● The Hmong of Laos: No Place to Run. By W. E. Garrett. 78-111, Jan. 1974
● One Family's Odyssey to America. By John Everingham. 642-661, May 1980
● Thailand: Refuge From Terror. By W.E. Garrett. 633-642, May 1980

HOABINHIAN CULTURE:
● New Light on a Forgotten Past (Southeast Asia). By Wilhelm G. Solheim II. 330-339, Mar. 1971

HOATZIN:
● Strange Little World of the Hoatzin. By J. Lear Grimmer. Photos by M. Woodbridge Williams. NGS research grant. 391-401, Sept. 1962

HOCHDORF, West Germany:
● Treasure From a Celtic Tomb. By Jörg Biel. Photos by Volkmar Wentzel. 428-438, Mar. 1980

HODGE, JOHN R.: Author:
● With the U. S. Army in Korea. 829-840, June 1947

HODGSON, BRYAN: Author:
● Exploring England's Canals. Photos by Linda Bartlett. 76-111, July 1974
● Irish Ways Live On in Dingle. Photos by Linda Bartlett. 551-576, Apr. 1976
● Montenegro: Yugoslavia's "Black Mountain." Photos by Linda Bartlett. 663-683, Nov. 1977

G H

• Mountain Voices, Mountain Days. Photos by Linda Bartlett. 118-146, July 1972
• Namibia: Nearly a Nation? Photos by Jim Brandenburg. 755-797, June 1982
• Natural Gas: The Search Goes On. Photos by Lowell Georgia. 632-651, Nov. 1978
• The Pipeline: Alaska's Troubled Colossus. Photos by Steve Raymer. 684-717, Nov. 1976
• Singapore: Mini-size Superstate. Photos by Dean Conger. 540-561, Apr. 1981
• Wales, the Lyric Land. Photos by Farrell Grehan. 36-63, July 1983
• War and Peace in Northern Ireland. Photos by Cary Wolinsky. 470-499, Apr. 1981

HOG RAISING:
• America's "Meat on the Hoof." By William H. Nicholas. 33-72, Jan. 1952
• The Diffident Truffle, France's Gift to Gourmets. Included: Truffle-hunting sows. 419-426, Sept. 1956
• The Family Farm Ain't What It Used To Be. By James A. Sugar. 391-411, Sept. 1974
• The Joy of Pigs. By Kent Britt. Photos by George F. Mobley. 398-415, Sept. 1978

HOGARTH, WILLIAM:
• The British Way. By Sir Evelyn Wrench. 421-541, Apr. 1949

HOHOKAM CULTURE:
• The Hohokam: First Masters of the American Desert. By Emil W. Haury. Photos by Helga Teiwes. 670-695, May 1967
• Magnetic Clues Help Date the Past. By Kenneth F. Weaver. 696-701, May 1967
• Pueblo Pottery–2,000 Years of Artistry. By David L. Arnold. 593-605, Nov. 1982

HOKKAIDO (Island), Japan:
• Hokkaido, Japan's Last Frontier. By Douglas Lee. Photos by Michael S. Yamashita. 62-93, Jan. 1980
• The Japanese Crane, Bird of Happiness. By Tsuneo Hayashida. 542-556, Oct. 1983
• Japan's "Sky People," the Vanishing Ainu. By Mary Inez Hilger. Photos by Eiji Miyazawa. 268-296, Feb. 1967
• Snow Festival in Japan's Far North. By Eiji Miyazawa. 824-833, Dec. 1968

HOKULE'A (Voyaging Canoe):
• A Canoe Helps Hawaii Recapture Her Past. By Herb Kawainui Kane. Photos by David Hiser. 468-489, Apr. 1976
• *Hokule'a* Follows the Stars to Tahiti. By David Lewis. Photos by Nicholas deVore III. 512-537, Oct. 1976
▪ Voyage of the *Hokule'a*. 575, Nov. 1976

HOLDEN, ANTHONY: Author:
• Windsor Castle. Photos by James L. Stanfield. 604-631, Nov. 1980

HOLGUÍN, NENA: Photographer:
• At My Limit–I Climbed Everest Alone. By Reinhold Messner. Photos by the author and Nena Holguín. 552-566, Oct. 1981

FARRELL GREHAN

Holland's Tulips: flowers at Keukenhof, *above;* anatomy of a tulip, *below*

PAINTING BY ROBERT HYNES

HOLIDAYS. *See* Christmas; Easter; Memorial Day Ceremonies; New Year Celebrations; *and* Festivals

HOLLAND, JAMES R.: Photographer:
• Tracking Danger With the Ice Patrol. By William S. Ellis. 780-793, June 1968

HOLLAND. *See* Netherlands

HOLLAND, Michigan:
• Work-hard, Play-hard Michigan. By Andrew H. Brown. 279-320, Mar. 1952

HOLLAND in the Caribbean: The Netherlands Antilles. By James Cerruti. Photos by Emory Kristof. 115-146, Jan. 1970

HOLLAND'S Beautiful Business: Tulips. By Elizabeth A. Moize. Photos by Farrell Grehan. 712-728, May 1978

HOLLIDAY, CLYDE T.: Author:
• Seeing the Earth From 80 Miles Up. 511-528, Oct. 1950

HOLMES, MIKE:
Author-Photographer:
• Nauru, the World's Richest Nation. 344-353, Sept. 1976
• Oil and Penguins Don't Mix. 384-397, Mar. 1973

HOLWAY, DONAL F.: Photographer:
• A Century Old, the Wonderful Brooklyn Bridge. By John G. Morris. 565-579, May 1983

HOLY ISLAND (Lindisfarne), England:
• Pilgrimage to Holy Island and the Farnes. By John E. H. Nolan. 547-570, Oct. 1952

HOLY LAND:
• Abraham, the Friend of God. By Kenneth MacLeish. Photos by Dean Conger. 739-789, Dec. 1966
• An Archeologist Looks at Palestine. By Nelson Glueck. 739-752, Dec. 1947
• Bringing Old Testament Times to Life. By G. Ernest Wright. Paintings by Henry J. Soulen. 833-864, Dec. 1957
• Crusader Lands Revisited. By Harold Lamb. Photos by David S. Boyer. Contents: Israel; Jordan; Lebanon; Syria; Turkey. 815-852, Dec. 1954
• Crusader Road to Jerusalem. By Franc Shor. Photos by Thomas Nebbia. 797-855, Dec. 1963
I. Desert Ordeal of the Knights. 797-837; II. Conquest of the Holy City. 839-855
◆ *Everyday Life in Bible Times.* Announced. 494-507, Oct. 1967; rev. ed. 1977
• Eyewitness to War in the Holy Land. By Charles Harbutt. 782-795, Dec. 1967
• Geographical Twins a World Apart. By David S. Boyer. Contents: Dead Sea, Sea of Galilee, Jordan River, Qumrān caves compared with counterparts in Utah. 848-859, Dec. 1958

● Holy Land, My Country. By His Majesty King Hussein of Jordan. 784-789, Dec. 1964
▲ *Holy Land Today,* Atlas series supplement. Dec. 1963
● Home to the Holy Land. By Maynard Owen Williams. 707-746, Dec. 1950
● In Search of Moses. By Harvey Arden. Photos by Nathan Benn. 2-37, Jan. 1976
● Israel: Land of Promise. By John Scofield. Photos by B. Anthony Stewart. 395-434, Mar. 1965
● Jerusalem to Rome in the Path of St. Paul. By David S. Boyer. 707-759, Dec. 1956
● Journey Into the Great Rift. By Helen and Frank Schreider. 254-290, Aug. 1965
● The Land of Galilee. By Kenneth MacLeish. Photos by B. Anthony Stewart. 832-865, Dec. 1965
▲ *Lands of the Bible Today,* supplement. Dec. 1956
▲ *Lands of the Bible Today,* supplement. Dec. 1967
● The Last Thousand Years Before Christ. By G. Ernest Wright. Paintings by H. J. Soulen and Peter V. Bianchi. 812-853, Dec. 1960
● The Living Dead Sea. By Harvey Arden. Photos by Nathan Benn. Included: Biblical history of the Dead Sea region; discovery site of the Dead Sea Scrolls. 225-245, Feb. 1978
● The Other Side of Jordan. By Luis Marden. 790-825, Dec. 1964
● Pilgrims Follow the Christmas Star. By Maynard Owen Williams. 831-840, Dec. 1952
● Sinai Sheds New Light on the Bible. By Henry Field. Photos by William B. and Gladys Terry. 795-815, Dec. 1948
● Where Jesus Walked. By Howard La Fay. Photos by Charles Harbutt. 739-781, Dec. 1967
● *See also* Exodus; Jericho; Jerusalem; Jordan; Khirbat Qumrān; Lebanon; Mesopotamia; Petra, Jordan; St. Catherine's Monastery, Sinai Peninsula; Syria

HOLY Land, My Country. By His Majesty King Hussein of Jordan. 784-789, Dec. 1964

HOLY ROMAN EMPIRE:
● The World of Martin Luther. By Merle Severy. Photos by James L. Amos. 418-463, Oct. 1983

HOLY WEEK:
● Andalusia, the Spirit of Spain. By Howard La Fay. Photos by Joseph J. Scherschel. 833-857, June 1975
● Brazil's Land of Minerals. By W. Robert Moore. Included: Holy Week in Ouro Prêto. 479-508, Oct. 1948
● Easter Week in Indian Guatemala. By John Scofield. 406-417, Mar. 1960
● Eternal Easter in a Greek Village. By Maria Nicolaidis-Karanikolas. Photos by James L. Stanfield. 768-777, Dec. 1983
● The Five Worlds of Peru. By Kenneth F. Weaver. Photos by Bates Littlehales. Included: Holy Week in Ayacucho. 213-265, Feb. 1964
● Guatemala, Maya and Modern. By Louis de la Haba. Photos by Joseph J. Scherschel. 661-689, Nov. 1974
● Holy Week and the Fair in Sevilla (Spain). By Luis Marden. 499-530, Apr. 1951
● Home to the Holy Land. By Maynard Owen Williams. Included: Holy Week in Jerusalem. 707-746, Dec. 1950
● Mesa del Nayar's Strange Holy Week. By Guillermo Aldana E. 780-795, June 1971

HOME Life in Paris Today. By Deena Clark. 43-72, July 1950

HOME to Arran, Scotland's Magic Isle. By J. Harvey Howells. 80-99, July 1965

HOME to Lonely Tristan da Cunha. By James P. Blair. 60-81, Jan. 1964

HOME to North Carolina. By Neil Morgan. Photos by Bill Weems. 333-359, Mar. 1980

HOME to the Enduring Berkshires. By Charles McCarry. Photos by Jonathan S. Blair. 196-221, Aug. 1970

HOME to the Heart of Kentucky. By Nadine Brewer. Photos by William Strode. 522-546, Apr. 1982

HOME to the Holy Land. By Maynard Owen Williams. 707-746, Dec. 1950

HOMER:
● Homeward With Ulysses. By Melville Bell Grosvenor. Photos by Edwin Stuart Grosvenor. 1-39, July 1973

HOMESTEADING:
● Alaskan Family Robinson. By Nancy Robinson. Photos by John Metzger and Peter Robinson. 55-75, Jan. 1973
● Brazil's Wild Frontier. By Loren McIntyre. 684-719, Nov. 1977

HOMETOWN Behind the Monuments: Washington, D. C. By Henry Mitchell. Photos by Adam Woolfitt. 84-125, Jan. 1983

HOMEWARD With Ulysses. By Melville Bell Grosvenor. Photos by Edwin Stuart Grosvenor. 1-39, July 1973

HONDURAS:
● Honduras: Eye of the Storm. By Mike Edwards. Photos by David Alan Harvey. 608-637, Nov. 1983
● "Pyramids" of the New World. By Neil Merton Judd. Included: Copán. 105-128, Jan. 1948
● Troubled Times for Central America. By Wilbur E. Garrett, Editor. 58-61, July 1981

HONDURAS, British. *See* Belize

HONEY ANTS:
● Living Honey Jars of the Ant World. By Ross E. Hutchins. 405-411, Mar. 1962

HONEY EATERS of Currumbin (Lorikeets). By Paul A. Zahl. 510-519, Oct. 1956

HONEY-GUIDE: The Bird That Eats Wax. By Herbert Friedmann. Paintings by Walter A. Weber. 551-560, Apr. 1954

HONEYBEES:
● Crossroads of the Insect World. By J. W. MacSwain. Photos by Edward S. Ross. 844-857, Dec. 1966
◆ *Honeybees.* Announced. 726-728, Nov. 1973
● Inside the World of the Honeybee. By Treat Davidson. 188-217, Aug. 1959
● Those Fiery Brazilian Bees. By Rick Gore. Photos by Bianca Lavies. 491-501, Apr. 1976

HONEYCUTT, BROOKS:
Photographer:
● Life 8,000 Years Ago Uncovered in an Alabama Cave. By Carl F. Miller. 542-558, Oct. 1956

HONG KONG:
● Eyes on the China Coast. By George W. Long. 505-512, Apr. 1953
■ Hong Kong: A Family Portrait. 1, Jan. 1979; cover, Feb. 1979
● Hong Kong, Saturday's Child. By Joseph Judge. Photos by Bruce Dale. 541-573, Oct. 1971
● Hong Kong Hangs On. By George W. Long. Photos by J. Baylor Roberts. 239-272, Feb. 1954
● Hong Kong Has Many Faces. By John Scofield. 1-41, Jan. 1962
● Hong Kong Restored. 483-490, Apr. 1947
● Hong Kong's Refugee Dilemma. By William S. Ellis. Photos by William Albert Allard. 709-732, Nov. 1979
● Round the World School (ISA). By Paul Antze. Photos by William Eppridge. 96-127, July 1962
● Those Outlandish Goldfish! By Paul A. Zahl. 514-533, Apr. 1973
● Trawling the China Seas. Photos by J. Charles Thompson. 381-395, Mar. 1950
● YWCA: International Success Story. By Mary French Rockefeller. Photos by Otis Imboden. 904-933, Dec. 1963
● *See also* Pacific Fleet, U. S.

HONOLULU, Oahu (Island), Hawaii:
● Because It Rains on Hawaii. By Frederick Simpich, Jr. 571-610, Nov. 1949
● Honolulu, Mid-ocean Capital. By Frederick Simpich, Jr. Photos by B. Anthony Stewart. 577-624, May 1954
● Look What's Happened to Honolulu! By Jim Becker. Photos by Bates Littlehales. 500-531, Oct. 1969
● Which Way Oahu? By Gordon Young. Photos by Robert W. Madden. 653-679, Nov. 1979

HONSHU (Island), Japan:
● Backwoods Japan During American Occupation. By M. A. Huberman. 491-518, Apr. 1947
● Japan's Amazing Inland Sea. By William S. Ellis. Photos by James L. Stanfield. 830-863, Dec. 1977
● Kayak Odyssey: From the Inland Sea to Tokyo. By Dan Dimancescu. Photos by Christopher G. Knight. 295-337, Sept. 1967

HOOGSTRAAL, HARRY: Author:
• South in the Sudan. 249-272, Feb. 1953
• Yemen Opens the Door to Progress. 213-244, Feb. 1952

HOOPER, THOMAS E.: Photographer:
• Probing the Mystery of the Medicine Wheels. By John A. Eddy. 140-146, Jan. 1977

HOOVER, HERBERT:
• The Living White House. By Lonnelle Aikman. 593-643, Nov. 1966
• Profiles of the Presidents: IV. America Enters the Modern Era. By Frank Freidel. 537-577, Oct. 1965

HOOVER, RICHARD B.:
Author-Photographer:
• Those Marvelous, Myriad Diatoms. 871-878, June 1979

HOPE for Big Cypress Swamp. By Rick Gore. Photos by Patricia Caulfield. 251-273, Aug. 1976

HOPE for the Bluebird. By Lawrence Zeleny. Photos by Michael L. Smith. 855-865, June 1977

HOPE-TAYLOR, BRIAN: Artist:
• Stonehenge–New Light on an Old Riddle. By Harold E. Edgerton. 846-866, June 1960

HOPEH (Province), China. *See* Peking

HOPES and Fears in Booming Thailand. By Peter T. White. Photos by Dean Conger. 76-125, July 1967

HOPES and Worries Along the Columbia River, Powerhouse of the Northwest. By David S. Boyer. 821-847, Dec. 1974

HOPEWELL CULTURE. *See* Mound Builders

HOPI INDIANS:
• Inside the Sacred Hopi Homeland. By Jake Page. Photos by Susanne Page. 607-629, Nov. 1982
• Kachinas: Masked Dancers of the Southwest. By Paul Coze. 219-236, Aug. 1957
▲ *The Southwest,* The Making of America series. Included: Arizona, New Mexico, and parts of California, Colorado, Texas, Utah; and in Mexico: Baja California Norte, Chihuahua, Sonora. On reverse: 12,000 Years of History; Spanish Conquest; Anglo-American Entry and Occupancy. Nov. 1982

HORCASITAS, FERNANDO: Author:
• Mexican Folk Art. Photos by David Hiser. 648-669, May 1978

HORGAN, THOMAS: Author:
• Down East Cruise (Maine). Photos by Luis Marden. 329-369, Sept. 1952
• *Nomad* Sails Long Island Sound. 295-338, Sept. 1957
• Windjamming Around New England. Photos by Robert F. Sisson. 141-169, Aug. 1950

HORMUZ, Strait of, Persian Gulf:
• Oman: Guardian of the Gulf. By Thomas J. Abercrombie. Photos by the author and Lynn Abercrombie. 344-377, Sept. 1981

HORN, Cape, South America:
• 'Round the Horn by Submarine. By Paul C. Stimson. 129-144, Jan. 1948

HORN OF AFRICA. *See* Djibouti; Ethiopia

HORNBEIN, THOMAS F.: Author:
• The First Traverse. By Thomas F. Hornbein and William F. Unsoeld. 509-513, Oct. 1963
• *See also* American Mount Everest Expedition

HORNBILLS, African Red-billed:
• Inside a Hornbill's Walled-up Nest. Photos by Joan and Alan Root. 846-855, Dec. 1969

HORNOCKER, MAURICE G.:
Author-Photographer:
• Stalking the Mountain Lion–to Save Him. 638-655, Nov. 1969

HORROR Strikes on Good Friday (Alaska Earthquake). By William P. E. Graves. 112-139, July 1964

HORSE FAIRS. *See* Appleby Fair

HORSE RACES:
• Heart of the Bluegrass (Kentucky). By Charles McCarry. Photos by J. Bruce Baumann. 634-659, May 1974
• The Palio of Siena (Italy). By Edgar Erskine Hume. 231-244, Aug. 1951

HORSE SHOWS:
• Dublin's Historic Horse Show. By Maynard Owen Williams. 115-132, July 1953
• New York Again Hails the Horse (National Horse Show). By Walter B. Devereux. 697-720, Nov. 1954

HORSEMEN. *See* Cowboys; Kazaks; Turkomans

HORSES:
• Heart of the Bluegrass (Kentucky). By Charles McCarry. Photos by J. Bruce Baumann. Contents: Thoroughbred racehorses. 634-659, May 1974
• King Ranch, Cattle Empire in Texas. 41-64, Jan. 1952
• The White Horses of Vienna. By Beverley M. Bowie. Photos by Volkmar Wentzel. 401-419, Sept. 1958

HORSES, Prehistoric:
• Ancient Ashfall Creates a Pompeii of Prehistoric Animals. By Michael R. Voorhies. Photos by Annie Griffiths. NGS research grant. 66-75, Jan. 1981

HORSES, Wild:
▪ The Animals Nobody Loved. Cover, Feb. 1976
• On the Track of the West's Wild Horses. By Hope Ryden. Photos by author and Dick Durrance II. 94-109, Jan. 1971
• Safe Landing on Sable, Isle of 500 Shipwrecks. By Melville Bell Grosvenor. 398-431, Sept. 1965
◆ *The Wild Ponies of Assateague Island.* Announced. 724-726, Nov. 1975

HORSESHOE CRABS:
• The Changeless Horseshoe Crab. By Anne and Jack Rudloe. Photos by Robert F. Sisson. 562-572, Apr. 1981

HORSTMAN, ROBERT and NINA:
Authors:
• Our Friend From the Sea (Seal). Photos by Robert F. Sisson. 728-736, Nov. 1968

HORTICULTURE:
• England's Scillies, the Flowering Isles. By Alan Villiers. Photos by Bates Littlehales. 126-145, July 1967
• The Flower Seed Growers: Gardening's Color Merchants. By Robert de Roos. Photos by Jack Fields. 720-738, May 1968
• Herbs for All Seasons. By Lonnelle Aikman. Photos by Sam Abell. Picture portfolio text by Larry Kohl. 386-409, Mar. 1983
• The Netherlands: Nation at War With the Sea. By Alan Villiers. Photos by Adam Woolfitt. 530-571, Apr. 1968
• Patent Plants Enrich Our World. By Orville H. Kneen. Photos from U. S. Plant Patents. 357-378, Mar. 1948
• *See also* Flowers; Fruit and Fruit Growing; Vegetables; *and* Gardens

HOSTELS:
• Europe Via the Hostel Route. By Joseph Nettis. 124-154, July 1955
• Lake District, Poets' Corner of England. By H. V. Morton. Photos by David S. Boyer. 511-545, Apr. 1956
• Thumbs Up Round the North Sea's Rim. By Frances James. Photos by Erica Koch. 685-704, May 1952

HOT-AIR Balloons Race on Silent Winds. By William R. Berry. Photos by Don W. Jones. 392-407, Mar. 1966

HOT SPRINGS, Seafloor. *See* Hydrothermal Vents

HOUOT, GEORGES S.: Author:
• Deep Diving off Japan. 138-150, Jan. 1960
• Two and a Half Miles Down. 80-86, July 1954
Author-Photographer:
• Four Years of Diving to the Bottom of the Sea. 715-731, May 1958
• *See also F.N.R.S. 3,* for dives

"HOUSE of Prayer for All People:" Washington Cathedral. By Robert Paul Jordan. Photos by Sisse Brimberg. 552-573, Apr. 1980

HOUSES:
• History Keeps House in Virginia. By Howell Walker. 441-484, Apr. 1956
• History Repeats in Old Natchez. By William H. Nicholas. Photos by Willard R. Culver. 181-208, Feb. 1949
• Inside the White House. By Lonnelle Aikman. Photos by B. Anthony Stewart and Thomas Nebbia. 3-43, Jan. 1961
• Land of Louisiana Sugar Kings. By Harnett T. Kane. Photos by Willard R. Culver. 531-567, Apr. 1958

• Land of the Pilgrims' Pride. By George W. Long. Photos by Robert F. Sisson. 193-219, Aug. 1947
• Literary Landmarks of Massachusetts. By William H. Nicholas. Photos by B. Anthony Stewart and John E. Fletcher. 279-310, Mar. 1950
• The Living White House. By Lonnelle Aikman. 593-643, Nov. 1966
• Mr. Jefferson's Charlottesville. By Anne Revis. 553-592, May 1950
• Philadelphia Houses a Proud Past. By Harold Donaldson Eberlein. Photos by Thomas Nebbia. 151-191, Aug. 1960
• Rhododendron Glories of Southwest Scotland. By David S. Boyer. Photos by B. Anthony Stewart and author. 641-664, May 1954
• Roving Maryland's Cavalier Country. By William A. Kinney. 431-470, Apr. 1954
• Stately Homes of Old Virginia. By Albert W. Atwood. 787-802, June 1953
• Vacation Tour Through Lincoln Land. By Ralph Gray. 141-184, Feb. 1952
• Washington: Home of the Nation's Great. By Albert W. Atwood. Contents: Ashburton House, Blair House, Clara Barton Home, Decatur House, Laird-Dunlop House, Madison Houses, Petersen House, Surratt House, Tayloe House, Tudor Place, The White House. 699-738, June 1947
• *See also* Hearst San Simeon State Historical Monument; Henry E. Huntington Library and Art Gallery; Henry Ford Museum; Monticello; Mount Vernon; White House

HOUSES, Underwater. *See* Conshelf Bases; Link Igloo; SPID; Tektite II

HOUSEWIFE at the End of the World. By Rae Natalie P. Goodall. Photos by James L. Stanfield. 130-150, Jan. 1971

HOUSTON, Texas:
• Houston, Prairie Dynamo. By Stuart E. Jones. Photos by William Albert Allard. 338-377, Sept. 1967
• Texas! By Howard La Fay. Photos by Gordon W. Gahan. 440-483, Apr. 1980

HOW Bats Hunt With Sound. By J. J. G. McCue. 571-578, Apr. 1961

HOW Earth and Moon Look to a Space Voyager. 53, July 1978

HOW Fruit Came to America. By J. R. Magness. Paintings by Else Bostelmann. 325-377, Sept. 1951

HOW Man-made Satellites Can Affect Our Lives. By Joseph Kaplan. 791-810, Dec. 1957

HOW Old Is It? By Lyman J. Briggs and Kenneth F. Weaver. 234-255, Aug. 1958

HOW One of the Society's Maps Saved a Precious Cargo. 844, June 1947

HOW Soon Will We Measure In Metric? By Kenneth F. Weaver. Drawings by Donald A. Mackay. 287-294, Aug. 1977

HOW the Decoy Fish Catches Its Dinner. Photos by Robert J. Shallenberger and William D. Madden. 224-227, Aug. 1974

HOW the Kazakhs Fled to Freedom. By Milton J. Clark. 621-644, Nov. 1954

HOW the Sun Gives Life to the Sea. By Paul A. Zahl. 199-225, Feb. 1961

HOW to Catch a Passing Comet. By Kenneth F. Weaver. 148-150, Jan. 1974

HOW to End a War: Grant and Lee at Appomattox. By Ulysses S. Grant 3rd. Photos by Bruce Dale. 435-469, Apr. 1965

HOW We Climbed Everest. By Barry C. Bishop. 477-507, Oct. 1963

HOW We Found the *Monitor.* By John G. Newton. 48-61, Jan. 1975

HOW We Plan to Put Men on the Moon. By Hugh L. Dryden. Paintings by Davis Meltzer and Pierre Mion. 357-401, Mar. 1964

HOW We Sailed the New *Mayflower* to America. By Alan Villiers. 627-672, Nov. 1957

HOWARD, ED: Author:
• Pitcairn and Norfolk–The Saga of *Bounty*'s Children. Photos by David Hiser and Melinda Berge. 510-541, Oct. 1983
Pitcairn Island. 512-529; Norfolk Island. 530-541

HOWARTH, WILLIAM: Author:
• The Country of Willa Cather. Photos by Farrell Grehan. 71-93, July 1982
• Thoreau, a Different Man. Photos by Farrell Grehan. 349-387, Mar. 1981

HOWE, JULIA WARD:
• Literary Landmarks of Massachusetts. By William H. Nicholas. Photos by B. Anthony Stewart and John E. Fletcher. 279-310, Mar. 1950

HOWELL, THOMAS R.: Author:
• What a Place to Lay an Egg! 414-419, Sept. 1971

HOWELLS, J. HARVEY: Author:
• Home to Arran, Scotland's Magic Isle. 80-99, July 1965

HOXIE BROS. GIGANTIC 3-RING CIRCUS:
• On the Road With an Old-time Circus. By John Fetterman. Photos by Jonathan Blair. 410-434, Mar. 1972

HSINKING, Manchuria. *See* Changchun

HUACA DE LA CRUZ, Virú Valley, Peru:
• Finding the Tomb of a Warrior-God. By William Duncan Strong. Photos by Clifford Evans, Jr. 453-482, Apr. 1947

HUASCARÁN NEVADO (Peak), Peru:
• Avalanche! By Bart McDowell. Photos by John E. Fletcher. 855-880, June 1962

HUASTEC INDIANS:
• Man's Eighty Centuries in Veracruz. By S. Jeffrey K. Wilkerson. Photos by David Hiser. Paintings by Richard Schlecht. NGS research grant. 203-231, Aug. 1980

HUBBARD, GARDINER GREENE:
• Clarke School for the Deaf. 382, 385, 386, 387, Mar. 1955
• First President of National Geographic Society and of Bell Telephone Company. 273, Mar. 1947; 517, 522, Oct. 1963; 1, 101, 103, 113, July 1965; 456, 458, Oct. 1966; 584, Apr. 1968
• A founder of the NGS. 387, Mar. 1955; 3, Jan. 1963; 459, Oct. 1963; 456, Oct. 1966

HUBBARD MEDAL:
• Medal designed by Laura Gardin Fraser; both sides shown. 564, Apr. 1953
Recipients:
• American Mount Everest Expedition: Medal presented to Norman G. Dyhrenfurth, leader of the expedition, with 21 gold-plated bronze replicas to individual members. 514-515, Oct. 1963; 1B, Jan. 1964; 331, Mar. 1964; 15, July 1965
• Apollo 8 and Apollo 11 astronauts. 859-861, June 1970
• Arnold, Henry H. 868, Dec. 1957; 583, Oct. 1963; 584, Apr. 1968
• Astronauts John W. Young and Robert L. Crippen, for the first flight of the Space Shuttle *Columbia.* 852, Dec. 1981
• Bartlett, Robert A. 787, June 1949; 470, Oct. 1953
• British Mount Everest Expedition: Medal presented to Sir John Hunt, with bronze replicas to Sir John, Sir Edmund Hillary, and Tenzing Norgay (in India). 64, July 1954; 846, June 1955; 867-868, Dec. 1957; 98, Jan. 1966; 584, Apr. 1968
• Byrd, Richard E. 250, Feb. 1948; 65H, July 1954; 38, 39, July 1957; 868, Dec. 1957; 574, 576, Apr. 1962; 556, Oct. 1963; 571, Oct. 1965; 584, Apr. 1968
• Ellsworth, Lincoln. 868, Dec. 1957; 583, Oct. 1963; 689, Nov. 1964; 847, June 1967; 584, Apr. 1968
• Fuchs, Sir Vivian. 589-590, Apr. 1959
• Glenn, John H., Jr. 827, June 1962; 904, 905, 906, Dec. 1962; 29, Jan. 1963; 584, Apr. 1968
• Leakey, Dr. and Mrs. Louis S. B. 903, 905, Dec. 1962; 197, 231, Feb. 1965
• Lindbergh, Anne Morrow. 562, Oct. 1963
• Lindbergh, Charles A. 868, Dec. 1957; 563, Oct. 1963; 584, 586, Apr. 1968
• MacMillan, Donald Baxter. 563-564, Apr. 1953
• Peary, Robert E. 867, Dec. 1957; 589, Apr. 1959; 905, Dec. 1962; 514, Oct. 1963; 584, Apr. 1968
• Shackleton, Sir Ernest H. 868, Dec. 1957
• Siple, Paul A. 792-793, June 1958
• Trippe, Juan. 584-586, Apr. 1968

• U. S. Navy Antarctic Expeditions of 1955-1959: Medal presented to Secretary of the Navy Thomas S. Gates, Jr., with gold duplicates to Adm. Arleigh A. Burke and Rear Adm. George Dufek. 589-590, Apr. 1959; 530, Oct. 1959
• Wetmore, Alexander. 151, Aug. 1975

HUBERMAN, M. A.: Author:
• Backwoods Japan During American Occupation. 491-518, Apr. 1947

HUDSON, HENRY:
• Henry Hudson's River. By Willard Price. Photos by Wayne Miller. 364-403, Mar. 1962
• North Through History Aboard *White Mist*. By Melville Bell Grosvenor. Photos by Edwin Stuart Grosvenor. 1-55, July 1970

HUDSON (River), New York:
• Henry Hudson's River. By Willard Price. Photos by Wayne Miller. 364-403, Mar. 1962
• Here's New York Harbor. By Stuart E. Jones. Photos by Robert F. Sisson and David S. Boyer. 773-813, Dec. 1954
• The Hudson: "That River's Alive." By Alice J. Hall. Photos by Ted Spiegel. 62-89, Jan. 1978
• The Mighty Hudson. By Albert W. Atwood. Photos by B. Anthony Stewart. 1-36, July 1948
• North Through History Aboard *White Mist*. By Melville Bell Grosvenor. Photos by Edwin Stuart Grosvenor. 1-55, July 1970
• Shad in the Shadow of Skyscrapers. By Dudley B. Martin. Photos by Luis Marden. 359-376, Mar. 1947

HUDSON BAY, and Region, Canada:
• Henry Hudson's Changing Bay. By Bill Richards. Photos by David Hiser. 380-405, Mar. 1982
■ Polar Bear Alert. 395, Cover, Mar. 1982
• Trailing Cosmic Rays in Canada's North. By Martin A. Pomerantz. NGS research grant. 99-115, Jan. 1953
• Vanished Mystery Men of Hudson Bay. By Henry B. Collins. NGS research grant. 669-687, Nov. 1956
• *See also* Igloolik; James Bay; McConnell River Region; Southampton Island

HUDSON'S BAY COMPANY:
• Henry Hudson's Changing Bay. By Bill Richards. Photos by David Hiser. 380-405, Mar. 1982

HUE, Viet Nam:
• Behind the Headlines in Viet Nam. By Peter T. White. Photos by Winfield Parks. 149-189, Feb. 1967
• Portrait of Indochina. By W. Robert Moore and Maynard Owen Williams. Paintings by Jean Despujols. 461-490, Apr. 1951

HUENS, JEAN-LEON: Artist:
• Ancient Bulgaria's Golden Treasures. By Colin Renfrew. Photos by James L. Stanfield. 112-129, July 1980
• Pioneers in Man's Search for the Universe. By Thomas Y. Canby. 627-633, May 1974

BOTH BY WINFIELD PARKS, NGS

Hue: General Thieu and Marshal Ky, *above;* sampan community, *below*

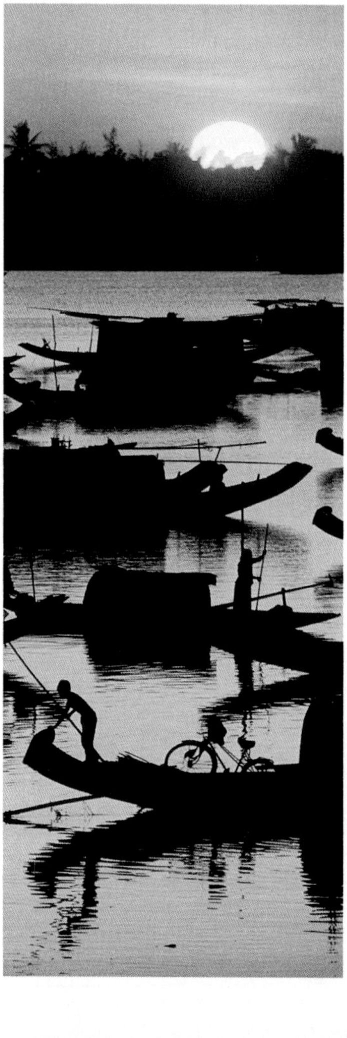

• Sir Francis Drake. By Alan Villiers. Photos by Gordon W. Gahan. 216-253, Feb. 1975

HUGHES, CAROL and DAVID:
Author-Photographers:
• Teeming Life of a Rain Forest. 49-65, Jan. 1983
Photographers:
• The Living Sands of the Namib. By William J. Hamilton III. 364-377, Sept. 1983

HUICHOL INDIANS:
• The Huichols, Mexico's People of Myth and Magic. By James Norman. Photos by Guillermo Aldana E. 832-853, June 1977

HUMAN BODY:
■ The Incredible Machine. 299, Sept. 1975; Cover announcement, Oct. 1975; 583, Nov. 1975; 575, Nov. 1976
◆ *Your Wonderful Body!* 1982
• *See also* Medicine and Health

HUMAN BRAIN:
■ Mysteries of the Mind. 1, Jan. 1980; cover, Feb. 1980

HUMAN-POWERED FLIGHT. *See Gossamer Albatross; Gossamer Condor*

HUMAN SACRIFICE:
• The Aztecs. 704-775, Dec. 1980
I. The Aztecs. By Bart McDowell. Photos by David Hiser. Paintings by Felipe Dávalos. 714-751; II. The Building of Tenochtitlan. By Augusto F. Molina Montes. Paintings by Felipe Dávalos. 753-765; III. New Finds in the Great Temple. By Eduardo Matos Moctezuma. Photos by David Hiser. 767-775
• Drama of Death in a Minoan Temple. By Yannis Sakellarakis and Efi Sapouna-Sakellaraki. Photos by Otis Imboden and Spyros Tsavdaroglou. 205-222, Feb. 1981
• Into the Well of Sacrifice (Chichén Itzá). NGS research grant. 540-561, Oct. 1961
I. Return to the Sacred Cenote. By Eusebio Dávalos Hurtado. 540-549; II. Treasure Hunt in the Deep Past. By Bates Littlehales. 550-561
• Joseph Alsop: A Historical Perspective (on Minoan Human Sacrifice). 223, Feb. 1981

HUMAN Treasures of Japan. By William Graves. Photos by James L. Stanfield. 370-379, Sept. 1972

HUMASON, MILTON L.: Author:
• First Photographs of Planets and Moon Taken with Palomar's 200-inch Telescope. 125-130, Jan. 1953

HUMBLE Masterpieces: Decoys. By George Reiger. Photos by Kenneth Garrett. 639-663, Nov. 1983

HUMBOLDT REDWOODS STATE PARK, California:
• Finding the Mt. Everest of All Living Things. By Paul A. Zahl. 10-51, July 1964
• World's Tallest Tree Discovered. By Melville Bell Grosvenor. Photos by George F. Mobley. 1-9, July 1964

HUME, EDGAR ERSKINE: Author:
● Italy Smiles Again. 693-732, June 1949
● The Palio of Siena. 231-244, Aug. 1951

HUME, IVOR NOËL. *See* Noël Hume, Ivor

HUMMINGBIRDS:
● Freezing the Flight of Hummingbirds. By Harold E. Edgerton, R. J. Niedrach, and Walker Van Riper. NGS research grant. 245-261, Aug. 1951
● The Hummingbirds. By Crawford H. Greenewalt. 658-679, Nov. 1960
● Hummingbirds: The Nectar Connection. By Paul W. Ewald. Photos by Robert A. Tyrrell. 223-227, Feb. 1982
● Hummingbirds in Action. By Harold E. Edgerton. 221-232, Aug. 1947
● The Man Who Talks to Hummingbirds (Augusto Ruschi). By Luis Marden. Photos by James Blair. 80-99, Jan. 1963
● The Marvelous Hummingbird Rediscovered. By Crawford H. Greenewalt. 98-101, July 1966
● Photographing Hummingbirds in Brazil. By Crawford H. Greenewalt. 100-115, Jan. 1963

HUMPBACK WHALES:
● Humpback Whales. NGS research grant. 2-25, Jan. 1979
I. The Gentle Giants. By Sylvia A. Earle. Photos by Al Giddings. 2-17; II. Their Mysterious Songs. By Roger Payne. Photos by Al Giddings. 18-25; III. Symphony of the Deep: "Songs of the Humpback Whale" (Sound sheet). 24-24B
● New Light on the Singing Whales. Introduction by Roger Payne. Photos by Flip Nicklin. NGS research grant. 463-477, Apr. 1982

HUNAN PROVINCE, People's Republic of China. *See* Ch'angsha

HUNGARIANS:
● Freedom Flight from Hungary. Photos by Robert F. Sisson. 424-436, Mar. 1957

HUNGARY:
● Down the Danube by Canoe. By William Slade Backer. Photos by Richard S. Durrance and Christopher G. Knight. 34-79, July 1965
● Hungary: Changing Homeland of a Tough, Romantic People. By Bart McDowell. Photos by Albert Moldvay and Joseph J. Scherschel. 443-483, Apr. 1971
● Hungary's New Way: A Different Communism. By John J. Putman. Photos by Bill Weems. 225-261, Feb. 1983
● *See also* Budapest

HUNT, CARLA: Author:
● Berber Brides' Fair. Photos by Nik Wheeler. 119-129, Jan. 1980

HUNT, SIR JOHN:
● President Eisenhower Presents the Hubbard Medal to Everest's Conquerors. 64, July 1954
● Triumph on Everest. 1-63, July 1954
Siege and Assault. By Sir John Hunt. 1-43

HUNTER, WILLIAM and JOHN:
● The British Way. By Sir Evelyn Wrench. 421-541, Apr. 1949

HUNTERS, Ice Age. *See* Paleo-Indians

HUNTERS of the Lost Spirit: Alaskans, Canadians, Greenlanders, Lapps. By Priit J. Vesilind. Photos by David Alan Harvey, Ivars Silis, and Sisse Brimberg. 150-197, Feb. 1983

HUNTING:
● Cliff Dwellers of the Bering Sea. By Juan Muñoz. Included: Seal and walrus hunting. 129-146, Jan. 1954
● Humble Masterpieces: Decoys. By George Reiger. Photos by Kenneth Garrett. 639-663, Nov. 1983
● Nomad in Alaska's Outback. By Thomas J. Abercrombie. Included: Walrus hunting. 540-567, Apr. 1969
● Spearing Lions with Africa's Masai. By Edgar Monsanto Queeny. 487-517, Oct. 1954
● We Dwelt in Kashgai Tents (Iran). By Jean and Franc Shor. 805-832, June 1952
● *See also* Falconry; Jaguar Hunting; Sealing; Whaling; *and* Bird Dogs; Paleo-Indians, for Ice Age hunters

HUNTING Africa's Smallest Game (Insects). By Edward S. Ross. 406-419, Mar. 1961

HUNTING Folk Songs in the Hebrides. By Margaret Shaw Campbell. 249-272, Feb. 1947

HUNTING Mexico's Buried Temples. Photos by Richard H. Stewart. 145-168, Feb. 1947

HUNTING Musical Game in West Africa. By Arthur S. Alberts. 262-282, Aug. 1951

HUNTING Prehistory in Panama Jungles. By Matthew W. Stirling. Photos by Richard H. Stewart. 271-290, Aug. 1953

HUNTING the Heartbeat of a Whale. By Paul Dudley White and Samuel W. Matthews. 49-64, July 1956

HUNTING Uranium Around the World. By Robert D. Nininger. Photos by Volkmar Wentzel. 533-558, Oct. 1954

HUNTINGTON, HENRY E., LIBRARY AND ART GALLERY, San Marino, California:
● Huntington Library, California Treasure House. By David S. Boyer. 251-276, Feb. 1958

HUNZA:
● At World's End in Hunza. By Jean and Franc Shor. 485-518, Oct. 1953
● "Every Day Is a Gift When You Are Over 100." By Alexander Leaf. Photos by John Launois. 93-119, Jan. 1973
● Sky Road East. By Tay and Lowell Thomas, Jr. 71-112, Jan. 1960
● Trek to Lofty Hunza–and Beyond. By Sabrina and Roland Michaud. 644-669, Nov. 1975

HUPEH (Province), China. *See* Hankow

HURLEY, FRANK: Photographer:
● Arab Land Beyond the Jordan. 753-768, Dec. 1947

HURON, Lake, Canada-U. S.:
● The Great Lakes: Is It Too Late? By Gordon Young. Photos by James L. Amos and Martin Rogers. 147-185, Aug. 1973

HURRICANES:
● Cajunland, Louisiana's French-speaking Coast. By Bern Keating. Photos by Charles Harbutt and Franke Keating. Included: Hurricane Audrey (1957); Hurricane Betsy (1965). 353-391, Mar. 1966
● Hurricane! By Ben Funk. Photos by Robert W. Madden. 346-379, Sept. 1980
Dominica. By Fred Ward. 357-359; Dynamics of a Hurricane. 370-371; Into the Eye of David. By John L. Eliot. 368-369; Paths of Fury–This Century's Worst American Storms. 360-361
● Men Against the Hurricane. By Andrew H. Brown. 537-560, Oct. 1950
● We're Doing Something About the Weather! By Walter Orr Roberts. 518-555, Apr. 1972

HURTADO, EUSEBIO DÁVALOS. *See* Dávalos Hurtado, Eusebio

HUSSEIN, King (Jordan):
● The Other Side of Jordan. By Luis Marden. 790-825, Dec. 1964
Author:
● Holy Land, My Country. 784-789, Dec. 1964

HUTCHINS, ROSS E.:
Author-Photographer:
● Living Honey Jars of the Ant World. 405-411, Mar. 1962

HUTCHISON, BRUCE: Author:
● Exploring Ottawa. 565-596, Nov. 1947

HUTCHISON, ISOBEL WYLIE: Author:
● From Barra to Butt in the Hebrides. 559-580, Oct. 1954
● Poets' Voices Linger in Scottish Shrines. Photos by Kathleen Revis. 437-488, Oct. 1957
● Shetland and Orkney, Britain's Far North. 519-536, Oct. 1953
● A Stroll to John o'Groat's. 1-48, July 1956
● A Stroll to London. Photos by B. Anthony Stewart. 171-204, Aug. 1950
● A Stroll to Venice. 378-410, Sept. 1951
● 2,000 Miles Through Europe's Oldest Kingdom. Photos by Maynard Owen Williams. 141-180, Feb. 1949

HUTSON, PAT: Author:
● Snow-mantled Stehekin: Where Solitude Is in Season. Photos by Bruce Dale. 572-588, Apr. 1974

GH

WILLIAM ALBERT ALLARD

Hutterites: Joe Stahl shears a ewe

The **HUTTERITES,** Plain People of the West. By William Albert Allard. 98-125, July 1970

HUTTON, JACQUELINE: Artist:
- Strange Babies of the Sea. By Hilary B. Moore. Paintings by Craig Phillips and Jacqueline Hutton. 41-56, July 1952

HUZZA for Otaheite! By Luis Marden. 435-459, Apr. 1962

HYBRIDS:
- Amateur Gardener Creates a New Rose. By Elizabeth A. Moize. Photos by Farrell Grehan. 286-294, Aug. 1972
- The Exquisite Orchids. By Luis Marden. 485-513, Apr. 1971
- Those Fiery Brazilian Bees. By Rick Gore. Photos by Bianca Lavies. 491-501, Apr. 1976

HYDROCARBON FUELS. *See* Coal; Natural Gas; Oil; Synfuels

HYDROELECTRIC POWER:
- Egypt's Desert of Promise. By Farouk El-Baz. Photos by Georg Gerster. Included: The proposed Qattara project. 190-221, Feb. 1982
- The Fire of Heaven. By Albert W. Atwood. 655-674, Nov. 1948
- Kitimat–Canada's Aluminum Titan. By David S. Boyer. 376-398, Sept. 1956. Included: Kemano power development.
- New St. Lawrence Seaway Opens the Great Lakes to the World. By Andrew H. Brown. 299-339, Mar. 1959
- Niagara Falls, Servant of Good Neighbors. Photos by Walter Meayers Edwards. 574-587, Apr. 1963
- Paraguay, Paradox of South America. By Gordon Young. Photos by O. Louis Mazzatenta. Included: Itaipú Dam. 240-269, Aug. 1982
- Powerhouse of the Northwest (Columbia River). By David S. Boyer. 821-847, Dec. 1974
- Quebec's Northern Dynamo. By Larry Kohl. Photos by Ottmar Bierwagen. Note: It is expected that nine powerhouses will produce 13,700 megawatts. 406-418, Mar. 1982

HYDROFOIL BOATS:
- Hydrofoil, *HD-4,* designed by Alexander Graham Bell. 493, 495, 496, Apr. 1957; 257, 264, Aug. 1959; 554-555, Oct. 1963
- Hydrofoil Ferry "Flies" the Strait of Messina. By Gilbert Grosvenor. Contents: *Arrow of the Sun, HD-4.* 493-496, Apr. 1957

HYDRO-QUÉBEC:
- Quebec's Northern Dynamo. By Larry Kohl. Photos by Ottmar Bierwagen. 406-418, Mar. 1982

HYDROTHERMAL ENERGY. *See* Geothermal Energy

HYDROTHERMAL VENTS:
- Incredible World of the Deep-sea Rifts. NGS research grant. 680-705, Nov. 1979
  I. Strange World Without Sun. The Editor. 680-688; II. Return to Oases of the Deep. By Robert D. Ballard and J. Frederick Grassle. 689-705
- Oases of Life in the Cold Abyss (Galapagos Rift). By John B. Corliss and Robert D. Ballard. 441-453, Oct. 1977
- *See also* Geothermal Energy

HYENAS:
- The Flamingo Eaters of Ngorongoro. By Richard D. Estes. 535-539, Oct. 1973
- Hyenas, the Hunters Nobody Knows. By Hans Kruuk. Photos by Baron Hugo van Lawick. 44-57, July 1968

I

IAGS. *See* Inter-American Geodetic Survey

IC. *See* Integrated Circuits

IGY. *See* International Geophysical Year

ISA. *See* International School of America

I BECOME a Bakhtiari. By Paul Edward Case. 325-358, Mar. 1947

I CLIMBED Everest Alone. By Reinhold Messner. Photos by the author and Nena Holguín. 552-566, Oct. 1981

I FLY the X-15. By Joseph A. Walker. Photos by Dean Conger. 428-450, Sept. 1962

I FOUND the Bones of the *Bounty.* By Luis Marden. 725-789, Dec. 1957

I JOINED a Sahara Salt Caravan. By Victor Englebert. 694-711, Nov. 1965

I LIVE With the Eskimos. By Guy Mary-Rousseliere. 188-217, Feb. 1971

I SAILED with Portugal's Captains Courageous. By Alan Villiers. 565-596, May 1952

I SEE America First. By Lynda Bird Johnson. Photos by William Albert Allard. 874-904, Dec. 1965

I WALKED Some Irish Miles. By Dorothea Sheats. 653-678, May 1951

"**I WILL** Fight No More Forever." By William Albert Allard. 409-434, Mar. 1977

IBAN (People):
- Brunei, Borneo's Abode of Peace. By Joseph Judge. Photos by Dean Conger. 207-225, Feb. 1974
- In Storied Lands of Malaysia. By Maurice Shadbolt. Photos by Winfield Parks. 734-783, Nov. 1963
- Jungle Journeys in Sarawak. By Hedda Morrison. 710-736, May 1956

IBERIAN PENINSULA:
- ▲ *Spain and Portugal,* Atlas series supplement. Mar. 1965
- *See also* Gibraltar; Portugal; Spain

IBISES:
- New Scarlet Bird in Florida Skies. By Paul A. Zahl. 874-882, Dec. 1967

• Search for the Scarlet Ibis in Venezuela. By Paul A. Zahl. NGS research grant. 633-661, May 1950
• Wildlife of Everglades National Park. By Daniel B. Beard. Paintings by Walter A. Weber. 83-116, Jan. 1949
• *See also* Wood Storks

IBIZA (Island), Balearics:
• Spain's Sun-blest Pleasure Isles. By Ethel A. Starbird. Photos by James A. Sugar. 679-701, May 1976

ICE AGE ANIMALS:
• Bison Kill By Ice Age Hunters. By Dennis Stanford. NGS research grant. 114-121, Jan. 1979
• The Search for the First Americans. By Thomas Y. Canby. Photos by Kerby Smith. Paintings by Roy Andersen. 330-363, Sept. 1979

ICE AGE MAN:
• A Bold New Look at Our Past. The Editor. NGS research grant. 62-63, Jan. 1975
• Exploring the Mind of Ice Age Man. By Alexander Marshack. NGS research grant. 64-89, Jan. 1975
• Ice Age Man, the First American. By Thomas R. Henry. Paintings by Andre Durenceau. 781-806, Dec. 1955
• Wyoming Muck Tells of Battle: Ice Age Man vs. Mammoth. By Cynthia Irwin, Henry Irwin, and George Agogino. NGS research grant. 828-837, June 1962
• *See also* Paleo-Indians

ICE AGES:
▲ "Ice Age Mammals of the Alaskan Tundra," painting supplement. Map of Canada. Mar. 1972
• On the Trail of Wisconsin's Ice Age. By Anne LaBastille. Photos by Cary Wolinsky. 182-205, Aug. 1977
• The Search for the First Americans. By Thomas Y. Canby. Photos by Kerby Smith. Paintings by Roy Andersen. 330-363, Sept. 1979
• A Visit to the Living Ice Age. By Rutherford Platt. 525-545, Apr. 1957
• What's Happening to Our Climate? By Samuel W. Matthews. 576-615, Nov. 1976
• *See also* Lascaux Cave

ICE BIRD (Sloop):
• Alone to Antarctica. By David Lewis. Drawings by Noel Sickles. 808-821, Dec. 1973
• *Ice Bird* Ends Her Lonely Odyssey. By David Lewis. 216-233, Aug. 1975

ICE CAVES:
• Probing Ice Caves of the Pyrenees. By Norbert Casteret. 391-404, Mar. 1953

ICE-CORE DATING:
• What's Happening to Our Climate? By Samuel W. Matthews. 576-615, Nov. 1976

ICE FISHING:
• Ice Fishing's Frigid Charms. By Thomas J. Abercrombie. 861-872, Dec. 1958

ICE ISLANDS:
• North Toward the Pole on Skis. By Bjørn O. Staib. 254-281, Feb. 1965
• Scientists Ride Ice Islands on Arctic Odysseys. By Lowell Thomas, Jr. Photos by Ted Spiegel. 670-691, Nov. 1965
• *See also* T-3

ICE SCULPTURE:
• Snow Festival in Japan's Far North. Photos by Eiji Miyazawa. 824-833, Dec. 1968

ICEBERGS:
• Far North with "Captain Mac." By Miriam MacMillan. 465-513, Oct. 1951
• Our Navy Explores Antarctica. By Richard E. Byrd. U. S. Navy official photos. 429-522, Oct. 1947
• Tracking Danger with the Ice Patrol. By William S. Ellis. Photos by James R. Holland. 780-793, June 1968
• Voyage to the Antarctic. By David Lewis. Included: The study of icebergs as a future water supply for the arid areas of the earth. 544-562, Apr. 1983

ICEBREAKERS:
• North for Oil: *Manhattan* Makes the Historic Northwest Passage. By Bern Keating. Photos by Tomas Sennett. 374-391, Mar. 1970
• Our Navy Explores Antarctica. By Richard E. Byrd. U. S. Navy official photos. 429-522, Oct. 1947
• Sea to Lakes on the St. Lawrence. By George W. Long. Photos by B. Anthony Stewart and John E. Fletcher. 323-366, Sept. 1950

ICELAND:
• "Around the World in Eighty Days." By Newman Bumstead. Included: Hekla Volcano; Reykjavík; Vatna Jökull. 705-750, Dec. 1951
• Atlantic Odyssey: Iceland to Antarctica. By Newman Bumstead. Photos by Volkmar Wentzel. 725-780, Dec. 1955
• Friendly Flight to Northern Europe. By Lyndon B. Johnson. Photos by Volkmar Wentzel. 268-293, Feb. 1964
• Iceland Tapestry. By Deena Clark. 599-630, Nov. 1951
• Sailing Iceland's Rugged Coasts. By Wright Britton. Photos by James A. Sugar. 228-265, Aug. 1969
• This Changing Earth. By Samuel W. Matthews. 1-37, Jan. 1973
• Vestmannaeyjar: Up From the Ashes. By Noel Grove. Photos by Robert S. Patton. 690-701, May 1977
• *See also* Heimaey; Surtsey; *and* Vikings

ICHAC, PIERRE: Photographer:
• Carefree People of the Cameroons. 233-248, Feb. 1947

ICONS:
• The Byzantine Empire. 709-777, Dec. 1983
I. Rome of the East. By Merle Severy. Photos by James L. Stanfield. 709-767; II. Mount Athos. 739-745; III. Eternal Easter in a Greek

JAMES R. HOLLAND (TOP); JAMES R. HOLLAND, WITH ARTWORK BELOW WATERLINE BY AN NGS STAFF ARTIST

Tracking Danger: iceberg's awesome tower, *top*, dwarfs ship, while water conceals an even larger ice mass, *above*

Village. By Maria Nicolaidis-Karanikolas. Photos by James L. Stanfield. 768-777
• Mount Sinai's Holy Treasures (St. Catherine's Monastery). By Kurt Weitzmann. Photos by Fred Anderegg. 109-127, Jan. 1964

IDA, DON:
• A Wild, Ill-fated Balloon Race. 778-797, Dec. 1983
I. Wild Launch. 778-787; II. The Fantastic Flight of *Cote d'Or*. By Cynthia Shields. 789-793; III. Last Ascent of a Heroic Team (Maxie Anderson and Don Ida). 794-797

IDAHO:
• Along the Great Divide. By Mike Edwards. Photos by Nicholas DeVore III. 483-515, Oct. 1979
• Chief Joseph. By William Albert Allard. 409-434, Mar. 1977
• Following the Trail of Lewis and Clark. By Ralph Gray. 707-750, June 1953
• Forest Fire: The Devil's Picnic. By Stuart E. Jones and Jay Johnston. Included: Blazes in Kaniksu National Forest and Nezperce National Forest. 100-127, July 1968
• High-stepping Idaho. By William S. Ellis. Photos by Dean Conger. 290-317, Mar. 1973
• Idaho Loggers Battle a River. 117-130, July 1951
• The Incredible Potato. By Robert E. Rhoades. Photos by Martin Rogers. Note: The Russet Burbank has allowed Idaho and Washington to surpass Maine's production lead. 668-694, May 1982
• Man on the Moon in Idaho. By William Belknap, Jr. 505-525, Oct. 1960
• A Map Maker Looks at the United States. By Newman Bumstead. Included: Coeur d'Alene; Lewiston; Pleasant Valley Rapids; Pocatello; Seven Devils country; Snake River; Weiser. 705-748, June 1951
• Stalking the Mountain Lion–to Save Him. By Maurice G. Hornocker. 638-655, Nov. 1969
• White-water Adventure on Wild Rivers of Idaho. By Frank Craighead, Jr. and John Craighead. 213-239, Feb. 1970
▥ Wild River. 239A-239B, Feb. 1970
• *See also* Grays Lake National Wildlife Refuge; Morgan Creek; Palouse Hills

IDITAROD TRAIL SLED DOG RACE, Alaska:
• Thousand-mile Race to Nome: A Woman's Icy Struggle. By Susan Butcher. Photos by Kerby Smith. 411-422, Mar. 1983

IDYLL, CLARENCE P.: Author:
• The Crab That Shakes Hands. Photos by Robert F. Sisson. 254-271, Feb. 1971
• Grunion, the Fish That Spawns on Land. Photos by Robert F. Sisson. 714-723, May 1969
• The Incredible Salmon. Photos by Robert F. Sisson. Paintings by Walter A. Weber. 195-219, Aug. 1968

BOTH BY BRUCE DALE, NGS

Île de la Cité: aerial view of island, *above*; diplomatic luncheon at Hôtel de Lauzun, *below*

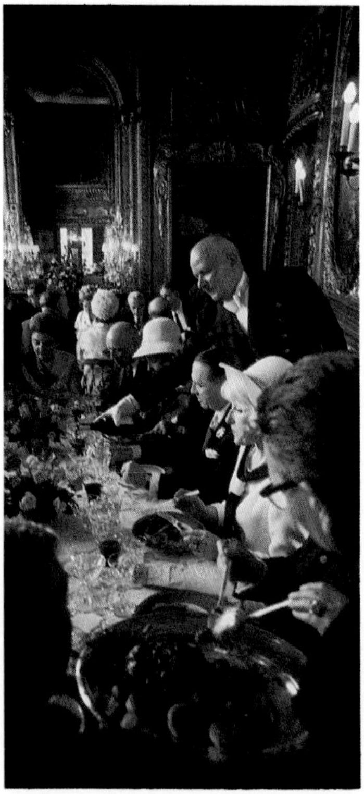

• New Florida Resident, the Walking Catfish. Photos by Robert F. Sisson. 847-851, June 1969
• Shrimp Nursery: Science Explores New Ways to Farm the Sea. Photos by Robert F. Sisson. 636-659, May 1965
• Shrimpers Strike Gold in the Gulf. Photos by Robert F. Sisson. 699-707, May 1957

The **IDYLLIC** Vale of Kashmir. By Volkmar Wentzel. 523-550, Apr. 1948

IFALIK, Lonely Paradise of the South Seas. By Marston Bates. 547-571, Apr. 1956

IGLOOLIK, Northwest Territories, Canada:
• Hunters of the Lost Spirit: Canadians. By Priit J. Vesilind. Photos by David Alan Harvey. 174-189, Feb. 1983
• I Live With the Eskimos. By Guy Mary-Rousseliere. 188-217, Feb. 1971

IGUANAS:
• The Galapagos, Eerie Cradle of New Species. By Roger Tory Peterson. Photos by Alan and Joan Root. 541-585, Apr. 1967
• In the Wilds of a City Parlor. By Paul A. Zahl. 645-672, Nov. 1954
• Lost World of the Galapagos. By Irving and Electa Johnson. 681-703, May 1959
• Undersea Wonders of the Galapagos. By Gerard Wellington. Photos by David Doubilet. 363-381, Sept. 1978

IKEYA-SEKI COMET:
• Giant Comet Grazes the Sun. By Kenneth F. Weaver. 259-261, Feb. 1966

ÎLE DE LA CITÉ, Birthplace of Paris. By Kenneth MacLeish. Photos by Bruce Dale. 680-719, May 1968

ILHA NOVA, Azores:
• A New Volcano Bursts from the Atlantic. By John Scofield. Photos by Robert F. Sisson. 735-757, June 1958

ILLINOIS:
▲ *Close-up: U.S.A., Illinois, Indiana, Ohio, and Kentucky*, supplement. Text on reverse. Feb. 1977
• Following the Trail of Lewis and Clark. By Ralph Gray. 707-750, June 1953
• Illinois–Healthy Heart of the Nation. By Leo A. Borah. Photos by B. Anthony Stewart and Willard R. Culver. 781-820, Dec. 1953
• Illinois: The City and the Plain. By Robert Paul Jordan. Photos by James L. Stanfield and Joseph J. Scherschel. 745-797, June 1967
• Mapping the Nation's Breadbasket. By Frederick Simpich. 831-849, June 1948
• "Pyramids" of the New World. By Neil Merton Judd. Included Cahokia. 105-128, Jan. 1948
• The Tallgrass Prairie: Can It Be Saved? By Dennis Farney. Photos by Jim Brandenburg. 37-61, Jan. 1980

• The Upper Mississippi. By Willard Price. 651-699, Nov. 1958
• Vacation Tour Through Lincoln Land. By Ralph Gray. 141-184, Feb. 1952
• Who Were the "Mound Builders"? By George E. Stuart. Included: Cahokia; Koster farm site; Monks Mound; East St. Louis. 783-801, Dec. 1972
• *See also* Chicago; East St. Louis; Shawneetown

ILLINOIS (River), Illinois:
• Down Mark Twain's River on a Raft. By Rex E. Hieronymus. Included: The Illinois and Mississippi rivers. 551-574, Apr. 1948

ILLUSTRATED LONDON NEWS:
• Witness to a War (U. S. Civil War): British Correspondent Frank Vizetelly. By Robert T. Cochran, Jr. 453-491, Apr. 1961

ILULÍSSAT, Greenland. *See* Jakobshavn

I'M From New Jersey. By John T. Cunningham. Photos by Volkmar Wentzel. 1-45, Jan. 1960

"**I'M OK,** I'm Alive!" Avalanche! By David Cupp. Photos by Lanny Johnson and Andre Benier. 282-289, Sept. 1982

IMAGING TECHNIQUES:
• Editorial. By Gilbert M. Grosvenor. 295, Mar. 1978
• Eyes of Science. By Rick Gore. Photos by James P. Blair. 360-389, Mar. 1978
• Heat Paints *Columbia*'s Portrait. By Cliff Tarpy. 650-653, Nov. 1982
▪ The Invisible World. 1, Jan. 1980; cover, Mar. 1980
• The Mystery of the Shroud. By Kenneth F. Weaver. Included: Density scans, stereometric photography, and ultraviolet photography. 730-753, June 1980
• The Once and Future Universe. By Rick Gore. Photos by James A. Sugar. Paintings by Barron Storey. Picture text by David Jeffery. 704-749, June 1983
• Satellites That Serve Us. By Thomas Y. Canby. Included: A portfolio, Images of Earth. 281-335, Sept. 1983
Spacelab 1: *Columbia*. By Michael E. Long. 301-307
• *See also* Fiber Optics; Photography; Photography, Underwater; Photomicrography; Thermograms

IMAZIGHEN. *See* Berbers

IMBODEN, OTIS: Photographer:
• Drama of Death in a Minoan Temple. By Yannis Sakellarakis and Efi Sapouna-Sakellaraki. Photos by Otis Imboden and Spyros Tsavdaroglou. 205-222, Feb. 1981
• Drowned Galleons Yield Spanish Gold. By Kip Wagner. 1-37, Jan. 1965
• First Flight Across the Bottom of the World. By James R. Reedy. 454-464, Mar. 1964
• Florida's Emerging Seminoles. By Louis Capron. 716-734, Nov. 1969
• Goal at the End of the Trail: Santa Fe. By William S. Ellis. Photos by Gordon W. Gahan and Otis Imboden. 323-345, Mar. 1982
• The Maya: Riddle of the Glyphs. By George E. Stuart. 768-791, Dec. 1975
• The People of Cades Cove. By William O. Douglas. Photos by Thomas Nebbia and Otis Imboden. 60-95, July 1962
• Thera, Key to the Riddle of Minos. By Spyridon Marinatos. 702-726, May 1972
• The Thousand-mile Glide. By Karl Striedieck. 431-438, Mar. 1978
• Threatened Glories of Everglades National Park. By Frederick Kent Truslow and Frederick G. Vosburgh. Photos by Frederick Kent Truslow and Otis Imboden. 508-553, Oct. 1967
• YWCA: International Success Story. By Mary French Rockefeller. 904-933, Dec. 1963

IMILCHIL PLATEAU, Morocco:
• Berber Brides' Fair. By Carla Hunt. Photos by Nik Wheeler. 119-129, Jan. 1980

IMMIGRANTS:
Australia:
• Coober Pedy: Opal Capital of Australia's Outback. By Kenny Moore. Photos by Penny Tweedie. 560-571, Oct. 1976
• The Making of a New Australia. By Howell Walker. 233-259, Feb. 1956
• South Australia, Gateway to the Great Outback. By Howell Walker. Photos by Joseph J. Scherschel. 441-481, Apr. 1970
Israel:
• Israel–The Seventh Day. By Joseph Judge. Photos by Gordon W. Gahan. 816-855, Dec. 1972
• Our Life on a Border Kibbutz. By Carol and Al Abrams. Photos by Al Abrams. 364-391, Sept. 1970
United States:
▲ *Atlantic Gateways,* The Making of America series. Included: Delaware, Maryland, New Jersey, New York, Pennsylvania, northern Virginia, West Virginia, and in Canada, southern Ontario and southern Quebec. On reverse: Indians and Trade, Nation in the Making, Peopling of the Gateways, Race for the Hinterlands, Growth of Industry, Spreading Urban Corridors. Mar. 1983
• Brooklyn: The Other Side of the Bridge. By Alice J. Hall. Photos by Robert W. Madden. Included: Caribbean Blacks, Germans, Hasidic Jews, Hispanics, Irish, Italians, Russian Jews, Sephardic Jews. 580-613, May 1983
• Chinatown, the Gilded Ghetto. By William Albert Allard. 627-643, Nov. 1975
• Cuba's Exiles Bring New Life to Miami. By Edward J. Linehan. Photos by Nathan Benn. 68-95, July 1973
• Florida–A Time for Reckoning. By William S. Ellis. Photos by Nathan Benn and Kevin Fleming. Included: Cubans; Haitians; Jamaicans; Jews of European origin; Puerto Ricans. 172-219, Aug. 1982
• Immigrants Still Flock to Liberty's Land. By Albert W. Atwood. 708-724, Nov. 1955
• The Incredible Potato. By Robert E. Rhoades. Photos by Martin Rogers. Included: Scotch-Irish. 668-694, May 1982
• New England's "Little Portugal." By O. Louis Mazzatenta. 90-109, Jan. 1975
• They'd Rather Be in Philadelphia. By Ethel A. Starbird. Photos by Ted Spiegel. Included: Asians, Germans, Irish, Italians, Jews, Poles. 314-343, Mar. 1983
• *See also* German Colonists; Hutterites; Moravians; Refugees; Russians; Swiss Colonists; Ukrainians

IMPERIAL Russia's Glittering Legacy. 24-33, Jan. 1978

The **IMPERILED** Everglades. By Fred Ward. 1-27, Jan. 1972

The **IMPERILED** Giants. By William Graves. 722-751, Dec. 1976

IMPERILED Gift of the Sea: Caribbean Green Turtle. By Archie Carr. Photos by Robert E. Schroeder. 876-890, June 1967

The **IMPERILED** Mountain Gorilla. By Dian Fossey. 501-523, Apr. 1981
Death of Marchessa. Photos by Peter G. Veit. 508-511

IMPERILED Phantom of Asian Peaks: First Photographs of Snow Leopards in the Wild. By George B. Schaller. 702-707, Nov. 1971

IMPRESSIONIST ART. *See* French Impressionists

IMPRINTING. *See* Snow Geese

IN Hawaii's Crystal Sea, A Galaxy of Life Fills the Night. By Kenneth Brower. Photos by William R. Curtsinger and Chris Newbert. 834-847, Dec. 1981

IN Long-Forbidden Tibet. By Fred Ward. 218-259, Feb. 1980

IN Manchuria Now. By W. Robert Moore. 389-414, Mar. 1947

IN Quest of Beauty. Text by Paul Mellon. 372-385, Mar. 1967

IN Quest of the Rarest Flamingo. By William G. Conway. Photos by Bates Littlehales. 91-105, July 1961

IN Quest of the World's Largest Frog. By Paul A. Zahl. 146-152, July 1967

IN Search of Arabia's Past. By Peter Bruce Cornwall. 493-522, Apr. 1948

IN Search of Man's Past at Lake Rudolf. By Richard E. Leakey. Photos by Gordon W. Gahan. 712-734, May 1970

IN Search of Moses. By Harvey Arden. Photos by Nathan Benn. 2-37, Jan. 1976

MUSEUM AND INSTITUTE OF ARCHAEOLOGY, UNIVERSITY OF SAN ANTONIO ABAD, CUZCO, BY LOREN MCINTYRE

Incas: gold figure of an Inca nobleman

IN Storied Lands of Malaysia. By Maurice Shadbolt. Photos by Winfield Parks. 734-783, Nov. 1963

IN the Crusaders' Footsteps. By Franc Shor. Photos by Thomas Nebbia and James P. Blair. 731-789, June 1962

IN the Footsteps of Alexander the Great. By Helen and Frank Schreider. Paintings by Tom Lovell. 1-65, Jan. 1968

IN the Gardens of Olympus. By Paul A. Zahl. 85-123, July 1955

IN the London of the New Queen. By H. V. Morton. 291-342, Sept. 1953

IN the Path of Destruction (Mount St. Helens). By Rowe Findley. 35-49, Jan. 1981

IN the Tracks of Thoreau. By William Howarth. Photos by Farrell Grehan. 349-387, Mar. 1981

IN the Wake of Darwin's *Beagle*. By Alan Villiers. Photos by James L. Stanfield. 449-495, Oct. 1969

IN the Wake of Sindbad. By Tim Severin. Photos by Richard Greenhill. 2-41, July 1982

IN the Wilds of a City Parlor. By Paul A. Zahl. 645-672, Nov. 1954

IN Touch With Nature. Text by Elizabeth A. Moize. Photos by Steve Raymer. 537-543, Apr. 1974

INADAN:
- The Inadan: Artisans of the Sahara. By Michael and Aubine Kirtley. 282-298, Aug. 1979

INCAS:
- The Five Worlds of Peru. By Kenneth F. Weaver. Photos by Bates Littlehales. 213-265, Feb. 1964
- Flamboyant Is the Word for Bolivia. By Loren McIntyre. 153-193, Feb. 1966

◆ *Incredible Incas and Their Timeless Land.* Announced. 870-874, June 1975

▲ *Indians of South America; Archaeology of South America,* double-sided supplement. Mar. 1982

- The Lost Empire of the Incas. By Loren McIntyre. Art by Ned and Rosalie Seidler. 729-787, Dec. 1973

A pictorial chronicle of the Incas. 747-753

- Peru, Homeland of the Warlike Inca. By Kip Ross. 421-462, Oct. 1950
- Titicaca, Abode of the Sun. By Luis Marden. Photos by Flip Schulke. 272-294, Feb. 1971
- The Two Souls of Peru. By Harvey Arden. Photos by William Albert Allard. 284-321, Mar. 1982

INCHWORMS:
- The Case of the Killer Caterpillars. By Steven L. Montgomery. Photos by Robert F. Sisson. 219-225, Aug. 1983

INCREDIBLE Andorra. By Lawrence L. Klingman. Photos by B. Anthony Stewart. 262-290, Aug. 1949

The **INCREDIBLE** Crawl of Ned Myers. 300-305, Mar. 1983

The **INCREDIBLE** Crystal: Diamonds. By Fred Ward. 85-113, Jan. 1979

The **INCREDIBLE** Helicopter. By Peter T. White. 533-557, Apr. 1959

The **INCREDIBLE** Kangaroo. By David H. Johnson. 487-500, Oct. 1955

INCREDIBLE Photograph Shows Earth From Pole to Pole. Photos by Nimbus I. 190-193, Feb. 1965

The **INCREDIBLE** Potato. By Robert E. Rhoades. Photos by Martin Rogers. 668-694, May 1982

The **INCREDIBLE** Rat. By Thomas Y. Canby. Photos by James L. Stanfield. 60-87, July 1977

The **INCREDIBLE** Salmon. By Clarence P. Idyll. Photos by Robert F. Sisson. Paintings by Walter A. Weber. 195-219, Aug. 1968

The **INCREDIBLE** Universe. By Kenneth F. Weaver. Photos by James P. Blair. 589-625, May 1974

INCREDIBLE World of the Deep-sea Rifts. 680-705, Nov. 1979

INDIA:
- Around the World and the Calendar with the Geographic. By Melville Bell Grosvenor. 832-866, Dec. 1959
- "Around the World in Eighty Days." By Newman Bumstead. Included: Agra, Calcutta, Delhi. 705-750, Dec. 1951
- A Bad Time to Be a Crocodile. By Rick Gore. Photos by Jonathan Blair. 90-115, Jan. 1978
- Bombay, the Other India. By John Scofield. Photos by Raghubir Singh. 104-129, July 1981
- Calcutta, India's Maligned Metropolis. By Peter T. White. Photos by Raghubir Singh. 534-563, Apr. 1973
- Can the World Feed Its People? By Thomas Y. Canby. Photos by Steve Raymer. 2-31, July 1975
- The Cobra, India's "Good Snake." By Harry Miller. Photos by author and Naresh and Rajesh Bedi. 393-409, Sept. 1970
- Delhi, Capital of a New Dominion. By Phillips Talbot. 597-630, Nov. 1947
- The Desert: An Age-old Challenge Grows. By Rick Gore. Photos by Georg Gerster and Bruce Dale. 586-639, Nov. 1979
- The Elephant and I. By M. D. Chaturvedi. 489-507, Oct. 1957
- Enchantress! (White Tigress). By Theodore H. Reed. Photos by Thomas J. Abercrombie. 628-641, May 1961
- Feudal Splendor Lingers in Rajputana. By Volkmar Wentzel. 411-458, Oct. 1948
- From the Hair of Siva (Ganges River). By Helen and Frank Schreider. 445-503, Oct. 1960
- The Ganges, River of Faith. By John J. Putman. Photos by Raghubir Singh. 445-483, Oct. 1971

• High Adventure in the Himalayas. By Thomas Weir. 193-234, Aug. 1952
• How Fruit Came to America. By J. R. Magness. Paintings by Else Bostelmann. Included: Mango, an Evergreen from India. 325-377, Sept. 1951
• India in Crisis. By John Scofield. 599-661, May 1963
• India Struggles to Save Her Wildlife. By John J. Putman. Paintings by Ned Seidler. 299-343, Sept. 1976
• India's Energetic Sikhs. By John E. Frazer. Photos by James P. Blair. 528-541, Oct. 1972
• India's Sculptured Temple Caves. By Volkmar Wentzel. 665-678, May 1953
• Mountaintop War in Remote Ladakh. By W. E. Garrett. 664-687, May 1963
• Mysore Celebrates the Death of a Demon. By Luc Bouchage. Photos by Ylla. 706-711, May 1958
• Nature's Gifts to Medicine. By Lonnelle Aikman. Paintings by Lloyd K. Townsend and Don Crowley. 420-440, Sept. 1974
• New Life for India's Villagers (Bastar). By Anthony and Georgette Dickey Chapelle. 572-588, Apr. 1956
• Orissa, Past and Promise in an Indian State. By Bart McDowell. Photos by James P. Blair. 546-577, Oct. 1970
• Our Vegetable Travelers. By Victor R. Boswell. Paintings by Else Bostelmann. Included: Pickles and Salads Owe a Debt to India. 145-217, Aug. 1949
• The Pageant of Rajasthan. By Raghubir Singh. 219-243, Feb. 1977
• Purdah in India: Life Behind the Veil. By Doranne Wilson Jacobson. 270-286, Aug. 1977
• The Rat, Lapdog of the Devil. By Thomas Y. Canby. Photos by James L. Stanfield. 60-87, July 1977
• Roaming India's Naga Hills. By S. Dillon Ripley. 247-264, Feb. 1955
• Round the World School. By Paul Antze. Photos by William Eppridge. 96-127, July 1962
• Royal Wedding at Jaisalmer. By Marilyn Silverstone. 66-79, Jan. 1965
• Silver: A Mineral of Excellent Nature. By Allen A. Boraiko. Photos by Fred Ward. 280-313, Sept. 1981
▲ *Southwest Asia, including India, Pakistan, and Northeast Africa,* supplement. June 1952
• Troubled Waters East of Suez. By Ernest M. Eller. 483-522, Apr. 1954
• When the President Goes Abroad (Eisenhower). By Gilbert M. Grosvenor. 588-649, May 1960
• Wild Elephant Roundup in India. By Harry Miller. Photos by author and James P. Blair. 372-385, Mar. 1969
• YWCA: International Success Story. By Mary French Rockefeller. Photos by Otis Imboden. 904-933, Dec. 1963
• *See also* Andaman Islands; Assam; Kashmir; Ladakh; Malabar Coast; Sikkim

INDIAN MOUNDS:
• Exploring Ancient Panama by Helicopter. By Matthew W. Stirling. Photos by Richard H. Stewart. NGS research grant. 227-246, Feb. 1950
• Exploring the Past in Panama. By Matthew W. Stirling. Photos by Richard H. Stewart. NGS research grant. 373-399, Mar. 1949
• "Pyramids" of the New World. By Neil Merton Judd. 105-128, Jan. 1948
• Who Were the "Mound Builders"? By George E. Stuart. 783-801, Dec. 1972

INDIAN OCEAN:
• *Calypso* Explores for Underwater Oil. By Jacques-Yves Cousteau. NGS research grant. 155-184, Aug. 1955
• Camera Under the Sea. By Luis Marden. NGS research grant. 162-200, Feb. 1956
• Crosscurrents Sweep the Indian Ocean. By Bart McDowell. Photos by Steve Raymer. 422-457, Oct. 1981
• Exploring Davy Jones's Locker with *Calypso.* By Jacques-Yves Cousteau. Photos by Luis Marden. NGS research grant. 149-161, Feb. 1956
• In the Wake of Sindbad. By Tim Severin. Photos by Richard Greenhill. 2-41, July 1982
▲ *Indian Ocean Floor,* supplement. Oct. 1967
• Science Explores the Monsoon Sea. By Samuel W. Matthews. Photos by Robert F. Sisson. 554-575, Oct. 1967
• *Yankee* Roams the Orient. By Irving and Electa Johnson. 327-370, Mar. 1951
• *See also* Andaman Islands; Madagascar; Maldives Republic; Seychelles (Islands); Sri Lanka; Zanzibar; *and* Dhows

INDIAN Shangri-La of the Grand Canyon. By Jay Johnston. Photos by Terry Eiler. 355-373, Mar. 1970

INDIANA:
▲ *Close-up: U.S.A., Illinois, Indiana, Ohio, and Kentucky,* supplement. Text on reverse. Feb. 1977
• Indiana's Self-reliant Uplanders. By James Alexander Thom. Photos by J. Bruce Baumann. 341-363, Mar. 1976
• Mapping the Nation's Breadbasket. By Frederick Simpich. 831-849, June 1948
• So Much Happens Along the Ohio River. By Frederick Simpich. Photos by Justin Locke. 177-212, Feb. 1950
• Vacation Tour Through Lincoln Land. By Ralph Gray. 141-184, Feb. 1952
• *See also* Columbus, Indiana

INDIANS OF CENTRAL AMERICA:
▲ *Archeological Map of Middle America, Land of the Feathered Serpent,* supplement. Text on reverse. Oct. 1968
• Christopher Columbus and the New World He Found. By John Scofield. Photos by Adam Woolfitt. Included: Guamis. 584-625, Nov. 1975
• Dzibilchaltun. NGS research grant. 91-129, Jan. 1959
I. Lost City of the Maya. By E. Wyllys Andrews. 91-109; II. Up From the Well of Time. By Luis Marden. 110-129
• Easter Week in Indian Guatemala. By John Scofield. 406-417, Mar. 1960
• Exploring Ancient Panama by Helicopter. By Matthew W. Stirling. Photos by Richard H. Stewart. Included: Pre-Columbian grave artifacts. NGS research grant. 227-246, Feb. 1950
• Exploring the Past in Panama. By Matthew W. Stirling. Photos by Richard H. Stewart. Included: Guaymi Indians, Coclé Indian culture, and pottery from the El Hatillo and Monagrillo sites. NGS research grant. 373-399, Mar. 1949
• Guatemala, Maya and Modern. By Louis de la Haba. Photos by Joseph J. Scherschel. 661-689, Nov. 1974
• Guatemala Revisited. By Luis Marden. Included: Itzas, Mayas, Quichés, Tzutuhiles. 525-564, Oct. 1947
• Hunting Prehistory in Panama Jungles. By Matthew W. Stirling. Photos by Richard H. Stewart. NGS research grant. 271-290, Aug. 1953
◆ *Indians of the Americas.* 418, Mar. 1957; 781, June 1959
• Into the Well of Sacrifice (Chichén Itzá). NGS research grant. 540-561, Oct. 1961
I. Return to the Sacred Cenote. By Eusebio Dávalos Hurtado. 540-549; II. Treasure Hunt in the Deep Past. By Bates Littlehales. 550-561
• The Maya. 729-811, Dec. 1975
I. Children of Time. By Howard La Fay. Photos by David Alan Harvey. 729-767; II. Riddle of the Glyphs. By George E. Stuart. Photos by Otis Imboden. 768-791; III. Resurrecting the Grandeur of Tikal. By William R. Coe. 792-798; IV. A Traveler's Tale of Ancient Tikal. Paintings by Peter Spier. Text by Alice J. Hall. 799-811
• Maya Art Treasures Discovered in Cave. By George E. Stuart. Photos by Wilbur E. Garrett. 220-235, Aug. 1981
◆ *The Mysterious Maya.* 1977
• "Pyramids" of the New World. By Neil Merton Judd. Included: Copán in Honduras; Piedras Negras and Tikal in Guatemala. 105-128, Jan. 1948
• Unearthing the Oldest Known Maya. By Norman Hammond. Photos by Lowell Georgia and Martha Cooper. NGS research grant. 126-140, July 1982
• We Drove Panama's Darién Gap. By Kip Ross. Included: Chocós, Cuna. 368-389, Mar. 1961

INDIANS OF NORTH AMERICA:
• Alaska: Rising Northern Star. By Joseph Judge. Photos by Bruce Dale. Included: Ahtena, Athapaskan, Haida, Nulato and Tlingit Indians. 730-767, June 1975
▲ *America's Federal Lands; The United States,* double-sided supple-

I
J

ment. Included: Indian reservations. Sept. 1982

● America's First Painters. By Dorothy Dunn. Contents: The art of the Apaches, Navajos, Pueblo, Sioux, Woodland and Plains tribes. 349-377, Mar. 1955

● Amid the Mighty Walls of Zion. By Lewis F. Clark. Photos by Justin Locke and author. Contents: Basket Makers, Paiutes, Pueblo. 37-70, Jan. 1954

● Arizona: Booming Youngster of the West. By Robert de Roos. Photos by Robert F. Sisson. Included: Apaches, Hopis, Navajos, Papagos. 299-343, Mar. 1963

▲ *Atlantic Gateways,* The Making of America series. Included: Delaware, Maryland, New Jersey, New York, Pennsylvania, northern Virginia, West Virginia, and in Canada, southern Ontario and southern Quebec. On reverse: Indians and Trade, Nation in the Making, Peopling of the Gateways, Race for the Hinterlands, Growth of Industry, Spreading Urban Corridors. Mar. 1983

● Baja's Murals of Mystery. By Harry Crosby. Photos by Charles O'Rear. 692-702, Nov. 1980

● Buffalo Bill and the Enduring West. By Alice J. Hall. Photos by James L. Amos. Included: Cheyenne, Pawnees, Sioux; and reenactments of the Indian wars of the 1860s. 76-103, July 1981

● Canada's Heartland, the Prairie Provinces. By W. E. Garrett. Included: Chipewyans, Crees. 443-489, Oct. 1970

● Canada's Window on the Pacific: The British Columbia Coast. By Jules B. Billard. Photos by Ted Spiegel. Included: Haida, Kwakiutl, Tsimshian. 338-375, Mar. 1972

● The Canadian North: Emerging Giant. By David S. Boyer. 1-43, July 1968

● Chief Joseph. By William Albert Allard. Included: Nez Perce. 409-434, Mar. 1977

▲ *Deep South,* The Making of America series. Included: Alabama, Florida, Georgia, Louisiana, Mississippi, South Carolina, and parts of Arkansas, North Carolina, and Tennessee. On reverse: Indian Legacy, Imperial Footholds, Three Empires and Three Races, Cotton Kingdom, Postbellum, New Deep South, Subtropical Playground. Aug. 1983

● A First American Views His Land. By N. Scott Momaday. 13-19, July 1976

● Following the Trail of Lewis and Clark. By Ralph Gray. Included: Arikara, Blackfeet, Flathead, Mandan, Minnetaree, Oto, Shoshoni, Sioux, Teton Sioux. 707-750, June 1953

● From Tucson to Tombstone. By Mason Sutherland. Included: Apaches, Hopi, Papagos; the San Carlos Apache, and the San Xavier Indian Reservations. 343-384, Sept. 1953

● Goal at the End of the Trail: Santa Fe. By William S. Ellis. Photos by Gordon W. Gahan and Otis Imboden. Included: Pueblo, San Ildefonso, Tesuque, Santa Clara. 323-345, Mar. 1982

● Grand Canyon: Nature's Story of Creation. By Louis Schellbach. Photos by Justin Locke. Included: Havasupai, Hopi, Navajos. 589-629, May 1955

● Hays, Kansas, at the Nation's Heart. By Margaret M. Detwiler. Photos by John E. Fletcher. Included: Cheyennes, Comanches, Kaws, Pawnees, Pueblo. 461-490, Apr. 1952

● Ice Age Man, the First American. By Thomas R. Henry. Paintings by Andre Durenceau. 781-806, Dec. 1955

● Indian Life Before the Colonists Came. By Stuart E. Jones. Engravings by Theodore de Bry, 1590. 351-368, Sept. 1947

▲ *Indians of North America; North America Before Columbus,* double-sided supplement. Dec. 1972

◆ *Indians of the Americas* (1955). 418, Mar. 1957; 781, June 1959

● Indians of the Far West. By Matthew W. Stirling. Paintings by W. Langdon Kihn. Contents: Cahuilla, Cayuse, Chemehuevi, Chumash, Costanoan, Dalles, Diegueño, Flatheads, Gabrieleño, Hidatsa, Hupa, Kamia, Klamath, Klikitat, Maidu, Miwok, Modoc, Mohave, Mono, Nez Percé, Paiute, Palus, Pomo, Shasta, Shoshoni, Tenino, Umatilla, Ute, Walla Walla, Wanapum, Wappo, Wintun, Yakima, Yokut, Yuki, Yuma, Yurok. 175-200, Feb. 1948

● Kachinas: Masked Dancers of the Southwest. By Paul Coze. 219-236, Aug. 1957

● Life 8,000 Years Ago Uncovered in an Alabama Cave. By Carl F. Miller. Photos by Brooks Honeycutt. 542-558, Oct. 1956

● Man's Eighty Centuries in Veracruz. By S. Jeffrey K. Wilkerson. Photos by David Hiser. Paintings by Richard Schlecht. Included: Huastec, Totonac, and the Paleo-Indians of Veracruz. 203-231, Aug. 1980

● Men, Moose, and Mink of Northwest Angle. By William H. Nicholas. Photos by J. Baylor Roberts. Included: Chippewa, Sioux. 265-284, Aug. 1947

● Mexican Folk Art. By Fernando Horcasitas. Photos by David Hiser. Included: Maya, Mayo, Nahua, Otomí, Seri, Tarascan, and Zapotec. 648-669, May 1978

● Mexico, the City That Founded a Nation. By Louis de la Haba. Photos by Albert Moldvay. Included: The Aztec capital, Tenochtitlan. 638-669, May 1973

● Mexico in Motion. By Bart McDowell. Photos by Kip Ross. Included: Aztecs; Chiapas, Mayas, Tarascans, Zinacantecos. 490-537, Oct. 1961

● Mexico's Booming Capital. By Mason Sutherland. Photos by Justin Locke. Included: Aztecs, Toltecs. 785-824, Dec. 1951

● Mexico's Window on the Past (National Museum). By Bart McDowell. by B. Anthony Stewart. Included: Aztecs, Maya, Mixtecs, Olmecs, Teotihuacanos, Toltecs, Zapotecs. 492-519, Oct. 1968

● Nature's Gifts to Medicine. By Lonnelle Aikman. Paintings by Lloyd K. Townsend and Don Crowley. 420-440, Sept. 1974

● New Day for Alaska's Pribilof Islanders. By Susan Hackley Johnson. Photos by Tim Thompson. Included: Tlingit Indians. 536-552, Oct. 1982

■ The New Indians. 575, Nov. 1976; cover, Feb. 1977

● New Mexico: The Golden Land. By Robert Laxalt. Photos by Adam Woolfitt. Included: Apache, Navajo, Pueblo (Santa Clara, Taos, Zuni). 299-345, Sept. 1970

● Nomads of the Far North. By Matthew W. Stirling. Contents: Algonquian and Athapascan linguistic stocks: Chipewyan, Cree, Kutchin, Micmac, Montagnais, Naskapi, Yellowknife. 471-504, Oct. 1949

Hearty Folk Defy Arctic Storms. Paintings by W. Langdon Kihn. 479-494

● North Dakota Comes into Its Own. By Leo A. Borah. Photos by J. Baylor Roberts. Included: Arikaras, Hidatsas, Mandans. 283-322, Sept. 1951

● Northwest Wonderland: Washington State. By Merle Severy. Photos by B. Anthony Stewart. Included: Hohs, Makahs, Yakimas. 445-493, Apr. 1960

● Oklahoma, the Adventurous One. By Robert Paul Jordan. Photos by Robert W. Madden. Included: Cherokees, Cheyennes, Choctaws, Creek-Seminoles, Quapaws, Shawnee-Peoria. 149-189, Aug. 1971

● On the Trail of La Venta Man. By Matthew W. Stirling. Photos by Richard H. Stewart. NGS research grant. 137-172, Feb. 1947

Hunting Mexico's Buried Temples. 145-168

● Peoples of the Arctic. 144-223, Feb. 1983

I. Introduction by Joseph Judge. 144-149; II. Hunters of the Lost Spirit: Alaskans, Canadians. By Priit J. Vesilind. Photos by David Alan Harvey. 150-189

▲ *Peoples of the Arctic; Arctic Ocean,* double-sided supplement. Feb. 1983

● Probing the Mystery of the Medicine Wheels. By John A. Eddy. Photos by Thomas E. Hooper. Included: Arapaho, Cheyenne, Crow, Shoshone. 140-146, Jan. 1977

● Puget Sound, Sea Gate of the Pacific Northwest. By William Graves. Photos by David Alan Harvey. Included: Fishing rights of the Duwamish, Lummi, Nisqually, and Puyallup. 71-97, Jan. 1977

• Rediscovering America's Forgotten Crops. By Noel D. Vietmeyer. Photos by Burgess Blevins. Paintings by Paul M. Breeden. 702-712, May 1981
• Seeking the Secret of the Giants. By Frank M. Setzler. Photos by Richard H. Stewart. Included: Maricopa, Pima, Yuma. 390-404, Sept. 1952
• So Long, St. Louis, We're Heading West. By William C. Everhart. Included: Apaches, Cheyennes, Mandans, Plains Indians, Shoshonis, Sioux. 643-669, Nov. 1965
• South to Mexico City. By W. E. Garrett. Included: Pre-Columbian civilizations; present-day Tarahumara and Tarascan Indians. 145-193, Aug. 1968
▲ *The Southwest,* The Making of America series. Included: Arizona, New Mexico, and parts of California, Colorado, Texas, Utah; and in Mexico: Baja California Norte, Chihuahua, Sonora. On reverse: 12,000 Years of History; Spanish Conquest; Anglo-American Entry and Occupancy. Nov. 1982
• That Dammed Missouri River. By Gordon Young. Photos by David Hiser. Included: The Arikaras, Hidatsas, and Mandans of Fort Berthold Indian Reservation; also Sioux of Standing Rock Reservation. 374-413, Sept. 1971
◆ *Three Little Indians.* Announced. 728-730, Nov. 1974
• 20th-century Indians Preserve Customs of the Cliff Dwellers. Photos by William Belknap, Jr. NGS research grant. 196-211, Feb. 1964
• Utah's Rock Art: Wilderness Louvre. A picture essay by Gary Smith, with Michael E. Long. Included: Anasazi Basket Maker, Anasazi Pueblo, Hopi, Ute. 97-117, Jan. 1980
• Warm Springs Indians Carve Out a Future. By David S. Boyer. Contents: Confederated Tribes of Warm Springs Indians, which include the Paiute, Wasco, and Warm Springs Tribes. 494-505, Apr. 1979
• Washington's Yakima Valley. By Mark Miller. Photos by Sisse Brimberg. Included: Yakima Indian Nation and Reservation. 609-631, Nov. 1978
• Will Oil and Tundra Mix? Alaska's North Slope Hangs in the Balance. By William S. Ellis. Photos by Emory Kristof. Included: Athapascan Indians of Arctic Village. 485-517, Oct. 1971
◆ *The World of the American Indian.* Announced. 584-586, Oct. 1974
• Wyoming Muck Tells of Battle: Ice Age Man vs. Mammoth. By Cynthia Irwin, Henry Irwin, and George Agogino. NGS research grant. 828-837, June 1962
• Yukon Fever: Call of the North. By Robert Booth. Photos by George F. Mobley. Included: Loucheaux, and the Council for Yukon Indians. 548-578, Apr. 1978
• *See also* Anasazi; Aztecs; Comanche; Cora; Crees; Havasupai; Hohokam Culture; Hopi; Huichol; Menominees; Miccosukees; Mohawks; Mound Builders; Navajos; Paleo-Indians; Powhatan Chiefdom; Pueblo; Seminoles; Sioux; Stoney; Tarahumara; Tarascans; Tlingit; White Mountain Apache

DAVID S. BOYER, NGS

Warm Springs Indians: tribal dance

INDIANS OF SOUTH AMERICA:
• Amazon–The River Sea. By Loren McIntyre. Included: Achual, Aguaruna, Auca, Kamayurá, Karajá, Kraho, Kréen-Akaróre, Kuikúro, Machiguenga, Shipibo, Txukahamẽi, Waiká, Waurá, Xavante. 456-495, Oct. 1972
• Animal Safari to British Guiana. By David Attenborough. Photos by Charles Lagus and author. Included: Acawai, Macushí. 851-874, June 1957
• Blue-eyed Indian: A City Boy's Sojourn with Primitive Tribesmen in Central Brazil. By Harald Schultz. Included: Carajás, Cayapós, Javahes, Shavantes, Tapirapés. 65-89, July 1961
• Brazil, Ôba! By Peter T. White. Photos by Winfield Parks. Included: Kashinaua, Pacaás Novos. 299-353, Sept. 1962
• Brazil's Wild Frontier. By Loren McIntyre. Included: Mato Grosso tribes: Erigpactsâ, Kabano Iáras and Kabano Pomons of the Cintas Largas, Xingu. 684-719, Nov. 1977
• Colombia, from Amazon to Spanish Main. By Loren McIntyre. Included: Arhuaco, Chibcha, Guajiro, Kogi, Tucano. 235-273, Aug. 1970
• Cruising Colombia's "Ol' Man River." By Amos Burg. Included: Chibchas, Motilones. 615-660, May 1947
• Ecuador–Low and Lofty Land Astride the Equator. By Loren McIntyre. Included: Auca, Cayapa, Cofán, Colorado, Inca, Jivaro, Secoya. 259-298, Feb. 1968
• El Sangay, Fire-breathing Giant of the Andes. By G. Edward Lewis. Included: Awishiras, Jivaros, Quechuas. 117-138, Jan. 1950
• The Five Worlds of Peru. By Kenneth F. Weaver. Photos by Bates Littlehales. Included: Aymará, Huanchaco, Inca, Shapra, Shipibo, Uru. 213-265, Feb. 1964
• Flamboyant Is the Word for Bolivia. By Loren McIntyre. Included: Aymará, Inca. 153-195, Feb. 1966
• Giant Insects of the Amazon. By Paul A. Zahl. Included: Galibi, Paricura. NGS research grant. 632-669, May 1959
• High, Wild World of the Vicuña. By William L. Franklin. Included: Indians of the Inca nation; present-day Indians. 77-91, Jan. 1973
• In the Wake of Darwin's *Beagle.* By Alan Villiers. Photos by James L. Stanfield. Included: Indians of Tierra del Fuego. 449-495, Oct. 1969
▲ *Indians of South America; Archaeology of South America,* double-sided supplement. Mar. 1982
◆ *Indians of the Americas* (1955). 418, Mar. 1957; 781, June 1959

I
J

• Jungle Jaunt on Amazon Headwaters. By Bernice M. Goetz. Included: Banivas and Cubeos. 371-388, Sept. 1952
• The Lost Empire of the Incas. By Loren McIntyre. Art by Ned and Rosalie Seidler. Included: Aymaras and Quechuas. 729-787, Dec. 1973
A pictorial chronicle of the Incas. 747-753
◆ *Lost Empires, Living Tribes.* 1982
• Man in the Amazon: Stone Age Present Meets Stone Age Past. By W. Jesco von Puttkamer. Included: Paleo-Indians; Wasúsu of the Nambicuara confederation. NGS research grant. 60-83, Jan. 1979
• Mystery of the Ancient Nazca Lines. By Loren McIntyre. NGS research grant. 716-728, May 1975
• Paraguay, Paradox of South America. By Gordon Young. Photos by O. Louis Mazzatenta. Included: Guaraní, Macá, Toba-Maskoy. 240-269, Aug. 1982
• Puya, the Pineapple's Andean Ancestor. By Mulford B. Foster. Included: Aymarás, Quechuas, Sibundoys. 463-480, Oct. 1950
• "Pyramids" of the New World. By Neil Merton Judd. Included: Pachacamac, Peru. 105-128, Jan. 1948
• The Search for the First Americans. By Thomas Y. Canby. Photos by Kerby Smith. Paintings by Roy Andersen. 330-363, Sept. 1979
• Seeking the Truth About the Feared Piranha. By Paul A. Zahl. Included: Karajá, Maká. 715-733, Nov. 1970
• Sky-high Bolivia. Photos by T. Ifor Rees and Carl S. Bell. Included: Aymarás, Quechuas, and the Bibundoys, part of a large tribal group called the Quillacingas. 481-496, Oct. 1950
• Titicaca, Abode of the Sun. By Luis Marden. Photos by Flip Schulke. Included: Aymarás, Incas, Quechuas, Urus. 272-294, Feb. 1971
• *See also* Aymará; Camaracoto; Chimor Empire; Cholo; Cinta Larga; Erigbaagtsa; Incas; Kraho; Kreen-Akarores; Machiguenga; Mochica Culture; Motilones; Peruvian Indians; Quechuas; Suyá; Tchikao; Tukuna; Txukahameis; Wai Wai; Waurá; Wayana Indians; Yanomamo

INDIANS OF THE CARIBBEAN:
• Christopher Columbus and the New World He Found. By John Scofield. Photos by Adam Woolfitt. Included: Caribs, Cunas. 584-625, Nov. 1975
• *See also* Carib Indians; Wayana Indians

INDIO (River), Panama:
• Hunting Prehistory in Panama Jungles. By Matthew W. Stirling. Photos by Richard H. Stewart. NGS research grant. 271-290, Aug. 1953

INDOCHINA:
• Indochina Faces the Dragon. By George W. Long. Photos by J. Baylor Roberts. 287-328, Sept. 1952
• The Lands and Peoples of Southeast Asia. 295-365, Mar. 1971
I. Mosaic of Cultures. By Peter T. White. Photos by W. E. Garrett. 296-329; II. New Light on a Forgotten Past. By Wilhelm G. Solheim II. 330-339; III. Pagan, on the Road to Mandalay. By W. E. Garrett. 343-365
▲ *The Peoples of Mainland Southeast Asia,* double-sided supplement. Mar. 1971
• Portrait of Indochina. By W. Robert Moore and Maynard Owen Williams. Paintings by Jean Despujols. 461-490, Apr. 1951
• Strife-torn Indochina. By W. Robert Moore. 499-510, Oct. 1950
• War and Quiet on the Laos Frontier. By W. Robert Moore. 665-680, May 1954
• *See also* Burma; Kampuchea; Laos; Malaysia; Thailand; Vietnam

The **INDOMITABLE** Cockroach. By Allen A. Boraiko. Photos by Bates Littlehales. 130-142, Jan. 1981

INDONESIA:
• The Bonanza Bean–Coffee. By Ethel A. Starbird. Photos by Sam Abell. 388-405, Mar. 1981
• East From Bali by Seagoing Jeep to Timor. By Helen and Frank Schreider. 236-279, Aug. 1962
• Indonesia, the Young and Troubled Island Nation. By Helen and Frank Schreider. 579-625, May 1961
• Indonesia Rescues Ancient Borobudur. By W. Brown Morton III. Photos by Dean Conger. 126-142, Jan. 1983
• New Guinea to Bali in *Yankee.* By Irving and Electa Johnson. 767-815, Dec. 1959
• Republican Indonesia Tries Its Wings. By W. Robert Moore. 1-40, Jan. 1951
• A Sumatran Journey. By Harvey Arden. Photos by David Alan Harvey. 406-430, Mar. 1981
• This Young Giant, Indonesia. By Beverley M. Bowie. Photos by J. Baylor Roberts. 351-392, Sept. 1955
• Tropical Rain Forests: Nature's Dwindling Treasures. By Peter T. White. Photos by James P. Blair. Paintings by Barron Storey. 2-47, Jan. 1983
• *See also* Bali; Irian Jaya (Indonesian New Guinea); Java; Lesser Sunda Islands; Moluccas; Sulawesi; Tanjung Puting Reserve

INDONESIAN INSTITUTE OF SCIENCES: Sponsorship:
• Orangutans. 835, June 1980

INDONESIAN NEW GUINEA (formerly, Netherlands New Guinea). *See* Irian Jaya, Indonesia

INDUSTRIAL MUSEUMS. *See* Corning Museum of Glass; Henry Ford Museum; John Woodman Higgins Armory

INDUSTRY:
• Acid Rain–How Great a Menace? By Anne LaBastille. Photos by Ted Spiegel. 652-681, Nov. 1981
• Barehanded Battle to Cleanse the Bay: San Francisco's Tragic Oil Spill Triggers Spontaneous Cooperation Between Industry and Concerned Citizens. By Peter T. White. Photos by Jonathan S. Blair. 866-881, June 1971
• Cities Like Worcester Make America. By Howell Walker. 189-214, Feb. 1955
• Crystals, Magical Servants of the Space Age. By Kenneth F. Weaver. Photos by James P. Blair. 278-296, Aug. 1968
• Dixie Spins the Wheel of Industry. By William H. Nicholas. Photos by J. Baylor Roberts. 281-324, Mar. 1949
• The Miracle Metal–Platinum. By Gordon Young. Photos by James L. Amos. 686-706, Nov. 1983
• Pollution, Threat to Man's Only Home. By Gordon Young. Photos by James P. Blair. 738-781, Dec. 1970
• A River Restored: Oregon's Willamette. By Ethel A. Starbird. Photos by Lowell J. Georgia. 816-835, June 1972
• Those Successful Japanese. By Bart McDowell. Photos by Fred Ward. 323-359, Mar. 1974
• Yesterday Lingers Along the Connecticut. By Charles McCarry. Photos by David L. Arnold. 334-369, Sept. 1972
• *See also* Aluminum; Automotive Industry; Cottage Industries; Cotton and Cotton Industry; Energy; Fishing (Industry); Hydroelectric Power; Lumber Industry; Mines and Mining; Paper and Pulp Industry; Steel Industry; Technology

INFLATABLE Ship Opens Era of Airborne Undersea Expeditions. By Jacques-Yves Cousteau. 142-148, July 1961

INFORMATION TRANSMISSION. *See* Chips; Communications; Radio

INFRARED IMAGERY:
• Heat Paints *Columbia's* Portrait. By Cliff Tarpy. 650-653, Nov. 1982

INFRARED RADIATION:
• Remote Sensing: New Eyes to See the World. By Kenneth F. Weaver. 46-73, Jan. 1969
• *See also* Photography, Infrared

INGALLS, HUNTLEY:
Author-Photographer:
• We Climbed Utah's Skyscraper Rock. Photos by author and Barry C. Bishop. 705-721, Nov. 1962

INGSTAD, HELGE: Author:
• Vinland Ruins Prove Vikings Found the New World. 708-734, Nov. 1964

INISHEER, INISHMAAN, INISHMORE (Islands), Ireland:
• The Arans, Ireland's Invincible Isles. By Veronica Thomas. Photos by Winfield Parks. 545-573, Apr. 1971

INLAND SEA, Japan:
• Cruising Japan's Inland Sea. By Willard Price. 619-650, Nov. 1953

• Japan's Amazing Inland Sea. By William S. Ellis. Photos by James L. Stanfield. 830-863, Dec. 1977
• Kayak Odyssey: From the Inland Sea to Tokyo. By Dan Dimancescu. Photos by Christopher G. Knight. 295-337, Sept. 1967
• Living in a Japanese Village. By William Graves. Photos by James L. Stanfield. 668-693, May 1972

INLAND WATERWAYS. *See* Canals; Inside Passage; Intracoastal Waterways; Rivers and River Trips; St. Lawrence Seaway

INLE (Lake), Burma:
• Burma's Leg Rowers and Floating Farms. Photos by W. E. Garrett. Text by David Jeffery. 826-845, June 1974

INNER HEBRIDES (Islands), Scotland:
• Scotland From Her Lovely Lochs and Seas. By Alan Villiers. Photos by Robert F. Sisson. 492-541, Apr. 1961
• Scotland's Inner Hebrides: Isles of the Western Sea. By Kenneth MacLeish. Photos by R. Stephen Uzzell III. 690-717, Nov. 1974
• *See also* Skye

INNSBRUCK, Austria:
• Occupied Austria, Outpost of Democracy. By George W. Long. Photos by Volkmar Wentzel. 749-790, June 1951
• A Stroll to Venice. By Isobel Wylie Hutchison. 378-410, Sept. 1951
• Tirol, Austria's Province in the Clouds. By Peter T. White. Photos by Volkmar Wentzel. 107-141, July 1961

INSECT CONTROL:
• Beltsville Brings Science to the Farm. By Samuel W. Matthews. 199-218, Aug. 1953
• Man's New Servant, the Friendly Atom. By F. Barrows Colton. Photos by Volkmar Wentzel. Included: Insects tagged with radioisotopes, easily identified; sterilizing of screwworm fly; experiments on effectiveness of insect poisons. 71-90, Jan. 1954
• Mosquitoes, the Mighty Killers. By Lewis T. Nielsen. 427-440, Sept. 1979
• New Tricks Outwit Our Insect Enemies. By Hal Higdon. Photos by Robert F. Sisson and Emory Kristof. 380-399, Sept. 1972
• The Pesticide Dilemma. By Allen A. Boraiko. Photos by Fred Ward. 145-183, Feb. 1980
• Pollution, Threat to Man's Only Home. By Gordon Young. Photos by James P. Blair. Included: The use of DDT during World War II against mosquitoes and body lice. 738-781, Dec. 1970
• The Revolution in American Agriculture. By Jules B. Billard. Photos by James P. Blair. 147-185, Feb. 1970
• *See also* Ladybugs; Locusts; Spiders (What's So Special)

INSECT-TRAPPING PLANTS. *See* Carnivorous Plants

INSECTICIDE POLLUTION:
• The Pesticide Dilemma. By Allen A. Boraiko. Photos by Fred Ward. Included: The harmful effects on beneficial insects and other forms of life. 145-183, Feb. 1980
• Pollution, Threat to Man's Only Home. By Gordon Young. Photos by James P. Blair. Included: DDT and the other chlorinated hydrocarbon insecticides are toxic to many forms of animal and marine life. 738-781, Dec. 1970

INSECTICIDES. *See* Insect Control

INSECTS:
• Amber: Golden Window on the Past. Photos by Paul A. Zahl. Text by Thomas J. O'Neill. 423-435, Sept. 1977
• Asian Insects in Disguise. By Edward S. Ross. NGS research grant. 433-439, Sept. 1965
• Back-yard Monsters in Color. By Paul A. Zahl. Contents: Black widow spider, Blister beetle, Broad-neck root borer, Bumblebee, Carpenter ant, Caterpillar, Cecropia moth, Colorado potato beetle, Housefly, Japanese beetle, Lacewing, Ladybird beetle, Locust, Long-horned grasshopper, Mosquito, Paper wasp, Parasitic fly, Polyphemus moth, Praying mantis, Queen butterfly, Scarab beetle, Scavenger beetle, Short-horned grasshopper, Soldier beetle, Sphinx moth, Sulphur butterfly, Tussock moth. 235-260, Aug. 1952
• Crossroads of the Insect World. By J. W. MacSwain. Photos by Edward S. Ross. Included: African katydid, Ambush bug, Bee fly, Blister beetle, *Ceratina* bee, Crab spider, Gnat, Halictine bee, *Hesperapis* bee, Honeybee, Malaysian mantis, *Megachile* bee, *Phyciodes* butterfly, Scarab beetle, Skipper, Syrphid fly. 844-857, Dec. 1966
• Deception: Formula for Survival. By Robert F. Sisson. 394-415, Mar. 1980
• Electronic Voyage Through an Invisible World. By Kenneth F. Weaver. Included: Ants, aphids, bees, mosquitoes. 274-290, Feb. 1977
• The Exquisite Orchids. By Luis Marden. Included: Pollination by insects. 485-513, Apr. 1971
• Giant Insects of the Amazon. By Paul A. Zahl. NGS research grant. 632-669, May 1959
▪ The Hidden World. 853A-853B, Dec. 1966
• The High World of the Rain Forest. By William Beebe. Paintings by Guy Neale. Included: Ant lion, Beetles, Butterflies, Caterpillars, Flies, Grasshoppers, Praying mantises, Spiders, Tree hoppers. 838-855, June 1958
• Hunting Africa's Smallest Game. By Edward S. Ross. NGS research grant. 406-419, Mar. 1961
• Life Around a Lily Pad. Photos by Bianca Lavies. Text by Charles R. Miller. 131-142, Jan. 1980

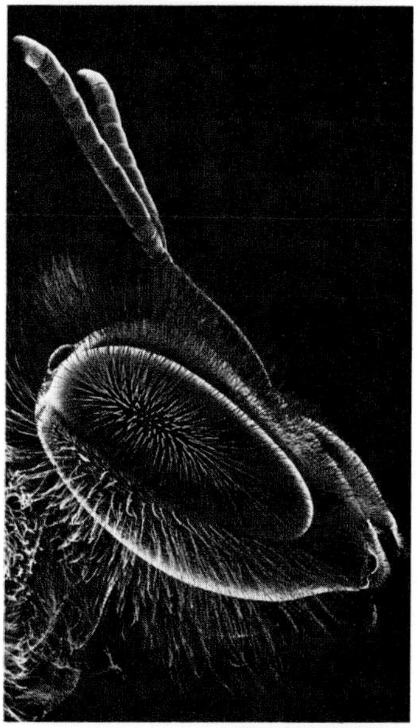

BOTH BY DAVID SCHARF

Insects: scanning electron microscope view of velvety tree ant, *top*; honeybee, *above*

• Life on a Rock Ledge. By William H. Amos. 558-566, Oct. 1980
• The Living Sand. By William H. Amos. Included: Ant lion, Digger wasp, Sand locust, Tiger beetle, Velvet ant (Wingless wasp), Yellow-banded wasp. 820-833, June 1965
▪ The Living Sands of Namib. 439, Oct. 1977; cover, Mar. 1978; 1, Jan. 1979
• The Living Sands of the Namib. By William J. Hamilton III. Photos by Carol and David Hughes. 364-377, Sept. 1983
• Malaysia's Giant Flowers and Insect-trapping Plants. By Paul A. Zahl. 680-701, May 1964
• Miracle of the Potholes. By Rowe Findley. Photos by Robert F. Sisson. 570-579, Oct. 1975
• Nature's Alert Eyes. By Constance P. Warner. Included: Horsefly, Praying mantis. 558-569, Apr. 1959
• Nature's Night Lights: Probing the Secrets of Bioluminescence. By Paul A. Zahl. 45-69, July 1971
• Nature's Year in Pleasant Valley. By Paul A. Zahl. 488-525, Apr. 1968
• The Pesticide Dilemma. By Allen A. Boraiko. Photos by Fred Ward. 145-183, Feb. 1980
• Plants That Eat Insects. By Paul A. Zahl. 643-659, May 1961
• Teeming Life of a Pond. By William H. Amos. 274-298, Aug. 1970
• Teeming Life of a Rain Forest. By Carol and David Hughes. 49-65, Jan. 1983
• Unseen Life of a Mountain Stream. By William H. Amos. 562-580, Apr. 1977
• The Wild World of Compost. By Cecil E. Johnson. Photos by Bianca Lavies. 273-284, Aug. 1980
• *See also* Ants; Aphids; Butterflies; Cicadas; Crickets; Cockroaches; Dragonflies; Fireflies; Honeybees; Inchworms; Ladybugs; Locusts; Mantis; Mosquitoes; Moths; Railroad Worm; Termites; Wasps; *and* Insect Control

INSIDE a Hornbill's Walled-up Nest. Photos by Joan and Alan Root. 846-855, Dec. 1969

INSIDE Cuba Today. By Fred Ward. 32-69, Jan. 1977

INSIDE Europe Aboard *Yankee*. By Irving and Electa Johnson. Photos by Joseph J. Scherschel. 157-195, Aug. 1964

INSIDE PASSAGE (Washington-British Columbia-Alaska):
• Alaska's Marine Highway: Ferry Route to the North. By W. E. Garrett. 776-819, June 1965
• Alaska's Warmer Side. By Elsie May Bell Grosvenor. 737-775, June 1956
• *Endeavour* Sails the Inside Passage. By Amos Burg. 801-828, June 1947
• Making Friends With a Killer Whale. By Edward I. Griffin. 418-446, Mar. 1966

INSIDE the Sacred Hopi Homeland. By Jake Page. Photos by Susanne Page. 607-629, Nov. 1982

INSIDE the White House. By Lonnelle Aikman. Photos by B. Anthony Stewart and Thomas Nebbia. 3-43, Jan. 1961

INSIDE the World of the Honeybee. By Treat Davidson. 188-217, Aug. 1959

INSTITUTE OF NAUTICAL ARCHEOLOGY: Expedition:
• Underwater Archaeology: Aegean Sea. 768, 774, June 1978

INSTITUTE OF NORTHERN AGRICULTURAL RESEARCH, Huntington Center, Vermont: Study Grant:
• Musk Ox. 863, 866, June 1970

INTEGRATED CIRCUITS:
• California's Silicon Valley. By Moira Johnston. Photos by Charles O'Rear. 459-477, Oct. 1982
• The Chip: Electronic Mini-marvel. By Allen A. Boraiko. Photos by Charles O'Rear. 421-457, Oct. 1982
• Crystals, Magical Servants of the Space Age. By Kenneth F. Weaver. Photos by James P. Blair. 278-296, Aug. 1968

INTER-AMERICAN GEODETIC SURVEY (IAGS):
• Expedition to Amazon source. 445, 459, 460, Oct. 1972
• Men Who Measure the Earth. By Robert Leslie Conly. Photos by John E. Fletcher. 335-362, Mar. 1956

INTER-AMERICAN HIGHWAY. *See* Pan American Highway

The **INTERNATIONAL** Committee of the Red Cross. *See* Red Cross

INTERNATIONAL GEOPHYSICAL YEAR (IGY):
• How Man-made Satellites Can Affect Our Lives. By Joseph Kaplan. 791-810, Dec. 1957
• The International Geophysical Year. By Hugh L. Dryden. 285-298, Feb. 1956
• Man's First Winter at the South Pole. By Paul A. Siple. 439-478, Apr. 1958
• Rockets Explore the Air Above Us. By Newman Bumstead. 562-580, Apr. 1957
• Space Satellites, Tools of Earth Research. By Heinz Haber. Paintings by William N. Palmstrom. 487-509, Apr. 1956
• To the Men at South Pole Station. By Richard E. Byrd. 1-4, July 1957
• We Are Living at the South Pole. By Paul A. Siple. Photos by David S. Boyer. Contents: The establishment of the first permanent base at the South Pole. 5-35, July 1957
• Year of Discovery Opens in Antarctica. By David S. Boyer. 339-381, Sept. 1957
• *See also* Expéditions Polaires Françaises; Operation Deep Freeze

INTERNATIONAL ICE PATROL:
• Tracking Danger With the Ice Patrol. By William S. Ellis. Photos by James R. Holland. 780-793, June 1968

INTERNATIONAL INDIAN OCEAN EXPEDITION:
• Science Explores the Monsoon Sea. By Samuel W. Matthews. Photos by Robert F. Sisson. 554-575, Oct. 1967

INTERNATIONAL PARK. *See* Waterton-Glacier International Peace Park

INTERNATIONAL SCHOOL OF AMERICA (ISA):
• Round the World School. By Paul Antze. Photos by William Eppridge. 96-127, July 1962

INTERNATIONAL UNION FOR CONSERVATION OF NATURE: Study Grant:
• Elephant Survey: Africa. 578, 584, Nov. 1980

INTERSTATE HIGHWAY SYSTEM:
• Our Growing Interstate Highway System. By Robert Paul Jordan. 195-219, Feb. 1968
• Trucks Race the Clock From Coast to Coast. By James A. Sugar. 226-243, Feb. 1974

INTERSTATE PARK. *See* Palisades Interstate Park

INTHA (People):
• Burma's Leg Rowers and Floating Farms. Photos by W. E. Garrett. Text by David Jeffery. 826-845, June 1974

INTO the Eye of David (Hurricane). By John L. Eliot. 368-369, Sept. 1980

INTO the Heart of Africa. By Gertrude S. Weeks. NGS research grant. 257-263, Aug. 1956

INTO the Lairs of "Sleeping" Sharks. By Eugenie Clark. Photos by David Doubilet. NGS research grant. 570-584, Apr. 1975

INTO the Well of Sacrifice (Chichén Itzá). By Eusebio Dávalos Hurtado and Bates Littlehales. Photos by Bates Littlehales. NGS research grant. 540-561, Oct. 1961

INTRACOASTAL WATERWAYS:
◆ *America's Inland Waterway.* Announced. 865-868, June 1973
• The Gulf's Workaday Waterway. By Gordon Young. Photos by Charles O'Rear. 200-223, Feb. 1978
• Slow Boat to Florida. By Dorothea and Stuart E. Jones. 1-65, Jan. 1958
• *See also* Florida Keys; Sea Islands

INUIT:
• Arctic Odyssey. By John Bockstoce. Photos by Jonathan Wright. Paintings by Jack Unruh. Contents: Umiak expedition tracing Thule Eskimo migration route from Alaska to Greenland. 100-127, July 1983
• Banks Island: Eskimo Life on the Polar Sea. By William O. Douglas. Photos by Clyde Hare. 703-735, May 1964
• Canada Counts Its Caribou. 261-268, Aug. 1952
• Canada's Caribou Eskimos. By Donald B. Marsh. 87-104, Jan. 1947
• The Canadian North: Emerging Giant. By David S. Boyer. 1-43, July 1968

● Eskimo and Viking Finds in the High Arctic: Ellesmere Island. By Peter Schledermann. Photos by Sisse Brimberg. Included: Artifacts of the Norse, the Dorset, the Thule. 575-601, May 1981
● Henry Hudson's Changing Bay. By Bill Richards. Photos by David Hiser. 380-405, Mar. 1982
● I Live With the Eskimos. By Guy Mary-Rousseliere. 188-217, Feb. 1971
● The Inuit of Umingmaktok: Still Eskimo, Still Free. By Yva Momatiuk and John Eastcott. 624-647, Nov. 1977
● Peoples of the Arctic. 144-223, Feb. 1983
I. Introduction by Joseph Judge. 144-149; II. Hunters of the Lost Spirit: Canadians, Greenlanders. By Priit J. Vesilind. Photos by David Alan Harvey and Ivars Silis. 174-193
▲ *Peoples of the Arctic; Arctic Ocean,* double-sided supplement. Feb. 1983
● Vanished Mystery Men of Hudson Bay. By Henry B. Collins. NGS research grant. 669-687, Nov. 1956

INUPIAT ESKIMOS:
● Peoples of the Arctic. 144-223, Feb. 1983
I. Introduction by Joseph Judge. 144-149; II. Hunters of the Lost Spirit: Alaskans. By Priit J. Vesilind. Photos by David Alan Harvey. 156-173
▲ *Peoples of the Arctic; Arctic Ocean,* double-sided supplement. Feb. 1983

INVENTORS AND INVENTIONS:
● Alexander Graham Bell Museum: Tribute to Genius. By Jean Lesage. 227-256, Aug. 1956
● Behold the Computer Revolution. By Peter T. White. Photos by Bruce Dale and Emory Kristof. 593-633, Nov. 1970
● The British Way: Great Britain's Major Gifts to Freedom, Democratic Government, Science, and Society. By Sir Evelyn Wrench. 421-541, Apr. 1949
● Cities Like Worcester Make America. By Howell Walker. Included: Bigelow (power carpet loom), Blanchard (lathe), Goddard (liquid-fueled rocket), Hawes (envelope-folding machine), Howe (sewing machine), piano wire, the steam calliope, Whitney (cotton gin). 189-214, Feb. 1955
● Eyes of Science. By Rick Gore. Photos by James P. Blair. Included: Harold Edgerton (strobe flash), William Herschel (infrared rays), Karl Jansky (radio waves from space), Joseph Niepce (world's first photographic image), Edweard Muybridge (photographic stop action), Johann Ritter (ultraviolet rays), Wilhelm Roentgen (X rays), Paul Villard (gamma rays), Vladimir Zworykin (television). 360-389, Mar. 1978
● Leonardo da Vinci: A Man for All Ages. By Kenneth MacLeish. Photos by James L. Amos. Included: Leonardo's ideas for self-propelled vehicles, automatic machines and tools, human-powered flying machines, military engines. 296-329, Sept. 1977

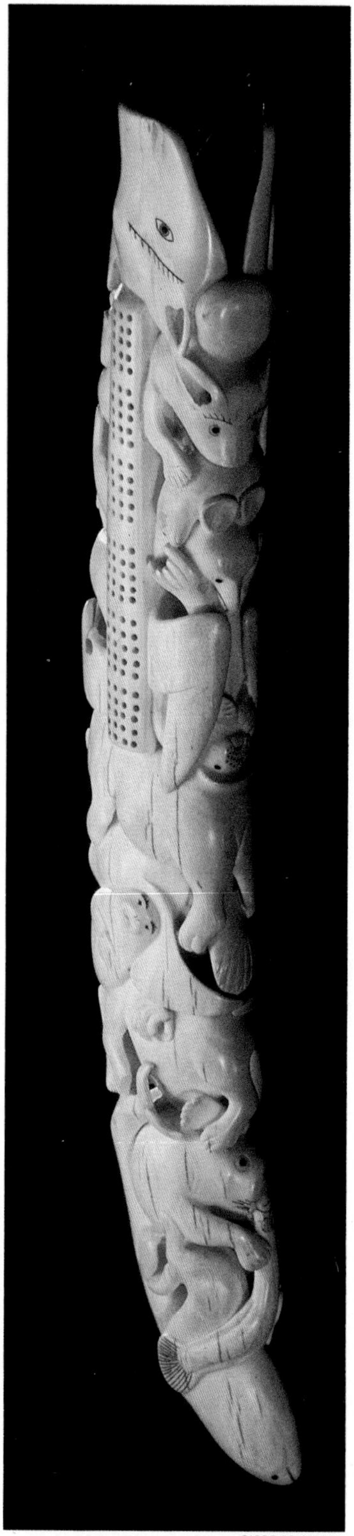
SISSE BRIMBERG
Peoples of the Arctic: carved tusk

● Miracle Men of the Telephone. By F. Barrows Colton. 273-316, Mar. 1947
● Swing Low, Sweet Chariot! By Noel Grove. Photos by Bruce Dale. 2-35, July 1983
◆ *Those Inventive Americans.* Announced. 880-884, June 1970
● Yesterday Lingers Along the Connecticut. By Charles McCarry. Photos by David L. Arnold. Included: Samuel Colt (six-shooter), John C. Garand (M-1 rifle), Samuel Morey (steamboat), James F. Tasker (bridges), Eli Whitney (interchangeable parts). 334-369, Sept. 1972
● *See also* Bell, Alexander Graham; Franklin, Benjamin; Henry Ford Museum; Jefferson, Thomas; Wright, Orville and Wilbur; *and* NGS: Inventions; Satellites; Solar-Powered Car; Technology; Ultralight Aircraft

The **INVESTITURE** of Great Britain's Prince of Wales. By Allan C. Fisher, Jr. Photos by James L. Stanfield and Adam Woolfitt. 698-715, Nov. 1969

INYO NATIONAL FOREST, California:
● Bristlecone Pine, Oldest Known Living Thing. By Edmund Schulman. Photos by W. Robert Moore. 355-372, Mar. 1958

IO (Jovian Satellite):
● What Voyager Saw: Jupiter's Dazzling Realm. By Rick Gore. Photos by NASA. 2-29, Jan. 1980

IONIAN ISLANDS, Greece:
● Homeward With Ulysses. By Melville Bell Grosvenor. Photos by Edwin Stuart Grosvenor. 1-39, July 1973

IONOSPHERE:
● Unlocking Secrets of the Northern Lights. By Carl W. Gartlein. Paintings by William Crowder. 673-704, Nov. 1947

IOS (Island), Greece:
● The Isles of Greece: Aegean Birthplace of Western Culture. By Melville Bell Grosvenor. Photos by Edwin Stuart Grosvenor and Winfield Parks. 147-193, Aug. 1972

IOWA:
● The Family Farm Ain't What It Used To Be. By James A. Sugar. 391-411, Sept. 1974
● Following the Trail of Lewis and Clark. By Ralph Gray. 707-750, June 1953
● Iowa, America's Middle Earth. By Harvey Arden. Photos by Craig Aurness. 603-629, May 1981
● Iowa's Enduring Amana Colonies. By Laura Longley Babb. Photos by Steve Raymer. 863-878, Dec. 1975
● Mapping the Nation's Breadbasket. By Frederick Simpich. 831-849, June 1948

IRAN:
● Coronations a World Apart. By the Editor. 299, Mar. 1968
● Darius Carved History on Ageless Rock. By George G. Cameron. 825-844, Dec. 1950

I
J

• The Desert: An Age-old Challenge Grows. By Rick Gore. Photos by Georg Gerster and Bruce Dale. 586-639, Nov. 1979
• I Become a Bakhtiari. By Paul Edward Case. 325-358, Mar. 1947
Beside the Persian Gulf. Photos by Maynard Owen Williams. 341-356
• In the Footsteps of Alexander the Great. By Helen and Frank Schreider. Paintings by Tom Lovell. 1-65, Jan. 1968
• Iran: Desert Miracle. By William Graves. Photos by James P. Blair. 2-47, Jan. 1975
• Iran's Shah Crowns Himself and His Empress. By Franc Shor. Photos by James L. Stanfield and Winfield Parks. 301-321, Mar. 1968
• Journey Into Troubled Iran. By George W. Long. Photos by J. Baylor Roberts. 425-464, Oct. 1951
• Oil, the Dwindling Treasure. By Noel Grove. Photos by Emory Kristof. 792-825, June 1974
• Old-new Iran, Next Door to Russia. By Edward J. Linehan. Photos by Thomas J. Abercrombie. 44-85, Jan. 1961
• Our Vegetable Travelers. By Victor R. Boswell. Paintings by Else Bostelmann. Included: Muskmelons Originated in Persia. 145-217, Aug. 1949
• Questing for Gems. By George S. Switzer. 835-863, Dec. 1971
• Sky Road East. By Tay and Lowell Thomas, Jr. 71-112, Jan. 1960
• Station Wagon Odyssey: Baghdad to Istanbul. By William O. Douglas. 48-87, Jan. 1959
• Troubled Waters East of Suez. By Ernest M. Eller. 483-522, Apr. 1954
• We Dwelt in Kashgai Tents. By Jean and Franc Shor. 805-832, June 1952
• We Lived in Turbulent Tehran. By Rebecca Shannon Cresson. 707-720, Nov. 1953
• West from the Khyber Pass. By William O. Douglas. Photos by Mercedes H. Douglas and author. 1-44, July 1958
• When the President Goes Abroad (Eisenhower). By Gilbert M. Grosvenor. 588-649, May 1960
• The World in Your Garden (Flowers). By W. H. Camp. Paintings by Else Bostelmann. Included: "In a Persian Garden" (Crown Imperial, Oriental Poppy). 1-65, July 1947

IRAQ:
• Abraham, the Friend of God. By Kenneth MacLeish. Photos by Dean Conger. 739-789, Dec. 1966
• Ancient Mesopotamia: A Light That Did Not Fail. By E. A. Speiser. Paintings by H. M. Herget. 41-105, Jan. 1951
• "Around the World in Eighty Days." By Newman Bumstead. Included: Baghdad; Basra; Tigris River. 705-750, Dec. 1951
• Beside the Persian Gulf. Photos by Maynard Owen Williams. Included: Port near Basra. 341-356, Mar. 1947
• Iraq–Where Oil and Water Mix. By Jean and Franc Shor. 443-489, Oct. 1958

WINFIELD PARKS, NGS

The Arans: getting water on Inishmaan

• The Kurds of Iraq: "We Who Face Death." By LeRoy Woodson, Jr. 364-387, Mar. 1975
• Marsh Dwellers of Southern Iraq. By Wilfred Thesiger. Photos by Gavin Maxwell. 205-239, Feb. 1958
• Report from the Locust Wars. By Tony and Dickey Chapelle. 545-562, Apr. 1953
• Station Wagon Odyssey: Baghdad to Istanbul. By William O. Douglas. 48-87, Jan. 1959
■ The *Tigris* Expedition. 826, Dec. 1978; 1, Jan. 1979; cover, Apr. 1979
• *Tigris* Sails Into the Past. By Thor Heyerdahl. Photos by Carlo Mauri and the crew of the *Tigris*. 806-827, Dec. 1978
• Troubled Waters East of Suez. By Ernest M. Eller. 483-522, Apr. 1954
• Water Dwellers in a Desert World. By Gavin Young. Photos by Nik Wheeler. 502-523, Apr. 1976
• West from the Khyber Pass. By William O. Douglas. Photos by Mercedes H. Douglas and author. 1-44, July 1958

IRAZÚ (Volcano), Costa Rica:
• Costa Rica, Free of the Volcano's Veil. By Robert de Roos. 125-152, July 1965

IRELAND, Northern:
• Editorial. By Wilbur E. Garrett. 431, Apr. 1981
• Ireland. 432-499, Apr. 1981
I. The Travail of Ireland. By Joseph Judge. Photos by Cotton Coulson. 432-441; II. A New Day for Ireland. By John J. Putman. Photos by Cotton Coulson. 442-469; III. War and Peace in Northern Ireland. By Bryan Hodgson. Photos by Cary Wolinsky. 470-499
▲ *Ireland and Northern Ireland: A Visitor's Guide; Historic Ireland* (Pre-Norman, Medieval, Modern), double-sided supplement, Apr. 1981
• Ireland's Rugged Coast Yields Priceless Relics of the Spanish Armada. By Robert Sténuit. Photos by Bates Littlehales. 745-777, June 1969
• The Magic Road Round Ireland. By H. V. Morton. Photos by Robert F. Sisson. 293-333, Mar. 1961
• Northern Ireland: From Derry to Down. By Robert L. Conly. 232-267, Aug. 1964

IRELAND, Republic of:
• The Arans, Ireland's Invincible Isles. By Veronica Thomas. Photos by Winfield Parks. 545-573, Apr. 1971
• *British Isles,* Atlas series supplement. July 1958
▲ *The British Isles,* supplement. Apr. 1949
• The Celts. By Merle Severy. Photos by James P. Blair. Paintings by Robert C. Magis. 582-633, May 1977
• Dublin's Historic Horse Show. By Maynard Owen Williams. 115-132, July 1953
• Editorial. By Wilbur E. Garrett. 431, Apr. 1981
• The Friendly Irish. By John Scofield. Photos by James A. Sugar. 354-391, Sept. 1969

• I Walked Some Irish Miles. By Dorothea Sheats. 653-678, May 1951
• The Incredible Potato. By Robert E. Rhoades. Photos by Martin Rogers. Included: The potato famine of 1845-1851; and the emigration to the United States. 668-694, May 1982
• Ireland. 432-499, Apr. 1981 I. The Travail of Ireland. By Joseph Judge. Photos by Cotton Coulson. 432-441; II. A New Day for Ireland. By John J. Putman. Photos by Cotton Coulson. 442-469; III. War and Peace in Northern Ireland. By Bryan Hodgson. Photos by Cary Wolinsky. 470-499
▲ *Ireland and Northern Ireland: A Visitor's Guide; Historic Ireland* (Pre-Norman, Medieval, Modern), double-sided supplement, Apr. 1981
• Irish Ways Live On in Dingle. By Bryan Hodgson. Photos by Linda Bartlett. Included: Efforts to preserve Gaelic language and literature. 551-576, Apr. 1976
• The Magic Road Round Ireland. By H. V. Morton. Photos by Robert F. Sisson. 293-333, Mar. 1961
• Playing 3,000 Golf Courses in Fourteen Lands. By Ralph A. Kennedy. 113-132, July 1952
▲ *A Traveler's Map of the British Isles,* supplement. Text on reverse. Apr. 1974
• Where the River Shannon Flows. By Allan C. Fisher, Jr. Photos by Adam Woolfitt. 652-679, Nov. 1978

IRIAN JAYA (Western New Guinea), Indonesia:
• The Asmat of New Guinea, Headhunters in Today's World. By Malcolm S. Kirk. 376-409, Mar. 1972
• Netherlands New Guinea. By John Scofield. 584-603, May 1962
• New Guinea. The Editor. 583, May 1962
• New Guinea to Bali in *Yankee*. By Irving and Electa Johnson. 767-815, Dec. 1959
• Strange Courtship of Birds of Paradise. By S. Dillon Ripley. Paintings by Walter A. Weber. 247-278, Feb. 1950
• To the Land of the Head-hunters. By E. Thomas Gilliard. NGS research grant. 437-486, Oct. 1955
• Tropical Rain Forests: Nature's Dwindling Treasures. By Peter T. White. Photos by James P. Blair. Paintings by Barron Storey. 2-47, Jan. 1983
• *Yankee* Roams the Orient. By Irving and Electa Johnson. 327-370, Mar. 1951

IRISES:
• History and Beauty Blend in a Concord Iris Garden (Buttrick). By Robert T. Cochran, Jr. Photos by M. Woodbridge Williams. 705-719, May 1959

The **IRISH:**
• The Voyage of *Brendan*. By Timothy Severin. Photos by Cotton Coulson. 770-797, Dec. 1977
• Who Discovered America? A New Look at an Old Question. The Editor. 769, Dec. 1977

IRISH REPUBLICAN ARMY:
• War and Peace in Northern Ireland. By Bryan Hodgson. Photos by Cary Wolinsky. 470-499, Apr. 1981

IRON AGE:
• The Celts. By Merle Severy. Photos by James P. Blair. Paintings by Robert C. Magis. 582-633, May 1977
• Finding West Africa's Oldest City. By Susan and Roderick McIntosh. Photos by Michael and Aubine Kirtley. Note: Jenne-jeno (site) in Mali is the oldest known city, and perhaps the most important Iron Age site in Africa south of the Sahara. 396-418, Sept. 1982
• Lifelike Man Preserved 2,000 Years in Peat. By P. V. Glob. 419-430, Mar. 1954
• Treasure From a Celtic Tomb. By Jörg Biel. Photos by Volkmar Wentzel. 428-438, Mar. 1980

IROQUOIS CONFEDERACY. *See* Mohawks

IRRIGATION:
• Behind the Veil of Troubled Yemen. By Thomas J. Abercrombie. 403-445, Mar. 1964
• Californians Escape to the Desert. By Mason Sutherland. Photos by Charles W. Herbert. 675-724, Nov. 1957
• The Desert: An Age-old Challenge Grows. By Rick Gore. Photos by Georg Gerster and Bruce Dale. 586-639, Nov. 1979
• Erosion, Trojan Horse of Greece. By F. G. Renner. 793-812, Dec. 1947
• From Sagebrush to Roses on the Columbia. By Leo A. Borah. 571-611, Nov. 1952
• The Hohokam: First Masters of the American Desert. By Emil W. Haury. Photos by Helga Teiwes. 670-695, May 1967
• I Become a Bakhtiari. By Paul Edward Case. 325-358, Mar. 1947
• North Dakota Comes into Its Own. By Leo A. Borah. Photos by J. Baylor Roberts. 283-322, Sept. 1951
• Sand in My Eyes. By Jinx Rodger. Photos by George Rodger. 664-705, May 1958
• Two Wheels Along the Mexican Border. By William Albert Allard. 591-635, May 1971
• Water for the World's Growing Needs. By Herbert B. Nichols and F. Barrows Colton. 269-286, Aug. 1952
• Western Australia, the Big Country. By Kenneth MacLeish. Photos by James L. Stanfield. 150-187, Feb. 1973

IRVINE RANCH, California:
• Orange, a Most California County. By Judith and Neil Morgan. Photos by Vince Streano. 750-779, Dec. 1981

IRVING, WASHINGTON:
▫ Washington Irving's Spain. 1966

IRWIN, COLIN: Author-Photographer:
• Trek Across Arctic America. 295-321, Mar. 1974

IRWIN, CYNTHIA and HENRY: Authors:
• Wyoming Muck Tells of Battle: Ice Age Man vs. Mammoth. By Cynthia Irwin, Henry Irwin, and George Agogino. 828-837, June 1962

IRWIN, JAMES B.:
• Apollo 15 Explores the Mountains of the Moon. By Kenneth F. Weaver. Photos from NASA. 233-265, Feb. 1972
• What Is It Like to Walk on the Moon? By David R. Scott. 326-331, Sept. 1973

IS This the Tomb of Philip of Macedon? By Manolis Andronicos. Photos by Spyros Tsavdaroglou. 55-77, July 1978

ISBJORN (Ketch):
• Wind, Wave, Star, and Bird. By David Lewis. Photos by Nicholas deVore III. 747-781, Dec. 1974

ISCHIA, Island of the Unexpected. By Dorothea and Stuart E. Jones. 531-550, Apr. 1954

ISLA GRANDE, Tierra del Fuego (Archipelago), South America:
• Guanacos: Wild Camels of South America. By William L. Franklin. 63-75, July 1981

ISLA RAZA, Gulf of California. *See* Raza, Isla

ISLAM:
• Abraham, the Friend of God. By Kenneth MacLeish. Photos by Dean Conger. 739-789, Dec. 1966
• The Arab World, Inc. By John J. Putman. Photos by Winfield Parks. 494-533, Oct. 1975
• Editorial. By Gilbert M. Grosvenor. 1, Jan. 1975
• From America to Mecca on Airborne Pilgrimage. By Abdul Ghafur. 1-60, July 1953
◆ *Great Religions of the World.* Announced. 587-590, Oct. 1971
• Islam's Heartland, Up in Arms. By Thomas J. Abercrombie. 335-345, Sept. 1980
▲ *Middle East, Eastern Mediterranean; Early Civilizations of the Middle East.* Sept. 1978
• Pakistan Under Pressure. By William S. Ellis. Photos by James L. Stanfield. 668-701, May 1981
▲ *The Peoples of the Middle East.* Text on reverse. July 1972
• Pilgrimage to Mecca. By Muhammad Abdul-Rauf. Photos by Mehmet Biber. 581-607, Nov. 1978
• Saudi Arabia: Beyond the Sands of Mecca. By Thomas J. Abercrombie. 1-53, Jan. 1966
• Saudi Arabia: The Kingdom and Its Power. By Robert Azzi. 286-333, Sept. 1980
• The Sword and the Sermon. By Thomas J. Abercrombie. 3-45, July 1972
• This Year in Jerusalem. By Joseph Judge. Photos by Jodi Cobb. 479-515, Apr. 1983
▲ *Two Centuries of Conflict in the Middle East; Mideast in Turmoil.* Sept. 1980

I
J

• *See also* Mosques; Muslims; *and* Afghanistan; Algeria; Bahrain; Chad; Djibouti; Egypt; Gambia; Indonesia; Iran; Iraq; Jordan; Kuwait; Lebanon; Mali; Mauritania; Morocco; Niger; Nigeria; Oman; Pakistan; Saudi Arabia; Senegal; Somalia; Sudan; Syria; Tunisia; Turkey; United Arab Emirates; Yemen Arab Republic

ISLAMIC ART:
• The Arab World, Inc. By John J. Putman. Photos by Winfield Parks. 494-533, Oct. 1975
• Glass Treasure From the Aegean. By George F. Bass. Photos by Jonathan Blair. 768-793, June 1978
• Iran: Desert Miracle. By William Graves. Photos by James P. Blair. 2-47, Jan. 1975
• Iran's Shah Crowns Himself and His Empress. By Franc Shor. Photos by James L. Stanfield and Winfield Parks. 301-321, Mar. 1968
• Saudi Arabia: Beyond the Sands of Mecca. By Thomas J. Abercrombie. 1-53, Jan. 1966
• Saudi Arabia: The Kingdom and Its Power. By Robert Azzi. 286-333, Sept. 1980
• The Sword and the Sermon. By Thomas J. Abercrombie. 3-45, July 1972
• *See also* Mosques

ISLAND, Prairie, Marsh, and Shore. By Charlton Ogburn. Photos by Bates Littlehales. 350-381, Mar. 1979

ISLAND of Faith in the Sinai Wilderness. By George H. Forsyth. Photos by Robert F. Sisson. 82-106, Jan. 1964

The **ISLAND** That's Still Hawaii: Kauai. By Ethel A. Starbird. Photos by Robert W. Madden. 584-613, Nov. 1977

ISLANDS, Formation of:
• This Changing Earth. By Samuel W. Matthews. 1-37, Jan. 1973
• *See also* the volcanic islands: Ilha Nova; Myojin; Surtsey

The **ISLANDS** Called Fiji. By Luis Marden. 526-561, Oct. 1958

ISLE OF MAN. *See* Man, Isle of

ISLE ROYALE, Michigan:
• Wolves Versus Moose on Isle Royale. By Durward L. Allen and L. David Mech. 200-219, Feb. 1963

The **ISLES** of Greece: Aegean Birthplace of Western Culture. By Melville Bell Grosvenor. Photos by Edwin Stuart Grosvenor and Winfield Parks. 147-193, Aug. 1972

The **ISLES** of the Pacific. By Kenneth P. Emory, David Lewis, Mary and Laurance S. Rockefeller. Photos by Nicholas deVore III and Thomas Nebbia. Paintings by Herb Kawainui Kane. 732-793, Dec. 1974

ISLES of the Western Sea: Scotland's Inner Hebrides. By Kenneth MacLeish. Photos by R. Stephen Uzzell III. 690-717, Nov. 1974

ISLES on the Edge of the Sea: Scotland's Outer Hebrides. By Kenneth MacLeish. Photos by Thomas Nebbia. 676-711, May 1970

ISMAILI (Muslims):
• Weighing the Aga Khan in Diamonds. Photos by David J. Carnegie. 317-324, Mar. 1947

ISRAEL:
• Abraham, the Friend of God. By Kenneth MacLeish. Photos by Dean Conger. Included: Abraham in Canaan; Beersheba; Gerar; Uru Salem (Jerusalem). 739-789, Dec. 1966
• An Archeologist Looks at Palestine. By Nelson Glueck. 739-752, Dec. 1947
• The Desert: An Age-old Challenge Grows. By Rick Gore. Photos by Georg Gerster and Bruce Dale. 586-639, Nov. 1979
• Eternal Sinai. By Harvey Arden. Photos by David Doubilet and Kevin Fleming. Included: Israeli withdrawal from the Sinai by April 25, 1982, as part of the Camp David accords. 420-461, Apr. 1982
Egyptian Sector. Photos by Kevin Fleming. 430-443; Israeli Sector. Photos by David Doubilet. 444-461
• Eyewitness to War in the Holy Land. By Charles Harbutt. 782-795, Dec. 1967
▲ *Holy Land Today,* Atlas series supplement. Dec. 1963
• Home to the Holy Land. By Maynard Owen Williams. 707-746, Dec. 1950
• Israel: Land of Promise. By John Scofield. Photos by B. Anthony Stewart. 395-434, Mar. 1965
• Israel–The Seventh Day. By Joseph Judge. Photos by Gordon W. Gahan. 816-855, Dec. 1972
• The Land of Galilee. By Kenneth MacLeish. Photos by B. Anthony Stewart. 832-865, Dec. 1965
▲ *Lands of the Bible Today,* supplement. Dec. 1956
▲ *Lands of the Bible Today,* supplement. Dec. 1967
• The Living Dead Sea. By Harvey Arden. Photos by Nathan Benn. 225-245, Feb. 1978
• Lost Outpost of the Egyptian Empire. By Trude Dothan. Photos by Sisse Brimberg. Paintings by Lloyd K. Townsend. Contents: Deir el-Balah, in the Gaza Strip. 739-769, Dec. 1982
• The Mediterranean–Sea of Man's Fate. By Rick Gore. Photos by Jonathan Blair. 694-737, Dec. 1982
▲ *Middle East, Eastern Mediterranean; Early Civilizations of the Middle East.* Sept. 1978
• New Life for the Troubled Suez Canal. By William Graves. Photos by Jonathan Blair. Included: The cross-canal fighting between Egypt and Israel, 1967-1973; Egypt's 1973 attack on Israel's Sinai fortifications, with photographs of the remains of those fortifications. 792-817, June 1975
• Our Life on a Border Kibbutz. By Carol and Al Abrams. Photos by Al Abrams. 364-391, Sept. 1970
▲ *The Peoples of the Middle East.* Text on reverse. July 1972
• Pilgrims Follow the Christmas Star. By Maynard Owen Williams. 831-840, Dec. 1952
• This Year in Jerusalem. By Joseph Judge. Photos by Jodi Cobb. 479-515, Apr. 1983
▲ *Two Centuries of Conflict in the Middle East; Mideast in Turmoil,* double-sided supplement. Sept. 1980
• Where Jesus Walked. By Howard La Fay. Photos by Charles Harbutt. 739-781, Dec. 1967
• *See also* Arab-Israeli Conflict; Jerusalem

ISRAELITES:
• Bringing Old Testament Times to Life. By G. Ernest Wright. Paintings by Henry J. Soulen. 833-864, Dec. 1957
• In Search of Moses. By Harvey Arden. Photos by Nathan Benn. 2-37, Jan. 1976
• The Last Thousand Years Before Christ. By G. Ernest Wright. Paintings by H. J. Soulen and Peter V. Bianchi. 812-853, Dec. 1960

ISTANBUL, Turkey:
• "Around the World in Eighty Days." By Newman Bumstead. 705-750, Dec. 1951
• Athens to Istanbul. By Jean and Franc Shor. 37-76, Jan. 1956
• The Byzantine Empire: Rome of the East. By Merle Severy. Photos by James L. Stanfield. 709-767, Dec. 1983
• Istanbul, the City That Links Europe and Asia. By William S. Ellis. Photos by Winfield Parks. 501-533, Oct. 1973
• A New Look at Medieval Europe. By Kenneth M. Setton. Paintings by Andre Durenceau and Birney Lettick. Included: Constantinople. 799-859, Dec. 1962
• Robert College, Turkish Gateway to the Future. By Franc Shor. 399-418, Sept. 1957
• Turkey Paves the Path of Progress. By Maynard Owen Williams. 141-186, Aug. 1951

ITAIPÚ HYDROELECTRIC DEVELOPMENT:
• Paraguay, Paradox of South America. By Gordon Young. Photos by O. Louis Mazzatenta. 240-269, Aug. 1982

ITALIAN RIVIERA, Land That Winter Forgot. By Howell Walker. 743-789, June 1963
• *See also* Portofino

ITALIANS:
• Brooklyn: The Other Side of the Bridge. By Alice J. Hall. Photos by Robert W. Madden. 580-613, May 1983

ITALY:
• Across the Alps in a Wicker Basket *(Bernina).* By Phil Walker. 117-131, Jan. 1963
• Across the Ridgepole of the Alps. By Walter Meayers Edwards. 410-419, Sept. 1960
• The Alps: Man's Own Mountains. By Ralph Gray. Photos by Walter Meayers Edwards and William Eppridge. 350-395, Sept. 1965
• Amalfi, Italy's Divine Coast. By Luis Marden. 472-509, Oct. 1959

• Ancient Shipwreck Yields New Facts–and a Strange Cargo. By Peter Throckmorton. Photos by Kim Hart and Joseph J. Scherschel. 282-300, Feb. 1969
• "Around the World in Eighty Days." By Newman Bumstead. Included: Anzio; Elba; Genoa; Larderello Valley; La Spezia; Otranto; Pisa; Rome; Turin; Vesuvius. 705-750, Dec. 1951
• A Buried Roman Town Gives Up Its Dead (Herculaneum). By Joseph Judge. Photos by Jonathan Blair. NGS research grant. 687-693, Dec. 1982
• Carrara Marble: Touchstone of Eternity. By Cathy Newman. Photos by Pierre Boulat. 42-59, July 1982
• Down the Ancient Appian Way. By James Cerruti. Photos by O. Louis Mazzatenta. 714-747, June 1981
• Fishing in the Whirlpool of Charybdis. By Paul A. Zahl. 579-618, Nov. 1953
• Hydrofoil Ferry "Flies" the Strait of Messina. By Gilbert Grosvenor. 493-496, Apr. 1957
• Italian Riviera, Land That Winter Forgot. By Howell Walker. 743-789, June 1963
▲ *Italy,* Atlas series supplement. Nov. 1961
• Italy Smiles Again. By Edgar Erskine Hume. 693-732, June 1949
• Leonardo da Vinci: A Man for All Ages. By Kenneth MacLeish. Photos by James L. Amos. 296-329, Sept. 1977
• Lombardy's Lakes, Blue Jewels in Italy's Crown. By Franc Shor. Photos by Joseph J. Scherschel. 58-99, July 1968
• The Mediterranean–Sea of Man's Fate. By Rick Gore. Photos by Jonathan Blair. 694-737, Dec. 1982
• A New Look at Medieval Europe. By Kenneth M. Setton. Paintings by Andre Durenceau and Birney Lettick. 799-859, Dec. 1962
• Periscope on the Etruscan Past. By Carlo M. Lerici. 337-350, Sept. 1959
• Restoration Reveals the "Last Supper." By Carlo Bertelli. Photos by Victor R. Boswell, Jr. 664-685, Nov. 1983
• Round the World School (ISA). By Paul Antze. Photos by William Eppridge. 96-127, July 1962
• A Stroll to Venice. By Isobel Wylie Hutchison. 378-410, Sept. 1951
▲ *A Traveler's Map of Italy,* supplement. Text on reverse. June 1970
• United Italy Marks Its 100th Year. By Nathaniel T. Kenney. 593-647, Nov. 1961
• Warriors From a Watery Grave (Bronze Sculptures). By Joseph Alsop. 821-827, June 1983
• When the President Goes Abroad. By Gilbert M. Grosvenor. 588-649, May 1960
• *See also* Florence; Marostica; Nettuno; Pompeii; Portofino; Rome; Siena; Trieste; Tuscany; Venice; *and* islands: Capri; Ischia; Sicily

ITHACA (Island), Greece:
• Homeward With Ulysses. By Melville Bell Grosvenor. Photos by Edwin Stuart Grosvenor. 1-39, July 1973

IT'S a Way of Life: Mexican Folk Art. By Fernando Horcasitas. Photos by David Hiser. 648-669, May 1978

IT'S Been a Banner Year! President's Report to Members. By Gilbert M. Grosvenor. 848-852, Dec. 1981

ITURI FOREST, Zaire:
• My Life With Africa's Little People. By Anne Eisner Putnam. 278-302, Feb. 1960

IVIZA (Island), Spain. *See* Ibiza

IVOR, HANCE ROY: Author:
• The Enigma of Bird Anting. 105-119, July 1956
Author-Photographer:
• Seeing Birds as Real Personalities. 523-530, Apr. 1954
Bluebirds on the Wing in Color. Photos by Bernard Corby and author. 527-530

IVORY:
• Where Magic Ruled: Art of the Bering Sea. By William W. Fitzhugh and Susan A. Kaplan. Photos by Sisse Brimberg. Contents: Eskimo art. 198-205, Feb. 1983

IVORY COAST, Republic of:
• Freedom Speaks French in Ouagadougou. By John Scofield. 153-203, Aug. 1966
• The Ivory Coast–African Success Story. By Michael and Aubine Kirtley. 94-125, July 1982

IVORY TRADE:
• Africa's Elephants: Can They Survive? By Oria Douglas-Hamilton. Photos by Oria and Iain Douglas-Hamilton. 568-603, Nov. 1980
• Wild Cargo: the Business of Smuggling Animals. By Noel Grove. Photos by Steve Raymer. Included: Illegal trade in elephant and walrus ivory. 287-315, Mar. 1981

IWO JIMA (Island), Volcano Islands:
• Adventures with the Survey Navy. By Irving Johnson. 131-148, July 1947
• The Bonins and Iwo Jima Go Back to Japan. By Paul Sampson. Photos by Joc Munroe. 128-144, July 1968

J

J. W. WESTCOTT, Postman for the Great Lakes. By Cy La Tour. 813-824, Dec. 1950

JACKALS of the Serengeti. By Patricia D. Moehlman. NGS research grant. 840-850, Dec. 1980

JACKSON, ANDREW:
• Inside the White House. By Lonnelle Aikman. Photos by B. Anthony Stewart and Thomas Nebbia. 3-43, Jan. 1961
• The Living White House. By Lonnelle Aikman. 593-643, Nov. 1966
• Profiles of the Presidents: II. A Restless Nation Moves West. By Frank Freidel. 80-121, Jan. 1965

DAVID HISER

It's a Way of Life: lacquered tray

Ivory Coast: dancers of the Dan tribe

MICHAEL AND AUBINE KIRTLEY

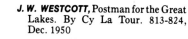

JONATHAN WRIGHT

Jackson Hole: jump off Crabtree Rock

• Today Along the Natchez Trace, Pathway Through History. By Bern Keating. Photos by Charles Harbutt. 641-667, Nov. 1968

JACKSON, CARMAULT B., Jr.: Author:
• The Flight of *Freedom* 7. 416-431, Sept. 1961

JACKSON HOLE, Wyoming:
• Grand Teton–A Winter's Tale. By François Leydet. 148-152, July 1979
• I See America First. By Lynda Bird Johnson. Photos by William Albert Allard. 874-904, Dec. 1965
• Jackson Hole: Good-bye to the Old Days? By François Leydet. Photos by Jonathan Wright. 768-789, Dec. 1976
• Wildlife Adventuring in Jackson Hole. By Frank and John Craighead. 1-36, Jan. 1956
• Wyoming: High, Wide, and Windy. By David S. Boyer. 554-594, Apr. 1966

JACOBS, FENNO: Photographer:
• Mid-century Holland Builds Her Future. By Sydney Clark. 747-778, Dec. 1950

JACOBSON, DORANNE WILSON: Author-Photographer:
• Purdah in India: Life Behind the Veil. 270-286, Aug. 1977

JACQUES-YVES COUSTEAU Receives National Geographic Society Medal at White House. 146-147, July 1961
• *See also* Cousteau, Jacques-Yves

JADE:
• China Unveils Her Newest Treasures. By Robert W. Madden. 848-857, Dec. 1974
• Exploring the World of Gems. By W. F. Foshag. 779-810, Dec. 1950

JAEGER, EDMUND C.: Author:
• Poorwill Sleeps Away the Winter. 273-280, Feb. 1953

JAFFA. *See* Tel Aviv-Jaffa

JAGANNATH FESTIVAL:
• Orissa, Past and Promise in an Indian State. By Bart McDowell. Photos by James P. Blair. 546-577, Oct. 1970

JAGUAR GOD:
• Gifts for the Jaguar God. By Philip Drucker and Robert F. Heizer. NGS research grant. 367-375, Sept. 1956

JAGUAR HUNTING:
• The Jungle Was My Home. By Sasha Siemel. 695-712, Nov. 1952

JAINS (Religious Sect):
• India's Sculptured Temple Caves. By Volkmar Wentzel. 665-678, May 1953

JAIPUR, India:
• Feudal Splendor Lingers in Rajputana. By Volkmar Wentzel. 411-458, Oct. 1948

JAISALMER, India:
• Feudal Splendor Lingers in Rajputana. By Volkmar Wentzel. 411-458, Oct. 1948
• Royal Wedding at Jaisalmer. By Marilyn Silverstone. 66-79, Jan. 1965

JAKARTA, Indonesia. *See* Djakarta

JAKOBSHAVN, Greenland:
• Greenland's "Place by the Icebergs." By Mogens Bloch Poulsen. Photos by Thomas Nebbia. 849-869, Dec. 1973

JALISCO (State), Mexico:
• The Most Mexican City, Guadalajara. By Bart McDowell. Photos by Volkmar Wentzel. 412-441, Mar. 1967
• *See also* Stone Spheres

JAMAICA (Island), West Indies:
• The Caribbean: Sun, Sea, and Seething. By Noel Grove. Photos by Steve Raymer. 244-271, Feb. 1981
• Exploring the Drowned City of Port Royal. By Marion Clayton Link. Photos by Luis Marden. NGS research grant. 151-183, Feb. 1960
• Jamaica–Hub of the Caribbean. By W. Robert Moore. 333-362, Mar. 1954
• Jamaica Goes It Alone. By James Cerruti. Photos by Thomas Nebbia. 843-873, Dec. 1967
• Reach for the New World. By Mendel Peterson. Photos by David L. Arnold. Paintings by Richard Schlecht. Included: Port Royal. 724-767, Dec. 1977
• Wing-borne Lamps of the Summer Night (Fireflies). By Paul A. Zahl. 48-59, July 1962

JAMBO–First Gorilla Raised by Its Mother in Captivity. By Ernst M. Lang. Photos by Paul Steinemann. 446-453, Mar. 1964

JAMES I, King (Great Britain):
• The British Way. By Sir Evelyn Wrench. Included: James I and the translation of the Bible (1611). 421-541, Apr. 1949

JAMES, FRANCES: Author:
• Keeping House in London. 769-792, Dec. 1947
• Thumbs Up Round the North Sea's Rim. Photos by Erica Koch. 685-704, May 1952

JAMES, THOMAS GARNER: Author:
• Kew: The Commoners' Royal Garden. Photos by B. Anthony Stewart. 479-506, Apr. 1950
• London's Zoo of Zoos. 771-786, June 1953
• Portsmouth, Britannia's Sally Port. Photos by B. Anthony Stewart. 513-544, Apr. 1952

JAMES (River), Virginia:
• Stately Homes of Old Virginia. By Albert W. Atwood. 787-802, June 1953

JAMES BAY, and Region, Canada:
• The Changing World of Canada's Crees. By Fred Ward. 541-569, Apr. 1975
• Quebec's Northern Dynamo. By Larry Kohl. Photos by Ottmar Bierwagen. 406-418, Mar. 1982

JAMESTOWN, Virginia:
• Captain Smith of Jamestown. By Bradford Smith. 581-620, May 1957

JAMMU AND KASHMIR (State), India:
● Ladakh–The Last Shangri-la. By Thomas J. Abercrombie. 332-359, Mar. 1978
● *See also* former name, Kashmir

JAN MAYEN (Island), Norwegian Sea:
● Seal Hunting Off Jan Mayen. By Ole Friele Backer. 57-72, Jan. 1948

JANE AND JUSTIN DART FOUNDATION: Study Grant:
● Orangutans. 835, June 1980

JANE GOODALL Finds Warfare and Cannibalism Among Gombe's Chimpanzees. By Jane Goodall. 592-621, May 1979

JANE M. SMITH AWARD:
● Ingram, Sir Bruce. 474, Apr. 1961
● Johnson, Lyndon B.: Vice President Johnson Accepts the Society's Jane Smith Award. 906, Dec. 1962; 113, Jan. 1966; 468, Oct. 1966

JANEL FISHERIES (Tuna Ranch), Canada:
● Plight of the Bluefin Tuna. By Michael J. A. Butler. Photos by David Doubilet. Paintings by Stanley Meltzoff. Included: Captive fattening of bluefin tuna for sale to Japanese market. 220-239, Aug. 1982

JANITZIO (Island), Lake Pátzcuaro, Mexico. *See* Pátzcuaro

JAPAN:
● Ama, Sea Nymphs of Japan. By Luis Marden. 122-135, July 1971
● Around the World and the Calendar with the Geographic: The President's Annual Message. By Melville Bell Grosvenor. 832-866, Dec. 1959
● Backwoods Japan During American Occupation. By M. A. Huberman. 491-518, Apr. 1947
● Bamboo, the Giant Grass. By Luis Marden. Photos by Jim Brandenburg. 502-529, Oct. 1980
● The Bonanza Bean–Coffee. By Ethel A. Starbird. Photos by Sam Abell. 388-405, Mar. 1981
● The Bonins and Iwo Jima Go Back to Japan. By Paul Sampson. Photos by Joe Munroe. 128-144, July 1968
● The Chip: Electronic Mini-marvel. By Allen A. Boraiko. Photos by Charles O'Rear. 421-457, Oct. 1982
● Day of the Rice God. Photos by H. Edward Kim. Text by Douglas Lee. Contents: The rice-transplanting festival in Chiyoda. 78-85, July 1978
● Human Treasures of Japan. By William Graves. Photos by James L. Stanfield. Contents: Ryujo Hori, doll maker; Gonroku Matsuda, lacquer artist; Tesshi Nagano, ironcaster; Utaemon Nakamura, Kabuki actor; Sadaichi Tsukiyama, samurai swordsmith. 370-379, Sept. 1972
● Japan, the Exquisite Enigma. By Franc Shor. Photos by John Launois. 733-777, Dec. 1960
▲ *Japan and Korea,* Atlas series supplement. Dec. 1960
● Japan Tries Freedom's Road. By Frederick G. Vosburgh. Photos by J. Baylor Roberts. 593-632, May 1950
● The Japanese Crane, Bird of Happiness. By Tsuneo Hayashida. 542-556, Oct. 1983

GEORGE F. MOBLEY, NGS

Kyoto and Nara: doll of lion dancer

Successful Japanese: student virtuoso

FRED WARD, BLACK STAR

● Japan's Warriors of the Wind. Photos by David Alan Harvey. Text by John Eliot. Contents: Annual kite festival in Hamamatsu. 551-561, Apr. 1977
● Kansai, Japan's Historic Heartland. By Thomas J. Abercrombie. Included: Expo '70. 295-339, Mar. 1970
● Kyoto and Nara: Keepers of Japan's Past. By Charles McCarry. Photos by George F. Mobley. 836-851, June 1976
Kyoto Says Happy New Year. 852-859
■ Living Treasures of Japan. 703, Dec. 1980
● The Lost Fleet of Kublai Khan. By Torao Mozai. Photos by Koji Nakamura. Paintings by Issho Yada. 634-649, Nov. 1982
● Nature's Night Lights: Probing the Secrets of Bioluminescence. By Paul A. Zahl. 45-69, July 1971
● Oil, the Dwindling Treasure. By Noel Grove. Photos by Emory Kristof. 792-825, June 1974
● Operation Eclipse: 1948. By William A. Kinney. 325-372, Mar. 1949
● Our Navy in the Far East. By Arthur W. Radford. Photos by J. Baylor Roberts. 537-577, Oct. 1953
● Our Vegetable Travelers. By Victor R. Boswell. Paintings by Else Bostelmann. Included: Native vegetables. 145-217, Aug. 1949
● Plight of the Bluefin Tuna. By Michael J. A. Butler. Photos by David Doubilet. Paintings by Stanley Meltzoff. 220-239, Aug. 1982
● Quicksilver and Slow Death. By John J. Putman. Photos by Robert W. Madden. Included: Japanese victims of methyl mercury poisoning. 507-527, Oct. 1972
● Round the World School (ISA). By Paul Antze. Photos by William Eppridge. 96-127, July 1962
● Shrimp Nursery: Science Explores New Ways to Farm the Sea. By Clarence P. Idyll. Photos by Robert F. Sisson. 636-659, May 1965
● Swing Low, Sweet Chariot! By Noel Grove. Photos by Bruce Dale. 2-35, July 1983
● Those Successful Japanese. By Bart McDowell. Photos by Fred Ward. 323-359, Mar. 1974
● The World in Your Garden (Flowers). By W. H. Camp. Paintings by Else Bostelmann. Included: Patient Gardeners of Old Japan (Japanese Wisteria, Bleeding heart, Japanese iris, Azalea). 1-65, July 1947
● YWCA: International Success Story. By Mary French Rockefeller. Photos by Otis Imboden. 904-933, Dec. 1963
● The Yankee Sailor Who Opened Japan (Commodore Perry). By Ferdinand Kuhn. 85-102, July 1953
● *See also* Hokkaido; Inland Sea; Japan Trench; Kansai; Myojin Island; Tokyo

JAPAN TRENCH, Pacific Ocean:
● Deep Diving off Japan. By Georges S. Houot. NGS research grant. 138-150, Jan. 1960

I J

JAPANESE ART:
● Human Treasures of Japan. By William Graves. Photos by James L. Stanfield. Included: Ironcasting, Kabuki, Lacquer working, Swordsmithing, Wood sculpture. 370-379, Sept. 1972
● Living Treasures of Japan. 703, Dec. 1980
● Kyoto and Nara: Keepers of Japan's Past. By Charles McCarry. Photos by George F. Mobley. 836-851, June 1976

The **JAPANESE** Crane, Bird of Happiness. By Tsuneo Hayashida. 542-556, Oct. 1983

JARAWAS (Negrito Tribe):
● The Last Andaman Islanders. By Raghubir Singh. 66-91, July 1975

JARCHÉ, JAMES: Photographer:
● In the London of the New Queen. By H. V. Morton. 291-342, Sept. 1953

JARI RIVER REGION, Brazil:
● Amazon–The River Sea. By Loren McIntyre. Included: Daniel K. Ludwig's planned paper pulp and food-production enterprise in Brazil's Amazon basin. 456-495, Oct. 1972
● Brazil's Wild Frontier. By Loren McIntyre. Included: Daniel K. Ludwig's three-million-acre agricultural and forestry experiment. 684-719, Nov. 1977
● Jari: A Billion-dollar Gamble. By Loren McIntyre. Contents: Daniel K. Ludwig's paper-pulp and food-production enterprise in Brazil's Amazon Basin. 686-711, May 1980

JASPER NATIONAL PARK, Canada:
● Heart of the Canadian Rockies. By Elizabeth A. Moize. Photos by Jim Brandenburg. 757-779, June 1980

JAVA (Island), Indonesia:
● Indonesia Rescues Ancient Borobudur. By W. Brown Morton III. Photos by Dean Conger. 126-142, Jan. 1983
● Java–Eden in Transition. By Kenneth MacLeish. Photos by Dean Conger. 1-43, Jan. 1971
● Postwar Journey Through Java. By Ronald Stuart Kain. 675-700, May 1948

JAVAHÉ INDIANS:
● Blue-eyed Indian: A city boy's sojourn with primitive tribesmen in central Brazil. By Harald Schultz. 65-89, July 1961

A **JAWBREAKER** for Sharks. By Valerie Taylor. 664-667, May 1981

JEEP, Amphibious. *See Tortuga II*

JEFFERSON, THOMAS:
● Inside the White House. By Lonnelle Aikman. Photos by B. Anthony Stewart and Thomas Nebbia. 3-43, Jan. 1961
● The Living White House. By Lonnelle Aikman. 593-643, Nov. 1966
● Mr. Jefferson's Charlottesville. By Anne Revis. 553-592, May 1950
● Mr. Jefferson's Monticello. By Joseph Judge. Photos by Dean Conger and Richard S. Durrance. 426-444, Sept. 1966
● Profiles of the Presidents: I. The Presidency and How It Grew. By Frank Freidel. 642-687, Nov. 1964
● Thomas Jefferson: Architect of Freedom. By Mike W. Edwards. Photos by Linda Bartlett. 231-259, Feb. 1976

JEFFERY, DAVID: Author:
● America's Auto Mania. Photos by Bruce Dale. 24-31, *Special Report on Energy* (Feb. 1981)
● Arizona's Suburbs of the Sun. Photos by H. Edward Kim. 486-517, Oct. 1977
● Audubon "On the Wing." Photos by Bates Littlehales. 149-177, Feb. 1977
● Burma's Leg Rowers and Floating Farms. Photos by W. E. Garrett. 826-845, June 1974
● The Grandeur of Windsor (Portfolio). 616-625, Nov. 1980
● A Most Uncommon Town: Columbus, Indiana. Photos by J. Bruce Baumann. 383-397, Sept. 1978
● The Once and Future Universe. By Rick Gore. Photos by James A. Sugar. Paintings by Barron Storey. Picture text by David Jeffery. 704-749, June 1983
● Preserving America's Last Great Wilderness (Alaska). 769-791, June 1975
● Royal House for Dolls. Photos by James L. Stanfield. 632-643, Nov. 1980

JEH (Tribe):
● Viet Nam's Montagnards. By Howard Sochurek. 443-487, Apr. 1968

JEHL, JOSEPH R., Jr.:
Author-Photographer:
● Mono Lake: A Vital Way Station for the Wilson's Phalarope. 520-525, Oct. 1981

JEKYLL ISLAND, Georgia:
● Sea Islands: Adventuring Along the South's Surprising Coast. By James Cerruti. Photos by Thomas Nebbia and James L. Amos. 366-393, Mar. 1971

JELLYFISHES:
● Glass Menageries of the Sea. By Paul A. Zahl. 797-822, June 1955
● Strange World of Palau's Salt Lakes. By William M. Hamner. Photos by David Doubilet. 264-282, Feb. 1982
● *See also* Portuguese Man-of-War

JENKINS, BARBARA:
Author-Photographer:
● A Walk Across America: Part II. By Peter and Barbara Jenkins. 194-229, Aug. 1979

JENKINS, PETER GORTON:
Author-Photographer:
● A Walk Across America. 466-499, Apr. 1977
● A Walk Across America: Part II. By Peter and Barbara Jenkins. 194-229, Aug. 1979

JENNE, Mali:
● Finding West Africa's Oldest City. By Susan and Roderick McIntosh. Photos by Michael and Aubine Kirtley. Contents: Jenne-jeno (site). 396-418, Sept. 1982

JENNER, EDWARD:
● The British Way. By Sir Evelyn Wrench. 421-541, Apr. 1949

JENNINGS, DEAN: Author:
● The Friendly Train Called Skunk. Photos by B. Anthony Stewart. 720-734, May 1959

JENNINGS, GARY: Author:
● Bavaria: Mod, Medieval–and Bewitching. Photos by George F. Mobley. 409-431, Mar. 1974
● Newfoundland Trusts in the Sea. Photos by Sam Abell. 112-141, Jan. 1974

JERICHO, Jordan:
● The Ghosts of Jericho. By James L. Kelso. 825-844, Dec. 1951
● Hashemite Jordan, Arab Heartland. By John Scofield. 841-856, Dec. 1952
● Jericho Gives Up Its Secrets. By Kathleen M. Kenyon and A. Douglas Tushingham. Photos by Nancy Lord. 853-870, Dec. 1953

JERSEY (Island), English Channel:
● Britain's "French" Channel Islands. By James Cerruti. Photos by James L. Amos. 710-740, May 1971

JERSTAD, LUTHER G.:
● American and Geographic Flags Top Everest. By Melvin M. Payne. Photos by Barry C. Bishop. 157-157C, Aug. 1963
● *See also* American Mount Everest Expedition

JERUSALEM:
● An Archeologist Looks at Palestine. By Nelson Glueck. 739-752, Dec. 1947
● Conquest of the Holy City (First Crusade). By Franc Shor. Photos by Thomas Nebbia. 839-855, Dec. 1963
● Crusader Lands Revisited. By Harold Lamb. Photos by David S. Boyer. 815-852, Dec. 1954
● Editorial. By Wilbur E. Garrett. 423, Apr. 1983
● Eyewitness to War in the Holy Land. By Charles Harbutt. 782-795, Dec. 1967
● Hashemite Jordan, Arab Heartland. By John Scofield. 841-856, Dec. 1952
● Holy Land, My Country. By His Majesty King Hussein of Jordan. 784-789, Dec. 1964
● Home to the Holy Land. By Maynard Owen Williams. 707-746, Dec. 1950
● Jerusalem, My Home. By Bertha Spafford Vester. 826-847, Dec. 1964
● Jerusalem, the Divided City. By John Scofield. Photos by Brian Brake. 492-531, Apr. 1959
● Jerusalem to Rome in the Path of St. Paul. By David S. Boyer. 707-759, Dec. 1956
● The Other Side of Jordan. By Luis Marden. 790-825, Dec. 1964
● Pilgrims Follow the Christmas Star. By Maynard Owen Williams. 831-840, Dec. 1952

• Reunited Jerusalem Faces Its Problems. By Kenneth MacLeish. Photos by Ted Spiegel. 835-871, Dec. 1968
• This Year in Jerusalem. By Joseph Judge. Photos by Jodi Cobb. 479-515, Apr. 1983
• Where Jesus Walked. By Howard La Fay. Photos by Charles Harbutt. 739-781, Dec. 1967
• YWCA: International Success Story. By Mary French Rockefeller. Photos by Otis Imboden. 904-933, Dec. 1963

JESUS:
• The Land of Galilee. By Kenneth MacLeish. Photos by B. Anthony Stewart. 832-865, Dec. 1965
• The Mystery of the Shroud. By Kenneth F. Weaver. 730-753, June 1980
• Where Jesus Walked. By Howard La Fay. Photos by Charles Harbutt. 739-781, Dec. 1967

JET AIRCRAFT:
• Aviation Looks Ahead on Its 50th Birthday. By Emory S. Land. 721-739, Dec. 1953
• Fact Finding for Tomorrow's Planes. By Hugh L. Dryden. Photos by Luis Marden. 757-780, Dec. 1953
• Flying in the "Blowtorch" Era. By Frederick G. Vosburgh. 281-322, Sept. 1950
• Of Planes and Men. By Kenneth F. Weaver. Photos by Emory Kristof and Albert Moldvay. 298-349, Sept. 1965
• Our Air Age Speeds Ahead. By F. Barrows Colton. 249-272, Feb. 1948
• The Solar Eclipse From a Jet. By Wolfgang B. Klemperer. 785-796, Nov. 1963
• They're Redesigning the Airplane. By Michael E. Long. Photos by James A. Sugar. 76-103, Jan. 1981

JET BOATS:
• Shooting Rapids in Reverse! Jet Boats Climb the Colorado's Torrent Through the Grand Canyon. By William Belknap, Jr. 552-565, Apr. 1962

JET PROPULSION LABORATORY, California Institute of Technology. *See* Mariner Missions; Ranger Spacecraft; Surveyor Spacecraft; Viking Spacecraft Missions; Voyager

JET SUBMARINES. *See DS-2; Denise*

JETHOU (Island), English Channel:
• Britain's "French" Channel Islands. By James Cerruti. Photos by James L. Amos. 710-740, May 1971

JEWELRY:
• Exploring the World of Gems. By W. F. Foshag. 779-810, Dec. 1950
• Gold, the Eternal Treasure. By Peter T. White. Photos by James L. Stanfield. 1-51, Jan. 1974
• Golden Window on the Past (Amber). Photos by Paul A. Zahl. Text by Thomas J. O'Neill. 423-435, Sept. 1977
• The Incredible Crystal: Diamonds. By Fred Ward. 85-113, Jan. 1979
• The Many-sided Diamond. By George S. Switzer. 568-586, Apr. 1958
• The Miracle Metal–Platinum. By Gordon Young. Photos by James L. Amos. 686-706, Nov. 1983
• Precious Corals, Hawaii's Deep-sea Jewels. By Richard W. Grigg. Photos by David Doubilet. 719-732, May 1979
• Questing for Gems. By George S. Switzer. Included: Gem mining in Africa, Brazil, and Colombia; samplings of the Crown Jewel collections of Great Britain, Iran, and tsarist Russia; the history of the Koh-i-noor, Hope, and Orloff diamonds. 835-863, Dec. 1971
• Silver: A Mineral of Excellent Nature. By Allen A. Boraiko. Photos by Fred Ward. 280-313, Sept. 1981
• *See also* Lapidary Work

Crown Jewels:
• Imperial Russia's Glittering Legacy. 24-33, Jan. 1978
• In the London of the New Queen (Elizabeth II). By H. V. Morton. 291-342, Sept. 1953
• The Incredible Crystal: Diamonds. By Fred Ward. Included: Iran. 85-113, Jan. 1979
• Iran's Shah Crowns Himself and His Empress. By Franc Shor. Photos by James L. Stanfield and Winfield Parks. 301-321, Mar. 1968
• The Many-sided Diamond. By George S. Switzer. Included: Great Britain's Imperial State Crown, the French crown jewels, and the crown jewel of the tsarist empire known as the Orloff Diamond. 568-586, Apr. 1958
• Questing for Gems. By George S. Switzer. Included: Great Britain; Iran; Tsarist Russia. 835-863, Dec. 1971

Salvaged Jewelry:
• Drowned Galleons Yield Spanish Gold. By Kip Wagner. Photos by Otis Imboden. 1-37, Jan. 1965
• Graveyard of the Quicksilver Galleons. By Mendel Peterson. Photos by Jonathan Blair. 850-876, Dec. 1979
• Priceless Relics of the Spanish Armada. By Robert Sténuit. Photos by Bates Littlehales. 745-777, June 1969
• Reach for the New World. By Mendel Peterson. Photos by David L. Arnold. Paintings by Richard Schlecht. 724-767, Dec. 1977
• Treasure From the Ghost Galleon: *Santa Margarita*. By Eugene Lyon. Photos by Don Kincaid. 228-243, Feb. 1982

JHELUM (River), Kashmir-Pakistan:
• The Idyllic Vale of Kashmir. By Volkmar Wentzel. 523-550, Apr. 1948

JIM (Diving Suit):
• A Walk in the Deep. By Sylvia A. Earle. Photos by Al Giddings and Chuck Nicklin. 624-631, May 1980

JODHPUR, India:
• Feudal Splendor Lingers in Rajputana. By Volkmar Wentzel. 411-458, Oct. 1948

Diamonds: Iran's crown of state

FRED WARD, BLACK STAR

DAVID DOUBILET

Precious Corals: pink coral jewelry

I
J

JOGJAKARTA, Java, Indonesia:
- Java–Eden in Transition. By Kenneth Macleish. Photos by Dean Conger. 1-43, Jan. 1971
- *See also* former name, Djokjakarta

JOHANSON, DONALD C.: Author:
- Ethiopia Yields First "Family" of Early Man. Photos by David Brill. 790-811, Dec. 1976

JOHN ELLIOTT PILLSBURY (Research Vessel):
- Squids: Jet-powered Torpedoes of the Deep. By Gilbert L. Voss. Photos by Robert F. Sisson. NGS research grant. 386-411, Mar. 1967

JOHN F. KENNEDY: The Last Full Measure. By Melville Bell Grosvenor. 307-355, Mar. 1964
- *See also* Kennedy, John F.

JOHN FRUM CULT:
- Tanna Awaits the Coming of John Frum. By Kal Muller. 706-715, May 1974

JOHN GLENN Receives the Society's Hubbard Medal. 827, June 1962

JOHN GLENN'S Three Orbits in *Friendship 7*. By Robert B. Voas. 792-827, June 1962

JOHN MUIR'S Wild America. By Harvey Arden. Photos by Dewitt Jones. 433-461, Apr. 1973

JOHN OLIVER LA GORCE Is Elected Vice-Chairman of the Board, Melville Bell Grosvenor President and Editor of the National Geographic Society. 419-423, Mar. 1957
- *See also* La Gorce, John Oliver

JOHN PAUL II, Pope:
- ▲ *The Face and Faith of Poland*, map, photo, and essay supplement. By Peter Miller. Essay by Czesław Miłosz. Photos by Bruno Barbey. Apr. 1982

JOHN PENNEKAMP CORAL REEF STATE PARK, Florida:
- Florida's Coral City Beneath the Sea. By Jerry Greenberg. 70-89, Jan. 1962
- Key Largo Coral Reef: America's First Undersea Park. By Charles M. Brookfield. Photos by Jerry Greenberg. 58-69, Jan. 1962
- The Lower Keys, Florida's "Out Islands." By John Scofield. Photos by Emory Kristof and Bates Littlehales. 72-93, Jan. 1971

JOHN WOODMAN HIGGINS ARMORY:
- Cities Like Worcester Make America. By Howell Walker. 189-214, Feb. 1955

JOHNS HOPKINS APPLIED PHYSICS LABORATORY. *See* DODGE Satellite

JOHNS HOPKINS UNIVERSITY:
Research:
- Torchbearers of the Twilight (Fireflies). By Frederick G. Vosburgh. Contents: The experiments of Dr. William D. McElroy with cold light, such as that of fireflies. 697-704, May 1951

JOHNS ISLAND, South Carolina:
- Sea Islands: Adventuring Along the South's Surprising Coast. By James Cerruti. Photos by Thomas Nebbia and James L. Amos. 366-393, Mar. 1971

JOHNSON, ANDREW:
- The Living White House. By Lonnelle Aikman. 593-643, Nov. 1966
- Profiles of the Presidents: III. The American Giant Comes of Age. By Frank Freidel. 660-711, May 1965

JOHNSON, CECIL E.: Author:
- The Wild World of Compost. Photos by Bianca Lavies. 273-284, Aug. 1980

JOHNSON, DAVID H.: Author:
- The Incredible Kangaroo. 487-500, Oct. 1955

JOHNSON, IRVING and ELECTA:
- Windjamming Around New England. By Tom Horgan. Photos by Robert F. Sisson. Contains information about Irving Johnson and his brigantine, *Yankee*. 141-169, Aug. 1950

Author-Photographers:
- Adventures with the Survey Navy. 131-148, July 1947
- Inside Europe Aboard *Yankee* (Ketch). Photos by Irving Johnson and Joseph J. Scherschel. 157-195, Aug. 1964
- Lost World of the Galapagos. 681-703, May 1959
- New Guinea to Bali in *Yankee* (Brigantine). 767-815, Dec. 1959
- Saga of a Ship, the *Yankee* (Brigantine). By Luis Marden. 263-269, Feb. 1966
- South Seas' Incredible Land Divers (New Hebrides Islanders). Photos by Arthur Johnson and Irving Johnson. 77-92, Jan. 1955
- *Yankee* (Ketch) Cruises the Storied Nile. Photos by Winfield Parks. 583-633, May 1965
- *Yankee* (Ketch) Cruises Turkey's History-haunted Coast. Photos by Joseph J. Scherschel. 798-845, Dec. 1969
- *Yankee* (Brigantine) Roams the Orient. 327-370, Mar. 1951
- The *Yankee*'s (Brigantine) Wander-world. 1-50, Jan. 1949

JOHNSON, LANNY: Photographer:
- Avalanche! "I'm OK, I'm Alive!" Photos by Lanny Johnson and Andre Benier. 282-289, Sept. 1982

JOHNSON, LYNDA BIRD: Author:
- I See America First. Photos by William Albert Allard. 874-904, Dec. 1965

JOHNSON, LYNDON B.:
- The Living White House. By Lonnelle Aikman. 593-643, Nov. 1966
- President Johnson Dedicates the Society's New Headquarters. 669-679, May 1964
- Profiles of the Presidents: V. The Atomic Age: Its Problems and Promises. By Frank Freidel. 66-119, Jan. 1966
- Vice President Johnson Accepts the Society's Jane M. Smith Award. 906, Dec. 1962
- Vice President Lyndon B. Johnson presents the Hubbard Medal to John H. Glenn, Jr. 827, June 1962

Author:
- Friendly Flight to Northern Europe. Photos by Volkmar Wentzel. 268-293, Feb. 1964

JOHNSON, NELSON T.: Author:
- Power Comes Back to Peiping. By Nelson T. Johnson and W. Robert Moore. 337-368, Sept. 1949

JOHNSON, SUSAN HACKLEY:
Author:
- New Day for Alaska's Pribilof Islanders. Photos by Tim Thompson. 536-552, Oct. 1982

JOHNSTON, DAVID:
- Eruption of Mount St. Helens. By Rowe Findley. 3-65, Jan. 1981
I. Mountain With a Death Wish. 3-33; II. In the Path of Destruction. 35-49; III. The Day the Sky Fell. Note: David Johnston lost his life in the eruption of Mount St. Helens. 50-65

JOHNSTON, JAY: Author:
- Forest Fire: The Devil's Picnic. By Stuart E. Jones and Jay Johnston. 100-127, July 1968
- Indian Shangri-La of the Grand Canyon. Photos by Terry Eiler. 355-373, Mar. 1970
- Staten Island Ferry, New York's Seagoing Bus. By John T. Cunningham and Jay Johnston. Photos by W. D. Vaughn. 833-843, June 1959
- Waterway to Washington, the C & O Canal. 419-439, Mar. 1960

JOHNSTON, MOIRA: Author:
- California's Silicon Valley. Photos by Charles O'Rear. 459-477, Oct. 1982
- Napa, California's Valley of the Vine. Photos by Charles O'Rear. 695-717, May 1979

JOINT HURRICANE WARNING CENTER, Miami, Florida:
- Men Against the Hurricane. By Andrew H. Brown. 537-560, Oct. 1950

JOINT OCEANOGRAPHIC INSTITUTIONS FOR DEEP EARTH SAMPLING (JOIDES). *See* Deep Sea Drilling Project

JOINT TASK FORCE I. *See* Operation Crossroads

JOJOBA:
- Rediscovering America's Forgotten Crops. By Noel D. Vietmeyer. Photos by Burgess Blevins. Paintings by Paul M. Breeden. Included: Oil from jojoba seeds. 702-712, May 1981

JONES, DEWITT:
- Editorial. By Gilbert M. Grosvenor. 437, Apr. 1976

Photographer:
- The Anasazi–Riddles in the Ruins. By Thomas Y. Canby. Photos by Dewitt Jones and David Brill. Paintings by Roy Andersen. 554-592, Nov. 1982

• Coal vs. Parklands. By François Leydet. 776-803, Dec. 1980
• John Muir's Wild America. By Harvey Arden. 433-461, Apr. 1973
• Look of a Land Beloved (New England). 444-467, Apr. 1976
• Redwoods, Rain, and Lots of Room: California's North Coast. By Judith and Neil Morgan. 330-363, Sept. 1977

JONES, DON W.: Photographer:
• Hot-air Balloons Race on Silent Winds. By William R. Berry. 392-407, Mar. 1966

JONES, DOROTHEA SHEATS: Author:
• Pennsylvania Avenue, Route of Presidents. By Dorothea and Stuart E. Jones. Photos by Volkmar Wentzel. 63-95, Jan. 1957
• Slow Boat to Florida *(Tradewinds)*. By Dorothea and Stuart E. Jones. 1-65, Jan. 1958
Author-Photographer:
• Ischia, Island of the Unexpected. By Dorothea and Stuart E. Jones. 531-550, Apr. 1954
• *See also* Sheats, Dorothea

JONES, LILIAN GROSVENOR. *See* Grosvenor, Lilian

JONES, STUART E.: Author:
• Central Park: Manhattan's Big Outdoors. Photos by Bates Littlehales. 781-811, Dec. 1960
• Charting Our Sea and Air Lanes (U. S. Coast and Geodetic Survey). Photos by J. Baylor Roberts. 189-209, Feb. 1957
• Copenhagen, Wedded to the Sea. Photos by Gilbert M. Grosvenor. 45-79, Jan. 1963
• Forest Fire: The Devil's Picnic. By Stuart E. Jones and Jay Johnston. 100-127, July 1968
• Fun Helped Them Fight. 95-104, Jan. 1948
• Here's New York Harbor. Photos by Robert F. Sisson and David S. Boyer. 773-813, Dec. 1954
• Houston, Prairie Dynamo. Photos by William Albert Allard. 338-377, Sept. 1967
• Indian Life Before the Colonists Came. Engravings by Theodore de Bry, 1590. 351-368, Sept. 1947
• Maryland on the Half Shell. Photos by Robert W. Madden. 188-229, Feb. 1972
• Oregon's Many Faces. Photos by Bates Littlehales. 74-115, Jan. 1969
• Pennsylvania Avenue, Route of Presidents. By Dorothea and Stuart E. Jones. Photos by Volkmar Wentzel. 63-95, Jan. 1957
• The President's Music Men (Marine Band). Photos by William W. Campbell III. 752-766, Dec. 1959
• Slow Boat to Florida *(Tradewinds)*. By Dorothea and Stuart E. Jones. 1-65, Jan. 1958
• Spices, the Essence of Geography. 401-420, Mar. 1949
• When in Rome. . . . Photos by Winfield Parks. 741-789, June 1970
Author-Photographer:
• Ischia, Island of the Unexpected. By Dorothea and Stuart E. Jones. 531-550, Apr. 1954

JONES, MRS. STUART E. *See* Jones, Dorothea Sheats

JORDAN, ROBERT PAUL: Author:
• Canada's "Now" Frontier. Photos by Lowell Georgia. 480-511, Oct. 1976
• Easter Greetings From the Ukrainians. Photos by James A. Sugar. 556-563, Apr. 1972
• Gettysburg and Vicksburg: the Battle Towns Today. Map notes by Carolyn Bennett Patterson. 4-57, July 1963
• High-Flying Tulsa. Photos by Annie Griffiths. 378-403, Sept. 1983
• Illinois: The City and the Plain. Photos by James L. Stanfield and Joseph J. Scherschel. 745-797, June 1967
• Nebraska . . . the Good Life. Photos by Lowell Georgia. 378-407, Mar. 1974
• Oklahoma, the Adventurous One. Photos by Robert W. Madden. 149-189, Aug. 1971
• Our Growing Interstate Highway System. 195-219, Feb. 1968
• The Proud Armenians. Photos by Harry N. Naltchayan. 846-873, June 1978
• St. Louis: New Spirit Soars in Mid-America's Proud Old City. Photos by Bruce Dale. 605-641, Nov. 1965
• Siberia's Empire Road, the River Ob. Photos by Dean Conger. 145-181, Feb. 1976
• Somalia's Hour of Need. Photos by Michael S. Yamashita and Kevin Fleming. 748-775, June 1981
• Sri Lanka: Time of Testing for an Ancient Land. Photos by Raghubir Singh. 123-150, Jan. 1979
• Turkey: Cross Fire at an Ancient Crossroads. Photos by Gordon W. Gahan. 88-123, July 1977
• Washington Cathedral: "House of Prayer for All People." Photos by Sisse Brimberg. 552-573, Apr. 1980
• Will Success Spoil Our Parks? 31-59, July 1979
• Yugoslavia: Six Republics in One. Photos by James P. Blair. 589-633, May 1970

JORDAN:
• Abraham, the Friend of God. By Kenneth MacLeish. Photos by Dean Conger. 739-789, Dec. 1966
• Arab Land Beyond the Jordan. Photos by Frank Hurley. 753-768, Dec. 1947
• Crusader Lands Revisited. By Harold Lamb. Photos by David S. Boyer. 815-852, Dec. 1954
• Eyewitness to War in the Holy Land. By Charles Harbutt. Included: The Arab-Israeli conflict. 782-795, Dec. 1967
• Holy Land, My Country. By His Majesty King Hussein of Jordan. 784-789, Dec. 1964
• Home to the Holy Land. By Maynard Owen Williams. 707-746, Dec. 1950
• Israel–The Seventh Day. By Joseph Judge. Photos by Gordon W. Gahan. Included: The Arab-Israeli conflict. 816-855, Dec. 1972

HARRY N. NALTCHAYAN

Armenians: patriarch replenishes sacred oil

I J

WESTON KEMP

***Joseph Conrad:* seamen silhouetted in rigging**

• Jerusalem, My Home. By Bertha Spafford Vester. 826-847, Dec. 1964
• Jerusalem, the Divided City. By John Scofield. Photos by Brian Brake. 492-531, Apr. 1959
• Journey Into the Great Rift: the Northern Half. By Helen and Frank Schreider. 254-290, Aug. 1965
• The Living Dead Sea. By Harvey Arden. Photos by Nathan Benn. 225-245, Feb. 1978
• The Other Side of Jordan. By Luis Marden. 790-825, Dec. 1964
• Our Life on a Border Kibbutz. By Carol and Al Abrams. Photos by Al Abrams. Included: Jordan-Israeli conflict. 364-391, Sept. 1970
• Pilgrims Follow the Christmas Star. By Maynard Owen Williams. 831-840, Dec. 1952
• Reunited Jerusalem Faces Its Problems. By Kenneth MacLeish. Photos by Ted Spiegel. Included: Israel-Jordan Armistice line. 835-871, Dec. 1968
• This Year in Jerusalem. By Joseph Judge. Photos by Jodi Cobb. Included: Administration of East Jerusalem (1948-1967). 479-515, Apr. 1983
• Where Jesus Walked. By Howard La Fay. Photos by Charles Harbutt. 739-781, Dec. 1967
• *See also* Jericho; Khirbat Qumrān; Petra; West Bank (Israeli-occupied Jordan)

JORDAN (River), Israel-Jordan:
• Geographical Twins a World Apart. By David S. Boyer. Included: A comparison of the Jordan River in the Holy Land with the Jordan River in Utah. 848-859, Dec. 1958

JORDAN (River), Utah. *See* article, *preceding*

JOSEPH, Chief:
• Chief Joseph. By William Albert Allard. 409-434, Mar. 1977

JOSEPH ALSOP: A Historical Perspective (on Minoan Human Sacrifice). 223, Feb. 1981
• *See also* Alsop, Joseph

JOSEPH CONRAD (Training Ship):
• The Age of Sail Lives On at Mystic. By Alan Villiers. Photos by Weston Kemp. 220-239, Aug. 1968

JOSÉPHINE, Empress (France):
• Napoleon. By John J. Putman. Photos by Gordon W. Gahan. 142-189, Feb. 1982

JOURNEY Into Stone Age New Guinea. By Malcolm S. Kirk. 568-592, Apr. 1969

JOURNEY Into the Great Rift: the Northern Half. By Helen and Frank Schreider. 254-290, Aug. 1965

JOURNEY Into Troubled Iran. By George W. Long. Photos by J. Baylor Roberts. 425-464, Oct. 1951

The **JOURNEY** of Burke and Wills: First Across Australia. By Joseph Judge. Photos by Joseph J. Scherschel. 152-191, Feb. 1979

JOURNEY Through Time: Papua New Guinea. By François Leydet. Photos by David Austen. 150-171, Aug. 1982

JOURNEY to China's Far West. By Rick Gore. Photos by Bruce Dale. 292-331, Mar. 1980

A **JOURNEY** to "Little Tibet" (Ladakh). By Enakshi Bhavnani. Photos by Volkmar Wentzel. 603-634, May 1951

JOURNEY to Mars. By Kenneth F. Weaver. Paintings by Ludek Pesek. 231-263, Feb. 1973

JOURNEY to Outer Mongolia. By William O. Douglas. Photos by Dean Conger. 289-345, Mar. 1962

The **JOY** of Pigs. By Kent Britt. Photos by George F. Mobley. 398-415, Sept. 1978

JUBILEES. *See* Grosvenor, Gilbert H.: Golden Jubilee; La Gorce, John Oliver: Golden Anniversary; *and* Diamond Jubilee (Aga Khan)

JUDAISM:
• Abraham, the Friend of God. By Kenneth MacLeish. Photos by Dean Conger. 739-789, Dec. 1966
• Bringing Old Testament Times to Life. By G. Ernest Wright. Paintings by Henry J. Soulen. 833-864, Dec. 1957
◆ *Great Religions of the World.* Announced. 587-590, Oct. 1971
▲ *Holy Land Today.* Atlas series. Dec. 1963
• In Search of Moses. By Harvey Arden. Photos by Nathan Benn. 2-37, Jan. 1976
▲ *Lands of the Bible Today.* Dec. 1956
▲ *Lands of the Bible Today.* Dec. 1967
• The Last Thousand Years Before Christ. By G. Ernest Wright. Paintings by H. J. Soulen and Peter V. Bianchi. 812-853, Dec. 1960
• The Men Who Hid the Dead Sea Scrolls. By A. Douglas Tushingham. Paintings by Peter V. Bianchi. 785-808, Dec. 1958
• Our Life on a Border Kibbutz. By Carol and Al Abrams. Photos by Al Abrams. 364-391, Sept. 1970
• The Pious Ones (Brooklyn's Hasidic Jews). By Harvey Arden. Photos by Nathan Benn. 276-298, Aug. 1975
• This Year in Jerusalem. By Joseph Judge. Photos by Jodi Cobb. 479-515, Apr. 1983
• *See also* Israel; Jerusalem

JUDD, NEIL MERTON: Author:
• "Pyramids" of the New World. 105-128, Jan. 1948

JUDGE, JOSEPH:
• Associate Editor (1978-). 427, Oct. 1980
Author:
• Alaska: Rising Northern Star. Photos by Bruce Dale. 730-767, June 1975

● Brunei, Borneo's Abode of Peace. Photos by Dean Conger. 207-225, Feb. 1974
● A Buried Roman Town Gives Up Its Dead (Herculaneum). Photos by Jonathan Blair. 687-693, Dec. 1982
● Florence Rises From the Flood. 1-43, July 1967
● Florida's Booming–and Beleaguered–Heartland. Photos by Jonathan Blair. 585-621, Nov. 1973
● Hong Kong, Saturday's Child. Photos by Bruce Dale. 541-573, Oct. 1971
● Israel–The Seventh Day. Photos by Gordon W. Gahan. 816-855, Dec. 1972
● The Journey of Burke and Wills: First Across Australia. Photos by Joseph J. Scherschel. 152-191, Feb. 1979
● Minoans and Mycenaeans: Greece's Brilliant Bronze Age. Photos by Gordon W. Gahan. Paintings by Lloyd K. Townsend. 142-185, Feb. 1978
● Mr. Jefferson's Monticello. Photos by Dean Conger and Richard S. Durrance. 426-444, Sept. 1966
● New Grandeur for Flowering Washington. Photos by James P. Blair. 500-539, Apr. 1967
● New Orleans and Her River. Photos by James L. Stanfield. 151-187, Feb. 1971
● Peoples of the Arctic. 144-223, Feb. 1983
I. Introduction by Joseph Judge. 144-149; II. Hunters of the Lost Spirit: Alaskans, Canadians, Greenlanders, Lapps. By Priit J. Vesilind. Photos by David Alan Harvey, Ivars Silis, and Sisse Brimberg. 150-197; III. Where Magic Ruled: Art of the Bering Sea. By William W. Fitzhugh and Susan A. Kaplan. Photos by Sisse Brimberg. 198-205; IV. People of the Long Spring (Chukchis). By Yuri Rytkheu. Photos by Dean Conger. 206-223
● Retracing John Wesley Powell's Historic Voyage Down the Grand Canyon. Photos by Walter Meayers Edwards. 668-713, May 1969
● This Year in Jerusalem. Photos by Jodi Cobb. 479-515, Apr. 1983
● Those Proper and Other Bostonians. Photos by Ted Spiegel. 352-381, Sept. 1974
● The Travail of Ireland. Photos by Cotton Coulson. 432-441, Apr. 1981
● Venice Fights for Life. Photos by Albert Moldvay. 591-631, Nov. 1972
● Williamsburg, City for All Seasons. Photos by James L. Amos. 790-823, Dec. 1968
● Wind River Range: Many-treasured Splendor. 198-205, Feb. 1974
● The Zulus: Black Nation in a Land of Apartheid. Photos by Dick Durrance II. 738-775, Dec. 1971

JUDITH RIVER BASIN, Montana. *See* Spring Creek Hutterite Colony

JUMP, World's Highest:
● The Long, Lonely Leap (Parachute Jump). By Joseph W. Kittinger, Jr. Photos by Volkmar Wentzel. 854-873, Dec. 1960

JUNEAU, Alaska:
● Avalanche! Battling the Juggernaut. By David Cupp. 290-305, Sept. 1982
● *Endeavour* Sails the Inside Passage. By Amos Burg. 801-828, June 1947

JUNEAU ICEFIELD, Alaska:
● Alaska's Mighty Rivers of Ice. By Maynard M. Miller. Photos by Christopher G. Knight. 194-217, Feb. 1967

JUNGE, CARL-JOHAN: Photographer:
● The Shy and Spectacular Kingfisher. Photos by Carl-Johan Junge and Emil Lütken. 413-419, Sept. 1974

JUNGFRAU (Peak), Switzerland:
● Switzerland Guards the Roof of Europe. By William H. Nicholas. Photos by Willard R. Culver. 205-246, Aug. 1950

JUNGLE Jaunt on Amazon Headwaters. By Bernice M. Goetz. 371-388, Sept. 1952

JUNGLE Journey to the World's Highest Waterfall. By Ruth Robertson. 655-690, Nov. 1949

JUNGLE Journeys in Sarawak. By Hedda Morrison. 710-736, May 1956

The **JUNGLE** Was My Home. By Sasha Siemel. 695-712, Nov. 1952

JUNGLES. *See* Tropical Rain Forests

JUNK SCULPTURE:
● The Fascinating World of Trash. By Peter T. White. Photos by Louie Psihoyos. 424-457, Apr. 1983

JUNKS (Boats):
● Hong Kong, Saturday's Child. By Joseph Judge. Photos by Bruce Dale. 541-573, Oct. 1971
● Return to Changing China. By Audrey Topping. 801-833, Dec. 1971
● Trawling the China Seas. Photos by J. Charles Thompson. 381-395, Mar. 1950
● Water War in Viet Nam. By Dickey Chapelle. 272-296, Feb. 1966

JUPITER (Planet):
● Mystery Shrouds the Biggest Planet. By Kenneth F. Weaver. 285-294, Feb. 1975
● Voyage to the Planets. By Kenneth F. Weaver. Paintings by Ludek Pesek. 147-193, Aug. 1970
● What Voyager Saw: Jupiter's Dazzling Realm. By Rick Gore. Photos by NASA. 2-29, Jan. 1980

JURUENA (River), Brazil:
● Indians of the Amazon Darkness. By Harald Schultz. NGS research grant. 737-758, May 1964

JUST a Hundred Years Ago (U. S. Civil War). By Carl Sandburg. 1-3, July 1963

JUTLAND (Peninsula), Denmark:
● 2,000 Miles Through Europe's Oldest Kingdom. By Isobel Wylie Hutchison. Photos by Maynard Owen Williams. 141-180, Feb. 1949

JUTLAND, Battle of (May 31, 1916):
● The British Way. By Sir Evelyn Wrench. 421-541, Apr. 1949

K

K2 (Peak), China-Pakistan:
● Americans Climb K2. Photos by members of the expedition. 623-649, May 1979
I. The Ultimate Challenge. By James W. Whittaker. 624-639; II. On to the Summit. By James Wickwire. 641-649

KABUKI:
● Human Treasures of Japan. By William Graves. Photos by James L. Stanfield. 370-379, Sept. 1972
● Kansai, Japan's Historic Heartland. By Thomas J. Abercrombie. 295-339, Mar. 1970

KACHINAS:
● Inside the Sacred Hopi Homeland. By Jake Page. Photos by Susanne Page. 607-629, Nov. 1982
● Kachinas: Masked Dancers of the Southwest. By Paul Coze. 219-236, Aug. 1957

KADAYAN (People):
● Brunei, Borneo's Abode of Peace. By Joseph Judge. Photos by Dean Conger. 207-225, Feb. 1974

KAFIRS (Tribespeople):
● In the Footsteps of Alexander the Great. By Helen and Frank Schreider. Paintings by Tom Lovell. 1-65, Jan. 1968

KAHL, M. PHILIP:
Author-Photographer:
● East Africa's Majestic Flamingos. 276-294, Feb. 1970

KAIN, RONALD STUART: Author:
● Postwar Journey Through Java. 675-700, May 1948

KALAHARI BUSHMEN:
● Africa's Bushman Art Treasures. By Alfred Friendly. Photos by Alex R. Willcox. 848-865, June 1963
● Bushmen of the Kalahari. By Elizabeth Marshall Thomas. 866-888, June 1963
■ Bushmen of the Kalahari. 578A-578B, Apr. 1973; 732A-732B, May 1974

KALASH TRIBE:
● Pakistan's Kalash: People of Fire and Fervor. By Debra Denker. Photos by Steve McCurry. 458-473, Oct. 1981

KALAVRYTA, Greece:
● Erosion, Trojan Horse of Greece. By F. G. Renner. 793-812, Dec. 1947

KALIMNOS (Island), Greece:
● The Isles of Greece: Aegean Birthplace of Western Culture. By

K L

Melville Bell Grosvenor. Photos by Edwin Stuart Grosvenor and Winfield Parks. 147-193, Aug. 1972

KALTENTHALER, HENRY:
Photographer:
• New Guinea's Rare Birds and Stone Age Men. By E. Thomas Gilliard. 421-488, Apr. 1953

KAMBITES, JERRY and SARAH:
Authors:
• Return to Uganda. Photos by Sarah Leen. 73-89, July 1980

KAMEHAMEHA THE GREAT, King (Hawaii):
• Kamehameha–Hawaii's Warrior King. By Louise E. Levathes. Photos by Steve Raymer. Paintings by Herb Kawainui Kane. 558-599, Nov. 1983

KAMIKAZE LEGEND:
• The Lost Fleet of Kublai Khan. By Torao Mozai. Photos by Koji Nakamura. Paintings by Issho Yada. 634-649, Nov. 1982

KAMMERMAN, EUGENE L.: Author:
• The Camargue, Land of Cowboys and Gypsies. 667-699, May 1956

KAMPUCHEA:
• Kampuchea Wakens From a Nightmare. By Peter T. White. Photos by David Alan Harvey. 590-623, May 1982
• The Temples of Angkor. 548-589, May 1982
I. Ancient Glory in Stone. By Peter T. White. Photos by Wilbur E. Garrett. 552-589; II. Will They Survive? Introduction by Wilbur E. Garrett. 548-551
• *See also* former name, Cambodia

KANDY, Sri Lanka:
• Ceylon, Island of the "Lion People." By Helen Trybulowski Gilles. 121-136, July 1948
• Ceylon, the Resplendent Land. By Donna K. and Gilbert M. Grosvenor. 447-497, Apr. 1966
• Sri Lanka: Time of Testing For an Ancient Land. By Robert Paul Jordan. Photos by Raghubir Singh. 123-150, Jan. 1979

KANE, HARNETT T.: Author:
• Land of Louisiana Sugar Kings. Photos by Willard R. Culver. 531-567, Apr. 1958
• New Orleans: Jambalaya on the Levee. Photos by Justin Locke. 143-184, Feb. 1953
• Rome: Eternal City with a Modern Air. Photos by B. Anthony Stewart. 437-491, Apr. 1957
• Trieste–Side Door to Europe. 824-857, June 1956

KANE, HERB KAWAINUI: Artist:
• Kamehameha–Hawaii's Warrior King. By Louise E. Levathes. Photos by Steve Raymer. 558-599, Nov. 1983
• The Pathfinders. 756-769, Dec. 1974
Author:
• A Canoe Helps Hawaii Recapture Her Past. Photos by David Hiser. 468-489, Apr. 1976

DAVID ALAN HARVEY, NGS

Kampuchea: soldier in Siem Reap

KANGAROOS:
• The Incredible Kangaroo. By David H. Johnson. 487-500, Oct. 1955
◆ *Koalas and Kangaroos: Strange Animals of Australia.* 1981
• Strange Animals of Australia. By David Fleay. Photos by Stanley Breeden. 388-411, Sept. 1963
• Those Kangaroos! They're a Marvelous Mob. By Geoffrey B. Sharman. Photos by Des and Jen Bartlett. 192-209, Feb. 1979

KANSAI, Japan's Historic Heartland, Hosts Expo '70. By Thomas J. Abercrombie. 295-339, Mar. 1970

KANSAS:
• Following the Trail of Lewis and Clark. By Ralph Gray. 707-750, June 1953
• Hays, Kansas, at the Nation's Heart. By Margaret M. Detwiler. Photos by John E. Fletcher. 461-490, Apr. 1952
• Mapping the Nation's Breadbasket. By Frederick Simpich. 831-849, June 1948
• Skyway Below the Clouds. By Carl R. Markwith. Photos by Ernest J. Cottrell. 85-108, July 1949
• The Tallgrass Prairie: Can It Be Saved? By Dennis Farney. Photos by Jim Brandenburg. Included: Pittsburg and Wichita. 37-61, Jan. 1980
• *See also* Missouri (River)

KANSAS CITY, Missouri:
• Kansas City, Heartland U.S.A. By Rowe Findley. Photos by Ted Spiegel. 112-139, July 1976

KANSU (Province), China:
• The Caves of the Thousand Buddhas. By Franc and Jean Shor. Contents: Ansi; Kiuchuan (Suchow); Yumen; and the Tunhwang Caves. 383-415, Mar. 1951

KAPINGAMARANGI (Atoll), Caroline Islands:
• Feast Day in Kapingamarangi. By W. Robert Moore. 523-537, Apr. 1950

KAPLAN, JOSEPH: Author:
• How Man-made Satellites Can Affect Our Lives. Paintings by Gilbert Emerson. 791-810, Dec. 1957

KAPLAN, MARION:
Author-Photographer:
• Twilight of the Arab Dhow. 330-351, Sept. 1974
Photographer:
• Djibouti, Tiny New Nation on Africa's Horn. 518-533, Oct. 1978
• Smallpox–Epitaph for a Killer? By Donald A. Henderson. 796-805, Dec. 1978

KAPLAN, SUSAN A.: Author:
• Where Magic Ruled: Art of the Bering Sea. By William W. Fitzhugh and Susan A. Kaplan. Photos by Sisse Brimberg. 198-205, Feb. 1983

KAPSIKI (Tribespeople):
• Carefree People of the Cameroons. Photos by Pierre Ichac. 233-248, Feb. 1947

KARACHI, Pakistan:
• Pakistan Under Pressure. By William S. Ellis. Photos by James L. Stanfield. 668-701, May 1981

KARAKORAM RANGE, Central Asia:
• Americans Climb K2. Photos by members of the expedition. 623-649, May 1979
I. The Ultimate Challenge. By James W. Whittaker. 624-639; II. On to the Summit. By James Wickwire. 641-649
• *See also* Hunza

KARAMOJONG (Tribespeople):
• Uganda, Africa's Uneasy Heartland. By Howard La Fay. Photos by George F. Mobley. 708-735, Nov. 1971

KARENS (Tribespeople):
• Spirits of Change Capture the Karens. By Peter Kunstadter. 267-285, Feb. 1972

KARISOKE RESEARCH CENTRE, Rwanda:
• The Imperiled Mountain Gorilla. By Dian Fossey. 501-523, Apr. 1981
Death of Marchessa. Photos by Peter G. Veit. 508-511

KARNAK, Egypt. *See* Akhenaten Temple Project

KARNALI (River), Nepal:
• Peerless Nepal–A Naturalist's Paradise. By S. Dillon Ripley. Photos by Volkmar Wentzel. NGS research grant. 1-40, Jan. 1950

KARNALI ZONE, Nepal:
• Karnali, Roadless World of Western Nepal. By Lila M. and Barry C. Bishop. NGS research grant. 656-689, Nov. 1971

KARNATKA (State), India. *See* former name, Mysore

KÁRPATHOS (Island), Greece:
• Eternal Easter in a Greek Village. By Maria Nicolaidis-Karanikolas. Photos by James L. Stanfield. 768-777, Dec. 1983

KARST FORMATIONS:
• Guilin, China's Beauty Spot. By W. E. Garrett. 536-563, Oct. 1979

KASHGAIS (Nomads):
• Journey into Troubled Iran. By George W. Long. Photos by J. Baylor Roberts. 425-464, Oct. 1951
• We Dwelt in Kashgai Tents. By Jean and Franc Shor. 805-832, June 1952

KASHI (Kashgar), and Region, China:
• American Skiers Find Adventure in Western China. By Ned Gillette. Photos by the author and Galen Rowell. 174-199, Feb. 1981
Skiing From the Summit of China's Ice Mountain. 192-199

KASHMIR:
• The Emperor's Private Garden: Kashmir. By Nigel Cameron. Photos by Brian Brake. 606-647, Nov. 1958
• Himalayan Pilgrimage. By Christopher Rand. 520-535, Oct. 1956
• How the Kazakhs Fled to Freedom. By Milton J. Clark. 621-644, Nov. 1954
• The Idyllic Vale of Kashmir. By Volkmar Wentzel. 523-550, Apr. 1948
• A Journey to "Little Tibet." By Enakshi Bhavnani. Photos by Volkmar Wentzel. 603-634, May 1951
• Mountaintop War in Remote Ladakh. By W. E. Garrett. 664-687, May 1963
• A Woman Paints the Tibetans. By Lafugie. 659-692, May 1949
• *See also* Gilgit; Hunza; Jammu and Kashmir

KATAHDIN, Mount, Maine:
• Mountains Top Off New England. By F. Barrows Colton. Photos by Robert F. Sisson. 563-602, May 1951
• Skyline Trail from Maine to Georgia. By Andrew H. Brown. Photos by Robert F. Sisson. 219-251, Aug. 1949

KATHMANDU, Nepal:
• Coronation in Katmandu. By E. Thomas Gilliard. Photos by Marc Riboud. 139-152, July 1957
• Kathmandu's Remarkable Newars. By John Scofield. 269-285, Feb. 1979
• Peerless Nepal–A Naturalist's Paradise. By S. Dillon Ripley. Photos by Volkmar Wentzel. NGS research grant. 1-40, Jan. 1950
• Temple Monkeys of Nepal. By Jane Teas. 575-584, Apr. 1980

KATMAI NATIONAL MONUMENT, Alaska:
• Lonely Wonders of Katmai. By Ernest Gruening. Photos by Winfield Parks. 800-831, June 1963

KATZEV, MICHAEL L.: Author:
• Last Harbor for the Oldest Ship. By Susan W. and Michael L. Katzev. 618-625, Nov. 1974
• Resurrecting the Oldest Known Greek Ship. Photos by Bates Littlehales. 841-857, June 1970

KATZEV, SUSAN W.: Author:
• Last Harbor for the Oldest Ship. By Susan W. and Michael L. Katzev. 618-625, Nov. 1974

KAUAI, the Island That's Still Hawaii. By Ethel A. Starbird. Photos by Robert W. Madden. 584-613, Nov. 1977

KAUFFMANN, JOHN MICHAEL: Author:
• Giant Sequoias Draw Millions to California Parks. Photos by B. Anthony Stewart. 147-187, Aug. 1959
• Our Wild and Scenic Rivers: The Noatak. Photos by Sam Abell. 52-59, July 1977

KAULONG (People):
• Blowgun Hunters of the South Pacific. By Jane C. Goodale. Photos by Ann Chowning. 793-817, June 1966

KAUTOKEINO, Norway:
• Hunters of the Lost Spirit: Lapps. By Priit J. Vesilind. Photos by Sisse Brimberg. 194-197, Feb. 1983

KAVANGOS (People):
• Namibia: Nearly a Nation? By Bryan Hodgson. Photos by Jim Brandenburg. 755-797, June 1982

KAYAKS:
• Kayak Odyssey: From the Inland Sea to Tokyo. By Dan Dimancescu. Photos by Christopher G. Knight. 295-337, Sept. 1967
• Kayaks Down the Nile. By John M. Goddard. 697-732, May 1955
• White-water Adventure on Wild Rivers of Idaho. By Frank Craighead, Jr., and John Craighead. 213-239, Feb. 1970

KAZAKS (People):
• How the Kazakhs Fled to Freedom. By Milton J. Clark. 621-644, Nov. 1954
• Journey to China's Far West. By Rick Gore. Photos by Bruce Dale. 292-331, Mar. 1980

KAZIRANGA WILD LIFE SANCTUARY, Assam, India:
• Stalking the Great Indian Rhino. By Lee Merriam Talbot. 389-398, Mar. 1957

KEA (Island), Greece:
• The Isles of Greece: Aegean Birthplace of Western Culture. By Melville Bell Grosvenor. Photos by Edwin Stuart Grosvenor and Winfield Parks. 147-193, Aug. 1972

KEACH, DONALD L.: Author:
• Down to *Thresher* by Bathyscaph. 764-777, June 1964

KEATING, BERN: Author:
• Cajunland, Louisiana's French-speaking Coast. Photos by Charles Harbutt and Franke Keating. 353-391, Mar. 1966
• North for Oil: *Manhattan* Makes the Historic Northwest Passage. Photos by Tomas Sennett. 374-391, Mar. 1970
• Pakistan: Problems of a Two-part Land. Photos by Albert Moldvay. 1-47, Jan. 1967
• Today Along the Natchez Trace, Pathway Through History. Photos by Charles Harbutt. 641-667, Nov. 1968

KEATING, FRANKE: Photographer:
• Cajunland, Louisiana's French-speaking Coast. By Bern Keating. Photos by Charles Harbutt and Franke Keating. 353-391, Mar. 1966

KEELING ISLANDS, Indian Ocean. *See* Cocos Islands

KEEPING House for a Biologist in Colombia. By Nancy Bell Fairchild Bates. Photos by Marston Bates. 251-274, Aug. 1948

KEEPING House for Tropical Butterflies. By Jocelyn Crane. Photos by M. Woodbridge Williams. NGS research grant. 193-217, Aug. 1957

KEEPING House in a Cappadocian Cave. By Jonathan S. Blair. 127-146, July 1970

KEEPING House in London. By Frances James. 769-792, Dec. 1947

K L

KEIJO, Korea. *See* Seoul

KEITH, DONALD H.: Author:
- Yellow Sea Yields Shipwreck Trove. Photos by H. Edward Kim. 231-243, Aug. 1979

KEKOPEY RANCH, Kenya:
- Life With the "Pumphouse Gang": New Insights Into Baboon Behavior. By Shirley C. Strum. Photos by Timothy W. Ransom. 672-691, May 1975

KELLEY, FRANCIS BEVERLY: Author:
- The Wonder City That Moves by Night. 289-324, Mar. 1948

KELP:
- Giant Kelp, Sequoias of the Sea. By Wheeler J. North. Photos by Bates Littlehales. 251-269, Aug. 1972
- Undersea World of a Kelp Forest. By Sylvia A. Earle. Photos by Al Giddings. 411-426, Sept. 1980

KELSO, JAMES L.:
Author-Photographer:
- The Ghosts of Jericho. 825-844, Dec. 1951

KEMANO POWER DEVELOPMENT:
- Kitimat–Canada's Aluminum Titan. By David S. Boyer. 376-398, Sept. 1956

KEMP, WESTON: Photographer:
- The Age of Sail Lives On at Mystic. By Alan Villiers. 220-239, Aug. 1968

KENETT, F. L.: Photographer:
- Tutankhamun's Golden Trove. By Christiane Desroches Noblecourt. 625-646, Oct. 1963

KENNEDY, JACQUELINE BOUVIER:
- Inside the White House. By Lonnelle Aikman. Photos by B. Anthony Stewart and Thomas Nebbia. 3-43, Jan. 1961
- The Last Full Measure. By Melville Bell Grosvenor. 307-355, Mar. 1964
- The Living White House. By Lonnelle Aikman. 593-643, Nov. 1966
- ◆ *The White House* (guidebook) presented to President and Mrs. John F. Kennedy. 888-889, 892, Dec. 1962

KENNEDY, JOHN F.:
- Distinguished Flying Cross awarded posthumously to Victor A. Prather, Jr. 684, 685, Nov. 1961
- Inside the White House. By Lonnelle Aikman. Photos by B. Anthony Stewart and Thomas Nebbia. 3-43, Jan. 1961
- Jacques-Yves Cousteau Receives National Geographic Society Medal at White House. 146-147, July 1961
- The Last Full Measure. By Melville Bell Grosvenor. 307-355, Mar. 1964
- The Living White House. By Lonnelle Aikman. 593-643, Nov. 1966
- President Kennedy Presents the Hubbard Medal (American Mount Everest Expedition). 514-515, Oct. 1963
- Profiles of the Presidents: V. The Atomic Age: Its Problems and Promises. By Frank Freidel. 66-119, Jan. 1966
- To the Memory of Our Beloved President, Friend to All Mankind. 1A-1B, Jan. 1964
- White House News Photographers Association's first-place award presented to Robert F. Sisson. 880, Dec. 1961
- ◆ *The White House* (guidebook) presented to President and Mrs. John F. Kennedy. 888-889, 892, Dec. 1962

KENNEDY, MRS. JOHN F. *See* Kennedy, Jacqueline Bouvier

KENNEDY, RALPH A.: Author:
- Playing 3,000 Golf Courses in Fourteen Lands. 113-132, July 1952

KENNEDY, ROBERT F.: Author:
- Canada's Mount Kennedy. II. A Peak Worthy of the President. 5-9, July 1965

KENNEDY, ROBERT S.: Author:
- Saving the Philippine Eagle. Photos by Alan R. Degen, Neil L. Rettig, and Wolfgang A. Salb. 847-856, June 1981

KENNEDY, Mount, Canada:
- Canada's Mount Kennedy. NGS research grant. 1-33, July 1965
  I. The Discovery. By Bradford Washburn. 1-3; II. A Peak Worthy of the President. By Robert F. Kennedy. 5-9; III. The First Ascent. By James W. Whittaker. Photos by William Albert Allard. 11-33
- ▲ *The Massif of Mount Hubbard, Mount Alverstone, and Mount Kennedy.* Announced. 736, Nov. 1968

KENNEDY SPACE CENTER, Cape Canaveral, Florida:
- Cape Canaveral's 6,000-mile Shooting Gallery. By Allan C. Fisher, Jr. Photos by Luis Marden and Thomas Nebbia. 421-471, Oct. 1959
- *Columbia's* Astronauts' Own Story: Our Phenomenal First Flight. By John W. Young and Robert L. Crippen. Paintings by Ken Dallison. 478-503, Oct. 1981
- "A Most Fantastic Voyage": The Story of Apollo 8's Rendezvous With the Moon. By Sam C. Phillips. 593-631, May 1969
- Reaching for the Moon. By Allan C. Fisher, Jr. Photos by Luis Marden. 157-171, Feb. 1959

KENNEY, NATHANIEL T.: Author:
- Africa: The Winds of Freedom Stir a Continent. Photos by W. D. Vaughn. 303-359, Sept. 1960
- Big Bend: Jewel in the Texas Desert. Photos by James L. Stanfield. 104-133, Jan. 1968
- Cape Cod, Where Sea Holds Sway Over Man and Land. Photos by Dean Conger. 149-187, Aug. 1962
- Chesapeake Country. Photos by Bates Littlehales. 370-411, Sept. 1964
- Chincoteague: Watermen's Island Home. Photos by James L. Amos. 810-829, June 1980
- Ethiopian Adventure. Photos by James P. Blair. 548-582, Apr. 1965
- Kings Point: Maker of Mariners. Photos by Volkmar Wentzel. 693-706, Nov. 1955
- Life in Walled-off West Berlin. By Nathaniel T. Kenney and Volkmar Wentzel. Photos by Thomas Nebbia. 735-767, Dec. 1961
- Maytime Miracle in Sherwood Gardens. 700-709, May 1956
- The Mighty *Enterprise*. Photos by Thomas J. Abercrombie. 431-448, Mar. 1963
- New Era on the Great Lakes. 439-490, Apr. 1959
- New National Park Proposed: The Spectacular North Cascades. Photos by James P. Blair. 642-667, May 1968
- A New Riviera: Mexico's West Coast. Photos by Charles O'Rear. 670-699, Nov. 1973
- The Other Yosemite. Photos by Dean Conger. 762-781, June 1974
- Our Changing Atlantic Coastline. Photos by B. Anthony Stewart. 860-887, Dec. 1962
- Our Green Treasury, the National Forests. Photos by J. Baylor Roberts. 287-324, Sept. 1956
- Our Wild and Scenic Rivers: The Rio Grande. Photos by Bank Langmore. 46-51, July 1977
- Sharks: Wolves of the Sea. 222-257, Feb. 1968
- Southern California's Trial by Mud and Water. Photos by Bruce Dale. 552-573, Oct. 1969
- United Italy Marks Its 100th Year. 593-647, Nov. 1961
- Where Falcons Wear Air Force Blue, United States Air Force Academy. Photos by William Belknap, Jr. 845-873, June 1959

KENTUCKY:
- Around the "Great Lakes of the South." By Frederick Simpich. Photos by J. Baylor Roberts. 463-491, Apr. 1948
- ▲ *Close-up: U.S.A., Illinois, Indiana, Ohio, and Kentucky,* supplement. Text on reverse. Feb. 1977
- Heart of the Bluegrass. By Charles McCarry. Photos by J. Bruce Baumann. 634-659, May 1974
- Home to the Heart of Kentucky. By Nadine Brewer. Photos by William Strode. 522-546, Apr. 1982
- The Ohio–River With a Job to Do. By Priit J. Vesilind. Photos by Martin Rogers. 245-273, Feb. 1977
- The People of Cumberland Gap. By John Fetterman. Photos by Bruce Dale. 591-621, Nov. 1971
- So Much Happens Along the Ohio River. By Frederick Simpich. Photos by Justin Locke. 177-212, Feb. 1950
- Vacation Tour Through Lincoln Land. By Ralph Gray. 141-184, Feb. 1952
- Whatever Happened to TVA? By Gordon Young. Photos by Emory Kristof. 830-863, June 1973
- Wrestlin' for a Livin' With King Coal. By Michael E. Long. Photos by Michael O'Brien. 793-819, June 1983

KENYA:
- Adventures in the Search for Man. By Louis S. B. Leakey. Photos by Hugo van Lawick. 132-152, Jan. 1963

• Africa's Elephants: Can They Survive? By Oria Douglas-Hamilton. Photos by Oria and Iain Douglas-Hamilton. 568-603, Nov. 1980
• Africa's Gentle Giants (Giraffes). By Bristol Foster. Photos by Bob Campbell and Thomas Nebbia. 402-417, Sept. 1977
• Africa's Uncaged Elephants. Photos by Quentin Keynes. 371-382, Mar. 1951
• Britain Tackles the East African Bush. By W. Robert Moore. 311-352, Mar. 1950
• East Africa's Majestic Flamingos. By M. Philip Kahl. NGS research grant. 276-294, Feb. 1970
• Freeing Flamingos From Anklets of Death (Lake Magadi). By John G. Williams. Photos by Alan Root. 934-944, Dec. 1963
• Kenya Says *Harambee!* By Allan C. Fisher, Jr. Photos by Bruce Dale. 151-205, Feb. 1969
■ Last Stand in Eden (Elephants). 1, Jan. 1979
• The Leakeys of Africa: Family in Search of Prehistoric Man. By Melvin M. Payne. NGS research grant. 194-231, Feb. 1965
• A New Look at Kenya's "Treetops." By Quentin Keynes. 536-541, Oct. 1956
• Rescuing the Rothschild (Giraffe). By Carolyn Bennett Patterson. 419-421, Sept. 1977
• Roaming Africa's Unfenced Zoos. By W. Robert Moore. Included: "Treetops Hotel," near Mount Kenya. 353-380, Mar. 1950
• Spearing Lions with Africa's Masai. By Edgar Monsanto Queeny. 487-517, Oct. 1954
• The Threatened Ways of Kenya's Pokot People. By Elizabeth L. Meyerhoff. Photos by Murray Roberts. NGS research grant. 120-140, Jan. 1982
• Where Elephants Have Right of Way. By George and Jinx Rodger. Photos by George Rodger. 363-389, Sept. 1960
• Wild Cargo: the Business of Smuggling Animals. By Noel Grove. Photos by Steve Raymer. 287-315, Mar. 1981
• *See also* Mzima Springs; Rudolf, Lake, and Region; Tsavo National Park; *and* Baboons; YWCA

KENYON, KARL W.: Author:
• Return of the Sea Otter. Photos by James A. Mattison, Jr. 520-539, Oct. 1971
Author-Photographer:
• The Fur Seal Herd Comes of Age. By Victor B. Scheffer and Karl W. Kenyon. 491-512, Apr. 1952

KENYON, KATHLEEN M.: Author:
• Jericho Gives Up Its Secrets. By Kathleen M. Kenyon and A. Douglas Tushingham. Photos by Nancy Lord. 853-870, Dec. 1953

KERN, JAMES A.:
Author-Photographer:
• Dragon Lizards of Komodo. 872-880, Dec. 1968

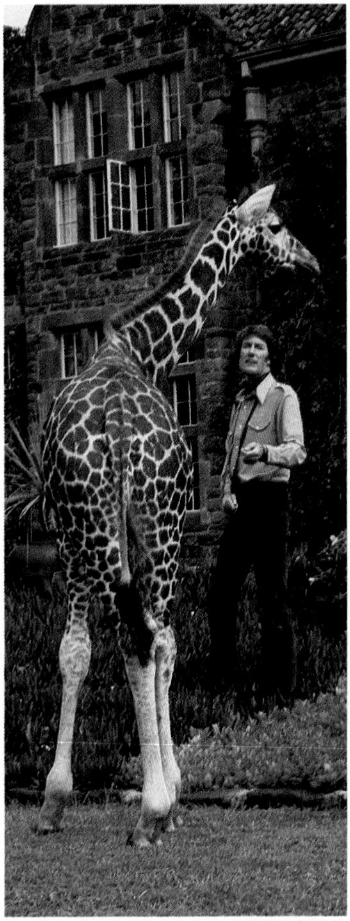

MARION GORDON

Rescuing the Rothschild: giraffe with adopted parent

KERNAN, MICHAEL: Author:
• There's More to Nashville than Music. Photos by Jodi Cobb. 692-711, May 1978

KERRY, County, Ireland. *See* Dingle Peninsula

KERTEZI, Greece:
• Erosion, Trojan Horse of Greece. By F. G. Renner. 793-812, Dec. 1947

KERWIN, JOSEPH P.:
• Skylab, Outpost on the Frontier of Space. By Thomas Y. Canby. Photos by the nine mission astronauts. 441-469, Oct. 1974

KESHISHIAN, JOHN M.: Author:
• Anatomy of a Burmese Beauty Secret. 798-801, June 1979

KETCHES. *See Betelgeuse; Carib; Great Britain II; Nomad; Tectona; Tradewinds; Yankee*

KEW: The Commoners' Royal Garden. By Thomas Garner James. Photos by B. Anthony Stewart. 479-506, Apr. 1950

KEY LARGO CORAL REEF, Florida:
• Florida's Coral City Beneath the Sea. By Jerry Greenberg. 70-89, Jan. 1962
• Key Largo Coral Reef: America's First Undersea Park. By Charles M. Brookfield. Photos by Jerry Greenberg. 58-69, Jan. 1962

KEY WEST, Florida:
• From Indian Canoes to Submarines at Key West. By Frederick Simpich. Photos by J. Baylor Roberts. 41-72, Jan. 1950
• The Lower Keys, Florida's "Out Islands." By John Scofield. Photos by Emory Kristof and Bates Littlehales. 72-93, Jan. 1971
• Our Navy's Long Submarine Arm. By Allan C. Fisher, Jr. 613-636, Nov. 1952
• Shrimpers Strike Gold in the Gulf. By Clarence P. Idyll. Photos by Robert F. Sisson. 699-707, May 1957
• Tropical Gardens of Key West. By Luis Marden. 116-124, Jan. 1953

KEYNES, QUENTIN:
Author-Photographer:
• Mauritius, Island of the Dodo. 77-104, Jan. 1956
• A New Look at Kenya's "Treetops." 536-541, Oct. 1956
• St. Helena: the Forgotten Island. 265-280, Aug. 1950
• Seychelles, Tropic Isles of Eden. 670-695, Nov. 1959
Photographer:
• Africa's Uncaged Elephants. 371-382, Mar. 1951

KHIRBAT QUMRĀN, Jordan:
• The Men Who Hid the Dead Sea Scrolls. By A. Douglas Tushingham. Paintings by Peter V. Bianchi. 785-808, Dec. 1958

KHMER (People):
• Angkor: Jewel of the Jungle. By W. Robert Moore. Paintings by Maurice Fiévet. 517-569, Apr. 1960

K L

ROBERT W. MADDEN, NGS

Hawaii: sampling Kilauea's lava

• Cambodia: Indochina's "Neutral" Corner. By Thomas J. Abercrombie. 514-551, Oct. 1964
• Kampuchea Wakens From a Nightmare. By Peter T. White. Photos by David Alan Harvey. 590-623, May 1982
• Portrait of Indochina. By W. Robert Moore and Maynard Owen Williams. Paintings by Jean Despujols. 461-490, Apr. 1951
• The Temples of Angkor. 548-589, May 1982
I. Ancient Glory in Stone. By Peter T. White. Photos by Wilbur E. Garrett. 552-589; II. Will They Survive? Introduction by Wilbur E. Garrett. 548-551

KHMER EMPIRE. *See* Angkor, Kampuchea

KHMER REPUBLIC. *See* Kampuchea

KHMER ROUGE:
• Kampuchea Wakens From a Nightmare. By Peter T. White. Photos by David Alan Harvey. 590-623, May 1982
• The Temples of Angkor. 548-589, May 1982
I. Ancient Glory in Stone. By Peter T. White. Photos by Wilbur E. Garrett. 552-589; II. Will They Survive? Introduction by Wilbur E. Garrett. 548-551

KHUMBU DISTRICT, Nepal:
• Park at the Top of the World: Mount Everest National Park. By Rick Ridgeway. Photos by Nicholas DeVore III. 704-725, June 1982
Preserving a Mountain Heritage. By Sir Edmund Hillary. 696-703

KIBBUTZIM:
• Israel: Land of Promise. By John Scofield. Photos by B. Anthony Stewart. 395-434, Mar. 1965
• The Land of Galilee. By Kenneth MacLeish. Photos by B. Anthony Stewart. 832-865, Dec. 1965
• Our Life on a Border Kibbutz. By Carol and Al Abrams. Photos by Al Abrams. 364-391, Sept. 1970

KIHN, W. LANGDON: Artist:
• Hearty Folk Defy Arctic Storms. 479-494, Oct. 1949
• Indians of the Far West. By Matthew W. Stirling. 175-200, Feb. 1948

KILAUEA VOLCANO, Hawaii:
• Fountain of Fire in Hawaii. By Frederick Simpich, Jr. Photos by Robert B. Goodman and Robert Wenkam. 303-327, Mar. 1960
• Hawaii, Island of Fire and Flowers. By Gordon Young. Photos by Robert W. Madden. 399-425, Mar. 1975
• Photographing a Volcano in Action. By Thomas J. Hargrave. 561-563, Oct. 1955
• Volcanic Fires of the 50th State: Hawaii National Park. By Paul A. Zahl. 793-823, June 1959

KILBON, ROLAND: Author:
• Born Hunters, the Bird Dogs. Paintings by Walter A. Weber. 369-398, Sept. 1947

KILBRACKEN, LORD (John Godley, Third Baron Kilbracken): Author:
• The Long, Deep Dive. Photos by Bates Littlehales. 718-731, May 1963

KILLARNEY, Lakes of, Ireland:
• Dublin's Historic Horse Show. By Maynard Owen Williams. 115-132, July 1953

KILLER BEES. *See* Africanized Honeybees

KILLER CATERPILLARS. *See* Inchworms

KILLER WHALES:
• Killer Whale Attack! Text by Cliff Tarpy. 542-545, Apr. 1979
• Making Friends With a Killer Whale. By Edward I. Griffin. 418-446, Mar. 1966
◆ *Namu.* Announced. 726-728, Nov. 1973
• Where Two Worlds Meet (Patagonia). Photos by Des and Jen Bartlett. 298-321, Mar. 1976

KIM, H. EDWARD:
Author-Photographer:
• Rare Look at North Korea. 252-277, Aug. 1974
• Seoul: Korean Showcase. 770-797, Dec. 1979
Photographer:
• Arizona's Suburbs of the Sun. By David Jeffery. 486-517, Oct. 1977
• China's Opening Door. By John J. Putman. 64-83, July 1983
• Day of the Rice God (Festival in Japan). By Douglas Lee. 78-85, July 1978
• Pennsylvania's Old-time Dutch Treat. By Kent Britt. 564-578, Apr. 1973
• South Korea: What Next? By Peter T. White. 394-427, Sept. 1975
• Yellow Sea Yields Shipwreck Trove. Introduction by Donald H. Keith. 231-243, Aug. 1979

KIMBERLEY (Region), Australia:
• Western Australia, the Big Country. By Kenneth MacLeish. Photos by James L. Stanfield. 150-187, Feb. 1975

KINCAID, DON: Photographer:
• Treasure From the Ghost Galleon: *Santa Margarita.* By Eugene Lyon. 228-243, Feb. 1982

KINDERZECHE (Festival):
• Dinkelsbühl (Germany) Rewards Its Children. By Charles Belden. 255-268, Feb. 1957

KING, ELIZABETH W.: Author:
• Flags of the Americas. 633-657, May 1949
• Flags of the United Nations. 213-238, Feb. 1951

KING, JOHN:
• The Journey of Burke and Wills. By Joseph Judge. Photos by Joseph J. Scherschel. 152-191, Feb. 1979

KING CRABS:
• The Crab That Shakes Hands. By Clarence P. Idyll. Photos by Robert F. Sisson. 254-271, Feb. 1971

KING ISLAND, Alaska:
● Cliff Dwellers of the Bering Sea. By Juan Muñoz. 129-146, Jan. 1954
● *North Star* Cruises Alaska's Wild West. By Amos Burg. 57-86, July 1952

KING RANCH, Texas:
● America's "Meat on the Hoof." By William H. Nicholas. 33-72, Jan. 1952
King Ranch, Cattle Empire in Texas. 41-64

KINGDON-WARD, F.:
Author-Photographer:
● Caught in the Assam-Tibet Earthquake. 403-416, Mar. 1952

KINGFISHERS:
● The Shy and Spectacular Kingfisher (European). Photos by Carl-Johan Junge and Emil Lütken. 413-419, Sept. 1974

KINGS CANYON NATIONAL PARK, California:
● Giant Sequoias Draw Millions to California Parks. By John Michael Kauffmann. Photos by B. Anthony Stewart. 147-187, Aug. 1959

KINGS COUNTY, New York:
● Brooklyn: The Other Side of the Bridge. By Alice J. Hall. Photos by Robert W. Madden. 580-613, May 1983

KINGS POINT, New York: U. S. Merchant Marine Academy:
● Kings Point: Maker of Mariners. By Nathaniel T. Kenney. Photos by Volkmar Wentzel. 693-706, Nov. 1955

KINGSTON, Massachusetts:
● Land of the Pilgrims' Pride. By George W. Long. Photos by Robert F. Sisson. 193-219, Aug. 1947

KINGSTON, Ontario, Canada:
● Sea to Lakes on the St. Lawrence. By George W. Long. Photos by B. Anthony Stewart and John E. Fletcher. 323-366, Sept. 1950

KINLOCH, BRUCE G.:
Author-Photographer:
● Orphans of the Wild. 683-699, Nov. 1962

KINNEY, WILLIAM A.: Author:
● Operation Eclipse: 1948. 325-372, Mar. 1949
● Roving Maryland's Cavalier Country. 431-470, Apr. 1954
● Washington's Historic Georgetown. 513-544, Apr. 1953

KIRGHIZ (People):
● We Took the Highroad in Afghanistan. By Jean and Franc Shor. 673-706, Nov. 1950
● Winter Caravan to the Roof of the World. By Sabrina and Roland Michaud. 435-465, Apr. 1972

KIRIN (Chilin), Manchuria:
● In Manchuria Now. By W. Robert Moore. 389-414, Mar. 1947

KIRK, MALCOLM S.:
Author-Photographer:
● The Asmat of New Guinea, Headhunters in Today's World. 376-409, Mar. 1972
● Change Ripples New Guinea's Sepik River. 354-381, Sept. 1973
● Journey Into Stone Age New Guinea. 568-592, Apr. 1969
● New Guinea Festival of Faces. 148-156, July 1969

KIRKJUFELL (Volcano), Heimaey, Iceland:
● A Village Fights for Its Life. By Noel Grove. 40-67, July 1973
● *See also* present name, Eldfell

KIRTLEY, MICHAEL and AUBINE:
Author-Photographers:
● The Inadan: Artisans of the Sahara. 282-298, Aug. 1979
● The Ivory Coast–African Success Story. 94-125, July 1982
Photographers:
● Finding West Africa's Oldest City. By Susan and Roderick McIntosh. Contents: Jenne-jeno (site), Mali. 396-418, Sept. 1982

KITES:
● Alexander Graham Bell Museum: Tribute to Genius. By Jean Lesage. 227-256, Aug. 1956
● Japan's Warriors of the Wind. Photos by David Alan Harvey. Text by John Eliot. 551-561, Apr. 1977
● Miracle Men of the Telephone. By F. Barrows Colton. Included: Illustrations of Alexander Graham Bell's multicelled and tetrahedral kites. 273-316, Mar. 1947

KITES (Birds):
● The Swallow-tailed Kite: Graceful Aerialist of the Everglades. Photos by Ray O. Green, Jr., Norman D. Reed, and Myron H. Wright, Jr. 496-505, Oct. 1972

KITIMAT–Canada's Aluminum Titan. By David S. Boyer. 376-398, Sept. 1956

KITTINGER, JOSEPH W., Jr.: Author:
● The Long, Lonely Leap. Photos by Volkmar Wentzel. 854-873, Dec. 1960

KITTY HAWK Floats Across North America. By Maxie and Kristian Anderson. 260-271, Aug. 1980

The **KIWI**, New Zealand's Wonder Bird. By Ron J. Anderson. 395-398, Sept. 1955

KLEMMER, HARVEY: Author:
● Belgium Comes Back. Photos by Maynard Owen Williams. 575-614, May 1948

KLEMPERER, WOLFGANG B.:
Author:
● The Solar Eclipse From a Jet. 785-796, Nov. 1963

KLINE, FRED: Author:
● Baltimore: The Hidden City. Photos by Martin Rogers. 188-215, Feb. 1975
● Library of Congress: The Nation's Bookcase. Photos by Dick Durrance II. 671-687, Nov. 1975
● San Antonio: "Texas, Actin' Kind of Natural." Photos by David Hiser. 524-549, Apr. 1976

KLINGEL, GILBERT C.: Author:
● One Hundred Hours Beneath the Chesapeake. Photos by Willard R. Culver. 681-696, May 1955

KLINGMAN, LAWRENCE L.: Author:
● Incredible Andorra. Photos by B. Anthony Stewart. 262-290, Aug. 1949

KLONDIKE DISTRICT, Canada:
● Yukon Fever: Call of the North. By Robert Booth. Photos by George F. Mobley. 548-578, Apr. 1978

KNEEN, ORVILLE H.: Author:
● Patent Plants Enrich Our World. 357-378, Mar. 1948

KNIGHT, CHRISTOPHER G.:
Photographer:
● Alaska's Mighty Rivers of Ice. By Maynard M. Miller. 194-217, Feb. 1967
● Americans Afoot in Rumania. By Dan Dimancescu. Photos by Dick Durrance II and Christopher G. Knight. 810-845, June 1969
● Down the Danube by Canoe. By William Slade Backer. Photos by Richard S. Durrance and Christopher G. Knight. 34-79, July 1965
● Kayak Odyssey: From the Inland Sea to Tokyo. By Dan Dimancescu. 295-337, Sept. 1967

KNIK GLACIER AND RIVER, Alaska:
● Alaska's Automatic Lake Drains Itself (Lake George). 835-844, June 1951

KNOCKING Out Grizzly Bears for Their Own Good. By Frank and John Craighead. NGS research grant. 276-291, Aug. 1960

KNOSSOS (Ancient City), Crete:
● Minoans and Mycenaeans: Greece's Brilliant Bronze Age. By Joseph Judge. Photos by Gordon W. Gahan. Paintings by Lloyd K. Townsend. 142-185, Feb. 1978

'KNOWN but to God' (Unknown Heroes). By Beverley M. Bowie. 593-605, Nov. 1958

KNUD PENINSULA, Ellesmere Island, Canada:
● Eskimo and Viking Finds in the High Arctic: Ellesmere Island. By Peter Schledermann. Photos by Sisse Brimberg. Included: Artifacts from Dorset sites. 575-601, May 1981

KNUDSEN, DON C.: Photographer:
● Alaska's Automatic Lake Drains Itself (Lake George). 835-844, June 1951

KNUTSEN, WILLIE: Author:
● Milestones in My Arctic Journeys. 543-570, Oct. 1949

KNUTSON, HAROLD A.:
Photographer:
● Nomads of China's West. By Galen Rowell. Photos by the author and Harold A. Knutson. 244-263, Feb. 1982

KOALAS:
◆ *Koalas and Kangaroos: Strange Animals of Australia.* 1981

K L

KOBLICK, IAN:
● Tektite II. 256-296, Aug. 1971
I. Science's Window on the Sea. By John G. VanDerwalker. Photos by Bates Littlehales. 256-289

KOCH, ERICA: Photographer:
● Thumbs Up Round the North Sea's Rim. By Frances James. 685-704, May 1952

KOFFLER, CAMILLA (Ylla): **Photographer:**
● Mysore Celebrates the Death of a Demon. By Luc Bouchage. 706-711, May 1958

KØGE, Denmark:
● 2,000 Miles Through Europe's Oldest Kingdom. By Isobel Wylie Hutchison. Photos by Maynard Owen Williams. 141-180, Feb. 1949

KOH-I-NOOR (Diamond):
● Questing for Gems. By George S. Switzer. 835-863, Dec. 1971

KOHL, LARRY: Author:
● British Columbia's Cold Emerald Sea. Photos by David Doubilet. 526-551, Apr. 1980
● Encampments of the Dispossessed (Somalis). 756-763, June 1981
● Herbs for All Seasons. By Lonnelle Aikman. Photos by Sam Abell. Picture portfolio text by Larry Kohl. 386-409, Mar. 1983
● Père David's Deer Saved From Extinction. Photos by Bates Littlehales. 478-485, Oct. 1982
● Quebec's Northern Dynamo. Photos by Ottmar Bierwagen. 406-418, Mar. 1982

KOHOUTEK (Comet):
● How to Catch a Passing Comet. By Kenneth F. Weaver. 148-150, Jan. 1974
● What You Didn't See in Kohoutek. By Kenneth F. Weaver. 214-223, Aug. 1974

KOKO (Gorilla):
● Conversations With a Gorilla. By Francine Patterson. Photos by Ronald H. Cohn. NGS research grant. 438-465, Oct. 1978

KOM, Kingdom of, Cameroon:
● Afo-A-Kom: A Sacred Symbol Comes Home. By William S. Ellis. Photos by James P. Blair. 141-148, July 1974

KOMARKOVA, VERA: Author:
● On the Summit (Annapurna). By Irene Miller, with Vera Komarkova. 312-313, Mar. 1979

KOMODO DRAGONS:
● Dragon Lizards of Komodo. By James A. Kern. 872-880, Dec. 1968

KONDOA (Region), Tanzania:
● Tanzania's Stone Age Art. By Mary D. Leakey. Photos by John Reader. 84-99, July 1983

KORDOFAN (Province), Sudan:
● With the Nuba Hillmen of Kordofan. By Robin Strachan. 249-278, Feb. 1951

KOREA:
▲ *Japan and Korea,* Atlas series supplement. Dec. 1960

North Korea: Communist youth corps

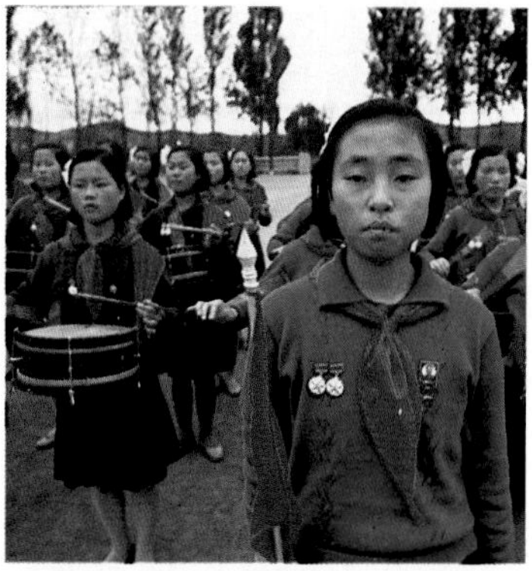

BOTH BY H. EDWARD KIM, NGS

Seoul: designer and his creations

KOREA, Democratic People's Republic of (North Korea):
● Rare Look at North Korea. By H. Edward Kim. 252-277, Aug. 1974

KOREA, Republic of (South Korea):
● Operation Eclipse: 1948. By William A. Kinney. NGS research grant. 325-372, Mar. 1949
● Roaming Korea South of the Iron Curtain. By Enzo de Chetelat. 777-808, June 1950
● Seoul: Korean Showcase. By H. Edward Kim. 770-797, Dec. 1979
● South Korea: Success Story in Asia. By Howard Sochurek. 301-345, Mar. 1969
● South Korea: What Next? By Peter T. White. Photos by H. Edward Kim. 394-427, Sept. 1975
● With the U. S. Army in Korea. By John R. Hodge. 829-840, June 1947
● YWCA: International Success Story. By Mary French Rockefeller. Photos by Otis Imboden. 904-933, Dec. 1963
● Yellow Sea Yields Shipwreck Trove. Photos by H. Edward Kim. Introduction by Donald H. Keith. 231-243, Aug. 1979

KOREA STRAIT, Pacific Ocean:
● The Lost Fleet of Kublai Khan. By Torao Mozai. Photos by Koji Nakamura. Paintings by Issho Yada. 634-649, Nov. 1982

KOREAN WAR:
● The GI and the Kids of Korea. By Robert H. Mosier. 635-664, May 1953
● Our Navy in the Far East. By Arthur W. Radford. Photos by J. Baylor Roberts. 537-577, Oct. 1953
● South Korea: Success Story in Asia. By Howard Sochurek. 301-345, Mar. 1969

KORNBLAU, GERALD: Photographer:
● The GI and the Kids of Korea. By Robert H. Mosier. 635-664, May 1953

KORONGO (Tribespeople):
● With the Nuba Hillmen of Kordofan. By Robin Strachan. Photos by George Rodger. 249-278, Feb. 1951

KOS (Island), Greece:
● The Isles of Greece: Aegean Birthplace of Western Culture. By Melville Bell Grosvenor. Photos by Edwin Stuart Grosvenor and Winfield Parks. 147-193, Aug. 1972

KRAHO INDIANS:
● Children of the Sun and Moon. By Harald Schultz; translated from German by Curtis T. Everett. 340-363, Mar. 1959

KRAKEL, DEAN, II: Photographer:
● The Untamed Yellowstone. By Bill Richards. 257-278, Aug. 1981

KRAWCZYK, JOHN J.: Photographer:
● Submarine Through the North Pole. By William G. Lalor, Jr. 1-20, Jan. 1959

KREEN-AKARORES (Indians):
● Brazil's Kreen-Akarores: Requiem for a Tribe? By W. Jesco von Puttkamer. 254-269, Feb. 1975

KREMLIN, Moscow, U.S.S.R.:
● An American in Russia's Capital. By Thomas T. Hammond. Photos by Dean Conger. 297-351, Mar. 1966
● Moscow: The City Around Red Square. By John J. Putman. Photos by Gordon W. Gahan. 2-45, Jan. 1978
Imperial Russia's Glittering Legacy. 24-33

KRESS COLLECTION:
● The Kress Collection: A Gift to the Nation. By Guy Emerson. 823-865, Dec. 1961
● The Nation's Newest Old Masters (National Gallery of Art). By John Walker. 619-657, Nov. 1956
● Your National Gallery of Art After 10 Years. By John Walker. 73-103, Jan. 1952

KRIST, BOB: Photographer:
● New Jersey: A State of Surprise. By Jim Hartz. Photos by Bob Krist and Michael S. Yamashita. 568-599, Nov. 1981

KRISTOF, EMORY:
● Designed shutterless camera. 492, Apr. 1975
Author-Photographer:
● The Last U. S. Whale Hunters. 346-353, Mar. 1973
Photographer:
● Behold the Computer Revolution. By Peter T. White. Photos by Bruce Dale and Emory Kristof. 593-633, Nov. 1970
● Bermuda–Balmy, British, and Beautiful. By Peter Benchley. 93-121, July 1971
● Can We Harness the Wind? By Roger Hamilton. 812-829, Dec. 1975
● Computer Helps Scholars Re-create an Egyptian Temple. By Ray Winfield Smith. 634-655, Nov. 1970
● Exploring a 140-year-old Ship Under Arctic Ice *(Breadalbane)*. By Joseph B. MacInnis. 104A-104D, July 1983
● From Sword to Scythe in Champlain Country. By Ethel A. Starbird. Photos by B. Anthony Stewart and Emory Kristof. 153-201, Aug. 1967
● Ghost Ships of the War of 1812: *Hamilton* and *Scourge*. By Daniel A. Nelson. Paintings by Richard Schlecht. 289-313, Mar. 1983
● Loch Ness: The Lake and the Legend. By William S. Ellis. Photos by Emory Kristof and David Doubilet. 759-779, June 1977
● Lonely Cape Hatteras, Besieged by the Sea. By William S. Ellis. 393-421, Sept. 1969
● The Lower Keys, Florida's "Out Islands." By John Scofield. Photos by Emory Kristof and Bates Littlehales. 72-93, Jan. 1971
● The Netherlands Antilles: Holland in the Caribbean. By James Cerruti. 115-146, Jan. 1970
● New Tricks Outwit Our Insect Enemies. By Hal Higdon. Photos by Robert F. Sisson and Emory Kristof. 380-399, Sept. 1972
● Of Planes and Men. By Kenneth F. Weaver. Photos by Emory Kristof and Albert Moldvay. 298-349, Sept. 1965
● Oil, the Dwindling Treasure. By Noel Grove. 792-825, June 1974
● Project FAMOUS. 586-615, May 1975
I. Where the Earth Turns Inside Out. By J. R. Heirtzler. 586-603; II. Dive Into the Great Rift. By Robert D. Ballard. 604-615
● The Promise and Peril of Nuclear Energy. By Kenneth F. Weaver. 459-493, Apr. 1979
● Sailors of the Sky. By Gordon Young. Photos by Emory Kristof and Jack Fields. Paintings by Davis Meltzer. 49-73, Jan. 1967
● The Search for Tomorrow's Power. By Kenneth F. Weaver. 650-681, Nov. 1972
● Solar Energy, the Ultimate Powerhouse. By John L. Wilhelm. 381-397, Mar. 1976
● Tanzania Marches to Its Own Drum. By Peter T. White. 474-509, Apr. 1975
● This Land of Ours–How Are We Using It? By Peter T. White. 20-67, July 1976
● Whatever Happened to TVA? By Gordon Young. 830-863, June 1973
● Will Oil and Tundra Mix? Alaska's North Slope Hangs in the Balance. By William S. Ellis. 485-517, Oct. 1971
● Window on Earth's Interior. By Robert D. Ballard. 228-249, Aug. 1976

KRUGER NATIONAL PARK, South Africa:
● Safari Through Changing Africa. By Elsie May Bell Grosvenor. Photos by Gilbert Grosvenor. 145-198, Aug. 1953

KRUNG THEP, Thailand. *See* Bangkok

KRUUK, HANS: Author:
● Hyenas, the Hunters Nobody Knows. Photos by Baron Hugo van Lawick. 44-57, July 1968

KUBASOV, VALERIY:
● Apollo-Soyuz: Handclasp in Space. By Thomas Y. Canby. 183-187, Feb. 1976

KUBLAI KHAN'S FLEET:
● The Lost Fleet of Kublai Khan. By Torao Mozai. Photos by Koji Nakamura. Paintings by Issho Yada. 634-649, Nov. 1982

KUEILIN, People's Republic of China. *See* Guilin

KUH, MICHAEL: Photographer:
● Growing Up With Snowflake. By Arthur J. Riopelle. 491-503, Oct. 1970

KUHN, DELIA: Author:
● Poland Opens Her Doors. By Delia and Ferdinand Kuhn. Photos by Erich Lessing. 354-398, Sept. 1958

KUHN, FERDINAND: Author:
● Poland Opens Her Doors. By Delia and Ferdinand Kuhn. Photos by Erich Lessing. 354-398, Sept. 1958
● Where Turk and Russian Meet. 743-766, June 1952
● The Yankee Sailor Who Opened Japan. 85-102, July 1953

KUNG (People):
● Bushmen of the Kalahari. By Elizabeth Marshall Thomas. Photos by Laurence K. Marshall. 866-888, June 1963
■ Bushmen of the Kalahari. 578A-578B, Apr. 1973; 732A-732B, May 1974
● Namibia: Nearly a Nation? By Bryan Hodgson. Photos by Jim Brandenburg. 755-797, June 1982

KUNMING, Yunnan, China:
● Kunming Pilgrimage. Photos by John Gutmann and Joseph Passantino. 213-226, Feb. 1950
● Letter From Kunming: Two American Teachers in China. By Elisabeth B. Booz. Photos by Thomas Nebbia. 793-813, June 1981

KUNSTADTER, PETER:
Author-Photographer:
● Living With Thailand's Gentle Lua. 122-152, July 1966
● Spirits of Change Capture the Karens. 267-285, Feb. 1972

KUNSTHISTORISCHES MUSEUM, Vienna, Austria:
● The Vienna Treasures and Their Collectors. By John Walker. 737-776, June 1950

KUNTZ, ROBERT E.: Photographer:
● Yemen Opens the Door to Progress. By Harry Hoogstraal. 213-244, Feb. 1952

KURDISTAN (Region), Asia:
● The Kurds of Iraq: "We Who Face Death." By LeRoy Woodson, Jr. 364-387, Mar. 1975
● *See also* Tepe Gawra

KURDS (People):
● Iraq–Where Oil and Water Mix. By Jean and Franc Shor. 443-489, Oct. 1958
● The Kurds of Iraq: "We Who Face Death." By LeRoy Woodson, Jr. 364-387, Mar. 1975

KUSH, Kingdom of:
● Sudan: Arab-African Giant. By Robert Caputo. 346-379, Mar. 1982

KUTZTOWN, Pennsylvania:
● Pennsylvania Dutch Folk Festival. By Maynard Owen Williams. 503-516, Oct. 1952
● Pennsylvania's Old-time Dutch Treat. By Kent Britt. Photos by H. Edward Kim. 564-578, Apr. 1973

KUUSAMO, Finland:
● Scenes of Postwar Finland. By La Verne Bradley. Photos by Jerry Waller. 233-264, Aug. 1947

KUWAIT:
● The Arab World, Inc. By John J. Putman. Photos by Winfield Parks. 494-533, Oct. 1975
● Boom Time in Kuwait. By Paul Edward Case. 783-802, Dec. 1952
● Kuwait, Aladdin's Lamp of the Middle East. By John E. Frazer. Photos by David F. Cupp. 636-667, May 1969
● Oil, the Dwindling Treasure. By Noel Grove. Photos by Emory Kristof. 792-825, June 1974

K L

PAINTING BY PIERRE MION

L-5: building a space habitat

KUYT, ERNIE: Author:
- Teamwork Helps the Whooping Crane. By Roderick C. Drewien, with Ernie Kuyt. 680-693, May 1979

KWAJALEIN (Atoll), Marshall Islands:
- Adventures with the Survey Navy. By Irving Johnson. 131-148, July 1947
- We Survive on a Pacific Atoll. By John and Frank Craighead. 73-94, Jan. 1948

KWAKIUTL INDIANS:
- Canada's Window on the Pacific: The British Columbia Coast. By Jules B. Billard. Photos by Ted Spiegel. 338-375, Mar. 1972

KWAZULU (Region), South Africa:
- Zulu King Weds a Swazi Princess. By Volkmar Wentzel. 47-61, Jan. 1978

KYOTO, Japan:
- Kansai, Japan's Historic Heartland. By Thomas J. Abercrombie. 295-339, Mar. 1970
- Kyoto and Nara: Keepers of Japan's Past. By Charles McCarry. Photos by George F. Mobley. 836-851, June 1976
  Kyoto Says Happy New Year. 852-859

KYRENIA SHIP:
- Last Harbor for the Oldest Ship. By Susan W. and Michael L. Katzev. NGS research grant. 618-625, Nov. 1974
- Resurrecting the Oldest Known Greek Ship. By Michael L. Katzev. Photos by Bates Littlehales. NGS research grant. 841-857, June 1970

KYUSHU (Island), Japan:
- Backwoods Japan During American Occupation. By M. A. Huberman. 491-518, Apr. 1947

L

L-5 (Space Colony, A.D. 2026):
- The Next Frontier? By Isaac Asimov. Paintings by Pierre Mion. 76-89, July 1976

LG 2 (Hydroelectric Site), Quebec (Province), Canada:
- Quebec's Northern Dynamo. By Larry Kohl. Photos by Ottmar Bierwagen. 406-418, Mar. 1982

L.S.B. LEAKEY FOUNDATION:
- Contributions invited; address given. 144, Jan. 1973

Study Grants:
- Chimpanzees. 598, May 1979
- Early-man research in Ethiopia. 805, Dec. 1976
- Orangutans. 835, June 1980
- Pokot People of Kenya. 122, Jan. 1982

LaBASTILLE, ANNE: Author:
- Acid Rain–How Great a Menace? Photos by Ted Spiegel. 652-681, Nov. 1981
- My Backyard, the Adirondacks. Photos by David Alan Harvey. 616-639, May 1975
- On the Trail of Wisconsin's Ice Age. Photos by Cary Wolinsky. 182-205, Aug. 1977
- *See also* Bowes, Anne LaBastille

La BEAUCE (Plain), France:
- Chartres: Legacy From the Age of Faith. By Kenneth MacLeish. Photos by Dean Conger. 857-882, Dec. 1969

LABORATORY in a Dirty Sky. By Rudolf J. Engelmann and Vera Simons. NGS research grant. 616-621, Nov. 1976

LABRADOR (Region), Newfoundland:
- Far North with "Captain Mac." By Miriam MacMillan. 465-513, Oct. 1951
- Labrador Canoe Adventure. By Andrew Brown and Ralph Gray. 65-99, July 1951
- Milestones in My Arctic Journeys. By Willie Knutsen. Included: Activities of the Search and Rescue section of the Air Force at Goose Bay. 543-570, Oct. 1949
- Newfoundland, Canada's New Province. By Andrew H. Brown. Photos by author and Robert F. Sisson. 777-812, June 1949
- School for Survival. By Curtis E. LeMay. 565-602, May 1953
- Sea Bird Cities Off Audubon's Labrador. By Arthur A. Allen. NGS research grant. 755-774, June 1948

LACQUER WARE:
- Human Treasures of Japan. By William Graves. Photos by James L. Stanfield. 370-379, Sept. 1972
- A Lady From China's Past. Photos from *China Pictorial.* Text by Alice J. Hall. 660-681, May 1974

La CRAU (Plain), France:
- Sheep Trek in the French Alps. By Maurice Moyal. Photos by Marcel Coen. 545-564, Apr. 1952

LADAKH (Region), China-India-Pakistan:
- A Journey to "Little Tibet." By Enakshi Bhavnani. Photos by Volkmar Wentzel. 603-634, May 1951
- Ladakh–The Last Shangri-la. By Thomas J. Abercrombie. 332-359, Mar. 1978
- Mountaintop War in Remote Ladakh. By W. E. Garrett. 664-687, May 1963
- A Woman Paints the Tibetans. By Lafugie. 659-692, May 1949

LADD, HARRY S.: Author:
- Fossils Lift the Veil of Time. By Harry S. Ladd and Roland W. Brown. 363-386, Mar. 1956

A **LADY** From China's Past. Photos from *China Pictorial.* Text by Alice J. Hall. 660-681, May 1974

LADYBUGS:
- Following the Ladybug Home. By Kenneth S. Hagen. Photos by Robert F. Sisson. 543-553, Apr. 1970
- New Tricks Outwit Our Insect Enemies. By Hal Higdon. Photos by Robert F. Sisson and Emory Kristof. 380-399, Sept. 1972

LAETOLI (Region), Tanzania:
● Footprints in the Ashes of Time. By Mary D. Leakey. NGS research grant. 446-457, Apr. 1979

La FAY, HOWARD:
● Editorial. By Wilbur E. Garrett. 709, Dec. 1981
Author:
● Alabama, Dixie to a Different Tune. Photos by Dick Durrance II. 534-569, Oct. 1975
● Algeria: France's Stepchild, Problem and Promise. Photos by Robert F. Sisson. 768-795, June 1960
● Andalusia, the Spirit of Spain. Photos by Joseph J. Scherschel. 833-857, June 1975
● "Be Ye Men of Valour" (Churchill's Life and Funeral). 159-197, Aug. 1965
● Carnival in Trinidad. Photos by Winfield Parks. 693-701, Nov. 1971
● DEW Line, Sentry of the Far North. 128-146, July 1958
● Easter Island and Its Mysterious Monuments. Photos by Thomas J. Abercrombie. 90-117, Jan. 1962
● Ebla: Splendor of an Unknown Empire. Photos by James L. Stanfield. Paintings by Louis S. Glanzman. 730-759, Dec. 1978
● The Eisenhower Story. 1-39, July 1969
● Freedom's Progress South of the Sahara. Photos by Joseph J. Scherschel. 603-637, Nov. 1962
● George Washington: The Man Behind the Myths. Photos by Ted Spiegel. 90-111, July 1976
● Gibraltar–Rock of Contention. Photos by Bates Littlehales. 102-121, July 1966
● Leningrad, Russia's Window on the West. Photos by Dick Durrance II. 636-673, May 1971
● The Maya, Children of Time. Photos by David Alan Harvey. 729-767, Dec. 1975
● Portugal at the Crossroads. Photos by Volkmar Wentzel. 453-501, Oct. 1965
● The St. Lawrence, River Key to Canada. Photos by John Launois. 622-667, May 1967
● Sicily, Where All the Songs Are Sad. Photos by Jonathan Blair. 407-436, Mar. 1976
● Syria Tests a New Stability. Photos by James L. Stanfield. 326-361, Sept. 1978
● Texas! Photos by Gordon W. Gahan. 440-483, Apr. 1980
● Uganda, Africa's Uneasy Heartland. Photos by George F. Mobley. 708-735, Nov. 1971
● The Vikings. Photos by Ted Spiegel. 492-541, Apr. 1970
● Where Jesus Walked. Photos by Charles Harbutt. 739-781, Dec. 1967

LAFAYETTE, Marquis de:
● Lafayette's Homeland, Auvergne. By Howell Walker. 419-436, Sept. 1957

LAFUGIE, Madame: Author-Artist:
● A Woman Paints the Tibetans. 659-692, May 1949

LA GORCE, GILBERT GROSVENOR:
● NGM advertising director. 442, 444, Mar. 1960
Author:
● Marineland, Florida's Giant Fish Bowl. Photos by Luis Marden. 679-694, Nov. 1952

LA GORCE, JOHN OLIVER:
● Board of Trustees, Vice Chairman. 419-423, Mar. 1957; 98, Jan. 1966
● Colleague of the Golden Years: John Oliver La Gorce (Memorial Tribute). By Gilbert Grosvenor. 440-444, Mar. 1960
● Editor (1954-1957). 65, 65D, July 1954; 441, 442, 444, Mar. 1960; 46-47, 67, July 1967
● Editor, Assistant. 418, Mar. 1957
● Editor, Associate. 65, 65C, July 1954; 418, Mar. 1957; 441, 443, Mar. 1960
● Golden Anniversary with the Society. 422, 423, Mar. 1957; 442, Mar. 1960
● Grosvenor Medal recipient. 422, 423, Mar. 1957
● President of NGS (1954-1957). 65, 65D, July 1954; 418, 419, 423, Mar. 1957; 440-444, Mar. 1960
● Vice President of NGS. 255, 260, 261, Aug. 1949; 65, 65C, July 1954; 441, 443, Mar. 1960
Author:
● Artists Look at Pennsylvania. 37-56, July 1948

LA GORCE, LOUISE PARKER:
Author:
● Christmas in Cookie Tree Land. Photos by B. Anthony Stewart. 844-851, Dec. 1955

LA GORCE MEDAL:
● First La Gorce Medal Honors Antarctic Expedition. Note: Melvin M. Payne guided the design of the medal, which was executed by Peter V. Bianchi and Howard E. Paine. NGS research grant. 864-867, June 1967

La GRANDE COMPLEX (Hydroelectric Sites), Quebec (Province), Canada:
● Quebec's Northern Dynamo. By Larry Kohl. Photos by Ottmar Bierwagen. Note: By the year 2000, it is expected that 63 turbines in nine power plants will produce 13,700 megawatts. 406-418, Mar. 1982

La GRANDE RIVER, Canada:
● Quebec's Northern Dynamo. By Larry Kohl. Photos by Ottmar Bierwagen. 406-418, Mar. 1982

LAGUS, CHARLES: Photographer:
● Animal Safari to British Guiana. By David Attenborough. Photos by Charles Lagus and author. 851-874, June 1957

LAHAINA RESTORATION FOUNDATION: Study Grants:
● Humpback Whales. 2, Jan. 1979; 466, Apr. 1982

LAHEY, CARLOTTA GONZALES:
Artist:
● Flags of the Americas. By Elizabeth W. King. 633-657, May 1949
● Flags of the United Nations. By Elizabeth W. King. 213-238, Feb. 1951

LAIRD, NORMAN: Photographer:
● Nature's Clown, the Penguin. By David Hellyer and Malcolm Davis. 405-428, Sept. 1952

LA JOLLA, California:
● Goggle Fishing in California Waters. By David Hellyer. Photos by Lamar Boren. 615-632, May 1949
● La Jolla, a Gem of the California Coast. By Deena Clark. Photos by J. Baylor Roberts. 755-782, Dec. 1952

LAKE CHARLES, Louisiana:
● Louisiana Trades With the World. By Frederick Simpich. Photos by J. Baylor Roberts. 705-738, Dec. 1947

LAKE DISTRICT, Poets' Corner of England. By H. V. Morton. Photos by David S. Boyer. 511-545, Apr. 1956

LAKE Erie's Bass Islands. By Terry and Lyntha Eiler. 86-101, July 1978

LAKE MANYARA NATIONAL PARK, Tanzania:
● Africa's Elephants: Can They Survive? By Oria Douglas-Hamilton. Photos by Oria and Iain Douglas-Hamilton. 568-603, Nov. 1980

LAKE OF THE WOODS, Canada-U. S.:
● Men, Moose, and Mink of Northwest Angle. By William H. Nicholas. Photos by J. Baylor Roberts. 265-284, Aug. 1947

LAKE Sunapee's Golden Trout (New Hampshire). Photos by Robert F. Sisson. 529-536, Oct. 1950

LAKEHURST, New Jersey. *See* Parachute Rigger School

LAKES:
● Around the "Great Lakes of the South." By Frederick Simpich. Photos by J. Baylor Roberts. 463-491, Apr. 1948
● Geographical Twins a World Apart. By David S. Boyer. Contents: Comparisons between the Dead Sea and Great Salt Lake; the Sea of Galilee and Utah Lake. 848-859, Dec. 1958
● Italy Smiles Again. By Edgar Erskine Hume. Included: Como, Garda, Maggiore. 693-732, June 1949
● Labrador Canoe Adventure. By Andrew Brown and Ralph Gray. Included: Dyke, Forget-me-not, Gabbro, Grand, Jacopie, Lake E, Lake Melville, Sandgirt, Winokapau. 65-99, July 1951
● Lake District, Poets' Corner of England. By H. V. Morton. Photos by David S. Boyer. 511-545, Apr. 1956
● Lombardy's Lakes, Blue Jewels in Italy's Crown. By Franc Shor. Photos by Joseph J. Scherschel. Included: Como, Garda, Maggiore. 58-99, July 1968
● A Map Maker Looks at the United States. By Newman Bumstead. Photos by U. S. Air Force. Included: Chelan, Crater, Diamond, Franklin Delano Roosevelt, Jackson, Kachess, Mead, Michigan, Tahoe, Utah. 705-748, June 1951
◆ *Nature's World of Wonders.* Included: The world's deepest, highest navigable, and largest lakes. 1983

K L

• New York's Land of Dreamers and Doers (Finger Lakes Region). By Ethel A. Starbird. Photos by Nathan Benn. Included: Canandaigua, Cayuga, Keuka, Owasco, Seneca, Skaneteles. 702-724, May 1977
• The Night the Mountains Moved (Montana's 1959 Earthquake). By Samuel W. Matthews. Photos by J. Baylor Roberts. Included: Hebgen Lake, Earthquake Lake. 329-359, Mar. 1960
◆ *Still Waters, White Waters.* 1977
• Strange World of Palau's Salt Lakes. By William M. Hamner. Photos by David Doubilet. 264-282, Feb. 1982
• *See also* Atitlán, Lake, Guatemala; Baykal, Lake, U.S.S.R.; Bras d'Or Lakes, Nova Scotia, Canada; Champlain, Lake, Canada-U.S.; Crater Lake, Oregon; Dead Sea, Israel-Jordan; George, Lake, Alaska; Grays Lake National Wildlife Refuge, Idaho; Great Lakes, and Region, Canada-U.S.; Great Salt Lake, Utah; Inle (Lake), Burma; Killarney, Lakes of, Ireland; Louise, Lake, Canada; Makat, Lake, Tanzania; Mono Lake, California; Moses, Lake, Washington; Natron, Lake, Tanzania; Ness, Loch, Scotland; Okeechobee, Lake, Florida; Pátzcuaro (City and Lake), Mexico; Powell, Lake, Arizona-Utah; Red Rock Lakes National Wildlife Refuge, Montana; Rudolf, Lake, and Region, Kenya; Sunapee Lake, New Hampshire; Te Anau, Lake, New Zealand; Titicaca, Lake, Bolivia-Peru; Victoria, Lake, Africa; Winnepesaukee, Lake, New Hampshire; Woods, Lake of the, Canada-U.S.

LALIBALA, Ethiopia:
• Searching Out Medieval Churches in Ethiopia's Wilds. By Georg Gerster. 856-884, Dec. 1970

LALOR, WILLIAM G., Jr.: Author:
• Submarine Through the North Pole. Photos by John J. Krawczyk. 1-20, Jan. 1959

LAMAISM. *See* Tibetan Buddhism

LAMB, HAROLD: Author:
• Crusader Lands Revisited. Photos by David S. Boyer. 815-852, Dec. 1954

LAMMER, ALFRED: Photographer:
• Children's Village in Switzerland, Pestalozzi. 268-282, Aug. 1959

LAMPREYS. *See* Sea Lampreys

LANCASTER COUNTY, Pennsylvania:
• Amish Folk: Plainest of Pennsylvania's Plain People. By Richard Gehman. Photos by William Albert Allard. 227-253, Aug. 1965
• Artists Look at Pennsylvania. By John Oliver La Gorce. 37-56, July 1948

LAND, EMORY S.: Author:
• Aviation Looks Ahead on Its 50th Birthday. 721-739, Dec. 1953

A **LAND** Apart–the Monterey Peninsula (California). By Mike W. Edwards. 682-703, Nov. 1972

KAL MULLER
Land Diving: Melanesian leaps off tower

LAND CLAIMS, Native-American:
• Alaska: Rising Northern Star. By Joseph Judge. Photos by Bruce Dale. Included: Alaska's land-use plan. 730-767, June 1975
• The Aleutians: Alaska's Far-out Islands. By Lael Morgan. Photos by Steven C. Wilson. 336-363, Sept. 1983
• Editorial. By Gilbert M. Grosvenor. 729, June 1975
• A First American Views His Land. By N. Scott Momaday. 13-19, July 1976
• Peoples of the Arctic. 144-223, Feb. 1983
I. Introduction by Joseph Judge. 144-149; II. Hunters of the Lost Spirit: Alaskans, Canadians, Greenlanders, Lapps. By Priit J. Vesilind. Photos by David Alan Harvey, Ivars Silis, and Sisse Brimberg. 150-197
▲ *Peoples of the Arctic; Arctic Ocean,* double-sided supplement. Feb. 1983

LAND DIVERS:
• Land Diving With the Pentecost Islanders. By Kal Muller. 799-817, Dec. 1970
• South Seas' Incredible Land Divers. By Irving and Electa Johnson. 77-92, Jan. 1955

LAND in the Middle: Thailand. By Bart McDowell. Photos by Steve Raymer. 500-535, Oct. 1982

The **LAND** of Galilee. By Kenneth MacLeish. Photos by B. Anthony Stewart. 832-865, Dec. 1965

LAND of Long Sunsets: Nebraska's Sand Hills. By John Madson. Photos by Jodi Cobb. 493-517, Oct. 1978

LAND of Louisiana Sugar Kings. By Harnett T. Kane. Photos by Willard R. Culver. 531-567, Apr. 1958

LAND of the Ancient Basques. By Robert Laxalt. Photos by William Albert Allard. 240-277, Aug. 1968

LAND of the Havasupai. By Jack Breed. 655-674, May 1948

LAND of the Pilgrims' Pride. By George W. Long. Photos by Robert F. Sisson. 193-219, Aug. 1947

LAND SNAILS. *See* Giant African Land Snails

LAND USE:
• Aldo Leopold: "A Durable Scale of Values." By Boyd Gibbons. Photos by Jim Brandenburg. 682-708, Nov. 1981
• Coal vs. Parklands. By François Leydet. Photos by Dewitt Jones. 776-803, Dec. 1980
• Egypt's Desert of Promise. By Farouk El-Baz. Photos by Georg Gerster. 190-221, Feb. 1982
• Five Noted Thinkers Explore the Future. Included: The ideas of Isaac Asimov, Richard F. Babcock, Edmund N. Bacon, Buckminster Fuller, Gerard Piel. 68-75, July 1976
• Orange, a Most California County. By Judith and Neil Morgan. Photos by Vince Streano. 750-779, Dec. 1981

• Sharing Alaska: How Much for Parks? Opposing views by Jay S. Hammond and Cecil D. Andrus. 60-65, July 1979
• The Tallgrass Prairie: Can It Be Saved? By Dennis Farney. Photos by Jim Brandenburg. 37-61, Jan. 1980
• This Land of Ours–How Are We Using It? By Peter T. White. Photos by Emory Kristof. Included: Maps showing land use, 1776 and 1976; megalopolises, from weather satellite, reflecting energy use; population density, 1776, 1876, 1976; transportation routes, 1776, 1876, 1976. 20-67, July 1976
• Tropical Rain Forests: Nature's Dwindling Treasures. By Peter T. White. Photos by James P. Blair. Paintings by Barron Storey. Included: The conversion of rain forest in South America and Southeast Asia to small-plot farms, lumber camps, and settlements. 2-47, Jan. 1983
• *See also* Agriculture; Federal Lands; Forests and Reforestation; Interstate Highway System; Landfills; National Parks; Strip Mining

LAND YACHTS:
• Dry-land Fleet Sails the Sahara. By Jean du Boucher. Photos by Jonathan S. Blair. 696-725, Nov. 1967
▪ Wind Raiders of the Sahara. 436A-436B, Sept. 1973

LANDELLS, GEORGE JAMES:
• The Journey of Burke and Wills: First Across Australia. By Joseph Judge. Photos by Joseph J. Scherschel. 152-191, Feb. 1979

LANDFILLS:
• The Fascinating World of Trash. By Peter T. White. Photos by Louie Psihoyos. 424-457, Apr. 1983

LANDMARKS of Literary England. By Leo A. Borah. Photos by Kathleen Revis. 295-350, Sept. 1955

The **LANDS** and Peoples of Southeast Asia. By Peter T. White, Wilhelm G. Solheim II, and W. E. Garrett. Photos by W. E. Garrett. 295-365, Mar. 1971

LANDSAT (Satellites):
• Editorial. By Gilbert M. Grosvenor. 1, July 1976
• Landsat Looks at Hometown Earth. By Barry C. Bishop. 140-147, July 1976
• Satellites That Serve Us. By Thomas Y. Canby. Included: A portfolio, Images of Earth. 281-335, Sept. 1983
• Studying Grizzly Habitat by Satellite. By John Craighead. NGS research grant. 148-158, July 1976

LANDSBERG, HANS H.:
• What Six Experts Say. 70-73, *Special Report on Energy* (Feb. 1981)

LANDSBURG, ROBERT:
• Mountain With a Death Wish (Mount St. Helens). By Rowe Findley. Included: Robert Landsburg's photos of the eruption of Mount St. Helens taken just before his death. 3-33, Jan. 1981

LANDSEER, EDWIN:
• The British Way. By Sir Evelyn Wrench. 421-541, Apr. 1949

LANDSLIDES. *See* Avalanches; Mudslides

LANE, CHARLES E.: Author:
• The Deadly Fisher. 388-397, Mar. 1963
Photographer:
• X-Rays Reveal the Inner Beauty of Shells. By Hilary B. Moore. 427-434, Mar. 1955

LANG, ERNST M.: Author:
• Jambo–First Gorilla Raised by Its Mother in Captivity. Photos by Paul Steinemann. 446-453, Mar. 1964

LANGMORE, BANK: Photographer:
• Our Wild and Scenic Rivers: The Rio Grande. By Nathaniel T. Kenney. 46-51, July 1977

LANGUEDOC (Region), France:
• France's Past Lives in Languedoc. By Walter Meayers Edwards. 1-43, July 1951

LANKA. *See* former name, Ceylon; and present name, Sri Lanka

L'ANSE AU MEADOW, Newfoundland:
• Vinland Ruins Prove Vikings Found the New World. By Helge Ingstad. 708-734, Nov. 1964

LANZAROTE, the Strangest Canary. By Stephanie Dinkins. 117-139, Jan. 1969

LANZHOU, China:
• Journey to China's Far West. By Rick Gore. Photos by Bruce Dale. 292-331, Mar. 1980

LAOS:
• The Hmong of Laos: No Place to Run. By W. E. Garrett. 78-111, Jan. 1974
• The Lands and Peoples of Southeast Asia. 295-365, Mar. 1971
I. Mosaic of Cultures. By Peter T. White. Photos by W. E. Garrett. 296-329; II. New Light on a Forgotten Past. By Wilhelm G. Solheim II. 330-339
• Little Laos, Next Door to Red China. By Elizabeth Perazic. 46-69, Jan. 1960
• The Mekong, River of Terror and Hope. By Peter T. White. Photos by W. E. Garrett. 737-787, Dec. 1968
• Report on Laos. By Peter T. White. Photos by W. E. Garrett. 241-275, Aug. 1961
▲ *Viet Nam, Cambodia, Laos, and Eastern Thailand,* supplement. Text on reverse. Jan. 1965
▲ *Viet Nam, Cambodia, Laos, and Thailand,* supplement. Feb. 1967
• War and Quiet on the Laos Frontier. By W. Robert Moore. 665-680, May 1954

LAOTIAN REFUGEES:
• One Family's Odyssey to America. By John Everingham. 642-661, May 1980
• Thailand: Refuge From Terror. By W. E. Garrett. 633-642, May 1980

LA PAZ, Baja California, Mexico:
• Baja California's Rugged Outback. By Michael E. Long. 543-567, Oct. 1972
• Rocks, Ruts, and Sand: Driving the Mexican 1000. By Michael E. Long. 569-575, Oct. 1972

LA PAZ, Bolivia:
• Flamboyant Is the Word for Bolivia. By Loren McIntyre. 153-195, Feb. 1965
• Sky-high Bolivia. 481-496, Oct. 1950

LAPIDARY WORK:
• The Glittering World of Rockhounds. By David S. Boyer. 276-294, Feb. 1974
• My Neighbors Hold to Mountain Ways. By Malcolm Ross. Photos by Flip Schulke. 856-880, June 1958
• "Rockhounds" Uncover Earth's Mineral Beauty. By George S. Switzer. 631-660, Nov. 1951

LA PITA, Panama:
• Exploring Ancient Panama by Helicopter. By Matthew W. Stirling. Photos by Richard H. Stewart. NGS research grant. 227-246, Feb. 1950

LAPLAND:
• Friendly Flight to Northern Europe. By Lyndon B. Johnson. Photos by Volkmar Wentzel. 268-293, Feb. 1964
• Hunters of the Lost Spirit: Lapps. By Priit J. Vesilind. Photos by Sisse Brimberg. 194-197, Feb. 1983
• Lapland's Reindeer Roundup. 109-116, July 1949
• North with Finland's Lapps. By Jean and Franc Shor. 249-280, Aug. 1954
• Norway, Land of the Generous Sea. By Edward J. Linehan. Photos by George F. Mobley. 1-43, July 1971
• Norway's Reindeer Lapps. By Sally Anderson. Photos by Erik Borg. 364-379, Sept. 1977

LARSEN, CALVIN L.: Photographer:
• Across the Frozen Desert to Byrd Station. By Paul W. Frazier. 383-398, Sept. 1957

LARSEN, THOR:
Author-Photographer:
• Polar Bear: Lonely Nomad of the North. 574-590, Apr. 1971

LARUE COUNTY, Kentucky:
• Home to the Heart of Kentucky. By Nadine Brewer. Photos by William Strode. 522-546, Apr. 1982

LARVAE, Insect:
• The Case of the Killer Caterpillars. By Steven L. Montgomery. Photos by Robert F. Sisson. 219-225, Aug. 1983
• Nature's Night Lights: Probing the Secrets of Bioluminescence. By Paul A. Zahl. 45-69, July 1971
• Nature's Toy Train, the Railroad Worm. By Darwin L. Tiemann. Photos by Robert F. Sisson. NGS research grant. 56-67, July 1970
• *See also* Silkworms

LASCAUX CAVE, Cradle of World Art (France). By Norbert Casteret. Photos by Maynard Owen Williams. 771-794, Dec. 1948

LASERS:
• Fiber Optics: Harnessing Light by a Thread. By Allen A. Boraiko. Photos by Fred Ward. 516-535, Oct. 1979
• The Laser's Bright Magic. By Thomas Meloy. Photos by Howard Sochurek. 858-881, Dec. 1966

LAS MARISMAS (Marshes), Spain:
• Rare Birds Flock to Spain's Marismas. By Roger Tory Peterson. 397-425, Mar. 1958

The **LAST** Andaman Islanders. By Raghubir Singh. 66-91, July 1975

LAST Ascent of a Heroic Team. 794-797, Dec. 1983

The **LAST** Full Measure. By Melville Bell Grosvenor. 307-355, Mar. 1964

The **LAST** Great Animal Kingdom: A Portfolio of Africa's Vanishing Wildlife. 390-409, Sept. 1960

LAST Harbor for the Oldest Ship. By Susan W. and Michael L. Katzev. NGS research grant. 618-625, Nov. 1974

LAST Moments of the Pompeians. By Amedeo Maiuri. Photos by Lee E. Battaglia. Paintings by Peter V. Bianchi. 651-669, Nov. 1961

LAST of a Breed, the Gauchos. By Robert Laxalt. Photos by O. Louis Mazzatenta. 478-501, Oct. 1980

LAST of the Black-footed Ferrets? By Tim W. Clark. Photos by Franz J. Camenzind and the author. NGS research grant. 828-838, June 1983

LAST of the Cape Horners *(Pamir).* By Alan Villiers. 701-710, May 1948

LAST Stand for the Bighorn. By James K. Morgan. 383-399, Sept. 1973

"LAST SUPPER" (Leonardo da Vinci):
• Restoration Reveals the "Last Supper." By Carlo Bertelli. Photos by Victor R. Boswell, Jr. 664-685, Nov. 1983

The **LAST** Thousand Years Before Christ. By G. Ernest Wright. Paintings by H. J. Soulen and Peter V. Bianchi. 812-853, Dec. 1960

The **LAST** U. S. Whale Hunters. By Emory Kristof. 346-353, Mar. 1973

LAS VEGAS, Nevada:
• The Other Nevada. By Robert Laxalt. Photos by J. Bruce Baumann. 733-761, June 1974

LATAH COUNTY, Idaho. *See* Palouse

LATEEN-RIGGED SHIP. *See Sohar*

LATHAM, MARTE: Author:
• Capturing Strange Creatures in Colombia. Photos by Tor Eigeland. 682-693, May 1966

LATIN AMERICA. *See* Central America; Cuba; Dominican Republic; Mexico; Puerto Rico; South America

LA TOUR, CY: Author-Photographer:
• *J. W. Westcott,* Postman for the Great Lakes. 813-824, Dec. 1950

LAUGHTER, ALBERT: Author:
• Navajo Ranger Interprets–Our People, Our Past. 81-85, July 1979

LAUNOIS, JOHN: Photographer:
• Bangkok, City of Angels. By William Graves. 96-129, July 1973
• "Every Day Is a Gift When You Are Over 100." By Alexander Leaf. 93-119, Jan. 1973
• Japan, the Exquisite Enigma. By Franc Shor. 733-777, Dec. 1960
• Liechtenstein: A Modern Fairy Tale. By Robert Booth. 273-284, Feb. 1981
• Martinique: Liberté, Egalité, and Uncertainty in the Caribbean. By Kenneth MacLeish. 124-148, Jan. 1975
• The St. Lawrence, River Key to Canada. By Howard La Fay. 622-667, May 1967
• The Tasadays, Stone Age Cavemen of Mindanao. By Kenneth MacLeish. 219-249, Aug. 1972
• Vienna, City of Song. By Peter T. White. 739-779, June 1968

LAVENBURG, JOSEPH D.: Photographer:
• Of Air and Space (National Air and Space Museum). By Michael Collins. 819-837, June 1978
Picture portfolio by Nathan Benn, Robert S. Oakes, and Joseph D. Lavenburg, with text by Michael E. Long. 825-837

LA VENTA, Mexico:
• Gifts for the Jaguar God. By Philip Drucker and Robert F. Heizer. NGS research grant. 367-375, Sept. 1956
• On the Trail of La Venta Man. By Matthew W. Stirling. Photos by Richard H. Stewart. NGS research grant. 137-172, Feb. 1947
Hunting Mexico's Buried Temples. 145-168

LAVIES, BIANCA: Photographer:
• The Astonishing Armadillo. By Eleanor E. Storrs. 820-830, June 1982
• Atlantic Salmon: The "Leaper" Struggles to Survive. By Art Lee. 600-615, Nov. 1981
• Found at Last: the Monarch's Winter Home. By Fred A. Urquhart. 161-173, Aug. 1976
• Life Around a Lily Pad. Text by Charles R. Miller. 131-142, Jan. 1980
• Manitoba's Fantastic Snake Pits. By Michael Aleksiuk. 715-723, Nov. 1975
• Those Fiery Brazilian Bees. By Rick Gore. 491-501, Apr. 1976
• Tireless Voyager, the Whistling Swan. By William J. L. Sladen. 134-147, July 1975
• The Tree Nobody Liked (Red Mangrove). By Rick Gore. 669-689, May 1977
• The Wild World of Compost. By Cecil E. Johnson. 273-284, Aug. 1980

LAVIGNE, DAVID M.: Author:
• Life or Death for the Harp Seal. Photos by William R. Curtsinger. 129-142, Jan. 1976

LAW:
• Ancient Mesopotamia: A Light That Did Not Fail. By E. A. Speiser. Paintings by H. M. Herget. Included: The Law Protects Zealously the Institution of Marriage.–Justice Catches Up With a Corrupt Magistrate. 41-105, Jan. 1951
• The British Way. By Sir Evelyn Wrench. Included: Jury System (1066-1086); Magna Carta (1215); The Mother of Parliaments (1295); William Blackstone (1723-1780). 421-541, Apr. 1949

LAW ENFORCEMENT:
• The FBI: Public Friend Number One. By Jacob Hay. Photos by Robert F. Sisson. 860-886, June 1961

LAWA (People). *See* Lua

LAWICK, HUGO VAN: Photographer:
• Adventures in the Search for Man. By Louis S. B. Leakey. 132-152, Jan. 1963
• Hyenas, the Hunters Nobody Knows. By Hans Kruuk. 44-57, July 1968
• The Leakeys of Africa: Family in Search of Prehistoric Man. By Melvin M. Payne. 194-231, Feb. 1965
• My Life Among Wild Chimpanzees. By Jane Goodall. Photos by Baron Hugo van Lawick and author. 272-308, Aug. 1963
• New Discoveries Among Africa's Chimpanzees. By Baroness Jane van Lawick-Goodall. 802-831, Dec. 1965
• Tool-using Bird: The Egyptian Vulture. By Baroness Jane van Lawick-Goodall. 631-641, May 1968

LAWICK-GOODALL, JANE VAN. *See* Goodall, Jane

LAWRENCE, Massachusetts:
• The Merrimack: River of Industry and Romance. By Albert W. Atwood. Photos by B. Anthony Stewart. 106-140, Jan. 1951

LAXALT, ROBERT: Author:
• The Enduring Pyrenees. Photos by Edwin Stuart Grosvenor. 794-819, Dec. 1974
• The Gauchos, Last of a Breed. Photos by O. Louis Mazzatenta. 478-501, Oct. 1980
• Golden Ghosts of the Lost Sierra. Photos by David Hiser. 332-353, Sept. 1973
• Land of the Ancient Basques. Photos by William Albert Allard. 240-277, Aug. 1968
• Lonely Sentinels of the American West: Basque Sheepherders. Photos by William Belknap, Jr. 870-888, June 1966
• New Mexico: The Golden Land. Photos by Adam Woolfitt. 299-345, Sept. 1970
• New Mexico's Mountains of Mystery. Photos by Craig Aurness. 416-436, Sept. 1978
• The Other Nevada. Photos by J. Bruce Baumann. 733-761, June 1974

LAYKAWKEY (Village), Thailand:
• Spirits of Change Capture the Karens. By Peter Kunstadter. 267-285, Feb. 1972

LAYSAN ISLAND, Leeward Islands, Hawaii:
• Hawaii's Far-flung Wildlife Paradise. By John L. Eliot. Photos by Jonathan Blair. 670-691, May 1978

LEA, JOHN S.: Co-Editor:
◆ *Research Reports* (NGS). 294, Feb. 1978; 298, Aug. 1979; 480, Mar. 1981; 830, June 1982
◆ *Research Reports* (NGS): *1973 Projects* and *1974 Projects*. 706, Nov. 1983

LEAF, ALEXANDER: Author:
• "Every Day Is a Gift When You Are Over 100." Photos by John Launois. 93-119, Jan. 1973

LEAKEY, LOUIS S. B.:
■ Dr. Leakey and the Dawn of Man. 703A-703B, Nov. 1966
• The Leakey Tradition Lives On. By Melvin M. Payne. 143-144, Jan. 1973
• The Leakeys of Africa: Family in Search of Prehistoric Man. By Melvin M. Payne. 194-231, Feb. 1965
■ The Legacy of L.S.B. Leakey. 439, Oct. 1977; cover, Jan. 1978
• Preserving the Treasures of Olduvai Gorge. By Melvin M. Payne. Photos by Joseph J. Scherschel. 701-709, Nov. 1966
Author:
• Adventures in the Search for Man. Photos by Hugo van Lawick. 132-152, Jan. 1963
• Exploring 1,750,000 Years Into Man's Past. Photos by Robert F. Sisson. 564-589, Oct. 1961
• Finding the World's Earliest Man. Photos by Des Bartlett. 420-435, Sept. 1960

LEAKEY, MARY D.: Author:
• Footprints in the Ashes of Time. 446-457, Apr. 1979
• Tanzania's Stone Age Art. Photos by John Reader. 84-99, July 1983

LEAKEY, RICHARD E.: Author:
• In Search of Man's Past at Lake Rudolf. Photos by Gordon W. Gahan. 712-734, May 1970
• Skull 1470. Photos by Bob Campbell. 819-829, June 1973

LEAKEY FAMILY:
• The Leakeys of Africa: Family in Search of Prehistoric Man. By Melvin M. Payne. NGS research grant. 194-231, Feb. 1965

LEARNING the Ways of the Walrus. By G. Carleton Ray. Photos by Bill Curtsinger. NGS research grant. 565-580, Oct. 1979

LEBANON:
• Beirut–Up From the Rubble. By William S. Ellis. Photos by Steve McCurry. 262-286, Feb. 1983
• Islam's Heartland, Up in Arms. By Thomas J. Abercrombie. 335-345, Sept. 1980

ROBERT F. SISSON, NGS

Exploring Man's Past: Leakey butchers ram with stone knife

Beirut: Palestinian at refugee camp

STEVE MCCURRY

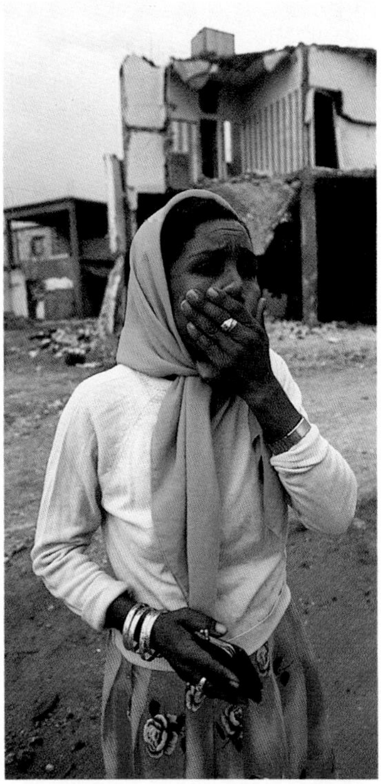

• Journey Into the Great Rift: The Northern Half. By Helen and Frank Schreider. 254-290, Aug. 1965
• Lebanon, Little Bible Land in the Crossfire of History. By William S. Ellis. Photos by George F. Mobley. 240-275, Feb. 1970
• The Phoenicians, Sea Lords of Antiquity. By Samuel W. Matthews. Photos by Winfield Parks. Paintings by Robert C. Magis. 149-189, Aug. 1974
• Troubled Waters East of Suez. By Ernest M. Eller. 483-522, Apr. 1954
• YWCA: International Success Story. By Mary French Rockefeller. Photos by Otis Imboden. 904-933, Dec. 1963
• Young-old Lebanon Lives by Trade. By Thomas J. Abercrombie. 479-523, Apr. 1958

LEE, ART: Author:
• Atlantic Salmon: The "Leaper" Struggles to Survive. Photos by Bianca Lavies. 600-615, Nov. 1981

LEE, DOUGLAS: Author:
• Day of the Rice God (Festival in Japan). Photos by H. Edward Kim. 78-85, July 1978
• Hokkaido, Japan's Last Frontier. Photos by Michael S. Yamashita. 62-93, Jan. 1980
• Mississippi Delta: The Land of the River. Photos by C. C. Lockwood. 226-253, Aug. 1983
• Slime Mold: The Fungus That Walks. Photos by Paul A. Zahl. 131-136, July 1981

LEE, ROBERT E.:
• Appomattox: Where Grant and Lee Made Peace With Honor a Century Ago. By Ulysses S. Grant 3rd. Photos by Bruce Dale. 435-469, Apr. 1965

LEEN, SARAH: Photographer:
• Return to Uganda. By Jerry and Sarah Kambites. 73-89, July 1980

LEEPER, JOHN and BLANCHE:
Authors:
• American Processional: History on Canvas. 173-212, Feb. 1951

LEEWARD ISLANDS, Hawaii:
• Hawaii's Far-flung Wildlife Paradise. By John L. Eliot. Photos by Jonathan Blair. 670-691, May 1978

LEEWARD ISLANDS, Lesser Antilles, West Indies:
• *Carib* Cruises the West Indies. By Carleton Mitchell. 1-56, Jan. 1948
• A Fresh Breeze Stirs the Leewards. By Carleton Mitchell. Photos by Winfield Parks. Included: Antigua; Dominica; Guadeloupe; Îles des Saintes; Nevis; Saba; St. Barthélemy; St. Christopher; St. Eustatius; St. Martin; Virgin Islands. 488-537, Oct. 1966
• *See also* Dominica; Guadeloupe; Nevis; Saba; St. Christopher; Sint Eustatius; Virgin Islands

LEGACY From the Age of Faith, Chartres. By Kenneth MacLeish. Photos by Dean Conger. 857-882, Dec. 1969

ENGRAVING BY THEODORE DE BRY, 1590

Indian Life: "Great Lordes of Virginia"

LEGACY From the Deep: Henry VIII's Lost Warship *(Mary Rose)*. By Margaret Rule. Introduction and picture text by Peter Miller. Paintings by Richard Schlecht. 646-675, May 1983

LEGACY of a Dazzling Past. By Alice J. Hall. 293-311, Mar. 1977

LEGACY of Lively Treasures: Sri Lanka's Wildlife. By Dieter and Mary Plage. 256-273, Aug. 1983

LEGENDS:
◆ *Amazing Mysteries of the World.* 1983
● *See also* Gilgamesh, Epic of; Hâ-âk Vâ-âk; Kamikaze Legend; Loch Ness; Marostica, Italy, for Chess Game (Living Pieces); Messina, Strait of, for Charybdis; St. Michael's Mount; Stonehenge

LEH, Ladakh (District), Jammu and Kashmir, now India:
● A Journey to "Little Tibet." By Enakshi Bhavnani. Photos by Volkmar Wentzel. 603-634, May 1951
● A Woman Paints the Tibetans. By Lafugie. 659-692, May 1949

LEIS:
● The Flowers That Say "Aloha." By Deena Clark. Photos by Robert B. Goodman. 121-131, Jan. 1967

LEM (Lunar Excursion Module). *See* Apollo Missions

LeMAY, CURTIS E.: Author:
● Artists Roam the World of the U. S. Air Force. 650-673, May 1960
● School for Survival. 565-602, May 1953
● U. S. Air Force: Power for Peace. 291-297, Sept. 1965

LE MOYNE DE MORGUES, JACQUES:
● Indian Life Before the Colonists Came. By Stuart E. Jones. Engravings by Theodore de Bry, 1590. Included: The artist, Jacques le Moyne de Morgues, and reproductions of his paintings from De Bry's engravings. 351-368, Sept. 1947

LEMURS, Flying:
● Seeking Mindanao's Strangest Creatures. By Charles Heizer Wharton. 389-408, Sept. 1948

LENDOMBWEY. *See* Malekula (Island)

LENINGRAD, U.S.S.R.:
● Leningrad, Russia's Window on the West. By Howard La Fay. Photos by Dick Durrance II. 636-673, May 1971

LEONARD CARMICHAEL: An Appreciation. By Melvin M. Payne. 871-874, Dec. 1973
● *See also* Carmichael, Leonard C.

LEONARDO DA VINCI:
● Leonardo da Vinci: A Man for All Ages. By Kenneth MacLeish. Photos by James L. Amos. 296-329, Sept. 1977
● Restoration Reveals the "Last Supper." By Carlo Bertelli. Photos by Victor R. Boswell, Jr. 664-685, Nov. 1983

LEONOV, ALEKSEY A.:
● Apollo-Soyuz: Handclasp in Space. By Thomas Y. Canby. 183-187, Feb. 1976

LEOPARDS. *See* Snow Leopards

LEOPOLD, ALDO:
● Aldo Leopold: "A Durable Scale of Values." By Boyd Gibbons. Photos by Jim Brandenburg. 682-708, Nov. 1981
● Editorial. By Wilbur E. Garrett. 567, Nov. 1981

LEPROSY. *See* Hansen's Disease

LERICI, CARLO M.: Author:
● Periscope on the Etruscan Past. 337-350, Sept. 1959

LERNER, IRA S.: Photographer:
● Getting to Know the Wild Burros of Death Valley. By Patricia des Roses Moehlman. Photos by Ira S. Lerner and author. 502-517, Apr. 1972

LERNER MARINE LABORATORY, Bahama Islands:
● The Bahamas, Isles of the Blue-green Sea. By Carleton Mitchell. Photos by B. Anthony Stewart. 147-203, Feb. 1958
● Man-of-War Fleet Attacks Bimini. By Paul A. Zahl. 185-212, Feb. 1952

LERWICK, Shetland Islands. *See* Up Helly Aa

LESAGE, JEAN: Author:
● Alexander Graham Bell Museum: Tribute to Genius. 227-256, Aug. 1956

LESBOS (Island), Greece:
● The Isles of Greece: Aegean Birthplace of Western Culture. By Melville Bell Grosvenor. Photos by Edwin Stuart Grosvenor and Winfield Parks. 147-193, Aug. 1972

LESLIE MELVILLE, JOCK and BETTY:
● Rescuing the Rothschild (Giraffe). By Carolyn Bennett Patterson. 419-421, Sept. 1977

LESSER ANTILLES. *See* Leeward Islands; Windward Islands

LESSER SUNDA ISLANDS:
● Dragon Lizards of Komodo. By James A. Kern. 872-880, Dec. 1968
● East From Bali by Seagoing Jeep to Timor. By Helen and Frank Schreider. 236-279, Aug. 1962
● *See also* Bali

LESSING, ERICH: Photographer:
● Firsthand Look at the Soviet Union. By Thomas T. Hammond. 352-407, Sept. 1959
● Modern Miracle, Made in Germany. By Robert Leslie Conly. 735-791, June 1959
● Poland Opens Her Doors. By Delia and Ferdinand Kuhn. 354-398, Sept. 1958

LESSON and Challenge. By James H. Wakelin, Jr. 759-763, June 1964

LETHBRIDGE, JOHN:
● The Treasure of Porto Santo. By Robert Sténuit. Photos by author and William R. Curtsinger. 260-275, Aug. 1975

LETTER From Kunming: Two American Teachers in China. By Elisabeth B. Booz. Photos by Thomas Nebbia. 793-813, June 1981

LETTICK, BIRNEY: Artist:
● A New Look at Medieval Europe. By Kenneth M. Setton. Paintings by Andre Durenceau and Birney Lettick. 799-859, Dec. 1962

LEVATHES, LOUISE E.: Author:
● The American Red Cross: A Century of Service. Photos by Annie Griffiths. 777-791, June 1981
● Gateway–Elbowroom for the Millions (Gateway National Recreation Area, New Jersey-New York). 86-97, July 1979
● Kamehameha–Hawaii's Warrior King. Photos by Steve Raymer. Paintings by Herb Kawainui Kane. 558-599, Nov. 1983
● Milwaukee: More Than Beer. Photos by Michael Mauney. 180-201, Aug. 1980
● Toledo–El Greco's Spain Lives On. Photos by James P. Blair. 726-753, June 1982

LEVEES. *See* Dikes and Levees

LEVKAS (Island), Greece:
● Homeward With Ulysses (Ionian Islands). By Melville Bell Grosvenor. Photos by Edwin Stuart Grosvenor. 1-39, July 1973

LEWIS, DAVID:
● Editorial. By Gilbert M. Grosvenor. 431, Oct. 1976
Author:
● Alone to Antarctica. Drawings by Noel Sickles. 808-821, Dec. 1973
● *Hokule'a* Follows the Stars to Tahiti. Photos by Nicholas deVore III. 512-537, Oct. 1976
● Voyage to the Antarctic. 544-562, Apr. 1983
● Wind, Wave, Star, and Bird. Photos by Nicholas deVore III. 747-781, Dec. 1974
Author-Photographer:
● *Ice Bird* Ends Her Lonely Odyssey. 216-233, Aug. 1975

LEWIS, G. EDWARD:
Author-Photographer:
● El Sangay, Fire-breathing Giant of the Andes. 117-138, Jan. 1950

LEWIS, LEWIS:
Author-Photographer:
● New Life for the "Loneliest Isle" (Tristan da Cunha). 105-116, Jan. 1950

LEWIS, M. LEE: Author:
● To 76,000 Feet by *Strato-Lab* Balloon. By Malcolm D. Ross and M. Lee Lewis. 269-282, Feb. 1957

LEWIS, Isle of, Scotland:
● Isles on the Edge of the Sea: Scotland's Outer Hebrides. By Kenneth MacLeish. Photos by Thomas Nebbia. 676-711, May 1970

LEWIS AND CLARK EXPEDITION:
● Following the Trail of Lewis and Clark. By Ralph Gray. 707-750, June 1953
◆ *In the Footsteps of Lewis and Clark.* Announced. 880-884, June 1970
● So Long, St. Louis, We're Heading West. By William C. Everhart. 643-669, Nov. 1965

LEXINGTON, Kentucky:
● Heart of the Bluegrass. By Charles McCarry. Photos by J. Bruce Baumann. 634-659, May 1974

LEYDET, FRANÇOIS: Author:
● Autumn Flames Along the Allagash. Photos by Farrell Grehan. 177-187, Feb. 1974
● Coal vs. Parklands. Photos by Dewitt Jones. 776-803, Dec. 1980
● Grand Teton–A Winter's Tale (Grand Teton National Park, Wyoming). 148-152, July 1979
● Jackson Hole: Good-bye to the Old Days? Photos by Jonathan Wright. 768-789, Dec. 1976
● Journey Through Time: Papua New Guinea. Photos by David Austen. 150-171, Aug. 1982
● The Mazatzal's Harsh but Lovely Land Between. Photos by Farrell Grehan. 161-167, Feb. 1974
● Okefenokee, the Magical Swamp. Photos by Farrell Grehan. 169-175, Feb. 1974
● The Olympics: Northwest Majesty. Photos by Farrell Grehan. 188-197, Feb. 1974

LHASA, Tibet:
● Editorial. By Gilbert M. Grosvenor. 143, Feb. 1980
● In Long-Forbidden Tibet. By Fred Ward. 218-259, Feb. 1980
● My Life in Forbidden Lhasa. By Heinrich Harrer. 1-48, July 1955

LI (River), People's Republic of China:
● Guilin, China's Beauty Spot. By W. E. Garrett. 536-563, Oct. 1979

LIBBY, ERNEST L.:
Author-Photographer:
● Miracle of the Mermaid's Purse (Skate). 413-420, Sept. 1957

LIBERIA:
● Africa: The Winds of Freedom Stir a Continent. By Nathaniel T. Kenney. Photos by W. D. Vaughn. 303-359, Sept. 1960
● Rubber-cushioned Liberia. By Henry S. Villard. Photos by Charles W. Allmon. 201-228, Feb. 1948

LIBRARIES:
● The DAR Story. By Lonnelle Aikman. Photos by B. Anthony Stewart and John E. Fletcher. Included: Genealogical Library. 565-598, Nov. 1951
● Florence Rises From the Flood. By Joseph Judge. Included: Biblioteca Nazionale Centrale, Gabinetto Vieusseux. 1-43, July 1967
● Literary Landmarks of Massachusetts. By William H. Nicholas. Photos by B. Anthony Stewart and John E. Fletcher. Included: Adams Library, The Athenaeum, Boston College Library, Boston Public Library, Converse Memorial Library, Houghton Library, Lamont Library. 279-310, Mar. 1950
● Miami's Expanding Horizons. By William H. Nicholas. Included: Brett Memorial Library, Miami Memorial Library, Montgomery Museum and Library, State Library, University of Miami Library. 561-594, Nov. 1950
● *See also* Folger; Henry E. Huntington Library and Art Gallery; Library of Congress

LIBRARY OF CONGRESS, Washington, D. C.:
● Library of Congress: The Nation's Bookcase. By Fred Kline. Photos by Dick Durrance II. 671-687, Nov. 1975
● The Nation's Library. By Albert W. Atwood. 663-684, May 1950

LICHENS:
● Life on a Rock Ledge. By William H. Amos. 558-566, Oct. 1980

LIECHTENSTEIN:
● Liechtenstein: A Modern Fairy Tale. By Robert Booth. Photos by John Launois. 273-284, Feb. 1981
● Liechtenstein Thrives on Stamps. By Ronald W. Clark. 105-112, July 1948

LIFE Among Mountain Gorillas. By Dian Fossey. NGS research grant. 501-523, Apr. 1981

LIFE Among the Wai Wai Indians. By Clifford Evans and Betty J. Meggers. 329-346, Mar. 1955

LIFE and Death at Gombe. By Jane Goodall. NGS research grant. 592-621, May 1979

LIFE and Death in Tana Toradja. By Pamela and Alfred Meyer. 793-815, June 1972

LIFE Around a Lily Pad. Photos by Bianca Lavies. Text by Charles R. Miller. 131-142, Jan. 1980

LIFE Ashore Beckons the Sea Gypsies. By Anne de Henning Singh. Photos by Raghubir Singh. 659-677, May 1976

LIFE by Night in a Desert Sea. By Kenneth Brower. Photos by William R. Curtsinger and Chris Newbert. 834-847, Dec. 1981

LIFE Cycle of a Coral. By Robert F. Sisson. 780-793, June 1973

LIFE 8,000 Years Ago Uncovered in an Alabama Cave. By Carl F. Miller. NGS research grant. 542-558, Oct. 1956

LIFE in a "Dead" Sea–Great Salt Lake. By Paul A. Zahl. 252-263, Aug. 1967

LIFE in an Undersea Desert. By Eugenie Clark. Photos by David Doubilet. 129-144, July 1983

LIFE in India Behind the Veil. By Doranne Wilson Jacobson. 270-286, Aug. 1977

LIFE in the Enduring Pyrenees. By Robert Laxalt. Photos by Edwin Stuart Grosvenor. 794-819, Dec. 1974

LIFE in the Land of the Basques. By John E. H. Nolan. Photos by Justin Locke. 147-186, Feb. 1954

LIFE in Walled-off West Berlin. By Nathaniel T. Kenney and Volkmar Wentzel. Photos by Thomas Nebbia. 735-767, Dec. 1961

FRED WARD, BLACK STAR

ARLAN R. WIKER, NGS

Light Technology: light is piped through optical fibers, *top;* laser light flashes across the Potomac, *above*

LIFE on a Rock Ledge. By William H. Amos. 558-566, Oct. 1980

LIFE or Death for the Harp Seal. By David M. Lavigne. Photos by William R. Curtsinger. 129-142, Jan. 1976

LIFE Slowly Changes in Remote Bhutan. By John Scofield. 658-683, Nov. 1976

LIFE Springs From Death in Truk Lagoon. By Sylvia A. Earle. Photos by Al Giddings. 578-613, May 1976

LIFE under Shellfire on Quemoy. By Franc Shor. Photos by Wilbur E. Garrett. 415-438, Mar. 1959

LIFE with the King of Beasts. By George B. Schaller. 494-519, Apr. 1969

LIFE with the "Pumphouse Gang": New Insights Into Baboon Behavior. By Shirley C. Strum. Photos by Timothy W. Ransom. 672-691, May 1975

LIFELIKE Man Preserved 2,000 Years in Peat. By P. V. Glob. 419-430, Mar. 1954

LIFE'S Tempo on Nantucket. By Peter Benchley. Photos by James L. Stanfield. 810-839, June 1970

LIGHT TECHNOLOGY:
- Fiber Optics: Harnessing Light by a Thread. By Allen A. Boraiko. Photos by Fred Ward. 516-535, Oct. 1979
- The Laser's Bright Magic. By Thomas Meloy. Photos by Howard Sochurek. 858-881, Dec. 1966
- *See also* Solar Energy

LIGHTHOUSES. *See* Devonshire, England, for Eddystone; Farne Islands, for Longstone Islet; Maine (Down East Cruise), for Boon Island, Neddick, Petit Manan Island, Portland Head, Seguin, Two Bush Island, West Quoddy Head; Outer Banks, for Cape Hatteras Light

LIGHTNING in Action. By F. Barrows Colton. 809-828, June 1950

The **LIGHTS** Are Up at Ford's Theatre. By Lonnelle Aikman. 392-401, Mar. 1970

LIGUUS FASCIATUS (Snail):
- Tree Snails, Gems of the Everglades. By Treat Davidson. 372-387, Mar. 1965

LILIENTHAL, OTTO:
- Happy Birthday, Otto Lilienthal! By Russell Hawkes. Photos by James Collison. 286-292, Feb. 1972

LILY PADS:
- Life Around a Lily Pad. Photos by Bianca Lavies. Text by Charles R. Miller. 131-142, Jan. 1980

LIMA, Peru:
- The Incredible Potato. By Robert E. Rhoades. Photos by Martin Rogers. 668-694, May 1982
- The Two Souls of Peru. By Harvey Arden. Photos by William Albert Allard. 284-321, Mar. 1982

LIMESTONE FORMATIONS:
- Guilin, China's Beauty Spot. By W. E. Garrett. 536-563, Oct. 1979

LIMESTONE SINKS:
- Manitoba's Fantastic Snake Pits. By Michael Aleksiuk. Photos by Bianca Lavies. 715-723, Nov. 1975

LIMNOLOGY. *See* Brook Life; Mzima Springs; Pond Life

LIMPKIN, the "Crying Bird" That Haunts Florida Swamps. By Frederick Kent Truslow. 114-121, Jan. 1958

LINCOLN, ABRAHAM:
- Inside the White House. By Lonnelle Aikman. Photos by B. Anthony Stewart and Thomas Nebbia. 3-43, Jan. 1961
- The Lights Are Up at Ford's Theatre. By Lonnelle Aikman. 392-401, Mar. 1970
- Lincoln, Man of Steel and Velvet. By Carl Sandburg. 239-241, Feb. 1960
- The Living White House. By Lonnelle Aikman. 593-643, Nov. 1966
- Our Land Through Lincoln's Eyes. By Carolyn Bennett Patterson. Photos by W. D. Vaughn. 243-277, Feb. 1960
- Profiles of the Presidents: III. The American Giant Comes of Age. By Frank Freidel. 660-711, May 1965
- Vacation Tour Through Lincoln Land. By Ralph Gray. 141-184, Feb. 1952
- Washington: Home of the Nation's Great. By Albert W. Atwood. 699-738, June 1947

LINCOLN, Nebraska:
- The West Through Boston Eyes. By Stewart Anderson. 733-776, June 1949

LINDBERGH, JON:
- The Deepest Days. By Robert Sténuit. 534-547, Apr. 1965
- Outpost Under the Ocean. By Edwin A. Link. Photos by Bates Littlehales. 530-533, Apr. 1965

LINDISFARNE (Island), England:
- Pilgrimage to Holy Island and the Farnes. By John E. H. Nolan. 547-570, Oct. 1952

LINE, FRANCIS R.:
Author-Photographer:
- Arizona Sheep Trek. 457-478, Apr. 1950

LINEHAN, EDWARD J.: Author:
- Colorado, the Rockies' Pot of Gold. Photos by James L. Amos. 157-201, Aug. 1969
- Cuba's Exiles Bring New Life to Miami. Photos by Nathan Benn. 68-95, July 1973
- Czechoslovakia: The Dream and the Reality. Photos by James P. Blair. 151-193, Feb. 1968
- Dogs Work for Man. Paintings by Edwin Megargee and R. E. Lougheed. 190-233, Aug. 1958
- Norway, Land of the Generous Sea. Photos by George F. Mobley. 1-43, July 1971
- Old-new Iran, Next Door to Russia. Photos by Thomas J. Abercrombie. 44-85, Jan. 1961
- The Trouble With Dolphins. Photos by Bill Curtsinger. 506-541, Apr. 1979

LINK, EDWIN A.:
- Exploring the Drowned City of Port Royal. By Marion Clayton Link. Photos by Luis Marden. 151-183, Feb. 1960

Author:
- Our Man-in-Sea Project. 713-717, May 1963
- Outpost Under the Ocean. Photos by Bates Littlehales. 530-533, Apr. 1965
- Tomorrow on the Deep Frontier. 778-801, June 1964

LINK, MARION CLAYTON: Author:
- Exploring the Drowned City of Port Royal. Photos by Luis Marden. 151-183, Feb. 1960

LINK IGLOO:
- Tomorrow on the Deep Frontier. By Edwin A. Link. NGS research grant. 778-801, June 1964

LIONS:
- Etosha: Namibia's Kingdom of Animals. By Douglas H. Chadwick. Photos by Des and Jen Bartlett. 344-385, Mar. 1983
- Family Life of Lions. By Des and Jen Bartlett. 800-819, Dec. 1982
- Life with the King of Beasts. By George B. Schaller. 494-519, Apr. 1969
- ◆ *Lion Cubs*. Announced. 736-738, Nov. 1972
- Spearing Lions with Africa's Masai. By Edgar Monsanto Queeny. 487-517, Oct. 1954
- ◆ *Wild Cats*. 1981

LIPAS (Sailing Craft):
- Sea Gypsies of the Philippines. By Anne de Henning Singh. Photos by Raghubir Singh. 659-677, May 1976

LIPIZZANERS:
- The White Horses of Vienna. By Beverley M. Bowie. Photos by Volkmar Wentzel. 401-419, Sept. 1958

LISBON, Portugal:
- Portugal at the Crossroads. By Howard La Fay. Photos by Volkmar Wentzel. 453-501, Oct. 1965
- Portugal Is Different. By Clement E. Conger. 583-622, Nov. 1948

LISTER, JOSEPH, LORD:
- The British Way. By Sir Evelyn Wrench. 421-541, Apr. 1949

LITERATURE:
- The Britain That Shakespeare Knew. By Louis B. Wright. Photos by Dean Conger. 613-665, May 1964
- The British Way. By Sir Evelyn Wrench. Included: Geoffrey Chaucer, William Shakespeare, James I and the Translation of the Bible, John Milton, Daniel Defoe, Some British Poets, Charles Dickens. 421-541, Apr. 1949
- Chelsea, London's Haven of Individualists. By James Cerruti. Photos by Adam Woolfitt. Included: Thomas Carlyle, George Eliot, George Meredith, R. J. Minney, Sir Thomas More, Tom Pocock, Dante Gabriel Rossetti, Jonathan Swift, Algernon Charles Swinburne, Mark Twain. 28-55, Jan. 1972

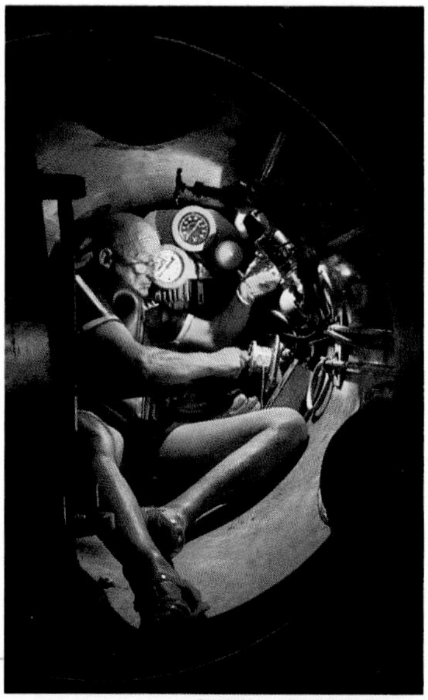

THOMAS J. ABERCROMBIE, NGS

PAINTING BY PIERRE MION

Man-in-Sea Project: Link checks capsule's controls, *top*; artist's conception of Link's diving chamber, *above*

- The Country of Willa Cather. By William Howarth. Photos by Farrell Grehan. 71-93, July 1982
- The England of Charles Dickens. By Richard W. Long. Photos by Adam Woolfitt. 443-483, Apr. 1974
- A First American Views His Land. By N. Scott Momaday. 13-19, July 1976
- The Fragile Beauty All About Us. By Harry S. C. Yen. Included: Chinese poetry, 6th century B.C.-A.D. 1269. 785-795, Dec. 1970
- Ghost Ships of the War of 1812: *Hamilton* and *Scourge*. By Daniel A. Nelson. Photos by Emory Kristof. Paintings by Richard Schlecht. Included: Excerpts from James Fenimore Cooper's naval classic, "Ned Myers; or A Life Before the Mast." 289-313, Mar. 1983
- Lake District, Poets' Corner of England. By H. V. Morton. Photos by David S. Boyer. 511-545, Apr. 1956
- Landmarks of Literary England. By Leo A. Borah. Photos by Kathleen Revis. 295-350, Sept. 1955
- Literary Landmarks of Massachusetts. By William H. Nicholas. Photos by B. Anthony Stewart and John E. Fletcher. Contents: Adams family, Alcott family, Nathaniel Bowditch, Anne Bradstreet, William Cullen Bryant, Dana family, Emily Dickinson, Ralph Waldo Emerson, Clyde Fitch, Louise Imogen Guiney, Sarah Josepha Hale, Nathaniel Hawthorne, Julia Ward Howe, Henry Wadsworth Longfellow, James Russell Lowell, Herman Melville, John Boyle O'Reilly, Harriet Beecher Stowe, Henry David Thoreau, Noah Webster, John Greenleaf Whittier. 279-310, Mar. 1950
- Mark Twain: Mirror of America. By Noel Grove. Photos by James L. Stanfield. 300-337, Sept. 1975
- Poets' Voices Linger in Scottish Shrines. By Isobel Wylie Hutchison. Photos by Kathleen Revis. Contents: Sir James Barrie, James Boswell, John Buchan, Robert Burns, Lord Byron, Thomas Carlyle, Sir Arthur Conan Doyle, James Hogg, Violet Jacob, Samuel Johnson, Allan Ramsay, Sir Walter Scott, William Shakespeare, Adam Smith, Tobias Smollett, Robert Louis Stevenson, William Wordsworth. 437-488, Oct. 1957
- Robert Frost and New England. By Archibald MacLeish. 438-467, Apr. 1976

Look of a Land Beloved. Photos by Dewitt Jones. 444-467
- A Stroll to John o' Groat's. By Isobel Wylie Hutchison. Included: Sir James Barrie, Michael Bruce, Thomas Carlyle, William Shakespeare, Adam Smith, Robert Louis Stevenson. 1-48, July 1956
- A Stroll to London. By Isobel Wylie Hutchison. Photos by B. Anthony Stewart. Included: James Boswell, Brontë sisters, Thomas Carlyle, Charles Dickens, George Eliot, Samuel Johnson, Sir Walter Scott, William Shakespeare, William Wordsworth. 171-204, Aug. 1950

• The Thames: That Noble River. By Ethel A. Starbird. Photos by O. Louis Mazzatenta. Included: Literary landmarks of southern England. 750-791, June 1983
• Thoreau, a Different Man. By William Howarth. Photos by Farrell Grehan. 349-387, Mar. 1981
• Tom Sawyer's Town. By Jerry Allen. 121-140, July 1956
• Wales, the Lyric Land. By Bryan Hodgson. Photos by Farrell Grehan. Included: Writings of Dafydd ap Gwilym and Dylan Thomas. 36-63, July 1983
Washington Irving's Spain. 1966
• *See also* Bible; Fairy Tales; Folger; Gilgamesh, Epic of; *Odyssey; Ramayana; The Thousand and One Nights*

LITTLE AMERICA, Antarctica:
• Admiral of the Ends of the Earth (Richard E. Byrd). By Melville Bell Grosvenor. 36-48, July 1957
• All-out Assault on Antarctica. By Richard E. Byrd. 141-180, Aug. 1956
• Our Navy Explores Antarctica. By Richard E. Byrd. U. S. Navy official photos. 429-522, Oct. 1947

LITTLE ANDAMAN ISLAND, India:
• The Last Andaman Islanders. By Raghubir Singh. 66-91, July 1975

LITTLE FALLS, New York:
• Drums to Dynamos on the Mohawk. By Frederick G. Vosburgh. Photos by B. Anthony Stewart. 67-110, July 1947

LITTLE Horses of the Sea. By Paul A. Zahl. 131-153, Jan. 1959

LITTLE Laos, Next Door to Red China. By Elizabeth Perazic. 46-69, Jan. 1960

LITTLE Tibet in Switzerland. By Laura Pilarski. Photos by Fred Mayer. 711-727, Nov. 1968

LITTLE TOBAGO (Island), West Indies:
• Feathered Dancers of Little Tobago. By E. Thomas Gilliard. Photos by Frederick Kent Truslow. Contents: Greater Birds of Paradise. NGS research grant. 428-440, Sept. 1958

LITTLEHALES, BATES:
• Designed OceanEye camera housing. 262, 271, 277, Aug. 1971
Author-Photographer:
• Into the Well of Sacrifice. II. Treasure Hunt in the Deep Past. 550-561, Oct. 1961
Photographer:
• Audubon "On the Wing." By David Jeffery. 149-177, Feb. 1977
• Back to the Historic Black Hills. By Leland D. Case. 479-509, Oct. 1956
• *Calypso* Explores an Undersea Canyon. By Jacques-Yves Cousteau. 373-396, Mar. 1958
• Central Park: Manhattan's Big Outdoors. By Stuart E. Jones. 781-811, Dec. 1960
• Channel Cruise to Glorious Devon. By Alan Villiers. 208-259, Aug. 1963
• Chesapeake Country. By Nathaniel T. Kenney. 370-411, Sept. 1964
• Cruising Florida's Western Waterways. By Rube Allyn. 49-76, Jan. 1955
• England's Scillies, the Flowering Isles. By Alan Villiers. 126-145, July 1967
• Fabled Mount of St. Michael. By Alan Villiers. 880-898, June 1964
• The Five Worlds of Peru. By Kenneth F. Weaver. 213-265, Feb. 1964
• Gettysburg and Vicksburg: the Battle Towns Today. By Robert Paul Jordan. Map notes by Carolyn Bennett Patterson. 4-57, July 1963
• Giant Kelp, Sequoias of the Sea. By Wheeler J. North. 251-269, Aug. 1972
• Giant Otters: "Big Water Dogs" in Peril. By Nicole Duplaix. Photos by the author and Bates Littlehales. 130-142, July 1980
• Gibraltar–Rock of Contention. By Howard La Fay. 102-121, July 1966
• In Quest of the Rarest Flamingo. By William G. Conway. 91-105, July 1961
• The Indomitable Cockroach. By Allen A. Boraiko. 130-142, Jan. 1981
• Island, Prairie, Marsh, and Shore. By Charlton Ogburn. 350-381, Mar. 1979
• The Long, Deep Dive. By Lord Kilbracken. 718-731, May 1963
• Look What's Happened to Honolulu! By Jim Becker. 500-531, Oct. 1969
• The Lower Keys, Florida's "Out Islands." By John Scofield. Photos by Emory Kristof and Bates Littlehales. 72-93, Jan. 1971
• New England, a Modern Pilgrim's Pride. By Beverley M. Bowie. 733-796, June 1955
• New Zealand's North Island: The Contented Land. By Charles McCarry. 190-213, Aug. 1974
• *Nomad* Sails Long Island Sound. By Thomas Horgan. 295-338, Sept. 1957
• Off Santa Barbara: California's Ranches in the Sea. By Earl Warren, Jr. 257-283, Aug. 1958
• Ohio Makes Its Own Prosperity. By Leo A. Borah. Photos by B. Anthony Stewart and Bates Littlehales. 435-484, Apr. 1955
• Ontario, Pivot of Canada's Power. By Andrew H. Brown. Photos by B. Anthony Stewart and Bates Littlehales. 823-852, Dec. 1953
• Oregon's Many Faces. By Stuart E. Jones. 74-115, Jan. 1969
• Outpost Under the Ocean. By Edwin A. Link. 530-533, Apr. 1965
• Père David's Deer Saved From Extinction. By Larry Kohl. 478-485, Oct. 1982
• Priceless Relics of the Spanish Armada. By Robert Sténuit. 745-777, June 1969
• Resurrecting the Oldest Known Greek Ship. By Michael L. Katzev. 841-857, June 1970
• Science's Window on the Sea. By John G. VanDerwalker. 256-289, Aug. 1971
• The Sunken Treasure of St. Helena. By Robert Sténuit. 562-576, Oct. 1978
• A Taxi for the Deep Frontier. By Kenneth MacLeish. 139-150, Jan. 1968
• Twenty Fathoms Down for Mother-of-Pearl. By Winston Williams. 512-529, Apr. 1962
• Working for Weeks on the Sea Floor. By Jacques-Yves Cousteau. Photos by Philippe Cousteau and Bates Littlehales. 498-537, Apr. 1966

LIVESTOCK:
• America Goes to the Fair. By Samuel W. Matthews. 293-333, Sept. 1954
• America's "Meat on the Hoof." By William H. Nicholas. 33-72, Jan. 1952
• Beltsville Brings Science to the Farm. By Samuel W. Matthews. 199-218, Aug. 1953
• Carnival in San Antonio. By Mason Sutherland. Photos by J. Baylor Roberts. 813-844, Dec. 1947
• Domesticating the Wild and Woolly Musk Ox. By John J. Teal, Jr. Photos by Robert W. Madden. 862-879, June 1970
• The Family Farm Ain't What It Used To Be. By James A. Sugar. 391-411, Sept. 1974
• 4-H Boys and Girls Grow More Food. By Frederick Simpich. 551-582, Nov. 1948
• The Goats of Thunder Hill. By Elizabeth Nicholds. Photos by Robert F. Sisson. 625-640, May 1954
• *See also* Cattle Raising; Hog Raising; Horses; Poultry; Sheep Raising

The **LIVING** Dead Sea. By Harvey Arden. Photos by Nathan Benn. 225-245, Feb. 1978

LIVING Honey Jars of the Ant World. By Ross E. Hutchins. 405-411, Mar. 1962

LIVING in a Japanese Village (Futagami Jima). By William Graves. Photos by James L. Stanfield. 668-693, May 1972

The **LIVING** Sand. By William H. Amos. 820-833, June 1965

The **LIVING** Sands of the Namib. By William J. Hamilton III. Photos by Carol and David Hughes. 364-377, Sept. 1983

LIVING the Good Life in Burgundy. By William Davenport. Photos by Robert Freson. 794-817, June 1978

LIVING Theater in New Guinea's Highlands. By Gillian Gillison. Photos by David Gillison. 147-169, Aug. 1983

The **LIVING** White House. By Lonnelle Aikman. 593-643, Nov. 1966

LIVING With Guanacos. By William L. Franklin. NGS research grant. 63-75, July 1981

LIVING With Thailand's Gentle Lua. By Peter Kunstadter. NGS research grant. 122-152, July 1966

LIVING With the Great Orange Apes: Indonesia's Orangutans. By Biruté M. F. Galdikas. Photos by Rod Brindamour. NGS research grant. 830-853, June 1980

LIZARDS:
◆ *Creepy Crawly Things: Reptiles and Amphibians*. Announced. 728-730, Nov. 1974
● In the Wilds of a City Parlor. By Paul A. Zahl. 645-672, Nov. 1954
● The Lure of the Changing Desert. 817-824, June 1954
■ Reptiles and Amphibians 875A-875B, Dec. 1968
● *See also* Iguanas; Komodo Dragons

LIZARRIETA, Col de, Pyrenees Mountains, Europe:
● Pigeon Netting–Sport of Basques. Photos by Irene Burdett-Scougall. 405-416, Sept. 1949

LOBSTERS AND LOBSTERING:
● The American Lobster, Delectable Cannibal. By Luis Marden. Photos by David Doubilet. 462-487, Apr. 1973
● Maine's Lobster Island, Monhegan. By William P. E. Graves. Photos by Kosti Ruohomaa. 285-298, Feb. 1959
● Martha's Vineyard. By William P. E. Graves. Photos by James P. Blair. 778-809, June 1961
● *See also* Spiny Lobsters

LOCH NESS: The Lake and the Legend. By William S. Ellis. Photos by Emory Kristof and David Doubilet. 759-779, June 1977

LOCKE, JUSTIN:
Author-Photographer:
● Lost Kingdom in Indian Mexico. 517-546, Oct. 1952
Photographer:
● Adobe New Mexico. By Mason Sutherland. 783-830, Dec. 1949
● Amid the Mighty Walls of Zion. By Lewis F. Clark. 37-70, Jan. 1954
● Appalachian Valley Pilgrimage. By Catherine Bell Palmer. 1-32, July 1949
● Grand Canyon: Nature's Story of Creation. By Louis Schellbach. 589-629, May 1955
● Growing Pains Beset Puerto Rico. By William H. Nicholas. 419-460, Apr. 1951
● High Road in the Pyrenees. By H. V. Morton. 299-334, Mar. 1956
● Life in the Land of the Basques. By John E. H. Nolan. 147-186, Feb. 1954
● Mexico's Booming Capital. By Mason Sutherland. 785-824, Dec. 1951
● Miami's Expanding Horizons. By William H. Nicholas. 561-594, Nov. 1950
● New Orleans: Jambalaya on the Levee. By Harnett T. Kane. 143-184, Feb. 1953
● Paris, Home Town of the World. By Donald William Dresden. 767-804, June 1952

DAVID DOUBILET

Lobsters: captive tries to escape trap, *above*; Monhegan Island buoys, *below*

LUIS MARDEN, NGS

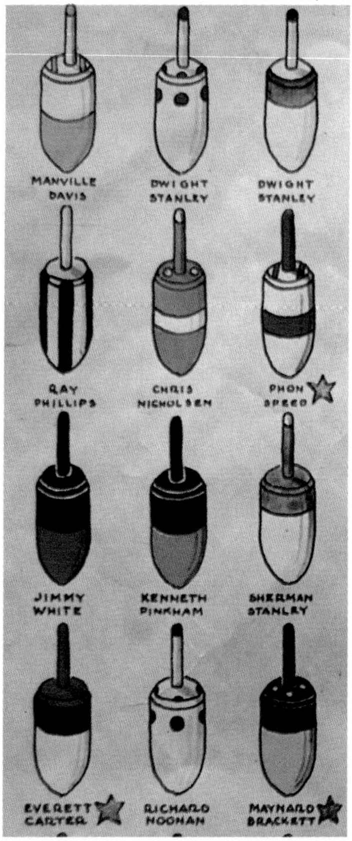

● Shooting Rapids in Dinosaur Country. By Jack Breed. Photos by author and Justin Locke. 363-390, Mar. 1954
● The Smithsonian Institution. By Thomas R. Henry. 325-348, Sept. 1948
● So Much Happens Along the Ohio River. By Frederick Simpich. 177-212, Feb. 1950
● Vizcaya: An Italian Palazzo in Miami. By William H. Nicholas. 595-604, Nov. 1950

LOCKLEY, R. M.: Author:
● The Solemn, Sociable Puffins. 414-422, Sept. 1954

LOCKWOOD, C. C.: Photographer:
● Mississippi Delta: The Land of the River. By Douglas Lee. 226-253, Aug. 1983
● Mississippi's Grand Reunion at the Neshoba County Fair. By Carolyn Bennett Patterson. 854-866, June 1980
● Trouble in Bayou Country: Louisiana's Atchafalaya. By Jack and Anne Rudloe. 377-397, Sept. 1979

LOCUSTS:
● Locusts: "Teeth of the Wind." By Robert A. M. Conley. Photos by Gianni Tortoli. 202-227, Aug. 1969
● Report from the Locust Wars. By Tony and Dickey Chapelle. 545-562, Apr. 1953

LOCUSTS, Seventeen-year:
● Rip Van Winkle of the Underground. By Kenneth F. Weaver. 133-142, July 1953

LOFOTEN (Islands), Norway:
● Fishing in the Lofotens. Photos by Lennart Nilsson. 377-388, Mar. 1947

LOGGERS:
● Idaho Loggers Battle a River. 117-130, July 1951

LOGGING:
● Tropical Rain Forests: Nature's Dwindling Treasures. By Peter T. White. Photos by James P. Blair. Paintings by Barron Storey. 2-47, Jan. 1983

LOIRE RIVER AND VALLEY, France:
● River of Counts and Kings: The Loire. By Kenneth MacLeish. Photos by Dean Conger. 822-869, June 1966

LOLOS (Tribespeople):
● Adventures in Lololand. By Rennold L. Lowy. 105-118, Jan. 1947

LOMBARDY'S Lakes, Blue Jewels in Italy's Crown. By Franc Shor. Photos by Joseph J. Scherschel. 58-99, July 1968

LOMPOC VALLEY, California:
● The Flower Seed Growers: Gardening's Color Merchants. By Robert de Roos. Photos by Jack Fields. 720-738, May 1968

LONDON, England:
● "Around the World in Eighty Days." By Newman Bumstead. 705-750, Dec. 1951

K
L

• "Be Ye Men of Valour" (Churchill's Life; Funeral). By Howard La Fay. 159-197, Aug. 1965
• Benjamin Franklin, Philosopher of Dissent. By Alice J. Hall. Photos by Linda Bartlett. 93-123, July 1975
• The Britain That Shakespeare Knew. By Louis B. Wright. Photos by Dean Conger. 613-665, May 1964
• The British Way. By Sir Evelyn Wrench. 421-541, Apr. 1949
• Chelsea, London's Haven of Individualists. By James Cerruti. Photos by Adam Woolfitt. 28-55, Jan. 1972
• "The City"–London's Storied Square Mile. By Allan C. Fisher, Jr. 735-777, June 1961
• The England of Charles Dickens. By Richard W. Long. Photos by Adam Woolfitt. 443-483, Apr. 1974
• The Final Tribute (Churchill's Funeral). Text by Carolyn Bennett Patterson. 199-225, Aug. 1965
• Founders of New England. By Sir Evelyn Wrench. Photos by B. Anthony Stewart. 803-838, June 1953
• Founders of Virginia. By Sir Evelyn Wrench. Photos by B. Anthony Stewart. 433-462, Apr. 1948
• In the London of the New Queen. By H. V. Morton. 291-342, Sept. 1953
• Keeping House in London. By Frances James. 769-792, Dec. 1947
• Landmarks of Literary England. By Leo A. Borah. Photos by Kathleen Revis. 295-350, Sept. 1955
• London's Zoo of Zoos. By Thomas Garner James. 771-786, June 1953
• One Man's London. By Allan C. Fisher, Jr. Photos by James P. Blair. 743-791, June 1966
• Queen Elizabeth Opens Parliament. By W. E. Roscher. Photos by Robert B. Goodman. 699-707, Nov. 1961
• A Stroll to London. By Isobel Wylie Hutchison. Photos by B. Anthony Stewart. 171-204, Aug. 1950
▪ The Thames. cover, Apr. 1982
• The Thames: That Noble River. By Ethel A. Starbird. Photos by O. Louis Mazzatenta. 750-791, June 1983
• The Thames Mirrors England's Varied Life. By Willard Price. Photos by Robert F. Sisson. 45-93, July 1958
• Two Englands. By Allan C. Fisher, Jr. Photos by Cary Wolinsky. 442-481, Oct. 1979
• The World of Elizabeth I. By Louis B. Wright. Photos by Ted Spiegel. 668-709, Nov. 1968
• *See also* Kew; Royal Academy of Arts

The **"LONE"** Coyote Likes Family Life. By Hope Ryden. Photos by author and David Hiser. 278-294, Aug. 1974

LONE Sailor Completes His Globe-girdling Voyage. By Robin Lee Graham. 504-545, Oct. 1970

LONELY Cape Hatteras, Besieged by the Sea. By William S. Ellis. Photos by Emory Kristof. 393-421, Sept. 1969

LONELY Sentinels of the American West: Basque Sheepherders. By Robert Laxalt. Photos by William Belknap, Jr. 870-888, June 1966

LONELY Wonders of Katmai. By Ernest Gruening. Photos by Winfield Parks. 800-831, June 1963

LONG, GEORGE W.:
• Memorial Tribute to George W. Long (1913-1958). 215, Feb. 1959
Author:
• Eyes on the China Coast. 505-512, Apr. 1953
• Hong Kong Hangs On. Photos by J. Baylor Roberts. 239-272, Feb. 1954
• Indochina Faces the Dragon. Photos by J. Baylor Roberts. 287-328, Sept. 1952
• Journey Into Troubled Iran. Photos by J. Baylor Roberts. 425-464, Oct. 1951
• Land of the Pilgrims' Pride. Photos by Robert F. Sisson. 193-219, Aug. 1947
• Macau, a Hole in the Bamboo Curtain. Photos by J. Baylor Roberts. 679-688, May 1953
• Malaya Meets Its Emergency. Photos by J. Baylor Roberts. 185-228, Feb. 1953
• Many-splendored Glacierland. Photos by Kathleen Revis. 589-636, May 1956
• New Rush to Golden California. 723-802, June 1954
• Occupied Austria, Outpost of Democracy. Photos by Volkmar Wentzel. 749-790, June 1951
• Rhode Island, Modern City-State. Photos by Willard R. Culver. 137-170, Aug. 1948
• Sea to Lakes on the St. Lawrence. Photos by B. Anthony Stewart and John E. Fletcher. 323-366, Sept. 1950
• Yugoslavia, Between East and West. Photos by Volkmar Wentzel. 141-172, Feb. 1951

LONG, MICHAEL E.: Author:
• The Air-Safety Challenge. Photos by Bruce Dale. 209-235, Aug. 1977
• Consider the Sponge. . . . Photos by David Doubilet. 392-407, Mar. 1977
• The Flight of the *Gossamer Condor*. 130-140, Jan. 1978
• Of Air and Space (National Air and Space Museum). By Michael Collins. 819-837, June 1978
Picture portfolio by Nathan Benn, Robert S. Oakes, and Joseph D. Lavenburg, with text by Michael E. Long. 825-837
• Rocks, Ruts, and Sand: Driving the Mexican 1000. 569-575, Oct. 1972
• Spacelab 1: *Columbia*. 301-307, Sept. 1983
• They're Redesigning the Airplane. Photos by James A. Sugar. 76-103, Jan. 1981
• Utah's Rock Art: Wilderness Louvre. A picture essay by Gary Smith, with Michael E. Long. 97-117, Jan. 1980
• Wrestlin' for a Livin' With King Coal. Photos by Michael O'Brien. 793-819, June 1983
Author-Photographer:
• Baja California's Rugged Outback. 543-567, Oct. 1972
• Oshkosh: America's Biggest Air Show. Photos by James A. Sugar and the author. 365-375, Sept. 1979
Photographer:
• Belize, the Awakening Land. By Louis de la Haba. 124-146, Jan. 1972

LONG, RICHARD W.: Author:
• The England of Charles Dickens. Photos by Adam Woolfitt. 443-483, Apr. 1974

The **LONG,** Deep Dive. By Lord Kilbracken. Photos by Bates Littlehales. 718-731, May 1963

The **LONG,** Lonely Leap. By Joseph W. Kittinger, Jr. Photos by Volkmar Wentzel. 854-873, Dec. 1960

LONG Distance Runners: Mexico's Tarahumaras. By James Norman. Photos by David Hiser. 702-718, May 1976

LONG-EARED Owls–Masters of the Night. By Art Wolfe. 31-35, Jan. 1980

A **LONG** History of New Beginnings (National Parks). By Melville Bell Grosvenor. 18-29, July 1979

LONG ISLAND, New York:
• Brooklyn: The Other Side of the Bridge. By Alice J. Hall. Photos by Robert W. Madden. 580-613, May 1983
• A Century Old, the Wonderful Brooklyn Bridge. By John G. Morris. Photos by Donal F. Holway. 565-579, May 1983
• Long Island Outgrows the Country. By Howell Walker. Photos by B. Anthony Stewart. 279-326, Mar. 1951
• Long Island's Quiet Side (East End). By Jane Snow. Photos by Sam Abell. 662-685, May 1980
• *See also* Kings Point (Merchant Marine Academy); Sagamore Hill

LONG ISLAND SOUND, Connecticut-New York:
• *Nomad* Sails Long Island Sound. By Thomas Horgan. 295-338, Sept. 1957

A **LONG** Life, a Good Life on the Potomac. By James L. Stanfield. 470-479, Oct. 1976

LONG-NECKED WOMEN:
• Anatomy of a Burmese Beauty Secret. By John M. Keshishian. 798-801, June 1979

The **LONGEST** Manned Balloon Flight. By Ed Yost. 208-217, Feb. 1977

LONGEVITY:
• "Every Day Is a Gift When You Are Over 100." By Alexander Leaf. Photos by John Launois. 93-119, Jan. 1973

LONGFELLOW, HENRY WADSWORTH:
• Literary Landmarks of Massachu-

setts. By William H. Nicholas. Photos by B. Anthony Stewart and John E. Fletcher. 279-310, Mar. 1950

LONGHORNS (Cattle):
• The Wichitas: Land of the Living Prairie. By M. Woodbridge Williams. 661-697, May 1957

LONGSHIPS:
• The Vikings. By Howard La Fay. Photos by Ted Spiegel. 492-541, Apr. 1970

LONGWOOD GARDENS, Kennett Square, Pennsylvania:
• Wonderland in Longwood Gardens. By Edward C. Ferriday, Jr. 45-64, July 1951

A **LOOK** at Alaska's Tundra. By Russell D. Guthrie and Paul A. Zahl. 294-337, Mar. 1972

LOOK of a Land Beloved. Photos by Dewitt Jones. 444-467, Apr. 1976

LOOK What's Happened to Honolulu! By Jim Becker. Photos by Bates Littlehales. 500-531, Oct. 1969

LOONEY, RALPH: Author:
• The Navajos. Photos by Bruce Dale. 740-781, Dec. 1972

LORD, NANCY: Photographer:
• Jericho Gives Up Its Secrets. By Kathleen M. Kenyon and A. Douglas Tushingham. 853-870, Dec. 1953

LORIKEETS:
• Honey Eaters of Currumbin. By Paul A. Zahl. 510-519, Oct. 1956

LOS ALAMOS, New Mexico:
• Adobe New Mexico. By Mason Sutherland. Photos by Justin Locke. 783-830, Dec. 1949

LOS ALAMOS SCIENTIFIC LABORATORY, New Mexico:
• The Search for Tomorrow's Power. By Kenneth F. Weaver. Photos by Emory Kristof. 650-681, Nov. 1972

LOS ANGELES, California:
• California, the Golden Magnet. 595-679, May 1966
I. The South. By William Graves. Photos by Thomas Nebbia. 595-639
• Los Angeles: City in Search of Itself. By William S. Ellis. Photos by Jodi Cobb. 26-59, Jan. 1979
• Los Angeles, City of the Angels. By Robert de Roos. Photos by Thomas Nebbia. 451-501, Oct. 1962
• The Mexican Americans: A People on the Move. By Griffin Smith, Jr. Photos by Stephanie Maze. 780-809, June 1980
• New Rush to Golden California. By George W. Long. 723-802, June 1954
• Southern California's Trial by Mud and Water. By Nathaniel T. Kenney. Photos by Bruce Dale. 552-573, Oct. 1969
• *See also* Los Angeles Aqueduct

LOS ANGELES AQUEDUCT:
• California's Parched Oasis, the Owens Valley. By Judith and Neil Morgan. Photos by Jodi Cobb and Galen Rowell. 98-127, Jan. 1976
• The Troubled Waters of Mono Lake. By Gordon Young. Photos by Craig Aurness. 504-519, Oct. 1981

LOS ANGELES BASIN, California:
• Southern California's Trial by Mud and Water. By Nathaniel T. Kenney. Photos by Bruce Dale. 552-573, Oct. 1969

LOST COLONY. *See* Roanoke Island, North Carolina

The **LOST** Empire of the Incas. By Loren McIntyre. Art by Ned and Rosalie Seidler. 729-787, Dec. 1973

The **LOST** Fleet of Kublai Khan. By Torao Mozai. Photos by Koji Nakamura. Paintings by Issho Yada. 634-649, Nov. 1982

LOST Kingdom in Indian Mexico. By Justin Locke. 517-546, Oct. 1952

LOST Outpost of the Egyptian Empire. By Trude Dothan. Photos by Sisse Brimberg. Paintings by Lloyd K. Townsend. NGS research grant. 739-769, Dec. 1982

LOST Ship Waits Under Arctic Ice *(Breadalbane).* By Joseph B. MacInnis. Photos by Emory Kristof. 104A-104D, July 1983

The **LOST SIERRA,** California:
• Golden Ghosts of the Lost Sierra. By Robert Laxalt. Photos by David Hiser. 332-353, Sept. 1973

LOST World of the Galapagos. By Irving and Electa Johnson. 681-703, May 1959

LOSTWOOD WILDLIFE REFUGE, North Dakota:
• Island, Prairie, Marsh, and Shore. By Charlton Ogburn. Photos by Bates Littlehales. 350-381, Mar. 1979

LOTUKA (Tribespeople):
• South in the Sudan. By Harry Hoogstraal. 249-272, Feb. 1953

LOUDER, MAX:
• North With the Wheat Cutters. By Noel Grove. Photos by James A. Sugar. 194-217, Aug. 1972

LOUGHEED, R. E.: Artist:
• Dogs Work for Man. By Edward J. Linehan. Paintings by Edwin Megargee and R. E. Lougheed. 190-233, Aug. 1958

LOUISBOURG (Fortress), Nova Scotia:
• Nova Scotia, the Magnificent Anchorage. By Charles McCarry. Photos by Gordon W. Gahan. 334-363, Mar. 1975
• The St. Lawrence, River Key to Canada. By Howard La Fay. Photos by John Launois. 622-667, May 1967

LOUISE, Lake, Canada:
• Canadian Rockies, Lords of a Beckoning Land. By Alan Phillips. Photos by James L. Stanfield. 353-393, Sept. 1966

LOUISIADE ARCHIPELAGO, Pacific Ocean:
• Adventures with the Survey Navy. By Irving Johnson. 131-148, July 1947

BOTH BY JODI COBB, NGS

Los Angeles: Dodger dugout clowns, *above;* downtown urban renewal, *below*

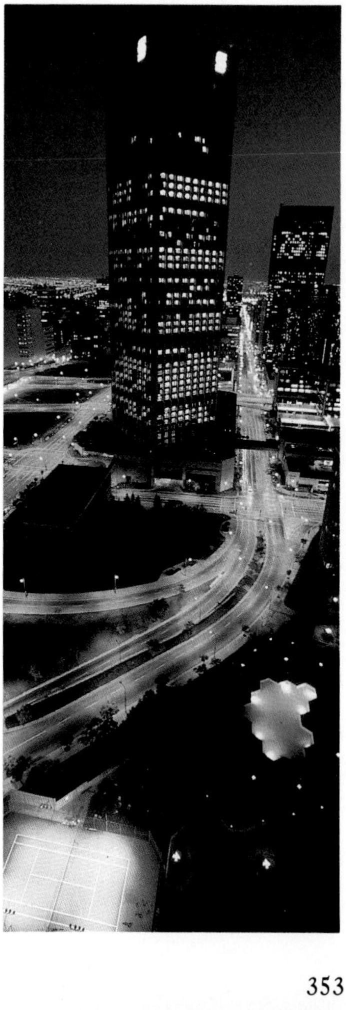

K L

BRUCE DALE, NGS

The Louvre: the "Venus de Milo"

LOUISIANA:
- Cajunland, Louisiana's French-speaking Coast. By Bern Keating. Photos by Charles Harbutt and Franke Keating. 353-391, Mar. 1966
- The Gulf's Workaday Waterway. By Gordon Young. Photos by Charles O'Rear. 200-223, Feb. 1978
- Land of Louisiana Sugar Kings. By Harnett T. Kane. Photos by Willard R. Culver. 531-567, Apr. 1958
- Louisiana Trades with the World. By Frederick Simpich. Photos by J. Baylor Roberts. 705-738, Dec. 1947
- The Lower Mississippi. By Willard Price. Photos by W. D. Vaughn. 681-725, Nov. 1960
- Skyway Below the Clouds. By Carl R. Markwith. Photos by Ernest J. Cottrell. Included: Monroe; Shreveport; Shreveport Municipal Airport. 85-108, July 1949
- Trouble in Bayou Country: Louisiana's Atchafalaya. By Jack and Anne Rudloe. Photos by C. C. Lockwood. 377-397, Sept. 1979
- A Walk Across America: Part II. By Peter and Barbara Jenkins. 194-229, Aug. 1979
- *See also* Mississippi River Delta; New Orleans

LOUSMA, JACK R.:
- Skylab, Outpost on the Frontier of Space. By Thomas Y. Canby. Photos by the nine mission astronauts. 441-469, Oct. 1974

The **LOUVRE,** Paris:
- The Louvre, France's Palace of the Arts. By Hereward Lester Cooke, Jr. 796-831, June 1971

LOVELL, JAMES A., Jr.:
- Hubbard Medal recipient. 861, June 1970
- "A Most Fantastic Voyage": The Story of Apollo 8's Rendezvous With the Moon. By Sam C. Phillips. 593-631, May 1969
- Space Rendezvous, Milestone on the Way to the Moon. By Kenneth F. Weaver. 539-553, Apr. 1966

LOVELL, TOM: Artist:
- In the Footsteps of Alexander the Great. By Helen and Frank Schreider. 1-65, Jan. 1968

LOVINS, AMORY B.:
- What Six Experts Say. 70-73, *Special Report on Energy* (Feb. 1981)

LOW COUNTRIES, Europe:
- ▲ *France, Belgium, and the Netherlands,* Atlas series supplement. June 1960
- *See also* Belgium; Luxembourg; Netherlands

LOWE, GEORGE: Photographer:
- The Crossing of Antarctica. By Sir Vivian Fuchs. 25-47, Jan. 1959
- Triumph on Everest. 1-63, July 1954

I. Siege and Assault. By Sir John Hunt. 1-43; II. The Conquest of the Summit. By Sir Edmund Hillary. 45-63

LOWELL, JAMES RUSSELL:
- Literary Landmarks of Massachusetts. By William H. Nicholas. Photos by B. Anthony Stewart and John E. Fletcher. 279-310, Mar. 1950

LOWELL, Massachusetts:
- The Merrimack: River of Industry and Romance. By Albert W. Atwood. Photos by B. Anthony Stewart. 106-140, Jan. 1951

LOWELL OBSERVATORY, Arizona: Expedition:
- New Light on the Changing Face of Mars. By E. C. Slipher. NGS research grant. 427-436, Sept. 1955

LOWER CALIFORNIA. *See* Baja California

The **LOWER** Keys, Florida's "Out Islands." By John Scofield. Photos by Emory Kristof and Bates Littlehales. 72-93, Jan. 1971

The **LOWER** Mississippi. By Willard Price. Photos by W. D. Vaughn. 681-725, Nov. 1960

LOWER SLAUGHTER, England:
- By Cotswold Lanes to Wold's End. By Melville Bell Grosvenor. 615-654, May 1948

LOWER SOURIS NATIONAL WILDLIFE REFUGE, North Dakota:
- Duck Hunting with a Color Camera. By Arthur A. Allen. 514-539, Oct. 1951

LOWMAN, PAUL D., Jr.: Author:
- The Earth From Orbit. 645-671, Nov. 1966

LOWREY, PERRY:
- Jungle Journey to the World's Highest Waterfall. By Ruth Robertson. 655-690, Nov. 1949

LOWY, RENNOLD L.:
Author-Photographer:
- Adventures in Lololand. 105-118, Jan. 1947

The **LOYALISTS** (Tories): Americans With a Difference. By Kent Britt. Photos by Ted Spiegel. 510-539, Apr. 1975

LUA (People):
- Living With Thailand's Gentle Lua. By Peter Kunstadter. NGS research grant. 122-152, July 1966

LUBUMBASHI, Zaire. *See* former name, Elisabethville, Democratic Republic of the Congo

LUCERNE, Switzerland:
- Switzerland Guards the Roof of Europe. By William H. Nicholas. Photos by Willard R. Culver. 205-246, Aug. 1950

LUDWIG, DANIEL KEITH:
- Amazon–The River Sea. By Loren McIntyre. Included: Daniel K. Ludwig's planned paper-pulp and food-production enterprise in Brazil's Amazon basin. 456-495, Oct. 1972
- Brazil's Wild Frontier. By Loren McIntyre. Included: Daniel K. Ludwig's three-million acre agricultural and forestry enterprise. 684-719, Nov. 1977
- Jari: A Billion-dollar Gamble. By Loren McIntyre. Contents: Daniel K. Ludwig's paper-pulp and food-production enterprise in Brazil's Amazon Basin. 686-711, May 1980

LUHIT (River), China-India:
● Caught in the Assam-Tibet Earthquake. By F. Kingdon-Ward. 403-416, Mar. 1952

LULLINGSTONE CASTLE, England:
● Silkworms in England Spin for the Queen. By John E. H. Nolan. 689-704, May 1953

LUMBER INDUSTRY:
● Backwoods Japan During American Occupation. By M. A. Huberman. 491-518, Apr. 1947
● Beauty and Bounty of Southern State Trees. By William A. Dayton. Paintings by Walter A. Weber. 508-552, Oct. 1957
● Canada's Dynamic Heartland, Ontario. By Marjorie Wilkins Campbell. Photos by Winfield Parks. 58-97, July 1963
● Canada's Window on the Pacific: The British Columbia Coast. By Jules B. Billard. Photos by Ted Spiegel. 338-375, Mar. 1972
● From Sagebrush to Roses on the Columbia. By Leo A. Borah. 571-611, Nov. 1952
● Louisiana Trades With the World. By Frederick Simpich. Photos by J. Baylor Roberts. 705-738, Dec. 1947
● Madawaska: Down East With a French Accent. By Perry Garfinkel. Photos by Cary Wolinsky. 380-409, Sept. 1980
● Ontario, Pivot of Canada's Power. By Andrew H. Brown. Photos by B. Anthony Stewart and Bates Littlehales. 823-852, Dec. 1953
● Oregon's Lovely, Lonely Coast. By Mark Miller. Photos by Cotton Coulson. 798-823, Dec. 1979
● Our National Forests: Problems in Paradise. By Rowe Findley. Photos by David Cupp. 306-339, Sept. 1982
■ Rain Forest. 824, Dec. 1982
● Redwoods, Rain, and Lots of Room: California's North Coast. By Judith and Neil Morgan. Photos by Dewitt Jones. 330-363, Sept. 1977
● Timber: How Much Is Enough? By John J. Putman. Photos by Bruce Dale. 485-511, Apr. 1974
● Tropical Rain Forests: Nature's Dwindling Treasures. By Peter T. White. Photos by James P. Blair. Paintings by Barron Storey. 2-47, Jan. 1983
● Versatile Wood Waits on Man. By Andrew H. Brown. 109-140, July 1951
● Wealth and Wonder of Northern State Trees. By William A. Dayton. Paintings by Walter A. Weber. 651-691, Nov. 1955

LUMINESCENCE. *See* Bioluminescence; *and* Fluorescent Gems

LUNAR ORBITERS (Satellites):
● Awesome Views of the Forbidding Moonscape. Contents: Photos by Lunar Orbiter 2, 4, 5. 233-239, Feb. 1969

LUNAR RESEARCH:
● And Now to Touch the Moon's Forbidding Face. By Kenneth F. Weaver. 633-635, May 1969
● Awesome Views of the Forbidding Moonscape. Contents: Photos by Lunar Orbiter 2, 4, 5. 233-239, Feb. 1969
● What the Moon Rocks Tell Us. By Kenneth F. Weaver. Included: Lunar Receiving Laboratory at the Manned Spacecraft Center in Houston, Texas. 788-791, Dec. 1969
● *See also* Apollo Missions; Ranger Spacecraft; Surveyor Spacecraft; *and* Moon

LUNDY (Island), England:
● Lundy, Treasure Island of Birds. By P. T. Etherton. Photos by J. Allan Cash. 675-698, May 1947

LUPE, RONNIE:
● The White Mountain Apache. 260-290, Feb. 1980
Coming of Age the Apache Way. By Nita Quintero. Photos by Bill Hess. 262-271; Seeking the Best of Two Worlds. By Bill Hess. 272-290
Author:
● At Peace With the Past, In Step With the Future. 260-261, Feb. 1980

LUQUE, MICHAEL H.:
Author-Photographer:
● Among Alaska's Brown Bears. By Allan L. Egbert and Michael H. Luque. 428-442, Sept. 1975

The **LURE** of the Changing Desert. 817-824, June 1954

LUTHER, MARTIN:
● The World of Martin Luther. By Merle Severy. Photos by James L. Amos. 418-463, Oct. 1983

LÜTKEN, EMIL: Photographer:
● The Shy and Spectacular Kingfisher. Photos by Carl-Johan Junge and Emil Lütken. 413-419, Sept. 1974

LUXEMBOURG:
● Luxembourg, Survivor of Invasions. By Sydney Clark. Photos by Maynard Owen Williams. 791-810, June 1948
● Luxembourg, the Quiet Fortress. By Robert Leslie Conly. Photos by Ted H. Funk. 69-97, July 1970

LUZ, HORST: Photographer:
● Proud Primitives, the Nuba People. By Oskar Luz. 673-699, Nov. 1966

LUZ, OSKAR: Author:
● Proud Primitives, the Nuba People. Photos by Horst Luz. 673-699, Nov. 1966

LYNDON B. JOHNSON SPACE CENTER, Houston, Texas. *See* former name, Manned Spacecraft Center

LYON, EUGENE: Author:
● *Atocha,* Tragic Treasure Galleon of the Florida Keys. 787-809, June 1976
● Treasure From the Ghost Galleon: *Santa Margarita.* Photos by Don Kincaid. 228-243, Feb. 1982

LYREBIRD, Australia's Meistersinger. By L. H. Smith. 849-857, June 1955

The **LYRIC** Land of Wales. By Bryan Hodgson. Photos by Farrell Grehan. 36-63, July 1983

M

MACAO (Macau):
● China's Opening Door. By John J. Putman. Photos by H. Edward Kim. Included: Zhuhai Special Economic Zone, adjoining Macau. 64-83, July 1983
● Eyes on the China Coast. By George W. Long. 505-512, Apr. 1953
● Macao Clings to the Bamboo Curtain. By Jules B. Billard. Photos by Joseph J. Scherschel. 521-539, Apr. 1969
● Macau, a Hole in the Bamboo Curtain. By George W. Long. Photos by J. Baylor Roberts. 679-688, May 1953

MacARTHUR, DOUGLAS:
● Japan Tries Freedom's Road. By Frederick G. Vosburgh. Photos by J. Baylor Roberts. 593-632, May 1950

McBAIN, DONALD: Photographer:
● Beltsville Brings Science to the Farm. By Samuel W. Matthews. 199-218, Aug. 1953
● Stately Homes of Old Virginia. By Albert W. Atwood. 787-802, June 1953
● The Wild Animals in My Life. By William M. Mann. 497-524, Apr. 1957
● Williamsburg: Its College and Its Cinderella City. By Beverley M. Bowie. 439-486, Oct. 1954

McBRIDE, HARRY A.: Author:
● Masterpieces on Tour. 717-750, Dec. 1948

McCARRY, CHARLES: Author:
● The Civilizing Seine. Photos by David L. Arnold. 478-511, Apr. 1982
● Heart of the Bluegrass. Photos by J. Bruce Baumann. 634-659, May 1974
● Home to the Enduring Berkshires. Photos by Jonathan S. Blair. 196-221, Aug. 1970
● Kyoto and Nara: Keepers of Japan's Past. Photos by George F. Mobley. 836-851, June 1976
● New Zealand's North Island: The Contented Land. Photos by Bates Littlehales. 190-213, Aug. 1974
● Nova Scotia, the Magnificent Anchorage. Photos by Gordon W. Gahan. 334-363, Mar. 1975
● Utah's Shining Oasis. Photos by James L. Amos. 440-473, Apr. 1975
● Yesterday Lingers Along the Connecticut. Photos by David L. Arnold. 334-369, Sept. 1972

McCLELLAN-KERR ARKANSAS RIVER NAVIGATION SYSTEM:
● Oklahoma, the Adventurous One. By Robert Paul Jordan. Photos by Robert W. Madden. 149-189, Aug. 1971

McCONNELL RIVER REGION, Canada:
● Beyond the North Wind With the Snow Goose. By Des and Jen Bartlett. 822-843, Dec. 1973
. . . And Then There Was Fred. . . . 843-847

McCRANE, MARION P.: Author:
• Zoo Animals Go to School. Photos by W. E. Garrett. 694-706, Nov. 1956

MacCREADY, PAUL B.:
• The Flight of the *Gossamer Condor*. By Michael E. Long. 130-140, Jan. 1978
• Winged Victory of *Gossamer Albatross*. By Bryan Allen. 640-651, Nov. 1979

McCUE, J. J. G.: Author:
• How Bats Hunt With Sound. 571-578, Apr. 1961

McCURDY, ARTHUR W.:
Photographer:
• 1898: The Bells on Sable. 408-409, 416-417, Sept. 1965

McCURRY, STEVE: Photographer:
• Beirut–Up From the Rubble. By William S. Ellis. 262-286, Feb. 1983
• Pakistan's Kalash: People of Fire and Fervor. By Debra Denker. 458-473, Oct. 1981

McDADE, MATT C.: Author:
• New York State's New Main Street. 567-618, Nov. 1956

McDIVITT, JAMES A.:
• America's 6,000-mile Walk in Space. 440-447, Sept. 1965

McDONALD, EDWIN A.: Author:
• Exploring Antarctica's Phantom Coast. Photos by W. D. Vaughn. 251-273, Feb. 1962

McDONALD, EUGENE F., Jr.:
• The Society's Hubbard Medal Awarded to Commander MacMillan. Note: Lieutenant Commander McDonald, present at the ceremony, was a member of the 1925 National Geographic Society–United States Navy MacMillan Arctic Expedition. 563-564, Apr. 1953

McDOWELL, BART: Author:
• Avalanche! Photos by John E. Fletcher. 855-880, June 1962
• The Aztecs. Photos by David Hiser. Paintings by Felipe Dávalos. 714-751, Dec. 1980
• Brazil's Golden Beachhead. Photos by Nicholas DeVore III. 246-277, Feb. 1978
• The Changing Face of Old Spain. Photos by Albert Moldvay. 291-339, Mar. 1965
• Crosscurrents Sweep the Indian Ocean. Photos by Steve Raymer. 422-457, Oct. 1981
• Deerfield Keeps a Truce With Time. Photos by Robert W. Madden. 780-809, June 1969
• Earthquake in Guatemala. Photos by W. E. Garrett and Robert W. Madden. 810-829, June 1976
• Hungary: Changing Homeland of a Tough, Romantic People. Photos by Albert Moldvay and Joseph J. Scherschel. 443-483, Apr. 1971
• Melville Bell Grosvenor, A Decade of Innovation, a Lifetime of Service. 270-278, Aug. 1982
• Mexico in Motion. Photos by Kip Ross. 490-537, Oct. 1961
• Mexico's Window on the Past. Photos by B. Anthony Stewart. 492-519, Oct. 1968
• The Most Mexican City, Guadalajara. Photos by Volkmar Wentzel. 412-441, Mar. 1967
• Orissa, Past and Promise in an Indian State. Photos by James P. Blair. 546-577, Oct. 1970
• The Panama Canal Today. Photos by George F. Mobley. 279-294, Feb. 1978
• Puerto Rico's Seven-league Bootstraps. Photos by B. Anthony Stewart. 755-793, Dec. 1962
• Thailand: Luck of a Land in the Middle. Photos by Steve Raymer. 500-535, Oct. 1982
• Theodore Roosevelt: a Centennial Tribute. 572-590, Oct. 1958
• Those Successful Japanese. Photos by Fred Ward. 323-359, Mar. 1974

MACEDON (Ancient Kingdom):
• Regal Treasures From a Macedonian Tomb. By Manolis Andronicos. Photos by Spyros Tsavdaroglou. 55-77, July 1978

MACEDONIA (Republic), Yugoslavia:
• Yugoslavia: Six Republics in One. By Robert Paul Jordan. Photos by James P. Blair. 589-633, May 1970

McELROY, WILLIAM D.:
• Torchbearers of the Twilight (Fireflies). By Frederick G. Vosburgh. 697-704, May 1951

MacFARLAND, CRAIG:
Author-Photographer:
• Giant Tortoises: Goliaths of the Galapagos. Photos by author and Jan MacFarland. 632-649, Nov. 1972

MacFARLAND, JAN: Photographer:
• Giant Tortoises: Goliaths of the Galapagos. By Craig MacFarland. Photos by author and Jan MacFarland. 632-649, Nov. 1972

McGAHAN, JERRY: Author:
• The Condor, Soaring Spirit of the Andes. Photos by Libby McGahan. 684-709, May 1971

McGAHAN, LIBBY: Photographer:
• The Condor, Soaring Spirit of the Andes. By Jerry McGahan. 684-709, May 1971

MACHIGUENGA INDIANS:
• Amazon–The River Sea. By Loren McIntyre. 456-495, Oct. 1972
• By Parachute Into Peru's Lost World. By G. Brooks Baekeland. Photos by author and Peter R. Gimbel. 268-296, Aug. 1964

MACHU PICCHU, Peru:
• The Five Worlds of Peru. By Kenneth F. Weaver. Photos by Bates Littlehales. 213-265, Feb. 1964
• Peru, Homeland of the Warlike Inca. By Kip Ross. Contents: National Geographic Society–Yale University expeditions. 421-462, Oct. 1950

MacINNIS, JOSEPH B.: Author:
• Diving Beneath Arctic Ice. Photos by William R. Curtsinger. 248-267, Aug. 1973
• Exploring a 140-year-old Ship Under Arctic Ice *(Breadalbane)*. Photos by Emory Kristof. 104A-104D, July 1983

McINTOSH, SUSAN and RODERICK:
Authors:
• Finding West Africa's Oldest City. Photos by Michael and Aubine Kirtley. 396-418, Sept. 1982

McINTYRE, LOREN:
• Editorials. By Gilbert M. Grosvenor. 295, Mar. 1975; By Wilbur E. Garrett. 553, Nov. 1982
Author-Photographer:
• Amazon–The River Sea. 456-495, Oct. 1972
• Brazil's Wild Frontier. 684-719, Nov. 1977
• Colombia, from Amazon to Spanish Main. 235-273, Aug. 1970
• Ecuador–Low and Lofty Land Astride the Equator. 259-298, Feb. 1968
• Flamboyant Is the Word for Bolivia. 153-195, Feb. 1966
• Jari: A Billion-dollar Gamble. Contents: Daniel K. Ludwig's paper-pulp and food-production enterprise in Brazil's Amazon Basin. 686-711, May 1980
• The Lost Empire of the Incas. Art by Ned and Rosalie Seidler. 729-787, Dec. 1973
• Which Way Now for Argentina? 296-333, Mar. 1975
Photographer:
• The Amazon. 445-455, Oct. 1972
• Mystery of the Ancient Nazca Lines. 716-728, May 1975
• Peru's Pilgrimage to the Sky. By Robert Randall. Photos by Loren McIntyre and Ira Block. 60-69, July 1982

MACKAY, DONALD A.: Artist:
• How Soon Will We Measure In Metric? By Kenneth F. Weaver. 287-294, Aug. 1977

MACKENZIE, ALEXANDER:
• Across Canada by Mackenzie's Track. By Ralph Gray. 191-239, Aug. 1955

MACKENZIE MOUNTAINS, Canada:
• Nahanni: Canada's Wilderness Park. By Douglas H. Chadwick. Photos by Matt Bradley. 396-420, Sept. 1981

MACKEY, CAROL J.: Author:
• Chan Chan, Peru's Ancient City of Kings. By Michael E. Moseley and Carol J. Mackey. Photos by David Brill. 318-345, Mar. 1973

McKINLEY, WILLIAM:
• Inside the White House. By Lonnelle Aikman. Photos by B. Anthony Stewart and Thomas Nebbia. 3-43, Jan. 1961
• The Living White House. By Lonnelle Aikman. 593-643, Nov. 1966
• Profiles of the Presidents: III. The American Giant Comes of Age. By Frank Freidel. 660-711, May 1965

McKINLEY, Mount, Alaska:
• Mount McKinley Conquered by New Route. By Bradford Washburn. 219-248, Aug. 1953

• New Mount McKinley Challenge–Trekking Around the Continent's Highest Peak. By Ned Gillette. 66-79, July 1979
• Wildlife of Mount McKinley National Park. By Adolph Murie. Paintings by Walter A. Weber. 249-270, Aug. 1953

McKNEW, THOMAS W.:
• Achievements and awards. 582, Apr. 1962; 588, 590, Oct. 1967
• Anniversary, twenty-fifth, with the Society: Board of Trustees dinner. 423, Mar. 1957
• Board of Trustees, Advisory Chairman. 576, 579, 588, 590, Oct. 1967; 529, Apr. 1968; 861, June 1970; 227, Aug. 1976
• Board of Trustees, Chairman. 484, Oct. 1966; 588, Oct. 1967
• Board of Trustees, Life Trustee. 588, Oct. 1967
• Board of Trustees, Vice Chairman. 579, 582, Apr. 1962; 583, 626, Oct. 1963; 484, Oct. 1966; 274, Aug. 1982
• Building Committee, Chairman. 673, May 1964; 588, Oct. 1967
• National Geographic Society Trustees Elect Key Executives. 576-590, Oct. 1967
• Secretary. 586, May 1947; 835, 836, Dec. 1959; 588, Oct. 1967
• Vice President of NGS. 419, 420, 421, 423, Mar. 1957; 866, 867, Dec. 1957; 793, June 1958
• Vice President, Executive, of NGS. 834, 835, 836, Dec. 1959; 882, 883, Dec. 1960; 881, Dec. 1961; 579, 580, 582, Apr. 1962; 588, Oct. 1967
Author:
• Fledgling Wings of the Air Force. 266-271, Aug. 1957
• Four-ocean Navy in the Nuclear Age. 145-187, Feb. 1965
• We Followed Peary to the Pole. By Gilbert Grosvenor and Thomas W. McKnew. 469-484, Oct. 1953

MacLEISH, ARCHIBALD:
• Editorial. By Gilbert M. Grosvenor. 437, Apr. 1976
Author:
• Robert Frost and New England. 438-444, Apr. 1976
• The Thrush on the Island of Barra. 692-693, May 1970

MacLEISH, KENNETH: Author:
• Abraham, the Friend of God. Photos by Dean Conger. 739-789, Dec. 1966
• Canterbury Cathedral. Photos by Thomas Nebbia. 364-379, Mar. 1976
• Chartres: Legacy From the Age of Faith. Photos by Dean Conger. 857-882, Dec. 1969
• Cyprus Under Four Flags: A Struggle for Unity. Photos by Jonathan Blair. 356-383, Mar. 1973
• Diving With Sea Snakes. Photos by Ben Cropp. 565-578, Apr. 1972
• Exploring Australia's Coral Jungle. 743-779, June 1973
• Help for Philippine Tribes in Trouble. Photos by Dean Conger. 220-255, Aug. 1971
• The Highlands, Stronghold of Scottish Gaeldom. Photos by Winfield Parks. 398-435, Mar. 1968
• Île de la Cité, Birthplace of Paris. Photos by Bruce Dale. 680-719, May 1968
• Isles on the Edge of the Sea: Scotland's Outer Hebrides. Photos by Thomas Nebbia. 676-711, May 1970
• Java–Eden in Transition. Photos by Dean Conger. 1-43, Jan. 1971
• The Land of Galilee. Photos by B. Anthony Stewart. 832-865, Dec. 1965
• Leonardo da Vinci: A Man for All Ages. Photos by James L. Amos. 296-329, Sept. 1977
• Martinique: Liberté, Egalité, and Uncertainty in the Caribbean. Photos by John Launois. 124-148, Jan. 1975
• Mont Saint Michel. Photos by Cotton Coulson. 820-831, June 1977
• Quebec: French City in an Anglo-Saxon World. Photos by James L. Stanfield and Declan Haun. 416-442, Mar. 1971
• Queensland: Young Titan of Australia's Tropic North. Photos by Winfield Parks. 593-639, Nov. 1968
• Reunited Jerusalem Faces Its Problems. Photos by Ted Spiegel. 835-871, Dec. 1968
• River of Counts and Kings: The Loire. Photos by Dean Conger. 822-869, June 1966
• Scotland's Inner Hebrides: Isles of the Western Sea. Photos by R. Stephen Uzzell III. 690-717, Nov. 1974
• Singapore, Reluctant Nation. Photos by Winfield Parks. 269-300, Aug. 1966
• The Tasadays, Stone Age Cavemen of Mindanao. Photos by John Launois. 219-249, Aug. 1972
• A Taxi for the Deep Frontier. Photos by Bates Littlehales. 139-150, Jan. 1968
• The Top End of Down Under. Photos by Thomas Nebbia. 145-174, Feb. 1973
• Western Australia, the Big Country. Photos by James L. Stanfield. 150-187, Feb. 1975

MacLEOD CLAN:
• Over the Sea to Scotland's Skye. By Robert J. Reynolds. 87-112, July 1952

MacMILLAN, DONALD BAXTER:
• Far North with "Captain Mac." By Miriam MacMillan. 465-513, Oct. 1951
• The Society's Hubbard Medal Awarded to Commander MacMillan. 563-564, Apr. 1953
• A Visit to the Living Ice Age. By Rutherford Platt. Included: MacMillan's route in the *Bowdoin*. 525-545, Apr. 1957

MacMILLAN, MIRIAM: Author:
• Far North with "Captain Mac." 465-513, Oct. 1951

McMURDO STATION, Antarctica:
• First Flight Across the Bottom of the World. By James R. Reedy. Photos by Otis Imboden. 454-464, Mar. 1964
• Flight Into Antarctic Darkness. By J. Lloyd Abbot, Jr. Photos by David S. Boyer. 732-738, Nov. 1967
• What We've Accomplished in Antarctica. By George J. Dufek. 527-557, Oct. 1959

MacNEIL, NORMAN M.:
Photographer:
• Square-rigger in a Tempest *(Pamir)*. 703-710, May 1948

McNEIL RIVER STATE GAME SANCTUARY, Alaska:
• Among Alaska's Brown Bears. By Allan L. Egbert and Michael H. Luque. 428-442, Sept. 1975

McPHEE, JOHN: Author:
• The People of New Jersey's Pine Barrens. Photos by William R. Curtsinger. 52-77, Jan. 1974

MACQUARIE ISLAND, South Pacific Ocean:
• Nature's Clown, the Penguin. By David Hellyer and Malcolm Davis. 405-428, Sept. 1952

MacSWAIN, J. W.: Author:
• Crossroads of the Insect World. Photos by Edward S. Ross. 844-857, Dec. 1966

MADAGASCAR:
• Crosscurrents Sweep the Indian Ocean. By Bart McDowell. Photos by Steve Raymer. 422-457, Oct. 1981
• Madagascar: Island at the End of the Earth. By Luis Marden. Photos by Albert Moldvay. 443-487, Oct. 1967
• Re-creating Madagascar's Giant Extinct Bird. By Alexander Wetmore. 488-493, Oct. 1967
• The World in Your Garden. By W. H. Camp. Paintings by Else Bostelmann. Included: Plant Marvels of Madagascar (Flamboyant or Royal Poinciana, Crown-of-thorns, Travelers-tree). 1-65, July 1947

MA'DAN (Tribespeople):
• Marsh Dwellers of Southern Iraq. By Wilfred Thesiger. Photos by Gavin Maxwell. 205-239, Feb. 1958
• Water Dwellers in a Desert World. By Gavin Young. Photos by Nik Wheeler. 502-523, Apr. 1976

MADAWASKA: Down East With a French Accent. By Perry Garfinkel. Photos by Cary Wolinsky. 380-409, Sept. 1980

MADDEN, ROBERT W.: Photographer:
• Antarctica: Icy Testing Ground for Space. By Samuel W. Matthews. 569-592, Oct. 1968
• Brooklyn: The Other Side of the Bridge. By Alice J. Hall. 580-613, May 1983
• China Unveils Her Newest Treasures. 848-857, Dec. 1974
• Deerfield Keeps a Truce With Time. By Bart McDowell. 780-809, June 1969
• Domesticating the Wild and Woolly Musk Ox. By John J. Teal, Jr. 862-879, June 1970
• Earthquake in Guatemala. By Bart McDowell. Photos by W. E. Garrett and Robert W. Madden. 810-829, June 1976
• Hawaii, Island of Fire and Flowers. By Gordon Young. 399-425, Mar. 1975

M N

• Hurricane! By Ben Funk. 346-379, Sept. 1980
Dominica. By Fred Ward. 357-359; Dynamics of a Hurricane. 370-371; Into the Eye of David. By John L. Eliot. 368-369; Paths of Fury–This Century's Worst American Storms. 360-361
• Kauai, the Island That's Still Hawaii. By Ethel A. Starbird. 584-613, Nov. 1977
• Maryland on the Half Shell. By Stuart E. Jones. 188-229, Feb. 1972
• Mobile, Alabama's City in Motion. By William Graves. Photos by Joseph J. Scherschel and Robert W. Madden. 368-397, Mar. 1968
• Oklahoma, the Adventurous One. By Robert Paul Jordan. 149-189, Aug. 1971
• Old Salem, Morning Star of Moravian Faith. By Rowe Findley. 818-837, Dec. 1970
• Quicksilver and Slow Death. By John J. Putman. 507-527, Oct. 1972
• Sydney: Big, Breezy, and a Bloomin' Good Show. By Ethel A. Starbird. 211-235, Feb. 1979
• Toronto: Canada's Dowager Learns to Swing. By Ethel A. Starbird. 190-215, Aug. 1975
• Venezuela's Crisis of Wealth. By Noel Grove. 175-209, Aug. 1976
• West Germany: Continuing Miracle. By John J. Putman. 149-181, Aug. 1977
• Which Way Oahu? By Gordon Young. 653-679, Nov. 1979

MADDEN, WILLIAM D.: Photographer:
• Something's Fishy About That Fin! Photos by Robert J. Shallenberger and William D. Madden. 224-227, Aug. 1974

MADEIRA ISLANDS, Atlantic Ocean:
• Madeira, Like Its Wine, Improves With Age. By Veronica Thomas. Photos by Jonathan Blair. 488-513, Apr. 1973
• Portugal's Gem of the Ocean: Madeira. By David S. Boyer. 364-394, Mar. 1959
• The Treasure of Porto Santo. By Robert Sténuit. Photos by author and William R. Curtsinger. 260-275, Aug. 1975

MADHYA PRADESH (State), India. *See* Nimkhera

MADISON, DOLLEY:
• Inside the White House. By Lonnelle Aikman. Photos by B. Anthony Stewart and Thomas Nebbia. 3-43, Jan. 1961
• The Living White House. By Lonnelle Aikman. 593-643, Nov. 1966

MADISON, JAMES:
• Profiles of the Presidents: I. The Presidency and How It Grew. By Frank Freidel. 642-687, Nov. 1964

MADOERA (Island), Java. *See* Madura

MADRID, Spain:
• "Around the World in Eighty Days." By Newman Bumstead. 705-750, Dec. 1951
• The Changing Face of Old Spain. By Bart McDowell. Photos by Albert Moldvay. 291-339, Mar. 1965
• Spain: It's a Changed Country. By Peter T. White. Photos by David Alan Harvey. 297-331, Mar. 1978
• Speaking of Spain. By Luis Marden. 415-456, Apr. 1950

MADRID CODEX:
• The Maya. 729-811, Dec. 1975

MADSON, JOHN: Author:
• Land of Long Sunsets: Nebraska's Sand Hills. Photos by Jodi Cobb. 493-517, Oct. 1978
• South Dakota's Badlands: Castles in Clay. Photos by Jim Brandenburg. 524-539, Apr. 1981

MADURA (Island), Indonesia:
• Postwar Journey Through Java. By Ronald Stuart Kain. 675-700, May 1948

MAGDALENA (River), Colombia:
• Cruising Colombia's "Ol' Man River." By Amos Burg. 615-660, May 1947

MAGELLAN, FERDINAND:
• Magellan: First Voyage Around the World. By Alan Villiers. Photos by Bruce Dale. Included: Strait of Magellan, discovered October 21, 1520. 721-753, June 1976
• *Triton* Follows Magellan's Wake. By Edward L. Beach. Photos by J. Baylor Roberts. 585-615, Nov. 1960

The **MAGIC** Lure of Sea Shells. By Paul A. Zahl. Photos by Victor R. Boswell, Jr. and author. 386-429, Mar. 1969

The **MAGIC** of Aluminum. By Thomas Y. Canby. Photos by James L. Amos. 186-211, Aug. 1978

The **MAGIC** Road Round Ireland. By H. V. Morton. Photos by Robert F. Sisson. 293-333, Mar. 1961

The **MAGIC** World of Hans Christian Andersen. By Harvey Arden. Photos by Sisse Brimberg. 825-849, Dec. 1979

The **MAGIC** Worlds of Walt Disney. By Robert de Roos. Photos by Thomas Nebbia. 159-207, Aug. 1963

MAGIS, ROBERT C.: Artist:
• The Celts. By Merle Severy. Photos by James P. Blair. 582-633, May 1977
• The Phoenicians, Sea Lords of Antiquity. By Samuel W. Matthews. Photos by Winfield Parks. 149-189, Aug. 1974
• The Tower of the Winds. By Derek J. de Solla Price. 587-596, Apr. 1967

MAGNA CARTA:
• The British Way. By Sir Evelyn Wrench. 421-541, Apr. 1949

MAGNESS, J. R.: Author:
• How Fruit Came to America. Paintings by Else Bostelmann. 325-377, Sept. 1951

MAGNETIC Clues Help Date the Past. By Kenneth F. Weaver. 696-701, May 1967

MAGNETIC STORMS:
• The Sun. By Herbert Friedman. 713-743, Nov. 1965
• Unlocking Secrets of the Northern Lights. By Carl W. Gartlein. Paintings by William Crowder. NGS research grant. 673-704, Nov. 1947

MAGNETISM DATING METHOD:
• Magnetic Clues Help Date the Past. By Kenneth F. Weaver. 696-701, May 1967

MAH JONG (Yawl):
• The Aegean Isles: Poseidon's Playground. By Gilbert M. Grosvenor. 733-781, Dec. 1958

MAHARASHTRA (State), India. *See* Shirala

MAHENDRA, King (Nepal):
• Coronation in Katmandu. By E. Thomas Gilliard. Photos by Marc Riboud. 139-152, July 1957

A **MAIDEN** Comes of Age (Apache). By Nita Quintero. 262-271, Feb. 1980

MAIL:
• So Long, St. Louis, We're Heading West. By William C. Everhart. 643-669, Nov. 1965
• *See also* Mail Boat; Pony Express; Postage Stamps; Postal Service; *and* Boston Post Roads; Natchez Trace

MAIL BOAT:
• *J. W. Westcott,* Postman for the Great Lakes. By Cy La Tour. 813-824, Dec. 1950

MAINE:
• The American Lobster, Delectable Cannibal. By Luis Marden. Photos by David Doubilet. 462-487, Apr. 1973
• Aroostook County, Maine, Source of Potatoes. By Howell Walker. 459-478, Oct. 1948
• Can We Save Our Salt Marshes? By Stephen W. Hitchcock. Photos by William R. Curtsinger. 729-765, June 1972
• Character Marks the Coast of Maine. By John Scofield. Photos by B. Anthony Stewart. 798-843, June 1968
▲ *Close-up: U.S.A., Maine, with the Maritime Provinces of Canada,* supplement. Text on reverse. Mar. 1975
• Down East Cruise *(Nomad).* By Tom Horgan. Photos by Luis Marden. 329-369, Sept. 1952
• The Incredible Potato. By Robert E. Rhoades. Photos by Martin Rogers. 668-694, May 1982
• Madawaska: Down East With a French Accent. By Perry Garfinkel. Photos by Cary Wolinsky. 380-409, Sept. 1980
• Mountains Top Off New England. By F. Barrows Colton. Photos by Robert F. Sisson. 563-602, May 1951
• Seashore Summer: One Mother's Recipe for Smallboy Bliss. By Arline Strong. 436-444, Sept. 1960
• Skyline Trail from Maine to Georgia. By Andrew H. Brown. Photos by Robert F. Sisson. 219-251, Aug. 1949
• Stalking Wild Foods on a Desert Isle. By Euell Gibbons. Photos by David Hiser. 47-63, July 1972

• Thoreau, a Different Man. By William Howarth. Photos by Farrell Grehan. 349-387, Mar. 1981
• A Way of Life Called Maine. By Ethel A. Starbird. Photos by David Hiser. 727-757, June 1977
• *See also* Allagash Wilderness Waterway; Monhegan Island

MAISEL, JAY: Photographer:
• Manhattan–Images of the City. By John J. Putman. 317-343, Sept. 1981

MAIURI, AMEDEO: Author:
• Last Moments of the Pompeians. Photos by Lee E. Battaglia. Paintings by Peter V. Bianchi. 651-669, Nov. 1961

MAJORCA (Island), Balearic Islands, Spain:
• The Balearics Are Booming. By Jean and Franc Shor. 621-660, May 1957
• Spain's Sun-blest Pleasure Isles. By Ethel A. Starbird. Photos by James A. Sugar. 679-701, May 1976

MAKAT, Lake, Tanzania:
• The Flamingo Eaters of Ngorongoro (Hyenas). By Richard D. Estes. 535-539, Oct. 1973

MAKING Friends With a Killer Whale. By Edward I. Griffin. 418-446, Mar. 1966

MAKING Friends With Mountain Gorillas. By Dian Fossey. Photos by Robert M. Campbell. NGS research grant. 48-67, Jan. 1970

The **MAKING** of a New Australia. By Howell Walker. 233-259, Feb. 1956

The **MAKING** of a West Pointer. By Howell Walker. 597-626, May 1952

THE MAKING OF AMERICA MAP SERIES:
• The Making of America: 17 New Maps Tie the Nation to Its Past. By Wilbur E. Garrett. 630-633, Nov. 1982
▲ *Atlantic Gateways,* The Making of America series. Included: Delaware, Maryland, New Jersey, New York, Pennsylvania, northern Virginia, West Virginia, and in Canada, southern Ontario and southern Quebec. On reverse: Indians and Trade, Nation in the Making, Peopling of the Gateways, Race for the Hinterlands, Growth of Industry, Spreading Urban Corridors. Mar. 1983
▲ *Deep South,* The Making of America series. Included: Alabama, Florida, Georgia, Louisiana, Mississippi, South Carolina, and parts of Arkansas, North Carolina, and Tennessee. On reverse: Indian Legacy, Imperial Footholds, Three Empires and Three Races, Cotton Kingdom, Postbellum, New Deep South, Subtropical Playground. Aug. 1983
• Editorial. By Wilbur E. Garrett. 145, Aug. 1983
▲ *Hawaii,* The Making of America series. Included: Polynesian Arrival, Hawaii in Transition, Labor for Sugar, Hawaii as Territory, Hawaii as State. Nov. 1983
▲ *The Southwest.* The Making of America series. Included: Arizona, New Mexico, and parts of California, Colorado, Texas, Utah; and in Mexico: Baja California Norte, Chihuahua, Sonora. On reverse: 12,000 Years of History; Spanish Conquest; Anglo-American Entry and Occupancy. Nov. 1982

The **MAKING** of an Astronaut. By Robert R. Gilruth. 122-144, Jan. 1965

MAKKAH, Saudi Arabia. *See* Mecca

MALABAR COAST, India:
• In the Wake of Sindbad. By Tim Severin. Photos by Richard Greenhill. 2-41, July 1982

MALAGASY REPUBLIC. *See* Madagascar

MALARIA:
• Mosquitoes, the Mighty Killers. By Lewis T. Nielsen. 427-440, Sept. 1979

MALAYA, Federation of:
• Malaya Meets Its Emergency. By George W. Long. Photos by J. Baylor Roberts. 185-228, Feb. 1953
• *See also* present name, Malaysia

MALAYS:
• Brunei, Borneo's Abode of Peace. By Joseph Judge. Photos by Dean Conger. 207-225, Feb. 1974
• Help for Philippine Tribes in Trouble. By Kenneth MacLeish. Photos by Dean Conger. Contents: The Higaonon, Mansaka, T'boli, and Ubo tribes of Malay stock (Southern Mongoloids) on Mindanao. 220-255, Aug. 1971
• Singapore, Reluctant Nation. By Kenneth MacLeish. Photos by Winfield Parks. 269-300, Aug. 1966

MALAYSIA:
• Asian Insects in Disguise. By Edward S. Ross. NGS research grant. 433-439, Sept. 1965
• In Storied Lands of Malaysia. By Maurice Shadbolt. Photos by Winfield Parks. 734-783, Nov. 1963
• Malaysia: Youthful Nation With Growing Pains. By William S. Ellis. Photos by David Alan Harvey. 635-667, May 1977
• Malaysia's Giant Flowers and Insect-trapping Plants. By Paul A. Zahl. 680-701, May 1964
• Tropical Rain Forests: Nature's Dwindling Treasures. By Peter T. White. Photos by James P. Blair. Paintings by Barron Storey. 2-47, Jan. 1983
• *See also* former name, Malaya, Federation of

MALDIVE ISLANDS, Indian Ocean:
• The Marvelous Maldive Islands. By Alan Villiers. 829-849, June 1957
• *See also* Maldives Republic

MALDIVES REPUBLIC, Indian Ocean:
• Crosscurrents Sweep the Indian Ocean. By Bart McDowell. Photos by Steve Raymer. 422-457, Oct. 1981
• *See also* Maldive Islands

MALEKULA (Island), New Hebrides:
• Taboos and Magic Rule Namba Lives. By Kal Muller. 57-83, Jan. 1972

BOTH BY DAVID ALAN HARVEY

Malaysia: country's richly varied wildlife includes the orangutan, *top;* Kerau Game Reserve's elephants, *above*

MALI:
• Finding West Africa's Oldest City. By Susan and Roderick McIntosh. Photos by Michael and Aubine Kirtley. Contents: Jenne-jeno (archaeological site), Mali. 396-418, Sept. 1982
• Foxes Foretell the Future in Mali's Dogon Country. By Pamela Johnson Meyer. 431-448, Mar. 1969
• Freedom Speaks French in Ouagadougou. By John Scofield. 153-203, Aug. 1966
• The Niger: River of Sorrow, River of Hope. By Georg Gerster. 152-189, Aug. 1975

The **MALIGNED** Coyote. By Hope Ryden. Photos by author and David Hiser. 278-294, Aug. 1974

MALLE, LOUIS: Photographer:
• *Calypso* Explores for Underwater Oil. By Jacques-Yves Cousteau. 155-184, Aug. 1955

MALLORCA (Island), Balearic Islands, Spain. *See* Majorca

MALTA:
• Democracy's Fortress: Unsinkable Malta. By Ernle Bradford. Photos by Ted H. Funk. 852-879, June 1969

MAMMALS:
• African Wildlife: Man's Threatened Legacy. By Allan C. Fisher, Jr. Photos by Thomas Nebbia. 147-187, Feb. 1972
A Continent's Living Treasure. Paintings by Ned Seidler. 164-167
◆ *Animals of East Africa: The Wild Realm.* Announced. 844-849, June 1968
• An Artist's Glimpses of Our Roadside Wildlife. Paintings by Walter A. Weber. Contents: Abert's Squirrel, Badgers, Black Bears, Coyotes, Moose, Pronghorn Antelopes, Skunks, Virginia Deer. 16-32, July 1950
◆ *Book of Mammals* (2 volumes). 1981
▪ Etosha: Place of Dry Water. 703, Dec. 1980; cover, Jan. 1981
▪ Last Stand in Eden. 1, Jan. 1979; cover, Mar. 1979
• London's Zoo of Zoos. By Thomas Garner James. 771-786, June 1953
• Mammals of the Alaskan Tundra. 329-337, Mar. 1972
▪ Man of the Serengeti. 179A-179B, Feb. 1972
▪ Monkeys, Apes, and Man. 585A-585B, Oct. 1971
• Orphans of the Wild. By Bruce G. Kinloch. 683-699, Nov. 1962
• Portrait of a Fierce and Fragile Land. By Paul A. Zahl. 303-314, Mar. 1972
• Roaming Africa's Unfenced Zoos. By W. Robert Moore. Contents: Antelopes, Buffaloes, Elephants, Gazelles, Giraffes, Gorillas, Hippopotamuses, Leopards, Lions, Okapi, Rhinoceroses, Wart Hogs, Zebras. 353-380, Mar. 1950
• The Romance of American Furs. By Wanda Burnett. Contents: Beaver, Chinchillas, Foxes, Minks, Muskrats, Seals. 379-402, Mar. 1948
• Seeking Mindanao's Strangest Creatures. By Charles Heizer Wharton. Contents: Cloud Rat, Flying Lemur, Tarsier, Tree Shrew. 389-408, Sept. 1948
• Stalking Central Africa's Wildlife. By T. Donald Carter. Paintings by Walter A. Weber. NGS research grant. 264-286, Aug. 1956
• The Wild Animals in My Life. By William M. Mann. Contents: Animals of the National Zoological Park. 497-524, Apr. 1957
◆ *Wild Animals of North America.* Announced. 554-557, Oct. 1960
◆ *Wild Animals of North America.* 1979
• Wildlife In and Near the Valley of the Moon. By H. H. Arnold. Photos by Paul J. Fair. Contents: Deer, Elk, Ground Squirrels, Raccoons. 401-414, Mar. 1950
• Wildlife of Everglades National Park. By Daniel B. Beard. Paintings by Walter A. Weber. Contents: Bobcat, Manatee, Marsh Rabbit, Otter, Porpoise, Puma, Raccoon. 83-116, Jan. 1949
• Wolves Versus Moose on Isle Royale. By Durward L. Allen and L. David Mech. 200-219, Feb. 1963
• The Wonder City That Moves by Night. By Francis Beverly Kelley. 289-324, Mar. 1948
• Zoo Animals Go to School. By Marion P. McCrane. Photos by W. E. Garrett. 694-706, Nov. 1956
◆ *Zoo Babies.* 1978
▪ Zoos of the World. 503A-503B, Oct. 1970
◆ *Zoos Without Cages.* 1981
• *See also* Antelopes; Armadillos; Baboons; Bats; *listing under* Bears; Beavers; Bighorn Sheep; Bison, American; Black-footed Ferrets; Burros, Wild; Caribou; Cats; Cheetahs; Chimpanzees; Coyotes; Deer; Dogs; Dolphins; Elephants; Flying Mammals; Gibbons; Giraffes; Goats; Gorillas; Guanacos; Hippopotamuses; Horses; Horses, Wild; Hyenas; Jackals; Kangaroos; Lions; Manatees; Monkeys; Mountain Goats; Mountain Lions; Musk Oxen; Opposums; Orangutans; Otters; Pandas, Giant; Pigs; Platypuses; Porcupines; Porpoises; Prairie Dogs; Raccoons; Rats; Reindeer; Rhinoceroses; Seals; Skunks; Snow Leopards; Tigers; Vicuñas; Walruses; Water Buffalo; Whales; Wolves; *and* Mammals, Prehistoric

MAMMALS, Prehistoric:
• Ancient Ashfall Creates a Pompeii of Prehistoric Animals. By Michael R. Voorhies. Photos by Annie Griffiths. Paintings by Jay Matternes. 66-75, Jan. 1981
• Big Game Hunting in the Land of Long Ago. By Joseph P. Connolly and James D. Bump. NGS research grant. 589-605, May 1947
• Bison Kill By Ice Age Hunters. By Dennis Stanford. NGS research grant. 114-121, Jan. 1979
• Exploring the Mind of Ice Age Man. By Alexander Marshack. Included: Mammals of the Ice Age as depicted in the art of Cro-Magnon man. NGS research grant. 64-89, Jan. 1975
◆ *Giants From the Past: The Age of Mammals.* 1983
▲ "Ice Age Mammals of the Alaskan Tundra," painting supplement. Map of Canada. Mar. 1972
• Wyoming Muck Tells of Battle: Ice Age Man vs. Mammoth. By Cynthia Irwin, Henry Irwin, and George Agogino. NGS research grant. 828-837, June 1962
• *See also* Man, Prehistoric

MAMMOTH:
• Wyoming Muck Tells of Battle: Ice Age Man vs. Mammoth. By Cynthia Irwin, Henry Irwin, and George Agogino. NGS research grant. 828-837, June 1962

MAN, Isle of, Irish Sea:
• The Manx and Their Isle of Man. By Veronica Thomas. Photos by Ted H. Funk. 426-444, Sept. 1972

MAN, Prehistoric:
• Adventures in the Search for Man *(Kenyapithecus wickeri).* By Louis S. B. Leakey. Photos by Hugo van Lawick. NGS research grant. 132-152, Jan. 1963
• A Bold New Look at Our Past. The Editor. NGS research grant. 62-63, Jan. 1975
▪ Dr. Leakey and the Dawn of Man. 703A-703B, Nov. 1966
• Ethiopia Yields First "Family" of Early Man. By Donald C. Johanson. Photos by David Brill. NGS research grant. 790-811, Dec. 1976
• Exploring 1,750,000 Years Into Man's Past. By L. S. B. Leakey. Photos by Robert F. Sisson. NGS research grant. 564-589, Oct. 1961
• Exploring the Mind of Ice Age Man. By Alexander Marshack. NGS research grant. 64-89, Jan. 1975
• Finding the World's Earliest Man *(Zinjanthropus boisei).* By L. S. B. Leakey. Photos by Des Bartlett. NGS research grant. 420-435, Sept. 1960
• Footprints in the Ashes of Time. By Mary D. Leakey. NGS research grant. 446-457, Apr. 1979
• Ice Age Man, the First American. By Thomas R. Henry. Paintings by Andre Durenceau. 781-806, Dec. 1955
• In Search of Man's Past at Lake Rudolf. By Richard E. Leakey. Photos by Gordon W. Gahan. NGS research grant. 712-734, May 1970
• The Leakey Tradition Lives On. By Melvin M. Payne. NGS research grant. 143-144, Jan. 1973
• The Leakeys of Africa: Family in Search of Prehistoric Man. By Melvin M. Payne. Included: *Homo habilis, Kenyapithecus, Proconsul, Zinjanthropus.* NGS research grant. 194-231, Feb. 1965
▪ The Legacy of L.S.B. Leakey. 439, Oct. 1977; cover, Jan. 1978

• Lifelike Man Preserved 2,000 Years in Peat. By P. V. Glob. 419-430, Mar. 1954
• Preserving the Treasures of Olduvai Gorge. By Melvin M. Payne. Photos by Joseph J. Scherschel. Included: *Homo erectus, Homo habilis, Kenyapithecus, Zinjanthropus.* NGS research grant. 701-709, Nov. 1966
• The Search for the First Americans. By Thomas Y. Canby. Photos by Kerby Smith. Paintings by Roy Andersen. 330-363, Sept. 1979
• Skull 1470. By Richard E. Leakey. Photos by Bob Campbell. NGS research grant. 819-829, June 1973
• Tanzania's Stone Age Art. By Mary D. Leakey. Photos by John Reader. 84-99, July 1983
• Vanished Mystery Men of Hudson Bay. By Henry B. Collins. Included: Dorset Eskimos, Sadlermiuts. NGS research grant. 669-687, Nov. 1956
• Wyoming Muck Tells of Battle: Ice Age Man vs. Mammoth. By Cynthia Irwin, Henry Irwin, and George Agogino. NGS research grant. 828-837, June 1962
• *See also* Paleo-Indians; Thule Inuit

The **MAN** Behind the Myths: George Washington. By Howard La Fay. Photos by Ted Spiegel. 90-111, July 1976

MAN-IN-SEA PROJECT:
• The Deepest Days. By Robert Sténuit. NGS research grant. 534-547, Apr. 1965
• The Long, Deep Dive. By Lord Kilbracken. Photos by Bates Littlehales. NGS research grant. 718-731, May 1963
• Our Man-in-Sea Project. By Edwin A. Link. NGS research grant. 713-717, May 1963
• Outpost Under the Ocean. By Edwin A. Link. Photos by Bates Littlehales. NGS research grant. 530-533, Apr. 1965
• A Taxi for the Deep Frontier. By Kenneth MacLeish. Photos by Bates Littlehales. 139-150, Jan. 1968

MAN in the Amazon: Stone Age Present Meets Stone Age Past. By W. Jesco von Puttkamer. NGS research grant. 60-83, Jan. 1979

MAN-OF-WAR:
• The Deadly Fisher. By Charles E. Lane. 388-397, Mar. 1963
• Man-of-war Fleet Attacks Bimini. By Paul A. Zahl. 185-212, Feb. 1952

MAN on the Moon in Idaho. By William Belknap, Jr. 505-525, Oct. 1960

MAN-POWERED FLIGHT. *See Gossamer Albatross; Gossamer Condor*

MAN Versus Nature. The Editor. 555, Oct. 1969

MAN Walks on Another World. By Neil A. Armstrong, Edwin E. Aldrin, Jr., and Michael Collins. 738-749, Dec. 1969

The **MAN** Who Talks to Hummingbirds. By Luis Marden. Photos by James Blair. 80-99, Jan. 1963

LENNART LARSEN

Lifelike Man: 2,000-year-old mummy found in peat tomb

BRUCE DALE, NGS

Philippines: Ilongot child spears fish

MANAMA, Bahrain:
• Bahrain: Hub of the Persian Gulf. By Thomas J. Abercrombie. Photos by Steve Raymer. 300-329, Sept. 1979

MANATEES:
• Florida's Manatees, Mermaids in Peril. By Daniel S. Hartman. Photos by James A. Sugar. NGS research grant. 342-353, Sept. 1969
• Guatemala Revisited. By Luis Marden. 525-564, Oct. 1947

MANAUS, Brazil:
• Sea Fever. By John E. Schultz. 237-268, Feb. 1949

MANCHURIA:
• In Manchuria Now. By W. Robert Moore. 389-414, Mar. 1947

MANDINGOS (Tribespeople):
• Rubber-cushioned Liberia. By Henry S. Villard. Photos by Charles W. Allmon. 201-228, Feb. 1948

MANGROVES. *See* Red Mangroves

MANHATTAN (Borough), New York, New York
• Manhattan–Images of the City. By John J. Putman. Photos by Jay Maisel. 317-343, Sept. 1981
▲ *Tourist Manhattan; Greater New York,* double-sided U. S. Atlas series supplement. July 1964
• The World in New York City. By Peter T. White. 52-107, July 1964
• *See also* Central Park; Harlem

MANHATTAN, S.S. (Tanker):
• North for Oil: *Manhattan* Makes the Historic Northwest Passage. By Bern Keating. Photos by Tomas Sennett. 374-391, Mar. 1970

MANILA, Philippines:
• The Philippines: Better Days Still Elude an Old Friend. By Don Moser. Photos by Bruce Dale. 360-391, Mar. 1977
• The Philippines, Freedom's Pacific Frontier. By Robert de Roos. Photos by Ted Spiegel. 301-351, Sept. 1966

MANITOBA (Province), Canada:
• Across Canada by Mackenzie's Track. By Ralph Gray. 191-239, Aug. 1955
• Canada's Heartland, the Prairie Provinces. By W. E. Garrett. 443-489, Oct. 1970
▲ *Close-up, Canada: Saskatchewan, Manitoba, Northwest Territories,* supplement. Text on reverse. May 1979
• Manitoba's Fantastic Snake Pits. By Michael Aleksiuk. Photos by Bianca Lavies. 715-723, Nov. 1975
• Western Grebes: The Birds That Walk on Water. By Gary L. Nuechterlein. 624-637, May 1982
• *See also* Churchill

MANKATO, Minnesota:
• Satellites Gave Warning of Midwest Floods. By Peter T. White. Photos by Thomas A. DeFeo. 574-592, Oct. 1969

MANN, WILLIAM M.: Author:
• The Wild Animals in My Life. 497-524, Apr. 1957

M
N

MANNED SPACECRAFT CENTER, Houston, Texas:
● First Explorers on the Moon: The Incredible Story of Apollo 11. 735-797, Dec. 1969
I. Man Walks on Another World. By Neil A. Armstrong, Edwin E. Aldrin, Jr., and Michael Collins. 738-749; III. The Flight of Apollo 11: "One giant leap for mankind." By Kenneth F. Weaver. 752-787; IV. What the Moon Rocks Tell Us. By Kenneth F. Weaver. 788-791
● Houston, Prairie Dynamo. By Stuart E. Jones. Photos by William Albert Allard. 338-377, Sept. 1967
● "A Most Fantastic Voyage": The Story of Apollo 8's Rendezvous With the Moon. By Sam C. Phillips. 593-631, May 1969

MAN'S Deepest Dive. By Jacques Piccard. Photos by Thomas J. Abercrombie. 224-239, Aug. 1960

MAN'S Eighty Centuries in Veracruz. By S. Jeffrey K. Wilkerson. Photos by David Hiser. Paintings by Richard Schlecht. NGS research grant. 203-231, Aug. 1980

MAN'S First Winter at the South Pole. By Paul A. Siple. 439-478, Apr. 1958

MAN'S Mightiest Ally. Photos by Willard R. Culver. 423-450, Apr. 1947

MAN'S New Frontier: The Continental Shelf. By Luis Marden. Photos by Ira Block. 495-531, Apr. 1978

MAN'S New Servant, the Friendly Atom. By F. Barrows Colton. Photos by Volkmar Wentzel. 71-90, Jan. 1954

MAN'S Own Mountains, the Alps. By Ralph Gray. Photos by Walter Meayers Edwards and William Eppridge. 350-395, Sept. 1965

MAN'S Wildlife Heritage Faces Extinction. By H. R. H. The Prince Philip, Duke of Edinburgh. 700-703, Nov. 1962

MANSAKA TRIBE:
● Help for Philippine Tribes in Trouble. By Kenneth MacLeish. Photos by Dean Conger. 220-255, Aug. 1971

MANSFIELD, Mount, Vermont:
● Mountains Top Off New England. By F. Barrows Colton. Photos by Robert F. Sisson. 563-602, May 1951

MANTA RAYS:
● A Strange Ride in the Deep (on Manta Rays). By Peter Benchley. 200-203, Feb. 1981

MANTFOMBI, Princess (Swazi):
● Zulu King Weds a Swazi Princess. By Volkmar Wentzel. 47-61, Jan. 1978

MANTIS:
● Praying Mantis. Photos by John G. Pitkin. 685-692, May 1950

MANUSCRIPTS, Medieval. *See* Henry E. Huntington Library and Art Gallery; Medieval Europe; St. Catherine's Monastery

The **MANX** and Their Isle of Man. By Veronica Thomas. Photos by Ted H. Funk. 426-444, Sept. 1972

The **MANY-SIDED** Diamond. By George S. Switzer. 568-586, Apr. 1958

MANY-SPLENDORED Glacierland. By George W. Long. Photos by Kathleen Revis. 589-636, May 1956

MAO TSE-TUNG:
● Return to Changing China. By Audrey Topping. 801-833, Dec. 1971

MAORIS:
● New Zealand: Gift of the Sea. By Maurice Shadbolt. Photos by Brian Brake. 465-511, Apr. 1962
● New Zealand, Pocket Wonder World. By Howell Walker. 419-460, Apr. 1952
● New Zealand's Cook Islands: Paradise in Search of a Future. By Maurice Shadbolt. Photos by William Albert Allard. 203-231, Aug. 1967
● New Zealand's North Island: The Contented Land. By Charles McCarry. Photos by Bates Littlehales. 190-213, Aug. 1974

A **MAP** Maker Looks at the United States. By Newman Bumstead. 705-748, June 1951

MAP MAKING. *See* Cartography

MAP SUPPLEMENTS:
Africa:
▲ *Africa.* Atlas series. Sept. 1960
▲ *Africa; Africa, Its Political Development.* Feb. 1980
▲ *Africa: Countries of the Nile.* Atlas series. Oct. 1963
▲ *Africa and the Arabian Peninsula.* Mar. 1950
▲ *The Heritage of Africa; The Peoples of Africa.* Dec. 1971
▲ *The Historic Mediterranean; The Mediterranean Seafloor.* Dec. 1982
▲ *Nile Valley, Land of the Pharaohs.* Atlas series. Text on reverse. May 1965
▲ *Northern Africa.* Dec. 1954
▲ *Northwestern Africa.* Atlas series. Aug. 1966
▲ *Southern Africa.* Atlas series. Nov. 1962
Antarctica:
▲ *Antarctica.* Sept. 1957
▲ *Antarctica.* Atlas series. Feb. 1963
Arctic:
▲ *Arctic Ocean; Arctic Ocean Floor.* Oct. 1971
▲ *Canada, Alaska, and Greenland.* June 1947
▲ *Peoples of the Arctic; Arctic Ocean,* double-sided supplement. Feb. 1983
▲ *The Top of the World.* Oct. 1949
▲ *Top of the World.* Atlas series. Nov. 1965
Asia:
▲ *Asia; The Peoples of Mainland Southeast Asia.* Mar. 1971
▲ *Asia and Adjacent Areas.* Mar. 1951
▲ *Asia and Adjacent Areas.* Atlas series. Dec. 1959
▲ *China.* Atlas series. Nov. 1964
▲ China: *The People's Republic of China; The Peoples of China.* July 1980
▲ *China Coast and Korea.* Oct. 1953
▲ *The Far East.* Sept. 1952
▲ *Japan and Korea.* Atlas series. Dec. 1960
▲ *Southeast Asia.* Sept. 1955
▲ *Southeast Asia.* Dec. 1968
▲ *Southeast Asia.* Atlas series. May 1961
▲ *Southwest Asia.* Atlas series. May 1963
▲ *Southwest Asia, including India, Pakistan, and Northeast Africa.* June 1952
▲ *Viet Nam, Cambodia, Laos, and Eastern Thailand.* Text on reverse. Jan. 1965
▲ *Viet Nam, Cambodia, Laos, and Thailand.* Feb. 1967
● *See also* Middle East; Union of Soviet Socialist Republics
Atlantic Ocean:
▲ *Atlantic Ocean.* Dec. 1955
▲ *Atlantic Ocean; Atlantic Ocean Floor.* Atlas series. June 1968
Australia:
▲ *Australia.* Mar. 1948
▲ *Australia.* Atlas series. Sept. 1963
▲ *Australia; Land of Living Fossils.* Feb. 1979
Canada:
▲ *British Columbia, Alberta, Yukon Territory.* Close-up series. Text on reverse. Apr. 1978
▲ *Canada.* Atlas series. Dec. 1961
▲ *Canada.* Text on reverse. Mar. 1972
▲ *Canada, Alaska, and Greenland.* June 1947
▲ *Central Canada.* Atlas series. July 1963
▲ *Eastern Canada.* Atlas series. May 1967
▲ *The Great Lakes Region of the United States and Canada.* Dec. 1953
▲ *Maine, with the Maritime Provinces of Canada.* Close-up series. Text on reverse. Included: New Brunswick, Nova Scotia, Prince Edward Island. Mar. 1975
▲ *National Parks, Monuments and Shrines of the United States and Canada.* Atlas series. Text on reverse. May 1958
▲ *Ontario.* Close-up series. Text on reverse. Dec. 1978
▲ *Quebec, Newfoundland.* Close-up series. Text on reverse, inset Southern Quebec. May 1980
▲ *Saskatchewan, Manitoba, Northwest Territories.* Close-up series. Text on reverse. May 1979
▲ *Vacationlands of the United States and Southern Canada.* Text on reverse. July 1966
▲ *Western Canada.* Atlas series. Sept. 1966
Caribbean Region:
▲ *Colonization and Trade in the New World.* Text on reverse. Dec. 1977
▲ *Countries of the Caribbean, including Mexico, Central America, and the West Indies.* Oct. 1947
▲ *Florida, with Puerto Rico and the Virgin Islands.* Close-up series. Text on reverse. Nov. 1973

▲ *Tourist Islands of the West Indies; West Indies and Central America.* Feb. 1981
▲ *West Indies.* Mar. 1954
▲ *West Indies* Atlas series. Dec. 1962
▲ *West Indies and Central America.* Jan. 1970

Central America:
▲ *Archeological Map of Middle America, Land of the Feathered Serpent.* Text on reverse. Oct. 1968
▲ *Central America; Mexico.* May 1973
▲ *Countries of the Caribbean, including Mexico, Central America, and the West Indies.* Oct. 1947
▲ *Mexico and Central America.* Mar. 1953
▲ *Mexico and Central America.* Atlas series. Oct. 1961
▲ *Tourist Islands of the West Indies; West Indies and Central America.* Feb. 1981
▲ *Visitor's Guide to the Aztec World; Mexico and Central America.* Dec. 1980
▲ *West Indies and Central America.* Jan. 1970

Ethnic Maps:
▲ *Celtic Europe.* May 1977
▲ *Discoverers of the Pacific.* Dec. 1974
▲ *Indians of North America.* Dec. 1972
▲ *Indians of South America.* Mar. 1982
▲ *The Peoples of Africa.* Dec. 1971
▲ *The Peoples of China.* July 1980
▲ *The Peoples of Mainland Southeast Asia.* Mar. 1971
▲ *The Peoples of the Arctic.* Feb. 1983
▲ *The Peoples of the Middle East.* July 1972
▲ *Peoples of the Soviet Union.* Feb. 1976
▲ *Two Centuries of Conflict in the Middle East.* Sept. 1980
▲ *Visitor's Guide to the Aztec World.* Dec. 1980

Europe:
▲ *The Balkans.* Atlas series. Feb. 1962
▲ *The British Isles.* Apr. 1949
▲ *British Isles.* Atlas series. July 1958
▲ British Isles: *Ireland and Northern Ireland: A Visitor's Guide; Historic Ireland* (Pre-Norman, Medieval, Modern). Apr. 1981
▲ British Isles: *Shakespeare's Britain.* May 1964
▲ British Isles: *A Traveler's Map of the British Isles.* Text on reverse. Apr. 1974
▲ *The British Isles; Medieval England.* Oct. 1979
▲ *Central Europe, including the Balkan States.* Sept. 1951
▲ *Europe.* June 1957
▲ *Europe.* June 1969
▲ *Europe.* Atlas series. June 1962
▲ *Europe; Celtic Europe.* May 1977
▲ *Europe; Historical Map of Europe,* double-sided supplement. Dec. 1983
▲ *Europe and the Near East.* June 1949
▲ France: *A Traveler's Map of France.* Text on reverse. June 1971
▲ *France, Belgium, and the Netherlands.* Atlas series. June 1960
▲ *Germany.* Atlas series. June 1959
▲ *Greece and the Aegean.* Atlas series. Dec. 1958
▲ *Italy.* Atlas series. Nov. 1961
▲ Italy: *A Traveler's Map of Italy.* Text on reverse. June 1970
▲ *Northern Europe.* Aug. 1954
▲ Poland: *The Face and Faith of Poland,* map, photo, and essay supplement. By Peter Miller. Essay by Czesław Miłosz. Photos by Bruno Barbey. Apr. 1982
▲ *Poland and Czechoslovakia.* Atlas series. Sept. 1958
▲ *Scandinavia.* Atlas series. Apr. 1963
▲ *Spain and Portugal.* Atlas series. Mar. 1965
▲ *Switzerland, Austria, and Northern Italy; The Alps–Europe's Backbone.* Atlas series. Sept. 1965
▲ *Western Europe.* Dec. 1950
● *See also* Mediterranean; Union of Soviet Socialist Republics

Indian Ocean:
▲ *Indian Ocean Floor.* Oct. 1967

Mediterranean:
▲ *Classical Lands of the Mediterranean.* Dec. 1949
▲ *The Historic Mediterranean; The Mediterranean Seafloor.* Dec. 1982
▲ *Lands of the Eastern Mediterranean.* Atlas series. Jan. 1959
▲ *Middle East, Eastern Mediterranean; Early Civilizations of the Middle East.* Sept. 1978

Mexico:
▲ *Archeological Map of Middle America, Land of the Feathered Serpent.* Text on reverse. Oct. 1968
▲ *Countries of the Caribbean, including Mexico, Central America, and the West Indies.* Oct. 1947
▲ *Mexico; Central America.* May 1973
▲ *Mexico and Central America.* Mar. 1953
▲ *Mexico and Central America.* Atlas series. Oct. 1961
▲ *Visitor's Guide to the Aztec World; Mexico and Central America.* Dec. 1980

Middle America:
▲ *Archeological Map of Middle America, Land of the Feathered Serpent.* Text on reverse. Oct. 1968
● *See also* Central America; Mexico

Middle East:
▲ *Europe and the Near East.* June 1949
▲ *The Historic Mediterranean; The Mediterranean Seafloor.* Dec. 1982
▲ *Holy Land Today.* Atlas series. Dec. 1963
▲ *Lands of the Bible Today.* Dec. 1956
▲ *Lands of the Bible Today.* Dec. 1967
▲ *Lands of the Eastern Mediterranean.* Atlas series. Jan. 1959
▲ *Middle East, Eastern Mediterranean; Early Civilizations of the Middle East.* Sept. 1978
▲ *The Peoples of the Middle East.* Text on reverse. July 1972
▲ *Two Centuries of Conflict in the Middle East; Mideast in Turmoil.* Sept. 1980

North America:
▲ *The Americas; Bird Migration in the Americas.* Aug. 1979
▲ *Colonization and Trade in the New World.* Text on reverse. Dec. 1977
▲ *North America.* Mar. 1952
▲ *North America.* Atlas series. Apr. 1964
▲ *North America Before Columbus; Indians of North America.* Dec. 1972
● *See also* Canada; Mexico; United States

Pacific Ocean:
▲ *Islands of the Pacific; Discoverers of the Pacific.* Dec. 1974
▲ *Pacific Ocean.* Dec. 1952
▲ *Pacific Ocean; Pacific Islands.* Atlas series. Apr. 1962
▲ *Pacific Ocean; Pacific Ocean Floor.* Oct. 1969

South America:
▲ *The Americas; Bird Migration in the Americas.* Aug. 1979
▲ *Eastern South America.* Mar. 1955
▲ *Eastern South America.* Atlas series. Sept. 1962
▲ *Indians of South America; Archaeology of South America.* Mar. 1982
▲ *Northwestern South America.* Atlas series. Feb. 1964
▲ *South America.* Oct. 1950
▲ *South America.* Atlas series. Feb. 1960
▲ *South America.* Text on reverse. Oct. 1972
▲ *Southern South America.* Atlas series. Mar. 1958

Union of Soviet Socialist Republics:
▲ *Eastern Soviet Union.* Atlas series. Mar. 1967
▲ *Soviet Union; Peoples of the Soviet Union.* Feb. 1976
▲ *Union of Soviet Socialist Republics.* Dec. 1960
▲ *Western Soviet Union.* Atlas series. Sept. 1959

United States:
▲ *Alaska.* June 1956
▲ *Alaska.* Close-up series. Text on reverse. June 1975
▲ Alaska: *State of Alaska.* Atlas series. July 1959
▲ *America's Federal Lands; The United States.* Sept. 1982
▲ *Atlantic Gateways,* The Making of America series. Included: Delaware, Maryland, New Jersey, New York, Pennsylvania, northern Virginia, West Virginia, and in Canada, southern Ontario and southern Quebec. On reverse: Indians and Trade, Nation in the Making, Peopling of the Gateways, Race for the Hinterlands, Growth of Industry, Spreading Urban Corridors. Mar. 1983
▲ *Battlefields of the Civil War; Cockpit of the Civil War.* Atlas series. Apr. 1961
▲ California: *A Map of California.* June 1954
▲ California: *Northern California; Southern California.* U. S. Atlas series. May 1966
▲ *California and Nevada.* Close-up series. Text on reverse. June 1974

M N

• Close-up: U.S.A.–a Fresh Look at Our Land and Its Heritage. By Gilbert M. Grosvenor. 287-289, Mar. 1973
▲ *Deep South,* The Making of America series. Included: Alabama, Florida, Georgia, Louisiana, Mississippi, South Carolina, and parts of Arkansas, North Carolina, and Tennessee. On reverse: Indian Legacy, Imperial Footholds, Three Empires and Three Races, Cotton Kingdom, Postbellum, New Deep South, Subtropical Playground. Aug. 1983
▲ *Florida, with Puerto Rico and U. S. Virgin Islands* and text on reverse. Close-up series. Nov. 1973
▲ *The Grand Canyon.* Photomosaic and text on reverse. NGS research grant. July 1978
▲ The Great Lakes: *Wisconsin, Michigan, and the Great Lakes.* Close-up series. Text on reverse. Aug. 1973
▲ *The Great Lakes Region of the United States and Canada.* Dec. 1953
▲ *Hawaii.* Atlas series. July 1960
▲ *Hawaii.* Close-up series. Text on reverse. Apr. 1976
▲ *Hawaii,* The Making of America series. Included: Polynesian Arrival, Hawaii in Transition, Labor for Sugar, Hawaii as Territory, Hawaii as State. Nov. 1983
▲ *Historical Map of the United States.* June 1953
▲ *Illinois, Indiana, Ohio, and Kentucky.* Close-up series. Text on reverse. Feb. 1977
▲ *Maine, with the Maritime Provinces of Canada.* Close-up series. Text on reverse. Mar. 1975
• The Making of America: 17 New Maps Tie the Nation to Its Past. By Wilbur E. Garrett. 630-633, Nov. 1982
▲ *The Mid-Atlantic States.* Close-up series. Text on reverse. Included: Delaware, Maryland, Virginia, West Virginia. Oct. 1976
▲ *National Parks, Monuments and Shrines of the United States and Canada.* Atlas series. Text on reverse. May 1958
▲ *New England.* Included: Connecticut, Maine, Massachusetts, New Hampshire, New Jersey, New York, Pennsylvania, Rhode Island, Vermont. June 1955
▲ New England: *Western New England.* Close-up series. Text on reverse. Included: Connecticut, Massachusetts, New Hampshire, Rhode Island, Vermont. July 1975
▲ New York City: *Greater New York; Tourist Manhattan.* U. S. Atlas series. July 1964
• New York City Map Launches United States Atlas Map Series. By Ralph E. McAleer. 108-110, July 1964
▲ *The North Central States.* Close-up series. Text on reverse. Included: Iowa, Kansas, Minnesota, Missouri, Nebraska, North Dakota, South Dakota. Mar. 1974
▲ *North Central United States.* Included: Illinois, Iowa, Kansas, Minnesota, Missouri, Nebraska, North Dakota, South Dakota, Wisconsin. June 1948
▲ *North Central United States.* Atlas series. Included: Illinois, Iowa, Kansas, Minnesota, Missouri, Nebraska, North Dakota, South Dakota, Wisconsin. Nov. 1958
▲ *The Northeast.* Close-up series. Text on reverse. Included: New Jersey, New York, Pennsylvania. Jan. 1978
▲ *Northeastern United States, including the Great Lakes Region.* Atlas series. Included: Connecticut, Delaware, Illinois, Indiana, Maine, Maryland, Massachusetts, Michigan, New Hampshire, New Jersey, New York, Ohio, Pennsylvania, Rhode Island, Vermont, Virginia, West Virginia, Wisconsin. Apr. 1959
▲ *The Northwest.* Close-up series. Text on reverse. Included: Idaho, Montana, Oregon, Washington, Wyoming. Mar. 1973
▲ *Northwestern United States.* Atlas series. Apr. 1960
▲ *Northwestern United States and Neighboring Canadian Provinces.* June 1950
▲ *The South Central States.* Close-up series. Text on reverse. Included: Arkansas, Louisiana, Oklahoma, Texas. Oct. 1974
▲ *South Central United States.* Included: Arkansas, Louisiana, Mississippi, New Mexico, Oklahoma, Texas. Dec. 1947
▲ *South Central United States.* Atlas series. Included: Arkansas, Louisiana, Mississippi, New Mexico, Oklahoma, Texas. Feb. 1961
▲ *The Southeast.* Close-up series. Text on reverse. Included: Alabama, Georgia, Mississippi, North Carolina, South Carolina, Tennessee. Oct. 1975
▲ *Southeastern United States.* Included: Alabama, Florida, Georgia, Kentucky, Maryland, Mississippi, North Carolina, South Carolina, Tennessee, Virginia, West Virginia. Feb. 1947
▲ *Southeastern United States.* Atlas series. Included: Alabama, Florida, Georgia, Kentucky, Maryland, Mississippi, North Carolina, South Carolina, Tennessee, Virginia, West Virginia. Jan. 1958
▲ *The Southwest.* Close-up series. Text on reverse. Included: Arizona, Colorado, New Mexico, Utah. Oct. 1977
▲ *The Southwest.* The Making of America series. Included: Arizona, New Mexico, and parts of California, Colorado, Texas, Utah; and in Mexico: Baja California Norte, Chihuahua, Sonora. On reverse: 12,000 Years of History; Spanish Conquest; Anglo-American Entry and Occupancy. Nov. 1982
▲ *Southwestern United States.* Included: Arizona, California, Colorado, Nevada, New Mexico, Utah. Dec. 1948
▲ *Southwestern United States.* Atlas series. Included: Arizona, California, Colorado, Nevada, New Mexico, Utah. Nov. 1959
▲ *The United States.* Sept. 1956
▲ *The United States.* Feb. 1968
▲ *The United States.* Atlas series. July 1961
▲ *The United States; Portrait U.S.A.* (photomosaic). July 1976
▲ *United States: Washington to Boston.* Atlas series. Aug. 1962
▲ *The United States of America.* June 1951
▲ *Vacationlands of the United States and Southern Canada.* Text on reverse. July 1966
▲ Washington, D. C.: *Heart of Our Nation's Capital; Washington Inside the Beltway.* Detachable. 93-98, Jan. 1983
▲ Washington, D. C.: *A Pocket Map of Central Washington; A Pocket Map of Suburban Washington.* Sept. 1948
▲ Washington, D. C.: *Round About the Nation's Capital.* Apr. 1956
▲ Washington, D. C.: *Tourist Washington; Suburban Washington.* U. S. Atlas series. Dec. 1964
▲ *Wild and Scenic Rivers of the United States.* July 1977
▲ *Wisconsin, Michigan, and the Great Lakes.* Close-up series. Text on reverse. Aug. 1973

Universe:
▲ *The Earth's Moon.* Feb. 1969
▲ *Journey Into the Universe Through Time and Space; National Geographic-Palomar Sky Survey Charting the Heavens,* double-sided supplement. June 1983
▲ *A Map of the Heavens.* Star charts on reverse. Dec. 1957; Aug. 1970
• Mapping the Unknown Universe. By F. Barrows Colton. NGS research grant. 401-420, Sept. 1950
▲ *The Red Planet Mars.* Text on reverse. Feb. 1973
▲ *The Solar System; Saturn.* July 1981

World:
• New Atlas Maps Announced by the Society: Expanded Map Program, Marking National Geographic's 70th Year. By James M. Darley. 66-68, Jan. 1958
▲ *The Political World; The Physical World.* Nov. 1975
▲ *The World.* Mar. 1957
▲ *The World.* Feb. 1965
▲ *The World.* Atlas series. Nov. 1960
▲ *The World.* Text on reverse. Dec. 1970
▲ World: *The Great Whales: Migration and Range.* Text on reverse. Dec. 1976
▲ *The World; The World Ocean Floor.* Dec. 1981
▲ *The World Map.* Dec. 1951

MAPLE SUGAR AND SYRUP:
• Sugar Weather in the Green Mountains. By Stephen Greene. Photos by Robert F. Sisson. 471-482, Apr. 1954

MAPPING the Nation's Breadbasket. By Frederick Simpich. 831-849, June 1948

MAPPING the Unknown Universe. By F. Barrows Colton. NGS research grant. 401-420, Sept. 1950

MARBLE:
- Carrara Marble: Touchstone of Eternity. By Cathy Newman. Photos by Pierre Boulat. 42-59, July 1982
- Mountains Top Off New England. By F. Barrows Colton. Photos by Robert F. Sisson. 563-602, May 1951

MARBLE CANYON NATIONAL MONUMENT, Arizona:
- Retracing John Wesley Powell's Historic Voyage Down the Grand Canyon. By Joseph Judge. Photos by Walter Meayers Edwards. 668-713, May 1969

MARBLEHEAD, Massachusetts:
- Windjamming Around New England. By Tom Horgan. Photos by Robert F. Sisson. 141-169, Aug. 1950

MARBLEHEAD-HALIFAX RACE:
- Down East to Nova Scotia. By Winfield Parks. 853-879, June 1964

MARBORÉ (Massif), France-Spain:
- Probing Ice Caves of the Pyrenees. By Norbert Casteret. 391-404, Mar. 1953

MARCHIONINI, ALFRED:
Author-Photographer:
- Peasants of Anatolia. 57-72, July 1948

MARDEN, LUIS:
- Editorial. By Gilbert M. Grosvenor. 439, Apr. 1978

Author:
- The American Lobster, Delectable Cannibal. Photos by David Doubilet. 462-487, Apr. 1973
- Bamboo, the Giant Grass. Photos by Jim Brandenburg. 502-529, Oct. 1980
- The Bird Men (Ultralight Fliers). Photos by Charles O'Rear. 198-217, Aug. 1983
- The Continental Shelf: Man's New Frontier. Photos by Ira Block. 495-531, Apr. 1978
- The Exquisite Orchids. Included: The newly discovered *Epistephium mardeni*. 485-513, Apr. 1971
- Guatemala Revisited. 525-564, Oct. 1947
- Madagascar: Island at the End of the Earth. Photos by Albert Moldvay. 443-487, Oct. 1967
- The Man Who Talks to Hummingbirds. Photos by James Blair. 80-99, Jan. 1963
- The Renaissance Lives On In Tuscany. Photos by Albert Moldvay. 626-659, Nov. 1974
- Saga of a Ship, the *Yankee* (Brigantine). 263-269, Feb. 1966
- The Sailing Oystermen of Chesapeake Bay. 798-819, Dec. 1967
- Titicaca, Abode of the Sun. Photos by Flip Schulke. 272-294, Feb. 1971

Author-Photographer:
- Ama, Sea Nymphs of Japan. 122-135, July 1971
- Amalfi, Italy's Divine Coast. 472-509, Oct. 1959
- Bruges, the City the Sea Forgot. 631-665, May 1955

LUIS MARDEN, NGS

GORDON W. GAHAN

Orchids: species discovered by Luis Marden, *top;* Peruvian flower attracts birds, *above*

- Camera Under the Sea. 162-200, Feb. 1956
- Dzibilchaltun: Up from the Well of Time. 110-129, Jan. 1959
- The Friendly Isles of Tonga. 345-367, Mar. 1968
- Gloucester Blesses Its Portuguese Fleet. 75-84, July 1953
- Holy Week and the Fair in Sevilla. 499-530, Apr. 1951
- Huzza for Otaheite! (*Bounty* Voyage). 435-459, Apr. 1962
- I Found the Bones of the *Bounty*. 725-789, Dec. 1957
- The Islands Called Fiji. 526-561, Oct. 1958
- The Other Side of Jordan. 790-825, Dec. 1964
- The Purple Land of Uruguay. 623-654, Nov. 1948
- Sicily the Three-cornered. 1-48, Jan. 1955
- Spain's Silkworm Gut. 100-108, July 1951
- Speaking of Spain. 415-456, Apr. 1950
- Tahiti, "Finest Island in the World." 1-47, July 1962
- Tropical Gardens of Key West. 116-124, Jan. 1953

Photographer:
- Aviation Looks Ahead on Its 50th Birthday. By Emory S. Land. 721-739, Dec. 1953
- Aviation Medicine on the Threshold of Space. By Allan C. Fisher, Jr. 241-278, Aug. 1955
- Cape Canaveral's 6,000-mile Shooting Gallery. By Allan C. Fisher, Jr. Photos by Luis Marden and Thomas Nebbia. 421-471, Oct. 1959
- Down East Cruise *(Nomad)*. By Tom Horgan. 329-369, Sept. 1952
- Exploring Davy Jones's Locker with *Calypso*. By Jacques-Yves Cousteau. 149-161, Feb. 1956
- Exploring the Drowned City of Port Royal. By Marion Clayton Link. 151-183, Feb. 1960
- Fact Finding for Tomorrow's Planes. By Hugh L. Dryden. 757-780, Dec. 1953
- Hydrofoil Ferry "Flies" the Strait of Messina. By Gilbert Grosvenor. 493-496, Apr. 1957
- Marineland, Florida's Giant Fish Bowl. By Gilbert Grosvenor La Gorce. 679-694, Nov. 1952
- Reaching for the Moon (Rockets). By Allan C. Fisher, Jr. 157-171, Feb. 1959
- Shad in the Shadow of Skyscrapers. By Dudley B. Martin. 359-376, Mar. 1947

MARDI GRAS:
- Mardi Gras in New Orleans. By Carolyn Bennett Patterson. Photos by Robert F. Sisson and John E. Fletcher. 726-732, Nov. 1960
- Mobile, Alabama's City in Motion. By William Graves. Photos by Joseph J. Scherschel and Robert W. Madden. 368-397, Mar. 1968
- New Orleans: Jambalaya on the Levee. By Harnett T. Kane. Photos by Justin Locke. 143-184, Feb. 1953
- New Orleans and Her River. By Joseph Judge. Photos by James L. Stanfield. 151-187, Feb. 1971

M N

BOTH BY DAVID DOUBILET

Emerald Sea: living wall of sea stars, *top;* strawberry anemones, *above*

MARE IMBRIUM, Moon:
● Have We Solved the Mysteries of the Moon? By Kenneth F. Weaver. Paintings by William H. Bond. 309-325, Sept. 1973

MARIANA ISLANDS, Pacific Ocean:
● Pacific Wards of Uncle Sam. By W. Robert Moore. 73-104, July 1948

MARIANA TRENCH, Pacific Ocean:
● Man's Deepest Dive (Challenger Deep). By Jacques Piccard. Photos by Thomas J. Abercrombie. 224-239, Aug. 1960

MARINATOS, SPYRIDON: Author:
● Thera, Key to the Riddle of Minos. Photos by Otis Imboden. 702-726, May 1972

MARINE BAND, U. S.:
● The President's Music Men. By Stuart E. Jones. Photos by William W. Campbell III. 752-766, Dec. 1959

MARINE BIOLOGY:
● Adrift on a Raft of Sargassum. Photos by Robert F. Sisson. 188-199, Feb. 1976
◆ *Amazing Animals of the Sea.* 1981
◆ *Animals That Live in the Sea.* 1978
● Antarctica's Nearer Side. By Samuel W. Matthews. Photos by William R. Curtsinger. 622-655, Nov. 1971
● At Home in the Sea. By Jacques-Yves Cousteau. 465-507, Apr. 1964
● Australia's Great Barrier Reef. Photos by Valerie and Ron Taylor. 728-741, June 1973
● Australia's Great Barrier Reef. 630-663, May 1981
I. A Marine Park Is Born. By Soames Summerhays. Photos by Ron and Valerie Taylor. 630-635; II. Paradise Beneath the Sea. By Ron and Valerie Taylor. 636-663
● British Columbia's Cold Emerald Sea. Photos by David Doubilet. Text by Larry Kohl. 526-551, Apr. 1980
● *Calypso* Explores an Undersea Canyon (Romanche Trench). By Jacques-Yves Cousteau. Photos by Bates Littlehales. NGS research grant. 373-396, Mar. 1958
● Camera Under the Sea. By Luis Marden. NGS research grant. 162-200, Feb. 1956
● Deep Diving off Japan. By Georges S. Houot. NGS research grant. 138-150, Jan. 1960
● *Deepstar* Explores the Ocean Floor. Photos by Ron Church. 110-129, Jan. 1971
■ Dive to the Edge of Creation. 682, Nov. 1979; 1, cover, Jan. 1980
● Diving Beneath Arctic Ice. By Joseph B. MacInnis. Photos by William R. Curtsinger. 248-267, Aug. 1973
● Diving Saucer Takes to the Deep. By Jacques-Yves Cousteau. NGS research grant. 571-586, Apr. 1960
● Exploring Davy Jones's Locker with *Calypso.* By Jacques-Yves Cousteau. Photos by Luis Marden. NGS research grant. 149-161, Feb. 1956
◆ *Exploring the Deep Frontier.* 1980
● Fishing in the Whirlpool of Charybdis. By Paul A. Zahl. 579-618, Nov. 1953
● Four Years of Diving to the Bottom of the Sea. By Georges S. Houot. NGS research grant. 715-731, May 1958
■ Galapagos Rift expedition. 682, Nov. 1979
● Glass Menageries of the Sea. By Paul A. Zahl. 797-822, June 1955
● Hatchetfish, Torchbearers of the Deep. By Paul A. Zahl. 713-714, May 1958
● Hidden Life of an Undersea Desert. By Eugenie Clark. Photos by David Doubilet. 129-144, July 1983
● How the Sun Gives Life to the Sea. By Paul A. Zahl. 199-225, Feb. 1961
● In Hawaii's Crystal Sea, A Galaxy of Life Fills the Night. By Kenneth Brower. Photos by William R. Curtsinger and Chris Newbert. 834-847, Dec. 1981
● Incredible World of the Deep-sea Rifts. NGS research grant. 680-705, Nov. 1979
I. Strange World Without Sun. The Editor. 680-688; II. Return to Oases of the Deep. By Robert D. Ballard and J. Frederick Grassle. 689-705
● Miami's Expanding Horizons. By William H. Nicholas. Included: University of Miami marine biology study and National Geographic Society–University of Miami long-range program to study plankton. 561-594, Nov. 1950
● My Chesapeake–Queen of Bays. By Allan C. Fisher, Jr. Photos by Lowell Georgia. 428-467, Oct. 1980
◆ *The Mysterious Undersea World.* 1980
● Nature's Night Lights: Probing the Secrets of Bioluminescence. By Paul A. Zahl. 45-69, July 1971
● New World of the Ocean. By Samuel W. Matthews. 792-832, Dec. 1981
● Night Life in the Gulf Stream. By Paul A. Zahl. 391-418, Mar. 1954
● Oases of Life in the Cold Abyss (Galapagos Rift). By John B. Corliss and Robert D. Ballard. 441-453, Oct. 1977
● The Ocean. By Jacques-Yves Cousteau. 780-791, Dec. 1981
◆ *The Ocean Realm.* 1978
● One Hundred Hours Beneath the Chesapeake. By Gilbert C. Klingel. Photos by Willard R. Culver. NGS research grant. 681-696, May 1955
● Oregon's Sidewalk on the Sea. By Paul A. Zahl. 708-734, Nov. 1961
● Patagonia. Photos by Des and Jen Bartlett. 290-339, Mar. 1976
I. Argentina Protects Its Wildlife Treasures. By William G. Conway. 290-297; II. Where Two Worlds Meet. 298-321; III. At Home With Right Whales. By Roger Payne. NGS research grant. 322-339
● Photographing the Sea's Dark Underworld. By Harold E. Edgerton. NGS research grant. 523-537, Apr. 1955
● Sailing a Sea of Fire (Phosphorescent Bay, Puerto Rico). By Paul A. Zahl. 120-129, July 1960
● Strange Babies of the Sea (Plankton). By Hilary B. Moore. Paintings by Craig Phillips and Jacqueline Hutton. NGS research grant. 41-56, July 1952

• Strange World of Palau's Salt Lakes. By William M. Hamner. Photos by David Doubilet. 264-282, Feb. 1982
• The Strangest Sea. By Eugenie Clark. Photos by David Doubilet. 338-365, Sept. 1975
Rainbow World Beneath the Red Sea. 344-365
• Tektite II. 256-296, Aug. 1971
I. Science's Window on the Sea. By John G. VanDerwalker. Photos by Bates Littlehales. 256-289; II. All-girl Team Tests the Habitat. By Sylvia A. Earle. Paintings by Pierre Mion. 291-296
• To the Depths of the Sea by Bathyscaphe. By Jacques-Yves Cousteau. NGS research grant. 67-79, July 1954
◆ *Treasures in the Sea*. Announced. 736-738, Nov. 1972
• Two and a Half Miles Down. By Georges S. Houot. NGS research grant. 80-86, July 1954
• Undersea Wonders of the Galapagos. By Gerard Wellington. Photos by David Doubilet. 363-381, Sept. 1978
• Undersea World of a Kelp Forest. By Sylvia A. Earle. Photos by Al Giddings. 411-426, Sept. 1980
• *See also* Algae; Corals and Coral Reefs; Crustaceans; Dolphins; Fishes; Octopuses; Plankton; Rotifers; Seals; Sharks; Sponges; Walruses; Whales

MARINE GARDENS. *See* Ras Muhammad

A **MARINE** Park Is Born. By Soames Summerhays. Photos by Ron and Valerie Taylor. 630-635, May 1981

MARINE PARKS. *See* Buck Island Reef National Monument, St. Croix, Virgin Islands; Great Barrier Reef, Australia; John Pennekamp Coral Reef State Park, Florida; Ras Muhammad, Sinai Peninsula

MARINE RESEARCH. *See* Airborne Undersea Expeditions; Marine Biology; Oceanography

MARINELAND, Florida's Giant Fish Bowl. By Gilbert Grosvenor La Gorce. Photos by Luis Marden. 679-694, Nov. 1952

MARINER MISSIONS:
• Journey to Mars (Mariner 9). By Kenneth F. Weaver. Paintings by Ludek Pesek. 231-263, Feb. 1973
• Mariner Scans a Lifeless Venus (Mariner 2). By Frank Sartwell. Paintings by Davis Meltzer. 733-742, May 1963
• Mariner Unveils Venus and Mercury (Mariner 10). By Kenneth F. Weaver. 858-869, June 1975
• Voyage to the Planets. By Kenneth F. Weaver. Paintings by Ludek Pesek. Included: Mariner 2, Mariner 4, Mariner 5, Mariner 6, Mariner 7. 147-193, Aug. 1970

MARINES, U. S. *See* U. S. Marine Corps

MARISMAS (Marshes), Spain:
• Rare Birds Flock to Spain's Marismas. By Roger Tory Peterson. 397-425, Mar. 1958

MARITIME ALPS, Europe:
• Sheep Trek in the French Alps. By Maurice Moyal. Photos by Marcel Coen. 545-564, Apr. 1952

MARITIME PROVINCES, Canada:
▲ *Close-up: U.S.A., Maine, with the Maritime Provinces of Canada,* supplement. Text on reverse. Mar. 1975
• *See also* New Brunswick; Nova Scotia

MARK TWAIN: Mirror of America. By Noel Grove. Photos by James L. Stanfield. 300-337, Sept. 1975
• *See also* Twain, Mark

MARKETS AND STORES:
• Keeping House in London. By Frances James. 769-792, Dec. 1947
• Paris Flea Market. By Franc Shor. Photos by Alexander Taylor. 318-326, Mar. 1957

MARKWITH, CARL R.: Author:
• Skyway Below the Clouds. Photos by Ernest J. Cottrell. 85-108, July 1949

MAROSTICA, Italy:
• Chessmen Come to Life in Marostica. By Alexander Taylor. 658-668, Nov. 1956

MARQUESAS ISLANDS, Pacific Ocean:
• Shores and Sails in the South Seas. By Charles Allmon. Included: Fatu Hiva; Fatu Huku; Hiva Oa; Nuku Hiva; Tahuata; Ua Huka; Ua Pu. 73-104, Jan. 1950

MARQUESAS KEYS, Florida:
• *Atocha,* Tragic Treasure Galleon of the Florida Keys. By Eugene Lyon. 787-809, June 1976
• Treasure From the Ghost Galleon: *Santa Margarita*. By Eugene Lyon. Photos by Don Kincaid. 228-243, Feb. 1982

MARS (Planet):
• Editorial. By Gilbert M. Grosvenor. 1, Jan. 1977
• Journey to Mars. By Kenneth F. Weaver. Paintings by Ludek Pesek. 231-263, Feb. 1973
• Mars: A New World to Explore. By Carl Sagan. 821-841, Dec. 1967
• Mars: Our First Close Look. 3-31, Jan. 1977
I. As Viking Sees It. 3-7; II. The Search For Life. By Rick Gore. 9-31
• New Light on the Changing Face of Mars. By E. C. Slipher. NGS research grant. 427-436, Sept. 1955
▲ *The Red Planet Mars;* "The Dusty Face of Mars," map-and-painting supplement. Feb. 1973
• The Search for Life on Mars. By Kenneth F. Weaver. 264-265, Feb. 1973
• Voyage to the Planets. By Kenneth F. Weaver. Paintings by Ludek Pesek. 147-193, Aug. 1970

MARS RESEARCH EXPEDITION: South Africa:
• New Light on the Changing Face of Mars. By E. C. Slipher. NGS research grant. 427-436, Sept. 1955

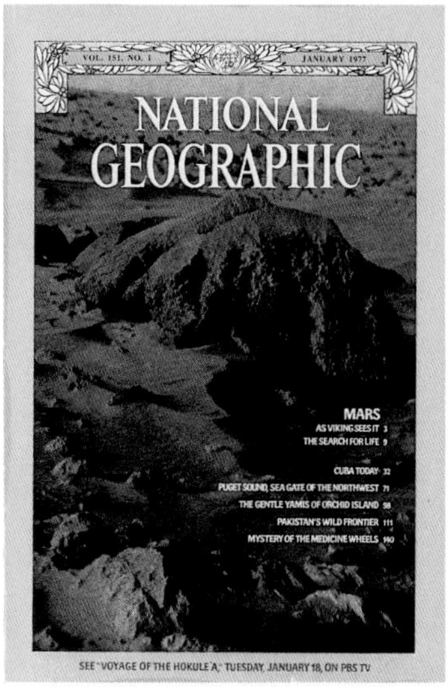

NASA

Mars: coating of rust gives desertscape its red color

MARSEILLE, France:
• French Riviera: Storied Playground on the Azure Coast. By Carleton Mitchell. Photos by Thomas Nebbia. 798-835, June 1967
• Provence, Empire of the Sun. By William Davenport. Photos by James A. Sugar. 692-715, May 1975

MARSH, DONALD B.:
Author-Photographer:
• Canada's Caribou Eskimos. 87-104, Jan. 1947

MARSH ARABS. *See* Ma'dan

MARSH DWELLERS of Southern Iraq. By Wilfred Thesiger. Photos by Gavin Maxwell. 205-239, Feb. 1958

MARSHACK, ALEXANDER:
• A Bold New Look at Our Past. The Editor. 62-63, Jan. 1975
Author:
• Exploring the Mind of Ice Age Man. 64-89, Jan. 1975

MARSHALL, GEORGE C.:
• Tribute to General George C. Marshall. 113, Jan. 1960
Author:
• Giant Effigies of the Southwest. 389, Sept. 1952
• Our War Memorials Abroad: A Faith Kept. 731-737, June 1957

MARSHALL, LAURENCE K.:
Photographer:
• Bushmen of the Kalahari. By Elizabeth Marshall Thomas. 866-888, June 1963

MARSHALL ISLANDS, Pacific Ocean:
• Pacific Wards of Uncle Sam. By W. Robert Moore. 73-104, July 1948
• *See also* Bikini; Kwajalein

MARSHALL KALAHARI EXPEDITIONS:
• Bushmen of the Kalahari. By Elizabeth Marshall Thomas. Photos by Laurence K. Marshall. 866-888, June 1963

MARSHES:
• Marsh Dwellers of Southern Iraq. By Wilfred Thesiger. Photos by Gavin Maxwell. 205-239, Feb. 1958
• Water Dwellers in a Desert World. By Gavin Young. Photos by Nik Wheeler. 502-523, Apr. 1976
• *See also* Abbotsbury Swannery, England; Delta Marsh, Manitoba, Canada; Everglades (Region), Florida; Marismas, Spain; Merritt Island National Wildlife Refuge, Florida; Mississippi River Delta, Louisiana; Salt Marshes; Swamps

MARSHFIELD, Massachusetts:
• Land of the Pilgrims' Pride. By George W. Long. Photos by Robert F. Sisson. 193-219, Aug. 1947

MARSUPIALS:
▪ Australia's Animal Mysteries. 824, Dec. 1982
• Eden in the Outback. By Kay and Stanley Breeden. 189-203, Feb. 1973
• Strange Animals of Australia. By David Fleay. Photos by Stanley Breeden. 388-411, Sept. 1963
• *See also* Kangaroos; Opossums

PAINTINGS BY RICHARD SCHLECHT

New Clues: attack on Virginia colonists

***Mary Rose:* panic as sea rushes in**

MARTHA'S VINEYARD, Massachusetts:
• Martha's Vineyard. By William P. E. Graves. Photos by James P. Blair. 778-809, June 1961
• Windjamming Around New England. By Tom Horgan. Photos by Robert F. Sisson. 141-169, Aug. 1950

MARTIN, DUDLEY B.: Author:
• Shad in the Shadow of Skyscrapers. Photos by Luis Marden. 359-376, Mar. 1947

MARTINIQUE (Island), West Indies:
• *Carib* Cruises the West Indies. By Carleton Mitchell. 1-56, Jan. 1948
• *Finisterre* Sails the Windward Islands. By Carleton Mitchell. Photos by Winfield Parks. 755-801, Dec. 1965
• Martinique: A Tropical Bit of France. By Gwen Drayton Allmon. Photos by Charles Allmon. 255-283, Feb. 1959
• Martinique: Liberté, Egalité, and Uncertainty in the Caribbean. By Kenneth MacLeish. Photos by John Launois. 124-148, Jan. 1975

MARTIN'S HUNDRED (Settlement Tract), Virginia:
• First Look at a Lost Virginia Settlement. By Ivor Noël Hume. Photos by Ira Block. Paintings by Richard Schlecht. 735-767, June 1979
• New Clues to an Old Mystery (Virginia's Wolstenholme Towne). By Ivor Noël Hume. Photos by Ira Block. Paintings by Richard Schlecht. 53-77, Jan. 1982

The **MARVELOUS** Hummingbird Rediscovered. By Crawford H. Greenewalt. 98-101, July 1966

The **MARVELOUS** Maldive Islands. By Alan Villiers. 829-849, June 1957

MARVELS of a Coral Realm. By Walter A. Starck II. NGS research grant. 710-738, Nov. 1966

MARY ROSE, H. M. S.:
• Henry VIII's Lost Warship: *Mary Rose.* By Margaret Rule. Introduction and picture text by Peter Miller. Paintings by Richard Schlecht. 646-675, May 1983

MARY-ROUSSELIERE, GUY:
Author-Photographer:
• I Live With the Eskimos. 188-217, Feb. 1971

MARYLAND:
• Appalachian Valley Pilgrimage. By Catherine Bell Palmer. Photos by Justin Locke. 1-32, July 1949
• Chesapeake Country. By Nathaniel T. Kenney. Photos by Bates Littlehales. 370-411, Sept. 1964
• "Delmarva," Gift of the Sea. By Catherine Bell Palmer. 367-399, Sept. 1950
• Down the Potomac by Canoe. By Ralph Gray. Photos by Walter Meayers Edwards. 213-242, Aug. 1948
• Down the Susquehanna by Canoe. By Ralph Gray. Photos by Walter Meayers Edwards. 73-120, July 1950

• Maryland on the Half Shell. By Stuart E. Jones. Photos by Robert W. Madden. 188-229, Feb. 1972
• My Chesapeake–Queen of Bays. By Allan C. Fisher, Jr. Photos by Lowell Georgia. 428-467, Oct. 1980
• The Nation's River. By Allan C. Fisher, Jr. Photos by James L. Stanfield. 432-469, Oct. 1976
• Nature's Year in Pleasant Valley. By Paul A. Zahl. 488-525, Apr. 1968
• Roving Maryland's Cavalier Country. By William A. Kinney. 431-470, Apr. 1954
• The Sailing Oystermen of Chesapeake Bay. By Luis Marden. 798-819, Dec. 1967
• Skyway Below the Clouds. By Carl R. Markwith. Photos by Ernest J. Cottrell. Included: Hyde Field, near Clinton. 85-108, July 1949
• Waterway to Washington, the C & O Canal. By Jay Johnston. 419-439, Mar. 1960
• *See also* Assateague Island; Baltimore; Beltsville; Eastern Shore

MASAI (Tribespeople):
▪ Man of the Serengeti. 179A-179B, Feb. 1972
• Preserving the Treasures of Olduvai Gorge. By Melvin M. Payne. Photos by Joseph J. Scherschel. 701-709, Nov. 1966
• Spearing Lions with Africa's Masai. By Edgar Monsanto Queeny. 487-517, Oct. 1954

MASCARENE ISLANDS, Indian Ocean. *See* Mauritius

MASQAT. *See* Muscat and Oman

MASSACHUSETTS:
• The American Lobster, Delectable Cannibal. By Luis Marden. Photos by David Doubilet. 462-487, Apr. 1973
• Captain Smith's New England . . . and the Pilgrims' Cape Cod. 765, June 1953
• Down East Cruise. By Tom Horgan. Photos by Luis Marden. 329-369, Sept. 1952
• Founders of New England. By Sir Evelyn Wrench. Photos by B. Anthony Stewart. 803-838, June 1953
• How Fruit Came to America. By J. R. Magness. Paintings by Else Bostelmann. 325-377, Sept. 1951
• Land of the Pilgrims' Pride. By George W. Long. Photos by Robert F. Sisson. 193-219, Aug. 1947
• Literary Landmarks of Massachusetts. By William H. Nicholas. Photos by B. Anthony Stewart and John E. Fletcher. 279-310, Mar. 1950
• Massachusetts Builds for Tomorrow. By Robert de Roos. Photos by B. Anthony Stewart. 790-843, Dec. 1966
• Massachusetts' North Shore: Harboring Old Ways. By Randall S. Peffer. Photos by Nathan Benn. 568-590, Apr. 1979
• The Merrimack: River of Industry and Romance. By Albert W. Atwood. Photos by B. Anthony Stewart. 106-140, Jan. 1951
• Mountains Top Off New England. By F. Barrows Colton. Photos by Robert F. Sisson. 563-602, May 1951
• New England's "Little Portugal." By O. Louis Mazzatenta. 90-109, Jan. 1975
• The Old Boston Post Roads. By Donald Barr Chidsey. 189-205, Aug. 1962
• Patriots in Petticoats. By Lonnelle Aikman. Paintings by Louis S. Glanzman. 475-493, Oct. 1975
• The Post Road Today. Photos by B. Anthony Stewart. 206-233, Aug. 1962
• Shrines of Each Patriot's Devotion. By Frederick G. Vosburgh. 51-82, Jan. 1949
• Windjamming Around New England. By Tom Horgan. Photos by Robert F. Sisson. Contents: Beverly; Cape Ann; Cape Cod; Gloucester; Hyannis; Marblehead; Martha's Vineyard; Nantucket; Provincetown; Rockport; Salem; Woods Hole. 141-169, Aug. 1950
• Yesterday Lingers Along the Connecticut. By Charles McCarry. Photos by David L. Arnold. 334-369, Sept. 1972
• *See also* Berkshires; Boston; Buttrick Garden; Cape Cod; Concord; Deerfield; Gloucester; Martha's Vineyard; Nantucket; Worcester; *and* Clarke School for the Deaf

MASSANUTTEN MOUNTAIN, Virginia:
• Appalachian Valley Pilgrimage. By Catherine Bell Palmer. Photos by Justin Locke. 1-32, July 1949

A **MASTER** Plan for Yellowstone: The Next 100 Years. By George B. Hartzog, Jr. 632-637, May 1972

MASTERPIECES on Tour. By Harry A. McBride. 717-750, Dec. 1948

MASTERWORK on the Mall. By J. Carter Brown. Photos by James A. Sugar. 680-701, Nov. 1978

MASTERWORKS of the Wild–a Portfolio From Our National Parks. Photos by David Alan Harvey. 3-17, July 1979

MASTIGIAS (Jellyfish):
• Strange World of Palau's Salt Lakes. By William M. Hamner. Photos by David Doubilet. 264-282, Feb. 1982

MATHEMATICIANS. *See* Bowditch, Nathaniel; Newton, Isaac

MATO GROSSO (State), Brazil:
• Indians of the Amazon Darkness. By Harald Schultz. NGS research grant. 737-758, May 1964
• The Jungle Was My Home. By Sasha Siemel. 695-712, Nov. 1952
• Man in the Amazon: Stone Age Present Meets Stone Age Past. By W. Jesco von Puttkamer. NGS research grant. 60-83, Jan. 1979
• *See also* Cinta Larga Indians; Kreen-Akarores; Txukahameis

MATOS MOCTEZUMA, EDUARDO: Author:
• New Finds in the Great Temple. Photos by David Hiser. 767-775, Dec. 1980

MATS: America's Long Arm of the Air. By Beverley M. Bowie. Photos by Robert F. Sisson. 283-317, Mar. 1957

MATTERNES, JAY: Artist:
• Ancient Ashfall Creates a Pompeii of Prehistoric Animals. By Michael R. Voorhies. Photos by Annie Griffiths. 66-75, Jan. 1981
▲ "Ice Age Mammals of the Alaskan Tundra," painting supplement. Map of Canada. Mar. 1972
• Skull 1470. By Richard E. Leakey. Photos by Bob Campbell. 819-829, June 1973

MATTHEWS, SAMUEL W.: Author:
• America Goes to the Fair. 293-333, Sept. 1954
• Antarctica: Icy Testing Ground for Space. Photos by Robert W. Madden. 569-592, Oct. 1968
• Antarctica's Nearer Side. Photos by William R. Curtsinger. 622-655, Nov. 1971
• Bali's Sacred Mountain Blows Its Top. Photos by Robert F. Sisson. 436-458, Sept. 1963
I. Disaster in Paradise. By Windsor P. Booth. 436-447; II. Devastated Land and Homeless People. By Samuel W. Matthews. 447-458
• Beltsville Brings Science to the Farm. 199-218, Aug. 1953
• Hunting the Heartbeat of a Whale. By Paul Dudley White and Samuel W. Matthews. 49-64, July 1956
• Nevada Learns to Live With the Atom. 839-850, June 1953
• Nevada's Mountain of Invisible Gold. Photos by David F. Cupp. 668-679, May 1968
• New World of the Ocean. 792-832, Dec. 1981
• The Night the Mountains Moved (Montana's 1959 Earthquake). Photos by J. Baylor Roberts. 329-359, Mar. 1960
• The Phoenicians, Sea Lords of Antiquity. Photos by Winfield Parks. Paintings by Robert C. Magis. 149-189, Aug. 1974
• Science Explores the Monsoon Sea. Photos by Robert F. Sisson. 554-575, Oct. 1967
• Scientists Drill at Sea to Pierce Earth's Crust (Project Mohole). Photos by J. Baylor Roberts. 686-697, Nov. 1961
• This Changing Earth. 1-37, Jan. 1973
• What's Happening to Our Climate? 576-615, Nov. 1976

MATTISON, JAMES A., Jr.: Photographer:
• Return of the Sea Otter. By Karl W. Kenyon. 520-539, Oct. 1971

MAUI (Island), Hawaii:
• Maui, Where Old Hawaii Still Lives. By Kenneth F. Weaver. Photos by Gordon W. Gahan. 514-543, Apr. 1971
• New Light on the Singing Whales. Introduction by Roger Payne. Photos by Flip Nicklin. NGS research grant. 463-477, Apr. 1982

M N

• Precious Corals, Hawaii's Deep-sea Jewels. By Richard W. Grigg. Photos by David Doubilet. 719-732, May 1979

MAUI WHALE WATCHERS:
Study Grant:
• Humpback Whales. 466, Apr. 1982

MAUNEY, MICHAEL: Photographer:
• Milwaukee: More Than Beer. By Louise Levathes. 180-201, Aug. 1980

MAURI, CARLO: Photographer:
• *Tigris* Sails Into the Past. By Thor Heyerdahl. Photos by Carlo Mauri and the crew of the *Tigris*. 806-827, Dec. 1978
• The Voyage of *Ra II*. By Thor Heyerdahl. Photos by Carlo Mauri and Georges Sourial. 44-71, Jan. 1971

MAURITANIA:
• The Desert: An Age-old Challenge Grows. By Rick Gore. Photos by Georg Gerster and Bruce Dale. 586-639, Nov. 1979
• Dry-land Fleet Sails the Sahara. By Jean du Boucher. Photos by Jonathan S. Blair. 696-725, Nov. 1967
• Freedom Speaks French in Ouagadougou. By John Scofield. 153-203, Aug. 1966

MAURITIUS (Island), Indian Ocean:
• Crosscurrents Sweep the Indian Ocean. By Bart McDowell. Photos by Steve Raymer. 422-457, Oct. 1981
• Mauritius, Island of the Dodo. By Quentin Keynes. 77-104, Jan. 1956

MAXWELL, GAVIN: Photographer:
• Marsh Dwellers of Southern Iraq. By Wilfred Thesiger. 205-239, Feb. 1958

MAYA (Indians):
• Belize, the Awakening Land. By Louis de la Haba. Photos by Michael E. Long. 124-146, Jan. 1972
◆ *Discovering Man's Past in the Americas*. Announced. 880-884, June 1969
• Dzibilchaltun. NGS research grant. 91-129, Jan. 1959
I. Lost City of the Maya. By E. Wyllys Andrews. 91-109; II. Up From the Well of Time. By Luis Marden. 110-129
• Editorial. By Gilbert M. Grosvenor. 727, Dec. 1975
• Guatemala, Maya and Modern. By Louis de la Haba. Photos by Joseph J. Scherschel. 661-689, Nov. 1974
• Into the Well of Sacrifice (Chichén Itzá). NGS research grant. 540-561, Oct. 1961
I. Return to the Sacred Cenote. By Eusebio Dávalos Hurtado. 540-549; II. Treasure Hunt in the Deep Past. By Bates Littlehales. 550-561
• The Maya. 729-811, Dec. 1975
I. Children of Time. By Howard La Fay. Photos by David Alan Harvey. 729-767; II. Riddle of the Glyphs. By George E. Stuart. Photos by Otis Imboden. 768-791; III. Resurrecting the Grandeur of Tikal. By William R. Coe. 792-798; IV. A Traveler's Tale of Ancient Tikal. Paintings by Peter Spier. Text by Alice J. Hall. 799-811
• Maya Art Treasures Discovered in Cave. By George E. Stuart. Photos by Wilbur E. Garrett. 220-235, Aug. 1981
◆ *The Mysterious Maya*. 1977
• "Pyramids" of the New World. By Neil Merton Judd. 105-128, Jan. 1948
• Unearthing the Oldest Known Maya. By Norman Hammond. Photos by Lowell Georgia and Martha Cooper. NGS research grant. 126-140, July 1982

MAYER, FRED: Photographer:
• Little Tibet in Switzerland. By Laura Pilarski. 711-727, Nov. 1968

MAYFLOWER (Ship):
• Founders of New England. By Sir Evelyn Wrench. Photos by B. Anthony Stewart. 803-838, June 1953

MAYFLOWER II (Ship):
• How We Sailed the New *Mayflower* to America. By Alan Villiers. 627-672, Nov. 1957
• "Mayflower II," painting supplement. Nov. 1957
• We're Coming Over on the *Mayflower*. By Alan Villiers. 708-728, May 1957

MAYTIME Miracle in Sherwood Gardens. By Nathaniel T. Kenney. 700-709, May 1956

MAZAMA, Mount, Oregon:
• Crater Lake Summer. By Walter Meayers Edwards. 134-148, July 1962
• When Mt. Mazama Lost Its Top: The Birth of Crater Lake. By Lyman J. Briggs. 128-133, July 1962

MAZATZAL WILDERNESS, Arizona:
• The Mazatzal's Harsh but Lovely Land Between. By François Leydet. Photos by Farrell Grehan. 161-167, Feb. 1974

MAZE, STEPHANIE: Photographer:
• The Mexican Americans: A People on the Move. By Griffin Smith, Jr. 780-809, June 1980
• The Uncertain State of Puerto Rico. By Bill Richards. 516-543, Apr. 1983

MAZZATENTA, O. LOUIS:
Author-Photographer:
• New England's "Little Portugal." 90-109, Jan. 1975
Photographer:
• The Azores, Nine Islands in Search of a Future. By Don Moser. 261-288, Feb. 1976
• Down the Ancient Appian Way. By James Cerruti. 714-747, June 1981
• The Gauchos, Last of a Breed. By Robert Laxalt. 478-501, Oct. 1980
• Paraguay, Paradox of South America. By Gordon Young. 240-269, Aug. 1982
• The Thames: That Noble River. By Ethel A. Starbird. 750-791, June 1983

MEANCO (Raft):
• Down Mark Twain's River on a Raft. By Rex E. Hieronymus. 551-574, Apr. 1948

MEASURES. *See* Metric System; National Bureau of Standards

MEAT INDUSTRY:
• America's "Meat on the Hoof." By William H. Nicholas. 33-72, Jan. 1952

MECCA, Saudi Arabia:
• From America to Mecca on Airborne Pilgrimage. By Abdul Ghafur. 1-60, July 1953
• Pilgrimage to Mecca. By Muhammad Abdul-Rauf. Photos by Mehmet Biber. 581-607, Nov. 1978
• Saudi Arabia: Beyond the Sands of Mecca. By Thomas J. Abercrombie. 1-53, Jan. 1966
• Saudi Arabia: The Kingdom and Its Power. By Robert Azzi. 286-333, Sept. 1980
• The Sword and the Sermon. By Thomas J. Abercrombie. 3-45, July 1972

MECH, L. DAVID: Author:
• Where Can the Wolf Survive? 518-537, Oct. 1977
• Wolves Versus Moose on Isle Royale. By Durward L. Allen and L. David Mech. 200-219, Feb. 1963

MEDALS. *See* Grosvenor Medal; Hubbard Medal; La Gorce Medal; Special Gold Medal

MEDELLÍN, Colombia:
• Cruising Colombia's "Ol' Man River." By Amos Burg. 615-660, May 1947

MEDICINE AND HEALTH:
• The American Red Cross: A Century of Service. By Louise Levathes. Photos by Annie Griffiths. 777-791, June 1981
• America's "Meat on the Hoof." By William H. Nicholas. Included: Pharmaceuticals from glandular byproducts–insulin, liver extract, thyroid, adrenocorticotrophic hormone (ACTH), epinephrine (suprarenalin). 33-72, Jan. 1952
• Ancient Mesopotamia: A Light That Did Not Fail. By E. A. Speiser. Paintings by H. M. Herget. Included: Medicine Teams Up With Religion and Magic. 41-105, Jan. 1951
• The Astonishing Armadillo. By Eleanor E. Storrs. Photos by Bianca Lavies. Included: Immunology research with leprosy bacilli provided by armadillos. 820-830, June 1982
• Beltsville Brings Science to the Farm. By Samuel W. Matthews. Included: Antibiotics, hormones. 199-218, Aug. 1953
• The British Way. By Sir Evelyn Wrench. Included: William Harvey, William Hunter, John Hunter, Edward Jenner, Florence Nightingale, Lord Lister, Sir Alexander Fleming. 421-541, Apr. 1949
• Electronic Voyage Through an Invisible World. By Kenneth F. Weaver. Included: Study, by means of the scanning electron microscope (SEM), of the origin and development of disease. 274-290, Feb. 1977

• Exploring Ancient Panama by Helicopter. By Matthew W. Stirling. Photos by Richard H. Stewart. Included: Gorgas Memorial Laboratory; yellow fever outbreak in Utivé and control measures taken. NGS research grant. 227-246, Feb. 1950
• Eyes of Science. By Rick Gore. Photos by James P. Blair. 360-389, Mar. 1978
• Fiber Optics: Harnessing Light by a Thread. By Allen A. Boraiko. Photos by Fred Ward. 516-535, Oct. 1979
• First Woman Across Greenland's Ice. By Myrtle Simpson. Photos by Hugh Simpson. Included: Study of the adrenal glands to learn the effects of stress on human beings. 264-279, Aug. 1967
• Herbs for All Seasons. By Lonnelle Aikman. Photos by Sam Abell. Picture portfolio text by Larry Kohl. 386-409, Mar. 1983
• Keeping House for a Biologist in Colombia. By Nancy Bell Fairchild Bates. Photos by Marston Bates. Included: Rockefeller Foundation laboratory; malaria and yellow fever research. 251-274, Aug. 1948
• Man's New Servant, the Friendly Atom. By F. Barrows Colton. Photos by Volkmar Wentzel. 71-90, Jan. 1954
• Minnesota, Where Water Is the Magic Word. By David S. Boyer. Photos by author and David Brill. Included: Mayo Clinic; University of Minnesota. 200-229, Feb. 1976
• Molokai–Forgotten Hawaii. By Ethel A. Starbird. Photos by Richard A. Cooke III. Included: Progress in treating leprosy at Kalaupapa. 188-219, Aug. 1981
• Mosquitoes, the Mighty Killers. By Lewis T. Nielsen. Included: The transmission of dengue fever, dog heartworm, encephalitis, filariasis, malaria, and yellow fever. 427-440, Sept. 1979
• Nature's Gifts to Medicine. By Lonnelle Aikman. Paintings by Lloyd K. Townsend and Don Crowley. 420-440, Sept. 1974
◆ *Nature's Healing Arts.* 1977
• The New Biology. 355-407, Sept. 1976
I. The Awesome Worlds Within a Cell. By Rick Gore. Photos by Bruce Dale. Paintings by Davis Meltzer. 355-395; II. The Cancer Puzzle. By Robert F. Weaver. 396-399; III. Seven Giants Who Led the Way. Paintings by Ned Seidler. Text by Rick Gore. 401-407
◆ *On the Brink of Tomorrow: Frontiers of Science.* 1982
• Our Navy's Long Submarine Arm. By Allan C. Fisher, Jr. Included: Research in night vision, color discernment, hearing, the physiological effects of air pressures, psychological factors in submarine life, the development of physical standards for personnel, and the psychological effect of color and color combinations in submarines. 613-636, Nov. 1952
• The Pesticide Dilemma. By Allen A. Boraiko. Photos by Fred Ward. 145-183, Feb. 1980

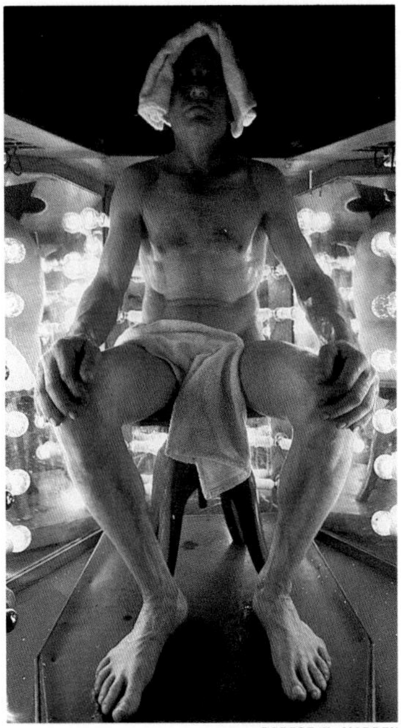
ROBERT W. MADDEN
Quicksilver: sweating out mercury

New Biology: DNA molecule
PAINTING BY DAVIS MELTZER
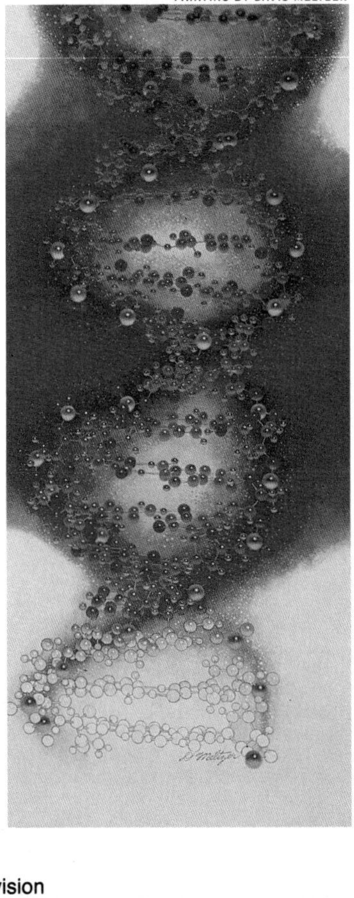

• Quicksilver and Slow Death. By John J. Putman. Photos by Robert W. Madden. Included: Mercury poisoning. 507-527, Oct. 1972
• The Rat, Lapdog of the Devil. By Thomas Y. Canby. Photos by James L. Stanfield. Included: Map showing known and suspected plague areas of the Americas, Africa, and Asia; the number of reported cases in 1975. 60-87, July 1977
• Safari Through Changing Africa. By Elsie May Bell Grosvenor. Photos by Gilbert Grosvenor. Included: The fight against malaria, tick fever, and trypanosomiasis (sleeping sickness). 145-198, Aug. 1953
• Salt–The Essence of Life. By Gordon Young. Photos by Volkmar Wentzel and Georg Gerster. 381-401, Sept. 1977
• Silver: A Mineral of Excellent Nature. By Allen A. Boraiko. Photos by Fred Ward. 280-313, Sept. 1981
• Six Months Alone in a Cave. By Michel Siffre. Included: Biorhythm research. 426-435, Mar. 1975
• Smallpox–Epitaph for a Killer? By Donald A. Henderson. Photos by Marion Kaplan. 796-805, Dec. 1978
• South in the Sudan. By Harry Hoogstraal. 249-272, Feb. 1953
• Those Successful Japanese. By Bart McDowell. Photos by Fred Ward. Included: Effects of pollution. 323-359, Mar. 1974
• White Magic in the Belgian Congo. By W. Robert Moore. 321-362, Mar. 1952
• Wintering on the Roof of the World (Himalayas). By Barry C. Bishop. NGS research grant. 503-547, Oct. 1962
Slow Death Threatens Man in the Thin Air of 19,000 Feet. 530-531
• With the Nuba Hillmen of Kordofan. By Robin Strachan. Included: Blackwater fever, cerebrospinal meningitis, jaundice, and control measures taken. 249-278, Feb. 1951
• Working for Weeks on the Sea Floor. By Jacques-Yves Cousteau. Photos by Philippe Cousteau and Bates Littlehales. NGS research grant. 498-537, Apr. 1966
• Yemen Opens the Door to Progress. By Harry Hoogstraal. 213-244, Feb. 1952
• You and the Obedient Atom. By Allan C. Fisher, Jr. Photos by B. Anthony Stewart and Thomas J. Abercrombie. 303-353, Sept. 1958
◆ *Your Wonderful Body.* 1982
• *See also* Aviation Medicine; The Bends; Coal, for black lung; Cook, James, for discoveries made in the relationship of diet and scurvy; Heart Research; Longevity; Man-in-Sea Project; Peace Corps; Space Medicine

MEDICINE MEN. *See* Shamanism

MEDICINE WHEELS:
• Probing the Mystery of the Medicine Wheels. By John A. Eddy. Photos by Thomas E. Hooper. NGS research grant. 140-146, Jan. 1977

MEDIEVAL EUROPE:
◆ *The Age of Chivalry.* Announced. 544-551, Oct. 1969
● The Byzantine Empire. 709-777, Dec. 1983
I. Rome of the East. By Merle Severy. Photos by James L. Stanfield. 709-767; II. Mount Athos. 739-745
● Canterbury Cathedral. By Kenneth MacLeish. Photos by Thomas Nebbia. 364-379, Mar. 1976
● Chartres: Legacy From the Age of Faith. By Kenneth MacLeish. Photos by Dean Conger. 857-882, Dec. 1969
▲ *Europe; Historical Map of Europe,* double-sided supplement. Dec. 1983
▲ *Ireland and Northern Ireland: A Visitor's Guide; Historic Ireland* (Pre-Norman, Medieval, Modern), double-sided supplement. Apr. 1981
▲ *Medieval England; British Isles,* double-sided supplement. Oct. 1979
● A New Look at Medieval Europe. By Kenneth M. Setton. Paintings by Andre Durenceau and Birney Lettick. 799-859, Dec. 1962
● 900 Years Ago: the Norman Conquest. By Kenneth M. Setton. Photos by George F. Mobley. 206-251, Aug. 1966
● The Travail of Ireland. By Joseph Judge. Photos by Cotton Coulson. 432-441, Apr. 1981
● The Vikings. By Howard La Fay. Photos by Ted Spiegel. 492-541, Apr. 1970
● The Voyage of *Brendan.* By Timothy Severin. Photos by Cotton Coulson. 770-797, Dec. 1977
● Who Discovered America? A New Look at an Old Question. The Editor. 769, Dec. 1977
● *See also* Crusades

MEDITERRANEAN REGION:
▲ *Classical Lands of the Mediterranean,* supplement. Dec. 1949
▲ *The Historic Mediterranean; The Mediterranean Seafloor,* double-sided supplement. Included: Phoenician, Greek, Roman, Byzantine, and Islamic eras; Heart of an Expanding World; The World of Homer; The World of Herodotus; The World of Strabo; Ptolemy's World; and The Hereford Map. Dec. 1982
● How Fruit Came to America. By J. R. Magness. Paintings by Else Bostelmann. Included: Olives, Oil-bearing Fruit from Southern Europe. 325-377, Sept. 1951
▲ *Lands of the Eastern Mediterranean.* Atlas series supplement. Jan. 1959
● The Mediterranean–Sea of Man's Fate. By Rick Gore. Photos by Jonathan Blair. 694-737, Dec. 1982
▲ *Middle East, Eastern Mediterranean; Early Civilizations of the Middle East,* double-sided supplement. Sept. 1978
● Our Vegetable Travelers. By Victor R. Boswell. Paintings by Else Bostelmann. Included: Green Gifts from the Mediterranean (Asparagus, Endive); Two Mediterranean Root Crops (Salsify and Parsnip). 145-217, Aug. 1949
● The Phoenicians, Sea Lords of Antiquity. By Samuel W. Matthews. Photos by Winfield Parks. Paintings by Robert C. Magis. 149-189, Aug. 1974
● The World in Your Garden. By W. H. Camp. Paintings by Else Bostelmann. 1-65, July 1947
● *See also* Balearic Islands; Capri; Corsica; Crete; Cyprus; Gibraltar; Ischia; Malta; Riviera; Sicily; *and* names of countries bordering the Mediterranean Sea: Albania; Algeria; Egypt; France; Greece; Israel; Italy; Lebanon; Monaco; Morocco; Spain; Syria; Tunisia; Turkey; Yugoslavia

MEDITERRANEAN SEA:
● Ancient Shipwreck Yields New Facts–and a Strange Cargo. By Peter Throckmorton. Photos by Kim Hart and Joseph J. Scherschel. 282-300, Feb. 1969
● Diving Through an Undersea Avalanche. By Jacques-Yves Cousteau. NGS research grant. 538-542, Apr. 1955
● Fish Men Discover a 2,200-year-old Greek Ship. By Jacques-Yves Cousteau. NGS research grant. 1-36, Jan. 1954
● Fish Men Explore a New World Undersea. By Jacques-Yves Cousteau. 431-472, Oct. 1952
● Four Years of Diving to the Bottom of the Sea. By Georges S. Houot. NGS research grant. 715-731, May 1958
▲ *The Historic Mediterranean; The Mediterranean Seafloor.* Dec. 1982
● The Mediterranean–Sea of Man's Fate. By Rick Gore. Photos by Jonathan Blair. 694-737, Dec. 1982
● New Tools for Undersea Archeology. By George F. Bass. Photos by Charles R. Nicklin, Jr. NGS research grant. 403-423, Sept. 1968
● Oldest Known Shipwreck Yields Bronze Age Cargo. By Peter Throckmorton. NGS research grant. 697-711, May 1962
● Photographing the Sea's Dark Underworld. By Harold E. Edgerton. NGS research grant. 523-537, Apr. 1955
● Thirty-three Centuries Under the Sea (Shipwreck). By Peter Throckmorton. 682-703, May 1960
● To the Depths of the Sea by Bathyscaphe. By Jacques-Yves Cousteau. NGS research grant. 67-79, July 1954
● Two and a Half Miles Down. By Georges S. Houot. NGS research grant. 80-86, July 1954
● Underwater Archeology: Key to History's Warehouse. By George F. Bass. Photos by Thomas J. Abercrombie and Robert B. Goodman. NGS research grant. 138-156, July 1963
● Working for Weeks on the Sea Floor. By Jacques-Yves Cousteau. Photos by Philippe Cousteau and Bates Littlehales. NGS research grant. 498-537, Apr. 1966
● *Yankee* Cruises Turkey's History-haunted Coast. By Irving and Electa Johnson. Photos by Joseph J. Scherschel. 798-845, Dec. 1969

MEEN, V. BEN: Author:
● Solving the Riddle of Chubb Crater (Quebec). Photos by Richard H. Stewart. 1-32, Jan. 1952

MEGALOPOLIS, U.S.A.:
▲ *Washington to Boston,* Atlas series supplement. Aug. 1962

MEGARGEE, EDWIN: Artist:
● Dogs Work for Man. By Edward J. Linehan. Paintings by Edwin Megargee and R. E. Lougheed. 190-233, Aug. 1958

MEGGERS, BETTY J.:
Author-Photographer:
● Life Among the Wai Wai Indians. By Clifford Evans and Betty J. Meggers. 329-346, Mar. 1955

MEGIDDO (Armageddon), Israel:
● An Archeologist Looks at Palestine. By Nelson Glueck. 739-752, Dec. 1947
● Bringing Old Testament Times to Life. By G. Ernest Wright. Paintings by Henry J. Soulen. 833-864, Dec. 1957

MEKONG (River), Southeast Asia:
● The Mekong, River of Terror and Hope. By Peter T. White. Photos by W. E. Garrett. 737-787, Dec. 1968
● Water War in Viet Nam. By Dickey Chapelle. 272-296, Feb. 1966

MELANESIA:
● *Yankee* Roams the Orient. By Irving and Electa Johnson. 327-370, Mar. 1951
● *See also* Fiji Islands; Louisiade Archipelago; Malekula; New Britain; New Caledonia; New Guinea; Pentecost Island; Solomon Islands; Tanna

MELBOURNE, Australia:
● Australia's Pacesetter State, Victoria. By Allan C. Fisher, Jr. Photos by Thomas Nebbia. 218-253, Feb. 1971
● Sports-minded Melbourne, Host to the Olympics. 688-693, Nov. 1956

MELHAM, TOM: Author:
● Cape Cod's Circle of Seasons. Photos by James P. Blair. 40-65, July 1975

MELLON, ANDREW:
● The National Gallery After a Quarter Century. By John Walker. 348-371, Mar. 1967

MELLON, MR. and MRS. PAUL: Art Collection:
● In Quest of Beauty. Text by Paul Mellon. 372-385, Mar. 1967

MELLON FAMILY:
● Pittsburgh, Pattern for Progress. By William J. Gill. Photos by Clyde Hare. 342-371, Mar. 1965
● Pittsburgh: Workshop of the Titans. By Albert W. Atwood. 117-144, July 1949

MELOY, THOMAS: Author:
● The Laser's Bright Magic. Photos by Howard Sochurek. 858-881, Dec. 1966

MELTZER, DAVIS: Artist:
● The Awesome Worlds Within a Cell. By Rick Gore. Photos by Bruce Dale. 355-395, Sept. 1976

• Footprints on the Moon. By Hugh L. Dryden. Paintings by Davis Meltzer and Pierre Mion. 357-401, Mar. 1964
• The Incredible Universe. By Kenneth F. Weaver. Photos by James P. Blair. 589-625, May 1974
• Mariner Scans a Lifeless Venus. By Frank Sartwell. 733-742, May 1963
• Project FAMOUS. 586-615, May 1975
• Sailors of the Sky. By Gordon Young. Photos by Emory Kristof and Jack Fields. 49-73, Jan. 1967

MELTZOFF, STANLEY: Artist:
• Plight of the Bluefin Tuna. By Michael J. A. Butler. Photos by David Doubilet. 220-239, Aug. 1982

MELVILLE, HERMAN:
• Literary Landmarks of Massachusetts. By William H. Nicholas. Photos by B. Anthony Stewart and John E. Fletcher. 279-310, Mar. 1950

MELVILLE BELL GROSVENOR, a Lifetime of Service. By Bart McDowell. 270-278, Aug. 1982

MELVILLE ISLAND, Australia:
• Expedition to the Land of the Tiwi. By Charles P. Mountford. NGS research grant. 417-440, Mar. 1956

MEMORIAL DAY CEREMONIES:
• 'Known but to God' (Unknown Heroes). By Beverley M. Bowie. 593-605, Nov. 1958

MEMORIAL TRIBUTES:
• Arnold, H. H.: 1886-1950. 400, Mar. 1950
• Bowie, Beverley M.: 1914-1958. 214, Feb. 1959
• Carmichael, Leonard: An Appreciation. By Melvin M. Payne. 871-874, Dec. 1973
• Chapelle, Dickey: What Was a Woman Doing There? By W. E. Garrett. 270-271, Feb. 1966
• Churchill, Winston. 153-225, Aug. 1965
The Churchill I Knew. By Dwight D. Eisenhower. 153-157; "Be Ye Men of Valour." By Howard La Fay. 159-197; The Final Tribute. Text by Carolyn Bennett Patterson. 199-225
• Eisenhower, Dwight D.: World's Last Salute to a Great American. By William Graves and other members of the National Geographic staff. 40-51, July 1969
• Fleming, Robert V.: 1890-1967. By Melville Bell Grosvenor. 526-529, Apr. 1968
• Grosvenor, Elsie May Bell: First Lady of the National Geographic. By Gilbert Hovey Grosvenor. 101-121, July 1965
• Grosvenor, Gilbert Hovey: To Gilbert Grosvenor: a Monthly Monument 25 Miles High. By Frederick G. Vosburgh and the staff of the National Geographic Society. 445-487, Oct. 1966
• Grosvenor, Melville Bell: Melville Bell Grosvenor, A Decade of Innovation, a Lifetime of Service. By Bart McDowell. 270-278, Aug. 1982
• Hildebrand, Jesse Richardson: 1888-1951. 104, Jan. 1952
• Kennedy, John F.: The Last Full Measure. By Melville Bell Grosvenor. 307-355, Mar. 1964
• Kennedy, John F.: To the Memory of Our Beloved President, Friend to All Mankind. 1A-1B, Jan. 1964
• La Gorce, John Oliver: Colleague of the Golden Years. By Gilbert Grosvenor. 440-444, Mar. 1960
• Leakey, Louis S. B.: The Leakey Tradition Lives On. By Melvin M. Payne. 143-144, Jan. 1973
• Long, George W.: 1913-1958. 215, Feb. 1959
• Marshall, George C.: 1880-1959. 113, Jan. 1960

MEMORIALS. *See* Monuments and Memorials; Shrines; War Memorials

MEN, Moose, and Mink of Northwest Angle. By William H. Nicholas. Photos by J. Baylor Roberts. 265-284, Aug. 1947

MEN Against the Hurricane. By Andrew H. Brown. 537-560, Oct. 1950

The **MEN** Who Hid the Dead Sea Scrolls. By A. Douglas Tushingham. Paintings by Peter V. Bianchi. 785-808, Dec. 1958

MEN Who Measure the Earth. By Robert Leslie Conly. Photos by John E. Fletcher. 335-362, Mar. 1956

MENEN, AUBREY: Author:
• St. Peter's, Rome's Church of Popes. Photos by Albert Moldvay. 865-879, Dec. 1971

MENÉNDEZ DE AVILÉS, DON PEDRO:
• St. Augustine, Nation's Oldest City, Turns 400. By Robert L. Conly. 196-229, Feb. 1966

MENHADEN–Uncle Sam's Top Commercial Fish. By Leonard C. Roy. Photos by Robert F. Sisson. 813-823, June 1949

MENNONITES (Sects):
• Amish Folk: Plainest of Pennsylvania's Plain People. By Richard Gehman. Photos by William Albert Allard. Contents: The Plain sects in Pennsylvania, including the Brethren (Dunkards), Mennonites, and Old Order Amish. 227-253, Aug. 1965
• Artists Look at Pennsylvania. By John Oliver La Gorce. 37-56, July 1948
• Pennsylvania: Faire Land of William Penn. By Gordon Young. Photos by Cary Wolinsky. 731-767, June 1978

MENOMINEES (Indians):
• Wisconsin's Menominees: Indians on a Seesaw. By Patricia Raymer. Photos by Steve Raymer. 228-251, Aug. 1974

MENZEL, DONALD H.:
• Devised Star Charts. 811, Dec. 1957
Author:
• Exploring Our Neighbor World, the Moon. 277-296, Feb. 1958

WILLIAM ALBERT ALLARD

Amish: one of Lancaster's Plain People

M N

• Solar Eclipse, Nature's Super Spectacular. By Donald H. Menzel and Jay M. Pasachoff. 222-233, Aug. 1970

MEO (Tribespeople). *See* Hmong

MERCHANT MARINE ACADEMY. *See* U. S. Merchant Marine Academy

MERCHANT MARINE TRAINING SHIPS. *See Dar Pomorza; Georg Stage; Joseph Conrad; and* U. S. Merchant Marine Academy

MERCHANTMAN, Nuclear. *See Savannah,* N. S.

MERCURY (Metal):
• Graveyard of the Quicksilver Galleons. By Mendel Peterson. Photos by Jonathan Blair. Note: The *Nuestra Señora de Guadalupe* and the *Conde de Tolosa* sank off the coast of the Dominican Republic in 1724 while carrying a cargo of mercury to the New World. 850-876, Dec. 1979
• Quicksilver and Slow Death. By John J. Putman. Photos by Robert W. Madden. 507-527, Oct. 1972

MERCURY (Planet):
• Mariner Unveils Venus and Mercury. By Kenneth F. Weaver. Included: First geological maps of Mercury. 858-869, June 1975
• Voyage to the Planets. By Kenneth F. Weaver. Paintings by Ludek Pesek. 147-193, Aug. 1970

MERCURY MISSIONS:
• Countdown for Space. By Kenneth F. Weaver. 702-734, May 1961
• The Earth From Orbit. By Paul D. Lowman, Jr. 645-671, Nov. 1966
• Exploring Tomorrow With the Space Agency. By Allan C. Fisher, Jr. Photos by Dean Conger. 48-89, July 1960
• The Flight of *Freedom 7*. By Carmault B. Jackson, Jr. 416-431, Sept. 1961
• John Glenn Receives the Society's Hubbard Medal. 827, June 1962
• John Glenn's Three Orbits in *Friendship 7:* A Minute-by-Minute Account of America's First Orbital Space Flight. By Robert B. Voas. 792-827, June 1962
• The Pilot's Story. By Alan B. Shepard, Jr. Photos by Dean Conger. 432-444, Sept. 1961
• Tracking America's Man in Orbit. By Kenneth F. Weaver. Photos by Robert F. Sisson. 184-217, Feb. 1962

MERMAID'S PURSE:
• Miracle of the Mermaid's Purse. By Ernest L. Libby. 413-420, Sept. 1959

The **MERRIMACK:** River of Industry and Romance. By Albert W. Atwood. Photos by B. Anthony Stewart. 106-140, Jan. 1951

MERRITT ISLAND NATIONAL WILDLIFE REFUGE, Florida:
• Island, Prairie, Marsh, and Shore. By Charlton Ogburn. Photos by Bates Littlehales. 350-381, Mar. 1979

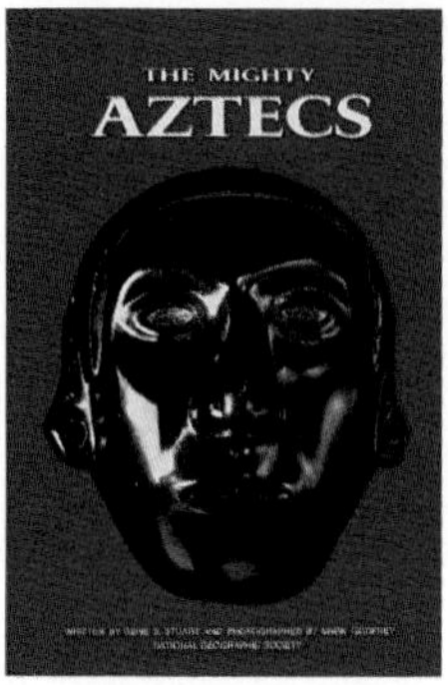

DAVID HISER

Mesoamerica: gold found off Veracruz

MESA DEL NAYAR, Mexico:
• Mesa del Nayar's Strange Holy Week. By Guillermo Aldana E. 780-795, June 1971

MESA VERDE NATIONAL PARK, Colorado:
• The Anasazi–Riddles in the Ruins. By Thomas Y. Canby. Photos by Dewitt Jones and David Brill. Paintings by Roy Andersen. 554-592, Nov. 1982
• Ancient Cliff Dwellers of Mesa Verde. By Don Watson. Photos by Willard R. Culver. 349-376, Sept. 1948
• I See America First. By Lynda Bird Johnson. Photos by William Albert Allard. 874-904, Dec. 1965
• Searching for Cliff Dwellers' Secrets. By Carroll A. Burroughs. NGS research grant. 619-625, Nov. 1959
• Solving the Riddles of Wetherill Mesa. By Douglas Osborne. Paintings by Peter V. Bianchi. NGS research grant. 155-195, Feb. 1964
▲ *The Southwest,* The Making of America series. Included: Arizona, New Mexico, and parts of California, Colorado, Texas, Utah; and in Mexico: Baja California Norte, Chihuahua, Sonora. On reverse: 12,000 Years of History; Spanish Conquest; Anglo-American Entry and Occupancy. Nov. 1982
• 20th-century Indians Preserve Customs of the Cliff Dwellers. Photos by William Belknap, Jr. NGS research grant. 196-211, Feb. 1964
• Your Society to Seek New Light on the Cliff Dwellers. NGS research grant. 154-156, Jan. 1959

MESOAMERICAN CIVILIZATIONS:
• Man's Eighty Centuries in Veracruz. By S. Jeffrey K. Wilkerson. Photos by David Hiser. Paintings by Richard Schlecht. NGS research grant. 203-231, Aug. 1980
▲ *Visitor's Guide to the Aztec World; Mexico and Central America,* double-sided supplement. Dec. 1980
• *See also* Aztecs; Maya

MESOPOTAMIA:
• Abraham, the Friend of God. By Kenneth MacLeish. Photos by Dean Conger. 739-789, Dec. 1966
• Ancient Mesopotamia: A Light That Did Not Fail. By E. A. Speiser. Paintings by H. M. Herget. 41-105, Jan. 1951
• Ebla: Splendor of an Unknown Empire. By Howard La Fay. Photos by James L. Stanfield. Paintings by Louis S. Glanzman. Included: Akkadian, Babylonian, and Sumerian city-kingdoms in southern Mesopotamia, and Assur in northern Mesopotamia. 730-759, Dec. 1978
▲ *Middle East, Eastern Mediterranean; Early Civilizations of the Middle East,* double-sided supplement. Sept. 1978
• Throne Above the Euphrates. By Theresa Goell. 390-405, Mar. 1961

• *Tigris* Sails Into the Past. By Thor Heyerdahl. Photos by Carlo Mauri and the crew of the *Tigris*. Included: Probable routes of ancient Sumerians from Mesopotamia through the Persian Gulf east to the Indus Valley, and southwest in the Indian Ocean to the Horn of Africa. 806-827, Dec. 1978

A **MESSAGE** From the President of the United States. By Dwight D. Eisenhower. 587, May 1960

MESSINA, Strait of, Italy-Sicily:
• Fishing in the Whirlpool of Charybdis. By Paul A. Zahl. 579-618, Nov. 1953
• Hydrofoil Ferry "Flies" the Strait of Messina. By Gilbert Grosvenor. 493-496, Apr. 1957

MESSNER, REINHOLD:
Author-Photographer:
• At My Limit–I Climbed Everest Alone. By Reinhold Messner. Photos by the author and Nena Holguín. 552-566, Oct. 1981

METALS. *See* Aluminum; Copper; Gold; Mercury; Platinum; Plutonium; Silver; Steel Industry; Uranium

METALWORK:
• The Inadan: Artisans of the Sahara. By Michael and Aubine Kirtley. 282-298, Aug. 1979
• Priceless Relics of the Spanish Armada. By Robert Sténuit. Photos by Bates Littlehales. 745-777, June 1969
• *See also* Aluminum; Bronzes; Dresden Treasures; Gold; Goldsmithing; Platinum; Silver; Silversmiths; Spanish Treasure

METASEQUOIA (Ancient Tree):
• Kew: The Commoners' Royal Garden. By Thomas Garner James. Photos by B. Anthony Stewart. 479-506, Apr. 1950

METEORITES:
• Apollo 15 Explores the Mountains of the Moon. By Kenneth F. Weaver. Photos from NASA. 233-265, Feb. 1972
• Have We Solved the Mysteries of the Moon? By Kenneth F. Weaver. Paintings by William H. Bond. 309-325, Sept. 1973
• "Rockhounds" Uncover Earth's Mineral Beauty. By George S. Switzer. 631-660, Nov. 1951
• *See also* Chubb Crater

METEOROLOGY. *See* Climate; Weather; Weather Satellites; Weather Stations and Research

METRIC SYSTEM:
• How Soon Will We Measure In Metric? By Kenneth F. Weaver. Drawings by Donald A. Mackay. 287-294, Aug. 1977

METROPOLIS Made to Order: Brasília. By Hernane Tavares de Sá. Photos by Thomas J. Abercrombie. 704-724, May 1960

METZGER, JOHN: Photographer:
• Alaskan Family Robinson. By Nancy Robinson. Photos by John Metzger and Peter Robinson. 55-75, Jan. 1973

MEUSE (River), France-Belgium:
• Paris to Antwerp With the Water Gypsies. By David S. Boyer. 530-559, Oct. 1955

MEXCALTITÁN, Mexico:
• Mexico's Little Venice. By W. E. Garrett. 876-888, June 1968

MEXICAN AMERICANS:
• The Mexican Americans: A People on the Move. By Griffin Smith, Jr. Photos by Stephanie Maze. 780-809, June 1980

MEXICO:
▲ *Archeological Map of Middle America, Land of the Feathered Serpent,* supplement. Text on reverse. Oct. 1968
• The Aztecs. 704-775, Dec. 1980
I. The Aztecs. By Bart McDowell. Photos by David Hiser. Paintings by Felipe Dávalos. 714-751; II. The Building of Tenochtitlan. By Augusto F. Molina Montes. Paintings by Felipe Dávalos. 753-765; III. New Finds in the Great Temple. By Eduardo Matos Moctezuma. Photos by David Hiser. 767-775
• The Disaster of El Chichón. By Boris Weintraub. Photos by Guillermo Aldana E. and Kenneth Garrett. 654-684, Nov. 1982
Volcanic Cloud May Alter Earth's Climate. By Robert I. Tilling. 672-675
• Dzibilchaltun. NGS research grant. 91-129, Jan. 1959
I. Lost City of the Maya. By E. Wyllys Andrews. 91-109; II. Up From the Well of Time. By Luis Marden. 110-129
• Editorials. By Gilbert M. Grosvenor. 579, May 1978; 585, May 1980
• Experiment in International Living. By Hugh M. Hamill, Jr. 323-350, Mar. 1953
• From Sun-clad Sea to Shining Mountains. By Ralph Gray. Photos by James P. Blair. 542-589, Apr. 1964
• Gifts for the Jaguar God. By Philip Drucker and Robert F. Heizer. NGS research grant. 367-375, Sept. 1956
• How Fruit Came to America. By J. R. Magness. Paintings by Else Bostelmann. Included: Avocado and Papaya, Gifts of the Aztecs. 325-377, Sept. 1951
• The Huichols, Mexico's People of Myth and Magic. By James Norman. Photos by Guillermo Aldana E. 832-853, June 1977
• Hunting the Heartbeat of a Whale. By Paul Dudley White and Samuel W. Matthews. NGS research grant. 49-64, July 1956
• Into the Well of Sacrifice (Chichén Itzá). NGS research grant. 540-561, Oct. 1961
I. Return to the Sacred Cenote. By Eusebio Dávalos Hurtado. 540-549; II. Treasure Hunt in the Deep Past. By Bates Littlehales. 550-561
• Lost Kingdom in Indian Mexico. By Justin Locke. 517-546, Oct. 1952
• The Maya. 729-811, Dec. 1975
I. Children of Time. By Howard La Fay. Photos by David Alan Harvey. Included: Archaeological sites: Becan; Bonampak; Chichén Itzá; Dzibilchaltún; Jaina Island; Palenque; Tancah; Tulum; Uxmal; and present-day Maya. 729-767; II. Riddle of the Glyphs. By George E. Stuart. Photos by Otis Imboden. Included: Cobá; Kohunlich; Palenque; Tancah; Yaxchilán. 768-791
• Mexican Folk Art. By Fernando Horcasitas. Photos by David Hiser. 648-669, May 1978
• Mexico: "A Very Beautiful Challenge." By Mike Edwards. Photos by Thomas Nebbia. 612-647, May 1978
▲ *Mexico; Central America,* double-sided supplement. May 1973
▲ *Mexico and Central America,* Atlas series supplement. Oct. 1961
▲ *Mexico and Central America,* supplement. Mar. 1953
• Mexico in Motion. By Bart McDowell. Photos by Kip Ross. 490-537, Oct. 1961
• Mexico's Little Venice. By W. E. Garrett. 876-888, June 1968
• Mexico's Window on the Past (National Museum). By Bart McDowell. Photos by B. Anthony Stewart. 492-519, Oct. 1968
◆ *The Mighty Aztecs.* 1981
◆ *The Mysterious Maya.* 1977
• A New Riviera: Mexico's West Coast. By Nathaniel T. Kenney. Photos by Charles O'Rear. 670-699, Nov. 1973
• On the Trail of La Venta Man. By Matthew W. Stirling. Photos by Richard H. Stewart. NGS research grant. 137-172, Feb. 1947
Hunting Mexico's Buried Temples. 145-168
• "Pyramids" of the New World. By Neil Merton Judd. Contents: Chichén Itzá, Cholula, Cuicuilco, Mexico City, Monte Albán, San Lorenzo, Tenayuca, Tenochtitlán, Teotihuacán, Texcoco, Tlaltelolco, Uxmal. 105-128, Jan. 1948
• Rediscovering America's Forgotten Crops. By Noel D. Vietmeyer. Photos by Burgess Blevins. Paintings by Paul M. Breeden. 702-712, May 1981
• Rocks, Ruts, and Sand: Driving the Mexican 1000. By Michael E. Long. 569-575, Oct. 1972
• Shells Take You Over World Horizons. By Rutherford Platt. 33-84, July 1949
• Silver: A Mineral of Excellent Nature. By Allen A. Boraiko. Photos by Fred Ward. 280-313, Sept. 1981
• Skyway Below the Clouds. By Carl R. Markwith. Photos by Ernest J. Cottrell. Included: Ciudad Juárez, Hermosillo. 85-108, July 1949
• Solar Eclipse, Nature's Super Spectacular. By Donald H. Menzel and Jay M. Pasachoff. NGS research grant. 222-233, Aug. 1970
• Solving the Mystery of Mexico's Great Stone Spheres. By Matthew W. Stirling. Photos by David F. Cupp. NGS research grant. 295-300, Aug. 1969
• South to Mexico City. By W. E. Garrett. 145-193, Aug. 1968

M N

KEVIN FLEMING

Florida: pitcher at old-timers ball game

▲ *The Southwest,* The Making of America series. Included: Arizona, New Mexico, and parts of California, Colorado, Texas, Utah; and in Mexico: Baja California Norte, Chihuahua, Sonora. On reverse: 12,000 Years of History; Spanish Conquest; Anglo-American Entry and Occupancy. Nov. 1982
• The Tarahumaras: Mexico's Long Distance Runners. By James Norman. Photos by David Hiser. 702-718, May 1976
• Two Wheels Along the Mexican Border. By William Albert Allard. 591-635, May 1971
▲ *Visitor's Guide to the Aztec World; Mexico and Central America,* double-sided supplement. Dec. 1980
• The World in Your Garden. By W. H. Camp. Paintings by Else Bostelmann. Included: Mexican Love of Flowers (Dahlia, Tiger-flower); Mexico, Happy Hunting Ground for Botanists (Cosmos, Zinnia, Poinsettias); More Native Mexicans (Frangipani, French and African Marigolds). 1-65, July 1947
• *See also* Acapulco; Baja California; Cozumel Island; Guadalajara; Mesa del Nayar; Mexico City; Mujeres, Isla; Raza, Isla; Sierra Madre Occidental; Sonora (State); Veracruz (State)

MEXICO, Gulf of:
• Shrimp Nursery: Science Explores New Ways to Farm the Sea. By Clarence P. Idyll. Photos by Robert F. Sisson. NGS research grant. 636-659, May 1965
• Shrimpers Strike Gold in the Gulf. By Clarence P. Idyll. Photos by Robert F. Sisson. 699-707, May 1957
• *See also* Dry Tortugas; Gulf Coast, U. S.; Key West, Florida

MEXICO, Valley of:
• Mexico's Window on the Past. By Bart McDowell. Photos by B. Anthony Stewart. 492-519, Oct. 1968

MEXICO CITY, Mexico:
• The Aztecs. 704-775, Dec. 1980
I. The Aztecs. By Bart McDowell. Photos by David Hiser. Paintings by Felipe Dávalos. 714-751; II. The Building of Tenochtitlan. By Augusto F. Molina Montes. Paintings by Felipe Dávalos. 753-765; III. New Finds in the Great Temple. By Eduardo Matos Moctezuma. Photos by David Hiser. 767-775
• Mexico, the City That Founded a Nation. By Louis de la Haba. Photos by Albert Moldvay. 638-669, May 1973
• Mexico in Motion. By Bart McDowell. Photos by Kip Ross. 490-537, Oct. 1961
• Mexico's Booming Capital. By Mason Sutherland. Photos by Justin Locke. 785-824, Dec. 1951
• Mexico's Window on the Past (National Museum). By Bart McDowell. Photos by B. Anthony Stewart. 492-519, Oct. 1968
• "Pyramids" of the New World. By Neil Merton Judd. Included: Tenochtitlán, predecessor of modern Mexico City; Gran Teocalli. 105-128, Jan. 1948
• South to Mexico City. By W. E. Garrett. 145-193, Aug. 1968
▲ *Visitor's Guide to the Aztec World; Mexico and Central America,* double-sided supplement. Dec. 1980

MEXICO to Canada on the Pacific Crest Trail. By Mike W. Edwards. Photos by David Hiser. 741-779, June 1971

MEYER, ALFRED: Author:
• Life and Death in Tana Toradja. By Pamela and Alfred Meyer. 793-815, June 1972

MEYER, CARL:
• Amateur Gardener Creates a New Rose. By Elizabeth A. Moize. Photos by Farrell Grehan. 286-294, Aug. 1972

MEYER, PAMELA JOHNSON: Author:
• Life and Death in Tana Toradja. By Pamela and Alfred Meyer. 793-815, June 1972
Author-Photographer:
• Foxes Foretell the Future in Mali's Dogon Country. 431-448, Mar. 1969

MEYERHOFF, ELIZABETH L.: Author:
• The Threatened Ways of Kenya's Pokot People. Photos by Murray Roberts. 120-140, Jan. 1982

MIAHUATLÁN, Mexico:
• Solar Eclipse, Nature's Super Spectacular. By Donald H. Menzel and Jay M. Pasachoff. NGS research grant. 222-233, Aug. 1970

MIAMI, Florida:
• Cuba's Exiles Bring New Life to Miami. By Edward J. Linehan. Photos by Nathan Benn. 68-95, July 1973
• Florida–A Time for Reckoning. By William S. Ellis. Photos by Nathan Benn and Kevin Fleming. 172-219, Aug. 1982
• Florida Rides a Space-age Boom. By Benedict Thielen. Photos by Winfield Parks and James P. Blair. 858-903, Dec. 1963
• Men Against the Hurricane. By Andrew H. Brown. 537-560, Oct. 1950
• Miami's Expanding Horizons. By William H. Nicholas. 561-594, Nov. 1950
• *See also* Vizcaya (Palace)

MIAMI SEAQUARIUM, Miami, Florida:
• Aha! It Really Works! (Bait-fishing Heron). By Robert F. Sisson. 143-147, Jan. 1974

MIAO TRIBE. *See* Hmong

MICARD, GASTON, Count:
• Milestones in My Arctic Journeys. By Willie Knutsen. 543-570, Oct. 1949

MICCOSUKEES (Indians):
• Florida's Emerging Seminoles. By Louis Capron. Photos by Otis Imboden. 716-734, Nov. 1969
• Threatened Glories of Everglades National Park. By Frederick Kent Truslow and Frederick G. Vosburgh. Photos by Frederick Kent Truslow and Otis Imboden. 508-553, Oct. 1967

MICHAUD, SABRINA and ROLAND: Author-Photographers:
● Bold Horsemen of the Steppes (Turkomans). 634-669, Nov. 1973
● Trek to Lofty Hunza–and Beyond. 644-669, Nov. 1975
● Winter Caravan to the Roof of the World. 435-465, Apr. 1972

MICHELANGELO:
● Carrara Marble: Touchstone of Eternity. By Cathy Newman. Photos by Pierre Boulat. 42-59, July 1982
● Florence Rises From the Flood. By Joseph Judge. 1-43, July 1967
● Rome: Eternal City With a Modern Air. By Harnett T. Kane. Photos by B. Anthony Stewart. Included: St. Peter's Dome and the Sistine Chapel. 437-491, Apr. 1957
● St. Peter's, Rome's Church of Popes. By Aubrey Menen. Photos by Albert Moldvay. 865-879, Dec. 1971
● When in Rome. . . . By Stuart E. Jones. Photos by Winfield Parks. Included: Sistine Chapel, Vatican. 741-789, June 1970

MICHIGAN:
▲ *Close-up: U.S.A., Wisconsin, Michigan, and the Great Lakes,* supplement. Text on reverse. Aug. 1973
● The Great Lakes: Is It Too Late? By Gordon Young. Photos by James L. Amos and Martin Rogers. 147-185, Aug. 1973
● Ice Fishing's Frigid Charms. By Thomas J. Abercrombie. 861-872, Dec. 1958
● The Past Is Present in Greenfield Village (Henry Ford Museum). By Beverley M. Bowie. Photos by Neal P. Davis and Willard R. Culver. 96-127, July 1958
● The Two Worlds of Michigan. By Noel Grove. Photos by James L. Amos. 802-843, June 1979
● Work-hard, Play-hard Michigan. By Andrew H. Brown. 279-320, Mar. 1952
● *See also* Isle Royale

MICHIGAN, Lake, U. S.:
● Wisconsin's Door Peninsula. By William S. Ellis. Photos by Ted Rozumalski. 347-371, Mar. 1969
● Work-hard, Play-hard Michigan. By Andrew H. Brown. 279-320, Mar. 1952

MICHIGAN STATE UNIVERSITY. *See* Summer Institute of Glaciological and Arctic Sciences

MICMAC INDIANS:
● Nomads of the Far North. By Matthew W. Stirling. Paintings by W. Langdon Kihn. 471-504, Oct. 1949

MICROBIOLOGY:
● The Awesome Worlds Within a Cell. By Rick Gore. Photos by Bruce Dale. Paintings by Davis Meltzer. 355-395, Sept. 1976

MICROELECTRONICS:
● The Chip: Electronic Mini-marvel. By Allen A. Boraiko. Photos by Charles O'Rear. 421-457, Oct. 1982
● Crystals, Magical Servants of the Space Age. By Kenneth F. Weaver. Photos by James P. Blair. 278-296, Aug. 1968

MICRONESIA:
● Feast Day in Kapingamarangi. By W. Robert Moore. Note: The natives of Kapingamarangi and Nukuoro are Polynesian and differ in language and customs from the people of other island groups in Micronesia. 523-537, Apr. 1950
● Micronesia: The Americanization of Eden. By David S. Boyer. 702-744, May 1967
● Pacific Wards of Uncle Sam. By W. Robert Moore. Contents: Trust Territory of Pacific Islands. 73-104, July 1948
● *See also* Bikini; Ifalik; Kwajalein; Nauru; Truk Lagoon; Ulithi; Yap Islands

MICROORGANISMS:
● Electronic Voyage Through an Invisible World. By Kenneth F. Weaver. 274-290, Feb. 1977
● Rotifers: Nature's Water Purifiers. By John Walsh. 287-292, Feb. 1979
● Those Marvelous, Myriad Diatoms. By Richard B. Hoover. 871-878, June 1979
● The Wild World of Compost. By Cecil E. Johnson. Photos by Bianca Lavies. 273-284, Aug. 1980

MICROPROCESSORS:
● California's Silicon Valley. By Moira Johnston. Photos by Charles O'Rear. 459-477, Oct. 1982
● The Chip: Electronic Mini-marvel. By Allen A. Boraiko. Photos by Charles O'Rear. 421-457, Oct. 1982

MICROSCOPY:
● A Bold New Look at Our Past. The Editor. NGS research grant. 62-63, Jan. 1975
● Electronic Voyage Through an Invisible World. By Kenneth F. Weaver. 274-290, Feb. 1977
● Exploring the Mind of Ice Age Man. By Alexander Marshack. NGS research grant. 64-89, Jan. 1975
● Finding Rare Beauty in Common Rocks. By Lorence G. Collins. 121-129, Jan. 1966
◆ *Hidden Worlds.* 1981
■ The Invisible World. 1, Jan. 1980; cover, Mar. 1980
● Life in a "Dead" Sea–Great Salt Lake. By Paul A. Zahl. 252-263, Aug. 1967
● *See also* Microbiology; Photography, Microscope

MICROWAVE RADIO RELAY:
● New Miracles of the Telephone Age. By Robert Leslie Conly. 87-120, July 1954

MID-ATLANTIC RIDGE:
● Exploring the Mid-Atlantic Ridge. By Maurice Ewing. NGS research grant. 275-294, Sept. 1948
● New Discoveries on the Mid-Atlantic Ridge. By Maurice Ewing. Photos by Robert F. Sisson. NGS research grant. 611-640, Nov. 1949

MID-ATLANTIC RIFT:
● Project FAMOUS. Photos by Emory Kristof. 586-615, May 1975
I. Where the Earth Turns Inside Out. By J. R. Heirtzler. 586-603; II. Dive Into the Great Rift. By Robert D. Ballard. 604-615

MID-ATLANTIC STATES:
▲ *Close-up: U.S.A., The Mid-Atlantic States,* supplement. Text on reverse. Included: Delaware; Maryland; Virginia; West Virginia. Oct. 1976

MID-CENTURY Holland Builds Her Future. By Sydney Clark. 747-778, Dec. 1950

MIDDLE AGES. *See* Byzantine Empire; Medieval Europe; *and* Crusades

MIDDLE AMERICA:
▲ *Archeological Map of Middle America, Land of the Feathered Serpent,* supplement. Text on reverse. Oct. 1968
● *See also* Central America; Mexico; *and* Aztecs; Maya

MIDDLE EAST:
● Ebla: Splendor of an Unknown Empire. By Howard La Fay. Photos by James L. Stanfield. Paintings by Louis S. Glanzman. Included: Akkad, Babylon, Ebla, Mari, Mesopotamia, Nippur, Sumer, Ugarit. 730-759, Dec. 1978
● Editorials. By Gilbert M. Grosvenor. 587, Nov. 1974; 1, Jan. 1975; 295, Mar. 1975; 291, Mar. 1977; 729, Dec. 1978; 285, Sept. 1980
▲ *Europe and the Near East,* supplement. June 1949
● Eyewitness to War in the Holy Land. By Charles Harbutt. 782-795, Dec. 1967
● Islam's Heartland, Up in Arms. By Thomas J. Abercrombie. 335-345, Sept. 1980
● Journey Into the Great Rift: the Northern Half. By Helen and Frank Schreider. 254-290, Aug. 1965
▲ *Lands of the Eastern Mediterranean,* Atlas series supplement. Jan. 1959
▲ *Middle East, Eastern Mediterranean; Early Civilizations of the Middle East,* double-sided supplement. Sept. 1978
● Our Vegetable Travelers. By Victor R. Boswell. Paintings by Else Bostelmann. Included: Near Eastern Plant in American Pies (Rhubarb); Garden Peas and Spinach from the Middle East. 145-217, Aug. 1949
▲ *The Peoples of the Middle East,* supplement. Text on reverse. July 1972
● Sailing with Sindbad's Sons. By Alan Villiers. 675-688, Nov. 1948
● *Tigris* Sails Into the Past. By Thor Heyerdahl. Photos by Carlo Mauri and the crew of the *Tigris*. Included: Probable trade routes of ancient Sumerians from Mesopotamia through the Persian Gulf east to the Indus Valley, and southwest in the Indian Ocean to the Horn of Africa. 806-827, Dec. 1978
● Troubled Waters East of Suez. By Ernest M. Eller. 483-522, Apr. 1954
● Twilight of the Arab Dhow. By Marion Kaplan. 330-351, Sept. 1974
▲ *Two Centuries of Conflict in the Middle East; Mideast in Turmoil,* double-sided supplement. Sept. 1980

• *See also* Bahrain; Crusades; Cyprus; Holy Land; Iran; Iraq; Israel; Jordan; Kurdistan; Lebanon; Oman; Red Sea; Saudi Arabia; Sinai Peninsula; Syria; Trucial Coast; Turkey; Yemen Arab Republic

MIDDLE FORK SALMON (River), Idaho:
• White-water Adventure on Wild Rivers of Idaho. By Frank Craighead, Jr. and John Craighead. 213-239, Feb. 1970
■ Wild River. 239A-239B, Feb. 1970

MIDDLE ISLAND, Quebec, Canada. *See* St. Mary Islands Sanctuary

MIDDLE MISSISSIPPI CULTURE. *See* Russell Cave, Alabama

The **MIDLANDS,** England:
• Exploring England's Canals. By Bryan Hodgson. Photos by Linda Bartlett. 76-111, July 1974

MIDNIGHT CAVE, Del Rio, Texas:
• Six Months Alone in a Cave (Biorhythm Research). By Michel Siffre. 426-435, Mar. 1975

MID-OCEANIC RIFT SYSTEM:
• Project FAMOUS. Photos by Emory Kristof. 586-615, May 1975
I. Where the Earth Turns Inside Out. By J. R. Heirtzler. 586-603; II. Dive Into the Great Rift. By Robert D. Ballard. 604-615
• This Changing Earth. By Samuel W. Matthews. 1-37, Jan. 1973

MIDSHIPMEN'S Cruise. By William J. Aston and Alexander G. B. Grosvenor. 711-754, June 1948

MIDWAY ISLANDS, Pacific Ocean:
• The Gooney Birds of Midway. By John W. Aldrich. 839-851, June 1964
• What a Place to Lay an Egg! By Thomas R. Howell. Contents: Fairy terns. NGS research grant. 414-419, Sept. 1971

MIDWEST (Region), U. S.:
▲ *Close-up: U.S.A., Illinois, Indiana, Ohio, and Kentucky,* supplement. Text on reverse. Feb. 1977
• The Hard Life of the Prairie Dog. By Tim W. Clark. Photos by Patricia Caulfield. NGS research grant. 270-281, Aug. 1979
• Last of the Black-footed Ferrets? By Tim W. Clark. Photos by Franz J. Camenzind and the author. NGS research grant. 828-838, June 1983
• A Map Maker Looks at the United States. By Newman Bumstead. Included: Illinois: Chicago and Rock Island; Indiana: South Bend and Gary; Iowa: Davenport and Muscatine; Lake Michigan. 705-748, June 1951
• Mapping the Nation's Breadbasket. By Frederick Simpich. 831-849, June 1948
▲ *The North Central States.* Close-up series. Text on reverse. Included: Iowa, Kansas, Minnesota, Missouri, Nebraska, North Dakota, South Dakota. Mar. 1974
▲ *North Central United States.* Included: Illinois, Iowa, Kansas, Minnesota, Missouri, Nebraska, North Dakota, South Dakota, Wisconsin. June 1948
▲ *North Central United States.* Atlas series. Included: Illinois, Iowa, Kansas, Minnesota, Missouri, Nebraska, North Dakota, South Dakota, Wisconsin. Nov. 1958
• North With the Wheat Cutters. By Noel Grove. Photos by James A. Sugar. 194-217, Aug. 1972
• The Parks in Your Backyard. By Conrad L. Wirth. 647-707, Nov. 1963
The Midlands. 691-697
• Satellites Gave Warning of Midwest Floods. By Peter T. White. Photos by Thomas A. DeFeo. 574-592, Oct. 1969
• The Tallgrass Prairie: Can It Be Saved? By Dennis Farney. Photos by Jim Brandenburg. 37-61, Jan. 1980
• That Dammed Missouri River. By Gordon Young. Photos by David Hiser. 374-413, Sept. 1971
• *See also* Great Lakes; *and* names of midwestern states

MIGHT Makes Right Among Alaska's Brown Bears. By Allan L. Egbert and Michael H. Luque. 428-442, Sept. 1975

The **MIGHTY** *Enterprise.* By Nathaniel T. Kenney. Photos by Thomas J. Abercrombie. 431-448, Mar. 1963

The **MIGHTY** Hudson. By Albert W. Atwood. Photos by B. Anthony Stewart. 1-36, July 1948

MIGRATING PEOPLES:
• Arctic Odyssey. By John Bockstoce. Photos by Jonathan Wright. Paintings by Jack Unruh. Contents: Umiak expedition tracing Thule Eskimo migration route from Alaska to Greenland. 100-127, July 1983
• Eskimo and Viking Finds in the High Arctic: Ellesmere Island. By Peter Schledermann. Photos by Sisse Brimberg. Included: Artifacts of the Norse, the Dorset, the Thule. 575-601, May 1981
• The Search for the First Americans. By Thomas Y. Canby. Photos by Kerby Smith. Paintings by Roy Andersen. Included: Theories of man's migration across the land bridge from Asia to America. 330-363, Sept. 1979
• *See also* Nomads

MIGRATION:
◆ *Animals that Travel.* 1982
• Arizona Sheep Trek. By Francis R. Line. 457-478, Apr. 1950
• Atlantic Salmon: The "Leaper" Struggles to Survive. By Art Lee. Photos by Bianca Lavies. 600-615, Nov. 1981
• Beyond the North Wind With the Snow Goose. By Des and Jen Bartlett. 822-843, Dec. 1973
▲ *Bird Migration in the Americas: The Americas,* double-sided supplement. Included: 67 paintings by Arthur Singer. Aug. 1979
• Canada Counts Its Caribou. 261-268, Aug. 1952
• Caribou: Hardy Nomads of the North. By Jim Rearden. 858-878, Dec. 1974
• The Crab That Shakes Hands. By Clarence P. Idyll. Photos by Robert F. Sisson. 254-271, Feb. 1971
• The Curlew's Secret. By Arthur A. Allen. NGS research grant. 751-770, Dec. 1948
• Editorial. By Gilbert M. Grosvenor. 153, Aug. 1979
• Etosha: Namibia's Kingdom of Animals. By Douglas H. Chadwick. Photos by Des and Jen Bartlett. 344-385, Mar. 1983
■ Etosha: Place of Dry Water. 703, Dec. 1980
• Following the Ladybug Home. By Kenneth S. Hagen. Photos by Robert F. Sisson. 543-553, Apr. 1970
• Found at Last: the Monarch's Winter Home. By Fred A. Urquhart. Photos by Bianca Lavies. NGS research grant. 161-173, Aug. 1976
• Humpbacks: The Gentle Whales. By Sylvia A. Earle. Photos by Al Giddings. NGS research grant. 2-17, Jan. 1979
• Imperiled Gift of the Sea: Caribbean Green Turtle. By Archie Carr. Photos by Robert E. Schroeder. 876-890, June 1967
• The Incredible Salmon. By Clarence P. Idyll. Photos by Robert F. Sisson. Paintings by Walter A. Weber. 195-219, Aug. 1968
• Island, Prairie, Marsh, and Shore. By Charlton Ogburn. Photos by Bates Littlehales. Included: Bear River Migratory Bird Refuge. 350-381, Mar. 1979
• Last Stand for the Bighorn. By James K. Morgan. 383-399, Sept. 1973
• Learning the Ways of the Walrus. By G. Carleton Ray. Photos by Bill Curtsinger. NGS research grant. 565-580, Oct. 1979
• Manitoba's Fantastic Snake Pits. By Michael Aleksiuk. Photos by Bianca Lavies. 715-723, Nov. 1975
• Mono Lake: A Vital Way Station for the Wilson's Phalarope. By Joseph R. Jehl, Jr. NGS research grant. 520-525, Oct. 1981
• Mysteries of Bird Migration. By Allan C. Fisher, Jr. Photos by Jonathan Blair. Included: A list of animals that migrate; an account of sea turtle migration. 154-193, Aug. 1979
• Mystery of the Monarch Butterfly. By Paul A. Zahl. 588-598, Apr. 1963
• New Light on the Singing Whales. Introduction by Roger Payne. Photos by Flip Nicklin. NGS research grant. 463-477, Apr. 1982
• Plight of the Bluefin Tuna. By Michael J. A. Butler. Photos by David Doubilet. Paintings by Stanley Meltzoff. 220-239, Aug. 1982
• Polar Bear: Lonely Nomad of the North. By Thor Larsen. 574-590, Apr. 1971
■ Polar Bear Alert. 395, cover, Mar. 1982
• Sheep Trek in the French Alps. By Maurice Moyal. Photos by Marcel Coen. 545-564, Apr. 1952

• Strange March of the Spiny Lobster. By William F. Herrnkind. Photos by Rick Frehsee and Bruce Mounier. NGS research grant. 819-831, June 1975
• Studying Wildlife by Satellite. By Frank Craighead, Jr. and John Craighead. NGS research grant. 120-123, Jan. 1973
• Tireless Voyager, the Whistling Swan. By William J. L. Sladen. Photos by Bianca Lavies. NGS research grant. 134-147, July 1975
▲ "Whales of the World." Painting supplement. Map on reverse, *The Great Whales: Migration and Range*. Dec. 1976
• White Storks, Vanishing Sentinels of the Rooftops. By Roger Tory Peterson. 838-853, June 1962
• *See also* Locusts (Migratory Grasshoppers)

MIKONOS, Aegean Islands, Greece:
• The Isles of Greece: Aegean Birthplace of Western Culture. By Melville Bell Grosvenor. Photos by Edwin Stuart Grosvenor and Winfield Parks. 147-193, Aug. 1972

MILAN, Italy:
• Italy Smiles Again. By Edgar Erskine Hume. 693-732, June 1949
• Leonardo da Vinci: A Man for All Ages. By Kenneth MacLeish. Photos by James L. Amos. 296-329, Sept. 1977
• Restoration Reveals the "Last Supper." By Carlo Bertelli. Photos by Victor R. Boswell, Jr. 664-685, Nov. 1983

MILESTONES in My Arctic Journeys. By Willie Knutsen. 543-570, Oct. 1949

MILFORD TRACK, New Zealand:
• New Zealand's Milford Track: "Walk of a Lifetime." By Carolyn Bennett Patterson. Photos by Robert E. Gilka. 117-129, Jan. 1978

The **MILITARY.** *See* U. S. Armed Forces

MILITARY ACADEMY. *See* U. S. Military Academy

MILITARY AIR TRANSPORT SERVICE:
• MATS: America's Long Arm of the Air. By Beverley M. Bowie. Photos by Robert F. Sisson. 283-317, Mar. 1957

MILITARY AIRLIFT COMMAND. *See* 3rd Aerospace Rescue and Recovery Group

MILITARY PARKS. *See* Gettysburg; Shiloh; Vicksburg

MILK:
• Deep in the Heart of "Swissconsin." By William H. Nicholas. Photos by J. Baylor Roberts. 781-800, June 1947
• *See also* Thunder Hill Goat Farm

MILKY WAY (Galaxy):
▲ *Journey Into the Universe Through Time and Space; National Geographic-Palomar Sky Survey Charting the Heavens,* double-sided supplement. June 1983
• The Once and Future Universe. By Rick Gore. Photos by James A. Sugar. Paintings by Barron Storey. Picture text by David Jeffery. 704-749, June 1983

MILLER, ARDEAN R., III:
Photographer:
• Through Europe by Trailer Caravan. By Norma Miller. 769-816, June 1957

MILLER, CARL F.: Author:
• Life 8,000 Years Ago Uncovered in an Alabama Cave. 542-558, Oct. 1956
• Russell Cave: New Light on Stone Age Life. 427-437, Mar. 1958

MILLER, CHARLES R.: Author:
• Life Around a Lily Pad. Photos by Bianca Lavies. 131-142, Jan. 1980

MILLER, HARRY:
Author-Photographer:
• The Cobra, India's "Good Snake." 393-409, Sept. 1970
• Wild Elephant Roundup in India. Photos by author and James P. Blair. 372-385, Mar. 1969

MILLER, HELEN HILL: Author:
• Rotterdam–Reborn From Ruins. Photos by James Blair. 526-553, Oct. 1960

MILLER, IRENE: Author:
• On the Summit (Annapurna). By Irene Miller, with Vera Komarkova. 312-313, Mar. 1979

MILLER, MARK: Author:
• Oregon's Lovely, Lonely Coast. Photos by Cotton Coulson. 798-823, Dec. 1979
• Washington's Yakima Valley. Photos by Sisse Brimberg. 609-631, Nov. 1978

MILLER, MAYNARD M.: Author:
• Alaska's Mighty Rivers of Ice. Photos by Christopher G. Knight. 194-217, Feb. 1967
• Our Restless Earth. 140-141, July 1964
Author-Photographer:
• First American Ascent of Mount St. Elias. 229-248, Feb. 1948

MILLER, NORMA: Author:
• Through Europe by Trailer Caravan. Photos by Ardean R. Miller III. 769-816, June 1957

MILLER, PETER: Author:
• Bali Celebrates a Festival of Faith. Photos by Fred and Margaret Eiseman. 416-427, Mar. 1980
▲ *The Face and Faith of Poland,* map, photo, and essay supplement. Essay by Czesław Miłosz. Photos by Bruno Barbey. Apr. 1982
• Henry VIII's Lost Warship: *Mary Rose.* By Margaret Rule. Introduction and picture text by Peter Miller. Paintings by Richard Schlecht. 646-675, May 1983

MILLER, WAYNE: Photographer:
• Henry Hudson's River. By Willard Price. 364-403, Mar. 1962

MILLER, WILLIAM C.:
Author-Photographer:
• First Color Portraits of the Heavens. 670-679, May 1959

BIANCA LAVIES, NGS

Life Around a Lily Pad: courting newts

M
N

MILLS, Silk:
• Silkworms in England Spin for the Queen. By John E. H. Nolan. 689-704, May 1953
MILOS (Island), Aegean Islands:
• The Isles of Greece: Aegean Birthplace of Western Culture. By Melville Bell Grosvenor. Photos by Edwin Stuart Grosvenor and Winfield Parks. 147-193, Aug. 1972
MIŁOSZ, CZESŁAW: Author:
▲ *The Face and Faith of Poland,* map, photo, and essay supplement. By Peter Miller. Essay by Czesław Miłosz. Photos by Bruno Barbey. Apr. 1982
MILTON, JOHN:
• The British Way. By Sir Evelyn Wrench. 421-541, Apr. 1949
MILWAUKEE, Wisconsin:
• Milwaukee: More Than Beer. By Louise Levathes. Photos by Michael Mauney. Included: Maps tracing Milwaukee's history: Three settlements (1835); ethnic divisions (1900); present-day Milwaukee. 180-201, Aug. 1980
MIMICRY:
• Deception: Formula for Survival. By Robert F. Sisson. Included: Insect mimicry. 394-415, Mar. 1980
MIN YUEN:
• Malaya Meets Its Emergency. By George W. Long. Photos by J. Baylor Roberts and author. 185-228, Feb. 1953
MINAS GERAIS (State), Brazil:
• Brazil's Land of Minerals. By W. Robert Moore. 479-508, Oct. 1948
• *See also* Bocaiuva
MINDANAO (Island), Philippines:
• First Glimpse of a Stone Age Tribe. 881-882, Dec. 1971
• Help for Philippine Tribes in Trouble. By Kenneth MacLeish. Photos by Dean Conger. 220-255, Aug. 1971
■ The Last Tribes of Mindanao. 882A-882B, Dec. 1971; 227, Aug. 1972
• Saving the Philippine Eagle. By Robert S. Kennedy. Photos by Alan R. Degen, Neil L. Rettig, and Wolfgang A. Salb. NGS research grant. 847-856, June 1981
• Seeking Mindanao's Strangest Creatures. By Charles Heizer Wharton. 389-408, Sept. 1948
• The Tasadays, Stone Age Cavemen of Mindanao. By Kenneth MacLeish. Photos by John Launois. 219-249, Aug. 1972
MINERALS AND METALS:
• Brazil's Land of Minerals. By W. Robert Moore. Contents: Bauxite, Beryls, Diamonds, Gold, Iron Ore, Iron Pyrites, Manganese, Mica, Quartz. 479-508, Oct. 1948
• The Canadian North: Emerging Giant. By David S. Boyer. Included: Asbestos, Copper, Gold, Iron, Lead, Nickel, Silver, Uranium, Zinc. 1-43, July 1968
• Colorado, the Rockies' Pot of Gold. By Edward J. Linehan. Photos by James L. Amos. Included: Gold, Lead, Molybdenum, Silver. 157-201, Aug. 1969
• Exploring the World of Gems. By W. F. Foshag. 779-810, Dec. 1950
• Finding Rare Beauty in Common Rocks. By Lorence G. Collins. 121-129, Jan. 1966
• The Glittering World of Rockhounds. By David S. Boyer. 276-294, Feb. 1974
• In Manchuria Now. By W. Robert Moore. Included: Aluminum, Coal, Copper, Gold, Iron, Lead, Magnesite, Molybdenum, Uranium, Zinc. 389-414, Mar. 1947
• Questing for Gems. By George S. Switzer. 835-863, Dec. 1971
• "Rockhounds" Uncover Earth's Mineral Beauty. By George S. Switzer. 631-660, Nov. 1951
• Sonora Is Jumping. By Mason Sutherland. Included: Cobalt, Copper, Gold, Graphite, Lead, Silver, Tungsten. 215-246, Feb. 1955
• *See also* Aluminum; Coal; Copper; Crystals; Diamonds; Gold; Mercury; Mines and Mining; Phosphate; Platinum; Plutonium; Salt; Silver; Steel Industry; Uranium
MINES AND MINING:
• Brazil's Land of Minerals. By W. Robert Moore. Included: Historic mines of Mariana; Ouro Prêto; Sabará; São João del Rei. 479-508, Oct. 1948
• The Canadian North: Emerging Giant. By David S. Boyer. Included: Asbestos, Copper, Gold, Iron, Lead, Nickel, Silver, Uranium, and Zinc mines. 1-43, July 1968
• Carrara Marble: Touchstone of Eternity. By Cathy Newman. Photos by Pierre Boulat. 42-59, July 1982
• Colorado by Car and Campfire. By Kathleen Revis. Included: Blackhawk mines; Camp Bird Mine; Climax Mine; Leadville mines; Placer mines near Ute Pass; Smuggler Mine. 207-248, Aug. 1954
• From Tucson to Tombstone. By Mason Sutherland. Included: The Mary G, Morenci open pit, Pearce mines, Tombstone mines. 343-384, Sept. 1953
• In Manchuria Now. By W. Robert Moore. Included: Open-pit coal mine of Fushun; Coal reserves, in general; and the following: Aluminum, Copper, Gold, Iron, Lead, Magnesite, Molybdenum, Shale, Uranium, Zinc. 389-414, Mar. 1947
• Minnesota Makes Ideas Pay. By Frederick G. Vosburgh. Photos by John E. Fletcher and B. Anthony Stewart. Included: Cuyuna, Mesabi, and Vermilion iron ranges; the Mountain Iron, Embarrass (mine in a lake), and Hull-Rust-Mahoning (Hibbing open-pit) mines; and research on the smelting of taconite and carbonate slate. 291-336, Sept. 1949
• Montana, Shining Mountain Treasureland. By Leo A. Borah. Included: Coal, Copper, Gold, Quartz, Silver, Zinc. 693-736, June 1950
• Newfoundland, Canada's New Province. By Andrew H. Brown. Photos by author and Robert F. Sisson. Included: Undersea iron mines and the lead-zinc-copper mine at Buchans. 777-812, June 1949
• Our National Forests: Problems in Paradise. By Rowe Findley. Photos by David Cupp. 306-339, Sept. 1982
• Questing for Gems. By George S. Switzer. Included: Mines in Africa; Asia; Australia. 835-863, Dec. 1971
• Should They Build a Fence Around Montana? By Mike W. Edwards. Photos by Nicholas deVore III. Included: Coal and Copper mines. 614-649, May 1976
• Synfuels: Fill 'er Up! With What? By Thomas Y. Canby. Photos by Jonathan Blair. Included: Oil-shale mines. 74-95, *Special Report on Energy* (Feb. 1981)
• White Magic in the Belgian Congo. By W. Robert Moore. Included: Cobalt, Copper, Diamond, Gold, Tin, and Uranium mines. 321-362, Mar. 1952
• Work-hard, Play-hard Michigan. By Andrew H. Brown. Included: Calumet and Hecla Consolidated Copper mines, Mather Iron Mine, Salt mines. 279-320, Mar. 1952
• Yukon Fever: Call of the North. By Robert Booth. Photos by George F. Mobley. Included: Gold, Lead, Silver, Copper, and Asbestos mines. 548-578, Apr. 1978
• *See also* Bauxite; Coal; Copper; Diamonds; Gold Mining; Mercury (Metal); Opal Mining; Phosphate; Prospectors; Salt Mines; Silver; Tin and Tin Mining; Uranium

MINIATURE Monaco. By Gilbert M. and Donna Kerkam Grosvenor. 546-573, Apr. 1963

MINK:
• Men, Moose, and Mink of Northwest Angle (Minnesota). By William H. Nicholas. Photos by J. Baylor Roberts. 265-284, Aug. 1947
• The Romance of American Furs. By Wanda Burnett. 379-402, Mar. 1948

MINNEAPOLIS, Minnesota:
• Minneapolis and St. Paul. By Thomas J. Abercrombie. Photos by Annie Griffiths. 665-691, Nov. 1980

MINNESOTA:
• Easter Greetings From the Ukrainians. By Robert Paul Jordan. Photos by James A. Sugar. 556-563, Apr. 1972
• I See America First. By Lynda Bird Johnson. Photos by William Albert Allard. 874-904, Dec. 1965
• Ice Fishing's Frigid Charms. By Thomas J. Abercrombie. 861-872, Dec. 1958
• Mapping the Nation's Breadbasket. By Frederick Simpich. 831-849, June 1948
• Men, Moose, and Mink of Northwest Angle. By William H. Nicholas. Photos by J. Baylor Roberts. 265-284, Aug. 1947
• Minneapolis and St. Paul. By Thomas J. Abercrombie. Photos by Annie Griffiths. 665-691, Nov. 1980
• Minnesota, Where Water Is the Magic Word. By David S. Boyer. Photos by author and David Brill. 200-229, Feb. 1976

● Minnesota Makes Ideas Pay. By Frederick G. Vosburgh. Photos by John E. Fletcher and B. Anthony Stewart. 291-336, Sept. 1949
● Our Bald Eagle: Freedom's Symbol Survives. By Thomas C. Dunstan. Photos by Jeff Foott. NGS research grant. 186-199, Feb. 1978
● Our Wild and Scenic Rivers: The St. Croix. By David S. Boyer. 30-37, July 1977
● Relics From the Rapids (Voyageurs). By Sigurd F. Olson. Photos by David S. Boyer. 413-435, Sept. 1963
● The Upper Mississippi. By Willard Price. 651-699, Nov. 1958
● Where Can the Wolf Survive? By L. David Mech. 518-537, Oct. 1977
● *See also* Mankato

MINNESOTA (River), Minnesota:
● Satellites Gave Warning of Midwest Floods. By Peter T. White. Photos by Thomas A. DeFeo. 574-592, Oct. 1969

MINOAN CIVILIZATION:
● Drama of Death in a Minoan Temple. By Yannis Sakellarakis and Efi Sapouna-Sakellaraki. Photos by Otis Imboden and Spyros Tsavdaroglou. 205-222, Feb. 1981
● Joseph Alsop: A Historical Perspective (on Minoan Human Sacrifice). 223, Feb. 1981
● Minoans and Mycenaeans: Greece's Brilliant Bronze Age. By Joseph Judge. Photos by Gordon W. Gahan. Paintings by Lloyd K. Townsend. 142-185. Feb. 1978
● Thera, Key to the Riddle of Minos. By Spyridon Marinatos. Photos by Otis Imboden. 702-726, May 1972

MINOT, North Dakota:
● North Dakota Comes into Its Own. By Leo A. Borah. Photos by J. Baylor Roberts. 283-322, Sept. 1951
● Satellites Gave Warning of Midwest Floods. By Peter T. White. Photos by Thomas A. DeFeo. 574-592, Oct. 1969

MINUTEMEN of the Civil Air Patrol. By Allan C. Fisher, Jr. Photos by John E. Fletcher. 637-665, May 1956

MION, PIERRE: Artist:
● Footprints on the Moon. By Hugh L. Dryden. Paintings by Davis Meltzer and Pierre Mion. 357-401, Mar. 1964
● The Next Frontier? By Isaac Asimov. 76-89, July 1976
● Robots to the Moon. By Frank Sartwell. 557-571, Oct. 1962
● "Teammates in Mankind's Greatest Adventure" (Apollo Astronauts), painting supplement. Sept. 1973
● Tektite II. 256-296, Aug. 1971
I. Science's Window on the Sea. By John G. VanDerwalker. Photos by Bates Littlehales. 256-289; II. All-girl Team Tests the Habitat. By Sylvia A. Earle. 291-296

MIQUELON (Island), Atlantic Ocean:
● *White Mist* Cruises to Wreck-haunted St. Pierre and Miquelon. By Melville Bell Grosvenor. 378-419, Sept. 1967

OTIS IMBODEN, NGS

NATIONAL GEOGRAPHIC ART DIVISION

Minoan Temple: figurine found in Cretan tomb

MIRACLE Men of the Telephone. By F. Barrows Colton. 273-316, Mar. 1947

The **MIRACLE** Metal–Platinum. By Gordon Young. Photos by James L. Amos. 686-706, Nov. 1983

MIRACLE of the Mermaid's Purse. By Ernest L. Libby. 413-420, Sept. 1959

MIRACLE of the Potholes. By Rowe Findley. Photos by Robert F. Sisson. 570-579, Oct. 1975

MIRACLES of Fiber Optics. By Allen A. Boraiko. Photos by Fred Ward. 516-535, Oct. 1979

MISHMI HILLS, Assam (State), India:
● Caught in the Assam-Tibet Earthquake. By F. Kingdon-Ward. 403-416, Mar. 1952

MISSILE RANGE. *See* Atlantic Missile Range

MISSILES. *See* Guided Missiles; Rockets

The **MISSION** Called 66: Today in Our National Parks. By Conrad L. Wirth. 7-47, July 1966

MISSIONARIES. *See* Mary-Rousseliere, Guy

MISSIONS:
● California, the Golden Magnet. By William Graves. Included: Spanish missions. 595-679, May 1966
I. The South. Photos by Thomas Nebbia. 595-639; II. Nature's North. Photos by James P. Blair and Jonathan S. Blair. 641-679
● Carnival in San Antonio. By Mason Sutherland. Photos by J. Baylor Roberts. Included: Espada, Mission Concepción, San José, San Juan Capistrano, and the Alamo. 813-844, Dec. 1947
● Cruise to Stone Age Arnhem Land. By Howell Walker. Included: Mission stations: Croker Island, Elcho Island, Milingimbi Island, South Goulburn Island, and Yirrkala. NGS research grant. 417-430, Sept. 1949
● Far North with "Captain Mac." By Miriam MacMillan. Included: Catholic, Church of England, and Moravian missions. 465-513, Oct. 1951
● From Tucson to Tombstone. By Mason Sutherland. 343-384, Sept. 1953
● I Live With the Eskimos (Canadian). By Guy Mary-Rousseliere. 188-217, Feb. 1971
● San Diego, California's Plymouth Rock. By Allan C. Fisher, Jr. Photos by James L. Amos. 114-147, July 1969
● *See also* Mesa del Nayar, Mexico; Sonora (State), Mexico

MISSISSIPPI:
● Dixie Spins the Wheel of Industry. By William H. Nicholas. Photos by J. Baylor Roberts. 281-324, Mar. 1949
● The Lower Mississippi. By Willard Price. Photos by W. D. Vaughn. 681-725, Nov. 1960

TOM HOOPER

ALVIN LANGDON COBURN, COURTESY MARK TWAIN MEMORIAL, HARTFORD, CONNECTICUT

Mark Twain: author Grove drifts past St. Louis, *top;* rare photo of Samuel Clemens, *above*

• Mississippi's Grand Reunion at the Neshoba County Fair. By Carolyn Bennett Patterson. Photos by C. C. Lockwood. 854-866, June 1980
• Skyway Below the Clouds. By Carl R. Markwith. Photos by Ernest J. Cottrell. Included: East Jackson Airport; Hawkins Field, Jackson; Vicksburg. 85-108, July 1949
• Today Along the Natchez Trace, Pathway Through History. By Bern Keating. Photos by Charles Harbutt. 641-667, Nov. 1968
• Troubled Odyssey of Vietnamese Fishermen. By Harvey Arden. Photos by Steve Wall. 378-395, Sept. 1981
• *See also* Natchez; Vicksburg

MISSISSIPPI (River), U. S.:
• Down Mark Twain's River on a Raft. By Rex E. Hieronymus. 551-574, Apr. 1948
• Gettysburg and Vicksburg: the Battle Towns Today. By Robert Paul Jordan. Map notes by Carolyn Bennett Patterson. 4-57, July 1963
• Land of Louisiana Sugar Kings. By Harnett T. Kane. Photos by Willard R. Culver. 531-567, Apr. 1958
• The Lower Mississippi. By Willard Price. Photos by W. D. Vaughn. 681-725, Nov. 1960
• Mark Twain: Mirror of America. By Noel Grove. Photos by James L. Stanfield. 300-337, Sept. 1975
◆ *The Mighty Mississippi.* Announced. 882-886, June 1971
• Minneapolis and St. Paul. By Thomas J. Abercrombie. Photos by Annie Griffiths. 665-691, Nov. 1980
• New Orleans: Jambalaya on the Levee. By Harnett T. Kane. Photos by Justin Locke. 143-184, Feb. 1953
• New Orleans and Her River. By Joseph Judge. Photos by James L. Stanfield. 151-187, Feb. 1971
• St. Louis: New Spirit Soars in Mid-America's Proud Old City. By Robert Paul Jordan. Photos by Bruce Dale. 605-641, Nov. 1965
• Trouble in Bayou Country: Louisiana's Atchafalaya. By Jack and Anne Rudloe. Photos by C. C. Lockwood. Note: The Atchafalaya Basin is a major element in controlling floods on the Mississippi. 377-397, Sept. 1979
• Troubled Odyssey of Vietnamese Fishermen. By Harvey Arden. Photos by Steve Wall. 378-395, Sept. 1981
• The Upper Mississippi. By Willard Price. 651-699, Nov. 1958
• *See also* Hannibal, Missouri; Mississippi River Delta

MISSISSIPPI RIVER DELTA, Louisiana:
• Mississippi Delta: The Land of the River. By Douglas Lee. Photos by C. C. Lockwood. 226-253, Aug. 1983

MISSISSIPPI VALLEY, U. S.:
• "Pyramids" of the New World. By Neil Merton Judd. Note: Hundreds of mounds were built including Cahokia, Illinois; Grave Creek Mound, Moundsville, West Virginia; "Great Serpent," Ohio; St. Louis ("Mound City"), Missouri; Spiro, Oklahoma. 105-128, Jan. 1948
• Who Were the "Mound Builders"? By George E. Stuart. Note: Hundreds of mounds were built including Cahokia, Illinois; Koster farm site, Illinois; Monks Mound, East St. Louis, Illinois; Serpent Mound, Ohio. 783-801, Dec. 1972

MISSISSIPPIAN CULTURE:
• Who Were the "Mound Builders"? By George E. Stuart. 783-801, Dec. 1972
• *See also* Russell Cave, Alabama

MISSOURI:
• Following the Trail of Lewis and Clark. By Ralph Gray. 707-750, June 1953
• Mapping the Nation's Breadbasket. By Frederick Simpich. 831-849, June 1948
• Skyway Below the Clouds. By Carl R. Markwith. Photos by Ernest J. Cottrell. Included: The Ozarks; St. Louis; Springfield. 85-108, July 1949
• Through Ozark Hills and Hollows. By Mike W. Edwards. Photos by Bruce Dale. 656-689, Nov. 1970
• The Upper Mississippi. By Willard Price. 651-699, Nov. 1958
• *See also* Hannibal; Kansas City; St. Louis

MISSOURI (River), U. S.:
• Following the Trail of Lewis and Clark. By Ralph Gray. 707-750, June 1953
• So Long, St. Louis, We're Heading West. By William C. Everhart. 643-669, Nov. 1965
• That Dammed Missouri River. By Gordon Young. Photos by David Hiser. 374-413, Sept. 1971

MR. JEFFERSON'S Charlottesville. By Anne Revis. 553-592, May 1950

MR. JEFFERSON'S Monticello. By Joseph Judge. Photos by Dean Conger and Richard S. Durrance. 426-444, Sept. 1966

MITCHELL, CARLETON: Author:
• The Bahamas, Isles of the Blue-green Sea. Photos by B. Anthony Stewart. 147-203, Feb. 1958
• Ballerinas in Pink. Photos by B. Anthony Stewart. 553-571, Oct. 1957
• Capri, Italy's Enchanted Rock. Photos by David F. Cupp. 795-809, June 1970
• *Finisterre* Sails the Windward Islands. Photos by Winfield Parks. 755-801, Dec. 1965
• French Riviera: Storied Playground on the Azure Coast. Photos by Thomas Nebbia. 798-835, June 1967
• A Fresh Breeze Stirs the Leewards. Photos by Winfield Parks. 488-537, Oct. 1966
• More of Sea Than of Land: The Bahamas. Photos by James L. Stanfield. 218-267, Feb. 1967
• Our Virgin Islands, 50 Years Under the Flag. Photos by James L. Stanfield. 67-103, Jan. 1968
• Time Turns Back in Picture-book Portofino. Photos by Winfield Parks. 232-253, Feb. 1965

● To Europe with a Racing Start (*Finisterre*). 758-791, June 1958
Author-Photographer:
● Baltic Cruise of the *Caribbee*. 605-646, Nov. 1950
● *Carib* Cruises the West Indies. 1-56, Jan. 1948

MITCHELL, EDGAR D.: Photographer:
● The Climb Up Cone Crater. By Alice J. Hall. Photos by Edgar D. Mitchell and Alan B. Shepard, Jr. 136-148, July 1971

MITCHELL, HENRY: Author:
● Washington, D. C.: Hometown Behind the Monuments. Photos by Adam Woolfitt. 84-125, Jan. 1983

MITES:
● The Wild World of Compost. By Cecil E. Johnson. Photos by Bianca Lavies. 273-284, Aug. 1980

MIURA RANCH, Spain:
● Holy Week and the Fair in Sevilla. By Luis Marden. 499-530, Apr. 1951

MIYAZAWA, EIJI: Photographer:
● Japan's "Sky People," the Vanishing Ainu. By Mary Inez Hilger. 268-296, Feb. 1967
● Scientist Studies Japan's Fantastic Long-tailed Fowl. By Frank X. Ogasawara. 845-855, Dec. 1970
● Snow Festival in Japan's Far North. 824-833, Dec. 1968

MNONG TRIBE:
● Viet Nam's Montagnards. By Howard Sochurek. 443-487, Apr. 1968

MOBILE, Alabama:
● Mobile, Alabama's City in Motion. By William Graves. Photos by Joseph J. Scherschel and Robert W. Madden. 368-397, Mar. 1968

MOBLEY, GEORGE F.: Photographer:
● Bavaria: Mod, Medieval–and Bewitching. By Gary Jennings. 409-431, Mar. 1974
● Chile, Republic on a Shoestring. By Gordon Young. 437-477, Oct. 1973
● Finland: Plucky Neighbor of Soviet Russia. By William Graves. 587-629, May 1968
● Firebrands of the Revolution. By Eric F. Goldman. 2-27, July 1974
● Greenland Feels the Winds of Change. By John J. Putman. 366-393, Sept. 1975
● The Joy of Pigs. By Kent Britt. 398-415, Sept. 1978
● Kyoto and Nara: Keepers of Japan's Past. By Charles McCarry. 836-859, June 1976
Kyoto Says Happy New Year. 852-859
● Lebanon, Little Bible Land in the Crossfire of History. By William S. Ellis. 240-275, Feb. 1970
● 900 Years Ago: the Norman Conquest. By Kenneth M. Setton. 206-251, Aug. 1966
● Norway, Land of the Generous Sea. By Edward J. Linehan. 1-43, July 1971
● The Panama Canal Today. By Bart McDowell. 279-294, Feb. 1978
● Parks, Plans, and People: How South America Guards Her Green Legacy. By Mary and Laurance Rockefeller. 74-119, Jan. 1967
● The Society Islands, Sisters of the Wind. By Priit J. Vesilind. 844-869, June 1979
● Uganda, Africa's Uneasy Heartland. By Howard La Fay. 708-735, Nov. 1971
● Under the Dome of Freedom: The United States Capitol. By Lonnelle Aikman. 4-59, Jan. 1964
● World's Tallest Tree Discovered. By Melville Bell Grosvenor. 1-9, July 1964
● Yukon Fever: Call of the North. By Robert Booth. 548-578, Apr. 1978

MOCHICA CULTURE:
● Finding the Tomb of a Warrior-God. By William Duncan Strong. Photos by Clifford Evans, Jr. 453-482, Apr. 1947

MODERN House, Ancient Architecture. 42-43, *Special Report on Energy* (Feb. 1981)

MODERN Miracle, Made in Germany. By Robert Leslie Conly. Photos by Erich Lessing. 735-791, June 1959

MOEHLMAN, PATRICIA DES ROSES:
Author-Photographer:
● Getting to Know the Wild Burros of Death Valley. Photos by Ira S. Lerner and author. 502-517, Apr. 1972
● Jackals of the Serengeti. 840-850, Dec. 1980

MOGADISHU, Somalia:
● Somalia's Hour of Need. By Robert Paul Jordan. Photos by Michael S. Yamashita and Kevin Fleming. 748-775, June 1981

MOGOLLON CULTURE:
● Pueblo Pottery–2,000 Years of Artistry. By David L. Arnold. 593-605, Nov. 1982

MOHAMMAD REZA PAHLAVI, Shah (Iran):
● Coronations a World Apart. By the Editor. 299, Mar. 1968
● Iran: Desert Miracle. By William Graves. Photos by James P. Blair. 2-47, Jan. 1975
● Iran's Shah Crowns Himself and His Empress. By Franc Shor. Photos by James L. Stanfield and Winfield Parks. 301-321, Mar. 1968

MOHAMMED (Prophet). *See* Muhammad

MOHAWK (River and Valley), New York:
● Drums to Dynamos on the Mohawk. By Frederick G. Vosburgh. Photos by B. Anthony Stewart. 67-110, July 1947
● *See also* New York State Thruway

MOHAWKS (Indians):
● Drums to Dynamos on the Mohawk. By Frederick G. Vosburgh. Photos by B. Anthony Stewart. 67-110, July 1947
● The Mohawks Scrape the Sky (High-iron Workers). By Robert L. Conly. Photos by B. Anthony Stewart. 133-142, July 1952

MOHOLE, Project:
● Scientists Drill at Sea to Pierce Earth's Crust. By Samuel W. Matthews. Photos by J. Baylor Roberts. 686-697, Nov. 1961

MOHR, CHARLES E.: Author:
● Exploring America Underground. 803-837, June 1964

MOIZE, ELIZABETH A.: Author:
● Amateur Gardener Creates a New Rose. Photos by Farrell Grehan. 286-294, Aug. 1972
● Heart of the Canadian Rockies. Photos by Jim Brandenburg. 757-779, June 1980
● In Touch With Nature. Photos by Steve Raymer. 537-543, Apr. 1974
● Tulips: Holland's Beautiful Business. Photos by Farrell Grehan. 712-728, May 1978
● Turnaround Time in West Virginia. Photos by Jodi Cobb. 755-785, June 1976

MOJAVE DESERT, California:
● Californians Escape to the Desert. By Mason Sutherland. Photos by Charles W. Herbert. 675-724, Nov. 1957
■ The Great Mojave Desert. 294A-294B, Feb. 1971
● The Lure of the Changing Desert. 817-824, June 1954
● *See also* Los Angeles Aqueduct

MOLDS:
● Slime Mold: The Fungus That Walks. By Douglas Lee. Photos by Paul A. Zahl. 131-136, July 1981

MOLDVAY, ALBERT: Photographer:
● The Changing Face of Old Spain. By Bart McDowell. 291-339, Mar. 1965
● Gotland: Sweden's Treasure Island. By James Cerruti. 268-288, Aug. 1973
● Hungary: Changing Homeland of a Tough, Romantic People. By Bart McDowell. Photos by Albert Moldvay and Joseph J. Scherschel. 443-483, Apr. 1971
● Italian Riviera, Land That Winter Forgot. By Howell Walker. 743-789, June 1963
● Madagascar: Island at the End of the Earth. By Luis Marden. 443-487, Oct. 1967
● Mexico, the City That Founded a Nation. By Louis de la Haba. 638-669, May 1973
● New Era in the Loneliest Continent. By David M. Tyree. 260-296, Feb. 1963
● Of Planes and Men. By Kenneth F. Weaver. Photos by Emory Kristof and Albert Moldvay. 298-349, Sept. 1965
● Pakistan: Problems of a Two-part Land. By Bern Keating. 1-47, Jan. 1967
● The Renaissance Lives On in Tuscany. By Luis Marden. 626-659, Nov. 1974
● St. Peter's, Rome's Church of Popes. By Aubrey Menen. 865-879, Dec. 1971

MN

BIANCA LAVIES, NGS

Monarch's Winter Home: butterfly drinks from stream

• Stockholm, Where "Kvalitet" Is a Way of Life. By James Cerruti. Photos by Albert Moldvay and Jonathan Blair. 43-69, Jan. 1976
• Venice Fights for Life. By Joseph Judge. 591-631, Nov. 1972

MOLECULAR BIOLOGY:
• The Awesome Worlds Within a Cell. By Rick Gore. Photos by Bruce Dale. Paintings by Davis Meltzer. 355-395, Sept. 1976

MOLENAAR, CORNELIUS and DEE: Photographers:
• First American Ascent of Mount St. Elias. By Maynard M. Miller. 229-248, Feb. 1948

MOLINA MONTES, AUGUSTO F.: Author:
• The Building of Tenochtitlan. Paintings by Felipe Dávalos. 753-765, Dec. 1980

MOLLUSKS:
• The Magic Lure of Sea Shells. By Paul A. Zahl. Photos by Victor R. Boswell, Jr., and author. 386-429, Mar. 1969
• Man-of-war Fleet Attacks Bimini. By Paul A. Zahl. Included: Sea hares. 185-212, Feb. 1952
• Shells Take You Over World Horizons. By Rutherford Platt. 33-84, July 1949
• X-Rays Reveal the Inner Beauty of Shells. By Hilary B. Moore. 427-434, Mar. 1955
• *See also* Abalone; Chambered Nautilus; Mother-of-Pearl; Nudibranchs; Octopuses; Oysters; Shipworms; Snails; Squids

MOLOKAI (Island), Hawaii:
• Molokai–Forgotten Hawaii. By Ethel A. Starbird. Photos by Richard A. Cooke III. 188-219, Aug. 1981

MOLUCCAS (Islands), Indonesia:
• Magellan: First Voyage Around the World. By Alan Villiers. Photos by Bruce Dale. 721-753, June 1976
• Shells Take You Over World Horizons. By Rutherford Platt. 33-84, July 1949
• Spices, the Essence of Geography. By Stuart E. Jones. 401-420, Mar. 1949
• *Yankee* Roams the Orient. By Irving and Electa Johnson. Included: Ternate (Island). 327-370, Mar. 1951

MOMADAY, N. SCOTT: Author:
• A First American Views His Land. 13-19, July 1976

MOMATIUK, YVA: Author-Photographer:
• New Zealand's High Country. By Yva Momatiuk and John Eastcott. 246-265, Aug. 1978
• Poland's Mountain People. By Yva Momatiuk and John Eastcott. 104-129, Jan. 1981
• Still Eskimo, Still Free: The Inuit of Umingmaktok. By Yva Momatiuk and John Eastcott. 624-647, Nov. 1977

"MONA LISA" (Leonardo da Vinci):
• Escorting Mona Lisa to America. By Edward T. Folliard. 838-847, June 1963

MONACO:
• Miniature Monaco. By Gilbert M. and Donna Kerkam Grosvenor. 546-573, Apr. 1963

MONARCH BUTTERFLY:
• Editorial. By Gilbert M. Grosvenor. 159, Aug. 1976
• Found at Last: the Monarch's Winter Home. By Fred A. Urquhart. Photos by Bianca Lavies. NGS research grant. 161-173, Aug. 1976
• Mystery of the Monarch Butterfly. By Paul A. Zahl. 588-598, Apr. 1963

MONASTERIES:
• An Archeologist Looks at Palestine. By Nelson Glueck. Included: St. Saba, St. George, Mount of Temptation. 739-752, Dec. 1947
• Caldy, the Monks' Island. By John E. H. Nolan. 564-578, Oct. 1955
• Gangtok, Cloud-wreathed Himalayan Capital. By John Scofield. Included: Rumtek Monastery, Sikkim. 689-713, Nov. 1970
• The Great St. Bernard Hospice Today. By George Pickow. 49-62, Jan. 1957
• India's Sculptured Temple Caves. By Volkmar Wentzel. 665-678, May 1953
• A Journey to "Little Tibet." By Enakshi Bhavnani. Photos by Volkmar Wentzel. 603-634, May 1951
• The Men Who Hid the Dead Sea Scrolls. By A. Douglas Tushingham. Paintings by Peter V. Bianchi. 785-808, Dec. 1958
• Mont Saint Michel. By Kenneth MacLeish. Photos by Cotton Coulson. 820-831, June 1977
• Mount Athos. Photos by James L. Stanfield. 739-745, Dec. 1983
• Searching Out Medieval Churches in Ethiopia's Wilds. By Georg Gerster. 856-884, Dec. 1970
• A Woman Paints the Tibetans. By Lafugie. 659-692, May 1949
• The World of Martin Luther. By Merle Severy. Photos by James L. Amos. 418-463, Oct. 1983
• *See also* St. Catherine's Monastery

MONGOLIAN PEOPLE'S REPUBLIC:
• Journey to Outer Mongolia. By William O. Douglas. Photos by Dean Conger. 289-345, Mar. 1962

MONGOLS:
• The Lost Fleet of Kublai Khan. By Torao Mozai. Photos by Koji Nakamura. Paintings by Issho Yada. 634-649, Nov. 1982

MONHEGAN ISLAND, Maine:
• Maine's Lobster Island, Monhegan. By William P. E. Graves. Photos by Kosti Ruohomaa. 285-298, Feb. 1959

MONITOR (Civil War Gunboat):
• How We Found the *Monitor*. By John G. Newton. NGS research grant. 48-61, Jan. 1975

MONITOR LIZARDS. *See* Komodo Dragons

MONKEY-EATING EAGLES. *See* Philippine Eagles

MONKEYS:
• Keeping House for a Biologist in Colombia. By Nancy Bell Fairchild Bates. Photos by Marston Bates. Included: Cebus, Douroucouli, Howler, Marmoset, Rhesus, Saimiri, Socay, Spider, Woolly. 251-272, Aug. 1948
• London's Zoo of Zoos. By Thomas Garner James. 771-786, June 1953
▪ Monkeys, Apes, and Man. 585A-585B, Oct. 1971
• Portraits of My Monkey Friends. By Ernest P. Walker. 105-119, Jan. 1956
• School for Space Monkeys. 725-729, May 1961
• Temple Monkeys of Nepal. By Jane Teas. Contents: Behavior study of rhesus monkeys. NGS research grant. 575-584, Apr. 1980
• *See also* Baboons

MONO LAKE, California:
• Editorial. By Wilbur E. Garrett. 421, Oct. 1981
• Mono Lake: A Vital Way Station for the Wilson's Phalarope. By Joseph R. Jehl, Jr. NGS research grant. 520-525, Oct. 1981
• The Troubled Waters of Mono Lake. By Gordon Young. Photos by Craig Aurness. 504-519, Oct. 1981

MONOLITHS. *See* Easter Island; Stone Spheres; Stonehenge

MONONGAHELA (River), Pennsylvania:
• Pittsburgh, Pattern for Progress. By William J. Gill. Photos by Clyde Hare. 342-371, Mar. 1965
• Pittsburgh: Workshop of the Titans. By Albert W. Atwood. 117-144, July 1949

MONROE, JAMES:
• Inside the White House. By Lonnelle Aikman. Photos by B. Anthony Stewart and Thomas Nebbia. 3-43, Jan. 1961
• The Living White House. By Lonnelle Aikman. 593-643, Nov. 1966
• Profiles of the Presidents: I. The Presidency and How It Grew. By Frank Freidel. 642-687, Nov. 1964

MONSOONS:
• Science Explores the Monsoon Sea. By Samuel W. Matthews. Photos by Robert F. Sisson. 554-575, Oct. 1967

MONT SAINT MICHEL, France:
• Mont Saint Michel. By Kenneth MacLeish. Photos by Cotton Coulson. 820-831, June 1977

MONTAGNARDS (Vietnamese Mountain People):
• American Special Forces in Action in Viet Nam. By Howard Sochurek. 38-65, Jan. 1965
• Viet Nam's Montagnards. By Howard Sochurek. 443-487, Apr. 1968

MONTANA:
• Along the Great Divide. By Mike Edwards. Photos by Nicholas DeVore III. 483-515, Oct. 1979
• Chief Joseph. By William Albert Allard. 409-434, Mar. 1977
• Following the Trail of Lewis and Clark. By Ralph Gray. 707-750, June 1953
• From Sun-clad Sea to Shining Mountains. By Ralph Gray. Photos by James P. Blair. 542-589, Apr. 1964
• Montana, Shining Mountain Treasureland. By Leo A. Borah. 693-736, June 1950
• The Night the Mountains Moved (1959 Earthquake). By Samuel W. Matthews. Photos by J. Baylor Roberts. 329-359, Mar. 1960
• Our Wild and Scenic Rivers: The Flathead. By Douglas H. Chadwick. Photos by Lowell Georgia. 13-19, July 1977
• Sharing the Lives of Wild Golden Eagles. By John Craighead. Photos by Charles and Derek Craighead. 420-439, Sept. 1967
• Should They Build a Fence Around Montana? By Mike W. Edwards. Photos by Nicholas deVore III. 614-657, May 1976
Growing Up in Montana. 650-657
• The Untamed Yellowstone. By Bill Richards. Photos by Dean Krakel II. 257-278, Aug. 1981
• *See also* Glacier National Park; Padlock Ranch; Pryor Mountain Wild Horse Range; Red Rock Lakes National Wildlife Refuge; Scapegoat Wilderness; Surprise Creek Hutterite Colony

MONTENEGRO (Republic), Yugoslavia:
• Montenegro: Yugoslavia's "Black Mountain." By Bryan Hodgson. Photos by Linda Bartlett. 663-683, Nov. 1977
• Yugoslavia: Six Republics in One. By Robert Paul Jordan. Photos by James P. Blair. 589-633, May 1970

MONTEREY PENINSULA, California:
• California's Land Apart–the Monterey Peninsula. By Mike W. Edwards. 682-703, Nov. 1972
• California's Wonderful One (State Highway No. 1). By Frank Cameron. Photos by B. Anthony Stewart. 571-617, Nov. 1959

MONTEVIDEO, Uruguay:
• The Purple Land of Uruguay. By Luis Marden. 623-654, Nov. 1948
• 'Round the Horn by Submarine. By Paul C. Stimson. 129-144, Jan. 1948

MONTGOMERY, STEVEN L.: Author:
• The Case of the Killer Caterpillars. Photos by Robert F. Sisson. 219-225, Aug. 1983

MONTICELLO (Estate), Virginia:
• Mr. Jefferson's Charlottesville. By Anne Revis. 553-592, May 1950
• Mr. Jefferson's Monticello. By Joseph Judge. Photos by Dean Conger and Richard S. Durrance. 426-444, Sept. 1966
• Thomas Jefferson: Architect of Freedom. By Mike W. Edwards. Photos by Linda Bartlett. 231-259, Feb. 1976

MONTREAL, Canada:
• Canada, My Country. By Alan Phillips. Photos by David S. Boyer and Walter Meayers Edwards. 769-819, Dec. 1961
• Montreal Greets the World (Expo 67). By Jules B. Billard. 600-621, May 1967
• Quebec's Forests, Farms, and Frontiers. By Andrew H. Brown. 431-470, Oct. 1949
• The St. Lawrence River: Canada's Highway to the Sea. By William S. Ellis. Photos by Bruce Dale. 586-623, May 1980
• Sea to Lakes on the St. Lawrence. By George W. Long. Photos by B. Anthony Stewart and John E. Fletcher. 323-366, Sept. 1950

MONUMENT VALLEY, Arizona-Utah:
• Better Days for the Navajos. By Jack Breed. Photos by Charles W. Herbert. 809-847, Dec. 1958
• I See America First. By Lynda Bird Johnson. Photos by William Albert Allard. 874-904, Dec. 1965

MONUMENTS, National. *See* National Monuments

MONUMENTS AND MEMORIALS:
• Gettysburg and Vicksburg: the Battle Towns Today. By Robert Paul Jordan. Map notes by Carolyn Bennett Patterson. 4-57, July 1963
• Literary Landmarks of Massachusetts. By William H. Nicholas. Photos by B. Anthony Stewart and John E. Fletcher. Included: Memorials to: John Adams, Peter Bulkeley, Mary Baker Eddy, Clyde Fitch, Benjamin Franklin, Louise Imogen Guiney, Henry David Thoreau. 279-310, Mar. 1950
• The Nation Honors Admiral Richard E. Byrd. 567-578, Apr. 1962
• Paris: Vibrant Heart of France. 285-302, Aug. 1958
• Pennsylvania Avenue, Route of Presidents. By Dorothea and Stuart E. Jones. Photos by Volkmar Wentzel. 63-95, Jan. 1957
• Shrines of Each Patriot's Devotion (United States). By Frederick G. Vosburgh. 51-82, Jan. 1949
• Vacation Tour Through Lincoln Land. By Ralph Gray. 141-184, Feb. 1952
• Washington: Home of the Nation's Great. By Albert W. Atwood. 699-738, June 1947
Our Magnificent Capital City. Photos by B. Anthony Stewart. 715-738
• The Washington National Monument Society. By Charles Warren. 739-744, June 1947
• *See also* Arlington National Cemetery, Virginia; Bell Museum; Harpers Ferry, West Virginia; Mount Vernon, Virginia; Shrines; War Memorials

MOON:
• And Now to Touch the Moon's Forbidding Face. By Kenneth F. Weaver. 633-635, May 1969
• Apollo 15 Explores the Mountains of the Moon. By Kenneth F. Weaver. Photos from NASA. 233-265, Feb. 1972

M N

• Apollo Missions. 289-331, Sept. 1973
I. Summing Up Mankind's Greatest Adventure. By Gilbert M. Grosvenor. 289; II. Exploring Taurus-Littrow. By Harrison H. Schmitt. Photos by the crew of Apollo 17. 290-307; III. Have We Solved the Mysteries of the Moon? By Kenneth F. Weaver. Paintings by William H. Bond. 309-325; IV. What Is It Like to Walk on the Moon? By David R. Scott. 326-331; V. "Teammates in Mankind's Greatest Adventure," painting supplement
• Apollo 16 Brings Us Visions From Space. 856-865, Dec. 1972
• Awesome Views of the Forbidding Moonscape. 233-239, Feb. 1969
• The Climb Up Cone Crater (Apollo 14). By Alice J. Hall. Photos by Edgar D. Mitchell and Alan B Shepard, Jr. 136-148, July 1971
▲ *The Earth's Moon,* supplement. Feb. 1969
• Exploring Our Neighbor World, the Moon. By Donald H. Menzel. 277-296, Feb. 1958
• First Explorers on the Moon: The Incredible Story of Apollo 11. 735-797, Dec. 1969
• First Photographs of Planets and Moon Taken with Palomar's 200-inch Telescope. By Milton L. Humason. 125-130, Jan. 1953
• Footprints on the Moon. By Hugh L. Dryden. Paintings by Davis Meltzer and Pierre Mion. 357-401, Mar. 1964
• How We Mapped the Moon. By David W. Cook. 240-245, Feb. 1969
◆ *Let's Go to the Moon.* 1977
• The Moon Close Up. By Eugene M. Shoemaker. Photos by Ranger 7. 690-707, Nov. 1964
• "A Most Fantastic Voyage": The Story of Apollo 8's Rendezvous With the Moon. By Sam C. Phillips. 593-631, May 1969
• Reaching for the Moon. By Allan C. Fisher, Jr. Photos by Luis Marden. 157-171, Feb. 1959
• Robots to the Moon. By Frank Sartwell. Paintings by Pierre Mion. 557-571, Oct. 1962
• Surveyor: Candid Camera on the Moon. By Homer E. Newell. 578-592, Oct. 1966
• That Orbèd Maiden . . . the Moon. By Kenneth F. Weaver. 207-230, Feb. 1969
• Voyager's Historic View of Earth and Moon. 53, July 1978

MOON ROCKS:
• What the Moon Rocks Tell Us. By Kenneth F. Weaver. 788-791, Dec. 1969

MOONQUAKES:
• Have We Solved the Mysteries of the Moon? By Kenneth F. Weaver. Paintings by William H. Bond. 309-325, Sept. 1973

MOORE, DAVID: Photographer:
• "The Alice" in Australia's Wonderland. By Alan Villiers. Photos by Jeff Carter and David Moore. 230-257, Feb. 1966
• New South Wales, the State That Cradled Australia. By Howell Walker. 591-635, Nov. 1967
• Okinawa, the Island Without a Country. By Jules B. Billard. Photos by Winfield Parks and David Moore. 422-448, Sept. 1969

MOORE, HILARY B.: Author:
• Strange Babies of the Sea (Plankton). Paintings by Craig Phillips and Jacqueline Hutton. 41-56, July 1952
• X-Rays Reveal the Inner Beauty of Shells. 427-434, Mar. 1955

MOORE, KENNY: Author:
• Coober Pedy: Opal Capital of Australia's Outback. Photos by Penny Tweedie. 560-571, Oct. 1976

MOORE, W. ROBERT: Author:
• Portrait of Indochina. By W. Robert Moore and Maynard Owen Williams. Paintings by Jean Despujols. 461-490, Apr. 1951
• Power Comes Back to Peiping. By Nelson T. Johnson and W. Robert Moore. 337-368, Sept. 1949
• The Spotlight Swings to Suez. 105-115, Jan. 1952
Author-Photographer:
• Alaska, the Big Land. 776-807, June 1956
• Along the Yangtze, Main Street of China. 325-356, Mar. 1948
• Angkor, Jewel of the Jungle. Paintings by Maurice Fiévet. 517-569, Apr. 1960
• Brazil's Land of Minerals. 479-508, Oct. 1948
• Britain Tackles the East African Bush. 311-352, Mar. 1950
• Burma, Gentle Neighbor of India and Red China. 153-199, Feb. 1963
• Cities of Stone in Utah's Canyonland. 653-677, May 1962
• Clove-scented Zanzibar. 261-278, Feb. 1952
• Escalante: Utah's River of Arches. 399-425, Sept. 1955
• Feast Day in Kapingamarangi. 523-537, Apr. 1950
• Grass-skirted Yap. 805-830, Dec. 1952
• In Manchuria Now. 389-414, Mar. 1947
• Jamaica–Hub of the Caribbean. 333-362, Mar. 1954
• Pacific Wards of Uncle Sam. 73-104, July 1948
• Progress and Pageantry in Changing Nigeria. 325-365, Sept. 1956
• Republican Indonesia Tries Its Wings. 1-40, Jan. 1951
• Roaming Africa's Unfenced Zoos. 353-380, Mar. 1950
• Scintillating Siam. 173-200, Feb. 1947
• Strife-torn Indochina. 499-510, Oct. 1950
• Thailand Bolsters Its Freedom. 811-849, June 1961
• War and Quiet on the Laos Frontier. 665-680, May 1954
• White Magic in the Belgian Congo. 321-362, Mar. 1952
Photographer:
• Alaska's Warmer Side. By Elsie May Bell Grosvenor. 737-775, June 1956
• Because It Rains on Hawaii. By Frederick Simpich, Jr. 571-610, Nov. 1949
• Bristlecone Pine, Oldest Known Living Thing. By Edmund Schulman. 355-372, Mar. 1958
• Operation Eclipse: 1948. By William A. Kinney. 325-372, Mar. 1949
• Pageantry of the Siamese Stage. By D. Sonakul. 201-212, Feb. 1947
• South in the Sudan. By Harry Hoogstraal. 249-272, Feb. 1953
• Three Whales That Flew. By Carleton Ray. 346-359, Mar. 1962

MOOREA (Island), Society Islands:
• Tahiti, "Finest Island in the World." By Luis Marden. 1-47, July 1962

MOORS (People):
• Portugal at the Crossroads. By Howard La Fay. Photos by Volkmar Wentzel. 453-501, Oct. 1965
• Portugal Is Different. By Clement E. Conger. 583-622, Nov. 1948
• Toledo–El Greco's Spain Lives On. By Louise E. Levathes. Photos by James P. Blair. 726-753, June 1982
• *See also* Alhambra

MOOSE:
• Men, Moose, and Mink of Northwest Angle (Minnesota). By William H. Nicholas. Photos by J. Baylor Roberts. 265-284, Aug. 1947
• Wolves Versus Moose on Isle Royale. By Durward L. Allen and L. David Mech. 200-219, Feb. 1963

MORAN, EDMOND J.: Author:
• Stop-and-Go Sail Around South Norway. Photos by Randi Kjekstad Bull and Andrew H. Brown. 153-192, Aug. 1954

MORAVIANS:
• Far North with "Captain Mac." By Miriam MacMillan. 465-513, Oct. 1951
• Old Salem, Morning Star of Moravian Faith. By Rowe Findley. Photos by Robert W. Madden. 818-837, Dec. 1970

MORE of Sea Than of Land: The Bahamas. By Carleton Mitchell. Photos by James L. Stanfield. 218-267, Feb. 1967

The **MORE** Paris Changes. . . . By Howell Walker. Photos by Gordon W. Gahan. 64-103, July 1972

MORE Years With Mountain Gorillas. By Dian Fossey. Photos by Robert M. Campbell. NGS research grant. 574-585, Oct. 1971

MORGAN, AUDREY and FRANK:
Photographers:
• Alaska's Russian Frontier: Little Diomede. 551-562, Apr. 1951

MORGAN, JAMES K.:
Author-Photographer:
• Last Stand for the Bighorn. 383-399, Sept. 1973

MORGAN, JUDITH: Author:
• California's Parched Oasis, the Owens Valley. By Judith and Neil Morgan. Photos by Jodi Cobb and Galen Rowell. 98-127, Jan. 1976

• California's Surprising Inland Delta. By Judith and Neil Morgan. Photos by Charles O'Rear. 409-430, Sept. 1976
• Orange, a Most California County. By Judith and Neil Morgan. Photos by Vince Streano. 750-779, Dec. 1981
• Redwoods, Rain, and Lots of Room: California's North Coast. By Judith and Neil Morgan. Photos by Dewitt Jones. 330-363, Sept. 1977

MORGAN, LAEL:
Author:
• The Aleutians: Alaska's Far-out Islands. Photos by Steven C. Wilson. 336-363, Sept. 1983
Author-Photographer:
• Atka, Rugged Home of My Aleut Friends. 572-583, Oct. 1974
• "Ocean Mammals Are to Us What the Buffalo Was to the Plains Indian." 354-355, Mar. 1973

MORGAN, NEIL: Author:
• California's Parched Oasis, the Owens Valley. By Judith and Neil Morgan. Photos by Jodi Cobb and Galen Rowell. 98-127, Jan. 1976
• California's Surprising Inland Delta. By Judith and Neil Morgan. Photos by Charles O'Rear. 409-430, Sept. 1976
• Home to North Carolina. Photos by Bill Weems. 333-359, Mar. 1980
• Orange, a Most California County. By Judith and Neil Morgan. Photos by Vince Streano. 750-779, Dec. 1981
• Redwoods, Rain, and Lots of Room: California's North Coast. By Judith and Neil Morgan. Photos by Dewitt Jones. 330-363, Sept. 1977

MORGAN CREEK, Idaho:
• Last Stand for the Bighorn. By James K. Morgan. 383-399, Sept. 1973

MORMONS:
• Amid the Mighty Walls of Zion. By Lewis F. Clark. 37-70, Jan. 1954
• First Motor Sortie into Escalante Land. By Jack Breed. 369-404, Sept. 1949
• Roaming the West's Fantastic Four Corners. By Jack Breed. 705-742, June 1952
• Utah's Shining Oasis. By Charles McCarry. Photos by James L. Amos. 440-473, Apr. 1975
The Family: A Mormon Shrine. 459-463

MOROCCO:
• Berber Brides' Fair. By Carla Hunt. Photos by Nik Wheeler. Contents: Annual event in Imilchil. 119-129, Jan. 1980
• From Sea to Sahara in French Morocco. By Jean and Franc Shor. 147-188, Feb. 1955
• Morocco, Land of the Farthest West. By Thomas J. Abercrombie. 834-865, June 1971
• Trek by Mule Among Morocco's Berbers. By Victor Englebert. 850-875, June 1968
• When the President Goes Abroad (Eisenhower). By Gilbert M. Grosvenor. 588-649, May 1960

NIK WHEELER, BLACK STAR

Berber Brides: Ait Hadiddou girl at fair

MORRIS, JOE ALEX: Author:
• Venice, City of Twilight Splendor. Photos by John Scofield. 543-569, Apr. 1961

MORRIS, JOHN G.: Author:
• A Century Old, the Wonderful Brooklyn Bridge. Photos by Donal F. Holway. 565-579, May 1983

MORRISON, HEDDA:
Author-Photographer:
• Jungle Journeys in Sarawak. 710-736, May 1956

MORRISTOWN, New Jersey:
• Shrines of Each Patriot's Devotion. By Frederick G. Vosburgh. 51-82, Jan. 1949

MORTON, H. V.: Author:
• High Road in the Pyrenees. Photos by Justin Locke. 299-334, Mar. 1956
• In the London of the New Queen. 291-342, Sept. 1953
• Lake District, Poets' Corner of England. Photos by David S. Boyer. 511-545, Apr. 1956
• The Magic Road Round Ireland. Photos by Robert F. Sisson. 293-333, Mar. 1961

MORTON, W. BROWN, III: Author:
• Indonesia Rescues Ancient Borobudur. Photos by Dean Conger. 126-142, Jan. 1983

MOSAIC of Cultures (Southeast Asia). By Peter T. White. Photos by W. E. Garrett. 296-329, Mar. 1971

MOSAICS:
• The Byzantine Empire. 709-777, Dec. 1983
I. Rome of the East. By Merle Severy. Photos by James L. Stanfield. 709-767; II. Mount Athos. 739-745
• Here Rest in Honored Glory. . . . By Howell Walker. 739-768, June 1957
• Mount Sinai's Holy Treasures (St. Catherine's Monastery). By Kurt Weitzmann. Photos by Fred Anderegg. 109-127, Jan. 1964
• A New Look at Medieval Europe. By Kenneth M. Setton. Paintings by Andre Durenceau and Birney Lettick. 799-859, Dec. 1962
• Roman Life in 1,600-year-old Color Pictures. By Gino Vinicio Gentili. Photos by Duncan Edwards. 211-229, Feb. 1957
• St. Peter's, Rome's Church of Popes. By Aubrey Menen. Photos by Albert Moldvay. 865-879, Dec. 1971

MOSCOW, U.S.S.R.:
• An American in Russia's Capital. By Thomas T. Hammond. Photos by Dean Conger. 297-351, Mar. 1966
• Five Times to Yakutsk. By Dean Conger. 256-269, Aug. 1977
• Moscow: The City Around Red Square. By John J. Putman. Photos by Gordon W. Gahan. 2-45, Jan. 1978

MOSELEY, MICHAEL E.: Author:
• Chan Chan, Peru's Ancient City of Kings. By Michael E. Moseley and Carol J. Mackey. Photos by David Brill. 318-345, Mar. 1973

MOHAMED AMIN

Mecca: worshipers circle the Kaaba

MOSER, DON: Author:
- The Azores, Nine Islands in Search of a Future. Photos by O. Louis Mazzatenta. 261-288, Feb. 1976
- Big Thicket of Texas. Photos by Blair Pittman. 504-529, Oct. 1974
- The Philippines: Better Days Still Elude an Old Friend. Photos by Bruce Dale. 360-391, Mar. 1977

MOSES:
- Eternal Sinai. By Harvey Arden. Photos by David Doubilet and Kevin Fleming. 420-461, Apr. 1982
- In Search of Moses. By Harvey Arden. Photos by Nathan Benn. 2-37, Jan. 1976
- Lost Outpost of the Egyptian Empire. By Trude Dothan. Photos by Sisse Brimberg. Paintings by Lloyd K. Townsend. NGS research grant. 739-769, Dec. 1982

MOSES, Lake, Washington:
- From Sagebrush to Roses on the Columbia. By Leo A. Borah. 571-611, Nov. 1952

MOSES SOLE (Fish):
- The Red Sea's Sharkproof Fish. By Eugenie Clark. Photos by David Doubilet. 718-727, Nov. 1974

MOSIER, ROBERT H.: Author-Photographer:
- The GI and the Kids of Korea. 635-664, May 1953

MOSLEMS. *See* Muslims

MOSQUES:
- From America to Mecca on Airborne Pilgrimage. By Abdul Ghafur. Included: The Kaaba, in the courtyard of the Great Mosque, Mecca; Masjid-al-Nabi (Mosque of the Prophet), in Medina; a mosque in Kuba; and Husain's tomb in Karbala. 1-60, July 1953
- Journey Into Troubled Iran. By George W. Long. Photos by J. Baylor Roberts. Included: Masjid-i-Shah, Masjid Sheik Lutf Ullah, and the mosque at Qum. 425-464, Oct. 1951
- Pilgrimage to Mecca. By Muhammad Abdul-Rauf. Photos by Mehmet Biber. Included: Mosque of Hudaybiyah, and al-Masjid al-Haram, the Sacred Mosque at Mecca. 581-607, Nov. 1978
- Saudi Arabia: The Kingdom and Its Power. By Robert Azzi. Included: The siege at Mecca. 286-333, Sept. 1980
- Turkey Paves the Path of Progress. By Maynard Owen Williams. Included: Beyazit, Blue Mosque, Eyüp Ansari, Suleiman the Magnificent, Yeni Cami (New Mosque), Yeşil Cami (Green Mosque). 141-186, Aug. 1951

MOSQUITOES:
- Exploring Ancient Panama by Helicopter. By Matthew W. Stirling. Photos by Richard H. Stewart. Included: *Aedes aegypti* and *Haemagogus* mosquitoes. NGS research grant. 227-246, Feb. 1950
- Keeping House for a Biologist in Colombia. By Nancy Bell Fairchild Bates. Photos by Marston Bates. Included: *Anopheles* and *Haemagogus* mosquitoes. 251-274, Aug. 1948
- Mosquitoes, the Mighty Killers. By Lewis T. Nielsen. 427-440, Sept. 1979

"A **MOST** Fantastic Voyage": The Story of Apollo 8's Rendezvous With the Moon. By Sam C. Phillips. 593-631, May 1969

The **MOST** Mexican City, Guadalajara. By Bart McDowell. Photos by Volkmar Wentzel. 412-441, Mar. 1967

A **MOST** Uncommon Town: Columbus, Indiana. By David Jeffery. Photos by J. Bruce Baumann. 383-397, Sept. 1978

MOTAGUA FAULT, Guatemala:
- Earthquake in Guatemala. By Bart McDowell. Photos by W. E. Garrett and Robert W. Madden. 810-829, June 1976

MOTH LARVAE. *See* Inchworms; Silkworms

MOTHER-OF-PEARL:
- Twenty Fathoms Down for Mother-of-Pearl. By Winston Williams. Photos by Bates Littlehales. 512-529, Apr. 1962
- *See also* Abalone

MOTHS:
- Moths That Behave Like Hummingbirds. Photos by Treat Davidson. 770-775, June 1965
- *See also* Gypsy Moths

MOTILONES (Indians):
- Venezuela Builds on Oil. By Thomas J. Abercrombie. 344-387, Mar. 1963

MOTORCYCLE RACES:
- The Manx and Their Isle of Man. By Veronica Thomas. Photos by Ted H. Funk. Included: International Tourist Trophy Races ("T.T."); Manx Grand Prix. 426-444, Sept. 1972

MOTORCYCLE TRIPS:
- Two Wheels Along the Mexican Border. By William Albert Allard. 591-635, May 1971

MOTZFELDT, JONATHAN:
- Hunters of the Lost Spirit: Greenlanders. By Priit J. Vesilind. Photos by Ivars Silis. 191-193, Feb. 1983

MOULIN, RAYMOND: Photographer:
- Saving Earth's Oldest Living Things. By Andrew H. Brown. Photos by Raymond Moulin and author. 679-695, May 1951

MOUND BUILDERS (Ancient Indians):
- "Pyramids" of the New World. By Neil Merton Judd. 105-128, Jan. 1948
- Who Were the "Mound Builders"? By George E. Stuart. 783-801, Dec. 1972

MOUNDS:
- Exploring Ancient Panama by Helicopter. By Matthew W. Stirling. Photos by Richard H. Stewart. Included: Archaeological sites in provinces of Chiriquí and Veraguas. NGS research grant. 227-246, Feb. 1950

• Exploring the Past in Panama. By Matthew W. Stirling. Photos by Richard H. Stewart. Included: Azuero Peninsula, Tambor region. NGS research grant. 373-399, Mar. 1949
• The Ghosts of Jericho. By James L. Kelso. 825-844, Dec. 1951
• Jericho Gives Up Its Secrets. By Kathleen M. Kenyon and A. Douglas Tushingham. Photos by Nancy Lord. 853-870, Dec. 1953
• *See also* La Venta, Mexico; Tell Mardikh Excavation; Tepe Gawra

MOUNIER, BRUCE: Photographer:
• Strange March of the Spiny Lobster. By William F. Herrnkind. Photos by Rick Frehsee and Bruce Mounier. 819-831, June 1975

MOUNT ATHOS (Monastic Republic), Greece:
• The Byzantine Empire. 709-777, Dec. 1983
I. Rome of the East. By Merle Severy. Photos by James L. Stanfield. 709-767; II. Mount Athos. 739-745

MOUNT EVEREST NATIONAL PARK, Nepal:
• Park at the Top of the World: Mount Everest National Park. By Rick Ridgeway. Photos by Nicholas DeVore III. 704-725, June 1982
• Preserving a Mountain Heritage. By Sir Edmund Hillary. 696-703, June 1982

MOUNT KENNEDY YUKON EXPEDITION:
• Canada's Mount Kennedy. NGS research grant. 1-33, July 1965
I. The Discovery. By Bradford Washburn. 1-3; II. A Peak Worthy of the President. By Robert F. Kennedy. 5-9; III. The First Ascent. By James W. Whittaker. Photos by William Albert Allard. 11-33

MOUNT McKINLEY NATIONAL PARK, Alaska:
• Mount McKinley Conquered by New Route. By Bradford Washburn. 219-248, Aug. 1953
• New Mount McKinley Challenge–Trekking Around the Continent's Highest Peak. By Ned Gillette. 66-79, July 1979
• Wildlife of Mount McKinley National Park. By Adolph Murie. Paintings by Walter A. Weber. 249-270, Aug. 1953

MOUNT RAINIER NATIONAL PARK, Washington. *See* Pacific Crest Trail; Rainier, Mount

MOUNT RUSHMORE NATIONAL MEMORIAL. *See* Rushmore, Mount

MOUNT ST. HELENS. By Rowe Findley. 3-65, Jan. 1981

MOUNT ST. HELENS Aftermath. By Rowe Findley. Photos by Steve Raymer. 713-733, Dec. 1981

MOUNT SINAI EXPEDITIONS:
• Island of Faith in the Sinai Wilderness (St. Catherine's Monastery). By George H. Forsyth. Photos by Robert F. Sisson. Sponsors: University of Michigan, Princeton University, University of Alexandria. 82-106, Jan. 1964
• Mount Sinai's Holy Treasures (St. Catherine's Monastery). By Kurt Weitzmann. Photos by Fred Anderegg. 109-127, Jan. 1964
• Sinai Sheds New Light on the Bible. By Henry Field. Photos by William B. and Gladys Terry. Sponsor: University of California African Expedition. 795-815, Dec. 1948

MOUNT VERNON, Virginia:
• Mount Vernon Lives On. By Lonnelle Aikman. 651-682, Nov. 1953

MOUNTAIN CLIMBING:
• American and Geographic Flags Top Everest. By Melvin M. Payne. Photos by Barry C. Bishop. NGS research grant. 157-157C, Aug. 1963
• American Skiers Find Adventure in Western China. By Ned Gillette. Photos by the author and Galen Rowell. 174-199, Feb. 1981
Skiing From the Summit of China's Ice Mountain. 192-199
• Americans Climb K2. Photos by members of the expedition. 623-649, May 1979
I. The Ultimate Challenge. By James W. Whittaker. 624-639; II. On to the Summit. By James Wickwire. 641-649
• At My Limit–I Climbed Everest Alone. By Reinhold Messner. Photos by the author and Nena Holguín. 552-566, Oct. 1981
• Beyond Everest. By Sir Edmund Hillary. 579-610, Nov. 1955
• Canada's Mount Kennedy. NGS research grant. 1-33, July 1965
I. The Discovery. By Bradford Washburn. 1-3; II. A Peak Worthy of the President. By Robert F. Kennedy. 5-9; III. The First Ascent. By James W. Whittaker. Photos by William Albert Allard. 11-33
• Climbing Our Northwest Glaciers. Photos by Bob and Ira Spring. 103-114, July 1953
• Cloud Gardens in the Tetons. By Frank and John Craighead. 811-830, June 1948
• Colorado by Car and Campfire. By Kathleen Revis. 207-248, Aug. 1954
• Colorado's Friendly Topland (Rocky Mountains). By Robert M. Ormes. 187-214, Aug. 1951
• El Sangay, Fire-breathing Giant of the Andes. By G. Edward Lewis. 117-138, Jan. 1950
• The Fabulous Sierra Nevada. By J. R. Challacombe. 825-843, June 1954
• First American Ascent of Mount St. Elias. By Maynard M. Miller. 229-248, Feb. 1948
• First Conquest of Antarctica's Highest Peaks. By Nicholas B. Clinch. NGS research grant. 836-863, June 1967
• The First Traverse (Everest). By Thomas F. Hornbein and William F. Unsoeld. NGS research grant. 509-513, Oct. 1963
• High Adventure in the Himalayas. By Thomas Weir. 193-234, Aug. 1952
• How We Climbed Everest. By Barry C. Bishop. NGS research grant. 477-507, Oct. 1963

SAMUEL C. SILVERSTEIN
Antarctica's Peaks: Ostenso's summit

M N

● Mount McKinley Conquered by New Route. By Bradford Washburn. 219-248, Aug. 1953
● Mount Rainier: Testing Ground for Everest. By Barry C. Bishop. NGS research grant. 688-711, May 1963
● New Guinea's Paradise of Birds. By E. Thomas Gilliard. Note: The true summit of Mount Wilhelm is reached. 661-688, Nov. 1951
● New Mount McKinley Challenge–Trekking Around the Continent's Highest Peak. By Ned Gillette. 66-79, July 1979
● Nomads of China's West. By Galen Rowell. Photos by the author and Harold A. Knutson. Included: An American expedition to Anyemaqen peak. 244-263, Feb. 1982
● Park at the Top of the World: Mount Everest National Park. By Rick Ridgeway. Photos by Nicholas DeVore III. 704-725, June 1982
Preserving a Mountain Heritage. By Sir Edmund Hillary. 696-703
● Sierra High Trip. By David R. Brower. 844-868, June 1954
● Six to the Summit (Everest). By Norman G. Dyhrenfurth. Photos by Barry C. Bishop. NGS research grant. 460-473, Oct. 1963
● Skyline Trail from Maine to Georgia. By Andrew H. Brown. Photos by Robert F. Sisson. 219-251, Aug. 1949
● Switzerland's Enchanted Val d'Hérens. By Georgia Engelhard Cromwell. 825-848, June 1955
● To Torre Egger's Icy Summit. By Jim Donini. 813-823, Dec. 1976
● Triumph and Tragedy on Annapurna. By Arlene Blum. 295-311, Mar. 1979
On the Summit. By Irene Miller, with Vera Komarkova. 312-313
● Triumph on Everest. 1-63, July 1954
I. Siege and Assault. By Sir John Hunt. 1-43; II. The Conquest of the Summit. By Sir Edmund Hillary. 45-63
● Wintering on the Roof of the World (Himalayas). By Barry C. Bishop. NGS research grant. 503-547, Oct. 1962
● *See also* Outward Bound School; Rock Climbing

MOUNTAIN GOATS:
● Mountain Goats: Daring Guardians of the Heights. By Douglas H. Chadwick. 284-296, Aug. 1978

MOUNTAIN GORILLAS:
● The Imperiled Mountain Gorilla. By Dian Fossey. NGS research grant. 501-523, Apr. 1981
Death of Marchessa. Photos by Peter G. Veit. 508-511
● Making Friends With Mountain Gorillas. By Dian Fossey. Photos by Robert M. Campbell. NGS research grant. 48-67, Jan. 1970
● More Years With Mountain Gorillas. By Dian Fossey. Photos by Robert M. Campbell. NGS research grant. 574-585, Oct. 1971
▯ Search for the Great Apes. cover, Jan. 1976

MAURICE G. HORNOCKER

Mountain Lion: lions take refuge in tree

MOUNTAIN LIONS:
● Stalking the Mountain Lion–to Save Him. By Maurice G. Hornocker. 638-655, Nov. 1969

MOUNTAIN PEOPLE, American:
◆ *American Mountain People.* Announced. 865-868, June 1973
● Chattooga River Country: Wild Water, Proud People. By Don Belt. Photos by Steve Wall. 458-477, Apr. 1983
● Wrestlin' for a Livin' With King Coal. By Michael E. Long. Photos by Michael O'Brien. 793-819, June 1983
● *See also* Adirondack Mountains; Blue Ridge; Cades Cove; Cumberland Country; Ozark Plateau; West Virginia

MOUNTAIN STREAM:
● Unseen Life of a Mountain Stream. By William H. Amos. 562-580, Apr. 1977

The **MOUNTAIN** That Was–and Will Be. By Rowe Findley. Photos by Steve Raymer. 713-733, Dec. 1981

MOUNTAIN VILLAGE, Alaska:
● The Curlew's Secret. By Arthur A. Allen. NGS research grant. 751-770, Dec. 1948

MOUNTAIN Voices, Mountain Days. By Bryan Hodgson. Photos by Linda Bartlett. 118-146, July 1972

MOUNTAIN With a Death Wish (Mount St. Helens). By Rowe Findley. 3-33, Jan. 1981

MOUNTAINBURG, Arkansas:
● An Ozark Family Carves a Living and a Way of Life. Photos by Bruce Dale. 124-133, July 1975

MOUNTAINS:
● Afoot in Roadless Nepal. By Toni Hagen. Contents: Himalaya, Mahabharat, and Siwalik Ranges. 361-405, Mar. 1960
◆ *American Mountain People.* Announced. 865-868, June 1973
◆ *America's Magnificent Mountains.* 1980
● A Map Maker Looks at the United States. By Newman Bumstead. Included: Big Hole, Blue, Cascades, Olympics, Rockies, Sawatch, Sierra Nevada, Tetons, Wasatch, Wenatchee. 705-748, June 1951
● Mountains Top Off New England. By F. Barrows Colton. Photos by Robert F. Sisson. Contents: Berkshires, Green Mountains, White Mountains. 563-602, May 1951
● New Guinea's Paradise of Birds. By E. Thomas Gilliard. Included: Bismarck Mountains (including the climbing of Mount Wilhelm); Hagen Range; Kubor Range. 661-688, Nov. 1951
● New Zealand, Pocket Wonder World. By Howell Walker. 419-460, Apr. 1952
● New Zealand's Bountiful South Island. By Peter Benchley. Photos by James L. Amos. 93-123, Jan. 1972
● New Zealand's High Country. By Yva Momatiuk and John Eastcott. 246-265, Aug. 1978

• New Zealand's Milford Track: "Walk of a Lifetime." By Carolyn Bennett Patterson. Photos by Robert E. Gilka. 117-129, Jan. 1978
• The Night the Mountains Moved (Montana's 1959 Earthquake). By Samuel W. Matthews. Photos by J. Baylor Roberts. 329-359, Mar. 1960
• Our Navy Explores Antarctica. By Richard E. Byrd. U. S. Navy official photos. 429-522, Oct. 1947
• Preserving America's Last Great Wilderness (Alaska). Text by David Jeffery. Included: Aniakchak Caldera; Brooks Range; Katmai; McKinley; Wrangell. 769-791, June 1975
• This Changing Earth. By Samuel W. Matthews. 1-37, Jan. 1973
• *See also* Alaska Range, Alaska; Aleutian Range, Alaska; Alps, Europe; Andes, South America; Anyemaqen (Peak), China; Appalachian Mountains, U. S.; Appenines, Italy; Blue Ridge Mountains, Virginia; Brooks Range, Alaska; Carpathian Mountains, Europe; Cascade Range, U. S.; Chugach Mountains, Alaska; High Atlas, Africa; Himalayas, Asia; Karakoram Range, Central Asia; Pamirs, Central Asia; Pennine Chain, England; Pyrenees, France-Spain; Rocky Mountains, Canada-U. S.; Ruwenzori, Africa; St. Elias, Mount, Canada; Sentinel Range, Antarctica; Sierra Madre Occidental, Mexico; Sierra Nevada, California; Sinai, Mount, Egypt; Virunga Mountains, Africa; *and* Karst Formations; Volcanoes

MOUNTAINS, Lunar:
• Apollo 15 Explores the Mountains of the Moon. By Kenneth F. Weaver. Photos from NASA. 233-265, Feb. 1972

MOUNTAINS, Submarine. *See* Ocean Floors

MOUNTAINS of the Moon (Ruwenzori). By Paul A. Zahl. 412-434, Mar. 1962

MOUNTAINTOP War in Remote Ladakh. By W. E. Garrett. 664-687, May 1963

MOUNTFORD, CHARLES P.: Author:
• Expedition to the Land of the Tiwi. 417-440, Mar. 1956
• Exploring Stone Age Arnhem Land. Photos by Howell Walker. 745-782, Dec. 1949

MOUSE RIVER, Canada-U. S.:
• Satellites Gave Warning of Midwest Floods. By Peter T. White. Photos by Thomas A. DeFeo. 574-592, Oct. 1969

MOYAL, MAURICE: Author:
• Sheep Trek in the French Alps. Photos by Marcel Coen. 545-564, Apr. 1952

MOYNIHAN, MICHAEL: Author:
• The Swans of Abbotsbury. Photos by Barnet Saidman. 563-570, Oct. 1959

MOZABITES:
• Oasis-hopping in the Sahara. By Maynard Owen Williams. 209-236, Feb. 1949

MOZAI, TORAO: Author:
• The Lost Fleet of Kublai Khan. Photos by Koji Nakamura. Paintings by Issho Yada. 634-649, Nov. 1982

MOZAMBIQUE:
• Mozambique: Land of the Good People. By Volkmar Wentzel. 197-231, Aug. 1964
• Safari Through Changing Africa. By Elsie May Bell Grosvenor. Photos by Gilbert Grosvenor. 145-198, Aug. 1953

MRU TRIBE:
• The Peaceful Mrus of Bangladesh. By Claus-Dieter Brauns. 267-286, Feb. 1973

MUD-PUDDLE FROGS:
• The Amazing Frog-Eating Bat. By Merlin D. Tuttle. NGS research grant. 78-91, Jan. 1982

MUDIE, COLIN:
• Braving the Atlantic by Balloon *(Small World)*. By Arnold Eiloart. 123-146, July 1959

MUDSKIPPERS:
• Who Says Fish Can't Climb Trees? By Ivan Polunin. 85-91, Jan. 1972

MUDSLIDES:
• Southern California's Trial by Mud and Water. By Nathaniel T. Kenney. Photos by Bruce Dale. 552-573, Oct. 1969

MUHAMMAD (Prophet):
• From America to Mecca on Airborne Pilgrimage. By Abdul Ghafur. 1-60, July 1953
• Pilgrimage to Mecca. By Muhammad Abdul-Rauf. Photos by Mehmet Biber. 581-607, Nov. 1978
• The Sword and the Sermon. By Thomas J. Abercrombie. 3-45, July 1972

MUIR, JOHN:
• John Muir's Wild America. By Harvey Arden. Photos by Dewitt Jones. 433-461, Apr. 1973
◆ *John Muir's Wild America.* Announced. 860-864, June 1976

MUJERES, Isla, Mexico:
• Into the Lairs of "Sleeping" Sharks. By Eugenie Clark. Photos by David Doubilet. NGS research grant. 570-584, Apr. 1975

MUKDEN, China. *See* Shenyang

MULES:
• Trek by Mule Among Morocco's Berbers. By Victor Englebert. 850-875, June 1968

MULLER, KAL: Author-Photographer:
• Land Diving With the Pentecost Islanders. 799-817, Dec. 1970
• Taboos and Magic Rule Namba Lives. 57-83, Jan. 1972
• Tanna Awaits the Coming of John Frum. 706-715, May 1974

MUMMIES:
• Ancient Cliff Dwellers of Mesa Verde. By Don Watson. Photos by Willard R. Culver. Contents: Mummification by natural dehydration; the famous mummy "Esther." 349-376, Sept. 1948
• A Lady From China's Past. Photos from *China Pictorial.* Text by Alice J. Hall. 660-681, May 1974
• Lifelike Man Preserved 2,000 Years in Peat. By P. V. Glob. 419-430, Mar. 1954
• The Lost Empire of the Incas. By Loren McIntyre. Art by Ned and Rosalie Seidler. Included: Mummified body of an Inca boy who froze to death 500 years ago. 729-787, Dec. 1973
A pictorial chronicle of the Incas. 747-753
• Tutankhamun's Golden Trove. By Christiane Desroches Noblecourt. Photos by F. L. Kenett. 625-646, Oct. 1963

MUNICH, Germany:
• Bavaria: Mod, Medieval–and Bewitching. By Gary Jennings. Photos by George F. Mobley. 409-431, Mar. 1974

MUÑOZ, JUAN: Author-Photographer:
• Cliff Dwellers of the Bering Sea. 129-146, Jan. 1954

MUNROE, JOE: Photographer:
• The Bonins and Iwo Jima Go Back to Japan. By Paul Sampson. 128-144, July 1968

MURCHISON MOUNTAINS, New Zealand:
• Finding an "Extinct" New Zealand Bird. By R. V. Francis Smith. 393-401, Mar. 1952

MURCIA, Spain:
• Spain's Silkworm Gut. By Luis Marden. 100-108, July 1951

MURIA GONDS (Tribespeople):
• New Life for India's Villagers. By Anthony and Georgette Dickey Chapelle. 572-588, Apr. 1956

MURIE, ADOLPH: Author:
• Wildlife of Mount McKinley National Park. Paintings by Walter A. Weber. 249-270, Aug. 1953

MUROC DRY LAKE, California:
• Flying in the "Blowtorch" Era. By Frederick G. Vosburgh. 281-322, Sept. 1950

MURPHY, GRACE E. BARSTOW: Photographer:
• Peru Profits from Sea Fowl. By Robert Cushman Murphy. Photos by author and Grace E. Barstow Murphy. 395-413, Mar. 1959

MURPHY, JOHN F., Jr.: Author:
• Ambassadors of Good Will: The Peace Corps. By Sargent Shriver and Peace Corps Volunteers. 297-345, Sept. 1964
Gabon. 325-329

MURPHY, ROBERT CUSHMAN: Author-Photographer:
• Peru Profits from Sea Fowl. Photos by author and Grace E. Barstow Murphy. 395-413, Mar. 1959

MURRES:
• Sea Bird Cities Off Audubon's Labrador. By Arthur A. Allen. NGS research grant. 755-774, June 1948

MURUNG (People):
• Bangladesh: Hope Nourishes a New Nation. By William S. Ellis. Photos by Dick Durrance II. 295-333, Sept. 1972

MÜSA, Gebel (Mountain), Egypt. *See* Sinai, Mount

MUSANDAM PENINSULA, Oman:
• Oman: Guardian of the Gulf. By Thomas J. Abercrombie. Photos by the author and Lynn Abercrombie. 344-377, Sept. 1981

MUSCAT AND OMAN:
• Troubled Waters East of Suez. By Ernest M. Eller. 483-522, Apr. 1954
• *See also* Oman

"MUSCLE and smoke, commerce and crowds." A Shanghai Portfolio by Bruce Dale. 2-13, July 1980

MUSEUM OF SCIENCE, Boston, Massachusetts: Study Grants:
• Cartography: Grand Canyon, Arizona. 37, July 1978
• Expeditions. *See* Mount Kennedy Yukon Expedition

MUSEUMS:
• The DAR Story. By Lonnelle Aikman. Photos by B. Anthony Stewart and John E. Fletcher. Included: Exhibits of early Americana in the DAR Museum. 565-598, Nov. 1951
• Florence Rises From the Flood. By Joseph Judge. Included: Archeological Museum, Bardini Museum, Bargello Museum, Horne Museum, Institute and Museum of the History of Science, Uffizi. 1-43, July 1967
• Washington, D. C.: Hometown Behind the Monuments. By Henry Mitchell. Photos by Adam Woolfitt. 84-125, Jan. 1983
• The World in New York City. By Peter T. White. 52-107, July 1964
• *See also* American Museum of Natural History; Bell Museum; Corning Museum of Glass; Desert Museum; Eastman, George, for Eastman House; Explorers Hall, NGS; Hearst San Simeon State Historical Monument; Henry E. Huntington Library and Art Gallery; Henry Ford Museum; Hermitage; Kunsthistorisches Museum; National Museum of Anthropology, Mexico City; Smithsonian Institution; *and* Mystic Seaport, for Maritime Museum; Worcester, Massachusetts, for arms and armor; *and* Art Galleries

MUSHERS (Dogsled Drivers):
• Solo to the Pole. By Naomi Uemura. Photos by the author and Ira Block. 298-325, Sept. 1978
• Thousand-mile Race to Nome: A Woman's Icy Struggle. By Susan Butcher. Photos by Kerby Smith. 411-422, Mar. 1983
• Trek Across Arctic America. By Colin Irwin. 295-321, Mar. 1974

"MUSHROOM ANIMALS." *See* Slime Mold

MUSHROOMS:
• Bizarre World of the Fungi. By Paul A. Zahl. 502-527, Oct. 1965

MUSIC AND MUSICIANS:
• The British Way. By Sir Evelyn Wrench. Included: Sir William Gilbert and Sir Arthur Sullivan. 421-541, Apr. 1949
• Building a New Austria. By Beverly M. Bowie. Photos by Volkmar Wentzel. 172-213, Feb. 1959
• Carnival in Trinidad. By Howard La Fay. Photos by Winfield Parks. 693-701, Nov. 1971
• Hunting Musical Game in West Africa. By Arthur S. Alberts. 262-282, Aug. 1951
• A Lady From China's Past. Photos from *China Pictorial.* Text by Alice J. Hall. 660-681, May 1974
• Miami's Expanding Horizons. By William H. Nicholas. Included: Barry College Department of Music, Miami Civic Music Association, Opera Guild of Miami, Philharmonic Society of Greater Miami, University of Miami School of Music. 561-594, Nov. 1950
• Old Salem, Morning Star of Moravian Faith. By Rowe Findley. Photos by Robert W. Madden. Included: Music of the Moravians. 818-837, Dec. 1970
• The President's Music Men (Marine Band). By Stuart E. Jones. Photos by William W. Campbell III. 752-766, Dec. 1959
• There's More to Nashville than Music. By Michael Kernan. Photos by Jodi Cobb. 692-711, May 1978
• Utah's Shining Oasis. By Charles McCarry. Photos by James L. Amos. Included: Ballet West, Mormon Tabernacle Choir, Utah Symphony Orchestra. 440-473, Apr. 1976
• Vienna, City of Song. By Peter T. White. Photos by John Launois. 739-779, June 1968
• *See also* Recording Supplements and Soundsheets; Songs; *and* Berkshires, for Berkshire Music Festival; Library of Congress; New Orleans, Louisiana, for jazz; Ozark Plateau, for folk music

MUSK OXEN:
• Domesticating the Wild and Woolly Musk Ox. By John J. Teal, Jr. Photos by Robert W. Madden. 862-879, June 1970

MUSKRATS:
• The Romance of American Furs. By Wanda Burnett. 379-402, Mar. 1948

MUSLIMS:
• Abraham, the Friend of God. By Kenneth MacLeish. Photos by Dean Conger. 739-789, Dec. 1966
• Crusader Lands Revisited. By Harold Lamb. Photos by David S. Boyer. 815-852, Dec. 1954
• From America to Mecca on Airborne Pilgrimage. By Abdul Ghafur. 1-60, July 1953
• How the Kazakhs Fled to Freedom. By Milton J. Clark. 621-644, Nov. 1954
• The Idyllic Vale of Kashmir. By Volkmar Wentzel. 523-550, Apr. 1948
• Islam's Heartland, Up in Arms. By Thomas J. Abercrombie. 335-345, Sept. 1980
• Jerusalem, My Home. By Bertha Spafford Vester. 826-847, Dec. 1964
• Jerusalem, the Divided City. By John Scofield. Photos by Brian Brake. 492-531, Apr. 1959
• Pilgrimage to Mecca. By Muhammad Abdul-Rauf. Photos by Mehmet Biber. 581-607, Nov. 1978
• Purdah in India: Life Behind the Veil. By Doranne Wilson Jacobson. Included: Muslim purdah of Nimkhera, India. 270-286, Aug. 1977
• Reunited Jerusalem Faces Its Problems. By Kenneth MacLeish. Photos by Ted Spiegel. 835-871, Dec. 1968
• This Year in Jerusalem. By Joseph Judge. Photos by Jodi Cobb. 479-515, Apr. 1983
• Weighing the Aga Khan in Diamonds. Photos by David J. Carnegie. Contents: Ismaili Muslims. 317-324, Mar. 1947
• *See also* Bedouin; Berbers; Ma'dan; Moors; Mozabites; Sikhs; Tuareg; Turkomans; *and* Islam

MUSTANG, Remote Realm in Nepal. By Michel Peissel. 579-604, Oct. 1965

MUTATIONS. *See* Albino Animals; Goldfish; Onagadori

MY Backyard, the Adirondacks. By Anne LaBastille. Photos by David Alan Harvey. 616-639, May 1975

MY Chesapeake–Queen of Bays. By Allan C. Fisher, Jr. Photos by Lowell Georgia. 428-467, Oct. 1980

MY Life Among Wild Chimpanzees. By Jane Goodall. Photos by Baron Hugo van Lawick and author. NGS research grant. 272-308, Aug. 1963

MY Life in Forbidden Lhasa. By Heinrich Harrer. 1-48, July 1955

MY Life in the Valley of the Moon. By H. H. Arnold. Photos by Willard R. Culver. 689-716, Dec. 1948

MY Life With Africa's Little People. By Anne Eisner Putnam. 278-302, Feb. 1960

MY Neighbors Hold to Mountain Ways. By Malcolm Ross. Photos by Flip Schulke. 856-880, June 1958

MYCENAEAN CIVILIZATION:
• Minoans and Mycenaeans: Greece's Brilliant Bronze Age. By Joseph Judge. Photos by Gordon W. Gahan. Paintings by Lloyd K. Townsend. 142-185, Feb. 1978

MYCETOZOA. *See* Slime Mold

MYCOLOGY:
• Bizarre World of the Fungi. By Paul A. Zahl. 502-527, Oct. 1965
• *See also* Slime Mold

MYKONOS (Island), Greece. *See* Mikonos

MYOJIN ISLAND (Volcano), Pacific Ocean:

• The Explosive Birth of Myojin Island. By Robert S. Dietz. 117-128, Jan. 1954

MYSORE (State), India:
• Mysore Celebrates the Death of a Demon. By Luc Bouchage. Photos by Ylla. 706-711, May 1958
• Wild Elephant Roundup in India. By Harry Miller. Photos by author and James P. Blair. 372-385, Mar. 1969

MYSTERIES of Bird Migration. By Allan C. Fisher, Jr. Photos by Jonathan Blair. 154-193, Aug. 1979

MYSTERY of the Ancient Nazca Lines. Photos by Loren McIntyre. NGS research grant. 716-728, May 1975

MYSTERY of the Medicine Wheels. By John A. Eddy. Photos by Thomas E. Hooper. 140-146, Jan. 1977

MYSTERY of the Monarch Butterfly. By Paul A. Zahl. 588-598, Apr. 1963

The **MYSTERY** of the Shroud. By Kenneth F. Weaver. 730-753, June 1980

MYSTERY Shrouds the Biggest Planet (Jupiter). By Kenneth F. Weaver. 285-294, Feb. 1975

MYSTIC SEAPORT, Connecticut:
• The Age of Sail Lives On at Mystic. By Alan Villiers. Photos by Weston Kemp. 220-239, Aug. 1968

MYXOMYCETES. *See* Slime Mold

MZABIS (People). *See* Mozabites

MZIMA SPRINGS, Tsavo National Park, Kenya:
• Mzima, Kenya's Spring of Life. By Joan and Alan Root. 350-373, Sept. 1971

N

NAGA HILLS, India-Burma:
• Roaming India's Naga Hills. By S. Dillon Ripley. 247-264, Feb. 1955

NAHA, Okinawa:
• Okinawa, the Island Without a Country. By Jules B. Billard. Photos by Winfield Parks and David Moore. 422-448, Sept. 1969

NAHANNI NATIONAL PARK, Canada:
• Nahanni: Canada's Wilderness Park. By Douglas H. Chadwick. Photos by Matt Bradley. 396-420, Sept. 1981

NAIROBI, Kenya:
• Kenya Says *Harambee!* By Allan C. Fisher, Jr. Photos by Bruce Dale. 151-205, Feb. 1969

NAIROBI NATIONAL PARK, Kenya:
• Africa's Gentle Giants (Giraffes). By Bristol Foster. Photos by Bob Campbell and Thomas Nebbia. 402-417, Sept. 1977

NAJ TUNICH (Cave), Guatemala:
• Maya Art Treasures Discovered in Cave. By George E. Stuart. Photos by Wilbur E. Garrett. 220-235, Aug. 1981

MATT BRADLEY

Nahanni: author camping at Hole-in-the-Wall Lake

Gentle Giants: giraffes at salt lick

BOB CAMPBELL

NAKAMURA, KOJI: Photographer:
• The Lost Fleet of Kublai Khan. By Torao Mozai. Paintings by Issho Yada. 634-649, Nov. 1982

NALTCHAYAN, HARRY N.:
• The Proud Armenians. By Robert Paul Jordan. 846-873, June 1978

NAMBAS (People):
• Taboos and Magic Rule Namba Lives. By Kal Muller. 57-83, Jan. 1972

NAMBICUARA INDIANS. *See* Wasúsu Indians

NAMGYAL, PALDEN THONDUP (Maharaja of Sikkim):
• Wedding of Two Worlds. By Lee E. Battaglia. 708-727, Nov. 1963

NAMIB DESERT, Angola-Namibia-South Africa:
▪ The Living Sands of Namib. 439, Oct. 1977; cover, Mar. 1978; 1, Jan. 1979
• The Living Sands of the Namib. By William J. Hamilton III. Photos by Carol and David Hughes. 364-377, Sept. 1983

NAMIBIA:
• Etosha: Namibia's Kingdom of Animals. By Douglas H. Chadwick. Photos by Des and Jen Bartlett. 344-385, Mar. 1983
▪ Etosha: Place of Dry Water. 703, Dec. 1980; cover, Jan. 1981
• Family Life of Lions. By Des and Jen Bartlett. 800-819, Dec. 1982
▪ The Living Sands of Namib. 439, Oct. 1977; cover, Mar. 1978; 1, Jan. 1979
• The Living Sands of the Namib. By William J. Hamilton III. Photos by Carol and David Hughes. 364-377, Sept. 1983
• Namibia: Nearly a Nation? By Bryan Hodgson. Photos by Jim Brandenburg. 755-797, June 1982

NAMU (Killer Whale):
• Making Friends With a Killer Whale. By Edward I. Griffin. 418-446, Mar. 1966
◆ *Namu.* Announced. 726-728, Nov. 1973

NANCY HANKS CENTER, Washington, D. C.:
• A Preservation Victory Saves Washington's Old Post Office. By Wolf Von Eckardt. Photos by Volkmar Wentzel. 407-416, Sept. 1983

NANKING, China:
• Along the Yangtze, Main Street of China. By W. Robert Moore. 325-356, Mar. 1948

NANTUCKET (Island), Massachusetts:
• Life's Tempo on Nantucket. By Peter Benchley. Photos by James L. Stanfield. 810-839, June 1970
• Windjamming Around New England. By Tom Horgan. Photos by Robert F. Sisson. 141-169, Aug. 1950

M N

JODI COBB, NGS

Nashville: Dolly Parton on tour

NAPA VALLEY, California:
• Napa, California's Valley of the Vine. By Moira Johnston. Photos by Charles O'Rear. 695-717, May 1979

NAPLES, Italy:
• Italy Smiles Again. By Edgar Erskine Hume. 693-732, June 1949

NAPO (River), Peru:
• Sea Fever. By John E. Schultz. 237-268, Feb. 1949

NAPOLEON I:
• Napoleon. By John J. Putman. Photos by Gordon W. Gahan. 142-189, Feb. 1982
• St. Helena: the Forgotten Island. By Quentin Keynes. 265-280, Aug. 1950
• Sunny Corsica: French Morsel in the Mediterranean. By Robert Cairns. Photos by Joseph J. Scherschel. 401-423, Sept. 1973

NARA, Japan:
• Kyoto and Nara: Keepers of Japan's Past. By Charles McCarry. Photos by George F. Mobley. 836-851, June 1976

NASA. *See* National Aeronautics and Space Administration

NASHVILLE, Tennessee:
• There's More to Nashville than Music. By Michael Kernan. Photos by Jodi Cobb. 692-711, May 1978

NASSAU, New Providence (Island), Bahamas:
• The Bahamas: Boom Times and Buccaneering. By Peter Benchley. Photos by Bruce Dale. 364-395, Sept. 1982
• The Bahamas, Isles of the Blue-green Sea. By Carleton Mitchell. Photos by B. Anthony Stewart. 147-203, Feb. 1958
• Ballerinas in Pink. By Carleton Mitchell. Photos by B. Anthony Stewart. Contents: Flamingos in Ardastra Gardens. 553-571, Oct. 1957
• More of Sea Than of Land: The Bahamas. By Carleton Mitchell. Photos by James L. Stanfield. 218-267, Feb. 1967

NASSER, Lake, Egypt:
• Abu Simbel's Ancient Temples Reborn. By Georg Gerster. 724-744, May 1969
• Saving the Ancient Temples at Abu Simbel. By Georg Gerster. Paintings by Robert W. Nicholson. 694-742, May 1966
• Threatened Treasures of the Nile. By Georg Gerster. 587-621, Oct. 1963
• *Yankee* Cruises the Storied Nile. By Irving and Electa Johnson. Photos by Winfield Parks. 583-633, May 1965

NATAL (Province), Republic of South Africa:
• The Zulus: Black Nation in a Land of Apartheid. By Joseph Judge. Photos by Dick Durrance II. 738-775, Dec. 1971

NATCHEZ, Mississippi:
• History Repeats in Old Natchez. By William H. Nicholas. Photos by Willard R. Culver. 181-208, Feb. 1949

NATCHEZ TRACE:
• Today Along the Natchez Trace, Pathway Through History. By Bern Keating. Photos by Charles Harbutt. 641-667, Nov. 1968

The **NATION** Honors Admiral Richard E. Byrd. 567-578, Apr. 1962

NATION in the Making: Papua New Guinea. By Robert J. Gordon. Photos by David Austen. 143-149, Aug. 1982

A **NATION** Named Zimbabwe. By Charles E. Cobb, Jr. Photos by James L. Stanfield and LeRoy Woodson, Jr. 616-651, Nov. 1981

A **NATION** Rises to the Challenge: Sri Lanka's Wildlife By Lyn de Alwis. Photos by Dieter and Mary Plage. 274-278, Aug. 1983

NATIONAL ADVISORY COMMITTEE FOR AERONAUTICS: United States:
• Fact Finding for Tomorrow's Planes. By Hugh L. Dryden. Photos by Luis Marden. 757-780, Dec. 1953

NATIONAL AERONAUTICS AND SPACE ADMINISTRATION (NASA):
• America's 6,000-mile Walk in Space. 440-447, Sept. 1965
• Countdown for Space (Project Mercury). By Kenneth F. Weaver. 702-734, May 1961
• Exploring Tomorrow With the Space Agency. By Allan C. Fisher, Jr. Photos by Dean Conger. 48-89, July 1960
• First Explorers on the Moon: The Incredible Story of Apollo 11. 735-797, Dec. 1969
I. Man Walks on Another World. By Neil A. Armstrong, Edwin E. Aldrin, Jr., and Michael Collins. 738-749; II. Sounds of the Space Age, From Sputnik to Lunar Landing. A record narrated by Frank Borman. 750-751; III. The Flight of Apollo 11: "One giant leap for mankind." By Kenneth F. Weaver. 752-787; IV. What the Moon Rocks Tell Us. By Kenneth F. Weaver. 788-791; V. Next Steps in Space. By Thomas O. Paine. 793-797
• The Flight of *Freedom 7*. By Carmault B. Jackson, Jr. 417-431, Sept. 1961
• Footprints on the Moon. By Hugh L. Dryden. Paintings by Davis Meltzer and Pierre Mion. 357-401, Mar. 1964
• John Glenn's Three Orbits in *Friendship 7:* A Minute-by-Minute Account of America's First Orbital Space Flight. By Robert B. Voas. 792-827, June 1962
• The Making of an Astronaut. By Robert R. Gilruth. 122-144, Jan. 1965
• The Pilot's Story: Astronaut Shepard's Firsthand Account of His Flight. Photos by Dean Conger. 432-444, Sept. 1961
• Satellites That Serve Us. By Thomas Y. Canby. Included: A portfolio: Images of Earth. 281-335, Sept. 1983
Spacelab 1: *Columbia*. By Michael E. Long. 301-307

• Space Rendezvous, Milestone on the Way to the Moon. By Kenneth F. Weaver. 539-553, Apr. 1966
• Surveyor: Candid Camera on the Moon. By Homer E. Newell. 578-592, Oct. 1966
• They're Redesigning the Airplane. By Michael E. Long. Photos by James A. Sugar. 76-103, Jan. 1981
• Tracking America's Man in Orbit. By Kenneth F. Weaver. Photos by Robert F. Sisson. 184-217, Feb. 1962
• Voyage to the Planets. By Kenneth F. Weaver. Paintings by Ludek Pesek. 147-193, Aug. 1970
• *See also* Kennedy Space Center; Manned Spacecraft Center; Rockets; Satellites; Skylab Missions; Space Flights and Research; Space Shuttles; Viking Spacecraft Missions; Voyager; Wind Power

NATIONAL AIR AND SPACE MUSEUM, Washington, D. C.:
• Of Air and Space. By Michael Collins. 819-837, June 1978
Picture portfolio by Nathan Benn, Robert S. Oakes, and Joseph D. Lavenburg, with text by Michael E. Long. 825-837

NATIONAL AUDUBON SOCIETY: United States:
• Corkscrew Swamp–Florida's Primeval Show Place. By Melville Bell Grosvenor. 98-113, Jan. 1958
• Saving Man's Wildlife Heritage. By John H. Baker. Photos by Robert F. Sisson. 581-620, Nov. 1954
• *See also* Roseate Spoonbills; Whooping Cranes

NATIONAL BUREAU OF STANDARDS, Washington, D. C.:
• Split-second Time Runs Today's World. By F. Barrows Colton and Catherine Bell Palmer. 399-428, Sept. 1947
• Uncle Sam's House of 1,000 Wonders. By Lyman J. Briggs and F. Barrows Colton. 755-784, Dec. 1951

NATIONAL CATHEDRAL, Washington, D. C. *See* Washington Cathedral

NATIONAL CIVIL WAR CENTENNIAL COMMISSION: United States:
• The Civil War. By Ulysses S. Grant 3rd. 437-449, Apr. 1961

NATIONAL ELK REFUGE, Wyoming:
• Jackson Hole: Good-bye to the Old Days? By François Leydet. Photos by Jonathan Wright. 768-789, Dec. 1976

NATIONAL FORESTS: United States:
• Adobe New Mexico. By Mason Sutherland. Photos by Justin Locke. Included: Carson, Santa Fe. 783-830, Dec. 1949
▲ *America's Federal Lands; The United States,* double-sided supplement. Sept. 1982
• Bristlecone Pine, Oldest Known Living Thing. By Edmund Schulman. Photos by W. Robert Moore. Contents: Inyo, California. 355-372, Mar. 1958
• Florida's Booming–and Beleaguered–Heartland. By Joseph Judge. Photos by Jonathan Blair. Included: Ocala. 585-621, Nov. 1973
• Forest Fire: The Devil's Picnic. By Stuart E. Jones and Jay Johnston. Included: Deschutes, Oregon; Kaniksu, Idaho; Nezperce, Idaho; Ochoco, Oregon; Snoqualmie, Washington; Wallowa-Whitman, Oregon; Willamette, Oregon. 100-127, July 1968
• Mexico to Canada on the Pacific Crest Trail. By Mike W. Edwards. Photos by David Hiser. Included: Deschutes, Oregon; Gifford Pinchot, Washington; Inyo, California; San Bernardino, California; Sierra, California; Trinity, California; Wenatchee, Washington; Willamette, Oregon. 741-779, June 1971
• Our Green Treasury, the National Forests. By Nathaniel T. Kenney. Photos by J. Baylor Roberts. Included: Angeles, California; Beaverhead, Montana; Bitterroot, Montana; Carson, New Mexico; Coconino, Arizona; Coronado, Arizona; Flathead, Montana; Gifford Pinchot, Washington; Inyo, California; Kisatchie, Louisiana; Lolo, Idaho; Mount Hood, Oregon; Ocala, Florida; Osceola, Florida; Ottawa, Michigan; Payette, Idaho; Pisgah, North Carolina; Priest River Experimental Forest, Idaho; Sequoia, California; Siuslaw, Oregon; Superior, Minnesota; and the U. S. Forest Service. 287-324, Sept. 1956
• Our National Forests: Problems in Paradise. By Rowe Findley. Photos by David Cupp. Included: Angeles, California; Bitterroot, Montana; Bridger-Teton, Wyoming; Caribbean, Puerto Rico; Caribou, Idaho; Chugach, Alaska; Cleveland, California; Deschutes, Oregon; Flathead, Montana; Gifford Pinchot, Washington; Hoosier, Indiana; Lewis and Clark, Montana; Lincoln, New Mexico; Los Padres, California; Manti-La Sal, Utah; Mark Twain, Missouri; Monongahela, West Virginia; Mount Hood, Oregon; Pisgah, North Carolina; Sawtooth, Idaho; Suislaw, Oregon; Toiyabe, Nevada; Tongass, Alaska; Tonto, Arizona; White Mountain, New Hampshire; White River, Colorado; Willamette, Oregon. 306-339, Sept. 1982
• Roosevelt Country: T. R.'s Wilderness Legacy. By John L. Eliot. Photos by Farrell Grehan. Included: Chugach, Alaska; Tongass, Alaska. 340-363, Sept. 1982
• Timber: How Much Is Enough? By John J. Putman. Photos by Bruce Dale. Included: Monongahela, West Virginia; Tongass, Alaska; Willamette, Oregon; and the U. S. Forest Service. 485-511, Apr. 1974
• Washington Wilderness, the North Cascades. By Edwards Park. Photos by Kathleen Revis. Included: Mt. Baker, Okanogan, Wenatchee. 335-367, Mar. 1961
• White-water Adventure on Wild Rivers of Idaho. By Frank Craighead, Jr. and John Craighead. Included: Bitterroot, Boise, Challis, Nezperce, Payette, Salmon. 213-239, Feb. 1970

NATIONAL FOUNDATION FOR THE INDIAN (FUNAI): Brazil. *See* Cinta Larga Indians; Kreen-Akarores; Txukahameis; Wasúsu Indians

NATIONAL 4-H COUNCIL:
• America Goes to the Fair. By Samuel W. Matthews. 293-333, Sept. 1954
• Down on the Farm, Soviet Style–a 4-H Adventure. By John Garaventa. Photos by James Tobin and Carol Schmidt. 768-797, June 1979
• 4-H Boys and Girls Grow More Food. By Frederick Simpich. 551-582, Nov. 1948

NATIONAL GALLERY OF ART, Washington, D. C.:
• American Masters in the National Gallery. By John Walker. 295-324, Sept. 1948
• Escorting Mona Lisa to America. By Edward T. Folliard. 838-847, June 1963
• Great Masters of a Brave Era in Art (Impressionist). By Hereward Lester Cooke, Jr. Included: The Chester Dale Collection. 661-697, May 1961
• In Quest of Beauty. Text by Paul Mellon. French Impressionist paintings from the collections of Mr. and Mrs. Paul Mellon and Mrs. Ailsa Mellon Bruce. 372-385, Mar. 1967
• The Kress Collection: A Gift to the Nation. By Guy Emerson. 823-865, Dec. 1961
• Masterpieces on Tour. By Harry A. McBride. 717-750, Dec. 1948
• The National Gallery After a Quarter Century. By John Walker. 348-371, Mar. 1967
• The National Gallery's New Masterwork on the Mall. By J. Carter Brown. Photos by James A. Sugar. Contents: The East Building, designed by I. M. Pei. 680-701, Nov. 1978
• The Nation's Newest Old Masters. By John Walker. Paintings from Kress Collection. 619-657, Nov. 1956
• The Vienna Treasures and Their Collectors. By John Walker. 737-776, June 1950
• Washington: Home of the Nation's Great. By Albert W. Atwood. 699-738, June 1947
• Your National Gallery of Art After 10 Years. By John Walker. Paintings from Kress Collection. 73-103, Jan. 1952

NATIONAL GEOGRAPHIC ATLAS OF THE WORLD. *See* Atlases, NGS: World Atlas

NATIONAL GEOGRAPHIC ATLAS SERIES MAPS:
• New Atlas Maps Announced by the Society: Expanded Map Program, Marking National Geographic's 70th Year. By James M. Darley. 66-68, Jan. 1958

NATIONAL GEOGRAPHIC MAGAZINE (NGM):
Atlases. *See* Atlases, NGS
Awards Received:

• Editorial. By Wilbur E. Garrett. 553, Nov. 1982
• Freedoms Foundation awards received by editor and two staff writers. 190, Feb. 1954
• In the tradition of excellence (Awards for 1980 and 1981). 850, Dec. 1981
• La Belle Award received by Franklin L. Fisher on behalf of the Society for outstanding contributions to the development of color photography in magazine illustration. 692, Nov. 1953
• National Geographic Photographers Win Top Magazine Awards. 830-831, June 1959
• Photographers amass national awards. 878, 880-881, Dec. 1961; 898, 901, Dec. 1962; 850, Dec. 1981
• Sigma Delta Chi award. 553, Nov. 1982
• U. S. Camera Achievement Award medal (1951). 481, Oct. 1966
• University of Missouri's Honor Award for Distinguished Service in Journalism (1954). 539, Oct. 1963
Editor. Gilbert Hovey Grosvenor (1899-1954); John Oliver La Gorce (1954-1957); Melville Bell Grosvenor (1957-1967); Frederick G. Vosburgh (1967-1970); Gilbert M. Grosvenor (1970-1980); Wilbur E. Garrett (1980-)
Editor, Associate. *See* Judge, Joseph
Editor, Associate, former. *See* Scofield, John; Shor, Franc
Editorial, first as regular feature. 587, Nov. 1974
Editorial Policy. 587, Nov. 1974; 1, Jan. 1978; 293, Mar. 1979; 427, Oct. 1980; 567, Nov. 1980; 279, Sept. 1981; 1, Jan. 1982; 553, Nov. 1982
History:
• First Lady of the National Geographic (Elsie May Bell Grosvenor). By Gilbert Hovey Grosvenor. 101-121, July 1965
• Melville Bell Grosvenor, A Decade of Innovation, a Lifetime of Service. By Bart McDowell. 270-278, Aug. 1982
◆ *The National Geographic Society and Its Magazine: A History.* By Gilbert H. Grosvenor. 582A, Oct. 1957; 880, Dec. 1964
• National Geographic Society Trustees Elect Key Executives. 576-590, Oct. 1967
• The Romance of the Geographic: National Geographic Magazine Observes Its Diamond Anniversary. By Gilbert Hovey Grosvenor. 516-585, Oct. 1963
• 75 Years Exploring Earth, Sea, and Sky: National Geographic Society Observes Its Diamond Anniversary. By Melvin M. Payne. 1-43, Jan. 1963
• To Gilbert Grosvenor: A Monthly Monument 25 Miles High. By Frederick G. Vosburgh and the staff of the National Geographic Society. 445-487, Oct. 1966
Indexes:
◆ *Cumulative Index, Volume I.* 879, 880, Dec. 1964; 738, May 1968; 442, Sept. 1970

KOLB BROTHERS
Photographs: dangerous attempt to photograph the Bright Angel Trail

◆ *Cumulative Index, Volume II.* 879-880, Dec. 1964; 580, 581, Oct. 1967; 442, Sept. 1970; 436-438, Sept. 1977
• Key to '83. 839A, Dec. 1983
◆ Six-Month Index, latest. 562, Apr. 1983; 144, July 1983
Issues, Early:
• First issue (October 1888). 1, Jan. 1963; 459, 517-518, Oct. 1963; 688-689, Nov. 1964; 587, Nov. 1974
Maps. *See* Map Supplements
Members Forum, introduced. 279, Sept. 1981
On Assignment, introduced. 709, Dec. 1981
Paintings. *See* Painting Supplements
Photographers:
• Editorials on. 295, Mar. 1975; 439, Apr. 1975; 1, July 1981; 553, Nov. 1982
• Number of color photographs made by NGM photographers (7,500,000). 149, July 1975
• *See also* NGM: Awards Received; NGM: Photographs, Notable; *and* names of individual photographers
Photographs, Notable:
• Autochromes: NGM's first published Autochrome (1914). 299, Sept. 1975; A never-before-published Autochrome of Mark Twain made in 1908. 299, 301, Sept. 1975
• Award-winning photos. 830-831, June 1959; 898, 901, Dec. 1962
• Doe and Twin Fawns. Flashlight photo by George Shiras, 3d. 297, Mar. 1952; 527, Oct. 1963
• First aerial photographs of the North Pole, published in October 1953. 478, 479, Oct. 1953; 10, Jan. 1959; 580, Oct. 1963; 485, Oct. 1966
• First color cover of the magazine (the American flag). July 1942
• First color series, hand-colored ("Scenes in Korea and China"), published in November 1910. 692, Nov. 1953; 65C, July 1954; 538-539, 574-575, Oct. 1963; 465, Oct. 1966
• First extensive use of photographs: Gilbert H. Grosvenor's policy. 421, Mar. 1957; 574, Oct. 1963
• First natural-color series ("The Land of the Best"), published in April 1916; Ted Shawn and Ruth St. Denis are shown. 576, May 1951; 550, 575-576, Oct. 1963; 466-467, Oct. 1966
• First photographic series: Eleven pages of pictures of the Forbidden City (Lhasa, Tibet), published in January 1905. 65, 65C, 65F, July 1954; 524-525, 565, Oct. 1963; 462-464, Oct. 1966
• First photographs taken from the stratosphere (*Explorer II* in 1935). 562, May 1947
• First successful natural-color photographs of life beneath the sea were made in 1926 and appeared in the January 1927 issue. 162, 180, Feb. 1956; 581, Oct. 1963; 135, Jan. 1964; 462, Oct. 1966; 92, Jan. 1971
• First use of High Speed Ektachrome film. 864, Dec. 1959
• Photographs appeared as a regular feature on the yellow-bordered cover during Melville Bell Grosvenor's tenure as Editor. 270, Aug. 1982

• Two NGM photographs were used in designing the Gadsden Purchase postage stamp. 135, July 1954
• *See also* NGM: Awards Received; *and* Photography
Printing and Printers:
• Beck Engraving Company, Philadelphia. 31, July 1952
• Gravure printing at W. F. Hall in Corinth, Mississippi. 224, 226, Aug. 1976; 583, Nov. 1977
• Judd & Detweiler, Inc., Washington, D. C. 559, Oct. 1951; 561, Oct. 1963
• Linofilm typesetting technique and high-speed web presses introduced. 836, Dec. 1959; 584, 588, Oct. 1967
• McClure, Phillips & Company, New York. 559, 561, Oct. 1963
• New presses printed an all-color magazine during Melville Bell Grosvenor's tenure. 270, Aug. 1982
• R. R. Donnelley & Sons, Chicago. 874-886, Dec. 1960; 878, 879, Dec. 1961; 582, Apr. 1962; 897, Dec. 1962; 772, June 1967; 529, Apr. 1968
Recordings:
• Recorded edition of NGM loaned by Library of Congress to the visually handicapped. 681, Nov. 1975
• *See also* Recording Supplements and Sound Sheets
Reprints:
• *The Last Full Measure* (Tribute to President Kennedy). By Melville Bell Grosvenor. 355, Mar. 1964
◆ *The National Geographic Society and Its Magazine: A History*. By Gilbert H. Grosvenor. 582A, Oct. 1957; 880, Dec. 1964
• Reprinting Brings Earliest Geographics to Life. By Melvin M. Payne. 688-689, Nov. 1964
• *Special Report on Energy* (Feb. 1981). 143, Feb. 1981; 849, 850, Dec. 1981; 553, Nov. 1982
Supplements. *See* Map Supplements; Painting Supplements; Photo Supplements; Recording Supplements and Sound Sheets
Writers:
• Editorials on. By Gilbert M. Grosvenor. 295, Mar. 1975; 439, Apr. 1975; By Wilbur E. Garrett. 1, July 1981; 709, Dec. 1981; 553, Nov. 1982

NATIONAL GEOGRAPHIC SOCIETY (NGS):
Atlases. *See* Atlases, NGS
Awards Presented:
• General Thomas D. White Space Trophy (USAF award) for 1973 presented to astronaut Henry W. Hartsfield, Jr., capsule communicator for Skylab I, at NGS headquarters. 452, Oct. 1974
• Jane M. Smith Award recipients: Ingram, Sir Bruce. 474, Apr. 1961; Johnson, Lyndon B. 906, Dec. 1962; 113, Jan. 1966; 468, Oct. 1966
• Tenzing Norkey presented with cash award and replica of the Hubbard Medal given to the British Mount Everest Expedition. 846, June 1955
• *See also* Grosvenor Medal; Hubbard Medal; La Gorce Medal; Special Gold Medal
Awards Received:
• Citation of Honor: Air Force Association's bronze plaque presented to the Society for providing cartographic aid to airmen during World War II. 846, Dec. 1949
• *See also* NGM: Awards Received; NGS: Book Service; NGS: Television and Educational Films
Board of Trustees:
• Chairman. *See* Grosvenor, Gilbert Hovey; Grosvenor, Melville Bell; McKnew, Thomas W.; Payne, Melvin M.
• Chairman, Advisory. *See* McKnew, Thomas W.
• Group Portraits. 65A-65B, July 1954; 834-835, Dec. 1959; 113, Jan. 1960; 883, Dec. 1960; 553, Oct. 1965; 484-485, Oct. 1966; 588-589, Oct. 1967; 226-227, Aug. 1976
• Vice Chairman. *See* Doyle, Robert E.; La Gorce, John Oliver; McKnew, Thomas W.
Book Service:
• Awards won. 848, 850, Dec. 1981
• Book Service Division. 851-852, Dec. 1981
• Established by Melville Bell Grosvenor in 1954. 897, Dec. 1962; 585-586, Oct. 1967; 275, Aug. 1982
• *See also* Books, NGS, for titles
Cartographic Division:
• Awarded U. S. Air Force Association's citation of honor for cartographic aid during World War II. 846, Dec. 1949
• Chamberlin Trimetric Projection. 841, June 1947; 826, June 1949; 399, Mar. 1950; 417, Mar. 1952; 591, Apr. 1964
• Established in 1915. 576, Oct. 1963; 463, Oct. 1966; 585, Oct. 1967
• First color photomosaic of the United States produced by combining Landsat imagery and the General Electric Company's color-mosaic expertise with the Society's map program. 140-147, July 1976
• First known use of Two Point Equidistant Projection in mapping Asia. 418, Mar. 1951; 751, Dec. 1959
• First use of Transverse Mercator Projection for mapping a long airplane flight (1921). 524, Oct. 1947
• Mapping the moon. 240-245, Feb. 1969
• *See also* Atlases, NGS; Globes, NGS; Map Supplements; Satellite Finder
Committee for Research and Exploration:
Chairman:
• Briggs, Lyman J. 326, 332, 355, Mar. 1949; 101, 108, 122, Jan. 1959
• Carmichael, Leonard C. 867, June 1967; 872, 873, Dec. 1973; 852, Dec. 1981; 275, Aug. 1982
• Payne, Melvin M. 159, 225, Aug. 1976
• Editorials. By Gilbert M. Grosvenor. 159, Aug. 1976; 729, June 1978
Vice Chairman:
• Wetmore, Alexander. 705, June 1947; 881-882, Dec. 1967
Dues:
• Use of funds. 566, Oct. 1963; 679, May 1964; 880, Dec. 1964; 102, 105, July 1965; 587, Oct. 1967
Educational Products. *See* Atlases; Books; Films and Filmstrips; Globes; Map Supplements; NGM: Indexes; Recording Supplements and Sound Sheets; Television Films; WORLD
Employees:
• Number of. 253, 261, Aug. 1949; 443, Mar. 1960; 585, Oct. 1963; 678, 679, May 1964; 102, 108, 112-113, 118, July 1965; 459, Oct. 1966; 208, Feb. 1972
Expeditions and Research. *See* NGS: Research and Exploration
Explorers Hall:
• Great Globe. 673-675, 677, 679, May 1964; 880, Dec. 1964; 578-579, Oct. 1967
• History. 91, Jan. 1957; 578-579, Oct. 1967
• President Johnson Dedicates the Society's New Headquarters. 669-679, May 1964
Films and Filmstrips:
• Number of filmstrips distributed. 851, Dec. 1981
• The World in Geographic Filmstrips. By Melvin M. Payne. 134-137, Jan. 1968
• *See also* Television Films
Flag, NGS:
• Designed by Elsie May Bell Grosvenor. 637, May 1949; 145, Aug. 1953; 459, 516, 557, 564, Oct. 1963; 100, 101, 116, 118, July 1965
Founders and Founding:
• 33 eminent men met at the Cosmos Club, January 13, 1888. 387, Mar. 1955; 807, 830, June 1960; 1-3, Jan. 1963; 518, 573-574, Oct. 1963; 880, Dec. 1964
Globes. *See* Globe, Great; Globes, NGS
Grants:
• Amount of annual funding. 889, 893, 899, Dec. 1962; 571, Oct. 1963; 163, Feb. 1964; 582, 586, Oct. 1967; 148, July 1971; 873, Dec. 1973; 226, Aug. 1976; 274, Aug. 1982; 824, Dec. 1982
• *See also* NGS: Research and Exploration; NGS: Land Grants
Headquarters, Washington, D. C.:
Hubbard Memorial Hall:
• First headquarters of the Society. 273, Mar. 1947; 65, July 1954; 564, Oct. 1963
• Laying of cornerstone (April 26, 1902). 420, Mar. 1957
• Mural and paintings by N. C. Wyeth. 38, July 1948; 105, July 1965
M Street Building.:
• Groundbreaking ceremony for third headquarters building. 848, Dec. 1981
16th Street Building:
• History. 410, Sept. 1948; 91, Jan. 1957; 669, May 1964; 588, Oct. 1967
17th Street Building:
• Dedication: President Johnson Dedicates the Society's New Headquarters. 669-679, May 1964
• *See also* NGS: Explorers Hall
History:
• Election of officers. 427, Oct. 1980
• First Lady of the National Geographic (Elsie May Bell Grosvenor). By Gilbert Hovey Grosvenor. 101-121, July 1965

M
N

• First transcontinental telephone conversation (January 25, 1915). 58, Jan. 1958
• First voice voyages via telephone taken to the four corners of the United States by 800 NGS members (January 7, 1916). 278, Mar. 1947
• Frederick G. Vosburgh Retires as Editor; Gilbert M. Grosvenor Succeeds Him. By Melvin M. Payne. 838-843, Dec. 1970
• Gilbert Grosvenor Is Elected Chairman of the Board, John Oliver La Gorce Chosen President and Editor of the National Geographic Society. 65, 65A-65H, 66, July 1954
• Gilbert Grosvenor's Golden Jubilee. By Albert W. Atwood. 253-261, Aug. 1949
• John Oliver La Gorce Is Elected Vice-Chairman of the Board, Melville Bell Grosvenor President and Editor of the National Geographic Society. 419-423, Mar. 1957
• Melville Bell Grosvenor: A Decade of Innovation, a Lifetime of Service. By Bart McDowell. 270-278, Aug. 1982
◆*The National Geographic Society and Its Magazine: A History*. By Gilbert H. Grosvenor. 582A, Oct. 1957; 880, Dec. 1964
• National Geographic Society Trustees Elect Key Executives. 576-590, Oct. 1967
• 90th Anniversary. 1, Jan. 1978
• On the Geographic's 75th Birthday–Our Best to You. Introduction to anniversary issue. By Melville Bell Grosvenor. 459, Oct. 1963
• Robert V. Fleming, 1890-1967. By Melville Bell Grosvenor. 526-529, Apr. 1968
• The Romance of the Geographic: National Geographic Magazine Observes Its Diamond Anniversary. By Gilbert Hovey Grosvenor. 516-585, Oct. 1963
• 75 Years Exploring Earth, Sea, and Sky: National Geographic Society Observes Its Diamond Anniversary. By Melvin M. Payne. 1-43, Jan. 1963
• To Gilbert Grosvenor: A Monthly Monument 25 Miles High. By Frederick G. Vosburgh and the staff of the National Geographic Society. 445-487, Oct. 1966
• Trustees Elect New Society Officers. 224-227, Aug. 1976

Illustrations Library:
• Franklin L. Fisher's contribution. 692, Nov. 1953
• World's largest library of color transparencies. 136, Jan. 1968; 149, July 1975

Inventions:
• Chamberlin Trimetric Projection. 841, June 1947; 826, June 1949; 399, Mar. 1950; 417, Mar. 1952; 591, Apr. 1964
• Compass invented by Albert H. Bumstead. 442, Oct. 1947; 469, Oct. 1953; 754, Dec. 1953; 160, Aug. 1956; 38, July 1957; 22, Jan. 1963
• "Geometer," used with NGS globes. 698-701, May 1961; 875, Dec. 1961; 897, Dec. 1962
• OceanEye camera housing, designed by Bates Littlehales. 271, 277, Aug. 1971
• Photo-composing machine, invented by Albert H. Bumstead and further developed by his son, Newman Bumstead. 419, Mar. 1953
• Shutterless camera designed by Emory Kristof. 492, Apr. 1975

Land Grants:
• Russell Cave, Alabama, presented to the people of the United States. 438, Mar. 1958; 614, May 1958; 36, Jan. 1963; 808, June 1964; 440, Sept. 1967; 851, June 1973
• Sequoia National Park, California: The NGS and its members contributed to the purchase of 2,239 acres. 679, 680, May 1951; 792, 794, June 1954; 552, Oct. 1957; 597, 614, May 1958; 162, 176, Aug. 1959; 38, Jan. 1963; 545, Oct. 1963; 107, July 1965; 627, 630, May 1966; 1, 2, July 1966
• Shenandoah National Park, Virginia, increased by gift of 1,000 acres in 1926. 18, July 1949; 40, Jan. 1963

Lecturers:
• Arnold, H. H. 400, Mar. 1950
• British Mount Everest Expedition members. 64, July 1954
• Byrd, Richard E. 42, 44, July 1957
• Fechtler, William H. 614-615, Nov. 1952
• Foster, John W. 549, Oct. 1963
• Leakey, Louis S. B. 194-195, Feb. 1965
• MacMillan, Donald B. 563, Apr. 1953
• Peary, Mrs. Robert E. 531, Oct. 1954
• Roosevelt, Theodore. 587, Oct. 1958; 542, 585, Oct. 1963; 732, Nov. 1963; 468, Oct. 1966
• Taft, William Howard. 585, Oct. 1963; 549, Oct. 1965

Lectures:
• Annual series of lectures has been given in Constitution Hall since 1933. 565, 573, Nov. 1951
• Chairman of Lecture Committee. 843, Dec. 1970
• First lecture (1888). 113, July 1965

Map Cases:
• Churchill, Winston, presented with NGS map case by Franklin D. Roosevelt. 576, Oct. 1963; 275, Feb. 1964; 468, Oct. 1966
• Eisenhower, Dwight D., during World War II, used NGS maps in a map rack made especially for him. 737, June 1947; 583, Oct. 1963
• Johnson, Lyndon B., presents map cases to rulers of Scandinavian countries. 274, 276, Feb. 1964
• Roosevelt, Franklin D., presented with map case. 576, Oct. 1963; 275, Feb. 1964
• Truman, Harry S., presented with map case. 850, June 1948

Maps. *See* Map Supplements

Medals. *See* Grosvenor Medal; Hubbard Medal; La Gorce Medal; Special Gold Medal

Media Diversification. 227, Aug. 1976

Members and Membership:
• Number of charter members (205). 689, Nov. 1964
• Number of members. 848, Dec. 1981
• One million new members joined for 1983. 1, Jan. 1983
• Our Society Welcomes Its 3,000,000th Member. By Melville Bell Grosvenor. 579-582, Apr. 1962

Membership Center Building, Gaithersburg, Maryland. 581, 585, 590, Oct. 1967; 209, Feb. 1972; 225, Aug. 1976; 214-215, Aug. 1983

Museum. *See* NGS: Explorers Hall

News Features:
• Sent to 2,500 editors of press, radio, and television. 836, Dec. 1959

Officers:
• Election of officers. 427, Oct. 1980
• Gilbert Grosvenor Is Elected Chairman of the Board, John Oliver La Gorce Chosen President and Editor of the National Geographic Society. 65, 65A-65H, 66, July 1954
• John Oliver La Gorce Is Elected Vice-Chairman of the Board, Melville Bell Grosvenor President and Editor of the National Geographic Society. 419-423, Mar. 1957
• National Geographic Society Trustees Elect Key Executives. 576-590, Oct. 1967
• Trustees Elect New Society Officers. 224-227, Aug. 1976

Photographic Laboratories. 308, Mar. 1948; 436, Apr. 1953; 567, Apr. 1959; 864, Dec. 1959; 540, 575, 581, Oct. 1963; 193, Feb. 1967; 729, Nov. 1967; 644, 675, May 1970; 785, Dec. 1970; 244, Feb. 1973; 237, 247, Aug. 1976

Photographic Library. *See* NGS: Illustrations Library

Photography. *See* NGM: Awards Received; NGM: Photographs, Notable; *and* Photography

President:
Gardiner Greene Hubbard (1888-1897); Alexander Graham Bell (1898-1903); Gilbert Hovey Grosvenor (1920-1954); John Oliver La Gorce (1954-1957); Melville Bell Grosvenor (1957-1967); Melvin M. Payne (1967-1976); Robert E. Doyle (1976-1980); Gilbert M. Grosvenor (1980-)

President's Report:
• Around the World and the Calendar with the Geographic: The President's Annual Message. By Melville Bell Grosvenor. 832-866, Dec. 1959
• Exploring an Epic Year. By Melville Bell Grosvenor. 874-886, Dec. 1960
• President's Report to Members. By Gilbert M. Grosvenor. 848-852, Dec. 1981; 820-824, Dec. 1982
• Your Society Takes Giant New Steps: The President's Annual Message to Members. By Melville Bell Grosvenor. 874-886, Dec. 1961
• Your Society's President Reports: A Year of Widening Horizons. By Melville Bell Grosvenor. 888-906, Dec. 1962

Public Service Publications:
◆*Equal Justice Under Law* (The U. S. Supreme Court). Published in cooperation with The Foundation of the Federal Bar Association. 411, Mar. 1966; 586, Oct. 1967

◆ *George Washington, Man and Monument.* Published in cooperation with the Washington National Monument Association. 586, Oct. 1967
◆ *The Living White House.* Published in cooperation with the White House Historical Association. 641, Nov. 1966; 586, Oct. 1967
◆ *We, the People* (U. S. Capitol guidebook). Published in cooperation with the United States Capitol Historical Society. 1-2, Jan. 1964; 411, Mar. 1966; 586, Oct. 1967
◆ *The White House* (Guidebook). Published in cooperation with the White House Historical Association. 888-893, Dec. 1962; 1, Jan. 1964; 331, Mar. 1964; 642, Nov. 1964; 108, Jan. 1966; 411, Mar. 1966; 59, July 1966; 585, 586, Oct. 1967; 274, Aug. 1982
Publications. *See* Atlases; Books; National Geographic Magazine; NGM: Indexes; NGS: News Features; School Bulletin; WORLD
Purpose of the Society:
65, July 1954; 459, 581, Oct. 1963; 677, May 1964; 880, Dec. 1964; 466, Oct. 1966; 227, Aug. 1976; 567, Nov. 1980
Recordings. *See* Recording Supplements and Sound Sheets
Research and Exploration:
• Amount spent annually. 889, 893, 899, Dec. 1962; 571, Oct. 1963; 163, Feb. 1964; 582, 586, Oct. 1967; 148, July 1971; 873, Dec. 1973; 226, Aug. 1976; 274, Aug. 1982; 824, Dec. 1982
• Number of projects. 729, June 1978; 852, Dec. 1981; 820, Dec. 1982
• *See also* NGS: Committee for Research and Exploration; Research Reports
Seal:
• The Seal of the National Geographic Society appears on one side of the Hubbard Medal. 564, Apr. 1953
Secretary:
• Anderson, Owen R. (1976-1980). 225, Aug. 1976
• Austin, O. P. (1904-1932). 565, 573, Oct. 1963
• Doyle, Robert E. (1967-1976). 577, 581, 587, 590, Oct. 1967
• McKnew, Thomas W. (1932-1962). 586, May 1947; 635, May 1949; 254, 256, 257, Aug. 1949; 413, Sept. 1951
• Payne, Melvin M. (1962-1967). 582, Apr. 1962; 1, Jan. 1964; 672, May 1964; 442, Sept. 1967; 274, Aug. 1982
Special Publications:
• Adventure, science, history, exploration spring to life in your Society's new program of Special Publications. By Melville Bell Grosvenor. 408-417, Mar. 1966
• Chief: Robert L. Breeden. 411, Mar. 1966; 884, June 1970
• Editorial Director: Gilbert M. Grosvenor. 843, Dec. 1970
• Number of copies distributed (nearly 8 million). 865, June 1973
• *See also* Books, NGS, for titles
Television and Educational Films:
• Awards Received. 848, 850, Dec. 1981; 824, Dec. 1982
• Emmy Awards. 731, Dec. 1974; 1, Jan. 1979; 848, 850, Dec. 1981; 275, Aug. 1982
• George Foster Peabody Award. 587, Oct. 1967; 850, Dec. 1981
• Director: Robert C. Doyle. 449-451, Sept. 1965; 586, 587, Oct. 1967
• Number of subjects available. 583, Nov. 1975
• *See also* Television Films, for titles
Treasurer:
• Fleming, Robert V. (1935-1967). 672, May 1964; 589, Oct. 1967
Trustees. *See* NGS: Board of Trustees
Vice President:
• Beers, Thomas M. 582, Apr. 1962; 28, July 1970
• Carmichael, Leonard C. 582, 589, Oct. 1967; 861, June 1970; 588, Oct. 1972; 143, Jan. 1973; 871, 873, Dec. 1973
• Doyle, Robert E. 577, 587, Oct. 1967
• Fleming, Robert V. 882, 883, Dec. 1960; 585, Oct. 1963; 672, May 1964; 589, Oct. 1967
• Grosvenor, Gilbert M. 576, 584, 587, 588, Oct. 1967; 136, Jan. 1968; 843, Dec. 1970
• Grosvenor, Melville Bell. 65, 65D, 66, July 1954; 419, Mar. 1957
• La Gorce, John Oliver. 255, 257, 258, 260, 261, Aug. 1949; 418, Mar. 1957; 441, 443, Mar. 1960; 866, June 1967
• McKnew, Thomas W. 793, June 1958
• Payne, Melvin M. 175, Feb. 1960
• Vosburgh, Frederick G. 585, Oct. 1963; 861, June 1970; 838, Dec. 1970
Vice President, Executive:
• McKnew, Thomas W. 882, 883, Dec. 1960; 579, Apr. 1962; 148, Feb. 1965; 588, Oct. 1967
• Payne, Melvin M. 582, Apr. 1962; 865, June 1967; 583, Oct. 1967; 274, Aug. 1982
Vice President for Research and Exploration:
• Carmichael, Leonard C. 525, Apr. 1965; 864, June 1967; 441, 442, Sept. 1967; 582, 586, Oct. 1967

NATIONAL GEOGRAPHIC-PALOMAR OBSERVATORY SKY SURVEYS:
• Completing the Atlas of the Universe. By Ira Sprague Bowen. NGS research grant. 185-190, Aug. 1955
Sky Survey Plates Unlock Secrets of the Stars. 186-187
• Exploring the Farthest Reaches of Space. By George O. Abell. NGS research grant. 782-790, Dec. 1956
▲ *Journey Into the Universe Through Time and Space; National Geographic-Palomar Sky Survey Charting the Heavens,* double-sided supplement. June 1983
• Mapping the Unknown Universe. By F. Barrows Colton. NGS research grant. 401-420, Sept. 1950
• Our Universe Unfolds New Wonders. By Albert G. Wilson. NGS research grant. 245-260, Feb. 1952
• Sky Survey Charts the Universe. By Ira Sprague Bowen. NGS research grant. 780-781, Dec. 1956

NATIONAL GEOGRAPHIC WORLD (Magazine for Young Readers):
• Circulation. 851, Dec. 1981
• Editorial. By Gilbert M. Grosvenor. The *School Bulletin* is retired after 56 years; replaced by WORLD. 299, Sept. 1975
• Start the World, I Want to Get On! 148-150, July 1975

NATIONAL INSTITUTES OF HEALTH, Bethesda, Maryland:
• Capturing Strange Creatures in Colombia. By Marte Latham. Photos by Tor Eigeland. 682-693, May 1966

NATIONAL MILITARY PARKS: United States:
• Echoes of Shiloh (Shiloh National Military Park, Tennessee). By Shelby Foote. 106-111, July 1979
• Gettysburg and Vicksburg: the Battle Towns Today. By Robert Paul Jordan. Map notes by Carolyn Bennett Patterson. 4-57, July 1963
• Heritage of Beauty and History. By Conrad L. Wirth. Included: Antietam, Chickamauga, Gettysburg, Kings Mountain, Shiloh, Vicksburg, Yorktown. 587-661, May 1958

NATIONAL MONUMENTS: United States:
• Alaska: Rising Northern Star. By Joseph Judge. Photos by Bruce Dale. Included: Katmai National Monument; *and* proposed monuments: Aniakchak Caldera, Cape Krusenstern, Harding Icefield-Kenai Fjords, Kobuk. 730-767, June 1975
• Alaska's Warmer Side. By Elsie May Bell Grosvenor. Included: Katmai National Monument, in which is located the Valley of Ten Thousand Smokes. 737-775, June 1956
▲ *America's Federal Lands; The United States,* double-sided supplement. Sept. 1982
• Blizzard of Birds: The Tortugas Terns. By Alexander Sprunt, Jr. Included: Fort Jefferson National Monument. 213-230, Feb. 1947
• Heritage of Beauty and History. By Conrad L. Wirth. Included: Aztec Ruins, Bandelier, Castillo de San Marcos, Cedar Breaks, Custer Battlefield, Death Valley, Devils Tower, Dinosaur, Edison Laboratory, El Morro, Fort Frederica, Fort Laramie, Fort McHenry, Fort Sumter, Great Sand Dunes, Harpers Ferry, Katmai, Lava Beds, Organ Pipe Cactus, Petrified Forest, Rainbow Bridge, Russell Cave, Saguaro, Scotts Bluff, Tuzigoot, Walnut Canyon National Monuments. 587-661, May 1958
• The Mission Called 66: Today in Our National Parks. By Conrad L. Wirth. Included: Death Valley, Dinosaur, Rainbow Bridge National Monuments. 7-47, July 1966
▲ *National Parks, Monuments and Shrines of the United States and Canada.* Atlas series supplement. Text on reverse. May 1958

M N

DAVID ALAN HARVEY, NGS

Our National Parks: Statue of Liberty

• Parkscape, U.S.A.: Tomorrow in Our National Parks. By George B. Hartzog, Jr. Included: Buck Island Reef, Chesapeake and Ohio Canal, Glacier Bay, Katmai, Muir Woods, Organ Pipe Cactus, Statue of Liberty. 48-93, July 1966

• Preserving America's Last Great Wilderness (Alaska). By David Jeffery. Included: Katmai; *and* proposed monuments: Aniakchak Caldera, Cape Krusenstern, Harding Icefield-Kenai Fjords, Kobuk. 769-791, June 1975

• Roosevelt Country: T. R.'s Wilderness Legacy. By John L. Eliot. Photos by Farrell Grehan. 340-363, Sept. 1982

• Shrines of Each Patriot's Devotion. By Frederick G. Vosburgh. Contents: Ackia Battleground, Andrew Johnson, Big Hole, Cabrillo, Custer Battlefield, El Morro, Father Millet Cross, Fort Matanzas, Fort Pulaski, Fort Vancouver, George Washington Birthplace, Homestead, Lava Beds, Perry's Victory and International Peace Memorial, Pipe Spring, Scotts Bluff, Statue of Liberty, Verendrye. 51-82, Jan. 1949

• Today and Tomorrow in Our National Parks. By Melville Bell Grosvenor. Included: Glacier Bay National Monument. 1-5, July 1966

• Utah's Arches of Stone. By Jack Breed. Contents: Arches National Monument. 173-192, Aug. 1947

• *See also* Arizona (From Tucson to Tombstone); Bandelier National Monument; Buck Island Reef National Monument; Castillo de San Marcos; Chesapeake and Ohio Canal; Craters of the Moon National Monument; Death Valley National Monument; Dinosaur National Monument; El Morro; Fort Jefferson National Monument; Glacier Bay National Monument; Harpers Ferry; Katmai National Monument; Marble Canyon National Monument; Natural Bridges National Monument; Navajo National Monument; Organ Pipe Cactus National Monument; Rainbow Bridge National Monument; Russell Cave; Santa Barbara Islands, for Channel Islands National Monument; White Sands National Monument; *and* Custer, George A., for Custer Battlefield National Monument

NATIONAL MUSEUM: United States. *See* Smithsonian Institution

NATIONAL MUSEUM OF ANTHROPOLOGY, Mexico City:

• Mexico's Window on the Past. By Bart McDowell. Photos by B. Anthony Stewart. 492-519, Oct. 1968

NATIONAL MUSEUM OF CANADA: Expeditions:

• Vanished Mystery Men of Hudson Bay. By Henry B. Collins. NGS research grant. 669-687, Nov. 1956

NATIONAL OCEANIC AND ATMOSPHERIC ADMINISTRATION: Study Grants:

• This Changing Earth. By Samuel W. Matthews. 1-37, Jan. 1973

• Underwater Exploration: Galapagos Rift. 685, Nov. 1979

• We're Doing Something About the Weather! By Walter Orr Roberts. 518-555, Apr. 1972

NATIONAL OCEANOGRAPHIC PROGRAM: United States:

• *Thresher:* Lesson and Challenge. By James H. Wakelin, Jr. Included: Interagency Committee on Oceanography, Federal Council for Science and Technology, TENOC. 759-763, June 1964

NATIONAL OUTDOOR LEADERSHIP SCHOOL:

• Wind River Range: Many-treasured Splendor. By Joseph Judge. 198-205, Feb. 1974

NATIONAL PARK SERVICE:

• Expeditions and Research. *See* Isle Royale; Wetherill Mesa; *and* Tree Snails

• Heritage of Beauty and History. By Conrad L. Wirth. Contents: *National Battlefield Parks:* Manassas; *National Battlefield Sites:* Antietam; *National Historic Sites:* Adams Mansion, Fort Raleigh; *National Historical Parks:* Appomattox Court House, Colonial, Cumberland Gap, Independence, Morristown, Saratoga; *National Memorials:* House Where Lincoln Died, Lincoln Memorial, Mount Rushmore, Washington Monument, Wright Brothers; *National Military Parks:* Antietam, Chickamauga, Gettysburg, Kings Mountain, Shiloh, Vicksburg; *National Monuments:* Aztec Ruins, Bandelier, Castillo de San Marcos, Cedar Breaks, Custer Battlefield, Death Valley, Devils Tower, Dinosaur, Edison Laboratory, El Morro, Fort Frederica, Fort Laramie, Fort McHenry, Fort Sumter, Great Sand Dunes, Harpers Ferry, Katmai, Lava Beds, Organ Pipe Cactus, Petrified Forest, Rainbow Bridge, Russell Cave, Saguaro, Scotts Bluff, Tuzigoot, Walnut Canyon; *National Parks:* Acadia, Big Bend, Bryce Canyon, Carlsbad Caverns, Crater Lake, Everglades, Glacier, Grand Canyon, Grand Teton, Great Smoky Mountains, Hawaii, Kings Canyon, Lassen Volcanic, Mammoth Cave, Mesa Verde, Mount McKinley, Mount Rainier, Olympic, Rocky Mountain, Sequoia, Shenandoah, Virgin Islands, Wind Cave, Yellowstone, Yosemite, Zion. 587-661, May 1958

• The Mission Called 66: Today in Our National Parks. By Conrad L. Wirth. Included: Achievements of Mission 66, ten-year program of National Park Service for improvement and expansion of national parks, 1956-1966. 7-47, July 1966

• The Next 100 Years: A Master Plan for Yellowstone. By George B. Hartzog, Jr. 632-637, May 1972

• Our National Parks. Photos by David Alan Harvey. 1-152, July 1979

• Parkscape, U. S. A.: Tomorrow in Our National Parks. By George B. Hartzog, Jr. Included: Future program of National Park Service. 48-93, July 1966

• Shrines of Each Patriot's Devotion. By Frederick G. Vosburgh. 51-82, Jan. 1949

• Today and Tomorrow in Our National Parks. By Melville Bell Grosvenor. Included: Golden anniversary of National Park Service; history of founding in 1916; plans for the future. 1-5, July 1966

• Yellowstone at 100: The Pitfalls of Success. By William S. Ellis. Photos by Jonathan Blair. 616-631, May 1972

NATIONAL PARKS:

Africa:

• African Wildlife: Man's Threatened Legacy. By Allan C. Fisher, Jr. Photos by Thomas Nebbia. Paintings by Ned Seidler. Included: Albert National Park, Zaire; Amboseli Game Reserve, Kenya; Etosha National Park, South-West Africa; Gorongosa National Park, Mozambique; Kidepo Valley National Park, Uganda; Kruger National Park, South Africa; Lake Manyara National Park, Tanzania; Marsabit National Reserve, Kenya; Mkuzi Game Reserve, South Africa; Mountain Zebra National Park, South Africa; Murchison Falls National Park, Uganda; Nairobi National Park, Kenya; Ngorongoro Conservation Area, Tanzania; Serengeti National Park, Tanzania; Tsavo National Park, Kenya; Volcanoes National Park, Rwanda; Wankie National Park, Rhodesia. 147-187, Feb. 1972

• Africa's Elephants: Can They Survive? By Oria Douglas-Hamilton. Photos by Oria and Iain Douglas-Hamilton. Included: Addo Elephant National Park, South Africa; Kabalega Falls National Park, Uganda; Kruger National Park, South Africa; Lake Manyara National Park, Tanzania; Niokolo Koba National Park, Senegal; Ruwenzori National Park, Uganda; Selous Game Reserve, Tanzania; Tsavo National Park, Kenya; Wankie National Park, Zimbabwe; Wonga Wongué Reserve, Gabon; Zambesi National Park, Zimbabwe. 568-603, Nov. 1980

• The Last Great Animal Kingdom. Included: Albert National Park, Congo; Amboseli National Reserve, Kenya; Kruger National Park, South Africa; Serengeti National Park, Tanganyika. 390-409, Sept. 1960

• Roaming Africa's Unfenced Zoos. By W. Robert Moore. Included: Hluhluwe Game Reserve, South Africa; Kruger National Park, South Africa; Nairobi National Park, Kenya; Parc National Albert, Congo; Umfolozi Reserve, South Africa. 353-380, Mar. 1950

• Uganda, Africa's Uneasy Heartland. By Howard La Fay. Photos by George F. Mobley. Included: Kidepo Valley National Park, Murchison Falls National Park, Queen Elizabeth National Park. 708-735, Nov. 1971

• Where Elephants Have Right of Way. By George and Jinx Rodger. Included: Amboseli National Reserve, Kenya; Garamba National Park, Congo; Murchison Falls National Park, Uganda; Nairobi Royal National Park, Kenya; Ngong National Reserve, Kenya; Queen Elizabeth National Park, Uganda; Tsavo Royal National Park, Kenya. 363-389, Sept. 1960

• White Magic in the Belgian Congo. By W. Robert Moore. 321-362, Mar. 1952

• *See also* Etosha National Park, Namibia; Gombe Stream National Park, Tanzania; Kruger National Park, South Africa; Lake Manyara National Park, Tanzania; Nairobi National Park, Kenya; Serengeti National Park, Tanzania; Tsavo National Park, Kenya

Asia:

• India Struggles to Save Her Wildlife. By John J. Putman. Included: Borivli National Park, Corbett National Park, Kanha National Park, Kaziranga National Park. 299-343, Sept. 1976

• Park at the Top of the World: Mount Everest National Park. By Rick Ridgeway. Photos by Nicholas DeVore III. 704-725, June 1982

Preserving a Mountain Heritage. By Sir Edmund Hillary. 696-703

• Sri Lanka's Wildlife. 254-278, Aug. 1983

I. Sri Lanka's Wildlife Heritage: A Personal Perspective. By Arthur C. Clarke. 254-255; II. Legacy of Lively Treasures. By Dieter and Mary Plage. 256-273; III. A Nation Rises to the Challenge. By Lyn de Alwis. Photos by Dieter and Mary Plage. 274-278

Australia:

• Australia's Great Barrier Reef. 630-663, May 1981

I. A Marine Park Is Born. By Soames Summerhays. Photos by Ron and Valerie Taylor. 630-635; II. Paradise Beneath the Sea. By Ron and Valerie Taylor. 636-663

• A Walk and Ride on the Wild Side: Tasmania. By Carolyn Bennett Patterson. Photos by David Hiser and Melinda Berge. Included: Franklin-Lower Gordon Wild Rivers National Park; Southwest National Park. 676-693, May 1983

Canada:

• Bikepacking Across Alaska and Canada. By Dan Burden. Included: Jasper. 682-695, May 1973

• Canada's Heartland, the Prairie Provinces. By W. E. Garrett. Included: Banff, Elk Island, Jasper, Wood Buffalo. 443-489, Oct. 1970

• Canadian Rockies, Lords of a Beckoning Land. By Alan Phillips. Photos by James L. Stanfield. Included: Banff, Jasper, Kootenay, Mount Robson, Waterton Lakes, Yoho. 353-393, Sept. 1966

• Heart of the Canadian Rockies. By Elizabeth A. Moize. Photos by Jim Brandenburg. Included: Banff, Jasper. 757-779, June 1980

• Hiking the Backbone of the Rockies; Canada's Great Divide Trail. By Mike W. Edwards. Photos by Lowell Georgia. Included: Banff, Jasper, Kootenay, Yoho. 795-817, June 1973

• On the Ridgepole of the Rockies. By Walter Meayers Edwards. Included: Banff, Jasper. 745-780, June 1947

Canada's Rocky Mountain Playground. 755-770

• *See also* Nahanni National Park; Waterton-Glacier International Peace Park, for Waterton Lakes National Park; Wood Buffalo National Park

Central America:

• Resurrecting the Grandeur of Tikal (Maya Ruin). By William R. Coe. 792-798, Dec. 1975

• Teeming Life of a Rain Forest. By Carol and David Hughes. 49-65, Jan. 1983

New Zealand. *See* Milford Track, for Fiordland National Park

South America:

• Parks, Plans, and People: How South America Guards Her Green Legacy. By Mary and Laurance Rockefeller. Photos by George F. Mobley. Included: Cabo Polonio, Iguaçu, Los Glaciares, Nahuel Huapí, Robinson Crusoe Island, Tierra del Fuego, Torres del Paine. 74-119, Jan. 1967

• *See also* Xingu National Park, Brazil

United States:

• Alaska: Rising Northern Star. By Joseph Judge. Photos by Bruce Dale. Included: Mount McKinley, Sitka; *and* proposed parks: Gates of the Arctic, Lake Clark, Wrangell-St. Elias. 730-767, June 1975

▲ *America's Federal Lands; The United States,* double-sided supplement. Included: Arches, Bryce Canyon, Canyonlands, Capitol Reef, Zion. Sept. 1982

◆ *America's Wonderlands, The National Parks.* Announced. 558-561, Oct. 1959; 562-563, Oct. 1961

■ America's Wonderlands: The National Parks. 549A-549B, Oct. 1968

• Coal vs. Parklands. By François Leydet. Photos by Dewitt Jones. 776-803, Dec. 1980

• Editorial. By Gilbert M. Grosvenor. 1-2, July 1979

• The Fabulous Sierra Nevada. By J. R. Challacombe. Included: Kings Canyon, Sequoia, Yosemite. 825-843, June 1954

• From Sun-clad Sea to Shining Mountains. By Ralph Gray. Photos by James P. Blair. Included: Parks and scenic wonders along highway, "International 89," from Sonora, Mexico, through western United States, to British Columbia, Canada. 542-589, Apr. 1964

MN

• From Tucson to Tombstone. By Mason Sutherland. 343-384, Sept. 1953
• Giant Sequoias Draw Millions to California Parks. By John Michael Kauffmann. Photos by B. Anthony Stewart. Included: Kings Canyon, Sequoia. 147-187, Aug. 1959
• Heritage of Beauty and History. By Conrad L. Wirth. Included: Acadia, Big Bend, Bryce Canyon, Carlsbad Caverns, Crater Lake, Everglades, Glacier, Grand Canyon, Grand Teton, Great Smoky Mountains, Hawaii, Kings Canyon, Lassen Volcanic, Mammoth Cave, Mesa Verde, Mount McKinley, Mount Rainier, Olympic, Rocky Mountain, Sequoia, Shenandoah, Virgin Islands, Wind Cave, Yellowstone, Yosemite, Zion. 587-661, May 1958
• I See America First. By Lynda Bird Johnson. Photos by William Albert Allard. Included: Grand Teton, Mesa Verde, Monument Valley, Yellowstone. 874-904, Dec. 1965
• John Muir's Wild America. By Harvey Arden. Photos by Dewitt Jones. Included: Petrified Forest, Sequoia, Yosemite. 433-461, Apr. 1973
• Mexico to Canada on the Pacific Crest Trail. By Mike W. Edwards. Photos by David Hiser. Included: Crater Lake, Lassen Volcanic, Mount Rainier, Sequoia, Yosemite. 741-779, June 1971
• The Mission Called 66: Today in Our National Parks. By Conrad L. Wirth. Included: Acadia, Bryce Canyon, Crater Lake, Everglades, Grand Canyon, Grand Teton, Mesa Verde, Mount Rainier, Sequoia, Shenandoah, Yellowstone, Yosemite. 7-47, July 1966
▲ *National Parks, Monuments and Shrines of the United States and Canada.* Atlas series supplement. Text on reverse. May 1958
▮ National Parks: Playground or Paradise. 703, Dec. 1980
◆ *The New America's Wonderlands.* Announced. 436-438, Mar. 1975
• New Rush to Golden California. By George W. Long. Included: Kings Canyon, Lassen Volcanic, Sequoia, Yosemite. 723-802, June 1954
• Our National Parks. Photos by David Alan Harvey. 1-152, July 1979
I. The Best of Our Land. By Gilbert M. Grosvenor. 1-2; II. Parks Grandeur in Pictures. 3-17; III. A Long History of New Beginnings. By Melville Bell Grosvenor. 18-30; IV. Will Success Spoil Our Parks? By Robert Paul Jordan. 31-59; V. Sharing Alaska: How Much for Parks? Opposing views by Jay S. Hammond and Cecil D. Andrus. 60-65; VI. Trekking Around the Continent's Highest Peak. By Ned Gillette. 66-79; VII. Our People, Our Past (Navajos). By Albert Laughter. 81-85; VIII. Gateway–Elbowroom for the Millions. By Louise Levathes. 86-97; IX. Golden Gate–Of City, Ships, and Surf. By David S. Boyer. 98-105; X. Echoes of Shiloh. By Shelby Foote. 106-111; XI. A Guide to Parklands. 111-123; XII. Spring Comes Late to Glacier. By Douglas Chadwick. 124-133; XIII. Guadalupe's Trails in Summer. By Edward Abbey. 135-141; XIV. Autumn–Season of the Smokies. By Gordon Young. 142-147; XV. Grand Teton–A Winter's Tale. By François Leydet. 148-152
• Parkscape, U.S.A.: Tomorrow in Our National Parks. By George B. Hartzog, Jr. Included: Canyonlands, Everglades, Great Smoky Mountains, Haleakala, Mount McKinley, North Cascades (Proposed), Redwood (Proposed), Shenandoah, Virgin Islands; *and* National Capital Parks. 48-93, July 1966
• Preserving America's Last Great Wilderness (Alaska). By David Jeffery. Included: Proposed parks: Gates of the Arctic, Katmai additional acreage, Lake Clark, Mount McKinley. 769-791, June 1975
• Roosevelt Country: T. R.'s Wilderness Legacy. By John L. Eliot. Photos by Farrell Grehan. 340-363, Sept. 1982
• Sierra High Trip. By David R. Brower. Included: Kings Canyon, Sequoia. 844-868, June 1954
• Skyline Trail from Maine to Georgia. By Andrew H. Brown. Photos by Robert F. Sisson. Included: Great Smoky Mountains, Shenandoah. 219-251, Aug. 1949
• Today and Tomorrow in Our National Parks. By Melville Bell Grosvenor. Included: Kings Canyon, Mount McKinley, Sequoia. 1-5, July 1966
◆ *Vacationland U.S.A.* Announced. 734-740, May 1970
▲ *Vacationlands of the United States and Southern Canada,* supplement. Text on reverse. July 1966
• The West Through Boston Eyes. By Stewart Anderson. Included: Bryce Canyon, Crater Lake, Glacier, Grand Canyon, Grand Teton, Yellowstone, Yosemite, Zion. 733-776, June 1949
◆ *Wilderness U.S.A.* Announced. 582-584, Oct. 1973
• Wyoming: High, Wide, and Windy. By David S. Boyer. Included: Grand Teton, Yellowstone. 554-594, Apr. 1966
• *See also* Badlands; Big Bend National Park; Bryce Canyon National Park; Canyonlands National Park; Carlsbad Caverns; Crater Lake; Everglades; Glacier National Park; Grand Canyon National Park; Grand Teton National Park; Great Smoky Mountains National Park; Guadalupe Mountains National Park; Haleakala National Park; Hawaii Volcanoes National Park; Isle Royale; Mesa Verde National Park; Mount McKinley National Park; North Cascades National Park; Olympic National Park; Redwood National Park; Sequoia National Park; Shenandoah National Park; Yellowstone National Park; Yosemite National Park; Zion National Park

NATIONAL PARKS: Proposed. *See* North Cascades National Park; Tallgrass Prairie National Park

NATIONAL PRESERVES: Proposed. *See* Big Cypress Swamp, Florida; Big Thicket, Texas

NATIONAL RECREATION AREAS. *See* Gateway National Recreation Area, New Jersey-New York; Glen Canyon National Recreation Area, Arizona-Utah; Golden Gate National Recreation Area, California

NATIONAL RIVER. *See* Buffalo National River

NATIONAL SCENIC TRAILS: United States. *See* Appalachian Trail; Continental Divide National Scenic Trail; Pacific Crest Trail

NATIONAL SCIENCE FOUNDATION:
• Animal Studies: Alaskan Brown Bear 433, Sept. 1975; Andean Condor 686, May 1971; Baboon 674, May 1975; Coral Reef 710, 712, Nov. 1966; Fiddler Crab 16, Jan. 1963; Galapagos Tortoise 639, Nov. 1972; Garden Eel 727, Nov. 1974; Green Turtle 879, 880, June 1967; Grizzly Bear 255, Aug. 1966; Lions 496, Apr. 1969; Moose and Wolves of Isle Royale 202, Feb. 1963; Porpoises 403, Sept. 1966; Salmon 205, Aug. 1968; Wild Burro 506, Apr. 1972
• Antarctic Research. *See* International Geophysical Year; U. S. Antarctic Research Program
• Anthropology: Ethiopia 805, Dec. 1976; Karnali Zone, Nepal 662, Nov. 1971; New Britain Tribes 795, June 1966; Papua New Guinea 128, July 1977; Polynesians 736, Dec. 1974; Skull 1470 829, June 1973
• Archaeology: Chan Chan 320, Mar. 1973; Dzibilchaltun 99, Jan. 1959; Jenne-jeno (site), Mali 408, Sept. 1982; *Monitor* search 49, Jan. 1975; Snaketown 675, 682, May 1967; Yassi Ada wrecks 404, Sept. 1968
• Bristlecone Pine. 361, Mar. 1958
• Deep Sea Drilling Project. 650, Nov. 1978
• Eclipse Expedition. 224, Aug. 1970
• Education: Science projects in Pittsburgh high schools. 365, 368, Mar. 1965
• Galapagos Rift Hydrothermal Expedition. 443, Oct. 1977; 682, 685, Nov. 1979
• Palau Lakes. 269, 271, Feb. 1982
• Programs supported: Cayman Expedition 230, Aug. 1976; International Biological Program (Tundra ecosystems) 305, Mar. 1972; Summer Institute of Glaciological and Arctic Sciences 796, June 1965; 201, Feb. 1967; University Corporation for Atmospheric Research 523, Apr. 1972
• *See also* American Mount Everest Expedition; Deep Sea Drilling Project; FAMOUS; Mohole, Project

NATIONAL SEASHORES: United States. *See* Assateague Island, Maryland-Virginia; Cape Cod, Massachusetts; Cape Hatteras National Seashore, North Carolina; Cumberland Island, Georgia; Padre Island National Seashore, Texas

NATIONAL TRAIL SYSTEM. *See listing under* National Scenic Trails

NATIONAL TRUST FOR HISTORIC PRESERVATION:
● Buildings Preserved. 93, Jan. 1957; 383, Mar. 1966; 834, Dec. 1970; 78, 83, Jan. 1978
● Study Grant. 1, July 1982

NATIONAL WEATHER SERVICE: United States:
● We're Doing Something About the Weather! By Walter Orr Roberts. 518-555, Apr. 1972
● The Year the Weather Went Wild. By Thomas Y. Canby. 799-829, Dec. 1977
● *See also* former name, U. S. Weather Bureau

NATIONAL WILD AND SCENIC RIVERS SYSTEM:
● America's Little Mainstream. By Harvey Arden. Photos by Matt Bradley. Note: In 1972, Congress created the Buffalo National River, a unique administrative unit. 344-359, Mar. 1977
◆ *America's Wild and Scenic Rivers.* 1983
● Our Wild and Scenic Rivers. 2-59, July 1977
I. Rivers Wild and Pure: A Priceless Legacy. By Robert E. Doyle. 2-11; II. The Flathead. By Douglas H. Chadwick. Photos by Lowell Georgia. 13-19; III. The Suwannee. By Jack and Anne Rudloe. Photos by Jodi Cobb. 20-29; IV. The St. Croix. By David S. Boyer. 30-37; V. The Skagit. By David S. Boyer. 38-45; VI. The Rio Grande. By Nathaniel T. Kenney. Photos by Bank Langmore. 46-51. VII. The Noatak. By John M. Kauffmann. Photos by Sam Abell. 52-59
● White-water Adventure on Wild Rivers of Idaho. By Frank Craighead, Jr. and John Craighead. Included: Middle Fork Salmon; Salmon; and rivers protected or proposed for protection under the Wild and Scenic Rivers Act of 1968. 213-239, Feb. 1970
▲ *Wild and Scenic Rivers of the United States,* double-sided supplement. July 1977
■ Wild River. Included: Middle Fork Salmon; Salmon. 239A-239B, Feb. 1970
● *See also* Allagash Wilderness Waterway, Maine; Chattooga River, Georgia-North Carolina-South Carolina; Clearwater (River), Idaho; Colorado River and Basin, U. S.; Hudson (River), New York; Mississippi (River), U. S.; Missouri (River), U. S.; Rio Grande (River), Mexico-U. S.; Salmon (River), Idaho; Snake (River), Idaho-Washington-Wyoming

NATIONAL WILDLIFE REFUGES: United States:
● Alaska: Rising Northern Star. By Joseph Judge. Photos by Bruce Dale. Included: Map showing existing and proposed refuges. 730-767, June 1975
▲ *America's Federal Lands; The United States,* double-sided supplement. Sept. 1982
● Beyond the North Wind With the Snow Goose. By Des and Jen Bartlett. Included: De Soto, Missouri River; Sand Lake, South Dakota; Squaw Creek, Missouri. 822-843, Dec. 1973
● Delaware–Who Needs to Be Big? By Jane Vessels. Photos by Kevin Fleming. Included: Bombay Hook National Wildlife Refuge. 171-197, Aug. 1983
● Hawaii's Far-flung Wildlife Paradise. By John L. Eliot. Photos by Jonathan Blair. Contents: Hawaiian Islands National Wildlife Refuge. 670-691, May 1978
● Our National Wildlife Refuges. 342-381, Mar. 1979
I. A Chance to Grow. By Robert E. Doyle. 342-349; II. Island, Prairie, Marsh, and Shore. By Charlton Ogburn. Photos by Bates Littlehales. 350-381; III. Wildlife Refuges of the United States. Tear-out guide with maps. 363-370
● Preserving America's Last Great Wilderness (Alaska). By David Jeffery. 769-791, June 1975
● Roosevelt Country: T. R.'s Wilderness Legacy. By John L. Eliot. Photos by Farrell Grehan. 340-363, Sept. 1982
● Teamwork Helps the Whooping Crane. By Roderick C. Drewien, with Ernie Kuyt. Included: Bosque del Apache National Wildlife Refuge, New Mexico; Grays Lake National Wildlife Refuge, Idaho; Monte Vista National Wildlife Refuge, Colorado. 680-693, May 1979
● Tireless Voyager, the Whistling Swan. By William J. L. Sladen. Photos by Bianca Lavies. Included: Back Bay, Virginia; Blackwater, Maryland; Eastern Neck, Maryland; Mattamuskeet, North Carolina; Pungo, North Carolina; Upper Mississippi River Wild Life and Fish Refuge. NGS research grant. 134-147, July 1975
● *See also* Aransas National Wildlife Refuge, Texas; Arctic National Wildlife Range, Alaska; National Elk Refuge, Wyoming; Okefenokee Swamp, Florida-Georgia; Red Rocks Lake National Wildlife Refuge, Montana; Wichita Mountains Wildlife Refuge, Oklahoma

NATIONAL ZOOLOGICAL PARK, Washington, D. C.:
● The Ape with Friends in Washington. By Margaretta Burr Wells. 61-74, July 1953
● Director: Theodore H. Reed. 630, May 1961; 875, Dec. 1968; 482, 484, 485, 487, Apr. 1970; 164, Feb. 1972; 803, 807, Dec. 1972

BATES LITTLEHALES, NGS

Our Wildlife Refuges: cattle egret

JONATHAN BLAIR

Hawaii's Paradise: frigatebird display

• Director, Acting: Theodore H. Reed. 524, Apr. 1957
• Enchantress! By Theodore H. Reed. Photos by Thomas J. Abercrombie. 628-641, May 1961
• Portraits of My Monkey Friends. By Ernest P. Walker. 105-119, Jan. 1956
• What's Black and White and Loved All Over? By Theodore H. Reed. Photos by Donna K. Grosvenor. 803-815, Dec. 1972
• White Tiger in My House. By Elizabeth C. Reed. Photos by Donna K. Grosvenor. 482-491, Apr. 1970
• The Wild Animals in My Life. By William M. Mann. 497-524, Apr. 1957

NATIONALIST CHINA. *See* Pescadores; Quemoy; Taiwan

The **NATION'S** Bookcase: Library of Congress. By Fred Kline. Photos by Dick Durrance II. 671-687, Nov. 1975

The **NATION'S** Capitol Revealed as Never Before. By Carl Hayden. 1-3, Jan. 1964

The **NATION'S** Library. By Albert W. Atwood. 663-684, May 1950

The **NATION'S** Newest Old Masters. By John Walker. Paintings from Kress Collection. 619-657, Nov. 1956

A **NATION'S** Quandary: Coal vs. Parklands. By François Leydet. Photos by Dewitt Jones. 776-803, Dec. 1980

The **NATION'S** River. By Allan C. Fisher, Jr. Photos by James L. Stanfield. 432-469, Oct. 1976

The **NATION'S** 200th Birthday. By Gilbert M. Grosvenor. 1, July 1974

NATIVE AMERICANS. *See* Aleuts; Eskimos; Indians of Central America; Indians of North America; Indians of South America; Inuit

NATIVE'S Return to Norway. By Arnvid Nygaard. Photos by Andrew H. Brown. 683-691, Nov. 1953

NATRON, Lake, Tanzania:
• East Africa's Majestic Flamingos. By M. Philip Kahl. NGS research grant. 276-294, Feb. 1970

NATURAL ARCHES AND BRIDGES. *See* Arches National Monument; Canyonlands National Park; Escalante Canyon, for Grosvenor Arch; *and* Natural Bridges National Monument; Rainbow Bridge National Monument; Zion National Park

NATURAL BRIDGES NATIONAL MONUMENT, Utah:
• Roaming the West's Fantastic Four Corners. By Jack Breed. 705-742, June 1952

NATURAL GAS:
• Alberta Unearths Her Buried Treasures. By David S. Boyer. 90-119, July 1960

JAMES L. STANFIELD, NGS

Nation's River: Potomac's South Branch

▲ *America's Federal Lands; The United States,* double-sided supplement. Sept. 1982
• An Atlas of Energy Resources. Included: Map locating natural gas resources of North America. 58-69, *Special Report on Energy* (Feb. 1981)
• Canada's "Now" Frontier. By Robert Paul Jordan. Photos by Lowell Georgia. Included: Map showing oil pipeline, proposed gas pipeline, and tar sands. 480-511, Oct. 1976
• Editorial. By Gilbert M. Grosvenor. 577, Nov. 1978
• The Eternal Flame. By Albert W. Atwood. 540-564, Oct. 1951
• Natural Gas: The Search Goes On. By Bryan Hodgson. Photos by Lowell Georgia. 632-651, Nov. 1978
• Oman: Guardian of the Gulf. By Thomas J. Abercrombie. Photos by the author and Lynn Abercrombie. 344-377, Sept. 1981
• The Pipeline: Alaska's Troubled Colossus. By Bryan Hodgson. Photos by Steve Raymer. Included: Diagram, anatomy of the pipeline; map showing potential and producing oil and gas areas. 684-717, Nov. 1976
• Turnaround Time in West Virginia. By Elizabeth A. Moize. Photos by Jodi Cobb. 755-785, June 1976

NATURAL HISTORY:
• In the Wake of Darwin's *Beagle.* By Alan Villiers. Photos by James L. Stanfield. 449-495, Oct. 1969
◆ *Our Continent: A Natural History of North America.* Announced. 572-574, Oct. 1976
• *See also* Nature Study; *and* Biology; Geology; Marine Biology; Paleontology; Plants

NATURAL RESOURCES:
▲ *America's Federal Lands; The United States,* double-sided supplement. Included: Managing Our Natural Heritage; Natural Resources Public and Private. Sept. 1982
• This Land of Ours–How Are We Using It? By Peter T. White. Photos by Emory Kristof. 20-67, July 1976
• *See also* Energy Sources; Forest Products; Minerals and Metals; Rain Forests; Water Resources

A **NATURALIST** in Penguin Land. By Niall Rankin. 93-116, Jan. 1955

NATURE Carves Fantasies in Bryce Canyon (Utah). By William Belknap, Jr. 490-511, Oct. 1958

NATURE PROTECTION AND WILDLIFE MANAGEMENT SERVICE: Study Grant:
• Orangutans. 449, Oct. 1975; 835, June 1980

NATURE STUDY:
• Buck Island–Underwater Jewel. By Jerry and Idaz Greenberg. 677-683, May 1971

• Businessman in the Bush. By Frederick Kent Truslow. 634-675, May 1970
◆ *A Day in the Woods*. Announced. 724-726, Nov. 1975
• The Fragile Beauty All About Us. Photos by Harry S. C. Yen. 785-795, Dec. 1970
• Frost, Nature's Icing. By Robert F. Sisson. 398-405, Mar. 1976
• In the Gardens of Olympus. By Paul A. Zahl. 85-123, July 1955
• In the Wilds of a City Parlor. By Paul A. Zahl. 645-672, Nov. 1954
• In Touch With Nature. Text by Elizabeth A. Moize. Photos by Steve Raymer. 537-543, Apr. 1974
• Life Around a Lily Pad. Photos by Bianca Lavies. Text by Charles R. Miller. 131-142, Jan. 1980
• Life on a Rock Ledge. By William H. Amos. 558-566, Oct. 1980
• The Living Sand. By William H. Amos. 820-833, June 1965
• Nature's Year in Pleasant Valley. By Paul A. Zahl. 488-525, Apr. 1968
• Photographing Northern Wild Flowers. By Virginia L. Wells. 809-823, June 1956
• Snowflakes to Keep. By Robert F. Sisson. 104-111, Jan. 1970
• Teeming Life of a Pond. By William H. Amos. 274-298, Aug. 1970
• The World of My Apple Tree. By Robert F. Sisson. 836-847, June 1972
• *See also* the natural sciences; *and* listings under Animals

NATURE'S Alert Eyes. By Constance P. Warner. 558-569, Apr. 1959

NATURE'S Aquatic Engineers, Beavers. By Des and Jen Bartlett. 716-732, May 1974

NATURE'S Clown, the Penguin. By David Hellyer and Malcolm Davis. 405-428, Sept. 1952

NATURE'S Dwindling Treasures: Tropical Rain Forests. By Peter T. White. Photos by James P. Blair. Paintings by Barron Storey. 2-47, Jan. 1983

NATURE'S Gifts to Medicine. By Lonnelle Aikman. Paintings by Lloyd K. Townsend and Don Crowley. 420-440, Sept. 1974

NATURE'S Kingdom on a Rock Ledge. By William H. Amos. 558-566, Oct. 1980

NATURE'S Living, Jumping Jewels. By Paul A. Zahl. 130-146, July 1973

NATURE'S Night Lights: Probing the Secrets of Bioluminescence. By Paul A. Zahl. 45-69, July 1971

NATURE'S Tank, the Turtle. By Doris M. Cochran. Paintings by Walter A. Weber. 665-684, May 1952

NATURE'S Toy Train, the Railroad Worm. By Darwin L. Tiemann. Photos by Robert F. Sisson. NGS research grant. 56-67, July 1970

NATURE'S "Whirling" Water Purifiers. By John Walsh. 287-292, Feb. 1979

NATURE'S Year in Pleasant Valley. By Paul A. Zahl. 488-525, Apr. 1968

NAURU, the World's Richest Nation. By Mike Holmes. 344-353, Sept. 1976

NAUTICAL Norfolk Turns to Azaleas. By William H. Nicholas. Photos by B. Anthony Stewart. 606-614, May 1947

NAUTILUS (Nuclear-powered Submarine):
• The Arctic as a Sea Route of the Future. By William R. Anderson. 21-24, Jan. 1959
• Submarine Through the North Pole. By William G. Lalor, Jr. Photos by John J. Krawczyk. 1-20, Jan. 1959

NAUTILUS, Chambered:
• The Chambered Nautilus, Exquisite Living Fossil. Photos by Douglas Faulkner. 38-41, Jan. 1976
• Shells Take You Over World Horizons. By Rutherford Platt. 33-84, July 1949

NAVAJO NATIONAL MONUMENT, Arizona:
• Navajo Ranger Interprets–Our People, Our Past. By Albert Laughter. 81-85, July 1979

NAVAJOS (Indians):
• Better Days for the Navajos. By Jack Breed. Photos by Charles W. Herbert. 809-847, Dec. 1958
• Desert River (San Juan) Through Navajo Land. By Alfred M. Bailey. Photos by author and Fred G. Brandenburg. 149-172, Aug. 1947
• Inside the Sacred Hopi Homeland. By Jake Page. Photos by Susanne Page. Included: Hopi-Navajo land dispute. 607-629, Nov. 1982
• Navajo Ranger Interprets–Our People, Our Past. By Albert Laughter. 81-85, July 1979
• The Navajos. By Ralph Looney. Photos by Bruce Dale. 740-781, Dec. 1972
▲ *The Southwest,* The Making of America series. Included: Arizona, New Mexico, and parts of California, Colorado, Texas, Utah; and in Mexico: Baja California Norte, Chihuahua, Sonora. On reverse: 12,000 Years of History; Spanish Conquest; Anglo-American Entry and Occupancy. Nov. 1982

NAVAL AIR TECHNICAL TRAINING UNIT. *See* Parachute Rigger School

NAVAL BASES:
• Crosscurrents Sweep the Indian Ocean. By Bart McDowell. Photos by Steve Raymer. 422-457, Oct. 1981
• Four-ocean Navy in the Nuclear Age. By Thomas W. McKnew. 145-187, Feb. 1965
• Our Navy in the Far East. By Arthur W. Radford. Photos by J. Baylor Roberts. 537-577, Oct. 1953
• *See also* Guantánamo (Cuba); Honolulu, Hawaii, for Pearl Harbor; Key West, Florida; Portsmouth; San Diego, California

NAVIGATION:
• Charting Our Sea and Air Lanes. By Stuart E. Jones. Photos by J. Baylor Roberts. 189-209, Feb. 1957
• Editorials. By Gilbert M. Grosvenor. 731, Dec. 1974; 431, Oct. 1976
• *See also Hokule'a; Mayflower II;* Radar; Sonar; Submarines, Nuclear-powered; *and* Graham, Robin Lee; Henry, Prince, the Navigator; Heyerdahl, Thor; Lewis, David; Schultz, John E.; Severin, Timothy; Vikings

NAVIGATION, Flight:
• Our Air Age Speeds Ahead. By F. Barrows Colton. 249-272, Feb. 1948
• Skyway Below the Clouds. By Carl R. Markwith. Photos by Ernest J. Cottrell. 85-108, July 1949
• *See also* Balloons

NAVIGATION SATELLITES:
• Satellites That Serve Us. By Thomas Y. Canby. Included: A portfolio: Images of Earth. 281-335, Sept. 1983
Spacelab 1: *Columbia*. By Michael E. Long. 301-307

NAVIGATORS. *See* Explorers, Discoverers, and Navigators

NAVSTAR. *See* Global Positioning System

NAVY. *See* U. S. Navy

NAVY HURRICANE WEATHER CENTRAL, Miami, Florida:
• Men Against the Hurricane. By Andrew H. Brown. 537-560, Oct. 1950

NAWANG GOMBU (Sherpa):
• American and Geographic Flags Top Everest. By Melvin M. Payne. Photos by Barry C. Bishop. 157-157C, Aug. 1963
• *See also* American Mount Everest Expedition

NAXOS (Island), Greece:
• The Isles of Greece: Aegean Birthplace of Western Culture. By Melville Bell Grosvenor. Photos by Edwin Stuart Grosvenor and Winfield Parks. 147-193, Aug. 1972

NAYARIT (State), Mexico. *See* Mesa del Nayar

NAZARÉ, Portugal:
• Portugal Is Different. By Clement E. Conger. 583-622, Nov. 1948

NAZARENOS (Penitents):
• Holy Week and the Fair in Sevilla. By Luis Marden. 499-530, Apr. 1951

NAZARETH, Israel:
• The Land of Galilee. By Kenneth MacLeish. Photos by B. Anthony Stewart. 832-865, Dec. 1965
• Where Jesus Walked. By Howard La Fay. Photos by Charles Harbutt. 739-781, Dec. 1967

NAZCA LINES (Figure Tracings):
• Mystery of the Ancient Nazca Lines. By Loren McIntyre. NGS research grant. 716-728, May 1975

NEALE, GUY: Artist:
• The High World of the Rain Forest. By William Beebe. 838-855, June 1958

LOWELL GEORGIA

Nebraska: harnessing the prairie wind

NEAR EAST. *See* Middle East

NEAVE, CHARLES:
Author-Photographer:
• Helping Holland Rebuild Her Land. By Gilbert M. Grosvenor and Charles Neave. 365-413, Sept. 1954

NEBBIA, THOMAS:
• National Geographic Photographers Win Top Magazine Awards. 830-831, June 1959
Photographer:
• African Wildlife: Man's Threatened Legacy. By Allan C. Fisher, Jr. Paintings by Ned Seidler. 147-187, Feb. 1972
• Africa's Gentle Giants (Giraffes). By Bristol Foster. Photos by Bob Campbell and Thomas Nebbia. 402-417, Sept. 1977
• Australia's Pacesetter State, Victoria. By Allan C. Fisher, Jr. 218-253, Feb. 1971
• California, the Golden Magnet: I. The South. By William Graves. 595-639, May 1966
• Canterbury Cathedral. By Kenneth MacLeish. 364-379, Mar. 1976
• Cape Canaveral's 6,000-mile Shooting Gallery. By Allan C. Fisher, Jr. Photos by Luis Marden and Thomas Nebbia. 421-471, Oct. 1959
• Crusader Road to Jerusalem. By Franc Shor. 797-855, Dec. 1963
• Denmark, Field of the Danes. By William Graves. 245-275, Feb. 1974
• The Fabulous State of Texas. By Stanley Walker. Photos by B. Anthony Stewart and Thomas Nebbia. 149-195, Feb. 1961
• French Riviera: Storied Playground on the Azure Coast. By Carleton Mitchell. 798-835, June 1967
• Greenland's "Place by the Icebergs." By Mogens Bloch Poulsen. 849-869, Dec. 1973
• Guantánamo: Keystone in the Caribbean. By Jules B. Billard. Photos by W. E. Garrett and Thomas Nebbia. 420-436, Mar. 1961
• Haiti: Beyond Mountains, More Mountains. By Carolyn Bennett Patterson. 70-97, Jan. 1976
• Hawaii, U.S.A. By Frederick Simpich, Jr. 1-45, July 1960
• In the Crusaders' Footsteps. By Franc Shor. Photos by Thomas Nebbia and James P. Blair. 731-789, June 1962
• Inside the White House. By Lonnelle Aikman. Photos by B. Anthony Stewart and Thomas Nebbia. 3-43, Jan. 1961
• Isles on the Edge of the Sea: Scotland's Outer Hebrides. By Kenneth MacLeish. 676-711, May 1970
• Jamaica Goes It Alone. By James Cerruti. 843-873, Dec. 1967
• Letter From Kunming: Two American Teachers in China. By Elisabeth B. Booz. 793-813, June 1981
• Life in Walled-off West Berlin. By Nathaniel T. Kenney and Volkmar Wentzel. 735-767, Dec. 1961
• Los Angeles, City of the Angels. By Robert de Roos. 451-501, Oct. 1962
• The Magic Worlds of Walt Disney. By Robert de Roos. 159-207, Aug. 1963
• Mexico: "A Very Beautiful Challenge." By Mike Edwards. 612-647, May 1978
• The People of Cades Cove. By William O. Douglas. Photos by Thomas Nebbia and Otis Imboden. 60-95, July 1962
• Philadelphia Houses a Proud Past. By Harold Donaldson Eberlein. 151-191, Aug. 1960
• Porpoises: Our Friends in the Sea. By Robert Leslie Conly. 396-425, Sept. 1966
• Prince Henry, the Explorer Who Stayed Home. By Alan Villiers. 616-656, Nov. 1960
• Problems in Paradise. By Mary and Laurance S. Rockefeller. 782-793, Dec. 1974
• Rhodesia, a House Divided. By Allan C. Fisher, Jr. 641-671, May 1975
• Sea Islands: Adventuring Along the South's Surprising Coast. By James Cerruti. Photos by Thomas Nebbia and James L. Amos. 366-393, Mar. 1971
• Seattle Fair Looks to the 21st Century. By Carolyn Bennett Patterson. 402-427, Sept. 1962
• Sweden, Quiet Workshop for the World. By Andrew H. Brown. Photos by Winfield Parks and Thomas Nebbia. 451-491, Apr. 1963
• The Top End of Down Under. By Kenneth MacLeish. 145-174, Feb. 1973
• The Two Acapulcos. By James Cerruti. 848-878, Dec. 1964
• Wales, Land of Bards. By Alan Villiers. 727-769, June 1965
• Washington: The City Freedom Built. By William Graves. Photos by Bruce Dale and Thomas Nebbia. 735-781, Dec. 1964

NEBRASKA:
• Ancient Ashfall Creates a Pompeii of Prehistoric Animals. By Michael R. Voorhies. Photos by Annie Griffiths. Paintings by Jay Matternes. Contents: Site of a ten-million-year-old ashfall near Orchard, Nebraska. NGS research grant. 66-75, Jan. 1981
• The Country of Willa Cather. By William Howarth. Photos by Farrell Grehan. 71-93, July 1982
• Following the Trail of Lewis and Clark. By Ralph Gray. 707-750, June 1953
• Land of Long Sunsets: Nebraska's Sand Hills. By John Madson. Photos by Jodi Cobb. 493-517, Oct. 1978
• Nebraska . . . the Good Life. By Robert Paul Jordan. Photos by Lowell Georgia. 378-407, Mar. 1974

NECK RINGS:
• Anatomy of a Burmese Beauty Secret. By John M. Keshishian. 798-801, June 1979

The **NECTAR** Connection. By Paul W. Ewald. Photos by Robert A. Tyrrell. 223-227, Feb. 1982

NEEDHAM, JAMES G.: Author:
• Dragonflies–Rainbows on the Wing. 215-229, Aug. 1951

NEEDLEWORK. *See* Bayeux Tapestry; Embroidery

NEFERTITI, Queen (Egypt):
• Computer Helps Scholars Re-create an Egyptian Temple. By Ray Winfield Smith. Photos by Emory Kristof. NGS research grant. 634-655, Nov. 1970

NEGRITOS (People):
• The Last Andaman Islanders. By Raghubir Singh. 66-91, July 1975

NELLIS AIR FORCE BASE, Nevada. *See* Nevada Wild Horse Range

NELSON, DANIEL A.: Author:
• Ghost Ships of the War of 1812: *Hamilton* and *Scourge*. Photos by Emory Kristof. Paintings by Richard Schlecht. 289-313, Mar. 1983

NELSON, EDWARD W.:
• Where Magic Ruled: Art of the Bering Sea. By William W. Fitzhugh and Susan A. Kaplan. Photos by Sisse Brimberg. Contents: The Nelson Collection of Eskimo artifacts. 198-205, Feb. 1983

NELSON, HORATIO, Viscount:
• The British Way. By Sir Evelyn Wrench. 421-541, Apr. 1949
• Portsmouth, Britannia's Sally Port. By Thomas Garner James. Photos by B. Anthony Stewart. 513-544, Apr. 1952

NEMRUD DAGH (Mountain), Turkey:
• Throne Above the Euphrates. By Theresa Goell. 390-405, Mar. 1961

NENE:
• Saving the Nene, World's Rarest Goose. By S. Dillon Ripley. Photos by Jerry Chong. 745-754, Nov. 1965

NENETS (People):
• People of the Long Spring. By Yuri Rytkheu. Photos by Dean Conger. 206-223, Feb. 1983

NEPAL:
• Afoot in Roadless Nepal (Geological Survey). By Toni Hagen. 361-405, Mar. 1960
• At My Limit–I Climbed Everest Alone. By Reinhold Messner. Photos by the author and Nena Holguín. 552-566, Oct. 1981
• Coronation in Katmandu. By E. Thomas Gilliard. Photos by Marc Riboud. 139-152, July 1957
• Karnali, Roadless World of Western Nepal. By Lila M. and Barry C. Bishop. NGS research grant. 656-689, Nov. 1971
• Kathmandu's Remarkable Newars. By John Scofield. 269-285, Feb. 1979
• Mustang, Remote Realm in Nepal. By Michel Peissel. 579-604, Oct. 1965
• Park at the Top of the World: Mount Everest National Park. By Rick Ridgeway. Photos by Nicholas DeVore III. 704-725, June 1982
Preserving a Mountain Heritage. By Sir Edmund Hillary. 696-703
• Peerless Nepal–A Naturalist's Paradise. By S. Dillon Ripley. Photos by Volkmar Wentzel. NGS research grant. 1-40, Jan. 1950
• Sherpaland, My Shangri-La. By Desmond Doig. 545-577, Oct. 1966
• Temple Monkeys of Nepal. By Jane Teas. NGS research grant. 575-584, Apr. 1980
• Trek to Nepal's Sacred Crystal Mountain. By Joel F. Ziskin. 500-517, Apr. 1977
• Triumph and Tragedy on Annapurna. By Arlene Blum. 295-311, Mar. 1979
On the Summit. By Irene Miller, with Vera Komarkova. 312-313
• We Build a School for Sherpa Children. By Sir Edmund Hillary. 548-551, Oct. 1962
• Wintering on the Roof of the World. By Barry C. Bishop. NGS research grant. 503-547, Oct. 1962
• *See also* Everest, Mount

NEPALESE:
• Gangtok, Cloud-wreathed Himalayan Capital. By John Scofield. 698-713, Nov. 1970

NEPENTHES (Pitcher Plants):
• Malaysia's Giant Flowers and Insect-trapping Plants. By Paul A. Zahl. 680-701, May 1964

NEPTUNE (Planet):
• Voyage to the Planets. By Kenneth F. Weaver. Paintings by Ludek Pesek. 147-193, Aug. 1970

NESHOBA COUNTY FAIR, Mississippi:
• Mississippi's Grand Reunion at the Neshoba County Fair. By Carolyn Bennett Patterson. Photos by C. C. Lockwood. 854-866, June 1980

NESS, Loch, Scotland:
• Loch Ness: The Lake and the Legend. By William S. Ellis. Photos by Emory Kristof and David Doubilet. 759-779, June 1977

NETHERLANDS:
• "Around the World in Eighty Days." By Newman Bumstead. Included: Amsterdam, Edam, The Hague, Hook of Holland, Leiden, Noordwijk ann Zee, Rotterdam, Zuider Zee. 705-750, Dec. 1951
▲ *France, Belgium, and the Netherlands,* Atlas series supplement. June 1960
• Helping Holland Rebuild Her Land. By Gilbert M. Grosvenor and Charles Neave. 365-413, Sept. 1954
■ Holland Against the Sea. 588A-588B, Apr. 1970
• Inside Europe Aboard *Yankee*. By Irving and Electa Johnson. Photos by Joseph J. Scherschel. 157-195, Aug. 1964
• Mid-century Holland Builds Her Future. By Sydney Clark. 747-778, Dec. 1950
• The Netherlands: Nation at War With the Sea. By Alan Villiers. Photos by Adam Woolfitt. 530-571, Apr. 1968
• Tulips: Holland's Beautiful Business. By Elizabeth A. Moize. Photos by Farrell Grehan. 712-728, May 1978
• Under Canvas in the Atomic Age. By Alan Villiers. Included: Amsterdam, Hilversum, Marken Island, Spakenburg, Volendam. 49-84, July 1955
• *See also* Amsterdam; Rotterdam

NETHERLANDS ANTILLES:
• A Fresh Breeze Stirs the Leewards. By Carleton Mitchell. Photos by Winfield Parks. 488-537, Oct. 1966
• The Netherlands Antilles: Holland in the Caribbean. By James Cerruti. Photos by Emory Kristof. 115-146, Jan. 1970

NETHERLANDS NEW GUINEA (now Irian Jaya, Indonesia):
• The Asmat of New Guinea, Headhunters in Today's World. By Malcolm S. Kirk. 376-409, Mar. 1972
• Netherlands New Guinea. By John Scofield. 584-603, May 1962
• New Guinea. The Editor. 583, May 1962
• New Guinea Festival of Faces. By Malcolm S. Kirk. 148-156, July 1969
• New Guinea to Bali in *Yankee*. By Irving and Electa Johnson. 767-815, Dec. 1959.
• Strange Courtship of Birds of Paradise. By S. Dillon Ripley. Paintings by Walter A. Weber. 247-278, Feb. 1950
• *Yankee* Roams the Orient. By Irving and Electa Johnson. 327-370, Mar. 1951

NETTIS, JOSEPH:
Author-Photographer:
• Europe Via the Hostel Route. 124-154, July 1955

NETTUNO, Italy:
• Here Rest in Honored Glory . . . The United States Dedicates Six New Battle Monuments in Europe to Americans Who Gave Their Lives During World War II. By Howell Walker. Included: Sicily–Rome American Cemetery and Memorial. 739-768, June 1957

NEVADA:
▲ *Close-up: U.S.A., California and Nevada,* supplement. Text on reverse. June 1974
• Lonely Sentinels of the American West: Basque Sheepherders. By Robert Laxalt. Photos by William Belknap, Jr. 870-888, June 1966
• A Map Maker Looks at the United States. By Newman Bumstead. Included: Carson City; Hoover Dam; Las Vegas; Mead, Lake; Reno; Tahoe, Lake. 705-748, June 1951
• Nevada Learns to Live with the Atom. By Samuel W. Matthews. 839-850, June 1953
• Nevada's Mountain of Invisible Gold. By Samuel W. Matthews. Photos by David F. Cupp. 668-679, May 1968
• The Other Nevada. By Robert Laxalt. Photos by J. Bruce Baumann. 733-761, June 1974
• Silver: A Mineral of Excellent Nature. By Allen A. Boraiko. Photos by Fred Ward. 280-313, Sept. 1981

M N

• The West Through Boston Eyes. By Stewart Anderson. 733-776, June 1949
• *See also* Nevada Wild Horse Range; Stead Air Force Base

NEVADA WILD HORSE RANGE, Nevada:
• On the Track of the West's Wild Horses. By Hope Ryden. Photos by author and Dick Durrance II. 94-109, Jan. 1971

NEVIS (Island), West Indies:
• A Fresh Breeze Stirs the Leewards. By Carleton Mitchell. Photos by Winfield Parks. 488-537, Oct. 1966

NEW BEDFORD, Massachusetts:
• New England's "Little Portugal." By O. Louis Mazzatenta. 90-109, Jan. 1975

The **NEW** Biology. 355-407, Sept. 1976
I. The Awesome Worlds Within a Cell. By Rick Gore. Photos by Bruce Dale. Paintings by Davis Meltzer. 355-395; II. The Cancer Puzzle. By Robert F. Weaver. 396-399; III. Seven Giants Who Led the Way. Paintings by Ned Seidler. Text by Rick Gore. 401-407

A **NEW** Bird Immigrant Arrives. By Roger Tory Peterson. 281-292, Aug. 1954

A **NEW** *Bounty* Sails to Tahiti. By Luis Marden. 435-459, Apr. 1962

NEW BRITAIN (Island), Bismarck Archipelago:
• Blowgun Hunters of the South Pacific. By Jane C. Goodale. Photos by Ann Chowning. 793-817, June 1966
• Exploring New Britain's Land of Fire. By E. Thomas Gilliard. NGS research grant. 260-292, Feb. 1961

NEW BRUNSWICK (Province), Canada:
• The Loyalists. By Kent Britt. Photos by Ted Spiegel. 510-539, Apr. 1975
• Madawaska: Down East With a French Accent. By Perry Garfinkel. Photos by Cary Wolinsky. 380-409, Sept. 1980
• *See also* Fundy, Bay of

NEW CALEDONIA (Island), Pacific Ocean:
• Problems in Paradise. By Mary and Laurance S. Rockefeller. Photos by Thomas Nebbia. 782-793, Dec. 1974
• Shells Take You Over World Horizons. By Rutherford Platt. 33-84, July 1949

NEW Clues to an Old Mystery (Virginia's Wolstenholme Towne). By Ivor Noël Hume. Photos by Ira Block. Paintings by Richard Schlecht. 53-77, Jan. 1982

NEW Course for Portugal. By William Graves. Photos by Bruno Barbey. 804-831, Dec. 1980

NEW Day for Alaska's Pribilof Islanders. By Susan Hackley Johnson. Photos by Tim Thompson. 536-552, Oct. 1982

A **NEW** Day for Ireland. By John J. Putman. Photos by Cotton Coulson. 442-469, Apr. 1981

NEW DELHI, India:
• Delhi, Capital of a New Dominion. By Phillips Talbot. 597-630, Nov. 1947
• India in Crisis. By John Scofield. 599-661, May 1963
• When the President Goes Abroad (Eisenhower Tour). By Gilbert M. Grosvenor. 588-649, May 1960

NEW Discoveries Among Africa's Chimpanzees. By Baroness Jane van Lawick-Goodall. Photos by Baron Hugo van Lawick. NGS research grant. 802-831, Dec. 1965

NEW Discoveries on the Mid-Atlantic Ridge. By Maurice Ewing. Photos by Robert F. Sisson. NGS research grant. 611-640, Nov. 1949

NEW Energy from an Old Source: the Wind. By Roger Hamilton. Photos by Emory Kristof. 812-829, Dec. 1975

NEW Energy Frontier: Powder River Basin. By Bill Richards. Photos by Louie Psihoyos. 96-113, *Special Report on Energy* (Feb. 1981)

NEW ENGLAND:
• Captain Smith of Jamestown. By Bradford Smith. Included: Exploration and mapping of Maine and Massachusetts. 581-620, May 1957
• Captain Smith's New England . . . and the Pilgrims' Cape Cod.–George Washington's Travels, Traced on the Arrowsmith Map. 765, 768, 769, June 1953
▲ *Close-up: U.S.A., Western New England,* supplement. Text on reverse. July 1975
• Founders of New England. By Sir Evelyn Wrench. Photos by B. Anthony Stewart. 803-838, June 1953
• The Incredible Potato. By Robert E. Rhoades. Photos by Martin Rogers. Note: Potatoes were first introduced in New England in 1719 by Scotch-Irish immigrants. 668-694, May 1982
• The Merrimack: River of Industry and Romance. By Albert W. Atwood. Photos by B. Anthony Stewart. 106-140, Jan. 1951
• Mountains Top Off New England. By F. Barrows Colton. Photos by Robert F. Sisson. 563-602, May 1951
▲ *New England,* supplement. June 1955
• New England, a Modern Pilgrim's Pride. By Beverley M. Bowie. 733-796, June 1955
• New England's "Little Portugal." By O. Louis Mazzatenta. 90-109, Jan. 1975
• The Old Boston Post Roads. By Donald Barr Chidsey. 189-205, Aug. 1962
• The Post Road Today. Photos by B. Anthony Stewart. 206-233, Aug. 1962
• Robert Frost and New England. By Archibald MacLeish. 438-467, Apr. 1976
Look of a Land Beloved. Photos by Dewitt Jones. 444-467
• Shells Take You Over World Horizons. By Rutherford Platt. 33-84, July 1949
• Skiing in the United States. By Kathleen Revis. 216-254, Feb. 1959
• Skyline Trail from Maine to Georgia. By Andrew H. Brown. Photos by Robert F. Sisson. 219-251, Aug. 1949
• Thoreau, a Different Man. By William Howarth. Photos by Farrell Grehan. 349-387, Mar. 1981
• Windjamming Around New England. By Tom Horgan. Photos by Robert F. Sisson. 141-169, Aug. 1950
• Yesterday Lingers Along the Connecticut. By Charles McCarry. Photos by David L. Arnold. Included: Connecticut; Massachusetts; New Hampshire; Vermont. 334-369, Sept. 1972
• *See also* Connecticut; Maine; Massachusetts; New Hampshire; Rhode Island; Vermont

NEW Era in the Loneliest Continent. By David M. Tyree. Photos by Albert Moldvay. 260-296, Feb. 1963

NEW Era on the Great Lakes. By Nathaniel T. Kenney. 439-490, Apr. 1959

NEW Finds at Aphrodisias. By Kenan T. Erim. Photos by David Brill. 527-551, Oct. 1981

NEW Finds in the Great Temple. By Eduardo Matos Moctezuma. Photos by David Hiser. 767-775, Dec. 1980

NEW Florida Resident, the Walking Catfish. By Clarence P. Idyll. Photos by Robert F. Sisson. 847-851, June 1969

NEW GLARUS, Wisconsin:
• Deep in the Heart of "Swissconsin." By William H. Nicholas. Photos by J. Baylor Roberts. 781-800, June 1947

NEW Grandeur for Flowering Washington. By Joseph Judge. Photos by James P. Blair. 500-539, Apr. 1967

NEW GUINEA:
• New Guinea. The Editor. 583, May 1962
• New Guinea to Bali in *Yankee*. By Irving and Electa Johnson. 767-815, Dec. 1959
• *Yankee* Roams the Orient. By Irving and Electa Johnson. 327-370, Mar. 1951
Irian Jaya (Indonesian New Guinea):
• The Asmat of New Guinea, Headhunters in Today's World. By Malcolm S. Kirk. 376-409, Mar. 1972
• Netherlands New Guinea. By John Scofield. 584-603, May 1962
• New Guinea. The Editor. 583, May 1962
• New Guinea Festival of Faces. By Malcolm S. Kirk. 148-156, July 1969
• New Guinea to Bali in *Yankee*. By Irving and Electa Johnson. 767-815, Dec. 1959

• Strange Courtship of Birds of Paradise. By S. Dillon Ripley. Paintings by Walter A. Weber. 247-278, Feb. 1950
• Tropical Rain Forests. 2-65, Jan. 1983
Nature's Dwindling Treasures. By Peter T. White. Photos by James P. Blair. Paintings by Barron Storey. 2-47; Teeming Life of a Rain Forest. By Carol and David Hughes. 49-65
• *Yankee* Roams the Orient. By Irving and Electa Johnson. 327-370, Mar. 1951

Papua New Guinea:
• Australian New Guinea. By John Scofield. 604-637, May 1962
• Change Ripples New Guinea's Sepik River. By Malcolm S. Kirk. 354-381, Sept. 1973
• Fertility Rites and Sorcery in a New Guinea Village (Gimi People). By Gillian Gillison. Photos by David Gillison. 124-146, July 1977
• Journey Into Stone Age New Guinea. By Malcolm S. Kirk. 568-592, Apr. 1969
• Living Theater in New Guinea's Highlands. By Gillian Gillison. Photos by David Gillison. 147-169, Aug. 1983
• New Guinea. The Editor. 583, May 1962
• New Guinea Festival of Faces. By Malcolm S. Kirk. 148-156, July 1969
• New Guinea to Bali in *Yankee*. By Irving and Electa Johnson. 767-815, Dec. 1959
• New Guinea's Paradise of Birds. By E. Thomas Gilliard. 661-688, Nov. 1951
• New Guinea's Rare Birds and Stone Age Men. By E. Thomas Gilliard. NGS research grant. 421-488, Apr. 1953
• Off the Beaten Track of Empire (Prince Philip's Tour). By Beverley M. Bowie. Photos by Michael Parker. 584-626, Nov. 1957
• Papua New Guinea. 143-171, Aug. 1982
I. Nation in the Making. By Robert J. Gordon. Photos by David Austen. 143-149; II. Journey Through Time. By François Leydet. Photos by David Austen. 150-171.
• Sheep Airlift in New Guinea. Photos by Ned Blood. Contents: The Hallstrom Trust's Nondugl Sheep Station in Australian New Guinea. 831-844, Dec. 1949
• To the Land of the Head-hunters. By E. Thomas Gilliard. NGS research grant. 437-486, Oct. 1955
• Tropical Rain Forests. 2-65, Jan. 1983
Nature's Dwindling Treasures. By Peter T. White. Photos by James P. Blair. Paintings by Barron Storey. 2-47; Teeming Life of a Rain Forest. By Carol and David Hughes. 49-65
• *Yankee* Roams the Orient. By Irving and Electa Johnson. 327-370, Mar. 1951

NEW HAMPSHIRE:
• Contrary New Hampshire. By Robert Booth. Photos by Sandy Felsenthal. 770-799, Dec. 1982

DAVID GILLISON
New Guinea: art imitates life

• Down East Cruise. By Tom Horgan. Photos by Luis Marden. Included: Gosport Harbor; Portsmouth. 369, Sept. 1952
• The Friendly Huts of the White Mountains. By William O. Douglas. Photos by Kathleen Revis. 205-239, Aug. 1961
• Lake Sunapee's Golden Trout. Photos by Robert F. Sisson. 529-536, Oct. 1950
• The Merrimack: River of Industry and Romance. By Albert W. Atwood. Photos by B. Anthony Stewart. 106-140, Jan. 1951
• Mountains Top Off New England. By F. Barrows Colton. Photos by Robert F. Sisson. 563-602, May 1951
• Robert Frost and New England. By Archibald MacLeish. 438-467, Apr. 1976
Look of a Land Beloved. Photos by Dewitt Jones. 444-467
• Skiing in the United States. By Kathleen Revis. 216-254, Feb. 1959
• Skyline Trail from Maine to Georgia. By Andrew H. Brown. Photos by Robert F. Sisson. 219-251, Aug. 1949
• Yesterday Lingers Along the Connecticut. By Charles McCarry. Photos by David L. Arnold. 334-369, Sept. 1972
• *See also* Maple Sugar and Syrup

NEW Harvests for Forgotten Crops. By Noel D. Vietmeyer. Photos by Burgess Blevins. Paintings by Paul M. Breeden. 702-712, May 1981

NEW HEBRIDES (Islands), Pacific Ocean:
• *Yankee* Roams the Orient. By Irving and Electa Johnson. 327-370, Mar. 1951
• *See also* Malekula; Pentecost Island; Tanna

NEW JERSEY:
• Can We Save Our Salt Marshes? By Stephen W. Hitchcock. Photos by William R. Curtsinger. 729-765, June 1972
▲ *Close-up: U.S.A., New York, New Jersey, and Pennsylvania,* supplement. Text on reverse. Jan. 1978
• Here's New York Harbor. By Stuart E. Jones. Photos by Robert F. Sisson and David S. Boyer. 773-813, Dec. 1954
• I'm From New Jersey. By John T. Cunningham. Photos by Volkmar Wentzel. 1-45, Jan. 1960
• New Jersey: A State of Surprise. By Jim Hartz. Photos by Bob Krist and Michael S. Yamashita. 568-599, Nov. 1981
• Our Changing Atlantic Coastline. By Nathaniel T. Kenney. Photos by B. Anthony Stewart. Included: Atlantic City; Brigantine; Harvey Cedars, Long Beach Island. 860-887, Dec. 1962
• Shad in the Shadow of Skyscrapers. By Dudley B. Martin. Photos by Luis Marden. 359-376, Mar. 1947
• Today on the Delaware, Penn's Glorious River. By Albert W. Atwood. Photos by Robert F. Sisson. 1-40, July 1952

MN

PAINTING BY ROY ANDERSEN

New Look at Dinosaurs: *Stegosaurus* beats heat with alternately placed back fins

• *See also* Bell Telephone Laboratories; Gateway National Recreation Area; Morristown; Parachute Rigger School, Lakehurst; Pine Barrens; *and* Perfume, for Delawanna

NEW Knowledge of Earth From Astronauts' Photographs. By Paul D. Lowman, Jr. 645-671, Nov. 1966

NEW Life for India's Villagers. By Anthony and Georgette Dickey Chapelle. 572-588, Apr. 1956

NEW Life for the "Loneliest Isle" (Tristan da Cunha). By Lewis Lewis. 105-116, Jan. 1950

NEW Life for the Old Post Office. By Wolf Von Eckardt. Photos by Volkmar Wentzel. 407-416, Sept. 1983

NEW Life for the Troubled Suez Canal. By William Graves. Photos by Jonathan Blair. 792-817, June 1975

A **NEW** Light Dawns on Bird Photography. By Arthur A. Allen. 774-790, June 1948

NEW Light on a Forgotten Past. By Wilhelm G. Solheim II. 330-339, Mar. 1971

NEW Light on an Old Riddle: Stonehenge. By Harold E. Edgerton. Paintings by Brian Hope-Taylor. 846-866, June 1960

NEW Light on the Changing Face of Mars. By E. C. Slipher. NGS research grant. 427-436, Sept. 1955

NEW Light on the Singing Whales. Introduction by Roger Payne. Photos by Flip Nicklin. NGS research grant. 463-477, Apr. 1982

NEW LONDON, Connecticut:
• Our Navy's Long Submarine Arm. By Allan C. Fisher, Jr. 613-636, Nov. 1952

A **NEW** Look at Dinosaurs. By John H. Ostrom. Paintings by Roy Andersen. 152-185, Aug. 1978

A **NEW** Look at Everest. By Dag Hammarskjöld. 87-93, Jan. 1961

A **NEW** Look at Kenya's "Treetops." By Quentin Keynes. 536-541, Oct. 1956

A **NEW** Look at Medieval Europe. By Kenneth M. Setton. Paintings by Andre Durenceau and Birney Lettick. 799-859, Dec. 1962

NEW Look at the Shuttle. By Cliff Tarpy. 650-653, Nov. 1982

A **NEW** Marine Park Is Born. By Soames Summerhays. Photos by Ron and Valerie Taylor. 630-635, May 1981

NEW MEXICO:
• Adobe New Mexico. By Mason Sutherland. Photos by Justin Locke. 783-830, Dec. 1949
• Along the Great Divide. By Mike Edwards. Photos by Nicholas DeVore III. 483-515, Oct. 1979
• The Anasazi–Riddles in the Ruins. By Thomas Y. Canby. Photos by Dewitt Jones and David Brill. Paintings by Roy Andersen. 554-592, Nov. 1982
• The Country of Willa Cather. By William Howarth. Photos by Farrell Grehan. 71-93, July 1982
• Hunting Uranium Around the World. By Robert D. Nininger. Photos by Volkmar Wentzel. 533-558, Oct. 1954
• The Long, Lonely Leap. By Joseph W. Kittinger, Jr. Photos by Volkmar Wentzel. 854-873, Dec. 1960
• A Map Maker Looks at the United States. By Newman Bumstead. Included: Acoma, San Ildefonso, Santa Fe. 705-748, June 1951
• The Mexican Americans: A People on the Move. By Griffin Smith, Jr. Photos by Stephanie Maze. 780-809, June 1980
• New Mexico: The Golden Land. By Robert Laxalt. Photos by Adam Woolfitt. 299-345, Sept. 1970
• New Mexico's Great White Sands. By William Belknap, Jr. 113-137, July 1957
• New Mexico's Mountains of Mystery. By Robert Laxalt. Photos by Craig Aurness. 416-436, Sept. 1978
• Pueblo Pottery–2,000 Years of Artistry. By David L. Arnold. 593-605, Nov. 1982
• Quicksilver and Slow Death. By John J. Putman. Photos by Robert W. Madden. 507-527, Oct. 1972
• Rockets Explore the Air Above Us. By Newman Bumstead. Included: Holloman Air Development Center. 562-580, Apr. 1957
• Teamwork Helps the Whooping Crane. By Roderick C. Drewien, with Ernie Kuyt. 680-693, May 1979
• 20th-century Indians Preserve Customs of the Cliff Dwellers. Photos by William Belknap, Jr. Included: Acoma, Jemez, Santa Ana, Santo Domingo, and Zia pueblos. 196-211, Feb. 1964
• *See also* Carlsbad Caverns; Chaco Canyon; El Morro; Four Corners Country; Los Alamos Scientific Laboratory; Navajos; Philmont Scout Ranch; Santa Fe; White Sands Proving Ground

NEW Microscopes Reveal an Invisible World. By Kenneth F. Weaver. 274-290, Feb. 1977

NEW MILLS, Braintree, England:
• Silkworms in England Spin for the Queen. By John E. H. Nolan. 689-704, May 1953

NEW Miracles of the Telephone Age. By Robert Leslie Conly. 87-120, July 1954

NEW Mount McKinley Challenge–Trekking Around the Continent's Highest Peak. By Ned Gillette. 66-79, July 1979

NEW National Park Proposed: The Spectacular North Cascades. By Nathaniel T. Kenney. Photos by James P. Blair. 642-667, May 1968

NEW ORLEANS, Louisiana:
• Louisiana Trades with the World. By Frederick Simpich. Photos by J. Baylor Roberts. 705-738, Dec. 1947

• Mardi Gras in New Orleans. By Carolyn Bennett Patterson. Photos by Robert F. Sisson and John E. Fletcher. 726-732, Nov. 1960
• New Orleans: Jambalaya on the Levee. By Harnett T. Kane. Photos by Justin Locke. 143-184, Feb. 1953
• New Orleans and Her River. By Joseph Judge. Photos by James L. Stanfield. 151-187, Feb. 1971

NEW PROVIDENCE (Island), Bahamas. *See* Nassau

A **NEW** Riviera: Mexico's West Coast. By Nathaniel T. Kenney. Photos by Charles O'Rear. 670-699, Nov. 1973

NEW Rush to Golden California. By George W. Long. 723-802, June 1954

NEW St. Lawrence Seaway Opens the Great Lakes to the World. By Andrew H. Brown. 299-339, Mar. 1959

NEW SALEM, Illinois:
• Vacation Tour Through Lincoln Land. By Ralph Gray. 141-184, Feb. 1952

NEW Scarlet Bird in Florida Skies. By Paul A. Zahl. 874-882, Dec. 1967

NEW SOUTH WALES (State), Australia:
• New South Wales, the State That Cradled Australia. By Howell Walker. Photos by David Moore. 591-635, Nov. 1967
• *See also* Sydney

NEW Stars for Old Glory. By Lonnelle Aikman. 86-121, July 1959

NEW Tools for Undersea Archeology. By George F. Bass. Photos by Charles R. Nicklin, Jr. NGS research grant. 403-423, Sept. 1968

The **NEW** Toronto. By Ethel A. Starbird. Photos by Robert W. Madden. 190-215, Aug. 1975

NEW Tricks Outwit Our Insect Enemies. By Hal Higdon. Photos by Robert F. Sisson and Emory Kristof. 380-399, Sept. 1972

A **NEW** Volcano Bursts from the Atlantic. By John Scofield. Photos by Robert F. Sisson. 735-757, June 1958

NEW WORLD. *See* The Americas; Explorers, Discoverers, and Navigators; Pre-Columbian Civilization; Pre-Hispanic Culture; Vinland

NEW World of the Ocean. By Samuel W. Matthews. 792-832, Dec. 1981

NEW YEAR CELEBRATIONS:
• Focusing on the Tournament of Roses. By B. Anthony Stewart and J. Baylor Roberts. 805-816, June 1954
• Kunming Pilgrimage. 213-226, Feb. 1950
• Kyoto Says Happy New Year. Photos by George F. Mobley. 852-859, June 1976
• Mustang, Remote Realm in Nepal. By Michel Peissel. 579-604, Oct. 1965
• My Life in Forbidden Lhasa. By Heinrich Harrer. 1-48, July 1955

NEW YORK:
▲ *Close-up: U.S.A., New York, New Jersey, and Pennsylvania,* supplement. Text on reverse. Jan. 1978
• Down the Susquehanna by Canoe. By Ralph Gray. Photos by Walter Meayers Edwards. 73-120, July 1950
• Drums to Dynamos on the Mohawk. By Frederick G. Vosburgh. Photos by B. Anthony Stewart. 67-110, July 1947
• Duck Hunting with a Color Camera. By Arthur A. Allen. 514-539, Oct. 1951
• From Sword to Scythe in Champlain Country. By Ethel A. Starbird. Photos by B. Anthony Stewart and Emory Kristof. 153-201, Aug. 1967
• Henry Hudson's River. By Willard Price. Photos by Wayne Miller. 364-403, Mar. 1962
• The Hudson: "That River's Alive." By Alice J. Hall. Photos by Ted Spiegel. 62-89, Jan. 1978
• The Mighty Hudson. By Albert W. Atwood. Photos by B. Anthony Stewart. 1-36, July 1948
• New York State's New Main Street (Thruway). By Matt C. McDade. 567-618, Nov. 1956
• New York's Land of Dreamers and Doers (Finger Lakes Region). By Ethel A. Starbird. Photos by Nathan Benn. 702-724, May 1977
• Niagara Falls, Servant of Good Neighbors. Photos by Walter Meayers Edwards. 574-587, Apr. 1963
• *Nomad* Sails Long Island Sound. By Thomas Horgan. 295-338, Sept. 1957
• North Through History Aboard *White Mist.* By Melville Bell Grosvenor. Photos by Edwin Stuart Grosvenor. 1-55, July 1970
• Sapsucker Woods, Cornell University's Exciting New Bird Sanctuary. By Arthur A. Allen. 530-551, Apr. 1962
• Shrines of Each Patriot's Devotion. By Frederick G. Vosburgh. 51-82, Jan. 1949
• Skyline Trail from Maine to Georgia. By Andrew H. Brown. Photos by Robert F. Sisson. 219-251, Aug. 1949
• Today on the Delaware, Penn's Glorious River. By Albert W. Atwood. Photos by Robert F. Sisson. 1-40, July 1952
• *See also* Adirondack Mountains; Long Island; New York, New York; Rochester; *and* Old Rhinebeck Aerodrome; Thunder Hill Goat Farm; U. S. Merchant Marine Academy; U. S. Military Academy

NEW YORK, New York:
• A Century Old, the Wonderful Brooklyn Bridge. By John G. Morris. Photos by Donal F. Holway. 565-579, May 1983
• The Fair Reopens (World's Fair, 1964-1965). Photos by James P. Blair. Text by Carolyn Bennett Patterson. 505-529, Apr. 1965
▲ *Greater New York; Tourist Manhattan,* double-sided U. S. Atlas series supplement. July 1964
• Here's New York Harbor. By Stuart E. Jones. Photos by Robert F. Sisson and David S. Boyer. 773-813, Dec. 1954
• Immigrants Still Flock to Liberty's Land. By Albert W. Atwood. 708-724, Nov. 1955
• In the Wilds of a City Parlor. By Paul A. Zahl. 645-672, Nov. 1954
• Manhattan–Images of the City. By John J. Putman. Photos by Jay Maisel. 317-343, Sept. 1981
• The Mohawks Scrape the Sky. By Robert L. Conly. Photos by B. Anthony Stewart. Contents: Brooklyn's steel-working Mohawk Indians. 133-142, July 1952
• New York Again Hails the Horse (National Horse Show). By Walter B. Devereux. 697-720, Nov. 1954
• The Romance of American Furs. By Wanda Burnett. 379-402, Mar. 1948
• Shad in the Shadow of Skyscrapers. By Dudley B. Martin. Photos by Luis Marden. 359-376, Mar. 1947
• Staten Island Ferry, New York's Seagoing Bus. By John T. Cunningham and Jay Johnston. Photos by W. D. Vaughn. 833-843, June 1959
• The World in New York City. By Peter T. White. 52-107, July 1964
• *See also* American Museum of Natural History; Bell Telephone Laboratories; Brooklyn; Central Park; Gateway National Recreation Area; Harlem; New York Aquarium; New York Zoological Park; United Nations; Westminster Kennel Club Dog Show

NEW YORK AQUARIUM, Coney Island, New York:
• Three Whales That Flew. By Carleton Ray. Photos by W. Robert Moore. 346-359, Mar. 1962

NEW YORK STATE BARGE CANAL:
• Drums to Dynamos on the Mohawk. By Frederick G. Vosburgh. Photos by B. Anthony Stewart. 67-110, July 1947

NEW YORK STATE THRUWAY:
• New York State's New Main Street. By Matt C. McDade. 567-618, Nov. 1956

NEW YORK ZOOLOGICAL PARK, New York:
• Biggest Worm Farm Caters to Platypuses. By W. H. Nicholas. 269-280, Feb. 1949
• Flight of the Platypuses. By David Fleay. 512-525, Oct. 1958
• Zoo Animals Go to School. By Marion P. McCrane. Photos by W. E. Garrett. 694-706, Nov. 1956

NEW YORK ZOOLOGICAL SOCIETY:
Animal Studies:
• Elephant Survey: Africa 578, 584, Nov. 1980; Giant Brazilian Otter 132, July 1980; Humpback Whale 2, Jan. 1979; 466, Apr. 1982; James's Flamingo 91, 93, July 1961; Lion 496, Apr. 1969; Mountain Lion 647, Nov. 1969; Orangutan 449, Oct. 1975; 835, June 1980; Patagonian Wildlife 297, Mar. 1976; Right Whale 578, 581, 584, Oct. 1972; 328, 329, Mar. 1976; Snow Leopard 706, Nov. 1971; Weddell Seal 56, Jan. 1966

M N

Field Station, Trinidad:
• Keeping House for Tropical Butterflies. By Jocelyn Crane. Photos by M. Woodbridge Williams. 193-217, Aug. 1957
Vilcabamba Expedition:
• By Parachute Into Peru's Lost World. By G. Brooks Baekeland. Photos by author and Peter R. Gimbel. 268-296, Aug. 1964

NEW ZEALAND:
• Captain Cook: The Man Who Mapped the Pacific. By Alan Villiers. Photos by Gordon W. Gahan. 297-349, Sept. 1971
• Finding an "Extinct" New Zealand Bird. By R. V. Francis Smith. 393-401, Mar. 1952
• First Flight Across the Bottom of the World (Cape Town to Christchurch). By James R. Reedy. Photos by Otis Imboden. 454-464, Mar. 1964
• In the Wake of Darwin's *Beagle*. By Alan Villiers. Photos by James L. Stanfield. 449-495, Oct. 1969
• The Kiwi, New Zealand's Wonder Bird. By Ron J. Anderson. 395-398, Sept. 1955
• New Zealand: Gift of the Sea. By Maurice Shadbolt. Photos by Brian Brake. 465-511, Apr. 1962
• New Zealand, Pocket Wonder World. By Howell Walker. 419-460, Apr. 1952
• New Zealand's Bountiful South Island. By Peter Benchley. Photos by James L. Amos. 93-123, Jan. 1972
• New Zealand's Cook Islands: Paradise in Search of a Future. By Maurice Shadbolt. Photos by William Albert Allard. 203-231, Aug. 1967
• New Zealand's High Country. By Yva Momatiuk and John Eastcott. 246-265, Aug. 1978
• New Zealand's Milford Track: "Walk of a Lifetime." By Carolyn Bennett Patterson. Photos by Robert E. Gilka. 117-129, Jan. 1978
• New Zealand's North Island: The Contented Land. By Charles McCarry. Photos by Bates Littlehales. 190-213, Aug. 1974
• Park at the Top of the World: Mount Everest National Park. By Rick Ridgeway. Photos by Nicholas DeVore III. Included: New Zealand's contribution to the establishment of Sagarmatha National Park, Nepal–funding for five years; construction of buildings; providing advisers; assisting the Nepalese in devising a plan of management. 704-725, June 1982
Preserving a Mountain Heritage. By Sir Edmund Hillary. 696-703
• *See also* Waitomo Caves

NEWARS (People):
• Kathmandu's Remarkable Newars. By John Scofield. 269-285, Feb. 1979

NEWBERT, CHRIS: Photographer:
• In Hawaii's Crystal Sea, A Galaxy of Life Fills the Night. By Kenneth Brower. Photos by William R. Curtsinger and Chris Newbert. 834-847, Dec. 1981

NEWELL, HOMER E.: Author:
• Surveyor: Candid Camera on the Moon. 578-592, Oct. 1966

NEWEST Leakey Discovery: Footprints 3.6 Million Years Old. By Mary D. Leakey. 446-457, Apr. 1979

NEWFOUNDLAND (Province), Canada:
• Atlantic Odyssey: Iceland to Antarctica. By Newman Bumstead. Photos by Volkmar Wentzel. 725-780, Dec. 1955
▲ *Close-up, Canada: Quebec, Newfoundland*, supplement. Text on reverse, inset Southern Quebec. May 1980
• I Sailed with Portugal's Captains Courageous. By Alan Villiers. 565-596, May 1952
• Newfoundland, Canada's New Province. By Andrew H. Brown. Photos by author and Robert F. Sisson. 777-812, June 1949
• Newfoundland Trusts in the Sea. By Gary Jennings. Photos by Sam Abell. 112-141, Jan. 1974
• Vinland Ruins Prove Vikings Found the New World. By Helge Ingstad. 708-734, Nov. 1964
• *See also* Labrador

NEWMAN, CATHY: Author:
• Carrara Marble: Touchstone of Eternity. Photos by Pierre Boulat. 42-59, July 1982
• Pompidou Center, Rage of Paris. Photos by Marc Riboud. 469-477, Oct. 1980

NEWMAN, LARRY: Author:
• *Double Eagle II* Has Landed! Crossing the Atlantic by Balloon. By Ben L. Abruzzo, with Maxie L. Anderson and Larry Newman. 858-882, Dec. 1978

NEWPORT, Rhode Island:
• By Square-rigger from Baltic to Bicentennial. By Kenneth Garrett. Note: Newport served as host to tall and small ships from 27 nations July 1-4, 1976. 824-857, Dec. 1976
• New England's "Lively Experiment," Rhode Island. By Robert de Roos. Photos by Fred Ward. 370-401, Sept. 1968
• Rhode Island, Modern City-State. By George W. Long. Photos by Willard R. Culver. 137-170, Aug. 1948
• Windjamming Around New England. By Tom Horgan. Photos by Robert F. Sisson. 141-169, Aug. 1950

NEWPORT BEACH, California:
• Happy Birthday, Otto Lilienthal! By Russell Hawkes. Photos by James Collison. 286-292, Feb. 1972

NEWTON, ISAAC:
• The British Way. By Sir Evelyn Wrench. 421-541, Apr. 1949

NEWTON, JOHN G.: Author:
• How We Found the *Monitor*. 48-61, Jan. 1975

The **NEXT** Frontier? By Isaac Asimov. Paintings by Pierre Mion. 76-89, July 1976

The **NEXT** 100 Years: A Master Plan for Yellowstone. By George B. Hartzog, Jr. 632-637, May 1972

NEXT Steps in Space. By Thomas O. Paine. 793-797, Dec. 1969

NEZ PERCE INDIANS:
• Chief Joseph. By William Albert Allard. 409-434, Mar. 1977

NGORONGORO CRATER, Tanzania:
• The Flamingo Eaters of Ngorongoro (Hyenas). By Richard D. Estes. 535-539, Oct. 1973
• Hyenas, the Hunters Nobody Knows. By Hans Kruuk. Photos by Baron Hugo van Lawick. 44-57, July 1968
• Tool-using Bird: The Egyptian Vulture. By Baroness Jane van Lawick-Goodall. Photos by Baron Hugo van Lawick. 631-641, May 1968

NIAGARA FALLS, Canada-U. S.:
• The Great Lakes: Is It Too Late? By Gordon Young. Photos by James L. Amos and Martin Rogers. 147-185, Aug. 1973
• Niagara Falls, Servant of Good Neighbors. Photos by Walter Meayers Edwards. 574-587, Apr. 1963

NICARAGUA:
• Troubled Times for Central America. By Wilbur E. Garrett, Editor. 58-61, July 1981

NICHOLAS, WILLIAM H.: Author:
• America's "Meat on the Hoof." 33-72, Jan. 1952
• Biggest Worm Farm Caters to Platypuses. 269-280, Feb. 1949
• Deep in the Heart of "Swissconsin." Photos by J. Baylor Roberts. 781-800, June 1947
• Dixie Spins the Wheel of Industry. Photos by J. Baylor Roberts. 281-324, Mar. 1949
• Growing Pains Beset Puerto Rico. Photos by Justin Locke. 419-460, Apr. 1951
• History Repeats in Old Natchez. Photos by Willard R. Culver. 181-208, Feb. 1949
• Literary Landmarks of Massachusetts. Photos by B. Anthony Stewart and John E. Fletcher. 279-310, Mar. 1950
• Men, Moose, and Mink of Northwest Angle. Photos by J. Baylor Roberts. 265-284, Aug. 1947
• Miami's Expanding Horizons. 561-594, Nov. 1950
• Nautical Norfolk Turns to Azaleas. Photos by B. Anthony Stewart. 606-614, May 1947
• Shawneetown Forsakes the Ohio. Photos by J. Baylor Roberts. 273-288, Feb. 1948
• Switzerland Guards the Roof of Europe. Photos by Willard R. Culver. 205-246, Aug. 1950
• Vizcaya: An Italian Palazzo in Miami. Photos by Justin Locke. 595-604, Nov. 1950

NICHOLDS, ELIZABETH: Author:
• The Goats of Thunder Hill. Photos by Robert F. Sisson. 625-640, May 1954

NICHOLS, HERBERT B.: Author:
• Water for the World's Growing Needs. By Herbert B. Nichols and F. Barrows Colton. 269-286, Aug. 1952

NICHOLSON, ROBERT W.: Artist:
• Saving the Ancient Temples at Abu Simbel. By Georg Gerster. 694-742, May 1966

NICKLIN, CHARLES R., Jr.:
Photographer:
• New Tools for Undersea Archeology. By George F. Bass. 403-423, Sept. 1968
• Swimming With Patagonia's Right Whales. By Roger Payne. Photos by William R. Curtsinger and Charles R. Nicklin, Jr. 576-587, Oct. 1972
• A Walk in the Deep. By Sylvia A. Earle. Photos by Al Giddings and Chuck Nicklin. 624-631, May 1980

NICKLIN, FLIP: Photographer:
• New Light on the Singing Whales. Introduction by Roger Payne. 463-477, Apr. 1982

NICOLAIDIS-KARANIKOLAS, MARIA:
Author:
• Eternal Easter in a Greek Village. Photos by James L. Stanfield. 768-777, Dec. 1983

NICOSIA, Cyprus:
• Cyprus Under Four Flags: A Struggle for Unity. By Kenneth MacLeish. Photos by Jonathan Blair. 356-383, Mar. 1973

NIEDRACH, R. J.:
Author-Photographer:
• Freezing the Flight of Hummingbirds. By Harold E. Edgerton, R. J. Niedrach, and Walker Van Riper. 245-261, Aug. 1951

NIELSEN, LEWIS T.: Author:
• Mosquitoes, the Mighty Killers. 427-440, Sept. 1979

NIGER:
• Drought Threatens the Tuareg World. By Victor Englebert. 544-571, Apr. 1974
• Freedom Speaks French in Ouagadougou. By John Scofield. 153-203, Aug. 1966
• I Joined a Sahara Salt Caravan. By Victor Englebert. 694-711, Nov. 1965
• The Inadan: Artisans of the Sahara. By Michael and Aubine Kirtley. 282-298, Aug. 1979
• Niger's Wodaabe: "People of the Taboo." By Carol Beckwith. 483-509, Oct. 1983

NIGER (River), West Africa:
• The Niger: River of Sorrow, River of Hope. By Georg Gerster. 152-189, Aug. 1975

NIGERIA:
• Beyond the Bight of Benin. By Jeannette and Maurice Fiévet. 221-253, Aug. 1959
• The Niger: River of Sorrow, River of Hope. By Georg Gerster. 152-189, Aug. 1975
• Nigeria Struggles With Boom Times. By Noel Grove. Photos by Bruno Barbey. 413-444, Mar. 1979
• Progress and Pageantry in Changing Nigeria. By W. Robert Moore. 325-365, Sept. 1956
• Safari Through Changing Africa. By Elsie May Bell Grosvenor. Photos by Gilbert Grosvenor. 145-198, Aug. 1953

NIGHT Life in the Gulf Stream. By Paul A. Zahl. 391-418, Mar. 1954

NIGHT of Terror (Alaska Earthquake). By Tay Pryor Thomas. 142-156, July 1964

The **NIGHT** the Mountains Moved. By Samuel W. Matthews. Photos by J. Baylor Roberts. 329-359, Mar. 1960

NIGHTINGALE, FLORENCE:
• The British Way. By Sir Evelyn Wrench. 421-541, Apr. 1949

The **NIGHTMARE** of Famine. Photos by Steve Raymer. 33-39, July 1975

NIKE (Guided Missile):
• New Miracles of the Telephone Age. By Robert Leslie Conly. 87-120, July 1954

NIKOLAEVSK: A Bit of Old Russia Takes Root in Alaska. By Jim Rearden. Photos by Charles O'Rear. 401-425, Sept. 1972

NILE (River and Valley), Africa:
• Abu Simbel's Ancient Temples Reborn. By Georg Gerster. 724-744, May 1969
▲ *Africa: Countries of the Nile,* Atlas series supplement. Oct. 1963
• Kayaks Down the Nile. By John M. Goddard. 697-732, May 1955
▲ *Nile Valley, Land of the Pharaohs,* Atlas series supplement. Text on reverse. May 1965
◆ *The River Nile.* Announced. 408-417, Mar. 1966
• Safari from Congo to Cairo. By Elsie May Bell Grosvenor. Photos by Gilbert Grosvenor. 721-771, Dec. 1954
• Saving the Ancient Temples at Abu Simbel. By Georg Gerster. Paintings by Robert W. Nicholson. 694-742, May 1966
• South in the Sudan. By Harry Hoogstraal. 249-272, Feb. 1953
• Threatened Treasures of the Nile. By Georg Gerster. 587-621, Oct. 1963
• *Yankee* Cruises the Storied Nile. By Irving and Electa Johnson. Photos by Winfield Parks. 583-633, May 1965

NILE CROCODILE:
• A Bad Time to Be a Crocodile. By Rick Gore. Photos by Jonathan Blair. 90-115, Jan. 1978

NILSSON, LENNART: Photographer:
• Fishing in the Lofotens. 377-388, Mar. 1947

NIMBUS (Weather Satellite Series):
• Extraordinary Photograph Shows Earth Pole to Pole. Photos by Nimbus I. 190-193, Feb. 1965
• Studying Wildlife by Satellite. By Frank Craighead, Jr. and John Craighead. 120-123, Jan. 1973

WINFIELD PARKS, NGS

Cruising the Nile: Ramesses II statue

M
N

NIMITZ, CHESTER W.:
• How One of The Society's Maps (Pacific Ocean) Saved a Precious Cargo. 844, June 1947

NIMKHERA (Village), Madhya Pradesh, India:
• Purdah in India: Life Behind the Veil. By Doranne Wilson Jacobson. 270-286, Aug. 1977

NIÑA (Schooner):
• Down East to Nova Scotia. By Winfield Parks. 853-879, June 1964

NINE-BANDED ARMADILLOS:
• The Astonishing Armadillo. By Eleanor E. Storrs. Photos by Bianca Lavies. 820-830, June 1982

900 Years Ago: the Norman Conquest. By Kenneth M. Setton. Photos by George F. Mobley. 206-251, Aug. 1966

NINEVEH (Ancient City):
• Ancient Mesopotamia: A Light That Did Not Fail. By E. A. Speiser. Paintings by H. M. Herget. 41-105, Jan. 1951

NININGER, ROBERT D.: Author:
• Hunting Uranium Around the World. Photos by Volkmar Wentzel. 533-558, Oct. 1954

NISBET, IAN: Author:
• Friend of the Wind: The Common Tern. Photos by Hope Alexander. 234-247, Aug. 1973

NIXON, RICHARD M.: Author:
• Russia as I Saw It. Photos by B. Anthony Stewart. 715-750, Dec. 1959

NO Place to Run: The Hmong of Laos. By W. E. Garrett. 78-111, Jan. 1974

NOAA. *See* National Oceanic and Atmospheric Administration

NOATAK RIVER, Alaska:
• Our Wild and Scenic Rivers: The Noatak. By John M. Kauffmann. Photos by Sam Abell. 52-59, July 1977

NOBLECOURT, CHRISTIANE DESROCHES: Author:
• Tutankhamun's Golden Trove. Photos by F. L. Kenett. 625-646, Oct. 1963

NOCTURNAL ANIMALS:
◆ *Creatures of the Night.* 1977
• In Hawaii's Crystal Sea, A Galaxy of Life Fills the Night. By Kenneth Brower. Photos by William R. Curtsinger and Chris Newbert. 834-847, Dec. 1981
• Nature's Night Lights: Probing the Secrets of Bioluminescence. By Paul A. Zahl. 45-69, July 1971
• Night Life in the Gulf Stream. By Paul A. Zahl. 391-418, Mar. 1954
• Photographing the Night Creatures of Alligator Reef. By Robert E. Schroeder. Photos by author and Walter A. Starck II. NGS research grant. 128-154, Jan. 1964
▪ Strange Creatures of the Night. 144A-144B, Jan. 1973
• Voices of the Night. By Arthur A. Allen. NGS research grant. 507-522, Apr. 1950
• *See also* Armadillos; Bats; Black-footed Ferrets; Fireflies; Frogs; Hyenas; Kangaroos; Oilbirds; Owls; Phalangers; Railroad Worm; Rats; Salamanders; Tarsiers; Termites

NOËL HUME, IVOR: Author:
• First Look at a Lost Virginia Settlement (Martin's Hundred). Photos by Ira Block. Paintings by Richard Schlecht. 735-767, June 1979
• New Clues to an Old Mystery (Virginia's Wolstenholme Towne). Photos by Ira Block. Paintings by Richard Schlecht. 53-77, Jan. 1982

"NOICEST Parrt o'England"–the Cotswolds. By James Cerruti. Photos by Adam Woolfitt. 846-869, June 1974

NOLAN, JOHN E. H.: Author:
• Life in the Land of the Basques. Photos by Justin Locke. 147-186, Feb. 1954
• Pilgrimage to Holy Island and the Farnes. 547-570, Oct. 1952
• Silkworms in England Spin for the Queen. 689-704, May 1953
Author-Photographer:
• Caldy, the Monks' Island. 564-578, Oct. 1955

NOMAD (Ketch):
• Down East Cruise. By Tom Horgan. Photos by Luis Marden. 329-369, Sept. 1952
• *Nomad* Sails Long Island Sound. By Thomas Horgan. 295-338, Sept. 1957
• Windjamming Around New England. By Tom Horgan. Photos by Robert F. Sisson. 141-169, Aug. 1950

NOMAD in Alaska's Outback. By Thomas J. Abercrombie. 540-567, Apr. 1969

NOMADS:
• Abraham, the Friend of God. By Kenneth MacLeish. Photos by Dean Conger. 739-789, Dec. 1966
• Afghanistan: Crossroad of Conquerors. By Thomas J. Abercrombie. 297-345, Sept. 1968
• The Danakil: Nomads of Ethiopia's Wasteland. By Victor Englebert. 186-211, Feb. 1970
• I Live With the Eskimos (Canadian). By Guy Mary-Rousseliere. 188-217, Feb. 1971
• Journey Into Troubled Iran. By George W. Long. Photos by J. Baylor Roberts. Included: Bakhtiari, Kashgais, Kurds, Lurs. 425-464, Oct. 1951
• Niger's Wodaabe: "People of the Taboo." By Carol Beckwith. 483-509, Oct. 1983
• Nomads of China's West. By Galen Rowell. Photos by the author and Harold A. Knutson. Contents: Gologs. 244-263, Feb. 1982
• Nomads of the Far North (Indians and Eskimos). By Matthew W. Stirling. Paintings by W. Langdon Kihn. 471-504, Oct. 1949
◆ *Nomads of the World.* Announced. 882-886, June 1971
• Saudi Arabia: Beyond the Sands of Mecca. By Thomas J. Abercrombie. 1-53, Jan. 1966
• We Dwelt in Kashgai Tents. By Jean and Franc Shor. 805-832, June 1952
• *See also* Aboriginals, Australian; Bakhtiari; Bedouin; Brahui; Bushmen; Gypsies; Ice Age Man; Kazaks; Kirghiz; Lapland, for Lapps; Masai; Tuareg; Turkomans

NONDUGL, Wahgi Valley, New Guinea:
• New Guinea's Paradise of Birds. By E. Thomas Gilliard. 661-688, Nov. 1951
• Sheep Airlift in New Guinea. Photos by Ned Blood. 831-844, Dec. 1949

NORFOLK, Virginia:
• Chesapeake Country. By Nathaniel T. Kenney. Photos by Bates Littlehales. 370-411, Sept. 1964

NORFOLK GARDENS, Norfolk, Virginia:
• Nautical Norfolk Turns to Azaleas. By William H. Nicholas. Photos by B. Anthony Stewart. 606-614, May 1947

NORFOLK ISLAND, South Pacific Ocean:
• *Bounty* Descendants Live on Remote Norfolk Island. By T. C. Roughley. Photos by J. Baylor Roberts. 559-584, Oct. 1960
• Pitcairn and Norfolk–The Saga of *Bounty*'s Children. By Ed Howard. Photos by David Hiser and Melinda Berge. 510-541, Oct. 1983
Pitcairn Island. 512-529; Norfolk Island. 530-541

NORKEY, TENZING. *See* Tenzing Norgay

NORMAN, JAMES: Author:
• The Huichols, Mexico's People of Myth and Magic. Photos by Guillermo Aldana E. 832-853, June 1977
• The Tarahumaras: Mexico's Long Distance Runners. Photos by David Hiser. 702-718, May 1976

NORMAN CONQUEST:
• The British Way. By Sir Evelyn Wrench. 421-541, Apr. 1949
• 900 Years Ago: the Norman Conquest. By Kenneth M. Setton. Photos by George F. Mobley. 206-251, Aug. 1966

NORMANDY (Region), France:
• The Civilizing Seine. By Charles McCarry. Photos by David L. Arnold. 478-511, Apr. 1982
• Here Rest in Honored Glory: The United States Dedicates Six New Battle Monuments in Europe to Americans Who Gave Their Lives During World War II. By Howell Walker. Included: Normandy American Cemetery and Memorial. 739-768, June 1957
• Normandy Blossoms Anew. By Howell Walker. 591-631, May 1959
• The Vikings. By Howard La Fay. Photos by Ted Spiegel. 492-541, Apr. 1970

NORSEMEN. *See* Vikings

NORTH, WHEELER J.: Author:
- Giant Kelp, Sequoias of the Sea. Photos by Bates Littlehales. 251-269, Aug. 1972

NORTH AFRICA:
- The Mediterranean–Sea of Man's Fate. By Rick Gore. Photos by Jonathan Blair. 694-737, Dec. 1982
- *See also* Algeria; Morocco; Tunisia; *and* Carthage

NORTH AMERICA:
- America in the Discovery Age: the Molineaux-Wright Chart. 757, June 1953
- The Anasazi–Riddles in the Ruins. By Thomas Y. Canby. Photos by Dewitt Jones and David Brill. Paintings by Roy Andersen. 554-592, Nov. 1982
- ▲ *Atlantic Gateways,* The Making of America series. Included: Delaware, Maryland, New Jersey, New York, Pennsylvania, northern Virginia, West Virginia, and in Canada, southern Ontario and southern Quebec. On reverse: Indians and Trade, Nation in the Making, Peopling of the Gateways, Race for the Hinterlands, Growth of Industry, Spreading Urban Corridors. Mar. 1983
- An Atlas of Energy Resources. 58-69, *Special Report on Energy* (Feb. 1981)
- ▲ *Bird Migration in the Americas; The Americas,* double-sided supplement. Aug. 1979
- ◆ *Clues to America's Past.* Announced. 860-864, June 1976
- ▲ *Colonization and Trade in the New World,* supplement. Painting and text on reverse. Dec. 1977
- ▲ *Deep South,* The Making of America series. Included: Alabama, Florida, Georgia, Louisiana, Mississippi, South Carolina, and parts of Arkansas, North Carolina, and Tennessee. On reverse: Indian Legacy, Imperial Footholds, Three Empires and Three Races, Cotton Kingdom, Postbellum, New Deep South, Subtropical Playground. Aug. 1983
- The Desert: An Age-old Challenge Grows. By Rick Gore. Photos by Georg Gerster and Bruce Dale. 586-639, Nov. 1979
- Editorial. By Gilbert M. Grosvenor. 733, Dec. 1979
- ◆ *Field Guide to Birds of North America.* 1983
- How Fruit Came to America. By J. R. Magness. Paintings by Else Bostelmann. Included: Native and imported varieties of fruit. 325-377, Sept. 1951
- Hurricane! By Ben Funk. Photos by Robert W. Madden. 346-379, Sept. 1980
  Dominica. By Fred Ward. 357-359; Dynamics of a Hurricane. 370-371; Into the Eye of David. By John L. Eliot. 368-369; Paths of Fury–This Century's Worst American Storms. 360-361
- The Incredible Potato. By Robert E. Rhoades. Photos by Martin Rogers. 668-694, May 1982
- ▲ *Indians of North America; North America Before Columbus,* double-sided supplement. Dec. 1972

JONATHAN BLAIR

Bird Migration: banded warblers

- ◆ *Into the Wilderness.* 1978
- The Making of America: 17 New Maps Tie the Nation to Its Past. By Wilbur E. Garrett, Editor. 630-633, Nov. 1982
- Mysteries of Bird Migration. By Allan C. Fisher, Jr. Photos by Jonathan Blair. 154-193, Aug. 1979
- ▲ *North America,* Atlas series supplement. Apr. 1964
- ▲ *North America,* supplement. Mar. 1952
- ◆ *Our Continent: A Natural History of North America.* Announced. 572-574, Oct. 1976
- Our Vegetable Travelers. By Victor R. Boswell. Paintings by Else Bostelmann. Included: Introduction of vegetable varieties to North America. 145-217, Aug. 1949
- Peoples of the Arctic. 144-223, Feb. 1983
  I. Introduction by Joseph Judge. 144-149; II. Hunters of the Lost Spirit: Alaskans, Canadians, Greenlanders, Lapps. By Priit J. Vesilind. Photos by David Alan Harvey, Ivars Silis, and Sisse Brimberg. 150-197; III. Where Magic Ruled: Art of the Bering Sea. By William W. Fitzhugh and Susan A. Kaplan. Photos by Sisse Brimberg. 198-205
- ▲ *Peoples of the Arctic; Arctic Ocean,* double-sided supplement. Feb. 1983
- Reach for the New World. By Mendel Peterson. Photos by David L. Arnold. Paintings by Richard Schlecht. 724-767, Dec. 1977
- The Search for the First Americans. By Thomas Y. Canby. Photos by Kerby Smith. Paintings by Roy Andersen. 330-363, Sept. 1979
- ◆ *Wild Animals of North America.* 1979
- ◆ *Wonder of Birds.* 1983
- The World in Your Garden (Flowers). By W. H. Camp. Paintings by Else Bostelmann. Included: Western North America as a Source (Clarkia, California poppy, Blanket-flower, Lupine). 1-65, July 1947
- *See also* Canada; Caribbean Region; Central America; Greenland; Mexico; United States; *and* Indians of North America; Wildlife

NORTH AMERICAN AIR DEFENSE COMMAND (NORAD):
- Of Planes and Men. By Kenneth F. Weaver. Photos by Emory Kristof and Albert Moldvay. Included: Air Defense Command, Military Air Transport Service, Pacific Air Forces, Strategic Air Command, Tactical Air Command. 298-349, Sept. 1965

NORTH American Decoys. By George Reiger. Photos by Kenneth Garrett. 639-663, Nov. 1983

NORTH BIMINI ISLAND, Bahamas. *See* Lerner Marine Laboratory

NORTH BORNEO. *See* Sabah

NORTH CALAVERAS GROVE (Sequoias), California. *See* Calaveras Big Trees State Park

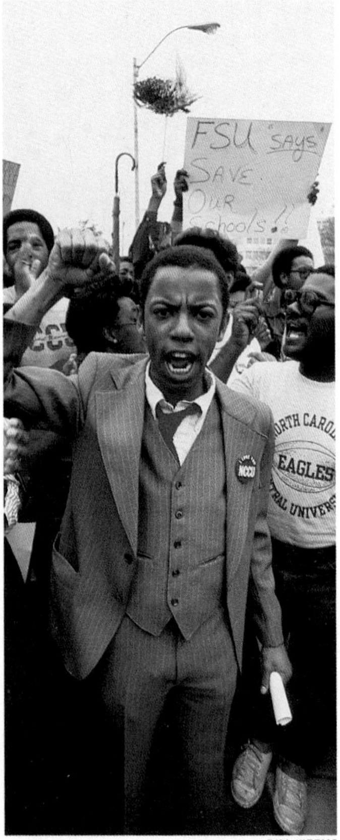

BILL WEEMS

North Carolina: 1978 student protest

NORTH CAROLINA:
- Around the "Great Lakes of the South." By Frederick Simpich. Photos by J. Baylor Roberts. 463-491, Apr. 1948
- Chattooga River Country: Wild Water, Proud People. By Don Belt. Photos by Steve Wall. 458-477, Apr. 1983
- Dixie Spins the Wheel of Industry. By William H. Nicholas. Photos by J. Baylor Roberts. 281-324, Mar. 1949
- Exploring America's Great Sand Barrier Reef. By Eugene R. Guild. Photos by John E. Fletcher and author. 325-350, Sept. 1947
- Here Come the Marines. By Frederick Simpich. Included: Cherry Point Air Station and Camp Lejeune. 647-672, Nov. 1950
- Home to North Carolina. By Neil Morgan. Photos by Bill Weems. 333-359, Mar. 1980
- Indian Life Before the Colonists Came. By Stuart E. Jones. Engravings by Theodore de Bry, 1590. 351-368, Sept. 1947
- Menhaden–Uncle Sam's Top Commercial Fish. By Leonard C. Roy. Photos by Robert F. Sisson. Included: Morehead City-Beaufort area on Bogue Sound. 813-823, June 1949
- My Neighbors Hold to Mountain Ways (Blue Ridge). By Malcolm Ross. Photos by Flip Schulke. 856-880, June 1958
- North Carolina, Dixie Dynamo. By Malcolm Ross. Photos by B. Anthony Stewart. 141-183, Feb. 1962
- Our Changing Atlantic Coastline. By Nathaniel T. Kenney. Photos by B. Anthony Stewart. Included: Bodie Island; Hatteras Island; Wash Woods. 860-887, Dec. 1962
- Pack Trip Through the Smokies. By Val Hart. Photos by Robert F. Sisson. 473-502, Oct. 1952
- Skyway Below the Clouds. By Carl R. Markwith. Photos by Ernest J. Cottrell. Included: Charlotte; High Rock Lake. 85-108, July 1949
- A Walk Across America. By Peter Gorton Jenkins. 466-499, Apr. 1977
- *See also* Great Smoky Mountains National Park; Old Salem; Outer Banks; Roan Mountain

NORTH CASCADES NATIONAL PARK, Washington:
- New National Park Proposed: The Spectacular North Cascades. By Nathaniel T. Kenney. Photos by James P. Blair. 642-667, May 1968

NORTH CENTRAL UNITED STATES:
- ▲ *Close-up: U.S.A., The North Central States,* supplement. Text on reverse. Mar. 1974
- A Map Maker Looks at the United States. By Newman Bumstead. Included: Illinois: Chicago and Rock Island; Indiana: South Bend and Gary; Iowa: Davenport and Muscatine; Lake Michigan. 705-748, June 1951
- Mapping the Nation's Breadbasket. By Frederick Simpich. 831-849, June 1948
- ▲ *North Central United States,* Atlas series supplement. Nov. 1958
- ▲ *North Central United States,* supplement. June 1948
- *See also* names of individual states

NORTH DAKOTA:
- Duck Hunting with a Color Camera. By Arthur A. Allen. 514-539, Oct. 1951
- Following the Trail of Lewis and Clark. By Ralph Gray. 707-750, June 1953
- North Dakota Comes into Its Own. By Leo A. Borah. Photos by J. Baylor Roberts. 283-322, Sept. 1951
- Roosevelt Country: T. R.'s Wilderness Legacy. By John L. Eliot. Photos by Farrell Grehan. 340-363, Sept. 1982
- *See also* Lostwood Wildlife Refuge; Minot

NORTH for Oil: *Manhattan* Makes the Historic Northwest Passage. By Bern Keating. Photos by Tomas Sennett. 374-391, Mar. 1970

NORTH ISLAND, New Zealand:
- New Zealand's North Island: The Contented Land. By Charles McCarry. Photos by Bates Littlehales. 190-213, Aug. 1974
- *See also* Waitomo Caves

NORTH KOREA. *See* Korea, Democratic People's Republic of

NORTH MANKATO, Minnesota:
- Satellites Gave Warning of Midwest Floods. By Peter T. White. Photos by Thomas A. DeFeo. 574-592, Oct. 1969

NORTH POLE:
- Circling Earth From Pole to Pole. By Sir Ranulph Fiennes. 464-481, Oct. 1983
- Editorial. By Gilbert M. Grosvenor. 297, Sept. 1978
- North Toward the Pole on Skis. By Bjørn O. Staib. 254-281, Feb. 1965
- The Peary Flag Comes to Rest. By Marie Peary Stafford. 519-532, Oct. 1954
- Solo to the Pole. By Naomi Uemura. Photos by the author and Ira Block. 298-325, Sept. 1978
- Submarine Through the North Pole *(Nautilus).* By William G. Lalor, Jr. Photos by John J. Krawczyk. 1-20, Jan. 1959
- Up Through the Ice of the North Pole *(Skate).* By James F. Calvert. 1-41, July 1959
- We Followed Peary to the Pole. By Gilbert Grosvenor and Thomas W. McKnew. 469-484, Oct. 1953

NORTH SEA:
- ▪ Holland Against the Sea. 588A-588B, Apr. 1970
- Oil, the Dwindling Treasure. By Noel Grove. Photos by Emory Kristof. 792-825, June 1974
- Pilgrimage to Holy Island and the Farnes. By John E. H. Nolan. 547-570, Oct. 1952

• Striking It Rich in the North Sea. By Rick Gore. Photos by Dick Durrance II. Included: Map showing five sectors of national rights over oil and gas reserves. 519-549, Apr. 1977
• Thumbs Up Round the North Sea's Rim. By Frances James. Photos by Erica Koch. 685-704, May 1952

NORTH SHORE, Massachusetts:
• Massachusetts' North Shore: Harboring Old Ways. By Randall S. Peffer. Photos by Nathan Benn. 568-590, Apr. 1979

NORTH SLOPE, Alaska:
• Alaska: Rising Northern Star. By Joseph Judge. Photos by Bruce Dale. 730-767, June 1975
• Oil, the Dwindling Treasure. By Noel Grove. Photos by Emory Kristof. 792-825, June 1974
• The Pipeline: Alaska's Troubled Colossus. By Bryan Hodgson. Photos by Steve Raymer. Included: Diagram, Anatomy of the pipeline; map showing potential and producing oil and gas areas. 684-717, Nov. 1976
• Will Oil and Tundra Mix? Alaska's North Slope Hangs in the Balance. By William S. Ellis. Photos by Emory Kristof. 485-517, Oct. 1971

NORTH STAR Cruises Alaska's Wild West. By Amos Burg. 57-86, July 1952

NORTH Through History Aboard *White Mist.* By Melville Bell Grosvenor. Photos by Edwin Stuart Grosvenor. NGS research grant. 1-55, July 1970

NORTH Toward the Pole on Skis. By Bjørn O. Staib. NGS research grant. 254-281, Feb. 1965

NORTH UIST (Island), Scotland:
• Isles on the Edge of the Sea: Scotland's Outer Hebrides. By Kenneth MacLeish. Photos by Thomas Nebbia. 676-711, May 1970

NORTH VIETNAM:
• Air Rescue Behind Enemy Lines. By Howard Sochurek. 346-369, Sept. 1968

NORTH With Finland's Lapps. By Jean and Franc Shor. 249-280, Aug. 1954

NORTH With the Snow Goose. By Des and Jen Bartlett. 822-843, Dec. 1973

NORTH With the Wheat Cutters. By Noel Grove. Photos by James A. Sugar. 194-217, Aug. 1972

NORTH YEMEN. By Noel Grove. Photos by Steve Raymer. 244-269, Aug. 1979

NORTHAMPTON, Massachusetts. *See* Clarke School for the Deaf

NORTHEAST (Region), U. S.:
▲ *Close-up: U.S.A., The Northeast,* supplement. Text on reverse. Included: New Jersey, New York, Pennsylvania. Jan. 1978
• The Incredible Potato. By Robert E. Rhoades. Photos by Martin Rogers. Note: Potatoes were first introduced in New England in 1719 by Scotch-Irish immigrants. 668-694, May 1982
• *See also* New England

NORTH-EAST NEW GUINEA (now part of Papua New Guinea):
• To the Land of the Head-hunters. By E. Thomas Gilliard. 437-486, Oct. 1955
• *See also* Papua New Guinea

NORTHERN IRELAND. *See* Ireland, Northern

NORTHERN LIGHTS. *See* Aurora Borealis

NORTHERN TERRITORY, Australia:
• Eden in the Outback. By Kay and Stanley Breeden. 189-203, Feb. 1973
• Rock Paintings of the Aborigines. By Kay and Stanley Breeden. 174-187, Feb. 1973
• The Top End of Down Under. By Kenneth MacLeish. Photos by Thomas Nebbia. 145-174, Feb. 1973
• *See also* Arnhem Land

NORTHWEST (Region), U. S.:
◆ *America's Spectacular Northwest.* 1982
• Climbing Our Northwest Glaciers. Photos by Bob and Ira Spring. 103-114, July 1953
▲ *Close-up: U.S.A., The Northwest,* supplement. Text on reverse. Mar. 1973
• Forest Fire: The Devil's Picnic. By Stuart E. Jones and Jay Johnston. Included: Worst blazes of 1967 in Northwest. 100-127, July 1968
• A Map Maker Looks at the United States. By Newman Bumstead. 705-748, June 1951
• Mexico to Canada on the Pacific Crest Trail. By Mike W. Edwards. Photos by David Hiser. 741-779, June 1971
▲ *Northwestern United States,* Atlas series supplement. Apr. 1960
▲ *Northwestern United States,* supplement. June 1950
• *See also* Idaho; Montana; Oregon; Washington

NORTHWEST ANGLE, Minnesota:
• Men, Moose, and Mink of Northwest Angle. By William H. Nicholas. Photos by J. Baylor Roberts. 265-284, Aug. 1947

NORTH-WEST FRONTIER PROVINCE, Pakistan:
• An Eye for an Eye: Pakistan's Wild Frontier. By Mike W. Edwards. Photos by J. Bruce Baumann. 111-139, Jan. 1977
• Pakistan's Kalash: People of Fire and Fervor. By Debra Denker. Photos by Steve McCurry. 458-473, Oct. 1981

NORTHWEST PASSAGE:
• North for Oil: *Manhattan* Makes the Historic Northwest Passage. By Bern Keating. Photos by Tomas Sennett. 374-391, Mar. 1970
• Trek Across Arctic America. By Colin Irwin. 295-321, Mar. 1974

NORTHWEST TERRITORIES, Canada:
• Across Canada by Mackenzie's Track. By Ralph Gray. 191-239, Aug. 1955
• Arctic Odyssey. By John Bockstoce. Photos by Jonathan Wright. Paintings by Jack Unruh. 100-127, July 1983
• Banks Island: Eskimo Life on the Polar Sea. By William O. Douglas. Photos by Clyde Hare. Included: Inuvik; Sachs Harbour, Banks Island. 703-735, May 1964
• Canada's Caribou Eskimos (Padlermiut). By Donald B. Marsh. 87-104, Jan. 1947
• Canada's "Now" Frontier. By Robert Paul Jordan. Photos by Lowell Georgia. 480-511, Oct. 1976
• The Canadian North: Emerging Giant. By David S. Boyer. 1-43, July 1968
▲ *Close-up, Canada: Saskatchewan, Manitoba, Northwest Territories,* supplement. Text on reverse. May 1979
• Far North with "Captain Mac." By Miriam MacMillan. Included: Baffin Island, Ellesmere Island. 465-513, Oct. 1951
• Henry Hudson's Changing Bay. By Bill Richards. Photos by David Hiser. 380-405, Mar. 1982
• I Live With the Eskimos. By Guy Mary-Rousseliere. 188-217, Feb. 1971
■ Journey to the High Arctic. 590A-590B, Apr. 1971
• Milestones in My Arctic Journeys. By Willie Knutsen. 543-570, Oct. 1949
• Peoples of the Arctic. 144-223, Feb. 1983
I. Introduction by Joseph Judge. 144-149; II. Hunters of the Lost Spirit: Canadians. By Priit J. Vesilind. Photos by David Alan Harvey. 174-189
▲ *Peoples of the Arctic; Arctic Ocean,* double-sided supplement. Feb. 1983
• Still Eskimo, Still Free: The Inuit of Umingmaktok. By Yva Momatiuk and John Eastcott. 624-647, Nov. 1977
• *See also* Ellesmere Island; Nahanni National Park; Northwest Passage; Southampton Island

NORTHWIND (Coast Guard Icebreaker):
• Our Navy Explores Antarctica. By Richard E. Byrd. U. S. Navy official photos. 429-522, Oct. 1947

NORWAY:
• "Around the World in Eighty Days." By Newman Bumstead. Included: Bergen, Frognerseteren, Hardanger Fjord, Holmenkollen, Oslo, Oslo Fjord. 705-750, Dec. 1951
• Baltic Cruise of the *Caribbee.* By Carleton Mitchell. 605-646, Nov. 1950
• Friendly Flight to Northern Europe. By Lyndon B. Johnson. Photos by Volkmar Wentzel. 268-293, Feb. 1964

M N

• Hunters of the Lost Spirit: Lapps. By Priit J. Vesilind. Photos by Sisse Brimberg. 194-197, Feb. 1983
• Midshipmen's Cruise. By William J. Aston and Alexander G. B. Grosvenor. 711-754, June 1948
• Native's Return to Norway (Mandal). By Arnvid Nygaard. Photos by Andrew H. Brown. 683-691, Nov. 1953
• Norway, Land of the Generous Sea. By Edward J. Linehan. Photos by George F. Mobley. 1-43, July 1971
• Norway Cracks Her Mountain Shell. By Sydney Clark. Photos by Gilbert Grosvenor and Ole Friele Backer. 171-211, Aug. 1948
• Norway's Fjords Pit Men Against Mountains. By Andrew H. Brown. 96-122, Jan. 1957
• Norway's Reindeer Lapps. By Sally Anderson. Photos by Erik Borg. 364-379, Sept. 1977
▲ *Peoples of the Arctic; Arctic Ocean,* double-sided supplément. Feb. 1983
• Stop-and-Go Sail Around South Norway. By Edmond J. Moran. Photos by Randi Kjekstad Bull and Andrew H. Brown. 153-192, Aug. 1954
• Striking It Rich in the North Sea. By Rick Gore. Photos by Dick Durrance II. 519-549, Apr. 1977
• Unlocking Secrets of the Northern Lights. By Carl W. Gartlein. Paintings by William Crowder. 673-704, Nov. 1947
• The Vikings. By Howard La Fay. Photos by Ted Spiegel. 492-541, Apr. 1970
• *See also* Jan Mayen (Island); Lofoten (Islands); Svalbard (Archipelago)

NORWEGIAN SEA:
• Seal Hunting Off Jan Mayen. By Ole Friele Backer. 57-72, Jan. 1948

NORWEGIANS:
▪ The Last Vikings. 434A-434B, Mar. 1972

NOTRE DAME DE CHARTRES (Cathedral). *See* Chartres

NOTRE DAME DE PARIS (Cathedral):
• Île de la Cité, Birthplace of Paris. By Kenneth MacLeish. Photos by Bruce Dale. 680-719, May 1968

NOVA AQUILAE 1982 (Star):
• The Once and Future Universe. By Rick Gore. Photos by James A. Sugar. Paintings by Barron Storey. Picture text by David Jeffery. 704-749, June 1983

NOVA SCOTIA (Province), Canada:
• Canada, My Country. By Alan Phillips. Photos by David S. Boyer and Walter Meayers Edwards. 769-819, Dec. 1961
• Canada's Winged Victory: the *Silver Dart.* By Gilbert M. Grosvenor. 254-267, Aug. 1959
• Down East to Nova Scotia. By Winfield Parks. Included: Baddeck, Boulaceet (Maskell's Harbour), Bras d'Or Lakes, Cape George Harbour, Halifax, Liscomb, Lunenburg, Peggy's Cove, St. Peters Canal. 853-879, June 1964
• Far North with "Captain Mac." By Miriam MacMillan. Included: Big Harbour (Port Bevis), Cape Breton Island, Cape Canso, Cape Sable, Halifax, Sydney. 465-513, Oct. 1951
• The Giant Tides of Fundy. By Paul A. Zahl. 153-192, Aug. 1957
• The Loyalists. By Kent Britt. Photos by Ted Spiegel. Included: Tories, American colonists who remained loyal to the British Empire and moved to Canada during and after the Revolution; their descendants today. 510-539, Apr. 1975
• Nova Scotia, the Magnificent Anchorage. By Charles McCarry. Photos by Gordon W. Gahan. 334-363, Mar. 1975
• Plight of the Bluefin Tuna. By Michael J. A. Butler. Photos by David Doubilet. Paintings by Stanley Meltzoff. 220-239, Aug. 1982
• *See also* Baddeck; Sable Island

NOVAE:
• The Once and Future Universe. By Rick Gore. Photos by James A. Sugar. Paintings by Barron Storey. Picture text by David Jeffery. 704-749, June 1983

NOVICK, ALVIN: Author:
• Bats Aren't All Bad. Photos by Bruce Dale. 615-637, May 1973

NOVOSIBIRSK, U.S.S.R.:
• Siberia's Empire Road, the River Ob. By Robert Paul Jordan. Photos by Dean Conger. 145-181, Feb. 1976

NOXONTOWN POND, Delaware:
• Teeming Life of a Pond. By William H. Amos. 274-298, Aug. 1970

NUBA (Tribespeople):
• Proud Primitives, the Nuba People. By Oskar Luz. Photos by Horst Luz. Contents: Masakin Qisar, Masakin Tiwal. 673-699, Nov. 1966
• With the Nuba Hillmen of Kordofan. By Robin Strachan. Contents: Fungor, Kau, Koalib, and Korongo. 249-278, Feb. 1951

NUBIA (Region), Africa:
• Threatened Treasures of the Nile. By Georg Gerster. 587-621, Oct. 1963
• *See also* Abu Simbel

NUCLEAR ENERGY:
• An Atlas of Energy Resources. 58-69, *Special Report on Energy* (Feb. 1981)
• Contrary New Hampshire. By Robert Booth. Photos by Sandy Felsenthal. Included: Seabrook nuclear power plant. 770-799, Dec. 1982
• Editorial. By Gilbert M. Grosvenor. 445, Apr. 1979
• Four-ocean Navy in the Nuclear Age. By Thomas W. McKnew. 145-187, Feb. 1965
• Man's New Servant, the Friendly Atom. By F. Barrows Colton. Photos by Volkmar Wentzel. 71-90, Jan. 1954
• New Era in the Loneliest Continent (Antarctica). By David M. Tyree. Photos by Albert Moldvay. 260-296, Feb. 1963
• Nuclear Power for the Polar Regions (Camp Century). By George J. Dufek. 712-730, May 1962
• Our Nuclear Navy. By George W. Anderson, Jr. 449-450, Mar. 1963
• Powerhouse of the Northwest (Columbia River). By David S. Boyer. 821-847, Dec. 1974
• The Promise and Peril of Nuclear Energy. By Kenneth F. Weaver. Photos by Emory Kristof. 459-493, Apr. 1979
• The Search for Tomorrow's Power. By Kenneth F. Weaver. Photos by Emory Kristof. 650-681, Nov. 1972
• Uncle Sam's House of 1,000 Wonders. By Lyman J. Briggs and F. Barrows Colton. 755-784, Dec. 1951
• Whatever Happened to TVA? By Gordon Young. Photos by Emory Kristof. 830-863, June 1973
• You and the Obedient Atom. By Allan C. Fisher, Jr. 303-353, Sept. 1958
• *See also* Atomic Bomb Tests; Cosmic Rays; *and Enterprise; Savannah,* N. S.; Submarines, Nuclear-powered

NUCLEAR WEAPONS:
• Four-ocean Navy in the Nuclear Age. By Thomas W. McKnew. 145-187, Feb. 1965
• Of Planes and Men. By Kenneth F. Weaver. Photos by Emory Kristof and Albert Moldvay. Included: Air Defense Command, Military Air Transport Service, Pacific Air Forces, Strategic Air Command, Tactical Air Command, U. S. Air Forces in Europe. 298-349, Sept. 1965
• Profiles of the Presidents: V. The Atomic Age: Its Problems and Promises. By Frank Freidel. 66-119, Jan. 1966
• South Carolina Rediscovered. By Herbert Ravenel Sass. Photos by Robert F. Sisson. Included: Savannah River Plant of the Atomic Energy Commission which produces H-bombs. 281-321, Mar. 1953
• *See also* Atomic Bomb Tests

NUCLEIC ACIDS:
• The Awesome Worlds Within a Cell. By Rick Gore. Photos by Bruce Dale. Paintings by Davis Meltzer. 355-395, Sept. 1976

NUDIBRANCHS (Sea Slugs):
• Unsung Beauties of Hawaii's Coral Reefs. By Paul A. Zahl. 510-525, Oct. 1959

NUECHTERLEIN, GARY L.:
Author-Photographer:
• Western Grebes: The Birds That Walk on Water. 624-637, May 1982

NUESTRA SEÑORA DE ATOCHA (Galleon):
• *Atocha,* Tragic Treasure Galleon of the Florida Keys. By Eugene Lyon. 787-809, June 1976
▪ Treasure! 575, Nov. 1976; cover, Dec. 1976
• Treasure From the Ghost Galleon: *Santa Margarita.* By Eugene Lyon. Photos by Don Kincaid. 228-243, Feb. 1982

NUNGS (Tribespeople):
• Cane Bridges of Asia. Photos from Paul Popper. 243-250, Aug. 1948

NURSING:
• The American Red Cross: A Century of Service. By Louise Levathes. Photos by Annie Griffiths. Included: A new role for home nursing. 777-791, June 1981

NUTRITION RESEARCH:
• The Incredible Potato. By Robert E. Rhoades. Photos by Martin Rogers. 668-694, May 1982

NYGAARD, ARNVID: Author:
• Native's Return to Norway. Photos by Andrew H. Brown. 683-691, Nov. 1953

O

OAHU (Island), Hawaii:
• A Walk in the Deep. By Sylvia A. Earle. Photos by Al Giddings and Chuck Nicklin. 624-631, May 1980
• Which Way Oahu? By Gordon Young. Photos by Robert W. Madden. 653-679, Nov. 1979
• *See also* Honolulu

OAK RIDGE, Tennessee:
• Man's New Servant, the Friendly Atom. By F. Barrows Colton. Photos by Volkmar Wentzel. 71-90, Jan. 1954
• Whatever Happened to TVA? By Gordon Young. Photos by Emory Kristof. 830-863, June 1973

OAKES, ROBERT S.: Photographer:
• Of Air and Space (National Air and Space Museum). By Michael Collins. 819-837, June 1978
Picture portfolio by Nathan Benn, Robert S. Oakes, and Joseph D. Lavenburg, with text by Michael E. Long. 825-837

OASES, Ocean-floor:
• Oases of Life in the Cold Abyss (Galapagos Rift). By John B. Corliss and Robert D. Ballard. 441-453, Oct. 1977
• Return to Oases of the Deep. By Robert D. Ballard and J. Frederick Grassle. 689-705, Nov. 1979

OASIS-HOPPING in the Sahara. By Maynard Owen Williams. 209-236, Feb. 1949

OATES, LAWRENCE EDWARD GRACE:
• The British Way. By Sir Evelyn Wrench. 421-541, Apr. 1949

OB (River), U.S.S.R.:
• Siberia's Empire Road, the River Ob. By Robert Paul Jordan. Photos by Dean Conger. 145-181, Feb. 1976

O'BRIEN, MICHAEL: Photographer:
• Wrestlin' for a Livin' With King Coal. By Michael E. Long. 793-819, June 1983

OBSERVATORIES, Astronomical:
▲ *Journey Into the Universe Through Time and Space; National Geographic-Palomar Sky Survey Charting the Heavens,* double-sided supplement. June 1983
• New Light on the Changing Face of Mars. By E. C. Slipher. Included: The Lamont-Hussey Observatory. 427-436, Sept. 1955
• The Once and Future Universe. By Rick Gore. Photos by James A. Sugar. Paintings by Barron Storey. Picture text by David Jeffery. 704-749, June 1983
• *See also* Lowell Observatory, Arizona; Palomar Observatory, California; U. S. Naval Observatory, Washington, D. C.

OCCUPIED Austria, Outpost of Democracy. By George W. Long. Photos by Volkmar Wentzel. 749-790, June 1951

OCEAN ENERGY:
• Conservation: Can We Live Better on Less? By Rick Gore. 34-57, *Special Report on Energy* (Feb. 1981)
• New World of the Ocean. By Samuel W. Matthews. 792-832, Dec. 1981
• The Promise of Ocean Energy. 51, *Special Report on Energy* (Feb. 1981)

OCEAN FARMING. *See* Aquaculture

OCEAN FLOORS:
▲ *Arctic Ocean Floor,* double-sided supplement. Oct. 1971
▲ *Atlantic Ocean Floor,* double-sided Atlas series supplement. June 1968
▪ Dive to the Edge of Creation: Galapagos Rift Expedition. 682, Nov. 1979; 1, Cover, Jan. 1980
◆ *Exploring Our Living Planet.* 1983; Announced. 824, Dec. 1982
• Four Years of Diving to the Bottom of the Sea. By Georges S. Houot. NGS research grant. 715-731, May 1958
▲ *The Historic Mediterranean; The Mediterranean Seafloor,* double-sided supplement. Dec. 1982
• Incredible World of the Deep-sea Rifts. NGS research grant. 680-705, Nov. 1979
▲ *Indian Ocean Floor,* supplement. Oct. 1967
▲ *Pacific Ocean Floor,* double-sided supplement. Oct. 1969
• This Changing Earth. By Samuel W. Matthews. 1-37, Jan. 1973
• Working for Weeks on the Sea Floor. By Jacques-Yves Cousteau. Photos by Philippe Cousteau and Bates Littlehales. NGS research grant. 498-537, Apr. 1966
▲ *The World; The World Ocean Floor,* double-sided supplement. Dec. 1981
• *See also* Cayman Trough; Japan Trench; Mariana Trench; Oases, Ocean-floor; Rifts, Ocean-floor; Romanche Trench

"OCEAN mammals are to us what the buffalo was to the Plains Indian." By Lael Morgan. 354-355, Mar. 1973

OCEANAUTS:
• Working for Weeks on the Sea Floor. By Jacques-Yves Cousteau. Photos by Philippe Cousteau and Bates Littlehales. 498-537, Apr. 1966
• *See also* Underwater Living

OCEANIA. *See* Palau Islands; Society Islands; South Pacific Islands

OCEANOGRAPHY:
• Antarctica's Nearer Side. By Samuel W. Matthews. Photos by William R. Curtsinger. 622-655, Nov. 1971
• At Home in the Sea (Underwater Lodge). By Jacques-Yves Cousteau. 465-507, Apr. 1964
• *Calypso* Explores an Undersea Canyon (Romanche Trench). By Jacques-Yves Cousteau. Photos by Bates Littlehales. NGS research grant. 373-396, Mar. 1958
• The Continental Shelf: Man's New Frontier. By Luis Marden. Photos by Ira Block. 495-531, Apr. 1978
• Deep Diving off Japan (Japan Trench). By Georges S. Houot. NGS research grant. 138-150, Jan. 1960
• The Deepest Days. By Robert Sténuit. NGS research grant. 534-547, Apr. 1965
• *Deepstar* Explores the Ocean Floor. Photos by Ron Church. 110-129, Jan. 1971
▪ Dive to the Edge of Creation: Galapagos Rift Expedition. 682, Nov. 1979; 1, Cover, Jan. 1980
• Diving Saucer Takes to the Deep. By Jacques-Yves Cousteau. NGS research grant. 571-586, Apr. 1960
• Diving Through an Undersea Avalanche. By Jacques-Yves Cousteau. NGS research grant. 538-542, Apr. 1955
• Exploring Davy Jones's Locker with *Calypso.* By Jacques-Yves Cousteau. Photos by Luis Marden. NGS research grant. 149-161, Feb. 1956
◆ *Exploring the Deep Frontier.* 1980
• Exploring the Mid-Atlantic Ridge. By Maurice Ewing. NGS research grant. 275-294, Sept. 1948
• Fish Men Explore a New World Undersea. By Jacques-Yves Cousteau. 431-472, Oct. 1952

O P

• Four Years of Diving to the Bottom of the Sea. By Georges S. Houot. NGS research grant. 715-731, May 1958
▲ *The Historic Mediterranean; The Mediterranean Seafloor,* double-sided supplement. Dec. 1982
• Incredible World of the Deep-sea Rifts. NGS research grant. 680-705, Nov. 1979
I. Strange World Without Sun. The Editor. 680-688; II. Return to Oases of the Deep. By Robert D. Ballard and J. Frederick Grassle. 689-705
• Inflatable Ship Opens New Era of Airborne Undersea Expeditions. By Jacques-Yves Cousteau. NGS research grant. 142-148, July 1961
• The Long, Deep Dive. By Lord Kilbracken. Photos by Bates Littlehales. NGS research grant. 718-731, May 1963
• Man's Deepest Dive (Challenger Deep in the Mariana Trench). By Jacques Piccard. Photos by Thomas J. Abercrombie. 224-239, Aug. 1960
• The Mediterranean–Sea of Man's Fate. By Rick Gore. Photos by Jonathan Blair. 694-737, Dec. 1982
◆ *The Mysterious Undersea World.* 1980
• New Discoveries on the Mid-Atlantic Ridge. By Maurice Ewing. Photos by Robert F. Sisson. 611-640, Nov. 1949
• New World of the Ocean. By Samuel W. Matthews. 792-832, Dec. 1981
• Oases of Life in the Cold Abyss (Galapagos Rift). By John B. Corliss and Robert D. Ballard. 441-453, Oct. 1977
• The Ocean. By Jacques-Yves Cousteau. 780-791, Dec. 1981
◆ *The Ocean Realm.* 1978
• Our Man-in-Sea Project. By Edwin A. Link. NGS research grant. 713-717, May 1963
• Outpost Under the Ocean. By Edwin A. Link. Photos by Bates Littlehales. NGS research grant. 530-533, Apr. 1965
• President's Report to Members: An Exciting Year of Discovery. By Gilbert M. Grosvenor. 820-824, Dec. 1982
• Project FAMOUS. Photos by Emory Kristof. 586-615, May 1975
I. Where the Earth Turns Inside Out. By J. R. Heirtzler. 586-603; II. Dive Into the Great Rift. By Robert D. Ballard. 604-615
• Science Explores the Monsoon Sea. By Samuel W. Matthews. Photos by Robert F. Sisson. 554-575, Oct. 1967
• Scientists Ride Ice Islands on Arctic Odysseys. By Lowell Thomas, Jr. Photos by Ted Spiegel. 670-691, Nov. 1965
• Stalking Seals Under Antarctic Ice. By Carleton Ray. 54-65, Jan. 1966
• Tektite II. 256-296, Aug. 1971
I. Science's Window on the Sea. By John G. VanDerwalker. Photos by Bates Littlehales. 256-289; II. All-girl Team Tests the Habitat. By Sylvia A. Earle. Paintings by Pierre Mion. 291-296

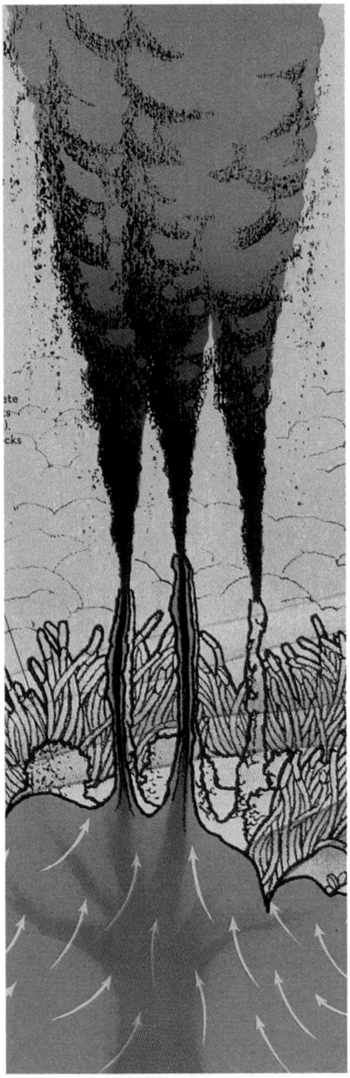

PAINTING BY WILLIAM H. BOND, NGS

Oases of the Deep: warm-water vents

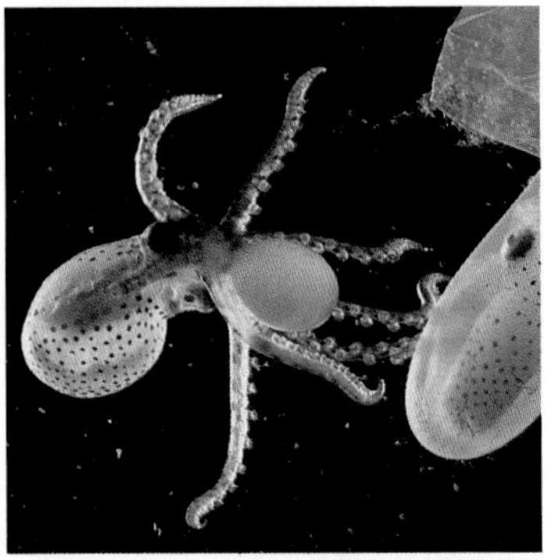

ROBERT F. SISSON, NGS

Shy Monster: newly hatched octopus

• This Changing Earth. By Samuel W. Matthews. 1-37, Jan. 1973
• Three Months on an Arctic Ice Island. By Joseph O. Fletcher. 489-504, Apr. 1953
• To the Depths of the Sea by Bathyscaphe. By Jacques-Yves Cousteau. NGS research grant. 67-79, July 1954
• Tomorrow on the Deep Frontier. By Edwin A. Link. NGS research grant. 778-801, June 1964
• Twelve National Geographic Society Scientific Projects Under Way. Included: *Calypso* oceanographic expedition, off Madagascar; French Navy's bathyscaphe dives. 869-870, June 1954
• Two and a Half Miles Down. By Georges S. Houot. NGS research grant. 80-86, July 1954
• A Walk in the Deep. By Sylvia A. Earle. Photos by Al Giddings and Chuck Nicklin. 624-631, May 1980
• What's Happening to Our Climate? By Samuel W. Matthews. 576-615, Nov. 1976
• Window on Earth's Interior. By Robert D. Ballard. Photos by Emory Kristof. Contents: Cayman Trough. 228-249, Aug. 1976
• Working for Weeks on the Sea Floor. By Jacques-Yves Cousteau. Photos by Philippe Cousteau and Bates Littlehales. NGS research grant. 498-537, Apr. 1966
▲ *The World; The World Ocean Floor,* double-sided supplement. Dec. 1981
◆ *World Beneath the Sea.* Announced. 868-875, June 1967
• *See also* Airborne Undersea Expeditions; Bathyscaphs; Ilha Nova (Volcanic Island); Marine Biology; Myojin Island (Volcano); National Oceanographic Program; Research Vessels; Scripps Institution of Oceanography; Tides and Tidal Bores

OCEANS:
• New World of the Ocean. By Samuel W. Matthews. 792-832, Dec. 1981
• The Ocean. By Jacques-Yves Cousteau. 780-791, Dec. 1981
▲ *The World; The World Ocean Floor,* double-sided supplement. Dec. 1981
• *See also* Arctic Ocean; Atlantic Ocean; Indian Ocean; Pacific Ocean

OCTOBER Holiday on the Outer Banks. By Nike Anderson. Photos by J. Baylor Roberts. 501-529, Oct. 1955

OCTOPUSES:
• Fish Men Explore a New World Undersea. By Jacques-Yves Cousteau. 431-472, Oct. 1952
• Shy Monster, the Octopus. By Gilbert L. Voss. Photos by Robert F. Sisson. 776-799, Dec. 1971

ODENSE, Denmark:
• The Magic World of Hans Christian Andersen. By Harvey Arden. Photos by Sisse Brimberg. 825-849, Dec. 1979
• 2,000 Miles Through Europe's Oldest Kingdom. By Isobel Wylie Hutchison. Photos by Maynard Owen Williams. 141-180, Feb. 1949

ODYSSEY (Homer):
• Homeward With Ulysses. By Melville Bell Grosvenor. Photos by Edwin Stuart Grosvenor. 1-39, July 1973

OEHSER, PAUL H.: Editor:
◆ *Research Reports* (NGS). 442, Sept. 1975; 296, Aug. 1976; 294, Feb. 1978; 298, Aug. 1979

OF Air and Space (National Air and Space Museum). By Michael Collins. 819-837, June 1978

OF City, Ships, and Surf (Golden Gate National Recreation Area, California). By David S. Boyer. 98-105, July 1979

OF Planes and Men. By Kenneth F. Weaver. Photos by Emory Kristof and Albert Moldvay. 298-349, Sept. 1965

OFF Santa Barbara: California's Ranches in the Sea. By Earl Warren, Jr. Photos by Bates Littlehales. 257-283, Aug. 1958

OFF the Beaten Track of Empire. By Beverley M. Bowie. Photos by Michael Parker. 584-626, Nov. 1957

OFFICE OF NAVAL RESEARCH (ONR):
• Study Grant: Underwater Exploration: Galapagos Rift. 682, 685, Nov. 1979
• To 76,000 Feet by *Strato-Lab* Balloon. By Malcolm D. Ross and M. Lee Lewis. 269-282, Feb. 1957

OFFICE OF SCIENTIFIC RESEARCH AND DEVELOPMENT (OSRD):
• Voices of the Night. By Arthur A. Allen. Included: OSRD's project on jungle acoustics. 507-522, Apr. 1950

OFFSHORE PETROLEUM LEASES:
▲ *America's Federal Lands; The United States,* double-sided supplement. Sept. 1982

OGADEN (Region), Ethiopia:
• Somalia's Hour of Need. By Robert Paul Jordan. Photos by Michael S. Yamashita and Kevin Fleming. Included: Refugees and guerrillas from the disputed Ogaden region now residing in Somalia. 748-775, June 1981
Encampments of the Dispossessed. By Larry Kohl. 756-763

OGALLALA AQUIFER, U. S.:
• Our Most Precious Resource: Water. By Thomas Y. Canby. Photos by Ted Spiegel. 144-179, Aug. 1980

OGASAWARA, FRANK X.: Author:
• Scientist Studies Japan's Fantastic Long-tailed Fowl. Photos by Eiji Miyazawa. 845-855, Dec. 1970

OGBURN, CHARLTON: Author:
• Island, Prairie, Marsh, and Shore. Photos by Bates Littlehales. 350-381, Mar. 1979

OHIO:
▲ *Close-up: U.S.A., Illinois, Indiana, Ohio, and Kentucky,* supplement. Text on reverse. Feb. 1977
• The Ohio–River With a Job to Do. By Priit J. Vesilind. Photos by Martin Rogers. 245-273, Feb. 1977
• Ohio Makes Its Own Prosperity. By Leo A. Borah. Photos by B. Anthony Stewart. 435-484, Apr. 1955
• "Pyramids" of the New World. By Neil Merton Judd. Included: Chillicothe, Cincinnati, "Great Serpent," Marietta. 105-128, Jan. 1948
• Skyway Below the Clouds. By Carl R. Markwith. Photos by Ernest J. Cottrell. Included: Dayton, Wright Field, and Zanesville. 85-108, July 1949
• So Much Happens Along the Ohio River. By Frederick Simpich. Photos by Justin Locke. 177-212, Feb. 1950
• Who Were the "Mound Builders"? By George E. Stuart. Included: The Adena culture at Chillicothe; the Hopewell culture at Fort Ancient and Newark; Serpent Mound. 783-801, Dec. 1972
• *See also* Bass Islands

OHIO (River), U. S.:
▲ *Close-up: U.S.A., Illinois, Indiana, Ohio, and Kentucky,* supplement. Text on reverse. Feb. 1977
• The Ohio–River With a Job to Do. By Priit J. Vesilind. Photos by Martin Rogers. 245-273, Feb. 1977
• Shawneetown Forsakes the Ohio. By William H. Nicholas. Photos by J. Baylor Roberts. 273-288, Feb. 1948
• So Much Happens Along the Ohio River. By Frederick Simpich. Photos by Justin Locke. 177-212, Feb. 1950

OHIO VALLEY, Ohio-West Virginia:
• Who Were the "Mound Builders"? By George E. Stuart. 783-801, Dec. 1972

OIL:
• Alberta Unearths Her Buried Treasures. By David S. Boyer. 90-119, July 1960
▲ *America's Federal Lands; The United States,* double-sided supplement. Included: Inset map showing drilling sites. Sept. 1982
• The Arab World, Inc. By John J. Putman. Photos by Winfield Parks. 494-533, Oct. 1975
• An Atlas of Energy Resources. 58-69, *Special Report on Energy* (Feb. 1981)
Oil: Lifeblood and Liability. 58-59
• Bahrain: Hub of the Persian Gulf. By Thomas J. Abercrombie. Photos by Steve Raymer. 300-329, Sept. 1979
• Boom Time in Kuwait. By Paul Edward Case. 783-802, Dec. 1952
• *Calypso* Explores for Underwater Oil. By Jacques-Yves Cousteau. NGS research grant. 155-184, Aug. 1955
• Canada's "Now" Frontier. By Robert Paul Jordan. Photos by Lowell Georgia. Included: Map showing oil pipeline, proposed gas pipeline, and tar sands. 480-511, Oct. 1976
• The Canadian North: Emerging Giant. By David S. Boyer. 1-43, July 1968
• The Continental Shelf: Man's New Frontier. By Luis Marden. Photos by Ira Block. 495-531, Apr. 1978
• Editorial. By Gilbert M. Grosvenor. 443, Oct. 1975

EMORY KRISTOF, NGS
Energy Report: **Kuwaiti with crude oil**

O P

• The Fabulous State of Texas. By Stanley Walker. Photos by B. Anthony Stewart and Thomas Nebbia. 149-195, Feb. 1961
• Giants That Move the World's Oil: Superships. By Noel Grove. Photos by Martin Rogers. 102-124, July 1978
• Happy-go-lucky Trinidad and Tobago. By Charles Allmon. 35-75, Jan. 1953
• High-Flying Tulsa. By Robert Paul Jordan. Photos by Annie Griffiths. 378-403, Sept. 1983
• Houston, Prairie Dynamo. By Stuart E. Jones. Photos by William Albert Allard. 338-377, Sept. 1967
• Iran: Desert Miracle. By William Graves. Photos by James P. Blair. 2-47, Jan. 1975
• Iraq–Where Oil and Water Mix. By Jean and Franc Shor. 443-489, Oct. 1958
• Journey into Troubled Iran. By George W. Long. Photos by J. Baylor Roberts. 425-464, Oct. 1951
• Kuwait, Aladdin's Lamp of the Middle East. By John E. Frazer. Photos by David F. Cupp. 636-667, May 1969
• Louisiana Trades with the World. By Frederick Simpich. Photos by J. Baylor Roberts. 705-738, Dec. 1947
• Mexico: "A Very Beautiful Challenge," By Mike Edwards. Photos by Thomas Nebbia. 612-647, May 1978
• Oil, the Dwindling Treasure. By Noel Grove. Photos by Emory Kristof. 792-825, June 1974
• Oklahoma, the Adventurous One. By Robert Paul Jordan. Photos by Robert W. Madden. 149-189, Aug. 1971
• Oman: Guardian of the Gulf. By Thomas J. Abercrombie. Photos by the author and Lynn Abercrombie. 344-377, Sept. 1981
• Oman, Land of Frankincense and Oil. By Robert Azzi. 205-229, Feb. 1973
• Pennsylvania: Faire Land of William Penn. By Gordon Young. Photos by Cary Wolinsky. 731-767, June 1978
• Sand in My Eyes (Algerian Sahara). By Jinx Rodger. 664-705, May 1958
• Saudi Arabia: Beyond the Sands of Mecca. By Thomas J. Abercrombie. 1-53, Jan. 1966
• Saudi Arabia, Oil Kingdom. Photos by Maynard Owen Williams. 497-512, Apr. 1948
• Saudi Arabia: The Kingdom and Its Power. By Robert Azzi. 286-333, Sept. 1980
• Siberia's Empire Road, the River Ob. By Robert Paul Jordan. Photos by Dean Conger. 145-181, Feb. 1976
• Striking It Rich in the North Sea. By Rick Gore. Photos by Dick Durrance II. 519-549, Apr. 1977
• A Sumatran Journey. By Harvey Arden. Photos by David Alan Harvey. 406-430, Mar. 1981
• This Young Giant, Indonesia. By Beverley M. Bowie. Photos by J. Baylor Roberts. 351-392, Sept. 1955
• Troubled Waters East of Suez. By Ernest M. Eller. 483-522, Apr. 1954
• Venezuela Builds on Oil. By Thomas J. Abercrombie. 344-387, Mar. 1963
• Venezuela's Crisis of Wealth. By Noel Grove. Photos by Robert W. Madden. 175-209, Aug. 1976
• Where Oil and Wildlife Mix. By Steven C. Wilson and Karen C. Hayden. 145-173, Feb. 1981
• *See also* North Slope, Alaska; *and* Conshelf Bases, for underwater oil wellhead experiment; Offshore Petroleum Leases; Oil Shale; Tankers

OIL, Vegetable:
• Rediscovering America's Forgotten Crops. By Noel D. Vietmeyer. Photos by Burgess Blevins. Paintings by Paul M. Breeden. Included: Jojoba oil. 702-712, May 1981

OIL and Penguins Don't Mix. Photos by Mike Holmes. 384-397, Mar. 1973

OIL SHALE:
• Synfuels: Fill 'er Up! With What? By Thomas Y. Canby. Photos by Jonathan Blair. 74-95, *Special Report on Energy* (Feb. 1981)
Wresting Oil From Reluctant Rock. 78-79

OIL SPILLS:
• Barehanded Battle to Cleanse the Bay. By Peter T. White. Photos by Jonathan S. Blair. 866-881, June 1971
• Editorial. By Gilbert M. Grosvenor. 1, July 1978
• Giants That Move the World's Oil: Superships. By Noel Grove. Photos by Martin Rogers. 102-124, July 1978
• Oil and Penguins Don't Mix. Photos by Mike Holmes. 384-397, Mar. 1973
• Superspill: Black Day for Brittany. Photos by Martin Rogers. Text by Noel Grove. 124-135, July 1978
• Where Oil and Wildlife Mix. By Steven C. Wilson and Karen C. Hayden. 145-173, Feb. 1981

OILBIRDS:
• Birds That "See" in the Dark with Their Ears. By Edward S. Ross. 282-290, Feb. 1965

OKEECHOBEE, Lake, Florida:
• The Imperiled Everglades. By Fred Ward. 1-27, Jan. 1972
• Threatened Glories of Everglades National Park. By Frederick Kent Truslow and Frederick G. Vosburgh. Photos by Frederick Kent Truslow and Otis Imboden. Included: Drainage from Lake Okeechobee in 1880, 1920, and 1967. 508-553, Oct. 1967

OKEFENOKEE SWAMP, Florida-Georgia:
• Okefenokee, the Magical Swamp. By François Leydet. Photos by Farrell Grehan. 169-175, Feb. 1974

OKINAWA (Island), Ryukyu Islands:
• Okinawa, Pacific Outpost. 538-552, Apr. 1950
• Okinawa, the Island Rebuilt. By Hope A. Diffenderfer. 265-288, Feb. 1955
• Okinawa, the Island Without a Country. By Jules B. Billard. Photos by Winfield Parks and David Moore. 422-448, Sept. 1969

OKLAHOMA:
• North With the Wheat Cutters. By Noel Grove. Photos by James A. Sugar. 194-217, Aug. 1972
• Oklahoma, the Adventurous One. By Robert Paul Jordan. Photos by Robert W. Madden. 149-189, Aug. 1971
• Skyway Below the Clouds. By Carl R. Markwith. Photos by Ernest J. Cottrell. Included: Monkey Island Airport, Lake O' The Cherokees, Oklahoma City, Tulsa. 85-108, July 1949
• Who Were the "Mound Builders"? By George E. Stuart. 783-801, Dec. 1972
• The Wichitas: Land of the Living Prairie. By M. Woodbridge Williams. 661-697, May 1957
• *See also* Tulsa

ÖLAND (Island), Sweden:
• Baltic Cruise of the *Caribbee*. By Carleton Mitchell. 605-646, Nov. 1950

OLD BELIEVERS:
• Nikolaevsk: A Bit of Old Russia Takes Root in Alaska. By Jim Rearden. Photos by Charles O'Rear. 401-425, Sept. 1972

OLD BERING SEA PEOPLE:
• Nomads of the Far North. By Matthew W. Stirling. Paintings by W. Langdon Kihn. 471-504, Oct. 1949

OLD Big Strong: The Lower Mississippi. By Willard Price. Photos by W. D. Vaughn. 681-725, Nov. 1960

The **OLD** Boston Post Roads. By Donald Barr Chidsey. 189-205, Aug. 1962

OLD-NEW Iran, Next Door to Russia. By Edward J. Linehan. Photos by Thomas J. Abercrombie. 44-85, Jan. 1961

OLD POST OFFICE, Washington, D. C.:
• A Preservation Victory Saves Washington's Old Post Office. By Wolf Von Eckardt. Photos by Volkmar Wentzel. 407-416, Sept. 1983

OLD Prague in Winter. By Peter T. White. Photos by Nathan Benn. 546-567, Apr. 1979

OLD RHINEBECK AERODROME, Rhinebeck, New York:
• World War I Aircraft Fly Again in Rhinebeck's Rickety Rendezvous. By Harvey Arden. Photos by Howard Sochurek. 578-587, Oct. 1970

OLD SALEM, North Carolina:
• Old Salem, Morning Star of Moravian Faith. By Rowe Findley. Photos by Robert W. Madden. 818-837, Dec. 1970

OLD Whaling Days Still Flavor Life on Sea-swept Martha's Vineyard. By William P. E. Graves. Photos by James P. Blair. 778-809, June 1961

OLDEST Known Shipwreck Yields Bronze Age Cargo. By Peter Throckmorton. NGS research grant. 697-711, May 1962

OLDEST PEOPLE:
- "Every Day Is a Gift When You Are Over 100." By Alexander Leaf. Photos by John Launois. 93-119, Jan. 1973

OLDUVAI GORGE, Tanzania:
- Adventures in the Search for Man. By Louis S. B. Leakey. Photos by Hugo van Lawick. NGS research grant. 132-152, Jan. 1963
- ■ Dr. Leakey and the Dawn of Man. 703A-703B, Nov. 1966
- Exploring 1,750,000 Years Into Man's Past. By L. S. B. Leakey. Photos by Robert F. Sisson. NGS research grant. 564-589, Oct. 1961
- Finding the World's Earliest Man (*Zinjanthropus boisei*). By L. S. B. Leakey. Photos by Des Bartlett. NGS research grant. 420-435, Sept. 1960
- The Leakey Tradition Lives On. By Melvin M. Payne. NGS research grant. 143-144, Jan. 1973
- The Leakeys of Africa: Family in Search of Prehistoric Man. By Melvin M. Payne. NGS research grant. 194-231, Feb. 1965
- Preserving the Treasures of Olduvai Gorge. By Melvin M. Payne. Photos by Joseph J. Scherschel. NGS research grant. 701-709, Nov. 1966

O'LEARY, JOHN F.:
- What Six Experts Say. 70-73, *Special Report on Energy* (Feb. 1981)

ÓLIMBOS, Kárpathos (Island), Greece:
- Eternal Easter in a Greek Village. By Maria Nicolaidis-Karanikolas. Photos by James L. Stanfield. 768-777, Dec. 1983

OLIVER, JAMES A.: Author:
- Behind New York's Window on Nature: The American Museum of Natural History. Photos by Robert F. Sisson. 220-259, Feb. 1963

OLIVES AND OLIVE OIL INDUSTRY:
- How Fruit Came to America. By J. R. Magness. Paintings by Else Bostelmann. 325-377, Sept. 1951
- Speaking of Spain. By Luis Marden. 415-456, Apr. 1950

OLMECS (Indians):
- Gifts for the Jaguar God. By Philip Drucker and Robert F. Heizer. 367-375, Sept. 1956
- On the Trail of La Venta Man. By Matthew W. Stirling. Photos by Richard H. Stewart. 137-172, Feb. 1947

OLMSTEAD, JUDITH: Author:
- Ethiopia's Artful Weavers. Photos by James A. Sugar. 125-141, Jan. 1973

OLSON, SIGURD F.: Author:
- Relics from the Rapids (Voyageurs). Photos by David S. Boyer. 413-435, Sept. 1963

OLYMPIC GAMES:
- Again–the Olympic Challenge. By Alan J. Gould. 488-513, Oct. 1964

THOMAS J. ABERCROMBIE, NGS

Oman: Bedouin woman masks face

- Sports-minded Melbourne, Host to the Olympics. 688-693, Nov. 1956
- Tokyo, the Peaceful Explosion. By William Graves. Photos by Winfield Parks. 445-487, Oct. 1964

OLYMPIC MOUNTAINS, Washington:
- A Map Maker Looks at the United States. By Newman Bumstead. 705-748, June 1951

OLYMPIC NATIONAL PARK, Washington:
- In the Gardens of Olympus. By Paul A. Zahl. 85-123, July 1955
- The Olympics: Northwest Majesty. By François Leydet. Photos by Farrell Grehan. 188-197, Feb. 1974

OLYMPIC PENINSULA, Washington. *See* Olympic National Park

OMAHA, Nebraska:
- Nebraska . . . the Good Life. By Robert Paul Jordan. Photos by Lowell Georgia. 378-407, Mar. 1974

OMAN:
- The Arab World, Inc. By John J. Putman. Photos by Winfield Parks. 494-533, Oct. 1975
- Editorial. By Wilbur E. Garrett. 279, Sept. 1981
- In the Wake of Sindbad. By Tim Severin. Photos by Richard Greenhill. Note: The Sindbad project was sponsored by Oman's Ministry of National Heritage and Culture. The project was financed by the sultan on behalf of Oman and the Arab world. 2-41, July 1982
- Oman: Guardian of the Gulf. By Thomas J. Abercrombie. Photos by the author and Lynn Abercrombie. 344-377, Sept. 1981
- Oman, Land of Frankincense and Oil. By Robert Azzi. 205-229, Feb. 1973
- *See also* Muscat and Oman; *and* Dhows

OMENS for a Better Tomorrow. By Thomas J. Abercrombie. 312-343, Mar. 1977

ON a Peaceful Good Friday, Alaskans Feel the Dread Earthquake! By William P. E. Graves. 112-139, July 1964

ON Australia's Coral Ramparts. By Paul A. Zahl. 1-48, Jan. 1957

ON the Geographic's 75th Birthday–Our Best to You. By Melville Bell Grosvenor. 459, Oct. 1963

ON the Ridgepole of the Rockies. By Walter Meayers Edwards. 745-780, June 1947

ON the Road With an Old-time Circus. By John Fetterman. Photos by Jonathan Blair. 410-434, Mar. 1972

ON the Slope of Vesuvius: A Buried Roman Town Gives Up Its Dead. By Joseph Judge. Photos by Jonathan Blair. 687-693, Dec. 1982

ON the Summit (Annapurna). By Irene Miller, with Vera Komarkova. 312-313, Mar. 1979

Onges: man's face decorated with paste of clay and turtle fat, *below;* Jarawa woman, *bottom*

BOTH BY RAGHUBIR SINGH

ON the Track of the West's Wild Horses. By Hope Ryden. Photos by author and Dick Durrance II. 94-109, Jan. 1971

ON the Trail of La Venta Man. By Matthew W. Stirling. Photos by Richard H. Stewart. NGS research grant. 137-172, Feb. 1947

ON the Trail of Wisconsin's Ice Age. By Anne LaBastille. Photos by Cary Wolinsky. 182-205, Aug. 1977

ON the Winds of the Dodecanese. By Jean and Franc Shor. 351-390, Mar. 1953

ON to the Summit (K2). By James Wickwire. 641-649, May 1979

ONAGADORI (Long-tailed Fowl):
• Scientist Studies Japan's Fantastic Long-tailed Fowl. By Frank X. Ogasawara. Photos by Eiji Miyazawa. 845-855, Dec. 1970

ONASSIS, JACQUELINE KENNEDY. *See* Kennedy, Jacqueline Bouvier

The **ONCE** and Future Universe. By Rick Gore. Photos by James A. Sugar. Paintings by Barron Storey. Picture text by David Jeffery. 704-749, June 1983

ONE Canada–or Two? By Peter T. White. Photos by Winfield Parks. 436-465, Apr. 1977

ONE Family's Odyssey to America. By John Everingham. 642-661, May 1980

ONE Hundred Hours Beneath the Chesapeake. By Gilbert C. Klingel. Photos by Willard R. Culver. NGS research grant. 681-696, May 1955

ONE Man's London. By Allan C. Fisher, Jr. Photos by James P. Blair. 743-791, June 1966

ONE Strange Night on Turtle Beach. By Paul A. Zahl. 570-581, Oct. 1973

O'NEILL, THOMAS J.: Author:
• Amber: Golden Window on the Past. Photos by Paul A. Zahl. 423-435, Sept. 1977
• Dazzling Corals of Palau. Photos by Douglas Faulkner. 136-150, July 1978
• The Four-eyed Fish Sees All. Photos by Paul A. Zahl. 390-395, Mar. 1978

ONELLI, LUIGI: Photographer:
• Italy Smiles Again. By Edgar Erskine Hume. 693-732, June 1949

ONGES (Negrito Tribe):
• The Last Andaman Islanders. By Raghubir Singh. 66-91, July 1975

ONTARIO (Province), Canada:
• Across Canada by Mackenzie's Track. By Ralph Gray. 191-239, Aug. 1955
• Canada, My Country. By Alan Phillips. Photos by David S. Boyer and Walter Meayers Edwards. 769-819, Dec. 1961
• Canada's Dynamic Heartland, Ontario. By Marjorie Wilkins Campbell. Photos by Winfield Parks. 58-97, July 1963
▲ *Close-up, Canada: Ontario,* supplement. Text on reverse. Dec. 1978
• The Great Lakes: Is It Too Late? By Gordon Young. Photos by James L. Amos and Martin Rogers. 147-185, Aug. 1973
• Ontario, Canada's Keystone. By David S. Boyer. Photos by Sam Abell and the author. 760-795, Dec. 1978
• Ontario, Pivot of Canada's Power. By Andrew H. Brown. Photos by B. Anthony Stewart and Bates Littlehales. 823-852, Dec. 1953
• Relics from the Rapids (Voyageurs). By Sigurd F. Olson. Photos by David S. Boyer. 413-435, Sept. 1963
• *See also* Kingston; Niagara Falls; Ottawa; St. Lawrence Seaway; Toronto

ONTARIO, Lake, Canada-U. S.:
• Ghost Ships of the War of 1812: *Hamilton* and *Scourge*. By Daniel A. Nelson. Photos by Emory Kristof. Paintings by Richard Schlecht. 289-313, Mar. 1983
• The Great Lakes: Is It Too Late? By Gordon Young. Photos by James L. Amos and Martin Rogers. 147-185, Aug. 1973

OPAL MINING:
• Coober Pedy: Opal Capital of Australia's Outback. By Kenny Moore. Photos by Penny Tweedie. 560-571, Oct. 1976
• South Australia, Gateway to the Great Outback. By Howell Walker. Photos by Joseph J. Scherschel. 441-481, Apr. 1970

OPEC. *See* Organization of Petroleum Exporting Countries

The **OPENING** of the American West: Burr's 1840 Map. 762-763, June 1953

OPERATION CROSSROADS (Atomic Bomb Tests). Photos by Joint Task Force I. Paintings by Charles Bittinger. 519-530, Apr. 1947

OPERATION DEEP FREEZE:
• Across the Frozen Desert to Byrd Station. By Paul W. Frazier. Photos by Calvin L. Larsen. 383-398, Sept. 1957
• All-out Assault on Antarctica. By Richard E. Byrd. 141-180, Aug. 1956
• Antarctica: Icy Testing Ground for Space. By Samuel W. Matthews. Photos by Robert W. Madden. 569-592, Oct. 1968
• Flight Into Antarctic Darkness. By J. Lloyd Abbot, Jr. Photos by David S. Boyer. 732-738, Nov. 1967
• Man's First Winter at the South Pole. By Paul A. Siple. 439-478, Apr. 1958
• New Era in the Loneliest Continent. By David M. Tyree. Photos by Albert Moldvay. 260-296, Feb. 1963
• We Are Living at the South Pole. By Paul A. Siple. Photos by David S. Boyer. 5-35, July 1957
• What We've Accomplished in Antarctica. By George J. Dufek. 527-557, Oct. 1959
• Year of Discovery Opens in Antarctica. By David S. Boyer. 339-381, Sept. 1957

OPERATION ECLIPSE: 1948. By William A. Kinney. NGS research grant. 325-372, Mar. 1949

OPERATION HIGHJUMP:
• Our Navy Explores Antarctica. By Richard E. Byrd. U. S. Navy official photos. 429-522, Oct. 1947

OPERATION SAIL:
• By Square-rigger from Baltic to Bicentennial. By Kenneth Garrett. 824-857, Dec. 1976

OPIUM:
• The Hmong of Laos: No Place to Run. By W. E. Garrett. 78-111, Jan. 1974
• Nature's Gifts to Medicine. By Lonnelle Aikman. Paintings by Lloyd K. Townsend and Don Crowley. 420-440, Sept. 1974
• Spirits of Change Capture the Karens. By Peter Kunstadter. 267-285, Feb. 1972

OPOSSUMS:
• Br'er Possum, Hermit of the Lowlands. By Agnes Akin Atkinson. Photos by Charles Philip Fox. 405-418, Mar. 1953
• *See also* Possums (Phalangers)

OPTICAL FIBERS:
• Fiber Optics: Harnessing Light by a Thread. By Allen A. Boraiko. Photos by Fred Ward. 516-535, Oct. 1979

OPTICS. *See* Fiber Optics; Lasers; Photography, Microscope; Telescopes; *and* Newton, Isaac, for his spectrum experiments

ORANGE COUNTY, California:
• Orange, a Most California County. By Judith and Neil Morgan. Photos by Vince Streano. 750-779, Dec. 1981

ORANGES AND ORANGE GROWING:
• Florida Rides a Space-age Boom. By Benedict Thielen. Photos by Winfield Parks and James P. Blair. 858-903, Dec. 1963
• How Fruit Came to America. By J. R. Magness. Paintings by Else Bostelmann. 325-377, Sept. 1951
• Orange, a Most California County. By Judith and Neil Morgan. Photos by Vince Streano. Included: Encroachment of commercial and residential development into former orange-grove land. 750-779, Dec. 1981

ORANGUTANS:
• Living with the Great Orange Apes: Indonesia's Orangutans. By Biruté M. F. Galdikas. Photos by Rod Brindamour. NGS research grant. 830-853, June 1980
• Orangutans, Indonesia's "People of the Forest." By Biruté Galdikas-Brindamour. Photos by Rod Brindamour. NGS research grant. 444-473, Oct. 1975
▪ Search for the Great Apes. cover, Jan. 1976

ORBITERS. *See* Space Shuttles

ORCHARD, Nebraska:
• Ancient Ashfall Creates a Pompeii of Prehistoric Animals. By Michael R. Voorhies. Photos by Annie Griffiths. Paintings by Jay Matternes. Contents: Site of a ten-million-year-old ashfall. 66-75, Jan. 1981

ORCHID ISLAND (Protectorate of Republic of China):
• The Gentle Yamis of Orchid Island. Photos by Chang Shuhua. 98-109, Jan. 1977

ORCHIDS:
• The Exquisite Orchids. By Luis Marden. 485-513, Apr. 1971
• Hawaii, Island of Fire and Flowers. By Gordon Young. Photos by Robert W. Madden. 399-425, Mar. 1975

O'REAR, CHARLES: Photographer:
• Baja's Murals of Mystery. By Harry Crosby. 692-702, Nov. 1980
• The Bird Men (Ultralight Flyers). By Luis Marden. 198-217, Aug. 1983
• The Bittersweet Waters of the Lower Colorado. By Rowe Findley. 540-569, Oct. 1973
• California's Silicon Valley. By Moira Johnston. 459-477, Oct. 1982
• California's Surprising Inland Delta. By Judith and Neil Morgan. 409-430, Sept. 1976
• The Chip: Electronic Mini-marvel. By Allen A. Boraiko. 421-457, Oct. 1982
• Dream On, Vancouver. By Mike Edwards. 467-491, Oct. 1978
• The Gulf's Workaday Waterway. By Gordon Young. 200-223, Feb. 1978
• Napa, California's Valley of the Vine. By Moira Johnston. 695-717, May 1979
• A New Riviera: Mexico's West Coast. By Nathaniel T. Kenney. 670-699, Nov. 1973
• Nikolaevsk: A Bit of Old Russia Takes Root in Alaska. By Jim Rearden. 401-425, Sept. 1972

OREGON:
• Chief Joseph. By William Albert Allard. 409-434, Mar. 1977
• Following the Trail of Lewis and Clark. By Ralph Gray. 707-750, June 1953
• Forest Fire: The Devil's Picnic. By Stuart E. Jones and Jay Johnston. Included: Big Lake Airstrip blaze in Willamette National Forest, Ochoco National Forest, Wallowa-Whitman National Forest. 100-127, July 1968
• From Sagebrush to Roses on the Columbia. By Leo A. Borah. 571-611, Nov. 1952
• A Map Maker Looks at the United States. By Newman Bumstead. Included: Albany, Astoria, Blue Mountains, Corvallis, Crater Lake, Diamond Lake, Eugene, Hells Canyon, Mount Hood, Oregon City, Portland, Rush Creek, Salem, Vanport City, Willamette Valley. 705-748, June 1951
• Oregon's Lovely, Lonely Coast. By Mark Miller. Photos by Cotton Coulson. 798-823, Dec. 1979
• Oregon's Many Faces. By Stuart E. Jones. Photos by Bates Littlehales. 74-115, Jan. 1969
• Oregon's Sidewalk on the Sea. By Paul A. Zahl. 708-734, Nov. 1961
• Powerhouse of the Northwest (Columbia River). By David S. Boyer. 821-847, Dec. 1974
• A River Restored: Oregon's Willamette. By Ethel A. Starbird. Photos by Lowell J. Georgia. 816-835, June 1972
• Sno-Cats Mechanize Oregon Snow Survey. By Andrew H. Brown. Photos by John E. Fletcher. 691-710, Nov. 1949
• Timber: How Much Is Enough? By John J. Putman. Photos by Bruce Dale. 485-511, Apr. 1974
• A Walk Across America: Part II. By Peter and Barbara Jenkins. 194-229, Aug. 1979
• Warm Springs Indians Carve Out a Future. By David S. Boyer. 494-505, Apr. 1979
• The West Through Boston Eyes. By Stewart Anderson. Included: Columbia River, Crater Lake, Klamath Falls. 733-776, June 1949
• *See also* Crater Lake

OREGON TERRITORY:
• The Opening of the American West: Burr's 1840 Map. 762-763, June 1953

O'REILLY, JOHN BOYLE:
• Literary Landmarks of Massachusetts. By William H. Nicholas. Photos by B. Anthony Stewart and John E. Fletcher. 279-310, Mar. 1950

ORGAN PIPE CACTUS NATIONAL MONUMENT, Arizona:
• Abundant Life in a Desert Land. By Walter Meayers Edwards. 424-436, Sept. 1973

ORGANIZATION OF PETROLEUM EXPORTING COUNTRIES (OPEC):
• The Arab World, Inc. By John J. Putman. Photos by Winfield Parks. 494-533, Oct. 1975

ORIENTAL, Cordillera, Andes Mountains, South America:
• El Sangay, Fire-breathing Giant of the Andes. By G. Edward Lewis. 117-138, Jan. 1950

The **ORIGINAL** Boston: St. Botolph's Town. By Veronica Thomas. Photos by James L. Amos. 382-389, Sept 1974

ORIOLES:
• An Exotic New Oriole (Spotted-breasted) Settles in Florida. By Charles M. Brookfield and Oliver Griswold. 261-264, Feb. 1956

ORISSA (State), India:
• Orissa, Past and Promise in an Indian State. By Bart McDowell. Photos by James P. Blair. 546-577, Oct. 1970

ORKNEY ISLANDS, Scotland:
• Shetland and Orkney, Britain's Far North. By Isobel Wylie Hutchison. 519-536, Oct. 1953

OP

ORLANDO, Florida:
• Florida's Booming–and Beleaguered–Heartland. By Joseph Judge. Photos by Jonathan Blair. 585-621, Nov. 1973

ORMES, ROBERT M.: Author:
• Colorado's Friendly Topland. 187-214, Aug. 1951

ORNITHOLOGY. *See* Birds

ORPHANS of the Wild. By Bruce G. Kinloch. 683-699, Nov. 1962

OSAKA, Japan:
• Kansai, Japan's Historic Heartland. By Thomas J. Abercrombie. 295-339, Mar. 1970

OSBORNE, DOUGLAS: Author:
• Solving the Riddles of Wetherill Mesa. Paintings by Peter V. Bianchi. 155-195, Feb. 1964

OSHKOSH, Wisconsin:
• Oshkosh: America's Biggest Air Show. By Michael E. Long. Photos by James A. Sugar and the author. 365-375, Sept. 1979

OSLO, Norway:
• "Around the World in Eighty Days." By Newman Bumstead. 705-750, Dec. 1951
• Baltic Cruise of the *Caribbee*. By Carleton Mitchell. 605-646, Nov. 1950
• Norway, Land of the Generous Sea. By Edward J. Linehan. Photos by George F. Mobley. 1-43, July 1971
• Norway Cracks Her Mountain Shell. By Sydney Clark. Photos by Gilbert Grosvenor and Ole Friele Backer. 171-211, Aug. 1948
• Stop-and-Go Sail Around South Norway. By Edmond J. Moran. Photos by Randi Kjekstad Bull and Andrew H. Brown. 153-192, Aug. 1954
• The Vikings. By Howard La Fay. Photos by Ted Spiegel. 492-541, Apr. 1970

OSPREYS:
• The Osprey, Endangered World Citizen. By Roger Tory Peterson. Photos by Frederick Kent Truslow. NGS research grant. 53-67, July 1969

OSSABAW (Island), Georgia:
• Sea Islands: Adventuring Along the South's Surprising Coast. By James Cerruti. Photos by Thomas Nebbia and James L. Amos. 366-393, Mar. 1971

OSTEND, Belgium:
• Belgium Comes Back. By Harvey Klemmer. Photos by Maynard Owen Williams. 575-614, May 1948

OSTIONAL BEACH, Costa Rica:
• One Strange Night on Turtle Beach. By Paul A. Zahl. 570-581, Oct. 1973

OSTROFF, EUGENE: Photographer:
• Vanished Mystery Men of Hudson Bay. By Henry B. Collins. 669-687, Nov. 1956

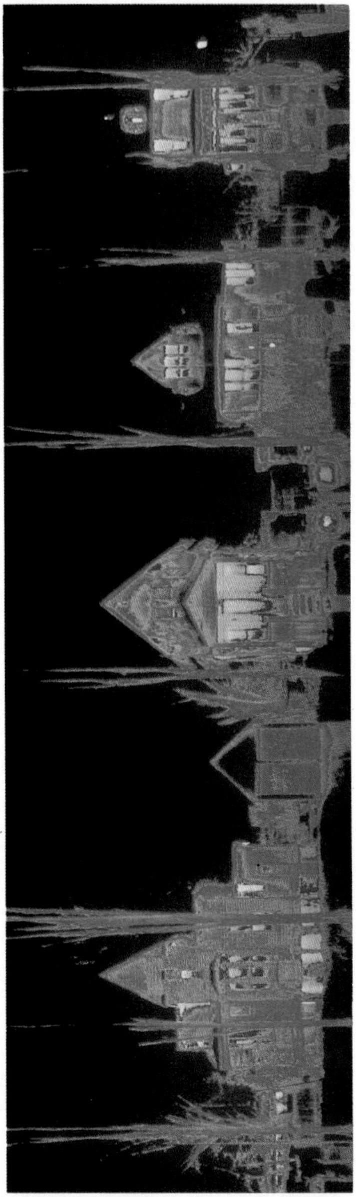

VANSCAN (TM) THERMOGRAM BY DAEDALUS ENTERPRISES, INC., ANN ARBOR, MICHIGAN

Our Energy Predicament: thermogram aids in analysis of heat loss in Michigan homes

OSTROM, JOHN H.: Author:
• A New Look at Dinosaurs. Paintings by Roy Andersen. 152-185, Aug. 1978

OTAHEITE. *See* Tahiti

The **OTHER** Nevada. By Robert Laxalt. Photos by J. Bruce Baumann. 733-761, June 1974

The **OTHER** Side of Jordan. By Luis Marden. 790-825, Dec. 1964

The **OTHER** Yosemite. By Nathaniel T. Kenney. Photos by Dean Conger. 762-781, June 1974

OTSEGO COUNTY, New York. *See* Thunder Hill Goat Farm

OTTAWA, Ontario, Canada:
• Exploring Ottawa. By Bruce Hutchison. 565-596, Nov. 1947
• Ontario, Canada's Keystone. By David S. Boyer. Photos by Sam Abell and the author. 760-795, Dec. 1978
• Queen of Canada (Elizabeth II). By Phyllis Wilson. Photos by Kathleen Revis. 825-829, June 1959

OTTERS:
• Giant Otters: "Big Water Dogs" in Peril. By Nicole Duplaix. Photos by the author and Bates Littlehales. Contents: River otters. 130-142, July 1980
• Return of the Sea Otter. By Karl W. Kenyon. Photos by James A. Mattison, Jr. 520-539, Oct. 1971

OUAGADOUGOU, Upper Volta:
• Freedom Speaks French in Ouagadougou. By John Scofield. 153-203, Aug. 1966

OUESSANT, Ile d', France:
• Atlantic Odyssey: Iceland to Antarctica. By Newman Bumstead. Photos by Volkmar Wentzel. 725-780, Dec. 1955

OUR Air Age Speeds Ahead. By F. Barrows Colton. 249-272, Feb. 1948

OUR Bald Eagle: Freedom's Symbol Survives. By Thomas C. Dunstan. Photos by Jeff Foott. NGS research grant. 186-199, Feb. 1978

OUR Best to You–On the Geographic's 75th Birthday. By Melville Bell Grosvenor. 459, Oct. 1963

OUR Changing Atlantic Coastline. By Nathaniel T. Kenney. Photos by B. Anthony Stewart. 860-887, Dec. 1962

OUR Earth as a Satellite Sees It. By W. G. Stroud. 293-302, Aug. 1960

OUR Ecological Crisis. By Gordon Young. Photos by James P. Blair and Harry S. C. Yen. 737-795, Dec. 1970

OUR Energy Predicament. By Kenneth F. Weaver. 2-23, *Special Report on Energy* (Feb. 1981)

OUR Friend From the Sea. By Robert and Nina Horstman. Photos by Robert F. Sisson. 728-736, Nov. 1968

OUR Green Treasury, the National Forests. By Nathaniel T. Kenney. Photos by J. Baylor Roberts. 287-324, Sept. 1956

OUR Growing Interstate Highway System. By Robert Paul Jordan. 195-219, Feb. 1968

OUR Home-town Planet, Earth. By F. Barrows Colton. 117-139, Jan. 1952

OUR LADY OF FÁTIMA, Shrine of, Portugal:
● Fátima: Beacon for Portugal's Faithful. By Jane Vessels. Photos by Bruno Barbey. 832-839, Dec. 1980

OUR Land Through Lincoln's Eyes. By Carolyn Bennett Patterson. Photos by W. D. Vaughn. 243-277, Feb. 1960

OUR Last Great Wilderness. By David Jeffery. 769-791, June 1975

OUR Life-giving Star, the Sun. By Herbert Friedman. 713-743, Nov. 1965

OUR Life on a Border Kibbutz. By Carol and Al Abrams. Photos by Al Abrams. 364-391, Sept. 1970

OUR Magnificent Capital City. Photos by B. Anthony Stewart. 715-738, June 1947

OUR Man-in-Sea Project. By Edwin A. Link. NGS research grant. 713-717, May 1963

OUR Most Precious Resource: Water. By Thomas Y. Canby. Photos by Ted Spiegel. 144-179, Aug. 1980

OUR National Forests: Problems in Paradise. By Rowe Findley. Photos by David Cupp. 306-339, Sept. 1982

OUR National Parks. Photos by David Alan Harvey. 1-152, July 1979

OUR National Wildlife Refuges. 342-381, Mar. 1979

OUR Navy Explores Antarctica. By Richard E. Byrd. U. S. Navy official photos. 429-522, Oct. 1947

OUR Navy in the Far East. By Arthur W. Radford. Photos by J. Baylor Roberts. 537-577, Oct. 1953

OUR Navy's Long Submarine Arm. By Allan C. Fisher, Jr. 613-636, Nov. 1952

OUR Nuclear Navy. By George W. Anderson, Jr. 449-450, Mar. 1963

OUR Only Native Stork, the Wood Ibis. By Robert Porter Allen. Photos by Frederick Kent Truslow. 294-306, Feb. 1964

OUR People, Our Past (Navajos). By Albert Laughter. 81-85, July 1979

OUR Phenomenal First Flight. By John W. Young and Robert L. Crippen. Paintings by Ken Dallison. 478-503, Oct. 1981

OUR Restless Earth. By Maynard M. Miller. 140-141, July 1964

OUR Search for British Paintings. By Franklin L. Fisher. 543-550, Apr. 1949

OUR Snake Friends and Foes. By Doris M. Cochran. Paintings by Walter A. Weber. 334-364, Sept. 1954

OUR Society Welcomes Its 3,000,000th Member. By Melville Bell Grosvenor. 579-582, Apr. 1962

OUR Society's 75 Years Exploring Earth, Sea, and Sky. By Melvin M. Payne. 1-43, Jan. 1963

OUR Universe Unfolds New Wonders. By Albert G. Wilson. NGS research grant. 245-260, Feb. 1952

OUR Vegetable Travelers. By Victor R. Boswell. Paintings by Else Bostelmann. 145-217, Aug. 1949

OUR Virgin Islands, 50 Years Under the Flag. By Carleton Mitchell. Photos by James L. Stanfield. 67-103, Jan. 1968

OUR War Memorials Abroad: A Faith Kept. By George C. Marshall. 731-737, June 1957

OUR Wild and Scenic Rivers. 2-59, July 1977

OUR Wildest Wilderness: Alaska's Arctic National Wildlife Range. By Douglas H. Chadwick. Photos by Lowell Georgia. 737-769, Dec. 1979

OURO PRÊTO, Minas Gerais, Brazil:
● Brazil's Land of Minerals. By W. Robert Moore. 479-508, Oct. 1948

OURSI, Upper Volta:
● Oursi, Magnet in the Desert. By Carole E. Devillers. 512-525, Apr. 1980

OUTER BANKS, North Carolina:
● Exploring America's Great Sand Barrier Reef. By Eugene R. Guild. Photos by John E. Fletcher and author. 325-350, Sept. 1947
● How We Found the *Monitor*. By John G. Newton. Note: *Monitor* was lost off the Outer Banks during the Civil War. 48-61, Jan. 1975
● Lonely Cape Hatteras, Besieged by the Sea. By William S. Ellis. Photos by Emory Kristof. Included: Foldout map, *Ghost Fleet of the Outer Banks*. 393-421, Sept. 1969
● October Holiday on the Outer Banks. By Nike Anderson. Photos by J. Baylor Roberts. 501-529, Oct. 1955
● Our Changing Atlantic Coastline. By Nathaniel T. Kenney. Photos by B. Anthony Stewart. 860-887, Dec. 1962

OUTER HEBRIDES (Islands), Scotland:
● From Barra to Butt in the Hebrides. By Isobel Wylie Hutchison. 559-580, Oct. 1954
● Hunting Folk Songs in the Hebrides. By Margaret Shaw Campbell. 249-272, Feb. 1947
● Isles on the Edge of the Sea. By Kenneth MacLeish. Photos by Thomas Nebbia. 676-711, May 1970
● Scotland From Her Lovely Lochs and Seas. By Alan Villiers. Photos by Robert F. Sisson. 492-541, Apr. 1961

OUTER MONGOLIA. *See* Mongolian People's Republic

OUTLAW TRAIL, U. S. West:
● Riding the Outlaw Trail. By Robert Redford. Photos by Jonathan Blair. 622-657, Nov. 1976

OUTPOST Under the Ocean. By Edwin A. Link. Photos by Bates Littlehales. NGS research grant. 530-533, Apr. 1965

OUTWARD BOUND SCHOOL:
▒ Journey to the Outer Limits. 150A-150B, Jan. 1974

OVAMBOS (People):
● Namibia: Nearly a Nation? By Bryan Hodgson. Photos by Jim Brandenburg. 755-797, June 1982

OVER and Under Chesapeake Bay. By David S. Boyer. 593-612, Apr. 1964

OVER Plains and Hills of South Dakota. Photos by J. Baylor Roberts. 563-586, May 1947

OVER the Sea to Scotland's Skye. By Robert J. Reynolds. 87-112, July 1952

OWENS VALLEY, California:
● California's Parched Oasis, the Owens Valley. By Judith and Neil Morgan. Photos by Jodi Cobb and Galen Rowell. 98-127, Jan. 1976

OWLS:
● Long-eared Owls–Masters of the Night. By Art Wolfe. 31-35, Jan. 1980

OXFORD, England:
● The Thames: That Noble River. By Ethel A. Starbird. Photos by O. Louis Mazzatenta. 750-791, June 1983

OYSTER FLEET:
● Chincoteague: Watermen's Island Home. By Nathaniel T. Kenney. Photos by James L. Amos. 810-829, June 1980
● The Sailing Oystermen of Chesapeake Bay. By Luis Marden. 798-819, Dec. 1967

OYSTERS:
● Chesapeake Country. By Nathaniel T. Kenney. Photos by Bates Littlehales. 370-411, Sept. 1964
● "Delmarva," Gift of the Sea. By Catherine Bell Palmer. 367-399, Sept. 1950
● My Chesapeake–Queen of Bays. By Allan C. Fisher, Jr. Photos by Lowell Georgia. 428-467, Oct. 1980

OZARK PLATEAU, Arkansas-Missouri:
● An Ozark Family Carves a Living and a Way of Life. Photos by Bruce Dale. 124-133, July 1975
● Through Ozark Hills and Hollows. By Mike W. Edwards. Photos by Bruce Dale. 656-689, Nov. 1970
● *See also* Buffalo National River

P

PLO. *See* Palestine Liberation Organization

P. T. GEORGIA-PACIFIC: Study Grant:
● Orangutans. 835, June 1980

PA PAE, Thailand:
● Living With Thailand's Gentle Lua. By Peter Kunstadter. 122-152, July 1966

PACIFIC COAST, U. S.:
◆ *America's Sunset Coast.* 1978
● California's Land Apart–the Monterey Peninsula. By Mike W. Edwards. 682-703, Nov. 1972
● California's Wonderful One (State Highway No. 1). By Frank Cameron. Photos by B. Anthony Stewart. 571-617, Nov. 1959
● Oregon's Sidewalk on the Sea. By Paul A. Zahl. 708-734, Nov. 1961

PACIFIC CREST TRAIL, U. S.:
● Mexico to Canada on the Pacific Crest Trail. By Mike W. Edwards. Photos by David Hiser. 741-779, June 1971
◆ *The Pacific Crest Trail.* Announced. 870-874, June 1974

PACIFIC FLEET, U. S.:
● Our Navy in the Far East. By Arthur W. Radford. Photos by J. Baylor Roberts. 537-577, Oct. 1953
● Pacific Fleet: Force for Peace. By Franc Shor. Photos by W. E. Garrett. 283-335, Sept. 1959

PACIFIC GROVE, California:
● Mystery of the Monarch Butterfly. By Paul A. Zahl. 588-598, Apr. 1963

PACIFIC ISLANDS:
● Adventures with the Survey Navy. By Irving Johnson. Contents: Deboyne Lagoon, Louisiade Archipelago; Florida Island, Solomon Islands; Funafuti, Ellice Islands; Guadalcanal, Solomon Islands; Iwo Jima, Volcano Islands; Kwajalein, Marshall Islands; Nukufetau, Ellice Islands; Tarawa, Gilbert Islands; Ulithi, Caroline Islands; Uvéa, Wallis Islands. 131-148, July 1947
● The Bonins and Iwo Jima Go Back to Japan. By Paul Sampson. Photos by Joe Munroe. 128-144, July 1968
● Captain Cook: The Man Who Mapped the Pacific. By Alan Villiers. Photos by Gordon W. Gahan. 297-349, Sept. 1971
▲ *Islands of the Pacific; Discoverers of the Pacific,* double-sided supplement. Dec. 1974
● Isles of the Pacific. 732-793, Dec. 1974
I. The Coming of the Polynesians. By Kenneth P. Emory. 732-745; II. Wind, Wave, Star, and Bird. By David Lewis. Photos by Nicholas deVore III. 747-781; III. The Pathfinders. Paintings by Herb Kawainui Kane. 756-769; IV. Problems in Paradise. By Mary and Laurance S. Rockefeller. Photos by Thomas Nebbia. 782-793
◆ *Isles of the South Pacific.* Announced. 868-875, June 1967
● Micronesia: The Americanization of Eden. By David S. Boyer. 702-744, May 1967
● New Guinea to Bali in *Yankee.* By Irving and Electa Johnson. 767-815, Dec. 1959
● Our Navy in the Far East. By Arthur W. Radford. Photos by J. Baylor Roberts. 537-577, Oct. 1953
▲ *Pacific Ocean,* supplement. Dec. 1952
▲ *Pacific Ocean; New Zealand, New Guinea and the Principal Islands of the Pacific,* double-sided Atlas series supplement. Apr. 1962
● Pacific Wards of Uncle Sam. By W. Robert Moore. 73-104, July 1948
▒ Polynesian Adventure. 592A-592B, Apr. 1969
● The Rat, Lapdog of the Devil. By Thomas Y. Canby. Photos by James L. Stanfield. 60-87, July 1977
● Shells Take You Over World Horizons. By Rutherford Platt. 33-84, July 1949
● A Teen-ager Sails the World Alone. By Robin Lee Graham. 445-491, Oct. 1968
▒ The Voyage of the Brigantine *Yankee.* 265A-265B, Feb. 1966
◆ *Voyages to Paradise: Exploring in the Wake of Captain Cook.* 1981
● *Yankee* Roams the Orient. By Irving and Electa Johnson. Included: New Guinea; New Hebrides; Solomon Islands; Trobriand Islands. 327-370, Mar. 1951
● The *Yankee*'s Wander-world. By Irving and Electa Johnson. 1-50, Jan. 1949
● *See also* Melanesia; Micronesia; Polynesia; *and* Galapagos Islands; Indonesia; Myojin Island; Okinawa; Philippines; Taiwan

PACIFIC MAP Played Providential Role: How One of the Society's Maps Saved a Precious Cargo. 844, June 1947

PACIFIC NORTHWEST. *See* Northwest (Region), U. S.

PACIFIC OCEAN:
● Adventures with the Survey Navy. By Irving Johnson. 131-148, July 1947
● Deep Diving off Japan. By Georges S. Houot. NGS research grant. 138-150, Jan. 1960
● Editorials. By Gilbert M. Grosvenor. 731, Dec. 1974; 431, Oct. 1976
● How One of the Society's Maps (Pacific Ocean) Saved a Precious Cargo. 844, June 1947
▲ *Islands of the Pacific; Discoverers of the Pacific,* double-sided supplement. Dec. 1974
● Magellan: First Voyage Around the World. By Alan Villiers. Photos by Bruce Dale. 721-753, June 1976
● Man's Deepest Dive (Mariana Trench). By Jacques Piccard. Photos by Thomas J. Abercrombie. 224-239, Aug. 1960
● New World of the Ocean. By Samuel W. Matthews. 792-832, Dec. 1981
● The Ocean. By Jacques-Yves Cousteau. 780-791, Dec. 1981
▲ *Pacific Ocean,* double-sided Atlas series supplement. Apr. 1962
▲ *Pacific Ocean,* supplement. Dec. 1952
▲ *Pacific Ocean; Pacific Ocean Floor,* double-sided supplement. Oct. 1969
● Scientists Drill at Sea to Pierce Earth's Crust (Project Mohole). By Samuel W. Matthews. Photos by J. Baylor Roberts. 686-697, Nov. 1961
▲ *The World; The World Ocean Floor,* double-sided supplement. Dec. 1981
● *See also* Galapagos Rift; Pacific Fleet, U. S.; Pacific Islands; *and Hokule'a; Triton*

PACIFIC OCEAN CROSSINGS:
● First Across the Pacific: The Flight of *Double Eagle V.* By Ben L. Abruzzo. 513-521, Apr. 1982

PACIFIC RIDLEY TURTLES:
● One Strange Night on Turtle Beach. By Paul A. Zahl. 570-581, Oct. 1973

PACK TRIPS:
● Pack Trip Through the Smokies. By Val Hart. Photos by Robert F. Sisson. 473-502, Oct. 1952

PADANARAM (Communal Village), Indiana:
● Indiana's Self-reliant Uplanders. By James Alexander Thom. Photos by J. Bruce Baumann. 341-363, Mar. 1976

PADAUNG (Tribespeople):
● Anatomy of a Burmese Beauty Secret. By John M. Keshishian. Contents: Long-necked women. 798-801, June 1979

PADLERMIUT (Eskimos):
● Canada's Caribou Eskimos. By Donald B. Marsh. 87-104, Jan. 1947

PADLOCK RANCH, Montana-Wyoming:
● Cowpunching on the Padlock Ranch. By William Albert Allard. 478-499, Oct. 1973

PADRE ISLAND NATIONAL SEASHORE, Texas:
● Where Oil and Wildlife Mix. By Steven C. Wilson and Karen C. Hayden. 145-173, Feb. 1981

PAGAN, Burma:
● Pagan, on the Road to Mandalay. By W. E. Garrett. 343-365, Mar. 1971

PAGE, JAKE: Author:
● Inside the Sacred Hopi Homeland. Photos by Susanne Page. 607-629, Nov. 1982

PAGE, SUSANNE: Photographer:
● Inside the Sacred Hopi Homeland. By Jake Page. 607-629, Nov. 1982

The **PAGEANT** of Rajasthan. By Raghubir Singh. 219-243, Feb. 1977

PAGEANTRY of the Siamese Stage. By D. Sonakul. Photos by W. Robert Moore. 201-212, Feb. 1947

PAGODAS:
● Pagan, on the Road to Mandalay. By W. E. Garrett. 343-365, Mar. 1971

PAHLAVI, MOHAMMAD REZA. *See* Mohammad Reza Pahlavi

PAINE, THOMAS:
● Firebrands of the Revolution. By Eric F. Goldman. Photos by George F. Mobley. 2-27, July 1974

PAINE, THOMAS O.: Author:
● Next Steps in Space. 793-797, Dec. 1969

PAINTERS. *See* Artists

PAINTING:

● American Processional: History on Canvas. By John and Blanche Leeper. 173-212, Feb. 1951
● America's First Painters: Indians. By Dorothy Dunn. 349-377, Mar. 1955
● Artists Look at Pennsylvania. By John Oliver La Gorce. 37-56, July 1948
● Audubon "On the Wing." By David Jeffery. Photos by Bates Littlehales. 149-177, Feb. 1977
● Belgium: One Nation Divisible. By James Cerruti. Photos by Martin Rogers. Included: Flemish techniques. 314-341, Mar. 1979
● The British Way: Great Britain's Major Gifts to Freedom, Democratic Government, Science, and Society. By Sir Evelyn Wrench. 421-541, Apr. 1949
● Children's Art Around the World. By Newman Bumstead. 365-387, Mar. 1957
● Early America Through the Eyes of Her Native Artists. By Hereward Lester Cooke, Jr. 356-389, Sept. 1962
● Escorting Mona Lisa to America. By Edward T. Folliard. 838-847, June 1963
● Florence Rises From the Flood. By Joseph Judge. 1-43, July 1967
● Fresh Treasures from Egypt's Ancient Sands. By Jefferson Caffery. Photos by David S. Boyer. 611-650, Nov. 1955
● Great Masters of a Brave Era in Art. By Hereward Lester Cooke, Jr. 661-697, May 1961
● In Quest of Beauty. Text by Paul Mellon. 372-385, Mar. 1967
● Last Moments of the Pompeians. By Amedeo Maiuri. Photos by Lee E. Battaglia. Paintings by Peter V. Bianchi. 651-669, Nov. 1961
● Leonardo da Vinci: A Man for All Ages. By Kenneth MacLeish. Photos by James L. Amos. 296-329, Sept. 1977
● The Lost Fleet of Kublai Khan. By Torao Mozai. Photos by Koji Nakamura. Paintings by Issho Yada. 634-649, Nov. 1982
● Masterpieces on Tour. By Harry A. McBride. 717-750, Dec. 1948
● The Maya. 729-811, Dec. 1975
I. Children of Time. By Howard La Fay. Photos by David Alan Harvey. 729-767; II. Riddle of the Glyphs. By George E. Stuart. Photos by Otis Imboden. 768-791; III. Resurrecting the Grandeur of Tikal. By William R. Coe. 792-798; IV. A Traveler's Tale of Ancient Tikal. Paintings by Peter Spier. Text by Alice J. Hall. 799-811
● Minoans and Mycenaeans: Greece's Brilliant Bronze Age. By Joseph Judge. Photos by Gordon W. Gahan. Paintings by Lloyd K. Townsend. 142-185. Feb. 1978
● Mount Sinai's Holy Treasures (St. Catherine's Monastery). By Kurt Weitzmann. Photos by Fred Anderegg. 109-127, Jan. 1964
● Our Search for British Paintings. By Franklin L. Fisher. 543-550, Apr. 1949
● Periscope on the Etruscan Past. By Carlo M. Lerici. 337-350, Sept. 1959
Profiles of the Presidents. By Frank Freidel:
● Part I. The Presidency and How It Grew. Contents: George Washington, John Adams, Thomas Jefferson, James Madison, James Monroe, John Quincy Adams. 642-687, Nov. 1964
● Part II. A Restless Nation Moves West. Contents: Andrew Jackson, Martin Van Buren, William Henry Harrison, John Tyler, James K. Polk, Zachary Taylor, Millard Fillmore, Franklin Pierce, James Buchanan. 80-121, Jan. 1965
● Part III. The American Giant Comes of Age. Contents: Abraham Lincoln, Andrew Johnson, Ulysses S. Grant, Rutherford B. Hayes, James A. Garfield, Chester A. Arthur, Grover Cleveland, Benjamin Harrison, William McKinley. 660-711, May 1965
● Part IV. America Enters the Modern Era. Contents: Theodore Roosevelt, William Howard Taft, Woodrow Wilson, Warren G. Harding, Calvin Coolidge, Herbert Hoover. 537-577, Oct. 1965
● Part V. The Atomic Age: Its Problems and Promises. Contents: Franklin D. Roosevelt, Harry S Truman, Dwight D. Eisenhower, John F. Kennedy, Lyndon B. Johnson. 66-119, Jan. 1966
● Regal Treasures From a Macedonian Tomb. By Manolis Andronicos. Photos by Spyros Tsavdaroglou. 55-77, July 1978
● Restoration Reveals the "Last Supper." By Carlo Bertelli. Photos by Victor R. Boswell, Jr. 664-685, Nov. 1983
● Roman Life in 1,600-year-old Color Pictures. By Gino Vinicio Gentili. Photos by Duncan Edwards. 211-229, Feb. 1957
● Ships Through the Ages: A Saga of the Sea. By Alan Villiers. 494-545, Apr. 1963
● So Long, St. Louis, We're Heading West. By William C. Everhart. 643-669, Nov. 1965
● Toledo–El Greco's Spain Lives On. By Louise E. Levathes. Photos by James P. Blair. 726-753, June 1982
The Genius of El Greco. Introduction by J. Carter Brown. 736-744
● U. S. Capitol, Citadel of Democracy. By Lonnelle Aikman. 143-192, Aug. 1952
● The World of Martin Luther. By Merle Severy. Photos by James L. Amos. 418-463, Oct. 1983
● *See also listing under* Art Galleries; Rock Art

PAINTING SUPPLEMENTS:

● "The Adoration of the Magi," a reproduction of the tondo by Fra Angelico and Fra Filippo Lippi. Jan. 1952
▲ "Australia; Land of Living Fossils," by Roy Andersen. Map on reverse. Feb. 1979

NATIONAL GALLERY, OSLO, NORWAY

Toledo: "St. Peter in Tears"

O P

▲ "Bird Migration in the Americas," by Arthur Singer. Map on reverse. Aug. 1979
▲ "The Dusty Face of Mars." Double-sided supplement. Feb. 1973
▲ "History Salvaged From the Sea," by Richard Schlecht. Map on reverse. Dec. 1977
▲ "How Man Pollutes His World." Map on reverse. Dec. 1970
▲ "Ice Age Mammals of the Alaskan Tundra." Map of Canada on reverse. Mar. 1972
▲ "Journey Into the Universe Through Time and Space," by Lloyd K. Townsend. Sky Survey photos on reverse. June 1983
● "Mayflower II." Nov. 1957
▲ "The Solar System," by Lloyd K. Townsend. NASA photo of Saturn on reverse. July 1981
▲ "Teammates in Mankind's Greatest Adventure" (Apollo Astronauts). Double-sided supplement. Sept. 1973
▲ "Whales of the World." Map on reverse. Dec. 1976

PAKISTAN:
● "Around the World in Eighty Days." By Newman Bumstead. Included: Karachi, Khyber Pass, Kohat Pass, Peshawar, Swat (State). 705-750, Dec. 1951
● An Eye for an Eye: Pakistan's Wild Frontier. By Mike W. Edwards. Photos by J. Bruce Baumann. 111-139, Jan. 1977
● Imperiled Phantom of Asian Peaks: First Photographs of Snow Leopards in the Wild. By George B. Schaller. NGS research grant. 702-707, Nov. 1971
● In the Footsteps of Alexander the Great. By Helen and Frank Schreider. Paintings by Tom Lovell. 1-65, Jan. 1968
● Pakistan, New Nation in an Old Land. By Jean and Franc Shor. 637-678, Nov. 1952
● Pakistan: Problems of a Two-part Land. By Bern Keating. Photos by Albert Moldvay. 1-47, Jan. 1967
● Pakistan Under Pressure. By William S. Ellis. Photos by James L. Stanfield. 668-701, May 1981
● Pakistan's Kalash: People of Fire and Fervor. By Debra Denker. Photos by Steve McCurry. 458-473, Oct. 1981
● Sky Road East. By Tay and Lowell Thomas, Jr. 71-112, Jan. 1960
● Troubled Waters East of Suez. By Ernest M. Eller. 483-522, Apr. 1954
● When the President Goes Abroad (Eisenhower Tour). By Gilbert M. Grosvenor. 588-649, May 1960
● *See also* Hunza; K2

PAKISTAN, East:
● East Pakistan Drives Back the Jungle. By Jean and Franc Shor. 399-426, Mar. 1955
● *See also* Bangladesh

PALAU ISLANDS, Pacific Ocean:
● Dazzling Corals of Palau. By Thomas O'Neill. Photos by Douglas Faulkner. 136-150, July 1978

BOTH BY DAVID DOUBILET

Palau's Salt Lakes: jellyfish, *Mastigias papua, top;* glass shrimp atop algae-encrusted mussels, *above*

● Strange World of Palau's Salt Lakes. By William M. Hamner. Photos by David Doubilet. 264-282, Feb. 1982

PALEN, COLE:
● World War I Aircraft Fly Again in Rhinebeck's Rickety Rendezvous. By Harvey Arden. Photos by Howard Sochurek. 578-587, Oct. 1970

PALEO-INDIANS:
● Bison Kill By Ice Age Hunters. By Dennis Stanford. NGS research grant. 114-121, Jan. 1979
● Ice Age Man, the First American. By Thomas R. Henry. Paintings by Andre Durenceau. 781-806, Dec. 1955
● Life 8,000 Years Ago Uncovered in an Alabama Cave. By Carl F. Miller. NGS research grant. 542-558, Oct. 1956
● Man's Eighty Centuries in Veracruz. By S. Jeffrey K. Wilkerson. Photos by David Hiser. Paintings by Richard Schlecht. NGS research grant. 203-231, Aug. 1980
● Probing the Mystery of the Medicine Wheels. By John A. Eddy. Photos by Thomas E. Hooper. NGS research grant. 140-146, Jan. 1977
● Russell Cave: New Light on Stone Age Life. By Carl F. Miller. NGS research grant. 427-437, Mar. 1958
● The Search for the First Americans. By Thomas Y. Canby. Photos by Kerby Smith. Paintings by Roy Andersen. 330-363, Sept. 1979
▲ *The Southwest,* The Making of America series. Included: 12,000 Years of History. Nov. 1982
● Wyoming Muck Tells of Battle: Ice Age Man vs. Mammoth. By Cynthia Irwin, Henry Irwin, and George Agogino. NGS research grant. 828-837, June 1962

PALEONTOLOGY:
● Adventures in the Search for Man. By Louis S. B. Leakey. Photos by Hugo van Lawick. Included: *Kenyapithecus wickeri; and* fossil remains of a giant rhinoceros, giant baboon, and antelope. NGS research grant. 132-152, Jan. 1963
● Ancient Ashfall Creates a Pompeii of Prehistoric Animals. By Michael R. Voorhies. Photos by Annie Griffiths. Paintings by Jay Matternes. NGS research grant. 66-75, Jan. 1981
● Big Game Hunting in the Land of Long Ago (South Dakota). By Joseph P. Connolly and James D. Bump. NGS research grant. 589-605, May 1947
● Bison Kill By Ice Age Hunters. By Dennis Stanford. NGS research grant. 114-121, Jan. 1979
■ Dr. Leakey and the Dawn of Man. 703A-703B, Nov. 1966
● Ethiopia Yields First "Family" of Early Man. By Donald C. Johanson. Photos by David Brill. Contents: *Australopithecus, Homo.* NGS research grant. 790-811, Dec. 1976
● Exploring 1,750,000 Years Into Man's Past. By L. S. B. Leakey. Photos by Robert F. Sisson. Included: Dinotherium, giant porcupine,

sabertoothed tiger, and swamp antelope. NGS research grant. 564-589, Oct. 1961
● Finding the World's Earliest Man. By L. S. B. Leakey. Photos by Des Bartlett. Included: *Afrochoerus* (prehistoric pig), *Pelorovis* (giant sheep), *Proconsul africanus* (primitive ape), *Simopithecus jonathani* (giant baboon), *Sivatherium* (short-necked giraffe), *Zinjanthropus boisei* (early man). NGS research grant. 420-435, Sept. 1960
● Footprints in the Ashes of Time. By Mary D. Leakey. NGS research grant. 446-457, Apr. 1979
● Fossils Lift the Veil of Time. By Harry S. Ladd and Roland W. Brown. 363-386, Mar. 1956
◆ *Giants From the Past: The Age of Mammals.* 1983
● Ice Age Man, the First American. By Thomas R. Henry. Paintings by Andre Durenceau. 781-806, Dec. 1955
● In Search of Man's Past at Lake Rudolf. By Richard E. Leakey. Photos by Gordon W. Gahan. NGS research grant. 712-734, May 1970
● The Leakey Tradition Lives On. By Melvin M. Payne. NGS research grant. 143-144, Jan. 1973
● The Leakeys of Africa: Family in Search of Prehistoric Man. By Melvin M. Payne. Included: *Kenyapithecus, Proconsul, Zinjanthropus; and* the discovery of *Homo habilis; also,* bantam rhinoceros jaw, rodent and bird bones. NGS research grant. 194-231, Feb. 1965
▪ The Legacy of L.S.B. Leakey. 439, Oct. 1977; cover, Jan. 1978
● Life 8,000 Years Ago Uncovered in an Alabama Cave. By Carl F. Miller. NGS research grant. 542-558, Oct. 1956
● A New Look at Dinosaurs. By John H. Ostrom. Paintings by Roy Andersen. NGS research grant. 152-185, Aug. 1978
● Preserving the Treasures of Olduvai Gorge. By Melvin M. Payne. Photos by Joseph J. Scherschel. Included: *Homo erectus, Homo habilis, Kenyapithecus,* Maiko Gully "George," *Zinjanthropus; and* the broken molar of a dinotherium; the tooth and bones of an extinct elephant. NGS research grant. 701-709, Nov. 1966
● Re-creating a Vanished World. By Russell D. Guthrie. 294-301, Mar. 1972
● The Search for the First Americans. By Thomas Y. Canby. Photos by Kerby Smith. Paintings by Roy Andersen. 330-363, Sept. 1979
● Skull 1470. By Richard E. Leakey. Photos by Bob Campbell. NGS research grant. 819-829, June 1973
● A Visit to the Living Ice Age. By Rutherford Platt. 525-545, Apr. 1957
● Wyoming Muck Tells of Battle: Ice Age Man vs. Mammoth. By Cynthia Irwin, Henry Irwin, and George Agogino. NGS research grant. 828-837, June 1962
● *See also Aepyornis;* Brontosaurs; *and* American Museum of Natural History; Dinosaur National Monument

PALERMO, Sicily:
● Sicily, Where All the Songs Are Sad. By Howard La Fay. Photos by Jonathan Blair. 407-436, Mar. 1976

PALESTINE. *See* Holy Land; Israel; Jordan

PALESTINE LIBERATION ORGANIZATION (PLO):
● Beirut–Up From the Rubble. By William S. Ellis. Photos by Steve McCurry. 262-286, Feb. 1983

PALESTINIAN REFUGEES:
● Beirut–Up From the Rubble. By William S. Ellis. Photos by Steve McCurry. 262-286, Feb. 1983

PALIO (Horse Race), Siena, Italy:
● The Palio of Siena. By Edgar Erskine Hume. 231-244, Aug. 1951
● The Renaissance Lives On in Tuscany. By Luis Marden. Photos by Albert Moldvay. 626-659, Nov. 1974

PALISADES, New York-New Jersey:
● The Mighty Hudson. By Albert W. Atwood. Photos by B. Anthony Stewart. 1-36, July 1948

PALISADES INTERSTATE PARK, New York-New Jersey:
● Skyline Trail from Maine to Georgia. By Andrew H. Brown. Photos by Robert F. Sisson. 219-251, Aug. 1949

PALM SPRINGS, California:
● Californians Escape to the Desert. By Mason Sutherland. Photos by Charles W. Herbert. 675-724, Nov. 1957

PALMAR, C. ERIC:
Author-Photographer:
● Scotland's Golden Eagles at Home. 273-286, Feb. 1954

PALMER, ALFRED MONROE:
● Yemen–Southern Arabia's Mountain Wonderland. By Harlan B. Clark. 631-672, Nov. 1947

PALMER, CATHERINE BELL: Author:
● Appalachian Valley Pilgrimage. 1-32, July 1949
● Crickets, Nature's Expert Fiddlers. 385-394, Sept. 1953
● "Delmarva," Gift of the Sea. 367-399, Sept. 1950
● Split-second Time Runs Today's World. By F. Barrows Colton and Catherine Bell Palmer. 399-428, Sept. 1947

PALMSTROM, WILLIAM N.: Artist:
● Space Satellites, Tools of Earth Research. By Heinz Haber. 487-509, Apr. 1956

PALOMAR OBSERVATORY, Mount Palomar, San Diego County, California:
● Completing the Atlas of the Universe (National Geographic Society-Palomar Observatory Sky Survey). By Ira Sprague Bowen. NGS research grant. 185-190, Aug. 1955
Sky Survey Plates Unlock Secrets of the Stars. 186-187
● Exploring the Farthest Reaches of Space. By George O. Abell. NGS research grant. 782-790, Dec. 1956
▲ *Journey Into the Universe Through Time and Space; National Geographic-Palomar Sky Survey Charting the Heavens,* double-sided supplement. June 1983
● Mapping the Unknown Universe. By F. Barrows Colton. 401-420, Sept. 1950
● Our Universe Unfolds New Wonders (National Geographic-Palomar Sky Survey). By Albert G. Wilson. 245-260, Feb. 1952
● Sky Survey Charts the Universe. By Ira Sprague Bowen. 780-781, Dec. 1956

PALOUSE HILLS, Idaho-Washington:
● A Paradise Called the Palouse. By Barbara Austin. Photos by Phil Schofield. 798-819, June 1982

PAMIR (Ship):
● Last of the Cape Horners. By Alan Villiers. 701-710, May 1948
Square-rigger in a Tempest. 703-710

PAMIRS (Mountains), Central Asia:
● American Skiers Find Adventure in Western China. By Ned Gillette. Photos by the author and Galen Rowell. 174-199, Feb. 1981
Skiing From the Summit of China's Ice Mountain. 192-199
● We Took the Highroad in Afghanistan. By Jean and Franc Shor. 673-706, Nov. 1950
● Winter Caravan to the Roof of the World. By Sabrina and Roland Michaud. 435-465, Apr. 1972

PAMPA GALERAS NATIONAL VICUÑA RESERVE, Peru:
● High, Wild World of the Vicuña. By William L. Franklin. 77-91, Jan. 1973

PAMPAS (Grasslands):
● High, Wild World of the Vicuña. By William L. Franklin. 77-91, Jan. 1973

PANAMA:
● The Amazing Frog-Eating Bat. By Merlin D. Tuttle. 78-91, Jan. 1982
● Exploring Ancient Panama by Helicopter. By Matthew W. Stirling. Photos by Richard H. Stewart. Included: Archaeological sites in provinces of Chiriquí and Veraguas. NGS research grant. 227-246, Feb. 1950
● Exploring the Past in Panama. By Matthew W. Stirling. Photos by Richard H. Stewart. Included: Azuero Peninsula, Tambor region. NGS research grant. 373-399, Mar. 1949
● Hunting Prehistory in Panama Jungles. By Matthew W. Stirling. Photos by Richard H. Stewart. NGS research grant. 271-290, Aug. 1953
● Panama, Link Between Oceans and Continents. By Jules B. Billard. Photos by Bruce Dale. 402-440, Mar. 1970
● The Panama Canal Today. By Bart McDowell. Photos by George F. Mobley. 279-294, Feb. 1978
● Robin Sails Home. By Robin Lee Graham. 504-545, Oct. 1970

OP

• Troubled Times for Central America. By Wilbur E. Garrett, Editor. 58-61, July 1981
• We Drove Panama's Darién Gap. By Kip Ross. 368-389, Mar. 1961

PANAMA CANAL:
• Editorial. By Gilbert M. Grosvenor. 141, Feb. 1978
• Panama, Link Between Oceans and Continents. By Jules B. Billard. Photos by Bruce Dale. 402-440, Mar. 1970
• The Panama Canal Today. By Bart McDowell. Photos by George F. Mobley. 279-294, Feb. 1978

PAN AMERICAN HIGHWAY:
• We Drove Panama's Darién Gap. By Kip Ross. 368-389, Mar. 1961

PANAMIN. *See* Presidential Arm for National Minorities (Philippines)

PANAMINT RANGE, California:
• Getting to Know the Wild Burros of Death Valley. By Patricia des Roses Moehlman. Photos by Ira S. Lerner and author. 502-517, Apr. 1972

PANDAS, Giant:
◆ *Pandas.* Announced. 726-728, Nov. 1973
• Pandas in the Wild. By George B. Schaller. 735-749, Dec. 1981
■ Save the Panda. 824, Dec. 1982
• What's Black and White and Loved All Over? By Theodore H. Reed. Photos by Donna K. Grosvenor. 803-815, Dec. 1972

PANTHERS. *See* Mountain Lions

PAPEETE, Tahiti, Society Islands:
• The Society Islands, Sisters of the Wind. By Priit J. Vesilind. Photos by George F. Mobley. 844-869, June 1979

PAPER AND PULP INDUSTRY:
• Amazon–The River Sea. By Loren McIntyre. Included: Daniel K. Ludwig's planned paper pulp and food-production enterprise in Brazil's Amazon basin. 456-495, Oct. 1972
• Brazil's Wild Frontier. By Loren McIntyre. Included: Daniel K. Ludwig's three-million-acre agricultural and forestry experiment. 684-719, Nov. 1977
• Dixie Spins the Wheel of Industry. By William H. Nicholas. Photos by J. Baylor Roberts. 281-324, Mar. 1949
• From Sagebrush to Roses on the Columbia. By Leo A. Borah. 571-611, Nov. 1952
• Jari: A Billion-dollar Gamble. By Loren McIntyre. Contents: Daniel K. Ludwig's paper-pulp and food-production enterprise in Brazil's Amazon basin. 686-711, May 1980
• Madawaska: Down East With a French Accent. By Perry Garfinkel. Photos by Cary Wolinsky. 380-409, Sept. 1980
• A River Restored: Oregon's Willamette. By Ethel A. Starbird. Photos by Lowell Georgia. 816-835, June 1972
• Timber: How Much Is Enough? By John J. Putman. Photos by Bruce Dale. 485-511, Apr. 1974

DAVID AUSTEN

Papua New Guinea: Yangome leader

• Versatile Wood Waits on Man. By Andrew H. Brown. 109-140, July 1951

PAPUA NEW GUINEA (Union of Australian New Guinea and North-East New Guinea):
• Australian New Guinea. By John Scofield. 604-637, May 1962
• Change Ripples New Guinea's Sepik River. By Malcolm S. Kirk. 354-381, Sept. 1973
• Fertility Rites and Sorcery in a New Guinea Village (Gimi People). By Gillian Gillison. Photos by David Gillison. 124-146, July 1977
• Journey Into Stone Age New Guinea. By Malcolm S. Kirk. 568-592, Apr. 1969
• Living Theater in New Guinea's Highlands. By Gillian Gillison. Photos by David Gillison. 147-169, Aug. 1983
• New Guinea. The Editor. 583, May 1962
• New Guinea to Bali in *Yankee*. By Irving and Electa Johnson. 767-815, Dec. 1959
• New Guinea's Rare Birds and Stone Age Men. By E. Thomas Gilliard. NGS research grant. 421-488, Apr. 1953
• Off the Beaten Track of Empire (Prince Philip's Tour). By Beverley M. Bowie. Photos by Michael Parker. 584-626, Nov. 1957
• Papua New Guinea. 143-171, Aug. 1982
I. Nation in the Making. By Robert J. Gordon. Photos by David Austen. 143-149; II. Journey Through Time. By François Leydet. Photos by David Austen. 150-171
• Sheep Airlift in New Guinea. Photos by Ned Blood. Contents: The Hallstrom Trust's Nondugl Sheep Station in Australian New Guinea. 831-844, Dec. 1949
• To the Land of the Head-hunters. By E. Thomas Gilliard. NGS research grant. 437-486, Oct. 1955
• Tropical Rain Forests: Nature's Dwindling Treasures. By Peter T. White. Photos by James P. Blair. Paintings by Barron Storey. 2-47, Jan. 1983
• *Yankee* Roams the Orient. By Irving and Electa Johnson. 327-370, Mar. 1951
• *See also* New Britain

PAPYRUS SHIP. *See Ra II*

PARACHUTE JUMPS:
• By Parachute Into Peru's Lost World. By G. Brooks Baekeland. Photos by author and Peter R. Gimbel. NGS research grant. 268-296, Aug. 1964
• Graduation by Parachute. By John E. Fletcher. 833-846, June 1952
• The Long, Lonely Leap. By Joseph W. Kittinger, Jr. Photos by Volkmar Wentzel. 854-873, Dec. 1960

PARACHUTE RIGGER SCHOOL, Lakehurst, New Jersey:
• Graduation by Parachute. By John E. Fletcher. 833-846, June 1952

PARADISE Beneath the Sea. By Ron and Valerie Taylor. 636-663, May 1981

A **PARADISE** Called the Palouse. By Barbara Austin. Photos by Phil Schofield. 798-819, June 1982

PARADISE Comes of Age: the U. S. Virgin Islands. By Thomas J. Colin. Photos by William Albert Allard and Cary Wolinsky. 225-243, Feb. 1981

PARA-EXPLORERS Challenge Peru's Unknown Vilcabamba. By G. Brooks Baekeland. Photos by author and Peter R. Gimbel. NGS research grant. 268-296, Aug. 1964

PARAGUAY:
• Paraguay, Paradox of South America. By Gordon Young. Photos by O. Louis Mazzatenta. 240-269, Aug. 1982

PARAGUAY (River), South America:
• The Jungle Was My Home. By Sasha Siemel. 695-712, Nov. 1952
• Paraguay, Paradox of South America. By Gordon Young. Photos by O. Louis Mazzatenta. 240-269, Aug. 1982

PARÍCUTIN (Volcano), Mexico:
• Lost Kingdom in Indian Mexico. By Justin Locke. 517-546, Oct. 1952

PARIS, France:
• The Civilizing Seine. By Charles McCarry. Photos by David L. Arnold. 478-511, Apr. 1982
• Home Life in Paris Today. By Deena Clark. 43-72, July 1950
• Île de la Cité, Birthplace of Paris. By Kenneth MacLeish. Photos by Bruce Dale. 680-719, May 1968
• The Louvre, France's Palace of the Arts. By Hereward Lester Cooke, Jr. 796-831, June 1971
• The More Paris Changes. . . . By Howell Walker. Photos by Gordon W. Gahan. 64-103, July 1972
• Paris, Home Town of the World. By Donald William Dresden. Photos by Justin Locke. 767-804, June 1952
• Paris: Vibrant Heart of France. 285-302, Aug. 1958
• Paris Flea Market. By Franc Shor. Photos by Alexander Taylor. 318-326, Mar. 1957
• Paris to Antwerp with the Water Gypsies. By David S. Boyer. 530-559, Oct. 1955
• Pompidou Center, Rage of Paris. By Cathy Newman. Photos by Marc Riboud. 469-477, Oct. 1980
• Round the World School (ISA). By Paul Antze. Photos by William Eppridge. 96-127, July 1962
• A Wild, Ill-fated Balloon Race. 778-797, Dec. 1983
I. Wild Launch. 778-787; II. The Fantastic Flight of *Cote d'Or*. By Cynthia Shields. 789-793; III. Last Ascent of a Heroic Team (Maxie Anderson and Don Ida). 794-797

PARITA, Panama:
• Exploring the Past in Panama. By Matthew W. Stirling. Photos by Richard H. Stewart. NGS research grant. 373-399, Mar. 1949

PARK, EDWARDS: Author:
• El Morro: Story in Stone (New Mexico). 237-244, Aug. 1957
• Washington Wilderness, the North Cascades. Photos by Kathleen Revis. 355-367, Mar. 1961

PARK at the Top of the World: Mount Everest National Park. By Rick Ridgeway. Photos by Nicholas DeVore III. 704-725, June 1982
Preserving a Mountain Heritage. By Sir Edmund Hillary. 696-703

A **PARK** to Save the Tallest Trees. By Melville Bell Grosvenor. 62-64, July 1966

PARKER, MICHAEL: Photographer:
• Off the Beaten Track of Empire (Prince Philip's Tour). By Beverley M. Bowie. 584-626, Nov. 1957

PARKS, WINFIELD: Author:
• Down East to Nova Scotia. 853-879, June 1964
Photographer:
• The Arab World, Inc. By John J. Putman. 494-533, Oct. 1975
• The Arans, Ireland's Invincible Isles. By Veronica Thomas. 545-573, Apr. 1971
• Behind the Headlines in Viet Nam. By Peter T. White. 149-189, Feb. 1967
• Brazil, Ôba! By Peter T. White. 299-353, Sept. 1962
• Buenos Aires, Argentina's Melting-pot Metropolis. By Jules B. Billard. 662-695, Nov. 1967
• Cairo, Troubled Capital of the Arab World. By William S. Ellis. 639-667, May 1972
• Canada's Dynamic Heartland, Ontario. By Marjorie Wilkins Campbell. 58-97, July 1963
• Carnival in Trinidad. By Howard La Fay. 693-701, Nov. 1971
• The Danube: River of Many Nations, Many Names. By Mike Edwards. 455-485, Oct. 1977
• *Finisterre* Sails the Windward Islands. By Carleton Mitchell. 755-801, Dec. 1965
• Florida Rides a Space-age Boom. By Benedict Thielen. Photos by Winfield Parks and James P. Blair. 858-903, Dec. 1963
• A Fresh Breeze Stirs the Leewards. By Carleton Mitchell. 488-537, Oct. 1966
• The Highlands, Stronghold of Scottish Gaeldom. By Kenneth MacLeish. 398-435, Mar. 1968
• In Storied Lands of Malaysia. By Maurice Shadbolt. 734-783, Nov. 1963
• Iran's Shah Crowns Himself and His Empress. By Franc Shor. Photos by James L. Stanfield and Winfield Parks. 301-321, Mar. 1968
• The Isles of Greece: Aegean Birthplace of Western Culture. By Melville Bell Grosvenor. Photos by Edwin Stuart Grosvenor and Winfield Parks. 147-193, Aug. 1972
• Istanbul, the City That Links Europe and Asia. By William S. Ellis. 501-533, Oct. 1973
• Lonely Wonders of Katmai. By Ernest Gruening. 800-831, June 1963
• Okinawa, the Island Without a Country. By Jules B. Billard. Photos by Winfield Parks and David Moore. 422-448, Sept. 1969
• One Canada–or Two? By Peter T. White. 436-465, Apr. 1977
• The Phoenicians, Sea Lords of Antiquity. By Samuel W. Matthews. Paintings by Robert C. Magis. 149-189, Aug. 1974
• Queensland: Young Titan of Australia's Tropic North. By Kenneth MacLeish. 593-639, Nov. 1968
• Romania: Maverick on a Tightrope. By William S. Ellis. 688-713, Nov. 1975
• Singapore, Reluctant Nation. By Kenneth MacLeish. 269-300, Aug. 1966
• Time Turns Back in Picture-book Portofino. By Carleton Mitchell. 232-253, Feb. 1965
• Tokyo, the Peaceful Explosion. By William Graves. 445-487, Oct. 1964
• When in Rome. . . . By Stuart E. Jones. 741-789, June 1970
• *Yankee* Cruises the Storied Nile. By Irving and Electa Johnson. 583-633, May 1965

PARKS:
• Parks, Plans, and People: How South America Guards Her Green Legacy. By Mary and Laurance Rockefeller. Photos by George F. Mobley. 74-119, Jan. 1967
• The Parks in Your Backyard (U. S.). By Conrad L. Wirth. 647-707, Nov. 1963
• *See also* Gardens; National Parks; National Recreation Areas; State Parks; Waterton-Glacier International Peace Park

PARKSCAPE, U.S.A.: Tomorrow in Our National Parks. By George B. Hartzog, Jr. 48-93, July 1966

PARROTS. *See* Lorikeets

PARSIS:
• Bombay, the Other India. By John Scofield. Photos by Raghubir Singh. 104-129, July 1981

PASACHOFF, JAY M.: Author:
• Solar Eclipse, Nature's Super Spectacular. By Donald H. Menzel and Jay M. Pasachoff. 222-233, Aug. 1970

PASADENA, California. *See* Tournament of Roses

PASSAGE to Freedom in Viet Nam. By Gertrude Samuels. 858-874, June 1955

PASSION PLAY:
• Mesa del Nayar's Strange Holy Week. By Guillermo Aldana E. 780-795, June 1971

The **PAST** Is Present in Greenfield Village. By Beverley M. Bowie. Photos by Neal P. Davis and Willard R. Culver. 96-127, July 1958

PATAGONIA (Region), Argentina-Chile:
• Guanacos: Wild Camels of South America. By William L. Franklin. 63-75, July 1981
• Magellan: First Voyage Around the World. By Alan Villiers. Photos by Bruce Dale. Included: Discovery and naming of Patagonia in 1520. 721-753, June 1976

O P

• Patagonia. Photos by Des and Jen Bartlett. 290-339, Mar. 1976
I. Argentina Protects Its Wildlife Treasures. By William G. Conway. 290-297; II. Where Two Worlds Meet. 298-321; III. At Home With Right Whales. By Roger Payne. NGS research grant. 322-339
• Swimming With Patagonia's Right Whales. By Roger Payne. Photos by William R. Curtsinger and Charles R. Nicklin, Jr. NGS research grant. 576-587, Oct. 1972

PATENT PLANTS:
• Patent Plants Enrich Our World. By Orville H. Kneen. Photos from U. S. Plant Patents. 357-378, Mar. 1948

PATHANS (Tribespeople):
• An Eye for an Eye: Pakistan's Wild Frontier. By Mike W. Edwards. Photos by J. Bruce Baumann. 111-139, Jan. 1977
• Pakistan Under Pressure. By William S. Ellis. Photos by James L. Stanfield. 668-701, May 1981

The **PATHFINDERS.** Paintings by Herb Kawainui Kane. 756-769, Dec. 1974

PATHS of Fury–This Century's Worst American Storms. 360-361, Sept. 1980

PATHWAY Through History: Today Along the Natchez Trace. By Bern Keating. Photos by Charles Harbutt. 641-667, Nov. 1968

PATMOS (Island), Greece:
• The Isles of Greece: Aegean Birthplace of Western Culture. By Melville Bell Grosvenor. Photos by Edwin Stuart Grosvenor and Winfield Parks. 147-193, Aug. 1972

PATRIOTS in Petticoats. By Lonnelle Aikman. Paintings by Louis S. Glanzman. 475-493, Oct. 1975

PATROLLING Troubled Formosa Strait. 573-588, Apr. 1955

PATTERSON, CAROLYN BENNETT:
Author:
• Date Line: United Nations, New York. Photos by B. Anthony Stewart and John E. Fletcher. 305-331, Sept. 1961
• The Fair Reopens (New York World's Fair, 1964-1965). Photos by James P. Blair. 505-529, Apr. 1965
• The Final Tribute (Churchill Funeral). 199-225, Aug. 1965
• Gettysburg and Vicksburg: the Battle Towns Today. By Robert Paul Jordan. Map notes by Carolyn Bennett Patterson. 4-57, July 1963
• Haiti: Beyond Mountains, More Mountains. Photos by Thomas Nebbia. 70-97, Jan. 1976
• Mardi Gras in New Orleans. Photos by Robert F. Sisson and John E. Fletcher. 726-732, Nov. 1960
• Mississippi's Grand Reunion at the Neshoba County Fair. Photos by C. C. Lockwood. 854-866, June 1980
• New Zealand's Milford Track: "Walk of a Lifetime." Photos by Robert E. Gilka. 117-129, Jan. 1978
• Our Land Through Lincoln's Eyes. Photos by W. D. Vaughn. 243-277, Feb. 1960
• Rescuing the Rothschild (Giraffe). 419-421, Sept. 1977
• Seattle Fair Looks to the 21st Century. Photos by Thomas Nebbia. 402-427, Sept. 1962
• Soaring on Skis in the Swiss Alps. Photos by Kathleen Revis. 94-121, Jan. 1961
• Travels With a Donkey–100 Years Later. Photos by Cotton Coulson. 535-561, Oct. 1978
• A Walk and Ride on the Wild Side: Tasmania. Photos by David Hiser and Melinda Berge. 676-693, May 1983

PATTERSON, FRANCINE (Penny):
Author:
• Conversations With a Gorilla. Photos by Ronald H. Cohn. 438-465, Oct. 1978

PATTON, GEORGE S., Jr.:
• Luxembourg, Survivor of Invasions. By Sydney Clark. Photos by Maynard Owen Williams. 791-810, June 1948

PATTON, ROBERT S.: Photographer:
• Vestmannaeyjar: Up From the Ashes. By Noel Grove. 690-701, May 1977

PÁTZCUARO (City and Lake), Mexico:
• Lost Kingdom in Indian Mexico. By Justin Locke. 517-546, Oct. 1952

PAUL, Saint:
• Jerusalem to Rome in the Path of St. Paul. By David S. Boyer. 707-759, Dec. 1956

PAXOS (Island), Greece:
• Homeward With Ulysses. By Melville Bell Grosvenor. Photos by Edwin Stuart Grosvenor. 1-39, July 1973

PAYNE, MELVIN M.:
• Board of Trustees, Chairman. 159, 225, 226, 227, Aug. 1976
• Committee for Research and Exploration. 433, Mar. 1958; 827, Dec. 1965; 872-873, Dec. 1973; Chairman. 159, 225, Aug. 1976; Secretary. 155, Jan. 1959; 4, Jan. 1963; Vice Chairman. 198, Feb. 1965
• Editorial. By Gilbert M. Grosvenor. 159, Aug. 1976
• NGS Offices. 852, Dec. 1981; 274, Aug. 1982
• Peak named for. 285, Aug. 1964
• President of NGS (1967-1976). 577, 583, 586, 589, 590, Oct. 1967; 843, Dec. 1970; 159, 225-227, Aug. 1976
• Secretary. 4, Jan. 1963; 1, Jan. 1964; 485, Oct. 1966
• Secretary, Assistant. 297, Sept. 1947
• Secretary, Associate. 834, Dec. 1959; 883, Dec. 1960
• Secretary, Senior Assistant. 420, 423, Mar. 1957; 867, Dec. 1957
• Vice President of NGS. 108, 155, Jan. 1959; 834, Dec. 1959; 175, Feb. 1960; 883, Dec. 1960; 485, 486, Oct. 1966
• Vice President, Executive, of NGS. 579, 582, Apr. 1962; 4, Jan. 1963; 1, Jan. 1964; 689, Nov. 1964; 865, 867, June 1967; 583, 590, Oct. 1967
Author:
• American and Geographic Flags Top Everest. Photos by Barry C. Bishop. 157-157C, Aug. 1963
• Frederick G. Vosburgh Retires as Editor; Gilbert M. Grosvenor Succeeds Him. 838-843, Dec. 1970
• The Leakey Tradition Lives On. 143-144, Jan. 1973
• The Leakeys of Africa: Family in Search of Prehistoric Man. 194-231, Feb. 1965
• Leonard Carmichael: An Appreciation. 871-874, Dec. 1973
• Preserving the Treasures of Olduvai Gorge. Photos by Joseph J. Scherschel. 701-709, Nov. 1966
• Reprinting Brings Earliest Geographics to Life. 688-689, Nov. 1964
• 75 Years Exploring Earth, Sea, and Sky: National Geographic Society Observes Its Diamond Anniversary. 1-43, Jan. 1963
• The World in Geographic Filmstrips. 134-137, Jan. 1968

PAYNE, ROGER: Author:
• At Home With Right Whales. Photos by Des and Jen Bartlett. 322-339, Mar. 1976
• Humpbacks: Their Mysterious Songs. Photos by Al Giddings. 18-25, Jan. 1979
Symphony of the Deep: "Songs of the Humpback Whale" (Sound sheet). 24-24B
• New Light on the Singing Whales. Photos by Flip Nicklin. 463-477, Apr. 1982
• Swimming With Patagonia's Right Whales. Photos by William R. Curtsinger and Charles R. Nicklin, Jr. 576-587, Oct. 1972

PEACE CORPS:
• Ambassadors of Good Will. By Sargent Shriver and Peace Corps Volunteers. Contents: Bolivia, Ecuador, Gabon, Sarawak, Tanganyika, Turkey. 297-345, Sept. 1964

PEACE PARK. *See* Waterton-Glacier International Peace Park

The **PEACEFUL** Mrus of Bangladesh. By Claus-Dieter Brauns. 267-286, Feb. 1973

PEANUTS. *See* Groundnut Scheme

PEARL INDUSTRY:
• Desert Sheikdoms of Arabia's Pirate Coast. By Ronald Codrai. 65-104, July 1956
• Exploring the World of Gems. By W. F. Foshag. 779-810, Dec. 1950
• The Philippines, Freedom's Pacific Frontier. By Robert de Roos. Photos by Ted Spiegel. 301-351, Sept. 1966

PEARY, JOSEPHINE D.:
• Gold Medal Awarded to Mrs. Robert E. Peary. 148, Jan. 1956
• Lecture by (1895). 531, Oct. 1954

PEARY, ROBERT E.:
• Far North with "Captain Mac." By Miriam MacMillan. Included: Battle Harbour, Labrador, where Peary gave his first interview to the press after reaching the North Pole; Eskimo friends and helpers. 465-513, Oct. 1951

• The Peary Flag Comes to Rest. By Marie Peary Stafford. 519-532, Oct. 1954
• Three Months on an Arctic Ice Island. By Joseph O. Fletcher. Included: Peary's description of the Ellesmere Island ice shelf and the Arctic "whiteout." 489-504, Apr. 1953
• We Followed Peary to the Pole. By Gilbert Grosvenor and Thomas W. McKnew. 469-484, Oct. 1953

The **PEARY FLAG** Comes to Rest. By Marie Peary Stafford. 519-532, Oct. 1954

PEASANTS of Anatolia. By Alfred Marchionini. 57-72, July 1948

PEAT-BOG BURIALS. *See* Tollund Man

PEAT SOIL:
• California's Surprising Inland Delta. By Judith and Neil Morgan. Photos by Charles O'Rear. 409-430, Sept. 1976

PEERLESS Nepal–A Naturalist's Paradise. By S. Dillon Ripley. Photos by Volkmar Wentzel. 1-40, Jan. 1950

PEFFER, RANDALL S.: Author:
• Massachusetts' North Shore: Harboring Old Ways. Photos by Nathan Benn. 568-590, Apr. 1979

PEISSEL, MICHEL:
Author-Photographer:
• Mustang, Remote Realm in Nepal. 579-604, Oct. 1965

PEKING, China:
• The City They Call Red China's Showcase. By Franc Shor. 193-223, Aug. 1960
Peking: a Pictorial Record. By Brian Brake. 194-197, 199-223
• Power Comes Back to Peiping. By Nelson T. Johnson and W. Robert Moore. 337-368, Sept. 1949
• Return to Changing China. By Audrey Topping. 801-833, Dec. 1971
• This Is the China I Saw. By Jørgen Bisch. 591-639, Nov. 1964

PELICANS. *See* Brown Pelicans

PELLY BAY, Northwest Territories, Canada:
• I Live With the Eskimos. By Guy Mary-Rousseliere. 188-217, Feb. 1971

PENGUINS:
• Antarctica's Nearer Side. By Samuel W. Matthews. Photos by William R. Curtsinger. 622-655, Nov. 1971
• A Naturalist in Penguin Land. By Niall Rankin. 93-116, Jan. 1955
• Nature's Clown, the Penguin. By David Hellyer and Malcolm Davis. 405-428, Sept. 1952
• Oil and Penguins Don't Mix. Photos by Mike Holmes. Included: Jackass penguins. 384-397, Mar. 1973
• Penguins and Their Neighbors. By Roger Tory Peterson. Photos by Des and Jen Bartlett. Included: Adélie, gentoo, and king penguins. 237-255, Aug. 1977
• People and Penguins of the Faraway Falklands. By Olin Sewall Pettingill, Jr. 387-416, Mar. 1956

DES AND JEN BARTLETT

Penguins: Adélies head for open sea

Antarctica: monitor records penguin's biological functions

WILLIAM R. CURTSINGER

PENITENTES (Religious Group):
• Adobe New Mexico. By Mason Sutherland. Photos by Justin Locke. 783-830, Dec. 1949
• New Mexico: The Golden Land. By Robert Laxalt. Photos by Adam Woolfitt. 299-345, Sept. 1970

PENITENTS:
• Easter Week in Indian Guatemala. By John Scofield. 406-417, Mar. 1960
• Holy Week and the Fair in Sevilla. By Luis Marden. 499-530, Apr. 1951

PENNINE CHAIN (Mountains), England:
• A Stroll to London. By Isobel Wylie Hutchison. Photos by B. Anthony Stewart. 171-204, Aug. 1950

PENNINGTON, JOHN: Author:
• Cumberland, My Island for a While. Photos by Jodi Cobb. 649-661, Nov. 1977

PENNSYLVANIA:
• Amish Folk: Plainest of Pennsylvania's Plain People. By Richard Gehman. Photos by William Albert Allard. 227-253, Aug. 1965
• Appalachian Valley Pilgrimage. By Catherine Bell Palmer. Photos by Justin Locke. 1-32, July 1949
• Artists Look at Pennsylvania. By John Oliver La Gorce. 37-56, July 1948
▲ *Close-up: U.S.A., New York, New Jersey, and Pennsylvania,* supplement. Text on reverse. Jan. 1978
• Down the Susquehanna by Canoe. By Ralph Gray. Photos by Walter Meayers Edwards. 73-120, July 1950
• Gettysburg and Vicksburg: the Battle Towns Today. By Robert Paul Jordan. Map notes by Carolyn Bennett Patterson. 4-57, July 1963
• Pennsylvania: Faire Land of William Penn. By Gordon Young. Photos by Cary Wolinsky. 731-767, June 1978
• Shrines of Each Patriot's Devotion. By Frederick G. Vosburgh. 51-82, Jan. 1949
• The Thousand-mile Glide. By Karl Striedieck. Photos by Otis Imboden. 431-438, Mar. 1978
• Today on the Delaware, Penn's Glorious River. By Albert W. Atwood. Photos by Robert F. Sisson. 1-40, July 1952
• *See also* Kutztown; Longwood Gardens; Philadelphia; Pittsburgh; Valley Forge

PENNSYLVANIA AVENUE, Washington, D. C.:
• New Grandeur for Flowering Washington. By Joseph Judge. Photos by James P. Blair. 500-539, Apr. 1967
• Pennsylvania Avenue, Route of Presidents. By Dorothea and Stuart E. Jones. Photos by Volkmar Wentzel. 63-95, Jan. 1957
• A Preservation Victory Saves Washington's Old Post Office. By Wolf Von Eckardt. Photos by Volkmar Wentzel. 407-416, Sept. 1983

OP

PENNSYLVANIA DUTCH (People):
• Pennsylvania Dutch Folk Festival. By Maynard Owen Williams. 503-516, Oct. 1952
• Pennsylvania's Old-time Dutch Treat. By Kent Britt. Photos by H. Edward Kim. 564-578, Apr. 1973
• *See also* Amish

PENNSYLVANIA'S Amish Folk. By Richard Gehman. Photos by William Albert Allard. 227-253, Aug. 1965

PENSAR (Island), Finland:
• Scenes of Postwar Finland. By La Verne Bradley. Photos by Jerry Waller. 233-264, Aug. 1947

PENTECOST ISLAND, New Hebrides:
• Land Diving With the Pentecost Islanders. By Kal Muller. 799-817, Dec. 1970
• South Seas' Incredible Land Divers. By Irving and Electa Johnson. 77-92, Jan. 1955

PEOPLE and Penguins of the Faraway Falklands. By Olin Sewall Pettingill, Jr. 387-416, Mar. 1956

The **PEOPLE** of Cades Cove. By William O. Douglas. Photos by Thomas Nebbia and Otis Imboden. 60-95, July 1962

The **PEOPLE** of Cumberland Gap. By John Fetterman. Photos by Bruce Dale. 591-621, Nov. 1971

PEOPLE of Fire and Fervor. By Debra Denker. Photos by Steve McCurry. 458-473, Oct. 1981

PEOPLE of Myth and Magic. By James Norman. Photos by Guillermo Aldana E. 832-853, June 1977

The **PEOPLE** of New Jersey's Pine Barrens. By John McPhee. Photos by William R. Curtsinger. 52-77, Jan. 1974

PEOPLE of the Long Spring. By Yuri Rytkheu. Photos by Dean Conger. 206-223, Feb. 1983

PEOPLE of the Reindeer. By Sally Anderson. Photos by Erik Borg. 364-379, Sept. 1977

PEOPLE of the Taboo. By Carol Beckwith. 483-509, Oct. 1983

The **PEOPLE** Who Made Saskatchewan. By Ethel A. Starbird. Photos by Craig Aurness. 651-679, May 1979

PEOPLES of the Arctic. 144-223, Feb. 1983
I. Introduction by Joseph Judge. 144-149; II. Hunters of the Lost Spirit: Alaskans, Canadians, Greenlanders, Lapps. By Priit J. Vesilind. Photos by David Alan Harvey, Ivars Silis, and Sisse Brimberg. 150-197; III. Where Magic Ruled: Art of the Bering Sea. By William W. Fitzhugh and Susan A. Kaplan. Photos by Sisse Brimberg. 198-205; IV. People of the Long Spring (Chukchis). By Yuri Rytkheu. Photos by Dean Conger. 206-223
▲ *Peoples of the Arctic; Arctic Ocean,* double-sided supplement. Feb. 1983

PEOPLE'S REPUBLIC OF CHINA. *See* China, People's Republic of

PERAZIC, ELIZABETH: Author:
• Little Laos, Next Door to Red China. 46-69, Jan. 1960

PÈRE David's Deer Saved From Extinction. By Larry Kohl. Photos by Bates Littlehales. 478-485, Oct. 1982

PERFUME, the Business of Illusion. By Lonnelle Aikman. 531-550, Apr. 1951

PERISCOPE on the Etruscan Past. By Carlo M. Lerici. 337-350, Sept. 1959

PERKINS, LARRY: Author:
• Across Australia by Sunpower. By Hans Tholstrup and Larry Perkins. Photos by David Austen. 600-607, Nov. 1983

PERÓN, JUAN DOMINGO:
• Which Way Now for Argentina? By Loren McIntyre. 296-333, Mar. 1975

PERRY, MATTHEW CALBRAITH:
• The Yankee Sailor Who Opened Japan. By Ferdinand Kuhn. 85-102, July 1953

PERSEPOLIS (Ruins), Iran:
• In the Footsteps of Alexander the Great. By Helen and Frank Schreider. Paintings by Tom Lovell. 1-65, Jan. 1968
• Iran: Desert Miracle. By William Graves. Photos by James P. Blair. 2-47, Jan. 1975
• Journey Into Troubled Iran. By George W. Long. Photos by J. Baylor Roberts. 425-464, Oct. 1951

PERSIAN EMPIRE:
• In the Footsteps of Alexander the Great. By Helen and Frank Schreider. Paintings by Tom Lovell. 1-65, Jan. 1968
• The Sword and the Sermon. By Thomas J. Abercrombie. Included: Conquest of the Persian Empire by Arab Moslems; the adoption of Persian arts and sciences by the conquerors. 3-45, July 1972

PERSIAN GULF:
• The Arab World, Inc. By John J. Putman. Photos by Winfield Parks. 494-533, Oct. 1975
• Bahrain: Hub Of the Persian Gulf. By Thomas J. Abercrombie. Photos by Steve Raymer. 300-329, Sept. 1979
• Beside the Persian Gurlf. Photos by Maynard Owen Williams. 341-356, Mar. 1947
• *Calypso* Explores for Underwater Oil. By Jacques-Yves Cousteau. 155-184, Aug. 1955
• In Search of Arabia's Past. By Peter Bruce Cornwall. 493-522, Apr. 1948
• In the Wake of Sindbad. By Tim Severin. Photos by Richard Greenhill. 2-41, July 1982
• Sailing with Sindbad's Sons. By Alan Villiers. 675-688, Nov. 1948
• *Tigris* Sails Into the Past. By Thor Heyerdahl. Photos by Carlo Mauri and the crew of the *Tigris*. 806-827, Dec. 1978
• Troubled Waters East of Suez. By Ernest M. Eller. 483-522, Apr. 1954
• Twilight of the Arab Dhow. By Marion Kaplan. 330-351, Sept. 1974
▪ The Voyage of the *Tigris*. 826, Dec. 1978; 1, Jan. 1979; cover, Apr. 1979
• *See also* Iran; Kuwait; Oman; Saudi Arabia; United Arab Emirates

PERTH, Australia:
• Perth–Fair Winds and Full Sails. By Thomas J. Abercrombie. Photos by Cary Wolinsky. 638-667, May 1982
• Western Australia, the Big Country. By Kenneth MacLeish. Photos by James L. Stanfield. 150-187, Feb. 1975

PERU:
• The Amazon. Photos by Loren McIntyre. 445-455, Oct. 1972
• Amazon–The River Sea. By Loren McIntyre. 456-495, Oct. 1972
• At Home in the High Andes. By Harry Tschopik, Jr. 133-146, Jan. 1955
• Avalanche! By Bart McDowell. Photos by John E. Fletcher. 855-880, June 1962
• Birds That "See" in the Dark With Their Ears. By Edward S. Ross. 282-290, Feb. 1965
• By Parachute Into Peru's Lost World. By G. Brooks Baekeland. Photos by author and Peter R. Gimbel. Included: Apurímac River, Cordillera Vilcabamba, Lake Parodi, Urubamba River. NGS research grant. 268-296, Aug. 1964
• Finding the Tomb of a Warrior-God. By William Duncan Strong. Photos by Clifford Evans, Jr. 453-482, Apr. 1947
• The Five Worlds of Peru. By Kenneth F. Weaver. Photos by Bates Littlehales. 213-265, Feb. 1964
• The Incredible Potato. By Robert E. Rhoades. Photos by Martin Rogers. 668-694, May 1982
▲ *Indians of South America; Archaeology of South America,* double-sided supplement. Mar. 1982
• The Marvelous Hummingbird Rediscovered. By Crawford H. Greenewalt. 98-101, July 1966
• Parks, Plans, and People: How South America Guards Her Green Legacy. By Mary and Laurance Rockefeller. Photos by George F. Mobley. 74-119, Jan. 1967
• Peru, Homeland of the Warlike Inca. By Kip Ross. 421-462, Oct. 1950
• Peru Profits from Sea Fowl. By Robert Cushman Murphy. Photos by author and Grace E. Barstow Murphy. 395-413, Mar. 1959
• Peru's Pilgrimage to the Sky. By Robert Randall. Photos by Loren McIntyre and Ira Block. 60-69, July 1982
• Sea Fever. By John E. Schultz. 237-268, Feb. 1949
• Silver: A Mineral of Excellent Nature. By Allen A. Boraiko. Photos by Fred Ward. 280-313, Sept. 1981
• Titicaca, Abode of the Sun. By Luis Marden. Photos by Flip Schulke. 272-294, Feb. 1971

• The Two Souls of Peru. By Harvey Arden. Photos by William Albert Allard. 284-321, Mar. 1982
• *See also* Condor; Vicuñas; *and* Nazca Lines

PERUVIAN INDIANS:
• Amazon–The River Sea. By Loren McIntyre. 456-495, Oct. 1972
• At Home in the High Andes. By Harry Tschopik, Jr. 133-146, Jan. 1955
• By Parachute Into Peru's Lost World. By G. Brooks Baekeland. Photos by author and Peter R. Gimbel. Included: Apurímac River, Cordillera Vilcabamba, Lake Parodi, Urubamba River. NGS research grant. 268-296, Aug. 1964
• Chan Chan, Peru's Ancient City of Kings. By Michael E. Moseley and Carol J. Mackey. Photos by David Brill. NGS research grant. 318-345, Mar. 1973
• The Five Worlds of Peru. By Kenneth F. Weaver. Photos by Bates Littlehales. 213-265, Feb. 1964
• The Incredible Potato. By Robert E. Rhoades. Photos by Martin Rogers. Included: *chuño,* a dehydrated potato product. 668-694, May 1982
• The Lost Empire of the Incas. By Loren McIntyre. Art by Ned and Rosalie Seidler. 729-787, Dec. 1973
A Pictorial Chronicle of the Incas. 747-753
• Mystery of the Ancient Nazca Lines. By Loren McIntyre. NGS research grant. 716-728, May 1975
• Peru's Pilgrimage to the Sky. By Robert Randall. Photos by Loren McIntyre and Ira Block. 60-69, July 1982
• Titicaca, Abode of the Sun. By Luis Marden. Photos by Flip Schulke. 272-294, Feb. 1971
• The Two Souls of Peru. By Harvey Arden. Photos by William Albert Allard. 284-321, Mar. 1982
• *See also* Incas

PESCADORES (Islands), Taiwan:
• Pescadores, Wind-swept Outposts of Formosa. By Horace Bristol, Sr. 265-284, Feb. 1956
• *See also* Formosa Strait

PESEK, LUDEK: Artist:
• Journey to Mars. By Kenneth F. Weaver. 231-263, Feb. 1973
▲ *The Red Planet Mars;* "The Dusty Face of Mars," supplement, Feb. 1973
• Voyage to the Planets. By Kenneth F. Weaver. 147-193, Aug. 1970

PESH MERGAS. *See* Kurds

PEST CONTROL:
• The Pesticide Dilemma. By Allen A. Boraiko. Photos by Fred Ward. 145-183, Feb. 1980
• The Rat, Lapdog of the Devil. By Thomas Y. Canby. Photos by James L. Stanfield. 60-87, July 1977
• *See also* Insect Control

PESTALOZZI, Switzerland:
• Children's Village in Switzerland, Pestalozzi. Photos by Alfred Lammer. 268-282, Aug. 1959

WILLIAM ALBERT ALLARD
Two Souls of Peru: prayer offering

PESTICIDE POLLUTION:
• Can the Cooper's Hawk Survive? By Noel Snyder. Photos by author and Helen Snyder. NGS research grant. 433-442, Mar. 1974
• The Osprey, Endangered World Citizen. By Roger Tory Peterson. Photos by Frederick Kent Truslow. NGS research grant. 53-67, July 1969
• The Pesticide Dilemma. By Allen A. Boraiko. Photos by Fred Ward. 145-183, Feb. 1980
• Pollution, Threat to Man's Only Home. By Gordon Young. Photos by James P. Blair. 738-781, Dec. 1970
• Quicksilver and Slow Death (Mercury). By John J. Putman. Photos by Robert W. Madden. 507-527, Oct. 1972

PETÉN, Department of the, Guatemala. *See* Naj Tunich; Tikal

PETER, Saint:
• St. Peter's, Rome's Church of Popes. By Aubrey Menen. Photos by Albert Moldvay. 865-879, Dec. 1971

PETERSON, ERNST: Photographer:
• Montana, Shining Mountain Treasureland. By Leo A. Borah. 693-736, June 1950

PETERSON, MENDEL: Author:
• Graveyard of the Quicksilver Galleons. Photos by Jonathan Blair. 850-876, Dec. 1979
• Reach for the New World. Photos by David L. Arnold. Paintings by Richard Schlecht. 724-767, Dec. 1977

PETERSON, ROGER TORY: Author:
• The Galapagos, Eerie Cradle of New Species. Photos by Alan and Joan Root. 541-585, Apr. 1967
• A New Bird Immigrant Arrives (Cattle Egret). 281-292, Aug. 1954
• The Osprey, Endangered World Citizen. Photos by Frederick Kent Truslow. 53-67, July 1969
• Penguins and Their Neighbors. Photos by Des and Jen Bartlett. 237-255, Aug. 1977
Author-Photographer:
• Rare Birds Flock to Spain's Marismas. 397-425, Mar. 1958
• White Storks, Vanishing Sentinels of the Rooftops. 838-853, June 1962

PETERSON, WILLIS:
Author-Photographer:
• Arizona's Operation Beaver Lift. 666-680, May 1955

PETRA, Jordan:
• Arab Land Beyond the Jordan. Photos by Frank Hurley. 753-768, Dec. 1947
• Petra, Rose-red Citadel of Biblical Edom. By David S. Boyer. 853-870, Dec. 1955

PETROGLYPHS:
• The Anasazi–Riddles in the Ruins. By Thomas Y. Canby. Photos by Dewitt Jones and David Brill. Paintings by Roy Andersen. Included: Sun dagger phenomenon. 554-592, Nov. 1982
• Baja's Murals of Mystery. By Harry Crosby. Photos by Charles O'Rear. 692-702, Nov. 1980

OP

PAINTING BY JOSEPH-SIFFRED DUPLESSIS, PRIVATE COLLECTION

Philadelphia: portrait of Franklin

• Tanzania's Stone Age Art. By Mary D. Leakey. Photos by John Reader. 84-99, July 1983
• Utah's Rock Art: Wilderness Louvre. A picture essay by Gary Smith, with Michael E. Long. 97-117, Jan. 1980
• *See also* Abrigo do Sol (Archaeological Site), Brazil

PETROGRAPHY:
• Finding Rare Beauty in Common Rocks. By Lorence G. Collins. 121-129, Jan. 1966

PETROLEUM. *See* Oil

PETSAMO REGION:
• Scenes of Postwar Finland. By La Verne Bradley. Photos by Jerry Waller. 233-264, Aug. 1947

PETTINGILL, OLIN SEWALL, Jr.:
Author-Photographer:
• People and Penguins of the Faraway Falklands. 387-416, Mar. 1956

PEYOTE CULT:
• The Huichols, Mexico's People of Myth and Magic. By James Norman. Photos by Guillermo Aldana E. 832-853, June 1977

PEYTON, CAROLINAS:
• A Long Life, a Good Life on the Potomac. By James L. Stanfield. 470-479, Oct. 1976

PFLEGER, MICHAEL: Photographer:
• Bicycles Are Back–and Booming! By Noel Grove. 671-681, May 1973

PHALANGERS:
• Strange Animals of Australia. By David Fleay. Photos by Stanley Breeden. 388-411, Sept. 1963

PHALAROPES:
• Mono Lake: A Vital Way Station for the Wilson's Phalarope. By Joseph R. Jehl, Jr. NGS research grant. 520-525, Oct. 1981

"PHANTOM COAST," Antarctica:
• Exploring Antarctica's Phantom Coast. By Edwin A. McDonald. Photos by W. D. Vaughn. 251-273 Feb. 1962

PHILADELPHIA, Pennsylvania:
• Artists Look at Pennsylvania. By John Oliver La Gorce. 37-56, July 1948
• Benjamin Franklin, Philosopher of Dissent. By Alice J. Hall. Photos by Linda Bartlett. 93-123, July 1975
• Pennsylvania: Faire Land of William Penn. By Gordon Young. Photos by Cary Wolinsky. 731-767, June 1978
• Philadelphia Houses a Proud Past. By Harold Donaldson Eberlein. Photos by Thomas Nebbia. 151-191, Aug. 1960
• They'd Rather Be in Philadelphia. By Ethel A. Starbird. Photos by Ted Spiegel. 314-343, Mar. 1983

PHILIP II, King (Macedon):
• Regal Treasures From a Macedonian Tomb. By Manolis Andronicos. Photos by Spyros Tsavdaroglou. 55-77, July 1978

PHILIP, Prince, Duke of Edinburgh:
• Off the Beaten Track of Empire. By Beverley M. Bowie. Photos by Michael Parker. 584-626, Nov. 1957
• President Eisenhower Presents to Prince Philip the National Geographic Society's Medal. 865-868, Dec. 1957
• Windsor Castle. By Anthony Holden. Photos by James L. Stanfield. 604-631, Nov. 1980
Author:
• H.R.H. The Prince Philip, Duke of Edinburgh, Introduces to Members the Narrative of His Round-the-world Tour. 583-584, Nov. 1957
• Man's Wildlife Heritage Faces Extinction. 700-703, Nov. 1962

PHILIPPINE EAGLES:
• Saving the Philippine Eagle. By Robert S. Kennedy. Photos by Alan R. Degen, Neil L. Rettig, and Wolfgang A. Salb. NGS research grant. 847-856, June 1981

PHILIPPINES, Republic of the:
• Magellan: First Voyage Around the World. By Alan Villiers. Photos by Bruce Dale. Note: Magellan was killed in a battle at Mactan Island. 721-753, June 1976
• The Philippines: Better Days Still Elude an Old Friend. By Don Moser. Photos by Bruce Dale. 360-391, Mar. 1977
• The Philippines, Freedom's Pacific Frontier. By Robert de Roos. Photos by Ted Spiegel. 301-351, Sept. 1966
• The Rat, Lapdog of the Devil. By Thomas Y. Canby. Photos by James L. Stanfield. 60-87, July 1977
• Sea Gypsies of the Philippines. By Anne de Henning Singh. Photos by Raghubir Singh. 659-677, May 1976
• *See also* Mindanao (Island); *and* YWCA

PHILLIPS, ALAN: Author:
• Canada, My Country. Photos by David S. Boyer and Walter Meayers Edwards. 769-819, Dec. 1961
• Canadian Rockies, Lords of a Beckoning Land. Photos by James L. Stanfield. 353-393, Sept. 1966

PHILLIPS, CRAIG: Artist:
• Solving Life Secrets of the Sailfish. By Gilbert Voss. Photos by B. Anthony Stewart. 859-872, June 1956
• Strange Babies of the Sea. By Hilary B. Moore. Paintings by Craig Phillips and Jacqueline Hutton. 41-56, July 1952

PHILLIPS, SAM C.: Author:
• "A Most Fantastic Voyage": The Story of Apollo 8's Rendezvous With the Moon. 593-631, May 1969

PHILMONT Scout Ranch Helps Boys Grow Up. By Andrew H. Brown. 399-416, Sept. 1956

PHILOSOPHER of Dissent, Benj. Franklin. By Alice J. Hall. Photos by Linda Bartlett. 93-123, July 1975

PHNOM PENH, Kampuchea:
• Kampuchea Wakens From a Nightmare. By Peter T. White. Photos by David Alan Harvey. 590-623, May 1982

The **PHOENICIANS,** Sea Lords of Antiquity. By Samuel W. Matthews. Photos by Winfield Parks. Paintings by Robert C. Magis. 149-189, Aug. 1974

PHOENIX, Arizona:
- Arizona's Suburbs of the Sun. By David Jeffery. Photos by H. Edward Kim. 486-517, Oct. 1977

PHOENIX ISLANDS. *See* Canton Island

PHOSPHATE:
- Nauru, the World's Richest Nation. By Mike Holmes. 344-353, Sept. 1976

PHOSPHORESCENT BAY, Puerto Rico:
- Sailing a Sea of Fire. By Paul A. Zahl. 120-129, July 1960

PHOTO SUPPLEMENTS:
▲ "The Earth From Space," double-sided supplement. Photo by Harrison H. Schmitt. Sept. 1973
▲ *The Face and Faith of Poland,* map, photo, and essay supplement. By Peter Miller. Essay by Czesław Miłosz. Photos by Bruno Barbey. Apr. 1982
▲ NASA photo of Saturn. "The Solar System," painting by Lloyd K. Townsend, on reverse. July 1981
▲ "Portrait U.S.A.," first color photomosaic of the 48 contiguous United States from Landsat satellite imagery. Map on reverse. July 1976

***PHOTOBLEPHARON*:**
- Flashlight Fish of the Red Sea. By Eugenie Clark. Photos by David Doubilet. 719-728, Nov. 1978

PHOTOGRAPHING a Volcano in Action. By Thomas J. Hargrave. 561-563, Oct. 1955

PHOTOGRAPHING Hummingbirds in Brazil. By Crawford H. Greenewalt. 100-115, Jan. 1963

PHOTOGRAPHING Northern Wild Flowers. By Virginia L. Wells. 809-823, June 1956

PHOTOGRAPHING the Night Creatures of Alligator Reef. By Robert E. Schroeder. Photos by author and Walter A. Starck II. 128-154, Jan. 1964

PHOTOGRAPHING the Sea's Dark Underworld. By Harold E. Edgerton. 523-537, Apr. 1955

PHOTOGRAPHY:
- Businessman in the Bush. By Frederick Kent Truslow. 634-675, May 1970
- Eastman of Rochester: Photographic Pioneer. By Allan C. Fisher, Jr. 423-438, Sept. 1954
- Editorials. By Gilbert M. Grosvenor. 299, Sept. 1975; 295, Mar. 1978
- Eyes of Science. By Rick Gore. Photos by James P. Blair. Contents: Photography and other imaging techniques. 360-389, Mar. 1978

◆ *Images of the World: Photography at the National Geographic.* Announced 709, 851, Dec. 1981
- National Geographic Photographers Win Top Magazine Awards. 830-831, June 1959
- The Romance of the Geographic: National Geographic Magazine Observes Its Diamond Anniversary. By Gilbert Hovey Grosvenor. 516-585, Oct. 1963
- Silver: A Mineral of Excellent Nature. By Allen A. Boraiko. Photos by Fred Ward. Note: The highest percentage of silver use in the United States is for photographic film. 280-313, Sept. 1981
- *See also* Imaging Techniques; *and* NGM: Photographs, Notable

PHOTOGRAPHY, Astronomical:
- First Color Portraits of the Heavens. By William C. Miller. 670-679, May 1959
- First Photographs of Planets and Moon Taken With Palomar's 200-inch Telescope. By Milton L. Humason. 125-130, Jan. 1953
- *See also* Sky Survey

PHOTOGRAPHY, Infrared:
- Heat Paints *Columbia's* Portrait. By Cliff Tarpy. 650-653, Nov. 1982
- Remote Sensing: New Eyes to See the World. By Kenneth F. Weaver. 46-73, Jan. 1969
- Skylab Looks at Earth. 471-493, Oct. 1974

PHOTOGRAPHY, Microscope:
- At Home With the Bulldog Ant. By Robert F. Sisson. 62-75, July 1974

Face-to-Face With a World of Ants (electron micrographs). 72-75
- Finding Rare Beauty in Common Rocks. By Lorence G. Collins. 121-129, Jan. 1966
- Snowflakes to Keep. By Robert F. Sisson. 104-111, Jan. 1970
- *See also* Crystals; Photosynthesis

PHOTOGRAPHY, Nature:
- Businessman in the Bush. By Frederick Kent Truslow. 634-675, May 1970
- Freezing the Trout's Lightning Leap. By Treat Davidson. 525-530, Apr. 1958

◆ *Hunting Wild Life with Camera and Flashlight* (1935). 296, Mar. 1952
◆ *Stalking Birds with Color Camera* (1951). 437, Oct. 1955; 562-563, Oct. 1961; 532, Apr. 1962; 147, Jan. 1969

PHOTOGRAPHY, Space:
▲ "The Earth From Space," double-sided supplement. Photo by Harrison H. Schmitt. Sept. 1973
- Extraordinary Photograph Shows Earth Pole to Pole. Photos by Nimbus I. 190-193, Feb. 1965
- Historic Color Portrait of Earth From Space. By Kenneth F. Weaver. Photos by DODGE Satellite. 726-731, Nov. 1967
- Our Earth as a Satellite Sees It. By W. G. Stroud. 293-302, Aug. 1960
- A Satellite Makes a Coast-to-Coast Picture. . . . By Barry C. Bishop. Contents: The Landsat Portrait of the United States. 140-147, July 1976
- Surveyor: Candid Camera on the Moon. By Homer E. Newell. 578-592, Oct. 1966

PHOTOGRAPHY, Underwater:
- British Columbia's Cold Emerald Sea. Photos by David Doubilet. Text by Larry Kohl. 526-551, Apr. 1980
- Camera Under the Sea. By Luis Marden. NGS research grant. 162-200, Feb. 1956
- Current Scientific Projects of the National Geographic Society. Included: "Aquascope"; Hand-held electronic flash equipment. 143-144, July 1953
- Ghost Ships of the War of 1812: *Hamilton* and *Scourge*. By Daniel A. Nelson. Photos by Emory Kristof. Paintings by Richard Schlecht. Included: The remotely piloted vehicle (RPV) which carried still-picture and videotape equipment. 289-313, Mar. 1983
- Incredible World of the Deep-sea Rifts. NGS research grant. 680-705, Nov. 1979

I. Strange World Without Sun. The Editor. 680-688; II. Return to Oases of the Deep. By Robert D. Ballard and J. Frederick Grassle. 689-705
- Oases of Life in the Cold Abyss (Galapagos Rift). By John B. Corliss and Robert D. Ballard. Included: ANGUS; "creature camera". 441-453, Oct. 1977
- Photographing the Night Creatures of Alligator Reef. By Robert E. Schroeder. Photos by author and Walter A. Starck II. NGS research grant. 128-154, Jan. 1964
- Photographing the Sea's Dark Underworld. By Harold E. Edgerton. NGS research grant. 523-537, Apr. 1955
- A Strange Ride in the Deep (on Manta Rays). By Peter Benchley. 200-203, Feb. 1981
- Strange World of Palau's Salt Lakes. By William M. Hamner. Photos by David Doubilet. 264-282, Feb. 1982
- Unseen Life of a Mountain Stream. By William H. Amos. 562-580, Apr. 1977
- Where the Earth Turns Inside Out (Project FAMOUS). By J. R. Heirtzler. Photos by Emory Kristof. Included: LIBEC (LIght BEhind Camera). 586-603, May 1975

PHOTOGRAPHY, X-Ray:
- Re-creating Madagascar's Giant Extinct Bird. By Alexander Wetmore. 488-493, Oct. 1967
- X-Rays Reveal the Inner Beauty of Shells. By Hilary B. Moore. 427-434, Mar. 1955

PHOTOMAPPING:
- Periscope on the Etruscan Past. By Carlo M. Lerici. 347-350, Sept. 1959
- *See also* Inter-American Geodetic Survey; Landsat; U. S. Coast and Geodetic Survey

PHOTOMICROGRAPHY:
- Electronic Voyage Through an Invisible World. By Kenneth F. Weaver. 274-290, Feb. 1977

■ The Invisible World. 1, Jan. 1980; cover, Mar. 1980
- The Mystery of the Shroud. By Kenneth F. Weaver. 730-753, June 1980

O P

• Rotifers: Nature's Water Purifiers. By John Walsh. 287-292, Feb. 1979
• Those Marvelous, Myriad Diatoms. By Richard B. Hoover. Included: Light and electron micrographs. 871-878, June 1979

PHOTOSYNTHESIS:
• How the Sun Gives Life to the Sea. By Paul A. Zahl. 199-225, Feb. 1961

PHYSICS:
• The British Way. By Sir Evelyn Wrench. 421-541, Apr. 1949
◆ *How Things Work.* 1983
• The Once and Future Universe. By Rick Gore. Photos by James A. Sugar. Paintings by Barron Storey. Picture text by David Jeffery. 704-749, June 1983
• The Search for Tomorrow's Power. By Kenneth F. Weaver. Photos by Emory Kristof. Included: Electromagnets, Fission, Fusion, Magnetohydrodynamics, Nuclear reactors. 650-681, Nov. 1972
• *See also* Electricity; Nuclear Energy; listing under Optics; *and* National Bureau of Standards

PHYTOPLANKTON. *See* Diatoms

PIAZZA ARMERINA, Sicily:
• Roman Life in 1,600-year-old Color Pictures. By Gino Vinicio Gentili. Photos by Duncan Edwards. 211-229, Feb. 1957

PICCARD, JACQUES: Author:
• Man's Deepest Dive. Photos by Thomas J. Abercrombie. 224-239, Aug. 1960

PICKERELL, JAMES H.:
Author-Photographer:
• Dory on the Banks: A Day in the Life of a Portuguese Fisherman. 573-583, Apr. 1968

PICKOW, GEORGE:
Author-Photographer:
• The Great St. Bernard Hospice Today. 49-62, Jan. 1957

PICTOGRAPHS (Indian Effigies). *See* Gravel Pictographs; Nazca Lines

A **PICTORIAL** Chronicle of the Incas. Paintings by Ned Seidler and drawings by Rosalie Seidler. 747-753, Dec. 1973

PICTORIAL SUPPLEMENTS. *See* Painting Supplements; Photo Supplements

PICTURE-BOOK Portofino. By Carleton Mitchell. Photos by Winfield Parks. 232-253, Feb. 1965

PIED-À-TERRE (Motorboat):
• French Riviera: Storied Playground on the Azure Coast. By Carleton Mitchell. Photos by Thomas Nebbia. 798-835, June 1967

PIEDRA PARADA, Chiapas, Mexico:
• On the Trail of La Venta Man. By Matthew W. Stirling. Photos by Richard H. Stewart. NGS research grant. 137-172, Feb. 1947
Hunting Mexico's Buried Temples. 145-168

PIEL, GERARD: Author:
• Five Noted Thinkers Explore the Future. 70-71, July 1976

Pine Barrens: bird flaps untried wings

WILLIAM R. CURTSINGER

GEORGE F. MOBLEY, NGS

Pigs: Porky hams it up with his trainer

PIERCE, FRANKLIN:
• Profiles of the Presidents: II. A Restless Nation Moves West. By Frank Freidel. 80-121, Jan. 1965

PIGEON NETTING:
• Land of the Ancient Basques. By Robert Laxalt. Photos by William Albert Allard. 240-277, Aug. 1968
• Pigeon Netting–Sport of Basques. Photos by Irene Burdett-Scougall. 405-416, Sept. 1949

PIGEONS:
• The Flying Telegraph. By Joseph F. Spears. Official U. S. Army Signal Corps photos. 531-554, Apr. 1947

PIGS:
• The Joy of Pigs. By Kent Britt. Photos by George F. Mobley. 398-415, Sept. 1978
• *See also* Hog Raising

PILARSKI, LAURA: Author:
• Little Tibet in Switzerland. Photos by Fred Mayer. 711-727, Nov. 1968

PILGRIMAGE Through Two Englands. By Allan C. Fisher, Jr. Photos by Cary Wolinsky. 442-481, Oct. 1979

PILGRIMAGES:
• Fátima: Beacon for Portugal's Faithful. By Jane Vessels. Photos by Bruno Barbey. 832-839, Dec. 1980
• From the Hair of Siva. By Helen and Frank Schreider. Included: Hindu pilgrimages to the Ganges. 445-503, Oct. 1960
• The Ganges, River of Faith. By John J. Putman. Photos by Raghubir Singh. 445-483, Oct. 1971
• Himalayan Pilgrimage. By Christopher Rand. Included: Hindu pilgrimage to Amarnath Cave, India. 520-535, Oct. 1956
• Home to the Holy Land. By Maynard Owen Williams. 707-746, Dec. 1950
• India's Sculptured Temple Caves. By Volkmar Wentzel. 665-678, May 1953
• Inside the Sacred Hopi Homeland. By Jake Page. Photos by Susanne Page. 607-629, Nov. 1982
• Kunming Pilgrimage. Contents: Buddhist New Year pilgrimage. 213-226, Feb. 1950
• Nomads of China's West. By Galen Rowell. Photos by the author and Harold A. Knutson. Included: Anyemaqen, a Tibetan holy mountain. 244-263, Feb. 1982
• Peru's Pilgrimage to the Sky. By Robert Randall. Photos by Loren McIntyre and Ira Block. Contents: Snow Star Pilgrimage, a Corpus Christi celebration. 60-69, July 1982
• Pilgrimage to Holy Island and the Farnes. By John E. H. Nolan. Included: Lindisfarne. 547-570, Oct. 1952
• Pilgrims Follow the Christmas Star. By Maynard Owen Williams. Included: Pilgrimage to the Holy Land. 831-840, Dec. 1952
• Searching Out Medieval Churches in Ethiopia's Wilds. By Georg Gerster. 856-844, Dec. 1970

• Trek to Nepal's Crystal Mountain. By Joel F. Ziskin. Included: Buddhist pilgrimage centers in Dolpo, Nepal. 500-517, Apr. 1977
• Vézelay, Hill of the Pilgrims. By Melvin Hall. 229-247, Feb. 1953
• Where Jesus Walked. By Howard La Fay. Photos by Charles Harbutt. 739-781, Dec. 1967
• *See also* Hajj

PILGRIMS:
• Founders of New England. By Sir Evelyn Wrench. Photos by B. Anthony Stewart. 803-838, June 1953

The **PILOT'S** Story. By Alan B. Shepard, Jr. Photos by Dean Conger. 432-444, Sept. 1961

PINE BARRENS (Region), New Jersey:
• The People of New Jersey's Pine Barrens. By John McPhee. Photos by William R. Curtsinger. 52-77, Jan. 1974

PINE RIDGE RESERVATION, South Dakota:
• South Dakota's Badlands: Castles in Clay. By John Madson. Photos by Jim Brandenburg. 524-539, Apr. 1981

PINEAPPLES AND PINEAPPLE GROWING:
• Because It Rains on Hawaii. By Frederick Simpich, Jr. 571-610, Nov. 1949
• Hawaii, U.S.A. By Frederick Simpich, Jr. Photos by Thomas Nebbia. 1-45, July 1960
• How Fruit Came to America. By J. R. Magness. Paintings by Else Bostelmann. 325-377, Sept. 1951
• *See also* Puya

The **PINK** Birds of Texas. By Paul A. Zahl. 641-654, Nov. 1949

PINKIANG, China. *See* Harbin

PIONEER PROBES:
• Mystery Shrouds the Biggest Planet (Jupiter). By Kenneth F. Weaver. Included: Pioneer 10, Pioneer 11. 285-294, Feb. 1975
• Reaching for the Moon. By Allan C. Fisher, Jr. Photos by Luis Marden. Included: Pioneer I, Pioneer II, Pioneer III. 157-171, Feb. 1959
• Voyage to the Planets. By Kenneth F. Weaver. Paintings by Ludek Pesek. Included: A Pioneer model; and plans for a future Pioneer F and Pioneer G. 147-193, Aug. 1970

PIONEERS Head North to Canada's "Now" Frontier. By Robert Paul Jordan. Photos by Lowell Georgia. 480-511, Oct. 1976

PIONEERS in Man's Search for the Universe. Paintings by Jean-Leon Huens. Text by Thomas Y. Canby. 627-633, May 1974

The **PIOUS** Ones (Brooklyn's Hasidic Jews). By Harvey Arden. Photos by Nathan Benn. 276-298, Aug. 1975

PIPELINES, Natural Gas:
• Canada's "Now" Frontier. By Robert Paul Jordan. Photos by Lowell Georgia. Included: Map showing oil pipeline, proposed gas pipeline, and tar sands. 480-511, Oct. 1976
• The Eternal Flame: Millions of Years Old, Natural Gas Now Is a New Servant of Man. By Albert W. Atwood. Included: Construction and cost of pipeline-network in the United States ("Big Inch," "Little Big Inch," "Super Inch," and "Toughest Inch"); the Trans-Arabian pipeline. 540-564, Oct. 1951
• Natural Gas: The Search Goes On. By Bryan Hodgson. Photos by Lowell Georgia. Included: Map of United States locating existing, future, and proposed gas pipelines. 632-651, Nov. 1978
• Striking It Rich in the North Sea. By Rick Gore. Photos by Dick Durrance II. Included: Map showing five sectors of national rights over oil and gas reserves; present and proposed oil and gas pipelines. 519-549, Apr. 1977

PIPELINES, Oil:
• Alaska: Rising Northern Star. By Joseph Judge. Photos by Bruce Dale. Included: Map of Trans-Alaska pipeline (under construction). 730-767, June 1975
• Canada's "Now" Frontier. By Robert Paul Jordan. Photos by Lowell Georgia. Included: Map showing oil pipeline, proposed gas pipeline, and tar sands. 480-511, Oct. 1976
• Colombia, from Amazon to Spanish Main. By Loren McIntyre. Included: The 194-mile Trans-Andean oil pipeline. 235-273, Aug. 1970
• Oil: Lifeblood and Liability. Included: Map of United States locating existing and proposed oil pipelines. 58-59, *Special Report on Energy* (Feb. 1981)
• Oil, the Dwindling Treasure. By Noel Grove. Photos by Emory Kristof. Included: Oil pipelines in the North Sea, on the North Slope, Alaska, and Saudi Arabia. 792-825, June 1974
• The Pipeline: Alaska's Troubled Colossus. By Bryan Hodgson. Photos by Steve Raymer. Included: Diagram, Anatomy of the pipeline; map showing potential and producing oil and gas areas. 684-717, Nov. 1976
• Striking It Rich in the North Sea. By Rick Gore. Photos by Dick Durrance II. Included: Map showing five sectors of national rights over oil and gas reserves; present and proposed oil and gas pipelines. 519-549, Apr. 1977
• Will Oil and Tundra Mix? Alaska's North Slope Hangs in the Balance. By William S. Ellis. Photos by Emory Kristof. Included: Map of Alaska and northern Canada showing existing pipeline which carries crude oil to refineries in Canada and the United States from Alberta, and proposed Trans-Alaska and Trans-Canada pipelines; map of United States showing existing major crude-oil pipelines, and proposed pipelines; diagram of pipeline. 485-517, Oct. 1971

PIRACY:
• The Vikings. By Howard La Fay. Photos by Ted Spiegel. 492-541, Apr. 1970

PIRANHAS:
• Seeking the Truth About the Feared Piranha. By Paul A. Zahl. 715-733, Nov. 1970

PISA, Italy:
• The Renaissance Lives On in Tuscany. By Luis Marden. Photos by Albert Moldvay. 626-659, Nov. 1974

PITCAIRN ISLAND, South Pacific Ocean:
• I Found the Bones of the *Bounty*. By Luis Marden. 725-789, Dec. 1957
• Pitcairn and Norfolk–The Saga of *Bounty*'s Children. By Ed Howard. Photos by David Hiser and Melinda Berge. 510-541, Oct. 1983
Pitcairn Island. 512-529; Norfolk Island. 530-541
• The *Yankee*'s Wander-world. By Irving and Electa Johnson. 1-50, Jan. 1949

The **PITFALLS** of Success: Yellowstone at 100. By William S. Ellis. Photos by Jonathan Blair. 616-631, May 1972

PITKIN, JOHN G.: Photographer:
• Praying Mantis. 685-692, May 1950

PITTMAN, BLAIR: Photographer:
• Big Thicket of Texas. By Don Moser. 504-529, Oct. 1974

PITTSBURGH, Pennsylvania:
• Artists Look at Pennsylvania. By John Oliver La Gorce. 37-56, July 1948
• Pennsylvania: Faire Land of William Penn. By Gordon Young. Photos by Cary Wolinsky. 731-767, June 1978
• Pittsburgh, Pattern for Progress. By William J. Gill. Photos by Clyde Hare. 342-371, Mar. 1965
• Pittsburgh: Workshop of the Titans. By Albert W. Atwood. 117-144, July 1949
• So Much Happens Along the Ohio River. By Frederick Simpich. Photos by Justin Locke. 177-212, Feb. 1950

PLAGE, DIETER and MARY: Photographers:
• Sri Lanka's Wildlife. 254-278, Aug. 1983
I. Sri Lanka's Wildlife Heritage: A Personal Perspective. By Arthur C. Clarke. 254-255; II. Legacy of Lively Treasures. 256-273; III. A Nation Rises to the Challenge. By Lyn de Alwis. 274-278

PLAGUE:
• The Rat, Lapdog of the Devil. By Thomas Y. Canby. Photos by James L. Stanfield. Included: Map showing known and suspected plague areas of the Americas, Africa, and Asia; cases reported in 1975. 60-87, July 1977

"PLAIN PEOPLE." *See* Amish; Hutterites; Mennonites

PLAINEST of Pennsylvania's Plain People: Amish Folk. By Richard Gehman. Photos by William Albert Allard. 227-253, Aug. 1965

PLANETS:
- First Photographs of Planets and Moon Taken with Palomar's 200-inch Telescope. By Milton L. Humason. 125-130, Jan. 1953
- ▲ *The Solar System; Saturn,* double-sided supplement. July 1981
- Voyage to the Planets. By Kenneth F. Weaver. Paintings by Ludek Pesek. 147-193, Aug. 1970
- Voyager's Historic View of Earth and Moon. Note: NASA's Voyager 1 spacecraft begins its flight toward Jupiter, Saturn, Uranus, and the interstellar space beyond. 53, July 1978
- *See also* Earth; Jupiter; Mars; Mercury; Saturn; Venus

PLANKTON:
- Blue-water Plankton: Ghosts of the Gulf Stream. By William M. Hamner. NGS research grant. 530-545, Oct. 1974
- How the Sun Gives Life to the Sea (Photosynthesis). By Paul A. Zahl. 199-225, Feb. 1961
- Night Life in the Gulf Stream. By Paul A. Zahl. 391-418, Mar. 1954
- Sailing a Sea of Fire. By Paul A. Zahl. 120-129, July 1960
- Strange Babies of the Sea. By Hilary B. Moore. Paintings by Craig Phillips and Jacqueline Hutton. NGS research grant. 41-56, July 1952
- Teeming Life of a Pond. By William H. Amos. 274-298, Aug. 1970
- *See also* Diatoms

PLANT EXPLORERS. *See* Agricultural and Botanical Explorers

PLANTATIONS. *See* Estates and Plantations

PLANTS:
- Abundant Life in a Desert Land. By Walter Meayers Edwards. 424-436, Sept. 1973
- Florida, Noah's Ark for Exotic Newcomers. By Rick Gore. Photos by David Doubilet. 538-559, Oct. 1976
- Herbs for All Seasons. By Lonnelle Aikman. Photos by Sam Abell. Picture portfolio text by Larry Kohl. 386-409, Mar. 1983
- In the Wilds of a City Parlor. By Paul A. Zahl. 645-672, Nov. 1954
- Kew: The Commoners' Royal Garden. By Thomas Garner James. Photos by B. Anthony Stewart. 479-506, Apr. 1950
- Malaysia's Giant Flowers and Insect-trapping Plants. By Paul A. Zahl. Included: Groundsels, Lichens, Lobelias. 680-701, May 1964
- Mountains of the Moon (Ruwenzori). By Paul A. Zahl. 412-434, Mar. 1962
- Nature's Gifts to Medicine. By Lonnelle Aikman. Paintings by Lloyd K. Townsend and Don Crowley. 420-440, Sept. 1974
- ◆ *Nature's Healing Arts.* 1977
- Nature's Year in Pleasant Valley. By Paul A. Zahl. 488-525, Apr. 1968
- Patent Plants Enrich Our World. By Orville H. Kneen. Photos from U. S. Plant Patents. 357-378, Mar. 1948
- Plants of the Alaskan Tundra. 315-321, Mar. 1972
- Plants That Eat Insects. By Paul A. Zahl. 643-659, May 1961
- Rediscovering America's Forgotten Crops. By Noel D. Vietmeyer. Photos by Burgess Blevins. Paintings by Paul M. Breeden. Included: Amaranths; Groundnuts; Guayule; Jojoba; Tepary beans. 702-712, May 1981
- Stalking the West's Wild Foods. By Euell Gibbons. Photos by David Hiser. 186-199, Aug. 1973
- Stalking Wild Foods on a Desert Isle. By Euell Gibbons. Photos by David Hiser. 47-63, July 1972
- The Tallgrass Prairie: Can It Be Saved? By Dennis Farney. Photos by Jim Brandenburg. 37-61, Jan. 1980
- A Visit to the Living Ice Age (Far North). By Rutherford Platt. 525-545, Apr. 1957
- *See also* Algae; Coffee; Flowers; Fungi; Gardens; Grasses; Lichens; Rain Forests; Seaweed; Trees; Vegetables; *and* Agriculture

PLAQUEMINES PARISH, Louisiana:
- New Orleans and Her River. By Joseph Judge. Photos by James L. Stanfield. 151-187, Feb. 1971

PLATE TECTONICS:
- ▲ *Arctic Ocean Floor,* double-sided supplement. Oct. 1971
- ▲ *Atlantic Ocean Floor,* double-sided Atlas series supplement. June 1968
- ■ Born of Fire. 824, Dec. 1982
- ■ Dive to the Edge of Creation: Galapagos II expedition. 682, Nov. 1979; 1, cover, Jan. 1980
- Editorial. By Gilbert M. Grosvenor. 585, May 1975
- ◆ *Exploring Our Living Planet.* Announced. 824, Dec. 1982
- Hawaii, U. S. A. By Frederick Simpich, Jr. Photos by Thomas Nebbia. Included: Kilauea; Mauna Loa. 1-45, July 1960
- Incredible World of the Deep-sea Rifts. 680-705, Nov. 1979
  I. Strange World Without Sun. The Editor. 680-688; II. Return to Oases of the Deep. By Robert D. Ballard and J. Frederick Grassle. 689-705
- ▲ *Indian Ocean Floor,* supplement. Oct. 1967
- The Mediterranean–Sea of Man's Fate. By Rick Gore. Photos by Jonathan Blair. Included: The unstable geologic history of its basin evidenced by volcanic eruptions, rising sea levels, and earthquakes; cross-section painting of African, Iberian, Apulian, and Eurasian Plates. 694-737, Dec. 1982
- New World of the Ocean. By Samuel W. Matthews. Included: Recent discoveries of forces at work in the ocean; rifting, crustal formation, drifting, and reabsorption; cross-section paintings of the anatomy of the seas, circulation of waters. 792-832, Dec. 1981
- Oases of Life in the Cold Abyss. By John B. Corliss and Robert D. Ballard. 441-453, Oct. 1977
- ◆ *Our Continent: A Natural History of North America.* 1976
- Our Hometown Planet, Earth. By F. Barrows Colton. Contents: An examination of earth's heaving crust; map of the "Belts of Fire"; drawing of earth's interior. 117-139, Jan. 1952
- ◆ *Our Violent Earth.* 1982
- ▲ *Pacific Ocean Floor,* double-sided supplement. Oct. 1969
- ◆ *Powers of Nature.* 1978
- Project FAMOUS. Photos by Emory Kristof. 586-615, May 1975
  I. Where the Earth Turns Inside Out. By J. R. Heirtzler. 586-603; II. Dive Into the Great Rift. By Robert D. Ballard. 604-615
- Science Explores the Monsoon Sea. By Samuel W. Matthews. Photos by Robert F. Sisson. Included: Magnetic profile of Mid-Oceanic ridge and rift in the Indian Ocean. 554-575, Oct. 1967
- Scientists Drill at Sea to Pierce Earth's Crust. By Samuel W. Matthews. Photos by J. Baylor Roberts. Contents: Project Mohole's attempt to drill through the Mohorovičić discontinuity to earth's mantle. 686-697, Nov. 1961
- This Changing Earth. By Samuel W. Matthews. 1-37, Jan. 1973
- ■ The Violent Earth. 286A-286B, Feb. 1973
- Volcano and Earthquake Show Nature's Awesome Power. The Editor. 303, Mar. 1960
- Window on Earth's Interior. By Robert D. Ballard. Photos by Emory Kristof. 228-249, Aug. 1976
- ▲ *The World; The World Ocean Floor,* double-sided supplement. Included: Trenches, rifts, faults, and fracture zones; Undersea ridges, continental shelves, abyssal plains, and basins. Dec. 1981
- *See also* Earthquakes; Volcanoes

PLATINUM:
- The Miracle Metal–Platinum. By Gordon Young. Photos by James L. Amos. 686-706, Nov. 1983

PLATT, RUTHERFORD:
Author-Photographer:
- Shells Take You Over World Horizons. 33-84, July 1949
- A Visit to the Living Ice Age. 525-545, Apr. 1957

PLATYPUSES:
- Biggest Worm Farm Caters to Platypuses. By W. H. Nicholas. 269-280, Feb. 1949
- Flight of the Platypuses. By David Fleay. 512-525, Oct. 1958

PLAYING 3,000 Golf Courses in Fourteen Lands. By Ralph A. Kennedy. 113-132, July 1952

PLEASANT VALLEY, Maryland:
- Nature's Year in Pleasant Valley. By Paul A. Zahl. 488-525, Apr. 1968

PLEISTOCENE EPOCH:
- In Search of Man's Past at Lake Rudolf. By Richard E. Leakey. Photos by Gordon W. Gahan. 712-734, May 1970
- *See also* Ice Ages

PLIGHT of the Bluefin Tuna. By Michael J. A. Butler. Photos by David Doubilet. Paintings by Stanley Meltzoff. 220-239, Aug. 1982

PLUMMETING Missile of Turquoise, the Shy and Spectacular Kingfisher. Photos by Carl-Johan Junge and Emil Lütken. 413-419, Sept. 1974

PLUTO (Planet):
● Voyage to the Planets. By Kenneth F. Weaver. Paintings by Ludek Pesek. 147-193, Aug. 1970

PLUTONIUM:
● The Promise and Peril of Nuclear Energy. By Kenneth F. Weaver. Photos by Emory Kristof. 459-493, Apr. 1979

PLYWOOD:
● Versatile Wood Waits on Man. By Andrew H. Brown. 109-140, July 1951

POACHING:
● African Wildlife: Man's Threatened Legacy. By Allan C. Fisher, Jr. Photos by Thomas Nebbia. 147-187, Feb. 1972
A Continent's Living Treasure. Paintings by Ned Seidler. 164-167
● Africa's Elephants: Can They Survive? By Oria Douglas-Hamilton. Photos by Oria and Iain Douglas-Hamilton. 568-603, Nov. 1980
● The Imperiled Mountain Gorilla. By Dian Fossey. NGS research grant. 501-523, Apr. 1981
Death of Marchessa. Photos by Peter G. Veit. 508-511
● Where Elephants Have Right of Way (Africa). By George and Jinx Rodger. Photos by George Rodger. 363-389, Sept. 1960
● Wild Cargo: the Business of Smuggling Animals. By Noel Grove. Photos by Steve Raymer. 287-315, Mar. 1981

PODHALE (Region), Poland:
● Poland's Mountain People. By Yva Momatiuk and John Eastcott. 104-129, Jan. 1981

POETS:
● The British Way. By Sir Evelyn Wrench. 421-541, Apr. 1949
● Lake District, Poets' Corner of England. By H. V. Morton. Photos by David S. Boyer. Included: Samuel Taylor Coleridge, Ralph Waldo Emerson, Thomas Gray, John Keats, Percy Bysshe Shelley, Robert Southey, Alfred, Lord Tennyson, William Wordsworth. 511-545, Apr. 1956
● Poets' Voices Linger in Scottish Shrines. By Isobel Wylie Hutchison. Photos by Kathleen Revis. Included: William E. Aytoun, John Barbour, Harold Boulton, Robert Burns, Lord Byron, William Douglas, James Hogg, Violet Jacob, Marjory Kennedy-Fraser, Andrew Lang, Allan Ramsay, Sir Walter Scott, William Shakespeare, Alexander Smith, Robert Louis Stevenson. 437-488, Oct. 1957
● *See also* Frost, Robert; MacLeish, Archibald; Momaday, N. Scott

POGUE, WILLIAM R.:
● Skylab, Outpost on the Frontier of Space. By Thomas Y. Canby. Photos by the nine mission astronauts. 441-469, Oct. 1974

POKOT PEOPLE:
● The Threatened Ways of Kenya's Pokot People. By Elizabeth L. Meyerhoff. Photos by Murray Roberts. NGS research grant. 120-140, Jan. 1982

POL POT:
● Kampuchea Wakens From a Nightmare. By Peter T. White. Photos by David Alan Harvey. 590-623, May 1982
● The Temples of Angkor. 548-589, May 1982
I. Ancient Glory in Stone. By Peter T. White. Photos by Wilbur E. Garrett. 552-589; II. Will They Survive? Introduction by Wilbur E. Garrett. 548-551

POLAND:
● By Square-rigger from Baltic to Bicentennial. By Kenneth Garrett. Included: The Polish Merchant Navy Academy's training ship, *Dar Pomorza*. 824-857, Dec. 1976
● Editorials. By Wilbur E. Garrett. 1, Jan. 1981; 419, Apr. 1982
▲ *The Face and Faith of Poland,* map, photo, and essay supplement. By Peter Miller. Essay by Czesław Miłosz. Photos by Bruno Barbey. Apr. 1982
▲ *Poland and Czechoslovakia,* Atlas series supplement. Sept. 1958
● Poland Opens Her Doors. By Delia and Ferdinand Kuhn. Photos by Erich Lessing. 354-398, Sept. 1958
● Poland's Mountain People. By Yva Momatiuk and John Eastcott. 104-129, Jan. 1981
● Salt–The Essence of Life. By Gordon Young. Photos by Volkmar Wentzel and Georg Gerster. Included: Wieliczka salt works. 381-401, Sept. 1977
● Springtime of Hope in Poland. By Peter T. White. Photos by James P. Blair. 467-501, Apr. 1972

POLAR BEARS:
● Henry Hudson's Changing Bay. By Bill Richards. Photos by David Hiser. 380-405, Mar. 1982
● Polar Bear: Lonely Nomad of the North. By Thor Larsen. 574-590, Apr. 1971
■ Polar Bear Alert. 395, cover, Mar. 1982

POLAR REGIONS:
● Nuclear Power for the Polar Regions. By George J. Dufek. 712-730, May 1962
● *See also* Antarctic Regions; Antarctica; Arctic Ocean; Arctic Regions; Greenland Icecap; North Pole; South Pole

POLK, JAMES K.:
● Profiles of the Presidents: II. A Restless Nation Moves West. By Frank Freidel. 80-121, Jan. 1965

YVA MOMATIUK AND JOHN EASTCOTT

Poland: Podhale home of góral people

Nomad of the North: bear on the prowl

THOR LARSEN

POLLINATION:
● Crossroads of the Insect World. By J. W. MacSwain. Photos by Edward S. Ross. 844-857, Dec. 1966
● The Flower Seed Growers: Gardening's Color Merchants. By Robert de Roos. Photos by Jack Fields. Included: The World of Flowers. Painting by Ned M. Seidler. 720-738, May 1968
● Hummingbirds: The Nectar Connection. By Paul W. Ewald. Photos by Robert A. Tyrrell. 223-227, Feb. 1982
● *See also* Bees; Fig Wasps; Orchids; Roses

POLLUTION:
● Acid Rain–How Great a Menace? By Anne LaBastille. Photos by Ted Spiegel. 652-681, Nov. 1981
◆ *As We Live and Breathe: The Challenge of Our Environment.* Announced. 882-886, June 1971
● Grand Canyon: Are We Loving It to Death? By W. E. Garrett. 16-51, July 1978
▲ "How Man Pollutes His World," painting supplement. Map on reverse. Dec. 1970
● The Pesticide Dilemma. By Allen A. Boraiko. Photos by Fred Ward. 145-183, Feb. 1980
● Pollution, Threat to Man's Only Home. By Gordon Young. Photos by James P. Blair. 738-781, Dec. 1970
● Problems in Paradise. By Mary and Laurance S. Rockefeller. Photos by Thomas Nebbia. 782-793, Dec. 1974
● Quicksilver and Slow Death (Mercury). By John J. Putman. Photos by Robert W. Madden. 507-527, Oct. 1972
● Those Successful Japanese. By Bart McDowell. Photos by Fred Ward. 323-359, Mar. 1974
● Venice Fights for Life. By Joseph Judge. Photos by Albert Moldvay. 591-631, Nov. 1972
● Water for the World's Growing Needs. By Herbert B. Nichols and F. Barrows Colton. 269-286, Aug. 1952
● *See also* Air Pollution; Oil Spills; Pesticide Pollution; Radioactive Wastes; Water Pollution

POLUNIN, IVAN:
Author-Photographer:
● Who Says Fish Can't Climb Trees? 85-91, Jan. 1972

POLYNESIA:
● A Canoe Helps Hawaii Recapture Her Past. By Herb Kawainui Kane. Photos by David Hiser. Contents: Proposed voyage by *Hokule'a* to Raiatea and Tahiti. 468-489, Apr. 1976
● Captain Cook: The Man Who Mapped the Pacific. By Alan Villiers. Photos by Gordon W. Gahan. 297-349, Sept. 1971
● Editorials. By Gilbert M. Grosvenor. 731, Dec. 1974; 431, Oct. 1976
● *Hokule'a* Follows the Stars to Tahiti. By David Lewis. Photos by Nicholas deVore III. 512-537, Oct. 1976
▲ *Islands of the Pacific; Discoverers of the Pacific,* double-sided supplement. Dec. 1974

TED SPIEGEL, BLACK STAR

Acid Rain: polluted air over St. Louis

Pollution: testing eye response to pollution

JAMES P. BLAIR, NGS

● Isles of the Pacific. 732-793, Dec. 1974
I. The Coming of the Polynesians. By Kenneth P. Emory. 732-745; II. Wind, Wave, Star, and Bird. By David Lewis. Photos by Nicholas deVore III. 747-781; III. The Pathfinders. Paintings by Herb Kawainui Kane. 756-769; IV. Problems in Paradise. By Mary and Laurance S. Rockefeller. Photos by Thomas Nebbia. 782-793
■ Polynesian Adventure. 592A-592B, Apr. 1969
■ Voyage of the *Hokule'a.* 575, Nov. 1976
● *Yankee* Roams the Orient. By Irving and Electa Johnson. Included: Tikopia and the Stewart Islands, two Polynesian outposts in Melanesia. 327-370, Mar. 1951
● *See also* Canton Island; Cook Islands; Easter Island; Ellice Islands; Hawaii; Marquesas Islands; New Zealand; Norfolk Island; Pitcairn Island; Samoa; Society Islands; Tahiti; Tonga; Tuamotu Archipelago; Uvéa

POLYNESIAN CANOE. *See Hokule'a*

POLYNESIANS:
● Feast Day in Kapingamarangi. By W. Robert Moore. 523-537, Apr. 1950

POMERANTZ, MARTIN A.: Author:
● Trailing Cosmic Rays in Canada's North. 99-115, Jan. 1953

POMPEII, Italy:
● Last Moments of the Pompeians. By Amedeo Maiuri. Photos by Lee E. Battaglia. Paintings by Peter V. Bianchi. 651-669, Nov. 1961

POMPEII of Prehistoric Animals in Nebraska. By Michael R. Voorhies. Photos by Annie Griffiths. Paintings by Jay Matternes. 66-75, Jan. 1981

POMPIDOU Center, Rage of Paris. Photos by Marc Riboud. Text by Cathy Newman. 469-477, Oct. 1980

PONCE, ROJAS: Artist:
● Finding the Tomb of a Warrior-God. By William Duncan Strong. Photos by Clifford Evans, Jr. 453-482, Apr. 1947

POND INLET, Baffin Island, Canada:
● I Live With the Eskimos. By Guy Mary-Rousseliere. 188-217, Feb. 1971

POND LIFE:
● Life Around a Lily Pad. Photos by Bianca Lavies. Text by Charles R. Miller. 131-142, Jan. 1980
◆ *Life in Ponds and Streams.* 1981
● Teeming Life of a Pond. By William H. Amos. 274-298, Aug. 1970
● *See also* Rotifers

PONIES:
◆ *The Wild Ponies of Assateague Island.* Announced. 724-726, Nov. 1975
● *See also* Devonshire, for Dartmoor ponies; Sable Island, for wild ponies; Shetland Islands, for Shetland ponies

PONTING, HERBERT G.:
Photographer:
● Nature's Clown, the Penguin. By

David Hellyer and Malcolm Davis. Included: Photos taken on the second Scott Antarctic expedition (1911). 405-428, Sept. 1952

PONY EXPRESS:
● The Pony Express. By Rowe Findley. Photos by Craig Aurness. 45-71, July 1980

POOR Little Rich Land–Formosa. By Frederick G. Vosburgh. Photos by J. Baylor Roberts. 139-176, Feb. 1950

POORWILL Sleeps Away the Winter. By Edmund C. Jaeger. 273-280, Feb. 1953

POPES:
● St. Peter's, Rome's Church of Popes. By Aubrey Menen. Photos by Albert Moldvay. Included: John XXIII, Julius II, Paul VI, Pius XII, and Saint Peter. 865-879, Dec. 1971

POPPER, PAUL: Photographer:
● Cane Bridges of Asia. 243-250, Aug. 1948

POPULATION:
● Census 1960: Profile of the Nation. By Albert W. Atwood and Lonnelle Aikman. 697-714, Nov. 1959
● Editorial. By Gilbert M. Grosvenor. 1, July 1975

PORCELAIN:
● The Sunken Treasure of St. Helena. By Robert Sténuit. Photos by Bates Littlehales. Included: Porcelain of the Ming Dynasty. 562-576, Oct. 1978
● Treasures of Dresden. By John L. Eliot. Photos by Victor R. Boswell, Jr. Included: Europe's first porcelain; Meissen porcelain. 702-717, Nov. 1978
● Yellow Sea Yields Shipwreck Trove. Photos by H. Edward Kim. Introduction by Donald H. Keith. 231-243, Aug. 1979

PORCUPINES, Rambling Pincushions. By Donald A. Spencer. 247-264, Aug. 1950

PORPOISES:
● Marineland, Florida's Giant Fish Bowl. By Gilbert Grosvenor La Gorce. Photos by Luis Marden. 679-694, Nov. 1952
◆ *The Playful Dolphins*. Announced. 718-720, Nov. 1976
● Porpoises: Our Friends in the Sea. By Robert Leslie Conly. Photos by Thomas Nebbia. 396-425, Sept. 1966
● The Trouble With Dolphins. By Edward J. Linehan. Photos by Bill Curtsinger. 506-541, Apr. 1979

PORT AU PRINCE, Haiti:
● Haiti: Beyond Mountains, More Mountains. By Carolyn Bennett Patterson. Photos by Thomas Nebbia. 70-97, Jan. 1976

PORT ROYAL, Jamaica:
● Exploring the Drowned City of Port Royal. By Marion Clayton Link. Photos by Luis Marden. NGS research grant. 151-183, Feb. 1960
● Reach for the New World. By Mendel Peterson. Photos by David L. Arnold. Paintings by Richard Schlecht. 724-767, Dec. 1977

PORT ROYAL SOUND, South Carolina:
● Sea Islands: Adventuring Along the South's Surprising Coast. By James Cerruti. Photos by Thomas Nebbia and James L. Amos. 366-393, Mar. 1971

PORTLAND, Oregon:
● Powerhouse of the Northwest (Columbia River). By David S. Boyer. 821-847, Dec. 1974
● A River Restored: Oregon's Willamette. By Ethel A. Starbird. Photos by Lowell J. Georgia. 816-835, June 1972

PORTO SANTO (Island), Atlantic Ocean:
● Madeira, Like Its Wine, Improves With Age. By Veronica Thomas. Photos by Jonathan Blair. 488-513, Apr. 1973
● The Treasure of Porto Santo. By Robert Sténuit. Photos by author and William R. Curtsinger. 260-275, Aug. 1975

PORTOFINO, Italy:
● Time Turns Back in Picture-book Portofino. By Carleton Mitchell. Photos by Winfield Parks. 232-253, Feb. 1965

PORTRAIT of a Fierce and Fragile Land (Alaskan Tundra). By Paul A. Zahl. 303-314, Mar. 1972

PORTRAIT of Indochina. By W. Robert Moore and Maynard Owen Williams. Paintings by Jean Despujols. 461-490, Apr. 1951

PORTRAIT of Planet Earth. 53, July 1978

PORTRAIT ROSE (All-America Rose Selection):
● Amateur Gardener Creates a New Rose. By Elizabeth A. Moize. Photos by Farrell Grehan. 286-294, Aug. 1972

PORTRAIT U.S.A., Landsat photomosaic. July 1976

PORTRAITS of My Monkey Friends. By Ernest P. Walker. 105-119, Jan. 1956

PORTSMOUTH, Britannia's Sally Port. By Thomas Garner James. Photos by B. Anthony Stewart. 513-544, Apr. 1952

PORTUGAL:
● After an Empire . . . Portugal. By William Graves. Photos by Bruno Barbey. 804-831, Dec. 1980
● Fátima: Beacon for Portugal's Faithful. By Jane Vessels. Photos by Bruno Barbey. 832-839, Dec. 1980
● Golden Beaches of Portugal. By Alan Villiers. 673-696, Nov. 1954
● Portugal at the Crossroads. By Howard La Fay. Photos by Volkmar Wentzel. 453-501, Oct. 1965
● Portugal Is Different. By Clement E. Conger. 583-622, Nov. 1948
● Prince Henry, the Explorer Who Stayed Home. By Alan Villiers. Photos by Thomas Nebbia. 616-656, Nov. 1960
▲ *Spain and Portugal,* Atlas series supplement. Mar. 1965
● *See also* Azores (Islands); Macao; Madeira Islands

PORTUGUESE:
● Macao Clings to the Bamboo Curtain. By Jules B. Billard. Photos by Joseph J. Scherschel. 521-539, Apr. 1969
● Macau, a Hole in the Bamboo Curtain. By George W. Long. Photos by J. Baylor Roberts. 679-688, May 1953
● New England's "Little Portugal." By O. Louis Mazzatenta. 90-109, Jan. 1975

PORTUGUESE FISHING FLEET:
● Dory on the Banks: A Day in the Life of a Portuguese Fisherman. By James H. Pickerell. 573-583, Apr. 1968
● Gloucester Blesses Its Portuguese Fleet. By Luis Marden. 75-84, July 1953
● I Sailed with Portugal's Captains Courageous. By Alan Villiers. 565-596, May 1952
■ The Lonely Dorymen. 579A-579B, Apr. 1968

PORTUGUESE MAN-OF-WAR:
● The Deadly Fisher. By Charles E. Lane. 388-397, Mar. 1963
● Man-of-war Fleet Attacks Bimini. By Paul A. Zahl. 185-212, Feb. 1952

POSSUMS (American). *See* Opossums

POSSUMS (Phalangers):
● Strange Animals of Australia. By David Fleay. Photos by Stanley Breeden. 388-411, Sept. 1963

POST OFFICE BUILDING, Washington, D. C.:
● A Preservation Victory Saves Washington's Old Post Office. By Wolf Von Eckardt. Photos by Volkmar Wentzel. 407-416, Sept. 1983

POST ROADS, U. S.:
● The Old Boston Post Roads. By Donald Barr Chidsey. 189-205, Aug. 1962
● The Post Road Today. Photos by B. Anthony Stewart. 206-233, Aug. 1962

POSTAGE STAMPS:
● Liechtenstein Thrives on Stamps. By Ronald W. Clark. 105-112, July 1948

POSTAL SERVICE, U. S.:
● Everyone's Servant, the Post Office. By Allan C. Fisher, Jr. Photos by Volkmar Wentzel. 121-152, July 1954
● *See also J. W. Westcott* (Mail Boat); Pony Express; Post Roads

POSTERS. *See* Painting Supplements; Photo Supplements

POSTWAR Journey Through Java. By Ronald Stuart Kain. 675-700, May 1948

POSTWAR RECOVERY:
● Airlift to Berlin. 595-614, May 1949
● Backwoods Japan During American Occupation. By M. A. Huberman. 491-518, Apr. 1947

MARTIN ROGERS

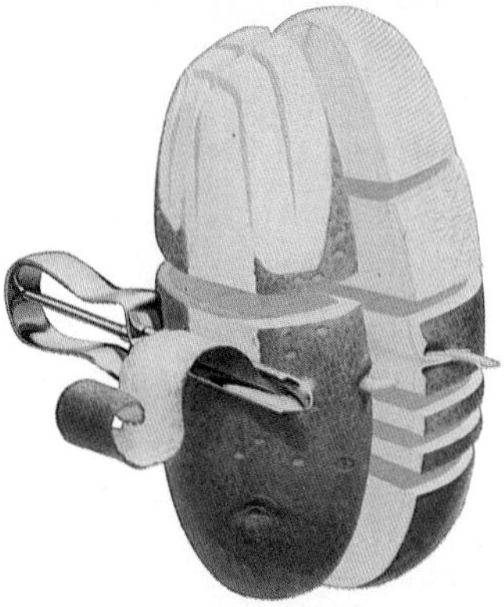

PAINTING BY DALE GUSTAFSON

The Incredible Potato: earth clings to potatoes bound for an Irish dinner table, *top;* dissected tuber, *above*

• Belgium Comes Back. By Harvey Klemmer. Photos by Maynard Owen Williams. 575-614, May 1948
• Berlin, Island in a Soviet Sea. By Frederick G. Vosburgh. Photos by Volkmar Wentzel. 689-704, Nov. 1951
• Italy Smiles Again. By Edgar Erskine Hume. 693-732, June 1949
• Japan Tries Freedom's Road. By Frederick G. Vosburgh. Photos by J. Baylor Roberts. 593-632, May 1950
• Keeping House in London. By Frances James. 769-792, Dec. 1947
• Luxembourg, Survivor of Invasions. By Sydney Clark. Photos by Maynard Owen Williams. 791-810, June 1948
• Mid-century Holland Builds Her Future. By Sydney Clark. 747-778, Dec. 1950
• Occupied Austria, Outpost of Democracy. By George W. Long. Photos by Volkmar Wentzel. 749-790, June 1951
• Okinawa, Pacific Outpost. 538-552, Apr. 1950
• Pacific Wards of Uncle Sam. By W. Robert Moore. 73-104, July 1948
• Scenes of Postwar Finland. By La Verne Bradley. Photos by Jerry Waller. 233-264, Aug. 1947
• Turkey Paves the Path of Progress. By Maynard Owen Williams. 141-186, Aug. 1951
• Uncle Sam Bends a Twig in Germany. By Frederick Simpich. Photos by J. Baylor Roberts. 529-550, Oct. 1948
• War-torn Greece Looks Ahead. By Maynard Owen Williams. 711-744, Dec. 1949
• What I Saw Across the Rhine. By J. Frank Dobie. 57-86, Jan. 1947
• With the U. S. Army in Korea. By John R. Hodge. 829-840, June 1947
• With Uncle Sam and John Bull in Germany. By Frederick Simpich. 117-140, Jan. 1949

POTALA (Palace), Lhasa, Tibet:
• In Long-Forbidden Tibet. By Fred Ward. 218-259, Feb. 1980
• My Life in Forbidden Lhasa. By Heinrich Harrer. 1-48, July 1955

POTASSIUM-ARGON DATING:
• A Clock for the Ages: Potassium-Argon. By Garniss H. Curtis. 590-592, Oct. 1961

POTATOES AND POTATO GROWING:
• Aroostook County, Maine, Source of Potatoes. By Howell Walker. 459-478, Oct. 1948
• The Incredible Potato. By Robert E. Rhoades. Photos by Martin Rogers. 668-694, May 1982
• Madawaska: Down East With a French Accent. By Perry Garfinkel. Photos by Cary Wolinsky. 380-409, Sept. 1980
• Our Vegetable Travelers. By Victor R. Boswell. Paintings by Else Bostelmann. 145-217, Aug. 1949

POTHOLES, Desert:
• Miracle of the Potholes. By Rowe Findley. Photos by Robert F. Sisson. 570-579, Oct. 1975

POTOMAC (River), U. S.:
• Across the Potomac from Washington. By Albert W. Atwood. 1-33, Jan. 1953
• Down the Potomac by Canoe. By Ralph Gray. Photos by Walter Meayers Edwards. 213-242, Aug. 1948
• The Nation's River. By Allan C. Fisher, Jr. Photos by James L. Stanfield. 432-479, Oct. 1976
A Good Life on the Potomac. 470-479
• New Grandeur for Flowering Washington. By Joseph Judge. Photos by James P. Blair. 500-539, Apr. 1967
• Waterway to Washington, the C & O Canal. By Jay Johnston. 419-439, Mar. 1960
• *See also* Harpers Ferry

POTTERY:
• Finding West Africa's Oldest City. By Susan and Roderick McIntosh. Photos by Michael and Aubine Kirtley. Included: Pottery of ancient and modern Jenne. 396-418, Sept. 1982
• Mexican Folk Art. By Fernando Horcasitas. Photos by David Hiser. 648-669, May 1978
• Pueblo Pottery–2,000 Years of Artistry. By David L. Arnold. 593-605, Nov. 1982
• 20th-century Indians Preserve Customs of the Cliff Dwellers. Photos by William Belknap, Jr. NGS research grant. 196-211, Feb. 1964

POUCH COVE, Newfoundland:
• Newfoundland, Canada's New Province. By Andrew H. Brown. Photos by author and Robert F. Sisson. 777-812, June 1949

POULSEN, MOGENS BLOCH: Author:
• Greenland's "Place by the Icebergs." Photos by Thomas Nebbia. 849-869, Dec. 1973

POULTRY:
• Delaware–Who Needs to Be Big? By Jane Vessels. Photos by Kevin Fleming. 171-197, Aug. 1983
• "Delmarva," Gift of the Sea. By Catherine Bell Palmer. 367-399, Sept. 1950
• Easter Egg Chickens. By Frederick G. Vosburgh. Photos by B. Anthony Stewart. 377-387, Sept. 1948
• Long Island Outgrows the Country. By Howell Walker. Photos by B. Anthony Stewart. Included: Duck raising. 279-326, Mar. 1951

POWARS, NANCY LINK: Co-Editor:
◆ *Research Reports* (NGS). 480, Mar. 1981; 830, June 1982
◆ *Research Reports* (NGS): *1973 Projects* and *1974 Projects.* 706, Nov. 1983

POWDER RIVER BASIN, Wyoming:
• Powder River Basin: New Energy Frontier. By Bill Richards. Photos by Louie Psihoyos. 96-113, *Special Report on Energy* (Feb. 1981)

POWELL, JOHN WESLEY:
• Retracing John Wesley Powell's Historic Voyage Down the Grand Canyon. By Joseph Judge. Photos by Walter Meayers Edwards. 668-713, May 1969

POWELL, Lake, Arizona-Utah:
● Lake Powell: Waterway to Desert Wonders. By Walter Meayers Edwards. 44-75, July 1967

POWER. *See* Energy Sources

POWER Comes Back to Peiping. By Nelson T. Johnson and W. Robert Moore. 337-368, Sept. 1949

The **POWER** of Letting Off Steam. By Kenneth F. Weaver. 566-579, Oct. 1977

POWER PLANTS:
● Coal vs. Parklands. By François Leydet. Photos by Dewitt Jones. 776-803, Dec. 1980
● Geothermal Energy: The Power of Letting Off Steam. By Kenneth F. Weaver. 566-579, Oct. 1977
● Jari: A Billion-dollar Gamble. By Loren McIntyre. Included: Daniel K. Ludwig's paper-pulp factory and the wood-burning plant that powers it. 686-711, May 1980
● The Search for Tomorrow's Power. By Kenneth F. Weaver. Photos by Emory Kristof. 650-681, Nov. 1972
● *See also* Hydroelectric Power; Nuclear Energy

POWERHOUSE of the Northwest (Columbia River). By David S. Boyer. 821-847, Dec. 1974

POWHATAN CHIEFDOM:
● New Clues to an Old Mystery (Virginia's Wolstenholme Towne). By Ivor Noël Hume. Photos by Ira Block. Paintings by Richard Schlecht. 53-77, Jan. 1982

PRAGUE, Czechoslovakia:
● Czechoslovakia: The Dream and the Reality. By Edward J. Linehan. Photos by James P. Blair. 151-193, Feb. 1968
● Old Prague in Winter. By Peter T. White. Photos by Nathan Benn. 546-567, Apr. 1979

PRAIRIE, Tallgrass:
● The Tallgrass Prairie: Can It Be Saved? By Dennis Farney. Photos by Jim Brandenburg. 37-61, Jan. 1980

PRAIRIE DOGS:
● The Hard Life of the Prairie Dog. By Tim W. Clark. Photos by Patricia Caulfield. NGS research grant. 270-281, Aug. 1979

PRAIRIE PROVINCES, Canada:
● Canada's Heartland, the Prairie Provinces. By W. E. Garrett. Contents: Alberta, Manitoba, Saskatchewan. 443-489, Oct. 1970

PRATHER, VICTOR A., Jr.:
● We Saw the World From the Edge of Space. By Malcolm D. Ross. Ground photos by Walter Meayers Edwards. 671-685, Nov. 1961

PRAYING MANTIS:
● Praying Mantis. Photos by John G. Pitkin. 685-692, May 1950

PRECIOUS Corals, Hawaii's Deep-sea Jewels. By Richard W. Grigg. Photos by David Doubilet. 719-732, May 1979

PRE-COLUMBIAN CIVILIZATION:
● The Hohokam: First Masters of the American Desert. By Emil W. Haury. Photos by Helga Teiwes. 670-695, May 1967
● Magnetic Clues Help Date the Past. By Kenneth F. Weaver. 696-701, May 1967
● *See also* Anasazi; Mound Builders

PRE-HISPANIC CULTURE:
Mexico:
● Mexico's Window on the Past (National Museum). By Bart McDowell. Photos by B. Anthony Stewart. 492-519, Oct. 1968
● "Pyramids" of the New World. By Neil Merton Judd. 105-128, Jan. 1948
● *See also* Aztecs; Maya; Olmecs; *and* Veracruz
South America:
● Chan Chan, Peru's Ancient City of Kings. By Michael E. Moseley and Carol J. Mackey. Photos by David Brill. NGS research grant. 318-345, Mar. 1973
● Gold, the Eternal Treasure. By Peter T. White. Photos by James L. Stanfield. 1-51, Jan. 1974
Golden Masterpieces. 29-39
● *See also* Incas; *and* Nazca Lines

PREHISTORIC CULTURES:
● Ancient Europe Is Older Than We Thought. By Colin Renfrew. Photos by Adam Woolfitt. 615-623, Nov. 1977
● New Light on a Forgotten Past (Southeast Asia). By Wilhelm G. Solheim II. 330-339, Mar. 1971
● *See also* Arctic Small Tool Culture; Bulgaria (Ancient); Ice Age Man; Paleo-Indians

PREHISTORY. *See* Anthropology; Archaeology; Paleontology; Prehistoric Cultures; *and* Lascaux Cave

PRELUDE to Gettysburg. Map notes by Carolyn Bennett Patterson. 14-21, July 1963

PRELUDE to Vicksburg. Map notes by Carolyn Bennett Patterson. 42-45, July 1963

PREMANA, Italy:
● Lombardy's Lakes, Blue Jewels in Italy's Crown. By Franc Shor. Photos by Joseph J. Scherschel. 58-99, July 1968

A **PRESERVATION** Victory Saves Washington's Old Post Office. By Wolf Von Eckardt. Photos by Volkmar Wentzel. 407-416, Sept. 1983

PRESERVING a Mountain Heritage. By Sir Edmund Hillary. 696-703, June 1982

PRESERVING America's Last Great Wilderness (Alaska). Text by David Jeffery. 769-791, June 1975

PRESERVING Our Wild and Scenic Rivers. 2-59, July 1977

PRESERVING the Treasures of Olduvai Gorge. By Melvin M. Payne. Photos by Joseph J. Scherschel. NGS research grant. 701-709, Nov. 1966

The **PRESIDENCY** and How It Grew. By Frank Freidel. 642-687, Nov. 1964

PRESIDENT Eisenhower Presents the Hubbard Medal to Everest's Conquerors. 64, July 1954

PRESIDENT Eisenhower Presents the Society's Hubbard Medal to the Conquerors of Antarctica. 589-590, Apr. 1959

PRESIDENT Eisenhower Presents to Prince Philip the National Geographic Society's Medal. 865-868, Dec. 1957

PRESIDENT Johnson Dedicates the Society's New Headquarters. 669-679, May 1964

PRESIDENT Kennedy Presents the Hubbard Medal (American Mount Everest Expedition). 514-515, Oct. 1963

PRESIDENTIAL ARM FOR NATIONAL MINORITIES (Panamin): Philippines:
● First Glimpse of a Stone Age Tribe. 881-882, Dec. 1971
● Help for Philippine Tribes in Trouble. By Kenneth MacLeish. Photos by Dean Conger. 220-255, Aug. 1971
● The Tasadays, Stone Age Cavemen of Mindanao. By Kenneth MacLeish. Photos by John Launois. 219-249, Aug. 1972

PRESIDENTS, U. S.:
● Inside the White House. By Lonnelle Aikman. Photos by B. Anthony Stewart and Thomas Nebbia. 3-43, Jan. 1961
● The Living White House. By Lonnelle Aikman. 593-643, Nov. 1966
◆ *Our Country's Presidents.* Announced. 408-417, Mar. 1966; 1981
Profiles of the Presidents. By Frank Freidel:
● Part I. The Presidency and How It Grew. Contents: George Washington, John Adams, Thomas Jefferson, James Madison, James Monroe, John Quincy Adams. 642-687, Nov. 1964
● Part II. A Restless Nation Moves West. Contents: Andrew Jackson, Martin Van Buren, William Henry Harrison, John Tyler, James K. Polk, Zachary Taylor, Millard Fillmore, Franklin Pierce, James Buchanan. 80-121, Jan. 1965
● Part III. The American Giant Comes of Age. Contents: Abraham Lincoln, Andrew Johnson, Ulysses S. Grant, Rutherford B. Hayes, James A. Garfield, Chester A. Arthur, Grover Cleveland, Benjamin Harrison, William McKinley. 660-711, May 1965
● Part IV. America Enters the Modern Era. Contents: Theodore Roosevelt, William Howard Taft, Woodrow Wilson, Warren G. Harding, Calvin Coolidge, Herbert Hoover. 537-577, Oct. 1965
● Part V. The Atomic Age: Its Problems and Promises. Contents: Franklin D. Roosevelt, Harry S Truman, Dwight D. Eisenhower, John F. Kennedy, Lyndon B. Johnson. 66-119, Jan. 1966

• *See also* Adams, John; Eisenhower, Dwight D.; Jackson, Andrew; Jefferson, Thomas; Johnson, Lyndon B.; Kennedy, John F.; Lincoln, Abraham; Roosevelt, Theodore; Washington, George

The **PRESIDENT'S** Music Men (U. S. Marine Band). By Stuart E. Jones. Photos by William W. Campbell III. 752-766, Dec. 1959

PRESIDENT'S REPORT TO MEMBERS (NGS):
• Around the World and the Calendar with the Geographic: The President's Annual Message. 832-866, Dec. 1959
• An Exciting Year of Discovery. By Gilbert M. Grosvenor. 820-824, Dec. 1982
• Exploring an Epic Year. By Melville Bell Grosvenor. 874-886, Dec. 1960
• It's Been a Banner Year! By Gilbert M. Grosvenor. 848-852, Dec. 1981
• Your Society Takes Giant New Steps: The President's Annual Message to Members. By Melville Bell Grosvenor. 874-886, Dec. 1961
• Your Society's President Reports: A Year of Widening Horizons. By Melville Bell Grosvenor. 888-906, Dec. 1962

PRESTWICH, GLENN D.:
Author-Photographer:
• Termites: Dwellers in the Dark. 532-547, Apr. 1978

PRETORIA, South Africa:
• South Africa Close-up. By Kip Ross. 641-681, Nov. 1962

PREWETT, GOLDA:
• Our Society Welcomes Its 3,000,000th Member. By Melville Bell Grosvenor. 579-582, Apr. 1962

PRIBILOF ISLANDS, Bering Sea:
• The Fur Seal Herd Comes of Age. By Victor B. Scheffer and Karl W. Kenyon. 491-512, Apr. 1952
• New Day for Alaska's Pribilof Islanders. By Susan Hackley Johnson. Photos by Tim Thompson. 536-552, Oct. 1982

PRICE, DEREK J. DE SOLLA: Author:
• The Tower of the Winds. Paintings by Robert C. Magis. 587-596, Apr. 1967

PRICE, EDWIN C., Jr.: Author:
• Ambassadors of Good Will: The Peace Corps. By Sargent Shriver and Peace Corps Volunteers. 297-345, Sept. 1964
Sarawak. 334-337

PRICE, WILLARD: Author:
• Cruising Japan's Inland Sea. 619-650, Nov. 1953
• Henry Hudson's River. Photos by Wayne Miller. 364-403, Mar. 1962
• The Lower Mississippi. Photos by W. D. Vaughn. 681-725, Nov. 1960
• The Thames Mirrors England's Varied Life. Photos by Robert F. Sisson. 45-93, July 1958
• The Upper Mississippi. 651-699, Nov. 1958

PRICELESS Relics of the Spanish Armada. By Robert Sténuit. Photos by Bates Littlehales. 745-777, June 1969

PRIMATES:
▪ Monkeys, Apes, and Man. 585A-585B, Oct. 1971
▪ Search for the Great Apes. cover, Jan. 1976
• *See also* Baboons; Chimpanzees; Gibbons; Gorillas; Lemurs; Man, Prehistoric; Monkeys; Orangutans; Tarsiers

PRIMITIVE SOCIETIES:
• Amazon–The River Sea. By Loren McIntyre. 456-495, Oct. 1972
▪ Bushmen of the Kalahari. 578A-578B, Apr. 1973; 732A-732B, May 1974
• Journey Into Stone Age New Guinea. By Malcolm S. Kirk. 568-592, Apr. 1969
• Jungle Jaunt on Amazon Headwaters. By Bernice M. Goetz. 371-388, Sept. 1952
▪ The Last Tribes of Mindanao. 882A-882B, Dec. 1971; 227, Aug. 1972
• New Guinea's Rare Birds and Stone Age Men. By E. Thomas Gilliard. NGS research grant. 421-488, Apr. 1953
◆ *Primitive Worlds.* Announced. 865-868, June 1973
• To the Land of the Head-hunters. By E. Thomas Gilliard. NGS research grant. 437-486, Oct. 1955
◆ *Vanishing Peoples of the Earth.* Announced. 844-849, June 1968
• *See also* Aboriginals; Asmat; Bushmen; Cinta Larga Indians; Dogon; Erigbaagtsa; Gimis; Kraho; Kreen-Akarores; Masai; Nambas; Negritos; Nuba; Suyá; Tarahumaras; Tasaday Tribe; Tchikao; Txukahameis; Wasúsu; Waurá; Wai Wai; Yanomamo

PRINCE HENRY, the Explorer Who Stayed Home. By Alan Villiers. Photos by Thomas Nebbia. 616-656, Nov. 1960

PRINCE OF WALES:
• The Investiture of Great Britain's Prince of Wales. By Allan C. Fisher, Jr. Photos by James L. Stanfield and Adam Woolfitt. 698-715, Nov. 1969

PRINCETON UNIVERSITY: Expeditions and Research. *See* Mount Sinai Expeditions (St. Catherine's Monastery)

PRISON AID:
• The American Red Cross: A Century of Service. By Louise Levathes. Photos by Annie Griffiths. Included: Run-A-Cross and first-aid teams. 777-791, June 1981

PROBING Ice Caves of the Pyrenees. By Norbert Casteret. 391-404, Mar. 1953

PROBING the Deep Reefs' Hidden Realm. By Walter A. Starck II and Jo D. Starck. NGS research grant. 867-886, Dec. 1972

PROBING the Mystery of the Medicine Wheels. By John A. Eddy. Photos by Thomas E. Hooper. NGS research grant. 140-146, Jan. 1977

PROBLEMS in Paradise. By Mary and Laurance S. Rockefeller. Photos by Thomas Nebbia. 782-793, Dec. 1974

PROBLEMS of a Two-part Land: Pakistan. By Bern Keating. Photos by Albert Moldvay. 1-47, Jan. 1967

PROFILES of the Presidents. By Frank Freidel:
• Part I. The Presidency and How It Grew. 642-687, Nov. 1964
• Part II. A Restless Nation Moves West. 80-121, Jan. 1965
• Part III. The American Giant Comes of Age. 660-711, May 1965
• Part IV. America Enters the Modern Era. 537-577, Oct. 1965
• Part V. The Atomic Age: Its Problems and Promises. 66-119, Jan. 1966

PROGRESS and Pageantry in Changing Nigeria. By W. Robert Moore. 325-365, Sept. 1956

PROJECT APOLLO. *See* Apollo Missions

PROJECT DA VINCI. *See* Da Vinci, Project

PROJECT FAMOUS. *See* FAMOUS, Project

PROJECT GEMINI. *See* Gemini Missions

PROJECT MERCURY. *See* Mercury Missions

PROJECT MOHOLE. *See* Mohole, Project

The **PROMISE** and Peril of Nuclear Energy. By Kenneth F. Weaver. Photos by Emory Kristof. 459-493, Apr. 1979

The **PROMISE** of Ocean Energy. 51, *Special Report on Energy* (Feb. 1981)

PROSPECTORS:
• Coober Pedy: Opal Capital of Australia's Outback. By Kenny Moore. Photos by Penny Tweedie. 560-571, Oct. 1976
• Golden Ghosts of the Lost Sierra. By Robert Laxalt. Photos by David Hiser. 332-353, Sept. 1973
• *See also* Death Valley National Monument; *and* Gold; Gold Mining

PROTESTANTISM:
• The British Way. By Sir Evelyn Wrench. Included: James I and the Translation of the Bible; The Pilgrim Fathers; Oliver Cromwell; John Wesley. 421-541, Apr. 1949
• The World of Martin Luther. By Merle Severy. Photos by James L. Amos. 418-463, Oct. 1983
• *See also* Amish; Hutterites; Mennonites; Moravians; Mormons; Puritans; Shakers

The **PROUD** Armenians. By Robert Paul Jordan. Photos by Harry N. Naltchayan. 846-873, June 1978

PROUD Primitives, the Nuba People. By Oskar Luz. Photos by Horst Luz. 673-699, Nov. 1966

PROVENCE (Region), France:
• Provence, Empire of the Sun. By William Davenport. Photos by James A. Sugar. 692-715, May 1975

• Sheep Trek in the French Alps. By Maurice Moyal. Photos by Marcel Coen. 545-564, Apr. 1952

PROVIDENCE, Rhode Island:
• New England's "Lively Experiment," Rhode Island. By Robert de Roos. Photos by Fred Ward. 370-401, Sept. 1968
• Rhode Island, Modern City-State. By George W. Long. Photos by Willard R. Culver. 137-170, Aug. 1948

PROVINCETOWN, Massachusetts:
• Cape Cod, Where Sea Holds Sway Over Man and Land. By Nathaniel T. Kenney. Photos by Dean Conger. 149-187, Aug. 1962
• Cape Cod's Circle of Seasons. By Tom Melham. Photos by James P. Blair. 40-65, July 1975

PRUDHOE BAY AREA, Alaska:
• Will Oil and Tundra Mix? Alaska's North Slope Hangs in the Balance. By William S. Ellis. Photos by Emory Kristof. 485-517, Oct. 1971

PRYOR, PAUL: Photographer:
• Exploring the World of Gems. By W. F. Foshag. 779-810, Dec. 1950

PRYOR, SAMUEL F.: Author:
• The World in Dolls. Photos by Kathleen Revis. 817-831, Dec. 1959

PRYOR MOUNTAIN WILD HORSE RANGE, Montana-Wyoming:
• On the Track of the West's Wild Horses. By Hope Ryden. Photos by author and Dick Durrance II. 94-109, Jan. 1971

PSIHOYOS, LOUIE: Photographer:
• The Fascinating World of Trash. By Peter T. White. 424-457, Apr. 1983
• Powder River Basin: New Energy Frontier. By Bill Richards. 96-113, *Special Report on Energy* (Feb. 1981)

PUBERTY RITES:
• Arnhem Land Aboriginals Cling to Dreamtime. By Clive Scollay. Photos by Penny Tweedie. 644-663, Nov. 1980
• Coming of Age the Apache Way. By Nita Quintero. Photos by Bill Hess. 262-271, Feb. 1980
• The Threatened Ways of Kenya's Pokot People. By Elizabeth L. Meyerhoff. Photos by Murray Roberts. 120-140, Jan. 1982
• Tukuna Maidens Come of Age. By Harald Schultz. 629-649, Nov. 1959

PUBLIC HEALTH SERVICE, U. S. *See* U. S. Public Health Service

PUEBLO INDIANS:
• Adobe New Mexico. By Mason Sutherland. Photos by Justin Locke. 783-830, Dec. 1949
• Ancient Cliff Dwellers of Mesa Verde. By Don Watson. Photos by Willard R. Culver. Included: Present-day Pueblo Indians. 349-376, Sept. 1948
• El Morro: Story in Stone. By Edwards Park. Photos by Willard R. Culver. 237-244, Aug. 1957
• Kachinas: Masked Dancers of the Southwest. By Paul Coze. 219-236, Aug. 1957
• Pueblo Pottery–2,000 Years of Artistry. By David L. Arnold. 593-605, Nov. 1982
▲ *The Southwest,* The Making of America series. Included: Arizona, New Mexico, and parts of California, Colorado, Texas, Utah; and in Mexico: Baja California Norte, Chihuahua, Sonora. On reverse: 12,000 Years of History; Spanish Conquest; Anglo-American Entry and Occupancy. Nov. 1982
• 20th-century Indians Preserve Customs of the Cliff Dwellers. Photos by William Belknap, Jr. NGS research grant. 196-211, Feb. 1964
• *See also* Anasazi, for ancient Pueblo Indians

PUEBLOS:
• The Anasazi–Riddles in the Ruins. By Thomas Y. Canby. Photos by Dewitt Jones and David Brill. Paintings by Roy Andersen. 554-592, Nov. 1982
• Searching for Cliff Dwellers' Secrets. By Carroll A. Burroughs. NGS research grant. 619-625, Nov. 1959
• Solving the Riddles of Wetherill Mesa. By Douglas Osborne. Paintings by Peter V. Bianchi. NGS research grant. 155-195, Feb. 1964
▲ *The Southwest,* The Making of America series. Included: Arizona, New Mexico, and parts of California, Colorado, Texas, Utah; and in Mexico: Baja California Norte, Chihuahua, Sonora. On reverse: 12,000 Years of History; Spanish Conquest; Anglo-American Entry and Occupancy. Nov. 1982
• Your Society to Seek New Light on the Cliff Dwellers. 154-156, Jan. 1959

PUERTO RICO:
▲ *Close-up U.S.A., Florida, with Puerto Rico and U.S. Virgin Islands.* Text on reverse. Close-up series. Nov. 1973
• Growing Pains Beset Puerto Rico. By William H. Nicholas. Photos by Justin Locke. 419-460, Apr. 1951
• Puerto Rico's Seven-league Bootstraps. By Bart McDowell. Photos by B. Anthony Stewart. 755-793, Dec. 1962
• Sailing a Sea of Fire. By Paul A. Zahl. 120-129, July 1960
• The Uncertain State of Puerto Rico. By Bill Richards. Photos by Stephanie Maze. 516-543, Apr. 1983

PUFFINS:
• Lundy, Treasure Island of Birds. By P. T. Etherton. Photos by J. Allan Cash. 675-698, May 1947
• The Solemn, Sociable Puffins. By R. M. Lockley. 414-422, Sept. 1954

PUGET SOUND, Washington:
• Making Friends With a Killer Whale. By Edward I. Griffin. 418-446, Mar. 1966
• Puget Sound, Sea Gate of the Pacific Northwest. By William Graves. Photos by David Alan Harvey. 71-97, Jan. 1977

PULPWOOD CULTIVATION:
• Jari: A Billion-dollar Gamble. By Loren McIntyre. Contents: Daniel

BOTH BY JERRY D. JACKA

Pueblo Pottery: worktable holding completed seed jar and painting supplies, *top;* 1890s jar crafted by Acoma Pueblo potter, *above*

O P

K. Ludwig's paper-pulp and food-production enterprise in Brazil's Amazon basin. 686-711, May 1980

PULPWOOD INDUSTRY. *See* Paper and Pulp Industry

PUMAS. *See* Mountain Lions

PUNAN (People):
• Brunei, Borneo's Abode of Peace. By Joseph Judge. Photos by Dean Conger. 207-225, Feb. 1974

PUNJAB, East, India:
• India's Energetic Sikhs. By John E. Frazer. Photos by James P. Blair. 528-541, Oct. 1972

PUNJAB, West, Pakistan:
• Pakistan, New Nation in an Old Land. By Jean and Franc Shor. 637-678, Nov. 1952
• Pakistan: Problems of a Two-part Land. By Bern Keating. Photos by Albert Moldvay. 1-47, Jan. 1967

PURDAH in India: Life Behind the Veil. By Doranne Wilson Jacobson. 270-286, Aug. 1977

PURDUE UNIVERSITY: Expeditions and Research:
• Wolves Versus Moose on Isle Royale. By Durward L. Allen and L. David Mech. 200-219, Feb. 1963

PURI, India:
• Orissa, Past and Promise in an Indian State. By Bart McDowell. Photos by James P. Blair. 546-577, Oct. 1970

PURITANS:
• Founders of New England. By Sir Evelyn Wrench. Photos by B. Anthony Stewart. 803-838, June 1953

The **PURPLE** Land of Uruguay. By Luis Marden. 623-654, Nov. 1948

PUSHTUNS. *See* Pathans

PUT-IN-BAY, Ohio:
• Yesterday Lingers on Lake Erie's Bass Islands. By Terry and Lyntha Eiler. 86-101, July 1978

PUTMAN, JOHN J.: Author:
• The Arab World, Inc. Photos by Winfield Parks. 494-533, Oct. 1975
• China's Opening Door. Photos by H. Edward Kim. 64-83, July 1983
• Denver, Colorado's Rocky Mountain High. Photos by David Cupp. 383-411, Mar. 1979
• East Germany: The Struggle to Succeed. Photos by Gordon W. Gahan. 295-329, Sept. 1974
• The Ganges, River of Faith. Photos by Raghubir Singh. 445-483, Oct. 1971
• Greenland Feels the Winds of Change. Photos by George F. Mobley. 366-393, Sept. 1975
• Hungary's New Way: A Different Communism. Photos by Bill Weems. 225-261, Feb. 1983
• India Struggles to Save Her Wildlife. 299-343, Sept. 1976
• Manhattan–Images of the City. Photos by Jay Maisel. 317-343, Sept. 1981
• Moscow: The City Around Red Square. Photos by Gordon W. Gahan. 2-45, Jan. 1978
• Napoleon. Photos by Gordon W. Gahan. 142-189, Feb. 1982
• A New Day for Ireland. Photos by Cotton Coulson. 442-469, Apr. 1981
• Quicksilver and Slow Death (Mercury). Photos by Robert W. Madden. 507-527, Oct. 1972
• Savannah to Charleston–A Good Life in the Low Country. Photos by Annie Griffiths. 798-829, Dec. 1983
• Timber: How Much Is Enough? Photos by Bruce Dale. 485-511, Apr. 1974
• West Germany: Continuing Miracle. Photos by Robert W. Madden. 149-181, Aug. 1977
• Yesterday's Congo, Today's Zaire. Photos by Eliot Elisofon. 398-432, Mar. 1973

PUTNAM, ANNE EISNER: Author:
• My Life With Africa's Little People. 278-302, Feb. 1960

PUTTKAMER, W. JESCO VON:
Author-Photographer:
• Brazil Protects Her Cinta Larga Indians. 420-444, Sept. 1971
• Brazil's Beleaguered Indians. 254-283, Feb. 1975
I. Requiem for a Tribe? (Kreen-Akarores). 254-269; II. Good-bye to the Stone Age (Txukahameis). 270-283
• Man in the Amazon: Stone Age Present Meets Stone Age Past. 60-83, Jan. 1979
Photographer:
• Saving Brazil's Stone Age Tribes From Extinction. By Orlando and Claudio Villas Boas. 424-444, Sept. 1968

PUYA, the Pineapple's Andean Ancestor. By Mulford B. Foster. 463-480, Oct. 1950

PYGMIES:
• Flight to Adventure. By Tay and Lowell Thomas, Jr. 49-112, July 1957
• My Life With Africa's Little People. By Anne Eisner Putnam. 278-302, Feb. 1960
• Yesterday's Congo, Today's Zaire. By John J. Putman. Photos by Eliot Elisofon. 398-432, Mar. 1973

PYONGYANG, North Korea:
• Rare Look at North Korea. By H. Edward Kim. 252-277, Aug. 1974

PYRAMIDS: The Americas:
• The Aztecs. Included: Great Temple at Tenochtitlan, a pyramid at a subway station, and the pyramid of Tlatelolco, all in Mexico City; reconstructed pyramid in the Aztec style in Santa Cecilia, north of Mexico City; Toltec pyramid at Tula, Mexico. 704-775, Dec. 1980
I. The Aztecs. By Bart McDowell. Photos by David Hiser. Paintings by Felipe Dávalos. 714-751; II. The Building of Tenochtitlan. By Augusto F. Molina Montes. Paintings by Felipe Dávalos. 753-765; III. New Finds in the Great Temple. By Eduardo Matos Moctezuma. Photos by David Hiser. 767-775
• Belize, the Awakening Land. By Louis de la Haba. Photos by Michael E. Long. Included: Maya Temple of the Masonry Altars. 124-146, Jan. 1972
• Man's Eighty Centuries in Veracruz. By S. Jeffrey K. Wilkerson. Photos by David Hiser. Paintings by Richard Schlecht. Included: El Tajín's Temple of the niches built by Maya-related Huastec people. NGS research grant. 203-231, Aug. 1980
• The Maya. Included: In Guatemala: El Mirador and Tikal; In Mexico: Cobá, Yucatan; Kohunlich; Pyramid of the Magician, Uxmal; and Temple of the Inscriptions (Pacal's pyramid tomb), Palenque. 729-811, Dec. 1975
I. Children of Time. By Howard La Fay. Photos by David Alan Harvey. 729-767; II. Riddle of the Glyphs. By George E. Stuart. Photos by Otis Imboden. 768-791; III. Resurrecting the Grandeur of Tikal. By William R. Coe. 792-798; IV. A Traveler's Tale of Ancient Tikal. Paintings by Peter Spier. Text by Alice J. Hall. 799-811
• "Pyramids" of the New World. By Neil Merton Judd. Included: Toltec, Aztec, and Maya pyramids in Mexico: Cholula Pyramid; Gran Teocalli, Mexico City; Monte Albán; Pyramid of Cuicuilco; Tenayuca; Tenochtitlán with the Great Pyramid; Teotihuacan with the Pyramids of the Sun and the Moon; Tlalelolco; Uxmal. 105-128, Jan. 1948
• Unearthing the Oldest Known Maya. By Norman Hammond. Photos by Lowell Georgia and Martha Cooper. Contents: Cuello site in northern Belize. 126-140, July 1982
▲ *Visitor's Guide to the Aztec World; Mexico and Central America,* double-sided supplement. Dec. 1980
• Who Were the "Mound Builders"? By George E. Stuart. 783-801, Dec. 1972

PYRAMIDS, Egyptian:
◆ *Ancient Egypt.* 1978
• Egypt: Two Perspectives. Included: Great Pyramid of Giza, Pyramid of Meidum near El Faiyum. 293-343, Mar. 1977
I. Legacy of a Dazzling Past. By Alice J. Hall. 293-311; II. Omens for a Better Tomorrow. By Thomas J. Abercrombie. 312-343
• Fresh Treasures from Egypt's Ancient Sands. By Jefferson Caffery. Photos by David S. Boyer. Included: Bent Pyramid, Dahshur; Great Pyramid of Khufu (Cheops), Giza; Northern Pyramid (first true pyramid), Dahshur; Seila, Faiyum; Step Pyramid, Djoser; Step Pyramid, Saqqara; unfinished pyramid at Zaqiyet el Aryan. 611-650, Nov. 1955
• Sudan: Arab-African Giant. By Robert Caputo. Note: The royal burial pyramids are to the east of the ancient city of Meroe, once capital of the Kingdom of Kush (flourished circa 800 B.C. to A.D. 350). 346-379, Mar. 1982

PYRENEES (Mountains), France-Spain:
• The Enduring Pyrenees. By Robert Laxalt. Photos by Edwin Stuart Grosvenor. 794-819, Dec. 1974
• High Road in the Pyrenees. By H. V. Morton. Photos by Justin Locke. 299-334, Mar. 1956

• Incredible Andorra. By Lawrence L. Klingman. Photos by B. Anthony Stewart. 262-290, Aug. 1949
• Land of the Ancient Basques. By Robert Laxalt. Photos by William Albert Allard. 240-277, Aug. 1968
• Life in the Land of the Basques. By John E. H. Nolan. Photos by Justin Locke. 147-186, Feb. 1954
• Pigeon Netting–Sport of Basques. Photos by Irene Burdett-Scougall. 405-416, Sept. 1949
• Probing Ice Caves of the Pyrenees. By Norbert Casteret. 391-404, Mar. 1953

Q

QATIF, Saudi Arabia:
• In Search of Arabia's Past. By Peter Bruce Cornwall. 493-522, Apr. 1948

QINGHAI PROVINCE, People's Republic of China:
• Nomads of China's West. By Galen Rowell. Photos by the author and Harold A. Knutson. 244-263, Feb. 1982

QIVIUT (Wool):
• Domesticating the Wild and Woolly Musk Ox. By John J. Teal, Jr. Photos by Robert W. Madden. 862-879, June 1970

QOMUL. *See* Hami, Sinkiang

QOYLLUR RITI (Star of the Snow), Peru:
• Peru's Pilgrimage to the Sky. By Robert Randall. Photos by Loren McIntyre and Ira Block. 60-69, July 1982

QUARRYING:
• Carrara Marble: Touchstone of Eternity. By Cathy Newman. Photos by Pierre Boulat. 42-59, July 1982

QUASARS:
• The Once and Future Universe. By Rick Gore. Photos by James A. Sugar. Paintings by Barron Storey. Picture text by David Jeffery. 704-749, June 1983

QUEBEC (Province), Canada:
• Canada, My Country. By Alan Phillips. Photos by David S. Boyer and Walter Meayers Edwards. 769-819, Dec. 1961
▲ *Close-up, Canada: Quebec, Newfoundland,* supplement. Text on reverse, inset Southern Quebec. May 1980
• Editorial. By Gilbert M. Grosvenor. 435, Apr. 1977
• Henry Hudson's Changing Bay. By Bill Richards. Photos by David Hiser. 380-405, Mar. 1982
• North Through History Aboard *White Mist.* By Melville Bell Grosvenor. Photos by Edwin Stuart Grosvenor. 1-55, July 1970
• One Canada–or Two? By Peter T. White. Photos by Winfield Parks. 436-465, Apr. 1977

TED SPIEGEL, BLACK STAR

Carrara Marble: Michelangelo's "Pietà"

• Quebec's Forests, Farms, and Frontiers. By Andrew H. Brown. 431-470, Oct. 1949
• Quebec's Northern Dynamo. By Larry Kohl. Photos by Ottmar Bierwagen. Contents: La Grande Complex, a hydroelectric project. 406-418, Mar. 1982
• The St. Lawrence, River Key to Canada. By Howard La Fay. Photos by John Launois. 622-667, May 1967
• The St. Lawrence River: Canada's Highway to the Sea. By William S. Ellis. Photos by Bruce Dale. 586-623, May 1980
• Sea Bird Cities Off Audubon's Labrador. By Arthur A. Allen. NGS research grant. 755-774, June 1948
• Sea to Lakes on the St. Lawrence. By George W. Long. Photos by B. Anthony Stewart and John E. Fletcher. 323-366, Sept. 1950
• Solving the Riddle of Chubb Crater. By V. Ben Meen. Photos by Richard H. Stewart. NGS research grant. 1-32, Jan. 1952
• *See also* James Bay; Montreal; Quebec (City); St. Lawrence Seaway

QUEBEC (City), Quebec, Canada:
• Quebec: French City in an Anglo-Saxon World. By Kenneth MacLeish. Photos by James L. Stanfield and Declan Haun. 416-442, Mar. 1971
• The St. Lawrence, River Key to Canada. By Howard La Fay. Photos by John Launois. 622-667, May 1967
• The St. Lawrence River: Canada's Highway to the Sea. By William S. Ellis. Photos by Bruce Dale. 586-623, May 1980
• Winter Brings Carnival Time to Quebec. By Kathleen Revis. 69-97, Jan. 1958

QUECHUAS (Indians):
• Ambassadors of Good Will: The Peace Corps. By Sargent Shriver and Peace Corps Volunteers. 297-345, Sept. 1964
Bolivia. By Edward S. Dennison. 315-319
• Peru, Homeland of the Warlike Inca. By Kip Ross. 421-462, Oct. 1950

QUEEN CHARLOTTE ISLANDS, British Columbia, Canada:
• Canada's Window on the Pacific: The British Columbia Coast. By Jules B. Billard. Photos by Ted Spiegel. 338-375, Mar. 1972

QUEEN ELIZABETH ISLANDS, Canada:
• Weather from the White North. By Andrew H. Brown. Photos by John E. Fletcher. 543-572, Apr. 1955

QUEEN ELIZABETH Opens Parliament. By W. E. Roscher. Photos by Robert B. Goodman. 699-707, Nov. 1961

QUEEN ELIZABETH'S Favorite Sea Dog: Sir Francis Drake. By Alan Villiers. Photos by Gordon W. Gahan. 216-253, Feb. 1975

QUEEN of Canada. By Phyllis Wilson. Photos by Kathleen Revis. 825-829, June 1959

QUEEN'S DOLLS' HOUSE, Windsor Castle, England:
• Royal House for Dolls. By David Jeffery. Photos by James L. Stanfield. 632-643, Nov. 1980

QUEENSLAND (State), Australia:
• Queensland: Young Titan of Australia's Tropic North. By Kenneth MacLeish. Photos by Winfield Parks. 593-639, Nov. 1968
• *See also* Great Barrier Reef

QUEENY, EDGAR MONSANTO: Author:
• Spearing Lions with Africa's Masai. 487-517, Oct. 1954

QUEMOY (Islands), China:
• Life under Shellfire on Quemoy. By Franc Shor. Photos by Wilbur E. Garrett. 415-438, Mar. 1959

QUESTING for Gems. By George S. Switzer. 835-863, Dec. 1971

The **QUETZAL,** Fabulous Bird of Maya Land. By Anne LaBastille Bowes. Photos by David G. Allen. 141-150, Jan. 1969

QUEZALTENANGO, Guatemala:
• Guatemala Revisited. By Luis Marden. 525-564, Oct. 1947

QUICKSILVER. *See* Mercury

QUICKSILVER and Slow Death. By John J. Putman. Photos by Robert W. Madden. 507-527, Oct. 1972

THE QUIET ACHIEVER (Solar-powered Car):
• Across Australia by Sunpower. By Hans Tholstrup and Larry Perkins. Photos by David Austen. 600-607, Nov. 1983

QUINTERO, NITA: Author:
• Coming of Age the Apache Way. Photos by Bill Hess. 262-271, Feb. 1980

QUITO, Ecuador:
• Ecuador–Low and Lofty Land Astride the Equator. By Loren McIntyre. 259-298, Feb. 1968

QUMRÂN. *See* Khirbat Qumrān, Jordan

R

RNA. *See* Ribonucleic Acid

RPV. *See* Remotely Piloted Vehicle

RA II (Papyrus Ship):
• The Voyage of *Ra II*. By Thor Heyerdahl. Photos by Carlo Mauri and Georges Sourial. 44-71, Jan. 1971

RACCOONS:
• Raccoon: Amiable Rogue in a Black Mask. By Melvin R. Ellis. 841-854, Dec. 1956

RACEHORSES:
• Heart of the Bluegrass. By Charles McCarry. Photos by J. Bruce Baumann. 634-659, May 1974

RACES. *See* Automobile Race; Balloon Races; Boat Races; Bull Derby; Horse Races; Iditarod Trail Sled Dog Race; Land Yachts; Motorcycle Races; Olympic Games; Tall-Ships Race

RADAR:
• Miracle Men of the Telephone. By F. Barrows Colton. 273-316, Mar. 1947
Birthplace of Telephone Magic. Photos by Willard R. Culver. 289-312
• Our Air Age Speeds Ahead. By F. Barrows Colton. 249-272, Feb. 1948
• *See also* DEW Line; Remote Sensing

RADFORD, ARTHUR W.: Author:
• Our Navy in the Far East. Photos by J. Baylor Roberts. 537-577, Oct. 1953

RADIATION:
• The Incredible Universe. By Kenneth F. Weaver. Photos by James P. Blair. 584-625, May 1974
• Remote Sensing: New Eyes to See the World. By Kenneth F. Weaver. Included: Cosmic Rays, Gamma Rays, Infrared Radiation, Microwaves, Radar and Sonar, Ultraviolet Rays. 46-73, Jan. 1969
• *See also* Lasers; Solar Energy

RADIO:
• Miracle Men of the Telephone. By F. Barrows Colton. 273-316, Mar. 1947
Birthplace of Telephone Magic. Photos by Willard R. Culver. 289-312
• Our Air Age Speeds Ahead. By F. Barrows Colton. 249-272, Feb. 1948
• Uncle Sam's House of 1,000 Wonders (National Bureau of Standards). By Lyman J. Briggs and F. Barrows Colton. 755-784, Dec. 1951
• Unlocking Secrets of the Northern Lights. By Carl W. Gartlein. Paintings by William Crowder. Included: The effect of magnetic storms on radio transmission. NGS research grant. 673-704, Nov. 1947
• *See also* Microwave Radio Relay

RADIOACTIVE WASTES:
• The Promise and Peril of Nuclear Energy. By Kenneth F. Weaver. Photos by Emory Kristof. 459-493, Apr. 1979

RADIOACTIVITY:
• Man's New Servant, the Friendly Atom. By F. Barrows Colton. Photos by Volkmar Wentzel. 71-90, Jan. 1954
• The Promise and Peril of Nuclear Energy. By Kenneth F. Weaver. Photos by Emory Kristof. 459-493, Apr. 1979
• Uncle Sam's House of 1,000 Wonders (National Bureau of Standards). By Lyman J. Briggs and F. Barrows Colton. 755-784, Dec. 1951
• You and the Obedient Atom. By Allan C. Fisher, Jr. 303-353, Sept. 1958
• *See also* Nuclear Energy; Potassium-Argon Dating; Radiocarbon Dating

RADIOCARBON DATING:
• Ancient Europe Is Older Than We Thought. By Colin Renfrew. Photos by Adam Woolfitt. Included: Calibration graph of radiocarbon dates corrected by tree-ring dates. 615-623, Nov. 1977
• How Old Is It? By Lyman J. Briggs and Kenneth F. Weaver. 234-255, Aug. 1958
• The Search for the First Americans. By Thomas Y. Canby. Photos by Kerby Smith. Paintings by Roy Andersen. Included: Radiocarbon dating; amino acid racemization; dentition; stratigraphy. 330-363, Sept. 1979

RADIOTELEMETRY:
• Antarctica's Nearer Side. By Samuel W. Matthews. Photos by William R. Curtsinger. Included: Radiotelemetering of penguins. 622-655, Nov. 1971
• Studying Wildlife by Satellite. By Frank Craighead, Jr., and John Craighead. NGS research grant. 120-123, Jan. 1973
• *See also* Bald Eagles; Bighorn Sheep; Brown Bears; Grizzly Bears; Polar Bears; Salmon (The Incredible); Whistling Swan; Wolves

RAFFLESIA (Flower):
• Malaysia's Giant Flowers and Insect-trapping Plants. By Paul A. Zahl. 680-701, May 1964

RAFT TRIPS:
• Chattooga River Country: Wild Water, Proud People. By Don Belt. Photos by Steve Wall. 458-477, Apr. 1983
• Down Mark Twain's River on a Raft. By Rex E. Hieronymus. 551-574, Apr. 1948
• Rafting Down the Yukon. By Keith Tryck. Photos by Robert Clark. 830-861, Dec. 1975
• Retracing John Wesley Powell's Historic Voyage Down the Grand Canyon. By Joseph Judge. Photos by Walter Meayers Edwards. 668-713, May 1969
• A Walk and Ride on the Wild Side: Tasmania. By Carolyn Bennett Patterson. Photos by David Hiser and Melinda Berge. 676-693, May 1983
• White-water Adventure on Wild Rivers of Idaho. By Frank Craighead, Jr., and John Craighead. 213-239, Feb. 1970

RAILROAD WORM:
• Nature's Toy Train, the Railroad Worm. By Darwin L. Tiemann. Photos by Robert F. Sisson. NGS research grant. 56-67, July 1970

RAILROADS:
◆ *Railroads: The Great American Adventure*. 1977. Announced. 860-864, June 1976
• Slow Train Through Viet Nam's War. By Howard Sochurek. 412-444, Sept. 1964
• *See also* California Western Railroad; Southern Railway System; *and* Trains

RAILS (Birds). *See* Takahe

RAIN FORESTS:
● Cock-of-the-Rock: Jungle Dandy. By Pepper W. Trail. NGS research grant. 831-839, Dec. 1983
● The High World of the Rain Forest (Trinidad). By William Beebe. Paintings by Guy Neale. 838-855, June 1958
● Malaysia's Giant Flowers and Insect-trapping Plants. By Paul A. Zahl. 680-701, May 1964
■ Rain Forest. 824, Dec. 1982; 49, cover, Jan. 1983
● Tropical Rain Forests. 2-65, Jan. 1983
Nature's Dwindling Treasures. By Peter T. White. Photos by James P. Blair. Paintings by Barron Storey. 2-47; Teeming Life of a Rain Forest. By Carol and David Hughes. 49-65
● What Future for the Wayana Indians? By Carole Devillers. 66-83, Jan. 1983
● *See also* Ituri Forest, Zaire; Olympic National Park, Washington; Ruwenzori, Africa; Tanjung Puting Reserve, Indonesia

RAINBOW BRIDGE NATIONAL MONUMENT, Utah:
● Desert River Through Navajo Land. By Alfred M. Bailey. Photos by author and Fred G. Brandenburg. 149-172, Aug. 1947
● Three Roads to Rainbow. By Ralph Gray. 547-561, Apr. 1957

RAINBOW World Beneath the Red Sea. By David Doubilet. 344-365, Sept. 1975

RAINIER, Mount, Washington:
● Climbing Our Northwest Glaciers. Photos by Bob and Ira Spring. 103-114, July 1953
● Mount Rainier: Testing Ground for Everest. By Barry C. Bishop. NGS research grant. 688-711, May 1963

RAJASTHAN (State), India:
● The Pageant of Rajasthan. By Raghubir Singh. 219-243, Feb. 1977
● *See also* Jaisalmer; Jodhpur

RAJPUTANA, India:
● Feudal Splendor Lingers in Rajputana. By Volkmar Wentzel. 411-458, Oct. 1948

RALEIGH, SIR WALTER:
● Founders of Virginia. By Sir Evelyn Wrench. Photos by B. Anthony Stewart. 433-462, Apr. 1948

RAMA IX, King (Thailand). *See* Bhumibol Adulyadej, King

RAMAYANA (Epic):
● Pageantry of the Siamese Stage. By D. Sonakul. Photos by W. Robert Moore. 201-212, Feb. 1947

RAMESSES II (Pharaoh):
● Abu Simbel's Ancient Temples Reborn. By Georg Gerster. 724-744, May 1969
● In Search of Moses. By Harvey Arden. Photos by Nathan Benn. 2-37, Jan. 1976
● Lost Outpost of the Egyptian Empire. By Trude Dothan. Photos by Sisse Brimberg. Paintings by Lloyd K. Townsend. NGS research grant. 739-769, Dec. 1982
● Saving the Ancient Temples at Abu Simbel. By Georg Gerster. Paintings by Robert W. Nicholson. 694-742, May 1966
● Threatened Treasures of the Nile. By Georg Gerster. 587-621, Oct. 1963
● *Yankee* Cruises the Storied Nile. By Irving and Electa Johnson. Photos by Winfield Parks. 583-633, May 1965

RAMSAY, SIR WILLIAM:
● The British Way. By Sir Evelyn Wrench. 421-541, Apr. 1949

RAMSES II (Pharaoh). *See* Ramesses II

RANCHES:
● America's "Meat on the Hoof." By William H. Nicholas. Included: The King Ranch. 33-72, Jan. 1952
● Buffalo Bill and the Enduring West. By Alice J. Hall. Photos by James L. Amos. Included: M Bar Ranch, Wyoming; Scout's Rest Ranch, Nebraska; TE Ranch, Wyoming. 76-103, July 1981
● The Camargue, Land of Cowboys and Gypsies. By Eugene L. Kammerman. Included: *Manades.* 667-699, May 1956
● Cowpunching on the Padlock Ranch. By William Albert Allard. 478-499, Oct. 1973
● From Tucson to Tombstone. By Mason Sutherland. Included: Boquillas Ranch, Cowan Ranch, Desert Treasures, San Rafael Ranch, and guest ranches: Double U, Flying V, Westward Look, Wild Horse. 343-384, Sept. 1953
● Holy Week and the Fair in Sevilla. By Luis Marden. Included: Miura Ranch. 499-530, Apr. 1951
● Housewife at the End of the World. By Rae Natalie P. Goodall. Photos by James L. Stanfield. Contents: Estancia Harberton, Tierra del Fuego, Argentina. 130-150, Jan. 1971
● The Hutterites, Plain People of the West. By William Albert Allard. 98-125, July 1970
● Land of Long Sunsets: Nebraska's Sand Hills. By John Madson. Photos by Jodi Cobb. Included: Abbott Ranch, Forney Ranch, Lord Ranch, Roth Ranch. 493-517, Oct. 1978
● New Zealand's High Country. By Yva Momatiuk and John Eastcott. Included: Birchwood Station, Black Forest Station, Glen Lyon Station, Godley Peaks Station, Irishman Creek Station, Lake Hawea Station. 246-265, Aug. 1978
● Orange, a Most California County. By Judith and Neil Morgan. Photos by Vince Streano. Included: The urbanization of Irvine Ranch. 750-779, Dec. 1981
● Philmont Scout Ranch Helps Boys Grow Up. By Andrew H. Brown. 399-416, Sept. 1956

FROM THE DAYAN COLLECTION, GIFT OF L. TISCH TO THE ISRAEL MUSEUM

BOTH BY SISSE BRIMBERG

Lost Outpost: coffin-lid mask from the Gaza Strip, *top;* carnelian seal showing Egyptian gods, *above*

Q R

• The Tallgrass Prairie: Can It Be Saved? By Dennis Farney. Photos by Jim Brandenburg. Included: Ferrell Ranch, Kansas; Hess Ranch, Kansas; Mahlberg Ranch, Minnesota. 37-61, Jan. 1980
• Texas! By Howard La Fay. Photos by Gordon W. Gahan. Included: O-6 Ranch. 440-483, Apr. 1980

RAND, CHRISTOPHER: Author:
• Himalayan Pilgrimage. 520-535, Oct. 1956

RANDALL, ROBERT: Author:
• Peru's Pilgrimage to the Sky. Photos by Loren McIntyre and Ira Block. 60-69, July 1982

RANGER SPACECRAFT:
• The Moon Close Up. By Eugene M. Shoemaker. Photos by Ranger 7. 690-707, Nov. 1964
• Robots to the Moon. By Frank Sartwell. Paintings by Pierre Mion. 557-571, Oct. 1962

RANKIN, NIALL:
Author-Photographer:
• A Naturalist in Penguin Land. 93-116, Jan. 1955

RANSOM, TIMOTHY W.:
Photographer:
• Life with the "Pumphouse Gang": New Insights Into Baboon Behavior. By Shirley C. Strum. 672-691, May 1975

RAPA (Island), Pacific Ocean:
• The *Yankee*'s Wander-world. By Irving and Electa Johnson. 1-50, Jan. 1949

RAPIDS:
• Relics from the Rapids. By Sigurd F. Olson. Photos by David S. Boyer. 413-435, Sept. 1963
• White-water Adventure on Wild Rivers of Idaho. By Frank Craighead, Jr. and John Craighead. 213-239, Feb. 1970
• *See also* Buffalo National River; Chattooga River; Colorado River; Franklin River; Hamilton (River); Noatak River; San Juan (River); Skagit River; South Nahanni River; Yampa (River)

RARE ANIMAL RELIEF EFFORT:
Study Grant:
• Giant Brazilian Otters. 132, July 1980

RARE Birds Flock to Spain's Marismas. By Roger Tory Peterson. 397-425, Mar. 1958

RARE Look at North Korea. By H. Edward Kim. 252-277, Aug. 1974

RAROTONGA (Island), Cook Islands:
• New Zealand's Cook Islands: Paradise in Search of a Future. By Maurice Shadbolt. Photos by William Albert Allard. 203-231, Aug. 1967

RAS MUHAMMAD, Sinai Peninsula:
• Hidden Life of an Undersea Desert. By Eugenie Clark. Photos by David Doubilet. 129-144, July 1983
• The Red Sea's Sharkproof Fish. By Eugenie Clark. Photos by David Doubilet. 718-727, Nov. 1974

TIMOTHY W. RANSOM

Baboons: baby Frodo on mom's back

• The Strangest Sea. By Eugenie Clark. Photos by David Doubilet. 338-365, Sept. 1975
Rainbow World Beneath the Red Sea. 344-365

RASSVET COLLECTIVE FARM, Byelorussian S.S.R., U.S.S.R.:
• Down on the Farm, Soviet Style–a 4-H Adventure. By John Garaventa. Photos by James Tobin and Carol Schmidt. 768-797, June 1979

RATELS:
• Honey-Guide: The Bird That Eats Wax. By Herbert Friedmann. Paintings by Walter A. Weber. 551-560, Apr. 1954

RATIONING:
• Keeping House in London. By Frances James. 769-792, Dec. 1947

RATS:
• The Rat, Lapdog of the Devil. By Thomas Y. Canby. Photos by James L. Stanfield. 60-87, July 1977

RAY, G. CARLETON: Author:
• Learning the Ways of the Walrus. Photos by Bill Curtsinger. 565-580, Oct. 1979
• Three Whales That Flew. Photos by W. Robert Moore. 346-359, Mar. 1962
Author-Photographer:
• Stalking Seals Under Antarctic Ice. 54-65, Jan. 1966

RAYLEIGH, LORD (John William Strutt):
• The British Way. By Sir Evelyn Wrench. 421-541, Apr. 1949

RAYMER, PATRICIA: Author:
• Wisconsin's Menominees: Indians on a Seesaw. Photos by Steve Raymer. 228-251, Aug. 1974

RAYMER, STEVE: Photographer:
• Bahrain: Hub of the Persian Gulf. By Thomas J. Abercrombie. 300-329, Sept. 1979
• Bangladesh: The Nightmare of Famine. 33-39, July 1975
• Can the World Feed Its People? By Thomas Y. Canby. 2-31, July 1975
• The Caribbean: Sun, Sea, and Seething. By Noel Grove. 244-271, Feb. 1981
• Chicago! By Harvey Arden. 463-493, Apr. 1978
• Crosscurrents Sweep the Indian Ocean. By Bart McDowell. 422-457, Oct. 1981
• In Touch With Nature. Text by Elizabeth A. Moize. 537-543, Apr. 1974
• Iowa's Enduring Amana Colonies. By Laura Longley Babb. 863-878, Dec. 1975
• Kamehameha–Hawaii's Warrior King. By Louise E. Levathes. Paintings by Herb Kawainui Kane. 558-599, Nov. 1983
• Mount St. Helens Aftermath: The Mountain That Was–and Will Be. By Rowe Findley. 713-733, Dec. 1981

• North Yemen. By Noel Grove. 244-269, Aug. 1979
• The Pipeline: Alaska's Troubled Colossus. By Bryan Hodgson. 684-717, Nov. 1976
• Risk and Reward on Alaska's Violent Gulf. By Boyd Gibbons. 237-267, Feb. 1979
• Thailand: Luck of a Land in the Middle. By Bart McDowell. 500-535, Oct. 1982
• Wild Cargo: the Business of Smuggling Animals. By Noel Grove. 287-315, Mar. 1981
• Wisconsin's Menominees: Indians on a Seesaw. By Patricia Raymer. 228-251, Aug. 1974

RAZA, Isla, Gulf of California:
• Sea Birds of Isla Raza. By Lewis Wayne Walker. 239-248, Feb. 1951

REACH for the New World. By Mendel Peterson. Photos by David L. Arnold. Paintings by Richard Schlecht. 724-767, Dec. 1977

REACHING for the Moon. By Allan C. Fisher, Jr. Photos by Luis Marden. 157-171, Feb. 1959

READER, JOHN: Photographer:
• Tanzania's Stone Age Art. By Mary D. Leakey. 84-99, July 1983

REARDEN, JIM: Author:
• Nikolaevsk: A Bit of Old Russia Takes Root in Alaska. Photos by Charles O'Rear. 401-425, Sept. 1972
Author-Photographer:
• Caribou: Hardy Nomads of the North. 858-878, Dec. 1974

RECLAMATION:
• Californians Escape to the Desert. By Mason Sutherland. Photos by Charles W. Herbert. 675-724, Nov. 1957
• California's Surprising Inland Delta. By Judith and Neil Morgan. Photos by Charles O'Rear. 409-430, Sept. 1976
• The Desert: An Age-old Challenge Grows. By Rick Gore. Photos by Georg Gerster and Bruce Dale. 586-639, Nov. 1979
• Egypt's Desert of Promise. By Farouk El-Baz. Photos by Georg Gerster. 190-221, Feb. 1982
• Helping Holland Rebuild Her Land. By Gilbert M. Grosvenor and Charles Neave. 365-413, Sept. 1954
■ Holland Against the Sea. 588A-588B, Apr. 1970
• Mid-century Holland Builds Her Future. By Sydney Clark. 747-778, Dec. 1950
• The Netherlands: Nation at War With the Sea. By Alan Villiers. Photos by Adam Woolfitt. 530-571, Apr. 1968
• Pennsylvania: Faire Land of William Penn. By Gordon Young. Photos by Cary Wolinsky. 731-767, June 1978
• A River Restored: Oregon's Willamette. By Ethel A. Starbird. Photos by Lowell J. Georgia. 816-835, June 1972
• Roosevelt Country: T. R.'s Wilderness Legacy. By John L. Eliot. Photos by Farrell Grehan. 340-363, Sept. 1982
• *See also* Recycling; Reforestation

RECORDING SUPPLEMENTS AND SOUND SHEETS:
◆ "Bird Songs of Garden, Woodland, and Meadow," record supplement to *Song and Garden Birds of North America*. 554, 557, Oct. 1964
◆ "Bird Sounds of Marsh, Upland, and Shore," record supplement to *Water, Prey, and Game Birds of North America*. 529, 530, 533, 534, 535, Oct. 1965
• "The Funeral of Sir Winston Churchill, with Excerpts from His Speeches," record supplement. 198A-198B, Aug. 1965; 580, 581, Oct. 1967
• "Sounds of the Space Age, from Sputnik to Lunar Landing," record supplement narrated by Frank Borman. 750A-750B, Dec. 1969
• "Sounds of the World" series. 701, Nov. 1971; 475, Apr. 1976
• Symphony of the Deep: "Songs of the Humpback Whale" (Sound Sheet). 24-24B, Jan. 1979

RE-CREATING a Vanished World. By Russell D. Guthrie. 294-301, Mar. 1972

RE-CREATING Madagascar's Giant Extinct Bird. By Alexander Wetmore. 488-493, Oct. 1967

RECREATIONAL AIRCRAFT:
• The Bird Men. By Luis Marden. Photos by Charles O'Rear. Contents: Ultralights. 198-217, Aug. 1983
• Electricity From the Sun. Contents: The solar-powered aircraft, *Gossamer Penguin*. 40-41, *Special Report on Energy* (Feb. 1981)
• The Flight of the *Gossamer Condor*. By Michael E. Long. Contents: Human-powered aircraft. 130-140, Jan. 1978
• Happy Birthday, Otto Lilienthal! By Russell Hawkes. Photos by James Collison. Contents: Hang gliders. 286-292, Feb. 1972
• Oshkosh: America's Biggest Air Show. By Michael E. Long. Photos by James A. Sugar and the author. Contents: The annual convention of the Experimental Aircraft Association. 365-375, Sept. 1979
• Sailors of the Sky. By Gordon Young. Photos by Emory Kristof and Jack Fields. Paintings by Davis Meltzer. Contents: Sailplanes. 49-73, Jan. 1967
• The Thousand-mile Glide. By Karl Striedieck. Photos by Otis Imboden. Contents: Sailplanes. 431-438, Mar. 1978
• Winged Victory of *Gossamer Albatross*. By Bryan Allen. Contents: Human-powered aircraft. 640-651, Nov. 1979
• World War I Aircraft Fly Again in Rhinebeck's Rickety Rendezvous. By Harvey Arden. Photos by Howard Sochurek. 578-587, Oct. 1970

RECYCLING:
• The Fascinating World of Trash. By Peter T. White. Photos by Louie Psihoyos. 424-457, Apr. 1983
• Pollution, Threat to Man's Only Home. By Gordon Young. Photos by James P. Blair. 738-781, Dec. 1970
• The Wild World of Compost. By Cecil E. Johnson. Photos by Bianca Lavies. 273-284, Aug. 1980

RED CROSS:
• The American Red Cross: A Century of Service. By Louise Levathes. Photos by Annie Griffiths. 777-791, June 1981
• Scenes of Postwar Finland. By La Verne Bradley. Photos by Jerry Waller. Included: American Red Cross, Finnish Red Cross. 233-264, Aug. 1947

RED MANGROVES:
• The Tree Nobody Liked. By Rick Gore. Photos by Bianca Lavies. 669-689, May 1977

RED ROCK LAKES NATIONAL WILDLIFE REFUGE, Montana:
• Return of the Trumpeter (Swan). By Frederick Kent Truslow. 134-150, July 1960

RED SEA:
• At Home in the Sea (Underwater Lodge). By Jacques-Yves Cousteau. 465-507, Apr. 1964
• *Calypso* Explores for Underwater Oil. By Jacques-Yves Cousteau. NGS research grant. 155-184, Aug. 1955
• Camera Under the Sea. By Luis Marden. NGS research grant. 162-200, Feb. 1956
• Exploring Davy Jones's Locker with *Calypso*. By Jacques-Yves Cousteau. Photos by Luis Marden. NGS research grant. 149-161, Feb. 1956
• Fish Men Explore a New World Undersea. By Jacques-Yves Cousteau. 431-472, Oct. 1952
• Flashlight Fish of the Red Sea. By Eugenie Clark. Photos by David Doubilet. 719-728, Nov. 1978
• Hidden Life of an Undersea Desert. By Eugenie Clark. Photos by David Doubilet. 129-144, July 1983
• The Red Sea's Gardens of Eels. By Eugenie Clark. Photos by James L. Stanfield and David Doubilet. NGS research grant. 724-735, Nov. 1972
• The Red Sea's Sharkproof Fish. By Eugenie Clark. Photos by David Doubilet. NGS research grant. 718-727, Nov. 1974
• The Strangest Sea. By Eugenie Clark. Photos by David Doubilet. 338-365, Sept. 1975
Rainbow World Beneath the Red Sea. 344-365

REDFORD, ROBERT: Author:
• Riding the Outlaw Trail. Photos by Jonathan Blair. 622-657, Nov. 1976

Q R

REDISCOVERING America's Forgotten Crops. By Noel D. Vietmeyer. Photos by Burgess Blevins. Paintings by Paul M. Breeden. 702-712, May 1981

REDWOOD NATIONAL PARK, California:
- Editorial. By Gilbert M. Grosvenor. 295, Sept. 1977
- A Park to Save the Tallest Trees. By Melville Bell Grosvenor. 62-64, July 1966

REDWOODS:
- Editorial. By Gilbert M. Grosvenor. 295, Sept. 1977
- Finding the Mt. Everest of All Living Things. By Paul A. Zahl. 10-51, July 1964
- A Park to Save the Tallest Trees. By Melville Bell Grosvenor. 62-64, July 1966
- Redwoods, Rain, and Lots of Room: California's North Coast. By Judith and Neil Morgan. Photos by Dewitt Jones. 330-363, Sept. 1977
- World's Tallest Tree Discovered. By Melville Bell Grosvenor. Photos by George F. Mobley. 1-9, July 1964

REED, ELIZABETH C.: Author:
- White Tiger in My House. Photos by Donna K. Grosvenor. 482-491, Apr. 1970

REED, NORMAN D.: Photographer:
- The Swallow-tailed Kite: Graceful Aerialist of the Everglades. 496-505, Oct. 1972

REED, THEODORE H.: Author:
- Enchantress! (White Tigress). Photos by Thomas J. Abercrombie. 628-641, May 1961
- What's Black and White and Loved All Over? Photos by Donna K. Grosvenor. 803-815, Dec. 1972

REED SHIPS. *See Ra II; Tigris*

REEDY, JAMES R.: Author:
- First Flight Across the Bottom of the World (Cape Town to Christchurch). Photos by Otis Imboden. 454-464, Mar. 1964

REEF SHARKS:
- Into the Lairs of "Sleeping" Sharks. By Eugenie Clark. Photos by David Doubilet. NGS research grant. 570-584, Apr. 1975

REEFS. *See* Corals and Coral Reefs; Great Bahama Bank; Great Sand Barrier Reef

REFORESTATION:
- Park at the Top of the World: Mount Everest National Park. By Rick Ridgeway. Photos by Nicholas DeVore III. 704-725, June 1982
- Timber: How Much Is Enough? By John J. Putman. Photos by Bruce Dale. 485-511, Apr. 1974

The **REFORMATION:**
- The World of Martin Luther. By Merle Severy. Photos by James L. Amos. 418-463, Oct. 1983

REFUGEES:
- Bangladesh: The Nightmare of Famine. By Steve Raymer. 33-39, July 1975
- Beirut–Up From the Rubble. By William S. Ellis. Photos by Steve McCurry. Included: Palestinian refugees. 262-286, Feb. 1983
- Editorial. By Wilbur E. Garrett. 713, June 1981
- Ethiopia: Revolution in an Ancient Empire. By Robert Caputo. 614-645, May 1983
- Florida–A Time for Reckoning. By William S. Ellis. Photos by Nathan Benn and Kevin Fleming. Included: Cubans, Haitians. 172-219, Aug. 1982
- Freedom Flight from Hungary. By Robert F. Sisson. 424-436, Mar. 1957
- Home to the Holy Land. By Maynard Owen Williams. 707-746, Dec. 1950
- Honduras: Eye of the Storm. By Mike Edwards. Photos by David Alan Harvey. Included: Nicaraguan and Salvadoran refugees. 608-637, Nov. 1983
- Hong Kong Hangs On. By George W. Long. Photos by J. Baylor Roberts. 239-272, Feb. 1954
- Hong Kong Has Many Faces. By John Scofield. 1-41, Jan. 1962
- Hong Kong's Refugee Dilemma. By William S. Ellis. Photos by William Albert Allard. Included: Ethnic Chinese from Vietnam. 709-732, Nov. 1979
- Jerusalem, the Divided City. By John Scofield. Photos by Brian Brake. 492-531, Apr. 1959
- Little Tibet in Switzerland. By Laura Pilarski. Photos by Fred Mayer. 711-727, Nov. 1968
- The Mekong, River of Terror and Hope. By Peter T. White. Photos by W. E. Garrett. 737-787, Dec. 1968
- One Family's Odyssey to America. By John Everingham. Contents: Laotians. 642-661, May 1980
- Pakistan Under Pressure. By William S. Ellis. Photos by James L. Stanfield. Included: Afghans. 668-701, May 1981
- Passage to Freedom in Viet Nam. By Gertrude Samuels. 858-874, June 1955
- Somalia's Hour of Need. By Robert Paul Jordan. Photos by Michael S. Yamashita and Kevin Fleming. 748-775, June 1981
Encampments of the Dispossessed (Ethiopians from Ogaden region). By Larry Kohl. 756-763
- Thailand: Refuge From Terror. By W. E. Garrett. Included: Cambodians, Laotians, Vietnamese. 633-642, May 1980
- Troubled Odyssey of Vietnamese Fishermen. By Harvey Arden. Photos by Steve Wall. 378-395, Sept. 1981
- *See also* Cuban Refugees; Hmong; Kazaks; *and* Berlin; Cyprus; Jerusalem; Jordan; Korea; Mali; Suez Canal; Taiwan; Vietnam

REFUGES. *See* Animal Orphanage; Bird Sanctuaries and Rookeries; Game Preserves; National Parks; Wildlife Refuges

REFUSE:
- The Fascinating World of Trash. By Peter T. White. Photos by Louie Psihoyos. 424-457, Apr. 1983

REGAL Treasures From a Macedonian Tomb. By Manolis Andronicos. Photos by Spyros Tsavdaroglou. 55-77, July 1978

REGATTAS. *See* Yachting

REGENT'S PARK, London England:
- London's Zoo of Zoos. By Thomas Garner James. Included: Regent's Park; Whipsnade. 771-786, June 1953

REGGIO CALABRIA, Italy:
- Warriors From a Watery Grave. By Joseph Alsop. Contents: The Riace bronzes, two heroic Greek sculptures, now at the museum in Reggio Calabria. 821-827, June 1983

REICHE, MARIA:
- Mystery of the Ancient Nazca Lines. By Loren McIntyre. 716-728, May 1975

REIGER, GEORGE: Author:
- Humble Masterpieces: Decoys. Photos by Kenneth Garrett. 639-663, Nov. 1983

REINDEER:
- Hunters of the Lost Spirit: Lapps. By Priit J. Vesilind. Photos by Sisse Brimberg. 194-197, Feb. 1983
- Lapland's Reindeer Roundup. 109-116, July 1949
- North with Finland's Lapps. By Jean and Franc Shor. 249-280, Aug. 1954
- Norway's Reindeer Lapps. By Sally Anderson. Photos by Erik Borg. 364-379, Sept. 1977
- People of the Long Spring. By Yuri Rytkheu. Photos by Dean Conger. 206-223, Feb. 1983
- *See also* Caribou

REKHI, JOGINDER SINGH:
Author-Photographer:
- A Sikh Discovers America. 558-590, Oct. 1964

RELICS, Religious. *See* Mount Athos, Greece; St. Catherine's Monastery; Shroud of Turin

RELICS From the Rapids. By Sigurd F. Olson. Photos by David S. Boyer. 413-435, Sept. 1963

RELIEF ORGANIZATIONS. *See* Red Cross

RELIGIONS AND RELIGIOUS GROUPS:
◆ *Great Religions of the World.* Announced. Included: Buddhism, Christianity, Hinduism, Islam, Judaism. 587-590, Oct. 1971
• *See also* Animism; Buddhism; Caodaism; Cargo Cults; Christianity; Hinduism; Islam; Judaism; Kalash; Shintoism

RELIGIOUS CEREMONIES AND FESTIVALS:
Animist:
• Expedition to the Land of the Tiwi (Melville Island). By Charles P. Mountford. Included: Australian Aboriginal funeral ceremonies. 417-440, Mar. 1956
• Foxes Foretell the Future in Mali's Dogon Country. By Pamela Johnson Meyer. 431-448, Mar. 1969
• Inside the Sacred Hopi Homeland. By Jake Page. Photos by Susanne Page. Included: Pilgrimages to sacred Hopi shrines. 607-629, Nov. 1982
• Taboos and Magic Rule Namba Lives. By Kal Muller. Included: Funeral ceremony. 57-83, Jan. 1972
• *See also* Kachinas
Buddhist:
• Cambodia: Indochina's "Neutral" Corner. By Thomas J. Abercrombie. 514-551, Oct. 1964
• Gangtok, Cloud-wreathed Himalayan Capital. By John Scofield. Included: Funeral of Princess Sonam Padaun. 689-713, Nov. 1970
• Kunming Pilgrimage. Included: New Year celebration. 213-226, Feb. 1950
• Mustang, Remote Realm in Nepal. By Michel Peissel. 579-604, Oct. 1965
• My Life in Forbidden Lhasa. By Heinrich Harrer. 1-48, July 1955
• Trek to Nepal's Sacred Crystal Mountain. By Joel F. Ziskin. Included: Pilgrimage centers in Dolpo. 500-517, Apr. 1977
Christian:
• Bruges, the City the Sea Forgot. By Luis Marden. Included: Play of the Holy Blood. 631-665, May 1955
• The Camargue, Land of Cowboys and Gypsies. By Eugene L. Kammerman. Included: Fete of the Two St. Marys and Gypsy Festival of St. Sarah. 667-699, May 1956
• Fátima: Beacon for Portugal's Faithful. By Jane Vessels. Photos by Bruno Barbey. Included: Annual pilgrimages to Fátima. 832-839, Dec. 1980
• France Meets the Sea in Brittany. By Howell Walker. Included: *pardons*. 470-503, Apr. 1965
• France's Wild, Watery South, the Camargue. By William Davenport. Included: Fete of the Two St. Marys and Gypsy Festival of St. Sarah. 696-726, May 1973
• Gloucester Blesses Its Portuguese Fleet. By Luis Marden. Contents: Blessing of the Fleet. 75-84, July 1953

BRUNO BARBEY, MAGNUM

Fátima: sacred statue on way to shrine

• Lost Kingdom in Indian Mexico. By Justin Locke. Included: Christmas celebrations. 517-546, Oct. 1952
• Pilgrimage to Holy Island and the Farnes. By John E. H. Nolan. Included: Lindisfarne, an English pilgrimage center. 547-570, Oct. 1952
• Pilgrims Follow the Christmas Star. By Maynard Owen Williams. Included: Pilgrimages to the Holy Land. 831-840, Dec. 1952
• South to Mexico City. By W. E. Garrett. Included: Day of the Dead, Feast of the Assumption of the Virgin. 145-193, Aug. 1968
• Sponge Fishermen of Tarpon Springs. By Jennie E. Harris. Included: Greek Orthodox "Feast of Lights" (Epiphany). 119-136, Jan. 1947
• Vézelay, Hill of the Pilgrims. By Melvin Hall. Note: Vézelay is a French pilgrimage center. 229-247, Feb. 1953
• *See also* Corpus Christi Celebration; Holy Week
Hindu:
• Angkor, Jewel of the Jungle. By W. Robert Moore. Paintings by Maurice Fiévet. 517-569, Apr. 1960
• Bali by the Back Roads. By Donna K. and Gilbert M. Grosvenor. Included: Trance dancers. 657-697, Nov. 1969
• Bali Celebrates a Festival of Faith. By Peter Miller. Photos by Fred and Margaret Eiseman. Contents: Eka Dasa Rudra. 416-427, Mar. 1980
• Ceylon, the Resplendent Land. By Donna K. and Gilbert M. Grosvenor. Included: Firewalking ceremony. 447-497, Apr. 1966
• The Cobra, India's "Good Snake." By Harry Miller. Photos by author and Naresh and Rajesh Bedi. Included: Naga Panchami (Serpent Festival). 393-409, Sept. 1970
• Disaster in Paradise (Bali). By Windsor P. Booth. Photos by Robert F. Sisson. Included: Ceremonies to halt a volcano's eruption. 436-447, Sept. 1963
• From the Hair of Siva. By Helen and Frank Schreider. Included: Pilgrimages to the Ganges for ritual bathing. 445-503, Oct. 1960
• The Ganges, River of Faith. By John J. Putman. Photos by Raghubir Singh. Included: Pilgrimages to the Ganges for ritual bathing. 445-483, Oct. 1971
• Himalayan Pilgrimage. By Christopher Rand. Contents: Pilgrimage to Amarnath Cave, India. 520-535, Oct. 1956
• India in Crisis. By John Scofield. Included: Pushkar Fair, Divali (Festival of Lights). 599-661, May 1963
• Mysore Celebrates the Death of a Demon. By Luc Bouchage. Photos by Ylla. Included: Dasara (Festival of Ten Days). 706-711, May 1958
• Orissa, Past and Promise in an Indian State. By Bart McDowell. Photos by James P. Blair. Included: Jagannath and Shivaratri. 546-577, Oct. 1970

SELF-PORTRAIT, 1512, BIBLIOTECA REALE, TURIN

CZARTÓRYSKI MUSEUM, KRAKÓW, POLAND

Leonardo da Vinci: a man for all ages, *top;* Cecilia Gallerani, *above*

Islam:
• Desert Sheikdoms of Arabia's Pirate Coast. By Ronald Codrai. Included: Sufi ceremony. 65-104, July 1956
• Weighing the Aga Khan in Diamonds. Photos by David J. Carnegie. 317-324, Mar. 1947
• *See also* Hajj
Kalash Religion:
• Pakistan's Kalash: People of Fire and Fervor. By Debra Denker. Photos by Steve McCurry. Included: Chaomos festival. 458-473, Oct. 1981
Shinto:
• Day of the Rice God. Photos by H. Edward Kim. Text by Douglas Lee. Contents: The rice-transplanting festival in Chiyoda. 78-85, July 1978
Taoist:
• Taiwan: The Watchful Dragon. By Helen and Frank Schreider. Included: *pai-pai,* a Taoist temple festival. 1-45, Jan. 1969

REMOTE SENSING:
• Remote Sensing: New Eyes to See the World. By Kenneth F. Weaver. 46-73, Jan. 1969
• Satellites That Serve Us. By Thomas Y. Canby. Included: A portfolio: Images of Earth. 281-335, Sept. 1983
Spacelab 1: *Columbia.* By Michael E. Long. 301-307
• *See also* Landsat

REMOTELY PILOTED VEHICLE (RPV):
• Exploring a 140-year-old Ship Under Arctic Ice *(Breadalbane).* By Joseph B. MacInnis. Photos by Emory Kristof. 104A-104D, July 1983
• Ghost Ships of the War of 1812: *Hamilton* and *Scourge.* By Daniel A. Nelson. Photos by Emory Kristof. Paintings by Richard Schlecht. 289-313, Mar. 1983

The **RENAISSANCE:**
• Florence Rises From the Flood. By Joseph Judge. Included: Renaissance art and architecture. 1-43, July 1967
• Henry VIII's Lost Warship: *Mary Rose.* By Margaret Rule. Introduction and picture text by Peter Miller. Paintings by Richard Schlecht. 646-675, May 1983
• Leonardo da Vinci: A Man for All Ages. By Kenneth MacLeish. Photos by James L. Amos. 296-329, Sept. 1977
◆ *The Renaissance: Maker of Modern Man.* Announced. 588-592, Oct. 1970; rev. ed. 1977
• The Renaissance Lives On in Tuscany. By Luis Marden. Photos by Albert Moldvay. 626-659, Nov. 1974
• Restoration Reveals the "Last Supper." By Carlo Bertelli. Photos by Victor R. Boswell, Jr. 664-685, Nov. 1983
• River of Counts and Kings: The Loire. By Kenneth MacLeish. Photos by Dean Conger. Included: Renaissance architecture. 822-869, June 1966
• *See also* The Reformation

RENFREW, COLIN: Author:
• Ancient Bulgaria's Golden Treasures. Photos by James L. Stanfield. Paintings by Jean-Leon Huens. 112-129, July 1980
• Ancient Europe Is Older Than We Thought. Photos by Adam Woolfitt. 615-623, Nov. 1977

RENNER, F. G.: Author:
• Erosion, Trojan Horse of Greece. 793-812, Dec. 1947

REPORT from the Locust Wars. By Tony and Dickey Chapelle. 545-562, Apr. 1953

REPORT on Laos. By Peter T. White. Photos by W. E. Garrett. 241-275, Aug. 1961

REPRINTING Brings Earliest Geographics to Life. By Melvin M. Payne. 688-689, Nov. 1964

REPTILES:
◆ *Creepy Crawly Things: Reptiles and Amphibians.* Announced. 728-730, Nov. 1974
• London's Zoo of Zoos. By Thomas Garner James. 771-786, June 1953
• The Lure of the Changing Desert. 817-824, June 1954
▪ Reptiles and Amphibians. 875A-875B, Dec. 1968
• Wild Cargo: the Business of Smuggling Animals. By Noel Grove. Photos by Steve Raymer. Included: Crocodiles, Lizards, Pythons, Sea Turtles. 287-315, Mar. 1981
• Zoo Animals Go to School. By Marion P. McCrane. Photos by W. E. Garrett. 694-706, Nov. 1956
• *See also* Alligators; Caimans; Crocodilians; Dinosaurs; Iguanas; Komodo Dragons; Lizards; Snakes; Tortoises; Turtles

REPUBLICAN Indonesia Tries Its Wings. By W. Robert Moore. 1-40, Jan. 1951

REQUIEM for a Tribe? Brazil's Kreen-Akarores. By W. Jesco von Puttkamer. 254-269, Feb. 1975

REQUIEM SHARKS:
• Into the Lairs of "Sleeping" Sharks. By Eugenie Clark. Photos by David Doubilet. NGS research grant. 570-584, Apr. 1975

RESCUE CRAFT:
• Tomorrow on the Deep Frontier. By Edwin A. Link. NGS research grant. 778-801, June 1964
• *See also* Helicopters

RESCUE WORK:
• The American Red Cross: A Century of Service. By Louise Levathes. Photos by Annie Griffiths. Included: Red Cross Certificates of Merit. 777-791, June 1981
• Earthquake in Guatemala. By Bart McDowell. Photos by W. E. Garrett and Robert W. Madden. Included: An international volunteer effort. 810-829, June 1976
• *See also* Air Rescue; Civil Air Patrol; Diving Bell; Great St. Bernard

Hospice; Military Air Transport Service; School for Survival; U. S. Coast Guard

RESCUING the Rothschild. By Carolyn Bennett Patterson. 419-421, Sept. 1977

RESEARCH REPORTS, NGS:
◆ Research Reports. Compiled and edited by Paul H. Oehser. *1890-1954 Projects*. 442, Sept. 1975; *1955-1960 Projects*. 444, Sept. 1972; *1963 Projects*. 296, Aug. 1968; *1964 Projects*. 300, Aug. 1969; *1965 Projects*. 148, July 1971; *1966 Projects*. 146, July 1973; *1967 Projects*. 148, July 1974; *1968 Projects*. 296, Aug. 1976
◆ Research Reports. Compiled and edited by Paul H. Oehser and John S. Lea. *1969 Projects*. 294, Feb. 1978; *1970 Projects*. 298, Aug. 1979
◆ Research Reports. Compiled and edited by John S. Lea and Nancy Link Powars. *1971 Projects*. 480, Mar. 1981; *1971 and 1972 Projects*. 830, June 1982; *1973 Projects* and *1974 Projects*. 706, Nov. 1983

RESEARCH VESSELS:
● Antarctica's Nearer Side. By Samuel W. Matthews. Photos by William R. Curtsinger. Included: *Alpha Helix, Bransfield, Endurance, Hero, Professor Viese*. 622-655, Nov. 1971
● How We Found the *Monitor*. By John G. Newton. Included: *Alcoa Seaprobe, Eastward*. NGS research grant. 48-61, Jan. 1975
● Project FAMOUS. Photos by Emory Kristof. Included: *Glomar Challenger; Knorr*, R.V.; *Mizar*, U.S.N.S.; and submersibles *Alvin; Archimède; Cyana; Lulu*. 586-615, May 1975
I. Where the Earth Turns Inside Out. By J. R. Heirtzler. 586-603; II. Dive Into the Great Rift. By Robert D. Ballard. 604-615
● Science Explores the Monsoon Sea. By Samuel W. Matthews. Photos by Robert F. Sisson. 554-575, Oct. 1967
● *Thresher:* Lesson and Challenge. By James H. Wakelin, Jr. Included: *Atlantis II, Conrad, Gilliss*. 759-763, June 1964
● *See also Alvin; Asherah; Calypso; Deepstar; Glomar Challenger; John Elliott Pillsbury; Sea Diver*

RESOLUTE BAY, Canada:
● Diving Beneath Arctic Ice. By Joseph B. MacInnis. Photos by William R. Curtsinger. 248-267, Aug. 1973

RESOLUTION (Sloop):
● Captain Cook: The Man Who Mapped the Pacific. By Alan Villiers. Photos by Gordon W. Gahan. 297-349, Sept. 1971

RESOURCE MANAGEMENT:
● Aldo Leopold: "A Durable Scale of Values." By Boyd Gibbons. Photos by Jim Brandenburg. 682-708, Nov. 1981
● *See also* Land Use

RESOURCE RECOVERY. *See* Recycling

A **RESTLESS** Nation Moves West. By Frank Freidel. 80-121, Jan. 1965

RESTORATION Reveals the "Last Supper." By Carlo Bertelli. Photos by Victor R. Boswell, Jr. 664-685, Nov. 1983

RESURRECTING the Grandeur of Tikal. By William R. Coe. 792-798, Dec. 1975

RESURRECTING the Oldest Known Greek Ship. By Michael L. Katzev. Photos by Bates Littlehales. NGS research grant. 841-857, June 1970

RETRACING John Wesley Powell's Historic Voyage Down the Grand Canyon. By Joseph Judge. Photos by Walter Meayers Edwards. 668-713, May 1969

RETTIG, NEIL L.:
Photographer:
● Saving the Philippine Eagle. By Robert S. Kennedy. Photos by Alan R. Degen, Neil L. Rettig, and Wolfgang A. Salb. 847-856, June 1981

THE RETURN OF DOVE (Sloop):
● Robin Sails Home. By Robin Lee Graham. 504-545, Oct. 1970

RETURN of the Sea Otter. By Karl W. Kenyon. Photos by James A. Mattison, Jr. 520-539, Oct. 1971

RETURN of the Trumpeter. By Frederick Kent Truslow. 134-150, July 1960

RETURN to Changing China. By Audrey Topping. 801-833, Dec. 1971

RETURN to Estonia. By Priit J. Vesilind. Photos by Cotton Coulson. 485-511, Apr. 1980

RETURN to Lonely Tristan da Cunha. By James P. Blair. 60-81, Jan. 1964

RETURN to Oases of the Deep. By Robert D. Ballard and J. Frederick Grassle. NGS research grant. 689-705, Nov. 1979

RETURN to Uganda. By Jerry and Sarah Kambites. Photos by Sarah Leen. 73-89, July 1980

RÉUNION (Island), Indian Ocean:
● Crosscurrents Sweep the Indian Ocean. By Bart McDowell. Photos by Steve Raymer. 422-457, Oct. 1981

REUNITED Jerusalem Faces Its Problems. By Kenneth MacLeish. Photos by Ted Spiegel. 835-871, Dec. 1968

REVIS, ANNE: Author:
● Mr. Jefferson's Charlottesville. 553-592, May 1950

REVIS, KATHLEEN:
Author-Photographer:
● Colorado by Car and Campfire. 207-248, Aug. 1954
● Skiing in the United States. 216-254, Feb. 1959
● Winter Brings Carnival Time to Quebec. 69-97, Jan. 1958

Photographer:
● The Friendly Huts of the White Mountains. By William O. Douglas. 205-239, Aug. 1961
● Landmarks of Literary England. By Leo A. Borah. 295-350, Sept. 1955
● Many-splendored Glacierland. By George W. Long. 589-636, May 1956
● Poets' Voices Linger in Scottish Shrines. By Isobel Wylie Hutchison. 437-488, Oct. 1957
● Queen of Canada (Elizabeth II). By Phyllis Wilson. 825-829, June 1959
● Soaring on Skis in the Swiss Alps. By Carolyn Bennett Patterson. 94-121, Jan. 1961
● Washington Wilderness, the North Cascades. By Edwards Park. 335-367, Mar. 1961
● Westminster, World Series of Dogdom. By John W. Cross, Jr. 91-116, Jan. 1954
● The World in Dolls. By Samuel F. Pryor. 817-831, Dec. 1959

REVOLUTION, American. *See* American Revolution

The **REVOLUTION** in American Agriculture. By Jules B. Billard. Photos by James P. Blair. 147-185, Feb. 1970

REVOLUTIONARY View of the 48 (Contiguous) States. By Barry C. Bishop. 140-147, July 1976

The **REWARDS** of Walrus-watching. By G. Carleton Ray. Photos by Bill Curtsinger. NGS research grant. 565-580, Oct. 1979

REWATI (White Tiger):
● White Tiger in My House. By Elizabeth C. Reed. Photos by Donna K. Grosvenor. 482-491, Apr. 1970

REYKJAVÍK, Iceland:
● Iceland Tapestry. By Deena Clark. 599-630, Nov. 1951
● Sailing Iceland's Rugged Coasts. By Wright Britton. Photos by James A. Sugar. 228-265, Aug. 1969

REYNOLDS, ROBERT J.:
Author-Photographer:
● Over the Sea to Scotland's Skye. 87-112, July 1952

RHESUS MONKEYS:
● Temple Monkeys of Nepal. By Jane Teas. 575-584, Apr. 1980

RHINE (River), Europe:
● The Rhine: Europe's River of Legend. By William Graves. Photos by Bruce Dale. 449-499, Apr. 1967

RHINEBECK, New York:
● World War I Aircraft Fly Again in Rhinebeck's Rickety Rendezvous. By Harvey Arden. Photos by Howard Sochurek. 578-587, Oct. 1970

RHINOCEROSES:
● Ancient Ashfall Creates a Pompeii of Prehistoric Animals. By Michael R. Voorhies. Photos by Annie Griffiths. Paintings by Jay Matternes. 66-75, Jan. 1981
● Stalking the Great Indian Rhino. By Lee Merriam Talbot. 389-398, Mar. 1957

• Where Elephants Have Right of Way. By George and Jinx Rodger. Included: Black Rhinoceros, White Rhinoceros. 363-389, Sept. 1960
• Wild Cargo: the Business of Smuggling Animals. By Noel Grove. Photos by Steve Raymer. Included: Black Rhinoceros, White Rhinoceros; and Rhino horn trade. 287-315, Mar. 1981

RHOADES, ROBERT E.: Author:
• The Incredible Potato. Photos by Martin Rogers. 668-694, May 1982

RHODE, CECIL E.:
Author-Photographer:
• When Giant Bears Go Fishing. 195-205, Aug. 1954

RHODE ISLAND:
• New England's "Little Portugal." By O. Louis Mazzatenta. 90-109, Jan. 1975
• New England's "Lively Experiment," Rhode Island. By Robert de Roos. Photos by Fred Ward. 370-401, Sept. 1968
• Rhode Island, Modern City-State. By George W. Long. Photos by Willard R. Culver. 137-170, Aug. 1948
• *See also* Newport

RHODE ISLAND (Sidewheeler):
• How We Found the *Monitor.* By John G. Newton. Note: A search area was established for the *Monitor* based on the log of *Rhode Island,* which had the *Monitor* in tow. 48-61, Jan. 1975

RHODES, CECIL:
• The British Way. By Sir Evelyn Wrench. 421-541, Apr. 1949

RHODES (Island), Greece:
• The Isles of Greece: Aegean Birthplace of Western Culture. By Melville Bell Grosvenor. Photos by Edwin Stuart Grosvenor and Winfield Parks. 147-193, Aug. 1972
• On the Winds of the Dodecanese. By Jean and Franc Shor. 351-390, Mar. 1953

RHODESIA:
• Africa: The Winds of Freedom Stir a Continent. By Nathaniel T. Kenney. Photos by W. D. Vaughn. 303-359, Sept. 1960
• Freedom's Progress South of the Sahara. By Howard La Fay. Photos by Joseph J. Scherschel. 603-637, Nov. 1962
• Rhodesia, a House Divided. By Allan C. Fisher, Jr. Photos by Thomas Nebbia. 641-671, May 1975
• Safari Through Changing Africa. By Elsie May Bell Grosvenor. Photos by Gilbert Grosvenor. 145-198, Aug. 1953
• *See also* present name, Zimbabwe

RHODODENDRONS:
• Pack Trip Through the Smokies. By Val Hart. Photos by Robert F. Sisson. 473-502, Oct. 1952
• Rhododendron Glories of Southwest Scotland. By David S. Boyer. Photos by B. Anthony Stewart and author. 641-664, May 1954
• Rhododendron Time on Roan Mountain. By Ralph Gray. 819-828, June 1957
• *See also* Azaleas

RHÔNE, France:
• Here Rest in Honored Glory; The United States Dedicates Six New Battle Monuments in Europe to Americans Who Gave Their Lives During World War II. By Howell Walker. Included: Rhône American Cemetery and Memorial. 739-768, June 1957

RHÔNE RIVER DELTA, France. *See* Camargue

RIACE BRONZES:
• Warriors From a Watery Grave (Bronze Sculptures). By Joseph Alsop. 821-827, June 1983

RIBONUCLEIC ACID (RNA):
• The Awesome Worlds Within a Cell. By Rick Gore. Photos by Bruce Dale. Paintings by Davis Meltzer. Included: The Language of Life, foldout showing replication of DNA and manufacture of RNA and proteins. 355-395, Sept. 1976

RIBOUD, MARC: Photographer:
• Cappadocia: Turkey's Country of Cones. 122-146, Jan. 1958
• Coronation in Katmandu. By E. Thomas Gilliard. 139-152, July 1957
• Pompidou Center, Rage of Paris. By Cathy Newman. 469-477, Oct. 1980

RICE GROWING:
• Backwoods Japan During American Occupation. By M. A. Huberman. 491-518, Apr. 1947
• Bangladesh: Hope Nourishes a New Nation. By William S. Ellis. Photos by Dick Durrance II. 295-333, Sept. 1972
• Day of the Rice God. Photos by H. Edward Kim. Text by Douglas Lee. Contents: Mibu Ohana-taue, a rice-transplanting festival. 78-85, July 1978
• Spirits of Change Capture the Karens. By Peter Kunstadter. 267-285, Feb. 1972

RICHARD THE LION-HEARTED:
• The British Way. By Sir Evelyn Wrench. 421-541, Apr. 1949

RICHARDS, BILL: Author:
• Henry Hudson's Changing Bay. Photos by David Hiser. 380-405, Mar. 1982
• Powder River Basin: New Energy Frontier. Photos by Louie Psihoyos. 96-113, *Special Report on Energy* (Feb. 1981)
• The Uncertain State of Puerto Rico. Photos by Stephanie Maze. 516-543, Apr. 1983
• The Untamed Yellowstone. Photos by Dean Krakel II. 257-278, Aug. 1981

RICHELIEU (River), Canada:
• North Through History Aboard *White Mist.* By Melville Bell Grosvenor. Photos by Edwin Stuart Grosvenor. 1-55, July 1970

RICKER, P. L.: Author-Photographer:
• American Wild Flower Odyssey. 603-634, May 1953

RIDDLE of the Glyphs. By George E. Stuart. Photos by Otis Imboden. 768-791, Dec. 1975

RIDGEWAY, RICK: Author:
• Park at the Top of the World: Mount Everest National Park. Photos by Nicholas DeVore III. 704-725, June 1982

RIDING SCHOOL. *See* Spanish Riding School

RIDING the Outlaw Trail. By Robert Redford. Photos by Jonathan Blair. 622-657, Nov. 1976

RIDLEY TURTLES. *See* Pacific Ridley Turtles

RIFLE BIRDS. *See* Birds of Paradise

RIFTS, Ocean-floor:
• New World of the Ocean. By Samuel W. Matthews. 792-832, Dec. 1981
• This Changing Earth. By Samuel W. Matthews. 1-37, Jan. 1973
• *See also* Cayman Trough; Galapagos Rift; Japan Trough; Mariana Trench; Mid-Atlantic Rift; Romanche Trench

RIGGERT, TOM: Author:
• Skylab's Fiery Finish. 581-584, Oct. 1979

RIGHT WHALES:
• At Home With Right Whales. By Roger Payne. Photos by Des and Jen Bartlett. NGS research grant. 322-339, Mar. 1976
• Swimming With Patagonia's Right Whales. By Roger Payne. Photos by William R. Curtsinger and Charles R. Nicklin, Jr. NGS research grant. 576-587, Oct. 1972

RINGLING BROS. AND BARNUM & BAILEY CIRCUS:
• The Wonder City That Moves by Night. By Francis Beverly Kelley. 289-324, Mar. 1948

RIO DE JANEIRO, Brazil:
• Brazil, Ôba! By Peter T. White. Photos by Winfield Parks. 299-353, Sept. 1962
• Brazil's Golden Beachhead. By Bart McDowell. Photos by Nicholas DeVore III. 246-277, Feb. 1978
• Spectacular Rio de Janeiro. By Hernane Tavares de Sá. Photos by Charles Allmon. 289-328, Mar. 1955

RIO GRANDE (River), U. S.-Mexico:
• Our Wild and Scenic Rivers: The Rio Grande. By Nathaniel T. Kenney. Photos by Bank Langmore. 46-51, July 1977
• Two Wheels Along the Mexican Border. By William Albert Allard. 591-635, May 1971
• *See also* Big Bend National Park, Texas

RÍO INDIO (Town and River), Panama:
• Hunting Prehistory in Panama Jungles. By Matthew W. Stirling. Photos by Richard H. Stewart. 271-290, Aug. 1953

RÍO MUNI (Spanish Province), Africa:
• In Quest of the World's Largest Frog. By Paul A. Zahl. 146-152, July 1967

• "Snowflake," the World's First White Gorilla. By Arthur J. Riopelle. Photos by Paul A. Zahl. NGS research grant. 443-448, Mar. 1967

RIOPELLE, ARTHUR J.: Author:
• Growing Up With Snowflake. Photos by Michael Kuh. 491-503, Oct. 1970
• "Snowflake," the World's First White Gorilla. Photos by Paul A. Zahl. 443-448, Mar. 1967

RIP VAN WINKLE of the Underground. By Kenneth F. Weaver. 133-142, July 1953

RIPLEY, S. DILLON: Author:
• Peerless Nepal–A Naturalist's Paradise. Photos by Volkmar Wentzel. 1-40, Jan. 1950
• Saving the Nene, World's Rarest Goose. Photos by Jerry Chong. 745-754, Nov. 1965
• Strange Courtship of Birds of Paradise. Paintings by Walter A. Weber. 247-278, Feb. 1950
Author-Photographer:
• Roaming India's Naga Hills. 247-264, Feb. 1955

RIPLEY, California:
• Seeking the Secret of the Giants. By Frank M. Setzler. Photos by Richard H. Stewart. 390-404, Sept. 1952

RISK and Reward on Alaska's Violent Gulf. By Boyd Gibbons. Photos by Steve Raymer. 237-267, Feb. 1979

RITUALS and Spells Shape Gimi Lives. By Gillian Gillison. Photos by David Gillison. 124-146, July 1977

RIVER GYPSY (Houseboat):
• The Jungle Was My Home. By Sasha Siemel. 695-712, Nov. 1952

RIVER of Counts and Kings: The Loire. By Kenneth MacLeish. Photos by Dean Conger. 822-869, June 1966

RIVER of Sorrow, River of Hope: The Niger. By Georg Gerster. 152-189, Aug. 1975

RIVER OTTERS:
• Giant Otters: "Big Water Dogs" in Peril. By Nicole Duplaix. Photos by the author and Bates Littlehales. 130-142, July 1980

RIVER PRESERVATION. *See* National Wild and Scenic Rivers System

A **RIVER** Restored: Oregon's Willamette. By Ethel A. Starbird. Photos by Lowell J. Georgia. 816-835, June 1972

RIVERS AND RIVER TRIPS:
◆ *America's Wild and Scenic Rivers.* 1983
• The Civilizing Seine. By Charles McCarry. Photos by David L. Arnold. 478-511, Apr. 1982
• The Coast Guard: Small Service With a Big Mission. By William S. Ellis. 113-139, July 1974
• Cruising Florida's Western Waterways. By Rube Allyn. Photos by Bates Littlehales. Contents: Chassahowitzka, Crystal, Homosassa, Suwannee, Weekiwachee, Withlacoochee. 49-76, Jan. 1955

HAROLD E. EDGERTON

Circus: performing unicyclists

• Desert River Through Navajo Land. By Alfred M. Bailey. Photos by author and Fred G. Brandenburg. Contents: A 200-mile journey down the swift San Juan and Colorado Rivers, from Mexican Hat, Utah, to Lees Ferry, Arizona. 149-172, Aug. 1947
• Following the Trail of Lewis and Clark. By Ralph Gray. 707-750, June 1953
• From Sagebrush to Roses on the Columbia. By Leo A. Borah. Contents: Columbia River and Basin, Willamette River and Valley, Yakima River region. 571-611, Nov. 1952
• Geographical Twins a World Apart. By David S. Boyer. Included: A comparison of the Jordan River in the Holy Land with its namesake in Utah. 848-859, Dec. 1958
• Hunting Prehistory in Panama Jungles. By Matthew W. Stirling. Photos by Richard H. Stewart. Included: Cascaja, Coclé del Norte, Coclecito, Indio. NGS research grant. 271-290, Aug. 1953
• Inside Europe Aboard *Yankee*. By Irving and Electa Johnson. Photos by Joseph J. Scherschel. 157-195, Aug. 1964
• Jungle Jaunt on Amazon Headwaters. By Bernice M. Goetz. Contents: Aiari, Querari, Vaupés. 371-388, Sept. 1952
• Jungle Journey to the World's Highest Waterfall. By Ruth Robertson. Included: Acanán, Carrao, and Churún Rivers. 655-690, Nov. 1949
• The Jungle Was My Home. By Sasha Siemel. Included: Cara Cara, Miranda, Paraguay, Paraguay-mirim (Estuary). 695-712, Nov. 1952
• Labrador Canoe Adventure. By Andrew Brown and Ralph Gray. Contents: Ashuanipi, Atikonak, Hamilton, Unknown. 65-99, July 1951
• A Map Maker Looks at the United States. By Newman Bumstead. Included: Arkansas, Chicago, Colorado, Columbia, Dosewallips, Duckabush, East (New York), Elwha, Gunnison, McCloud, Mississippi, Niagara, Pit, Potomac, Rock, Sacramento, Snake, Spokane. 705-748, June 1951
• My Chesapeake–Queen of Bays. By Allan C. Fisher, Jr. Photos by Lowell Georgia. Included: Choptank; Elizabeth; Goldsborough Creek; James; Potomac; Spa Creek; Susquehanna; Town Creek; Tred Avon. 428-467, Oct. 1980
• Nahanni: Canada's Wilderness Park. By Douglas H. Chadwick. Photos by Matt Bradley. Included: Kayaking down the Flat and South Nahanni Rivers. 396-420, Sept. 1981
• New St. Lawrence Seaway Opens the Great Lakes to the World. By Andrew H. Brown. 299-339, Mar. 1959
• North Through History Aboard *White Mist*. By Melville Bell Grosvenor. Photos by Edwin Stuart Grosvenor. Included: Hudson, Richelieu, Saguenay, St. Lawrence. 1-55, July 1970

QR

• Oklahoma, the Adventurous One. By Robert Paul Jordan. Photos by Robert W. Madden. Included: McClellan-Kerr Arkansas River Navigation System. 149-189, Aug. 1971
• Our Wild and Scenic Rivers. 2-59, July 1977
I. Rivers Wild and Pure: A Priceless Legacy. By Robert E. Doyle. 2-11; II. The Flathead. By Douglas H. Chadwick. Photos by Lowell Georgia. 13-19; III. The Suwannee. By Jack and Anne Rudloe. Photos by Jodi Cobb. 20-29; IV. The St. Croix. By David S. Boyer. 30-37; V. The Skagit. By David S. Boyer. 38-45; VI. The Rio Grande. By Nathaniel T. Kenney. Photos by Bank Langmore. 46-51; VII. The Noatak. By John M. Kauffmann. Photos by Sam Abell. 52-59
• Paris to Antwerp with the Water Gypsies. By David S. Boyer. Contents: Aisne, Meuse, Oise. 530-559, Oct. 1955
• Pittsburgh, Pattern for Progress. By William J. Gill. Photos by Clyde Hare. Included: Allegheny, Monongahela, Ohio. 342-371, Mar. 1965
• Pittsburgh: Workshop of the Titans. By Albert W. Atwood. Included: Allegheny, Monongahela, Ohio. 117-144, July 1949
• Pollution, Threat to Man's Only Home. By Gordon Young. Photos by James P. Blair. Included: Cuyahoga, Nile, Potomac, Rhine. 738-781, Dec. 1970
• Probing Ice Caves of the Pyrenees. By Norbert Casteret. 391-404, Mar. 1953
• Quebec's Northern Dynamo. By Larry Kohl. Photos by Ottmar Bierwagen. 406-418, Mar. 1982
• Relics from the Rapids. By Sigurd F. Olson. Photos by David S. Boyer. Included: Wild waters of the Minnesota-Ontario border. 413-435, Sept. 1963
• Sea Fever. By John E. Schultz. Contents: The author's journey on the Napo and Amazon, with detail of the tidal flood, or bore, of the latter. 237-268, Feb. 1949
• Shooting Rapids in Dinosaur Country. By Jack Breed. Photos by author and Justin Locke. Contents: Yampa and Green River gorges. 363-390, Mar. 1954
• Skylab Looks at Earth. Included: Drainage patterns and configurations for the Amazon, Atchafalaya, Colorado, Mississippi, Ohio, Salween, Uncompahgre, and White Rivers. 471-493, Oct. 1974
◆ *Still Waters, White Waters.* 1977
• A Walk and Ride on the Wild Side: Tasmania. By Carolyn Bennett Patterson. Photos by David Hiser and Melinda Berge. Included: Franklin, Lower Gordon. 676-693, May 1983
• Whatever Happened to TVA? By Gordon Young. Photos by Emory Kristof. 830-863, June 1973
• White-water Adventure on Wild Rivers of Idaho. By Frank Craighead, Jr., and John Craighead. Included: Middle Fork Salmon, Salmon, and rivers protected or proposed for protection under the Wild and Scenic Rivers Act of 1968. 213-239, Feb. 1970
▲ *Wild and Scenic Rivers of the United States,* double-sided supplement. July 1977
▮ Wild River. Included: Hudson, Middle Fork Salmon, Potomac, Salmon. 239A-239B, Feb. 1970
• *See also* Allagash Wilderness Waterway; Amazon Basin; Arno; Bow; Buffalo National River; Chattooga River; Clearwater; Colorado; Columbia River and Basin; Congo River; Connecticut River and Valley; Danube; Delaware; Detroit; Escalante Canyon, for Escalante; Euphrates; Ganges; Hudson; James; Jhelum; Juruena; Knik; Li; Loire River and Valley; Magdalena; Mekong; Merrimack; Mississippi; Missouri; Mohawk; Niger; Nile; Ob; Ohio; Potomac; Rhine; Rio Grande; Saint John River and Valley; St. Lawrence River; Sepik River; Shannon; Snake; Susquehanna; Thames; Virgin; Volga; Willamette; Yangtze; Yellowstone River; Yukon

RIVIERA (Region), Mediterranean:
• French Riviera: Storied Playground on the Azure Coast. By Carleton Mitchell. Photos by Thomas Nebbia. 798-835, June 1967
• Italian Riviera, Land That Winter Forgot. By Howell Walker. 743-789, June 1963
• *See also* Monaco; Portofino

RIYADH, Saudi Arabia:
• Saudi Arabia: The Kingdom and Its Power. By Robert Azzi. 286-333, Sept. 1980

ROACHES. *See* Cockroaches

ROADRUNNERS:
• The Roadrunner–Clown of the Desert. By Martha A. Whitson. Photos by Bruce Dale. 694-702, May 1983

ROADS. *See* Highways and Roads

ROAMING Africa's Unfenced Zoos. By W. Robert Moore. 353-380, Mar. 1950

ROAMING India's Naga Hills. By S. Dillon Ripley. 247-264, Feb. 1955

ROAMING Korea South of the Iron Curtain. By Enzo de Chetelat. 777-808, June 1950

ROAMING the West's Fantastic Four Corners. By Jack Breed. 705-742, June 1952

ROAN MOUNTAIN, Tennessee-North Carolina:
• Rhododendron Time on Roan Mountain. By Ralph Gray. 819-828, June 1957

ROANOKE ISLAND, North Carolina:
• Exploring America's Great Sand Barrier Reef. By Eugene R. Guild. Photos by John E. Fletcher and author. 325-350, Sept. 1947
• Indian Life Before the Colonists Came. By Stuart E. Jones. Engravings by Theodore de Bry, 1590. 351-368, Sept. 1947
• Lonely Cape Hatteras, Besieged by the Sea. By William S. Ellis. Photos by Emory Kristof. 393-421, Sept. 1969
• October Holiday on the Outer Banks. By Nike Anderson. Photos by J. Baylor Roberts. 501-529, Oct. 1955

ROBERT COLLEGE, Turkish Gateway to the Future. By Franc Shor. 399-418, Sept. 1957

ROBERT FROST and New England. By Archibald MacLeish. 438-444, Apr. 1976

ROBERT REDFORD Rides the Outlaw Trail. By Robert Redford. Photos by Jonathan Blair. 622-657, Nov. 1976

ROBERT V. FLEMING, 1890-1967. By Melville Bell Grosvenor. 526-529, Apr. 1968
• *See also* Fleming, Robert V.

ROBERTS, J. BAYLOR:
Author-Photographer:
• Focusing on the Tournament of Roses. By B. Anthony Stewart and J. Baylor Roberts. 805-816, June 1954
Photographer:
• Across Canada by Mackenzie's Track. By Ralph Gray. 191-239, Aug. 1955
• America Goes to the Fair. By Samuel W. Matthews. 293-333, Sept. 1954
• Around the "Great Lakes of the South." By Frederick Simpich. 463-491, Apr. 1948
• "Around the World in Eighty Days." By Newman Bumstead. 705-750, Dec. 1951
• *Bounty* Descendants Live on Remote Norfolk Island. By T. C. Roughley. 559-584, Oct. 1960
• Carnival in San Antonio. By Mason Sutherland. 813-844, Dec. 1947
• Charting Our Sea and Air Lanes. By Stuart E. Jones. 189-209, Feb. 1957
• Cruising Japan's Inland Sea. By Willard Price. 619-650, Nov. 1953
• Deep in the Heart of "Swissconsin." By William H. Nicholas. 781-800, June 1947
• Dixie Spins the Wheel of Industry. By William H. Nicholas. 281-324, Mar. 1949
• Dog Mart Day in Fredericksburg. By Frederick G. Vosburgh. 817-832, June 1951
• Formosa–Hot Spot of the East. By Frederick G. Vosburgh. 139-176, Feb. 1950
• From Indian Canoes to Submarines at Key West. By Frederick Simpich. 41-72, Jan. 1950
• Heritage of Beauty and History. By Conrad L. Wirth. 587-661, May 1958
• Hong Kong Hangs On. By George W. Long. 239-272, Feb. 1954
• Hunting the Heartbeat of a Whale. By Paul Dudley White and Samuel W. Matthews. 49-64, July 1956
• Indochina Faces the Dragon. By George W. Long. 287-328, Sept. 1952
• Iraq–Where Oil and Water Mix. By Jean and Franc Shor. 443-489, Oct. 1958

• Japan Tries Freedom's Road. By Frederick G. Vosburgh. 593-632, May 1950
• Journey Into Troubled Iran. By George W. Long. 425-464, Oct. 1951
• La Jolla, a Gem of the California Coast. By Deena Clark. 755-782, Dec. 1952
• Louisiana Trades with the World. By Frederick Simpich. 705-738, Dec. 1947
• Macau, a Hole in the Bamboo Curtain. By George W. Long. 679-688, May 1953
• Malaya Meets Its Emergency. By George W. Long. 185-228, Feb. 1953
• Men, Moose, and Mink of Northwest Angle. By William H. Nicholas. 265-284, Aug. 1947
• New Rush to Golden California. By George W. Long. 723-802, June 1954
• The Night the Mountains Moved. By Samuel W. Matthews. 329-359, Mar. 1960
• North Dakota Comes into Its Own. By Leo A. Borah. 283-322, Sept. 1951
• October Holiday on the Outer Banks. By Nike Anderson. 501-529, Oct. 1955
• Our Green Treasury, the National Forests. By Nathaniel T. Kenney. 287-324, Sept. 1956
• Our Navy in the Far East. By Arthur W. Radford. 537-577, Oct. 1953
• Over Plains and Hills of South Dakota. 563-586, May 1947
• Pittsburgh: Workshop of the Titans. By Albert W. Atwood. 117-144, July 1949
• Saving Man's Wildlife Heritage. By John H. Baker. 581-620, Nov. 1954
• Scientists Drill at Sea to Pierce Earth's Crust (Project Mohole). By Samuel W. Matthews. 686-697, Nov. 1961
• Seeing the Earth from 80 Miles Up. By Clyde T. Holliday. 511-528, Oct. 1950
• Shawneetown Forsakes the Ohio. By William H. Nicholas. 273-288, Feb. 1948
• Slow Boat to Florida. By Dorothea and Stuart E. Jones. 1-65, Jan. 1958
• This Young Giant, Indonesia. By Beverley M. Bowie. 351-392, Sept. 1955
• *Triton* Follows Magellan's Wake. By Edward L. Beach. 585-615, Nov. 1960
• Uncle Sam Bends a Twig in Germany. By Frederick Simpich. 529-550, Oct. 1948
• The Wonder City That Moves by Night. By Francis Beverly Kelley. 289-324, Mar. 1948

ROBERTS, MURRAY: Photographer:
• The Threatened Ways of Kenya's Pokot People. By Elizabeth L. Meyerhoff. 120-140, Jan. 1982

ROBERTS, WALTER ORR: Author:
• We're Doing Something About the Weather! 518-555, Apr. 1972

ROBERTSON, RUTH:
Author-Photographer:
• Jungle Journey to the World's Highest Waterfall. 655-690, Nov. 1949

ROBIN Sails Home. By Robin Lee Graham. 504-545, Oct. 1970

ROBINSON, ANNE GROSVENOR:
Author:
• Seattle, City of Two Voices. Photos by B. Anthony Stewart. 494-513, Apr. 1960

ROBINSON, G. D.: Author:
• Exploring Aleutian Volcanoes. 509-528, Oct. 1948

ROBINSON, NANCY: Author:
• Alaskan Family Robinson. Photos by John Metzger and Peter Robinson. 55-75, Jan. 1973

ROBINSON, PETER: Photographer:
• Alaskan Family Robinson. By Nancy Robinson. Photos by John Metzger and Peter Robinson. 55-75, Jan. 1973

ROBOTS:
• The Chip: Electronic Mini-marvel. By Allen A. Boraiko. Photos by Charles O'Rear. 421-457, Oct. 1982

ROBOTS to the Moon. By Frank Sartwell. Paintings by Pierre Mion. 557-571, Oct. 1962

ROCHESTER, New York:
• Eastman of Rochester: Photographic Pioneer. By Allan C. Fisher, Jr. 423-438, Sept. 1954

ROCK ART:
• Africa's Bushman Art Treasures. By Alfred Friendly. Photos by Alex R. Willcox. 848-865, June 1963
• Baja's Murals of Mystery. By Harry Crosby. Photos by Charles O'Rear. 692-702, Nov. 1980
• A Bold New Look at Our Past. The Editor. NGS research grant. 62-63, Jan. 1975
• Exploring Stone Age Arnhem Land (Australia). By Charles P. Mountford. Photos by Howell Walker. Included: Cave paintings of Oenpelli and Groote Eylandt. NGS research grant. 745-782, Dec. 1949
• Exploring the Mind of Ice Age Man. By Alexander Marshack. NGS research grant. 64-89, Jan. 1975
• Lascaux Cave, Cradle of World Art. By Norbert Casteret. Photos by Maynard Owen Williams. Contents: La Baume Ladrone, La Henne Morte, La Mouthe, Lascaux, Montespan, Niaux, Trois Frères, Tuc D'Audoubert, in France; and Altamira in Spain. NGS research grant. 771-794, Dec. 1948
• Man in the Amazon: Stone Age Present Meets Stone Age Past. By W. Jesco von Puttkamer. NGS research grant. 60-83, Jan. 1979
• Maya Art Treasures Discovered in Cave. By George E. Stuart. Photos by Wilbur E. Garrett. 220-235, Aug. 1981
• Rock Paintings of the Aborigines. By Kay and Stanley Breeden. 174-187, Feb. 1973

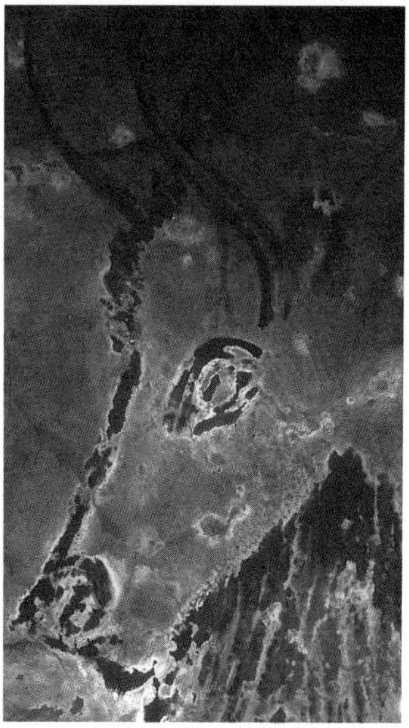

ALEXANDER MARSHACK

Ice Age Man: French rock art

Lascaux Cave: prehistoric art gallery

MAYNARD OWEN WILLIAMS, NGS

QR

PAINTING BY NED M. SEIDLER, NGS

Rock-ledge Life: animals visit ledge's rich habitat

• Tanzania's Stone Age Art. By Mary D. Leakey. Photos by John Reader. 84-99, July 1983
• Utah's Rock Art: Wilderness Louvre. A picture essay by Gary Smith, with Michael E. Long. 97-117, Jan. 1980
• *See also* Petroglyphs

ROCK CARVINGS:
• The Caves of the Thousand Buddhas. By Franc and Jean Shor. 383-415, Mar. 1951
• Darius Carved History on Ageless Rock. By George G. Cameron. 825-844, Dec. 1950
• India's Sculptured Temple Caves. By Volkmar Wentzel. 665-678, May 1953
• Searching Out Medieval Churches in Ethiopia's Wilds. By Georg Gerster. 856-884, Dec. 1970
• *See also* Cappadocia; Petra

ROCK CLIMBING:
• Climbing Half Dome the Hard Way. By Galen Rowell. 782-791, June 1974
• We Climbed Utah's Skyscraper Rock. By Huntley Ingalls. Photos by author and Barry C. Bishop. 705-721, Nov. 1962

ROCK-LEDGE LIFE:
• Life on a Rock Ledge. By William H. Amos. 558-566, Oct. 1980

ROCK PAINTINGS. *See* Rock Art

ROCKEFELLER, LAURANCE S.:
• Board of Trustees, member. 647, 655, May 1958; 5, 46, 55, July 1966; 531, 533, Oct. 1966; 80, Jan. 1967; 588, Oct. 1967; 542, Apr. 1971; 227, Aug. 1976
Author:
• Parks, Plans, and People: How South America Guards Her Green Legacy. By Mary and Laurance Rockefeller. Photos by George F. Mobley. 74-119, Jan. 1967
• Problems in Paradise. By Mary and Laurance S. Rockefeller. Photos by Thomas Nebbia. 782-793, Dec. 1974

ROCKEFELLER, MARY FRENCH:
Author:
• Parks, Plans, and People: How South America Guards Her Green Legacy. By Mary and Laurance Rockefeller. Photos by George F. Mobley. 74-119, Jan. 1967
• Problems in Paradise. By Mary and Laurance S. Rockefeller. Photos by Thomas Nebbia. 782-793, Dec. 1974
• YWCA: International Success Story. Photos by Otis Imboden. 904-933, Dec. 1963

ROCKEFELLER FOUNDATION:
• Yellow fever research in Colombia. 626, May 1947; 251, 254, 258, 261, 265, 266, 268, 269, 273, Aug. 1948

ROCKEFELLER UNIVERSITY:
Study Grant:
• Humpback Whales. 466, Apr. 1982

ROCKET PLANES:
• Flying in the "Blowtorch" Era. By Frederick G. Vosburgh. 281-322, Sept. 1950
• *See also* X-15

ROCKETS:
• Aviation Medicine on the Threshold of Space. By Allan C. Fisher, Jr. Photos by Luis Marden. 241-278, Aug. 1955
• Cape Canaveral's 6,000-mile Shooting Gallery. By Allan C. Fisher, Jr. Photos by Luis Marden and Thomas Nebbia. 421-471, Oct. 1959
• Exploring Tomorrow With the Space Agency. By Allan C. Fisher, Jr. Photos by Dean Conger. 48-89, July 1960
• Reaching for the Moon. By Allan C. Fisher, Jr. Photos by Luis Marden. 157-171, Feb. 1959
• Rockets Explore the Air Above Us. By Newman Bumstead. 562-580, Apr. 1957
• Seeing the Earth from 80 Miles Up. By Clyde T. Holliday. 511-528, Oct. 1950
• Space Satellites, Tools of Earth Research. By Heinz Haber. Paintings by William N. Palmstrom. 487-509, Apr. 1956
• *See also* Apollo Missions; Gemini Missions; Mercury Missions

The **ROCKIES'** Pot of Gold, Colorado. By Edward J. Linehan. Photos by James L. Amos. 157-201, Aug. 1969

ROCKS:
• Finding Rare Beauty in Common Rocks. By Lorence G. Collins. 121-129, Jan. 1966
• The Glittering World of Rockhounds. By David S. Boyer. 276-294, Feb. 1974
• "Rockhounds" Uncover Earth's Mineral Beauty. By George S. Switzer. 631-660, Nov. 1951
• *See also* Moon Rocks

ROCKS, Ruts, and Sand: Driving the Mexican 1000. By Michael E. Long. 569-575, Oct. 1972

ROCKY MOUNTAINS, Canada-U. S.:
◆ *Along the Continental Divide.* 1981
• Along the Great Divide. By Mike Edwards. Photos by Nicholas DeVore III. 483-515, Oct. 1979
• Bikepacking Across Alaska and Canada. By Dan Burden. 682-695, May 1973
• Canadian Rockies, Lords of a Beckoning Land. By Alan Phillips. Photos by James L. Stanfield. 353-393, Sept. 1966
• Colorado, the Rockies' Pot of Gold. By Edward J. Linehan. Photos by James L. Amos. 157-201, Aug. 1969
• Colorado by Car and Campfire. By Kathleen Revis. Included: Longs Peak, Pikes Peak. 207-248, Aug. 1954
• Colorado's Friendly Topland. By Robert M. Ormes. Contents: Elk Mountains, Front Range, Mosquito Range, Park Range, Pikes Peak, San

Juan Mountains, San Miguel Mountains, Sangre de Cristo Mountains, Sawatch Mountains. 187-214, Aug. 1951
• Denver, Colorado's Rocky Mountain High. By John J. Putman. Photos by David Cupp. 383-411, Mar. 1979
• Heart of the Canadian Rockies. By Elizabeth A. Moize. Photos by Jim Brandenburg. 757-779, June 1980
• Hiking the Backbone of the Rockies: Canada's Great Divide Trail. By Mike W. Edwards. Photos by Lowell Georgia. 795-817, June 1973
• Last Stand for the Bighorn. By James K. Morgan. 383-399, Sept. 1973
◆ *The Majestic Rocky Mountains.* Announced. 870-874, June 1975
• Nahanni: Canada's Wilderness Park. By Douglas H. Chadwick. Photos by Matt Bradley. 396-420, Sept. 1981
• The Night the Mountains Moved (Montana's 1959 Earthquake). By Samuel W. Matthews. Photos by J. Baylor Roberts. 329-359, Mar. 1960
• On the Ridgepole of the Rockies. By Walter Meayers Edwards. 745-780, June 1947
Canada's Rocky Mountain Playground. 755-770
• Teamwork Helps the Whooping Crane. By Roderick C. Drewien, with Ernie Kuyt. 680-693, May 1979
• *See also* Aspen, Colorado; Glacier National Park; Kennedy, Mount; Teton Range; Wasatch Front

RODENTS:
• In the Wilds of a City Parlor. By Paul A. Zahl. 645-672, Nov. 1954
• *See also* Beavers; Porcupines; Prairie Dogs; Rats; Squirrels

RODEOS:
• Buffalo Bill and the Enduring West. By Alice J. Hall. Photos by James L. Amos. 76-103, July 1981

RODGER, GEORGE:
Author-Photographer:
• Where Elephants Have Right of Way. By George and Jinx Rodger. 363-389, Sept. 1960
Photographer:
• Boom Time in Kuwait. By Paul Edward Case. 783-802, Dec. 1952
• Sand in My Eyes. By Jinx Rodger. 664-705, May 1958
• With the Nuba Hillmen of Kordofan. By Robin Strachan. 249-278, Feb. 1951

RODGER, JINX: Author:
• Sand in My Eyes. 664-705, May 1958
• Where Elephants Have Right of Way. By George and Jinx Rodger. Photos by George Rodger. 363-389, Sept. 1960

ROEBLING, JOHN A.:
• A Century Old, the Wonderful Brooklyn Bridge. By John G. Morris. Photos by Donal F. Holway. 565-579, May 1983

ROEBLING, WASHINGTON A.:
• A Century Old, the Wonderful Brooklyn Bridge. By John G. Morris. Photos by Donal F. Holway. 565-579, May 1983

ROGERS, MARTIN: Photographer:
• Baltimore: The Hidden City. By Fred Kline. 188-215, Feb. 1975
• Belgium: One Nation Divisible. By James Cerruti. 314-341, Mar. 1979
• The Dominican Republic: Caribbean Comeback. By James Cerruti. 538-565, Oct. 1977
• Giants That Move the World's Oil: Superships. By Noel Grove. 102-124, July 1978
• The Great Lakes: Is It Too Late? By Gordon Young. Photos by James L. Amos and Martin Rogers. 147-185, Aug. 1973
• The Incredible Potato. By Robert E. Rhoades. 668-694, May 1982
• Norway's Strategic Arctic Islands (Svalbard). By Gordon Young. 267-283, Aug. 1978
• The Ohio–River With a Job to Do. By Priit J. Vesilind. 245-273, Feb. 1977
• Superspill: Black Day for Brittany. Text by Noel Grove. 124-135, July 1978

ROLAND, ARTHUR (Pseudonym). *See* Kilbon, Roland

ROMAN CATHOLICISM:
• Caldy, the Monks' Island (Wales). By John E. H. Nolan. 564-578, Oct. 1955
▲ *The Face and Faith of Poland,* map, photo, and essay supplement. By Peter Miller. Essay by Czesław Miłosz. Photos by Bruno Barbey. Apr. 1982
• Fátima: Beacon for Portugal's Faithful. By Jane Vessels. Photos by Bruno Barbey. 832-839, Dec. 1980
• Mesa del Nayar's Strange Holy Week. By Guillermo Aldana E. Included: Syncretism with Cora Indians' ancient religion. 780-795, June 1971
• New Mexico's Mountains of Mystery. By Robert Laxalt. Photos by Craig Aurness. Included: Penitente sect of Sangre de Cristo. 416-436, Sept. 1978
• Peru's Pilgrimage to the Sky. By Robert Randall. Photos by Loren McIntyre and Ira Block. Included: Syncretism of Indian beliefs and Roman Catholicism. 60-69, July 1982
• Rome: Eternal City with a Modern Air. By Harnett T. Kane. Photos by B. Anthony Stewart. 437-491, Apr. 1957
• St. Peter's, Rome's Church of Popes. By Aubrey Menen. Photos by Albert Moldvay. 865-879, Dec. 1971
• Toledo–El Greco's Spain Lives On. By Louise E. Levathes. Photos by James P. Blair. 726-753, June 1982
• The World of Martin Luther. By Merle Severy. Photos by James L. Amos. 418-463, Oct. 1983

ROMAN EMPIRE:
• Ancient Aphrodisias Lives Through Its Art. By Kenan T. Erim. Photos by David Brill. NGS research grant. 527-551, Oct. 1981
• A Buried Roman Town Gives Up Its Dead (Herculaneum). By Joseph Judge. Photos by Jonathan Blair. NGS research grant. 687-693, Dec. 1982
▲ *Classical Lands of the Mediterranean,* supplement. Dec. 1949
• Down the Ancient Appian Way. By James Cerruti. Photos by O. Louis Mazzatenta. 714-747, June 1981
◆ *Greece and Rome: Builders of Our World.* Announced. 550-567, Oct. 1968
• A New Look at Medieval Europe. By Kenneth M. Setton. Paintings by Andre Durenceau and Birney Lettick. 799-859, Dec. 1962
• Roman Life in 1,600-year-old Color Pictures. By Gino Vinicio Gentili. Photos by Duncan Edwards. 211-229, Feb. 1957
• *See also* Byzantine Empire

ROMAN RUINS:
• The British Way: Great Britain's Major Gifts to Freedom, Democratic Government, Science, and Society. By Sir Evelyn Wrench. 421-541, Apr. 1949
• A Stroll to London. By Isobel Wylie Hutchison. Photos by B. Anthony Stewart. 171-204, Aug. 1950
• *Yankee* Cruises the Storied Nile. By Irving and Electa Johnson. Photos by Winfield Parks. 583-633, May 1965
• *See also* Aphrodisias; Appian Way; Herculaneum; Languedoc; Pompeii

The **ROMANCE** of American Furs. By Wanda Burnett. 379-402, Mar. 1948

The **ROMANCE** of the Geographic: National Geographic Magazine Observes Its Diamond Anniversary. By Gilbert Hovey Grosvenor. 516-585, Oct. 1963

ROMANCHE TRENCH, Atlantic Ocean:
• *Calypso* Explores an Undersea Canyon. By Jacques-Yves Cousteau. Photos by Bates Littlehales. NGS research grant. 373-396, Mar. 1958

ROMANIA:
• Americans Afoot in Rumania. By Dan Dimancescu. Photos by Dick Durrance II and Christopher G. Knight. 810-845, June 1969
▲ *The Balkans,* Atlas series supplement. Feb. 1962
• The Danube: River of Many Nations, Many Names. By Mike Edwards. Photos by Winfield Parks. 455-485, Oct. 1977
• Down the Danube by Canoe. By William Slade Backer. Photos by Richard S. Durrance and Christopher G. Knight. 34-79, July 1965
• Romania: Maverick on a Tightrope. By William S. Ellis. Photos by Winfield Parks. 688-713, Nov. 1975

ROMANIES. *See* Gypsies

ROME, Italy:
● Italy Smiles Again. By Edgar Erskine Hume. 693-732, June 1949
● Jerusalem to Rome in the Path of St. Paul. By David S. Boyer. 707-759, Dec. 1956
● Rome: Eternal City with a Modern Air. By Harnett T. Kane. Photos by B. Anthony Stewart. 437-491, Apr. 1957
● St. Peter's, Rome's Church of Popes. By Aubrey Menen. Photos by Albert Moldvay. 865-879, Dec. 1971
▲ *A Traveler's Map of Italy,* supplement. Text on reverse. June 1970
● When in Rome. . . . By Stuart E. Jones. Photos by Winfield Parks. 741-789, June 1970

ROME of the East. By Merle Severy. Photos by James L. Stanfield. 709-767, Dec. 1983

RONNING, CHESTER:
● Return to Changing China. By Audrey Topping. 801-833, Dec. 1971

ROOKERIES. *See* Bird Sanctuaries and Rookeries; Pribilof Islands, for Polovina Seal Rookery

ROOSEVELT, FRANKLIN D.:
● Inside the White House. By Lonnelle Aikman. Photos by B. Anthony Stewart and Thomas Nebbia. 3-43, Jan. 1961
● The Living White House. By Lonnelle Aikman. 593-643, Nov. 1966
● Profiles of the Presidents: V. The Atomic Age: Its Problems and Promises. By Frank Freidel. 66-119, Jan. 1966

ROOSEVELT, THEODORE:
● Inside the White House. By Lonnelle Aikman. Photos by B. Anthony Stewart and Thomas Nebbia. 3-43, Jan. 1961
● The Living White House. By Lonnelle Aikman. 593-643, Nov. 1966
● North Dakota Comes into Its Own. By Leo A. Borah. Photos by J. Baylor Roberts. Included: Roosevelt's log cabin, now a museum on the State Capitol grounds. 283-322, Sept. 1951
● Profiles of the Presidents: IV. America Enters the Modern Era. By Frank Freidel. 537-577, Oct. 1965
● Roosevelt Country: T. R.'s Wilderness Legacy. By John L. Eliot. Photos by Farrell Grehan. 340-363, Sept. 1982
● Theodore Roosevelt: a Centennial Tribute. By Bart McDowell. 572-590, Oct. 1958

ROOT, ALAN: Photographer:
● Freeing Flamingos From Anklets of Death. By John G. Williams. 934-944, Dec. 1963
● The Galapagos, Eerie Cradle of New Species. By Roger Tory Peterson. Photos by Alan and Joan Root. 541-585, Apr. 1967
● Inside a Hornbill's Walled-up Nest. By Joan and Alan Root. 846-855, Dec. 1969
● Mzima, Kenya's Spring of Life. By Joan and Alan Root. 350-373, Sept. 1971

ROOT, JOAN: Photographer:
● The Galapagos, Eerie Cradle of New Species. By Roger Tory Peterson. Photos by Alan and Joan Root. 541-585, Apr. 1967
● Inside a Hornbill's Walled-up Nest. By Joan and Alan Root. 846-855, Dec. 1969
● Mzima, Kenya's Spring of Life. By Joan and Alan Root. 350-373, Sept. 1971

ROSCHER, W. E.: Author:
● Queen Elizabeth Opens Parliament. Photos by Robert B. Goodman. 699-707, Nov. 1961

ROSE APHIDS. By Treat Davidson. 851-859, June 1961

ROSEATE SPOONBILLS:
● The Pink Birds of Texas. By Paul A. Zahl. 641-654, Nov. 1949
● Roseate Spoonbills, Radiant Birds of the Gulf Coast. By Robert Porter Allen. Photos by Frederick Kent Truslow. 274-288, Feb. 1962
● Saving Man's Wildlife Heritage. By John H. Baker. Photos by Robert F. Sisson. 581-620, Nov. 1954

ROSENQUIST, GARY:
● Mountain With a Death Wish (Mount St. Helens). By Rowe Findley. Included: Gary Rosenquist's photos of Mount St. Helens' eruption taken just before he fled the area. 3-33, Jan. 1981

ROSENSTIEL SCHOOL OF MARINE SCIENCE. *See* University of Miami: Marine Research

ROSES:
● Amateur Gardener Creates a New Rose (Portrait). By Elizabeth A. Moize. Photos by Farrell Grehan. 286-294, Aug. 1972
● Patent Plants Enrich Our World. By Orville H. Kneen. Photos from U. S. Plant Patents. 357-378, Mar. 1948
● *See also* Tournament of Roses

ROSIER CREEK, Virginia:
● A Good Life on the Potomac. By James L. Stanfield. 470-479, Oct. 1976

ROSS, EDWARD S.: Author:
● Hunting Africa's Smallest Game. 406-419, Mar. 1961
Author-Photographer:
● Asian Insects in Disguise. 433-439, Sept. 1965
● Birds That "See" in the Dark With Their Ears. 282-290, Feb. 1965
Photographer:
● Crossroads of the Insect World. By J. W. MacSwain. 844-857, Dec. 1966

ROSS, KIP: Author-Photographer:
● Chile, the Long and Narrow Land. 185-235, Feb. 1960
● Peru, Homeland of the Warlike Inca. 421-462, Oct. 1950
● South Africa Close-up. 641-681, Nov. 1962
● We Drove Panama's Darién Gap. 368-389, Mar. 1961
Photographer:
● Mexico in Motion. By Bart McDowell. 490-537, Oct. 1961

ROSS, MALCOLM D.: Author:
● My Neighbors Hold to Mountain Ways. Photos by Flip Schulke. 856-880, June 1958
● North Carolina, Dixie Dynamo. Photos by B. Anthony Stewart. 141-183, Feb. 1962
● To 76,000 Feet by *Strato-Lab* Balloon. By Malcolm D. Ross and M. Lee Lewis. 269-282, Feb. 1957
● We Saw the World From the Edge of Space. Ground photos by Walter Meayers Edwards. 671-685, Nov. 1961

ROTH, TOM and TOMMY:
● Down Mark Twain's River on a Raft. By Rex E. Hieronymus. 551-574, Apr. 1948

ROTHSCHILD'S GIRAFFE:
● Rescuing the Rothschild. By Carolyn Bennett Patterson. 419-421, Sept. 1977

ROTIFERS: Nature's Water Purifiers. By John Walsh. 287-292, Feb. 1979

ROTTERDAM, Netherlands:
● Rotterdam–Reborn From Ruins. By Helen Hill Miller. Photos by James Blair. 526-553, Oct. 1960

ROUGHEST Road Race: the Mexican 1000. By Michael E. Long. 569-575, Oct. 1972

ROUGHLEY, T. C.: Author:
● *Bounty* Descendants Live on Remote Norfolk Island. Photos by J. Baylor Roberts. 559-584, Oct. 1960

ROUMANIA. *See* Romania

The **ROUND** *Earth on Flat Paper.* By Wellman Chamberlin. 399, Mar. 1950

'ROUND the Horn by Submarine. By Paul C. Stimson. 129-144, Jan. 1948

ROUND THE WORLD SCHOOL. By Paul Antze. Photos by William Eppridge. 96-127, July 1962

ROUNDUPS. *See* Cattle Raising; Elephants (Wild Elephant Roundup); Reindeer

ROVER (Lunar Vehicle):
● Apollo 15 Explores the Mountains of the Moon. By Kenneth F. Weaver. Photos from NASA. 233-265, Feb. 1972
● Detailed diagram of Rover. 148, July 1971
● Exploring Taurus-Littrow. By Harrison H. Schmitt. Photos by the crew of Apollo 17. 290-307, Sept. 1973
● What Is It Like to Walk on the Moon? By David R. Scott. 326-331, Sept. 1973

ROVING Maryland's Cavalier Country. By William A. Kinney. 431-470, Apr. 1954

ROWELL, GALEN:
Author-Photographer:
● Climbing Half Dome the Hard Way. 782-791, June 1974
● Nomads of China's West. By Galen Rowell. Photos by the author and Harold A. Knutson. 244-263, Feb. 1982

Photographer:
• American Skiers Find Adventure in Western China. By Ned Gillette. Photos by the author and Galen Rowell. 174-199, Feb. 1981
Skiing From the Summit of China's Ice Mountain. 192-199
• California's Parched Oasis, the Owens Valley. By Judith and Neil Morgan. Photos by Jodi Cobb and Galen Rowell. 98-127, Jan. 1976

ROY, LEONARD C.: Author:
• Menhaden–Uncle Sam's Top Commercial Fish. Photos by Robert F. Sisson. 813-823, June 1949

ROYAL ACADEMY OF ARTS, London:
• Our Search for British Paintings. By Franklin L. Fisher. 543-550, Apr. 1949

ROYAL AIR FORCE (RAF). *See* Airlift to Berlin

ROYAL BOTANIC GARDENS, England:
• Kew: The Commoners' Royal Garden. By Thomas Garner James. Photos by B. Anthony Stewart. 479-506, Apr. 1950

ROYAL GEOGRAPHICAL SOCIETY: Expeditions. *See* British Mount Everest Expedition

ROYAL House for Dolls. By David Jeffery. Photos by James L. Stanfield. 632-643, Nov. 1980

ROYAL ONTARIO MUSEUM OF GEOLOGY AND MINERALOGY, Canada: Expeditions. *See* Chubb Crater

ROYAL Wedding at Jaisalmer. By Marilyn Silverstone. 66-79, Jan. 1965

ROYALTY at Work. Photos by John Everingham. 486-499, Oct. 1982

ROZUMALSKI, TED: Photographer:
• Wisconsin's Door Peninsula. By William S. Ellis. 347-371, Mar. 1969

RUBBER:
• Rediscovering America's Forgotten Crops. By Noel D. Vietmeyer. Photos by Burgess Blevins. Paintings by Paul M. Breeden. Included: Guayule rubber. 702-712, May 1981

RUBBER-CUSHIONED Liberia. By Henry S. Villard. Photos by Charles W. Allmon. 201-228, Feb. 1948

RUBIES:
• Questing for Gems. By George S. Switzer. 835-863, Dec. 1971
• *See also* Lasers

RUDLOE, ANNE and JACK: Authors:
• The Changeless Horseshoe Crab. Photos by Robert F. Sisson. 562-572, Apr. 1981
• Our Wild and Scenic Rivers: The Suwannee. Photos by Jodi Cobb. 20-29, July 1977
• Trouble in Bayou Country: Louisiana's Atchafalaya. Photos by C. C. Lockwood. 377-397, Sept. 1979

RUDOLF, Lake (Lake Turkana), Kenya:
• In Search of Man's Past at Lake Rudolf. By Richard E. Leakey. Photos by Gordon W. Gahan. NGS research grant. 712-734, May 1970
• Skull 1470. By Richard E. Leakey. Photos by Bob Campbell. 819-829, June 1973

RUGGED Is the Word for Bravo (Weather Station). By Phillip M. Swatek. 829-843, Dec. 1955

RUGS AND RUG MAKING:
• Afghanistan: Crossroad of Conquerors. By Thomas J. Abercrombie. 297-345, Sept. 1968
• The Idyllic Vale of Kashmir. By Volkmar Wentzel. 523-550, Apr. 1948
• Journey into Troubled Iran. By George W. Long. Photos by J. Baylor Roberts. 425-464, Oct. 1951
• *See also* Kashgais; Navajos; Turkomans

RUHR (Region), Germany:
• With Uncle Sam and John Bull in Germany. By Frederick Simpich. 117-140, Jan. 1949

RUINS:
• Athens: Her Golden Past Still Lights the World. By Kenneth F. Weaver. Photos by Phillip Harrington. 100-137, July 1963
• From Sea to Sahara in French Morocco. By Jean and Franc Shor. 147-188, Feb. 1955
• *See also* Angkor; Pagan; Persepolis; Roman Ruins; Stonehenge; Zimbabwe (Ruins); *and* Archaeology

RULE, MARGARET: Author:
• Henry VIII's Lost Warship: *Mary Rose*. Introduction and picture text by Peter Miller. Paintings by Richard Schlecht. 646-675, May 1983

RUMANIA. *See* Romania

RUMBUR VALLEY, Pakistan:
• Pakistan's Kalash: People of Fire and Fervor. By Debra Denker. Photos by Steve McCurry. 458-473, Oct. 1981

RUMTEK MONASTERY, Sikkim:
• Gangtok, Cloud-wreathed Himalayan Capital. By John Scofield. 698-713, Nov. 1970

RUOHOMAA, KOSTI: Photographer:
• Maine's Lobster Island, Monhegan. By William P. E. Graves. 285-298, Feb. 1959

RUPERT HOUSE, Quebec, Canada:
• The Changing World of Canada's Crees. By Fred Ward. 541-569, Apr. 1975

RUSCHI, AUGUSTO:
• The Man Who Talks to Hummingbirds. By Luis Marden. Photos by James Blair. 80-99, Jan. 1963

RUSHMORE, Mount, South Dakota:
• Back to the Historic Black Hills. By Leland D. Case. Photos by Bates Littlehales. 479-509, Oct. 1956
• South Dakota Keeps Its West Wild. By Frederick Simpich. 555-588, May 1947

RUSSELL, Kansas:
• Hays, Kansas, at the Nation's Heart. By Margaret M. Detwiler. Photos by John E. Fletcher. 461-490, Apr. 1952

RUSSELL CAVE, Alabama:
• Life 8,000 Years Ago Uncovered in an Alabama Cave. By Carl F. Miller. NGS research grant. 542-558, Oct. 1956
• National Geographic Society Presents Russell Cave to the American People. By Melville Bell Grosvenor. NGS research grant. 438, Mar. 1958
• Russell Cave: New Light on Stone Age Life. By Carl F. Miller. NGS research grant. 427-437, Mar. 1958
• Russell Cave Dedicated; New Visitor Center Named for Gilbert H. Grosvenor. NGS research grant. 440-442, Sept. 1967

RUSSIA:
• Imperial Russia's Glittering Legacy. 24-33, Jan. 1978
• *See also* Union of Soviet Socialist Republics

RUSSIAN ORTHODOX CHURCH:
• The Byzantine Empire: Rome of the East. By Merle Severy. Photos by James L. Stanfield. 709-767, Dec. 1983
• Nikolaevsk: A Bit of Old Russia Takes Root in Alaska. By Jim Rearden. Photos by Charles O'Rear. Contents: Old Believers. 401-425, Sept. 1972

RUSSIANS:
• Nikolaevsk: A Bit of Old Russia Takes Root in Alaska. By Jim Rearden. Photos by Charles O'Rear. 401-425, Sept. 1972

RUSSIA'S Mighty River Road, the Volga. By Howard Sochurek. 579-613, May 1973

RUSSIA'S Window on the West: Leningrad. By Howard La Fay. Photos by Dick Durrance II. 636-673, May 1971

RUTHERFORD, ERNEST, LORD:
• The British Way. By Sir Evelyn Wrench. 421-541, Apr. 1949

RUWENZORI (Mountains of the Moon), Africa:
• Mountains of the Moon. By Paul A. Zahl. 412-434, Mar. 1962

RWANDA:
• The Imperiled Mountain Gorilla. By Dian Fossey. 501-523, Apr. 1981
Death of Marchessa. Photos by Peter G. Veit. 508-511
• *See also* Virunga Mountains

RYDEN, HOPE:
Author-Photographer:
• The "Lone" Coyote Likes Family Life. Photos by author and David Hiser. 278-294, Aug. 1974
• On the Track of the West's Wild Horses. Photos by author and Dick Durrance II. 94-109, Jan. 1971

RYTKHEU, YURI: Author:
• People of the Long Spring. Photos by Dean Conger. 206-223, Feb. 1983

RYUKYU ISLANDS. *See* Okinawa

S

SÁ, HERNANE TAVARES DE: Author:
- Brasília, Metropolis Made to Order. Photos by Thomas J. Abercrombie. 704-724, May 1960
- Spectacular Rio de Janeiro. Photos by Charles Allmon. 289-328, Mar. 1955

SAAMI. *See* Lapland, for Lapps

SAAR:
- Coal Makes the Saar a Prize. By Franc Shor. 561-576, Apr. 1954

SAARINEN, EERO:
- St. Louis: New Spirit Soars in Mid-America's Proud Old City. By Robert Paul Jordan. Photos by Bruce Dale. Included: Saarinen's Gateway Arch. 605-641, Nov. 1965

SABA (Island), West Indies:
- A Fresh Breeze Stirs the Leewards. By Carleton Mitchell. Photos by Winfield Parks. 488-537, Oct. 1966
- The Netherlands Antilles: Holland in the Caribbean. By James Cerruti. Photos by Emory Kristof. 115-146, Jan. 1970

SABAH (North Borneo):
- In Storied Lands of Malaysia. By Maurice Shadbolt. Photos by Winfield Parks. 734-783, Nov. 1963
- Malaysia's Giant Flowers and Insect-trapping Plants. By Paul A. Zahl. 680-701, May 1964

SABLE ISLAND, Nova Scotia:
- Safe Landing on Sable, Isle of 500 Shipwrecks. By Melville Bell Grosvenor. Included: Maps, 1766 to 1964, indicating eastward shift of the island; map of known shipwreck sites. 398-431, Sept. 1965
  1898: The Bells on Sable. Photos by Arthur W. McCurdy. 408-409, 416-417

SACRAMENTO, California:
- California, Horn of Plenty. By Frederick Simpich. Photos by Willard R. Culver. 553-594, May 1949
- California, the Golden Magnet. By William Graves. 595-679, May 1966
  Nature's North. Photos by James P. Blair and Jonathan S. Blair. 641-679
- New Rush to Golden California. By George W. Long. 723-802, June 1954

SACRAMENTO-SAN JOAQUIN RIVER DELTA, California:
- California's Surprising Inland Delta. By Judith and Neil Morgan. Photos by Charles O'Rear. 409-430, Sept. 1976
- San Francisco Bay: The Beauty and the Battles. By Cliff Tarpy. Photos by James A. Sugar. 814-845, June 1981

A **SACRED** Symbol Comes Home: Afo-A-Kom. By William S. Ellis. Photos by James P. Blair. 141-148, July 1974

SACRIFICE. *See* Animal Sacrifice; Human Sacrifice

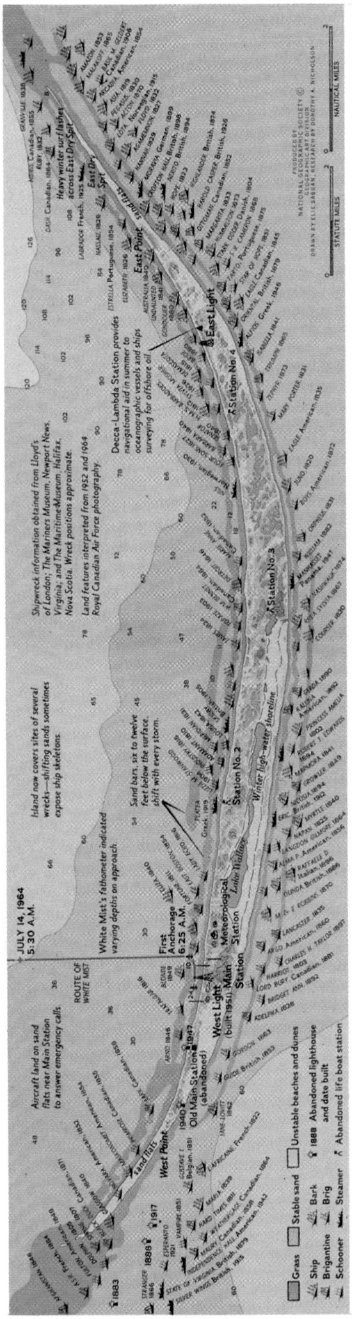

NGS CARTOGRAPHIC DIVISION

Sable Island: graveyard of the Atlantic

SADAT, ANWAR:
- Egypt's Desert of Promise. By Farouk El-Baz. Photos by Georg Gerster. Included: Anwar Sadat's five-year plan to expand desert agriculture. 190-221, Feb. 1982
- Eternal Sinai. By Harvey Arden. Photos by David Doubilet and Kevin Fleming. Included: First-hand account of Anwar Sadat's assassination. 420-461, Apr. 1982
  Egyptian Sector. Photos by Kevin Fleming. 430-443; Israeli Sector. Photos by David Doubilet. 444-461

SADLERMIUTS (Eskimos):
- Vanished Mystery Men of Hudson Bay. By Henry B. Collins. NGS research grant. 669-687, Nov. 1956

SAFARI from Congo to Cairo. By Elsie May Bell Grosvenor. Photos by Gilbert Grosvenor. 721-771, Dec. 1954

SAFARI Through Changing Africa. By Elsie May Bell Grosvenor. Photos by Gilbert Grosvenor. 145-198, Aug. 1953

SAFE Landing on Sable, Isle of 500 Shipwrecks. By Melville Bell Grosvenor. 398-431, Sept. 1965

SAGA of a Ship, the *Yankee* (Brigantine). By Luis Marden. 263-269, Feb. 1966

SAGAMORE HILL, Long Island, N.Y.:
- Roosevelt Country: T. R.'s Wilderness Legacy. By John L. Eliot. Photos by Farrell Grehan. 340-363, Sept. 1982

SAGAN, CARL: Author:
- Mars: a New World to Explore. 821-841, Dec. 1967

SAGARMATHA NATIONAL PARK, Nepal:
- Park at the Top of the World: Mount Everest National Park. By Rick Ridgeway. Photos by Nicholas DeVore III. 704-725, June 1982
  Preserving a Mountain Heritage. By Sir Edmund Hillary. 696-703

SAGUARO (Cactus):
- Abundant Life in a Desert Land. By Walter Meayers Edwards. 424-436, Sept. 1973

SAGUENAY RIVER REGION, Canada:
- North Through History Aboard *White Mist.* By Melville Bell Grosvenor. Photos by Edwin Stuart Grosvenor. 1-55, July 1970
- Quebec's Forests, Farms, and Frontiers. By Andrew H. Brown. 431-470, Oct. 1949
- Sea to Lakes on the St. Lawrence. By George W. Long. Photos by B. Anthony Stewart and John E. Fletcher. 323-366, Sept. 1950

SAHARA (Desert), Africa:
- Algeria: France's Stepchild, Problem and Promise. By Howard La Fay. Photos by Robert F. Sisson. 768-795, June 1960
- Algeria: Learning to Live With Independence. By Thomas J. Abercrombie. 200-233, Aug. 1973

• The Desert: An Age-old Challenge Grows. By Rick Gore. Photos by Georg Gerster and Bruce Dale. 586-639, Nov. 1979
• Drought Threatens the Tuareg World. By Victor Englebert. 544-571, Apr. 1974
• Dry-land Fleet Sails the Sahara. By Jean du Boucher. Photos by Jonathan S. Blair. 696-725, Nov. 1967
• Egypt's Desert of Promise. By Farouk El-Baz. Photos by Georg Gerster. 190-221, Feb. 1982
• Freedom Speaks French in Ouagadougou. By John Scofield. 153-203, Aug. 1966
• I Joined a Sahara Salt Caravan. By Victor Englebert. 694-711, Nov. 1965
• The Inadan: Artisans of the Sahara. By Michael and Aubine Kirtley. 282-298, Aug. 1979
• Oasis-hopping in the Sahara. By Maynard Owen Williams. 209-236, Feb. 1949
• Oursi, Magnet in the Desert. By Carole E. Devillers. 512-525, Apr. 1980
• Sand in My Eyes. By Jinx Rodger. 664-705, May 1958
• The Sword and the Sermon. By Thomas J. Abercrombie. 3-45, July 1972
▪ Wind Raiders of the Sahara. 436A-436B, Sept. 1973

SAHEL (Southern Sahara Region), Africa:
• The Desert: An Age-old Challenge Grows. By Rick Gore. Photos by Georg Gerster and Bruce Dale. 586-639, Nov. 1979
• Drought Threatens the Tuareg World. By Victor Englebert. 544-571, Apr. 1974
• The Inadan: Artisans of the Sahara. By Michael and Aubine Kirtley. 282-298, Aug. 1979
• The Niger: River of Sorrow, River of Hope. By Georg Gerster. 152-189, Aug. 1975
• Niger's Wodaabe: "People of the Taboo." By Carol Beckwith. 483-509, Oct. 1983
• Oursi, Magnet in the Desert. By Carole E. Devillers. 512-525, Apr. 1980

SAIDMAN, BARNET: Photographer:
• The Swans of Abbotsbury (Dorsetshire, England). By Michael Moynihan. 563-570, Oct. 1959

SAIGON, Vietnam:
• Indochina Faces the Dragon. By George W. Long. Photos by J. Baylor Roberts. 287-328, Sept. 1952
• Portrait of Indochina. By W. Robert Moore and Maynard Owen Williams. Paintings by Jean Despujols. 461-490, Apr. 1951
• Saigon: Eye of the Storm. By Peter T. White. Photos by W. E. Garrett. 834-872, June 1965
• Slow Train Through Viet Nam's War. By Howard Sochurek. 412-444, Sept. 1964
• South Viet Nam Fights the Red Tide. By Peter T. White. Photos by W. E. Garrett. 445-489, Oct. 1961

SAILFISH:
• Solving Life Secrets of the Sailfish. By Gilbert Voss. Photos by B. Anthony Stewart. Paintings by Craig Phillips. NGS research grant. 859-872, June 1956

SAILING. *See* Cruises and Voyages; Sailing Vessels; Yachting

SAILING a Sea of Fire. By Paul A. Zahl. 120-129, July 1960

SAILING CARS:
• Dry-land Fleet Sails the Sahara. By Jean du Boucher. Photos by Jonathan S. Blair. 696-725, Nov. 1967
▪ Wind Raiders of the Sahara. 436A-436B, Sept. 1973

SAILING Iceland's Rugged Coasts. By Wright Britton. Photos by James A. Sugar. 228-265, Aug. 1969

The **SAILING** Oystermen of Chesapeake Bay. By Luis Marden. 798-819, Dec. 1967

SAILING VESSELS:
• The Age of Sail Lives On at Mystic. By Alan Villiers. Photos by Weston Kemp. Included: *Alice, Charles W. Morgan, Joseph Conrad, L. A. Dunton.* 220-239, Aug. 1968
• By Square-rigger from Baltic to Bicentennial. By Kenneth Garrett. Included: The tall-ships race. 824-857, Dec. 1976
• Last of the Cape Horners *(Pamir).* By Alan Villiers. Contents: *Abraham Rydberg, Archibald Russell, Grace Harwar, Kjøbenhavn, Kommodore Johnsen, Lawhill, Moshulu, Padua, Pamir, Parma, Passat, Pommern, Viking.* 701-710, May 1948
Square-rigger in a Tempest *(Pamir).* 703-710
• Life's Tempo on Nantucket. By Peter Benchley. Photos by James L. Stanfield. 810-839, June 1970
• The Sailing Oystermen of Chesapeake Bay. By Luis Marden. 798-819, Dec. 1967
• Windjamming Around New England. By Tom Horgan. Photos by Robert F. Sisson. Included: *Abigail Chandler, Bluenose, Bolero, Bowdoin, Charles W. Morgan, Daniel I. Tenny, Fiddlers' Green, Gertrude L. Thebaud, Great Republic, Hannah, Hero, Joseph Conrad, Lagoda, Malabar XIII, Manxman, Nomad, Regina M., Telegraph, Wanderer, Yankee.* 141-169, Aug. 1950
• *See also* Dhows; Fishing (Industry); Galleons and Galleasses; Junks; *Lipas;* Longships; Square-riggers; Training Ships; listing under Yachts; *and Beagle,* H.M.S.; *Bounty,* H.M.S.; *Breadalbane; Brendan; Dick Smith Explorer; Dove; Endeavour; Hamilton* and *Scourge; Hokule'a; Ice Bird; Isbjorn;* Kublai Khan's Fleet; *Mary Rose,* H.M.S.; *Mayflower II; Ra II; Sohar; Tigris; Vasa; Witte Leeuw*

SAILING with Sindbad's Sons. By Alan Villiers. 675-688, Nov. 1948

SAILING With the Supertankers. By Noel Grove. Photos by Martin Rogers. 102-124, July 1978

The **SAILOR** Who Gave Us the New World: Christopher Columbus. By John Scofield. Photos by Adam Woolfitt. 584-625, Nov. 1975

SAILORS in the Sky: Fifty Years of Naval Aviation. By Patrick N. L. Bellinger. 276-296, Aug. 1961

SAILPLANES:
• Sailors of the Sky. By Gordon Young. Photos by Emory Kristof and Jack Fields. Paintings by Davis Meltzer. 49-73, Jan. 1967
• The Thousand-mile Glide. By Karl Striedieck. Photos by Otis Imboden. 431-438, Mar. 1978

ST. AUBYN, SIR FRANCIS CECIL. *See* St. Levan, Baron

ST. AUGUSTINE, Florida:
• St. Augustine, Nation's Oldest City, Turns 400. By Robert L. Conly. 196-229, Feb. 1966

ST. BERNARD DOGS:
• The Great St. Bernard Hospice Today. By George Pickow. 49-62, Jan. 1957

ST. BERNARD HOSPICE, Switzerland:
• The Great St. Bernard Hospice Today. By George Pickow. 49-62, Jan. 1957

ST. BOTOLPH'S Town: the Original Boston. By Veronica Thomas. Photos by James L. Amos. 382-389, Sept. 1974

ST. CATHERINES (Island), Georgia:
• Sea Islands: Adventuring Along the South's Surprising Coast. By James Cerruti. Photos by Thomas Nebbia and James L. Amos. 366-393, Mar. 1971

ST. CATHERINE'S MONASTERY, Sinai (Peninsula):
• Island of Faith in the Sinai Wilderness. By George H. Forsyth. Photos by Robert F. Sisson. 82-106, Jan. 1964
• Mount Sinai's Holy Treasures. By Kurt Weitzmann. Photos by Fred Anderegg. 109-127, Jan. 1964
• Sinai Sheds New Light on the Bible. By Henry Field. Photos by William B. and Gladys Terry. 795-815, Dec. 1948

ST. CHRISTOPHER (Island), West Indies:
• A Fresh Breeze Stirs the Leewards. By Carleton Mitchell. Photos by Winfield Parks. 488-537, Oct. 1966

ST. CROIX (Island), U. S. Virgin Islands:
• Buck Island–Underwater Jewel. By Jerry and Idaz Greenberg. 677-683, May 1971
• The U. S. Virgin Islands. By Thomas J. Colin. Photos by William Albert Allard and Cary Wolinsky. 225-243, Feb. 1981

ST. CROIX RIVER, Minnesota-Wisconsin:
• Our Wild and Scenic Rivers: The St. Croix. By David S. Boyer. 30-37, July 1977

ST

ST. ELIAS, Mount, Alaska-Canada:
• First American Ascent of Mount St. Elias. By Maynard M. Miller. 229-248, Feb. 1948

ST. EUSTATIUS (Island). *See* Sint Eustatius

ST. HELENA (Island), Atlantic Ocean:
• Napoleon. By John J. Putman. Photos by Gordon W. Gahan. 142-189, Feb. 1982
• St. Helena: the Forgotten Island. By Quentin Keynes. 265-280, Aug. 1950
• The Sunken Treasure of St. Helena. By Robert Sténuit. Photos by Bates Littlehales. 562-576, Oct. 1978

ST. HELENS, Mount, Washington:
• Editorial. By Wilbur E. Garrett. 1, Jan. 1981
• Eruption of Mount St. Helens. By Rowe Findley. 3-65, Jan. 1981
I. Mountain With a Death Wish. 3-33; II. In the Path of Destruction. 35-49; III. The Day the Sky Fell. 50-65
• Mount St. Helens Aftermath: The Mountain That Was–and Will Be. By Rowe Findley. Photos by Steve Raymer. 713-733, Dec. 1981

ST. JOHN ISLAND, U. S. Virgin Islands:
• Tektite II (Sea and Space Research Project). 256-296, Aug. 1971
• The U. S. Virgin Islands. By Thomas J. Colin. Photos by William Albert Allard and Cary Wolinsky. 225-243, Feb. 1981

SAINT JOHN RIVER AND VALLEY, Canada-U. S.:
• Madawaska: Down East With a French Accent. By Perry Garfinkel. Photos by Cary Wolinsky. 380-409, Sept. 1980

ST. JOHN'S, Newfoundland:
• Newfoundland, Canada's New Province. By Andrew H. Brown. Photos by author and Robert F. Sisson. 777-812, June 1949
• Newfoundland Trusts in the Sea. By Gary Jennings. Photos by Sam Abell. 112-141, Jan. 1974

ST. KITTS (Island). *See* St. Christopher

ST. LAWRENCE, Gulf of, Canada:
• Sea Bird Cities Off Audubon's Labrador. By Arthur A. Allen. NGS research grant. 755-774, June 1948

ST. LAWRENCE RIVER, Canada-U. S.:
• North Through History Aboard *White Mist.* By Melville Bell Grosvenor. Photos by Edwin Stuart Grosvenor. 1-55, July 1970
• Quebec's Forests, Farms, and Frontiers. By Andrew H. Brown. 431-470, Oct. 1949
• The St. Lawrence, River Key to Canada. By Howard La Fay. Photos by John Launois. 622-667, May 1967
• The St. Lawrence River: Canada's Highway to the Sea. By William S. Ellis. Photos by Bruce Dale. 586-623, May 1980
• Sea to Lakes on the St. Lawrence. By George W. Long. Photos by B. Anthony Stewart and John E. Fletcher. 323-366, Sept. 1950
• *See also* Montreal; Quebec (City)

ST. LAWRENCE SEAWAY, Canada-U. S.:
• New St. Lawrence Seaway Opens the Great Lakes to the World. By Andrew H. Brown. 299-339, Mar. 1959
• The St. Lawrence River: Canada's Highway to the Sea. By William S. Ellis. Photos by Bruce Dale. 586-623, May 1980

ST. LEVAN, BARON and BARONESS:
• Fabled Mount of St. Michael. By Alan Villiers. Photos by Bates Littlehales. 880-898, June 1964

ST. LOUIS, Île, Paris, France:
• Île de la Cité, Birthplace of Paris. By Kenneth MacLeish. Photos by Bruce Dale. 680-719, May 1968
• The More Paris Changes.... By Howell Walker. Photos by Gordon W. Gahan. 64-103, July 1972

ST. LOUIS, Missouri:
• "Pyramids" of the New World. By Neil Merton Judd. Included: "The Mound City." 105-128, Jan. 1948
• St. Louis: New Spirit Soars in Mid-America's Proud Old City. By Robert Paul Jordan. Photos by Bruce Dale. 605-641, Nov. 1965
• So Long, St. Louis, We're Heading West. By William C. Everhart. 643-669, Nov. 1965

ST. LUCIA (Island), West Indies:
• *Finisterre* Sails the Windward Islands. By Carleton Mitchell. Photos by Winfield Parks. 755-801, Dec. 1965

ST. MARGARETS BAY, Canada:
• Plight of the Bluefin Tuna. By Michael J. A. Butler. Photos by David Doubilet. Paintings by Stanley Meltzoff. 220-239, Aug. 1982

ST. MARTIN (Island), Netherlands Antilles. *See* Sint Maarten

ST. MARY ISLANDS SANCTUARY, Quebec, Canada:
• Sea Bird Cities Off Audubon's Labrador. By Arthur A. Allen. Contents: Birds on Cliff, Harbour, and Middle Islands. NGS research grant. 755-774, June 1948

ST. MARYS, West Virginia:
• So Much Happens Along the Ohio River. By Frederick Simpich. Photos by Justin Locke. 177-212, Feb. 1950

ST. MICHAEL'S MOUNT, England:
• Fabled Mount of St. Michael. By Alan Villiers. Photos by Bates Littlehales. 880-898, June 1964

ST. PAUL (Apostle). *See* Paul, Saint

ST. PAUL, Minnesota:
• Minneapolis and St. Paul. By Thomas J. Abercrombie. Photos by Annie Griffiths. 665-691, Nov. 1980
• Minnesota, Where Water Is the Magic Word. By David S. Boyer. Photos by author and David Brill. 200-229, Feb. 1976
• Minnesota Makes Ideas Pay. By Frederick G. Vosburgh. Photos by John E. Fletcher and B. Anthony Stewart. 291-336, Sept. 1949
• The Upper Mississippi. By Willard Price. 651-699, Nov. 1958

ST. PETER'S (Basilica), Vatican City:
• Rome: Eternal City with a Modern Air. By Harnett T. Kane. Photos by B. Anthony Stewart. 437-491, Apr. 1957
• St. Peter's, Rome's Church of Popes. By Aubrey Menen. Photos by Albert Moldvay. 865-879, Dec. 1971
• When in Rome.... By Stuart E. Jones. Photos by Winfield Parks. 741-789, June 1970

ST. PIERRE, Martinique:
• Martinique: A Tropical Bit of France. By Gwen Drayton Allmon. Photos by Charles Allmon. 255-283, Feb. 1959

ST. PIERRE AND MIQUELON (Archipelago), North Atlantic Ocean:
• *White Mist* Cruises to Wreck-haunted St. Pierre and Miquelon. By Melville Bell Grosvenor. 378-419, Sept. 1967

ST. SIMONS (Island), Georgia:
• Sea Islands: Adventuring Along the South's Surprising Coast. By James Cerruti. Photos by Thomas Nebbia and James L. Amos. 366-393, Mar. 1971

ST. THOMAS (Island), U. S. Virgin Islands:
• A Fresh Breeze Stirs the Leewards. By Carleton Mitchell. Photos by Winfield Parks. 488-537, Oct. 1966
• The U. S. Virgin Islands. By Thomas J. Colin. Photos by William Albert Allard and Cary Wolinsky. 225-243, Feb. 1981
• Virgin Islands: Tropical Playland, U.S.A. By John Scofield. Photos by Charles Allmon. 201-232, Feb. 1956

SAINT VÉRAN, France's Highest Village. By Robert K. Burns, Jr. 571-588, Apr. 1959

ST. VINCENT (Island), West Indies:
• *Finisterre* Sails the Windward Islands. By Carleton Mitchell. Photos by Winfield Parks. 755-801, Dec. 1965
• St. Vincent, the Grenadines, and Grenada: Taking It as It Comes. By Ethel A. Starbird. Photos by Cotton Coulson. 399-425, Sept. 1979

STE. CÉCILE, Cathedral of, Albi, France:
• France's Past Lives in Languedoc. By Walter Meayers Edwards. 1-43, July 1951

SAKELLARAKIS, YANNIS: Author:
• Drama of Death in a Minoan Temple. By Yannis Sakellarakis and Efi Sapouna-Sakellaraki. Photos by Otis Imboden and Spyros Tsavdaroglou. 205-222, Feb. 1981

SALAMANDERS:
• In the Wilds of a City Parlor. By Paul A. Zahl. 645-672, Nov. 1954
• The Shadowy World of Salamanders. By Paul A. Zahl. 104-117, July 1972

SALB, WOLFGANG A.: Photographer:
• Saving the Philippine Eagle. By Robert S. Kennedy. Photos by Alan R. Degen, Neil L. Rettig, and Wolfgang A. Salb. 847-856, June 1981

SALEM, Massachusetts:
● Literary Landmarks of Massachusetts. By William H. Nicholas. Photos by B. Anthony Stewart and John E. Fletcher. 279-310, Mar. 1950

SALERNO, Gulf of:
● Amalfi, Italy's Divine Coast. By Luis Marden. 472-509, Oct. 1959

SALERNO, Italy:
● Italy Smiles Again. By Edgar Erskine Hume. 693-732, June 1949

SALISBURY, Rhodesia:
● Rhodesia, a House Divided. By Allan C. Fisher, Jr. Photos by Thomas Nebbia. 641-671, May 1975

SALMON (River), Idaho:
● White-water Adventure on Wild Rivers of Idaho. By Frank Craighead, Jr. and John Craighead. 213-239, Feb. 1970
■ Wild River. 239A-239B, Feb. 1970
● *See also* Morgan Creek

SALMON:
● Atlantic Salmon: The "Leaper" Struggles to Survive. By Art Lee. Photos by Bianca Lavies. 600-615, Nov. 1981
● The Columbia River, Powerhouse of the Northwest. By David S. Boyer. 821-847, Dec. 1974
● *Endeavour* Sails the Inside Passage. By Amos Burg. 801-828, June 1947
● The Incredible Salmon. By Clarence P. Idyll. Photos by Robert F. Sisson. Paintings by Walter A. Weber. 195-219, Aug. 1968
Life portraits of a famous family: Pacific salmon. 214-216
● A River Restored: Oregon's Willamette. By Ethel A. Starbird. Photos by Lowell J. Georgia. 816-835, June 1972
● When Giant Bears Go Fishing. By Cecil E. Rhode. 195-205, Aug. 1954

SALT:
● I Joined a Sahara Salt Caravan. By Victor Englebert. 694-711, Nov. 1965
● Salt–The Essence of Life. By Gordon Young. Photos by Volkmar Wentzel and Georg Gerster. 381-401, Sept. 1977
● *See also* Danakil Depression; Salt Lakes; Salzkammergut

SALT LAKE CITY, Utah:
● Utah's Shining Oasis. By Charles McCarry. Photos by James L. Amos. 440-473, Apr. 1975

SALT LAKES:
● Strange World of Palau's Salt Lakes. By William M. Hamner. Photos by David Doubilet. 264-282, Feb. 1982
● *See also* Dead Sea; Great Salt Lake; Mono Lake

SALT MARSHES:
● Can We Save Our Salt Marshes? By Stephen W. Hitchcock. Photos by William R. Curtsinger. 729-765, June 1972
● Sea Islands: Adventuring Along the South's Surprising Coast. By James Cerruti. Photos by Thomas Nebbia and James L. Amos. 366-393, Mar. 1971

SALT MINES:
● Salt–The Essence of Life. By Gordon Young. Photos by Volkmar Wentzel and Georg Gerster. 381-401, Sept. 1977
● Salzkammergut, Austria's Alpine Playground. By Beverley M. Bowie. Photos by Volkmar Wentzel. 246-275, Aug. 1960

SALUT, Îles du, French Guiana. *See* Devil's Island

SALVAGE:
● Exploring a 140-year-old Ship Under Arctic Ice *(Breadalbane).* By Joseph B. MacInnis. Photos by Emory Kristof. 104A-104D, July 1983
● Ghost Ships of the War of 1812: *Hamilton* and *Scourge*. By Daniel A. Nelson. Photos by Emory Kristof. Paintings by Richard Schlecht. 289-313, Mar. 1983
● Graveyard of the Quicksilver Galleons. By Mendel Peterson. Photos by Jonathan Blair. Contents: The *Nuestra Señora de Guadalupe* and the *Conde de Tolosa*. 850-876, Dec. 1979
● Henry VIII's Lost Warship: *Mary Rose*. By Margaret Rule. Introduction and picture text by Peter Miller. Paintings by Richard Schlecht. 646-675, May 1983
▲ "History Salvaged From the Sea," painting supplement. Map on reverse. Dec. 1977
● The Lost Fleet of Kublai Khan. By Torao Mozai. Photos by Koji Nakamura. Paintings by Issho Yada. 634-649, Nov. 1982
● New Life for the Troubled Suez Canal. By William Graves. Photos by Jonathan Blair. 792-817, June 1975
● Reach for the New World. By Mendel Peterson. Photos by David L. Arnold. Paintings by Richard Schlecht. 724-767, Dec. 1977
■ Treasure! 575, Nov. 1976; cover, Dec. 1976
● Treasure From the Ghost Galleon: *Santa Margarita*. By Eugene Lyon. Photos by Don Kincaid. Contents: *Atocha; Santa Margarita*. 228-243, Feb. 1982
● Warriors From a Watery Grave (Bronze Sculptures). By Joseph Alsop. 821-827, June 1983
● *See also* Ceramics; Glass; Spanish Treasure; *and* Kyrenia Ship; *Monitor; Slot ter Hooge; Thresher; Vasa; Witte Leeuw;* Yassi Ada

SALZBURG, Austria:
● Occupied Austria, Outpost of Democracy. By George W. Long. Photos by Volkmar Wentzel. 749-790, June 1951

SALZKAMMERGUT, Austria's Alpine Playground. By Beverley M. Bowie. Photos by Volkmar Wentzel. 246-275, Aug. 1960

JONATHAN BLAIR

Suez Canal: Egyptian soldier detonates mines

S T

SAMARITANS:
• Hashemite Jordan, Arab Heartland. By John Scofield. 841-856, Dec. 1952

SAMOA:
• Problems in Paradise. By Mary and Laurance S. Rockefeller. Photos by Thomas Nebbia. 782-793, Dec. 1974
• A Teen-ager Sails the World Alone. By Robin Lee Graham. 445-491, Oct. 1968
• Western Samoa, the Pacific's Newest Nation. By Maurice Shadbolt. Photos by Robert B. Goodman. 573-602, Oct. 1962

SAMPSON, PAUL: Author:
• The Bonins and Iwo Jima Go Back to Japan. Photos by Joe Munroe. 128-144, July 1968

SAMUELS, GERTRUDE: Author:
• Passage to Freedom in Viet Nam. 858-874, June 1955

SAN (People). *See* Bushmen (Namibia)

SAN ANDREAS FAULT, California:
• California's San Andreas Fault. By Thomas Y. Canby. Photos by James P. Blair. 38-53, Jan. 1973

SAN ANTONIO, Texas:
• Carnival in San Antonio. By Mason Sutherland. Photos by J. Baylor Roberts. 813-844, Dec. 1947
• The Fabulous State of Texas. By Stanley Walker. Photos by B. Anthony Stewart and Thomas Nebbia. 149-195, Feb. 1961
• The Mexican Americans: A People on the Move. By Griffin Smith, Jr. Photos by Stephanie Maze. 780-809, June 1980
• San Antonio: "Texas, Actin' Kind of Natural." By Fred Kline. Photos by David Hiser. 524-549, Apr. 1976

SAN DIEGO, California:
• California, Horn of Plenty. By Frederick Simpich. Photos by Willard R. Culver. 553-594, May 1949
• California, the Golden Magnet. By William Graves. 595-679, May 1966
I. The South. Photos by Thomas Nebbia. 595-639
• New Rush to Golden California. By George W. Long. 723-802, June 1954
• San Diego, California's Plymouth Rock. By Allan C. Fisher, Jr. Photos by James L. Amos. 114-147, July 1969

SAN FRANCISCO (City and Bay), California:
• Barehanded Battle to Cleanse the Bay. By Peter T. White. Photos by Jonathan S. Blair. 866-881, June 1971
• Boom on San Francisco Bay. By Franc Shor. Photos by David S. Boyer. 181-226, Aug. 1956
• California, Horn of Plenty. By Frederick Simpich. Photos by Willard R. Culver. 553-594, May 1949
• California, the Golden Magnet. By William Graves. 595-679, May 1966
II. Nature's North. Photos by James P. Blair and Jonathan S. Blair. 641-679

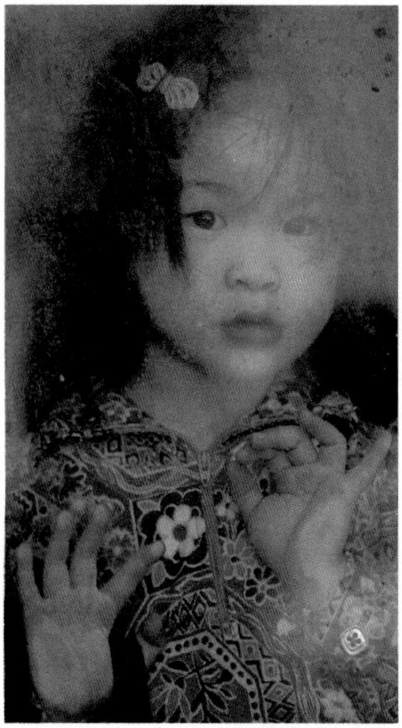

WILLIAM ALBERT ALLARD

Chinatown: child of the ghetto

San Francisco Bay: cable-car ride

JAMES L. STANFIELD, NGS.

• Chinatown, the Gilded Ghetto. By William Albert Allard. 627-643, Nov. 1975
• New Rush to Golden California. By George W. Long. 723-802, June 1954
▲ *Northern California; Southern California,* double-sided U. S. Atlas series supplement. May 1966
• San Francisco Bay: The Beauty and the Battles. By Cliff Tarpy. Photos by James A. Sugar. 814-845, June 1981
• San Francisco Bay, the Westward Gate. By William Graves. Photos by James L. Stanfield. 593-637, Nov. 1969
• This Changing Earth. By Samuel W. Matthews. Included: 1906 earthquake. 1-37, Jan. 1973

SAN FRANCISCO BAY, California:
• Barehanded Battle to Cleanse the Bay. By Peter T. White. Photos by Jonathan S. Blair. 866-881, June 1971
• Boom on San Francisco Bay. By Franc Shor. Photos by David S. Boyer. 181-226, Aug. 1956
• San Francisco Bay: The Beauty and the Battles. By Cliff Tarpy. Photos by James A. Sugar. 814-845, June 1981
• San Francisco Bay, the Westward Gate. By William Graves. Photos by James L. Stanfield. 593-637, Nov. 1969
• *See also* Golden Gate National Recreation Area

SAN JACINTO WEEK (Fiesta):
• Carnival in San Antonio. By Mason Sutherland. Photos by J. Baylor Roberts. 813-844, Dec. 1947

SAN JUAN, Puerto Rico:
• Growing Pains Beset Puerto Rico. By William H. Nicholas. Photos by Justin Locke. 419-460, Apr. 1951
• Puerto Rico's Seven-league Bootstraps. By Bart McDowell. Photos by B. Anthony Stewart. 755-793, Dec. 1962
• The Uncertain State of Puerto Rico. By Bill Richards. Photos by Stephanie Maze. 516-543, Apr. 1983

SAN JUAN (River), U. S.:
• Desert River Through Navajo Land. By Alfred M. Bailey. Photos by author and Fred G. Brandenburg. 149-172, Aug. 1947
• *See also* Powell, Lake, Arizona-Utah

SAN JUAN ISLANDS, Washington:
• Puget Sound, Sea Gate of the Pacific Northwest. By William Graves. Photos by David Alan Harvey. 71-97, Jan. 1977

SAN JUAN MOUNTAINS, Colorado-New Mexico:
• Colorado's Friendly Topland. By Robert M. Ormes. 187-214, Aug. 1951

SAN LORENZO, Veracruz, Mexico:
• On the Trail of La Venta Man. By Matthew W. Stirling. Photos by Richard H. Stewart. NGS research grant. 137-172, Feb. 1947
Hunting Mexico's Buried Temples. 145-168

SAN MARCOS, Castillo de, St. Augustine, Florida. *See* Castillo de San Marcos

SAN MARINO (Republic):
● San Marino, Little Land of Liberty. By Donna Hamilton Shor. Photos by Ted H. Funk. 233-251, Aug. 1967
● United Italy Marks Its 100th Year. By Nathaniel T. Kenney. 593-647, Nov. 1961

SAN MARINO, California. *See* Henry E. Huntington Library and Art Gallery

SAN MIGUEL MOUNTAINS, Colorado:
● Colorado's Friendly Topland. By Robert M. Ormes. 187-214, Aug. 1951

SAN SIMEON, California. *See* Hearst San Simeon State Historical Monument

SANCTUARIES. *See* Bird Sanctuaries and Rookeries; Pribilof Islands, for Polovina Seal Rookery; Wildlife Refuges

SAND DUNES:
● The Desert: An Age-old Challenge Grows. By Rick Gore. Photos by Georg Gerster and Bruce Dale. 586-639, Nov. 1979
● Egypt's Desert of Promise. By Farouk El-Baz. Photos by Georg Gerster. 190-221, Feb. 1982
● The Living Sand. By William H. Amos. 820-833, June 1965
● *See also* Namib Desert

SAND HILLS (Region), Nebraska:
● Land of Long Sunsets: Nebraska's Sand Hills. By John Madson. Photos by Jodi Cobb. 493-517, Oct. 1978

SAND in My Eyes. By Jinx Rodger. 664-705, May 1958

SAND YACHTS:
● Dry-land Fleet Sails the Sahara. By Jean du Boucher. Photos by Jonathan S. Blair. 696-725, Nov. 1967
■ Wind Raiders of the Sahara. 436A-436B, Sept. 1973

SANDBURG, CARL: Author:
● Just a Hundred Years Ago (U. S. Civil War). 1-3, July 1963
● Lincoln, Man of Steel and Velvet. 239-241, Feb. 1960

SANDHILL CRANES:
● Beyond the North Wind With the Snow Goose. By Des and Jen Bartlett. 822-843, Dec. 1973
. . . And Then There Was Fred. . . . 843-847
● *See also* Greater Sandhill Cranes

SANDYS, SIR EDWIN:
● Founders of Virginia. By Sir Evelyn Wrench. Photos by B. Anthony Stewart. 433-462, Apr. 1948

SANGER, RICHARD H.: Photographer:
● Ancient "Skyscrapers" of the Yemen. 645-668, Nov. 1947

SANGRE DE CRISTO MOUNTAINS, New Mexico:
● New Mexico's Mountains of Mystery. By Robert Laxalt. Photos by Craig Aurness. 416-436, Sept. 1978

SANTA BARBARA ISLANDS, California:
● Off Santa Barbara: California's Ranches in the Sea. By Earl Warren, Jr. Photos by Bates Littlehales. 257-283, Aug. 1958

SANTA CATALINA ISLAND, California:
● Undersea World of a Kelp Forest. By Sylvia A. Earle. Photos by Al Giddings. 411-426, Sept. 1980

SANTA CLARA COUNTY, California:
● California's Silicon Valley. By Moira Johnston. Photos by Charles O'Rear. 459-477, Oct. 1982

SANTA CRUZ ISLAND, California:
● Off Santa Barbara: California's Ranches in the Sea. By Earl Warren, Jr. Photos by Bates Littlehales. 257-283, Aug. 1958

SANTA FE, New Mexico:
● Adobe New Mexico. By Mason Sutherland. Photos by Justin Locke. 783-830, Dec. 1949
● Goal at the End of the Trail: Santa Fe. By William S. Ellis. Photos by Gordon W. Gahan and Otis Imboden. 323-345, Mar. 1982
● New Mexico: The Golden Land. By Robert Laxalt. Photos by Adam Woolfitt. 299-345, Sept. 1970

SANTA LUISA (Site), Mexico:
● Man's Eighty Centuries in Veracruz. By S. Jeffrey K. Wilkerson. Photos by David Hiser. Paintings by Richard Schlecht. NGS research grant. 203-231, Aug. 1980

SANTA MARGARITA (Galleon):
● Treasure From the Ghost Galleon: *Santa Margarita*. By Eugene Lyon. Photos by Don Kincaid. 228-243, Feb. 1982

SANTA ROSA ISLAND, California:
● Off Santa Barbara: California's Ranches in the Sea. By Earl Warren, Jr. Photos by Bates Littlehales. 257-283, Aug. 1958

SANTANDER, Spain:
● Under Canvas in the Atomic Age (United States Coast Guard Cadets). By Alan Villiers. 49-84, July 1955

SANTIAGO, Chile:
● Chile, Republic on a Shoestring. By Gordon Young. Photos by George F. Mobley. 437-477, Oct. 1973
● Chile, the Long and Narrow Land. By Kip Ross. 185-235, Feb. 1960

SANTIAGO ATITLÁN, Guatemala:
● Guatemala, Maya and Modern. By Louis de la Haba. Photos by Joseph J. Scherschel. 661-689, Nov. 1974
● Guatemala Revisited. By Luis Marden. 525-564, Oct. 1947

SANTORINI (Island), Greece. *See* Thera

SÃO PAULO, Brazil:
● Brazil's Golden Beachhead. By Bart McDowell. Photos by Nicholas DeVore III. 246-277, Feb. 1978

SAPELO (Island), Georgia:
● Sea Islands: Adventuring Along the South's Surprising Coast. By James Cerruti. Photos by Thomas Nebbia and James L. Amos. 366-393, Mar. 1971

SAPOUNA-SAKELLARAKI, EFI: **Author:**
● Drama of Death in a Minoan Temple. By Yannis Sakellarakis and Efi Sapouna-Sakellaraki. Photos by Otis Imboden and Spyros Tsavdaroglou. 205-222, Feb. 1981

SAPPORO, Japan:
● Snow Festival in Japan's Far North. By Eiji Miyazawa. 824-833, Dec. 1968

SAPSUCKER WOODS, Cornell University's Exciting New Bird Sanctuary. By Arthur A. Allen. 530-551, Apr. 1962

SARA (Tribespeople):
● Into the Heart of Africa. By Gertrude S. Weeks. NGS research grant. 257-263, Aug. 1956

SARAWAK:
● Ambassadors of Good Will: The Peace Corps. By Sargent Shriver and Peace Corps Volunteers. 297-345, Sept. 1964
Sarawak. By Edwin C. Price, Jr. 334-337
● In Storied Lands of Malaysia. By Maurice Shadbolt. Photos by Winfield Parks. 734-783, Nov. 1963
● Jungle Journeys in Sarawak. By Hedda Morrison. 710-736, May 1956

SARCOPHAGI:
● Ancient Shipwreck Yields New Facts–and a Strange Cargo. By Peter Throckmorton. Photos by Kim Hart and Joseph J. Scherschel. 282-300, Feb. 1969
● Fresh Treasures from Egypt's Ancient Sands. By Jefferson Caffery. Photos by David S. Boyer. 611-650, Nov. 1955

SARGASSO SEA:
● Night Life in the Gulf Stream. By Paul A. Zahl. 391-418, Mar. 1954

SARGASSUM:
● Adrift on a Raft of Sargassum. Photos by Robert F. Sisson. 188-199, Feb. 1976

SARGASSUM FISH:
● Adrift on a Raft of Sargassum. Photos by Robert F. Sisson. 188-199, Feb. 1976

SARGON II, King (Assyria):
● Ancient Mesopotamia: A Light That Did Not Fail. By E. A. Speiser. Paintings by H. M. Herget. 41-105, Jan. 1951

SARK (Island), English Channel:
● Britain's "French" Channel Islands. By James Cerruti. Photos by James L. Amos. 710-740, May 1971

SARTWELL, FRANK: Author:
● Mariner Scans a Lifeless Venus. Paintings by Davis Meltzer. 733-742, May 1963
● Robots to the Moon. Paintings by Pierre Mion. 557-571, Oct. 1962

SASKATCHEWAN (Province), Canada:
● Canada's Heartland, the Prairie Provinces. By W. E. Garrett. 443-489, Oct. 1970
● The Canadian North: Emerging Giant. By David S. Boyer. 1-43, July 1968
▲ *Close-up, Canada: Saskatchewan, Manitoba, Northwest Territories,* supplement. Text on reverse. May 1979
● Hunting Uranium Around the World. By Robert D. Nininger. Photos by Volkmar Wentzel. 533-558, Oct. 1954
● The People Who Made Saskatchewan. By Ethel A. Starbird. Photos by Craig Aurness. 651-679, May 1979

SASS, HERBERT RAVENEL: Author:
● South Carolina Rediscovered. Photos by Robert F. Sisson. 281-321, Mar. 1953

SATELLITE FINDER:
▲ The National Geographic Society Satellite Finder (Map overlay). 808-809, Dec. 1957

SATELLITES:
● How Man-made Satellites Can Affect Our Lives. By Joseph Kaplan. 791-810, Dec. 1957
● The Next Frontier? By Isaac Asimov. Paintings by Pierre Mion. 76-89, July 1976
● Satellites Gave Warning of Midwest Floods. By Peter T. White. Photos by Thomas A. DeFeo. 574-592, Oct. 1969
● Satellites That Serve Us. By Thomas Y. Canby. Included: A portfolio: Images of Earth. 281-335, Sept. 1983
Spacelab 1: *Columbia.* By Michael E. Long. 301-307
● Space Satellites, Tools of Earth Research. By Heinz Haber. Paintings by William N. Palmstrom. 487-509, Apr. 1956
● Telephone a Star: the Story of Communications Satellites. By Rowe Findley. 638-651, May 1962
● *See also* DODGE Satellite; Landsat; Mariner Missions; Nimbus; Spacelab

The **SATIN** Bowerbird, Australia's Feathered Playboy. By Philip Green. 865-872, Dec. 1977

SATMAR HASIDIM. *See* Hasidic Jews

SATURN (Planet):
▲ *The Solar System; Saturn,* double-sided supplement. July 1981
● Voyage to the Planets. By Kenneth F. Weaver. Paintings by Ludek Pesek. 147-193, Aug. 1970
● Voyager 1 at Saturn: Riddles of the Rings. By Rick Gore. Photos by NASA. Included: Saturnian satellites Dione, Enceladus, Hyperion, Iapetus, Mimas, Rhea, Tethys, Titan. 3-31, July 1981

SATURN V (Rocket):
● First Explorers on the Moon: The Incredible Story of Apollo 11. 735-797, Dec. 1969
III. The Flight of Apollo 11: "One giant leap for mankind." By Kenneth F. Weaver. 752-787; V. Next Steps in Space. By Thomas O. Paine. 793-797
● "A Most Fantastic Voyage": The Story of Apollo 8's Rendezvous With the Moon. By Sam C. Phillips. 593-631, May 1969

MEHMET BIBER

Mecca: Kaaba's gold-and-silver door

SAUD, House of:
● Saudi Arabia: The Kingdom and Its Power. By Robert Azzi. Included: The royal lineage from King Abdulaziz Al Saud (1880-1953). 286-333, Sept. 1980

SAUDI ARABIA:
▲ *Africa and the Arabian Peninsula,* supplement. Mar. 1950
● The Arab World. 712-732, Nov. 1958
● The Arab World, Inc. By John J. Putman. Photos by Winfield Parks. 494-533, Oct. 1975
● From America to Mecca on Airborne Pilgrimage. By Abdul Ghafur. 1-60, July 1953
● In Search of Arabia's Past. By Peter Bruce Cornwall. 493-522, Apr. 1948
Saudi Arabia, Oil Kingdom. Photos by Maynard Owen Williams. 497-512
● Oil, the Dwindling Treasure. By Noel Grove. Photos by Emory Kristof. 792-825, June 1974
● Pilgrimage to Mecca. By Muhammad Abdul-Rauf. Photos by Mehmet Biber. 581-607, Nov. 1978
● Saudi Arabia: Beyond the Sands of Mecca. By Thomas J. Abercrombie. 1-53, Jan. 1966
● Saudi Arabia: The Kingdom and Its Power. By Robert Azzi. 286-333, Sept. 1980
● The Sword and the Sermon. By Thomas J. Abercrombie. Included: Mecca, Medina. 3-45, July 1972
● Troubled Waters East of Suez. By Ernest M. Eller. 483-522, Apr. 1954

SAVANNAH, N. S.:
● Aboard the N. S. *Savannah:* World's First Nuclear Merchantman. By Alan Villiers. Photos by John E. Fletcher. 280-298, Aug. 1962

SAVANNAH to Charleston–A Good Life in the Low Country. By John J. Putman. Photos by Annie Griffiths. 798-829, Dec. 1983

SAVE-THE-REDWOODS League. 682, May 1951; 510, Oct. 1957; 658, Nov. 1963; 15, 28, 44, July 1964; 60, 63, 67, July 1966

SAVING Brazil's Stone Age Tribes From Extinction. By Orlando and Claudio Villas Boas. Photos by W. Jesco von Puttkamer. 424-444, Sept. 1968

SAVING Earth's Oldest Living Things. By Andrew H. Brown. Photos by Raymond Moulin and author. 679-695, May 1951

SAVING Man's Wildlife Heritage. By John H. Baker. Photos by Robert F. Sisson. 581-620, Nov. 1954

SAVING Père David's Deer. By Larry Kohl. Photos by Bates Littlehales. 478-485, Oct. 1982

SAVING the Ancient Temples at Abu Simbel. By Georg Gerster. Paintings by Robert W. Nicholson. 694-742, May 1966

SAVING the Nene, World's Rarest Goose. By S. Dillon Ripley. Photos by Jerry Chong. 745-754, Nov. 1965

SAVING the Philippine Eagle. By Robert S. Kennedy. Photos by Alan R. Degen, Neil L. Rettig, and Wolfgang A. Salb. NGS research grant. 847-856, June 1981

SAVING the Rothschild's Giraffe. By Carolyn Bennett Patterson. 419-421, Sept. 1977

SAXONY (Region), East Germany:
● Treasures of Dresden. By John L. Eliot. Photos by Victor R. Boswell, Jr. 702-717, Nov. 1978

SCALLOPS:
● The Magic Lure of Sea Shells. By Paul A. Zahl. Photos by Victor R. Boswell, Jr. and author. 386-429, Mar. 1969
● Shells Take You Over World Horizons. By Rutherford Platt. 33-84, July 1949

SCAMMON LAGOON, Baja California, Mexico:
● The California Gray Whale Comes Back. By Theodore J. Walker. 394-415, Mar. 1971
● Hunting the Heartbeat of a Whale. By Paul Dudley White and Samuel W. Matthews. NGS research grant. 49-64, July 1956

SCANDINAVIA:
● Friendly Flight to Northern Europe. By Lyndon B. Johnson. Photos by Volkmar Wentzel. 268-293, Feb. 1964
● Hunters of the Lost Spirit: Lapps. By Priit J. Vesilind. Photos by Sisse Brimberg. 194-197, Feb. 1983
■ The Last Vikings. 434A-434B, Mar. 1972
▲ *Northern Europe,* supplement. Aug. 1954
▲ *Peoples of the Arctic; Arctic Ocean,* double-sided supplement. Feb. 1983
▲ *Scandinavia,* Atlas series supplement. Apr. 1963
● *See also* Denmark; Finland; Iceland; Norway; Sweden

SCAPEGOAT WILDERNESS, Montana:
● Studying Grizzly Habitat by Satellite. By John Craighead. NGS research grant. 148-158, July 1976

SCARLET IBIS:
● New Scarlet Bird in Florida Skies. By Paul A. Zahl. 874-882, Dec. 1967
● Search for the Scarlet Ibis in Venezuela. By Paul A. Zahl. NGS research grant. 633-661, May 1950

SCAVENGERS:
● The Fascinating World of Trash. By Peter T. White. Photos by Louie Psihoyos. 424-457, Apr. 1983

SCENES of Postwar Finland. By La Verne Bradley. Photos by Jerry Waller. 233-264, Aug. 1947

SCENIC Guilin Links China's Past and Present. By W. E. Garrett. 536-563, Oct. 1979

SCHALLER, GEORGE B.:
Author-Photographer:
● Imperiled Phantom of Asian Peaks: First Photographs of Snow Leopards in the Wild. 702-707, Nov. 1971
● Life with the King of Beasts. 494-519, Apr. 1969
● Pandas in the Wild. 735-749, Dec. 1981

SCHEFFER, VICTOR B.: Author:
● Exploring the Lives of Whales. 752-767, Dec. 1976
Author-Photographer:
● The Fur Seal Herd Comes of Age. By Victor B. Scheffer and Karl W. Kenyon. 491-512, Apr. 1952

SCHELLBACH, LOUIS: Author:
● Grand Canyon: Nature's Story of Creation. Photos by Justin Locke. 589-629, May 1955

SCHERSCHEL, JOSEPH J.:
Photographer:
● Ancient Shipwreck Yields New Facts–and a Strange Cargo. By Peter Throckmorton. Photos by Kim Hart and Joseph J. Scherschel. 282-300, Feb. 1969
● Andalusia, the Spirit of Spain. By Howard La Fay. 833-857, June 1975
● Freedom's Progress South of the Sahara. By Howard La Fay. 603-637, Nov. 1962
● Guatemala, Maya and Modern. By Louis de la Haba. 661-689, Nov. 1974
● Hungary: Changing Homeland of a Tough, Romantic People. By Bart McDowell. Photos by Albert Moldvay and Joseph J. Scherschel. 443-483, Apr. 1971
● Illinois: The City and the Plain. By Robert Paul Jordan. Photos by James L. Stanfield and Joseph J. Scherschel. 745-797, June 1967
● Inside Europe Aboard *Yankee.* By Irving and Electa Johnson. 157-195, Aug. 1964
● The Journey of Burke and Wills: First Across Australia. By Joseph Judge. 152-191, Feb. 1979
● Lombardy's Lakes, Blue Jewels in Italy's Crown. By Franc Shor. 58-99, July 1968
● Macao Clings to the Bamboo Curtain. By Jules B. Billard. 521-539, Apr. 1969
● Mobile, Alabama's City in Motion. By William Graves. Photos by Joseph J. Scherschel and Robert W. Madden. 368-397, Mar. 1968
● Preserving the Treasures of Olduvai Gorge. By Melvin M. Payne. 701-709, Nov. 1966
● South Australia, Gateway to the Great Outback. By Howell Walker. 441-481, Apr. 1970
● Sunny Corsica: French Morsel in the Mediterranean. By Robert Cairns. 401-423, Sept. 1973
● *Yankee* Cruises Turkey's History-haunted Coast. By Irving and Electa Johnson. 798-845, Dec. 1969

SCHIRRA, WALTER M., Jr.:
● Space Rendezvous, Milestone on the Way to the Moon. By Kenneth F. Weaver. 539-553, Apr. 1966

SCHLECHT, RICHARD: Artist:
● First Look at a Lost Virginia Settlement (Martin's Hundred). By Ivor Noël Hume. Photos by Ira Block. 735-767, June 1979
● Ghost Ships of the War of 1812: *Hamilton* and *Scourge.* By Daniel A. Nelson. Photos by Emory Kristof. 289-313, Mar. 1983
● Henry VIII's Lost Warship: *Mary Rose.* By Margaret Rule. Introduction and picture text by Peter Miller. 646-675, May 1983
▲ "History Salvaged From the Sea," painting supplement. Map on reverse. Dec. 1977
● Man's Eighty Centuries in Veracruz. By S. Jeffrey K. Wilkerson. Photos by David Hiser. 203-231, Aug. 1980
▲ "Medieval England," painting supplement. Map on reverse. Oct. 1979
● New Clues to an Old Mystery (Virginia's Wolstenholme Towne). By Ivor Noël Hume. Photos by Ira Block. 53-77, Jan. 1982
● Reach for the New World. By Mendel Peterson. Photos by David L. Arnold. 724-767, Dec. 1977

SCHLEDERMANN, PETER: Author:
● Eskimo and Viking Finds in the High Arctic: Ellesmere Island. Photos by Sisse Brimberg. Included: Artifacts of the Norse, the Dorset, the Thule. 575-601, May 1981

SCHMIDT, BERNHARD:
● Mapping the Unknown Universe. By F. Barrows Colton. Note: Bernhard Schmidt invented the "Big Schmidt" telescope. 401-420, Sept. 1950

SCHMIDT, CAROL: Photographer:
● Down on the Farm, Soviet Style–a 4-H Adventure. By John Garaventa. Photos by James Tobin and Carol Schmidt. 768-797, June 1979

SCHMITT, HARRISON H.:
Author-Photographer:
● Exploring Taurus-Littrow. 290-307, Sept. 1973
Photographer:
▲ "The Earth From Space," photo supplement. Painting on reverse. Sept. 1973

SCHNEEBERGER, JON:
Author-Photographer:
● Escalante Canyon–Wilderness at the Crossroads. 270-285, Aug. 1972
Photographer:
● When the Space Shuttle Finally Flies. By Rick Gore. Paintings by Ken Dallison. 317-347, Mar. 1981

SCHOFIELD, PHIL: Photographer:
● A Paradise Called the Palouse. By Barbara Austin. 798-819, June 1982

SCHOOL BULLETIN, NGS:
● The *School Bulletin* is retired after 56 years; replaced by *WORLD.* 299, Sept. 1975

SCHOOL for Space Monkeys. 725-729, May 1961

SCHOOL for Survival. By Curtis E. LeMay. 565-602, May 1953

SCHOOLS:
● The DAR Story. By Lonnelle Aikman. Photos by B. Anthony Stewart and John E. Fletcher. Note: DAR partially supports a dozen schools and colleges in this country, maintains a large student-loan fund, presents annual awards for high

S
T

standing in certain subjects, and operates two schools of its own, the Kate Duncan Smith School, Grant, Alabama, and Tamassee School, South Carolina. 565-598, Nov. 1951
• Round the World School (International School of America). By Paul Antze. Photos by William Eppridge. 96-127, July 1962
• We Build a School for Sherpa Children. By Sir Edmund Hillary. 548-551, Oct. 1962
• Zoo Animals Go to School. By Marion P. McCrane. Photos by W. E. Garrett. 694-706, Nov. 1956
• *See also* The Deaf, Schools for; National Outdoor Leadership School; Outward Bound School; U. S. Air Force Academy; U. S. Merchant Marine Academy; U. S. Military Academy; Universities and Colleges

SCHOONERS:
• Down East Cruise. By Tom Horgan. Photos by Luis Marden. 329-369, Sept. 1952
• *See also: Georg Stage;* Portuguese Fishing Fleet; *Vaitere*

SCHREIBER, RALPH W.:
Author-Photographer:
• Bad Days for the Brown Pelican. Photos by William R. Curtsinger and author. 111-123, Jan. 1975

SCHREIDER, HELEN and FRANK:
Author-Photographers:
• East From Bali by Seagoing Jeep to Timor. 236-279, Aug. 1962
• From the Hair of Siva (Ganges River, India). 445-503, Oct. 1960
• In the Footsteps of Alexander the Great. Paintings by Tom Lovell. 1-65, Jan. 1968
• Indonesia, the Young and Troubled Island Nation. 579-625, May 1961
• Journey Into the Great Rift: the Northern Half. 254-290, Aug. 1965
• Taiwan: The Watchful Dragon. 1-45, Jan. 1969

SCHROEDER, ROBERT E.:
Author-Photographer:
• Photographing the Night Creatures of Alligator Reef (Florida). Photos by author and Walter A. Starck. 124-154, Jan. 1964
Photographer:
• Imperiled Gift of the Sea: Caribbean Green Turtle. By Archie Carr. 876-890, June 1967

SCHULKE, FLIP: Photographer:
• My Neighbors Hold to Mountain Ways (Blue Ridge, North Carolina). By Malcolm Ross. 856-880, June 1958
• Titicaca, Abode of the Sun. By Luis Marden. 272-294, Feb. 1971

SCHULMAN, EDMUND: Author:
• Bristlecone Pine, Oldest Known Living Thing. Photos by W. Robert Moore. 355-372, Mar. 1958

SCHULTZ, HARALD:
Author-Photographer:
• Blue-eyed Indian. 65-89, July 1961
• Brazil's Big-lipped Indians. 118-133, Jan. 1962
• Children of the Sun and Moon (Kraho Indians). Translated from German by Curtis T. Everett. 340-363, Mar 1959
• Indians of the Amazon Darkness. 737-758, May 1964
• Tukuna Maidens Come of Age. 629-649, Nov. 1959
• The Waurá: Brazilian Indians of the Hidden Xingu. 130-152, Jan. 1966

SCHULTZ, JOHN E.: Author:
• Sea Fever. 237-268, Feb. 1949

SCIENCE:
◆ *Amazing Mysteries of the World.* 1983
◆ *Far-Out Facts.* 1980
◆ *More Far-Out Facts.* 1982
◆ *On the Brink of Tomorrow: Frontiers of Science.* 1982
• *See also* Archaeology; Astronomy; Biology; Chemistry; Ecology; Geology; Meteorology; Paleontology; Physics; Technology

SCIENCE Explores the Monsoon Sea. By Samuel W. Matthews. Photos by Robert F. Sisson. 554-575, Oct. 1967

SCIENCE Finds New Clues to Our Climates in Alaska's Mighty Rivers of Ice. By Maynard M. Miller. Photos by Christopher G. Knight. NGS research grant. 194-217, Feb. 1967

SCIENCE Seeks to Solve . . . The Mystery of the Shroud. By Kenneth F. Weaver. 730-753, June 1980

SCIENCE'S Window on the Sea. By John G. VanDerwalker. Photos by Bates Littlehales. 256-289, Aug. 1971

SCIENTIST Studies Japan's Fantastic Long-tailed Fowl. By Frank X. Ogasawara. Photos by Eiji Miyazawa. 845-855, Dec. 1970

A **SCIENTIST** Visits Some of the World's Oldest People. By Alexander Leaf. Photos by John Launois. 93-119, Jan. 1973

SCIENTISTS Drill at Sea to Pierce Earth's Crust. By Samuel W. Matthews. Photos by J. Baylor Roberts. 686-697, Nov. 1961

SCIENTISTS Ride Ice Islands on Arctic Odysseys. By Lowell Thomas, Jr. Photos by Ted Spiegel. 670-691, Nov. 1965

SCILLY, Isles of, England:
• England's Scillies, the Flowering Isles. By Alan Villiers. Photos by Bates Littlehales. 126-145, July 1967

SCINTILLATING Siam. By W. Robert Moore. 173-200, Feb. 1947

SCOFIELD, JOHN:
• Editor, Associate. 698, Nov. 1970; 73, Jan. 1971; 546, Oct. 1974; 584, Nov. 1975; 658, Nov. 1976
Author:
• Bombay, the Other India. Photos by Raghubir Singh. 104-129, July 1981
• Character Marks the Coast of Maine. Photos by B. Anthony Stewart. 798-843, June 1968
• Christopher Columbus and the New World He Found. Photos by Adam Woolfitt. 584-625, Nov. 1975
• The Friendly Irish. Photos by James A. Sugar. 354-391, Sept. 1969
• Israel: Land of Promise. Photos by B. Anthony Stewart. 395-434, Mar. 1965
• Jerusalem, the Divided City. Photos by Brian Brake. 492-531, Apr. 1959
• The Lower Keys, Florida's "Out Islands." Photos by Emory Kristof and Bates Littlehales. 72-93, Jan. 1971
• A New Volcano Bursts from the Atlantic (Ilha Nova). Photos by Robert F. Sisson. 735-757, June 1958
• Virgin Islands: Tropical Playland, U.S.A. Photos by Charles Allmon. 201-232, Feb. 1956
Author-Photographer:
• Australian New Guinea. 604-637, May 1962
• Bhutan Crowns a New Dragon King. 546-571, Oct. 1974
• Easter Week in Indian Guatemala. 406-417, Mar. 1960
• Freedom Speaks French in Ouagadougou. 153-203, Aug. 1966
• Gangtok, Cloud-wreathed Himalayan Capital. 698-713, Nov. 1970
• Haiti–West Africa in the West Indies. 226-259, Feb. 1961
• Hashemite Jordan, Arab Heartland. 841-856, Dec. 1952
• Hong Kong Has Many Faces. 1-41, Jan. 1962
• India in Crisis. 599-661, May 1963
• Kathmandu's Remarkable Newars. 269-285, Feb. 1979
• Life Slowly Changes in Remote Bhutan. 658-683, Nov. 1976
• Netherlands New Guinea. 584-603, May 1962
Photographer:
• Venice, City of Twilight Splendor. By Joe Alex Morris. 543-569, Apr. 1961

SCOLLAY, CLIVE: Author:
• Arnhem Land Aboriginals Cling to Dreamtime. Photos by Penny Tweedie. 644-663, Nov. 1980

SCORPIONFISH:
• Something's Fishy About That Fin! (Decoy Fish). Photos by Robert J. Shallenberger and William D. Madden. 224-227, Aug. 1974

SCORPIONS: Living Fossils of the Sands. By Paul A. Zahl. 436-442, Mar. 1968

SCOTLAND:
• The Britain That Shakespeare Knew. By Louis B. Wright. Photos by Dean Conger. 613-665, May 1964
• British Castles, History in Stone. By Norman Wilkinson. 111-129, July 1947
▲ *British Isles,* Atlas series supplement. July 1958
▲ *The British Isles,* supplement. Apr. 1949
• The British Way. By Sir Evelyn Wrench. Included: James I, James Watt. 421-541, Apr. 1949
• The Celts. By Merle Severy. Photos by James P. Blair. Paintings by Robert C. Magis. 582-633, May 1977
• The Highlands, Stronghold of Scottish Gaeldom. By Kenneth MacLeish. Photos by Winfield Parks. 398-435, Mar. 1968
• Midshipmen's Cruise. By William J. Aston and Alexander G. B. Grosvenor. 711-754, June 1948

• Playing 3,000 Golf Courses in Fourteen Lands. By Ralph A. Kennedy. 113-132, July 1952
• Poets' Voices Linger in Scottish Shrines. By Isobel Wylie Hutchison. Photos by Kathleen Revis. 437-488, Oct. 1957
• Rhododendron Glories of Southwest Scotland. By David S. Boyer. Photos by B. Anthony Stewart and author. 641-664, May 1954
• Scotland From Her Lovely Lochs and Seas. By Alan Villiers. Photos by Robert F. Sisson. 492-541, Apr. 1961
• Scotland's Golden Eagles at Home. By C. Eric Palmar. 273-286, Feb. 1954
• Striking It Rich in the North Sea. By Rick Gore. Photos by Dick Durrance II. 519-549, Apr. 1977
• A Stroll to John o'Groat's. By Isobel Wylie Hutchison. 1-48, July 1956
• A Stroll to London. By Isobel Wylie Hutchison. Photos by B. Anthony Stewart. 171-204, Aug. 1950
▲ *A Traveler's Map of the British Isles,* supplement. Text on reverse. Apr. 1974
• *See also* Arran, Island of; Edinburgh; Hebrides; Ness, Loch; Orkney Islands; Shetland Islands

SCOTT, DAVID R.:
• Apollo 15 Explores the Mountains of the Moon. By Kenneth F. Weaver. Photos from NASA. 233-265, Feb. 1972
Author:
• What Is It Like to Walk on the Moon? 326-331, Sept. 1973

SCOTT, DOUGLAS: Photographer:
• High Adventure in the Himalayas. By Thomas Weir. 193-234, Aug. 1952

SCOTT, ROBERT F.:
• All-out Assault on Antarctica. By Richard E. Byrd. 141-180, Aug. 1956
• The British Way. By Sir Evelyn Wrench. 421-541, Apr. 1949
• Our Navy Explores Antarctica. By Richard E. Byrd. U. S. Navy official photos. 429-522, Oct. 1947

SCOTT, SIR WALTER:
• The British Way. By Sir Evelyn Wrench. 421-541, Apr. 1949
• Poets' Voices Linger in Scottish Shrines. By Isobel Wylie Hutchison. Photos by Kathleen Revis. 437-488, Oct. 1957
• A Stroll to London. By Isobel Wylie Hutchison. Photos by B. Anthony Stewart. 171-204, Aug. 1950

SCOTT EXPEDITION:
• The British Way. By Sir Evelyn Wrench. Included: A Very Gallant Gentleman–Lawrence Edward Grace Oates (1880-1912). 421-541, Apr. 1949
• *See also* Scott, Robert F.

SCOTTISH TRANS-GREENLAND EXPEDITION:
• First Woman Across Greenland's Ice. By Myrtle Simpson. Photos by Hugh Simpson. 264-279, Aug. 1967

SCOUGALL, IRENE. *See* Burdett-Scougall, Irene

SCOURGE (Warship):
• Ghost Ships of the War of 1812: *Hamilton* and *Scourge*. By Daniel A. Nelson. Photos by Emory Kristof. Paintings by Richard Schlecht. 289-313, Mar. 1983

SCOUTS AND SCOUTING. *See* Boy Scouts

SCRIPPS INSTITUTION OF OCEANOGRAPHY:
• Expeditions. *See* Deep Sea Drilling Project
• La Jolla, a Gem of the California Coast. By Deena Clark. Photos by J. Baylor Roberts. 755-782, Dec. 1952

SCROLLS. *See* Dead Sea Scrolls

SCULPTURE:
• Ancient Aphrodisias and Its Marble Treasures. By Kenan T. Erim. Photos by Jonathan S. Blair. NGS research grant. 280-294, Aug. 1967
• Ancient Aphrodisias Lives Through Its Art. By Kenan T. Erim. Photos by David Brill. 527-551, Oct. 1981
• Aphrodisias, Awakened City of Ancient Art. By Kenan T. Erim. Photos by Jonathan S. Blair. NGS research grant. 766-791, June 1972
• The British Way. By Sir Evelyn Wrench. Included: Landseer Lions. 421-541, Apr. 1949
• Carrara Marble: Touchstone of Eternity. By Cathy Newman. Photos by Pierre Boulat. 42-59, July 1982
• The Caves of the Thousand Buddhas (Tunhwang, China). By Franc and Jean Shor. 383-415, Mar. 1951
• China Unveils Her Newest Treasures. Photos by Robert W. Madden. 848-857, Dec. 1974
• China's Incredible Find. By Audrey Topping. Paintings by Yang Hsien-min. Included: The first emperor's burial mound, with guardian army of terra-cotta men and horses. 440-459, Apr. 1978
• Darius Carved History on Ageless Rock. By George G. Cameron. 825-844, Dec. 1950
• India's Sculptured Temple Caves. By Volkmar Wentzel. 665-678, May 1953
• Indonesia Rescues Ancient Borobudur. By W. Brown Morton III. Photos by Dean Conger. 126-142, Jan. 1983
• Lascaux Cave, Cradle of World Art (France). By Norbert Casteret. Photos by Maynard Owen Williams. Included: Clay statues of the Old Stone Age. 771-794, Dec. 1948
• The Louvre, France's Palace of the Arts. By Hereward Lester Cooke, Jr. 796-831, June 1971
• The Maya. 729-811, Dec. 1975
I. Children of Time. By Howard La Fay. Photos by David Alan Harvey. 729-767; II. Riddle of the Glyphs. By George E. Stuart. Photos by Otis Imboden. 768-791; III. Resurrecting the Grandeur of Tikal. By William R. Coe. 792-798
• The National Gallery's New Masterwork on the Mall. By J. Carter Brown. Photos by James A. Sugar. 680-701, Nov. 1978

BOTH BY ROBERT HARDING ASSOCIATES, TIMES NEWSPAPERS LTD.

China Unveils Treasures: flying horse, *top;* pottery figurine from Chiaotso, *above*

S T

• Petra, Rose-red Citadel of Biblical Edom. By David S. Boyer. 853-870, Dec. 1955
• Searching Out Medieval Churches in Ethiopia's Wilds. By Georg Gerster. 856-884, Dec. 1970
• Warriors From a Watery Grave (Bronze Sculptures). By Joseph Alsop. 821-827, June 1983
• *See also* Afo-A-Kom; Akhenaten Temple Project; Ceramics; Dreyfus Collection; War Memorials; *and* Abu Simbel; Athens; Florence; Rome; Tuscany; Washington, D. C.; *and* Goldsmithing; Wood Carving

SCULPTURE, Gravel. *See* Gravel Pictographs

SCULPTURE, Ice:
• Snow Festival in Japan's Far North. By Eiji Miyazawa. 824-833, Dec. 1968

SEA AND SPACE RESEARCH PROJECT. *See* Tektite II

SEA ANEMONES:
• Camera Under the Sea. By Luis Marden. NGS research grant. 162-200, Feb. 1956
• Oregon's Sidewalk on the Sea. By Paul A. Zahl. 708-734, Nov. 1961

SEA-CORE DATING:
• What's Happening to Our Climate? By Samuel W. Matthews. 576-615, Nov. 1976

SEA COWS. *See* Manatees

SEA DIVER (Research Vessel):
• The Deepest Days. By Robert Sténuit. NGS research grant. 534-547, Apr. 1965
• The Long, Deep Dive. By Lord Kilbracken. Photos by Bates Littlehales. NGS research grant. 718-731, May 1963
• Our Man-in-Sea Project. By Edwin A. Link. NGS research grant. 713-717, May 1963
• Outpost Under the Ocean. By Edwin A. Link. Photos by Bates Littlehales. NGS research grant. 530-533, Apr. 1965
• A Taxi for the Deep Frontier. By Kenneth MacLeish. Photos by Bates Littlehales. 139-150, Jan. 1968
• Tomorrow on the Deep Frontier. By Edwin A. Link. NGS research grant. 778-801, June 1964

SEA DRAGONS:
• Dragons of the Deep. Photos by Paul A. Zahl. 838-845, June 1978

SEA DYAKS (Tribespeople). *See* Iban

SEA ELEPHANTS:
• Off Santa Barbara: California's Ranches in the Sea. By Earl Warren, Jr. Photos by Bates Littlehales. 257-283, Aug. 1958

SEA Fever. By John E. Schultz. 237-268, Feb. 1949

SEA Gate of the Pacific Northwest, Puget Sound. By William Graves. Photos by David Alan Harvey. 71-97, Jan. 1977

SEA Gypsies of the Philippines. By Anne de Henning Singh. Photos by Raghubir Singh. 659-677, May 1976

DAVID DOUBILET

Galapagos: sea lions in aquatic ballet

SEA HORSES:
• Little Horses of the Sea. By Paul A. Zahl. 131-153, Jan. 1959

SEA ISLANDS, South Carolina-Georgia-Florida:
• Sea Islands: Adventuring Along the South's Surprising Coast. By James Cerruti. Photos by Thomas Nebbia and James L. Amos. Included: Blackbeard, Cumberland, Jekyll, Ossabaw, St. Catherines, St. Simons, Sapelo, Sea Island, Wassaw, in Georgia; Daufuskie, Hilton Head, Johns, Port Royal Sound, in South Carolina. 366-393, Mar. 1971
• *See also* Cumberland Island

SEA LAMPREYS:
• New Era on the Great Lakes. By Nathaniel T. Kenney. 439-490, Apr. 1959

SEA LIONS:
• The Galapagos, Eerie Cradle of New Species. By Roger Tory Peterson. Photos by Alan and Joan Root. 541-585, Apr. 1967
• Lost World of the Galapagos. By Irving and Electa Johnson. 681-703, May 1959
• Undersea Wonders of the Galapagos. By Gerard Wellington. Photos by David Doubilet. 363-381, Sept. 1978
• Where Two Worlds Meet (Patagonia). Photos by Des and Jen Bartlett. 298-321, Mar. 1976

SEA Nymphs of Japan. By Luis Marden. 122-135, July 1971

SEA OTTERS:
• Return of the Sea Otter. By Karl W. Kenyon. Photos by James A. Mattison, Jr. 520-539, Oct. 1971

SEA ROBIN (Submarine):
• 'Round the Horn by Submarine. By Paul C. Stimson. 129-144, Jan. 1948

SEA SLUGS. *See* Nudibranchs

SEA SNAKES:
• Diving With Sea Snakes. By Kenneth MacLeish. Photos by Ben Cropp. 565-578, Apr. 1972

SEA to Lakes on the St. Lawrence. By George W. Long. Photos by B. Anthony Stewart and John E. Fletcher. 323-366, Sept. 1950

SEA TURTLES:
• Wild Cargo: the Business of Smuggling Animals. By Noel Grove. Photos by Steve Raymer. Included: Green Sea Turtle, Hawksbill Turtle, Pacific Ridley Turtle; and Turtle farming, Turtle shell trade. 287-315, Mar. 1981
• *See also* Green Turtles

SEA URCHINS:
• Giant Kelp, Sequoias of the Sea. By Wheeler J. North. Photos by Bates Littlehales. Included: Destruction of kelp by sea urchins. 251-269, Aug. 1972

SEABIRDS:
• The Galapagos, Eerie Cradle of New Species. By Roger Tory Peterson. Photos by Alan and Joan Root. 541-585, Apr. 1967

• Hawaii's Far-flung Wildlife Paradise. By John L. Eliot. Photos by Jonathan Blair. 760-791, May 1978
• Lundy, Treasure Island of Birds. By P. T. Etherton. Photos by J. Allan Cash. 675-698, May 1947
• New Day for Alaska's Pribilof Islanders. By Susan Hackley Johnson. Photos by Tim Thompson. 536-552, Oct. 1982
• Penguins and Their Neighbors. By Roger Tory Peterson. Photos by Des and Jen Bartlett. Included: Albatrosses, Gulls, Penguins, Wilson's storm petrel. 237-255, Aug. 1977
• Peru Profits from Sea Fowl. By Robert Cushman Murphy. Photos by author and Grace E. Barstow Murphy. 395-413, Mar. 1959
• Sea Bird Cities Off Audubon's Labrador. By Arthur A. Allen. NGS research grant. 755-774, June 1948
• Sea Birds of Isla Raza. By Lewis Wayne Walker. 239-248, Feb. 1951
• *See also* Albatrosses; Brown Pelicans; Puffins; Terns

SEAFARING. *See* Cruises and Voyages; Shipwrecks

SEAFLOORS:
◆ *Exploring Our Living Planet.* 1983
• Hidden Life of an Undersea Desert. By Eugenie Clark. Photos by David Doubilet. 129-144, July 1983
▲ *The Historic Mediterranean; The Mediterranean Seafloor*, double-sided supplement. Dec. 1982
• Working for Weeks on the Sea Floor. By Jacques-Yves Cousteau. Photos by Philippe Cousteau and Bates Littlehales. NGS research grant. 498-537, Apr. 1966
• *See also* Ocean Floors

SEAFOOD INDUSTRY:
• Cajunland, Louisiana's French-speaking Coast. By Bern Keating. Photos by Charles Harbutt and Franke Keating. 353-391, Mar. 1966
• Chesapeake Country. By Nathaniel T. Kenney. Photos by Bates Littlehales. 370-411, Sept. 1964
• "Delmarva," Gift of the Sea. By Catherine Bell Palmer. 367-399, Sept. 1950
• The Sailing Oystermen of Chesapeake Bay. By Luis Marden. 798-819, Dec. 1967
• *See also* Crabs; Lobsters and Lobstering; Shrimp Fishing

SEAGO, EDWARD: Artist:
• Off the Beaten Track of Empire (Prince Philip's Tour). By Beverley M. Bowie. Photos by Michael Parker. 584-626, Nov. 1957

SEALING:
• Cliff Dwellers of the Bering Sea. By Juan Muñoz. 129-146, Jan. 1954
• Life or Death for the Harp Seal. By David M. Lavigne. Photos by William R. Curtsinger. 129-142, Jan. 1976
• New Day for Alaska's Pribilof Islanders. By Susan Hackley Johnson. Photos by Tim Thompson. 536-552, Oct. 1982
• The Romance of American Furs. By Wanda Burnett. 379-402, Mar. 1948
• Seal Hunting Off Jan Mayen. By Ole Friele Backer. 57-72, Jan. 1948
• Where Magic Ruled: Art of the Bering Sea. By William W. Fitzhugh and Susan A. Kaplan. Photos by Sisse Brimberg. Included: Eskimo hunting implements and tactics. 198-205, Feb. 1983

SEALS:
• The Fur Seal Herd Comes of Age. By Victor B. Scheffer and Karl W. Kenyon. 491-512, Apr. 1952
• A Naturalist in Penguin Land. By Niall Rankin. Included: Atlantic, crabeater, elephant, leopard, and Weddell seals. 93-116, Jan. 1955
• Nature's Clown, the Penguin. By David Hellyer and Malcolm Davis. Included: Elephant seal, fur seal, and sea leopard. 405-428, Sept. 1952
• Our Friend From the Sea. By Robert and Nina Horstman. Photos by Robert F. Sisson. 728-736, Nov. 1968
• Penguins and Their Neighbors. By Roger Tory Peterson. Photos by Des and Jen Bartlett. Included: Elephant seals, Leopard seals, Southern fur seals. 237-255, Aug. 1977
• Seal Hunting Off Jan Mayen. By Ole Friele Backer. Contents: Harp (Greenland) seal, hooded seal ("Blueback"). 57-72, Jan. 1948
• Stalking Seals Under Antarctic Ice. By Carleton Ray. 54-65, Jan. 1966
• *See also* Fur Seals; Harp Seals; Sea Elephants; Sea Lions; Sealing

SEAMANS, ROBERT C., Jr.:
• Board of Trustees, member. 860, June 1970; 289, Mar. 1976

The **SEARCH** for Life. By Rick Gore. 9-31, Jan. 1977

The **SEARCH** for Life on Mars. By Kenneth F. Weaver. 264-265, Feb. 1973

The **SEARCH** for *Mary Rose*. By Margaret Rule. Introduction and picture text by Peter Miller. Paintings by Richard Schlecht. 646-675, May 1983

The **SEARCH** for the First Americans. By Thomas Y. Canby. Photos by Kerby Smith. Paintings by Roy Andersen. 330-363, Sept. 1979

SEARCH for the Oldest People. By Alexander Leaf. Photos by John Launois. 93-119, Jan. 1973

SEARCH for the Scarlet Ibis in Venezuela. By Paul A. Zahl. NGS research grant. 633-661, May 1950

The **SEARCH** for Tomorrow's Power. By Kenneth F. Weaver. Photos by Emory Kristof. 650-681, Nov. 1972

SEARCHING for Cliff Dwellers' Secrets. By Carroll A. Burroughs. NGS research grant. 619-625, Nov. 1959

SEARCHING Out Medieval Churches in Ethiopia's Wilds. By Georg Gerster. 856-884, Dec. 1970

SEASHELLS. *See* Shells

SEASHORE:
• The Living Sand. By William H. Amos. 820-833, June 1965
• Oregon's Sidewalk on the Sea. By Paul A. Zahl. 708-734, Nov. 1961
• Our Changing Atlantic Coastline (U. S.). By Nathaniel T. Kenney. Photos by B. Anthony Stewart. 860-887, Dec. 1962
• Seashore Summer. By Arline Strong. 436-444, Sept. 1960
• A Wild Shore Where Two Worlds Meet (Patagonia). Photos by Des and Jen Bartlett. 298-321, Mar. 1976
• *See also* Cape Cod; Outer Banks

SEATTLE, Washington:
• Making Friends With a Killer Whale. By Edward I. Griffin. 418-446, Mar. 1966
• Puget Sound, Sea Gate of the Pacific Northwest. By William Graves. Photos by David Alan Harvey. 71-97, Jan. 1977
• Seattle, City of Two Voices. By Anne Grosvenor Robinson. Photos by B. Anthony Stewart. 494-513, Apr. 1960
• Seattle Fair Looks to the 21st Century. By Carolyn Bennett Patterson. Photos by Thomas Nebbia. 402-427, Sept. 1962

SEAWEED:
• Algae: the Life-givers. By Paul A. Zahl. 361-377, Mar. 1974
• Undersea World of a Kelp Forest. By Sylvia A. Earle. Photos by Al Giddings. 411-426, Sept. 1980
• *See also* Giant Kelp; Sargassum

SECRET of the Discus Fish. By Gene Wolfsheimer. 675-681, May 1960

The **SECRETS** of Nature's Night Lights. By Paul A. Zahl. 45-69, July 1971

SEED INDUSTRY:
• The Flower Seed Growers: Gardening's Color Merchants. By Robert de Roos. Photos by Jack Fields. 720-738, May 1968

SEEING Birds as Real Personalities. By Hance Roy Ivor. 523-530, Apr. 1954

SEEING-EYE DOGS:
• Dogs Work for Man. By Edward J. Linehan. Paintings by Edward Megargee and R. E. Lougheed. 190-233, Aug. 1958

SEEING the Earth from 80 Miles Up. By Clyde T. Holliday. 511-528, Oct. 1950

SEEKING Mindanao's Strangest Creatures. By Charles Heizer Wharton. 389-408, Sept. 1948

SEEKING the Best of Two Worlds (Apache). By Bill Hess. 272-290, Feb. 1980

SEEKING the Oldest Known Maya. By Norman Hammond. Photos by Lowell Georgia and Martha Cooper. NGS research grant. 126-140, July 1982

SEEKING the Secret of the Giants. By Frank M. Setzler. Photos by Richard H. Stewart. 390-404, Sept. 1952

SEEKING the Tomb of Philip of Macedon. By Manolis Andronicos. Photos by Spyros Tsavdaroglou. 55-77, July 1978

SEEKING the Truth About the Feared Piranha. By Paul A. Zahl. 715-733, Nov. 1970

The **SEETHING** Caribbean. By Noel Grove. Photos by Steve Raymer. 244-271, Feb. 1981

SEIDLER, NED: Artist:
- A Continent's Living Treasure. 164-167, Feb. 1972
- India's Wildlife Vanishes As Man Alters the Land. 307-309, Sept. 1976
- The Lost Empire of the Incas. By Loren McIntyre. Art by Ned and Rosalie Seidler. 729-787, Dec. 1973
- Seven Giants Who Led the Way. Text by Rick Gore. 401-407, Sept. 1976

SEIDLER, ROSALIE: Artist:
- The Lost Empire of the Incas. By Loren McIntyre. Art by Ned and Rosalie Seidler. 729-787, Dec. 1973

SEINE (River), France:
- The Civilizing Seine. By Charles McCarry. Photos by David L. Arnold. 478-511, Apr. 1982

SEINE FISHING:
- Golden Beaches of Portugal. By Alan Villiers. 673-696, Nov. 1954
- Menhaden–Uncle Sam's Top Commercial Fish. By Leonard C. Roy. Photos by Robert F. Sisson. 813-823, June 1949
- Scenes of Postwar Finland. By La Verne Bradley. Photos by Jerry Waller. 233-264, Aug. 1947

SEISMIC SEA WAVES. *See* Tsunamis

SEISMOLOGY:
- First Explorers on the Moon: The Incredible Story of Apollo 11. 735-797, Dec. 1969
- Have We Solved the Mysteries of the Moon? By Kenneth F. Weaver. Paintings by William H. Bond. 309-325, Sept. 1973
- *See also* Earthquakes

SEMINOLES (Indians):
- Florida's Emerging Seminoles. By Louis Capron. Photos by Otis Imboden. 716-734, Nov. 1969
- Florida's "Wild" Indians, the Seminole. By Louis Capron. Photos by Willard R. Culver. 819-840, Dec. 1956
- Haunting Heart of the Everglades. By Andrew H. Brown. Photos by author and Willard R. Culver. 145-173, Feb. 1948

SENEGAL:
- Freedom Speaks French in Ouagadougou. By John Scofield. 153-203, Aug. 1966

SENGSENG (People):
- Blowgun Hunters of the South Pacific. By Jane C. Goodale. Photos by Ann Chowning. 793-817, June 1966

SENNETT, TOMAS: Photographer:
- North for Oil: *Manhattan* Makes the Historic Northwest Passage. By Bern Keating. 374-391, Mar. 1970

SENTINEL RANGE, Antarctica:
- First Conquest of Antarctica's Highest Peaks. By Nicholas B. Clinch. NGS research grant. 836-863, June 1967

SENTINELESE (Negrito Tribe):
- The Last Andaman Islanders. By Raghubir Singh. 66-91, July 1975

SEOUL, Republic of Korea:
- Roaming Korea South of the Iron Curtain. By Enzo de Chetelat. 777-808, June 1950
- Seoul: Korean Showcase. By H. Edward Kim. 770-797, Dec. 1979
- South Korea: Success Story in Asia. By Howard Sochurek. 301-345, Mar. 1969
- South Korea: What Next? By Peter T. White. Photos by H. Edward Kim. 394-427, Sept. 1975
- With the U. S. Army in Korea. By John R. Hodge. 829-840, June 1947

SEPIK RIVER, and Region, New Guinea:
- Change Ripples New Guinea's Sepik River. By Malcolm S. Kirk. 354-381, Sept. 1973
- To the Land of the Head-hunters. By E. Thomas Gilliard. NGS research grant. 437-486, Oct. 1955

SEPTEMBER, remember . . . Atlantic Waters Spawn the Deadly, Unpredictable Hurricane! By Ben Funk. Photos by Robert W. Madden. 346-379, Sept. 1980

SEQUOIA GIGANTEA:
- The General Sherman: Earth's Biggest Living Thing. 605-608, May 1958

SEQUOIA NATIONAL PARK, California:
- Giant Sequoias Draw Millions to California Parks. By John Michael Kauffmann. Photos by B. Anthony Stewart. 147-187, Aug. 1959
- Saving Earth's Oldest Living Things. By Andrew H. Brown. Photos by Raymond Moulin and author. 679-695, May 1951

SEQUOIA SEMPERVIRENS. *See* Redwoods

SEQUOIAS of the Sea: Giant Kelp. By Wheeler J. North. Photos by Bates Littlehales. 251-269, Aug. 1972

SERBIA (Republic), Yugoslavia:
- Yugoslavia: Six Republics in One. By Robert Paul Jordan. Photos by James P. Blair. 589-633, May 1970

SERÇE LIMANI, Turkey:
- Glass Treasure From the Aegean. By George F. Bass. Photos by Jonathan Blair. 768-793, June 1978

SERENGETI NATIONAL PARK, Tanzania:
- African Wildlife: Man's Threatened Legacy. By Allan C. Fisher, Jr. Photos by Thomas Nebbia. Paintings by Ned Seidler. 147-187, Feb. 1972
- Cheetahs: In a Race for Survival. By George W. and Lory Herbison Frame. 712-728, May 1980
- Hyenas, the Hunters Nobody Knows. By Hans Kruuk. Photos by Baron Hugo van Lawick. 44-57, July 1968
- Life With the King of Beasts. By George B. Schaller. 494-519, Apr. 1969
- Man of the Serengeti. 179A-179B, Feb. 1972
- Tool-using Bird: The Egyptian Vulture. By Baroness Jane van Lawick-Goodall. Photos by Baron Hugo van Lawick. 631-641, May 1968

SERENGETI PLAIN, Tanzania:
- Jackals of the Serengeti. By Patricia D. Moehlman. NGS research grant. 840-850, Dec. 1980

SERTÃO (Brazilian Backland):
- Drought Bedevils Brazil's Sertão. By John Wilson. Photos by Gordon W. Gahan. 704-723, Nov. 1972

SETO NAIKAI. *See* Inland Sea, Japan

SETTON, KENNETH M.: Author:
- A New Look at Medieval Europe. Paintings by Andre Durenceau and Birney Lettick. 799-859, Dec. 1962
- 900 Years Ago: the Norman Conquest. Photos by George F. Mobley. 206-251, Aug. 1966

SETÚBAL CANYON, Atlantic Ocean:
- Four Years of Diving to the Bottom of the Sea. By Georges S. Houot. NGS research grant. 715-731, May 1958

SETZLER, FRANK M.: Author:
- Seeking the Secret of the Giants (Gravel Figures). Photos by Richard H. Stewart. 390-404, Sept. 1952

SEVEN Giants Who Led the Way. Paintings by Ned Seidler. Text by Rick Gore. 401-407, Sept. 1976

SEVEN Men Who Solved Riddles of the Cosmos. Paintings by Jean-Leon Huens. Text by Thomas Y. Canby. 627-633, May 1974

SEVENTH FLEET, U. S.:
- Crosscurrents Sweep the Indian Ocean. By Bart McDowell. Photos by Steve Raymer. 422-457, Oct. 1981
- Our Navy in the Far East. By Arthur W. Radford. Photos by J. Baylor Roberts. 537-577, Oct. 1953
- Pacific Fleet: Force for Peace. By Franc Shor. Photos by W. E. Garrett. 283-335, Sept. 1959
- Patrolling Troubled Formosa Strait. 573-588, Apr. 1955

75 YEARS Exploring Earth, Sea, and Sky: National Geographic Society Observes Its Diamond Anniversary. By Melvin M. Payne. 1-43, Jan. 1963

SEVERIN, TIMOTHY: Author:
- In the Wake of Sindbad. Photos by Richard Greenhill. 2-41, July 1982
- The Voyage of *Brendan*. Photos by Cotton Coulson. 770-797, Dec. 1977

SEVERY, MERLE: Author:
- The Byzantine Empire: Rome of the East. Photos by James L. Stanfield. 709-767, Dec. 1983
- The Celts. Photos by James P. Blair. Paintings by Robert C. Magis. 582-633, May 1977
- Northwest Wonderland: Washington State. Photos by B. Anthony Stewart. 445-493, Apr. 1960
- The World of Martin Luther. Photos by James L. Amos. 418-463, Oct. 1983

SEVILLA, Spain:
- Andalusia, the Spirit of Spain. By Howard La Fay. Photos by Joseph J. Scherschel. 833-857, June 1975
- Holy Week and the Fair in Sevilla. By Luis Marden. 499-530, Apr. 1951

SEYCHELLES (Islands), Indian Ocean:
● Crosscurrents Sweep the Indian Ocean. By Bart McDowell. Photos by Steve Raymer. 422-457, Oct. 1981
● Seychelles, Tropic Isles of Eden. By Quentin Keynes. 670-695, Nov. 1959

'S GRAVENHAGE (The Hague), Netherlands:
● Mid-century Holland Builds Her Future. By Sydney Clark. 747-778, Dec. 1950
● The Netherlands: Nation at War With the Sea. By Alan Villiers. Photos by Adam Woolfitt. 530-571, Apr. 1968

SHA'AB RÜMI (Reef), Red Sea:
● At Home in the Sea. By Jacques-Yves Cousteau. 465-507, Apr. 1964

SHACKLETON, SIR ERNEST H.:
● Our Navy Explores Antarctica. By Richard E. Byrd. U. S. Navy official photos. 429-522, Oct. 1947

SHAD in the Shadow of Skyscrapers. By Dudley B. Martin. Photos by Luis Marden. 359-376, Mar. 1947

SHADBOLT, MAURICE: Author:
● In Storied Lands of Malaysia. Photos by Winfield Parks. 734-783, Nov. 1963
● New Zealand: Gift of the Sea. Photos by Brian Brake. 465-511, Apr. 1962
● New Zealand's Cook Islands: Paradise in Search of a Future. Photos by William Albert Allard. 203-231, Aug. 1967
● Western Samoa, the Pacific's Newest Nation. Photos by Robert B. Goodman. 573-602, Oct. 1962

The **SHADOWY** World of Salamanders. By Paul A. Zahl. 104-117, July 1972

SHAKERS (Religious Sect):
● Home to the Enduring Berkshires. By Charles McCarry. Photos by Jonathan S. Blair. 196-221, Aug. 1970

SHAKESPEARE, WILLIAM:
● The Britain That Shakespeare Knew. By Louis B. Wright. Photos by Dean Conger. 613-665, May 1964
● The British Way. By Sir Evelyn Wrench. 421-541, Apr. 1949
● Founders of Virginia. By Sir Evelyn Wrench. Photos by B. Anthony Stewart. Included: Stratford on Avon and *The Tempest*. 433-462, Apr. 1948
▲ *Shakespeare's Britain*, supplement. May 1964
● A Stroll to London. By Isobel Wylie Hutchison. Photos by B. Anthony Stewart. 171-204, Aug. 1950
● The World of Elizabeth I. By Louis B. Wright. 668-709, Nov. 1968
● *See also* Folger; Henry E. Huntington Library and Art Gallery

SHALE OIL:
● Synfuels: Fill 'er Up! With What? By Thomas Y. Canby. Photos by Jonathan Blair. 74-95, *Special Report on Energy* (Feb. 1981)
Wresting Oil From Reluctant Rock. 78-79

SHALLENBERGER, ROBERT J.: Photographer:
● Something's Fishy About That Fin! Photos by Robert J. Shallenberger and William D. Madden. 224-227, Aug. 1974

SHAMANISM:
● Better Days for the Navajos. By Jack Breed. Photos by Charles W. Herbert. 809-847, Dec. 1958
● Bushmen of the Kalahari. By Elizabeth Marshall Thomas. Photos by Laurence K. Marshall. 866-888, June 1963
■ Bushmen of the Kalahari. 578A-578B, Apr. 1973; 732A-732B, May 1974
● The Huichols, Mexico's People of Myth and Magic. By James Norman. Photos by Guillermo Aldana E. 832-853, June 1977
● Nomads of the Far North. By Matthew W. Stirling. 471-504, Oct. 1949
● The White Mountain Apache. 260-290, Feb. 1980
I. At Peace With the Past, In Step With the Future. By Ronnie Lupe. 260-261; II. Coming of Age the Apache Way. By Nita Quintero. Photos by Bill Hess. 262-271; III. Seeking the Best of Two Worlds. By Bill Hess. 272-290

SHAN STATE, Burma. *See* Inle (Lake)

SHANGHAI, China:
● Along the Yangtze, Main Street of China. By W. Robert Moore. 325-356, Mar. 1948
● Eyes on the China Coast. By George W. Long. 505-512, Apr. 1953
● Shanghai: Born-again Giant. By Mike Edwards. Photos by Bruce Dale. 2-43, July 1980
"Muscle and smoke, commerce and crowds." A Shanghai portfolio by Bruce Dale. 2-13
● This Is the China I Saw. By Jørgen Bisch. 591-639, Nov. 1964

SHANNON, River, Ireland:
● Where the River Shannon Flows. By Allan C. Fisher, Jr. Photos by Adam Woolfitt. 652-679, Nov. 1978

SHANTOU SPECIAL ECONOMIC ZONE, China:
● China's Opening Door. By John J. Putman. Photos by H. Edward Kim. 64-83, July 1983

SHARING Alaska: How Much for Parks? Opposing views by Jay S. Hammond and Cecil D. Andrus. 60-65, July 1979

SHARING the Lives of Wild Golden Eagles. By John Craighead. Photos by Charles and Derek Craighead. 420-439, Sept. 1967

SHARKS:
● *Calypso* Explores for Underwater Oil. By Jacques-Yves Cousteau. Included: Aqualung divers' war on sharks in the Indian Ocean. NGS research grant. 155-184, Aug. 1955
● Fish Men Explore a New World Undersea. By Jacques-Yves Cousteau. 431-472, Oct. 1952

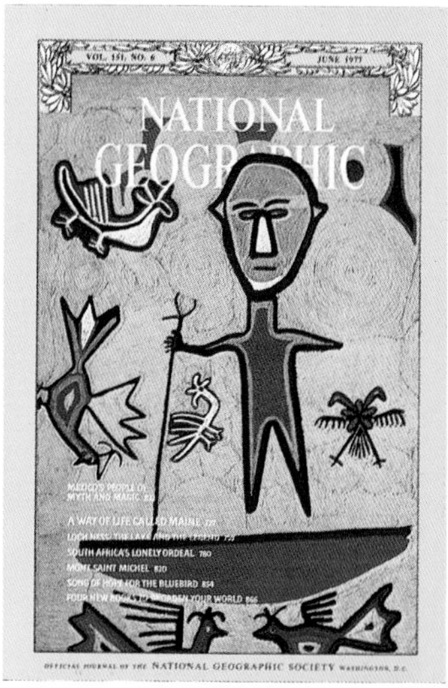

GUILLERMO ALDANA E.

Huichols: makeup paints a prayer

WILLIAM BELKNAP, JR.

Lonely Sentinels: lamb rescued by sheepherder

• Into the Lairs of "Sleeping" Sharks. By Eugenie Clark. Photos by David Doubilet. NGS research grant. 570-584, Apr. 1975
• A Jawbreaker for Sharks. By Valerie Taylor. Contents: A chain-mail diving suit. 664-667, May 1981
• Marineland, Florida's Giant Fish Bowl. By Gilbert Grosvenor La Gorce. Photos by Luis Marden. 679-694, Nov. 1952
• The Red Sea's Sharkproof Fish. By Eugenie Clark. Photos by David Doubilet. 718-727, Nov. 1974
▪ The Sharks. cover, Jan. 1982
• Sharks: Magnificent and Misunderstood. By Eugenie Clark. Photos by David Doubilet. 138-187, Aug. 1981
• Sharks: Wolves of the Sea. By Nathaniel T. Kenney. 222-257, Feb. 1968

SHARMAN, GEOFFREY B.: Author:
• Those Kangaroos! They're a Marvelous Mob. Photos by Des and Jen Bartlett. 192-209, Feb. 1979

SHAWNEETOWN Forsakes the Ohio. By William H. Nicholas. Photos by J. Baylor Roberts. 273-288, Feb. 1948

SHEATS, DOROTHEA: Author-Photographer:
• I Walked Some Irish Miles. 653-678, May 1951
• *See also* Jones, Dorothea

SHEEP RAISING:
• America's "Meat on the Hoof." By William H. Nicholas. 33-72, Jan. 1952
• Better Days for the Navajos. By Jack Breed. Photos by Charles W. Herbert. 809-847, Dec. 1958
• Housewife at the End of the World. By Rae Natalie P. Goodall. Photos by James L. Stanfield. 130-150, Jan. 1971
• Land of the Ancient Basques. By Robert Laxalt. Photos by William Albert Allard. 240-277, Aug. 1968
• Lonely Sentinels of the American West: Basque Sheepherders. By Robert Laxalt. Photos by William Belknap, Jr. 870-888, June 1966
• The Navajos. By Ralph Looney. Photos by Bruce Dale. 740-781, Dec. 1972
• New South Wales, the State That Cradled Australia. By Howell Walker. Photos by David Moore. 591-635, Nov. 1967
• New Zealand: Gift of the Sea. By Maurice Shadbolt. Photos by Brian Brake. 465-511, Apr. 1962
• New Zealand's Bountiful South Island. By Peter Benchley. Photos by James L. Amos. 93-123, Jan. 1972
• New Zealand's High Country. By Yva Momatiuk and John Eastcott. 246-265, Aug. 1978
• New Zealand's North Island: The Contented Land. By Charles McCarry. Photos by Bates Littlehales. 190-213, Aug. 1974
• People and Penguins of the Faraway Falklands. By Olin Sewall Pettingill, Jr. 387-416, Mar. 1956
• Perth–Fair Winds and Full Sails. By Thomas J. Abercrombie. Photos by Cary Wolinsky. 638-667, May 1982
• Scotland's Inner Hebrides: Isles of the Western Sea. By Kenneth MacLeish. Photos by R. Stephen Uzzell III. 690-717, Nov. 1974
• Sheep Airlift in New Guinea. Photos by Ned Blood. 831-844, Dec. 1949
• Winter Caravan to the Roof of the World. By Sabrina and Roland Michaud. 435-465, Apr. 1972
• Yugoslavia: Six Republics in One. By Robert Paul Jordan. Photos by James P. Blair. 589-633, May 1970
• *See also* Bighorn Sheep

SHEEP TREK:
• Arizona Sheep Trek. By Francis R. Line. 457-478, Apr. 1950
• Sheep Trek in the French Alps. By Maurice Moyal. Photos by Marcel Coen. 545-564, Apr. 1952

SHELLFISH. *See* Crustaceans; Mollusks; *and* Shellfish Industry

SHELLFISH INDUSTRY:
• My Chesapeake–Queen of Bays. By Allan C. Fisher, Jr. Photos by Lowell Georgia. 428-467, Oct. 1980
• *See also* Crayfish; Shrimp Fishing

SHELLS (Mollusks):
• Little Horses of the Sea. By Paul A. Zahl. Note: Sanibel Island, Florida, is one of the most famous shelling centers in the world. 131-153, Jan. 1959
• The Magic Lure of Sea Shells. By Paul A. Zahl. Photos by Victor R. Boswell, Jr. and author. Contents: More than 100 kinds of shells. 386-429, Mar. 1969
• On Australia's Coral Ramparts. By Paul A. Zahl. 1-48, Jan. 1957
• Shells Take You Over World Horizons. By Rutherford Platt. Contents: *Conus, Helicostyla, Liguus, Murex, Patella, Pecten, Pelecypoda, Tellina, Terebra, Thais, Tridacna, Trochus, Voluta*. 33-84, July 1949
• X-Rays Reveal the Inner Beauty of Shells. By Hilary B. Moore. 427-434, Mar. 1955
• *See also* Abalone; Mother-of-Pearl; Nautilus, Chambered

SHELTER OF THE SUN (Archaeological Site), Brazil. *See* Abrigo do Sol

SHENANDOAH NATIONAL PARK, Virginia:
• Skyline Trail from Maine to Georgia. By Andrew H. Brown. Photos by Robert F. Sisson. 219-251, Aug. 1949

SHENANDOAH VALLEY, Virginia-West Virginia:
• Appalachian Valley Pilgrimage. By Catherine Bell Palmer. Photos by Justin Locke. 1-32, July 1949
• Shenandoah, I Long to Hear You. By Mike W. Edwards. Photos by Thomas Anthony DeFeo. 554-588, Apr. 1970

SHENYANG (Mukden), Manchuria:
• In Manchuria Now. By W. Robert Moore. 389-414, Mar. 1947

SHENZEN SPECIAL ECONOMIC ZONE, China:
• China's Opening Door. By John J. Putman. Photos by H. Edward Kim. 64-83, July 1983

SHEPARD, ALAN B., Jr.:
• The Flight of *Freedom 7*. By Carmault B. Jackson, Jr. 416-431, Sept. 1961
Author:
• The Pilot's Story. Photos by Dean Conger. 432-444, Sept. 1961
Photographer:
• The Climb Up Cone Crater. By Alice J. Hall. Photos by Edgar D. Mitchell and Alan B. Shepard, Jr. 136-148, July 1971

SHEPARD, OLIVER:
• Circling Earth From Pole to Pole. By Sir Ranulph Fiennes. 464-481, Oct. 1983

SHERPAS:
• Park at the Top of the World: Mount Everest National Park. By Rick Ridgeway. Photos by Nicholas DeVore III. 704-725, June 1982
Preserving a Mountain Heritage. By Sir Edmund Hillary. 696-703
• Sherpaland, My Shangri-La. By Desmond Doig. 545-577, Oct. 1966
• We Build a School for Sherpa Children. By Sir Edmund Hillary. 548-551, Oct. 1962
• *See also* American Mount Everest Expedition; British Mount Everest Expedition

SHERWOOD GARDENS, Baltimore, Maryland:
• Maytime Miracle in Sherwood Gardens. By Nathaniel T. Kenney. 700-709, May 1956

SHETLAND ISLANDS, Scotland:
• Shetland and Orkney, Britain's Far North. By Isobel Wylie Hutchison. 519-536, Oct. 1953
• Striking It Rich in the North Sea. By Rick Gore. Photos by Dick Durrance II. 519-549, Apr. 1977
• Viking Festival in the Shetlands. Photos by Karl W. Gullers. 853-862, Dec. 1954

SHIELDS, CYNTHIA: Author:
• The Fantastic Flight of *Cote d'Or*. 789-793, Dec. 1983

SHILOH NATIONAL MILITARY PARK, Tennessee:
• Echoes of Shiloh. By Shelby Foote. 106-111, July 1979

SHINTOISM:
• Cruising Japan's Inland Sea. By Willard Price. 619-650, Nov. 1953
• Day of the Rice God (Festival in Japan). Photos by H. Edward Kim. Text by Douglas Lee. 78-85, July 1978
• Kansai, Japan's Historic Heartland. By Thomas J. Abercrombie. Included: Expo '70. 295-339, Mar. 1970
• Kayak Odyssey: From the Inland Sea to Tokyo. By Dan Dimancescu. Photos by Christopher G. Knight. 295-337, Sept. 1967
• Kyoto and Nara: Keepers of Japan's Past. By Charles McCarry. Photos by George F. Mobley. 836-851, June 1976

SHIP CRAFTING:
• In the Wake of Sindbad. By Tim Severin. Photos by Richard Greenhill. 2-41, July 1982
• *See also Brendan; Tigris*

SHIPBUILDING:
• Helsinki: City With Its Heart in the Country. By Priit J. Vesilind. Photos by Jodi Cobb. Included: Icebreakers; Ice-breaking freighters; Drydock operations. 237-255, Aug. 1981
• Ships Through the Ages: A Saga of the Sea. By Alan Villiers. 494-545, Apr. 1963
• *See also* Kyrenia Ship; *Mayflower II;* Vikings; *and* Ship Crafting

SHIPLIFT:
• Passage to Freedom in Viet Nam. By Gertrude Samuels. 858-874, June 1955

SHIPPING:
• The Coming Revolution in Transportation. By Fredric C. Appel. Photos by Dean Conger. Included: Containerized cargo, Hovercraft, hydrofoils, supertankers. 301-341, Sept. 1969
• Crosscurrents Sweep the Indian Ocean. By Bart McDowell. Photos by Steve Raymer. 422-457, Oct. 1981
• Here's New York Harbor. By Stuart E. Jones. Photos by Robert F. Sisson and David S. Boyer. 773-813, Dec. 1954
• Louisiana Trades with the World. By Frederick Simpich. Photos by J. Baylor Roberts. 705-738, Dec. 1947
• New Era on the Great Lakes. By Nathaniel T. Kenney. 439-490, Apr. 1959
• New Orleans: Jambalaya on the Levee. By Harnett T. Kane. Photos by Justin Locke. 143-184, Feb. 1953
• Norway, Land of the Generous Sea. By Edward J. Linehan. Photos by George F. Mobley. 1-43, July 1971
• Portsmouth, Britannia's Sally Port. By Thomas Garner James. Photos by B. Anthony Stewart. 513-544, Apr. 1952
• The Thames: That Noble River. By Ethel A. Starbird. Photos by O. Louis Mazzatenta. 750-791, June 1983
• Work-hard, Play-hard Michigan. By Andrew H. Brown. 279-320, Mar. 1952
• *See also* Tankers; U. S. Merchant Marine Academy; *and* Intracoastal Waterway, Gulf Coast; Panama Canal; St. Lawrence Seaway, Canada–U. S.; Suez Canal

SHIPS:
• Editorial. By Gilbert M. Grosvenor. 149, Feb. 1975
• The Marvelous Maldive Islands. By Alan Villiers. Included: Indian and Maldivian *baggalas*. 829-849, June 1957
◆ *Men, Ships, and the Sea*. Announced. 552-555, Oct. 1962
• Milestones in My Arctic Journeys. By Willie Knutsen. Included: *Effie M. Morrissey, Endurance, Northland, Polarbjörn, Quest, Ringsel (En Avant)*. 543-570, Oct. 1949
• *North Star* Cruises Alaska's Wild West. By Amos Burg. 57-86, July 1952
◆ *Romance of the Sea*. 1981
• Ships Through the Ages: A Saga of the Sea. By Alan Villiers. 494-545, Apr. 1963
■ The Superliners: Twilight of an Era. 1, Jan. 1980; cover, Apr. 1980
◆ *Voyages to Paradise: Exploring in the Wake of Captain Cook*. 1981
• The Yankee Sailor Who Opened Japan. By Ferdinand Kuhn. 85-102, July 1953
• *See also* Dhows; Galleons and Galleasses; Junks; Longships; Mohole, Project; Research Vessels; Sailing Vessels; Shipping; Shipwrecks; Submarines; Tall-Ships Race; Tankers; U. S. Coast Guard; U. S. Navy; listing under Yachts; *and Af Chapman; Amphitrite; Beagle,* H.M.S.; *Benjamin Bowring; Bounty; Dick Smith Explorer; Endeavour; Hickory; J. W. Westcott; Mayflower II; Ra II; Savannah,* N.S.; *Sohar; Tigris*

SHIPWORMS, Saboteurs of the Sea. By F. G. Walton Smith. 559-566, Oct. 1956

SHIPWRECKS:
• Ancient Shipwreck Yields New Facts–and a Strange Cargo. By Peter Throckmorton. Photos by Kim Hart and Joseph J. Scherschel. 282-300, Feb. 1969
• *Atocha,* Tragic Treasure Galleon of the Florida Keys. By Eugene Lyon. Included: *Santa Margarita* wreck. 787-809, June 1976
• Bermuda–Balmy, British, and Beautiful. By Peter Benchley. Photos by Emory Kristof. 93-121, July 1971
• Drowned Galleons Yield Spanish Gold. By Kip Wagner. Photos by Otis Imboden. 1-37, Jan. 1965
• England's Scillies, the Flowering Isles. By Alan Villiers. Photos by Bates Littlehales. 126-145, July 1967
• Exploring a 140-year-old Ship Under Arctic Ice *(Breadalbane)*. By Joseph B. MacInnis. Photos by Emory Kristof. 104A-104D, July 1983
• Fish Men Discover a 2,200-year-old Greek Ship. By Jacques-Yves Cousteau. NGS research grant. 1-36, Jan. 1954
• Ghost Ships of the War of 1812: *Hamilton* and *Scourge*. By Daniel A. Nelson. Photos by Emory Kristof. Paintings by Richard Schlecht. 289-313, Mar. 1983
• Glass Treasure From the Aegean. By George F. Bass. Photos by Jonathan Blair. 768-793, June 1978
• Graveyard of the Quicksilver Galleons. By Mendel Peterson. Photos by Jonathan Blair. Included: The *Nuestra Señora de Guadalupe* and the *Conde de Tolosa*. 850-876, Dec. 1979
• Henry VIII's Lost Warship: *Mary Rose*. By Margaret Rule. Introduction and picture text by Peter Miller. Paintings by Richard Schlecht. 646-675, May 1983

▲ "History Salvaged From the Sea," painting supplement by Richard Schlecht. Map on reverse. Dec. 1977
• Life Springs From Death in Truk Lagoon. By Sylvia A. Earle. Photos by Al Giddings. 578-613, May 1976
• Lonely Cape Hatteras, Besieged by the Sea. By William S. Ellis. Photos by Emory Kristof. Included: Foldout map, Ghost Fleet of the Outer Banks. 393-421, Sept. 1969
• The Lost Fleet of Kublai Khan. By Torao Mozai. Photos by Koji Nakamura. Paintings by Issho Yada. 634-649, Nov. 1982
• The Lower Keys, Florida's "Out Islands." By John Scofield. Photos by Emory Kristof and Bates Littlehales. 72-93, Jan. 1971
• New Tools for Undersea Archeology. By George F. Bass. Photos by Charles R. Nicklin, Jr. NGS research grant. 403-423, Sept. 1968
• Oldest Known Shipwreck Yields Bronze Age Cargo. By Peter Throckmorton. NGS research grant. 697-711, May 1962
• Priceless Relics of the Spanish Armada. By Robert Sténuit. Photos by Bates Littlehales. 745-777, June 1969
• Reach for the New World. By Mendel Peterson. Photos by David L. Arnold. Paintings by Richard Schlecht. Included: *Le Chameau,* H.M.S. *Looe, Machault, "Manilla Wreck," Nuestra Señora de la Concepción, Nuestra Señora de las Maravillas, Nuestra Señora de los Milagros, San Antonio, Sea Venture, Winchester.* 724-767, Dec. 1977
• Safe Landing on Sable, Isle of 500 Shipwrecks. By Melville Bell Grosvenor. 398-431, Sept. 1965
• That Dammed Missouri River. By Gordon Young. Photos by David Hiser. 374-413, Sept. 1971
• Thirty-three Centuries Under the Sea. By Peter Throckmorton. 682-703, May 1960
▪ Treasure! 575, Nov. 1976; cover, Dec. 1976
• Treasure From the Ghost Galleon: *Santa Margarita.* By Eugene Lyon. Photos by Don Kincaid. Included: *Atocha; Santa Margarita.* 228-243, Feb. 1982
• Underwater Archeology: Key to History's Warehouse. By George F. Bass. Photos by Thomas J. Abercrombie and Robert B. Goodman. NGS research grant. 138-156, July 1963
• *White Mist* Cruises to Wreck-haunted St. Pierre and Miquelon. By Melville Bell Grosvenor. 378-419, Sept. 1967
• Yellow Sea Yields Shipwreck Trove. Photos by H. Edward Kim. Introduction by Donald H. Keith. 231-243, Aug. 1979
• *See also Amoco Cadiz;* Kyrenia Ship; *Monitor; Slot ter Hooge; Thresher; Vasa; Witte Leeuw*

SHIRALA, Maharashtra (State), India:
• The Cobra, India's "Good Snake." By Harry Miller. Photos by author and Naresh and Rajesh Bedi. 393-409, Sept. 1970

NATIONAL GEOGRAPHIC
TRUK LAGOON
A SUNKEN JAPANESE FLEET BECOMES A SCIENTIFIC LABORATORY

AL GIDDINGS

Truk Lagoon: diver with working compass on wreck of *Seiko Maru*

SHOEMAKER, EUGENE M.: Author:
• The Moon Close Up. Photos by Ranger 7. 690-707, Nov. 1964

SHOOTING Rapids in Dinosaur Country. By Jack Breed. Photos by author and Justin Locke. 363-390, Mar. 1954

SHOOTING Rapids in Reverse! By William Belknap, Jr. 552-565, Apr. 1962

SHOR, DONNA HAMILTON: Author:
• San Marino, Little Land of Liberty. Photos by Ted H. Funk. 233-251, Aug. 1967

SHOR, FRANC:
• Editor, Associate. 583, Oct. 1967; 299, Mar. 1968; 309, Sept. 1968
• Editor, Senior Assistant. 864, Dec. 1959; 193, Aug. 1960; 890, Dec. 1962; 857, Dec. 1963
• Executive Editorial Council meeting. 586-587, Oct. 1967

Author:
• Boom on San Francisco Bay. Photos by David S. Boyer. 181-226, Aug. 1956
• The City They Call Red China's Showcase. Photos by Brian Brake. 193-223, Aug. 1960
• Crusader Road to Jerusalem. Photos by Thomas Nebbia. 797-855, Dec. 1963
I. Desert Ordeal of the Knights. 797-837; II. Conquest of the Holy City. 839-855
• Cyprus, Geography's Stepchild. 873-884, June 1956
• In the Crusaders' Footsteps. Photos by Thomas Nebbia and James P. Blair. 731-789, June 1962
• Iran's Shah Crowns Himself and His Empress. Photos by James L. Stanfield and Winfield Parks. 301-321, Mar. 1968
• Japan, the Exquisite Enigma. Photos by John Launois. 733-777, Dec. 1960
• Life under Shellfire on Quemoy. Photos by Wilbur E. Garrett. 415-438, Mar. 1959
• Lombardy's Lakes, Blue Jewels in Italy's Crown. Photos by Joseph J. Scherschel. 58-99, July 1968
• Pacific Fleet: Force for Peace. Photos by W. E. Garrett. 283-335, Sept. 1959
• Paris Flea Market. Photos by Alexander Taylor. 318-326, Mar. 1957

Author-Photographer:
• Argentina: Young Giant of the Far South. By Jean and Franc Shor. 297-352, Mar. 1958
• At World's End in Hunza. By Jean and Franc Shor. 485-518, Oct. 1953
• Athens to Istanbul. By Jean and Franc Shor. 37-76, Jan. 1956
• The Balearics Are Booming. By Jean and Franc Shor. 621-660, May 1957
• The Caves of the Thousand Buddhas. By Franc and Jean Shor. 383-415, Mar. 1951
• Coal Makes the Saar a Prize. 561-576, Apr. 1954
• Cyprus, Idyllic Island in a Troubled Sea. By Jean and Franc Shor. 627-664, May 1952

• East Pakistan Drives Back the Jungle. By Jean and Franc Shor. 399-426, Mar. 1955
• From Sea to Sahara in French Morocco. By Jean and Franc Shor. 147-188, Feb. 1955
• Iraq–Where Oil and Water Mix. By Jean and Franc Shor. 443-489, Oct. 1958
• North with Finland's Lapps. By Jean and Franc Shor. 249-280, Aug. 1954
• On the Winds of the Dodecanese. By Jean and Franc Shor. 351-390, Mar. 1953
• Pakistan, New Nation in an Old Land. By Jean and Franc Shor. 637-678, Nov. 1952
• Robert College, Turkish Gateway to the Future. 399-418, Sept. 1957
• Spain's "Fortunate Isles," the Canaries. By Jean and Franc Shor. 485-522, Apr. 1955
• Surprising Switzerland. By Jean and Franc Shor. 427-478, Oct. 1956
• Switzerland's Once-in-a-generation Festival (Vevey). By Jean and Franc Shor. 563-571, Oct. 1958
• We Dwelt in Kashgai Tents (Iran). By Jean and Franc Shor. 805-832, June 1952
• We Took the Highroad in Afghanistan. By Jean and Franc Shor. 673-706, Nov. 1950
Photographer:
• Camargue, Land of Cowboys and Gypsies. By Eugene L. Kammerman. 667-699, May 1956

SHOR, JEAN: Author-Photographer:
• Argentina: Young Giant of the Far South. By Jean and Franc Shor. 297-352, Mar. 1958
• At World's End in Hunza. By Jean and Franc Shor. 485-518, Oct. 1953
• Athens to Istanbul. By Jean and Franc Shor. 37-76, Jan. 1956
• The Balearics Are Booming. By Jean and Franc Shor. 621-660, May 1957
• The Caves of the Thousand Buddhas. By Franc and Jean Shor. 383-415, Mar. 1951
• Cyprus, Idyllic Island in a Troubled Sea. By Jean and Franc Shor. 627-664, May 1952
• East Pakistan Drives Back the Jungle. By Jean and Franc Shor. 399-426, Mar. 1955
• From Sea to Sahara in French Morocco. By Jean and Franc Shor. 147-188, Feb. 1955
• Iraq–Where Oil and Water Mix. By Jean and Franc Shor. 443-489, Oct. 1958
• North with Finland's Lapps. By Jean and Franc Shor. 249-280, Aug. 1954
• On the Winds of the Dodecanese. By Jean and Franc Shor. 351-390, Mar. 1953
• Pakistan, New Nation in an Old Land. By Jean and Franc Shor. 637-678, Nov. 1952
• Spain's "Fortunate Isles," the Canaries. By Jean and Franc Shor. 485-522, Apr. 1955
• Surprising Switzerland. By Jean and Franc Shor. 427-478, Oct. 1956
• Switzerland's Once-in-a-generation Festival (Vevey). By Jean and Franc Shor. 563-571, Oct. 1958
• We Dwelt in Kashgai Tents (Iran). By Jean and Franc Shor. 805-832, June 1952
• We Took the Highroad in Afghanistan. By Jean and Franc Shor. 673-706, Nov. 1950
Photographer:
• The Camargue, Land of Cowboys and Gypsies. By Eugene L. Kammerman. 667-699, May 1956

SHORES and Sails in the South Seas. By Charles Allmon. 73-104, Jan. 1950

SHOSHONEAN LINGUISTIC STOCK:
• Indians of the Far West (United States). By Matthew W. Stirling. Paintings by W. Langdon Kihn. 175-200, Feb. 1948

SHOSHONI INDIANS:
• Following the Trail of Lewis and Clark. By Ralph Gray. 707-750, June 1953

SHOULD They Build a Fence Around Montana? By Mike W. Edwards. Photos by Nicholas deVore III. 614-649, May 1976

SHOWCASE of Red China (Peking). By Franc Shor. Photos by Brian Brake. 193-223, Aug. 1960

SHREWS. *See* Tree Shrews

SHRIMP:
• Life in a "Dead" Sea–Great Salt Lake. By Paul A. Zahl. Included: Brine shrimp. 252-263, Aug. 1967
• Miracle of the Potholes. By Rowe Findley. Photos by Robert F. Sisson. 570-579, Oct. 1975
• Night Life in the Gulf Stream. By Paul A. Zahl. 391-418, Mar. 1954
• Shrimp Nursery: Science Explores New Ways to Farm the Sea. By Clarence P. Idyll. Photos by Robert F. Sisson. NGS research grant. 636-659, May 1965

SHRIMP FISHING:
• Greenland's "Place by the Icebergs." By Mogens Bloch Poulsen. Photos by Thomas Nebbia. 849-869, Dec. 1973
• Shrimpers Strike Gold in the Gulf. By Clarence P. Idyll. Photos by Robert F. Sisson. 699-707, May 1957
• Troubled Odyssey of Vietnamese Fishermen. By Harvey Arden. Photos by Steve Wall. 378-395, Sept. 1981

SHRINES, Historic:
◆ *America's Historylands, Landmarks of Liberty.* Announced. 360-363, Mar. 1962
• Dog Mart Day in Fredericksburg (Virginia). By Frederick G. Vosburgh. Included: Kenmore, Mary Washington House, Ferry Farm, James Monroe Law Office, the John Paul Jones house, and Civil War battlesites. 817-832, June 1951
• Founders of Virginia. By Sir Evelyn Wrench. Photos by B. Anthony Stewart. Included: Historic and hallowed places in England. 433-462, Apr. 1948
• Shrines of Each Patriot's Devotion (United States). By Frederick G. Vosburgh. 51-82, Jan. 1949
• Vacation Tour Through Lincoln Land. By Ralph Gray. 141-184, Feb. 1952
• *See also* Monticello, Virginia; Monuments and Memorials; National Monuments

SHRIVER, SARGENT: Author:
• Ambassadors of Good Will: The Peace Corps. By Sargent Shriver and Peace Corps Volunteers. 297-345, Sept. 1964

SHROUD OF TURIN:
• Editorial. By Gilbert M. Grosvenor. 729, June 1980
• The Mystery of the Shroud. By Kenneth F. Weaver. Note: The Shroud of Turin is believed by some to be the burial shroud of Jesus. 730-753, June 1980

SHUHUA, CHANG: Photographer:
• The Gentle Yamis of Orchid Island. 98-109, Jan. 1977

The **SHY** and Spectacular Kingfisher. Photos by Carl-Johan Junge and Emil Lütken. 413-419, Sept. 1974

SHY Monster, the Octopus. By Gilbert L. Voss. Photos by Robert F. Sisson. 776-799, Dec. 1971

SIAM. *See* Thailand

SIBERIA (Region), U.S.S.R.:
▲ *Eastern Soviet Union,* Atlas series supplement. Mar. 1967
• Five Times to Yakutsk. By Dean Conger. 256-269, Aug. 1977
• People of the Long Spring. By Yuri Rytkheu. Photos by Dean Conger. 206-223, Feb. 1983
▲ *Peoples of the Arctic; Arctic Ocean,* double-sided supplement. Feb. 1983
• Siberia: Russia's Frozen Frontier. By Dean Conger. 297-345, Mar. 1967
■ Siberia: The Endless Horizon. 734A-734B, Nov. 1969
• Siberia's Empire Road, the River Ob. By Robert Paul Jordan. Photos by Dean Conger. 145-181, Feb. 1976

SICHUAN PROVINCE, China:
• Pandas in the Wild. By George B. Schaller. 735-749, Dec. 1981
• *See also* former spelling, Szechwan

SICILY (Island), Italy:
• Fishing in the Whirlpool of Charybdis. By Paul A. Zahl. 579-618, Nov. 1953
• Roman Life in 1,600-year-old Color Pictures (Mosaics). By Gino Vinicio Gentili. Photos by Duncan Edwards. 211-229, Feb. 1957
• Sicily, Where All the Songs Are Sad. By Howard La Fay. Photos by Jonathan Blair. 407-436, Mar. 1976
• Sicily the Three-cornered. By Luis Marden. 1-48, Jan. 1955

SICKLES, NOEL: Artist:
• Alone to Antarctica. By David Lewis. 808-821, Dec. 1973

SIDEWHEELER. *See Rhode Island*

ST

SIEMEL, SASHA:
Author-Photographer:
• The Jungle Was My Home. 695-712, Nov. 1952

SIENA, Italy:
• The Palio of Siena. By Edgar Erskine Hume. 231-244, Aug. 1951
• The Renaissance Lives On in Tuscany. By Luis Marden. Photos by Albert Moldvay. Included: The Palio. 626-659, Nov. 1974

SIERRA LEONE:
• The Loyalists. By Kent Britt. Photos by Ted Spiegel. Note: Slaves of Patriot colonists, liberated by the British during the American Revolution, founded Freetown after the war. 510-539, Apr. 1975

SIERRA MADRE OCCIDENTAL (Mountain Range), Mexico:
• Found at Last: the Monarch's Winter Home. By Fred A. Urquhart. Photos by Bianca Lavies. NGS research grant. 161-173, Aug. 1976
• The Tarahumaras: Mexico's Long Distance Runners. By James Norman. Photos by David Hiser. 702-718, May 1976

SIERRA NEVADA (Mountains), California:
• Avalanche! "I'm OK, I'm Alive!" By David Cupp. Photos by Lanny Johnson and Andre Benier. 282-289, Sept. 1982
• The Fabulous Sierra Nevada. By J. R. Challacombe. 825-843, June 1954
• Giant Sequoias Draw Millions to California Parks. By John Michael Kauffmann. Photos by B. Anthony Stewart. 147-187, Aug. 1959
• Golden Ghosts of the Lost Sierra. By Robert Laxalt. Photos by David Hiser. 332-353, Sept. 1973
• John Muir's Wild America. By Harvey Arden. Photos by Dewitt Jones. 433-461, Apr. 1973
• Mexico to Canada on the Pacific Crest Trail. By Mike W. Edwards. Photos by David Hiser. 741-779, June 1971
• School for Survival. By Curtis E. LeMay. 565-602, May 1953
• Sierra High Trip. By David R. Brower. 844-868, June 1954
• The Troubled Waters of Mono Lake. By Gordon Young. Photos by Craig Aurness. 504-519, Oct. 1981
• *See also* Yosemite National Park

SIFFRE, MICHEL:
Author-Photographer:
• Six Months Alone in a Cave (Biorhythm Research). 426-435, Mar. 1975

SIFTING for Life in the Sands of Mars. By Rick Gore. 9-31, Jan. 1977

SIKANG (Former Chinese Province):
• Adventures in Lololand. By Rennold L. Lowy. 105-118, Jan. 1947

A **SIKH** Discovers America. By Joginder Singh Rekhi. 558-590, Oct. 1964

SIKHS:
• India's Energetic Sikhs. By John E. Frazer. Photos by James P. Blair. 528-541, Oct. 1972

SIKKIM:
• Gangtok, Cloud-wreathed Himalayan Capital. By John Scofield. 698-713, Nov. 1970
• Sikkim. By Desmond Doig. 398-429, Mar. 1963
• Wedding of Two Worlds. By Lee E. Battaglia. 708-727, Nov. 1963

SILICON VALLEY (Industrial District), California:
• California's Silicon Valley. By Moira Johnston. Photos by Charles O'Rear. 459-477, Oct. 1982
• The Chip: Electronic Mini-marvel. By Allen A. Boraiko. Photos by Charles O'Rear. 421-457, Oct. 1982

SILIS, IVARS:
Photographer:
• Hunters of the Lost Spirit: Greenlanders. By Priit J. Vesilind. 191-193, Feb. 1983

SILK:
• A Lady From China's Past. Photos from *China Pictorial.* Text by Alice J. Hall. 660-681, May 1974
• Thailand Bolsters Its Freedom. By W. Robert Moore. 811-849, June 1961

SILKWORMS:
• Silkworms in England Spin for the Queen. By John E. H. Nolan. 689-704, May 1953
• Spain's Silkworm Gut. By Luis Marden. 100-108, July 1951
• This Is the China I Saw. By Jørgen Bisch. 591-639, Nov. 1964

SILVER:
• Silver: A Mineral of Excellent Nature. By Allen A. Boraiko. Photos by Fred Ward. 280-313, Sept. 1981
• *See also Slot ter Hooge;* Spanish Treasure

SILVER-BACKED JACKALS:
• Jackals of the Serengeti. By Patricia D. Moehlman. NGS research grant. 840-850, Dec. 1980

SILVER DART I* and *II (Airplanes):
• Canada's Winged Victory: the *Silver Dart.* By Gilbert M. Grosvenor. 254-267, Aug. 1959

SILVER FOX (Balloon):
• The Longest Manned Balloon Flight. By Ed Yost. 208-217, Feb. 1977

SILVERSMITHS:
• Better Days for the Navajos. By Jack Breed. Photos by Charles W. Herbert. 809-847, Dec. 1958

SILVERSTONE, MARILYN:
Photographer:
• Royal Wedding at Jaisalmer. 66-79, Jan. 1965

SIMLA, Trinidad:
• Keeping House for Tropical Butterflies. By Jocelyn Crane. Photos by M. Woodbridge Williams. NGS research grant. 193-217, Aug. 1957

SIMONS, VERA: Author:
• Laboratory in a Dirty Sky. By Rudolf J. Engelmann and Vera Simons. 616-621, Nov. 1976

SIMPICH, FREDERICK: Author:
• Around the "Great Lakes of the South." Photos by J. Baylor Roberts. 463-491, Apr. 1948
• California, Horn of Plenty. Photos by Willard R. Culver. 553-594, May 1949
• 4-H Boys and Girls Grow More Food. 551-582, Nov. 1948
• From Indian Canoes to Submarines at Key West. Photos by J. Baylor Roberts. 41-72, Jan. 1950
• Here Come the Marines. 647-672, Nov. 1950
• Louisiana Trades with the World. Photos by J. Baylor Roberts. 705-738, Dec. 1947
• Mapping the Nation's Breadbasket. 831-849, June 1948
• So Much Happens Along the Ohio River. Photos by Justin Locke. 177-212, Feb. 1950
• South Dakota Keeps Its West Wild. 555-588, May 1947
• Uncle Sam Bends a Twig in Germany. Photos by J. Baylor Roberts. 529-550, Oct. 1948
• With Uncle Sam and John Bull in Germany. 117-140, Jan. 1949

SIMPICH, FREDERICK, Jr.: Author:
• Because It Rains on Hawaii. 571-610, Nov. 1949
• Changing Formosa, Green Island of Refuge. Photos by Horace Bristol. 327-364, Mar. 1957
• Fountain of Fire in Hawaii. Photos by Robert B. Goodman and Robert Wenkam. 303-327, Mar. 1960
• Hawaii, U.S.A. Photos by Thomas Nebbia. 1-45, July 1960
• Honolulu, Mid-ocean Capital. Photos by B. Anthony Stewart. 577-624, May 1954

SIMPSON, HUGH: Photographer:
• First Woman Across Greenland's Ice. By Myrtle Simpson. 264-279, Aug. 1967

SIMPSON, MYRTLE: Author:
• First Woman Across Greenland's Ice. Photos by Hugh Simpson. 264-279, Aug. 1967

SINAI, Mount, Egypt:
• In Search of Moses. By Harvey Arden. Photos by Nathan Benn. 2-37, Jan. 1976
• Island of Faith in the Sinai Wilderness (St. Catherine's Monastery). By George H. Forsyth. Photos by Robert F. Sisson. 82-106, Jan. 1964
• Mount Sinai's Holy Treasures (St. Catherine's Monastery). By Kurt Weitzmann. Photos by Fred Anderegg. 109-127, Jan. 1964
• Sinai Sheds New Light on the Bible. By Henry Field. Photos by William B. and Gladys Terry. 795-815, Dec. 1948

SINAI PENINSULA, Egypt:
• Eternal Sinai. By Harvey Arden. Photos by David Doubilet and Kevin Fleming. Included: Israeli withdrawal from the Sinai Peninsula by

April 25, 1982, as part of the Camp David accords. 420-461, Apr. 1982
Egyptian Sector. Photos by Kevin Fleming. 430-443; Israeli Sector. Photos by David Doubilet. 444-461
• In Search of Moses. By Harvey Arden. Photos by Nathan Benn. 2-37, Jan. 1976
• Island of Faith in the Sinai Wilderness (St. Catherine's Monastery). By George H. Forsyth. Photos by Robert F. Sisson. 82-106, Jan. 1964
• Mount Sinai's Holy Treasures (St. Catherine's Monastery). By Kurt Weitzmann. Photos by Fred Anderegg. 109-127, Jan. 1964
• New Life for the Troubled Suez Canal. By William Graves. Photos by Jonathan Blair. 792-817, June 1975
• Sinai Sheds New Light on the Bible. By Henry Field. Photos by William B. and Gladys Terry. 795-815, Dec. 1948
• *See also* Ras Muhammad

SINAN (District), Republic of Korea:
• Yellow Sea Yields Shipwreck Trove. Photos by H. Edward Kim. Introduction by Donald H. Keith. 231-243, Aug. 1979

SINDBAD THE SAILOR:
• In the Wake of Sindbad. By Tim Severin. Photos by Richard Greenhill. 2-41, July 1982
• Sailing with Sindbad's Sons. By Alan Villiers. 675-688, Nov. 1948

SINDONOLOGY. *See* Shroud of Turin

SING-SING (Fair):
• Australian New Guinea. By John Scofield. 604-637, May 1962
• Blowgun Hunters of the South Pacific. By Jane C. Goodale. Photos by Ann Chowning. 793-817, June 1966
• New Guinea Festival of Faces. By Malcolm S. Kirk. 148-156, July 1969
• New Guinea's Rare Birds and Stone Age Men. By E. Thomas Gilliard. NGS research grant. 421-488, Apr. 1953
• To the Land of the Head-hunters. By E. Thomas Gilliard. NGS research grant. 437-486, Oct. 1955

SINGAPORE:
• In Storied Lands of Malaysia. By Maurice Shadbolt. Photos by Winfield Parks. 734-783, Nov. 1963
• Malaya Meets Its Emergency. By George W. Long. Photos by J. Baylor Roberts and author. 185-228, Feb. 1953
• Singapore: Mini-size Superstate. By Bryan Hodgson. Photos by Dean Conger. 540-561, Apr. 1981
• Singapore, Reluctant Nation. By Kenneth MacLeish. Photos by Winfield Parks. 269-300, Aug. 1966

SINGER, ARTHUR: Artist:
▲ "Bird Migration in the Americas," painting supplement. Map on reverse. Aug. 1979

SINGH, ANNE DE HENNING: Author:
• Sea Gypsies of the Philippines. Photos by Raghubir Singh. 659-677, May 1976

RICHARD GREENHILL

PAINTING BY ARTHUR SZYK FROM THE ARABIAN NIGHTS ENTERTAINMENTS, COURTESY HERITAGE PRESS, NORWALK, CONNECTICUT

Sindbad: sailing the Indian Ocean, *top*; in the wake of Sindbad, *above*

SINGH, RAGHUBIR:
Author-Photographer:
• The Last Andaman Islanders. 66-91, July 1975
• The Pageant of Rajasthan. 219-243, Feb. 1977
Photographer:
• Bombay, the Other India. By John Scofield. 104-129, July 1981
• Calcutta, India's Maligned Metropolis. By Peter T. White. 534-563, Apr. 1973
• The Ganges, River of Faith. By John J. Putman. 445-483, Oct. 1971
• Sea Gypsies of the Philippines. By Anne de Henning Singh. 659-677, May 1976
• Sri Lanka: Time of Testing for an Ancient Land. By Robert Paul Jordan. 123-150, Jan. 1979

SINHALESE:
• Sri Lanka: Time of Testing for an Ancient Land. By Robert Paul Jordan. Photos by Raghubir Singh. 123-150, Jan. 1979

SINKIANG (Autonomous Region), People's Republic of China:
• The Caves of the Thousand Buddhas. By Franc and Jean Shor. Included: Urumchi, Turfan, and Qomul (Hami), visited on way to the caves in Kansu Province. 383-415, Mar. 1951
• How the Kazakhs Fled to Freedom. By Milton J. Clark. 621-644, Nov. 1954
• *See also* present name, Xinjiang Uygur Autonomous Region

SINT EUSTATIUS (Island), Netherlands Antilles:
• A Fresh Breeze Stirs the Leewards. By Carleton Mitchell. Photos by Winfield Parks. 488-537, Oct. 1966
• The Netherlands Antilles: Holland in the Caribbean. By James Cerruti. Photos by Emory Kristof. 115-146, Jan. 1970

SINT MAARTEN (Island), Netherlands Antilles:
• The Netherlands Antilles: Holland in the Caribbean. By James Cerruti. Photos by Emory Kristof. 115-146, Jan. 1970

SIOUX FALLS, South Dakota:
• Satellites Gave Warning of Midwest Floods. By Peter T. White. Photos by Thomas A. DeFeo. 574-592, Oct. 1969

SIOUX INDIANS:
• Back to the Historic Black Hills. By Leland D. Case. Photos by Bates Littlehales. 479-509, Oct. 1956
• South Dakota Keeps Its West Wild. By Frederick Simpich. 555-588, May 1947
• South Dakota's Badlands: Castles in Clay. By John Madson. Photos by Jim Brandenburg. Included: Miniconjou Sioux and Oglala Sioux. 524-539, Apr. 1981

SIPLE, GREG and JUNE:
• Bikepacking Across Alaska and Canada. By Dan Burden. 682-695, May 1973

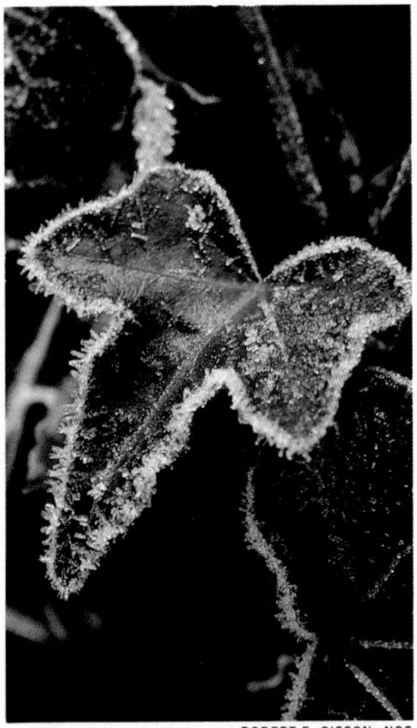

ROBERT F. SISSON, NGS

Nature's Icing: frost on ivy leaf

SIPLE, PAUL A.:
- All-out Assault on Antarctica. By Richard E. Byrd. 141-180, Aug. 1956
- Antarctic Scientist Honored by the Society. 792-793, June 1958
- Our Navy Explores Antarctica. By Richard E. Byrd. U. S. Navy official photos. 429-522, Oct. 1947
- To the Men at South Pole Station. By Richard E. Byrd. 1-4, July 1957

Author:
- Man's First Winter at the South Pole. 439-478, Apr. 1958
- We Are Living at the South Pole. Photos by David S. Boyer. 5-35, July 1957

SIR FRANCIS DRAKE. By Alan Villiers. Photos by Gordon W. Gahan. 216-253, Feb. 1975

SIRIKIT, Queen (Thailand):
- Thailand's Working Royalty. Photos by John Everingham. 486-499, Oct. 1982

SISSON, ROBERT F.:
- Octopus-training experiments. 788-789, 792, 794-795, Dec. 1971
- Photographic feats. 880, Dec. 1961; 901, Dec. 1962; 107, Jan. 1970; 692, Nov. 1970; 265, 266, Feb. 1971; 727, 748, June 1973

Author-Photographer:
- Aha! It Really Works! 143-147, Jan. 1974
- At Home With the Bulldog Ant. 62-75, July 1974

Face-to-Face With a World of Ants. 72-75
- Deception: Formula for Survival. 394-415, Mar. 1980
- Frost, Nature's Icing. 398-405, Mar. 1976
- Life Cycle of a Coral. 780-793, June 1973
- Snowflakes to Keep. 104-111, Jan. 1970
- The Spider That Lives Under Water. 694-701, May 1972
- The Wasp That Plays Cupid to a Fig. 690-697, Nov. 1970
- The World of My Apple Tree. 836-847, June 1972

Photographer:
- Adrift on a Raft of Sargassum. 188-199, Feb. 1976
- Algeria: France's Stepchild, Problem and Promise. By Howard La Fay. 768-795, June 1960
- Arizona: Booming Youngster of the West. By Robert de Roos. 299-343, Mar. 1963
- Behind New York's Window on Nature: The American Museum of Natural History. By James A. Oliver. 220-259, Feb. 1963
- The Case of the Killer Caterpillars. By Steven L. Montgomery. 219-225, Aug. 1983
- The Changeless Horseshoe Crab. By Anne and Jack Rudloe. 562-572, Apr. 1981
- The Crab That Shakes Hands. By Clarence P. Idyll. 254-271, Feb. 1971
- "Delmarva," Gift of the Sea. By Catherine Bell Palmer. 367-399, Sept. 1950
- Disaster in Paradise (Bali). By Windsor P. Booth and Samuel W. Matthews. 436-458, Sept. 1963
- Eastman of Rochester: Photographic Pioneer. By Allan C. Fisher, Jr. 423-438, Sept. 1954
- Exploring 1,750,000 Years Into Man's Past. By L.S.B. Leakey. 564-589, Oct. 1961
- The FBI: Public Friend Number One. By Jacob Hay. 860-886, June 1961
- Following the Ladybug Home. By Kenneth S. Hagen. 543-553, Apr. 1970
- 4-H Boys and Girls Grow More Food. By Frederick Simpich. 551-582, Nov. 1948
- Freedom Flight from Hungary. 424-436, Mar. 1957
- Friendless Squatters of the Sea (Barnacles). By Ethel A. Starbird. 623-633, Nov. 1973
- The Goats of Thunder Hill. By Elizabeth Nicholds. 625-640, May 1954
- Grunion, the Fish That Spawns on Land. By Clarence P. Idyll. 714-723, May 1969
- Here's New York Harbor. By Stuart E. Jones. Photos by Robert F. Sisson and David S. Boyer. 773-813, Dec. 1954
- The Incredible Salmon. By Clarence P. Idyll. Paintings by Walter A. Weber. 195-219, Aug. 1968
- Island of Faith in the Sinai Wilderness. By George H. Forsyth. 82-106, Jan. 1964
- Lake Sunapee's Golden Trout. 529-536, Oct. 1950
- Land of the Pilgrims' Pride. By George W. Long. 193-219, Aug. 1947
- The Magic Road Round Ireland. By H. V. Morton. 293-333, Mar. 1961
- Mardi Gras in New Orleans. By Carolyn Bennett Patterson. Photos by Robert F. Sisson and John E. Fletcher. 726-732, Nov. 1960
- MATS: America's Long Arm of the Air. By Beverley M. Bowie. 283-317, Mar. 1957
- Menhaden–Uncle Sam's Top Commercial Fish. By Leonard C. Roy. 813-823, June 1949
- Miracle of the Potholes. By Rowe Findley. 570-579, Oct. 1975
- Mountains Top Off New England. By F. Barrows Colton. 563-602, May 1951
- Nature's Toy Train, the Railroad Worm. By Darwin L. Tiemann. 56-67, July 1970
- New Discoveries on the Mid-Atlantic Ridge. By Maurice Ewing. 611-640, Nov. 1949
- New Florida Resident, the Walking Catfish. By Clarence P. Idyll. 847-851, June 1969
- New Tricks Outwit Our Insect Enemies. By Hal Higdon. Photos by Robert F. Sisson and Emory Kristof. 380-399, Sept. 1972
- A New Volcano Bursts from the Atlantic (Ilha Nova). By John Scofield. 735-757, June 1958
- New York State's New Main Street. By Matt C. McDade. 567-618, Nov. 1956

• Newfoundland, Canada's New Province. By Andrew H. Brown. 777-812, June 1949
• *Nomad* Sails Long Island Sound. By Thomas Horgan. 295-338, Sept. 1957
• Our Friend From the Sea (Seal). By Robert and Nina Horstman. 728-736, Nov. 1968
• Pack Trip Through the Smokies. By Val Hart. 473-502, Oct. 1952
• Saving Man's Wildlife Heritage. By John H. Baker. 581-620, Nov. 1954
• Science Explores the Monsoon Sea. By Samuel W. Matthews. 554-575, Oct. 1967
• Scotland From Her Lovely Lochs and Seas. By Alan Villiers. 492-541, Apr. 1961
• Shipworms, Saboteurs of the Sea. By F. G. Walton Smith. 559-566, Oct. 1956
• Shrimp Nursery: Science Explores New Ways to Farm the Sea. By Clarence P. Idyll. 636-659, May 1965
• Shrimpers Strike Gold in the Gulf (Gulf of Mexico). By Clarence P. Idyll. 699-707, May 1957
• Shy Monster, the Octopus. By Gilbert L. Voss. 776-799, Dec. 1971
• Skyline Trail from Maine to Georgia. By Andrew H. Brown. 219-251, Aug. 1949
• South Carolina Rediscovered. By Herbert Ravenel Sass. 281-321, Mar. 1953
• Squids: Jet-powered Torpedoes of the Deep. By Gilbert L. Voss. 386-411, Mar. 1967
• Stately Homes of Old Virginia. By Albert W. Atwood. 787-802, June 1953
• Sugar Weather in the Green Mountains. By Stephen Greene. 471-482, Apr. 1954
• The Thames Mirrors England's Varied Life. By Willard Price. 45-93, July 1958
• Today on the Delaware, Penn's Glorious River. By Albert W. Atwood. 1-40, July 1952
• Tracking America's Man in Orbit. By Kenneth F. Weaver. 184-217, Feb. 1962
• The Upper Mississippi. By Willard Price. 651-699, Nov. 1958
• Westminster, World Series of Dogdom. By John W. Cross, Jr. 91-116, Jan. 1954
• The Wild Animals in My Life. By William M. Mann. 497-524, Apr. 1957
• Windjamming Around New England. By Tom Horgan. 141-169, Aug. 1950

SISTINE CHAPEL, Vatican City:
• When in Rome. . . . By Stuart E. Jones. Photos by Winfield Parks. 741-789, June 1970

SIX Months Alone in a Cave. By Michel Siffre. 426-435, Mar. 1975

SIX to the Summit (Everest). By Norman G. Dyhrenfurth. Photos by Barry C. Bishop. NGS research grant. 460-473, Oct. 1963

SKAGIT RIVER, Washington:
• Our Wild and Scenic Rivers: The Skagit. By David S. Boyer. 38-45, July 1977

SKAGWAY, Alaska:
• Along the Yukon Trail. By Amos Burg. 395-416, Sept. 1953

SKATE (Nuclear-powered Submarine):
• The Arctic as a Sea Route of the Future. By William R. Anderson. 21-24, Jan. 1959
• Up Through the Ice of the North Pole. By James F. Calvert. 1-41, July 1959

SKATES (Fish):
• Miracle of the Mermaid's Purse. By Ernest L. Libby. 413-420, Sept. 1959

SKIING:
• American Skiers Find Adventure in Western China. By Ned Gillette. Photos by the author and Galen Rowell. 174-199, Feb. 1981
Skiing From the Summit of China's Ice Mountain. 192-199
• Avalanche! Battling the Juggernaut. By David Cupp. 290-305, Sept. 1982
• First Woman Across Greenland's Ice. By Myrtle Simpson. Photos by Hugh Simpson. 264-279, Aug. 1967
• Golden Ghosts of the Lost Sierra. By Robert Laxalt. Photos by David Hiser. Included: Long-board skiing. 332-353, Sept. 1973
• New Mount McKinley Challenge–Trekking Around the Continent's Highest Peak. By Ned Gillette. 66-79, July 1979
• North Toward the Pole on Skis. By Bjørn O. Staib. NGS research grant. 254-281, Feb. 1965
• Rafting Down the Yukon. By Keith Tryck. Photos by Robert Clark. Note: Three of the four men finished the trek on skis along 150 miles of the frozen Yukon to the Bering Sea. 830-861, Dec. 1975
• Skiing in the United States. By Kathleen Revis. 216-254, Feb. 1959
• Soaring on Skis in the Swiss Alps. By Carolyn Bennett Patterson. Photos by Kathleen Revis. 94-121, Jan. 1961
• A Town . . . a Mountain . . . a Way of Life (Aspen, Colorado). By Jill Durrance and Dick Durrance II. 788-807, Dec. 1973
• Yosemite National Park. 491-498, Apr. 1951

SKINGLE, DEREK:
• Journey Into Stone Age New Guinea. By Malcolm S. Kirk. 568-592, Apr. 1969

SKOMER (Island), Wales:
• The Solemn, Sociable Puffins. By R. M. Lockley. 414-422, Sept. 1954

SKOPJE, Yugoslavia:
• Yugoslavia: Six Republics in One. By Robert Paul Jordan. Photos by James P. Blair. Included: 1963 Earthquake. 589-633, May 1970

SKRAELING ISLAND, Canada:
• Eskimo and Viking Finds in the High Arctic: Ellesmere Island. By Peter Schledermann. Photos by Sisse Brimberg. Included: Artifacts from Thule sites. 575-601, May 1981

SKULL 1470. By Richard E. Leakey. Photos by Bob Campbell. NGS research grant. 819-829, June 1973

"SKUNK" (Train):
• The Friendly Train Called Skunk. By Dean Jennings. Photos by B. Anthony Stewart. 720-734, May 1959

SKUNKS Want Peace–or Else! By Melvin R. Ellis. Photos by Charles Philip Fox. 279-294, Aug. 1955

SKY-HIGH Bolivia. 481-496, Oct. 1950

"SKY PEOPLE." *See* Ainu

SKY Road East. By Tay and Lowell Thomas, Jr. 71-112, Jan. 1960

SKY SURVEY:
• Completing the Atlas of the Universe (National Geographic Society-Palomar Observatory Sky Survey). By Ira Sprague Bowen. NGS research grant. 185-190, Aug. 1955
Sky Survey Plates Unlock Secrets of the Stars. 186-187
• Current Scientific Projects of the National Geographic Society. NGS research grant. 143-144, July 1953
• Exploring the Farthest Reaches of Space. By George O. Abell. NGS research grant. 782-790, Dec. 1956
▲ *Journey Into the Universe Through Time and Space; National Geographic-Palomar Sky Survey Charting the Heavens,* double-sided supplement. June 1983
• Mapping the Unknown Universe. By F. Barrows Colton. NGS research grant. 401-420, Sept. 1950
• Our Universe Unfolds New Wonders (National Geographic-Palomar Sky Survey). By Albert G. Wilson. NGS research grant. 245-260, Feb. 1952
• Sky Survey Charts the Universe. By Ira Sprague Bowen. NGS research grant. 780-781, Dec. 1956
• Twelve National Geographic Society Scientific Projects Under Way. 869-870, June 1954

SKYE, Isle of, Inner Hebrides:
• Over the Sea to Scotland's Skye. By Robert J. Reynolds. 87-112, July 1952

SKYLAB MISSIONS:
• Skylab. Photos by the nine mission astronauts. 441-503, Oct. 1974
I. Outpost in Space. By Thomas Y. Canby. 441-469; II. Its View of Earth. 471-493; III. The Sun Unveiled. By Edwin G. Gibson. 494-503
• Skylab's Fiery Finish. By Tom Riggert. 581-584, Oct. 1979

SKYLINE Trail from Maine to Georgia. By Andrew H. Brown. Photos by Robert F. Sisson. 219-251, Aug. 1949

SKYSCRAPERS:
• The Mohawks Scrape the Sky. By Robert L. Conly. Photos by B. Anthony Stewart. 133-142, July 1952

S
T

SKYWAY Below the Clouds. By Carl R. Markwith. Photos by Ernest J. Cottrell. Contents: Skyway 1 (Wright Way), a route planned and marked especially for the use of private flyers. 85-108, July 1949

SLADEN, WILLIAM J. L.: Author:
- Tireless Voyager, the Whistling Swan. Photos by Bianca Lavies. 134-147, July 1975

SLAYTON, DONALD K.:
- Apollo-Soyuz: Handclasp in Space. By Thomas Y. Canby. 183-187, Feb. 1976

SLED DOG RACE:
- Thousand-mile Race to Nome: A Woman's Icy Struggle. By Susan Butcher. Photos by Kerby Smith. 411-422, Mar. 1983

SLED DOGS:
- Solo to the Pole. By Naomi Uemura. Photos by the author and Ira Block. 298-325, Sept. 1978
- Thousand-mile Race to Nome: A Woman's Icy Struggle. By Susan Butcher. Photos by Kerby Smith. 411-422, Mar. 1983
- Trek Across Arctic America. By Colin Irwin. 295-321, Mar. 1974

SLIME MOLD: The Fungus That Walks. By Douglas Lee. Photos by Paul A. Zahl. 131-136, July 1981

SLIPHER, E. C.: Author:
- New Light on the Changing Face of Mars. 427-436, Sept. 1955

SLOT TER HOOGE (Dutch East Indiaman):
- The Treasure of Porto Santo. By Robert Sténuit. Photos by author and William R. Curtsinger. 260-275, Aug. 1975

SLOVENIA (Republic), Yugoslavia:
- Yugoslavia: Six Republics in One. By Robert Paul Jordan. Photos by James P. Blair. 589-633, May 1970

SLOW Boat to Florida. By Dorothea and Stuart E. Jones. 1-65, Jan. 1958

SLOW Death Threatens Man in the Thin Air of 19,000 Feet. 530-531, Oct. 1962

SLOW Train Through Viet Nam's War. By Howard Sochurek. 412-444, Sept. 1964

SMALL NAMBAS (People):
- Taboos and Magic Rule Namba Lives. By Kal Muller. 57-83, Jan. 1972

SMALL Service With a Big Mission: The Coast Guard. By William S. Ellis. 113-139, July 1974

SMALL WORLD (Balloon):
- Braving the Atlantic by Balloon. By Arnold Eiloart. 123-146, July 1959

SMALLPOX–Epitaph for a Killer? By Donald A. Henderson. Photos by Marion Kaplan. 796-805, Dec. 1978

SMART, MAXWELL:
- Journey Into Stone Age New Guinea. By Malcolm S. Kirk. 568-592, Apr. 1969

SMITH, BRADFORD: Author:
- Captain Smith of Jamestown. 581-620, May 1957

SMITH, BRADFORD A.: Author:
▲ *The Solar System; Saturn,* double-sided supplement. July 1981

SMITH, F. G. WALTON: Author:
- Shipworms, Saboteurs of the Sea. 559-566, Oct. 1956

SMITH, GARY: Author-Photographer:
- Utah's Rock Art: . Wilderness Louvre. A picture essay by Gary Smith, with Michael E. Long. 97-117, Jan. 1980

SMITH, GRIFFIN, Jr.: Author:
- The Mexican Americans: A People on the Move. Photos by Stephanie Maze. 780-809, June 1980

SMITH, HERVEY GARRETT: Artist:
- "Mayflower II," painting supplement. Nov. 1957
- Ships Through the Ages: A Saga of the Sea. By Alan Villiers. 494-545, Apr. 1963

SMITH, JANE M., AWARD: Recipients:
- Ingram, Sir Bruce. 474, Apr. 1961
- Johnson, Lyndon B. 906, Dec. 1962; 113, Jan. 1966; 468, Oct. 1966

SMITH, JOHN:
- Captain Smith of Jamestown. By Bradford Smith. 581-620, May 1957
- Eight Maps of Discovery. Included: Capt. John Smith's Map of Virginia; Captain Smith's New England...and the Pilgrims' Cape Cod. 757-769, June 1953
- Founders of Virginia. By Sir Evelyn Wrench. Photos by B. Anthony Stewart. 433-462, Apr. 1948

SMITH, KERBY: Photographer:
- The Search for the First Americans. By Thomas Y. Canby. Paintings by Roy Andersen. 330-363, Sept. 1979
- Thousand-mile Race to Nome: A Woman's Icy Struggle. By Susan Butcher. 411-422, Mar. 1983

SMITH, L. H.: Author-Photographer:
- Lyrebird, Australia's Meistersinger. 849-857, June 1955

SMITH, MICHAEL L.: Photographer:
- Song of Hope for the Bluebird. By Lawrence Zeleny. 855-865, June 1977

SMITH, R. V. FRANCIS: Author:
- Finding an "Extinct" New Zealand Bird (Takahe). 393-401, Mar. 1952

SMITH, RAY WINFIELD: Author:
- Computer Helps Scholars Re-create an Egyptian Temple. Photos by Emory Kristof. 634-655, Nov. 1970
- History Revealed in Ancient Glass. Photos by B. Anthony Stewart and Lee E. Battaglia. 346-369, Sept. 1964

SMITHSON, JAMES:
- The Smithsonian, Magnet on the Mall. By Leonard Carmichael. Photos by Volkmar Wentzel. 796-845, June 1960
- The Smithsonian Institution. By Thomas R. Henry. 325-348, Sept. 1948

SMITHSONIAN ASTROPHYSICAL OBSERVATORY:
- Cambridge, Massachusetts. 190, Feb. 1962; 808, 812, Dec. 1966; Ikeya-Seki comet. 260, 261, Feb. 1966; Kohoutek comet. 148, Jan. 1974
- Solar Eclipse, Nature's Super Spectacular. By Donald H. Menzel and Jay M. Pasachoff. 222-233, Aug. 1970
- Solar studies. 334, 343, 344, 346, Sept. 1948

SMITHSONIAN INSTITUTION, Washington, D. C.:
- Canal Zone Biological Area: Sea level canal study. 772, Dec. 1970; Tropical Research Institute. 417, 440, Mar. 1970; 575, Apr. 1972; 282, 288, 292, Feb. 1978; 78, 80, Jan. 1982
- Center for Short-Lived Phenomena, Cambridge, Massachusetts. 286B, Feb. 1973
- Chesapeake Bay Center for Environmental Studies: Whistling swan. 140, 141, 144, July 1975
- "Contributions to Knowledge" (1848): Indian mounds. 106, Jan. 1948
- International Exchange Service. 798, 816, June 1960
- "Science City," Maui. 515, 527, Apr. 1971
- Science Information Exchange. 614, Nov. 1970
- The Smithsonian, Magnet on the Mall. By Leonard Carmichael. Photos by Volkmar Wentzel. 796-845, June 1960
- The Smithsonian Institution. By Thomas R. Henry. 325-348, Sept. 1948

Bureau of American Ethnology. 339, 341, Sept. 1948; 798, 827-829, June 1960
- American Indians: Bering Sea Expedition, 1936. 339, Sept. 1948; Broken Bow, Oklahoma. 189, Aug. 1971; Fort Berthold, North Dakota. 721, 731, June 1953; Gravel pictographs. 389-404, Sept. 1952; Lindenmeier valley site, Colorado. 340, Sept. 1948, 793, Dec. 1955; Missouri River, North Dakota: Indian villages submerged in 1946. 385, 387, Sept. 1971; Olmec culture: Mexico. 137-172, Feb. 1947, 736, June 1947, 117, Jan. 1948, 341, Sept. 1948, 807, Dec. 1950, 816, Dec. 1951, 420, Mar. 1953, 367-375, Sept. 1956, 505, 521, Oct. 1968; Panama. 373-399, Mar. 1949, 227-246, Feb. 1950, 420, Mar. 1953, 143, 144, July 1953, 271-290, Aug. 1953; Pueblo Bonito, Chaco Canyon, New Mexico. 340-341, Sept. 1948, 785, Dec. 1950, 34-35, 36, Jan. 1963, 332, Sept. 1970; Russell Cave, Alabama. 542-558, Oct. 1956, 427-438, Mar. 1958, 614, May 1958, 34-36, Jan. 1963, 440, Sept. 1967
- Eskimos: Sadlermiut. 669, 672, Nov. 1956; Sadlermiut and Dorset. 870, June 1954; Thule and Dorset. 562, Apr. 1955

Expeditions and Research. 328, Sept. 1948; 13-16, 34-35, 36, 37, 38, Jan. 1963
• Akhenaten Temple Project, Egypt. 636, 637, Nov. 1970
• Arnhem Land, Australia: Aborigines. 430, Mar. 1948, 637, May 1949, 417-430, Sept. 1949, 745-782, Dec. 1949, 870, June 1954, 828, June 1960, 37, Jan. 1963; Cattle egret. 292, Aug. 1954
• "Around the World for Animals" (1937). 497, 504, 505, 516, Apr. 1957
• Bering Sea Eskimos. 198, Feb. 1983
• British Guiana: Hoatzin. 825, June 1960, 391-401, Sept. 1962, 42, Jan. 1963; Wai Wai Indians. 329-346, Mar. 1955
• *Glomar Challenger:* Ocean samples. 597, May 1975
• Kalahari Desert, Africa: Bushmen. 877, June 1963
• Lake Champlain, New York: Search for Benedict Arnold's fleet. 72, Jan. 1969
• Marine biology: Mollusks. 397, Mar. 1969; Shark-attack file. 224, 256, Feb. 1968
• Mud-puddle frogs. 78, 80, Jan. 1982
• Nanmatol, Ponape: Archaeology. 735, May 1967
• Nicaragua: Cerro Negro 1968 volcanic eruption. 497, Oct. 1969
• Paleo-Indians. 60, 69, 116, 121, Jan. 1979; 26, July 1979; 332, 354, Sept. 1979
• Port Royal, Jamaica. 151-183, Feb. 1960; 871, Dec. 1967
• Powell Grand Canyon Expedition, 1869. 686, May 1969
• Red Sea. 727, Nov. 1972
• Spiny babbler: Nepal. 1-40, Jan. 1950
• Stone spheres: Costa Rica. 142, 144, July 1965; Mexico. 300, Aug. 1969
• Sudan: Giraffes. 725, June 1947
• *Tecumseh,* U.S.S. 380, 382, Mar. 1968
• Veracruz, Mexico: New birds discovered. 344, Sept. 1948
• Virú Valley, Peru: Archaeology. 454, 464, Apr. 1947
Museums:
• Freer Gallery of Art. 348, Sept. 1948; 798, 805, 832-833, 838, June 1960; 363, Sept. 1964
• Museum of History and Technology. 741, 743, Dec. 1964; 873, 874, Dec. 1973; 95-97, 99, July 1975
• National Air and Space Museum: Of Air and Space. By Michael Collins. 819-837, June 1978
Picture portfolio by Nathan Benn, Robert S. Oakes, and Joseph D. Lavenburg, with text by Michael E. Long. 825-837
• National Collection of Fine Arts. 798, 831, 838, June 1960; 508, 511, Apr. 1967
• National Herbarium. 477, Oct. 1950
• Natural History Museum. 874, Dec. 1973; Hall of Gems and Minerals. 568, 575, 579, 584, Apr. 1958; 835-839, 852-853, 858-863, Dec.

BOTH BY NATHAN BENN

Of Air and Space: Milestones of Flight gallery, *above;* lunar module, *below*

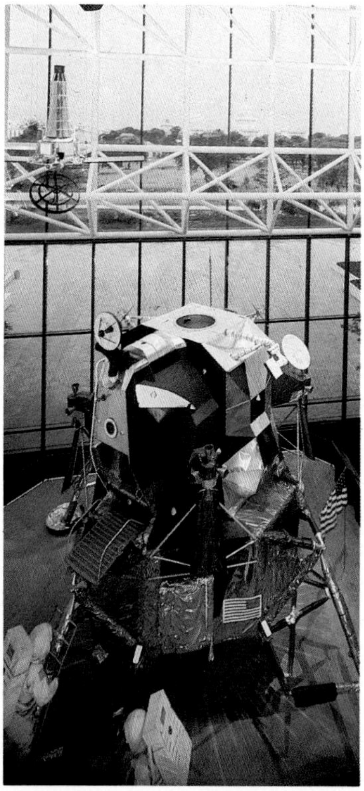

1971; Ice Age "Mummy." 297, Mar. 1972; Mural. 294-295, Mar. 1972
• The Smithsonian, Magnet on the Mall. By Leonard Carmichael. Photos by Volkmar Wentzel. 796-845, June 1960
• The Smithsonian Institution. By Thomas R. Henry. 325-348, Sept. 1948
• U. S. National Museum. 792, 798, 800, 803, 805, 806, Dec. 1950; 367, Mar. 1954; 90, Jan. 1956; 264, Feb. 1956; 276, Aug. 1956; 829, 832, Dec. 1956; First Lady exhibit. 328, 347, Sept. 1948; 90, Jan. 1957; Fossil collection. 363, 365, 376, 379, 381, Mar. 1956; Mineral collection. 631, 638-641, Nov. 1951; Shell collection. 39, 68, 71, July 1949; Eskimo artifacts. 198, Feb. 1983
• *See also* National Gallery of Art; National Zoological Park, Washington, D. C.; Smithsonian Astrophysical Observatory

SMOKEJUMPING:
• Forest Fire: The Devil's Picnic. By Stuart E. Jones and Jay Johnston. 100-127, July 1968

SMOKY MOUNTAINS, North Carolina-Tennessee. *See* Great Smoky Mountains

SMOLAN, RICK: Photographer:
• Alone Across the Outback. By Robyn Davidson. 581-611, May 1978

SMUGGLING:
• Wild Cargo: the Business of Smuggling Animals. By Noel Grove. Photos by Steve Raymer. 287-315, Mar. 1981

SNAILS:
• Blue-water Plankton: Ghosts of the Gulf Stream. By William M. Hamner. Included: Planktonic snails. NGS research grant. 530-545, Oct. 1974
• Shells Take You Over World Horizons. By Rutherford Platt. Included: Land, marine, and tree snails. 33-84, July 1949
• *See also* Giant African Land Snails; Tree Snails

SNAKE (River), Wyoming-Idaho-Washington:
• A Map Maker Looks at the United States. By Newman Bumstead. 705-748, June 1951
• Wildlife Adventuring in Jackson Hole. By Frank and John Craighead. 1-36, Jan. 1956

SNAKES:
• The Lure of the Changing Desert. 817-824, June 1954
• Our Snake Friends and Foes. By Doris M. Cochran. Paintings by Walter A. Weber. 334-364, Sept. 1954
• The People of Cumberland Gap. By John Fetterman. Photos by Bruce Dale. Included: Snake hunting. 591-621, Nov. 1971
• Wildlife of Everglades National Park. By Daniel B. Beard. Paintings by Walter A. Weber. Included: Indigo snake, rattlesnake, water snake. 83-116, Jan. 1949

ST

BOTH BY BRUCE DALE, NGS

Stehekin: mule deer await breakfast, *above;* Judy Breeze hauls water, *below*

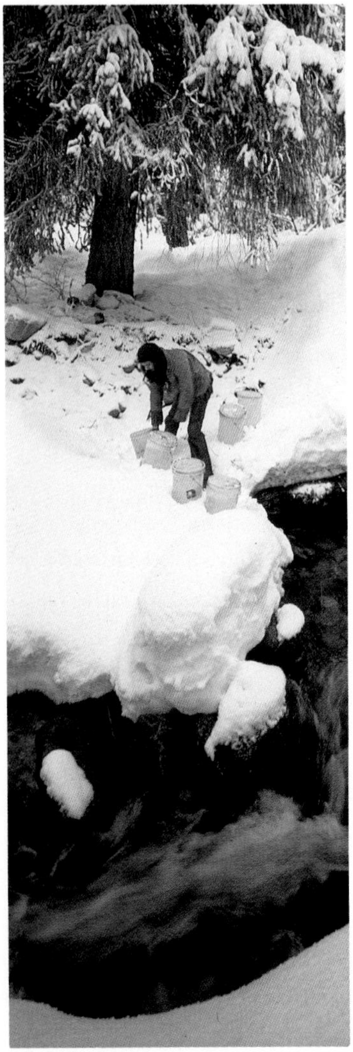

• Zoo Animals Go to School. By Marion P. McCrane. Photos by W. E. Garrett. 694-706, Nov. 1956
• *See also* Cobras; Garter Snakes; Sea Snakes

SNAKETOWN (Excavation Site), Arizona:
• The Hohokam: First Masters of the American Desert. By Emil W. Haury. Photos by Helga Teiwes. 670-695, May 1967
• Magnetic Clues Help Date the Past. By Kenneth F. Weaver. 696-701, May 1967

SNO-CATS Mechanize Oregon Snow Survey. By Andrew H. Brown. Photos by John E. Fletcher. 691-710, Nov. 1949

SNOW, JANE: Author:
• Long Island's Quiet Side (East End). Photos by Sam Abell. 662-685, May 1980

SNOW:
• Avalanche! By David Cupp. 280-305, Sept. 1982
I. Winter's White Death. 280-281; II. "I'm OK, I'm Alive!" Photos by Lanny Johnson and Andre Benier. 282-289; III. Battling the Juggernaut. 290-305
• *See also* Snowflakes

SNOW FESTIVAL in Japan's Far North. By Eiji Miyazawa. 824-833, Dec. 1968

SNOW GEESE:
• Beyond the North Wind With the Snow Goose. By Des and Jen Bartlett. 822-843, Dec. 1973

SNOW LEOPARDS:
• Imperiled Phantom of Asian Peaks: First Photographs of Snow Leopards in the Wild. By George B. Schaller. NGS research grant. 702-707, Nov. 1971

SNOW-MANTLED Stehekin: Where Solitude Is in Season. Photos by Bruce Dale. Text by Pat Hutson. 572-588, Apr. 1974

SNOW STAR PILGRIMAGE:
• Peru's Pilgrimage to the Sky. By Robert Randall. Photos by Loren McIntyre and Ira Block. 60-69, July 1982

SNOW SURVEY:
• Sno-Cats Mechanize Oregon Snow Survey. By Andrew H. Brown. Photos by John E. Fletcher. 691-710, Nov. 1949

SNOWFLAKE (Albino Gorilla):
• Growing Up With Snowflake. By Arthur J. Riopelle. Photos by Michael Kuh. NGS research grant. 491-503, Oct. 1970
• "Snowflake," the World's First White Gorilla. By Arthur J. Riopelle. Photos by Paul A. Zahl. NGS research grant. 443-448, Mar. 1967

SNOWFLAKES to Keep. By Robert F. Sisson. 104-111, Jan. 1970

SNYDER, HELEN: Photographer:
• Can the Cooper's Hawk Survive? By Noel Snyder. Photos by author and Helen Snyder. 433-442, Mar. 1974

SNYDER, NOEL:
Author-Photographer:
• Can the Cooper's Hawk Survive? Photos by author and Helen Snyder. 433-442, Mar. 1974

"SO Empty, Yet So Full" (Alaska's Arctic National Wildlife Range). By Douglas H. Chadwick. Photos by Lowell Georgia. 737-769, Dec. 1979

SO Long, St. Louis, We're Heading West. By William C. Everhart. 643-669, Nov. 1965

SO Much Happens Along the Ohio River. By Frederick Simpich. Photos by Justin Locke. 177-212, Feb. 1950

SOARING:
• Happy Birthday, Otto Lilienthal! By Russell Hawkes. Photos by James Collison. 286-292, Feb. 1972
• Sailors of the Sky. By Gordon Young. Photos by Emory Kristof and Jack Fields. Paintings by Davis Meltzer. 49-73, Jan. 1967
• The Thousand-mile Glide. By Karl Striedieck. Photos by Otis Imboden. 431-438, Mar. 1978

SOARING on Skis in the Swiss Alps. By Carolyn Bennett Patterson. Photos by Kathleen Revis. 94-121, Jan. 1961

SOBHUZA II, King (Swaziland):
• Swaziland Tries Independence. By Volkmar Wentzel. 266-293, Aug. 1969

SOC (Sub-ice Observation Chamber):
• Stalking Seals Under Antarctic Ice. By Carleton Ray. 54-65, Jan. 1966

SOCHUREK, HOWARD:
Author-Photographer:
• Air Rescue Behind Enemy Lines (North Viet Nam). 346-369, Sept. 1968
• American Special Forces in Action in Viet Nam. 38-65, Jan. 1965
• Berlin, on Both Sides of the Wall. 1-47, Jan. 1970
• Slow Train Through Viet Nam's War. 412-444, Sept. 1964
• South Korea: Success Story in Asia. 301-345, Mar. 1969
• Viet Nam's Montagnards. 443-487, Apr. 1968
• The Volga, Russia's Mighty River Road. 579-613, May 1973
Photographer:
• The Laser's Bright Magic. By Thomas Meloy. 858-881, Dec. 1966
• World War I Aircraft Fly Again in Rhinebeck's Rickety Rendezvous. By Harvey Arden. 578-587, Oct. 1970

SOCIAL INSECTS. *See* Ants; Bees; Termites

SOCIÉTÉ D'ÉNERGIE DE LA BAIE JAMES: Quebec (Province), Canada:
• Quebec's Northern Dynamo. By Larry Kohl. Photos by Ottmar Bierwagen. 406-418, Mar. 1982

SOCIETY Honors the Conquerors of Antarctica. 589-590, Apr. 1959

SOCIETY ISLANDS, South Pacific Ocean:

• The Society Islands, Sisters of the Wind. By Priit J. Vesilind. Photos by George F. Mobley. 844-869, June 1979
• The *Yankee*'s Wander-world. By Irving and Electa Johnson. 1-50, Jan. 1949
• *See also* Tahiti

The **SOCIETY** Reports to Its Members on Russia Today. The Editor. 351, Sept. 1959

The **SOCIETY'S** Great 75th Anniversary Issue. Introduction by Melville Bell Grosvenor. 459, Oct. 1963

The **SOCIETY'S** Hubbard Medal Awarded to Commander MacMillan. 563-564, Apr. 1953

SOCKEYE SALMON:
• The Incredible Salmon. By Clarence P. Idyll. Photos by Robert F. Sisson. Paintings by Walter A. Weber. 195-219, Aug. 1968

SOHAR (Dhow):
• In the Wake of Sindbad. By Tim Severin. Photos by Richard Greenhill. 2-41, July 1982

SOIL EROSION:
• Erosion, Trojan Horse of Greece. By F. G. Renner. 793-812, Dec. 1947
• This Land of Ours–How Are We Using It? By Peter T. White. Photos by Emory Kristof. 20-67, July 1976
• Water for the World's Growing Needs. By Herbert B. Nichols and F. Barrows Colton. 269-286, Aug. 1952
• *See also* Forests; Reforestation; U. S. Soil Conservation Service

SOLAR ECLIPSES:
• Burr Prizes Awarded to Dr. Edgerton and Dr. Van Biesbroeck. 705-706, May 1953
• Eclipse Hunting in Brazil's Ranchland. By F. Barrows Colton. Photos by Richard H. Stewart and Guy W. Starling. NGS research grant. 285-324, Sept. 1947
• Operation Eclipse: 1948. By William A. Kinney. Contents: Eclipse observation stations in Burma; Thailand; China; Korea; Japan; Aleutian Islands. NGS research grant. 325-372, Mar. 1949
• Solar Eclipse, Nature's Super Spectacular. By Donald H. Menzel and Jay M. Pasachoff. NGS research grant. 222-233, Aug. 1970
• The Solar Eclipse From a Jet. By Wolfgang B. Klemperer. Included: Path of totality of eclipse from Hokkaido, Japan, to beyond Bar Harbor, Maine. NGS research grant. 785-796, Nov. 1963
• South in the Sudan. By Harry Hoogstraal. Included: Khartoum, 1952 eclipse site. 249-272, Feb. 1953
• The Sun. By Herbert Friedman. 713-743, Nov. 1965
• Your Society Observes Eclipse in Brazil. NGS research grant. 661, May 1947

SOLAR ENERGY:
• Across Australia by Sunpower. By Hans Tholstrup and Larry Perkins. Photos by David Austen. 600-607, Nov. 1983
• An Atlas of Energy Resources. Included: Maps of the United States showing the average daily radiation. 58-69, *Special Report on Energy* (Feb. 1981)
• Conservation: Can We Live Better on Less? By Rick Gore. 34-57, *Special Report on Energy* (Feb. 1981)
• Editorial. By Gilbert M. Grosvenor. 289, Mar. 1976
• Electricity From the Sun. 40-41, *Special Report on Energy* (Feb. 1981)
• The Next Frontier? By Isaac Asimov. Paintings by Pierre Mion. 76-89, July 1976
• The Search for Tomorrow's Power. By Kenneth F. Weaver. Photos by Emory Kristof. 650-681, Nov. 1972
• Silver: A Mineral of Excellent Nature. By Allen A. Boraiko. Photos by Fred Ward. 280-313, Sept. 1981
• Solar Energy, the Ultimate Powerhouse. By John L. Wilhelm. Photos by Emory Kristof. 381-397, Mar. 1976
• The Sun. By Herbert Friedman. 713-743, Nov. 1965
• What's Happening to Our Climate? By Samuel W. Matthews. 576-615, Nov. 1976

SOLAR-POWERED CAR:
• Across Australia by Sunpower. By Hans Tholstrup and Larry Perkins. Photos by David Austen. 600-607, Nov. 1983

SOLAR SYSTEM:
▲ *The Solar System; Saturn,* double-sided supplement. July 1981
• Voyage to the Planets. By Kenneth F. Weaver. Paintings by Ludek Pesek. 147-193, Aug. 1970
• *See also* Comets; Moon; Planets; Sun

SOLE:
• The Red Sea's Sharkproof Fish. By Eugenie Clark. Photos by David Doubilet. Contents: Moses sole. NGS research grant. 718-727, Nov. 1974

The **SOLEMN,** Sociable Puffins. By R. M. Lockley. 414-422, Sept. 1954

SOLHEIM, WILHELM G., II: Author:
• New Light on a Forgotten Past. 330-339, Mar. 1971

SOLIDARITY (Trade Union):
▲ *The Face and Faith of Poland,* map, photo, and essay supplement. By Peter Miller. Essay by Czesław Miłosz. Photos by Bruno Barbey. Apr. 1982

SOLO to the Pole. By Naomi Uemura. Photos by the author and Ira Block. 298-325, Sept. 1978

SOLOMON ISLANDS, South Pacific Ocean:
• Adventures with the Survey Navy. By Irving Johnson. 131-148, July 1947
• A Teen-ager Sails the World Alone. By Robin Lee Graham. 445-491, Oct. 1968
• *Yankee* Roams the Orient. By Irving and Electa Johnson. 327-370, Mar. 1951

SOLVING Life Secrets of the Sailfish. By Gilbert Voss. Photos by B. Anthony Stewart. Paintings by Craig Phillips. 859-872, June 1956

SOLVING the Mystery of Mexico's Great Stone Spheres. By Matthew W. Stirling. Photos by David F. Cupp. 295-300, Aug. 1969

SOLVING the Riddle of Chubb Crater. By V. Ben Meen. Photos by Richard H. Stewart. 1-32, Jan. 1952

SOLVING the Riddles of Wetherill Mesa. By Douglas Osborne. Paintings by Peter V. Bianchi. 155-195, Feb. 1964

SOMALIA:
• Somalia's Hour of Need. By Robert Paul Jordan. Photos by Michael S. Yamashita and Kevin Fleming. 748-775, June 1981
Encampments of the Dispossessed. By Larry Kohl. 756-763

SOMETHING'S Fishy About That Fin! Photos by Robert J. Shallenberger and William D. Madden. 224-227, Aug. 1974

SONAKUL, D.: Author:
• Pageantry of the Siamese Stage. Photos by W. Robert Moore. 201-212, Feb. 1947

SONAR (Sound Navigation and Ranging):
• Down to *Thresher* by Bathyscaph. By Donald L. Keach. 764-777, June 1964
• From Indian Canoes to Submarines at Key West. By Frederick Simpich. Photos by J. Baylor Roberts. 41-72, Jan. 1950
• Our Navy's Long Submarine Arm. By Allan C. Fisher, Jr. 613-636, Nov. 1952

SONAR ABILITY. *See* Bats; Killer Whales; Oilbirds; Porpoises; Weddell Seals

SONG of Hope for the Bluebird. By Lawrence Zeleny. Photos by Michael L. Smith. 855-865, June 1977

SONGHAIS (Tribespeople):
• The Niger: River of Sorrow, River of Hope. By Georg Gerster. 152-189, Aug. 1975

SONGS:
• Hunting Folk Songs in the Hebrides. By Margaret Shaw Campbell. 249-272, Feb. 1947
• Hunting Musical Game in West Africa. By Arthur S. Alberts. 262-282, Aug. 1951

SONOMA VALLEY, California. *See* Valley of the Moon

SONORA (State), Mexico:
• From Sun-clad Sea to Shining Mountains. By Ralph Gray. Photos by James P. Blair. 542-589, Apr. 1964
• Sonora Is Jumping. By Mason Sutherland. 215-246, Feb. 1955

SONORAN DESERT, Arizona-Mexico:
• Abundant Life in a Desert Land. By Walter Meayers Edwards. 424-436, Sept. 1973

• Arizona's Suburbs of the Sun. By David Jeffery. Photos by H. Edward Kim. 486-517, Oct. 1977

SORCERY:

• American Special Forces in Action in Viet Nam. By Howard Sochurek. Included: Rhadé tribe sorcerers. 38-65, Jan. 1965

• Fertility Rites and Sorcery in a New Guinea Village. By Gillian Gillison. Photos by David Gillison. Included: Sorcery trials, involving divination, to affix guilt in cases of illness and death among the Gimis. 124-146, July 1977

• Journey Into Stone Age New Guinea. By Malcolm S. Kirk. Included: Sorcerers of Nomad River, and Oksapmin. 568-592, Apr. 1969

• Viet Nam's Montagnards. By Howard Sochurek. Included: Mnong tribe sorcerers. 443-487, Apr. 1968

The **SOUL** of a Tribe Returns to Africa. By William S. Ellis. Photos by James P. Blair. 141-148, July 1974

SOULEN, HENRY J.: Artist:

• Bringing Old Testament Times to Life. By G. Ernest Wright. 833-864, Dec. 1957

• The Last Thousand Years Before Christ. By G. Ernest Wright. Paintings by H. J. Soulen and Peter V. Bianchi. 812-853, Dec. 1960

SOUND SHEETS:

◆ "Bird Songs of Garden, Woodland, and Meadow," record supplement to *Song and Garden Birds of North America*. 554, 557, Oct. 1964

◆ "Bird Sounds of Marsh, Upland, and Shore," record supplement to *Water, Prey, and Game Birds of North America*. 529, 530, 533, 534, 535, Oct. 1965

• "The Funeral of Sir Winston Churchill, with Excerpts from His Speeches," record supplement. 198A-198B, Aug. 1965; 580, 581, Oct. 1967

• "Sounds of the Space Age, from Sputnik to Lunar Landing," record supplement narrated by Frank Borman. 750A-750B, Dec. 1969

• "Sounds of the World" series. 701, Nov. 1971; 475, Apr. 1976

• Symphony of the Deep: "Songs of the Humpback Whale" (Sound Sheet). 24-24B, Jan. 1979

SOURIAL, GEORGES: Photographer:

• The Voyage of *Ra II*. By Thor Heyerdahl. Photos by Carlo Mauri and Georges Sourial. 44-71, Jan. 1971

The **SOUTH** (Region), U. S.:

• Around the "Great Lakes of the South." By Frederick Simpich. Photos by J. Baylor Roberts. 463-491, Apr. 1948

• Beauty and Bounty of Southern State Trees. By William A. Dayton. Paintings by Walter A. Weber. 508-552, Oct. 1957

• Chattooga River Country: Wild Water, Proud People. By Don Belt. Photos by Steve Wall. 458-477, Apr. 1983

▲ *Close-up: U.S.A., The South Central States,* supplement. Text on reverse. Oct. 1974

▲ *Close-up: U.S.A., The Southeast,* supplement. Text on reverse. Oct. 1975

▲ *Deep South,* The Making of America series. Included: Alabama, Florida, Georgia, Louisiana, Mississippi, South Carolina, and parts of Arkansas, North Carolina, and Tennessee. On reverse: Indian Legacy, Imperial Footholds, Three Empires and Three Races, Cotton Kingdom, Postbellum, New Deep South, Subtropical Playground. Aug. 1983

• Dixie Spins the Wheel of Industry. By William H. Nicholas. Photos by J. Baylor Roberts. 281-324, Mar. 1949

• Mississippi Delta: The Land of the River. By Douglas Lee. Photos by C. C. Lockwood. 226-253, Aug. 1983

• Savannah to Charleston–A Good Life in the Low Country. By John J. Putman. Photos by Annie Griffiths. 798-829, Dec. 1983

• Sea Islands: Adventuring Along the South's Surprising Coast. By James Cerruti. Photos by Thomas Nebbia and James L. Amos. 366-393, Mar. 1971

▲ *South Central United States,* Atlas series supplement. Feb. 1961

▲ *South Central United States,* supplement. Dec. 1947

▲ *Southeastern United States,* Atlas series supplement. Jan. 1958

▲ *Southeastern United States,* supplement. Feb. 1947

• A Walk Across America. By Peter Gorton Jenkins. 466-499, Apr. 1977

• *See also* Gulf Coast; Intracoastal Waterways; *and* names of individual states

SOUTH AFRICA, Republic of:

• Adventures With South Africa's Black Eagles. By Jeanne Cowden. Photos by author and Arthur Bowland. 533-543, Oct. 1969

• Africa: The Winds of Freedom Stir a Continent. By Nathaniel T. Kenney. Photos by W. D. Vaughn. 303-359, Sept. 1960

• Editorial. By Gilbert M. Grosvenor. 725, June 1977

• First Flight Across the Bottom of the World. By James R. Reedy. Photos by Otis Imboden. 454-464, Mar. 1964

• Freedom's Progress South of the Sahara. By Howard La Fay. Photos by Joseph J. Scherschel. 603-637, Nov. 1962

• Gold, the Eternal Treasure. By Peter T. White. Photos by James L. Stanfield. 1-51, Jan. 1974

• The Incredible Crystal: Diamonds. By Fred Ward. 85-113, Jan. 1979

• The Many-sided Diamond. By George Switzer. 568-586, Apr. 1958

• Namibia: Nearly a Nation? By Bryan Hodgson. Photos by Jim Brandenburg. Included: Namibia's efforts to establish independence from South Africa. 755-797, June 1982

• Questing for Gems. By George S. Switzer. 835-863, Dec. 1971

• Roaming Africa's Unfenced Zoos. By W. Robert Moore. Included: Hluhluwe, Kruger, and Umfolozi reserves. 353-380, Mar. 1950

• Safari Through Changing Africa. By Elsie May Bell Grosvenor. Photos by Gilbert Grosvenor. 145-198, Aug. 1953

• South Africa Close-up. By Kip Ross. 641-681, Nov. 1962

• South Africa's Lonely Ordeal. By William S. Ellis. Photos by James P. Blair. 780-819, June 1977

• World-roaming Teen-ager Sails On. By Robin Lee Graham. 449-493, Apr. 1969

• The Zulus: Black Nation in a Land of Apartheid. By Joseph Judge. Photos by Dick Durrance II. 738-775, Dec. 1971

• *See also* Dassen Island; Good Hope, Cape of; Kwazulu

SOUTH AMERICA:

• The Amazon. Photos by Loren McIntyre. 445-455, Oct. 1972

• Amazon–The River Sea. By Loren McIntyre. 456-495, Oct. 1972

• Ambassadors of Good Will: The Peace Corps. By Sargent Shriver and Peace Corps Volunteers. Included: Bolivia; Ecuador. 297-345, Sept. 1964

▲ *Bird Migration in the Americas; The Americas,* double-sided supplement. Aug. 1979

• The Desert: An Age-old Challenge Grows. By Rick Gore. Photos by Georg Gerster and Bruce Dale. 586-639, Nov. 1979

▲ *Eastern South America,* Atlas series supplement. Sept. 1962

▲ *Eastern South America,* supplement. Mar. 1955

• Editorial. By Gilbert M. Grosvenor. 295, Mar. 1975

• Flags of the Americas. By Elizabeth W. King. Included: Argentina; Bolivia; Brazil; Chile; Colombia; Ecuador; Paraguay; Peru; Uruguay; Venezuela. 633-657, May 1949

• The Gauchos, Last of a Breed. By Robert Laxalt. Photos by O. Louis Mazzatenta. 478-501, Oct. 1980

• Gold, the Eternal Treasure. By Peter T. White. Photos by James L. Stanfield. 1-51, Jan. 1974

• How Fruit Came to America. By J. R. Magness. Paintings by Else Bostelmann. Included: Origin of the pineapple; Development of the strawberry. 325-377, Sept. 1951

• In the Wake of Darwin's *Beagle*. By Alan Villiers. Photos by James L. Stanfield. Included: Argentina; Brazil; Chile; Peru; Uruguay. 449-495, Oct. 1969

• The Incredible Potato. By Robert E. Rhoades. Photos by Martin Rogers. 668-694, May 1982

▲ *Indians of South America; Archaeology of South America,* double-sided supplement. Mar. 1982

• Jungle Jaunt on Amazon Headwaters. By Bernice M. Goetz. 371-388, Sept. 1952

• Magellan: First Voyage Around the World. By Alan Villiers. Photos by Bruce Dale. 721-753, June 1976

• Mysteries of Bird Migration. By Allan C. Fisher, Jr. Photos by Jonathan Blair. 154-193, Aug. 1979
▲ *Northwestern South America,* Atlas series supplement. Feb. 1964
• Our Vegetable Travelers. By Victor R. Boswell. Paintings by Else Bostelmann. Included: Vegetables native to South America (Corn, Potato, Sweet Potato). 145-217, Aug. 1949
• Parks, Plans, and People: How South America Guards Her Green Legacy. By Mary and Laurance Rockefeller. Photos by George F. Mobley. 74-119, Jan. 1967
• Playing 3,000 Golf Courses in Fourteen Lands. By Ralph A. Kennedy. 113-132, July 1952
• Sea Fever. By John E. Schultz. Contents: The author's 6,000-mile trip from Quito, Ecuador, to Miami, Florida, by way of the Napo and Amazon Rivers and the West Indies. 237-268, Feb. 1949
• The Search for the First Americans. By Thomas Y. Canby. Photos by Kerby Smith. Paintings by Roy Andersen. Included: Paleo-Indian sites in Argentina, Chile, Peru, and Venezuela. 330-363, Sept. 1979
• Sir Francis Drake. By Alan Villiers. 216-253, Feb. 1975
▲ *South America,* Atlas series supplement. Feb. 1960
▲ *South America,* supplement. Oct. 1950
▲ *South America,* supplement. Text on reverse. Oct. 1972
▲ *Southern South America,* Atlas series supplement. Mar. 1958
• Theodore Roosevelt: a Centennial Tribute. By Bart McDowell. Included: Travels in South America. 572-590, Oct. 1958
• Tropical Rain Forests: Nature's Dwindling Treasures. By Peter T. White. Photos by James P. Blair. Paintings by Barron Storey. 2-47, Jan. 1983
• The World in Your Garden (Flowers). By W. H. Camp. Paintings by Else Bostelmann. Included: South America Rich in Plant Life (Fuchsia, Petunia, Cupflower, Garden verbena, Scarlet sage); From South American Jungles (Spider flower, Morning glory, Cypress vine, Nasturtium, Victoria waterlily, Canna). 1-65, July 1947
• *See also* Argentina; Bolivia; Brazil; British Guiana; Chile; Colombia; Ecuador; Netherlands Antilles; Paraguay; Peru; Suriname; Trinidad and Tobago; Uruguay; Venezuela; *and* Indians of South America

SOUTH AUSTRALIA (State), Australia:
• South Australia, Gateway to the Great Outback. By Howell Walker. Photos by Joseph J. Scherschel. 441-481, Apr. 1970
• *See also* Coober Pedy

SOUTH CALAVERAS GROVE, California:
• Saving Earth's Oldest Living Things (Sequoias). By Andrew H. Brown. Photos by Raymond Moulin and author. 679-695, May 1951

SOUTH CAROLINA:
• Chattooga River Country: Wild Water, Proud People. By Don Belt. Photos by Steve Wall. 458-477, Apr. 1983
• Dixie Spins the Wheel of Industry. By William H. Nicholas. Photos by J. Baylor Roberts. 281-324, Mar. 1949
• Here Come the Marines. By Frederick Simpich. Included: Parris Island. 647-672, Nov. 1950
• Savannah to Charleston–A Good Life in the Low Country. By John J. Putman. Photos by Annie Griffiths. 798-829, Dec. 1983
• Sea Islands: Adventuring Along the South's Surprising Coast. By James Cerruti. Photos by Thomas Nebbia and James L. Amos. 366-393, Mar. 1971
• South Carolina Rediscovered. By Herbert Ravenel Sass. Photos by Robert F. Sisson. 281-321, Mar. 1953

SOUTH CENTRAL STATES:
▲ *Close-up: U.S.A., The South Central States,* supplement. Text on reverse. Oct. 1974
▲ *South Central United States,* Atlas series supplement. Feb. 1961
▲ *South Central United States,* supplement. Dec. 1947
• *See also* names of individual states

SOUTH CHINA SEA VOYAGE:
• In the Wake of Sindbad. By Tim Severin. Photos by Richard Greenhill. 2-41, July 1982

SOUTH DAKOTA:
• Back to the Historic Black Hills. By Leland D. Case. Photos by Bates Littlehales. 479-509, Oct. 1956
• Big Game Hunting in the Land of Long Ago. By Joseph P. Connolly and James D. Bump. NGS research grant. 589-605, May 1947
• Following the Trail of Lewis and Clark. By Ralph Gray. 707-750, June 1953
• South Dakota Keeps Its West Wild. By Frederick Simpich. 555-588, May 1947
Over Plains and Hills of South Dakota. Photos by J. Baylor Roberts. 563-586
• South Dakota's Badlands: Castles in Clay. By John Madson. Photos by Jim Brandenburg. 524-539, Apr. 1981
• *See also* Sioux Falls; Stratobowl

SOUTH GEORGIA ISLAND, South Atlantic Ocean:
• A Naturalist in Penguin Land. By Niall Rankin. 93-116, Jan. 1955

SOUTH in the Sudan. By Harry Hoogstraal. 249-272, Feb. 1953

SOUTH ISLAND, New Zealand:
• New Zealand's Bountiful South Island. By Peter Benchley. Photos by James L. Amos. 93-123, Jan. 1972
• New Zealand's High Country. By Yva Momatiuk and John Eastcott. 246-265, Aug. 1978

THOMAS NEBBIA

Sea Islands: centuries-old Angel Oak

S T

• New Zealand's Milford Track: "Walk of a Lifetime." By Carolyn Bennett Patterson. Photos by Robert E. Gilka. 117-129, Jan. 1978

SOUTH KOREA. *See* Korea, Republic of

SOUTH NAHANNI RIVER, Canada:
• Nahanni: Canada's Wilderness Park. By Douglas H. Chadwick. Photos by Matt Bradley. 396-420, Sept. 1981

SOUTH PACIFIC ISLANDS:
• Adventures with the Survey Navy. By Irving Johnson. Contents: The surveying and charting of Deboyne Lagoon, Louisiade Archipelago; Florida Island and Guadalcanal, Solomon Islands; Funafuti and Nukufetau, Ellice Islands; Kwajalein, Marshall Islands; Tarawa, Gilbert Islands; Ulithi, Caroline Islands; Uvéa, Wallis Islands. 131-148, July 1947
• Pacific Wards of Uncle Sam. By W. Robert Moore. Contents: The United States Trust Territory of Pacific Islands comprising the Carolines with Palau, the Marshalls, and the Marianas. 73-104, July 1948
• A Teen-ager Sails the World Alone. By Robin Lee Graham. Included: Fiji Islands; Samoa Islands; Solomon Islands; Tonga. 445-491, Oct. 1968
• The *Yankee*'s Wander-world. By Irving and Electa Johnson. Included: Ahé; Bora Bora; Easter Island; Mooréa; Pitcairn; Raïvavaé; Rapa; Tahiti. 1-50, Jan. 1949
• *See also* Melanesia; Micronesia; Norfolk; Pitcairn; Polynesia

SOUTH POLE:
• All-out Assault on Antarctica. By Richard E. Byrd. 141-180, Aug. 1956
• Antarctica: Icy Testing Ground for Space. By Samuel W. Matthews. Photos by Robert W. Madden. 569-592, Oct. 1968
• Circling Earth From Pole to Pole. By Sir Ranulph Fiennes. 464-481, Oct. 1983
• The Crossing of Antarctica. By Sir Vivian Fuchs. Photos by George Lowe. 25-47, Jan. 1959
• Man's First Winter at the South Pole. By Paul A. Siple. 439-478, Apr. 1958
• Our Navy Explores Antarctica. By Richard E. Byrd. U. S. Navy official photos. 429-522, Oct. 1947
• To the Men at South Pole Station. By Richard E. Byrd. 1-4, July 1957
• We Are Living at the South Pole. By Paul A. Siple. Photos by David S. Boyer. 5-35, July 1957
• What We've Accomplished in Antarctica. By George J. Dufek. 527-557, Oct. 1959
• Year of Discovery Opens in Antarctica. By David S. Boyer. 339-381, Sept. 1957

SOUTH SHETLAND ISLANDS, Antarctica. *See* Deception Island

SOUTH to Mexico City. By W. E. Garrett. 145-193, Aug. 1968

SOUTH UIST (Island), Scotland:
• Isles on the Edge of the Sea: Scotland's Outer Hebrides. By Kenneth MacLeish. Photos by Thomas Nebbia. 676-711, May 1970

SOUTH VIETNAM. *See* Vietnam, South

SOUTHAMPTON, THIRD EARL OF (Henry Wriothesley):
• Founders of Virginia. By Sir Evelyn Wrench. Photos by B. Anthony Stewart. 433-462, Apr. 1948

SOUTHAMPTON ISLAND, Northwest Territories, Canada:
• Twelve National Geographic Society Scientific Projects Under Way. 869-870, June 1954
• Vanished Mystery Men of Hudson Bay. By Henry B. Collins. NGS research grant. 669-687, Nov. 1956

SOUTHEAST (Region), U. S.:
▲ *Close-up: U.S.A., The Southeast,* supplement. Text on reverse. Oct. 1975
▲ *Southeastern United States,* Atlas series supplement. Jan. 1958
▲ *Southeastern United States,* supplement. Feb. 1947
• *See also* names of individual states

SOUTHEAST ASIA:
• The Lands and Peoples of Southeast Asia. 295-365, Mar. 1971
1. Mosaic of Cultures. By Peter T. White. Photos by W. E. Garrett. 296-329; 2. New Light on a Forgotten Past. By Wilhelm G. Solheim II. 330-339; 3. Pagan, on the Road to Mandalay. By W. E. Garrett. 343-365
• The Mekong, River of Terror and Hope. By Peter T. White. Photos by W. E. Garrett. 737-787, Dec. 1968
▲ *The Peoples of Mainland Southeast Asia,* double-sided supplement. Mar. 1971
▲ *Southeast Asia,* Atlas series supplement. May 1961
▲ *Southeast Asia,* supplement. Sept. 1955
▲ *Southeast Asia,* supplement. Dec. 1968
• Tropical Rain Forests: Nature's Dwindling Treasures. By Peter T. White. Photos by James P. Blair. Paintings by Barron Storey. 2-47, Jan. 1983
▲ *Viet Nam, Cambodia, Laos, and Eastern Thailand,* supplement. Text on reverse. Jan. 1965
▲ *Viet Nam, Cambodia, Laos, and Thailand,* supplement. Feb. 1967
• *See also* Burma; Hong Kong; Indochina; Indonesia; Kampuchea; Laos; Macao; Malaysia; Philippines; Singapore; Taiwan; Thailand; Vietnam

SOUTHERN ALPS, New Zealand:
• New Zealand, Pocket Wonder World. By Howell Walker. 419-460, Apr. 1952
• New Zealand's Bountiful South Island. By Peter Benchley. Photos by James L. Amos. 93-123, Jan. 1972
• New Zealand's High Country. By Yva Momatiuk and John Eastcott. 246-265, Aug. 1978

SOUTHERN California's Trial by Mud and Water. By Nathaniel T. Kenney. Photos by Bruce Dale. 552-573, Oct. 1969

SOUTHERN RAILWAY SYSTEM:
• Dixie Spins the Wheel of Industry. By William H. Nicholas. Photos by J. Baylor Roberts. 281-324, Mar. 1949

SOUTHWEST (Region), U. S.:
• The Anasazi–Riddles in the Ruins. By Thomas Y. Canby. Photos by Dewitt Jones and David Brill. Paintings by Roy Andersen. 554-592, Nov. 1982
▲ *Close-up: U.S.A., The Southwest,* supplement. Text on reverse. Included: Arizona, Colorado, New Mexico, Utah. Oct. 1977
• The Country of Willa Cather. By William Howarth. Photos by Farrell Grehan. 71-93, July 1982
◆ *The Great Southwest.* 1980
• Inside the Sacred Hopi Homeland. By Jake Page. Photos by Susanne Page. 607-629, Nov. 1982
• The Mexican Americans: A People on the Move. By Griffin Smith, Jr. Photos by Stephanie Maze. 780-809, June 1980
• Pueblo Pottery–2,000 Years of Artistry. By David L. Arnold. 593-605, Nov. 1982
• Rediscovering America's Forgotten Crops. By Noel D. Vietmeyer. Photos by Burgess Blevins. Paintings by Paul M. Breeden. 702-712, May 1981
▲ *The Southwest,* The Making of America series. Included: Arizona, New Mexico, and parts of California, Colorado, Texas, Utah; and in Mexico: Baja California Norte, Chihuahua, Sonora. On reverse: 12,000 Years of History; Spanish Conquest; Anglo-American Entry and Occupancy. Nov. 1982
▲ *Southwestern United States,* Atlas series supplement. Nov. 1959
▲ *Southwestern United States,* supplement. Dec. 1948
• Two Wheels Along the Mexican Border. By William Albert Allard. 591-635, May 1971
• *See also* names of individual states; *and* Colorado (River); Four Corners Country; *and* Pre-Columbian Civilization

SOUTH-WEST AFRICA. *See* Namibia

SOUTH-WEST AFRICA PEOPLE'S ORGANIZATION. *See* SWAPO

SOUTHWEST ASIA:
▲ *Southwest Asia,* Atlas series supplement. May 1963
▲ *Southwest Asia, including India, Pakistan, and Northeast Africa,* supplement, June 1952

SOUTHWEST AUSTRALIA'S Wild Gardens: Bizarre and Beautiful. By Paul A. Zahl. 858-868, Dec. 1976

The **SOVIET UNION** Is My Beat. By Dean Conger. 256-269, Aug. 1977
• *See also* Union of Soviet Socialist Republics

SOYUZ-APOLLO MISSION:
• Apollo-Soyuz: Handclasp in Space. By Thomas Y. Canby. 183-187, Feb. 1976

SPACE COLONIES:
• The Next Frontier? By Isaac Asimov. Paintings by Pierre Mion. 76-89, July 1976

SPACE FLIGHTS AND RESEARCH:
• Awesome Views of the Forbidding Moonscape. 233-239, Feb. 1969
• Behold the Computer Revolution. By Peter T. White. Photos by Bruce Dale and Emory Kristof. 593-633, Nov. 1970
• I Fly the X-15. By Joseph A. Walker. Photos by Dean Conger. 428-450, Sept. 1962
• The Long, Lonely Leap. By Joseph W. Kittinger, Jr. Photos by Volkmar Wentzel. 854-873, Dec. 1960
◆ *Man's Conquest of Space.* Announced. 844-849, June 1968; rev. ed. 1975
• Satellites That Serve Us. By Thomas Y. Canby. Included: A portfolio: Images of Earth. 281-335, Sept. 1983
Spacelab 1: *Columbia.* By Michael E. Long. 301-307
• The Sun. By Herbert Friedman. Included: U. S. Naval Research Laboratory studies. 713-743, Nov. 1965
• We Saw the World From the Edge of Space. By Malcolm D. Ross. Ground photos by Walter Meayers Edwards. 671-685, Nov. 1961
• *See also* Apollo Missions; Gemini Missions; Mariner Missions; Mercury Missions; Pioneer Probes; Ranger Spacecraft; Rockets; Satellites; Skylab Missions; Space Shuttles; Spacelab; Surveyor Spacecraft; Viking Spacecraft Missions; Voyager

SPACE MEDICINE:
• Aviation Medicine on the Threshold of Space. By Allan C. Fisher, Jr. Photos by Luis Marden. 241-278, Aug. 1955
• The Flight of *Freedom 7.* By Carmault B. Jackson, Jr. 416-431, Sept. 1961
• The Making of an Astronaut. By Robert R. Gilruth. 122-144, Jan. 1965
• School for Space Monkeys. 725-729, May 1961
• Skylab, Outpost on the Frontier of Space. By Thomas Y. Canby. Photos by the nine mission astronauts. 441-469, Oct. 1974
• Spacelab 1: *Columbia.* By Michael E. Long. 301-307, Sept. 1983
• We Saw the World From the Edge of Space. By Malcolm D. Ross. Ground photos by Walter Meayers Edwards. 671-685, Nov. 1961
• *See also* Biorhythm Research; Tektite II

SPACE PIONEERS of NASA Journey Into Tomorrow. By Allan C. Fisher, Jr. Photos by Dean Conger. 48-89, July 1960

SPACE RENDEZVOUS, Milestone on the Way to the Moon. By Kenneth F. Weaver. 539-553, Apr. 1966

SPACE SATELLITES. *See* Satellites

SPACE SHUTTLES:
• *Columbia*'s Astronauts' Own Story: Our Phenomenal First Flight. By John W. Young and Robert L. Crippen. Paintings by Ken Dallison. 478-503, Oct. 1981
• *Columbia*'s Landing Closes a Circle. By Tom Wolfe. 474-477, Oct. 1981
• Heat Paints *Columbia*'s Portrait. By Cliff Tarpy. 650-653, Nov. 1982
• Satellites That Serve Us. By Thomas Y. Canby. Included: A portfolio: Images of Earth. 281-335, Sept. 1983
Spacelab 1: *Columbia.* By Michael E. Long. 301-307
• When the Space Shuttle Finally Flies. By Rick Gore. Photos by Jon Schneeberger. Paintings by Ken Dallison. Note: The space shuttle *Columbia* will be joined in the future by *Challenger, Discovery,* and *Atlantis.* 317-347, Mar. 1981

SPACE STATIONS:
• The Next Frontier? By Isaac Asimov. Paintings by Pierre Mion. 76-89, July 1976
• Solar Energy, the Ultimate Powerhouse. By John L. Wilhelm. Photos by Emory Kristof. 381-397, Mar. 1976
• *See also* Skylab Missions

SPACE WALK:
• America's 6,000-mile Walk in Space. 440-447, Sept. 1965

SPACECRAFT:
• Of Air and Space (National Air and Space Museum). By Michael Collins. 819-837, June 1978
Picture portfolio by Nathan Benn, Robert S. Oakes, and Joseph D. Lavenburg, with text by Michael E. Long. 825-837
• *See also* Apollo Missions; Gemini Missions; Mariner Missions; Mercury Missions; Pioneer Probes; Ranger Spacecraft; Skylab Missions; Space Shuttles; Spacelab; Surveyor Spacecraft; Viking Spacecraft Missions; Voyager; *and* Satellites: DODGE Satellite; Nimbus I (Extraordinary); Telstar; *Tiros I*

SPACELAB:
• Spacelab 1: *Columbia.* By Michael E. Long. 301-307, Sept. 1983
• When the Space Shuttle Finally Flies. By Rick Gore. Photos by Jon Schneeberger. Paintings by Ken Dallison. Note: Spacelab is a European-built laboratory for use aboard the space shuttle. 317-347, Mar. 1981

SPAFFORD MEMORIAL CHILDREN'S HOSPITAL, Jerusalem:
• Jerusalem, My Home. By Bertha Spafford Vester. 826-847, Dec. 1964

SPAIN:
• "Around the World in Eighty Days." By Newman Bumstead. Included: Barcelona; Cape Creus; Madrid. 705-750, Dec. 1951
• The Changing Face of Old Spain. By Bart McDowell. Photos by Albert Moldvay. Included: Barcelona; Madrid; Pamplona; Segovia; Seville; Toledo; Valencia. 291-339, Mar. 1965

NASA, SHUTTLE MISSION 7

Satellites: the shuttle *Challenger*

ST

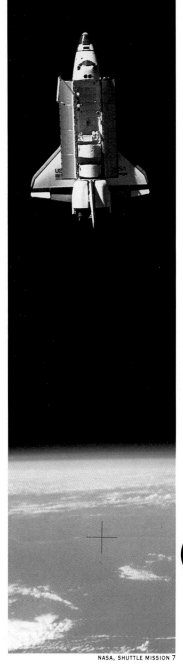

Atocha: salvaged gold whistle, manicure set, and ear spoon

ROBERT S. PATTON, NGS

DON KINCAID

***Santa Margarita*: partial treasure hoard recovered from the galleon**

• Christopher Columbus and the New World He Found. By John Scofield. Photos by Adam Woolfitt. 584-625, Nov. 1975
• Spain: It's a Changed Country. By Peter T. White. Photos by David Alan Harvey. 297-331, Mar. 1978
▲ *Spain and Portugal,* Atlas series supplement. Mar. 1965
• Spain's Silkworm Gut. By Luis Marden. 100-108, July 1951
• Speaking of Spain. By Luis Marden. 415-456, Apr. 1950
• The Sword and the Sermon (Islam). By Thomas J. Abercrombie. 3-45, July 1972
▥ Washington Irving's Spain. 1966
• When the President Goes Abroad (Eisenhower Tour). By Gilbert M. Grosvenor. 588-649, May 1960
• *See also* Andalusia; Córdoba; Marismas; Pyrenees; Santander; Sevilla; Toledo; *and* Balearic Islands; Canary Islands

SPANISH-AMERICAN WAR:
• Guantánamo: Keystone in the Caribbean. By Jules B. Billard. Photos by W. E. Garrett and Thomas Nebbia. 420-436, Mar. 1961

SPANISH ARMADA:
• Priceless Relics of the Spanish Armada. By Robert Sténuit. Photos by Bates Littlehales. 745-777, June 1969
• Sir Francis Drake. By Alan Villiers. Photos by Gordon W. Gahan. 216-253, Feb. 1975

SPANISH GALLEONS. *See* Galleons and Galleasses

SPANISH RIDING SCHOOL, Vienna, Austria:
• The White Horses of Vienna. By Beverley M. Bowie. Photos by Volkmar Wentzel. 401-419, Sept. 1958

SPANISH SAHARA:
• Dry-land Fleet Sails the Sahara. By Jean du Boucher. Photos by Jonathan S. Blair. 696-725, Nov. 1967

SPANISH TREASURE:
• *Atocha,* Tragic Treasure Galleon of the Florida Keys. By Eugene Lyon. 787-809, June 1976
▲ *Colonization and Trade in the New World;* "History Salvaged From the Sea," supplement. Painting and text on reverse. Dec. 1977
• Drowned Galleons Yield Spanish Gold. By Kip Wagner. Photos by Otis Imboden. 1-37, Jan. 1965
• Priceless Relics of the Spanish Armada. By Robert Sténuit. Photos by Bates Littlehales. 745-777, June 1969
• Reach for the New World. By Mendel Peterson. Photos by David L. Arnold. Paintings by Richard Schlecht. 724-767, Dec. 1977
▥ Treasure! 575, Nov. 1976; cover, Dec. 1976
• Treasure From the Ghost Galleon: *Santa Margarita.* By Eugene Lyon. Photos by Don Kincaid. 228-243, Feb. 1982

SPARROWS POINT, Maryland:
• Man's Mightiest Ally (Steel). Photos by Willard R. Culver. 432-450, Apr. 1947

SPAWNING. *See* Grunion; Salmon

SPEAKING of Spain. By Luis Marden. 415-456, Apr. 1950

SPEARING Lions with Africa's Masai. By Edgar Monsanto Queeny. 487-517, Oct. 1954

SPEARS, JOSEPH F.: Author:
• The Flying Telegraph. Official U. S. Army Signal Corps photos. 531-554, Apr. 1947

SPECIAL Economic Zones: China's Opening Door. By John J. Putman. Photos by H. Edward Kim. 64-83, July 1983

SPECIAL FORCES, U. S. Army. *See* U. S. Army Special Forces

SPECIAL GOLD MEDAL, NGS:
• Designs by: Peter V. Bianchi. 146, July 1961; Felix W. deWeldon. 868, Dec. 1957; Laura Gardin Fraser. 45, July 1957
Recipients:
Amundsen, Roald:
• Received Special Gold Medal for discovery of the South Pole; presentation by Robert E. Peary. 65F, July 1954
Bennett, Floyd:
• Awarded Gold Medal; presentation by President Coolidge. 868, Dec. 1957
Byrd, Richard E.:
• Awarded Society's Special Medal of Honor; presentation by President Hoover. 38, 45, July 1957; 868, Dec. 1957; 574, 576, Apr. 1962
Cousteau, Jacques-Yves:
• Jacques-Yves Cousteau Receives National Geographic Society Medal at White House; presentation by President Kennedy. 146-147, July 1961
Earhart, Amelia:
• Awarded Gold Medal; presentation by President Hoover in 1932. 566, Nov. 1951; 868, Dec. 1957; 571, 582, Oct. 1963; 619, Nov. 1966
Goethals, George W.:
• Awarded Gold Medal; presentation by President Wilson in 1914. 868, Dec. 1957; 585, Oct. 1963; 141, Feb. 1978
Peary, Robert E.:
• Awarded the Society's Special Gold Medal for being the first to reach the North Pole. 18, Jan. 1963; Medal in the Smithsonian Institution. 347, Sept. 1948
Peary, Mrs. Robert E.:
• Gold Medal Awarded to Mrs. Robert E. Peary. 148, Jan. 1956
Philip, Prince:
• President Eisenhower Presents to Prince Philip the National Geographic Society's Medal. 865-868, Dec. 1957
Poulter, Thomas C.:
• Awarded Special Gold Medal for Antarctic research from 1933-1935. 205, Feb. 1967

The **SPECTACULAR** North Cascades: New National Park Proposed. By Nathaniel T. Kenney. Photos by James P. Blair. 642-667, May 1968

SPECTACULAR Rio de Janeiro. By Hernane Tavares de Sá. Photos by Charles Allmon. 289-328, Mar. 1955

SPECTACULAR Treasures From a Chinese Tomb. Photos from *China Pictorial*. Text by Alice J. Hall. 660-681, May 1974

SPEISER, E. A.: Author:
- Ancient Mesopotamia: A Light That Did Not Fail. Paintings by H. M. Herget. 41-105, Jan. 1951

SPELEOLOGY:
- Exploring America Underground. By Charles E. Mohr. 803-837, June 1964
- Probing Ice Caves of the Pyrenees. By Norbert Casteret. 391-404, Mar. 1953

SPENCER, DONALD A.: Author-Photographer:
- Porcupines, Rambling Pincushions. 247-264, Aug. 1950

SPICE ISLANDS. *See* Moluccas

SPICES:
- Clove-scented Zanzibar. By W. Robert Moore. 261-278, Feb. 1952
- Herbs for All Seasons. By Lonnelle Aikman. Photos by Sam Abell. Picture portfolio text by Larry Kohl. 386-409, Mar. 1983
- Spices, the Essence of Geography. By Stuart E. Jones. 401-420, Mar. 1949

SPID (Submersible Portable Inflatable Dwelling):
- The Deepest Days. By Robert Sténuit. 534-547, Apr. 1965
- Outpost Under the Ocean. By Edwin A. Link. Photos by Bates Littlehales. 530-533, Apr. 1965

SPIDERS:
- The Spider That Lives Under Water. By Robert F. Sisson. 694-701, May 1972
- ◆ *Spiders*. Announced. 728-730, Nov. 1974
- What's So Special About Spiders? By Paul A. Zahl. 190-219, Aug. 1971

SPIEGEL, TED: Photographer:
- Acid Rain–How Great a Menace? By Anne LaBastille. 652-681, Nov. 1981
- Canada's Window on the Pacific: The British Columbia Coast. By Jules B. Billard. 338-375, Mar. 1972
- George Washington: The Man Behind the Myths. By Howard La Fay. 90-111, July 1976
- The Hudson: "That River's Alive." By Alice J. Hall. 62-89, Jan. 1978
- Kansas City, Heartland U.S.A. By Rowe Findley. 112-139, July 1976
- The Loyalists. By Kent Britt. 510-539, Apr. 1975
- Our Most Precious Resource: Water. By Thomas Y. Canby. 144-179, Aug. 1980
- The Philippines, Freedom's Pacific Frontier. By Robert de Roos. 301-351, Sept. 1966
- Reunited Jerusalem Faces Its Problems. By Kenneth MacLeish. 835-871, Dec. 1968
- Scientists Ride Ice Islands on Arctic Odysseys. By Lowell Thomas, Jr. 670-691, Nov. 1965
- They'd Rather Be in Philadelphia. By Ethel A. Starbird. 314-343, Mar. 1983
- Those Proper and Other Bostonians. By Joseph Judge. 352-381, Sept. 1974
- The Vikings. By Howard La Fay. 492-541, Apr. 1970
- The World of Elizabeth I. By Louis B. Wright. 668-709, Nov. 1968

SPIER, PETER: Artist:
- A Traveler's Tale of Ancient Tikal. Text by Alice J. Hall. 799-811, Dec. 1975

SPINY BABBLER (Bird):
- Peerless Nepal–A Naturalist's Paradise. By S. Dillon Ripley. Photos by Volkmar Wentzel. NGS research grant. 1-40, Jan. 1950

SPINY LOBSTERS:
- New Life for the "Loneliest Isle" (Tristan da Cunha). By Lewis Lewis. 105-116, Jan. 1950
- Strange March of the Spiny Lobster. By William F. Herrnkind. Photos by Rick Frehsee and Bruce Mounier. NGS research grant. 819-831, June 1975
- Tektite II: Science's Window on the Sea. By John G. VanDerwalker. Photos by Bates Littlehales. 256-289, Aug. 1971

SPIRITS of Change Capture the Karens. By Peter Kunstadter. 267-285, Feb. 1972

SPITSBERGEN (Island), Norway:
- Spitsbergen, Norway's Arctic Hot Spot. By Gordon Young. Photos by Martin Rogers. 267-283, Aug. 1978
- Spitsbergen Mines Coal Again. 113-120, July 1948
- *See also* Edgeøya

SPLENDOR of an Unknown Empire: Ebla. By Howard La Fay. Photos by James L. Stanfield. Paintings by Louis S. Glanzman. 730-759, Dec. 1978

SPLIT, Yugoslavia:
- Yugoslavia, Between East and West. By George W. Long. Photos by Volkmar Wentzel. 141-172, Feb. 1951
- Yugoslavia's Window on the Adriatic. By Gilbert M. Grosvenor. 219-247, Feb. 1962

SPLIT-SECOND Time Runs Today's World. By F. Barrows Colton and Catherine Bell Palmer. 399-428, Sept. 1947

SPLIT Seconds in the Lives of Birds. By Arthur A. Allen. 681-706, May 1954

SPONGE-FISHING INDUSTRY:
- On the Winds of the Dodecanese. By Jean and Franc Shor. 351-390, Mar. 1953
- Sponge Fishermen of Tarpon Springs. By Jennie E. Harris. 119-136, Jan. 1947

SPONGES:
- Consider the Sponge. . . . Photos by David Doubilet. Text by Michael E. Long. 392-407, Mar. 1977
- *See also* Sponge-Fishing Industry

SPOOKY LAKE, Eil Malk (Island), Palau Islands:
- Strange World of Palau's Salt Lakes. By William M. Hamner. Photos by David Doubilet. 264-282, Feb. 1982

SPOONBILLS. *See* Roseate Spoonbills

SPORANGIA:
- Slime Mold: The Fungus That Walks. By Douglas Lee. Photos by Paul A. Zahl. 131-136, July 1981

SPORTS:
- Around the "Great Lakes of the South." By Frederick Simpich. Photos by J. Baylor Roberts. Included: Boating, Fishing, Horseback riding, Swimming. 463-491, Apr. 1948
- Long Island Outgrows the Country. By Howell Walker. Photos by B. Anthony Stewart. Included: Baseball, Fishing, Golf, Lawn bowling, Sailing, Swimming, Tennis. 279-326, Mar. 1951
- Mexico's Booming Capital. By Mason Sutherland. Photos by Justin Locke. Included: Baseball, Bowling, Bullfighting, Football, Swimming. 785-824, Dec. 1951
- *See also* Olympic Games

SPORTS-MINDED Melbourne, Host to the Olympics. 688-693, Nov. 1956

The **SPOTLIGHT** Swings to Suez. By W. Robert Moore. 105-115, Jan. 1952

SPRING, BOB and IRA: Photographers:
- Climbing Our Northwest Glaciers. 103-114, July 1953

SPRING:
- Spring Comes Late to Glacier (Glacier National Park, Montana). By Douglas H. Chadwick. 125-133, July 1979
- Springtime Comes to Yellowstone National Park. By Paul A. Zahl. 761-779, Dec. 1956
- ◆ *What Happens in the Spring*. 1977

SPRING CREEK HUTTERITE COLONY, Montana:
- The Hutterites, Plain People of the West. By William Albert Allard. 98-125, July 1970

SPRINGBOKS:
- Etosha: Namibia's Kingdom of Animals. By Douglas H. Chadwick. Photos by Des and Jen Bartlett. 344-385, Mar. 1983

SPRINGFIELD, Illinois:
- Illinois–Healthy Heart of the Nation. By Leo A. Borah. Photos by B. Anthony Stewart and Willard R. Culver. 781-820, Dec. 1953
- Vacation Tour Through Lincoln Land. By Ralph Gray. 141-184, Feb. 1952

SPRINGTAILS:
- The Wild World of Compost. By Cecil E. Johnson. Photos by Bianca Lavies. 273-284, Aug. 1980

SPRINGTIME Comes to Yellowstone National Park. By Paul A. Zahl. 761-779, Dec. 1956

SPRINGTIME of Hope in Poland. By Peter T. White. Photos by James P. Blair. 467-501, Apr. 1972

SPRUNT, ALEXANDER, Jr.: Author:
• Blizzard of Birds: The Tortugas Terns. 213-230, Feb. 1947

SQUARE-RIGGERS:
• By Square-rigger from Baltic to Bicentennial. By Kenneth Garrett. Included: *Amerigo Vespucci, Christian Radich, Danmark, Dar Pomorza, Eagle, Esmeralda, Gazela Primeiro, Gloria, Gorch Fock, Juan Sebastián de Elcano, Kruzenshtern, Libertad, Mircea, Nippon Maru, Sagres II, Tovarishch.* 824-857, Dec. 1976
• Windjamming Around New England. By Tom Horgan. Photos by Robert F. Sisson. 141-169, Aug. 1950
• *See also Breadalbane; Charles W. Morgan; Eagle; Georg Stage; Joseph Conrad; Pamir; Vasa; Yankee* (Brigantine)

SQUAWS Along the Yukon. By Ginny Hill Wood. 245-265, Aug. 1957

SQUIDS:
• Nature's Night Lights: Probing the Secrets of Bioluminescence. By Paul A. Zahl. 45-69, July 1971
• Squids: Jet-powered Torpedoes of the Deep. By Gilbert L. Voss. Photos by Robert F. Sisson. NGS research grant. 386-411, Mar. 1967

SQUIRRELS, Flying:
• "Flying" Squirrels, Nature's Gliders. By Ernest P. Walker. 663-674, May 1947

SRI LANKA:
• Sri Lanka: Time of Testing For an Ancient Land. By Robert Paul Jordan. Photos by Raghubir Singh. 123-150, Jan. 1979
• Sri Lanka's Wildlife. 254-278, Aug. 1983
I. Sri Lanka's Wildlife Heritage: A Personal Perspective. By Arthur C. Clarke. 254-255; II. Legacy of Lively Treasures. By Dieter and Mary Plage. 256-273; III. A Nation Rises to the Challenge. By Lyn de Alwis. Photos by Dieter and Mary Plage. 274-278
• *See also* former name, Ceylon

SRINAGAR, Kashmir:
• The Idyllic Vale of Kashmir. By Volkmar Wentzel. 523-550, Apr. 1948

STAFFORD, MARIE PEARY:
• Gold Medal Awarded to Mrs. Robert E. Peary. Note: Mrs. Stafford accepted the Special Gold Medal on behalf of her mother. 148, Jan. 1956
Author:
• The Peary Flag Comes to Rest. 519-532, Oct. 1954

STAFFORD, THOMAS P.:
• Apollo-Soyuz: Handclasp in Space. By Thomas Y. Canby. 183-187, Feb. 1976
• Space Rendezvous, Milestone on the Way to the Moon. By Kenneth F. Weaver. 539-553, Apr. 1966

STAIB, BJØRN O.: Author:
• North Toward the Pole on Skis. 254-281, Feb. 1965

STAINED GLASS:
• Chartres: Legacy From the Age of Faith. By Kenneth MacLeish. Photos by Dean Conger. 857-882, Dec. 1969
• Washington Cathedral: "House of Prayer for All People." By Robert Paul Jordan. Photos by Sisse Brimberg. 552-573, Apr. 1980

STALINGRAD, U.S.S.R. *See* Volgograd

STALKING Central Africa's Wildlife. By T. Donald Carter. Paintings by Walter A. Weber. 264-286, Aug. 1956

STALKING Seals Under Antarctic Ice. By Carleton Ray. 54-65, Jan. 1966

STALKING the Great Indian Rhino. By Lee Merriam Talbot. 389-398, Mar. 1957

STALKING the Mountain Lion–to Save Him. By Maurice G. Hornocker. 638-655, Nov. 1969

STALKING the West's Wild Foods. By Euell Gibbons. Photos by David Hiser. 186-199, Aug. 1973

STALKING Wild Foods on a Desert Isle. By Euell Gibbons. Photos by David Hiser. 47-63, July 1972

STAMPS, Postage:
• Everyone's Servant, the Post Office. By Allan C. Fisher, Jr. Photos by Volkmar Wentzel. 121-152, July 1954
• Liechtenstein Thrives on Stamps. By Ronald W. Clark. 105-112, July 1948

STANDARD OIL COMPANY OF CALIFORNIA:
• Barehanded Battle to Cleanse the Bay. By Peter T. White. Photos by Jonathan S. Blair. 866-881, June 1971

STANDARD WEIGHTS AND MEASURES:
• Uncle Sam's House of 1,000 Wonders (U. S. Bureau of Standards). By Lyman J. Briggs and F. Barrows Colton. 755-784, Dec. 1951

STANFIELD, JAMES L.:
Photographer:
• After Rhodesia, a Nation Named Zimbabwe. By Charles E. Cobb, Jr. Photos by James L. Stanfield and LeRoy Woodson, Jr. 616-651, Nov. 1981
• Ancient Bulgaria's Golden Treasures. By Colin Renfrew. Paintings by Jean-Leon Huens. 112-129, July 1980
• Big Bend: Jewel in the Texas Desert. By Nathaniel T. Kenney. 104-133, Jan. 1968
• The Bulgarians. By Boyd Gibbons. 91-111, July 1980
• The Byzantine Empire. 709-777, Dec. 1983
I. Rome of the East. By Merle Severy. 709-767; II. Mount Athos. 739-745; III. Eternal Easter in a Greek Village. By Maria Nicolaidis-Karanikolas. 768-777
• Canadian Rockies, Lords of a Beckoning Land. By Alan Phillips. 353-393, Sept. 1966
• Ebla: Splendor of an Unknown Empire. By Howard La Fay. Paintings by Louis S. Glanzman. 730-759, Dec. 1978
• Gold, the Eternal Treasure. By Peter T. White. 1-51, Jan. 1974
Golden Masterpieces. 29-39
• Housewife at the End of the World. By Rae Natalie P. Goodall. 130-150, Jan. 1971
• Human Treasures of Japan. By William Graves. 370-379, Sept. 1972
• Illinois: The City and the Plain. By Robert Paul Jordan. Photos by James L. Stanfield and Joseph J. Scherschel. 745-797, June 1967
• In the Wake of Darwin's *Beagle.* By Alan Villiers. 449-495, Oct. 1969
• The Investiture of Great Britain's Prince of Wales. By Allan C. Fisher, Jr. Photos by James L. Stanfield and Adam Woolfitt. 698-715, Nov. 1969
• Iran's Shah Crowns Himself and His Empress. By Franc Shor. Photos by James L. Stanfield and Winfield Parks. 301-321, Mar. 1968
• Japan's Amazing Inland Sea. By William S. Ellis. 830-863, Dec. 1977
• Life's Tempo on Nantucket. By Peter Benchley. 810-839, June 1970
• Living in a Japanese Village. By William Graves. 668-693, May 1972
• Mark Twain: Mirror of America. By Noel Grove. 300-337, Sept. 1975
• More of Sea Than of Land: The Bahamas. By Carleton Mitchell. 218-267, Feb. 1967
• The Nation's River. By Allan C. Fisher, Jr. 432-469, Oct. 1976
A Good Life on the Potomac. 470-479
• New Orleans and Her River. By Joseph Judge. 151-187, Feb. 1971
• Our Virgin Islands, 50 Years Under the Flag. By Carleton Mitchell. 67-103, Jan. 1968
• Pakistan Under Pressure. By William S. Ellis. 668-701, May 1981
• Quebec: French City in an Anglo-Saxon World. By Kenneth MacLeish. Photos by James L. Stanfield and Declan Haun. 416-442, Mar. 1971
• The Rat, Lapdog of the Devil. By Thomas Y. Canby. 60-87, July 1977
• The Red Sea's Gardens of Eels. By Eugenie Clark. Photos by James L. Stanfield and David Doubilet. 724-735, Nov. 1972
• Royal House for Dolls. By David Jeffery. 632-643, Nov. 1980
• San Francisco Bay, the Westward Gate. By William Graves. 593-637, Nov. 1969
• Syria Tests a New Stability. By Howard La Fay. 326-361, Sept. 1978
• Western Australia, the Big Country. By Kenneth MacLeish. 150-187, Feb. 1975
• Windsor Castle. By Anthony Holden. 604-631, Nov. 1980

STANFORD, DENNIS: Author:
• Bison Kill By Ice Age Hunters. 114-121, Jan. 1979

STANFORD UNIVERSITY, California:
Research:
• Primate Communication. 440, Oct. 1978

STAR CHARTS:
▲ Star charts, supplement. *A Map of the Heavens*. Dec. 1957
▲ Star charts, supplement. *Map of the Heavens*. Aug. 1970

"STAR OF GLADNESS." *See Hokule'a*

STAR OF THE SNOW (Sacred Place), Peru:
• Peru's Pilgrimage to the Sky. By Robert Randall. Photos by Loren McIntyre and Ira Block. 60-69, July 1982

STAR II (Submersible):
• Precious Corals, Hawaii's Deep-sea Jewels. By Richard W. Grigg. Photos by David Doubilet. 719-732, May 1979
• A Walk in the Deep. By Sylvia A. Earle. Photos by Al Giddings and Chuck Nicklin. 624-631, May 1980

STARBIRD, ETHEL A.: Author:
• The Bonanza Bean–Coffee. Photos by Sam Abell. 388-405, Mar. 1981
• Friendless Squatters of the Sea. Photos by Robert F. Sisson. 623-633, Nov. 1973
• From Sword to Scythe in Champlain Country. Photos by B. Anthony Stewart and Emory Kristof. 153-201, Aug. 1967
• Kauai, the Island That's Still Hawaii. Photos by Robert W. Madden. 584-613, Nov. 1977
• Molokai–Forgotten Hawaii. Photos by Richard A. Cooke III. 188-219, Aug. 1981
• New York's Land of Dreamers and Doers (Finger Lakes Region). Photos by Nathan Benn. 702-724, May 1977
• The People Who Made Saskatchewan. Photos by Craig Aurness. 651-679, May 1979
• A River Restored: Oregon's Willamette. Photos by Lowell J. Georgia. 816-835, June 1972
• St. Vincent, the Grenadines, and Grenada: Taking It as It Comes. Photos by Cotton Coulson. 399-425, Sept. 1979
• Spain's Sun-blest Pleasure Isles. Photos by James A. Sugar. 679-701, May 1976
• Sydney: Big, Breezy, and a Bloomin' Good Show. Photos by Robert W. Madden. 211-235, Feb. 1979
• The Thames: That Noble River. Photos by O. Louis Mazzatenta. 750-791, June 1983
• They'd Rather Be in Philadelphia. Photos by Ted Spiegel. 314-343, Mar. 1983
• Toronto: Canada's Dowager Learns to Swing. Photos by Robert W. Madden. 190-215, Aug. 1975
• Vermont–a State of Mind and Mountains. Photos by Nathan Benn. 28-61, July 1974
• A Way of Life Called Maine. Photos by David Hiser. 727-757, June 1977

STARCK, JO D.:
Author-Photographer:
• Probing the Deep Reefs' Hidden Realm. By Walter A. Starck II and Jo D. Starck. 867-886, Dec. 1972

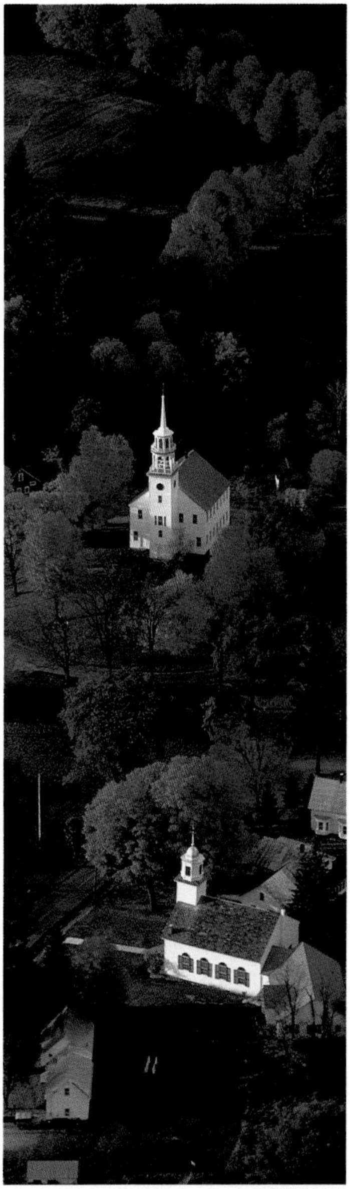

NATHAN BENN

Vermont: autumn colors of Strafford

STARCK, WALTER A., II:
Author-Photographer:
• Marvels of a Coral Realm. 710-738, Nov. 1966
• Probing the Deep Reefs' Hidden Realm. By Walter A. Starck II and Jo D. Starck. 867-886, Dec. 1972
Photographer:
• Photographing the Night Creatures of Alligator Reef. By Robert E. Schroeder. Photos by author and Walter A. Starck II. 128-154, Jan. 1964

STARFISH:
• Starfish Threaten Pacific Reefs. By James A. Sugar. Contents: Crown-of-thorns starfish. 340-353, Mar. 1970

STARFISH HOUSE (Conshelf Two):
• At Home in the Sea. By Jacques-Yves Cousteau. 465-507, Apr. 1964

STARK BROOK, Vermont:
• Unseen Life of a Mountain Stream. By William H. Amos. 562-580, Apr. 1977

STARLING, GUY W.: Photographer:
• Eclipse Hunting in Brazil's Ranchland. By F. Barrows Colton. Photos by Richard H. Stewart and Guy W. Starling. 285-324, Sept. 1947

STARS:
• The Incredible Universe. By Kenneth F. Weaver. Photos by James P. Blair. 589-625, May 1974
▲ *Journey Into the Universe Through Time and Space; National Geographic-Palomar Sky Survey Charting the Heavens,* double-sided supplement. June 1983
• The Once and Future Universe. By Rick Gore. Photos by James A. Sugar. Paintings by Barron Storey. Picture text by David Jeffery. 704-749, June 1983
• Our Universe Unfolds New Wonders. By Albert G. Wilson. NGS research grant. 245-260, Feb. 1952
• Wind, Wave, Star, and Bird. By David Lewis. Photos by Nicholas deVore III. Included: Navigating by the stars. 747-781, Dec. 1974
• *See also* Star Charts; Sun

STARTLING New Look at Dinosaurs. By John H. Ostrom. Paintings by Roy Andersen. 152-185, Aug. 1978

STATE FARMS:
• Down on the Farm, Soviet Style–a 4-H Adventure. By John Garaventa. Photos by James Tobin and Carol Schmidt. 768-797, June 1979
• In Long-Forbidden Tibet. By Fred Ward. 218-259, Feb. 1980

STATE PARKS:
• Finding the Mt. Everest of All Living Things (Redwood Tree). By Paul A. Zahl. Included: California state parks: Del Norte Coast State Park; Humboldt Redwoods State Park; Jedediah Smith Redwoods State Park; Prairie Creek Redwoods State Park; Richardson Grove State Park. 10-51, July 1964

S T

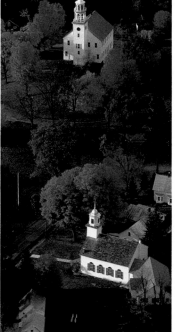

• Mexico to Canada on the Pacific Crest Trail. By Mike W. Edwards. Photos by David Hiser. 741-779, June 1971
• The Parks in Your Backyard. By Conrad L. Wirth. 647-707, Nov. 1963
The East. 675-689; The Midlands. 691-697; The West. 699-707
▲ *Vacationlands of the United States and Southern Canada,* supplement. Text on reverse. July 1966
• *See also* Adirondack Mountains, for Adirondack State Park; Calaveras Big Trees State Park; John Pennekamp Coral Reef State Park; Palisades Interstate Park; Valley Forge

STATELY Homes of Old Virginia. By Albert W. Atwood. 787-802, June 1953

STATEN ISLAND FERRY, New York's Seagoing Bus. By John T. Cunningham and Jay Johnston. Photos by W. D. Vaughn. 833-843, June 1959

STATIA (Island). *See* Sint Eustatius

STATION WAGON Odyssey: Baghdad to Istanbul. By William O. Douglas. 48-87, Jan. 1959

STATUES:
• The Nation Honors Admiral Richard E. Byrd. Included: Byrd Memorial statue. 567-578, Apr. 1962
• Warriors From a Watery Grave (Bronze Sculptures). By Joseph Alsop. 821-827, June 1983
• *See also* Blessing of the Fleet, for Our Lady of Good Voyage; Buddhism, for Buddhas; Carrara Marble; Sculpture; War Memorials; *and* Abu Simbel; Aegean Islands; Aphrodisias; Athens; Easter Island; Florence; Rome

STAVANGER, Norway:
• Norway, Land of the Generous Sea. By Edward J. Linehan. Photos by George F. Mobley. 1-43, July 1971
• Striking It Rich in the North Sea. By Rick Gore. Photos by Dick Durrance II. 519-549, Apr. 1977

STEAD AIR FORCE BASE, Nevada:
• School for Survival. By Curtis E. LeMay. 565-602, May 1953

STEAMBOATS:
• Henry Hudson's River. By Willard Price. Photos by Wayne Miller. 364-403, Mar. 1962
• Mark Twain: Mirror of America. By Noel Grove. Photos by James L. Stanfield. 300-337, Sept. 1975
• The Mighty Hudson. By Albert W. Atwood. Photos by B. Anthony Stewart. 1-36, July 1948
• Ships Through the Ages: A Saga of the Sea. By Alan Villiers. 494-545, Apr. 1963
• Squaws Along the Yukon. By Ginny Hill Wood. 245-265, Aug. 1957
• That Dammed Missouri River. By Gordon Young. Photos by David Hiser. Included: The discovery of sunken steamer, *Bertrand*. 374-413, Sept. 1971
• Tom Sawyer's Town. By Jerry Allen. 121-140, July 1956
• The Upper Mississippi. By Willard Price. 651-699, Nov. 1958
• *See also Rhode Island; and* Magdalena (River), Colombia

STEEL BANDS:
• Carnival in Trinidad. By Howard La Fay. Photos by Winfield Parks. 693-701, Nov. 1971
• "The Music of Trinidad." NGS recording announced. 701, Nov. 1971

STEEL INDUSTRY:
• Coal Makes the Saar a Prize. By Franc Shor. 561-576, Apr. 1954
• Luxembourg, the Quiet Fortress. By Robert Leslie Conly. Photos by Ted H. Funk. 69-97, July 1970
• Ohio Makes Its Own Prosperity. By Leo A. Borah. Photos by B. Anthony Stewart. 435-484, Apr. 1955
• Pennsylvania: Faire Land of William Penn. By Gordon Young. Photos by Cary Wolinsky. 731-767, June 1978
• Pittsburgh: Workshop of the Titans. By Albert W. Atwood. 117-144, July 1949
• Pittsburgh, Pattern for Progress. By William J. Gill. Photos by Clyde Hare. 342-371, Mar. 1965
• Steel: Master of Them All. By Albert W. Atwood. 415-452, Apr. 1947
Man's Mightiest Ally. Photos by Willard R. Culver. 423-450
• Today on the Delaware, Penn's Glorious River. By Albert W. Atwood. Photos by Robert F. Sisson. 1-40, July 1952

STEHEKIN, Washington:
• Snow-mantled Stehekin: Where Solitude Is in Season. Photos by Bruce Dale. Text by Pat Hutson. 572-588, Apr. 1974

STEINEMANN, PAUL: Photographer:
• Jambo–First Gorilla Raised by Its Mother in Captivity. By Ernst M. Lang. 446-453, Mar. 1964

STÉNUIT, ROBERT:
• The Long, Deep Dive. By Lord Kilbracken. Photos by Bates Littlehales. 718-731, May 1963
• Outpost Under the Ocean. By Edwin A. Link. Photos by Bates Littlehales. 530-533, Apr. 1965
Author:
• The Deepest Days. 534-547, Apr. 1965
• Priceless Relics of the Spanish Armada. Photos by Bates Littlehales. 745-777, June 1969
• The Sunken Treasure of St. Helena. Photos by Bates Littlehales. 562-576, Oct. 1978
Author-Photographer:
• The Treasure of Porto Santo. Photos by author and William R. Curtsinger. 260-275, Aug. 1975

STEVENSON, ADLAI E.: Author:
• The United Nations: Capital of the Family of Man. Photos by B. Anthony Stewart and John E. Fletcher. 297-303, Sept. 1961

STEVENSON, ROBERT LOUIS:
• Poets' Voices Linger in Scottish Shrines. By Isobel Wylie Hutchison. Photos by Kathleen Revis. 437-488, Oct. 1957
• Travels With a Donkey–100 Years Later. By Carolyn Bennett Patterson. Photos by Cotton Coulson. 535-561, Oct. 1978

STEWART, B. ANTHONY:
• National Geographic Photographers Win Top Magazine Awards. 830-831, June 1959
Author-Photographer:
• Focusing on the Tournament of Roses. By B. Anthony Stewart and J. Baylor Roberts. 805-816, June 1954
Photographer:
• Across the Potomac from Washington. By Albert W. Atwood. 1-33, Jan. 1953
• The Bahamas, Isles of the Blue-green Sea. By Carleton Mitchell. 147-203, Feb. 1958
• Ballerinas in Pink. By Carleton Mitchell. 553-571, Oct. 1957
• California's Wonderful One (State Highway No. 1). By Frank Cameron. 571-617, Nov. 1959
• Captain Smith of Jamestown. By Bradford Smith. 581-620, May 1957
• Character Marks the Coast of Maine. By John Scofield. 798-843, June 1968
• Christmas in Cookie Tree Land. By Louise Parker La Gorce. 844-851, Dec. 1955
• The DAR Story. By Lonnelle Aikman. Photos by B. Anthony Stewart and John E. Fletcher. 565-598, Nov. 1951
• Date Line: United Nations, New York. By Carolyn Bennett Patterson. Photos by B. Anthony Stewart and John E. Fletcher. 305-331, Sept. 1961
• Dog Mart Day in Fredericksburg. By Frederick G. Vosburgh. 817-832, June 1951
• Drums to Dynamos on the Mohawk. By Frederick G. Vosburgh. 67-110, July 1947
• Easter Egg Chickens. By Frederick G. Vosburgh. 377-387, Sept. 1948
• The Fabulous State of Texas. By Stanley Walker. Photos by B. Anthony Stewart and Thomas Nebbia. 149-195, Feb. 1961
• Folger: Biggest Little Library in the World. By Joseph T. Foster. Photos by B. Anthony Stewart and John E. Fletcher. 411-424, Sept. 1951
• Fossils Lift the Veil of Time. By Harry S. Ladd and Roland W. Brown. 363-386, Mar. 1956
• Founders of New England. By Sir Evelyn Wrench. 803-838, June 1953
• Founders of Virginia. By Sir Evelyn Wrench. 433-462, Apr. 1948
• The Friendly Train Called Skunk. By Dean Jennings. 720-734, May 1959
• From Sword to Scythe in Champlain Country. By Ethel A. Starbird. Photos by B. Anthony Stewart and Emory Kristof. 153-201, Aug. 1967
• Giant Sequoias Draw Millions to California Parks. By John Michael Kauffmann. 147-187, Aug. 1959
• The Greener Fields of Georgia. By Howell Walker. Photos by author and B. Anthony Stewart. 287-330, Mar. 1954

• History Revealed in Ancient Glass. By Ray Winfield Smith. Photos by B. Anthony Stewart and Lee E. Battaglia. 346-369, Sept. 1964
• Honolulu, Mid-ocean Capital. By Frederick Simpich, Jr. 577-624, May 1954
• Illinois–Healthy Heart of the Nation. By Leo A. Borah. Photos by B. Anthony Stewart and Willard R. Culver. 781-820, Dec. 1953
• Incredible Andorra. By Lawrence L. Klingman. 262-290, Aug. 1949
• Inside the White House. By Lonnelle Aikman. Photos by B. Anthony Stewart and Thomas Nebbia. 3-43, Jan. 1961
• Israel: Land of Promise. By John Scofield. 395-434, Mar. 1965
• Kew: The Commoners' Royal Garden. By Thomas Garner James. 479-506, Apr. 1950
• The Land of Galilee. By Kenneth MacLeish. 832-865, Dec. 1965
• Literary Landmarks of Massachusetts. By William H. Nicholas. Photos by B. Anthony Stewart and John E. Fletcher. 279-310, Mar. 1950
• London's Zoo of Zoos. By Thomas Garner James. 771-786, June 1953
• Long Island Outgrows the Country. By Howell Walker. 279-326, Mar. 1951
• The Making of a West Pointer. By Howell Walker. 597-626, May 1952
• Massachusetts Builds for Tomorrow. By Robert de Roos. 790-843, Dec. 1966
• The Merrimack: River of Industry and Romance. By Albert W. Atwood. 106-140, Jan. 1951
• Mexico's Window on the Past (National Museum). By Bart McDowell. 492-519, Oct. 1968
• Midshipmen's Cruise. By William J. Aston and Alexander G. B. Grosvenor. 711-754, June 1948
• The Mighty Hudson. By Albert W. Atwood. 1-36, July 1948
• Minnesota Makes Ideas Pay. By Frederick G. Vosburgh. Photos by John E. Fletcher and B. Anthony Stewart. 291-336, Sept. 1949
• Mr. Jefferson's Charlottesville. By Anne Revis. 553-592, May 1950
• The Mohawks Scrape the Sky. By Robert L. Conly. 133-142, July 1952
• Nautical Norfolk Turns to Azaleas. By William H. Nicholas. 606-614, May 1947
• New England, a Modern Pilgrim's Pride. By Beverley M. Bowie. 733-796, June 1955
• New Rush to Golden California. By George W. Long. 723-802, June 1954
• New York State's New Main Street. By Matt C. McDade. 567-618, Nov. 1956
• North Carolina, Dixie Dynamo. By Malcolm Ross. 141-183, Feb. 1962
• Northwest Wonderland: Washington State. By Merle Severy. 445-493, Apr. 1960
• Ohio Makes Its Own Prosperity. By Leo A. Borah. 435-484, Apr. 1955
• Ontario, Pivot of Canada's Power. By Andrew H. Brown. Photos by B. Anthony Stewart and Bates Littlehales. 823-852, Dec. 1953
• Our Changing Atlantic Coastline. By Nathaniel T. Kenney. 860-887, Dec. 1962
• Our Magnificent Capital City. 715-738, June 1947
• Pittsburgh: Workshop of the Titans. By Albert W. Atwood. 117-144, July 1949
• Portsmouth, Britannia's Sally Port. By Thomas Garner James. 513-544, Apr. 1952
• Portugal's Gem of the Ocean: Madeira. By David S. Boyer. 364-394, Mar. 1959
• The Post Road Today. 206-233, Aug. 1962
• Puerto Rico's Seven-league Bootstraps. By Bart McDowell. 755-793, Dec. 1962
• Rhododendron Glories of Southwest Scotland. By David S. Boyer. Photos by B. Anthony Stewart and author. 641-664, May 1954
• Rome: Eternal City with a Modern Air. By Harnett T. Kane. 437-491, Apr. 1957
• Roving Maryland's Cavalier Country. By William A. Kinney. 431-470, Apr. 1954
• Russia as I Saw It. By Richard M. Nixon. 715-750, Dec. 1959
• Sea to Lakes on the St. Lawrence. By George W. Long. Photos by B. Anthony Stewart and John E. Fletcher. 323-366, Sept. 1950
• Seattle, City of Two Voices. By Anne Grosvenor Robinson. 494-513, Apr. 1960
• Solving Life Secrets of the Sailfish. By Gilbert Voss. Paintings by Craig Phillips. 859-872, June 1956
• A Stroll to John o'Groat's. By Isobel Wylie Hutchison. 1-48, July 1956
• A Stroll to London. By Isobel Wylie Hutchison. 171-204, Aug. 1950
• Trieste–Side Door to Europe. By Harnett T. Kane. 824-857, June 1956
• The United Nations: Capital of the Family of Man. By Adlai E. Stevenson. Photos by B. Anthony Stewart and John E. Fletcher. 297-303, Sept. 1961
• Vacation Tour Through Lincoln Land. By Ralph Gray. 141-184, Feb. 1952
• Washington's Historic Georgetown. By William A. Kinney. 513-544, Apr. 1953
• We're Coming Over on the *Mayflower*. By Alan Villiers. 708-728, May 1957
• Williamsburg: Its College and Its Cinderella City. By Beverley M. Bowie. 439-486, Oct. 1954
• Wonderland in Longwood Gardens (Du Pont Estate). By Edward C. Ferriday, Jr. 45-64, July 1951
• You and the Obedient Atom. By Allan C. Fisher, Jr. 303-353, Sept. 1958

STEWART, RICHARD H.:
Photographer:
• Eclipse Hunting in Brazil's Ranchland. By F. Barrows Colton. Photos by Richard H. Stewart and Guy W. Starling. 285-324, Sept. 1947

BOTH BY B. ANTHONY STEWART, NGS

Rome: dome of St. Peter's, *above;* Bernini's Pluto and Persephone, *below*

S T

• Exploring Ancient Panama by Helicopter. By Matthew W. Stirling. 227-246, Feb. 1950
• Exploring the Past in Panama. By Matthew W. Stirling. 373-399, Mar. 1949
• Hunting Prehistory in Panama Jungles. By Matthew W. Stirling. 271-290, Aug. 1953
• On the Trail of La Venta Man. By Matthew W. Stirling. 137-172, Feb. 1947
Hunting Mexico's Buried Temples. 145-168
• Seeking the Secret of the Giants (Gravel Figures). By Frank M. Setzler. 390-404, Sept. 1952
• Solving the Riddle of Chubb Crater (Quebec). By V. Ben Meen. 1-32, Jan. 1952

STILL Eskimo, Still Free: The Inuit of Umingmaktok. By Yva Momatiuk and John Eastcott. 624-647, Nov. 1977

STILTS (Birds):
• The Dauntless Little Stilt. By Frederick Kent Truslow. 241-245, Aug. 1960

STIMSON, PAUL C.: Author:
• 'Round the Horn by Submarine. 129-144, Jan. 1948

STIRLING, MATTHEW W.: Author:
• Exploring Ancient Panama by Helicopter. Photos by Richard H. Stewart. 227-246, Feb. 1950
• Exploring the Past in Panama. Photos by Richard H. Stewart. 373-399, Mar. 1949
• Hunting Prehistory in Panama Jungles. Photos by Richard H. Stewart. 271-290, Aug. 1953
• Indians of the Far West (United States). Paintings by W. Langdon Kihn. 175-200, Feb. 1948
• Nomads of the Far North. Paintings by W. Langdon Kihn. 471-504, Oct. 1949
• On the Trail of La Venta Man. Photos by Richard H. Stewart. 137-172, Feb. 1947
• Solving the Mystery of Mexico's Great Stone Spheres. Photos by David F. Cupp. 295-300, Aug. 1969

STOBAUGH, ROBERT B.:
• What Six Experts Say. 70-73, *Special Report on Energy* (Feb. 1981)

STOCKHOLM, Sweden:
• Baltic Cruise of the *Caribbee*. By Carleton Mitchell. 605-646, Nov. 1950
• Stockholm, Where "Kvalitet" Is a Way of Life. By James Cerruti. Photos by Albert Moldvay and Jonathan Blair. 43-69, Jan. 1976
• Sweden, Quiet Workshop for the World. By Andrew H. Brown. 451-491, Apr. 1963
• Thumbs Up Round the North Sea's Rim. By Frances James. Photos by Erica Koch. 685-704, May 1952
• *See also Vasa*

STONE. *See* Marble; Rocks

STONE AGE:
• Bison Kill By Ice Age Hunters. By Dennis Stanford. 114-121, Jan. 1979
• Man in the Amazon: Stone Age Present Meets Stone Age Past. By W. Jesco von Puttkamer. 60-83, Jan. 1979
• The Search for the First Americans. By Thomas Y. Canby. Photos by Kerby Smith. Paintings by Roy Andersen. 330-363, Sept. 1979
• Stone Age Art of Tanzania. By Mary D. Leakey. Photos by John Reader. 84-99, July 1983
• Vanished Mystery Men of Hudson Bay. By Henry B. Collins. 669-687, Nov. 1956
• *See also* Ice Age Man; Russell Cave, Alabama

STONE AGE PEOPLES of Today. *See* Arnhem Land; Cinta Larga Indians; Gimis; Kreen-Akarores; Negritos; New Guinea; Tasaday Tribe; Xingu National Park; Wasúsu

STONE CIRCLES. *See* Medicine Wheels

STONE SPHERES:
• Solving the Mystery of Mexico's Great Stone Spheres. By Matthew W. Stirling. Photos by David F. Cupp. NGS research grant. 295-300, Aug. 1969

STONEHENGE–New Light on an Old Riddle. By Harold E. Edgerton. Paintings by Brian Hope-Taylor. 846-866, June 1960

STONES, Precious and Semiprecious. *See* Gems

STONEY INDIANS:
• On the Ridgepole of the Rockies. By Walter Meayers Edwards. 745-780, June 1947

STOP-AND-GO Sail Around South Norway. By Edmond J. Moran. Photos by Randi Kjekstad Bull and Andrew H. Brown. 153-192, Aug. 1954

STOREY, BARRON: Artist:
• The Once and Future Universe. By Rick Gore. Photos by James A. Sugar. Picture text by David Jeffery. 704-749, June 1983
• Tropical Rain Forests: Nature's Dwindling Treasures. By Peter T. White. Photos by James P. Blair. 2-47, Jan. 1983

STORIED Lands of Malaysia. By Maurice Shadbolt. Photos by Winfield Parks. 734-783, Nov. 1963

STORKS:
• Our Only Native Stork, the Wood Ibis. By Robert Porter Allen. Photos by Frederick Kent Truslow. 294-306, Feb. 1964
• White Storks, Vanishing Sentinels of the Rooftops. By Roger Tory Peterson. 838-853, June 1962

STORMS:
• Our Changing Atlantic Coastline (U. S.). By Nathaniel T. Kenney. Photos by B. Anthony Stewart. 860-887, Dec. 1962
◆ *Our Violent Earth*. 1982
◆ *Powers of Nature*. 1978
• The Year the Weather Went Wild. By Thomas Y. Canby. 799-829, Dec. 1977
• We're Doing Something About the Weather! By Walter Orr Roberts. 518-555, Apr. 1972
• *See also* Hurricanes; Monsoons; Typhoons

STORRS, ELEANOR E.: Author:
• The Astonishing Armadillo. Photos by Bianca Lavies. 820-830, June 1982

STRACHAN, ROBIN: Author:
• With the Nuba Hillmen of Kordofan. 249-278, Feb. 1951

STRANGE Animals of Australia. By David Fleay. Photos by Stanley Breeden. 388-411, Sept. 1963

STRANGE Babies of the Sea. By Hilary B. Moore. Paintings by Craig Phillips and Jacqueline Hutton. 41-56, July 1952

STRANGE Courtship of Birds of Paradise. By S. Dillon Ripley. Paintings by Walter A. Weber. 247-278, Feb. 1950

STRANGE Courtship of the Cock-of-the-Rock. By E. Thomas Gilliard. 134-140, Jan. 1962

STRANGE Little World of the Hoatzin. By J. Lear Grimmer. Photos by M. Woodbridge Williams. 391-401, Sept. 1962

STRANGE March of the Spiny Lobster. By William F. Herrnkind. Photos by Rick Frehsee and Bruce Mounier. 819-831, June 1975

A **STRANGE** Ride in the Deep (on Manta Rays). By Peter Benchley. 200-203, Feb. 1981

STRANGE World of Palau's Salt Lakes. By William M. Hamner. Photos by David Doubilet. 264-282, Feb. 1982

STRANGE World Without Sun (Deep-sea Rifts). The Editor. 680-688, Nov. 1979

The **STRANGEST** Sea. By Eugenie Clark. Photos by David Doubilet. 338-343, Sept. 1975

STRASBOURG, France:
• The Rhine: Europe's River of Legend. By William Graves. Photos by Bruce Dale. 449-499, Apr. 1967

STRATEGIC AIR COMMAND (SAC):
• Of Planes and Men (U. S. Air Force). By Kenneth F. Weaver. Photos by Emory Kristof and Albert Moldvay. 298-349, Sept. 1965
• School for Survival. By Curtis E. LeMay. 565-602, May 1953
• *See also* DEW Line

STRATEGIC Spitsbergen (Svalbard). By Gordon Young. Photos by Martin Rogers. 267-283, Aug. 1978

STRATFORD-UPON-AVON, England:
• The Britain That Shakespeare Knew. By Louis B. Wright. Photos by Dean Conger. 613-665, May 1964

STRATOBOWL, South Dakota:
• To 76,000 Feet by *Strato-Lab* Balloon. By Malcolm D. Ross and M. Lee Lewis. 269-282, Feb. 1957

STRATO-LAB (Balloon):
• To 76,000 Feet by *Strato-Lab* Balloon. By Malcolm D. Ross and M. Lee Lewis. 269-282, Feb. 1957
• We Saw the World From the Edge of Space. By Malcolm D. Ross. Ground photos by Walter Meayers Edwards. 671-685, Nov. 1961

STREANO, VINCE: Photographer:
• Orange, a Most California County. By Judith and Neil Morgan. 750-779, Dec. 1981

STRIEDIECK, KARL: Author:
• The Thousand-mile Glide. Photos by Otis Imboden. 431-438, Mar. 1978

STRIFE-TORN Indochina. By W. Robert Moore. 499-510, Oct. 1950

STRIKING It Rich in the North Sea. By Rick Gore. Photos by Dick Durrance II. 519-549, Apr. 1977

STRIP MINING:
• Coal vs. Parklands. By François Leydet. Photos by Dewitt Jones. 776-803, Dec. 1980
• Illinois–Healthy Heart of the Nation. By Leo A. Borah. Photos by B. Anthony Stewart and Willard R. Culver. 781-820, Dec. 1953
• The People of Cumberland Gap. By John Fetterman. Photos by Bruce Dale. 591-621, Nov. 1971
• Should They Build a Fence Around Montana? By Mike W. Edwards. Photos by Nicholas deVore III. 614-649, May 1976
• This Land of Ours–How Are We Using It? By Peter T. White. Photos by Emory Kristof. 20-67, July 1976
• Will Coal Be Tomorrow's "Black Gold"? By Gordon Young. Photos by James P. Blair. 234-259, Aug. 1975

STRODE, WILLIAM: Photographer:
• Home to the Heart of Kentucky. By Nadine Brewer. 522-546, Apr. 1982

A **STROLL** to John o' Groat's. By Isobel Wylie Hutchison. 1-48, July 1956

A **STROLL** to London. By Isobel Wylie Hutchison. Photos by B. Anthony Stewart. 171-204, Aug. 1950

A **STROLL** to Venice. By Isobel Wylie Hutchison. Note: The author trekked from Innsbruck, Austria, through the Tyrol and Dolomites, to Venice, Italy. 378-410, Sept. 1951

STRONG, ARLINE:
Author-Photographer:
• Seashore Summer. 436-444, Sept. 1960

STRONG, WILLIAM DUNCAN: Author:
• Finding the Tomb of a Warrior-God. Photos by Clifford Evans, Jr. 453-482, Apr. 1947

STROUD, W. G.: Author:
• Our Earth as a Satellite Sees It. 293-302, Aug. 1960

STRUM, SHIRLEY C.: Author:
• Life with the "Pumphouse Gang": New Insights Into Baboon Behavior. Photos by Timothy W. Ransom. 672-691, May 1975

NICHOLAS DEVORE III

Montana: strip-mining coal

STRUTT, JOHN WILLIAM (Third Baron Rayleigh):
• The British Way. By Sir Evelyn Wrench. 421-541, Apr. 1949

STUART, GEORGE E.: Author:
• The Maya: Riddle of the Glyphs. Photos by Otis Imboden. 768-791, Dec. 1975
• Maya Art Treasures Discovered in Cave. Photos by Wilbur E. Garrett. 220-235, Aug. 1981
• Who Were the "Mound Builders"? 783-801, Dec. 1972

STUBENRAUCH, ROBERT:
Photographer:
• Okinawa, Pacific Outpost. 538-552, Apr. 1950

STUDENTS:
• Helping Holland Rebuild Her Land. By Gilbert M. Grosvenor and Charles Neave. 365-413, Sept. 1954
• Norway Cracks Her Mountain Shell. By Sydney Clark. Photos by Gilbert H. Grosvenor and Ole Friele Backer. 171-211, Aug. 1948
• *See also* Experiment in International Living; Schools; Universities and Colleges; YWCA

STUDYING Grizzly Habitat by Satellite. By John Craighead. 148-158, July 1976

STUDYING Wildlife by Satellite. By Frank Craighead, Jr. and John Craighead. 120-123, Jan. 1973

SUB-IGLOO (Underwater Workshop):
• Diving Beneath Arctic Ice. By Joseph B. MacInnis. Photos by William R. Curtsinger. 248-267, Aug. 1973

SUBMARINES:
• From Indian Canoes to Submarines at Key West. By Frederick Simpich. Photos by J. Baylor Roberts. 41-72, Jan. 1950
• Our Navy's Long Submarine Arm. By Allan C. Fisher, Jr. 613-636, Nov. 1952
• Pacific Fleet: Force for Peace. By Franc Shor. Photos by W. E. Garrett. Included: *Grayback, Gudgeon, Sterlet.* 283-335, Sept. 1959
• *See also* Submarines, Nuclear-powered; Submersibles; *and Sea Robin*

SUBMARINES, Nuclear-powered:
• Four-ocean Navy in the Nuclear Age. By Thomas W. McKnew. Included: *Nautilus, Shark, Skate, Triton.* 145-187, Feb. 1965
• Man's New Servant, the Friendly Atom. By F. Barrows Colton. Photos by Volkmar Wentzel. Included: *Nautilus, Seawolf.* 71-90, Jan. 1954
• Our Nuclear Navy. By George W. Anderson, Jr. 449-450, Mar. 1963
• You and the Obedient Atom. By Allan C. Fisher, Jr. Included: *Nautilus, Seawolf.* 303-353, Sept. 1958
• *See also Nautilus; Skate; Thresher; Triton*

SUBMERSIBLES:
• Diving Saucer *(Denise)* Takes to the Deep. By Jacques-Yves Cousteau. NGS research grant. 571-586, Apr. 1960

ROBERT CAPUTO

Sudan: Zande man displaying his World War II medals

• Exploring a 140-year-old Ship Under Arctic Ice *(Breadalbane)*. By Joseph B. MacInnis. Photos by Emory Kristof. Included: WASP submersible. 104A-104D, July 1983
• Incredible World of the Deep-sea Rifts. NGS research grant. 680-705, Nov. 1979
I. Strange World Without Sun. The Editor. 680-688; II. Return to Oases of the Deep. By Robert D. Ballard and J. Frederick Grassle. 689-705
• Oases of Life in the Cold Abyss (Galapagos Rift). By John B. Corliss and Robert D. Ballard. 441-453, Oct. 1977
• Project FAMOUS. Included: *Alvin, Archimède, Cyana.* 586-615, May 1975
I. Where the Earth Turns Inside Out. By J. R. Heirtzler. Photos by Emory Kristof. 586-603; II. Dive Into the Great Rift. By Robert D. Ballard. Photos by Emory Kristof. 604-615
• Window on Earth's Interior. By Robert D. Ballard. Photos by Emory Kristof. 228-249, Aug. 1976
• *See also Asherah;* Bathyscaphs; *DS-2; Deep Diver; Deepstar; Star II;* Submarines

SUDAN:
▲ *Africa: Countries of the Nile,* Atlas series supplement. Oct. 1963
• Journey Into the Great Rift: the Northern Half. By Helen and Frank Schreider. 254-290, Aug. 1965
• Kayaks Down the Nile. By John M. Goddard. 697-732, May 1955
• Locusts: "Teeth of the Wind." By Robert A. M. Conley. Photos by Gianni Tortoli. 202-227, Aug. 1969
• Proud Primitives, the Nuba People. By Oskar Luz. Photos by Horst Luz. 673-699, Nov. 1966
• Safari from Congo to Cairo. By Elsie May Bell Grosvenor. Photos by Gilbert Grosvenor. 721-771, Dec. 1954
• South in the Sudan. By Harry Hoogstraal. 249-272, Feb. 1953
• Sudan: Arab-African Giant. By Robert Caputo. 346-379, Mar. 1982
• *See also* Kordofan; Nubia (Region)

The **SUDD** (Swamp), Sudan:
• Sudan: Arab-African Giant. By Robert Caputo. 346-379, Mar. 1982

SUEHSDORF, ADOLPH: Author:
• The Cats in Our Lives. Photos by Walter Chandoha. 508-541, Apr. 1964

SUEZ CANAL:
• An Engineer's View of the Suez Canal. By Glen E. Edgerton. 123-140, Jan. 1957
• New Life for the Troubled Suez Canal. By William Graves. Photos by Jonathan Blair. 792-817, June 1975
• The Spotlight Swings to Suez. By W. Robert Moore. 105-115, Jan. 1952

SUGAR, JAMES A.:
Author-Photographer:
• The Family Farm Ain't What It Used to Be. 391-411, Sept. 1974
• Starfish Threaten Pacific Reefs. 340-353, Mar. 1970
• Trucks Race the Clock From Coast to Coast. 226-243, Feb. 1974
Photographer:
• Easter Greetings From the Ukrainians. By Robert Paul Jordan. 556-563, Apr. 1972
• Ethiopia's Artful Weavers. By Judith Olmstead. 125-141, Jan. 1973
• Florida's Manatees, Mermaids in Peril. By Daniel S. Hartman. 342-353, Sept. 1969
• The Friendly Irish. By John Scofield. 354-391, Sept. 1969
• The National Gallery's New Masterwork on the Mall. By J. Carter Brown. 680-701, Nov. 1978
• North With the Wheat Cutters. By Noel Grove. 194-217, Aug. 1972
• The Once and Future Universe. By Rick Gore. Paintings by Barron Storey. Picture text by David Jeffery. 704-749, June 1983
• Oshkosh: America's Biggest Air Show. By Michael E. Long. Photos by James A. Sugar and the author. 365-375, Sept. 1979
• Provence, Empire of the Sun. By William Davenport. 692-715, May 1975
• Sailing Iceland's Rugged Coasts. By Wright Britton. 228-265, Aug. 1969
• San Francisco Bay: The Beauty and the Battles. By Cliff Tarpy. 814-845, June 1981
• Spain's Sun-blest Pleasure Isles. By Ethel A. Starbird. 679-701, May 1976
• They're Redesigning the Airplane. By Michael E. Long. 76-103, Jan. 1981

SUGAR INDUSTRY:
• Barbados, Outrider of the Antilles. By Charles Allmon. 363-392, Mar. 1952
• Because It Rains on Hawaii. By Frederick Simpich, Jr. 571-610, Nov. 1949
• Cuba–American Sugar Bowl. By Melville Bell Grosvenor. 1-56, Jan. 1947
• Growing Pains Beset Puerto Rico. By William H. Nicholas. Photos by Justin Locke. 419-460, Apr. 1951
• Hawaii, U.S.A. By Frederick Simpich, Jr. Photos by Thomas Nebbia. 1-45, July 1960
• Inside Cuba Today. By Fred Ward. 32-69, Jan. 1977
• Land of Louisiana Sugar Kings. By Harnett T. Kane. Photos by Willard R. Culver. 531-567, Apr. 1958
• Mauritius, Island of the Dodo. By Quentin Keynes. 77-104, Jan. 1956
• Puerto Rico's Seven-league Bootstraps. By Bart McDowell. Photos by B. Anthony Stewart. 755-793, Dec. 1962
• Sugar Weather in the Green Mountains. By Stephen Greene. Photos by Robert F. Sisson. 471-482, Apr. 1954

SULAWESI (Island), Indonesia:
• Life and Death in Tana Toradja. By Pamela and Alfred Meyer. 793-815, June 1972

SULFUR DIOXIDE:
• Acid Rain–How Great a Menace? By Anne LaBastille. Photos by Ted Spiegel. 652-681, Nov. 1981

SULLIVAN, SIR ARTHUR:
• The British Way. By Sir Evelyn Wrench. 421-541, Apr. 1949

SULU ARCHIPELAGO, Philippines:
• Sea Gypsies of the Philippines. By Anne de Henning Singh. Photos by Raghubir Singh. 659-677, May 1976

SUMATRA (Island), Indonesia:
• Indonesia, the Young and Troubled Island Nation. By Helen and Frank Schreider. 579-625, May 1961
• Republican Indonesia Tries Its Wings. By W. Robert Moore. 1-40, Jan. 1951
• A Sumatran Journey. By Harvey Arden. Photos by David Alan Harvey. 406-430, Mar. 1981
• This Young Giant, Indonesia. By Beverley M. Bowie. Photos by J. Baylor Roberts. 351-392, Sept. 1955

SUMERIANS (People):
• Ancient Mesopotamia: A Light That Did Not Fail. By E. A. Speiser. Paintings by H. M. Herget. 41-105, Jan. 1951
▪ The *Tigris* Expedition. 826, Dec. 1978; 1, Jan. 1979; cover, Apr. 1979
• *Tigris* Sails Into the Past. By Thor Heyerdahl. Photos by Carlo Mauri and the crew of the *Tigris*. 806-827, Dec. 1978

SUMMER INSTITUTE OF GLACIOLOGICAL AND ARCTIC SCIENCES, Alaska:
• Alaska's Mighty Rivers of Ice. By Maynard M. Miller. Photos by Christopher G. Knight. NGS research grant. 194-217, Feb. 1967

SUMMERHAYS, SOAMES: Author:
• A Marine Park Is Born: Australia's Great Barrier Reef. Photos by Ron and Valerie Taylor. 630-635, May 1981

SUMNER, U.S.S. (Survey Ship):
• Adventures with the Survey Navy. By Irving Johnson. 131-148, July 1947

SUN:
• The Incredible Universe. By Kenneth F. Weaver. Photos by James P. Blair. 589-625, May 1974
• Skylab, Outpost on the Frontier of Space. By Thomas Y. Canby. 441-469, Oct. 1974
• The Sun. By Herbert Friedman. 713-743, Nov. 1965
• The Sun As Never Seen Before. By Edward G. Gibson. 494-503, Oct. 1974
• Unlocking Secrets of the Northern Lights. By Carl W. Gartlein. Paintings by William Crowder. NGS research grant. 673-704, Nov. 1947
• *See also* Photosynthesis; Solar Eclipses; Solar Energy

SUN Car Crosses Australia. By Hans Tholstrup and Larry Perkins. Photos by David Austen. 600-607, Nov. 1983

"SUN DAGGER" (Petroglyph):
• The Anasazi–Riddles in the Ruins. By Thomas Y. Canby. Photos by Dewitt Jones and David Brill. Paintings by Roy Andersen. 554-592, Nov. 1982

SUNAPEE LAKE, New Hampshire:
• Lake Sunapee's Golden Trout. Photos by Robert F. Sisson. 529-536, Oct. 1950

SUNBELT. *See* The South; Southwest

A **SUNKEN** Japanese Fleet Becomes a Scientific Laboratory: Truk Lagoon. By Sylvia A. Earle. Photos by Al Giddings. 578-613, May 1976

The **SUNKEN** Treasure of St. Helena (*Witte Leeuw*). By Robert Sténuit. Photos by Bates Littlehales. 562-576, Oct. 1978

SUNNY Corsica: French Morsel in the Mediterranean. By Robert Cairns. Photos by Joseph J. Scherschel. 401-423, Sept. 1973

SUNRISE DANCE (Puberty Rites):
• Coming of Age the Apache Way. By Nita Quintero. Photos by Bill Hess. 262-271, Feb. 1980

SUPERFORTRESSES:
• Flying in the "Blowtorch" Era. By Frederick G. Vosburgh. Included: B-29; B-50. 281-322, Sept. 1950
• Operation Eclipse: 1948. By William A. Kinney. NGS research grant. 325-372, Mar. 1949

SUPERIOR, Lake, Canada-U. S.:
• The Great Lakes: Is It Too Late? By Gordon Young. Photos by James L. Amos and Martin Rogers. 147-185, Aug. 1973
• Work-hard, Play-hard Michigan. By Andrew H. Brown. 279-320, Mar. 1952

SUPERNOVAE:
• The Once and Future Universe. By Rick Gore. Photos by James A. Sugar. Paintings by Barron Storey. Picture text by David Jeffery. 704-749, June 1983

SUPERPORTS, Tanker:
• Giants That Move the World's Oil: Superships. By Noel Grove. Photos by Martin Rogers. 102-124, July 1978
• Nova Scotia, the Magnificent Anchorage. By Charles McCarry. Photos by Gordon W. Gahan. Included: Gulf Oil deepwater port. 334-363, Mar. 1975
• Oil, the Dwindling Treasure. By Noel Grove. Photos by Emory Kristof. Included: Plans for superports in Alabama, Louisiana, Texas. 792-825, June 1974

SUPERTANKERS:
• Editorial. By Gilbert M. Grosvenor. 1, July 1978
• Giants That Move the World's Oil: Superships. By Noel Grove. Photos by Martin Rogers. 102-124, July 1978
• Superspill: Black Day for Brittany. Photos by Martin Rogers. Text by Noel Grove. 124-135, July 1978

SUPPLEMENTS. *See* Map Supplements; Painting Supplements; Photo Supplements; Sound Sheets

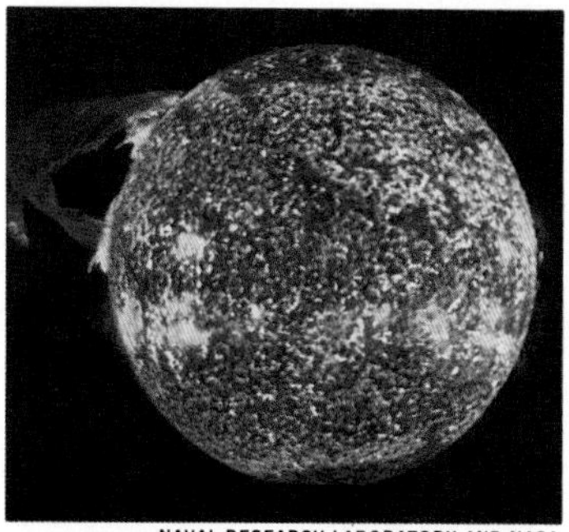

NAVAL RESEARCH LABORATORY AND NASA

As Never Seen Before: sun's hot spots

MARTIN ROGERS

Superships: oil tanker on test run

ST

SURINAME:
• Cock-of-the-Rock: Jungle Dandy. By Pepper W. Trail. NGS research grant. 831-839, Dec. 1983
• Giant Otters: "Big Water Dogs" in Peril. By Nicole Duplaix. Photos by the author and Bates Littlehales. NGS research grant. 130-142, July 1980
• Tracking the Shore Dwellers (Sandpipers): From Canada to Suriname. 175-179, Aug. 1979
• World-roaming Teen-ager Sails On. By Robin Lee Graham. 449-493, Apr. 1969

SURINAME NATURE CONSERVATION FOUNDATION: Study Sponsorship:
• Giant Brazilian Otters. 132, July 1980

SURPRISE CREEK HUTTERITE COLONY, Montana:
• The Hutterites, Plain People of the West. By William Albert Allard. 98-125, July 1970

SURPRISING Switzerland. By Jean and Franc Shor. 427-478, Oct. 1956

SURTSEY (Island), North Atlantic Ocean:
• Surtsey: Island Born of Fire. By Sigurdur Thorarinsson. 713-726, May 1965

"SURVEY NAVY":
• Adventures with the Survey Navy. By Irving Johnson. 131-148, July 1947

SURVEY SHIP, U. S. *See Sumner,* U.S.S.

SURVEYOR SPACECRAFT:
• Surveyor: Candid Camera on the Moon. By Homer E. Newell. 578-592, Oct. 1966
• That Orbèd Maiden . . . the Moon. By Kenneth F. Weaver. 207-230, Feb. 1969

SURVIVAL TRAINING:
▪ Journey to the Outer Limits. Contents: Outward Bound School. 150A-150B, Jan. 1974
• The Making of an Astronaut. By Robert R. Gilruth. 122-144, Jan. 1965
• Nevada Learns to Live with the Atom. By Samuel W. Matthews. 839-850, June 1953
• Philmont Scout Ranch Helps Boys Grow Up. By Andrew H. Brown. 399-416, Sept. 1956
• School for Survival. By Curtis E. LeMay. 565-602, May 1953
• We Survive on a Pacific Atoll. By John and Frank Craighead. 73-94, Jan. 1948
• Wind River Range: Many-treasured Splendor. By Joseph Judge. 198-205, Feb. 1974
• *See also* Wild Foods

SUSPENSION BRIDGES:
• A Century Old, the Wonderful Brooklyn Bridge. By John G. Morris. Photos by Donal F. Holway. 565-579, May 1983

SUSQUEHANNA (River), New York-Pennsylvania-Maryland:
• Down the Susquehanna by Canoe. By Ralph Gray. Photos by Walter Meayers Edwards. 73-120, July 1950

SUTHERLAND, MASON: Author:
• Adobe New Mexico. Photos by Justin Locke. 783-830, Dec. 1949
• Californians Escape to the Desert. Photos by Charles W. Herbert. 675-724, Nov. 1957
• Carlsbad Caverns in Color. Photos by E. "Tex" Helm. 433-468, Oct. 1953
• Carnival in San Antonio. Photos by J. Baylor Roberts. 813-844, Dec. 1947
• From Tucson to Tombstone (Arizona). 343-384, Sept. 1953
• Mexico's Booming Capital. Photos by Justin Locke. 785-824, Dec. 1951
• Sonora (Mexico) Is Jumping. 215-246, Feb. 1955

SUWANNEE RIVER, Florida-Georgia:
• Our Wild and Scenic Rivers: The Suwannee. By Jack and Anne Rudloe. Photos by Jodi Cobb. 20-29, July 1977

SUYÁ INDIANS:
• Brazil's Big-lipped Indians. By Harald Schultz. 118-133, Jan. 1962

SVALBARD (Archipelago), Arctic Ocean:
• Norway's Strategic Arctic Islands. By Gordon Young. Photos by Martin Rogers. 267-283, Aug. 1978
• Polar Bear: Lonely Nomad of the North. By Thor Larsen. 574-590, Apr. 1971
• Spitsbergen Mines Coal Again. 113-120, July 1948

The **SWALLOW-TAILED KITE:** Graceful Aerialist of the Everglades. Photos by Ray O. Green, Jr., Norman D. Reed, and Myron H. Wright, Jr. 496-505, Oct. 1972

SWAMPS:
◆ *Explore a Spooky Swamp.* 1978
• *See also* Atchafalaya Basin; Big Cypress Swamp; Northern Territory, Australia; Okefenokee Swamp; Pine Barrens; The Sudd

SWANS:
• The Swans of Abbotsbury (England). By Michael Moynihan. Photos by Barnet Saidman. 563-570, Oct. 1959
• *See also* Trumpeter Swans; Whistling Swans

SWAPO (South-West Africa People's Organization):
• Namibia: Nearly a Nation? By Bryan Hodgson. Photos by Jim Brandenburg. Note: SWAPO members are recognized by the United States as representatives of Namibia. 755-797, June 1982

SWAT (State), Pakistan:
• Pakistan, New Nation in an Old Land. By Jean and Franc Shor. 637-678, Nov. 1952

SWATEK, PHILLIP M.: Author:
• Rugged Is the Word for Bravo. 829-843, Dec. 1955

SWAZILAND:
• Swaziland Tries Independence. By Volkmar Wentzel. 266-293, Aug. 1969
• Zulu King Weds a Swazi Princess. By Volkmar Wentzel. 47-61, Jan. 1978

SWEDEN:
• Baltic Cruise of the *Caribbee*. By Carleton Mitchell. 605-646, Nov. 1950
• Friendly Flight to Northern Europe. By Lyndon B. Johnson. Photos by Volkmar Wentzel. 268-293, Feb. 1964
• Ghost From the Depths: the Warship *Vasa*. By Anders Franzén. 42-57, Jan. 1962
• Sweden, Quiet Workshop for the World. By Andrew H. Brown. 451-491, Apr. 1963
• Thumbs Up Round the North Sea's Rim. By Frances James. Photos by Erica Koch. 685-704, May 1952
• The Vikings. By Howard La Fay. Photos by Ted Spiegel. 492-541, Apr. 1970
• *See also* Gotland; Stockholm

SWEET, O. C.: Photographer:
• Busy Fairbanks Sets Alaska's Pace. By Bruce A. Wilson. 505-523, Oct. 1949

SWIMMING. *See* Water Safety

SWIMMING With Patagonia's Right Whales. By Roger Payne. Photos by William R. Curtsinger and Charles R. Nicklin, Jr. NGS research grant. 576-587, Oct. 1972

SWINE. *See* Hog Raising

SWING Low, Sweet Chariot! By Noel Grove. Photos by Bruce Dale. 2-35, July 1983

SWISS COLONISTS: United States:
• Deep in the Heart of "Swissconsin." By William H. Nicholas. Photos by J. Baylor Roberts. 781-800, June 1947

SWITZER, GEORGE S.: Author:
• The Many-sided Diamond. 568-586, Apr. 1958
• Questing for Gems. 835-863, Dec. 1971
• "Rockhounds" Uncover Earth's Mineral Beauty. 631-660, Nov. 1951

SWITZERLAND:
• Across the Alps in a Wicker Basket *(Bernina).* By Phil Walker. 117-131, Jan. 1963
• The Alps: Man's Own Mountains. By Ralph Gray. Photos by Walter Meayers Edwards and William Eppridge. 350-395, Sept. 1965
• "Around the World in Eighty Days." By Newman Bumstead. Included: Geneva; Jungfraujoch, in the Alps. 705-750, Dec. 1951
• Avalanche! Battling the Juggernaut. By David Cupp. 290-305, Sept. 1982
• Children's Village in Switzerland, Pestalozzi. Photos by Alfred Lammer. 268-282, Aug. 1959
• Europe Via the Hostel Route. By Joseph Nettis. 124-154, July 1955

• The Great St. Bernard Hospice Today. By George Pickow. 49-62, Jan. 1957
• Little Tibet in Switzerland. By Laura Pilarski. Photos by Fred Mayer. 711-727, Nov. 1968
• The Rhine: Europe's River of Legend. By William Graves. Photos by Bruce Dale. 449-499, Apr. 1967
• Soaring on Skis in the Swiss Alps. By Carolyn Bennett Patterson. Photos by Kathleen Revis. 94-121, Jan. 1961
• Surprising Switzerland. By Jean and Franc Shor. 427-478, Oct. 1956
▲ *Switzerland, Austria, and Northern Italy,* double-sided Atlas series supplement. Sept. 1965
• Switzerland, Europe's High-rise Republic. By Thomas J. Abercrombie. 68-113, July 1969
• Switzerland Guards the Roof of Europe. By William H. Nicholas. Photos by Willard R. Culver. 205-246, Aug. 1950
• Switzerland's Enchanted Val d'Hérens. By Georgia Engelhard Cromwell. 825-848, June 1955
• Switzerland's Once-in-a-generation Festival (Vevey). By Jean and Franc Shor. 563-571, Oct. 1958

The **SWORD** and the Sermon. By Thomas J. Abercrombie. 3-45, July 1972

SYDNEY, Australia:
• Australia. By Alan Villiers. 309-385, Sept. 1963
• The Making of a New Australia. By Howell Walker. 233-259, Feb. 1956
• New South Wales, the State That Cradled Australia. By Howell Walker. Photos by David Moore. 591-635, Nov. 1967
• Sydney: Big, Breezy, and a Bloomin' Good Show. By Ethel A. Starbird. Photos by Robert W. Madden. 211-235, Feb. 1979

SYMPHONY of the Deep: "Songs of the Humpback Whale" (Sound Sheet). 24-24B, Jan. 1979

SYNFUELS:
• Synfuels: Fill 'er Up! With What? By Thomas Y. Canby. Photos by Jonathan Blair. 74-95, *Special Report on Energy* (Feb. 1981)

SYRIA:
• Abraham, the Friend of God. By Kenneth MacLeish. Photos by Dean Conger. 739-789, Dec. 1966
• The Arab World. 712-732, Nov. 1958
• Damascus, Syria's Uneasy Eden. By Robert Azzi. 512-535, Apr. 1974
• Ebla: Splendor of an Unknown Empire. By Howard La Fay. Photos by James L. Stanfield. Paintings by Louis S. Glanzman. 730-759, Dec. 1978
• Journey Into the Great Rift: the Northern Half. By Helen and Frank Schreider. 254-290, Aug. 1965
• Syria Tests a New Stability. By Howard La Fay. Photos by James L. Stanfield. 326-361, Sept. 1978

SZECHWAN (Province), China:
• Adventures in Lololand. By Rennold L. Lowy. 105-118, Jan. 1947
• *See also* Yangtze (River and Basin)

T

T-3 (Fletcher's Ice Island), Arctic Region:
• Scientists Ride Ice Islands on Arctic Odysseys. By Lowell Thomas, Jr. Photos by Ted Spiegel. 670-691, Nov. 1965
• Three Months on an Arctic Ice Island. By Joseph O. Fletcher. 489-504, Apr. 1953
• We Followed Peary to the Pole. By Gilbert Grosvenor and Thomas W. McKnew. 469-484, Oct. 1953

TCDD (Poison):
• The Pesticide Dilemma. By Allen A. Boraiko. Photos by Fred Ward. 145-183, Feb. 1980

TDRS. *See* Tracking and Data Relay Satellites

T. R.'S Wilderness Legacy. By John L. Eliot. Photos by Farrell Grehan. 340-363, Sept. 1982

TABLETS. *See* Cuneiform

TABOOS:
• Niger's Wodaabe: "People of the Taboo." By Carol Beckwith. 483-509, Oct. 1983
• Taboos and Magic Rule Namba Lives. By Kal Muller. 57-83, Jan. 1972

TACTICAL AIR COMMAND (TAC):
• Of Planes and Men. By Kenneth F. Weaver. Photos by Emory Kristof and Albert Moldvay. 298-349, Sept. 1965

TAFT, WILLIAM HOWARD:
• Profiles of the Presidents: IV. America Enters the Modern Era. By Frank Freidel. 537-577, Oct. 1965

TAHITI (Island), Society Islands:
• Captain Cook: The Man Who Mapped the Pacific. By Alan Villiers. Photos by Gordon W. Gahan. 297-349, Sept. 1971
• Huzza for Otaheite! By Luis Marden. 435-459, Apr. 1962
• In the Wake of Darwin's *Beagle*. By Alan Villiers. Photos by James L. Stanfield. 449-495, Oct. 1969
• The Society Islands, Sisters of the Wind. By Priit J. Vesilind. Photos by George F. Mobley. 844-869, June 1979
• Tahiti, "Finest Island in the World." By Luis Marden. 1-47, July 1962
• The *Yankee*'s Wander-world. By Irving and Electa Johnson. 1-50, Jan. 1949

TAHOE, Lake, and Region, California-Nevada:
• Avalanche! By David Cupp. 280-305, Sept. 1982
I. Winter's White Death. 280-281; II.

BOTH BY GORDON W. GAHAN

Captain Cook: Tahitian dancer, *above*; navigating off Tahiti, *below*

S T

"I'm OK, I'm Alive!" Photos by Lanny Johnson and Andre Benier. 282-289; III. Battling the Juggernaut. 290-305

TAIF, Saudi Arabia:
● Saudi Arabia, Oil Kingdom. Photos by Maynard Owen Williams. 497-512, Apr. 1948

TAIPEI, Taiwan:
● Taiwan: The Watchful Dragon. By Helen and Frank Schreider. 1-45, Jan. 1969

TAIWAN (Formosa):
● Changing Formosa, Green Island of Refuge. By Frederick Simpich, Jr. Photos by Horace Bristol. 327-364, Mar. 1957
▲ *China,* Atlas series supplement. Nov. 1964
● Eyes on the China Coast. By George W. Long. 505-512, Apr. 1953
● Formosa–Hot Spot of the East. By Frederick G. Vosburgh. Photos by J. Baylor Roberts. 139-176, Feb. 1950
● The Gentle Yamis of Orchid Island. By Chang Shuhua. 98-109, Jan. 1977
● Our Navy in the Far East. By Arthur W. Radford. Photos by J. Baylor Roberts. 537-577, Oct. 1953
● Taiwan: The Watchful Dragon. By Helen and Frank Schreider. 1-45, Jan. 1969
● Taiwan Confronts a New Era. By Noel Grove. Photos by John Chao. 93-119, Jan. 1982
● *See also* Formosa Strait; Pescadores

TAIYALS (Aborigines):
● Formosa–Hot Spot of the East. By Frederick G. Vosburgh. Photos by J. Baylor Roberts. 139-176, Feb. 1950

TA'IZZ, Yemen Arab Republic:
● Behind the Veil of Troubled Yemen. By Thomas J. Abercrombie. 403-445, Mar. 1964

TAJ MAHAL, Agra, India:
● Around the World and the Calendar with the Geographic: The President's Annual Message. By Melville Bell Grosvenor. 832-866, Dec. 1959
● "Around the World in Eighty Days." By Newman Bumstead. 705-750, Dec. 1951
● From the Hair of Siva (Ganges River). By Helen and Frank Schreider. 445-503, Oct. 1960
● India in Crisis. By John Scofield. 599-661, May 1963
● When the President Goes Abroad (Eisenhower Tour). By Gilbert M. Grosvenor. 588-649, May 1960

TAKAHE:
● Finding an "Extinct" New Zealand Bird. By R. V. Francis Smith. 393-401, Mar. 1952

TAKAROA (Atoll), Tuamotu Archipelago:
● Twenty Fathoms Down for Mother-of-Pearl. By Winston Williams. Photos by Bates Littlehales. 512-529, Apr. 1962

BOTH BY KENNETH GARRETT

Tall-Ships Race: cadets furl sails aboard *Dar Pomorza, above;* the Polish training vessel scuds before the wind, *below*

TAKASHIMA (Island), Japan:
● The Lost Fleet of Kublai Khan. By Torao Mozai. Photos by Koji Nakamura. Paintings by Issho Yada. 634-649, Nov. 1982

TAKING It as It Comes: St. Vincent, the Grenadines, and Grenada. By Ethel A. Starbird. Photos by Cotton Coulson. 399-425, Sept. 1979

TALBOT, LEE MERRIAM: Author-Photographer:
● Stalking the Great Indian Rhino. 389-398, Mar. 1957

TALBOT, PHILLIPS: Author:
● Delhi, Capital of a New Dominion. 597-630, Nov. 1947

A **TALE** of Twin Cities: Minneapolis and St. Paul. By Thomas J. Abercrombie. Photos by Annie Griffiths. 665-691, Nov. 1980

TALL-SHIPS RACE:
● By Square-rigger from Baltic to Bicentennial. By Kenneth Garrett. Included: Training ships from Argentina, Chile, Colombia, Denmark, England, Italy, Japan, Norway, Poland, Portugal, Romania, Spain, Union of Soviet Socialist Republics, United States, West Germany. 824-857, Dec. 1976

TALLGRASS PRAIRIE NATIONAL PARK (Proposed):
● The Tallgrass Prairie: Can It Be Saved? By Dennis Farney. Photos by Jim Brandenburg. 37-61, Jan. 1980

TAMILS:
● Sri Lanka: Time of Testing for an Ancient Land. By Robert Paul Jordan. Photos by Raghubir Singh. 123-150, Jan. 1979

TAMPA, Florida:
● America Goes to the Fair. By Samuel W. Matthews. Included: Florida State Fair, Gasparilla Celebration. 293-333, Sept. 1954

TAMPA BAY, Gulf of Mexico:
● Cruising Florida's Western Waterways. By Rube Allyn. Photos by Bates Littlehales. 49-76, Jan. 1955

TANA TORADJA (Region), Sulawesi:
● Life and Death in Tana Toradja. By Pamela and Alfred Meyer. 793-815, June 1972

TANGANYIKA:
● Ambassadors of Goodwill: The Peace Corps. By Sargent Shriver and Peace Corps Volunteers. 297-345, Sept. 1964
Tanganyika. By Ruth E. Dygert. 321-323
● Britain Tackles the East African Bush. By W. Robert Moore. 311-352, Mar. 1950
● The Last Great Animal Kingdom. 390-409, Sept. 1960
● Roaming Africa's Unfenced Zoos. By W. Robert Moore. 353-380, Mar. 1950
● Spearing Lions with Africa's Masai. By Edgar Monsanto Queeny. 487-517, Oct. 1954

• Weighing the Aga Khan in Diamonds. Photos by David J. Carnegie. 317-324, Mar. 1947
• *See also* Tanzania

TANGIER ISLAND, Virginia:
• This Is My Island, Tangier. By Harold G. Wheatley. Photos by David Alan Harvey. 700-725, Nov. 1973

TANJUNG PUTING RESERVE, Indonesia:
• Living with the Great Orange Apes: Indonesia's Orangutans. By Biruté M. F. Galdikas. Photos by Rod Brindamour. NGS research grant. 830-853, June 1980
• Orangutans, Indonesia's "People of the Forest." By Biruté Galdikas-Brindamour. Photos by Rod Brindamour. NGS research grant. 444-473, Oct. 1975

TANKERS, Oil:
• Giants That Move the World's Oil: Superships. By Noel Grove. Photos by Martin Rogers. 102-124, July 1978
• Oil, the Dwindling Treasure. By Noel Grove. Photos by Emory Kristof. 792-825, June 1974
• Oman: Guardian of the Gulf. By Thomas J. Abercrombie. Photos by the author and Lynn Abercrombie. 344-377, Sept. 1981
• Superspill: Black Day for Brittany. Photos by Martin Rogers. Text by Noel Grove. 124-135, July 1978
• *See also Manhattan,* S.S.; Oil Spills

TANNA (Island), New Hebrides:
• Tanna Awaits the Coming of John Frum. By Kal Muller. 706-715, May 1974

TANZANIA, United Republic of:
• Africa's Elephants: Can They Survive? By Oria Douglas-Hamilton. Photos by Oria and Iain Douglas-Hamilton. 568-603, Nov. 1980
• Footprints in the Ashes of Time. By Mary D. Leakey. NGS research grant. 446-457, Apr. 1979
• Tanzania Marches to Its Own Drum. By Peter T. White. Photos by Emory Kristof. 474-509, Apr. 1975
• Tanzania's Stone Age Art. By Mary D. Leakey. Photos by John Reader. 84-99, July 1983
• *See also* Gombe Stream Game National Park; Natron, Lake; Ngorongoro Crater; Olduvai Gorge; Serengeti National Park; Tanganyika; Zanzibar

TAOIST SHRINES:
• Kunming Pilgrimage. 213-226, Feb. 1950

TAPESTRIES. *See* Bayeux Tapestry

TARAHUMARAS (Indians):
• South to Mexico City. By W. E. Garrett. 145-193, Aug. 1968
• The Tarahumaras: Mexico's Long Distance Runners. By James Norman. Photos by David Hiser. 702-718, May 1976

TARANTO, Gulf of, Italy:
• Ancient Shipwreck Yields New Facts–and a Strange Cargo. By Peter Throckmorton. Photos by Kim Hart and Joseph J. Scherschel. 282-300, Feb. 1969

TARANTULAS:
• What's So Special About Spiders? By Paul A. Zahl. 190-219, Aug. 1971

TARASCANS (Indians):
• Lost Kingdom in Indian Mexico. By Justin Locke. 517-546, Oct. 1952
• Mexican Folk Art. By Fernando Horcasitas. Photos by David Hiser. 648-669, May 1978
• South to Mexico City. By W. E. Garrett. 145-193, Aug. 1968

TARAWA (Atoll), Gilbert Islands:
• Adventures with the Survey Navy. By Irving Johnson. 131-148, July 1947

TARPON KEY, Florida:
• Bad Days for the Brown Pelican. By Ralph W. Schreiber. Photos by William R. Curtsinger and author. 111-123, Jan. 1975

TARPON SPRINGS, Florida:
• Sponge Fishermen of Tarpon Springs. By Jennie E. Harris. 119-136, Jan. 1947

TARPY, CLIFF: Author:
• Heat Paints *Columbia's* Portrait. 650-653, Nov. 1982
• Killer Whale Attack! 542-545, Apr. 1979
• San Francisco Bay: The Beauty and the Battles. Photos by James A. Sugar. 814-845, June 1981

TARSIERS:
• Seeking Mindanao's Strangest Creatures. By Charles Heizer Wharton. 389-408, Sept. 1948

TASADAY TRIBE:
• First Glimpse of a Stone Age Tribe. 881-882, Dec. 1971
▪ The Last Tribes of Mindanao. 882A-882B, Dec. 1971; 227, Aug. 1972
• The Tasadays, Stone Age Cavemen of Mindanao. By Kenneth MacLeish. Photos by John Launois. 219-249, Aug. 1972

TASMANIA (Island), Australia:
• Tasmania, Australia's Island State. By Howell Walker. 791-818, Dec. 1956
• A Walk and Ride on the Wild Side: Tasmania. By Carolyn Bennett Patterson. Photos by David Hiser and Melinda Berge. 676-693, May 1983

TATRA MOUNTAINS, Czechoslovakia-Poland:
• Poland's Mountain People. By Yva Momatiuk and John Eastcott. 104-129, Jan. 1981

TAUFA'AHAU TUPOU IV, King (Tonga):
• South Seas' Tonga Hails a King. By Melville Bell Grosvenor. Photos by Edwin Stuart Grosvenor. 322-343, Mar. 1968

TAURUS-LITTROW (Valley), Moon:
• Exploring Taurus-Littrow. By Harrison H. Schmitt. 290-307, Sept. 1973

TAVARES DE SÁ, HERNANE: Author:
• Brasília, Metropolis Made to Order. Photos by Thomas J. Abercrombie. 704-724, May 1960
• Spectacular Rio de Janeiro. Photos by Charles Allmon. 289-328, Mar. 1955

A **TAXI** for the Deep Frontier. By Kenneth MacLeish. Photos by Bates Littlehales. 139-150, Jan. 1968

TAYLOR, ALEXANDER:
Author-Photographer:
• Chessmen Come to Life in Marostica. 658-668, Nov. 1956
Photographer:
• By Full-rigged Ship to Denmark's Fairyland. By Alan Villiers. Photos by Alexander Taylor and author. 809-828, Dec. 1955
• Paris Flea Market. By Franc Shor. 318-326, Mar. 1957

TAYLOR, RON: Author-Photographer:
• Paradise Beneath the Sea: Australia's Great Barrier Reef. By Ron and Valerie Taylor. 636-663, May 1981
Photographer:
• Australia's Great Barrier Reef. 728-741, June 1973
• Exploring Australia's Coral Jungle. By Kenneth MacLeish. 743-779, June 1973
• A Marine Park Is Born: Australia's Great Barrier Reef. By Soames Summerhays. Photos by Ron and Valerie Taylor. 630-635, May 1981

TAYLOR, VALERIE: Author:
• A Jawbreaker for Sharks (Chain-Mail Diving Suit). 664-667, May 1981
Author-Photographer:
• Paradise Beneath the Sea: Australia's Great Barrier Reef. By Ron and Valerie Taylor. 636-663, May 1981
Photographer:
• Australia's Great Barrier Reef. 728-741, June 1973
• Exploring Australia's Coral Jungle. By Kenneth MacLeish. 743-779, June 1973
• A Marine Park Is Born: Australia's Great Barrier Reef. By Soames Summerhays. Photos by Ron and Valerie Taylor. 630-635, May 1981

TAYLOR, ZACHARY:
• Profiles of the Presidents: II. A Restless Nation Moves West. By Frank Freidel. 80-121, Jan. 1965

TAYLOR COUNTY, Kentucky:
• Home to the Heart of Kentucky. By Nadine Brewer. Photos by William Strode. 522-546, Apr. 1982

T'BOLI TRIBE:
• Help for Philippine Tribes in Trouble. By Kenneth MacLeish. Photos by Dean Conger. 220-255, Aug. 1971
▪ The Last Tribes of Mindanao. 882A-882B, Dec. 1971; 227, Aug. 1972

S
T

TCHIKAO INDIANS:
• Saving Brazil's Stone Age Tribes From Extinction. By Orlando and Claudio Villas Boas. Photos by W. Jesco von Puttkamer. 424-444, Sept. 1968

TE ANAU (Lake), New Zealand:
• Finding an "Extinct" New Zealand Bird. By R. V. Francis Smith. 393-401, Mar. 1952

TEAL, JOHN J., Jr.: Author:
• Domesticating the Wild and Wooly Musk Ox. Photos by Robert W. Madden. 862-879, June 1970

TEAMWORK Helps the Whooping Crane. By Roderick C. Drewien, with Ernie Kuyt. 680-693, May 1979

TEAS, JANE: Author:
• Temple Monkeys of Nepal. 575-584, Apr. 1980

TECHNOLOGY:
• Behold the Computer Revolution. By Peter T. White. Photos by Bruce Dale and Emory Kristof. 593-633, Nov. 1970
• Can We Harness the Wind? By Roger Hamilton. Photos by Emory Kristof. 812-829, Dec. 1975
• Crystals, Magical Servants of the Space Age. By Kenneth F. Weaver. Photos by James P. Blair. 278-296, Aug. 1968
• Editorial. By Gilbert M. Grosvenor. 295, Mar. 1978
• Eyes of Science. By Rick Gore. Photos by James P. Blair. 360-389, Mar. 1978
• Fiber Optics: Harnessing Light by a Thread. By Allen A. Boraiko. Photos by Fred Ward. 516-535, Oct. 1979
• Five Noted Thinkers Explore the Future. Included: Isaac Asimov, Richard F. Babcock, Edmund N. Bacon, Buckminster Fuller, Gerard Piel. 68-75, July 1976
• Landsat. 140-158, July 1976
I. Landsat Looks at Hometown Earth. By Barry C. Bishop. Contents: How the satellite photomosaic, *Portrait U.S.A.*, was made. 140-147; II. Studying Grizzly Habitat by Satellite. By John Craighead. NGS research grant. 148-158
• The Miracle Metal–Platinum. By Gordon Young. Photos by James L. Amos. 686-706, Nov. 1983
◆ *On the Brink of Tomorrow: Frontiers of Science*. 1982
• Remote Sensing: New Eyes to See the World. By Kenneth F. Weaver. 46-73, Jan. 1969
• The Revolution in American Agriculture. By Jules B. Billard. Photos by James P. Blair. 147-185, Feb. 1970
• Satellites That Serve Us. By Thomas Y. Canby. Included: A portfolio, Images of Earth. 281-335, Sept. 1983
Spacelab 1: *Columbia*. By Michael E. Long. 301-307
• Solar Energy, the Ultimate Powerhouse. By John L. Wilhelm. Photos by Emory Kristof. 381-397, Mar. 1976

CAROL AND DAVID HUGHES

Rain Forest: poison-arrow frogs

• What's Happening to Our Climate? By Samuel W. Matthews. Included: Advanced satellites, computers, microscopes, lasers, spectrometers. 576-615, Nov. 1976
• *See also* names of specific applied sciences; *and* Aluminum; Automotive Industry; Aviation; Computer Applications; Computer Technology; Energy; Energy Sources; Imaging Techniques; Space Flights and Research

TECTONA (Ketch):
• Channel Cruise to Glorious Devon (England). By Alan Villiers. Photos by Bates Littlehales. 208-259, Aug. 1963

TEDDY ROOSEVELT'S Wilderness Legacy. By John L. Eliot. Photos by Farrell Grehan. 340-363, Sept. 1982

TEEMING Life of a Pond. By William H. Amos. 274-298, Aug. 1970

TEEMING Life of a Rain Forest. By Carol and David Hughes. 49-65, Jan. 1983

A **TEEN-AGER** Sails the World Alone. By Robin Lee Graham. 445-491, Oct. 1968

TEGRE PROVINCE, Ethiopia:
• Searching Out Medieval Churches in Ethiopia's Wilds. By Georg Gerster. 856-884, Dec. 1970

TEHRAN, Iran:
• Beside the Persian Gulf. Photos by Maynard Owen Williams. 341-356, Mar. 1947
• Iran: Desert Miracle. By William Graves. Photos by James P. Blair. 2-47, Jan. 1975
• Iran's Shah Crowns Himself and His Empress. By Franc Shor. Photos by James L. Stanfield and Winfield Parks. 301-321, Mar. 1968
• Journey Into Troubled Iran. By George W. Long. Photos by J. Baylor Roberts. 425-464, Oct. 1951
• Old-New Iran, Next Door to Russia. By Edward J. Linehan. Photos by Thomas J. Abercrombie. 44-85, Jan. 1961
• We Lived in Turbulent Tehran. By Rebecca Shannon Cresson. 707-720, Nov. 1953

TEIWES, HELGA: Photographer:
• The Hohokam: First Masters of the American Desert. By Emil W. Haury. 670-695, May 1967

TEKTITE II (Sea and Space Research Project):
• Tektite II. 256-296, Aug. 1971
I. Science's Window on the Sea. By John G. VanDerwalker. Photos by Bates Littlehales. 256-289; II. All-girl Team Tests the Habitat. By Sylvia A. Earle. Paintings by Pierre Mion. 291-296

TEL AVIV-JAFFA, Israel:
• Eyewitness to War in the Holy Land. By Charles Harbutt. 782-795, Dec. 1967
• Home to the Holy Land. By Maynard Owen Williams. 707-746, Dec. 1950

● Israel: Land of Promise. By John Scofield. Photos by B. Anthony Stewart. 395-434, Mar. 1965
● Israel–The Seventh Day. By Joseph Judge. Photos by Gordon W. Gahan. 816-855, Dec. 1972

TELEPHONE:
● Fiber Optics: Harnessing Light by a Thread. By Allen A. Boraiko. Photos by Fred Ward. 516-535, Oct. 1979
● Miracle Men of the Telephone. By F. Barrows Colton. 273-316, Mar. 1947
Birthplace of Telephone Magic. Photos by Willard R. Culver. 289-312
● New Miracles of the Telephone Age. By Robert Leslie Conly. 87-120, July 1954

TELEPHONE a Star: the Story of Communications Satellites. By Rowe Findley. 638-651, May 1962

TELESCOPES:
● First Photographs of Planets and Moon Taken with Palomar's 200-inch Telescope. By Milton L. Humason. 125-130, Jan. 1953
● The Incredible Universe. By Kenneth F. Weaver. Photos by James P. Blair. 589-625, May 1974
● Mapping the Unknown Universe. By F. Barrows Colton. Included: "Big Schmidt" and the 200-inch Hale telescope or "Big Eye." NGS research grant. 401-420, Sept. 1950
● The Once and Future Universe. By Rick Gore. Photos by James A. Sugar. Paintings by Barron Storey. Picture text by David Jeffery. 704-749, June 1983
● Pioneers in Man's Search for the Universe. Paintings by Jean-Leon Huens. Text by Thomas Y. Canby. 627-633, May 1974
● *See also* Sky Survey; Skylab Missions

TELEVISION:
● Fish Men Discover a 2,200-year-old Greek Ship. By Jacques-Yves Cousteau. NGS research grant. 1-36, Jan. 1954
● New Miracles of the Telephone Age. By Robert Leslie Conly. 87-120, July 1954
● Your Society Observes Eclipse in Brazil. NGS research grant. 661, May 1947

TELEVISION FILMS, NGS:
● National Geographic's Newest Adventure: a Color Television Series. By Melville Bell Grosvenor. Note: The first program was "Americans on Everest." 448-452, Sept. 1965
Awards:
● Emmy. 731, Dec. 1974; 1, Jan. 1979; 848, 850, Dec. 1981; 275, Aug. 1982
● George Foster Peabody Award. 587, Oct. 1967; 848, 850, Dec. 1981
Editorials:
● Editorial. By Wilbur E. Garrett. 703, Dec. 1980
● Editorials. By Gilbert M. Grosvenor. 731, Dec. 1974; 299, Sept. 1975; 583, Nov. 1975; 575, Nov. 1976; 439, Oct. 1977; 1, Jan. 1979; 1, Jan. 1980
Specials:
■ Alaska! 215A-215B, Feb. 1967
■ Amazon. 295A-295B, Feb. 1968
■ Americans on Everest. 448-452, Sept. 1965; 575, Nov. 1976
■ America's Wonderlands: The National Parks. 549A-549B, Oct. 1968
■ The Animals Nobody Loved. cover, Feb. 1976
■ Australia: The Timeless Land. 300A-300B, Feb. 1969
■ Australia's Animal Mysteries. 824, Dec. 1982; cover, Feb. 1983
■ The Big Cats. 442A-442B, Mar. 1974
■ Born of Fire. 824, Dec. 1982; cover, Apr. 1983
■ Bushmen of the Kalahari. 578A-578B, Apr. 1973; 732A-732B, May 1974
■ Dive to the Edge of Creation: Galapagos Rift expedition (II). 682, Nov. 1979; 1, cover, Jan. 1980
■ Dr. Leakey and the Dawn of Man. 703A-703B, Nov. 1966
■ Egypt, Quest for Eternity. cover, Feb. 1982
■ Ethiopia: The Hidden Empire. 884A-884B, Dec. 1970
■ Etosha: Place of Dry Water. 703, Dec. 1980; cover, Jan. 1981
■ Gold! 1, cover, Jan. 1979
■ Gorilla. 703, Dec. 1980; cover, Apr. 1981
■ The Great Mojave Desert. 294A-294B, Feb. 1971
■ The Great Whales. 439, Oct. 1977; cover, Feb. 1978; Emmy Award. 1, Jan. 1979
■ Grizzly! 639A-639B, Nov. 1967
■ The Haunted West. 1972
■ The Hidden World. 853A-853B, Dec. 1966
■ Holland Against the Sea. 588A-588B, Apr. 1970
■ Hong Kong: A Family Portrait. 1, Jan. 1979; cover, Feb. 1979
■ The Incredible Machine. 299, Sept. 1975; cover, Oct. 1975; 583, Nov. 1975; 575, Nov. 1976
■ The Invisible World. 1, Jan. 1980; cover, Mar. 1980
■ Journey to the High Arctic. 590A-590B, Apr. 1971
■ Journey to the Outer Limits. 150A-150B, Jan. 1974
■ Last Stand in Eden. 1, Jan. 1979, cover, Mar. 1979
■ The Last Tribes of Mindanao. 882A-882B, Dec. 1971; 227, Aug. 1972
■ The Last Vikings. 434A-434B, Mar. 1972
■ The Legacy of L. S. B. Leakey. 439, Oct. 1977; cover, Jan. 1978
■ The Living Sands of Namib. 439, Oct. 1977; cover, Mar. 1978; 1, Jan. 1979
■ Living Treasures of Japan. 703, Dec. 1980; cover, Feb. 1981
■ The Lonely Dorymen. 579A-579B, Apr. 1968
■ Man of the Serengeti. 179A-179B, Feb. 1972
■ Miss Goodall and the Wild Chimpanzees. 448, 451, Sept. 1965; 831A-831B, Dec. 1965
■ Monkeys, Apes, and Man. 585A-585B, Oct. 1971
■ Mysteries of the Mind. 1, Jan. 1980; cover, Feb. 1980
■ The Mystery of Animal Behavior. 592A-592B, Oct. 1969
■ National Parks: Playground or Paradise. 703, Dec. 1980; cover, Mar. 1981
■ The New Indians. 575, Nov. 1976; cover, Feb. 1977
■ Polar Bear Alert. 395, cover, Mar. 1982
■ Polynesian Adventure. 592A-592B, Apr. 1969
■ Rain Forest. 824, Dec. 1982; 49, cover, Jan. 1983
■ Reptiles and Amphibians. 875A-875B, Dec. 1968
■ Save the Panda. 824, Dec. 1982; cover, Mar. 1983
■ Search for the Great Apes. cover, Jan. 1976
■ The Sharks. cover, Jan. 1982
■ Siberia: The Endless Horizon. 734A-734B, Nov. 1969
■ Strange Creatures of the Night. 144A-144B, Jan. 1973
■ The Superliners: Twilight of an Era. 1, Jan. 1980; cover, Apr. 1980
■ The Thames. cover, Apr. 1982
■ This Britain. 583, Nov. 1975; cover, Dec. 1975
■ The *Tigris* Expedition. 826, Dec. 1978; 1, Jan. 1979; cover, Apr. 1979
■ Treasure! 575, Nov. 1976; cover, Dec. 1976
■ The Violent Earth. 286A-286B, Feb. 1973
■ The Volga. 575, Nov. 1976; cover, Mar. 1977
■ The Voyage of the Brigantine *Yankee*. 449, 451, Sept. 1965; 265A-265B, Feb. 1966
■ Voyage of the *Hokule'a*. 575, Nov. 1976
■ Washington Irving's Spain. 1966
■ Wild River. 239A-239B, Feb. 1970
■ Wind Raiders of the Sahara. 436A-436B, Sept. 1973
■ Winged World. 877A-877B, Dec. 1967
■ The World of Jacques-Yves Cousteau. 449, 451, Sept. 1965; 529A-529B, Apr. 1966
■ *Yankee* Sails Across Europe. 469A-469B, Apr. 1967
■ Yukon Passage. 439, Oct. 1977; cover, Dec. 1977
■ Zoos of the World. 503A-503B, Oct. 1970

TELL EL MUTASALLIM, Israel. *See* Megiddo

TELL MARDIKH EXCAVATION, Syria:
● Ebla: Splendor of an Unknown Empire. By Howard La Fay. Photos by James L. Stanfield. Paintings by Louis S. Glanzman. 730-759, Dec. 1978

TELSTAR:
● Telephone a Star: the Story of Communications Satellites. By Rowe Findley. 638-651, May 1962

TEMPLE CAVES:
● The Caves of the Thousand Buddhas. By Franc and Jean Shor. 383-415, Mar. 1951

S
T

• India's Sculptured Temple Caves. By Volkmar Wentzel. 665-678, May 1953
• *See also* Amarnath Cave

TEMPLE Monkeys of Nepal. By Jane Teas. NGS research grant. 575-584, Apr. 1980

TEMPLES:
• Computer Helps Scholars Re-create an Egyptian Temple. By Ray Winfield Smith. Photos by Emory Kristof. NGS research grant. 634-655, Nov. 1970
• Drama of Death in a Minoan Temple. By Yannis Sakellarakis and Efi Sapouna-Sakellaraki. Photos by Otis Imboden and Spyros Tsavdaroglou. 205-222, Feb. 1981
• Indonesia Rescues Ancient Borobudur. By W. Brown Morton III. Photos by Dean Conger. 126-142, Jan. 1983
• Kyoto and Nara: Keepers of Japan's Past. By Charles McCarry. Photos by George F. Mobley. Included: Chion-in, Daisen-in, Daitoku-ji, Gyokurin-in, Heian Shrine, Jinko-in, Todai-ji, To-ji. 836-859, June 1976
Kyoto Says Happy New Year. 852-859
• "Pyramids" of the New World. By Neil Merton Judd. 105-128, Jan. 1948
• Republican Indonesia Tries Its Wings. By W. Robert Moore. Included: Borobudur, Prambanan, Temple of Agriculture, and Temple of Irrigation. 1-40, Jan. 1951
• Temple Monkeys of Nepal. By Jane Teas. Included: Pashupati Hindu temple, Swayambhu Buddhist temple. NGS research grant. 575-584, Apr. 1980
• The Temples of Angkor. 548-589, May 1982
I. Ancient Glory in Stone. By Peter T. White. Photos by Wilbur E. Garrett. 552-589; II. Will They Survive? Introduction by Wilbur E. Garrett. 548-551
• Thailand Bolsters Its Freedom. By W. Robert Moore. 811-849, June 1961
• Who Were the "Mound Builders"? By George E. Stuart. 783-801, Dec. 1972
• *See also* Abu Simbel, Egypt; El Tajín (Archaeological Site), Mexico; Great Temple of Tenochtitlan, Mexico; *and* Pagodas

TENNESSEE:
• Around the "Great Lakes of the South." By Frederick Simpich. Photos by J. Baylor Roberts. 463-491, Apr. 1948
▲ *Deep South,* The Making of America series. Included: Alabama, Florida, Georgia, Louisiana, Mississippi, South Carolina, and parts of Arkansas, North Carolina, and Tennessee. On reverse: Indian Legacy, Imperial Footholds, Three Empires and Three Races, Cotton Kingdom, Postbellum, New Deal South, Subtropical Playground. Aug. 1983

PAINTING BY FELIPE DÁVALOS

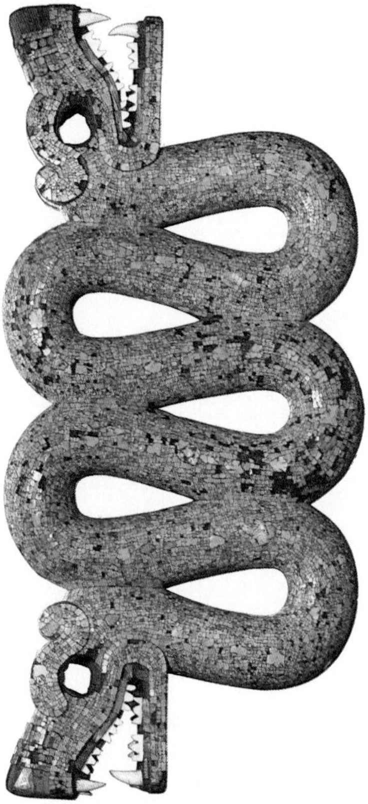

BRITISH MUSEUM, LONDON; BOTH BY VICTOR R. BOSWELL, JR., NGS

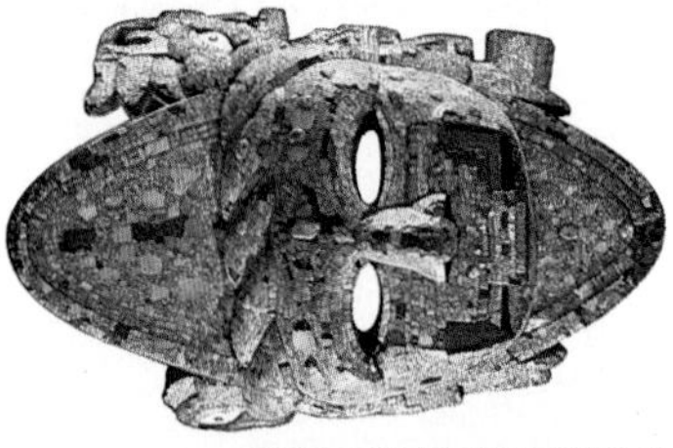

MUSEO NAZIONALE PREISTORICO ED ETNOGRAFICO LUIGI PIGORINI, ROME

Tenochtitlan: Stone of the Fifth Sun, *top;* Aztec turquoise serpent, *middle;* mosaic mask, *above*

• Dixie Spins the Wheel of Industry. By William H. Nicholas. Photos by J. Baylor Roberts. 281-324, Mar. 1949
• The Lower Mississippi. By Willard Price. Photos by W. D. Vaughn. 681-725, Nov. 1960
• Pack Trip Through the Smokies. By Val Hart. Photos by Robert F. Sisson. 473-502, Oct. 1952
• Skyline Trail from Maine to Georgia. By Andrew H. Brown. Photos by Robert F. Sisson. 219-251, Aug. 1949
• There's More to Nashville than Music. By Michael Kernan. Photos by Jodi Cobb. 692-711, May 1978
• Today Along the Natchez Trace, Pathway Through History. By Bern Keating. Photos by Charles Harbutt. 641-667, Nov. 1968
• A Walk Across America. By Peter Gorton Jenkins. 466-499, Apr. 1977
• Whatever Happened to TVA? By Gordon Young. Photos by Emory Kristof. 830-863, June 1973
• *See also* Cades Cove; Great Smoky Mountains National Park; Oak Ridge; Roan Mountain; Shiloh National Military Park

TENNESSEE VALLEY AUTHORITY:
• Around the "Great Lakes of the South." By Frederick Simpich. Photos by J. Baylor Roberts. 463-491, Apr. 1948
• Whatever Happened to TVA? By Gordon Young. Photos by Emory Kristof. 830-863, June 1973

TENOC (Ten-year Oceanographic Program). *See* National Oceanographic Program

TENOCHTITLAN (Aztec Capital):
• The Aztecs. 704-775, Dec. 1980
I. The Aztecs. By Bart McDowell. Photos by David Hiser. Paintings by Felipe Dávalos. 714-751; II. The Building of Tenochtitlan. By Augusto F. Molina Montes. Paintings by Felipe Dávalos. 753-765; III. New Finds in the Great Temple. By Eduardo Matos Moctezuma. Photos by David Hiser. 767-775
▲ *Visitor's Guide to the Aztec World; Mexico and Central America,* double-sided supplement. Dec. 1980

TENZING NORGAY:
• President Eisenhower Presents the Hubbard Medal to Everest's Conquerors. 64, July 1954
• Triumph on Everest. 1-63, July 1954
I. Siege and Assault. By Sir John Hunt. 1-43; II. The Conquest of the Summit. By Sir Edmund Hillary. 45-63

TEOTIHUACÁN, Mexico:
• Mexico's Booming Capital. By Mason Sutherland. Photos by Justin Locke. 785-824, Dec. 1951
• "Pyramids" of the New World. By Neil Merton Judd. 105-128, Jan. 1948
• South to Mexico City. By W. E. Garrett. 145-193, Aug. 1968

TEPARY BEANS:
- Rediscovering America's Forgotten Crops. By Noel D. Vietmeyer. Photos by Burgess Blevins. Paintings by Paul M. Breeden. 702-712, May 1981

TEPE GAWRA (Archaeological Site), Iraq:
- Ancient Mesopotamia: A Light That Did Not Fail. By E. A. Speiser. Paintings by H. M. Herget. 41-105, Jan. 1951

TEREDOS. *See* Shipworms

TERMITES:
- Termites: Dwellers in the Dark. By Glenn D. Prestwich. 532-547, Apr. 1978

TERNATE (Island), Moluccas, Indonesia:
- *Yankee* Roams the Orient. By Irving and Electa Johnson. 327-370, Mar. 1951

TERNS:
- Blizzard of Birds: The Tortugas Terns. By Alexander Sprunt, Jr. Included: Noddy terns; Sooty terns. 213-230, Feb. 1947
- Friend of the Wind: The Common Tern. By Ian Nisbet. Photos by Hope Alexander. 234-247, Aug. 1973
- Sea Birds of Isla Raza. By Lewis Wayne Walker. Included: Elegant terns; Royal terns. 239-248, Feb. 1951
- What A Place to Lay an Egg! By Thomas R. Howell. Contents: Fairy terns. NGS research grant. 414-419, Sept. 1971

TERRA-COTTA ARMY:
- China's Incredible Find. By Audrey Topping. Paintings by Yang Hsien-min. Included: The first emperor's burial mound, with guardian army of terra-cotta men and horses. 440-459, Apr. 1978

TERRY, WILLIAM B. and GLADYS: Photographers:
- Sinai Sheds New Light on the Bible. By Henry Field. 795-815, Dec. 1948

TETON RANGE, Wyoming:
- Cloud Gardens in the Tetons. By Frank and John Craighead. 811-830, June 1948
- *See also* Grand Teton National Park

TEXAS:
- America Goes to the Fair. By Samuel W. Matthews. Included: Texas State Fair at Dallas. 293-333, Sept. 1954
- America's "Meat on the Hoof." By William H. Nicholas. 33-72, Jan. 1952

  King Ranch, Cattle Empire in Texas. 41-64
- Big Thicket of Texas. By Don Moser. Photos by Blair Pittman. 504-529, Oct. 1974
- Boundary changes between Texas and Mexico due to the shifting of the Rio Grande; El Chamizal restored to Mexico; map. 590, Apr. 1964
- The Fabulous State of Texas. By Stanley Walker. Photos by B. Anthony Stewart and Thomas Nebbia. 149-195, Feb. 1961
- The Gulf's Workaday Waterway. By Gordon Young. Photos by Charles O'Rear. 200-223, Feb. 1978
- The Mexican Americans: A People on the Move. By Griffin Smith, Jr. Photos by Stephanie Maze. 780-809, June 1980
- North With the Wheat Cutters. By Noel Grove. Photos by James A. Sugar. 194-217, Aug. 1972
- Our Wild and Scenic Rivers: The Rio Grande. By Nathaniel T. Kenney. Photos by Bank Langmore. 46-51, July 1977
- The Pink Birds of Texas. By Paul A. Zahl. 641-654, Nov. 1949
- Roseate Spoonbills, Radiant Birds of the Gulf Coast. By Robert Porter Allen. Photos by Frederick Kent Truslow. 274-288, Feb. 1962
- Saving Man's Wildlife Heritage. By John H. Baker. Photos by Robert F. Sisson. Included: Audubon sanctuaries in Texas. 581-620, Nov. 1954
- Skyway Below the Clouds. By Carl R. Markwith. Photos by Ernest J. Cottrell. Included: Abilene, Big Spring, Dallas, El Paso, Fort Worth, Guadalupe Peak, Salt Flat CAA Intermediate Field, Tyler, Wink Municipal Airport. 85-108, July 1949
- Texas! By Howard La Fay. Photos by Gordon W. Gahan. 440-483, Apr. 1980
- Two Wheels Along the Mexican Border. By William Albert Allard. 591-635, May 1971
- A Walk Across America: Part II. By Peter and Barbara Jenkins. 194-229, Aug. 1979
- We Captured a 'Live' Brontosaur. By Roland T. Bird. 707-722, May 1954
- Where Oil and Wildlife Mix. By Steven C. Wilson and Karen C. Hayden. 145-173, Feb. 1981
- *See also* Aransas National Wildlife Refuge; Big Bend National Park; Guadalupe Mountains National Park; Houston; Midnight Cave; San Antonio

TEXAS A & M UNIVERSITY: Study Grant:
- Underwater Archaeology: Aegean Sea. 774, June 1978

TEXTILE INDUSTRY:
- Dixie Spins the Wheel of Industry. By William H. Nicholas. Photos by J. Baylor Roberts. 281-324, Mar. 1949
- The Merrimack: River of Industry and Romance. By Albert W. Atwood. Photos by B. Anthony Stewart. Included: Cotton and wool. 106-140, Jan. 1951
- North Carolina, Dixie Dynamo. By Malcolm Ross. Photos by B. Anthony Stewart. 141-183, Feb. 1962
- South Carolina Rediscovered. By Herbert Ravenel Sass. Photos by Robert F. Sisson. 281-321, Mar. 1953
- *See also Qiviut;* Tweed; Weaving

THAILAND:
- Around the World and the Calendar with the Geographic: The President's Annual Message. By Melville Bell Grosvenor. 832-866, Dec. 1959
- "Around the World in Eighty Days." By Newman Bumstead. 705-750, Dec. 1951
- Hopes and Fears in Booming Thailand. By Peter T. White. Photos by Dean Conger. 76-125, July 1967
- The Lands and Peoples of Southeast Asia. 295-365, Mar. 1971

  I. Mosaic of Cultures. By Peter T. White. Photos by W. E. Garrett. 296-329; II. New Light on a Forgotten Past. By Wilhelm G. Solheim II. 330-339
- Living With Thailand's Gentle Lua. By Peter Kunstadter. NGS research grant. 122-152, July 1966
- The Mekong, River of Terror and Hope. By Peter T. White. Photos by W. E. Garrett. 737-787, Dec. 1968
- Operation Eclipse: 1948. By William A. Kinney. NGS research grant. 325-372, Mar. 1949
- Pageantry of the Siamese Stage. By D. Sonakul. Photos by W. Robert Moore. 201-212, Feb. 1947

▲ *The Peoples of Mainland Southeast Asia; Asia,* double-sided supplement. Mar. 1971
- Round the World School. By Paul Antze. Photos by William Eppridge. 96-127, July 1962
- Scintillating Siam. By W. Robert Moore. 173-200, Feb. 1947
- Spirits of Change Capture the Karens. By Peter Kunstadter. 267-285, Feb. 1972
- Thailand: Luck of a Land in the Middle. By Bart McDowell. Photos by Steve Raymer. 500-535, Oct. 1982
- Thailand: Refuge From Terror. By W. E. Garrett. Contents: Refugees from Cambodia, Laos, and Vietnam. 633-642, May 1980
- Thailand Bolsters Its Freedom. By W. Robert Moore. 811-849, June 1961
- Thailand's Working Royalty. Photos by John Everingham. 486-499, Oct. 1982

▲ *Viet Nam, Cambodia, Laos, and Eastern Thailand,* supplement. Text on reverse. Jan. 1965

▲ *Viet Nam, Cambodia, Laos, and Thailand,* supplement. Feb. 1967
- War and Quiet on the Laos Frontier. By W. Robert Moore. Included: Eastern Thailand. 665-680, May 1954
- YWCA: International Success Story. By Mary French Rockefeller. Photos by Otis Imboden. 904-933, Dec. 1963
- *Yankee* Roams the Orient. By Irving and Electa Johnson. 327-370, Mar. 1951
- *See also* Bangkok

THAMES (River), England:
- One Man's London. By Allan C. Fisher, Jr. Photos by James P. Blair. 743-791, June 1966

■ The Thames. cover, Apr. 1982

● The Thames: That Noble River. By Ethel A. Starbird. Photos by O. Louis Mazzatenta. 750-791, June 1983
● The Thames Mirrors England's Varied Life. By Willard Price. Photos by Robert F. Sisson. 45-93, July 1958

THAMES BARRIER, Woolwich, England:
● The Thames: That Noble River. By Ethel A. Starbird. Photos by O. Louis Mazzatenta. 750-791, June 1983

THARUS (People):
● Peerless Nepal–A Naturalist's Paradise. By S. Dillon Ripley. Photos by Volkmar Wentzel. NGS research grant. 1-40, Jan. 1950

THAT Dammed Missouri River. By Gordon Young. Photos by David Hiser. 374-413, Sept. 1971

THAT Noble River: The Thames. By Ethel A. Starbird. Photos by O. Louis Mazzatenta. 750-791, June 1983

THAT Orbèd Maiden . . . the Moon. By Kenneth F. Weaver. 207-230, Feb. 1969

THEATER:
● The Britain That Shakespeare Knew. By Louis B. Wright. Photos by Dean Conger. 613-665, May 1964
● The British Way. By Sir Evelyn Wrench. Included: William Shakespeare; Sir William Gilbert and Sir Arthur Sullivan. 421-541, Apr. 1949
● Chelsea, London's Haven of Individualists. By James Cerruti. Photos by Adam Woolfitt. Included: Brendan Behan, Julie Christie, R. J. Minney, Sir Laurence Olivier, John Osborne, Vanessa Redgrave, George Bernard Shaw, Dame Sybil Thorndike, Oscar Wilde. 28-55, Jan. 1972
● The Lights Are Up at Ford's Theatre. By Lonnelle Aikman. 392-401, Mar. 1970
● Living Theater in New Guinea's Highlands. By Gillian Gillison. Photos by David Gillison. 147-169, Aug. 1983
● Miami's Expanding Horizons. By William H. Nicholas. Included: Barry College Dramatic Department; University of Miami Drama Department. 561-594, Nov. 1950
● Pageantry of the Siamese Stage. By D. Sonakul. Photos by W. Robert Moore. 201-212, Feb. 1947
● Wonderland in Longwood Gardens. By Edward C. Ferriday, Jr. Included: Indoor and outdoor theaters. 45-64, July 1951
● *See also* Folger, for Elizabethan theater; Kabuki

THEBES (Ancient City), Egypt:
● Computer Helps Scholars Re-create an Egyptian Temple. By Ray Winfield Smith. Photos by Emory Kristof. NGS research grant. 634-655, Nov. 1970

THEODORE ROOSEVELT: a Centennial Tribute. By Bart McDowell. 572-590, Oct. 1958
● *See also* Roosevelt, Theodore

THEODORE ROOSEVELT NATIONAL MEMORIAL PARK, North Dakota:
● North Dakota Comes into Its Own. By Leo A. Borah. Photos by J. Baylor Roberts. 283-322, Sept. 1951

THEOTOKOPOULOS, DOMENIKOS. *See* El Greco

THERA (Island), Greece:
● The Isles of Greece: Aegean Birthplace of Western Culture. By Melville Bell Grosvenor. Photos by Edwin Stuart Grosvenor and Winfield Parks. 147-193, Aug. 1972
● Minoans and Mycenaeans: Greece's Brilliant Bronze Age. By Joseph Judge. Photos by Gordon W. Gahan. Paintings by Lloyd K. Townsend. 142-185, Feb. 1978
● Thera, Key to the Riddle of Minos. By Spyridon Marinatos. Photos by Otis Imboden. 702-726, May 1972

THERE'S More to Nashville than Music. By Michael Kernan. Photos by Jodi Cobb. 692-711, May 1978

THERMAL ENERGY. *See* Geothermal Energy

THERMOGRAMS:
● Heat Paints *Columbia*'s Portrait. By Cliff Tarpy. 650-653, Nov. 1982
● Our Energy Predicament. By Kenneth F. Weaver. Included: Thermograms showing heat loss from cities, clothing, and housing. 2-23, *Special Report on Energy* (Feb. 1981)

THESIGER, WILFRED: Author:
● Marsh Dwellers of Southern Iraq. Photos by Gavin Maxwell. 205-239, Feb. 1958

THEY Crossed Australia First: The Tragic Burke-Wills Journey. By Joseph Judge. Photos by Joseph J. Scherschel. 152-191, Feb. 1979

THEY'D Rather Be in Philadelphia. By Ethel A. Starbird. Photos by Ted Spiegel. 314-343, Mar. 1983

THEY'RE Redesigning the Airplane. By Michael E. Long. Photos by James A. Sugar. 76-103, Jan. 1981

THIELEN, BENEDICT: Author:
● Florida Rides a Space-age Boom. Photos by Winfield Parks and James P. Blair. 858-903, Dec. 1963

THIMPHU, Bhutan:
● Bhutan Crowns a New Dragon King. Photos by John Scofield. 546-571, Oct. 1974

3RD AEROSPACE RESCUE AND RECOVERY GROUP:
● Air Rescue Behind Enemy Lines. By Howard Sochurek. 346-369, Sept. 1968

THIRTY-THREE Centuries Under the Sea. By Peter Throckmorton. 682-703, May 1960

THIS Changing Earth. By Samuel W. Matthews. 1-37, Jan. 1973

THIS Is My Island, Tangier. By Harold G. Wheatley. Photos by David Alan Harvey. 700-725, Nov. 1973

THIS Is the China I Saw. By Jørgen Bisch. 591-639, Nov. 1964

THIS Is the World's Richest Nation–All of It! By Mike Holmes. 344-353, Sept. 1976

"THIS land is your land . . ." (A Portfolio). 2-11, July 1976

THIS Land of Ours (Bicentennial Issue). 1-158, July 1976

THIS Year in Jerusalem. By Joseph Judge. Photos by Jodi Cobb. 479-515, Apr. 1983

THIS Young Giant, Indonesia. By Beverley M. Bowie. Photos by J. Baylor Roberts. 351-392, Sept. 1955

THOLSTRUP, HANS: Author:
● Across Australia by Sunpower. By Hans Tholstrup and Larry Perkins. Photos by David Austen. 600-607, Nov. 1983

THOM, JAMES ALEXANDER: Author:
● Indiana's Self-reliant Uplanders. Photos by J. Bruce Baumann. 341-363, Mar. 1976

THOMAS, DYLAN:
● Wales, the Lyric Land. By Bryan Hodgson. Photos by Farrell Grehan. 36-63, July 1983

THOMAS, ELIZABETH MARSHALL:
Author:
● Bushmen of the Kalahari. Photos by Laurence K. Marshall and other members of the expeditions. 866-888, June 1963

THOMAS, LOWELL, Jr.: Author:
● Scientists Ride Ice Islands on Arctic Odysseys. Photos by Ted Spiegel. 670-691, Nov. 1965
Author-Photographer:
● Flight to Adventure. By Tay and Lowell Thomas, Jr. 49-112, July 1957
● Sky Road East. By Tay and Lowell Thomas, Jr. 71-112, Jan. 1960

THOMAS, MARJORY C.: Author:
● Copra-ship Voyage to Fiji's Outlying Islands. 121-140, July 1950

THOMAS, TAY: Author:
● An Alaskan Family's Night of Terror (Earthquake). 142-156, July 1964
Author-Photographer:
● Flight to Adventure. By Tay and Lowell Thomas, Jr. 49-112, July 1957
● Sky Road East. By Tay and Lowell Thomas, Jr. 71-112, Jan. 1960

THOMAS, VERONICA: Author:
● The Arans, Ireland's Invincible Isles. Photos by Winfield Parks. 545-573, Apr. 1971
● Madeira, Like Its Wine, Improves With Age. Photos by Jonathan Blair. 488-513, Apr. 1973
● The Manx and Their Isle of Man. Photos by Ted H. Funk. 426-444, Sept. 1972
● The Original Boston: St. Botolph's Town (England). Photos by James L. Amos. 382-389, Sept. 1974

THOMAS JEFFERSON: Architect of Freedom. By Mike W. Edwards. Photos by Linda Bartlett. 231-259, Feb. 1976
● *See also* Jefferson, Thomas

THOMPSON, J. CHARLES: **Photographer:**
• Trawling the China Seas. 381-395, Mar. 1950

THOMPSON, TIM: Photographer:
• New Day for Alaska's Pribilof Islanders. By Susan Hackley Johnson. 536-552, Oct. 1982

THOMSON, DONALD F.: **Author-Photographer:**
• An Arnhem Land Adventure. 403-430, Mar. 1948

THOMSON, SIR J. J.:
• The British Way. By Sir Evelyn Wrench. 421-541, Apr. 1949

THOR HEYERDAHL Sails in the Wake of Sumerian Voyagers. By Thor Heyerdahl. Photos by Carlo Mauri and the crew of the *Tigris*. 806-827, Dec. 1978

THOR HEYERDAHL'S Own Story of *Ra II*. Photos by Carlo Mauri and Georges Sourial. 44-71, Jan. 1971

THORARINSSON, SIGURDUR: Author:
• Surtsey: Island Born of Fire. 713-726, May 1965

THOREAU, HENRY DAVID:
• Literary Landmarks of Massachusetts. By William H. Nicholas. Photos by B. Anthony Stewart and John E. Fletcher. 279-310, Mar. 1950
• Thoreau, a Different Man. By William Howarth. Photos by Farrell Grehan. 349-387, Mar. 1981

THOROUGHBREDS:
• Heart of the Bluegrass (Kentucky). By Charles McCarry. Photos by J. Bruce Baumann. 634-659, May 1974

THOSE Fiery Brazilian Bees. By Rick Gore. Photos by Bianca Lavies. 491-501, Apr. 1976

THOSE Kangaroos! They're a Marvelous Mob. By Geoffrey B. Sharman. Photos by Des and Jen Bartlett. 192-209, Feb. 1979

THOSE Marvelous, Myriad Diatoms. By Richard B. Hoover. 871-878, June 1979

THOSE Outlandish Goldfish! By Paul A. Zahl. 514-533, Apr. 1973

THOSE Popular Pandas. By Theodore H. Reed. Photos by Donna K Grosvenor. 803-815, Dec. 1972

THOSE Proper and Other Bostonians. By Joseph Judge. Photos by Ted Spiegel. 352-381, Sept. 1974

THOSE Successful Japanese. By Bart McDowell. Photos by Fred Ward. 323-359, Mar. 1974

The ***THOUSAND AND ONE NIGHTS*** *(The Arabian Nights Entertainments):*
• In the Wake of Sindbad. By Tim Severin. Photos by Richard Greenhill. 2-41, July 1982

The **THOUSAND-MILE** Glide. By Karl Striedieck. Photos by Otis Imboden. 431-438, Mar. 1978

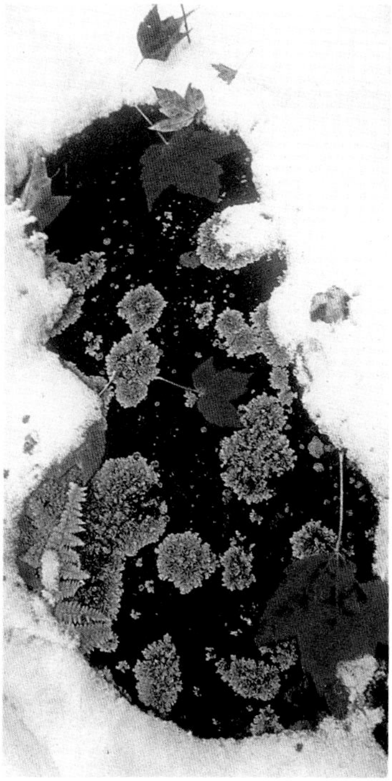

FARRELL GREHAN

Thoreau: early snowfall

THOUSAND-MILE Race to Nome: A Woman's Icy Struggle. By Susan Butcher. Photos by Kerby Smith. 411-422, Mar. 1983

THRACIANS:
• Ancient Bulgaria's Golden Treasures. By Colin Renfrew. Photos by James L. Stanfield. Paintings by Jean-Leon Huens. 112-129, July 1980

THREATENED Glories of Everglades National Park. By Frederick Kent Truslow and Frederick G. Vosburgh. Photos by Frederick Kent Truslow and Otis Imboden. 508-553, Oct. 1967

THREATENED Treasures of the Nile. By Georg Gerster. 587-621, Oct. 1963

The **THREATENED** Ways of Kenya's Pokot People. By Elizabeth L. Meyerhoff. Photos by Murray Roberts. NGS research grant. 120-140, Jan. 1982

THREE Months on an Arctic Ice Island. By Joseph O. Fletcher. 489-504, Apr. 1953

THREE Roads to Rainbow. By Ralph Gray. 547-561, Apr. 1957

THREE Whales That Flew. By Carleton Ray. Photos by W. Robert Moore. 346-359, Mar. 1962

THRESHER, U.S.S. (Submarine):
• *Thresher* Tragedy Spurs Deep-sea Research. 759-777, June 1964
I. Lesson and Challenge. By James H. Wakelin, Jr. 759-763; II. Down to *Thresher* by Bathyscaph. By Donald L. Keach. 764-777

THROCKMORTON, PETER: Author:
• Ancient Shipwreck Yields New Facts–and a Strange Cargo. Photos by Kim Hart and Joseph J. Scherschel. 282-300, Feb. 1969
• Oldest Known Shipwreck Yields Bronze Age Cargo. 697-711, May 1962
• Thirty-three Centuries Under the Sea. 682-703, May 1960

THRONE Above the Euphrates. By Theresa Goell. 390-405, Mar. 1961

THROUGH Europe by Trailer Caravan. By Norma Miller. Photos by Ardean R. Miller III. 769-816, June 1957

THROUGH Ozark Hills and Hollows. By Mike W. Edwards. Photos by Bruce Dale. 656-689, Nov. 1970

THROUGH the Northwest Passage for Oil. By Bern Keating. Photos by Tomas Sennett. 374-391, Mar. 1970

The **THRUSH** on the Island of Barra. By Archibald MacLeish. 692-693, May 1970

THULE AIR BASE, Greenland:
• We Followed Peary to the Pole. By Gilbert Grosvenor and Thomas W. McKnew. 469-484, Oct. 1953
• Weather from the White North. By Andrew H. Brown. Photos by John E. Fletcher. 543-572, Apr. 1955

S
T

THULE INUIT:
• Arctic Odyssey. By John Bockstoce. Photos by Jonathan Wright. Paintings by Jack Unruh. Contents: Umiak expedition tracing Thule Eskimo migration route from Alaska to Greenland. 100-127, July 1983
• Eskimo and Viking Finds in the High Arctic: Ellesmere Island. By Peter Schledermann. Photos by Sisse Brimberg. 575-601, May 1981

THUMB MOVIE:
• What Voyager Saw: Jupiter's Dazzling Realm. By Rick Gore. Photos by NASA. Included: Thumb movie showing movements in the atmosphere of Jupiter. 2-29, Jan. 1980

THUMBS Up Round the North Sea's Rim. By Frances James. Photos by Erica Koch. 685-704, May 1952

THUNDER HILL GOAT FARM, New York:
• The Goats of Thunder Hill. By Elizabeth Nicholds. Photos by Robert F. Sisson. 625-640, May 1954

THURBER, MURIEL: Photographer:
• Squaws Along the Yukon. By Ginny Hill Wood. 245-265, Aug. 1957

TIBET:
• Caught in the Assam-Tibet Earthquake. By F. Kingdon-Ward. 403-416, Mar. 1952
• Editorial. By Gilbert M. Grosvenor. 143, Feb. 1980
• In Long-Forbidden Tibet. By Fred Ward. 218-259, Feb. 1980
• A Woman Paints the Tibetans. By Lafugie. 659-692, May 1949
• *See also* Lhasa

TIBETAN BUDDHISM:
• Bhutan, Land of the Thunder Dragon. By Burt Kerr Todd. 713-754, Dec. 1952
• Bhutan Crowns a New Dragon King. By John Scofield. 546-571, Oct. 1974
• Gangtok, Cloud-wreathed Himalayan Capital. By John Scofield. 698-713, Nov. 1970
• In Long-Forbidden Tibet. By Fred Ward. 218-259, Feb. 1980
• A Journey to "Little Tibet" (Ladakh). By Enakshi Bhavnani. Photos by Volkmar Wentzel. Included: Yellow Hat lamas and Red lamas. 603-634, May 1951
• Ladakh–The Last Shangri-la. By Thomas J. Abercrombie. 332-359, Mar. 1978
• Little Tibet in Switzerland. By Laura Pilarski. Photos by Fred Mayer. 711-727, Nov. 1968
• Mountaintop War in Remote Ladakh. By W. E. Garrett. 664-687, May 1963
• Mustang, Remote Realm in Nepal. By Michel Peissel. 579-604, Oct. 1965
• My Life in Forbidden Lhasa. By Heinrich Harrer. 1-48, July 1955
• Sherpaland, My Shangri-La. By Desmond Doig. 545-577, Oct. 1966
• Sikkim. By Desmond Doig. 398-429, Mar. 1963
• Trek to Nepal's Sacred Crystal Mountain. By Joel F. Ziskin. 500-517, Apr. 1977
• A Woman Paints the Tibetans. By Lafugie. 659-692, May 1949

TIBETANS:
• A Journey to "Little Tibet" (Ladakh). By Enakshi Bhavnani. Photos by Volkmar Wentzel. 603-634, May 1951
• Little Tibet in Switzerland. By Laura Pilarski. Photos by Fred Mayer. 711-727, Nov. 1968
• A Woman Paints the Tibetans. By Lafugie. 659-692, May 1949

TICONDEROGA, New York:
• From Sword to Scythe in Champlain Country. By Ethel A. Starbird. Photos by B. Anthony Stewart and Emory Kristof. 153-201, Aug. 1967
• North Through History Aboard *White Mist.* By Melville Bell Grosvenor. Photos by Edwin Stuart Grosvenor. 1-55, July 1970

TIDES AND TIDAL BORES:
• Amazon–The River Sea. By Loren McIntyre. Included: Amazon tidal bore, the *pororoca.* 456-495, Oct. 1972
• Cruising Japan's Inland Sea. By Willard Price. Included: The tidal whirlpools of Naruto Strait. 619-650, Nov. 1953
• The Giant Tides of Fundy. By Paul A. Zahl. 153-192, Aug. 1957
• Sea Fever. By John E. Schultz. Included: Amazon tidal bore, the *pororoca.* 237-268, Feb. 1949
• Venice Fights for Life. By Joseph Judge. Photos by Albert Moldvay. 591-631, Nov. 1972
• *See also* Blue Holes; Farne Islands; Messina, Strait of; St. Michael's Mount; Wight, Isle of

TIDEWATER AREA. *See* Chesapeake Bay

TIEMANN, DARWIN L.: Author:
• Nature's Toy Train, the Railroad Worm. Photos by Robert F. Sisson. 56-67, July 1970

TIERRA DEL FUEGO (Archipelago), South America:
• Argentina: Young Giant of the Far South. By Jean and Franc Shor. 297-352, Mar. 1958
• Chile, the Long and Narrow Land. By Kip Ross. 185-235, Feb. 1960
• Guanacos: Wild Camels of South America. By William L. Franklin. NGS research grant. 63-75, July 1981
• Housewife at the End of the World. By Rae Natalie P. Goodall. Photos by James L. Stanfield. 130-150, Jan. 1971
• In the Wake of Darwin's *Beagle.* By Alan Villiers. Photos by James L. Stanfield. 449-495, Oct. 1969

TIGERS:
• Enchantress! (White Tigress). By Theodore H. Reed. Photos by Thomas J. Abercrombie. 628-641, May 1961
• India Struggles to Save Her Wildlife. By John J. Putman. 299-343, Sept. 1976
• White Tiger in My House. By Elizabeth C. Reed. Photos by Donna K. Grosvenor. 482-491, Apr. 1970

TIGRIS (Reed Ship):
• *Tigris* Sails Into the Past. By Thor Heyerdahl. Photos by Carlo Mauri and the crew of the *Tigris.* 806-827, Dec. 1978
▪ The Voyage of the *Tigris.* 826, Dec. 1978; 1, Jan. 1979; cover, Apr. 1979

TIHWA, Sinkiang, China. *See* Urumchi

TIJUANA, Mexico:
• Two Wheels Along the Mexican Border. By William Albert Allard. 591-635, May 1971

TIKAL (Maya Ruin), Guatemala:
• Guatemala, Maya and Modern. By Louis de la Haba. Photos by Joseph J. Scherschel. 661-689, Nov. 1974
• The Maya. 729-811, Dec. 1975
III. Resurrecting the Grandeur of Tikal. By William R. Coe. 792-798; IV. A Traveler's Tale of Ancient Tikal. Paintings by Peter Spier. Text by Alice J. Hall. 799-811

TIKOPIA (Island), Santa Cruz Islands:
• *Yankee* Roams the Orient. By Irving and Electa Johnson. 327-370, Mar. 1951

TILLING, ROBERT I.: Author:
• Volcanic Cloud May Alter Earth's Climate. 672-675, Nov. 1982

TIMBER INDUSTRY:
• Timber: How Much Is Enough? By John J. Putman. Photos by Bruce Dale. 485-511, Apr. 1974
• *See also* Lumber Industry

TIMBER WOLF. *See* Gray Wolf

TIME of Testing for Sri Lanka. By Robert Paul Jordan. Photos by Raghubir Singh. 123-150, Jan. 1979

TIME Turns Back in Picture-book Portofino. By Carleton Mitchell. Photos by Winfield Parks. 232-253, Feb. 1965

TIMEKEEPING:
• Split-second Time Runs Today's World. By F. Barrows Colton and Catherine Bell Palmer. 399-428, Sept. 1947
• The Tower of the Winds. By Derek J. de Solla Price. Paintings by Robert C. Magis. NGS research grant. 587-596, Apr. 1967

TIMOR (Island), Malay Archipelago:
• East From Bali by Seagoing Jeep to Timor. By Helen and Frank Schreider. 236-279, Aug. 1962

TIN AND TIN MINING:
• Malaya Meets Its Emergency. By George W. Long. Photos by J. Baylor Roberts. 185-228, Feb. 1953

TIN TRADE. *See* St. Michael's Mount

TINKERS, Irish. *See* Appleby Fair

TINOS (Island), Greece:
• The Isles of Greece: Aegean Birthplace of Western Culture. By Melville Bell Grosvenor. Photos by Edwin Stuart Grosvenor and Winfield Parks. 147-193, Aug. 1972

TIRELESS Voyager, the Whistling Swan. By William J. L. Sladen. Photos by Bianca Lavies. NGS research grant. 134-147, July 1975

TIROL, Austria's Province in the Clouds. By Peter T. White. Photos by Volkmar Wentzel. 107-141, July 1961
• *See also* Tyrol

TIROS I (Weather Satellite):
• Our Earth as a Satellite Sees It. By W. G. Stroud. 293-302, Aug. 1960

TITAN (Rock Spire), Fisher Towers, Utah:
• We Climbed Utah's Skyscraper Rock. By Huntley Ingalls. Photos by author and Barry C. Bishop. 705-721, Nov. 1962

TITAN II (Rocket). *See* Gemini Missions

TITICACA, Lake, Bolivia-Peru:
• Flamboyant Is the Word for Bolivia. By Loren McIntyre. 153-195, Feb. 1966
• The Lost Empire of the Incas. By Loren McIntyre. Art by Ned and Rosalie Seidler. 729-787, Dec. 1973
• Sky-high Bolivia. 481-496, Oct. 1950
• Titicaca, Abode of the Sun. By Luis Marden. Photos by Flip Schulke. 272-294, Feb. 1971

TITO, JOSIP BROZ:
• Yugoslavia: Six Republics in One. By Robert Paul Jordan. Photos by James P. Blair. 589-633, May 1970
• Yugoslavia's Window on the Adriatic. By Gilbert M. Grosvenor. 219-247, Feb. 1962

TIVOLI, Copenhagen, Denmark:
• Copenhagen, Wedded to the Sea. By Stuart E. Jones. Photos by Gilbert M. Grosvenor. 45-79, Jan. 1963
• Denmark, Field of the Danes. By William Graves. Photos by Thomas Nebbia. 245-275, Feb. 1974

TIWI (People):
• Expedition to the Land of the Tiwi. By Charles P. Mountford. NGS research grant. 417-440, Mar. 1956

TLINGIT INDIANS:
• Alaska's Marine Highway: Ferry Route to the North. By W. E. Garrett. 776-819, June 1965
• New Day for Alaska's Pribilof Islanders. By Susan Hackley Johnson. Photos by Tim Thompson. 536-552, Oct. 1982

"**TO** Be Indomitable, To be Joyous": Greece. By Peter T. White. Photos by James P. Blair. 360-393, Mar. 1980

TO Europe with a Racing Start. By Carleton Mitchell. 758-791, June 1958

TO Gilbert Grosvenor: a Monthly Monument 25 Miles High. By Frederick G. Vosburgh and the staff of the National Geographic Society. 445-487, Oct. 1966

TO Live in Harlem. . . . By Frank Hercules. Photos by LeRoy Woodson, Jr. 178-207, Feb. 1977

TO 76,000 Feet by *Strato-Lab* Balloon. By Malcolm D. Ross and M. Lee Lewis. 269-282, Feb. 1957

TO the Depths of the Sea by Bathyscaphe. By Jacques-Yves Cousteau. NGS research grant. 67-79, July 1954

TO the Land of the Head-hunters. By E. Thomas Gilliard. NGS research grant. 437-486, Oct. 1955

TO the Memory of Our Beloved President, Friend to All Mankind. 1A-1B, Jan. 1964

TO the Men at South Pole Station. By Richard E. Byrd. 1-4, July 1957

TO the Mountains of the Moon. By Kenneth F. Weaver. Photos from NASA. 233-265, Feb. 1972

TO Torre Egger's Icy Summit. By Jim Donini. 813-823, Dec. 1976

TOADS:
• Voices of the Night. By Arthur A. Allen. Included: Canadian toad, Common toad, Common tree toad, Oak toad, Spadefoot toad, Western toad. NGS research grant. 507-522, Apr. 1950

TOADSTOOLS:
• Bizarre World of the Fungi. By Paul A. Zahl. 502-527, Oct. 1965

TOBACCO GROWING:
• The Bulgarians. By Boyd Gibbons. Photos by James L. Stanfield. 91-111, July 1980
• Cuba–American Sugar Bowl. By Melville Bell Grosvenor. 1-56, Jan. 1947
• Heart of the Bluegrass. By Charles McCarry. Photos by J. Bruce Baumann. 634-659, May 1974
• Home to North Carolina. By Neil Morgan. Photos by Bill Weems. 333-359, Mar. 1980
• Inside Cuba Today. By Fred Ward. 32-69, Jan. 1977
• North Carolina, Dixie Dynamo. By Malcolm Ross. Photos by B. Anthony Stewart. 141-183, Feb. 1962
• Yesterday Lingers Along the Connecticut. By Charles McCarry. Photos by David L. Arnold. 334-369, Sept. 1972

TOBAGO (Island), West Indies:
• Feathered Dancers of Little Tobago. By E. Thomas Gilliard. Photos by Frederick Kent Truslow. NGS research grant. 428-440, Sept. 1958
• Happy-go-lucky Trinidad and Tobago. By Charles Allmon. 35-75, Jan. 1953

TOBIN, JAMES: Photographer:
• Down on the Farm, Soviet Style–a 4-H Adventure. By John Garaventa. Photos by James Tobin and Carol Schmidt. 768-797, June 1979

TODAY Along the Natchez Trace, Pathway Through History. By Bern Keating. Photos by Charles Harbutt. 641-667, Nov. 1968

JAMES P. BLAIR, NGS

Indomitable Greece: woman on Crete

BOTH BY JONATHAN BLAIR

Tolosa:* crystal wine decanter, *top;*. fortune in jewels recovered, *above

TODAY and Tomorrow in Our National Parks. By Melville Bell Grosvenor. 1-5, July 1966

TODAY on the Delaware, Penn's Glorious River. By Albert W. Atwood. Photos by Robert F. Sisson. 1-40, July 1952

TODD, BURT KERR:
Author-Photographer:
• Bhutan, Land of the Thunder Dragon. 713-754, Dec. 1952

TOKYO, Japan:
• Japan, the Exquisite Enigma. By Franc Shor. 733-777, Dec. 1960
• Japan Tries Freedom's Road. By Frederick G. Vosburgh. Photos by J. Baylor Roberts. 593-632, May 1950
• Operation Eclipse: 1948. By William A. Kinney. Note: Tokyo's location error was discovered by expedition scientists. NGS research grant. 325-372, Mar. 1949
• Those Successful Japanese. By Bart McDowell. Photos by Fred Ward. 323-359, Mar. 1974
• Tokyo, the Peaceful Explosion. By William Graves. Photos by Winfield Parks. 445-487, Oct. 1964

TOKYO BAY, Japan:
• The Yankee Sailor Who Opened Japan. By Ferdinand Kuhn. 85-102, July 1953

TOLEDO, Spain:
• Toledo–El Greco's Spain Lives On. By Louise E. Levathes. Photos by James P. Blair. 726-753, June 1982
The Genius of El Greco. Introduction by J. Carter Brown. 736-744

TOLLUND MAN:
• Lifelike Man Preserved 2,000 Years in Peat. By P. V. Glob. 419-430, Mar. 1954

TOLOSA, CONDE DE (Spanish Galleon):
• Graveyard of the Quicksilver Galleons. By Mendel Peterson. Photos by Jonathan Blair. 850-876, Dec. 1979

TOLTEC CULTURE. *See* Teotihuacán

TOM SAWYER'S Town. By Jerry Allen. 121-140, July 1956

TOMBS:
• Ancient Bulgaria's Golden Treasures. By Colin Renfrew. Photos by James L. Stanfield. Paintings by Jean-Leon Huens. 112-129, July 1980
• An Archeologist Looks at Palestine. By Nelson Glueck. 739-752, Dec. 1947
• China's Incredible Find. By Audrey Topping. Paintings by Yang Hsien-min. Included: The first emperor's burial mound, with guardian army of terra-cotta men and horses. 440-459, Apr. 1978
• Finding the Tomb of a Warrior-God. By William Duncan Strong. Photos by Clifford Evans, Jr. 453-482, Apr. 1947
• Fresh Treasures from Egypt's Ancient Sands. By Jefferson Caffery. Photos by David S. Boyer. 611-650, Nov. 1955
• Regal Treasures From a Macedonian Tomb. By Manolis Andronicos. Photos by Spyros Tsavdaroglou. 55-77, July 1978
• Treasure From a Celtic Tomb. By Jörg Biel. Photos by Volkmar Wentzel. 428-438, Mar. 1980
• *See also* Arlington National Cemetery; Etruscans; Han Dynasty Tombs; La Venta; Maya; Petra; Pyramids; Tutankhamun; Ur

TOMBSTONE, Arizona:
• From Tucson to Tombstone. By Mason Sutherland. 343-384, Sept. 1953

TOMORROW on the Deep Frontier. By Edwin A. Link. NGS research grant. 778-801, June 1964

TONGA:
• Coronations a World Apart. By the Editor. 299, Mar. 1968
• The Friendly Isles of Tonga. By Luis Marden. 345-367, Mar. 1968
• Problems in Paradise. By Mary and Laurance S. Rockefeller. Photos by Thomas Nebbia. 782-793, Dec. 1974
• South Seas' Tonga Hails a King. By Melville Bell Grosvenor. Photos by Edwin Stuart Grosvenor. 322-343, Mar. 1968

TONLÉ SAP (Lake and River), Kampuchea:
• Angkor, Jewel of the Jungle. By W. Robert Moore. Paintings by Maurice Fiévet. 517-569, Apr. 1960
• Cambodia: Indochina's "Neutral" Corner. By Thomas J. Abercrombie. 514-551, Oct. 1964
• The Temples of Angkor. 548-589, May 1982
I. Ancient Glory in Stone. By Peter T. White. Photos by Wilbur E. Garrett. 552-589; II. Will They Survive? Introduction by Wilbur E. Garrett. 548-551

TOOL-USING ANIMALS:
• Aha! It Really Works! By Robert F. Sisson. Note: A heron fishes with bait. 143-147, Jan. 1974
• The Galapagos, Eerie Cradle of New Species. By Roger Tory Peterson. Photos by Alan and Joan Root. Included: Tool-using finches. 541-585, Apr. 1967
• Tool-using Bird: The Egyptian Vulture. By Baroness Jane van Lawick-Goodall. Photos by Baron Hugo van Lawick. 631-641, May 1968
• *See also* Chimpanzees; Sea Otters

TOOLS, Primitive:
• First Glimpse of a Stone Age Tribe. 881-882, Dec. 1971
• The Search for the First Americans. By Thomas Y. Canby. Photos by Kerby Smith. Paintings by Roy Andersen. 330-363, Sept. 1979
• The Tasadays, Stone Age Cavemen of Mindanao. By Kenneth MacLeish. Photos by John Launois. 219-249, Aug. 1972

• *See also* Asmat; Cinta Larga Indians; Hoabinhian Culture; Ice Age Man; Weapons, Primitive

The **TOP** End of Down Under. By Kenneth MacLeish. Photos by Thomas Nebbia. 145-174, Feb. 1973

TOPPING, AUDREY: Author:
• China's Incredible Find. Paintings by Yang Hsien-min. 440-459, Apr. 1978
Author-Photographer:
• Return to Changing China. 801-833, Dec. 1971

TORADJALAND (Region), Sulawesi. *See* Tana Toradja

TORCHBEARERS of the Twilight. By Frederick G. Vosburgh. 697-704, May 1951

TORIES. *See* The Loyalists

TORNADOES:
• We're Doing Something About the Weather! By Walter Orr Roberts. 518-555, Apr. 1972

TORONTO, Ontario, Canada:
• Canada's Dynamic Heartland, Ontario. By Marjorie Wilkins Campbell. Photos by Winfield Parks. 58-97, July 1963
• Ontario, Canada's Keystone. By David S. Boyer. Photos by Sam Abell and the author. 760-795, Dec. 1978
• Ontario, Pivot of Canada's Power. By Andrew H. Brown. Photos by B. Anthony Stewart and Bates Littlehales. 823-852, Dec. 1953
• Royal Ontario Museum of Geology and Mineralogy: Expedition. *See* Chubb Crater
• Toronto: Canada's Dowager Learns to Swing. By Ethel A. Starbird. Photos by Robert W. Madden. 190-215, Aug. 1975

TORRE EGGER (Mountain), Argentina-Chile:
• To Torre Egger's Icy Summit. By Jim Donini. 813-823, Dec. 1976

TORRE SGARRATA EXPEDITION: Italy:
• Ancient Shipwreck Yields New Facts–and a Strange Cargo. By Peter Throckmorton. Photos by Kim Hart and Joseph J. Scherschel. 282-300, Feb. 1969

TÓRSHAVN, Faeroe Islands:
• The Faeroes, Isles of Maybe. By Ernle Bradford. Photos by Adam Woolfitt. 410-442, Sept. 1970

TORTOISES:
• Giant Tortoises: Goliaths of the Galapagos. By Craig MacFarland. Photos by author and Jan MacFarland. 632-649, Nov. 1972

TORTOLI, GIANNI: Photographer:
• Locusts: "Teeth of the Wind." By Robert A. M. Conley. 202-227, Aug. 1969

TORTUGA II (Amphibious Jeep):
• East From Bali by Seagoing Jeep to Timor. By Helen and Frank Schreider. 236-279, Aug. 1962
• From the Hair of Siva (Ganges River, India). By Helen and Frank Schreider. 445-503, Oct. 1960
• Indonesia, the Young and Troubled Island Nation. By Helen and Frank Schreider. 579-625, May 1961

TORTUGAS (Islands), Florida. *See* Dry Tortugas

TORTUGUERO BEACH, Costa Rica:
• Imperiled Gift of the Sea: Caribbean Green Turtle. By Archie Carr. Photos by Robert E. Schroeder. 876-890, June 1967

TOTAL Victory Over Smallpox? By Donald A. Henderson. Photos by Marion Kaplan. 796-805, Dec. 1978

TOTONAC INDIANS:
• Man's Eighty Centuries in Veracruz. By S. Jeffrey K. Wilkerson. Photos by David Hiser. Paintings by Richard Schlecht. 203-231, Aug. 1980

TOULON CANYON, Mediterranean Sea:
• Diving Through an Undersea Avalanche. By Jacques-Yves Cousteau. NGS research grant. 538-542, Apr. 1955
• To the Depths of the Sea by Bathyscaphe. By Jacques-Yves Cousteau. NGS research grant. 67-79, July 1954

TOULOUSE, France:
• France's Past Lives in Languedoc. By Walter Meayers Edwards. Included: Academy of the Floral Games, Canal du Midi, Cathedral of St. Etienne, and St. Sernin. 1-43, July 1951

TOURNAMENT OF ROSES: Pasadena, California:
• Focusing on the Tournament of Roses. By B. Anthony Stewart and J. Baylor Roberts. 805-816, June 1954

TOWBOATS:
• The Gulf's Workaday Waterway. By Gordon Young. Photos by Charles O'Rear. 200-223, Feb. 1978
• The Ohio–River With a Job to Do. By Priit J. Vesilind. Photos by Martin Rogers. Included: The *Northern,* working the 981-mile length of the Ohio River. 245-273, Feb. 1977
• That Dammed Missouri River. By Gordon Young. Photos by David Hiser. 374-413, Sept. 1971

The **TOWER** of the Winds. By Derek J. de Solla Price. Paintings by Robert C. Magis. NGS research grant. 587-596, Apr. 1967

TOWERS, Rock. *See* Fisher Towers, Utah

A **TOWN** . . . a Mountain . . . a Way of Life. By Jill Durrance and Dick Durrance II. 788-807, Dec. 1973

TOWNSEND, LLOYD K.: Artist:
▲ "Early Civilizations," painting supplement. Map on reverse. Sept. 1978
• Lost Outpost of the Egyptian Empire. By Trude Dothan. Photos by Sisse Brimberg. 739-769, Dec. 1982
• Minoans and Mycenaeans: Greece's Brilliant Bronze Age. By Joseph Judge. Photos by Gordon W. Gahan. 142-185, Feb. 1978
• Nature's Gifts to Medicine. By Lonnelle Aikman. Paintings by Lloyd K. Townsend and Don Crowley. 420-440, Sept. 1974
▲ "The Solar System," painting supplement. NASA photo of Saturn on reverse. July 1981

TRACKING America's Man in Orbit. By Kenneth F. Weaver. Photos by Robert F. Sisson. 184-217, Feb. 1962

TRACKING AND DATA RELAY SATELLITES (TDRS):
• Satellites That Serve Us. By Thomas Y. Canby. 281-335, Sept. 1983
Spacelab 1: *Columbia.* By Michael E. Long. 301-307

TRACKING Danger With the Ice Patrol. By William S. Ellis. Photos by James R. Holland. 780-793, June 1968

TRACKING the Shore Dwellers (Sandpipers): From Canada to Suriname. 175-179, Aug. 1979

TRADE:
• The Bonanza Bean–Coffee. By Ethel A. Starbird. Photos by Sam Abell. 388-405, Mar. 1981
▲ *Colonization and Trade in the New World,* supplement. Painting and text on reverse. Dec. 1977
• Louisiana Trades with the World. By Frederick Simpich. Photos by J. Baylor Roberts. 705-738, Dec. 1947
• Reach for the New World. By Mendel Peterson. Photos by David L. Arnold. Paintings by Richard Schlecht. 724-767, Dec. 1977
• Spices, the Essence of Geography. By Stuart E. Jones. 401-420, Mar. 1949
• Wild Cargo: the Business of Smuggling Animals. By Noel Grove. Photos by Steve Raymer. 287-315, Mar. 1981
• With Uncle Sam and John Bull in Germany. By Frederick Simpich. 117-140, Jan. 1949
• *See also* Shipping; *and Witte Leeuw,* for East Indies trade

TRADE ROUTES:
• Crosscurrents Sweep the Indian Ocean. By Bart McDowell. Photos by Steve Raymer. 422-457, Oct. 1981
• *See also* Persian Gulf; St. Lawrence Seaway
Historical:
• In the Wake of Sindbad. By Tim Severin. Photos by Richard Greenhill. 2-41, July 1982
• Journey to China's Far West. By Rick Gore. Photos by Bruce Dale. Included: Silk Road. 292-331, Mar. 1980
• *See also* Mesopotamia; *and* Phoenicians; Vikings

TRADEWINDS (Ketch):
• Slow Boat to Florida. By Dorothea and Stuart E. Jones. 1-65, Jan. 1958

TRAFALGAR, Battle of:
• The British Way. By Sir Evelyn Wrench. 421-541, Apr. 1949
• Portsmouth, Britannia's Sally Port. By Thomas Garner James. Photos by B. Anthony Stewart. 513-544, Apr. 1952

S T

The **TRAGIC** Journey of Burke and Wills. By Joseph Judge. Photos by Joseph J. Scherschel. 152-191, Feb. 1979

TRAIL, PEPPER W.:
Author-Photographer:
• Cock-of-the-Rock: Jungle Dandy. 831-839, Dec. 1983

TRAILING Cosmic Rays in Canada's North. By Martin A. Pomerantz. NGS research grant. 99-115, Jan. 1953

TRAILING Yellowstone's Grizzlies by Radio. By Frank Craighead, Jr., and John Craighead. NGS research grant. 252-267, Aug. 1966

TRAILS:
• Along the Yukon Trail. By Amos Burg. 395-416, Sept. 1953
• On the Trail of Wisconsin's Ice Age. By Anne LaBastille. Photos by Cary Wolinsky. Contents: A tour of the state's glacial features. 182-205, Aug. 1977
◆ *Trails West.* 1979
• *See also* Appalachian Trail; Continental Divide National Scenic Trail; Great Divide Trail; Lewis and Clark Expedition; Natchez Trace; Outlaw Trail; Pacific Crest Trail; *and* Sheep Trek

TRAINING SHIPS:
• By Full-rigged Ship to Denmark's Fairyland. By Alan Villiers. Photos by Alexander Taylor and author. Included: *Arken, Danmark, Georg Stage, Lilla Dan, Peder Most.* 809-828, Dec. 1955
• By Square-rigger from Baltic to Bicentennial. By Kenneth Garrett. Included: *Amerigo Vespucci, Christian Radich, Danmark, Dar Pomorza, Eagle, Esmeralda, Gazela Primeiro, Gloria, Gorch Fock, Juan Sebastián de Elcano, Kruzenshtern, Libertad, Mircea, Nippon Maru, Sagres II, Tovarishch.* 824-857, Dec. 1976
• *See also Eagle;* Midshipmen's Cruise; *and* Portsmouth; *and* listing under Merchant Marine Training Ships

TRAINS:
• The Coming Revolution in Transportation. By Fredric C. Appel. Photos by Dean Conger. Included: Air-cushion trains, High-speed trains, Pneumatic trains, "Unit trains". 301-341, Sept. 1969
• Freedom Train Tours America. 529-542, Oct. 1949
• The Friendly Train Called Skunk. By Dean Jennings. Photos by B. Anthony Stewart. 720-734, May 1959
◆ *Railroads: The Great American Adventure.* 1977. Announced. 860-864, June 1976
• Slow Train Through Viet Nam's War. By Howard Sochurek. 412-444, Sept. 1964
• *See also* Southern Railway System

TRANS-ANDEAN PIPELINE:
• Colombia, from Amazon to Spanish Main. By Loren McIntyre. 235-273, Aug. 1970

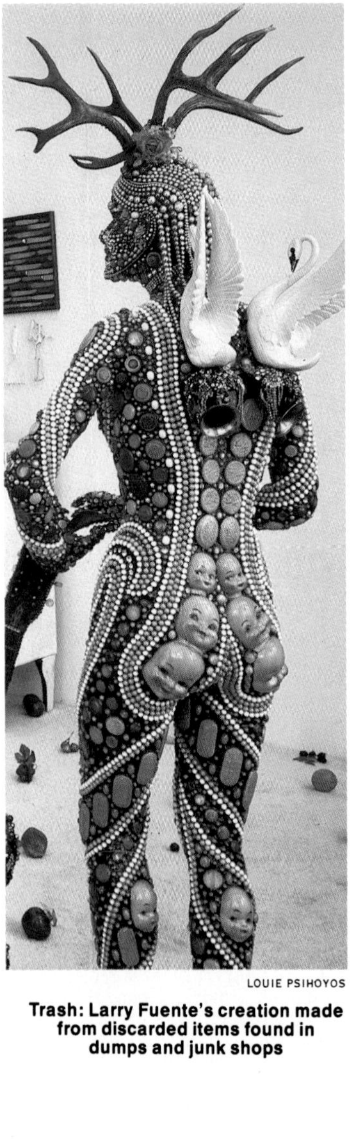

LOUIE PSIHOYOS

Trash: Larry Fuente's creation made from discarded items found in dumps and junk shops

TRANSATLANTIC BALLOON FLIGHT:
• *Double Eagle II* Has Landed! By Ben L. Abruzzo, with Maxie L. Anderson and Larry Newman. 858-882, Dec. 1978
• *See also Silver Fox,* for Ed Yost's attempt

TRANSCONTINENTAL BALLOON FLIGHT:
• *Kitty Hawk* Floats Across North America. By Maxie and Kristian Anderson. 260-271, Aug. 1980

TRANS-DARIÉN EXPEDITION:
• We Drove Panama's Darién Gap. By Kip Ross. 368-389, Mar. 1961

TRANSPORTATION:
• The Coming Revolution in Transportation. By Fredric C. Appel. Photos by Dean Conger. 301-341, Sept. 1969
• *See also* Automobiles; Aviation; Boats; Caravans; Ships; Space Flights and Research; Trains

TRANS-SAHARA SAND AND LAND YACHT RALLY:
• Dry-land Fleet Sails the Sahara. By Jean du Boucher. Photos by Jonathan S. Blair. 696-725, Nov. 1967
■ Wind Raiders of the Sahara. 436A-436B, Sept. 1973

TRASH:
• The Fascinating World of Trash. By Peter T. White. Photos by Louie Psihoyos. 424-457, Apr. 1983

TRASH DISPOSAL:
• The Fascinating World of Trash. By Peter T. White. Photos by Louie Psihoyos. 424-457, Apr. 1983

The **TRAVAIL** of Ireland. By Joseph Judge. Photos by Cotton Coulson. 432-441, Apr. 1981

A **TRAVELER'S** Tale of Ancient Tikal. Paintings by Peter Spier. Text by Alice J. Hall. 799-811, Dec. 1975

TRAVELS With a Donkey–100 Years Later. By Carolyn Bennett Patterson. Photos by Cotton Coulson. 535-561, Oct. 1978

TRAWLERS. *See* Oyster Fleet; Shrimp Fishing

TRAWLING the China Seas. Photos by J. Charles Thompson. 381-395, Mar. 1950

TREASURE, Sunken:
• *Atocha,* Tragic Treasure Galleon of the Florida Keys. By Eugene Lyon. 787-809, June 1976
• Bermuda–Balmy, British, and Beautiful. By Peter Benchley. Photos by Emory Kristof. 93-121, July 1971
▲ *Colonization and Trade in the New World;* "History Salvaged From the Sea," supplement. Dec. 1977
• Drowned Galleons Yield Spanish Gold. By Kip Wagner. Photos by Otis Imboden. 1-37, Jan. 1965
• Glass Treasure From the Aegean. By George F. Bass. Photos by Jonathan Blair. NGS research grant. 768-793, June 1978
• Graveyard of the Quicksilver Galleons. By Mendel Peterson. Photos by Jonathan Blair. 850-876, Dec. 1979

● The Lost Fleet of Kublai Khan. By Torao Mozai. Photos by Koji Nakamura. Paintings by Issho Yada. 634-649, Nov. 1982
● Priceless Relics of the Spanish Armada. By Robert Sténuit. Photos by Bates Littlehales. 745-777, June 1969
● Reach for the New World. By Mendel Peterson. Photos by David L. Arnold. Paintings by Richard Schlecht. 724-767, Dec. 1977
● The Sunken Treasure of St. Helena. By Robert Sténuit. Photos by Bates Littlehales. Included: Porcelain of the Ming Dynasty. 562-576, Oct. 1978
■ Treasure! 575, Nov. 1976; cover, Dec. 1976
● Treasure From the Ghost Galleon: *Santa Margarita*. By Eugene Lyon. Photos by Don Kincaid. 228-243, Feb. 1982
● The Treasure of Porto Santo. By Robert Sténuit. Photos by author and William R. Curtsinger. 260-275, Aug. 1975
◆ *Treasures in the Sea.* Announced. 736-738, Nov. 1972
◆ *Undersea Treasures.* Announced. 870-874, June 1974
● Yellow Sea Yields Shipwreck Trove. Photos by H. Edward Kim. Introduction by Donald H. Keith. Included: Earthenware, porcelain, and stoneware. 231-243, Aug. 1979

TREASURE Chest or Pandora's Box? Brazil's Wild Frontier. By Loren McIntyre. 684-719, Nov. 1977

TREASURE From a Celtic Tomb. By Jörg Biel. Photos by Volkmar Wentzel. 428-438, Mar. 1980

TREASURE From the Ghost Galleon: *Santa Margarita*. By Eugene Lyon. Photos by Don Kincaid. 228-243, Feb. 1982

TREASURES of Dresden. By John L. Eliot. Photos by Victor R. Boswell, Jr. 702-717, Nov. 1978

TREASURES of the Tsars. 24-33, Jan. 1978

TREE FROGS:
● Voices of the Night. By Arthur A. Allen. 507-522, Apr. 1950

TREE PLANTATIONS:
● Amazon–The River Sea. By Loren McIntyre. Included: Daniel K. Ludwig's planned paper pulp and food-production enterprise in Brazil's Amazon basin. 456-495, Oct. 1972
● Brazil's Wild Frontier. By Loren McIntyre. Included: Daniel K. Ludwig's three-million-acre agricultural and forestry experiment. 684-719, Nov. 1977
● Jari: A Billion-dollar Gamble. By Loren McIntyre. Contents: Daniel K. Ludwig's paper-pulp and food-production enterprise in Brazil's Amazon basin. 686-711, May 1980
● Tropical Rain Forests: Nature's Dwindling Treasures. By Peter T. White. Photos by James P. Blair. Paintings by Barron Storey. 2-47, Jan. 1983

TREE-RING DATING:
● Bristlecone Pine, Oldest Known Living Thing. By Edmund Schulman. Photos by W. Robert Moore. 355-372, Mar. 1958
● What's Happening to Our Climate? By Samuel W. Matthews. 576-615, Nov. 1976

TREE SHREWS:
● Seeking Mindanao's Strangest Creatures. By Charles Heizer Wharton. 389-408, Sept. 1948

TREE SNAILS, Gems of the Everglades. By Treat Davidson. 372-387, Mar. 1965

TREES:
● Beauty and Bounty of Southern State Trees. By William A. Dayton. Paintings by Walter A. Weber. Contents: Cottonwood, Eastern (Kansas); Dogwood (Missouri, Virginia); Live Oak (Georgia); Magnolia (Mississippi); Palmetto, Cabbage (Florida, South Carolina); Paloverde, Blue (Arizona); Pecan (Texas); Pine, Longleaf (Alabama); Pine, Shortleaf (Arkansas); Piñon (New Mexico); Piñon, Singleleaf (Nevada); Redbud, Eastern (Oklahoma); Redwood, Coast (California); Spruce, Blue (Colorado, Utah); Tulip (Indiana, Kentucky, Tennessee); White Oak (Connecticut, Maryland). 508-552, Oct. 1957
● Brazil's Wild Frontier. By Loren McIntyre. Included: Daniel K. Ludwig's three-million-acre agricultural and forestry experiment. 684-719, Nov. 1977
● Jari: A Billion-dollar Gamble. By Loren McIntyre. Contents: Daniel K. Ludwig's paper-pulp and food-production enterprise in Brazil's Amazon basin. 686-711, May 1980
● A Tree Is an Amazing Mechanism. 672-673, Nov. 1955
● Wealth and Wonder of Northern State Trees. By William A. Dayton. Paintings by Walter A. Weber. Contents: Birch (New Hampshire); Buckeye (Ohio); Douglas Fir (Oregon); Elm, American (Massachusetts, Nebraska, North Dakota); Hemlock, Eastern (Pennsylvania); Hemlock, Western (Washington); Holly (Delaware); Maple, Red (Rhode Island); Maple, Sugar (New York, Vermont, West Virginia, Wisconsin); Oak, Bur (Illinois); Oak, Northern Red (New Jersey); Pine, Ponderosa (Montana); Pine, Red (Minnesota); Pine, Western White (Idaho); Pine, White (Maine); Poplar, Balsam (Wyoming); Spruce (South Dakota). 651-691, Nov. 1955
● *See also* Apple Tree; Bristlecone Pine; *Metasequoia;* National Forests; Rain Forests; Red Mangroves; Redwoods; *Sequoia gigantea; and* Big Cypress Swamp; Sequoia National Park; *and* Forests and Reforestation

TREES, Oldest Known. *See* Bristlecone Pine

TREES, World's Tallest. *See* Redwoods

"TREETOPS" (Game-observation Lodge), Kenya:
● A New Look at Kenya's "Treetops." By Quentin Keynes. 536-541, Oct. 1956

TREK Across Arctic America. By Colin Irwin. 295-321, Mar. 1974

TREK by Mule Among Morocco's Berbers. By Victor Englebert. 850-875, June 1968

TREK to Lofty Hunza–and Beyond. By Sabrina and Roland Michaud. 644-669, Nov. 1975

TREK to Nepal's Sacred Crystal Mountain. By Joel F. Ziskin. 500-517, Apr. 1977

TREKKING:
● Park at the Top of the World: Mount Everest National Park. By Rick Ridgeway. Photos by Nicholas DeVore III. 704-725, June 1982
Preserving a Mountain Heritage. By Sir Edmund Hillary. 696-703
● Trekking Around the Continent's Highest Peak (Mount McKinley). By Ned Gillette. 66-79, July 1979

TRENCHES, Undersea. *See* Cayman Trough; Japan Trench; Mariana Trench; Romanche Trench

TRIBAL FAIRS. *See* Sing-Sing

TRIBESPEOPLE. *See* Ethnology

TRIESTE–Side Door to Europe. By Harnett T. Kane. 824-857, June 1956

TRIESTE (Bathyscaph):
● Down to *Thresher* by Bathyscaph. By Donald L. Keach. 764-777, June 1964
● Man's Deepest Dive. By Jacques Piccard. Photos by Thomas J. Abercrombie. 224-239, Aug. 1960

TRINIDAD, Cuba:
● Cuba–American Sugar Bowl. By Melville Bell Grosvenor. 1-56, Jan. 1947

TRINIDAD AND TOBAGO, West Indies:
● *Carib* Cruises the West Indies. By Carleton Mitchell. 1-56, Jan. 1948
● Carnival in Trinidad. By Howard La Fay. Photos by Winfield Parks. 693-701, Nov. 1971
● Feathered Dancers of Little Tobago. By E. Thomas Gilliard. Photos by Frederick Kent Truslow. NGS research grant. 428-440, Sept. 1958
● Happy-go-lucky Trinidad and Tobago. By Charles Allmon. 35-75, Jan. 1953
● The High World of the Rain Forest. By William Beebe. Paintings by Guy Neale. 838-855, June 1958
● "The Music of Trinidad." NGS recording announced. 701, Nov. 1971
● Sea Fever. By John E. Schultz. 237-268, Feb. 1949
● *See also* Caroni Swamp Sanctuary; Simla

TRIPPE, JUAN T.:
● National Geographic Society Honors Air Pioneer Juan Trippe. 584-586, Apr. 1968

TRISTAN DA CUNHA (Island), South Atlantic Ocean:
• Death of an Island, Tristan da Cunha. By P.J.F. Wheeler. 678-695, May 1962
• Home to Lonely Tristan da Cunha. By James P. Blair. 60-81, Jan. 1964
• New Life for the "Loneliest Isle." By Lewis Lewis. 105-116, Jan. 1950

TRITON Follows Magellan's Wake. By Edward L. Beach. Photos by J. Baylor Roberts. 585-615, Nov. 1960

TRIUMPH and Tragedy on Annapurna. By Arlene Blum. 295-311, Mar. 1979
On the Summit. By Irene Miller, with Vera Komarkova. 312-313

TRIUMPH of the First Crusade to the Holy Land. By Franc Shor. Photos by Thomas Nebbia. 797-855, Dec. 1963

TRIUMPH on Everest. By Sir John Hunt and Sir Edmund Hillary. 1-63, July 1954

TROPICAL Gardens of Key West. By Luis Marden. 116-124, Jan. 1953

TROPICAL Rain Forests: Nature's Dwindling Treasures. By Peter T. White. Photos by James P. Blair. Paintings by Barron Storey. 2-47, Jan. 1983

TROUBLE in Bayou Country: Louisiana's Atchafalaya. By Jack and Anne Rudloe. Photos by C. C. Lockwood. 377-397, Sept. 1979

The **TROUBLE** With Dolphins. By Edward J. Linehan. Photos by Bill Curtsinger. 506-541, Apr. 1979

The **TROUBLE** With Treasure *(Atocha)*. By Eugene Lyon. 787-809, June 1976

TROUBLED Capital of the Arab World: Cairo. By William S. Ellis. Photos by Winfield Parks. 639-667, May 1972

TROUBLED Odyssey of Vietnamese Fishermen. By Harvey Arden. Photos by Steve Wall. 378-395, Sept. 1981

TROUBLED Times for Central America. By Wilbur E. Garrett. 58-61, July 1981

TROUBLED Waters East of Suez. By Ernest M. Eller. 483-522, Apr. 1954

The **TROUBLED** Waters of Mono Lake. By Gordon Young. Photos by Craig Aurness. 504-519, Oct. 1981

TROUT:
• Freezing the Trout's Lightning Leap. By Treat Davidson. 525-530, Apr. 1958
• *See also* Golden Trout

TRUCIAL COAST:
• Desert Sheikdoms of Arabia's Pirate Coast. By Ronald Codrai. 65-104, July 1956
• Troubled Waters East of Suez. By Ernest M. Eller. 483-522, Apr. 1954
• *See also* United Arab Emirates

TRUCKS AND TRUCKING:
• North With the Wheat Cutters. By Noel Grove. Photos by James A. Sugar. 194-217, Aug. 1972
• Trucks Race the Clock From Coast to Coast. By James A. Sugar. 226-243, Feb. 1974

"TRUE PEOPLE" of the Jungle (Yanomamo). By Napoleon A. Chagnon. 211-223, Aug. 1976

TRUFFLES:
• The Diffident Truffle, France's Gift to Gourmets. 419-426, Sept. 1956

TRUK ISLANDS, Caroline Islands, Pacific Ocean:
• Micronesia: The Americanization of Eden. By David S. Boyer. 702-744, May 1967
• Pacific Wards of Uncle Sam. By W. Robert Moore. 73-104, July 1948
• *See also* Truk Lagoon

TRUK LAGOON, Truk Islands, Pacific Ocean:
• Life Springs From Death in Truk Lagoon. By Sylvia A. Earle. Photos by Al Giddings. 578-613, May 1976
From Graveyard to Garden. Included: Japanese ships sunk in two 1944 attacks by U. S. Navy carrier-launched planes. 604-613

TRUMAN, HARRY R.:
• Mount St. Helens Aftermath: The Mountain That Was–and Will Be. By Rowe Findley. Photos by Steve Raymer. 713-733, Dec. 1981
• Mountain With a Death Wish (Mount St. Helens). By Rowe Findley. Note: Harry R. Truman was a casualty of the eruption of Mount St. Helens. 3-33, Jan. 1981

TRUMAN, HARRY S.:
• Inside the White House. By Lonnelle Aikman. Photos by B. Anthony Stewart and Thomas Nebbia. 3-43, Jan. 1961
• The Living White House. By Lonnelle Aikman. 593-643, Nov. 1966
• Profiles of the Presidents: V. The Atomic Age: Its Problems and Promises. By Frank Freidel. 66-119, Jan. 1966

TRUMPETER SWANS:
• Return of the Trumpeter. By Frederick Kent Truslow. 134-150, July 1960

TRUSLOW, FREDERICK KENT:
Author-Photographer:
• Businessman in the Bush. 634-675, May 1970
• The Dauntless Little Stilt. 241-245, Aug. 1960
• Eye to Eye With Eagles. 123-148, Jan. 1961
• Limpkin, the "Crying Bird" That Haunts Florida Swamps. 114-121, Jan. 1958
• Return of the Trumpeter. 134-150, July 1960
• Threatened Glories of Everglades National Park. By Frederick Kent Truslow and Frederick G. Vosburgh. Photos by Frederick Kent Truslow and Otis Imboden. 508-553, Oct. 1967
• When Disaster Struck a Woodpecker's Home. 882-884, Dec. 1966
Photographer:
• Feathered Dancers of Little Tobago (Greater Birds of Paradise). By E. Thomas Gilliard. 428-440, Sept. 1958
• The Osprey, Endangered World Citizen. By Roger Tory Peterson. 53-67, July 1969
• Our Only Native Stork, the Wood Ibis. By Robert Porter Allen. 294-306, Feb. 1964
• Roseate Spoonbills, Radiant Birds of the Gulf Coast. By Robert Porter Allen. 274-288, Feb. 1962
• Whooping Cranes Fight for Survival. By Robert Porter Allen. 650-669, Nov. 1959

TRUST TERRITORY OF NEW GUINEA. *See* Australian New Guinea; New Britain

TRUST TERRITORY OF THE PACIFIC ISLANDS:
• Micronesia: The Americanization of Eden. By David S. Boyer. 702-744, May 1967
• Pacific Wards of Uncle Sam. By W. Robert Moore. 73-104, July 1948
• *See also* Ifalik; Kapingamarangi; Kwajalein; Truk Lagoon; Yap Islands

TRYCK, KEITH: Author:
• Rafting Down the Yukon. Photos by Robert Clark. 830-861, Dec. 1975

TSAVDAROGLOU, SPYROS:
Photographer:
• Drama of Death in a Minoan Temple. By Yannis Sakellarakis and Efi Sapouna-Sakellaraki. Photos by Otis Imboden and Spyros Tsavdaroglou. 205-222, Feb. 1981
• Regal Treasures From a Macedonian Tomb. By Manolis Andronicos. 55-77, July 1978

TSAVO NATIONAL PARK, Kenya:
• Africa's Elephants: Can They Survive? By Oria Douglas-Hamilton. Photos by Oria and Iain Douglas-Hamilton. 568-603, Nov. 1980
• Inside a Hornbill's Walled-up Nest. By Joan and Alan Root. 846-855, Dec. 1969
• *See also* Mzima Springs

TSCHOPIK, HARRY, Jr.:
Author-Photographer:
• At Home in the High Andes. 133-146, Jan. 1955

TSETSE FLY:
• Britain Tackles the East African Bush. By W. Robert Moore. 311-352, Mar. 1950
• Safari Through Changing Africa. By Elsie May Bell Grosvenor. Photos by Gilbert H. Grosvenor. 145-198, Aug. 1953

TSUNAMIS:
• Earthquake! By William P. E. Graves. 112-139, July 1964
• Hawaii, Island of Fire and Flowers. By Gordon Young. Photos by Robert W. Madden. 399-425, Mar. 1975
• Thera, Key to the Riddle of Minos. By Spyridon Marinatos. Photos by Otis Imboden. 702-726, May 1972

TUAMOTU ARCHIPELAGO, South Pacific Ocean:
● Twenty Fathoms Down for Mother-of-Pearl. By Winston Williams. Photos by Bates Littlehales. 512-529, Apr. 1962

TUAREG (Tribespeople):
● Drought Threatens the Tuareg World. By Victor Englebert. 544-571, Apr. 1974
● I Joined a Sahara Salt Caravan. By Victor Englebert. 694-711, Nov. 1965
● The Inadan: Artisans of the Sahara. By Michael and Aubine Kirtley. Contents: A study of the symbiotic relationship between Tuareg nobles and artisans. 282-298, Aug. 1979
● The Niger: River of Sorrow, River of Hope. By Georg Gerster. 152-189, Aug. 1975
● Oursi, Magnet in the Desert. By Carole E. Devillers. 512-525, Apr. 1980
● Sand in My Eyes. By Jinx Rodger. 664-705, May 1958

TUCK, JOHN, Jr.:
● Man's First Winter at the South Pole. By Paul A. Siple. 439-478, Apr. 1958
● We Are Living at the South Pole. By Paul A. Siple. Photos by David S. Boyer. 5-35, July 1957

TUCSON, Arizona:
● Arizona's Suburbs of the Sun. By David Jeffery. Photos by H. Edward Kim. 486-517, Oct. 1977
● From Tucson to Tombstone. By Mason Sutherland. 343-384, Sept. 1953
● *See also* Desert Museum

TUKUNA INDIANS:
● Tukuna Maidens Come of Age. By Harald Schultz. 629-649, Nov. 1959

TULANE UNIVERSITY:
● Delta Regional Primate Research Center. *See* Snowflake (White Gorilla)
● Expedition. *See* Dzibilchaltun, Yucatán, Mexico

TULIPS: Holland's Beautiful Business. By Elizabeth A. Moize. Photos by Farrell Grehan. 712-728, May 1978

TULSA, Oklahoma:
● High-Flying Tulsa. By Robert Paul Jordan. Photos by Annie Griffiths. 378-403, Sept. 1983
● Oklahoma, the Adventurous One. By Robert Paul Jordan. Photos by Robert W. Madden. 149-189, Aug. 1971

TUNA:
● Golden Beaches of Portugal. By Alan Villiers. 673-696, Nov. 1954
● Quicksilver and Slow Death. By John J. Putman. Photos by Robert W. Madden. Included: Mercury found in tuna. 507-527, Oct. 1972
● The *Yankee*'s Wander-world. By Irving and Electa Johnson. Included: Portuguese fishermen, out from San Diego, tuna fishing in Tagus Cove, Galapagos Islands. 1-50, Jan. 1949
● *See also* Bluefin Tuna

TUNDRA: North America:
● Beyond the North Wind With the Snow Goose. By Des and Jen Bartlett. 822-843, Dec. 1973
. . . And Then There Was Fred. . . . 843-847
● Caribou: Hardy Nomads of the North. By Jim Rearden. 858-878, Dec. 1974
● North to the Tundra. 293-337, Mar. 1972
I. Re-creating a Vanished World. By Russell D. Guthrie. 294-301; "Ice Age Mammals of the Alaskan Tundra." Painting supplement by Jay H. Matternes; II. Portrait of a Fierce and Fragile Land. By Paul A. Zahl. 303-314; III. Plants of the Alaskan Tundra. 315-321; IV. Birds of the Alaskan Tundra. 322-327; V. Mammals of the Alaskan Tundra. 329-337
● Our Wildest Wilderness: Alaska's Arctic National Wildlife Range. By Douglas H. Chadwick. Photos by Lowell Georgia. 737-769, Dec. 1979
● The Pipeline: Alaska's Troubled Colossus. By Bryan Hodgson. Photos by Steve Raymer. 684-717, Nov. 1976
● Will Oil and Tundra Mix? Alaska's North Slope Hangs in the Balance. By William S. Ellis. Photos by Emory Kristof. 485-517, Oct. 1971

TUNDRA SWAN. *See* Whistling Swan

TUNHWANG, Kansu, China:
● The Caves of the Thousand Buddhas. By Franc and Jean Shor. 383-415, Mar. 1951

TUNISIA:
● Tunisia: Sea, Sand, Success. By Mike Edwards. Photos by David Alan Harvey. 184-217, Feb. 1980
● When the President Goes Abroad (Eisenhower). By Gilbert M. Grosvenor. 588-649, May 1960

TUNNELS:
● The Alps: Man's Own Mountains. By Ralph Gray. Photos by Walter Meayers Edwards and William Eppridge. Included: Mont Blanc Tunnel. 350-395, Sept. 1965
● Inside Europe Aboard *Yankee*. By Irving and Electa Johnson. Photos by Joseph J. Scherschel. 157-195, Aug. 1964
● *See also* Chesapeake Bay Bridge-Tunnel; Kitimat

TURKEY:
● Ambassadors of Good Will: The Peace Corps. By Sargent Shriver and Peace Corps Volunteers. 297-345, Sept. 1964
Turkey. By Nan and James W. Borton. 331-333
● "Around the World in Eighty Days." By Newman Bumstead. Included: Anatolia, Ankara, The Bosporus, Istanbul, Konya, Rumeli Hissar, Sea of Marmara. 705-750, Dec. 1951
● The Byzantine Empire: Rome of the East. By Merle Severy. Photos by James L. Stanfield. 709-767, Dec. 1983

LOWELL GEORGIA

Our Wildest Wilderness: snow geese

S T

• Greece: "To Be Indomitable, To Be Joyous." By Peter T. White. Photos by James P. Blair. Included: A history of the continuing conflicts between Greece and Turkey. 360-393, Mar. 1980
• In the Footsteps of Alexander the Great. By Helen and Frank Schreider. Paintings by Tom Lovell. 1-65, Jan. 1968
• Jerusalem to Rome in the Path of St. Paul. By David S. Boyer. 707-759, Dec. 1956
• Oldest Known Shipwreck Yields Bronze Age Cargo. By Peter Throckmorton. NGS research grant. 697-711, May 1962
• The Proud Armenians. By Robert Paul Jordan. Photos by Harry N. Naltchayan. 846-873, June 1978
• Round the World School. By Paul Antze. Photos by William Eppridge. 96-127, July 1962
• Station Wagon Odyssey: Baghdad to Istanbul. By William O. Douglas. 48-87, Jan. 1959
• Throne Above the Euphrates. By Theresa Goell. 390-405, Mar. 1961
• Turkey: Cross Fire at an Ancient Crossroads. By Robert Paul Jordan. Photos by Gordon W. Gahan. 88-123, July 1977
• Turkey Paves the Path of Progress. By Maynard Owen Williams. 141-186, Aug. 1951
• When the President Goes Abroad (Eisenhower). By Gilbert M. Grosvenor. 588-649, May 1960
• Where Turk and Russian Meet. By Ferdinand Kuhn. 743-766, June 1952
• YWCA: International Success Story. By Mary French Rockefeller. Photos by Otis Imboden. 904-933, Dec. 1963
• *Yankee* Cruises Turkey's History-haunted Coast. By Irving and Electa Johnson. Photos by Joseph J. Scherschel. 798-845, Dec. 1969
• *See also* Anatolia; Aphrodisias; Cappadocia; Istanbul; Serçe Limanı; Yassi Ada

TURKEYS, Wild:
• The Wichitas: Land of the Living Prairie. By M. Woodbridge Williams. 661-697, May 1957

TURKOMANS:
• Bold Horsemen of the Steppes. By Sabrina and Roland Michaud. 634-669, Nov. 1973

TURKS:
• Cyprus Under Four Flags: A Struggle for Unity. By Kenneth MacLeish. Photos by Jonathan Blair. 356-383, Mar. 1973
• The Isles of Greece: Aegean Birthplace of Western Culture. By Melville Bell Grosvenor. Photos by Edwin Stuart Grosvenor and Winfield Parks. 147-193, Aug. 1972

TURKU ARCHIPELAGO, Finland:
• Scenes of Postwar Finland. By La Verne Bradley. Photos by Jerry Waller. 233-264, Aug. 1947

TURNAROUND Time in West Virginia. By Elizabeth A. Moize. Photos by Jodi Cobb. 755-785, June 1976

BOTH BY F. L. KENETT, © GEORGE RAINBIRD LTD.

Tutankhamun's Golden Trove: statue of king with the mace of rule and rod of majesty, *top;* decoration from throne, *above*

TURPAN DEPRESSION (Region), China:
• Journey to China's Far West. By Rick Gore. Photos by Bruce Dale. 292-331, Mar. 1980

TURTLE BOGUE. *See* Tortuguero Beach, Costa Rica

TURTLES:
• Imperiled Gift of the Sea: Caribbean Green Turtle. By Archie Carr. Photos by Robert E. Schroeder. 876-890, June 1967
• In the Wilds of a City Parlor. By Paul A. Zahl. 645-672, Nov. 1954
• Nature's Tank, the Turtle. By Doris M. Cochran. Paintings by Walter A. Weber. 665-684, May 1952
• One Strange Night on Turtle Beach. By Paul A. Zahl. 570-581, Oct. 1973
• *See also* Green Turtles; Sea Turtles; Tortoises

TUSCANY (Region), Italy:
• Carrara Marble: Touchstone of Eternity. By Cathy Newman. Photos by Pierre Boulat. 42-59, July 1982
• Leonardo da Vinci: A Man for All Ages. By Kenneth MacLeish. Photos by James L. Amos. 296-329, Sept. 1977
• The Renaissance Lives On in Tuscany. By Luis Marden. Photos by Albert Moldvay. 626-659, Nov. 1974
• *See also* Florence; Siena

TUSHINGHAM, A. DOUGLAS: Author:
• Jericho Gives Up Its Secrets. By Kathleen M. Kenyon and A. Douglas Tushingham. Photos by Nancy Lord. 853-870, Dec. 1953
• The Men Who Hid the Dead Sea Scrolls. Paintings by Peter V. Bianchi. 785-808, Dec. 1958

TUTANKHAMUN:
◆ *Ancient Egypt.* 1978
• Dazzling Legacy of an Ancient Quest. By Alice J. Hall. 293-311, Mar. 1977
• Golden Masterpieces. 36-39, Jan. 1974
• Tutankhamun's Golden Trove. By Christiane Desroches Noblecourt. Photos by F. L. Kenett. 625-646, Oct. 1963

TUTTLE, MERLIN D.:
Author-Photographer:
• The Amazing Frog-Eating Bat. 78-91, Jan. 1982

TUVALU. *See* former name, Ellice Islands

TWAIN, MARK:
• Editorials. By Gilbert M. Grosvenor. 299, Sept. 1975; 577, May 1976
• Mark Twain: Mirror of America. By Noel Grove. Photos by James L. Stanfield. 300-337, Sept. 1975
• Tom Sawyer's Town. By Jerry Allen. 121-140, July 1956
• The West Through Boston Eyes. By Stewart Anderson. Included: Today in Mark Twain's Home Town; Exploring Tom Sawyer's Cave. 733-776, June 1949

TWEED:
• From Barra to Butt in the Hebrides. By Isobel Wylie Hutchison. 559-580, Oct. 1954
• Over the Sea to Scotland's Skye. By Robert J. Reynolds. 87-112, July 1952

TWEEDIE, PENNY: Photographer:
• Arnhem Land Aboriginals Cling to Dreamtime. By Clive Scollay. 644-663, Nov. 1980
• Coober Pedy: Opal Capital of Australia's Outback. By Kenny Moore. 560-571, Oct. 1976

TWELVE National Geographic Society Scientific Projects Under Way. 869-870, June 1954

TWENTIETH Anniversary of the Epoch-making Stratosphere Flight by *Explorer II*. NGS research grant. 707, Nov. 1955

20TH-CENTURY Indians Preserve Customs of the Cliff Dwellers. Photos by William Belknap, Jr. NGS research grant. 196-211, Feb. 1964

TWENTY Fathoms Down for Mother-of-Pearl. By Winston Williams. Photos by Bates Littlehales. 512-529, Apr. 1962

TWILIGHT Hope for Big Cypress. By Rick Gore. Photos by Patricia Caulfield. 251-273, Aug. 1976

TWILIGHT of the Arab Dhow. By Marion Kaplan. 330-351, Sept. 1974

TWIN CITIES, Minnesota:
• Minneapolis and St. Paul. By Thomas J. Abercrombie. Photos by Annie Griffiths. 665-691, Nov. 1980

2, 4, 5-T (Herbicide):
• The Pesticide Dilemma. By Allen A. Boraiko. Photos by Fred Ward. 145-183, Feb. 1980

The **TWO** Acapulcos. By James Cerruti. Photos by Thomas Nebbia. 848-878, Dec. 1964

TWO American Teachers in China. By Elisabeth B. Booz. Photos by Thomas Nebbia. 793-813, June 1981

TWO and a Half Miles Down. By Georges S. Houot. NGS research grant. 80-86, July 1954

TWO Berlins–A Generation Apart. By Priit J. Vesilind. Photos by Cotton Coulson. 2-51, Jan. 1982

TWO Englands. By Allan C. Fisher, Jr. Photos by Cary Wolinsky. 442-481, Oct. 1979

The **TWO** Souls of Peru. By Harvey Arden. Photos by William Albert Allard. 284-321, Mar. 1982

2,000 Miles Through Europe's Oldest Kingdom. By Isobel Wylie Hutchison. Photos by Maynard Owen Williams. 141-180, Feb. 1949

2,300-YEAR-OLD Greek Ship Reaches Port at Last. By Susan W. and Michael L. Katzev. NGS research grant. 618-625, Nov. 1974

TWO Wheels Along the Mexican Border. By William Albert Allard. 591-635, May 1971

The **TWO** Worlds of Michigan. By Noel Grove. Photos by James L. Amos. 802-843, June 1979

TXUKAHAMEIS (Indians):
• Amazon–The River Sea. By Loren McIntyre. 456-495, Oct. 1972
• Brazil's Txukahameis: Good-bye to the Stone Age. Photos by W. Jesco von Puttkamer. 270-283, Feb. 1975

TYLER, JOHN:
• Profiles of the Presidents: II. A Restless Nation Moves West. By Frank Freidel. 80-121, Jan. 1965

TYPHOONS:
• The Lost Fleet of Kublai Khan. By Torao Mozai. Photos by Koji Nakamura. Paintings by Issho Yada. 634-649, Nov. 1982

TYREE, DAVID M.: Author:
• New Era in the Loneliest Continent (Antarctica). Photos by Albert Moldvay. 260-296, Feb. 1963

TYROL (Region), Austria-Italy:
• Occupied Austria, Outpost of Democracy. By George W. Long. Photos by Volkmar Wentzel. 749-790, June 1951
• A Stroll to Venice. By Isobel Wylie Hutchison. 378-410, Sept. 1951
• Tirol, Austria's Province in the Clouds. By Peter T. White. Photos by Volkmar Wentzel. 107-141, July 1961

TYRRELL, ROBERT A.: Photographer:
• Hummingbirds: The Nectar Connection. By Paul W. Ewald. 223-227, Feb. 1982

TYRRHENIAN SEA:
• Fishing in the Whirlpool of Charybdis. By Paul A. Zahl. 579-618, Nov. 1953

TYUMEN OBLAST (Region), U.S.S.R.:
• Siberia's Empire Road, the River Ob. By Robert Paul Jordan. Photos by Dean Conger. 145-181, Feb. 1976

U

U.S.S.R. *See* Union of Soviet Socialist Republics

UAUPÉS (River), South America. *See* Vaupés River

UBAIGUBI, Papua New Guinea:
• Fertility Rites and Sorcery in a New Guinea Village. By Gillian Gillison. Photos by David Gillison. 124-146, July 1977

"UBANGI" (Tribespeople). *See* Sara

UBO TRIBE:
• Help for Philippine Tribes in Trouble. By Kenneth MacLeish. Photos by Dean Conger. 220-255, Aug. 1971
■ The Last Tribes of Mindanao. 882A-882B, Dec. 1971

UDORN ROYAL THAI AIR FORCE BASE, Thailand:
• Air Rescue Behind Enemy Lines. By Howard Sochurek. 346-369, Sept. 1968

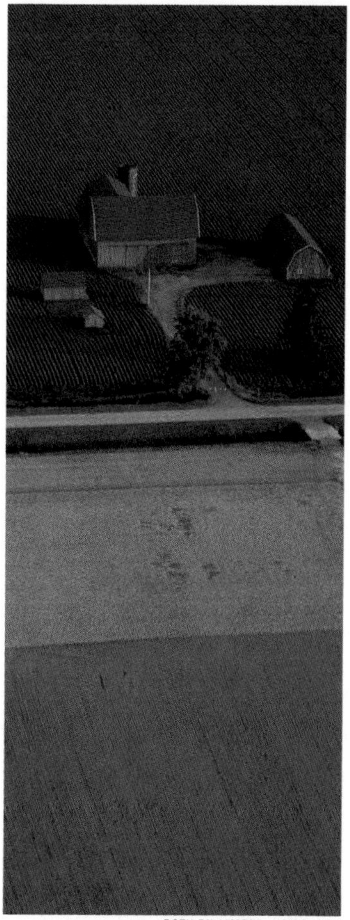

BOTH BY JAMES L. AMOS, NGS

Two Worlds: Michigan farm, *above*; World War I veterans, *below*

U V

ROBERT S. OAKES, NGS

Ukrainians: Easter-egg keepsakes

UEMURA, NAOMI:
Author-Photographer:
• Solo to the Pole. Photos by the author and Ira Block. 298-325, Sept. 1978

UGANDA:
• Britain Tackles the East African Bush. By W. Robert Moore. 311-352, Mar. 1950
• Kayaks Down the Nile. By John M. Goddard. 697-732, May 1955
• Orphans of the Wild. By Bruce G. Kinloch. 683-699, Nov. 1962
• Return to Uganda. By Jerry and Sarah Kambites. Photos by Sarah Leen. 73-89, July 1980
• Roaming Africa's Unfenced Zoos. By W. Robert Moore. 353-380, Mar. 1950
• Safari from Congo to Cairo. By Elsie May Bell Grosvenor. Photos by Gilbert Grosvenor. 721-771, Dec. 1954
• Uganda, Africa's Uneasy Heartland. By Howard La Fay. Photos by George F. Mobley. 708-735, Nov. 1971
• Where Elephants Have Right of Way. By George and Jinx Rodger. Photos by George Rodger. 363-389, Sept. 1960
• *See also* Ruwenzori; Virunga Mountains

UIGHURS (People). *See* Uygurs

UIST, North, and South Uist (Islands), Scotland:
• Isles on the Edge of the Sea: Scotland's Outer Hebrides. By Kenneth MacLeish. Photos by Thomas Nebbia. 676-711, May 1970

UKRAINIAN S.S.R., U.S.S.R. *See* Crimean Peninsula

UKRAINIANS: United States and Canada:
• Easter Greetings From the Ukrainians. By Robert Paul Jordan. Photos by James A. Sugar. 556-563, Apr. 1972

ULITHI (Atoll), Caroline Islands:
• Adventures with the Survey Navy. By Irving Johnson. 131-148, July 1947

ULSTER. *See* Ireland, Northern

The **ULTIMATE** Challenge (K2 expedition). By James Whittaker. 624-639, May 1979

ULTRALIGHT AIRCRAFT:
• The Bird Men. By Luis Marden. Photos by Charles O'Rear. 198-217, Aug. 1983
• *See also* Hang Gliders

ULYSSES. *See Odyssey*

UMIAKS:
• Arctic Odyssey. By John Bockstoce. Photos by Jonathan Wright. Paintings by Jack Unruh. Contents: Umiak expedition tracing Thule Eskimo migration route from Alaska to Greenland. 100-127, July 1983

UMINGMAKTOK SETTLEMENT, Northwest Territories, Canada:
• Still Eskimo, Still Free: The Inuit of Umingmaktok. By Yva Momatiuk and John Eastcott. 624-647, Nov. 1977

UMNAK (Island), Alaska:
• The Aleutians: Alaska's Far-out Islands. By Lael Morgan. Photos by Steven C. Wilson. 336-363, Sept. 1983

UNALASKA (Island), Alaska:
• The Aleutians: Alaska's Far-out Islands. By Lael Morgan. Photos by Steven C. Wilson. 336-363, Sept. 1983

The **UNBALANCED** World. By National Geographic Society President Gilbert M. Grosvenor. 1, *Special Report on Energy* (Feb. 1981)

The **UNCERTAIN** State of Puerto Rico. By Bill Richards. Photos by Stephanie Maze. 516-543, Apr. 1983

UNCLE Sam Bends a Twig in Germany. By Frederick Simpich. Photos by J. Baylor Roberts. 529-550, Oct. 1948

UNCLE Sam's House of 1,000 Wonders. By Lyman J. Briggs and F. Barrows Colton. 755-784, Dec. 1951

UNCLE Sam's Museum with Wings (National Air and Space Museum). By Michael Collins. 819-837, June 1978

UNDER Canvas in the Atomic Age. By Alan Villiers. 49-84, July 1955

UNDER the Dome of Freedom: The United States Capitol. By Lonnelle Aikman. Photos by George F. Mobley. 4-59, Jan. 1964

UNDERSEA Wonders of the Galapagos. By Gerard Wellington. Photos by David Doubilet. 363-381, Sept. 1978

UNDERSEA World of a Kelp Forest. By Sylvia A. Earle. Photos by Al Giddings. 411-426, Sept. 1980

UNDERWATER Archeology: Key to History's Warehouse. By George F. Bass. Photos by Thomas J. Abercrombie and Robert B. Goodman. NGS research grant. 138-156, July 1963
• *See also* Archaeology, Underwater

UNDERWATER DEMOLITION TEAMS:
• Goggle Fishing in California Waters. By David Hellyer. Photos by Lamar Boren. 615-632, May 1949
• New Life for the Troubled Suez Canal. By William Graves. Photos by Jonathan Blair. 792-817, June 1975

UNDERWATER EXPLORATION:
• The Continental Shelf: Man's New Frontier. By Luis Marden. Photos by Ira Block. 495-531, Apr. 1978
• Deep Diving off Japan. By Georges S. Houot. NGS research grant. 138-150, Jan. 1960
▪ Dive to the Edge of Creation: Galapagos Rift expedition. 682, Nov. 1979; 1, Cover, Jan. 1980
• Diving Into the Blue Holes of the Bahamas. By George J. Benjamin. 347-363, Sept. 1970

• Exploring Davy Jones's Locker with *Calypso*. By Jacques-Yves Cousteau. Photos by Luis Marden. NGS research grant. 149-161, Feb. 1956
◆ *Exploring the Deep Frontier.* 1980
• Four Years of Diving to the Bottom of the Sea. By Georges S. Houot. NGS research grant. 715-731, May 1958
• Incredible World of the Deep-sea Rifts. NGS research grant. 680-705, Nov. 1979
I. Strange World Without Sun. The Editor. 680-688; II. Return to Oases of the Deep. By Robert D. Ballard and J. Frederick Grassle. 689-705
• Inflatable Ship Opens New Era of Airborne Undersea Expeditions. By Jacques-Yves Cousteau. NGS research grant. 142-148, July 1961
◆ *The Mysterious Undersea World.* 1980
• Oases of Life in the Cold Abyss (Galapagos Rift). By John B. Corliss and Robert D. Ballard. 441-453, Oct. 1977
◆ *The Ocean Realm.* 1978
• Our Man-in-Sea Project. By Edwin A. Link. NGS research grant. 713-717, May 1963
• Project FAMOUS. Photos by Emory Kristof. 586-615, May 1975
I. Where the Earth Turns Inside Out. By J. R. Heirtzler. 586-603; II. Dive Into the Great Rift. By Robert D. Ballard. 604-615
• Tomorrow on the Deep Frontier. By Edwin A. Link. NGS research grant. 778-801, June 1964
• Unexpected Glory in Canada's Cold Seas. Photos by David Doubilet. Text by Larry Kohl. 526-551, Apr. 1980
• A Walk in the Deep. By Sylvia A. Earle. Photos by Al Giddings and Chuck Nicklin. Included: First open-ocean use of diving suit "Jim" for scientific research; deepest exploration of its kind. 624-631, May 1980
• Window on Earth's Interior. By Robert D. Ballard. Photos by Emory Kristof. Contents: Cayman Trough. 228-249, Aug. 1976
• *See also* Archaeology, Underwater; Divers and Diving; Submersibles; Treasure, Sunken

UNDERWATER LIVING:
• The Deepest Days. By Robert Sténuit. NGS research grant. 534-547, Apr. 1965
• Diving Beneath Arctic Ice. By Joseph B. MacInnis. Photos by William R. Curtsinger. 248-267, Aug. 1973
• Outpost Under the Ocean. By Edwin A. Link. Photos by Bates Littlehales. NGS research grant. 530-533, Apr. 1965
• Tomorrow on the Deep Frontier. By Edwin A. Link. NGS research grant. 778-801, June 1964
• Working for Weeks on the Sea Floor. By Jacques-Yves Cousteau. Photos by Philippe Cousteau and Bates Littlehales. NGS research grant. 498-537, Apr. 1966
• *See also* Conshelf Bases; Tektite II

UNDERWATER PARKS. *See* Buck Island Reef National Monument; Great Barrier Reef, Australia; John Pennekamp Coral Reef State Park; Ras Muhammad

UNEARTHING the Oldest Known Maya. By Norman Hammond. Photos by Lowell Georgia and Martha Cooper. NGS research grant. 126-140, July 1982

UNEXPECTED Glory in Canada's Cold Seas. Photos by David Doubilet. Text by Larry Kohl. 526-551, Apr. 1980

UNFAMILIAR Glories of the West. 733-791, June 1974

UNGAVA (Region), Quebec, Canada. *See* Chubb Crater

UNION OF SOUTH AFRICA. *See* South Africa, Republic of

UNION OF SOVIET SOCIALIST REPUBLICS:
• An American in Russia's Capital. By Thomas T. Hammond. Photos by Dean Conger. 297-351, Mar. 1966
• Down on the Farm, Soviet Style–a 4-H Adventure. By John Garaventa. Photos by James Tobin and Carol Schmidt. 768-797, June 1979
• Down the Danube by Canoe. By William Slade Backer. Photos by Richard S. Durrance and Christopher G. Knight. 34-79, July 1965
▲ *Eastern Soviet Union,* Atlas series supplement. Mar. 1967
• Editorials. By Gilbert M. Grosvenor. 143, Feb. 1976; 733, June 1979
• Firsthand Look at the Soviet Union. By Thomas T. Hammond. Photos by Erich Lessing. 352-407, Sept. 1959
• Five Times to Yakutsk. By Dean Conger. 256-269, Aug. 1977
◆ *Journey Across Russia: The Soviet Union Today.* 1977
• Leningrad, Russia's Window on the West. By Howard La Fay. Photos by Dick Durrance II. 636-673, May 1971
• Moscow: The City Around Red Square. By John J. Putman. Photos by Gordon W. Gahan. 2-45, Jan. 1978
• People of the Long Spring. By Yuri Rytkheu. Photos by Dean Conger. Contents: Soviet Arctic Regions. 206-223, Feb. 1983
▲ *Peoples of the Arctic; Arctic Ocean,* double-sided supplement. Feb. 1983
• The Proud Armenians. By Robert Paul Jordan. Photos by Harry N. Naltchayan. 846-873, June 1978
• Questing for Gems. By George S. Switzer. Included: The Kremlin's Hall of Facets. 835-863, Dec. 1971
• Russia as I Saw It. By Richard M. Nixon. Photos by B. Anthony Stewart. 715-750, Dec. 1959
• The Society Reports to Its Members on Russia Today. The Editor. 351, Sept. 1959
▲ *Soviet Union; Peoples of the Soviet Union,* double-sided supplement. Feb. 1976

DEAN CONGER, NGS

People of the Long Spring: arctic camp

▲ *Union of Soviet Socialist Republics.* Announced. 887, Dec. 1960
■ The Volga. 575, Nov. 1976; cover, Mar. 1977
● The Volga, Russia's Mighty River Road. By Howard Sochurek. 579-613, May 1973
▲ *Western Soviet Union,* Atlas series supplement. Sept. 1959
● Where Turk and Russian Meet. By Ferdinand Kuhn. 743-766, June 1952
● *See also* Abkhazian A.S.S.R.; Estonian S.S.R.; Siberia; *and* Soyuz-Apollo Mission

UNITED ARAB EMIRATES:
● The Arab World, Inc. By John J. Putman. Photos by Winfield Parks. 494-533, Oct. 1975
▲ *The Peoples of the Middle East,* supplement. Text on reverse. July 1972
● *See also* former designation, Trucial Coast

UNITED ARAB REPUBLIC:
▲ *Africa: Countries of the Nile,* Atlas series supplement. Oct. 1963
● *See also* Egypt; *and* Syria, a former member

UNITED Italy Marks Its 100th Year. By Nathaniel T. Kenney. 593-647, Nov. 1961

UNITED KINGDOM OF GREAT BRITAIN AND NORTHERN IRELAND. *See* England; Ireland, Northern; Scotland; Wales

UNITED NATIONS:
● Date Line: United Nations, New York. By Carolyn Bennett Patterson. Photos by B. Anthony Stewart and John E. Fletcner. 305-331, Sept. 1961
● Flags of the United Nations (60 Member States). By Elizabeth W. King. 213-238, Feb. 1951
● Flags of the United Nations (99 Member States). 332-345, Sept. 1961
● The United Nations: Capital of the Family of Man. By Adlai E. Stevenson. Photos by B. Anthony Stewart and John E. Fletcher. 297-303, Sept. 1961

UNITED NATIONS: World Health Organization (WHO):
● Malaria Eradication Campaign. 436, Sept. 1979
● Plague-control effort. 86, July 1977
● Smallpox–Epitaph for a Killer? By Donald A. Henderson. Photos by Marion Kaplan. 796-805, Dec. 1978

UNITED NATIONS EDUCATIONAL, SCIENTIFIC AND CULTURAL ORGANIZATION (UNESCO): Preservation effort. *See* Abu Simbel

UNITED NATIONS FOOD AND AGRICULTURE ORGANIZATION (FAO):
● Can the World Feed Its People? By Thomas Y. Canby. Photos by Steve Raymer. Included: World Food Conference in Rome (1974). 2-31, July 1975
● Locusts: "Teeth of the Wind." By Robert A. M. Conley. Photos by Gianni Tortoli. 202-227, Aug. 1969

UNITED NATIONS TRUST TERRITORY, Pacific Ocean. *See* Palau Islands

UNITED STATES:
● America Goes to the Fair. By Samuel W. Matthews. 293-333, Sept. 1954
◆ *The American Cowboy in Life and Legend.* 1972. Announced. 882-886, June 1971
◆ *American Mountain People.* Announced. 865-868, June 1973
● The American Red Cross: A Century of Service. By Louise Levathes. Photos by Annie Griffiths. 777-791, June 1981
● American Wild Flower Odyssey. By P. L. Ricker. 603-634, May 1953
▲ *America's Federal Lands; The United States,* double-sided supplement. Sept. 1982
◆ *America's Hidden Corners.* 1983
◆ *America's Inland Waterway.* Announced. 865-868, June 1973
● America's "Meat on the Hoof." By William H. Nicholas. 33-72, Jan. 1952
◆ *America's Wild and Scenic Rivers.* 1983
◆ *The Appalachian Trail.* Announced. 870-874, June 1972
◆ *As We Live and Breathe: The Challenge of Our Environment.* Announced. 882-886, June 1971
▲ *Atlantic Gateways,* The Making of America series. Included: Delaware, Maryland, New Jersey, New York, Pennsylvania, northern Virginia, West Virginia, and in Canada, southern Ontario and southern Quebec. On reverse: Indians and Trade, Nation in the Making, Peopling of the Gateways, Race for the Hinterlands, Growth of Industry, Spreading Urban Corridors. Mar. 1983
● Atlas of the Fifty United States: Bringing America Into Your Home. By Melville Bell Grosvenor. 130-133, July 1960
● Avalanche! By David Cupp. 280-305, Sept. 1982
I. Winter's White Death. 280-281; II. "I'm OK, I'm Alive!" Photos by Lanny Johnson and Andre Benier. 282-289; III. Battling the Juggernaut. 290-305
◆ *Back Roads America.* 1980
● Census 1960: Profile of the Nation. By Albert W. Atwood and Lonnelle Aikman. 697-714, Nov. 1959
● Chattooga River Country: Wild Water, Proud People. By Don Belt. Photos by Steve Wall. 458-477, Apr. 1983
● The Chip: Electronic Mini-marvel. By Allen A. Boraiko. Photos by Charles O'Rear. 421-457, Oct. 1982
● Close-up: U.S.A.–a Fresh Look at Our Land and Its Heritage. By Gilbert M. Grosvenor. 287-289, Mar. 1973
▲ *Close-up: U.S.A., Alaska,* supplement. Text on reverse. June 1975
▲ *Close-up: U.S.A., California and Nevada,* supplement. Text on reverse. June 1974
▲ *Close-up: U.S.A., Florida, with Puerto Rico and U. S. Virgin Islands,* supplement. Text on reverse. Nov. 1973
▲ *Close-up: U.S.A., Hawaii,* supplement. Text on reverse. Apr. 1976
▲ *Close-up: U.S.A., Illinois, Indiana, Ohio, and Kentucky,* supplement. Text on reverse. Feb. 1977
▲ *Close-up: U.S.A., Maine, with the Maritime Provinces of Canada,* supplement. Text on reverse. Mar. 1975
▲ *Close-up: U.S.A., The Mid-Atlantic States,* supplement. Text on reverse. Included: Delaware, Maryland, Virginia, West Virginia. Oct. 1976
▲ *Close-up: U.S.A., The North Central States,* supplement. Text on reverse. Included: Iowa, Kansas, Minnesota, Missouri, Nebraska, North Dakota, South Dakota. Mar. 1974
▲ *Close-up: U.S.A., The Northeast,* supplement. Text on reverse. Included: New Jersey, New York, Pennsylvania. Jan. 1978
▲ *Close-up: U.S.A., The Northwest,* supplement. Text on reverse. Included: Idaho, Montana, Oregon, Washington, Wyoming. Mar. 1973
▲ *Close-up: U.S.A., The South Central States,* supplement. Text on reverse. Included: Arkansas, Louisiana, Oklahoma, Texas. Oct. 1974
▲ *Close-up: U.S.A., The Southeast,* supplement. Text on reverse. Included: Alabama, Georgia, Mississippi, North Carolina, South Carolina, Tennessee. Oct. 1975
▲ *Close-up: U.S.A., The Southwest,* supplement. Text on reverse. Included: Arizona, Colorado, New Mexico, Utah. Oct. 1977
▲ *Close-up: U.S.A., Western New England,* supplement. Text on reverse. Included: Connecticut, Massachusetts, New Hampshire, Rhode Island, Vermont. July 1975
▲ *Close-up: U.S.A., Wisconsin, Michigan, and the Great Lakes,* supplement. Text on reverse. Aug. 1973
● Coal vs. Parklands. By François Leydet. Photos by Dewitt Jones. 776-803, Dec. 1980
● The Continental Shelf: Man's New Frontier. By Luis Marden. Photos by Ira Block. 495-531, Apr. 1978
◆ *The Craftsman in America.* Announced. 870-874, June 1975
▲ *Deep South,* The Making of America series. Included: Alabama, Florida, Georgia, Louisiana, Mississippi, South Carolina, and parts of Arkansas, North Carolina, and Tennessee. On reverse: Indian Legacy, Imperial Footholds, Three Empires and Three Races, Cotton Kingdom, Postbellum, New Deep South, Subtropical Playground. Aug. 1983
● The Desert: An Age-old Challenge Grows. By Rick Gore. Photos by Georg Gerster and Bruce Dale. 586-639, Nov. 1979
● Editorial. By Gilbert M. Grosvenor. 1, July 1976
● Eight Maps of Discovery. 757-769, June 1953
● Exploring America Underground. By Charles E. Mohr. 803-837, June 1964

◆ *Exploring America's Backcountry.* 1979
● The Fascinating World of Trash. By Peter T. White. Photos by Louie Psihoyos. 424-457, Apr. 1983
● Flags of the Americas. By Elizabeth W. King. Included: The Flag of the United States, the President, the Vice President, Executive Agencies and Departments, and the United States Armed Forces. 633-657, May 1949
● Following the Trail of Lewis and Clark. By Ralph Gray. 707-750, June 1953
● 4-H Boys and Girls Grow More Food. By Frederick Simpich. 551-582, Nov. 1948
● Freedom Train Tours America. 529-542, Oct. 1949
● From Sea to Shining Sea. By Ralph Gray. Photos by Dean Conger and author. 1-61, July 1961
● From Sun-clad Sea to Shining Mountains (U. S. 89). By Ralph Gray. Photos by James P. Blair. 542-589, Apr. 1964
● Geothermal Energy: The Power of Letting Off Steam. By Kenneth F. Weaver. 566-579, Oct. 1977
● The Glittering World of Rockhounds. By David S. Boyer. 276-294, Feb. 1974
◆ *Great American Deserts.* Announced. 870-874, June 1972
● The Gulf's Workaday Waterway. By Gordon Young. Photos by Charles O'Rear. 200-223, Feb. 1978
● Herbs for All Seasons. By Lonnelle Aikman. Photos by Sam Abell. Picture portfolio text by Larry Kohl. 386-409, Mar. 1983
● How Fruit Came to America. By J. R. Magness. Paintings by Else Bostelmann. Included: American Plums–Fruit of the Pioneers. 325-377, Sept. 1951
● How Soon Will We Measure in Metric? By Kenneth F. Weaver. Drawings by Donald A. Mackay. 287-294, Aug. 1977
● Humble Masterpieces: Decoys. By George Reiger. Photos by Kenneth Garrett. Included: Waterfowl hunting in the United States. 639-663, Nov. 1983
● Hurricane! By Ben Funk. Photos by Robert W. Madden. 346-379, Sept. 1980
Dominica. By Fred Ward. 357-359; Dynamics of a Hurricane. 370-371; Into the Eye of David. By John L. Eliot. 368-369; Paths of Fury–This Century's Worst American Storms. 360-361
● I See America First. By Lynda Bird Johnson. Photos by William Albert Allard. 874-904, Dec. 1965
● The Incredible Potato. By Robert E. Rhoades. Photos by Martin Rogers. 668-694, May 1982
● John Muir's Wild America. By Harvey Arden. Photos by Dewitt Jones. 433-461, Apr. 1973
◆ *John Muir's Wild America.* Announced. 860-864, June 1976
◆ *Life in Rural America.* Announced. 870-874, June 1974

KENNETH GARRETT
Humble Masterpieces: duck decoy

● The Making of America: 17 New Maps Tie the Nation to Its Past. By Wilbur E. Garrett, Editor. 630-633, Nov. 1982
● A Map Maker Looks at the United States. By Newman Bumstead. 705-748, June 1951
● Mapping the Nation's Breadbasket. By Frederick Simpich. 831-849, June 1948
● Mark Twain: Mirror of America. By Noel Grove. Photos by James L. Stanfield. 300-337, Sept. 1975
● Mexico to Canada on the Pacific Crest Trail. By Mike W. Edwards. Photos by David Hiser. 741-779, June 1971
● Natural Gas: The Search Goes On. By Bryan Hodgson. Photos by Lowell Georgia. 632-651, Nov. 1978
▲ *North Central United States,* Atlas series supplement. Nov. 1958
▲ *North Central United States,* supplement. June 1948
● North With the Wheat Cutters. By Noel Grove. Photos by James A. Sugar. 194-217, Aug. 1972
▲ *Northeastern United States, including the Great Lakes Region,* Atlas series supplement. Apr. 1959
▲ *Northwestern United States,* Atlas series supplement. Apr. 1960
▲ *Northwestern United States and Neighboring Canadian Provinces,* supplement. June 1950
● Our Changing Atlantic Coastline. By Nathaniel T. Kenney. Photos by B. Anthony Stewart. 860-887, Dec. 1962
◆ *Our Continent: A Natural History of North America.* Announced. 572-574, Oct. 1976
● Our Growing Interstate Highway System. By Robert Paul Jordan. 195-219, Feb. 1968
● Our Land Through Lincoln's Eyes. By Carolyn Bennett Patterson. Photos by W. D. Vaughn. 243-277, Feb. 1960
● Our Most Precious Resource: Water. By Thomas Y. Canby. Photos by Ted Spiegel. 144-179, Aug. 1980
● Our Wild and Scenic Rivers. 2-59, July 1977
◆ *The Pacific Crest Trail.* 1975. Announced. 870-874, June 1974
● The Parks in Your Backyard. By Conrad L. Wirth. 647-707, Nov. 1963
The East. 675-689; The Midlands. 691-697; The West. 699-707
● The Pesticide Dilemma. By Allen A. Boraiko. Photos by Fred Ward. 145-183, Feb. 1980
◆ *Picture Atlas of Our Fifty States.* 1978
● Playing 3,000 Golf Courses in Fourteen Lands. By Ralph A. Kennedy. 113-132, July 1952
▲ *Portrait U.S.A.,* first satellite photomosaic of the contiguous 48 states; *The United States,* supplement. July 1976
◆ *Preserving America's Past.* 1983
● The Promise and Peril of Nuclear Energy. By Kenneth F. Weaver. Photos by Emory Kristof. 459-493, Apr. 1979

BRUCE DALE, NGS

Sweet Chariot: four-level L.A. freeway

◆ *Railroads: The Great American Adventure.* 1977. Announced. 860-864, June 1976
• The Revolution in American Agriculture. By Jules B. Billard. Photos by James P. Blair. 147-185, Feb. 1970
• Satellites That Serve Us. By Thomas Y. Canby. Included: Images of Earth. 281-335, Sept. 1983
• The Search for Tomorrow's Power. By Kenneth F. Weaver. Photos by Emory Kristof. 650-681, Nov. 1972
• A Sikh Discovers America. By Joginder Singh Rekhi. 558-590, Oct. 1964
• Silver: A Mineral of Excellent Nature. By Allen A. Boraiko. Photos by Fred Ward. 280-313, Sept. 1981
• Skiing in the United States. By Kathleen Revis. 216-254, Feb. 1959
• Skyway Below the Clouds. By Carl R. Markwith. Photos by Ernest J. Cottrell. 85-108, July 1949
• Solar Energy, the Ultimate Powerhouse. By John L. Wilhelm. Photos by Emory Kristof. Included: Map of average annual hours of sunshine. 381-397, Mar. 1976
▲ *South Central United States,* Atlas series supplement. Feb. 1961
▲ *South Central United States,* supplement. Dec. 1947
▲ *Southeastern United States,* Atlas series supplement. Jan. 1958
▲ *Southeastern United States,* supplement. Feb. 1947
▲ *The Southwest,* The Making of America series. Nov. 1982
▲ *Southwestern United States,* Atlas series supplement. Nov. 1959
▲ *Southwestern United States,* supplement. Dec. 1948
• *Special Report on Energy.* (Feb. 1981)
• Swing Low, Sweet Chariot! By Noel Grove. Photos by Bruce Dale. 2-35, July 1983
• This Land of Ours (Bicentennial issue). 1-158, July 1976
◆ *Those Inventive Americans.* 1971. Announced. 880-884, June 1970
• The Thousand-mile Glide. By Karl Striedieck. Photos by Otis Imboden. 431-438, Mar. 1978
• Trucks Race the Clock From Coast to Coast. By James A. Sugar. 226-243, Feb. 1974
• Two Wheels Along the Mexican Border. By William Albert Allard. 591-635, May 1971
▲ *The United States,* Atlas series supplement. July 1961
▲ *The United States,* supplement. Sept. 1956
▲ *The United States,* supplement. Feb. 1968
▲ *United States: Washington to Boston,* Atlas series supplement. Aug. 1962
▲ *The United States of America,* supplement. June 1951
• Vacation Tour Through Lincoln Land. By Ralph Gray. 141-184, Feb. 1952
◆ *Vacationland U.S.A.* Announced. 734-740, May 1970; 573, Apr. 1973
▲ *Vacationlands of the United States and Southern Canada,* supplement. Text on reverse. July 1966
• A Walk Across America. By Peter Gorton Jenkins. 466-499, Apr. 1977
• A Walk Across America: Part II. By Peter and Barbara Jenkins. 194-229, Aug. 1979
◆ *We Americans.* Announced. 580-582, Oct. 1975; rev. ed. 1981
• The West Through Boston Eyes. By Stewart Anderson. 733-776, June 1949
• What's Happening to Our Climate? By Samuel W. Matthews. 576-615, Nov. 1976
▲ *Wild and Scenic Rivers of the United States,* double-sided supplement. July 1977
• Wild Cargo: the Business of Smuggling Animals. By Noel Grove. Photos by Steve Raymer. 287-315, Mar. 1981
◆ *Wilderness U.S.A.* Announced. 582-584, Oct. 1973
• The World in Your Garden. By W. H. Camp. Paintings by Else Bostelmann. Included: Gems from the Southeastern United States (Catawba Rhododendron, Flame Azalea). 1-65, July 1947
• Wrestlin' for a Livin' With King Coal. By Michael E. Long. Photos by Michael O'Brien. 793-819, June 1983
• The Year the Weather Went Wild. By Thomas Y. Canby. 799-829, Dec. 1977
• You Can't Miss America by Bus. By Howell Walker. Paintings by Walter A. Weber. 1-42, July 1950
• *See also* names of cities, lakes, mountains, rivers, and states; *and* Federal Lands; Great Lakes and Region; History, U. S.; Immigrants; Indians of North America; Presidents, U. S.; Space Flights and Research; West (Region); Wilderness; Wildlife

U. S. AGRICULTURAL RESEARCH CENTER. *See* Beltsville, Maryland

U. S. AIR FORCE:
• Across the Frozen Desert to Byrd Station. By Paul W. Frazier. Photos by Calvin L. Larsen. 383-398, Sept. 1957
• Air Rescue Behind Enemy Lines. By Howard Sochurek. 346-369, Sept. 1968
• Airlift to Berlin. 595-614, May 1949
• Artists Roam the World of the U. S. Air Force. By Curtis E. LeMay. 650-673, May 1960
• Cape Canaveral's 6,000-mile Shooting Gallery. By Allan C. Fisher, Jr. Photos by Luis Marden and Thomas Nebbia. 421-471, Oct. 1959
• *Columbia*'s Landing Closes a Circle. By Tom Wolfe. 474-477, Oct. 1981
• Fact Finding for Tomorrow's Planes. By Hugh L. Dryden. Photos by Luis Marden. 757-780, Dec. 1953
• Flags of the Americas. By Elizabeth W. King. 633-657, May 1949
• Fledgling Wings of the Air Force. By Thomas W. McKnew. 266-271, Aug. 1957

● Flying in the "Blowtorch" Era. By Frederick G. Vosburgh. 281-322, Sept. 1950
● History Written in the Skies. 273-294, Aug. 1957
● The Long, Lonely Leap. By Joseph W. Kittinger, Jr. Photos by Volkmar Wentzel. 854-873, Dec. 1960
● A Map Maker Looks at the United States. By Newman Bumstead. 705-748, June 1951
● Men Against the Hurricane. By Andrew H. Brown. 537-560, Oct. 1950
● Of Planes and Men. By Kenneth F. Weaver. Photos by Emory Kristof and Albert Moldvay. Included: Air Defense Command, Military Air Transport Service, Pacific Air Forces, Strategic Air Command, Tactical Air Command, U. S. Air Forces in Europe. 298-349, Sept. 1965
● Patrolling Troubled Formosa Strait. 573-588, Apr. 1955
● Reaching for the Moon. By Allan C. Fisher, Jr. Photos by Luis Marden. Included: First lunar probe by U. S. Air Force's rocket, *Pioneer I*. 157-171, Feb. 1959
● School for Survival. By Curtis E. LeMay. 565-602, May 1953
● They're Redesigning the Airplane. By Michael E. Long. Photos by James A. Sugar. 76-103, Jan. 1981
● Three Months on an Arctic Ice Island. By Joseph O. Fletcher. 489-504, Apr. 1953
● Uncle Sam Bends a Twig in Germany. By Frederick Simpich. Photos by J. Baylor Roberts. 529-550, Oct. 1948
● U. S. Air Force: Power for Peace. By Curtis E. LeMay. 291-297, Sept. 1965
● We Are Living at the South Pole. By Paul A. Siple. Photos by David S. Boyer. 5-35, July 1957
● Your Society Observes Eclipse in Brazil. NGS research grant. 661, May 1947
● *See also* Air Bases; Air Rescue Squadrons; Aviation Medicine; MATS; U. S. Air Force Academy; X-15; *and* former designation, U. S. Army Air Forces

U. S. AIR FORCE ACADEMY, Colorado:
● Where Falcons Wear Air Force Blue, United States Air Force Academy. By Nathaniel T. Kenney. Photos by William Belknap, Jr. 845-873, June 1959

U. S. ANTARCTIC RESEARCH PROGRAM (USARP):
● Antarctica: Icy Testing Ground for Space. By Samuel W. Matthews. Photos by Robert W. Madden. 569-592, Oct. 1968
● Antarctica's Nearer Side. By Samuel W. Matthews. Photos by William R. Curtsinger. 622-655, Nov. 1971
● First Conquest of Antarctica's Highest Peaks. By Nicholas B. Clinch. NGS research grant. 836-863, June 1967
● First Flight Across the Bottom of the World. By James R. Reedy. Photos by Otis Imboden. 454-464, Mar. 1964
● First La Gorce Medal Honors Antarctic Expedition. NGS research grant. 864-867, June 1967
● Flight Into Antarctic Darkness. By J. Lloyd Abbot, Jr. Photos by David S. Boyer. 732-738, Nov. 1967
● New Era in the Loneliest Continent. By David M. Tyree. Photos by Albert Moldvay. 260-296, Feb. 1963
● Stalking Seals Under Antarctic Ice. By Carleton Ray. 54-65, Jan. 1966

U. S. ARMED FORCES:
● The American Red Cross: A Century of Service. By Louise Levathes. Photos by Annie Griffiths. 777-791, June 1981
● Flags of the Americas. By Elizabeth W. King. Included: Flags of the United States Air Force, Army, Coast Guard, Marine Corps, Navy. 633-657, May 1949
● The Incredible Helicopter. By Peter T. White. 533-557, Apr. 1959
● *See also* U. S. Air Force; U. S. Army; U. S. Marine Corps; U. S. Navy; *and* Unknown Servicemen; War Memorials

U. S. ARMY:
● Across the Frozen Desert to Byrd Station. By Paul W. Frazier. Photos by Calvin L. Larsen. 383-398, Sept. 1957
● The Eisenhower Story. By Howard La Fay. 1-39, July 1969
● Flags of the Americas. By Elizabeth W. King. 633-657, May 1949
● The GI and the Kids of Korea. By Robert H. Mosier. 635-664, May 1953
● Masterpieces on Tour. By Harry A. McBride. 717-750, Dec. 1948
● Reaching for the Moon. By Allan C. Fisher, Jr. Photos by Luis Marden. Included: U. S. Army's first lunar probe *(Pioneer III)*. 157-171, Feb. 1959
● Uncle Sam Bends a Twig in Germany. By Frederick Simpich. Photos by J. Baylor Roberts. 529-550, Oct. 1948
● With the U. S. Army in Korea. By John R. Hodge. 829-840, June 1947
● *See also* Camp Century, Greenland; U. S. Military Academy; Vietnam, South; War Memorials; *and* Fifth Army; Unknown Servicemen

U. S. ARMY AIR FORCES:
● Adventures in Lololand. By Rennold L. Lowy. 105-118, Jan. 1947
● Carnival in San Antonio. By Mason Sutherland. Photos by J. Baylor Roberts. Included: Duncan Field, Fort Sam Houston, Kelly Field, Randolph Field. 813-844, Dec. 1947
● Eclipse Hunting in Brazil's Ranchland. By F. Barrows Colton. Photos by Richard H. Stewart and Guy W. Starling. NGS research grant. 285-324, Sept. 1947
● Fun Helped Them Fight. By Stuart E. Jones. 95-104, Jan. 1948
● Milestones in My Arctic Journeys. By Willie Knutsen. Included: The Arctic Search and Rescue section at Frobisher Bay, Baffin Island and at Goose Bay, Labrador. 543-570, Oct. 1949
● *See also* U. S. Air Force

U. S. ARMY CORPS OF ENGINEERS:
● The Imperiled Everglades. By Fred Ward. 1-27, Jan. 1972
● The Lower Mississippi. By Willard Price. Photos by W. D. Vaughn. 681-725, Nov. 1960
● Satellites Gave Warning of Midwest Floods. By Peter T. White. Photos by Thomas A. DeFeo. 574-592, Oct. 1969
● Trouble in Bayou Country: Louisiana's Atchafalaya. By Jack and Anne Rudloe. Photos by C. C. Lockwood. 377-397, Sept. 1979

U. S. ARMY QUARTERMASTER CORPS:
● First American Ascent of Mount St. Elias. By Maynard M. Miller. 229-248, Feb. 1948

U. S. ARMY SIGNAL CORPS:
● The Flying Telegraph (Pigeons). By Joseph F. Spears. Official U. S. Army Signal Corps photos. 531-554, Apr. 1947

U. S. ARMY SPECIAL FORCES:
● American Special Forces in Action in Viet Nam. By Howard Sochurek. 38-65, Jan. 1965
● Viet Nam's Montagnards. By Howard Sochurek. 443-487, Apr. 1968

UNITED STATES ATLAS. *See* Atlases, NGS

U. S. ATOMIC ENERGY COMMISSION:
● Hunting Uranium Around the World. By Robert D. Nininger. Photos by Volkmar Wentzel. 533-558, Oct. 1954
● South Carolina Rediscovered. By Herbert Ravenel Sass. Photos by Robert F. Sisson. Included: H-Bomb Project. 281-321, Mar. 1971
● *See also* Atomic Bomb Tests

U. S. BUREAU OF STANDARDS. *See* National Bureau of Standards

U. S. CAPITOL, Washington, D. C.:
● The Last Full Measure (Tribute to President Kennedy). By Melville Bell Grosvenor. 307-355, Mar. 1964
● The Nation's Capitol Revealed as Never Before. By Carl Hayden. 1-3, Jan. 1964
● Under the Dome of Freedom: The United States Capitol. By Lonnelle Aikman. Photos by George F. Mobley. 4-59, Jan. 1964
● U. S. Capitol, Citadel of Democracy. By Lonnelle Aikman. 143-192, Aug. 1952
◆ *We, the People,* Capitol guidebook. Published in cooperation with the United States Capitol Historical Society. 1, 2, Jan. 1964; 411, Mar. 1966; 586, Oct. 1967

U. S. CENSUS BUREAU:
● Census 1960: Profile of the Nation. By Albert W. Atwood and Lonnelle Aikman. 697-714, Nov. 1959

FRED WARD, BLACK STAR

Pesticides: crop dusting a Texas field

U. S. COAST AND GEODETIC SURVEY:
• Charting Our Sea and Air Lanes. By Stuart E. Jones. Photos by J. Baylor Roberts. 189-209, Feb. 1957

U. S. COAST GUARD:
• The Coast Guard: Small Service With a Big Mission. By William S. Ellis. 113-139, July 1974
• Flags of the Americas. By Elizabeth W. King. 633-657, May 1949
• Lonely Cape Hatteras, Besieged by the Sea. By William S. Ellis. Photos by Emory Kristof. 393-421, Sept. 1969
• Rugged Is the Word for Bravo. By Phillip M. Swatek. 829-843, Dec. 1955
• Tracking Danger With the Ice Patrol. By William S. Ellis. Photos by James R. Holland. 780-793, June 1968
• Under Canvas in the Atomic Age. By Alan Villiers. Included: U. S. Coast Guard Academy training ship *Eagle*. 49-84, July 1955

U. S. CONGRESS:
• Under the Dome of Freedom: The United States Capitol. By Lonnelle Aikman. Photos by George F. Mobley. 4-59, Jan. 1964

U. S. DEPARTMENT OF AGRICULTURE:
• How Fruit Came to America. By J. R. Magness. Paintings by Else Bostelmann. 325-377, Sept. 1951
• New Tricks Outwit Our Insect Enemies. By Hal Higdon. Photos by Robert F. Sisson and Emory Kristof. 380-399, Sept. 1972
• The Pesticide Dilemma. By Allen A. Boraiko. Photos by Fred Ward. 145-183, Feb. 1980
• Report from the Locust Wars. By Tony and Dickey Chapelle. Included: U. S. Department of Agriculture's Bureau of Entomology and Plant Quarantine. 545-562, Apr. 1953
• The Revolution in American Agriculture. By Jules B. Billard. Photos by James P. Blair. 147-185, Feb. 1970
• *See also* Beltsville, Maryland, for U. S. Agricultural Research Center; U. S. Forest Service; U. S. Soil Conservation Service

U. S. DEPARTMENT OF COMMERCE. *See* National Bureau of Standards; National Weather Service; U. S. Census Bureau; U. S. Coast and Geodetic Survey; U. S. Patent Office

U. S. DEPARTMENT OF DEFENSE. *See* Civil Air Patrol; DEW Line; DODGE Satellite; U. S. Armed Forces

U. S. DEPARTMENT OF JUSTICE. *See* Federal Bureau of Investigation

U. S. DEPARTMENT OF THE INTERIOR:
• Expeditions and Research. *See* Starfish; Tektite II
• Sharing Alaska: How Much for Parks? Opposing views by Jay S. Hammond and Cecil D. Andrus. 60-65, July 1979
• *See also* National Park Service; U. S. Fish and Wildlife Service

U. S. DEPARTMENT OF TRANSPORTATION:
• The Coming Revolution in Transportation. By Fredric C. Appel. Photos by Dean Conger. 301-341, Sept. 1969
• *See also* Interstate Highway System; U. S. Coast Guard

U. S. EXECUTIVE DEPARTMENTS:
• Flags of the Americas. By Elizabeth W. King. Included: Flags of the President of the United States, the Vice President of the United States, Secretary of Agriculture, Secretary of the Air Force, Secretary of the Army, Secretary of Commerce, Secretary of Defense, Secretary of the Interior, Attorney General, Secretary of Labor, Secretary of the Navy, Postmaster General, Secretary of State, Secretary of the Treasury. 633-657, May 1949

U. S. FISH AND WILDLIFE SERVICE:
• An Exotic New Oriole Settles in Florida. By Charles M. Brookfield and Oliver Griswold. 261-264, Feb. 1956
• The Gooney Birds of Midway. By John W. Aldrich. 839-851, June 1964
• Teamwork Helps the Whooping Crane. By Roderick C. Drewien, with Ernie Kuyt. Contents: A U. S.-Canadian effort to establish a second breeding flock of wild whoopers among close-kin sandhill cranes. 680-693, May 1979
• *See also* Aransas National Wildlife Refuge; Bear River Migratory Bird Refuge; National Elk Refuge; National Wildlife Refuges; *and* listing under Woods Hole Oceanographic Institution

U. S. FOOD AND DRUG ADMINISTRATION:
• Quicksilver and Slow Death. By John J. Putman. Photos by Robert W. Madden. 507-527, Oct. 1972

U. S. FOREST SERVICE:
• Forest Fire: The Devil's Picnic. By Stuart E. Jones and Jay Johnston. Included: Northern regional headquarters, Missoula, Montana; Smokejumper Center; Northern Forest Fire Laboratory. 100-127, July 1968
• Mexico to Canada on the Pacific Crest Trail. By Mike W. Edwards. Photos by David Hiser. 741-779, June 1971
• Our Green Treasury, the National Forests. By Nathaniel T. Kenney. Photos by J. Baylor Roberts. 287-324, Sept. 1956
• Our National Forests: Problems in Paradise. By Rowe Findley. Photos by David Cupp. 306-339, Sept. 1982
• Timber: How Much Is Enough? By John J. Putman. Photos by Bruce Dale. 485-511, Apr. 1974
• Washington Wilderness, the North Cascades. By Edwards Park. Photos by Kathleen Revis. 335-367, Mar. 1961

U. S. GEOLOGICAL SURVEY:
● California's San Andreas Fault. By Thomas Y. Canby. Photos by James P. Blair. 38-53, Jan. 1973
● Can We Predict Quakes? By Thomas Y. Canby. 830-835, June 1976
● Fountain of Fire in Hawaii. By Frederick Simpich, Jr. Photos by Robert B. Goodman and Robert Wenkam. Included: The Hawaiian Volcano Observatory. 303-327, Mar. 1960
● Hunting Uranium Around the World. By Robert D. Nininger. Photos by Volkmar Wentzel. 533-558, Oct. 1954

U. S. GOVERNMENT AGENCIES:
● Flags of the Americas. By Elizabeth W. King. Included: U. S. Coast and Geodetic Survey, U. S. Customs Service, U. S. Fish and Wildlife Service, U. S. Foreign Service, U. S. Geological Survey, U. S. Immigration and Naturalization Service, U. S. Maritime Commission, U. S. Public Health Service. 633-657, May 1949
● *See also* names of government agencies

U. S. IMMIGRATION AND NATURALIZATION SERVICE:
● Immigrants Still Flock to Liberty's Land. By Albert W. Atwood. 708-724, Nov. 1955

U. S. MARINE CORPS:
● Behind the Headlines in Viet Nam. By Peter T. White. Photos by Winfield Parks. 149-189, Feb. 1967
● Flags of the Americas. By Elizabeth W. King. 633-657, May 1949
● Four-ocean Navy in the Nuclear Age. By Thomas W. McKnew. 145-187, Feb. 1965
● Freedom Train Tours America. Included: U. S. Marine Corps guards. 529-542, Oct. 1949
● The GI and the Kids of Korea. By Robert H. Mosier. 635-664, May 1953
● Helicopter War in South Viet Nam. By Dickey Chapelle. 723-754, Nov. 1962
● Here Come the Marines. By Frederick Simpich. 647-672, Nov. 1950
● The President's Music Men. By Stuart E. Jones. Photos by William W. Campbell III. 752-766, Dec. 1959
● *See also* Unknown Servicemen

U. S. MERCHANT MARINE ACADEMY, Kings Point, New York:
● Kings Point: Maker of Mariners. By Nathaniel T. Kenney. Photos by Volkmar Wentzel. 693-706, Nov. 1955
● Long Island Outgrows the Country. By Howell Walker. Photos by B. Anthony Stewart. 279-326, Mar. 1951

U. S. MILITARY ACADEMY, West Point, New York:
● The Making of a West Pointer. By Howell Walker. 597-626, May 1952
● The Mighty Hudson. By Albert W. Atwood. Photos by B. Anthony Stewart. 1-36, July 1948

U. S. NAVAL ACADEMY, Annapolis, Maryland:
● Midshipmen's Cruise. By William J. Aston and Alexander G. B. Grosvenor. 711-754, June 1948

U. S. NAVAL AIR STATION, Lakehurst, New Jersey. *See* Parachute Rigger School

U. S. NAVAL OBSERVATORY, Washington, D. C.:
● Split-second Time Runs Today's World. By F. Barrows Colton and Catherine Bell Palmer. 399-428, Sept. 1947

U. S. NAVY:
● Adventures with the Survey Navy. By Irving Johnson. 131-148, July 1947
● Crosscurrents Sweep the Indian Ocean. By Bart McDowell. Photos by Steve Raymer. 422-457, Oct. 1981
● Expeditions and Research. *See* American Antarctic Mountaineering Expedition; Operation Deep Freeze; Operation Highjump
● First Flight Across the Bottom of the World. By James R. Reedy. Photos by Otis Imboden. 454-464, Mar. 1964
● Flags of the Americas. By Elizabeth W. King. 633-657, May 1949
● Flying in the "Blowtorch" Era. By Frederick G. Vosburgh. 281-322, Sept. 1950
● Four-ocean Navy in the Nuclear Age. By Thomas W. McKnew. 145-187, Feb. 1965
● From Indian Canoes to Submarines at Key West. By Frederick Simpich. Photos by J. Baylor Roberts. Included: U. S. Naval Station Submarine Base, Air Station, and Fleet Sonar School. 41-72, Jan. 1950
● The Gooney Birds of Midway. By John W. Aldrich. 839-851, June 1964
● Men Against the Hurricane. By Andrew H. Brown. 537-560, Oct. 1950
● Midshipmen's Cruise. By William J. Aston and Alexander G. B. Grosvenor. 711-754, June 1948
● Our Navy Explores Antarctica. By Richard E. Byrd. U. S. Navy official photos. 429-522, Oct. 1947
● Our Navy in the Far East. By Arthur W. Radford. Photos by J. Baylor Roberts. 537-577, Oct. 1953
● Our Navy's Long Submarine Arm. By Allan C. Fisher, Jr. 613-636, Nov. 1952
● Our Nuclear Navy. By George W. Anderson, Jr. 449-450, Mar. 1963
● Pacific Fleet: Force for Peace. By Franc Shor. Photos by W. E. Garrett. 283-335, Sept. 1959
● Patrolling Troubled Formosa Strait. 573-588, Apr. 1955
● 'Round the Horn by Submarine. By Paul C. Stimson. 129-144, Jan. 1948
● Sailors in the Sky: Fifty Years of Naval Aviation. By Patrick N. L. Bellinger. 276-296, Aug. 1961
● Troubled Waters East of Suez. By Ernest M. Eller. 483-522, Apr. 1954
● We Survive on a Pacific Atoll. By John and Frank Craighead. 73-94, Jan. 1948
● The Yankee Sailor Who Opened Japan. By Ferdinand Kuhn. 85-102, July 1953
● Yemen Opens the Door to Progress. By Harry Hoogstraal. Included: A United States Navy team of medical research workers. 213-244, Feb. 1952
● *See also* Guantánamo; Honolulu, Hawaii, for Pearl Harbor; San Diego, California; *and* Aviation Medicine; *Enterprise;* MATS; Office of Naval Research; Shiplift; *Strato-Lab;* Submarines; *Trieste;* Unknown Servicemen; War Memorials
Medals awarded the Navy:
● Replica of first La Gorce Medal for support of American Antarctic Mountaineering Expedition. 865, 867, June 1967
● Society Honors the Conquerors of Antarctica (U. S. Navy Antarctic Expeditions, 1955-1959). 589-590, Apr. 1959

U. S. PATENT OFFICE:
● Patent Plants Enrich Our World. By Orville H. Kneen. 357-378, Mar. 1948

U. S. POSTAL SERVICE:
● Everyone's Servant, the Post Office. By Allan C. Fisher, Jr. Photos by Volkmar Wentzel. 121-152, July 1954
● *See also J. W. Westcott* (Mail Boat); Pony Express; Post Roads

U. S. PUBLIC HEALTH SERVICE:
● Immigrants Still Flock to Liberty's Land. By Albert W. Atwood. 708-724, Nov. 1955

U. S. ROUTE 40:
● From Sea to Shining Sea. By Ralph Gray. Photos by Dean Conger and author. 1-61, July 1961

U. S. ROUTE 89:
● From Sun-clad Sea to Shining Mountains. By Ralph Gray. Photos by James P. Blair. 542-589, Apr. 1964

U. S. SOIL CONSERVATION SERVICE:
● Sno-Cats Mechanize Oregon Snow Survey. By Andrew H. Brown. Photos by John E. Fletcher. 691-710, Nov. 1949

UNITED STATES-SOVIET UNION 4-H EXCHANGE PROGRAM. *See* National 4-H Council

U. S. SUBMARINE SCHOOL, New London, Connecticut:
● Our Navy's Long Submarine Arm. By Allan C. Fisher, Jr. 613-636, Nov. 1952

U. S. TRUST TERRITORY OF THE PACIFIC ISLANDS. *See* Trust Territory of the Pacific Islands

U. S. VIRGIN ISLANDS:
▲ *Close-up: U.S.A., Florida, with Puerto Rico and U. S. Virgin Islands,* supplement. Text on reverse. Nov. 1973
● A Fresh Breeze Stirs the Leewards. By Carleton Mitchell. Photos by Winfield Parks. 488-537, Oct. 1966

• Our Virgin Islands, 50 Years Under the Flag. By Carleton Mitchell. Photos by James L. Stanfield. 67-103, Jan. 1968
• The U. S. Virgin Islands. By Thomas J. Colin. Photos by William Albert Allard and Cary Wolinsky. 225-243, Feb. 1981
• Virgin Islands: Tropical Playland, U.S.A. By John Scofield. Photos by Charles Allmon. 201-232, Feb. 1956
• *See also* Buck Island Reef National Monument, St. Croix; St. John Island

U. S. WEATHER BUREAU:
• Men Against the Hurricane. By Andrew H. Brown. 537-560, Oct. 1950
• Milestones in My Arctic Journeys. By Willie Knutsen. 543-570, Oct. 1949
• Rugged Is the Word for Bravo. By Phillip M. Swatek. 829-843, Dec. 1955
• Weather from the White North. By Andrew H. Brown. Photos by John E. Fletcher. 543-572, Apr. 1955
• *See also* National Weather Service

UNIVERSE:
◆ *The Amazing Universe.* Announced. 870-874, June 1975
• Completing the Atlas of the Universe (National Geographic Society-Palomar Observatory Sky Survey). By Ira Sprague Bowen. NGS research grant. 185-190, Aug. 1955
Sky Survey Plates Unlock Secrets of the Stars. 186-187
• The Incredible Universe. By Kenneth F. Weaver. Photos by James P. Blair. 589-625, May 1974
▲ *Journey Into the Universe Through Time and Space; National Geographic-Palomar Sky Survey Charting the Heavens,* double-sided supplement. June 1983
• Mapping the Unknown Universe. By F. Barrows Colton. NGS research grant. 401-420, Sept. 1950
• The Once and Future Universe. By Rick Gore. Photos by James A. Sugar. Paintings by Barron Storey. Picture text by David Jeffery. 704-749, June 1983
• Our Universe Unfolds New Wonders. By Albert G. Wilson. NGS research grant. 245-260, Feb. 1952
◆ *Picture Atlas of Our Universe.* 1980
• Pioneers in Man's Search for the Universe. Paintings by Jean-Leon Huens. Text by Thomas Y. Canby. 627-633, May 1974
• Sky Survey Charts the Universe. By Ira Sprague Bowen. NGS research grant. 780-781, Dec. 1956

UNIVERSITIES AND COLLEGES:
• Atlanta, Pacesetter City of the South. By William S. Ellis. Photos by James L. Amos. Included: Atlanta University Center (Atlanta University, Clark, Interdenominational Theological Center, Morehouse, Morris Brown, Spelman); Emory University; Georgia Institute of Technology. 246-281, Feb. 1969
• California, the Golden Magnet. By William Graves. Included: Stanford University, University of California, University of Southern California. 595-679, May 1966
• Literary Landmarks of Massachusetts. By William H. Nicholas. Photos by B. Anthony Stewart and John E. Fletcher. Included: Amherst College, Boston College, College of the Holy Cross, Harvard University, Smith College. 279-310, Mar. 1950
• Pittsburgh, Pattern for Progress. By William J. Gill. Photos by Clyde Hare. Included: Carnegie Institute of Technology, University of Pittsburgh. 342-371, Mar. 1965
• Pittsburgh: Workshop of the Titans. By Albert W. Atwood. Included: Carnegie Institute of Technology, University of Pittsburgh. 117-144, July 1949
• Robert College, Turkish Gateway to the Future. By Franc Shor. Included: American College for Girls, Robert Academy. 399-418, Sept. 1957
• Washington's Historic Georgetown. By William A. Kinney. 513-544, Apr. 1953
• Young-Old Lebanon Lives by Trade. By Thomas J. Abercrombie. Included: American University of Beirut. 479-523, Apr. 1958
• *See also* California Institute of Technology; Cornell University; William and Mary College; *and* the following universities

UNIVERSITY OF ALASKA:
Arctic Research Laboratory:
• Scientists Ride Ice Islands on Arctic Odysseys. By Lowell Thomas, Jr. Photos by Ted Spiegel. 670-691, Nov. 1965

UNIVERSITY OF ALEXANDRIA:
Expeditions and Research:
• Island of Faith in the Sinai Wilderness. By George H. Forsyth. Photos by Robert F. Sisson. 82-106, Jan. 1964

UNIVERSITY OF ARIZONA-ARIZONA STATE MUSEUM EXPEDITION. *See* Snaketown, Arizona

UNIVERSITY OF CALIFORNIA:
Expeditions and Research:
• Giant Kelp, Sequoias of the Sea. By Wheeler J. North. Photos by Bates Littlehales. 251-269, Aug. 1972
• Gifts for the Jaguar God. By Philip Drucker and Robert F. Heizer. Contents: Olmec archaeological expedition. NGS research grant. 367-375, Sept. 1956
• La Jolla, a Gem of the California Coast. By Deena Clark. Photos by J. Baylor Roberts. Included: Scripps Institution of Oceanography. 755-782, Dec. 1952
• Mono Lake Study. 511, Oct. 1981
• Sinai Sheds New Light on the Bible. By Henry Field. Photos by William B. and Gladys Terry. 795-815, Dec. 1948

UNIVERSITY OF COSTA RICA:
Research:
• One Strange Night on Turtle Beach. By Paul A. Zahl. 570-581, Oct. 1973

UNIVERSITY OF FLORIDA: Research:
• Imperiled Gift of the Sea: Caribbean Green Turtle. By Archie Carr. Photos by Robert E. Schroeder. 876-890, June 1967

UNIVERSITY OF HAWAII: Sea Grant Program:
• Precious corals. 720, May 1979

UNIVERSITY OF MIAMI:
• Miami's Expanding Horizons. By William H. Nicholas. Included: College of Arts and Sciences, Drama Department, Food Technology Department, Graduate School, Marine Biology Department, Medical Research Unit, School of Business Administration, School of Education, School of Engineering, School of Law, School of Music. 561-594, Nov. 1950
Marine Research:
• The Changeless Horseshoe Crab. By Anne and Jack Rudloe. Photos by Robert F. Sisson. Note: These arthropods are not true crabs. 562-572, Apr. 1981
• The Deadly Fisher. By Charles E. Lane. 388-397, Mar. 1963
• The Incredible Salmon. By Clarence P. Idyll. Photos by Robert F. Sisson. Paintings by Walter A. Weber. 195-219, Aug. 1968
• New Florida Resident, the Walking Catfish. By Clarence P. Idyll. Photos by Robert F. Sisson. 847-851, June 1969
• Shipworms, Saboteurs of the Sea. By F. G. Walton Smith. 559-566, Oct. 1956
• Shrimp Nursery: Science Explores New Ways to Farm the Sea. By Clarence P. Idyll. Photos by Robert F. Sisson. NGS research grant. 636-659, May 1965
• Shrimpers Strike Gold in the Gulf. By Clarence P. Idyll. Photos by Robert F. Sisson. 699-707, May 1957
• Shy Monster, the Octopus. By Gilbert L. Voss. Photos by Robert F. Sisson. 776-799, Dec. 1971
• Squids: Jet-powered Torpedoes of the Deep. By Gilbert L. Voss. Photos by Robert F. Sisson. NGS research grant. 386-411, Mar. 1967
• Strange Babies of the Sea. By Hilary B. Moore. Paintings by Craig Phillips and Jacqueline Hutton. Contents: Plankton study and other marine life. NGS research grant. 41-56, July 1952
• X-Rays Reveal the Inner Beauty of Shells. By Hilary B. Moore. 427-434, Mar. 1955

UNIVERSITY OF MICHIGAN:
Expeditions and Research:
• Island of Faith in the Sinai Wilderness. By George H. Forsyth. Photos by Robert F. Sisson. 82-106, Jan. 1964

UNIVERSITY OF MINNESOTA:
Bell Museum of Natural History: Study Grant:
• Western Grebes. 630, May 1982

UNIVERSITY OF MISSOURI SCHOOL OF JOURNALISM:
• Photography awards. 830-831, June 1959; 898, 901, Dec. 1962; 539, Oct. 1963

UNIVERSITY OF PENNSYLVANIA:
Museum: Expeditions and Research:
• Computer Helps Scholars Re-create an Egyptian Temple. By Ray Winfield Smith. Photos by Emory Kristof. NGS research grant. 634-655, Nov. 1970
• The Maya: Resurrecting the Grandeur of Tikal. By William R. Coe. 792-798, Dec. 1975
• Medical Research: Undersea Living (Man-in-Sea Project). 530, 541, Apr. 1965
• New Tools for Undersea Archeology. By George F. Bass. Photos by Charles R. Nicklin, Jr. NGS research grant. 403-423, Sept. 1968
• Oldest Known Shipwreck Yields Bronze Age Cargo. By Peter Throckmorton. NGS research grant. 697-711, May 1962
• Underwater Archeology: Key to History's Warehouse. By George F. Bass. Photos by Thomas J. Abercrombie and Robert B. Goodman. NGS research grant. 138-156, July 1963

UNIVERSITY OF SOUTHERN CALIFORNIA: Study Grant:
• Kelp. 414, Sept. 1980

UNIVERSITY OF VIRGINIA:
• Mr. Jefferson's Charlottesville. By Anne Revis. 553-592, May 1950
• Thomas Jefferson: Architect of Freedom. By Mike W. Edwards. Photos by Linda Bartlett. 231-259, Feb. 1976

UNIVERSITY OF WISCONSIN:
Study Grant:
• Jackals of the Serengeti. 840, Dec. 1980

UNKNOWN FALLS, Upper and Lower, Labrador:
• Labrador Canoe Adventure. By Andrew H. Brown and Ralph Gray. 65-99, July 1951

UNKNOWN SERVICEMEN: World War II and Korea:
• 'Known But to God.' By Beverley M. Bowie. 593-605, Nov. 1958

UNLOCKING Secrets of the Northern By Carl W. Gartlein. Paintings by William Crowder. NGS research grant. 673-704, Nov. 1947

UNOTO (Masai Ceremony):
• Spearing Lions with Africa's Masai. By Edgar Monsanto Queeny. 487-517, Oct. 1954

UNRUH, JACK: Artist:
• Arctic Odyssey. By John Bockstoce. Photos by Jonathan Wright. 100-127, July 1983

UNSEEN Life of a Mountain Stream. By William H. Amos. 562-580, Apr. 1977

UNSINKABLE Malta. By Ernle Bradford. Photos by Ted H. Funk. 852-879, June 1969

UNSOELD, WILLIAM F.: Author:
• The First Traverse. By Thomas F. Hornbein and William F. Unsoeld. 509-513, Oct. 1963
• *See also* American Mount Everest Expedition

UNSUNG Beauties of Hawaii's Coral Reefs. By Paul A. Zahl. 510-525, Oct. 1959

The **UNTAMED** Yellowstone. By Bill Richards. Photos by Dean Krakel II. 257-278, Aug. 1981

UP HELLY AA (Festival):
• Viking Festival in the Shetlands. Photos by Karl W. Gullers. 853-862, Dec. 1954

UP Through the Ice of the North Pole. By James F. Calvert. 1-41, July 1959

The **UPPER** Mississippi. By Willard Price. 651-699, Nov. 1958

UPPER VOLTA:
• Freedom Speaks French in Ouagadougou. By John Scofield. 153-203, Aug. 1966
• Oursi, Magnet in the Desert. By Carole E. Devillers. 512-525, Apr. 1980

Al **'UQAYR,** Saudi Arabia. *See* Gerrha

UR (Ancient City):
• Abraham, the Friend of God. By Kenneth MacLeish. Photos by Dean Conger. 739-789, Dec. 1966

URANIUM:
• An Atlas of Energy Resources. 58-69, *Special Report on Energy* (Feb. 1981)
• The Canadian North: Emerging Giant. By David S. Boyer. Included: Eldorado Mining and Refining Ltd.'s uranium mine in Saskatchewan. 1-43, July 1968
• Hunting Uranium Around the World. By Robert D. Nininger. Photos by Volkmar Wentzel. 533-558, Oct. 1954
• Man's New Servant, the Friendly Atom. By F. Barrows Colton. Photos by Volkmar Wentzel. 71-90, Jan. 1954
• The Promise and Peril of Nuclear Energy. By Kenneth F. Weaver. Photos by Emory Kristof. 459-493, Apr. 1979
• White Magic in the Belgian Congo. By W. Robert Moore. 321-362, Mar. 1952
• *See also* Nuclear Energy

URANUS (Planet):
• Voyage to the Planets. By Kenneth F. Weaver. Paintings by Ludek Pesek. 147-193, Aug. 1970

URBAN LIFE:
• Five Noted Thinkers Explore the Future. Included: Isaac Asimov, Richard F. Babcock, Edmund N. Bacon, Buckminster Fuller, Gerard Piel. 68-75, July 1976

BOTH BY EMORY KRISTOF, NGS

Promise and Peril of Nuclear Energy: project to test components for breeder reactors, *top;* dummy uranium and plutonium pellets, *above*

U V

URBAN NATIONAL PARKS. *See* Gateway National Recreation Area, New Jersey-New York; Golden Gate National Recreation Area, California

"URBAN ORE":
• The Fascinating World of Trash. By Peter T. White. Photos by Louie Psihoyos. 424-457, Apr. 1983

URBAN RENEWAL. *See* Atlanta, Georgia; Baltimore, Maryland; Brooklyn, New York; Kansas City, Missouri; Philadelphia, Pennsylvania; Pittsburgh, Pennsylvania; St. Louis, Missouri; Stockholm, Sweden; Tulsa, Oklahoma; Venice, Italy; Washington, D. C.; Wilmington, Delaware

URICK, FRANK, and Family:
• Growing Up in Montana. Photos by Nicholas deVore III. 650-657, May 1976

URQUHART, FRED A.: Author:
• Found at Last: the Monarch's Winter Home. Photos by Bianca Lavies. 161-173, Aug. 1976

URU INDIANS:
• Titicaca, Abode of the Sun. By Luis Marden. Photos by Flip Schulke. 272-294, Feb. 1971

URUGUAY:
• Parks, Plans, and People: How South America Guards Her Green Legacy. By Mary and Laurance Rockefeller. Photos by George F. Mobley. 74-119, Jan. 1967
• The Purple Land of Uruguay. By Luis Marden. 623-654, Nov. 1948

URUMCHI (Wulumuchi), Sinkiang:
• The Caves of the Thousand Buddhas. By Franc and Jean Shor. 383-415, Mar. 1951

USE and Abuse of Our National Forests: Problems in Paradise. By Rowe Findley. Photos by David Cupp. 306-339, Sept. 1982

UTAH:
• The Anasazi–Riddles in the Ruins. By Thomas Y. Canby. Photos by Dewitt Jones and David Brill. Paintings by Roy Andersen. 554-592, Nov. 1982
▲ *Close-up: U.S.A., The Southwest,* supplement. Text on reverse. Oct. 1977
• Coal vs. Parklands. By François Leydet. Photos by Dewitt Jones. 776-803, Dec. 1980
• From Sun-clad Sea to Shining Mountains. By Ralph Gray. Photos by James P. Blair. 542-589, Apr. 1964
• A Map Maker Looks at the United States. By Newman Bumstead. Included: Arches National Monument, Bryce Canyon, Price, Provo, Roan (Brown) Cliffs, Salt Lake City. 705-748, June 1951
• Miracle of the Potholes. By Rowe Findley. Photos by Robert F. Sisson. 570-579, Oct. 1975
• Riding the Outlaw Trail. By Robert Redford. Photos by Jonathan Blair. 622-657, Nov. 1976
• Skiing in the United States. By Kathleen Revis. 216-254, Feb. 1959

PAINTINGS BY LOUIS S. GLANZMAN

Patriots: writer of the Revolution, *above;* volunteer helps artillery crew, *below*

• Utah's Rock Art: Wilderness Louvre. A picture essay by Gary Smith, with Michael E. Long. 97-117, Jan. 1980
• Utah's Shining Oasis. By Charles McCarry. Photos by James L. Amos. 440-473, Apr. 1975
• *See also* Arches National Monument; Bear River Migratory Bird Refuge; Bryce Canyon National Park; Canyonlands National Park; Dinosaur National Monument; Escalante Canyon; Fisher Towers; Four Corners Country; Great Salt Lake; Powell, Lake; Rainbow Bridge National Monument; San Juan (River); Wasatch Range; Zion National Park

UVÉA (Island), Wallis Islands, Pacific Ocean:
• Adventures with the Survey Navy. By Irving Johnson. 131-148, July 1947

UYGURS (People):
• Journey to China's Far West. By Rick Gore. Photos by Bruce Dale. 292-331, Mar. 1980

UZZELL, R. STEPHEN, III: Photographer:
• Scotland's Inner Hebrides: Isles of the Western Sea. By Kenneth MacLeish. 690-717, Nov. 1974

V

V-2 (Rocket):
• Seeing the Earth from 80 Miles Up. By Clyde T. Holliday. 511-528, Oct. 1950

VACATION Tour Through Lincoln Land. By Ralph Gray. 141-184, Feb. 1952

VACCINATIONS:
• Smallpox–Epitaph for a Killer? By Donald A. Henderson. Photos by Marion Kaplan. 796-805, Dec. 1978

VADUZ, Liechtenstein:
• Liechtenstein Thrives on Stamps. By Ronald W. Clark. 105-112, July 1948

VAITERE (Schooner):
• Shores and Sails in the South Seas. By Charles Allmon. 73-104, Jan. 1950

VAL D'HÉRENS, Switzerland:
• Switzerland's Enchanted Val d'Hérens. By Georgia Engelhard Cromwell. 825-848, June 1955

VALENCIA, Spain:
• The Changing Face of Old Spain. By Bart McDowell. Photos by Albert Moldvay. 291-339, Mar. 1965
• Speaking of Spain. By Luis Marden. 415-456, Apr. 1950

VALLEY FORGE, Pennsylvania:
• Patriots in Petticoats. By Lonnelle Aikman. Paintings by Louis S. Glanzman. 475-493, Oct. 1975
• Washington Lives Again at Valley Forge. By Howell Walker. 187-202, Feb. 1954

VALLEY OF TEN THOUSAND SMOKES, Alaska:
● Lonely Wonders of Katmai. By Ernest Gruening. Photos by Winfield Parks. 800-831, June 1963

VALLEY OF THE MOON (Sonoma Valley), California:
● My Life in the Valley of the Moon. By H. H. Arnold. Photos by Willard R. Culver. 689-716, Dec. 1948
● Wildlife In and Near the Valley of the Moon. By H. H. Arnold. Photos by Paul J. Fair. 401-414, Mar. 1950

VALPARAÍSO, Chile:
● Chile, the Long and Narrow Land. By Kip Ross. 185-235, Feb. 1960

VAN BIESBROECK, GEORGE:
● Burr Prizes Awarded to Dr. Edgerton and Dr. Van Biesbroeck. 705-706, May 1953
● Eclipse Hunting in Brazil's Ranchland. By F. Barrows Colton. Photos by Richard H. Stewart and Guy W. Starling. 285-324, Sept. 1947
● Operation Eclipse: 1948. By William A. Kinney. 325-372, Mar. 1949
● South in the Sudan. By Harry Hoogstraal. 249-272, Feb. 1953

VAN BUREN, MARTIN:
● Profiles of the Presidents: II. A Restless Nation Moves West. By Frank Freidel. 80-121, Jan. 1965

VANCOUVER, British Columbia, Canada:
● Dream On, Vancouver. By Mike Edwards. Photos by Charles O'Rear. 467-491, Oct. 1978

VANCOUVER AQUARIUM:
Study Grant:
● Humpback Whales. 466, Apr. 1982

VANCOUVER ISLAND, British Columbia, Canada:
● British Columbia: Life Begins at 100. By David S. Boyer. 147-189, Aug. 1958
● Canada's Window on the Pacific: The British Columbia Coast. By Jules B. Billard. Photos by Ted Spiegel. 338-375, Mar. 1972

VANDERWALKER, JOHN G.: Author:
● Tektite II: Science's Window on the Sea. Photos by Bates Littlehales. 256-289, Aug. 1971

VANISHED Mystery Men of Hudson Bay. By Henry B. Collins. NGS research grant. 669-687, Nov. 1956

VAN LAWICK, HUGO. *See* Lawick, Hugo van

VAN LAWICK-GOODALL, JANE. *See* Goodall, Jane

VAN RIPER, WALKER:
Author-Photographer:
● Freezing the Flight of Hummingbirds. By Harold E. Edgerton, R. J. Niedrach, and Walker Van Riper. 245-261, Aug. 1951

VAN TIENHOVEN FOUNDATION OF THE NETHERLANDS: Study Grant:
● Orangutans. 835, June 1980

VASA (Swedish Warship):
● Ghost From the Depths: the Warship *Vasa*. By Anders Franzén. 42-57, Jan. 1962

VATICAN CITY:
● Rome: Eternal City with a Modern Air. By Harnett T. Kane. Photos by B. Anthony Stewart. 437-491, Apr. 1957
● St. Peter's, Rome's Church of Popes. By Aubrey Menen. Photos by Albert Moldvay. 865-879, Dec. 1971
● When in Rome. . . . By Stuart E. Jones. Photos by Winfield Parks. 741-789, June 1970
● When the President Goes Abroad (Eisenhower Tour). By Gilbert M. Grosvenor. 588-649, May 1960

VAUGHN, W. D.: Photographer:
● Africa: The Winds of Freedom Stir a Continent. By Nathaniel T. Kenney. 303-359, Sept. 1960
● Exploring Antarctica's Phantom Coast. By Edwin S. McDonald. 251-273, Feb. 1962
● The Lower Mississippi. By Willard Price. 681-725, Nov. 1960
● New Era on the Great Lakes. By Nathaniel T. Kenney. 439-490, Apr. 1959
● Our Land Through Lincoln's Eyes. By Carolyn Bennett Patterson. 243-277, Feb. 1960
● Staten Island Ferry, New York's Seagoing Bus. By John T. Cunningham and Jay Johnston. 833-843, June 1959

VAUPÉS RIVER, Colombia-Brazil:
● Jungle Jaunt on Amazon Headwaters. By Bernice M. Goetz. 371-388, Sept. 1952

VEGETABLES:
● California, Horn of Plenty. By Frederick Simpich. Photos by Willard R. Culver. 553-594, May 1949
● Our Vegetable Travelers. By Victor R. Boswell. Paintings by Else Bostelmann. Contents: Artichoke, Asparagus, Beans (Great Northern, Kidney, Lima, Marrow, Navy or Pea, Pinto, Stringless or Snap, Yellow), Broccoli, Brussels Sprouts, Cabbage, Cardoon, Carrots, Cauliflower, Celery, Chard, Chinese Cabbage, Collards, Corn, Cowpea, Cucumber, Eggplant, Endive, Kale, Kohlrabi, Lettuce, Muskmelons (Banana Melon, Cantaloupe, Casaba, Honey Dew, Montreal, Santa Claus), Mustard, Okra, Onions (Chive, Garlic, Leek), Parsnip, Peas, Peppers (Garden Pepper, Pimiento), Potato, Radish, Rhubarb, Romaine, Rutabaga, Salsify, Soybeans, Spinach, Squash (Acorn, Boston Marrow, Cocozelle, Crookneck, Cushaw, Cymling, Delicious, Hubbard, Marblehead, Pumpkin, Straightneck, Turks Turban, White Bush Scallop, Zucchini), Sweet Potato, Tomato, Turnip, Watermelon. 145-217, Aug. 1949
◆ *The World in Your Garden.* Announced. 729-730, May 1957
● *See also* Beltsville, Maryland, for Agricultural Research Center; Corn Growing; Potatoes and Potato Growing

VEILED WOMEN. *See* Purdah

VEIT, PETER G.: Photographer:
● Death of Marchessa (Mountain Gorilla). 508-511, Apr. 1981

VENEZUELA:
● Search for the Scarlet Ibis in Venezuela. By Paul A. Zahl. NGS research grant. 633-661, May 1950
● Venezuela Builds on Oil. By Thomas J. Abercrombie. 344-387, Mar. 1963
● Venezuela's Crisis of Wealth. By Noel Grove. Photos by Robert W. Madden. 175-209, Aug. 1976
● Yanomamo, the True People. By Napoleon A. Chagnon. 211-223, Aug. 1976
● *See also* Angel Falls

VENICE, Italy:
● Italy Smiles Again. By Edgar Erskine Hume. 693-732, June 1949
● A Stroll to Venice. By Isobel Wylie Hutchison. 378-410, Sept. 1951
● Venice, City of Twilight Splendor. By Joe Alex Morris. Photos by John Scofield. 543-569, Apr. 1961
● Venice Fights for Life. By Joseph Judge. Photos by Albert Moldvay. 591-631, Nov. 1972
Venice's Golden Legacy. Photos by Victor R. Boswell, Jr. 609-619

VENUS (Planet):
● Mariner Scans a Lifeless Venus. By Frank Sartwell. Paintings by Davis Meltzer. 733-742, May 1963
● Mariner Unveils Venus and Mercury. By Kenneth F. Weaver. 858-869, June 1975
● Voyage to the Planets. By Kenneth F. Weaver. Paintings by Ludek Pesek. 147-193, Aug. 1970

VENUS FLYTRAP:
● Plants That Eat Insects. By Paul A. Zahl. 643-659, May 1961

VERACRUZ (State), Mexico:
● Man's Eighty Centuries in Veracruz. By S. Jeffrey K. Wilkerson. Photos by David Hiser. Paintings by Richard Schlecht. NGS research grant. 203-231, Aug. 1980
● *See also* San Lorenzo

VERAGUAS (Province), Panama. *See* La Pita

VERMONT:
● Life on a Rock Ledge. By William H. Amos. 558-566, Oct. 1980
● New England, a Modern Pilgrim's Pride. By Beverley M. Bowie. 733-796, June 1955
● Robert Frost and New England. By Archibald MacLeish. 438-467, Apr. 1976
Look of a Land Beloved. Photos by Dewitt Jones. 444-467
● Skiing in the United States. By Kathleen Revis. 216-254, Feb. 1959
● Vermont–a State of Mind and Mountains. By Ethel A. Starbird. Photos by Nathan Benn. 28-61, July 1974
● *See also* Champlain, Lake; Connecticut River and Valley; Green Mountains; Stark Brook

VERONA, Italy:
• Italy Smiles Again. By Edgar Erskine Hume. 693-732, June 1949

VERREAUX'S EAGLES. *See* Black Eagles

VERSATILE Wood Waits on Man. By Andrew H. Brown. 109-140, July 1951

VESILIND, PRIIT J.: Author:
• Helsinki: City With Its Heart in the Country. Photos by Jodi Cobb. 237-255, Aug. 1981
• Hunters of the Lost Spirit: Alaskans, Canadians, Greenlanders, Lapps. Photos by David Alan Harvey, Ivars Silis, and Sisse Brimberg. 150-197, Feb. 1983
• The Ohio–River With a Job to Do. Photos by Martin Rogers. 245-273, Feb. 1977
• Return to Estonia. Photos by Cotton Coulson. 485-511, Apr. 1980
• The Society Islands, Sisters of the Wind. Photos by George F. Mobley. 844-869, June 1979
• Two Berlins–A Generation Apart. Photos by Cotton Coulson. 2-51, Jan. 1982

VESSELS, JANE: Author:
• Delaware–Who Needs to Be Big? Photos by Kevin Fleming. 171-197, Aug. 1983
• Fátima: Beacon for Portugal's Faithful. Photos by Bruno Barbey. 832-839, Dec. 1980

VEST SPITSBERGEN (Island), Svalbard:
• Spitsbergen Mines Coal Again. 113-120, July 1948

VESTER, BERTHA SPAFFORD: Author-Photographer-Artist:
• Jerusalem, My Home. 826-847, Dec. 1964

VESTFJORDEN, Norway:
• Fishing in the Lofotens. Photos by Lennart Nilsson. 377-388, Mar. 1947

VESTMANNAEYJAR, Heimaey, Iceland:
• Vestmannaeyjar: Up From the Ashes. By Noel Grove. Photos by Robert S. Patton. 690-701, May 1977
• A Village Fights for Its Life. By Noel Grove. 40-67, July 1973

VESUVIUS, Mount, Italy:
• A Buried Roman Town Gives Up Its Dead (Herculaneum). By Joseph Judge. Photos by Jonathan Blair. NGS research grant. 687-693, Dec. 1982

VEVEY, Switzerland:
• Switzerland's Once-in-a-generation Festival. By Jean and Franc Shor. 563-571, Oct. 1958

VÉZELAY, Hill of the Pilgrims. By Melvin Hall. 229-247, Feb. 1953

VIA APPIA, Italy. *See* Appian Way

VICKSBURG, Mississippi:
• Gettysburg and Vicksburg: the Battle Towns Today. By Robert Paul Jordan. Map notes by Carolyn Bennett Patterson. 4-57, July 1963

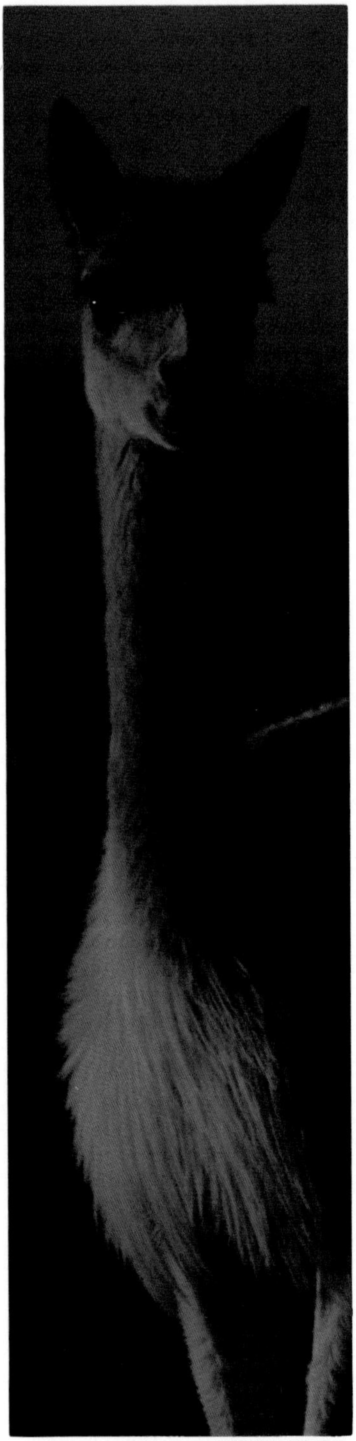

WILLIAM L. FRANKLIN

Vicuña: the camel's endangered Andean cousin

VICTOR, PAUL-EMILE: Author:
• Wringing Secrets from Greenland's Icecap. 121-147, Jan. 1956

VICTORIA, Queen (Great Britain and Ireland):
• The British Way. By Sir Evelyn Wrench. 421-541, Apr. 1949

VICTORIA (State), Australia:
• Australia's Pacesetter State, Victoria. By Allan C. Fisher, Jr. Photos by Thomas Nebbia. 218-253, Feb. 1971
• *See also* Melbourne

VICTORIA, British Columbia, Canada:
• British Columbia: Life Begins at 100. By David S. Boyer. 147-189, Aug. 1958
• Canada's Window on the Pacific: The British Columbia Coast. By Jules B. Billard. Photos by Ted Spiegel. 338-375, Mar. 1972

VICTORIA, Kansas:
• Hays, Kansas, at the Nation's Heart. By Margaret M. Detwiler. Photos by John E. Fletcher. 461-490, Apr. 1952

VICTORIA, Lake, Africa:
• Adventures in the Search for Man. By Louis S. B. Leakey. Photos by Hugo van Lawick. NGS research grant. 132-152, Jan. 1963
• Britain Tackles the East African Bush. By W. Robert Moore. 311-353, Mar. 1950
• Uganda, Africa's Uneasy Heartland. By Howard La Fay. Photos by George F. Mobley. 708-735, Nov. 1971

VICTORIA FALLS, Zambia-Zimbabwe:
• Africa: The Winds of Freedom Stir a Continent. By Nathaniel T. Kenney. Photos by W. D. Vaughn. 303-359, Sept. 1960
• Rhodesia, a House Divided. By Allan C. Fisher, Jr. Photos by Thomas Nebbia. 641-671, May 1975

VICTORIAN AGE:
• The England of Charles Dickens. By Richard W. Long. Photos by Adam Woolfitt. 443-483, Apr. 1974

VICUÑAS:
• High, Wild World of the Vicuña. By William L. Franklin. 77-91, Jan. 1973

VIENNA, Austria:
• Building a New Austria. By Beverley M. Bowie. Photos by Volkmar Wentzel. 172-213, Feb. 1959
• Occupied Austria, Outpost of Democracy. By George W. Long. Photos by Volkmar Wentzel. 749-790, June 1951
• Vienna, City of Song. By Peter T. White. Photos by John Launois. 739-779, June 1968
• The Vienna Treasures and Their Collectors. By John Walker. Included: Kunsthistorisches Museum. 737-776, June 1950
• What I Saw Across the Rhine. By J. Frank Dobie. 57-86, Jan. 1947
• *See also* Spanish Riding School

VIETMEYER, NOEL D.: Author:
• Rediscovering America's Forgotten Crops. Photos by Burgess Blevins. Paintings by Paul M. Breeden. 702-712, May 1981

VIETNAM:
• Indochina Faces the Dragon. By George W. Long. Photos by J. Baylor Roberts. 287-328, Sept. 1952
• Kampuchea Wakens From a Nightmare. By Peter T. White. Photos by David Alan Harvey. Included: Vietnam's occupation of Kampuchea. 590-623, May 1982
• The Lands and Peoples of Southeast Asia. 295-365, Mar. 1971
I. Mosaic of Cultures. By Peter T. White. Photos by W. E. Garrett. 296-329; II. New Light on a Forgotten Past. By Wilhelm G. Solheim II. 330-339
• Passage to Freedom in Viet Nam. By Gertrude Samuels. 858-874, June 1955
▲ *The Peoples of Mainland Southeast Asia; Asia,* double-sided supplement. Mar. 1971
• Portrait of Indochina. By W. Robert Moore and Maynard Owen Williams. Paintings by Jean Despujols. 461-490, Apr. 1951
• Strife-torn Indochina. By W. Robert Moore. 499-510, Oct. 1950
▲ *Viet Nam, Cambodia, Laos, and Eastern Thailand,* supplement. Text on reverse. Jan. 1965
▲ *Viet Nam, Cambodia, Laos, and Thailand,* supplement. Feb. 1967
• *See also* Vietnam, North; Vietnam, South

VIETNAM, North:
• Air Rescue Behind Enemy Lines. By Howard Sochurek. 346-369, Sept. 1968

VIETNAM, South:
• American Special Forces in Action in Viet Nam. By Howard Sochurek. 38-65, Jan. 1965
• Behind the Headlines in Viet Nam. By Peter T. White. Photos by Winfield Parks. 149-189, Feb. 1967
• Helicopter War in South Viet Nam. By Dickey Chapelle. 723-754, Nov. 1962
• The Mekong, River of Terror and Hope. By Peter T. White. Photos by W. E. Garrett. 737-787, Dec. 1968
• Of Planes and Men. By Kenneth F. Weaver. Photos by Emory Kristof and Albert Moldvay. Included: Bien Hoa and Tan Son Nhut air bases at Saigon; Da Nang Air Base; and outposts at Khe Sahn and Vinh Long. 298-349, Sept. 1965
• Slow Train Through Viet Nam's War. By Howard Sochurek. 412-444, Sept. 1964
• South Viet Nam Fights the Red Tide. By Peter T. White. Photos by W. E. Garrett. 445-489, Oct. 1961
• Viet Nam's Montagnards. By Howard Sochurek. 443-487, Apr. 1968
• Water War in Viet Nam. By Dickey Chapelle. 272-296, Feb. 1966
• *See also* Saigon

VIETNAMESE REFUGEES:
• Hong Kong's Refugee Dilemma. By William S. Ellis. Photos by William Albert Allard. Included: Ethnic Chinese refugees expelled from Vietnam. 709-732, Nov. 1979
• Thailand: Refuge From Terror. By W. E. Garrett. 633-642, May 1980
• Troubled Odyssey of Vietnamese Fishermen. By Harvey Arden. Photos by Steve Wall. 378-395, Sept. 1981

VIGOROUS Young Nation in the South Sea. By Alan Villiers. 309-385, Sept. 1963

VIKING FESTIVAL in the Shetlands. Photos by Karl W. Gullers. 853-862, Dec. 1954

VIKING LANDER (Spacecraft):
• The Search for Life on Mars. By Kenneth F. Weaver. 264-265, Feb. 1973
• *See also* Viking Spacecraft Missions; Voyager

VIKING MARU (Balloon):
• Last Ascent of a Heroic Team (Maxie Anderson and Don Ida). 794-797, Dec. 1983

VIKING SPACECRAFT MISSIONS:
• Mars: Our First Close Look. 3-31, Jan. 1977
I. As Viking Sees It. 3-7; II. The Search for Life. By Rick Gore. 9-31

VIKINGS:
• Eskimo and Viking Finds in the High Arctic: Ellesmere Island. By Peter Schledermann. Photos by Sisse Brimberg. 575-601, May 1981
• A New Look at Medieval Europe. By Kenneth M. Setton. Paintings by Andre Durenceau and Birney Lettick. 799-859, Dec. 1962
• The Vikings. By Howard La Fay. Photos by Ted Spiegel. 492-541, Apr. 1970
◆ *The Vikings.* Announced. 870-874, June 1972
• Vinland Ruins Prove Vikings Found the New World. By Helge Ingstad. NGS research grant. 708-734, Nov. 1964

VILCABAMBA, Cordillera, Peru:
• By Parachute Into Peru's Lost World. By G. Brooks Baekeland. Photos by author and Peter R. Gimbel. NGS research grant. 268-296, Aug. 1964

VILCABAMBA, Ecuador:
• "Every Day Is a Gift When You Are Over 100." By Alexander Leaf. Photos by John Launois. 93-119, Jan. 1973

A **VILLAGE** Fights for Its Life. By Noel Grove. 40-67, July 1973

VILLAGE From the Past. By Maria Nicolaidis-Karanikolas. Photos by James L. Stanfield. 768-777, Dec. 1983

A **VILLAGE** Rises From Ashes. By Noel Grove. Photos by Robert S. Patton. 690-701, May 1977

VILLARD, HENRY S.: Author:
• Rubber-cushioned Liberia. Photos by Charles W. Allmon. 201-228, Feb. 1948

VILLAS BOAS, CLAUDIO and ORLANDO: Authors:
• Saving Brazil's Stone Age Tribes From Extinction. Photos by W. Jesco von Puttkamer. 424-444, Sept. 1968

VILLAVICENCIO, Colombia:
• Keeping House for a Biologist in Colombia. By Nancy Bell Fairchild Bates. Photos by Marston Bates. 251-274, Aug. 1948

VILLIERS, ALAN:
• Editorial. By Gilbert M. Grosvenor. 149, Feb. 1975
Author:
• Aboard the N.S. *Savannah:* World's First Nuclear Merchantman. Photos by John E. Fletcher. 280-298, Aug. 1962
• The Age of Sail Lives On at Mystic. Photos by Weston Kemp. 220-239, Aug. 1968
• "The Alice" in Australia's Wonderland. Photos by Jeff Carter and David Moore. 230-257, Feb. 1966
• Australia. 309-385, Sept. 1963
• Captain Cook: The Man Who Mapped the Pacific. Photos by Gordon W. Gahan. 297-349, Sept. 1971
• Channel Cruise to Glorious Devon. Photos by Bates Littlehales. 208-259, Aug. 1963
• Cowes to Cornwall. Photos by Robert B. Goodman. 149-201, Aug. 1961
• England's Scillies, the Flowering Isles. Photos by Bates Littlehales. 126-145, July 1967
• Fabled Mount of St. Michael. Photos by Bates Littlehales. 880-898, June 1964
• In the Wake of Darwin's *Beagle.* Photos by James L. Stanfield. 449-495, Oct. 1969
• Last of the Cape Horners. 701-710, May 1948
• Magellan: First Voyage Around the World. Photos by Bruce Dale. 721-753, June 1976
• The Netherlands: Nation at War With the Sea. Photos by Adam Woolfitt. 530-571, Apr. 1968
• Prince Henry, the Explorer Who Stayed Home. Photos by Thomas Nebbia. 616-656, Nov. 1960
• Scotland From Her Lovely Lochs and Seas. Photos by Robert F. Sisson. 492-541, Apr. 1961
• Ships Through the Ages: A Saga of the Sea. 494-545, Apr. 1963
• Sir Francis Drake. Photos by Gordon W. Gahan. 216-253, Feb. 1975
• Wales, Land of Bards. Photos by Thomas Nebbia. 727-769, June 1965
• We're Coming Over on the *Mayflower.* 708-728, May 1957
Author-Photographer:
• By Full-rigged Ship to Denmark's Fairyland. Photos by Alexander Taylor and author. 809-828, Dec. 1955
• Golden Beaches of Portugal. 673-696, Nov. 1954
• How We Sailed the New *Mayflower* to America. 627-672, Nov. 1957

U V

• I Sailed with Portugal's Captains Courageous. 565-596, May 1952
• The Marvelous Maldive Islands. 829-849, June 1957
• Sailing with Sindbad's Sons. 675-688, Nov. 1948
• Under Canvas in the Atomic Age. 49-84, July 1955

VINCI, LEONARDO DA:
• Leonardo da Vinci: A Man for All Ages. By Kenneth MacLeish. Photos by James L. Amos. 296-329, Sept. 1977
• Restoration Reveals the "Last Supper." By Carlo Bertelli. Photos by Victor R. Boswell, Jr. 664-685, Nov. 1983

VINEYARDS. *See* Grapes and Grape Culture

VINLAND Ruins Prove Vikings Found the New World. By Helge Ingstad. NGS research grant. 708-734, Nov. 1964

The **VIOLENT** Gulf of Alaska. By Boyd Gibbons. Photos by Steve Raymer. 237-267, Feb. 1979

VIRGIN ISLANDS, West Indies:
• A Fresh Breeze Stirs the Leewards. By Carleton Mitchell. Photos by Winfield Parks. 488-537, Oct. 1966
• Our Virgin Islands, 50 Years Under the Flag. By Carleton Mitchell. Photos by James L. Stanfield. 67-103, Jan. 1968
• The U. S. Virgin Islands. By Thomas J. Colin. Photos by William Albert Allard and Cary Wolinsky. 225-243, Feb. 1981
• Virgin Islands: Tropical Playland, U.S.A. By John Scofield. Photos by Charles Allmon. 201-232, Feb. 1956
• *See also* Buck Island Reef National Monument, St. Croix; St. John Island

VIRGIN RIVER, Arizona-Nevada-Utah:
• Amid the Mighty Walls of Zion. By Lewis F. Clark. 37-70, Jan. 1954

VIRGINIA:
• Capt. John Smith's Map of Virginia.–George Washington's Travels, Traced on the Arrowsmith Map. 760, 768, June 1953
• Chesapeake Country. By Nathaniel T. Kenney. Photos by Bates Littlehales. 370-411, Sept. 1964
• Exploring America's Great Sand Barrier Reef. By Eugene R. Guild. Photos by author and John E. Fletcher. 325-350, Sept. 1947
• Firebrands of the Revolution. By Eric F. Goldman. Photos by George F. Mobley. 2-27, July 1974
• First Look at a Lost Virginia Settlement (Martin's Hundred). By Ivor Noël Hume. Photos by Ira Block. Paintings by Richard Schlecht. NGS research grant. 735-767, June 1979
• Founders of Virginia. By Sir Evelyn Wrench. Photos by B. Anthony Stewart. 433-462, Apr. 1948
• History Keeps House in Virginia. By Howell Walker. 441-484, Apr. 1956

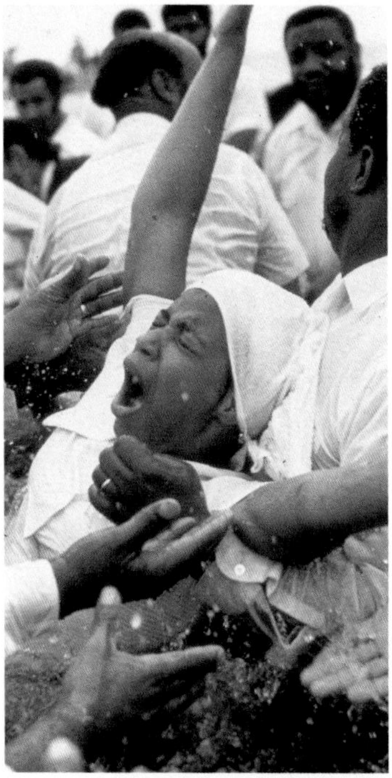

DAVID ALAN HARVEY

Virginians: mass baptism

• Indian Life Before the Colonists Came. By Stuart E. Jones. Engravings by Theodore de Bry, 1590. 351-368, Sept. 1947
• My Chesapeake–Queen of Bays. By Allan C. Fisher, Jr. Photos by Lowell Georgia. 428-467, Oct. 1980
• The Nation's River. By Allan C. Fisher, Jr. Photos by James L. Stanfield. 432-469, Oct. 1976
A Good Life on the Potomac. 470-479
• New Clues to an Old Mystery (Virginia's Wolstenholme Towne). By Ivor Noël Hume. Photos by Ira Block. Paintings by Richard Schlecht. 53-77, Jan. 1982
• Over and Under Chesapeake Bay. By David S. Boyer. 593-612, Apr. 1964
▲ *A Pocket Map of Suburban Washington; Central Washington,* double-sided supplement. Sept. 1948
▲ *Round About the Nation's Capital,* supplement. Apr. 1956
• Shrines of Each Patriot's Devotion. By Frederick G. Vosburgh. 51-82, Jan. 1949
• Stately Homes of Old Virginia. By Albert W. Atwood. 787-802, June 1953
▲ *Suburban Washington; Tourist Washington,* double-sided Atlas series supplement. Dec. 1964
• The Virginians. By Mike W. Edwards. Photos by David Alan Harvey. 588-617, Nov. 1974
• Witness to a War: British Correspondent Frank Vizetelly. By Robert T. Cochran, Jr. 453-491, Apr. 1961
• Wrestlin' for a Livin' With King Coal. By Michael E. Long. Photos by Michael O'Brien. 793-819, June 1983
• *See also* Appomattox; Arlington County; Arlington National Cemetery; Chincoteague Island; Delmarva Peninsula; Fredericksburg; Harmony Hollow; Jamestown; Monticello; Mount Vernon; Norfolk; Shenandoah National Park; Tangier Island; Williamsburg

VIRÚ VALLEY, Peru:
• Finding the Tomb of a Warrior-God. By William Duncan Strong. Photos by Clifford Evans, Jr. 453-482, Apr. 1947

VIRUNGA MOUNTAINS, Rwanda-Uganda-Zaire:
• The Imperiled Mountain Gorilla. By Dian Fossey. NGS research grant. 501-523, Apr. 1981
Death of Marchessa. Photos by Peter G. Veit. 508-511
• Making Friends With Mountain Gorillas. By Dian Fossey. Photos by Robert M. Campbell. NGS research grant. 48-67, Jan. 1970
• More Years With Mountain Gorillas. By Dian Fossey. Photos by Robert M. Campbell. NGS research grant. 574-585, Oct. 1971

VISBY, Gotland, Sweden:
• Gotland: Sweden's Treasure Island. By James Cerruti. Photos by Albert Moldvay. 268-288, Aug. 1973

A **VISIT** From House Doctors. 48-49, *Special Report on Energy* (Feb. 1981)

VISIT to Forbidden Tibet. By Fred Ward. 218-259, Feb. 1980

A **VISIT** to the Living Ice Age. By Rutherford Platt. 525-545, Apr. 1957

A **VISITORS'** Guide to All 320 Park Sites (United States National Parks). 111-123, July 1979

VISOKE, Mount, Rwanda-Zaire:
• The Imperiled Mountain Gorilla. By Dian Fossey. NGS research grant. 501-523, Apr. 1981
Death of Marchessa. Photos by Peter G. Veit. 508-511

VIZCAYA: An Italian Palazzo in Miami. By William H. Nicholas. Photos by Justin Locke. 595-604, Nov. 1950

VIZETELLY, FRANK:
• Witness to a War: British Correspondent Frank Vizetelly. By Robert T. Cochran, Jr. 453-491, Apr. 1961

VOAS, ROBERT B.: Author:
• John Glenn's Three Orbits in *Friendship 7:* A Minute-by-Minute Account of America's First Orbital Space Flight. 792-827, June 1962

VOICES of the Night. By Arthur A. Allen. 507-522, Apr. 1950

VOLATILE North Yemen. By Noel Grove. Photos by Steve Raymer. 244-269, Aug. 1979

VOLCANIC ACTIVITY, Subsea. *See* Ilha Nova; Myojin Island; Surtsey

VOLCANIC Cloud May Alter Earth's Climate. By Robert I. Tilling. 672-675, Nov. 1982

VOLCANO ISLANDS, Pacific Ocean. *See* Iwo Jima

VOLCANOES:
■ Born of Fire. 824, Dec. 1982
• Death of an Island, Tristan da Cunha. By P. J. F. Wheeler. 678-695, May 1962
• Disaster in Paradise. By Windsor P. Booth and Samuel W. Matthews. Photos by Robert F. Sisson. Contents: The eruption of Mount Agung, Bali. 436-458, Sept. 1963
• El Sangay, Fire-breathing Giant of the Andes. By G. Edward Lewis. Contents: El Antisana, El Cayambe, El Chimborazo, El Cotopaxi, El Pichincha, El Sangay, El Tulabug, and Imbabura. 117-138, Jan. 1950
• Exploring Aleutian Volcanoes. By G. D. Robinson. 509-528, Oct. 1948
◆ *Exploring Our Living Planet.* Announced. 824, Dec. 1982
• Have We Solved the Mysteries of the Moon? By Kenneth F. Weaver. Paintings by William H. Bond. 309-325, Sept. 1973
• Hawaii, U.S.A. By Frederick Simpich, Jr. Photos by Thomas Nebbia. Included: Kilauea; Mauna Loa. 1-45, July 1960
• Iceland Tapestry. By Deena Clark. Included: Hekla. 599-630, Nov. 1951
• Journey to Mars. By Kenneth F. Weaver. Paintings by Ludek Pesek. Included: Discovery of nineteen volcanic features, the largest being Nix Olympica. 231-263, Feb. 1973

ROBERT S. PATTON, NGS

Icelandic Village: Kirkjufell volcano erupts

• Lost Kingdom in Indian Mexico. By Justin Locke. Included: El Pilon, Parícutin. 517-546, Oct. 1952
• The Mediterranean–Sea of Man's Fate. By Rick Gore. Photos by Jonathan Blair. Included: Etna; Phlegraean Fields; Stromboli; Thera; Vesuvius; Vulcano. 694-737, Dec. 1982
• Our Home-town Planet, Earth. By F. Barrows Colton. 117-139, Jan. 1952
◆ *Our Violent Earth.* 1982
◆ *Powers of Nature.* 1978
• Sicily the Three-cornered. By Luis Marden. Included: Etna, Stromboli. 1-48, Jan. 1955
• This Changing Earth. By Samuel W. Matthews. 1-37, Jan. 1973
■ The Violent Earth. 286A-286B, Feb. 1973
• Volcano and Earthquake Show Nature's Awesome Power. The Editor. 303, Mar. 1960
• Volcano Overwhelms an Icelandic Village. By Noel Grove. Contents: The eruption of Kirkjufell. 40-67, July 1973
• What's Happening to Our Climate? By Samuel W. Matthews. 576-615, Nov. 1976
• *See also* Crater Lake, Oregon; Craters of the Moon National Monument, Idaho; Deception Island, Antarctica; El Chichón; Haleakala National Park, Hawaii; Ilha Nova, Azores; Io, a moon of Jupiter; Irazú, Costa Rica; Katmai National Monument, Alaska; Kilauea Volcano, Hawaii; Lanzarote, Canary Islands; Myojin Island, Pacific Ocean; Pompeii, Italy; St. Helens, Mount; Surtsey (Island), North Atlantic Ocean; Thera (Island), Greece; Vesuvius, Mount; Vestmannaeyjar

VOLGA (River), U.S.S.R.:
■ The Volga. 575, Nov. 1976; Cover, Mar. 1977
• The Volga, Russia's Mighty River Road. By Howard Sochurek. 579-613, May 1973

VOLGOGRAD, U.S.S.R.:
• The Volga, Russia's Mighty River Road. By Howard Sochurek. 579-613, May 1973

VOLTA BUREAU, Georgetown, Washington, D. C.:
• Washington's Historic Georgetown. By William A. Kinney. 513-544, Apr. 1953

VOLUNTEER ORGANIZATIONS. *See* Red Cross

VON ECKARDT, WOLF: Author:
• A Preservation Victory Saves Washington's Old Post Office. Photos by Volkmar Wentzel. 407-416, Sept. 1983

VON PUTTKAMER, W. JESCO:
Author-Photographer:
• Brazil Protects Her Cinta Larga Indians. 420-444, Sept. 1971
• Brazil's Beleaguered Indians. 254-283, Feb. 1975
I. Requiem for a Tribe? (Kreen-Akarores). 254-269; II. Good-bye to the Stone Age (Txukahameis). 270-283

• Man in the Amazon: Stone Age Present Meets Stone Age Past. 60-83, Jan. 1979
Photographer:
• Saving Brazil's Stone Age Tribes From Extinction. By Orlando and Claudio Villas Boas. 424-444, Sept. 1968

VOODOO:
• Haiti: Beyond Mountains, More Mountains. By Carolyn Bennett Patterson. Photos by Thomas Nebbia. 70-97, Jan. 1976
• Haiti–West Africa in the West Indies. By John Scofield. 226-259, Feb. 1961

VOORHIES, MICHAEL R.: Author:
• Ancient Ashfall Creates a Pompeii of Prehistoric Animals. Photos by Annie Griffiths. Paintings by Jay Matternes. 66-75, Jan. 1981

VOSBURGH, FREDERICK G.:
• Board of Trustees, member. 867, Dec. 1957; 485, Oct. 1966; 589, Oct. 1967; 838, Dec. 1970; 226, Aug. 1976
• Editor (1967-1970). 576, 577, 579, 586, 588, Oct. 1967; 861, June 1970; 841, Dec. 1970; 270, 276, Aug. 1982
• Editor, Assistant. 841, Dec. 1970
• Editor, Associate. 419, 420, 423, Mar. 1957; 867, Dec. 1957; 834, Dec. 1959; 585, Oct. 1963; 485, Oct. 1966; 579, Oct. 1967; 841, Dec. 1970
• Vice President of NGS. 585, Oct. 1963; 485, Oct. 1966; 576, 577, 588, Oct. 1967; 861, June 1970; 838, Dec. 1970
Author:
• Berlin, Island in a Soviet Sea. Photos by Volkmar Wentzel. 689-704, Nov. 1951
• Dog Mart Day in Fredericksburg. 817-832, June 1951
• Drums to Dynamos on the Mohawk. Photos by B. Anthony Stewart. 67-110, July 1947
• Easter Egg Chickens. Photos by B. Anthony Stewart. 377-387, Sept. 1948
• Flying in the "Blowtorch" Era. 281-322, Sept. 1950
• Formosa–Hot Spot of the East. Photos by J. Baylor Roberts. 139-176, Feb. 1950
• Japan Tries Freedom's Road. Photos by J. Baylor Roberts. 593-632, May 1950
• Minnesota Makes Ideas Pay. Photos by John E. Fletcher and B. Anthony Stewart. 291-336, Sept. 1949
• Shrines of Each Patriot's Devotion. 51-82, Jan. 1949
• Threatened Glories of Everglades National Park. By Frederick Kent Truslow and Frederick G. Vosburgh. Photos by Frederick Kent Truslow and Otis Imboden. 508-553, Oct. 1967
• To Gilbert Grosvenor: a Monthly Monument 25 Miles High. By Frederick G. Vosburgh and the staff of the National Geographic Society. 445-487, Oct. 1966
• Torchbearers of the Twilight. 697-704, May 1951

VOSS, GILBERT L.: Author:
• Shy Monster, the Octopus. Photos by Robert F. Sisson. 776-799, Dec. 1971
• Solving Life Secrets of the Sailfish. Photos by B. Anthony Stewart. Paintings by Craig Phillips. 859-872, June 1956
• Squids: Jet-powered Torpedoes of the Deep. Photos by Robert F. Sisson. 386-411, Mar. 1967

VOURAIKOS RIVER WATERSHED, Greece:
• Erosion, Trojan Horse of Greece. By F. G. Renner. 793-812, Dec. 1947

A **VOYAGE** Into the Unknown Changed Man's Understanding of His World. By Alan Villiers. Photos by Bruce Dale. 721-753, June 1976

The **VOYAGE** of *Brendan*–Did Irish Monks Discover America? By Timothy Severin. Photos by Cotton Coulson. 770-797, Dec. 1977

The **VOYAGE** of *Ra II*. By Thor Heyerdahl. Photos by Carlo Mauri and Georges Sourial. 44-71, Jan. 1971

VOYAGE Through an Invisible World. By Kenneth F. Weaver. 274-290, Feb. 1977

VOYAGE to the Antarctic. By David Lewis. 544-562, Apr. 1983

VOYAGE to the Planets. By Kenneth F. Weaver. Paintings by Ludek Pesek. 147-193, Aug. 1970

VOYAGE to Venus: The Story of Mariner II. By Frank Sartwell. Paintings by Davis Meltzer. 733-742, May 1963

VOYAGER (Spacecraft):
• Mars: A New World to Explore. By Carl Sagan. Note: Spacecraft later named Viking. 821-841, Dec. 1967
• Voyager 1 at Saturn: Riddles of the Rings. By Rick Gore. Photos by NASA. 3-31, July 1981
• Voyager's Historic View of Earth and Moon. 53, July 1978
• What Voyager Saw: Jupiter's Dazzling Realm. By Rick Gore. Photos by NASA. 2-29, Jan. 1980

VOYAGERS, Solo. *See* Graham, Robin Lee; *Ice Bird,* for David Lewis; Schultz, John E.

VOYAGES. *See* Cruises and Voyages

The **VOYAGES** and Historic Discoveries of Capt. Jas. Cook. By Alan Villiers. Photos by Gordon W. Gahan. 297-349, Sept. 1971

VOYAGEURS:
• Relics from the Rapids. By Sigurd F. Olson. Photos by David S. Boyer. 413-435, Sept. 1963

VULTURES. *See* Andean Condors; Egyptian Vulture

W

WAGNER, KIP: Author:
• Drowned Galleons Yield Spanish Gold. Photos by Otis Imboden. 1-37, Jan. 1965

WAHGI VALLEY, New Guinea:
• New Guinea's Paradise of Birds. By E. Thomas Gilliard. 661-688, Nov. 1951
• New Guinea's Rare Birds and Stone Age Men. By E. Thomas Gilliard. NGS research grant. 421-488, Apr. 1953
• Sheep Airlift in New Guinea. Photos by Ned Blood. 831-844, Dec. 1949

WAI WAI INDIANS:
• Life Among the Wai Wai Indians. By Clifford Evans and Betty J. Meggers. 329-346, Mar. 1955

WAIKIKI, Oahu (Island), Hawaii:
• Which Way Oahu? By Gordon Young. Photos by Robert W. Madden. 653-679, Nov. 1979

WAITOMO CAVES, New Zealand:
• Nature's Night Lights: Probing the Secrets of Bioluminescence. By Paul A. Zahl. 45-69, July 1971

WAKELIN, JAMES H., Jr.: Author:
• *Thresher:* Lesson and Challenge. 759-763, June 1964

WAKHAN (Region), Afghanistan:
• Afghanistan: Crossroad of Conquerors. By Thomas J. Abercrombie. 297-345, Sept. 1968
• We Took the Highroad in Afghanistan. By Jean and Franc Shor. 673-706, Nov. 1950
• Winter Caravan to the Roof of the World. By Sabrina and Roland Michaud. 435-465, Apr. 1972

WAKHI (People):
• Winter Caravan to the Roof of the World. By Sabrina and Roland Michaud. 435-465, Apr. 1972

WALDEN POND, Massachusetts:
• Thoreau, a Different Man. By William Howarth. Photos by Farrell Grehan. 349-387, Mar. 1981

WALES:
• British Castles, History in Stone. By Norman Wilkinson. 111-129, July 1947
• The Celts. By Merle Severy. Photos by James P. Blair. Paintings by Robert C. Magis. 582-633, May 1977
• The Investiture of Great Britain's Prince of Wales. By Allan C. Fisher, Jr. Photos by James L. Stanfield and Adam Woolfitt. Included: Caernarvon Castle. 698-715, Nov. 1969
▲ *A Traveler's Map of the British Isles,* supplement. Text on reverse. Apr. 1974
• Wales, Land of Bards. By Alan Villiers. Photos by Thomas Nebbia. 727-769, June 1965
• Wales, the Lyric Land. By Bryan Hodgson. Photos by Farrell Grehan. 36-63, July 1983
• *See also* Caldy; Skomer

A **WALK** Across America. By Peter Gorton Jenkins. 466-499, Apr. 1977

A **WALK** Across America: Part II. By Peter and Barbara Jenkins. 194-229, Aug. 1979

A **WALK** and Ride on the Wild Side: Tasmania. By Carolyn Bennett Patterson. Photos by David Hiser and Melinda Berge. 676-693, May 1983

A **WALK** in the Deep. By Sylvia A. Earle. Photos by Al Giddings and Chuck Nicklin. 624-631, May 1980

A **WALK** Through the Wilderness: Yellowstone at 100. By Karen and Derek Craighead. Photos by Sam Abell. 579-603, May 1972

WALKER, ERNEST P.: Author:
- "Flying" Squirrels, Nature's Gliders. 663-674, May 1947

Author-Photographer:
- Portraits of My Monkey Friends. 105-119, Jan. 1956

Photographer:
- The Wild Animals in My Life. By William M. Mann. 497-524, Apr. 1957

WALKER, HOWELL: Author:
- Italian Riviera, Land That Winter Forgot. 743-789, June 1963
- Long Island Outgrows the Country. Photos by B. Anthony Stewart. 279-326, Mar. 1951
- The Making of a West Pointer. 597-626, May 1952
- The More Paris Changes. . . . Photos by Gordon W. Gahan. 64-103, July 1972
- New South Wales, the State That Cradled Australia. Photos by David Moore. 591-635, Nov. 1967
- South Australia, Gateway to the Great Outback. Photos by Joseph J. Scherschel. 441-481, Apr. 1970
- Washington Lives Again at Valley Forge. 187-202, Feb. 1954

Author-Photographer:
- Air Age Brings Life to Canton Island. 117-132, Jan. 1955
- Aroostook County, Maine, Source of Potatoes. 459-478, Oct. 1948
- Belgium Welcomes the World (1958 World's Fair). 795-837, June 1958
- Cities Like Worcester Make America. 189-214, Feb. 1955
- Cruise to Stone Age Arnhem Land. 417-430, Sept. 1949
- France Meets the Sea in Brittany. 470-503, Apr. 1965
- From Spear to Hoe on Groote Eylandt. 131-142, Jan. 1953
- The Greener Fields of Georgia. Photos by author and B. Anthony Stewart. 287-330, Mar. 1954
- Here Rest in Honored Glory . . . (War Memorials). 739-768, June 1957
- History Keeps House in Virginia. 441-484, Apr. 1956
- Lafayette's Homeland, Auvergne. 419-436, Sept. 1957
- The Making of a New Australia. 233-259, Feb. 1956
- New Zealand, Pocket Wonder World. 419-460, Apr. 1952
- Normandy Blossoms Anew. 591-631, May 1959
- Tasmania, Australia's Island State. 791-818, Dec. 1956
- You Can't Miss America by Bus. Paintings by Walter A. Weber. 1-42, July 1950

Photographer:
- Exploring Stone Age Arnhem Land. By Charles P. Mountford. 745-782, Dec. 1949
- King Ranch, Cattle Empire in Texas. 41-64, Jan. 1952

WALKER, JOHN: Author:
- American Masters in the National Gallery. 295-324, Sept. 1948
- The National Gallery After a Quarter Century. 348-371, Mar. 1967
- The Nation's Newest Old Masters. Paintings from Kress Collection. 619-657, Nov. 1956
- The Vienna Treasures and Their Collectors. 737-776, June 1950
- Your National Gallery of Art After 10 Years. Paintings from Kress Collection. 73-103, Jan. 1952

WALKER, JOSEPH A.: Author:
- I Fly the X-15. Photos by Dean Conger. 428-450, Sept. 1962

WALKER, LEWIS WAYNE:

Author-Photographer:
- Arizona's Window on Wildlife. 240-250, Feb. 1958
- Sea Birds of Isla Raza. 239-248, Feb. 1951

WALKER, PHIL: Author:
- Across the Alps in a Wicker Basket *(Bernina)*. 117-131, Jan. 1963

WALKER, STANLEY: Author:
- The Fabulous State of Texas. Photos by B. Anthony Stewart and Thomas Nebbia. 149-195, Feb. 1961

WALKER, THEODORE J.: Author:
- The California Gray Whale Comes Back. 394-415, Mar. 1971

WALKING CATFISH:
- New Florida Resident, the Walking Catfish. By Clarence P. Idyll. Photos by Robert F. Sisson. 847-851, June 1969

WALKING TOURS:
- From Barra to Butt in the Hebrides. By Isobel Wylie Hutchison. 559-580, Oct. 1954
- I Walked Some Irish Miles. By Dorothea Sheats. 653-678, May 1951
- A Stroll to John o'Groat's. By Isobel Wylie Hutchison. 1-48, July 1956
- A Stroll to London. By Isobel Wylie Hutchison. Photos by B. Anthony Stewart. 171-204, Aug. 1950
- A Stroll to Venice. By Isobel Wylie Hutchison. 378-410, Sept. 1951
- *See also* Hiking Trips; *and* Hostels

WALL, STEVE: Photographer:
- Chattooga River Country: Wild Water, Proud People. By Don Belt. 458-477, Apr. 1983
- Troubled Odyssey of Vietnamese Fishermen. By Harvey Arden. 378-395, Sept. 1981

WALLER, JERRY: Photographer:
- Scenes of Postwar Finland. By La Verne Bradley. 233-264, Aug. 1947

WALLIS ISLANDS, Pacific Ocean. *See* Uvéa

WALLO PROVINCE, Ethiopia. *See* Lalibala

NATIONAL GALLERY OF ART

National Gallery: Fragonard's "A Young Girl Reading"

W X

WALLONIA (Region), Belgium:
• Belgium: One Nation Divisible. By James Cerruti. Photos by Martin Rogers. 314-341, Mar. 1979

WALLOONS:
• Belgium: One Nation Divisible. By James Cerruti. Photos by Martin Rogers. 314-341, Mar. 1979

WALRUS HUNTING:
• Cliff Dwellers of the Bering Sea. By Juan Muñoz. 129-146, Jan. 1954
• Nomad in Alaska's Outback. By Thomas J. Abercrombie. 540-567, Apr. 1969

WALRUSES:
• Learning the Ways of the Walrus. By G. Carleton Ray. Photos by Bill Curtsinger. NGS research grant. 565-580, Oct. 1979

WALSH, JOHN: Author-Photographer:
• Rotifers: Nature's Water Purifiers. 287-292, Feb. 1979

WALT DISNEY: Genius of Laughter and Learning. By Melville Bell Grosvenor. 157D, Aug. 1963
• *See also* Disney, Walt

WALT DISNEY WORLD, Florida:
• Florida's Booming–and Beleaguered–Heartland. By Joseph Judge. Photos by Jonathan Blair. 585-621, Nov. 1973

The **WANDERERS** From Vung Tau. By Harvey Arden. Photos by Steve Wall. 378-395, Sept. 1981

WANGCHUCK DYNASTY (Bhutan):
• Bhutan, Land of the Thunder Dragon. By Burt Kerr Todd. 713-754, Dec. 1952
• Bhutan Crowns a New Dragon King. By John Scofield. 546-571, Oct. 1974
• Life Slowly Changes in a Remote Himalayan Kingdom. By John Scofield. 658-683, Nov. 1976

WAR and Peace in Northern Ireland. By Bryan Hodgson. Photos by Cary Wolinsky. 470-499, Apr. 1981

WAR and Quiet on the Laos Frontier. By W. Robert Moore. 665-680, May 1954

WAR MEMORIALS:
• Gettysburg and Vicksburg: the Battle Towns Today. By Robert Paul Jordan. Map notes by Carolyn Bennett Patterson. 4-57, July 1963
• Here Rest in Honored Glory . . . The United States Dedicates Six New Battle Monuments in Europe to Americans Who Gave Their Lives During World War II. By Howell Walker. Contents: Cambridge, England; Brittany, Épinal, Normandy, and Rhône in France; Sicily-Rome at Nettuno, Italy. 739-768, June 1957
• Our War Memorials Abroad: A Faith Kept. By George C. Marshall. 731-737, June 1957
• *See also* Arlington National Cemetery, Virginia; Civil War, U. S.

WAR OF 1812:
• Ghost Ships of the War of 1812: *Hamilton* and *Scourge*. By Daniel A. Nelson. Photos by Emory Kristof. Paintings by Richard Schlecht. 289-313, Mar. 1983

LIBERTO PERUGI

Warriors From Grave: a Riace bronze

WAR-TORN Greece Looks Ahead. By Maynard Owen Williams. 711-744, Dec. 1949

WARBLERS:
• The Bird's Year. By Arthur A. Allen. Included: Chestnut-sided, Kentucky, Magnolia, Mourning, and Yellow warblers. 791-816, June 1951

WARD, FRED:
• Editorial. By Gilbert M. Grosvenor. 143, Feb. 1980
Author-Photographer:
• The Changing World of Canada's Crees. 541-569, Apr. 1975
• Hurricane! Dominica. 357-359, Sept. 1980
• The Imperiled Everglades. 1-27, Jan. 1972
• In Long-Forbidden Tibet. 218-259, Feb. 1980
• The Incredible Crystal: Diamonds. 85-113, Jan. 1979
• Inside Cuba Today. 32-69, Jan. 1977
Photographer:
• Fiber Optics: Harnessing Light by a Thread. By Allen A. Boraiko. 516-535, Oct. 1979
• New England's "Lively Experiment," Rhode Island. By Robert de Roos. 370-401, Sept. 1968
• The Pesticide Dilemma. By Allen A. Boraiko. 145-183, Feb. 1980
• Silver: A Mineral of Excellent Nature. By Allen A. Boraiko. 280-313, Sept. 1981
• Those Successful Japanese. By Bart McDowell. 323-359, Mar. 1974

WARM SPRINGS INDIANS, Confederated Tribes of:
• Warm Springs Indians Carve Out a Future. By David S. Boyer. 494-505, Apr. 1979

WARNER, CONSTANCE P.:
Author-Photographer:
• Nature's Alert Eyes. 558-569, Apr. 1959

WARREN, CHARLES: Author:
• The Washington National Monument Society. 739-744, June 1947

WARREN, EARL:
• Board of Trustees, member. 422, Mar. 1957; 258, Aug. 1958; 835, Dec. 1959; 880, Dec. 1961; 670, 671, May 1964; 751, Dec. 1964; 485, Oct. 1966; 589, Oct. 1967; 860, June 1970
Hubbard Medal Presentations:
• Paul A. Siple. 792-793, June 1958; Dr. and Mrs. Louis S. B. Leakey. 903, 905, Dec. 1962; 197, 231, Feb. 1965; Juan Trippe. 584-586, Apr. 1968
La Gorce Medal Presentation:
• Antarctic Expedition. 864-867, June 1967

WARREN, EARL, Jr.: Author:
• Off Santa Barbara: California's Ranches in the Sea. 257-283, Aug. 1958

WARRIORS From a Watery Grave (Bronze Sculptures). By Joseph Alsop. 821-827, June 1983

WARROAD, Minnesota:
• Men, Moose, and Mink of Northwest Angle. By William H. Nicholas. Photos by J. Baylor Roberts. 265-284, Aug. 1947

WARSAW, Poland:
• Poland Opens Her Doors. By Delia and Ferdinand Kuhn. Photos by Erich Lessing. 354-398, Sept. 1958
• Springtime of Hope in Poland. By Peter T. White. Photos by James P. Blair. 467-501, Apr. 1972

WARSHIPS:
• Ghost Ships of the War of 1812: *Hamilton* and *Scourge*. By Daniel A. Nelson. Photos by Emory Kristof. Paintings by Richard Schlecht. 289-313, Mar. 1983
• Henry VIII's Lost Warship: *Mary Rose*. By Margaret Rule. Introduction and picture text by Peter Miller. Paintings by Richard Schlecht. 646-675, May 1983
• Ships Through the Ages: A Saga of the Sea. By Alan Villiers. 494-545, Apr. 1963
• *See also Monitor;* Spanish Armada; *Vasa; and* Battleships

WASATCH FRONT (Valleys), Utah:
• Utah's Shining Oasis. By Charles McCarry. Photos by James L. Amos. 440-473, Apr. 1975

WASATCH RANGE, Utah:
• Avalanche! Winter's White Death. 280-281, Sept. 1982

WASHBURN, BRADFORD: Author:
• Canada's Mount Kennedy: I. The Discovery. 1-3, July 1965
Author-Photographer:
• Mount McKinley Conquered by New Route. 219-248, Aug. 1953

WASHINGTON, GEORGE:
• Across the Potomac from Washington. By Albert W. Atwood. 1-33, Jan. 1953
◆ *George Washington–Man and Monument.* Published in cooperation with the Washington National Monument Association. 586, Oct. 1967
• George Washington: The Man Behind the Myths. By Howard La Fay. Photos by Ted Spiegel. 90-111, July 1976
• George Washington's Travels, Traced on the Arrowsmith Map. 768-769, June 1953
• The Living White House. By Lonnelle Aikman. 593-643, Nov. 1966
• Mount Vernon Lives On. By Lonnelle Aikman. 651-682, Nov. 1953
• Profiles of the Presidents: I. The Presidency and How It Grew. By Frank Freidel. 642-687, Nov. 1964
• Shrines of Each Patriot's Devotion. By Frederick G. Vosburgh. Included: George Washington's birthplace; Mount Vernon; Valley Forge Park. 51-82, Jan. 1949
• Washington Lives Again at Valley Forge. By Howell Walker. 187-202, Feb. 1954

WASHINGTON, MARTHA:
• Patriots in Petticoats. By Lonnelle Aikman. Paintings by Louis S. Glanzman. 475-493, Oct. 1975

WASHINGTON:
• Chief Joseph. By William Albert Allard. 409-434, Mar. 1977
• Climbing Our Northwest Glaciers. Photos by Bob and Ira Spring. 103-114, July 1953
• *Endeavour* Sails the Inside Passage. By Amos Burg. 801-828, June 1947
• Following the Trail of Lewis and Clark. By Ralph Gray. 707-750, June 1953
• From Sagebrush to Roses on the Columbia. By Leo A. Borah. 571-611, Nov. 1952
• The Incredible Potato. By Robert E. Rhoades. Photos by Martin Rogers. Note: The Russet Burbank has allowed Idaho and Washington to surpass Maine's production lead. 668-694, May 1982
• A Map Maker Looks at the United States. By Newman Bumstead. Included: Aberdeen; Adams, Mount; Blewett; Bremerton; Chelan, Lake; Cle Elum; Cle Elum Lake; Dosewallips River; Duckabush River; Dungeness Spit; Ediz Hook; Franklin Delano Roosevelt Lake; Gifford Pinchot National Forest; Grand Coulee Dam; Greenacres; Hoh River Valley; Hood Canal; Hoquiam; Kachess Lake; Olympic National Park; Olympic Peninsula; Opportunity; Port Angeles; Port Orchard; Port Townsend; Puget Sound; Rosalia; St. Helens, Mount; Seattle; Sequim; Snoqualmie Pass; Spokane; Walla Walla; Wenatchee; Wenatchee Mountains; Yakima; Zenith. 705-748, June 1951
• Mexico to Canada on the Pacific Crest Trail. By Mike W. Edwards. Photos by David Hiser. 741-779, June 1971
• Mount Rainier: Testing Ground for Everest. By Barry C. Bishop. NGS research grant. 688-711, May 1963
• New National Park Proposed: The Spectacular North Cascades. By Nathaniel T. Kenney. Photos by James P. Blair. 642-667, May 1968
• Northwest Wonderland: Washington State. By Merle Severy. Photos by B. Anthony Stewart. 445-493, Apr. 1960
• A Paradise Called the Palouse. By Barbara Austin. Photos by Phil Schofield. 798-819, June 1982
• Powerhouse of the Northwest (Columbia River). By David S. Boyer. 821-847, Dec. 1974
• Snow-mantled Stehekin: Where Solitude Is in Season. Photos by Bruce Dale. Text by Pat Hutson. 572-588, Apr. 1974
• Timber: How Much Is Enough? By John J. Putman. Photos by Bruce Dale. 485-511, Apr. 1974
• Washington Wilderness, the North Cascades. By Edwards Park. Photos by Kathleen Revis. 335-367, Mar. 1961
• Washington's Yakima Valley. By Mark Miller. Photos by Sisse Brimberg. 609-631, Nov. 1978
• *See also* Georgia, Strait of; Olympic National Park; Puget Sound; St. Helens, Mount; Seattle; Skagit River

WASHINGTON, D. C.:
• Across the Potomac from Washington. By Albert W. Atwood. 1-33, Jan. 1953
• American Processional: History on Canvas. By John and Blanche Leeper. 173-212, Feb. 1951
• The DAR Story. By Lonnelle Aikman. Photos by B. Anthony Stewart and John E. Fletcher. Included: Headquarters of the National Society of Daughters of the American Revolution. 565-598, Nov. 1951
• Editorials. By Wilbur E. Garrett. 1, Jan. 1983; 557, Nov. 1983
▲ *Heart of Our Nation's Capital; Washington Inside the Beltway,* double-sided tear-out. Jan. 1983
• The Last Full Measure (Tribute to President Kennedy). By Melville Bell Grosvenor. 307-355, Mar. 1964
• New Grandeur for Flowering Washington. By Joseph Judge. Photos by James P. Blair. 500-539, Apr. 1967
• Parkscape, U.S.A.: Tomorrow in Our National Parks. By George B. Hartzog, Jr. Included: National Capital Parks; Pennsylvania Avenue. 48-93, July 1966
• Pennsylvania Avenue, Route of Presidents. By Dorothea and Stuart E. Jones. Photos by Volkmar Wentzel. 63-95, Jan. 1957
▲ *A Pocket Map of Central Washington; Suburban Washington,* double-sided supplement. Sept. 1948
• A Preservation Victory Saves Washington's Old Post Office. By Wolf Von Eckardt. Photos by Volkmar Wentzel. 407-416, Sept. 1983
▲ *Round About the Nation's Capital,* supplement. Apr. 1956
▲ *Tourist Washington; Suburban Washington,* double-sided U. S. Atlas series supplement. Dec. 1964
• Washington: Home of the Nation's Great. By Albert W. Atwood. 699-738, June 1947
Our Magnificent Capital City. Photos by B. Anthony Stewart. 715-738
• Washington: The City Freedom Built. By William Graves. Photos by Bruce Dale and Thomas Nebbia. 735-781, Dec. 1964
• Washington, D. C.: Hometown Behind the Monuments. By Henry Mitchell. Photos by Adam Woolfitt. 84-125, Jan. 1983
• Washington's Historic Georgetown. By William A. Kinney. 513-544, Apr. 1953
• Waterway to Washington, the C & O Canal. By Jay Johnston. 419-439, Mar. 1960
• World's Last Salute to a Great American (Dwight D. Eisenhower). By William Graves and other members of the NGS staff. 40-51, July 1969
• *See also* Folger; Ford's Theatre; Library of Congress; National Bureau of Standards; National Gallery of Art; National Zoological Park; Presidents, U. S.; Smithsonian Institution; U. S. Capitol; Washington Cathedral; Washington Monument; White House; *and* names of U. S. government agencies

WX

WASHINGTON, Mount, New Hampshire:
● The Friendly Huts of the White Mountains. By William O. Douglas. Photos by Kathleen Revis. 205-239, Aug. 1961
● Mountains Top Off New England. By F. Barrows Colton. Photos by Robert F. Sisson. 563-602, May 1951
● Skyline Trail (Appalachian Trail) from Maine to Georgia. By Andrew H. Brown. Photos by Robert F. Sisson. 219-251, Aug. 1949

WASHINGTON CATHEDRAL, Washington, D. C.:
● Washington Cathedral: "House of Prayer for All People." By Robert Paul Jordan. Photos by Sisse Brimberg. 552-573, Apr. 1980

WASHINGTON MONUMENT, Washington, D. C.:
◆ *George Washington–Man and Monument.* Published in cooperation with the Washington National Monument Association. 586, Oct. 1967
● The Washington National Monument Society. By Charles Warren. 739-744, June 1947

WASP (Submersible):
● Exploring a 140-year-old Ship Under Arctic Ice *(Breadalbane).* By Joseph B. MacInnis. Photos by Emory Kristof. 104A-104D, July 1983

WASPS:
● New Tricks Outwit Our Insect Enemies. By Hal Higdon. Photos by Robert F. Sisson and Emory Kristof. 380-399, Sept. 1972
● The Wasp That Plays Cupid to a Fig. By Robert F. Sisson. 690-697, Nov. 1970

WASSAW (Island), Georgia:
● Sea Islands: Adventuring Along the South's Surprising Coast. By James Cerruti. Photos by Thomas Nebbia and James L. Amos. 366-393, Mar. 1971

WASTE DISPOSAL:
● The Fascinating World of Trash. By Peter T. White. Photos by Louie Psihoyos. 424-457, Apr. 1983

WASÚSU INDIANS:
● Man in the Amazon: Stone Age Present Meets Stone Age Past. By W. Jesco von Puttkamer. NGS research grant. 60-83, Jan. 1979

WATCH INDUSTRY:
● Switzerland, Europe's High-rise Republic. By Thomas J. Abercrombie. 68-113, July 1969
● Switzerland Guards the Roof of Europe. By William H. Nicholas. Photos by Willard R. Culver. 205-246, Aug. 1950

WATCHING a Baby Gorilla Grow Up. By Ernst M. Lang. Photos by Paul Steinemann. 446-453, Mar. 1964

WATER BIRDS:
● Barehanded Battle to Cleanse the Bay. By Peter T. White. Photos by Jonathan S. Blair. Included: Oil-crippled birds. 866-881, June 1971
▲ *Bird Migration in the Americas,* double-sided supplement. Aug. 1979
● Can We Save Our Salt Marshes? By Stephen W. Hitchcock. Photos by William R. Curtsinger. 729-765, June 1972
● Corkscrew Swamp–Florida's Primeval Show Place. By Melville Bell Grosvenor. 98-113, Jan. 1958
● The Curlew's Secret. By Arthur A. Allen. Included: Alaska longspur, Alaska yellow wagtail, Baird's sandpiper, Black-bellied plover, Bristle-thighed curlew, Cackling goose, Cranes, Ducks, Emperor goose, Frigate bird, Geese, Golden plover, Hoary redpoll, Hudsonian curlew, Little brown crane, Northern phalarope, Old-squaw, Pacific godwit, Parasitic jaeger, Pectoral sandpiper, Ruddy turnstone, Sabine's gull, Savannah sparrow, Snow bunting, Spectacled eider, Tree sparrow, Varied thrush, Western sandpiper, Whistling swan, White-fronted goose, Wilson's snipe. 751-770, Dec. 1948
● Island, Prairie, Marsh, and Shore. By Charlton Ogburn. Photos by Bates Littlehales. 350-381, Mar. 1979
● Mysteries of Bird Migration. By Allan C. Fisher, Jr. Photos by Jonathan Blair. 154-193, Aug. 1979
Tracking the Shore Dwellers: From Canada to Suriname. 175-179
● Saving Man's Wildlife Heritage. By John H. Baker. Photos by Robert F. Sisson. 581-620, Nov. 1954
● Threatened Glories of Everglades National Park. By Frederick Kent Truslow and Frederick G. Vosburgh. Photos by Frederick Kent Truslow and Otis Imboden. 508-553, Oct. 1967
◆ *Water, Prey, and Game Birds of North America.* Announced. 529-535, Oct. 1965
● Where Oil and Wildlife Mix. By Steven C. Wilson and Karen C. Hayden. 145-173, Feb. 1981
◆ *Wildlife Alert: The Struggle to Survive.* 1980
● Wildlife of Everglades National Park. By Daniel B. Beard. Paintings by Walter A. Weber. 83-116, Jan. 1949
● *See also* Ducks; Flamingos; Geese; Herons; Ibises; Limpkin; Penguins; Roseate Spoonbills; Swans; Western Grebes; Whooping Cranes; Wilson's Phalarope; *and* Seabirds; Waterfowl Hunting

WATER BUFFALO:
● Life and Death in Tana Toradja. By Pamela and Alfred Meyer. 793-815, June 1972
● Marsh Dwellers of Southern Iraq. By Wilfred Thesiger. Photos by Gavin Maxwell. 205-239, Feb. 1958
● The Top End of Down Under. By Kenneth MacLeish. Photos by Thomas Nebbia. 145-174, Feb. 1973
● Water Dwellers in a Desert World. By Gavin Young. Photos by Nik Wheeler. 502-523, Apr. 1976

WATER CLOCKS. *See* The Tower of the Winds

WATER Dwellers in a Desert World. By Gavin Young. Photos by Nik Wheeler. 502-523, Apr. 1976

SISSE BRIMBERG
Washington Cathedral: the high altar

WATER LILIES:
• Life Around a Lily Pad. Photos by Bianca Lavies. Text by Charles R. Miller. 131-142, Jan. 1980

WATER POLLUTION:
• Can We Save Our Salt Marshes? By Stephen W. Hitchcock. Photos by William R. Curtsinger. 729-765, June 1972
• The Continental Shelf: Man's New Frontier. By Luis Marden. Photos by Ira Block. 495-531. Apr. 1978
• The Great Lakes: Is It Too Late? By Gordon Young. Photos by James L. Amos and Martin Rogers. 147-185, Aug. 1973
• The Hudson: "That River's Alive." By Alice J. Hall. Photos by Ted Spiegel. 62-89, Jan. 1978
• The Mediterranean–Sea of Man's Fate. By Rick Gore. Photos by Jonathan Blair. 694-737, Dec. 1982
• My Chesapeake–Queen of Bays. By Allan C. Fisher, Jr. Photos by Lowell Georgia. 428-467, Oct. 1980
• North Through History Aboard *White Mist*. By Melville Bell Grosvenor. Photos by Edwin Stuart Grosvenor. Included: Hudson River. 1-55, July 1970
• Our Most Precious Resource: Water. By Thomas Y. Canby. Photos by Ted Spiegel. 144-179, Aug. 1980
• Pollution, Threat to Man's Only Home. By Gordon Young. Photos by James P. Blair. 738-781, Dec. 1970
• Quicksilver and Slow Death (Mercury). By John J. Putman. Photos by Robert W. Madden. 507-527, Oct. 1972
• A River Restored: Oregon's Willamette. By Ethel A. Starbird. Photos by Lowell J. Georgia. 816-835, June 1972
• San Francisco Bay: The Beauty and the Battles. By Cliff Tarpy. Photos by James A. Sugar. 814-845, June 1981
• Yesterday Lingers Along the Connecticut. By Charles McCarry. Photos by David L. Arnold. 334-369, Sept. 1972
• *See also* Oil Spills; Pesticide Pollution

WATER POWER. *See* Hydroelectric Power

WATER RESOURCES:
• Arizona's Suburbs of the Sun. By David Jeffery. Photos by H. Edward Kim. 486-517, Oct. 1977
• Editorials. By Gilbert M. Grosvenor. 143, Aug. 1980; By Wilbur E. Garrett. 421, Oct. 1981
• Egypt's Desert of Promise. By Farouk El-Baz. Photos by Georg Gerster. 190-221, Feb. 1982
• Our Most Precious Resource: Water. By Thomas Y. Canby. Photos by Ted Spiegel. 144-179, Aug. 1980
• Paraguay, Paradox of South America. By Gordon Young. Photos by O. Louis Mazzatenta. Included: Itaipú Development. 240-269, Aug. 1982
• Quebec's Northern Dynamo. By Larry Kohl. Photos by Ottmar Bierwagen. 406-418, Mar. 1982

CRAIG AURNESS

Mono Lake: ghostly islands of tufa

• San Francisco Bay: The Beauty and the Battles. By Cliff Tarpy. Photos by James A. Sugar. 814-845, June 1981
• Sno-Cats Mechanize Oregon Snow Survey. By Andrew H. Brown. Photos by John E. Fletcher. 691-710, Nov. 1949
• The Troubled Waters of Mono Lake. By Gordon Young. Photos by Craig Aurness. Note: The Los Angeles Aqueduct annually diverts 32 billion gallons of Mono basin water. 504-519, Oct. 1981
• The Untamed Yellowstone. By Bill Richards. Photos by Dean Krakel II. Included: Water allocation controversy between irrigation and coal-recovery. 257-278, Aug. 1981
• Water for the World's Growing Needs. By Herbert B. Nichols and F. Barrows Colton. 269-286, Aug. 1952
• The Year the Weather Went Wild. By Thomas Y. Canby. 799-829, Dec. 1977
• *See also* Dams; Dikes and Levees; Floods and Flood Control; Irrigation; *and* Los Angeles Aqueduct

WATER SAFETY:
• The American Red Cross: A Century of Service. By Louise Levathes. Photos by Annie Griffiths. 777-791, June 1981

WATER SKIING:
• The Booming Sport of Water Skiing. By Wilbur E. Garrett. 700-711, Nov. 1958

WATER War in Viet Nam. By Dickey Chapelle. 272-296, Feb. 1966

WATERFALLS:
• Labrador Canoe Adventure. By Andrew H. Brown and Ralph Gray. Included: Grand Falls of the Hamilton River, Lower Unknown Falls, Upper Unknown Falls. 65-99, July 1951
• Land of the Havasupai. By Jack Breed. Included: Beaver Falls, Fifty-foot Falls, Havasu or Bridal Veil Falls, Mooney Falls, Navajo Falls. 655-674, May 1948
• *See also* Angel Falls, Venezuela; Niagara Falls, Canada-U. S.; Victoria Falls, Zambia-Zimbabwe

WATERFOWL HUNTING:
• Born Hunters, the Bird Dogs. By Roland Kilbon. Paintings by Walter A. Weber. 369-398, Sept. 1947
• Humble Masterpieces: Decoys. By George Reiger. Photos by Kenneth Garrett. 639-663, Nov. 1983

WATERMEN:
• Chincoteague: Watermen's Island Home. By Nathaniel T. Kenney. Photos by James L. Amos. 810-829, June 1980
• My Chesapeake–Queen of Bays. By Allan C. Fisher, Jr. Photos by Lowell Georgia. 428-467, Oct. 1980
• The Sailing Oystermen of Chesapeake Bay. By Luis Marden. 798-819, Dec. 1967
• This Is My Island, Tangier. By Harold G. Wheatley. Photos by David Alan Harvey. 700-725, Nov. 1973

WATERTON-GLACIER INTERNATIONAL PEACE PARK, Canada-U. S.:
● Canadian Rockies, Lords of a Beckoning Land. By Alan Phillips. Photos by James L. Stanfield. 353-393, Sept. 1966
● Many-splendored Glacierland. By George W. Long. Photos by Kathleen Revis. 589-636, May 1956

WATERWAY to Washington, the C & O Canal. By Jay Johnston. 419-439, Mar. 1960

WATERWAYS. *See* Canals; Chesapeake Bay; Great Lakes; Inland Sea, Japan; Inside Passage; Intracoastal Waterways; Panama Canal; St. Lawrence Seaway; *and* Rivers and River Trips

WATSON, DON: Author:
● Ancient Cliff Dwellers of Mesa Verde. Photos by Willard R. Culver. 349-376, Sept. 1948

WATT, JAMES:
● The British Way. By Sir Evelyn Wrench. 421-541, Apr. 1949

WAURÁ (Indians):
● Amazon–The River Sea. By Loren McIntyre. 456-495, Oct. 1972
● The Waurá: Brazilian Indians of the Hidden Xingu. By Harald Schultz. 130-152, Jan. 1966

WAVES (Women's Reserve of the U. S. Naval Reserve). *See* Parachute Rigger School

A **WAY** of Life Called Maine. By Ethel A. Starbird. Photos by David Hiser. 727-757, June 1977

WAY of the Jackal. By Patricia D. Moehlman. 840-850, Dec. 1980

WAY Station for the Wilson's Phalarope. By Joseph R. Jehl, Jr. 520-525, Oct. 1981

WAYANA INDIANS:
● What Future for the Wayana Indians? By Carole Devillers. 66-83, Jan. 1983

WE're Coming Over on the *Mayflower*. By Alan Villiers. 708-728, May 1957

WE're Doing Something About the Weather! By Walter Orr Roberts. 518-555, Apr. 1972

WE Are Living at the South Pole. By Paul A. Siple. Photos by David S. Boyer. 5-35, July 1957

WE Build a School for Sherpa Children. By Sir Edmund Hillary. 548-551, Oct. 1962

WE Captured a 'Live' Brontosaur. By Roland T. Bird. 707-722, May 1954

WE Climbed Utah's Skyscraper Rock. By Huntley Ingalls. Photos by author and Barry C. Bishop. 705-721, Nov. 1962

WE Drove Panama's Darién Gap. By Kip Ross. 368-389, Mar. 1961

WE Dwelt in Kashgai Tents. By Jean and Franc Shor. 805-832, June 1952

WE Followed Peary to the Pole. By Gilbert Grosvenor and Thomas W. McKnew. 469-484, Oct. 1953

ANTHONY A. BOCCACCIO

Doing Something About the Weather: laboratory twister

WE Lived in Turbulent Tehran. By Rebecca Shannon Cresson. 707-720, Nov. 1953

WE Saw the World From the Edge of Space. By Malcolm D. Ross. Ground photos by Walter Meayers Edwards. 671-685, Nov. 1961

WE Survive on a Pacific Atoll. By John and Frank Craighead. 73-94, Jan. 1948

WE Took the Highroad in Afghanistan. By Jean and Franc Shor. 673-706, Nov. 1950

"WE Who Face Death." By LeRoy Woodson, Jr. 364-387, Mar. 1975

WEALTH and Wonder of Northern State Trees. By William A. Dayton. Paintings by Walter A. Weber. 651-691, Nov. 1955

WEAPONS, Primitive:
● Bison Kill By Ice Age Hunters. By Dennis Stanford. NGS research grant. 114-121, Jan. 1979
● The Search for the First Americans. By Thomas Y. Canby. Photos by Kerby Smith. Paintings by Roy Andersen. 330-363, Sept. 1979

WEATHER:
● Acid Rain–How Great a Menace? By Anne LaBastille. Photos by Ted Spiegel. 652-681, Nov. 1981
● The Air-Safety Challenge. By Michael E. Long. Photos by Bruce Dale. 209-235, Aug. 1977
● Alaska's Mighty Rivers of Ice. By Maynard M. Miller. Photos by Christopher G. Knight. 194-217, Feb. 1967
● Extraordinary Photograph Shows Earth Pole to Pole. Photos by Nimbus I. 190-193, Feb. 1965
● The Mediterranean–Sea of Man's Fate. By Rick Gore. Photos by Jonathan Blair. 694-737, Dec. 1982
● Our Changing Atlantic Coastline (March 1962 Storm). By Nathaniel T. Kenney. Photos by B. Anthony Stewart. 860-887, Dec. 1962
◆ *Our Violent Earth.* 1982
◆ *Powers of Nature.* 1978
● Volcanic Cloud May Alter Earth's Climate. By Robert I. Tilling. 672-675, Nov. 1982
● We're Doing Something About the Weather! By Walter Orr Roberts. 518-555, Apr. 1972
● What's Happening to Our Climate? By Samuel W. Matthews. 576-615, Nov. 1976
● The Year the Weather Went Wild. By Thomas Y. Canby. Included: Eight maps depicting the unusual aspects of weather in the United States (1976-1977). 799-829, Dec. 1977
● *See also* Drought; Lightning; Storms

WEATHER SATELLITES:
● The Earth From Orbit. By Paul D. Lowman, Jr. 645-671, Nov. 1966
● Extraordinary Photograph Shows Earth Pole to Pole. Photos by Nimbus I. 190-193, Feb. 1965
● How Man-made Satellites Can Affect Our Lives. By Joseph Kaplan. Paintings by Gilbert Emerson. 791-810, Dec. 1957

• Our Earth as a Satellite (*Tiros I*) Sees It. By W. G. Stroud. 293-302, Aug. 1960
• Remote Sensing: New Eyes to See the World. By Kenneth F. Weaver. 46-73, Jan. 1969
• Satellites Gave Warning of Midwest Floods. By Peter T. White. Photos by Thomas A. DeFeo. 574-592, Oct. 1969
• Satellites That Serve Us. By Thomas Y. Canby. Included: A portfolio, Images of Earth. 281-335, Sept. 1983
Spacelab 1: *Columbia*. By Michael E. Long. 301-307
• Space Satellites, Tools of Earth Research. By Heinz Haber. Paintings by William N. Palmstrom. 487-509, Apr. 1956

WEATHER STATIONS AND RESEARCH:
• Man's First Winter at the South Pole. By Paul A. Siple. 439-478, Apr. 1958
• Men Against the Hurricane. By Andrew H. Brown. Included: Joint Hurricane Warning Center, Miami. 537-560, Oct. 1950
• Milestones in My Arctic Journeys. By Willie Knutsen. Included: Weather stations in Arctic Canada. 543-570, Oct. 1949
• Our Navy Explores Antarctica. By Richard E. Byrd. U. S. Navy official photos. 429-522, Oct. 1947
• Rugged Is the Word for Bravo (Weather Patrol). By Phillip M. Swatek. 829-843, Dec. 1955
• Three Months on an Arctic Ice Island. By Joseph O. Fletcher. 489-504, Apr. 1953
• We Followed Peary to the Pole. By Gilbert Grosvenor and Thomas W. McKnew. 469-484, Oct. 1953
• Weather from the White North. By Andrew H. Brown. Photos by John E. Fletcher. 543-572, Apr. 1955
• We're Doing Something About the Weather! By Walter Orr Roberts. 518-555, Apr. 1972
• Year of Discovery Opens in Antarctica. By David S. Boyer. 339-381, Sept. 1957

WEATHERIZATION PROGRAMS:
• Conservation: Can We Live Better on Less? By Rick Gore. 34-57, *Special Report on Energy* (Feb. 1981)

WEAVER, KENNETH F.:
• Editorial. By Gilbert M. Grosvenor. 729, June 1980
Author:
• And Now to Touch the Moon's Forbidding Face. 633-635, May 1969
• Apollo 15 Explores the Mountains of the Moon. Photos from NASA. 233-265, Feb. 1972
• Athens: Her Golden Past Still Lights the World. Photos by Phillip Harrington. 100-137, July 1963
• Countdown for Space. 702-734, May 1961
• Crystals, Magical Servants of the Space Age. Photos by James P. Blair. 278-296, Aug. 1968
• Electronic Voyage Through an Invisible World. 274-290, Feb. 1977
• The Five Worlds of Peru. Photos by Bates Littlehales. 213-265, Feb. 1964
• The Flight of Apollo 11: "One giant leap for mankind." 752-787, Dec. 1969
• Geothermal Energy: The Power of Letting Off Steam. 566-579, Oct. 1977
• Giant Comet Grazes the Sun. 259-261, Feb. 1966
• Have We Solved the Mysteries of the Moon? Paintings by William H. Bond. 309-325, Sept. 1973
• Historic Color Portrait of Earth From Space. Photos by DODGE Satellite. 726-731, Nov. 1967
• How Old Is It? By Lyman J. Briggs and Kenneth F. Weaver. 234-255, Aug. 1958
• How Soon Will We Measure In Metric? Drawings by Donald A. Mackay. 287-294, Aug. 1977
• How to Catch a Passing Comet. 148-150, Jan. 1974
• The Incredible Universe. Photos by James P. Blair. 589-625, May 1974
• Journey to Mars. Paintings by Ludek Pesek. 231-263, Feb. 1973
• Magnetic Clues Help Date the Past. 696-701, May 1967
• Mariner Unveils Venus and Mercury. 858-869, June 1975
• Maui, Where Old Hawaii Still Lives. Photos by Gordon W. Gahan. 514-543, Apr. 1971
• The Mystery of the Shroud. 730-753, June 1980
• Mystery Shrouds the Biggest Planet (Jupiter). 285-294, Feb. 1975
• Of Planes and Men. Photos by Emory Kristof and Albert Moldvay. 298-349, Sept. 1965
• Our Energy Predicament. 2-23, *Special Report on Energy* (Feb. 1981)
• The Promise and Peril of Nuclear Energy. Photos by Emory Kristof. 459-493, Apr. 1979
• Remote Sensing: New Eyes to See the World. 46-73, Jan. 1969
• Rip Van Winkle of the Underground (Cicada). 133-142, July 1953
• The Search for Life on Mars. 264-265, Feb. 1973
• The Search for Tomorrow's Power. Photos by Emory Kristof. 650-681, Nov. 1972
• Space Rendezvous, Milestone on the Way to the Moon. 539-553, Apr. 1966
• That Orbèd Maiden . . . the Moon. 207-230, Feb. 1969
• Tracking America's Man in Orbit. Photos by Robert F. Sisson. 184-217, Feb. 1962
• Voyage to the Planets. Paintings by Ludek Pesek. 147-193, Aug. 1970
• What the Moon Rocks Tell Us. 788-791, Dec. 1969
• What You Didn't See in Kohoutek. 214-223, Aug. 1974

WEAVER, ROBERT F.: Author:
• The Cancer Puzzle. 396-399, Sept. 1976

WEAVING:
• Ethiopia's Artful Weavers. By Judith Olmstead. Photos by James A. Sugar. 125-141, Jan. 1973
• *See also* Rugs and Rug Making; Tweed

WEBBER, JOHN:
• Captain Cook: The Man Who Mapped the Pacific. By Alan Villiers. Photos by Gordon W. Gahan. Included: Oil painting of Captain Cook (1776) and sketches by *Resolution* artist John Webber. 297-349, Sept. 1971

WEBER, WALTER A.: Artist:
• An Artist's Glimpses of Our Roadside Wildlife. 16-32, July 1950
• Beauty and Bounty of Southern State Trees. By William A. Dayton. 508-552, Oct. 1957
• Born Hunters, the Bird Dogs. By Roland Kilbon. 369-398, Sept. 1947
• Honey-Guide: The Bird That Eats Wax. By Herbert Friedmann. 551-560, Apr. 1954
• Life Portraits of a Famous Family: Pacific Salmon. 214-216, Aug. 1968
• Nature's Tank, the Turtle. By Doris M. Cochran. 665-684, May 1952
• Our Snake Friends and Foes. By Doris M. Cochran. 334-364, Sept. 1954
• Stalking Central Africa's Wildlife. By T. Donald Carter. 264-286, Aug. 1956
• Strange Courtship of Birds of Paradise. By S. Dillon Ripley. 247-278, Feb. 1950
• Wealth and Wonder of Northern State Trees. By William A. Dayton. 651-691, Nov. 1955
• Wildlife of Everglades National Park. By Daniel B. Beard. 83-116, Jan. 1949
• Wildlife of Mount McKinley National Park. By Adolph Murie. 249-270, Aug. 1953

WEBSTER, NOAH:
• Literary Landmarks of Massachusetts. By William H. Nicholas. Photos by B. Anthony Stewart and John E. Fletcher. 279-310, Mar. 1950

WEDDELL SEALS:
• Stalking Seals Under Antarctic Ice. By Carleton Ray. 54-65, Jan. 1966

WEDDINGS:
• Berber Brides' Fair. By Carla Hunt. Photos by Nik Wheeler. 119-129, Jan. 1980
• Purdah in India: Life Behind the Veil. By Doranne Wilson Jacobson. 270-286, Aug. 1977
• Royal Wedding at Jaisalmer. By Marilyn Silverstone. 66-79, Jan. 1965
• Wedding of Two Worlds. By Lee E. Battaglia. Contents: The wedding uniting Hope Cooke of New York and Palden Thondup Namgyal, Crown Prince of Sikkim. 708-727, Nov. 1963
• Zulu King Weds a Swazi Princess. By Volkmar Wentzel. 47-61, Jan. 1978

WEEDS, Aquatic:
● Adrift on a Raft of Sargassum. Photos by Robert F. Sisson. 188-199, Feb. 1976
● Algae: the Life-givers. By Paul A. Zahl. 361-377, Mar. 1974
● Florida, Noah's Ark for Exotic Newcomers. By Rick Gore. Photos by David Doubilet. 538-559, Oct. 1976
● Giant Kelp, Sequoias of the Sea. By Wheeler J. North. Photos by Bates Littlehales. 251-269, Aug. 1972

WEEKS, GERTRUDE S.: Author:
● Into the Heart of Africa. 257-263, Aug. 1956

WEEKS EXPEDITION:
● Into the Heart of Africa. By Gertrude S. Weeks. 257-263, Aug. 1956
● Stalking Central Africa's Wildlife. By T. Donald Carter. Paintings by Walter A. Weber. 264-286, Aug. 1956

WEEMS, BILL:
Photographer:
● Georgia, Unlimited. By Alice J. Hall. 212-245, Aug. 1978
● Home to North Carolina. By Neil Morgan. 333-359, Mar. 1980
● Hungary's New Way: A Different Communism. By John J. Putman. 225-261, Feb. 1983

WEEVILS. *See* Boll Weevils

WEIGHING the Aga Khan in Diamonds. Photos by David J. Carnegie. 317-324, Mar. 1947

WEIGHTS AND MEASURES. *See* Metric System; National Bureau of Standards, Washington, D. C.

WEINTRAUB, BORIS: Author:
● The Disaster of El Chichón. Photos by Guillermo Aldana E. and Kenneth Garrett. 654-684, Nov. 1982

WEIR, THOMAS:
Author:
● High Adventure in the Himalayas. 193-234, Aug. 1952

WEITZ, PAUL J.:
● Skylab, Outpost on the Frontier of Space. By Thomas Y. Canby. Photos by the nine mission astronauts. 441-469, Oct. 1974

WEITZMANN, KURT: Author:
● Mount Sinai's Holy Treasures. Photos by Fred Anderegg. 109-127, Jan. 1964

WELLINGTON, GERARD: Author:
● Undersea Wonders of the Galapagos. Photos by David Doubilet. 363-381, Sept. 1978

WELLINGTON, New Zealand:
● New Zealand: Gift of the Sea. By Maurice Shadbolt. Photos by Brian Brake. 465-511, Apr. 1962
● New Zealand, Pocket Wonder World. By Howell Walker. 419-460, Apr. 1952
● New Zealand's North Island: The Contented Land. By Charles McCarry. Photos by Bates Littlehales. 190-213, Aug. 1974

WELLS, MARGARETTA BURR:
Author:
● The Ape with Friends in Washington. 61-74, July 1953

WELLS, VIRGINIA L.:
Author-Photographer:
● Photographing Northern Wild Flowers. 809-823, June 1956

WELLS, Natural. *See* Chichén Itzá, Mexico; Dzibilchaltun, Mexico

WENKAM, ROBERT: Photographer:
● Fountain of Fire in Hawaii. By Frederick Simpich, Jr. Photos by Robert B. Goodman and Robert Wenkam. 303-327, Mar. 1960

WENTZEL, VOLKMAR:
Author-Photographer:
● Angola, Unknown Africa. 347-383, Sept. 1961
● Feudal Splendor Lingers in Rajputana. 411-458, Oct. 1948
● History Awakens at Harpers Ferry. 399-416, Mar. 1957
● The Idyllic Vale of Kashmir. 523-550, Apr. 1948
● India's Sculptured Temple Caves. 665-678, May 1953
● Life in Walled-off West Berlin. By Nathaniel T. Kenney and Volkmar Wentzel. 735-767, Dec. 1961
● Mozambique: Land of the Good People. 197-231, Aug. 1964
● Swaziland Tries Independence. 266-293, Aug. 1969
● Zulu King Weds a Swazi Princess. 47-61, Jan. 1978
Photographer:
● Atlantic Odyssey: Iceland to Antarctica. By Newman Bumstead. 725-780, Dec. 1955
● Berlin, Island in a Soviet Sea. By Frederick G. Vosburgh. 689-704, Nov. 1951
● Building a New Austria. By Beverley M. Bowie. 172-213, Feb. 1959
● Delhi, Capital of a New Dominion. By Phillips Talbot. 597-630, Nov. 1947
● Everyone's Servant, the Post Office. By Allan C. Fisher, Jr. 121-152, July 1954
● Friendly Flight to Northern Europe. By Lyndon B. Johnson. 268-293, Feb. 1964
● Hunting Uranium Around the World. By Robert D. Nininger. 533-558, Oct. 1954
● I'm From New Jersey. By John T. Cunningham. 1-45, Jan. 1960
● A Journey to "Little Tibet." By Enakshi Bhavnani. 603-634, May 1951
● Kings Point: Maker of Mariners. By Nathaniel T. Kenney. 693-706, Nov. 1955
● The Long, Lonely Leap (Parachute Jump). By Joseph W. Kittinger, Jr. 854-873, Dec. 1960
● Man's New Servant, the Friendly Atom. By F. Barrows Colton. 71-90, Jan. 1954
● The Most Mexican City, Guadalajara. By Bart McDowell. 412-441, Mar. 1967
● Occupied Austria, Outpost of Democracy. By George W. Long. 749-790, June 1951
● Peerless Nepal–A Naturalist's Paradise. By S. Dillon Ripley. 1-40, Jan. 1950
● Pennsylvania Avenue, Route of Presidents. By Dorothea and Stuart E. Jones. 63-95, Jan. 1957
● Portugal at the Crossroads. By Howard La Fay. 453-501, Oct. 1965
● A Preservation Victory Saves Washington's Old Post Office. By Wolf Von Eckardt. 407-416, Sept. 1983
● Salt–The Essence of Life. By Gordon Young. Photos by Volkmar Wentzel and Georg Gerster. 381-401, Sept. 1977
● Salzkammergut, Austria's Alpine Playground. By Beverley M. Bowie. 246-275, Aug. 1960
● School for Survival. By Curtis E. LeMay. 565-602, May 1953
● The Smithsonian, Magnet on the Mall. By Leonard Carmichael. 796-845, June 1960
● A Stroll to Venice. By Isobel Wylie Hutchison. 378-410, Sept. 1951
● Tirol, Austria's Province in the Clouds. By Peter T. White. 107-141, July 1961
● Treasure From a Celtic Tomb. By Jörg Biel. 428-438, Mar. 1980
● The White Horses of Vienna. By Beverley M. Bowie. 401-419, Sept. 1958
● Wisconsin, Land of the Good Life. By Beverley M. Bowie. 141-187, Feb. 1957
● Yugoslavia, Between East and West. By George W. Long. 141-172, Feb. 1951

WESLEY, JOHN and CHARLES:
● The British Way. By Sir Evelyn Wrench. 421-541, Apr. 1949

The **WEST** (Region), U. S.:
◆ *Along the Continental Divide.* 1981
● Along the Great Divide. By Mike Edwards. Photos by Nicholas DeVore III. 483-515, Oct. 1979
◆ *America's Majestic Canyons.* 1979
◆ *America's Spectacular Northwest.* 1982
◆ *America's Sunset Coast.* 1978
● Avalanche! By David Cupp. 280-305, Sept. 1982
I. Winter's White Death. 280-281; II. "I'm OK, I'm Alive!" Photos by Lanny Johnson and Andre Benier. 282-289; III. Battling the Juggernaut. 290-305
● Buffalo Bill and the Enduring West. By Alice J. Hall. Photos by James L. Amos. 76-103, July 1981
● Chief Joseph. By William Albert Allard. 409-434, Mar. 1977
▲ *Close-up: U.S.A., California and Nevada,* supplement. Text on reverse. June 1974
▲ *Close-up: U.S.A., The Northwest,* supplement. Text on reverse. Mar. 1973
▲ *Close-up: U.S.A., The Southwest,* supplement. Text on reverse. Included: Arizona, Colorado, New Mexico, Utah. Oct. 1977
● Coal vs. Parklands. By François Leydet. Photos by Dewitt Jones. 776-803, Dec. 1980

• The Country of Willa Cather. By William Howarth. Photos by Farrell Grehan. 71-93, July 1982
• Cowpunching on the Padlock Ranch. By William Albert Allard. 478-499, Oct. 1973
• Eruption of Mount St. Helens. By Rowe Findley. 3-65, Jan. 1981
I. Mountain With a Death Wish. 3-33; II. In the Path of Destruction. 35-49; III. The Day the Sky Fell. 50-65
• From Sun-clad Sea to Shining Mountains. By Ralph Gray. Photos by James P. Blair. 542-589, Apr. 1964
• Geothermal Energy: The Power of Letting Off Steam. By Kenneth F. Weaver. 566-579, Oct. 1977
◆ *The Great Southwest.* 1980
■ The Haunted West. 1972.
• The Hutterites, Plain People of the West. By William Albert Allard. 98-125, July 1970
• I See America First. By Lynda Bird Johnson. Photos by William Albert Allard. 874-904, Dec. 1965
• Indians of the Far West. By Matthew W. Stirling. Paintings by W. Langdon Kihn. 175-200, Feb. 1948
• Lonely Sentinels of the American West: Basque Sheepherders. By Robert Laxalt. Photos by William Belknap, Jr. 870-888, June 1966
• A Map Maker Looks at the United States. By Newman Bumstead. Included: Bremerton Shipyards; Columbia River; Continental Divide; Denver; Dry Falls; El Morro; Hells Canyon; Los Angeles; Mojave Desert; Mount Shasta; Olympic Peninsula rain forest; Provo; San Francisco; Tetons; Tillamook Burn. 705-748, June 1951
• The Mexican Americans: A People on the Move. By Griffin Smith, Jr. Photos by Stephanie Maze. 780-809, June 1980
• Mexico to Canada on the Pacific Crest Trail. By Mike W. Edwards. Photos by David Hiser. 741-779, June 1971
• Mount St. Helens Aftermath: The Mountain That Was–and Will Be. By Rowe Findley. Photos by Steve Raymer. 713-733, Dec. 1981
▲ *Northwestern United States,* Atlas series supplement. Apr. 1960
▲ *Northwestern United States and Neighboring Canadian Provinces,* supplement. June 1950
• The Opening of the American West: Burr's 1840 Map. 763, June 1953
• Our Most Precious Resource: Water. By Thomas Y. Canby. Photos by Ted Spiegel. 144-179, Aug. 1980
◆ *The Pacific Crest Trail.* 1975. Announced. 870-874, June 1974
• The Parks in Your Backyard. By Conrad L. Wirth. 647-707, Nov. 1963
The West. 699-707
• The Pony Express. By Rowe Findley. Photos by Craig Aurness. 45-71, July 1980
• Profiles of the Presidents: II. A Restless Nation Moves West. By Frank Freidel. 80-121, Jan. 1965

PONY EXPRESS STABLES MUSEUM, ST. JOSEPH, MO.

Pony Express: Richard Erastus Egan

Cowpunching: reflection of a harsh life

WILLIAM ALBERT ALLARD

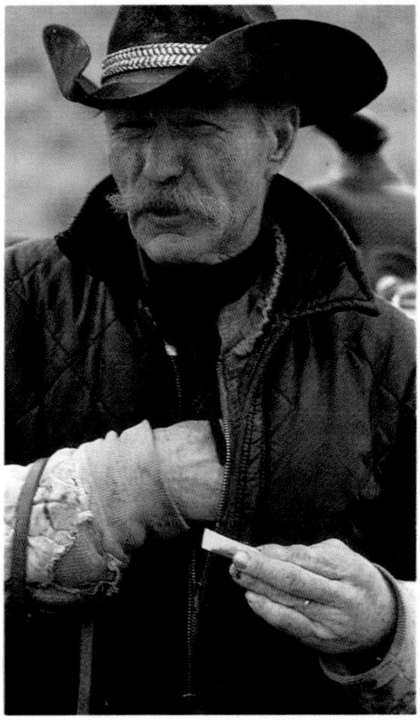

• Rediscovering America's Forgotten Crops. By Noel D. Vietmeyer. Photos by Burgess Blevins. Paintings by Paul M. Breeden. 702-712, May 1981
• Riding the Outlaw Trail. By Robert Redford. Photos by Jonathan Blair. 622-657, Nov. 1976
• Roaming the West's Fantastic Four Corners. By Jack Breed. 705-742, June 1952
• A Sikh Discovers America. By Joginder Singh Rekhi. 558-590, Oct. 1964
• So Long, St. Louis, We're Heading West. By William C. Everhart. 643-669, Nov. 1965
▲ *The Southwest,* The Making of America series. Included: Arizona, New Mexico, and parts of California, Colorado, Texas, Utah. On reverse: 12,000 Years of History; Spanish Conquest; Anglo-American Entry and Occupancy. Nov. 1982
▲ *Southwestern United States,* Atlas series supplement. Nov. 1959
▲ *Southwestern United States,* supplement. Dec. 1948
• Stalking the West's Wild Foods. By Euell Gibbons. Photos by David Hiser. 186-199, Aug. 1973
• Theodore Roosevelt: a Centennial Tribute. By Bart McDowell. 572-590, Oct. 1958
◆ *Trails West.* 1979
• Two Wheels Along the Mexican Border. By William Albert Allard. 591-635, May 1971
• The Untamed Yellowstone. By Bill Richards. Photos by Dean Krakel II. 257-278, Aug. 1981
• A Walk Across America: Part II. By Peter and Barbara Jenkins. 194-229, Aug. 1979
• The West Through Boston Eyes. By Stewart Anderson. 733-776, June 1949

WEST AFRICA:
• Freedom Speaks French in Ouagadougou. By John Scofield. 153-203, Aug. 1966
• Hunting Musical Game in West Africa. By Arthur S. Alberts. 262-282, Aug. 1951
• *See also* Cameroon; Ghana; Ivory Coast; Liberia; Mali; Mauritania; Niger; Nigeria; Sierra Leone; *and* Tuareg

WEST BANK, Israeli-occupied Jordan:
• The Living Dead Sea. By Harvey Arden. Photos by Nathan Benn. 225-245, Feb. 1978
• This Year in Jerusalem. By Joseph Judge. Photos by Jodi Cobb. 479-515, Apr. 1983

WEST from the Khyber Pass. By William O. Douglas. Photos by Mercedes H. Douglas and author. 1-44, July 1958

WEST GERMANY: Continuing Miracle. By John J. Putman. Photos by Robert W. Madden. 149-181, Aug. 1977
• *See also* Germany, Federal Republic of

BOTH BY GARY L. NUECHTERLEIN

Western Grebes: courtship maneuver known as "rushing," ***top;*** **chick on its mother's back,** ***above***

WEST INDIES:
● Cape Canaveral's 6,000-mile Shooting Gallery. By Allan C. Fisher, Jr. Photos by Luis Marden and Thomas Nebbia. Included: Antigua, Bahama Islands, Dominican Republic, Grand Turk, Puerto Rico, St. Lucia. 421-471, Oct. 1959
● *Carib* Cruises the West Indies. By Carleton Mitchell. 1-56, Jan. 1948
● The Caribbean: Sun, Sea, and Seething. By Noel Grove. Photos by Steve Raymer. 244-271, Feb. 1981
● Christopher Columbus and the New World He Found. By John Scofield. Photos by Adam Woolfitt. 584-625, Nov. 1975
▲ *Countries of the Caribbean, including Mexico, Central America, and the West Indies,* supplement. Oct. 1947
● *Finisterre* Sails the Windward Islands. By Carleton Mitchell. Photos by Winfield Parks. 755-801, Dec. 1965
● Flags of the Americas. By Elizabeth W. King. Included: Cuba, Dominican Republic, Haiti. 633-657, May 1949
● A Fresh Breeze Stirs the Leewards. By Carleton Mitchell. Photos by Winfield Parks. 488-537, Oct. 1966
● How Fruit Came to America. By J. R. Magness. Paintings by Else Bostelmann. 325-377, Sept. 1951
◆ *Isles of the Caribbean.* 1980
◆ *Isles of the Caribbees.* Announced. 408-417, Mar. 1966
● Our Vegetable Travelers. By Victor R. Boswell. Paintings by Else Bostelmann. 145-217, Aug. 1949
● Reach for the New World. By Mendel Peterson. Photos by David L. Arnold. Paintings by Richard Schlecht. 724-767, Dec. 1977
● Robin Sails Home. By Robin Lee Graham. 504-545, Oct. 1970
● St. Vincent, the Grenadines, and Grenada: Taking It as It Comes. By Ethel A. Starbird. Photos by Cotton Coulson. 399-425, Sept. 1979
● Sea Fever. By John E. Schultz. 237-268, Feb. 1949
▲ *Tourist Islands of the West Indies; West Indies and Central America,* double-sided supplement. Feb. 1981
▲ *West Indies,* Atlas series supplement. Dec. 1962
▲ *West Indies,* supplement. Mar. 1954
▲ *West Indies and Central America,* supplement. Jan. 1970
● *See also* Bahama Islands; Barbados; Bimini Islands; Cuba; Dominica; Dominican Republic; Haiti; Jamaica; Martinique; Netherlands Antilles; Puerto Rico; Trinidad and Tobago; Virgin Islands

WEST IRIAN (Indonesian New Guinea). *See* Irian Jaya

WEST POINT, New York:
● The Making of a West Pointer. By Howell Walker. 597-626, May 1952
● The Mighty Hudson (River). By Albert W. Atwood. Photos by B. Anthony Stewart. 1-36, July 1948

WEST VIRGINIA:
● Appalachian Valley Pilgrimage. By Catherine Bell Palmer. Photos by Justin Locke. 1-32, July 1949
● Down the Potomac by Canoe. By Ralph Gray. Photos by Walter Meayers Edwards. 213-242, Aug. 1948
● Mountain Voices, Mountain Days. By Bryan Hodgson. Photos by Linda Bartlett. 118-146, July 1972
● The Nation's River. By Allan C. Fisher, Jr. Photos by James L. Stanfield. 432-469, Oct. 1976
● Shenandoah, I Long to Hear You. By Mike W. Edwards. Photos by Thomas Anthony DeFeo. 554-588, Apr. 1970
● So Much Happens Along the Ohio River. By Frederick Simpich. Photos by Justin Locke. 177-212, Feb. 1950
● Turnaround Time in West Virginia. By Elizabeth A. Moize. Photos by Jodi Cobb. 755-785, June 1976
● Wrestlin' for a Livin' With King Coal. By Michael E. Long. Photos by Michael O'Brien. 793-819, June 1983
● *See also* Harpers Ferry

WESTCOTT (Mail Boat). *See J. W. Westcott*

WESTERN AUSTRALIA (State), Australia:
● Perth–Fair Winds and Full Sails. By Thomas J. Abercrombie. Photos by Cary Wolinsky. 638-667, May 1982
● Western Australia, the Big Country. By Kenneth MacLeish. Photos by James L. Stanfield. 150-187, Feb. 1975

WESTERN DESERT, Egypt:
● The Desert: An Age-old Challenge Grows. By Rick Gore. Photos by Georg Gerster and Bruce Dale. 586-639, Nov. 1979
● Egypt's Desert of Promise. By Farouk El-Baz. Photos by Georg Gerster. 190-221, Feb. 1982

WESTERN GREBES:
● Western Grebes: The Birds That Walk on Water. By Gary L. Nuechterlein. NGS research grant. 624-637, May 1982

WESTERN Indian Ocean: Crosscurrents Sweep a Strategic Sea. By Bart McDowell. Photos by Steve Raymer. 422-457, Oct. 1981

WESTERN SAMOA, the Pacific's Newest Nation. By Maurice Shadbolt. Photos by Robert B. Goodman. 573-602, Oct. 1962

WESTMANN ISLANDS, Iceland. *See* Vestmannaeyjar

WESTMINSTER KENNEL CLUB DOG SHOW, New York City:
● Westminster, World Series of Dogdom. By John W. Cross, Jr. 91-116, Jan. 1954

WETHERILL MESA, Colorado:
● Searching for Cliff Dwellers' Secrets. By Carroll A. Burroughs. NGS research grant. 619-625, Nov. 1959

• Solving the Riddles of Wetherill Mesa. By Douglas Osborne. Paintings by Peter V. Bianchi. NGS research grant. 155-195, Feb. 1964
• 20th-century Indians Preserve Customs of the Cliff Dwellers. Photos by William Belknap, Jr. NGS research grant. 196-211, Feb. 1964
• Your Society to Seek New Light on the Cliff Dwellers. NGS research grant. 154-156, Jan. 1959

WETLANDS:
• Can We Save Our Salt Marshes? By Stephen W. Hitchcock. Photos by William R. Curtsinger. 729-765, June 1972
◆ *Explore a Spooky Swamp.* 1978
• Florida's Booming–and Beleaguered–Heartland. By Joseph Judge. Photos by Jonathan Blair. 585-621, Nov. 1973
• Island, Prairie, Marsh, and Shore. By Charlton Ogburn. Photos by Bates Littlehales. 350-381, Mar. 1979
• Marsh Dwellers of Southern Iraq. By Wilfred Thesiger. Photos by Gavin Maxwell. 205-239, Feb. 1958
• Mississippi Delta: The Land of the River. By Douglas Lee. Photos by C. C. Lockwood. 226-253, Aug. 1983
• The People of New Jersey's Pine Barrens. By John McPhee. Photos by William R. Curtsinger. 52-77, Jan. 1974
• Rare Birds Flock to Spain's Marismas. By Roger Tory Peterson. 397-425, Mar. 1958
• San Francisco Bay: The Beauty and the Battles. By Cliff Tarpy. Photos by James A. Sugar. 814-845, June 1981
• Sea Islands: Adventuring Along the South's Surprising Coast. By James Cerruti. Photos by Thomas Nebbia and James L. Amos. 366-393, Mar. 1971
• Sudan: Arab-African Giant. By Robert Caputo. Included: The Sudd swamp. 346-379, Mar. 1982
• The Swans of Abbotsbury. By Michael Moynihan. Photos by Barnet Saidman. 563-570, Oct. 1959
• Trouble in Bayou Country. By Jack and Anne Rudloe. Photos by C. C. Lockwood. 377-397, Sept. 1979
• Water Dwellers in a Desert World. By Gavin Young. Photos by Nik Wheeler. 502-523, Apr. 1976
• Western Grebes: The Birds That Walk on Water. By Gary L. Nuechterlein. NGS research grant. 624-637, May 1982
• *See also* Corkscrew Swamp; Everglades; Okefenokee Swamp

WETMORE, ALEXANDER:
• Board of Trustees, member. 595, May 1947; 344, Sept. 1948; 65A-65B, July 1954; 364, Mar. 1956; 835, Dec. 1959; 883, Dec. 1960; 555, Oct. 1964; 485, Oct. 1966; 839, Dec. 1970; 151, Aug. 1975; 227, Aug. 1976
• Board of Trustees: Trustee Emeritus. 672, May 1978
• Committee for Research and Exploration, Vice Chairman. 705, June 1947; 175, Feb. 1960; 532, Oct. 1965; 489, Oct. 1967; 881-882, Dec. 1967
• Editorial. By Gilbert M. Grosvenor. 151, Aug. 1975
• Hubbard Medal recipient (1975). 151, Aug. 1975
Author:
• Re-creating Madagascar's Giant Extinct Bird. 488-493, Oct. 1967

WHALES:
• *Calypso* Explores for Underwater Oil. By Jacques-Yves Cousteau. Photos by Louis Malle. NGS research grant. 155-184, Aug. 1955
• Editorial. By Gilbert M. Grosvenor. 721, Dec. 1976
▪ The Great Whales. 439, Oct. 1977; cover, Feb. 1978; Emmy Award. 1, Jan. 1979
• Hunting the Heartbeat of a Whale. By Paul Dudley White and Samuel W. Matthews. NGS research grant. 49-64, July 1956
◆ *Namu.* Announced. 726-728, Nov. 1973
• Whales of the World. 722-767, Dec. 1976
I. The Imperiled Giants. By William Graves. 722-751; II. Exploring the Lives of Whales. By Victor B. Scheffer. 752-767
▲ "Whales of the World." Painting supplement. Map on reverse, *The Great Whales: Migration and Range.* Dec. 1976
• *See also* Belugas; Blue Whales; Bowhead Whales; Gray Whales; Humpback Whales; Killer Whales; Right Whales; *and* Dolphins

WHALING:
• The Azores, Nine Islands in Search of a Future. By Don Moser. Photos by O. Louis Mazzatenta. 261-288, Feb. 1976
• Editorial. By Gilbert M. Grosvenor. 721, Dec. 1976
• The Last U. S. Whale Hunters. By Emory Kristof. 346-353, Mar. 1973
"Ocean mammals are to us what the buffalo was to the Plains Indian." By Lael Morgan. 354-355
• Martha's Vineyard. By William P. E. Graves. Photos by James P. Blair. 778-809, June 1961
• A Naturalist in Penguin Land. By Niall Rankin. 93-116, Jan. 1955
• *Nomad* Sails Long Island Sound. By Thomas Horgan. 295-338, Sept. 1957
• Off the Beaten Track of Empire. By Beverley M. Bowie. Photos by Michael Parker. 584-626, Nov. 1957
• Peoples of the Arctic. 144-223, Feb. 1983
I. Introduction by Joseph Judge. 144-149; II. Hunters of the Lost Spirit: Alaskans. By Priit J. Vesilind. Photos by David Alan Harvey. 150-197; III. People of the Long Spring. By Yuri Rytkheu. Photos by Dean Conger. 206-223, Feb. 1983
▲ *Peoples of the Arctic; Arctic Ocean,* double-sided supplement. Feb. 1983
• To Europe with a Racing Start. By Carleton Mitchell. 758-791, June 1958
• Whales of the World. 722-767, Dec. 1976
The Imperiled Giants. By William Graves. 722-751
• *See also* Faeroe Islands; Nantucket; Western Australia

WHARTON, CHARLES HEIZER:
Author:
• Seeking Mindanao's Strangest Creatures. 389-408, Sept. 1948

WHAT a Place to Lay an Egg! By Thomas R. Howell. NGS research grant. 414-419, Sept. 1971

WHAT About Nuclear Energy? By Kenneth F. Weaver. Photos by Emory Kristof. 459-493, Apr. 1979

WHAT Causes Earthquakes. By Maynard M. Miller. 140-141, July 1964

WHAT Future for the Wayana Indians? By Carole Devillers. 66-83, Jan. 1983

WHAT I Saw Across the Rhine. By J. Frank Dobie. 57-86, Jan. 1947

WHAT'S Black and White and Loved All Over? By Theodore H. Reed. Photos by Donna K. Grosvenor. 803-815, Dec. 1972

WHAT'S Happening to Our Climate? By Samuel W. Matthews. 576-615, Nov. 1976

WHAT Is It Like to Walk on the Moon? By David R. Scott. 326-331, Sept. 1973

WHAT'S So Special About Spiders? By Paul A. Zahl. 190-219, Aug. 1971

WHAT Six Experts Say. Contents: Statements from John F. O'Leary, Hans H. Landsberg, Steven C. Wilson, Robert B. Stobaugh, Fred L. Hartley, Amory B. Lovins. 70-73, *Special Report on Energy* (Feb. 1981)

WHAT the Moon Rocks Tell Us. By Kenneth F. Weaver. 788-791, Dec. 1969

WHAT Voyager Saw: Jupiter's Dazzling Realm. By Rick Gore. Photos by NASA. 2-29, Jan. 1980

WHAT Was a Woman Doing There? By W. E. Garrett. 270-271, Feb. 1966

WHAT We've Accomplished in Antarctica. By George J. Dufek. 527-557, Oct. 1959

WHAT You Didn't See in Kohoutek. By Kenneth F. Weaver. 214-223, Aug. 1974

WHATEVER Happened to TVA? By Gordon Young. Photos by Emory Kristof. 830-863, June 1973

WHEAT AND WHEAT GROWING:
• Can the World Feed Its People? By Thomas Y. Canby. Photos by Steve Raymer. 2-31, July 1975
• Canada's Heartland, the Prairie Provinces. By W. E. Garrett. 443-489, Oct. 1970
• North Dakota Comes into Its Own. By Leo A. Borah. Photos by J. Baylor Roberts. 283-322, Sept. 1951
• North With the Wheat Cutters. By Noel Grove. Photos by James A. Sugar. 194-217, Aug. 1972

WHEATLEY, HAROLD G.: Author:
• This Is My Island, Tangier. Photos by David Alan Harvey. 700-725, Nov. 1973

WHEELER, NIK: Photographer:
- Berber Brides' Fair. By Carla Hunt. 119-129, Jan. 1980
- Water Dwellers in a Desert World. By Gavin Young. 502-523, Apr. 1976

WHEELER, P. J. F.: Author:
- Death of an Island, Tristan da Cunha. 678-695, May 1962

WHEELER MOUNTAIN, Vermont:
- Life on a Rock Ledge. By William H. Amos. 558-566, Oct. 1980

WHEELING, West Virginia:
- So Much Happens Along the Ohio River. By Frederick Simpich. Photos by Justin Locke. 177-212, Feb. 1950

WHEN Disaster Struck a Woodpecker's Home. By Frederick Kent Truslow. 882-884, Dec. 1966

WHEN Giant Bears Go Fishing. By Cecil E. Rhode. 195-205, Aug. 1954

WHEN Gypsies Gather at Appleby Fair. Photos by Bruce Dale. 848-869, June 1972

WHEN in Rome. . . . By Stuart E. Jones. Photos by Winfield Parks. 741-789, June 1970

WHEN Mt. Mazama Lost Its Top: The Birth of Crater Lake. By Lyman J. Briggs. 128-133, July 1962

WHEN the President Goes Abroad. By Gilbert M. Grosvenor. 588-649, May 1960

WHEN the Space Shuttle Finally Flies. By Rick Gore. Photos by Jon Schneeberger. Paintings by Ken Dallison. 317-347, Mar. 1981

WHEN Will We Measure In Metric? By Kenneth F. Weaver. Drawings by Donald A. Mackay. 287-294, Aug. 1977

WHERE Bald Eagles Soar. By Thomas C. Dunstan. Photos by Jeff Foott. 186-199, Feb. 1978

WHERE Can the Wolf Survive? By L. David Mech. 518-537, Oct. 1977

WHERE Do Society Members Stand? 52-53, *Special Report on Energy* (Feb. 1981)

WHERE Elephants Have Right of Way. By George and Jinx Rodger. 363-389, Sept. 1960

WHERE Falcons Wear Air Force Blue, United States Air Force Academy. By Nathaniel T. Kenney. Photos by William Belknap, Jr. 845-873, June 1959

WHERE Jesus Walked. By Howard La Fay. Photos by Charles Harbutt. 739-781, Dec. 1967

WHERE Magic Ruled: Art of the Bering Sea. By William W. Fitzhugh and Susan A. Kaplan. Photos by Sisse Brimberg. 198-205, Feb. 1983

WHERE Oil and Wildlife Mix. By Steven C. Wilson and Karen C. Hayden. 145-173, Feb. 1981

WHERE Old Hawaii Still Lives: Maui. By Kenneth F. Weaver. Photos by Gordon W. Gahan. 514-543, Apr. 1971

WHERE Solitude Is in Season: Snow-mantled Stehekin. Photos by Bruce Dale. Text by Pat Hutson. 572-588, Apr. 1974

WHERE the Earth Turns Inside Out. By J. R. Heirtzler. Photos by Emory Kristof. 586-603, May 1975

WHERE the River Shannon Flows. By Allan C. Fisher, Jr. Photos by Adam Woolfitt. 652-679, Nov. 1978

WHERE Turk and Russian Meet. By Ferdinand Kuhn. 743-766, June 1952

WHERE Two Worlds Meet. Photos by Des and Jen Bartlett. 298-321, Mar. 1976

WHERE Would We Be Without Algae? By Paul A. Zahl. 361-377, Mar. 1974

WHICH Way Now for Argentina? By Loren McIntyre. 296-333, Mar. 1975

WHICH Way Oahu? By Gordon Young. Photos by Robert W. Madden. 653-679, Nov. 1979

WHIPSNADE ZOOLOGICAL PARK, Dunstable Downs, England:
- London's Zoo of Zoos. By Thomas Garner James. Included: Regent's Park; Whipsnade. 771-786, June 1953

WHISTLING SWANS:
- Tireless Voyager, the Whistling Swan. By William J. L. Sladen. Photos by Bianca Lavies. NGS research grant. 134-147, July 1975

WHITE, EDWARD H.:
- America's 6,000-mile Walk in Space. 440-447, Sept. 1965

WHITE, JOHN:
- Indian Life Before the Colonists Came. By Stuart E. Jones. Engravings by Theodore de Bry, 1590. Included: John White, one of Sir Walter Raleigh's colonists on Roanoke Island, 1585, and reproductions of his paintings from De Bry's copper plate engravings. 351-368, Sept. 1947

WHITE, PAUL DUDLEY: Author:
- Hunting the Heartbeat of a Whale. By Paul Dudley White and Samuel W. Matthews. 49-64, July 1956

WHITE, PETER T.: Author:
- Barehanded Battle to Cleanse the Bay. Photos by Jonathan S. Blair. 866-881, June 1971
- Behind the Headlines in Viet Nam. Photos by Winfield Parks. 149-189, Feb. 1967
- Behold the Computer Revolution. Photos by Bruce Dale and Emory Kristof. 593-633, Nov. 1970
- Brazil, Ôba! Photos by Winfield Parks. 299-353, Sept. 1962
- Calcutta, India's Maligned Metropolis. Photos by Raghubir Singh. 534-563, Apr. 1973
- The Fascinating World of Trash. Photos by Louie Psihoyos. 424-457, Apr. 1983
- Gold, the Eternal Treasure. Photos by James L. Stanfield. 1-51, Jan. 1974
- Greece: "To Be Indomitable, To Be Joyous." Photos by James P. Blair. 360-393, Mar. 1980
- Hopes and Fears in Booming Thailand. Photos by Dean Conger. 76-125, July 1967
- The Incredible Helicopter. 533-557, Apr. 1959
- Kampuchea Wakens From a Nightmare. Photos by David Alan Harvey. 590-623, May 1982
- The Mekong, River of Terror and Hope. Photos by W. E. Garrett. 737-787, Dec. 1968
- Mosaic of Cultures (Southeast Asia). Photos by W. E. Garrett. 296-329, Mar. 1971
- Old Prague in Winter. Photos by Nathan Benn. 546-567, Apr. 1979
- One Canada–or Two? Photos by Winfield Parks. 436-465, Apr. 1977
- Report on Laos. Photos by W. E. Garrett. 241-275, Aug. 1961
- Saigon: Eye of the Storm. Photos by W. E. Garrett. 834-872, June 1965
- Satellites Gave Warning of Midwest Floods. Photos by Thomas A. DeFeo. 574-592, Oct. 1969
- South Korea: What Next? Photos by H. Edward Kim. 394-427, Sept. 1975
- South Viet Nam Fights the Red Tide. Photos by W. E. Garrett. 445-489, Oct. 1961
- Spain: It's a Changed Country. Photos by David Alan Harvey. 297-331, Mar. 1978
- Springtime of Hope in Poland. Photos by James P. Blair. 467-501, Apr. 1972
- Tanzania Marches to Its Own Drum. Photos by Emory Kristof. 474-509, Apr. 1975
- The Temples of Angkor: Ancient Glory in Stone. Photos by Wilbur E. Garrett. 552-589, May 1982
- This Land of Ours–How Are We Using It? Photos by Emory Kristof. 20-67, July 1976
- Tirol, Austria's Province in the Clouds. Photos by Volkmar Wentzel. 107-141, July 1961
- Tropical Rain Forests: Nature's Dwindling Treasures. Photos by James P. Blair. Paintings by Barron Storey. 2-47, Jan. 1983
- Vienna, City of Song. Photos by John Launois. 739-779, June 1968
- The World in New York City. 52-107, July 1964

The **WHITE HORSES** of Vienna. By Beverley M. Bowie. Photos by Volkmar Wentzel. 401-419, Sept. 1958

WHITE HOUSE, Washington, D. C.:
- Inside the White House. By Lonnelle Aikman. Photos by B. Anthony Stewart and Thomas Nebbia. 3-43, Jan. 1961
- The Last Full Measure (Tribute to President Kennedy). By Melville Bell Grosvenor. 307-355, Mar. 1964
- The Living White House. By Lonnelle Aikman. 593-643, Nov. 1966

◆*The Living White House.* Published in cooperation with the White House Historical Association. 641, Nov. 1966; 586, Oct. 1967
• Washington: Home of the Nation's Great. By Albert W. Atwood. 699-738, June 1947
◆*The White House* (Guidebook). Published in cooperation with the White House Historical Association. 888-893, Dec. 1962; Presentation ceremony. 274, Aug. 1982
• *See also* Presidents, U. S.

WHITE LION (Dutch East Indiaman). *See Witte Leeuw*

WHITE MAGIC in the Belgian Congo. By W. Robert Moore. 321-362, Mar. 1952

WHITE MIST (Yawl):
• Homeward With Ulysses. By Melville Bell Grosvenor. Photos by Edwin Stuart Grosvenor. 1-39, July 1973
• The Isles of Greece: Aegean Birthplace of Western Culture. By Melville Bell Grosvenor. Photos by Edwin Stuart Grosvenor and Winfield Parks. 147-193, Aug. 1972
• North (U. S. and Canada) Through History Aboard *White Mist.* By Melville Bell Grosvenor. Photos by Edwin Stuart Grosvenor. 1-55, July 1970
• Safe Landing on Sable, Isle of 500 Shipwrecks. By Melville Bell Grosvenor. 398-431, Sept. 1965
• *White Mist* Cruises to Wreck-haunted St. Pierre and Miquelon. By Melville Bell Grosvenor. 378-419, Sept. 1967

WHITE MOUNTAIN APACHE:
• The White Mountain Apache. 260-290, Feb. 1980
I. At Peace With the Past, In Step With the Future. By Ronnie Lupe. 260-261; II. Coming of Age the Apache Way. By Nita Quintero. Photos by Bill Hess. 262-271; III. Seeking the Best of Two Worlds. By Bill Hess. 272-290

WHITE MOUNTAINS, California:
• Bristlecone Pine, Oldest Known Living Thing. By Edmund Schulman. Photos by W. Robert Moore. 355-372, Mar. 1958

WHITE MOUNTAINS, New Hampshire:
• The Friendly Huts of the White Mountains. By William O. Douglas. Photos by Kathleen Revis. 205-239, Aug. 1961
• Mountains Top Off New England. By F. Barrows Colton. Photos by Robert F. Sisson. 563-602, May 1951
• Skyline Trail (Appalachian Trail) from Maine to Georgia. By Andrew H. Brown. Photos by Robert F. Sisson. 219-251, Aug. 1949

WHITE SANDS NATIONAL MONUMENT, New Mexico:
• New Mexico: The Golden Land. By Robert Laxalt. Photos by Adam Woolfitt. 299-345, Sept. 1970
• New Mexico's Great White Sands. By William Belknap, Jr. 113-137, July 1957

WHITE SANDS PROVING GROUND, New Mexico:
• Seeing the Earth from 80 Miles Up. By Clyde T. Holliday. 511-528, Oct. 1950

WHITE STORKS, Vanishing Sentinels of the Rooftops. By Roger Tory Peterson. 838-853, June 1962

WHITE TIGERS:
• Enchantress! By Theodore H. Reed. Photos by Thomas J. Abercrombie. 628-641, May 1961
• White Tiger in My House. By Elizabeth C. Reed. Photos by Donna K. Grosvenor. 482-491, Apr. 1970

WHITE-WATER RIVERS:
◆*America's Wild and Scenic Rivers.* 1983
• Chattooga River Country: Wild Water, Proud People. By Don Belt. Photos by Steve Wall. 458-477, Apr. 1983
• White-water Adventure on Wild Rivers of Idaho. By Frank Craighead, Jr. and John Craighead. 213-239, Feb. 1970
• White Water, Proud People. By Don Belt. Photos by Steve Wall. 458-477, Apr. 1983
• White Water Yields Relics of Canada's Voyageurs. By Sigurd F. Olson. Photos by David S. Boyer. 413-435, Sept. 1963
◆*Still Waters, White Waters.* 1977
• *See also* Rapids; Waterfalls

WHITEFISH. *See* Menhaden

WHITEHORSE, Canada:
• Yukon Fever: Call of the North. By Robert Booth. Photos by George F. Mobley. 548-578, Apr. 1978

WHITMAN COUNTY, Washington:
• A Paradise Called the Palouse. By Barbara Austin. Photos by Phil Schofield. 798-819, June 1982

WHITNEY, Mount, California:
• Sierra High Trip. By David R. Brower. 844-868, June 1954

WHITSON, MARTHA A.: Author:
• The Roadrunner–Clown of the Desert. Photos by Bruce Dale. 694-702, May 1983

WHITTAKER, JAMES W.:
• Six to the Summit. By Norman G. Dyhrenfurth. Photos by Barry C. Bishop. Note: Jim Whittaker was the first American to reach the summit of Everest. 460-473, Oct. 1963
Author:
• Americans Climb K2: The Ultimate Challenge. 624-639, May 1979
• Canada's Mount Kennedy: III. The First Ascent. Photos by William Albert Allard. 11-33, July 1965
• *See also* American Mount Everest Expedition

WHITTIER, JOHN GREENLEAF:
• Literary Landmarks of Massachusetts. By William H. Nicholas. Photos by B. Anthony Stewart and John E. Fletcher. 279-310, Mar. 1950

WHO Are Earth's Richest People? By Mike Holmes. 344-353, Sept. 1976

PHIL SCHOFIELD

Whitman County: snow in the Palouse

WHO Discovered America? A New Look at an Old Question. The Editor. 769, Dec. 1977

WHO Says Fish Can't Climb Trees? By Ivan Polunin. 85-91, Jan. 1972

WHO Were the "Mound Builders"? By George E. Stuart. 783-801, Dec. 1972

WHOOPING CRANES:
• Teamwork Helps the Whooping Crane. By Roderick C. Drewien, with Ernie Kuyt. 680-693, May 1979
• Where Oil and Wildlife Mix. By Steven C. Wilson and Karen C. Hayden. 145-173, Feb. 1981
• Whooping Cranes Fight for Survival. By Robert Porter Allen. Photos by Frederick Kent Truslow. 650-669, Nov. 1959

WHY Is It That Calcutta–the World's Most Maligned Metropolis–Is Where So Many People Want To Be? By Peter T. White. Photos by Raghubir Singh. 534-563, Apr. 1973

WICHITA MOUNTAINS WILDLIFE REFUGE, Oklahoma:
• The Wichitas: Land of the Living Prairie. By M. Woodbridge Williams. 661-697, May 1957

WICKWIRE, JAMES: Author:
• Americans Climb K2: On to the Summit. 641-649, May 1979

WIGHT, Isle of, England:
• Portsmouth, Britannia's Sally Port. By Thomas Garner James. Photos by B. Anthony Stewart. 513-544, Apr. 1952
• *See also* Cowes

The **WILD ANIMALS** in My Life. By William M. Mann. 497-524, Apr. 1957

WILD BUNCH:
• Riding the Outlaw Trail. By Robert Redford. Photos by Jonathan Blair. 622-657, Nov. 1976

The **WILD BURROS** of Death Valley. By Patricia des Roses Moehlman. Photos by Ira S. Lerner and author. NGS research grant. 502-517, Apr. 1972

WILD Cargo: the Business of Smuggling Animals. By Noel Grove. Photos by Steve Raymer. 287-315, Mar. 1981

WILD ELEPHANT Roundup in India. By Harry Miller. Photos by author and James P. Blair. 372-385, Mar. 1969

WILD FLOWERS:
• American Wild Flower Odyssey. By P. L. Ricker. 603-634, May 1953
• Australia's Bizarre Wild Flowers. By Paul A. Zahl. 858-868, Dec. 1976
• Cloud Gardens in the Tetons. By Frank and John Craighead. 811-830, June 1948
• Eden in the Outback. By Kay and Stanley Breeden. 189-203, Feb. 1973
• The Fragile Beauty All About Us. Photos by Harry S. C. Yen. 785-795, Dec. 1970

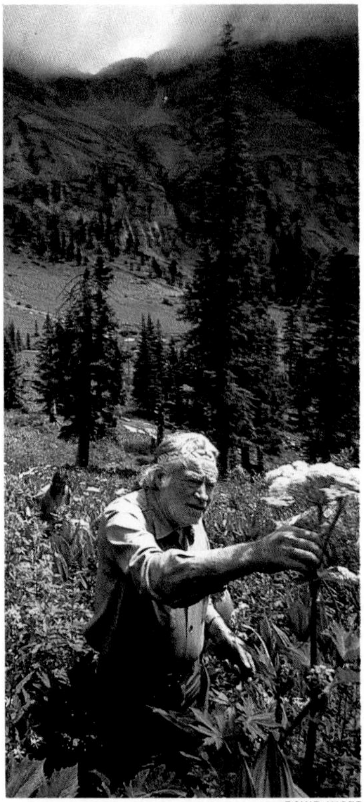

DAVID HISER

West's Wild Foods: author picks cow parsnip

Wild Flowers: Australia's *Banksia*

PAUL A. ZAHL

• Hummingbirds: The Nectar Connection. By Paul W. Ewald. Photos by Robert A. Tyrrell. 223-227, Feb. 1982
• In the Gardens of Olympus. By Paul A. Zahl. 85-123, July 1955
• Photographing Northern Wild Flowers. By Virginia L. Wells. 809-823, June 1956
• Plants of the Alaskan Tundra. 315-321, Mar. 1972
• Saving Man's Wildlife Heritage. By John H. Baker. Photos by Robert F. Sisson. 581-620, Nov. 1954
• The Tallgrass Prairie: Can It Be Saved? By Dennis Farney. Photos by Jim Brandenburg. Included: Blazing star, Mead's milkweed, Pasqueflower, Prairie orchid, Shooting star; Search for and rescue of rare species; Seed gleaning. 37-61, Jan. 1980
• A Visit to the Living Ice Age. By Rutherford Platt. 525-545, Apr. 1957

WILD FOODS:
• The Making of an Astronaut. By Robert R. Gilruth. 122-144, Jan. 1965
• Philmont Scout Ranch Helps Boys Grow Up. By Andrew H. Brown. 399-416, Sept. 1956
• Stalking the West's Wild Foods. By Euell Gibbons. Photos by David Hiser. 186-199, Aug. 1973
• Stalking Wild Foods on a Desert Isle. By Euell Gibbons. Photos by David Hiser. 47-63, July 1972
• We Survive on a Pacific Atoll. By John and Frank Craighead. 73-94, Jan. 1948

A **WILD,** Ill-fated Balloon Race. 778-797, Dec. 1983
I. Wild Launch. 778-787; II. The Fantastic Flight of *Cote d'Or*. By Cynthia Shields. 789-793; III. Last Ascent of a Heroic Team (Maxie Anderson and Don Ida). 794-797

WILD Nursery of the Mangroves. By Rick Gore. Photos by Bianca Lavies. 669-689, May 1977

WILD RIVERS: Preservation:
◆ *America's Wild and Scenic Rivers.* 1983
• Autumn Flames Along the Allagash. By François Leydet. Photos by Farrell Grehan. 177-187, Feb. 1974
• Chattooga River Country: Wild Water, Proud People. By Don Belt. Photos by Steve Wall. 458-477, Apr. 1983
• Editorial. By Gilbert M. Grosvenor. 723, Dec. 1977
• Idaho Loggers Battle a River. 117-130, July 1951
• Nahanni: Canada's Wilderness Park. By Douglas H. Chadwick. Photos by Matt Bradley. 396-420, Sept. 1981
• Our Wild and Scenic Rivers. 2-59, July 1977
I. Rivers Wild and Pure: A Priceless Legacy. By Robert E. Doyle. 2-11; II. The Flathead. By Douglas H.Chadwick. Photos by Lowell Georgia. 13-19; III. The Suwannee. By Jack and Anne Rudloe. Photos by Jodi Cobb. 20-29; IV. The St. Croix.

By David S. Boyer. 30-37; V. The Skagit. By David S. Boyer. 38-45; VI. The Rio Grande. By Nathaniel T. Kenney. Photos by Bank Langmore. 46-51; VII. The Noatak. By John M. Kauffmann. Photos by Sam Abell. 52-59
● The Untamed Yellowstone. By Bill Richards. Photos by Dean Krakel II. 257-278, Aug. 1981
● A Walk and Ride on the Wild Side: Tasmania. By Carolyn Bennett Patterson. Photos by David Hiser and Melinda Berge. Included: The Franklin-Lower Gordon Wild Rivers National Park. 676-693, May 1983
● White-water Adventure on Wild Rivers of Idaho. By Frank Craighead, Jr. and John Craighead. Included: Middle Fork Salmon; Salmon; and rivers protected or proposed for protection under the Wild and Scenic Rivers Act of 1968. 213-239, Feb. 1970
▲ *Wild and Scenic Rivers of the United States,* double-sided supplement. July 1977
■ Wild River. Included: Middle Fork Salmon; Salmon. 239A-239B, Feb. 1970
● Wildlife Adventuring in Jackson Hole. By Frank and John Craighead. 1-36, Jan. 1956
● *See also* Colorado River

A **WILD SHORE** Where Two Worlds Meet. Photos by Des and Jen Bartlett. 298-321, Mar. 1976

WILD Water, Proud People. By Don Belt. Photos by Steve Wall. 458-477, Apr. 1983

WILD WEST:
● Riding the Outlaw Trail. By Robert Redford. Photos by Jonathan Blair. 622-657, Nov. 1976

WILD WEST EXHIBITION:
● Buffalo Bill and the Enduring West. By Alice J. Hall. Photos by James L. Amos. 76-103, July 1981

The **WILD** World of Compost. By Cecil E. Johnson. Photos by Bianca Lavies. 273-284, Aug. 1980

WILDERNESS: North America:
● Alaskan Family Robinson. By Nancy Robinson. Photos by John Metzger and Peter Robinson. 55-75, Jan. 1973
● Aldo Leopold: "A Durable Scale of Values." By Boyd Gibbons. Photos by Jim Brandenburg. 682-708, Nov. 1981
▲ *America's Federal Lands; The United States,* double-sided supplement. Sept. 1982
● America's Wilderness: How Much Can We Save? By Gilbert M. Grosvenor, François Leydet, and Joseph Judge. Photos by Farrell Grehan. Included: Allagash Wilderness Waterway, Maine; Mazatzal Wilderness, Arizona; Okefenokee Swamp, Georgia; Olympic National Park, Washington; Wind River Range, Wyoming. 151-205, Feb. 1974
◆ *Canada's Wilderness Lands.* 1982
● Escalante Canyon–Wilderness at the Crossroads. By Jon Schneeberger. 270-285, Aug. 1972
◆ *Exploring America's Backcountry.* 1979
◆ *Into the Wilderness.* 1978
● John Muir's Wild America. By Harvey Arden. Photos by Dewitt Jones. 433-461, Apr. 1973
◆ *John Muir's Wild America.* Announced. 860-864, June 1976
● Mexico to Canada on the Pacific Crest Trail. By Mike W. Edwards. Photos by David Hiser. Included: Glacier Peak Wilderness, Washington; Goat Rocks Wilderness, Washington; John Muir Wilderness, California; Mount Jefferson Wilderness, Oregon; Pasayten Wilderness, Washington. 741-779, June 1971
● Nahanni: Canada's Wilderness Park. By Douglas H. Chadwick. Photos by Matt Bradley. 396-420, Sept. 1981
● New National Park Proposed: The Spectacular North Cascades. By Nathaniel T. Kenney. Photos by James P. Blair. Included: Glacier Peak Wilderness, Washington; Pasayten Wilderness, Washington. 642-667, May 1968
● The Noatak. By John M. Kauffmann. Photos by Sam Abell. 52-59, July 1977
● Our National Forests: Problems in Paradise. By Rowe Findley. Photos by David Cupp. 306-339, Sept. 1982
● Our Wildest Wilderness: Alaska's Arctic National Wildlife Range. By Douglas H. Chadwick. Photos by Lowell Georgia. 737-769, Dec. 1979
● Preserving America's Last Great Wilderness (Alaska). By David Jeffery. 769-791, June 1975
● Roosevelt Country: T. R.'s Wilderness Legacy. By John L. Eliot. Photos by Farrell Grehan. 340-363, Sept. 1982
● South Dakota's Badlands: Castles in Clay. By John Madson. Photos by Jim Brandenburg. 524-539, Apr. 1981
● Studying Grizzly Habitat by Satellite. By John Craighead. NGS research grant. 148-158, July 1976
● White-water Adventure on Wild Rivers of Idaho. By Frank Craighead, Jr. and John Craighead. 213-239, Feb. 1970
◆ *Wilderness Challenge.* 1980
◆ *Wilderness U.S.A.* Announced. 582-584, Oct. 1973
● Yellowstone at 100: A Walk Through the Wilderness. By Karen and Derek Craighead. Photos by Sam Abell. 579-603, May 1972

WILDLIFE:
● Florida, Noah's Ark for Exotic Newcomers. By Rick Gore. Photos by David Doubilet. 538-559, Oct. 1976
● Man's Wildlife Heritage Faces Extinction. By H.R.H. The Prince Philip, Duke of Edinburgh. 700-703, Nov. 1962
● Studying Wildlife by Satellite. By Frank Craighead, Jr. and John Craighead. NGS research grant. 120-123, Jan. 1973
● *See also* Birds; Fishes; Mammals; *and* Endangered and Threatened Species

Africa:
● African Termites, Dwellers in the Dark. By Glenn D. Prestwich. 532-547, Apr. 1978
● African Wildlife: Man's Threatened Legacy. By Allan C. Fisher, Jr. Photos by Thomas Nebbia. 147-187, Feb. 1972
A Continent's Living Treasure. Paintings by Ned Seidler. 164-167
● Africa's Elephants: Can They Survive? By Oria Douglas-Hamilton. Photos by Oria and Iain Douglas-Hamilton. 568-603, Nov. 1980
● Africa's Gentle Giants (Giraffes). By Bristol Foster. Photos by Bob Campbell and Thomas Nebbia. 402-417, Sept. 1977
● Africa's Uncaged Elephants. Photos by Quentin Keynes. 371-382, Mar. 1951
◆ *Animals of East Africa: The Wild Realm.* 1969. Announced. 844-849, June 1968
● A Bad Time to Be a Crocodile. By Rick Gore. Photos by Jonathan Blair. 90-115, Jan. 1978
● East Africa's Majestic Flamingos. By M. Philip Kahl. Included: Greater flamingo; Lesser flamingo. NGS research grant. 276-294, Feb. 1970
● Etosha: Namibia's Kingdom of Animals. By Douglas H. Chadwick. Photos by Des and Jen Bartlett. 344-385, Mar. 1983
■ Etosha: Place of Dry Water. 703, Dec. 1980
● Face to Face With Gorillas in Central Africa. By Paul A. Zahl. 114-137, Jan. 1960
● Family Life of Lions. By Des and Jen Bartlett. 800-819, Dec. 1982
● The Flamingo Eaters of Ngorongoro. By Richard D. Estes. Contents: Flamingos as hyenas' prey. 535-539, Oct. 1973
● Freeing Flamingos From Anklets of Death. By John G. Williams. Photos by Alan Root. 934-944, Dec. 1963
■ Gorilla. 703, Dec. 1980
● Hunting Africa's Smallest Game (Insects). By Edward S. Ross. 406-419, Mar. 1961
● Hyenas, the Hunters Nobody Knows. By Hans Kruuk. Photos by Baron Hugo van Lawick. Included: Lions, Wildebeests, Zebras. 44-57, July 1968
● The Imperiled Mountain Gorilla. By Dian Fossey. 501-523, Apr. 1981
● Jackals of the Serengeti. By Patricia D. Moehlman. 840-850, Dec. 1980
● The Last Great Animal Kingdom. 390-409, Sept. 1960
■ Last Stand in Eden. 1, Jan. 1979
● Life and Death at Gombe (Chimpanzees). By Jane Goodall. 592-621, May 1979
● Life With the King of Beasts. By George B. Schaller. 494-519, Apr. 1969
■ The Living Sands of Namib. 439, Oct. 1977; cover, Mar. 1978; 1, Jan. 1979
● The Living Sands of the Namib. By William J. Hamilton III. Photos by Carol and David Hughes. Contents: Unique desert creatures. 364-377, Sept. 1983

● Locusts: "Teeth of the Wind." By Robert A. M. Conley. Photos by Gianni Tortoli. 202-227, Aug. 1969
● Making Friends With Mountain Gorillas. Photos by Robert M. Campbell. 48-67, Jan. 1970
■ Miss Goodall and the Wild Chimpanzees. 831A-831B, Dec. 1965
● More Years With Mountain Gorillas. Photos by Robert M. Campbell. 574-585, Oct. 1971
◆ *My Friends the Wild Chimpanzees*. 1967. Announced. 408-417, Mar. 1966
● My Life Among Wild Chimpanzees. By Jane Goodall. Photos by Baron Hugo van Lawick and author. 272-308, Aug. 1963
● Mzima, Kenya's Spring of Life. By Joan and Alan Root. 350-373, Sept. 1971
● Namibia: Nearly a Nation? By Bryan Hodgson. Photos by Jim Brandenburg. 755-797, June 1982
● New Discoveries Among Africa's Chimpanzees. By Baroness Jane van Lawick-Goodall. Photos by Baron Hugo van Lawick. 802-831, Dec. 1965
● A New Look at Kenya's "Treetops." By Quentin Keynes. 536-541, Oct. 1956
● Orphans of the Wild (Animal Orphanage, Uganda). By Bruce G. Kinloch. 683-699, Nov. 1962
● Rescuing the Rothschild. By Carolyn Bennett Patterson. 419-421, Sept. 1977
● Roaming Africa's Unfenced Zoos. By W. Robert Moore. 353-380, Mar. 1950
◆ *Safari!* 1982
● Safari from Congo to Cairo. By Elsie May Bell Grosvenor. Photos by Gilbert Grosvenor. 721-771, Dec. 1954
● Safari Through Changing Africa. By Elsie May Bell Grosvenor. Photos by Gilbert Grosvenor. 145-198, Aug. 1953
● Spearing Lions with Africa's Masai. By Edgar Monsanto Queeny. 487-517, Oct. 1954
● Stalking Central Africa's Wildlife. By T. Donald Carter. Paintings by Walter A. Weber. NGS research grant. 264-286, Aug. 1956
● Tanzania Marches to Its Own Drum. By Peter T. White. Photos by Emory Kristof. 474-509, Apr. 1975
● Where Elephants Have Right of Way. By George and Jinx Rodger. Included: Buffaloes, Giraffes, Hippopotamuses, Lyrehorned ankoles, Rhinoceroses. 363-389, Sept. 1960
● *See also* Baboons; Black Eagles; Cattle Egrets; Cheetahs; Egyptian Vulture; Flamingos; Giant Frogs; Honey-Guide; Hornbills; *and* National Parks (Africa)

Antarctic Regions:

● Antarctica's Nearer Side. By Samuel W. Matthews. Photos by William R. Curtsinger. 622-655, Nov. 1971
● Penguins and Their Neighbors. By Roger Tory Peterson. Photos by Des and Jen Bartlett. 237-255, Aug. 1977
● *See also* Penguins; Weddell Seals

Arctic:

TSUNEO HAYASHIDA

Japanese Crane: male braces against the cold

▲ "Ice Age Mammals of the Alaskan Tundra," painting supplement. Map of Canada. Mar. 1972
■ Journey to the High Arctic. 590A-590B, Apr. 1971
● Learning the Ways of the Walrus. By G. Carleton Ray. Photos by Bill Curtsinger. 565-580, Oct. 1979
● Nomad in Alaska's Outback. By Thomas J. Abercrombie. 540-567, Apr. 1969
● Our Wildest Wilderness: Alaska's Arctic National Wildlife Range. By Douglas H. Chadwick. Photos by Lowell Georgia. 737-769, Dec. 1979
● *See also* Harp Seals; Musk Oxen; Polar Bears; Reindeer

Asia:

● Bhutan, Land of the Thunder Dragon. By Burt Kerr Todd. 713-754, Dec. 1952
● The Elephant and I. By M. D. Chaturvedi. 489-507, Oct. 1957
● India Struggles to Save Her Wildlife. By John J. Putman. Paintings by Ned Seidler. 299-343, Sept. 1976
● The Japanese Crane, Bird of Happiness. By Tsuneo Hayashida. 542-556, Oct. 1983
● Seeking Mindanao's Strangest Creatures. By Charles Heizer Wharton. 389-408, Sept. 1948
● Sri Lanka's Wildlife. 254-278, Aug. 1983
I. Sri Lanka's Wildlife Heritage: A Personal Perspective. By Arthur C. Clarke. 254-255; II. Legacy of Lively Treasures. By Dieter and Mary Plage. 256-273; III. A Nation Rises to the Challenge. By Lyn de Alwis. Photos by Dieter and Mary Plage. 274-278
● Stalking the Great Indian Rhino. By Lee Merriam Talbot. 389-398, Mar. 1957
● Wild Elephant Roundup in India. By Harry Miller. Photos by author and James P. Blair. 372-385, Mar. 1969
● *See also* Cattle Egrets; Crocodilians; Komodo Dragons; Orangutans; Pandas, Giant; Père David's Deer; Philippine Eagles; Rhesus Monkeys; Spiny Babbler; *and* Red Sea

Australia:

■ Australia's Animal Mysteries. 824, Dec. 1982
● Eden in the Outback. By Kay and Stanley Breeden. 189-203, Feb. 1973
▲ "Land of Living Fossils," painting supplement. Map on reverse. Feb. 1979
● Strange Animals of Australia. By David Fleay. Photos by Stanley Breeden. 388-411, Sept. 1963
● *See also* Bowerbirds; Crocodilians; Kangaroos; Lorikeets; Lyrebird; Platypuses; *and* Great Barrier Reef

Central America:

● The Amazing Frog-Eating Bat. By Merlin D. Tuttle. NGS research grant. 78-91, Jan. 1982
● The Hummingbirds. By Crawford H. Greenewalt. 658-679, Nov. 1960
● Nature's Living, Jumping Jewels. By Paul A. Zahl. 130-146, July 1973
● One Strange Night on Turtle Beach. By Paul A. Zahl. 570-581, Oct. 1973

• The Quetzal, Fabulous Bird of Maya Land. By Anne LaBastille Bowes. Photos by David G. Allen. 141-150, Jan. 1969
• *See also* Crocodilians
Desert:
• The Desert: An Age-old Challenge Grows. By Rick Gore. Photos by Georg Gerster and Bruce Dale. 586-639, Nov. 1979
■ The Living Sands of Namib. 439, Oct. 1977; cover, Mar. 1978; 1, Jan. 1979
• The Living Sands of the Namib. By William J. Hamilton III. Photos by Carol and David Hughes. Contents: Unique desert creatures. 364-377, Sept. 1983
• The Lure of the Changing Desert. 817-824, June 1954
• *See also* Locusts; Scorpions
Europe:
• Rare Birds Flock to Spain's Marismas. By Roger Tory Peterson. 397-425, Mar. 1958
• Scotland's Golden Eagles at Home. By C. Eric Palmar. 273-286, Feb. 1954
• The Swans of Abbotsbury (England). By Michael Moynihan. Photos by Barnet Saidman. 563-570, Oct. 1959
• *See also* Cattle Egrets; Kingfishers; Puffins; Reindeer; White Storks; *and* Zoos
Galapagos Islands:
• The Galapagos, Eerie Cradle of New Species. By Roger Tory Peterson. Photos by Alan and Joan Root. 541-585, Apr. 1967
• Lost World of the Galapagos. By Irving and Electa Johnson. 681-703, May 1959
• Undersea Wonders of the Galapagos. By Gerard Wellington. Photos by David Doubilet. 363-381, Sept. 1978
Hawaii:
• Hawaii's Far-flung Wildlife Paradise. By John L. Eliot. Photos by Jonathan Blair. 670-691, May 1978
• In Hawaii's Crystal Sea, A Galaxy of Life Fills the Night. By Kenneth Brower. Photos by William R. Curtsinger and Chris Newbert. 834-847, Dec. 1981
• *See also* Humpback Whales; Nene
Midway Islands:
• *See* Albatrosses; Fairy Terns
New Guinea:
• *See* Birds of Paradise
New Zealand:
• *See* Kiwi; Takahe
North America:
• Arizona's Window on Wildlife. By Lewis Wayne Walker. 240-250, Feb. 1958
• An Artist's Glimpses of Our Roadside Wildlife. Paintings by Walter A. Weber. 16-32, July 1950
• Audubon "On the Wing." By David Jeffery. Photos by Bates Littlehales. 149-177, Feb. 1977
• Businessman in the Bush. By Frederick Kent Truslow. 634-675, May 1970
• Cajunland, Louisiana's French-speaking Coast. By Bern Keating. Photos by Charles Harbutt and Franke Keating. 353-391, Mar. 1966
• Can We Save Our Salt Marshes? By Stephen W. Hitchcock. Photos by William R. Curtsinger. 729-765, June 1972
• Corkscrew Swamp–Florida's Primeval Show Place. By Melville Bell Grosvenor. 98-113, Jan. 1958
◆ *Field Guide to the Birds of North America.* 1983
• Florida, Noah's Ark for Exotic Newcomers. By Rick Gore. Photos by David Doubilet. Included: The introduction of tropical birds: budgerigar, bulbul, myna, parakeet, and parrot. 538-559, Oct. 1976
• Freezing the Flight of Hummingbirds. By Harold E. Edgerton, R. J. Niedrach, and Walker Van Riper. NGS research grant. 245-261, Aug. 1951
• Haunting Heart of the Everglades. By Andrew H. Brown. Photos by author and Willard R. Culver. 145-173, Feb. 1948
• Heart of the Canadian Rockies. By Elizabeth A. Moize. Photos by Jim Brandenburg. 757-779, June 1980
• Henry Hudson's Changing Bay. By Bill Richards. Photos by David Hiser. Included: Arctic fox, Beluga whales, Caribou, Murres, Polar bears. 380-405, Mar. 1982
• The Hummingbirds. By Crawford H. Greenewalt. 658-679, Nov. 1960
• Last of the Black-footed Ferrets? By Tim W. Clark. Photos by Franz J. Camenzind and the author. NGS research grant. 828-838, June 1983
• Last Stand for the Bighorn. By James K. Morgan. 383-399, Sept. 1973
• Men, Moose, and Mink of Northwest Angle. By William H. Nicholas. Photos by J. Baylor Roberts. 265-284, Aug. 1947
• Mysteries of Bird Migration. By Allan C. Fisher, Jr. Photos by Jonathan Blair. 154-193, Aug. 1979
Tracking the Shore Dwellers: From Canada to Suriname. 175-179
• Nature's Year in Pleasant Valley. By Paul A. Zahl. 488-525, Apr. 1968
◆ *Our Continent: A Natural History of North America.* Announced. 572-574, Oct. 1976
• Our National Wildlife Refuges. 342-381. Mar. 1979
• Preserving America's Last Great Wilderness (Alaska). By David Jeffery. 769-791, June 1975
• The Roadrunner–Clown of the Desert. By Martha A. Whitson. Photos by Bruce Dale. 694-702, May 1983
• Saving Man's Wildlife Heritage. By John H. Baker. Photos by Robert F. Sisson. 581-620, Nov. 1954
• Sharing the Lives of Wild Golden Eagles. By John Craighead. Photos by Charles and Derek Craighead. 420-439, Sept. 1967
◆ *Song and Garden Birds of North America.* Announced. 553-557, Oct. 1964; rev. ed. 1975
• Springtime Comes to Yellowstone National Park. By Paul A. Zahl. 761-779, Dec. 1956

DOUG BROWN
Black-footed Ferrets: rare mammal

WX

• Stalking the Mountain Lion–to Save Him. By Maurice G. Hornocker. 638-655, Nov. 1969
• Studying Grizzly Habitat by Satellite. By John Craighead. 148-158, July 1976
• Threatened Glories of Everglades National Park. By Frederick Kent Truslow and Frederick G. Vosburgh. Photos by Frederick Kent Truslow and Otis Imboden. 508-553, Oct. 1967
• Twilight Hope for Big Cypress. By Rick Gore. Photos by Patricia Caulfield. 251-273, Aug. 1976
◆ *Vanishing Wildlife of North America*. Announced. 865-868, June 1973
◆ *Water, Prey, and Game Birds of North America*. Announced. 529-535, Oct. 1965
• White-water Adventure on Wild Rivers of Idaho. By Frank Craighead, Jr. and John Craighead. 213-239, Feb. 1970
• The Wichitas: Land of the Living Prairie. By M. Woodbridge Williams. 661-697, May 1957
◆ *Wild Animals of North America*. Announced. 554-557, Oct. 1960
◆ *Wild Animals of North America*. 1979
• Wildlife Adventuring in Jackson Hole. By Frank and John Craighead. 1-36, Jan. 1956
• Wildlife In and Near the Valley of the Moon. By H. H. Arnold. Photos by Paul J. Fair. 401-414, Mar. 1950
• Wildlife of Everglades National Park. By Daniel B. Beard. Paintings by Walter A. Weber. 83-116, Jan. 1949
• Wildlife of Mount McKinley National Park. By Adolph Murie. Paintings by Walter A. Weber. 249-270, Aug. 1953
• Wolves Versus Moose on Isle Royale. By Durward L. Allen and L. David Mech. 200-219, Feb. 1963
◆ *Wonder of Birds*. 1983
• Yellowstone at 100: A Walk Through the Wilderness. By Karen and Derek Craighead. Photos by Sam Abell. 579-603, May 1972
• Yellowstone Wildlife in Winter. By William Albert Allard. 637-661, Nov. 1967
• *See also* Armadillos; Caribou; Crocodilians; Grizzly Bears; Mountain Goats; Prairie Dogs; Seals; Walruses; Wolves; *and* Bird Sanctuaries and Rookeries; Birds; National Parks (Canada; United States); Tundra

South America:
• Animal Safari to British Guiana. By David Attenborough. Photos by Charles Lagus and author. 851-874, June 1957
▲ *Bird Migration in the Americas: The Americas*, double-sided supplement. Included: 67 paintings by Arthur Singer. Aug. 1979
• Capturing Strange Creatures in Colombia. By Marte Latham. Photos by Tor Eigeland. 682-693, May 1966
• The Hummingbirds. By Crawford H. Greenewalt. 658-679, Nov. 1960
• In Quest of the Rarest Flamingo (James's Flamingo). By William G. Conway. Photos by Bates Littlehales. 91-105, July 1961
• The Jungle Was My Home. By Sasha Siemel. 695-712, Nov. 1952
• Keeping House for a Biologist in Colombia. By Nancy Bell Fairchild Bates. Photos by Marston Bates. 251-274, Aug. 1948
• The Man Who Talks to Hummingbirds (Augusto Ruschi). By Luis Marden. Photos by James Blair. 80-99, Jan. 1963
• The Marvelous Hummingbird Rediscovered. By Crawford H. Greenewalt. 98-101, July 1966
• Mysteries of Bird Migration. By Allan C. Fisher, Jr. Photos by Jonathan Blair. 154-193, Aug. 1979
• Patagonia. 290-339, Mar. 1976
• Peru Profits from Sea Fowl. By Robert Cushman Murphy. Photos by author and Grace E. Barstow Murphy. 395-413, Mar. 1959
• Photographing Hummingbirds in Brazil. By Crawford H. Greenewalt. 100-115, Jan. 1963
• *See also* Cocks-of-the-Rock; Four-eyed Fish; Giant Brazilian Otters; Giant Earthworms; Guanacos; Hoatzin; Oilbirds; Scarlet Ibis; Tortoises; *and* National Parks (South America); Tierra del Fuego

West Indies:
• *See* Flamingos; Greater Birds of Paradise

World:
• Man's Wildlife Heritage Faces Extinction. By H.R.H. The Prince Philip, Duke of Edinburgh. 700-703, Nov. 1962
• Nature's Alert Eyes (Animal Eyes). By Constance P. Warner. 558-569, Apr. 1959
• Tropical Rain Forests. 2-65, Jan. 1983
Nature's Dwindling Treasures. By Peter T. White. Photos by James P. Blair. Paintings by Barron Storey. 2-47; Teeming Life of a Rain Forest. By Carol and David Hughes. 49-65
◆ *Wildlife Alert!* 1980
• *See also* Birds; Crocodilians; Dolphins; Fishes; Mammals; Whales; *and* Wildlife Refuges

WILDLIFE MANAGEMENT:
• Etosha: Namibia's Kingdom of Animals. By Douglas H. Chadwick. Photos by Des and Jen Bartlett. 344-385, Mar. 1983
• Sri Lanka's Wildlife: A Nation Rises to the Challenge. By Lyn de Alwis. Photos by Dieter and Mary Plage. 274-278, Aug. 1983

WILDLIFE MANAGEMENT INSTITUTE: Expeditions and Research. *See* Isle Royale, Michigan

WILDLIFE REFUGES:
Africa. *See* Entebbe Animal Refuge, Uganda; Etosha National Park, Namibia; Serengeti National Park, Tanzania; *and* National Parks
Asia. *See* Kaziranga Wild Life Sanctuary, India; Sri Lanka's Wildlife; Tanjung Puting Reserve, Indonesia; Wolong Natural Reserve, China; *and* National Parks
Australia. *See* National Parks
Caribbean. *See* Little Tobago (Island)
Europe. *See* Abbotsbury Swannery, England; The Camargue, France; Marismas, Spain
South America. *See* Pampa Galeras National Vicuña Reserve, Peru; *and* National Parks

United States:
• Alaska: Rising Northern Star. By Joseph Judge. Photos by Bruce Dale. Included: Mount McKinley, Sitka; *and* proposed parks: Gates of the Arctic, Lake Clark, Wrangell-St. Elias. 730-767, June 1975
• The Aleutians: Alaska's Far-out Islands. By Lael Morgan. Photos by Steven C. Wilson. Note: 95 percent of the islands are claimed by the federal government as wildlife refuges and military sites. 336-363, Sept. 1983
▲ *America's Federal Lands; The United States*, double-sided supplement. Sept. 1982
• Beyond the North Wind With the Snow Goose. By Des and Jen Bartlett. 822-843, Dec. 1973
• Delaware–Who Needs to Be Big? By Jane Vessels. Photos by Kevin Fleming. Included: Bombay Hook National Wildlife Refuge. 171-197, Aug. 1983
• Hawaii's Far-flung Wildlife Paradise. By John L. Eliot. Photos By Jonathan Blair. 670-691, May 1978
• Our National Forests: Problems in Paradise. By Rowe Findley. Photos by David Cupp. 306-339, Sept. 1982
• Our National Wildlife Refuges. 342-381, Mar. 1979
I. A Chance to Grow. By Robert E. Doyle. 342-349; II. Island, Prairie, Marsh, and Shore. By Charlton Ogburn. Photos by Bates Littlehales. 350-381; III. Wildlife Refuges of the United States. Tear-out guide with maps. 363-370
• Preserving America's Last Great Wilderness (Alaska). By David Jeffery. Included: Proposed parks: Gates of the Arctic, Katmai additional acreage, Lake Clark, Mount McKinley. 769-791, June 1975
• Roosevelt Country: T. R.'s Wilderness Legacy. By John L. Eliot. Photos by Farrell Grehan. 340-363, Sept. 1982
• Teamwork Helps the Whooping Crane. By Roderick C. Drewien, with Ernie Kuyt. 680-693, May 1979
• Tireless Voyager, the Whistling Swan. By William J. L. Sladen. Photos by Bianca Lavies. NGS research grant. 134-147, July 1975
• *See also* Aransas National Wildlife Refuge, Texas; Arctic National Wildlife Range, Alaska; Bear River Migratory Bird Refuge, Utah; Chincoteague Island, Virginia; Corkscrew Swamp, Florida; Desert Museum, Arizona; Everglades, Florida; McNeil River State Game Sanctuary, Alaska; National Elk Refuge, Wyoming; Okefenokee Swamp, Georgia; Pribilof Islands, Alaska; Red Rock Lakes National Wildlife Refuge, Montana; Santa Barbara Islands, California; Sapsucker Woods, New York; Wichita Mountains Wildlife Refuge, Oklahoma; *and* Bird Sanctuaries and Rookeries; Game Preserves; National Parks

WILDLIFE TRADE:
• Wild Cargo: the Business of Smuggling Animals. By Noel Grove. Photos by Steve Raymer. 287-315, Mar. 1981

WILES, WILBUR:
• Stalking the Mountain Lion–to Save Him. By Maurice G. Hornocker. 638-655, Nov. 1969

WILHELM, JOHN L.: Author:
• Solar Energy, the Ultimate Powerhouse. Photos by Emory Kristof. 381-397, Mar. 1976

WILKERSON, S. JEFFREY K.: Author:
• Man's Eighty Centuries in Veracruz. Photos by David Hiser. Paintings by Richard Schlecht. 203-231, Aug. 1980

WILKIE BROTHERS FOUNDATION:
Study Grant:
• Orangutans. 835, June 1980

WILKINSON, NORMAN: Author-Artist:
• British Castles, History in Stone. 111-129, July 1947

WILL Brazil's Fiery Bees Reach the U. S.? By Rick Gore. Photos by Bianca Lavies. 491-501, Apr. 1976

WILL Coal Be Tomorrow's "Black Gold"? By Gordon Young. Photos by James P. Blair. 234-259, Aug. 1975

WILL Oil and Tundra Mix? Alaska's North Slope Hangs in the Balance. By William S. Ellis. Photos by Emory Kristof. 485-517, Oct. 1971

WILL Success Spoil Our Parks? By Robert Paul Jordan. 31-59, July 1979

WILLA CATHER: Voice of the Frontier. By William Howarth. Photos by Farrell Grehan. 71-93, July 1982

WILLAMETTE RIVER AND VALLEY, Oregon:
• A River Restored: Oregon's Willamette. By Ethel A. Starbird. Photos by Lowell J. Georgia. 816-835, June 1972

WILLCOX, ALEX R.: Photographer:
• Africa's Bushman Art Treasures. By Alfred Friendly. 848-865, June 1963

WILLEMSTAD, Curaçao, Netherlands Antilles:
• The Netherlands Antilles: Holland in the Caribbean. By James Cerruti. Photos by Emory Kristof. 115-146, Jan. 1970

WILLIAM THE CONQUEROR:
• The British Way. By Sir Evelyn Wrench. 421-541, Apr. 1949
• A New Look at Medieval Europe. By Kenneth M. Setton. Paintings by Andre Durenceau and Birney Lettick. 799-859, Dec. 1962
• 900 Years Ago: the Norman Conquest. By Kenneth M. Setton. Photos by George F. Mobley. 206-251, Aug. 1966

WILLIAM AND MARY COLLEGE, Williamsburg, Virginia:
• Williamsburg: Its College and Its Cinderella City. By Beverley M. Bowie. 439-486, Oct. 1954

WILLIAM PENN'S Faire Land. By Gordon Young. Photos by Cary Wolinsky. 731-767, June 1978

WILLIAM T. GRANT FOUNDATION:
Study Grant:
• Chimpanzees. 598, May 1979

WILLIAMS, JOHN G.: Author:
• Freeing Flamingos From Anklets of Death. Photos by Alan Root. 934-944, Dec. 1963

WILLIAMS, M. WOODBRIDGE:
Author-Photographer:
• The Wichitas: Land of the Living Prairie. 661-697, May 1957
Photographer:
• History and Beauty Blend in a Concord Iris Garden. By Robert T. Cochran, Jr. 705-719, May 1959
• Keeping House for Tropical Butterflies. By Jocelyn Crane. 193-217, Aug. 1957
• Strange Little World of the Hoatzin. By J. Lear Grimmer. 391-401, Sept. 1962

WILLIAMS, MAYNARD OWEN:
• Chief of the NGS Foreign Staff for 20 years; total service, 34 years. 627, Oct. 1963
Author:
• Pilgrims Follow the Christmas Star. 831-840, Dec. 1952
• Portrait of Indochina. By W. Robert Moore and Maynard Owen Williams. Paintings by Jean Despujols. 461-490, Apr. 1951
• Turkey Paves the Path of Progress. 141-186, Aug. 1951
• War-torn Greece Looks Ahead. 711-744, Dec. 1949
Author-Photographer:
• Crete, Cradle of Western Civilization. 693-706, Nov. 1953
• Dublin's Historic Horse Show. 115-132, July 1953
• Home to the Holy Land. 707-746, Dec. 1950
• Oasis-hopping in the Sahara. 209-236, Feb. 1949
• Pennsylvania Dutch Folk Festival. 503-516, Oct. 1952
Photographer:
• Belgium Comes Back. By Harvey Klemmer. 575-614, May 1948
• Beside the Persian Gulf. 341-356, Mar. 1947
• Lascaux Cave, Cradle of World Art. By Norbert Casteret. 771-794, Dec. 1948
• Luxembourg, Survivor of Invasions. By Sydney Clark. 791-810, June 1948
• Operation Eclipse: 1948. By William A. Kinney. 325-372, Mar. 1949
• Saudi Arabia, Oil Kingdom. 497-512, Apr. 1948
• 2,000 Miles Through Europe's Oldest Kingdom (Denmark). By Isobel Wylie Hutchison. 141-180, Feb. 1949

WILLIAMS, WINSTON: Author:
• Twenty Fathoms Down for Mother-of-Pearl. Photos by Bates Littlehales. 512-529, Apr. 1962

WILLIAMSBURG, Brooklyn, New York:
• The Pious Ones (Hasidic Jews). By Harvey Arden. Photos by Nathan Benn. 276-298, Aug. 1975

BOTH BY NATHAN BENN

Williamsburg: Hasid offers a blessing, *above;* boy in his prayer shawl, *below*

WX

WILLIAMSBURG, Virginia:
• Firebrands of the Revolution. By Eric F. Goldman. Photos by George F. Mobley. 2-27, July 1974
• Williamsburg, City for All Seasons. By Joseph Judge. Photos by James L. Amos. 790-823, Dec. 1968
• Williamsburg: Its College and Its Cinderella City. By Beverley M. Bowie. 439-486, Oct. 1954

WILLM, PIERRE HENRI:
• Two and a Half Miles Down. By Georges S. Houot. NGS research grant. 80-86, July 1954

WILLS, WILLIAM JOHN:
• The Journey of Burke and Wills: First Across Australia. By Joseph Judge. Photos by Joseph J. Scherschel. 152-191, Feb. 1979

WILMINGTON, Delaware:
• Delaware–Who Needs to Be Big? By Jane Vessels. Photos by Kevin Fleming. 171-197, Aug. 1983

WILSON, ALBERT G.: Author:
• Our Universe Unfolds New Wonders. 245-260, Feb. 1952

WILSON, BRUCE A.: Author:
• Busy Fairbanks Sets Alaska's Pace. 505-523, Oct. 1949

WILSON, JAY: Photographer:
• To Torre Egger's Icy Summit. By Jim Donini. 813-823, Dec. 1976

WILSON, JOHN: Author:
• Drought Bedevils Brazil's Sertão. Photos by Gordon W. Gahan. 704-723, Nov. 1972

WILSON, PHYLLIS: Author:
• Queen of Canada (Elizabeth II). Photos by Kathleen Revis. 825-829, June 1959

WILSON, STEVEN C.:
• What Six Experts Say. 70-73, *Special Report on Energy* (Feb. 1981)
Author-Photographer:
• Where Oil and Wildlife Mix. By Steven C. Wilson and Karen C. Hayden. 145-173, Feb. 1981
Photographer:
• The Aleutians: Alaska's Far-out Islands. By Lael Morgan. 336-363, Sept. 1983

WILSON, WOODROW:
• Inside the White House. By Lonnelle Aikman. Photos by B. Anthony Stewart and Thomas Nebbia. 3-43, Jan. 1961
• The Living White House. By Lonnelle Aikman. 593-643, Nov. 1966
• Profiles of the Presidents: IV. America Enters the Modern Era. By Frank Freidel. 537-577, Oct. 1965

WILSON'S PHALAROPE:
• Mono Lake: A Vital Way Station for the Wilson's Phalarope. By Joseph R. Jehl, Jr. 520-525, Oct. 1981

WIND, Wave, Star, and Bird. By David Lewis. Photos by Nicholas deVore III. 747-781, Dec. 1974

WIND POWER:
• Can We Harness the Wind? By Roger Hamilton. Photos by Emory Kristof. 812-829, Dec. 1975
• Harnessing the Wind. 34-57, *Special Report on Energy* (Feb. 1981)

WIND RIVER RANGE, Wyoming:
• Wind River Range: Many-treasured Splendor. By Joseph Judge. 198-205, Feb. 1974

WINDJAMMING Around New England. By Tom Horgan. Photos by Robert F. Sisson. 141-169, Aug. 1950

WINDMILLS:
• Can We Harness the Wind? By Roger Hamilton. Photos by Emory Kristof. 812-829, Dec. 1975

WINDOW on Earth's Interior. By Robert D. Ballard. Photos by Emory Kristof. 228-249, Aug. 1976

WINDOW on Nature: The American Museum of Natural History. By James A. Oliver. Photos by Robert F. Sisson. 220-259, Feb. 1963

The **WINDS** of Freedom Stir a Continent. By Nathaniel T. Kenney. Photos by W. D. Vaughn. 303-359, Sept. 1960

WINDSOR CASTLE, England:
• Royal House for Dolls. By David Jeffery. Photos by James L. Stanfield. 632-643, Nov. 1980
• Windsor Castle. By Anthony Holden. Photos by James L. Stanfield. 604-631, Nov. 1980
The Grandeur of Windsor. Text by David Jeffery. 616-625

WINDWARD ISLANDS, West Indies:
• *Carib* Cruises the West Indies. By Carleton Mitchell. 1-56, Jan. 1948
• *Finisterre* Sails the Windward Islands. By Carleton Mitchell. Photos by Winfield Parks. 755-801, Dec. 1965
• St. Vincent, the Grenadines, and Grenada: Taking It as It Comes. By Ethel A. Starbird. Photos by Cotton Coulson. 399-425, Sept. 1979
• *See also* Martinique

WINE MAKING:
• Bordeaux: Fine Wines and Fiery Gascons. By William Davenport. Photos by Adam Woolfitt. 233-259, Aug. 1980
• Italian Riviera, Land That Winter Forgot. By Howell Walker. 743-789, June 1963
• Living the Good Life in Burgundy. By William Davenport. Photos by Robert Freson. 794-817, June 1978
• Madeira, Like Its Wine, Improves With Age. By Veronica Thomas. Photos by Jonathan Blair. 488-513, Apr. 1973
• My Life in the Valley of the Moon (California). By H. H. Arnold. Photos by Willard R. Culver. Included: Vineyards and wineries of the Sonoma, Napa, and Petaluma Valleys. 689-716, Dec. 1948
• Napa, California's Valley of the Vine. By Moira Johnston. Photos by Charles O'Rear. 695-717, May 1979
• Portugal at the Crossroads. By Howard La Fay. Photos by Volkmar Wentzel. 458-501, Oct. 1965
• Provence, Empire of the Sun. By William Davenport. Photos by James A. Sugar. 692-715, May 1975
• The Renaissance Lives On in Tuscany. By Luis Marden. Photos by Albert Moldvay. 626-659, Nov. 1974

WINEGROWERS' FESTIVAL:
• Switzerland's Once-in-a-generation Festival. By Jean and Franc Shor. 563-571, Oct. 1958

WING-BORNE Lamps of the Summer Night. By Paul A. Zahl. 48-59, July 1962

WINGED Victory of *Gossamer Albatross*. By Bryan Allen. 640-651, Nov. 1979

WINNIPESAUKEE, Lake, New Hampshire:
• Contrary New Hampshire. By Robert Booth. Photos by Sandy Felsenthal. 770-799, Dec. 1982
• The Merrimack: River of Industry and Romance. By Albert W. Atwood. Photos by B. Anthony Stewart. 106-140, Jan. 1951

WINSTON-SALEM, North Carolina:
• Old Salem, Morning Star of Moravian Faith. By Rowe Findley. Photos by Robert W. Madden. 818-837, Dec. 1970

WINTER:
◆ *Animals in Winter.* 1982
• Yellowstone Wildlife in Winter. By William Albert Allard. 637-661, Nov. 1967

WINTER Caravan to the Roof of the World. By Sabrina and Roland Michaud. 435-465, Apr. 1972

WINTER FESTIVALS:
• Pakistan's Kalash: People of Fire and Fervor. By Debra Denker. Photos by Steve McCurry. Included: Chaomos. 458-473, Oct. 1981
• Snow Festival in Japan's Far North. By Eiji Miyazawa. 824-833, Dec. 1968
• A Town . . . a Mountain . . . a Way of Life. By Jill Durrance and Dick Durrance II. Included: Aspen Winterskol. 788-807, Dec. 1973
• Winter Brings Carnival Time to Quebec. By Kathleen Revis. 69-97, Jan. 1958

WINTER in Snowy Stehekin. Photos by Bruce Dale. Text by Pat Hutson. 572-588, Apr. 1974

WINTER 1976-'77: United States:
• The Year the Weather Went Wild. By Thomas Y. Canby. 799-829, Dec. 1977

WINTERING on the Roof of the World. By Barry C. Bishop. NGS research grant. 503-547, Oct. 1962

WINTERKEEPING in Yellowstone. By R. Steven Fuller. 829-857, Dec. 1978

WINTER'S White Death: Avalanche! 280-281, Sept. 1982

WIRE SUSPENSION BRIDGE:
• A Century Old, the Wonderful Brooklyn Bridge. By John G. Morris. Photos by Donal F. Holway. 565-579, May 1983

WIRTH, CONRAD L.: Author:
• Heritage of Beauty and History (National Parks). 587-661, May 1958

• The Mission Called 66: Today in Our National Parks. 7-47, July 1966
• The Parks in Your Backyard. 647-707, Nov. 1963

WISCONSIN:
• Aldo Leopold: "A Durable Scale of Values." By Boyd Gibbons. Photos by Jim Brandenburg. 682-708, Nov. 1981
▲ *Close-up: U.S.A., Wisconsin, Michigan, and the Great Lakes,* supplement. Text on reverse. Aug. 1973
• Deep in the Heart of "Swissconsin." By William H. Nicholas. Photos by J. Baylor Roberts. 781-800, June 1947
• The Great Lakes: Is It Too Late? By Gordon Young. Photos by James L. Amos and Martin Rogers. 147-185, Aug. 1973
• In Touch With Nature. By Elizabeth A. Moize. Photos by Steve Raymer. Contents: Towering Pines and Woodland Camps, Eagle River. 537-543, Apr. 1974
• Mapping the Nation's Breadbasket. By Frederick Simpich. 831-849, June 1948
• On the Trail of Wisconsin's Ice Age. By Anne LaBastille. Photos by Cary Wolinsky. 182-205, Aug. 1977
• Our Wild and Scenic Rivers: The St. Croix. By David S. Boyer. 30-37, July 1977
• Wisconsin, Land of the Good Life. By Beverley M. Bowie. Photos by Volkmar Wentzel. 141-187, Feb. 1957
• Wisconsin's Door Peninsula. By William S. Ellis. Photos by Ted Rozumalski. 347-371, Mar. 1969
• Wisconsin's Menominees: Indians on a Seesaw. By Patricia Raymer. Photos by Steve Raymer. 228-251, Aug. 1974
• *See also* Milwaukee; Oshkosh

WISCONSIN, U.S.S. *See* Midshipmen's Cruise

WISHERD, EDWIN L.: Photographer:
• The Wonder City That Moves by Night. By Francis Beverly Kelley. 289-324, Mar. 1948

WITH the Nuba Hillmen of Kordofan. By Robin Strachan. 249-278, Feb. 1951

WITH the U. S. Army in Korea. By John R. Hodge. 829-840, June 1947

WITH Uncle Sam and John Bull in Germany. By Frederick Simpich. 117-140, Jan. 1949

WITNESS to a War: British Correspondent Frank Vizetelly. By Robert T. Cochran, Jr. 453-491, Apr. 1961

WITTE LEEUW (Dutch East Indiaman):
• The Sunken Treasure of St. Helena. By Robert Sténuit. Photos by Bates Littlehales. 562-576, Oct. 1978

WIZARD ISLAND (Volcano), Oregon:
• Crater Lake Summer. By Walter Meayers Edwards. 134-148, July 1962

WOBURN ABBEY (Estate), England:
• Père David's Deer Saved From Extinction. By Larry Kohl. Photos by Bates Littlehales. 478-485, Oct. 1982

WODAABE (People):
• Niger's Wodaabe: "People of the Taboo." By Carol Beckwith. 483-509, Oct. 1983

WOLFE, ART: Author-Photographer:
• Long-eared Owls–Masters of the Night. 31-35, Jan. 1980

WOLFE, JAMES:
• The British Way. By Sir Evelyn Wrench. 421-541, Apr. 1949

WOLFE, TOM: Author:
• *Columbia's* Landing Closes a Circle. 474-477, Oct. 1981

WOLFSHEIMER, GENE:
Author-Photographer:
• The Discus Fish Yields a Secret. 675-681, May 1960

WOLINSKY, CARY: Photographer:
• Madawaska: Down East With a French Accent. By Perry Garfinkel. 380-409, Sept. 1980
• On the Trail of Wisconsin's Ice Age. By Anne LaBastille. 182-205, Aug. 1977
• Pennsylvania: Faire Land of William Penn. By Gordon Young. 731-767, June 1978
• Perth–Fair Winds and Full Sails. By Thomas J. Abercrombie. 638-667, May 1982
• Two Englands. By Allan C. Fisher, Jr. 442-481, Oct. 1979
• The U. S. Virgin Islands. By Thomas J. Colin. Photos by William Albert Allard and Cary Wolinsky. 225-243, Feb. 1981
• War and Peace in Northern Ireland. By Bryan Hodgson. 470-499, Apr. 1981

WOLONG NATURAL RESERVE, Sichuan Province, China:
• Pandas in the Wild. By George B. Schaller. 735-749, Dec. 1981

WOLSTENHOLME TOWNE (Site), Virginia:
• First Look at a Lost Virginia Settlement. By Ivor Noël Hume. Photos by Ira Block. Paintings by Richard Schlecht. NGS research grant. 735-767, June 1979
• New Clues to an Old Mystery (Virginia's Wolstenholme Towne). By Ivor Noël Hume. Photos by Ira Block. Paintings by Richard Schlecht. 53-77, Jan. 1982

WOLVES:
• Where Can the Wolf Survive? By L. David Mech. 518-537, Oct. 1977
• Wolves Versus Moose on Isle Royale. By Durward L. Allen and L. David Mech. 200-219, Feb. 1963

WOLVES of the Sea (Sharks). By Nathaniel T. Kenney. 222-257, Feb. 1968

A **WOMAN** Paints the Tibetans. By Lafugie. 659-692, May 1949

A **WOMAN'S** Icy Struggle: Thousand-mile Race to Nome. By Susan Butcher. Photos by Kerby Smith. 411-422, Mar. 1983

WOMEN, Long-necked. *See* Padaung

CAROL BECKWITH

Wodaabe: preparing for *yaake* dance

W X

MUSEUM OF THE CITY OF NEW YORK

Brooklyn Bridge: Roebling's masterpiece, *above;* portal to Brooklyn, *below*

ROBERT W. MADDEN, NGS

WOMEN DIVERS:
• Ama, Sea Nymphs of Japan. By Luis Marden. 122-135, July 1971
• Tektite II. 256-296, Aug. 1971
II. All-girl Team Tests the Habitat. By Sylvia A. Earle. Paintings by Pierre Mion. 291-296

WOMEN of the Revolution: Patriots in Petticoats. By Lonnelle Aikman. Paintings by Louis S. Glanzman. 475-493, Oct. 1975

WOMEN'S RESERVE OF THE U.S. NAVAL RESERVE (WAVES). *See* Parachute Rigger School

The **WONDER** City That Moves by Night. By Francis Beverly Kelley. 289-324, Mar. 1948

The **WONDERFUL** Brooklyn Bridge. By John G. Morris. Photos by Donal F. Holway. 565-579, May 1983

WONDERLAND in Longwood Gardens. By Edward C. Ferriday, Jr. 45-64, July 1951

The **WONDROUS** Eyes of Science. By Rick Gore. Photos by James P. Blair. 360-389, Mar. 1978

WOOD, GINNY HILL: Author:
• Squaws Along the Yukon. 245-265, Aug. 1957

WOOD:
• Versatile Wood Waits on Man. By Andrew H. Brown. 109-140, July 1951
• *See also* Lumber Industry; Paper and Pulp Industry

WOOD BUFFALO NATIONAL PARK, Canada:
• Teamwork Helps the Whooping Crane. By Roderick C. Drewien, with Ernie Kuyt. 680-693, May 1979

WOOD CARVING:
• An Ozark Family Carves a Living and a Way of Life. By Bruce Dale. 124-133, July 1975
• *See also* Afo-A-Kom; Decoys

WOOD IBIS. *See* Wood Storks

WOOD STORKS:
• Our Only Native Stork, the Wood Ibis. By Robert Porter Allen. Photos by Frederick Kent Truslow. 294-306, Feb. 1964

WOODLAND PERIOD. *See* Russell Cave, Alabama

WOODPECKERS:
• The Bird's Year. By Arthur A. Allen. Included: Gila, Golden-fronted, Red-bellied woodpeckers. 791-816, June 1951
• When Disaster Struck a Woodpecker's Home. By Frederick Kent Truslow. 882-884, Dec. 1966

WOODS, Lake of the, Canada-U. S.:
• Men, Moose, and Mink of Northwest Angle. By William H. Nicholas. Photos by J. Baylor Roberts. 265-284, Aug. 1947

WOODS HOLE, Massachusetts:
• Cape Cod, Where Sea Holds Sway Over Man and Land. By Nathaniel T. Kenney. Photos by Dean Conger. 149-187, Aug. 1962
• Windjamming Around New England. By Tom Horgan. Photos by Robert F. Sisson. 141-169, Aug. 1950

WOODS HOLE OCEANOGRAPHIC INSTITUTION:
• Expeditions and Research. *See* Galapagos Rift; Mid-Atlantic Ridge; Mid-Atlantic Rift; *and* Weddell Seals

WOODSON, LeROY, Jr.:
• Editorial. By Gilbert M. Grosvenor. 295, Mar. 1975
Author-Photographer:
• The Kurds of Iraq: "We Who Face Death." 364-387, Mar. 1975
Photographer:
• After Rhodesia, a Nation Named Zimbabwe. By Charles E. Cobb, Jr. Photos by James L. Stanfield and LeRoy Woodson, Jr. 616-651, Nov. 1981
• To Live in Harlem. . . . By Frank Hercules. 178-207, Feb. 1977

WOOL:
• The Cotswolds, "Noicest Parrt o'England." By James Cerruti. Photos by Adam Woolfitt. 846-869, June 1974
• High, Wild World of the Vicuña. By William L. Franklin. 77-91, Jan. 1973
• *See also Qiviut;* Tweed

WOOLFITT, ADAM: Photographer:
• Amiable Amsterdam. By William Davenport. 683-705, May 1974
• Ancient Europe Is Older Than We Thought. By Colin Renfrew. 615-623, Nov. 1977
• Bordeaux: Fine Wines and Fiery Gascons. By William Davenport. 233-259, Aug. 1980
• Chelsea, London's Haven of Individualists. By James Cerruti. 28-55, Jan. 1972
• Christopher Columbus and the New World He Found. By John Scofield. 584-625, Nov. 1975
• The Cotswolds, "Noicest Parrt o'England." By James Cerruti. 846-869, June 1974
• Edinburgh: Capital in Search of a Country. By James Cerruti. 274-296, Aug. 1976
• The England of Charles Dickens. By Richard W. Long. 443-483, Apr. 1974
• The Faeroes, Isles of Maybe. By Ernle Bradford. 410-442, Sept. 1970
• The Investiture of Great Britain's Prince of Wales. By Allan C. Fisher, Jr. Photos by James L. Stanfield and Adam Woolfitt. 698-715, Nov. 1969
• The Netherlands: Nation at War With the Sea. By Alan Villiers. 530-571, Apr. 1968
• New Mexico: The Golden Land. By Robert Laxalt. 299-345, Sept. 1970
• Washington, D. C.: Hometown Behind the Monuments. By Henry Mitchell. 84-125, Jan. 1983
• Where the River Shannon Flows. By Allan C. Fisher, Jr. 652-679, Nov. 1978

WORCESTER, Massachusetts:
• Cities Like Worcester Make America. By Howell Walker. 189-214, Feb. 1955

WORDEN, ALFRED M.:
- Apollo 15 Explores the Mountains of the Moon. By Kenneth F. Weaver. Photos from NASA. 233-265, Feb. 1972

WORDSWORTH, WILLIAM:
- The British Way. By Sir Evelyn Wrench. 421-541, Apr. 1949
- Lake District, Poets' Corner of England. By H. V. Morton. Photos by David S. Boyer. 511-545, Apr. 1956

WORK-HARD, Play-hard Michigan. By Andrew H. Brown. 279-320, Mar. 1952

WORKING for Weeks on the Sea Floor. By Jacques-Yves Cousteau. Photos by Philippe Cousteau and Bates Littlehales. NGS research grant. 498-537, Apr. 1966

WORLD:
◆ *Amazing Mysteries of the World.* 1983
- The Bonanza Bean–Coffee. By Ethel A. Starbird. Photos by Sam Abell. 388-405, Mar. 1981
- The Desert: An Age-old Challenge Grows. By Rick Gore. Photos by Georg Gerster and Bruce Dale. 586-639, Nov. 1979

◆ *The Desert Realm, Lands of Majesty and Mystery.* 1982
◆ *Exploring Our Living Planet.* 1983
- The Incredible Potato. By Robert E. Rhoades. Photos by Martin Rogers. Included: Genetic and nutrition research around the world. 668-694, May 1982

◆ *Nature's World of Wonders.* 1983
- New World of the Ocean. By Samuel W. Matthews. 792-832, Dec. 1981
- The Ocean. By Jacques-Yves Cousteau. 780-791, Dec. 1981
- Our Vegetable Travelers. By Victor R. Boswell. Paintings by Else Bostelmann. 145-217, Aug. 1949

▲ *The Political World; The Physical World,* double-sided supplement. Nov. 1975
■ Rain Forest. 824, Dec. 1982; 49, cover, Jan. 1983
◆ *Secret Corners of the World.* 1982
- Tropical Rain Forests: Nature's Dwindling Treasures. By Peter T. White. Photos by James P. Blair. Paintings by Barron Storey. 2-47, Jan. 1983

▲ *The World,* Atlas series supplement. Nov. 1960
▲ *The World,* supplement. Mar. 1957; Feb. 1965
▲ *The World,* supplement. Painting and text on reverse. Dec. 1970; Dec. 1976
▲ *The World; The World Ocean Floor,* double-sided supplement. Dec. 1981
- World Energy Resources. Contents: Map locating major resources of oil, coal, natural gas, and uranium. 20-21, *Special Report on Energy* (Feb. 1981)
- The World in Dolls. By Samuel F. Pryor. Photos by Kathleen Revis. 817-831, Dec. 1959
- The World in Your Garden (Flowers). By W. H. Camp. Paintings by Else Bostelmann. Contents: Gardens of Africa, Australia, China, Colonial America, Egypt, England, France, Greece, India, Iran, Japan, the Mediterranean Region, Mexico, the Netherlands, Rome, South America, Spain. 1-65, July 1947

▲ *The World Map,* supplement. Dec. 1951
- *See also* Earth; *and* Atlases, NGS

WORLD (Magazine for Young Readers):
- Circulation. 851, Dec. 1981
- Editorial: The *School Bulletin* is retired after 56 years; replaced by WORLD. By Gilbert M. Grosvenor. 299, Sept. 1975
- Start the World, I Want to Get On! Text announcing National Geographic WORLD. 148-150, July 1975

WORLD ATLAS. *See* Atlases, NGS: World

WORLD CRUISES AND VOYAGES:
- "Around the World in Eighty Days." By Newman Bumstead. 705-750, Dec. 1951
- Captain Cook: The Man Who Mapped the Pacific. By Alan Villiers. Photos by Gordon W. Gahan. 297-349, Sept. 1971
- Circling Earth From Pole to Pole. By Sir Ranulph Fiennes. 464-481, Oct. 1983
- In the Wake of Darwin's *Beagle.* By Alan Villiers. Photos by James L. Stanfield. 449-495, Oct. 1969
- Magellan: First Voyage Around the World. By Alan Villiers. Photos by Bruce Dale. 721-753, June 1976
- Off the Beaten Track of Empire (Prince Philip's Tour). By Beverley M. Bowie. Photos by Michael Parker. 584-626, Nov. 1957
- Robin Sails Home. By Robin Lee Graham. 504-545, Oct. 1970
- Saga of a Ship, the *Yankee.* By Luis Marden. 263-269, Feb. 1966
- Sir Francis Drake. By Alan Villiers. Photos by Gordon W. Gahan. 216-253, Feb. 1975
- A Teen-ager Sails the World Alone. By Robin Lee Graham. 445-491, Oct. 1968
- *Triton* Follows Magellan's Wake. By Edward L. Beach. Photos by J. Baylor Roberts. 585-616, Nov. 1960

■ The Voyage of the Brigantine *Yankee.* 265A-265B, Feb. 1966
◆ *Voyages to Paradise: Exploring in the Wake of Captain Cook.* 1981
- World-roaming Teen-ager Sails On. By Robin Lee Graham. 449-493, Apr. 1969

WORLD HEALTH ORGANIZATION (WHO). *See* United Nations: World Health Organization

WORLD HERITAGE FUND: Grant:
- Buddhist temple restoration: Nepal. 716, June 1982

WORLD HERITAGE SITES (UNESCO-Designated):
- A Walk and Ride on the Wild Side: Tasmania. By Carolyn Bennett Patterson. Photos by David Hiser and Melinda Berge. Contents: Franklin-Lower Gordon Wild Rivers National Park and the Southwest National Park. 676-693, May 1983
- *See also* Nahanni National Park, Canada

The **WORLD** in Dolls. By Samuel F. Pryor. Photos by Kathleen Revis. 817-831, Dec. 1959

The **WORLD** in New York City. By Peter T. White. 52-107, July 1964

The **WORLD** in Your Garden. By W. H. Camp. Paintings by Else Bostelmann. 1-65, July 1947

The **WORLD** of Elizabeth I. By Louis B. Wright. Photos by Ted Spiegel. 668-709, Nov. 1968

The **WORLD** of Martin Luther. By Merle Severy. Photos by James L. Amos. 418-463, Oct. 1983

The **WORLD** of My Apple Tree. By Robert F. Sisson. 836-847, June 1972

The **WORLD** Pays Final Tribute (Churchill Funeral). Text by Carolyn Bennett Patterson. 199-225, Aug. 1965

WORLD WAR I Aircraft Fly Again in Rhinebeck's Rickety Rendezvous. By Harvey Arden. Photos by Howard Sochurek. 578-587, Oct. 1970

WORLD WAR II:
- Adventures with the Survey Navy. By Irving Johnson. 131-148, July 1947
- Belgium Comes Back. By Harvey Klemmer. Photos by Maynard Owen Williams. Included: Bastogne; Battle of the Bulge. 575-614, May 1948
- The Bonins and Iwo Jima Go Back to Japan. By Paul Sampson. Photos by Joe Munroe. 128-144, July 1968
- The British Way. By Sir Evelyn Wrench. Included: Sinking of the *Bismarck,* May 27, 1941; Winston Churchill. 421-541, Apr. 1949
- The Eisenhower Story. By Howard La Fay. 1-39, July 1969
- Fun Helped Them Fight. By Stuart E. Jones. Contents: Army Air Forces' informal method of naming and decorating combat aircraft. 95-104, Jan. 1948
- Here Come the Marines. By Frederick Simpich. 647-672, Nov. 1950
- History Written in the Skies (U. S. Air Force). 273-294, Aug. 1957
- How One of The Society's Maps (Pacific Ocean) Saved a Precious Cargo. 844, June 1947
- Italy Smiles Again. By Edgar Erskine Hume. 693-732, June 1949
- Life Springs From Death in Truk Lagoon. By Sylvia A. Earle. Photos by Al Giddings. Included: Japanese ships sunk in two 1944 attacks by U. S. Navy carrier-launched planes. 578-613, May 1976

From Graveyard to Garden. 604-613
- Luxembourg, Survivor of Invasions. By Sydney Clark. Photos by Maynard Owen Williams. 791-810, June 1948
- Okinawa, Pacific Outpost. 538-552, Apr. 1950
- Sailors in the Sky: Fifty Years of Naval Aviation. By Patrick N. L. Bellinger. 276-296, Aug. 1961

WX

• *See also* Churchill, Sir Winston; Profiles of the Presidents: V; U. S. Army Signal Corps; Unknown Servicemen; War Memorials

WORLD WILDLIFE FUND:
• Man's Wildlife Heritage Faces Extinction. By H.R.H. The Prince Philip. 700-703, Nov. 1962
Grants:
• African Elephant survey. 578, 584, Nov. 1980
• Giant Brazilian Otters. 132, July 1980
• Humpback Whales. 1, Jan. 1979; 466, Apr. 1982
• Orangutans. 835, June 1980
• Pandas. 735, Dec. 1981
• TRAFFIC (Monitoring of Wildlife Shipments). 296, Mar. 1981

WORLD'S FAIRS:
• Belgium Welcomes the World. By Howell Walker. 795-837, June 1958
• The Fair Reopens (New York). Photos by James P. Blair. Text by Carolyn Bennett Patterson. 505-529, Apr. 1965
• Kansai, Japan's Historic Heartland, Hosts Expo '70. By Thomas J. Abercrombie. 295-339, Mar. 1970
• Montreal Greets the World. By Jules B. Billard. 600-621, May 1967
• Seattle Fair Looks to the 21st Century. By Carolyn Bennett Patterson. Photos by Thomas Nebbia. 402-427, Sept. 1962

WORLD'S Last Salute to a Great American (Dwight D. Eisenhower). By William Graves and other members of the NGS staff. 40-51, July 1969

WORLD'S Tallest Tree Discovered. By Melville Bell Grosvenor. Photos by George F. Mobley. 1-9, July 1964

WORLD'S Worst Spill. Photos by Martin Rogers. Text by Noel Grove. 124-135, July 1978

WORMS AND WORMLIKE ANIMALS:
• Biggest Worm Farm Caters to Platypuses. By W. H. Nicholas. 269-280, Feb. 1949
• Capturing Strange Creatures in Colombia. By Marte Latham. Photos by Tor Eigeland. 682-693, May 1966
• The Wild World of Compost. By Cecil E. Johnson. Photos by Bianca Lavies. Included: Earthworms; nematodes; red worms. 273-284, Aug. 1980
• *See also* Glowworms; Inchworms; Railroad Worm; Shipworms

WRASSES:
• Finned Doctors of the Deep. By Douglas Faulkner. 867-873, Dec. 1965

WREN, CHRISTOPHER:
• The British Way. By Sir Evelyn Wrench. 421-541, Apr. 1949

WRENCH, SIR EVELYN: Author:
• The British Way. 421-541, Apr. 1949
• Founders of New England. Photos by B. Anthony Stewart. 803-838, June 1953
• Founders of Virginia. Photos by B. Anthony Stewart. 433-462, Apr. 1948

WRESTING Oil From Reluctant Rock. 78-79, *Special Report on Energy* (Feb. 1981)

WRESTLIN' for a Livin' With King Coal. By Michael E. Long. Photos by Michael O'Brien. 793-819, June 1983

WRIGHT, BELINDA: Photographer:
• India Struggles to Save Her Wildlife. By John J. Putman. 299-343, Sept. 1976

WRIGHT, G. ERNEST: Author:
• Bringing Old Testament Times to Life. Paintings by Henry J. Soulen. 833-864, Dec. 1957
• The Last Thousand Years Before Christ. Paintings by H. J. Soulen and Peter V. Bianchi. 812-853, Dec. 1960

WRIGHT, JONATHAN: Photographer:
• Arctic Odyssey. By John Bockstoce. Paintings by Jack Unruh. 100-127, July 1983
• Jackson Hole: Good-bye to the Old Days? By François Leydet. 768-789, Dec. 1976

WRIGHT, LOUIS B.: Author:
• The Britain That Shakespeare Knew. Photos by Dean Conger. 613-665, May 1964
• The World of Elizabeth I. Photos by Ted Spiegel. 668-709, Nov. 1968

WRIGHT, MYRON H., Jr.: Photographer:
• The Swallow-tailed Kite: Graceful Aerialist of the Everglades. 496-505, Oct. 1972

WRIGHT, ORVILLE and WILBUR:
• Aviation Looks Ahead on Its 50th Birthday. By Emory S. Land. 721-739, Dec. 1953
• Fifty Years of Flight. 740-756, Dec. 1953
• Fledgling Wings of the Air Force. By Thomas W. McKnew. 266-271, Aug. 1957
• Lonely Cape Hatteras, Besieged by the Sea. By William S. Ellis. Photos by Emory Kristof. 393-421, Sept. 1969

WRIGHT, WILLIAM:
• The Journey of Burke and Wills: First Across Australia. By Joseph Judge. Photos by Joseph J. Scherschel. 152-191, Feb. 1979

WRIGHT WAY (Skyway 1):
• Skyway Below the Clouds. By Carl R. Markwith. Photos by Ernest J. Cottrell. Contents: A round-trip flight over Skyway 1, an airway route planned and marked especially for the use of private flyers. 85-108, July 1949

WRINGING Secrets from Greenland's Icecap. By Paul-Emile Victor. 121-147, Jan. 1956

WRIOTHESLEY, HENRY (Third Earl of Southampton):
• Founders of Virginia. By Sir Evelyn Wrench. Photos by B. Anthony Stewart. 433-462, Apr. 1948

WRITING:
• Ancient Mesopotamia: A Light That Did Not Fail. By E. A. Speiser. Paintings by H. M. Herget. Included: How Seal Engraving Led to the Invention of Writing. 41-105, Jan. 1951
• Ebla: Splendor of an Unknown Empire. By Howard La Fay. Photos by James L. Stanfield. Paintings by Louis S. Glanzman. 730-759, Dec. 1978
• The Phoenicians, Sea Lords of Antiquity. By Samuel W. Matthews. Photos by Winfield Parks. Paintings by Robert C. Magis. 149-189, Aug. 1974
• *See also* Cuneiform Script; Glyphs

WULUMUCHI, Sinkiang. *See* Urumchi

WYOMING:
• Along the Great Divide. By Mike Edwards. Photos by Nicholas DeVore III. 483-515, Oct. 1979
• Beavers, Nature's Aquatic Engineers. By Des and Jen Bartlett. Included: Granite Creek in Teton National Forest. 716-732, May 1974
• Buffalo Bill and the Enduring West. By Alice J. Hall. Photos by James L. Amos. 76-103, July 1981
• Cloud Gardens in the Tetons. By Frank and John Craighead. 811-830, June 1948
• From Sun-clad Sea to Shining Mountains. By Ralph Gray. Photos by James P. Blair. 542-589, Apr. 1964
• Last of the Black-footed Ferrets? By Tim W. Clark. Photos by Franz J. Camenzind and the author. NGS research grant. 828-838, June 1983
• A Map Maker Looks at the United States. By Newman Bumstead. Included: Grand Teton National Park, Jackson, Jackson Hole, Jackson Lake, Jenny Lake, Teton Range. 705-748, June 1951
• Powder River Basin: New Energy Frontier. By Bill Richards. Photos by Louie Psihoyos. 96-113, *Special Report on Energy* (Feb. 1981)
• Riding the Outlaw Trail. By Robert Redford. Photos by Jonathan Blair. 622-657, Nov. 1976
• The Untamed Yellowstone. By Bill Richards. Photos by Dean Krakel II. 257-278, Aug. 1981
• Wyoming: High, Wide, and Windy. By David S. Boyer. 554-594, Apr. 1966
• Wyoming Muck Tells of Battle: Ice Age Man vs. Mammoth. By Cynthia Irwin, Henry Irwin, and George Agogino. NGS research grant. 828-837, June 1962
• *See also* Bighorn Medicine Wheel; Grand Teton National Park; Jackson Hole; Padlock Ranch; Pryor Mountain Wild Horse Range; Wind River Range; Yellowstone National Park

X

X-1:
• Flying in the "Blowtorch" Era. By Frederick G. Vosburgh. 281-322, Sept. 1950

X-15:
● I Fly the X-15. By Joseph A. Walker. Photos by Dean Conger. 428-450, Sept. 1962

X RAYS:
● The Incredible Universe. By Kenneth F. Weaver. Photos by James P. Blair. 589-625, May 1974
● Rockets Explore the Air Above Us. By Newman Bumstead. 562-580, Apr. 1957
● The Sun. By Herbert Friedman. 713-743, Nov. 1965
● The Sun As Never Seen Before. By Edward G. Gibson. 494-503, Oct. 1974
● *See also* Photography, X-Ray

XENARTHRANS:
● The Astonishing Armadillo. By Eleanor E. Storrs. Photos by Bianca Lavies. 820-830, June 1982

XIAMEN SPECIAL ECONOMIC ZONE, China:
● China's Opening Door. By John J. Putman. Photos by H. Edward Kim. 64-83, July 1983

XINGU NATIONAL PARK, Brazil:
● Amazon–The River Sea. By Loren McIntyre. 456-495, Oct. 1972
● Brazil's Txukahameis: Good-bye to the Stone Age. Photos by W. Jesco von Puttkamer. 270-283, Feb. 1975
● Saving Brazil's Stone Age Tribes From Extinction. By Orlando and Claudio Villas Boas. Photos by W. Jesco von Puttkamer. 424-444, Sept. 1968
● The Waurá: Brazilian Indians of the Hidden Xingu. By Harald Schultz. 130-152, Jan. 1966

XINJIANG UYGUR AUTONOMOUS REGION, China:
● Journey to China's Far West. By Rick Gore. Photos by Bruce Dale. NGS research grant. 292-331, Mar. 1980
● *See also* former name, Sinkiang

XIONG FAMILY:
● One Family's Odyssey to America. By John Everingham. 642-661, May 1980

Y

YWCA: International Success Story. By Mary French Rockefeller. Photos by Otis Imboden. 904-933, Dec. 1963
● *See also* Young Women's Christian Association

YACHTING:
● Baltic Cruise of the *Caribbee*. By Carleton Mitchell. Included: Sandhamn Regatta Week. 605-646, Nov. 1950
● The British Way. By Sir Evelyn Wrench. Included: Cowes: Cradle of Yachting. 421-541, Apr. 1949
● "Delmarva," Gift of the Sea. By Catherine Bell Palmer. Included: Cambridge Yacht Club's championship races for Hampton-class sloops; and log canoe, *Jay Dee,* racing on the Choptank. 367-399, Sept. 1950
● Down East Cruise. By Tom Horgan. Photos by Luis Marden. 329-369, Sept. 1952
● Down East to Nova Scotia. By Winfield Parks. Included: Marblehead-Halifax race, Bras d'Or McCurdy Cup race, Jones Trophy. 853-879, June 1964
● Inside Europe Aboard *Yankee*. By Irving and Electa Johnson. Photos by Joseph J. Scherschel. Included: Fastnet race. 157-195, Aug. 1964
● More of Sea Than of Land: The Bahamas. By Carleton Mitchell. Photos by James L. Stanfield. Included: Out-Island Regatta. 218-267, Feb. 1967
● To Europe with a Racing Start. By Carleton Mitchell. Included: Newport-to-Bermuda race. 758-791, June 1958
● Windjamming Around New England. By Tom Horgan. Photos by Robert F. Sisson. Contents: Weekly regattas of Cape Cod in the summer, the annual Provincetown-Wellfleet competition, Squam Day Regatta on Ipswich Bay, and Race Week at Marblehead. 141-169, Aug. 1950

YACHTS. *See Argyll; Betelgeuse; Britannia; Carib; Caribbee; Delight; Elsie; Finisterre; Great Britain II; Mah Jong; Nomad; Tectona; Tradewinds; White Mist; Yankee* (Brigantine); *Yankee* (Ketch)

YACHTS, Sand. *See* Sand Yachts

YADA, ISSHO: Artist:
● The Lost Fleet of Kublai Khan. By Torao Mozai. Photos by Koji Nakamura. 634-649, Nov. 1982

YAKIMA VALLEY, Washington:
● The Day the Sky Fell. By Rowe Findley. Included: Ashfall and cleanup after the eruption of Mount St. Helens. 50-65, Jan. 1981
● Mount St. Helens Aftermath: The Mountain That Was–and Will Be. By Rowe Findley. Photos by Steve Raymer. 713-733, Dec. 1981
● Washington's Yakima Valley. By Mark Miller. Photos by Sisse Brimberg. 609-631, Nov. 1978

YAKUTSK, U.S.S.R.:
● Five Times to Yakutsk. By Dean Conger. 256-269, Aug. 1977

YAMASHITA, MICHAEL S.: Photographer:
● Hokkaido, Japan's Last Frontier. By Douglas Lee. 62-93, Jan. 1980
● New Jersey: A State of Surprise. By Jim Hartz. Photos by Bob Krist and Michael S. Yamashita. 568-599, Nov. 1981
● Somalia's Hour of Need. By Robert Paul Jordan. Photos by Michael S. Yamashita and Kevin Fleming. 748-775, June 1981

BOTH BY SISSE BRIMBERG

Yakima: ice-covered pear blossoms, *top*; transplanted Sioux cowboy, *above*

YAMIS (People):
• The Gentle Yamis of Orchid Island. Photos by Chang Shuhua. 98-109, Jan. 1977

YAMPA (River), Colorado:
• Shooting Rapids in Dinosaur Country. By Jack Breed. Photos by author and Justin Locke. 363-390, Mar. 1954

YANG HSIEN-MIN: Artist:
• China's Incredible Find. By Audrey Topping. 440-459, Apr. 1978

YANGTZE (River and Basin), China:
• Along the Yangtze, Main Street of China. By W. Robert Moore. 325-356, Mar. 1948

YANKEE (Brigantine):
• Lost World of the Galapagos. By Irving and Electa Johnson. 681-703, May 1959
• New Guinea to Bali in *Yankee*. By Irving and Electa Johnson. 767-815, Dec. 1959
• Saga of a Ship, the *Yankee*. By Luis Marden. 263-269, Feb. 1966
▪ The Voyage of the Brigantine *Yankee*. 265A-265B, Feb. 1966
• *Yankee* Roams the Orient. By Irving and Electa Johnson. 327-370, Mar. 1951
• The *Yankee*'s Wander-world. By Irving and Electa Johnson. 1-50, Jan. 1949

YANKEE (Ketch):
• Inside Europe Aboard *Yankee*. By Irving and Electa Johnson. Photos by Joseph J. Scherschel. 157-195, Aug. 1964
• *Yankee* Cruises the Storied Nile. By Irving and Electa Johnson. Photos by Winfield Parks. 583-633, May 1965
• *Yankee* Cruises Turkey's History-haunted Coast. By Irving and Electa Johnson. Photos by Joseph J. Scherschel. 798-845, Dec. 1969
▪ *Yankee* Sails Across Europe. 469A-469B, Apr. 1967

The **YANKEE** Sailor Who Opened Japan: Commodore Perry. By Ferdinand Kuhn. 85-102, July 1953

YANOMAMO, the True People. By Napoleon A. Chagnon. 211-223, Aug. 1976

YAP ISLANDS, Caroline Islands, Pacific Ocean:
• Grass-skirted Yap. By W. Robert Moore. 805-830, Dec. 1952
• Micronesia: The Americanization of Eden. By David S. Boyer. 702-744, May 1967
• Pacific Wards of Uncle Sam. By W. Robert Moore. 73-104, July 1948

YASSI ADA (Island), Turkey:
• New Tools for Undersea Archeology. By George F. Bass. Photos by Charles R. Nicklin, Jr. NGS research grant. 403-423, Sept. 1968
• Thirty-three Centuries Under the Sea. By Peter Throckmorton. 682-703, May 1960

JONATHAN BLAIR

Yellowstone's Birthday: Castle Geyser, *above;* Lower Falls, *below*

JOSEPH J. SCHERSCHEL, NGS

• Underwater Archeology: Key to History's Warehouse. By George F. Bass. Photos by Thomas J. Abercrombie and Robert B. Goodman. NGS research grant. 138-156, July 1963

YAWLS. *See Argyll; Caribbee; Delight; Elsie; Finisterre; Mah Jong; White Mist*

YEAGER, CHUCK:
• *Columbia*'s Landing Closes a Circle. By Tom Wolfe. 474-477, Oct. 1981

YEAR of Discovery Opens in Antarctica. By David S. Boyer. 339-381, Sept. 1957

A **YEAR** of Widening Horizons: The President's Message to Members. By Melville Bell Grosvenor. 888-906, Dec. 1962

The **YEAR** the Weather Went Wild. By Thomas Y. Canby. 799-829, Dec. 1977

YELLOW FEVER:
• Exploring Ancient Panama by Helicopter. By Matthew W. Stirling. Photos by Richard H. Stewart. NGS research grant. 227-246, Feb. 1950
• Keeping House for a Biologist in Colombia. By Nancy Bell Fairchild Bates. Photos by Marston Bates. 251-274, Aug. 1948
• Mosquitoes, the Mighty Killers. By Lewis T. Nielsen. 427-440, Sept. 1979

YELLOW SEA Yields Shipwreck Trove. Photos by H. Edward Kim. Introduction by Donald H. Keith. 231-243, Aug. 1979

YELLOWSTONE NATIONAL PARK, Wyoming-Montana-Idaho:
▪ Grizzly! 639A-639B, Nov. 1967
• Knocking Out Grizzly Bears for Their Own Good. By Frank and John Craighead. NGS research grant. 276-291, Aug. 1960
• The "Lone" Coyote Likes Family Life. By Hope Ryden. Photos by author and David Hiser. 278-294, Aug. 1974
• The Night the Mountains Moved. By Samuel W. Matthews. Photos by J. Baylor Roberts. 329-359, Mar. 1960
• Springtime Comes to Yellowstone National Park. By Paul A. Zahl. 761-779, Dec. 1956
• Studying Wildlife by Satellite. By Frank Craighead, Jr. and John Craighead. NGS research grant. 120-123, Jan. 1973
• Trailing Yellowstone's Grizzlies by Radio. By Frank Craighead, Jr. and John Craighead. NGS research grant. 252-267, Aug. 1966
• The Untamed Yellowstone. By Bill Richards. Photos by Dean Krakel II. 257-278, Aug. 1981
• The West Through Boston Eyes. By Stewart Anderson. 733-776, June 1949
• Winterkeeping in Yellowstone. By R. Steven Fuller. 829-857, Dec. 1978

• Wyoming: High, Wide, and Windy. By David S. Boyer. 554-594, Apr. 1966
• Yellowstone Wildlife in Winter. By William Albert Allard. 637-661, Nov. 1967
• Yellowstone's Hundredth Birthday: A Four-part Report. 579-637, May 1972
I. A Walk Through the Wilderness. By Karen and Derek Craighead. Photos by Sam Abell. 579-603; II. Ageless Splendors of Our Oldest Park. 604-615; III. The Pitfalls of Success. By William S. Ellis. Photos by Jonathan Blair. 616-631; IV. The Next 100 Years: A Master Plan for Yellowstone. By George B. Hartzog, Jr. 632-637

YEMEN. *See* Yemen Arab Republic

YEMEN, Democratic Republic of. *See* former name, Aden Protectorate

YEMEN, North. *See* Yemen Arab Republic

YEMEN, South. *See* former name, Aden Protectorate

YEMEN ARAB REPUBLIC (North Yemen):
• Behind the Veil of Troubled Yemen. By Thomas J. Abercrombie. 403-445, Mar. 1964
• North Yemen. By Noel Grove. Photos by Steve Raymer. 244-269, Aug. 1979
• Yemen–Southern Arabia's Mountain Wonderland. By Harlan B. Clark. 631-672, Nov. 1947
Ancient "Skyscrapers" of the Yemen. Photos by Richard H. Sanger. 645-668
• Yemen Opens the Door to Progress. By Harry Hoogstraal. 213-244, Feb. 1952

YEN, HARRY S. C.: Photographer:
• The Fragile Beauty All About Us. 785-795, Dec. 1970

YEREVAN, Soviet Armenia, U.S.S.R.:
• The Proud Armenians. By Robert Paul Jordan. Photos by Harry N. Naltchayan. 846-873, June 1978

YESTERDAY Lingers Along the Connecticut. By Charles McCarry. Photos by David L. Arnold. 334-369, Sept. 1972

YESTERDAY Lingers on Lake Erie's Bass Islands. By Terry and Lyntha Eiler. 86-101, July 1978

YESTERDAY'S Congo, Today's Zaire. By John J. Putman. Photos by Eliot Elisofon. 398-432, Mar. 1973

YLLA (Camilla Koffler): Photographer:
• Mysore Celebrates the Death of a Demon. By Luc Bouchage. 706-711, May 1958

YOGYAKARTA, Java. *See* Djokjakarta

YOHO NATIONAL PARK, British Columbia, Canada. *See* Great Divide Trail

YOSEMITE NATIONAL PARK, California:
• Climbing Half Dome the Hard Way. By Galen Rowell. 782-791, June 1974
• John Muir's Wild America. By Harvey Arden. Photos by Dewitt Jones. 433-461, Apr. 1973
• New Rush to Golden California. By George W. Long. 723-802, June 1954
• The Other Yosemite. By Nathaniel T. Kenney. Photos by Dean Conger. 762-781, June 1974
• Yosemite National Park. 491-498, Apr. 1951

YOST, ED: Author:
• The Longest Manned Balloon Flight. 208-217, Feb. 1977

YOU and the Obedient Atom. By Allan C. Fisher, Jr. 303-353, Sept. 1958

YOU Can't Miss America by Bus. By Howell Walker. Paintings by Walter A. Weber. 1-42, July 1950

YOUNG, GAVIN: Author:
• Water Dwellers in a Desert World. Photos by Nik Wheeler. 502-523, Apr. 1976

YOUNG, GORDON: Author:
• Autumn–Season of the Smokies (Great Smoky Mountains National Park). 142-147, July 1979
• Chile, Republic on a Shoestring. Photos by George F. Mobley. 437-477, Oct. 1973
• The Great Lakes: Is It Too Late? Photos by James L. Amos and Martin Rogers. 147-185, Aug. 1973
• Great Smokies National Park: Solitude for Millions. Photos by James. L. Amos. 522-549, Oct. 1968
• The Gulf's Workaday Waterway. Photos by Charles O'Rear. 200-223, Feb. 1978
• Hawaii, Island of Fire and Flowers. Photos by Robert W. Madden. 399-425, Mar. 1975
• "How Man Pollutes His World," painting supplement. Map on reverse. Dec. 1970
• The Miracle Metal–Platinum. Photos by James L. Amos. 686-706, Nov. 1983
• Norway's Strategic Arctic Islands (Svalbard). Photos by Martin Rogers. 267-283, Aug. 1978
• Paraguay, Paradox of South America. Photos by O. Louis Mazzatenta. 240-269, Aug. 1982
• Pennsylvania: Faire Land of William Penn. Photos by Cary Wolinsky. 731-767, June 1978
• Pollution, Threat to Man's Only Home. Photos by James P. Blair. 738-781, Dec. 1970
• Sailors of the Sky. Photos by Emory Kristof and Jack Fields. Paintings by Davis Meltzer. 49-73, Jan. 1967
• Salt–The Essence of Life. Photos by Volkmar Wentzel and Georg Gerster. 381-401, Sept. 1977
• That Dammed Missouri River. Photos by David Hiser. 374-413, Sept. 1971
• The Troubled Waters of Mono Lake. Photos by Craig Aurness. 504-519, Oct. 1981
• Whatever Happened to TVA? Photos by Emory Kristof. 830-863, June 1973
• Which Way Oahu? Photos by Robert W. Madden. 653-679, Nov. 1979
• Will Coal Be Tomorrow's "Black Gold"? Photos by James P. Blair. 234-259, Aug. 1975

YOUNG, JOHN W.:
• *Columbia*'s Landing Closes a Circle. By Tom Wolfe. 474-477, Oct. 1981
• NGS Hubbard Medal Recipient. 852, Dec. 1981
• When the Space Shuttle Finally Flies. By Rick Gore. Photos by Jon Schneeberger. Paintings by Ken Dallison. 317-347, Mar. 1981
Author:
• *Columbia*'s Astronauts' Own Story: Our Phenomenal First Flight. By John W. Young and Robert L. Crippen. Paintings by Ken Dallison. 478-503, Oct. 1981

YOUNG-OLD Lebanon Lives by Trade. By Thomas J. Abercrombie. 479-523, Apr. 1958

YOUNG WOMEN'S CHRISTIAN ASSOCIATION (YWCA):
• Parks, Plans, and People: How South America Guards Her Green Legacy. By Mary and Laurance Rockefeller. Photos by George F. Mobley. 74-119, Jan. 1967
• YWCA: International Success Story. By Mary French Rockefeller. Photos by Otis Imboden. 904-933, Dec. 1963

YOUR National Gallery of Art After 10 Years. By John Walker. Paintings from Kress Collection. 73-103, Jan. 1952

YOUR Society Observes Eclipse in Brazil. NGS research grant. 661, May 1947

YOUR Society Takes Giant New Steps: The President's Annual Message to Members. By Melville Bell Grosvenor. 874-886, Dec. 1961

YOUR Society to Seek New Light on the Cliff Dwellers. NGS research grant. 154-156, Jan. 1959

YOUR Society's President Reports: A Year of Widening Horizons. By Melville Bell Grosvenor. 888-906, Dec. 1962

YOUTH. *See* Boy Scouts; 4-H Clubs; Hostels; Peace Corps; Students; Young Women's Christian Association; *and* Graham, Robin Lee; Jenkins, Peter Gorton

YUCATÁN PENINSULA, Mexico:
• The Maya. 729-811, Dec. 1975
I. Children of Time. By Howard La Fay. Photos by David Alan Harvey. Included: Archeological sites: Becan, Chichén Itzá, Dzibilchaltún, Jaina Island, Tancah, Tulum, Uxmal; present-day Maya of Xcobenhaltun and elsewhere. 729-767; II. Riddle of the Glyphs. By George E. Stuart. Photos by Otis Imboden. Included: Cobá; Kohunlich; Tancah. 768-791
• *See also* Chichén Itzá; Dzibilchaltun; Mujeres, Isla; Pyramids: The Americas

YUGOSLAVIA:
▲ *The Balkans,* Atlas series supplement. Feb. 1962
• The Danube: River of Many Nations, Many Names. By Mike Edwards. Photos by Winfield Parks. 455-485, Oct. 1977
• Down the Danube by Canoe. By William Slade Backer. Photos by Richard S. Durrance and Christopher G. Knight. 34-79, July 1965
• Montenegro: Yugoslavia's "Black Mountain." By Bryan Hodgson. Photos by Linda Bartlett. 663-683, Nov. 1977
• Yugoslavia, Between East and West. By George W. Long. Photos by Volkmar Wentzel. 141-172, Feb. 1951
• Yugoslavia: Six Republics in One. By Robert Paul Jordan. Photos by James P. Blair. Contents: Bosnia-Hercegovina; Croatia; Macedonia; Montenegro; Serbia; Slovenia. 589-633, May 1970
• Yugoslavia's Window on the Adriatic. By Gilbert M. Grosvenor. 219-247, Feb. 1962
• *See also* Trieste

YUKAGHIRS:
• People of the Long Spring. By Yuri Rytkheu. Photos by Dean Conger. 206-223, Feb. 1983

YUKON (River), Canada-Alaska:
• Rafting Down the Yukon. By Keith Tryck. Photos by Robert Clark. 830-861, Dec. 1975
• Squaws Along the Yukon. By Ginny Hill Wood. 245-265, Aug. 1957
■ Yukon Passage. 439, Oct. 1977; cover, Dec. 1977

YUKON TERRITORY, Canada:
• Along the Yukon Trail. By Amos Burg. 395-416, Sept. 1953
• The Canadian North: Emerging Giant. By David S. Boyer. 1-43, July 1968
▲ *Close-up, Canada: British Columbia, Alberta, Yukon Territory,* supplement. Text on reverse. Apr. 1978
• Peoples of the Arctic. 144-223, Feb. 1983
I. Introduction by Joseph Judge. 144-149; II. Hunters of the Lost Spirit: Canadians. By Priit J. Vesilind. Photos by David Alan Harvey. 150-197
• Rafting Down the Yukon. By Keith Tryck. Photos by Robert Clark. 830-861, Dec. 1975
• Squaws Along the Yukon. By Ginny Hill Wood. 245-265, Aug. 1957
• Yukon Fever: Call of the North. By Robert Booth. Photos by George F. Mobley. 548-578, Apr. 1978
■ Yukon Passage. 439, Oct. 1977; cover, Dec. 1977
• *See also* Kennedy, Mount; St. Elias, Mount

YUNGKI (Kirin), China. *See* Chilin

YUNNAN PROVINCE, China:
• Kunming Pilgrimage. Photos by John Gutmann and Joseph Passantino. 213-226, Feb. 1950
• Letter From Kunming: Two American Teachers in China. By Elisabeth B. Booz. Photos by Thomas Nebbia. 793-813, June 1981

Z

ZAGREB, Yugoslavia:
• Yugoslavia, Between East and West. By George W. Long. Photos by Volkmar Wentzel. 141-172, Feb. 1951
• Yugoslavia: Six Republics in One. By Robert Paul Jordan. Photos by James P. Blair. 589-633, May 1970

ZAHL, PAUL A.:
Author-Photographer:
• Algae: the Life-givers. 361-377, Mar. 1974
• Australia's Bizarre Wild Flowers. 858-868, Dec. 1976
• Back-yard Monsters in Color. 235-260, Aug. 1952
• Bizarre World of the Fungi. 502-527, Oct. 1965
• Exotic Birds in Manhattan's Bowery. 77-98, Jan. 1953
• Face to Face With Gorillas in Central Africa. 114-137, Jan. 1960
• Finding the Mt. Everest of All Living Things. 10-51, July 1964
• Fishing in the Whirlpool of Charybdis. 579-618, Nov. 1953
• Flamingos' Last Stand on Andros Island. 635-652, May 1951
• Fluorescent Gems From Davy Jones's Locker. 260-271, Aug. 1963
• Giant Insects of the Amazon. 632-669, May 1959
• The Giant Tides of Fundy. 153-192, Aug. 1957
• Glass Menageries of the Sea. 797-822, June 1955
• Hatchetfish, Torchbearers of the Deep. 713-714, May 1958
• Hidden Worlds in the Heart of a Plant. 389-397, Mar. 1975
• Honey Eaters of Currumbin. 510-519, Oct. 1956
• How the Sun Gives Life to the Sea. 199-225, Feb. 1961
• In Quest of the World's Largest Frog. 146-152, July 1967
• In the Gardens of Olympus. 85-123, July 1955
• In the Wilds of a City Parlor. 645-672, Nov. 1954
• Life in a "Dead" Sea–Great Salt Lake. 252-263, Aug. 1967
• Little Horses of the Sea. 131-153, Jan. 1959
• The Magic Lure of Sea Shells. Photos by Victor R. Boswell, Jr. and author. 386-429, Mar. 1969
• Malaysia's Giant Flowers and Insect-trapping Plants. 680-701, May 1964
• Man-of-war Fleet Attacks Bimini. 185-212, Feb. 1952
• Mountains of the Moon. 412-434, Mar. 1962
• Mystery of the Monarch Butterfly. 588-598, Apr. 1963
• Nature's Living, Jumping Jewels. 130-146, July 1973
• Nature's Night Lights: Probing the Secrets of Bioluminescence. 45-69, July 1971
• Nature's Year in Pleasant Valley. 488-525, Apr. 1968
• New Scarlet Bird in Florida Skies. 874-882, Dec. 1967
• Night Life in the Gulf Stream. 391-418, Mar. 1954
• On Australia's Coral Ramparts. 1-48, Jan. 1957
• One Strange Night on Turtle Beach. 570-581, Oct. 1973
• Oregon's Sidewalk on the Sea. 708-734, Nov. 1961
• The Pink Birds of Texas. 641-654, Nov. 1949
• Plants That Eat Insects. 643-659, May 1961
• Portrait of a Fierce and Fragile Land. 303-314, Mar. 1972
• Sailing a Sea of Fire. 120-129, July 1960
• Scorpions: Living Fossils of the Sands. 436-442, Mar. 1968
• Search for the Scarlet Ibis in Venezuela. 633-661, May 1950
• Seeking the Truth About the Feared Piranha. 715-733, Nov. 1970
• The Shadowy World of Salamanders. 104-117, July 1972
• Springtime Comes to Yellowstone National Park. 761-779, Dec. 1956
• Those Outlandish Goldfish! 514-533, Apr. 1973
• Unsung Beauties of Hawaii's Coral Reefs. 510-525, Oct. 1959
• Volcanic Fires of the 50th State: Hawaii National Park. 793-823, June 1959
• What's So Special About Spiders? 190-219, Aug. 1971
• Wing-borne Lamps of the Summer Night. 48-59, July 1962
Photographer:
• Amber: Golden Window on the Past. Text by Thomas J. O'Neill. 423-435, Sept. 1977
• Dragons of the Deep. 838-845, June 1978
• The Four-eyed Fish Sees All. Text by Thomas O'Neill. 390-395, Mar. 1978
• Slime Mold: The Fungus That Walks. By Douglas Lee. 131-136, July 1981
• "Snowflake," the World's First White Gorilla. By Arthur J. Riopelle. 443-448, Mar. 1967

ZAIRE, Republic of:
• The Imperiled Mountain Gorilla. By Dian Fossey. NGS research grant. 501-523, Apr. 1981
Death of Marchessa. Photos by Peter G. Veit. 508-511
• Tropical Rain Forests: Nature's Dwindling Treasures. By Peter T. White. Photos by James P. Blair. Paintings by Barron Storey. 2-47, Jan. 1983
• Yesterday's Congo, Today's Zaire. By John J. Putman. Photos by Eliot Elisofon. 398-432, Mar. 1973
• *See also* Virunga Mountains; *and* former name, Congo, Democratic Republic of the

ZANTE (Island), Greece:
• Homeward With Ulysses. By Melville Bell Grosvenor. Photos by Edwin Stuart Grosvenor. 1-39, July 1973

ZANZIBAR:
• Clove-scented Zanzibar. By W. Robert Moore. 261-278, Feb. 1952

• Safari from Congo to Cairo. By Elsie May Bell Grosvenor. Photos by Gilbert Grosvenor. 721-771, Dec. 1954
• Tanzania Marches to Its Own Drum. By Peter T. White. Photos by Emory Kristof. 474-509, Apr. 1975
• *Yankee* Roams the Orient. By Irving and Electa Johnson. 327-370, Mar. 1951

ZELENY, LAWRENCE: Author:
• Song of Hope for the Bluebird. Photos by Michael L. Smith. 855-865, June 1977

ZEN BUDDHISM:
• Kyoto and Nara: Keepers of Japan's Past. By Charles McCarry. Photos by George F. Mobley. 836-859, June 1976
Kyoto Says Happy New Year. 852-859

ZHUHAI SPECIAL ECONOMIC ZONE, China:
• China's Opening Door. By John J. Putman. Photos by H. Edward Kim. 64-83, July 1983

ZIMBABWE:
• After Rhodesia, a Nation Named Zimbabwe. By Charles E. Cobb, Jr. Photos by James L. Stanfield and LeRoy Woodson, Jr. 616-651, Nov. 1981
• Editorial. By Wilbur E. Garrett. 567, Nov. 1981
• *See also* former name, Rhodesia

ZIMBABWE (Ruins), Zimbabwe:
• Safari Through Changing Africa. By Elsie May Bell Grosvenor. Photos by Gilbert Grosvenor. 145-198, Aug. 1953

ZINJANTHROPUS (Near-man):
• Finding the World's Earliest Man. By L. S. B. Leakey. Photos by Des Bartlett. NGS research grant. 420-435, Sept. 1960
• Preserving the Treasures of Olduvai Gorge. By Melvin M. Payne. Photos by Joseph J. Scherschel. NGS research grant. 701-709, Nov. 1966
• *See also Australopithecus*

ZION NATIONAL PARK, Utah:
• Amid the Mighty Walls of Zion. By Lewis F. Clark. 37-70, Jan. 1954

ZISKIN, JOEL F.:
Author-Photographer:
• Trek to Nepal's Sacred Crystal Mountain. 500-517, Apr. 1977

ZOOS:
• The Ape with Friends in Washington. By Margaretta Burr Wells. Included: The National Zoological Park, Washington, D. C. 61-74, July 1953
• Biggest Worm Farm Caters to Platypuses. By W. H. Nicholas. Note: Bronx zookeepers (New York Zoological Park) learned to raise 25,000 worms needed as food each month. 269-280, Feb. 1949
• Enchantress! By Theodore H. Reed. Photos by Thomas J. Abercrombie. Included: Albino tigress at the National Zoological Park, Washington, D. C. 628-641, May 1961

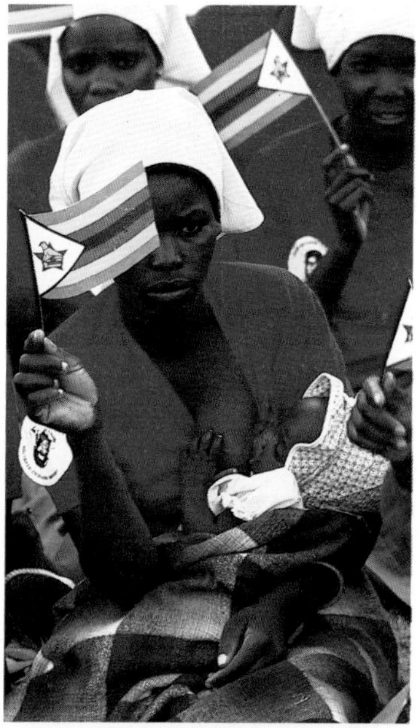

BOTH BY JAMES L. STANFIELD, NGS

Zimbabwe: salute to a nation's birth, *top*; boy harvests cotton crop, *above*

• Growing Up With Snowflake. By Arthur J. Riopelle. Photos by Michael Kuh. Contents: Albino gorilla at zoo in Barcelona, Spain. NGS research grant. 491-503, Oct. 1970
• Jambo–First Gorilla Raised by Its Mother in Captivity. By Ernst M. Lang. Photos by Paul Steinemann. Included: The Zoological Gardens of Basel, Switzerland. 446-453, Mar. 1964
• London's Zoo of Zoos. By Thomas Garner James. Included: Regent's Park; Whipsnade. 771-786, June 1953
• Portraits of My Monkey Friends. By Ernest P. Walker. Included: Primates at the National Zoological Park, Washington, D. C. 105-119, Jan. 1956
• What's Black and White and Loved All Over? By Theodore H. Reed. Photos by Donna K. Grosvenor. Contents: Giant pandas at the National Zoological Park, Washington, D. C. 803-815, Dec. 1972
• The Wild Animals in My Life. By William M. Mann. Included: Establishment and growth of the National Zoological Park, Washington, D. C. 497-524, Apr. 1957
• Zoo Animals Go to School. By Marion P. McCrane. Photos by W. E. Garrett. Contents: Animals from New York Zoological Park (Bronx Zoo). 694-706, Nov. 1956
◆ *Zoo Babies.* 1978
■ Zoos of the World. 503A-503B, Oct. 1970
◆ *Zoos Without Cages.* 1981
• *See also* Animal Orphanage; Animal Safari

ZULULAND (Region), South Africa:
• Roaming Africa's Unfenced Zoos. By W. Robert Moore. 353-380, Mar. 1950
• Safari Through Changing Africa. By Elsie May Bell Grosvenor. Photos by Gilbert Grosvenor. 145-198, Aug. 1953
• The Zulus: Black Nation in a Land of Apartheid. By Joseph Judge. Photos by Dick Durrance II. 738-775, Dec. 1971

ZULUS:
• Zulu King Weds a Swazi Princess. By Volkmar Wentzel. 47-61, Jan. 1978
• The Zulus: Black Nation in a Land of Apartheid. By Joseph Judge. Photos by Dick Durrance II. 738-775, Dec. 1971

ZUMBACH, EARL:
• The Family Farm Ain't What It Used to Be. By James A. Sugar. 391-411, Sept. 1974

ZÜRICH, Switzerland:
• Switzerland, Europe's High-rise Republic. By Thomas J. Abercrombie. 68-113, July 1969

ZWELITHINI, GOODWILL, King of the Zulus:
• Zulu King Weds a Swazi Princess. By Volkmar Wentzel. 47-61, Jan. 1978

Expeditions and Scientific Research

By MELVIN M. PAYNE
CHAIRMAN, BOARD OF TRUSTEES,
AND CHAIRMAN, COMMITTEE FOR RESEARCH AND EXPLORATION

AT ITS FOUNDING in 1888, the National Geographic Society proclaimed a two-fold mission: "the increase and diffusion of geographic knowledge." Its official journal, the NATIONAL GEOGRAPHIC, first published in 1888, has won a worldwide reputation for its excellence in the *diffusion* of geographic knowledge. In its earliest years the magazine served as a scholarly publication but was later more broadly directed to its growing membership—that is, to anyone, scholar or not, interested in the full panoply of the world and its peoples. Over the years the Society has supplemented the magazine through a variety of other media such as maps, atlases, books, filmstrips, and educational programming on television and radio.

Actions by the Society to *increase* geographic knowledge, while dating from 1890, are less well known to our membership or to the general public—with some notable exceptions, such as support of Peary's polar expedition in 1908-09, of major archaeological discoveries in Middle and South America, and of the more recent search by the Leakeys for human origins in East Africa.

Yet over the years, and through its Committee for Research and Exploration, the Society has made more than 2,700 grants to aid the efforts of scholars and scientists around the world in increasing the knowledge of our planet, its environment, and its inhabitants—and even of the cosmos beyond. In 1983 more than 170 grants were made with a total budget in excess of three million dollars.

The scientists and scholars who receive these grants communicate the results of their work primarily in specialized journals that are seldom read by the general public. Consequently, to record in one place and to make more generally accessible the extent and results of this Society-sponsored research, the *National Geographic Society Research Reports* were undertaken in 1968. To date 16 volumes, covering grants made in the years 1890-1975, have been issued, and five more are in preparation.*

The wide variety of projects reported in this series is exemplified by the volume covering research and exploration supported by Society grants in 1975. A sampling of subjects covered that year are: anthropology, archaeology, geology, botany, entomology, ecology, vertebrate paleontology, and zoology.

In order to communicate even more effectively and rapidly the extensive findings of Society-sponsored research and exploration, a refereed scientific journal, *National Geographic Research,* will replace the Society's *Research Reports* early in 1985.

The pages that follow illustrate in their abbreviated listings the scope and variety of subjects that scientists and scholars of widely diverse training and nationalities have been able to address, thanks to financial support ultimately derived from Society members. Perhaps the findings of fewer than one in twenty-five of these will appear in NATIONAL GEOGRAPHIC. Yet they have contributed to that interconnected aquifer of knowledge that remains ready to tap when the older wells of wisdom seem to have run dry.

*Copies of the first 16 volumes of the series may be obtained for $7.50 each, postpaid, by writing to Dept. 63, National Geographic Society, Washington, D. C. 20036. Request later billing if desired.

As part of a Society-sponsored research project, a diver raises an artifact of Maya civilization from a well in Mexico.

LUIS MARDEN, NGS

...for the increase and

OTIS IMBODEN, NGS

Ballooning in the dirty air over St. Louis, Rudolf J. Engelmann and Vera Simons release a small balloon to track air motion during a study of pollution.

Aeronautics and Atmospheric Science

Air-quality measurement device: development. John S. Hall. 1974

Da Vinci–Trans-America Manned Scientific Balloon Flight. Rudolf J. Engelmann. 1973

Explorer I (balloon). William E. Kepner, Albert W. Stevens, and Orvil A. Anderson. 1934

Explorer II (balloon): altitude record. Albert W. Stevens and Orvil A. Anderson. 1935

Pollution: basic standards of air quality from telephotometer measurements. John S. Hall. 1977

Stratosphere sampling. Bismarck, North Dakota. National Bureau of Standards. 1940-41

Anthropology

ARCHAEOLOGY

General

Dating, archaeological ceramics: electron spin resonance spectroscopy. Thomas J. Riley. 1978

Fire: man's use to shape earths and metals. Theodore A. Wertime. 1968, 1970, 1972

North America

Agate Basin ancient Indian camp. Wyoming. Frank H. H. Roberts and William M. Bass. 1959, 1961

American Southwest: bat cave and early agriculture. Richard I. Ford and John D. Speth. 1982

Arizona, central: prehistoric human adaptation in an environmental transition zone. George J. Gumerman. 1973

Baffin Island, Northwest Territories, Canada. Lorna M. McKenzie-Pollock. 1968-69

Balankanche Cave, Chichén Itzá, Mexico. E. Wyllys Andrews IV. 1959

Barker Creek Village: high-altitude desert ecology. Nevada. David H. Thomas. 1981

Basket Maker occupation, Upper Grand Gulch, Utah. William D. Lipe. 1968-69

Basque whaling stations: 16th century. Labrador. James A. Tuck. 1978

Bering Strait, Alaska. Henry B. Collins. 1936

Bison-kill site, Jones-Miller Paleo-Indian. Colorado. Dennis J. Stanford. 1973-76

Blackwater Draw site. New Mexico. Dennis J. Stanford. 1983

Bourbon Field site. Georgia. Morgan Ray Crook, Jr. 1980

Campeche, southeastern: hieroglyphic inscriptions and figurative art. Mexico. Ian J. A. Graham. 1977

diffusion of geographic knowledge

Carter's Grove, Virginia. Ivor Noël Hume. 1976-78

Chaco Canyon, New Mexico: Holocene paleoecology. Paul S. Martin. 1981

——— remote-sensing analysis of prehistoric human occupations. Thomas R. Lyons. 1973

Chalcatzingo, Morelos, Mexico. David C. Grove. 1971-72

Chiapas, Mexico: coastal humid tropics. Barbara Voorhies. 1978, 1980, 1982

Chichén Itzá, Yucatán, Mexico. Charles E. Lincoln. 1983

Cobá Mapping Project. Quintana Roo, Mexico. George E. Stuart. 1974-75, 1978

Colima, Mexico. Isabel T. Kelly. 1968, 1970

Coxcatlán, Puebla, Mexico. Richard S. MacNeish. 1971-73

Cuicuilco ruins, Mexico. Byron Cummings. 1924-25

Cultural ecology. Mexican Gulf Coast. S. Jeffrey K. Wilkerson. 1973-75, 1977, 1979

Dorset Eskimo sites. Southampton Island, Hudson Bay. Henry B. Collins. 1954

Dry Creek, central Alaska. William R. Powers. 1976

Dzibilchaltún, Yucatán, Mexico. E. Wyllys Andrews IV. 1957-66

——— E. Wyllys Andrews V. 1978

Engelbert site: Indian burials. Nichols, New York. William D. Lipe. 1968

Environmental archaeology and cultural systems. Hamilton Inlet, Labrador. William W. Fitzhugh. 1971-72

Etzna: prehistoric house mounds and canals. Campeche, Mexico. Ray T. Matheny. 1974

Exploration of Early Man Sites in Alaska Project. National Park Service. 1976

Finger Lakes region, New York. Marian E. White. 1975

Four Corners: pre-Columbian towers. Colorado and Utah. Ray A. Williamson and Florence H. Ellis. 1977

Fox Islands: faunal remains. Penobscot Bay, Maine. Bruce J. Bourque. 1978

Gatecliff Shelter. Nevada. David H. Thomas. 1975-76

Grand Canyon, Arizona: North Rim. Douglas W. Schwartz. 1968-71

Grasshopper Pueblo habitat. Arizona. William A. Longacre. 1974

Hell Gap site. Wyoming. Cynthia and Henry T. Irwin and George A. Agogino. 1962-66

Hirundo site. Maine. David Sanger. 1972-73, 1975

Hontoon Island, Florida: identification of woods from a wet site. Barbara A. Purdy. 1982-83

Jeffrey-Harris Rock-shelter. Virginia. Charles W. McNett, Jr. 1978

Kagati Lake, southwestern Alaska. Robert E. Ackerman. 1979

Katmai National Monument, Alaska: ancient Aleut and Eskimo site. Donald E. Dummond. 1967-68

Kimmswick: Clovis adaptations in the Midwest. Missouri. Russell W. Graham. 1980

King site. Floyd County, Georgia. David J. Hally. 1973

Kuskokwim region, Alaska. Robert E. Ackerman. 1978, 1981-82

Lahonton Lake, Nevada. Phil C. Orr. 1957

Larsen site. South Dakota. William M. Bass. 1970

Lehner Paleo-Indian site. San Pedro Valley, Arizona. C. Vance Haynes and Emil W. Haury. 1973, 1975

Manis Mastodon Archaeological Project. Washington. Carl E. Gustafson. 1979

Maya, Cozumel: animal utilization. William L. Rathje. 1977

Maya sites. Becan, Campeche, Mexico. Prentice M. Thomas, Jr. 1972-73

——— Yucatán Peninsula, Mexico. E. Wyllys Andrews IV. 1968, 1970

Maya writing. Mexico. George E. Stuart. 1983

Meadowcroft Rock-shelter and Cross Creek drainage. Pennsylvania. James M. Adovasio. 1976-77

Mimbres Mogollon. New Mexico. Harry J. Shafer. 1978

Mississippi, southwestern. Stephen Williams. 1970, 1972

Mississippi Valley: protohistoric and early 18th-century period. Jeffrey P. Brain. 1974

Mohawk Valley Project. Oak Hill, New York. Dean R. Snow. 1983

Mount Jasper mine, New Hampshire. Richard M. Gramly. 1979

Mummy Cave, Wyoming. Harold McCracken. 1965

Natchez Indians. Mississippi. Stephen Williams. 1981-82

Oaxaca: pre-Hispanic murals. Mexico. Arthur G. Miller. 1983

Olmec sites. La Venta, Tres Zapotes, and San Lorenzo, Mexico. Philip Drucker, 1955; Robert F. Heizer, 1955, 1965-69; Matthew W. Stirling, 1938-46

Paleo-Indian habitation area. Little Salt Spring, Florida. Carl J. Clausen. 1977

Paleo-Indian quarry and living sites. Shenandoah Valley, Virginia. William M. Gardner. 1970

Paleo-Indian site. Little Salt Spring, Florida. Arthur D. Cohen. 1980

Pilcher Creek Project. Oregon. David R. Brauner. 1983

Porcupine River, Alaska: Pleistocene cave deposits and alluvial sediments. Edward J. Dixon, Jr. 1979-81

Port Royal, Jamaica. Edwin A. Link. 1959

Post-Hopewell culture subsistence change: testing a model for. Stuart Struever. 1973

Potomac Valley: prehistoric shell middens. Gregory A. Waselkov. 1979

Potts Farm Clovis site. New York. Richard M. Gramly. 1982

Prehistoric cave art. Tennessee. Charles H. Faulkner. 1982

Pryor Mountain, Montana: environmental archaeological project. Robson Bonnichsen. 1979, 1982

Pueblo Bonito, New Mexico. Andrew Ellicott Douglass, 1923-29; Neil M. Judd, 1920-27, 1929

Puerco River Valley, New Mexico: resettlement of Pueblo populations. Cynthia Irwin-Williams. 1970-73

Quintana Roo: murals and architecture. Mexico. Arthur G. Miller. 1972-75

Río Bec region: ecological change and cultural history. Yucatán Peninsula, Mexico. Richard E. W. Adams. 1972

Rocky Dell Rock-shelter: archaeology and geomorphology. Allegheny County, Pennsylvania. James M. Adovasio. 1980

Russell Cave, Jackson County, Alabama. Carl F. Miller, 1956-58

Salts Cave, Mammoth Cave National Park, Kentucky. Patty Jo Watson. 1968-69

San Juan County, Utah. Neil M. Judd. 1923

Sandia Cave, New Mexico. George A. Agogino. 1961

Santa Elena, Parris Island, South Carolina. 16-century Spanish occupation. Stanley A. South. 1979

——— Robert L. Stephenson. 1981

——— Stanley A. South and Robert L. Stephenson. 1982

Santa Rosa Island, California. Phil C. Orr. 1957

"Spanish Diggings": aboriginal flint quarries. Southeastern Wyoming. John M. Saul. 1964

Stone spheres. Jalisco, Mexico. Matthew W. Stirling. 1967-68

Tellico Reservoir, Tennessee. Jefferson Chapman. 1976

Tetzcotzingo, Mexico: mapping of ritual hill. Richard F. Townsend. 1979

Towers of Hovenweep National Monument. Mesa Verde, Colorado. Ray A. Williamson. 1976

Tunica Treasure Project. Louisiana. Jeffrey P. Brain. 1977

Turner Farm site. North Haven, Maine. Bruce J. Bourque. 1974-75

Upper Delaware Valley Early Man Project. Charles W. McNett, Jr. 1974-76

Vail Paleo-Indian site. Oxford County, Maine. Richard M. Gramly. 1980

Viking site. L'Anse aux Meadows, Newfoundland. Helge Ingstad. 1963-65

Voyageurs: Fort Charlotte Underwater Project. Grand Portage National Monument, Minnesota. Robert C. Wheeler. 1975

——— fur-trade materials. Minnesota-Ontario border. Robert C. Wheeler. 1963-66

Water distribution systems, preclassical. Mexico. Melvin L. Fowler. 1983

Well of Sacrifice probe. Chichén Itzá, Mexico. William J. Folan. 1960-61

Wetherill Mesa, Colorado. Douglas Osborne. 1958-63

Xitle (volcano) and Cuicuilco (pyramid), Mexico. Robert F. Heizer. 1957

Xochicalco Mapping Project. Mexico. Kenneth G. Hirth. 1978

Xochicalco site. Mexico. Richard F. Townsend. 1980

Yucatán Peninsula, Mexico: settlement patterns, pre-Columbian. Edward B. Kurjack. 1975

Central and South America

Abaj Takalik, Guatemala. John A. Graham. 1975-79

Abrigo do Sol Rock-shelter. Mato Grosso, Brazil. Eurico T. Miller. 1977

Agronomy potential. Bajo de Santa Fe, Petén, Guatemala. Bruce H. Dahlin. 1975

Andes: cultivation. Augusto R. Cardich. 1979, 1982

——— metallurgy. Batan Grande, Peru. Izumi Shimada. 1981-82

——— ruins. Johan G. Reinhard. 1982

——— Titicaca Basin. South-Central Andes. Elias J. Mujica. 1981

Architectural stones and sculpture. Peru and Bolivia. Robert F. Heizer. 1963

Arenal area: settlement and volcanism. Costa Rica. Payson D. Sheets. 1983

Arenal Lake and volcano region, Costa Rica. Carlos Aguilar P. 1977

Ariari River Basin, Colombia: archaeological chronology. John P. Marwitt. 1973-74

Belize, southern. Richard M. Leventhal. 1979

Beni, Bolivia. Bernardo Dougherty. 1982

Callejon de Huaylas, Peru. Richard L. Burger. 1978-79, 1982

Caves and rock-shelters: art. Chile. Calogero M. Santoro. 1983

——— Dominican Republic. Marcio Veloz Maggiolo. 1976

Chan Chan-Moche Valley Project. Peru. Carol J. Mackey and Michael E. Moseley. 1969-74

Chicama-Moche Canal Project. Peru. James S. Kus. 1968-69

Chotuna and Chornancap, Peru. Christopher B. Donnan. 1981-82

Colha, Belize: main pyramidal mound. Thomas R. Hester. 1983

Cuello site. Belize. Norman Hammond. 1978-80

Culebra, Bay of, Costa Rica. Frederick W. Lange. 1976

Cupisnique culture: Caballo Muerto complex. Peru. Thomas G. Pozorski. 1973

Ecuador Indians: pre-Columbian sites. Matthew W. Stirling. 1957

El Mirador Project. Petén, Guatemala. Bruce H. Dahlin and Ray T. Matheny. 1979, 1981-82

Gold artifacts, pre-Columbian: catalog. Panama. Reina Torres de Araúz. 1971

Honduras cultural change (pre-Columbian Mesoamerican frontier). Paul F. Healy. 1975-76

Incas. Machu Picchu, Peru. Hiram Bingham. 1912, 1914-15

Macal-Tipu Project. Belize. Robert R. Kautz and Grant D. Jones. 1982

Maya: classic settlement organization and internal function. Belize. Joseph W. Ball. 1980

——— highlands. Guatemala. Robert J. Sharer. 1972-73

——— housing. El Salvador. Payson D. Sheets. 1979

——— search for evidence of seaborne contact with highland cultures of Mesoamerica. Nancy M. Farriss. 1974-75

Middle American Research Institute archaeological publications. New Orleans, Louisiana. E. Wyllys Andrews V. 1975, 1977

Monte Alto, Guatemala. Lee A. Parsons, 1968-70

——— Edwin Martin Shook. 1972

Monte Verde, Chile. Tom D. Dillehay. 1978

Nazca lines. Peru. Gerald S. Hawkins. 1967

——— Maria Reiche. 1974

——— geometric and astronomical order. Anthony F. Aveni. 1981

Nohmul Project. Belize. Norman Hammond. 1981-83

Pacatnamu, Peru. Christopher B. Donnan. 1983

Pachamachay Cave, Peru. Ramiro Matos. 1981

Paleo-Indian technology. South America. Clifford Evans. 1978

Panama. Matthew W. Stirling. 1948-49, 1951, 1953

Pedernales Province, Dominican Republic. Marcio E. Veloz M. 1978

Peruvian highlands. Ruth M. Shady. 1982

——— Ruth M. Shady and Hermilio Rosas. 1978

Petén savanna. Guatemala. Don S. Rice. 1978

Preceramic sites. Eastern Venezuela. Mario J. Sanoja. 1977

Prehistoric maize spread, ceramic evidence of. Peru. Mary Eubanks Dunn. 1975

Quereo, Los Vilos: Paleo-Indian archaeology, paleoclimate, and paleontology. Chile. Lautaro Nuñez A. 1977-78

Quichean civilization. Central Guatemala. Kenneth L. Brown. 1976-77

Quiriguá, Guatemala. William R. Coe, 1974-75; Robert J. Sharer, 1976-79

Río Azul Project. Guatemala. Richard E. W. Adams. 1983

Sangay site. Morona-Santiago Province, Ecuador. P. Pedro I. Porras G. 1980, 1983

Santa Barbara Project. Honduras. Edward M. Schortman. 1983

Sican metallurgy. Peru. Izumi Shimada. 1983

Textiles, pre-Columbian. Los Rios Province, Ecuador. Joan S. Gardner. 1977, 1979

Tiahuanacoid Temple. Huari, Peru. William H. Isbell. 1980

Túnel site. Argentina. Luis Abel Orquera. 1981, 1983

Williamsburg and Palmar Sur, Costa Rica. Matthew W. Stirling. 1964

Pacific

Huahine, Society Islands. Yosihiko H. Sinoto. 1974-75, 1977

Lau Island, Fiji. Roger C. Green. 1976

Lelu stone ruins. Kosrae, Micronesia. Ross H. Cordy. 1982

Micronesia: origins of human settlement. Guam. Hiro Kurashina. 1983

Nam Madol site. Ponape Island, Micronesia. William S. Ayres. 1983

Torres Strait: recent paleoenvironmental history. Northern Australia. Anthony J. Barham and David R. Harris. 1982

Asia

Abu Salabikh, Iraq (Sumerian city). John N. Postgate. 1976, 1978, 1980, 1982

Aegean Dendrochronology Project. Turkey. Peter I. Kuniholm. 1979-80, 1982-83

Ain Dara. Syria. Elizabeth C. Stone. 1983

Ain Ghazal. Jordan. Gary O. Rollefson. 1983

Animal domestication. China. Stanley J. Olsen. 1981

Antiochus I: tomb. Nemrud Dagh, Turkey. Theresa Goell. 1963-64

Aphrodisias, Turkey. Kenan T. Erim. 1966-83

Asia, southern: trade. Janice M. Stargardt. 1979

Bakhtiari Mountains, Iran: routes through. Allen Zagarell. 1976

Baqcah Valley Project: test soundings of magnetometer and resistivity anomalies. Jordan. Patrick E. McGovern. 1979-81

Bronze Age: life patterns. Dead Sea, Jordan. Walter E. Rast. 1979, 1981

——— settlement. Cyprus. James R. Carpenter. 1974

Caesarea Maritima: ancient harbors. Israel. Robert L. Hohlfelder. 1983

Camel: early domestication. China. Stanley J. Olsen. 1983

Cyprus. James M. Adovasio. 1973

Deir el-Balah Regional Project. Gaza Strip. Trude Dothan. 1980-82

Dishon Basin, upper. Israel. Milla Y. Ohel. 1979

DIAN FOSSEY

BOB CAMPBELL

Digit (top) and Uncle Bert (above) were among the mountain gorillas studied by Dian Fossey in central Africa. Another, Macho, is carried to her grave (below). All three were killed by poachers.

A. WILLIAM WEBER

B. B. FULTON

Robert F. Griggs struggles in Alaskan quicksand on a Society study of the effects of Mount Katmai's 1912 eruption.

En-Nabratein, Israel. Eric M. Meyers. 1980

Erbaba, south-central Turkey: Neolithic site. Jacques Bordaz and Louise A. Bordaz. 1977-78

Farming communities. Jordan Valley. Ofer Bar-Yosef. 1982

Jericho, Jordan: Hasmonean and Herodian winter palace complexes. Ehud Netzer. 1979

Jerusalem, Israel. Kathleen M. Kenyon. 1962-67

Malay Peninsula and Indonesia. Janice M. Stargardt. 1978

Negev Desert: prehistoric farming societies. Israel. Thomas E. Levy. 1982-83

Nestorian archives. Anatolia. James Hamilton Charlesworth. 1982

Palawan caves. Palawan Island, Philippines. Robert B. Fox. 1965-66

Pella, Jordan. Robert H. Smith. 1979-80, 1982

Radiometric dating of Paleolithic sites. Israel and Hungary. Henry P. Schwarcz. 1975

Samosata Mound, Turkey. Theresa Goell. 1967, 1969

Sarepta (Zarephath), Lebanon: Phoenician and biblical city. James B. Pritchard. 1968-72

Shahr-i Qumis: lost capital of Parthian Iran. John F. Hansman. 1970, 1975

Shanidar Cave, northern Iraq. Ralph S. Solecki. 1978

Sri Lanka: 10th-12th century trading site. John Carswell. 1978

Susa, Iran: early fourth millennium strata. Henry T. Wright. 1978

Syria. Trevor F. Watkins. 1975

——— northeastern: London Institute of Archaeology expedition. David Oates. 1983

Tal-i Malyan, Fars, Iran. Robert H. Dyson, Jr. 1976, 1978

Tell el-Hayyat Project. Jordan. William G. Dever. 1983

Tell Hadidi, Syria. Rudolph H. Dornemann. 1977-78

Tell Jemmeh, Israel. Gus W. Van Beek. 1975-78

——— Paula Wapnish-Hesse. 1980

Tell Keisan, Israel. Roland DeVaux. 1971

Thailand, prehistoric. Douglas D. Anderson. 1983

Turkey, northwestern. Mehmet C. Ozdogan. 1979, 1981

——— southeastern: early village site. Robert J. Braidwood. 1980-81

Yagi site: social dynamics and subsistence strategies. Japan. William M. Hurley and Peter Bleed. 1978-80

Yemen Arab Republic archaeological-environmental survey. McGuire Gibson. 1978

Europe

Amber: prehistoric trade. A. Colin Renfrew and Curt W. Beck. 1975

——— spectroscopic provenance analysis. Curt W. Beck. 1973

Anglo-Saxon royal burial ground. Sutton Hoo, Suffolk, England. Rupert L. S. Bruce-Mitford. 1968, 1970

Apollo sanctuary. Halieis, Greece. Michael H. Jameson. 1973-74

Architecture and village layout: ancient Greece. William A. McDonald. 1971

Argolid Peninsula, Greece. Michael H. Jameson. 1979

——— Greece: postglacial environmental history. Donald R. Whitehead. 1972-73

Britain: search for earliest humans. Ronald Singer. 1978-79

"Camelot." South Cadbury, Somerset, England. Leslie Alcock. 1970

Caves. Jumilla, Yecla, and Villena, southeastern Spain. Michael J. Walker. 1979

——— Quaternary and Holocene origins. Spain. William H. Waldren. 1971, 1973

Central Russian Plain: Upper Paleolithic settlements and exchange networks. Olga Soffer-Bobyshev. 1982

Chalosse district, southwestern France. Lawrence G. Straus. 1980

Classical marble: stable isotopic signatures applied. Norman Herz. 1979, 1981-82

Cretan Exploration Project. Livingston V. Watrous. 1983

Franchthi Cave, Greece. John A. Gifford. 1981, 1983

Great Hungarian Plain: prehistoric settlement history. Andrew G. Sherratt. 1980

Greece: society, culture, economy in the later Roman period. Timothy E. Gregory. 1974

Guipúzcoa Province, Spain. Lawrence G. Straus. 1979

Hascherkeller site: prehistoric economy. West Germany. Peter S. Wells. 1980, 1983

Helice, Greece. Harold E. Edgerton and Peter Throckmorton. 1970-71

Herculaneum: ancient Roman population. Italy. Sara C. Bisel. 1982-83

——— boat. Italy. J. Richard Steffy. 1983

Ice Age Franco-Cantabrian caves: photography and analysis. Alexander Marshack. 1973

Koukounaries: Mycenaean acropolis. Demetrius U. Schilardi. 1977

Lucania, Italy. Sterling P. Vinson. 1978-79

Mezhirichi, Ukrainian S.S.R. Olga Soffer. 1979

Mirobriga Project. Portugal. William R. Biers. 1982-83

Mochlos field survey. Crete. Jeffrey S. Soles. 1983

Molise Project. Biferno Valley, Italy. Graeme W. Barker. 1977-78

Monastery, seventh-century. Jarrow, England. Rosemary J. Cramp. 1973

Morava Valley, Yugoslavia: ecology and cultural change. H. Arthur Bankoff. 1977, 1980-81

Mycenaean palace. Páros, Greece. Demetrius U. Schilardi. 1978

Neolithic fortress site and rock paintings. Sierra de Taibilla, Spain. Michael J. Walker. 1968-70

Pantelleria. David P. S. Peacock. 1977

Porto Longo Harbor, Sapienza Island, Greece. Harold E. Edgerton and Peter Throckmorton. 1970

O. C. HAVENS

The expedition car mires in Chaco Canyon during a 1921 investigation of New Mexico's pre-Columbian Pueblo Bonito.

Stonehenge, England, and Callanish, Scotland. Gerald S. Hawkins. 1965

Thisbe Basin, Greece: Ohio Boeotia Expedition. Timothy E. Gregory. 1981

Tower of the Winds. Athens. Derek J. de Solla Price. 1964

Ukrina Valley, Yugoslavia: paleoliths. Anta Montet-White. 1980

Voidokoilia, Greece: pre-Mycenaean tumulus. George S. Korres. 1977-8, 1982

Africa

Akhmim, Upper Egypt. Naguib Kanawati. 1979-83

Aten, temple of: computerized study. Karnak, Egypt. Ray W. Smith. 1968-69

Bamenda-Koumbo area, West Cameroon. Donald D. Hartle. 1967

Cambyses, Lost Army of. Egypt. Gary S. Chafetz. 1983

Carthage: port and sacrificial precinct. Lawrence Stager. 1978

Caves. Mali. Johan Huizinga. 1970

Chad and Libya: archaeological reconnaissance. Carleton S. Coon. 1966-67

Colossi of Memnon, Egypt. Robert F. Heizer. 1971

Engaruka, Tanzania: cultural site of early man. Hamo Sassoon. 1967

Gebel Adda, Egypt. Nicholas B. Millet. 1963-65

Iron Age settlement survey. Upper Zambezi Valley, Zambia. Joseph O. Vogel. 1976

Karamoja District, Uganda. Hamo Sassoon. 1972

Kramo excavation. Begho, Ghana. Merrick Posnansky. 1978

Lake Ndutu Research Project. Tanzania. Amini A. Mturi. 1983

Libyan Desert, Egypt: geological-anthropological survey. C. Vance Haynes. 1974-76

Madagascar, southwest. Robert E. Dewar. 1979

Megaliths. Central Africa. Nicholas C. David. 1974

Pre-Columbian Panamanian gold artifacts were photographed for cataloging under the direction of Reina Torres de Araúz.

BOTH BY VICTOR R. BOSWELL, JR., NGS

Mosaics. Tunisia. Margaret A. Alexander. 1973, 1976

Ngamiland, Botswana. John E. Yellen. 1973

Northern Volta Basin, Ghana. Emmanuel K. Agorsah. 1983

Pyramids: cosmic-ray research in. Egypt. Luis W. Alvarez. 1968

Quseir Project. Egypt. Janet H. Johnson. 1977, 1979, 1981

Serengeti National Park, Tanzania: Middle Stone Age. John R. F. Bower. 1979

Timbuktu, Mali. Roderick McIntosh. 1983

Underwater

American Revolutionary gunboat. Lake Champlain. Philip K. Lundeberg. 1968

Battle of Lepanto shipwrecks: Greece. Spyridon Marinatos. 1971

Bermuda waters. Mendel L. Peterson. 1965-67

Breadalbane: scientific and photographic survey. Barrow Strait, Canada. Joseph B. MacInnis. 1981

Byzantine shipwrecks. Turkey. George F. Bass. 1961-69, 1976

Defence: Revolutionary War privateer. David C. Switzer. 1977

Greek cargo ship, seventh-century. Sicilian waters. Edwin A. Link. 1962

Iron Age shipwreck. Turkey. George F. Bass. 1974-75

Kyrenia, Cyprus: shipwreck. Michael L. Katzev. 1967-72

Kyrenia Ship Project: film documentary. Susan W. Katzev. 1975

Medieval Islamic shipwreck. Turkey. George F. Bass. 1978-79

Mediterranean Sea search. Peter Throckmorton. 1975

——— survey. George F. Bass. 1973

Molasses Reef shipwreck, 16th-century. Caribbean. Donald H. Keith. 1983

Mombasa wreck excavation. Kenya. Robin C. M. Piercy. 1979

***Monitor* search.** Cape Hatteras area, North Carolina. John J. Newton and Harold E. Edgerton. 1973-74

Ottoman shipwreck, 16th-century. Turkey. George F. Bass. 1982

Porto Longo, Greece: sonar search. Peter Throckmorton. 1968-69

Portuguese frigate search. Mombasa Harbor, Kenya. Hamo Sassoon. 1975

Program of nautical archaeology. New World. George F. Bass. 1981

Punic ship, third-century B.C. Sicily. Honor E. Frost. 1973

Sonar gear. Eastern Mediterranean. Harold E. Edgerton. 1968

Spanish Plate Fleet. Florida. Kip L. Wagner. 1965

Turkey: survey of ancient shipwrecks. George F. Bass. 1980

ETHNOLOGY

Chewing sticks. West Africa, Egypt, and Pakistan. Memory P. Elvin-Lewis and Walter H. Lewis. 1975

Facial expressions: cross-cultural comparison of patterns. Wolfgang M. Schleidt. 1980

North America

Aleutian survivors of the Bering land bridge. William S. Laughlin. 1972

Aleuts: Russian influence on ecology, culture, and physical anthropology. Christy G. Turner II. 1972-73

Eskimos: linguistics and religion. Canada. Svend Frederiksen. 1965

——— prehistoric Thule culture. Northwest Hudson Bay, Canada. Charles F. Merbs. 1968-70

Hinds Cave, Val Verde County, Texas. Vaughn M. Bryant, Jr. 1975

Indian ethnobotany. California. Lowell J. Bean. 1975

Maya textile designs. Chiapas, Mexico. Walter F. Morris, Jr. 1977, 1979

Mesoamerica: food and cosmology. Mexico. Nancy M. Farriss. 1983

——— textile traditions. Mexico and Guatemala. Patricia R. Anawalt. 1982

——— and Southwestern cosmology. Evon Z. Vogt. 1982

Otomi Indians: resource cognition. Mexico. Kirsten J. Haring. 1973

Preceramic culture. Chiapas, Mexico. Philip Drucker. 1947

Pre-Columbian cultural change. Cozumel, Mexico. Jeremy A. Sabloff. 1971-73

Rock art, prehistoric. Nevada caves. Robert F. Heizer. 1975

Tarahumara people. Mexico. Robert A. Bye, Jr. 1972

Tlapanec Indians. Tlacoapa, Mexico. Marion Oettinger, Jr. 1971

Washo Indians: art. Nevada. Norval C. Kern, Jr. 1970

Zinacantan. Mexico. John B. Haviland. 1983

Central and South America

***Afkodre* magic and religion:** Creoles. Suriname. Benjamin E. Pierce. 1971

Amazonia: aboriginal animal domestication. Daniel W. Gade. 1977

——— Mestizo floodplain subsistence. Peru. Mario Hiraoka. 1982-83

——— relationships between the Tukanoan fishing and Maduan hunting tribes. Katharine Milton. 1980

Ayoreo Indians. Southeastern Bolivia. Paul E. Bugos, Jr. 1980

Black Caribs. Central America. William V. Davidson. 1973-74

Brazilian Indian fabrics. Berta G. Ribeiro. 1980

Chickens, black-boned: distribution and use. Central and South America. Carl L. Johannessen. 1976-77

Chimu Empire. Peru. Carol J. Mackey. 1982

Copablanca Festival: ethnographic and ethnomusicological survey. Bolivia. Edwin E. Erickson. 1973

Maya salt trade. Guatemala and Mexico. Anthony P. Andrews. 1975

Mesoamerican pottery techniques. Lewis A. Krevolin. 1972

Peasant livelihood behavior. Trinidad. Bonham C. Richardson. 1971

Peruvian highlands: prehistoric cultural development. Clifford Evans and Betty Meggers. 1968-69

Quechua communities: subsistence economy. North Peruvian Andes. Cesar A. Fonseca. 1980

Tooth extraction. Peru and Colombia. Memory P. Elvin-Lewis and Walter H. Lewis. 1982

Waurá Indians. Mato Grosso, Brazil. Harald Schultz. 1961-64

Welsh colony. Patagonia. Glyn Williams. 1968-69

Pacific

Caroline Islanders: ethnohistory. Saul H. Riesenberg. 1973

Child behavior. New Hebrides. E. Richard Sorenson. 1971

Dani people: material culture. Netherlands New Guinea. Robert G. Gardner. 1962

Diseases and cures. Torres Strait Islands. George J. Simeon. 1974

Foragers: Pacific nutritional adaptation. Papua New Guinea. Carol L. Jenkins. 1983

Fore and Bahinemo peoples: facial expression of emotions. New Guinea. E. Richard Sorenson. 1968-69

Maoris. New Zealand. William N. Fenton. 1974

New Guinea natives: religious symbolism. Wilson G. Wheatcroft. 1968-70

Polynesian dances. Cook Island. E. Richard Sorenson. 1975

Polynesian origins. Roger C. Green. 1977

Tanna Island, New Hebrides. Kalman A. Muller. 1974

Trade, migration, and marriage. New Guinea. Deborah Gewertz. 1974

Australia

Aborigines. Arnhem Land, northern Australia. Charles P. Mountford. 1948

Art sanctuary. Koonalda Cave, South Australia. Christine Elvera Sharpe. 1975

Tiwi culture. Melville Island, Australia. Jane C. Goodale. 1980

——— Melville Island, Australia. Charles P. Mountford. 1954

Asia

Ainu of Hokkaido. Japan. M. Inez Hilger. 1965-66

Arab potters. Israel. Owen S. Rye. 1976

Bakhtiari tribe: role in history. Iran. Gene R. Garthwaite. 1971

Buddhist monasticism. Melvyn C. Goldstein. 1980

Burial ritual. North Borneo. Peter A. Metcalf. 1975

Hindu pilgrimage: cultural symbolism. Muktinath, Nepal. Donald A. Messerschmidt. 1980

Karnali zone: cultural-ecological analysis. Western Nepal. Barry C. Bishop. 1968-69, 1971

——— livelihood strategies and seasonal rhythms. Nepal. Barry C. Bishop. 1980

Kenyah Dayaks: religion and social organization. Sarawak, Malaysia. Herbert L. Whittier. 1973

Kinship and marriage: hierarchy and amity. South Asia. Anthony T. Carter. 1973

Kurds. Khorasan, Iran. Robert E. Peck. 1967

Lua tribe. Northern Thailand. Peter Kunstadter. 1963-64

Man, protohistoric and early historic: interaction with the environment. Isthmian Thailand. Janice M. Stargardt. 1973

Mesolithic occupations. Cyprus. James M. Adovasio. 1972-73

Nagas: cultural development. Southeast Asia. Vikuosa O. Nienu. 1977

Pashtoon: pastoral nomadism. Afghanistan. Asen Balikci. 1972

Pastoralism. Southern Sinai. Ofer Bar-Yosef. 1976

Religious centers. Himalayas. Barbara N. Aziz. 1975

Shabakites. Northern Iraq. Sami Said Ahmed. 1973

Sherpa culture. Nepal and Sikkim. Luther G. Jerstad. 1965

Tugitils, highland: ethnobiology. Halmahera Island, Indonesia. Paul M. Taylor. 1980-81

Yazidi religious group. Middle East. Sami Said Ahmed. 1967

Europe

Depopulation and cultural change. Islands of western Ireland. Kevin C. Kearns. 1975

Symbol systems, Paleolithic. East Europe and the Soviet Union. Alexander Marshack. 1975-76

Africa

Afar nomadism. Ethiopia. Robert G. Gardner. 1965

Bani-Niger people: African migrants. Johan Huizinga. 1974

Fulani people: social system with their cattle. Northern Nigeria. Dale F. Lott. 1973

Kipsigis. Kenya. Monique Borgerhoff-Mulder. 1983

Kisii, Kenya: migration and communication. Ronald D. Garst. 1975

Kwanyama linguistic group: ethnobotany. Ovamboland, Namibia. Robert J. Rodin. 1972

Malagasy: origins and prehistory. Robert E. Dewar, Jr. 1978

Mandinko people: history, social structure, and ethnobotany. Pakao, southern Senegal. David M. Schaffer. 1973, 1975

Mbuti Pygmies. Ituri Forest, Zaire. Robert C. Bailey. 1979

Ngamiland peoples: demography. Okavango River and delta, Africa. Thomas J. Larson. 1971

Pokot tribe: women's role. Kenya. Elizabeth L. Meyerhoff. 1976

Rural migration: relationship to expansion of commercial agriculture. Tanzania. Marilyn Silberfein. 1973

West African settlement geography along a linguistic and environmental transect. Reed F. Stewart. 1976

Yoruba geophagy. Nigeria. Donald E. Vermeer. 1975

PHYSICAL ANTHROPOLOGY and PALEO-ANTHROPOLOGY

Adaptive strategies of primates and evolution of suspensory locomotion. John G. H. Cant. 1981

African sites: Fort Ternan, Kenya; Lake Turkana, Kenya; Olduvai Gorge, Tanzania; Omo Valley, Ethiopia. Louis S. B. Leakey, Mary Leakey, and Richard E. Leakey. 1960-69, 1971

CHARLES P. MOUNTFORD

A Tiwi man of Melville Island, Australia, prepares for a ritual funeral dance in the mid-1950s.

——— Louis S. B. Leakey. 1971-72.

Aging, biological. Nepal. Cynthia M. Beall. 1983

Ambrona. Soria Province, Spain. F. Clark Howell. 1981

Americans, first: dental evidence. Christy G. Turner II. 1978-80, 1982

Arikara burial sites. South Dakota. T. Dale Stewart. 1971

——— Indian skeletons. North Dakota. William M. Bass. 1968-69

Buluk: Miocene hominid site. Kenya. Alan C. Walker. 1983

Calico Mountains, Mojave Desert, California. Louis S. B. Leakey, Thomas Clements, Gerald A. Smith, and Ruth D. Simpson. 1964-67

Centre for Prehistory and Palaeontology, Nairobi, Kenya. Louis S. B. Leakey. 1971

Cerebral function at extreme high altitude. Thomas F. Hornbein. 1981

Colonsay and Jura: historical demography. Scotland. John W. Sheets II. 1983

Disease, pre-Columbian American. Marvin J. Allison. 1971, 1973-74, 1976-77, 1979-81, 1983

Early man: taphonomic perspectives. Gary A. Haynes. 1982

Ecuador, coastal: demography. Douglas H. Ubelaker. 1974

Ethiopia: Upper Pliocene localities. Francis H. Brown and F. Clark Howell. 1974

Extinct fauna and early man. Mojave Desert, California. Emma Lou Davis. 1970-71

Fossil bones: amino-acid dating. East Africa. Jeffrey L. Bada. 1978

Hadar, central Afar, Ethiopia. Donald C. Johanson. 1975-76, 1980

Hominid corridor: Plio-Pleistocene deposits. Malawi. Timothy G. Bromage. 1983

Homo erectus. Olduvai Gorge, Africa. G. Philip Rightmire. 1978

Hubei Province, China. Frank E. Poirier. 1981

Kathmandu Valley, Nepal. Elwyn L. Simons. 1974

Laetolil Beds. Tanzania. Raymonde Bonnefille. 1976

——— Mary D. Leakey. 1975-82

Lamb Springs Early Man Project. Douglas County, Colorado. Dennis J. Stanford. 1980-81

Makau and Olduvai, and continued preparation of Laetoli monograph. Tanzania. Mary D. Leakey. 1982

Men: physiological responses to hypoxia and cold at altitude. John B. West. 1980

Middle Awash Valley. Ethiopia. John D. Clark. 1982

Nomads, pastoral: desert physiology. Northern Kenya. Geoffrey M. O. Maloiy. 1977

Olduvai Gorge, Tanzania. Raymonde Bonnefille. 1976

——— Mary D. Leakey. 1970-75, 1983

——— publication. Philip V. Tobias. 1977

——— reevaluation of putative bone tools. Patty L. Shipman. 1982

Paleomagnetic dating of the earliest human occupations. Italy. Alan L. McPherron. 1981

Primates. Outamba-Kilimi National Park, Sierra Leone. Robert S. O. Harding. 1981

Sahabi, northern Libya. Noel T. Boaz. 1978

Semliki Valley, Zaire. Noel T. Boaz. 1983

Sherpas: high-altitude adaptation and genetics. Georgio P. Morpurgo. 1976

Skeletal biology. Bahrain. Bruno Frøhlich. 1980

——— Corinth, Greece. Henry S. Robinson. 1975

——— Maya. Cozumel, Mexico. Frank P. Saul. 1979

——— Mehrgarh, Pakistan. John R. Lukacs. 1982

——— Neanderthal. Egypt. T. Dale Stewart. 1982

——— prehistoric human. Easter Island. George W. Gill. 1980

Toromoja: potential Early Man site. Alison S. Brooks. 1980

Turkana (Rudolf), Lake, Kenya. Richard E. Leakey. 1965-81

——— hominid locality. Kenya. John M. Harris. 1982

——— report of discoveries. F. Clark Howell. 1974

Women: physiological responses to hypoxia and cold at altitude. Barbara L. Drinkwater. 1980

Astronomy and Astrophysics

Asteroid geography: a study of asteroid topography. A.M.J. Gehrels. 1980

Asteroids: Geographos (1620). Betty F. Mintz. 1968-69

——— Geographos orbit study. Samuel Herrick. 1968-69

——— Geographos and others. A.M.J. Gehrels. 1971

Astronomical alignment: Canadian Indian cairns and medicine wheels. John A. Eddy. 1975

Atlas of the Andromeda Galaxy. Paul W. Hodge. 1977, 1979

Auroras: observations on brightness, color, variety, and sequence. Carl W. Gartlein. 1938-56

Beta Scorpii and companion: occultation by Jupiter. David S. Evans. 1971

Cosmic-ray monitoring. Martin A. Pomerantz. 1946-53, 1956-58, 1964

Disk characteristics of Sc I galaxies. Gregory O. Boeshaar. 1979

"Einstein Shift" verification: 1952 solar eclipse. Khartoum, Sudan. George A. Van Biesbroeck. 1952

Epsilon Aurigae: polarimetry of the eclipsing star system. James C. Kemp. 1983

Galaxy clusters: size. Hale Observatories. Thomas W. Noonan. 1974

Gravitational light-deflection effect: improved measurement. Bryce S. DeWitt. 1973

Interstellar deuterium. Jay M. Pasachoff. 1974

Interstellar molecular clouds: exploration by submillimeter polarimetry. Roger H. Hildebrand. 1979

Kohoutek, comet, and the annular solar eclipse. Donald H. Menzel. 1973

Mars: greenish patches and mysterious "canals." Bloemfontein Observatory, South Africa. E. C. Slipher. 1954-56

Mars and Jupiter: spectroscopic studies. Mauna Loa, Hawaii. C. C. Kiess and C. H. Corliss. 1956-57

"Martian Pavilion," Georgetown College Observatory, presented by the National Geographic Society. 1956

Planetary systems search. A.M.J. Gehrels and Krzysztof M. Serkowski. 1974-76

——— Krzysztof M. Serkowski. 1978, 1980

Planets: brighter, photographic atlas. E. C. Slipher and John S. Hall. 1962-63

Sky survey: infrared photographs. Eric R. Craine. 1976

——— Palomar Observatory–National Geographic Society: photomapping. 1949-58

——— Palomar Observatory–National Geographic Society: transparent overlay map preparation. John D. Kraus. 1976

——— Palomar Observatory. Wallace L. W. Sargent. 1980

——— radio-telescope monitoring of infrared emissions. James N. Douglas. 1973-75

Solar corona: heating studies, 1980 eclipse. Jay M. Pasachoff. 1979

——— photography of the spectrum, polarization, and form. Donald H. Menzel. 1972

——— spectrographic study, 1970 eclipse. Donald H. Menzel. 1969

——— temperature and density studies, 1977 eclipse. Jay M. Pasachoff. 1977

Solar eclipse: aerial photographs. Bocaiúva, Brazil. Lyman J. Briggs. 1947

——— Africa. Donald H. Menzel. 1972

——— Australia. Donald H. Menzel. 1976

——— Burma to the Aleutian Islands. Lyman J. Briggs. 1948

——— Canton Island, Pacific. Samuel A. Mitchell. 1937

——— Maine-New Hampshire. Albert W. Stevens and Paul A. McNally. 1932

——— Norfolk, Virginia. Simon Newcomb and Alexander Graham Bell. 1900

DAVID BRILL

Statue of a priest at Aphrodisias, Turkey, is bound during a restoration gluing of its cracked torso and limbs.

——— Northern Canada. Wolfgang B. Klemperer. 1963

——— Patos, Brazil. Irvine C. Gardner. 1940

——— Trans-African baseline. Jay M. Pasachoff. 1973

——— U.S.S.R. Irvine C. Gardner. 1936

——— U.S.S.R. Paul A. McNally and W. Robert Moore. 1936

——— and occultation by Neptune. Indonesia. Jay M. Pasachoff. 1982

Solar radiation. Mount Brukkaros, Namibia. Charles G. Abbot. 1925-29

Spacewatch Camera: microwave data link. A.M.J. Gehrels. 1983

Stars: peculiar early-type. Deane M. Peterson. 1974

Structure of the early universe. Richard A. Matzner. 1980

Sunlike stars: synoptic observation of magnetically induced chromospheric variations. Arthur H. Vaughan, George W. Preston, and Robert W. Noyes. 1982

Uranus occultation: 1977. William B. Hubbard, Jr. 1976

Zodiacal light. Colorado-Nebraska border. George A. Van Biesbroeck. 1954

Biology

Animal hard parts: biological destruction of, in marine environment. Peter M. Kranz. 1973

Aquatic animals: behavior in relation to polarized light. Talbot H. Waterman. 1970-71

Biogeography, vicariance: empirical test. Spain and Morocco. Stephen D. Busack. 1983

Biological and archaeological expedition. Southeast Oceania. John E. Randall. 1969

Biological colonization of a recently formed volcanic island. Motmot, Papua New Guinea. Eldon E. Ball. 1972, 1974, 1976, 1978, 1980, 1983

Biological investigation: disease study. Bolivia. Richard G. Van Gelder. 1964

Biological studies of the northern Cordillera Vilcabamba. Peru. John W. Terborgh. 1966-68

Bioluminescent and optical attenuation measurements. Maui Basin, Hawaii. Guy C. McLeod. 1977

Bird and plant communities: convergent evolution. Africa and North America. Martin L. Cody. 1977

Central Australia: biological exploration of remote mountain chains. G. Alan Solem. 1982

Cerro Tacarcuna, Panama-Colombia border: biological exploration. Alwyn H. Gentry. 1974

Cordella Bank Expedition. Pacific Ocean. Robert W. Schmieder. 1979

Deep reefs: ecology. Western Caribbean. Walter A. Starck II. 1970

Deep-sea fauna: biology and distribution. Tropical Atlantic Ocean. Gilbert L. Voss. 1963-73

——— hydrothermal-vent: photographic documentation. Pacific. Robert R. Hessler. 1983

——— pressure tolerance. Bermuda. Alister G. MacDonald. 1980

Gombe National Park: establishment. Tanzania. 1968

——— support. D. N. Bryceson. 1973

Hudson Bay and Labrador: biological expedition. W. E. Clyde Todd. 1912, 1914, 1917

Lake Baikal: freshwater fauna. U.S.S.R. Ralph W. Brauer. 1977-79

Lizard malaria: ecology. Sierra Leone. Joseph J. Schall. 1982

Magnetic bacteria search. Southern Hemisphere. Richard P. Blakemore. 1979

Natural history collection. Inner Mongolia, China. Frederick R. Wulsin. 1923-24

Netherlands Indies: collection of rare species for zoos. Sumatra. William M. Mann. 1937

Organisms from simple environments. Nicholas C. Collins. 1976

Photorefraction and penguin vision. Falkland Islands. Jacob G. Sivak. 1980

Prochloron and ascidian symbioses. Palau. Rosevelt L. Pardy. 1981

Río Camuy Cave, northwestern Puerto Rico. Russell H. Gurnee, Brother G. Nicholas, and John V. Thrailkill. 1963

Tambopata Reserve: flora and fauna. Peru. David L. Pearson. 1979

Tierra del Fuego: natural history. Argentina-Chile. Rae Natalie P. Goodall. 1977-79, 1982

Urubamba Valley: biological expedition. Peru. Frank M. Chapman. 1916

BOTANY

Agave sebastiana: pollination ecology. Cedros Island, Mexico. James H. Brown. 1981

Algae. Australia. Ralph A. Lewin. 1976

——— calcareous. North Atlantic Ocean. Walter H. Adey. 1964-65

Algal communities in tide pools. New England coast. Philip Sze. 1981

Alpine cushion plants. George G. Spomer. 1974

Andean desert loma formations: botanical response to El Niño. Peru and Chile. Michael O. Dillon. 1983

Angiosperms: pollination mechanisms. New Caledonia. Leonard B. Thien. 1983

Anthurium. Central America. Thomas B. Croat. 1977

Araucarian cones. Southern Argentina. Thomas N. Taylor. 1973

Asteraceae: biosystematic studies. South America. Robert Merrill King. 1973

Bahama, Turks, and Caicos Islands. William Thomas Gillis, Jr. 1973

Bali and Celebes Islands. Willem Meijer. 1976

Bamboos. Costa Rica. Richard W. Pohl. 1982

——— and bambusoid grasses. Brazil. Thomas R. Soderstrom. 1971, 1975

Beach heather. Ralph P. Collins. 1980

Bracken-fern gametophytes: comparative normal and abnormal development. Carl R. Partanen. 1971

Bromeliads. Brazilian mountains. Margaret U. Mee. 1966

——— carnivorism. South America. Thomas J. Givnish. 1983

Bryophytes. South America. John J. Engel. 1975, 1981

——— Southern Africa. R. E. Magill. 1983

***Capsicum pubescens* complex:** biosystematics and evolution. W. Hardy Eshbaugh. 1970-71

Cerro de la Neblina. Venezuela. Thomas B. Croat. 1983

Cerro Sumaco. Ecuador. Michael T. Madison. 1978

Chenopodium germplasm. South America. Hugh D. Wilson. 1978

***Chondrus crispus* alga.** Esther L. McCandless. 1970

Cycad *(Zamia)*. Knut Norstog. 1975

Death Valley, California. Frederick V. Coville. 1931

Desert Plants. Chile. Harold A. Mooney and Sherry L. Gulmon. 1978

——— *(Welwitschia)*. Namibia. Chris H. Bornman. 1968

Euphorbiaceae. New Caledonia. Gordon D. McPherson. 1983

Ferns, tropical. Eastern United States. Donald R. Farrar. 1981

Flax *(Linum)*. Mediterranean region. Claude M. Rogers. 1971

Forest reserves in the "Green Plan." Austria. Else A. Schmidt. 1968-69

Forest types. North Cascade Range, Washington. Richard N. Mack. 1973

Forests: conservation. Malawi. Françoise B. Dowsett-Lemaire. 1982

——— establishment. Celebes. Willem Meijer. 1975

——— evergreen. Cameroon. Duncan W. Thomas. 1983

——— Paleotropical. Africa and Asia. Alwyn H. Gentry. 1981

——— tropical: regeneration. Panama. Nicholas V. L. Brokaw. 1982

Fungi. Brazil. Gary J. Samuels. 1983

Grasses: biosystematic investigation. Oaxaca and Chiapas, Mexico. Frank W. Gould. 1973

Gustavia superba: population ecology. Panama. Victoria L. Sork. 1983

Hanging gardens. Colorado Plateau. Stanley L. Welsh. 1972

Hawaiian Islands. Ron Scogin. 1978

Heliconia, Melanesian. Walter J. E. Kress. 1982

Kakabekia: microorganism with Precambrian affinities. Iceland. Sanford M. Siegel. 1971

Kokechik Bay area, Alaska. Charles M. Kirkpatrick. 1972

Krakatoa: resurvey of flora. John R. Flenley. 1979

Kwangsi, China. G. Weidman Groff. 1937

Lepidoptera: host plants. Aldabra Atoll, Indian Ocean. Jay C. Shaffer. 1967

Lichen growths on Maya ruins. Mason E. Hale. 1975, 1978-79

Lichens, rain-forest. Australia. Mason E. Hale, Jr. 1983

——— *(Stereocaulon paschale)* as caribou fodder. K. A. Kershaw. 1976

——— (Thelotremataceae): systematics and evolution. Lesser Antilles. Mason E. Hale. 1971

——— and bryophytes. Galapagos Islands. William A. Weber. 1975

Lodgepole pine forests: biotic succession following fire. Yellowstone National Park. Dale L. Taylor. 1971

Log-fern hybrids *(Dryopteris)*. Great Dismal Swamp, Virginia. Lytton J. Musselman. 1976-77

Madagascar. Peter Goldblatt. 1973

Mangroves: evolutionary mechanisms. Philip B. Tomlinson. 1976.

——— Old World. Indo-Pacific. Philip B. Tomlinson. 1973

——— Oriental. A. Malcolm Gill. 1968-69

Marquesas Islands. Marie-Helene Sachet. 1974

Maya Mountains, British Honduras. John D. Dwyer. 1972

Microflora: composition, variation, and ecology. Arctic Sea. Spencer Apollonio. 1971

Mistletoes: biogeographical affinities and chromosomal relationships. Africa. Delbert Wiens. 1971

Mosses. Society Islands. Henry O. Whittier. 1979

Mount Mulanje Massif. Malawi. J. D. Chapman. 1983

Orchids, terrestrial: pollination. Australia. Warren P. Stoutamire. 1972-73

CRAIG AND JAN MACFARLAND

Zoologist Craig MacFarland and his wife, Jan (below), trekked across the Galapagos Islands to study 11 surviving native subspecies of threatened giant tortoises (above).

ROBERT W. MADDEN

Dragging a hapless centipede to its under-leaf nest, an Indonesian Myrmoteras ant (right) will share the prey. The African naked mole rat (far right) lives in a termite-like, queen-dominated society.

Palms: key to Neotropical mammal abundance. Peru. Louise H. Emmons. 1979

——— taxonomic studies. Papua New Guinea. Frederick B. Essig. 1977

Pandanaceae: floral evolution. South Pacific. Paul A. Cox. 1982

Phytogeographic studies. Burica Peninsula, Panama and Costa Rica. Thomas B. Croat. 1972

Plankton, blue-water. William M. Hamner. 1970

Plant collecting. China. Robert Ornduff. 1980

——— Costa Rica. Gerrit Davidse. 1983

——— Japan. John L. Creech. 1978

——— Sierra de San Lazaro, Baja California. Amy Jean Gilmartin. 1968-69

Plant communities: distribution and diversity. Amazonian Peru. Alwyn H. Gentry. 1979

——— effects of pollinating bats. Costa Rica and Arizona. Donna J. Howell. 1974

Plant species: *Beagle* voyage. Duncan M. Porter. 1980, 1982

——— Cook and Flinders voyages. Society Islands and Australia. Francis R. Fosberg. 1981

——— Cook voyages. Society Islands. Francis R. Fosberg. 1982

Plant succession on Soufrière. St. Vincent, Leeward Islands. John Stanley Beard. 1971

Plants and landforms. Tristan da Cunha and St. Helena Islands. Nigel M. Wace. 1975

Psilotum: classical culture, mutants, and wild occurrences. Japan. Albert S. Rouffa. 1972

Pteridophytic plants: phytogeography. Chocó, Colombia. David B. Lellinger. 1968-69

Rafflesiaceae. Southeast Asia. Willem Meijer. 1982

Rattan–palm collection. Asian rain forests. Jack B. Fisher. 1976

Redwoods: preservation. California. Chester C. Brown. 1963

Sage *(Salvia)*. James L. Reveal. 1974

Sichuan Province, China. Bruce M. Bartholomew. 1983

Solanaceae. Madagascar. William G. D'Arcy. 1982

Spore research. West Indies and northern South and Central America. Fred C. Meier. 1935

Stromatolites and algal carbonate structures of the Recent Epoch: ecology. Shark Bay, Australia. Stjepko Golubic. 1973

Subarctic plant systems and water conservation. Wayne R. Rouse. 1971

Sunflower family (Compositae): as source of fish poisons. Tod F. Stuessy. 1976

Tariquia Forest: botanical inventory. Bolivia. James C. Solomon. 1981

Tibet: botanical expedition. Ronald H. Petersen. 1979

Tierra del Fuego, Argentina and Chile: study, collection, and illustration of flora. Rae Natalie P. Goodall. 1970-72.

Tiliaceae. Cameroon, West Africa. Willem Meijer. 1981

Tree-limit ecotone: vegetational dynamics. Central Brooks Range, Alaska. Ann M. Odasz. 1981

Tree-species diversity. Upper Amazonia, Peru. Alwyn H. Gentry. 1983

Trigger plants: pollinating mechanisms. Australia. Sherwin J. Carlquist. 1977

Tristan da Cunha Islands: atmospheric pollen and spores. Nigel M. Wace. 1982

Viticulture. South Africa. Harm J. de Blij. 1983

Wheats, cultivated: origin and ancestry. B. Lennart Johnson. 1972

Wildflowers of the United States. New York Botanical Garden. 1965

Witchweeds: fertility patterns. Lytton J. Musselman. 1979

ECOLOGY

Amazon Basin: ecosystem rehabilitation. Brazil. Christopher Uhl. 1983

Amazonian Brazil: species area requirements. David C. Oren. 1979-80

Ants and giant anteaters: ecologic interaction. Venezuela. Yael D. Lubin. 1977

Camera equipment for marine biology research. Harold E. Edgerton. 1974

Computer extrapolation of Landsat spectral signatures to classify vegetation. John J. Craighead. 1981

Dead Sea system: limnology and ecology. Joel R. Gat. 1976-77

Desert buttes: testing island biogeography theories. David M. Armstrong. 1981

Dugongs and sea turtles: exploitation. Torres Strait. Bernard Nietschmann. 1976

Ecological influences of the Tarahumara Indians on three plants. Mexico. Robert A. Bye, Jr. 1977

Ecological surveying in East Lake Rudolf, Kenya. Michael Norton-Griffiths. 1976

Everglades ecology. Everglades National Park, Florida. Frank C. Craighead, Sr. 1966, 1970

Falkland Islands: natural history and ecology. Olin S. Pettingill, Jr. 1970

Forests, semideciduous: ecology of the canopy. Panama. Pedro Galindo. 1973

Great Plains: comparative competition and diversity of herbivores. Gary E. Belovsky. 1979

Hawaii: introduced avifauna. Stuart L. Pimm. 1982

Island factors and density regulation on land-bird populations in Hawaii. John T. Emlen. 1977

Kruger National Park: biomass production of selected woody species utilized by browsing game. South Africa. Bruce R. Dayton. 1977

Little Dunk's Bay, Great Lakes system: ecosystem. Joseph B. MacInnis and Alan R. Emery. 1970

Masai land: ecology. Tanzania. Tepilit Ole-Saitoti. 1978

Mono Lake. California. John M. Melack. 1979-80

Moose and wolf relationships. Isle Royale, Michigan. Rolf O. Peterson. 1980, 1983

——— Isle Royale, Michigan. Durward L. Allen and Peter A. Jordan. 1964-65.

New Guinea mountains. J. Linsley Gressitt. 1968-69

Northern Thailand: highland land use and environmental change. Peter Kunstadter. 1982

MARK W. MOFFETT

CHRISTOPHER SPRINGMANN

Northern Waterfowl Project: U. S.-U.S.S.R. Environmental Protection Agreement. William J. L. Sladen. 1977

Panama: recovery of vegetation from earthquake-caused landslides. Nancy C. Garwood. 1980

Papyrus swamps: effect on ecology. Lake Naivasha, Kenya. John J. Gaudet. 1971, 1973, 1975, 1977

Plant-insect interactions in a tropical herb. Mexico. Carol C. Horvitz. 1982

Pollution: 70-year evaluation. Dry Tortugas, Florida. Richard H. Chesher. 1972

Protozoan communities: ecology. Lake Waiau, Hawaii. Raymond D. Dillon. 1970

Rain forests: fruit and vertebrate frugivore interaction. Gabon. Louise H. Emmons. 1980

——— production and nutrient cycling. Sarawak. John Proctor. 1977-78

——— Valdivian: gap dynamics. Chile. Thomas T. Veblen. 1983

Saltville Valley: paleoecology. Virginia. Jerry N. McDonald. 1982

Submarine limnological study. Great Lakes. Joseph B. MacInnis. 1968-69

Tidal marsh: ecosystem. Trenton, New Jersey. Dennis F. Whigham. 1974

Titicaca, Lake. Peru-Bolivia. Carl Widmer. 1972

United States-Mexico boundary: vegetation and landform study. Robert R. Humphrey. 1983

Water conservation in desert animals. Israel. Knut Schmidt-Nielsen. 1977, 1979

Web-spider resource partitioning. California and Costa Rica. Matthew H. Greenstone. 1979

Wildlife-habitat classification by satellite imagery. John J. Craighead. 1975

Wolf-elk and wolf-cattle relationships. Alberta, Canada. Robert R. Ream. 1982

ZOOLOGY

Actinians symbiotic with pomacentrid fishes. Daphne F. Dunn. 1977

Animals with algal endosymbionts: defense against photosynthetic oxygen toxicity. Australia. J. Malcolm Shick. 1983

Cave fauna. Yucatán Peninsula. Robert W. Mitchell. 1974-75

Cetacean fauna and former dolphin fishery of St. Helena: taxonomy investigation. William F. Perrin. 1982

Madeira and Deserta Islands: fauna evolution. Laurence M. Cook. 1980

Marine fish eggs: chorion microstructure and sculpturing. George W. Boehlert. 1982

Marine organisms, complex: sensory information processing and visual behavior. Talbot H. Waterman. 1968-69, 1973-77

Moths and bats: behavioral ecology. Tanzania and Hawaii. James H. Fullard. 1979, 1982

Parthenogenetic organisms in the arid zone of Western Australia. Michael J. D. White. 1982

Reptiles, amphibians, and insects. Ethiopia. Thomas P. Monath. 1964

Vertebrate genetic systems: comparative population cytogenetics and evolutionary roles. William P. Hall, 3d. 1971

Vertebrates: locomotion. East Africa. Charles R. Taylor. 1976

——— Neotropical: seasonal patterns. Sinaloa, Mexico. Terry A. Vaughan. 1970

——— populations in strip-mine areas. Frederick J. Brenner. 1971, 1973-74

Wildlife survey. Sarpo National Park, Liberia. Phillip T. Robinson. 1981

——— and collection of specimens. Nepal. S. Dillon Ripley. 1948-49

Vertebrate Zoology

HERPETOLOGY

Alligators, American: thermoregulation and ecology. Frederick R. Gehlbach. 1971

——— Chinese *(Alligator sinensis).* Myrna E. Watanabe. 1981

——— thermoregulation. Clifford Ray Johnson. 1974

Amphibians: ecology. Chaco Boreal, Paraguay. Lon L. McClanahan. 1983

——— Seychelles Islands, Indian Ocean. Ronald A. Nussbaum. 1976-77

——— West Africa. Victor H. Hutchison. 1980

——— and reptiles. Andes. William E. Duellman. 1974

——— and reptiles. Colombia. Victor H. Hutchison. 1965

Chameleons: distribution. Kenya. James J. Hebrard. 1980

Crocodiles, American: ecology. Jamaica. Leslie D. Garrick. 1983

——— Northern Australia. Grahame J. W. Webb. 1979

Frogs, Cascades: sibling recognition. Oregon. Andrew R. Blaustein. 1982

——— Neotropical. Kentwood D. Wells. 1978

——— relation of activity periods to phototactic behavior. Robert G. Jaeger. 1972

——— telmatobiid; physiological ecology. Lake Titicaca, Peru-Bolivia. Victor H. Hutchison. 1973

——— tree *(Hyla meridionalis* and *H. arborea):* mating calls. Canary Islands. H. Carl Gerhardt. 1978

——— tree *(Litoria):* communication. Australia. Howard C. Gerhardt. 1983

——— vocalizations. Panama. Michael J. Ryan. 1983

——— and reptiles. New Guinea. Richard G. Zweifel. 1968

Geckos, mourning: behavioral ecology. Hawaii. David P. Crews. 1983

Herpetofauna. Argentina. Raymond F. Laurent. 1977

Iguanas, land *(Conolophus pallidus* and *C. subcristatus):* conservation survey. Galapagos Islands. Dagmar I. Werner. 1975-78, 1980.

Lizards *(Anolis).* Bahamas and West Indies. Thomas W. Schoener. 1968-70

——— *(Anolis):* island ecology. Caribbean. George C. Gorman. 1971

——— *(Anolis limifrons):* functions and social displays. Thomas A. Jenssen. 1971

——— collared: hybridization. Richard R. Montanucci. 1979

——— desert. Western Australia. Eric R. Pianka. 1977, 1979

——— giant *(Sauromalus):* behavioral ecology. Gulf of California. Ted J. Case. 1977, 1979

——— iguanid *(Sceloporus grammicus):* biogeography of karyotype variation. William P. Hall, 3d. 1970

——— iguanid. South America. Richard E. Etheridge. 1982

——— Kalahari Desert, Africa. Raymond B. Huey. 1975

——— shiny: unisexual clones. Suriname and West Indies. Charles J. Cole. 1980, 1983

Rattlesnakes, prairie *(Crotalus viridis viridis)*: ethology and movement. Wyoming. David J. Duvall. 1982-83

——— eastern diamondback. D. Bruce Means. 1977

——— timber: population ecology. New York. William S. Brown. 1982-83

Reptiles. Gunong Mulu National Park, Sarawak. Ian R. Swingland. 1977

——— desert: orientation and navigation. Arizona. Kraig Adler. 1979

Salamanders, tropical: behavioral defense mechanisms. Edmund D. Brodie, Jr. 1973, 1975

Sea snakes, Philippine. George C. Gorman. 1977-78

Snakes and amphibians. French Guiana. Thomas P. Monath. 1963

Toads, Yosemite *(Bufo canorus)*: energetics and natural history. Martin L. Morton. 1973

——— *(Bufo marinus)*: evolutionary genetics. Latin America and Caribbean. Simon Easteal. 1982

——— *(Bufo marinus)*: evolutionary response. Michael D. Sabath. 1980

Tortoises, Galapagos. James L. Patton. 1976

——— Galapagos: population ecology. William G. Reeder and Craig G. MacFarland. 1968-69

Turtles. Africa. Roger C. Wood. 1967

——— fresh-water chelid: taxonomy, distribution, and ecology. Australia. John M. Legler. 1972, 1974, 1976

——— giant leatherback: taxonomic study. Suriname. Wayne F. Frair. 1968-69

——— green. Ascension Island. Archie F. Carr. 1976

——— green *(Chelonia mydas)*. Caribbean. John C. Ogden. 1981, 1983

——— green. Galapagos Islands. William G. Reeder. 1981

——— Hawaiian basking green sea. G. Causey Whittow. 1977

DAVID DOUBILET

While studying "sleeping" sharks, Eugenie Clark inspects a bull shark, temporarily made docile when hooked by a fisherman.

——— Pacific green. Galapagos Islands. Craig G. MacFarland. 1975-77

——— Pacific ridley: nesting biology. David A. Hughes. 1971

——— pleurodiran: systematics, evolution, and ecology. South America. Roger C. Wood. 1970

——— sea, hawksbill: exploitation and ecology. Bernard Nietschmann. 1972

——— sea, olive ridley: population ecology. Mexico. John G. Frazier. 1980-81

——— slider *(Pseudemys scripta)*. Panama. John M. Legler. 1966

ICHTHYOLOGY

Anglerfishes: feeding mechanisms. Theodore W. Pietsch. 1977

Characid, splashing *(Copeina arnoldi)*: reproductive and parental behavior. Guyana. Charles O. Krekorian. 1973

Coelacanth *(Latimeria chalumnae)*. Indian Ocean. Keith Stewart Thomson. 1972

Eels, American: breeding area. James D. McCleave. 1980

——— American and European: migratory mechanisms in larvae and adults. James D. McCleave. 1977

——— garden: ecological and behavioral study. Red Sea. Eugenie Clark. 1971.

Fishes: collection. Río Nichare, Venezuela. James E. Böhlke. 1976

——— coral-reef. Bahamas. Raymond D. Clarke. 1974

——— coral-reef. Moluccas, Indonesia. Victor G. Springer. 1973

——— coral-reef. Solomon Islands. John E. Randall. 1973

——— electric. Walter F. Heiligenberg. 1976, 1981-82

——— electric, mormyriform. Peter Moller. 1975, 1977

——— electric, mormyriform. Gabon. Carl D. Hopkins. 1976, 1979, 1981

——— genetics. Atlantic and Pacific Oceans. Dennis A. Powers. 1975

——— glandulocaudin: zoogeography. South America. Stanley H. Weitzman. 1977

——— labrid. David R. Robertson. 1975

——— Lord Howe Island. New South Wales, Australia. Frank H. Talbot. 1972

——— marine invertebrates, and algae. Southeast Oceania. John E. Randall. 1969.

——— Neotropical stream: community structure and convergent ecomorphological trends. Venezuela. Kirk O. Winemiller. 1983

——— osteoglossid. South America. Joan Dorothy Fuller. 1972

——— pelagic. F. G. Walton Smith and Hilary B. Moore. 1953-60

——— pelagic. North Atlantic. Frank J. Mather 3d. 1962

——— *(Poecilia):* color-pattern convergences. Trinidad and Venezuela. John A. Endler. 1979

——— *(Poecilia):* ethology. Mexico. Joseph S. Balsano and Ellen M. Rasch. 1976

——— *(Poecilia formosa):* evolutionary genetics. Mexico. Bruce J. Turner. 1980

——— St. Helena Island, South Atlantic. Alasdair J. Edwards. 1983

——— survey. Congo River's lower rapids. Tyson R. Roberts. 1972

——— toxic-repellent effect of certain species on sharks. Red Sea. Eugenie Clark. 1972.

——— *(Trichonotus nikii):* massive swarming and lek behavior. Red Sea. Eugenie Clark. 1982

——— tropical reef. Caribbean. Robert R. Warner. 1976

——— tropical sand-diving. Red Sea. Eugenie Clark. 1977

Killifish, annual: systematics, ecology, and distribution. Northern South America. Jamie E. Thomerson. 1971

Lungfish *(Clarias)* and *Tilapia*. East Africa. Geoffrey Moriaso Ole Maloiy. 1974-75

River fishes. Australia. Tim M. Berra. 1968-69

Sharks, bull: speciation. Lake Nicaragua. Jack D. Burke. 1970

——— gray reef: social behavior and aggression. Donald R. Nelson. 1971-72

——— reef. Rangiroa, French Polynesia. Donald R. Nelson. 1973

RONALD H. COHN

Senior Assistant Editor Mary G. Smith shares a moment with the gorilla Koko, whose language abilities are studied by Francine Patterson.

——— scalloped hammerhead. Gulf of California. Peter Klimley and Donald R. Nelson. 1980

——— "sleeping." Mexican caves. Eugenie Clark. 1973-74.

——— teleost symbionts. Japan. Eugenie Clark. 1975

Shore fishes. Easter Island. John E. Randall. 1968-69

Stingrays: freshwater adaptation. Thomas B. Thorson. 1974, 1976-79

Surgeonfishes: spawning. Atlantic Ocean. Patrick L. Colin. 1977-78

Tuna. Francis G. Carey. 1967-69

MAMMALOGY

Animal tracking by satellite. Frank C. Craighead, Jr. 1970

Anteaters, giant. Brazil. Kent H. Redford. 1980

Antelopes. East Africa. Richard Despard Estes. 1974

——— bongo: search for. Kenya. Theodore H. Reed. 1968

——— sable. Angola and Kenya. Richard Despard Estes. 1968-70, 1975

——— topi. Mara Game Preserve, Tanzania. Geoffrey Moriaso Ole Maloiy. 1972

Armadillos: habitat utilization. Brazil. Tracy S. Carter. 1979

Asses, feral: distribution and ecological impact. Galapagos Islands. Patricia D. Moehlman. 1980

Baboons, olive: ecology and behavior. Kenya. Robert S. O. Harding. 1974

Bats, African megadermatid: communication. Kenya. Terry A. Vaughan. 1982

——— false vampire: social, foraging, and roosting behavior. Terry A. Vaughan. 1972

——— frog-eating. Panama and Kenya. Merlin D. Tuttle. 1979-80, 1983.

——— fruit: cooperative foraging and harem evolution. Douglas W. Morrison. 1979

——— fruit. Ivory Coast. Donald W. Thomas. 1980

——— mouse-tailed: echolocation. James A. Simmons. 1979

——— mustache: acoustic basis of prey selection. Jamaica. O'Dell W. Henson, Jr. 1982

JONATHAN BLAIR

Found near Kyrenia, Cyprus, an ancient Greek ship is rebuilt.

——— Neotropical: echolocation. Trinidad. Patricia E. Brown. 1979

——— Neotropical: mating and kinship. Trinidad. Gary F. McCracken. 1980

——— West African: energetics. Roger E. Carpenter. 1977

Bears, black: satellite monitoring during winter sleep. John J. Craighead. 1971

——— brown. Alaska Peninsula. Allen W. Stokes. 1972-73

——— grizzly. Yellowstone National Park, Wyoming. Frank C. Craighead, Jr., and John J. Craighead. 1959-67

——— grizzly: habitat survey by Landsat. John J. Craighead. 1976, 1979

——— polar: behavior and ecology. Northwest Territories, Canada. Brian M. Knudsen. 1970-71

——— polar: survey of dens. Svalbard, Arctic Ocean. Thor Larsen. 1971

Biotelemetry systems for wildlife research. Frank C. Craighead, Jr., and John J. Craighead. 1968-69

Bison, American: social and sexual behavior. Montana. Dale F. Lott. 1967-71

Bobcats: ecology. Idaho. Maurice G. Hornocker. 1983

Burros, wild: social organization and communication behavior. Patricia D. Moehlman. 1970, 1972

Bushbaby, thick-tailed: ecology and behavior. South Africa. Gerald A. Doyle. 1968, 1970

Camels, one-humped: locomotion. Kenya. Geoffrey Moriaso Ole Maloiy. 1982

——— temperature regulation and dehydration. Australia. Knut Schmidt-Nielsen. 1982

Caribou. Labrador. Dietland Muller-Schwarze. 1980

——— telemetry tracking. Idaho. Donald R. Johnson. 1974

Cats, farm: nursing coalitions and infanticide. David W. MacDonald. 1979

——— Iriomote *(Mayailurus iriomotensis):* ecology and conservation. Japan. Paul Leyhausen. 1973

Cetacea: neurologic disease in. Nicholas R. Hall. 1978

——— of southern South America. Argentina. Rae Natalie P. Goodall. 1983

Cheetahs. Botswana. Mark J. Owens and Delia Owens. 1974

——— male coalitions. Tanzania. Timothy M. Caro. 1982-83

Chimpanzees: communicative capacity. R. Allen Gardner and Beatrice T. Gardner. 1968-69

——— Gombe Stream, Tanzania. Jane Goodall. 1961-71, 1976, 1978

——— pygmy *(Pan paniscus):* comparison with common chimpanzee. San Diego Zoo, California. Frans B. M. de Waal. 1983

——— pygmy: feeding ecology. Zaire. Randall L. Susman. 1979

Deer, Key. Florida. Willard D. Klimstra. 1968-71

Dolphins, dusky. Argentina. Roger S. Payne. 1974

——— dusky and southern common. Argentina. Charles Walcott. 1975-76

——— Franciscana: life history, behavior, and acoustics. Uruguay. Robert L. Brownell, Jr. 1972-73

——— Uruguay. Ricardo Praderi. 1980-82

Dugongs. Australia. Paul K. Anderson. 1975, 1980

Elephants, African. Iain Douglas-Hamilton. 1981

——— African. Phyllis C. Lee. 1982-83

Ferrets, black-footed, and prairie dogs. Wyoming. Timothy W. Clark. 1973

——— black-footed: conservation. Wyoming. Timothy W. Clark. 1977, 1982-83

Gazelles, desert. Charles R. Taylor. 1971

Gophers, pocket: zoogeography and systematics. Florida. S. David Webb. 1979

Gorillas, lowland: ecology. West Africa. Julie C. Webb. 1974-75

——— lowland: interrelationships with chimpanzees. Río Muni, West Africa. Arthur J. Riopelle. 1966-69

——— lowland: linguistic and cognitive capacities. Francine G. Patterson. 1976-82

——— mountain: behavior and ecology. Virunga Mountains, Rwanda. Dian Fossey. 1967-78, 1981, 1983

——— mountain. Rwanda and Zaire. Alexander H. Harcourt. 1979

——— white ("Snowflake"): adolescent development. Barcelona, Spain. Arthur J. Riopelle. 1970

Guanacos. South America. William L. Franklin. 1976, 1978

Horses, wild: social biology. Nevada. Joel Berger. 1982-83

Hutia, Haitian. Charles A. Woods. 1974-75

Hyenas, spotted *(Crocuta crocuta):* social behavior. Kenya. Laurence G. Frank. 1980, 1982

Jackals. Serengeti Plain, Tanzania. Patricia D. Moehlman. 1975-76

Jaguars. Brazil. George B. Schaller. 1976, 1980

——— Pantanal region, Brazil. Howard B. Quigley and George B. Schaller. 1983

Kangaroos, rat: nutritional physiology. Australia. Ian D. Hume. 1983

Kobs: conventionality of territorial leks. Uganda. Helmut K. Buechner. 1971

——— white-eared, migratory: ecology. Boma region, Sudan. Anthony R. E. Sinclair. 1982

Lemurs: ecology, conservation, and management. Madagascar. Sheila M. O'Connor. 1983

——— *(Varecia variegatus).* Madagascar and Comoro Archipelago, Indian Ocean. Ian Tattersall. 1974, 1976

Leopards, snow: radiotracking. Himalayas, Nepal. Rodney M. Jackson. 1981, 1983

Lions: ecology. Kitengela Conservation Area, Kenya. Judith Ann Rudnai. 1974

——— male coalitions. Tanzania. Craig Packer. 1981

Macaques. Sri Lanka. Wolfgang P. J. Dittus. 1975

——— wild bonnet. South India. Paul E. Simonds. 1975

Mammals: distribution and taxonomy. Chilean coastal islands. Bruce D. Patterson. 1982

——— effects of kinship on social behavior. Paul W. Sherman. 1979

——— highland. Papua New Guinea. Michael Archer. 1983

——— large, high-altitude. Pakistan and Nepal. George B. Schaller. 1971-73.

——— Neotropical. Ralph M. Wetzel. 1968-69

——— nocturnal. Botswana. Reay H. N. Smithers. 1969

——— Paraguay. Ralph M. Wetzel. 1973-75, 1977, 1981

——— small. Cameroon. Duane A. Schlitter. 1978

——— small: of open-pit mine waste dumps. Gordon L. Kirkland, Jr. 1973

——— small: microdistribution at the coniferous-deciduous interface. Gordon L. Kirkland, Jr. 1972

——— small: speciation. Apostle Islands, Lake Superior. Richard R. Meierotto. 1970-71, 1973

——— Uinta Mountains, Utah. Gordon L. Kirkland, Jr. 1976-77

Mammals and birds: collecting. Central Africa. Carnes Weeks and Gertrude S. Weeks. 1952

Manatees, Florida: behavior and ecology. Daniel S. Hartman. 1968

Marine mammals. Guadalupe and Cedros Islands, Baja California. G. Dallas Hanna and A. W. Anthony. 1922

Marsupials, arboreal: utilization of eucalyptus foliage. Australia. Ian D. Hume. 1980, 1982

——— evolution. South America. Larry G. Marshall. 1974

——— reproductive biology. South America. C. H. Tyndale-Biscoe. 1971

Martens: ecology. Grand Teton National Park, Wyoming. Timothy W. Clark. 1975

Moles. North America. Robert J. Baker. 1977

Mongoose, dwarf *(Helogale parvula)* and banded *(Mungos mungo):* ecology and social organization. Uganda. Jonathan P. Rood. 1973

Monkeys, capuchin *(Cebus nigrivittatus):* influences of neighboring groups. Venezuela. John G. Robinson. 1980

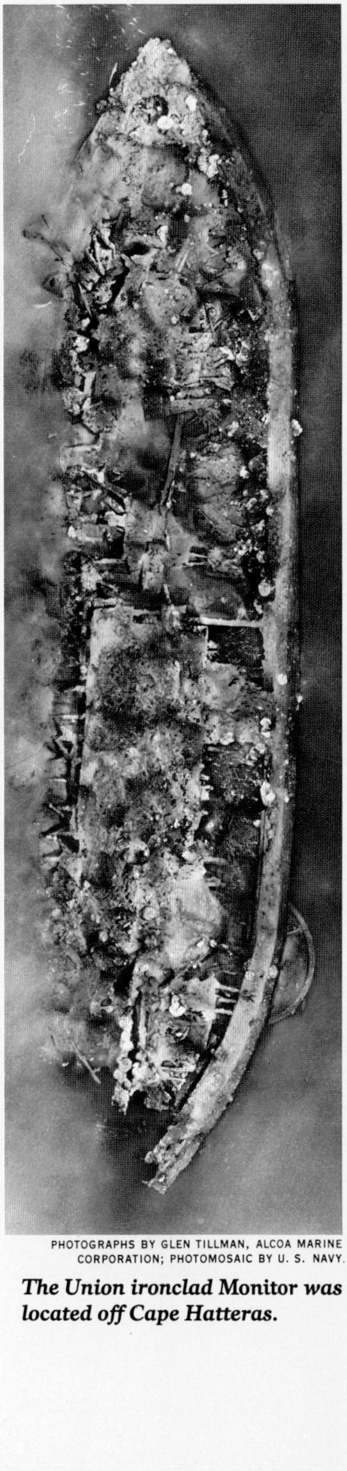

PHOTOGRAPHS BY GLEN TILLMAN, ALCOA MARINE CORPORATION; PHOTOMOSAIC BY U. S. NAVY.

The Union ironclad Monitor was located off Cape Hatteras.

——— red colobus and agile mangabey. Kenya. Colin P. Groves. 1972

——— red howler *(Alouatta seniculus):* population. Venezuela. Carolyn M. Crockett. 1982

——— rhesus: ecology and behavior. Nepal. Charles H. Southwick. 1973, 1975

——— talapoin: mating behavior. Reserved Forest of Maolmayo, Cameroon. Thelma E. Rowell. 1973

——— and lesser primates. Tigoni Primate Research Centre, Limuru, Kenya. Cynthia P. Booth. 1963

——— and loris. Sri Lanka. John F. Eisenberg. 1968

Ngorongoro Crater: aerial census of ungulates. Tanzania. Richard Despard Estes. 1977-78

Nyala, mountain. Ethiopia. Leslie H. Brown. 1965

Ocelots: ecology and behavior. Venezuela. Melvin E. Sunquist. 1983

Opossum, brush-tailed *(Trichosurus vulpecula).* Ian D. Hume. 1975

Orangutans. Mount Looser Reserve, Sumatra, and Tanjung Puting Reserve, Borneo. Biruté M. F. Galdikas. 1971, 1973-77, 1979, 1981, 1983

Otters, giant Brazilian. Suriname. Nicole Duplaix-Hall. 1976-77

Pandas, giant: behavioral ecology. China. John F. Eisenberg. 1981

Peccaries *(Catagonus wagneri).* Lyle K. Sowls. 1980

——— Peru. John W. Terborgh. 1976

Pigs, domestic and wild: cultural and ecological aspects. New Guinea. James A. Baldwin. 1973, 1976

Pikas, Asian *(Ochotona):* behavioral ecology. China. Andrew T. Smith. 1983

——— ecological study. Western United States. Richard D. Bates. 1970-71

Prairie dogs, black-tailed: dispersal. Kansas. Zuleyma T. Halpin. 1980

——— black-tailed: sociobiology. John L. Hoogland. 1978-79

Primates: Neotropical. Manu National Park, Peru. John W. Terborgh. 1974-75

——— nonhuman. East Borneo. Peter S. Rodman. 1974

——— vocal communication. Kenya. Peter R. Marler. 1977

Prosimians, nocturnal: competition and adaptation. Kenya. Caroline S. Harcourt. 1981

Raccoons, tropical: ecology and relationships. James D. Lazell, Jr. 1972

Rats, kangaroo: comparison of social structure and communication. Arizona. Janet A. Randall. 1982

——— kangaroo: radiotelemetry study. California. Martin Daly. 1983

——— naked mole: behavior and ecology. Africa. Paul W. Sherman. 1979

——— naked mole: influence of ecological factors on sociality. Kenya. Jennifer U. M. Jarvis. 1979

Rhinoceros, black: calf survival. Kenya. Vaughan A. Langman. 1982

Sea lions: sonar. Thomas C. Poulter. 1970

——— Steller's. H. Dean Fisher. 1972

Seals, fur, and sea lions. Galapagos Islands. Gerald L. Kooyman. 1980

——— fur: feeding behavior. South America. Gerald L. Kooyman. 1982

——— harbor and gray: feeding habits and population dynamics. Maine. David T. Richardson. 1972

——— Hawaiian monk *(Monachus schauinslandi).* Hawaii. G. Causey Whittow. 1976

——— Juan Fernandez fur. Daniel N. Torres. 1977

Sheep, bighorn. Nez Perce Creek, Wyoming. E. Earl Willard. 1974-75

——— desert bighorn: environmental and physiological biology. Jack Chardon Turner. 1972

——— urial, and markhor goats. Pakistan. George B. Schaller. 1970

Shrews, elephant, golden-rumped. Kenya. Galen B. Rathbun. 1971, 1974, 1976

——— giant African otter: thermoregulatory biology. Martin E. Nicoll. 1982

Squirrels, Kaibab. Joseph G. Hall. 1970-71

Tamarins, golden lion: behavioral ecology and reintroduction studies. Brazil. Devra G. Kleiman. 1982

Tenrecs. Madagascar. Edwin Gould. 1963

Topi. East Africa. Richard Despard Estes. 1977

Walrus: female-calf bond. Edward H. Miller. 1980

Walrus and whale studies: observation cruise of the U. S. Coast Guard Cutter *Glacier.* G. Carleton Ray. 1977

Whales, bowhead: population. Arctic. John R. Bockstoce. 1976

——— California gray: tracking. John E. Schultz. 1968-69

——— gray. San Ignacio Lagoon, Baja California. Steven L. Swartz. 1978-81

——— gray. Scammon Lagoon, Baja California. Merrill P. Spencer. 1966

——— heartbeat. Scammon Lagoon, Baja California. Paul Dudley White. 1956

——— humpback. Roger S. Payne. 1976, 1979-80

——— right: vocalizations and behavior. Argentina. Roger S. Payne. 1971-73

——— right. Charles Walcott. 1976-77

——— sperm: bioacoustic research. Kenneth S. Norris. 1970

——— sperm: identification. Caribbean. William A. Watkins. 1983

Wildebeests. Ngorongoro Crater, Tanzania. Richard Despard Estes. 1963-66, 1972

Wolverines: ecology in an Arctic ecosystem. Brooks Range, Alaska. Philip S. Gipson. 1979

——— ecology. Northwestern Montana. Maurice G. Hornocker. 1973-75

Wolves, red, and coyotes: comparative study of vocalization. Howard McCarley. 1973

Yaks. Richard P. Palmieri. 1971, 1973

Zebras, Grevy's: behavioral ecology. Kenya. Joshua R. Ginsberg. 1983

ORNITHOLOGY

Accipiters. North America. Noel F. R. Snyder. 1970-71

Albatrosses, Laysan: survival, longevity, and turnover in breeding populations. Harvey I. Fisher. 1971

Anis: male incubation and communal nesting. Sandra L. Vehrencamp. 1978

Avian ecology expedition. Falkland Islands. Robin W. Woods. 1983

Bananaquits: foraging behavior on artificial flowers. Grenada. Joseph M. Wunderle, Jr. 1981

Bee-eaters, African: cooperative breeding. Stephen T. Emlen. 1973-74

——— European. Fred N. White. 1975

Bird-fossil comparative study. Trindade Island, South Atlantic Ocean. Storrs L. Olson. 1974

Birds: adaptations for tropical survival. North America. Eugene S. Morton. 1973

——— ant-following. South America and Africa. Edwin O. Willis. 1974, 1979, 1981-82

——— behavior. Bahama Islands. John T. Emlen. 1979

——— Chinese: museum study. Zheng Bao-Lai. 1983

——— collection. New Britain. E. Thomas Gilliard. 1958-59

——— community structure, lowland forest. David L. Pearson. 1974, 1976

——— Dominican rain-forest: conservation. Peter G. H. Evans. 1983

——— ecological studies. Amazon forest. Thomas E. Lovejoy III. 1971

——— Ethiopian: library study. Emil K. Urban. 1966, 1968

——— field studies and collecting specimens. New Guinea. Jared M. Diamond. 1965-68

——— high-Andean. François Vuilleumier. 1975

——— marine: significance of feeding in mixed-species flocks. Spencer G. Sealy. 1978

——— montane forest. Nyika Plateau, Malawi. Françoise B. Dowsett-Lemaire. 1979

——— New Guinea. E. Thomas Gilliard. 1953-54

——— New Guinea, West Irian mountain ranges. Jared M. Diamond. 1980, 1982

——— New Zealand. Charles G. Sibley. 1982

——— North American. Hudson Bay, Gulf of St. Lawrence, southern United States, Mexico, Georgia, Florida, North Dakota, New York. Arthur A. Allen. 1944-49

——— Patagonian: speciation. Chile. François Vuilleumier. 1983

——— piscivorous: effects of human disturbance on breeding success. Eagle Lake, California. James R. Koplin. 1971

——— post-fire competition among hole nesters. Dale L. Taylor. 1973

——— Procellariiformes: olfactory behavior and neurophysiology. Bernice M. Wenzel. 1977, 1980-81

——— radar study of transpacific migration. Timothy C. and Janet M. Williams. 1979

——— recolonization of exploded volcanic islands. New Guinea. Jared M. Diamond. 1972

——— Rift Valley lakes, Ethiopia. Emil K. Urban. 1970

——— Rio Grande do Sul, Brazil. William Belton. 1976

——— São Paulo, Brazil. Yoshika Oniki Willis. 1978

——— Simen Mountains, Ethiopia. Michel Desfayes. 1970

——— small mammals, and bat distribution. Peru. Asa C. Thoresen. 1964-65

——— social systems. Africa. J. David Ligon. 1975

——— songs. John R. Krebs. 1977

——— songs. John R. Krebs and Malcolm L. Hunter, Jr. 1976

——— stranded on land-bridge islands. Jared M. Diamond. 1974

——— Sudan: Dinder Park and Lake Kundi expedition. Stewart M. Evans. 1980

——— survey. Brazil and Venezuela. Ernest G. Holt. 1929-30

——— systematics. South America. Ned K. Johnson. 1974

——— tropical-forest communities. James Richard Karr. 1975-76

——— tropical Pacific islands. Jared M. Diamond. 1976

——— UHF radiolocation system. Frank C. Craighead, Jr. 1973

——— visual mimicry. New Guinea and Australia. Jared M. Diamond. 1979

——— wetland: distribution. West Africa. Patrick J. Dugan. 1983

Birds of paradise. Papua New Guinea. Bruce M. Beehler. 1980

CAROLYN M. CROCKETT

Red howler monkeys have been studied by Carolyn M. Crockett.

ROD BRINDAMOUR

An orangutan searches a visitor for food in the Borneo study area of Biruté M. F. Galdikas.

DARLA HILLARD

Biologist Rodney M. Jackson examines a snow leopard, one of the rarest of the world's big cats.

BIANCA LAVIES, NGS

Timber rattlesnakes have a friend in William Brown, who studies their population ecology.

——— Lawes's six-wired: social organization and ecology. Papua New Guinea. Frank A. Pitelka. 1981-82

——— Little Tobago, West Indies. E. Thomas Gilliard. 1958

Birds of prey: survey. South Africa. C.W.R. Knight. 1937

Blackbirds, red-winged: transplant experiments. Mexico. Frances C. James. 1983

Bowerbirds: comparative socioecology. Australia. Alan Lill. 1977-79

——— golden-fronted *(Amblyornis flavifrons):* search for. New Guinea. E. Thomas Gilliard. 1963

Brazil and Venezuela jungles: specimen collection. Orinoco headwaters. Ernest G. Holt. 1929-31

Cock-of-the-rock: dancing courtship. British Guiana. E. Thomas Gilliard. 1961

——— *(Rupicola rupicola):* lek mating system. Suriname. Kurt M. Fristrup. 1980

——— *(Rupicola rupicola):* lek mating system. Suriname. Pepper W. Trail. 1979, 1981

Condors: number and range; preservation. California. National Audubon Society. 1961-64

Cranes: coiled tracheae. Wisconsin. Abbot S. Gaunt. 1983

Cuckoos, parasitic: social organization and mating. Robert B. Payne. 1982

Ducks, dabbling. Australia and New Zealand. Frank McKinney. 1980

——— torrent: reproduction dynamics and behavior. South America. Marvin C. Cecil. 1968-70

Eagles, bald: post-fledgling activities. Thomas C. Dunstan. 1971.

——— golden. Montana. John J. Craighead. 1973

——— golden: nesting behavior. Texas. W. Grainger Hunt. 1975

——— Philippine: population and breeding. Robert S. Kennedy. 1977, 1979-80

——— satellite tracking. Alaska. Frank C. Craighead, Jr. 1981

Falcons, Eleanora's: territory and aggression. Morocco. Hartmut Walter. 1968-69

——— gregarious: sociobiological studies. Hartmut Walter. 1977

——— laughing. Venezuela. William J. Mader. 1977

——— Patagonian. David H. Ellis. 1981

——— peregrine: migration. North and South America. William W. Cochran. 1975

——— peregrine. Chihuahuan Desert, Mexico. Wilmer G. Hunt. 1977

Finches: courtship behavior. Africa. Robert B. Payne. 1971

——— foraging behavior. Cocos Island, Costa Rica. Thomas W. Sherry and Tracey K. Warner. 1983

——— Galapagos: genetic analysis of evolution patterns. Robert I. Bowman. 1973

——— Mexican. John W. Hardy and Bertram G. Murray, Jr. 1977

——— song mimicry. Cameroon. Robert B. Payne. 1980

Flamingos: ecology and reproductive biology. Florida. M. Philip Kahl. 1972

——— limnological studies of diets and distributions. Chile and Bolivia. Stuart H. Hurlbert. 1973, 1975

——— New World: population ecology. M. Philip Kahl. 1971

——— photographic study. Andros Island, Bahama Islands. John Oliver La Gorce and Louis Agassiz Fuertes. 1920

——— salt lakes of the Andean puna. Stuart H. Hurlbert. 1978-79, 1981-82

——— worldwide survey of population dynamics. M. Philip Kahl. 1974

Fowl, long-tailed. Japan. Frank X. Ogasawara. 1969

Geese, cackling: breeding ecology. Yukon and Kuskokwim river deltas, Alaska. Peter G. Mickelson. 1971-72

——— Canada: breeding biology. Yukon and Kuskokwim river deltas, Alaska. Peter G. Mickelson. 1970

Grassquits, blue-black: thermal consequences of territorial displays. Panama. Wesley W. Weathers. 1982

Grebes, hooded. Gary L. Nuechterlein. Argentina. 1980-81

——— hooded. Argentina. Gary L. Nuechterlein and Robert W. Storer. 1982

——— hooded. Patagonia. Robert W. Storer. 1975

——— pied-billed. Lake Atitlán, Guatemala. Anne LaBastille. 1967-68

——— western. Gary L. Nuechterlein. 1975-78

Grosbeaks, evening. Colorado. Marc Bekoff. 1983

Grouse, spruce *(Canachites canadensis).* Montana. Stanley S. Frissell. 1975

Gyrfalcons: population ecology. Iceland. Thomas J. Cade. 1981-83

Hawks, savanna. Venezuela. William J. Mader. 1979

Hemipode *(Turnix sylvatica):* ecological relations, reproduction, and distribution. Andalusia, Spain. Gerald Collier. 1973

Herons, goliath. South Africa. Douglas W. Mock. 1977

History of ornithology in the Western Hemisphere. Keir B. Sterling. 1977

Hoatzin. British Guiana. J. Lear Grimmer. 1959-60

Honeyeaters (Meliphagidae). Australia. Richard E. MacMillen. 1983

Hoopoes, green wood. Kenya. J. David Ligon. 1976-77

Hornbills, African. Fred N. White. 1976

Hummingbirds: ecology. Mexico, Central America, South America. Augusto Ruschi. 1974

——— heat exchanges in nesting. Rocky Mountains. William A. Calder, III. 1972

——— migration and population dynamics. Colorado. William A. Calder, III. 1983

——— rufous: utilization of time and microhabitat. William A. Calder, III. 1973, 1975

——— South America. Augusto Ruschi. 1962

Ibises, scarlet: search for rookery. Venezuela. Paul A. Zahl. 1949

Jays, Florida scrub. Glen E. Woolfenden and John W. Fitzpatrick. 1978

——— green: ecology. Colombia. Humberto Alvarez. 1974

——— Yucatán: social and reproductive biology. John William Hardy. 1973

Kakapos. Stewart Island, New Zealand. Margaret B. Shepard. 1979-80

Kites, hook-billed. Stanley A. Temple. 1979-80

Kiwi: olfactory sense. Bernice M. Wenzel. 1967

Loons, common. Saskatchewan, Canada. Judith W. McIntyre. 1980

Manakins, swallow-tailed. Paraguay. Mercedes S. Foster. 1977

Nightjars. Peru. John W. Hardy. 1981

Oilbirds. Colombia. Masakazu Konishi. 1975-76

——— Venezuela. Bernice Tannenbaum. 1976

Ospreys: ecology. Connecticut River. Roger Tory Peterson and Peter Ames. 1962

——— pesticide influence on reproductive function. Flathead Lake, Montana, and northwestern California. James R. Koplin. 1968-70, 1972

——— West Africa. Yves A. Prevost. 1978

Palila. Hawaii. Charles van Riper III. 1979

Pelicans, brown: embryos and chicks. Panama. George A. Bartholomew. 1982

——— great white *(Pelecanus onocrotalus):* breeding behavior. Ralph W. Schreiber. 1977

Penguins, gentoo and macaroni. South Georgia Island. Randall W. Davis. 1983

——— jackass. Southern Africa. Walter R. Siegfried. 1973, 1976, 1979

Petrels, Leach's and ashy: nocturnal orientation. Robert I. Bowman. 1971

Phalaropes, Wilson's. Mono Lake, California. Joseph R. Jehl, Jr. 1980

Pheasants, mikado and Swinhoe's. Taiwan. Sheldon R. Severinghaus. 1971

Pigeons, homing: navigation analysis. Charles Walcott. 1968-69

——— homing: role of gravity in navigation. Charles Walcott. 1982

——— pink. Mauritius. Anthony S. Cheke. 1973

Plovers, Egyptian. Thomas R. Howell. 1976

——— golden: wintering behavior. Hawaii. Oscar W. Johnson. 1982

Prairie chickens and sharp-tailed grouse. North Dakota. Donald W. Sparling, Jr. 1976

Quails *(Coturnix):* calling behavior patterns. Wolfgang M. Schleidt. 1974

Raptors: tracking by satellite. Frank C. Craighead, Jr. 1976

Ruffs, male *(Philomachus pugnax).* Julia Marian Wentworth-Shepard. 1974-75

Seabirds: ecology and reproductive behavior. Thomas R. Howell. 1969

——— ecology and tick distribution. Indian Ocean. Christopher J. Feare. 1976

——— ecology, numbers, and distribution. Aegean Sea. George E. Watson. 1966

——— population biology. Midway Island. Robert E. Ricklefs. 1981-83

——— population ecology. Christmas Island. Robert E. Ricklefs. 1980

——— recovery from population failure, 1982. Christmas Island. Ralph W. Schreiber. 1983

Shorebirds, desert *(Peltohyas* and *Stiltia).* Australia. Gordon Lindsay Maclean. 1973

Sparrows, rufous-collared *(Zonotrichia capensis).* Bolivia. Kendall W. Corbin. 1979-80

Spoonbills, African: reproductive biology. M. Philip Kahl. 1980

Storks: worldwide study of the 17 species. Asia and Africa. M. Philip Kahl. 1966-69.

Swallows, cave. Texas. Charles F. Martin. 1974, 1977

Swans, mute. Chesapeake Bay. Jan G. Reese. 1976-78

——— whistling: migrations. Alaska breeding grounds. William J. L. Sladen. 1972-74.

Taiko: search for. Chatham Island, New Zealand. David E. Crockett. 1980.

Tinamous, crested. Argentina. Hannon B. Graves. 1979-80

Vultures, Cape. Africa. Joan C. Dobbs. 1980

Weaverbirds, sociable: ecological role of the nest. George A. Bartholomew. 1972-73

BOTH BY MERLIN D. TUTTLE

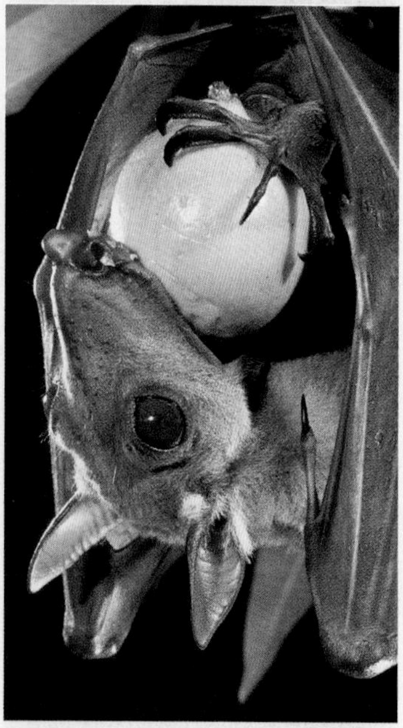

Merlin D. Tuttle holds two of his bat subjects (top). His studies have included such species as the fruit bat (above) and the role of sound in predatory relationships.

——— sparrow, white-browed: determinants of population structure. Zambia. Dale M. Lewis. 1979

Woodpeckers: behavior, ecology, and taxonomy. Asia. Lester L. Short. 1971

——— ivory-billed, search for. Louisiana and east Texas. John V. Dennis. 1967

Wrens: variation in communication, Panama. Eugene S. Morton. 1978.

Invertebrate Zoology

ENTOMOLOGY

Ants, African weaver. Bert Hölldobler. 1977

——— Australian: social behavior and communication. Bert Hölldobler. 1979

——— division of labor. Florida. Prassede Calabi. 1982

——— giant Amazon. Brazil. Paul A. Zahl. 1957

——— *(Pheidologeton).* Asia. Mark W. Moffett. 1981-82

——— *(Polyergus breviceps):* slave-making behavior. Arizona. Howard Topoff. 1983

Army ant mites and leafhoppers. Paraguay. Richard J. Elzinga. 1975

Bagworms: distribution and host-tree orientation of the eggs and parasites. Herbert M. Kulman. 1970

Bees (Anthophoridae): territorial and mating behavior. Costa Rica. Gordon W. Frankie. 1979, 1981

——— euglossine: thermoregulation and flight energetics. Panama. Michael L. Lay. 1980

——— (Panurginae). Jerome G. Rozen, Jr. 1978

Beetles, dung. Bernd Heinrich and George A. Bartholomew. 1977

Butterflies, Alaskan: survey. Victoria Island, Canada. Kenelm W. Philip. 1974-75

——— cabbage. Morocco. Frances S. Chew. 1981

——— ecology and specimen collection. Aldabra Atoll, Indian Ocean. Jay C. Shaffer. 1967

——— equatorial alpine. Colombia. Arthur M. Shapiro. 1976

——— *(Heliconius).* Costa Rica. James L. B. Mallet. 1980

——— (Hesperiidae): systematic and distributional study. Mexico. Hugh A. Freeman. 1973-75

——— monarch: migration. Texas, Florida, California, Australia, Mexico. Fred A. Urquhart. 1968-71, 1975-76, 1978

——— monarch: soaring flight and navigation. David L. Gibo. 1982

——— Neotropical. Trinidad. William Beebe and Jocelyn Crane. 1957

——— pierid: population ecology. Ward B. Watt. 1972

——— swallowtail, Brazilian *(Eurytides lysithous).* David A. West. 1981

——— *(Tatochila sterodice).* Argentina. Arthur M. Shapiro. 1980

Crickets, Hawaiian: song evolution in relation to species formation. Daniel Otte. 1978

Fireflies: luminescence. Far East. John B. Buck. 1965-68

——— *(Pteroptyx).* Asia. Ivan Polunin. 1971

——— *(Pteroptyx).* Thailand. James E. Lloyd. 1980

Flies (Tabanidae). Thailand. John J. S. Burton. 1968-69

——— snail-killing: Pacific Northwest. Benjamin A. Foote. 1971

Grasshoppers, desert: reproductive behavior. California. Michael D. Greenfield. 1983

Halobates. Lanna Cheng. 1977.

Honeybees. Thailand. Thomas D. Seeley. 1978

——— use of the earth's magnetic field. New Jersey. James L. Gould. 1983

Hymenoptera, Neotropical Ichneumonidae. Charles C. Porter. 1974-75, 1979

——— stinging: phenology, mimics, and insectivorous birds. Gilbert P. Waldbauer. 1972

——— systematics and zoogeography. Charles C. Porter. 1973-75

——— tropical and spiders, salticid: visual adaptations. Panama. Andrew D. Blest. 1982

Insects, glacial stream. Washington. Stamford D. Smith. 1982

——— water balance. Namib Desert, Namibia. Eric B. Edney. 1973

Lepidoptera, Neotropical: life history. Panama. Annette Aiello. 1982

Mosquitoes, Holarctic *(Aedes)*. Lewis T. Nielsen. Newfoundland, Canada. 1979, 1981

Moths. Balkans. John B. Heppner. 1980

——— *(Microlepidoptera)*. Chile. Don R. Davis. 1981

——— *(Microlepidoptera)*. South America. John B. Heppner. 1977, 1979

Neuroptera. South America. Lionel A. Stange. 1974-76

——— aquatic. Ecuador. Paul J. Spangler. 1975

——— aquatic: zoogeographical connections. New Caledonia. William L. Peters. 1972

——— collection. Africa. Edward S. Ross. 1957-58

——— collection. Southern Asia and Australia. Edward S. Ross. 1961-62

——— dispersal of. Ethiopia. Jørgen Birket-Smith. 1966

Orthoptera. Gulf of California islands. David B. Weissman. 1983

———Madeira. S. K. Gangwere. 1975

Saldidae: zoogeographical studies. Southern Hemisphere. John T. Polhemus. 1979

Spiders: funnel-web builders: niche analysis. Carrizozo Malpais, New Mexico. Susan E. Riechert. 1972, 1974

——— moth-attracting. United States. Mark K. Stowe. 1982

——— Neotropical *(Anelosimus eximus)*: population genetics. Panama and Suriname. Deborah R. Smith. 1983

——— *(Nephila clavipes)*: foraging behavior. Peru. Ann L. Rypstra. 1983

——— web-building jumping. Asia and Africa. Robert R. Jackson. 1981

——— web-building. Mexico. George W. Uetz. 1978

Treehopper, membracid *(Umbonia crassicornis)*. Florida. Thomas K. Wood. 1974

Triatominae. Central and South America. Pedro W. Wygodzinsky. 1963

Wasps, eumenid: biosystematic studies. Argentina and Chile. Abraham Willink. 1978

——— solitary: biosystematics. Australia. Howard E. Evans. 1979

——— spider *(Trypoxylon)*: behavioral ecology. Costa Rica. Rollin E. Coville. 1981

——— (Thyreodon): biosystematics and zoogeography. Mexico. Charles C. Porter. 1981

Worms, railroad *(Phrixothrix)*: life history. Brazil. Darwin L. Tiemann. 1968-69

MALACOLOGY

Clams, giant: ecology. Samoa. Richard L. Radtke. 1983

——— giant: Zooxanthellae influence on metamorphosis. Robert K. Trench. 1979

Marine invertebrates: biogeography and history. Moluccas. Joseph Rosewater and Barry R. Wilson. 1969

Marine mollusks: ecology and distribution. South Pacific. Harald A. Rehder. 1965, 1967, 1973, 1976

——— shallow-water. Yucatán Peninsula, Mexico. Walter E. Vokes. 1974

Mollusks. Maumee River Valley, Ohio and Indiana. Mark J. Camp. 1982

——— Peruvian: effect of 1982-83 El Niño. Harold B. Rollins. 1983

Nautilus, chambered: growth rate determined using natural radionuclides. James K. Cochran. 1982

——— long-term growth and movement. Palau. W. Bruce Saunders. 1977-79

Snails *(Dyakia striata)*: bioluminescence. Singapore. Jonathan Copeland. 1983

——— heat, desiccation, and starvation. Middle East. Knut Schmidt-Nielsen. 1968-69

——— high-intertidal: crab predation and shell architecture. Geerat J. Vermeij. 1974

——— land: Hispaniolan urocoptid. Fred G. Thompson. 1975, 1978

——— polymorphic: population survey. North Africa. Geoffrey Lewis. 1977

OTHER INVERTEBRATES

Brachiopods: marine environment. Joyce R. Richardson. 1976, 1978, 1981

Bryozoans. Florida. Judith E. Winston. 1983

Cephalopods, deep-sea: photographic record. Noel Peter Dilly. 1971, 1973

Corals, blue *(Heliopora coerula)*. Branko Velimirov. 1978

——— non-symbiotic. Gerard Wellington and Robert K. Trench. 1982

Coral reefs. Lizard Island, Australia. Michel Pichon. 1976

——— destruction and later recolonization. American Samoa. Austin E. Lamberts. 1974, 1978

——— Florida. Gilbert L. Voss. 1961-63

———Jamaica. Judith C. Lang. 1975

Crabs, brachyuran. Gulf of Guinea. Raymond B. Manning. 1972

——— fiddler. Europe. Jocelyn Crane. 1959

——— hermit: ethology. Alex Henderson and Syd Radinovsky. 1971

——— *(Ocypode)*: acoustic-signal processing. Kenneth W. Horah. 1977

——— tropical land. Charles L. Hogue and Donald B. Bright. 1970

Crustaceans, deep-sea: live retrieval. James J. Childress. 1980

——— deep-sea: live retrieval for physiological study. U.S.S.R. Ralph W. Brauer. 1983

Echinoderms, crinoid. Great Barrier Reef, Australia. David L. Meyer. 1982

Foraminifera, large calcareous: ecology. Queensland Shelf and Great Barrier Reef, Australia. Charles A. Ross. 1970

Invertebrate predation and crustacean zooplankton. English Lake District. W. Gary Sprules. 1976

Jellyfish. Palau. Leonard Muscatine. 1981

——— mangrove: zooxanthellae contribution to respiration. Richard S. Blanquet. 1979

Lobster, spiny: mass migrations. William F. Herrnkind. 1973

Ostracods, marine: bioluminescent communication. Panama. James G. Morin. 1983

Plankton: Florida Current. University of Miami Institute of Marine Sciences. 1950-52

Reef dynamics: anatomy and growth. Antigua. H. Gray Multer. 1982

Rotifers. Patagonia. David Kuczynski. 1983

Sea anemones (Actiniidae). Lisbeth Francis. 1980

Shrimp. Bermuda. Raymond B. Manning. 1982

——— Florida. Clarence P. Idyll and David A. Hughes. 1964-69

——— *Macrobrachium:* migration mechanisms. David A. Hughes. 1970

——— mantis: predation on prawns. Gulf of California. Marea E. Hatziolos. 1979

——— symbiotic: local and long-distance dispersal of larvae. Jamaica. Nancy Knowlton. 1982

Sponges: morphological and ecological studies. Pacific reef caves. Willard D. Hartman. 1971

Squid fisheries. North Atlantic. Gilbert L. Voss. 1965

Starfish, coral-reef. Guam. Masashi Yamaguchi. 1974

——— crown-of-thorns *(Acenthaster planci):* biology and epidemiology. Walter A. Starck II. 1971.

Zooplankton: nocturnal study. Laurence P. Madin. 1981

——— demersal: distribution on coral reefs. Alice L. Alldredge. 1978

——— freshwater. Indonesia. Constantine H. Fernando. 1977

Geography

Aerial survey: Washington to Buenos Aires. Albert W. Stevens, Frederick Simpich, and Jacob Gayer. 1930

Africa: a history of exploration by Americans. James A. Casada. 1976

Agricultural development: semiarid drainage basin potential. Central Tanzania. John W. Pawling. 1973

Alaska: ancient environments and age of nonglaciated terrain. Ian A. Worley. 1971

Alaska Peninsula and Aleutian Islands. Bernard R. Hubbard. 1934

Ankara: population changes since 1969. Turkey. John R. Clark. 1978

Antarctica: air exploration. Lincoln Ellsworth. 1934

——— first expedition, 1928-30; second expedition, 1933-35. Richard E. Byrd, Jr.

Arctic: Franz Josef Land islands. Walter Wellman. 1898, 1906

——— MacMillan expedition. Donald B. MacMillan and Richard E. Byrd, Jr. 1925

——— survey, area north of Alaska. Robert A. Bartlett. 1924

Bali: tourism and small-scale indigenous enterprise. Antonio Hussey. 1983

Bolivia: access to the sea. Martin I. Glassner. 1981

Cape Horn region, South America. Amos Burg. 1934

Carlsbad Caverns: exploration, mapping, and photographing. New Mexico. Willis T. Lee. 1924

China-Tibet frontier. Joseph F. Rock. 1923-30

Citröen-Haardt Trans-Asiatic Expedition, Beirut to Peking. Georges-Marie Haardt. 1931

Cocos Island: geologic, geophysical, and biologic study. Costa Rica. Rodey Batiza. 1983

Delaware Bay: baseline study. William S. Gaither. 1970

Estonia: urban transportation and structure in a planned society. Siim Sööt. 1983

Everest, Mount: first American ascent. Nepal. Norman G. Dyhrenfurth and Barry C. Bishop. 1962-63

France: nuclear energy development and implications. James R. McDonald. 1981

Franco-Italian borderland: impact of two decades of integration. Julian V. Minghi. 1979

Geographic education assistance. Association of American Geographers. 1962

Green River: landscape change. Utah-Colorado. William L. Graf. 1976

Hengduan Shan: reconnaissance of highland-lowland interaction systems. China. Barry C. Bishop. 1982

Himalayas. Sir Edmund Hillary and Barry C. Bishop. 1960, 1962

——— Bhutan. Pradyumna P. Karan. 1964-65

Hudson Bay lowlands: potential climatic modifications. Canada. Wayne R. Rouse. 1977

Ice caves. Canadian Cordillera. Derek C. Ford. 1973

Indonesia and the Philippines: mobility behavior and employment characteristics. Richard Ulack and Thomas R. Leinbach. 1982

International Geographical Congresses, 1871-1976: bibliography of papers. George Kish. 1977

Japan: three decades of change in two rural townships. Forrest R. Pitts. 1983

Katmai, Mount: Valley of Ten Thousand Smokes. Alaska. Robert F. Griggs. 1915-20, 1930

Kenya: tropical agriculture and socioeconomic and physical factors. Ernestine Cary. 1982

Leeward Islands: land-use intensity and labor migration. St. Kitts and Nevis. Bonham C. Richardson. 1975

McKinley, Mount: aerial photo survey. Bradford Washburn. 1936

Mexico: prehispanic wetland agriculture. Alfred H. Siemens. 1983

Micronesia: role of urban growth centers in economic development. John D. Eyre. 1983

Nepal: Tilicho Lake alpine-zone research project. Barry C. Bishop. 1983

New Guinea: eastern mountains. J. Linsley Gressitt. 1968-69

North America: history of geography. Geoffrey J. Martin. 1981

North Pole: attempt to reach. Walter Wellman. 1898

——— attempt to reach. William Ziegler, Anthony Fiala, and William J. Peters. 1903

——— attempt to reach, by dirigible balloon. Walter Wellman and Henry E. Hersey. 1906-07

——— attempt to reach, on skis. Bjørn O. Staib. 1964

——— first successful effort to reach. Robert E. Peary. 1908-09

Northwest Mexico: traditional water-harvesting systems. Gerald Fish. 1980

Norway: Jotunheimen research expedition. John A. Matthews. 1982

Pakistan: northern mountain agro-ecosystems. Nigel J. R. Allan. 1982

KATHRYN KOSTOW

Studying grebe behavior, Gary L. Nuechterlein mimics a courtship ritual and gets a like response from a subject bird.

Reventazon and General Valleys: river terraces. Costa Rica. Richard H. Kesel. 1974, 1977

Rock, Joseph F.: biography. Stephanne B. Sutton. 1971

Saharan expansion. Southern Tunisia. Ian A. Campbell. 1970

St. Elias, Mount: first National Geographic Society expedition. Alaska-Canada. Israel C. Russell. 1890-91

St. Elias Mountains: Mount St. Elias-Mount Logan aerial photography. Alaska and Canada. Bradford Washburn. 1938

——— Yukon Territory, Canada. Bradford Washburn. 1935

Santa Inés. Tierra del Fuego, Chile. E. Jack Miller and Paul H. Dix. 1964

Southern Colorado Plateau: transport and storage of natural mercury in stream sediments. William L. Graf. 1980, 1982

Taiwan: impact of industrial estates on rural areas. Roger M. Selya. 1981

Theodore Roosevelt National Memorial Park: feasibility study for expansion. North Dakota. Paul B. Kannowski. 1972

Torres Strait: traditional knowledge of marine environments and biota. Australia. Bernard Q. Nietschmann. 1980

United States: landscapes of the western interior. Thomas R. Vale. 1983

United States and Europe: emergency evacuation of cities. Wilbur Zelinsky. 1983

Vilcabamba Range: plateau between the Apurímac and Urubamba Rivers. Peru. G. Brooks Baekeland and Peter R. Gimbel. 1963

Vinson Massif ascent. Sentinel Range, Ellsworth Mountains, Antarctica. Nicholas B. Clinch. 1966

West African grain coast: ports. William R. Stanley. 1974

Yunnan-Sichuan: mountains and gorges. China. Joseph R. Rock. 1923, 1927, 1929

CARTOGRAPHY

American Revolution: military map sources. Douglas W. Marshall. 1976

Antarctica: mapping. Lincoln Ellsworth. 1934

Chan Chan-Moche Valley site: maps published. Peru. Carol J. Mackey and Michael E. Moseley. 1973

Grand Canyon of the Colorado: South Rim mapping. Bradford Washburn. 1971-72, 1974

Grand Canyon map: final revision. Bradford Washburn. 1979

Historical map testing. Roland E. Chardon. 1976

Kennedy, Mount, and Mount Hubbard: mapping. Canada. Bradford Washburn. 1965

——— mapping. Canada. Paul Ulmer. 1966

Roads Through History: map catalog publication. Peabody Institute Library. 1965

Sikkim: physical-cultural map. Pradyumna P. Karan. 1968

Geology

Ai (Et-Tell), Israel: soils, construction, and geologic materials. George R. Glenn. 1970

Alaska Range Quaternary Mapping Program. United States. Norman W. Ten Brink. 1981

Alpine chain: geological exploration. Southern Italy. Walter Alvarez. 1975

Aluminous laterite and bauxite: origin. Palau, western Pacific Ocean. Samuel S. Goldich. 1978

Andes: climatic and vegetational changes. Peru. Herbert E. Wright, Jr. 1978

——— mapping of eastern slope. Quito region, Ecuador. Tomas Feininger. 1979

——— metamorphic rocks. Colombia and Ecuador. Tomas Feininger. 1971

Archaean rocks: tectonic and thermal history. West Greenland. Robert F. Dymek. 1979

Avalon Peninsula: biostratigraphy and depositional tectonics, Lower Cambrian. Newfoundland, Canada. Ed Landing. 1982-83

Basalts: petrology and geochemistry. Snake River Plain, Idaho. William P. Leeman. 1969

Bentonite dating: Lower Paleozoic. Britain. Reuben J. Ross, Jr. 1976

Calcalkaline rocks: isotopic tracer studies. Mitsunobu Tatsumoto. 1979

Caledonites. Norway. William B. Size. 1976

Carboniferous deposits: statistical analysis. Fife, Scotland. Edward S. Belt. 1972

Chubb Crater. Quebec. V. Ben Meen. 1951.

Clay sediments: mineralogy and distribution. Turnagain Arm region, Alaska. Neal R. O'Brien. 1973

Cumberland Peninsula, Baffin Island: south-coast reconnaissance, late Quaternary. Canada. William W. Locke III. 1982

Española Island: volcanic and biologic study. Galapagos Islands. Minard L. Hall. 1979

Evaporites: Triassic, first deposits of the rifting Atlantic. Morocco. William T. Holser. 1982

Gem study. Asia. V. Ben Meen. 1964-65

Geomorphology: Baltit area. Karakoram Mountains, Pakistan. Andrew S. Goudie. 1980

Geothermal activity: remote sensing. East African Rift. Kathleen Crane. 1980

Glacial and floral changes: climatic history, last 140 centuries. Argentina. John H. Mercer. 1974

Glacial indicator fan: from Reindeer Lake Cretaceous shale. Saskatchewan, Canada. William G. Johnston. 1983

Glacial sediments: Precambrian. Sierra Leone and Senegal. Stephen J. Culver. 1983

Great Rift Valley: structural origin of the Ethiopian section. George H. Megrue and Paul A. Mohr. 1968-69

Hydrographic evolution: late Glacial to Recent. Western Mediterranean. Daniel J. Stanley. 1970

Indus suture zone and Karakoram Mountains: radiometric dating of rocks. Michael E. Brookfield. 1979, 1980, 1983

NATALIE J. DEMONG

Stephen T. Emlen found that these African bee-eaters have one of the most complex of avian societies.

WILLIAM F. KUYKENDALL, NGS

Jared Diamond displays a hornbill, one of his finds in New Guinea.

Iron formation. Disko Island, western Greenland. John M. Bird. 1977, 1980-81

Italy: Plio-Pleistocene boundary. Charles W. Naeser. 1979

Karst: development and archaeology. Belize. Thomas E. Miller. 1983

Kenya, Mount: Quaternary history. East Africa. William C. Mahaney. 1976, 1981, 1983

Labrador Crater. Canada. V. Ben Meen. 1953-54

Laetolil Beds and footprint tuffs: geologic history. Tanzania. Richard L. Hay. 1976, 1978-82

Landslide history. Gros Ventre mountains, Wyoming. Robert C. Palmquist. 1980, 1982

Magma intrusion: geochemical monitoring. Long Valley caldera, California. Stanley N. Williams. 1983

Marble Canyon quadrangle. Death Valley, California. Edward A. Johnson. 1973

Metamorphic rocks: petrographic mapping. New Caledonia. Philippa M. Black. 1970

Meteorite and tektite collection. Australia. Brian H. Mason and E. P. Henderson. 1963-67

Meteorite craters. Mauritania. Robert F. Fudali. 1969-70

Messina earthquake study. Sicily. Charles Will Wright. 1909

Mineralogical research. Prince of Wales Island, Alaska. George S. Switzer. 1967

Miocene rocks: stratigraphy and faunas. Northwestern Nebraska. Robert M. Hunt, Jr. 1972

Mirror Lake: magnetic studies of lake sediments and sources. New Hampshire. Frank Oldfield. 1981-82

Molokai, windward coast: geology and botany. Hawaii. Robert R. Compton. 1980

Morrison and Cloverly Formations: study of sediments in Big Horn Basin. Wyoming. Carl F. Vondra. 1983

Olduvai Gorge, Tanzania: geologic history. Richard L. Hay. 1962, 1968-70, 1972.

Paleoclimatic and geologic studies. Nubian and Western Deserts, Sudan and Egypt. C. Vance Haynes, Jr. 1977-80

Palsa development in permafrost. Yukon Territory, Canada. Ann M. Tallman. 1977

Patrick Buttes: Miocene rocks and fauna. Wyoming. Robert M. Hunt, Jr. 1979

Pegmatite mineral studies. Black Hills, South Dakota. George Rapp, Jr. 1964

Recent Nile cone history based on sediment-core analysis. Daniel J. Stanley. 1974

Salmon River: batholith. Idaho. Philip J. Shenon and John C. Reed. 1935

Saltpeter conversion and cave nitrate origins. Carol A. Hill. 1974

Sedimentation patterns: submarine. Wilmington Canyon, Atlantic Ocean. Daniel J. Stanley. 1966

Sedimentological study. Volta Delta, West Africa. John K. Adams. 1972

Sediments, internal: interrelationships with submarine lithification. Robert L. Eutsler. 1973

Skaergaard region, Greenland. Alexander R. McBirney. 1974

Speleothems: paleoenvironmental analysis. Carlsbad Caverns, New Mexico. Brooks B. Ellwood. 1982

Strontium and lead isotopes: dating of metamorphosed sediments. California and Baja California. Russell G. Gastil. 1980

Stuart, Mount: batholith petrology and geochemistry. Cascade Range, Washington. Erik R. Erickson, Jr. 1971-72, 1974

Submerged beach-rock pavements. Bimini, Bahama Islands. Mahlon M. Ball. 1971

Tektites. Bosumtwi Crater, Ivory Coast. John Saul. 1964

Trondhjemites: development and the earth's early sialic crust. Fred Barker. 1972

Troodos ophiolite: controls of metamorphism. Cyprus. Judith L. Hannah. 1981-82

Turbidity maximum. Westerschelde Estuary, Netherlands. Richard W. Faas. 1973

Ultramafic inclusions: origin and relationship to basalt genesis. A. William Laughlin. 1972

West Spitsbergen Island: geology and glaciology. Norway. George H. Sutton and P. C. Parks. 1952

Zeolite distribution: in relation to lung cancer. Central Turkey. Frederick A. Mumpton. 1978

GLACIOLOGY

Alaska: glaciers. Ralph S. Tarr and Lawrence Martin. 1909-11

——— glacier studies. Maynard M. Miller. 1961-67

Alaska-British Columbia Coast Mountains: glacier differentiation. Maynard M. Miller. 1968-69

Atlin Park glaciers. British Columbia. Maynard M. Miller. 1974

Austrian Alps: glaciation chronology. Henry W. Posamentier. 1975

Baffin Island: glacial erosion. Canada. David E. Sugden. 1975

Glacier Bay: late Wisconsin and neoglacial history. Alaska. George M. Haselton. 1975

Glaciers: presurge dynamics. Sam G. Collins. 1971

Lewis Glacier. Mount Kenya, East Africa. Stefan L. Hastenrath. 1980

Norway: (Jotunheimen) model of periglacial landscapes. Colin E. Thorn. 1983

St. Elias Mountains. Alaska. Richard L. Cameron. 1968

——— Alaska-Yukon Territory. Walter A. Wood. 1964-67

PALEONTOLOGY

Actinopterygian fishes: Jurassic. Western United States. Bobb Schaeffer. 1980

Agate National Monument: Miocene mammals. Nebraska. Robert M. Hunt, Jr. 1977

Alamosa Formation: Plio-Pleistocene flora and fauna. Colorado. Karel L. Rogers. 1979-81

Amphibians and reptiles: Lower Pliocene. Kansas. J. Alan Holman. 1972-73

——— Upper Miocene. Nebraska. J. Alan Holman. 1975

Angiosperm flowers: Oligocene. East Texas. William L. Crepet. 1979

Appalachian caves: Pleistocene paleoecology. John E. Guilday. 1978

Arctic steppe-mammoth biome: symposium. David M. Hopkins. 1978

Billfish. Philippines. Harry L. Fierstine. 1980

Biostratigraphy: Tertiary molluscan. Tierra del Fuego and Patagonia. William J. Zinsmeister. 1975

Birds, earliest: cranial anatomy, brain size, and flight capabilities. British Museum, London. Larry D. Martin. 1980

——— evolution of extinct teratorns. Argentina. Kenneth E. Campbell. 1981

——— Pleistocene. Puerto Rico. Storrs L. Olson. 1977

——— terrestrial: Upper Cretaceous. Baja California. William J. Morris. 1973

Bivalve mollusks: Neogene mass extinction. Western Atlantic. Steven M. Stanley. 1981

——— Permo-Triassic crisis. Nevada-Idaho. Norman D. Newell. 1982

Blacktail Cave: fossils and associated artifacts. Montana. William G. Melton, Jr. 1978

Bovidae. Tanzania and Kenya. Alan W. Gentry. 1964-65

Calvert Cliffs. Maryland. Robert E. Gernant and A. Lincoln Dryden. 1968

Catfish. Green River Formation, Wyoming. H. Paul Buchheim and Ronald C. Surdam. 1976

Cave with scavengers. Villafranca de los Barros, Spain. Emiliano Aguirre. 1971-72

Cetaceans: Oligocene. South Carolina. Albert E. Sanders. 1972.

——— Oligocene. U.S.S.R. Albert E. Sanders. 1979

Coral reefs: Cretaceous. Europe and Caribbean. Anthony G. Coates. 1975

——— Cretaceous. Middle East. Anthony G. Coates. 1978-9

——— history: clonal growth. Anthony G. Coates. 1982

Crabs: late Cretaceous. North America. Gale A. Bishop. 1976

Desmostylia and its mammalian relations. Roy H. Reinhart. 1973

Dinosaurs: comparative study of North American and Mongolian fossils. John H. Ostrom. 1977

——— Gadoufaoua, Niger. Philippe Taquet. 1973

——— Jurassic. Colorado. James A. Jensen. 1975.

——— Jurassic and Cretaceous. Colorado and Utah. James A. Jensen. 1977

——— Morrison Formation. Western United States. Peter Dodson. 1974-75

——— (Psittacosauridae). China. Paul C. Sereno. 1983

Dry Cave: Pleistocene paleoecology. New Mexico. Arthur H. Harris. 1971

Dutton fauna: late Pleistocene. Colorado. Russell W. Graham. 1978

Early man and extinct animals. China Lake, California. Emma Lou Davis. 1971

Fish fauna: Cenozoic. Green River, Wyoming. R. Lance Grande. 1981

Flamingos: Eocene, nesting area. Wyoming. Paul O. McGrew. 1971, 1975

Floras and vertebrate faunas: Tertiary terrestrial. Canadian high Arctic. Mary R. Dawson. 1979

——— Tertiary terrestrial. Canadian high Arctic. Mary R. Dawson and Robert M. West. 1976

Footprint castings: Oligocene. Presidio County, Texas. John A. Wilson. 1975

Foraminifera: Jurassic and Cretaceous. Pacific Ocean. Robert G. Douglas. 1970, 1974

Fossil grasses. Ash Hollow Canyon, Nebraska. Joseph R. Thomasson. 1978

Fossil plants. Antelope and Garden Counties, Nebraska. Joseph R. Thomasson. 1980

Fossils: collecting. Kenya. Vincent J. Maglio. 1968-69, 1972

——— dating, using racemization of amino acids from Africa. Jeffrey L. Bada. 1973

——— dating, using racemization of amino acids from caves. John H. Ostrom. 1970

——— exploration. Central Australia. Patricia V. Rich. 1982-83

Geomagnetic chronology: land mammals. South America. Larry G. Marshall. 1974, 1976, 1978

Glossina fossils. Florissant, Colorado. Frank L. Lambrecht. 1981

Gondwana: Cretaceous mammals and birds. South Africa. Thomas H. Rich. 1977, 1980

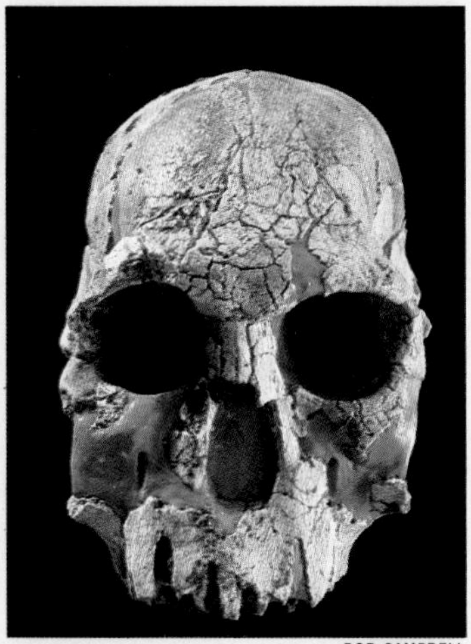

BOB CAMPBELL

"Skull 1470," found in Kenya in 1972 and now dated at about two million years, led Richard E. Leakey to reassess the origin of early man.

Graptolite biostratigraphy: Ordovician. Bolivia. Stanley C. Finney. 1981

Herbivore taphonomy: Kenya. Diane P. Gifford. 1976

Judith River Formation: vertebrates and paleoecological history. Montana. William A. Clemens. 1980-82

Kayenta and Moenave Formations: biostratigraphy and paleoenvironments. Arizona. Kevin Padian. 1982

Kayenta Formation: biostratigraphic and sedimentologic exploration. Arizona. Kevin Padian. 1981

La Venta Formation: paleontological investigation. Colombia. Kubet E. Luchterhand. 1980

Labrador, southeastern: glacial and vegetational history. Herbert E. Wright, Jr. 1979

Ladds Quarry: Pleistocene fauna and ecology. Georgia. J. Alan Holman. 1978, 1980-82

Limestone reef: mid-Cretaceous flora and fauna. Puebla, Mexico. George L. Callison. 1982

Madagascar: mammalian evolutionary history. Ross D. E. MacPhee. 1983

Magnetostratigraphy: Eureka Sound Formation, lithostratigraphic, biostratigraphic, paleoclimatic correlations. Canadian Arctic. Robert M. West. 1980

Malagasy lemur subfossils: crania and dentitions. Ian M. Tattersall. 1969

Mammal bones. Amboseli National Park, Kenya. Anna K. Behrensmeyer. 1975-76

Mammals. James S. Mellett. 1975

——— Cretaceous. Greenwood Canyon, Montague County, Texas. Bob H. Slaughter. 1973

——— earliest in the New World. Arizona. Farish A. Jenkins, Jr. 1981-83

——— early Cenozoic. Montana. David W. Krause. 1983

——— early Cretaceous. North America. Farish A. Jenkins, Jr. and A. W. Crompton. 1974-75

——— Eocene, anatomy and adaptations. Kenneth D. Rose. 1981

——— Paleocene. Bear Tooth region, Wyoming and Montana. Charles R. Schaff. 1979

——— small: biologic and geologic relationships. Austria. Robert W. Wilson. 1973, 1978, 1982

——— South Dakota. Robert W. Wilson. 1965, 1974

Mammoth-kill sites, Selby and Dutton, Colorado. Dennis J. Stanford. 1976-77

——— Wyoming and New Mexico. George A. Agogino. 1959-65, 1977

——— Murray Springs, Arizona. C. Vance Haynes, Jr. 1966-72.

Mammoth site: late Pleistocene. Hot Springs, South Dakota. Larry D. Agenbroad. 1975, 1977-79, 1982

Mammoth skeleton: 11,000-year-old *Mammuthus columbi.* Wyoming. George A. Agogino. 1960-61.

Megafauna: extinct Pleistocene animals. Utah. Paul S. Martin. 1983

Mesozoic and Tertiary fauna. Australia and New Zealand. Thomas H. Rich. 1973, 1975

Microvertebrates: Chadron Formation. Nebraska and South Dakota. Philip R. Bjork. 1978

——— Chinle Formation. Arizona. Louis L. Jacobs. 1979

——— first from Miocene of Central America. Bob H. Slaughter. 1977

——— late Cretaceous and early Tertiary fauna. Bolivia. Larry G. Marshall. 1982

——— Miocene and Pliocene. South Dakota. Morton Green. 1973

Mollusks: radiocarbon dating and climatic significance. Ohio and Indiana. Barry B. Miller. 1982

Natural Trap Cave: Pleistocene and Recent flora and fauna. Wyoming. B. Miles Gilbert. 1978

Nearctylodon: taxonomy of mammal-like reptiles. G. Edward Lewis. 1982

Old World monkey fossils *(Cercopithecoidea).* Mediterranean region. Eric Delson. 1971

Oldman Formation: Cretaceous paleoecology. Dinosaur Provincial Park, Alberta, Canada. Peter Dodson. 1981-83

Paleofauna from caves in the Dominican Republic. Renato O. Rimoli M. 1977, 1979

Paleontology and archaeology. Lubbock Lake site. Texas. Craig C. Black. 1973-74

Paraguay: stratigraphy and paleontological exploration. Rafael Herbst. 1979

Paraguay and Uruguay: paleobotanical research. Rafael Herbst. 1982

Permian conodont paleoecology. Wyoming. Fred H. Behnken. 1976

Pliocene fauna. Nebraska. Michael R. Voorhies. 1965

Pliocene fossil localities. Rift Valley, Kenya. Vincent J. Maglio. 1972

Plio-Pleistocene fossils. Iran. Douglas M. Lay. 1976

Pre-Carboniferous coal swamps: paleoecology. Southern Appalachia. Stephen E. Scheckler. 1981

Primates: late Oligocene. Chubut region, Argentina. John G. Fleagle. 1982

Pterosaurs, giant. Texas. Douglas A. Lawson. 1975

Rhinoceros herd: Miocene, buried in volcanic ash. Michael R. Voorhies. 1978-79

Rhinoceros and pig bones. South Dakota. Joseph P. Connolly and James D. Bump. 1940

Rocks, minerals, and fossils: collecting for conservation. Badlands, South Dakota. Robert W. Wilson. 1965, 1968-69

Salamander and frog fossils: paleogeography. Richard Dean Estes. 1973

Sangamon interglacial deposits. Natural Trap Cave, Wyoming. Larry D. Martin. 1983

Semionotus: adaptive radiations, Mesozoic lakes. Amy R. McCune. 1981

Siwalik Group: Neogene vertebrate paleontology and geology. Western Nepal. Robert M. West. 1981

Stanton's Cave: Pleistocene paleoclimatology. Grand Canyon, Arizona. Robert C. Euler. 1969-70

Taphonomy: Miocene. Flint Hill, South Dakota. James E. Martin. 1983

Tarija Basin: Pleistocene vertebrates and chronology. Bolivia. Bruce J. MacFadden. 1983

Tetrapods: Upper Devonian. Australia. Richard C. Fox. 1983

——— Upper Permian and Triassic. Southern Brazil. Mario C. Barberena. 1978, 1980

Tobago: zoogeographical implications of recent and fossil vertebrates. West Indies. Ralph E. Eshelman. 1980

Trace fossils: Proterozoic. Godavari Valley, India. James D. Howard. 1981

Turtles, African and South American: paleoecology and plate tectonics. Roger C. Wood. 1978

Underwater paleontology. Florida. S. David Webb. 1968-69

Vertebrate biostratigraphy: Miocene sediments. Western Nebraska. John A. Breyer. 1977

Vertebrates. Australia. Thomas H. Rich. 1975

——— and geology: Pliocene and Pleistocene. Eastern Lake Eyre Basin, South Australia. Richard H. Tedford. 1980, 1982-83

——— Baja California. Theodore Downs. 1974

——— Baja California. William J. Morris. 1965-71

——— Cenozoic. Eastern Canadian high Arctic. Mary R. Dawson and Robert M. West. 1973

——— Cenozoic. Pilbara and Canning Basins, Australia. William D. Turnbull. 1976

——— Cenozoic, and stratigraphy. Nepal. Jens Munthe. 1980

——— Central America and Great American interchange. S. David Webb. 1976

——— Cockpit Caves, Jamaica. Gregory K. Pregill. 1982

——— comparison of late Pleistocene fauna with living species. San Salvador, Bahama Islands. Storrs L. Olson. 1980

——— early and middle Tertiary. Canadian high Arctic. Mary R. Dawson and Robert M. West. 1977, 1982

——— Galapagos Islands. David W. Steadman. 1979

——— Jurassic and Cretaceous, terrestrial. South America. José F. Bonaparte. 1975-79, 1981-83

——— late Arikarean. Nebraska. Margery C. Coombs. 1975

——— late Cenozoic: biochronology and magnetostratigraphy. Europe. Everett H. Lindsay. 1979-80

——— late Cretaceous, longitudinal study in western United States. J. David Archibald. 1982

——— late Pliocene, marine. California. Thomas A. Deméré. 1983

——— late Tertiary. Peru. Kenneth E. Campbell. 1977

——— late Triassic, Popo Agie Formation. Wyoming. Nicholas Hotton III. 1981

——— Lower Eocene. Namibia. John A. Van Couvering. 1975

——— Lower Triassic. Tasmania. John W. Cosgriff. 1970

——— mid-Tertiary. Charleston, South Carolina. Albert E. Sanders. 1971-72

——— Miocene. Southeastern Peru. Kenneth E. Campbell. 1979

——— Miocene marine. Orange County, California. Lawrence G. Barnes. 1982

——— Pleistocene, paleoecology. Lake Bonneville deposits, Utah. Wade E. Miller. 1973

——— terrestrial, present and fossil. Fernando de Noronha Island, South Atlantic. Storrs L. Olson. 1972

——— Triassic, taphonomy and paleoecology. West Texas. Sankar Chatterjee. 1980, 1982-83

——— tropical. South America. Bryan Patterson. 1974

Geophysics

Archeomagnetic chronology: New World. Robert Lee DuBois. 1969-70

Joint and fracture patterns. Israel and Iceland. Amos A. Nur. 1974

Landscape viewed in ultraviolet. Arizona. William C. Livingston. 1983

OCEANOGRAPHY

Aquascope: designed, built, and used in study of Chesapeake Bay. Gilbert C. Klingel. 1952-53

Doe-eyed cousins to camels, guanacos of South America were studied in Tierra del Fuego by wildlife ecologist William L. Franklin. WILLIAM L. FRANKLIN

ARGO/JASON vehicle: exploration of the Mid-Ocean Ridge. Robert D. Ballard. 1983

Bathymetry: physiography. Northeastern Indian Ocean. Joseph R. Curray. 1980

Bathysphere: record depth and observations. Bermuda. William Beebe and Otis Barton. 1934

***Calypso* expeditions.** Jacques-Yves Cousteau. 1952-67

Deep-sea exploration: large-area imaging. Robert D. Ballard. 1981

Freshwater streams in the sea. Cephalonia, Ionian Sea. T. Nicholas Panay. 1953

Galapagos Rift: hydrothermal vents investigation by remote camera. Robert D. Ballard. 1978

"Knee-line" depths and positions: seismic study. Mediterranean Sea. Harold E. Edgerton. 1969

Man-in-Sea Project: test of an underwater sea habitat. Mediterranean Sea, off Villefranche, France. Edwin A. Link and Robert Sténuit. 1963

Marine aerosols: chemical composition sampled worldwide from a sailing boat. Rene E. Van Grieken. 1979

Mid-Atlantic Ridge: topography, geology, and sea life. Maurice Ewing. 1947-48

Mid-Atlantic Ridge Rift Valley: sonar exploration. Harold E. Edgerton. 1969

Ocean floors: global physiographical study. Bruce C. Heezen. 1970

Photographic and echo-sounding research and equipment. Harold E. Edgerton. 1950, 1952-62, 1966, 1974

Photographic equipment. Walter A. Starck II. 1964

Photographic equipment: for study of living plankton in the sea. Harold E. Edgerton. 1978

Sediments: bioturbation. Puerto Rico. Jack Morelock. 1973

Underwater instrumentation: for geology, archaeology, and biology. Harold E. Edgerton. 1980

VOLCANOLOGY

Arenal volcano: eruption dynamics and petrology. Costa Rica. William G. Melson. 1969

Basement rock and volcanic correlations: Tertiary. Gulf of California. R. Gordon Gastil. 1972

Katmai, Mount: examination following eruption. Alaska. George C. Martin. 1912

Nunivak Island: volcanic ejecta. Alaska. John Sloan Dickey, Jr. 1974

Pavlof volcano. Alaska Peninsula. Thomas A. Jaggar. 1928

Pelée, Mount: eruption. Martinique. Robert T. Hill, Israel C. Russell, and Thomas A. Jaggar. 1902

Ranier, Mount: summit crater geophysical and volcanological investigation. Washington. Barry W. Prather and Maynard M. Miller. 1970-71

Thera: before eruption of 1450 B.C. Greece. Grant H. Heiken. 1981

——— eruption date, Bronze Age. Aegean Sea. Charles J. Vitaliano. 1974

——— Minoan ash, downwind island distribution and relation to caldera size. Greece. Floyd W. McCoy. 1982

Tonga Islands volcanoes: survey of recent activity. William G. Melson and W. B. Bryan. 1968

Vesuvius A.D. 79 **and El Chichón 1982:** impact of pyroclastic flows on human populations. Haraldur Sigurdsson. 1982

Volcanic flames and fumes: spectroscopy. Hawaii. Dale P. Cruikshank. 1971

Volcanic gas and fumes: spectroscopy. Hawaii. Dale P. Cruikshank and Jay M. Pasachoff. 1981

Volcanic gas and petrology. Galapagos Islands. Bert E. Nordlie. 1971

Volcanic rocks. Micronesia. Fred Barker. 1976

Volcanism. Austral Islands. Rockne H. Johnson. 1971

——— Zuni Centers volcanic field, late Cenozoic. New Mexico. A. William Laughlin. 1973

Volcanoes, submarine. Near Samoa. Rockne H. Johnson. 1975

Volcanologic studies: evidence for mantle upwelling. Azores. Martin F. J. Flower. 1983

Social Sciences

HISTORY

Hydraulic cement, early. Greece and Cyprus. Theodore A. Wertime. 1980

Llanos: tropical plains frontier. Northern South America. Jane M. Loy. 1973

Manuscript collections: survey. Nepal, Sikkim, and Bhutan monasteries. John F. Staal and Lewis R. Lancaster. 1973

Manuscripts: St. Mpatsis Monastery. Andros Island, Aegean Sea. Antonia Tripolitis. 1968-69

Metallurgic zones: descriptions by Homer and Strabo. Northern Turkey. Theodore A. Wertime. 1970

Naval documents: cataloging and indexing. Naval Historical Foundation. 1965

Persian Royal Road Survey. Anatolia, Turkey. S. Frederick Starr. 1961

SOCIOLOGY

City street life. New York City. William H. Whyte. 1972-73

Library of Congress CIP Data

Main entry under title:

National geographic index, 1947-1983.

Includes essays.
1. National geographic—Indexes. I. National Geographic Society (U. S.) II. National geographic.
G1.N27 Suppl. 910'.5 84-7130
ISBN 0-87044-510-3

NATIONAL GEOGRAPHIC SOCIETY

WASHINGTON, D. C.

Organized "for the increase and diffusion of geographic knowledge"

GILBERT HOVEY GROSVENOR
Editor, 1899-1954; President, 1920-1954
Chairman of the Board, 1954-1966

THE NATIONAL GEOGRAPHIC SOCIETY is chartered in Washington, D. C., in accordance with the laws of the United States, as a nonprofit scientific and educational organization. Since 1890 the Society has supported more than 2,450 explorations and research projects, adding immeasurably to man's knowledge of earth, sea, and sky. It diffuses this knowledge through its monthly journal, NATIONAL GEOGRAPHIC; its books, globes, atlases, filmstrips, and educational films; *National Geographic WORLD,* a magazine for children age 8 and older; information services; technical reports; exhibits in Explorers Hall; and television.

MELVIN M. PAYNE *Chairman of the Board*

NATIONAL GEOGRAPHIC MAGAZINE

GILBERT M. GROSVENOR *President*
WILBUR E. GARRETT *Editor*
JOSEPH JUDGE *Associate Editor*

SENIOR ASSISTANT EDITORS

John B. Garver, Jr., *Cartography* Robert E. Gilka, *Photography*
William Graves, *Expeditions* Robert P. Jordan, *Special Projects*
H. Edward Kim, *Layout* Edward J. Linehan, *Manuscripts*
Samuel W. Matthews, *Production* O. Louis Mazzatenta, *Control Center*
Charles McCarry, *Contract Writers* Howard E. Paine, *Art*
Carolyn Bennett Patterson, *Legends* Thomas R. Smith, *Illustrations*
Mary G. Smith, *Research Grant Projects* Kenneth F. Weaver, *Science*
Ann K. Wendt, *Research*

TEXT

ASSISTANT EDITORS: Kent Britt, Thomas Y. Canby, Rowe Findley, Bart McDowell, Elizabeth A. Moize, Merle Severy
SENIOR WRITERS: Thomas J. Abercrombie, David S. Boyer, Mike Edwards, William S. Ellis, Rick Gore, Noel Grove, John J. Putman, Peter T. White
SENIOR EDITORIAL STAFF: Harvey Arden, Robert Booth, Allen A. Boraiko, John L. Eliot, Boyd Gibbons, Alice J. Hall, Bryan Hodgson, David Jeffery, Michael E. Long, Priit J. Vesilind, Gordon Young. *Production:* John L. McIntosh
EDITORIAL STAFF: Judith Brown, Larry Kohl, Douglas Lee, Louise E. Levathes, Peter Miller, Cathy Newman, Cliff Tarpy, Jane Vessels
RESEARCH: Lesley B. Rogers (Assoc. Dir.); Michaeline A. Sweeney (Asst. Dir.); *Researcher-Editor:* Susan L. Anderson. *Researchers:* Carolyn H. Anderson, Rebecca Beall, Julia G. Grover, Ann B. Henry, Jan Holderness, Patricia B. Kellogg, Kathy B. Maher, Barbara W. McConnell, Jean B. McConville, Margaret S. Nottingham, Jeanne E. Peters, Frances W. Shaffer. *Geography:* Bette Joan Goss. *Legends:* Victoria C. Ducheneaux, Abigail A. Tipton. *Planning Council:* Gaither G. Kyhos, Mary McPeak

ILLUSTRATIONS

PHOTOGRAPHERS: Dean Conger, Joseph J. Scherschel (Assistant Directors); James L. Amos, Joseph H. Bailey, James P. Blair, Victor R. Boswell, Jr., Jodi Cobb, Bruce Dale, David Alan Harvey, Otis Imboden, Emory Kristof, Joseph D. Lavenburg, Bianca Lavies, Bates Littlehales, Robert W. Madden, George F. Mobley, Robert S. Oakes, Steve Raymer, Robert F. Sisson *(Nat. Science),* James L. Stanfield. *Administration:* Claude E. Petrone, Susan A. Smith
ILLUSTRATIONS EDITORS: W. Allan Royce (Assistant Director); David L. Arnold, Taylor Gregg, Bruce A. McElfresh, Charlene Murphy, Robert S. Patton, Elie S. Rogers, Jon Schneeberger, Susan Welchman
LAYOUT: Constance H. Phelps, William T. Douthitt
ART: Jan Adkins, J. Robert Teringo (Assoc. Directors); *Artists:* William H. Bond, Ned M. Seidler. *Design:* Charles C. Uhl (Asst. Dir.); Betty Clayman
ENGRAVING AND PRINTING: William W. Smith (Director); James R. Whitney (Assoc. Dir.); Bill M. Aldridge, John T. Dunn, Judy L. Garvey, John W. Gergel

CARTOGRAPHY

Richard J. Darley (Senior Assoc. Director); John F. Shupe (Assoc. Director); Walter Q. Crowe, John F. Dorr, Harold A. Hanson, Harry D. Kauhane, Richard K. Rogers, Elie Sabban (Asst. Dirs.). *Map Editors:* Thomas A. Walsh (Supvr.); John T. Blozis, Russel G. Fritz, Charles W. Gotthardt, Jr., Thomas L. Gray, Mary Anne McAleer, Gus Platis. *Artists:* Lisa Biganzoli, John W. Lothers, Nancy Schweickart, Sally Suominen-Summerall, Tibor G. Toth. *Archaeologist:* George E. Stuart. *Geographer:* Ted Dachtera. *Researchers:* Timothy J. Carter, Ross M. Emerson, Marguerite B. Hunsiker, Mary C. Latham, Dorothy A. Nicholson, Douglas A. Strobel, Susan Young. *Map Artists:* Roland R. Nichols, Leo B. Zebarth (Supvrs.); Iskandar Baday, Alfred L. Zebarth. *Specialists:* Charles F. Case, Martin J. Golden, Thomas A. Wall. *Scheduling:* Charles L. Miller, Henri A. Delanghe. *Admin:* Catherine M. Hart, Patricia M. Oakes

EDITORIAL SERVICES

ADMINISTRATION: M. Jean Vile (Asst. to the Editor), Elaine Rice Ames, Marie L. Barnes, G. Merrill Clift, Neva L. Folk, Lilian Davidson, Virginia H. Finnegan, Eleanor W. Hahne, Mary F. Klemann, Ellen E. Kohlberg, Liisa Maurer, Lucille L. McInerney, Carol D. Rhoads. *Picture Requests:* Barbara A. Shattuck. *Correspondence:* Carolyn F. Clewell, Gwendolyn C. Blackman, Joseph M. Blanton, Jr. *Indexes:* Jolene M. Blozis. *Travel:* Virginia A. Bachant
LIBRARIES: *Publications:* Susan Fifer Canby (Director); Patricia Murphy Smith, Margery K. Barkdull, Karen F. Carrick, Carolyn Locke, Louise A. Robinson, Marta Strada. *Records & Illustrations:* Lorie Northrop (Director); L. Fern Dame, Mary Anne McMillen, M. Scott Bolden, Carolyn J. Harrison, Marguerite S. Northwood, Mennen M. Smith. *Photo Archivist:* Volkmar Wentzel. *Films:* Betty G. Kotcher
NEWS SERVICE: Paul Sampson (Director); Joy Aschenbach, Kenneth C. Danforth, Donald J. Frederick, Rebecca R. Kirtland, Barbara S. Moffet, William J. O'Neill. *Radio:* Robert C. Radcliffe
PHOTOGRAPHIC LABORATORIES AND TYPESETTING: Carl M. Shrader (Director); Milton A. Ford (Associate Director); Lawrence F. Ludwig (Asst. Director); Herbert Altemus, Jr., Billy R. Barnett, Richard A. Bredeck, David H. Chisman, Ellwood M. Kohler, Jr., Geoffrey T. McConnell, William S. Petrini, Bernard G. Quarrick, Joan S. Simms, James H. Trott, Alfred M. Yee

RELATED EDUCATIONAL SERVICES OF THE SOCIETY

ROBERT L. BREEDEN *Vice President*

SENIOR ASSISTANT EDITORS: Donald J. Crump, *Special Publications and School Services;* Charles O. Hyman, *Book Service*
BOOK SERVICE: Greta Arnold, Ross Bennett, Mary Dickinson, Karen F. Edwards, Suzanne Kane, Anne D. Kobor, J. Edward Lanouette, Carol B. Lutyk, Linda B. Meyerriecks, Elizabeth Newhouse, David F. Robinson, Shirley Scott, David M. Seager, Margaret Sedeen, Susan Sidman, Penelope Timbers, Jonathan Tourtellot, Anne Withers
SPECIAL PUBLICATIONS AND SCHOOL SERVICES: Philip B. Silcott (Assoc. Dir.); William L. Allen, William R. Gray (Asst. Dirs.); John G. Agnone, Jody Bolt, Jane H. Buxton, Marilyn W. Clement, Margery G. Dunn, Toni Eugene, Seymour L. Fishbein, Ron Fisher, Patricia F. Frakes, Barbara Grazzini, Mary Ann Harrell, Suzanne J. Jacobson, Bonnie S. Lawrence, Christine E. Lee, Jane R. McCauley, Tom Melham, Robert Messer, H. Robert Morrison, Thomas O'Neill, Thomas B. Powell III, Cynthia Ramsay, Jennifer C. Urquhart, George V. White, Merrill Windsor. *National Geographic WORLD:* Ralph Gray (Editor); Pat Robbins (Mng. Ed.); Jacqueline Geschickter, Pat Holland, Joan Hurst, Tee Loftin, Margaret McKelway, Veronica Morrison, Judith Rinard, Eleanor Shannahan, Ursula Vosseler. *Educational Media:* George Peterson (Editor); Jimmie Abercrombie, David F. Beacom, James B. Caffrey
PUBLICATIONS ART: John D. Garst, Jr. (Director); Virginia L. Baza (Asst. Dir.). *Map Artists:* Isaac Ortiz, Peter J. Balch
TELEVISION AND FILMS: Dennis B. Kane (Director); Sidney Platt (Director, Educational Films); Donald M. Cooper, Anne B. K. Krumbhaar, Yeorgos N. Lampathakis, Karen S. Marsh, Louise C. Millikan, Marjorie M. Moomey, Nola L. Shrewsberry, Kathleen F. Teter, Carl E. Ziebe
AUDIOVISUAL: Joanne M. Hess (Director); Jon H. Larimore (Tech. Director); Ronald S. Altemus, Robert G. Fleegal, Paul Gorski, Gerald L. Wiley